WEEK 1 - 13-45 & 46-62

Making Literature Matter

AN ANTHOLOGY FOR
READERS AND WRITERS

Making Literature Matter

AN ANTHOLOGY FOR READERS AND WRITERS

SECOND EDITION

John Schilb

Indiana University

John Clifford

University of North Carolina at Wilmington

BEDFORD/ST. MARTIN'S   Boston • New York

For Bedford/St. Martin's
Executive Editor: Stephen A. Scipione
Production Editor: Bridget Leahy
Senior Production Supervisor: Dennis J. Conroy
Editorial Assistant: Emily Goodall
Copyeditor: Rosemary Winfield
Text Design: Geri Davis, The Davis Group, Inc.
Cover Design: Mark McKie
Cover Art: The Bar IV, 1993. © Bill Jacklin, courtesy Marlborough Gallery, New York
Composition: Stratford Publishing Services, Inc.
Printing and Binding: Quebecor World Kingsport

President: Joan E. Feinberg
Editor in Chief: Karen S. Henry
Director of Marketing: Karen Melton
Director of Editing, Design, and Production: Marcia Cohen
Managing Editor: Elizabeth M. Schaaf

Library of Congress Control Number: 2002102565

Copyright © 2003 by Bedford/St. Martin's

All rights reserved. No part of this book may be reproduced, stored in a retrieval system, or transmitted in any form or by any means, electronic, mechanical, photocopying, recording, or otherwise, except as may be expressly permitted by the applicable copyright statutes or in writing by the Publisher.

Manufactured in the United States of America.

7   6   5   4
f   e

For information, write: Bedford/St. Martin's, 75 Arlington Street, Boston, MA 02116
(617-399-4000)

ISBN: 0-312-39460-8

Acknowledgments

Diane Ackerman. "Plato: The Perfect Union." From *A Natural History of Love* by Diane Ackerman. Copyright © 1994 by Diane Ackerman. Reprinted by permission of Random House, Inc.

James Agee. "A Mother's Tale." Reprinted by permission of the James Agee Trust.

Sherman Alexie. "Capital Punishment." From *The Summer of Black Widows* by Sherman Alexie. Copyright © 1996 by Sherman Alexie. Reprinted by permission of Hanging Loose Press.

Julia Alvarez. "How I Learned to Sweep." From *Homecoming* by Julia Alvarez. Copyright © 1984, 1996 by Julia Alvarez. Published by Plume, an imprint of Dutton Signet, a division of Penguin USA. Originally published by Grove Press. Reprinted by permission of Susan Bergholz Literary Services, New York. All rights reserved.

Acknowledgments and copyrights are continued at the back of the book on pages 1643–1650, which constitute an extension of the copyright page. It is a violation of the law to reproduce these selections by any means whatsoever without the written permission of the copyright holder.

For Wendy and Janet

Preface for Instructors

Heartened by the popularity of the first edition of *Making Literature Matter*, we preserve its mission in the second—to combine an exceptionally diverse selection of literary works with unusually thorough writing instruction that helps students read and write about literature thoughtfully. Integrating literature and composition has long been a goal of our pedagogy, and we continue to explore ways of achieving this aim in our classrooms. What is distinctive about our approach is that we see reading and writing as acts of comparison, through which students make explicit or implicit connections between texts. Therefore, we still cluster thematically related works of literature and invite students to examine them in light of one another. At the same time, the book continues to set literary criticism in a robust rhetorical framework, emphasizing strategies for *arguing* about literature. As in our first edition, we urge students to see argument not as combat but as inquiry. We depict it as a civil process of deliberation through which writers clarify, support, and revise their claims.

We retain the basic structure and much of the content of the first edition. As before, a substantial part of the book is a writing text that discusses how to compose arguments about literature. In Part One, "Working with Literature," we explain the elements of argument, introducing students to terms such as *issue*, *claim*, *audience*, and *warrant*, and paying particular attention to the kinds of issues that literary critics habitually raise. We also refer to actual literary texts, analyze sample student drafts, and identify the distinct characteristics of the four literary genres represented here—short stories, poems, essays, and plays. Later, in an appendix, we turn to the research paper, guiding students through its challenges by discussing a particular case study.

Part Two, "Literature and Its Issues," is again an anthology that contains most of the book's literary selections, where they are organized into thematically focused chapters. Given students' keen interest in our original chapter topics, most of these have been retained, including Living in Families, Teaching and Learning, Loving, and Confronting Mortality. Within each chapter, readers will continue to find issue-based clusters—that is, groupings of texts that prompt careful comparison, often between famous and lesser-known works. The groupings include three special kinds of clusters, which instructors report to be especially

useful: a set of works by one author; a single work accompanied by critical observations about it; and a single work accompanied by documents reflecting the
work's cultural context. Each cluster in Part Two still provides plenty of guidance
for students' own writing through questions and assignments that deal with the
cluster's texts separately and together.

An instructor's manual, *Resources for Teaching* MAKING LITERATURE MATTER:
AN ANTHOLOGY FOR READERS AND WRITERS, Second Edition, includes suggestions for organizing a course and teaching with the book. As before, this resource
provides sample syllabi, detailed commentary on the literary selections, and an
annotated bibliography of scholarship on integrating literary study with composition. Overall, the manual remains one of the most extensive and informative of
such guides.

New to the Second Edition

We have tried to make the second edition a better vehicle of instruction for
the kinds of writing and reading that students will do in the course. In Part One,
for example, we have replaced all the student writing with drafts that will provide better opportunities for analysis. In chapter 3, we have added advice on
how to write comparative essays, a genre often scanted by literature textbooks.
With the aid of a student's rough and final drafts, we show how to go beyond a
mere listing of similarities and differences and instead recommend that students
write *weighted* comparisons — essays that make one work primary while noting
others akin to it.

Other changes in Part One involve its literature. For example, we now begin
this section by juxtaposing James Wright's famous poem "Lying in a Hammock
at William Duffy's Farm in Pine Island, Minnesota" with one by Michael Lohre
that reflects on it, thus emphasizing immediately the value of putting literary
works in dialogue. We also have greatly increased the number of literary texts in
Part One and centered them all on one theme — *work*, a subject bound to engage
students' interest. The part's new title, "Working with Literature," also signals that
interpreting literature is an active process. In effect, Part One anticipates the thematic chapters in Part Two, presenting as they do an opportunity for students to
explore a body of literature on a certain topic. Indeed, Part One now previews
Part Two in another way. Chapters 8 through 11 introduce and explain the special kinds of clusters that appear throughout the book's second part so that students will see the purpose and value of, for example, reading criticism about a
particular literary work, or understanding its cultural context.

Of the book's 174 literary selections, fifty are new. As we noted, most of
the book's literature remains in Part Two's anthology. Responding to surveys of
instructors who used the first edition, we have deleted a number of literary selections while adding others. For example, there is a new cluster of poems by Countee Cullen, Langston Hughes, Audre Lorde, and Cornelius Eady on the issue of
racial injustice. We have kept Matthew Arnold's classic "Dover Beach" but now
pair it with a contemporary poem, Mark Doty's "Night Ferry," to examine the

notion of people's using love as a refuge. And although we have kept most of the chapter topics originally in Part Two, we have dropped one, "Considering Outsiders," while redistributing its popular selections by Nathaniel Hawthorne, Flannery O'Connor, and Maxine Hong Kingston. We have slightly modified another chapter and retitled it "Doing Justice."

Within Part Two, we have also shifted some works into clusters where they are even more likely to stimulate thought. For instance, Sophocles' play *Antigone* is now paired with his drama *Oedipus the King* so that students can better grasp the issues addressed by this crucial tragedian and the techniques he used to do so. Similarly, William Shakespeare's *Hamlet* now appears with Susan Glaspell's twentieth-century play *Trifles*, so that students can compare a Renaissance classic about revenge with a modern feminist's handling of the subject. Flannery O'Connor's short story "A Good Man is Hard to Find" is now followed by critical commentaries that provide students with more tools for analyzing its enigmas. The grouping of Nathaniel Hawthorne's "Young Goodman Brown," "The Minister's Black Veil," and "Ethan Brand" allows students to explore Hawthorne's preoccupation with sin.

Another significant change in Part Two is the addition of a fourth special cluster to each chapter. This new kind of grouping emphasizes "re-visions," showing how authors adapt or reconceive earlier texts. For example, although we have carried over from the first edition Tennessee Williams's play *The Glass Menagerie*, we now pair it with his earlier short story "Portrait of a Girl in Glass," in which he began to explore Laura Wingfield's plight. Similarly, we follow Anton Chekhov's well-known story "The Lady with the Pet Dog" with variations on it by Joyce Carol Oates and Beth Lordan. We also group three versions of the Red Riding Hood story: Charles Perrault's, the Grimm Brothers', and Angela Carter's contemporary short story "The Company of Wolves." Part Two's concluding chapter on "Confronting Mortality" features three versions of "Richard Cory": Edwin Arlington Robinson's classic poem, the lyrics to Paul Simon's song version of it, and W. D. Snodgrass's recent "de/composition" of Robinson's text.

Part Two includes two new instructional aids. Each chapter now begins with a set of brief quotations on the chapter's topic, which classes can use as springboards for prewriting or for other informal reflections. Each special cluster concludes with a writing assignment based on Web research and a link to the *Making Literature Matter* companion Web site, where students will find further links needed to complete the activity.

Also helpful, we think, is a new appendix on critical approaches to literature. In this appendix we explain as clearly as possible various schools of thought in contemporary literary criticism. Then, we show how each can be applied to two stories of physical abuse in families, James Joyce's "Counterparts" and Ann Petry's "Like a Winding Sheet." From our demonstrations of theory in practice, students will better glimpse directions they can pursue in their own writing about literature.

Acknowledgments

In working on this second edition, we have continued to enjoy and learn from our collaboration with the staff at Bedford/St. Martin's. Our editor, Steve Scipione, remains a wonderful partner and friend; we rely on his patience, experience, and wisdom. We continue to value the support of Joan Feinberg, now president of the company. Still a source of inspiration, too, is former president Charles Christensen, who seems anything but "retired." Other staff members we especially want to thank are Bridget Leahy, who supervised copyediting and production; Emily Goodall, who not only pulled the manuscript together but also developed the book's Web site; and Karen Melton, Richard Cadman, and Jenna Bookin Barry, who have been hard at work on the marketing of the book.

Again, we thank Janet E. Gardner of the University of Massachusetts at Dartmouth for her fine work on the research appendix. We appreciate Susan Doheny's photo research and Sandy Schechter's work on clearing permissions. We also remain indebted to Joyce Hollingsworth from the University of North Carolina at Wilmington, who again has gone far beyond the call of duty in contributing to the instructor's manual. For this edition, Jennifer Raspet from the same university has ably assisted John Cliffford with research and editorial work. As before, John Schilb thanks his former colleagues at the University of Maryland, especially ace rhetorician Jeanne Fahnestock. He also continues to be grateful for the support given him by his present colleagues at Indiana University. In particular, Christine Farris and Kathy Smith have been constant resources. For this edition, Kenneth Johnston and David Wojahn made valuable suggestions.

As always, we appreciate and thank those who reviewed our manuscript at its various stages and those who adopted and taught from the book and shared with us their impressions of it. Their observations and suggestions were extremely useful. They include Julie Aipperspach Anderson, Texas A&M University; Jonathan Alexander, University of Southern Colorado; Virginia Anderson, University of Texas at Austin; Carolyn Baker, San Antonio College; Rance G. Baker, San Antonio College; Barbara Barnard, Hunter College; Charles Bateman, Essex County College; Linda Bensel-Meyers, University of Tennessee, Knoxville; Elizabeth L. Cobb, Chapman University; Michael A. Cronin, Northern Oklahoma College; Thomas Deans, Kansas State University; Kevin J. H. Dettmar, Southern Illinois University at Carbondale; Michael Doyle, Blue Ridge Community College; Thomas Dukes, University of Akron; Irene R. Fairley, Northeastern University; Martha K. Goodman, Central Virginia Community College; Iris Rose Hart, Santa Fe Community College; Carol Peterson Haviland, California State University, San Bernardino; John Heyda, Miami University-Middletown; Richard Dean Hovey, Pima Community College; Karen Howard, Volunteer State Community College; Sabine A. Klein, Purdue University; Kasee Clifton Laster, Ashland University; Margaret Lindgren, University of Cincinnati; Phillip Mayfield, Fullerton College; Miles S. McCrimmon, J. Sargeant Reynolds Community College; Christopher McDermott, University of Georgia; Steven Newman, University of Nebraska–Omaha; Meryl F. Schwartz, Lakeland Community College; Julie Segedy, Chabot College; Jason Skipper, Miami University at Oxford; Jennifer Smith, Miami University at Oxford; Larry A. VanMeter, Texas A&M University; Sharon Winn, Northeastern State University; Bertha Wise, Oklahoma City Community College; Pauline G. Woodward, Endicott College.

We said it before, and we say it again: What matters most to John Schilb is Wendy Elliot; what matters most to John Clifford is Janet Ellerby. Once more, we dedicate this book to our wives, whose love and support remain steadfast.

J.S.
J.C.

Brief Contents

Contents

PART TWO
Literature and Its Issues

Sample Student Research Paper   1626

Making Literature Matter

An Anthology for Readers and Writers

Working with Literature

What Is Literature? How and Why Does It Matter?

The title of this book, *Making Literature Matter*, may seem curious to you. Presumably your school assumes that literature already matters, for otherwise it would hardly offer courses in the subject. Quite possibly you are taking this course because you think literature is important or hope it will become so for you. But with our title, we want to emphasize that literature does not exist in a social vacuum. Rather, literature is part of human relationships; people *make* literature matter to other people. We will be especially concerned with how you can make literature matter to others as well as to yourself. Above all, we will point out ways you can argue about literature, both in class discussions and in your own writing.

Here is a poem that has engaged many readers, judging by how often it has appeared in literature anthologies since its first publication in 1963. The author is James Wright (1927–1980), who was born and raised in the industrial town of Martin's Ferry, Ohio. Many of Wright's poems deal with the working-class life he experienced there. Early in his career as a poet, he wrote in conventional forms, but later he became much more experimental. The following poem, perhaps Wright's most famous, is a case in point.

JAMES WRIGHT
Lying in a Hammock at William Duffy's Farm in Pine Island, Minnesota

Over my head, I see the bronze butterfly,
Asleep on the black trunk,
Blowing like a leaf in green shadow.
Down the ravine behind the empty house,
The cowbells follow one another   5
Into the distances of the afternoon.
To my right,
In a field of sunlight between two pines,
The droppings of last year's horses

Blaze up into golden stones.   10
I lean back, as the evening darkens and comes on.
A chicken hawk floats over, looking for home.
I have wasted my life.   [1963]

Did the last line startle you? For many readers, Wright's poem is memorable because its conclusion is unexpected, even jarring. At first glance, nothing in the speaker's description of his surroundings justifies his blunt self-condemnation at the end. If anything, the previous lines evoke rural tranquility, so that a more predictable finish would be "I am now at peace." Instead, the speaker suddenly criticizes himself. Intrigued by this mysterious move, readers usually look at the whole poem again, studying it for signs of growing despair. Often they debate with one another how the ending does relate to preceding lines. Thus, although the poem's speaker implies his life hasn't mattered, the poem itself has mattered to readers, plunging them into lively exchanges over how to interpret Wright's text.

We present Wright's poem to begin pointing out how literature can matter to people. We will keep referring to the poem in this Introduction. But now we turn to three big questions:

- How have people defined literature?
- What about literature has mattered to people?
- What can you do to make literature matter to others?

How Have People Defined Literature?

Asked to define *literature*, most people would include Wright's text, along with other poems. In addition to poetry, they would say *literature* encompasses fiction (novels as well as short stories) and drama. But limiting the term's scope to these genres can be misleading, for they are rooted in everyday life. Often they employ ordinary forms of talk, although they may play with such expressions and blend them with less common ones. Someone lying in a hammock may, in fact, recite details of the landscape — especially if he or she is talking to someone else on a cell phone, as is common nowadays. And quite possibly you have heard someone proclaim "I have wasted my life" or make a similar declaration. In any case, surely much of Wright's language is familiar to you, even if you haven't seen it arranged into these particular phrases and lines.

The genres regarded as literary are tied in other ways to everyday behavior. For instance, things function as symbols not only in poems but also in daily conversation. Even people who aren't poets have little trouble associating shadows, evening, darkness, and hawks with death. (In the case of Wright's poem, the issue then becomes whether the text supports or complicates this association.) Hammocks, too, are often treated as meaningful images. Recently, the newspaper in John Schilb's town printed an article with the following headline: "Hammocks are familiar symbols of taking it easy." (With Wright's poem, the issue again becomes whether the speaker's hammock signifies *more* than just leisure.)

Throughout the day, then, it can be said that people put literary genres into practice. Perhaps you have commented on certain situations by quoting a song lyric or citing words from a poem, story, or play. Surely you are poetic in the sense that you use metaphors in your everyday conversations. After all, most of us are capable, as Wright's speaker is, of comparing a butterfly to a leaf (even if we aren't apt to compare horse droppings to "golden stones"). Probably you are often theatrical as well, carrying out various kinds of scripts and performing any number of roles. Furthermore, probably you are engaged in storytelling no matter how little fiction you actually write. Imagine this familiar situation: You are late for a meeting with friends because you got stuck in traffic, and now you must explain to them your delay. Your explanation may well become a tale of suspense, with you the hero racing against time to escape the bumper-to-bumper horde. As writer Joan Didion has observed, "We tell ourselves stories in order to live." Almost all of us spin narratives day after day because doing so helps us meaningfully frame our lives. (Unfortunately, the story that Wright's speaker tells is "I have wasted my life." Nevertheless, it's a means for interpreting his existence, and maybe somehow it helps him keep on living.)

You may admit that literature is grounded in real life and yet still tend to apply the term only to written texts of fiction, poetry, and drama. But this tendency is distinctly modern, for the term *literature* has not always been applied so restrictively. *Literature* was at first a characteristic of *readers.* From the term's emergence in the fourteenth century to the middle of the eighteenth, *literature* was more or less a synonym for *literacy.* People of literature were assumed to be well read.

In the late eighteenth century, however, the term's meaning changed. Increasingly it referred to books and other printed texts rather than to people who read them. At the beginning of this shift, the scope of literature was broad, encompassing nearly all public writing. But as the nineteenth century proceeded, the term's range shrank. More and more people considered literature to be imaginative or creative writing, which they distinguished from nonfiction. This trend did take years to build; in the early 1900s, literature anthologies still featured essays as well as excerpts from histories and biographies. By the mid-1900s, though, the narrower definition of literature prevailed.

This limited definition has become newly vulnerable. From the early 1970s, a number of literature faculty have called for widening it. In 1979, for instance, a National Endowment for the Humanities–Modern Language Association institute entitled "Women's Nontraditional Literature" applied the term *literature* to genres that had not been thought of as such. Participants studied essays, letters, diaries, autobiographies, and oral testimonies. To each of these genres, women have contributed much; in fact, the institute's participants concluded that a literature curriculum slights many works by women if it focuses on fiction, poetry, and drama alone.

Of course, even within these three categories, the term *literature* has been selectively applied. Take the case of novelist and short-story writer Stephen King, whose books have sold millions of copies. Despite his commercial success, a lot of readers — including some of his fans — refuse to call King's writing literature. They assume that to call something literature is to say that it has artistic merit, and for them King's tales of horror fall short.

Yet people who use the term *literature* as a compliment may still disagree about whether a certain text deserves it. Plenty of readers do praise King's writing as literature, even as others deem it schlock. In short, artistic standards differ. To be sure, some works have been constantly admired through the years; regarded as classics, they are frequently taught in literature classes. *Hamlet* and other plays by William Shakespeare are the most obvious examples. But in the last twenty years, much controversy has arisen over the *literary canon*, those works taught again and again. Are there good reasons why the canon has consisted mostly of works by white men? Or have the principles of selection been skewed by sexism and racism? Should the canon be changed to accommodate a greater range of authors? Or should literary studies resist having any canon at all? These questions have provoked various answers and continued debate.

Also in question are attempts to separate literature from *nonfiction*. Much nonfiction shows imagination and relies on devices found in novels, short stories, poems, and plays. The last few years have seen the emergence of the term *creative nonfiction* as a synonym for essays, autobiographies, histories, and journalistic accounts that use evocative language and strong narratives. Conversely, works of fiction, poetry, and drama may center on real-life events. For example, beginning with James Wright's "Lying in a Hammock," several of the poems in our book can easily be seen as autobiographical. Perhaps you have suspected already that the speaker in Wright's poem is Wright himself. In numerous interviews, Wright admitted as much. He acknowledged that he based the poem on his own experience of lying in a hammock, which really did lead him to think "I have wasted my life."

A note of caution is in order. While testimony such as Wright's can be illuminating, it should be used prudently. In crucial respects, Wright's poem still differs from Wright's life. The text is a representation of his experience, not the experience itself. His particular choice and arrangement of words continue to merit study, especially because he could have depicted his experience in plenty of other ways. As critic Charles Altieri notes, important to specify are the ways in which a poem is "binding the forms of syntax to the possibilities of feeling." Keep in mind, too, that not always is the author of a work the ideal guide to it. After all, the work may matter to its readers by raising for them issues and ideas that the author did not foresee. Besides, often the author's comments about the text leave certain aspects of it unexplained. Though Wright disclosed his poem's origins, readers must still decide how to connect its various images to its final line. Even so, "Lying in a Hammock" confirms that a literary work can stem from actual circumstances, whatever use the reader makes of facts about them.

Some people argue, however, that literature about real events is still "literary" because it inspires contemplation rather than action. This view of literature has traditionally been summed up as "art for art's sake." This notion brushes aside, however, all the poems, novels, short stories, and plays that encourage audiences to undertake certain acts. Included in our book, for example, is Sherman Alexie's "Capital Punishment," a poem obviously designed to spark resistance to the death penalty. True, not every poem is so conspicuously action-oriented. Wright's "Lying in a Hammock" seems more geared toward reflection, especially because the speaker is physically reclining while he observes nature and ponders his life. But readers may take even this poem as an incitement to change their behavior, so that they can feel they have not wasted their own lives.

In our book, we resist endorsing a single definition of *literature*. Rather, we encourage you to review and perhaps rethink what the term means to you. At the same time, to expand the realm of literature, we include several essays in addition to short stories, poems, and plays. We also present numerous critical commentaries as well as various historical documents. Throughout the book, we invite you to make connections among these different kinds of texts. You need not treat them as altogether separate species.

What about *Literature Has Mattered to People?*

People have studied literature for all sorts of reasons. You may be surprised to learn that in the late 1800s, English departments in American colleges taught Shakespeare's plays mainly by having students trace the origins of particular words he used. His plots, characters, and themes received little attention. Today, by contrast, most Shakespeare classes consider these things important; they are not content to use his plays as a springboard for dictionary research. In fact, literary history can be seen as a history of changing responses to literature. Nevertheless, if you were to ask several people today why they read literature, probably you would get several common answers. The following are some we have heard. As we enumerate them, compare them with what you might say.

One common reason for reading literature has to do with seeming sophisticated. Since the eighteenth century, people have sought to join cultural elites by proving their familiarity with literature. Read Shakespeare's plays, their thinking goes, and then you can impress high society by quoting him. The desire to raise one's status is understandable. Still, this motive is rarely enough to sustain a person's interest in literature. Frankly, we hope you find other reasons for reading it. At the same time, we invite you to analyze how knowledge of literature has served as *cultural capital*: that is, as a sign of a person's worth. In coining the term *cultural capital*, sociologist Pierre Bourdieu suggested there is something wrong when a society makes literature a means of achieving status. Do you agree?

Another common reason for reading literature has to do with institutional requirements. Millions of students read literature simply because they have to take courses in it. Probably Roland Barthes, the French critic, had this situation in mind when he wryly defined *literature* as "what gets taught in schools." Barthes was being provocatively reductive; if pressed, perhaps he would have conceded that people read literature outside school, too. Across the United States, college graduates and others meet regularly in book discussion groups, studying literature together. Even if you are taking this course only because you must, the obligation may turn out to be enjoyable. When required to read literature, students have found value in it. While inevitably they end up preferring some works to others, they learn that literature provides them with pleasures and insights that they had not anticipated. Stay open to the possibility that you will find it much more than a waste of time.

Still another popular reason for reading literature is, in fact, the enjoyment it provides. Quite simply, lots of people find the experience entertaining. They may revel in literature's ability to render human existence concretely. They may delight in its often eloquent and evocative language. They may like finding all the various patterns in a literary text. They may prize the moments when literature makes them think, laugh, or cry.

People have also turned to literature because, as scholar and critic Kenneth Burke has noted, it serves as "equipment for living." Perhaps you have found that a certain story, poem, play, or essay helped you understand your life and conduct it better. Of course, even readers who look to literature for guidance may have different tastes. While some readers prefer literature that reflects their own lives, others like it most when it explores situations they have not lived through or pondered. Perhaps you would never say to yourself "I have wasted my life"; all the same, you may find it worthwhile to analyze how Wright's speaker reaches this conclusion. "When it's the real thing," critic Frank Lentricchia suggests, "literature enlarges us, strips the film of familiarity from the world; creates bonds of sympathy with all kinds, even with evil characters, who we learn are all in the family."

Some people *dislike* literature because they find it too vague and indirect. They resent that it often forces them to figure out symbols and implications when they would rather have ideas presented outright. Perhaps you wish the speaker in Wright's poem had made clear why his observations prompted him to criticize himself. But in life, truth can be complicated and elusive. In many ways, literature is most realistic when it suggests the same. Besides, many readers — perhaps including you — appreciate literature most when it resists simple decoding, forcing them to adopt new assumptions and learn new methods of analysis. Indeed, throughout this book we suggest that the most interesting and profitable conversations about literature are those in which the issues are not easily resolved. One of the best things your course can provide you and your classmates is the chance to exchange insights about texts such as Wright's.

We hope that any literature you read in this book strikes you as "equipment for living." If a particular selection leaves you cold, try at least to identify and review the standards by which you are judging it. Even if you like a piece, think about the values you are applying to it. Probably these will grow clearer to you in class debates, especially if you have to support your own view of a text.

What Can You Do to Make Literature Matter to Others?

In an 1895 essay called "The Art of Fiction," the American novelist, short-story writer, and critic Henry James wrote, "Art lives upon discussion, upon experiment, upon curiosity, upon variety of attempt, upon the exchange of views and the comparison of standpoints." Certainly James was suggesting that the creators of literature play a big role in making it matter. But he was suggesting, too, that plenty of other people contribute to literature's impact. Today, these people include publishers, printers, agents, advertisers, librarians, professional reviewers, bookstore staff, Internet chat groups, and even show business figures such as Oprah Winfrey, who has interested millions of viewers in participating in her "book club." Teachers of literature also make it matter—or at least they try to. Perhaps your parents or other family members have contributed to your appreciation of certain literary texts; many adults introduce their children and grandchildren to books they loved when young. Moreover, friends often recommend works of literature to one another.

Again, we concede that some people think of literature negatively, believing that it matters in a way they don't like. The ancient Greek philosopher Plato wanted to ban poets from his ideal republic because he thought they merely imitated truth. Throughout subsequent history, various groups have tried to abolish or censor much literature. In communities across the contemporary United States, pressure groups have succeeded in removing particular novels from library shelves, including classics such as Mark Twain's *Adventures of Huckleberry Finn* and J. D. Salinger's *The Catcher in the Rye*. History has also seen many writers killed, jailed, or harassed for their work. In recent years, the most conspicuous example of such persecution has been the Ayatollah Khomeini's indictment of author Salman Rushdie. In 1989, the ayatollah was so enraged by the portrayal of Islam in Rushdie's novel *The Satanic Verses* that he commanded his followers to hunt Rushdie down and slay him. Even after the ayatollah died, Rushdie was in danger, for the *fatwa* against him remained in effect. Not until eight years after the original edict did the Iranian government back away from it. At present, Rushdie still enjoys only a limited measure of safety, and the whole affair stands as a reminder that some writers risk their lives. Ironically, the ayatollah's execution order was a sort of homage to literature, a fearsome way of crediting it with the power to shape thinking.

Our book aims to help you join the conversations that Henry James saw as nourishing literature. More specifically, our book focuses on helping you argue about literature, whether your audience is your classmates, your teacher, or other people. While arguments involve real or potential disagreement, they need not be waged like wars. When we use the term *argument* in this book, we have in mind civilized efforts through which people try to make their views persuasive. When you argue about literature, you are carefully reasoning with others, helping them see how a certain text should matter to them.

In particular, we have much to say about you as a writer. A key goal of your course, we assume, is to help you compose more effective texts of your own. By writing arguments about literature, you make it matter to others. Moreover, you learn about yourself as you analyze a literary text and negotiate other readers' views of it. We emphasize that, at its best, arguing is a process of inquiry for everyone involved. Both you and your audience may wind up changing your minds.

A WRITING ASSIGNMENT

We would like you to continue exploring the concept of "making literature matter" by writing about the following poem. First published in the summer 2001 issue of the magazine *DoubleTake*, the poem is by Michael Lohre, who teaches English at the Ohio State University's Marion campus. The poem's speaker expresses appreciation for James Wright's "Lying in a Hammock." That text and its author matter to her. Therefore, we suggest that you first reread Wright's poem and then keep it in mind as you turn to Lohre's. Throughout our book, we bring literary works together in pairs, trios, and other clusters, emphasizing that you can learn much about a text by comparing it with another.

MICHAEL LOHRE
Dear Michael, Love Pam

Just walked home for my 2-hour break
& I want to take a nap before I go back
at noon. Exhausted. Went to the Grain Bin
last night for a dance lesson in the Western Swing.
I learned to Barrel-turn and Dip, but I stayed out   5
too late. A chemical salesman disguised as my dance
partner asked me out to supper on Valentine's Day.
I'm going but am not thrilled over the guy.
My guts say don't trust a 44-year-old wearing
sneakers & sideburns. Hope you are doing better   10
than this old divorcée. Thank you for the letter,
pictures, and my goodness the poetry.
The one poem brought tears to my eyes —
the hammock one & he's wasted his life.
That and Charlie Walhof's death last Tuesday   15
had me thinking about making every day
count for something. Charlie was our local
entertainer who never found his star in Nashville
during his younger days but was giving music another
go now at 51. His Dodge van was halved by a train   20
in Maynard, MN, on a business trip that he'd hoped
might create an Opry near the lakes — in Alexandria, I think.
For the tourists. Charlie was a good man, Mike. Reminded
me of Dad. Same blue eyes, kind, & smile. He used to
hold my hand for a second after I passed his mail   25
to him. Lonely, I think. I wish you'd have
met him. I wonder . . . I know this will sound odd . . .
could you write something for Charlie? I guess that must
seem silly. I don't know how all that poetry stuff works.
Maybe if I sent a picture? That might not be the way   30
either. Somehow I just thought you might find the right
words? Anyway, I'm going to have to lie down now.
The kids and I miss you, Michael, and I want you to know
— I don't believe that James Wright wasted his life.   [2001]

In your writing, feel free to discuss anything that strikes you about this poem. You might address one or more of the following questions:

+ The poem is in the form of a letter—one that the poet's sister sent him or might have sent him. What specific characteristics of a letter appear here?
+ Pam asks Michael to write a poem for Charlie. She thinks that Michael, rather than she herself, "might find the right / words" to commemorate her dead friend. Yet evidently Michael has responded by turning Pam's own letter into a poem. What do you think the poet is suggesting about "how all that poetry stuff works"? Do *you* see his text as a poem? What definition of *poetry* are you working with as you answer this question?
+ When you compare this poem with James Wright's, which strike you more—similarities or differences?
+ In certain respects, this poem differs from a letter. Most notably, the sentence isn't the key unit. Like most poems, this one is divided into lines. In fact, many of the sentences in this poem run from one line to another (a process that is called *enjambment*). For instance, the first sentence spans three lines. What does the poet achieve by stretching sentences across lines? What is the effect of the last word of each line? (For instance, in dividing the first sentence into three lines, the poet ends line 1 with "break" and line 2 with "back." What effects do these words have? How do they relate to each other?)
+ Although the poem is in a single continuous stanza, it still can be divided into sections. What would you say are its main parts? Where does the poem shift from one subject to another? What are the effects of these shifts?
+ This poem refers much to work. Evidently Pam works as a mail deliverer—a job that leaves her "Exhausted." She reports that Charlie was killed "on a business trip." She even identifies her would-be date as "A chemical salesman." On a related note, Pam doesn't seem to have much time for leisure. She writes the letter on her break from work, and she must use some of this time to sleep. Furthermore, surely she is busy as a single mother. And yet Pam doesn't seem to fault James Wright for lying in a hammock. Quite the opposite: she likes his poem. Apparently it *matters* to her. Why, do you think? What conceivably leads Pam to say, "I don't believe that James Wright wasted his life"?

ADDITIONAL WRITING ASSIGNMENTS

1. Write a brief essay in which you explain what you value in literature by focusing on a literary work you have liked and why you like it. Don't worry about whether you are defining *literature* correctly. The aim of this exercise is for you to begin reviewing the values you hold as you read a work that you regard as literary.

2. Sometimes a literary work matters to you in one way, and when you read it again, it matters to you in another way. Write a brief essay in which you

discuss a work that did matter to you differently when you reread it. In what way did it matter to you the first time? What significance did it have for you later? What about your life had changed in the meantime? If you cannot think of a literary work, choose a film you have seen.

3. Write a brief essay in which you identify the values that a previous literature teacher of yours seemed to hold. Be sure to identify, too, ways in which the teacher expressed these values. You may want to bring up one or more specific events that took place in the teacher's classroom.

4. Many bookstores sell computer instruction manuals. Examine one of these. Do you consider it literature? Write a brief essay answering this question. Be sure to explain how you are defining *literature* and to refer to the manual's specific features.

5. Visit your school's bookstore or another bookstore. Spend at least half an hour looking at books in various sections of the store, noting how the publishers of these works try to make them matter. Look at such things as the books' physical formats, the language on their covers, and any introductory material they include. Write a brief essay in which you identify and evaluate the strategies for "mattering" used by at least three of these books.

6. Visit a Web site that includes readers' comments about particular works of fiction. A good example is www.amazon.com, a commercial online "bookstore." Another good site is Oprah Winfrey's, www.oprah.com, which features extensive exchanges about novels she has chosen for her "book club." At whatever site you visit, choose a novel or short-story collection that has attracted many reader comments. Write a brief essay in which you identify the values that seem reflected in the comments. In what respects does literature seem to matter to these readers? What do they evidently hope to find in it?

Diff between essay &
Argument.

Can't 2 issues in any poem
included

what words about
this reading

2

Reading and Thinking about Literature

This book presents many poems, short stories, plays, and essays. You may feel that you grasp some right away. Others, however, may puzzle you at first. If this happens, take heart. Few people make brilliant observations about a work of literature when they first read it. Examining literature is best seen as a process during which you gradually construct, test, revise, and refine your sense of a text. We think literature is most worth reading when it does challenge your current understanding of the world, pressing you to expand your knowledge and review your beliefs.

Here in Part One of the book, we focus on making several key points about the study of literature. At the same time, we present several literary texts, applying our points to them. These selections, too, deal with the same subject—in this case, work. We start off with this topic because we suspect it is very much on your mind. Though you may be in college for several reasons, probably a big one is to improve your chances to secure a good job. Because work has long been central to most people's lives, much literature has been written about it. Yet you may find that some of the selections we include in Part One complicate your views on this subject.

Part Two consists of five chapters filled with literary selections for you to read and think about. Each chapter's selections treat the same general subject and its various issues. In Chapter 12, the subject is "Living in Families"; in Chapter 13, "Teaching and Learning"; in Chapter 14, "Loving"; in Chapter 15, "Doing Justice"; and in Chapter 16, "Confronting Mortality." Within each chapter, the selections are arranged in clusters that address aspects of the chapter's subject.

A WRITING EXERCISE

Quite likely you have been employed in various capacities already. Without stopping, write for ten minutes about your work history. Note the jobs you have had, and explain how they have influenced your notion of the kind of career you want to have in the future. Don't feel that you have to pour forth terrific insights right away. This exercise, often called **freewriting**, simply helps you begin thinking about a subject.

13

Approaching Literature

If any of the selections in this book puzzle you, keep in mind that you need not read in isolation, relying solely on yourself. If you have trouble understanding a literary work, try consulting other readers. In the course you are taking, you will have plenty of chances to exchange insights with your classmates and teacher. All these people are resources for your thinking. Encourage them to see you as a resource, too.

Often, the process of reading literature is collective in another sense. Consciously or not, you may compare the text you are focused on with those you have previously read. By recalling your experience with other texts, you grow more able to identify typical features of the present one, along with ways it is distinctive. Because such comparisons are useful, we seek to encourage them throughout this book. This is why we group texts together and invite you to compare works within each cluster.

Still another good way to ponder a literary work is to write about it. Again, do not feel obliged to churn out a polished, profound **analysis** of the text right away. If reading literature is best seen as a process, so too is writing about it. To begin your study of a work, you might freewrite in a notebook or journal. Then you might try extended drafts in which you experiment with sustained analysis. Only later might you attempt a whole formal paper on the text, aiming to show others that you have arrived at a solid, credible view of it. In each of these activities, your thinking might be helped by class discussions. Perhaps classmates will even be able to give you direct feedback on your writing, including the freewriting you have just done.

In your course, you will read many of the literary selections we present. Naturally, we hope that you will find them emotionally engaging as well as thought-provoking. Moreover, we hope the course helps you become a more learned and thoughtful reader of whatever literature you read later. But we have yet another goal. With the texts we present, the background information we provide, the questions we raise, and the assignments we suggest, we seek to help you become a more thoughtful and effective writer.

Probably you have already taken courses that required you to write a great deal. On your own, perhaps you have enjoyed writing poems, short stories, plays, essays, or other kinds of texts. Actually, almost everyone does some kind of writing outside of school, whether it's merely a letter or a full-fledged essay. Nevertheless, you may hesitate to call yourself a writer out of a belief that your writing is often flawed. Yet everyone brings strengths to the act of writing, and we hope this course helps you recognize yours. While obviously the course is a chance for you to improve as a writer, believing that you deserve to be called a writer is an important step in your growth.

A WRITING EXERCISE

Introduce yourself to the rest of the class through a letter that describes your career as a writer. You might recall particular works you have written and memorable writing teachers you have had. You also might identify whatever kinds of writing you like to do, your current strengths as a writer, and aspects of your writing that you hope to strengthen in this course.

Thinking Critically: The Value of Argument

Our writing assignments are designed to help you reflect on the literature you read. Although these assignments are varied, mostly we encourage you to argue about literature. We do so for three reasons. First, the term **argument** refers to a kind of talk as well as a kind of writing; thus, focusing on this term can help you relate your own written work to discussions in class. Second, you will read a work of literature with greater direction and purpose if you are working toward the goal of constructing arguments about it. Finally, when you argue, you learn a lot, because you have to ponder things you may have taken for granted as well as things unfamiliar to you.

Specifically, *arguing* is a process in which you identify a subject of current or possible debate; you take a position on that subject; you analyze why you view the subject the way you do; and you try to persuade others that your view is worth sharing or is at least reasonable. Often the process of arguing is not straightforward. Just when you think you have decided how you feel about a subject, class discussion may lead you to change your position or shift to a completely different topic. Whatever the case, to argue well means to engage in self-examination. Also, it means attending to the world around you: especially to the ways that other people think differently from you.

For many, *argument* is a negative term. Perhaps it makes you think of unpleasant shouting matches you have been in or witnessed — times when people have bitterly disagreed with one another and refused to compromise. Almost everyone has experienced arguments of this sort. Moreover, they are a kind of argument that the media promote. On talk radio, hosts as well as callers are often brutally argumentative, mixing strong opinion with outright insult. Similarly, television's political talk shows regularly become sheer quarrels; on *Crossfire*, *The McLaughlin Group*, and *The Capital Gang* panelists fall again and again into nasty, noisy debate. Spats are even more spectacular on daytime talk shows like Jerry Springer's, which invite friends and family members to clash in public on such high-voltage topics as "You Stole Him from Me and I Want Him Back!" On occasion, the participants turn from words to fists. No wonder many people see argument as fierce competition, even as a form of war.

A WRITING EXERCISE

Although this book emphasizes arguments about literature, a good way to start thinking about argument is to consider how it may come up in everyday situations. Read the following excerpt, which is about work in fast-food restaurants and appears in Eric Schlosser's recent book on this industry, *Fast Food Nation: The Dark Side of the American Meal.* Then write an informal essay in which you identify one or two elements of Schlosser's piece that you suspect people will disagree about. Examine not only *what* Schlosser is reporting but also *how* he apparently feels about what he describes. Feel free to express and support your own views of the elements on which you focus.

Every Saturday Elisa Zamot gets up at 5:15 in the morning. It's a struggle, and her head feels groggy as she steps into the shower. Her little sisters, Cookie and Sabrina, are fast asleep in their beds. By 5:30, Elisa's showered, done her hair, and put on her McDonald's uniform. She's sixteen, bright-eyed and olive-skinned, pretty and petite, ready for another day of work. Elisa's mother usually drives her the half-mile or so to the restaurant, but sometimes Elisa walks, leaving home before the sun rises. Her family's modest townhouse sits beside a busy highway on the south side of Colorado Springs, in a largely poor and working-class neighborhood. Throughout the day, sounds of traffic fill the house, the steady whoosh of passing cars. But when Elisa heads for work, the streets are quiet, the sky's still dark, and the lights are out in the small houses and rental apartments along the road.

When Elisa arrives at McDonald's, the manager unlocks the door and lets her in. Sometimes the husband-and-wife cleaning crew are just finishing up. More often, it's just Elisa and the manager in the restaurant, surrounded by an empty parking lot. For the next hour or so, the two of them get everything ready. They turn on the ovens and grills. They go downstairs into the basement and get food and supplies for the morning shift. They get the paper cups, wrappers, cardboard containers, and packets of condiments. They step into the big freezer and get the frozen bacon, the frozen pancakes, and the frozen cinnamon rolls. They get the frozen hash browns, the frozen biscuits, the frozen McMuffins. They get the cartons of scrambled egg mix and orange juice mix. They bring the food upstairs and start preparing it before any customers appear, thawing some things in the microwave and cooking other things on the grill. They put the cooked food in special cabinets to keep it warm.

The restaurant opens for business at seven o'clock, and for the next hour or so, Elisa and the manager hold down the fort, handling all the orders. As the place starts to get busy, other employees arrive. Elisa works behind the counter. She takes orders and hands food to customers from breakfast through lunch. When she finally walks home, after seven hours of standing at a cash register, her feet hurt. She's wiped out. She comes through the front door, flops onto the living room couch, and turns on the TV. And the next morning she gets up at 5:15 again and starts the same routine.

Up and down Academy Boulevard, along South Nevada, Circle Drive, and Woodman Road, teenagers like Elisa run the fast food restaurants of Colorado Springs. Fast food kitchens often seem like a scene from *Bugsy Malone*, a film in which all the actors are children pretending to be adults. No other industry in the United States has a workforce so dominated by adolescents. About two-thirds of the nation's fast food workers are under the age of twenty. Teenagers open the fast food outlets in the morning, close them at night, and keep them going at all hours in between. Even the managers and assistant managers are sometimes in their late teens. Unlike Olympic gymnastics — an activity in which teenagers consistently perform at a higher level than adults — there's nothing about the work in a fast food kitchen that requires young employees. Instead of relying upon a small, stable, well-paid, and well-trained workforce, the fast food industry seeks out part-time, unskilled workers who are willing to accept low pay. Teenagers have been the perfect candidates for these jobs, not only because they are less expensive to hire than adults, but also because their youthful inexperience makes them easier to control. (67–68)

Although many people view argument as war, we encourage you to argue in a more positive sense. In any meaning of the term, to *argue* is to disagree with others or to set forth a view that you suspect not everyone holds. But argument need not be a competition in which you aim to prove that only you are right. For one thing, at times you might collaborate with someone else in arguing a position. Also, in an argument you can concede that several views on the subject are possible, even as you develop your own position. You are in fact more likely to persuade your audience if you treat fairly opinions other than yours. Furthermore, successful arguers establish common ground with their audience; they identify and honor at least some of the beliefs that their readers or listeners hold.

Keep in mind, too, that participants in an argument ought to learn from one another. If you take seriously other people's responses to your position, you will find yourself reexamining why and how you express that view. As we have already noted, you may even change your mind. Above all, we hope you will see argument as *inquiry*, a process in which you think hard about your beliefs rather than just declare them.

Responding to Four Poems about Work

As we discuss the process of arguing about literature, we mention arguments that might be made about the following set of four poems, each of which features a speaker reflecting on his or her work experience. Also, we stress how useful it can be for you to **compare** these texts. Indeed, we continue to emphasize comparison in subsequent chapters. As you read each poem, take a few moments to reflect on the questions we ask after each one, perhaps jotting down your responses to keep in mind as you read the rest of the chapter.

Three of the poems in this set are by contemporary writers. The first poem, however, is from the eighteenth century. It is a famous one by William Blake (1757–1827), who, though dismissed by many of his contemporaries as eccentric and even mad, is now regarded as a major figure in British Romanticism. Besides being a writer, Blake was a painter and engraver, lavishly illustrating his own editions of his poems. These volumes included his 1789 collection *Songs of Innocence*, where "The Chimney Sweeper" first appeared.

WILLIAM BLAKE
The Chimney Sweeper

When my mother died I was very young,
And my father sold me while yet my tongue
Could scarcely cry "'weep! 'weep! 'weep! 'weep!"
So your chimneys I sweep, and in soot I sleep.

There's little Tom Dacre, who cried when his head,   5
That curled like a lamb's back, was shaved: so I said
"Hush, Tom! never mind it, for when your head's bare
You know that the soot cannot spoil your white hair."

And so he was quiet, and that very night,
As Tom was a-sleeping, he had such a sight!   10
That thousands of sweepers, Dick, Joe, Ned, and Jack,
Were all of them locked up in coffins of black.

And by came an Angel who had a bright key,
And he opened the coffins and set them all free;
Then down a green plain leaping, laughing, they run,   15
And wash in the river, and shine in the sun.

Then naked and white, all their bags left behind,
They rise upon clouds and sport in the wind;
And the Angel told Tom, if he'd be a good boy,
He'd have God for his father, and never want joy.   20

And so Tom awoke; and we rose in the dark,
And got with our bags and our brushes to work.
Though the morning was cold, Tom was happy and warm;
So if all do their duty they need not fear harm.   [1789]

THINKING ABOUT THE TEXT

1. Blake wrote his poem at a time when many children in London indeed
   labored in filth as chimney sweepers and were even sold by family members
   for this service. What are possible counterparts to such child workers today?

2. The speaker of the poem tells us a dream related to him by Tom, another
   chimney sweeper, which the speaker proceeded to interpret. Is the poem
   more about Tom, or more about the speaker, or about both of them
   equally?

3. Tom's dream is a religious vision. To what extent do you think Blake himself endorses it?

4. At the end, the speaker seems resigned to his lot, but what's *your* view of
   it? How inclined are you to agree with the last line: "So if all do their duty
   they need not fear harm"?

The next poem is by Stephen Dunn (b. 1939). In addition to being Trustee Fellow in the Arts and Professor of Creative Writing at Richard Stockton College of New Jersey, Dunn is a much-published poet. In 2001 he won the Pulitzer Prize for his sixteenth book of verse, *Different Hours*. The following poem is from his earlier collection, *Work and Love* (1981).

STEPHEN DUNN

Hard Work

1956

At the Coke plant, toting empties
in large crates to the assembly line,
I envied my friends away at camp,
but the money was good
and hard work, my father said,   5
was how you became a man.
I saw a man for no special reason
piss into a coke bottle
and put it back onto the line.
After a while I, too, hated   10
the bottles enough to break some
deliberately, and smile
and share with the other workers
a petty act of free will.
When I came home at night my body   15
hurt with that righteous hurt
men have brought home for centuries,
the hurt that demands
food and solicitation, that makes men
separate, lost.   20
I quit before the summer was over,
exercised the prerogatives of my class
by playing ball all August
and spent the money I'd earned
on Barbara Winokur, who was beautiful.   25
And now I think my job
must be phased out, a machine must
do it, though someone for sure
still does the hard work of boredom
and that person can't escape,   30
goes there each morning
and comes home each night
and probably has no opportunity

to say who he is
through destruction, some big   35
mechanical eye watching him
or some time and motion man
or just something hesitant, some father
or husband, in himself.   [1981]

THINKING ABOUT THE TEXT

1. Evidently the speaker in this poem is recollecting a job he held several years ago. What may have provoked him to remember it now?

2. He indicates that in part, he took the job in obedience to his father's notion that "hard work . . . / was how you became a man." What meanings of *manhood* does this poem touch on? What possible definitions of *hard work*?

3. On the job, a fellow worker and eventually the speaker himself rebelled "through destruction." In what ways, if any, have you witnessed or done the same sort of thing at work?

4. Although at first the speaker refers to his vandalism as "a petty act of free will," later in the poem he seems to mourn the lost "opportunity" for such "destruction." How do you explain this apparent change in attitude?

The next poem is by Dorianne Laux (b. 1952), a native of Maine whose ancestry includes Irish, French, and Algonquin Indian strands. This selection comes from her second collection of poetry, *What We Carry* (1994). Laux's other volumes include *Awake* (1990) and *Smoke* (2000), as well as a book coauthored with Kim Addonnizio, *The Poet's Companion: A Guide to the Pleasures of Writing Poetry* (1997). Like the speaker in the poem, Laux has been a sanatorium cook, gas station manager, maid, and donut holer. Presently she is a professor of creative writing at the University of Oregon.

DORIANNE LAUX
What I Wouldn't Do

The only job I didn't like, quit
after the first shift, was selling
subscriptions to *TV Guide* over the phone.
Before that it was fast food, all
the onion rings I could eat, handing   5
sacks of deep fried burritos through
the sliding window, the hungry hands
grabbing back. And at the laundromat,
plucking bright coins from a palm
or pressing them into one, kids   10

screaming from the bathroom and twenty
dryers on high. Cleaning houses was fine,
polishing the knick-knacks of the rich.
I liked holding the hand-blown glass bell
from Czechoslovakia up to the light,   15
the jewelled clapper swinging lazily
from side to side, its foreign,
A-minor ping. I drifted, an itinerant,
from job to job, the sanatorium
where I pureed peas and carrots   20
and stringy beets, scooped them,
like pudding, onto flesh-colored
plastic plates, or the gas station
where I dipped the ten-foot measuring stick
into the hole in the blacktop,   25
pulled it up hand over hand
into the twilight, dripping
its liquid gold, pink-tinged.
I liked the donut shop best, 3 AM,
alone in the kitchen, surrounded   30
by sugar and squat mounds of dough,
the flashing neon sign strung from wire
behind the window, gilding my white uniform
yellow, then blue, then drop-dead red.
It wasn't that I hated calling them, hour   35
after hour, stuck in a booth with a list
of strangers' names, dialing their numbers
with the eraser end of a pencil and them
saying hello. It was that moment
of expectation, before I answered back,   40
the sound of their held breath,
their disappointment when they realized
I wasn't who they thought I was,
the familiar voice, or the voice they loved
and had been waiting all day to hear.   [1994]   45

THINKING ABOUT THE TEXT

1. Make a list of the jobs you've had, and compare your list with the speaker's. To what extent have your work experiences been similar?

2. The speaker seems to move chronologically through her work history. What, if anything, do some of her jobs have in common? What does the fact that she "liked the donut shop best" say about her?

3. Although the speaker begins by referring to "The only job I didn't like," she postpones explaining it until she abruptly returns to it and spends the

poem's last eleven lines on it. What is the effect of the delay? Again, what does her dislike of this particular job say about her?

4. What would you say to someone who argued that the speaker deserves no sympathy at the end because telemarketers are a nuisance?

The next poem is by Maura Stanton (b. 1946), a professor of creative writing at Indiana University, Bloomington, who has published collections of short stories as well as verse. Her volumes of poetry include *Snow on Snow* (1975), *Tales of the Supernatural* (1988), *Life Among the Trolls* (1998), and *Glacier Wine* (2001). The following selection first appeared in *Atlantic Monthly* and then became part of Stanton's second book of poems, *Cries of Swimmers* (1984).

MAURA STANTON
Shoplifters

I'd smoke in the freezer
among the hooked beefsides,
wondering about the shoplifters
who wept when the manager's
nephew tugged them to his office.   5
He made me search the women.
I found twenty cans of tuna fish
under the skirt of a mother whose son
drowned in a flash flood out west.
Now he haunted her,   10
begging for mouthfuls of fish.
Candles fell from a nun's sleeves.
She meant to light the route
for tobogganists on the convent hill.
Two old sisters emptied beans   15
from their big apron pockets,
claiming they cured rheumatism.
Soon I recognized snow
drifting across faces at the door,
watching in the round mirrors   20
the way hands snatched out
unhesitatingly at onions.
In the mirrors everyone stole,
buttoning coats again, looking
once over their shoulders   25
while eggs bulged in a mitten
or salt sifted from their hems.
Did they think me an angel

when I glided in my white uniform
down the soap aisle, preventing   30
some clutch of fingers?
An old man I caught last year
stuffing baloney down his trousers
lived alone in a dim bedroom.
The manager said cupcake papers   35
blew across his floor—
hundreds, yellow, white & pink.
Now he peers through the window,
watching me bag groceries
for hours until my hands sweat.   [1984]   40

THINKING ABOUT THE TEXT

1. This poem seems to be about not only shoplifters but also the speaker's attitude toward them. Does her attitude change, or does it seem consistent throughout the poem? Support your answer with specific details.

2. How much do *you* sympathize with the shoplifters depicted here? Again, note details that affect your attitude toward them.

3. What, if anything, do the shoplifters have in common?

4. In what ways is this poem about acts of watching? What moral problems do these acts raise?

5. The poem ends with the speaker's hands sweating. Why do you suppose Stanton chose to end with this particular image?

A WRITING EXERCISE

Once you have read the four poems as a group, write brief responses to at least two. You might jot down things you especially notice about them, feelings they evoke in you, and questions you have about them. You might also note your own work experiences that they lead you to recall. With each poem, write for ten minutes without stopping. Again, this useful exercise is usually called freewriting.

THE ELEMENTS OF ARGUMENT

We turn now to specific elements of argument. An argument involves six basic elements. When you argue, you attempt to **persuade** an **audience** to accept your **claims** regarding an **issue** by presenting **evidence** and relying on **warrants**. The boldfaced words are key to this book; we mention them often. Here we explain what we mean by each, beginning with *issue* and then moving to *claims*, *persuasion*, *audience*, *evidence*, and *warrants*. Throughout our discussion, we refer to the poems by Blake, Dunn, Laux, and Stanton.

Issues

An **issue** is something about which people have disagreed or might disagree. Even as you read a text, you can try to guess what features of it will lead to disagreements in class. You may sense that your own reaction to certain aspects of the text is heavily influenced by your background and values, which other students may not share. Some parts of the text may leave you with conflicting ideas or mixed feelings, as if half of you disagrees with the other half. At moments like these, you come to realize what topics are issues for you, and next you can urge the rest of your class to see these topics as issues, too.

An issue is best defined as a question with no obvious, immediate answer. Thus, you can start identifying issues by noting questions that occur to you as you read. Perhaps this question-posing approach to texts is new for you. Often readers demand that a text be clear, and they get annoyed if it leaves them puzzled. Of course, certain writing ought to be immediately clear in meaning; think of operating instructions on a plane's emergency doors. But the value of a literary work often lies in the work's complexities, which can lead readers to reexamine their own ways of perceiving the world. Also, your discussions and papers about literature are likely to be most useful when they go beyond the obvious to deal with more challenging matters. When your class begins talking about a work, you may feel obliged to stay quiet if you have no firm statements to make. But you can contribute a lot by bringing up questions that occurred to you as you read. Especially worth raising are questions that continue to haunt you.

In the case of William Blake's "The Chimney Sweeper," one possible issue concerns its ending. From Tom's dream of the chimney sweepers' release, the speaker concludes that "if all do their duty they need not fear harm." Should readers accept this interpretation, or is there a better way of understanding both the dream and the sweepers' grueling daily life? A possible issue with Stephen Dunn's "Hard Work" concerns its numerous references to manhood. To what extent are the ideas and feelings expressed in the poem indeed gender-specific? An issue related to Dorianne Laux's poem has to do with its form. Though the speaker begins by referring to "The only job I didn't like," she waits until the end of the poem to elaborate on the job. What conceivably is the effect of postponing such details? An issue concerning Maura Stanton's poem involves the speaker's attitude toward the shoplifters. To what extent does she sympathize with them?

You may feel unable to answer questions like these. But again, you achieve much when you simply formulate questions and bring them up in class. As other students help you ponder them, you will grow better able to explore issues through writing as well as through conversation.

You are more likely to come up with questions about a text if you do not assume that the text had to be written exactly the way it was. For every move the writer made, alternatives existed. Blake might have presented his own interpretation of the dream more directly instead of having his poem's speaker be another chimney sweeper. Dunn might have consistently referred to all humanity instead of referring so much to men. Laux might have immediately provided details of the unpleasant job. Stanton might have had her poem's speaker express clearer judgments about the shoplifters. When you bear in mind writers' options, you grow more inclined to explore why they made the choices they did and what the effects of those choices may be.

You will recognize writers' options more easily if you compare their texts with others. As we have said, we invite comparison throughout this book. For instance, Blake's mention of an angel is more apt to strike you as a calculated decision if you note Stanton's use of this figure. In Blake's poem, Tom dreams of an angel who frees him and other chimney sweepers. At least within Tom's dream, then, the angel is real. In Stanton's poem, the speaker wonders if would-be shoplifters saw her as an angel when she stopped them from stealing. This text, then, depicts at most a *metaphorical* angel. Of course, in both cases we can ultimately see the angel image as a projection of human hopes. Nevertheless, Blake's poem first confronts us with an angel's literal presence, whereas Stanton's poem does not.

Next we identify ten kinds of issues that arise in literature courses. Our list will help you detect the issues that come up in your class and discover others to bring up in discussions or in your writing. The list does not include every kind of issue; you may think of others. Moreover, you may find that an issue can fit into more than one of the categories we name. But when you do have an issue that seems hard to classify, try nevertheless to assign it to a single category, if only for the time being. You will then have some initial guidance for your reading, class discussions, and writing. If you later feel that the issue belongs to another category, you can shift your focus.

1. *Issues of fact.* Rarely does a work of literature provide complete information about its characters and events. Rather, literature is usually marked by what literary theorist Wolfgang Iser calls "gaps," moments when certain facts are omitted or obscured. At such times, readers may give various answers to the question, What is happening in this text? For instance, Dunn's poem "Hard Work" does not specify the speaker's present circumstances. Although we learn some of the thoughts he has "now," we do not know what in his current life prompted him to recall a job he had back in 1956. Of course, readers tackle questions of fact only if they suspect that the answers will affect their overall view of a text. Imagine a reader who believes that Dunn's speaker recalls his 1956 job because he also hates his present one. Imagine a second reader who supposes the speaker's recollection is a result of current insecurities about his masculinity. How might these two readers see the whole poem differently because of their different assumptions?

2. *Issues of theme.* You may be familiar with the term **theme** from other literature courses. By *theme* critics usually mean the main claim that an author seems to be making with his or her text. Sometimes a theme is defined in terms of a single word — for example, *work* or *love*. But such words are really mere topics. Identifying the topics addressed by a text can be a useful way of starting to analyze that text, and later in Part One we list several topics that currently preoccupy literary studies. A text's theme, however, is best seen as an assertion that you need at least one whole sentence to express.

With many texts, an issue of theme arises because readers can easily disagree over what the text's main idea is. In literature classes, such disagreements often occur, in part because literary works tend to express their themes indirectly. Readers of Stanton's poem may give several different answers to the question, What is Stanton ultimately saying? Perhaps some readers will take her to imply that our dislike of crime often conflicts with our sense of the criminal's physical or emotional neediness. Other readers may conclude that her poem is much more than a list of petty crimes and instead is a call for recognizing how isolated many human beings are.

If you try to express a text's theme, avoid making it a statement so general that it could apply to an enormous number of works. Arguing that Stanton's theme is "Refrain from quickly judging others" hardly gets at the details of her poem. On the other hand, do not let the text's details restrict you so much that you wind up making the theme seem relevant only to a tiny group. If you argue that Stanton's theme is "Store employees shouldn't let managers make them spy on customers," then the many readers who are *not* store employees will wonder why they should care. In short, try to express themes as midlevel generalizations. With Stanton's poem, one possibility is "When people do wrong out of desperation, we may sympathize with them, but our compassion may leave us feeling conflicted rather than purely angelic." A statement like this seems both attentive to Stanton's specific text and applicable to a large portion of humanity. Of course, you are free to challenge this version of Stanton's theme by proposing an alternative. Moreover, even if you do accept this statement as her theme, you are then free to decide whether it is a sound observation. Identifying a theme is one thing; evaluating it is another.

Sometimes an author will appear to state the theme explicitly in his or her text. Such moments are worth studying as you try to determine what the theme is. For instance, you may believe that Blake's theme is his concluding line: "So if all do their duty they need not fear harm." Yet a poem's author may not share the views of its speaker; perhaps Blake disagrees with the chimney sweeper's declaration. Recognize, too, that a theme ties together various parts of a text. Focusing on a single passage, even if it seems thematic, may lead you to ignore other passages that a statement of theme should encompass. With Blake's poem, someone may argue that the last line does *not* state the theme, for it neglects the hard, dirty labor that these children must perform.

Often you will sense a work's theme but still have to decide whether to state it as an **observation** or as a **recommendation**. You would be doing the first if, for example, you expressed Stanton's theme as we did above: "When people do wrong out of desperation, we may sympathize with them, but our compassion may leave us feeling conflicted rather than purely angelic." You would be doing the second if you said Stanton's theme is "One should consider criminals' circumstances rather than automatically condemn them." Indeed, when they depict a theme as a recommendation, people often use a word like *should*. Neither way of expressing a theme is necessarily better than the other. But notice that each way conjures up a particular image of the author. Reporting Stanton's theme as an observation suggests that she is writing as a psychologist, a philosopher, or some other analyst of human nature. Reporting her theme as a recommendation suggests that she is writing as a teacher, preacher, manager, or coach: someone who is telling her readers what to do. Your decision about how to phrase a theme will depend in part on which of these two images of the author you think appropriate.

You risk obscuring the intellectual, emotional, and stylistic richness of a text if you insist on reducing it to a single message. Try stating the text's theme as a problem for which there is no easy solution. This way you will suggest that the text is, in fact, complex. For instance, if you incorporate into Stanton's theme the idea that "our compassion may leave us feeling conflicted," you position yourself to address various elements of her poem.

Also weigh the possibility that a text is conveying more than one theme. If you plan to associate the text with any theme at all, you might refer to *a* theme of the text rather than *the* theme of the text. To be sure, your use of the term *theme* would still have implications. Above all, you would still be suggesting that you have identified one of the text's major points. Subsequently, you might have to defend this claim, showing how the point you have identified is indeed central to the text.

Issues of theme have loomed large in literary studies. We hope that you will find them useful to pursue. But because references to theme are so common in literary studies, students sometimes forget that there are other kinds of issues. As you move through this list, you may find some that interest you more.

3. *Issues of definition.*   In arguments about literature, issues of **definition** arise most often when readers try to decide what an author means by a particular word. Look at the ending of Dunn's poem, where the speaker suggests that his present-day counterpart holds back from rebelling at work because of "some father / or husband, in himself." What, conceivably, does Dunn mean here by *father* and *husband*? Evidently we are to consider more than these figures' official family roles, associating such men with particular qualities. But which? Perhaps Dunn wants us to see fathers and husbands as horribly domineering patriarchs, who inhibit us from engaging in worthwhile revolt. Perhaps Dunn respects these figures and wants us to see them as enforcing a desirable prudence. Or perhaps Dunn is ambivalent toward them, believing they blend tyranny with wisdom.

An issue of definition looms especially when a word or phrase appears to shift meaning as the text proceeds. A good example is the very title of Dunn's poem, "Hard Work." When this term first appears in the poem itself, it seems to refer to arduous physical labor; at least, this is what the speaker's father seems to have had in mind when declaring that "hard work . . . / was how you became a man." Later in the poem, though, comes a reference to "the hard work of boredom," which associates the term *hard work* with a tedium that seems mostly psychological. We can even identify the main subject of the poem as sons' struggles to fit their fathers' standards of manhood, in which case *hard work* takes on yet another sense.

4. *Issues of symbolism.*   In literary studies, an issue of **symbolism** is often a question about the meaning and purpose of a particular image. Blake's poem is

filled with evocative images, including soot, a lamb, white hair, black coffins, an angel, a green plain, a river, the sun, nakedness, clouds, and the dark. What do you usually associate with each? What new associations, if any, does the poem prompt you to make? An issue of symbolism is also involved if you find yourself wondering whether some element of a text is symbolic in the first place. At the start of Dunn's poem, the speaker reports that his job was "toting empties." In what ways might this mention of emptiness relate to other things in the text?

5. *Issues of pattern.*   With issues of **pattern**, you observe how a text is organized. More precisely, you try to determine how certain parts of the text are related to other parts of it. But keep in mind the meaning and purpose of any pattern you find, especially since readers may disagree about the pattern's significance. Also ponder the implications of any moment when a text *breaks* with a pattern it has been following. Disruptions of a pattern may be as important as the pattern itself.

Many poems exhibit patterns in their rhymes and stanza lengths. Blake's poem is six stanzas, with four lines each. In each of the first four stanzas, the first two lines rhyme, and the next two lines rhyme in a different way. The last two stanzas slightly break with this pattern. They feature what literary critics term **off-rhymes**. In stanza 5, "wind" does not exactly rhyme with "behind." In stanza 6, "work" does not exactly rhyme with "dark," and the same goes for "harm" and "warm." Worth considering, then, is the relation between the form and content of these last stanzas. What about their ideas might have led Blake to make their rhymes a bit awkward?

Another common pattern in literature is **repetition**. Perhaps you have noticed already that the speaker of Laux's poem "What I Didn't Like" refers often to acts performed with hands as she recites her work history. She remembers "handing / sacks of deep fried burritos through / the sliding window, the hungry hands / grabbing back." She recalls "plucking bright coins from a palm / or pressing them into one." She "liked holding the hand-blown glass bell / from Czechoslovakia up to the light." At the sanatorium, she "scooped"; at the gas station, she "dipped the ten-foot measuring stick / into the hole in the blacktop, / pulled it up hand over hand." What do you think Laux aims to convey with this chain of references? Even when repetition is easy to detect, readers may have different ideas about its function. The issue then becomes not so much whether the author is repeating words but how this repetition contributes to the work as a whole.

Stanton's poem also refers many times to acts of touching. Such acts are committed by the shoplifters, including those whose "hands snatched out / unhesitatingly at onions." In addition, the manager's nephew "tugged" the would-be thieves and made the speaker "search" them. Furthermore, much to her distress, she found herself "preventing / some clutch of fingers." Continuing this pattern right to the end, the poem concludes with the speaker's acknowledgment that "my hands sweat." Yet while Stanton and Laux resort to a rather similar pattern, perhaps it functions differently in their respective poems. What do you think?

Again, just as important to consider is any divergence from a pattern. Toward the end of her poem, for example, Laux moves away from an emphasis on touch-

ing. The job that Laux's speaker enjoyed most left her "alone in the kitchen"—
that is, without human contact. But next we learn that the job she hated most did
not involve touching at all. Rather, she telephoned people, "dialing their numbers / with the eraser end of a pencil." If any holding occurred on the job, it was
done by the people she called, who disturbed her when they responded with
"held breath." What do you conclude from the poem's climactic shift in *this*
direction?

A text's apparent oppositions are also patterns to be debated. An example in
Laux's poem is the opposition that the speaker establishes when she notes her
most favorite and least favorite jobs. In one respect, these jobs resemble each
other: both deemphasize the human touch. How, then, do you explain the
speaker's quite different attitudes toward them? Maybe the key difference is that
the phone job cruelly frustrated people who longed for human warmth.

6. *Issues of evaluation.*   Consciously or unconsciously, **evaluation** always
plays a central role in reading. When you read a work of literature, you evaluate
its ideas and the actions of its characters. You judge, too, the views you assume
the author is promoting. Moreover, you gauge the artistic quality of the text.

Specifically, you engage in three kinds of evaluation as you read. One kind is
philosophical: you decide whether a particular idea or action is wise. Another
kind is *ethical:* you decide whether an idea or action is morally good. The third
kind is *aesthetic:* you decide whether parts of the text, or the work as a whole, succeed as art. Another reader may disagree with your criteria for wisdom, morality,
and art; people's standards often differ. It is not surprising, then, that in the study
of literature issues of evaluation come up frequently.

As we suggested earlier, philosophical differences may arise when Blake's
speaker claims, "So if all do their duty they need not fear harm." Some readers
may like his attitude, others may accuse him of being too passive, and others may
disagree with his view but feel that a child can perceive only so much. Different
ethical judgments may arise as readers contemplate the society evoked by the
poem. While few readers approve of all child labor, some may condone certain
uses of it. And even those readers who would ban it may disagree about what kind
of economy best prevents it. Some may look to capitalism for salvation, while others may condemn capitalism as the most exploitative of all economic systems.
Finally, different aesthetic judgments are possible as readers decide the artistic
value of Blake's poem. Some readers may simply be stirred by the poignancy of
the chimney sweepers' life. Others may enjoy the poem's interplay of images.
Still others may find the poem interesting chiefly because its speaker is a child, so
that we must guess what the poem's adult author really believes. Meanwhile,
another group of readers may dislike the poem for the very same reasons.

Sometimes you may have trouble distinguishing the three types of judgments from each other. Philosophical evaluation, ethical evaluation, and aesthetic evaluation can overlap. Probably all three operate in the mind of a reader
who disagrees with the chimney sweeper's concluding view, believes that Blake
shares that view, and therefore dislikes the whole poem. Keep in mind, however,
that you can admire many aspects of a literary work even if you disagree with

ideas you see the author promoting. Again, someone may relish the imagery of
"The Chimney Sweeper" regardless of its author's thinking.

If you disputed the artistic value of Blake's poem, you would be challenging
countless admirers of it. Increasingly, though, the status of Blake's poem and
other literary classics is being questioned. Many scholars argue that literary studies have focused too much on white male authors. They refuse to assume that
Blake's works are great and universally relevant; they criticize the long neglect of
women and minority authors. Yet other people continue to prize more well-
known writers such as Blake. The result is ongoing debate about whose works
should be taught in the classroom.

7. Issues of historical and cultural context. Because works of literature are
written by people living in particular times and places, issues of **historical and
cultural context** arise. Eventually these works may engage a wide variety of readers, including members of much-later generations and inhabitants of distant
lands. Yet these works often continue to reflect the circumstances of their creation. You can tell just by the title of Blake's poem "The Chimney Sweeper" that
he wrote at a time when a certain form of child labor was more common in England than it now is. With this fact in mind, you might address the question, To
what extent does the situation described in this poem apply to more than just
chimney sweepers? Although the poems of Dunn, Laux, and Stanton seem much
closer to the present, you can examine from a historical perspective the specific
aspects of contemporary life that each of these texts mentions. For example,
Dunn's poem explicitly notes that a certain kind of assembly-line job in 1956 no
longer exists nowadays. Therefore, you might address the question, What contemporary forms of "hard work" does Dunn conceivably have in mind as he looks
back to the 1950s? Meanwhile, phone jobs like the one mentioned in Laux's
poem have proliferated, especially now that computers enable salespeople to ring
potential customers easily. Therefore, an issue to address is, To what extent does
Laux's poem suggest that this kind of job is the wave of the future?

We provide some background for each literary work we present, thereby
helping you begin to situate it historically and culturally. In Appendix 2, we
explain how to keep putting literature in context, especially by doing research in
the library and on the World Wide Web. For now, we want to emphasize that
contextualizing a work involves more than just piling up facts about its origin. In
the study of literature, often issues of historical and cultural context are issues of
relevance. The questions become, *Which* facts about a work's creation are important for readers to know? and *How* would awareness of these facts help readers
better understand the work? For instance, while readers can inform themselves
about a particular author's life, they may disagree about the extent to which a
given text by that author is autobiographical.

Perhaps you like to connect a literary work with its author's own life. Since
all three of the contemporary poems we have been discussing use the first person
("I"), you may feel that they strongly invite you to make such a link. Yet you are
almost always engaging in a debatable move when you assert that a work is thoroughly autobiographical. Among other things, you risk overlooking aspects of the

text that depart from the author's own experiences, impressions, and beliefs. Like the three contemporary poems, certain texts do seem windows into the author's life. We are not urging you to refrain from ever making this connection. Rather, we are pointing out that whatever links you draw may be the subject of debate.

It is also important to note that the term *history* can be defined in various ways. When you refer to a work's historical context, you need to clarify what you have in mind. After all, you may be examining one or more of the following: (1) the life of the work's author; (2) the time period in which it was written; (3) any time period mentioned within the text; (4) its subsequent reception, including responses to it by later generations; (5) the forms in which the work has been published, which may involve changes in its spelling, punctuation, wording, and overall appearance.

8. *Issues of genre.* So far we have been identifying categories of issues. Issues of **genre** are *about* categorization, for they involve efforts to determine what *kind* of text a particular work is. If you were asked to identify the genres of the works by Blake, Dunn, Laux, and Stanton, you might logically call each a poem. But you do not have to stop there. You can try to classify each poem more precisely, aiming for a term that better sums up its specific content and form. Issues of genre often arise with such further classification. And as you come up with more exact labels for the poems, other readers may label them differently. Because Blake's speaker is obviously trying to soothe the distress that he and his friend Tom feel as chimney sweepers, you may see the poem as an act of self-consolation. Meanwhile, a number of readers may be more inclined to see the poem as a sermon, with Blake using the speaker to exemplify and advance his own religious views. Still others may see the poem mainly as social criticism, believing that Blake scorns a world in which child laborers accept their lot. You may find that two or more labels for the poem are appropriate, in which case you must decide whether they are *equally* so. Much of the time, issues of genre are issues of priority. Readers debate not whether a certain label for a work is possible but whether that label is the best.

9. *Issues of social policy.* Many works of literature have been attempts at social reform, exposing defects of their cultures and encouraging specific cures. A famous example is Upton Sinclair's 1906 novel *The Jungle*; by vividly depicting horrible working conditions in Chicago's stockyards, it led the meat processing industry to adopt more humane practices. Even when a work of literature is not blatantly political or seems rooted in the distant past, it may make you conscious of your own society's problems and possible solutions to them. Yet you and your classmates may propose different solutions and even disagree about what is a problem in the first place. The result is what we call issues of **social policy**.

Sometimes your position on a current issue of social policy will affect how you read a certain work. If you have been interrupted by telephone pitches at dinnertime and have welcomed various states' efforts to limit these, you may empathize immediately with the people called in Laux's poem. Similarly, your view on whether religion should play a central role in contemporary American society may affect your response to Blake's text. Even if current issues of social policy do not influence your original reading of a work, you can still use the work to raise such issues in your writing or in class discussion. Imagine discussing Stanton's poem "Shoplifters" at a police convention. What policies might the poem be used to promote there?

10. *Issues of cause and effect.*   Issues of **causality** are common in literary studies. Often they arise as readers present different explanations for a certain character's behavior. Remember that even the speaker in a poem can be thought of as a character with motives worth analyzing. You can pursue questions like these: Why does Blake's chimney sweeper draw the conclusion he does? Why does Dunn's speaker recall a job he held back in 1956? Why was Laux's speaker especially disturbed by her phone job? Why do the hands of Stanton's speaker "sweat"?

These questions can be rephrased to center on the author. For example, you can ask why Blake has his speaker end by affirming "duty." Actually, if you look back at all the questions we have brought up in discussing the various types of issues, you may see that most can be phrased as questions about the author's purposes. But keep in mind your options. You may not find it useful to focus on authorial intention in a given case. Often you will be better off sticking with one of the other types of issues. Or you may prefer to turn a question about authorial intention into a question about authorial effect. For instance, how should readers react when Blake has his speaker defer to "duty"? You can address questions like this without sounding as if you know exactly what the author intended.

Claims

You may not be used to calling things you say or write *claims*. But even when you utter a simple observation about the weather—for instance, "It's beginning to rain"—you are making a claim. Basically, a **claim** is a statement that is spoken or written in the hope that it will be considered true. With this definition in mind, you may start noticing claims everywhere. Most of us make lots of them every day. Furthermore, most of our claims are accepted as true by the people to whom we make them. Imagine how difficult life would be if the opposite were the case; human beings would be perpetually anxious if they distrusted almost everything they were told.

At times, though, claims do conflict with other claims. In a literature course, disagreements inevitably arise. Again, try not to let disagreements scare you. You can learn a lot from encountering views other than yours and from having to support your own. Moreover, exciting talk can occur as your class negotiates differences of opinion.

Recall that we defined an *issue* as a question with various debatable answers. *Claims*, as we will be using the term, are the debatable answers. For examples of claims in literary studies, look back at our explanations of various kinds of issues. Along the way, we mentioned a host of claims: that the conclusion reached by Blake's speaker is misguided but understandable; that Dunn's speaker feels insecure about his masculinity; that Laux's speaker disliked her phone job because it meanly disappointed people seeking contact; and that Stanton's theme is that our compassion may leave us feeling torn. These claims are debatable because in each case at least one other position is possible.

Not every claim is a firm, sweeping generalization. In some instances, you may want to *qualify* a claim of yours, which involves expressing the claim in words that make it less than absolute. The terms available for qualifying a claim are numerous. You might use words such as *perhaps, maybe, seems, appears, probably,* and *most likely* to indicate that you are not reporting a definite fact. Similarly, words such as *some, many, most,* and *several* allow you to acknowledge that your claim is limited in scope, applicable to just a portion of whatever you are discussing.

In literature classes, two types of claims are especially common. To criticize Laux's choice of images is to engage in **evaluation**. To identify the main ideas of her poem is to engage in **interpretation**. Conventionally, interpretation is the kind of analysis that depends on hypotheses rather than simple observation of plain fact. Throughout this book, we refer to the practice of interpreting a work or certain aspects of it. Admittedly, sometimes you may have trouble distinguishing interpretation from evaluation. When you evaluate some feature of a work or make an overall judgment of that work, probably you are operating with a certain interpretation as well, even if you do not make that interpretation explicit. Similarly, when you interpret part of a work or the text as a whole, probably you have already decided whether the text is worth figuring out. Nevertheless, the two types of claims differ in their emphases. When you attempt to interpret a work, you are mostly analyzing it; when you attempt to evaluate the work, you are mostly judging it.

In class discussions, other students may resist a claim you make about a literary work. Naturally, you may choose to defend your view at length. But remain open to the possibility of changing your mind, either by modifying your claim somehow or by shifting completely to another one. Also, entertain the possibility that a view different from yours is just as reasonable, even if you do not share it.

In much of your writing for your course, you will be identifying an issue and making one main claim about it, which can be called your **thesis**. Then, as you attempt to support your main claim, you will make a number of smaller claims. In drafts of your paper, welcome opportunities to test the claims you make in it. Review your claims with classmates to help you determine how persuasive your thinking is. You will be left with a stronger sense of what you must do to make your paper credible.

Persuasion

As we have noted, argument is often associated with arrogant insistence. Many assume that if two people are arguing, they are each demanding to be seen as correct. At its best, however, argument involves careful efforts to persuade. When you make such an effort, you indicate that you believe your claims, even if you remain open to revising them. You indicate as well that you would like others to agree with you. Yet to attempt **persuasion** is to concede that you must support your claims if others are to value them.

The art of persuasion has been studied for centuries under the name of **rhetoric**. Today, often the term *rhetoric* is used negatively: politicians accuse one another of indulging in "mere rhetoric," as if the term meant deceptive exaggeration. But human beings habitually resort to persuasion; hence, rhetoric deserves more esteem. Besides, only in modern times has rhetoric not been regarded as a central part of education. In ancient Greece and Rome as well as in Renaissance Europe, rhetoric was an important academic subject. It was viewed, too, as a body of thought that people could actually put to use, especially in the realm of public affairs. Much of the advice we give you about writing looks back to this history. Over and over, we convey to you principles drawn from the rhetorical tradition.

As you have probably discovered on many occasions, it can be hard for you to sway people who hold views different from yours. Not always will you be able to change their minds. Yet you may still convince them that your claims are at least reasonable. Moreover, the process of trying to persuade others will force you to clarify your ideas, to review why you hold them, and to analyze the people you aim to affect.

Audience

When you hear the word **audience**, perhaps you think first of people attending plays, concerts, movies, or lectures. Yet *audience* also describes readers, including the people who read your writing. Not everything you write is for other people's eyes; in this course, you may produce notes, journal entries, and even full-length drafts that only you will see. From time to time in the course, however, you will do public writing. On these occasions, you will be trying to persuade your audience to accept whatever claims you make.

These occasions will require you to consider more than just your subject matter. If you are truly to persuade your readers, you must take them into account. Unfortunately, you will not be able to find out everything about your audience beforehand. Moreover, you will have to study the ways in which your readers differ from one another. Usually, though, you will be able to identify some of their common values, experiences, and assumptions. Having this knowledge will strengthen your ability to make a case they appreciate.

In analyzing a work of literature, you may try to identify its *implied reader:* that is, the type of person that the work seems to address. Remember, too, that people may have read the work in manuscript or when it was first published. Finally, the work may have had innumerable readers since. Often we ask you to write about a text's effect on you and to compare your reaction with your classmates'.

Evidence

Evidence is the support that you give your claims so that others will accept them. What sort of evidence you must provide depends on what your audience requires to be persuaded. When you make claims during class discussions, your classmates and instructor might ask you follow-up questions, thereby suggesting what you must do to convince them. As a writer, you might often find yourself having to guess your readers' standards of evidence. Naturally, your guesses will be influenced by any prior experiences you have had with your audience. Moreover, you may have opportunities to review drafts with some of its members.

When you make an argument about literature, the evidence most valued by your audience is likely to be details of the work itself. Direct quotations from the text are an especially powerful means of indicating that your claims are well grounded. But when you quote, you need to avoid seeming willfully selective. If you merely quote Dunn's reference to "hard work" of lifting crates without acknowledging his later phrase "the hard work of boredom," you may come across as distorting his poem. In general, quoting from various parts of a text will help you give your readers the impression that you are being accurate.

If you make claims about the historical or cultural context of a work, your evidence may include facts about its original circumstances. You may be drawn to the author's own experiences and statements, believing these shed light on the text. But again, use such materials cautiously, for not always will they seem strong evidence for your claims. Even if the author of a text explicitly declared what he or she was up to in writing it, people are not obliged to accept that declaration as a guide to the finished work. Some people may feel that the author's statement of intention was deliberately misleading, while others may claim that the author failed to understand his or her own achievement.

Another kind of evidence for your arguments about literature is your **ethos**. This is a traditional term in rhetoric; it refers to the image of you that your audience gets as you attempt to persuade. Actually, there are two kinds of ethos. One is the image of you that your audience holds even before you present your analysis. Often your audience will not know much about you beforehand. In general, this kind of ethos plays a role when the speaker or writer has a prior reputation. When Secretary of State Colin Powell gives a speech, he can expect much of his audience to start off trusting him, since millions of Americans admire him already as a retired army general.

Even if you are not well known, the second kind of ethos may greatly influence how people respond to your argument. This is the image of you that your audience develops in hearing or reading your actual words. To secure your audience's trust, you ought to give the impression that you are calmly and methodically laying out your claims as well as your reasons for them. Making concessions to views different from yours is also a good strategy, indicating that you aim to be fair. On the other hand, if your presentation is disorganized or your tone self-righteous, you may put your audience on guard. You may come across as someone not committed to serious inquiry.

Warrants

Of all the elements of argument, **warrants** may be the least familiar to you. You have heard of search warrants and arrest warrants, documents that indicate the police are justified in searching a place or jailing a person. More generally, warrants are the beliefs that lead people to call certain things evidence for their claims. Imagine that you have just made a claim to your classmates and are now trying to support it. Imagine further that your listeners are reluctant to call your supporting information *evidence*; they want you to explain why you do so. In effect, your audience is asking you to identify your warrants: that is, the assumptions that make you think the information you have given reinforces your case. Throughout this book, we use the terms *warrants* and *assumptions* interchangeably.

Let's say you claim that when Stanton's speaker refers twice to the mirrors that revealed shoplifting, she is concerned as well about the image of *herself* that her policing of them "reflects," for she can be accused of insensitivity to their circumstances. Asked to provide evidence for your claim, you might point out the following things: (1) that her repetition of the mirror reference suggests troubled thoughts lurk within her; (2) that mirrors can be associated with *self*-reflection; (3) that at other moments in the poem, the speaker notes the shoplifters' desperate conditions; and (4) that the poem ends with an image of her hands sweating, which implies feelings of guilt. But then you may be asked for your warrants, the assumptions that lead you to see your evidence as support for your claim. Some of your assumptions might be about literature itself: for instance, that repetition in a poem is significant; that the final image of a poem is also important; and that characters are most interesting when they express emotions indirectly. Some of your assumptions might be about human nature: for example, that people often sweat when they feel ashamed. Some of your assumptions might be about specific historical periods and cultures: for instance, that contemporary American society often sees mirrors as devices for revealing the self. Often literature classes are most enlightening when students discuss with one another their assumptions about literature, about human nature, and about particular times and places. If your classmates differ in their assumptions, that may be because they differ in the ways they grew up, the experiences they have had, the reading they have done, and the authorities that have influenced them.

Once you state your warrants for a claim you are making, your audience may go further, asking you to identify assumptions supporting the warrants themselves. But more frequently you will have to decide how much you should mention your warrants in the first place. In class discussion, usually your classmates' and instructor's responses to your claims will indicate how much you have to spell out your assumptions. When you write, you have to rely more on your own judgment of what your audience requires. If you suspect that your readers will find your evidence unusual, you should identify your warrants at length. If, however, your readers are bound to accept your evidence, then a presentation of warrants may simply distract them. Again, reviewing drafts of your paper with potential readers will help you determine what to do.

LITERATURE AS ARGUMENT

Much of this book concerns arguing *about* literature. But sometimes literary works can be said to present arguments themselves. In some of the works we have included, certain characters make claims, often in debate with one another, while other works give the impression that the author is arguing for a certain position. Admittedly, not all works of literature are best seen as containing or making arguments, but occasionally, you will find that associating a literary text with argument opens up productive lines of inquiry. Moreover, as you argue about literature, arguments *within* literature can help you see how you might persuade others.

For an example of such arguments, let us turn to the following poem. Written around 1652, it is by John Milton (1608–1674), a poet who played a leading role in England's Puritan revolution. Seeking to make dominant their own version of Christianity, the Puritans executed King Charles I and installed their leader, Oliver Cromwell, as head of state. Milton wrote "When I consider how my light is spent" while working as an official in Cromwell's government. This is an autobiographical poem and refers to Milton's growing blindness, which threatened to prevent him from serving both his political leader and his religious one, God.

JOHN MILTON

When I consider how my light is spent

When I consider how my light is spent,
    Ere half my days in this dark world and wide,
    And that one talent which is death to hide
Lodged with me useless, though my soul more bent
To serve therewith my Maker, and present   5
    My true account, lest He returning chide;
    "Doth God exact day-labor, light denied?"
I fondly ask. But Patience, to prevent
That murmur, soon replies, "God doth not need
    Either man's work or His own gifts. Who best   10
    Bear His mild yoke, they serve Him best. His state
Is kingly: thousands at His bidding speed,
    And post o'er land and ocean without rest;
    They also serve who only stand and wait."   [c. 1652]

The speaker does not actually spell out his warrants. Consider, however, his reference to Christ's parable of the talents (Luke 19:12–27). In the ancient Middle East, a *talent* was a unit of money. In the parable, a servant is scolded by his master for hoarding the one talent that his master had given him. By telling this story, Christ implies that people should make use of the gifts afforded them by God. For the speaker in Milton's poem, the parable has a lot of authority. Evidently he feels that he should carry out its lesson. In effect, then, the parable has indeed become a warrant for him: that is, a basis for finding his blindness cause for lament.

Who, exactly, is the speaker's audience? Perhaps he is not addressing anyone in particular. Or perhaps the speaker's mind is divided and one side of it is addressing the other. Or perhaps the speaker is addressing God, even though he refers to God in the third person. Given that the speaker is answered by Patience, perhaps he means to address *that* figure, although Patience may actually be just a part of him rather than an altogether separate being.

At any rate, Patience takes the speaker for an audience in responding. And while Patience does not provide evidence, let alone warrants, Patience does make claims about God and His followers. Furthermore, Milton as author seems to endorse Patience's claims; apparently he is using the poem to advance them. Besides pointing out how God is served, Milton suggests that God ought to be served, even if God lets bad things happen to good people like Milton.

Every author can be considered an audience for his or her own writing, but some authors write expressly to engage in a dialogue with themselves. Perhaps Milton wrote his poem partly to convince himself that his religion was still valid and his life still worth living. Significantly, he did not publish the poem until about twenty years later. Yet because he did publish it eventually, at some point he must have contemplated a larger audience for it. The first readers of the poem would have been a relatively small segment of the English population: those literate and prosperous enough to have access to books of poetry. In addition, a number of the poem's first readers would have shared Milton's religious beliefs. Perhaps, however, Milton felt that even the faith of this band had to be bolstered. For one thing, not every Protestant of the time would have shared Milton's enthusiasm for the Puritan government. Recall that this regime executed the king, supposedly replacing him with the rule of God. Milton's words "His state / Is kingly" can be seen as an effort to persuade readers that the Puritans did put God on England's throne.

Most works of literature do not incorporate each element of argument we have discussed. Rarely do they feature arguments that do everything: acknowledge an audience, specify an issue, articulate claims, and carefully support these claims with substantial evidence and identified warrants. When characters argue, typically they do so in dramatic situations, not the sort of circumstances that permit elaborate debate. Also, traditionally literature has been a way for authors to make their own arguments indirectly: that is, to persuade with characterization, plot, and image rather than with straightforward development of claims. Do register the "gaps" as well as the strengths of any argument you find in a literary work. If the argument seems incomplete, however, a more drawn-out argument may have made the work less compelling.

Investigating Topics of Literary Criticism

To generate ideas about a literary text, try considering how it deals with **topics** that have preoccupied literary studies as a profession. Some of these topics have interested the discipline for many years. One example is work, a common subject of the poems by Blake, Dunn, Laux, Stanton, and Milton. Traditionally, literary studies has also been concerned with the chapter topics in Part Two: family relations, teaching and learning, love, justice, and mortality. Moreover, the discipline has long called attention to topics that are essentially classic conflicts: for example, innocence versus experience, free will versus fate or determinism, the individual versus society, nature versus culture, and eternity versus the passing time.

Over the last few years, however, literary studies has turned to several new concerns. For instance, quite a few literary critics now consider the ways in which literary texts are often *about* reading, writing, interpretation, and evaluation. Critics increasingly refer to some of the following subjects in their analysis of literature:

- Traits that significantly shape human identity, including gender, race, ethnic background, social class, sexual orientation, cultural background, nationality, and historical context;
- Representations of groups, including stereotypes held by others;
- Acknowledgments — or denials — of differences among human beings;
- Divisions, conflicts, and multiple forces *within* the self;
- Boundaries, including the processes through which these are created, preserved, and challenged;
- Politics and ideology, including the various forms that power and authority can take; acts of domination, oppression, exclusion, and appropriation; and acts of subversion, resistance, and parody;
- Ways that carnivals and other festivities challenge or preserve social order;
- Distinctions between what's universal and what's historically or culturally specific;
- Relations between the public and the private; the social and the personal;
- Relations between the apparently central and the apparently marginal;
- Relations between what's supposedly normal and what's supposedly abnormal;
- Relations between "high" culture and "low" (that is, mass or popular) culture;
- Economic and technological developments, as well as their effects;
- The role of performance in everyday life;
- Values — ethical, aesthetic, religious, professional, and institutional;
- Desire and pleasure;
- The body;
- The unconscious;
- Memory, including public commemorations as well as personal memory.

If you find that a literary text touches on one of these topics, try next to determine how the work specifically addresses that topic. Perhaps you will consider the topic an element of the text's theme. In any case, remember that by itself, a topic is not the same as a theme. While a topic can usually be expressed in a word or short phrase, a theme is a whole claim or assertion that you believe the text makes.

Actually, the topics we have identified may be most worth consulting when you have just begun analyzing a literary text and are far from establishing its theme. By using these topics, you can generate preliminary questions about the text, various issues you can then explore.

To demonstrate how these topics can stimulate inquiry, we apply some of them to the following poem, "Night Waitress." It is from the 1986 book *Ghost Memory*, by the late American poet Lynda Hull (1954–1994). Hull had been developing an impressive career in literature when she died in a car accident. This poem is also about work, the speaker being the night waitress of the title.

LYNDA HULL

Night Waitress

Reflected in the plate glass, the pies
look like clouds drifting off my shoulder.
I'm telling myself my face has character,
not beauty. It's my mother's Slavic face.
She washed the floor on hands and knees   5
below the Black Madonna, praying
to her god of sorrows and visions
who's not here tonight when I lay out the plates,
small planets, the cups and moons of saucers.
At this hour the men all look   10
as if they'd never had mothers.
They do not see me. I bring the cups.
I bring the silver. There's the man
who leans over the jukebox nightly
pressing the combinations   15
of numbers. I would not stop him
if he touched me, but it's only songs
of risky love he leans into. The cook sings
with the jukebox, a moan and sizzle
into the grill. On his forehead   20
a tattooed cross furrows,
diminished when he frowns. He sings words
dragged up from the bottom of his lungs.
I want a song that rolls
through the night like a big Cadillac   25
past factories to the refineries
squatting on the bay, round and shiny
as the coffee urn warming my palm.
Sometimes when coffee cruises my mind
visiting the most remote way stations,   30
I think of my room as a calm arrival
each book and lamp in its place. The calendar
on my wall predicts no disaster
only another white square waiting
to be filled like the desire that fills   35

jail cells, the old arrest
that makes me stare out the window or want
to try every bar down the street.
When I walk out of here in the morning
my mouth is bitter with sleeplessness.   40
Men surge to the factories and I'm too tired
to look. Fingers grip lunch box handles,
belt buckles gleam, wind riffles my uniform
and it's not romantic when the sun unlids
the end of the avenue. I'm fading   45
in the morning's insinuations
collecting in the crevices of buildings,
in wrinkles, in every fault
of this frail machinery.   [1986]

A WRITING EXERCISE

After you read "Night Waitress," do a ten-minute freewrite in which you try to identify how the poem relates to one or more of the topics mentioned on page 39. You might also find it helpful to compare this poem about work to the poems by Blake, Dunn, Laux, Stanton, and Milton on pages 18 to 23 and 37.

We think that several of the topics now popular in literary studies are relevant to Hull's poem. Here are a few possibilities, along with questions that these topics can generate:

Gender. The speaker alludes to conventional roles through which men and women relate to each other. When the speaker declares that "at this hour the men all look / as if they'd never had mothers," she indicates that women have often played a maternal role for men. Furthermore, she implies that often women have been the primary caretaker of their sons. (Notice that she makes no reference to fathers.) What is the effect of this attention to women as mothers of men? In most of the poem, the speaker refers to men as potential lovers. Yet even as she suggests she would like a sexual relationship with a man, she suggests as well that she has had trouble establishing worthwhile attachments. Why has she had such difficulty, do you think? Does the problem seem due to her personality alone, or do you sense larger forces shaping her situation? Notice, too, that the poem refers to the factory workers as male, while the woman who speaks is a waitress. To what extent does American society perpetuate a gendered division of labor?

Ethnic background. Near the start of the poem, the speaker refers to her "mother's Slavic face" and points out that her mother served "the Black Madonna," a religious icon popular in Central European countries like the Czech Republic and Poland. What is the effect of these particular ethnic references? To pursue this line of inquiry, probably you will need to do research into the Black Madonna, whether in a library or on the Internet.

Social class.   In part, considering social class means thinking about people's ability to obtain material goods. When the speaker compares her ideal song to "a big Cadillac," she implies that she doesn't currently possess such a luxurious car. At the same time, she is expressing her desire for the song, not the car. Why might the first item be more important to her right now? Social class is also a matter of how various workplaces are related to one another. This poem evokes a restaurant, factories, refineries, and bars. How are these settings connected as parts of American society? Think, too, about how you would label the social class of the various occupations the poem mentions. What would you say is the social class of a waitress? To what classes would you assign people who work in factories and refineries? Who, for the most part, are the social classes that have to work at night?

Sexual orientation.   The speaker of "Night Waitress" seems heterosexual, an orientation often regarded as the only legitimate one. Because almost all societies have made heterosexuality the norm, a lot of people forget that it is a particular orientation and that not everyone practices it. Within literary studies, gay and lesbian critics have pointed out that a literary work may seem to deal with sexuality in general but may actually refer just to heterosexuality. Perhaps "Night Waitress" is examining heterosexuality as a specific social force. If so, how might the speaker's discontent be related to heterosexuality's influence as a particular institution? Keep in mind that you don't have to assume anything about the author's sexuality as you pursue such a question. In fact, heterosexuality may be a more important topic in Hull's poem than she intended.

Divisions, conflicts, and multiple forces within the self.   The poem's beginning indicates that the speaker experiences herself as divided. The first four lines reveal that she feels pride and disappointment in her mirror image: "telling myself my face has character, / not beauty." Later she indicates that within her mind are "remote way stations" that she visits only on occasion. Furthermore, she seems to contradict herself. Although she initially refers to her room as "a calm arrival," she goes on to describe that place negatively, as empty and confined. Early in the evening, she seems sexually attracted to the man playing the jukebox ("I would not stop him / if he touched me"), but by morning her mood is "not romantic" and she is "too tired / to look" at the male factory workers. What may be the significance of these paradoxes?

Boundaries.   In the first line the speaker is apparently looking at a window, and later, she reveals that at times she feels driven to "stare out the window" of her room. What should a reader make of these two references to such a common boundary? When the speaker observes that the men in the restaurant "do not see me," she indicates that a boundary exists between them and her. Do you think she is merely being paranoid, or do you suspect that the men are indeed ignoring her? If they *are* oblivious to her, how do you explain their behavior? Still another boundary explored in the poem is the line between night and day. What happens when the speaker crosses this line? What can night, day, and the boundary between them signify? You might also consider what the author of a literary work does with its technical boundaries. Often a poem creates boundaries in its breaks between stanzas. Yet "Night Waitress" is a continuous, unbroken text; what is the effect of Hull's making it so? At the same time, Hull doesn't always respect sentence boundaries in her lines. At several points in the poem, sentences spill over from one line to another. This poetic technique is called **enjambment**; what is its effect here?

Politics and ideology. When, in referring to the jukebox man, the speaker declares that "I would not stop him / if he touched me," she can be taken to imply that often male customers flirt with waitresses. How might flirtation be seen as involving power, authority, and even outright domination? Do you see the poem as commenting on such things? Earlier we raised issues of social class; these can be seen as political issues, too. How would you describe a society in which some people have "a big Cadillac" and others do not?

Carnivals and other festivities. Although the poem does not refer to a "carnival" in any sense of that word, it does mention bars, which today are regarded by many people as places of festive retreat from work. What adjectives would you use to describe the speaker when she says that sometimes she wants "to try every bar down the street"?

Distinctions between what is universal and what is historically or culturally specific. Try to identify anything that is historically or culturally specific about this poem's setting. Certainly the word *Slavic* and the reference to the Black Madonna indicate that the speaker has a particular background. You might also note her description of the restaurant, her use of the Cadillac as a metaphor, and her mention of the "factories" and the "refineries" that "are squatting on the bay." Although a wide range of places might fit these details, the poem's setting does not seem universal. Indeed, many readers are attracted to literature *because* it deals with specific landscapes, people, and plots. Nevertheless, these same readers usually expect to get some larger, more widely applicable meanings out of literature even as they are engaged by its specific details. Are you inclined to draw general conclusions from "Night Waitress"? If so, what general meanings do you find in it? What sorts of people do you think might learn something about themselves from reading this poem?

Relations between the public and the private, the social and the personal. The speaker of "Night Waitress" works in a very public place, a restaurant. Yet she seems to feel isolated there, trapped in her own private world. How did she come to experience public life this way, do you think? Later, she initially seems to value her room as a private retreat, calling it a "calm arrival," but then she describes it as a place so lonely that it leads her to "stare out the window or want / to try every bar down the street." How, then, would you ultimately describe the relations between the speaker's public life and her private one? In addressing this issue, probably you need to consider whether the speaker's difficulties are merely personal or reflect a larger social disorder. When, at the end of the poem, she refers to "this frail machinery," is she referring just to herself, or is she suggesting that this phrase applies to her society in general? If she is indeed making a social observation, what do you sense are the "faults" in her society? Who else might be "fading"?

Relations between "high" culture and "low" culture.   Although the speaker does not identify the "songs / of risky love" playing on the jukebox, surely they are examples of what is called low, mass, or popular culture. Just as a lot of us are moved by such music when we hear it, so the jukebox player and the cook are engaged by it. In contrast, the poem itself can be considered an example of high culture. Often poetry is regarded as a serious art even by people who don't read it. In what ways, if any, does this poem conceivably resemble the songs it mentions? Given that author Lynda Hull is in essence playing with combinations of words, can we compare her with "the man / who leans over the jukebox nightly / pressing the combinations / of numbers"? (Actually, *numbers* has been a poetic term; centuries ago, it was commonly used as a synonym for the rhythms of poems.)

The role of performance in everyday life.   The most conspicuous performer in this poem is the cook, who "sings words / dragged up from the bottom of his lungs." But in everyday life, people often perform in the sense of taking on certain roles, even disguising their real personalities. Do you see such instances of performing in this poem? If so, where? Notice that the speaker wears a uniform; can that be considered a costume she wears while performing as a waitress?

Religious values.   The speaker clearly refers to religion when she recalls her mother's devotion to the Black Madonna, behavior that involved "praying / to her god of sorrows and visions." And although that god is "not here tonight," the speaker's description of waitressing has ritualistic overtones reminiscent of religious ceremonies. When she says, "I bring the cups. / I bring the silver," she could almost be describing preparations for Communion. In fact, she depicts the cook as wearing a religious emblem: "On his forehead / a tattooed cross furrows, / diminished when he frowns." What do you make of all this religious imagery? Might the speaker be trying to pursue certain religious values? Can she be reasonably described as looking for salvation?

Desire and pleasure.   The speaker explicitly mentions the word *desire* when she describes the emptiness she feels in her room, a feeling of desolation "that makes me stare out the window or want / to try every bar down the street." These lines may lead you to believe that her desire is basically sexual. Yet when the speaker uses the words *I want* earlier in the poem, she expresses her wish for "a song that rolls / through the night like a big Cadillac." Here, her longing does not appear sexual in nature. Is the speaker referring to at least two kinds of desire, then? Or do you see her as afflicted with basically one kind?

The body.   A notable feature of this poem is its attention to body parts. The speaker mentions her "shoulder," her "face," her mother's "face," her mother's "hands and knees," the cook's "forehead," his "lungs," her "palm," the "way stations" of her "mind," her "mouth," the factory workers' "fingers," and their "belt buckles." At the same time, the speaker never describes any particular body as a whole. What is the effect of this emphasis on mere parts? Does it connect in any way to the speaker's ultimate "fading"?

Memory.   Already we have noted the speaker's reference to her mother at the start of the poem. In what way, if any, is it significant that she engages in recollection? What circumstances in her life might have prompted the speaker to look back at the past?

A WRITING EXERCISE

We have applied several topics from our list to Lynda Hull's poem "Night Waitress." Now see how you can apply topics from the list to another poem about work in Part One. Try to come up with several questions about the poem you choose, referring to topics on our list. Then select one of the questions you have formulated, and freewrite for ten minutes in response to it.

3

The Writing Process

In Chapters 4 through 7, we discuss how to write about each of the four literary genres featured in this book. Here, however, we suggest how to write about a literary work of any genre. To make our advice concrete, we trace what one student did as she worked on a writing assignment for a course much like yours. The assignment was given to a class that had been reading and discussing several poems about work, including the poems we included in Chapter 2. Each student chose a single poem from the syllabus and wrote a 600-word argument paper on it for a general audience. We focus on the writing process of a student named Abby Hazelton.

Ultimately, Abby chose to write about William Wordsworth's "The Solitary Reaper." In his own day, Wordsworth (1770–1850) was poet laureate of England, and he continues to be regarded as a major British Romantic poet. He and fellow poet Samuel Taylor Coleridge collaborated on *Lyrical Ballads* (1798), a collection of verse that became a landmark of Romantic poetry. In his preface to the second edition two years later, Wordsworth famously defined *poetry* as "emotion recollected in tranquillity," contended that it should draw on "common life," and called for it to incorporate "language really used by men." Like many other Romantics, Wordsworth celebrated scenes of nature and country life, while deploring the increasing spread of cities. "The Solitary Reaper" appeared in his 1807 *Poems in Two Volumes*.

Before examining Abby's writing process, read Wordsworth's poem.

WILLIAM WORDSWORTH
The Solitary Reaper

Behold her, single in the field,
   Yon solitary Highland Lass!
Reaping and singing by herself;
   Stop here, or gently pass!
Alone she cuts and binds the grain,

5

And sings a melancholy strain;
O listen! for the Vale profound
Is overflowing with the sound.

No Nightingale did ever chaunt
    More welcome notes to weary bands   10
Of travellers in some shady haunt,
    Among Arabian sands:
A voice so thrilling ne'er was heard
In spring-time from the Cuckoo-bird,
Breaking the silence of the seas   15
Among the farthest Hebrides.

Will no one tell me what she sings? —
    Perhaps the plaintive numbers flow
For old, unhappy, far-off things,
    And battles long ago: 20
Or is it some more humble lay,
Familiar matter of to-day?
Some natural sorrow, loss, or pain,
That has been, and may be again?

Whate'er the theme, the Maiden sang   25
    As if her song could have no ending;
I saw her singing at her work,
    And o'er the sickle bending; —
I listen'd, motionless and still;
And, as I mounted up the hill,   30
The music in my heart I bore,
Long after it was heard no more.   [1807]

Once she chose to write about Wordsworth's poem for her paper, Abby engaged in four sorts of activities: (1) exploring, (2) planning, (3) composing, and (4) revising. As we describe each, keep in mind that these activities need not be consecutive. Abby moved back and forth among them as she worked on her assignment.

Exploring

As you read a literary work, you are bound to interpret and judge it. Yet not all reading is **critical reading**, which involves carefully and self-consciously analyzing various aspects of a text, including its meanings, its effects, and its treatment of typical elements of its genre. When you read a work critically, you also note questions it raises for you — issues you might explore further in class discussion and writing. Indeed, critical reading is a process of self-reflection. During this process, you monitor your own response to the text and try to identify why you see the text the way you do.

Perhaps you assume that literature contains hidden meanings that only an elite group of readers can spot. This is a common belief, but most people are quite capable of analyzing a literary work, especially if they know certain strategies for getting ideas about it. In rhetorical theory, these strategies are called *methods of invention.* Here we list some that Abby used, including a few strategies that we have mentioned already. Try out any that are unfamiliar to you, even as you first read a text. Again, critical reading does not require divine inspiration. The following techniques have helped many a mortal:

1. *Make predictions as you read a text, guessing how it will turn out.*   If you wind up being surprised, fine. You may gain several insights into the text and into yourself as you reflect on the ways in which the text defies your expectations. Even if the text proceeds as you anticipated, making predictions about it is worthwhile, for at least you will have considered its possible lines of development.

2. *Read the text more than once.*   You greatly increase your chances of getting ideas about it if you do. The first time around, you may be preoccupied with following the plot or with figuring out the text's basic meaning. Only by looking at the text repeatedly may you notice several of its other aspects, including features that really stir your thoughts. Given the busy schedule of a college student, you may be tempted to read a work just once before your class discusses it. But a single reading may leave you with relatively little to say, whereas multiple readings may give you several ideas to share.

3. *Note whatever changes of mind you go through as you read and reread the text.*

4. *Describe the audience that the author apparently had in mind, and note features of the text that support your image of its implied audience.*   At the same time, consider how real readers of the text—past, present, and future—might react to it and why they might respond so. Also reflect on your own response to the text, noting anything in your own life that affects your reading of it.

5. *Read at least part of the text aloud, even if you are alone.*   Doing this will give you a better sense of how the text manipulates language.

6. *Consciously focus on the text's content and on its form.*   If you can focus on both content and form at the same time, fine, but many readers have trouble paying attention to the two simultaneously. In this case, deliberately alternate your focus first on content and then on form. This way you increase your chances of noticing things that the text is saying and doing.

7. *Consult a dictionary when you come across words in the text that you do not understand.*   Keep in mind that a text may make a familiar word ambiguous, leaving you with the impression that the author is attaching more than one meaning to it. An example might be Dunn's use of the words *hard work,* which seem to take on various definitions as his poem proceeds. Furthermore, a text may define a commonly used word in a way unfamiliar to you. As we noted earlier, an example would be Milton's use of the word *fondly,* which in his time

meant "foolishly," not "affectionately." If you suspect that a writer is using a common word in what for you is an uncommon way, turn to a dictionary to check the word's possible meanings.

8. *Note patterns within the text.*   At the same time, pay attention to elements of the text that appear to threaten its unity — for instance, apparent contradictions or digressions.

9. *Try to identify the text's most important word, image, or scene.*   At the same time, consider how to justify your choice.

10. *Identify moments where the text makes a significant shift in meaning, imagery, tone, plot, narrator, or point of view.*   These moments may very well occur at typographic breaks in the text. In a poem, for example, significant changes may occur when one stanza ends and another begins. Similarly, a play may change significantly as it moves from scene to scene. Short stories and essays may also engage in important shifts as they go from paragraph to paragraph. But you may find turning points anywhere in the text, so do not look solely at its obvious moments of transition.

11. *Mark passages in the text that strike you as especially memorable.*   These passages would include any that you might quote in a paper about the text.

12. *Aim to complicate the views you take of characters in the text.*   If you tend to see a character as thoroughly mistaken, evil, or "sick," look for potentially redeeming qualities of that person. Similarly, if you tend to see a character as thoroughly good, look for qualities that suggest the person is less than perfect. Furthermore, consider whether you or the author are inclined to stereotype people. Note, too, any ways in which the characters fail to fit stereotypes.

13. *Raise questions about the text even as you read.*   For help, you can turn to our list of ten different types of issues (pp. 25–32). In effect, the list indicates some aspects of the text that might be especially worth pondering. Recall that these include the following:

- Facts obscured or absent in the text
- The text's theme
- Possible definitions of key words in the text
- The symbols it employs
- Its patterns
- Evaluations that might be made in response to it
- Its historical and cultural context
- Its genre
- Its relevance to current political debates
- Causes and effects of its characters' behavior; the author's aims and effects

14. *Note whether and how the text addresses topics of particular interest to professional literary critics today.*   (For a discussion of such topics, refer to the last section of Chapter 2, pp. 38–45.)

15. Think about the writer's alternatives: things the writer could have done and yet didn't do. Then, imagine that the writer had pursued these alternatives. How would the effect of the text have been different?

16. Consider whether and how the text itself features elements of argument. (Refer back to pp. 23–36 in Chapter 2.)

17. Compare the text with others on the same subject. So far, we have encouraged you to compare various poems about work. Going beyond the world of literature, you might compare whatever text you are focusing on to certain films, television shows, songs, advertisements, and articles in newspapers and magazines.

18. Discuss the text with your instructor, your classmates, and other people you know. If differences emerge between their views and yours, try to identify the exact issues at hand, as well as the possible reasons for those differences. Perhaps you will talk about the text with people who have not read it at all. If so, note the questions these people have about the text. Note, too, what you find yourself emphasizing as you describe the text to them.

You can also develop and pull together your thoughts about a text by informally writing about it. And the sooner you plunge into the rhythms of composing, the more comfortable you will feel producing a full-length paper. Your informal, preliminary writing can take various shapes. The following are just some of the things you might do.

1. Make notes in the text itself. A common method is to mark key passages, either by underlining these passages or running a magic marker through them. Both ways of marking are popular because they help readers recall main features of the text. But use these techniques moderately if you use them at all, for marking lots of passages will leave you unable to distinguish the really important parts of the text. Also, try "talking back" to the text in its margins. Next to particular passages, you might jot down words of your own, indicating any feelings and questions you have about those parts. On any page of the text, you might circle related words and then draw lines between these words to emphasize their connection. If a word or an idea shows up on numerous pages, you might circle it each time. Furthermore, try cross-referencing, by listing on at least one page the numbers of all those pages where the word or idea appears.

2. As you read the text, occasionally look away from it, and jot down anything in it you recall. This memory exercise lets you review your developing impressions of the text. When you turn back to its actual words, you may find that you have distorted or overlooked aspects of it that you should take into account.

3. At various moments in your reading, freewrite about the text for ten minutes or so. Spontaneously explore your preliminary thoughts and feelings about it, as well as any personal experiences the text leads you to recall. One logical moment to do freewriting is when you have finished reading the text. But you do not have to wait until then; as you read, you might pause occasionally to freewrite. This way, you give yourself an opportunity to develop and review your thoughts about the text early on.

4. Create a "dialectical notebook."   So named by composition theorist Ann Berthoff, it involves using pages of your regular notebook in a particular way. On each page, draw a line down the middle to create two columns. In the left column, list various details of the text: specifically, words, images, characters, and events that strike you. In the right column, jot down for each detail one or more sentences indicating *why* you were drawn to it. Take as many pages as you need to record and reflect on your observations. You can also use the two-column format to carry out a dialogue with yourself about the text. This is an especially good way to ponder aspects of the text that you find confusing, mysterious, or complex.

5. Play with the text by revising it.   Doing so will make you more aware of options that the author rejected and give you a better sense of the moves that the author chose to make. Specifically, you might rearrange parts of the text, add to it, change some of its words, or shift its narrative point of view. After you revise the text, compare your alternative version with the original, considering especially differences in their effects.

A WRITING EXERCISE

Do at least ten minutes of freewriting about Wordsworth's poem, keeping it nearby so that you can consult it if you need to. In particular, try to raise questions about the poem, and consider which of these may be worth addressing in a more formal paper.

Here is an excerpt from Abby's freewriting:

```
    I see that this poem consists of four stanzas, each
of which is eight lines long. But these stanzas have dif-
ferent emphases. The first stanza is a series of com-
mands. The speaker tells people to "Behold," "Stop here,
or gently pass," and "listen." The second stanza mainly
describes the reaper. The third stanza is basically a
bunch of questions. The fourth is the speaker's recollec-
tion of his experience in general. So I could write a
paper about how this poem changes as it moves along and
why the stanzas shift in emphasis. But one problem with a
paper like that is that it might get me bogged down in
mechanically moving from stanza to stanza. I don't want
that to happen. Another thing I could do is answer one of
the speaker's own questions, which are about what kind
of song the reaper is singing. Evidently this "Highland
```

Lass" is using a Scottish dialect that he doesn't understand. But I'm just as ignorant as he is about the song.
I guess I'm more likely to contribute some analysis of
my own if I come up with a question myself. I'm struck
by the fact that he doesn't give us much sense of the
reaper's song. There's no way that a printed poem could
convey the reaper's tune, but still. And the words are
foreign to the speaker. But I'm surprised that he doesn't
make a little effort to convey at least some of the
song's lyrics even if they're foreign words that he might
hear wrong or misspell. How can I as a reader join him in
experiencing the beauty of her song if I don't learn any
of its words? I wonder if we're supposed to see the poem
as being more about the speaker than about the reaper.
More specifically, maybe we're supposed to be a little
disturbed that he's a British intellectual who is making
a spectacle out of a foreign woman from the working
class. At any rate, he seems bent on controlling this
experience even as he invites us to share it. Another
question for me is, Why does he shift from present tense
to past tense in the last stanza? This change is really
curious to me. I don't see anything earlier on that prepares me for it. First, we're led to believe that the
speaker is observing the reaper right then and there,
but at the end he speaks as if this occurred in the past,
though maybe the recent past. This inconsistency in the
time frame makes me think that in some important way the
overall poem is about time. At any rate, I'm drawn to
the inconsistency because it's so blatant. If I wrote
about it, I might still devote a paragraph to each stanza,
but I'd be starting with the last one and referring back
to the others in order to explain that stanza. What I
still have to figure out, though, is what exactly the poem
is saying about time when it makes the shift of tense.

Freewriting enabled Abby to raise several questions. At the same time, she
realized that her paper could not deal with everything that puzzled her. When
you first get an assignment like hers, you may fear that you will have nothing
to say. But you will come up with a lot of material if, like Abby, you take time

for exploration. As we have suggested, it's a process of examining potential subjects through writing, discussion, and just plain thinking. One of your challenges will be to choose among the various issues you have formulated. At the end of the above excerpt from her freewriting, Abby is on the verge of choosing to analyze the poem's shift of tense in its final stanza. For her, this shift is an interesting change from a pattern, the poem's previous uses of present tense. Abby has not yet decided how to explain this shift; at the moment, it remains for her a mystery. But her paper would achieve little if it focused just on aspects of the poem that are easy to interpret. Though Abby has more thinking to do about the poem's shift of tense, it seems a promising subject for her precisely because it puzzles her.

Planning

Planning for an assignment like Abby's involves five main activities:

1. Choosing the text you will analyze;
2. Identifying your audience;
3. Identifying the main issue, claim, and evidence you will present;
4. Identifying particular challenges you will face and warrants you will use;
5. Determining how you will organize your argument.

Abby considered several poems before choosing one for her paper. She settled on Wordsworth's for five reasons. First, it was a text that left her with plenty of questions. Second, she believed that these questions could be issues for other readers. Third, she felt increasingly able to *argue* about the poem—that is, to make and support claims about it. Fourth, she believed that she could adequately analyze the poem within the assignment's word limit. Finally, Wordsworth's poem drew her because she had heard about the Romantic movement in English literature and was curious to study an example of it.

Faced with the same assignment, you might choose a different poem than Abby did. Still, the principles that she followed are useful. Think about them whenever you are free to decide which texts you will write about. With some assignments, of course, you may need a while to decide which text is best for you. And later, after you have made your decision, you may want to make a switch. For example, you may find yourself changing your mind once you have done a complete draft. Frustrated by the text you have chosen, you may realize that another inspires you more. If so, consider making a substitution. Naturally, you will feel more able to switch if you have ample time left to write the paper, so avoid waiting to start your paper just before it is due.

To determine what your readers will see as an issue and to make your claims about it persuasive to them, you need to develop an audience profile. Perhaps your instructor will specify your audience. You may be asked, for example, to imagine yourself writing for a particular group in a particular situation. If you were Abby, how would you analyze "The Solitary Reaper" for an orchestra wanting to know what this poem implies about music? Even when not required of you, such an exercise can be fun and thought-provoking for you as you plan a paper.

Most often, though, instructors ask students to write for a "general" audience, the readership that Abby was asked to address. Assume that a general audience is one that will want evidence for your claims. While this audience will include your instructor, let it also include your classmates, since in class discussions they will be an audience for you whenever you speak. Besides, your class may engage in peer review, with students giving one another feedback on their drafts.

If your audience is indeed supposed to be a general group of readers, what can you assume about their prior knowledge? You may not be sure. Above all, you may wonder how familiar your readers already are with the text you are analyzing. Perhaps your teacher will resolve your uncertainty, telling you exactly how much your audience knows about the text. Then again, you may be left to guess. Should you presume that your audience is totally unfamiliar with the text? This approach is risky, for it may lead you to spend a lot of your paper merely summarizing the text rather than analyzing it. A better move is to write as if your audience is at least a bit more knowledgeable. Here is a good rule of thumb: assume that your audience has, in fact, read the text but that you need to recall for this group any features of the text that are crucial to your argument. Although probably your paper will still include summary, the amount you provide will be limited, and your own ideas will be more prominent.

When you have written papers for previous classes, you may have been most concerned with coming up with a thesis. Maybe you did not encounter the term *issue* at all. But good planning for a paper does entail identifying the main issue you will address. Once you have sensed what that issue is, try phrasing it as a question. If the answer would be obvious to your readers, be cautious, for you really do not have an issue if the problem you are raising can be easily resolved.

Also, try to identify what *kind* of issue you will focus on. For help, look at our list of various types (pp. 24–32). Within "The Solitary Reaper," the speaker raises an issue of fact: he wants to know what sort of song the reaper is singing. But as someone writing about Wordsworth's poem, Abby wanted to focus on another kind of issue, which she decided is best regarded as an issue of pattern. More precisely, she thought her main question might be, What should we conclude from the inconsistency in pattern that occurs when the final stanza shifts to past tense? To be sure, Abby recognized that addressing this issue would lead to issues of theme and of cause and effect, for she would have to consider why Wordsworth shifts tenses and how the shift relates to his overall subject.

Now that she had identified her main issue, Abby had to determine her main claim. Perhaps you have grown comfortable with the term *thesis* and want to keep using it. Fine. Bear in mind, though, that your thesis is the main *claim* you will make and proceed to support. And when, as Abby did, you put your main issue as a question, then your main claim is your answer to that question. Sometimes you will come up with question and answer simultaneously. Once in a while, you may even settle on your answer first, not being certain yet how to word the question. Whatever the case, planning for your paper involves articulating both the question (the issue) and the answer (your main claim). Try actually writing both down, making sure to phrase your main issue as a question and your main claim as the answer. Again, Abby's main issue was, What should we conclude from the inconsistency in pattern that occurs when the final stanza shifts to past tense? After much thought, she expressed her main claim this way:

```
One possible justification for the shift to past tense is
that it reminds us of the speaker's inability to halt the
passage of time. He would like to freeze his encounter
with the reaper, keeping it always in the present. But as
the shift in tense indicates, time goes on, making the
encounter part of the speaker's past. Perhaps, therefore,
the poem's real subject is the idea that time is always
in flux.
```

Audiences usually want evidence, and as we noted earlier, most arguments you write about literature will need to cite details of the work itself. Because direct quotation is usually an effective move, Abby planned to elaborate her claim by citing several of Wordsworth's references to time. Remember, though, that you need to avoid seeming willfully selective when you quote. While Abby expected to quote from Wordsworth's last stanza, she also knew she had to relate it to earlier lines, so that her readers would see her as illuminating the basic subject of the whole poem. In particular, she looked for language in the first three stanzas that might hint at the speaker's lack of control over time, thereby previewing the last stanza's emphasis.

Often, to think about particular challenges of your paper is to think about your warrants. Remember that warrants are assumptions; they are what lead you to call certain things evidence for your claims. Abby knew that one of her warrants was an assumption about Wordsworth himself—that he was not being sloppy when he shifted tenses in his last stanza. Rarely will your paper need to admit all the warrants on which it relies. Most of the time, your task will be to guess which warrants your readers do want stated. Abby felt there was at least one warrant she would have to spell out—her belief that the poem's verb tenses reveal something about the speaker's state of mind.

To make sure their texts seem organized, most writers first do an **outline**, a list of their key points in the order they will appear. Outlines are indeed a good idea, but bear in mind that there are various kinds. One popular type, which you may already know, is the **sentence outline**. As the name implies, it lists the writer's key points in sentence form. Its advantages are obvious: this kind of outline forces you to develop a detailed picture of your argument's major steps, and it leaves you with sentences you can then incorporate into your paper. Unfortunately, sentence outlines tend to discourage flexibility. Because they demand much thought and energy, you may hesitate to revise them, even if you come to feel your paper would work better with a new structure.

A second, equally familiar outline is the **topic outline**, a list in which the writer uses a few words to signify the main subjects that he or she will discuss. Because it is sketchy, this kind of outline allows writers to go back and change plans if necessary. Nevertheless, a topic outline may fail to provide all the guidance a writer needs.

We find a third type useful: a **rhetorical purpose outline**. As with the first two, you list the major sections of your paper. Next, you briefly indicate two things for each section: the effect you want it to have on your audience, and how you will achieve that effect. Here is the rhetorical purpose outline that Abby devised for her paper.

```
                        INTRODUCTION
    The audience needs to know      I'll identify Wordsworth's
        the text I'll discuss.          poem.
    The audience must know my       I'll point out that the
        main issue.                     poem is puzzling in its
                                        shift of tenses at the
                                        end.
    The audience must know my       I'll argue that the shift
        main claim.                     to past tense suggests
                                        that the poem's real
                                        subject is the inability
                                        of human beings to halt
                                        the passage of time.

            ANALYSIS OF THE POEM'S FINAL STANZA
    The audience needs to see       I will point out not only
        in detail how the final         the shift of tense but
        stanza's shift to past          also other words in the
        tense signals the               last stanza that imply
        speaker's inability to          time moves on. I will
        control the passage             note as well that music
        of time.                        is an especially fleet-
                                        ing medium, so the
                                        reaper's song was bound
                                        to fade.

            ANALYSIS OF THE PRECEDING STANZAS
    To accept that the passage      I will analyze the first
        of time is the poem's           three stanzas in turn,
        real concern, the               showing how each implies
        audience must see that          the speaker is frus-
        the preceding stanzas           trated over his inabil-
        hint at this subject.           ity to control time.
```

CONCLUSION

The audience may need to be clearer about what I consider the ultimate <u>tone</u> of the poem.	I will say that although the poem can be thought of as a warm tribute to the singing reaper, the final emphasis on the passage of time is pessimistic in tone, and the speaker winds up as "solitary" as the reaper.

For your own rhetorical purpose outlines, you may want to use phrases rather than sentences. If you do use sentences, as Abby did, you do not have to write all that many. Note that Abby wrote relatively few as she stated the effects she would aim for and her strategies for achieving those effects. Thus, she was not tremendously invested in preserving her original outline. She felt free to change it if it failed to prove helpful.

Composing

Composing is not always distinguishable from exploring, planning, and revising. As you prepare for your paper, you may jot down words or whole sentences. Once you begin a draft, you may alter that draft in several ways before you complete it. You may be especially prone to making changes in drafts if you use a computer, for word processing enables you to jump around in your text, revisiting and revising what you have written.

Still, most writers feel that doing a draft is an activity in its own right, and a major one at that. The next four chapters present various tips for writing about specific genres, and Appendix 2 discusses writing research papers. Meanwhile, here are some tips to help you with composing in general.

Title

You may be inclined to let your **title** be the same as that of the text you discuss. Were you to write about Wordsworth's poem, then, you would be calling your own paper "The Solitary Reaper." But often such mimicry backfires. For one thing, it may lead your readers to think that you are unoriginal and perhaps even lazy. Also, you risk confusing your audience, since your paper would actually be about Wordsworth's poem rather than being the poem itself. So take the time to come up with a title of your own. Certainly it may announce the text you will focus on, but let it do more. In particular, use your title to indicate the main claim you will be making. With just a few words, you can preview the argument to come.

Style

Perhaps you have been told to "sound like yourself" when you write. Yet that can be a difficult demand (especially if you are not sure what your "self" is really like). Above all, the **style** you choose depends on your audience and purpose. In writing an argument for a general audience, probably you would do best to avoid the extremes of pomposity and breezy informality. Try to stick with words you know well, and if you do want to use some that are only hazily familiar to you, check their dictionary definitions first.

At some point in our lives, probably all of us have been warned not to use *I* in our writing. In the course you are taking, however, you may be asked to write about your experiences. If so, you will find *I* hard to avoid. Whether to use it does become a real question when you get assignments like Abby's, which require you chiefly to make an argument about a text. Since you are supposed to focus on that text, your readers may be disconcerted if you keep referring to yourself. Even so, you need not assume that your personal life is irrelevant to the task. Your opening paragraph might refer to your personal encounters with the text, as a way of establishing the issue you will discuss. A personal anecdote might serve as a forceful conclusion to your paper. Moreover, before you reach the conclusion, you might orient your readers to the structure of your paper by using certain expressions that feature the word *I*: for example, *As I suggested earlier, As I have noted, As I argue later*. In general, you may be justified in saying *I* at certain moments. When tempted to use this pronoun, though, consider whether it really is your best move.

In a paper, the expressions *I think* and *I feel* are rarely effective. Often writers resort to such phrasing because they sense they are offering nothing more than their own opinion. The audience may view such expressions as indications of a weak argument or limited evidence. You might make the claim more persuasive by avoiding *I think* and *I feel* and by qualifying it through words such as *probably, possibly, maybe,* and *perhaps*. If you believe that you have little evidence for a claim you want to make, take time out from writing and go back to exploring your ideas. If you can, come up with additional means of support.

Arguments about literature are most compelling when supported by quotations, but be careful not to quote excessively. If you constantly repeat other people's words, providing few of your own, your readers will hardly get a sense of you as an author. Moreover, a paper full of quotation marks is hard to read. Make sure to quote selectively, remembering that sometimes you can simply paraphrase. When you do quote, try to cite only the words you need. You do not have to reproduce a whole line or sentence if one word is enough to support your point.

When summarizing what happens in a literary work, be careful not to shift tenses as you go along. Your reader may be confused if you shift back and forth between past and present. We suggest that you stick primarily to the present tense, which is the tense that literary critics customarily employ. For example, instead of saying that the speaker *praised* the lass, say that he *praises* her.

Introduction

Many writers aim to impress their audience right away. You may be tempted, then, to begin your paper with a grand philosophical statement, hoping your readers will find such an **introduction** profound. Often, however, this approach results in broad, obvious generalities. Here are some examples:

> Society doesn't always appreciate the work that everyone does.

> Over the centuries, there has been a lot of literature, and much of it has been about work.

> William Wordsworth was a great British Romantic poet.

As writing theorist William Coles points out, statements like these are mere "throat-clearing." They may lead your audience to think that you are delaying, not introducing, your real argument. Rather than beginning your paper with such statements, try mentioning the specific text you will analyze. Start by making assertions about that text.

Usually, your introduction will identify the main issue that you will discuss. Perhaps you will be able to assume that your audience is already aware of this issue and sees it as important. Abby felt that her audience would wonder, as she did, why Wordsworth shifts to the past tense. Sometimes, however, your introduction will need to set out your issue at greater length. It will need to identify the issue as a significant question with no obvious answer.

A classic way to establish the importance of an issue is to show that other critics have grappled with it or wrongly ignored it. You may, however, get assignments in your course that do not push you to consider what previous critics have said. An alternative method of establishing your issue's significance is personal anecdote. By describing how the issue came to matter to you, you may persuade your readers to see it as mattering to them. If you do not want to be autobiographical, you have at least one other option. You can show that if your issue is left unaddressed, your readers will remain puzzled by other key aspects of the text you are discussing.

Development

When you write a paper, naturally you want the parts of each sentence to hang together. But make sure, too, that each sentence connects clearly to the one before and the one after. Smooth transitions from one paragraph to the next encourage your reader to follow the **development** of your argument. Certain words can help you signal relations between sentences. Here are just a few examples. Each could appear at the beginning of a sentence, where it would indicate how that sentence relates to the one before.

- Numerical order: *first, second, third,* etc.
- Temporal order: *then, next, earlier, previously, before, later, subsequently, afterward*
- Addition: *also, in addition to, furthermore, moreover, another*
- Degree: *more/less important, more/less often*
- Effect: *thus, therefore, as a result, consequently, hence, so*
- Opposition: *but, yet, however, nevertheless, still, even so, by contrast, on the contrary, conversely, on the other hand*

- Exemplarity: *for example, for instance*
- Emphasis: *indeed, in fact*
- Restatement: *that is, in other words*
- Specificity: *specifically, more precisely, in particular*

Do not fall into the habit of relying on *and* as a connective. As a means of linking sentences or of bridging ideas within them, *and* may seem a safe choice; besides being a common word, it looks too little to cause trouble. Nevertheless, as a connective *and* is often vague, failing to show how words actually relate. Note the following sentence:

The speaker loves the reaper's song, and he does not know what it is.

The word *and* does little to fuse the sentence's two halves. A more precise way to connect the halves would be with language that shows their relation to be contrast:

The speaker loves the reaper's song, *but* he does not know what it is.

Whatever the merits of this revision, it is more coherent than the sentence using *and*, which hardly conveys relation at all. Also, if your paper constantly uses *and* or any other particular word, your prose may come across as monotonous.

The word *and* often becomes a prime means of transition in papers that mostly just summarize plots of texts. Presumably, though, your goal in a paper is to *analyze* whatever text you are discussing, not simply outline it. If you see that you are using *and* a lot in your writing, consider the possibility that you are, in fact, summarizing more than analyzing. In our experience, writers are most apt to lapse into plot summary toward the middle of their paper. At that point, they may grow tired of developing and keeping track of their own ideas. The easiest thing to do then is to coast, simply paraphrasing their chosen text line by line. Pause in your writing from time to time to see if you have lapsed into this practice. Remember that you can analyze details of a text without sticking to their original order.

How coherent a paper seems depends in part on the length of its paragraphs. Usually, a paragraph should be at least three sentences long. When readers confront one very short paragraph after another, they are apt to feel that they are seeing random, fragmented observations rather than a well-organized argument. Of course, paragraphs can also be too long. Readers have trouble following the structure of one that runs a full page. If you find yourself writing a lengthy paragraph, stop and check to see if there is any place in it where starting a new paragraph makes sense.

Emphasis

Many people assume that academic writing consists of long, dense statements. Furthermore, they assume that such prose is virtually unreadable. Whether or not they are right about the kind of writing favored in college, your own readers may get tired and lost if each of your sentences seems endless. On the other hand, your writing may strike your readers as choppy if each sentence contains just a few words. Usually, your papers will be most effective if you vary the lengths of your sentence for **emphasis**. In any paper you write for your course, aim for a mixture of sentence lengths, blending long, medium, and short.

But in any of your sentences, use only the amount of words you need to make your point. For example, do not resort to sixteen words when eight will suffice. Your readers are likely to become impatient, even bored, if your prose seems padded. Also, they may doubt your credibility, suspecting that you are pretending to have more ideas than you do.

Perhaps you fear that if you economize with your language, all your sentences will wind up short. But a concise sentence is not always brief; a sentence can be long and yet tightly edited, with every word in it deserving a place. Another possible fear has to do with writer's block. You may worry that you will have trouble getting words down if you must justify every single one of them. A good solution is to postpone editing for a while, perhaps even waiting until you have finished a draft. Simply remember that at some point you should review whatever you have written, looking for words you might trim.

Your sentences will have more impact if you use active rather than passive verbs. To grasp the difference, read the following two sentences:

> In the final stanza, tenses are shifted by the speaker.
>
> In the final stanza, the speaker shifts tenses.

Certainly both sentences are grammatical. The second, however, is more concise and dynamic. That is because it uses the active form of the verb *to shift* and indicates right away the agent performing the action. The first sentence uses the passive form, *are shifted by*. The word *is* can serve as a tip-off: passive verbs always feature some version of *to be*.

Passive verbs are not always bad. Sometimes a sentence will work better if it uses one. We can even envision a situation where our first sample sentence would perhaps make more sense. Imagine that up to this point, the writer has repeatedly referred to the "you." Imagine, too, that the writer had left off mentioning the speaker several paragraphs back. By making the "you" the grammatical subject of the sentence, the writer can maintain consistency, whereas suddenly switching to "the speaker" might throw readers off. Usually, however, passive verbs are unnecessary and counterproductive. Make them an exception, not the rule.

Usually, a sentence will seem better paced if you keep the main subject and verb close together. When several words come between subject and verb, readers may have trouble following along. This pair of sentences illustrates what we mean:

> The speaker, hoping to make other people abandon all motion and gaze at the reaper, commands them to "Behold her."
>
> Hoping to make other people abandon all motion and gaze at the reaper, the speaker commands them to "Behold her."

Neither sentence is bad. But the first forces the reader to slow down right in the middle, since it puts several words between subject and verb. By keeping them together, the second sentence flows more.

Sentences are easier to read when they include at most one negative expression: words such as *not, never, don't,* and *won't.* On the other hand, a sentence is often hard to follow when it features several negatives. Look at the following pair of examples:

> Not able to halt the passage of time, because no human being ever can, the speaker does not stick to the present tense.

> Because, like other human beings, he cannot halt the passage of time, the speaker shifts to the past tense.

While the first sentence is grammatically correct and makes a logical point, its blizzard of negatives will confuse many readers. The second sentence makes basically the same point, but because it minimizes negatives, it is easier to read.

A point can have greater or less emphasis depending on where you place it. If you want to call attention to a paragraph's main idea, try beginning the paragraph with it. In any case, most likely your readers will assume that a paragraph's opening sentence is important. Usually they will pay special attention to its last sentence, too. Therefore, try not to fill either of these slots with relatively trivial points. Also, remember that you may obscure an important idea if you put it in the middle of a paragraph. There, the idea will have trouble getting the prominence it deserves.

Conclusion

You can always end your paper by summarizing the argument you have made. In fact, many readers will welcome a recap. Yet a conclusion that merely restates your argument risks boring your audience. Therefore, try to keep any final summary brief, using your **conclusion** to do additional things.

For example, the conclusion is a good place to make concessions. Even if you have already indicated ways in which people may reasonably disagree with you, you may use the close of your paper to acknowledge that you have no monopoly on truth. Your conclusion is also an opportunity for you to evaluate the text you have been discussing or to identify questions that the text still leaves in your mind. Consider as well the possibility of using your conclusion to bring up some personal experience that relates to the text. Yet another option is to have your conclusion identify implications of your argument that you have not so far announced: How might people apply your method of analysis to other texts? What, in effect, have you suggested about how people should live? What image have you given of the author that you have been discussing?

You might also end your paper by indicating further research you would like to do. Admittedly, this sort of conclusion is more typical of the sciences and social sciences. Literary critics tend to conclude their arguments as if there is nothing more they need to investigate. But if you do suggest you have more work to do, your readers may admire you for remaining curious and ambitious.

Sample Student Paper: First Draft

The following is Abby's first complete draft of her paper. Eventually, she revised this draft after a group of her classmates reviewed it and after she reflected further on it herself. For the moment, though, read this first version, and decide what you would have said to her about it.

Abby Hazelton

Professor Ramsey

English 102

4 March —

The Passage of Time in

"The Solitary Reaper"

William Wordsworth, one of the most famous writers in the movement known as British Romanticism, liked to write about beautiful features of the countryside. In his poem "The Solitary Reaper," the speaker enthuses over a girl who sings as she works in the fields. Yet although he is enraptured by her "melancholy strain," he is unsure what it is about because she is using a Scottish dialect that he cannot understand. By contrast, the subject of the poem itself seems much clearer. The very title of the poem refers to the singing girl, and the subsequent lines repeatedly praise her song as wonderfully haunting. Nevertheless, the poem has puzzling aspects. Many readers are likely to wonder if they are supposed to find the speaker guilty of cultural and class superiority when he, as a British intellectual, treats a Scottish peasant girl as a spectacle. Another issue, the one I focus on in my paper, arises when the final stanza shifts to past tense. In the first three stanzas, the speaker uses present tense, as if he is currently observing the singer whom he describes. In the concluding stanza, however, the speaker uses verbs such as "sang," "saw," and "listen'd," as if he is recalling his encounter with her. How can we explain this inconsistency? One possible justification for the final shift to past tense is that it reminds us of the speaker's inability to halt the passage of time.

Even though he would like to freeze the encounter, time goes on. Perhaps, therefore, the poem's real subject is the idea that time is always in flux. Indeed, even before the final stanza, the speaker betrays an awareness that he can't bend time to his will.

Simply by virtue of the shift to past tense, the last stanza indicates that time goes on despite the speaker's wishes. But other elements of this stanza convey the same notion. Recalling his experience of the girl's singing, the speaker reports that he was "motionless and still," yet in the very next line he admits that he eventually moved: "I mounted up the hill." When the speaker says that "The Maiden sang / As if her song could have no ending," the words "As if" are significant, implying that the song did end for him in reality. Similarly, the poem itself has to end at some point. In fact, it concludes with the words "no more," which stress that the singer and her song now belong to the speaker's past. Only in his "heart," apparently, can he retain them. Furthermore, the medium of print can never convey the sound of music. In fact, prior to recording technology, music was the most fleeting of media, its notes fading with each new moment. By seeking to transmit music, the speaker ensures that he will wind up being frustrated by time.

Even if the final stanza's shift of tense is jarring, the first three stanzas give hints that the speaker will end up defeated by time. Significantly, the poem's very first word is "Behold." In issuing this command, the speaker evidently hopes that other people will abandon all motion and gaze at the singer, basking in her song. The speaker reinforces this call for paralysis with the command that begins line 4: "Stop here." Yet, as if acknowledging limits to his control, he adds "or gently pass!" Besides referring to other human beings, these commands seem directed at time itself. The speaker hopes that time, too, will "Stop" and "Behold." Even at this point in the poem, however, he realizes that time is inclined to "pass," in which case he hopes that it will at least move on "gently."

The second stanza is chiefly concerned with space. Comparing the girl's song to other sounds, the speaker ranges from "Arabian sands" to "the seas / Among the far-thest Hebrides." In the third stanza, however, he focuses again on time. Trying to determine the subject of the song, he expresses uncertainty about its time frame. He wonders whether the song concerns "old, unhappy, far-off things / And battles long ago" or instead deals with "Familiar matter of to-day." Moreover, even if he sus-pects the song's subject is "Some natural sorrow, loss, or pain," he is unsure whether this experience of despair is confined to the past ("has been") or will reoccur ("may be again"). Whichever of the possibilities he raises is true, the speaker is clearly limited in his ability to figure out the song's relation to time. In other words, he cannot force time into a meaningful pat-tern, let alone prevent its passing.

By the end of the poem, the speaker seems as "soli-tary" as the reaper. In addition to losing his experience with her as time moves on, he is isolated in other ways. Throughout the poem, actually, we don't see him in the company of others. His opening "Behold" is directed at no one in particular. Furthermore, we can't be sure he is speaking to actual passers-by or, rather, to the poem's hypothetical future readers. Nor, for all his praise of the singer, does he apparently talk to her. Rather, he gives the impression that he keeps at a distance. Even if he did try to converse with the reaper, he himself would still be "solitary" in the sense of failing to understand her language and failing to communicate her song to his readers. He does not even bother trying to reproduce some of the song's words. Therefore, despite the speaker's enchantment over the reaper, this poem is ultimately pes-simistic. The speaker is left only with his memories of a wonderful experience. He has lost the experience itself.

Revising

Most first drafts are far from perfect. Even experienced professional writers often have to revise their work. Besides making changes on their own, many of them solicit feedback from others. In various workplaces, writing is collaborative, with coauthors exchanging ideas as they try to improve a piece. Remain open to the possibility that your draft needs changes, perhaps several. Of course, you are more apt to revise extensively if you have given yourself enough time. Conversely, you will not feel able to change much of your paper if it is due the next day. You will also limit your ability to revise if you work only with your original manuscript, scribbling possible changes between the lines. This practice amounts to conservatism, for it encourages you to keep passages that really ought to be overhauled.

You may have trouble, however, improving a draft if you are checking many things in it at once. Therefore, read the draft repeatedly, looking at a different aspect of it each time. A good way to begin is to outline the paper you have written and then compare that outline with your original one. If the two outlines differ, your draft may or may not need adjusting; perhaps you were wise to swerve from your original plan. In any case, you should ponder your departures from that plan, considering whether they were for the best.

If, like Abby, you are writing an argument paper, here are some topics and questions you might apply as you review your first draft. Some of these considerations overlap. Nevertheless, take them in turn rather than all at once.

Logic

- Will my audience see that the issue I am focusing on is indeed an issue?
- Will the audience be able to follow the logic of my argument?
- Is the logic as persuasive as it might be? Is there more evidence I can provide? Do I need to identify more of my warrants?
- Have I addressed all of my audience's potential concerns?

Organization

- Does my introduction identify the issue that I will focus on? Does it state my main claim?
- Will my audience be able to detect and follow the stages of my argument?
- Does the order of my paragraphs seem purposeful rather than arbitrary?
- Have I done all I can to signal connections within and between sentences? Within and between paragraphs?
- Have I avoided getting bogged down in mere summary?
- Will my conclusion satisfy readers? Does it leave any key questions dangling?

Clarity

- Does my title offer a good preview of my argument?
- Will each of my sentences be immediately clear?
- Am I sure how to define each word that I have used?

Emphasis

* Have I put key points in prominent places?
* Have I worded each sentence for maximum impact? In particular, is each sentence as concise as possible? Do I use active verbs whenever I can?

Style

* Are my tone and level of vocabulary appropriate?
* Will my audience think me fair-minded? Should I make any more concessions?
* Do I use any mannerisms that may distract my readers?
* Have I used any expressions that may annoy or offend?
* Is there anything else I can do to make my paper readable and interesting?

Grammar

* Is each of my sentences grammatically correct?
* Have I punctuated properly?

Physical Appearance

* Have I followed the proper format for quotations, notes, and bibliography?
* Are there any typographical errors?

We list these considerations from most to least important. When revising a draft, think first about matters of logic, organization, and clarity. There is little point in fixing the grammar of particular sentences if you are going to drop them later because they fail to advance your argument.

As we noted, a group of Abby's classmates discussed her draft. Most of these students seemed to like her overall argument, including her main issue and claim. Having been similarly confused by the poem's shift of tense, they appreciated the light that Abby shed on it. They were impressed by her willingness to examine the poem's specific words. They especially liked her closing analogy between the reaper and the speaker himself. Nevertheless, the group made several comments about Abby's paper that she took as suggestions for improvement. Ultimately, she decided that the following changes were in order.

1. *She should make her introduction more concise.* The first draft is so long and dense that it may confuse readers instead of helping them sense the paper's main concerns. This problem is common to first drafts. In this preliminary phase, many writers worry that they will fail to generate *enough* words; they are hardly thinking about how to restrain themselves. Moreover, the writer of a first draft may still be unsure about the paper's whole argument, so the introduction often lacks a sharp focus. After Abby finished and reviewed her first draft, she saw ways of making her introduction tighter.

2. *She should rearrange paragraphs.* After her introduction, Abby discussed the poem's last stanza in more detail. Then she moved back to stanza 1. Next, just before her paper's conclusion, she analyzed stanzas 2 and 3. Abby thought that the structure of her paper moved logically from the obvious to the hidden:

the poem's last stanza emphasized the passage of time, and the earlier stanzas touched on this subject more subtly. Yet Abby's method of organization frustrated her classmates. They thought her paper would be easier to follow if, after the introduction, it moved chronologically through the poem. For them, her discussion of stanzas 2 and 3 seemed especially mislocated. Though she had positioned this discussion as her paper's climax, her classmates did not sense it to be her most significant and compelling moment of insight. Most important, they believed, were her comments on the *final* stanza, for that seemed to them the most important part of Wordsworth's poem. In other words, they thought the climax of the paper would be stronger if it focused on the climax of the poem. Abby hesitated to adopt her classmates' recommendation, but eventually she did so. When you read her final version, see if you like her rearrangement of paragraphs. Sometimes, though not always, a paper about a literary work seems more coherent if it does follow the work's chronological structure. And papers should indeed build to a climax, even if readers disagree about what its content should be.

3. *She should reconsider her claim that "the poem is ultimately pessimistic."* Abby's classmates thought this claim did not fully account for the poem's last two lines: "The music in my heart I bore, / Long after it was heard no more." While they agreed with her that the words "no more" emphasize that the singer has faded into the past, they disagreed that her song is lost as well, for it remains in the speaker's "heart." They noted that Abby had acknowledged this fact, but they felt she had done so too briefly and dismissively. In addition, one student encouraged her to think about poetry and music as ways of keeping memories alive. More specifically, he suggested that the speaker of "The Solitary Reaper" is Wordsworth himself, who is using this poem to preserve his memory of an actual encounter. After studying the poem again, Abby decided her classmates' ideas had merit, and she incorporated them into her revision. Of course, such advice is not always worth heeding. Still, writers should accept the invitation to look more closely at whatever text they are analyzing.

Sample Student Paper: Revised Draft

Here is the new version of her paper that Abby wrote. Again, decide what you think of it.

```
Abby Hazelton

Professor Ramsey

English 102

11 March —
```

                    The Passage of Time in

                "The Solitary Reaper"

        In William Wordsworth's poem "The Solitary Reaper,"

    the speaker enthuses over a girl who sings as she works

in the fields. Throughout the poem, his rapture is evident. Yet in the last stanza, he makes a puzzling move,
shifting to past tense after using present tense in the
previous three stanzas. No longer does he seem to be currently observing the singer he describes; rather, now
he seems to be <u>recalling</u> his encounter with her. One possible justification for this shift in tense is that it
reminds us of the speaker's inability to halt the passage of time. Even though he would like to freeze the
encounter, time goes on. Perhaps, therefore, the poem's
real theme is that time is always in flux. Indeed, even
before the final stanza, the speaker betrays an awareness
that he can't bend time to his will.

Significantly, the poem's very first word is "Behold."
In issuing this command, the speaker evidently hopes that
other people will abandon all motion and gaze at the
singer, basking in her song. The speaker reinforces this
call for paralysis with the command that begins line 4:
"Stop here." Yet, as if acknowledging limits to his control, he adds "or gently pass!" Besides referring to
other human beings, these commands seem directed at time
itself. The speaker hopes that time, too, will "Stop" and
"Behold." Even at this point in the poem, however, he
realizes that time is inclined to "pass," in which case
he hopes that it will at least move on "gently."

The second stanza is chiefly concerned with space.
Comparing the girl's song to other sounds, the speaker
ranges from "Arabian sands" to "the seas / among the farthest Hebrides." In the third stanza, however, he focuses
again on time. Trying to determine the subject of the
song, he expresses uncertainty about its time frame. He
wonders whether the song concerns "old, unhappy, far-off
things / And battles long ago" or instead deals with
"Familiar matter of to-day." Moreover, even if he suspects
the song's subject is "Some natural sorrow, loss, or
pain," he is unsure whether this experience of despair is
confined to the past ("has been") or will reoccur ("may

be again"). Whichever of the possibilities he raises is
true, the speaker is clearly limited in his ability to
figure out the song's relation to time. In other words,
he cannot force time into a meaningful pattern, let alone
prevent its passing.

Simply by virtue of the shift to past tense, the last
stanza indicates that time goes on despite the speaker's
wishes. But other elements of this stanza convey the same
notion. Recalling his experience of the girl's singing,
the speaker reports that he was "motionless and still,"
yet in the very next line he admits that he eventually
moved: "I mounted up the hill." When the speaker says
that "The Maiden sang / As if her song could have no ending," the words "As if" are significant, implying that
the song did end for him in reality. Similarly, the poem
itself has to end at some point. In fact, it concludes
with the words "no more," which stress that the singer
and her song now belong to the speaker's past. Only in
his "heart," apparently, can he retain them.

This situation seems to leave the speaker as "solitary" as the reaper. Throughout the poem, actually, we
don't see him in the company of others. His opening
"Behold" is directed at no one in particular. Furthermore, we can't be sure he is speaking to actual passers-
by or, rather, to the poem's hypothetical future readers.
Nor, for all his praise of the singer, does he apparently
talk to her. Rather, he gives the impression that he
keeps at a distance. Even if he did converse with the
reaper, he himself would still be "solitary" in the sense
of failing to understand her dialect and failing to communicate her words to his readers. As things stand, he
is apparently unable or unwilling to reproduce any of
the song's lyrics. Just as important, the medium of print
can never convey the sound of music. In fact, prior to
recording technology, music was the most fleeting of
media, its notes fading with each new moment. By seeking

```
to transmit music, the speaker ensures that he will wind
up being frustrated by time.
    Yet perhaps the singer and her song are preserved in
more than just the speaker's "heart." It can be argued
that they are also preserved by the poem, if only to a
limited extent. More generally, we can say that litera-
ture is a means by which human beings partially succeed
in perpetuating things. This idea seems quite relevant to
"The Solitary Reaper" if we suppose that the speaker is
the poet himself and that he actually witnessed the scene
he describes. If we make such assumptions, we can see
Wordsworth as analogous to the speaker. After all, both
engage in commemorative verbal art. Because time passes,
the "strains" that Wordsworth and the singer produce in
their efforts to preserve time are bound to be "melan-
choly." Still, their art matters, for through it they can
imaginatively "reap" experiences that would otherwise
fade.
```

To us, Abby's revision is more persuasive and compelling than her first draft. In particular, she has nicely complicated her claim about the poem's "pessimism." Nevertheless, we would hesitate to call this revision the definitive version of her paper. Maybe you have thought of things Abby could do to make it even more effective. In presenting her two drafts, we mainly want to emphasize the importance of revision. We hope, too, that you will remember our specific tips as you work on your own writing.

Writing a Comparative Paper

Much writing about literature *compares* two or more texts. After all, you can gain many insights into a text by noting how it resembles and differs from others. Throughout this book, therefore, we cluster texts, encouraging you to trace similarities and differences within each set. For instance, the chapters in Part One repeatedly present clusters that treat various aspects of work. At the moment, we offer suggestions for writing a comparative paper, a task you may be assigned in your course.

To aid our discussion, we ask you to reread Wordsworth's "The Solitary Reaper" and then read the following poem, which is by the contemporary American poet Ted Kooser (b. 1939). Though born in Iowa, Kooser has spent much of his life in Nebraska. There he has not only produced several volumes of poetry but also worked for an insurance company, from which he eventually retired as vice president. This selection is from Kooser's book *Weather Central* (1994).

TED KOOSER
Four Secretaries

All through the day I hear or overhear
their clear, light voices calling
from desk to desk, young women whose fingers
play casually over their documents,

setting the incoming checks to one side,   5
the thick computer reports to the other,
tapping the correspondence into stacks
while they sing to each other, not intending

to sing nor knowing how beautiful
their voices are as they call back and forth,   10
singing their troubled marriage ballads,
their day-care, car-park, landlord songs.

Even their anger with one another
is lovely: the color rising in their throats,
their white fists clenched in their laps,   15
the quiet between them that follows.

And their sadness—how deep and full of love
is their sadness when one among them
is hurt, and they hear her calling
and gather about her to cry.   [1994]   20

A class like yours sensed value in comparing Wordsworth's poem with Kooser's. So the students proceeded to brainstorm lists of specific similarities and differences—something you might do to start analyzing texts you bring together. For these two poems, the class came up with the following comparisons:

SIMILARITIES

"Reaper" and "Secretaries" both have titles that refer to
    women at work.
Both poems describe women <u>singing</u> at work.
The speakers in both poems "hear or overhear" the singing
    rather than being its direct audience.
In general, the speakers in both poems seem alone or
    detached as they observe their subjects.

Both speakers seem to find beauty in the people they
    observe.
Both speakers refer to sorrow: the speaker of "Reaper"
    detecting "a melancholy strain," the speaker of "Sec-
    retaries" noting "sadness."
Both poems use fairly simple language for their time
    period.

DIFFERENCES

The speaker of "Reaper" observes one woman; the speaker
    of "Secretaries" four.
The reaper is literally singing; the secretaries only
    metaphorically so.
The speaker of "Reaper" is referring to a particular
    event of singing, whereas the speaker of "Secre-
    taries" describes singing that occurs daily.
"Reaper" is set in the countryside; "Secretaries" in an
    office.
The woman in "Reaper" seems to sing to herself, whereas
    the women in "Secretaries" sing to one another.
The speaker of "Reaper" cannot understand the singer's
    words, but the speaker of "Secretaries" seems to know
    what the women are singing about.
The speaker of "Reaper" refers consistently to the
    woman's singing, but the speaker of "Secretaries"
    gives more attention to the four women's "calling,"
    using that word in the first and last stanzas.
While each stanza of "Reaper" ends with a period, the
    first two stanzas of "Secretaries" end with sentences
    that spill over into the next sentences.
"Reaper" ends by focusing on the speaker's "heart," but
    "Secretaries" ends with an expression of heartfelt
    sympathy by the women whom the speaker has been
    observing.

As you plan your own comparative paper, lists such as these can help you
organize your thoughts. To be sure, this class did not immediately think of all the
similarities and differences it ended up noting. Usually, going beyond obvious

points of comparison is a gradual process, for which you should give yourself plenty of time. Similarly, once you have made lists such as the above, take time to decide which similarities and differences truly merit your attention. At most, only a few can be part of your paper's main issue and claim.

Unfortunately, many students writing a comparative analysis are content to put forth main claims such as these:

> There are many similarities and differences between "The
> Solitary Reaper" and "Four Secretaries."
> While "The Solitary Reaper" and "Four Secretaries" have
> many similarities, in many ways they are also dif-
> ferent.
> While "The Solitary Reaper" and "Four Secretaries" are
> different in many ways, they are similar in others.

Several problems arise with these common methods of introducing a comparative paper. For one thing, they give the reader no preview of the specific ideas to come. Indeed, they could have been written by someone who never bothered to read the two poems, for any two texts are similar in certain ways and different in others. Furthermore, these sorts of claims leave no meaningful and compelling way of organizing the paper. Rather, they encourage the writer to proceed arbitrarily, noting miscellaneous similarities and differences on impulse. More precisely, claims such as these fail to identify the *issue* driving the paper. Why compare Wordsworth's and Kooser's poems in the first place? Comparison is a means to an end, not an end in itself. What important question is the writer using these two texts to answer? In short, what's at stake?

A more fruitful approach, we think, is to write a *weighted* comparative analysis—that is, an argument chiefly concerned with *one* text more than others. When professional literary critics compare two texts, often they mainly want to answer a question about just one of them. They bring in the second text because they believe that doing so helps them address the issue they are raising about their key text. True, a good paper can result even when you treat equally all texts you discuss. But you are more apt to write a paper that seems purposeful and coherent if you focus basically on one work, using comparisons to resolve some issue concerning it.

Sample Comparative Paper

The following paper by student Marla Tracy demonstrates weighted comparative analysis. The author refers to Wordsworth's "The Solitary Reaper" as well as Kooser's "Four Secretaries," but she is mainly concerned with Kooser's poem. She brings up Wordsworth's poem not to do comparison for its own sake but to address a question she has about Kooser's text.

Marla Tracy

Professor James

English 12

23 February —

When Singing Is Not Singing

In Ted Kooser's poem "Four Secretaries," the speaker praises the "singing" of the title characters, whose voices he listens to as they perform their daily clerical duties nearby. His admiration for the music of women workers has precedent in poetry. In William Wordsworth's "The Solitary Reaper," a poem from the early nineteenth century, the speaker glories in the tune that a Scottish country girl produces as she "cuts and binds the grain." But whereas the reaper of Wordsworth's poem really does sing, such is not the case with Kooser's secretaries. When the speaker in Kooser's poem refers to their "singing," he is being metaphorical. Given that he more or less <u>imagines</u> the women's singing, what should we conclude? We may be tempted to see the poem as chiefly exposing the speaker's own warped mind. But a more plausible interpretation is that the speaker reveals how the secretaries really interact. Though his reference to their "singing" is figurative, his imaginative use of the word enables him to convey the sensitivity they show one another.

Some elements of Kooser's poem do encourage readers to see it as a psychological case study of the speaker. Rather than mind his own business, he clearly likes to "hear or overhear" the secretaries' conversations and thus seems at least a bit nosey. Perhaps he is even indulging the power of observation typically granted a boss. (Kooser has been an insurance executive, and maybe the poem is about his own office.) At the same time, the speaker can be thought emotionally detached, especially when he reports the women's occasional sadness, notes that they console one another, and yet apparently does not offer them comfort himself. Moreover, he risks seeming sadistic when he declares that "their anger with one another / is lovely," for here he appears to find beauty in their pain. His claim that the women are "singing," then, can be considered another sign that his own idiosyncrasies are the poem's main concern.

Ultimately, though, the poem seems much more about the secretaries than about the speaker. If the speaker has quirks, they are rather understated; throughout the poem, his tone remains calm. Again, Wordsworth's "Solitary Reaper" provides an instructive contrast, for its speaker puts his emotions blatantly on display. Besides declaring that the reaper's song is "welcome," "thrilling," and "plaintive," he beseeches passers-by to "Behold her" and "tell me what she sings." Compared with Wordsworth's speaker, Kooser's is fairly reticent, focusing on the secretaries' behavior rather than his own personal passions.

The speaker admits that the secretaries are "not intending / to sing." Indeed, this phrase spills over from the second to the third stanza, thereby emphasizing the speaker's confession. At the same time, the speaker's claim that they are in some sense "singing" enables him to consider the various possible actions that this word can entail. In fact, because "singing" here is metaphorical rather than literal, the poem can more easily raise an issue of definition: What do we <u>want</u> "singing" to mean?

The speaker answers this question by focusing largely on the interplay of the women's voices. In the first stanza, he describes their "light voices calling / from desk to desk"; in the third, he observes that "they call back and forth." With these references to "calling," the speaker defines and praises "singing" as the vocal building of relationships. Perhaps Kooser even wants us to think of the "call and response" tradition of African American religious music, which helped keep that community together during years of oppression. In any case, the poem's emphasis on the social nature of singing differs yet again from the focus of "The Solitary Reaper," where singing is a solo affair.

Of course, Kooser's fourth stanza complicates the poem's emphasis on the secretaries' emotional bonds. By noting that sometimes the secretaries experience "anger with one another," the speaker seems to put their feeling of community in question. But "the quiet" mentioned in the stanza's last line seems merely a typical pause in a song, not the ceasing of it. While the singing of Wordsworth's reaper is eventually "no more," the singing of these secretaries seems bound to resume. Furthermore, anger can be considered another form of emotional commitment. Often, people are angry with someone precisely because they expect a lot from that person. Actually, when the speaker asserts that "Even their anger with one another / is lovely," perhaps "lovely" here means "full of love," a phrase that the speaker subsequently uses to describe the secretaries' "sadness."

However we interpret the wording of the fourth stanza, the poem's basic drift is clear. It ends with a concrete image of the secretaries' bonding. More specifically, three of the secretaries comfort the fourth. Rather than make her "cry" alone, they join her in her tears, reminding us that "singing" in this poem is collective.

Marla gains much from comparing Kooser's poem with Wordsworth's. By bringing up "The Solitary Reaper" in her first paragraph, she establishes that "Four Secretaries" belongs to a poetic tradition, while also pointing out this contemporary text's distinctiveness (its references to "singing" are metaphorical). In paragraph 3, she contrasts Kooser's speaker with Wordsworth's to reinforce her claim that Kooser's poem is more about the secretaries. In paragraphs 5 and 6, she contrasts the two poems again, as part of her argument that "singing" in Kooser's poem is an ongoing social relationship. Clearly, though, Marla focuses her paper on Kooser's poem, not both. By concentrating chiefly on "Four Secretaries," she enables herself to develop a logical analysis, whereas focusing on both poems would encourage her to wander through various similarities and differences at random.

Perhaps you know the advice usually given about how to organize a comparative paper. Traditionally, writers aiming to compare two texts learn of two options: (1) discuss one text and then move to the other, comparing it with the first; (2) discuss the texts together, noting each of their similarities and differences in turn. Both of these alternatives make sense and provide a ready-made structure for your paper; either can result in a coherent essay. Still, a weighted analysis such as Marla's—an analysis that focuses on one text more than another—is more likely than either of the alternatives to seem the logical evolution of a pointed claim.

4

Writing about Stories

Short stories can be said to resemble novels. Above all, both are works of fiction. Yet the difference in length matters. As William Trevor, a veteran writer of short stories, has observed, short fiction is "the art of the glimpse; it deals in echoes and reverberations; craftily it withholds information. Novels tell all. Short stories tell as little as they dare." Maybe Trevor overstates the situation when he claims that novels reveal everything. All sorts of texts feature what literary theorist Wolfgang Iser calls "gaps." Still, Trevor is right to emphasize that short stories usually tell much less than novels do. They demand that you understand and evaluate characters on the basis of just a few details and events. In this respect, short stories resemble poems. Both tend to rely on compression rather than expansion, seeking to affect their audience with a sharply limited number of words.

Short stories' focused use of language can make the experience of reading them wonderfully intense. Furthermore, you may end up considering important human issues as you try to interpret the "glimpses" they provide. Precisely because short stories "tell as little as they dare," they offer you much to ponder as you proceed to write about them.

In discussing that writing process, we refer often to the three stories that follow. The stories tell of the work that a healthy person does as he or she encounters someone physically suffering. The first story, "The Use of Force," is by a writer more known for his poetry, William Carlos Williams (1883–1963). Even as he produced literature, Williams served as a doctor in his hometown of Rutherford, New Jersey, as well as in the nearby city of Paterson. The story presented here, which appeared in Williams's 1938 collection *Life along the Passaic River*, is one of several based on his medical work during America's Great Depression. The second selection, "A Visit of Charity," is by a pioneer of the modern American short story, Eudora Welty (1909–2001), who spent most of her life in her hometown of Jackson, Mississippi. This particular piece appeared in Welty's first collection, *A Curtain of Green and Other Stories*, published in 1941. The final story, "The Gift of Sweat," is by a contemporary American writer, Rebecca Brown (b. 1956). It is the lead-off piece in her 1994 book *The Gifts of the Body*, a sequence of short stories narrated by a woman who does housekeeping for people with AIDS—a kind of service work that Brown, too, has done.

WILLIAM CARLOS WILLIAMS
The Use of Force

They were new patients to me, all I had was the name, Olson. Please come down as soon as you can, my daughter is very sick. When I arrived I was met by the mother, a big startled looking woman, very clean and apologetic who merely said, Is this the doctor? and let me in. In the back, she added. You must excuse us, doctor, we have her in the kitchen where it is warm. It is very damp here sometimes.

The child was fully dressed and sitting on her father's lap near the kitchen table. He tried to get up, but I motioned for him not to bother, took off my overcoat and started to look things over. I could see that they were all very nervous, eyeing me up and down distrustfully. As often, in such cases, they weren't telling me more than they had to, it was up to me to tell them; that's why they were spending three dollars on me.

The child was fairly eating me up with her cold, steady eyes, and no expression to her face whatever. She did not move and seemed, inwardly, quiet; an unusually attractive little thing, and as strong as a heifer in appearance. But her face was flushed, she was breathing rapidly, and I realized that she had a high fever. She had magnificent blond hair, in profusion. One of those picture children often reproduced in advertising leaflets and the photogravure sections of the Sunday papers.

She's had a fever for three days, began the father and we don't know what it comes from. My wife has given her things, you know, like people do, but it don't do no good. And there's been a lot of sickness around. So we tho't you'd better look her over and tell us what is the matter.

As doctors often do I took a trial shot at it as a point of departure. Has she had   5
a sore throat?

Both parents answered me together, No . . . No, she says her throat don't hurt her.

Does your throat hurt you? added the mother to the child. But the little girl's expression didn't change nor did she move her eyes from my face.

Have you looked?

I tried to, said the mother, but I couldn't see.

As it happens we had been having a number of cases of diphtheria in the   10
school to which the child went during that month and we were all, quite apparently, thinking of that, though no one had as yet spoken of the thing.

Well, I said, suppose we take a look at the throat first. I smiled in my best professional manner and asking for the child's first name I said, come on, Mathilda, open your mouth and let's take a look at your throat.

Nothing doing.

Aw, come on, I coaxed, just open your mouth wide and let me take a look. Look, I said opening both hands wide, I haven't anything in my hands. Just open up and let me see.

Such a nice man, put in the mother. Look how kind he is to you. Come on, do what he tells you to, he won't hurt you.

At that I ground my teeth in disgust. If only they wouldn't use the word 15
"hurt" I might be able to get somewhere. But I did not allow myself to be hurried
or disturbed but speaking quietly and slowly I approached the child again.

As I moved my chair a little nearer suddenly with one catlike movement
both her hands clawed instinctively for my eyes and she almost reached them too.
In fact she knocked my glasses flying and they fell, though unbroken, several feet
away from me on the kitchen floor.

Both the mother and father almost turned themselves inside out in embarrassment and apology. You bad girl, said the mother, taking her and shaking her
by one arm. Look what you've done. The nice man . . .

For heaven's sake, I broke in. Don't call me a nice man to her. I'm here to
look at her throat on the chance that she might have diphtheria and possibly die
of it. But that's nothing to her. Look here, I said to the child, we're going to look
at your throat. You're old enough to understand what I'm saying. Will you open it
now by yourself or shall we have to open it for you?

Not a move. Even her expression hadn't changed. Her breaths however were
coming faster and faster. Then the battle began. I had to do it. I had to have a
throat culture for her own protection. But first I told the parents that it was
entirely up to them. I explained the danger but said that I would not insist on a
throat examination so long as they would take the responsibility.

If you don't do what the doctor says you'll have to go to the hospital, the 20
mother admonished her severely.

Oh yeah? I had to smile to myself. After all, I had already fallen in love with
the savage brat, the parents were contemptible to me. In the ensuing struggle
they grew more and more abject, crushed, exhausted while she surely rose to
magnificent heights of insane fury of effort bred of her terror of me.

The father tried his best, and he was a big man but the fact that she was his
daughter, his shame at her behavior and his dread of hurting her made him
release her just at the critical times when I had almost achieved success, till I
wanted to kill him. But his dread also that she might have diphtheria made him
tell me to go on, go on though he himself was almost fainting, while the mother
moved back and forth behind us raising and lowering her hands in an agony of
apprehension.

Put her in front of you on your lap, I ordered, and hold both her wrists.

But as soon as he did the child let out a scream. Don't, you're hurting me.
Let go of my hands. Let them go I tell you. Then she shrieked terrifyingly, hysterically. Stop it! Stop it! You're killing me!

Do you think she can stand it, doctor! said the mother. 25

You get out, said the husband to his wife. Do you want her to die of diphtheria?

Come on now, hold her, I said.

Then I grasped the child's head with my left hand and tried to get the
wooden tongue depressor between her teeth. She fought, with clenched teeth,
desperately! But now I also had grown furious — at a child. I tried to hold myself
down but I couldn't. I know how to expose a throat for inspection. And I did my
best. When finally I got the wooden spatula behind the last teeth and just the

point of it into the mouth cavity, she opened up for an instant but before I could see anything she came down again and gripped the wooden blade between her molars. She reduced it to splinters before I could get it out again.

Aren't you ashamed, the mother yelled at her. Aren't you ashamed to act like that in front of the doctor?

Get me a smooth-handled spoon of some sort, I told the mother. We're going through with this. The child's mouth was already bleeding. Her tongue was cut and she was screaming in wild hysterical shrieks. Perhaps I should have desisted and come back in an hour or more. No doubt it would have been better. But I have seen at least two children lying dead in bed of neglect in such cases, and feeling that I must get a diagnosis now or never I went at it again. But the worst of it was that I too had got beyond reason. I could have torn the child apart in my own fury and enjoyed it. It was a pleasure to attack her. My face was burning with it. 30

The damned little brat must be protected against her own idiocy, one says to one's self at such times. Others must be protected against her. It is a social necessity. And all these things are true. But a blind fury, a feeling of adult shame, bred of a longing for muscular release are the operatives. One goes on to the end.

In the final unreasoning assault I overpowered the child's neck and jaws. I forced the heavy silver spoon back of her teeth and down her throat till she gagged. And there it was—both tonsils covered with membrane. She had fought valiantly to keep me from knowing her secret. She had been hiding that sore throat for three days at least and lying to her parents in order to escape just such an outcome as this.

Now truly she was furious. She had been on the defensive before but now she attacked. Tried to get off her father's lap and fly at me while tears of defeat blinded her eyes.   [1938]

EUDORA WELTY
A Visit of Charity

It was mid-morning—a very cold, bright day. Holding a potted plant before her, a girl of fourteen jumped off the bus in front of the Old Ladies' Home, on the outskirts of town. She wore a red coat, and her straight yellow hair was hanging down loose from the pointed white cap all the little girls were wearing that year. She stopped for a moment beside one of the prickly dark shrubs with which the city had beautified the Home, and then proceeded slowly toward the building, which was of whitewashed brick and reflected the winter sunlight like a block of ice. As she walked vaguely up the steps she shifted the small pot from hand to hand; then she had to set it down and remove her mittens before she could open the heavy door.

"I'm a Campfire Girl. . . . I have to pay a visit to some old lady," she told the nurse at the desk. This was a woman in a white uniform who looked as if she were cold; she had close-cut hair which stood up on the very top of her head exactly like a sea wave. Marian, the little girl, did not tell her that this visit would give her a minimum of only three points in her score.

"Acquainted with any of our residents?" asked the nurse. She lifted one eyebrow and spoke like a man.

"With any old ladies? No—but—that is, any of them will do," Marian stammered. With her free hand she pushed her hair behind her ears, as she did when it was time to study Science.

The nurse shrugged and rose. "You have a nice *multiflora cineraria*° there," she remarked as she walked ahead down the hall of closed doors to pick out an old lady.   5

There was loose, bulging linoleum on the floor. Marian felt as if she were walking on the waves, but the nurse paid no attention to it. There was a smell in the hall like the interior of a clock. Everything was silent until, behind one of the doors, an old lady of some kind cleared her throat like a sheep bleating. This decided the nurse. Stopping in her tracks, she first extended her arm, bent her elbow, and leaned forward from the hips—all to examine the watch strapped to her wrist; then she gave a loud double-rap on the door.

"There are two in each room," the nurse remarked over her shoulder.

"Two what?" asked Marian without thinking. The sound like a sheep's bleating almost made her turn around and run back.

One old woman was pulling the door open in short, gradual jerks, and when she saw the nurse a strange smile forced her old face dangerously awry. Marian, suddenly propelled by the strong, impatient arm of the nurse, saw next the side-face of another old woman, even older, who was lying flat in bed with a cap on and a counterpane° drawn up to her chin.

"Visitor," said the nurse, and after one more shove she was off up the hall.   10

Marian stood tongue-tied; both hands held the potted plant. The old woman, still with that terrible, square smile (which was a smile of welcome) stamped on her bony face, was waiting. . . . Perhaps she said something. The old woman in bed said nothing at all, and she did not look around.

Suddenly Marian saw a hand, quick as a bird claw, reach up in the air and pluck the white cap off her head. At the same time, another claw to match drew her all the way into the room, and the next moment the door closed behind her.

"My, my, my," said the old lady at her side.

Marian stood enclosed by a bed, a washstand and a chair; the tiny room had altogether too much furniture. Everything smelled wet—even the bare floor. She held on to the back of the chair, which was wicker and felt soft and damp. Her heart beat more and more slowly, her hands got colder and colder, and she could not hear whether the old women were saying anything or not. She could not see them very clearly. How dark it was! The window shade was down, and the only door was shut. Marian looked at the ceiling. . . . It was like being caught in a robbers' cave, just before one was murdered.

"Did you come to be our little girl for a while?" the first robber asked.   15

---

multiflora cineraria: A house plant with brightly colored flowers and heart-shaped leaves.
counterpane: Bedspread.

Then something was snatched from Marian's hand—the little potted plant.

"Flowers!" screamed the old woman. She stood holding the pot in an unde-
cided way. "Pretty flowers," she added.

Then the old woman in bed cleared her throat and spoke. "They are not
pretty," she said, still without looking around, but very distinctly.

Marian suddenly pitched against the chair and sat down in it.

"Pretty flowers," the first old woman insisted. "Pretty—pretty . . ."   20

Marian wished she had the little pot back for just a moment—she had forgotten to look at the plant herself before giving it away. What did it look like?

"Stinkweeds," said the other old woman sharply. She had a bunchy white
forehead and red eyes like a sheep. Now she turned them toward Marian. The
fogginess seemed to rise in her throat again, and she bleated, "Who—are—you?"

To her surprise, Marian could not remember her name. "I'm a Campfire
Girl," she said finally.

"Watch out for the germs," said the old woman like a sheep, not addressing
anyone.

"One came out last month to see us," said the first old woman.   25

A sheep or a germ? wondered Marian dreamily, holding on to the chair.

"Did not!" cried the other old woman.

"Did so! Read to us out of the Bible, and we enjoyed it!" screamed the first.

"Who enjoyed it!" said the woman in bed. Her mouth was unexpectedly
small and sorrowful, like a pet's.

"We enjoyed it," insisted the other. "You enjoyed it—I enjoyed it."   30

"We all enjoyed it," said Marian, without realizing that she had said a word.

The first old woman had just finished putting the potted plant high, high on
the top of the wardrobe, where it could hardly be seen from below. Marian wondered how she had ever succeeded in placing it there, how she could ever have
reached so high.

"You mustn't pay any attention to old Addie," she now said to the little girl.
"She's ailing today."

"Will you shut your mouth?" said the woman in bed. "I am not."

"You're a story."   35

"I can't stay but a minute—really, I can't," said Marian suddenly. She looked
down at the wet floor and thought that if she were sick in here they would have to
let her go.

With much to-do the first old woman sat down in a rocking chair—still
another piece of furniture!—and began to rock. With the fingers of one hand she
touched a very dirty cameo pin on her chest. "What do you do at school?" she
asked.

"I don't know . . ." said Marian. She tried to think but she could not.

"Oh, but the flowers are beautiful," the old woman whispered. She seemed
to rock faster and faster; Marian did not see how anyone could rock so fast.

"Ugly," said the woman in bed.   40

"If we bring flowers—" Marian began, and then fell silent. She had almost said
that if Campfire Girls brought flowers to the Old Ladies' Home, the visit would
count one extra point, and if they took a Bible with them on the bus and read it to

the old ladies, it counted double. But the old woman had not listened, anyway; she was rocking and watching the other one, who watched back from the bed.

"Poor Addie is ailing. She has to take medicine — see?" she said, pointing a horny finger at a row of bottles on the table, and rocking so high that her black comfort shoes lifted off the floor like a little child's.

"I am no more sick than you are," said the woman in bed.

"Oh, yes you are!"

"I just got more sense than you have, that's all," said the other old woman, nodding her head.   45

"That's only the contrary way she talks when *you all* come," said the first old lady with sudden intimacy. She stopped the rocker with a neat pat of her feet and leaned toward Marian. Her hand reached over — it felt like a petunia leaf, clinging and just a little sticky.

"Will you hush! Will you hush!" cried the other one.

Marian leaned back rigidly in her chair.

"When I was a little girl like you, I went to school and all," said the old woman in the same intimate, menacing voice. "Not here — another town . . ."

"Hush!" said the sick woman. "You never went to school. You never came   50
and you never went. You never were anything — only here. You never were born! You don't know anything. Your head is empty, your heart and hands and your old black purse are all empty, even that little old box that you brought with you you brought empty — you showed it to me. And yet you talk, talk, talk, talk, talk all the time until I think I'm losing my mind! Who are you? You're a stranger — a perfect stranger! Don't you know you're a stranger? Is it possible that they have actually done a thing like this to anyone — sent them in a stranger to talk, and rock, and tell away her whole long rigmarole? Do they seriously suppose that I'll be able to keep it up, day in, day out, night in, night out, living in the same room with a terrible old woman — forever?"

Marian saw the old woman's eyes grow bright and turn toward her. This old woman was looking at her with despair and calculation in her face. Her small lips suddenly dropped apart, and exposed a half circle of false teeth with tan gums.

"Come here, I want to tell you something," she whispered. "Come here!"

Marian was trembling, and her heart nearly stopped beating altogether for a moment.

"Now, now, Addie," said the first old woman. "That's not polite. Do you know what's really the matter with old Addie today?" She, too, looked at Marian; one of her eyelids dropped low.

"The matter?" the child repeated stupidly. "What's the matter with her?"   55

"Why, she's mad because it's her birthday!" said the first old woman, beginning to rock again and giving a little crow as though she had answered her own riddle.

"It is not, it is not!" screamed the old woman in bed. "It is not my birthday, no one knows when that is but myself, and will you please be quiet and say nothing more, or I'll go straight out of my mind!" She turned her eyes toward Marian again, and presently she said in the soft, foggy voice, "When the worst comes to the worst, I ring this bell, and the nurse comes." One of her hands was drawn out from under the patched counterpane—a thin little hand with enormous black freckles. With a finger which would not hold still she pointed to a little bell on the table among the bottles.

"How old are you?" Marian breathed. Now she could see the old woman in bed very closely and plainly, and very abruptly, from all sides, as in dreams. She wondered about her—she wondered for a moment as though there was nothing else in the world to wonder about. It was the first time such a thing had happened to Marian.

"I won't tell!"

The old face on the pillow, where Marian was bending over it, slowly gath-   60
ered and collapsed. Soft whimpers came out of the small open mouth. It was a sheep that she sounded like—a little lamb. Marian's face drew very close, the yellow hair hung forward.

"She's crying!" She turned a bright, burning face up to the first old woman.

"That's Addie for you," the old woman said spitefully.

Marian jumped up and moved toward the door. For the second time, the claw almost touched her hair, but it was not quick enough. The little girl put her cap on.

"Well, it was a real visit," said the old woman, following Marian through the doorway and all the way out into the hall. Then from behind she suddenly clutched the child with her sharp little fingers. In an affected, high-pitched whine she cried, "Oh, little girl, have you a penny to spare for a poor old woman that's not got anything of her own? We don't have a thing in the world—not a penny for candy—not a thing! Little girl, just a nickel—a penny—"

Marian pulled violently against the old hands for a moment before she was   65
free. Then she ran down the hall, without looking behind her and without looking at the nurse, who was reading *Field & Stream* at her desk. The nurse, after another triple motion to consult her wrist watch, asked automatically the question put to visitors in all institutions: "Won't you stay and have dinner with *us?*"

Marian never replied. She pushed the heavy door open into the cold air and ran down the steps.

Under the prickly shrub she stooped and quickly, without being seen, retrieved a red apple she had hidden there.

Her yellow hair under the white cap, her scarlet coat, her bare knees all flashed in the sunlight as she ran to meet the big bus rocketing through the street.

"Wait for me!" she shouted. As though at an imperial command, the bus ground to a stop.

She jumped on and took a big bite out of the apple.   [1941]   70

REBECCA BROWN
The Gift of Sweat

I went to Rick's every Tuesday and Thursday morning. I usually called before I went to see if he wanted me to pick up anything for him on the way. He never used to ask me for anything until once when I hadn't had breakfast and I stopped at this place a couple blocks from him, the Hostess with the Mostest, to get a cinnamon roll and I got two, one for him. I didn't really think he'd eat it because he was so organic. He had this incredible garden on the side of the apartment with tomatoes and zucchinis and carrots and he used to do all his own baking. I also got two large coffees with milk. I could have eaten it all if he didn't want his. But when I got to his place and asked him if he'd had breakfast and showed him what I'd brought, he squealed. He said those cinnamon rolls were his absolute favorite things in the world and he used to go to the Hostess on Sunday mornings. He said he'd try to be there when they were fresh out of the oven and get the best ones, the ones from the center of the pan, which are the stickiest and softest. It was something he used to do for himself on Sunday, which was not his favorite day.

So after that when I called him before I went over and asked if he wanted anything, he'd still say no thanks, and then I would say, "How about the usual," meaning the rolls and coffee, and he'd say he'd love it.

So one morning when I called and asked him if he wanted "the usual" and he said he didn't, I was surprised.

He said, "Not today!" He sounded really chirpy. "Just get your sweet self over here. I got a surprise for you."

I said OK and that I'd see him in a few. I made a quick cup of coffee and   5
downed the end of last night's pizza and went over. I was at his place in half an hour.

I always knocked on the door. When he was there he'd always shout, "Hello! Just a minute!" and come let me in. It took him a while to get to the door but he liked being able to answer it himself, he liked still living in his own place. If he wasn't at home I let myself in and read the note he would have left me — that he had an appointment or something, or if there was some special thing he wanted me to do. Then I would clean or do chores. I used to like being there alone sometimes. I could do surprises for him, like leave him notes under his pillow or rearrange his wind-up toys so they were kissing or other silly things. Rick loved surprises.

But this one morning when I knocked on the door it took him a long time to answer. Then I heard him trying to shout, but he sounded small. "Can you let yourself in?"

I unlocked the door and went in. He was in the living room on the futon. It was usually up like a couch to sit on, but it was flat like a bed and he was lying on it.

I went over and sat on the floor by the futon. He was lying on his side, facing away from me, curled up. His knees were near his chest.

"Rick?" I said. I put my hand on his back.   10
He didn't move, but said, "Hi," very quietly.
"What's going on?" I said.
He made a noise like a little animal.
"You want me to call your doc?"
He swallowed a couple of times. Then he said, "I called UCS. Margaret is   15
coming over to take me to the hospital."
"Good," I said, "she'll be here soon."

"Yeah," he said. Then he made that animal noise again. He was holding his stomach. "I meant to call you back," he said, "to tell you you didn't need to come over today."

"That's OK, Rick. I'm glad I'm here. I'm glad I'm with you right now."

"I didn't feel bad when you called." He sounded apologetic. "It was so sudden."

"Your stomach?"   20

He tried to nod. "Uh-huh. But everywhere some."

He was holding the corner of his quilt, squeezing it.

"I was about to get in the shower. I wanted to be all clean before you came over. It was so sudden."

"Oh, Rick," I said, "I'm sorry you hurt so much."

"Thank you."   25

"Is there anything I can do before Margaret gets here?"

"No." He swallowed again. I could smell his breath. "No thank you."

Then his mouth got tight and he squeezed the quilt corner, then he was pulsing it, then more like stabs. He started to shake. "I'm cold," he said.

I pulled the quilt over most of him. It had a pattern of moon and stars. "I'm gonna go get another blanket," I said.

"Don't go," he said really fast. "Please don't go."   30

"OK," I said, "I'll stay here."

"I'm so cold," he said again.

I touched his back. It was sweaty and hot.

I got onto the futon. I slid on very carefully so I wouldn't jolt him. I lay on my side behind him. I could feel him shaking. I put my left arm around his middle. I slipped my right hand under his head and touched his forehead. It was wet and hot. I held my hand on his forehead a couple of seconds to cool it. Then I petted his forehead and up through his hair. His hair was wet too. I combed my fingers through his wet hair to his ponytail. I said, "Poor Rick. Poor Ricky."

He was still shaking. I pulled my body close to him so his butt was in my lap   35
and my breasts and stomach were against his back. I pressed against him to warm him. He pulled my hand onto his stomach. I opened my hand so my palm was flat across him, my fingers spread. He held his hand on top of mine, squeezing it like the quilt. I could feel the sweat of his hand on the back of mine, and of his stomach, through his shirt, against my palm. I could feel his pulse all through him; it was fast.

I tightened my arms around him as if I could press the sickness out.

After a while he started to shake less. He was still sweating and I could feel more wet on the side of his face from crying.

When Margaret came we wrapped his coat around him and helped him, one on either side of him, to the car. Rick hunched and kept making noises. I helped him get in and closed the door behind him while Margaret got in the driver's side. While she was fumbling for her keys I ran around to her and asked her, "You want me to come with you?"

She said, "You don't need to. We'll be OK."

Rick didn't say anything.   40

I leaned in and said, "Your place will be all clean when you come back home, Rick."

He tried to smile.

"I'll call you later," said Margaret. She put her hand up and touched the side of my face. "You're wet," she told me.

I touched my face. It was wet. "I'll talk to you later," I said to her.

"I'll see you later, Rick," I said.   45

He nodded but didn't say anything. His face was splotched. Margaret found her keys and started the car.

I went back into his apartment. When I closed the door behind me I could smell it. It was a slight smell, sour, but also partly sweet. It was the smell of Rick's sweat.

I started cleaning. I usually started in the kitchen, but as soon as I set foot in there and saw the kitchen table I couldn't. I turned around and stood in the hall a second and held my breath. After a while I let it out.

I did everything else first. I stripped the bed and put a load of laundry in. I vacuumed and dusted. I dusted all his fairy gear, his stones and incense burners and little statues and altars. I straightened clothes in his closet he hadn't worn in ages. I untangled ties and necklaces. I put cassettes back in their cases and reshelved them. I took out the trash. I did it all fast because I wanted to get everything done, but I also wished I could stretch it out and still be doing it and be here when he came home as if he would come home soon.

I cleaned the bathroom. I shook cleanser in the shower and sink and cleaned   50
them. I sprayed Windex on the mirror. When I was wiping it off I saw myself. My face was splotched. My t-shirt had a dark spot. I put my hands to it and sniffed them. They smelled like me, but also him. It was Rick's sweat. I put my hands up to my face and I could smell him in my hands. I put my face in my hands and closed my eyes. I stood there like that a while then I went to the kitchen.

What was on the kitchen table was this: his two favorite coffee mugs, his and what used to be Barry's. There was a Melitta over one full of ground coffee, all ready to go. There were two dessert plates with a pair of cinnamon rolls from the Hostess, the soft sticky ones from the center of the pan.

I thought of Rick going down there, how long it took him to get down the street, how early he had to go to get the best ones. I thought of him planning a nice surprise, of him trying to do what he couldn't.

Rick told me once how one of the things he missed most was Sunday breakfast in bed. Every Saturday night he and Barry would watch a movie on the VCR in the living room. They'd pull the futon out like a bed and watch it from there and pretend they were at a bed-and-breakfast on vacation. Rick would make something fabulous and they'd eat it together. That was when he was still trying to help Barry eat. After Barry died Rick started going to the Hostess, especially on Sundays, because he had to get out of the apartment. He used to go to the Hostess all the time until it got to be too much for him. That's about the time I started coming over.

I sat at the table he'd laid for us. I put my elbows on the table and folded my hands. I closed my eyes and lowered my head and put my forehead in my hands. I tried to think how Rick would think, I tried to imagine Barry.

After a while I opened my eyes. He'd laid the table hopefully. I took the food he meant for me, I ate.   55
                                                                     [1994]

A WRITING EXERCISE

Once you have read the three stories, write your reaction to them off the top of your head, spending at least ten minutes on each. For each story, note any personal experience affecting your response as well as one or more questions that you have about the story even after you have finished reading it. Remember that question-posing is a good way to prepare for a formal paper on the story, enabling you to identify issues worth writing about at length.

Students' Personal Responses to the Stories

Here is some freewriting that students did about the three stories you have just read.

Alison Caldwell on Williams's "The Use of Force":

```
     I can understand why the doctor got furious at the
girl. He was asking her to open her mouth for her own
good, and she started physically attacking him. On the
other hand, I can sympathize with the girl. I can remem-
ber being scared of doctors when I was that young. I
dreaded having to get various shots. The girl in the
story is probably not used to seeing doctors in the first
place, so this one is bound to seem especially frighten-
ing to her. I can sympathize with her parents, too,
because they only want what's best for their daughter and
they're doing everything they can to assist the doctor. I
was kind of shocked to see the doctor fuming with anger
at them. Of course, his reaction to them is one of the
interesting things about this story, along with the
strange respect that he feels in a way for the girl. I
guess the biggest issue for me is what we're to make of
the doctor's sort of identification with the girl even as
he gets mad at her and she strongly resists him. There's
some connection between these two characters that I need
to figure out. I notice that at the end her eyes are
```

"blinded" and not long before he's possessed by a "blind fury." Probably I should explore this particular similarity more.

Monica Albertson on Welty's "A Visit of Charity":

I'm not sure which character I should be sympathizing with in Welty's story. Right away I disliked the girl because she wasn't really interested in seeing the old women. I don't know why the story is called "A Visit of Charity," since she just wanted to get more points. And yet I have to admit that when I was younger I was sort of like her. I remember one time that my church youth group had to sing Christmas carols at an old folks' home, and I was uneasy about having to meet all these ancient men and women I didn't know, some of whom could barely walk or talk. It's funny, because I was always comfortable around my grandparents, but I have to confess that being around all those old people at once spooked me a little. I smiled a lot at them and joined in the singing and helped hand out candy canes afterward. But I couldn't wait to leave. Once I did, I felt proud of myself for going there, but I guess I also felt a little guilty because I didn't really want to be there at all. So, maybe I'm being hypocritical when I criticize the girl in Welty's story for insensitivity. Anyway, I expected that Welty would present in a good light any old women that Marian encountered, just to emphasize that Marian was being unkind and that it's really sad for people to have to live in a retirement home (or senior citizens center or whatever they're calling such places nowadays). And yet the two old women she meets are cranky and unpleasant. Even the receptionist doesn't come off all that good. If I were Marian, I probably would have left even sooner than she did! Maybe Welty didn't want us to sympathize with anyone in the story, and maybe that's OK. I tend to want a story to make at least some of the characters sympathetic, but maybe it's unfair of me to demand that.

Still, I'm wondering if I'm not appreciating Welty's
characters enough. When the two old women argue, should
we side with one of them, or are we supposed to be bothered by them both? Are we supposed to think any better of
the girl by the time she leaves? The apple she eats immediately made me think of the Adam and Eve story, but I
don't know what I'm supposed to do with that parallel.

Jon Pike on Brown's "The Gift of Sweat":

The narrator's tone in this story is very quiet, very
matter-of-fact and understated, but the story moved me
all the same. I can't help feeling sorry for poor Ricky,
who seems to be dying from AIDS and wanted to give the
narrator a really good breakfast in return for the work
she's done for him and the friendship she's given him.
But I think the story is mostly about the narrator's
helplessness, especially when Ricky is taken off to the
hospital and she's left with nothing directly to do for
him. I think it's interesting that we're not told right
away what she seeks in the kitchen. Instead, she tells
about how she thoroughly cleaned Ricky's apartment, as if
that was the only way she could think of to help him at
this point. When she finally reveals that what's in the
kitchen is the breakfast he has prepared for her, I wonder why she the sight of it originally disturbed her and
even made her leave the room, plunging herself into her
cleaning work. It's as if she couldn't bear taking this
"gift" from him when he risked his health to get it for
her. I wonder, though, why the story is called "The Gift
of Sweat" rather than "The Gift of Breakfast." Maybe it's
because the breakfast is the result of Ricky's sweat, in
the sense that he physically struggled to prepare it. In
the same way, the narrator sweats as she cleans the
apartment. So which is more important, the similarities
between these two people or their differences?

Before any of these students could produce a full-length paper on the story
they freewrote on, they had to do more writing and thinking. Yet simply by jotting

down some observations and questions, they provided themselves with seeds of a paper. Compare your thoughts to theirs. To what extent did you react to the stories as they did? In what ways, if any, did your responses differ from theirs? What would you say to them if they were your classmates, especially as they proceeded to write more developed arguments?

The Elements of Short Fiction

Whether discussing them in class or writing about them, you will improve your ability to analyze stories like Williams's, Welty's, and Brown's if you grow familiar with typical elements of short fiction. These elements include plot and structure, point of view, characterization, setting, imagery, language, and theme.

Plot and Structure

For many readers, the most important element in any work of fiction is **plot**. As they turn the pages of a short story, their main question is, What will happen next? In reading Williams's story, probably you were curious, as the narrator is, to know whether the girl is concealing an infected throat. In reading Welty's story, quite possibly you wanted to know how Marian's visit to the rest home would turn out. In reading Brown's story, most likely you hoped to learn why Rick was unable to let the narrator into his home. Furthermore, if a friend unfamiliar with Williams's, Welty's, and Brown's stories asked you what each was about, probably you would begin by summarizing their plots.

A WRITING EXERCISE

In one or two sentences, summarize what you take to be the plot of Welty's story. Then read the following three summaries of her plot, which were written by three other students. Finally, list a few similarities and differences you notice as you compare the three summaries with one another and with yours.

> *Jerry's summary:* A girl visits an Old Ladies' Home just so she can add some points to her record as a Campfire Girl. Much to her dismay, she encounters two roommates who fight a lot with each other, and their unpleasantness eventually causes her to flee.
>
> *Carla's summary:* A young girl named Marian who starts off basically interested in only herself is forced to consider the suffering of old people when she spends time with two old women at a retirement home. Eventually she leaves in fear and disgust, but as she leaves she eats an apple, which implies that she is no longer as innocent as she was and that she is maybe a little more prepared to acknowledge what goes on in the wider world.
>
> *Matt's summary:* A really insensitive girl meets two old women, and though in many respects she is put off by both of them, she can't help being intrigued by the one who is sick in bed. Maybe she becomes

more aware of mortality at this point, but if so she has trouble facing it and in the end runs away.

To an extent, the students point out different things. For instance, only Carla mentions the apple, and only Matt observes that Marian is momentarily interested in the bedridden woman. Also, these two students are more willing than Jerry is to speculate about Marian's final state of mind. At the same time, Carla's summary ends on a slightly more upbeat note than Matt's. She emphasizes that Marian has perhaps become more open-minded, while Matt concludes by pointing out that Marian nevertheless flees.

Any summary of Welty's story will be somewhat personal. It is bound to reflect the reader's own sense of who the story's main characters are, which of their actions are significant, how these actions are connected, and what principles these actions illustrate. Were you to compare summaries with Jerry, Carla, and Matt in class, each of you might learn much from discussing experiences and beliefs that influenced your accounts.

Even so, you do not have to treat every summary of Welty's story as merely subjective. Probably some accounts of it are more attentive than others to actual details of Welty's text. If a reader declared that Marian loves visiting the Old Ladies' Home, many other readers would rightfully disagree, pointing out that Marian dashes off. If you discussed Welty's story with Jerry, Carla, and Matt, the four of you would probably consider which summary of it is best. Furthermore, probably each of you would argue for your respective candidates by pointing to specific passages in Welty's text. Ultimately, you might still prefer your own summary. On the other hand, you might wind up adopting someone else's, or you might want to combine aspects of various summaries you have read.

Jerry's, Carla's, and Matt's summaries do have some features in common, indicating that there are certain basic things for you to consider when you examine a short story's plot. For example, plots usually center on human beings, who can be seen as engaging in actions, as being acted upon, or both. In recounting the plot of Welty's story, each of the three students focuses on Marian. Furthermore, each describes her as acting (she "encounters," "flees," "spends time," "leaves," "eats," "meets," "runs away") *and* as being affected by other forces (the "unpleasantness" of the old women "causes her to flee"; she is "forced to consider" their pain; she is "put off" as well as "intrigued"). Also, most short stories put characters into a high-pressure situation, whether for dark or comic effect. To earn the merit points she desires, Marian has to contend with the feuding roommates.

Besides physical events, a short story may involve psychological developments. Each student here points to mental changes in Welty's heroine. According to Jerry, Marian experiences "dismay." According to Carla, she "starts off basically interested in only herself" but perhaps becomes "a little more prepared to acknowledge what goes on in the wider world." According to Matt, she starts off "really insensitive," perhaps grows "more aware of mortality," yet then "has trouble facing it." Many stories do show characters undergoing complete or partial conversions. Meanwhile, a number of stories include characters who stick to their beliefs but gain a new perspective on them.

Jerry, Carla, and Matt connect Marian's visit to the rest home with her subsequent behavior. Like most plot summaries, in other words, theirs bring up relations of cause and effect. The novelist and short-story writer E. M. Forster refers to cause and effect in his famous definition of plot. To Forster, a plot is not simply one incident after another, such as "the king died and then the queen died." Rather, it is a situation or a whole chain of events in which there are reasons *why* characters behave as they do. Forster's example: "The king died, and then the queen died of grief."

Writers of short stories do not always make cause and effect immediately clear. Another possible plot, Forster suggests, is "The queen died, no one knew why, until it was discovered that it was through grief at the death of the king." In this scenario, all of the characters lack information about the queen's true psychology for a while, and perhaps the reader is in the dark as well. Indeed, many short stories leave the reader ignorant for a spell. For instance, only near the conclusion of her story does Welty reveal that prior to entering the rest home, Marian had put an apple under the shrub. Why does the author withhold this key fact from you? Perhaps Welty was silent about the apple because, had she reported it right away, its echoes of Eve might have overshadowed your interpretation of the story as you read. Worth considering are issues of effect: what the characters' behavior makes you think of them and what impact the author's strategies have on you.

When you summarize a story's plot, you may be inclined to put events in chronological order. But remember that short stories are not always linear. Often they depart from strict chronology, moving back and forth in time. Consider the following opening sentences, both of which deal with a funeral ceremony. They come from two of the stories featured in this book, William Faulkner's "A Rose for Emily," reprinted in Chapter 14, and Andre Dubus's "Killings," reprinted in Chapter 15:

> When Miss Emily Grierson died, our whole town went to her funeral: the men through a sort of respectful affection for a fallen monument, the women mostly out of curiosity to see the inside of her house, which no one save an old manservant—a combined gardener and cook—had seen in at least ten years.

> On the August morning when Matt Fowler buried his youngest son, Frank, who had lived for twenty-one years, eight months, and four days, Matt's older son, Steve, turned to him as the family left the grave and walked between their friends, and said: "I should kill him."

Probably Faulkner's opening makes you wonder why Emily Grierson kept people out of her house. Probably Dubus's opening makes you wonder how Frank died and whom Steve means by "him." Eventually the authors do answer these questions by moving their stories back in time. Faulkner presents episodes in Emily's life, returning only at the end of the story to the time after her death. Dubus spends much of his story's first half on flashbacks that inform you about Frank's murder; then, Dubus returns to the present and shows Matt's effort to avenge his son. Many literary critics use the term **discourse** for a text's actual ordering of events. Chronologically, Emily Grierson's funeral comes near the end of Faulkner's short story. Yet it appears at the beginning of his discourse. Chronologically, Frank's funeral is sandwiched between several events. Yet it is the start of Dubus's discourse.

Alice Adams, author of many short stories, offers a more detailed outline of their typical **structure**. She has proposed the formula ABDCE: these letters stand for **action, background, development, climax,** and **ending**. More precisely, Adams has said that she sometimes begins a story with an action, follows that action with some background information, and then moves the plot forward in time through a major turning point and toward some sort of resolution. Not all writers of short stories follow this scheme. In fact, Adams does not always stick to it. Certainly a lot of short stories combine her background and development stages, moving the plot along while offering details of their characters' pasts. And sometimes a story will have several turning points rather than a single distinct climax. But if you keep Adams's formula in mind, if only as a common way to construct short stories, you will be better prepared to recognize how a story departs from chronological order.

The first paragraph of Welty's story seems to be centered on *action*. Marian arrives at the Old Ladies' Home and prepares to enter it. Even so, Welty provides some basic information in this paragraph, describing Marian and the rest home as if the reader is unfamiliar with both. Yet only in the second paragraph do you learn Marian's name and the purpose of her visit. Therefore, Welty can be said to obey Adams's formula, beginning with *action* and then moving to *background*. Note, however, that the second paragraph features *development* as well. By explaining to the receptionist who she is and why she is there, Marian takes a step closer to the central event, her meeting with the two roommates. The remainder of the story keeps moving forward in time.

Williams's story "The Use of Force" begins with a paragraph that establishes the *background* to the narrator's visit. Nevertheless, the paragraph is brief and the background slight, with the narrator acknowledging that "They were new patients to me, all I had was the name, Olson." Then we are quickly plunged into *action*, as the narrator starts to describe his experience at the Olson house. Even as the story proceeds, we continue to receive some background information, as when the narrator tells us of an outbreak of diphtheria at the child's school. Yet, for the most part, we sense *development* as the narrator wages an increasingly violent struggle to open the child's mouth.

Brown's story "The Gift of Sweat" begins with two paragraphs mostly devoted to background. They tell you about the arrangements between the narrator and Rick prior to the particular day that will be the story's focus. With the opening words of her third paragraph—"So one morning when I called"— Brown signals that she has spent the previous two on background material. Now, she implies, she will turn to developing the story's main situation.

What about *climax*, Adams's fourth term? Traditionally, the climax of a story has been defined as a peak moment of drama appearing near the end. Also, it is usually thought of as a point when at least one character commits a significant act, experiences a significant change, makes a significant discovery, learns a significant lesson, or perhaps does all these things. With Welty's story, you could argue that the climax is when Marian asks Addie her age, meets with refusal, sees Addie crying, and tries to bolt. Certainly this is a dramatic moment, involving intense display of emotion resulting in Marian's departure. But Welty indicates, too, that Marian here experiences inner change. When she looks on Addie "as though there was nothing else in the world to wonder about," this is "the first time such a thing had happened to Marian."

Adams's term *ending* may seem unnecessary. Why would anyone have to be reminded that stories end? Yet a story's climax may engage readers so much that they overlook whatever follows. If the climax of Welty's story is Marian's conversation with tearful Addie, then the ending is basically in four parts: the plea that Addie's roommate makes to Marian as she is leaving; Marian's final encounter with the receptionist; Marian's retrieval of the apple; and her escape on the bus, where she bites into the apple. Keep in mind that the ending of a story may relate somehow to its beginning. The ending of Welty's "A Visit of Charity," for instance, brings the story full circle. Whereas at the start Marian gets off a bus, hides the apple, and meets the receptionist, at the conclusion she rushes by the receptionist, recovers the apple, and boards another bus. However a story ends, ask yourself if any of the characters has changed at some point between start and finish. Does the conclusion of the story indicate that at least one person has developed in some way, or does it leave you with the feeling of lives frozen since the start? As Welty's story ends, readers may have various opinions about Marian. Some may find that she has not been changed all that much by her visit to the home, while others may feel that it has helped her mature.

A common organizational device in short stories is **repetition**. It takes various forms. First, a story may repeat various words; in Williams's story, for example, the word "look" appears again and again. Second, a story may involve repeated actions. In Welty's story, the two roommates repeatedly argue; Marian travels by bus at beginning and end; and the receptionist consults her wristwatch both when Marian arrives and when she leaves. Third, a story may echo previous events. In Brown's story, the narrator mentions her earlier visits to Rick and his past trips to the Hostess. Of course, in various ways a story's current situation will be new. In Brown's story, Rick's present condition makes his trek to the Hostess a big step for him, and he winds up in pain.

Point of View

A short story may be told from a particular character's perspective or **point of view**. Probably you have noticed that Williams's and Brown's stories are written in the **first person**; each is narrated by someone using the pronoun *I*. With every first-person story, you have to decide how much to accept the narrator's point of view, keeping in mind that the narrator may be psychologically complex. How objective does the narrator seem in depicting other people and events? In what ways, if any, do the narrator's perceptions seem influenced by his or her personal experiences, circumstances, feelings, values, and beliefs? Does the narrator seem to have changed in any way since the events recalled? How reasonable do the narrator's judgments seem? At what moments, if any, do you find yourself disagreeing with the narrator's view of things?

Not every short story is narrated by an identifiable person. Many of them are told by what has been traditionally called an **omniscient narrator**. The word *omniscient* means "all-knowing" and is often used as an adjective for God. An omniscient narrator is usually a seemingly all-knowing, objective voice. This is the kind of voice operating in the first paragraph of Welty's story. There, Marian is described in an authoritatively matter-of-fact tone that appears detached from her: "Holding a potted plant before her, a girl of fourteen jumped off the bus in front of the Old Ladies' Home." Keep in mind, though, that a story may primarily rely on an omniscient narrator and yet at some points seem immersed in a character's perspective. This, too, is the case with Welty's story. Consider the following passage about Marian:

> Everything smelled wet — even the bare floor. She held on to the back of the chair, which was wicker and felt soft and damp. Her heart beat more and more slowly, her hands got colder and colder, and she could not hear whether the old women were saying anything or not. She could not see them very clearly. How dark it was! The window shade was down, and the only door was shut. Marian looked at the ceiling. . . . It was like being caught in a robbers' cave, just before one was murdered.

The passage remains in the third person, referring to "she" rather than to "I." Nevertheless, the passage seems intimately in touch with Marian's physical sensations. Indeed, the sentence "How dark it was!" seems something that Marian would say to herself. Similarly, the analogy to the robbers' cave may be Marian's own personal perception, and as such, the analogy may reveal more about her own state of mind than about the room. Many literary critics use the term **free indirect style** for moments like this, when a narrator otherwise omniscient conveys a particular character's viewpoint by resorting to the character's own language.

First-person singular narration and omniscient narration are not the only methods for telling a story. For instance, William Faulkner's "A Rose for Emily" (in Chapter 14) is narrated by "we," the first-person plural. Even more striking is the technique that Pam Houston uses in her short story "How to Talk to a Hunter" (Chapter 13). The story seems to be narrated from an unnamed woman's point of view, but she avoids the word *I* and instead consistently refers to *you*. While Houston's method is unusual, it serves as a reminder that short stories can be told in all sorts of ways.

Throughout this book, we encourage you to analyze an author's strategies by considering the options that he or she faced. You may better understand a short story's point of view if you think about the available alternatives. For example, how would you have reacted to Welty's story if it had focused on Addie's perceptions more than on Marian's? With Williams's or Brown's story, how would you have felt if the narrator had been omniscient?

A WRITING EXERCISE

Choose a passage from Williams's, Welty's, or Brown's story and rewrite it from another point of view. Then exchange your rewritten passage with a classmate's response to this assignment. Finally, write a paragraph analyzing your classmate's revision. Specifically, compare the revision with the original passage that your classmate chose, noting any differences in effect.

Characters

Although we have been discussing plots, we have also referred to the people caught up in them. Any analysis you do of a short story will reflect your understanding and evaluation of its **characters**. Rarely does the author of a story provide you with extended, enormously detailed biographies. Rather, you see the story's characters at select moments of their lives. To quote William Trevor again, the short story is "the art of the glimpse."

A WRITING EXERCISE

Choose any character from the three stories featured here. Off the top of your head, jot down at least five adjectives you think apply to that character. Next, exchange lists with a classmate. When you look at your classmate's list, circle the adjective that surprises you most, even if it deals with another character. Finally, write a brief essay in which you consider how applicable that adjective is. Do you agree with your classmate that it suits the character he or she chose? Why, or why not?

You may want to judge characters according to how easily you can identify with them. Yet there is little reason for you to read works that merely reinforce your prejudices. Furthermore, you may overlook the potential richness of a story if you insist that its characters fit your usual standards of behavior. An author can teach you much by introducing you to the complexity of people you might automatically praise or condemn in real life. If you tend to admire home-care providers, Brown's portrayal of one can be thought-provoking for you, since this particular provider is not sure what to do with the breakfast that Rick has set out in his kitchen. You may be tempted to dismiss the roommates in Welty's story as unpleasant, even "sick"; in any case, take the story as an opportunity to explore *why* women in a rest home may express discontent.

One thing to consider about the characters in a story is what each basically desires. At the beginning of Welty's story, for example, Marian is hardly visiting the Old Ladies' Home out of "charity," despite that word's presence in the story's title. Rather, Marian hopes to earn points as a Campfire Girl. Again, characters in a story may change, so consider whether the particular characters you are examining alter their thinking. Perhaps you feel that Marian's visit broadens her vision of life; then again, perhaps you conclude that she remains much the same.

Reading a short story involves relating its characters to one another. In part, you will be determining their relative importance in the story. When a particular character seems to be the story's focus, he or she is referred to as the story's **protagonist**. Many readers would say that the doctor is the protagonist of Williams's story, Marian is the protagonist of Welty's, and the home-care worker is the protagonist of Brown's. When the protagonist is in notable conflict with another character, the latter is referred to as the **antagonist**. In Williams's story, the child seems to assume this role, since the narrator winds up fighting her. To be sure, the relationship between a protagonist and an antagonist may show nuances worth exploring. For example, Williams's narrator does not simply hate his patient. Rather, he wants to help her, and he grudgingly admires her stubbornness while harboring scorn for her parents.

Even a seemingly minor character can perform some noteworthy function in a story. Take Brown's character Margaret, who is apparently the narrator's supervisor. On the surface, Margaret seems much less important to the story than the narrator and Rick do. For one thing, Margaret's appearance is brief: she arrives, she exchanges some words with the narrator, and then she drives off with Rick. Before she goes, though, Margaret points out that the narrator is sweaty, and thus she makes the reader aware of this fact. Furthermore, Brown uses Margaret to put the narrator in a psychologically complex situation. Once Margaret takes Rick away, the narrator must figure out how to express her concern for him, which she ultimately does by thoroughly cleaning his home. On the whole, Margaret is more a plot device than a fully developed personality. Nevertheless, she merits study if only as an example of author Brown's craft.

In many short stories, characters are allies or enemies. But as the story proceeds, they may alter their relationships, forging new bonds or developing new conflicts. Although Welty's Marian initially finds both roommates unpleasant, she grows more conscious of the tension *between* them, and then for a moment she sympathizes with Addie. It is possible, too, for one character to be ambivalent about another, feeling both drawn and opposed to that person. We have already suggested that such is the case with Williams's narrator as he struggles with the child. One might argue, too, that the two roommates in Welty's story have a love-hate relationship, needing each other's company even as they bicker. As perhaps you have found in your own experience, human relationships are often far from simple. Works of literature can prove especially interesting when they suggest as much.

What power and influence people can achieve have often depended on particular traits of theirs. These include their gender, social class, race, ethnic background, nationality, sexual orientation, and the kind of work they do. Because these attributes can greatly affect a person's life, pay attention to them if an author refers to them in describing a character. For instance, in Brown's story, the narrator indicates her gender as she recalls how she lay down with pain-stricken Rick: "I pulled my body close to him so his butt was in my lap and my breasts and stomach were against his back." But would the story be significantly different if she were a man? Perhaps. Certainly it is interesting that she has become a caretaker of what was formerly the home of a male couple. Also, note that the physical position described in the quoted passage is that of mother with fetus. In fact, just before the passage, the narrator addresses Rick as if he were her child, changing his name to "Ricky." Remember, too, that for many people, Mother is the original Hostess with the Mostest. Still, you may feel that we are making too much of gender here. If so, what would you point to in arguing that view?

Typically, characters express views of one another, and you have to decide how accurate these are. Some characters will seem wise observers of humanity. Others will strike you as making distorted statements about the world, revealing little more than their own biases and quirks. And some characters will seem to fall in the middle, coming across as partly objective and partly subjective. On occasion, you and your classmates may find yourselves debating which category a particular character fits. One interesting case is Welty's character Addie. Look again at the speech in which she berates her roommate:

> "Hush!" said the sick woman. "You never went to school. You never came and you never went. You never were anything—only here. You never were born! You don't know anything. Your head is empty, your heart and hands and your old black purse are all empty, even that little old box that you brought with you you brought empty—you showed it to me. And yet you talk, talk, talk, talk, talk all the time until I think I'm losing my mind! Who are you? You're a stranger—a perfect stranger! Don't you know you're a stranger? Is it possible that they have actually done a thing like this to anyone—sent them in a stranger to talk, and rock, and tell away her whole long rigmarole? Do they seriously suppose that I'll be able to keep it up, day in, day out, night in, night out, living in the same room with a terrible old woman—forever?"

Some may argue that this speech is merely an unreasonable rant, indicating Addie's dour mood rather than her roommate's true nature. (For one thing, contrary to Addie's declaration, the roommate must have been born!) Yet it can also be argued that Addie shrewdly diagnoses her situation. Perhaps statements like "you never were born," "your head is empty," and "you're a stranger" are true in a metaphorical sense.

Setting

Usually a short story enables readers to examine how people behave in concrete circumstances. The characters are located in a particular place or **setting**. Moreover, they are shown at particular moments in their personal histories. Sometimes the story goes further, referring to them as living at a certain point in world history.

As the word *sometimes* implies, short stories vary in the precision with which they identify their settings. At one extreme is Haruki Murakami's "Another Way to Die," featured in Chapter 15. The story's place and time are sharply defined: The action occurs in a Manchurian zoo in August 1945, when the Russian army was about to seize the region from its Japanese occupiers. On the other hand, the setting of Williams's "The Use of Force" is much less exact. Most of the action occurs in the Olsons' kitchen, but we get practically no details of it. Mainly we learn that "it is warm," while the rest of the house can be "very damp." And though the Olsons are evidently from the working class, the text does not situate them within a particular region or era. Even when a story's setting is rather vague, certain details may seem historically or geographically specific. Brown's story says little about Rick's apartment and events in the larger world, but since he has AIDS, the time frame can be no earlier than the 1980s.

Short stories differ as well in the importance of their setting. Sometimes, as with "The Use of Force," location serves as a mere backdrop for the plot. At other times, the setting can be a looming presence. When Welty's character Marian visits the Old Ladies' Home, we get her vivid impressions of it. Even when a story's setting seems ordinary, it may become filled with drama and meaning as the plot develops. For most people, a kitchen is a mundane place, but there Brown's narrator must decide whether to accept the breakfast that Rick has assembled.

Stories may focus on one site and show it changing over time. This is the case with Faulkner's "A Rose for Emily" (Chapter 14), in which Emily's town comes to view her differently over the years. Of course, a story may take place in more than one setting, and when it does, the differences between its various sites may be notable. In Katherine Mansfield's story "The Garden-Party" (Chapter 16), the young protagonist struggles to understand the sharp contrast between two events she witnesses—the garden party of the title, which is on her family's estate, and another family's mourning for a dead workman, which occurs in a nearby house.

One way of analyzing characters is to consider how they accommodate themselves—or fail to accommodate themselves—to their surroundings. The two roommates in Welty's story are evidently frustrated with living in the Old Ladies' Home, and they take out this frustration on each other. In Brown's story, the narrator's cleaning of Rick's home may leave you with mixed feelings. When, in his absence, she strips his bed, washes his laundry, vacuums his floor, dusts his objects, straightens his clothes, stores his cassettes, removes his garbage, and scrubs his bathroom, she is certainly caring for him. At the same time, her actions signify that he has lost all privacy. Though it is his own apartment, she has taken charge.

A WRITING EXERCISE

To become more aware of how setting may function in a short story, write a two- to three-page description of a setting you associate with someone you know. Choose a particular room, building, or landscape in which you have seen that person. In your description, use details of the setting to reveal something about his or her life.

Imagery

Just like poems, short stories often use **imagery** to convey meaning. Sometimes a character in the story may interpret a particular image just the way you do. Some stories, though, include images that you and the characters may analyze quite differently. One example is the apple in Welty's story. Whereas Marian probably views the apple as just something to eat, many readers would make other associations with it, thinking in particular of the apple that Adam and Eve ate from the Tree of Knowledge in Eden. By the end of Welty's story, perhaps Marian has indeed become like Adam and Eve, in that she has lost her innocence and grown more aware that human beings age. At any rate, many readers would call Marian's apple a **symbol**. Traditionally, that is the term for an image seen as representing some concept or concepts. Again, probably Marian herself does not view her apple as symbolic; indeed, characters within stories rarely use the word *symbol* at all.

Images may appear in the form of metaphors or other figures of speech. For example, when Marian enters the Old Ladies' Home, she experiences "a smell in the hall like the interior of a clock." Welty soon builds on the clock image as she describes the receptionist checking her wristwatch, an action that this character repeats near the end. Welty's whole story can be said to deal with time and its effects, both on the old and on the young.

Images in short stories usually appeal to the reader's visual sense. Most often, they are things you can picture in your mind. Yet stories are not limited to rendering visual impressions. They may refer and appeal to other senses, too. In Brown's story, the narrator is struck by how Rick's sweat smells. Similarly, Welty's young heroine notes the odor of the hall.

A WRITING EXERCISE

Write a brief essay in which you analyze how a particular advertisement uses imagery. The ad may come from any medium, including a newspaper, a magazine, television, or radio. What specific associations do you make with the ad's imagery? Why do you think the advertiser used it? Would you say that this use of imagery is successful? Why, or why not?

Language

Everything about short stories we have discussed so far concerns **language**. After all, works of literature are constructed entirely out of words. Here, however, we call your attention to three specific uses of language in stories: title, predominant style, and dialogue.

A story's **title** may be just as important as any words in the text. Not always will the relevance of the title be immediately clear to you. Usually you have to read a story all the way through before you can sense fully how its title applies. In any case, play with the title in your mind, considering its various possible meanings and implications.

A WRITING EXERCISE

Write a brief essay in which you focus on Williams's, Welty's, or Brown's story and examine how the title relates to the actual text. Consider the writer's alternatives. If you choose to discuss Welty's "A Visit of Charity," you may find it helpful to think about this famous passage from the New

Testament: "And now abideth faith, hope, charity, these three; but the greatest of these is charity" (I Corinthians 13:13). You may also want to look up the word *charity* in a dictionary.

Not all short stories have a uniform **style**. Some feature various tones, dialects, vocabularies, and levels of formality. Stories that do have a predominant style are often narrated in the first person, thus giving the impression of a presiding "voice." Brown's story "The Gift of Sweat," with its matter-of-fact, conversational tone, comes across as an anecdote that someone is relating to a friend.

Dialogue may serve more than one purpose in a short story. By reporting various things, characters may provide you with necessary background for the plot. In Welty's story, it's only from the roommates' fragmentary remarks that Marian—and the reader—can learn anything about their lives up until now. Also, by saying certain things to one another, characters may advance the plot. When, in Brown's story, suffering Rick says to the narrator "please don't go," she winds up in a physical intimacy with him that they may not have had together before. Actually, dialogue can be thought of as action in itself. Try to identify the particular kinds of acts that characters perform when they speak. For instance, Rick's "please don't go" can be labeled a plea.

Another plea occurs when the mother in "The Use of Force" begs her daughter to open her mouth for the narrator: "Such a nice man. . . . Look how kind he is to you. Come on, do what he tells you to. He won't hurt you." Just a bit later, though, the narrator scolds the mother herself: "For heaven's sake, I broke in. Don't call me a nice man to her." To the narrator, no longer are the girl's parents his partners; instead, he feels contempt for them. Indeed, dialogue may function to reveal shifts in characters' relations with one another.

Theme

We have already discussed the term **theme** on pages 25 to 27. There, we identified issues of theme as one kind of issue that comes up in literary studies. At the same time, we suggested that term *theme* applies to various literary genres, not just short stories. Later, in Chapters 5, 6, and 7, we examine theme in connection with poems, plays, and essays. Here, though, we consider theme as an element of short fiction. In doing so, we review some points from our earlier discussion, applying them now to the three stories you have just read.

Recall that we defined the theme of a work as the main claim it seems to make. Furthermore, we identified it as an assertion, proposition, or statement rather than as a single word. "Charity" is obviously a *topic* of Welty's story, but because it is just one word, it is not an adequate expression of the story's *theme*. The following exercise invites you to consider just what that theme may be.

A WRITING EXERCISE

Here we list possible statements of theme for Williams's, Welty's, and Brown's stories. Choose one of these stories, and rank the statements listed for it, placing at the top whatever sentence you think most accurately expresses the story's theme. Then, in two or three pages, explain your reasoning, referring at least once to each statement you have ranked. Propose your own statement of the story's theme if none of those listed seem adequate to you.

Statements of Theme for Williams's "The Use of Force"

1. Force against people is justified when it is used to halt disease.
2. Though we like to think doctors are kind, they may actually scorn us.
3. Doctors should be especially sensitive when their patient is a child.
4. Children are capable of stubborn fury.
5. The desire to help may be met with resistance.
6. Working-class life is different from the life of middle-class professionals.
7. We should cooperate with doctors, even if they seem threatening to us.
8. People may secretly admire those who resist them.
9. All of us are "blind" in one way or another.
10. The cure may be worse than the disease.

Statements of Theme for Welty's "A Visit of Charity"

1. Be nice to old people, for many of them have it tough.
2. None of us can escape the passage of time.
3. Searching for merit points is incompatible with a true spirit of charity.
4. Everyone has to give up dreams of innocence and paradise, just as Adam and Eve did.
5. Although we are tempted to repress our awareness of mortality, we should maintain that awareness.
6. We should all behave charitably toward one another.
7. We can tell how charitable we are by the way we treat people we find strange or irritable.
8. Old age homes need to be made more pleasant, both for the residents and for their visitors.
9. Whenever we become strongly aware of mortality, we tend to repress that awareness, thus robbing ourselves of any benefit we may gain from it.
10. Young people are capable of showing interest in others, if only for a moment, but for better or worse they're basically self-centered.

Statement of Theme for Brown's "The Gift of Sweat"

1. We should be compassionate toward people with AIDS.
2. Even when we sympathize with others, we may not be sure how to help them.
3. Simple acts, such as cleaning and eating, may be ways of coping.

4. We should give one another a lot more gifts.
5. Gifts may take various forms.
6. Live life to the fullest, for it is the greatest gift of all.
7. We may feel guilt as well as gratitude in accepting a person's gift.
8. Risking one's health may be worthwhile.
9. Sweat is a sign of our humanity.
10. We may do more for people when we accept *their* work rather than work *for* them.

Think about the other points we made when we discussed theme in Chapter 2. To see how these apply to short fiction, we can start by relating each point to the stories by Williams, Welty, and Brown.

1. *Try to state a text's theme as a midlevel generalization.*   If you were to put it in very broad terms, your audience would see it as fitting a great many works besides the one you have read. If you went to the opposite extreme, tying the theme completely to specific details of the text, your audience might think the theme irrelevant to their own lives.

The phrase "the moral of the story" suggests that a story can usually be reduced to a single message, often a principle of ethics or religion. Plenty of examples can be cited to support this suggestion. In the New Testament, for instance, Jesus tells stories — they are called *parables* — to convey some of his key ideas. In any number of cultures today, stories are used to teach children elements of good conduct. Moreover, people often determine the significance of a real-life event by building a story from it and by drawing a moral from it at the same time. These two processes conspicuously dovetailed when England's Princess Diana was killed in a car crash. Given that she died fleeing photographers, many people saw her entire life story as that of a woman hounded by media. The moral was simultaneous and clear: thou shalt honor the right to privacy.

It is possible to lose sight of a story's theme by placing too much emphasis on minor details of the text. The more common temptation, however, is to turn a story's theme into an all-too-general cliché. Actually, a story is often most interesting when it *complicates* some widely held idea that it seemed ready to endorse. Therefore, a useful exercise is to start with a general thematic statement about the story and then make it increasingly specific. With "The Gift of Sweat," for example, you might begin by supposing that the theme is "We should do whatever we can for sick people." Your next step would be to identify the specific spin that Brown's story puts on this idea. How does her story differ from others on this theme? Note, for instance, that Brown's narrator evidently wants to help sick people right from the beginning of the story, whereas other stories might trace how a character gradually becomes committed to charity. Also, not every story about helping sick people would emphasize sweat and cleaning as Brown's does. With these two observations and others in mind, try now to restate our version of Brown's theme so that it seems more in touch with the specific details of her text.

2. The theme of a text may be related to its title.   It may also be expressed by some statement made within the text. But often various parts of the text merit consideration as you try to determine its theme.

In our discussion of a short story's language, we called attention to the potential significance of its title. The title may serve as a guide to the story's theme. What clues, if any, do you find in the three story titles in this chapter — "The Use of Force," "A Visit of Charity," and "The Gift of Sweat"? Of course, determining a story's theme entails going beyond the title. You have to read, and usually reread, the entire text. In doing so, you may come across a statement that seems a candidate for the theme because it is a philosophical generalization. Nevertheless, take the time to consider whether the story's essence is indeed captured by this statement alone.

3. You can state a text's theme either as an observation or as a recommendation.   Each way of putting it evokes a certain image of the text's author. When you state the theme as an **observation**, you depict the author as a psychologist, a philosopher, or some other kind of analyst. When you state the theme as a **recommendation** — which often involves your using the word *should* — you depict the author as a teacher, preacher, manager, or coach. That is, the author comes across as telling readers what to do.

As we have noted, stories are often used to teach lessons. Moreover, often the lessons are recommendations for action, capable of being phrased as "Do X" or "Do not do X." The alternative is to make a generalization about some state of affairs. When you try to express a particular story's theme, which of these two options should you follow? There are several things to consider in making your decision. First is your personal comfort: do you feel at ease with both ways of stating the theme, or is one of these ways more to your taste? Also worth pondering is the impression you want to give of the author: do you want to portray this person as a maker of recommendations, or do you want to assign the author a more modest role? Because Brown has helped people with AIDS, you may want to state the theme of her story as a prescription for physical and spiritual health. Yet maybe Brown is out to remind her audience that home-care providers have human frailties; hence, expressing her theme as an observation may be the more appropriate move.

4. Consider stating a text's theme as a problem.   That way, you are more apt to convey the complexity and drama of the text.

We have suggested that short stories often pivot around conflicts between people and conflicts within people. Perhaps the most interesting stories are ones that pose conflicts not easily resolved. Probably you will be more faithful to such a text if you phrase its theme as a problem. In the case of Brown's story, for example, you might state the theme as follows: "When we try to help people, we may find ourselves resisting the gifts they want to give us because our guilt over their suffering interferes with our ability to accept things they do for us."

5. Rather than refer to the *theme of a text, you might refer to* a *theme of the text, implying that the text has more than one.*   You would still be suggesting that you have identified a central idea of the text. Subsequently, you might have to defend your claim.

Unlike the average novel, the typical short story pivots around only a few ideas. Yet you need not insist that the story you are analyzing has a single theme; in fact, even the shortest piece of short fiction may have a number of them. Besides, your audience is apt to think you nicely open-minded if you suggest that the theme you have discovered is not the only one. We believe, for example, that Brown's story has at least two themes. One is that people with AIDS deserve more understanding, appreciation, and attention than many of them now get. A second theme is that care of the ill may involve more than helping them keep their life "clean"; it may also mean sharing their "sweat," by making bodily contact with them and accepting whatever they achieve in their pain. Although we are labeling each of these ideas *a* theme of Brown's story rather than *the* theme of it, we are still making strong claims. To use the term *theme* at all implies that we are identifying key principles of the text. You might disagree with our claims about Brown's themes, and if you did, we would have to support our position in order to change your mind.

Perhaps the biggest challenge you will face in writing about short stories is to avoid long stretches of plot summary. Selected details of the plot will often serve as key evidence for you. You will need to describe such moments from the story you are discussing, even if your audience has already read it. But your readers are apt to be frustrated if you just repeat plot at length. They will feel that they may as well turn back to the story itself rather than linger with your rehash. Your paper is worth your readers' time only if you provide insights of your own, *analyzing* the story rather than just *summarizing* it.

To understand what analysis of a short story involves, let's return to Alison Caldwell, whose freewriting on "The Use of Force" you read earlier. Assigned to write an argument paper about a short story, Alison decided to focus on Williams's. She realized that for her paper to be effective, she had to come up with an issue worth addressing, a claim about that issue, and evidence for that claim. Moreover, she had to be prepared to identify the warrants or assumptions behind her evidence.

For most writing assignments, settling on an issue will be your most important preliminary step. Without a driving question, you will have difficulty producing fresh, organized, and sustained analysis. For her paper on "The Use of Force," Alison chose to address an issue that she had raised in her freewriting: What's the most important connection between the narrator and the child? Ultimately, she saw this as an issue of pattern because she would have to identify, analyze, and rank in order of importance whatever sets of words link the two characters. Again, building on her freewriting, Alison thought in particular about the narrator's closing reference to the child's "blindness." In her paper, she came to argue that "blindness" was the most important similarity between these two people. She realized, of course, that she would have to explore various possible meanings of the term, especially since neither character was literally blind. To a certain extent, then, she would have to address an issue of definition, even as the issue of pattern remained her key concern. Moreover, she felt obliged to justify her emphasis on the narrator's final words. You will see that in her paper she states her warrant for taking them as evidence. The narrator's concluding reference to "blindness" is significant, she contends, because the last words of a character often are. To be sure, Alison also assumed that Williams was deliberate rather than arbitrary in having the narrator speak this way at the end.

A paper about a short story need not explicitly mention the elements of short fiction we have identified. Nevertheless, thinking of these elements can help you plan such a paper, providing you with some preliminary terms for your analysis. Alison perceived that her paper would be very much about two characters who on the surface are protagonist and antagonist but who actually have features in common. Also, the paper would attend much to the story's ending. It would deal as well with a particular symbol, blindness.

When you plan a paper about a short story, keep in mind that you are more apt to persuade readers if you include quotations from the text you discuss. Before you attempt a complete draft, copy in your notebook any words from the story that might figure in your analysis. Alison, for example, was pretty sure that her paper on "The Use of Force" would incorporate the narrator's final words, "tears of defeat blinded her eyes," as well as his interesting declaration that "I had already fallen in love with the savage brat, the parents were contemptible to me." Yet, as with plot summary, quoting should be limited, so that the paper seems to be an original argument about the story instead of a mere recycling of it. Alison sensed that practically every sentence of Williams's story could be quoted and then plumbed for meaning. At the same time, she realized that she should quote only some words rather than all.

Sample Student Paper: Final Draft

Here is Alison's final draft of her paper about "The Use of Force." As you read it, keep in mind that it emerged only after she had done several preliminary drafts, in consultation with some of her classmates as well as her instructor. Although Alison's paper is a good example of how to write about a short story, most drafts can stand to be revised further. What do you think Alison has done well in her paper? If she planned to do yet another version, what suggestions would you make?

```
Alison Caldwell
Professor Stein
English 1A
November 3, —
            Forms of Blindness in "The Use of Force"
    In William Carlos Williams's story "The Use of
Force," the narrator is a doctor frustrated by one of his
patients, a young girl who refuses to let him determine
```

if her throat is infected. After violently struggling
with the child, he finally manages to pry open her mouth
and does find her tonsils diseased. In an important
sense, therefore, the child is the narrator's antagonist,
over whom he eventually triumphs. Yet throughout the
story, the narrator seems to identify with the child,
almost as if she is his secret self or double. At the
same time, we readers must decide which of her characteristics he shares most. To answer this question, we should
consider the narrator's very last words, which seem significant just because they serve as his conclusion. After
his victory over the girl, he reports, "tears of defeat
blinded her eyes." These final words suggest that he,
too, has been "blind," in various senses of the term.
Most important, his anger at the child has obscured for
him her humanity. Even at the end, perhaps, he does not
fully "see" the limits of his compassion.

     To understand the narrator's identification with the
child, we should note his relationship with her parents.
Though her mother and father are allies in his fight
against her, he feels increasing scorn for them. When the
mother says to the child "He won't hurt you," the narrator must conceal his "disgust." Later, he openly snarls
at the mother: "For heaven's sake, I broke in. Don't call
me a nice man." Although the child accuses the narrator
of "killing me," he is actually homicidal toward her
ineffective father: "I wanted to kill him."

     With the child, the narrator has a different rela-
tionship. At several moments, he is negative about her,
too. When she resists his effort to open her mouth with a
wooden tongue depressor, he gets "furious," even though
he realizes that he is angry at a mere girl. Eventually,
his wrath becomes so intense that "I could have torn the
child apart in my own fury and enjoyed it." Nevertheless,
his anger is mixed with admiration. The child's sheer
force of resistance makes him think highly of her. After
he triumphs, he admits to himself that "She had fought

valiantly to keep me from knowing her secret." More important, midway through the story he contrasts her quite favorably with her parents: "I had already fallen in love with the savage brat, the parents were contemptible to me. In the ensuing struggle they grew more and more abject, crushed, exhausted while she surely rose to magnificent heights of insane fury of effort bred of her terror of me."

The narrator's identification with the child is not simply one person's respect for another. In various ways, he comes to resemble her. For example, both find her parents unhelpful as allies. If she shows "insane fury of effort," he feels "my own fury." She violently resists him; he violently attacks her. If "her face was flushed," eventually he feels a "pleasure" in combat with her that leaves his face "burning." Perhaps the narrator finds the child compelling precisely because they mirror each other.

But which of their similarities is most important? By announcing at the end that the girl has been "blinded," the narrator invites us to suppose that he has been "blind" as well and to believe that this is their most noteworthy connection. Significantly, the narrator wears glasses, which the girl knocks off. Literally, he lacks clear vision. For much of the story, though, the narrator has been "blind" in that he lacks the opportunity to see what disease lurks behind the girl's mouth. His earnestly repeated use of the word "look" suggests what a struggle it is for him to view his patient's secret. After proposing to the parents that "we take a look at the throat first," he pleads with the girl to "open your mouth and let's take a look at your throat." When she refuses, he begs her to "let me take a look," "Just open up and let me see." He even resorts to the word "look" as he tries to reassure her: "Look, I said opening both hands wide, I haven't anything in my hands." Once he gets more exasperated with the child, he uses the word "look" more

sternly: "Look here, I said to the child, we're going to
look at your throat."

Yet the narrator seems "blind" in a psychological
sense, too. As he intensifies his attack on the girl, he
tells himself that he is doing so for her own and society's good: "The damned little brat must be protected
against her own idiocy, one says to one's self at such
times. Others must be protected against her." At some
point, though, he realizes that his rationalizations protect himself. In reality, he comes to acknowledge, he has
been driven by "a blind fury" which leads him to a "final
unreasoning assault." Here, the word "blind" refers to
obsession with victory, regardless of its human consequences. For the narrator, helping the girl becomes less
crucial than conquering her.

Nevertheless, the narrator doesn't seem "blind" as he
looks back on his own conduct. Notice that he tells the
story in the past tense, which means that he is analyzing
how he behaved on a previous occasion. As he reviews what
he did and felt when he visited the Olsons, he comes
across as remarkably candid about his own base motives.
We readers do not have to infer that he acted mainly out
of "a blind fury"; he himself informs us of this fact. If
anything, we may conclude that he is now a man of vision,
bursting with true insights about himself.

We need not accept all of his self-analysis, however.
By acknowledging his more negative feelings, he may win
points with us for honesty without really changing his
behavior or mindset. Even as he notes his "blind fury,"
for example, he concludes that "One goes on to the end,"
as if humanity in general would inevitably have acted as
he did. When he makes this fatalistic declaration, he may
be protecting himself yet again by refusing to see ways
in which he must still take personal responsibility.

Perhaps he is using a strategy that many middle-class
professionals have used when confronted with lower-class
suffering. Although Williams provides few details of the

Olsons' life, clearly they belong at best to the working class. Their house can get "very damp," they seem unused to doctors, and the narrator points out that the mother is "clean," as if she might well have been living in filth. The narrator is not blatantly prejudiced against the lower classes. After all, he has responded when the Olsons' summoned him. But he seems disposed to think of the parents as stupid, and his concern about their daughter stems in part from his effort to stop a diphtheria outbreak. His tone of ironic wisdom in telling the story is consistent with a basic detachment from such people. By summarizing his visit to the Olsons with the world-weary statement "One goes on to the end," he may still be "blinding" himself to the possibility of forming a genuine bond with this specific family.

5

Writing about Poems

Some students are put off by poetry, perhaps because their early experiences with it were discouraging. They imagine poems have deep hidden meanings that they can't uncover. Maybe their high-school English teacher always had the right interpretation, and they rarely did. This need not be the case. Poetry can be accessible to all readers.

The problem is often a confusion about the nature of poetry, since poetry is more compressed than prose. It focuses more on connotative, emotional, or associative meanings and conveys meaning more through suggestion, indirection, and the use of metaphor, symbol, and imagery than prose does. Poetry seldom hands us a specific meaning. Poetic texts suggest certain possibilities, but the reader completes the transaction. Part of the meaning comes from the writer, part from the text itself, and part from the reader. Even if students are the same age, race, religion, and ethnicity, they are not exact duplicates of each other. All of them have their own experiences, their own family histories, their own emotional lives. If thirty people are reading a poem about conformity or responsibility, all thirty will have varying views about these concepts, even though there will probably be commonalities. (Our culture is so saturated with media images that it is nearly impossible to avoid some overlap in responses.)

In a good class discussion, then, we should be aware that even though we might be members of the same culture, each of us reads from a unique perspective, a perspective that might also shift from time to time. If a woman reads a poem about childbirth, her identity as a female will seem more relevant than if she were reading a poem about death, a more universal experience. In other words, how we read a poem and how significant and meaningful the poem is for us depends both on the content of the poem and our specific circumstances. Suppose you are fourteen when you first read a poem about dating; you would likely have very different responses rereading it at nineteen, twenty-five, and fifty. We read poems through our experiences. As we gain new experiences, our readings change.

That is one reason that it is important to respond in writing to your first reading. You want to be able to separate your first thoughts from those of your classmates; they too will be bringing their own experiences, values, and ideas to the discussion. In the give-and-take of open discussion, it may be difficult to remember what you first said. Of course, the point of a classroom discussion is not simply to defend your initial response, for then you would be denying yourself the benefit of other people's ideas. A good discussion should open up the poem, allow you to see it from multiple viewpoints, and enable you to expand your perspective, to see how others make sense of the world.

This rich mixture of the poet's text, the reader's response, and discussion among several readers can create new possibilities of meaning. Even more than fiction or drama, poetry encourages creative readings that can be simultaneously true to the text and to the reader. A lively class discussion can uncover a dozen or more plausible interpretations of a poem, each backed up with valid evidence both from the poem and the reader's experience. You may try to persuade others that your views about the poem are correct; others may do the same to you. This negotiation is at the heart of a liberal, democratic education. In fact, maybe the most respected and repeated notion about being well-educated is the ability to empathize with another's point of view, to see as another sees. Reading, discussing, and writing about poetry can help you become a person who can both create meaning and understand and appreciate how others do. This is one important way literature matters.

We have chosen six poems about work—about the joys and sorrows, the satisfactions and frustrations of physical labor. Some people might think of poets as intellectuals far removed from the experiences of the working class, but this is not the case. Indeed, many poets were themselves brought up in working-class homes and know firsthand the dignity and value of such work. Even among poets who do not themselves toil with their hands, few lack the imaginative empathy that would allow them to write perceptively about firefighters and factory workers, cleaning women and mill workers. These six poems are especially relevant today when physical work is becoming less and less a reality among middle-class Americans. Poems that matter are poems about real life—about love and death, about pain and loss, about beauty and hope. These six poems about work are about all of these and more.

The first poem, "In Creve Coeur, Missouri," is by Rosanna Warren (b. 1953), a contemporary poet and scholar who teaches at Boston University. Charles Fort (b. 1951), the author of "We Did Not Fear the Father," is an African American poet who grew up in New Britain, Connecticut, taught in the South for a number of years, and now lives and teaches in Nebraska. His poem first appeared in *The Georgia Review*. Philip Levine (b. 1928) grew up in Detroit. Much of his poetry, including "What Work Is," recalls his youth in his native city, where he worked as a laborer in Detroit factories. Mary Oliver's (b. 1935) "Singapore" appeared in *House of Light* (1992). She has won a Pulitzer prize for her poetry. "Blackberries" is by Yusef Komunyakaa (b. 1947), who has become known for exploring various aspects of African American experience; the poem is from *Magic City* (1992). Edwin Arlington Robinson's "The Mill" is the oldest poem in the cluster. Robinson (1869–1935) is considered the first major poet of twentieth-century America.

ROSANNA WARREN
In Creve Coeur, Missouri

Only in Creve Coeur
would an amateur photographer
firebug snap a shot so
unconsolable: fireman bent low

over the rag of body held   5
like impossible laundry pulled
too soon from the line, too pale,
too sodden with smoke to flail

in his huge, dark, crumpled embrace.
He leans to the tiny face.   10
Her hair stands out like flame.
She is naked, she has no name.

No longer a baby, almost
a child, not yet a ghost,
she presses a doll-like fist   15
to his professional chest.

Her head falls back to his hand.
Tell us that she will stand
again, quarrel and misbehave.
He is trying to make her breathe.   20

Strong man, you know how it's done,
you've done it again and again
sucking the spirit back
to us from its lair of smoke.

We'll call it a fine surprise.   25
The snapshot won a prize
though it couldn't revive *her*
that night in Creve Coeur.   [1993]

CHARLES FORT
We Did Not Fear the Father

We did not fear the father as the barber who stood
like a general in a white jacket with a green visor cap.
For six long days he held a straight razor like a sword
until his porcelain-chrome chariot became a down-home chair.
The crop-eared son learned to see how the workingman's   5

day job after the night shift filled the son's small pockets
with licorice, filled the offering plate, and paid for the keeper
who clipped our grape vines under his own pageant.

We did not fear the father as landlord in our three-story tenement
who took charge of four apartments and the attic dwellers.   10
We searched each corner of the dirt cellar for a fuse box
while he broke out plasterboard upstairs with a sledgehammer.
We peeled out paper from wire mesh and read the headline news
a century old before he lifted us like birds into our bunk beds.

We did not fear the father until he entered the tomb of noise   15
for his night job, shaping molten steel into ball bearings
as we stared into the barbed grate where he stood
before the furnace sending smoke into the trees.
Fear became the eight-hour echo and glow inside his skull,
the high-pitched metal scraping our ears as our provider   20
left the factory floor with oil and sawdust inside his mouth
and punched out as fermented daylight burned his eyes.
We did not fear our father until he stooped in the dark.   [1999]

PHILIP LEVINE
What Work Is

We stand in the rain in a long line
waiting at Ford Highland Park. For work.
You know what work is — if you're
old enough to read this you know what
work is, although you may not do it.   5
Forget you. This is about waiting,
shifting from one foot to another.
Feeling the light rain falling like mist
into your hair, blurring your vision
until you think you see your own brother   10
ahead of you, maybe ten places.
You rub your glasses with your fingers,
and of course its someone else's brother,
narrower across the shoulders than
yours but with the same sad slouch, the grin   15
that does not hide the stubbornness,
the sad refusal to give in to
rain, to the hours wasted waiting,
to the knowledge that somewhere ahead
a man is waiting who will say, "No,   20
we're not hiring today," for any

reason he wants. You love your brother,
now suddenly you can hardly stand
the love flooding you for your brother,
who's not beside you or behind or   25
ahead because he's home trying to
sleep off a miserable night shift
at Cadillac so he can get up
before noon to study his German.
Works eight hours a night so he can sing   30
Wagner, the opera you hate most,
the worst music ever invented.
How long has it been since you told him
you loved him, held his wide shoulders,
opened your eyes wide and said those words,   35
and maybe kissed his cheek? You've never
done something so simple, so obvious,
not because you're too young or too dumb,
not because you're jealous or even mean
or incapable of crying in   40
the presence of another man, no,
just because you don't know what work is.   [1991]

MARY OLIVER
Singapore

In Singapore, in the airport,
a darkness was ripped from my eyes.
In the women's restroom, one compartment stood open.
A woman knelt there, washing something
          in the white bowl.   5

Disgust argued in my stomach
and I felt, in my pocket, for my ticket.

A poem should always have birds in it.
Kingfishers, say, with their bold eyes and gaudy wings.
Rivers are pleasant, and of course trees.   10
A waterfall, or if that's not possible, a fountain
          rising and falling.
A person wants to stand in a happy place, in a poem.

When the woman turned I could not answer her face.
Her beauty and her embarrassment struggled together, and   15
          neither could win.
She smiled and I smiled. What kind of nonsense is this?
Everybody needs a job.

Yes, a person wants to stand in a happy place, in a poem.
But first we must watch her as she stares down at her labor,   20
    which is dull enough.
She is washing the tops of the airport ashtrays, as big as
    hubcaps, with a blue rag.
Her small hands turn the metal, scrubbing and rinsing.
She does not work slowly, nor quickly, but like a river.   25
Her dark hair is like the wing of a bird.

I don't doubt for a moment that she loves her life.
And I want her to rise up from the crust and the slop
    and fly down to the river.
This probably won't happen.   30
But maybe it will.
If the world were only pain and logic, who would want it?

Of course, it isn't.
Neither do I mean anything miraculous, but only
the light that can shine out of a life. I mean   35
the way she unfolded and refolded the blue cloth,
the way her smile was only for my sake; I mean
the way this poem is filled with trees, and birds.   [1992]

YUSEF KOMUNYAKAA
Blackberries

They left my hands like a printer's
Or thief's before a police blotter
& pulled me into early morning's
Terrestrial sweetness, so thick
The damp ground was consecrated   5
Where they fell among a garland of thorns.

Although I could smell old lime-covered
History, at ten I'd still hold out my hands
& berries fell into them. Eating from one
& filling a half gallon with the other,   10
I ate the mythology & dreamt
Of pies & cobbler, almost

Needful as forgiveness. My bird dog Spot
Eyed blue jays & thrashers. The mud frogs
In rich blackness, hid from daylight.   15
An hour later, beside City Limits Road
I balanced a gleaming can in each hand,
Limboed between worlds, repeating *one dollar.*

The big blue car made me sweat.
Wintertime crawled out of the windows.   20
When I leaned closer I saw the boy
& girl my age, in the wide back seat
Smirking, & it was then I remembered my fingers
Burning with thorns among berries too ripe to touch.   [1992]

EDWIN ARLINGTON ROBINSON
The Mill

The miller's wife had waited long,
    The tea was cold, the fire was dead;
And there might yet be nothing wrong
    In how he went and what he said;
"There are no millers any more,"   5
    Was all that she had heard him say;
And he had lingered at the door
    So long that it seemed yesterday.

Sick with fear that had no form
    She knew that she was there at last;   10
And in the mill there was a warm
    And mealy fragrance of the past.
What else there was would only seem
    To say again what he had meant;
And what was hanging from a beam   15
    Would not have heeded where she went.

And if she thought it followed her,
    She may have reasoned in the dark
That one way of the few there were
    Would hide her and would leave no mark: 20
Black water, smooth above the weir
    Like starry velvet in the night,
Though ruffled once, would soon appear
    The same as ever to the sight.   [1920]

A WRITING EXERCISE

Look again at the Topics of Literary Criticism (p. 38), selecting one that
seems promising as an interpretive lens through which to view the six work
poems in this cluster. Freewrite for a few minutes on all six, but don't worry if
your topic doesn't seem to fit all the poems. A later exercise will eventually
ask you to pick the three poems that work the best.

A Student's Personal Responses to the Poems

The following are selections from the response journal of Michaela Fiorucci, a nineteen-year-old sophomore from Cape May, New Jersey, who chose to focus on boundaries—on the various divisions we set up between ourselves and other people, such as income, race, gender, sexual preference, and religion. It seemed to her an interesting way to talk about work since Michaela had observed barriers of all kinds between workers at her job at the university.

As an explorative strategy, Michaela did some freewriting on the six poems, hoping to discover an argument about boundaries that might fit at least three of the poems. The following are selections from her response journal.

In "In Creve Coeur, Missouri," there are the obvious boundaries between life and death, between the firefighter and the girl, between the photograph and reality, but I think the biggest boundary is between an acceptance of what is actually the case--that the little girl is dead--and the poet's desire for another reading of the photo. Since the boundary between life and death cannot be crossed by imagination or desire, she must admit the stark reality of the firefighter's failure.

In "We Did Not Fear the Father," the poet begins with a division between his father as a normal man and his own image of him as a general in a chariot. Mostly there is the father's separation from the family during his day job, his night job, and his landlord job. In the last stanza we can see the real separation that the poet has been leading up to--the separation of the father as he enters "the tomb of noise" where he might lose his health. The boundary the poet really fears is between a robust and a "stooped" father, between his protection and his loss.

Although the boundary in "What Work Is" seems to be between those who know what hard work is and those who don't, the narrator shifts his focus when he thinks he sees his brother in line, waiting for work. The most significant boundary in the poem is emotional intimacy or honesty. The poet laments our inability to cross that psychological boundary.

In "Singapore," there is a clear boundary between the
middle-class American tourist and the cleaning lady, so
much so that at first the narrator says, "Disgust argued
in my stomach." The cleaning woman also seems to believe
in a barrier and continues to work in a steady way. The
narrator finally sees beauty in her dedication to her
work. When the narrator does see beauty in her work
habits, it helps close the barrier between them. There
are also the issues of boundaries between fantasy and
reality and between a world of pain and logic and one
with birds and rivers. But at the end these boundaries
also seem to be closing.

In "Blackberries," the young boy seems to be living
in a rural paradise, beyond the city boundaries, outside
the usual urban and suburban environment. He lives in a
land of bird dogs, jays, thrashers, and mud frogs. He
makes comparisons between blackness and light that seem
to anticipate the economic boundary that appears in the
last stanza, the one between the poor boy and the rich
kids in the car. It is this division between the children
in air conditioned comfort and the narrator on the outside looking in that seems to be the main point of this
poem. Some boundaries cause us pain.

"The Mill" tells the sad story of a miller who could
not see a boundary between himself and his job. When he
tells his wife "there are no millers any more," he is
really saying that his life is over; he has no reason to
live. And so he crosses the boundary between life and
death. Tragically, his wife also has difficulty seeing
herself outside her role as wife and housekeeper, and so
she also crosses that ultimate boundary. She does so,
however, in a completely different way: she drowns herself, so no one will know. She passes through life's
boundary without leaving a trace.

After reading these six brief freewrites to her response group, Michaela
decided that "Blackberries, "Singapore," and "The Mill" were the most promis-

ing. Michaela still didn't have a focus, but she liked the idea that boundaries, like walls, sometimes serve a purpose and sometimes they don't. She remembered a discussion of Robert Frost's "Mending Wall" from another course that focused on negotiating the walls we build between us. Her professor liked this idea since it helped her considerably narrow the concept of boundaries.

After reviewing her freewriting, Michaela wrote the following first draft and read it to her response group. She then discussed with her instructor her plans for a revision. Her instructor made a number of specific and general comments. After reading her first draft, what feedback would you give Michaela? Her revision appears at the end of the chapter.

Sample Student Paper: First Draft

Michaela Fiorucci

Mr. Hardee

English 102

Boundaries in Robinson,

Komunyakaa, and Oliver

Although most sophomores I know at school value their privacy, they also want to create intimate relationships. It is often hard to reconcile these two impulses. Most middle-class students are lucky enough to have their own rooms, private enclaves against annoying sisters and brothers, intrusive mothers and fathers. But a room is also more than a physical boundary; it is also a symbolic assertion of identity. It says, "I'm separate from others, even within the closeness of the family." Such a commitment to physical privacy might be innocent enough, but it does contain dangerous seeds, especially when extended beyond the home to neighborhoods. When different ethnic groups want boundaries between them, it is no longer innocent. When the upper classes need to be separated from workers because they see each other as radically different, a dangerous boundary has been erected.

It would be reductive, however, to say all boundaries need to be erased. Edwin Arlington Robinson's "The Mill" is a good example of the dangerous consequences of a missing boundary. The poem narrates the sad story of a farm couple who commit suicide--the husband because he

feels useless, the wife because she can't imagine life
without her husband. During my first few readings, I was
struck by the lack of communication between the couple.
He must have been depressed for a long time, but it seems
they never discussed his feelings. Keeping an emotional
distance from others was probably a typical part of the
way men and women dealt with each other a hundred years
ago. It was a boundary not to be crossed. Apparently he
could not say, "I feel terrible that I am going to lose
my job." And his wife accepts his reticence, even though
he might have been having second thoughts as he "lingered
at the door." Clearly this is a boundary that should have
been breached. But after several readings I began to
realize that the boundary that should have been established wasn't--the idea that a person's value or worth is
synonymous with their identity is dehumanizing. And it
probably isn't something that just happened in the past.
Nor is the equally dehumanizing idea that a wife is nothing without her husband. When the miller's wife decides
to "leave no mark" by jumping into the pond, she is
admitting she is not a worthwhile person by herself. Both
identify totally with a role that in my view should only
be one aspect of a complex human life. The final barrier
she crosses, from life to death, is symbolically represented in the poem as a feminine domestic gesture: she
doesn't want to leave a mess. The boundaries of person
and occupation should be made clear; the arbitrary boundaries between genders should not.

When the narrator in "Blackberries" claims that he is
"Limboed between two worlds," he means the rural paradise
of "Terrestrial sweetness" and "rich blackness" he temporarily lives in versus the commercial, urban work that
"made him sweat." He has constructed a boundary between
the ancient picking of berries and the technology of
automobiles, between a natural closeness with nature and
the artificial "Wintertime crawled out of the windows."
Even though the narrator is only ten, he senses the sen-

sual joys of being one with nature. He seems to reject
"old lime-covered / History" in favor of "mythology,"
which seems to suggest a conscious rejection or maybe
repression of the contemporary world. But this boundary
cannot stand. He needs the outside world to survive, and
when the car approaches, it is the modern world and all
its pluses and minuses that draw near. When he looks in
he sees "Smirking" children; he sees class prejudice,
hierarchy, and economic reality. The smirkers of the
world are in charge. This realization dissolves the protective boundary around his garden of Eden, and he feels
physical pain. But really he feels the pain of initiation, the pain of having to cross a boundary he wanted to
delay as long as possible. Although we can sympathize
with the young narrator, he would probably have fared
better by not making his boundary so extreme.

   The narrator in Mary Oliver's "Singapore" at first
sees a significant boundary between herself as a middle-
class traveler and a cleaning woman washing a toilet. It
is a separation we might all make, given our socialization to see this kind of physical labor is degrading.
College-educated people in America have a tendency to see
themselves as distinct from workers. For most, a woman
washing something in a compartment is beyond the pale, a
clear indication that the woman is other. But Oliver does
have some conflicting ideas since she says a "Disgust
argued in my stomach." Since we are also socialized to be
tolerant and open-minded, she knows she shouldn't think
this way. And since she is also a writer with ideas about
how poems should "always have birds in it," she looks
harder at the cleaning woman, finally seeing in her face,
in her hair, and in the way she works slowly, "like a
river," the positive aspects she probably wants to find.
Oliver does not simply accept the boundaries that her
culture constructs but negotiates with herself, eventually seeing that "light can shine out of a life" even
where we do not expect it. In the woman's careful folding

```
and unfolding of her blue work cloth and in her smile,
Oliver eclipses the social boundary and ends up with a
life affirming vision "filled with trees, with birds."
```

The Elements of Poetry

Speaker and Tone

The voice we hear in a poem could be the poet's, but it is better to think of the speaker as a sort of poetic construction — perhaps a **persona** (mask) for the poet or perhaps a complete fiction. The speaker's tone or attitude is sometimes difficult to discern. It could be ironic or sentimental, joyful or morose, or a combination. In "In Creve Coeur, Missouri," for example, we can get at the tone of the speaker by noticing the ironic comment in the town's name (broken/sad heart). Content is not always a reliable guide to tone, since writers can be trying to be satiric. But as with Swift's essay "A Modest Proposal," in which he suggests that babies be cooked and eaten to relieve the famine in Ireland, we use our own moral sense to figure out that he could not really be suggesting such a monstrously aberrant solution. So too in the content of this poem we sense a bitter irony in the opening stanzas that changes to images ("rag of body," "tiny face") that directly suggest the speaker's sadness. But her description of a static photo becomes a kind of narrative as the speaker sees in the position of the child in the firefighter's "huge, dark, crumpled embrace" a glimmer of hope. Using the present tense, the speaker imagines the child's "head falls back to his hand," giving us the possibility that "she will stand / again." The strength and professionalism of the firefighter give the poet confidence and pride and change her bitter irony and sadness to hope for a miracle. But in the final stanza, she must move from wishing for "a fine surprise" to the harsh realization that, regardless of the artistic quality of the photo, finally and irrevocably a child died in a place called broken heart.

A WRITING EXERCISE

Each of the poems in this cluster has a distinctive tone. Sometimes the narrator speaks in the first person; sometimes, in the third person as an observer. Compare the tone of the narrators in Charles Fort's or Mary Oliver's poem to the tone of Edwin Arlington Robinson's "The Mill," noting if it is easier to sense the narrator's tone when *I* or *we* is used.

Diction and Syntax

In "We Did Not Fear the Father," we initially assume that "fear" in the first line carries the usual negative **denotation** of anxiety, but the image that follows — the "general in a white jacket with a green visor" — doesn't seem threatening. In line three, "razor" and "sword" might cause concern, but that quickly dissolves under the positive **connotations** of "chariot" and "down-home chair." Except for the similes and metaphors, throughout the first stanza the diction and syntax seem almost colloquial and straightforward, mostly with the usual subject-verb-object pattern. The second half of the first stanza is also filled with positive connotations ("licorice," "offering plate," and "grape vines") that continue to undercut the worrisome "fear" of the first line.

But Fort repeats "We did not fear the father," this time referring to him not as barber but as landlord. Again the narrator's syntax and diction belie any threat. On the contrary, the poetic simile "lifted us like birds" suggests a gentle and strong provider.

In the last stanza, he again repeats the opening phrase but adds the simple but critical "until." Now we anticipate that there might actually be a reason for "fear" in its usual denotation. But again we see the father at work. Now as factory worker, "shaping molten steel ball bearings." The diction becomes more menacing ("barbed grate," "glow inside his skull," "metal scraping our ears," "punched out," "burned his eyes"). Now we are prepared for the simple declarative sentence: "We did not fear our father until he stooped in the dark." The poignant image of the father "stooped" dramatically clarifies the meaning of the ambiguous "fear": the children fear that his hard work has seriously weakened their general. Fort is actually fearful for his father and, of course, by extension fearful that his protector will be taken from him.

WRITING EXERCISE

Compare the diction and syntax in "Singapore" and "Blackberries." How do the denotation and connotation of the words convey the poet's attitude? How does the syntax?

Figures of Speech

When we use figures of speech, we mean something other than the words' literal meaning. In the first sentence of "Singapore," Mary Oliver writes that a "darkness was ripped from my eyes." This direct comparison is a **metaphor**. Had she been more indirect, she might have written "it was like a darkness . . . ," a common literary device called a **simile**. Poets use metaphors and similes to help us to see in a fresh perspective. Comparing love to a rose encourages us to think differently about love, helping us to see its delicate beauty. Of course, today that comparison is no longer novel and can even be a cliché, suggesting that a writer is not trying to be original and is settling instead for an easy comparison. When Robert Burns wrote "my love is like a red, red rose" over two hundred years ago, it was a fresh comparison that excited new ways of looking at love. Indeed, some thinkers, like the contemporary American philosopher Richard Rorty, think that metaphors can change our ways of looking at the world. Our thinking about time, for example, might be different if we didn't think with linear metaphors about the past being behind us and the future up ahead. What if, like some American Indian languages, we used a circular metaphor, having just one day that constantly repeated itself? Would our perceptions of time change?

What if Mary Oliver had begun her poem by saying that a misunderstanding was corrected, instead of "a darkness was ripped from my eyes"? Her metaphor is not only more dramatic and memorable but more suggestive. Darkness deepens the idea of lack of knowledge, suggesting not only intellectual blindness but a host of negative connotations that readers might associate with the dark. Fresh metaphors can be expansive and illuminating. They help us understand the world differently.

Oliver creatively uses metaphors and similes throughout "Singapore." "Disgust argued" is an interesting metaphor or perhaps a personification, where her stomach is given the ability to argue. Oliver interrupts her observation of the cleaning woman in the third stanza to make a comment on the function of poetry itself, claiming that poems should have birds, rivers, and trees in them. Is she suggesting metaphorically that poems should be pleasant? Is that the only thing birds, rivers, and trees suggest to you?

She returns to the woman, and they exchange glances. Apparently Oliver is struggling with her own socialization that sees this kind of physical labor as demeaning. She directly describes the woman's "scrubbing and rinsing" but then returns to similes, describing her work as "like a river" and her hair "like the wing of a bird." These comparisons seem for a moment to clarify the event for Oliver, helping her see this seemingly oppressive job positively. Amazingly, she wants the woman actually to become a bird and "rise up from the crust and the slop and fly."

But she reminds us in the final stanza that she isn't really expecting that kind of physical miracle; instead, she wants to remind us that how we describe the woman working controls how we feel about her. If we see the folding and unfolding of her wash cloth metaphorically, then we might see her differently; we might see her natural dignity, her beauty, and how her "light" was able to illuminate Mary Oliver's "darkness."

Although students often seem perplexed when professors find hidden **symbols** in poems, writers rarely plant such puzzling images deep in the recesses of their texts. The best symbols grow naturally out of the meaning-making process that readers go through. In the context of a particular poem, symbols are usually objects that can stand for general ideas. And like metaphors and similes, they suggest different things to different readers. The whale in *Moby-Dick*, for example, can be read as a symbol for implacable evil or perhaps the mysteries of the universe. The glass unicorn in *The Glass Menagerie* is often read as a symbol for Laura's fragility, but it might also suggest her uniqueness or maybe her isolation from real life. In "Singapore," the specific event of the poet watching a woman washing a toilet could be symbolic of anything we find unpleasant or strange or alien. And the whole event, including her eventual understanding, could easily be an **allegory** or extended symbol for the necessity for all of us to transcend our cultural socialization to understand other cultures and other attitudes toward working.

WRITING EXERCISE

Look at several of the poems in this cluster, noting the metaphors, similes, symbols, and allegories that you notice. Do they enhance the meaning of the poem? Do they help you see the situation in a fresh way?

Sound

The English poet Alexander Pope hoped that poetry's **sound** could become "an echo to [its] sense," that what the ear hears would reinforce what the mind understands. To many people, **rhyme** is the most recognizable aspect of poetry. The matching of final vowel and consonant sounds can make a poem trite or interesting. The now-familiar rhyming of "moon" and "June" with "swoon" suggests a poet that will settle for a cliché rather than do the hard work of being fresh. Rhyme, of course, is pleasing to the ear and makes the poem easier to remember, but it also gives the poem psychological force. Most contemporary poets choose not to rhyme, preferring the flexibility and freedom of free verse. But sound is still a high priority.

In Philip Levine's "What Work Is," for example, sound is used in subtle ways to reinforce meaning. Poets use *alliteration,* for example, to connect words near each other by repeating the initial consonant sound. A variation, *assonance,* repeats vowel sounds. Levine focuses on the shifting meaning of work, claiming first that "You know what work is" and then in the last line that "you don't know what work is." Levine begins by talking about the difficulties of physical labor and concludes by noting the difficult work of emotional intimacy. He creates patterns of sound that prepares us for this shift. A number of words are repeated: *work, stand, know, waiting, rain, long, love, sad, ahead, man, wide, not,* and *because,* as well as the phrase "You know what work is." And a number of words are alliteratively connected:

forget, foot, feeling, falling, fingers

someone, shoulders, same sad slouch, stubbornness, sad

wasted waiting, wants, somewhere

brother beside, behind

works, worst, wide, words

never, not

Although these sounds probably affect readers unconsciously, they do prepare us for a shift from people waiting for a job to the job of brotherly love. The repeated sounds connect both halves of the poem. Note the way *stand* first means being in line but later ("you can hardly stand / the love") connects with a brotherly bond. Similarly, *shift* first describes restless behavior in line but later the night job of the sleeping brother. The word *long* also fits this pattern, as it initially means the length of the line and later refers to the duration of their relationship: "How long has it been since you told him / you loved him." In these and other ways, Levine uses sound to enhance meaning.

WRITING EXERCISE

Note the use of alliteration in "In Creve Coeur." How might this and other sound devices enhance meaning?

Rhythm and Meter

Many poets in the early twentieth century chose to have their poems rhyme. Edwin Arlington Robinson's "The Mill" employs a typical **rhyme scheme** in which in each stanza the last words in lines 1 and 3 sound the same and the last words in lines 2 and 4 sound the same. We indicate such a pattern with letters — abab. The second half of the first stanza would then be cdcd and so forth.

Rhythm in poetry refers to the beat, a series of stresses, pauses, and accents. We are powerfully attuned to rhythm, whether it is our own heartbeat or the throb of the bass guitar in a rock band. When we pronounce a word, we give more **stress** (breath, emphasis) to some syllables than to others. When these stresses occur at a regular interval over, say, a line of poetry, we refer to it as **meter**. When we scan a line of poetry, we try to mark its stresses and pauses. We use ´ to indicate a stressed syllable and ˘ for an unstressed one. The basic measuring unit for these stressed and unstressed syllables in English is the **foot**. There are four usual feet: *iambic, trochaic, anapestic,* and *dactylic*. An **iamb** is an unstressed syllable followed by a stressed one, as in "the woods." Reversed we have a **trochee,** as in "tiger." An **anapest** contains three syllables that are unstressed, then unstressed, then stressed, as in "When the blue / wave rolls nightly / on deep Galilee." The reverse, the **dactyl,** can be heard in the Mother Goose rhyme, "Pussy cat, / pussy cat / where have you / been?" If you look at the first four lines of "The Mill" again, you can hear a regular beat of iambs:

> The mill / er's wife / had wait / ed long,
> The tea / was cold, / the fire / was dead
> And there / might yet / be noth / ing wrong
> In how / he went / and what / he said:

Depending on the number of feet, we give lines various names. If a line contains one foot, it is a **monometer;** two is a **dimeter;** three a **trimeter;** four a **tetrameter;** five a **pentameter;** six a **hexameter;** seven a **heptameter;** and eight an **octometer.** So Robinson's lines are iambic tetrameter. Most lines in Shakespeare's sonnets are iambic pentameter, or five iambs.

Note the punctuation in Robinson's poem. When a line ends with a comma, we are meant to pause very briefly; when a line ends with a period (end stop), we pause a bit longer. But when there is no punctuation (line 7), we are meant to continue on until the end of the next line. This is known as *enjambment*. These poetic techniques improve the sound and flow of the poem and enhance the thoughts and feelings that give poetry its memorable depth and meaningfulness.

A WRITING EXERCISE

Finish marking the rhythm and meter of "The Mill." Why do you think the poet chose these patterns rather than free verse? Does the rhyme add to the poem's somber, rather grim conclusion?

Theme

Some readers are fond of extracting **theme statements** from poems, claiming, for example, that the theme of "Blackberries" is the loss of innocence or that "What Work Is" is the emotional reticence of men. In a sense, these thematic observations are plausible enough, but they are limiting and misleading. "Blackberries" certainly seems to have something to do with the interruption of a certain view about physical labor, but the significance for each reader might be much more specific, having to do with the noble savage, the Garden of Eden, hierarchy in society, with the arrogance of the rich, with sensitivity, cruelty, and dignity. Reducing a complex, ambiguous poem to a bald statement robs the poem of its evocative power, its mystery, and its art.

Some critics stress the response of readers; others care only for what the text itself says; still others are concerned with the social and cultural implications of the poem's meaning. There are psychoanalytic readers who see poems as reflections of the psychological health or illness of the poet; source-hunting or intertextual readers want to find references and hints of other literary works hidden deep within the poem. Feminist readers may find sexism, Marxists may find economic injustice, and gay and lesbian readers may find heterosexual bias. Readers can and will find in texts a whole range of issues. Perhaps we find what we are looking for, or we find what matters most to us.

This does not mean that we should think of committed readers as biased or as distorting the text to fulfill their own agenda, although biased or distorted readings are not rare. In a literature course, readers are entitled to read poems according to their own interpretations as long as they follow the general convention of academic discourse. That is, it is possible to make a reasonable case that "Blackberries" is really about rejecting contemporary technology in favor of rural life. The reason that some themes sound more plausible than others is that these critics marshal their evidence from the text and their own experience. Usually the evidence that fits best wins: if you can persuade others that you have significant textual support for your theme and if you present a balanced and judicious persona, you can usually carry the day. Poems almost always have several reasonable themes. The critic's job is to argue for a theme that seems to make the most sense in relation to the support. Often the same evidence can be used to bolster different themes because themes are really just higher-level generalizations than the particulars found in the text. Critics use the concrete elements of a poem to make more general abstract statements. In "Blackberries," for example, the same textual support could be used to support the theme of the cruelty of children or the more general notion of an initiation in a class-conscious culture or the even more general idea of the inevitable loss of innocence.

WRITING EXERCISE

What are some possible themes introduced in "The Mill"? How might the theme change if read from the context of gender? Culture? Economics? Psychology?

Sample Student Paper: Revised Draft

Michaela Fiorucci
Mr. Hardee
English 102

Negotiating Boundaries

Although most college students value their privacy,
they also want to create intimate relationships; it is
often hard to reconcile these two impulses. Most middle-
class students are lucky enough to have their own bedrooms, private enclaves against annoying sisters and
brothers, intrusive mothers and fathers. But such boundaries are more than physical barriers; they are also a
symbolic assertion of identity. They say, "I'm separate
from you even within the closeness of our family." Such a
commitment to physical privacy might be innocent enough,
but it does contain dangerous seeds, especially when
extended beyond the home to neighborhoods. When different
ethnic groups want boundaries between them, it is no
longer innocent. When the upper classes want to be separated from workers because they see each other as radically different, a dangerously undemocratic boundary has
been erected. Boundaries clearly serve a protective function, but unneeded ones can also prevent us from helping
and understanding each other. Writers like Edwin Arlington Robinson, Yusef Komunyakaa, and Mary Oliver understand that we must negotiate boundaries, building them
when they increase privacy and self-worth and bridging
them when human solidarity can be enhanced.

It would be reductive to say that boundaries are
either good or bad, since their value depends so much on
context. Robinson's "The Mill" is a good example of the
dangerous consequences of a failure to cross a boundary
that should not exist and then a failure to establish a
boundary where one should exist. The poem narrates the
sad story of a farm couple who commit suicide--the husband because he feels useless, the wife because she can't

imagine life without her husband. A contemporary reader
is struck by the lack of communication between the couple.
He must have been depressed for a long time, but it seems
they never discussed his feelings. Keeping such an emotional boundary between husband and wife was probably
typical of the way men and women dealt with each other
one hundred years ago. Apparently it was a constructed
barrier that few could cross. He simply could not bare
his heart by saying, "I feel terrible that I am going to
lose my job." And his wife accepts his reticence, even
though he might have been having second thoughts as he
"lingered at the door." Clearly this is a boundary that
should have been breached. The time for their solidarity
was before he kills himself, not after.

After several readings it is clear that the boundary
that should have been established wasn't. The miller is
the victim of the demeaning idea that a person's worth is
synonymous with his or her occupation. When his job disappears, so must he. Although Robinson's tone is flat, we
sense his frustration with the inevitability of this grim
tragedy, one that is compounded by the equally dehumanizing idea that a wife cannot exist without her husband.
When the miller's wife decides to "leave no mark" by
jumping into the pond, she is admitting that she is useless outside her matrimonial role. Both identify with a
role that should only be one aspect of a complex human
life. The final barrier she crosses, from life to death,
is symbolically represented in the poem as a feminine
domestic gesture: she doesn't want to leave a mess. She
continues as a housewife even in death. The boundaries
between a person and occupation should be clear, but the
arbitrary boundaries between husbands and wives should
continue to be eradicated.

When the ten-year-old narrator in "Blackberries"
claims that he is "Limboed between two worlds," he means
the rural paradise of "Terrestrial sweetness" and "rich
blackness" he temporarily lives in versus the commercial

urban world that seems to make him anxious. He has constructed a boundary between the ancient task of picking
berries and the modern technology of automobiles, between
a closeness with nature and the artificial air-condition-
ing of the car. Although the narrator enjoys being one
with nature, he seems to be cutting himself off from the
realities of the world. He seems to reject "old lime-
covered / History" in favor of "mythology," which seems to
suggest a conscious rejection of the present. But this is
a boundary that cannot stand. He needs the outside world
to survive financially, and so when the car approaches,
it is the modern world and all its complexity that draws
near. When he looks into the car, he sees "smirking children"; he sees class prejudice, hierarchy, and economic
reality. The smirkers of the world are in charge. It is
this realization that dissolves the protective boundary
around his Garden of Eden; consequently, he feels physical pain, but it is really the pain of initiation into
reality that he feels. He must now cross a boundary he
tried to delay. Although we can sympathize with the young
narrator, like the couple in "The Mill," he would have
been better off not making his boundary so extreme.

The narrator in Mary Oliver's "Singapore" also imagines that she sees a significant boundary, here between
herself as a middle-class traveler and a cleaning woman
laboring over a toilet. It is a separation we might all
make, given our socialization in America to consider this
kind of physical labor as degrading. College-educated
people have a tendency to see themselves as distinct from
the working class. For many, a woman washing an ashtray
in a toilet bowl is beyond the pale, a clear indication
that the woman is Other. But Oliver does not simply give
into her cultural conditioning; she contests the boundary, asserting that a "Disgust argued in my stomach."
Since part of our democratic socialization is also to be
tolerant and open-minded, Oliver knows that she shouldn't
stereotype workers. And since she is also a writer with

ideas about how a poem should "always have birds in it,"
she looks hard at the cleaning woman, finally seeing in
her face, in her hair, and in the way she works, slowly
"like a river," the positive aspects of the woman that
most of us would probably miss.

Oliver does not simply accept the boundaries that her
culture constructs. Instead, she negotiates internally,
eventually seeing that a "light can shine out of a life"
even where we would not expect it. In the woman's careful
folding and unfolding of her blue work cloth and in her
smile, Oliver sees a beauty that helps her eclipse a
social boundary, ending with a life-affirming vision
"filled with trees, with birds." Such an insight does not
come easily to us because we usually accept our given
cultural boundaries. The miller and his wife are tragically unequipped to bridge the divide between them. Likewise, the boy in "Blackberries" is unable to sustain his
fantasy boundaries. Oliver's traveler, however, struggles to negotiate boundaries and is thereby able to
increase human solidarity even across class structures
and cultures.

6

Writing about Plays

Most plays incorporate elements also found in short fiction, such as plot, characterization, dialogue, setting, and theme. But unlike short fiction and other literary genres, plays are typically enacted live, in front of an audience. Theater professionals distinguish between the written *script* of a play and its actual *performances*. When you write about a play, you may wind up saying little or nothing about performances of it. When you first read and analyze a play, however, try to imagine ways of staging it. You might even research past productions of the play, noting how scenery, costumes, and lighting—as well as particular actors—were used.

Because a play is usually meant to be staged, its readers are rarely its only interpreters. Theater audiences also ponder its meanings. So, too, do cast members; no doubt you have heard of actors "interpreting" their parts. When a play is put on, even members of the backstage team are involved in interpreting it. The technical designers' choices of sets, costumes, and lighting reflect their ideas about the play, while the director works with cast and crew to implement a particular vision of it. No matter what the author of the script intended, theater is a collaborative art: All of the key figures involved in a play's production are active interpreters of the play in that they influence the audience's understanding and experience of it. Therefore, you can develop good ideas when you read a play if you imagine yourself directing a production of it. More specifically, think what you would say to the actors as you guided them through their parts. As you engage in this thought experiment, you will see that you have options, for even directors keen on staying faithful to the script know it can be staged in any number of ways. Perhaps your course will give you and other students the chance to perform a scene together; if so, you will be deciding what interpretation of the scene to set forth.

To help you understand how to write about plays, we refer often to the following two scenes, which come from plays later in the book. Each of these scenes involves a mother and her grown daughter, who reports frustrations with the world of work.

Our first scene is an early one in Tennessee Williams's *The Glass Menagerie*, a 1945 play about a family struggling to survive in St. Louis. (The complete play is presented in Chapter 12, Living in Families, where the scene appears on pp. 422–45.) Long ago, Amanda Wingfield's husband fled, leaving her to raise their children, Laura and Tom, alone. The scene we present involves Amanda and the now adult Laura. Laura is painfully shy, in part because she is physically disabled. Believing that Laura must eventually become self-supporting, Amanda has insisted that her daughter attend business school. At the beginning of this scene, however, Amanda returns home to report an embarrassing discovery: Laura has been skipping classes without telling her.

TENNESSEE WILLIAMS
From *The Glass Menagerie*

Scene 2

"Laura, Haven't You Ever Liked Some Boy?"

On the dark stage the screen is lighted with the image of blue roses.

> *Gradually Laura's figure becomes apparent and the screen goes out.*
> *The music subsides.*
> *Laura is seated in the delicate ivory chair at the small clawfoot table.*
> *She wears a dress of soft violet material for a kimono — her hair tied back from her forehead with a ribbon.*
> *She is washing and polishing her collection of glass.*
> *Amanda appears on the fire-escape steps. At the sound of her ascent, Laura catches her breath, thrusts the bowl of ornaments away, and seats herself stiffly before the diagram of the typewriter keyboard as though it held her spellbound. Something has happened to Amanda. It is written in her face as she climbs to the landing: a look that is grim and hopeless and a little absurd.*
> *She has on one of those cheap or imitation velvety-looking cloth coats with imitation fur collar. Her hat is five or six years old, one of those dreadful cloche hats that were worn in the late twenties, and she is clasping an enormous black patent-leather pocketbook with nickel clasp and initials. This is her full-dress outfit, the one she usually wears to the D.A.R.°*
> *Before entering she looks through the door.*
> *She purses her lips, opens her eyes wide, rolls them upward, and shakes her head.*
> *Then she slowly lets herself in the door. Seeing her mother's expression Laura touches her lips with a nervous gesture.*

LAURA: Hello, Mother, I was — *(She makes a nervous gesture toward the chart on the wall. Amanda leans against the shut door and stares at Laura with a martyred look.)*

D.A.R.: Daughters of the American Revolution; members must document that they have ancestors who served the patriots' cause in the Revolutionary War.

AMANDA: Deception? Deception? *(She slowly removes her hat and gloves, continuing the swift suffering stare. She lets the hat and gloves fall on the floor — a bit of acting.)*

LAURA *(shakily)*:   How was the D.A.R. meeting? *(Amanda slowly opens her purse and removes a dainty white handkerchief, which she shakes out delicately and delicately touches to her lips and nostrils.)* Didn't you go to the D.A.R. meeting, Mother?

AMANDA *(faintly, almost inaudibly)*:   —No.—No. *(Then more forcibly.)* I did not have the strength—to go to the D.A.R. In fact, I did not have the courage! I wanted to find a hole in the ground and hide myself in it forever! *(She crosses slowly to the wall and removes the diagram of the typewriter keyboard. She holds it in front of her for a second, staring at it sweetly and sorrowfully — then bites her lips and tears it in two pieces.)*

LAURA *(faintly)*:   Why did you do that, Mother? *(Amanda repeats the same procedure with the chart of the Gregg Alphabet.°)* Why are you—

AMANDA: Why? Why? How old are you, Laura?

LAURA: Mother, you know my age.

AMANDA: I thought that you were an adult; it seems that I was mistaken. *(She crosses slowly to the sofa and sinks down and stares at Laura.)*

LAURA: Please don't stare at me, Mother.

Amanda closes her eyes and lowers her head. Count ten.

AMANDA: What are we going to do, what is going to become of us, what is the future?

Count ten.

LAURA: Has something happened, Mother? *(Amanda draws a long breath and takes out the handkerchief again. Dabbing process.)* Mother, has—something happened?

AMANDA: I'll be all right in a minute. I'm just bewildered—*(count five)*—by life. . . .

LAURA: Mother, I wish that you would tell me what's happened.

AMANDA: As you know, I was supposed to be inducted into my office at the D.A.R. this afternoon. *(Image: A swarm of typewriters.)* But I stopped off at Rubicam's Business College to speak to your teachers about your having a cold and ask them what progress they thought you were making down there.

LAURA: Oh. . . .

AMANDA: I went to the typing instructor and introduced myself as your mother. She didn't know who you were. Wingfield, she said. We don't have any such student enrolled at the school! I assured her she did, that you had been going to classes since early in January. "I wonder," she said, "if you could be talking about that terribly shy little girl who dropped out of school after only a few days' attendance?" "No," I said, "Laura, my daughter, has been going to school every day for the past six weeks!" "Excuse me," she said. She took the

---

Gregg Alphabet: System of shorthand symbols invented by John Robert Gregg.

attendance book out and there was your name, unmistakably printed, and all the dates you were absent until they decided that you had dropped out of school. I still said, "No, there must have been some mistake! There must have been some mix-up in the records!" And she said, "No—I remember her perfectly now. Her hand shook so that she couldn't hit the right keys! The first time we gave a speed-test, she broke down completely—was sick at the stomach and almost had to be carried into the wash-room! After that morning she never showed up any more. We phoned the house but never got any answer"—while I was working at Famous and Barr, I suppose, demonstrating those—Oh! I felt so weak I could barely keep on my feet. I had to sit down while they got me a glass of water! Fifty dollars' tuition, all of our plans—my hopes and ambitions for you—just gone up the spout, just gone up the spout like that. *(Laura draws a long breath and gets awkwardly to her feet. She crosses to the Victrola, and winds it up.)* What are you doing?

LAURA: Oh! *(She releases the handle and returns to her seat.)*

AMANDA: Laura, where have you been going when you've gone out pretending that you were going to business college?

LAURA: I've just been going out walking.

AMANDA: That's not true.

LAURA: It is. I just went walking.

AMANDA: Walking? Walking? In winter? Deliberately courting pneumonia in that light coat? Where did you walk to, Laura?

LAURA: It was the lesser of two evils, Mother. *(Image: Winter scene in park.)* I couldn't go back up. I—threw up—on the floor!

AMANDA: From half past seven till after five every day you mean to tell me you walked around in the park, because you wanted to make me think that you were still going to Rubicam's Business College?

LAURA: It wasn't as bad as it sounds. I went inside places to get warmed up.

AMANDA: Inside where?

LAURA: I went in the art museum and the bird-houses at the Zoo. I visited the penguins every day! Sometimes I did without lunch and went to the movies. Lately I've been spending most of my afternoons in the Jewel-box, that big glass house where they raise the tropical flowers.

AMANDA: You did all this to deceive me, just for the deception? *(Laura looks down.)* Why?

LAURA: Mother, when you're disappointed, you get that awful suffering look on your face, like the picture of Jesus' mother in the museum!

AMANDA: Hush!

LAURA: I couldn't face it.

Pause. A whisper of strings.
(Legend: "The Crust of Humility.")

AMANDA *(hopelessly fingering the huge pocketbook)*:   So what are we going to do the rest of our lives? Stay home and watch the parades go by? Amuse ourselves with the glass menagerie, darling? Eternally play those worn-out phonograph records your father left as a painful reminder of him? We won't have a business career — we've given that up because it gave us nervous indigestion! *(Laughs wearily.)* What is there left but dependency all our lives? I know so well what becomes of unmarried women who aren't prepared to occupy a position. I've seen such pitiful cases in the South — barely tolerated spinsters living upon the grudging patronage of sister's husband or brother's wife! — stuck away in some little mousetrap of a room — encouraged by one in-law to visit another — little birdlike women without any nest — eating the crust of humility all their life! Is that the future that we've mapped out for ourselves? I swear it's the only alternative I can think of! It isn't a very pleasant alternative, is it? Of course — some girls *do marry. (Laura twists her hands nervously.)* Haven't you ever liked some boy?

LAURA: Yes. I liked one once. *(Rises.)* I came across his picture a while ago.

AMANDA *(with some interest)*:   He gave you his picture?

LAURA: No, it's in the year-book.

AMANDA *(disappointed)*:   Oh — a high-school boy.

(Screen image: Jim as a high-school hero bearing a silver cup.)

LAURA: Yes. His name was Jim. *(Laura lifts the heavy annual from the clawfoot table.)* Here he is in *The Pirates of Penzance.*

AMANDA *(absently)*:   The what?

LAURA: The operetta the senior class put on. He had a wonderful voice and we sat across the aisle from each other Mondays, Wednesdays, and Fridays in the Aud. Here he is with the silver cup for debating! See his grin?

AMANDA *(absently)*:   He must have had a jolly disposition.

LAURA: He used to call me — Blue Roses.

(Image: Blue roses.)

AMANDA: Why did he call you such a name as that?

LAURA: When I had that attack of pleurosis — he asked me what was the matter when I came back. I said pleurosis — he thought that I said Blue Roses! So that's what he always called me after that. Whenever he saw me, he'd holler, "Hello, Blue Roses!" I didn't care for the girl that he went out with. Emily Meisenbach. Emily was the best-dressed girl at Soldan. She never struck me, though, as being sincere. . . . It says in the Personal Section — they're engaged. That's — six years ago! They must be married by now.

AMANDA: Girls that aren't cut out for business careers usually wind up married to some nice man. *(Gets up with a spark of revival.)* Sister, that's what you'll do!

Laura utters a startled, doubtful laugh. She reaches quickly for a piece of glass.

LAURA: But, Mother —

AMANDA: Yes? *(Crossing to photograph.)*

LAURA *(in a tone of frightened apology)*:   I'm — crippled!

(Image: Screen.)

AMANDA: Nonsense! Laura, I've told you never, never to use that word. Why, you're not crippled, you just have a little defect — hardly noticeable, even! When people have some slight disadvantage like that, they cultivate other things to make up for it — develop charm — and vivacity — and — *charm!*

That's all you have to do! (*She turns again to the photograph.*) One thing your father had *plenty of* — was *charm!*

Tom *motions to the fiddle in the wings.*
(*The scene fades out with music.*)   [1945]

A WRITING EXERCISE

In three to five sentences, write a summary of the scene from *The Glass Menagerie* that you have just read. Do not attempt to *evaluate* the two characters' behavior. Rather, focus on identifying the most important things they say and do.

Our second scene is from Marsha Norman's 1983 two-character play *'night, Mother*. (The complete play is presented in Chapter 16, Confronting Mortality, where the scene appears on pp. 1508–10.) This drama as a whole is distinctive in two respects. One has to do with form: basically, the play takes ninety minutes to perform, and what goes on *within* the play is a ninety-minute conversation at night between Thelma Cates and her adult daughter, Jessie. Indeed, in most evening performances of the play, the time shown by clocks on the set is the same as the audience's own. Just as striking is the play's subject matter. Soon after their conversation begins, Jessie tells her mother that she intends to shoot herself at the end of the night. Jessie mentions several motives for committing suicide, including her epilepsy, the break-up of her marriage, the delinquency of her son, and her general despair. For much of the play, though, she bustles around, attempting to put her mother's house physically in order before she dies. Meanwhile, Thelma tries to talk her daughter out of ending her life. In the following excerpt, the two women discuss Jessie's inability to keep a job, though ironically Jessie is doing household work for her mother on this fateful night.

MARSHA NORMAN
From 'night, Mother

JESSIE (*going back into the kitchen*):   I called this morning and canceled the papers, except for Sunday, for your puzzles; you'll still get that one.

MAMA: Let's get another dog, Jessie! You liked a big dog, now, didn't you? That King dog, didn't you?

JESSIE (*washing her hands*):   I did like that King dog, yes.

MAMA: I'm so dumb. He's the one run under the tractor.

JESSIE: That makes him dumb, not you.

MAMA: For bringing it up.

JESSIE: It's O.K. Handi-Wipes and sponges under the sink.

MAMA: We could get a new dog and keep him in the house. Dogs are cheap!

JESSIE (*getting big pill jars out of the cabinet*):   No.

MAMA: Something for you to take care of.

JESSIE: I've had you, Mama.

MAMA *(frantically starting to fill pill bottles)*:   You do too much for me. I can fill pill bottles all day, Jessie, and change the shelf paper and wash the floor when I get through. You just watch me. You don't have to do another thing in this house if you don't want to. You don't have to take care of me, Jessie.

JESSIE: I know that. You've just been letting me do it so I'll have something to do, haven't you?

MAMA *(realizing this was a mistake)*:   I don't do it as well as you. I just meant if it tires you out or makes you feel used . . .

JESSIE: Mama, I know you used to ride the bus. Riding the bus and it's hot and bumpy and crowded and too noisy and more than anything in the world you want to get off and the only reason in the world you don't get off is it's still fifty blocks from where you're going? Well, I can get off right now if I want to, because even if I ride fifty more years and get off then, it's the same place when I step down to it. Whenever I feel like it, I can get off. As soon as I've had enough, it's my stop. I've had enough.

MAMA: You're feeling sorry for yourself!

JESSIE: The plumber's helper is under the sink, too.

MAMA: You're not having a good time! Whoever promised you a good time? Do you think I've had a good time?

JESSIE: I think you're pretty happy, yeah. You have things you like to do.

MAMA: Like what?

JESSIE: Like crochet.

MAMA: I'll teach you to crochet.

JESSIE: I can't do any of that nice work, Mama.

MAMA: Good time don't come looking for you, Jessie. You could work some puzzles or put in a garden or go to the store. Let's call a taxi and go to the A&P!

JESSIE: I shopped you up for about two weeks already. You're not going to need toilet paper till Thanksgiving.

MAMA *(interrupting)*:   You're acting like some little brat, Jessie. You're mad and everybody's boring and you don't have anything to do and you don't like me and you don't like going out and you don't like staying in and you never talk on the phone and you don't watch TV and you're miserable and it's your own sweet fault.

JESSIE: And it's time I did something about it.

MAMA: Not something like killing yourself. Something like . . . buying us all new dishes! I'd like that. Or maybe the doctor would let you get a driver's license now, or I know what let's do right this minute, let's rearrange the furniture.

JESSIE: I'll do that. If you want. I always thought if the TV was somewhere else, you wouldn't get such a glare on it during the day. I'll do whatever you want before I go.

MAMA *(badly frightened by those words)*:   You could get a job!

JESSIE: I took that telephone sales job and I didn't even make enough money to pay the phone bill, and I tried to work at the gift shop at the hospital and they said I made people real uncomfortable smiling at them the way I did.

MAMA: You could keep books. You kept your dad's books.

JESSIE: But nobody ever checked them.

MAMA: When he died, they checked them.

JESSIE: And that's when they took the books away from me.

MAMA: That's because without him there wasn't any business, Jessie!

JESSIE *(putting the pill bottles away)*:   You know I couldn't work. I can't do anything. I've never been around people my whole life except when I went to the hospital. I could have a seizure any time. What good would a job do? The kind of job I could get would make me feel worse.

MAMA: Jessie!

JESSIE: It's true!

MAMA: It's what you think is true!

JESSIE *(struck by the clarity of that)*:   That's right. It's what I think is true.

MAMA *(hysterically)*:   But I can't do anything about that!

JESSIE *(quietly)*:   No. You can't. *(Mama slumps, if not physically, at least emotionally.)* And I can't do anything either, about my life, to change it, make it better, make me feel better about it. Like it better, make it work. But I can stop it. Shut it down, turn it off like the radio when there's nothing on I want to listen to. It's all I really have that belongs to me and I'm going to say what happens to it. And it's going to stop. And I'm going to stop it. So. Let's just have a good time.

MAMA: Have a good time.

JESSIE: We can't go on fussing all night. I mean, I could ask you things I always wanted to know and you could make me some hot chocolate. The old way.

MAMA *(in despair)*:   It takes cocoa, Jessie.

JESSIE *(gets it out of the cabinet)*:   I bought cocoa, Mama. And I'd like to have a caramel apple and do your nails.

MAMA: You didn't eat a bite of supper.

JESSIE: Does that mean I can't have a caramel apple?

MAMA: Of course not. I mean . . . *(Smiling a little.)* Of course you can have a caramel apple.

JESSIE: I thought I could.

MAMA: I make the best caramel apples in the world.

JESSIE: I know you do.

MAMA: Or used to. And you don't get cocoa like mine anywhere anymore.

JESSIE: It takes time, I know, but . . .

MAMA: The salt is the trick.

JESSIE: Trouble and everything.

MAMA *(backing away toward the stove)*:   It's no trouble. What trouble? You put it in the pan and stir it up. All right. Fine. Caramel apples. Cocoa. O.K.

Jessie walks to the counter to retrieve her cigarettes as Mama looks for the right pan. There are brief near-smiles, and maybe Mama clears her throat. We have a truce, for the moment. A genuine but nevertheless uneasy one. Jessie, who has been in constant motion since the beginning, now seems content to sit.

Mama starts looking for a pan to make the cocoa, getting out all the pans in the cabinets in the process. It looks like she's making a mess on purpose so Jessie will have to put them all away again. Mama is buying time, or trying to, and entertaining.

[1983]

A WRITING EXERCISE

In three to five sentences, write a summary of the scene from *'night, Mother* that you have just read. Do not attempt to *evaluate* the two characters' behavior. Rather, focus on identifying the most important things they say and do.

The Elements of Drama

You will strengthen your ability to write about plays like Williams's and Norman's if you grow familiar with typical elements of drama. These elements include plot and structure, characters, stage directions and setting, imagery, language, and theme.

Plot and Structure

After each of the scenes you have read, we have asked you to write a summary because doing so moves you into considerations of **plot**. Most plays, like most short stories, do have a plot. When you read them, you find yourself following a **narrative**, a sequence of interrelated events. As with short fiction, the reader of a play is often anxious to know how events will turn out. Will *The Glass Menagerie*'s Laura Wingfield find a rewarding relationship, especially now that she seems too scared to pursue a business career? Will *'night, Mother*'s Jessie actually kill herself? In fact, there are various ways you can describe the plot; just bear in mind that your account should be grounded in actual details of the text. Perhaps you will want to emphasize characters' emotional conflicts, for often a play's plot involves psychological tension as well as physical acts. In any case, if you focus on character at all, your summary of the play's **structure** will reflect your understanding of which people are central to it. As you may have guessed, we think the characters in our excerpts are major figures throughout their respective plays. Sometimes, though, a character's status is less immediately clear.

Summarizing the plot of a play can mean arranging its events chronologically. Yet bear in mind that some of the play's important events may have occurred in the characters' distant or immediate past. In the scene from *The Glass Menagerie*, for example, Amanda tells a long anecdote about her visit to the business school, where a teacher told her that Laura was no longer attending. Actually, many plays feature acts of recollection and revelation that lead characters to come to a new understanding of their history. When Jessie recalls her history of failed jobs, in the scene from *'night, Mother*, she draws a conclusion that perhaps she reached only recently: "I can't do anything." You may, like Thelma, disagree with this judgment, but significantly it gives Jessie an incentive to end her life.

A WRITING EXERCISE

Reread at least one of the scenes we have presented, noting moments when the characters are engaged basically in remembrance. Then write a paragraph in which you make and support a claim about the extent to which the scene is concerned with the past rather than with the present or future.

In discussing the structure of short stories, we said that many of them follow Alice Adams's formula ABDCE (**action**, **background**, **development**, **climax**, and **ending**). This scheme, however, does not fit many plays. In one sense, the average play is entirely action, for its performers constantly make physical movements of various sorts. Furthermore, as we have been suggesting, information about background can surface often as characters talk. Yet the terms *development*, *climax*, and *ending* do seem appropriate for many plays.

Certainly, each of the two scenes we have excerpted develop the play as a whole. The mother-daughter conversation from *The Glass Menagerie* reveals that Amanda is a Southern "lady" in two crucial respects: the scene begins with Amanda's social embarrassment upon finding Laura a truant and ends with Amanda calling for Laura to rely on "charm." When the mother-daughter conversation from *'night, Mother* concludes with a truce, this moment of peace is temporary, for Jessie has declared that suicide is her only remaining means of power: though her life has been miserable, at least now she can "Shut it down, turn it off." In other words, both scenes bring up important matters but leave them for the rest of the play to resolve.

We will not reveal how the terms *climax* and *ending* fit the two dramas' overall plots, for you might prefer to discover on your own how both plays turn out. But in the case of *'night, Mother,* at any rate, probably you can imagine that the climax is Thelma's final attempt to prevent her daughter's suicide. After all, their debate about this move has been the play's central conflict. Similarly, the play is bound to end with the success or failure of Thelma's effort, though the specific details of the final moment deserve close analysis. Always consider what, exactly, characters are doing when the curtain falls.

Like short stories, plays often use repetition as an organizational device. Characters may repeat certain words; for example, notice how Amanda ends the *Glass Menagerie* scene by using the word *charm* three times. Also, a play may show repeated actions, as *'night, Mother* does when it shows Jessie performing numerous household chores. In addition, a play may suggest that the onstage situation echoes previous events. On many an occasion, Amanda probably has pushed Laura to take charge of her own life. No doubt Jessie and Thelma have quarreled about subjects other than suicide.

Through the centuries, plays have been subdivided in all sorts of ways. Sophocles' ancient Greek dramas *Oedipus the King* and *Antigone*, which appear in Chapter 12, Living in Families, alternate choral sections with scenes that involve only two characters. All of Shakespeare's plays (such as *Hamlet* in Chapter 15, Doing Justice), and most modern ones, are divided into acts, which are often further divided into scenes. For example, *Raisin in the Sun* (in Chapter 11, Working with Cultural Contexts) has three acts, which vary in their number of scenes: Act One includes two, Act Two has three, and Act Three is one scene only. But not all modern plays feature multiple acts. *'night, Mother* is just a single act long, and *The Glass Menagerie* consists of seven scenes. Of course, you may see a play as having other divisions than its official ones. In fact, a good exercise is to break a play down into segments that more precisely reflect the development of the plot.

Characters

As with short stories, a good step toward analyzing a play's characters is to consider what each desires. The drama or comedy of many plays arises when the desires of one character conflict with those of another. A strong example can be found in the scene from *'night, Mother*, where Jessie seeks to end her life and Thelma tries to preserve it. Also important to analyze, of course, is whether and how characters eventually alter their desires, perhaps coming to share the values of people whom they have opposed.

A WRITING EXERCISE

Choose one of the scenes we have excerpted and write a brief, informal essay in which you examine the scene for signs that either or both of the characters will eventually change.

The main character of a play is referred to as its **protagonist**, and a character who notably opposes this person is referred to as the **antagonist**. As you might guess even without reading Shakespeare's play, Hamlet is the protagonist of *Hamlet*, while his uncle Claudius serves as his antagonist. Applying these terms may be tricky or impossible in some instances. In *The Glass Menagerie*, Amanda's son Tom repeatedly argues with her and ultimately leaves her, but either of these characters might be called the protagonist. A similar difficulty arises with the characters who argue in the scene from *'night, Mother*. Of course, a play may be interesting precisely because it makes the terms *protagonist* and *antagonist* hard to apply.

In discussing the elements of short fiction, we referred to point of view, the perspective from which a story is told. But very few plays are narrated. One of the rare cases is *The Glass Menagerie*, which is framed through monologues by Amanda's son Tom. In general, the play supposedly presents his memories. Even in this instance, however, at plenty of moments the narrator is *not* observing or interpreting the action. Similarly, while it is possible to claim that much of Shakespeare's *Hamlet* reflects the title character's point of view, he is offstage for stretches, and the audience may focus on other characters even when he appears. In general, therefore, the term *point of view* fits plays less well than it does short fiction. In fact, worth thinking about is the possible significance of characters who are not physically present. A character may be important even if he or she never appears onstage. Such is the case with Amanda Wingfield's husband, who is available to her now only in a photograph. Such, too, is the case with numerous people whom Jessie and Thelma refer to in *'night, Mother*, including Jessie's father, former husband, brother, and son.

In most plays, characters' lives are influenced by their social standing, which in turn is influenced by particular traits of theirs. These may include their gender, social class, race, ethnic background, nationality, and sexual orientation and the kind of work they do. For instance, *The Glass Menagerie*'s Amanda Wingfield is still affected by her upbringing as a Southern lady, though now she must struggle to survive financially in St. Louis, a modern city in a border state.

A WRITING EXERCISE

In almost all productions of *The Glass Menagerie* and *'night, Mother*, the characters have been played by white performers. Choose either the *Glass Menagerie* scene we have excerpted or the *'night, Mother* scene. Do you think there would be significantly different effects and implications if the actors in the scene were of another race? Address this issue in a brief, informal essay.

Stage Directions and Setting

When analyzing a script, pay attention to the stage directions it gives. Through a slight physical movement, performers can indicate important developments in their characters' thoughts. Look, for example, at the conclusion of our scene from *'night, Mother*. Through stage directions, playwright Marsha Norman suggests how the mother and daughter may be seen as momentarily resting before resuming their conflict. Always, you can imagine additional ways that a play's performers might move around. What else, for instance, might you have the actors in Norman's play do at this point?

You can learn much about a play's characters by studying how they accommodate themselves—or fail to accommodate themselves—to the places in which you find them. Notice what Thelma does at the end of the scene we have excerpted from *'night, Mother*: "*Mama starts looking for a pan to make the cocoa, getting out all the pans in the cabinets in the process. It looks like she's making a mess on purpose so Jessie will have to put them all away again.*" Is Thelma controlling the kitchen space in an effort to control Jessie—creating chaos so that her daughter will be distracted from thoughts of suicide?

To understand better how a play might be staged, you can research its actual production history. Granted, finding out about its previous stagings may be difficult. But at the very least, you can discover some of the theatrical conventions that must have shaped presentations of the play, even one that is centuries old. Take the case of Sophocles' *Oedipus Rex* and *Antigone*, both of which appear in Chapter 12, "Living in Families." While classical scholars would like to learn more about early performances of these dramas, they already know that ancient Greek plays were staged in open-air arenas. They know, too, that Sophocles' chorus turned in unison at particular moments and that the whole cast wore large masks.

Most of the modern plays we include in this book were first staged in a style most often called **realism**. Not every modern play fits this description, though. Introducing his script for *The Glass Menagerie*, Tennessee Williams calls for a different rendition of the Wingfield apartment: "The scene is memory and therefore nonrealistic. Memory takes a lot of poetic license. It omits some details; others are exaggerated, according to the emotional values of the articles it touches, for memory is seated predominantly in the heart. The interior is therefore rather dim and poetic." As you can tell from the particular scene we have excerpted, the nonrealistic atmosphere that Williams urges is reinforced by the highly theatrical use of slides. Realism, by contrast, is typified by the set for *'night, Mother* as author Marsha Norman envisions it. The Cates house, Norman writes, should be depicted as the home "of very specific real people who happen to live in a particular part of the country" (presumably an area of the South). To achieve this realistic impression, Norman calls for a set with various lifelike features. For example, "The living room is cluttered with magazines and needlework catalogues, ashtrays and candy dishes."

When a production is quite true-to-life, audiences may think it has no style at all. Nevertheless, even realism uses identifiable conventions. A common one is what theater professionals refer to as the *illusion of the fourth wall*, which is essentially what Norman recommends for *'night, Mother*. She suggests that the actors pretend the "house" is fully enclosed, whereas the set has just three walls, and the audience looks in.

Some plays can be staged in any number of styles and still work well. Shakespeare wrote *Hamlet* (in Chapter 15, Doing Justice) back in Renaissance England, but quite a few successful productions of it have been set in later times, such as late nineteenth-century England. Indeed, very few modern productions of *Hamlet* follow the Renaissance tradition of an all-male cast. Since the first production of *The Glass Menagerie*, the play has been successfully mounted with various degrees of realism. Some versions strictly follow Williams's guidelines, striving to be "nonrealistic" and "poetic," whereas others make the Wingfield apartment as lifelike as Thelma Cates's house. You may feel that any divergence from a playwright's directives is wrong; nevertheless, remember that productions of a play may be more diverse in style than the script indicates.

A WRITING EXERCISE

A particular theater's architecture may affect a production team's decisions. Realism's illusion of the fourth wall works best on a **proscenium stage**, which is the kind probably most familiar to you. A proscenium stage is a boxlike space where the actors perform in front of the entire audience. In a proscenium production of *'night, Mother*, the Cates home can be depicted in great detail. The performing spaces at some theaters, however, are "in the round"—that is, the audience completely encircles the stage. What would have to be done with the *'night, Mother* setting then? List some items in it that an in-the-round staging could accommodate. Or, if you prefer, do this listing for *The Glass Menagerie*.

Imagery

When plays use images to convey meaning, sometimes they do so through a title. A clear example is *The Glass Menagerie*, where the title refers to Laura's collection of figurines but also signifies the fragility of her family's life and dreams.

As you have seen, this image also comes up in the play's conversations; often, dialogue enables symbols to emerge and develop. Just as often, a play's meaningful images are physically presented in the staging—through gestures, costumes, lighting, and props. When Amanda Wingfield enters wearing "one of those cheap or imitation velvety-looking cloth coats with imitation fur collar," her clothes imply a futile effort to conceal her dire financial condition. When she proceeds to shred her daughter's typewriting charts, she dramatically acknowledges that her plan for Laura's schooling has been destroyed.

You may interpret an image differently than characters within the play do. Take the gesture that Jessie Cates makes as she tells her mother, "You know I couldn't work." At this moment, Jessie is putting pill bottles away, an action that mirrors her insistence that nothing will remedy her miserable life. Although Jessie herself probably does not make this connection, you may very well do so.

A WRITING EXERCISE

Imagine that you have been asked to stage the scene from *The Glass Menagerie* or the one from *'night, Mother*. List gestures not mentioned in the script that you would have the actors perform. Then compare lists with a classmate working with the same scene.

Language

You can learn much about a play's meaning and impact from studying the **language** in its script. Try starting with the play's title. As we have already discussed, the title of *The Glass Menagerie* seems symbolically important, but even the apparently ordinary title of *'night, Mother* carries weight. Although Jessie has commonly said these two words at the end of an evening, on this occasion they have chilling significance, since she intends to leave her mother for eternal rest.

In most plays, language is a matter of dialogue. The audience tries to figure out the play by focusing on how the characters address one another. A revealing use of language occurs, for example, near the end of our scene from *The Glass Menagerie*. Resisting Amanda's dream of marrying her off, Laura points out that "I'm—crippled!" But Amanda continues to show optimism, by objecting to Laura's self-description: "Nonsense! Laura, I've told you never, never to use that word. Why, you're not crippled, you just have a little defect—hardly noticeable, even!" To be sure, Amanda is not always so optimistic; earlier in the scene, she is frustrated by Laura's failure to attend business school. Her dismissal of Laura's term "crippled," however, reveals how capable she is of wishful thinking, too. Meanwhile, Laura's instant labeling of herself emphasizes her tendency to recoil from life.

A character's style of speaking can be revealing as well, often indicating something about the character's social background. Actresses playing Amanda Wingfield usually adopt a Southern accent to emphasize how much her upbringing in that region has influenced her. It is also plausible for Thelma and Jessie in *'night, Mother* to speak with Southern inflections. Significantly, though, Marsha

Norman's introduction to the script explicitly warns against making their accents "heavy," which Norman fears "would further distance the audience from [them]."

Remember that the pauses or silences within a play may be just as important as its dialogue. Notice that at the beginning of the scene from *The Glass Menagerie,* Amanda hesitates before she enters the apartment and speaks to Laura; evidently, she is pained at the prospect of confronting her daughter about Laura's absence from school. Actually, directors of plays often add moments of silence that the script does not explicitly demand, giving the performers another means of expressing their characters' feelings.

Theme

We have already discussed **theme** on pages 25 to 27, and here we build on some points from our earlier discussion. A theme is the main claim—an assertion, proposition, or statement—that a literary work seems to make. As with other literary genres, try to state a play's theme as a midlevel generalization. If expressed in very broad terms, it will seem to fit many other works besides the one you have read. If narrowly tied to the play's characters and their particular situation, it will seem irrelevant to most other people's lives. With *'night, Mother,* an example of a very broad theme would be "Mothers should try to understand their daughters better." At the opposite extreme, a too-narrow theme would be "Southern women who fail at their jobs and relationships might resolve to commit suicide, especially if they are also epileptic." If, after reading Marsha Norman's entire play, you want to identify a theme of it, you might start with the broad generalization we have cited and then try to narrow it down to a midlevel one. You might even think of ways that Norman's play *complicates* that broad generalization.

You can state a play's theme as an **observation** or as a **recommendation**. With Norman's play, an observation-type theme would be "Despair might drive someone to see suicide as a rational choice." A recommendation-type theme would be "People who want to commit suicide should be allowed to do so if their life will otherwise probably be bleak." Neither way of stating the theme is automatically preferable, but remain aware of the different tones and effects they may carry. Consider, too, the possibility of stating the theme as a problem, in this example: "People may seem to have strong justification for killing themselves, but their loved ones will understandably have difficulty letting them commit suicide." Furthermore, consider referring to *a* theme of the play rather than *the* theme, thereby acknowledging the possibility that the play is making several important claims.

When you write about a play, certainly you will refer to the text of it, its **script**. But probably the play was meant to be staged, and most likely it has been. Thus, you might refer to actual productions of it and to ways it can be performed. Remember, though, that different productions of the play may stress different meanings and create different effects. In your paper, you might discuss how much room for interpretation the script allows those who would stage it. For any paper you write about the play, look beyond the characters' dialogue and study whatever stage directions the script gives.

Undoubtedly, your paper will have to offer some plot summary, even if your audience has already read the play. After all, certain details of the plot will be important support for your points. But as with papers about short fiction, keep the amount of plot summary small, mentioning only events in the play that are crucial to your overall argument. Your reader should feel that you are analyzing the play rather than just recounting it.

To show you better what analysis of a play involves, we present the final draft of a paper by student Chuck Thornburgh. Required to write about a particular scene in a play read by his class, he chose the scene from *The Glass Menagerie* that we have been examining. Chuck realized that although he would be dealing with just one scene, he would have to be even more selective—identifying a particular issue, developing a particular claim, and referring to particular elements of the scene. He decided pretty quickly that he would analyze how the scene illuminated aspects of Amanda and Laura's relationship. After all, they are the only characters in the scene, and they reveal some of their key beliefs and feelings as they discuss Laura's future. On reading this scene several times, Chuck became aware that at the end of it the two Wingfield women seem to switch positions. Whereas at the start Amanda was basically urging Laura to be more realistic, the scene concludes with Amanda dreaming of Laura's marriage, apparently more gripped by blind faith than Laura is. Chuck saw that he could address an issue of pattern by identifying and explaining the significance of the characters' shift in roles. The more he studied the ending, however, the more he realized that even here, Amanda shows a bit of realism, while Laura is still inclined to hold the world at bay. And earlier in the scene, Amanda's realism is mixed with a fondness of her own for pretense, while Laura can be viewed as having a pragmatic streak. In his paper, Chuck did proceed to claim that the ending suggested a shift of roles but also that the shift was not necessarily complete; rather, it indicated that each woman is capable of confronting reality, evading it, or simultaneously doing both. In other words, Chuck was determined not to simplify Amanda and Laura's conversation. His main claim became a complex observation, taking into account various nuances of the scene. As you will see, his paper shows this commitment to detail by quoting a lot from dialogue and stage directions, while allowing Chuck's own argument to emerge clearly.

Sample Student Paper: Final Draft

Here is Chuck's final draft. It emerged after several drafts and after he had consulted classmates as well as his instructor. As you read this version of his paper, note its strengths, but also think of any suggestions that might help him make the paper even better.

Chuck Thornburgh

Professor Mancuso

English 102

14 April —

Like Mother, Like Daughter:

Amanda's and Laura's Attitudes

toward Reality in Scene 2

of <u>The Glass Menagerie</u>

In the second scene of Tennessee Williams's play <u>The
Glass Menagerie</u>, Amanda Wingfield's first word is "Deception." For her, this word fits the behavior of her daughter Laura, who has been pretending to attend business
school. Actually, Amanda does not straightforwardly
accuse Laura of deception. Rather, she turns the word
into a question: "Deception? Deception?" Clearly, though,
she thinks the word applies, and her repetition of it
gives it emphasis. In fact, later in the scene, she
utters the word again. After Laura reveals what she has
actually been doing while supposedly going to school,
Amanda's response is, "You did all this to deceive me,
just for the deception?" Therefore, the scene could be
viewed in general as Amanda's effort to make Laura
acknowledge reality.

Nevertheless, this summary would be misleading. It
does not convey Amanda's own love of dreamy pretense and
Laura's own capacity to recognize truth. As they talk,
the two women even seem to switch attitudes. Indeed,
their conversation ends with Laura admitting her disability while Amanda expresses faith in the powers of
"charm." This pattern of reversal suggests that, to a
significant extent, mother and daughter are ultimately
alike. Each of them blends awareness of reality with
fondness for illusion.

For the first two-thirds of the scene, Amanda seems
devoted to reality while Laura apparently wants to avoid
it. Basically, Amanda expresses to Laura her dismay at
learning that Laura had stopped attending school. Amanda

is concerned not only that Laura has lied to her but that by dropping out of school Laura has abandoned a means of survival: "So what are we going to do the rest of our lives? Stay home and watch the parades go by? Amuse ourselves with the glass menagerie, darling? Eternally play those worn-out phonograph records your father left as a painful reminder of him?" Quite reasonably, Amanda believes these are not strategies for living. More specifically, she worries about Laura's falling into "dependency," a common plight for "unmarried women who aren't prepared to occupy a position." When Amanda tears Laura's typing charts, she dramatically declares that she wants illusion to cease.

By contrast, Laura resorts to evasion. As the scene begins, she _is_ preoccupied with her collection of glass animals. In "washing and polishing" it, she seems to be nurturing her own dreams of escape. Moreover, just as significant as her "deception" is her reason for it: Amanda's disappointment is something she "couldn't face." Laura's desire to avoid reality surfaces even during this conversation with her mother. As Amanda confronts her about her hoax, Laura tries to play her father's records, thereby escaping the pressures of the real world.

As the scene proceeds, however, Amanda comes to seem dreamier than Laura. Although Laura recalls enthusiastically her high school friendship with Jim, she acknowledges that he is probably married by now. Laura can also be seen as valuing commitment to reality when she criticizes Jim's girlfriend Emily for not "being sincere." By contrast, Amanda shows wishful thinking. After concluding that, "Girls that aren't cut out for business careers usually wind up being married to some nice man," she abruptly announces "Sister, that's what you'll do!" Here, Amanda seems to confuse ambition with reality, taking Laura's marriage as a done deal. When Laura acknowledges that she is "crippled," Amanda is blindly optimistic: "Nonsense! Laura, I've told you never, never to use that

word. Why, you're not crippled, you just have a little
defect--hardly noticeable, even!" Although it can be
argued that Laura should not let her disability control
her life, Amanda seems utterly oblivious to it. Next,
Amanda seems willfully simplistic when she tells Laura
that "all you have to do" is develop "charm." Finally,
although Amanda has suffered from her husband's escape
and mocked Laura's attachment to her father's records,
Amanda now turns to the man's photograph and expresses
admiration for his "charm." Thus, the scene ends with
mother and daughter apparently switching the roles they
occupied at the start.

   Still, we should not conclude that Amanda is essentially a dreamer and Laura a realist. The apparent reversal at the end of the scene should, rather, prompt us to
realize the similarity of these two women. At any given
moment, each is capable of being realistic, evasive, or
some combination of the two. The reversal is not necessarily total. Although the scene ends with Amanda cheerily proclaiming that "One thing your father had plenty
of--was charm!," her use of the word "one" may be an
acknowledgment that he lacked many other things his family needed. Meanwhile, Laura's reasonable skepticism
toward Amanda's talk of marriage is accompanied by a gesture indicating Laura's own lingering fondness for illusion. She "reaches quickly for a piece of glass," part of
the collection that is her substitute for the real world.
Moreover, subtle signs of each character's psychological
complexity appear early in the scene. For example, even
as Amanda enters the apartment determined to expose the
truth, she is wearing "one of those cheap or imitation
velvety-looking cloth coats with imitation fur collar."
As she recounts her visit to the school, she makes the
phrase "all of our plans" equivalent to "my hopes and
ambitions for you," not admitting the difference between
"our" and "my." Meanwhile, Laura can be seen as realistic

about her prospects for business school, and her deception did require thought.

Of course, Scene 2 is only one scene in The Glass Menagerie, and an early one at that. Relationships among the characters remain to be developed, including the two women's relationship with son and brother Tom. But with this scene, Tennessee Williams establishes that Amanda and Laura waver in their commitment to reality. Sometimes they recognize it, sometimes they flee it, and sometimes they mix realism with fantasy. Williams calls our attention to these multiple tendencies in each woman by structuring the scene so that it ends with them apparently exchanging the roles they took at the outset. This conclusion to the scene implies, however, that their attitudes may shift yet again, as the play continues.

7

Writing about Essays

Many readers do not think of nonfiction as a literary genre. They believe dealing with information and facts, science and technology, history and biography, memories and arguments is too ordinary, too far from traditional literary works such as sonnets, short stories, and plays. But what counts as literature is often more a matter of tradition and perspective than content, language, or merit. Many contemporary critics have noticed that definitions of literature are quite subjective, even arbitrary. We are told that literature must move us emotionally; it must contain imaginative, extraordinary language; it must deal with profound, timeless, and universal themes. If all of these claims are true of poems, stories, and plays, they might also be true of essays, autobiographies, memoirs, and historical writing.

Essays demand as much of a reader's attention as fiction, drama, and poetry. They also demand a reader's active participation. And, as with more conventional literature, the intellectual, emotional, and aesthetic rewards of attentively reading essays are significant.

Writing about essays in college is best done as a process, one that begins with a first response and ends with editing and proofreading. Author Henry David Thoreau once noted that books should be read with the same care and deliberation with which they were written. This is as true for essays as it is for complex modern poetry. One's understanding is enhanced by careful reading and a composing process that calls for a cycle of reading, writing, and reflecting. Few people, even professionals, can read a text and write cogently about it the first time. Writing well about essays takes as much energy and discipline as writing about other genres. And the results are always worth it.

The two essays here deal with women and work—more specifically, with the struggles of gifted African American women in a context of poverty and oppression. Both essays were originally speeches. "Many Rivers to Cross" by June Jordan (b. 1936) was the keynote address at a 1981 conference on "Women and Work" held at Barnard College in New York City. In the speech, Jordan recalls the suicide of her mother fifteen years earlier. Alice Walker's was given at a May 1973 conference on "The Black Woman: Myths and Realities" held at Radcliffe College in large part as a response to the 1965 Moynihan report that argued that women-headed families were a major cause of poverty among African Americans. Walker (b. 1944) made additions when it appeared in the May 1974 issue of *Ms* and then in the essay collection *In Search of Our Mothers' Gardens: Womanist Prose* (1983).

JUNE JORDAN
Many Rivers to Cross

When my mother killed herself I was looking for a job. That was fifteen years ago. I had no money and no food. On the pleasure side I was down to my last pack of Pall Malls plus half a bottle of J & B. I needed to find work because I needed to be able fully to support myself and my eight-year-old son, very fast. My plan was to raise enough big bucks so that I could take an okay apartment inside an acceptable public school district, by September. That deadline left me less than three months to turn my fortunes right side up.

It seemed that I had everything to do at once. Somehow, I must move all of our things, mostly books and toys, out of the housing project before the rent fell due, again. I must do this without letting my neighbors know because destitution and divorce added up to personal shame, and failure. Those same neighbors had looked upon my husband and me as an ideal young couple, in many ways: inseparable, doting, ambitious. They had kept me busy and laughing in the hard weeks following my husband's departure for graduate school in Chicago; they had been the ones to remember him warmly through teasing remarks and questions all that long year that I remained alone, waiting for his return while I became the "temporary," sole breadwinner of our peculiar long-distance family by telephone. They had been the ones who kindly stopped the teasing and the queries when the year ended and my husband, the father of my child, did not come back. They never asked me and I never told them what that meant, altogether. I don't think I really knew.

I could see how my husband would proceed more or less naturally from graduate school to a professional occupation of his choice, just as he had shifted rather easily from me, his wife, to another man's wife — another woman. What I could not see was how I should go forward, now, in any natural, coherent way. As a mother without a husband, as a poet without a publisher, a freelance journalist without assignment, a city planner without a contract, it seemed to me that several incontestable and conflicting necessities had suddenly eliminated the whole realm of choice from my life.

My husband and I agreed that he would have the divorce that he wanted, and I would have the child. This ordinary settlement is, as millions of women will testify, as absurd as saying, "I'll give you a call, you handle everything else." At any rate, as my lawyer explained, the law then was the same as the law today; the courts would surely award me a reasonable amount of the father's income as child support, but the courts would also insist that they could not enforce their own decree. In other words, according to the law, what a father owes to his child is not serious compared to what a man owes to the bank for a car, or a vacation. Hence, as they say, it is extremely regrettable but nonetheless true that the courts cannot garnish a father's salary, nor freeze his account, nor seize his property on behalf of his children, in our society. Apparently this is because a child is not a car or a couch or a boat. (I would suppose this is the very best available definition of the difference between an American child and a car.)

Anyway, I wanted to get out of the projects as quickly as possible. But I was going to need help because I couldn't bend down and I couldn't carry anything heavy and I couldn't let my parents know about these problems because I didn't want to fight with them about the reasons behind the problems—which was the same reason I couldn't walk around or sit up straight to read or write without vomiting and acute abdominal pain. My parents would have evaluated that reason as a terrible secret compounded by a terrible crime; once again an unmarried woman, I had, nevertheless, become pregnant. What's more I had tried to interrupt this pregnancy even though this particular effort required not only one but a total of three abortions—each of them illegal and amazingly expensive, as well as, evidently, somewhat poorly executed. 5

My mother, against my father's furious rejections of me and what he viewed as my failure, offered what she could; she had no money herself but there was space in the old brownstone of my childhood. I would live with them during the summer while I pursued my crash schedule for cash, and she would spend as much time with Christopher, her only and beloved grandchild, as her worsening but partially undiagnosed illness allowed.

After she suffered a stroke, her serenely imposing figure had shrunk into an unevenly balanced, starved shell of chronic disorder. In the last two years, her physical condition had forced her retirement from nursing, and she spent most of her days on a makeshift cot pushed against the wall of the dining room next to the kitchen. She could do very few things for herself, besides snack on crackers, or pour ready-made juice into a cup and then drink it.

In June, 1966, I moved from the projects into my parents' house with the help of a woman named Mrs. Hazel Griffin. Since my teens, she had been my hairdresser. Every day, all day, she stood on her feet, washing and straightening hair in her crowded shop, the Arch of Beauty. Mrs. Griffin had never been married, had never finished high school, and she ran the Arch of Beauty with an imperturbable and contagious sense of success. She had a daughter as old as I who worked alongside her mother, coddling customer fantasy into confidence. Gradually, Mrs. Griffin and I became close; as my own mother became more and more bedridden and demoralized, Mrs. Griffin extended herself—dropping by my parents' house to make dinner for them, or calling me to wish me good luck on a special freelance venture, and so forth. It was Mrs. Griffin who closed her shop for a whole day and drove all the way from Brooklyn to my housing project apartment in Queens. It was Mrs. Griffin who packed me up, so to speak, and carried me and the boxes back to Brooklyn, back to the house of my parents. It was Mrs. Griffin who ignored my father standing hateful at the top of the stone steps of the house and not saying a word of thanks and not once relieving her of a single load she wrestled up the stairs and past him. My father hated Mrs. Griffin because he was proud and because she was a stranger of mercy. My father hated Mrs. Griffin because he was like that sometimes: hateful and crazy.

My father alternated between weeping bouts of self-pity and storm explosions of wrath against the gods apparently determined to ruin him. These were his alternating reactions to my mother's increasing enfeeblement, her stoic depression. I think he was scared; who would take care of him? Would she get well again and make everything all right again?

This is how we organized the brownstone; I fixed a room for my son on the   10
top floor of the house. I slept on the parlor floor in the front room. My father slept on the same floor, in the back. My mother stayed downstairs.

About a week after moving in, my mother asked me about the progress of my plans. I told her things were not terrific but that there were two different planning jobs I hoped to secure within a few days. One of them involved a study of new towns in Sweden and the other one involved an analysis of the social consequences of a huge hydro-electric dam under construction in Ghana. My mother stared at me uncomprehendingly and then urged me to look for work in the local post office. We bitterly argued about what she dismissed as my "high-falutin" ideas and, I believe, that was the last substantial conversation between us.

From my first memory of him, my father had always worked at the post office. His favorite was the night shift, which brought him home usually between three and four o'clock in the morning.

It was hot. I finally fell asleep that night, a few nights after the argument between my mother and myself. She seemed to be rallying; that afternoon, she and my son had spent a long time in the backyard, oblivious to the heat and the mosquitoes. They were both tired but peaceful when they noisily re-entered the house, holding hands awkwardly.

But someone was knocking at the door to my room. Why should I wake up? It would be impossible to fall asleep again. It was so hot. The knocking continued. I switched on the light by the bed: 3:30 A.M. It must be my father. Furious, I pulled on a pair of shorts and a t-shirt. "What do you want? What's the matter?" I asked him, through the door. Had he gone berserk? What could he have to talk about at that ridiculous hour?

"OK, all right," I said, rubbing my eyes awake as I stepped to the door and   15
opened it. "What?"

To my surprise, my father stood there looking very uncertain.

"It's your mother," he told me, in a burly, formal voice. "I think she's dead, but I'm not sure." He was avoiding my eyes.

"What do you mean," I answered.

"I want you to go downstairs and figure it out."

I could not believe what he was saying to me. "You want me to figure out if   20
my mother is dead or alive?"

"I can't tell! I don't know!!" he shouted angrily.

"Jesus Christ," I muttered, angry and beside myself.

I turned and glanced about my room, wondering if I could find anything to carry with me on this mission; what do you use to determine a life or a death? I couldn't see anything obvious that might be useful.

"I'll wait up here," my father said. "You call up and let me know."

I could not believe it; a man married to a woman more than forty years and he can't tell if she's alive or dead and he wakes up his kid and tells her, "You figure it out." 25

I was at the bottom of the stairs. I halted just outside the dining room where my mother slept. Suppose she really was dead? Suppose my father was not just being crazy and hateful? "Naw," I shook my head and confidently entered the room.

"Momma?!" I called, aloud. At the edge of the cot, my mother was leaning forward, one arm braced to hoist her body up. She was trying to stand up! I rushed over. "Wait. Here, I'll help you!" I said.

And I reached out my hands to give her a lift. The body of my mother was stiff. She was not yet cold, but she was stiff. Maybe I had come downstairs just in time! I tried to loosen her arms, to change her position, to ease her into lying down.

"Momma!" I kept saying. "Momma, listen to me! It's OK! I'm here and everything. Just relax. Relax! Give me a hand, now. I'm trying to help you lie down!"

Her body did not relax. She did not answer me. But she was not cold. Her eyes were not shut. 30

From upstairs my father was yelling, "Is she dead? Is she dead?"

"No!" I screamed at him. "No! She's not dead!"

At this, my father tore down the stairs and into the room. Then he braked.

"Milly?" he called out, tentative. Then he shouted at me and banged around the walls. "You damn fool. Don't you see now she's gone. Now she's gone!" We began to argue.

"She's alive! Call the doctor!" 35

"No!"

"Yes!"

At last my father left the room to call the doctor.

I straightened up. I felt completely exhausted from trying to gain a response from my mother. There she was, stiff on the edge of her bed, just about to stand up. Her lips were set, determined. She would manage it, but by herself. I could not help. Her eyes fixed on some point below the floor.

"Momma!" I shook her hard as I could to rouse her into focus. Now she fell back on the cot, but frozen and in the wrong position. It hit me that she might be dead. She might be dead. 40

My father reappeared at the door. He would not come any closer. "Dr. Davis says he will come. And he call the police."

The police? Would they know if my mother was dead or alive? Who would know?

I went to the phone and called my aunt. "Come quick," I said. "My father thinks Momma has died but she's here but she's stiff."

Soon the house was weird and ugly and crowded and I thought I was losing my mind.

Three white policemen stood around telling me my mother was dead. "How   45
do you know?" I asked, and they shrugged and then they repeated themselves.
And the doctor never came. But my aunt came and my uncle and they said she
was dead.

After a conference with the cops, my aunt disappeared and when she came
back she held a bottle in one of her hands. She and the police whispered together
some more. Then one of the cops said, "Don't worry about it. We won't say anything." My aunt signalled me to follow her into the hallway where she let me
understand that, in fact, my mother had committed suicide.

I could not assimilate this information: suicide.

I broke away from my aunt and ran to the telephone. I called a friend of
mine, a woman who talked back loud to me so that I could realize my growing
hysteria, and check it. Then I called my cousin Valerie who lived in Harlem; she
woke up instantly and urged me to come right away.

I hurried to the top floor and stood my sleeping son on his feet. I wanted to
get him out of this house of death more than I ever wanted anything. He could
not stand by himself so I carried him down the two flights to the street and laid
him on the backseat and then took off.

At Valerie's, my son continued to sleep, so we put him to bed, closed the   50
door, and talked. My cousin made me eat eggs, drink whiskey, and shower. She
would take care of Christopher, she said. I should go back and deal with the situation in Brooklyn.

When I arrived, the house was absolutely full of women from the church
dressed as though they were going to Sunday communion. It seemed to me they
were, every one of them, wearing hats and gloves and drinking coffee and
solemnly addressing invitations to a funeral and I could not find my mother anywhere and I could not find an empty spot in the house where I could sit down
and smoke a cigarette.

My mother was dead.

Feeling completely out of place, I headed for the front door, ready to leave.
My father grabbed my shoulder from behind and forcibly spun me around.

"You see this?" he smiled, waving a large document in the air. "This am
insurance paper for you!" He waved it into my face. "Your mother, she left you
insurance, see?"

I watched him.   55

"But I gwine burn it in the furnace before I give it you to t'row away on trash!"

"Is that money?" I demanded. "Did my mother leave me money?"

"Eh-heh!" he laughed. "And you don't get it from me. Not today, not tomorrow. Not until I dead and buried!"

My father grabbed for my arm and I swung away from him. He hit me on my
head and I hit back. We were fighting.

Suddenly, the ladies from the church bustled about and pushed, horrified,   60
between us. This was a sin, they said, for a father and a child to fight in the
house of the dead and the mother not yet in the ground! Such a good woman she
was, they said. She was a good woman, a good woman, they all agreed. Out of
respect for the memory of this good woman, in deference to my mother who had

committed suicide, the ladies shook their hats and insisted we should not fight; I should not fight with my father.

Utterly disgusted and disoriented, I went back to Harlem. By the time I reached my cousin's place I had begun to bleed, heavily. Valerie said I was hemorrhaging so she called up her boyfriend and the two of them hobbled me into Harlem Hospital.

I don't know how long I remained unconscious, but when I opened my eyes I found myself on the women's ward, with an intravenous setup feeding into my arm. After a while, Valerie showed up. Christopher was fine, she told me; my friends were taking turns with him. Whatever I did, I should not admit I'd had an abortion or I'd get her into trouble, and myself in trouble. Just play dumb and rest. I'd have to stay on the ward for several days. My mother's funeral was tomorrow afternoon. What did I want her to tell people to explain why I wouldn't be there? She meant, what lie?

I thought about it and I decided I had nothing to say; if I couldn't tell the truth then the hell with it.

I lay in that bed at Harlem Hospital, thinking and sleeping. I wanted to get well.

I wanted to be strong. I never wanted to be weak again as long as I lived. I   65 thought about my mother and her suicide and I thought about how my father could not tell whether she was dead or alive.

I wanted to get well and what I wanted to do as soon as I was strong again, actually, what I wanted to do was I wanted to live my life so that people would know unmistakably that I am alive, so that when I finally die people will know the difference for sure between my living and my death.

And I thought about the idea of my mother as a good woman and I rejected that, because I don't see why it's a good thing when you give up, or when you cooperate with those who hate you or when you polish and iron and mend and endlessly mollify for the sake of the people who love the way that you kill yourself day by day silently.

And I think all of this is really about women and work. Certainly this is all about me as a woman and my life work. I mean I am not sure my mother's suicide was something extraordinary. Perhaps most women must deal with a similar inheritance, the legacy of a woman whose death you cannot possibly pinpoint because she died so many, many times and because, even before she became your mother, the life of that woman was taken; I say it was taken away.

And really it was to honor my mother that I did fight with my father, that man who could not tell the living from the dead.

And really it is to honor Mrs. Hazel Griffin and my cousin Valerie and all the   70 women I love, including myself, that I am working for the courage to admit the truth that Bertolt Brecht has written; he says, "It takes courage to say that the good were defeated not because they were good, but because they were weak."

I cherish the mercy and the grace of women's work. But I know there is new work that we must undertake as well: that new work will make defeat detestable to us. That new women's work will mean we will not die trying to stand up: we will live that way: standing up.

I came too late to help my mother to her feet.

By way of everlasting thanks to all of the women who have helped me to stay alive I am working never to be late again.   [1985]

ALICE WALKER
In Search of Our Mothers' Gardens

> I described her own nature and temperament. Told how they needed a larger life for their expression. . . . I pointed out that in lieu of proper channels, her emotions had overflowed into paths that dissipated them. I talked, beautifully I thought, about an art that would be born, an art that would open the way for women the likes of her. I asked her to hope, and build up an inner life against the coming of that day. . . . I sang, with a strange quiver in my voice, a promise song.
>
> — "Avey," Jean Toomer, *Cane*
> *The poet speaking to a prostitute who falls asleep while he's talking*

When the poet Jean Toomer walked through the South in the early twenties, he discovered a curious thing: black women whose spirituality was so intense, so deep, so *unconscious*, they were themselves unaware of the richness they held. They stumbled blindly through their lives: creatures so abused and mutilated in body, so dimmed and confused by pain, that they considered themselves unworthy even of hope. In the selfless abstractions their bodies became to the men who used them, they became more than "sexual objects," more even than mere women: they became "Saints." Instead of being perceived as whole persons, their bodies became shrines: what was thought to be their minds became temples suitable for worship. These crazy Saints stared out at the world, wildly, like lunatics — or quietly, like suicides; and the "God" that was in their gaze was as mute as a great stone.

Who were these Saints? These crazy, loony, pitiful women?

Some of them, without a doubt, were our mothers and grandmothers.

In the still heat of the post-Reconstruction South, this is how they seemed to Jean Toomer: exquisite butterflies trapped in an evil honey, toiling away their lives in an era, a century, that did not acknowledge them, except as "the *mule* of the world." They dreamed dreams that no one knew — not even themselves, in any coherent fashion — and saw visions no one could understand. They wandered or sat about the countryside crooning lullabies to ghosts, and drawing the mother of Christ in charcoal on courthouse walls.

They forced their minds to desert their bodies and their striving spirits sought   5
to rise, like frail whirlwinds from the hard red clay. And when those frail whirlwinds fell, in scattered particles, upon the ground, no one mourned. Instead, men lit candles to celebrate the emptiness that remained, as people do who enter a beautiful but vacant space to resurrect a God.

Our mothers and grandmothers, some of them: moving to music not yet written. And they waited.

They waited for a day when the unknown thing that was in them would be made known; but guessed, somehow in their darkness, that on the day of their revelation they would be long dead. Therefore to Toomer they walked, and even ran, in slow motion. For they were going nowhere immediate, and the future was not yet within their grasp. And men took our mothers and grandmothers, "but got no pleasure from it." So complex was their passion and their calm.

To Toomer, they lay vacant and fallow as autumn fields, with harvest time never in sight: and he saw them enter loveless marriages, without joy; and become prostitutes, without resistance; and become mothers of children, without fulfillment.

For these grandmothers and mothers of ours were not Saints, but Artists; driven to a numb and bleeding madness by the springs of creativity in them for which there was no release. They were Creators, who lived lives of spiritual waste, because they were so rich in spirituality—which is the basis of Art—that the strain of enduring their unused and unwanted talent drove them insane. Throwing away this spirituality was their pathetic attempt to lighten the soul to a weight their work-worn, sexually abused bodies could bear.

What did it mean for a black woman to be an artist in our grandmothers' time? In our great-grandmothers' day? It is a question with an answer cruel enough to stop the blood.   10

Did you have a genius of a great-great-grandmother who died under some ignorant and depraved white overseer's lash? Or was she required to bake biscuits for a lazy backwater tramp, when she cried out in her soul to paint watercolors of sunsets, or the rain falling on the green and peaceful pasturelands? Or was her body broken and forced to bear children (who were more often than not sold away from her)—eight, ten, fifteen, twenty children—when her one joy was the thought of modeling heroic figures of rebellion, in stone or clay?

How was the creativity of the black woman kept alive, year after year and century after century, when for most of the years black people have been in America, it was a punishable crime for a black person to read or write? And the freedom to paint, to sculpt, to expand the mind with action did not exist. Consider, if you can bear to imagine it, what might have been the result if singing, too, had been forbidden by law. Listen to the voices of Bessie Smith, Billie Holiday, Nina Simone, Roberta Flack, and Aretha Franklin, among others, and imagine those voices muzzled for life. Then you may begin to comprehend the lives of our "crazy," "Sainted" mothers and grandmothers. The agony of the lives of women who might have been Poets, Novelists, Essayists, and Short-Story Writers (over a period of centuries), who died with their real gifts stifled within them.

And, if this were the end of the story, we would have cause to cry out in my paraphrase of Okot p'Bitek's great poem:

> O, my clanswoman
> Let us all cry together!
> Come,
> Let us mourn the death of our mother,
> The death of a Queen

The ash that was produced
By a great fire!
O, this homestead is utterly dead
Close the gates
With *lacari* thorns,
For our mother
The creator of the Stool is lost!
And all the young men
Have perished in the wilderness!

But this is not the end of the story, for all the young women—our mothers and grandmothers, *ourselves*—have not perished in the wilderness. And if we ask ourselves why, and search for and find the answer, we will know beyond all efforts to erase it from our minds, just exactly who, and of what, we black American women are.

One example, perhaps the most pathetic, most misunderstood one, can provide a backdrop for our mothers' work: Phillis Wheatley, a slave in the 1700s.

Virginia Woolf, in her book *A Room of One's Own*, wrote that in order for a woman to write fiction she must have two things, certainly: a room of her own (with key and lock) and enough money to support herself.

What then are we to make of Phillis Wheatley, a slave, who owned not even herself? This sickly, frail black girl who required a servant of her own at times—her health was so precarious—and who, had she been white, would have been easily considered the intellectual superior of all the women and most of the men in the society of her day.

Virginia Woolf wrote further, speaking of course not of our Phillis, that "any woman born with a great gift in the sixteenth century [insert "eighteenth century," insert "black woman," insert "born or made a slave"] would certainly have gone crazed, shot herself, or ended her days in some lonely cottage outside the village, half witch, half wizard [insert "Saint"], feared and mocked at. For it needs little skill and psychology to be sure that a highly gifted girl who had tried to use her gift of poetry would have been so thwarted and hindered by contrary instincts [add "chains, guns, the lash, the ownership of one's body by someone else, submission to an alien religion"], that she must have lost her health and sanity to a certainty."

The key words, as they relate to Phillis, are "contrary instincts." For when we read the poetry of Phillis Wheatley—as when we read the novels of Nella Larsen or the oddly false-sounding autobiography of that freest of all black women writers, Zora Hurston—evidence of "contrary instincts" is everywhere. Her loyalties were completely divided, as was, without question, her mind.

But how could this be otherwise? Captured at seven, a slave of wealthy, doting whites who instilled in her the "savagery" of the Africa they "rescued" her from . . . one wonders if she was even able to remember her homeland as she had known it, or as it really was.

Yet, because she did try to use her gift for poetry in a world that made her a slave, she was "so thwarted and hindered by . . . contrary instincts, that she . . . lost her health. . . ." In the last years of her brief life, burdened not only with the

15

20

need to express her gift but also with a penniless, friendless "freedom" and several small children for whom she was forced to do strenuous work to feed, she lost her health, certainly. Suffering from malnutrition and neglect and who knows what mental agonies, Phillis Wheatley died.

So torn by "contrary instincts" was black, kidnapped, enslaved Phillis that her description of "the Goddess" — as she poetically called the Liberty she did not have — is ironically, cruelly humorous. And, in fact, has held Phillis up to ridicule for more than a century. It is usually read prior to hanging Phillis's memory as that of a fool. She wrote:

> The Goddess comes, she moves divinely fair,
> Olive and laurel binds her *golden* hair.
> Wherever shines this native of the skies,
> Unnumber'd charms and recent graces rise. [My italics]

It is obvious that Phillis, the slave, combed the "Goddess's" hair every morning; prior, perhaps, to bringing in the milk, or fixing her mistress's lunch. She took her imagery from the one thing she saw elevated above all others.

With the benefit of hindsight we ask, "How could she?"

But at last, Phillis, we understand. No more snickering when your stiff, struggling, ambivalent lines are forced on us. We know now that you were not an idiot or a traitor; only a sickly little black girl, snatched from your home and country and made a slave; a woman who still struggled to sing the song that was your gift, although in a land of barbarians who praised you for your bewildered tongue. It is not so much what you sang, as that you kept alive, in so many of our ancestors, *the notion of song.*

Black women are called, in the folklore that so aptly identifies one's status in society, "the *mule* of the world," because we have been handed the burdens that everyone else — *everyone* else — refused to carry. We have also been called "Matriarchs," "Superwomen," and "Mean and Evil Bitches." Not to mention "Castraters" and "Sapphire's Mama." When we have pleaded for understanding, our character has been distorted; when we have asked for simple caring, we have been handed empty inspirational appellations, then stuck in the farthest corner. When we have asked for love, we have been given children. In short, even our plainer gifts, our labors of fidelity and love, have been knocked down our throats. To be an artist and a black woman, even today, lowers our status in many respects, rather than raises it: and yet, artists we will be.

Therefore we must fearlessly pull out of ourselves and look at and identify with our lives the living creativity some of our great-grandmothers were not allowed to know. I stress *some* of them because it is well known that the majority of our great-grandmothers knew, even without "knowing" it, the reality of their spirituality, even if they didn't recognize it beyond what happened in the singing at church — and they never had any intention of giving it up.

How they did it — those millions of black women who were not Phillis Wheatley, or Lucy Terry or Frances Harper or Zora Hurston or Nella Larsen or

25

Bessie Smith; or Elizabeth Catlett, or Katherine Dunham, either—brings me to the title of this essay, "In Search of Our Mothers' Gardens," which is a personal account that is yet shared, in its theme and its meaning, by all of us. I found, while thinking about the far-reaching world of the creative black woman, that often the truest answer to a question that really matters can be found very close.

In the late 1920s my mother ran away from home to marry my father. Marriage, if not running away, was expected of seventeen-year-old girls. By the time she was twenty, she had two children and was pregnant with a third. Five children later, I was born. And this is how I came to know my mother: she seemed a large, soft, loving-eyed woman who was rarely impatient in our home. Her quick, violent temper was on view only a few times a year, when she battled with the white landlord who had the misfortune to suggest to her that her children did not need to go to school.

She made all the clothes we wore, even my brothers' overalls. She made all   30
the towels and sheets we used. She spent the summers canning vegetables and fruits. She spent the winter evenings making quilts enough to cover all our beds.

During the "working" day, she labored beside—not behind—my father in the fields. Her day began before sunup, and did not end until late at night. There was never a moment for her to sit down, undisturbed, to unravel her own private thoughts; never a time free from interruption—by work or the noisy inquiries of her many children. And yet, it is to my mother—and all our mothers who were not famous—that I went in search of the secret of what has fed that muzzled and often mutilated, but vibrant, creative spirit that the black woman has inherited, and that pops out in wild and unlikely places to this day.

But when, you will ask, did my overworked mother have time to know or care about feeding the creative spirit?

The answer is so simple that many of us have spent years discovering it. We have constantly looked high, when we should have looked high—and low.

For example: in the Smithsonian Institution in Washington, D.C., there hangs a quilt unlike any other in the world. In fanciful, inspired, and yet simple and identifiable figures, it portrays the story of the Crucifixion. It is considered rare, beyond price. Though it follows no known pattern of quiltmaking, and though it is made of bits and pieces of worthless rags, it is obviously the work of a person of powerful imagination and deep spiritual feeling. Below this quilt I saw a note that says it was made by "an anonymous Black woman in Alabama, a hundred years ago."

If we could locate this "anonymous" black woman from Alabama, she would   35
turn out to be one of our grandmothers—an artist who left her mark in the only materials she could afford, and in the only medium her position in society allowed her to use.

As Virginia Woolf wrote further, in *A Room of One's Own:*

> Yet genius of a sort must have existed among women as it must have existed among the working class. [Change this to "slaves" and "the wives and daughters of sharecroppers."] Now and again an Emily Brontë or a Robert

Burns [change this to "a Zora Hurston or a Richard Wright"] blazes out and proves its presence. But certainly it never got itself on to paper. When, however, one reads of a witch being ducked, of a woman possessed by devils [or "Sainthood"], of a wise woman selling herbs [or root workers], or even a very remarkable man who had a mother, then I think we are on the track of a lost novelist, a suppressed poet, or some mute and inglorious Jane Austen. . . . Indeed, I would venture to guess that Anon, who wrote so many poems without signing them, was often a woman. . . .

And so our mothers and grandmothers have, more often than not anonymously, handed on the creative spark, the seed of the flower they themselves never hoped to see: or like a sealed letter they could not plainly read.

And so it is, certainly, with my own mother. Unlike "Ma" Rainey's songs, which retained their creator's name even while blasting forth from Bessie Smith's mouth, no song or poem will bear my mother's name. Yet so many of the stories that I write, that we all write, are my mother's stories. Only recently did I fully realize this: that through years of listening to my mother's stories of her life, I have absorbed not only the stories themselves, but something of the manner in which she spoke, something of the urgency that involves the knowledge that her stories—like her life—must be recorded. It is probably for this reason that so much of what I have written is about characters whose counterparts in real life are so much older than I am.

But the telling of these stories, which came from my mother's lips as naturally as breathing, was not the only way my mother showed herself as an artist. For stories, too, were subject to being distracted, to dying without conclusion. Dinners must be started, and cotton must be gathered before the big rains. The artist that was and is my mother showed itself to me only after many years. This is what I finally noticed:

Like Mem, a character in *The Third Life of Grange Copeland*, my mother   40 adorned with flowers whatever shabby house we were forced to live in. And not just your typical straggly country stand of zinnias, either. She planted ambitious gardens—and still does—with over fifty different varieties of plants that bloom profusely from early March until late November. Before she left home for the fields, she watered her flowers, chopped up the grass, and laid out new beds. When she returned from the fields she might divide clumps of bulbs, dig a cold pit, uproot and replant roses, or prune branches from her taller bushes or trees— until night came and it was too dark to see.

Whatever she planted grew as if by magic, and her fame as a grower of flowers spread over three counties. Because of her creativity with her flowers, even my memories of poverty are seen through a screen of blooms—sunflowers, petunias, roses, dahlias, forsythia, spirea, delphiniums, verbena . . . and so on.

And I remember people coming to my mother's yard to be given cuttings from her flowers; I hear again the praise showered on her because whatever rocky soil she landed on, she turned into a garden. A garden so brilliant with colors, so original in its design, so magnificent with life and creativity, that to this day people drive by our house in Georgia—perfect strangers and imperfect strangers—and ask to stand or walk among my mother's art.

I notice that it is only when my mother is working in her flowers that she is radiant, almost to the point of being invisible — except as Creator: hand and eye. She is involved in work her soul must have. Ordering the universe in the image of her personal conception of Beauty.

Her face, as she prepares the Art that is her gift, is a legacy of respect she leaves to me, for all that illuminates and cherishes life. She has handed down respect for the possibilities — and the will to grasp them.

For her, so hindered and intruded upon in so many ways, being an artist has   45
still been a daily part of her life. This ability to hold on, even in very simple ways, is work black women have done for a very long time.

This poem is not enough, but it is something, for the woman who literally covered the holes in our walls with sunflowers:

> They were women then
> My mama's generation
> Husky of voice — Stout of
> Step
> With fists as well as
> Hands
> How they battered down
> Doors
> And ironed
> Starched white
> Shirts
> How they led
> Armies
> Headragged Generals
> Across mined
> Fields
> Booby-trapped
> Kitchens
> To discover books
> Desks
> A place for us
> How they knew what we
> *Must* know
> Without knowing a page
> Of it
> Themselves.

Guided by my heritage of a love of beauty and a respect for strength — in search of my mother's garden, I found my own.

And perhaps in Africa over two hundred years ago, there was just such a mother; perhaps she painted vivid and daring decorations in oranges and yellows and greens on the walls of her hut; perhaps she sang — in a voice like Roberta Flack's — *sweetly* over the compounds of her village; perhaps she wove the most stunning mats or told the most ingenious stories of all the village storytellers. Perhaps she was herself a poet — though only her daughter's name is signed to the poems that we know.

Perhaps Phillis Wheatley's mother was also an artist.

Perhaps in more than Phillis Wheatley's biological life is her mother's signa- 50
ture made clear.   [1974]

A WRITING EXERCISE

Read Jordan's "Many Rivers to Cross," jotting down your notes and comments in the margin. Consider your immediate reactions, and don't ignore personal associations. Then freewrite a response to her essay for ten minutes.

A Student's Personal Response

Isla Bravo wrote in her journal:

> It was shocking to read about Jordan's mother's sui-
> cide in the first sentence of "Many Rivers to Cross." I
> expected the rest of the essay to be about only that one
> event, but she went on to talk about everything else that
> was going on in her life around that time first. It is
> hard to understand how she managed everything in her
> life. She is out of money and needs to find a way to
> improve her financial status in just three months. My
> family may not have everything we've ever wanted, but
> we've always done pretty well, and I never worried about
> where we lived.
>
> Even though I have never had to struggle the way Jor-
> dan did, I can relate to her descriptions of her friends
> and neighbors. They all help her out the best they can
> when her husband leaves her and then when her mother
> dies. These are the people that she really appreciates in
> her life. They are the same kind of people that brought
> food to my parents when my grandmother died. These are
> the people that she loves and creates her own sort of
> family despite the fact that her father is so mean to
> her. These are people with whom she creates relationships
> that aren't defined by specific standards created by
> society.
>
> When Jordan says that her mother's death may not be
> extraordinary, that maybe every woman watches someone die
> over and over, she is really talking about all the little

things that can wear a lot of women down and cause their deaths a long time before they actually die. She can't even tell that her mother is dead because she's been wearing down for so long. The image of her mother looking as if she was "just about to stand up" made me think of my grandmother's funeral and how she looked like she was sleeping rather than dead. For Jordan the image of her mother in that sort of stasis is also an image of her possible future. It is strange to think of someone whose life has been so hard on them that their death doesn't create a jarring difference.

Jordan seems to be trying to keep herself from wearing down just like her mother at the end. Women are given roles by society that prevent them from being able to really enjoy their lives. She uses her other friends and family as models for how to survive. She has a friend who calms her down on the phone, a cousin that gives her advice in the hospital, and more that take care of her son when she can't. Mrs. Griffin is a good example of the type of person she wants to be. She has to work hard to avoid becoming her mother. It seems as if she is motivated by guilt because she wasn't able to help her mother when she says, "I came too late to help my mother to her feet." Even though it wasn't her fault that her mother put up with so much, it certainly makes her determined to prevent her life from ending up the same way her mother's did.

The Elements of Essays

First impressions are valuable, but writing intelligently about essays should not be completely spontaneous. We can be personal and insightful, but persuading others about the validity of our reading takes a more focused and textually informed presentation. The following discussion of the basic elements of the essay is meant to increase your ability to analyze and write about essays. The elements include **voice**, **style**, **structure**, and **ideas**.

Voice

When we read the first few sentences of an essay, we usually hear the narrator's **voice**: we hear a person speaking to us, and we begin to notice if he or she sounds friendly or hostile, stuffy or casual, self-assured or tentative. The voice might be austere and technical or personal and flamboyant. The voice may be intimate or remote. It may be sincere, hectoring, hysterical, meditative, or ironic. The possibilities are endless.

We usually get a sense of the writer's voice from the **tone** the writer projects. In the first paragraph of Walker's essay, we get a sense of the speaker's voice through the informed and serious tone that she takes. We also sense some irony and anger especially when she asks, "Who were . . . these crazy, loony, pitiful women?" There also seems a note of lyrical sadness in her tone in paragraph 6: "Our mothers and grandmothers, some of them: moving to music not yet written. And they waited." Writing about such complex matters as racism and art, Walker's voice is equally complex. At times her tone is alternately angry ("When we have pleaded," paragraph 26); hopeful ("Therefore we must fearlessly pull out of ourselves," paragraph 27); thoughtful (paragraph 28); admiring (paragraph 29), and honestly self-reflective ("Only recently did I fully realize this," paragraph 38). And there are numerous examples of her employing a celebratory tone, especially when she discusses the matriarchal artists she so admires. The tone of her speculative conclusion is dramatic as she uses "perhaps" seven times, a rhetorically satisfying ending to an essay meant to be a moving argument about the ability of oppressed women to keep their artistic spirit alive. When we speak of a writer's persona, we mean a kind of performance mask or stance the writer assumes. Writers are trying to construct a persona that will serve their purposes. Voice and tone are techniques that help writers create a persona.

A WRITING EXERCISE

Read June Jordan's essay "Many Rivers to Cross," and make some notes about the voice you hear. Like Walker, Jordan is also concerned with injustice and racism. Is her tone angrier? More determined? And like Walker, Jordan employs the rhetorical technique of repetition to conclude her essay. How would you compare the effectiveness of repeating "I" with Walker's "perhaps"?

Style

We all have stylish friends. They look good. Their shoes and pants and shirts seem to complement each other perfectly. It's not that they are color-coordinated — that would be too obvious for them — it's something more subtle. They seem to make just the right choices. When they go to a party, to the movies, or to school, they have a personal style that is their own.

Writers also have **style**. They make specific choices in words, in syntax and sentence length, in diction, in metaphors, even in sentence beginnings and endings. Writers use parallelism, balance, formal diction, poetic language, even sentence fragments to create their own styles.

Review each of the two essays with an eye to comparing the styles of Walker and Jordan. Notice the interesting use of the colon in Walker's first sentence and the dramatic repetition of "so intense, so deep, so *unconscious.*" Actually, Walker's first paragraph makes creative use of the colon and dash. She writes sophisticated, complex sentences, varying the usual subject/verb/object pattern. In the second and third paragraphs, she varies the length of her sentences with short questions and statements before returning in the fourth, fifth, and sixth paragraphs to a literary style employing metaphors ("exquisite butterflies"), similes ("like frail whirlwinds"), and analogies ("moving to music"). It is an impassioned style, moving, evocative, and committed. Filled with literary devices, rhetorical flourishes, and emotional honesty, Walker writes her own rules for how a persuasive essay works.

A WRITING EXERCISE

Note any literary techniques in Jordan's style. Focus especially on the last dozen paragraphs or so. Are her sentences as complex as Walker's? Is her style appropriate to her purpose? Explain.

Structure

The way essayists put their work together is not mysterious. The best writers create a **structure** to fit their needs. Most do not have a prearranged structure in mind or feel the need to obey the composition rules many students think they have to follow: topic sentence first and three examples following. Writers of essays aren't inclined to follow formulas. Essayists begin and end as they see fit; they give explicit topic sentences or create narratives that imply themes; they begin with an assertion and support it, or vice versa. Essayists are inventors of structures that fit the occasion and their own way of seeing the world. The thought of the essay significantly influences its structure. Like the relationship between mind and body, form and thought are inseparable.

Walker's essay is an argument and its structure is part of her persuasive intent. In "Literature as Argument" (36), we note that writers sometimes specify an issue, make claims, and then explicitly support these claims with substantial evidence, hoping to persuade a particular audience. Most literary texts usually make arguments indirectly, but essays are often more direct. Walker directly uses personal experience in the service of her argument. Although students are sometimes taught that one's own experience is too subjective to persuade others, experienced writers like Walker and Jordan do use personal and literary experiences to call for certain changes in the attitudes of their readers.

In her first paragraph, Walker reveals some of her **assumptions** or warrants, especially the idea that black women were not aware of their capabilities, were "abused and mutilated," and were misread. After establishing common ground with her audience — that these women are the mothers and grandmothers of the speaker and her audience — Walker comes eventually to her thesis in paragraph 9, in which she asserts that these women were "not Saints, but Artists." After asking how these women kept their creativity from disappearing, she notes that African American women of her mother's generation found a way through song and other strategies to keep an artistic heritage alive in spite of the barriers they faced. Most of the essay then develops this idea more concretely.

Walker's essay does not use a thesis statement and then a point-by-point argument. Instead, she leads us into her main idea gradually, interweaving examples, letting one idea lead to another, coming back to ideas mentioned earlier, and developing them further. She ends by returning to her Phillis Wheatley example to make a connection to the deep past, as just one of the many ways she achieves coherence and unity in this quilt-like essay, sewn together with carefully crafted transitions.

A WRITING EXERCISE

As you read through Jordan's essay, describe the structure or organizing strategies that she uses. How does her extended personal narrative support her main idea?

Ideas

All writers have something on their minds when they write. That seems especially true when writers decide to put their **ideas** into a nonfictional form such as the essay. Of course, lots of ideas fill poems and short stories too, but they are usually expressed more indirectly. Although essays seem more idea-driven, this does not mean that as readers we have a responsibility to extract the precise idea or argument the writer had in mind. That may not even be possible since in the creative process of all writing, ideas get modified or changed. Sometimes a writer's original intention is significantly transformed; sometimes writers are not fully conscious of all their hidden intentions. Regardless, readers of essays are not simply miners unearthing hidden meanings; they are more like coproducers. And in creating that meaning, ideas are central.

"In Search of Our Mothers' Gardens" is an argument based on the idea that Walker's ancestors were not really the strange "crazy, loony, pitiful women" that Jean Toomer thought—not "exquisite butterflies" but artists "driven to a numb and bleeding madness by the springs of creativity in them for which there was no release." They could not do the work that was in their hearts and minds, and yet they managed to survive. They did so, Walker claims, through a psychological process Freud might call sublimation, by channeling their unacceptable creative drive into such acceptable ordinary paths as singing, quilting, and gardening. Phillis Wheatley is used as an example of an artist whose natural creativity was so thwarted that her health deteriorated as a result. And after reviewing her main ideas of heritage, love of beauty, and respect for the strength of her creative ancestors, Walker concludes with the speculation that perhaps the artistic tradition goes back even further than Wheatley, back to Wheatley's African mother and beyond.

A WRITING EXERCISE

Ideas are often more powerful and more dramatic when they seem to evolve as a result of personal experience and not simply from political beliefs or ideological conviction. There seems to be a considerable difference between starkly asserting that black women were not able to live up to their potential and enveloping that idea that Walker does here. What do you think are some ideas that June Jordan develops? Comment on the effectiveness of her extended narrative in enhancing her ideas.

Sample Student Paper: Final Draft

After writing journal entries and a freewrite, Isla planned her essay and then wrote a draft. She used responses from several students in a small-group workshop and from her instructor to help her revise her essay, sharpening her focus and supporting her claims more explicitly. Here is Isla's final version.

Isla Bravo

Ms. Hollingsworth

English 201

21 April —

Resisting Women's Roles

June Jordan takes a strongly feminist stance against the roles women are forced to contend with in her essay "Many Rivers to Cross." She begins the essay from her experience as a woman who has conformed to the social expectations of a wife, daughter, and mother. Her commitment to these roles have left her as a single mother who is contending with an unwanted pregnancy, forced to care for a dying mother and a belligerent father, and without a place of her own to live or work. This essay is Jordan's own testimonial to why women need to establish their independence and not allow society to control their lives. She makes this statement by exploring her own defiance of society's conventions regarding the roles for women as wife, daughter, and mother in an attempt to preserve herself from the restrictions that destroyed her mother.

Women are expected by society to place their families before their careers, and part of this sacrifice includes aiding their husband's careers in lieu of their own. Jordan portrays herself as an example of how this convention is detrimental to a woman's ability to survive on her own. Jordan sacrifices her own professional ambition to

her husband's pursuit of his career. The ensuing complications depict the limitations and perils of the idea
that women must always place their own careers behind
their husbands. Rather than specifically condemn this
social expectation, she provides an illustration of the
destruction it can cause. Her own career is a secondary
priority, subjugated to her roles as a supportive wife
and mother, while her husband pursues graduate school in
another city and has an affair with another man's wife.
Jordan squanders a year of her life waiting for her husband's return and becomes "a mother without a husband, as
a poet without a publisher, a freelance journalist without assignment, a city planner without a contract." She
abides by the social conventions that insist she support
her husband, and her life remains in stasis until he
steps out of his own commitments. By living her life
under the social guidelines for a wife, she allows herself to be exploited for her husband's convenience. Her
needs are supplanted by her husband's, and his abandonment leaves her embarrassed and destitute.

Jordan's depiction of her parent's relationship
illustrates the generational quality of these social
conventions. Her parent's relationship foreshadows
the potential outcome of her marriage if it continues.
Her parents' relationship is wholly restricted to the
typical gender roles they both inherit from society. Her
mother subjugates her own life only to the needs of her
husband, a sacrifice he expects from her. This historical
relationship becomes clear when Jordan describes her
father's response to her mother's fatal illness when she
says, "I think he was scared; who would take care of him?
Would she get well again and make everything all right
again?" The fact that his concern was about his own
life--"who would take care of him?"--makes it clear that
their relationship revolved around only his own comfort.
Jordan is desperate to prevent her own life from following
this path.

Jordan's relationship with her father explores another aspect of the expectations placed on women by society, that of a daughter. Jordan's father's reliance on her mother for all of his comfort turns onto Jordan when her mother is no longer able to fulfill these duties. Jordan's role as his daughter, her most important function, is dynamically portrayed when her father forces her to check her mother's body to see if she is alive because he is incapable or unwilling to do it himself. He says to her, "I'll wait up here. . . . You call up and let me know," only to yell at her inaccurate determination. His anger appears to stem more from the disruption to his own life rather than the loss of his wife; he is angry rather than sad. He appears almost offended by her death and his daughter's failure to provide him with the level of comfort he craves for his life. His own expectations for the superior role in the household have been created by a male-dominated society and have been enforced by the manner in which his wife seems to have fulfilled those expectations as well. The role of a dutiful child is not by itself destructive until it begins to take precedence in this destructive manner. His expectation is that Jordan should take on the role of caregiver, waiting on him despite any reluctance on her part and regardless of the animosity that exists between them.

Jordan also defies social conventions by her unwillingness to become a mother again to the new baby she's carrying. She attempts to abort the child several times until she finally does lose the baby. Jordan describes the advice she receives from a friend in the hospital, "Whatever I did, I should not admit I'd had an abortion or I'd get her into trouble, and myself in trouble." The possibility that Jordan does not want to be a mother to another child is abhorrent to the social standards that have formed her life and surroundings. Motherhood is the expected career for a woman, and her choice to not have another baby is a direct rejection of those standards.

As a woman in this particular culture, she has certain designated assignments of work that include being a
daughter, wife, and mother. She rejects a caretaker role
for her father, her marriage has dissolved, and she has
an abortion. These portrayals do not suggest a rejection
of these roles in their entirety; rather, they explicitly
show how they can become harmful if they force women into
situations they might have avoided if not for these societal pressures. From this point, she is able to look
toward her own career and her own needs. The role society
imposes on her as a woman puts her in a position that
deemphasizes her own ambitions and preferences. The end
of her mother's life is the catalyst that forces her to
fully recognize the restrictions that she has been living
with and that her mother succumbed to until her death.
Jordan says, "I came too late to help my mother to her
feet. . . . I am working never to be late again." She wants
to free herself from the limiting standards for women in
society and hopefully free other women as well.

8

Working with a Collection of Writings

In each chapter in Part Two, we devote one cluster to a single author, someone whose writing merits special consideration. From the plays of Sophocles and the poetry of Emily Dickinson to the fiction of Nathaniel Hawthorne, Jamaica Kincaid, and Kate Chopin, we present multiple works to demonstrate a writer's range, style, or thematic variation.

In these clusters, after a brief introduction and biography, we present the texts—the Collection of Writings. Each text is followed by questions to help you think about the text and to compare it to the others. At the end of the cluster are four suggested writing assignments. The following cluster, focusing on the poetry of Marge Piercy, is typical of the single-author clusters you will find in each chapter.

WORKING WOMEN: FOUR POEMS BY MARGE PIERCY

MARGE PIERCY, "To Be of Use"
MARGE PIERCY, "For Strong Women"
MARGE PIERCY, "The Market Economy"
MARGE PIERCY, "What's That Smell in the Kitchen?"

The Austrian psychoanalyst Sigmund Freud thought work and love were crucial to our well being, especially our sense of self-worth. Most people want to do meaningful work, and most of us want to feel our contributions at work matter. Freud was probably referring to the work of men since most of the women of his time worked only at home, an occupation that most men did not consider to be real work.

That cultures historically fail to see that both men and women need and want to be engaged in satisfying work is one of the topics that engages the poet and activist, Marge Piercy (b. 1936), a veteran of the modern civil rights and women's movements. Concerned with promoting various social causes, she has focused primarily on feminist issues such as the effects of patriarchal oppression on women's lives. In the four poems given here, Piercy focuses on various aspects of work. In "To Be of Use," perhaps her most famous poem, she extols the virtues of committed work. "For Strong Women" affirms the dignity of struggling against demeaning stereotypes of women. Piercy indicts capitalism's neglect of consumer safety in "The Market Economy" then turns a critical feminist eye on the anger some wives feel toward their husband's expectations in "What's That Smell in the Kitchen?"

Piercy is a provocative writer, often making an argument she probably doesn't expect her readers to agree with fully. Primarily concerned with issues of social policy, she wants to jolt you into intense discussion about where you stand on some of the controversial topics of the day. Indeed, her four poems on work are hard to ignore. In her introduction to *Circles on the Water*, a 1982 collection of her poems, Piercy hopes that her readers "will find poems that speak to each other and put them up on the bathroom wall and remember bits and pieces of them in stressful or quiet moments" (xii).

BEFORE YOU READ

Do you believe that there is a task or job to which you can entirely commit yourself? Do you think corporations are concerned enough with product safety? Do you think that most women eventually become disenchanted with their husbands?

MARGE PIERCY
To Be of Use

Born in 1936, Marge Piercy was a child of the Great Depression, and her roots are thoroughly working class. She grew up Jewish in Detroit, Michigan, a city that was "black and white by blocks." When she won a scholarship to the University of Michigan, Piercy became the first member of her family to go to college. She went on to earn a master of arts degree from Northwestern University. Piercy has worked as a secretary, a switchboard operator, a department store clerk, an artist's model, and a low-paid part-time instructor. She has also been actively involved in political work, participating in the civil rights, antiwar, feminist, and environmentalist movements. In both her poems and her fiction, her goal is to portray ordinary working people who are also thinking people. She has published fourteen books of poetry, fifteen novels, and a book of essays about the work of writing poetry. Her recent work includes the poetry collection, What Are Big Girls Made Of?, *the novels* Storm Tide *(with Ira Wood) and* Three Women, *and a memoir,* Sleeping with Cats.

(Ira Wood.)

The people I love the best
jump into work head first
without dallying in the shallows
and swim off with sure strokes almost out of sight.
They seem to become natives of that element,   5
the black sleek heads of seals
bouncing like half-submerged balls.

I love people who harness themselves, an ox to a heavy cart,
who pull like water buffalo, with massive patience,
who strain in the mud and the muck to move things forward,   10
who do what has to be done, again and again.

I want to be with people who submerge
in the task, who go into the fields to harvest
and work in a row and pass the bags along,
who are not parlor generals and field deserters   15
but move in a common rhythm
when the food must come in or the fire be put out.

The work of the world is common as mud.
Botched, it smears the hands, crumbles to dust.
But the thing worth doing well done　　　　　　　　　20
has a shape that satisfies, clean and evident.
Greek amphoras for wine or oil,
Hopi vases that held corn, are put in museums
but you know they were made to be used.
The pitcher cries for water to carry　　　　　　　　　25
and a person for work that is real.　　　　　　　[1974]

THINKING ABOUT THE TEXT

1. Do you think Piercy is talking only about people who do physical work? What is your idea of the "the thing worth doing well done"?
2. Is the swimming analogy effective? What other analogies, similes, and metaphors does she use?
3. Is the key idea here one's attitude, the kind of work available in a society, or something else?
4. What do you think she is referring to in the phrase "parlor generals and field deserters"?
5. What is your reading of "real" in the last line? What are some examples of such work in our society?

MARGE PIERCY
For Strong Women

A strong woman is a woman who is straining.
A strong woman is a woman standing
on tiptoe and lifting a barbell
while trying to sing Boris Godunov.
A strong woman is a woman at work　　　　　　　　5
cleaning out the cesspool of the ages,
and while she shovels, she talks about
how she doesn't mind crying, it opens
the ducts of the eyes, and throwing up
develops the stomach muscles, and　　　　　　　　10
she goes on shoveling with tears
in her nose.

A strong woman is a woman in whose head
a voice is repeating, I told you so,
ugly, bad girl, bitch, nag, shrill, witch,　　　　　　15
ballbuster, nobody will ever love you back,
why aren't you feminine, why aren't

you soft, why aren't you quiet, why
aren't you dead?

A strong woman is a woman determined   20
to do something others are determined
not be done. She is pushing up on the bottom
of a lead coffin lid. She is trying to raise
a manhole cover with her head, she is trying
to butt her way through a steel wall.   25
Her head hurts. People waiting for the hole
to be made say, hurry, you're so strong.

A strong woman is a woman bleeding
inside. A strong woman is a woman making
herself strong every morning while her teeth   30
loosen and her back throbs. Every baby,
a tooth, midwives used to say, and now
every battle a scar. A strong woman
is a mass of scar tissue that aches
when it rains and wounds that bleed   35
when you bump them and memories that get up
in the night and pace in boots to and fro.

A strong woman is a woman who craves love
like oxygen or she turns blue choking.
A strong woman is a woman who loves   40
strongly and weeps strongly and is strongly
terrified and has strong needs. A strong woman is strong
in words, in action, in connection, in feeling;
she is not strong as a stone but as a wolf
suckling her young. Strength is not in her, but she   45
enacts it as the wind fills a sail.

What comforts her is others loving
her equally for the strength and for the weakness
from which it issues, lightning from a cloud.
Lightning stuns. In rain, the clouds disperse.   50
Only water of connection remains,
flowing through us. Strong is what we make
each other. Until we are all strong together,
a strong woman is a woman strongly afraid.   [1980]

THINKING ABOUT THE TEXT

1. What would your definition of a strong woman be? Which of Piercy's
   examples would you agree with? Are any confusing or odd? Do you know
   any women who you think Piercy would call strong?

2. How might this poem be specifically connected to work in our society?

3. Is Piercy contradicting herself when she says at the end of stanza 5, "Strength is not in her"?

4. How would you make concrete and specific the lines that begin, "A strong woman / is a mass of scar tissue"?

5. What do you think Piercy is getting at with the elaborate climate analogy in the last stanza? Is it a rallying cry? A plea? How might her suggestion affect social policy?

MAKING COMPARISONS

1. Is it possible that Piercy is talking about the same people in both poems? Could "To Be of Use" be an answer to this poem?

2. What lines in the first poem might be comparable to "A strong woman . . . is trying / to butt her way through a steel wall"?

3. Compare the analogies and metaphors used in both poems.

MARGE PIERCY
The Market Economy

Suppose some peddler offered
you can have a color TV
but your baby will be
born with a crooked spine;
you can have polyvinyl cups   5
and wash and wear
suits but it will cost
you your left lung
rotted with cancer; suppose
somebody offered you   10
a frozen precooked dinner
every night for ten years
but at the end
your colon dies
and then you do,   15
slowly and with much pain.
You get a house in the suburbs
but you work in a new plastics
factory and die at fifty-one
when your kidneys turn off.   20

But where else will you
work? where else can
you rent but Smog City?
The only houses for sale

are under the yellow sky.   25
You've been out of work for
a year and they're hiring
at the plastics factory.
Don't read the fine
print, there isn't any.   [1982]   30

THINKING ABOUT THE TEXT

1. Even though they are probably rhetorical, how would you answer Piercy's question in the second stanza? In stanza 1, does she mean for you to "Suppose," or is this also rhetorical?

2. What is the relationship between the two stanzas?

3. Is Piercy being hyperbolic? Provocative? Sincere?

4. Is it effective for poems to speak directly to readers? What is gained or lost?

5. If this poem concerns social policy, what might Piercy's arguments be?

MAKING COMPARISONS

1. There seems to be fewer poetic devices (like metaphors and analogies) in this poem than in the other two. Why might this be?

2. If the assumptions of this poem are true, is it still possible to be "strong" and "of use"?

3. How would you describe the attitude (tone, voice) of the poet in these three poems?

MARGE PIERCY

What's That Smell in the Kitchen?

All over America women are burning dinners.
It's lambchops in Peoria; it's haddock
in Providence; it's steak in Chicago
tofu delight in Big Sur; red
rice and beans in Dallas.   5
All over America women are burning
food they're supposed to bring with calico
smile on platters glittering like wax.
Anger sputters in her brainpan, confined
but spewing out missiles of hot fat.   10
Carbonized despair presses like a clinker
from a barbecue against the back of her eyes.
If she wants to grill anything, it's

her husband spitted over a slow fire.
If she wants to serve him anything   15
it's a dead rat with a bomb in its belly
ticking like the heart of an insomniac.
Her life is cooked and digested,
nothing but leftovers in Tupperware.
Look, she says, once I was roast duck   20
on your platter with parsley but now I am Spam.
Burning dinner is not incompetence but war.   [1976]

THINKING ABOUT THE TEXT

1. Are women all over America burning dinners on purpose? Is this just a metaphor for something else? What?

2. What is meant by a "calico / smile"? Is this an expectation men have of women?

3. What is "Carbonized despair"? What is meant by "roast duck" and "Spam"?

4. If you were Piercy's editor, which line or image would you suggest she soften? To what? Why?

5. Who or what are these women at war with? How can the war be won? Can there be a negotiated settlement? A truce?

MAKING COMPARISONS

1. Is Piercy's attitude here different than in the other three poems? In what ways?

2. Are there any lines in the previous three poems that are thematically similar to the last one here?

3. Which simile, metaphor, or analogy in the four poems is the most effective? The least? The funniest? The most accurate?

WRITING ABOUT ISSUES

1. Which of the four poems by Piercy comes closest to describing a situation in America that you might agree with? Write an essay that explains why this is so.

2. Write an essay that describes an attitude of the poet you think is the best example of contemporary feminism.

3. Argue that finding meaningful work is or is not the secret of happiness.

4. Should poets be as committed to gender equality as Piercy? Does it affect the quality of her work? Should poets be, as Shelley suggests "the unacknowledged legislators of the world"? Argue that poets should or should not try to change the world.

--- A WEB ASSIGNMENT ---

Marge Piercy has a number of interesting links on her home page. Visit the Web Assignments section of the *Making Literature Matter* Web site to link to her page. Listed under Essays are three pieces Piercy has written about her life and work. "Looking at Myself" specifically comments on her poetry. After reading this selection, discuss what insights or information Piercy provided about "To Be of Use" that might assist you in expanding your understanding of that poem.

--- Visit www.bedfordstmartins.com/makinglitmatter ---

9

Working with Critical Commentaries

Each chapter of Part Two includes a cluster that features a literary text, scholars' remarks about it, questions encouraging you to analyze the text in light of these remarks, and writing assignments that help you take your analysis farther. In all cases, we present just a sample of the existing commentaries on the text. Yet we have tried to include the positions and issues that are most often raised by critics. Here, we offer a preview of our Critical Commentaries sections by leading you through Robert Frost's poem "After Apple-Picking" and various statements about it. At the same time, we continue Part One's emphasis on literature about work. A recent Frost biographer, Jay Parini, contends that he was "one of the few poets in the [English] language to make good poems out of real work" (78). From its title alone, you can tell "After Apple-Picking" refers to a certain form of labor, but the poem suggests this work is a metaphor for other things. As you will see, interpreters of the poem have differed over what the labor in it exactly represents, as well as how worthwhile this labor is in the overall context of human life.

WORK AS METAPHOR:
CRITICAL COMMENTARIES ON ROBERT FROST'S
"AFTER APPLE-PICKING"

ROBERT FROST, "After Apple-Picking"

CRITICAL COMMENTARIES:
ROBERT PENN WARREN, From "The Themes of Robert Frost"
JOHN J. CONDER, From "'After Apple-Picking': Frost's Troubled Sleep"
MARIE BORROFF, From "Robert Frost: 'To Earthward'"
ROBERT FAGGEN, From *Robert Frost and the Challenge of Darwin*

Like Frost's poem, many of the literary texts you will study have already been analyzed in books, articles, and lectures. Perhaps you fear prior commentaries, suspecting they have definitively explained the text you wish to examine. Most times, however, analyses of the text have multiplied precisely because none are authoritative and several conflict. In a sense, these analyses form an ongoing conversation, one in which you do have a role to play. Especially worth noting are the various *issues* that previous commentators on the text have raised—that is, the key questions they have pursued. Worth knowing, too, are their answers to these questions, especially if their responses diverge. Developing your own argument about the text, then, involves sorting through the issues and claims already expressed in the conversation about it. During this process, try to refrain from simple pro and con judgments. You may get more analytical leverage out of a previously expressed view when you seek to refine it rather than just praise or condemn it. In general, prepare your own argument by carefully deciding which issues and claims to value, which to challenge, which to complicate, which to deemphasize, and which to extend. You might also bring up points missing from the conversation so far.

BEFORE YOU READ

Recall or imagine the experience of picking apples, and then write a paragraph describing this activity. Which of the details you have noted could be used as symbols? With what possible meanings?

ROBERT FROST
After Apple-Picking

Robert Frost (1874–1963) became one of the United States's best-known and beloved poets. During his lifetime, he was such a public figure that he was asked to read his poetry at the 1961 inauguration of President John F. Kennedy. In particular, Frost has been celebrated for his poems about New England farm life. Clearly, "After Apple-Picking" reflects work that Frost himself did in that setting. When he wrote the poem in 1913, however, he was living temporarily in England, so that the poem reflects his memories of farm work more than his current experience of it. Indeed, Frost hardly spent all his life on farms. He was born in the city of San Francisco, and as an adult he taught at numerous colleges, including Amherst College and the University of Michigan. Nor was he immediately acclaimed as a poet. He was thirty-eight years old when his first book of verse, A Boy's Will, appeared in 1912, and it came out in England rather than the United States. His American reputation soared only with the 1914 publication of his second volume, North of Boston, which included "After Apple-Picking."

My long two-pointed ladder's sticking through a tree
Toward heaven still,
And there's a barrel that I didn't fill

(Rauner Library, Special Collections, Dartmouth College.)

Beside it, and there may be two or three
Apples I didn't pick upon some bough.   5
But I am done with apple-picking now.
Essence of winter sleep is on the night,
The scent of apples: I am drowsing off.
I cannot rub the strangeness from my sight
I got from looking through a pane of glass   10
I skimmed this morning from the drinking trough
And held against the world of hoary grass.
It melted, and I let it fall and break.
But I was well
Upon my way to sleep before it fell,   15
And I could tell
What form my dreaming was about to take.
Magnified apples appear and disappear,
Stem end and blossom end,
And every fleck of russet showing clear.   20
My instep arch not only keeps the ache,
It keeps the pressure of a ladder-round.
I feel the ladder sway as the boughs bend.
And I keep hearing from the cellar bin
The rumbling sound   25
Of load on load of apples coming in.

For I have had too much
Of apple-picking: I am overtired
Of the great harvest I myself desired.
There were ten thousand thousand fruit to touch,   30
Cherish in hand, lift down, and not let fall.
For all
That struck the earth,
No matter if not bruised or spiked with stubble,
Went surely to the cider-apple heap   35
As of no worth.
One can see what will trouble
This sleep of mine, whatever sleep it is.
Were he not gone,
The woodchuck could say whether it's like his   40
Long sleep, as I describe its coming on,
Or just some human sleep.   [1914]

In each Critical Commentaries cluster, the literary text is immediately followed by several questions about it, under the heading Thinking about the Text.
These questions will help you begin to develop an interpretation of your own.
Next, we present existing commentaries about the text, in the form of excerpts
from books, articles, and lectures. If you wish, you can move to these statements
right away, using them to catalyze your own ideas. In any case, the cluster ends by
inviting you to join the conversation that these statements have established. More
precisely, we ask questions about these remarks in a section called Making Comparisons, and we suggest how you can enter the conversation through your own
writing.

THINKING ABOUT THE TEXT

1. What details in this poem can be taken to indicate that it deals with matters of religion and the afterlife? In your own view, to what extent *does* it
   concern such matters? In what ways, if any, might it refer to the writing of
   poetry? Are there other subjects that the poem seems to address? If so,
   what?

2. If you find the verb tenses in this poem a bit confusing, you are not alone.
   Frost seems deliberately to make past, present, and future hard to distinguish here. Why, do you think? Try, at any rate, to figure out the chronological order of the speaker's day. What happened in the morning, what
   happened later on, and what may occur when the speaker falls asleep?

3. In lines 28 and 29, the speaker declares that "I am overtired / Of the great
   harvest I myself desired." What do you think the speaker really wanted?
   What do you think he really wants now?

4. Which of his physical senses does the speaker refer to? Identify specific
   lines where these come up. How realistic is his description of his physical

experience? Do any of his sensory details seem exaggerated or distorted? If so, which?

5. At the end, the speaker wonders if "human sleep" resembles that of a woodchuck. More generally, he encourages us to compare human beings with animals. What other details of the poem seem relevant to this comparison? How close a connection between humans and animals are you inclined to make after reading Frost's poem?

Critical Commentaries

Our first commentary on Frost's poem is by Robert Penn Warren (1905–1989). He himself was a notable writer, in 1985 becoming the first poet laureate of the United States. In fact, Warren received Pulitzer Prizes not only for poetry (*Promises: Poems, 1954–1956*) but also for fiction (his 1946 novel *All the King's Men*). Warren excelled, too, at analyzing other people's writing. For example, in 1938 he coauthored the textbook *Understanding Poetry*, which influenced how several generations of students looked at the genre. The following observations by Warren on "After Apple-Picking" are from a 1947 lecture he gave at the University of Michigan entitled "The Themes of Robert Frost," which can be found in his *New and Selected Essays*. Here Warren expresses a sunny view of the speaker's "dream" and, indeed, does not seem troubled by the speaker's use of the word "troubled."

ROBERT PENN WARREN
From *"The Themes of Robert Frost"*

The [speaker's] dream will relive the world of effort, even to the ache of the instep arch where the ladder rung was pressed. But is this a cause for regret or for self-congratulation? Is it a good dream or a bad dream? . . .

[W]e must look for the answer in the temper of the description he gives of the dream — the apples, stem end and blossom end, and every fleck of russet showing clear. The richness and beauty of the harvest — magnified now — is what is dwelt upon. . . . For instance, we have the delicious rhythm of the line

I feel the ladder sway as the boughs bend.

It is not the rhythm of nightmare, but of the good dream. Or we find the same temper in the next few lines in which the poet returns to the fact that he, in the real world, the world of effort, had carefully handled and cherished each fruit, and *cherished* is not the word to use if the labor is mere labor, the brutal act. So even though we find the poet saying that his sleep will be troubled, the word *troubled* comes to us colored by the whole temper of the passage, ironically qualified by that temper. . . .

[I]t may be well to ask ourselves if the poet is really talking about immortality and heaven — if he is really trying to define the heaven he wants and expects after this mortal life. No, he is only using that as an image for his meaning, a way to define his attitude. And that attitude is an attitude toward the here and now, toward man's conduct of his life in the literal world. . . .

This attitude has many implications. And this leads us to a rather important   5
point about poetry. When we read a poem merely in terms of a particular application of the attitude involved in it, we almost always read it as a kind of cramped and mechanical allegory. A poem defines an attitude, a basic view, which can have many applications. It defines, if it is a good poem, a sort of strategic point for the spirit from which experience of all sorts may be freshly viewed.

But to return to this poem: What would be some of the implied applications? First, let us take it in reference to the question of any sort of ideal which man sets up for himself, in reference to his dream. By this application the valid ideal would be that which stems from and involves the literal world, which is arrived at in terms of the literal world and not by violation of man's nature as an inhabitant of that literal world. Second, let us take it in reference to man's reward in this literal world. By this application we would arrive at a statement like this: Man must seek his reward in his fulfillment through effort and must not expect reward as something coming at the end of effort, like the oats for the dray horse in the trough at the end of the day's pull. He must cherish each thing in his hand. Third, let us take it in reference to poetry, or the arts. By this application, which is really a variant of the first, we would find that art must stem from the literal world, from the common body of experience, and must be a magnified "dream" of that experience as it has achieved meaning, and not a thing set apart, a mere decoration.

These examples, chosen from among many, are intended merely to point us back into the poem — to the central impulse of the poem itself. But they are all summed up in this line from "Mowing," another of Frost's poems: "The fact is the sweetest dream that labor knows."   [1947]

The following is from a commentary published in the 1974 collection *Frost: Centennial Essays*. At the time he wrote this piece, John J. Conder was a professor of English at Vanderbilt University. A distinctive feature of Conder's commentary on the poem is his willingness to sift through various possible meanings of the speaker's "sleep." In other words, Conder demonstrates how an interpretation might reveal the interpreter's *process* of thought rather than simply put forth definite opinions. Notice, too, that Conder views the speaker's situation more pessimistically than Warren does. For Conder, the speaker is not simply about to enter "the happy sleep of contemplation."

JOHN J. CONDER
From "'After Apple-Picking': Frost's Troubled Sleep"

. . . The sense of discipline associated with value during the apple-picking is not present in the dream. The apples are unrelated to the speaker, moving of their own accord, without his direction, his sense of purpose. Furthermore, they are all magnified; the distinction between those harvested and those lost does not exist. Gone is the speaker's sense of relative values. Associated with the statement ". . . I am overtired / Of the great harvest I myself desired," their magnification and autonomy bring into bold relief the very doubts surfacing toward the end of his description of the actual venture of picking apples. He has literally lost sight of all the values of the harvest. If this *is* a happy sleep of contemplation, the happiness is highly qualified.

Concerned about his values, the speaker is also concerned about the nature of his sleep, a concern imaged in the contrast between himself and the woodchuck. As part of nature the woodchuck will automatically be renewed. But the speaker may need, for renewal, not simply rest, some period of dormancy, but also some certain knowledge of human values. And where is such knowledge to come from? Recall, this is a poem about what happens after apple-picking. Hardly an allegory either supporting or denouncing Christian doctrine, the work nonetheless relies on overtones of the Fall to enrich its complex meaning. When man first picked the apple, he was expelled from Eden to labor by the sweat of his brow, a consequence of his newly found knowledge of good and evil. The speaker lives in a fallen world where he has labored and sweated. But he gains no sure knowledge as Adam did. His ladder is pointed toward heaven only, and he has had to descend from it. Man can climb the ladder toward heaven, toward certainty, but when he returns, he discovers how little he has learned with certainty. He cannot even know the nature of his sleep, although the possibilities seem clear.

Perhaps his will be like the woodchuck's sleep, the sleep of nature, in the limited sense that his creative powers are subject to the same kind of cyclical movement observed in the seasons. At worst, this sleep would be like nature's in its duration, though not in its character (unlike nature, man can dream). Such a sleep, induced by physical and mental fatigue, is not a function of man's uncertain values. His values are certain; his ability to act on them, limited. This is the sleep of renewal.

This meaning of "sleep," though possible in the poem, seems obviated by the apparent failure of the analogy between man and nature. Although Frost allows for its possibility in the reference to the woodchuck, such a sleep seems inconsistent with his larger view of man and nature. A second possible sleep, not far removed from the first, is also ascribable to a straining of the physical and mental powers, a strain just severe enough to confuse the speaker's sense of values and to blur his sense of purpose. But if he originally possessed a firmly grounded sense of value and purpose, he can be reasonably certain he will awaken from this sleep, from this confusion about values. A good rest, a night's or a month's, will settle the matter. . . .

But in the world of "After Apple-Picking," recovery is not certain. . . . If the   5 speaker's encounter with the apples has led him to question not just the nature, but the source of his values, then his sleep may be longer, even permanent. It is one matter to recover values lost because of fatigue. It is another to be forced to return to their source, particularly if the source is only the "I myself" who "desired." For when desire fails and values falter, what source outside the self can restore desire? In "After Apple-Picking," the ladder only points *toward* heaven.

What will trouble the speaker's sleep, whatever sleep it is? He is only falling asleep in this poem, and he does not know yet which sleep his will be. Its duration will determine its nature. It is his uncertainty as to when (or whether) he will awaken which will be carried into his sleep, troubling it. Ironically enough, only when he awakens will he know what sleep it is—or, rather, was.   [1974]

Our next selection is an excerpt from an essay that appeared in the 1976 volume *Frost: Centennial Essays II*. Now Sterling Emeritus Professor of English at Yale University, Marie Borroff has been known mostly as a scholar of medieval literature. Here, though, she analyzes Frost's twentieth-century poem. Borroff emphasizes that the speaker's labor is analogous to many other human activities. More specifically, for her the poem is about anxieties that stem from any number of responsibilities that human beings face. This view of the poem may or may not be considered as dark as Conder's.

MARIE BORROFF
From *"Robert Frost: 'To Earthward'* "

. . . The dream the speaker uneasily looks forward to is the kind of dream we all experience after working at anything too hard and too long, in which we continue vainly to try to cope with the minutiae of the preceding day's task. It is, in other words, an anxiety dream of the occupational sort; and, to the degree that anxiety is a peculiarly human state, it is a peculiarly human kind of dream. . . .

What has made the speaker "overtired" is not simply the gathering of an enormously large crop of apples but the necessity of "cherishing" each one, of lifting it down and not letting it fall, lest it be judged worthless and so lost from the harvest. (We might note that the exact wording is "cherish *in hand*.") The symbolic purport of these lines needs scarcely be made explicit. For apples, substitute any series of things—or persons—with which one is responsibly concerned, each of which must be not merely handled but handled with love. This is the source of the kind of tiredness that is peculiarly human, the kind of tiredness that leads to a troubled, not a dreamless, sleep. . . .

The woodchuck's "long sleep" is of course the dreamless oblivion referred to in Anglo-Saxon diction early in the poem as "winter sleep," i.e., hibernation. If he were there to be asked, the woodchuck would have to say that the night's sleep to which the speaker looks forward is not at all like hibernation, or even the daily sleep of animals. It *is* "just some human sleep," a restless sleep of poor quality. What vitiates it is the anxiety bound up with the responsibilities to which only human beings are subject, the ideals of behavior making them at once less fortunate than animals and—I think Frost would agree—more interesting and important. But . . . the end of the poem leads us to look beyond the time-scope of one harvest season, and even beyond the scope of human life itself, when the endless carrying out of the task under the pressure of altruistic responsibility will be over for good. This wider dimension, transcending mortality, is, I think, alluded to by the pane of ice lifted from the drinking-trough, through which the speaker sees the world as through a glass darkly; it has left "a strangeness on his sight" that cannot be rubbed off. Yet the New Testament promise of a life beyond this, in which we will see face to face, has no part in the meaning of the poem or in Frost's sceptical vision generally. The pane of ice is there, rather, to remind us that the nature of human life, the inescapable imposition of the ideal upon fleshly being, is a mystery, and that here on earth it will remain so.

. . . In "After Apple-Picking," satisfaction in the completion of the task is marred by a weariness that comes from having worked too long under the pressure of the responsibility of cherishing each object.   [1976]

Our final excerpt is from a 1997 book by Robert Faggen, associate professor of literature at Claremont McKenna College. Faggen sees Frost's poetry as, in part, responding to Charles Darwin's theory of evolution. Darwin argued that species evolve through chance variations and not necessarily according to the careful plans of a God who favors humanity. According to Faggen, much of Frost's poetry explores the implications of Darwin's view. More specifically, Faggen believes that in "After Apple-Picking," Frost grants the speaker little power to transcend, control, or even understand his fate.

ROBERT FAGGEN

From *Robert Frost and the Challenge of Darwin*

. . . Unlike Jacob's, this ladder is a human construct that rests and depends on the tree and is left to nature as an artifact of human effort. And the speaker's oncoming dream is not of angels but, rather, of the details of apples and of labor. If anything is retained in the allusion to Jacob, it is the sense of an impending struggle.

. . . [The speaker's] dreams are not of angels or of heaven but of the troubling abundance and waste of apples that are beyond his "picking," expressing the physical "ache" of his foot, his sensuous desire to touch. Moreover, the preponderance of first-person pronouns expresses an ego inspired and burdened by its own desire. . . .

Close examination of nature in its great plurality and in its waste ultimately diminishes the significance of the observer. At once he sees the massive abundance and waste of nature, which overwhelm his own desire. . . .

If man is a laborer, Darwin tells us, then nature is a far greater one. Our "view" is "imperfect." The laborer of "After Apple-Picking" works in a state that is a continual confusion of dream and knowledge, between the human idea of nature and its elusive reality always on the verge of transformation. A consciousness of a limited view and of a larger process of selection to which we are subjected is the darker fruit of our own knowledge. And what are wasted apples for humans who select for beauty and perfection become food for a hibernating woodchuck or further the spread of apple seeds.

The apple tree evokes the loss and displacement of the Fall—the Tree of Knowledge. But it also becomes the dominant metaphor of life and death in the new scripture of Darwin. Darwin's Tree of Life represents both nature's diversity as well as the common descent and destiny of all living creatures including man. In his emphasis on survival no creature or branch is given certain privilege in the hierarchy; no future is certain. It is therefore not surprising that, after considering the apples "as of no worth," the apple picker wonders about the relation of his own "sleep," a metaphor for loss of control and death in our self-consciousness, to that of another creature, "the woodchuck," for whom sleep hibernation is at least protection against the environment. . . .

The apple picker, however, turns to another creature at the end of his labor only in hope of finding a way out of his troubling isolation and fears—and there may be no way out of what he can "describe.". . . *Just* in the final line expresses a diminished view of "*human* sleep," a diminished sense of the labor, knowledge, and aspiration by which our species once thought itself elect. . . .

Frost's poetry invites us to see a human enterprise of labor, struggle, and waste. And this is because we are the products of a blind and wasteful creator.

[1997]

In each Critical Commentaries cluster, we follow the interpretations with questions. These will help you relate the commentaries not only to one another but also to the literary text they analyze.

MAKING COMPARISONS

1. Warren is willing to equate the speaker with the poet, Frost himself. Furthermore, Warren raises the possibility that this poem about apple-picking is also about the writing of poetry. To what extent does Warren's view account for significant details of the poem? How useful for you is his association of the speaker with Frost?

2. Warren, Conder, and Faggen all refer to "man" as they explore the larger relevance of the speaker's situation. Evidently they intend "man" to include women, too. To what extent does their use of the word indeed reflect women's lives as well? In what ways, if any, does their use of "man" seem actually gender-specific?

3. Each commentator sees the poem as expressing a particular view of human life. They differ, though, over how pessimistic the view is. Which interpreter strikes you as summarizing the view most accurately? Support your choice.

We conclude each Critical Commentaries cluster with a set of writing assignments. These give you the opportunity to continue examining the literary text and to keep addressing issues raised by the commentaries on it.

WRITING ABOUT ISSUES

1. Whatever general ideas about human life we draw from Frost's poem, on a literal level it is about apple-picking. What does Frost gain from focusing his poem on this particular form of work? Write an essay in which you address this issue of cause and effect. In your essay, you may refer to associations that people commonly make with apples.

2. At the end of the poem, the speaker wonders if his "sleep" will be like the woodchuck's or "just some human sleep." Which of these two possibilities does the poem seem to support more? Write an essay in which you address this issue. In the course of your analysis, you will need to make specific comparisons between "woodchuck sleep" and "human sleep." Also refer to at least one of the commentaries you have read. It need not be one with which you fully agree.

3. Write an essay recalling an occasion when your engagement in a specific form of labor made you think about a larger issue. What particular details got you thinking in larger terms? To what extent were you left with questions rather than answers?

4. Faggen's commentary touches on the possible role of Darwinism in Frost's poem. Pursue this subject further by finding another article dealing with Darwin's views. Then write an essay in which you explain the extent to which this article helps you understand "After Apple-Picking." If you wish, you may refer to the excerpt from Faggen as well.

A WEB ASSIGNMENT

Visit the Web Assignments section of the *Making Literature Matter* Web site, where you will find a link to poet Amy Lowell's November 7, 1914, *New Republic* review of Frost's book *North of Boston*, which contained "After Apple-Picking." Lowell's review played a key role in establishing Frost's American reputation while he lived in England and after he returned home. Write an essay in which you (1) summarize what Lowell finds interesting or admirable about Frost's poetry and (2) explain the extent to which her ideas about his work help you analyze "After Apple-Picking."

Visit www.bedfordstmartins.com/makinglitmatter

10

Working with
Re-visions

Each chapter of Part Two includes a cluster that features a literary text and one or more "re-visions" of it. No doubt you are familiar with *revision* as a term for the rewriting of a text. Most writing teachers will encourage you to revise your own papers, so that you take each through numerous drafts. Notice, however, that we hyphenate the word. We do so to emphasize that rewriting a text may involve adopting a whole new view of it, rather than just fiddling with a few of its details. In a now-famous 1971 essay, poet Adrienne Rich usefully defines "re-vision" as "the act of looking back, of seeing with fresh eyes, of entering an old text from a new critical direction." Rich calls for her audience to engage in re-vision not only of their own writing but also of others' work. She especially encourages women to critique and transform classic texts that have perpetuated male supremacy. Throughout the centuries, writers have indeed created new versions of earlier literature, for reasons like Rich's and for other reasons, as well.

Actually, no text is entirely original. Deliberately or not, each appropriates elements of previous writing, including plot situations, character types, metaphors, and phrases. A fancy, but useful, term for this derivation is **intertextuality** (the prefix *inter* meaning "between"). When literary scholars do intertextual analysis, they trace how a piece of writing is connected to one or more predecessors. In our "re-vision" clusters, we present cases where the connections are strong, with writers consciously refashioning a certain earlier work.

When you compare multiple forms of a text, inevitably you will consider which version is best. And certainly this issue of evaluation is worth raising. But you have plenty of other things to ponder when you compare versions. Whatever judgments you make of their relative merits, looking at them together can help you better see — and perhaps appreciate — the distinct qualities of each. Also, much room for analysis lies in considering why, how, and with what effects the original text has changed.

A Disgruntled Worker:
Re-Visions of a Raymond Carver Story

RAYMOND CARVER, "The Bath"
RAYMOND CARVER, "A Small, Good Thing"

Here we offer a sample "re-vision" cluster by showing how Raymond Carver rewrote one of his own short stories about a disgruntled worker who harasses a grieving family. The first story we present is Carver's story "The Bath"; the second is his re-vision, "A Small, Good Thing." Carver was an influential practitioner of a kind of fiction that has been called *minimalism*. The style of such fiction is often spare, plain, and cool. The characters may be going through a crisis, but often their dialogue is mundane, packed with references to small everyday details. Although Carver did not especially care for the term *minimalism* himself, it can be applied to "The Bath," which appeared in Carver's 1981 collection *What We Talk about When We Talk about Love* and won *Columbia* magazine's Carlos Fuentes Fiction Award. But Carver then began writing more warmly and expansively, perhaps in part because his personal life had improved. (He had begun a relationship with the poet Tess Gallagher and given up drinking, after a marriage that had been wrecked by his alcoholism.) His change of style is reflected in "A Small, Good Thing," which was published in a 1982 issue of the literary journal *Ploughshares* and then appeared in Carver's 1983 book *Cathedral*. This story was selected for the top prize in the 1983 O. Henry Awards. Carver preferred the second story to the first; when he compiled his retrospective collection *Where I'm Calling From: New and Selected Stories* (1988), he included "A Small, Good Thing" but not "The Bath." Still, he admitted in a 1984 interview that "I've had people tell me that they much prefer 'The Bath.'" Decide whether *you* like one of these stories more, but whatever your judgment, use your comparison of them to analyze in detail how one particular writer changed his text.

BEFORE YOU READ

Recall an occasion when you significantly revised something you had written. What specific changes did you make? Why did you make them? In what respects, if any, do you think you could have improved the final text even more?

RAYMOND CARVER
The Bath

Brought up in the Pacific Northwest in a working-class family, Raymond Carver (1938–1988) began writing in high school and married early. While both he and his young wife worked at low-paying jobs, Carver took college courses and struggled

(Marion Ettlinger.)

to find time to write. In 1958, he studied fiction writing with John Gardner and graduated from what is now the California State University at Humboldt in 1963. He received national recognition in 1967 when a story was included in the Best American Short Stories *annual anthology. Although Carver was a National Endowment for the Arts fellow in poetry in 1971, fiction remained his primary genre, earning him numerous awards and fellowships, including O. Henry awards in 1974, 1975, and 1980. Despite his success as a writer, alcoholism plagued Carver for most of his life until with the help of Alcoholics Anonymous he stopped drinking in 1982, soon after his divorce. His second marriage to the poet and short story writer, Tess Gallagher lasted until his death by cancer, at the height of his fame and influence.*

Saturday afternoon the mother drove to the bakery in the shopping center. After looking through a loose-leaf binder with photographs of cakes taped onto the pages, she ordered chocolate, the child's favorite. The cake she chose was decorated with a spaceship and a launching pad under a sprinkling of white stars. The name SCOTTY would be iced on in green as if it were the name of the spaceship.

The baker listened thoughtfully when the mother told him Scotty would be eight years old. He was an older man, this baker, and he wore a curious apron, a heavy thing with loops that went under his arms and around his back and then crossed in front again where they were tied in a very thick knot. He kept wiping his hands on the front of the apron as he listened to the woman, his wet eyes examining her lips as she studied the samples and talked.

He let her take her time. He was in no hurry.

The mother decided on the spaceship cake, and then she gave the baker her name and her telephone number. The cake would be ready Monday morning, in plenty of time for the party Monday afternoon. This was all the baker was willing to say. No pleasantries, just this small exchange, the barest information, nothing that was not necessary.

Monday morning, the boy was walking to school. He was in the company of another boy, the two boys passing a bag of potato chips back and forth between them. The birthday boy was trying to trick the other boy into telling what he was going to give in the way of a present.   5

At an intersection, without looking, the birthday boy stepped off the curb, and was promptly knocked down by a car. He fell on his side, his head in the gutter, his legs in the road moving as if he were climbing a wall.

The other boy stood holding the potato chips. He was wondering if he should finish the rest or continue on to school.

The birthday boy did not cry. But neither did he wish to talk anymore. He would not answer when the other boy asked what it felt like to be hit by a car. The birthday boy got up and turned back for home, at which time the other boy waved good-bye and headed off for school.

The birthday boy told his mother what had happened. They sat together on the sofa. She held his hands in her lap. This is what she was doing when the boy pulled his hands away and lay down on his back.

Of course, the birthday party never happened. The birthday boy was in the hospital instead. The mother sat by the bed. She was waiting for the boy to wake up. The father hurried over from his office. He sat next to the mother. So now the both of them waited for the boy to wake up. They waited for hours, and then the father went home to take a bath.   10

The man drove home from the hospital. He drove the streets faster than he should. It had been a good life till now. There had been work, fatherhood, family. The man had been lucky and happy. But fear made him want a bath.

He pulled into the driveway. He sat in the car trying to make his legs work. The child had been hit by a car and he was in the hospital, but he was going to be all right. The man got out of the car and went up to the door. The dog was barking and the telephone was ringing. It kept ringing while the man unlocked the door and felt the wall for the light switch.

He picked up the receiver. He said, "I just got in the door!"

"There's a cake that wasn't picked up."

This is what the voice on the other end said.   15

"What are you saying?" the father said.

"The cake," the voice said. "Sixteen dollars."

The husband held the receiver against his ear, trying to understand. He said, "I don't know anything about it."

"Don't hand me that," the voice said.

The husband hung up the telephone. He went into the kitchen and poured   20
himself some whiskey. He called the hospital.

The child's condition remained the same.

While the water ran into the tub, the man lathered his face and shaved. He was in the tub when he heard the telephone again. He got himself out and hurried through the house, saying, "Stupid, stupid," because he wouldn't be doing this if he'd stayed where he was in the hospital. He picked up the receiver and shouted, "Hello!"

The voice said, "It's ready."

The father got back to the hospital after midnight. The wife was sitting in the chair by the bed. She looked up at the husband and then she looked back at the child. From an apparatus over the bed hung a bottle with a tube running from the bottle to the child.

"What's this?" the father said.   25

"Glucose," the mother said.

The husband put his hand to the back of the woman's head.

"He's going to wake up," the man said.

"I know," the woman said.

In a little while the man said, "Go home and let me take over."   30

She shook her head. "No," she said.

"Really," he said. "Go home for a while. You don't have to worry. He's sleeping, is all."

A nurse pushed open the door. She nodded to them as she went to the bed. She took the left arm out from under the covers and put her fingers on the wrist. She put the arm back under the covers and wrote on the clipboard attached to the bed.

"How is he?" the mother said.

"Stable," the nurse said. Then she said, "Doctor will be in again shortly."   35

"I was saying maybe she'd want to go home and get a little rest," the man said. "After the doctor comes."

"She could do that," the nurse said.

The woman said, "We'll see what the doctor says." She brought her hand up to her eyes and leaned her head forward.

The nurse said, "Of course."

◆   ◆   ◆

The father gazed at his son, the small chest inflating and deflating under the   40
covers. He felt more fear now. He began shaking his head. He talked to himself
like this. The child is fine. Instead of sleeping at home, he's doing it here. Sleep is
the same wherever you do it.

The doctor came in. He shook hands with the man. The woman got up from
the chair.
"Ann," the doctor said and nodded. The doctor said, "Let's just see how he's
doing." He moved to the bed and touched the boy's wrist. He peeled back an eyelid and then the other. He turned back the covers and listened to the heart. He
pressed his fingers here and there on the body. He went to the end of the bed and
studied the chart. He noted the time, scribbled on the chart, and then he considered the mother and the father.
This doctor was a handsome man. His skin was moist and tan. He wore a
three-piece suit, a vivid tie, and on his shirt were cufflinks.
The mother was talking to herself like this. He has just come from somewhere with an audience. They gave him a special medal.
The doctor said, "Nothing to shout about, but nothing to worry about. He   45
should wake up pretty soon." The doctor looked at the boy again. "We'll know
more after the tests are in."
"Oh, no," the mother said.
The doctor said, "Sometimes you see this."
The father said, "You wouldn't call this a coma, then?"
The father waited and looked at the doctor.
"No, I don't want to call it that," the doctor said. "He's sleeping. It's restora-   50
tive. The body is doing what it has to do."
"It's a coma," the mother said. "A kind of coma."
The doctor said, "I wouldn't call it that."
He took the woman's hands and patted them. He shook hands with the
husband.

The woman put her fingers on the child's forehead and kept them there for a
while. "At least he doesn't have a fever," she said. Then she said, "I don't know.
Feel his head."
The man put his fingers on the boy's forehead. The man said, "I think he's   55
supposed to feel this way."
The woman stood there awhile longer, working her lip with her teeth. Then
she moved to her chair and sat down.
The husband sat in the chair beside her. He wanted to say something else.
But there was no saying what it should be. He took her hand and put it in his lap.
This made him feel better. It made him feel he was saying something. They sat
like that for a while, watching the boy, not talking. From time to time he
squeezed her hand until she took it away.
"I've been praying," she said.
"Me too," the father said. "I've been praying too."

◆   ◆   ◆

A nurse came back in and checked the flow from the bottle.   60

A doctor came in and said what his name was. This doctor was wearing loafers.

"We're going to take him downstairs for more pictures," he said. "And we want to do a scan."

"A scan?" the mother said. She stood between this new doctor and the bed.

"It's nothing," he said.

"My God," she said.   65

Two orderlies came in. They wheeled a thing like a bed. They unhooked the boy from the tube and slid him over onto the thing with wheels.

It was after sunup when they brought the birthday boy back out. The mother and father followed the orderlies into the elevator and up to the room. Once more the parents took up their places next to the bed.

They waited all day. The boy did not wake up. The doctor came again and examined the boy again and left after saying the same things again. Nurses came in. Doctors came in. A technician came in and took blood.

"I don't understand this," the mother said to the technician.

"Doctor's orders," the technician said.   70

The mother went to the window and looked out at the parking lot. Cars with their lights on were driving in and out. She stood at the window with her hands on the sill. She was talking to herself like this. We're into something now, something hard.

She was afraid.

She saw a car stop and a woman in a long coat get into it. She made believe she was that woman. She made believe she was driving away from here to some-place else.

The doctor came in. He looked tanned and healthier than ever. He went to the bed and examined the boy. He said, "His signs are fine. Everything's good."

The mother said, "But he's sleeping."   75

"Yes," the doctor said.

The husband said, "She's tired. She's starved."

The doctor said, "She should rest. She should eat. Ann," the doctor said.

"Thank you," the husband said.

He shook hands with the doctor and the doctor patted their shoulders   80 and left.

"I suppose one of us should go home and check on things," the man said. "The dog needs to be fed."

"Call the neighbors," the wife said. "Someone will feed him if you ask them to."

She tried to think who. She closed her eyes and tried to think anything at all. After a time she said, "Maybe I'll do it. Maybe if I'm not here watching, he'll wake up. Maybe it's because I'm watching that he won't."

"That could be it," the husband said.

"I'll go home and take a bath and put on something clean," the woman said.   85

"I think you should do that," the man said.

She picked up her purse. He helped her into her coat. She moved to the door, and looked back. She looked at the child, and then she looked at the father. The husband nodded and smiled.

She went past the nurses' station and down to the end of the corridor, where she turned and saw a little waiting room, a family in there, all sitting in wicker chairs, a man in a khaki shirt, a baseball cap pushed back on his head, a large woman wearing a housedress, slippers, a girl in jeans, hair in dozens of kinky braids, the table littered with flimsy wrappers and styrofoam and coffee sticks and packets of salt and pepper.

"Nelson," the woman said. "Is it about Nelson?"

The woman's eyes widened.   90

"Tell me now, lady," the woman said. "Is it about Nelson?"

The woman was trying to get up from her chair. But the man had his hand closed over her arm.

"Here, here," the man said.

"I'm sorry," the mother said. "I'm looking for the elevator. My son is in the hospital. I can't find the elevator."

"Elevator is down that way," the man said, and he aimed a finger in the right   95
direction.

"My son was hit by a car," the mother said. "But he's going to be all right. He's in shock now, but it might be some kind of coma too. That's what worries us, the coma part, I'm going out for a little while. Maybe I'll take a bath. But my husband is with him. He's watching. There's a chance everything will change when I'm gone. My name is Ann Weiss."

The man shifted in his chair. He shook his head.

He said, "Our Nelson."

She pulled into the driveway. The dog ran out from behind the house. He ran in circles on the grass. She closed her eyes and leaned her head against the wheel. She listened to the ticking of the engine.

She got out of the car and went to the door. She turned on lights and put on   100
water for tea. She opened a can and fed the dog. She sat down on the sofa with her tea.

The telephone rang.

"Yes!" she said. "Hello!" she said.

"Mrs. Weiss," a man's voice said.

"Yes," she said. "This is Mrs. Weiss. Is it about Scotty?" she said.

"Scotty," the voice said. "It is about Scotty," the voice said. "It has to do with   105
Scotty, yes."   [1981]

THINKING ABOUT THE TEXT

1. Why do you think Carver called this story "The Bath"? What other possible titles can you imagine?

2. How would you describe the style of this story? In what ways does it seem minimalist, according to whatever you associate with the term? Refer to specific passages.

3. This story features limited use of names. For example, only at the beginning and end do we get the child's name, Scotty. Although we learn that the mother's name is Ann Weiss, most of the time she is referred to simply as "the mother," just as other characters are called "the father," "the doctor," and "the baker." What is the effect of this stylistic device? What is the effect when Carver breaks with it by giving us the name Nelson?

4. Although Carver does not explicitly identify the mysterious caller, he encourages us to believe that it is the baker. What is the effect of Carver's not identifying him more clearly? Why do you think the baker calls?

5. The last sentence of this story is "It has to do with Scotty, yes." To what extent is this story indeed about Scotty? Whom or what else does it seem about?

RAYMOND CARVER

A *Small, Good Thing*

Saturday afternoon she drove to the bakery in the shopping center. After looking through a loose-leaf binder with photographs of cakes taped onto the pages, she ordered chocolate, the child's favorite. The cake she chose was decorated with a space ship and launching pad under a sprinkling of white stars, and a planet made of red frosting at the other end. His name, SCOTTY, would be in green letters beneath the planet. The baker, who was an older man with a thick neck, listened without saying anything when she told him the child would be eight years old next Monday. The baker wore a white apron that looked like a smock. Straps cut under his arms, went around in back and then to the front again, where they were secured under his heavy waist. He wiped his hands on his apron as he listened to her. He kept his eyes down on the photographs and let her talk. He let her take her time. He'd just come to work and he'd be there all night, baking, and he was in no real hurry.

She gave the baker her name, Ann Weiss, and her telephone number. The cake would be ready on Monday morning, just out of the oven, in plenty of time for the child's party that afternoon. The baker was not jolly. There were no pleasantries between them, just the minimum exchange of words, the necessary information. He made her feel uncomfortable, and she didn't like that. While he was bent over the counter with the pencil in his hand, she studied his coarse features and wondered if he'd ever done anything else with his life besides be a baker. She was a mother and thirty-three years old, and it seemed to her that everyone, especially someone the baker's age — a man old enough to be her father — must have children who'd gone through this special time of cakes and birthday parties. There must be that between them, she thought. But he was abrupt with her — not rude, just abrupt. She gave up trying to make friends with him. She looked into the back of the bakery and could see a long, heavy wooden table with aluminum pie pans stacked at one end; and beside the table a metal container filled with empty racks. There was an enormous oven. A radio was playing country-Western music.

The baker finished printing the information on the special order card and closed up the binder. He looked at her and said, "Monday morning." She thanked him and drove home.

On Monday morning, the birthday boy was walking to school with another boy. They were passing a bag of potato chips back and forth and the birthday boy was trying to find out what his friend intended to give him for his birthday that afternoon. Without looking, the birthday boy stepped off the curb at an intersection and was immediately knocked down by a car. He fell on his side with his head in the gutter and his legs out in the road. His eyes were closed, but his legs moved back and forth as if he were trying to climb over something. His friend dropped the potato chips and started to cry. The car had gone a hundred feet or so and stopped in the middle of the road. The man in the driver's seat looked back over his shoulder. He waited until the boy got unsteadily to his feet. The boy wobbled a little. He looked dazed, but okay. The driver put the car into gear and drove away.

The birthday boy didn't cry, but he didn't have anything to say about any-   5
thing either. He wouldn't answer when his friend asked him what it felt like to be hit by a car. He walked home, and his friend went on to school. But after the birthday boy was inside his house and was telling his mother about it—she sitting beside him on the sofa, holding his hands in her lap, saying, "Scotty, honey, are you sure you feel all right, baby?" thinking she would call the doctor anyway—he suddenly lay back on the sofa, closed his eyes, and went limp. When she couldn't wake him up, she hurried to the telephone and called her husband at work. Howard told her to remain calm, remain calm, and then he called an ambulance for the child and left for the hospital himself.

Of course, the birthday party was canceled. The child was in the hospital with a mild concussion and suffering from shock. There'd been vomiting, and his lungs had taken in fluid which needed pumping out that afternoon. Now he simply seemed to be in a very deep sleep—but no coma, Dr. Francis had emphasized, no coma, when he saw the alarm in the parents' eyes. At eleven o'clock that night, when the boy seemed to be resting comfortably enough after the many X-rays and the lab work, and it was just a matter of his waking up and coming around, Howard left the hospital. He and Ann had been at the hospital with the child since that afternoon, and he was going home for a short while to bathe and change clothes. "I'll be back in an hour," he said. She nodded. "It's fine," she said. "I'll be right here." He kissed her on the forehead, and they touched hands. She sat in the chair beside the bed and looked at the child. She was waiting for him to wake up and be all right. Then she could begin to relax.

Howard drove home from the hospital. He took the wet, dark streets very fast, then caught himself and slowed down. Until now, his life had gone smoothly and to his satisfaction — college, marriage, another year of college for the advanced degree in business, a junior partnership in an investment firm. Fatherhood. He was happy and, so far, lucky — he knew that. His parents were still living, his brothers and his sister were established, his friends from college had gone out to take their places in the world. So far, he had kept away from any real harm, from those forces he knew existed and that could cripple or bring down a man if the luck went bad, if things suddenly turned. He pulled into the driveway and parked. His left leg began to tremble. He sat in the car for a minute and tried to deal with the present situation in a rational manner. Scotty had been hit by a car and was in the hospital, but he was going to be all right. Howard closed his eyes and ran his hand over his face. He got out of the car and went up to the front door. The dog was barking inside the house. The telephone rang and rang while he unlocked the door and fumbled for the light switch. He shouldn't have left the hospital, he shouldn't have. "Goddamn it!" he said. He picked up the receiver and said, "I just walked in the door!"

"There's a cake here that wasn't picked up," the voice on the other end of the line said.

"What are you saying?" Howard asked.

"A cake," the voice said. "A sixteen-dollar cake."   10

Howard held the receiver against his ear, trying to understand. "I don't know anything about a cake," he said. "Jesus, what are you talking about?"

"Don't hand me that," the voice said.

Howard hung up the telephone. He went into the kitchen and poured himself some whiskey. He called the hospital. But the child's condition remained the same; he was still sleeping and nothing had changed there. While water poured into the tub, Howard lathered his face and shaved. He'd just stretched out in the tub and closed his eyes when the telephone rang again. He hauled himself out, grabbed a towel, and hurried through the house, saying, "Stupid, stupid," for having left the hospital. But when he picked up the receiver and shouted, "Hello!" there was no sound at the other end of the line. Then the caller hung up.

He arrived back at the hospital a little after midnight. Ann still sat in the chair beside the bed. She looked up at Howard, and then she looked back at the child. The child's eyes stayed closed, the head was still wrapped in bandages. His breathing was quiet and regular. From an apparatus over the bed hung a bottle of glucose with a tube running from the bottle to the boy's arm.

"How is he?" Howard said. "What's all this?" waving at the glucose and the   15
tube.

"Dr. Francis's orders," she said. "He needs nourishment. He needs to keep up his strength. Why doesn't he wake up, Howard? I don't understand, if he's all right."

Howard put his hand against the back of her head. He ran his fingers through her hair. "He's going to be all right. He'll wake up in a little while. Dr. Francis knows what's what."

After a time, he said, "Maybe you should go home and get some rest. I'll stay here. Just don't put up with this creep who keeps calling. Hang up right away."

"Who's calling?" she asked.

"I don't know who, just somebody with nothing better to do than call up   20
people. You go on now."

She shook her head. "No," she said, "I'm fine."

"Really," he said. "Go home for a while, and then come back and spell me in
the morning. It'll be all right. What did Dr. Francis say? He said Scotty's going to
be all right. We don't have to worry. He's just sleeping now, that's all."

A nurse pushed the door open. She nodded at them as she went to the bedside. She took the left arm out from under the covers and put her fingers on the
wrist, found the pulse, then consulted her watch. In a little while, she put the arm
back under the covers and moved to the foot of the bed, where she wrote something on a clipboard attached to the bed.

"How is he?" Ann said. Howard's hand was a weight on her shoulder. She
was aware of the pressure from his fingers.

"He's stable," the nurse said. Then she said, "Doctor will be in again shortly.   25
Doctor's back in the hospital. He's making rounds right now."

"I was saying maybe she'd want to go home and get a little rest," Howard said.
"After the doctor comes," he said.

"She could do that," the nurse said. "I think you should both feel free to do
that, if you wish." The nurse was a big Scandinavian woman with blond hair.
There was the trace of an accent in her speech.

"We'll see what the doctor says," Ann said. "I want to talk to the doctor. I
don't think he should keep sleeping like this. I don't think that's a good sign." She
brought her hand up to her eyes and let her head come forward a little. Howard's
grip tightened on her shoulder, and then his hand moved up to her neck, where
his fingers began to knead the muscles there.

"Dr. Francis will be here in a few minutes," the nurse said. Then she left the
room.

Howard gazed at his son for a time, the small chest quietly rising and falling   30
under the covers. For the first time since the terrible minutes after Ann's telephone call to him at his office, he felt a genuine fear starting in his limbs. He
began shaking his head. Scotty was fine, but instead of sleeping at home in his
own bed, he was in a hospital bed with bandages around his head and a tube in
his arm. But this help was what he needed right now.

Dr. Francis came in and shook hands with Howard, though they'd just seen
each other a few hours before. Ann got up from the chair. "Doctor?"

"Ann," he said and nodded. "Let's just first see how he's doing," the doctor
said. He moved to the side of the bed and took the boy's pulse. He peeled back
one eyelid and then the other. Howard and Ann stood beside the doctor and
watched. Then the doctor turned back the covers and listened to the boy's heart
and lungs with his stethoscope. He pressed his fingers here and there on the
abdomen. When he was finished, he went to the end of the bed and studied the
chart. He noted the time, scribbled something on the chart, and then looked at
Howard and Ann.

"Doctor, how is he?" Howard said. "What's the matter with him exactly?"

"Why doesn't he wake up?" Ann said.

The doctor was a handsome, big-shouldered man with a tanned face. He   35
wore a three-piece blue suit, a striped tie, and ivory cufflinks. His gray hair was

combed along the sides of his head, and he looked as if he had just come from a concert. "He's all right," the doctor said. "Nothing to shout about, he could be better, I think. But he's all right. Still, I wish he'd wake up. He should wake up pretty soon." The doctor looked at the boy again. "We'll know some more in a couple of hours, after the results of a few more tests are in. But he's all right, believe me, except for the hairline fracture of the skull. He does have that."

"Oh, no," Ann said.

"And a bit of a concussion, as I said before. Of course, you know he's in shock," the doctor said. "Sometimes you see this in shock cases. This sleeping."

"But he's out of any real danger?" Howard said. "You said before he's not in a coma. You wouldn't call this a coma, then — would you, doctor?" Howard waited. He looked at the doctor.

"No, I don't want to call it a coma," the doctor said and glanced over at the boy once more. "He's just in a very deep sleep. It's a restorative measure the body is taking on its own. He's out of any real danger, I'd say that for certain, yes. But we'll know more when he wakes up and the other tests are in," the doctor said.

"It's a coma," Ann said. "Of sorts." 40

"It's not a coma yet, not exactly," the doctor said. "I wouldn't want to call it coma. Not yet, anyway. He's suffered shock. In shock cases, this kind of reaction is common enough; it's a temporary reaction to bodily trauma. Coma. Well, coma is a deep, prolonged unconsciousness, something that could go on for days, or weeks even. Scotty's not in that area, not as far as we can tell. I'm certain his condition will show improvement by morning. I'm betting that it will. We'll know more when he wakes up, which shouldn't be long now. Of course, you may do as you like, stay here or go home for a time. But by all means feel free to leave the hospital for a while if you want. This is not easy, I know." The doctor gazed at the boy again, watching him, and then he turned to Ann and said, "You try not to worry, little mother. Believe me, we're doing all that can be done. It's just a question of a little more time now." He nodded at her, shook hands with Howard again, and then he left the room.

Ann put her hand over the child's forehead. "At least he doesn't have a fever," she said. Then she said, "My God, he feels so cold, though. Howard? Is he supposed to feel like this? Feel his head."

Howard touched the child's temples. His own breathing had slowed. "I think he's supposed to feel this way right now," he said. "He's in shock, remember? That's what the doctor said. The doctor was just in here. He would have said something if Scotty wasn't okay."

Ann stood there a while longer, working her lip with her teeth. Then she moved over to her chair and sat down.

Howard sat in the chair next to her chair. They looked at each other. He 45 wanted to say something else and reassure her, but he was afraid, too. He took her hand and put it in his lap, and this made him feel better, her hand being there. He picked up her hand and squeezed it. Then he just held her hand. They sat like that for a while, watching the boy and not talking. From time to time, he squeezed her hand. Finally, she took her hand away.

"I've been praying," she said.

He nodded.

She said, "I almost thought I'd forgotten how, but it came back to me. All I had to do was close my eyes and say, 'Please God, help us — help Scotty,' and then the rest was easy. The words were right there. Maybe if you prayed, too," she said to him.

"I've already prayed," he said. "I prayed this afternoon — yesterday afternoon, I mean — after you called, while I was driving to the hospital. I've been praying," he said.

"That's good," she said. For the first time, she felt they were together in it,   50
this trouble. She realized with a start that, until now, it had only been happening to her and to Scotty. She hadn't let Howard into it, though he was there and needed all along. She felt glad to be his wife.

The same nurse came in and took the boy's pulse again and checked the flow from the bottle hanging above the bed.

In an hour, another doctor came in. He said his name was Parsons, from Radiology. He had a bushy mustache. He was wearing loafers, a Western shirt, and a pair of jeans.

"We're going to take him downstairs for more pictures," he told them. "We need to do some more pictures, and we want to do a scan."

"What's that?" Ann said. "A scan?" She stood between this new doctor and the bed. "I thought you'd already taken all your X-rays."

"I'm afraid we need some more," he said. "Nothing to be alarmed about. We   55
just need some more pictures, and we want to do a brain scan on him."

"My God," Ann said.

"It's perfectly normal procedure in cases like this," this new doctor said. "We just need to find out for sure why he isn't back awake yet. It's normal medical procedure, and nothing to be alarmed about. We'll be taking him down in a few minutes," this doctor said.

In a little while, two orderlies came into the room with a gurney. They were black-haired, dark-complexioned men in white uniforms, and they said a few words to each other in a foreign tongue as they unhooked the boy from the tube and moved him from his bed to the gurney. Then they wheeled him from the room. Howard and Ann got on the same elevator. Ann gazed at the child. She closed her eyes as the elevator began its descent. The orderlies stood at either end of the gurney without saying anything, though once one of the men made a comment to the other in their own language, and the other man nodded slowly in response.

Later that morning, just as the sun was beginning to lighten the windows in the waiting room outside the X-ray department, they brought the boy out and moved him back up to his room. Howard and Ann rode up on the elevator with him once more, and once more they took up their places beside the bed.

They waited all day, but still the boy did not wake up. Occasionally, one of   60
them would leave the room to go downstairs to the cafeteria to drink coffee and then, as if suddenly remembering and feeling guilty, get up from the table and hurry back to the room. Dr. Francis came again that afternoon and examined the boy once more and then left after telling them he was coming along and could

wake up at any minute now. Nurses, different nurses from the night before, came in from time to time. Then a young woman from the lab knocked and entered the room. She wore white slacks and a white blouse and carried a little tray of things which she put on the stand beside the bed. Without a word to them, she took blood from the boy's arm. Howard closed his eyes as the woman found the right place on the boy's arm and pushed the needle in.

"I don't understand this," Ann said to the woman.

"Doctor's orders," the young woman said. "I do what I'm told. They say draw that one, I draw. What's wrong with him, anyway?" she said. "He's a sweetie."

"He was hit by a car," Howard said. "A hit-and-run."

The young woman shook her head and looked again at the boy. Then she took her tray and left the room.

"Why won't he wake up?" Ann said. "Howard? I want some answers from these people."

Howard didn't say anything. He sat down again in the chair and crossed one leg over the other. He rubbed his face. He looked at his son and then he settled back in the chair, closed his eyes, and went to sleep.

Ann walked to the window and looked out at the parking lot. It was night, and cars were driving into and out of the parking lot with their lights on. She stood at the window with her hands gripping the sill, and knew in her heart that they were into something now, something hard. She was afraid, and her teeth began to chatter until she tightened her jaws. She saw a big car stop in front of the hospital and someone, a woman in a long coat, get into the car. She wished she were that woman and somebody, anybody, was driving her away from here to somewhere else, a place where she would find Scotty waiting for her when she stepped out of the car, ready to say *Mom* and let her gather him in her arms.

In a little while, Howard woke up. He looked at the boy again. Then he got up from the chair, stretched, and went over to stand beside her at the window. They both stared out at the parking lot. They didn't say anything. But they seemed to feel each other's insides now, as though the worry had made them transparent in a perfectly natural way.

The door opened and Dr. Francis came in. He was wearing a different suit and tie this time. His gray hair was combed along the sides of his head, and he looked as if he had just shaved. He went straight to the bed and examined the boy. "He ought to have come around by now. There's just no good reason for this," he said. "But I can tell you we're all convinced he's out of any danger. We'll just feel better when he wakes up. There's no reason, absolutely none, why he shouldn't come around. Very soon. Oh, he'll have himself a dilly of a headache when he does, you can count on that. But all of his signs are fine. They're as normal as can be."

"It is a coma, then?" Ann said.

The doctor rubbed his smooth cheek. "We'll call it that for the time being, until he wakes up. But you must be worn out. This is hard. I know this is hard. Feel free to go out for a bite," he said. "It would do you good. I'll put a nurse in here while you're gone if you'll feel better about going. Go and have yourselves something to eat."

"I couldn't eat anything," Ann said.

"Do what you need to do, of course," the doctor said. "Anyway, I wanted to tell you that all the signs are good, the tests are negative, nothing showed up at all, and just as soon as he wakes up he'll be over the hill."

"Thank you, doctor," Howard said. He shook hands with the doctor again. The doctor patted Howard's shoulder and went out.

"I suppose one of us should go home and check on things," Howard said.   75
"Slug needs to be fed, for one thing."

"Call one of the neighbors," Ann said. "Call the Morgans. Anyone will feed a dog if you ask them to."

"All right," Howard said. After a while, he said, "Honey, why don't you do it? Why don't you go home and check on things, and then come back? It'll do you good. I'll be right here with him. Seriously," he said. "We need to keep up our strength on this. We'll want to be here for a while even after he wakes up."

"Why don't *you* go?" she said. "Feed Slug. Feed yourself."

"I already went," he said. "I was gone for exactly an hour and fifteen minutes. You go home for an hour and freshen up. Then come back."

She tried to think about it, but she was too tired. She closed her eyes and   80
tried to think about it again. After a time, she said, "Maybe I will go home for a few minutes. Maybe if I'm not just sitting right here watching him every second, he'll wake up and be all right. You know? Maybe he'll wake up if I'm not here. I'll go home and take a bath and put on clean clothes. I'll feed Slug. Then I'll come back."

"I'll be right here," he said. "You go on home, honey. I'll keep an eye on things here." His eyes were bloodshot and small, as if he'd been drinking for a long time. His clothes were rumpled. His beard had come out again. She touched his face; and then she took her hand back. She understood he wanted to be by himself for a while, not have to talk or share his worry for a time. She picked her purse up from the nightstand, and he helped her into her coat.

"I won't be gone long," she said.

"Just sit and rest for a little while when you get home," he said. "Eat something. Take a bath. After you get out of the bath, just sit for a while and rest. It'll do you a world of good, you'll see. Then come back," he said. "Let's try not to worry. You heard what Dr. Francis said."

She stood in her coat for a minute trying to recall the doctor's exact words, looking for any nuances, any hint of something behind his words other than what he had said. She tried to remember if his expression had changed any when he bent over to examine the child. She remembered the way his features had composed themselves as he rolled back the child's eyelids and then listened to his breathing.

She went to the door, where she turned and looked back. She looked at the   85
child, and then she looked at the father. Howard nodded. She stepped out of the room and pulled the door closed behind her.

She went past the nurses' station and down to the end of the corridor, looking for the elevator. At the end of the corridor, she turned to her right and entered a little waiting room where a Negro family sat in wicker chairs. There was a middle-aged man in a khaki shirt and pants, a baseball cap pushed back on his head. A large woman wearing a housedress and slippers was slumped in one of the chairs. A teenaged girl in jeans, hair done in dozens of little braids, lay stretched out in one of the chairs smoking a cigarette, her legs crossed at the ankles. The family swung their eyes to Ann as she entered the room. The little table was littered with hamburger wrappers and Styrofoam cups.

"Franklin," the large woman said as she roused herself. "Is it about Franklin?" Her eyes widened. "Tell me now, lady," the woman said. "Is it about Franklin?" She was trying to rise from her chair, but the man had closed his hand over her arm.

"Here, here," he said. "Evelyn."

"I'm sorry," Ann said. "I'm looking for the elevator. My son is in the hospital, and now I can't find the elevator."

"Elevator is down that way, turn left," the man said as he aimed a finger.   90

The girl drew on her cigarette and stared at Ann. Her eyes were narrowed to slits, and her broad lips parted slowly as she let the smoke escape. The Negro woman let her head fall on her shoulder and looked away from Ann, no longer interested.

"My son was hit by a car," Ann said to the man. She seemed to need to explain herself. "He has a concussion and a little skull fracture, but he's going to be all right. He's in shock now, but it might be some kind of coma, too. That's what really worries us, the coma part. I'm going out for a little while, but my husband is with him. Maybe he'll wake up while I'm gone."

"That's too bad," the man said and shifted in the chair. He shook his head. He looked down at the table, and then he looked back at Ann. She was still standing there. He said, "Our Franklin, he's on the operating table. Somebody cut him. Tried to kill him. There was a fight where he was at. At this party. They say he was just standing and watching. Not bothering nobody. But that don't mean nothing these days. Now he's on the operating table. We're just hoping and praying, that's all we can do now." He gazed at her steadily.

Ann looked at the girl again, who was still watching her, and at the older woman, who kept her head down, but whose eyes were now closed. Ann saw the lips moving silently, making words. She had an urge to ask what those words were. She wanted to talk more with these people who were in the same kind of waiting she was in. She was afraid, and they were afraid. They had that in common. She would have liked to have said something else about the accident, told them more about Scotty, that it had happened on the day of his birthday, Monday, and that he was still unconscious. Yet she didn't know how to begin. She stood looking at them without saying anything more.

She went down the corridor the man had indicated and found the elevator.   95
She waited a minute in front of the closed doors, still wondering if she was doing the right thing. Then she put out her finger and touched the button.

She pulled into the driveway and cut the engine. She closed her eyes and leaned her head against the wheel for a minute. She listened to the ticking sounds the engine made as it began to cool. Then she got out of the car. She could hear the dog barking inside the house. She went to the front door, which was unlocked. She went inside and turned on lights and put on a kettle of water for tea. She opened some dogfood and fed Slug on the back porch. The dog ate in hungry little smacks. It kept running into the kitchen to see that she was going to stay. As she sat down on the sofa with her tea, the telephone rang.

"Yes!" she said as she answered. "Hello!"

"Mrs. Weiss," a man's voice said. It was five o'clock in the morning, and she thought she could hear machinery or equipment of some kind in the background.

"Yes, yes! What is it?" she said. "This is Mrs. Weiss. This is she. What is it, please?" She listened to whatever it was in the background. "Is it Scotty, for Christ's sake?"

"Scotty," the man's voice said. "It's about Scotty, yes. It has to do with Scotty, that problem. Have you forgotten about Scotty?" the man said. Then he hung up.   100

She dialed the hospital's number and asked for the third floor. She demanded information about her son from the nurse who answered the telephone. Then she asked to speak to her husband. It was, she said, an emergency.

She waited, turning the telephone cord in her fingers. She closed her eyes and felt sick at her stomach. She would have to make herself eat. Slug came in from the back porch and lay down near her feet. He wagged his tail. She pulled at his ear while he licked her fingers. Howard was on the line.

"Somebody just called here," she said. "She twisted the telephone cord. "He said it was about Scotty," she cried.

"Scotty's fine," Howard told her. "I mean, he's still sleeping. There's been no change. The nurse has been in twice since you've been gone. A nurse or else a doctor. He's all right."

"This man called. He said it was about Scotty," she told him.   105

"Honey, you rest for a little while, you need the rest. It must be that same caller I had. Just forget it. Come back down here after you've rested. Then we'll have breakfast or something."

"Breakfast," she said. "I don't want any breakfast."

"You know what I mean," he said. "Juice, something. I don't know. I don't know anything, Ann. Jesus, I'm not hungry, either. Ann, it's hard to talk now. I'm standing here at the desk. Dr. Francis is coming again at eight o'clock this morning. He's going to have something to tell us then, something more definite. That's what one of the nurses said. She didn't know any more than that. Ann? Honey, maybe we'll know something more then. At eight o'clock. Come back here before eight. Meanwhile, I'm right here and Scotty's all right. He's still the same," he added.

"I was drinking a cup of tea," she said, "when the telephone rang. They said it was about Scotty. There was a noise in the background. Was there a noise in the background on that call you had, Howard?"

"I don't remember," he said. "Maybe the driver of the car, maybe he's a psy-   110
chopath and found out about Scotty somehow. But I'm here with him. Just rest like you were going to do. Take a bath and come back by seven or so, and we'll talk to the doctor together when he gets here. It's going to be all right, honey. I'm here, and there are doctors and nurses around. They say his condition is stable."

"I'm scared to death," she said.

She ran water, undressed, and got into the tub. She washed and dried quickly, not taking the time to wash her hair. She put on clean underwear, wool slacks, and a sweater. She went into the living room, where the dog looked up at her and let its tail thump once against the floor. It was just starting to get light outside when she went out to the car.

She drove into the parking lot of the hospital and found a space close to the front door. She felt she was in some obscure way responsible for what had happened to the child. She let her thoughts move to the Negro family. She remembered the name Franklin and the table that was covered with hamburger papers, and the teenaged girl staring at her as she drew on her cigarette. "Don't have children," she told the girl's image as she entered the front door of the hospital. "For God's sake, don't."

She took the elevator up to the third floor with two nurses who were just going on duty. It was Wednesday morning, a few minutes before seven. There was a page for a Dr. Madison as the elevator doors slid open on the third floor. She got off behind the nurses, who turned in the other direction and continued the conversation she had interrupted when she'd gotten into the elevator. She walked down the corridor to the little alcove where the Negro family had been waiting. They were gone now, but the chairs were scattered in such a way that it looked as if people had just jumped up from them the minute before. The tabletop was cluttered with the same cups and papers, the ashtray was filled with cigarette butts.

She stopped at the nurses' station. A nurse was standing behind the counter, 115 brushing her hair and yawning.

"There was a Negro boy in surgery last night," Ann said. "Franklin was his name. His family was in the waiting room. I'd like to inquire about his condition."

A nurse who was sitting at a desk behind the counter looked up from a chart in front of her. The telephone buzzed and she picked up the receiver, but she kept her eyes on Ann.

"He passed away," said the nurse at the counter. The nurse held the hairbrush and kept looking at her. "Are you a friend of the family or what?"

"I met the family last night," Ann said. "My own son is in the hospital. I guess he's in shock. We don't know for sure what's wrong. I just wondered about Franklin, that's all. Thank you." She moved down the corridor. Elevator doors the same color as the walls slid open and a gaunt, bald man in white pants and white canvas shoes pulled a heavy cart off the elevator. She hadn't noticed these doors last night. The man wheeled the cart out into the corridor and stopped in front of the room nearest the elevator and consulted a clipboard. Then he reached down and slid a tray out of the cart. He rapped lightly on the door and entered the room. She could smell the unpleasant odors of warm food as she passed the cart. She hurried on without looking at any of the nurses and pushed open the door to the child's room.

Howard was standing at the window with his hands behind his back. He 120 turned around as she came in.

"How is he?" she said. She went over to the bed. She dropped her purse on the floor beside the nightstand. It seemed to her she had been gone a long time. She touched the child's face. "Howard?"

"Dr. Francis was here a little while ago," Howard said. She looked at him closely and thought his shoulders were bunched a little.

"I thought he wasn't coming until eight o'clock this morning," she said quickly.

"There was another doctor with him. A neurologist."

"A neurologist," she said.   125

Howard nodded. His shoulders were bunching, she could see that. "What'd they say, Howard? For Christ's sake, what'd they say? What is it?"

"They said they're going to take him down and run more tests on him, Ann. They think they're going to operate, honey. Honey, they *are* going to operate. They can't figure out why he won't wake up. It's more than just shock or concussion, they know that much now. It's in his skull, the fracture, it has something, something to do with that, they think. So they're going to operate. I tried to call you, but I guess you'd already left the house."

"Oh, God," she said. "Oh, please, Howard, please," she said, taking his arms.

"Look!" Howard said. "Scotty! Look, Ann!" He turned her toward the bed.

The boy had opened his eyes, then closed them. He opened them again   130
now. The eyes stared straight ahead for a minute, then moved slowly in his head until they rested on Howard and Ann, then traveled away again.

"Scotty," his mother said, moving to the bed.

"Hey, Scott," his father said. "Hey, son."

They leaned over the bed. Howard took the child's hand in his hands and began to pat and squeeze the hand. Ann bent over the boy and kissed his forehead again and again. She put her hands on either side of his face. "Scotty, honey, it's Mommy and Daddy," she said. "Scotty?"

The boy looked at them, but without any sign of recognition. Then his mouth opened, his eyes scrunched closed, and he howled until he had no more air in his lungs. His face seemed to relax and soften then. His lips parted as his last breath was puffed through his throat and exhaled gently through the clenched teeth.

The doctors called it a hidden occlusion and said it was a one-in-a-million   135
circumstance. Maybe if it could have been detected somehow and surgery undertaken immediately, they could have saved him. But more than likely not. In any case, what would they have been looking for? Nothing had shown up in the tests or in the X-rays.

Dr. Francis was shaken. "I can't tell you how badly I feel. I'm so very sorry, I can't tell you," he said as he led them into the doctors' lounge. There was a doctor sitting in a chair with his legs hooked over the back of another chair, watching an early-morning TV show. He was wearing a green delivery-room outfit, loose green pants and green blouse, and a green cap that covered his hair. He looked at Howard and Ann and then looked at Dr. Francis. He got to his feet and turned off the set and went out of the room. Dr. Francis guided Ann to the sofa, sat down beside her, and began to talk in a low, consoling voice. At one point, he leaned over and embraced her. She could feel his chest rising and falling evenly against her shoulder. She kept her eyes open and let him hold her. Howard went into the bathroom, but he left the door open. After a violent fit of weeping, he ran water and washed his face. Then he came out and sat down at the little table that held a telephone. He looked at the telephone as though deciding what to do first. He made some calls. After a time, Dr. Francis used the telephone.

"Is there anything else I can do for the moment?" he asked them.

Howard shook his head. Ann stared at Dr. Francis as if unable to comprehend his words.

The doctor walked them to the hospital's front door. People were entering and leaving the hospital. It was eleven o'clock in the morning. Ann was aware of how slowly, almost reluctantly, she moved her feet. It seemed to her that Dr. Francis was making them leave when she felt they should stay, when it would be more the right thing to do to stay. She gazed out into the parking lot and then turned around and looked back at the front of the hospital. She began shaking her head. "No, no," she said. "I can't leave him here, no." She heard herself say that and thought how unfair it was that the only words that came out were the sort of words used on TV shows where people were stunned by violent or sudden deaths. She wanted her words to be her own. "No," she said, and for some reason the memory of the Negro woman's head lolling on the woman's shoulder came to her. "No," she said again.

"I'll be talking to you later in the day," the doctor was saying to Howard.   140 "There are still some things that have to be done, things that have to be cleared up to our satisfaction. Some things that need explaining."

"An autopsy," Howard said.

Dr. Francis nodded.

"I understand," Howard said. Then he said, "Oh, Jesus. No, I don't understand, doctor. I can't, I can't. I just can't."

Dr. Francis put his arm around Howard's shoulders. "I'm sorry. God, how I'm sorry." He let go of Howard's shoulders and held out his hand. Howard looked at the hand, and then he took it. Dr. Francis put his arms around Ann once more. He seemed full of some goodness she didn't understand. She let her head rest on his shoulder, but her eyes stayed open. She kept looking at the hospital. As they drove out of the parking lot, she looked back at the hospital.

At home, she sat on the sofa with her hands in her coat pockets. Howard   145 closed the door to the child's room. He got the coffee-maker going and then he found an empty box. He had thought to pick up some of the child's things that were scattered around the living room. But instead he sat down beside her on the sofa, pushed the box to one side, and leaned forward, arms between his knees. He began to weep. She pulled his head over into her lap and patted his shoulder. "He's gone," she said. She kept patting his shoulder. Over his sobs, she could hear the coffee-maker hissing in the kitchen. "There, there," she said tenderly. "Howard, he's gone. He's gone and now we'll have to get used to that. To being alone."

In a little while, Howard got up and began moving aimlessly around the room with the box, not putting anything into it, but collecting some things together on the floor at one end of the sofa. She continued to sit with her hands in her coat pockets. Howard put the box down and brought coffee into the living room. Later, Ann made calls to relatives. After each call had been placed and the party had answered, Ann would blurt out a few words and cry for a minute. Then she would quietly explain, in a measured voice, what had happened and tell them about arrangements. Howard took the box out to the garage, where he saw the child's bicycle. He dropped the box and sat down on the pavement beside the bicycle. He took hold of the bicycle awkwardly so that it leaned against his chest. He held it, the rubber pedal sticking into his chest. He gave the wheel a turn.

Ann hung up the telephone after talking to her sister. She was looking up another number when the telephone rang. She picked it up on the first ring.

"Hello," she said, and she heard something in the background, a humming noise. "Hello!" she said. "For God's sake," she said. "Who is this? What is it you want?"

"Your Scotty, I got him ready for you," the man's voice said. "Did you forget him?"

"You evil bastard!" she shouted into the receiver. "How can you do this, you 150
evil son of a bitch?"

"Scotty," the man said. "Have you forgotten about Scotty?" Then the man hung up on her.

Howard heard the shouting and came in to find her with her head on her arms over the table, weeping. He picked up the receiver and listened to the dial tone.

Much later, just before midnight, after they had dealt with many things, the telephone rang again.

"You answer it," she said. "Howard, it's him, I know." They were sitting at the kitchen table with coffee in front of them. Howard had a small glass of whiskey beside his cup. He answered on the third ring.

"Hello," he said. "Who is this? Hello! Hello!" The line went dead. "He hung 155
up," Howard said. "Whoever it was."

"It was him," she said. "That bastard. I'd like to kill him," she said. "I'd like to shoot him and watch him kick," she said.

"Ann, my God," he said.

"Could you hear anything?" she said. "In the background? A noise, machinery, something humming?"

"Nothing, really. Nothing like that," he said. "There wasn't much time. I think there was some radio music. Yes, there was a radio going, that's all I could tell. I don't know what in God's name is going on," he said.

She shook her head. "If I could, could get my hands on him." It came to her 160
then. She knew who it was. Scotty, the cake, the telephone number. She pushed the chair away from the table and got up. "Drive me down to the shopping center," she said. "Howard."

"What are you saying?"

"The shopping center. I know who it is who's calling. I know who it is. It's the baker, the son-of-a-bitching baker, Howard. I had him bake a cake for Scotty's birthday. That's who's calling. That's who has the number and keeps calling us. To harass us about that cake. The baker, that bastard."

◆ ◆ ◆

They drove down to the shopping center. The sky was clear and stars were out. It was cold, and they ran the heater in the car. They parked in front of the bakery. All of the shops and stores were closed, but there were cars at the far end of the lot in front of the movie theater. The bakery windows were dark, but when they looked through the glass they could see a light in the back room and, now and then, a big man in an apron moving in and out of the white, even light. Through the glass, she could see the display cases and some little tables with chairs. She tried the door. She rapped on the glass. But if the baker heard them, he gave no sign. He didn't look in their direction.

They drove around behind the bakery and parked. They got out of the car. There was a lighted window too high up for them to see inside. A sign near the back door said THE PANTRY BAKERY, SPECIAL ORDERS. She could hear faintly a radio playing inside and something creak—an oven door as it was pulled down? She knocked on the door and waited. Then she knocked again, louder. The radio was turned down and there was a scraping sound now, the distinct sound of something, a drawer, being pulled open and then closed.

Someone unlocked the door and opened it. The baker stood in the light and peered out at them. "I'm closed for business," he said. "What do you want at this hour? It's midnight. Are you drunk or something?"

She stepped into the light that fell through the open door. He blinked his heavy eyelids as he recognized her. "It's you," he said.

"It's me," she said. "Scotty's mother. This is Scotty's father. We'd like to come in."

The baker said, "I'm busy now. I have work to do."

She had stepped inside the doorway anyway. Howard came in behind her. The baker moved back. "It smells like a bakery in here. Doesn't it smell like a bakery in here, Howard?"

"What do you want?" the baker said. "Maybe you want your cake? That's it, you decided you want your cake. You ordered a cake, didn't you?"

"You're pretty smart for a baker," she said. "Howard, this is the man who's been calling us." She clenched her fists. She stared at him fiercely. There was a deep burning inside her, an anger that made her feel larger than herself, larger than either of these men.

"Just a minute here," the baker said. "You want to pick up your three-day-old cake? That it? I don't want to argue with you, lady. There it sits over there, getting stale. I'll give it to you for half of what I quoted you. No. You want it? You can have it. It's no good to me, no good to anyone now. It cost me time and money to make that cake. If you want it, okay, if you don't, that's okay, too. I have to get back to work." He looked at them and rolled his tongue behind his teeth.

"More cakes," she said. She knew she was in control of it, of what was increasing in her. She was calm.

"Lady, I work sixteen hours a day in this place to earn a living," the baker said. He wiped his hands on his apron. "I work night and day in here, trying to make ends meet." A look crossed Ann's face that made the baker move back and say, "No trouble, now." He reached to the counter and picked up a rolling pin

165

170

with his right hand and began to tap it against the palm of his other hand. "You want the cake or not? I have to get back to work. Bakers work at night," he said again. His eyes were small, mean-looking, she thought, nearly lost in the bristly flesh around his cheeks. His neck was thick with fat.

"I know bakers work at night," Ann said. "They make phone calls at night,   175 too. You bastard," she said.

The baker continued to tap the rolling pin against his hand. He glanced at Howard. "Careful, careful," he said to Howard.

"My son's dead," she said with a cold, even finality. "He was hit by a car Monday morning. We've been waiting with him until he died. But, of course, you couldn't be expected to know that, could you? Bakers can't know every- thing—can they, Mr. Baker? But he's dead. He's dead, you bastard!" Just as sud- denly as it had welled in her, the anger dwindled, gave way to something else, a dizzy feeling of nausea. She leaned against the wooden table that was sprinkled with flour, put her hands over her face, and began to cry, her shoulders rocking back and forth. "It isn't fair," she said. "It isn't, isn't fair."

Howard put his hand at the small of her back and looked at the baker. "Shame on you," Howard said to him. "Shame."

The baker put the rolling pin back on the counter. He undid his apron and threw it on the counter. He looked at them, and then he shook his head slowly. He pulled a chair out from under the card table that held papers and receipts, an adding machine, and a telephone directory. "Please sit down," he said. "Let me get you a chair," he said to Howard. "Sit down now, please." The baker went into the front of the shop and returned with two little wrought-iron chairs. "Please sit down, you people."

Ann wiped her eyes and looked at the baker. "I wanted to kill you," she said.   180 "I wanted you dead."

The baker had cleared a space for them at the table. He shoved the adding machine to one side, along with the stacks of notepaper and receipts. He pushed the telephone directory onto the floor, where it landed with a thud. Howard and Ann sat down and pulled their chairs up to the table. The baker sat down, too.

"Let me say how sorry I am," the baker said, putting his elbows on the table. "God alone knows how sorry. Listen to me. I'm just a baker. I don't claim to be anything else. Maybe once, maybe years ago, I was a different kind of human being. I've forgotten, I don't know for sure. But I'm not any longer, if I ever was. Now I'm just a baker. That don't excuse my doing what I did, I know. But I'm deeply sorry. I'm sorry for your son, and sorry for my part in this," the baker said. He spread his hands out on the table and turned them over to reveal his palms. "I don't have any children myself, so I can only imagine what you must be feeling. All I can say to you now is that I'm sorry. Forgive me, if you can," the baker said. "I'm not an evil man, I don't think. Not evil, like you said on the phone. You got to understand what it comes down to is I don't know how to act anymore, it would seem. Please," the man said, "let me ask you if you can find it in your hearts to for- give me?"

It was warm inside the bakery. Howard stood up from the table and took off his coat. He helped Ann from her coat. The baker looked at them for a minute and then nodded and got up from the table. He went to the oven and turned off some switches. He found cups and poured coffee from an electric coffee-maker. He put a carton of cream on the table, and a bowl of sugar.

"You probably need to eat something," the baker said. "I hope you'll eat some of my hot rolls. You have to eat and keep going. Eating is a small, good thing in a time like this," he said.

He served them warm cinnamon rolls just out of the oven, the icing still   185 runny. He put butter on the table and knives to spread the butter. Then the baker sat down at the table with them. He waited. He waited until they each took a roll from the platter and began to eat. "It's good to eat something," he said, watching them. "There's more. Eat up. Eat all you want. There's all the rolls in the world in here."

They ate rolls and drank coffee. Ann was suddenly hungry, and the rolls were warm and sweet. She ate three of them, which pleased the baker. Then he began to talk. They listened carefully. Although they were tired and in anguish, they listened to what the baker had to say. They nodded when the baker began to speak of loneliness, and of the sense of doubt and limitation that had come to him in his middle years. He told them what it was like to be childless all these years. To repeat the days with the ovens endlessly full and endlessly empty. The party food, the celebrations he'd worked over. Icing knuckle-deep. The tiny wedding couples stuck into cakes. Hundreds of them, no, thousands by now. Birthdays. Just imagine all those candles burning. He had a necessary trade. He was a baker. He was glad he wasn't a florist. It was better to be feeding people. This was a better smell anytime than flowers.

"Smell this," the baker said, breaking open a dark loaf. "It's a heavy bread, but rich." They smelled it, then he had them taste it. It had the taste of molasses and coarse grains. They listened to him. They ate what they could. They swallowed the dark bread. It was like daylight under the fluorescent trays of light. They talked on into the early morning, the high, pale cast of light in the windows, and they did not think of leaving.   [1983]

THINKING ABOUT THE TEXT

1. What do you conclude about Ann and Howard's relationship from their behavior in this crisis? To what extent might you behave the same way?

2. Much of this story involves the couple and the medical staff brooding about why Scotty will not wake up. In what way(s) might his sleep be *symbolically* significant?

3. What do you learn about the baker? What *don't* you learn about him? How much does his account of himself explain his phone calls?

4. Why do you think Carver included the African American family in this story?

5. The story ends with the words "they did not think of leaving." Why do Ann and Howard stay at the baker's? Of course, eventually they *will* leave. What kind of lasting effect, if any, do you think their visit to the baker will have on them? Meanwhile, would you say this is a happy ending? Why or why not?

MAKING COMPARISONS

1. What elements of "The Bath" does "A Small, Good Thing" retain? What are the main differences between the two stories?

2. To what extent, and in what ways, did your attitude toward the characters change when you read the second story?

3. In your view, is one of these stories better than the other one? Refer to specific aspects of both.

WRITING ABOUT ISSUES

1. Choose "The Bath" or "A Small, Good Thing" and write an essay in which you respond to the claim that the baker is the most important character in the story.

2. Write an essay in which you focus on a difference between the two stories that someone might not immediately notice — a small change in wording, perhaps. In your essay, explain why this difference is significant.

3. Write an essay in which you recall and analyze how your family behaved in a crisis. More specifically, focus on describing and explaining some action by a family member that surprised you. If you prefer, write about a family other than yours. Feel free to refer to one or both of Carver's stories.

4. Interview a baker or another kind of worker who makes something and sells it to the public. Then write an essay in which you specify the extent to which this person feels that he or she has "a necessary trade" (words from the next-to-last paragraph of "A Small, Good Thing.") If you wish, you can express your own view of how "necessary" this person's work is.

─────────── A WEB ASSIGNMENT ───────────

Numerous sites are dedicated to Raymond Carver and feature documents related to his work. Visit the Web Assignments section of the *Making Literature Matter* Web site, where you will find links to some of these sites. From one of these sites, choose a document that helps you analyze "The Bath" and/or "A Small, Good Thing." Then, write an essay in which you explain precisely how the document is helpful.

─────────── Visit www.bedfordstmartins.com/makinglitmatter ───────────

11

Working with
Cultural Contexts

Many literary texts, especially those labeled classics, are credited with universal appeal. The situations they depict and the insights they offer are supposedly relevant to everyone. Yet when people read a text from another time or place, surely their view of it is influenced by beliefs and values of their own society. In addition, most works of literature reflect in some way the environment of their author. Probably you will decode a literary text better if you try to pinpoint differences between its original culture and yours. Of course, not all of these differences may be significant. You will need to determine which are noteworthy, and why. To help you with this kind of analysis, each chapter of Part Two includes a Cultural Contexts cluster, where a literary selection is joined by documents illuminating the social conditions of its birth.

The selection in our preview here is Lorraine Hansberry's 1959 play *A Raisin in the Sun*. Following the play are four texts that help you place it within cultural history. The first, a short article about Lorraine Hansberry's own family, comes from a 1941 issue of *The Crisis*, the journal of the National Association for the Advancement of Colored People (NAACP). The second text is an excerpt from a letter to the *New York Times* that Hansberry wrote in 1964 when the civil rights movement was gaining momentum. Next comes a set of excerpts from Alan Ehrenhalt's 1995 book, *The Lost City: Discovering the Forgotten Virtues of Community in the Chicago of the 1950s*. In these passages, Ehrenhalt describes Bronzeville, the segregated community where Hansberry grew up and where she set her play. Finally, to give you a sense of forces affecting *Raisin's* first performances, we present an excerpt from actor Sidney Poitier's recent memoir. Poitier originated the role of Walter Lee Younger, and he recalls arguments he had with other members of the company during the play's initial production.

WORKERS' DREAMS: CULTURAL CONTEXTS FOR LORRAINE HANSBERRY'S *A RAISIN IN THE SUN*

LORRAINE HANSBERRY, *A Raisin in the Sun*

CULTURAL CONTEXTS:

THE CRISIS, "The Hansberrys of Chicago: They Join Business Acumen
with Social Vision"
LORRAINE HANSBERRY, *April 23, 1964, Letter to the* New York Times
ALAN EHRENHALT, From *The Lost City: Discovering the Forgotten Virtues
of Community in the Chicago of the 1950s*
SIDNEY POITIER, From *The Measure of a Man: A Spiritual Autobiography*

Hansberry's title comes from African American poet Langston Hughes's 1951 poem "Harlem," which begins by asking "What happens to a dream deferred? / Does it dry up / Like a raisin in the sun?" Hughes had in mind white America's continued thwarting of his own race's hopes for freedom, equality, and prosperity. This is a situation painfully familiar to the Youngers, the African American family of Hansberry's play, who live in a Chicago ghetto during the 1950s. Like other texts in Part One, the play deals with the topic of work. Most of the Youngers have survived by laboring for white people, though they have been stuck in near poverty all the same. Now, a large inheritance promises to fulfill their dreams at last—but these dreams conflict. Whereas Lena wants to buy a house, her son Walter Lee wants to invest in a liquor store to escape his degrading job as a chauffeur. Much of the play's drama occurs as these two characters clash.

BEFORE YOU READ

Think of your own family or another you know well. For outsiders to get a sense of this family, what do they have to know about its social and historical background? Do you think the phrase *a dream deferred* applies to this family? Why, or why not?

LORRAINE HANSBERRY
A Raisin in the Sun

The life of Lorraine Hansberry (1930–1965) was brief. She died of cancer the day that her second play, The Sign in Sidney Brustein's Window *(1964), closed on Broadway. But even by then, she had been immensely productive as a writer and gained a considerable reputation for her work. In 1959, her first play,* A Raisin in the Sun, *was the first by an African American woman to be produced on Broadway. Later that year, it became the first play by an African American to win the New York*

(AP/Wide World.)

Drama Critics Circle Award. In part, the play was based on an experience that Hansberry's own family endured while she was growing up in Chicago. Her father, Carl Hansberry, a prominent realtor and banker, made history in 1938 when he moved his family to an all-white section of Chicago's Hyde Park neighborhood. After encountering white resistance there, he fought a series of legal battles that went all the way to the Supreme Court. In 1940, the Court ruled in his favor, but its decision largely was not enforced; housing remained basically segregated in Chicago and in most of the country. Embittered, Carl Hansberry considered moving his family permanently to Mexico, but before he could, he died of a cerebral hemorrhage there in 1946.

After attending the University of Wisconsin, Lorraine Hansberry moved to New York City. Besides plays, she wrote essays, articles, and pieces of journalism on a variety of subjects, including homophobia and racism. She also wrote the screenplay for the 1961 film version of A Raisin in the Sun, which featured the original Broadway cast (including Sidney Poitier as Walter Lee Younger). In 1969, her husband Robert Nemiroff combined various writings of hers into a play called To Be Young, Gifted, and Black. *In 1970, a book version of it was published, and that same year there was a Broadway production of Hansberry's final play,* Les Blancs.

Harlem (A Dream Deferred)

What happens to a dream deferred?

Does it dry up
Like a raisin in the sun?
Or fester like a sore—
And then run?
Does it stink like rotten meat?
Or crust and sugar over—
Like a syrupy sweet?

Maybe it just sags
Like a heavy load.

Or does it explode?
                                            —Langston Hughes

CHARACTERS (in order of appearance)

RUTH YOUNGER
TRAVIS YOUNGER
WALTER LEE YOUNGER, *brother*
BENEATHA YOUNGER
LENA YOUNGER, MAMA
JOSEPH ASAGAI
GEORGE MURCHISON
MRS. JOHNSON
KARL LINDNER
BOBO
MOVING MEN

The action of the play is set in Chicago's Southside, sometime between World War II and the present.

ACT 1, Scene 1

[Friday morning.]

The Younger living room would be a comfortable and well-ordered room if it were not for a number of indestructible contradictions to this state of being. Its furnishings are typical and undistinguished and their primary feature now is that they have clearly had to accommodate the living of too many people for too many years — and they are tired. Still, we can see that at some time, a time probably no longer remembered by the family (except perhaps for Mama), the furnishings of this room were actually selected with care and love and even hope — and brought to this apartment and arranged with taste and pride.

That was a long time ago. Now the once loved pattern of the couch upholstery has to fight to show itself from under acres of crocheted doilies and couch covers which have themselves finally come to be more important than the upholstery. And here a table or a chair has been moved to disguise the worn places in the carpet; but the carpet has fought back by showing its weariness, with depressing uniformity, elsewhere on its surface.

Weariness has, in fact, won in this room. Everything has been polished, washed, sat on, used, scrubbed too often. All pretenses but living itself have long since vanished from the very atmosphere of this room.

Moreover, a section of this room, for it is not really a room unto itself, though the landlord's lease would make it seem so, slopes backward to provide a small kitchen area, where the family prepares the meals that are eaten in the living room proper, which must also serve as dining room. The single window that has been provided for these "two" rooms is located in this kitchen area. The sole natural light the family may enjoy in the course of a day is only that which fights its way through this little window.

At left, a door leads to a bedroom which is shared by Mama and her daughter, Beneatha. At right, opposite, is a second room (which in the beginning of the life of this apartment was probably a breakfast room) which serves as a bedroom for Walter and his wife, Ruth.

Time: Sometime between World War II and the present.

Place: Chicago's Southside.

At Rise: It is morning dark in the living room. Travis is asleep on the make-down bed at center. An alarm clock sounds from within the bedroom at right, and presently Ruth enters from that room and closes the door behind her. She crosses sleepily toward the window. As she passes her sleeping son she reaches down and shakes him a little. At the window she raises the shade and a dusky Southside morning light comes in feebly. She fills a pot with water and puts it on to boil. She calls to the boy, between yawns, in a slightly muffled voice.

Ruth is about thirty. We can see that she was a pretty girl, even exceptionally so, but now it is apparent that life has been little that she expected, and disappointment has already begun to hang in her face. In a few years, before thirty-five even, she will be known among her people as a "settled woman."

She crosses to her son and gives him a good, final, rousing shake.

RUTH: Come on now, boy, it's seven thirty! *(Her son sits up at last, in a stupor of sleepiness.)* I say hurry up, Travis! You ain't the only person in the world got to use a bathroom! *(The child, a sturdy, handsome little boy of ten or eleven, drags himself out of the bed and almost blindly takes his towels and "today's clothes" from drawers and a closet and goes out to the bathroom, which is in an outside hall and which is shared by another family or families on the same floor. Ruth crosses to the bedroom door at right and opens it and calls in to her husband.)* Walter Lee! . . . It's after seven thirty! Lemme see you do some waking up in there now! *(She waits.)* You better get up from there, man! It's after seven thirty I tell you. *(She waits again.)* All right, you just go ahead and lay there and next thing you know Travis be finished and Mr. Johnson'll be in there and you'll be fussing and cussing round here like a madman! And be late too! *(She waits, at the end of patience.)* Walter Lee — it's time for you to GET UP!

She waits another second and then starts to go into the bedroom, but is apparently satisfied that her husband has begun to get up. She stops, pulls the door to, and returns to the kitchen area. She wipes her face with a moist cloth and runs her fingers through her sleep-disheveled hair in a vain effort and ties an apron around her housecoat. The bedroom door at right opens and her husband stands in the doorway in his pajamas, which are rumpled and mismated. He is a lean, intense young man in his middle thirties, inclined to quick nervous movements and erratic speech habits — and always in his voice there is a quality of indictment.

WALTER: Is he out yet?

RUTH: What you mean *out?* He ain't hardly got in there good yet.

WALTER *(wandering in, still more oriented to sleep than to a new day):*   Well, what was you doing all that yelling for if I can't even get in there yet? *(Stopping and thinking.)* Check coming today?

RUTH: They *said* Saturday and this is just Friday and I hopes to God you ain't going to get up here first thing this morning and start talking to me 'bout no money — 'cause I 'bout don't want to hear it.

WALTER: Something the matter with you this morning?

RUTH: No — I'm just sleepy as the devil. What kind of eggs you want?

WALTER: Not scrambled. *(Ruth starts to scramble eggs.)* Paper come? *(Ruth points impatiently to the rolled up* Tribune *on the table, and he gets it and spreads it out and vaguely reads the front page.)* Set off another bomb yesterday.

RUTH *(maximum indifference):*   Did they?

WALTER *(looking up):*   What's the matter with you?

RUTH: Ain't nothing the matter with me. And don't keep asking me that this morning.

WALTER: Ain't nobody bothering you. *(Reading the news of the day absently again.)* Say Colonel McCormick is sick.

RUTH *(affecting tea-party interest):*   Is he now? Poor thing.

WALTER *(sighing and looking at his watch):*   Oh, me. *(He waits.)* Now what is that boy doing in that bathroom all this time? He just going to have to start getting up earlier. I can't be being late to work on account of him fooling around in there.

RUTH *(turning on him):*   Oh, no he ain't going to be getting up no earlier no such thing! It ain't his fault that he can't get to bed no earlier nights 'cause he got a bunch of crazy good-for-nothing clowns sitting up running their mouths in what is supposed to be his bedroom after ten o'clock at night . . .

WALTER: That's what you mad about, ain't it? The things I want to talk about with my friends just couldn't be important in your mind, could they?

He rises and finds a cigarette in her handbag on the table and crosses to the little window and looks out, smoking and deeply enjoying this first one.

RUTH *(almost matter of factly, a complaint too automatic to deserve emphasis):* Why you always got to smoke before you eat in the morning?

WALTER *(at the window):*   Just look at 'em down there . . . Running and racing to work . . . *(He turns and faces his wife and watches her a moment at the stove, and then, suddenly.)* You look young this morning, baby.

RUTH (*indifferently*):   Yeah?

WALTER: Just for a second—stirring them eggs. Just for a second it was—you looked real young again. (*He reaches for her; she crosses away. Then, drily.*) It's gone now—you look like yourself again!

RUTH: Man, if you don't shut up and leave me alone.

WALTER (*looking out to the street again*):   First thing a man ought to learn in life is not to make love to no colored woman first thing in the morning. You all some eeeevil people at eight o'clock in the morning.

Travis appears in the hall doorway, almost fully dressed and quite wide awake now, his towels and pajamas across his shoulders. He opens the door and signals for his father to make the bathroom in a hurry.

TRAVIS (*watching the bathroom*):   Daddy, come on!

Walter gets his bathroom utensils and flies out to the bathroom.

RUTH: Sit down and have your breakfast, Travis.

TRAVIS: Mama, this is Friday. (*Gleefully.*) Check coming tomorrow, huh?

RUTH: You get your mind off money and eat your breakfast.

TRAVIS (*eating*):   This is the morning we supposed to bring the fifty cents to school.

RUTH: Well, I ain't got no fifty cents this morning.

TRAVIS: Teacher say we have to.

RUTH: I don't care what teacher say. I ain't got it. Eat your breakfast, Travis.

TRAVIS: I *am* eating.

RUTH: Hush up now and just eat!

The boy gives her an exasperated look for her lack of understanding, and eats grudgingly.

TRAVIS: You think Grandmama would have it?

RUTH: No! And I want you to stop asking your grandmother for money, you hear me?

TRAVIS (*outraged*):   Gaaaleee! I don't ask her, she just gimme it sometimes!

RUTH: Travis Willard Younger—I got too much on me this morning to be—

TRAVIS: Maybe Daddy—

RUTH: *Travis!*

The boy hushes abruptly. They are both quiet and tense for several seconds.

TRAVIS (*presently*):   Could I maybe go carry some groceries in front of the supermarket for a little while after school then?

RUTH: Just hush, I said. (*Travis jabs his spoon into his cereal bowl viciously, and rests his head in anger upon his fists.*) If you through eating, you can get over there and make up your bed.

The boy obeys stiffly and crosses the room, almost mechanically, to the bed and more or less folds the bedding into a heap, then angrily gets his books and cap.

TRAVIS (*sulking and standing apart from her unnaturally*):   I'm gone.

RUTH (*looking up from the stove to inspect him automatically*):   Come here. (*He crosses to her and she studies his head.*) If you don't take this comb and fix this here head, you better! *(Travis puts down his books with a great sigh of oppres-sion, and crosses to the mirror. His mother mutters under her breath about his "slubbornness.")* 'Bout to march out of here with that head looking just like chickens slept in it! I just don't know where you get your slubborn ways . . . And get your jacket, too. Looks chilly out this morning.

TRAVIS *(with conspicuously brushed hair and jacket):* I'm gone.

RUTH: Get carfare and milk money — *(Waving one finger.)* — and not a single penny for no caps, you hear me?

TRAVIS *(with sullen politeness):* Yes'm.

He turns in outrage to leave. His mother watches after him as in his frustration he approaches the door almost comically. When she speaks to him, her voice has become a very gentle tease.

RUTH *(mocking; as she thinks he would say it):* Oh, Mama makes me so mad sometimes, I don't know what to do! *(She waits and continues to his back as he stands stock-still in front of the door.)* I wouldn't kiss that woman good-bye for nothing in this world this morning! *(The boy finally turns around and rolls his eyes at her, knowing the mood has changed and he is vindicated; he does not, however, move toward her yet.)* Not for nothing in this world! *(She finally laughs aloud at him and holds out her arms to him and we see that it is a way between them, very old and practiced. He crosses to her and allows her to embrace him warmly but keeps his face fixed with masculine rigidity. She holds him back from her presently and looks at him and runs her fingers over the features of his face. With utter gentleness — .)* Now — whose little old angry man are you?

TRAVIS *(the masculinity and gruffness start to fade at last):* Aw gaalee — Mama . . .

RUTH *(mimicking):* Aw — gaaaaalleeeee, Mama! *(She pushes him, with rough playfulness and finality, toward the door.)* Get on out of here or you going to be late.

TRAVIS *(in the face of love, new aggressiveness):* Mama, could I *please* go carry groceries?

RUTH: Honey, it's starting to get so cold evenings.

WALTER *(coming in from the bathroom and drawing a make-believe gun from a make-believe holster and shooting at his son):* What is it he wants to do?

RUTH: Go carry groceries after school at the supermarket.

WALTER: Well, let him go . . .

TRAVIS *(quickly, to the ally):* I *have* to — she won't gimme the fifty cents . . .

WALTER *(to his wife only):* Why not?

RUTH *(simply, and with flavor):* 'Cause we don't have it.

WALTER *(to Ruth only):* What you tell the boy things like that for? *(Reaching down into his pants with a rather important gesture.)* Here, son —

He hands the boy the coin, but his eyes are directed to his wife's. Travis takes the money happily.

TRAVIS: Thanks, Daddy.

He starts out. Ruth watches both of them with murder in her eyes. Walter stands and stares back at her with defiance, and suddenly reaches into his pocket again on an afterthought.

WALTER (*without even looking at his son, still staring hard at his wife*):   In fact, here's another fifty cents . . . Buy yourself some fruit today—or take a taxicab to school or something!

TRAVIS: Whoopee—

He leaps up and clasps his father around the middle with his legs, and they face each other in mutual appreciation; slowly Walter Lee peeks around the boy to catch the violent rays from his wife's eyes and draws his head back as if shot.

WALTER: You better get down now—and get to school, man.

TRAVIS (*at the door*):   O.K. Good-bye.

He exits.

WALTER (*after him, pointing with pride*):   That's *my* boy. (*She looks at him in disgust and turns back to her work.*) You know what I was thinking 'bout in the bathroom this morning?

RUTH: No.

WALTER: How come you always try to be so pleasant!

RUTH: What is there to be pleasant 'bout!

WALTER: You want to know what I was thinking 'bout in the bathroom or not!

RUTH: I know what you thinking 'bout.

WALTER (*ignoring her*):   'Bout what me and Willy Harris was talking about last night.

RUTH (*immediately—a refrain*):   Willy Harris is a good-for-nothing loudmouth.

WALTER: Anybody who talks to me has got to be a good-for-nothing loudmouth, ain't he? And what you know about who is just a good-for-nothing loudmouth? Charlie Atkins was just a "good-for-nothing loudmouth" too, wasn't he! When he wanted me to go in the dry-cleaning business with him. And now—he's grossing a hundred thousand a year. A hundred thousand dollars a year! You still call *him* a loudmouth!

RUTH (*bitterly*):   Oh, Walter Lee . . .

She folds her head on her arms over the table.

WALTER (*rising and coming to her and standing over her*):   You tired, ain't you? Tired of everything. Me, the boy, the way we live—this beat-up hole—everything. Ain't you? (*She doesn't look up, doesn't answer.*) So tired—moaning and groaning all the time, but you wouldn't do nothing to help, would you? You couldn't be on my side that long for nothing, could you?

RUTH: Walter, please leave me alone.

WALTER: A man needs for a woman to back him up . . .

RUTH: Walter—

WALTER: Mama would listen to you. You know she listen to you more than she do me and Bennie. She think more of you. All you have to do is just sit down with her when you drinking your coffee one morning and talking 'bout things like you do and—(*He sits down beside her and demonstrates graphically what he thinks her methods and tone should be.*)—you just sip your coffee, see, and say easy like that you been thinking 'bout that deal Walter Lee is so interested in, 'bout the store and all, and sip some more coffee, like what you saying ain't really that important to you—And the next thing you know, she be listening good and asking you questions and when I come home—I can tell her the details. This ain't no fly-by-night proposition, baby. I mean we figured it out, me and Willy and Bobo.

RUTH *(with a frown)*:　Bobo?

WALTER:　Yeah. You see, this little liquor store we got in mind cost seventy-five thousand and we figured the initial investment on the place be 'bout thirty thousand, see. That be ten thousand each. Course, there's a couple of hundred you got to pay so's you don't spend your life just waiting for them clowns to let your license get approved—

RUTH:　You mean graft?

WALTER *(frowning impatiently)*:　Don't call it that. See there, that just goes to show you what women understand about the world. Baby, don't *nothing* happen for you in the world 'less you pay *somebody* off!

RUTH:　Walter, leave me alone! *(She raises her head and stares at him vigorously—then says, more quietly.)* Eat your eggs, they gonna be cold.

WALTER *(straightening up from her and looking off)*:　That's it. There you are. Man say to his woman: I got me a dream. His woman say: Eat your eggs. *(Sadly, but gaining in power.)* Man say: I got to take hold of this here world, baby! And a woman will say: Eat your eggs and go to work. *(Passionately now.)* Man say: I got to change my life, I'm choking to death, baby! And his woman say—*(In utter anguish as he brings his fists down on his thighs.)*—Your eggs is getting cold!

RUTH *(softly)*:　Walter, that ain't none of our money.

WALTER *(not listening at all or even looking at her)*:　This morning, I was lookin' in the mirror and thinking about it . . . I'm thirty-five years old; I been married eleven years and I got a boy who sleeps in the living room—*(Very, very quietly.)*—and all I got to give him is stories about how rich white people live . . .

RUTH:　Eat your eggs, Walter.

WALTER *(slams the table and jumps up)*:　—DAMN MY EGGS—DAMN ALL THE EGGS THAT EVER WAS!

RUTH:　Then go to work.

WALTER *(looking up at her)*:　See—I'm trying to talk to you 'bout myself—*(Shaking his head with the repetition.)*—and all you can say is eat them eggs and go to work.

RUTH *(wearily)*:　Honey, you never say nothing new. I listen to you every day, every night and every morning, and you never say nothing new. *(Shrugging.)* So you would rather *be* Mr. Arnold than be his chauffeur. So—I would *rather* be living in Buckingham Palace.

WALTER:　That is just what is wrong with the colored woman in this world . . . Don't understand about building their men up and making 'em feel like they somebody. Like they can do something.

RUTH *(drily, but to hurt)*:　There *are* colored men who do things.

WALTER:　No thanks to the colored woman.

RUTH:　Well, being a colored woman, I guess I can't help myself none.

She rises and gets the ironing board and sets it up and attacks a huge pile of rough-dried clothes, sprinkling them in preparation for the ironing and then rolling them into tight fat balls.

WALTER (*mumbling*):   We one group of men tied to a race of women with small minds!

His sister Beneatha enters. She is about twenty, as slim and intense as her brother. She is not as pretty as her sister-in-law, but her lean, almost intellectual face has a handsomeness of its own. She wears a bright-red flannel nightie, and her thick hair stands wildly about her head. Her speech is a mixture of many things; it is different from the rest of the family's insofar as education has permeated her sense of English — and perhaps the Midwest rather than the South has finally — at last — won out in her inflection; but not altogether, because over all of it is a soft slurring and transformed use of vowels which is the decided influence of the Southside. She passes through the room without looking at either Ruth or Walter and goes to the outside door and looks, a little blindly, out to the bathroom. She sees that it has been lost to the Johnsons. She closes the door with a sleepy vengeance and crosses to the table and sits down a little defeated.

BENEATHA: I am going to start timing those people.

WALTER: You should get up earlier.

BENEATHA (*her face in her hands. She is still fighting the urge to go back to bed*):   Really — would you suggest dawn? Where's the paper?

WALTER (*pushing the paper across the table to her as he studies her almost clinically, as though he has never seen her before*):   You a horrible-looking chick at this hour.

BENEATHA (*drily*):   Good morning, everybody.

WALTER (*senselessly*):   How is school coming?

BENEATHA (*in the same spirit*):   Lovely. Lovely. And you know, biology is the greatest. (*Looking up at him.*) I dissected something that looked just like you yesterday.

WALTER: I just wondered if you've made up your mind and everything.

BENEATHA (*gaining in sharpness and impatience*):   And what did I answer yesterday morning — and the day before that?

RUTH (*from the ironing board, like someone disinterested and old*):   Don't be so nasty, Bennie.

BENEATHA (*still to her brother*):   And the day before that and the day before that!

WALTER (*defensively*):   I'm interested in you. Something wrong with that? Ain't many girls who decide —

WALTER AND BENEATHA (*in unison*):   — "to be a doctor."

Silence.

WALTER: Have we figured out yet just exactly how much medical school is going to cost?

RUTH: Walter Lee, why don't you leave that girl alone and get out of here to work?

BENEATHA (*exits to the bathroom and bangs on the door*):   Come on out of there, please!

She comes back into the room.

WALTER (*looking at his sister intently*):   You know the check is coming tomorrow.

BENEATHA (*turning on him with a sharpness all her own*):   That money belongs to Mama, Walter, and it's for her to decide how she wants to use it. I don't care if she wants to buy a house or a rocket ship or just nail it up somewhere and look at it. It's hers. Not ours — *hers.*

WALTER (*bitterly*):   Now ain't that fine! You just got your mother's interest at heart, ain't you, girl? You such a nice girl — but if Mama got that money she can always take a few thousand and help you through school too — can't she?

BENEATHA: I have never asked anyone around here to do anything for me!

WALTER: No! And the line between asking and just accepting when the time comes is big and wide — ain't it!

BENEATHA (*with fury*):   What do you want from me, Brother — that I quit school or just drop dead, which!

WALTER: I don't want nothing but for you to stop acting holy 'round here. Me and Ruth done made some sacrifices for you — why can't you do something for the family?

RUTH: Walter, don't be dragging me in it.

WALTER: You are in it — Don't you get up and go work in somebody's kitchen for the last three years to help put clothes on her back?

RUTH: Oh, Walter — that's not fair . . .

WALTER: It ain't that nobody expects you to get on your knees and say thank you, Brother; thank you, Ruth; thank you, Mama — and thank you, Travis, for wearing the same pair of shoes for two semesters —

BENEATHA (*dropping to her knees*):   Well — I *do* — all right? — thank everybody! And forgive me for ever wanting to be anything at all! (*Pursuing him on her knees across the floor.*) FORGIVE ME, FORGIVE ME, FORGIVE ME!

RUTH: Please stop it! Your mama'll hear you.

WALTER: Who the hell told you you had to be a doctor? If you so crazy 'bout messing 'round with sick people — then go be a nurse like other women — or just get married and be quiet . . .

BENEATHA: Well — you finally got it said . . . It took you three years but you finally got it said. Walter, give up; leave me alone — it's Mama's money.

WALTER: *He was my father, too!*

BENEATHA: So what? He was mine, too — and Travis' grandfather — but the insurance money belongs to Mama. Picking on me is not going to make her give it to you to invest in any liquor stores — (*Under breath, dropping into a chair.*) — and I for one say, God bless Mama for that!

WALTER (*to Ruth*):   See — did you hear? Did you hear!

RUTH: Honey, please go to work.

WALTER: Nobody in this house is ever going to understand me.

BENEATHA: Because you're a nut.

WALTER: Who's a nut?

BENEATHA: You — you are a nut. Thee is mad, boy.

WALTER (*looking at his wife and his sister from the door, very sadly*):   The world's most backward race of people, and that's a fact.

BENEATHA (*turning slowly in her chair*):   And then there are all those prophets who would lead us out of the wilderness — (*Walter slams out of the house.*) — into the swamps!

RUTH: Bennie, why you always gotta be pickin' on your brother? Can't you be a little sweeter sometimes? (*Door opens. Walter walks in. He fumbles with his cap, starts to speak, clears throat, looks everywhere but at Ruth. Finally:*)

WALTER (*to Ruth*):   I need some money for carfare.

RUTH (*looks at him, then warms; teasing, but tenderly*):   Fifty cents? (*She goes to her bag and gets money.*) Here — take a taxi!

Walter exits. Mama enters. She is a woman in her early sixties, full-bodied and strong. She is one of those women of a certain grace and beauty who wear it so unobtrusively that it takes a while to notice. Her dark-brown face is surrounded by the total whiteness of her hair, and, being a woman who has adjusted to many things in life and overcome many more, her face is full of strength. She has, we can see, wit and faith of a kind that keep her eyes lit and full of interest and expectancy. She is, in a word, a beautiful woman. Her bearing is perhaps most like the noble bearing of the women of the Hereros of Southwest Africa — rather as if she imagines that as she walks she still bears a basket or a vessel upon her head. Her speech, on the other hand, is as careless as her carriage is precise — she is inclined to slur everything — but her voice is perhaps not so much quiet as simply soft.

MAMA: Who that 'round here slamming doors at this hour?

She crosses through the room, goes to the window, opens it, and brings in a feeble little plant growing doggedly in a small pot on the window sill. She feels the dirt and puts it back out.

RUTH: That was Walter Lee. He and Bennie was at it again.

MAMA: My children and they tempers. Lord, if this little old plant don't get more sun than it's been getting it ain't never going to see spring again. (*She turns from the window.*) What's the matter with you this morning, Ruth? You looks right peaked. You aiming to iron all them things? Leave some for me. I'll get to 'em this afternoon. Bennie honey, it's too drafty for you to be sitting 'round half dressed. Where's your robe?

BENEATHA: In the cleaners.

MAMA: Well, go get mine and put it on.

BENEATHA: I'm not cold, Mama, honest.

MAMA: I know — but you so thin . . .

BENEATHA (*irritably*):   Mama, I'm not cold.

MAMA (*seeing the make-down bed as Travis has left it*):   Lord have mercy, look at that poor bed. Bless his heart — he tries, don't he?

She moves to the bed Travis has sloppily made up.

RUTH: No — he don't half try at all 'cause he knows you going to come along behind him and fix everything. That's just how come he don't know how to do nothing right now — you done spoiled that boy so.

MAMA (*folding bedding*):   Well—he's a little boy. Ain't supposed to know 'bout housekeeping. My baby, that's what he is. What you fix for his breakfast this morning?

RUTH (*angrily*):   I feed my son, Lena!

MAMA: I ain't meddling—(*Under breath; busy-bodyish.*) I just noticed all last week he had cold cereal, and when it starts getting this chilly in the fall a child ought to have some hot grits or something when he goes out in the cold—

RUTH (*furious*):   I gave him hot oats—is that all right!

MAMA: I ain't meddling. (*Pause.*) Put a lot of nice butter on it? (*Ruth shoots her an angry look and does not reply.*) He likes lots of butter.

RUTH (*exasperated*):   Lena—

MAMA (*to Beneatha. Mama is inclined to wander conversationally sometimes*): What was you and your brother fussing 'bout this morning?

BENEATHA: It's not important, Mama.

She gets up and goes to look out at the bathroom, which is apparently free, and she picks up her towels and rushes out.

MAMA: What was they fighting about?

RUTH: Now you know as well as I do.

MAMA (*shaking her head*):   Brother still worrying hisself sick about that money?

RUTH: You know he is.

MAMA: You had breakfast?

RUTH: Some coffee.

MAMA: Girl, you better start eating and looking after yourself better. You almost thin as Travis.

RUTH: Lena—

MAMA: Un-hunh?

RUTH: What are you going to do with it?

MAMA: Now don't you start, child. It's too early in the morning to be talking about money. It ain't Christian.

RUTH: It's just that he got his heart set on that store—

MAMA: You mean that liquor store that Willy Harris want him to invest in?

RUTH: Yes—

MAMA: We ain't no business people, Ruth. We just plain working folks.

RUTH: Ain't nobody business people till they go into business. Walter Lee say colored people ain't never going to start getting ahead till they start gambling on some different kinds of things in the world—investments and things.

MAMA: What done got into you, girl? Walter Lee done finally sold you on investing.

RUTH: No. Mama, something is happening between Walter and me. I don't know what it is—but he needs something—something I can't give him any more. He needs this chance, Lena.

MAMA (*frowning deeply*):   But liquor, honey—

RUTH: Well—like Walter say—I spec people going to always be drinking themselves some liquor.

MAMA: Well—whether they drinks it or not ain't none of my business. But whether I go into business selling it to 'em *is*, and I don't want that on my ledger this late in life. *(Stopping suddenly and studying her daughter-in-law.)* Ruth Younger, what's the matter with you today? You look like you could fall over right there.

RUTH: I'm tired.

MAMA: Then you better stay home from work today.

RUTH: I can't stay home. She'd be calling up the agency and screaming at them, "My girl didn't come in today—send me somebody! My girl didn't come in!" Oh, she just have a fit . . .

MAMA: Well, let her have it. I'll just call her up and say you got the flu—

RUTH *(laughing):* Why the flu?

MAMA: 'Cause it sounds respectable to 'em. Something white people get, too. They know 'bout the flu. Otherwise they think you been cut up or something when you tell 'em you sick.

RUTH: I got to go in. We need the money.

MAMA: Somebody would of thought my children done all but starved to death the way they talk about money here late. Child, we got a great big old check coming tomorrow.

RUTH *(sincerely, but also self-righteously):* Now that's your money. It ain't got nothing to do with me. We all feel like that—Walter and Bennie and me— even Travis.

MAMA *(thoughtfully, and suddenly very far away):* Ten thousand dollars—

RUTH: Sure is wonderful.

MAMA: Ten thousand dollars.

RUTH: You know what you should do, Miss Lena? You should take yourself a trip somewhere. To Europe or South America or someplace—

MAMA *(throwing up her hands at the thought):* Oh, child!

RUTH: I'm serious. Just pack up and leave! Go on away and enjoy yourself some. Forget about the family and have yourself a ball for once in your life—

MAMA *(drily):* You sound like I'm just about ready to die. Who'd go with me? What I look like wandering 'round Europe by myself?

RUTH: Shoot—these here rich white women do it all the time. They don't think nothing of packing up they suitcases and piling on one of them big steamships and—swoosh!—they gone, child.

MAMA: Something always told me I wasn't no rich white woman.

RUTH: Well—what are you going to do with it then?

MAMA: I ain't rightly decided. *(Thinking. She speaks now with emphasis.)* Some of it got to be put away for Beneatha and her schoolin'—and ain't nothing going to touch that part of it. Nothing. *(She waits several seconds, trying to make up her mind about something, and looks at Ruth a little tentatively before going on.)* Been thinking that we maybe could meet the notes on a little old two-story somewhere, with a yard where Travis could play in the summertime, if we use part of the insurance for a down payment and everybody kind of pitch in. I could maybe take on a little day work again, few days a week—

RUTH *(studying her mother-in-law furtively and concentrating on her ironing, anxious to encourage without seeming to):* Well, Lord knows, we've put enough rent into this here rat trap to pay for four houses by now . . .

MAMA *(looking up at the words "rat trap" and then looking around and leaning back and sighing—in a suddenly reflective mood—):* "Rat trap"—yes, that's all it is. *(Smiling.)* I remember just as well the day me and Big Walter moved in here. Hadn't been married but two weeks and wasn't planning on living here no more than a year. *(She shakes her head at the dissolved dream.)* We was going to set away, little by little, don't you know, and buy a little place out in Morgan Park. We had even picked out the house. *(Chuckling a little.)* Looks right dumpy today. But Lord, child, you should know all the dreams I had 'bout buying that house and fixing it up and making me a little garden in the back—*(She waits and stops smiling.)* And didn't none of it happen.

Dropping her hands in a futile gesture.

RUTH *(keeps her head down, ironing):* Yes, life can be a barrel of disappointments, sometimes.

MAMA: Honey, Big Walter would come in here some nights back then and slump down on that couch there and just look at the rug, and look at me and look at the rug and then back at me—and I'd know he was down then . . . really down. *(After a second very long and thoughtful pause; she is seeing back to times that only she can see.)* And then, Lord, when I lost that baby—little Claude—I almost thought I was going to lose Big Walter too. Oh, that man grieved hisself! He was one man to love his children.

RUTH: Ain't nothin' can tear at you like losin' your baby.

MAMA: I guess that's how come that man finally worked hisself to death like he done. Like he was fighting his own war with this here world that took his baby from him.

RUTH: He sure was a fine man, all right. I always liked Mr. Younger.

MAMA: Crazy 'bout his children! God knows there was plenty wrong with Walter Younger—hard-headed, mean, kind of wild with women—plenty wrong with him. But he sure loved his children. Always wanted them to have something—be something. That's where Brother gets all these notions, I reckon. Big Walter used to say, he'd get right wet in the eyes sometimes, lean his head back with the water standing in his eyes and say, "Seem like God didn't see fit to give the black man nothing but dreams—but He did give us children to make them dreams seem worthwhile." *(She smiles.)* He could talk like that, don't you know.

RUTH: Yes, he sure could. He was a good man, Mr. Younger.

MAMA: Yes, a fine man—just couldn't never catch up with his dreams, that's all.

Beneatha comes in, brushing her hair and looking up to the ceiling, where the sound of a vacuum cleaner has started up.

BENEATHA: What could be so dirty on that woman's rugs that she has to vacuum them every single day?

RUTH: I wish certain young women 'round here who I could name would take inspiration about certain rugs in a certain apartment I could also mention.

BENEATHA *(shrugging):* How much cleaning can a house need, for Christ's sakes.

MAMA *(not liking the Lord's name used thus):*   Bennie!

RUTH: Just listen to her — just listen!

BENEATHA: Oh, God!

MAMA: If you use the Lord's name just one more time —

BENEATHA *(a bit of a whine):*   Oh, Mama —

RUTH: Fresh — just fresh as salt, this girl!

BENEATHA *(drily):*   Well — if the salt loses its savor —

MAMA: Now that will do. I just ain't going to have you 'round here reciting the scriptures in vain — you hear me?

BENEATHA: How did I manage to get on everybody's wrong side by just walking into a room?

RUTH: If you weren't so fresh —

BENEATHA: Ruth, I'm twenty years old.

MAMA: What time you be home from school today?

BENEATHA: Kind of late. *(With enthusiasm.)* Madeline is going to start my guitar lessons today.

Mama and Ruth look up with the same expression.

MAMA: Your *what* kind of lessons?

BENEATHA: Guitar.

RUTH: Oh, Father!

MAMA: How come you done taken it in your mind to learn to play the guitar?

BENEATHA: I just want to, that's all.

MAMA *(smiling):*   Lord, child, don't you know what to do with yourself? How long it going to be before you get tired of this now — like you got tired of that little play-acting group you joined last year? *(Looking at Ruth.)* And what was it the year before that?

RUTH: The horseback-riding club for which she bought that fifty-five-dollar riding habit that's been hanging in the closet ever since!

MAMA *(to Beneatha):*   Why you got to flit so from one thing to another, baby?

BENEATHA *(sharply):*   I just want to learn to play the guitar. Is there anything wrong with that?

MAMA: Ain't nobody trying to stop you. I just wonders sometimes why you has to flit so from one thing to another all the time. You ain't never done nothing with all that camera equipment you brought home —

BENEATHA: I don't flit! I — I experiment with different forms of expression —

RUTH: Like riding a horse?

BENEATHA: — People have to express themselves one way or another.

MAMA: What is it you want to express?

BENEATHA *(angrily):*   Me! *(Mama and Ruth look at each other and burst into raucous laughter.)* Don't worry — I don't expect you to understand.

MAMA *(to change the subject):*   Who you going out with tomorrow night?

BENEATHA *(with displeasure):*   George Murchison again.

MAMA *(pleased):*   Oh — you getting a little sweet on him?

RUTH: You ask me, this child ain't sweet on nobody but herself — *(Under breath.)* Express herself!

They laugh.

BENEATHA: Oh—I like George all right, Mama. I mean I like him enough to go
out with him and stuff, but—

RUTH *(for devilment)*:   What does *and stuff* mean?

BENEATHA: Mind your own business.

MAMA: Stop picking at her now, Ruth. *(She chuckles—then a suspicious sudden
look at her daughter as she turns in her chair for emphasis.)* What DOES it
mean?

BENEATHA *(wearily)*:   Oh, I just mean I couldn't ever really be serious about
George. He's—he's so shallow.

RUTH: Shallow—what do you mean he's shallow? He's *rich!*

MAMA: Hush, Ruth.

BENEATHA: I know he's rich. He knows he's rich, too.

RUTH: Well—what other qualities a man got to have to satisfy you, little girl?

BENEATHA: You wouldn't even begin to understand. Anybody who married
Walter could not possibly understand.

MAMA *(outraged)*:   What kind of way is that to talk about your brother?

BENEATHA: Brother is a flip—let's face it.

MAMA *(to Ruth, helplessly)*:   What's a flip?

RUTH *(glad to add kindling)*:   She's saying he's crazy.

BENEATHA: Not crazy. Brother isn't really crazy yet—he—he's an elaborate
neurotic.

MAMA: Hush your mouth!

BENEATHA: As for George. Well. George looks good—he's got a beautiful car
and he takes me to nice places and, as my sister-in-law says, he is probably
the richest boy I will ever get to know and I even like him sometimes—but if
the Youngers are sitting around waiting to see if their little Bennie is going to
tie up the family with the Murchisons, they are wasting their time.

RUTH: You mean you wouldn't marry George Murchison if he asked you someday? That pretty, rich thing? Honey, I knew you was odd—

BENEATHA: No I would not marry him if all I felt for him was what I feel now.
Besides, George's family wouldn't really like it.

MAMA: Why not?

BENEATHA: Oh, Mama—The Murchisons are honest-to-God-real-*live*-rich colored people, and the only people in the world who are more snobbish than
rich white people are rich colored people. I thought everybody knew that.
I've met Mrs. Murchison. She's a scene!

MAMA: You must not dislike people 'cause they well off, honey.

BENEATHA: Why not? It makes just as much sense as disliking people 'cause
they are poor, and lots of people do that.

RUTH *(a wisdom-of-the-ages manner. To Mama)*:   Well, she'll get over some of
this—

BENEATHA: Get over it? What are you talking about, Ruth? Listen, I'm going to
be a doctor. I'm not worried about who I'm going to marry yet—if I ever get
married.

MAMA and RUTH: *If!*

MAMA: Now, Bennie —

BENEATHA: Oh, I probably will . . . but first I'm going to be a doctor, and George, for one, still thinks that's pretty funny. I couldn't be bothered with that. I am going to be a doctor and everybody around here better understand that!

MAMA *(kindly):*   'Course you going to be a doctor, honey, God willing.

BENEATHA *(drily):*   God hasn't got a thing to do with it.

MAMA: Beneatha — that just wasn't necessary.

BENEATHA: Well — neither is God. I get sick of hearing about God.

MAMA: Beneatha!

BENEATHA: I mean it! I'm just tired of hearing about God all the time. What has He got to do with anything? Does He pay tuition?

MAMA: You 'bout to get your fresh little jaw slapped!

RUTH: That's just what she needs, all right!

BENEATHA: Why? Why can't I say what I want to around here, like everybody else?

MAMA: It don't sound nice for a young girl to say things like that — you wasn't brought up that way. Me and your father went to trouble to get you and Brother to church every Sunday.

BENEATHA: Mama, you don't understand. It's all a matter of ideas, and God is just one idea I don't accept. It's not important. I am not going out and be immoral or commit crimes because I don't believe in God. I don't even think about it. It's just that I get tired of Him getting credit for all the things the human race achieves through its own stubborn effort. There simply is no blasted God — there is only man and it is *He* who makes miracles!

Mama absorbs this speech, studies her daughter, and rises slowly and crosses to Beneatha and slaps her powerfully across the face. After, there is only silence and the daughter drops her eyes from her mother's face, and Mama is very tall before her.

MAMA: Now — you say after me, in my mother's house there is still God. *(There is a long pause and Beneatha stares at the floor wordlessly. Mama repeats the phrase with precision and cool emotion.)* In my mother's house there is still God.

BENEATHA: In my mother's house there is still God.

A long pause.

MAMA *(walking away from Beneatha, too disturbed for triumphant posture. Stopping and turning back to her daughter):*   There are some ideas we ain't going to have in this house. Not long as I am at the head of this family.

BENEATHA: Yes, ma'am.

Mama walks out of the room.

RUTH *(almost gently, with profound understanding):*   You think you a woman, Bennie — but you still a little girl. What you did was childish — so you got treated like a child.

BENEATHA: I see. *(Quietly.)* I also see that everybody thinks it's all right for
 Mama to be a tyrant. But all the tyranny in the world will never put a God in
 the heavens!

She picks up her books and goes out. Pause.

RUTH *(goes to Mama's door):*   She said she was sorry.

MAMA *(coming out, going to her plant):*   They frightens me, Ruth. My children.

RUTH: You got good children, Lena. They just a little off sometimes — but
 they're good.

MAMA: No — there's something come down between me and them that don't let
 us understand each other and I don't know what it is. One done almost lost
 his mind thinking 'bout money all the time and the other done commence
 to talk about things I can't seem to understand in no form or fashion. What is
 it that's changing, Ruth.

RUTH *(soothingly, older than her years):*   Now . . . you taking it all too seriously.
 You just got strong-willed children and it takes a strong woman like you to
 keep 'em in hand.

MAMA *(looking at her plant and sprinkling a little water on it):*   They spirited all
 right, my children. Got to admit they got spirit — Bennie and Walter. Like
 this little old plant that ain't never had enough sunshine or nothing — and
 look at it . . .

*She has her back to Ruth, who has had to stop ironing and lean against something
and put the back of her hand to her forehead.*

RUTH *(trying to keep Mama from noticing):*   You . . . sure . . . loves that little old
 thing, don't you? . . .

MAMA: Well, I always wanted me a garden like I used to see sometimes at the
 back of the houses down home. This plant is close as I ever got to having one.
 (She looks out of the window as she replaces the plant.) Lord, ain't nothing as
 dreary as the view from this window on a dreary day, is there? Why ain't you
 singing this morning, Ruth? Sing that "No Ways Tired." That song always
 lifts me up so — *(She turns at last to see that Ruth has slipped quietly to the
 floor, in a state of semiconsciousness.)* Ruth! Ruth honey — what's the matter
 with you . . . Ruth!

Curtain.

Scene 2

*It is the following morning; a Saturday morning, and house cleaning is in progress
at the Youngers'. Furniture has been shoved hither and yon and Mama is giving the
kitchen-area walls a washing down. Beneatha, in dungarees, with a handkerchief
tied around her face, is spraying insecticide into the cracks in the walls. As they
work, the radio is on and a Southside disk-jockey program is inappropriately filling
the house with a rather exotic saxophone blues. Travis, the sole idle one, is leaning
on his arms, looking out of the window.*

TRAVIS: Grandmama, that stuff Bennie is using smells awful. Can I go down-stairs, please?

MAMA: Did you get all them chores done already? I ain't seen you doing much.

TRAVIS: Yes'm — finished early. Where did Mama go this morning?

MAMA *(looking at Beneatha):* She had to go on a little errand.

The phone rings. Beneatha runs to answer it and reaches it before Walter, who has entered from bedroom.

TRAVIS: Where?

MAMA: To tend to her business.

BENEATHA: Haylo . . . *(Disappointed.)* Yes, he is. *(She tosses the phone to Walter, who barely catches it.)* It's Willie Harris again.

WALTER *(as privately as possible under Mama's gaze):* Hello, Willie. Did you get the papers from the lawyer? . . . No, not yet. I told you the mailman doesn't get here till ten-thirty . . . No, I'll come there . . . Yeah! Right away. *(He hangs up and goes for his coat.)*

BENEATHA: Brother, where did Ruth go?

WALTER *(as he exits):* How should I know!

TRAVIS: Aw come on, Grandma. Can I go outside?

MAMA: Oh, I guess so. You stay right in front of the house, though, and keep a good lookout for the postman.

TRAVIS: Yes'm. *(He darts into bedroom for stickball and bat, reenters, and sees Beneatha on her knees spraying under sofa with behind upraised. He edges closer to the target, takes aim, and lets her have it. She screams.)* Leave them poor little cockroaches alone, they ain't bothering you none! *(He runs as she swings the spraygun at him viciously and playfully.)* Grandma! Grandma!

MAMA: Look out there, girl, before you be spilling some of that stuff on that child!

TRAVIS *(safely behind the bastion of Mama):* That's right — look out, now! *(He exits.)*

BENEATHA *(drily):* I can't imagine that it would hurt him — it has never hurt the roaches.

MAMA: Well, little boys' hides ain't as tough as Southside roaches. You better get over there behind the bureau. I seen one marching out of there like Napoleon yesterday.

BENEATHA: There's really only one way to get rid of them, Mama —

MAMA: How?

BENEATHA: Set fire to this building! Mama, where did Ruth go?

MAMA *(looking at her with meaning):* To the doctor, I think.

BENEATHA: The doctor? What's the matter? *(They exchange glances.)* You don't think —

MAMA *(with her sense of drama):* Now I ain't saying what I think. But I ain't never been wrong 'bout a woman neither.

The phone rings.

BENEATHA *(at the phone):* Hay-lo . . . *(Pause, and a moment of recognition.)* Well — when did you get back! . . . And how was it? . . . Of course I've missed you—in my way . . . This morning? No . . . house cleaning and all that and Mama hates it if I let people come over when the house is like this . . . You *have?* Well, that's different . . . What is it—Oh, what the hell, come on over . . . Right, see you then. *Arrividerci.*

She hangs up.

MAMA *(who has listened vigorously, as is her habit):*   Who is that you inviting over here with this house looking like this? You ain't got the pride you was born with!

BENEATHA: Asagai doesn't care how houses look, Mama—he's an intellectual.

MAMA: Who?

BENEATHA: Asagai—Joseph Asagai. He's an African boy I met on campus. He's been studying in Canada all summer.

MAMA: What's his name?

BENEATHA: Asagai, Joseph. Ah-sah-guy . . . He's from Nigeria.

MAMA: Oh, that's the little country that was founded by slaves way back . . .

BENEATHA: No, Mama—that's Liberia.

MAMA: I don't think I never met no African before.

BENEATHA: Well, do me a favor and don't ask him a whole lot of ignorant questions about Africans. I mean, do they wear clothes and all that—

MAMA: Well, now, I guess if you think we so ignorant 'round here maybe you shouldn't bring your friends here—

BENEATHA: It's just that people ask such crazy things. All anyone seems to know about when it comes to Africa is Tarzan—

MAMA *(indignantly):*   Why should I know anything about Africa?

BENEATHA: Why do you give money at church for the missionary work?

MAMA: Well, that's to help save people.

BENEATHA: You mean save them from *heathenism*—

MAMA *(innocently):*   Yes.

BENEATHA: I'm afraid they need more salvation from the British and the French.

Ruth comes in forlornly and pulls off her coat with dejection. They both turn to look at her.

RUTH *(dispiritedly):*   Well, I guess from all the happy faces—everybody knows.

BENEATHA: You pregnant?

MAMA: Lord have mercy, I sure hope it's a little old girl. Travis ought to have a sister.

Beneatha and Ruth give her a hopeless look for this grandmotherly enthusiasm.

BENEATHA: How far along are you?

RUTH: Two months.

BENEATHA: Did you mean to? I mean did you plan it or was it an accident?

MAMA: What do you know about planning or not planning?

BENEATHA: Oh, Mama.

RUTH *(wearily):*   She's twenty years old, Lena.

BENEATHA: Did you plan it, Ruth?

RUTH: Mind your own business.

BENEATHA: It is my business—where is he going to live, on the *roof? (There is silence following the remark as the three women react to the sense of it.)* Gee— I didn't mean that, Ruth, honest. Gee, I don't feel like that at all. I—I think it is wonderful.

RUTH *(dully):* Wonderful.

BENEATHA: Yes—really.

MAMA *(looking at Ruth, worried):* Doctor say everything going to be all right?

RUTH *(far away):* Yes—she says everything is going to be fine . . .

MAMA *(immediately suspicious):* "She"—What doctor you went to?

Ruth folds over, near hysteria.

MAMA *(worriedly hovering over Ruth):* Ruth honey—what's the matter with you—you sick?

Ruth has her fists clenched on her thighs and is fighting hard to suppress a scream that seems to be rising in her.

BENEATHA: What's the matter with her, Mama?

MAMA *(working her fingers in Ruth's shoulders to relax her):* She be all right. Women gets right depressed sometimes when they get her way. *(Speaking softly, expertly, rapidly.)* Now you just relax. That's right . . . just lean back, don't think 'bout nothing at all . . . nothing at all—

RUTH: I'm all right . . .

The glassy-eyed look melts and then she collapses into a fit of heavy sobbing. The bell rings.

BENEATHA: Oh, my God—that must be Asagai.

MAMA *(to Ruth):* Come on now, honey. You need to lie down and rest awhile . . . then have some nice hot food.

They exit, Ruth's weight on her mother-in-law. Beneatha, herself profoundly disturbed, opens the door to admit a rather dramatic-looking young man with a large package.

ASAGAI: Hello, Alaiyo—

BENEATHA *(holding the door open and regarding him with pleasure):* Hello . . . *(Long pause.)* Well—come in. And please excuse everything. My mother was very upset about my letting anyone come here with the place like this.

ASAGAI *(coming into the room):* You look disturbed too . . . Is something wrong?

BENEATHA *(still at the door, absently):* Yes . . . we've all got acute ghetto-itus. *(She smiles and comes toward him, finding a cigarette and sitting.)* So—sit down! No! Wait! *(She whips the spraygun off sofa where she had left it and puts the cushions back. At last perches on arm of sofa. He sits.)* So, how was Canada?

ASAGAI *(a sophisticate):* Canadian.

BENEATHA *(looking at him):* Asagai, I'm very glad you are back.

ASAGAI *(looking back at her in turn):* Are you really?

BENEATHA: Yes—very.

ASAGAI: Why?—you were quite glad when I went away. What happened?

BENEATHA: You went away.

ASAGAI: Ahhhhhhhh.

BENEATHA: Before—you wanted to be so serious before there was time.

ASAGAI: How much time must there be before one knows what one feels?

BENEATHA *(stalling this particular conversation. Her hands pressed together, in a deliberately childish gesture)*:   What did you bring me?

ASAGAI *(handing her the package)*:   Open it and see.

BENEATHA *(eagerly opening the package and drawing out some records and the colorful robes of a Nigerian woman)*:   Oh Asagai! . . . You got them for me! . . . How beautiful . . . and the records too! *(She lifts out the robes and runs to the mirror with them and holds the drapery up in front of herself.)*

ASAGAI *(coming to her at the mirror)*:   I shall have to teach you how to drape it properly. *(He flings the material about her for the moment and stands back to look at her.)* Ah—Oh-pay-gay-day, oh-gbah-mu-shay. *(A Yoruba exclamation for admiration.)* You wear it well . . . very well . . . mutilated hair and all.

BENEATHA *(turning suddenly)*:   My hair—what's wrong with my hair?

ASAGAI *(shrugging)*:   Were you born with it like that?

BENEATHA *(reaching up to touch it)*:   No . . . of course not.

She looks back to the mirror, disturbed.

ASAGAI *(smiling)*:   How then?

BENEATHA: You know perfectly well how . . . as crinkly as yours . . . that's how.

ASAGAI: And it is ugly to you that way?

BENEATHA *(quickly)*:   Oh, no—not ugly . . . *(More slowly, apologetically.)* But it's so hard to manage when it's, well—raw.

ASAGAI: And so to accommodate that—you mutilate it every week?

BENEATHA: It's not mutilation!

ASAGAI *(laughing aloud at her seriousness)*:   Oh . . . please! I am only teasing you because you are so very serious about these things. *(He stands back from her and folds his arms across his chest as he watches her pulling at her hair and frowning in the mirror.)* Do you remember the first time you met me at school? . . . *(He laughs.)* You came up to me and you said—and I thought you were the most serious little thing I had ever seen—you said: *(He imitates her.)* "Mr. Asagai—I want very much to talk with you. About Africa. You see, Mr. Asagai, I am looking for my *identity!*"

He laughs.

BENEATHA *(turning to him, not laughing)*:   Yes—

Her face is quizzical, profoundly disturbed.

ASAGAI *(still teasing and reaching out and taking her face in his hands and turning her profile to him)*:   Well . . . it is true that this is not so much a profile of a Hollywood queen as perhaps a queen of the Nile—*(A mock dismissal of the importance of the question.)* But what does it matter? Assimilationism is so popular in your country.

BENEATHA *(wheeling, passionately, sharply)*:   I am not an assimilationist!

ASAGAI *(the protest hangs in the room for a moment and Asagai studies her, his laughter fading):*   Such a serious one. *(There is a pause.)* So—you like the robes? You must take excellent care of them—they are from my sister's personal wardrobe.

BENEATHA *(with incredulity):*   You—you sent all the way home—for me?

ASAGAI *(with charm):*   For you—I would do much more . . . Well, that is what I came for. I must go.

BENEATHA: Will you call me Monday?

ASAGAI: Yes . . . We have a great deal to talk about. I mean about identity and time and all that.

BENEATHA: Time?

ASAGAI: Yes. About how much time one needs to know what one feels.

BENEATHA: You see! You never understood that there is more than one kind of feeling which can exist between a man and a woman—or, at least, there should be.

ASAGAI *(shaking his head negatively but gently):*   No. Between a man and a woman there need be only one kind of feeling. I have that for you . . . Now even . . . right this moment . . .

BENEATHA: I know—and by itself—it won't do. I can find that anywhere.

ASAGAI: For a woman it should be enough.

BENEATHA: I know—because that's what it says in all the novels that men write. But it isn't. Go ahead and laugh—but I'm not interested in being someone's little episode in America or—*(With feminine vengeance.)*—one of them! *(Asagai has burst into laughter again.)* That's funny as hell, huh!

ASAGAI: It's just that every American girl I have known has said that to me. White—black—in this you are all the same. And the same speech, too!

BENEATHA *(angrily):*   Yuk, yuk, yuk!

ASAGAI: It's how you can be sure that the world's most liberated women are not liberated at all. You all talk about it too much!

Mama enters and is immediately all social charm because of the presence of a guest.

BENEATHA: Oh—Mama—this is Mr. Asagai.

MAMA: How do you do?

ASAGAI *(total politeness to an elder):*   How do you do, Mrs. Younger. Please forgive me for coming at such an outrageous hour on a Saturday.

MAMA: Well, you are quite welcome. I just hope you understand that our house don't always look like this. *(Chatterish.)* You must come again. I would love to hear all about—*(Not sure of the name.)*—your country. I think it's so sad the way our American Negroes don't know nothing about Africa 'cept Tarzan and all that. And all that money they pour into these churches when they ought to be helping you people over there drive out them French and Englishmen done taken away your land.

The mother flashes a slightly superior look at her daughter upon completion of the recitation.

ASAGAI *(taken aback by this sudden and acutely unrelated expression of sympathy):*   Yes . . . yes . . .

MAMA (*smiling at him suddenly and relaxing and looking him over*):   How many
    miles is it from here to where you come from?

ASAGAI: Many thousands.

MAMA (*looking at him as she would Walter*):   I bet you don't half look after your-
    self, being away from your mama either. I spec you better come 'round here
    from time to time to get yourself some decent homecooked meals . . .

ASAGAI (*moved*):   Thank you. Thank you very much. (*They are all quiet, then—*)
    Well . . . I must go. I will call you Monday, Alaiyo.

MAMA: What's that he call you?

ASAGAI: Oh—"Alaiyo." I hope you don't mind. It is what you would call a nick-
    name, I think. It is a Yoruba word. I am a Yoruba.

MAMA (*looking at Beneatha*):   I—I thought he was from—(*Uncertain.*)

ASAGAI (*understanding*):   Nigeria is my country. Yoruba is my tribal origin—

BENEATHA: You didn't tell us what Alaiyo means . . . for all I know, you might be
    calling me Little Idiot or something . . .

ASAGAI: Well . . . let me see . . . I do not know how just to explain it . . . The
    sense of a thing can be so different when it changes languages.

BENEATHA: You're evading.

ASAGAI: No—really it is difficult . . . (*Thinking.*) It means . . . it means One for
    Whom Bread—Food—Is Not Enough. (*He looks at her.*) Is that all right?

BENEATHA (*understanding, softly*):   Thank you.

MAMA (*looking from one to the other and not understanding any of it*):   Well . . .
    that's nice . . . You must come see us again—Mr.—

ASAGAI: Ah-sah-guy . . .

MAMA: Yes . . . Do come again.

ASAGAI: Good-bye.

He exits.

MAMA (*after him*):   Lord, that's a pretty thing just went out here! (*Insinuatingly,
    to her daughter.*) Yes, I guess I see why we done commence to get so inter-
    ested in Africa 'round here. Missionaries my aunt Jenny!

She exits.

BENEATHA: Oh, Mama! . . .

*She picks up the Nigerian dress and holds it up to her in front of the mirror again.
She sets the headdress on haphazardly and then notices her hair again and
clutches at it and then replaces the headdress and frowns at herself. Then she starts
to wriggle in front of the mirror as she thinks a Nigerian woman might. Travis
enters and stands regarding her.*

TRAVIS: What's the matter, girl, you cracking up?

BENEATHA: Shut up.

*She pulls the headdress off and looks at herself in the mirror and clutches at her
hair again and squinches her eyes as if trying to imagine something. Then, suddenly, she gets her raincoat and kerchief and hurriedly prepares for going out.*

MAMA (*coming back into the room*):   She's resting now. Travis, baby, run next
    door and ask Miss Johnson to please let me have a little kitchen cleanser.
    This here can is empty as Jacob's kettle.

TRAVIS: I just came in.

MAMA: Do as you told. *(He exits and she looks at her daughter.)* Where you going?

BENEATHA *(halting at the door)*:   To become a queen of the Nile!

She exits in a breathless blaze of glory. Ruth appears in the bedroom doorway.

MAMA: Who told you to get up?

RUTH: Ain't nothing wrong with me to be lying in no bed for. Where did Bennie go?

MAMA *(drumming her fingers)*:   Far as I could make out—to Egypt. *(Ruth just looks at her.)* What time is it getting to?

RUTH: Ten twenty. And the mailman going to ring that bell this morning just like he done every morning for the last umpteen years.

Travis comes in with the cleanser can.

TRAVIS: She say to tell you that she don't have much.

MAMA *(angrily)*:   Lord, some people I could name sure is tight-fisted! *(Directing her grandson.)* Mark two cans of cleanser on the list there. If she that hard up for kitchen cleanser, I sure don't want to forget to get her none!

RUTH: Lena—maybe the woman is just short on cleanser—

MAMA *(not listening)*:   —Much baking powder as she done borrowed from me all these years, she could of done gone into the baking business!

The bell sounds suddenly and sharply and all three are stunned—serious and silent—midspeech. In spite of all the other conversations and distractions of the morning, this is what they have been waiting for, even Travis, who looks helplessly from his mother to his grandmother. Ruth is the first to come to life again.

RUTH *(to Travis)*:   Get down them steps, boy!

Travis snaps to life and flies out to get the mail.

MAMA *(her eyes wide, her hand to her breast)*:   You mean it done really come?

RUTH *(excited)*:   Oh, Miss Lena!

MAMA *(collecting herself)*:   Well . . . I don't know what we all so excited about 'round here for. We known it was coming for months.

RUTH: That's a whole lot different from having it come and being able to hold it in your hands . . . a piece of paper worth ten thousand dollars . . . *(Travis bursts back into the room. He holds the envelope high above his head, like a little dancer, his face is radiant and he is breathless. He moves to his grandmother with sudden slow ceremony and puts the envelope into her hands. She accepts it, and then merely holds it and looks at it.)* Come on! Open it . . . Lord have mercy, I wish Walter Lee was here!

TRAVIS: Open it, Grandmama!

MAMA *(staring at it)*:   Now you all be quiet. It's just a check.

RUTH: Open it . . .

MAMA *(still staring at it)*:   Now don't act silly . . . We ain't never been no people to act silly 'bout no money—

RUTH *(swiftly)*:   We ain't never had none before—OPEN IT!

Mama finally makes a good strong tear and pulls out the thin blue slice of paper and inspects it closely. The boy and his mother study it raptly over Mama's shoulders.

MAMA: *Travis! (She is counting off with doubt.)* Is that the right number of zeros?

TRAVIS: Yes'm . . . ten thousand dollars. Gaalee, grandmama, you rich.

MAMA *(She holds the check away from her, still looking at it. Slowly her face sobers into a mask of unhappiness):* Ten thousand dollars. *(She hands it to Ruth.)* Put it away somewhere, Ruth. *(She does not look at Ruth; her eyes seem to be seeing something somewhere very far off.)* Ten thousand dollars they give you. Ten thousand dollars.

TRAVIS *(to his mother, sincerely):* What's the matter with Grandmama — don't she want to be rich?

RUTH *(distractedly):* You go on out and play now, baby. *(Travis exits. Mama starts wiping dishes absently, humming intently to herself. Ruth turns to her, with kind exasperation.)* You've gone and got yourself upset.

MAMA *(not looking at her):* I spec if it wasn't for you all . . . I would just put that money away or give it to the church or something.

RUTH: Now what kind of talk is that. Mr. Younger would just be plain mad if he could hear you talking foolish like that.

MAMA *(stopping and staring off):* Yes . . . he sure would. *(Sighing.)* We got enough to do with that money, all right. *(She halts then, and turns and looks at her daughter-in-law hard; Ruth avoids her eyes and Mama wipes her hands with finality and starts to speak firmly to Ruth.)* Where did you go today, girl?

RUTH: To the doctor.

MAMA *(impatiently):* Now, Ruth . . . you know better than that. Old Doctor Jones is strange enough in his way but there ain't nothing 'bout him make somebody slip and call him "she" — like you done this morning.

RUTH: Well, that's what happened — my tongue slipped.

MAMA: You went to see that woman, didn't you?

RUTH *(defensively, giving herself away):* What woman you talking about?

MAMA *(angrily):* That woman who —

Walter enters in great excitement.

WALTER: Did it come?

MAMA *(quietly):* Can't you give people a Christian greeting before you start asking about money?

WALTER *(to Ruth):* Did it come? *(Ruth unfolds the check and lays it quietly before him, watching him intently with thoughts of her own. Walter sits down and grasps it close and counts off the zeros.)* Ten thousand dollars — *(He turns suddenly, frantically to his mother and draws some papers out of his breast pocket.)* Mama — look. Old Willy Harris put everything on paper —

MAMA: Son — I think you ought to talk to your wife . . . I'll go on out and leave you alone if you want —

WALTER: I can talk to her later — Mama, look —

MAMA: Son —

WALTER: WILL SOMEBODY PLEASE LISTEN TO ME TODAY!

MAMA *(quietly):* I don't 'low no yellin' in this house, Walter Lee, and you know it — *(Walter stares at them in frustration and starts to speak several times.)* And there ain't going to be no investing in no liquor stores.

WALTER: But, Mama, you ain't even looked at it.

MAMA: I don't aim to have to speak on that again.

A long pause.

WALTER: You ain't looked at it and you don't aim to have to speak on that again? You ain't even looked at it and *you* have decided — *(Crumpling his papers.)* Well, *you* tell that to my boy tonight when you put him to sleep on the living-room couch . . . *(Turning to Mama and speaking directly to her.)* Yeah — and tell it to my wife, Mama, tomorrow when she has to go out of here to look after somebody else's kids. And tell it to *me*, Mama, every time we need a new pair of curtains and I have to watch *you* go out and work in somebody's kitchen. Yeah, you tell me then!

Walter starts out.

RUTH: Where you going?

WALTER: I'm going out!

RUTH: Where?

WALTER: Just out of this house somewhere —

RUTH *(getting her coat):*   I'll come too.

WALTER: I don't want you to come!

RUTH: I got something to talk to you about, Walter.

WALTER: That's too bad.

MAMA *(still quietly):*   Walter Lee — *(She waits and he finally turns and looks at her.)* Sit down.

WALTER: I'm a grown man, Mama.

MAMA: Ain't nobody said you wasn't grown. But you still in my house and my presence. And as long as you are — you'll talk to your wife civil. Now sit down.

RUTH *(suddenly):*   Oh, let him go on out and drink himself to death! He makes me sick to my stomach! *(She flings her coat against him and exits to bedroom.)*

WALTER *(violently flinging the coat after her):*   And you turn mine too, baby! *(The door slams behind her.)* That was my biggest mistake —

MAMA *(still quietly):*   Walter, what is the matter with you?

WALTER: Matter with me? Ain't nothing the matter with *me!*

MAMA: Yes there is. Something eating you up like a crazy man. Something more than me not giving you this money. The past few years I been watching it happen to you. You get all nervous acting and kind of wild in the eyes — *(Walter jumps up impatiently at her words.)* I said sit there now, I'm talking to you!

WALTER: Mama — I don't need no nagging at me today.

MAMA: Seem like you getting to a place where you always tied up in some kind of knot about something. But if anybody ask you 'bout it you just yell at 'em and bust out the house and go out and drink somewheres. Walter Lee, people can't live with that. Ruth's a good, patient girl in her way — but you getting to be too much. Boy, don't make the mistake of driving that girl away from you.

WALTER: Why—what she do for me?

MAMA: She loves you.

WALTER: Mama—I'm going out. I want to go off somewhere and be by myself for a while.

MAMA: I'm sorry 'bout your liquor store, son. It just wasn't the thing for us to do. That's what I want to tell you about—

WALTER: I got to go out, Mama—

He rises.

MAMA: It's dangerous, son.

WALTER: What's dangerous?

MAMA: When a man goes outside his home to look for peace.

WALTER *(beseechingly):*   Then why can't there never be no peace in this house then?

MAMA: You done found it in some other house?

WALTER: No—there ain't no woman! Why do women always think there's a woman somewhere when a man gets restless. *(Picks up the check.)* Do you know what this money means to me? Do you know what this money can do for us? *(Puts it back.)* Mama—Mama—I want so many things . . .

MAMA: Yes, son—

WALTER: I want so many things that they are driving me kind of crazy . . . Mama—look at me.

MAMA: I'm looking at you. You a good-looking boy. You got a job, a nice wife, a fine boy, and—

WALTER: A job. *(Looks at her.)* Mama, a job? I open and close car doors all day long. I drive a man around in his limousine and I say, "Yes, sir; no, sir; very good, sir; shall I take the Drive, sir?" Mama, that ain't no kind of job . . . that ain't nothing at all. *(Very quietly.)* Mama, I don't know if I can make you understand.

MAMA: Understand what, baby?

WALTER *(quietly):*   Sometimes it's like I can see the future stretched out in front of me—just plain as day. The future, Mama. Hanging over there at the edge of my days. Just waiting for me—a big, looming blank space—full of *nothing*. Just waiting for *me*. But it don't have to be. *(Pause. Kneeling beside her chair.)* Mama—sometimes when I'm downtown and I pass them cool, quiet-looking restaurants where them white boys are sitting back and talking 'bout things . . . sitting there turning deals worth millions of dollars . . . sometimes I see guys don't look much older than me—

MAMA: Son—how come you talk so much 'bout money?

WALTER *(with immense passion):*   Because it is life, Mama!

MAMA *(quietly):*   Oh—*(Very quietly.)* So now it's life. Money is life. Once upon a time freedom used to be life—now it's money. I guess the world really do change . . .

WALTER: No—it was always money, Mama. We just didn't know about it.

MAMA: No . . . something has changed. *(She looks at him.)* You something new, boy. In my time we was worried about not being lynched and getting to the

North if we could and how to stay alive and still have a pinch of dignity too . . . Now here come you and Beneatha—talking 'bout things we ain't never even thought about hardly, me and your daddy. You ain't satisfied or proud of nothing we done. I mean that you had a home; that we kept you out of trouble till you was grown; that you don't have to ride to work on the back of nobody's streetcar—You my children—but how different we done become.

WALTER *(a long beat. He pats her hand and gets up):*   You just don't understand, Mama, you just don't understand.

MAMA: Son—do you know your wife is expecting another baby? *(Walter stands, stunned, and absorbs what his mother has said.)* That's what she wanted to talk to you about. *(Walter sinks down into a chair.)* This ain't for me to be telling—but you ought to know. *(She waits.)* I think Ruth is thinking 'bout getting rid of that child.

WALTER *(slowly understanding):*   —No—no—Ruth wouldn't do that.

MAMA: When the world gets ugly enough—a woman will do anything for her family. *The part that's already living.*

WALTER: You don't know Ruth, Mama, if you think she would do that.

Ruth opens the bedroom door and stands there a little limp.

RUTH *(beaten):*   Yes I would too, Walter. *(Pause.)* I gave her a five-dollar down payment.

There is total silence as the man stares at his wife and the mother stares at her son.

MAMA *(presently):*   Well—*(Tightly.)* Well—son, I'm waiting to hear you say something . . . *(She waits.)* I'm waiting to hear how you be your father's son. Be the man he was . . . *(Pause. The silence shouts.)* Your wife say she going to destroy your child. And I'm waiting to hear you talk like him and say we a people who give children life, not who destroys them—*(She rises.)* I'm waiting to see you stand up and look like your daddy and say we done give up one baby to poverty and that we ain't going to give up nary another one . . . I'm waiting.

WALTER: Ruth—*(He can say nothing.)*

MAMA: If you a son of mine, tell her! *(Walter picks up his keys and his coat and walks out. She continues, bitterly.)* You . . . you are a disgrace to your father's memory. Somebody get me my hat!

Curtain.

ACT 2, Scene 1

Time: Later the same day.

At rise: Ruth is ironing again. She has the radio going. Presently Beneatha's bedroom door opens and Ruth's mouth falls and she puts down the iron in fascination.

RUTH: What have we got on tonight!

BENEATHA *(emerging grandly from the doorway so that we can see her thoroughly robed in the costume Asagai brought):*   You are looking at what a well-dressed Nigerian woman wears—*(She parades for Ruth, her hair completely hidden by the headdress; she is coquettishly fanning herself with an ornate*

oriental fan, mistakenly more like Butterfly than any Nigerian that ever was.)
Isn't it beautiful? *(She promenades to the radio and, with an arrogant flourish,
turns off the good loud blues that is playing.)* Enough of this assimilationist
junk! *(Ruth follows her with her eyes as she goes to the phonograph and puts
on a record and turns and waits ceremoniously for the music to come up. Then,
with a shout—)* OCOMOGOSIAY!

*Ruth jumps. The music comes up, a lovely Nigerian melody. Beneatha listens, enrap-
tured, her eyes far way—"back to the past." She begins to dance. Ruth is dumfounded.*

RUTH: What kind of dance is that?

BENEATHA: A folk dance.

RUTH *(Pearl Bailey):*   What kind of folks do that, honey?

BENEATHA: It's from Nigeria. It's a dance of welcome.

RUTH: Who you welcoming?

BENEATHA: The men back to the village.

RUTH: Where they been?

BENEATHA: How should I know—out hunting or something. Anyway, they are
    coming back now . . .

RUTH: Well, that's good.

BENEATHA *(with the record):*

Alundi, alundi

Alundi alunya

Jop pu a jeepua

Ang gu soooooooooo

Ai yai yae . . .

Ayehaye—alundi . . .

*Walter comes in during this performance; he has obviously been drinking. He leans
against the door heavily and watches his sister, at first with distaste. Then his eyes
look off—"back to the past"—as he lifts both his fists to the roof, screaming.*

WALTER: YEAH . . . AND ETHIOPIA STRETCH FORTH HER HANDS
    AGAIN! . . .

RUTH *(drily, looking at him):*   Yes—and Africa sure is claiming her own tonight.
    (She gives them both up and starts ironing again.)

WALTER *(all in a drunken, dramatic shout):*   Shut up! . . . I'm diggin them
    drums . . . them drums move me! . . . *(He makes his weaving way to his wife's
    face and leans in close to her.)* In my *heart of hearts*—*(He thumps his
    chest.)*—I am much warrior!

RUTH *(without even looking up):*   In your heart of hearts you are much drunkard.

WALTER *(coming away from her and starting to wander around the room, shouting):*
    Me and Jomo . . . *(Intently, in his sister's face. She has stopped dancing to
    watch him in this unknown mood.)* That's my man, Kenyatta. *(Shouting and
    thumping his chest.)* FLAMING SPEAR! HOT DAMN! *(He is suddenly in
    possession of an imaginary spear and actively spearing enemies all over the
    room.)* OCOMOGOSIAY . . .

BENEATHA *(to encourage Walter, thoroughly caught up with this side of him):*
    OCOMOGOSIAY, FLAMING SPEAR!

WALTER: THE LION IS WAKING . . . OWIMOWEH!

He pulls his shirt open and leaps up on the table and gestures with his spear.

BENEATHA: OWIMOWEH!

WALTER *(on the table, very far gone, his eyes pure glass sheets. He sees what we cannot, that he is a leader of his people, a great chief, a descendant of Chaka, and that the hour to march has come):*   Listen, my black brothers—

BENEATHA: OCOMOGOSIAY!

WALTER: —Do you hear the waters rushing against the shores of the coastlands—

BENEATHA: OCOMOGOSIAY!

WALTER: —Do you hear the screeching of the cocks in yonder hills beyond where the chiefs meet in council for the coming of the mighty war—

BENEATHA: OCOMOGOSIAY!

And now the lighting shifts subtly to suggest the world of Walter's imagination, and the mood shifts from pure comedy. It is the inner Walter speaking: the South-side chauffeur has assumed an unexpected majesty.

WALTER: —Do you hear the beating of the wings of the birds flying low over the mountains and the low places of our land—

BENEATHA: OCOMOGOSIAY!

WALTER: —Do you hear the singing of the women, singing the war songs of our fathers to the babies in the great houses? Singing the sweet war songs! *(The doorbell rings.)* OH, DO YOU HEAR, MY *BLACK* BROTHERS!

BENEATHA *(completely gone):*   We hear you, Flaming Spear—

Ruth shuts off the phonograph and opens the door. George Murchison enters.

WALTER: Telling us to prepare for the GREATNESS OF THE TIME! *(Lights back to normal. He turns and sees George.)* Black Brother!

He extends his hand for the fraternal clasp.

GEORGE: Black Brother, hell!

RUTH *(having had enough, and embarrassed for the family):*   Beneatha, you got company—what's the matter with you? Walter Lee Younger, get down off that table and stop acting like a fool . . .

Walter comes down off the table suddenly and makes a quick exit to the bathroom.

RUTH: He's had a little to drink . . . I don't know what her excuse is.

GEORGE *(to Beneatha):*   Look honey, we're going to the theater—we're not going to be *in* it . . . so go change, huh?

Beneatha looks at him and slowly, ceremoniously, lifts her hands and pulls off the headdress. Her hair is close-cropped and unstraightened. George freezes mid-sentence and Ruth's eyes all but fall out of her head.

GEORGE: What in the name of—

RUTH *(touching Beneatha's hair):*   Girl, you done lost your natural mind? Look at your head!

GEORGE: What have you done to your head—I mean your hair!

BENEATHA: Nothing—except cut it off.

RUTH:　Now that's the truth — it's what ain't been done to it! You expect this boy to go out with you with your head all nappy like that?

BENEATHA *(looking at George):*　That's up to George. If he's ashamed of his heritage —

GEORGE:　Oh, don't be so proud of yourself, Bennie — just because you look eccentric.

BENEATHA:　How can something that's natural be eccentric?

GEORGE:　That's what being eccentric means — being natural. Get dressed.

BENEATHA:　I don't like that, George.

RUTH:　Why must you and your brother make an argument out of everything people say?

BENEATHA:　Because I hate assimilationist Negroes!

RUTH:　Will somebody please tell me what assimila-whoever means!

GEORGE:　Oh, it's just a college girl's way of calling people Uncle Toms — but that isn't what it means at all.

RUTH:　Well, what does it mean?

BENEATHA *(cutting George off and staring at him as she replies to Ruth):*　It means someone who is willing to give up his own culture and submerge himself completely in the dominant, and in this case *oppressive* culture!

GEORGE:　Oh, dear, dear, dear! Here we go! A lecture on the African past! On our Great West African Heritage! In one second we will hear all about the great Ashanti empires; the great Songhay civilizations; and the great sculpture of Bénin — and then some poetry in the Bantu — and the whole monologue will end with the word *heritage! (Nastily.)* Let's face it, baby, your heritage is nothing but a bunch of raggedy-assed spirituals and some grass huts!

BENEATHA:　GRASS HUTS! *(Ruth crosses to her and forcibly pushes her toward the bedroom.)* See there . . . you are standing there in your splendid ignorance talking about people who were the first to smelt iron on the face of the earth! *(Ruth is pushing her through the door.)* The Ashanti were performing surgical operations when the English — *(Ruth pulls the door to, with Beneatha on the other side, and smiles graciously at George. Beneatha opens the door and shouts the end of the sentence defiantly at George.)* — were still tatooing themselves with blue dragons! *(She goes back inside.)*

RUTH:　Have a seat, George. *(They both sit. Ruth folds her hands rather primly on her lap, determined to demonstrate the civilization of the family.)* Warm, ain't it? I mean for September. *(Pause.)* Just like they always say about Chicago weather: if it's too hot or cold for you, just wait a minute and it'll change. *(She smiles happily at this cliché of clichés.)* Everybody say it's got to do with them bombs and things they keep setting off. *(Pause.)* Would you like a nice cold beer?

GEORGE:　No, thank you. I don't care for beer. *(He looks at his watch.)* I hope she hurries up.

RUTH:　What time is the show?

GEORGE:　It's an eight-thirty curtain. That's just Chicago, though. In New York standard curtain time is eight forty.

He is rather proud of this knowledge.

RUTH (*properly appreciating it*):   You get to New York a lot?

GEORGE (*offhand*):   Few times a year.

RUTH: Oh—that's nice. I've never been to New York.

Walter enters. We feel he has relieved himself, but the edge of unreality is still with him.

WALTER: New York ain't got nothing Chicago ain't. Just a bunch of hustling people all squeezed up together—being "Eastern."

He turns his face into a screw of displeasure.

GEORGE: Oh—you've been?

WALTER: *Plenty* of times.

RUTH (*shocked at the lie*):   Walter Lee Younger!

WALTER (*staring her down*):   Plenty! (*Pause.*) What we got to drink in this house? Why don't you offer this man some refreshment. (*To George.*) They don't know how to entertain people in this house, man.

GEORGE: Thank you—I don't really care for anything.

WALTER (*feeling his head; sobriety coming*):   Where's Mama?

RUTH: She ain't come back yet.

WALTER (*looking Murchison over from head to toe, scrutinizing his carefully casual tweed sports jacket over cashmere V-neck sweater over soft eyelet shirt and tie, and soft slacks, finished off with white buckskin shoes*):   Why all you college boys wear them faggoty-looking white shoes?

RUTH: Walter Lee!

George Murchison ignores the remark.

WALTER (*to Ruth*):   Well, they look crazy as hell—white shoes, cold as it is.

RUTH (*crushed*):   You have to excuse him—

WALTER: No he don't! Excuse me for what? What you always excusing me for! I'll excuse myself when I needs to be excused! (*A pause.*) They look as funny as them black knee socks Beneatha wears out of here all the time.

RUTH: It's the college *style*, Walter.

WALTER: Style, hell. She looks like she got burnt legs or something!

RUTH: Oh, Walter—

WALTER (*an irritable mimic*):   Oh, Walter! Oh, Walter! (*To Murchison.*) How's your old man making out? I understand you all going to buy that big hotel on the Drive? (*He finds a beer in the refrigerator, wanders over to Murchison, sipping and wiping his lips with the back of his hand, and straddling a chair backwards to talk to the other man.*) Shrewd move. Your old man is all right, man. (*Tapping his head and half winking for emphasis.*) I mean he knows how to operate. I mean he thinks *big*, you know what I mean, I mean for a *home*, you know? But I think he's kind of running out of ideas now. I'd like to talk to him. Listen, man, I got some plans that could turn this city upside down. I mean think like he does. *Big*. Invest big, gamble big, hell, lose *big* if you have to, you know what I mean. It's hard to find a man on this whole Southside who understands my kind of thinking—you dig? (*He scrutinizes Murchison again, drinks his beer, squints his eyes and leans in close, confidential, man to man.)* Me and you ought to sit down and talk sometimes, man. Man, I got me some ideas . . .

MURCHISON *(with boredom):*　Yeah — sometimes we'll have to do that, Walter.

WALTER *(understanding the indifference, and offended):*　Yeah — well, when you get the time, man. I know you a busy little boy.

RUTH:　Walter, please —

WALTER *(bitterly, hurt):*　I know ain't nothing in this world as busy as you colored college boys with your fraternity pins and white shoes . . .

RUTH *(covering her face with humiliation):*　Oh, Walter Lee —

WALTER:　I see you all all the time — with the books tucked under your arms — going to your *(British A — a mimic.)* "clahsses." And for what! What the hell you learning over there? Filling up your heads — *(Counting off on his fingers.)* — with the sociology and the psychology — but they teaching you how to be a man? How to take over and run the world? They teaching you how to run a rubber plantation or a steel mill? Naw — just to talk proper and read books and wear them faggoty-looking white shoes . . .

GEORGE *(looking at him with distaste, a little above it all):*　You're all wacked up with bitterness, man.

WALTER *(intently, almost quietly, between the teeth, glaring at the boy):*　And you — ain't you bitter, man? Ain't you just about had it yet? Don't you see no stars gleaming that you can't reach out and grab? You happy? — You contented son-of-a-bitch — you happy? You got it made? Bitter? Man, I'm a volcano. Bitter? Here I am a giant — surrounded by ants! Ants who can't even understand what it is the giant is talking about.

RUTH *(passionately and suddenly):*　Oh, Walter — ain't you with nobody!

WALTER *(violently):*　No! 'Cause ain't nobody with me! Not even my own mother!

RUTH:　Walter, that's a terrible thing to say!

Beneatha enters, dressed for the evening in a cocktail dress and earrings, hair natural.

GEORGE:　Well — hey — *(Crosses to Beneatha; thoughtful, with emphasis, since this is a reversal.)* You look great!

WALTER *(seeing his sister's hair for the first time):*　What's the matter with your head?

BENEATHA *(tired of the jokes now):*　I cut it off, Brother.

WALTER *(coming close to inspect it and walking around her):*　Well, I'll be damned. So that's what they mean by the African bush . . .

BENEATHA:　Ha ha. Let's go, George.

GEORGE *(looking at her):*　You know something? I like it. It's sharp. I mean it really is. *(Helps her into her wrap.)*

RUTH:　Yes — I think so, too. *(She goes to the mirror and starts to clutch at her hair.)*

WALTER:　Oh no! You leave yours alone, baby. You might turn out to have a pin-shaped head or something!

BENEATHA:　See you all later.

RUTH:　Have a nice time.

GEORGE:　Thanks. Good night. *(Half out the door, he reopens it. To Walter.)* Good night, Prometheus!

Beneatha and George exit.

WALTER *(to Ruth):*   Who is Prometheus?

RUTH: I don't know. Don't worry about it.

WALTER *(in fury, pointing after George):*   See there — they get to a point where they can't insult you man to man — they got to go talk about something ain't nobody never heard of!

RUTH: How do you know it was an insult? *(To humor him.)* Maybe Prometheus is a nice fellow.

WALTER: Prometheus! I bet there ain't even no such thing! I bet that simple-minded clown —

RUTH: Walter —

She stops what she is doing and looks at him.

WALTER *(yelling):*   Don't start!

RUTH: Start what?

WALTER: Your nagging! Where was I? Who was I with? How much money did I spend?

RUTH *(plaintively):*   Walter Lee — why don't we just try to talk about it . . .

WALTER *(not listening):*   I been out talking with people who understand me. People who care about the things I got on my mind.

RUTH *(wearily):*   I guess that means people like Willy Harris.

WALTER: Yes, people like Willy Harris.

RUTH *(with a sudden flash of impatience):*   Why don't you all just hurry up and go into the banking business and stop talking about it!

WALTER: Why? You want to know why? 'Cause we all tied up in a race of people that don't know how to do nothing but moan, pray and have babies!

The line is too bitter even for him and he looks at her and sits down.

RUTH: Oh, Walter . . . *(Softly.)* Honey, why can't you stop fighting me?

WALTER *(without thinking):*   Who's fighting you? Who even cares about you?

This line begins the retardation of his mood.

RUTH: Well — *(She waits a long time, and then with resignation starts to put away her things.)* I guess I might as well go on to bed . . . *(More or less to herself.)* I don't know where we lost it . . . but we have . . . *(Then, to him.)* I — I'm sorry about this new baby, Walter. I guess maybe I better go on and do what I started . . . I guess I just didn't realize how bad things was with us . . . I guess I just didn't really realize — *(She starts out to the bedroom and stops.)* You want some hot milk?

WALTER: Hot milk?

RUTH: Yes — hot milk.

WALTER: Why hot milk?

RUTH: 'Cause after all that liquor you come home with you ought to have something hot in your stomach.

WALTER: I don't want no milk.

RUTH: You want some coffee then?

WALTER: No, I don't want no coffee. I don't want nothing hot to drink. *(Almost plaintively.)* Why you always trying to give me something to eat?

RUTH *(standing and looking at him helplessly)*:   What *else* can I give you, Walter Lee Younger?

She stands and looks at him and presently turns to go out again. He lifts his head and watches her going away from him in a new mood which began to emerge when he asked her "Who cares about you?"

WALTER: It's been rough, ain't it, baby? *(She hears and stops but does not turn around and he continues to her back.)* I guess between two people there ain't never as much understood as folks generally thinks there is. I mean like between me and you — *(She turns to face him.)* How we gets to the place where we scared to talk softness to each other. *(He waits, thinking hard himself.)* Why you think it got to be like that? *(He is thoughtful, almost as a child would be.)* Ruth, what is it gets into people ought to be close?

RUTH: I don't know, honey. I think about it a lot.

WALTER: On account of you and me, you mean? The way things are with us. The way something done come down between us.

RUTH: There ain't so much between us, Walter . . . Not when you come to me and try to talk to me. Try to be with me . . . a little even.

WALTER *(total honesty)*:   Sometimes . . . sometimes . . . I don't even know how to try.

RUTH: Walter —

WALTER: Yes?

RUTH *(coming to him, gently and with misgiving, but coming to him)*:   Honey . . . life don't have to be like this. I mean sometimes people can do things so that things are better . . . You remember how we used to talk when Travis was born . . . about the way we were going to live . . . the kind of house . . . *(She is stroking his head.)* Well, it's all starting to slip away from us . . .

He turns her to him and they look at each other and kiss, tenderly and hungrily. The door opens and Mama enters — Walter breaks away and jumps up. A beat.

WALTER: Mama, where have you been?

MAMA: My — them steps is longer than they used to be. Whew! *(She sits down and ignores him.)* How you feeling this evening, Ruth?

Ruth shrugs, disturbed at having been interrupted and watching her husband knowingly.

WALTER: Mama, where have you been all day?

MAMA *(still ignoring him and leaning on the table and changing to more comfortable shoes)*:   Where's Travis?

RUTH: I let him go out earlier and he ain't come back yet. Boy, is he going to get it!

WALTER: Mama!

MAMA *(as if she has heard him for the first time)*:   Yes, son?

WALTER: Where did you go this afternoon?

MAMA: I went downtown to tend to some business that I had to tend to.

WALTER: What kind of business?

MAMA: You know better than to question me like a child, Brother.

WALTER *(rising and bending over the table):*   Where were you, Mama? *(Bringing his fists down and shouting.)* Mama, you didn't go do something with that insurance money, something crazy?

The front door opens slowly, interrupting him, and Travis peeks his head in, less than hopefully.

TRAVIS *(to his mother):*   Mama, I—

RUTH: "Mama I" nothing! You're going to get it, boy! Get on in that bedroom and get yourself ready!

TRAVIS: But I—

MAMA: Why don't you all never let the child explain hisself.

RUTH: Keep out of it now, Lena.

Mama clamps her lips together, and Ruth advances toward her son menacingly.

RUTH: A thousand times I have told you not to go off like that—

MAMA *(holding out her arms to her grandson):*   Well—at least let me tell him something. I want him to be the first one to hear . . . Come here, Travis. *(The boy obeys, gladly.)* Travis—*(She takes him by the shoulder and looks into his face.)*—you know that money we got in the mail this morning?

TRAVIS: Yes'm—

MAMA: Well—what you think your grandmama gone and done with that money?

TRAVIS: I don't know, Grandmama.

MAMA *(putting her finger on his nose for emphasis):*   She went out and she bought you a house! *(The explosion comes from Walter at the end of the revelation and he jumps up and turns away from all of them in a fury. Mama continues, to Travis.)* You glad about the house? It's going to be yours when you get to be a man.

TRAVIS: Yeah—I always wanted to live in a house.

MAMA: All right, gimme some sugar then—*(Travis puts his arms around her neck as she watches her son over the boy's shoulder. Then, to Travis, after the embrace.)* Now when you say your prayers tonight, you thank God and your grandfather—'cause it was him who give you the house—in his way.

RUTH *(taking the boy from Mama and pushing him toward the bedroom):*   Now you get out of here and get ready for your beating.

TRAVIS: Aw, Mama—

RUTH: Get on in there—*(Closing the door behind him and turning radiantly to her mother-in-law.)* So you went and did it!

MAMA *(quietly, looking at her son with pain):*   Yes, I did.

RUTH *(raising both arms classically):*   PRAISE GOD! *(Looks at Walter a moment, who says nothing. She crosses rapidly to her husband.)* Please, honey—let me be glad . . . you be glad too. *(She has laid her hands on his shoulders, but he shakes himself free of her roughly, without turning to face her.)* Oh, Walter . . . a home . . . a home. *(She comes back to Mama.)* Well— where is it? How big is it? How much it going to cost?

MAMA: Well—

RUTH: When we moving?

MAMA *(smiling at her):*   First of the month.

RUTH *(throwing back her head with jubilance):*   *Praise God!*

MAMA *(tentatively, still looking at her son's back turned against her and Ruth):* It's—it's a nice house too . . . *(She cannot help speaking directly to him. An imploring quality in her voice, her manner, makes her almost like a girl now.)* Three bedrooms—nice big one for you and Ruth . . . Me and Beneatha still have to share our room, but Travis have one of his own—and *(With difficulty.)* I figure if the—new baby—is a boy, we could get one of them double-decker outfits . . . And there's a yard with a little patch of dirt where I could maybe get to grow me a few flowers . . . And a nice big basement . . .

RUTH: Walter honey, be glad—

MAMA *(still to his back, fingering things on the table):*   'Course I don't want to make it sound fancier than it is . . . It's just a plain little old house—but it's made good and solid—and it will be *ours.* Walter Lee—it makes a difference in a man when he can walk on floors that belong to *him* . . .

RUTH: Where is it?

MAMA *(frightened at this telling):*   Well—well—it's out there in Clybourne Park—

Ruth's radiance fades abruptly, and Walter finally turns slowly to face his mother with incredulity and hostility.

RUTH: Where?

MAMA *(matter-of-factly):*   Four o six Clybourne Street, Clybourne Park.

RUTH: Clybourne Park? Mama, there ain't no colored people living in Clybourne Park.

MAMA *(almost idiotically):*   Well, I guess there's going to be some now.

WALTER *(bitterly):*   So that's the peace and comfort you went out and bought for us today!

MAMA *(raising her eyes to meet his finally):*   Son—I just tried to find the nicest place for the least amount of money for my family.

RUTH *(trying to recover from the shock):*   Well—well—'course I ain't one never been 'fraid of no crackers, mind you—but—well, wasn't there no other houses nowhere?

MAMA: Them houses they put up for colored in them areas way out all seem to cost twice as much as other houses. I did the best I could.

RUTH *(struck senseless with the news, in its various degrees of goodness and trouble, she sits a moment, her fists propping her chin in thought, and then she starts to rise, bringing her fists down with vigor, the radiance spreading from cheek to cheek again):*   Well—well—All I can say is—if this is my time in life—MY TIME—to say good-bye—*(And she builds with momentum as she starts to circle the room with an exuberant, almost tearfully happy release.)*—to these Goddamned cracking walls!—*(She pounds the walls.)*—and these marching roaches!—*(She wipes at an imaginary army of marching roaches.)*—and this cramped little closet which ain't now or never was no kitchen! . . . then I say it loud and good, HALLELUJAH! AND GOOD-BYE MISERY . . . I DON'T NEVER WANT TO SEE YOUR UGLY FACE AGAIN! *(She laughs joyously, having practically destroyed the apartment, and flings her arms up and lets them come down happily, slowly, reflectively, over her abdomen, aware for the first time perhaps that the life therein pulses with happiness and not despair.)* Lena?

MAMA *(moved, watching her happiness):*   Yes, honey?

RUTH *(looking off):*   Is there — is there a whole lot of sunlight?

MAMA *(understanding):*   Yes, child, there's a whole lot of sunlight.

Long pause.

Ruth *(collecting herself and going to the door of the room Travis is in):*   Well — I guess I better see 'bout Travis. *(To Mama.)* Lord, I sure don't feel like whipping nobody today!

She exits.

Mama *(the mother and son are left alone now and the mother waits a long time, considering deeply, before she speaks):*   Son — you — you understand what I done, don't you? *(Walter is silent and sullen.)* I — I just seen my family falling apart today . . . just falling to pieces in front of my eyes . . . We couldn't of gone on like we was today. We was going backwards 'stead of forwards — talking 'bout killing babies and wishing each other was dead . . . When it gets like that in life — you just got to do something different, push on out and do something bigger . . . *(She waits.)* I wish you say something, son . . . I wish you'd say how deep inside you you think I done the right thing —

WALTER *(crossing slowly to his bedroom door and finally turning there and speaking measuredly):*   What you need me to say you done right for? You the head of this family. You run our lives like you want to. It was your money and you did what you wanted with it. So what you need for me to say it was all right for? *(Bitterly, to hurt her as deeply as he knows is possible.)* So you butchered up a dream of mine — you — who always talking 'bout your children's dreams . . .

MAMA: Walter Lee —

He just closes the door behind him. Mama sits alone, thinking heavily.

Curtain.

Scene 2

Time: Friday night, a few weeks later.

   At rise: Packing crates mark the intention of the family to move. Beneatha and George come in, presumably from an evening out again.

GEORGE: O.K. . . . O.K., whatever you say . . . *(They both sit on the couch. He tries to kiss her. She moves away.)* Look, we've had a nice evening; let's not spoil it, huh? . . .

He again turns her head and tries to nuzzle in and she turns away from him, not with distaste but with momentary lack of interest; in a mood to pursue what they were talking about.

BENEATHA: I'm *trying* to talk to you.

GEORGE: We always talk.

BENEATHA: Yes — and I love to talk.

GEORGE *(exasperated; rising):*   I know it and I don't mind it sometimes ... I want you to cut it out, see — The moody stuff, I mean. I don't like it. You're a nice-looking girl ... all over. That's all you need, honey, forget the atmosphere. Guys aren't going to go for the atmosphere — they're going to go for what they see. Be glad for that. Drop the Garbo routine. It doesn't go with you. As for myself, I want a nice — *(Groping.)* — simple *(Thoughtfully.)* — sophisticated girl ... not a poet — O.K.?

He starts to kiss her, she rebuffs him again and he jumps up.

BENEATHA: Why are you angry, George?

GEORGE: Because this is stupid! I don't go out with you to discuss the nature of "quiet desperation" or to hear all about your thoughts — because the world will go on thinking what it thinks regardless —

BENEATHA: Then why read books? Why go to school?

GEORGE *(with artificial patience, counting on his fingers):*   It's simple. You read books — to learn facts — to get grades — to pass the course — to get a degree. That's all — it has nothing to do with thoughts.

A long pause.

BENEATHA: I see. *(He starts to sit.)* Good night, George.

George looks at her a little oddly, and starts to exit. He meets Mama coming in.

GEORGE: Oh — hello, Mrs. Younger.

MAMA: Hello, George, how you feeling?

GEORGE: Fine — fine, how are you?

MAMA: Oh, a little tired. You know them steps can get you after a day's work. You all have a nice time tonight?

GEORGE: Yes — a fine time. A fine time.

MAMA: Well, good night.

GEORGE: Good night. *(He exits. Mama closes the door behind her.)* Hello, honey. What you sitting like that for?

BENEATHA: I'm just sitting.

MAMA: Didn't you have a nice time?

BENEATHA: No.

MAMA: No? What's the matter?

BENEATHA: Mama, George is a fool — honest. *(She rises.)*

MAMA *(hustling around unloading the packages she has entered with. She stops):* Is he, baby?

BENEATHA: Yes.

Beneatha makes up Travis's bed as she talks.

MAMA: You sure?

BENEATHA: Yes.

MAMA: Well — I guess you better not waste your time with no fools.

Beneatha looks up at her mother, watching her put groceries in the refrigerator. Finally she gathers up her things and starts into the bedroom. At the door she stops and looks back at her mother.

BENEATHA: Mama—

MAMA: Yes, baby—

BENEATHA: Thank you.

MAMA: For what?

BENEATHA: For understanding me this time.

She exits quickly and the mother stands, smiling a little, looking at the place where Beneatha just stood. Ruth enters.

RUTH: Now don't you fool with any of this stuff, Lena—

MAMA: Oh, I just thought I'd sort a few things out. Is Brother here?

RUTH: Yes.

MAMA *(with concern)*: Is he—

RUTH *(reading her eyes)*: Yes.

Mama is silent and someone knocks on the door. Mama and Ruth exchange weary and knowing glances and Ruth opens it to admit the neighbor, Mrs. Johnson,° who is a rather squeaky wide-eyed lady of no particular age, with a newspaper under her arm.

Mama *(changing her expression to acute delight and a ringing cheerful greeting)*: Oh—hello there, Johnson.

JOHNSON *(this is a woman who decided long ago to be enthusiastic about EVERY-THING in life and she is inclined to wave her wrist vigorously at the height of her exclamatory comments)*: Hello there, yourself! H'you this evening, Ruth?

RUTH *(not much of a deceptive type)*: Fine, Mis' Johnson, h'you?

JOHNSON: Fine. *(Reaching out quickly, playfully, and patting Ruth's stomach.)* Ain't you starting to poke out none yet! *(She mugs with delight at the over familiar remark and her eyes dart around looking at the crates and packing preparation; Mama's face is a cold sheet of endurance.)* Oh, ain't we getting ready round here, though! Yessir! Lookathere! I'm telling you the Youngers is really getting ready to "move on up a little higher!"—Bless God!

MAMA *(a little drily, doubting the total sincerity of the Blesser)*: Bless God.

JOHNSON: He's good, ain't He?

MAMA: Oh yes, He's good.

JOHNSON: I mean sometimes He works in mysterious ways . . . but He works, don't He!

MAMA *(the same)*: Yes, he does.

JOHNSON: I'm just sooooooo happy for y'all. And this here child—*(About Ruth.)* looks like she could just pop open with happiness, don't she. Where's all the rest of the family?

MAMA: Bennie's gone to bed—

JOHNSON: Ain't no . . . *(The implication is pregnancy.)* sickness done hit you—I hope . . . ?

MAMA: No—she just tired. She was out this evening.

JOHNSON *(all is a coo, an emphatic coo)*: Aw—ain't that lovely. She still going out with the little Murchison boy?

Mrs. Johnson: This character and the scene of her visit were cut from the original production and early editions of the play.

MAMA *(drily):*   Ummmm huh.

JOHNSON: That's lovely. You sure got lovely children, Younger. Me and Isaiah talks all the time 'bout what fine children you was blessed with. We sure do.

MAMA: Ruth, give Mis' Johnson a piece of sweet potato pie and some milk.

JOHNSON: Oh honey, I can't stay hardly a minute—I just dropped in to see if there was anything I could do. *(Accepting the food easily.)* I guess y'all seen the news what's all over the colored paper this week . . .

MAMA: No—didn't get mine yet this week.

JOHNSON *(lifting her head and blinking with the spirit of catastrophe):*   You mean you ain't read 'bout them colored people that was bombed out their place out there?

Ruth straightens with concern and takes the paper and reads it. Johnson notices her and feeds commentary.

JOHNSON: Ain't it something how bad these here white folks is getting here in Chicago! Lord, getting so you think you right down in Mississippi! *(With a tremendous and rather insincere sense of melodrama.)* 'Course I thinks it's wonderful how our folk keeps on pushing out. You hear some of these Negroes round here talking 'bout how they don't go where they ain't wanted and all that—but not me, honey! *(This is a lie.)* Wilhemenia Othella Johnson goes anywhere, any time she feels like it! *(With head movement for emphasis.)* Yes I do! Why if we left it up to these here crackers, the poor niggers wouldn't have nothing—*(She clasps her hand over her mouth.)* Oh, I always forgets you don't 'low that word in your house.

MAMA *(quietly, looking at her):*   No—I don't 'low it.

JOHNSON *(vigorously again):*   Me neither! I was just telling Isaiah yesterday when he come using it in front of me—I said, "Isaiah, it's just like Mis' Younger says all the time—"

MAMA: Don't you want some more pie?

JOHNSON: No—no thank you; this was lovely. I got to get on over home and have my midnight coffee. I hear some people say it don't let them sleep but I finds I can't close my eyes right lessen I done had that laaaast cup of coffee . . . *(She waits. A beat. Undaunted.)* My Goodnight coffee, I calls it!

MAMA *(with much eye-rolling and communication between herself and Ruth):*   Ruth, why don't you give Mis' Johnson some coffee.

Ruth gives Mama an unpleasant look for her kindness.

JOHNSON *(accepting the coffee):*   Where's Brother tonight?

MAMA: He's lying down.

JOHNSON: MMmmmmm, he sure gets his beauty rest, don't he? Good-looking man. Sure is a good-looking man! *(Reaching out to pat Ruth's stomach again.)* I guess that's how come we keep on having babies around here. *(She winks at Mama.)* One thing 'bout Brother, he always know how to have a *good* time. And soooooo ambitious! I bet it was his idea y'all moving out to Clybourne Park. Lord—I bet this time next month y'all's names will have been in the papers plenty—*(Holding up her hands to mark off each word of the headline she can see in front of her.)* "NEGROES INVADE CLYBOURNE PARK— BOMBED!"

MAMA *(she and Ruth look at the woman in amazement):*   We ain't exactly moving out there to get bombed.

JOHNSON: Oh honey—you know I'm praying to God every day that don't noth-ing like that happen! But you have to think of life like it is—and these here Chicago peckerwoods is some baaaad peckerwoods.

MAMA *(wearily):*   We done thought about all that Mis' Johnson.

Beneatha comes out of the bedroom in her robe and passes through to the bath-room. Mrs. Johnson turns.

JOHNSON: Hello there, Bennie!

BENEATHA *(crisply):*   Hello, Mrs. Johnson.

JOHNSON: How is school?

BENEATHA *(crisply):*   Fine, thank you. *(She goes out.)*

JOHNSON *(insulted):*   Getting so she don't have much to say to nobody.

MAMA: The child was on her way to the bathroom.

JOHNSON: I know—but sometimes she act like ain't got time to pass the time of day with nobody ain't been to college. Oh—I ain't criticizing her none. It's just—you know how some of our young people gets when they get a little education. *(Mama and Ruth say nothing, just look at her.)* Yes—well. Well, I guess I better get on home. *(Unmoving.)* 'Course I can understand how she must be proud and everything—being the only one in the family to make something of herself. I know just being a chauffeur ain't never satisfied Brother none. He shouldn't feel like that, though. Ain't nothing wrong with being a chauffeur.

MAMA: There's plenty wrong with it.

JOHNSON: What?

MAMA: Plenty. My husband always said being any kind of a servant wasn't a fit thing for a man to have to be. He always said a man's hands was made to make things, or to turn the earth with—not to drive nobody's car for 'em—or—*(She looks at her own hands.)* carry they slop jars. And my boy is just like him—he wasn't meant to wait on nobody.

JOHNSON *(rising, somewhat offended):*   Mmmmmmmmmm. The Youngers is too much for me! *(She looks around.)* You sure one proud-acting bunch of col-ored folks. Well—I always thinks like Booker T. Washington said that time—"Education has spoiled many a good plow hand"—

MAMA: Is that what old Booker T. said?

JOHNSON: He sure did.

MAMA: Well, it sounds just like him. The fool.

JOHNSON *(indignantly):*   Well—he was one of our great men.

MAMA: Who said so?

JOHNSON *(nonplussed):*   You know, me and you ain't never agreed about some things, Lena Younger. I guess I better be going—

RUTH *(quickly):*   Good night.

JOHNSON: Good night. Oh—*(Thrusting it at her.)* You can keep the paper! *(With a trill.)* 'Night.

MAMA: Good night, Mis' Johnson.

Mrs. Johnson exits.

RUTH: If ignorance was gold . . .

MAMA: Shush. Don't talk about folks behind their backs.

RUTH: You do.

MAMA: I'm old and corrupted. *(Beneatha enters.)* You was rude to Mis' Johnson, Beneatha, and I don't like it at all.

BENEATHA *(at her door):* Mama, if there are two things we, as a people, have got to overcome, one is the Klu Klux Klan — and the other is Mrs. Johnson. *(She exits.)*

MAMA: Smart aleck.

The phone rings.

RUTH: I'll get it.

MAMA: Lord, ain't this a popular place tonight.

RUTH *(at the phone):* Hello — Just a minute. *(Goes to door.)* Walter, it's Mrs. Arnold. *(Waits. Goes back to the phone. Tense.)* Hello. Yes, this is his wife speaking . . . He's lying down now. Yes . . . well, he'll be in tomorrow. He's been very sick. Yes — I know we should have called, but we were so sure he'd be able to come in today. Yes — yes, I'm very sorry. Yes . . . Thank you very much. *(She hangs up. Walter is standing in the doorway of the bedroom behind her.)* That was Mrs. Arnold.

WALTER *(indifferently):* Was it?

RUTH: She said if you don't come in tomorrow that they are getting a new man . . .

WALTER: Ain't that sad — ain't that crying sad.

RUTH: She said Mr. Arnold has had to take a cab for three days . . . Walter, you ain't been to work for three days! *(This is a revelation to her.)* Where you been, Walter Lee Younger? *(Walter looks at her and starts to laugh.)* You're going to lose your job.

WALTER: That's right . . . *(He turns on the radio.)*

RUTH: Oh, Walter, and with your mother working like a dog every day —

A steamy, deep blues pours into the room.

WALTER: That's sad too — Everything is sad.

MAMA: What you been doing for these three days, son?

WALTER: Mama — you don't know all the things a man what got leisure can find to do in this city . . . What's this — Friday night? Well — Wednesday I borrowed Willy Harris' car and I went for a drive . . . just me and myself and I drove and drove . . . Way out . . . way past South Chicago, and I parked the car and I sat and looked at the steel mills all day long. I just sat in the car and looked at them big black chimneys for hours. Then I drove back and I went to the Green Hat. *(Pause.)* And Thursday — Thursday I borrowed the car again and I got in it and I pointed it the other way and I drove the other way — for hours — way, way up to Wisconsin, and I looked at the farms. I just drove and looked at the farms. Then I drove back and I went to the Green Hat. *(Pause.)* And today — today I didn't get the car. Today I just walked. All over the Southside. And I looked at the Negroes and they looked at me and finally I just sat down on the curb at Thirty-ninth and South Parkway and I just sat there and watched the Negroes go by. And then I went to the Green Hat. You all sad? You all depressed? And you know where I am going right now —

Ruth goes out quietly.

MAMA: Oh, Big Walter, is this the harvest of our days?

WALTER: You know what I like about the Green Hat? I like this little cat they got there who blows a sax . . . He blows. He talks to me. He ain't but 'bout five feet tall and he's got a conked head and his eyes is always closed and he's all music —

MAMA *(rising and getting some papers out of her handbag):*   Walter —

WALTER: And there's this other guy who plays the piano . . . and they got a sound. I mean they can work on some music . . . They got the best little combo in the world in the Green Hat . . . You can just sit there and drink and listen to them three men play and you realize that don't nothing matter worth a damn, but just being there —

MAMA: I've helped do it to you, haven't I, son? Walter, I been wrong.

WALTER: Naw — you ain't never been wrong about nothing, Mama.

MAMA: Listen to me, now. I say I been wrong, son. That I been doing to you what the rest of the world been doing to you. *(She turns off the radio.)* Walter — *(She stops and he looks up slowly at her and she meets his eyes pleadingly.)* What you ain't never understood is that I ain't got nothing, don't own nothing, ain't never really wanted nothing that wasn't for you. There ain't nothing as precious to me . . . There ain't nothing worth holding on to, money, dreams, nothing else — if it means — if it means it's going to destroy my boy. *(She takes an envelope out of her handbag and puts it in front of him and he watches her without speaking or moving.)* I paid the man thirty-five hundred dollars down on the house. That leaves sixty-five hundred dollars. Monday morning I want you to take this money and take three thousand dollars and put it in a savings account for Beneatha's medical schooling. The rest you put in a checking account — with your name on it. And from now on any penny that come out of it or that go in it is for you to look after. For you to decide. *(She drops her hands a little helplessly.)* It ain't much, but it's all I got in the world and I'm putting it in your hands. I'm telling you to be the head of this family from now on like you supposed to be.

WALTER *(stares at the money):*   You trust me like that, Mama?

MAMA: I ain't never stop trusting you. Like I ain't never stop loving you.

She goes out, and Walter sits looking at the money on the table. Finally, in a decisive gesture, he gets up, and, in mingled joy and desperation, picks up the money. At the same moment, Travis enters for bed.

TRAVIS: What's the matter, Daddy? You drunk?

WALTER *(sweetly, more sweetly than we have ever known him):*   No, Daddy ain't drunk. Daddy ain't going to never be drunk again . . .

TRAVIS: Well, good night, Daddy.

The father has come from behind the couch and leans over, embracing his son.

WALTER: Son, I feel like talking to you tonight.

TRAVIS: About what?

WALTER: Oh, about a lot of things. About you and what kind of man you going to be when you grow up . . . Son — son, what do you want to be when you grow up?

TRAVIS: A bus driver.

WALTER *(laughing a little):*   A what? Man, that ain't nothing to want to be!

TRAVIS: Why not?

WALTER: 'Cause, man — it ain't big enough — you know what I mean.

TRAVIS: I don't know then. I can't make up my mind. Sometimes Mama asks me that too. And sometimes when I tell her I just want to be like you — she says she don't want me to be like that and sometimes she says she does. . . .

WALTER *(gathering him up in his arms):*   You know what, Travis? In seven years you going to be seventeen years old. And things is going to be very different with us in seven years, Travis. . . . One day when you are seventeen I'll come home — home from my office downtown somewhere —

TRAVIS: You don't work in no office, Daddy.

WALTER: No — but after tonight. After what your daddy gonna do tonight, there's going to be offices — a whole lot of offices. . . .

TRAVIS: What you gonna do tonight, Daddy?

WALTER: You wouldn't understand yet, son, but your daddy's gonna make a transaction . . . a business transaction that's going to change our lives. . . . That's how come one day when you 'bout seventeen years old I'll come home and I'll be pretty tired, you know what I mean, after a day of conferences and secretaries getting things wrong the way they do . . .'cause an executive's life is hell, man — *(The more he talks the farther away he gets.)* And I'll pull the car up on the driveway . . . just a plain black Chrysler, I think, with white walls — no — black tires. More elegant. Rich people don't have to be flashy . . . though I'll have to get something a little sportier for Ruth — maybe a Cadillac convertible to do her shopping in. . . . And I'll come up the steps to the house and the gardener will be clipping away at the hedges and he'll say, "Good evening, Mr. Younger." And I'll say, "Hello, Jefferson, how are you this evening?" And I'll go inside and Ruth will come downstairs and meet me at the door and we'll kiss each other and she'll take my arm and we'll go up to your room to see you sitting on the floor with the catalogues of all the great schools in America around you. . . . All the great schools in the world! And — and I'll say, all right son — it's your seventeenth birthday, what is it you've decided? . . . Just tell me where you want to go to school and you'll *go.* Just tell me, what it is you want to be — and you'll *be* it. . . . Whatever you want to be — Yessir! *(He holds his arms open for Travis.)* You just name it, son . . . *(Travis leaps into them.)* and I hand you the world!

Walter's voice has risen in pitch and hysterical promise and on the last line he lifts Travis high.

Blackout.

Scene 3

Time: Saturday, moving day, one week later.

   Before the curtain rises, Ruth's voice, a strident, dramatic church alto, cuts through the silence.

It is, in the darkness, a triumphant surge, a penetrating statement of expectation: "Oh, Lord, I don't feel no ways tired! Children, oh, glory hallelujah!"

As the curtain rises we see that Ruth is alone in the living room, finishing up the family's packing. It is moving day. She is nailing crates and tying cartons. Beneatha enters, carrying a guitar case, and watches her exuberant sister-in-law.

RUTH: Hey!

BENEATHA *(putting away the case):* Hi.

RUTH *(pointing at a package):* Honey—look in that package there and see what I found on sale this morning at the South Center. *(Ruth gets up and moves to the package and draws out some curtains.)* Lookahere—hand-turned hems!

BENEATHA: How do you know the window size out there?

RUTH *(who hadn't thought of that):* Oh—Well, they bound to fit something in the whole house. Anyhow, they was too good a bargain to pass up. *(Ruth slaps her head, suddenly remembering something.)* Oh, Bennie—I meant to put a special note on that carton over there. That's your mama's good china and she wants 'em to be very careful with it.

BENEATHA: I'll do it.

Beneatha finds a piece of paper and starts to draw large letters on it.

RUTH: You know what I'm going to do soon as I get in that new house?

BENEATHA: What?

RUTH: Honey—I'm going to run me a tub of water up to here . . . *(With her fingers practically up to her nostrils.)* And I'm going to get in it—and I am going to sit . . . and sit . . . and sit in that hot water and the first person who knocks to tell *me* to hurry up and come out—

BENEATHA: Gets shot at sunrise.

RUTH *(laughing happily):* You said it, sister! *(Noticing how large Beneatha is absent-mindedly making the note):* Honey, they ain't going to read that from no airplane.

BENEATHA *(laughing herself):* I guess I always think things have more emphasis if they are big, somehow.

RUTH *(looking up at her and smiling):* You and your brother seem to have that as a philosophy of life. Lord, that man—done changed so 'round here. You know—you know what we did last night? Me and Walter Lee?

BENEATHA: What?

RUTH *(smiling to herself):* We went to the movies. *(Looking at Beneatha to see if she understands.)* We went to the movies. You know the last time me and Walter went to the movies together?

BENEATHA: No.

RUTH: Me neither. That's how long it been. *(Smiling again.)* But we went last night. The picture wasn't much good, but that didn't seem to matter. We went—and we held hands.

BENEATHA: Oh, Lord!

RUTH: We held hands—and you know what?

BENEATHA: What?

RUTH:　　When we come out of the show it was late and dark and all the stores and
　　　things was closed up . . . and it was kind of chilly and there wasn't many
　　　people on the streets . . . and we was still holding hands, me and Walter.

BENEATHA:　　You're killing me.

*Walter enters with a large package. His happiness is deep in him; he cannot keep
still with his newfound exuberance. He is singing and wiggling and snapping his
fingers. He puts his package in a corner and puts a phonograph record, which he
has brought in with him, on the record player. As the music, soulful and sensuous,
comes up he dances over to Ruth and tries to get her to dance with him. She gives in
at last to his raunchiness and in a fit of giggling allows herself to be drawn into his
mood. They dip and she melts into his arms in a classic, body-melting "slow drag."*

BENEATHA *(regarding them a long time as they dance, then drawing in her breath
　　　for a deeply exaggerated comment which she does not particularly mean):*
　　　Talk about — olddddddddddd-fashionedddddddd — Negroes!

WALTER *(stopping momentarily):*　　What kind of Negroes?

*He says this in fun. He is not angry with her today, nor with anyone. He starts to
dance with his wife again.*

BENEATHA:　　Old-fashioned.

WALTER *(as he dances with Ruth):*　　You know, when these *New Negroes* have
　　　their convention — *(Pointing at his sister.)* — that is going to be the chairman
　　　of the Committee on Unending Agitation. *(He goes on dancing, then stops.)*
　　　Race, race, race! . . . Girl, I do believe you are the first person in the history
　　　of the entire human race to successfully brainwash yourself. *(Beneatha
　　　breaks up and he goes on dancing. He stops again, enjoying his tease.)* Damn,
　　　even the N double A C P takes a holiday sometimes! *(Beneatha and Ruth
　　　laugh. He dances with Ruth some more and starts to laugh and stops and pan-
　　　tomimes someone over an operating table.)* I can just see that chick someday
　　　looking down at some poor cat on an operating table and before she starts to
　　　slice him, she says . . . *(Pulling his sleeves back maliciously.)* "By the way,
　　　what are your views on civil rights down there? . . ."

He laughs at her again and starts to dance happily. The bell sounds.

BENEATHA:　　Sticks and stones may break my bones but . . . words will never
　　　hurt me!

*Beneatha goes to the door and opens it as Walter and Ruth go on with the clown-
ing. Beneatha is somewhat surprised to see a quiet-looking middle-aged white man
in a business suit holding his hat and a briefcase in his hand and consulting a
small piece of paper.*

MAN:　　Uh — how do you do, miss. I am looking for a Mrs. — *(He looks at the slip
　　　of paper.)* Mrs. Lena Younger? *(He stops short, struck dumb at the sight of the
　　　oblivious Walter and Ruth.)*

BENEATHA *(smoothing her hair with slight embarrassment):*　　Oh — yes, that's my
　　　mother. Excuse me. *(She closes the door and turns to quiet the other two.)*
　　　Ruth! Brother! *(Enunciating precisely but soundlessly: "There's a white man
　　　at the door!" They stop dancing, Ruth cuts off the phonograph, Beneatha*

opens the door. The man casts a curious quick glance at all of them.) Uh —
come in please.

MAN *(coming in):* Thank you.

BENEATHA: My mother isn't here just now. Is it business?

MAN: Yes . . . well, of a sort.

WALTER *(freely, the Man of the House):* Have a seat. I'm Mrs. Younger's son. I
look after most of her business matters.

Ruth and Beneatha exchange amused glances.

MAN *(regarding Walter, and sitting):* Well — My name is Karl Lindner . . .

WALTER *(stretching out his hand):* Walter Younger. This is my wife — *(Ruth nods
politely.)* — and my sister.

LINDNER: How do you do.

WALTER *(amiably, as he sits himself easily on a chair, leaning forward on his knees
with interest and looking expectantly into the newcomer's face):* What can
we do for you, Mr. Lindner!

LINDNER *(some minor shuffling of the hat and briefcase on his knees):* Well — I
am a representative of the Clybourne Park Improvement Association —

WALTER *(pointing):* Why don't you sit your things on the floor?

LINDNER: Oh — yes. Thank you. *(He slides the briefcase and hat under the chair.)*
And as I was saying — I am from the Clybourne Park Improvement Association and we have had it brought to our attention at the last meeting that you
people — or at least your mother — has bought a piece of residential property
at — *(He digs for the slip of paper again.)* — four o six Clybourne Street . . .

WALTER: That's right. Care for something to drink? Ruth, get Mr. Lindner a
beer.

LINDNER *(upset for some reason):* Oh — no, really. I mean thank you very much,
but no thank you.

RUTH *(innocently):* Some coffee?

LINDNER: Thank you, nothing at all.

Beneatha is watching the man carefully.

LINDNER: Well, I don't know how much you folks know about our organization.
(He is a gentle man; thoughtful and somewhat labored in his manner.) It is
one of these community organizations set up to look after — oh, you know,
things like block upkeep and special projects and we also have what we call
our New Neighbors Orientation Committee . . .

BENEATHA *(drily):* Yes — and what do they do?

LINDNER *(turning a little to her and then returning the main force to Walter):*
Well — it's what you might call a sort of welcoming committee, I guess. I
mean they, we — I'm the chairman of the committee — go around and see
the new people who move into the neighborhood and sort of give them the
low-down on the way we do things out in Clybourne Park.

BENEATHA *(with appreciation of the two meanings, which escape Ruth and Walter):* Un-huh.

LINDNER: And we also have the category of what the association calls — *(He
looks elsewhere.)* — uh — special community problems . . .

BENEATHA: Yes—and what are some of those?

WALTER: Girl, let the man talk.

LINDNER *(with understated relief)*:   Thank you. I would sort of like to explain this thing in my own way. I mean I want to explain to you in a certain way.

WALTER: Go ahead.

LINDNER: Yes. Well. I'm going to try to get right to the point. I'm sure we'll all appreciate that in the long run.

BENEATHA: Yes.

WALTER: Be still now!

LINDNER: Well—

RUTH *(still innocently)*:   Would you like another chair—you don't look comfortable.

LINDNER *(more frustrated than annoyed)*:   No, thank you very much. Please. Well—to get right to the point, I—*(A great breath, and he is off at last.)* I am sure you people must be aware of some of the incidents which have happened in various parts of the city when colored people have moved into certain areas—*(Beneatha exhales heavily and starts tossing a piece of fruit up and down in the air.)* Well—because we have what I think is going to be a unique type of organization in American community life—not only do we deplore that kind of thing—but we are trying to do something about it. *(Beneatha stops tossing and turns with a new and quizzical interest to the man.)* We feel—*(gaining confidence in his mission because of the interest in the faces of the people he is talking to.)*—we feel that most of the trouble in this world, when you come right down to it—*(He hits his knee for emphasis.)*—most of the trouble exists because people just don't sit down and talk to each other.

RUTH *(nodding as she might in church, pleased with the remark)*:   You can say that again, mister.

LINDNER *(more encouraged by such affirmation)*:   That we don't try hard enough in this world to understand the other fellow's problem. The other guy's point of view.

RUTH: Now that's right.

Beneatha and Walter merely watch and listen with genuine interest.

LINDNER: Yes—that's the way we feel out in Clybourne Park. And that's why I was elected to come here this afternoon and talk to you people. Friendly like, you know, the way people should talk to each other and see if we couldn't find some way to work this thing out. As I say, the whole business is a matter of *caring* about the other fellow. Anybody can see that you are a nice family of folks, hard working and honest I'm sure. *(Beneatha frowns slightly, quizzically, her head tilted regarding him.)* Today everybody knows what it means to be on the outside of *something*. And of course, there is always somebody who is out to take advantage of people who don't always understand.

WALTER: What do you mean?

LINDNER: Well—you see our community is made up of people who've worked hard as the dickens for years to build up that little community. They're not rich and fancy people; just hard-working, honest people who don't really have much but those little homes and a dream of the kind of community they want to raise their children in. Now, I don't say we are perfect and there is a lot wrong in some of the things they want. But you've got to admit that a man, right or wrong, has the right to want to have the neighborhood he lives in a certain kind of way. And at the moment the overwhelming majority of our people out there feel that people get along better, take more of a common interest in the life of the community, when they share a common background. I want you to believe me when I tell you that race prejudice simply doesn't enter into it. It is a matter of the people of Clybourne Park believing, rightly or wrongly, as I say, that for the happiness of all concerned that our Negro families are happier when they live in their *own* communities.

BENEATHA *(with a grand and bitter gesture):*   This, friends, is the Welcoming Committee!

WALTER *(dumfounded, looking at Lindner):*   Is this what you came marching all the way over here to tell us?

LINDNER: Well, now we've been having a fine conversation. I hope you'll hear me all the way through.

WALTER *(tightly):*   Go ahead, man.

LINDNER: You see — in the face of all the things I have said, we are prepared to make your family a very generous offer . . .

BENEATHA: Thirty pieces and not a coin less!

WALTER: Yeah?

LINDNER *(putting on his glasses drawing a form out of the briefcase):*   Our association is prepared, through the collective effort of our people, to buy the house from you at a financial gain to your family.

RUTH: Lord have mercy, ain't this the living gall!

WALTER: All right, you through?

LINDNER: Well, I want to give you the exact terms of the financial arrangement—

WALTER: We don't want to hear no exact terms of no arrangements. I want to know if you got any more to tell us 'bout getting together?

LINDNER *(taking off his glasses):*   Well — I don't suppose that you feel . . .

WALTER: Never mind how I feel — you got any more to say 'bout how people ought to sit down and talk to each other? . . . Get out of my house, man.

He turns his back and walks to the door.

LINDNER *(looking around at the hostile faces and reaching and assembling his hat and briefcase):*   Well — I don't understand why you people are reacting this way. What do you think you are going to gain by moving into a neighborhood where you just aren't wanted and where some elements — well — people can get awful worked up when they feel that their whole way of life and everything they've ever worked for is threatened.

WALTER: Get out.

LINDNER *(at the door, holding a small card):*   Well — I'm sorry it went like this.

WALTER: Get out.

LINDNER *(almost sadly regarding Walter):*   You just can't force people to change their hearts, son.

He turns and puts his card on a table and exits. Walter pushes the door to with stinging hatred, and stands looking at it. Ruth just sits and Beneatha just stands. They say nothing. Mama and Travis enter.

MAMA: Well — this all the packing got done since I left out of here this morning. I testify before God that my children got all the energy of the *dead!* What time the moving men due?

BENEATHA: Four o'clock. You had a caller, Mama.

She is smiling, teasingly.

MAMA: Sure enough — who?

BENEATHA *(her arms folded saucily):*   The Welcoming Committee.

Walter and Ruth giggle.

MAMA *(innocently):*   Who?

BENEATHA: The Welcoming Committee. They said they're sure going to be glad to see you when you get there.

WALTER *(devilishly):*   Yeah, they said they can't hardly wait to see your face.

Laughter.

MAMA *(sensing their facetiousness):*   What's the matter with you all?

WALTER: Ain't nothing the matter with us. We just telling you 'bout the gentleman who came to see you this afternoon. From the Clybourne Park Improvement Association.

MAMA: What he want?

RUTH *(in the same mood as Beneatha and Walter):*   To welcome you, honey.

WALTER: He said they can't hardly wait. He said the one thing they don't have, that they just *dying* to have out there is a fine family of fine colored people! *(To Ruth and Beneatha.)* Ain't that right!

RUTH *(mockingly):*   Yeah! He left his card —

BENEATHA *(handing card to Mama):*   In case.

Mama reads and throws it on the floor — understanding and looking off as she draws her chair up to the table on which she has put her plant and some sticks and some cord.

MAMA: Father, give us strength. *(Knowingly — and without fun.)* Did he threaten us?

BENEATHA: Oh — Mama — they don't do it like that any more. He talked Brotherhood. He said everybody ought to learn how to sit down and hate each other with good Christian fellowship.

She and Walter shake hands to ridicule the remark.

MAMA *(sadly):*   Lord, protect us . . .

RUTH: You should hear the money those folks raised to buy the house from us. All we paid and then some.

BENEATHA: What they think we going to do — eat 'em?

RUTH: No, honey, marry 'em.

MAMA *(shaking her head):*   Lord, Lord, Lord . . .

RUTH: Well — that's the way the crackers crumble. *(A beat.)* Joke.

BENEATHA (*laughingly noticing what her mother is doing*):   Mama, what are you doing?

MAMA: Fixing my plant so it won't get hurt none on the way . . .

BENEATHA: Mama, you going to take *that* to the new house?

MAMA: Un-huh —

BENEATHA: That raggedy-looking old thing?

MAMA (*stopping and looking at her*):   It expresses ME!

RUTH (*with delight, to Beneatha*):   So there, Miss Thing!

Walter comes to Mama suddenly and bends down behind her and squeezes her in his arms with all his strength. She is overwhelmed by the suddenness of it and, though delighted, her manner is like that of Ruth and Travis.

MAMA: Look out now, boy! You make me mess up my thing here!

WALTER (*his face lit, he slips down on his knees beside her, his arms still about her*):   Mama . . . you know what it means to climb up in the chariot?

MAMA (*gruffly, very happy*):   Get on away from me now . . .

RUTH (*near the gift-wrapped package, trying to catch Walter's eye*):   Psst —

WALTER: What the old song say, Mama . . .

RUTH: Walter — Now?

She is pointing at the package.

WALTER (*speaking the lines, sweetly, playfully, in his mother's face*):
I got wings . . . you got wings . . .
All God's children got wings . . .

MAMA: Boy — get out of my face and do some work . . .

WALTER:
When I get to heaven gonna put on my wings,
Gonna fly all over God's heaven . . .

BENEATHA (*teasingly, from across the room*):   Everybody talking 'bout heaven ain't going there!

WALTER (*to Ruth, who is carrying the box across to them*):   I don't know, you think we ought to give her that . . . Seems to me she ain't been very appreciative around here.

MAMA (*eying the box, which is obviously a gift*):   What is that?

WALTER (*taking it from Ruth and putting it on the table in front of Mama*):   Well — what you all think? Should we give it to her?

RUTH: Oh — she was pretty good today.

MAMA: I'll good you —

She turns her eyes to the box again.

BENEATHA: Open it, Mama.

She stands up, looks at it, turns and looks at all of them, and then presses her hands together and does not open the package.

WALTER (*sweetly*):   Open it, Mama. It's for you. (*Mama looks in his eyes. It is the first present in her life without its being Christmas. Slowly she opens her package and lifts out, one by one, a brand-new sparkling set of gardening tools. Walter continues, prodding.*) Ruth made up the note — read it . . .

MAMA (*picking up the card and adjusting her glasses*): "To our own Mrs. Miniver—Love from Brother, Ruth, and Beneatha." Ain't that lovely . . .

TRAVIS (*tugging at his father's sleeve*): Daddy, can I give her mine now?

WALTER: All right, son. (*Travis flies to get his gift.*)

MAMA: Now I don't have to use my knives and forks no more . . .

WALTER: Travis didn't want to go in with the rest of us, Mama. He got his own. (*Somewhat amused.*) We don't know what it is . . .

TRAVIS (*racing back in the room with a large hatbox and putting it in front of his grandmother*): Here!

MAMA: Lord have mercy, baby. You done gone and bought your grandmother a hat?

TRAVIS (*very proud*): Open it!

She does and lifts out an elaborate, but very elaborate, wide gardening hat, and all the adults break up at the sight of it.

RUTH: Travis, honey, what is that?

TRAVIS (*who thinks it is beautiful and appropriate*): It's a gardening hat! Like the ladies always have on in the magazines when they work in their gardens.

BENEATHA (*giggling fiercely*): Travis—we were trying to make Mama Mrs. Miniver—not Scarlett O'Hara!

MAMA (*indignantly*): What's the matter with you all! This here is a beautiful hat! (*Absurdly.*) I always wanted me one just like it!

She pops it on her head to prove it to her grandson, and the hat is ludicrous and considerably oversized.

RUTH: Hot dog! Go, Mama!

WALTER (*doubled over with laughter*): I'm sorry, Mama—but you look like you ready to go out and chop you some cotton sure enough!

They all laugh except Mama, out of deference to Travis's feelings.

MAMA (*gathering the boy up to her*): Bless your heart—this is the prettiest hat I ever owned—(*Walter, Ruth, and Beneatha chime in—noisily, festively, and insincerely congratulating Travis on his gift.*) What are we all standing around here for? We ain't finished packin' yet. Bennie, you ain't packed one book.

The bell rings.

BENEATHA: That couldn't be the movers . . . it's not hardly two good yet—

Beneatha goes into her room. Mama starts for door.

WALTER (*turning, stiffening*): Wait—wait—I'll get it.

He stands and looks at the door.

MAMA: You expecting company, son?

WALTER (*just looking at the door*): Yeah—yeah . . .

Mama looks at Ruth, and they exchange innocent and unfrightened glances.

MAMA (*not understanding*): Well, let them in, son.

BENEATHA (*from her room*): We need some more string.

MAMA: Travis — you run to the hardware and get me some string cord.

Mama goes out and Walter turns and looks at Ruth. Travis goes to a dish for money.

RUTH: Why don't you answer the door, man?

WALTER *(suddenly bounding across the floor to embrace her)*:   'Cause sometimes it hard to let the future begin! *(Stooping down in her face.)*
     I got wings! You got wings!
     All God's children got wings!

He crosses to the door and throws it open. Standing there is a very slight little man in a not-too-prosperous business suit and with haunted frightened eyes and a hat pulled down tightly, brim up, around his forehead. Travis passes between the men and exits. Walter leans deep in the man's face, still in his jubilance.

     When I get to heaven gonna put on my wings,
     Gonna fly all over God's heaven . . .

The little man just stares at him.

     Heaven —

Suddenly he stops and looks past the little man into the empty hallway.

     Where's Willy, man?

BOBO: He ain't with me.

WALTER *(not disturbed)*:   Oh — come on in. You know my wife.

BOBO *(dumbly, taking off his hat)*:   Yes — h'you, Miss Ruth.

RUTH *(quietly, a mood apart from her husband already, seeing Bobo)*:   Hello, Bobo.

WALTER: You right on time today . . . Right on time. That's the way! *(He slaps Bobo on his back.)* Sit down . . . lemme hear.

Ruth stands stiffly and quietly in back of them, as though somehow she senses death, her eyes fixed on her husband.

BOBO *(his frightened eyes on the floor, his hat in his hands)*:   Could I please get a drink of water, before I tell you about it, Walter Lee?

Walter does not take his eyes off the man. Ruth goes blindly to the tap and gets a glass of water and brings it to Bobo.

WALTER: There ain't nothing wrong, is there?

BOBO: Lemme tell you —

WALTER: Man — didn't nothing go wrong?

BOBO: Lemme tell you — Walter Lee. *(Looking at Ruth and talking to her more than to Walter.)* You know how it was. I got to tell you how it was. I mean first I got to tell you how it was all the way . . . I mean about the money I put in, Walter Lee . . .

WALTER *(with taut agitation now)*:   What about the money you put in?

BOBO: Well — it wasn't much as we told you — me and Willy — *(He stops.)* I'm sorry, Walter. I got a bad feeling about it. I got a real bad feeling about it . . .

WALTER: Man, what you telling me about all this for? . . . Tell me what happened in Springfield . . .

BOBO: Springfield.

RUTH *(like a dead woman):*   What was supposed to happen in Springfield?

BOBO *(to her):*   This deal that me and Walter went into with Willy—Me and
Willy was going to go down to Springfield and spread some money 'round
so's we wouldn't have to wait so long for the liquor license . . . That's what we
were going to do. Everybody said that was the way you had to do, you understand, Miss Ruth?

WALTER: Man—what happened down there?

BOBO *(a pitiful man, near tears):*   I'm trying to tell you, Walter.

WALTER *(screaming at him suddenly):*   THEN TELL ME, GODDAMMIT . . .
WHAT'S THE MATTER WITH YOU?

BOBO: Man . . . I didn't go to no Springfield, yesterday.

WALTER *(halted, life hanging in the moment):*   Why not?

BOBO *(the long way, the hard way to tell):*   'Cause I didn't have no reasons to . . .

WALTER: Man, what are you talking about!

BOBO: I'm talking about the fact that when I got to the train station yesterday morning—eight o'clock like we planned . . . Man—*Willy didn't never show up.*

WALTER: Why . . . where was he . . . where is he?

BOBO: That's what I'm trying to tell you . . . I don't know . . . I waited six
hours . . . I called his house . . . and I waited . . . six hours . . . I waited in
that train station six hours . . . *(Breaking into tears.)* That was all the extra
money I had in the world . . . *(Looking up at Walter with the tears running
down his face.)* Man, *Willy is gone.*

WALTER: Gone, what you mean Willy is gone? Gone where? You mean he went
by himself. You mean he went off to Springfield by himself—to take care of
getting the license—*(Turns and looks anxiously at Ruth.)* You mean maybe he
didn't want too many people in on the business down there? *(Looks to Ruth
again, as before.)* You know Willy got his own ways. *(Looks back to Bobo.)*
Maybe you was late yesterday and he just went on down there without you.
Maybe—maybe—he's been callin' you at home tryin' to tell you what happened or something. Maybe—maybe—he just got sick. He's somewhere—
he's got to be somewhere. We just got to find him—me and you got to find
him. *(Grabs Bobo senselessly by the collar and starts to shake him.)* We got to!

BOBO *(in sudden angry, frightened agony):*   What's the matter with you, Walter!
When a cat take off with your money he don't leave you no road maps!

WALTER *(turning madly, as though he is looking for Willy in the very room):*
Willy! . . . Willy . . . don't do it . . . Please don't do it . . . Man, not with that
money . . . Man, please, not with that money . . . Oh, God . . . Don't let it be
true . . . *(He is wandering around, crying out for Willy and looking for him or
perhaps for help from God.)* Man . . . I trusted you . . . Man, I put my life in
your hands . . . *(He starts to crumple down on the floor as Ruth just covers her
face in horror. Mama opens the door and comes into the room, with Beneatha
behind her.)* Man . . . *(He starts to pound the floor with his fists, sobbing wildly.)*
THAT MONEY IS MADE OUT OF MY FATHER'S FLESH—

BOBO *(standing over him helplessly):*   I'm sorry, Walter . . . *(only Walter's sobs
reply. Bobo puts on his hat.)* I had my life staked on this deal, too . . .

He exits.

MAMA *(to Walter)*:   Son — *(She goes to him, bends down to him, talks to his bent head.)* Son . . . Is it gone? Son, I gave you sixty-five hundred dollars. Is it gone? All of it? Beneatha's money too?

WALTER *(lifting his head slowly)*:   Mama . . . I never . . . went to the bank at all . . .

MAMA *(not wanting to believe him)*:   You mean . . . your sister's school money . . . you used that too . . . Walter? . . .

WALTER: Yessss! All of it . . . It's all gone . . .

There is total silence. Ruth stands with her face covered with her hands; Beneatha leans forlornly against a wall, fingering a piece of red ribbon from the mother's gift. Mama stops and looks at her son without recognition and then, quite without thinking about it, starts to beat him senselessly in the face. Beneatha goes to them and stops it.

BENEATHA: Mama!

Mama stops and looks at both of her children and rises slowly and wanders vaguely, aimlessly away from them.

MAMA: I seen . . . him . . . night after night . . . come in . . . and look at that rug . . . and then look at me . . . the red showing in his eyes . . . the veins moving in his head . . . I seen him grow thin and old before he was forty . . . working and working and working like somebody's old horse . . . killing himself . . . and you — you give it all away in a day — *(She raises her arms to strike him again.)*

BENEATHA: Mama —

MAMA: Oh, God . . . *(She looks up to Him.)* Look down here — and show me the strength.

BENEATHA: Mama —

MAMA *(folding over)*:   Strength . . .

BENEATHA *(plaintively)*:   Mama . . .

MAMA: Strength!

Curtain.

ACT 3

Time: An hour later.

At curtain, there is a sullen light of gloom in the living room, gray light not unlike that which began the first scene of Act 1. At left we can see Walter within his room, alone with himself. He is stretched out on the bed, his shirt out and open, his arms under his head. He does not smoke, he does not cry out, he merely lies there, looking up at the ceiling, much as if he were alone in the world.

In the living room Beneatha sits at the table, still surrounded by the now almost ominous packing crates. She sits looking off. We feel that this is a mood struck perhaps an hour before, and it lingers now, full of the empty sound of profound disappointment. We see on a line from her brother's bedroom the sameness of *their attitudes. Presently the bell rings and Beneatha rises without ambition or interest in answering. It is Asagai, smiling broadly, striding into the room with energy and happy expectation and conversation.*

ASAGAI: I came over . . . I had some free time. I thought I might help with the packing. Ah, I like the look of packing crates! A household in preparation for a journey! It depresses some people . . . but for me . . . it is another feeling. Something full of the flow of life, do you understand? Movement, progress . . . It makes me think of Africa.

BENEATHA: Africa!

ASAGAI: What kind of a mood is this? Have I told you how deeply you move me?

BENEATHA: He gave away the money, Asagai . . .

ASAGAI: Who gave away what money?

BENEATHA: The insurance money. My brother gave it away.

ASAGAI: Gave it away?

BENEATHA: He made an investment! With a man even Travis wouldn't have trusted with his most worn-out marbles.

ASAGAI: And it's gone?

BENEATHA: Gone!

ASAGAI: I'm very sorry . . . And you, now?

BENEATHA: Me? . . . Me? . . . Me, I'm nothing . . . Me. When I was very small . . . we used to take our sleds out in the wintertime and the only hills we had were the ice-covered stone steps of some houses down the street. And we used to fill them in with snow and make them smooth and slide down them all day . . . and it was very dangerous, you know . . . far too steep . . . and sure enough one day a kid named Rufus came down too fast and hit the sidewalk and we saw his face just split open right there in front of us . . . And I remember standing there looking at his bloody open face thinking that was the end of Rufus. But the ambulance came and they took him to the hospital and they fixed the broken bones and they sewed it all up . . . and the next time I saw Rufus he just had a little line down the middle of his face . . . I never got over that . . .

ASAGAI: What?

BENEATHA: That that was what one person could do for another, fix him up — sew up the problem, make him all right again. That was the most marvelous thing in the world . . . I wanted to do that. I always thought it was the one concrete thing in the world that a human being could do. Fix up the sick, you know — and make them whole again. This was truly being God . . .

ASAGAI: You wanted to be God?

BENEATHA: No — I wanted to cure. It used to be so important to me. I wanted to cure. It used to matter. I used to care. I mean about people and how their bodies hurt . . .

ASAGAI: And you've stopped caring?

BENEATHA: Yes — I think so.

ASAGAI: Why?

BENEATHA *(bitterly):*   Because it doesn't seem deep enough, close enough to
    what ails mankind! It was a child's way of seeing things — or an idealist's.

ASAGAI: Children see things very well sometimes — and idealists even better.

BENEATHA: I know that's what you think. Because you are still where I left off.
    You with all your talk and dreams about Africa! You still think you can patch
    up the world. Cure the Great Sore of Colonialism — *(Loftily, mocking it.)*
    with the Penicillin of Independence —!

ASAGAI: Yes!

BENEATHA: Independence *and then what?* What about all the crooks and
    thieves and just plain idiots who will come into power and steal and plunder
    the same as before — only now they will be black and do it in the name of the
    new Independence — WHAT ABOUT THEM?!

ASAGAI: That will be the problem for another time. First we must get there.

BENEATHA: And where does it end?

ASAGAI: End? Who even spoke of an end? To life? To living?

BENEATHA: An end to misery! To stupidity! Don't you see there isn't any real
    progress, Asagai, there is only one large circle that we march in, around and
    around, each of us with our own little picture in front of us — our own little
    mirage that we think is the future.

ASAGAI: That is the mistake.

BENEATHA: What?

ASAGAI: What you just said — about the circle. It isn't a circle — it is simply a long
    line — as in geometry, you know, one that reaches into infinity. And because
    we cannot see the end — we also cannot see how it changes. And it is very odd
    but those who see the changes — who dream, who will not give up — are called
    idealists . . . and those who see only the circle — we call *them* the "realists"!

BENEATHA: Asagai, while I was sleeping in that bed in there, people went out
    and took the future right out of my hands! And nobody asked me, nobody
    consulted me — they just went out and changed my life!

ASAGAI: Was it your money?

BENEATHA: What?

ASAGAI: Was it your money he gave away?

BENEATHA: It belonged to all of us.

ASAGAI: But did you earn it? Would you have had it at all if your father had not
    died?

BENEATHA: No.

ASAGAI: Then isn't there something wrong in a house — in a world — where all
    dreams, good or bad, must depend on the death of a man? I never thought to
    see *you* like this, Alaiyo. You! Your brother made a mistake and you are grate-
    ful to him so that now you can give up the ailing human race on account of
    it! You talk about what good is struggle, what good is anything! Where are we
    all going and why are we bothering!

BENEATHA: AND YOU CANNOT ANSWER IT!

ASAGAI *(shouting over her):*   *I LIVE THE ANSWER! (Pause.)* In my village at
    home it is the exceptional man who can even read a newspaper . . . or who
    ever sees a book at all. I will go home and much of what I will have to say will

seem strange to the people of my village. But I will teach and work and things will happen, slowly and swiftly. At times it will seem that nothing changes at all . . . and then again the sudden dramatic events which make history leap into the future. And then quiet again. Retrogression even. Guns, murder, revolution. And I even will have moments when I wonder if the quiet was not better than all that death and hatred. But I will look about my village at the illiteracy and disease and ignorance and I will not wonder long. And perhaps . . . perhaps I will be a great man . . . I mean perhaps I will hold on to the substance of truth and find my way always with the right course . . . and perhaps for it I will be butchered in my bed some night by the servants of empire . . .

BENEATHA: *The martyr!*

ASAGAI *(he smiles):* . . . or perhaps I shall live to be a very old man, respected and esteemed in my new nation . . . And perhaps I shall hold office and this is what I'm trying to tell you, Alaiyo: perhaps the things I believe now for my country will be wrong and outmoded, and I will not understand and do terrible things to have things my way or merely to keep my power. Don't you see that there will be young men and women — not British soldiers then, but my own black countrymen — to step out of the shadows some evening and slit my then useless throat? Don't you see they have always been there . . . that they always will be. And that such a thing as my own death will be an advance? They who might kill me even . . . actually replenish all that I was.

BENEATHA: Oh, Asagai, I know all that.

ASAGAI: Good! Then stop moaning and groaning and tell me what you plan to do.

BENEATHA: Do?

ASAGAI: I have a bit of a suggestion.

BENEATHA: What?

ASAGAI *(rather quietly for him):* That when it is all over — that you come home with me —

BENEATHA *(staring at him and crossing away with exasperation):* Oh — Asagai — at this moment you decide to be romantic!

ASAGAI *(quickly understanding the misunderstanding):* My dear, young creature of the New World — I do not mean across the city — I mean across the ocean: home — to Africa.

BENEATHA *(slowly understanding and turning to him with murmured amazement):* To Africa?

ASAGAI: Yes! . . . *(smiling and lifting his arms playfully.)* Three hundred years later the African Prince rose up out of the seas and swept the maiden back across the middle passage over which her ancestors had come —

BENEATHA *(unable to play):* To — to Nigeria?

ASAGAI: Nigeria. Home. *(Coming to her with genuine romantic flippancy.)* I will show you our mountains and our stars; and give you cool drinks from gourds and teach you the old songs and the ways of our people — and, in time, we will pretend that — *(Very softly.)* — you have only been away for a day. Say that you'll come — *(He swings her around and takes her full in his arms in a kiss which proceeds to passion.)*

BENEATHA *(pulling away suddenly):*   You're getting me all mixed up —

ASAGAI: Why?

BENEATHA: Too many things — too many things have happened today. I must sit down and think. I don't know what I feel about anything right this minute.

She promptly sits down and props her chin on her fist.

ASAGAI *(charmed):*   All right, I shall leave you. No — don't get up. *(Touching her, gently, sweetly.)* Just sit awhile and think . . . Never be afraid to sit awhile and think. *(He goes to door and looks at her.)* How often I have looked at you and said, "Ah — so this is what the New World hath finally wrought . . ."

He exits. Beneatha sits on alone. Presently Walter enters from his room and starts to rummage through things, feverishly looking for something. She looks up and turns in her seat.

BENEATHA *(hissingly):*   Yes — just look at what the New World hath wrought! . . . Just look! *(She gestures with bitter disgust.)* There he is! *Monsieur le petit bourgeois noir°* — himself! There he is — Symbol of a Rising Class! Entrepreneur! Titan of the system! *(Walter ignores her completely and continues frantically and destructively looking for something and hurling things to floor and tearing things out of their place in his search. Beneatha ignores the eccentricity of his actions and goes on with the monologue of insult.)* Did you dream of yachts on Lake Michigan, Brother? Did you see yourself on that Great Day sitting down at the Conference Table, surrounded by all the mighty bald-headed men in America? All halted, waiting, breathless, waiting for your pronouncements on industry? Waiting for you — Chairman of the Board! *(Walter finds what he is looking for — a small piece of white paper — and pushes it in his pocket and puts on his coat and rushes out without ever having looked at her. She shouts after him.)* I look at you and I see the final triumph of stupidity in the world!

The door slams and she returns to just sitting again. Ruth comes quickly out of Mama's room.

RUTH: Who was that?

BENEATHA: Your husband.

RUTH: Where did he go?

BENEATHA: Who knows — maybe he has an appointment at U.S. Steel.

RUTH *(anxiously, with frightened eyes):*   You didn't say nothing bad to him, did you?

BENEATHA: Bad? Say anything bad to him? No — I told him he was a sweet boy and full of dreams and everything is strictly peachy keen, as the ofay kids say!

Mama enters from her bedroom. She is lost, vague, trying to catch hold, to make some sense of her former command of the world, but it still eludes her. A sense of waste overwhelms her gait; a measure of apology rides on her shoulders. She goes to her plant, which has remained on the table, looks at it, picks it up and takes it to the window sill and sits it outside, and she stands and looks at it a long moment. Then she closes the window, straightens her body with effort and turns around to her children.

Monsieur le petit bourgeois noir: Mr. Black Bourgoisie (French).

MAMA: Well—ain't it a mess in here, though? (*A false cheerfulness, a beginning of something.*) I guess we all better stop moping around and get some work done. All this unpacking and everything we got to do. (*Ruth raises her head slowly in response to the sense of the line; and Beneatha in similar manner turns very slowly to look at her mother.*) One of you all better call the moving people and tell 'em not to come.

RUTH: Tell 'em not to come?

MAMA: Of course, baby. Ain't no need in 'em coming all the way here and having to go back. They charges for that too. (*She sits down, fingers to her brow, thinking.*) Lord, ever since I was a little girl, I always remembers people saying, "Lena—Lena Eggleston, you aims too high all the time. You needs to slow down and see life a little more like it is. Just slow down some." That's what they always used to say down home—"Lord, that Lena Eggleston is a high-minded thing. She'll get her due one day!"

RUTH: No, Lena . . .

MAMA: Me and Big Walter just didn't never learn right.

RUTH: Lena, no! We gotta go. Bennie—tell her . . .

She rises and crosses to Beneatha with her arms outstretched. Beneatha doesn't respond.

Tell her we can still move . . . the notes ain't but a hundred and twenty-five a month. We got four grown people in this house—we can work . . .

MAMA (*to herself*):   Just aimed too high all the time—

RUTH (*turning and going to Mama fast—the words pouring out with urgency and desperation*):   Lena—I'll work . . . I'll work twenty hours a day in all the kitchens in Chicago . . . I'll strap my baby on my back if I have to and scrub all the floors in America and wash all the sheets in America if I have to—but we got to MOVE! We got to get OUT OF HERE!!

Mama reaches out absently and pats Ruth's hand.

MAMA: No—I sees things differently now. Been thinking 'bout some of the things we could do to fix this place up some. I seen a second-hand bureau over on Maxwell Street just the other day that could fit right there. (*She points to where the new furniture might go. Ruth wanders away from her.*) Would need some new handles on it and then a little varnish and it look like something brand-new. And—we can put up them new curtains in the kitchen . . . Why this place be looking fine. Cheer us all up so that we forget trouble ever come . . . (*To Ruth.*) And you could get some nice screens to put up in your room round the baby's bassinet . . . (*She looks at both of them pleadingly.*) Sometimes you just got to know when to give up some things . . . and hold on to what you got . . .

Walter enters from the outside, looking spent and leaning against the door, his coat hanging from him.

MAMA: Where you been, son?

WALTER (*breathing hard*):   Made a call.

MAMA: To who, son?

WALTER: To The Man. *(He heads for his room.)*

MAMA: What man, baby?

WALTER *(stops in the door):*   The Man, Mama. Don't you know who The Man is?

RUTH: Walter Lee?

WALTER: *The Man.* Like the guys in the streets say—The Man. Captain Boss— Mistuh Charley . . . Old Cap'n Please Mr. Bossman . . .

BENEATHA *(suddenly):*   Lindner!

WALTER: That's right! That's good. I told him to come right over.

BENEATHA *(fiercely, understanding):*   For what? What do you want to see him for!

WALTER *(looking at his sister):*   We going to do business with him.

MAMA: What you talking 'bout, son?

WALTER: Talking 'bout life, Mama. You all always telling me to see life like it is. Well—I laid in there on my back today . . . and I figured it out. Life just like it is. Who gets and who don't get. *(He sits down with his coat on and laughs.)* Mama, you know it's all divided up. Life is. Sure enough. Between the takers and the "tooken." *(He laughs.)* I've figured it out finally. *(He looks around at them.)* Yeah. Some of us always getting "tooken." *(He laughs.)* People like Willy Harris, they don't never get "tooken." And you know why the rest of us do? 'Cause we all mixed up. Mixed up bad. We get to looking 'round for the right and the wrong; and we worry about it and cry about it and stay up nights trying to figure out 'bout the wrong and the right of things all the time . . . And all the time, man, them takers is out there operating, just taking and taking. Willy Harris? Shoot—Willy Harris don't even count. He don't even count in the big scheme of things. But I'll say one thing for old Willy Harris . . . he's taught me something. He's taught me to keep my eye on what counts in this world. Yeah—*(Shouting out a little.)* Thanks, Willy!

RUTH: What did you call that man for, Walter Lee?

WALTER: Called him to tell him to come on over to the show. Gonna put on a show for the man. Just what he wants to see. You see, Mama, the man came here today and he told us that them people out there where you want us to move—well they so upset they willing to pay us *not* to move! *(He laughs again.)* And—and oh, Mama—you would of been proud of the way me and Ruth and Bennie acted. We told him to get out . . . Lord have mercy! We told the man to get out! Oh, we was some proud folks this afternoon, yeah. *(He lights a cigarette.)* We were still full of that old-time stuff . . .

RUTH *(coming toward him slowly):*   You talking 'bout taking them people's money to keep us from moving in that house?

WALTER: I ain't just talking 'bout it, baby—I'm telling you that's what's going to happen!

BENEATHA: Oh, God! Where is the bottom! Where is the real honest-to-God bottom so he can't go any farther!

WALTER: See—that's the old stuff. You and that boy that was here today. You all want everybody to carry a flag and a spear and sing some marching songs, huh? You wanna spend your life looking into things and trying to find the right and the wrong part, huh? Yeah. You know what's going to happen to that boy someday—he'll find himself sitting in a dungeon, locked in forever — and the takers will have the key! Forget it, baby! There ain't no causes — there ain't nothing but taking in this world, and he who takes most is smartest — and it don't make a damn bit of difference *how*.

MAMA: You making something inside me cry, son. Some awful pain inside me.

WALTER: Don't cry, Mama. Understand. That white man is going to walk in that door able to write checks for more money than we ever had. It's important to him and I'm going to help him . . . I'm going to put on the show, Mama.

MAMA: Son — I come from five generations of people who was slaves and share-croppers — but ain't nobody in my family never let nobody pay 'em no money that was a way of telling us we wasn't fit to walk the earth. We ain't never been that poor. *(Raising her eyes and looking at him.)* We ain't never been that — dead inside.

BENEATHA: Well — we are dead now. All the talk about dreams and sunlight that goes on in this house. It's all dead now.

WALTER: What's the matter with you all! I didn't make this world! It was give to me this way! Hell, yes, I want me some yachts someday! Yes, I want to hang some real pearls 'round my wife's neck. Ain't she supposed to wear no pearls? Somebody tell me — tell me, who decides which women is suppose to wear pearls in this world. I tell you I am a *man* — and I think my wife should wear some pearls in this world!

This last line hangs a good while and Walter begins to move about the room. The word "Man" has penetrated his consciousness; he mumbles it to himself repeatedly between strange agitated pauses as he moves about.

MAMA: Baby, how you going to feel on the inside?

WALTER: Fine! . . . Going to feel fine . . . a man . . .

MAMA: You won't have nothing left then, Walter Lee.

WALTER *(coming to her)*: I'm going to feel fine, Mama. I'm going to look that son-of-a-bitch in the eyes and say — *(He falters.)* — and say, "All right, Mr. Lindner — *(He falters even more.)* — that's *your* neighborhood out there! You got the right to keep it like you want! You got the right to have it like you want! Just write the check and — the house is yours." And — and I am going to say — *(His voice almost breaks.)* "And you — you people just put the money in my hand and you won't have to live next to this bunch of stinking niggers! . . ." *(He straightens up and moves away from his mother, walking around the room.)* And maybe — maybe I'll just get down on my black knees . . . *(He does so; Ruth and Bennie and Mama watch him in frozen horror.)* "Captain, Mistuh, Bossman — *(Groveling and grinning and wringing his hands in profoundly anguished imitation of the slow-witted movie stereo-type.)* A-hee-hee-hee! Oh, yassuh boss! Yassssuh! Great white — *(Voice breaking, he forces himself to go on.)* — Father, just gi' ussen de money, fo' God's sake, and we's — we's ain't gwine come out deh and dirty up yo' white folks neighborhood . . ." *(He breaks down completely.)* And I'll feel fine! Fine! FINE! *(He gets up and goes into the bedroom.)*

BENEATHA: That is not a man. That is nothing but a toothless rat.

MAMA: Yes — death done come in this here house. *(She is nodding, slowly, reflectively.)* Done come walking in my house on the lips of my children. You what supposed to be my beginning again. You — what supposed to be my harvest. *(To Beneatha.)* You — you mourning your brother?

BENEATHA: He's no brother of mine.

MAMA: What you say?

BENEATHA: I said that that individual in that room is no brother of mine.

MAMA: That's what I thought you said. You feeling like you better than he is today? *(Beneatha does not answer.)* Yes? What you tell him a minute ago? That he wasn't a man? Yes? You give him up for me? You done wrote his epitaph too — like the rest of the world? Well, who give you the privilege?

BENEATHA: Be on my side for once! You saw what he just did, Mama! You saw him — down on his knees. Wasn't it you who taught me to despise any man who would do that? Do what he's going to do?

MAMA: Yes — I taught you that. Me and your daddy. But I thought I taught you something else too . . . I thought I taught you to love him.

BENEATHA: Love him? There is nothing left to love.

MAMA: There is *always* something left to love. And if you ain't learned that, you ain't learned nothing. *(Looking at her.)* Have you cried for that boy today? I don't mean for yourself and for the family 'cause we lost the money. I mean for him: what he been through and what it done to him. Child, when do you think is the time to love somebody the most? When they done good and made things easy for everybody? Well then, you ain't through learning — because that ain't the time at all. It's when he's at his lowest and can't believe in hisself 'cause the world done whipped him so! When you starts measuring somebody, measure him right, child, measure him right. Make sure you done taken into account what hills and valleys he come through before he got to wherever he is.

Travis bursts into the room at the end of the speech, leaving the door open.

TRAVIS: Grandmama — the moving men are downstairs! The truck just pulled up.

MAMA *(turning and looking at him)*:   Are they, baby? They downstairs?

She sighs and sits. Lindner appears in the doorway. He peers in and knocks lightly, to gain attention, and comes in. All turn to look at him.

LINDNER *(hat and briefcase in hand)*:   Uh — hello . . .

Ruth crosses mechanically to the bedroom door and opens it and lets it swing open freely and slowly as the lights come up on Walter within, still in his coat, sitting at the far corner of the room. He looks up and out through the room to Lindner.

RUTH: He's here.

A long minute passes and Walter slowly gets up.

LINDNER *(coming to the table with efficiency, putting his briefcase on the table and starting to unfold papers and unscrew fountain pens)*:   Well, I certainly was glad to hear from you people. *(Walter has begun the trek out of the room, slowly and awkwardly, rather like a small boy, passing the back of his sleeve across his mouth from time to time.)* Life can really be so much simpler than people let it be most of the time. Well — with whom do I negotiate? You, Mrs. Younger, or your son here? *(Mama sits with her hands folded on her lap and her eyes closed as Walter advances. Travis goes closer to Lindner and looks at the papers curiously.)* Just some official papers, sonny.

RUTH: Travis, you go downstairs —

MAMA *(opening her eyes and looking into Walter's):*   No. Travis, you stay right here. And you make him understand what you doing, Walter Lee. You teach him good. Like Willy Harris taught you. You show where our five generations done come to. *(Walter looks from her to the boy, who grins at him innocently.)* Go ahead, son — *(She folds her hands and closes her eyes.)* Go ahead.

WALTER *(at last crosses to Lindner, who is reviewing the contract):*   Well, Mr. Lindner. *(Beneatha turns away.)* We called you — *(There is a profound, simple groping quality in his speech.)* — because, well, me and my family *(He looks around and shifts from one foot to the other.)* Well — we are very plain people . . .

LINDNER: Yes —

WALTER: I mean — I have worked as a chauffeur most of my life — and my wife here, she does domestic work in people's kitchens. So does my mother. I mean — we are plain people . . .

LINDNER: Yes, Mr. Younger —

WALTER *(really like a small boy, looking down at his shoes and then up at the man):*   And — uh — well, my father, well, he was a laborer most of his life. . . .

LINDNER *(absolutely confused):*   Uh, yes — yes, I understand. *(He turns back to the contract.)*

WALTER *(a beat; staring at him):*   And my father — *(With sudden intensity.)* My father almost *beat a man to death* once because this man called him a bad name or something, you know what I mean?

LINDNER *(looking up, frozen):*   No, no, I'm afraid I don't —

WALTER *(a beat. The tension hangs; then Walter steps back from it):*   Yeah. Well — what I mean is that we come from people who had a lot of *pride*. I mean — we are very proud people. And that's my sister over there and she's going to be a doctor — and we are very proud —

LINDNER: Well — I am sure that is very nice, but —

WALTER: What I am telling you is that we called you over here to tell you that we are very proud and that this — *(Signaling to Travis.)* Travis, come here. *(Travis crosses and Walter draws him before him facing the man.)* This is my son, and he makes the sixth generation our family in this country. And we have all thought about your offer —

LINDNER: Well, good . . . good —

WALTER: And we have decided to move into our house because my father — my father — he earned it for us brick by brick. *(Mama has her eyes closed and is rocking back and forth as though she were in church, with her head nodding the Amen yes.)* We don't want to make no trouble for nobody or fight no causes, and we will try to be good neighbors. And that's *all* we got to say about that. *(He looks the man absolutely in the eyes.)* We don't want your money. *(He turns and walks away.)*

LINDNER *(looking around at all of them):*   I take it then — that you have decided to occupy . . .

BENEATHA: That's what the man said.

LINDNER *(to Mama in her reverie):*   Then I would like to appeal to you, Mrs. Younger. You are older and wiser and understand things better I am sure . . .

MAMA: I am afraid you don't understand. My son said we was going to move and there ain't nothing left for me to say. *(Briskly.)* You know how these young folks is nowadays, mister. Can't do a thing with 'em! *(As he opens his mouth, she rises.)* Good-bye.

LINDNER *(folding up his materials):*   Well — if you are that final about it . . . there is nothing left for me to say. *(He finishes, almost ignored by the family, who are concentrating on Walter Lee. At the door Lindner halts and looks around.)* I sure hope you people know what you're getting into.

He shakes his head and exits.

RUTH *(looking around and coming to life):*   Well, for God's sake — if the moving men are here — LET'S GET THE HELL OUT OF HERE!

MAMA *(into action):*   Ain't it the truth! Look at all this here mess. Ruth, put Travis' good jacket on him . . . Walter Lee, fix your tie and tuck your shirt in, you look like somebody's hoodlum! Lord have mercy, where is my plant? *(She flies to get it amid the general bustling of the family, who are deliberately trying to ignore the nobility of the past moment.)* You all start on down . . . Travis child, don't go empty-handed . . . Ruth, where did I put that box with my skillets in it? I want to be in charge of it myself . . . I'm going to make us the biggest dinner we ever ate tonight . . . Beneatha, what's the matter with them stockings? Pull them things up, girl . . .

The family starts to file out as two moving men appear and begin to carry out the heavier pieces of furniture, bumping into the family as they move about.

BENEATHA: Mama, Asagai asked me to marry him today and go to Africa —

MAMA *(in the middle of her getting-ready activity):*   He did? You ain't old enough to marry nobody — *(Seeing the moving men lifting one of her chairs precariously.)* Darling, that ain't no bale of cotton, please handle it so we can sit in it again! I had that chair twenty-five years . . .

The movers sigh with exasperation and go on with their work.

BENEATHA *(girlishly and unreasonably trying to pursue the conversation):*   To go to Africa, Mama — be a doctor in Africa . . .

MAMA *(distracted):*   Yes, baby —

WALTER: *Africa!* What he want you to go to Africa for?

BENEATHA: To practice there . . .

WALTER: Girl, if you don't get all them silly ideas out your head! You better marry yourself a man with some loot . . .

BENEATHA *(angrily, precisely as in the first scene of the play):*   What have you got to do with who I marry!

WALTER: Plenty. Now I think George Murchison —

BENEATHA: *George Murchison!* I wouldn't marry him if he was Adam and I was Eve!

Walter and Beneatha go out yelling at each other vigorously and the anger is loud and real till their voices diminish. Ruth stands at the door and turns to Mama and smiles knowingly.

MAMA *(fixing her hat at last):*   Yeah—they something all right, my children . . .

RUTH: Yeah—they're something. Let's go, Lena.

MAMA *(stalling, starting to look around at the house):*   Yes—I'm coming. Ruth—

RUTH: Yes?

MAMA *(quietly, woman to woman):*   He finally come into his manhood today, didn't he? Kind of like a rainbow after the rain . . .

RUTH *(biting her lip lest her own pride explode in front of Mama):*   Yes, Lena.

Walter's voice calls for them raucously.

WALTER *(offstage):*   Y'all come on! These people charges by the hour, you know!

MAMA *(waving Ruth out vaguely):*   All right, honey—go on down. I be down directly.

Ruth hesitates, then exits. Mama stands, at last alone in the living room, her plant on the table before her as the lights start to come down. She looks around at all the walls and ceilings and suddenly, despite herself, while the children call below, a great heaving thing rises in her and she puts her fist to her mouth to stifle it, takes a final desperate look, pulls her coat about her, pats her hat, and goes out. The lights dim down. The door opens and she comes back in, grabs her plant, and goes out for the last time.

Curtain.   [1959]

THINKING ABOUT THE TEXT

1. The play's main characters are Walter Lee, Mama, Ruth, and Beneatha. List three or more adjectives to describe each of these characters. What basic values does each character seem to express during the arguments that occur in their family? Do you sympathize with them equally? Why, or why not? What, evidently, was Walter Lee's father like?

2. At the end of the play, speaking to Ruth about Walter Lee, Mama says "He finally come into his manhood today, didn't he"? How does Mama appear to be defining *manhood*? What other possible definitions of *manhood* come up directly or indirectly in the play? Identify places where characteristics of *womanhood* are brought up. In general, would you say that gender is at least as important in this play as race is? Why, or why not?

3. Analyze Asagai's conversations with Beneatha and the rest of her family. What does Hansberry suggest about the relations of Africans and African Americans in the late 1950s?

4. Although there is a white character, he makes only two relatively brief appearances, and no other white characters are shown. Why do you suppose Hansberry keeps the presence of whites minimal?

5. Do you think this play is universal in its truths and concerns, or are you more inclined to see it as specifically about African Americans? Explain. In what ways is this 1959 play relevant to life in the United States today?

THE CRISIS

The Hansberrys of Chicago:
They Join Business Acumen
with Social Vision

The following article appeared in the April 1941 issue of The Crisis, *the journal of the National Association for the Advancement of Colored People (NAACP). The photographs to which the article refers are omitted. The NAACP was established in 1909 and* The Crisis *a year later, its founder and first editor being the noted African American intellectual W. E. B. Du Bois. This article pays tribute to Lorraine Hansberry's parents; it notes their successful real estate business, the foundation they established to get civil rights laws enforced, and their 1940 Supreme Court victory. The Court's decision was meant to erode at least some racial covenants, policies by which white neighborhoods kept out blacks. However, the decision lacked enforcement and very little changed.*

Mr. and Mrs. Carl A. Hansberry of Chicago, Ill., have the distinction not only of conducting one of the largest real estate enterprises in the country operated by Negroes but they are unique business people because they are spending much of their wealth to safeguard the civil rights of colored citizens in their city, state, and nation.

The properties shown on these pages are a part of the $250,000.00 worth of Chicago real estate from which The Hansberry Enterprises and The Hansberry Foundation receive a gross annual income of $100,000.00. The real estate firm makes available to Negroes with limited income apartments within their economic reach, while the profits from this enterprise are used to safeguard the Negro's civil rights and to make additional housing available to him. The Hansberrys played a very significant role in the recent Chicago restrictive covenant case before the United States Supreme Court whose decision opened blocks of houses and apartment buildings from which Negroes formerly had been excluded.

THE HANSBERRY ENTERPRISES

The Hansberry Enterprises is a real estate syndicate founded by Mr. Hansberry in 1929. From a very modest beginning, the business has grown to be one of the largest in the Mid-West. The property owned and controlled by the company is in excess of $250,000 in value and accommodates four hundred families. During the past ten years the payroll and commissions have aggregated more than $350,000.00.

The offices of the Hansberry Enterprises are located at 4247 Indiana Avenue, Chicago, Ill.

THE HANSBERRY FOUNDATION

The Hansberry Foundation was established in 1936 by Mrs. N. Louise   5
Hansberry, and her husband, Carl A. Hansberry, with substantial grants of the interest from the Hansberry Enterprises. Mr. Hansberry is the Director. The Foundation was set up as a Trust Fund and only the members of the immediate Hansberry family may contribute to this Fund. A provision of the Trust provides "That during the first ten (10) years only 60 percent of the income of the trust may be used, thereafter, both the income and the principal may be used, but at no time shall the principal be reduced to less than Ten Thousand ($10,000.00) dollars."

The purpose of the Foundation is to encourage and promote respect for all laws, and especially those laws as related to the Civil Rights of American citizens. The following paragraph taken from a letter to the Cook County Bar Association under date of April 27, 1937, gives a precise statement of the purpose and scope of the Hansberry Foundation:

> The Creators of the Hansberry Foundation believe that the Illinois Civil Rights Law represents the crystallized views of the best citizens of Illinois and were made in the best interest of the whole people of Illinois. They therefore believed, that the Civil Rights Code should be enforced; that the passiveness of any citizen should cease. Because of and in view of the foregoing premises, the Hansberry Foundation was created and now therefore announces its desire to cooperate with sympathetic public officials, associations, or organizations, likewise interested in the active enforcement of the Civil Rights Laws of Illinois and throughout the Nation. The Foundation will assume (at its discretion) a part, or all of the costs of prosecuting violations of the law wherever, and/or whenever, the authorities willfully neglect or refuse to act; and where the victims are financially unable to protect themselves.

[1941]

THINKING ABOUT THE TEXT

1. What do you sense is the main rhetorical purpose of *The Crisis* in publishing this article? Does anyone in *A Raisin in the Sun* share the values expressed by the article? To what extent do you aim to "join business acumen with social vision"?

2. Much of the article consists of quotations from legal documents associated with the Hansberry Foundation. What do you think of this rhetorical strategy?

3. The article makes clear that when Lorraine Hansberry's family sought to live in an all-white part of Chicago, they were wealthier than the Youngers.

What would you say to someone who argued that it would have been more honest of Hansberry to focus her play on a family as well-off as hers?

LORRAINE HANSBERRY

April 23, 1964, Letter to
the New York Times

Here is part of a letter by Lorraine Hansberry written five years after A Raisin in the Sun. *Once again, she quotes the poem by Langston Hughes containing her play's title. Now, however, she is expressing approval of civil rights activists' aggressive tactics, including attempts by the Congress of Racial Equality (CORE) to block traffic. In her letter, Hansberry also recalls her family's fight against racial covenants and her father's subsequent death in Mexico. Although the* New York Times *never published Hansberry's letter, some of it was included by her husband Robert Nemiroff in his 1969 compilation of her writings,* To Be Young, Gifted, and Black.

April 23, 1964

To the Editor,
The New York Times:

    . . . My father was typical of a generation of Negroes who believed that the "American way" could successfully be made to work to democratize the United States. Thus, twenty-five years ago, he spent a small personal fortune, his considerable talents, and many years of his life fighting, in association with NAACP attorneys, Chicago's "restrictive covenants" in one of this nation's ugliest ghettoes.

    That fight also required that our family occupy the disputed property in a hellishly hostile "white neighborhood" in which, literally, howling mobs surrounded our house. One of their missiles almost took the life of the then eight-year-old signer of this letter. My memories of this "correct" way of fighting white supremacy in America include being spat at, cursed and pummeled in the daily trek to and from school. And I also remember my desperate and courageous mother, patrolling our house all night with a loaded German luger, doggedly guarding her four children, while my father fought the respectable part of the battle in the Washington court.

    The fact that my father and the NAACP "won" a Supreme Court decision, in a now famous case which bears his name in the lawbooks, is — ironically — the sort of "progress" our satisfied friends allude to when they presume to deride the more radical means of struggle. The cost, in emotional turmoil, time and money, which led to my father's early death as a permanently embittered exile in a foreign country when he saw that after such sacrificial efforts the Negroes of Chicago were as ghetto-locked as ever, does not seem to figure in their calculations.

    That is the reality that I am faced with when I now read that some Negroes my own age and younger say that we must now lie down in the streets, tie up traffic, do whatever we can — take to the hills with guns if necessary — and fight back. Fatuous people remark these days on our "bitterness." Why, of course we are bitter. The entire situation suggests that the nation be reminded of the too little noted final lines of Langston Hughes' mighty poem:

What happens to a dream deferred?

Does it dry up
Like a raisin in the sun?
Or fester like a sore —
And then run?
Does it stink like rotten meat?
Or crust and sugar over —
Like a syrupy sweet?

Maybe it just sags
Like a heavy load.

Or does it explode?

Sincerely,
Lorraine Hansberry
[1964]

THINKING ABOUT THE TEXT

1. Hansberry indicates that she is "bitter." Is *bitter* a word that you associate with the author of *A Raisin in the Sun*? Why, or why not? Do you get the sense that the bitterness she refers to in her letter is justified? Why, or why not?

2. Does Hansberry's play give you the impression that the family in it will suffer the same kinds of things described in the second paragraph of Hansberry's letter? Support your answer with details from the play.

3. In the letter, Hansberry seems to condone acts of civil disobedience. In what kinds of cases, if any, do you think people are justified in breaking the law?

ALAN EHRENHALT

From *The Lost City: Discovering the Forgotten Virtues of Community in the Chicago of the 1950s*

Alan Ehrenhalt (b. 1947) is the executive editor of Governing *magazine and was formerly political editor of* Congressional Quarterly. *In much of his writing, he argues that Americans will achieve true democracy only if they regain the sense of community they once had. This is the basic claim of Ehrenhalt's first book,* The United States of Ambition: Politicians, Power, and the Pursuit of Office *(1991). In his second,* The Lost City: Discovering the Forgotten Virtues of Community in the Chicago of the 1950s *(1995), he extends his concern with community spirit by focusing on the role it played in Chicago during the 1950s. The following excerpts deal with Bronzeville, the South Side ghetto where Lorraine Hansberry grew up and where her 1959 play* A Raisin in the Sun *takes place.*

If St. Nick's parish° was a world of limited choices, a far more limited world existed five miles further east, where the bulk of Chicago's black community — hundreds of thousands of people — lived together in Bronzeville, a neighborhood they were all but prohibited from escaping.

Any discussion of the city we have lost during the past generation must eventually confront the issue of Bronzeville, and the question that may be most troublesome of all: Have we lost something important that existed even in the worst place that the Chicago of the 1950s had to offer?

Anybody who did not live in a black ghetto is bound to be leery of asking the question, with its implied assumption that segregation hid its good points. But the fact remains, long after Bronzeville's disappearance from the map, that a remarkable number of people who did live there find themselves asking it.

"Fifty-first and Dearborn was a bunch of shacks," Alice Blair wrote thirty years later, after she had become Chicago's deputy superintendent of education. "We didn't have hot water — and the houses were torn down for slum clearance to build Robert Taylor Homes. But in those shacks, there was something different from what is there now."

What was it, exactly? Several things. "People took a great deal of pride in just　　5 being where they were," says John Stroger, the first black president of the Cook County Board of Commissioners. "It was economically poor, but spiritually and socially rich. People had hope that things would be better." Stroger echoes what Vernon Jarrett, the longtime Chicago newspaper columnist, said rather hauntingly a few years ago. "The ghetto used to have something going for it. It had a beat, it had a certain rhythm, and it was all hope. I don't care how rough things were."

Then there is the bluntness of Timuel Black, a lifelong civil rights activist, looking back at age seventy-five on the South Side as it used to be and as it has become: "I would say," he declares at the end of a long conversation, "at this point in my life and experience, that we made a mistake leaving the ghetto."

These fragments prove nothing. To many who read them, they will suggest merely that nostalgia is not only powerful but dangerous, that late in life it can generate a fondness for times and places that should be properly remembered with nothing more than relief that they are gone. And yet something valuable did die with Bronzeville, and we can learn something about community and authority, faith and hope, by tracing their presence even in what was, by common agreement, an unjust and constricted corner of the world.

What Bronzeville had, and so many of its graduates continue to mourn, was a sense of posterity — a feeling that, however difficult the present might be, the

---

St. Nick's parish: St. Nicholas of Tolentine parish, a postimmigrant, working-class neighborhood of Chicago.

future was worth thinking about and planning for in some detail. Most of the inhabitants of Bronzeville were farsighted people, able to focus on events and ideas whose outlines were hazy and whose arrival might still be very far away. They were looking forward to a time in which it would be possible to break free of the constrictions and indignities of the moment.

Forty years later, in a time-shortened world hooked on fax machines, microwave popcorn, and MTV, the word *posterity* carries far less meaning than it once did. Its gradual disappearance is one of the genuine losses of modern life. To find the concept so vibrant and well entrenched in a place as deprived as Bronzeville in the 1950s seems to mock the freer but far less anchored world that most of us inhabit today.

The indignities of life for a black person on the South Side in the 1950s are   10
unlikely to come as news to very many readers of any race, but some details are worth dredging up. They reveal the triumphs and comforts of Bronzeville society to have been that much more impressive.

It was, for example, uncommonly dangerous for a black Chicagoan to get sick. Of the seventy-seven hospitals in the metropolitan area, only six would accept black patients at all, and five of those had quotas, so that once a certain small number of beds were occupied by blacks, the next black patient would be turned away, no matter how ill he or she was. It was not unusual for blacks who could perfectly well afford private hospital care to be taken to Cook County Hospital, the spartan and overcrowded charity institution on the West Side.

Most of the time, though, even in an emergency, they would be rushed to Provident, the city's only "black" hospital, sometimes speeding past one white facility after another to get to the Provident emergency room. In 1956, Provident saw an emergency patient every nineteen minutes, five times the average for the city's other hospitals. And it was, of course, the only place where a black doctor could aspire to practice; the other hospitals did their hiring on a strict Jim Crow basis.

Getting stopped for a traffic ticket on the South Side was not the same experience for blacks that it was for whites. Until 1958, all traffic tickets in Chicago mentioned the race of the driver. The police maintained a special task force, known to just about everybody as the "flying squad," which was supposed to zero in on high-crime neighborhoods but in fact spent a good deal of its time harassing black citizens, middle-class as well as poor. It was standard practice for flying squad officers to stop black motorists for traffic violations, frisk them, and search their cars before writing the ticket, often abusing them verbally and physically in the process. The abuses nearly always took place when someone was driving alone, so there were rarely any witnesses.

The force that patrolled these neighborhoods was still mostly white, and the supervisors were essentially all white. There were 1,200 black police officers in Chicago in 1957, but only one black captain, and no lieutenants. In the Englewood district, where many of the new recruits were sent, black patrolmen were nearly always given the most tedious assignments: guard duty night after night, or a motorcycle beat in the depths of winter. The two-man teams were all segregated; blacks and whites were not allowed to work together.

Meanwhile, the public schools were not only segregated but demonstrably　15
unequal. Most of the white elementary schools on the South Side were under-
used, while the black ones were jammed far beyond capacity. Some black schools
in Bronzeville were handling more than 2,000 pupils a day on a double-shift
basis, with one set of children in attendance from 8 A.M. to noon and another
from noon to 4 P.M. At the same time, there were nearly 300 vacant classrooms
elsewhere in the city and more than 1,000 classrooms being used for nonessential
activities of one sort or another. But the school board did not want to adjust the
district lines to permit black kids to take advantage of the space that existed
beyond the racial borders.

The incidents of hospital bias, police harassment, and school inequity
pointed up just how indifferent Jim Crow was to class distinctions in the 1950s:
having money was simply no help in these situations. There was a fourth indignity that somehow makes this point even clearer, and it had to do with travel and
vacations.

For $20 a year in 1957, a black family could join an organization called the
Tourist Motor Club. What they received in return was a list of hotels and restaurants where blacks would be allowed inside the door, and a guarantee of $500 in
bond money in case they found themselves being arrested for making the wrong
choice. "Are you ready for any traveling emergency — even in a hostile town?" the
Tourist Motor Club asked in its ads, and not unreasonably. "What would you do
if you were involved in a highway accident in a hostile town — far away from
home. You could lose your life savings — you could be kept in jail without adequate reason. You could lose your entire vacation fighting unjust prejudice."

Vacations were for those who could afford them. The problem that united
everyone in the black community — wealthy, working class, and poor — was housing. Unlike St. Nick's or any other white community in Chicago, the ghetto was
almost impossible to move out of. The rules of segregation simply made it difficult for a black family to live anywhere else, whether it could afford to or not.

By 1957, that had begun to change. Chicago's South Side black population
was expanding, block by block, into what had been white working-class territory
on its southern and western borders, and a new, separate black enclave had
emerged a few miles west of downtown. But as a practical matter, the number of
decent housing opportunities opening up for blacks was far smaller than the
number needed. Thus, most of the city's black community remained where it
had been since the 1920s: in a narrow strip south of Twenty-third Street, roughly
eight miles long and still no more than two or three miles wide.

This ghetto had been badly overcrowded by the time of World War II, and in　20
the years since then it had grown more crowded still. The number of black people
in Chicago had increased nearly 40 percent between 1950 and 1956, while the
white population was declining. And the newcomers were simply stacking up on
top of one another. The Kenwood-Oakland neighborhood, centered around Forty-
seventh Street, had gone from 13,000 white residents to 80,000 blacks in a matter of
a few years. "A new Negro reaches this sprawling city every fifteen minutes," the
young black journalist Carl Rowan wrote in 1957, seeming a little overwhelmed

himself. Parts of the South Side that had once been relatively spacious and comfortable now held more people than anyone had imagined possible.

The physical world that those migrants confronted was the world of the infamous "kitchenette" — a one-room flat with an icebox, a bed, and a hotplate, typically in an ancient building that once held a few spacious apartments but had been cut up into the tiniest possible pieces to bring the landlord more money. The bathroom and stove were shared with neighbors, a dozen or more people taking turns with the same meager facilities. . . .

In Bronzeville, hope and authority tended to come out of the same package. If the ultimate authority figures were wealthy white people somewhere far away, the most familiar and important ones were right there, inside the community. They were people who had maneuvered their way through the currents of segregated life, made careers and often fortunes for themselves, and remained in the neighborhood, hammering home the message that there were victories to strive for. They were employers and entrepreneurs of all sorts: businessmen, politicians, and entertainers, gambling czars and preachers of the Gospel. They were people whose moral flaws and weaknesses were no secret to those around them, and those weaknesses were a frequent topic of discussion in the community. But they were leaders nevertheless. They led by command, sometimes rather crudely, and they also led by example.

It is easy to forget, forty years later, just how many successful black-owned businesses there were in Chicago. There were black entrepreneurs all up and down the commercial streets in the 1950s, able to stay afloat because they were guaranteed a clientele. They provided services that white businesses simply did not want to provide to blacks. They ran barber shops and beauty parlors, restaurants and taverns, photography studios and small hotels. Many of them were mom-and-pop operations but quite a few evolved into sizable corporations. "Business," as Dempsey Travis says, "was the pillar of optimism."

The nation's largest black-owned bank was at Forty-seventh Street and Cottage Grove Avenue. Parker House Sausage Company, at Forty-sixth and State, called itself the "Jackie Robinson of meat-packing." At Twenty-seventh and Wabash, S. B. Fuller operated a giant cosmetics business that touted three hundred different products, maintained thirty-one branches all over the country, and employed five thousand salesmen. "Anyone can succeed," Fuller used to say, "if he has the desire."

But the great symbols of the entrepreneurial spirit in Bronzeville were the funeral parlors and the insurance companies. In many cases they were related businesses, a legacy of the burial insurance associations that had existed among black sharecroppers in Mississippi and Arkansas early in the century. Undertakers were the largest single source of advertising in the *Defender*; they were also, like their white counterparts elsewhere in the city, mainstays of every community organization: lodges, churches, social clubs.

The opening of a new funeral parlor was a community event in itself. In the spring of 1957, the Jackson funeral home opened a state-of-the art facility on Cottage Grove Avenue, complete, with three large chapels, slumber rooms, a powder room, and a smoking lounge. On the first day, three thousand people came to see it. The Jackson family also owned Jackson Mutual, the fifth largest insurance

25

company in Bronzeville, employing one hundred and twenty people and writing nearly $2 million worth of policies every year.

Insurance actually was a service that white corporations were willing to provide to black customers. Thousands of Bronzeville residents had policies with Metropolitan Life, paying a dollar or two every month to an agent who came by door-to-door to collect. But this was one case where black firms could compete fairly easily. Met Life charged black families more than it charged whites for the same policies, its agents didn't like to come at night when customers were home, and they often seemed to resent having to be there at all. There were billboards all over the neighborhood urging people to buy their insurance from a Negro company.

The result was that by the mid-1950s, the five largest black-owned insurance companies in Chicago had nearly $50 million in assets and more than two thousand employees among them. "Negro life insurance companies," said Walter Lowe, one of the leading agents, "represent the core of Negro economic life. It is the axis upon which are revolved the basic financial activities of a world constricted by the overpowering forces of discrimination."

But it was more than that. It was the underwriter of the extended time horizons that made life in Bronzeville tolerable in the first place. It was the primary symbol of hope for people burdened with a difficult present but unwilling to abandon their focus on the future. In 1954, *Ebony* magazine, published in Chicago, took a survey of its black readership and found that 42 percent owned washing machines, 44 percent owned cars, and 60 percent owned television sets. But 86 percent said they carried life insurance.

The *Defender*'s tribute to the life insurance companies was reprinted every year to coincide with National Negro Insurance Week: "I am the destroyer of poverty and the enemy of crime," it said. "I bring sunshine and happiness wherever I am given half the welcome I deserve. I do not live for the day nor for the morrow but for the unfathomable future. I am your best friend—I am life insurance." . . .

Overcoming evil was a job at which most of Bronzeville worked very hard every Sunday, in congregations that ranged in size from tiny to immense. There were five churches whose sanctuary had a seating capacity of two thousand or more, and at least two churches had more than ten thousand people on their membership rolls. But a majority of the churches in the community, even in the late 1950s, were basically storefront operations—often a couple of dozen worshipers or even fewer than that.

In the bigger churches, Sunday worship was an all-day affair: Sunday school at nine in the morning and the main service at eleven; an evening musicale later on, with the full choir and Gospel chorus; and then, for many of the faithful, a radio sermon from one of the big-name Bronzeville preachers before retiring for the night. Music was at the heart of the experience. Most churches had choirs that accompanied the pastor when he preached as a guest in another pulpit, which all of them did. Some choirs spent considerable time traveling outside the city.

Between Sundays, the odds were that a larger congregation would be busy with some social activity every single night. All these churches had a wide variety of auxiliary organizations—youth groups, missionary societies, sewing circles—

30

and some had as many as two dozen different ones in existence at the same time. Of all the Bronzeville social institutions of the 1950s, the churches were the most uniformly successful and self-reliant. "In their own churches in their own denominational structures," the historian C. Eric Lincoln was to write in retrospect, "black Christians had become accustomed to a sense of dignity and self-fulfillment impossible even to contemplate in the white church in America. . . . To be able to say that 'I belong to Mount Nebo Baptist' or 'We go to Mason's Chapel Methodist' was the accepted way of establishing identity and status."

The storefront churches had to make do without the elaborate network of groups and social involvement. But the key distinction was not the size of the facility; it was the style of worship and particularly the level of emotion. Many of the storefronts, perhaps most, were Holiness or Pentecostal churches — Holy Rollers, as the outside world had already come to know them. The service combined shouting, faith healing, and speaking in tongues; as much as three hours of singing, accompanied by guitar, drum, and tambourine; and vivid story-telling sermons about such things as the fiery furnace or the prodigal son. Some churches employed attendants in white uniforms to calm the shouting worshipers when they became too excited. In a liturgy that devoted a great deal of its time to discussing the nature and consequences of sin — and the specific sins of alcohol, tobacco, profanity, gambling, and adultery — there was intense joy as well. "I have known the sisters and the brothers to become so happy," one woman told Horace Cayton and St. Clair Drake in *Black Metropolis*, "that persons around them are in actual danger of getting knocked in the face."

The popularity of these storefronts was something of a problem for the main- 35
line Baptist and African Methodist Episcopal (AME) congregations that aimed for what they saw as a higher level of decorum and dignity. Some ministers used to upbraid their worshipers for becoming too emotional during the service. By the mid-1950s, however, the liturgical distinction between the storefronts and the mainline institutions was blurring. Dozens of preachers who had begun with nothing had built their churches into successful operations, all without departing significantly from the Holiness or Pentecostal script.

The mid-1950s were an exciting time for Bronzeville churches of all varieties. Congregations were growing, debts were being paid, and churches everywhere seemed to be moving into larger, more elaborate facilities: the shouters as well as the elite. . . .

Bronzeville no longer exists. That is not merely because no one would use such a name anymore, but because most of the buildings that comprised the neighborhood have long since been leveled. With the completion in 1962 of Robert Taylor Homes, the nation's largest public housing project and quite possibly its most squalid, the area once called Bronzeville ceased to run the gamut from worn-out but respectable apartment buildings to gruesome kitchenettes. It became a much more uniform high-rise slum, punctuated every half-mile or so by decrepit commercial strips, hosting intermittent taverns, barbecues, and convenience stores and suggesting only a remnant of the much more thriving business streets that once existed.

Bronzeville is long gone not only physically but socially; it passed out of existence as a community as soon as the middle class left, which was as soon as it was permitted to leave with the lifting of segregation. By 1960, the middle-class exodus had already begun, and by 1970, it was virtually complete. Thousands of families who had been the pillars of Bronzeville society returned at most once a week, for church on Sunday.

So much his been written about the impact of middle-class departure on the life of the ghetto that it seems unnecessary to belabor the point. Perhaps it is sufficient to say that Bronzeville was a community unique in America, that its uniqueness depended on the presence of people from all classes and with all sorts of values, living and struggling together, and that with the disappearance of that diversity, the community could not have continued to exist, even if there had been no physical changes at all.

In thinking about what has disappeared, however, there is no shortage of ironies to ponder. The policy racket is legal now, run neither by local black gamblers nor by the Mafia but by the state of Illinois, which calls it a lottery. The game that was once considered an emblem of sin by much of white Chicago is now depended upon as a contributor to the financing of public education. Policy is merely a business now, managed by a colorless bureaucracy far away—it is no longer a cult or a neighborhood institution. There is no demand for dream books anymore on the South Side, no circus-like drawings in crowded basements with a light over the entrance. People play the legal numbers game with a humorless compulsiveness that has little in common with the old-fashioned emotional experience. 40

Legal businesses have fared almost as badly as illegal ones. Notwithstanding Earl Dickerson's prediction that Supreme Liberty Life would thrive under integration to become a billion-dollar insurance business by the end of the century, the company was simply absorbed into United of America, becoming a piece of a gigantic white institution, and a rather small and inconspicuous piece at that. Not that there was anything racist about such a consolidation; plenty of smaller white-owned insurance companies suffered the same fate. But the cumulative effect on black economic life was powerful: the old life insurance companies were the one significant engine of capital in Chicago's black community, and by 1990, not a single firm was left.

The *Chicago Defender* remains in business at the same location it occupied in the 1950s, published by the same man, John Sengstacke. But it never really found a coherent role to play as a voice of its people in an integrated city. Once the white newspapers began printing news about blacks on the South Side, the paper lost its franchise as virtually the sole source of information within the community. It played a surprisingly passive role in the civil rights confrontations of the 1960s, serving neither as a conspicuous engine of militant activism nor as a persistent critic. By the 1970s, the *Defender* had essentially been superseded as a forum for political debate by the plethora of black radio stations that had sprung up on the South Side. The Bud Billiken parade is still held each summer in Washington Park, attracting a huge contingent of Chicago politicians, white as well as black, but it is no longer the signature event of a powerful black journalistic institution: it is a reminder of the influence that institution once had.

Of all the fixtures of Bronzeville life, the churches come the closest to having survived in recognizable form. Olivet Baptist stands as an impressive edifice at Thirty-first Street and King Drive, its front lawn dominated by a statue of the Reverend J. H. Jackson, pugnacious in stone as he was in life, along with quotations from some of his sermons and praise for him from around the world. Olivet, South Park Baptist, and some of the other Bronzeville churches still turn out crowds at services on Sunday morning, attracting families who return from the far South Side and the suburbs, senior citizens who have remained in the neighborhood, and a sprinkling of children and adults from the projects nearby.

Some of the churches still maintain choirs, Sunday schools, Bible study groups, and social outreach programs, struggling rather heroically against the social disorganization that is all around them. But they have ceased to be voices of clear authority. No preacher can deliver instruction and expect compliance in the way that J. H. Jackson could in his prime. And while sin remains a familiar topic in the South Side black churches on Sundays—a more important topic than at St. Nick's or Elmhurst Presbyterian—the subject no longer has the hold over its listeners that it had a generation ago.

Only in politics can one really argue that Bronzeville has gained more than 45 it has lost. William L. Dawson was a power broker and even a role model of sorts, but he was a leader whose rewards from the white machine were disappointingly meager, somehow not commensurate with the job he did in guaranteeing the election of Richard J. Daley and other white politicians. Dawson's machine yielded in the 1980s to something truly remarkable—a citywide coalition that made possible the election of Harold Washington as the city's first black mayor. Washington's victory in 1983, in a campaign with "Our Turn" as its most conspicuous slogan, was a psychological triumph far beyond anything the old Dawson organization could possibly accomplish, perhaps beyond anything blacks had experienced in any American city. And while the extent of Washington's tangible achievements in office can be debated, the fact that he died in 1987 with his heroic status in the black community intact, and his respect growing even among whites, represented a victory comparable in its way to the first one.

Black political power in Chicago, however, seemed to disappear almost as suddenly as it emerged. Ten years after Washington's first election, Chicago was again being governed by a white mayor, Richard M. Daley, son of the old boss, and by a majority coalition in which Hispanics, not blacks, were the significant minority partner. Meanwhile, the black community was deeply divided over whom to follow and how to proceed, seemingly years away from the level of influence it had had in city politics in the mid-1980s.

In the black community, unlike the white working-class neighborhoods or white suburbia, it may seem perverse—or at least misleading—to dwell on the losses of the past generation. At the individual level, there have been so many gains—in personal freedom, in job opportunities, in income. Today's black middle class is far larger in proportional terms than the one that existed in Bronzeville in the 1950s, much of it living comfortably in neighborhoods scattered all across the Chicago metropolitan area.

When it comes to community institutions, however, the losses are no less real for Chicago's blacks than for white ethnics or for the split-level suburbanites of the 1950s generation. If anything, they are more real. Nearly all of the things that gave texture and coherence to life in Bronzeville, demeaning as that life often was, are simply not reproducible in the freer, more individualistic, more bewildering world of the 1990s.   [1995]

THINKING ABOUT THE TEXT

1. Does reading these passages from Ehrenhalt's book make you think differently about any of the events and characters in *A Raisin in the Sun?* Why, or why not?

2. To what extent does the neighborhood described by Ehrenhalt resemble where you grew up? Identify specific similarities and differences.

3. Note Ehrenhalt's last sentence. While he recognizes that Bronzeville was segregated, evidently he feels some regret over its passing, mourning in particular what he sees as the death of its community spirit. Does his attitude make sense to you? Explain your reasoning. What do you think he might say about the Younger family's decision to leave the neighborhood? How much does it matter to you that this historian of Bronzeville is white?

SIDNEY POITIER

From *The Measure of a Man:*
A Spiritual Autobiography

Raised in the Bahamas, Sidney Poitier (b. 1927) became the leading African American film star of his generation. For his 1963 movie Lilies of the Field, *he won the Academy Award for best actor, the first African American to do so. He has also acted in such important films as* The Blackboard Jungle *(1955),* The Defiant Ones *(1958),* A Patch of Blue *(1965),* Guess Who's Coming to Dinner *(1967),* In the Heat of the Night *(1967),* To Sir, With Love *(1967), and* A Raisin in the Sun *(1961), where he again portrayed Walter Lee Younger, his role in the play's original production. In the following excerpt from his memoir* The Measure of a Man: A Spiritual Autobiography *(2000), Poitier recalls that first staging, especially his struggle in getting other members of the company to accept his view of the play.*

I finished a six-month run, but by the time I left the production the actress who played the mother wasn't speaking to me. She hated me. Need I tell you that this is a difficult position to find yourself in as the member of an ensemble of actors?

Claudia McNeil, a fine performer, was in complete dominance over most of the other members of the cast. Naturally enough, she perceived the play as being best when it unfolded from the mother's point of view. I perceived the play as being best when it unfolded from the son's point of view, however, and I argued that position. In fact, we argued constantly.

I prevailed, I guess because I was considered the principal player who was responsible for getting the piece mounted. I suppose there might have been some who didn't agree with me but simply acquiesced to my position. But I wasn't just throwing my weight around. I was not, and am not, in the habit of doing that. I genuinely felt that when tragedy fell on the family in *Raisin*, the most devastating effects were visited upon the son, because the mother was such a towering figure.

In my opinion, it was the son who carried the theatrical obligation as the force between the audience and the play. The eyes of those watching were on the son to see if the tragedy would destroy him, would blow him apart beyond recovery. And it was also my opinion that there was no such feeling between the audience and the mother. The audience witnessed the sadness that was visited on her. They saw that her family was in disarray, but they also saw her as a force beyond that kind of vulnerability. If they were to vote, they would say, "Oh, but she's going to be okay."

So where's the drama in the piece?   5

The drama asks an audience to *care*. This was my argument to the playwright and the director and the producer, all of whom were my friends. If you're going to ask that audience to care, you're going to have to take them to the place where the most damage is possible so they can feel that pain.

If you keep them focused on the mother, they're going to say, "Oh, that's too bad that happened — but listen, that family's going to be okay."

Well, I had learned in my experience as an actor and as a theater participant that wherever there's threatened destruction of a human being, that's where the focus is; and the only existence that was threatened in *Raisin* was the son's. There was simply no guarantee that he would survive. It was fifty-fifty that this boy couldn't do it, wouldn't be able to bounce back. It was highly probable that he wouldn't have the resilience, the guts, the stamina, or the determination. Or, looked at another way, it was possible that he wouldn't be able to experience the catharsis as fully as necessary for him to be reborn. That's what the audience had to see to be fully engaged: the rebirth of this person.

Now, there was no ego in that. I mean, I was a theater person. I had spent most of my early years in theater — not on Broadway necessarily, but I had done many, many off-Broadway shows. I'd seen dozens and dozens of plays, I'd *worked* in dozens of plays, so I felt comfortable in my sense of what drama is made of, both in theatrical terms and in life terms.

So that was my position, and I was fought tooth and nail on it by the director   10
and the writer and the producer. Ruby Dee and I saw more eye to eye than did either of us with the others, so it was my intent, and she concurred, that I would play the drama on opening night the way I believed it *should* be played. That didn't require changing the words, only making a fundamental change in the attitude of the individual.

Now, this gets to the very core of what acting is. How do you shift the emphasis of a play when, as is the case in A *Raisin in the Sun*, there are two characters who are very forceful and quite strong? Here's how: if you see the son's need as not just personal but a need on behalf of his family, then the emotional center shifts, and it becomes a different play.

The action of the play turns on the death of the father, and the fact that the mother receives ten thousand dollars in insurance money because her husband was killed in an accident on the job. The son wants to use the money in the most constructive way he can think of, which is to start a business, to move the family in some structural way up from where they are.

The mother, on the other hand, wants to use the money to buy a house. But the son says to her, in effect. "The money used to buy a house wouldn't affect the family circumstances in that I'd still chauffeur for somebody else, my wife still works as a maid, and you'd still work as a maid. There'd be no shifting of dynamics here. But there could be, with some sweat and tears, there could be some shifting of dynamics if that money were used as down payment for a business that we could all work at. Then in two years or five years, what we'd have done would be substantial enough for us to be thinking about getting a house and, hopefully, then the business would grow and we could have two such businesses or three such businesses in ten years by the time my son is ready for college."

That's his argument, and the mother's argument runs something like, "You want to spend that money to open a liquor store?" She insists, "My husband's memory is not going to be tied in with the selling of liquor. I'm going to use that money to buy a house, to put a roof over our heads."

He says to his mother, "Isn't it better that my father's death advances the fam- 15
ily? You have a daughter who's going off to college, hopefully, but where is the money coming from? I have a son who is going to be soon a young man. What are the lessons in this for him? I am a chauffeur. Where are we going to be down the line? Am I going to be a chauffeur at the age of sixty, and is my son going to take over chauffeuring?"

So that's the heart of it. Therefore, the playing of this man has to be such that the audience believes that his need for his family is absolutely elemental, and that this is the last chance, *his* last chance. If he fails now, he'll never be able to gather the steam, gather the courage and the determination to spend himself again in a losing effort. He just won't be able to.

It's this sense of possible destruction that prepares the audience for tragedy when the mother *does* give him the money, after he really fights and struggles for it, and the money is lost. All of it.

The audience is primed to see either total destruction of this man or his resurrection, you follow? But there's no resurrection for the mother, regardless. She gives the money to her son because she finally decides to let him have his shot at being a man, his own man — and then he fucks it up. Well, sad as it might be for her as a mother, there's no great tragedy in that for her as an individual. She loses ten grand that she didn't really have in the first place.

But this young man — he's destroyed. That's what the audience assumes. But in the third act he comes out of the ashes, and that's where the real drama is, because he looks at that boy of his, and he talks to him. In fact, he's talking to the audience *through* the boy; and when he speaks, the audience just goes nuts. I mean, it's so *dramatic*.

Well, that was my position — the position I acted from. The other position, as 20
I said, was held very strongly by the actress who played the mother, as well as by the producer, the director, and the playwright — my friends. When I left the fold to go make movies and they had to replace me, the several men who, over time, took the part had to play it the other way, the mother's way, because the continued success of the play depended on having Claudia McNeil.

Well, the audiences didn't seem to mind one bit. The play continued to work well because it had garnered such recognition by then. And the guys who took over the part were all very fine actors, all extremely fine actors, one of whom was Ruby Dee's husband, Ossie Davis.

So what was the lesson in all this?

I would say that sometimes convictions firmly held can cost more than we're willing to pay. And irrevocable change occurs when we're not up to paying, and irrevocable change occurs when we *are* up to paying. Either way, we have to live with the consequences. If I'm up to paying the price in a certain situation, I walk away from the experience with some kind of self-respect because I took the heat. And if I go the other way, feeling that the cost is too high, then however bright the situation turns out, I feel that something is missing.

For an actor to go onstage every night with the sort of hostile undercurrent we experienced with *A Raisin in the Sun* — it can only be described as being like a bad marriage. I felt that Claudia McNeil wasn't giving me what I needed. She knew where my big moments were, and she knew when to hold back and take the air out — and I lived through that opposition for months.

It was very painful for me to know the effect our disagreement was having on   25
my colleagues. If you're a producer, certainly you're irritated by dissension that threatens to interrupt the life of a hit play. Now, my friend Philip Rose, the producer, disagreed with me completely, and I believe that his disagreement was genuine, because I've known the man all these years, and today he's still one of my closest friends. But at the time, I was leaving his play. He had a play that would run, if he could hold it together and keep Claudia McNeil happy, for years and years. So he wasn't especially sympathetic to my concerns.

The playwright's sympathies were completely against me. She saw the play as weighted toward the mother; that's how she'd *written* it. She was a very intelligent young black woman, and she came from a family of achievers. Her whole family were achievers, especially the women, and she had a certain mindset about women and their potential, especially black women in America. So she wrote a play about a matriarch faced with this dilemma. But in that formulation the son is just a ne'er-do-well. He's a fuckup, not a tragic figure, not a man whose life is on the line. I simply couldn't do it that way, because in my mind the dramatic possibilities were so much greater the other way.

Then, of course, there was the director, Lloyd Richards. Again, a very close friend with whom I had very little quarrel on the question, because his first responsibility was to the work by the playwright. He had gone inside the play with her; she had taken him on an excursion into the inner selves of these characters. So he saw the play as she conceived it, and when he put it together, he put it together that way. He didn't have any conflict with it. But I did — because I had to face an audience, you know? — and I just couldn't face an audience playing it with less than the attitude I thought was necessary for this drama.

Out of town in New Haven I played it their way, but I was looking for answers. I wasn't altogether comfortable. We went on to Philadelphia. Same thing. The play was working fine, but there was something missing. It was working overall, but I wasn't really there. We went to Chicago. Same thing. So Ruby Dee and I started exploring, and in Chicago magic started to happen. Wham! And I started to play differently.

Then we went to New York, and on opening night the energy was at its apex. The director saw it, but he wouldn't characterize the added excitement he sensed as coming from the way I had played the role. The producer saw it too, but he said it was just a great night. The playwright was in the audience, and I went out and helped her up on the stage so that all the world could see this magnificent young woman, this gifted person. She assumed that the incredible night of theater we'd all just experienced was as she wrote it.

Well, I say it played well because there was something special in the conviction I held, and I carried it from Chicago to New York. 30

There's a special moment in the third act, just before the end. They had put a down payment on a house before they lost the money, but a man comes to tell them that they're not wanted in that neighborhood. My character, the son, has to stand up and talk to this man. He's talking to this man about his family. After a given point in the speech, he says, "This is my mother." Then he says, "This is my sister." And then he says. "This is my wife, — and she is"— pride, pain, and love overpower him and he's not able to get her name out. And by the time he turns to his son, his emotions are more than any words could express. The tears roll down his cheeks and he begins to cry. He gestures to the boy, but the words won't come out, and finally he forces out the words. He says, "This is my son," and the house goes nuts, you hear me?

I know from my own experience that when a guy is just afraid, and he wishes to succeed *because he's afraid of failure*, that's not much of a commitment. But there's another kind of drive to succeed. I think of my father, going from bar to bar selling his cigars, probing my arm because he's worried that I'm not getting enough to eat. Then sitting down to write a letter to his eldest son, telling him that he's no longer able to control and guide his youngest, that he needs help. You find a man like that, with a need to do something that's over and above his own ego-requirement—a need that's for his *family*, as he sees it—and you get every ounce of his energy. When a man says, "This is for my *child*," you get over and above that which he thinks he's capable of.

My father was with me every moment as I performed in *A Raisin in the Sun*. The themes, too, seemed like so many threads from my own life. The days in Nassau and Miami and New York when I seemed to be in such a downward spiral and there was no promise of resurrection. All the risks I took, all the brushes with destruction. I know how much it pained my family, but there was nothing they could do. It was this art form that saved me. Ultimately, by taking even greater risks—by going to New York and then by choosing a life in the theater—I came through. And it wasn't just for myself. It was for Reggie too.

THINKING ABOUT THE TEXT

1. Poitier's experience with the play was very much that of an actor involved in performing it. Does his account make you aware of anything that you did not realize when you simply *read* the play? If so, what?

2. Poitier reports that even author Hansberry disagreed with his view of the play. In such cases, do you think the performer should usually defer to the playwright? Why or why not?

3. Does Poitier succeed in persuading you that his view of the play made more sense than its rival? Specify things that affect your response to his argument.

WRITING ABOUT ISSUES

1. Choose a particular moment in *A Raisin in the Sun* when characters disagree. Then write an essay analyzing their disagreement. More specifically, identify the different positions they take, the warrants or assumptions that seem to underlie their positions, the outcome of their disagreement, your own evaluation of their views, and the relationship of this moment to the rest of the play. Be sure to quote from the text.

2. Imagine that Hansberry's play is being republished and that you are asked to edit it. Imagine further that the publisher asks you to introduce the play with one of the four background documents in this cluster. Write an essay stating which document you would choose and why.

3. Choose a family you know well, and write an essay comparing it with the Younger family. Above all, consider whether your chosen family, too, has conflicting dreams.

4. Spend time in the library examining newspapers and magazines from 1959, the year *A Raisin in the Sun* opened on Broadway. In particular, try to identify a variety of events and trends that might have affected an American family that year. Next, imagine a specific American family living in 1959. Finally, write an essay describing a play that might be written about your imagined family's reaction to a specific event or trend back then. Give details of the plot, the family's social background, and its members' personalities. If you wish, present some dialogue.

A WEB ASSIGNMENT

Visit the Web Assignments section of the *Making Literature Matter* Web site, where you will find a link to a site entitled "Racial Restrictive Covenants in the United States." At this site, historian Wendy Plotkin has assembled various documents related to community agreements ("covenants") that kept African Americans out of white neighborhoods. Many of Plotkin's documents deal with legal efforts to get these agreements invalidated. One such struggle she chronicles is the case of *Hansberry v. Lee, et al.*, which went all the way to the Supreme Court. The "Hansberry" of the case was Lorraine Hansberry's father Carl, who had moved his family to a white neighborhood that was now trying to evict him. The playwright had this case in mind when she later wrote *A Raisin in the Sun*. Choose at least two of the documents that Plotkin has gathered for this case, and write an essay relating them to specific conversations in the play. You may be especially interested in the articles that Plotkin has transcribed from the *Chicago Defender*, the city's leading black-owned newspaper at the time.

Visit www.bedfordstmartins.com/makinglitmatter

Literature
and Its Issues

12

Living in Families

Blood's thicker than water, and when one's in trouble
Best to seek out a relative's open arms.
— Euripides

Cruel is the strife of brothers.
— Aristotle

Happy families are all alike; every unhappy family is unhappy in its
own way.
— Leo Tolstoy

Happy or unhappy, families are all mysterious.
— Gloria Steinem

The family in the West is finished. . . . Its origin was economic, not biological. . . . The odd group of strangers that make up every family no
longer have any reason to live together, to suffer from one another's
jagged edges.
— Gore Vidal

A man's women folk, whatever their outward show of respect for his
merit and authority, always regard him secretly as an ass, and with something akin to pity.
— H. L. Mencken

In the not-too-distant past, family life was the focal point of our emotional
existence, the center of all our important psychological successes and failures. It
was common for several generations to live together in the same town and even
the same home. Grandparents, aunts, and uncles were an intimate part of daily
life, not just relatives one saw during the holidays. Besides the usual emotional

315

drama that always takes place between parents and children, there were the additional tensions that inevitably arise when the values of the old clash with those of the young. Of course, there was also the comforting emotional support available from more than just a mother and father as well as the sense of belonging and bonding with the many aunts, uncles, and cousins that usually lived nearby.

As extended families become less common, the emotional stakes of home life seem higher than ever. Since we rely on each other more in today's nuclear family, our sense of disappointment, our sense of rejection, and our sense of unworthiness can be more acute. During childhood, the drama of family life can stamp an indelible mark on our psyches, leaving psychological scars that make safe passage into adulthood difficult. Our status within the family can also offer us a sense of worth and confidence that leads to contentment and success later on. For all of us, however, family life is not composed of psychological and sociological generalities but, rather, of our one-to-one relationships with fathers, sisters, grandmothers. Writers often give us imaginative, honest, and illuminating charts of their successes and failures in negotiating both the calm and choppy waters of our family journeys. The following clusters do not hope to be complete or representative of your experiences. We do hope, however, that in reading and discussing these poems and stories, you will find them an interesting and provocative catalyst for you to delve into the joys and sorrows of your own life in a family.

The chapter opens with contemporary writers who give autobiographical accounts of their childhood memories — of people and events that taught them valuable lessons about life (p. 317). Fathers are the focus of the second cluster as four poets paint memorable but not always positive portraits of their fathers (p. 343). The third cluster groups Sylvia Plath's "Daddy" with four critical commentaries on the poet's brilliant and haunting attempt to come to grips with her father's death when she was a girl (p. 349). The next cluster examines the tensions between mothers and daughters as they try to work out questions of identity and responsibility (p. 367). The fifth cluster sharply contrasts the relationship of brothers in different socioeconomic settings (p. 390). In the next cluster, a story and a play dramatize one episode in Tennessee Williams's life and explore a troubled family (p. 427). In the next cluster, five poets give us loving, humorous, and honest snapshots of their grandparents (p. 485). A famously flawed ancient family is the focus of the eighth cluster as Oedipus's discovery leads to tragedy in both *Oedipus the King* and *Antigone* (p. 494). Gwendolyn Brooks's controversial poem, "The Mother," is the topic of this chapter's cultural context (p. 581). The next-to-last cluster explores the circumstances influencing young parents who make fateful decisions about their newborn children (p. 603). The feelings of gays and lesbians within families are the concern of the poets in the final cluster (p. 626).

MEMORIES OF FAMILY

BELL HOOKS, "Inspired Eccentricity"
BRENT STAPLES, "The Runaway Son"
N. SCOTT MOMADAY, "The Way to Rainy Mountain"
LOREN EISELEY, "The Running Man"

We all tell stories about our lives in families. Perhaps the first are those about our relationships with our parents and about our contradictory impulses for understanding and independence. When we tell these tales to others, we might be trying to give meaning to our experiences, perhaps trying to give narrative shape to what seemed confusing and random at the time. Because our childhood memories may seem a disparate series of anecdotes and snapshots, it is probably natural to order them into coherent narratives with definite beginnings and ends. But memories are puzzling. Do we really remember these events, or do we remember someone else telling us about them? Or, more mysteriously, are we remembering earlier memories? The four writers in this cluster create narratives out of their experience, giving a sense of meaning to their futures.

BEFORE YOU READ

Are there members of your immediate or extended family you want to forget? Are there family members you always want to remember? Do the stories you tell about family members have a recurring theme? Why do you tell these stories? How do you feel about the stories members of your family tell about you?

BELL HOOKS
Inspired Eccentricity

Writer, professor, and social critic, bell hooks, born Gloria Jean Watkins in 1952, adopted the name of her maternal great-grandmother, a woman known for speaking her mind. Her books reflect her position as a bold interpreter of contemporary culture in terms of race, class, and gender: Ain't I a Woman *(1981),* Talking Back: Thinking Feminist, Thinking Black *(1989),* Yearning: Race, Gender and Cultural Politics *(1990),* Outlaw Culture: Resisting Representation *(1994), among others. She recently published a memoir,* Bone Black: Memories of Girlhood *(1996). Her most recent book is* Remembered Rapture: The Writer at Work *(1999). She has taught literature, women's studies, and African American studies at Yale University, Oberlin College, and City College of New York and continues to teach and to write poetry and social criticism. The selection that follows is from* Family: American Writers Remember Their Own *(1996), edited by Sharon Sloan Fiffer and Steve Fiffer.*

There are family members you try to forget and ones that you always remember, that you can't stop talking about. They may be dead — long gone — but their presence lingers and you have to share who they were and who they still are with the world. You want everyone to know them as you did, to love them as you did.

All my life I have remained enchanted by the presence of my mother's parents, Sarah and Gus Oldham. When I was a child they were already old. I did not see that then, though. They were Baba and Daddy Gus, together for more than seventy years at the time of his death. Their marriage fascinated me. They were strangers and lovers — two eccentrics who created their own world.

More than any other family members, together they gave me a worldview that sustained me during a difficult and painful childhood. Reflecting on the eclectic writer I have become, I see in myself a mixture of these two very different but equally powerful figures from my childhood. Baba was tall, her skin so white and her hair so jet black and straight that she could have easily "passed" denying all traces of blackness. Yet the man she married was short and dark, and sometimes his skin looked like the color of soot from burning coal. In our childhood the fireplaces burned coal. It was bright heat, luminous and fierce. If you got too close it could burn you.

Together Baba and Daddy Gus generated a hot heat. He was a man of few words, deeply committed to silence — so much so that it was like a religion to him. When he spoke you could hardly hear what he said. Baba was just the opposite. Smoking an abundance of cigarettes a day, she talked endlessly. She preached. She yelled. She fussed. Often her vitriolic rage would heap itself on Daddy Gus, who would sit calmly in his chair by the stove, as calm and still as the Buddha sits. And when he had enough of her words, he would reach for his hat and walk.

Neither Baba nor Daddy Gus drove cars. Rarely did they ride in them. They   5
preferred walking. And even then their styles were different. He moved slow, as though carrying a great weight; she with her tall, lean, boyish frame moved swiftly, as though there was never time to waste. Their one agreed-upon passion was fishing. Though they did not do even that together. They lived close but they created separate worlds.

In a big two-story wood frame house with lots of rooms they constructed a world that could contain their separate and distinct personalities. As children one of the first things we noticed about our grandparents was that they did not sleep in the same room. This arrangement was contrary to everything we understood about marriage. While Mama never wanted to talk about their separate worlds, Baba would tell you in a minute that Daddy Gus was nasty, that he smelled like tobacco juice, that he did not wash enough, that there was no way she would want him in her bed. And while he would say nothing nasty about her, he would merely say why would he want to share somebody else's bed when he could have his own bed to himself, with no one to complain about anything.

I loved my granddaddy's smells. Always, they filled my nostrils with the scent of happiness. It was sheer ecstasy for me to be allowed into his inner sanctum. His room was a small Van Gogh–like space off from the living room. There was no door. Old-fashioned curtains were the only attempt at privacy. Usually the curtains were closed. His room reeked of tobacco. There were treasures everywhere in that small room. As a younger man Daddy Gus did odd jobs, and sometimes even in his old age he would do a chore for some needy lady. As he went about his work, he would pick up found objects, scraps. All these objects would lie about his room, on the dresser, on the table near his bed. Unlike all other grown-ups he never cared about children looking through his things. Anything we wanted he gave to us.

Daddy Gus collected beautiful wooden cigar boxes. They held lots of the important stuff—the treasures. He had tons of little diaries that he made notes in. He gave me my first wallet, my first teeny little book to write in, my first beautiful pen, which did not write for long, but it was still a found and shared treasure. When I would lie on his bed or sit close to him, sometimes just standing near, I would feel all the pain and anxiety of my troubled childhood leave me. His spirit was calm. He gave me the unconditional love I longed for.

"Too calm," his grown-up children thought. That's why he had let this old woman rule him, my cousin BoBo would say. Even as children we knew that grown-ups felt sorry for Daddy Gus. At times his sons seemed to look upon him as not a "real man." His refusal to fight in wars was another sign to them of weakness. It was my grandfather who taught me to oppose war. They saw him as a man controlled by the whims of others, by this tall, strident, demanding woman he had married. I saw him as a man of profound beliefs, a man of integrity. When he heard their put-downs—for they talked on and on about his laziness—he merely muttered that he had no use for them. He was not gonna let anybody tell him what to do with his life.

Daddy Gus was a devout believer, a deacon at his church; he was one of the right-hand men of God. At church, everyone admired his calmness. Baba had no use for church. She liked nothing better than to tell us all the ways it was one big hypocritical place: "Why, I can find God anywhere I want to—I do not need a church." Indeed, when my grandmother died, her funeral could not take place in a church, for she had never belonged. Her refusal to attend church bothered some of her daughters, for they thought she was sinning against God, setting a bad example for the children. We were not supposed to listen when she began to damn the church and everybody in it.   10

Baba loved to "cuss." There was no bad word she was not willing to say. The improvisational manner in which she would string those words together was awesome. It was the goddamn sons of bitches who thought that they could fuck with her when they could just kiss her black ass. A woman of strong words and powerful metaphors, she could not read or write. She lived in the power of language. Her favorite sayings were a prelude for storytelling. It was she who told me, "Play with a puppy, he'll lick you in the mouth." When I heard this saying, I knew what was coming—a long polemic about not letting folks get too close, 'cause they will mess with you.

Baba loved to tell her stories. And I loved to hear them. She called me Glory. And in the midst of her storytelling she would pause to say, "Glory, are ya listenin'. Do you understand what I'm telling ya." Sometimes I would have to repeat the lessons I had learned. Sometimes I was not able to get it right and she would start again. When Mama felt I was learning too much craziness "over home" (that is what we called Baba's house), my visits were curtailed. As I moved into my teens I learned to keep to myself all the wisdom of the old ways I picked up over home.

Baba was an incredible quilt maker, but by the time I was old enough to really understand her work, to see its beauty; she was already having difficulty with her eyesight. She could not sew as much as in the old days, when her work was on everybody's bed. Unwilling to throw anything away, she loved to make crazy quilts, 'cause they allowed every scrap to be used. Although she would one day order patterns and make perfect quilts with colors that went together, she always collected scraps.

Long before I read Virginia Woolf's *A Room of One's Own* I learned from Baba that a woman needed her own space to work. She had a huge room for her quilting. Like every other space in the private world she created upstairs, it had her treasures, an endless array of hatboxes, feathers, and trunks filled with old clothes she had held on to. In room after room there were feather tick mattresses; when they were pulled back, the wooden slats of the bed were revealed, lined with exquisite hand-sewn quilts.

In all these trunks, in crevices and drawers were braided tobacco leaves to   15
keep away moths and other insects. A really hot summer could make cloth sweat, and stains from tobacco juice would end up on quilts no one had ever used. When I was a young child, a quilt my grandmother had made kept me warm, was my solace and comfort. Even though Mama protested when I dragged that old raggedy quilt from Kentucky to Stanford, I knew I needed that bit of the South, of Baba's world, to sustain me.

Like Daddy Gus, she was a woman of her word. She liked to declare with pride, "I mean what I say and I say what I mean." "Glory," she would tell me, "nobody is better than their word—if you can't keep ya word you ain't worth nothin' in this world." She would stop speaking to folk over the breaking of their word, over lies. Our mama was not given to loud speech or confrontation. I learned all those things from Baba—"to stand up and speak up" and not to "give a good goddamn" what folk who "ain't got a pot to pee in" think. My parents were concerned with their image in the world. It was pure blasphemy for Baba to teach that it did not matter what other folks thought—"Ya have to be right with yaself in ya own heart—that's all that matters." Baba taught me to listen to my heart—to follow it. From her we learned as small children to remember our dreams in the night and to share them when we awakened. They would be interpreted by her. She taught us to listen to the knowledge in dreams. Mama would say this was all nonsense, but she too was known to ask the meaning of a dream.

In their own way my grandparents were rebels, deeply committed to radical individualism. I learned how to be myself from them. Mama hated this. She thought it was important to be liked, to conform. She had hated growing up in such an eccentric, otherworldly household. This world where folks made their own wine, their own butter, their own soap; where chickens were raised, and huge gardens were grown for canning everything. This was the world Mama wanted to leave behind. She wanted store-bought things.

Baba lived in another time, a time when all things were produced in the individual household. Everything the family needed was made at home. She loved to tell me stories about learning to trap animals, to skin, to soak possum and coon in brine, to fry up a fresh rabbit. Though a total woman of the outdoors who could shoot and trap as good as any man, she still believed every woman should sew — she made her first quilt as a girl. In her world, women were as strong as men because they had to be. She had grown up in the country and knew that country ways were the best ways to live. Boasting about being able to do anything that a man could do and better, this woman who could not read or write was confident about her place in the universe.

My sense of aesthetics came from her. She taught me to really look at things, to see underneath the surface, to see the different shades of red in the peppers she had dried and hung in the kitchen sunlight. The beauty of the ordinary, the everyday, was her feast of light. While she had no use for the treasures in my granddaddy's world, he too taught me to look for the living spirit in things — the things that are cast away but still need to be touched and cared for. Picking up a found object he would tell me its story or tell me how he was planning to give it life again.

Connected in spirit but so far apart in the life of everydayness, Baba and   20
Daddy Gus were rarely civil to each other. Every shared talk begun with goodwill ended in disagreement and contestation. Everyone knew Baba just loved to fuss. She liked a good war of words. And she was comfortable using words to sting and hurt, to punish. When words would not do the job, she could reach for the strap, a long piece of black leather that would leave tiny imprints on the flesh.

There was no violence in Daddy Gus. Mama shared that he had always been that way, a calm and gentle man, full of tenderness. I remember clinging to his tenderness when nothing I did was right in my mother's eyes, when I was constantly punished. Baba was not an ally. She advocated harsh punishment. She had no use for children who would not obey. She was never ever affectionate. When we entered her house, we gave her a kiss in greeting and that was it. With Daddy Gus we could cuddle, linger in his arms, give as many kisses as desired. His arms and heart were always open.

In the back of their house were fruit trees, chicken coops, and gardens, and in the front were flowers. Baba could make anything grow. And she knew all about herbs and roots. Her home remedies healed our childhood sicknesses. Of course she thought it crazy for anyone to go to a doctor when she could tell them just what they needed. All these things she had learned from her mother, Bell Blair Hooks, whose name I would choose as my pen name. Everyone agreed that I had the temperament of this great-grandmother I would not remember. She was a sharp-tongued woman. Or so they said. And it was believed I had inherited my way with words from her.

Families do that. They chart psychic genealogies that often overlook what is right before our eyes. I may have inherited my great-grandmother Bell Hook's way with words, but I learned to use those words listening to my grandmother. I learned to be courageous by seeing her act without fear. I learned to risk because she was daring. Home and family were her world. While my grandfather journeyed downtown, visited at other folks' houses, went to church, and conducted affairs in the world, Baba rarely left home. There was nothing in the world she needed. Things out there violated her spirit.

As a child I had no sense of what it would mean to live a life, spanning so many generations, unable to read or write. To me Baba was a woman of power. That she would have been extraordinarily powerless in a world beyond 1200 Broad Street was a thought that never entered my mind. I believed that she stayed home because it was the place she liked best. Just as Daddy Gus seemed to need to walk — to roam.

After his death it was easier to see the ways that they complemented and   25
completed each other. For suddenly, without him as a silent backdrop, Baba's spirit was diminished. Something in her was forever lonely and could not find solace. When she died, tulips, her favorite flower, surrounded her. The preacher told us that her death was not an occasion for grief, for "it is hard to live in a world where your choicest friends are gone." Daddy Gus was the companion she missed most. His presence had always been the mirror of memory. Without it there was so much that could not be shared. There was no witness.

Seeing their life together, I learned that it was possible for women and men to fashion households arranged around their own needs. Power was shared. When there was an imbalance, Baba ruled the day. It seemed utterly alien to me to learn about black women and men not making families and homes together. I had not been raised in a world of absent men. One day I knew I would fashion a life using the patterns I inherited from Baba and Daddy Gus. I keep treasures in my cigar box, which still smells after all these years. The quilt that covered me as a child remains, full of ink stains and faded colors. In my trunks are braided tobacco leaves, taken from over home. They keep evil away — keep bad spirits from crossing the threshold, like the ancestors they guard and protect.   [1996]

THINKING ABOUT THE TEXT

1. Do you think hooks is right, that we learn specific life lessons from people in our families? What lessons were you explicitly taught? Are there other, more indirect lessons that you learned from members of your family?

2. Explain the title. What attitude does hooks take toward her grandparents? Does she convince you? What would you think if they were your grandparents?

3. Hooks begins her memoir with a generalization that Baba and Daddy Gus gave her a "worldview that sustained [her] during a difficult and painful childhood" (para. 3). Does she adequately support this idea? How?

4. Writers use specific details about their characters to make them come alive. What are some concrete details or images that you remember about Baba or Daddy Gus? Do these details seem authentic? Is that important?

5. Often a tension exists in families between the roles and personalities members present in their public lives and those they have in their families. Is that the case in this memoir? In what ways might these tensions be good or bad for individual family members? For our culture?

BRENT STAPLES
The Runaway Son

As an editorial writer for the New York Times, *Brent Staples (b. 1951) is an influential commentator on American politics and culture. A proponent of individual effort, Staples resists being reduced to a symbol of African American progress, remembering his childhood as economically stable until marred by his father's alcoholism. After a chaotic family life during his high-school years, he had such little hope of attending college that he did not take the SAT; however, a special program at Philadelphia Military College and Penn Morton College provided needed skills. He earned a B.A. with honors from Widener University (1973) and received a Danforth Fellowship for graduate study at the University of Chicago, where he earned a* Ph.D. in psychology (1977). "The Runaway Son" comes from Staples's memoir, Parallel Time: Growing Up in Black and White (1994).

The mother at the beach was supernaturally pale, speaking that blunt Canadian French with a couple on the next blanket. At the market, she wore a business suit and was lost in a dream at the cheese counter. At the museum, the mother was tan and grimly thin, wearing ink-black shades and hissing furiously into a pocket phone. I was watching when each of these women let a small child wander away. The events were years and cities apart, but basically the same each time. I shadowed the child and waited for its absence to hit home. A mother who loses her cub—even for a moment—displays a seizure of panic unique to itself. Those seizures of panic are a specialty of mine. I guess you could say I collect them.

This morning I am walking to the doctor's office, brooding about mortality and the yearly finger up the butt. Today's mother has flaming red hair and is standing on the steps, riffling her bag for keys. Her little girl is no more than four—with the same creamy face, trimmed in ringlets of red. The mother's hair is thick and shoulder length, blocking her view as she leans over the bag. The child drifts down the steps and stands on the sidewalk. Idling as children do, she crosses to the curb and stares dreamily into traffic. Three people pass her without breaking stride. A pair of teenagers with backpacks. A homeless man pushing a junk-laden shopping cart. A businessman, who glances up at the woman's legs and marches onward.

For some people a four-year-old beyond its mother's reach is invisible. For me that child is the axis of the world. Should I run to her, pull her back from the curb? Should I yell in crude Brooklynese, "Hey lady, look out for the friggin' kid!" Nearing the child, I croon in sweet falsetto, "Hey honey, let's wait for Mommy before you cross." The mention of Mommy freezes her. Up on the steps, the red mane of hair whips hysterically into the air. "Patty, get back here! I told you: Don't go near the street!" The woman thanks me and flushes with embarrassment. I smile—"No trouble at all"—and continue on my way.

Most men past forty dream of muscle tone and sex with exotic strangers. Mine is a constant fantasy of rescue, with a sobbing child as the star. What I tell now is how this came to be.

◆ ◆ ◆

My parents were children when they married. She was eighteen. He was 5
twenty-two. The ceremony was performed in the log house where my mother was
born and where she, my grandmother Mae, and my great-grandmother Luella
still lived, in the foothills of the Blue Ridge Mountains. I visited the house often
as a small child. The only surviving picture shows a bewildered toddler sitting in
the grass, staring fixedly at an unknown something in the distance. My great-
grandmother Luella was a tall, raw-boned woman with a mane of hair so long she
had to move it aside to sit down. Her daughter, my Grandma Mae, wore tight
dresses that showed off her bosoms and a string of dead foxes that trailed from her
shoulder. The beady eyes of the foxes were frightening when she bent to kiss me.

The log house had no running water, no electricity. At night I bathed in a
metal washtub set near the big, wood-burning stove. Once washed, I got into my
white dressing gown and prepared for the trip to the outhouse. My grandmother
held a hurricane lamp out of the back door to light the way. The path was long
and dark and went past the cornfield where all the monsters were. I could tell
they were there, hidden behind the first row, by the way the corn squeaked and
rustled as I passed. Most feared among them were the snakes that turned themselves into hoops and rolled after you at tremendous speed, thrashing through the
corn as they came.

The outhouse itself was dank and musty. While sitting on the toilet I tried as
much as possible to keep the lamp in view through cracks in the outhouse wall. The
trip back to the log house was always the worst; the monsters gathered in the corn to
ambush me, their groaning, growling reaching a crescendo as they prepared to
spring. I ran for the light and landed in the kitchen panting and out of breath.

My father's clan, the Staples of Troutville, had an indoor toilet. My paternal
great-grandparents, John Wesley and Eliza Staples, were people of substance in
the Roanoke valley. In the 1920s, when folks still went about on horseback, John
Wesley burst on the scene in a Model T Ford with all the extras — and let it be
known that he paid for the car in cash. Though not an educated man, he could
read and write. He was vain of his writing: he scribbled even grocery lists with
flourish, pausing often to lick the pencil point. There was no school for black
children at that time. And so John Wesley and his two immediate neighbors built
one at the intersection of their three properties. Then they retained the teacher
who worked in it.

The Pattersons were rich in love, but otherwise broke. This made my
mother's marriage to a Staples man seem a fine idea. But domestic stability was
not my father's experience, the role of husband and father not one that he could
play. His own father, John Wesley's son Marshall, had routinely disappeared on
payday and reappeared drunk and broke several days later. He abandoned the
family at the start of the Depression, leaving Grandma Ada with four children in
hand and one — my father — on the way. Ada had no choice but to place her children with relatives and go north, looking for work.

The luckiest of my uncles landed with John Wesley and Eliza. My father 10
came to rest in hell on earth: the home of Ada's father, Tom Perdue. Three wives
preceded Tom into the grave and the family lore was that he worked them to
death. He hired out his sons for farmwork and collected their pay, leaving them

with nothing. My father was beaten for wetting the bed and forced to sleep on a pallet under the kitchen sink. He left school at third grade and became part of Tom's dark enterprise. Birthdays went by unnoted. Christmas meant a new pair of work boots — if that. Had it not been for my father and a younger cousin, Tom would have died with no one to note his passing.

This childhood left its mark. My father distrusted affection and what there was of it he pushed away. He looked suspicious when you hugged or kissed him — as though doubting that affection was real. The faculty for praising us was dead in him. I could choose any number of examples from childhood, but permit me to skip ahead to college. I was obsessed with achievement and made the dean's list nearly every semester. My father was mute on the subject — and never once said "good job." Finally, I achieved the perfect semester — an A in every subject — with still not a word from him. Years later, I found that he had carried my grades in his wallet and bragged on them to strangers at truck stops.

My father worked as a truck driver; he earned a handsome salary, then tried to drink it up. My mother mishandled what was left. How could she do otherwise when money was a mystery to her? She grew up in a barter economy, where one farmer's milk bought another's eggs and the man who butchered the hogs was paid in port. She stared at dollar bills as though awaiting divine instruction on how to spend them.

I grew up in a household on the verge of collapse, the threat of eviction ever present, the utilities subject to cutoff at any moment. Gas was cheap and therefore easy to regain. The water company had pity on us and relented when we made even token efforts to pay. But the electric company had no heart to harden. We lived in darkness for weeks at a time. While our neighbors' houses were blazing with light, we ate, played, and bathed in the sepia glow of hurricane lamps. My mother made the darkness into a game. Each night before bed, she assembled us in a circle on the floor, with a hurricane lamp at the center. First she told a story, then had each of us tell one. Those too young to tell stories sang songs. I looked forward to the circle and my brothers' and sisters' faces in the lamplight. The stories I told were the first stirrings of the writer in me.

On Saturday night my father raged through the house hurling things at the walls. Sunday morning would find him placid, freshly shaven, and in his favorite chair, the air around him singing with Mennon Speed Stick and Old Spice Cologne. At his feet were stacked the Sunday papers, *The Philadelphia Bulletin* and *The Philadelphia Inquirer*. I craved his attention but I was wary of him; it was never clear who he would be.

On a table nearby was a picture of him when he was in the navy and not yet   15
twenty years old. He was wearing dress whites, with his cap tilted snappily back on his head, his hand raised in a salute. He smiled a rich expansive smile that spread to every corner of his face. A hardness had undermined the smile and limited its radius. His lips — full and fleshy in the picture — were tense and narrow by comparison. The picture showed a carefree boy — free of terrible Tom — on the verge of a life filled with possibility. Ten years later those possibilities had all been exhausted. He was knee-deep in children, married to a woman he no longer loved but lacked the courage to leave. The children were coming fast. We were three, then five, then nine.

Our first neighborhood was called The Hill, a perfect place for a young mother with a large family and an unreliable husband. The men went to work at the shipyard and brought home hefty paychecks that easily supported an entire household. The women stayed home to watch and dote on the children. Not just their own, but all of us. Many of these women were no happier than my mother. They had husbands who beat them; husbands who took lovers within full view of their neighbors; husbands who drove them crazy in any number of ways. The women submerged their suffering in love for children. There was no traffic to speak of, and we played for hours in the streets. A child five years old passed easily from its mother's arms into the arms of the neighborhood. Eyes were on us at every moment. We'd be playing with broken glass when a voice rang out from nowhere: "Y'all stop that and play nice!" We'd be transfixed by the sight of wet cement, ripe for writing curse words, when the voice rang out again: "Y'all get away from that cement. Mr. Prince paid good money to have that done!" Women on errands patroled the sidewalks and made them unsafe for fighting. Every woman had license to discipline a child caught in the wrong. We feigned the deepest remorse, hopeful that the report would not reach our mothers.

Everyone on The Hill grew some kind of fruit; my gang was obsessed with stealing it. We prowled hungrily at people's fences, eyeing their apples, pears, and especially their peaches. We were crazed to get at them, even when they were tiny and bitter and green. We turned surly when there was no fruit at all. Then we raided gardens where people grew trumpet flowers, which gave a sweet nectar when you sucked them. The flowers were enormous and bright orange. When the raid was finished, the ground would be covered with them.

I lost The Hill when my family was evicted. We landed miles away in the Polish West End. The Poles and Ukrainians had once ruled much of the city. They had surrendered it street by street and were now confined to the westernmost neighborhood, their backs pressed to the city limits.

My family had crossed the color line. The people who lived in the house before us had been black as well. But they were all adults. After them, my brothers and sisters must have seemed an invading army.

The Polish and Ukrainian kids spelled their names exotically and ate unpronounceable foods. They were Catholics and on certain Wednesdays wore ashes on their foreheads. On Fridays they were forbidden to eat meat. When you walked by their churches you caught a glimpse of a priest swinging incense at the end of a chain. I wanted to know all there was to know about them. That I was their neighbor entitled me to it.

The Polish and Ukrainian boys did not agree. The first week was a series of fights, one after another. They despised us, as did their parents and grandparents. I gave up trying to know them and played alone. Deprived of friends, I retreated into comic books. My favorite hero was the Silver Surfer, bald and naked to his silver skin, riding a surfboard made of the same silver stuff. The comic's most perfect panels showed the seamless silver body flashing through space on the board. No words; just the long view of the Surfer hurtling past planets and stars.

My fantasies of escape centered on airplanes; I was drunk with the idea of flying. At home, I labored over model planes until the glue made me dizzy. At school,

20

I made planes out of notebook paper and crammed them into my pockets and books. I was obsessed with movies about aerial aces and studied them carefully, prepping for the acehood that I'd been born to and that was destined to be mine. I planned to join the air force when I graduated from high school. The generals would already have heard of me; my jet would be warming up on the runway.

My favorite plane was a wooden Spitfire with British Air Force markings and a propeller powered by a rubber band. I was flying it one day when it landed in the yard of a Ukrainian boy whose nose I had bloodied. His grandfather was gardening when the plane touched down on the neatly kept lawn. He seized the plane, sputtered at me in Ukrainian, and disappeared into the house. A few minutes later one of his older grandsons delivered what was left of it. The old man had destroyed it with malevolent purpose. The wings and fuselage were broken the long way, twice. The pieces were the width of popsicle sticks and wrapped in the rubber band. This was the deepest cruelty I had known.

My mother suffered too. She missed her friends on The Hill, but we were too far west for them to reach us easily. She was learning how difficult it was to care for us on her own, especially since there were few safe places to play. The new house sat on a truck route. Forty-foot semis thundered by, spewing smoke and rattling windows. My mother lived in terror of the traffic and forbade us to roller-skate even on the sidewalk. On The Hill, she had swept off on errands confident that we would be fine. In the Polish West End, she herded us into the house and told us to stay there until she got back.

The house had become a prison. My eldest sister, Yvonne, was thirteen years old — and the first to escape. She stayed out later and later and finally disappeared for days at a time. My mother strapped her. My father threatened her with the juvenile home. But Yvonne met their anger with steeliness. When they questioned her she went dumb and stared into space. I knew the look from prisoner-of-war movies; do your worst, it said, I will tell you nothing. She lied casually and with great skill. But I was an expert listener, determined to break the code. The lie had a strained lightness, the quality of cotton candy. I recognized that sound when she said, "Mom, I'll be right back, I'm going out to the store." I followed her. She passed the store and started across town just as I thought she would. I trotted after her, firing questions. "Where do you think you're going? What is on your mind? What are you trying to do to yourself?" I was my mother's son and accepted all she told me about the dangers of the night. Girls became sluts at night. Boys got into fights and went to jail. These hazards meant nothing to Yvonne; she ignored me and walked on. I yelled "Slut! Street dog!" She lunged at me, but I dodged out of reach. "Slut" I had gotten from my mother. But "street dog" was an original, I'd made it up on the spur of the moment. I had become the child parent. I could scold and insult — but I was too young and ill-formed to instruct. I relished the role; it licensed me to be judge and disparage people I envied but lacked the courage to imitate.

Yvonne was wild to get away. You turned your back and — POOF! — she was gone. Finally she stayed away for days that stretched into weeks and then months. There was no sign or word of her. My mother was beaten up with worry. By night she walked the floors, tilting at every sound in the street.

25

What is it like to be one of nine children, to be tangled in arms and legs in bed and at the dinner table? My brothers and sisters were part of my skin; you only notice your skin when something goes wrong with it. My youngest brother, Blake, got infections that dulled his hearing and closed his ears to the size of pinholes. Bruce broke his arm — while playing in the safety of our treeless and boring backyard. Sherri began to sleepwalk, once leaping down a flight of stairs. Every illness and injury and visit to the hospital involved me. I was first assistant mother now, auxiliary parent in every emergency.

My five-year-old sister Christi was burned nearly to death. Her robe caught fire at the kitchen stove. I was upstairs in my room when it happened. First I heard the scream. Then came thunder of feet below me, and soon after the sound of the ambulance. The doctors did the best they could and gave the rest up to God.

The sign at the nurses' station said that no one under sixteen could visit. I was only eleven; with Yvonne missing, I was as close to sixteen as the children got. I knew that Christi had been brought back from the dead. What I saw the first day added mightily to that awareness. A domed frame had been built over the bed to keep the sheets from touching the burns. Peering under the dome, I saw her wrapped in gauze, round and round the torso, round and round each leg, like a mummy. Blood seeped through the bandages where the burns were deepest. The burns that I could see outside the bandages didn't look too bad. The skin was blackened, but bearable.

Eventually she was allowed to sit up. I would arrive to find her in her bright white gauze suit, sitting in a child's rocking chair. I got used to the gauze. Then they took it off to air out the wounds. Her body was raw from the breast to below the knee. The flesh was wet and bloody in places; I could see the blood pulsing beneath what had been her skin. The room wobbled, but I kept smiling and tried to be natural. I walked in a wide circle around her that day, afraid that I would brush against her. I got past even this, because Christi smiled interminably. The nerve endings were dead and she felt nothing. In time I grew accustomed to flesh without skin.

Christi's injuries were the worst on the ward. Next to the burns everything else was easy to look at. I was especially interested in the boy with the steel rods jutting out of his leg. He'd been hit by a car, and the bone was shattered. He didn't talk much, but the rods in his legs were fascinating. The skin clung to them like icing to the candies on a cake.

The children's ward was sparsely visited on weekdays. I cruised the room, cooing at toddlers and making jokes with frightened newcomers. On weekends the ward filled up with parents, highlighting the fact that I was eleven years old — and that my own parents were elsewhere. When real parents visited, I felt like a fraud. I clung to Christi's bedside and did not stray. I wished that the scene at Christi's bed was like the scene around the other beds: fathers, mothers, relatives. But that was not to be.

Christi's accident made the world dangerous. When left in charge, I gathered the children in the living room and imprisoned them there. Trips to the bathroom were timed and by permission only. Now and then I imagined the

30

smell of gas and trotted into the kitchen to check the stove. I avoided looking out of windows for fear of daydreaming. Staring at the sky, I punched through it into space and roamed the galaxy with my hero, the Silver Surfer.

I was daydreaming one day when my brother Brian cried out in pain. He had taken a pee and gotten his foreskin snarled in his zipper. He had given a good yank, too, and pulled it nearly halfway up. Every step tugged at the zipper and caused him to scream. I cut off the pants and left just the zipper behind. To keep his mind off his troubles and kill time until my parents got home, I plunked out a tune on the piano. The longer they stayed away the more crazed I became.

The days were too full for an eleven-year-old who needed desperately to   35 dream. The coal-fired boiler that heated our house was part of the reason. The fire went out at night, which meant that I built a new fire in the morning: chop kindling; haul ashes; shovel coal. Then it was up from the basement, to iron shirts, polish shoes, make sandwiches, and pack the school lunches. My mother tried to sweeten the jobs by describing them as "little": "Build a little fire to throw the chill off of the house." But there was no such thing as a "little" fire. Every fire required the same backbreaking work. Chop kindling. Chop wood. Shovel coal. Haul ashes. One morning she said, "Put a little polish on the toe of your brother's shoes." I dipped the applicator into the liquid polish and dabbed the tiniest spot on the top of each shoe. Yvonne's departure had left my mother brittle and on the edge of violence. I knew this but couldn't stop myself. She was making breakfast when I presented her with the shoes, which were still scuffed and unpolished. "I told you to polish those shoes," she said. "No, you didn't," I said, "you said 'put a little polish on the toe.'" She snapped at me. I snapped back. Then she lifted the serving platter and smashed it across my head.

My father was drinking more than ever. Debt mounted in the customary pattern. We pushed credit to the limit at one store, then abandoned the bills and moved on to the next. Mine was the face of the family's debt. I romanced the shop owners into giving us food and coal on time, then tiptoed past their windows to put the bite on the next guy. When gas and electricity were cut off, I traveled across town to plead with the utility companies. The account executives were mainly women with soft spots for little boys. I conned them, knowing we would never pay. We were behind in the rent and would soon be evicted. Once settled elsewhere, we would apply for gas and electricity, under a fictitious name.

The only way to get time to myself was to steal it. During the summer, I got up early, dressed with the stealth of a burglar, and tiptoed out of the house. The idea was to get in a full day's play unencumbered by errands or housework. Most days I escaped. On other days my mother's radar was just too good, and her rich contralto came soaring out of the bedroom. "Brent, make sure you're back here in time to . . ." to go shopping, to visit Christi at the hospital, to go a thousand places on a thousand errands.

Inevitably I thought of running away — to Florida. In Florida you could sleep outside, live on fruit from the orange groves, and never have to work. I decided to do it on a snowy Saturday at the start of a blizzard. Thought and impulse were one: I took an orange from the fruit bowl, grabbed my parka from the coat rack, and ran from the house.

I did not get to Florida. In my haste, I had grabbed the coat belonging to my younger brother Brian. It was the same color as mine but too small even to zip up. The freight train I planned to take never left the rail yard. The snow thickened and began to freeze. Numb and disheartened, I headed home.

Five years later I succeeded in running away—this time to college. Widener   40 University was two miles from where my family lived. For all that I visited them, two miles could have been two thousand. I lived at school year round—through holidays, semester breaks, and right through the summer. Alone in bed for the first time, I recognized how crowded my life had been. I enjoyed the campus most when it was deserted. I wandered the dormitory drinking in the space. At night I sat in the stadium, smoking pot and studying the constellations. I never slept with my brothers again.

Years later youngest sister, Yvette, accused me of abandoning the family. But the past is never really past; what we have lived is who we are. I am still the frightened ten-year-old tending babies and waiting for my parents. The sight of a child on its own excludes everything else from view. No reading. No idle conversation. No pretending not to see. I follow and watch and intervene because I have no choice. When next you see a child beyond its mother's reach, scan the crowd for me. I am there, watching you watch the child.   [1994]

THINKING ABOUT THE TEXT

1. If you hadn't read the first and last sections (paras. 1–4, 41), what would you say Staples's theme is? What generalizations does his narrative evidence point to?

2. Race and class figure in this essay in varying degrees. Explain. Do they figure in your experiences? In those of your friends?

3. Staples begins with three anecdotes about mothers and children, then concludes his first section with his "fantasy of rescue" (para. 4). Is his last paragraph a satisfactory conclusion to this idea?

4. Re-creating the past in nonfiction often involves the same techniques as fiction writing: using the five senses. Find examples of creative touches that you think make the essay real.

5. Do you agree that "the past is never really past" (para. 41)? Are you still somehow a ten-year-old? Is Staples's idea of having "no choice" one you identify with? Since the last paragraph cannot be literally true, what is Staples driving at?

MAKING COMPARISONS

1. Is there something typically male or female about hooks's and Staples's memoirs? For example, how might Staples's childhood experiences have been different for a female?

2. Do you think hooks and Staples would have chosen their childhoods? Be specific about what each might keep or change.

3. What do you think is hooks's and Staples's sense of themselves in these first two essays? Do they seem secure? Happy? Defensive? Proud? Bitter?

N. SCOTT MOMADAY
The Way to Rainy Mountain

Born in 1934 into a Native American family in Oklahoma next to Rainy Mountain, Momaday grew up on a family farm and later on several reservations. Momaday graduated from the University of New Mexico and earned his Ph.D. at Stanford University. He has taught writing at the University of California at Berkeley and at Stanford, and currently teaches at the University of Arizona. Momaday is a poet and novelist as well as an accomplished essayist and painter. He won the Pulitzer Prize in 1969 for House Made of Dawn. *Momaday's work celebrates his Native American heritage, about which he writes with reverence and artistic subtlety. The following essay appeared as the introduction to* The Way to Rainy Mountain *(1969), a collection of Kiowa legends.*

A single knoll rises out of the plain in Oklahoma, north and west of the Wichita range. For my people, the Kiowas, it is an old landmark, and they gave it the name Rainy Mountain. The hardest weather in the world is there. Winter brings blizzards, hot tornadic winds arise in the spring, and in summer the prairie is an anvil's edge. The grass turns brittle and brown, and it cracks beneath your feet. There are green belts along the rivers and creeks, linear groves of hickory and pecan, willow and witch hazel. At a distance in July or August the steaming foliage seems almost to writhe in fire. Great green and yellow grasshoppers are everywhere in the tall grass, popping up like corn to sting the flesh, and tortoises crawl about on the red earth, going nowhere in the plenty of time. Loneliness is an aspect of the land. All things in the plain are isolate; there is no confusion of objects in the eye, but *one* hill or *one* tree or *one* man. To look upon that landscape in the early morning, with the sun at your back, is to lose the sense of proportion. Your imagination comes to life, and this, you think, is where Creation was begun.

I returned to Rainy Mountain in July. My grandmother had died in the spring, and I wanted to be at her grave. She had lived to be very old and at last infirm. Her only living daughter was with her when she died, and I was told that in death her face was that of a child.

I like to think of her as a child. When she was born, the Kiowas were living the last great moment of their history. For more than a hundred years they had controlled the open range from the Smoky Hill River to the Red, from the headwaters of the Canadian to the fork of the Arkansas and Cimarron. In alliance with the Comanches, they had ruled the whole of the Southern Plains. War was their sacred business, and they were the finest horsemen the world has ever known. But warfare for the Kiowas was pre-eminently a matter of disposition rather than of survival, and they never understood the grim, unrelenting advance of the U.S. Cavalry. When at last, divided and ill provisioned, they were driven onto the Staked Plains in the cold of autumn, they fell into panic. In Palo Duro Canyon they abandoned their crucial stores to pillage and had nothing then but their lives. In order to save themselves, they surrendered to the soldiers at Fort Sill and were imprisoned in the old stone corral that now stands as a military museum. My grandmother was spared the humiliation of those high gray walls by eight or ten years, but she must have known from birth the affliction of defeat, the dark brooding of old warriors.

Her name was Aho, and she belonged to the last culture to evolve in North America. Her forebears came down from the high country in western Montana nearly three centuries ago. They were a mountain people, a mysterious tribe of hunters whose language has never been classified in any major group. In the late seventeenth century they began a long migration to the south and east. It was a journey toward the dawn, and it led to a golden age. Along the way the Kiowas were befriended by the Crows, who gave them the culture and religion of the Plains. They acquired horses, and their ancient nomadic spirit was suddenly free of the ground. They acquired Tai-me, the sacred sun-dance doll, from that moment the object and symbol of their worship, and so shared in the divinity of the sun. Not least, they acquired the sense of destiny, therefore courage and pride. When they entered upon the Southern Plains they had been transformed. No longer were they slaves to the simple necessity of survival; they were a lordly and dangerous society of fighters and thieves, hunters and priests of the sun. According to their origin myth, they entered the world through a hollow log. From one point of view, their migration was the fruit of an old prophecy, for indeed they emerged from a sunless world.

Though my grandmother lived out her long life in the shadow of Rainy   5
Mountain, the immense landscape of the continental interior lay like memory in her blood. She could tell of the Crows, whom she had never seen, and of the Black Hills, where she had never been. I wanted to see in reality what she had seen more perfectly in the mind's eye, and drove fifteen hundred miles to begin my pilgrimage.

A dark mist lay over the Black Hills, and the land was like iron. At the top of a ridge I caught sight of Devil's Tower upthrust against the gray sky as if in the birth of time the core of the earth had broken through its crust and the motion of the world was begun. There are things in nature that engender an awful quiet in the heart of man; Devil's Tower is one of them. Two centuries ago, because of their need to explain it, the Kiowas made a legend at the base of the rock. My grandmother said:

"Eight children were there at play, seven sisters and their brother. Suddenly the boy was struck dumb; he trembled and began to run upon his hands and feet. His fingers became claws, and his body was covered with fur. There was a bear where the boy had been. The sisters were terrified; they ran, and the bear after them. They came to the stump of a great tree, and the tree spoke to them. It bade them climb upon it, and as they did so, it began to rise into the air. The bear came to kill them, but they were just beyond its reach. It reared against the tree and scored the bark all around with its claws. The seven sisters were borne into the sky, and they became the stars of the Big Dipper." From that moment, and so long as the legend lives, the Kiowas have kinsmen in the night sky. Whatever they were in the mountains, they could be no more. However tenuous their well-being, however much they had suffered and would suffer again, they had found a way out of the wilderness.

My grandmother had a reverence for the sun, a holy regard that now is all but gone out of mankind. There was a wariness in her, and an ancient awe. She was a Christian in her later years, but she had come a long way about, and she never forgot her birthright. As a child she had been to the sun dances; she had taken part in that annual rite, and by it she had learned the restoration of her people in the presence of Tai-me. She was about seven when the last Kiowa sun dance was held in 1887 on the Washita River above Rainy Mountain Creek. The buffalo were gone. In order to consummate the ancient sacrifice — to impale the head of a buffalo bull upon the Tai-me tree — a delegation of old men journeyed into Texas, there to beg and barter for an animal from the Goodnight herd. She was ten when the Kiowas came together for the last time as a living sun-dance culture. They could find no buffalo; they had to hang an old hide from the sacred tree. Before the dance could begin, a company of soldiers rode out from Fort Sill under orders to disperse the tribe. Forbidden without cause the essential act of their faith, having seen the wild herds slaughtered and left to rot upon the ground, the Kiowas backed away forever from the tree. That was July 20, 1890, at the great bend of the Washita. My grandmother was there. Without bitterness, and for as long as she lived, she bore a vision of deicide.

Now that I can have her only in memory, I see my grandmother in the several postures that were peculiar to her: standing at the wood stove on a winter morning and turning meat in a great iron skillet; sitting at the south window, bent above her beadwork, and afterwards, when her vision failed, looking down for a long time into the fold of her hands; going out upon a cane, very slowly as she did when the weight of age came upon her; praying. I remember her most often at prayer. She made long, rambling prayers out of suffering and hope, having seen many things. I was never sure that I had the right to hear, so exclusive were they of all mere custom and company. The last time I saw her she prayed standing by the side of the bed at night, naked to the waist, the light of a kerosene lamp moving upon her dark skin. Her long black hair, always drawn and braided in the day, lay upon her shoulders and against her breasts like a shawl. I do not speak Kiowa, and I never understood her prayers, but there was something inherently sad in the sound, some merest hesitation upon the syllables of sorrow. She began in a high and descending pitch, exhausting her breath to silence; then again and again — and always the same intensity of effort, of something that is, and is not, like urgency in the human voice. Transported so in the dancing light among the shadows of her room, she seemed beyond the reach of time. But that was illusion; I think I knew then that I should not see her again.

Houses are like sentinels in the plain, old keepers of the weather watch. There, in a very little while, wood takes on the appearance of great age. All colors wear soon away in the wind and rain, and then the wood is burned gray and the grain appears and the nails turn red with rust. The window panes are black and opaque; you imagine there is nothing within, and indeed there are many ghosts, bones given up to the land. They stand here and there against the sky, and you approach them for a longer time than you expect. They belong in the distance; it is their domain.

Once there was a lot of sound in my grandmother's house, a lot of coming and going, feasting and talk. The summers there were full of excitement and reunion. The Kiowas are a summer people; they abide the cold and keep to themselves, but when the season turns and the land becomes warm and vital they cannot hold still; an old love of going returns upon them. The aged visitors who came to my grandmother's house when I was a child were made of lean and leather, and they bore themselves upright. They wore great black hats and bright ample shirts that shook in the wind. They rubbed fat upon their hair and wound their braids with strips of colored cloth. Some of them painted their faces and carried the scars of old and cherished enmities. They were an old council of warlords, come to remind and be reminded of who they were. Their wives and daughters served them well. The women might indulge themselves; gossip was at once the mark and compensation of their servitude. They made loud and elaborate talk among themselves, full of jest and gesture, fright and false alarm. They went abroad in fringed and flowered shawls, bright beadwork and German silver. They were at home in the kitchen, and they prepared meals that were banquets.

There were frequent prayer meetings, and nocturnal feasts. When I was a child I played with my cousins outside, where the lamplight fell upon the ground and the singing of the old people rose up around us and carried away into the darkness. There were a lot of good things to eat, a lot of laughter and surprise. And afterwards, when the quiet returned, I lay down with my grandmother and could hear the frogs away by the river and feel the motion of the air.

Now there is a funereal silence in the rooms, the endless wake of some final word. The walls have closed in upon my grandmother's house. When I returned to it in mourning, I saw for the first time in my life how small it was. It was late at night, and there was a white moon, nearly full. I sat for a long time on the stone steps by the kitchen door. From there I could see out across the land; I could see the long row of trees by the creek, the low light upon the rolling plains, and the stars of the Big Dipper. Once I looked at the moon and caught sight of a strange thing. A cricket had perched upon the handrail, only a few inches away. My line of vision was such that the creature filled the moon like a fossil. It had gone there, I thought to live and die, for there, of all places, was its small definition made whole and eternal. A warm wind rose up and purled like the longing within me.

The next morning, I awoke at dawn and went out on the dirt road to Rainy Mountain. It was already hot and the grasshoppers began to fill the air. Still, it was early in the morning, and birds sang out of the shadows. The long yellow grass on the mountain shone in the bright light, and a scissortail hied above the land. There, where it ought to be, at the end of a long and legendary way, was my grandmother's grave. She had at last succeeded to that holy ground. Here and there on the dark stones were ancestral names. Looking back once, I saw the mountain and came away.   [1969]

THINKING ABOUT THE TEXT

1. Momaday wants to "see in reality" the things his grandmother described, so he travels "fifteen hundred miles to begin [his] pilgrimage" (para. 5). Is he successful in this quest? What does it mean to see as someone else has seen? How would you know if you had succeeded?

2. Momaday mixes memoir, folklore, myth, history, and personal reflections in this essay. Does he successfully blend these genres? What is Momaday's aim in each? How does he achieve coherence?

3. Critics claim that Momaday treats his grandmother's memory with tenderness and reverence. Can you cite specific examples of this attitude?

4. What specific attitudes or values of his grandmother's world does Momaday seem to miss? Does he share some of these values? Would our culture benefit from adopting the attitudes of the Kiowas, or is that impossible now?

5. How would you describe Momaday's attitude in the beginning of the penultimate paragraph?

MAKING COMPARISONS

1. Does Momaday seem to reveal his own feelings as much as bell hooks and Brent Staples do?

2. Make a brief list of what you think hooks, Staples, and Momaday learn from members of their families.

3. How would you characterize these three writers' attitudes toward the past? Does sentimentality play a role? Nostalgia? Resentment? Regret?

LOREN EISELEY

The Running Man

Loren Eiseley (1907–1977), born in Nebraska early in the twentieth century, spent a lonely childhood in a difficult family. As he roamed the plains as a young boy and rode freight trains during the Depression, he must have been developing his keen sense of nature, space, and time; however, he did not find his vocation as a scientist until he was a young man in college. He graduated from the University of Nebraska in 1933 and went on to receive a graduate degree from the University of Pennsylvania, where, after teaching at other colleges, he returned to serve on the faculty for over thirty years. He was an essayist, poet, anthropologist, professor, and "curator of early man" at his university's museum; he published eleven books, two of which were volumes of poems. His first book was The Immense Journey *(1946). In 1975, he wrote the autobiographical* All the Strange Hours, *from which the essay here is taken.*

While I endured the months in the Colorado cabin, my mother, who had been offered a safe refuge in the home of her sister, quarreled and fought with everyone. Finally, in her own inelegant way of putting things, she had "skipped town," to work as a seamstress, domestic, or housekeeper upon farms. She was stone deaf. I admired her courage, but I also knew by then that she was paranoid, neurotic, and unstable. What ensued on these various short-lived adventures I neither know to this day, nor wish to know.

It comes to me now in retrospect that I never saw my mother weep: it was her gift to make others suffer instead. She was an untutored, talented artist, and she left me, if anything, a capacity for tremendous visual impressions just as my father, a one-time itinerant actor, had in that silenced household of the stone age—a house of gestures, of daylong facial contortion—produced for me the miracle of words when he came home. My mother had once been very beautiful. It is only thus that I can explain the fatal attraction that produced me. I have never known how my parents chanced to meet.

There will be those to say, in this mother-worshipping culture, that I am harsh, embittered. They will be quite wrong. Why should I be embittered? It is far too late. A month ago, after a passage of many years, I stood above her grave in a place called Wyuka. We, she and I, were close to being one now, lying like the skeletons of last year's leaves in a fence corner. And it was all nothing. Nothing, do you understand? All the pain, all the anguish. Nothing. We were, both of us, merely the debris life always leaves in its passing, like the maimed, discarded chicks in the hatchery trays—no more than that. For a little longer I would see and hear, but it was nothing, and to the world it would mean nothing.

I murmured to myself and tried to tell her this belatedly: Nothing, mama, nothing. Rest. You could never rest. That was your burden. But now, sleep. Soon I will join you, although, forgive me, not here. Neither of us then would rest. I will go far to lie down; the time draws on; it is unlikely that I will return. Now you will understand, I said, touching the October warmth of the gravestone. It was for nothing. It has taken me all my life to grasp this one fact.

I am, it is true, wandering out of time and place. This narrative is faltering. To tell the story of a life one is bound to linger above gravestones where memory blurs and doors can be pushed ajar, but never opened. Listen, or do not listen, it is all the same.

I am every man and no man, and will be so to the end. This is why I must tell the story as I may. Not for the nameless name upon the page, not for the trails behind me that faded or led nowhere, not for the rooms at nightfall where I slept from exhaustion or did not sleep at all, not for the confusion of where I was to go, or if I had a destiny recognizable by any star. No, in retrospect it was the loneliness of not knowing, not knowing at all.

5

I was a child of the early century, American man, if the term may still be tolerated. A creature molded of plains' dust and the seed of those who came west with the wagons. The names Corey, Hollister, Appleton, McKee lie strewn in graveyards from New England to the broken sticks that rotted quickly on the Oregon trail. That ancient contingent, with a lost memory and a gene or two from the Indian, is underscored by the final German of my own name.

How, among all these wanderers, should I have absorbed a code by which to live? How should I have answered in turn to the restrained Puritan, and the long hatred of the beaten hunters? How should I have curbed the flaring rages of my maternal grandfather? How should—

But this I remember out of deepest childhood—I remember the mad Shepards as I heard the name whispered among my mother's people. I remember the pacing, the endless pacing of my parents after midnight, while I lay shivering in the cold bed and tried to understand the words that passed between my mother and my father.

Once, a small toddler, I climbed from bed and seized their hands, pleading   10
wordlessly for sleep, for peace, peace. And surprisingly they relented, even my unfortunate mother. Terror, anxiety, ostracism, shame; I did not understand the words. I learned only the feelings they represent. I repeat, I am an American whose profession, even his life, is no more than a gambler's throw by the firelight of a western wagon.

What have I to do with the city in which I live? Why, far to the west, does my mind still leap to great windswept vistas of grass or the eternal snows of the Cascades? Why does the sight of wolves in cages cause me to avert my eyes?

I will tell you only because something like this was at war in the heart of every American at the final closing of the westward trails. One of the most vivid memories I retain from my young manhood is of the wagon ruts of the Oregon trail still visible on the unplowed short-grass prairie. They stretched half a mile in width and that was only yesterday. In his young years, my own father had carried a gun and remembered the gamblers at the green tables in the cow towns. I dream inexplicably at times of a gathering of wagons, of women in sunbonnets and black-garbed, bewhiskered men. Then I wake and the scene dissolves.

I have strayed from the Shepards. It was a name to fear but this I did not learn for a long time. I thought they were the people pictured in the family Bible, men with white beards and long crooks with which they guided sheep.

In that house, when my father was away and my mother's people came to visit, the Shepards were spoken of in whispers. They were the mad Shepards, I slowly gathered, and they lay somewhere in my line of descent. When I was recalcitrant, the Shepards were spoken of and linked with my name.

In that house there was no peace, yet we loved each other fiercely. Perhaps   15
the adults were so far on into the midcountry that mistakes were never rectifiable, flight disreputable. We were Americans of the middle border where the East was forgotten and the one great western road no longer crawled with wagons.

A silence had fallen. I was one of those born into that silence. The bison had perished; the Sioux no longer rode. Only the yellow dust of the cyclonic twisters still marched across the landscape. I knew the taste of that dust in my youth. I knew it in the days of the dust bowl. No matter how far I travel it will be a fading memory upon my tongue in the hour of my death. It is the taste of one dust only, the dust of a receding ice age.

So much for my mother, the mad Shepards, and the land, but this is not all, certainly not. Some say a child's basic character is formed by the time he is five. I can believe it, I who begged for peace at four and was never blessed for long by its presence.

The late W. H. Auden once said to me over a lonely little dinner in New York before he left America, "What public event do you remember first from child-hood?" I suppose the massive old lion was in his way encouraging a shy man to speak. Being of the same age we concentrated heavily upon the subject.

"I think for me, the *Titanic* disaster," he ventured thoughtfully.

"Of course," I said. "That would be 1912. She was a British ship, and you   20
British have always been a sea people."

"And you?" he questioned, holding me with his seamed features that always gave him the aspect of a seer.

I dropped my gaze. Was it 1914? Was it Pancho Villa's raid into New Mexico in 1916? All westerners remembered that. We wandered momentarily among dead men and long-vanished events. Auden waited patiently.

"Well," I ventured, for it was a long-held personal secret. "It was an escape, just an escape from prison."

"Your own?" Auden asked with a trace of humor.

"No," I began, "it was the same year as the *Titanic* sinking. He blew the gates   25
with nitroglycerin. I was five years old, like you." Then I paused, considering the time. "You are right," I admitted hesitantly, "I was already old enough to know one should flee from the universe, but I did not know where to run." I identified with the man as I always had across the years. "We never made it," I added glumly, and shrugged. "You see, there was a warden, a prison, and a blizzard. Also there was an armed posse and a death." I could feel the same snow driving beside the window in New York. "We never made it," I repeated unconsciously.

Auden sighed and looked curiously at me. I knew he was examining the pro-noun. "There are other things that constitute a child," I added hastily. "Sand-piles, for example. There was a lot of building being done then on our street. I used to spend hours turning over the gravel. Why, I wouldn't know. Finally I had a box of pretty stones and some fossils. I prospected for hours alone. It was like today in book stores, old book stores," I protested defensively.

Auden nodded in sympathy.

"I still can't tell what started it," I went on. "I was groping, I think, childishly into time, into the universe. It was to be my profession, but I never understood in the least, not till much later. No other child on the block wasted his time like that. I have never understood my precise motivation, never. For actually I was retarded in the reading of clock time. Was it because, in the things found in the sand, I was already lost and wandering instinctively — amidst the debris of van-ished eras?"

"Ah," Auden said kindly, "who knows these things?"

"Then there was the period of the gold crosses," I added. "Later, in another   30
house, I had found a little bottle of liquid gilt my mother used on picture frames.
I made some crosses, carefully whittled out of wood, and gilded them till they
were gold. Then I placed them over an occasional dead bird I buried. Or, if I read
of a tragic, heroic death like those of the war aces, I would put the clipping—I
could read by then—into a little box and bury it with a gold cross to mark the
spot. One day a mower in the empty lot beyond our backyard found the little
cemetery and carried away all of my carefully carved crosses. I cried but I never
told anyone. How could I? I had sought in my own small way to preserve the
memory of what always in the end perishes: life and great deeds. I wonder what
the man with the scythe did with my crosses. I wonder if they still exist."

"Yes, it was a child's effort against time," commented Auden. "And perhaps
the archaeologist is just that child grown up."

It was time for Auden to go. We stood and exchanged polite amenities while
he breathed in that heavy, sad way he had. "Write me at Oxford," he had said at
the door. But then there was Austria and soon he was gone. Besides one does not
annoy the great. Their burdens are too heavy. They listen kindly with their eyes
far away.

After that dinner I was glumly despondent for days. Finally a rage possessed
me, started unwittingly by that gentle, gifted man who was to die happily after a
recitation of his magnificent verse. For nights I lay sleepless in a New York hotel
room and all my memories in one gigantic catharsis were bad, spewed out of
hell's mouth, invoked by that one dinner, that one question, *what do you remember first?* My God, they were all firsts. My brain was so scarred it was a miracle it
had survived in any fashion.

For example, I remembered for the first time a ruined farmhouse that I had
stumbled upon in my solitary ramblings after school. The road was one I had
never taken before. Rain was falling. Leaves lay thick on the abandoned road.
Hesitantly I approached and stood in the doorway. Plaster had collapsed from the
ceiling; wind mourned through the empty windows. I crunched tentatively over
shattered glass upon the floor. Papers lay scattered about in wild disorder. Some
looked like school examination papers. I picked one up in curiosity, but this, my
own mature judgment tells me, no one will believe. The name Eiseley was
scrawled across the cover. I was too shocked even to read the paper. No such family had ever been mentioned by my parents. We had come from elsewhere. But
here, in poverty like our own, at the edge of town, had subsisted in this ruined
house a boy with my own name. Gingerly I picked up another paper. There was
the scrawled name again, not too unlike my own rough signature. The date was
what might have been expected in that tottering clapboard house. It read from
the last decade of the century before. They were gone, whoever they were, and
another Eiseley was tiptoeing through the ruined house.

All that remained in a room that might in those days have been called the   35
parlor were two dice lying forlornly amidst the plaster, forgotten at the owners'
last exit. I picked up the pretty cubes uncertainly in the growing sunset through
the window and on impulse cast them. I did not know how adults played. I

merely cast and cast again, making up my own game as I played. Sometimes I thought I won and murmured to myself as children will. Sometimes I thought I lost, but I liked the clicking sound before I rolled the dice. For what stakes did I play, with my childish mind gravely considering? I think I was too naive for such wishes as money and fortune. I played, and here memory almost fails me. I think I played against the universe as the universe was represented by the wind, stirring papers on the plaster-strewn floor. I played against time, remembering my stolen crosses, I played for adventure and escape. Then, clutching the dice, but not the paper with my name, I fled frantically down the leaf-sodden unused road, never to return. One of the dice survives still in my desk drawer. The time is sixty years away.

I have said that, though almost ostracized, we loved each other fiercely there in the silent midcountry because there was nothing else to love, but was it true? Was the hour of departure nearing? My mother lavished affection upon me in her tigerish silent way, giving me cakes when I should have had bread, attempting protection when I was already learning without brothers the grimness and realities of the street.

There had been the time I had just encountered the neighborhood bully. His father's shoulder had been long distorted and rheumatic from the carrying of ice, and the elder son had just encountered the law and gone to prison. My antagonist had inherited his brother's status in the black Irish gang that I had heretofore succeeded in avoiding by journeying homeward from school through alleys and occasional thickets best known to me. But now brother replaced brother. We confronted each other on someone's lawn.

"Get down on your knees," he said contemptuously, knowing very well what was coming. He had left me no way out. At that moment I hit him most inexpertly in the face, whereupon he began very scientifically, as things go in childish circles, to cut me to ribbons. My nose went first.

But then came the rage, the utter fury, summoned up from a thousand home repressions, adrenalin pumped into me from my Viking grandfather, the throwback from the long ships, the berserk men who cared nothing for living when the mood came on them and they stormed the English towns. It comes to me now that the Irishman must have seen it in my eyes. By nature I was a quiet reclusive boy, but then I went utterly mad.

The smashed nose meant nothing, the scientific lefts and rights slicing up my features meant nothing. I went through them with body punches and my eyes. When I halted, we were clear across the street and the boy was gone, running for home. Typically I, too, turned homeward but not for succor. All I wanted was access to the outside watertap to wash off the blood cascading down my face. This I proceeded to do with the stoical indifference of one who expected no help.

As I went about finishing my task, my mother, peering through the curtains, saw my face and promptly had hysterics. I turned away then. I always turned away. In the end, not too far distant, there would be an unbridgeable silence between us. Slowly I was leaving the world she knew and desperation marked her face.

I was old enough that I obeyed my father's injunction, reluctantly given out of his own pain. "Your mother is not responsible, son. Do not cross her. Do you

40

understand?" He held me with his eyes, a man I loved, who could have taken the poor man's divorce, desertion, at any moment. The easy way out. He stayed for me. That was the simple reason. He stayed when his own closest relatives urged him to depart.

I cast down my eyes. "Yes, father," I promised, but I could not say for always. I think he knew it, but work and growing age were crushing him. We looked at each other in a blind despair.

I was like a rag doll upon whose frame skins were tightening in a distorted crippling sequence; the toddler begging for peace between his parents at midnight; the lad suppressing fury till he shook with it; the solitary with his books; the projected fugitive running desperately through the snows of 1912; the dice player in the ruined house of his own name. Who was he, really? The man, so the psychologists would say, who had to be shaped or found in five years' time. I was inarticulate but somewhere, far forward, I would meet the running man; the peace I begged for between my parents would, too often, leave me sleepless. There was another thing I could not name to Auden. The fact that I remember it at all reveals the beginning of adulthood and a sense of sin beyond my years.

To grow is a gain, an enlargement of life; is not this what they tell us? Yet it is also a departure. There is something lost that will not return. We moved one fall to Aurora, Nebraska, a sleepy country town near the Platte. A few boys gathered to watch the van unload. "Want to play?" ventured one. "Sure," I said. I followed them off over a rise to a creek bed. "We're making a cave in the bank," they explained. It was a great raw gaping hole obviously worked on by more than one generation of troglodytes. They giggled. "But first you've got to swear awful words. We'll all swear."

I was a silent boy, who went by reading. My father did not use these words. I was, in retrospect, a very funny little boy. I was so alone I did not know how to swear, but clamoring they taught me. I wanted to belong, to enter the troglodytes' existence. I shouted and mouthed the uncouth, unfamiliar words with the rest.

Mother was restless in the new environment, though again my father had wisely chosen a house at the edge of town. The population was primarily Scandinavian. She exercised arbitrary judgment. She drove good-natured, friendly boys away if they seemed big, and on the other hand encouraged slighter youngsters whom I had every reason to despise.

Finally, because it was farmland over which children roamed at will, mother's ability to keep track of my wide-ranging absences faltered. On one memorable occasion her driving, possessive restlessness passed out of bounds. She pursued us to a nearby pasture and in the rasping voice of deafness ordered me home.

My comrades of the fields stood watching. I was ten years old by then. I sensed my status in this gang was at stake. I refused to come. I had refused a parental order that was arbitrary and uncalled for and, in addition, I was humiliated. My mother was behaving in the manner of a witch. She could not hear, she was violently gesticulating without dignity, and her dress was somehow appropriate to the occasion.

Slowly I turned and looked at my companions. Their faces could not be read. They simply waited, doubtless waited for me to break the apron strings that rested

45

50

lightly and tolerably upon themselves. And so in the end I broke my father's injunction; I ran, and with me ran my childish companions, over fences, tumbling down haystacks, chuckling, with the witch, her hair flying, her clothing disarrayed, stumbling after. Escape, escape, the first stirrings of the running man. Miles of escape.

Of course she gave up. Of course she never caught us. Walking home alone in the twilight I was bitterly ashamed. Ashamed for the violation of my promise to my father. Ashamed at what I had done to my savage and stone-deaf mother who could not grasp the fact that I had to make my way in a world unknown to her. Ashamed for the story that would penetrate the neighborhood. Ashamed for my own weakness. Ashamed, ashamed.

I do not remember a single teacher from that school, a single thing I learned there. Men were then drilling in a lot close to our house. I watched them every day. Finally they marched off. It was 1917. I was ten years old. I wanted to go. Either that or back to sleeping the troglodyte existence we had created in the cave bank. But never home, not ever. Even today, as though in a far-off crystal, I can see my running, gesticulating mother and her distorted features cursing us. And they laughed, you see, my companions. Perhaps I, in anxiety to belong, did also. That is what I could not tell Auden. Only an unutterable savagery, my savagery at myself, scrawls it once and once only on this page.   [1975]

THINKING ABOUT THE TEXT

1. It seems to take a while before the reader gets at the real answer to Auden's question. Why doesn't Eiseley state his point much earlier? Is something gained by his indirection?

2. How important is the context Eiseley gives — his parents, his geography, his historical moment, his personality, and so forth? Do we need more? Or maybe less?

3. At the start of this essay, Eiseley seems to be wandering. Why does he do this? What is his real focus? Himself? His mother? His memories? His guilt?

4. Eiseley (para. 7) claims he is an "American man, if the term may still be tolerated." Why does he say this? Is his story part of a mainstream American narrative?

5. What specifically did Eiseley do as a child that so upsets him? Do you think this is a literal story? Is it perhaps symbolic of something he did over time?

MAKING COMPARISONS

1. In what ways are the three other memoirs in this cluster also part of an American story?

2. Compare the purposes of each of the four memoirs. How do you read the last sentence of Eiseley's essay? Can bitterness against oneself be a motivating force for writing?

3. Compare the tone you hear in Eiseley's essay with the tone in the essays by hooks and Staples.

WRITING ABOUT ISSUES

1. Argue in a brief essay that one can or cannot get beyond the past. Use concrete examples.

2. Argue that difficulties in one's childhood are not necessarily a negative influence.

3. Write a personal essay that imitates the general structure of one of the essays in this cluster.

4. In paragraph 45 Eiseley writes, "To grow is a gain, an enlargement of life. . . . Yet it is also a departure. There is something lost that will not return." Write an essay that argues that this is or is not true. Make reference to Eiseley and Staples, as well as other texts (novels, films, memoirs) you think are appropriate. You might also want to include your own experience for support.

RECONCILING WITH FATHERS

LUCILLE CLIFTON, "forgiving my father"
ROBERT HAYDEN, "Those Winter Sundays"
THEODORE ROETHKE, "My Papa's Waltz"
SHIRLEY GEOK-LIN LIM, "Father from Asia"

In childhood, our emotions are often intense. Fears about life arise because we feel so powerless. For some of us, our fathers held all the power. Fathers may use their power in various ways—some to control or abuse, others to comfort and protect. We form perceptions about our fathers from these early memories. Often we become judgmental about their failures in the world or their failures as parents. As we grow older, we sometimes come to terms with our fathers and see them simply as human beings with strengths and weaknesses. But it is not always so simple; some wounds may be too deep for us to reconcile. The four poets in this cluster approach memories of their fathers with different perspectives and purposes: some want to forgive, others will not.

BEFORE YOU READ

Make a list of four strong memories about your father from your childhood. Are the memories positive or not? Can you remember how you felt then? Is it different from how you feel now? How can you explain the difference?

LUCILLE CLIFTON
forgiving my father

*Born in 1936 in a small town near Buffalo, New York, Lucille Clifton attended
Howard University and Fredonia State Teacher's College and has taught poetry at
a number of universities. Her numerous awards for writing include two creative writing fellowships from the National Endowment for the Arts (1970 and 1973), two
Pulitzer Prize nominations (for* Good Woman: Poems and a Memoir *and for* Next,
*both in 1988), several major poetry awards, and an Emmy. The mother of six,
Clifton's works include fifteen children's books. She is a former poet laureate of Maryland and has been the Distinguished Professor of Humanities at St. Mary's College
since 1991. "Forgiving my father" is from her 1980 book,* Two-Headed Woman.*

it is friday. we have come
to the paying of the bills.
all week you have stood in my dreams
like a ghost, asking for more time
but today is payday, payday old man,   5
my mother's hand opens in her early grave
and i hold it out like a good daughter.

there is no more time for you. there will
never be time enough daddy daddy old lecher
old liar. i wish you were rich so i could take it all   10
and give the lady what she was due
but you were the son of a needy father,
the father of a needy son,
you gave her all you had
which was nothing. you have already given her   15
all you had.

you are the pocket that was going to open
and come up empty any friday.
you were each other's bad bargain, not mine.
daddy old pauper   old prisoner,   old dead man   20
what am i doing here collecting?
you lie side by side in debtor's boxes
and no accounting will open them up.   [1980]

THINKING ABOUT THE TEXT

1. How might you answer the question in line 21? Are the last two lines
   of the poem a kind of answer? Is there some way we can "collect" from
   the dead?

2. Should we bury the dead — that is, should we let the past go and let bygones be bygones? Or is it necessary to settle old scores? What do you think Clifton's answer would be?

3. How consistently does Clifton use the payday analogy? Make a list of words that reinforce her overall scheme.

4. Would you think differently about the speaker's father if Clifton had written "elderly one" instead of "old man" (line 5) or "old playboy / old fibber" instead of "old lecher / old liar" (lines 9–10)?

5. Some readers look for tensions or contradictions early in a poem, hoping they will be resolved at the end. Does this poem end in a resolution of paying up and forgiving?

ROBERT HAYDEN
Those Winter Sundays

Born in Detroit, Michigan, African American poet Robert Hayden (1913–1980) grew up in a poor neighborhood where his natural parents left him with family friends. He grew up with the Hayden name, not discovering his original name until he was forty. Hayden attended Detroit City College (now Wayne State University) from 1932 to 1936, worked in the Federal Writer's Project, and later earned his M.A. at the University of Michigan in 1944. He taught at Fisk University from 1946 to 1968 and at the University of Michigan from 1968 to 1980 and published several collections of poetry. Although his poems sometimes contain autobiographical elements, Hayden is primarily a formalist poet who preferred that his poems not be limited to personal or ethnic interpretations. "Those Winter Sundays" is from Angle of Ascent (1966).

Sundays too my father got up early
and put his clothes on in the blueblack cold,
then with cracked hands that ached
from labor in the weekday weather made
banked fires blaze. No one ever thanked him.   5

I'd wake and hear the cold splintering, breaking.
When the rooms were warm, he'd call,
and slowly I would rise and dress,
fearing the chronic angers of that house,

Speaking indifferently to him,   10
who had driven out the cold
and polished my good shoes as well.
What did I know, what did I know
of love's austere and lonely offices?   [1962]

THINKING ABOUT THE TEXT

1. Is the concluding question meant rhetorically—that is, is the answer so obvious no real reply is expected? Write a response you think the son would give now.

2. Why did the children never thank their father? Is this common? What specific things might you thank your father (or mother) for? Do parents have basic responsibilities to their children that do not warrant thanks?

3. Is there evidence that the son loves his father now? Did he then? Why did he speak "indifferently" to his father? Is it clear what the "chronic angers" are? Should it be?

4. How might you fill in the gaps here? For example, how old do you think the boy is? How old is the father? What kind of a job might he have? What else can you infer?

5. What is the speaker's tone? Is he hoping for your understanding? Your sympathy? Are we responsible for the things we do in childhood? Is this speaker repentant or simply explaining?

MAKING COMPARISONS

1. What degrees of forgiveness do you see in Clifton's and Hayden's poems?

2. Writing a poem for one's father seems different from writing a poem about him. Explain this statement in reference to these poems.

3. Compare the purpose of the questions in each poem. How might each poet answer the other poet's questions?

THEODORE ROETHKE
My Papa's Waltz

Born in Saginaw, Michigan, Theodore Roethke (1908–1963) was strongly influenced by childhood experiences with his father, a usually stern man who sold plants and flowers and who kept a large greenhouse, the setting for many of Roethke's poems. Theodore Roethke was educated at the University of Michigan, took courses at Harvard, and taught at several universities before becoming poet-in-residence at the University of Washington in 1948. Roethke's books include The Lost Son and Other Poems *(1949), the source for "My Papa's Waltz";* The Waking *(1953), which won a Pulitzer Prize; and* Words for the Wind *(1958), which won the National Book Award. Roethke's intensely personal style insures his place among the most influential postmodern American poets.*

The whiskey on your breath
Could make a small boy dizzy;

But I hung on like death:
Such waltzing was not easy.

We romped until the pans   5
Slid from the kitchen shelf;
My mother's countenance
Could not unfrown itself.

The hand that held my wrist
Was battered on one knuckle;   10
At every step you missed
My right ear scraped a buckle.

You beat time on my head
With a palm caked hard by dirt,
Then waltzed me off to bed   15
Still clinging to your shirt.   [1948]

THINKING ABOUT THE TEXT

1. Is the narrator looking back at his father with fondness? Bitterness?
2. Would the poem make a different impression if we changed "romped" to "fought" and "waltzing" to "dancing"?
3. Why did the boy hang on and cling to his father? From fear? From affection?
4. What is the mother's role here? How would you characterize her frown?
5. Readers often have a negative view of the relationship represented here, but many change their minds, seeing some positive aspects to the father and son's waltz. How might you account for this revision?

MAKING COMPARISONS

1. Would you have read this poem differently if the poet had used Clifton's title "forgiving my father"?
2. How would you compare the tone of Roethke's poem with that of Hayden's? Do they miss their fathers?
3. Would you say that Roethke has more complex feelings about his father, whereas Clifton and Hayden seem clearer?

SHIRLEY GEOK-LIN LIM
Father from Asia

Born in 1944 in Malacca, Malaysia, Shirley Geok-lin Lim attended the University of Malaysia and came to study in the United States in the 1960s; she earned a Ph.D. from Brandeis University in 1971. Of her four published books of poetry,

Crossing the Peninsula *won the Commonwealth Poetry Prize in 1980, a first both for an Asian and for a woman. Her published works include two short-story collections and several editions of critical studies and anthologies focusing on gender and Asian American issues, including* The Forbidden Stitch: An Asian American Women's Anthology *(1989), which won an American Book Award. Her most recent work is* Among the White Moonfaces: Memoirs of a Nyonya Feminist *(1996). She is a professor of English at the University of California at Santa Barbara. The poem that follows is from* Crossing the Peninsula.

Father, you turn your hands toward me.
Large hollow bowls, they are empty
stigmata of poverty. Light pours
through them, and I back away,
for you are dangerous, father   5
of poverty, father of ten children,
father of nothing, from whose life
I have learned nothing for myself.
You are the father of childhood,
father from Asia, father of sacrifice.   10
I renounce you, keep you in my sleep,
keep you two oceans away, ghost
who eats his own children,
Asia who loved his children,
who didn't know abandonment,   15
father who lived at the center of the world,
whose life I dare not remember,
for memory is a wheel that crushes,
and Asia is dust, is dust.   [1980]

THINKING ABOUT THE TEXT

1. What does "I renounce you" (line 11) mean? If the speaker renounces her father, why does the line end with "keep you in my sleep"?

2. If you were to write a poem about your father, would it be for you? For him? For someone else? Do you think poets write for a specific audience or only for themselves? Which does Lim do?

3. "Father of nothing" (line 7) seems harsh. Does Lim mean it to be? Is "ghost / who eats his own children" (lines 12–13) hyperbolic — that is, a deliberate overstatement?

4. Why does Lim compare the father's hands to bowls? What other metaphors does she use? Rewrite the last line, being explicit about what you think she means.

5. Lim's speaker says she "learned nothing" (line 8) from her father's life. Is this possible? Is memory "a wheel that crushes" (line 18)? Is this poem a remembrance? Can we escape the past? Should we? Does the speaker?

MAKING COMPARISONS

1. Is Lim's speaker angrier than Clifton's, Hayden's, or Roethke's? Is there a resolution in Lim's poem? Is there in the other three poems?
2. Clifton's speaker seems to be forgiving her father for something. Is Lim's forgiving her father? Is Hayden's? Roethke's?
3. Which speaker's attitude seems the healthiest? Which the least?

WRITING ABOUT ISSUES

1. Choose one of the four preceding poems to argue that our feelings for our fathers are complex, not simple.
2. Jean-Paul Sartre writes in *Words* (1964) that "there is no good father, that is the rule." Use examples from the four poems to argue that this is, or is not, the case.
3. Do you think all children leave childhood or adolescence with unresolved tensions in their relationships with their fathers? Write a personal narrative that confronts this idea.
4. Locate at least six more poems that deal with memories of fathers. Write a brief report, noting the similarities to the four poems given here.

Exorcising the Dead:
Critical Commentaries on Sylvia Plath's "Daddy"

SYLVIA PLATH, "Daddy"

Critical Commentaries:
MARY LYNN BROE, From *Protean Poetic: The Poetry of Sylvia Plath*
LYNDA K. BUNDTZEN, From *Plath's Incarnations*
STEVEN GOULD AXELROD, From *Sylvia Plath: The Wound and the Cure of Words*
TIM KENDALL, From *Sylvia Plath: A Critical Study*

As contradictory as it might seem, we sometimes get angry when someone close to us dies. Psychologists tell us that anger is a healthy emotion in the mourning process, following sorrow and preceding acceptance: it is painful to miss loved ones, and we resent it. We might even direct the anger at them, feeling as if they are responsible for depriving us of their love. Sometimes, however, this anger lingers on long after the normal grieving process is over. Perhaps the attachment was abnormally strong, or the person's own life is too unstable to follow through to reach the final acceptance stage.

In the following poem, Sylvia Plath writes about her dead father as if he were a terrible person, even though as a young girl she seems to have adored him. Perhaps she is trying to expel his memory so she can find peace; perhaps she is using the

(© Bettmann/CORBIS.)

poem as an occasion to express a deeper meaning about authority or influence from the past. Regardless, the poem is a powerful, strange, and passionate work of art.

BEFORE YOU READ

Does it make sense to you that we might get angry at those who die because they have somehow deserted us? Do you think we have to "work out" the tensions between us and our parents before we can move into adulthood? Might it be healthy to exaggerate the difficulties of our childhood in poems and stories?

SYLVIA PLATH
Daddy

Born to middle-class parents in suburban New York, Sylvia Plath (1932–1963) became known as an intensely emotional "confessional" poet whose work is primarily autobiographical. Her father, a professor of biology and German, died when she was eight, the year her first poem was published. She graduated with honors from Smith College in 1950, after an internship at Mademoiselle *and a suicide attempt in her junior year, experiences described in her novel* The Bell Jar *(1963). She won a Fulbright Scholarship to study at Cambridge, England, where she met and married poet Ted Hughes. The couple had two children; the marriage ended the year before her suicide in 1963. "Daddy" is from* Ariel, *published posthumously in 1965.*

You do not do, you do not do
Any more, black shoe
In which I have lived like a foot
For thirty years, poor and white,
Barely daring to breathe or Achoo.   5

Daddy, I have had to kill you.
You died before I had time —
Marble-heavy, a bag full of God,
Ghastly statue with one gray toe
Big as a Frisco seal   10

And a head in the freakish Atlantic
Where it pours bean green over blue
In the waters off beautiful Nauset.°   *Cape Cod inlet*
I used to pray to recover you.
Ach, du.°   *Oh, you*   15

In the German tongue, in the Polish Town°
Scraped flat by the roller
Of wars, wars, wars.
But the name of the town is common.
My Polack friend   20

Says there are a dozen or two.
So I never could tell where you
Put your foot, your root,
I never could talk to you.
The tongue stuck in my jaw.   25

It stuck in a barb wire snare.
Ich, ich, ich, ich,°   *I, I, I, I*
I could hardly speak.
I thought every German was you.
And the language obscene   30

An engine, an engine
Chuffing me off like a Jew.

16 Polish town: Plath's father was born in Granbow, Poland.

A Jew to Dachau, Auschwitz, Belsen.°
I began to talk like a Jew.
I think I may well be a Jew.   35

The snows of the Tyrol, the clear beer of Vienna
Are not very pure or true.
With my gypsy-ancestress and my weird luck
And my Taroc° pack and my Taroc pack
I may be a bit of a Jew.   40

I have always been scared of *you*,
With your Luftwaffe,° your gobbledygoo.
And your neat mustache
And your Aryan eye, bright blue.
Panzer-man, panzer-man,° O You —   45

Not God but a swastika
So black no sky could squeak through.
Every woman adores a Fascist,
The boot in the face, the brute
Brute heart of a brute like you.   50

You stand at the blackboard, daddy,
In the picture I have of you,
A cleft in your chin instead of your foot
But no less a devil for that, no not
Any less the black man who   55

Bit my pretty red heart in two.
I was ten when they buried you.
At twenty I tried to die
And get back, back, back to you.
I thought even the bones would do   60

But they pulled me out of the sack,
And they stuck me together with glue.
And then I knew what to do.
I made a model of you,
A man in black with a Meinkampf° look   65

And a love of the rack and the screw.
And I said I do, I do.
So daddy, I'm finally through.
The black telephone's off at the root,
The voices just can't worm through.   70

---

33 Dachau . . . Belsen: Nazi death camps in World War II.   **39 Taroc:** Tarot cards used to tell fortunes. The practice may have originated among the early Jewish Cabalists and was then widely adopted by European Gypsies during the Middle Ages.   **42 Luftwaffe:** World War II German air force.   **45 panzer-man:** A member of the German armored vehicle division.   **65 Meinkampf:** Hitler's autobiography (*My Struggle*).

If I've killed one man, I've killed two—
The vampire who said he was you
And drank my blood for a year,
Seven years, if you want to know.
Daddy, you can lie back now.   75

There's a stake in your fat black heart
And the villagers never liked you.
They are dancing and stamping on you.
They always *knew* it was you.
Daddy, daddy, you bastard, I'm through.   [1962]   80

THINKING ABOUT THE TEXT

1. Can this poem be seen as a series of arguments for why Plath has to forget her father? What complaints does the speaker seem to have against her father?

2. Some psychologists claim that we all have a love-hate relationship with our parents. Do you agree? Would Plath's speaker agree?

3. How effective is it for the speaker to compare herself to a Jew in Hitler's Germany? What other similes and metaphors are used to refer to her father? Do they work, or are they too extreme? Perhaps Plath wants them to be outrageous. Why might she?

4. Plath combines childhood rhymes and words with brutal images. What effect does this have on you? Why do you think Plath does this? What odd stylistic features can you point to here?

5. Why do you think it is necessary for the speaker to be finally "through" with her father? Is it normal young adult rebelliousness? What else might it be?

MARY LYNN BROE
From *Protean Poetic: The Poetry of Sylvia Plath*

Mary Lynn Broe (b. 1946) was educated at St. Louis University, where she received her B.A. in 1967, and the University of Connecticut, where she earned an M.A. in 1970 and a Ph.D. in 1976. She currently teaches English at the State University of New York at Binghamton. She publishes and travels extensively and is an international voice in the fields of women's studies and modern literature.

Among the other poems that display the performing self, "Daddy" and "Lady Lazarus" are two of the most often quoted, but most frequently misunderstood, poems in the Plath canon. The speaker in "Daddy" performs a mock poetic exorcism of an event that has already happened—the death of her father who she feels withdrew his love from her by dying prematurely: "Daddy, I have had to kill you. / You died before I had time —."

The speaker attempts to exorcise not just the memory of her father but her own *Mein Kampf* model of him as well as her inherited behavioral traits that lead her graveward under the Freudian banner of death instinct or Thanatos's libido. But her ritual reenactment simply does not take. The event comically backfires as pure self-parody: the metaphorical murder of the father dwindles into Hollywood spectacle, while the poet is lost in the clutter of the collective unconscious.

Early in the poem, the ritual gets off on the wrong foot both literally and figuratively. A sudden rhythmic break midway through the first stanza interrupts the insistent and mesmeric chant of the poet's own freedom:

> You do not do, you do not do
> Any more, black shoe
> In which I have lived like a foot
> For thirty years, poor and white,
> Barely daring to breathe or Achoo.

The break suggests, on the one hand, that the nursery-rhyme world of contained terror is here abandoned; on the other, that the poet-exorcist's mesmeric control is superficial, founded in a shaky faith and an unsure heart — the worst possible state for the strong, disciplined exorcist.

At first, she kills her father succinctly with her own words, demythologizing him to a ludicrous piece of statuary that is hardly a Poseidon or the Colossus of Rhodes:

> Marble-heavy, a bag full of God,
> Ghastly statue with one grey toe
> Big as a Frisco seal
>
> And a head in the freakish Atlantic
> Where it pours bean green over blue
> In the waters off beautiful Nauset.
> I used to pray to recover you.
> Ach, du.

Then as she tries to patch together the narrative of him, his tribal myth (the "common" town, the "German tongue," the war-scraped culture), she begins to lose her own powers of description to a senseless Germanic prattle ("The tongue stuck in my jaw. / It stuck in a barb wire snare. / Ich, ich, ich, ich"). The individual man is absorbed by his inhuman archetype, the "panzer-man," "an engine / Chuffing me off like a Jew." Losing the exorcist's power that binds the spirit and then casts out the demon, she is the classic helpless victim of the swastika man. As she culls up her own picture of him as a devil, he refuses to adopt this stereotype. Instead he jumbles his trademark:

> A cleft in your chin instead of your foot
> But no less a devil for that, no not
> Any less the black man who
>
> Bit my pretty red heart in two.

The overt Nazi-Jew allegory throughout the poem suggests that, by a simple inversion of power, father and daughter grow more alike. But when she tries to imitate his action of dying, making all the appropriate grand gestures, she once again fails: "But they pulled me out of the sack, / And they stuck me together with glue." She retreats to a safe world of icons and replicas, but even the doll image she constructs turns out to be "the vampire who said he was you." At last, she abandons her father to the collective unconscious where it is *he* who is finally recognized ("They always *knew* it was you"). *She* is lost, impersonally absorbed by his irate persecutors, bereft of both her power and her conjurer's discipline, and possessed by the incensed villagers. The exorcist's ritual, one of purifying, cleansing, commanding silence, and then ordering the evil spirit's departure, has dwindled to a comic picture from the heart of darkness. Mad villagers stamp on the devil-vampire creation.

In the course of performing the imaginative "killing," the speaker moves through a variety of emotions, from viciousness ("a stake in your fat black heart"), to vengefulness ("you bastard, I'm through"), finally to silence ("The black telephone's off at the root"). It would seem that the real victim is the poet-performer who, despite her straining toward identification with the public events of holocaust and destruction of World War II, becomes more murderously persecuting than the "panzer-man" who smothered her, and who abandoned her with a paradoxical love, guilt, and fear. Unlike him, she kills three times: the original subject, the model to whom she said "I do, I do," and herself, the imitating victim. But each of these killings is comically inverted. Each backfires. Instead of successfully binding the spirits, commanding them to remain silent and cease doing harm, and then ordering them to an appointed place, the speaker herself is stricken dumb.

The failure of the exorcism and the emotional ambivalence are echoed in the curious rhythm. The incantatory safety of the nursery-rhyme thump (seemingly one of controlled, familiar terrors) also suggests some sinister brooding by its repetition. The poem opens with a suspiciously emphatic protest, a kind of psychological whistling-in-the-dark. As it proceeds, "Daddy"'s continuous life-rhythms — the assonance, consonance, and especially the sustained *oo* sounds — triumph over either the personal or the cultural-historical imagery. The sheer sense of organic life in the interwoven sounds carries the verse forward in boisterous spirit and communicates an underlying feeling of comedy that is also echoed in the repeated failure of the speaker to perform her exorcism.

Ultimately, "Daddy" is like an emotional, psychological, and historical autopsy, a final report. There is no real progress. The poet is in the same place in the beginning as in the end. She begins the poem as a hesitant but familiar fairy-tale daughter who parodies her attempt to reconstruct the myth of her father. Suffocating in her shoe house, she is unable to do much with that "bag full of God." She ends as a murderous member of a mythical community enacting the ritual or vampire killing, but only for a surrogate vampire, not the real thing ("The vampire who said he was you"). Although it seems that the speaker has moved from identification with the persecuted to identify as persecutor, Jew to vampire-killer, powerless to powerful, she has simply enacted a performance that allows her to live with what is unchangeable. She has used her art to stave off suffocation and performs her self-contempt with a degree of bravado.   [1980]

LYNDA K. BUNDTZEN
From *Plath's Incarnations*

Educated at the University of Minnesota, where she earned a B.A. in 1968, and the University of Chicago, where she earned a Ph.D. in 1972, Lynda Bundtzen (b. 1947) teaches at Williams College. A Renaissance scholar with a strong interest in women's issues, she teaches and writes on subjects that range from Shakespeare to Thelma and Louise. Plath's Incarnations was published in 1983.

In "Daddy," Plath is conscious of her complicity in creating and worshiping a father-colossus.

> You stand at the blackboard, daddy,
> In the picture I have of you,
> A cleft in your chin instead of your foot
> But no less a devil for that, no not
> Any less the black man who
>
> Bit my pretty red heart in two.
> I was ten when they buried you.
> At twenty I tried to die
> And get back, back, back to you.
> I thought even the bones would do.

The photograph is of an ordinary man, a teacher, with a cleft chin. She imaginatively transforms him into a devil who broke her heart, and she tells her audience precisely what she is doing. As Plath describes "Daddy," it is "spoken by a girl with an Electra complex. Her father died while she thought he was God. Her case is complicated by the fact that her father was also a Nazi and her mother very possibly part Jewish. In the daughter the two strains marry and paralyze each other—she has to act out the awful little allegory once over before she is free of it." The poem is a figurative drama about mourning—about the human impulse to keep a dead loved one alive emotionally. And it is about mourning gone haywire—a morbid inability to let go of the dead. The child was unready for her father's death, which is why, she says, she must kill him a second time. She resurrected Daddy and sustained his unnatural existence in her psyche as a vampire, sacrificing her own life's blood, her vitality, to a dead man. The worship of this father-god, she now realizes, is self-destructive.

There is nothing unconscious about the poem; instead it seems to force into consciousness the child's dread and love for the father, so that these feelings may be resolved. Plath skillfully evokes the child's world with her own versions of Mother Goose rhymes. Like the "old woman who lived in a shoe and had so many children she didn't know what to do," she has tried to live in the confines of the black shoe that is Daddy. Like Chicken Little, waiting for the sky to fall in, she lives under an omnipresent swastika "So black no sky could squeak through." And Daddy is a fallen giant toppled over and smothering, it seems, the entire United States. He has one grey toe (recalling Otto Plath's gangrened appendage) dangling like a Frisco seal in the Pacific and his head lies in the Atlantic.

The Mother Goose rhythms gradually build to a goose step march as the mourning process turns inward. She feels more than sorrow, now guilt, for Daddy's death and this guilt leads to feelings of inadequacy, acts of self-abasement, and finally self-murder. Nothing she can do will appease the guilt: she tries to learn his language; she tries to kill herself; she marries a man in his image. It will not do.

The self-hatred must be turned outward again into "*You* do not do" by a very self-conscious transformation of a mild-mannered professor into an active oppressor. Her emotional paralysis is acted out as a struggle between Nazi man and Jewess, and, I would argue, the Jewess wins. The poem builds toward the imaginary stake driving, the dancing and stamping and "Daddy, daddy, you bastard, I'm through." Not necessarily through with life, as many critics have read this line, but through with the paralysis, powerlessness, guilt. At last Daddy—the Nazi Daddy she frightened herself with, and not the real one, the professor—is at rest.

Plath's control over ambivalent feelings toward her father is probably the   5
result of their availability for conscious artistic manipulation. She had already written several poems about her dead father when she composed "Daddy," and we also know from a conversation recorded by Steiner that she had "worked through" her emotions in therapy. "She talked freely about her father's death when she was nine and her reactions to it. 'He was an autocrat,' she recalled. 'I adored and despised him, and I probably wished many times that he were dead. When he obliged me and died, I imagined that I had killed him.' " The result in "Daddy" is a powerful and remarkably accessible allegory about her adoration and dread, which ends in emotional catharsis.   [1983]

STEVEN GOULD AXELROD
From *Sylvia Plath: The Wound and the Cure of Words*

An expert in nineteenth- and twentieth-century American poetry, Steven Gould Axelrod (b. 1944) was educated at the University of California at Los Angeles and currently serves as chair of the English Department at the University of California at Riverside, where he received a Distinguished Teaching Award in 1989. His publications include book-length works on modern and contemporary poets. Sylvia Plath: The Wound and the Cure of Words was published in 1990.

The covert protest of "The Colossus" eventually transformed itself into the overt rebellion of "Daddy." Although this poem too has traditionally been read as "personal" or "confessional," Margaret Homans has more recently suggested that it concerns a woman's dislocated relations to speech. Plath herself introduced it on the BBC as the opposite of confession, as a constructed fiction: "Here is a poem spoken by a girl with an Electra complex. Her father died while she thought he was God. Her case is complicated by the fact that her father was also a Nazi and her mother very possibly part Jewish. In the daughter the two strains marry and paralyze each other—she has to act out the awful little allegory once over before she is free of it." We might interpret this preface as an accurate retelling of the poem; or we might regard it as a case of an author's estrangement from her text, on the order of Coleridge's preface to "Kubla Khan" in which he claims to be unable to finish the poem, having forgotten what it was about. However we interpret Plath's preface, we must agree that "Daddy" is dramatic and allegorical, since its details depart freely from the facts of her biography. In this poem she again figures her unresolved conflicts with paternal authority as a textual issue. Significantly, her father was a published writer, and his successor, her husband, was also a writer. Her preface asserts that the poem concerns a young woman's paralyzing self-division, which she can defeat only through allegorical representation. Recalling that paralysis was one of Plath's main tropes for literary incapacity, we begin to see that the poem evokes the female poet's anxiety of authorship and specifically Plath's strategy of delivering herself from that anxiety by making it the topic of her discourse. Viewed from this perspective, "Daddy" enacts the woman poet's struggle with "daddy-poetry." It represents her effort to eject the "buried male muse" from her invention process and the "jealous gods" from her audience.

Plath wrote "Daddy" several months after Hughes left her, on the day she learned that he had agreed to a divorce. George Brown and Tirril Harris have shown that early loss makes one especially vulnerable to subsequent loss, and Plath seems to have defended against depression by almost literally throwing herself into her poetry. She followed "Daddy" with a host of poems that she considered her greatest achievement to date: "Medusa," "The Jailer," "Lady Lazarus," "Ariel," the bee sequence, and others. The letters she wrote to her mother and brother on the day of "Daddy," and then again four days later, brim with a sense of artistic self-discovery: "Writing like mad. . . . Terrific stuff, as if domesticity had choked me." Composing at the "still blue, almost eternal hour before the baby's cry, before the glassy music of the milkman, settling his bottles," she experienced an "enormous surge in creative energy. Yet she also expressed feelings of misery: "The half year ahead seems like a lifetime, and the half behind an endless hell." She was again contemplating things German: a trip to the Austrian Alps, a renewed effort to learn the language. If "German" was Randall Jarrell's "favorite country," it was not hers, yet it returned to her discourse like clockwork at times of psychic distress. Clearly Plath was attempting to find and to evoke in her art what she could not find or communicate in her life. She wished to compensate for her fragmenting social existence by investing herself in her texts: "Hope, when free, to write myself out of this hole." Desperately eager to sacrifice her "flesh," which was "wasted," to her "mind and spirit," which were "fine," she wrote "Daddy" to demonstrate the existence of her voice, which had been silent or subservient for so long. She wrote it to prove her "genius."

Plath projected her struggle for textual identity onto the figure of a partly Jewish young woman who learns to express her anger at the patriarch and at his language of male mastery, which is as foreign to her as German, as "obscene" as murder, and as meaningless as "gobbledygoo." The patriarch's death "off beautiful Nauset" recalls Plath's journal entry in which she associated the "green sea-weeded water" at "Nauset Light" with "the deadness of a being . . . who no longer creates." Daddy's deadness—suggesting Plath's unwillingness to let her father, her education, her library, or her husband inhibit her any longer—inspires the poem's speaker to her moment of illumination. At a basic level, "Daddy" concerns its own violent, transgressive birth as a text, its origin in a culture that regards it as illegitimate—a judgment the speaker hurls back on the patriarch himself when she labels *him* a bastard. Plath's unaccommodating worldview, which was validated by much in her childhood and adult experience, led her to understand literary tradition not as an expanding universe of beneficial influence . . . but as a closed universe in which every addition required a corresponding subtraction—a Spencerian agon in which only the fittest survived. If Plath's speaker was to be born as a poet, a patriarch must die.

As in "The Colossus," the father here appears as a force or an object rather than as a person. Initially he takes the form of an immense "black shoe," capable of stamping on his victim. Immediately thereafter he becomes a marble "statue," cousin to the monolith of the earlier poem. He then transforms into Nazi Germany, the archetypal totalitarian state. When the protagonist mentions Daddy's "boot in the face," she may be alluding to Orwell's comment in 1984, "If you want a picture of the future, imagine a boot stomping on a human face—forever." Eventually the father declines in stature from God to a devil to a dying vampire. Perhaps he shrinks under the force of his victim's denunciation, which de-creates him as a power as it creates him as figure. But whatever his size, he never assumes human dimensions, aspirations, and relations—except when posing as a teacher in a photograph. Like the colossus, he remains figurative and symbolic, not individual.

Nevertheless, the male figure of "Daddy" does differ significantly from that of "The Colossus." In the earlier poem, which emphasizes his lips, mouth, throat, tongue, and voice, the colossus allegorically represents the power of speech, however fragmented and resistant to the protagonist's ministrations. In the later poem Daddy remains silent, apart from the gobbledygoo attributed to him once. He uses his mouth primarily for biting and for drinking blood. The poem emphasizes his feet and, implicitly, his phallus. He is a "black shoe," a statue with "one gray toe," a "boot." The speaker, estranged from him by fear, could never tell where he put his "foot," his "root." Furthermore, she is herself silenced by his shoe: "I never could talk to you." Daddy is no "male muse," not even one in ruins, but frankly a male censor. His boot in the face of "every woman" is presumably lodged in her mouth. He stands for all the elements in the literary situation and in the female ephebe's internalization of it, that prevent her from producing any words at all, even copied or subservient ones. Appropriately, Daddy can be killed only by being stamped on: he lives and dies by force, not language. If "The Colossus" tells a tale of the patriarch's speech, his grunts and brays, "Daddy" tells a tale of the daughter's effort to speak.

Thus we are led to another important difference between the two poems. The "I" of "The Colossus" acquires her identity only through serving her "father," whereas the "I" of "Daddy" actuates her gift only through opposition to him. The latter poem precisely inscribes the plot of Plath's dream novel of 1958: "a girl's search for her dead father—for an outside authority which must be developed,

5

instead, from the inside." As the child of a Nazi, the girl could "hardly speak," but as a Jew she begins "to talk" and to acquire an identity. In Plath's allegory, the outsider Jew corresponds to "the rebel, the artist, the odd," and particularly to the woman artist. Otto Rank's *Beyond Psychology*, which had a lasting influence on her, explicitly compares women to Jews, since "woman . . . has suffered from the very beginning a fate similar to that of the Jew, namely, suppression, slavery, confinement, and subsequent persecution." Rank, whose discourse I would consider tainted by anti-Semitism, argues that Jews speak a language of pessimistic "self-hatred" that differs essentially from the language of the majority cultures in which they find themselves. He analogously, though more sympathetically, argues that woman speaks in a language different from man's, and that as a result of man's denial of woman's world, "woman's 'native tongue' has hitherto been unknown or at least unheard." Although Rank's essentializing of woman's "nature" lapses into the sexist clichés of his time ("intuitive," "irrational"), his idea of linguistic difference based on gender and his analogy between Jewish and female speech seem to have embedded themselves in the substructure of "Daddy" (and in many of Plath's other texts as well). For Plath, as later for Adrienne Rich, the Holocaust and the patriarchy's silencing of women were linked outcomes of the masculinist interpretation of the world. Political insurrection and female self-assertion also interlaced symbolically. In "Daddy," Plath's speaker finds her voice and motive by identifying herself as antithetical to her Fascist father. Rather than getting the colossus "glued" and properly jointed, she wishes to stick herself "together with glue," an act that seems to require her father's dismemberment. Previously devoted to the patriarch — both in "The Colossus" and in memories evoked in "Daddy" of trying to "get back" to him — she now seeks only to escape from him and to see him destroyed.

Plath has unleashed the anger, normal in mourning as well as in revolt, that she suppressed in the earlier poem. But she has done so at a cost. Let us consider her childlike speaking voice. The language of "Daddy," beginning with its title, is often regressive. The "I" articulates herself by moving backward in time, using the language of nursery rhymes and fairy tales (the little old woman who lived in a shoe, the black man of the forest). Such language accords with a child's conception of the world, not an adult's. Plath's assault on the language of "daddy-poetry" has turned inward, on the language of her own poem, which teeters precariously on the edge of a preverbal abyss — represented by the eerie, keening "oo" sound with which a majority of the verses end. And then let us consider the play on "through" at the poem's conclusion. Although that last line allows for multiple readings, one interpretation is that the "I" has unconsciously carried out her father's wish: her discourse, by transforming itself into cathartic oversimplifications, has undone itself.

Yet the poem does contain its verbal violence by means more productive than silence. In a letter to her brother, Plath referred to "Daddy" as "gruesome," while on almost the same day she described it to A. Alvarez as a piece of "light verse." She later read it on the BBC in a highly ironic tone of voice. The poem's unique spell derives from its rhetorical complexity: its variegated and perhaps bizarre fusion of the horrendous and the comic. . . . [I]t both shares and remains detached from the fixation of its protagonist. The protagonist herself seems detached from her own fixation. She is "split in the most complex fashion," as Plath wrote of Ivan Karamazov in her Smith College honors thesis. Plath's speaker uses potentially self-mocking melodramatic terms to describe both her opponent ("so black no sky could squeak through") and herself ("poor and white"). While this aboriginal speaker quite literally expresses black-and-white thinking, her civilized double possesses a sensibility sophisticated enough to subject such thinking to irony. Thus the poem expresses feelings that it simultaneously parodies—it may be parodying the very idea of feeling. The tension between erudition and simplicity in the speaker's voice appears in her pairings that juxtapose adult with childlike diction: "breathe or Achoo," "your Luftwaffe, your gobbledygoo." She can expound such adult topics as Taroc packs, Viennese beer, and Tyrolean snowfall; can specify death camps by name; and can employ an adult vocabulary of "recover," "ancestress," "Aryan," "*Meinkampf*," "obscene," and "bastard." Yet she also has recourse to a more primitive lexicon that includes "chuffing," "your fat black heart," and "my pretty red heart." She proves herself capable of careful intellectual discriminations ("so I never could tell"), conventionalized description ("beautiful Nauset"), and moral analogy ("if I've killed one man, I've killed two"), while also exhibiting regressive fantasies (vampires), repetitions ("wars, wars, wars"), and inarticulateness ("panzer-man, panzer-man, O You—"). She oscillates between calm reflection ("You stand at the blackboard, daddy, / In the picture I have of you") and mad incoherence ("Ich, ich, ich, ich"). Her sophisticated language puts her wild language in an ironic perspective, removing the discourse from the control of the archaic self who understands experience only in extreme terms.

The ironies in "Daddy" proliferate in unexpected ways, however. When the speaker proclaims categorically that "every woman adores a Fascist," she is subjecting her victimization to irony by suggesting that sufferers choose, or at least accommodate themselves to, their suffering. But she is also subjecting her authority to irony, since her claim about "every woman" is transparently false. It simply parodies patriarchal commonplaces, such as those advanced . . . concerning "feminine masochism." The adult, sophisticated self seems to be speaking here: Who else would have the confidence to make a sociological generalization? Yet the content of the assertion, if taken straightforwardly, returns us to the regressive self who is dominated by extravagant emotions she cannot begin to understand. Plath's mother wished that Plath would write about "decent, courageous people," and she herself heard an inner voice demanding that she be a perfect "paragon" in her language and feeling. But in the speaker of "Daddy," she inscribed the opposite of such a paragon: a divided self whose veneer of civilization is breached and infected by unhealthy instincts.

Plath's irony cuts both ways. At the same time that the speaker's sophisticated voice undercuts her childish voice, reducing its melodrama to comedy, the childish or maddened voice undercuts the pretensions of the sophisticated voice, revealing the extremity of suffering masked by its ironies. While demonstrating the inadequacy of thinking and feeling in opposites, the poem implies that such a mode can locate truths denied more complex cognitive and affective systems.

10

The very moderation of the normal adult intelligence, its tolerance of ambiguity, its defenses against the primal energies of the id, results in falsification. Reflecting Schiller's idea that the creative artist experiences a "momentary and passing madness" (quoted by Freud in a passage of *The Interpretation of Dreams* that Plath underscored), "Daddy" gives voice to that madness. Yet the poem's sophisticated awareness, its comic vision, probably wins out in the end, since the poem concludes by curtailing the power of its extreme discourse. . . . Furthermore, Plath distanced herself from the poem's aboriginal voice by introducing her text as "a poem spoken by a girl with an Electra complex" — that is, as a study of the *girl's* pathology rather than her father's — and as an allegory that will "free" her from that pathology. She also distanced herself by reading the poem in a tone that emphasized its irony. And finally, she distanced herself by laying the poem's wild voice permanently to rest after October. The aboriginal vision was indeed purged. "Daddy" represents not Dickinson's madness that is divinest sense, but rather an entry into a style of discourse and a mastery of it. The poem realizes the trope of suffering by means of an inherent irony that both questions and validates the trope in the same gestures, and that finally allows the speaker to conclude the discourse and to remove herself from the trope with a sense of completion rather than wrenching, since the irony was present from the very beginning.

Plath's poetic revolt in "Daddy" liberated her pent-up creativity, but the momentary success sustained her little more than self-sacrifice had done. "Daddy" became another stage in her development, an unrepeatable experiment, a vocal opening that closed itself at once. The poem is not only an elegy for the power of "daddy-poetry" but for the powers of speech Plath discovered in composing it.

When we consider "Daddy" generically, a further range of implications presents itself. Although we could profitably consider the poem as the dramatic monologue Plath called it in her BBC broadcast, let us regard it instead as the kind of poem most readers have taken it to be: a domestic poem. I have chosen this term, rather than M. L. Rosenthal's better-known "confessional poem" or the more neutral "autobiographical poem," because "confessional poem" implies a confession rather than a making (though Steven Hoffman and Lawrence Kramer have recently indicated the mode's conventions) and because "autobiographical poem" is too general for our purpose. I shall define the domestic poem as one that represents and comments on a protagonist's relationship to one or more family members, usually a parent, child, or spouse. To focus our discussion even further, I shall emphasize poetry that specifically concerns a father.   [1990]

TIM KENDALL

From *Sylvia Plath: A Critical Study*

Tim Kendall edits Thumbscrew *and is author of* Paul Muldoon. *He received an Eric Gregory Award for his poetry in 1997 and appears in the* Oxford Poets 2000 *anthology. He teaches at the University of Bristol and is the Thomas Chatterton British Academy Lecturer for 2001. This selection is from a book he published in 2001.*

Plath's journals . . . indicate that as late as December 1958, the poet was seriously considering a Ph.D. in psychology: "Awesome to confront a program of study which is so monumental: all human experience."[1] The previous day Plath had discovered in Freud's *Mourning and Melancholia* "an almost exact description of my feelings and reasons for suicide."[2] She felt creatively vindicated when she found parallels between her own life and writings and those of Freud and Jung: "All this relates in a most meaningful way my instinctive images with perfectly valid psychological analysis. However, I am the victim, rather than the analyst."[3] In these examples, experience precedes the psychoanalytical explanation; Freud and Jung confirm what Plath already knows. Despite her emphasis on victimhood, such passages show how she transforms herself into her own case history, becoming simultaneously victim and analyst. The same dual role is apparent in "Daddy," which Plath introduces for BBC radio in terms of Freudian allegory:

> Here is a poem spoken by a girl with an Electra complex. Her father died while she thought he was God. Her case is complicated by the fact that her father was also a Nazi and her mother very possibly part Jewish. In the daughter the two strains marry and paralyse each other—she has to act out the awful little allegory once over before she is free of it.

"Daddy," built on poetic repetition, is therefore a poem about a compulsion to repeat, and its psychology is characterised according to Freudian principles. Repetition necessitates performance—the speaker must "*act out* the awful little allegory once over" in order to escape it. Whether she does succeed in escaping depends on the poem's ambivalent last line: "Daddy, daddy, you bastard, I'm through." "I'm through" can mean (especially to an American ear) "I've had enough of you," but it also means "I've got away from you, I'm free of you," or "I'm done for, I'm beaten," or even "I've finished what I have to say." The speaker's ability to free herself from the urge to repeat remains in the balance.

These dilemmas and uncertainties can be traced back, as Plath suggests, to Freud's accounts of compulsive behaviour. "Daddy" adopts a Freudian understanding of infantile sexuality (the Electra complex), a Freudian belief in transference (the vampire-husband "said he was you," and the father also shifts identities), and a Freudian attitude towards repetitive behaviour. In a passage from *Beyond the Pleasure Principle* which might conveniently serve to diagnose the speaker of "Daddy," Freud argues that,

> The patient cannot remember the whole of what is repressed in him, and what he cannot remember may be precisely the essential part of it. Thus he acquires no sense of the conviction of the correctness of the construction that has been communicated to him. He is obliged to *repeat* the repressed material as a contemporary experience instead of, as the physician would prefer to see, *remembering* it as something belonging to the past. These reproductions, which emerge with such unwished-for exactitude, always have as their subject some portion of infantile sexual life—of the Oedipus complex, that is, and its derivatives; and they are invariably acted out in the sphere of the transference, of the patient's relation to the physician.[4]

This illuminates Plath's attempts to persuade the dead father to communicate. The refusal of the father-figure, in his various transferred roles of colossus, Nazi, teacher and vampire, to become "something belonging to the past" is evident in the speaker's need to kill him repeatedly. He must be imaginatively disinterred in order to be killed again, and even as one of the undead, he must be destroyed with a stake in his heart. This repetitive pattern of disappearance and return represents Plath's version of the *fort-da* game as famously described in *Beyond the Pleasure Principle*, where the child's repeated and "long-drawn-out 'o-o-o-o'" is only a slight vowel modulation away from the "oo" repetitions of "Daddy." The father-figure is a "contemporary experience," not a memory; and, as Freud explains, the reason for his continuing presence lies in the speaker's "infantile sexual life." The father's early death ensures that she cannot progress, and her sense of selfhood is stutteringly confined within a compulsion to repeat:

> I never could talk to you.
> The tongue stuck in my jaw.
>
> It stuck in a barb wire snare.
> Ich, ich, ich, ich,
> I could hardly speak.

Repetition occurs when Plath's speaker gets stuck in the barb wire snare of communication with her father. She is unable to move beyond the self. This proposes a more fundamental understanding of repetitive words and phrases than those suggested by Blessing or Shapiro. "Daddy" implies that each local repetition, whatever its microcosmic effects, symptomises a larger behavioural pattern of repetition compulsion. The poem's title, the "oo" rhymes, and the nursery-rhyme rhythms all reinforce this suggestion of a mind struggling to free itself from the need to repeat infantile trauma. Such infantilism, exhibited by an adult persona, contributes to the poem's transgressive humour: Plath read "Daddy" aloud to a friend, reports Anne Stevenson, "in a mocking, comical voice that made both women fall about with laughter."[5]

Psychoanalysing the speaker of "Daddy" in the Freudian terms proposed by Plath herself is a valuable exercise which carries important implications for *Ariel*'s use of repetition, but it still does not settle the nature of the poet's complex relationship to the "girl with an Electra complex." Plath's introduction for radio seems to reverse the pattern in her journals: now Freud becomes a source as much as an explanation. Her introduction also reverses the reader's experience of the poem. "Daddy" conveys a power and an intimacy which challenge any hygienic separation of poet and poetic voice. With such contradictory evidence, the gulf between poet and persona, cold-blooded technique and blood-hot emotion, analyst and victim, seems unbridgeable. If these divisions can be successfully reconciled, it is through Plath's emphasis on performance and repetition. Freud's account of repetition compulsion shares with Plath's description of "Daddy" a crucial verb: just as Plath's persona must "act out the awful little allegory," so Freud notes that the Oedipus complex and its derivatives are "invariably acted out in the sphere of the transference." Repetition guarantees performance, and performance requires an audience. Freud notes, as if glossing "Daddy," that "the artistic play and artistic imitation carried out by adults, which, unlike children's, are aimed at an audience, do not spare the spectators (for instance, in tragedy) the most painful experiences and can yet be felt by them as highly enjoyable." Plath categorised "Daddy" as "light verse,"[6] a genre which W. H. Auden considered to be "written for performance."[7] "Daddy" may be written for performance, but it pushes the "painful experiences" and the entertainment value to extremes which many readers find intolerable. Freud's Aristotelian concern — why is tragedy pleasurable? — also seems a valid question to ask of Plath's poem: "Daddy" derives its aesthetic pleasures from incest, patricide, suicide, and the Nazi extermination camps.

These taboo-breaking juxtapositions of personal and private realms help explain the poem's notoriety. However, controversy over "Daddy" always returns eventually to Plath's relationship with her persona. Seamus Heaney's principled objection, for example, discerns no difference at all:

> A poem like "Daddy," however brilliant a *tour de force* it can be acknowledged to be, and however its violence and vindictiveness can be understood or excused in light of the poet's parental and marital relations, remains, nevertheless, so entangled in biographical circumstances and rampages so permissively in the history of other people's sorrows that it simply withdraws its rights to our sympathy.[8]

Heaney's pointed phrase "rampages so permissively" might be disputed as an unfair rhetorical flourish, especially in the context of Plath's hard-earned Emersonian desire to assimilate and her wider theological explorations. But Heaney's most revealing word is his last: "sympathy." Heaney refers to one aspect of Aristotelian catharsis — pity for the suffering of others — which he claims that "Daddy" fails to earn. It is not surprising that his critical decorum should come into conflict with a poem which is so consciously and manifestly indecorous. Heaney reads "Daddy" purely as the protest of the poet-victim, who behaves vindictively because of her difficult parental and marital relations. This fails to credit Plath with the self-awareness to be acting deliberately — to be performing. In "Daddy" Plath seeks no one's "sympathy"; she has once more become victim and analyst, the girl with the Electra complex and the physician who diagnoses her condition. Plath wonders in her journal whether "our desire to investigate psychology [is] a desire to get Beuscher's [her psychiatrist's] power and handle it ourselves."[9] "Daddy," as her introduction makes clear, represents a poetic handling of that power. Freud states that the patient must acquire "some degree of aloofness."[10] "Daddy" is the work of a poet so aloof as to render allegorical, act out, and psychoanalyse, her own mental history. [2001]

Notes

1. Plath, Sylvia, *The Journals of Sylvia Plath, 1950–1962*, ed. Karen V. Kukil (London: Faber & Faber, 2000), p. 452.
2. Ibid., p. 447.
3. Ibid., p. 514.

4. Freud, S., *Beyond the Pleasure Principle*, tr. and ed. J. Strachey (Hogarth, 1961), p. 12.
5. Stevenson, A., *Bitter Fame: A Life of Sylvia Plath* (Viking, 1989), p. 277.
6. Alvarez, A., "Sylvia Plath," in C. Newman (ed.), *The Art of Sylvia Plath* (Indiana UP, 1970), p. 66.
7. Auden, W. H. (ed.), *The Oxford Book of Light Verse* (OUP, 1938), p. ix.
8. Heaney, S., "The Indefatigable Hoof-taps: Sylvia Plath," *The Government of the Tongue* (Faber, 1988), p. 165.
9. *Journals*, p. 449.
10. *Beyond the Pleasure Principle*, p. 13.

MAKING COMPARISONS

1. "Daddy" seems to be a protest, but some critics see it as more than that. Which of the four commentaries makes the best case that it is more than a revolt against the speaker's father?

2. Which critic seems to answer most of the perplexing questions of this poem—for example, the father as Nazi, the father as vampire, the childlike rhythms, the speaker's vengefulness, her viciousness?

3. Do these critics make any similar points? How might you describe them? What is their most striking difference?

WRITING ABOUT ISSUES

1. Argue that the textual evidence Axelrod provides for his assertions is, or is not, adequate.

2. Imagine you are Sylvia Plath. After reading these four essays, write a letter to a literary journal either attacking or praising these critics.

3. Write an essay arguing that your own reading of "Daddy" makes more sense than those of Broe, Bundtzen, Axelrod, and Kendall. Assume that the audience for the criticism is your class.

4. There are dozens of critical commentaries on Plath's "Daddy." Some were written soon after the poem's publication; others are quite recent. Locate an early piece of criticism, and compare it to one published in the past two years. Do these critics make similar or different points? Is one more concerned with the text, with gender issues, with cultural concerns, or with what other critics say? Write a brief comparison of the two, explaining your evidence.

A WEB ASSIGNMENT

Sylvia Plath is the focus of several Web sites. Visit the Web Assignments section of the *Making Literature Matter* Web site to find the link to one of these sites. Find the essay on "Daddy" and vampires. Write a brief assessment of how this essay alters your opinion about the four pieces of criticism given here.

Visit www.bedfordstmartins.com/makinglitmatter

MOTHERS AND DAUGHTERS

TILLIE OLSEN, "I Stand Here Ironing"
AMY TAN, "Two Kinds"
ALICE WALKER, "Everyday Use"

We all know stories of parents who want to mold their children, mothers and fathers who push their reluctant children to be fashion models or beauty queens or little league stars. Some studies of adults playing musical instruments in orchestras say the biggest factor in their success was the commitment of their parents. But we also hear about tennis prodigies who burn out at sixteen because of parental pressure. Mothers and daughters have always struggled with each other over life goals and identity. How much guidance is enough? How much is too much? What is a reasonable balance between preparing a child for life's challenges and shaping a child to act out the mother's fantasy or her internal vision of what the good life is? And no matter where parents fall on this continuum, are there childhood events so powerful that we cannot get beyond them? The following three stories chart the difficulties mothers and daughters have with each other and with the social and cultural forces that influence our destiny.

BEFORE YOU READ

Are your parents responsible for your successes? Your failures? Do you wish that your parents had pushed you to succeed more insistently? Are you annoyed that your parents set unreasonable standards for you?

TILLIE OLSEN

I Stand Here Ironing

Born in Omaha, Nebraska, to Russian immigrants of Jewish descent and socialist views, Tillie Olsen (b. 1913) has been an activist in social and political causes all of her life, often choosing family, work, union, feminist, or other political causes over writing. Although her publishing record is short, its quality is greatly admired. In addition to critically respected short stories, Olsen has written a novel, Yonnondio *(1974), which paints a vivid picture of a coal-mining family during the Depression. Her essay collection,* Silences *(1978), stimulated debate about class and gender as factors in the creation of literature and led both directly and indirectly to the revived interest in works by women writers. The mother of four daughters, Olsen often writes about generational relationships within families. "I Stand Here Ironing" is from her 1961 collection of stories,* Tell Me a Riddle.

I stand here ironing, and what you asked me moves tormented back and forth with the iron.

"I wish you would manage the time to come in and talk with me about your daughter. I'm sure you can help me understand her. She's a youngster who needs help and whom I'm deeply interested in helping."

"Who needs help." . . . Even if I came, what good would it do? You think because I am her mother I have a key, or that in some way you could use me as a key? She has lived for nineteen years. There is all that life that has happened outside of me, beyond me.

And when is there time to remember, to sift, to weigh, to estimate, to total? I will start and there will be an interruption and I will have to gather it all together again. Or I will become engulfed with all I did or did not do, with what should have been and what cannot be helped.

She was a beautiful baby. The first and only one of our five that was beautiful   5
at birth. You do not guess how new and uneasy her tenancy in her now-loveliness. You did not know her all those years she was thought homely, or see her poring over her baby pictures, making me tell her over and over how beautiful she had been—and would be, I would tell her—and was now, to the seeing eye. But the seeing eyes were few or nonexistent. Including mine.

I nursed her. They feel that's important nowadays, I nursed all the children, but with her, with all the fierce rigidity of first motherhood, I did like the books then said. Though her cries battered me to trembling and my breasts ached with swollenness, I waited till the clock decreed.

Why do I put that first? I do not even know if it matters, or if it explains anything.

She was a beautiful baby. She blew shining bubbles of sound. She loved motion, loved light, loved color and music and textures. She would lie on the floor in her blue overalls patting the surface so hard in ecstasy her hands and feet would blur. She was a miracle to me, but when she was eight months old I had to leave her daytimes with the woman downstairs to whom she was no miracle at all, for I worked or looked for work and for Emily's father, who "could no longer endure" (he wrote in his good-bye note) "sharing want with us."

I was nineteen. It was the pre-relief, pre-WPA world of the depression. I would start running as soon as I got off the streetcar, running up the stairs, the place smelling sour, and awake or asleep to startle awake, when she saw me she would break into a clogged weeping that could not be comforted, a weeping I can hear yet.

After a while I found a job hashing at night so I could be with her days, and it   10
was better. But it came to where I had to bring her to his family and leave her.

It took a long time to raise the money for her fare back. Then she got chicken pox and I had to wait longer. When she finally came, I hardly knew her, walking quick and nervous like her father, looking like her father, thin, and dressed in a shoddy red that yellowed her skin and glared at the pockmarks. All the baby loveliness gone.

She was two. Old enough for nursery school they said, and I did not know then what I know now—the fatigue of the long day, and the lacerations of group life in the kinds of nurseries that are only parking places for children.

Except that it would have made no difference if I had known. It was the only place there was. It was the only way we could be together, the only way I could hold a job.

And even without knowing, I knew. I knew the teacher that was evil because all these years it has curdled into my memory, the little boy hunched in the corner, her rasp, "why aren't you outside, because Alvin hits you? that's no reason, go out, scaredy." I knew Emily hated it even if she did not clutch and implore "don't go Mommy" like the other children, mornings.

She always had a reason why we should stay home. Momma, you look sick. 15 Momma, I feel sick. Momma, the teachers aren't there today, they're sick. Momma, we can't go, there was a fire there last night. Momma, it's a holiday today, no school, they told me.

But never a direct protest, never rebellion. I think of our others in their three-, four-year-oldness — the explosions, the tempers, the denunciations, the demands — and I feel suddenly ill. I put the iron down. What in me demanded that goodness in her? And what was the cost, the cost to her of such goodness?

The old man living in the back once said in his gentle way: "You should smile at Emily more when you look at her." What *was* in my face when I looked at her? I loved her. There were all the acts of love.

It was only with the others I remembered what he said, and it was the face of joy, and not of care or tightness or worry I turned to them — too late for Emily. She does not smile easily, let alone almost always as her brothers and sisters do. Her face is closed and sombre, but when she wants, how fluid. You must have seen it in her pantomimes, you spoke of her rare gift for comedy on the stage that rouses laughter out of the audience so dear they applaud and applaud and do not want to let her go.

Where does it come from, that comedy? There was none of it in her when she came back to me that second time, after I had to send her away again. She had a new daddy now to learn to love, and I think perhaps it was a better time.

Except when we left her alone nights, telling ourselves she was old enough. 20

"Can't you go some other time, Mommy, like tomorrow?" she would ask. "Will it be just a little while you'll be gone? Do you promise?"

The time we came back, the front door open, the clock on the floor in the hall. She rigid awake. "It wasn't just a little while. I didn't cry. Three times I called you, just three times, and then I ran downstairs to open the door so you could come faster. The clock talked loud. I threw it away, it scared me what it talked."

She said the clock talked loud again that night I went to the hospital to have Susan. She was delirious with the fever that comes before red measles, but she was fully conscious all the week I was gone and the week after we were home when she could not come near the new baby or me.

She did not get well. She stayed skeleton thin, not wanting to eat, and night after night she had nightmares. She would call for me, and I would rouse from exhaustion to sleepily call back: "You're all right, darling, go to sleep, it's just a dream," and if she still called, in a sterner voice, "now go to sleep, Emily, there's nothing to hurt you." Twice, only twice, when I had to get up for Susan anyhow, I went in to sit with her.

Now when it is too late (as if she would let me hold her and comfort her like 25 I do the others) I get up and go to her at once at her moan or restless stirring. "Are you awake, Emily? Can I get you something?" And the answer is always the same: "No, I'm all right, go back to sleep, Mother."

They persuaded me at the clinic to send her away to a convalescent home in the country where "she can have the kind of food and care you can't manage for her, and you'll be free to concentrate on the new baby." They still send children to that place. I see pictures on the society page of sleek young women planning affairs to raise money for it, or dancing at the affairs, or decorating Easter eggs or filling Christmas stockings for the children.

They never have a picture of the children so I do not know if the girls still wear those gigantic red bows and the ravaged looks on the every other Sunday when parents can come to visit "unless otherwise notified" — as we were notified the first six weeks.

Oh it is a handsome place, green lawns and tall trees and fluted flower beds. High up on the balconies of each cottage the children stand, the girls in their red bows and white dresses, the boys in white suits and giant red ties. The parents stand below shrieking up to be heard and the children shriek down to be heard, and between them the invisible wall "Not To Be Contaminated by Parental Germs or Physical Affection."

There was a tiny girl who always stood hand in hand with Emily. Her parents never came. One visit she was gone. "They moved her to Rose Cottage," Emily shouted in explanation. "They don't like you to love anybody here."

She wrote once a week, the labored writing of a seven-year-old. "I am fine.   30
How is the baby. If I write my leter nicly I will have a star. Love." There never was a star. We wrote every other day, letters she could never hold or keep but only hear read — once. "We simply do not have room for children to keep any personal possessions," they patiently explained when we pieced one Sunday's shrieking together to plead how much it would mean to Emily, who loved so to keep things, to be allowed to keep her letters and cards.

Each visit she looked frailer. "She isn't eating," they told us.

(They had runny eggs for breakfast or mush with lumps, Emily said later, I'd hold it in my mouth and not swallow. Nothing ever tasted good, just when they had chicken.)

It took us eight months to get her released home, and only the fact that she gained back so little of her seven lost pounds convinced the social worker.

I used to try to hold and love her after she came back, but her body would stay stiff, and after a while she'd push away. She ate little. Food sickened her, and I think much of life too. Oh she had physical lightness and brightness, twinkling by on skates, bouncing like a ball up and down up and down over the jump rope, skimming over the hill; but these were momentary.

She fretted about her appearance, thin and dark and foreign-looking at a   35
time when every little girl was supposed to look or thought she should look a chubby blonde replica of Shirley Temple. The doorbell sometimes rang for her, but no one seemed to come and play in the house or to be a best friend. Maybe because we moved so much.

There was a boy she loved painfully through two school semesters. Months later she told me how she had taken pennies from my purse to buy him candy. "Licorice was his favorite and I brought him some every day, but he still liked Jennifer better'n me. Why, Mommy?" The kind of question for which there is no answer.

School was a worry for her. She was not glib or quick in a world where glibness and quickness were easily confused with ability to learn. To her overworked and exasperated teachers she was an overconscientious "slow learner" who kept trying to catch up and was absent entirely too often.

I let her be absent, though sometimes the illness was imaginary. How different from my now-strictness about attendance with the others. I wasn't working. We had a new baby. I was home anyhow. Sometimes, after Susan grew old enough, I would keep her home from school, too, to have them all together.

Mostly Emily had asthma, and her breathing, harsh and labored, would fill the house with a curiously tranquil sound. I would bring the two old dresser mirrors and her boxes of collections to her bed. She would select beads and single earrings, bottle tops and shells, dried flowers and pebbles, old postcards and scraps, all sorts of oddments; then she and Susan would play Kingdom, setting up landscapes and furniture, peopling them with action.

Those were the only times of peaceful companionship between her and Susan. I have edged away from it, that poisonous feeling between them, that terrible balancing of hurts and needs I had to do between the two, and did so badly, those earlier years.

Oh there were conflicts between the others too, each one human, needing, demanding, hurting, taking—but only between Emily and Susan, no, Emily toward Susan that corroding resentment. It seems so obvious on the surface, yet it is not obvious; Susan, the second child, Susan, golden- and curly-haired and chubby, quick and articulate and assured, everything in appearance and manner Emily was not; Susan, not able to resist Emily's precious things, losing or sometimes clumsily breaking them; Susan telling jokes and riddles to company for applause while Emily sat silent (to say to me later: that was *my* riddle, Mother, I told it to Susan); Susan, who for all the five years' difference in age was just a year behind Emily in developing physically.

I am glad for that slow physical development that widened the difference between her and her contemporaries, though she suffered over it. She was too vulnerable for that terrible world of youthful competition, of preening and parading, of constant measuring of yourself against every other, of envy, "If I had that copper hair," "If I had that skin. . . ." She tormented herself enough about not looking like the others, there was enough of unsureness, the having to be conscious of words before you speak, the constant caring—what are they thinking of me? without having it all magnified by the merciless physical drives.

Ronnie is calling. He is wet and I change him. It is rare there is such a cry now. That time of motherhood is almost behind me when the ear is not one's own but must always be racked and listening for the child cry, the child call. We sit for a while and I hold him, looking out over the city spread in charcoal with its soft aisles of light. "Shoogily," he breathes and curls closer. I carry him back to bed, asleep. Shoogily. A funny word, a family word, inherited from Emily, invented by her to say: *comfort.*

In this and other ways she leaves her seal, I say aloud. And startle at my saying it. What do I mean? What did I start to gather together, to try and make coherent? I was at the terrible, growing years. War years. I do not remember them well. I was working, there were four smaller ones now, there was not time for her. She had to help be a mother, and housekeeper, and shopper. She had to get her seal. Mornings of crisis and near hysteria trying to get lunches packed, hair combed, coats and shoes found, everyone to school or Child Care on time, the baby ready for transportation. And always the paper scribbled on by a smaller one, the book looked at by Susan then mislaid, the homework not done. Running out to that huge school where she was one, she was lost, she was a drop; suffering over the unpreparedness, stammering and unsure in her classes.

There was so little time left at night after the kids were bedded down. She   45
would struggle over books, always eating (it was in those years she developed her enormous appetite that is legendary in our family) and I would be ironing, or preparing food for the next day, or writing V-mail to Bill, or tending the baby. Sometimes, to make me laugh, or out of her despair, she would imitate happenings or types at school.

I think I said once: "Why don't you do something like this in the school amateur show?" One morning she phoned me at work, hardly understandable through the weeping: "Mother, I did it. I won, I won; they gave me first prize; they clapped and clapped and wouldn't let me go."

Now suddenly she was Somebody, and as imprisoned in her difference as she had been in anonymity.

She began to be asked to perform at other high schools, even in colleges, then at city and statewide affairs. The first one we went to, I only recognized her that first moment when thin, shy, she almost drowned herself into the curtains. Then: Was this Emily? The control, the command, the convulsing and deadly clowning, the spell, then the roaring, stamping audience, unwilling to let this rare and precious laughter out of their lives.

Afterwards: You ought to do something about her with a gift like that—but without money or knowing how, what does one do? We have left it all to her, and the gift has so often eddied inside, clogged and clotted, as been used and growing.

She is coming. She runs up the stairs two at a time with her light graceful   50
step, and I know she is happy tonight. Whatever it was that occasioned your call did not happen today.

"Aren't you ever going to finish the ironing, Mother? Whistler painted his mother in a rocker. I'd have to paint mine standing over an ironing board." This is one of her communicative nights and she tells me everything and nothing as she fixes herself a plate of food out of the icebox.

She is so lovely. Why did you want me to come in at all? Why were you concerned? She will find her way.

She starts up the stairs to bed. "Don't get me up with the rest in the morning." "But I thought you were having midterms." "Oh, those," she comes back in, kisses me, and says quite lightly, "in a couple of years when we'll all be atom-dead they won't matter a bit."

She has said it before. She *believes* it. But because I have been dredging the past, and all that compounds a human being is so heavy and meaningful in me, I cannot endure it tonight.

I will never total it all. I will never come in to say: She was a child seldom   55
smiled at. Her father left me before she was a year old. I had to work her first six
years when there was work, or I sent her home and to his relatives. There were
years she had care she hated. She was dark and thin and foreign-looking in a world
where the prestige went to blondeness and curly hair and dimples, she was slow
where glibness was prized. She was a child of anxious, not proud, love. We were
poor and could not afford for her the soil of easy growth. I was a young mother, I
was a distracted mother. There were other children pushing up, demanding. Her
younger sister seemed all that she was not. There were years she did not want me
to touch her. She kept too much in herself, her life was such she had to keep too
much in herself. My wisdom came too late. She has much to her and probably
little will come of it. She is a child of her age, of depression, of war, of fear.

Let her be. So all that is in her will not bloom — but in how many does it?
There is still enough left to live by. Only help her to know — help make it so there
is cause for her to know — that she is more than this dress on the ironing board,
helpless before the iron.   [1961]

THINKING ABOUT THE TEXT

1. Is Olsen's last paragraph optimistic or pessimistic about personal destiny?
   Is there some support in the story for both perspectives?

2. There is an old expression: "To know all is to forgive all." Do you agree
   with this statement in regards to "I Stand Here Ironing"? Some critics
   want to privilege personal responsibility; others, social conditions. Do you
   blame Emily's mother? Or is she just a victim?

3. How might this story be different if told from Emily's perspective? From
   Susan's? From Emily's teacher's? What are the advantages and disadvantages of writing a story from one character's point of view?

4. How would you describe the voice or voices we hear in the story? What
   qualities, dimensions, or emotions can you infer? Does one dominate?
   Are you sympathetic to this voice? Is that what Olsen wanted?

5. Do you agree with the mother's decision not to visit the school for a conference? What are her reasons? Are they sound? What do you think the
   teacher wants to discuss? How involved in a child's life should a teacher be?

AMY TAN

Two Kinds

*Born to Chinese immigrants in Oakland, California, Amy Tan (b. 1952) weaves
intricate stories about generational and intercultural relationships among women
in families, basing much of her writing on her own family history. She earned
a B.A. in English and an M.A. in linguistics at San Jose State University. Her novels dealing with mother-daughter relationships,* The Joy Luck Club *(1989) and*
The Kitchen God's Wife *(1991), have received awards and critical acclaim. The*

Hundred Secret Senses *(1996) explores the relationship between sisters who grew up in different cultures. At the age of twenty-six, Tan herself learned that she had three half-sisters in China. Her latest novel is* The Bonesetter's Daughter *(2001). "Two Kinds" is excerpted from* The Joy Luck Club.

My mother believed you could be anything you wanted to be in America. You could open a restaurant. You could work for the government and get good retirement. You could buy a house with almost no money down. You could become rich. You could become instantly famous.

"Of course you can be prodigy, too," my mother told me when I was nine. "You can be best anything. What does Auntie Lindo know? Her daughter, she is only best tricky."

America was where all my mother's hopes lay. She had come here in 1949 after losing everything in China: her mother and father, her family home, her first husband, and two daughters, twin baby girls. But she never looked back with regret. There were so many ways for things to get better.

We didn't immediately pick the right kind of prodigy. At first my mother thought I could be a Chinese Shirley Temple. We'd watch Shirley's old movies on TV as though they were training films. My mother would poke my arm and say, "Ni *kan*"—You watch. And I would see Shirley tapping her feet, or singing a sailor song, or pursing her lips into a very round O while saying, "Oh my goodness."

"Ni *kan*," said my mother as Shirley's eyes flooded with tears. "You already know how. Don't need talent for crying!"   5

Soon after my mother got this idea about Shirley Temple, she took me to a beauty training school in the Mission district and put me in the hands of a student who could barely hold the scissors without shaking. Instead of getting big fat curls, I emerged with an uneven mass of crinkly black fuzz. My mother dragged me off to the bathroom and tried to wet down my hair.

"You look like Negro Chinese," she lamented, as if I had done this on purpose.

The instructor of the beauty training school had to lop off these soggy clumps to make my hair even again. "Peter Pan is very popular these days," the instructor assured my mother. I now had hair the length of a boy's, with straight-across bangs that hung at a slant two inches above my eyebrows. I liked the haircut and it made me actually look forward to my future fame.

In fact, in the beginning, I was just as excited as my mother, maybe even more so. I pictured this prodigy part of me as many different images, trying each one on for size. I was a dainty ballerina girl standing by the curtains, waiting to hear the right music that would send me floating on my tiptoes. I was like the Christ child lifted out of the straw manger, crying with holy indignity. I was Cinderella stepping from her pumpkin carriage with sparkly cartoon music filling the air.

In all of my imaginings, I was filled with a sense that I would soon become   10
perfect. My mother and father would adore me. I would be beyond reproach. I would never feel the need to sulk for anything.

But sometimes the prodigy in me became impatient. "If you don't hurry up and get me out of here, I'm disappearing for good," it warned. "And then you'll always be nothing."

Every night after dinner, my mother and I would sit at the Formica kitchen table. She would present new tests, taking her examples from stories of amazing children she had read in *Ripley's Believe It or Not,* or *Good Housekeeping, Reader's Digest,* and a dozen other magazines she kept in a pile in our bathroom. My mother got these magazines from people whose houses she cleaned. And since she cleaned many houses each week, we had a great assortment. She would look through them all, searching for stories about remarkable children.

The first night she brought out a story about a three-year-old boy who knew the capitals of all the states and even most of the European countries. A teacher was quoted as saying the little boy could also pronounce the names of the foreign cities correctly.

"What's the capital of Finland?" my mother asked me, looking at the magazine story.

All I knew was the capital of California, because Sacramento was the name of the street we lived on in Chinatown. "Nairobi!" I guessed, saying the most foreign word I could think of. She checked to see if that was possibly one way to pronounce "Helsinki" before showing me the answer.

The tests got harder — multiplying numbers in my head, finding the queen of hearts in a deck of cards, trying to stand on my head without using my hands, predicting the daily temperatures in Los Angeles, New York, and London.

One night I had to look at a page from the Bible for three minutes and then report everything I could remember. "Now Jehoshaphat had riches and honor in abundance and . . . that's all I remember, Ma," I said.

And after seeing my mother's disappointed face once again, something inside of me began to die. I hated the tests, the raised hopes and failed expectations. Before going to bed that night, I looked in the mirror above the bathroom sink and when I saw only my face staring back — and that it would always be this ordinary face — I began to cry. Such a sad, ugly girl! I made high-pitched noises like a crazed animal, trying to scratch out the face in the mirror.

And then I saw what seemed to be the prodigy side of me — because I had never seen that face before. I looked at my reflection, blinking so I could see more clearly. The girl staring back at me was angry, powerful. This girl and I were the same. I had new thoughts, willful thoughts, or rather thoughts filled with lots of won'ts. I won't let her change me, I promised myself. I won't be what I'm not.

So now on nights when my mother presented her tests, I performed listlessly, my head propped on one arm. I pretended to be bored. And I was. I got so bored I started counting the bellows of the foghorns out on the bay while my mother drilled me in other areas. The sound was comforting and reminded me of the cow jumping over the moon. And the next day, I played a game with myself, seeing if my mother would give up on me before eight bellows. After a while I usually counted only one, maybe two bellows at most. At last she was beginning to give up hope.

♦ ♦ ♦

Two or three months had gone by without any mention of my being a prodigy again. And then one day my mother was watching *The Ed Sullivan Show* on TV. The TV was old and the sound kept shorting out. Every time my mother got halfway up from the sofa to adjust the set, the sound would go back on and Ed would be talking. As soon as she sat down, Ed would go silent again. She got up, the TV broke into loud piano music. She sat down. Silence. Up and down, back and forth, quiet and loud. It was like a stiff embraceless dance between her and the TV set. Finally she stood by the set with her hand on the sound dial.

She seemed entranced by the music, a little frenzied piano piece with this mesmerizing quality, sort of quick passages and then teasing lilting ones before it returned to the quick playful parts.

"Ni kan," my mother said, calling me over with hurried hand gestures. "Look here."

I could see why my mother was fascinated by the music. It was being pounded out by a little Chinese girl, about nine years old, with a Peter Pan haircut. The girl had the sauciness of a Shirley Temple. She was proudly modest like a proper Chinese child. And she also did this fancy sweep of a curtsy, so that the fluffy skirt of her white dress cascaded slowly to the floor like the petals of a large carnation.

In spite of these warning signs, I wasn't worried. Our family had no piano   25 and we couldn't afford to buy one, let alone reams of sheet music and piano lessons. So I could be generous in my comments when my mother bad-mouthed the little girl on TV.

"Play note right, but doesn't sound good! No singing sound," complained my mother.

"What are you picking on her for?" I said carelessly. "She's pretty good. Maybe she's not the best, but she's trying hard." I knew almost immediately I would be sorry I said that.

"Just like you," she said. "Not the best. Because you not trying." She gave a little huff as she let go of the sound dial and sat down on the sofa.

The little Chinese girl sat down also to play an encore of "Anitra's Dance" by Grieg. I remember the song, because later on I had to learn how to play it.

Three days after watching *The Ed Sullivan Show*, my mother told me what   30 my schedule would be for piano lessons and piano practice. She had talked to Mr. Chong, who lived on the first floor of our apartment building. Mr. Chong was a retired piano teacher and my mother had traded housecleaning services for weekly lessons and a piano for me to practice on every day, two hours a day, from four until six.

When my mother told me this, I felt as though I had been sent to hell. I whined and then kicked my foot a little when I couldn't stand it anymore.

"Why don't you like me the way I am? I'm *not* a genius! I can't play the piano. And even if I could, I wouldn't go on TV if you paid me a million dollars!" I cried.

My mother slapped me. "Who ask you be genius?" she shouted. "Only ask you be your best. For you sake. You think I want you be genius? Hnnh! What for! Who ask you!"

"So ungrateful," I heard her mutter in Chinese. "If she had as much talent as she has temper, she would be famous now."

Mr. Chong, whom I secretly nicknamed Old Chong, was very strange, always tapping his fingers to the silent music of an invisible orchestra. He looked ancient in my eyes. He had lost most of the hair on top of his head and he wore thick glasses and had eyes that always looked tired and sleepy. But he must have been younger than I thought, since he lived with his mother and was not yet married. 35

I met Old Lady Chong once and that was enough. She had this peculiar smell like a baby that had done something in its pants. And her fingers felt like a dead person's, like an old peach I once found in the back of the refrigerator; the skin just slid off the meat when I picked it up.

I soon found out why Old Chong had retired from teaching piano. He was deaf. "Like Beethoven!" he shouted to me. "We're both listening only in our head!" And he would start to conduct his frantic silent sonatas.

Our lessons went like this. He would open the book and point to different things, explaining their purpose: "Key! Treble! Bass! No sharps or flats! So this is C major! Listen now and play after me!"

And then he would play the C scale a few times, a simple chord, and then, as if inspired by an old, unreachable itch, he gradually added more notes and running trills and a pounding bass until the music was really something quite grand.

I would play after him, the simple scale, the simple chord, and then I just played some nonsense that sounded like a cat running up and down on top of garbage cans. Old Chong smiled and applauded and then said, "Very good! But now you must learn to keep time!" 40

So that's how I discovered that Old Chong's eyes were too slow to keep up with the wrong notes I was playing. He went through the motions in half-time. To help me keep rhythm, he stood behind me, pushing down on my right shoulder for every beat. He balanced pennies on top of my wrists so I would keep them still as I slowly played scales and arpeggios. He had me curve my hand around an apple and keep that shape when playing chords. He marched stiffly to show me how to make each finger dance up and down, staccato like an obedient little soldier.

He taught me all these things, and that was how I also learned I could be lazy and get away with mistakes, lots of mistakes. If I hit the wrong notes because I hadn't practiced enough, I never corrected myself. I just kept playing in rhythm. And Old Chong kept conducting his own private reverie.

So maybe I never really gave myself a fair chance. I did pick up the basics pretty quickly, and I might have become a good pianist at that young age. But I was so determined not to try, not to be anybody different that I learned to play only the most ear-splitting preludes, the most discordant hymns.

Over the next year, I practiced like this, dutifully in my own way. And then one day I heard my mother and her friend Lindo Jong both talking in a loud bragging tone of voice so others could hear. It was after church, and I was leaning against the brick wall wearing a dress with stiff white petticoats. Auntie Lindo's daughter, Waverly, who was about my age, was standing farther down the wall about five feet away. We had grown up together and shared all the closeness of two sisters squabbling over crayons and dolls. In other words, for the most part, we hated each other. I thought she was snotty. Waverly Jong had gained a certain amount of fame as "Chinatown's Littlest Chinese Chess Champion."

"She bring home too many trophy," lamented Auntie Lindo that Sunday.   45 "All day she play chess. All day I have no time do nothing but dust off her winnings." She threw a scolding look at Waverly, who pretended not to see her.

"You lucky you don't have this problem," said Auntie Lindo with a sigh to my mother.

And my mother squared her shoulders and bragged: "Our problem worser than yours. If we ask Jing-mei wash dish, she hear nothing but music. It's like you can't stop this natural talent."

And right then, I was determined to put a stop to her foolish pride.

A few weeks later, Old Chong and my mother conspired to have me play in a talent show which would be held in the church hall. By then, my parents had saved up enough to buy me a secondhand piano, a black Wurlitzer spinet with a scarred bench. It was the showpiece of our living room.

For the talent show, I was to play a piece called "Pleading Child" from   50 Schumann's *Scenes from Childhood*. It was a simple, moody piece that sounded more difficult than it was. I was supposed to memorize the whole thing, playing the repeat parts twice to make the piece sound longer. But I dawdled over it, playing a few bars and then cheating, looking up to see what notes followed. I never really listened to what I was playing. I daydreamed about being somewhere else, about being someone else.

The part I liked to practice best was the fancy curtsy: right foot out, touch the rose on the carpet with a pointed foot, sweep to the side, left leg bends, look up and smile.

My parents invited all the couples from the Joy Luck Club to witness my debut. Auntie Lindo and Uncle Tin were there. Waverly and her two older brothers had also come. The first two rows were filled with children both younger and older than I was. The littlest ones got to go first. They recited simple nursery rhymes, squawked out tunes on miniature violins, twirled Hula Hoops, pranced in pink ballet tutus, and when they bowed or curtsied, the audience would sigh in unison, "Awww," and then clap enthusiastically.

When my turn came, I was very confident. I remember my childish excitement. It was as if I knew, without a doubt, that the prodigy side of me really did exist. I had no fear whatsoever, no nervousness. I remember thinking to myself, This is it! This is it! I looked out over the audience, at my mother's blank face, my father's yawn, Auntie Lindo's stiff-lipped smile, Waverly's sulky expression. I had on a white dress layered with sheets of lace, and a pink bow in my Peter Pan haircut. As I sat down I envisioned people jumping to their feet and Ed Sullivan rushing up to introduce me to everyone on TV.

And I started to play. It was so beautiful. I was so caught up in how lovely I looked that at first I didn't worry how I would sound. So it was a surprise to me when I hit the first wrong note and I realized something didn't sound quite right.

And then I hit another and another followed that. A chill started at the top of my head and began to trickle down. Yet I couldn't stop playing, as though my hands were bewitched. I kept thinking my fingers would adjust themselves back, like a train switching to the right track. I played this strange jumble through two repeats, the sour notes staying with me all the way to the end.

When I stood up, I discovered my legs were shaking. Maybe I had just been   55
nervous and the audience, like Old Chong, had seen me go through the right motions and had not heard anything wrong at all. I swept my right foot out, went down on my knee, looked up and smiled. The room was quiet, except for Old Chong, who was beaming and shouting, "Bravo! Bravo! Well done!" But then I saw my mother's face, her stricken face. The audience clapped weakly, and as I walked back to my chair, with my whole face quivering as I tried not to cry, I heard a little boy whisper loudly to his mother, "That was awful," and the mother whispered back, "Well, she certainly tried."

And now I realized how many people were in the audience, the whole world it seemed. I was aware of eyes burning into my back. I felt the shame of my mother and father as they sat stiffly throughout the rest of the show.

We could have escaped during intermission. Pride and some strange sense of honor must have anchored my parents to their chairs. And so we watched it all: the eighteen-year-old boy with a fake mustache who did a magic show and juggled flaming hoops while riding a unicycle. The breasted girl with white makeup who sang from *Madama Butterfly* and got honorable mention. And the eleven-year-old boy who won first prize playing a tricky violin song that sounded like a busy bee.

After the show, the Hsus, the Jongs, and the St. Clairs from the Joy Luck Club came up to my mother and father.

"Lots of talented kids," Auntie Lindo said vaguely, smiling broadly.

"That was somethin' else," said my father, and I wondered if he was referring   60
to me in a humorous way, or whether he even remembered what I had done.

Waverly looked at me and shrugged her shoulders. "You aren't a genius like me," she said matter-of-factly. And if I hadn't felt so bad, I would have pulled her braids and punched her stomach.

But my mother's expression was what devastated me: a quiet, blank look that said she had lost everything. I felt the same way, and it seemed as if everybody were now coming up, like gawkers at the scene of an accident, to see what parts were actually missing. When we got on the bus to go home, my father was humming the busy-bee tune and my mother was silent. I kept thinking she wanted to wait until we got home before shouting at me. But when my father unlocked the door to our apartment, my mother walked in and then went to the back, into the bedroom. No accusations. No blame. And in a way, I felt disappointed. I had been waiting for her to start shouting, so I could shout back and cry and blame her for all my misery.

I assumed my talent-show fiasco meant I never had to play the piano again. But two days later, after school, my mother came out of the kitchen and saw me watching TV.

"Four clock," she reminded me as if it were any other day. I was stunned, as though she were asking me to go through the talent-show torture again. I wedged myself more tightly in front of the TV.

"Turn off TV," she called from the kitchen five minutes later.   65

I didn't budge. And then I decided. I didn't have to do what my mother said anymore. I wasn't her slave. This wasn't China. I had listened to her before and look what happened. She was the stupid one.

She came out from the kitchen and stood in the arched entryway of the living room. "Four clock," she said once again, louder.

"I'm not going to play anymore," I said nonchalantly. "Why should I? I'm not a genius."

She walked over and stood in front of the TV. I saw her chest was heaving up and down in an angry way.

"No!" I said, and I now felt stronger, as if my true self had finally emerged. So   70
this was what had been inside me all along.

"No! I won't!" I screamed.

She yanked me by the arm, pulled me off the floor, snapped off the TV. She was frighteningly strong, half pulling, half carrying me toward the piano as I kicked the throw rugs under my feet. She lifted me up and onto the hard bench. I was sobbing by now, looking at her bitterly. Her chest was heaving even more and her mouth was open, smiling crazily as if she were pleased I was crying.

"You want me to be someone that I'm not!" I sobbed. "I'll never be the kind of daughter you want me to be!"

"Only two kinds of daughters," she shouted in Chinese. "Those who are obedient and those who follow their own mind! Only one kind of daughter can live in this house. Obedient daughter!"

"Then I wish I wasn't your daughter. I wish you weren't my mother," I   75
shouted. As I said these things I got scared. I felt like worms and toads and slimy things were crawling out of my chest, but it also felt good, as if this awful side of me had surfaced, at last.

"Too late change this," said my mother shrilly.

And I could sense her anger rising to its breaking point. I wanted to see it spill over. And that's when I remembered the babies she had lost in China, the ones we never talked about. "Then I wish I'd never been born!" I shouted. "I wish I were dead! Like them."

It was as if I had said the magic words, Alakazam! — and her face went blank, her mouth closed, her arms went slack, and she backed out of the room, stunned, as if she were blowing away like a small brown leaf, thin, brittle, lifeless.

It was not the only disappointment my mother felt in me. In the years that followed, I failed her so many times, each time asserting my own will, my right to fall short of expectations. I didn't get straight As. I didn't become class president. I didn't get into Stanford. I dropped out of college.

For unlike my mother, I did not believe I could be anything I wanted to be. I   80
could only be me.

And for all those years, we never talked about the disaster at the recital or my terrible accusations afterward at the piano bench. All that remained unchecked, like a betrayal that was now unspeakable. So I never found a way to ask her why she had hoped for something so large that failure was inevitable.

And even worse, I never asked her what frightened me the most: Why had she given up hope?

For after our struggle at the piano, she never mentioned my playing again. The lessons stopped, the lid to the piano was closed, shutting out the dust, my misery, and her dreams.

So she surprised me. A few years ago, she offered to give me the piano, for my thirtieth birthday. I had not played in all those years. I saw the offer as a sign of forgiveness, a tremendous burden removed.

"Are you sure?" I asked shyly. "I mean, won't you and Dad miss it?"   85

"No, this your piano," she said firmly. "Always your piano. You only one can play."

"Well, I probably can't play anymore," I said. "It's been years."

"You pick up fast," said my mother, as if she knew this was certain. "You have natural talent. You could been genius if you want to."

"No I couldn't."

"You just not trying," said my mother. And she was neither angry nor sad. She   90
said it as if to announce a fact that could never be disproved. "Take it," she said.

But I didn't at first. It was enough that she had offered it to me. And after that, every time I saw it in my parents' living room, standing in front of the bay windows, it made me feel proud, as if it were a shiny trophy I had won back.

Last week I sent a tuner over to my parents' apartment and had the piano reconditioned, for purely sentimental reasons. My mother had died a few months before and I had been getting things in order for my father, a little bit at a time. I put the jewelry in special silk pouches. The sweaters she had knitted in yellow, pink, bright orange — all the colors I hated — I put those in moth-proof boxes. I found some old Chinese silk dresses, the kind with little slits up the sides. I rubbed the old silk against my skin, then wrapped them in tissue and decided to take them home with me.

After I had the piano tuned, I opened the lid and touched the keys. It sounded even richer than I remembered. Really, it was a very good piano. Inside the bench were the same exercise notes with handwritten scales, the same secondhand music books with their covers held together with yellow tape.

I opened up the Schumann book to the dark little piece I had played at the recital. It was on the left-hand side of the page, "Pleading Child." It looked more difficult than I remembered. I played a few bars, surprised at how easily the notes came back to me.

And for the first time, or so it seemed, I noticed the piece on the right-hand   95
side. It was called "Perfectly Contented." I tried to play this one as well. It had a lighter melody but the same flowing rhythm and turned out to be quite easy. "Pleading Child" was shorter but slower; "Perfectly Contented" was longer but faster. And after I played them both a few times, I realized they were two halves of the same song.   [1989]

THINKING ABOUT THE TEXT

1. Most sons and daughters struggle to establish their own identities. Does this seem true in "Two Kinds"? Does the cultural difference between the immigrant mother and Americanized daughter intensify their struggle? Do you think you have different goals in life than your parents do?

2. Do you agree with the mother's belief that "you could be anything you wanted to be in America" (para. 1)? Does race matter? Gender? Ethnicity? Religion? Sexual orientation?

3. What do you believe each character learned from the argument at the piano bench the day after the recital?

4. How does Tan establish the differing personalities of her characters? Through details? Dialogue? Anecdotes? Do the main characters change significantly? Does she tell us or show us?

5. Do you sympathize with the mother or the daughter? Should parents channel their children toward selected activities? Or should parents let their children choose their own paths? Can parents push their children too much? Why would they do this?

MAKING COMPARISONS

1. Do you think Emily's mother in Olsen's story would want to be like the Chinese mother if given the opportunity? Which mother would you prefer to have? Why?

2. One mother seems to do too little, one too much. Is this your reading of the two stories? Is the lesson of Olsen's and Tan's stories that mothers can't win no matter what they do? Or do you have a more optimistic interpretation?

3. Which daughter's life seems more difficult? How possible is it to say from the outside looking in?

ALICE WALKER
Everyday Use

A native of Eatonton, Georgia, Alice Walker attended Spelman College and received her B.A. from Sarah Lawrence College in 1965. During the 1960s she was active in the civil rights movement, an experience reflected in her 1976 novel Meridian *and in her autobiographical 2000 book,* The Way Forward Is with a Broken Heart. *Walker is accomplished in many genres, and her essays, short stories, novels, and poems are widely read. She is perhaps best known for the novel* The Color Purple *(1976), which earned her both a Pulitzer Prize and an American Book Award and was made into a movie. Terming herself a "womanist" rather than a feminist in the essays of* In Search of Our Mothers' Gardens *(1983), Walker has confronted many issues concerning women, including abusive relationships, lesbian love, and the horrors of ritual genital mutilation in some African societies. Her daughter, Rebecca, has written her own memoir,* Black, White and Jewish, *dealing with her childhood and adolescence as the daughter of Alice Walker and activist lawyer Mel Leventhal, to whom Walker was married for nine years, after meeting him during voter registration drives in Mississippi in 1967. The short story "Everyday Use" from the collection* In Love and Trouble: Stories of Black Women *(1973) deals with definitions of history, heritage, and value in a changing world for African Americans in the mid-twentieth century.*

I will wait for her in the yard that Maggie and I made so clean and wavy yesterday afternoon. A yard like this is more comfortable than most people know. It is not just a yard. It is like an extended living room. When the hard clay is swept clean as a floor and the fine sand around the edges lined with tiny, irregular grooves anyone can come and sit and look up into the elm tree and wait for the breezes that never come inside the house.

Maggie will be nervous until after her sister goes: she will stand hopelessly in corners homely and ashamed of the burn scars down her arms and legs, eyeing her sister with a mixture of envy and awe. She thinks her sister has held life always in the palm of one hand, that "no" is a word the world never learned to say to her.

You've no doubt seen those TV shows where the child who has "made it" is confronted, as a surprise, by her own mother and father, tottering in weakly from backstage. (A pleasant surprise, of course: What would they do if parent and child came on the show only to curse out and insult each other?) On TV mother and child embrace and smile into each other's faces. Sometimes the mother and father weep, the child wraps them in her arms and leans across the table to tell how she would not have made it without their help. I have seen these programs.

Sometimes I dream a dream in which Dee and I are suddenly brought together on a TV program of this sort. Out of a dark and soft-seated limousine I am ushered into a bright room filled with many people. There I meet a smiling, gray, sporty man like Johnny Carson who shakes my hand and tells me what a fine girl I have. Then we are on the stage and Dee is embracing me with tears in her eyes. She pins on my dress a large orchid, even though she has told me once that she thinks orchids are tacky flowers.

In real life I am a large, big-boned woman with rough, man-working hands.   5
In the winter I wear flannel nightgowns to bed and overalls during the day. I can kill and clean a hog as mercilessly as a man. My fat keeps me hot in zero weather. I can work outside all day, breaking ice to get water for washing; I can eat pork liver cooked over the open fire minutes after it comes steaming from the hog. One winter I knocked a bull calf straight in the brain between the eyes with a sledge hammer and had the meat hung up to chill before nightfall. But of course all this does not show on television. I am the way my daughter would want me to

be: a hundred pounds lighter, my skin like an uncooked barley pancake. My hair glistens in the hot bright lights. Johnny Carson has much to do to keep up with my quick and witty tongue.

But that is a mistake. I know even before I wake up. Who ever knew a Johnson with a quick tongue? Who can even imagine me looking a strange white man in the eye? It seems to me I have talked to them always with one foot raised in flight, with my head turned in whichever way is farthest from them. Dee, though. She would always look anyone in the eye. Hesitation was no part of her nature.

"How do I look, Mama?" Maggie says, showing just enough of her thin body enveloped in pink skirt and red blouse for me to know she's there, almost hidden by the door.

"Come out into the yard," I say.

Have you ever seen a lame animal, perhaps a dog run over by some careless person rich enough to own a car, sidle up to someone who is ignorant enough to be kind to him? That is the way my Maggie walks. She has been like this, chin on chest, eyes on ground, feet in shuffle, ever since the fire that burned the other house to the ground.

Dee is lighter than Maggie, with nicer hair and a fuller figure. She's a woman now, though sometimes I forget. How long ago was it that the other house burned? Ten, twelve years? Sometimes I can still hear the flames and feel Maggie's arms sticking to me, her hair smoking and her dress falling off her in little black papery flakes. Her eyes seemed stretched open, blazed open by the flames reflected in them. And Dee. I see her standing off under the sweet gum tree she used to dig gum out of; a look of concentration on her face as she watched the last dingy gray board of the house fall in toward the red-hot brick chimney. Why don't you do a dance around the ashes? I'd wanted to ask her. She had hated the house that much.

I used to think she hated Maggie, too. But that was before we raised the money, the church and me, to send her to Augusta to school. She used to read to us without pity; forcing words, lies, other folks' habits, whole lives upon us two, sitting trapped and ignorant underneath her voice. She washed us in a river of make-believe, burned us with a lot of knowledge we didn't necessarily need to know. Pressed us to her with the serious way she read, to shove us away at just the moment, like dimwits, we seemed about to understand.

Dee wanted nice things. A yellow organdy dress to wear to her graduation from high school; black pumps to match a green suit she'd made from an old suit somebody gave me. She was determined to stare down any disaster in her efforts. Her eyelids would not flicker for minutes at a time. Often I fought off the temptation to shake her. At sixteen she had a style of her own: and knew what style was.

I never had an education myself. After second grade the school was closed down. Don't ask me why: in 1927 colored asked fewer questions than they do now. Sometimes Maggie reads to me. She stumbles along good-naturedly but can't see well. She knows she is not bright. Like good looks and money, quick-

10

ness passed her by. She will marry John Thomas (who has mossy teeth in an earnest face) and then I'll be free to sit here and I guess just sing church songs to myself. Although I never was a good singer. Never could carry a tune. I was always better at a man's job. I used to love to milk till I was hooked in the side in '49. Cows are soothing and slow and don't bother you, unless you try to milk them the wrong way.

I have deliberately turned my back on the house. It is three rooms, just like the one that burned, except the roof is tin; they don't make shingle roofs any more. There are no real windows, just some holes cut in the sides, like the port-holes in a ship, but not round and not square, with rawhide holding the shutters up on the outside. This house is in a pasture, too, like the other one. No doubt when Dee sees it she will want to tear it down. She wrote me once that no matter where we "choose" to live, she will manage to come see us. But she will never bring her friends. Maggie and I thought about this and Maggie asked me, "Mama, when did Dee ever *have* any friends?"

She had a few. Furtive boys in pink shirts hanging about on washday after   15
school. Nervous girls who never laughed. Impressed with her they worshiped the well-turned phrase, the cute shape, the scalding humor that erupted like bubbles in lye. She read to them.

When she was courting Jimmy T she didn't have much time to pay to us, but turned all her faultfinding power on him. He *flew* to marry a cheap gal from a family of ignorant flashy people. She hardly had time to recompose herself.

When she comes I will meet — but there they are!

Maggie attempts to make a dash for the house, in her shuffling way, but I stay her with my hand. "Come back here," I say. And she stops and tries to dig a well in the sand with her toe.

It is hard to see them clearly through the strong sun. But even the first glimpse of leg out of the car tells me it is Dee. Her feet were always neat-looking, as if God himself had shaped them with a certain style. From the other side of the car comes a short, stocky man. Hair is all over his head a foot long and hanging from his chin like a kinky mule tail. I hear Maggie suck in her breath. "Uhnnnh," is what it sounds like. Like when you see the wriggling end of a snake just in front of your foot on the road. "Uhnnnh."

Dee next. A dress down to the ground, in this hot weather. A dress so loud it   20
hurts my eyes. There are yellows and oranges enough to throw back the light of the sun. I feel my whole face warming from the heat waves it throws out. Earrings gold, too, and hanging down to her shoulders. Bracelets dangling and making noises when she moves her arm up to shake the folds of the dress out of her armpits. The dress is loose and flows, and as she walks closer, I like it. I hear Maggie go "Uhnnnh" again. It is her sister's hair. It stands straight up like the wool on a sheep. It is black as night and around the edges are two long pigtails that rope about like small lizards disappearing behind her ears.

"Wa-su-zo-Tean-o!" she says, coming on in that gliding way the dress makes her move. The short stocky fellow with the hair to his navel is all grinning and he follows up with "Asalamalakim, my mother and sister!" He moves to hug Maggie but she falls back, right up against the back of my chair. I feel her trembling there and when I look up I see the perspiration falling off her chin.

"Don't get up," says Dee. Since I am stout it takes something of a push. You can see me trying to move a second or two before I make it. She turns, showing white heels through her sandals, and goes back to the car. Out she peeks next with a Polaroid. She stoops down quickly and lines up picture after picture of me sitting there in front of the house with Maggie cowering behind me. She never takes a shot without making sure the house is included. When a cow comes nibbling around the edge of the yard she snaps it and me and Maggie *and* the house. Then she puts the Polaroid in the back seat of the car, and comes up and kisses me on the forehead.

Meanwhile Asalamalakim is going through the motions with Maggie's hand. Maggie's hand is as limp as a fish, and probably as cold, despite the sweat, and she keeps trying to pull it back. It looks like Asalamalakim wants to shake hands but wants to do it fancy. Or maybe he don't know how people shake hands. Anyhow, he soon gives up on Maggie.

"Well," I say. "Dee."

"No, Mama," she says. "Not 'Dee,' Wangero Leewanika Kemanjo!"   25

"What happened to 'Dee'?" I wanted to know.

"She's dead," Wangero said. "I couldn't bear it any longer being named after the people who oppress me."

"You know as well as me you was named after your aunt Dicie," I said. Dicie is my sister. She named Dee. We called her "Big Dee" after Dee was born.

"But who was *she* named after?" asked Wangero.

"I guess after Grandma Dee," I said.   30

"And who was she named after?" asked Wangero.

"Her mother," I said, and saw Wangero was getting tired. "That's about as far back as I can trace it," I said. Though, in fact, I probably could have carried it back beyond the Civil War through the branches.

"Well," said Asalamalakim, "there you are."

"Uhnnnh," I heard Maggie say.

"There I was not," I said, "before 'Dicie' cropped up in our family, so why   35
should I try to trace it that far back?"

He just stood there grinning, looking down on me like somebody inspecting a Model A car. Every once in a while he and Wangero sent eye signals over my head.

"How do you pronounce this name?" I asked.

"You don't have to call me by it if you don't want to," said Wangero.

"Why shouldn't I?" I asked. "If that's what you want us to call you, we'll call you."

"I know it might sound awkward at first," said Wangero.   40

"I'll get used to it," I said. "Ream it out again."

Well, soon we got the name out of the way. Asalamalakim had a name twice as long and three times as hard. After I tripped over it two or three times he told me to just call him Hakim-a-barber. I wanted to ask him was he a barber, but I didn't really think he was, so I didn't ask.

"You must belong to those beef-cattle peoples down the road," I said. They said "Asalamalakim" when they met you, too, but they didn't shake hands. Always too busy: feeding the cattle, fixing the fences, putting up salt-lick shelters, throwing down hay. When the white folks poisoned some of the herd the men stayed up all night with rifles in their hands. I walked a mile and a half just to see the sight.

Hakim-a-barber said, "I accept some of their doctrines, but farming and raising cattle is not my style." (They didn't tell me, and I didn't ask, whether Wangero [Dee] had really gone and married him.)

We sat down to eat and right away he said he didn't eat collards and pork was   45
unclean. Wangero, though, went on through the chitlins and corn bread, the greens and everything else. She talked a blue streak over the sweet potatoes. Everything delighted her. Even the fact that we still used the benches her daddy made for the table when we couldn't afford to buy chairs.

"Oh, Mama!" she cried. Then turned to Hakim-a-barber. "I never knew how lovely these benches are. You can feel the rump prints," she said, running her hands underneath her and along the bench. Then she gave a sigh and her hand closed over Grandma Dee's butter dish. "That's it!" she said. "I knew there was something I wanted to ask you if I could have." She jumped up from the table and went over in the corner where the churn stood, the milk in it clabber by now. She looked at the churn and looked at it.

"This churn top is what I need," she said. "Didn't Uncle Buddy whittle it out of a tree you all used to have?"

"Yes," I said.

"Uh huh," she said happily. "And I want the dasher, too."

"Uncle Buddy whittle that, too?" asked the barber.   50

Dee (Wangero) looked up at me.

"Aunt Dee's first husband whittled the dash," said Maggie so low you almost couldn't hear her. "His name was Henry, but they called him Stash."

"Maggie's brain is like all elephant's," Wangero said, laughing. "I can use the churn top as a centerpiece for the alcove table," she said, sliding a plate over the churn, "and I'll think of something artistic to do with the dasher."

When she finished wrapping the dasher the handle stuck out. I took it for a moment in my hands. You didn't even have to look close to see where hands pushing the dasher up and down to make butter had left a kind of sink in the wood. In fact, there were a lot of small sinks; you could see where thumbs and fingers had sunk into the wood. It was beautiful light yellow wood, from a tree that grew in the yard where Big Dee and Stash had lived.

After dinner Dee (Wangero) went to the trunk at the foot of my bed and   55
started rifling through it. Maggie hung back in the kitchen over the dishpan. Out came Wangero with two quilts. They had been pieced by Grandma Dee and then Big Dee and me had hung them on the quilt frames on the front porch and quilted them. One was in the Lone Star pattern. The other was Walk Around the Mountain. In both of them were scraps of dresses Grandma Dee had worn fifty and more years ago. Bits and pieces of Grandpa Jarrell's paisley shirts. And one teeny faded blue piece, about the size of a penny matchbox, that was from Great Grandpa Ezra's uniform that he wore in the Civil War.

"Mama," Wangero said sweet as a bird. "Can I have these old quilts?"

I heard something fall in the kitchen, and a minute later the kitchen door slammed.

"Why don't you take one or two of the others?" I asked. "These old things was just done by me and Big Dee from some tops your grandma pieced before she died."

"No," said Wangero. "I don't want those. They are stitched around the borders by machine."

"That'll make them last better," I said.   60

"That's not the point," said Wangero. "These are all pieces of dresses Grandma used to wear. She did all this stitching by hand. Imagine!" She held the quilts securely in her arms, stroking them.

"Some of the pieces, like those lavender ones, come from old clothes her mother handed down to her," I said, moving up to touch the quilts. Dee (Wangero) moved back just enough so that I couldn't reach the quilts. They already belonged to her.

"Imagine!" she breathed again, clutching them closely to her bosom.

"The truth is," I said, "I promised to give them quilts to Maggie, for when she marries John Thomas."

She gasped like a bee had stung her.   65

"Maggie can't appreciate these quilts!" she said. "She'd probably be backward enough to put them to everyday use."

"I reckon she would," I said. "God knows I been saving 'em for long enough with nobody using 'em. I hope she will!" I didn't want to bring up how I had offered Dee (Wangero) a quilt when she went away to college. Then she had told me they were old-fashioned, out of style.

"But they're *priceless!*" she was saying now, furiously; for she has a temper. "Maggie would put them on the bed and in five years they'd be in rags. Less than that!"

"She can always make some more," I said. "Maggie knows how to quilt."

Dee (Wangero) looked at me with hatred. "You just will not understand. The   70
point is these quilts, *these* quilts!"

"Well," I said, stumped. "What would *you* do with them?"

"Hang them," she said. As if that was the only thing you *could* do with quilts.

Maggie by now was standing in the door. I could almost hear the sound her feet made as they scraped over each other.

"She can have them, Mama," she said, like somebody used to never winning anything, or having anything reserved for her. "I can 'member Grandma Dee without the quilts."

I looked at her hard. She had filled her bottom lip with checkerberry snuff   75
and it gave her face a kind of dopey, hangdog look. It was Grandma Dee and Big Dee who taught her how to quilt herself. She stood there with her scarred hands hidden in the folds of her skirt. She looked at her sister with something like fear but she wasn't mad at her. This was Maggie's portion. This was the way she knew God to work.

When I looked at her like that something hit me in the top of my head and ran down to the soles of my feet. Just like when I'm in church and the spirit of

God touches me and I get happy and shout. I did something I never had done before: hugged Maggie to me, then dragged her on into the room, snatched the quilts out of Miss Wangero's hands and dumped them into Maggie's lap. Maggie just sat there on my bed with her mouth open.

"Take one or two of the others," I said to Dee.

But she turned without a word and went out to Hakim-a-barber.

"You just don't understand," she said, as Maggie and I came out to the car.

"What don't I understand?" I wanted to know.

"Your heritage," she said. And then she turned to Maggie, kissed her, and said, "You ought to try to make something of yourself, too, Maggie. It's really a new day for us. But from the way you and Mama still live you'd never know it."

She put on some sunglasses that hid everything above the tip of her nose and her chin.

Maggie smiled; maybe at the sunglasses. But a real smile, not scared. After we watched the car dust settle I asked Maggie to bring me a dip of snuff. And then the two of us sat there just enjoying, until it was time to go in the house and go to bed.   [1973]

80

THINKING ABOUT THE TEXT

1. Be specific in arguing that Mama is more sympathetic to Maggie than to Dee. Is Mama hostile to Dee? What values are involved in the tension between Mama and Dee and Maggie?

2. Although many students seem to prefer Maggie to Dee, most would probably rather be Dee than Maggie. Is this true for you? Why?

3. Do you think Walker is against "getting back to one's roots"? Does she give a balanced characterization of Maggie? Of Dee? How might she portray Dee if she wanted to be more positive about her? Less positive?

4. Do you think it helps or hinders the social fabric to affirm ethnic differences? Do you think America is a melting pot? Is a quilt a better symbol to capture our diversity? Can you suggest another metaphor?

5. Do you think most mothers would side with daughters that they are more politically or culturally sympathetic with? What might be the deciding factor? Are most mothers equally supportive of each of their children?

MAKING COMPARISONS

1. How do you think Maggie would fare if she were the first child in "I Stand Here Ironing"? In "Two Kinds"?

2. Might either Emily or the daughter in "Two Kinds" adopt attitudes similar to Dee?

3. Which one of the four daughters seems the kindest? The smartest? The most ambitious? The most troubled? The most likely to succeed? To find love? Do you think the mothers are responsible for how their daughters turn out?

WRITING ABOUT ISSUES

1. As Emily's teacher, write a letter to Emily's mother persuading her that she should still come in for a conference. Acknowledge her excuses and her side of the issue, but offer objections.

2. Write a brief essay arguing that each of the mothers presented in Olsen's, Tan's, and Walker's stories is either a good or bad model for parenting.

3. Write a personal experience narrative about a time when your parents pushed you too hard or too little or wanted you to be someone you thought you were not. Conclude with your present view of the consequences of their action.

4. Ask six males and six females if they feel their parents tried to shape their personalities, behavior, choice of friends, and so forth. Were the parents' efforts successful? Do the sons and daughters resent it now? Conclude your brief report with some generalizations, including how relevant gender is.

Siblings in Conflict

TOBIAS WOLFF, "The Rich Brother"
JAMES BALDWIN, "Sonny's Blues"

Although the expression "blood is thicker than water" suggests that brothers and sisters should support each other, the reality is often more complex. Children growing up together share intense emotional ties, but affection and loyalty sometimes conflict with hostility and jealousy. Children often feel they are competing for their parents' attention and love, a rivalry often played out over a lifetime and intensified as siblings choose different lifestyles. Well into adulthood, brothers and sisters often find their relationships with each other conflicted by unresolved issues of mutual responsibility and disparities in values as well as individual issues of financial success, self-esteem, and guilt. The siblings in the following two stories, separated by age and disparate occupations, engage in a psychologically complex dance that ebbs and flows over their lives. They struggle to understand each other and ultimately themselves, for, as with all of us, healthy relationships with siblings start with a healthy relationship with oneself.

BEFORE YOU READ

How would you describe your relationship with your siblings? Did rivalry ever play a part? Does it now? Do you consider your siblings' futures as similar to yours? Is it important for brothers and sisters to look after each other? Or might that create more problems than it solves?

TOBIAS WOLFF
The Rich Brother

Tobias Wolff (b. 1945) is known chiefly for his short stories. The following piece comes from his second collection, Back in the World *(1985). He has produced two other volumes of stories,* In the Garden of the North American Martyrs *(1981) and* The Night in Question *(1996), and a short novel,* The Barracks Thief *(1984). Wolff is also the author of two memoirs. In the first,* This Boy's Life *(1989), he recalls his parents' divorce and subsequent family dramas. These include wanderings with his mother through the West and Northwest; arguments with his abusive stepfather; occasional contact with his real father, who was a habitual liar later imprisoned for fraud; and years of separation from his brother Geoffrey, who eventually became a writer himself.* This Boy's Life *won the* Los Angeles Times *Book Award for Biography and later became a movie starring Robert De Niro as the stepfather and Leonardo DiCaprio as the young Toby. Wolff's second memoir,* In Pharaoh's Army: Memories of the Lost War *(1994), mostly deals with his military service in Vietnam. Today, Wolff teaches creative writing at Stanford University.*

There were two brothers, Pete and Donald.

Pete, the older brother, was in real estate. He and his wife had a Century 21 franchise in Santa Cruz. Pete worked hard and made a lot of money, but not any more than he thought he deserved. He had two daughters, a sailboat, a house from which he could see a thin slice of the ocean, and friends doing well enough in their own lives not to wish bad luck on him. Donald, the younger brother, was still single. He lived alone, painted houses when he found the work, and got deeper in debt to Pete when he didn't.

No one would have taken them for brothers. Where Pete was stout and hearty and at home in the world, Donald was bony, grave, and obsessed with the fate of his soul. Over the years Donald had worn the images of two different Perfect Masters around his neck. Out of devotion to the second of these he entered an ashram in Berkeley, where he nearly died of undiagnosed hepatitis. By the time Pete finished paying the medical bills Donald had become a Christian. He drifted from church to church, then joined a pentecostal community that met somewhere in the Mission District to sing in tongues and swap prophecies.

Pete couldn't make sense of it. Their parents were both dead, but while they were alive neither of them had found it necessary to believe in anything. They managed to be decent people without making fools of themselves, and Pete had the same ambition. He thought that the whole thing was an excuse for Donald to take himself seriously.

The trouble was that Donald couldn't content himself with worrying about his own soul. He had to worry about everyone else's, and especially Pete's. He handed down his judgments in ways that he seemed to consider subtle: through significant silence, innuendo, looks of mild despair that said, *Brother, what have*   5 *you come to?* What Pete had come to, as far as he could tell, was prosperity. That was the real issue between them. Pete prospered and Donald did not prosper.

At the age of forty Pete took up sky diving. He made his first jump with two friends who'd started only a few months earlier and were already doing stunts. He never would have used the word *mystical,* but that was how Pete felt about the experience. Later he made the mistake of trying to describe it to Donald, who kept asking how much it cost and then acted appalled when Pete told him.

"At least I'm trying something new," Pete said. "At least I'm breaking the pattern."

Not long after that conversation Donald also broke the pattern, by going to live on a farm outside Paso Robles. The farm was owned by several members of Donald's community, who had bought it and moved there with the idea of forming a family of faith. That was how Donald explained it in the first letter he sent. Every week Pete heard how happy Donald was, how "in the Lord." He told Pete that he was praying for him, he and the rest of Pete's brothers and sisters on the farm.

"I only have one brother," Pete wanted to answer, "and that's enough." But he kept this thought to himself.

In November the letters stopped. Pete didn't worry about this at first, but when he called Donald at Thanksgiving Donald was grim. He tried to sound upbeat but he didn't try hard enough to make it convincing. "Now listen," Pete said, "you don't have to stay in that place if you don't want to."

"I'll be all right," Donald answered.

"That's not the point. Being all right is not the point. If you don't like what's going on up there, then get out."

"I'm all right," Donald said again, more firmly. "I'm doing fine."

But he called Pete a week later and said that he was quitting the farm. When Pete asked him where he intended to go, Donald admitted that he had no plan. His car had been repossessed just before he left the city, and he was flat broke.

"I guess you'll have to stay with us," Pete said.

Donald put up a show of resistance. Then he gave in. "Just until I get my feet on the ground," he said.

"Right," Pete said. "Check out your options." He told Donald he'd send him money for a bus ticket, but as they were about to hang up Pete changed his mind. He knew that Donald would try hitchhiking to save the fare. Pete didn't want him out on the road all alone where some head case would pick him up, where anything could happen to him.

"Better yet," he said, "I'll come and get you."

"You don't have to do that. I didn't expect you to do that," Donald said. He added, "It's a pretty long drive."

"Just tell me how to get there."

But Donald wouldn't give him directions. He said that the farm was too depressing, that Pete wouldn't like it. Instead, he insisted on meeting Pete at a service station called Jonathan's Mechanical Emporium.

"You must be kidding," Pete said.

10

15

20

"It's close to the highway," Donald said. "I didn't name it."

"That's one for the collection," Pete said.

The day before he left to bring Donald home, Pete received a letter from a 25
man who described himself as "head of household" at the farm where Donald
had been living. From this letter Pete learned that Donald had not quit the farm,
but had been asked to leave. The letter was written on the back of a mimeo-
graphed survey form asking people to record their response to a ceremony of
some kind. The last question said:

> *What did you feel during the liturgy?*
> *a) Being*
> *b) Becoming*
> *c) Being and Becoming*
> *d) None of the Above*
> *e) All of the Above*

Pete tried to forget the letter. But of course he couldn't. Each time he
thought of it he felt crowded and breathless, a feeling that came over him again
when he drove into the service station and saw Donald sitting against a wall with
his head on his knees. It was late afternoon. A paper cup tumbled slowly past
Donald's feet, pushed by the damp wind.

Pete honked and Donald raised his head. He smiled at Pete, then stood and
stretched. His arms were long and thin and white. He wore a red bandanna across
his forehead, a T-shirt with a couple of words on the front. Pete couldn't read
them because the letters were inverted.

"Grow up," Pete yelled. "Get a Mercedes."

Donald came up to the window. He bent down and said, "Thanks for coming. You must be totally whipped."

"I'll make it." Pete pointed at Donald's T-shirt. "What's that supposed to say?" 30

Donald looked down at his shirt front. "Try God. I guess I put it on backwards. Pete, could I borrow a couple of dollars? I owe these people for coffee and
sandwiches."

Pete took five twenties from his wallet and held them out the window.

Donald stepped back as if horrified. "I don't need that much."

"I can't keep track of all these nickels and dimes," Pete said. "Just pay me
back when your ship comes in." He waved the bills impatiently. "Go on—
take it."

"Only for now." Donald took the money and went into the service station 35
office. He came out carrying two orange sodas, one of which he gave to Pete as he
got into the car. "My treat," he said.

"No bags?"

"Wow, thanks for reminding me." Donald balanced his drink on the dashboard, but the slight rocking of the car as he got out tipped it onto the passenger's
seat, where half its contents foamed over before Pete could snatch it up again.
Donald looked on while Pete held the bottle out the window, soda running down
his fingers.

"Wipe it up," Pete told him. "Quick!"

"With what?"

Pete stared at Donald. "That shirt. Use the shirt." 40

Donald pulled a long face but did as he was told, his pale skin puckering against the wind.

"Great, just great," Pete said. "We haven't even left the gas station yet."

Afterwards, on the highway, Donald said, "This is a new car, isn't it?"

"Yes. This is a new car."

"Is that why you're so upset about the seat?" 45

"Forget it, okay? Let's just forget about it."

"I said I was sorry."

Pete said, "I just wish you'd be more careful. These seats are made of leather. That stain won't come out, not to mention the smell. I don't see why I can't have leather seats that smell like leather instead of orange pop."

"What was wrong with the other car?"

Pete glanced over at Donald. Donald had raised the hood of the blue sweat- 50 shirt he'd put on. The peaked hood above his gaunt, watchful face gave him the look of an inquisitor.

"There wasn't anything wrong with it," Pete said. "I just happened to like this one better."

Donald nodded.

There was a long silence between them as Pete drove on and the day darkened toward evening. On either side of the road lay stubble-covered fields. A line of low hills ran along the horizon, topped here and there with trees black against the grey sky. In the approaching line of cars a driver turned on his headlights. Pete did the same.

"So what happened?" he asked. "Farm life not your bag?"

Donald took some time to answer, and at last he said, simply, "It was my 55 fault."

"What was your fault?"

"The whole thing. Don't play dumb, Pete. I know they wrote to you." Donald looked at Pete, then stared out the windshield again.

"I'm not playing dumb."

Donald shrugged.

"All I really know is they asked you to leave," Pete went on. "I don't know any 60 of the particulars."

"I blew it," Donald said. "Believe me, you don't want to hear the gory details."

"Sure I do," Pete said. He added, "Everybody likes the gory details."

"You mean everybody likes to hear how someone messed up."

"Right," Pete said. "That's the way it is here on Spaceship Earth."

Donald bent one knee onto the front seat and leaned against the door so that 65 he was facing Pete instead of the windshield. Pete was aware of Donald's scrutiny. He waited. Night was coming on in a rush now, filling the hollows of the land. Donald's long cheeks and deep-set eyes were dark with shadow. His brow was white. "Do you ever dream about me?" Donald asked.

"Do I ever dream about you? What kind of a question is that? Of course I don't dream about you," Pete said, untruthfully.

"What do you dream about?"

"Sex and money. Mostly money. A nightmare is when I dream I don't have any."

"You're just making that up," Donald said.

Pete smiled.

"Sometimes I wake up at night," Donald went on, "and I can tell you're dreaming about me."

"We were talking about the farm," Pete said. "Let's finish that conversation and then we can talk about our various out-of-body experiences and the interesting things we did during previous incarnations."

For a moment Donald looked like a grinning skull; then he turned serious again. "There's not much to tell," he said. "I just didn't do anything right."

"That's a little vague," Pete said.

"Well, like the groceries. Whenever it was my turn to get the groceries I'd blow it somehow. I'd bring the groceries home and half of them would be missing, or I'd have all the wrong things, the wrong kind of flour or the wrong kind of chocolate or whatever. One time I gave them away. It's not funny, Pete."

Pete said, "Who did you give the groceries to?"

"Just some people I picked up on the way home. Some fieldworkers. They had about eight kids with them and they didn't even speak English—just nodded their heads. Still, I shouldn't have given away the groceries. Not all of them, anyway. I really learned my lesson about that. You have to be practical. You have to be fair to yourself." Donald leaned forward, and Pete could sense his excitement. "There's nothing actually wrong with being in business," he said. "As long as you're fair to other people you can still be fair to yourself. I'm thinking of going into business, Pete."

"We'll talk about it," Pete said. "So, that's the story? There isn't any more to it than that?"

"What did they tell you?" Donald asked.

"Nothing."

"They must have told you something."

Pete shook his head.

"They didn't tell you about the fire?" When Pete shook his head again Donald regarded him for a time, then folded his arms across his chest and slumped back into the corner. "Everybody had to take turns cooking dinner. I usually did tuna casserole or spaghetti with garlic bread. But this one night I thought I'd do something different, something really interesting." Donald looked sharply at Pete. "It's all a big laugh to you, isn't it?"

"I'm sorry," Pete said.

"You don't know when to quit. You just keep hitting away."

"Tell me about the fire, Donald."

Donald kept watching him. "You have this compulsion to make me look foolish."

"Come off it, Donald. Don't make a big thing out of this."

"I know why you do it. It's because you don't have any purpose in life. You're afraid to relate to people who do, so you make fun of them."

"Relate," Pete said.

"You're basically a very frightened individual," Donald said. "Very threatened. You've always been like that. Do you remember when you used to try to kill me?"

"I don't have any compulsion to make you look foolish, Donald—you do it yourself. You're doing it right now."

"You can't tell me you don't remember," Donald said. "It was after my operation. You remember that?"

"Sort of." Pete shrugged. "Not really."

"Oh yes," Donald said. "Do you want to see the scar?"

"I remember you had an operation. I don't remember the specifics, that's all. And I sure as hell don't remember trying to kill you."

"Oh yes," Donald repeated, maddeningly. "You bet your life you did. All the time. The thing was, I couldn't have anything happen to me where they sewed me up because then my intestines would come apart again and poison me. That was a big issue, Pete. Mom was always in a state about me climbing trees and so on. And you used to hit me there every chance you got."

"Mom was in a state every time you burped," Pete said. "I don't know. Maybe I bumped into you accidentally once or twice. I never did it deliberately."

"Every chance you got," Donald said. "Like when the folks went out at night and left you to baby-sit. I'd hear them say good night, and then I'd hear the car start up, and when they were gone I'd lie there and listen. After a while I would hear you coming down the hall, and I would close my eyes and pretend to be asleep. There were nights when you would stand outside the door, just stand there, and then go away again. But most nights you'd open the door and I would hear you in the room with me, breathing. You'd come over and sit next to me on the bed—you remember, Pete, you have to—you'd sit next to me on the bed and pull the sheets back. If I was on my stomach you'd roll me over. Then you would lift up my pajama shirt and start hitting me on my stitches. You'd hit me as hard as you could, over and over. I was afraid that you'd get mad if you knew I was awake. Is that strange or what? I was afraid that you'd get mad if you found out that I knew you were trying to kill me." Donald laughed. "Come on, you can't tell me you don't remember that."

"It might have happened once or twice. Kids do those things. I can't get all excited about something I maybe did twenty-five years ago."

"No maybe about it. You did it."

Pete said, "You're wearing me out with this stuff. We've got a long drive ahead of us and if you don't back off pretty soon we aren't going to make it. You aren't, anyway."

Donald turned away.

"I'm doing my best," Pete said. The self-pity in his own voice made the words sound like a lie. But they weren't a lie! He was doing his best.

The car topped a rise. In the distance Pete saw a cluster of lights that blinked out when he started downhill. There was no moon. The sky was low and black.

"Come to think of it," Pete said, "I did have a dream about you the other night." Then he added, impatiently, as if Donald were badgering him, "A couple of other nights, too. I'm getting hungry," he said.

"The same dream?"

"Different dreams. I only remember one of them. There was something wrong with me, and you were helping out. Taking care of me. Just the two of us. I don't know where everyone else was supposed to be."

Pete left it at that. He didn't tell Donald that in this dream he was blind.

"I wonder if that was when I woke up," Donald said. He added, "I'm sorry I   110 got into that thing about my scar. I keep trying to forget it but I guess I never will. Not really. It was pretty strange, having someone around all the time who wanted to get rid of me."

"Kid stuff," Pete said. "Ancient history."

They ate dinner at a Denny's on the other side of King City. As Pete was paying the check he heard a man behind him say, "Excuse me, but I wonder if I might ask which way you're going?" and Donald answer, "Santa Cruz."

"Perfect," the man said.

Pete could see him in the fish-eye mirror above the cash register: a red blazer with some kind of crest on the pocket, little black moustache, glossy black hair combed down on his forehead like a Roman emperor's. A rug, Pete thought. Definitely a rug.

Pete got his change and turned. "Why is that perfect?" he asked.   115

The man looked at Pete. He had a soft, ruddy face that was doing its best to express pleasant surprise, as if this new wrinkle were all he could have wished for, but the eyes behind the aviator glasses showed signs of regret. His lips were moist and shiny. "I take it you're together," he said.

"You got it," Pete told him.

"All the better, then," the man went on. "It so happens I'm going to Santa Cruz myself. Had a spot of car trouble down the road. The old Caddy let me down."

"What kind of trouble?" Pete asked.

"Engine trouble," the man said. "I'm afraid it's a bit urgent. My daughter is sick.   120 Urgently sick. I've got a telegram here." He patted the breast pocket of his blazer.

Before Pete could say anything Donald got into the act again. "No problem," Donald said. "We've got tons of room."

"Not that much room," Pete said.

Donald nodded. "I'll put my things in the trunk."

"The trunk's full," Pete told him.

"It so happens I'm traveling light," the man said. "This leg of the trip anyway.   125 In fact, I don't have any luggage at this particular time."

Pete said, "Left it in the old Caddy, did you?"

"Exactly," the man said.

"No problem," Donald repeated. He walked outside and the man went with him. Together they strolled across the parking lot, Pete following at a distance. When they reached Pete's car Donald raised his face to the sky, and the man did the same. They stood there looking up. "Dark night," Donald said.

"Stygian," the man said.

Pete still had it in his mind to brush him off, but he didn't do that. Instead he   130
unlocked the door for him. He wanted to see what would happen. It was an
adventure, but not a dangerous adventure. The man might steal Pete's ashtrays
but he wouldn't kill him. If Pete got killed on the road it would be by some spiritual person in a sweatsuit, someone with his eyes on the far horizon and a wet Try
God T-shirt in his duffel bag.

As soon as they left the parking lot the man lit a cigar. He blew a cloud of
smoke over Pete's shoulder and sighed with pleasure. "Put it out," Pete told him.

"Of course," the man said. Pete looked in the rearview mirror and saw the
man take another long puff before dropping the cigar out the window. "Forgive
me," he said. "I should have asked. Name's Webster, by the way."

Donald turned and looked back at him. "First name or last?"

The man hesitated. "Last," he said finally.

"I know a Webster," Donald said. "Mick Webster."   135

"There are many of us," Webster said.

"Big fellow, wooden leg," Pete said.

Donald gave Pete a look.

Webster shook his head. "Doesn't ring a bell. Still, I wouldn't deny the connection. Might be one of the cousinry."

"What's your daughter got?" Pete asked.   140

"That isn't clear," Webster answered. "It appears to be a female complaint of
some nature. Then again it may be tropical." He was quiet for a moment, and
added: "If indeed it *is* tropical, I will have to assume some of the blame myself. It
was my own vaulting ambition that first led us to the tropics and kept us in the
tropics all those many years, exposed to every evil. Truly I have much to answer
for. I left my wife there."

Donald said quietly, "You mean she died?"

"I buried her with these hands. The earth will be repaid, gold for gold."

"Which tropics?" Pete asked.

"The tropics of Peru."   145

"What part of Peru are they in?"

"The lowlands," Webster said.

"What's it like down there? In the lowlands."

"Another world," Webster said. His tone was sepulchral. "A world better
imagined than described."

"Far out," Pete said.   150

The three men rode in silence for a time. A line of trucks went past in the
other direction, trailers festooned with running lights, engines roaring.

"Yes," Webster said at last, "I have much to answer for."

Pete smiled at Donald, but Donald had turned in his seat again and was gazing at Webster. "I'm sorry about your wife," Donald said.

"What did she die of?" Pete asked.

"A wasting illness," Webster said. "The doctors have no name for it, but I do."   155
He leaned forward and said, fiercely, "*Greed.* My greed, not hers. She wanted no
part of it."

Pete bit his lip. Webster was a find and Pete didn't want to scare him off by hooting at him. In a voice low and innocent of knowingness, he asked, "What took you there?"

"It's difficult for me to talk about."

"Try," Pete told him.

"A cigar would make it easier."

Donald turned to Pete and said, "It's okay with me."   160

"All right," Pete said. "Go ahead. Just keep the window rolled down."

"Much obliged." A match flared. There were eager sucking sounds.

"Let's hear it," Pete said.

"I am by training an engineer," Webster began. "My work has exposed me to all but one of the continents, to desert and alp and forest, to every terrain and season of the earth. Some years ago I was hired by the Peruvian government to search for tungsten in the tropics. My wife and daughter accompanied me. We were the only white people for a thousand miles in any direction, and we had no choice but to live as the Indians lived—to share their food and drink and even their culture."

Pete said, "You knew the lingo, did you?"   165

"We picked it up." The ember of the cigar bobbed up and down. "We were used to learning as necessity decreed. At any rate, it became evident after a couple of years that there was no tungsten to be found. My wife had fallen ill and was pleading to be taken home. But I was deaf to her pleas, because by then I was on the trail of another metal—a metal far more valuable than tungsten."

"Let me guess," Pete said. "Gold?"

Donald looked at Pete, then back at Webster.

"Gold," Webster said. "A vein of gold greater than the Mother Lode itself. After I found the first traces of it nothing could tear me away from my search—not the sickness of my wife or anything else. I was determined to uncover the vein, and so I did—but not before I laid my wife to rest. As I say, the earth will be repaid."

Webster was quiet. Then he said, "But life must go on. In the years since my   170
wife's death I have been making the arrangements necessary to open the mine. I could have done it immediately, of course, enriching myself beyond measure, but I knew what that would mean—the exploitation of our beloved Indians, the brutal destruction of their environment. I felt I had too much to atone for already." Webster paused, and when he spoke again his voice was dull and rushed, as if he had used up all the interest he had in his own words. "Instead I drew up a program for returning the bulk of the wealth to the Indians themselves. A kind of trust fund. The interest alone will allow them to secure their ancient lands and rights in perpetuity. At the same time, our investors will be rewarded a thousandfold. Two-thousandfold. Everyone will prosper together."

"That's great," said Donald. "That's the way it ought to be."

Pete said, "I'm willing to bet that you just happen to have a few shares left. Am I right?"

Webster made no reply.

"Well?" Pete knew that Webster was on to him now, but he didn't care. The story had bored him. He'd expected something different, something original, and

Webster had let him down. He hadn't even tried. Pete felt sour and stale. His eyes
burned from cigar smoke and the high beams of road-hogging truckers. "Douse
the stogie," he said to Webster. "I told you to keep the window down."

"Got a little nippy back here."   175

Donald said, "Hey, Pete. Lighten up."

"Douse it!"

Webster sighed. He got rid of the cigar.

"I'm a wreck," Pete said to Donald. "You want to drive for a while?"

Donald nodded.   180

Pete pulled over and they changed places.

Webster kept his counsel in the back seat. Donald hummed while he drove,
until Pete told him to stop. Then everything was quiet.

Donald was humming again when Pete woke up. Pete stared sullenly at the
road, at the white lines sliding past the car. After a few moments of this he turned
and said, "How long have I been out?"

Donald glanced at him. "Twenty, twenty-five minutes."

Pete looked behind him and saw that Webster was gone. "Where's our   185
friend?"

"You just missed him. He got out in Soledad. He told me to say thanks and
good-bye."

"Soledad? What about his sick daughter? How did he explain her away?"

"He has a brother living there. He's going to borrow a car from him and drive
the rest of the way in the morning."

"I'll bet his brother's living there," Pete said. "Doing fifty concurrent life sentences. His brother and his sister and his mom and his dad."

"I kind of liked him," Donald said.   190

"I'm sure you did," Pete said wearily.

"He was interesting. He's been places."

"His cigars had been places, I'll give you that."

"Come on, Pete."

"Come on yourself. What a phony."   195

"You don't know that."

"Sure I do."

"How? How do you know?"

Pete stretched. "Brother, there are some things you're just born knowing.
What's the gas situation?"

"We're a little low."   200

"Then why didn't you get some more?"

"I wish you wouldn't snap at me like that," Donald said.

"Then why don't you use your head? What if we run out?"

"We'll make it," Donald said. "I'm pretty sure we've got enough to make it.
You didn't have to be so rude to him," Donald added.

Pete took a deep breath. "I don't feel like running out of gas tonight, okay?"   205

Donald pulled in at the next station they came to and filled the tank while
Pete went to the men's room. When Pete came back, Donald was sitting in the

passenger's seat. The attendant came up to the driver's window as Pete got in behind the wheel. He bent down and said, "Twelve fifty-five."

"You heard the man," Pete said to Donald.

Donald looked straight ahead. He didn't move.

"Cough up," Pete said. "This trip's on you."

"I can't."   210

"Sure you can. Break out that wad."

Donald glanced up at the attendant, then at Pete. "Please," he said, "Pete, I don't have it anymore."

Pete took this in. He nodded, and paid the attendant.

Donald began to speak when they left the station but Pete cut him off. He said, "I don't want to hear from you right now. You just keep quiet or I swear to God I won't be responsible."

They left the fields and entered a tunnel of tall trees. The trees went on and   215 on. "Let me get this straight," Pete said at last. "You don't have the money I gave you."

"You treated him like a bug or something," Donald said.

"You don't have the money," Pete said again.

Donald shook his head.

"Since I bought dinner, and since we didn't stop anywhere in between, I assume you gave it to Webster. Is that right? Is that what you did with it?"

"Yes."   220

Pete looked at Donald. His face was dark under the hood but he still managed to convey a sense of remove, as if none of this had anything to do with him.

"Why?" Pete asked. "Why did you give it to him?" When Donald didn't answer, Pete said, "A hundred dollars. Gone. Just like that. I *worked* for that money, Donald."

"I know, I know," Donald said.

"You don't know! How could you? You get money by holding out your hand."

"I work too," Donald said.   225

"You work too. Don't kid yourself, brother."

Donald leaned toward Pete, about to say something, but Pete cut him off again.

"You're not the only one on the payroll, Donald. I don't think you understand that. I have a family."

"Pete, I'll pay you back."

"Like hell you will. A hundred dollars!" Pete hit the steering wheel with the   230 palm of his hand. "Just because you think I hurt some goofball's feelings. Jesus, Donald."

"That's not the reason," Donald said. "And I didn't just *give* him the money."

"What do you call it, then? What do you call what you did?"

"I *invested* it. I wanted a share, Pete." When Pete looked over at him Donald nodded and said again, "I wanted a share."

Pete said, "I take it you're referring to the gold mine in Peru."

"Yes," Donald said.   235

"You believe that such a gold mine exists?"

Donald looked at Pete, and Pete could see him just beginning to catch on. "You'll believe anything," Pete said. "Won't you? You really will believe anything at all."

"I'm sorry," Donald said, and turned away.

Pete drove on between the trees and considered the truth of what he had just said—that Donald would believe anything at all. And it came to him that it would be just like this unfair life for Donald to come out ahead in the end, by believing in some outrageous promise that would turn out to be true and that he, Pete, would reject out of hand because he was too wised up to listen to anybody's pitch anymore except for laughs. What a joke. What a joke if there really was a blessing to be had, and the blessing didn't come to the one who deserved it, the one who did all the work, but to the other.

And as if this had already happened Pete felt a shadow move upon him, dark-   240
ening his thoughts. After a time he said, "I can see where all this is going, Donald."

"I'll pay you back," Donald said.

"No," Pete said. "You won't pay me back. You can't. You don't know how. All you've ever done is take. All your life."

Donald shook his head.

"I see exactly where this is going," Pete went on. "You can't work, you can't take care of yourself, you believe anything anyone tells you. I'm stuck with you, aren't I?" He looked over at Donald. "I've got you on my hands for good."

Donald pressed his fingers against the dashboard as if to brace himself. "I'll   245
get out," he said.

Pete kept driving.

"Let me out," Donald said. "I mean it, Pete."

"Do you?"

Donald hesitated. "Yes," he said.

"Be sure," Pete told him. "This is it. This is for keeps."   250

"I mean it."

"All right. You made the choice." Pete braked the car sharply and swung it to the shoulder of the road. He turned off the engine and got out. Trees loomed on both sides, shutting out the sky. The air was cold and musty. Pete took Donald's duffel bag from the back seat and set it down behind the car. He stood there, fac-ing Donald in the red glow of the taillights. "It's better this way," Pete said.

Donald just looked at him.

"Better for you," Pete said.

Donald hugged himself. He was shaking. "You don't have to say all that," he   255
told Pete. "I don't blame you."

"Blame me? What the hell are you talking about? Blame me for what?"

"For anything," Donald said.

"I want to know what you mean by blame me."

"Nothing. Nothing, Pete. You'd better get going. God bless you."

"That's it," Pete said. He dropped to one knee, searching the packed dirt with   260
his hands. He didn't know what he was looking for, his hands would know when
they found it.

Donald touched Pete's shoulder. "You'd better go," he said.

Somewhere in the trees Pete heard a branch snap. He stood up. He looked at
Donald, then went back to the car and drove away. He drove fast, hunched over
the wheel, conscious of the way he was hunched and the shallowness of his
breathing, refusing to look in the mirror above his head until there was nothing
behind him but darkness.

Then he said, "A hundred dollars," as if there were someone to hear.

The trees gave way to fields. Metal fences ran beside the road, plastered with
windblown scraps of paper. Tule fog hung above the ditches, spilling into the
road, dimming the ghostly halogen lights that burned in the yards of the farms
Pete passed. The fog left beads of water rolling up the windshield.

Pete rummaged among his cassettes. He found Pachelbel's Canon and   265
pushed it into the tape deck. When the violins began to play he leaned back and
assumed an attentive expression as if he were really listening to them. He smiled
to himself like a man at liberty to enjoy music, a man who has finished his work
and settled his debts, done all things meet and due.

And in this way, smiling, nodding to the music, he went another mile or so
and pretended that he was not already slowing down, that he was not going to
turn back, that he would be able to drive on like this, alone, and have the right
answer when his wife stood before him in the doorway of his home and asked,
Where is he? Where is your brother?   [1985]

THINKING ABOUT THE TEXT

1. Are you more sympathetic to Donald's side or to Pete's side in this story?
   Do you agree with the comment that "everybody likes to hear how someone messed up" (para. 63)? Does Donald get conned by Webster? Would
   you be angry with Donald for giving Webster your money? Does Pete
   want Donald to look foolish? Is Donald foolish?

2. How do you interpret Donald's story about Pete hitting his stitches? Is
   Pete trying to get rid of Donald? What could his reason be?

3. Why doesn't Pete tell Donald he was blind in his dream? How do you
   interpret this dream? Is the heart of their dispute "prosperity," or is it
   something else?

4. Your response to the Webster episode might say something about your
   own level of credulity. Were you skeptical of Webster from the first?
   Would you have given him a ride? Will Donald believe "anything" (para.
   237)? Is it sometimes a good thing to be skeptical? Is it sometimes a good
   thing to believe in "some outrageous promise" (para. 239)?

5. Why would Pete turn around to get Donald? Why would he keep going?
   What would you do? Why?

JAMES BALDWIN
Sonny's Blues

James Baldwin (1924–1987) wanted to be a writer since he was a boy growing up in Harlem. He continued his writing through high school while also following in his foster father's footsteps by doing some preaching. On his own since he was eighteen, Baldwin left Greenwich Village in 1948 and moved to Paris. He lived in France for eight years before returning to New York, where he wrote widely about the civil rights movement. Indeed, passionate and eloquent essays like those in Notes of a Native Son *(1955) and* The Fire Next Time *(1963) exploring the place of African Americans in contemporary society are considered among the best nonfiction of Baldwin's generation.*

Being an artist and an African American were lifelong central issues for Baldwin. His fiction confronts the psychological challenges that were inevitable for black writers searching for identity in America. Themes of responsibility, pain, identity, frustration, and bitterness are woven into his fiction along with understanding, equanimity, love, and tolerance. "Sonny's Blues," from Going to Meet the Man *(1965), is one of his strongest dramatizations of the struggles and achievements of black artists.*

I read about it in the paper, in the subway, on my way to work. I read it, and I couldn't believe it, and I read it again. Then perhaps I just stared at it, at the newsprint spelling out his name, spelling out the story. I stared at it in the swinging lights of the subway car, and in the faces and bodies of the people, and in my own face, trapped in the darkness which roared outside.

It was not to be believed and I kept telling myself that, as I walked from the subway station to the high school. And at the same time I couldn't doubt it. I was scared, scared for Sonny. He became real to me again. A great block of ice got settled in my belly and kept melting there slowly all day long, while I taught my classes algebra. It was a special kind of ice. It kept melting, sending trickles of ice water all up and down my veins, but it never got less. Sometimes it hardened and seemed to expand until I felt my guts were going to come spilling out or that I was going to choke or scream. This would always be at a moment when I was remembering some specific thing Sonny had once said or done.

When he was about as old as the boys in my classes his face had been bright and open, there was a lot of copper in it; and he'd had wonderfully direct brown eyes, and great gentleness and privacy. I wondered what he looked like now. He had been picked up, the evening before, in a raid on an apartment downtown, for peddling and using heroin.

I couldn't believe it: but what I mean by that is that I couldn't find any room for it anywhere inside me. I had kept it outside me for a long time. I hadn't wanted to know. I had had suspicions, but I didn't name them, I kept putting them away. I told myself that Sonny was wild, but he wasn't crazy. And he'd always been a good boy, he hadn't ever turned hard or evil or disrespectful, the way kids can, so quick, so quick, especially in Harlem. I didn't want to believe that I'd ever see my brother going down, coming to nothing, all that light in his face gone out, in the condition I'd already seen so many others. Yet it had happened and here I was, talking about algebra to a lot of boys who might, every one of them for all I knew, be popping off needles every time they went to the head. Maybe it did more for them than algebra could.

I was sure that the first time Sonny had ever had horse, he couldn't have 5
been much older than these boys were now. These boys, now, were living as we'd been living then, they were growing up with a rush and their heads bumped abruptly against the low ceiling of their actual possibilities. They were filled with rage. All they really knew were two darknesses, the darkness of their lives, which was now closing in on them, and the darkness of the movies, which had blinded them to that other darkness, and in which they now, vindictively, dreamed, at once more together than they were at any other time, and more alone.

When the last bell rang, the last class ended, I let out my breath. It seemed I'd been holding it for all that time. My clothes were wet — I may have looked as though I'd been sitting in a steam bath, all dressed up, all afternoon. I sat alone in the classroom a long time. I listened to the boys outside, downstairs, shouting and cursing and laughing. Their laughter struck me for perhaps the first time. It was not the joyous laughter which — God knows why — one associates with children. It was mocking and insular, its intent to denigrate. It was disenchanted, and in this, also, lay the authority of their curses. Perhaps I was listening to them because I was thinking about my brother and in them I heard my brother. And myself.

One boy was whistling a tune, at once very complicated and very simple, it seemed to be pouring out of him as though he were a bird, and it sounded very cool and moving through all that harsh, bright air, only just holding its own through all those other sounds.

I stood up and walked over to the window and looked down into the courtyard. It was the beginning of the spring and the sap was rising in the boys. A teacher passed through them every now and again, quickly, as though he or she couldn't wait to get out of that courtyard, to get those boys out of their sight and off their minds. I started collecting my stuff. I thought I'd better get home and talk to Isabel.

The courtyard was almost deserted by the time I got downstairs. I saw this boy standing in the shadow of a doorway, looking just like Sonny. I almost called his name. Then I saw that it wasn't Sonny, but somebody we used to know, a boy from around our block. He'd been Sonny's friend. He'd never been mine, having been too young for me, and, anyway, I'd never liked him. And now, even though he was a grown-up man, he still hung around that block, still spent hours on the street corners, was always high and raggy. I used to run into him from time to time and he'd often work around to asking me for a quarter or fifty cents. He always had some real good excuse, too, and I always gave it to him, I don't know why.

But now, abruptly, I hated him. I couldn't stand the way he looked at me, 10
partly like a dog, partly like a cunning child. I wanted to ask him what the hell he was doing in the school courtyard.

He sort of shuffled over to me, and he said, "I see you got the papers. So you already know about it."

"You mean about Sonny? Yes, I already know about it. How come they didn't get you?"

He grinned. It made him repulsive and it also brought to mind what he'd looked like as a kid. "I wasn't there. I stay away from them people."

"Good for you." I offered him a cigarette and I watched him through the smoke. "You come all the way down here just to tell me about Sonny?"

"That's right." He was sort of shaking his head and his eyes looked strange, as 15
though they were about to cross. The bright sun deadened his damp dark brown skin and it made his eyes look yellow and showed up the dirt in his kinked hair. He smelled funky. I moved a little away from him and I said, "Well, thanks. But I already know about it and I got to get home."

"I'll walk you a little ways," he said. We started walking. There were a couple of kids still loitering in the courtyard and one of them said goodnight to me and looked strangely at the boy beside me.

"What're you going to do?" he asked me. "I mean, about Sonny?"

"Look. I haven't seen Sonny for over a year. I'm not sure I'm going to do anything. Anyway, what the hell *can* I do?"

"That's right," he said quickly, "ain't nothing you can do. Can't much help old Sonny no more, I guess."

It was what I was thinking and so it seemed to me he had no right to say it. 20

"I'm surprised at Sonny, though," he went on — he had a funny way of talking, he looked straight ahead as though he were talking to himself — "I thought Sonny was a smart boy, I thought he was too smart to get hung."

"I guess he thought so too," I said sharply, "and that's how he got hung. And now about you? You're pretty goddamn smart, I bet."

Then he looked directly at me, just for a minute. "I ain't smart," he said. "If I was smart, I'd have reached for a pistol a long time ago."

"Look. Don't tell *me* your sad story, if it was up to me, I'd give you one." Then I felt guilty — guilty, probably, for never having supposed that the poor bastard *had* a story of his own, much less a sad one, and I asked, quickly, "What's going to happen to him now?"

He didn't answer this. He was off by himself some place. "Funny thing," he 25
said, and from his tone we might have been discussing the quickest way to get to Brooklyn, "when I saw the papers this morning, the first thing I asked myself was if I had anything to do with it. I felt sort of responsible."

I began to listen more carefully. The subway station was on the corner, just before us, and I stopped. He stopped, too. We were in front of a bar and he ducked slightly, peering in, but whoever he was looking for didn't seem to be there. The juke box was blasting away with something black and bouncy and I half watched the barmaid as she danced her way from the juke box to her place behind the bar. And I watched her face as she laughingly responded to something someone said to her, still keeping time to the music. When she smiled one saw the little girl, one sensed the doomed, still-struggling woman beneath the battered face of the semi-whore.

"I never *give* Sonny nothing," the boy said finally, "but a long time ago I come to school high and Sonny asked me how it felt." He paused, I couldn't bear to watch

him, I watched the barmaid, and I listened to the music which seemed to be causing the pavement to shake. "I told him it felt great." The music stopped, the barmaid paused and watched the juke box until the music began again. "It did."

All this was carrying me some place I didn't want to go. I certainly didn't
want to know how it felt. It filled everything, the people, the houses, the music,
the dark, quicksilver barmaid, with menace; and this menace was their reality.

"What's going to happen to him now?" I asked again.

"They'll send him away some place and they'll try to cure him." He shook his   30
head. "Maybe he'll even think he's kicked the habit. Then they'll let him
loose" — he gestured, throwing his cigarette into the gutter. "That's all."

"What do you mean, that's *all*?"

But I knew what he meant.

"I *mean*, that's *all*." He turned his head and looked at me, pulling down the
corners of his mouth. "Don't you know what I mean?" he asked, softly.

"How the hell *would* I know what you mean?" I almost whispered it, I don't
know why.

"That's right," he said to the air, "how would *he* know what I mean?" He   35
turned toward me again, patient and calm, and yet I somehow felt him shaking,
shaking as though he were going to fall apart. I felt that ice in my guts again, the
dread I'd felt all afternoon; and again I watched the barmaid, moving about the
bar, washing glasses, and singing. "Listen. They'll let him out and then it'll just
start all over again. That's what I mean."

"You mean — they'll let him out. And then he'll just start working his way
back in again. You mean he'll never kick the habit. Is that what you mean?"

"That's right," he said, cheerfully. "*You* see what I mean."

"Tell me," I said at last, "why does he want to die? He must want to die, he's
killing himself, why does he want to die?"

He looked at me in surprise. He licked his lips. "He don't want to die. He
wants to live. Don't nobody want to die, ever."

Then I wanted to ask him — too many things. He could not have answered,   40
or if he had, I could not have borne the answers. I started walking. "Well, I guess
it's none of my business."

"It's going to be rough on old Sonny," he said. We reached the subway station. "This is your station?" he asked. I nodded. I took one step down. "Damn!"
he said, suddenly. I looked up at him. He grinned again. "Damn it if I didn't
leave all my money home. You ain't got a dollar on you, have you? Just for a
couple of days, is all."

All at once something inside gave and threatened to come pouring out of
me. I didn't hate him any more. I felt that in another moment I'd start crying like
a child.

"Sure," I said. "Don't sweat." I looked in my wallet and didn't have a dollar, I
only had a five. "Here," I said. "That hold you?"

He didn't look at it — he didn't want to look at it. A terrible closed look came
over his face, as though he were keeping the number on the bill a secret from
him and me. "Thanks," he said, and now he was dying to see me go. "Don't worry
about Sonny. Maybe I'll write him or something."

"Sure," I said. "You do that. So long."   45
"Be seeing you," he said. I went on down the steps.

And I didn't write Sonny or send him anything for a long time. When I
finally did, it was just after my little girl died, he wrote me back a letter which
made me feel like a bastard.

Here's what he said:

> Dear brother,
> You don't know how much I needed to hear from you. I wanted to write
> you many a time but I dug how much I must have hurt you and so I didn't
> write. But now I feel like a man who's been trying to climb up out of some
> deep, real deep and funky hole and just saw the sun up there, outside. I got
> to get outside.
> I can't tell you much about how I got here. I mean I don't know how to
> tell you. I guess I was afraid of something or I was trying to escape from
> something and you know I have never been very strong in the head (smile).
> I'm glad Mama and Daddy are dead and can't see what's happened to their
> son and I swear if I'd known what I was doing I would never have hurt you
> so, you and a lot of other fine people who were nice to me and who believed
> in me.
> I don't want you to think it had anything to do with me being a musi-
> cian. It's more than that. Or maybe less than that. I can't get anything
> straight in my head down here and I try not to think about what's going to
> happen to me when I get outside again. Sometime I think I'm going to flip
> and *never* get outside and sometime I think I'll come straight back. I tell you
> one thing, though, I'd rather blow my brains out than go through this again.
> But that's what they all say, so they tell me. If I tell you when I'm coming to
> New York and if you could meet me, I sure would appreciate it. Give my
> love to Isabel and the kids and I was sure sorry to hear about little Gracie. I
> wish I could be like Mama and say the Lord's will be done, but I don't know
> it seems to me that trouble is the one thing that never does get stopped and I
> don't know what good it does to blame it on the Lord. But maybe it does
> some good if you believe it.
>
> > Your brother,
> > Sonny

Then I kept in constant touch with him and I sent him whatever I could and
I went to meet him when he came back to New York. When I saw him many
things I thought I had forgotten came flooding back to me. This was because I
had begun, finally, to wonder about Sonny, about the life that Sonny lived inside.
This life, whatever it was, had made him older and thinner and it had deepened
the distant stillness in which he had always moved. He looked very unlike my
baby brother. Yet, when he smiled, when we shook hands, the baby brother I'd
never known looked out from the depths of his private life, like an animal waiting
to be coaxed into the light.

"How you been keeping?" he asked me.   50
"All right. And you?"
"Just fine." He was smiling all over his face. "It's good to see you again."

"It's good to see you."

The seven years' difference in our ages lay between us like a chasm: I wondered if these years would ever operate between us as a bridge. I was remembering, and it made it hard to catch my breath, that I had been there when he was born; and I had heard the first words he had ever spoken. When he started to walk, he walked from our mother straight to me. I caught him just before he fell when he took the first steps he ever took in this world.

"How's Isabel?"   55

"Just fine. She's dying to see you."

"And the boys?"

"They're fine, too. They're anxious to see their uncle."

"Oh, come on. You know they don't remember me."

"Are you kidding? Of course they remember you."   60

He grinned again. We got into a taxi. We had a lot to say to each other, far too much to know how to begin.

As the taxi began to move, I asked, "You still want to go to India?"

He laughed. "You still remember that. Hell, no. This place is Indian enough for me."

"It used to belong to them," I said.

And he laughed again. "They damn sure knew what they were doing when   65
they got rid of it."

Years ago, when he was around fourteen, he'd been all hipped on the idea of going to India. He read books about people sitting on rocks, naked, in all kinds of weather, but mostly bad, naturally, and walking barefoot through hot coals and arriving at wisdom. I used to say that it sounded to me as though they were getting away from wisdom as fast as they could. I think he sort of looked down on me for that.

"Do you mind," he asked, "if we have the driver drive alongside the park? On the west side — I haven't seen the city in so long."

"Of course not," I said. I was afraid that I might sound as though I were humoring him, but I hoped he wouldn't take it that way.

So we drove along, between the green of the park and the stony, lifeless elegance of hotels and apartment buildings, toward the vivid, killing streets of our childhood. These streets hadn't changed, though housing projects jutted up out of them now like rocks in the middle of a boiling sea. Most of the houses in which we had grown up had vanished, as had the stores from which we had stolen, the basements in which we had first tried sex, the rooftops from which we had hurled tin cans and bricks. But houses exactly like the houses of our past yet dominated the landscape, boys exactly like the boys we once had been found themselves smothering in these houses, came down into the streets for light and air and found themselves encircled by disaster. Some escaped the trap, most didn't. Those who got out always left something of themselves behind, as some animals amputate a leg and leave it in the trap. It might be said, perhaps, that I had escaped, after all, I was a school teacher; or that Sonny had, he hadn't lived in Harlem for years. Yet, as the cab moved uptown through streets which seemed, with a rush, to darken with dark people, and as I covertly studied Sonny's face, it came to me that what we both were seeking through our separate cab windows was that part of ourselves which had been left behind. It's always at the hour of trouble and confrontation that the missing member aches.

We hit 110th Street and started rolling up Lenox Avenue. And I'd known this avenue all my life, but it seemed to me again, as it had seemed on the day I'd first heard about Sonny's trouble, filled with a hidden menace which was its very breath of life.

"We almost there," said Sonny.

"Almost." We were both too nervous to say anything more.

We live in a housing project. It hasn't been up long. A few days after it was up it seemed uninhabitably new, now, of course, it's already rundown. It looks like a parody of the good, clean, faceless life—God knows the people who live in it do their best to make it a parody. The beat-looking grass lying around isn't enough to make their lives green, the hedges will never hold out the streets, and they know it. The big windows fool no one, they aren't big enough to make space out of no space. They don't bother with the windows, they watch the TV screen instead. The playground is most popular with the children who don't play at jacks, or skip rope, or roller skate, or swing, and they can be found in it after dark. We moved in partly because it's not too far from where I teach, and partly for the kids; but it's really just like the houses in which Sonny and I grew up. The same things happen, they'll have the same things to remember. The moment Sonny and I started into the house I had the feeling that I was simply bringing him back into the danger he had almost died trying to escape.

Sonny has never been talkative. So I don't know why I was sure he'd be dying to talk to me when supper was over the first night. Everything went fine, the oldest boy remembered him, and the youngest boy liked him, and Sonny had remembered to bring something for each of them; and Isabel, who is really much nicer than I am, more open and giving, had gone to a lot of trouble about dinner and was genuinely glad to see him. And she's always been able to tease Sonny in a way that I haven't. It was nice to see her face so vivid again and to hear her laugh and watch her make Sonny laugh. She wasn't, or, anyway, she didn't seem to be, at all uneasy or embarrassed. She chatted as though there were no subject which had to be avoided and she got Sonny past his first, faint stiffness. And thank God she was there, for I was filled with that icy dread again. Everything I did seemed awkward to me, and everything I said sounded freighted with hidden meaning. I was trying to remember everything I'd heard about dope addiction and I couldn't help watching Sonny for signs. I wasn't doing it out of malice. I was trying to find out something about my brother. I was dying to hear him tell me he was safe.

"Safe!" my father grunted, whenever Mama suggested trying to move to a neighborhood which might be safer for children. "Safe, hell! Ain't no place safe for kids, nor nobody."

He always went on like this, but he wasn't, ever, really as bad as he sounded, not even on weekends, when he got drunk. As a matter of fact, he was always on the lookout for "something a little better," but he died before he found it. He died suddenly, during a drunken weekend in the middle of the war, when Sonny was fifteen. He and Sonny hadn't ever got on too well. And this was partly because

70

75

Sonny was the apple of his father's eye. It was because he loved Sonny so much and was frightened for him, that he was always fighting with him. It doesn't do any good to fight with Sonny. Sonny just moves back, inside himself, where he can't be reached. But the principal reason that they never hit it off is that they were so much alike. Daddy was big and rough and loud-talking, just the opposite of Sonny, but they both had — that same privacy.

Mama tried to tell me something about this, just after Daddy died. I was home on leave from the army.

This was the last time I ever saw my mother alive. Just the same, this picture gets all mixed up in my mind with pictures I had of her when she was younger. The way I always see her is the way she used to be on a Sunday afternoon, say, when the old folks were talking after the big Sunday dinner. I always see her wearing pale blue. She'd be sitting on the sofa. And my father would be sitting in the easy chair, not far from her. And the living room would be full of church folks and relatives. There they sit, in chairs all around the living room, and the night is creeping up outside, but nobody knows it yet. You can see the darkness growing against the windowpanes and you hear the street noises every now and again, or maybe the jangling beat of a tambourine from one of the churches close by, but it's real quiet in the room. For a moment nobody's talking, but every face looks darkening, like the sky outside. And my mother rocks a little from the waist, and my father's eyes are closed. Everyone is looking at something a child can't see. For a minute they've forgotten the children. Maybe a kid is lying on the rug, half asleep. Maybe somebody's got a kid in his lap and is absent-mindedly stroking the kid's head. Maybe there's a kid, quiet and big-eyed, curled up in a big chair in the corner. The silence, the darkness coming, and the darkness in the faces frightens the child obscurely. He hopes that the hand which strokes his forehead will never stop — will never die. He hopes that there will never come a time when the old folks won't be sitting around the living room, talking about where they've come from, and what they've seen, and what's happened to them and their kinfolk.

But something deep and watchful in the child knows that this is bound to end, is already ending. In a moment someone will get up and turn on the light. Then the old folks will remember the children and they won't talk any more that day. And when light fills the room, the child is filled with darkness. He knows that every time this happens he's moved just a little closer to that darkness outside. The darkness outside is what the old folks have been talking about. It's what they've come from. It's what they endure. The child knows that they won't talk any more because if he knows too much about what's happened to *them*, he'll know too much too soon, about what's going to happen to *him*.

The last time I talked to my mother, I remember I was restless. I wanted to get out and see Isabel. We weren't married then and we had a lot to straighten out between us.   80

There Mama sat, in black, by the window. She was humming an old church song, *Lord, you brought me from a long ways off.* Sonny was out somewhere. Mama kept watching the streets.

"I don't know," she said, "if I'll ever see you again, after you go off from here. But I hope you'll remember the things I tried to teach you."

"Don't talk like that," I said, and smiled. "You'll be here a long time yet."

She smiled, too, but she said nothing. She was quiet for a long time. And I said, "Mama, don't you worry about nothing. I'll be writing all the time, and you be getting the checks. . . ."

"I want to talk to you about your brother," she said, suddenly. "If anything happens to me he ain't going to have nobody to look out for him."   85

"Mama," I said, "ain't nothing going to happen to you *or* Sonny. Sonny's all right. He's a good boy and he's got good sense."

"It ain't a question of his being a good boy," Mama said, "nor of his having good sense. It ain't only the bad ones, nor yet the dumb ones that gets sucked under." She stopped, looking at me. "Your Daddy once had a brother," she said, and she smiled in a way that made me feel she was in pain. "You didn't never know that, did you?"

"No," I said, "I never knew that," and I watched her face.

"Oh, yes," she said, "your Daddy had a brother." She looked out of the window again. "I know you never saw your Daddy cry. But *I* did — many a time, through all these years."

I asked her, "What happened to his brother? How come nobody's ever talked   90 about him?"

This was the first time I ever saw my mother look old.

"His brother got killed," she said, "when he was just a little younger than you are now. I knew him. He was a fine boy. He was maybe a little full of the devil, but he didn't mean nobody no harm."

Then she stopped and the room was silent, exactly as it had sometimes been on those Sunday afternoons. Mama kept looking out into the streets.

"He used to have a job in the mill," she said, "and, like all young folks, he just liked to perform on Saturday nights. Saturday nights, him and your father would drift around to different places, go to dances and things like that, or just sit around with people they knew, and your father's brother would sing, he had a fine voice, and play along with himself on his guitar. Well, this particular Saturday night, him and your father was coming home from some place, and they were both a little drunk and there was a moon that night, it was bright like day. Your father's brother was feeling kind of good, and he was whistling to himself, and he had his guitar slung over his shoulder. They was coming down a hill and beneath them was a road that turned off from the highway. Well, your father's brother, being always kind of frisky, decided to run down this hill, and he did, with that guitar banging and clanging behind him, and he ran across the road, and he was making water behind a tree. And your father was sort of amused at him and he was still coming down the hill, kind of slow. Then he heard a car motor and that same minute his brother stepped from behind the tree, into the road, in the moonlight. And he started to cross the road. And your father started to run down the hill, he says he don't know why. This car was full of white men. They was all drunk, and when they seen your father's brother they let out a great whoop and holler and they aimed the car straight at him. They was having fun, they just wanted to scare him, the way they do sometimes, you know. But they was drunk. And I guess the boy, being drunk, too, and scared, kind of lost his head. By the time he jumped it was too late. Your father says he heard his brother scream when the car rolled over him, and he heard the wood of that guitar when it give, and he heard them strings go flying, and he heard them white men shouting, and the car kept on a-going and it ain't stopped till this day. And, time your father got down the hill, his brother weren't nothing but blood and pulp."

Tears were gleaming on my mother's face. There wasn't anything I could say.   95

"He never mentioned it," she said, "because I never let him mention it before you children. Your Daddy was like a crazy man that night and for many a night thereafter. He says he never in his life seen anything as dark as that road after the lights of that car had gone away. Weren't nothing, weren't nobody on that road, just your Daddy and his brother and that busted guitar. Oh, yes. Your Daddy never did really get right again. Till the day he died he weren't sure but that every white man he saw was the man that killed his brother."

She stopped and took out her handkerchief and dried her eyes and looked at me.

"I ain't telling you all this," she said, "to make you scared or bitter or to make you hate nobody. I'm telling you this because you got a brother. And the world ain't changed."

I guess I didn't want to believe this. I guess she saw this in my face. She turned away from me, toward the window again, searching those streets.

"But I praise my Redeemer," she said at last, "that He called your Daddy   100
home before me. I ain't saying it to throw no flowers at myself, but, I declare, it keeps me from feeling too cast down to know I helped your father get safely through this world. Your father always acted like he was the roughest, strongest man on earth. And everybody took him to be like that. But if he hadn't had *me* there — to see his tears!"

She was crying again. Still, I couldn't move. I said, "Lord, Lord, Mama, I didn't know it was like that."

"Oh, honey," she said, "there's a lot that you don't know. But you are going to find it out." She stood up from the window and came over to me. "You got to hold on to your brother," she said, "and don't let him fall, no matter what it looks like is happening to him and no matter how evil you gets with him. You going to be evil with him many a time. But don't you forget what I told you, you hear?"

"I won't forget," I said. "Don't you worry, I won't forget. I won't let nothing happen to Sonny."

My mother smiled as though she were amused at something she saw in my face. Then, "You may not be able to stop nothing from happening. But you got to let him know you's *there*."

Two days later I was married, and then I was gone. And I had a lot of things   105
on my mind and I pretty well forgot my promise to Mama until I got shipped home on a special furlough for her funeral.

And, after the funeral, with just Sonny and me alone in the empty kitchen, I tried to find out something about him.

"What do you want to do?" I asked him.

"I'm going to be a musician," he said.

For he had graduated, in the time I had been away, from dancing to the juke box to finding out who was playing what, and what they were doing with it, and he had bought himself a set of drums.

"You mean, you want to be a drummer?" I somehow had the feeling that being a drummer might be all right for other people but not for my brother Sonny. 110

"I don't think," he said, looking at me very gravely, "that I'll ever be a good drummer. But I think I can play a piano."

I frowned. I'd never played the role of the older brother quite so seriously before, had scarcely ever, in fact, *asked* Sonny a damn thing. I sensed myself in the presence of something I didn't really know how to handle, didn't understand. So I made my frown a little deeper as I asked: "What kind of musician do you want to be?"

He grinned. "How many kinds do you think there are?"

"Be *serious*," I said.

He laughed, throwing his head back, and then looked at me. "I *am* serious." 115

"Well, then, for Christ's sake, stop kidding around and answer a serious question. I mean, do you want to be a concert pianist, you want to play classical music and all that, or — or what?" Long before I finished he was laughing again. "For Christ's *sake*, Sonny!"

He sobered, but with difficulty. "I'm sorry. But you sound so — *scared!*" and he was off again.

"Well, you may think it's funny now, baby, but it's not going to be so funny when you have to make your living at it, let me tell you *that*." I was furious because I knew he was laughing at me and I didn't know why.

"No," he said, very sober now, and afraid, perhaps, that he'd hurt me, "I don't want to be a classical pianist. That isn't what interests me. I mean" — he paused, looking hard at me, as though his eyes would help me to understand, and then gestured helplessly, as though perhaps his hand would help — "I mean, I'll have a lot of studying to do, and I'll have to study *everything*, but, I mean, I want to play *with* — jazz musicians." He stopped. "I want to play jazz," he said.

Well, the word had never before sounded as heavy, as real, as it sounded that afternoon in Sonny's mouth. I just looked at him and I was probably frowning a real frown by this time. I simply couldn't see why on earth he'd want to spend his time hanging around nightclubs, clowning around on bandstands, while people pushed each other around a dance floor. It seemed — beneath him, somehow. I had never thought about it before, had never been forced to, but I suppose I had always put jazz musicians in a class with what Daddy called "good-time people." 120

"Are you *serious*?"

"Hell, *yes*, I'm serious."

He looked more helpless than ever, and annoyed, and deeply hurt.

I suggested, helpfully: "You mean — like Louis Armstrong?"

His face closed as though I'd struck him. "No. I'm not talking about none of that old-time, down home crap." 125

"Well, look, Sonny, I'm sorry, don't get mad. I just don't altogether get it, that's all. Name somebody — you know, a jazz musician you admire."

"Bird."

"Who?"

"Bird! Charlie Parker! Don't they teach you nothing in the goddamn army?"

I lit a cigarette. I was surprised and then a little amused to discover that I was   130
trembling. "I've been out of touch," I said. "You'll have to be patient with me.
Now. Who's this Parker character?"

"He's just one of the greatest jazz musicians alive," said Sonny, sullenly, his
hands in his pockets, his back to me. "Maybe *the* greatest," he added, bitterly,
"that's probably why *you* never heard of him."

"All right," I said, "I'm ignorant. I'm sorry. I'll go out and buy all the cat's
records right away, all right?"

"It don't," said Sonny, with dignity, "make any difference to me. I don't care
what you listen to. Don't do me no favors."

I was beginning to realize that I'd never seen him so upset before. With
another part of my mind I was thinking that this would probably turn out to be
one of those things kids go through and that I shouldn't make it seem important
by pushing it too hard. Still, I didn't think it would do any harm to ask: "Doesn't
all this take a lot of time? Can you make a living at it?"

He turned back to me and half leaned, half sat, on the kitchen table. "Every-   135
thing takes time," he said, "and—well, yes, sure, I can make a living at it. But
what I don't seem to be able to make you understand is that it's the only thing I
want to do."

"Well, Sonny," I said, gently, "you know people can't always do exactly what
they *want* to do—"

"No, I don't know that," said Sonny, surprising me. "I think people *ought* to
do what they want to do, what else are they alive for?"

"You getting to be a big boy," I said desperately, "it's time you started thinking
about your future."

"I'm thinking about my future," said Sonny, grimly. "I think about it all the
time."

I gave up. I decided, if he didn't change his mind, that we could always talk   140
about it later. "In the meantime," I said, "you got to finish school." We had
already decided that he'd have to move in with Isabel and her folks. I knew this
wasn't the ideal arrangement because Isabel's folks are inclined to be dicty and
they hadn't especially wanted Isabel to marry me. But I didn't know what else to
do. "And we have to get you fixed up at Isabel's."

There was a long silence. He moved from the kitchen table to the window.
"That's a terrible idea. You know it yourself."

"Do you have a *better* idea?"

He just walked up and down the kitchen for a minute. He was as tall as I
was. He had started to shave. I suddenly had the feeling that I didn't know him
at all.

He stopped at the kitchen table and picked up my cigarettes. Looking at me
with a kind of mocking, amused defiance, he put one between his lips. "You
mind?"

"You smoking already?"   145

He lit the cigarette and nodded, watching me through the smoke. "I just wanted to see if I'd have the courage to smoke in front of you." He grinned and blew a great cloud of smoke to the ceiling. "It was easy." He looked at my face. "Come on, now. I bet you was smoking at my age, tell the truth."

I didn't say anything but the truth was on my face, and he laughed. But now there was something very strained in his laugh. "Sure. And I bet that ain't all you was doing."

He was frightening me a little. "Cut the crap," I said. "We already decided that you was going to go and live at Isabel's. Now what's got into you all of a sudden?"

"*You* decided it," he pointed out. "*I* didn't decide nothing." He stopped in front of me, leaning against the stove, arms loosely folded. "Look, brother. I don't want to stay in Harlem no more, I really don't." He was very earnest. He looked at me, then over toward the kitchen window. There was something in his eyes I'd never seen before, some thoughtfulness, some worry all his own. He rubbed the muscle of one arm. "It's time I was getting out of here."

"Where do you want to go, Sonny?"   150

"I want to join the army. Or the navy, I don't care. If I say I'm old enough, they'll believe me."

Then I got mad. It was because I was so scared. "You must be crazy. You goddamn fool, what the hell do you want to go and join the *army* for?"

"I just told you. To get out of Harlem."

"Sonny, you haven't even finished *school*. And if you really want to be a musician, how do you expect to study if you're in the *army*?"

He looked at me, trapped, and in anguish. "There's ways. I might be able to   155
work out some kind of deal. Anyway, I'll have the G.I. Bill when I come out."

"*If* you come out." We stared at each other. "Sonny, please. Be reasonable. I know the setup is far from perfect. But we got to do the best we can."

"I ain't learning nothing in school," he said. "Even when I go." He turned away from me and opened the window and threw his cigarette out into the narrow alley. I watched his back. "At least, I ain't learning nothing you'd want me to learn." He slammed the window so hard I thought the glass would fly out, and turned back to me. "And I'm sick of the stink of these garbage cans!"

"Sonny," I said, "I know how you feel. But if you don't finish school now, you're going to be sorry later that you didn't." I grabbed him by the shoulders. "And you only got another year. It ain't so bad. And I'll come back and I swear I'll help you do *whatever* you want to do. Just try to put up with it till I come back. Will you please do that? For me?"

He didn't answer and he wouldn't look at me.

"Sonny. You hear me?"   160

He pulled away. "I hear you. But you never hear anything *I* say."

I didn't know what to say to that. He looked out of the window and then back at me. "OK," he said, and sighed. "I'll try."

Then I said, trying to cheer him up a little, "They got a piano at Isabel's. You can practice on it."

And as a matter of fact, it did cheer him up for a minute. "That's right," he said to himself. "I forgot that." His face relaxed a little. But the worry, the thoughtfulness, played on it still, the way shadows play on a face which is staring into the fire.

But I thought I'd never hear the end of that piano. At first, Isabel would write   165
me, saying how nice it was that Sonny was so serious about his music and how, as soon as he came in from school, or wherever he had been when he was supposed to be at school, he went straight to that piano and stayed there until suppertime. And, after supper, he went back to that piano and stayed there until everybody went to bed. He was at the piano all day Saturday and all day Sunday. Then he bought a record player and started playing records. He'd play one record over and over again, all day long sometimes, and he'd improvise along with it on the piano. Or he'd play one section of the record, one chord, one change, one progression, then he'd do it on the piano. Then back to the record. Then back to the piano.

Well, I really don't know how they stood it. Isabel finally confessed that it wasn't like living with a person at all, it was like living with sound. And the sound didn't make any sense to her, didn't make any sense to any of them—naturally. They began, in a way, to be afflicted by this presence that was living in their home. It was as though Sonny were some sort of god, or monster. He moved in an atmosphere which wasn't like theirs at all. They fed him and he ate, he washed himself, he walked in and out of their door; he certainly wasn't nasty or unpleasant or rude, Sonny isn't any of those things; but it was as though he were all wrapped up in some cloud, some fire, some vision all his own; and there wasn't any way to reach him.

At the same time, he wasn't really a man yet, he was still a child, and they had to watch out for him in all kinds of ways. They certainly couldn't throw him out. Neither did they dare to make a great scene about that piano because even they dimly sensed, as I sensed, from so many thousands of miles away, that Sonny was at that piano playing for his life.

But he hadn't been going to school. One day a letter came from the school board and Isabel's mother got it—there had, apparently, been other letters but Sonny had torn them up. This day, when Sonny came in, Isabel's mother showed him the letter and asked where he'd been spending his time. And she finally got it out of him that he'd been down in Greenwich Village, with musicians and other characters, in a white girl's apartment. And this scared her and she started to scream at him and what came up, once she began—though she denies it to this day—was what sacrifices they were making to give Sonny a decent home and how little he appreciated it.

Sonny didn't play the piano that day. By evening, Isabel's mother had calmed down but then there was the old man to deal with, and Isabel herself. Isabel says she did her best to be calm but she broke down and started crying. She says she just watched Sonny's face. She could tell, by watching him, what was happening with him. And what was happening was that they penetrated his cloud, they had reached him. Even if their fingers had been a thousand times more gentle than human fingers ever are, he could hardly help feeling that they had stripped him naked and were spitting on that nakedness. For he also had to see that his presence, that music, which was life or death to him, had been torture for them and that they had endured it, not at all for his sake, but only for mine. And Sonny couldn't take that. He can take it a little better today than he could then but he's still not very good at it and, frankly, I don't know anybody who is.

The silence of the next few days must have been louder than the sound of all   170
the music ever played since time began. One morning, before she went to work, Isabel was in his room for something and she suddenly realized that all of his records were gone. And she knew for certain that he was gone. And he was. He went as far as the navy would carry him. He finally sent me a postcard from some place in Greece and that was the first I knew that Sonny was still alive. I didn't see him any more until we were both back in New York and the war had long been over.

He was a man by then, of course, but I wasn't willing to see it. He came by the house from time to time, but we fought almost every time we met. I didn't like the way he carried himself, loose and dreamlike all the time, and I didn't like his friends, and his music seemed to be merely an excuse for the life he led. It sounded just that weird and disordered.

Then we had a fight, a pretty awful fight, and I didn't see him for months. By and by I looked him up, where he was living, in a furnished room in the Village, and I tried to make it up. But there were lots of people in the room and Sonny just lay on his bed, and he wouldn't come downstairs with me, and he treated these other people as though they were his family and I weren't. So I got mad and then he got mad, and then I told him that he might just as well be dead as live the way he was living. Then he stood up and he told me not to worry about him any more in life, that he *was* dead as far as I was concerned. Then he pushed me to the door and the other people looked on as though nothing were happening, and he slammed the door behind me. I stood in the hallway, staring at the door. I heard somebody laugh in the room and then the tears came to my eyes. I started down the steps, whistling to keep from crying, I kept whistling to myself, *You going to need me, baby, one of these cold, rainy days.*

I read about Sonny's trouble in the spring. Little Grace died in the fall. She was a beautiful little girl. But she only lived a little over two years. She died of polio and she suffered. She had a slight fever for a couple of days, but it didn't seem like anything and we just kept her in bed. And we would certainly have called the doctor, but the fever dropped, she seemed to be all right. So we thought it had just been a cold. Then, one day, she was up, playing, Isabel was in the kitchen fixing lunch for the two boys when they'd come in from school, and she heard Grace fall down in the living room. When you have a lot of children you don't always start running when one of them falls, unless they start screaming or something. And, this time, Grace was quiet. Yet, Isabel says that when she heard that *thump* and then that silence, something happened in her to make her afraid. And she ran to the living room and there was little Grace on the floor, all twisted up, and the reason she hadn't screamed was that she couldn't get her breath. And when she did scream, it was the worst sound, Isabel says, that she'd ever heard in all her life, and she still hears it sometimes in her dreams. Isabel will sometimes wake me up with a low, moaning, strangled sound and I have to be quick to awaken her and hold her to me and where Isabel is weeping against me seems a mortal wound.

I think I may have written Sonny the very day that little Grace was buried. I was sitting in the living room in the dark, by myself, and I suddenly thought of Sonny. My trouble made his real.

One Saturday afternoon, when Sonny had been living with us, or, anyway, 175 been in our house, for nearly two weeks, I found myself wandering aimlessly about the living room, drinking from a can of beer, and trying to work up the courage to search Sonny's room. He was out, he was usually out whenever I was home, and Isabel had taken the children to see their grandparents. Suddenly I was standing still in front of the living room window, watching Seventh Avenue. The idea of searching Sonny's room made me still. I scarcely dared to admit to myself what I'd be searching for. I didn't know what I'd do if I found it. Or if I didn't.

On the sidewalk across from me, near the entrance to a barbecue joint, some people were holding an old-fashioned revival meeting. The barbecue cook, wearing a dirty white apron, his conked hair reddish and metallic in the pale sun, and a cigarette between his lips, stood in the doorway, watching them. Kids and older people paused in their errands and stood there, along with some older men and a couple of very tough-looking women who watched everything that happened on the avenue, as though they owned it, or were maybe owned by it. Well, they were watching this, too. The revival was being carried on by three sisters in black, and a brother. All they had were their voices and their Bibles and a tambourine. The brother was testifying and while he testified two of the sisters stood together, seeming to say, amen, and the third sister walked around with the tambourine outstretched and a couple of people dropped coins into it. Then the brother's testimony ended and the sister who had been taking up the collection dumped the coins into her palm and transferred them to the pocket of her long black robe. Then she raised both hands, striking the tambourine against the air, and then against one hand, and she started to sing. And the two other sisters and the brother joined in.

It was strange, suddenly, to watch, though I had been seeing these street meetings all my life. So, of course, had everybody else down there. Yet, they paused and watched and listened and I stood still at the window. *"Tis the old ship of Zion,"* they sang, and the sister with the tambourine kept a steady, jangling beat, *"it has rescued many a thousand!"* Not a soul under the sound of their voices was hearing this song for the first time, not one of them had been rescued. Nor had they seen much in the way of rescue work being done around them. Neither did they especially believe in the holiness of the three sisters and the brother, they knew too much about them, knew where they lived, and how. The woman with the tambourine, whose voice dominated the air, whose face was bright with joy, was divided by very little from the woman who stood watching her, a cigarette between her heavy, chapped lips, her hair a cuckoo's nest, her face scarred and swollen from many beatings, and her black eyes glittering like coal. Perhaps they both knew this, which was why, when, as rarely, they addressed each other, they addressed each other as Sister. As the singing filled the air the watching, listening faces underwent a change, the eyes focusing on something within; the music seemed to soothe a poison out of them; and time seemed, nearly, to fall away from the sullen, belligerent, battered faces, as though they were fleeing back to their first condition, while dreaming of their last. The barbecue cook half shook his head and smiled, and dropped his cigarette and disappeared into his joint. A man fumbled in his pockets for change and stood holding it in his hand impatiently, as though he had just remembered a pressing appointment further up the avenue. He looked furious. Then I saw Sonny, standing on the edge of the crowd. He was carrying a wide, flat notebook with a green cover, and it made him look, from where I was standing, almost like a schoolboy. The coppery sun brought out the copper in his skin, he was very faintly smiling, standing very still. Then the singing stopped, the tambourine turned into a collection plate again. The furious man dropped in his coins and vanished, so did a couple of the women, and Sonny dropped some change in the plate, looking directly at the woman with a little smile. He started across the avenue, toward the house. He has a slow, loping walk, something like the way Harlem hipsters walk, only he's imposed on this his own half-beat. I had never really noticed it before.

I stayed at the window, both relieved and apprehensive. As Sonny disappeared from my sight, they began singing again. And they were still singing when his key turned in the lock.

"Hey," he said.

"Hey, yourself. You want some beer?"   180

"No. Well, maybe." But he came up to the window and stood beside me, looking out. "What a warm voice," he said.

They were singing *If I could only hear my mother pray again!*

"Yes," I said, "and she can sure beat that tambourine."

"But what a terrible song," he said, and laughed. He dropped his notebook on the sofa and disappeared into the kitchen. "Where's Isabel and the kids?"

"I think they went to see their grandparents. You hungry?"   185

"No." He came back into the living room with his can of beer. "You want to come some place with me tonight?"

I sensed, I don't know how, that I couldn't possibly say no. "Sure. Where?"

He sat down on the sofa and picked up his notebook and started leafing through it. "I'm going to sit in with some fellows in a joint in the Village."

"You mean, you're going to play, tonight?"

"That's right." He took a swallow of his beer and moved back to the window.   190
He gave me a sidelong look. "If you can stand it."

"I'll try," I said.

He smiled to himself and we both watched as the meeting across the way broke up. The three sisters and the brother, heads bowed, were singing *God be with you till we meet again*. The faces around them were very quiet. Then the song ended. The small crowd dispersed. We watched the three women and the lone man walk slowly up the avenue.

"When she was singing before," said Sonny, abruptly, "her voice reminded me for a minute of what heroin feels like sometimes—when it's in your veins. It makes you feel sort of warm and cool at the same time. And distant. And—and sure." He sipped his beer, very deliberately not looking at me. I watched his face. "It makes you feel—in control. Sometimes you've got to have that feeling."

"Do you?" I sat down slowly in the easy chair.

"Sometimes." He went to the sofa and picked up his notebook again. "Some people do." 195

"In order," I asked, "to play?" And my voice was very ugly, full of contempt and anger.

"Well"—he looked at me with great, troubled eyes, as though, in fact, he hoped his eyes would tell me things he could never otherwise say—"they *think* so. And *if* they think so—!"

"And what do *you* think?" I asked.

He sat on the sofa and put his can of beer on the floor. "I don't know," he said, and I couldn't be sure if he were answering my question or pursuing his thoughts. His face didn't tell me. "It's not so much to *play*. It's to *stand* it, to be able to make it at all. On any level." He frowned and smiled: "In order to keep from shaking to pieces."

"But these friends of yours," I said, "they seem to shake themselves to pieces pretty goddamn fast." 200

"Maybe." He played with the notebook. And something told me that I should curb my tongue, that Sonny was doing his best to talk, that I should listen. "But of course you only know the ones that've gone to pieces. Some don't—or at least they haven't *yet* and that's just about all *any* of us can say." He paused. "And then there are some who just live, really, in hell, and they know it and they see what's happening and they go right on. I don't know." He sighed, dropped the notebook, folded his arms. "Some guys, you can tell from the way they play, they on something *all* the time. And you can see that, well, it makes something real for them. But of course," he picked up his beer from the floor and sipped it and put the can down again, "they *want* to, too, you've got to see that. Even some of them that say they don't—*some*, not all."

"And what about you?" I asked—I couldn't help it. "What about you? Do *you* want to?"

He stood up and walked to the window and remained silent for a long time. Then he sighed. "Me," he said. Then: "While I was downstairs before, on my way here, listening to that woman sing, it struck me all of a sudden how much suffering she must have had to go through—to sing like that. It's *repulsive* to think you have to suffer that much."

I said: "But there's no way not to suffer—is there, Sonny?"

"I believe not," he said and smiled, "but that's never stopped anyone from trying." He looked at me. "Has it?" I realized, with this mocking look, that there stood between us, forever, beyond the power of time or forgiveness, the fact that I had held silence—so long!—when he had needed human speech to help him. He turned back to the window. "No, there's no way not to suffer. But you try all kinds of ways to keep from drowning in it, to keep on top of it, and to make it seem—well, like *you*. Like you did something, all right, and now you're suffering for it. You know?" I said nothing. "Well you know," he said, impatiently, 205 "why *do* people suffer? Maybe it's better to do something to give it a reason, *any* reason."

"But we just agreed," I said, "that there's no way not to suffer. Isn't it better, then, just to—take it?"

"But nobody just takes it," Sonny cried, "that's what I'm telling you! *Everybody* tries not to. You're just hung up on the *way* some people try—it's not *your* way!"

The hair on my face began to itch, my face felt wet. "That's not true," I said, "that's not true. I don't give a damn what other people do, I don't even care how they suffer. I just care how *you* suffer." And he looked at me. "Please believe me," I said, "I don't want to see you—die—trying not to suffer."

"I won't," he said, flatly, "die trying not to suffer. At least, not any faster than anybody else."

"But there's no need," I said, trying to laugh, "is there? in killing yourself."   210

I wanted to say more, but I couldn't. I wanted to talk about will power and how life could be—well, beautiful. I wanted to say that it was all within; but was it? or, rather, wasn't that exactly the trouble? And I wanted to promise that I would never fail him again. But it would all have sounded—empty words and lies.

So I made the promise to myself and prayed that I would keep it.

"It's terrible sometimes, inside," he said, "that's what's the trouble. You walk these streets, black and funky and cold, and there's not really a living ass to talk to, and there's nothing shaking, and there's no way of getting it out—that storm inside. You can't talk it and you can't make love with it, and when you finally try to get with it and play it, you realize *nobody's* listening. So *you've* got to listen. You got to find a way to listen."

And then he walked away from the window and sat on the sofa again, as though all the wind had suddenly been knocked out of him. "Sometimes you'll do *anything* to play, even cut your mother's throat." He laughed and looked at me. "Or your brother's." Then he sobered. "Or your own." Then: "Don't worry. I'm all right now and I think I'll *be* all right. But I can't forget—where I've been. I don't mean just the physical place I've been, I mean where I've *been*. And *what* I've been."

"What have you been, Sonny?" I asked.   215

He smiled—but sat sideways on the sofa, his elbow resting on the back, his fingers playing with his mouth and chin, not looking at me. "I've been something I didn't recognize, didn't know I could be. Didn't know anybody could be." He stopped, looking inward, looking helplessly young, looking old. "I'm not talking about it now because I feel *guilty* or anything like that—maybe it would be better if I did, I don't know. Anyway, I can't really talk about it. Not to you, not to anybody," and now he turned and faced me. "Sometimes, you know, and it was actually when I was most *out* of the world, I felt that I was in it, that I was *with* it, really, and I could play or I didn't really have to *play*, it just came out of me, it was there. And I don't know how I played, thinking about it now, but I know I did awful things, those times, sometimes, to people. Or it wasn't that I *did* anything to them—it was that they weren't real." He picked up the beer can; it was empty; he rolled it between his palms: "And other times—well, I needed a fix, I needed to find a place to lean, I needed to clear a space to *listen*—and I couldn't find it, and I—went crazy, I did terrible things to *me*, I was terrible *for* me." He began pressing the beer can between his hands, I watched the metal begin to give. It glittered, as he played with it, like a knife, and I was afraid he would cut himself, but I said nothing. "Oh well. I can never tell you. I was all by myself at the bottom of something, stinking and sweating and crying and shaking, and I smelled it, you know? *my* stink, and I thought I'd die if I couldn't get away from it and yet, all the same, I knew that everything I was doing was just locking me in with it. And I didn't know," he paused, still flattening the beer can, "I didn't know, I still *don't* know, something kept telling me that maybe it was good to smell your own stink, but I didn't think that *that* was what I'd been trying to do—and—who can stand it?" and he abruptly dropped the ruined beer can, looking at me with a small, still smile, and then rose, walking to the window as though it were the lodestone rock. I watched his face, he watched the avenue. "I couldn't tell you when Mama died—but the reason I wanted to leave Harlem so bad was to get away from drugs. And then, when I ran away, that's what I was running from—really. When I came back, nothing had changed, *I* hadn't changed, I was just—older." And he stopped, drumming with his fingers on the windowpane. The sun had vanished, soon darkness would fall. I watched his face. "It can come again," he said, almost as though speaking to himself. Then he turned to me. "It can come again," he repeated. "I just want you to know that."

"All right," I said, at last. "So it can come again, All right."

He smiled, but the smile was sorrowful. "I had to try to tell you," he said.

"Yes," I said. "I understand that."

"You're my brother," he said, looking straight at me, and not smiling at all.   220

"Yes," I repeated, "yes. I understand that."

He turned back to the window, looking out. "All that hatred down there," he said, "all that hatred and misery and love. It's a wonder it doesn't blow the avenue apart."

We went to the only nightclub on a short, dark street, downtown. We squeezed through the narrow, chattering, jam-packed bar to the entrance of the big room, where the bandstand was. And we stood there for a moment, for the lights were very dim in this room and we couldn't see. Then, "Hello, boy," said a voice and an enormous black man, much older than Sonny or myself, erupted out of all that atmospheric lighting and put an arm around Sonny's shoulder. "I been sitting right here," he said, "waiting for you."

He had a big voice, too, and heads in the darkness turned toward us.

Sonny grinned and pulled a little away, and said, "Creole, this is my brother.   225
I told you about him."

Creole shook my hand. "I'm glad to meet you, son," he said, and it was clear that he was glad to meet me *there*, for Sonny's sake. And he smiled, "You got a real musician in *your* family," and he took his arm from Sonny's shoulder and slapped him, lightly, affectionately, with the back of his hand.

"Well. Now I've heard it all," said a voice behind us. This was another musician, and a friend of Sonny's, a coal-black, cheerful-looking man, built close to the ground. He immediately began confiding to me, at the top of his lungs, the most terrible things about Sonny, his teeth gleaming like a lighthouse and his laugh coming up out of him like the beginning of an earthquake. And it turned out that everyone at the bar knew Sonny, or almost everyone; some were musicians, working there, or nearby, or not working, some were simply hangers-on, and some were there to hear Sonny play. I was introduced to all of them and they were all very polite to me. Yet, it was clear that, for them, I was only Sonny's brother. Here, I was in Sonny's world. Or, rather: his kingdom. Here, it was not even a question that his veins bore royal blood.

They were going to play soon and Creole installed me, by myself, at a table in a dark corner. Then I watched them, Creole, and the little black man, and Sonny, and the others, while they horsed around, standing just below the bandstand. The light from the bandstand spilled just a little short of them and, watching them laughing and gesturing and moving about, I had the feeling that they, nevertheless, were being most careful not to step into that circle of light too suddenly: that if they moved into the light too suddenly, without thinking, they would perish in flame. Then, while I watched, one of them, the small, black man, moved into the light and crossed the bandstand and started fooling around with his drums. Then — being funny and being, also, extremely ceremonious — Creole took Sonny by the arm and led him to the piano. A woman's voice called Sonny's name and a few hands started clapping. And Sonny, also being funny and being ceremonious, and so touched, I think, that he could have cried, but neither hiding it nor showing it, riding it like a man, grinned, and put both hands to his heart and bowed from the waist.

Creole then went to the bass fiddle and a lean, very bright-skinned brown man jumped up on the bandstand and picked up his horn. So there they were, and the atmosphere on the bandstand and in the room began to change and tighten. Someone stepped up to the microphone and announced them. Then there were all kinds of murmurs. Some people at the bar shushed others. The waitress ran around, frantically getting in the last orders, guys and chicks got closer to each other, and the lights on the bandstand, on the quartet, turned to a kind of indigo. Then they all looked different there. Creole looked about him for the last time, as though he were making certain that all his chickens were in the coop, and then he — jumped and struck the fiddle. And there they were.

All I know about music is that not many people ever really hear it. And even then, on the rare occasions when something opens within, and the music enters, what we mainly hear, or hear corroborated, are personal, private, vanishing evocations. But the man who creates the music is hearing something else, is dealing with the roar rising from the void and imposing order on it as it hits the air. What is evoked in him, then, is of another order, more terrible because it has no words, and triumphant, too, for that same reason. And his triumph, when he triumphs, is ours. I just watched Sonny's face. His face was troubled, he was working hard, but he wasn't with it. And I had the feeling that, in a way, everyone on the bandstand was waiting for him, both waiting for him and pushing him along. But as I began to watch Creole, I realized that it was Creole who held them all back. He had them on a short rein. Up there, keeping the beat with his whole body, wailing

230

on the fiddle, with his eyes half closed, he was listening to everything, but he was listening to Sonny. He was having a dialogue with Sonny. He wanted Sonny to leave the shoreline and strike out for the deep water. He was Sonny's witness that deep water and drowning were not the same thing—he had been there, and he knew. And he wanted Sonny to know. He was waiting for Sonny to do the things on the keys which would let Creole know that Sonny was in the water.

And, while Creole listened, Sonny moved, deep within, exactly like someone in torment. I had never before thought of how awful the relationship must be between the musician and his instrument. He has to fill it, this instrument, with the breath of life, his own. He has to make it do what he wants it to do. And a piano is just a piano. It's made out of so much wood and wires and little hammers and big ones, and ivory. While there's only so much you can do with it, the only way to find this out is to try; to try and make it do everything.

And Sonny hadn't been near a piano for over a year. And he wasn't on much better terms with his life, not the life that stretched before him now. He and the piano stammered, started one way, got scared, stopped; started another way, panicked, marked time, started again; then seemed to have found a direction, panicked again, got stuck. And the face I saw on Sonny I'd never seen before. Everything had been burned out of it, and, at the same time, things usually hidden were being burned in, by the fire and fury of the battle which was occurring in him up there.

Yet, watching Creole's face as they neared the end of the first set, I had the feeling that something had happened, something I hadn't heard. Then they finished, there was scattered applause, and then, without an instant's warning, Creole started into something else, it was almost sardonic, it was *Am I Blue*. And, as though he commanded, Sonny began to play. Something began to happen. And Creole let out the reins. The dry, low, black man said something awful on the drums, Creole answered, and the drums talked back. Then the horn insisted, sweet and high, slightly detached perhaps, and Creole listened, commenting now and then, dry, and driving, beautiful and calm and old. Then they all came together again, and Sonny was part of the family again. I could tell this from his face. He seemed to have found, right there beneath his fingers, a damn brand-new piano. It seemed that he couldn't get over it. Then, for awhile, just being happy with Sonny, they seemed to be agreeing with him that brand-new pianos certainly were a gas.

Then Creole stepped forward to remind them that what they were playing was the blues. He hit something in all of them, he hit something in me, myself, and the music tightened and deepened, apprehension began to beat the air. Creole began to tell us what the blues were all about. They were not about anything very new. He and his boys up there were keeping it new, at the risk of ruin, destruction, madness, and death, in order to find new ways to make us listen. For, while the tale of how we suffer, and how we are delighted, and how we may triumph is never new, it always must be heard. There isn't any other tale to tell, it's the only light we've got in all this darkness.

And this tale, according to that face, that body, those strong hands on those strings, has another aspect in every country, and a new depth in every generation. Listen, Creole seemed to be saying, listen. Now these are Sonny's blues. He made the little black man on the drums know it, and the bright, brown man on the horn. Creole wasn't trying any longer to get Sonny in the water. He was wishing him Godspeed. Then he stepped back, very slowly, filling the air with the immense suggestion that Sonny speak for himself.

Then they all gathered around Sonny and Sonny played. Every now and again one of them seemed to say, amen. Sonny's fingers filled the air with life, his life. But that life contained so many others. And Sonny went all the way back, he really began with the spare, flat statement of the opening phrase of the song. Then he began to make it his. It was very beautiful because it wasn't hurried and it was no longer a lament. I seemed to hear with what burning he had made it his, with what burning we had yet to make it ours, how we could cease lamenting. Freedom lurked around us and I understood, at last, that he could help us to be free if we would listen, that he would never be free until we did. Yet, there was no battle in his face now. I heard what he had gone through, and would continue to go through until he came to rest in earth. He had made it his: that long line, of which we knew only Mama and Daddy. And he was giving it back, as everything must be given back, so that, passing through death, it can live forever. I saw my mother's face again, and felt, for the first time, how the stones of the road she had walked on must have bruised her feet. I saw the moonlit road where my father's brother died. And it brought something else back to me, and carried me past it. I saw my little girl again and felt Isabel's tears again, and I felt my own tears begin to rise. And I was yet aware that this was only a moment, that the world waited outside, as hungry as a tiger, and that trouble stretched above us, longer than the sky.

Then it was over. Creole and Sonny let out their breath, both soaking wet, and grinning. There was a lot of applause and some of it was real. In the dark, the girl came by and I asked her to take drinks to the bandstand. There was a long pause, while they talked up there in the indigo light and after awhile I saw the girl put a Scotch and milk on top of the piano for Sonny. He didn't seem to notice it, but just before they started playing again, he sipped from it and looked toward me, and nodded. Then he put it back on top of the piano. For me, then, as they began to play again, it glowed and shook above my brother's head like the very cup of trembling.   [1957]

THINKING ABOUT THE TEXT

1. Were you sympathetic to the older brother in the beginning of the story? Did this become more so or less so as the story progressed? Is Sonny a sympathetic character in the beginning? At the end?

2. In real life, what do you believe is the role of an older brother? Do you have a responsibility to the members of your family regardless of their behavior? Explain. What is Sonny's mother's view of this?

3. Baldwin refers to the "darkness outside" several times. What do you think this means for Sonny? For Sonny's mother and father? For the older brother?

4. Listening seems to play an important function for Sonny and his brother. Cite specific examples of how they do or do not listen to each other. What might be some definitions of "listening" in this context?

5. One might think that brothers would understand each other better than outsiders. But is that the case here? In your experience? In other stories or movies? How might you account for this difficulty?

MAKING COMPARISONS

1. The older brothers in "The Rich Brother" and "Sonny's Blues" struggle to understand their younger brothers. Which one seems more successful? Why?
2. Both younger brothers in these two stories seem to march to different drummers. How would you describe their variations from the norm?
3. Some critics claim that these two stories are about responsibility; others claim they are about tolerance; still others see sibling rivalry, blind faith, or ego as the focus. What do you think, and why?

WRITING ABOUT ISSUES

1. Baldwin shows us the letter Sonny writes to his older brother, but we do not see any of the older brother's letters to Sonny. Based on the older brother's insights about Sonny in the closing scene, write a letter to Sonny from the older brother's point of view, explaining the substance of his new understanding of Sonny's life and music.
2. Write an essay that compares the relationship between Pete and Donald to the one between Sonny and his brother. Be sure to comment on similarities and differences.
3. Write a personal essay based on a conflict you had with a sibling, explaining how the relationship evolved. Use at least two specific incidents, and describe how they fit into a larger pattern.
4. Do some library research on birth order as it affects sibling rivalry, especially between brothers. Write a report comparing your findings to the relationships depicted in these two stories.

ART OR FAMILY?
RE-VISIONS OF *THE GLASS MENAGERIE*

TENNESSEE WILLIAMS, "Portrait of a Girl in Glass"
TENNESSEE WILLIAMS, *The Glass Menagerie*

Tennessee Williams's own troubled life became the source for a series of stories and plays he wrote in the early 1940s. The 1943 story "Portrait of a Girl in Glass," a narrative close to his own circumstances, describes an episode from his late twenties when he was living with his mother and sister and working in a

(Photography Collection, Harry Ransom Humanities Research Center, The University of Texas at Austin.)

factory, a life he later described as requiring "endurance, a life of clawing and scratching along a sheer surface and holding on tight with raw fingers." The story is set in the Depression, a time of deep insecurity in America. Although the story does not develop the sociopolitical context as fully as the play does, we do get the sense, from a disturbing anecdote about a dog, that the world of the story is dangerous and cruel. In the story, his sister retreats from this world into fantasy and perhaps mental illness. And Tom, Williams's alter ego, is torn between protecting her and seeking his destiny as a writer. Williams later wrote a screenplay, *The Gentleman Caller,* and then revised it into *The Glass Menagerie.* He makes a number of interesting changes, filling out the context of the Depression and giving his sister a physical disability. But the idea of lost innocence remains a theme in both as Williams (Tom) struggles to reconcile his duty to a sister he loves and a vocation he is compelled to follow. He must decide between them and live with the painful consequences for the rest of his life.

BEFORE YOU READ

Should your first loyalty be to yourself or to your family? What if you were expected to quit college and work in a factory to help support your mother and disabled sibling. Would you do it? Why?

TENNESSEE WILLIAMS
Portrait of a Girl in Glass

Thomas Lanier "Tennessee" Williams (1911–1983) wrote some of the most famous plays of the American stage. The Glass Menagerie (1945), A Streetcar Named Desire *(1948),* Cat on a Hot Tin Roof *(1955),* Suddenly Last Summer *(1958), and* The Night of the Iguana *(1961) were made into popular and acclaimed films. His plays were considered shocking at the time since they dealt frankly with adultery, mental illness, homosexuality, and incest. His childhood was "lonely and miserable" largely because of his domineering, alcoholic father and because of the taunts he endured for being small, sickly, and bookish. After many difficulties, he graduated from the University of Iowa in 1939 and immediately began writing fiction and drama.*

We lived in a third floor apartment on Maple Street in Saint Louis, on a block which also contained the Ever-ready Garage, a Chinese laundry, and a bookie shop disguised as a cigar store.

Mine was an anomalous character, one that appeared to be slated for radical change or disaster, for I was a poet who had a job in a warehouse. As for my sister Laura, she could be classified even less readily than I. She made no positive motion toward the world but stood at the edge of the water, so to speak, with feet that anticipated too much cold to move. She'd never have budged an inch, I'm pretty sure, if my mother who was a relatively aggressive sort of woman had not shoved her roughly forward, when Laura was twenty years old, by enrolling her as a student in a nearby business college. Out of her "magazine money" (she sold subscriptions to women's magazines), Mother had paid my sister's tuition for a term of six months. It did not work out. Laura tried to memorize the typewriter keyboard, she had a chart at home, she used to sit silently in front of it for hours, staring at it while she cleaned and polished her infinite number of little glass ornaments. She did this every evening after dinner. Mother would caution me to be very quiet. "Sister is looking at her typewriter chart!" I felt somehow that it would do her no good, and I was right. She would seem to know the positions of the keys until the weekly speed-drill got under way, and then they would fly from her mind like a bunch of startled birds.

At last she couldn't bring herself to enter the school any more. She kept this failure a secret for a while. She left the house each morning as before and spent six hours walking around the park. This was in February, and all the walking outdoors regardless of weather brought on influenza. She was in bed for a couple of weeks with a curiously happy little smile on her face. Of course Mother phoned the business college to let them know she was ill. Whoever was talking on the other end of the line had some trouble, it seems, in remembering who Laura was, which annoyed my mother and she spoke up pretty sharply. "Laura has been attending that school of yours for two months, you certainly ought to recognize her name!" Then came the stunning disclosure. The person sharply retorted, after a moment or two, that now she *did* remember the Wingfield girl, and that she had not been at the business college *once* in about a month. Mother's voice became strident. Another person was brought to the phone to verify the statement of the first. Mother hung up and went to Laura's bedroom where she lay with a tense and frightened look in place of the faint little smile. Yes, admitted my sister, what they said was true. "I couldn't go any longer, it scared me too much, it made me sick at the stomach!"

After this fiasco, my sister stayed at home and kept in her bedroom mostly. This was a narrow room that had two windows on a dusky areaway between two wings of the building. We called this areaway Death Valley for a reason that seems worth telling. There were a great many alley-cats in the neighborhood and one particularly vicious dirty white Chow who stalked them continually. In the open or on the fire-escapes they could usually elude him but now and again he cleverly contrived to run some youngster among them into the cul-de-sac of this narrow areaway at the far end of which, directly beneath my sister's bedroom windows, they made the blinding discovery that what had appeared to be an avenue of escape was really a locked arena, a gloomy vault of concrete and brick with walls too high for any cat to spring, in which they must suddenly turn to spit at their death until it was hurled upon them. Hardly a week went by without a repetition of this violent drama. The areaway had grown to be hateful to Laura because she could not look out on it without recalling the screams and the snarls of killing. She kept the shades drawn down, and as Mother would not permit the use of electric current except when needed, her days were spent almost in perpetual twilight. There were three pieces of dingy ivory furniture in the room, a bed, a bureau, a chair. Over the bed was a remarkably bad religious painting, a very effeminate head of Christ with teardrops visible just below the eyes. The charm of the room was produced by my sister's collection of glass. She loved colored glass and had covered the walls with shelves of little glass articles, all of them light and delicate in color. These she washed and polished with endless care. When you entered the room there was always this soft, transparent radiance in it which came from the glass absorbing whatever faint light came through the shades on Death Valley. I have no idea how many articles there were of this delicate glass. There must have been hundreds of them. But Laura could tell you exactly. She loved each one.

She lived in a world of glass and also a world of music. The music came from a 1920 victrola and a bunch of records that dated from about the same period, pieces such as *Whispering* or *The Love Nest* or *Dardanella*. These records were souvenirs of our father, a man whom we barely remembered, whose name was spoken rarely. Before his sudden and unexplained disappearance from our lives, he had made this gift to the household, the phonograph and the records, whose music remained as a sort of apology for him. Once in a while, on pay-day at the warehouse, I would bring home a new record. But Laura seldom cared for these new records, maybe because they reminded her too much of the noisy tragedies in Death Valley or the speed-drills at the business college. The tunes she loved were the ones she had always heard. Often she sang to herself at night in her bedroom. Her voice was thin, it usually wandered off-key. Yet it had a curious childlike sweetness. At eight o'clock in the evening I sat down to write in my own mouse-trap of a room. Through the closed doors, through the walls, I would hear my sister singing to herself, a piece like *Whispering* or *I Love You* or *Sleepy Time Gal*, losing the tune now and then but always preserving the minor atmosphere of the music. I think that was why I always wrote such strange and sorrowful poems in those days. Because I had in my ears the wispy sound of my sister serenading her pieces of colored glass, washing them while she sang or merely looking down at them with her vague blue eyes until the points of gem-like radiance in them gently drew the aching particles of reality from her mind and finally produced a state of hypnotic calm in which she even stopped singing or washing the glass and merely sat without motion until my mother knocked at the door and warned her against the waste of electric current.

I don't believe that my sister was actually foolish. I think the petals of her mind had simply closed through fear, and it's no telling how much they had closed upon in the way of secret wisdom. She never talked very much, not even to me, but once in a while she did pop out with something that took you by surprise.

After work at the warehouse or after I'd finished my writing in the evening, I'd drop in her room for a little visit because she had a restful and soothing effect on nerves that were worn rather thin from trying to ride two horses simultaneously in two opposite directions.

I usually found her seated in the straight-back ivory chair with a piece of glass cupped tenderly in her palm.

"What are you doing? Talking to it?" I asked.

"No," she answered gravely, "I was just looking at it." 10

On the bureau were two pieces of fiction which she had received as Christmas or birthday presents. One was a novel called the *Rose-Garden Husband* by someone whose name escapes me. The other was *Freckles* by Gene Stratton Porter. I never saw her reading the *Rose-Garden Husband*, but the other book was one that she actually lived with. It had probably never occurred to Laura that a book was something you read straight through and then laid aside as finished. The character Freckles, a one-armed orphan youth who worked in a lumber-camp, was someone that she invited into her bedroom now and then for a friendly visit just as she did me. When I came in and found this novel open upon her lap, she would gravely remark that Freckles was having some trouble with the foreman of the lumber-camp or that he had just received an injury to his spine when a tree fell on him. She frowned with genuine sorrow when she reported these misadventures of her story-book hero, possibly not recalling how successfully he came through them all, that the injury to the spine fortuitously resulted in the discovery of rich parents and that the bad-tempered foreman had a heart of gold at the end of the book. Freckles became involved in romance with a girl he called The Angel, but my sister usually stopped reading when this girl became too prominent in the story. She closed the book or turned back to the lonelier periods in the orphan's story. I only remember her making one reference to this heroine of the novel. "The Angel is nice," she said, "but seems to be kind of conceited about her looks."

◆　◆　◆

Then one time at Christmas, while she was trimming the artificial tree, she picked up the Star of Bethlehem that went on the topmost branch and held it gravely toward the chandelier.

"Do stars have five points really?" she enquired.

This was the sort of thing that you didn't believe and that made you stare at Laura with sorrow and confusion.

"No," I told her, seeing she really meant it, "they're round like the earth and   15
most of them much bigger."

She was gently surprised by this new information. She went to the window to look up at the sky which was, as usual during Saint Louis winters, completely shrouded by smoke.

"It's hard to tell," she said, and returned to the tree.

So time passed on till my sister was twenty-three. Old enough to be married, but the fact of the matter was she had never even had a date with a boy. I don't believe this seemed as awful to her as it did to Mother.

At breakfast one morning Mother said to me, "Why don't you cultivate some nice young friends? How about down at the warehouse? Aren't there some young men down there you could ask to dinner?"

This suggestion surprised me because there was seldom quite enough food   20
on her table to satisfy three people. My mother was a terribly stringent house-keeper, God knows we were poor enough in actuality, but my mother had an almost obsessive dread of becoming even poorer. A not unreasonable fear since the man of the house was a poet who worked in a warehouse, but one which I thought played too important a part in all her calculations.

Almost immediately Mother explained herself.

"I think it might be nice," she said, "for your sister."

I brought Jim home to dinner a few nights later. Jim was a big red-haired Irishman who had the scrubbed and polished look of well-kept chinaware. His big square hands seemed to have a direct and very innocent hunger for touching his friends. He was always clapping them on your arms or shoulders and they burned through the cloth of your shirt like plates taken out of an oven. He was the best-liked man in the warehouse and oddly enough he was the only one that I was on good terms with. He found me agreeably ridiculous I think. He knew of my secret practice of retiring to a cabinet in the lavatory and working on rhyme schemes when work was slack in the warehouse, and of sneaking up on the roof now and then to smoke my cigarette with a view across the river at the undulant open country of Illinois. No doubt I was classified as screwy in Jim's mind as much as in the others', but while their attitude was suspicious and hostile when they first knew me, Jim's was warmly tolerant from the beginning. He called me Slim, and gradually his cordial acceptance drew the others around, and while he remained the only one who actually had anything to do with me, the others had now begun to smile when they saw me as people smile at an oddly fashioned dog who crosses their path at some distance.

Nevertheless it took some courage for me to invite Jim to dinner. I thought about it all week and delayed the action till Friday noon, the last possible moment, as the dinner was set for that evening.

"What are you doing tonight?" I finally asked him. 25

"Not a God damn thing," said Jim. "I had a date but her Aunt took sick and she's hauled her freight to Centralia!"

"Well," I said, "why don't you come over for dinner?"

"Sure!" said Jim. He grinned with astonishing brightness.

I went outside to phone the news to Mother.

Her voice that was never tired responded with an energy that made the wires 30 crackle.

"I suppose he's Catholic?" she said.

"Yes," I told her, remembering the tiny silver cross on his freckled chest.

"Good!" she said. "I'll bake a salmon loaf!"

And so we rode home together in his jalopy.

I had a curious feeling of guilt and apprehension as I led the lamb-like Irish- 35 man up three flights of cracked marble steps to the door of Apartment F, which was not thick enough to hold inside it the odor of baking salmon.

Never having a key, I pressed the bell.

"Laura!" came Mother's voice. "That's Tom and Mr. Delaney! Let them in!"

There was a long, long pause.

"Laura?" she called again. "I'm busy in the kitchen, you answer the door!"

Then at last I heard my sister's footsteps. They went right past the door at 40 which we were standing and into the parlor. I heard the creaking noise of the phonograph crank. Music commenced. One of the oldest records, a march of Sousa's, put on to give her the courage to let in a stranger.

The door came timidly open and there she stood in a dress from Mother's wardrobe, a black chiffon ankle-length and high-heeled slippers on which she balanced uncertainly like a tipsy crane of melancholy plumage. Her eyes stared back at us with a glass brightness and her delicate wing-like shoulders were hunched with nervousness.

"Hello!" said Jim, before I could introduce him.

He stretched out his hand. My sister touched it only for a second.

"Excuse me!" she whispered, and turned with a breathless rustle back to her bedroom door, the sanctuary beyond it briefly revealing itself with the tinkling, muted radiance of glass before the door closed rapidly but gently on her wraith-like figure.

Jim seemed to be incapable of surprise. 45

"Your sister?" he asked.

"Yes, that was her," I admitted. "She's terribly shy with strangers."

"She looks like you," said Jim, "except she's pretty."

Laura did not reappear till called to dinner. Her place was next to Jim at the drop-leaf table and all through the meal her figure was slightly tilted away from his. Her face was feverishly bright and one eyelid, the one on the side toward Jim, had developed a nervous wink. Three times in the course of the dinner she

dropped her fork on her plate with a terrible clatter and she was continually raising the water-glass to her lips for hasty little gulps. She went on doing this even
after the water was gone from the glass. And her handling of the silver became
more awkward and hurried all the time.

I thought of nothing to say. 50

To Mother belonged the conversational honors, such as they were. She
asked the caller about his home and family. She was delighted to learn that his
father had a business of his own, a retail shoe store somewhere in Wyoming. The
news that he went to night-school to study accounting was still more edifying.
What was his heart set on beside the warehouse? Radio-engineering? My, my,
my! It was easy to see that here was a very up-and-coming young man who was
certainly going to make his place in the world!

Then she started to talk about her children. Laura, she said, was not cut out for
business. She was domestic, however, and making a home was really a girl's best bet.

Jim agreed with all this and seemed not to sense the ghost of an implication.
I suffered through it dumbly, trying not to see Laura trembling more and more
beneath the incredible unawareness of Mother.

And bad as it was, excruciating in fact, I thought with dread of the moment
when dinner was going to be over, for then the diversion of food would be taken
away, we would have to go into the little steam-heated parlor. I fancied the four of
us having run out of talk, even Mother's seemingly endless store of questions
about Jim's home and his job all used up finally — the four of us, then, just sitting
there in the parlor, listening to the hiss of the radiator and nervously clearing our
throats in the kind of self-consciousness that gets to be suffocating.

But when the blanc-mange was finished, a miracle happened. 55

Mother got up to clear the dishes away. Jim gave me a clap on the shoulders
and said, "Hey, Slim, let's go have a look at those old records in there!"

He sauntered carelessly into the front room and flopped down on the floor
beside the victrola. He began sorting through the collection of worn-out records
and reading their titles aloud in a voice so hearty that it shot like beams of sunlight through the vapors of self-consciousness engulfing my sister and me.

He was sitting directly under the floor-lamp and all at once my sister jumped
up and said to him, "Oh — you have freckles!"

Jim grinned. "Sure that's what my folks call me — Freckles!"

"Freckles?" Laura repeated. She looked toward me as if for the confirmation 60
of some too wonderful hope. I looked away quickly, not knowing whether to feel
relieved or alarmed at the turn that things were taking.

Jim had wound the victrola and put on *Dardanella*.

He grinned at Laura.

"How about you an' me cutting the rug a little?"

"What?" said Laura breathlessly, smiling and smiling.

"Dance!" he said, drawing her into his arms. 65

As far as I knew she had never danced in her life. But to my everlasting wonder she slipped quite naturally into those huge arms of Jim's, and they danced
round and around the small steam-heated parlor, bumping against the sofa and
chairs and laughing loudly and happily together. Something opened up in my

sister's face. To say it was love is not too hasty a judgment, for after all he had
freckles and that was what his folks called him. Yes, he had undoubtedly assumed
the identity — for all practical purposes — of the one-armed orphan youth who
lived in the Limberlost, that tall and misty region to which she retreated whenever the walls of Apartment F became too close to endure.

Mother came back in with some lemonade. She stopped short as she entered
the portieres.

"Good heavens! Laura? Dancing?"

Her look was absurdly grateful as well as startled.

"But isn't she stepping all over you, Mr. Delaney?"   70

"What if she does?" said Jim, with bearish gallantry. "I'm not made of eggs!"

"Well, well, well!" said Mother, senselessly beaming.

"She's light as a feather!" said Jim. "With a little more practice she'd dance as
good as Betty!"

There was a little pause of silence.

"Betty?" said Mother.   75

"The girl I go out with!" said Jim.

"Oh!" said Mother.

She set the pitcher of lemonade carefully down and with her back to the
caller and her eyes on me, she asked him just how often he and the lucky young
lady went out together.

"Steady!" said Jim.

Mother's look, remaining on my face, turned into a glare of fury.   80

"Tom didn't mention that you went out with a girl!"

"Nope," said Jim. "I didn't mean to let the cat out of the bag. The boys at the
warehouse'll kid me to death when Slim gives the news away."

He laughed heartily but his laughter dropped heavily and awkwardly away as
even his dull senses were gradually penetrated by the unpleasant sensation the
news of Betty had made.

"Are you thinking of getting married?" said Mother.

"First of next month!" he told her.   85

It took her several moments to pull herself together. Then she said in a dismal tone, "How nice! If Tom had only told us we could have asked you *both*!"

Jim had picked up his coat.

"Must you be going?" said Mother.

"I hope it don't seem like I'm rushing off," said Jim, "but Betty's gonna get
back on the eight o'clock train an' by the time I get my jalopy down to the
Wabash depot —"

"Oh, then, we mustn't keep you."   90

Soon as he'd left, we all sat down, looking dazed.

Laura was the first to speak.

"Wasn't he nice?" she said. "And all those freckles!"

"Yes," said Mother. Then she turned on me.

"You didn't mention that he was engaged to be married!"   95

"Well, how did I know that he was engaged to be married?"

"I thought you called him your best friend down at the warehouse?"

"Yes, but I didn't know he was going to be married!"

"How peculiar!" said Mother. "How very peculiar!"

"No," said Laura gently, getting up from the sofa. "There's nothing peculiar   100
about it."

She picked up one of the records and blew on its surface a little as if it were
dusty, then set it softly back down.

"People in love," she said, "take everything for granted."

What did she mean by that? I never knew.

She slipped quietly back to her room and closed the door.

Not very long after that I lost my job at the warehouse. I was fired for writing   105
a poem on the lid of a shoe-box. I left Saint Louis and took to moving around.
The cities swept about me like dead leaves, leaves that were brightly colored but
torn away from the branches. My nature changed. I grew to be firm and sufficient.

In five years' time I had nearly forgotten home. I had to forget it, I couldn't
carry it with me. But once in a while, usually in a strange town before I have
found companions, the shell of deliberate hardness is broken through. A door
comes softly and irresistibly open. I hear the tired old music my unknown father
left in the place he abandoned as faithlessly as I. I see the faint and sorrowful radiance of the glass, hundreds of little transparent pieces of it in very delicate colors.
I hold my breath, for if my sister's face appears among them — the night is hers!

[1943]

THINKING ABOUT THE TEXT

1. It is said that the purpose of family is to give roots first and then wings.
   Can family also be a trap? Is that the conflict in this story — between being
   free and being trapped?

2. What are some ways to interpret the significance of Laura's glass collection? What, for example, might it tell us about Laura's connection to reality? About her personality?

3. Why does Williams tell us the story of the vicious Chow (para. 4)? What is
   the significance of leading the "lamb-like Irishman" (para. 35) up to the
   apartment?

4. What do you think Williams is trying to do by having Laura reading *Freckles* (para. 11)? By having her ask about stars (paras. 13–17)? By having her
   forget the keyboard (para. 2)?

5. From his biography, we can reasonably speculate that Williams felt guilty
   about leaving his family. Is his purpose here to persuade the reader that he
   made the right decision? To persuade himself? To replay the trauma of
   leaving? Something else?

TENNESSEE WILLIAMS
The Glass Menagerie

In The Glass Menagerie, *Laura is based on Williams's sister, Rose, who had numerous mental problems. Tom, of course, is modeled on Williams and reflects his desire to escape the responsibilities of his family and live a life of adventure. Williams noted that leaving Rose was the most traumatic event of his life, one from which, like Tom, he never fully recovered.*

> nobody,not even the rain,has such small hands
> — e. e. cummings

LIST OF CHARACTERS

AMANDA WINGFIELD, *the mother. A little woman of great but confused vitality clinging frantically to another time and place. Her characterization must be carefully created, not copied from type. She is not paranoiac, but her life is paranoia. There is much to admire in Amanda, and as much to love and pity as there is to laugh at. Certainly she has endurance and a kind of heroism, and though her foolishness makes her unwittingly cruel at times, there is tenderness in her slight person.*

LAURA WINGFIELD, *her daughter. Amanda, having failed to establish contact with reality, continues to live vitally in her illusions, but Laura's situation is even graver. A childhood illness has left her crippled, one leg slightly shorter than the other, and held in a brace. This defect need not be more than suggested on the stage. Stemming from this, Laura's separation increases till she is like a piece of her own glass collection, too exquisitely fragile to move from the shelf.*

TOM WINGFIELD, *her son. And the narrator of the play. A poet with a job in a warehouse. His nature is not remorseless, but to escape from a trap he has to act without pity.*

JIM O'CONNOR, *the gentleman caller. A nice, ordinary, young man.*

SCENE: *An alley in St. Louis.*
PART I: *Preparation for a Gentleman Caller.*
PART II: *The Gentleman Calls.*
TIME: *Now and the Past.*

Scene 1

The Wingfield apartment is in the rear of the building, one of those vast hivelike conglomerations of cellular living-units that flower as warty growths in overcrowded urban centers of lower middle-class population and are symptomatic of the impulse of this largest and fundamentally enslaved section of American society to avoid fluidity and differentiation and to exist and function as one interfused mass of automatism.

The apartment faces an alley and is entered by a fire-escape, a structure whose name is a touch of accidental poetic truth, for all of these huge buildings are always

*burning with the slow and implacable fires of human desperation. The fire-escape
is included in the set — that is, the landing of it and steps descending from it.*

*The scene is memory and is therefore nonrealistic. Memory takes a lot of poetic
license. It omits some details; others are exaggerated, according to the emotional
value of the articles it touches, for memory is seated predominantly in the heart. The
interior is therefore rather dim and poetic.*

*At the rise of the curtain, the audience is faced with the dark, grim rear wall of
the Wingfield tenement. This building, which runs parallel to the footlights, is
flanked on both sides by dark, narrow alleys which run into murky canyons of
tangled clotheslines, garbage cans, and the sinister latticework of neighboring fire-
escapes. It is up and down these side alleys that exterior entrances and exits are
made, during the play. At the end of Tom's opening commentary, the dark tenement
wall slowly reveals (by means of a transparency) the interior of the ground floor
Wingfield apartment.*

*Downstage is the living room, which also serves as a sleeping room for Laura,
the sofa unfolding to make her bed. Upstage, center, and divided by a wide arch or
second proscenium with transparent faded portieres (or second curtain), is the dining room. In an old-fashioned what-not in the living room are seen scores of transparent glass animals. A blown-up photograph of the father hangs on the wall of the
living room, facing the audience, to the left of the archway. It is the face of a very
handsome young man in a doughboy's First World War cap. He is gallantly smiling, ineluctably smiling, as if to say, "I will be smiling forever."*

*The audience hears and sees the opening scene in the dining room through
both the transparent fourth wall of the building and the transparent gauze portieres
of the dining-room arch. It is during this revealing scene that the fourth wall slowly
ascends, out of sight. This transparent exterior wall is not brought down again until
the very end of the play, during Tom's final speech.*

*The narrator is an undisguised convention of the play. He takes whatever
license with dramatic convention as is convenient to his purposes.*

*Tom enters dressed as a merchant sailor from alley, stage left, and strolls across
the front of the stage to the fire-escape. There he stops and lights a cigarette. He
addresses the audience.*

TOM: Yes, I have tricks in my pocket, I have things up my sleeve. But I am the
opposite of a stage magician. He gives you illusion that has the appearance of
truth. I give you truth in the pleasant disguise of illusion. To begin with, I turn
back time. I reverse it to that quaint period, the thirties, when the huge
middle class of America was matriculating in a school for the blind. Their
eyes had failed them, or they had failed their eyes, and so they were having
their fingers pressed forcibly down on the fiery Braille alphabet of a dissolving
economy. In Spain there was revolution. Here there was only shouting and
confusion. In Spain there was Guernica.° Here there were disturbances of

----

Guernica: A town in northern Spain destroyed by German bombers in 1937 during the Spanish Civil War.

labor, sometimes pretty violent, in otherwise peaceful cities such as Chicago, Cleveland, Saint Louis. . . . This is the social background of the play.

(Music.)

The play is memory. Being a memory play, it is dimly lighted, it is sentimental, it is not realistic. In memory everything seems to happen to music. That explains the fiddle in the wings. I am the narrator of the play, and also a character in it. The other characters are my mother, Amanda, my sister, Laura, and a gentleman caller who appears in the final scenes. He is the most realistic character in the play, being an emissary from a world of reality that we were somehow set apart from. But since I have a poet's weakness for symbols, I am using this character also as a symbol; he is the long delayed but always expected something that we live for. There is a fifth character in the play who doesn't appear except in this larger-than-life photograph over the mantel. This is our father who left us a long time ago. He was a telephone man who fell in love with long distances; he gave up his job with the telephone company and skipped the light fantastic out of town. . . . The last we heard of him was a picture post-card from Mazatlán, on the Pacific coast of Mexico, containing a message of two words — "Hello — Good-bye!" and no address. I think the rest of the play will explain itself. . . .

Amanda's voice becomes audible through the portieres.

(Legend on screen: "Où sont les neiges."°)

He divides the portieres and enters the upstage area.
Amanda and Laura are seated at a drop-leaf table. Eating is indicated by gestures without food or utensils. Amanda faces the audience.
Tom and Laura are seated in profile.
The interior has lit up softly and through the scrim we see Amanda and Laura seated at the table in the upstage area.

AMANDA *(calling):*   Tom?

TOM: Yes, Mother.

AMANDA: We can't say grace until you come to the table!

TOM: Coming, Mother. *(He bows slightly and withdraws, reappearing a few moments later in his place at the table.)*

AMANDA *(to her son):*   Honey, don't *push* with your *fingers.* If you have to push with something, the thing to push with is a crust of bread. And chew — chew! Animals have sections in their stomachs which enable them to digest food without mastication, but human beings are supposed to chew their food before they swallow it down. Eat food leisurely, son, and really enjoy it. A well-cooked meal has lots of delicate flavors that have to be held in the mouth for appreciation. So chew your food and give your salivary glands a chance to function!

Où sont les neiges: Part of a line from a poem by the French medieval writer François Villon; the full line translates, "Where are the snows of yesteryear?"

Tom deliberately lays his imaginary fork down and pushes his chair back from the table.

TOM: I haven't enjoyed one bite of this dinner because of your constant direc-
        tions on how to eat it. It's you that makes me rush through meals with your
        hawklike attention to every bite I take. Sickening—spoils my appetite—all
        this discussion of animals' secretion—salivary glands—mastication!

AMANDA *(lightly)*:   Temperament like a Metropolitan star! *(He rises and crosses
        downstage.)* You're not excused from the table.

TOM: I am getting a cigarette.

AMANDA: You smoke too much.

Laura rises.

LAURA: I'll bring in the blanc mange.

He remains standing with his cigarette by the portieres during the following.

AMANDA *(rising)*:   No, sister, no, sister—you be the lady this time and I'll be the
        darky.

LAURA: I'm already up.

AMANDA: Resume your seat, little sister—I want you to stay fresh and pretty—
        for gentlemen callers!

LAURA: I'm not expecting any gentlemen callers.

AMANDA *(crossing out to kitchenette. Airily)*:   Sometimes they come when they
        are least expected! Why, I remember one Sunday afternoon in Blue Moun-
        tain—*(Enters kitchenette.)*

TOM: I know what's coming!

LAURA: Yes. But let her tell it.

TOM: Again?

LAURA: She loves to tell it.

Amanda returns with bowl of dessert.

AMANDA: One Sunday afternoon in Blue Mountain—your mother received—
        seventeen!—gentlemen callers! Why, sometimes there weren't chairs enough
        to accommodate them all. We had to send the nigger over to bring in folding
        chairs from the parish house.

TOM *(remaining at portieres)*:   How did you entertain those gentlemen callers?

AMANDA: I understood the art of conversation!

TOM: I bet you could talk.

AMANDA: Girls in those days knew how to talk, I can tell you.

TOM: Yes?

(Image: Amanda as a girl on a porch greeting callers.)

AMANDA: They knew how to entertain their gentlemen callers. It wasn't enough
        for a girl to be possessed of a pretty face and a graceful figure—although I
        wasn't slighted in either respect. She also needed to have a nimble wit and a
        tongue to meet all occasions.

TOM: What did you talk about?

AMANDA: Things of importance going on in the world! Never anything coarse or
        common or vulgar. *(She addresses Tom as though he were seated in the vacant*

chair at the table though he remains by portieres. He plays this scene as though he held the book.) My callers were gentlemen—all! Among my callers were some of the most prominent young planters of the Mississippi Delta—planters and sons of planters!

Tom motions for music and a spot of light on Amanda.
Her eyes lift, her face glows, her voice becomes rich and elegiac.
(Screen legend: "Où sont les neiges.")

There was young Champ Laughlin who later became vice-president of the Delta Planters Bank. Hadley Stevenson who was drowned in Moon Lake and left his widow one hundred and fifty thousand in Government bonds. There were the Cutrere brothers, Wesley and Bates. Bates was one of my bright particular beaux! He got in a quarrel with that wild Wainright boy. They shot it out on the floor of Moon Lake Casino. Bates was shot through the stomach. Died in the ambulance on his way to Memphis. His widow was also well-provided for, came into eight or ten thousand acres, that's all. She married him on the rebound—never loved her—carried my picture on him the night he died! And there was that boy that every girl in the Delta had set her cap for! That beautiful, brilliant young Fitzhugh boy from Green County!

TOM: What did he leave his widow?

AMANDA: He never married! Gracious, you talk as though all of my old admirers had turned up their toes to the daisies!

TOM: Isn't this the first you mentioned that still survives?

AMANDA: That Fitzhugh boy went North and made a fortune—came to be known as the Wolf of Wall Street! He had the Midas touch, whatever he touched turned to gold! And I could have been Mrs. Duncan J. Fitzhugh, mind you! But—I picked your *father!*

LAURA *(rising):*   Mother, let me clear the table.

AMANDA: No dear, you go in front and study your typewriter chart. Or practice your shorthand a little. Stay fresh and pretty!—It's almost time for our gentlemen callers to start arriving. *(She flounces girlishly toward the kitchenette.)* How many do you suppose we're going to entertain this afternoon?

Tom throws down the paper and jumps up with a groan.

LAURA *(alone in the dining room):*   I don't believe we're going to receive any, Mother.

AMANDA *(reappearing, airily):*   What? No one—not one? You must be joking! *(Laura nervously echoes her laugh. She slips in a fugitive manner through the half-open portieres and draws them gently behind her. A shaft of very clear light is thrown on her face against the faded tapestry of the curtains.) (Music: "The Glass Menagerie" under faintly.) (Lightly.)* Not one gentleman caller? It can't be true! There must be a flood, there must have been a tornado!

LAURA: It isn't a flood, it's not a tornado, Mother. I'm just not popular like you were in Blue Mountain. . . . *(Tom utters another groan. Laura glances at him with a faint, apologetic smile. Her voice catching a little.)* Mother's afraid I'm going to be an old maid.

(The scene dims out with "Glass Menagerie" music.)

Scene 2

"Laura, Haven't You Ever Liked Some Boy?"

On the dark stage the screen is lighted with the image of blue roses.

> Gradually Laura's figure becomes apparent and the screen goes out.
>
> The music subsides.
>
> Laura is seated in the delicate ivory chair at the small clawfoot table.
>
> She wears a dress of soft violet material for a kimono — her hair tied back from her forehead with a ribbon.
>
> She is washing and polishing her collection of glass.
>
> Amanda appears on the fire-escape steps. At the sound of her ascent, Laura catches her breath, thrusts the bowl of ornaments away, and seats herself stiffly before the diagram of the typewriter keyboard as though it held her spellbound. Something has happened to Amanda. It is written in her face as she climbs to the landing: a look that is grim and hopeless and a little absurd.
>
> She has on one of those cheap or imitation velvety-looking cloth coats with imitation fur collar. Her hat is five or six years old, one of those dreadful cloche hats that were worn in the late twenties, and she is clasping an enormous black patent-leather pocketbook with nickel clasp and initials. This is her full-dress outfit, the one she usually wears to the D.A.R.°
>
> Before entering she looks through the door.
>
> She purses her lips, opens her eyes wide, rolls them upward, and shakes her head.
>
> Then she slowly lets herself in the door. Seeing her mother's expression Laura touches her lips with a nervous gesture.

LAURA: Hello, Mother, I was — *(She makes a nervous gesture toward the chart on the wall. Amanda leans against the shut door and stares at Laura with a martyred look.)*

AMANDA: Deception? Deception? *(She slowly removes her hat and gloves, continuing the swift suffering stare. She lets the hat and gloves fall on the floor — a bit of acting.)*

LAURA *(shakily):*   How was the D.A.R. meeting? *(Amanda slowly opens her purse and removes a dainty white handkerchief, which she shakes out delicately and delicately touches to her lips and nostrils.)* Didn't you go to the D.A.R. meeting, Mother?

AMANDA *(faintly, almost inaudibly):*   —No. —No. *(Then more forcibly.)* I did not have the strength — to go to the D.A.R. In fact, I did not have the courage! I wanted to find a hole in the ground and hide myself in it forever! *(She crosses slowly to the wall and removes the diagram of the typewriter keyboard. She holds it in front of her for a second, staring at it sweetly and sorrowfully — then bites her lips and tears it in two pieces.)*

D.A.R.: Daughters of the American Revolution; members must document that they have ancestors who served the patriots' cause in the Revolutionary War.

LAURA *(faintly):*   Why did you do that, Mother? *(Amanda repeats the same procedure with the chart of the Gregg Alphabet.°)* Why are you —

AMANDA: Why? Why? How old are you, Laura?

LAURA: Mother, you know my age.

AMANDA: I thought that you were an adult; it seems that I was mistaken. *(She crosses slowly to the sofa and sinks down and stares at Laura.)*

LAURA: Please don't stare at me, Mother.

Amanda closes her eyes and lowers her head. Count ten.

AMANDA: What are we going to do, what is going to become of us, what is the future?

Count ten.

LAURA: Has something happened, Mother? *(Amanda draws a long breath and takes out the handkerchief again. Dabbing process.)* Mother, has — something happened?

AMANDA: I'll be all right in a minute. I'm just bewildered — *(count five)* — by life. . . .

LAURA: Mother, I wish that you would tell me what's happened.

AMANDA: As you know, I was supposed to be inducted into my office at the D.A.R. this afternoon. *(Image: A swarm of typewriters.)* But I stopped off at Rubicam's Business College to speak to your teachers about your having a cold and ask them what progress they thought you were making down there.

LAURA: Oh. . . .

AMANDA: I went to the typing instructor and introduced myself as your mother. She didn't know who you were. Wingfield, she said. We don't have any such student enrolled at the school! I assured her she did, that you had been going to classes since early in January. "I wonder," she said, "if you could be talking about that terribly shy little girl who dropped out of school after only a few days' attendance?" "No," I said, "Laura, my daughter, has been going to school every day for the past six weeks!" "Excuse me," she said. She took the attendance book out and there was your name, unmistakably printed, and all the dates you were absent until they decided that you had dropped out of school. I still said, "No, there must have been some mistake! There must have been some mix-up in the records!" And she said, "No — I remember her perfectly now. Her hand shook so that she couldn't hit the right keys! The first time we gave a speed-test, she broke down completely — was sick at the stomach and almost had to be carried into the wash-room! After that morning she never showed up any more. We phoned the house but never got any answer" — while I was working at Famous and Barr, I suppose, demonstrating those — Oh! I felt so weak I could barely keep on my feet. I had to sit down while they got me a glass of water! Fifty dollars' tuition, all of our plans — my hopes and ambitions for you — just gone up the spout, just gone

---

Gregg Alphabet: System of shorthand symbols invented by John Robert Gregg.

up the spout like that. *(Laura draws a long breath and gets awkwardly to her feet. She crosses to the Victrola, and winds it up.)* What are you doing?

LAURA: Oh! *(She releases the handle and returns to her seat.)*

AMANDA: Laura, where have you been going when you've gone out pretending that you were going to business college?

LAURA: I've just been going out walking.

AMANDA: That's not true.

LAURA: It is. I just went walking.

AMANDA: Walking? Walking? In winter? Deliberately courting pneumonia in that light coat? Where did you walk to, Laura?

LAURA: It was the lesser of two evils, Mother. *(Image: Winter scene in park.)* I couldn't go back up. I — threw up — on the floor!

AMANDA: From half past seven till after five every day you mean to tell me you walked around in the park, because you wanted to make me think that you were still going to Rubicam's Business College?

LAURA: It wasn't as bad as it sounds. I went inside places to get warmed up.

AMANDA: Inside where?

LAURA: I went in the art museum and the bird-houses at the Zoo. I visited the penguins every day! Sometimes I did without lunch and went to the movies. Lately I've been spending most of my afternoons in the Jewel-box, that big glass house where they raise the tropical flowers.

AMANDA: You did all this to deceive me, just for the deception? *(Laura looks down.)* Why?

LAURA: Mother, when you're disappointed, you get that awful suffering look on your face, like the picture of Jesus' mother in the museum!

AMANDA: Hush!

LAURA: I couldn't face it.

Pause. A whisper of strings.
(Legend: "The Crust of Humility.")

AMANDA *(hopelessly fingering the huge pocketbook)*: So what are we going to do the rest of our lives? Stay home and watch the parades go by? Amuse ourselves with the glass menagerie, darling? Eternally play those worn-out phonograph records your father left as a painful reminder of him? We won't have a business career — we've given that up because it gave us nervous indigestion! *(Laughs wearily.)* What is there left but dependency all our lives? I know so well what becomes of unmarried women who aren't prepared to occupy a position. I've seen such pitiful cases in the South — barely tolerated spinsters living upon the grudging patronage of sister's husband or brother's wife! — stuck away in some little mousetrap of a room — encouraged by one in-law to visit another — little birdlike women without any nest — eating the crust of humility all their life! Is that the future that we've mapped out for ourselves? I swear it's the only alternative I can think of! It isn't a very pleasant alternative, is it? Of course — some girls *do marry.* *(Laura twists her hands nervously.)* Haven't you ever liked some boy?

LAURA: Yes. I liked one once. *(Rises.)* I came across his picture a while ago.

AMANDA (*with some interest*):   He gave you his picture?

LAURA: No, it's in the year-book.

AMANDA (*disappointed*):   Oh — a high-school boy.

(*Screen image: Jim as a high-school hero bearing a silver cup.*)

LAURA: Yes. His name was Jim. (*Laura lifts the heavy annual from the clawfoot table.*) Here he is in *The Pirates of Penzance.*

AMANDA (*absently*):   The what?

LAURA: The operetta the senior class put on. He had a wonderful voice and we sat across the aisle from each other Mondays, Wednesdays, and Fridays in the Aud. Here he is with the silver cup for debating! See his grin?

AMANDA (*absently*):   He must have had a jolly disposition.

LAURA: He used to call me — Blue Roses.

(*Image: Blue roses.*)

AMANDA: Why did he call you such a name as that?

LAURA: When I had that attack of pleurosis — he asked me what was the matter when I came back. I said pleurosis — he thought that I said Blue Roses! So that's what he always called me after that. Whenever he saw me, he'd holler, "Hello, Blue Roses!" I didn't care for the girl that he went out with. Emily Meisenbach. Emily was the best-dressed girl at Soldan. She never struck me, though, as being sincere.... It says in the Personal Section — they're engaged. That's — six years ago! They must be married by now.

AMANDA: Girls that aren't cut out for business careers usually wind up married to some nice man. (*Gets up with a spark of revival.*) Sister, that's what you'll do!

Laura utters a startled, doubtful laugh. She reaches quickly for a piece of glass.

LAURA: But, Mother —

AMANDA: Yes? (*Crossing to photograph.*)

LAURA (*in a tone of frightened apology*):   I'm — crippled!

(*Image: Screen.*)

AMANDA: Nonsense! Laura, I've told you never, never to use that word. Why, you're not crippled, you just have a little defect — hardly noticeable, even! When people have some slight disadvantage like that, they cultivate other things to make up for it — develop charm — and vivacity — and — *charm!* That's all you have to do! (*She turns again to the photograph.*) One thing your father had *plenty of* — was *charm!*

Tom motions to the fiddle in the wings.
    (*The scene fades out with music.*)

Scene 3

(*Legend on the screen: "After the Fiasco —"*)
    Tom speaks from the fire-escape landing.

TOM: After the fiasco at Rubicam's Business College, the idea of getting a gentleman caller for Laura began to play a more important part in Mother's calculations. It became an obsession. Like some archetype of the universal unconscious, the image of the gentleman caller haunted our small apartment. . . . (*Image: Young man at door with flowers.*) An evening at home rarely passed without some allusion to this image, this specter, this hope. . . . Even when he wasn't mentioned, his presence hung in Mother's preoccupied look and in my sister's frightened, apologetic manner—hung like a sentence passed upon the Wingfields! Mother was a woman of action as well as words. She began to take logical steps in the planned direction. Late that winter and in the early spring—realizing that extra money would be needed to properly feather the nest and plume the bird—she conducted a vigorous campaign on the telephone, roping in subscribers to one of those magazines for matrons called *The Home-maker's Companion*, the type of journal that features the serialized sublimations of ladies of letters who think in terms of delicate cuplike breasts, slim, tapering waists, rich, creamy thighs, eyes like wood-smoke in autumn, fingers that soothe and caress like strains of music, bodies as powerful as Etruscan sculpture.

(*Screen image:* Glamour *magazine cover.*)

Amanda enters with phone on long extension cord. She is spotted in the dim stage.

AMANDA: Ida Scott? This is Amanda Wingfield! We *missed* you at the D.A.R. last Monday! I said to myself: She's probably suffering with that sinus condition! How is that sinus condition? Horrors! Heaven have mercy!—You're a Christian martyr, yes, that's what you are, a Christian martyr! Well, I just now happened to notice that your subscription to the *Companion*'s about to expire! Yes, it expires with the next issue, honey!—just when that wonderful new serial by Bessie Mae Hopper is getting off to such an exciting start. Oh, honey, it's something that you can't miss! You remember how *Gone with the Wind* took everybody by storm? You simply couldn't go out if you hadn't read it. All everybody *talked* was Scarlett O'Hara. Well, this is a book that critics already compare to *Gone with the Wind*. It's the *Gone with the Wind* of the post–World War generation!—What?—Burning?—Oh, honey, don't let them burn, go take a look in the oven and I'll hold the wire! Heavens—I think she's hung up!

(*Dim out.*)

(*Legend on screen: "You think I'm in love with Continental Shoemakers?"*)

Before the stage is lighted, the violent voices of Tom and Amanda are heard. They are quarreling behind the portieres. In front of them stands Laura with clenched hands and panicky expression.

A clear pool of light on her figure throughout this scene.

TOM: What in Christ's name am I—

AMANDA (*shrilly*):   Don't you use that—

TOM: Supposed to do!

AMANDA: Expression! Not in my—

TOM: Ohhh!

AMANDA: Presence! Have you gone out of your senses?

TOM: I have, that's true, *driven* out!

AMANDA: What is the matter with you, you—big—big—IDIOT!

TOM: Look—I've got *no thing*, no single thing—
AMANDA: Lower your voice!
TOM: In my life here that I can call my own! Everything is—
AMANDA: Stop that shouting!
TOM: Yesterday you confiscated my books! You had the nerve to—
AMANDA: I took that horrible novel back to the library—yes! That hideous book by that insane Mr. Lawrence.° *(Tom laughs wildly.)* I cannot control the output of diseased minds or people who cater to them—*(Tom laughs still more wildly.)* BUT I WON'T ALLOW SUCH FILTH BROUGHT INTO MY HOUSE! No, no, no, no, no!
TOM: House, house! Who pays rent on it, who makes a slave of himself to—
AMANDA *(fairly screeching)*:   Don't you DARE to—
TOM: No, no, I mustn't say things! *I've* got to just—
AMANDA: Let me tell you—
TOM: I don't want to hear any more! *(He tears the portieres open. The upstage area is lit with a turgid smoky red glow.)*

Amanda's hair is in metal curlers and she wears a very old bathrobe, much too large for her slight figure, a relic of the faithless Mr. Wingfield.

An upright typewriter and a wild disarray of manuscripts are on the drop-leaf table. The quarrel was probably precipitated by Amanda's interruption of his creative labor. A chair lying overthrown on the floor.

Their gesticulating shadows are cast on the ceiling by the fiery glow.

AMANDA: You *will* hear more, you—
TOM: No, I won't hear more, I'm going out!
AMANDA: You come right back in—
TOM: Out, out, out! Because I'm—
AMANDA: Come back here, Tom Wingfield! I'm not through talking to you!
TOM: Oh, go—
LAURA *(desperately)*:   Tom!
AMANDA: You're going to listen, and no more insolence from you! I'm at the end of my patience! *(He comes back toward her.)*
TOM: What do you think I'm at? Aren't I supposed to have any patience to reach the end of, Mother? I know, I know. It seems unimportant to you, what I'm *doing*—what I *want* to do—having a little *difference* between them! You don't think that—
AMANDA: I think you've been doing things that you're ashamed of. That's why you act like this. I don't believe that you go every night to the movies. Nobody goes to the movies night after night. Nobody in their right minds goes to the movies as often as you pretend to. People don't go to the movies at nearly midnight, and movies don't let out at two A.M. Come in stumbling. Muttering to yourself like a maniac! You get three hours' sleep and then go to work. Oh, I can picture the way you're doing down there. Moping, doping, because you're in no condition.

Mr. Lawrence: D. H. Lawrence (1885–1930), English poet and novelist who advocated sexual freedom.

TOM *(wildly)*:   No, I'm in no condition!

AMANDA: What right have you got to jeopardize your job? Jeopardize the security of us all? How do you think we'd manage if you were —

TOM: Listen! You think I'm crazy *about* the *warehouse!* *(He bends fiercely toward her slight figure.)* You think I'm in love with the Continental Shoemakers? You think I want to spend fifty-five *years* down there in that — *celotex interior!* with — *fluorescent — tubes!* Look! I'd rather somebody picked up a crowbar and battered out my brains — than go back mornings! I *go!* Every time you come in yelling that God damn *"Rise and Shine!" "Rise and Shine!"* I say to myself "How *lucky dead* people are!" But I get up. I *go!* For sixty-five dollars a month I give up all that I dream of doing and being *ever!* And you say self — *self's* all I ever think of. Why, listen, if self is what I thought of, Mother, I'd be where he is — ! *(Pointing to father's picture.)* As far as the system of transportation reaches! *(He starts past her. She grabs his arm.)* Don't grab at me, Mother!

AMANDA: Where are you going?

TOM: I'm going to the *movies!*

AMANDA: I don't believe that lie!

TOM *(crouching toward her, overtowering her tiny figure. She backs away, gasping)*: I'm going to opium dens! Yes, opium dens, dens of vice and criminals' hang-outs, Mother. I've joined the Hogan gang, I'm a hired assassin, I carry a tommy-gun in a violin case! I run a string of cat-houses in the Valley! They call me Killer, Killer Wingfield, I'm leading a double-life, a simple, honest ware-house worker by day, by night a dynamic *czar* of the *underworld*, Mother. I go to gambling casinos, I spin away fortunes on the roulette table! I wear a patch over one eye and a false mustache, sometimes I put on green whiskers. On those occasions they call me — *El Diablo!*° Oh, I could tell you things to make you sleepless! My enemies plan to dynamite this place. They're going to blow us all sky-high some night! I'll be glad, very happy, and so will you! You'll go up, up on a broomstick, over Blue Mountain with seventeen gentlemen callers! You ugly — babbling old — *witch.* . . . *(He goes through a series of violent, clumsy movements, seizing his overcoat, lunging to the door, pulling it fiercely open. The women watch him, aghast. His arm catches in the sleeve of the coat as he struggles to pull it on. For a moment he is pinioned by the bulky garment. With an outraged groan he tears the coat off again, splitting the shoulders of it, and hurls it across the room. It strikes against the shelf of Laura's glass collection, there is a tinkle of shattering glass. Laura cries out as if wounded.)*

(Music legend: "The Glass Menagerie.")

LAURA *(shrilly)*:   My glass! — menagerie. . . . *(She covers her face and turns away.)*

But Amanda is still stunned and stupefied by the "ugly witch" so that she barely notices this occurrence. Now she recovers her speech.

AMANDA *(in an awful voice)*:   I won't speak to you — until you apologize! *(She crosses through portieres and draws them together behind her. Tom is left with Laura. Laura clings weakly to the mantel with her face averted. Tom stares at her*

El Diablo: The devil (Spanish).

stupidly for a moment. Then he crosses to shelf. Drops awkwardly to his knees to collect the fallen glass, glancing at Laura as if he would speak but couldn't.)

"The Glass Menagerie" steals in as
(The scene dims out.)

Scene 4

The interior is dark. Faint light in the alley.

A deep-voiced bell in a church is tolling the hour of five as the scene commences.

Tom appears at the top of the alley. After each solemn boom of the bell in the tower, he shakes a little noise-maker or rattle as if to express the tiny spasm of man in contrast to the sustained power and dignity of the Almighty. This and the unsteadiness of his advance make it evident that he has been drinking.

As he climbs the few steps to the fire-escape landing light steals up inside. Laura appears in night-dress, observing Tom's empty bed in the front room.

Tom fishes in his pockets for the door-key, removing a motley assortment of articles in the search, including a perfect shower of movie-ticket stubs and an empty bottle. At last he finds the key, but just as he is about to insert it, it slips from his fingers. He strikes a match and crouches below the door.

TOM *(bitterly):*   One crack—and it falls through!

Laura opens the door.

LAURA: Tom! Tom, what are you doing?

TOM: Looking for a door-key.

LAURA: Where have you been all this time?

TOM: I have been to the movies.

LAURA: All this time at the movies?

TOM: There was a very long program. There was a Garbo picture and a Mickey Mouse and a travelogue and a newsreel and a preview of coming attractions. And there was an organ solo and a collection for the milk-fund—simultaneously—which ended up in a terrible fight between a fat lady and an usher!

LAURA *(innocently):*   Did you have to stay through everything?

TOM: Of course! And, oh, I forgot! There was a big stage show! The headliner on this stage show was Malvolio the Magician. He performed wonderful tricks, many of them, such as pouring water back and forth between pitchers. First it turned to wine and then it turned to beer and then it turned to whiskey. I know it was whiskey it finally turned into because he needed somebody to come up out of the audience to help him, and I came up— both shows! It was Kentucky Straight Bourbon. A very generous fellow, he gave souvenirs. *(He pulls from his back pocket a shimmering rainbow-colored scarf.)* He gave me this. This is his magic scarf. You can have it, Laura. You wave it over a canary cage and you get a bowl of gold-fish. You wave it over the gold-fish bowl and they fly away canaries. . . . But the wonderfullest trick of all was the coffin trick. We nailed him into a coffin and he got out of the coffin without removing one nail. *(He has come inside.)* There is a trick that would come in handy for me—get me out of this 2 by 4 situation! *(Flops onto bed and starts removing shoes.)*

LAURA: Tom—Shhh!

TOM: What you shushing me for?

LAURA: You'll wake up Mother.

TOM: Goody, goody! Pay 'er back for all those "Rise an' Shines." *(Lies down, groaning.)* You know it don't take much intelligence to get yourself into a nailed-up coffin, Laura. But who in hell ever got himself out of one without removing one nail?

As if in answer, the father's grinning photograph lights up.
      (Scene dims out.)
      Immediately following: The church bell is heard striking six. At the sixth stroke the alarm clock goes off in Amanda's room, and after a few moments we hear her calling: "Rise and Shine! Rise and Shine! Laura, go tell your brother to rise and shine!"

TOM *(sitting up slowly)*:   I'll rise—but I won't shine.

The light increases.

AMANDA: Laura, tell your brother his coffee is ready.

Laura slips into front room.

LAURA: Tom! it's nearly seven. Don't make Mother nervous. *(He stares at her stupidly. Beseechingly.)* Tom, speak to Mother this morning. Make up with her, apologize, speak to her!

TOM: She won't to me. It's her that started not speaking.

LAURA: If you just say you're sorry she'll start speaking.

TOM: Her not speaking—is that such a tragedy?

LAURA: Please—please!

AMANDA *(calling from kitchenette)*:   Laura, are you going to do what I asked you to do, or do I have to get dressed and go out myself?

LAURA: Going, going—soon as I get on my coat! *(She pulls on a shapeless felt hat with nervous, jerky movement, pleadingly glancing at Tom. Rushes awkwardly for coat. The coat is one of Amanda's, inaccurately made-over, the sleeves too short for Laura.)* Butter and what else?

AMANDA *(entering upstage)*:   Just butter. Tell them to charge it.

LAURA: Mother, they make such faces when I do that.

AMANDA: Sticks and stones may break my bones, but the expression on Mr. Garfinkel's face won't harm us! Tell your brother his coffee is getting cold.

LAURA *(at door)*:   Do what I asked you, will you, will you, Tom?

He looks sullenly away.

AMANDA: Laura, go now or just don't go at all!

LAURA *(rushing out)*:   Going—going! *(A second later she cries out. Tom springs up and crosses to the door. Amanda rushes anxiously in. Tom opens the door.)*

TOM: Laura?

LAURA: I'm all right. I slipped, but I'm all right.

AMANDA *(peering anxiously after her)*:   If anyone breaks a leg on those fire-escape steps, the landlord ought to be sued for every cent he possesses! *(She shuts door. Remembers she isn't speaking and returns to other room.)*

As Tom enters listlessly for his coffee, she turns her back to him and stands rigidly facing the window on the gloomy gray vault of the areaway. Its light on her face with its aged but childish features is cruelly sharp, satirical as a Daumier° print. *(Music under: "Ave Maria.")*

Tom glances sheepishly but sullenly at her averted figure and slumps at the table. The coffee is scalding hot; he sips it and gasps and spits it back in the cup. At his gasp, Amanda catches her breath and half turns. Then catches herself and turns back to window.

Tom blows on his coffee, glancing sidewise at his mother. She clears her throat. Tom clears his. He starts to rise. Sinks back down again, scratches his head, clears his throat again. Amanda coughs. Tom raises his cup in both hands to blow on it, his eyes staring over the rim of it at his mother for several moments. Then he slowly sets the cup down and awkwardly and hesitantly rises from the chair.

TOM *(hoarsely)*:   Mother. I—I apologize. Mother. *(Amanda draws a quick, shuddering breath. Her face works grotesquely. She breaks into childlike tears.)* I'm sorry for what I said, for everything that I said, I didn't mean it.

AMANDA *(sobbingly)*:   My devotion has made me a witch and so I make myself hateful to my children!

TOM: No, you *don't.*

AMANDA: I worry so much, don't sleep, it makes me nervous!

TOM *(gently)*:   I understand that.

AMANDA: I've had to put up a solitary battle all these years. But you're my right-hand bower! Don't fall down, don't fail!

TOM *(gently)*:   I try, Mother.

AMANDA *(with great enthusiasm)*:   Try and you will SUCCEED! *(The notion makes her breathless.)* Why, you—you're just *full* of natural endowments! Both of my children—they're *unusual* children! Don't you think I know it? I'm so—proud! Happy and—feel I've—so much to be thankful for but—Promise me one thing, son!

TOM: What, Mother?

AMANDA: Promise, son, you'll—never be a drunkard!

TOM *(turns to her grinning)*:   I will never be a drunkard, Mother.

AMANDA: That's what frightened me so, that you'd be drinking! Eat a bowl of Purina!

TOM: Just coffee, Mother.

AMANDA: Shredded wheat biscuit?

TOM: No. No, Mother, just coffee.

Daumier: Honoré Daumier (1808–1879), French caricaturist, lithographer, and painter who mercilessly satirized bourgeois society.

AMANDA: You can't put in a day's work on an empty stomach. You've got ten minutes—don't gulp! Drinking too-hot liquids makes cancer of the stomach. . . . Put cream in.

TOM: No, thank you.

AMANDA: To cool it.

TOM: No! No, thank you, I want it black.

AMANDA: I know, but it's not good for you. We have to do all that we can to build ourselves up. In these trying times we live in, all that we have to cling to is— each other. . . . That's why it's so important to—Tom, I—I sent out your sister so I could discuss something with you. If you hadn't spoken I would have spoken to you. *(Sits down.)*

TOM *(gently):*   What is it, Mother, that you want to discuss?

AMANDA: Laura!

Tom puts his cup down slowly.
     (Legend on screen: "Laura.")
     (Music: "The Glass Menagerie.")

TOM: —Oh.—Laura . . .

AMANDA *(touching his sleeve):*   You know how Laura is. So quiet but—still water runs deep! She notices things and I think she—broods about them. *(Tom looks up.)* A few days ago I came in and she was crying.

TOM: What about?

AMANDA: You.

TOM: Me?

AMANDA: She has an idea that you're not happy here.

TOM: What gave her that idea?

AMANDA: What gives her any idea? However, you do act strangely. I—I'm not criticizing, understand *that!* I know your ambitions do not lie in the warehouse, that like everybody in the whole wide world—you've had to—make sacrifices, but—Tom—Tom—life's not easy, it calls for—Spartan endurance! There's so many things in my heart that I cannot describe to you! I've never told you but I—*loved* your father. . . .

TOM *(gently):*   I know that, Mother.

AMANDA: And you—when I see you taking after his ways! Staying out late— and—well, you *had* been drinking the night you were in that—terrifying condition! Laura says that you hate the apartment and that you go out nights to get away from it! Is that true, Tom?

TOM: No. You say there's so much in your heart that you can't describe to me. That's true of me, too. There's so much in my heart that I can't describe to *you!* So let's respect each other's—

AMANDA: But, why—*why,* Tom—are you always so *restless?* Where do you go to, nights?

TOM: I—go to the movies.

AMANDA: Why do you go to the movies so much, Tom?

TOM: I go to the movies because—I like adventure. Adventure is something I don't have much of at work, so I go to the movies.

AMANDA: But, Tom, you go to the movies *entirely too much!*

TOM: I like a lot of adventure.

Amanda looks baffled, then hurt. As the familiar inquisition resumes he becomes hard and impatient again. Amanda slips back into her querulous attitude toward him.
   (Image on screen: Sailing vessel with Jolly Roger.)

AMANDA: Most young men find adventure in their careers.

TOM: Then most young men are not employed in a warehouse.

AMANDA: The world is full of young men employed in warehouses and offices and factories.

TOM: Do all of them find adventure in their careers?

AMANDA: They do or they do without it! Not everybody has a craze for adventure.

TOM: Man is by instinct a lover, a hunter, a fighter, and none of those instincts are given much play at the warehouse!

AMANDA: Man is by instinct! Don't quote instinct to me! Instinct is something that people have got away from! It belongs to animals! Christian adults don't want it!

TOM: What do Christian adults want, then, Mother?

AMANDA: Superior things! Things of the mind and the spirit! Only animals have to satisfy instincts! Surely your aims are somewhat higher than theirs! Than monkeys — pigs —

TOM: I reckon they're not.

AMANDA: You're joking. However, that isn't what I wanted to discuss.

TOM *(rising):*   I haven't much time.

AMANDA *(pushing his shoulders):*   Sit down.

TOM: You want me to punch in red° at the warehouse, Mother?

AMANDA: You have five minutes. I want to talk about Laura.

(Legend: "Plans and Provisions.")

TOM: All right! What about Laura?

AMANDA: We have to be making plans and provisions for her. She's older than you, two years, and nothing has happened. She just drifts along doing nothing. It frightens me terribly how she just drifts along.

TOM: I guess she's the type that people call home girls.

AMANDA: There's no such type, and if there is, it's a pity! That is unless the home is hers, with a husband!

TOM: What?

AMANDA: Oh, I can see the handwriting on the wall as plain as I see the nose in front of my face! It's terrifying! More and more you remind me of your father! He was out all hours without explanation — Then *left! Good-bye!* And me with the bag to hold. I saw that letter you got from the Merchant Marine. I know what you're dreaming of. I'm not standing here blindfolded. Very well, then. Then *do* it! But not till there's somebody to take your place.

TOM: What do you mean?

punch in red: Be late for work.

AMANDA: I mean that as soon as Laura has got somebody to take care of her, married, a home of her own, independent — why, then you'll be free to go wherever you please, on land, on sea, whichever way the wind blows! But until that time you've got to look out for your sister. I don't say me because I'm old and don't matter! I say for your sister because she's young and dependent. I put her in business college — a dismal failure! Frightened her so it made her sick to her stomach. I took her over to the Young People's League at the church. Another fiasco. She spoke to nobody, nobody spoke to her. Now all she does is fool with those pieces of glass and play those worn-out records. What kind of a life is that for a girl to lead!

TOM: What can I do about it?

AMANDA: Overcome selfishness! Self, self, self is all that you ever think of! *(Tom springs up and crosses to get his coat. It is ugly and bulky. He pulls on a cap with earmuffs.)* Where is your muffler? Put your wool muffler on! *(He snatches it angrily from the closet and tosses it around his neck and pulls both ends tight.)* Tom! I haven't said what I had in mind to ask you.

TOM: I'm too late to —

AMANDA *(catching his arms — very importunately. Then shyly.)*:   Down at the warehouse, aren't there some — nice young men?

TOM: No!

AMANDA: There *must* be — *some*.

TOM: Mother —

Gesture.

AMANDA: Find out one that's clean-living — doesn't drink and — ask him out for sister!

TOM: What?

AMANDA: For *sister!* To *meet!* Get *acquainted!*

TOM *(stamping to door)*:   Oh, my go-osh!

AMANDA: Will you? *(He opens door. Imploringly.)* Will you? *(He starts down.)* Will you? *Will* you, dear?

TOM *(calling back)*:   YES!

*Amanda closes the door hesitantly and with a troubled but faintly hopeful expression.
(Screen image: Glamour magazine cover.)
Spot Amanda at phone.*

AMANDA: Ella Cartwright? This is Amanda Wingfield! How are you, honey? How is that kidney condition? *(Count five.)* Horrors! *(Count five.)* You're a Christian martyr, yes, honey, that's what you are, a Christian martyr! Well, I just happened to notice in my little red book that your subscription to the *Companion* has just run out! I knew that you wouldn't want to miss out on the wonderful serial starting in this new issue. It's by Bessie Mae Hopper, the first thing she's written since *Honeymoon for Three*. Wasn't that a strange and interesting story? Well, this one is even lovelier, I believe. It has a sophisticated society background. It's all about the horsey set on Long Island!

(Fade out.)

Scene 5

(Legend on screen: "Annunciation.") Fade with music.

   It is early dusk of a spring evening. Supper has just been finished in the Wingfield apartment. Amanda and Laura in light-colored dresses are removing dishes from the table, in the upstage area, which is shadowy, their movements formalized almost as a dance or ritual, their moving forms as pale and silent as moths.

   Tom, in white shirt and trousers, rises from the table and crosses toward the fire-escape.

AMANDA *(as he passes her)*:   Son, will you do me a favor?

TOM: What?

AMANDA: Comb your hair! You look so pretty when your hair is combed! *(Tom slouches on sofa with evening paper. Enormous caption "Franco Triumphs."°)* There is only one respect in which I would like you to emulate your father.

TOM: What respect is that?

AMANDA: The care he always took of his appearance. He never allowed himself to look untidy. *(He throws down the paper and crosses to fire-escape.)* Where are you going?

TOM: I'm going out to smoke.

AMANDA: You smoke too much. A pack a day at fifteen cents a pack. How much would that amount to in a month? Thirty times fifteen is how much, Tom? Figure it out and you will be astounded at what you could save. Enough to give you a night-school course in accounting at Washington U! Just think what a wonderful thing that would be for you, son!

Tom is unmoved by the thought.

TOM: I'd rather smoke. *(He steps out on landing, letting the screen door slam.)*

AMANDA *(sharply)*:   I know! That's the tragedy of it. . . . *(Alone, she turns to look at her husband's picture.)*

(Dance music: "All the World Is Waiting for the Sunrise!")

TOM *(to the audience)*:   Across the alley from us was the Paradise Dance Hall. On evenings in spring the windows and doors were open and the music came outdoors. Sometimes the lights were turned out except for a large glass sphere that hung from the ceiling. It would turn slowly about and filter the dusk with delicate rainbow colors. Then the orchestra played a waltz or a tango, something that had a slow and sensuous rhythm. Couples would come outside, to the relative privacy of the alley. You could see them kissing behind ash-pits and telephone poles. This was the compensation for lives that passed like mine, without any change or adventure. Adventure and change were imminent in this year. They were waiting around the corner for all these kids. Suspended in the mist over the Berchtesgaden,° caught in the

---

"Franco Triumphs": In January 1939, the Republican forces of Francisco Franco (1892–1975) defeated the Loyalists, ending the Spanish Civil War.   **Berchtesgaden:** A resort in the German Alps where Adolf Hitler had a heavily protected villa.

folds of Chamberlain's° umbrella—In Spain there was Guernica! But here there was only hot swing music and liquor, dance halls, bars, and movies, and sex that hung in the gloom like a chandelier and flooded the world with brief, deceptive rainbows. . . . All the world was waiting for bombardments!

Amanda turns from the picture and comes outside.

AMANDA (*sighing*): A fire-escape landing's a poor excuse for a porch. (*She spreads a newspaper on a step and sits down, gracefully and demurely as if she were settling into a swing on a Mississippi veranda.*) What are you looking at?

TOM: The moon.

AMANDA: Is there a moon this evening?

TOM: It's rising over Garfinkel's Delicatessen.

AMANDA: So it is! A little silver slipper of a moon. Have you made a wish on it yet?

TOM: Um-hum.

AMANDA: What did you wish for?

TOM: That's a secret.

AMANDA: A secret, huh? Well, I won't tell mine either. I will be just as mysterious as you.

TOM: I bet I can guess what yours is.

AMANDA: Is my head so transparent?

TOM: You're not a sphinx.

AMANDA: No, I don't have secrets. I'll tell you what I wished for on the moon. Success and happiness for my precious children! I wish for that whenever there's a moon, and when there isn't a moon, I wish for it, too.

TOM: I thought perhaps you wished for a gentleman caller.

AMANDA: Why do you say that?

TOM: Don't you remember asking me to fetch one?

AMANDA: I remember suggesting that it would be nice for your sister if you brought home some nice young man from the warehouse. I think I've made that suggestion more than once.

TOM: Yes, you have made it repeatedly.

AMANDA: Well?

TOM: We are going to have one.

AMANDA: *What?*

TOM: A gentleman caller!

(*The Annunciation is celebrated with music.*)
   Amanda rises.
   (*Image on screen: Caller with bouquet.*)

AMANDA: You mean you have asked some nice young man to come over?

TOM: Yep. I've asked him to dinner.

AMANDA: You really did?

TOM: I did!

AMANDA: You did, and did he—*accept?*

Chamberlain: Neville Chamberlain (1869–1940), British prime minister who sought to avoid war with Hitler through a policy of appeasement.

TOM: He did!

AMANDA: Well, well — well, well! That's — lovely!

TOM: I thought that you would be pleased.

AMANDA: It's definite, then?

TOM: Very definite.

AMANDA: Soon?

TOM: Very soon.

AMANDA: For heaven's sake, stop putting on and tell me some things, will you?

TOM: What things do you want me to tell you?

AMANDA: Naturally I would like to know when he's *coming!*

TOM: He's coming tomorrow.

AMANDA: *Tomorrow?*

TOM: Yep. Tomorrow.

AMANDA: But, Tom!

TOM: Yes, Mother?

AMANDA: Tomorrow gives me no time!

TOM: Time for what?

AMANDA: Preparations! Why didn't you phone me at once, as soon as you asked him, the minute that he accepted? Then, don't you see, I could have been getting ready!

TOM: You don't have to make any fuss.

AMANDA: Oh, Tom, Tom, Tom, of course I have to make a fuss! I want things nice, not sloppy! Not thrown together. I'll certainly have to do some fast thinking, won't I?

TOM: I don't see why you have to think at all.

AMANDA: You just don't know. We can't have a gentleman caller in a pig-sty! All my wedding silver has to be polished, the monogrammed table linen ought to be laundered! The windows have to be washed and fresh curtains put up. And how about clothes? We have to *wear* something, don't we?

TOM: Mother, this boy is no one to make a fuss over!

AMANDA: Do you realize he's the first young man we've introduced to your sister? It's terrible, dreadful, disgraceful that poor little sister has never received a single gentleman caller! Tom, come inside! *(She opens the screen door.)*

TOM: What for?

AMANDA: I want to ask you some things.

TOM: If you're going to make such a fuss, I'll call it off, I'll tell him not to come.

AMANDA: You certainly won't do anything of the kind. Nothing offends people worse than broken engagements. It simply means I'll have to work like a Turk! We won't be brilliant, but we'll pass inspection. Come on inside. *(Tom follows, groaning.)* Sit down.

TOM: Any particular place you would like me to sit?

AMANDA: Thank heavens I've got that new sofa! I'm also making payments on a floor lamp I'll have sent out! And put the chintz covers on, they'll brighten things up! Of course I'd hoped to have these walls re-papered. . . . What is the young man's name?

TOM: His name is O'Connor.

AMANDA: That, of course, means fish — tomorrow is Friday! I'll have that salmon
    loaf — with Durkee's dressing! What does he do? He works at the warehouse?

TOM: Of course! How else would I —

AMANDA: Tom, he — doesn't drink?

TOM: Why do you ask me that?

AMANDA: Your father *did!*

TOM: Don't get started on that!

AMANDA: He *does* drink, then?

TOM: Not that I know of!

AMANDA: Make sure, be certain! The last thing I want for my daughter's a boy
    who drinks!

TOM: Aren't you being a little premature? Mr. O'Connor has not yet appeared
    on the scene!

AMANDA: But will tomorrow. To meet your sister, and what do I know about his
    character? Nothing! Old maids are better off than wives of drunkards!

TOM: Oh, my God!

AMANDA: Be still!

TOM *(leaning forward to whisper):*   Lots of fellows meet girls whom they don't
    marry!

AMANDA: Oh, talk sensibly, Tom — and don't be sarcastic! *(She has gotten a
    hairbrush.)*

TOM: What are you doing?

AMANDA: I'm brushing that cow-lick down! What is this young man's position at
    the warehouse?

TOM *(submitting grimly to the brush and the interrogation):*   This young man's
    position is that of a shipping clerk, Mother.

AMANDA: Sounds to me like a fairly responsible job, the sort of a job *you* would
    be in if you just had more *get-up.* What is his salary? Have you got any idea?

TOM: I would judge it to be approximately eighty-five dollars a month.

AMANDA: Well — not princely, but —

TOM: Twenty more than I make.

AMANDA: Yes, how well I know! But for a family man, eighty-five dollars a month
    is not much more than you can just get by on. . . .

TOM: Yes, but Mr. O'Connor is not a family man.

AMANDA: He might be, mightn't he? Some time in the future?

TOM: I see. Plans and provisions.

AMANDA: You are the only young man that I know of who ignores the fact that
    the future becomes the present, the present the past, and the past turns into
    everlasting regret if you don't plan for it!

TOM: I will think that over and see what I can make of it.

AMANDA: Don't be supercilious with your mother! Tell me some more about
    this — what do you call him?

TOM: James D. O'Connor. The D. is for Delaney.

AMANDA: Irish on *both* sides! *Gracious!* And doesn't drink?

TOM: Shall I call him up and ask him right this minute?

AMANDA: The only way to find out about those things is to make discreet inquiries at the proper moment. When I was a girl in Blue Mountain and it was suspected that a young man drank, the girl whose attentions he had been receiving, if any girl *was*, would sometimes speak to the minister of his church, or rather her father would if her father was living, and sort of feel him out on the young man's character. That is the way such things are discreetly handled to keep a young woman from making a tragic mistake!

TOM: Then how did you happen to make a tragic mistake?

AMANDA: That innocent look of your father's had everyone fooled! He *smiled*— the world was *enchanted*! No girl can do worse than put herself at the mercy of a handsome appearance! I hope that Mr. O'Connor is not too good-looking.

TOM: No, he's not too good-looking. He's covered with freckles and hasn't too much of a nose.

AMANDA: He's not right-down homely, though?

TOM: Not right-down homely. Just medium homely, I'd say.

AMANDA: Character's what to look for in a man.

TOM: That's what I've always said, Mother.

AMANDA: You've never said anything of the kind and I suspect you would never give it a thought.

TOM: Don't be suspicious of me.

AMANDA: At least I hope he's the type that's up and coming.

TOM: I think he really goes in for self-improvement.

AMANDA: What reason have you to think so?

TOM: He goes to night school.

AMANDA *(beaming)*:   Splendid! What does he do, I mean study?

TOM: Radio engineering and public speaking!

AMANDA: Then he has visions of being advanced in the world! Any young man who studies public speaking is aiming to have an executive job some day! And radio engineering? A thing for the future! Both of these facts are very illuminating. Those are the sort of things that a mother should know concerning any young man who comes to call on her daughter. Seriously or—not.

TOM: One little warning. He doesn't know about Laura. I didn't let on that we had dark ulterior motives. I just said, why don't you come have dinner with us? He said okay and that was the whole conversation.

AMANDA: I bet it was! You're eloquent as an oyster. However, he'll know about Laura when he gets here. When he sees how lovely and sweet and pretty she is, he'll thank his lucky stars he was asked to dinner.

TOM: Mother, you mustn't expect too much of Laura.

AMANDA: What do you mean?

TOM: Laura seems all those things to you and me because she's ours and we love her. We don't even notice she's crippled any more.

AMANDA: Don't say crippled! You know that I never allow that word to be used!

TOM: But face facts, Mother. She is and—that's not all—

AMANDA: What do you mean "not all"?

TOM: Laura is very different from other girls.

AMANDA: I think the difference is all to her advantage.

TOM: Not quite all—in the eyes of others—strangers—she's terribly shy and lives in a world of her own and those things make her seem a little peculiar to people outside the house.

AMANDA: Don't say peculiar.

TOM: Face the facts. She is.

(The dance-hall music changes to a tango that has a minor and somewhat ominous tone.)

AMANDA: In what way is she peculiar—may I ask?

TOM *(gently)*:   She lives in a world of her own—a world of—little glass ornaments, Mother. . . . *(Gets up. Amanda remains holding brush, looking at him, troubled.)* She plays old phonograph records and—that's about all—*(He glances at himself in the mirror and crosses to door.)*

AMANDA *(sharply)*:   Where are you going?

TOM: I'm going to the movies. *(Out screen door.)*

AMANDA: Not to the movies, every night to the movies! *(Follows quickly to screen door.)* I don't believe you always go to the movies! *(He is gone. Amanda looks worriedly after him for a moment. Then vitality and optimism return and she turns from the door. Crossing to portieres.)* Laura! Laura! *(Laura answers from kitchenette.)*

LAURA: Yes, Mother.

AMANDA: Let those dishes go and come in front! *(Laura appears with dish towel. Gaily.)* Laura, come here and make a wish on the moon!

LAURA *(entering)*:   Moon—moon?

AMANDA: A little silver slipper of a moon. Look over your left shoulder, Laura, and make a wish! *(Laura looks faintly puzzled as if called out of sleep. Amanda seizes her shoulders and turns her at angle by the door.)* Now! Now, darling, *wish!*

LAURA: What shall I wish for, Mother?

AMANDA *(her voice trembling and her eyes suddenly filling with tears)*:   Happiness! Good Fortune!

The violin rises and the stage dims out.

Scene 6

(Image: High-school hero.)

TOM: And so the following evening I brought Jim home to dinner. I had known Jim slightly in high school. In high school Jim was a hero. He had tremendous Irish good nature and vitality with the scrubbed and polished look of white chinaware. He seemed to move in a continual spotlight. He was a star in basketball, captain of the debating club, president of the senior class and the glee club and he sang the male lead in the annual light operas. He was always running or bounding, never just walking. He seemed always at the point of defeating the law of gravity. He was shooting with such velocity through his adolescence that you would logically expect him to arrive at nothing short of the White House by the time he was thirty. But Jim apparently ran into more interference after his graduation from Soldan. His speed had definitely slowed. Six years after he left high school he was holding a job that wasn't much better than mine.

(Image: Clerk.)

He was the only one at the warehouse with whom I was on friendly terms. I was valuable to him as someone who could remember his former glory, who had seen him win basketball games and the silver cup in debating. He knew of my secret practice of retiring to a cabinet of the washroom to work on poems when business was slack in the warehouse. He called me Shakespeare. And while the other boys in the warehouse regarded me with suspicious hostility, Jim took a humorous attitude toward me. Gradually his attitude affected the others, their hostility wore off, and they also began to smile at me as people smile at an oddly fashioned dog who trots across their paths at some distance.

I knew that Jim and Laura had known each other at Soldan, and I had heard Laura speak admiringly of his voice. I didn't know if Jim remembered her or not. In high school Laura had been as unobtrusive as Jim had been astonishing. If he did remember Laura, it was not as my sister, for when I asked him to dinner, he grinned and said, "You know, Shakespeare, I never thought of you as having folks!"

He was about to discover that I did. . . .

(Light upstage.)

(Legend on screen: "The Accent of a Coming Foot.")

Friday evening. It is about five o'clock of a late spring evening which comes "scattering poems in the sky."

A delicate lemony light is in the Wingfield apartment.

Amanda has worked like a Turk in preparation for the gentleman caller. The results are astonishing. The new floor lamp with its rose-silk shade is in place, a colored paper lantern conceals the broken light fixture in the ceiling, new billowing white curtains are at the windows, chintz covers are on chairs and sofa, a pair of new sofa pillows make their initial appearance.

Open boxes and tissue paper are scattered on the floor.

Laura stands in the middle with lifted arms while Amanda crouches before her, adjusting the hem of the new dress, devout and ritualistic. The dress is colored and designed by memory. The arrangement of Laura's hair is changed; it is softer and more becoming. A fragile, unearthly prettiness has come out in Laura: she is like a piece of translucent glass touched by light, given a momentary radiance, not actual, not lasting.

AMANDA *(impatiently)*: Why are you trembling?

LAURA: Mother, you've made me so nervous!

AMANDA: How have I made you nervous?

LAURA: By all this fuss! You make it seem so important!

AMANDA: I don't understand you, Laura. You couldn't be satisfied with just sitting home, and yet whenever I try to arrange something for you, you seem to resist it. *(She gets up.)* Now take a look at yourself. No, wait! Wait just a moment—I have an idea!

LAURA: What is it now?

Amanda produces two powder puffs which she wraps in handkerchiefs and stuffs in Laura's bosom.

LAURA: Mother, what are you doing?

AMANDA: They call them "Gay Deceivers"!

LAURA: I won't wear them!

AMANDA: You will!

LAURA: Why should I?

AMANDA: Because, to be painfully honest, your chest is flat.

LAURA: You make it seem like we were setting a trap.

AMANDA: All pretty girls are a trap, a pretty trap, and men expect them to be. *(Legend: "A Pretty Trap.")* Now look at yourself, young lady. This is the prettiest you will ever be! I've got to fix myself now! You're going to be surprised by your mother's appearance! *(She crosses through portieres, humming gaily.)*

Laura moves slowly to the long mirror and stares solemnly at herself.

A wind blows the white curtains inward in a slow, graceful motion and with a faint, sorrowful sighing.

AMANDA *(offstage):* It isn't dark enough yet. *(She turns slowly before the mirror with a troubled look).*

(Legend on screen: "This Is My Sister: Celebrate Her with Strings!" Music.)

AMANDA *(laughing, off):* I'm going to show you something. I'm going to make a spectacular appearance!

LAURA: What is it, Mother?

AMANDA: Possess your soul in patience—you will see! Something I've resurrected from that old trunk! Styles haven't changed so terribly much after all. . . . *(She parts the portieres.)* Now just look at your mother! *(She wears a girlish frock of yellowed voile with a blue silk sash. She carries a bunch of jonquils—the legend of her youth is nearly revived. Feverishly.)* This is the dress in which I led the cotillion. Won the cakewalk twice at Sunset Hill, wore one spring to the Governor's ball in Jackson! See how I sashayed around the ballroom, Laura? *(She raises her skirt and does a mincing step around the room.)* I wore it on Sundays for my gentlemen callers! I had it on the day I met your father—I had malaria fever all that spring. The change of climate from East Tennessee to the Delta—weakened resistance—I had a little temperature all the time—not enough to be serious—just enough to make me restless and giddy! Invitations poured in—parties all over the Delta!—"Stay in bed," said Mother, "you have fever!"—but I just wouldn't.—I took quinine but kept on going, going!—Evenings, dances!—Afternoons, long, long rides! Picnics—lovely!—So lovely, that country in May.—All lacy with dogwood, literally flooded with jonquils!—That was the spring I had the craze for jonquils. Jonquils became an absolute obsession. Mother said, "Honey, there's no more room for jonquils." And still I kept bringing in more jonquils. Whenever, wherever I saw them, I'd say, "Stop! Stop! I see jonquils!" I made the young men help me gather the jonquils! It was a joke, Amanda and her jonquils! Finally there were no more vases to hold them, every available space was filled with jonquils. No vases to hold them? All right, I'll hold them myself! And then I—*(She stops in front of the picture.) (Music.)* met your father! Malaria fever and jonquils and then—this—boy. . . . *(She switches on the rose-colored lamp.)* I hope they get here before it starts to rain. *(She crosses upstage and places the jonquils in bowl on table.)* I gave your brother a little extra change so he and Mr. O'Connor could take the service car home.

LAURA *(with altered look):*　What did you say his name was?

AMANDA:　O'Connor.

LAURA:　What is his first name?

AMANDA:　I don't remember. Oh, yes, I do. It was—Jim!

Laura sways slightly and catches hold of a chair.
　　(Legend on screen: "Not Jim!")

LAURA *(faintly):*　Not—Jim!

AMANDA:　Yes, that was it, it was Jim! I've never known a Jim that wasn't nice!

(Music: Ominous.)

LAURA:　Are you sure his name is Jim O'Connor?

AMANDA:　Yes. Why?

LAURA:　Is he the one that Tom used to know in high school?

AMANDA:　He didn't say so. I think he just got to know him at the warehouse.

LAURA:　There was a Jim O'Connor we both knew in high school—*(Then, with effort.)* If that is the one that Tom is bringing to dinner—you'll have to excuse me, I won't come to the table.

AMANDA:　What sort of nonsense is this?

LAURA:　You asked me once if I'd ever liked a boy. Don't you remember I showed you this boy's picture?

AMANDA:　You mean the boy you showed me in the year-book?

LAURA:　Yes, that boy.

AMANDA:　Laura, Laura, were you in love with that boy?

LAURA:　I don't know, Mother. All I know is I couldn't sit at the table if it was him!

AMANDA:　It won't be him! It isn't the least bit likely. But whether it is or not, you will come to the table. You will not be excused.

LAURA:　I'll have to be, Mother.

AMANDA:　I don't intend to humor your silliness, Laura. I've had too much from you and your brother, both! So just sit down and compose yourself till they come. Tom has forgotten his key so you'll have to let them in, when they arrive.

LAURA *(panicky):*　Oh, Mother—*you* answer the door!

AMANDA *(lightly):*　I'll be in the kitchen—busy!

LAURA:　Oh, Mother, please answer the door, don't make me do it!

AMANDA *(crossing into kitchenette):*　I've got to fix the dressing for the salmon. Fuss, fuss—silliness!—over a gentleman caller!

Door swings shut. Laura is left alone.
　　(Legend: "Terror!")

She utters a low moan and turns off the lamp—sits stiffly on the edge of the sofa, knotting her fingers together.
(Legend on screen: "The Opening of a Door!")
Tom and Jim appear on the fire-escape steps and climb to landing. Hearing their approach, Laura rises with a panicky gesture. She retreats to the portieres.
The doorbell. Laura catches her breath and touches her throat. Low drums.

AMANDA *(calling)*:   Laura, sweetheart! The door!

Laura stares at it without moving.

JIM: I think we just beat the rain.

TOM: Uh-huh. *(He rings again, nervously. Jim whistles and fishes for a cigarette.)*

AMANDA *(very, very gaily)*:   Laura, that is your brother and Mr. O'Connor! Will you let them in, darling?

Laura crosses toward kitchenette door.

LAURA *(breathlessly)*:   Mother—you go to the door!

Amanda steps out of kitchenette and stares furiously at Laura. She points imperiously at the door.

LAURA: Please, please!

AMANDA *(in a fierce whisper)*:   What is the matter with you, you silly thing?

LAURA *(desperately)*:   Please, you answer it, *please!*

AMANDA: I told you I wasn't going to humor you, Laura. Why have you chosen this moment to lose your mind?

LAURA: Please, please, please, you go!

AMANDA: You'll have to go to the door because I can't!

LAURA *(despairingly)*:   I can't either!

AMANDA: Why?

LAURA: I'm *sick!*

AMANDA: I'm sick, too—of your nonsense! Why can't you and your brother be normal people? Fantastic whims and behavior! *(Tom gives a long ring.)* Preposterous goings on! Can you give me one reason—*(Calls out lyrically.)* COMING! JUST ONE SECOND!—why should you be afraid to open a door? Now you answer it, Laura!

LAURA: Oh, oh, oh . . . *(She returns through the portieres. Darts to the Victrola and winds it frantically and turns it on.)*

AMANDA: Laura Wingfield, you march right to that door!

LAURA: Yes—yes, Mother!

A faraway, scratchy rendition of "Dardanella" softens the air and gives her strength to move through it. She slips to the door and draws it cautiously open.
Tom enters with the caller, Jim O'Connor.

TOM: Laura, this is Jim. Jim, this is my sister, Laura.

JIM *(stepping inside)*:   I didn't know that Shakespeare had a sister!

LAURA *(retreating stiff and trembling from the door)*:   How—how do you do?

JIM *(heartily extending his hand)*:   Okay!

Laura touches it hesitantly with hers.

JIM: Your hand's *cold*, Laura!

LAURA: Yes, well — I've been playing the Victrola . . .

JIM: Must have been playing classical music on it! You ought to play a little hot swing music to warm you up!

LAURA: Excuse me — I haven't finished playing the Victrola . . .

She turns awkwardly and hurries into the front room. She pauses a second by the Victrola. Then catches her breath and darts through the portieres like a frightened deer.

JIM *(grinning)*:   What was the matter?

TOM: Oh — with Laura? Laura is — terribly shy.

JIM: Shy, huh? It's unusual to meet a shy girl nowadays. I don't believe you ever mentioned you had a sister.

TOM: Well, now you know. I have one. Here is the *Post Dispatch*. You want a piece of it?

JIM: Uh-huh.

TOM: What piece? The comics?

JIM: Sports! *(Glances at it.)* Ole Dizzy Dean is on his bad behavior.

TOM *(disinterest)*:   Yeah? *(Lights cigarette and crosses back to fire-escape door.)*

JIM: Where are *you* going?

TOM: I'm going out on the terrace.

JIM *(goes after him)*:   You know, Shakespeare — I'm going to sell you a bill of goods!

TOM: What goods?

JIM: A course I'm taking.

TOM: Huh?

JIM: In public speaking! You and me, we're not the warehouse type.

TOM: Thanks — that's good news. But what has public speaking got to do with it?

JIM: It fits you for — executive positions!

TOM: Awww.

JIM: I tell you it's done a helluva lot for me.

(Image: Executive at desk.)

TOM: In what respect?

JIM: In every! Ask yourself what is the difference between you an' me and men in the office down front? Brains? — No! — Ability? — No! Then what? Just one little thing —

TOM: What is that one little thing?

JIM: Primarily it amounts to — social poise! Being able to square up to people and hold your own on any social level!

AMANDA *(offstage)*:   Tom?

TOM: Yes, Mother?

AMANDA: Is that you and Mr. O'Connor?

TOM: Yes, Mother.

AMANDA: Well, you just make yourselves comfortable in there.

TOM: Yes, Mother.

AMANDA: Ask Mr. O'Connor if he would like to wash his hands.

JIM: Aw—no—no—thank you—I took care of that at the warehouse. Tom—

TOM: Yes?

JIM: Mr. Mendoza was speaking to me about you.

TOM: Favorably?

JIM: What do you think?

TOM: Well—

JIM: You're going to be out of a job if you don't wake up.

TOM: I am waking up—

JIM: You show no signs.

TOM: The signs are interior.

(Image on screen: The sailing vessel with Jolly Roger again.)

TOM: I'm planning to change. (*He leans over the rail speaking with quiet exhila-
       ration. The incandescent marquees and signs of the first-run movie houses light
       his face from across the alley. He looks like a voyager.*) I'm right at the point of
       committing myself to a future that doesn't include the warehouse and Mr.
       Mendoza or even a night-school course in public speaking.

JIM: What are you gassing about?

TOM: I'm tired of the movies.

JIM: Movies!

TOM: Yes, movies! Look at them—(*A wave toward the marvels of Grand Avenue.*)
       All of those glamorous people—having adventures—hogging it all, gobbling
       the whole thing up! You know what happens? People go to the *movies* instead
       of *moving*! Hollywood characters are supposed to have all the adventures for
       everybody in America, while everybody in America sits in a dark room and
       watches them have them! Yes, until there's a war. That's when adventure
       becomes available to the masses! *Everyone's* dish, not only Gable's! Then the
       people in the dark room come out of the dark room to have some adventures
       themselves—Goody, goody—It's our turn now, to go to the South Sea
       Island—to make a safari—to be exotic, far-off—But I'm not patient. I don't
       want to wait till then. I'm tired of the *movies* and I am *about* to *move*!

JIM (*incredulously*):   Move?

TOM: Yes.

JIM: When?

TOM: Soon!

JIM: Where? Where?

*(Theme three: Music seems to answer the question, while Tom thinks it over. He
searches among his pockets.)*

TOM: I'm starting to boil inside. I know I seem dreamy, but inside—well, I'm
       boiling! Whenever I pick up a shoe, I shudder a little thinking how short life
       is and what I am doing!—Whatever that means. I know it doesn't mean
       shoes—except as something to wear on a traveler's feet! (*Finds paper.*)
       Look—

JIM: What?

TOM: I'm a member.

JIM (*reading*):   The Union of Merchant Seamen.

TOM: I paid my dues this month, instead of the light bill.

JIM: You will regret it when they turn the lights off.

TOM: I won't be here.

JIM: How about your mother?

TOM: I'm like my father. The bastard son of a bastard! See how he grins? And he's been absent going on sixteen years!

JIM: You're just talking, you drip. How does your mother feel about it?

TOM: Shhh—Here comes Mother! Mother is not acquainted with my plans!

AMANDA *(enters portieres):*   Where are you all?

TOM: On the terrace, Mother.

They start inside. She advances to them. Tom is distinctly shocked at her appearance. Even Jim blinks a little. He is making his first contact with girlish Southern vivacity and in spite of the night-school course in public speaking is somewhat thrown off the beam by the unexpected outlay of social charm.

    Certain responses are attempted by Jim but are swept aside by Amanda's gay laughter and chatter. Tom is embarrassed but after the first shock Jim reacts very warmly. Grins and chuckles, is altogether won over.

    (Image: Amanda as a girl.)

AMANDA *(coyly smiling, shaking her girlish ringlets):*   Well, well, well, so this is Mr. O'Connor. Introductions entirely unnecessary. I've heard so much about you from my boy. I finally said to him, Tom—good gracious!—why don't you bring this paragon to supper? I'd like to meet this nice young man at the warehouse!—Instead of just hearing him sing your praises so much! I don't know why my son is so stand-offish—that's not Southern behavior! Let's sit down and—I think we could stand a little more air in here! Tom, leave the door open. I felt a nice fresh breeze a moment ago. Where has it gone? Mmm, so warm already! And not quite summer, even. We're going to burn up when summer really gets started. However, we're having—we're having a very light supper. I think light things are better fo' this time of year. The same as light clothes are. Light clothes an' light food are what warm weather calls fo'. You know our blood gets so thick during th' winter—it takes a while fo' us to *adjust* ou'selves!—when the season changes. . . . It's come so quick this year. I wasn't prepared. All of a sudden—heavens! Already summer!—I ran to the trunk an' pulled out this light dress—Terribly old! Historical almost! But feels so good—so good an' co-ol, y'know. . . .

TOM: Mother—

AMANDA: Yes, honey?

TOM: How about—supper?

AMANDA: Honey, you go ask Sister if supper is ready! You know that Sister is in full charge of supper! Tell her you hungry boys are waiting for it. *(To Jim.)* Have you met Laura?

JIM: She—

AMANDA: Let you in? Oh, good, you've met already! It's rare for a girl as sweet an' pretty as Laura to be domestic! But Laura is, thank heavens, not only pretty but also very domestic. I'm not at all. I never was a bit. I never could make a thing but angel-food cake. Well, in the South we had so many servants. Gone, gone, gone. All vestiges of gracious living! Gone completely! I wasn't prepared for what the future brought me. All of my gentlemen callers were sons of planters and so of course I assumed that I would be married to one and raise my family on a large piece of land with plenty of servants. But man proposes—and woman accepts the proposal!—To vary that old, old saying a little bit—I married no planter! I married a man who worked for the telephone company!—that gallantly smiling gentleman over there! *(Points to the picture.)* A telephone man who—fell in love with long distance!— Now he travels and I don't even know where!—But what am I going on for about my—tribulations! Tell me yours—I hope you don't have any! Tom?

TOM *(returning)*: Yes, Mother?

AMANDA: Is supper nearly ready?

TOM: It looks to me like supper is on the table.

AMANDA: Let me look—*(She rises prettily and looks through portieres.)* Oh, lovely—But where is Sister?

TOM: Laura is not feeling well and she says that she thinks she'd better not come to the table.

AMANDA: What?—Nonsense!—Laura? Oh, Laura!

LAURA *(offstage, faintly)*: Yes, Mother.

AMANDA: You really must come to the table. We won't be seated until you come to the table! Come in, Mr. O'Connor. You sit over there and I'll—Laura? Laura Wingfield! You're keeping us waiting, honey! We can't say grace until you come to the table!

The back door is pushed weakly open and Laura comes in. She is obviously quite faint, her lips trembling, her eyes wide and staring. She moves unsteadily toward the table.
(Legend: "Terror!")
Outside a summer storm is coming abruptly. The white curtains billow inward at the windows and there is a sorrowful murmur and deep blue dusk.
Laura suddenly stumbles—She catches at a chair with a faint moan.

TOM: Laura!

AMANDA: Laura! *(There is a clap of thunder.)* *(Legend: "Ah!")* *(Despairingly.)* Why, Laura, you *are* sick, darling! Tom, help your sister into the living room, dear! Sit in the living room, Laura—rest on the sofa. Well! *(To the gentleman caller.)* Standing over the hot stove made her ill!—I told her that it was just too warm this evening, but—*(Tom comes back in. Laura is on the sofa.)* Is Laura all right now?

TOM: Yes.

AMANDA: What *is* that? Rain? A nice cool rain has come up! *(She gives the gentleman caller a frightened look.)* I think we may—have grace—now . . . *(Tom looks at her stupidly.)* Tom, honey—you say grace!

TOM: Oh . . . "For these and all thy mercies—" *(They bow their heads, Amanda stealing a nervous glance at Jim. In the living room Laura, stretched on the sofa, clenches her hand to her lips, to hold back a shuddering sob.)* God's Holy Name be praised—

(The scene dims out.)

Scene 7

A Souvenir

Half an hour later. Dinner is just being finished in the upstage area, which is concealed by the drawn portieres.

As the curtain rises Laura is still huddled upon the sofa, her feet drawn under her, her head resting on a pale blue pillow, her eyes wide and mysteriously watchful. The new floor lamp with its shade of rose-colored silk gives a soft, becoming light to her face, bringing out the fragile, unearthly prettiness which usually escapes attention. There is a steady murmur of rain, but it is slackening and stops soon after the scene begins; the air outside becomes pale and luminous as the moon breaks out.

A moment after the curtain rises, the lights in both rooms flicker and go out.

JIM: Hey, there, Mr. Light Bulb!

Amanda laughs nervously.

   (Legend: "Suspension of a Public Service.")

AMANDA: Where was Moses when the lights went out? Ha-ha. Do you know the answer to that one, Mr. O'Connor?

JIM: No, Ma'am, what's the answer?

AMANDA: In the dark! *(Jim laughs appreciatively.)* Everybody sit still. I'll light the candles. Isn't it lucky we have them on the table? Where's a match? Which of you gentlemen can provide a match?

JIM: Here.

AMANDA: Thank you, sir.

JIM: Not at all, Ma'am!

AMANDA: I guess the fuse has burnt out. Mr. O'Connor, can you tell a burnt-out fuse? I know I can't and Tom is a total loss when it comes to mechanics. *(Sound: Getting up: Voices recede a little to kitchenette.)* Oh, be careful you don't bump into something. We don't want our gentleman caller to break his neck. Now wouldn't that be a fine howdy-do?

JIM: Ha-ha! Where is the fuse-box?

AMANDA: Right here next to the stove. Can you see anything?

JIM: Just a minute.

AMANDA: Isn't electricity a mysterious thing? Wasn't it Benjamin Franklin who tied a key to a kite? We live in such a mysterious universe, don't we? Some people say that science clears up all the mysteries for us. In my opinion it only creates more! Have you found it yet?

JIM: No, Ma'am. All these fuses look okay to me.

AMANDA: Tom!

TOM: Yes, Mother?

AMANDA: That light bill I gave you several days ago. The one I told you we got the notices about?

TOM: Oh. — Yeah.

(Legend: "Ha!")

AMANDA: You didn't neglect to pay it by any chance?

TOM: Why, I —

AMANDA: Didn't! I might have known it!

JIM: Shakespeare probably wrote a poem on that light bill, Mrs. Wingfield.

AMANDA: I might have known better than to trust him with it! There's such a high price for negligence in this world!

JIM: Maybe the poem will win a ten-dollar prize.

AMANDA: We'll just have to spend the remainder of the evening in the nineteenth century, before Mr. Edison made the Mazda lamp!

JIM: Candlelight is my favorite kind of light.

AMANDA: That shows you're romantic! But that's no excuse for Tom. Well, we got through dinner. Very considerate of them to let us get through dinner before they plunged us into everlasting darkness, wasn't it, Mr. O'Connor?

JIM: Ha-ha!

AMANDA: Tom, as a penalty for your carelessness you can help me with the dishes.

JIM: Let me give you a hand.

AMANDA: Indeed you will not!

JIM: I ought to be good for something.

AMANDA: Good for something? *(Her tone is rhapsodic.)* You? Why, Mr. O'Connor, nobody, *nobody's* given me this much entertainment in years — as you have!

JIM: Aw, now, Mrs. Wingfield!

AMANDA: I'm not exaggerating, not one bit! But Sister is all by her lonesome. You go keep her company in the parlor! I'll give you this lovely old candelabrum that used to be on the altar at the church of the Heavenly Rest. It was melted a little out of shape when the church burnt down. Lightning struck it one spring. Gypsy Jones was holding a revival at the time and he intimated that the church was destroyed because the Episcopalians gave card parties.

JIM: Ha-ha.

AMANDA: And how about coaxing Sister to drink a little wine? I think it would be good for her! Can you carry both at once?

JIM: Sure. I'm Superman!

AMANDA: Now, Thomas, get into this apron!

The door of kitchenette swings closed on Amanda's gay laughter; the flickering light approaches the portieres.

Laura sits up nervously as he enters. Her speech at first is low and breathless from the almost intolerable strain of being alone with a stranger.

(Legend: "I Don't Suppose You Remember Me at All!")

In her first speeches in this scene, before Jim's warmth overcomes her paralyzing shyness, Laura's voice is thin and breathless as though she has run up a steep flight of stairs.

Jim's attitude is gently humorous. In playing this scene it should be stressed that while the incident is apparently unimportant, it is to Laura the climax of her secret life.

JIM: Hello, there, Laura.

LAURA *(faintly)*:   Hello. *(She clears her throat.)*

JIM: How are you feeling now? Better?

LAURA: Yes. Yes, thank you.

JIM: This is for you. A little dandelion wine. *(He extends it toward her with extravagant gallantry.)*

LAURA: Thank you.

JIM: Drink it—but don't get drunk! *(He laughs heartily. Laura takes the glass uncertainly; laughs shyly.)* Where shall I set the candles?

LAURA: Oh—oh, anywhere . . .

JIM: How about here on the floor? Any objections?

LAURA: No.

JIM: I'll spread a newspaper under to catch the drippings. I like to sit on the floor. Mind if I do?

LAURA: Oh, no.

JIM: Give me a pillow?

LAURA: What?

JIM: A pillow!

LAURA: Oh . . . *(Hands him one quickly.)*

JIM: How about you? Don't you like to sit on the floor?

LAURA: Oh—yes.

JIM: Why don't you, then?

LAURA: I—will.

JIM: Take a pillow! *(Laura does. Sits on the other side of the candelabrum. Jim crosses his legs and smiles engagingly at her.)* I can't hardly see you sitting way over there.

LAURA: I can—see you.

JIM: I know, but that's not fair, I'm in the limelight. *(Laura moves her pillow closer.)* Good! Now I can see you! Comfortable?

LAURA: Yes.

JIM: So am I. Comfortable as a cow. Will you have some gum?

LAURA: No, thank you.

JIM: I think that I will indulge, with your permission. *(Musingly unwraps it and holds it up.)* Think of the fortune made by the guy that invented the first piece of chewing gum. Amazing, huh? The Wrigley Building is one of the sights of Chicago.—I saw it summer before last when I went up to the Century of Progress. Did you take in the Century of Progress?

LAURA: No, I didn't.

JIM: Well, it was quite a wonderful exposition. What impressed me most was the Hall of Science. Gives you an idea of what the future will be in America, even more wonderful than the present time is! *(Pause. Smiling at her.)* Your brother tells me you're shy. Is that right, Laura?

LAURA: I—don't know.

JIM: I judge you to be an old-fashioned type of girl. Well, I think that's a pretty good type to be. Hope you don't think I'm being too personal—do you?

LAURA *(hastily, out of embarrassment):*   I believe I *will* take a piece of gum, if you—don't mind. *(Clearing her throat.)* Mr. O'Connor, have you—kept up with your singing?

JIM: Singing? Me?

LAURA: Yes. I remember what a beautiful voice you had.

JIM: When did you hear me sing?

(Voice offstage in the pause.)

VOICE *(offstage)*:   O blow, ye winds, heigh-ho,
                A-roving I will go!
                I'm off to my love
                With a boxing glove—
                Ten thousand miles away!

JIM: You say you've heard me sing?

LAURA: Oh, yes! Yes, very often . . . I—don't suppose you remember me—at all?

JIM *(smiling doubtfully)*:   You know I have an idea I've seen you before. I had that idea soon as you opened the door. It seemed almost like I was about to remember your name. But the name that I started to call you—wasn't a name! And so I stopped myself before I said it.

LAURA: Wasn't it—Blue Roses?

JIM *(springs up, grinning)*:   Blue Roses! My gosh, yes—Blue Roses! That's what I had on my tongue when you opened the door! Isn't it funny what tricks your memory plays? I didn't connect you with the high school somehow or other. But that's where it was; it was high school. I didn't even know you were Shakespeare's sister! Gosh, I'm sorry.

LAURA: I didn't expect you to. You—barely knew me!

JIM: But we did have a speaking acquaintance, huh?

LAURA: Yes, we—spoke to each other.

JIM: When did you recognize me?

LAURA: Oh, right away!

JIM: Soon as I came in the door?

LAURA: When I heard your name I thought it was probably you. I knew that Tom used to know you a little in high school. So when you came in the door—Well, then I was—sure.

JIM: Why didn't you *say* something, then?

LAURA *(breathlessly)*:   I didn't know what to say, I was—too surprised!

JIM: For goodness' sakes! You know, this sure is funny!

LAURA: Yes! Yes, isn't it, though . . .

JIM: Didn't we have a class in something together?

LAURA: Yes, we did.

JIM: What class was that?

LAURA: It was—singing—Chorus!

JIM: Aw!

LAURA: I sat across the aisle from you in the Aud.

JIM: Aw.

LAURA: Mondays, Wednesdays, and Fridays.

JIM: Now I remember—you always came in late.

LAURA: Yes, it was so hard for me, getting upstairs. I had that brace on my leg—it clumped so loud!

JIM: I never heard any clumping.

LAURA *(wincing in the recollection):*   To me it sounded like — thunder!

JIM: Well, well, well. I never even noticed.

LAURA: And everybody was seated before I came in. I had to walk in front of all those people. My seat was in the back row. I had to go clumping all the way up the aisle with everyone watching!

JIM: You shouldn't have been self-conscious.

LAURA: I know, but I was. It was always such a relief when the singing started.

JIM: Aw, yes, I've placed you now! I used to call you Blue Roses. How was it that I got started calling you that?

LAURA: I was out of school a little while with pleurosis. When I came back you asked me what was the matter. I said I had pleurosis — you thought I said Blue Roses. That's what you always called me after that!

JIM: I hope you didn't mind.

LAURA: Oh, no — I liked it. You see, I wasn't acquainted with many — people. . . .

JIM: As I remember you sort of stuck by yourself.

LAURA: I — I — never had much luck at — making friends.

JIM: I don't see why you wouldn't.

LAURA: Well, I — started out badly.

JIM: You mean being —

LAURA: Yes, it sort of — stood between me —

JIM: You shouldn't have let it!

LAURA: I know, but it did, and —

JIM: You were shy with people!

LAURA: I tried not to be but never could —

JIM: Overcome it?

LAURA: No, I — I never could!

JIM: I guess being shy is something you have to work out of kind of gradually.

LAURA *(sorrowfully):*   Yes — I guess it —

JIM: Takes time!

LAURA: Yes —

JIM: People are not so dreadful when you know them. That's what you have to remember! And everybody has problems, not just you, but practically everybody has got some problems. You think of yourself as having the only problems, as being the only one who is disappointed. But just look around you and you will see lots of people as disappointed as you are. For instance, I hoped when I was going to high school that I would be further along at this time, six years later, than I am now — You remember that wonderful write-up I had in *The Torch?*

LAURA: Yes! *(She rises and crosses to table.)*

JIM: It said I was bound to succeed in anything I went into! *(Laura returns with the annual.)* Holy Jeez! The Torch! *(He accepts it reverently. They smile across it with mutual wonder. Laura crouches beside him and they begin to turn through it. Laura's shyness is dissolving in his warmth.)*

LAURA: Here you are in *Pirates of Penzance!*

JIM *(wistfully):*   I sang the baritone lead in that operetta.

LAURA *(rapidly):*   So—*beautifully!*

JIM *(protesting):*   Aw—

LAURA: Yes, yes—beautifully—beautifully!

JIM: You heard me?

LAURA: All three times!

JIM: No!

LAURA: Yes!

JIM: All three performances?

LAURA *(looking down):*   Yes.

JIM: Why?

LAURA: I—wanted to ask you to—autograph my program.

JIM: Why didn't you ask me to?

LAURA: You were always surrounded by your own friends so much that I never had a chance to.

JIM: You should have just—

LAURA: Well, I—thought you might think I was—

JIM: Thought I might think you was—what?

LAURA: Oh—

JIM *(with reflective relish):*   I was beleaguered by females in those days.

LAURA: You were terribly popular!

JIM: Yeah—

LAURA: You had such a—friendly way—

JIM: I was spoiled in high school.

LAURA: Everybody—liked you!

JIM: Including you?

LAURA: I—yes, I—I did, too—*(She gently closes the book in her lap.)*

JIM: Well, well, well!—Give me that program, Laura. *(She hands it to him. He signs it with a flourish.)* There you are—better late than never!

LAURA: Oh, I—what a—surprise!

JIM: My signature isn't worth very much right now. But some day—maybe—it will increase in value! Being disappointed is one thing and being discouraged is something else. I am disappointed but I'm not discouraged. I'm twenty-three years old. How old are you?

LAURA: I'll be twenty-four in June.

JIM: That's not old age.

LAURA: No, but—

JIM: You finished high school?

LAURA *(with difficulty):*   I didn't go back.

JIM: You mean you dropped out?

LAURA: I made bad grades in my final examinations. *(She rises and replaces the book and the program. Her voice strained.)* How is—Emily Meisenbach getting along?

JIM: Oh, that kraut-head!

LAURA: Why do you call her that?

JIM: That's what she was.

LAURA: You're not still—going with her?

JIM: I never see her.

LAURA: It said in the Personal Section that you were — engaged!

JIM: I know, but I wasn't impressed by that — propaganda!

LAURA: It wasn't — the truth?

JIM: Only in Emily's optimistic opinion!

LAURA: Oh —

(Legend: "What Have You Done Since High School?")

Jim lights a cigarette and leans indolently back on his elbows smiling at Laura with a warmth and charm which light her inwardly with altar candles. She remains by the table and turns in her hands a piece of glass to cover her tumult.

JIM *(after several reflective puffs on a cigarette)*:   What have you done since high school? *(She seems not to hear him.)* Huh? *(Laura looks up.)* I said what have you done since high school, Laura?

LAURA: Nothing much.

JIM: You must have been doing something these six long years.

LAURA: Yes.

JIM: Well, then, such as what?

LAURA: I took a business course at business college —

JIM: How did that work out?

LAURA: Well, not very — well — I had to drop out, it gave me — indigestion —

Jim laughs gently.

JIM: What are you doing now?

LAURA: I don't do anything — much. Oh, please don't think I sit around doing nothing! My glass collection takes up a good deal of my time. Glass is something you have to take good care of.

JIM: What did you say — about glass?

LAURA: Collection I said — I have one — *(She clears her throat and turns away again, acutely shy.)*

JIM *(abruptly)*:   You know what I judge to be the trouble with you? Inferiority complex! Know what that is? That's what they call it when someone low-rates himself! I understand it because I had it, too. Although my case was not so aggravated as yours seems to be. I had it until I took up public speaking, developed my voice, and learned that I had an aptitude for science. Before that time I never thought of myself as being outstanding in any way whatsoever! Now I've never made a regular study of it, but I have a friend who says I can analyze people better than doctors that make a profession of it. I don't claim that to be necessarily true, but I can sure guess a person's psychology, Laura! *(Takes out his gum.)* Excuse me, Laura. I always take it out when the flavor is gone. I'll use this scrap of paper to wrap it in. I know how it is to get it stuck on a shoe. Yep — that's what I judge to be your principal trouble. A lack of confidence in yourself as a person. You don't have the proper amount of faith in yourself. I'm basing that fact on a number of your remarks and also on certain observations I've made. For instance that clumping you thought was so awful in high school. You say that you even dreaded to walk into class. You see what you did? You dropped out of school, you gave up an education because of a clump, which as far as I know was practically nonexistent! A little physical defect is what you have. Hardly noticeable even! Magnified thousands of times by imagination! You know what my strong advice to you is? Think of yourself as *superior* in some way!

LAURA: In what way would I think?

JIM: Why, man alive, Laura! Just look about you a little. What do you see? A world full of common people! All of 'em born and all of 'em going to die! Which of them has one-tenth of your good points! Or mine! Or anyone else's, as far as that goes—Gosh! Everybody excels in some one thing. Some in many! *(Unconsciously glances at himself in the mirror.)* All you've got to do is discover in *what!* Take me, for instance. *(He adjusts his tie at the mirror.)* My interest happened to lie in electrodynamics. I'm taking a course in radio engineering at night school, Laura, on top of a fairly responsible job at the warehouse. I'm taking that course and studying public speaking.

LAURA: Ohhhh.

JIM: Because I believe in the future of television! *(Turning back to her.)* I wish to be ready to go up right along with it. Therefore I'm planning to get in on the ground floor. In fact, I've already made the right connections and all that remains is for the industry itself to get under way! Full steam—*(His eyes are starry.)* Knowledge—Zzzzzp! Money—Zzzzzzp!—Power! That's the cycle democracy is built on! *(His attitude is convincingly dynamic. Laura stares at him, even her shyness eclipsed in her absolute wonder. He suddenly grins.)* I guess you think I think a lot of myself!

LAURA: No—o-o-o, I—

JIM: Now how about you? Isn't there something you take more interest in than anything else?

LAURA: Well, I do—as I said—have my—glass collection—

A peal of girlish laughter from the kitchen.

JIM: I'm not right sure I know what you're talking about. What kind of glass is it?

LAURA: Little articles of it, they're ornaments mostly! Most of them are little animals made out of glass, the tiniest little animals in the world. Mother calls them a glass menagerie! Here's an example of one, if you'd like to see it! This one is one of the oldest. It's nearly thirteen. *(He stretches out his hand.)* *(Music: "The Glass Menagerie.")* Oh, be careful—if you breathe, it breaks!

JIM: I'd better not take it. I'm pretty clumsy with things.

LAURA: Go on, I trust you with him! *(Places it in his palm.)* There now—you're holding him gently! Hold him over the light, he loves the light! You see how the light shines through him?

JIM: It sure does shine!

LAURA: I shouldn't be partial, but he is my favorite one.

JIM: What kind of thing is this one supposed to be?

LAURA: Haven't you noticed the single horn on his forehead?

JIM: A unicorn, huh?

LAURA: Mmm-hmmm!

JIM: Unicorns, aren't they extinct in the modern world?

LAURA: I know!

JIM: Poor little fellow, he must feel sort of lonesome.

LAURA *(smiling)*:   Well, if he does he doesn't complain about it. He stays on a shelf with some horses that don't have horns and all of them seem to get along nicely together.

JIM: How do you know?

LAURA *(lightly)*:   I haven't heard any arguments among them!

JIM *(grinning)*:   No arguments, huh? Well, that's a pretty good sign! Where shall I set him?

LAURA: Put him on the table. They all like a change of scenery once in a while!

JIM *(stretching)*:   Well, well, well, well—Look how big my shadow is when I stretch!

LAURA: Oh, oh, yes—it stretches across the ceiling!

JIM *(crossing to door)*:   I think it's stopped raining. *(Opens fire-escape door.)* Where does the music come from?

LAURA: From the Paradise Dance Hall across the alley.

JIM: How about cutting the rug a little, Miss Wingfield?

LAURA: Oh, I—

JIM: Or is your program filled up? Let me have a look at it. *(Grasps imaginary card.)* Why, every dance is taken! I'll have to scratch some out. *(Waltz music: "La Golondrina.")* Ahhh, a waltz! *(He executes some sweeping turns by himself then holds his arms toward Laura.)*

LAURA *(breathlessly)*:   I—can't dance!

JIM: There you go, that inferiority stuff!

LAURA: I've never danced in my life!

JIM: Come on, try!

LAURA: Oh, but I'd step on you!

JIM: I'm not made out of glass.

LAURA: How—how—how do we start?

JIM: Just leave it to me. You hold your arms out a little.

LAURA: Like this?

JIM: A little bit higher. Right. Now don't tighten up, that's the main thing about it—relax.

LAURA *(laughing breathlessly)*:   It's hard not to.

JIM: Okay.

LAURA: I'm afraid you can't budge me.

JIM: What do you bet I can't? *(He swings her into motion.)*

LAURA: Goodness, yes, you can!

JIM: Let yourself go, now, Laura, just let yourself go.

LAURA: I'm—

JIM: Come on!

LAURA: Trying.

JIM: Not so stiff—Easy does it!

LAURA: I know but I'm—

JIM: Loosen th' backbone! There now, that's a lot better.

LAURA: Am I?

JIM: Lots, lots better! *(He moves her about the room in a clumsy waltz.)*

LAURA: Oh, my!

JIM: Ha-ha!

LAURA: Goodness, yes you can!

JIM: Ha-ha-ha! *(They suddenly bump into the table. Jim stops.)* What did we hit on?

LAURA: Table.

JIM: Did something fall off it? I think—

LAURA: Yes.

JIM: I hope it wasn't the little glass horse with the horn!

LAURA: Yes.

JIM: Aw, aw, aw. Is it broken?

LAURA: Now it is just like all the other horses.

JIM: It's lost its—

LAURA: Horn! It doesn't matter. Maybe it's a blessing in disguise.

JIM: You'll never forgive me. I bet that that was your favorite piece of glass.

LAURA: I don't have favorites much. It's no tragedy, Freckles. Glass breaks so easily. No matter how careful you are. The traffic jars the shelves and things fall off them.

JIM: Still I'm awfully sorry that I was the cause.

LAURA *(smiling)*:   I'll just imagine he had an operation. The horn was removed to make him feel less—freakish! *(They both laugh.)* Now he will feel more at home with the other horses, the ones that don't have horns . . .

JIM: Ha-ha, that's very funny! *(Suddenly serious.)* I'm glad to see that you have a sense of humor. You know—you're—well—very different! Surprisingly different from anyone else I know! *(His voice becomes soft and hesitant with a genuine feeling.)* Do you mind me telling you that? *(Laura is abashed beyond speech.)* You make me feel sort of—I don't know how to put it! I'm usually pretty good at expressing things, but—This is something that I don't know how to say! *(Laura touches her throat and clears it—turns the broken unicorn in her hands.)* *(Even softer.)* Has anyone ever told you that you were pretty?

Pause: Music.

(Laura looks up slowly, with wonder, and shakes her head.) Well, you are! In a very different way from anyone else. And all the nicer because of the difference, too. *(His voice becomes low and husky. Laura turns away, nearly faint with the novelty of her emotions.)* I wish that you were my sister. I'd teach you to have some confidence in yourself. The different people are not like other people, but being different is nothing to be ashamed of. Because other people are not such wonderful people. They're one hundred times one thousand. You're one times one! They walk all over the earth. You just stay here. They're common as—weeds, but—you—well, you're—*Blue Roses!*

(Image on screen: Blue Roses.)
    (Music changes.)

LAURA: But blue is wrong for — roses . . .

JIM: It's right for you — You're — pretty!

LAURA: In what respect am I pretty?

JIM: In all respects — believe me! Your eyes — your hair — are pretty! Your hands
are pretty! *(He catches hold of her hand.)* You think I'm making this up
because I'm invited to dinner and have to be nice. Oh, I could do that! I
could put on an act for you, Laura, and say lots of things without being very
sincere. But this time I am. I'm talking to you sincerely. I happened to notice
you had this inferiority complex that keeps you from feeling comfortable
with people. Somebody needs to build your confidence up and make you
proud instead of shy and turning away and — blushing — Somebody ought
to — ought to — *kiss* you, Laura! *(His hand slips slowly up her arm to her
shoulder.) (Music swells tumultuously.) (He suddenly turns her about and
kisses her on the lips. When he releases her Laura sinks on the sofa with a
bright, dazed look. Jim backs away and fishes in his pocket for a cigarette.)
(Legend on screen: "Souvenir.")* Stumble-john! *(He lights the cigarette, avoiding her look. There is a peal of girlish laughter from Amanda in the kitchen.
Laura slowly raises and opens her hand. It still contains the little broken glass
animal. She looks at it with a tender, bewildered expression.)* Stumble-john! I
shouldn't have done that — That was way off the beam. You don't smoke, do
you? *(She looks up, smiling, not hearing the question. He sits beside her a little
gingerly. She looks at him speechlessly — waiting. He coughs decorously and
moves a little farther aside as he considers the situation and senses her feelings,
dimly, with perturbation. Gently.)* Would you — care for a — mint? *(She doesn't
seem to hear him but her look grows brighter even.)* Peppermint — Life Saver?
My pocket's a regular drug store — wherever I go . . . *(He pops a mint in his
mouth. Then gulps and decides to make a clean breast of it. He speaks slowly
and gingerly.)* Laura, you know, if I had a sister like you, I'd do the same thing
as Tom. I'd bring out fellows — introduce her to them. The right type of boys
of a type to — appreciate her. Only — well — he made a mistake about me.
Maybe I've got no call to be saying this. That may not have been the idea in
having me over. But what if it was? There's nothing wrong about that. The
only trouble is that in my case — I'm not in a situation to — do the right thing.
I can't take down your number and say I'll phone. I can't call up next week
and — ask for a date. I thought I had better explain the situation in case you
misunderstood it and — hurt your feelings. . . . *(Pause. Slowly, very slowly,
Laura's look changes, her eyes returning slowly from his to the ornament in her
palm.)*

Amanda utters another gay laugh in the kitchen.

LAURA *(faintly)*:   You — won't — call again?

JIM: No, Laura, I can't. *(He rises from the sofa.)* As I was just explaining, I've —
got strings on me, Laura, I've — been going steady! I go out all the time with a
girl named Betty. She's a home-girl like you, and Catholic, and Irish, and in
a great many ways we — get along fine. I met her last summer on a moonlight
boat trip up the river to Alton, on the *Majestic*. Well — right away from the

start it was—love! *(Legend: Love!) (Laura sways slightly forward and grips the arm of the sofa. He fails to notice, now enrapt in his own comfortable being.)* Being in love has made a new man of me! *(Leaning stiffly forward, clutching the arm of the sofa, Laura struggles visibly with her storm. But Jim is oblivious, she is a long way off.)* The power of love is really pretty tremendous! Love is something that—changes the whole world, Laura! *(The storm abates a little and Laura leans back. He notices her again.)* It happened that Betty's aunt took sick, she got a wire and had to go to Centralia. So Tom—when he asked me to dinner—I naturally just accepted the invitation, not knowing that you—that he—that I—*(He stops awkwardly.)* Huh—I'm a stumble-john! *(He flops back on the sofa. The holy candles in the altar of Laura's face have been snuffed out! There is a look of almost infinite desolation. Jim glances at her uneasily.)* I wish that you would—say something. *(She bites her lip which was trembling and then bravely smiles. She opens her hand again on the broken glass ornament. Then she gently takes his hand and raises it level with her own. She carefully places the unicorn in the palm of his hand, then pushes his fingers closed upon it.)* What are you—doing that for? You want me to have him?—Laura? *(She nods.)* What for?

LAURA: A—souvenir . . .

She rises unsteadily and crouches beside the Victrola to wind it up.
(Legend on screen: "Things Have a Way of Turning Out So Badly.")
(Or image: "Gentleman caller waving good-bye!—Gaily.")
At this moment Amanda rushes brightly back in the front room. She bears a pitcher of fruit punch in an old-fashioned cut-glass pitcher and a plate of macaroons. The plate has a gold border and poppies painted on it.

AMANDA: Well, well, well! Isn't the air delightful after the shower? I've made you children a little liquid refreshment. *(Turns gaily to the gentleman caller.)* Jim, do you know that song about lemonade?
"Lemonade, lemonade
Made in the shade and stirred with a spade—
Good enough for any old maid!"

JIM *(uneasily):*   Ha-ha! No—I never heard it.

AMANDA: Why, Laura! You look so serious!

JIM: We were having a serious conversation.

AMANDA: Good! Now you're better acquainted!

JIM *(uncertainly):*   Ha-ha! Yes.

AMANDA: You modern young people are much more serious-minded than my generation. I was so gay as a girl!

JIM: You haven't changed, Mrs. Wingfield.

AMANDA: Tonight I'm rejuvenated! The gaiety of the occasion, Mr. O'Connor! *(She tosses her head with a peal of laughter. Spills lemonade.)* Oooo! I'm baptizing myself!

JIM: Here—let me—

AMANDA *(setting the pitcher down):*   There now. I discovered we had some maraschino cherries. I dumped them in, juice and all!

JIM: You shouldn't have gone to that trouble, Mrs. Wingfield.

AMANDA: Trouble, trouble? Why it was loads of fun! Didn't you hear me cutting up in the kitchen? I bet your ears were burning! I told Tom how outdone with him I was for keeping you to himself so long a time! He should have brought you over much, much sooner! Well, now that you've found your way, I want you to be a very frequent caller! Not just occasional but all the time. Oh, we're going to have a lot of gay times together! I see them coming! Mmm, just breathe that air! So fresh, and the moon's so pretty! I'll skip back out—I know where my place is when young folks are having a—serious conversation!

JIM: Oh, don't go out, Mrs. Wingfield. The fact of the matter is I've got to be going.

AMANDA: Going, now? You're joking! Why, it's only the shank of the evening, Mr. O'Connor!

JIM: Well, you know how it is.

AMANDA: You mean you're a young workingman and have to keep working-men's hours. We'll let you off early tonight. But only on the condition that next time you stay later. What's the best night for you? Isn't Saturday night the best night for you workingmen?

JIM: I have a couple of time-clocks to punch, Mrs. Wingfield. One at morning, another one at night!

AMANDA: My, but you *are* ambitious! You work at night, too?

JIM: No, Ma'am, not work but—Betty! (*He crosses deliberately to pick up his hat. The band at the Paradise Dance Hall goes into a tender waltz.*)

AMANDA: Betty? Betty? Who's—Betty! (*There is an ominous cracking sound in the sky.*)

JIM: Oh, just a girl. The girl I go steady with! (*He smiles charmingly. The sky falls.*)

(*Legend: "The Sky Falls."*)

AMANDA (*a long-drawn exhalation*):   Ohhhh . . . Is it a serious romance, Mr. O'Connor?

JIM: We're going to be married the second Sunday in June.

AMANDA: Ohhhh—how nice! Tom didn't mention that you were engaged to be married.

JIM: The cat's not out of the bag at the warehouse yet. You know how they are. They call you Romeo and stuff like that. (*He stops at the oval mirror to put on his hat. He carefully shapes the brim and the crown to give a discreetly dashing effect.*) It's been a wonderful evening, Mrs. Wingfield. I guess this is what they mean by Southern hospitality.

AMANDA: It really wasn't anything at all.

JIM: I hope it don't seem like I'm rushing off. But I promised Betty I'd pick her up at the Wabash depot, an' by the time I get my jalopy down there her train'll be in. Some women are pretty upset if you keep 'em waiting.

AMANDA: Yes, I know—The tyranny of women! (*Extends her hand.*) Good-bye, Mr. O'Connor. I wish you luck—and happiness—and success! All three of them, and so does Laura—Don't you, Laura?

LAURA: Yes!

JIM *(taking her hand):*   Good-bye, Laura. I'm certainly going to treasure that
    souvenir. And don't you forget the good advice I gave you. *(Raises his
    voice to a cheery shout.)* So long, Shakespeare! Thanks again, ladies — Good
    night!

He grins and ducks jauntily out.

    *Still bravely grimacing, Amanda closes the door on the gentleman caller. Then
she turns back to the room with a puzzled expression. She and Laura don't dare to
face each other. Laura crouches beside the Victrola to wind it.*

AMANDA *(faintly):*   Things have a way of turning out so badly. I don't believe that
    I would play the Victrola. Well, well — well — Our gentleman caller was
    engaged to be married! Tom!

TOM *(from back):*   Yes, Mother?

AMANDA: Come in here a minute. I want to tell you something awfully funny.

TOM *(enters with macaroon and a glass of the lemonade):*   Has the gentleman
    caller gotten away already?

AMANDA: The gentleman caller has made an early departure. What a wonderful
    joke you played on us!

TOM: How do you mean?

AMANDA: You didn't mention that he was engaged to be married.

TOM: Jim? Engaged?

AMANDA: That's what he just informed us.

TOM: I'll be jiggered! I didn't know about that.

AMANDA: That seems very peculiar.

TOM: What's peculiar about it?

AMANDA: Didn't you call him your best friend down at the warehouse?

TOM: He is, but how did I know?

AMANDA: It seems extremely peculiar that you wouldn't know your best friend
    was going to be married!

TOM: The warehouse is where I work, not where I know things about people!

AMANDA: You don't know things anywhere! You live in a dream; you manufac-
    ture illusions! *(He crosses to door.)* Where are you going?

TOM: I'm going to the movies.

AMANDA: That's right, now that you've had us make such fools of ourselves. The
    effort, the preparations, all the expense! The new floor lamp, the rug, the
    clothes for Laura! All for what? To entertain some other girl's fiancé! Go to
    the movies, go! Don't think about us, a mother deserted, an unmarried sister
    who's crippled and has no job! Don't let anything interfere with your selfish
    pleasure! Just go, go, go — to the movies!

TOM: All right, I will! The more you shout about my selfishness to me the
    quicker I'll go, and I won't go to the movies!

AMANDA: Go, then! Then go to the moon — you selfish dreamer!

*Tom smashes his glass on the floor. He plunges out on the fire-escape, slamming the
door. Laura screams — cut by door.*

    *Dance-hall music up. Tom goes to the rail and grips it desperately, lifting his
face in the chill white moonlight penetrating the narrow abyss of the alley.*

    (Legend on screen: "And So Good-Bye . . .")

Tom's closing speech is timed with the interior pantomime. The interior scene is played as though viewed through sound-proof glass. Amanda appears to be making a comforting speech to Laura who is huddled upon the sofa. Now that we cannot hear the mother's speech, her silliness is gone and she has dignity and tragic beauty. Laura's dark hair hides her face until at the end of the speech she lifts it to smile at her mother. Amanda's gestures are slow and graceful, almost dancelike, as she comforts the daughter. At the end of her speech she glances a moment at the father's picture — then withdraws through the portieres. At close of Tom's speech, Laura blows out the candles, ending the play.

TOM: I didn't go to the moon, I went much further—for time is the longest distance between two places — Not long after that I was fired for writing a poem on the lid of a shoe-box. I left Saint Louis. I descended the steps of this fire-escape for a last time and followed, from then on, in my father's footsteps, attempting to find in motion what was lost in space — I traveled around a great deal. The cities swept about me like dead leaves, leaves that were brightly colored but torn away from the branches. I would have stopped, but I was pursued by something. It always came upon me unawares, taking me altogether by surprise. Perhaps it was a familiar bit of music. Perhaps it was only a piece of transparent glass — Perhaps I am walking along a street at night, in some strange city, before I have found companions. I pass the lighted window of a shop where perfume is sold. The window is filled with pieces of colored glass, tiny transparent bottles in delicate colors, like bits of a shattered rainbow. Then all at once my sister touches my shoulder. I turn around and look into her eyes. . . . Oh, Laura, Laura, I tried to leave you behind me, but I am more faithful than I intended to be! I reach for a cigarette, I cross the street, I run into the movies or a bar, I buy a drink, I speak to the nearest stranger—anything that can blow your candles out! *(Laura bends over the candles)* — for nowadays the world is lit by lightning! Blow out your candles, Laura — and so good-bye . . .

She blows the candles out.
(The Scene Dissolves.)   [1945]

THINKING ABOUT THE TEXT

1. Is Amanda just overprotective, or is there something seriously wrong with her devotion to Laura's eventual marriage? If you were a close friend of Amanda, how would you advise her to behave toward Laura?

2. Why does Laura keep the glass menagerie? Why does she give Jim her broken unicorn? Is this a positive sign?

3. This is a play about love, guilt, pity, regret, cruelty, and self-loathing. Can you cite concrete examples of these emotions in this play? Are there other emotions that you noticed? Is this a realistic portrait of family life, or is it an exaggeration?

4. Critics are divided over Williams's motivation in this play. Is he trying to get rid of Laura's memory (based on his sister Rose who went mad and whom Williams deserted), or is he replaying the traumatic leaving?

Which makes the most sense to you? How do you read the last line, "Blow out your candles, Laura—and so good-bye . . ."?

5. Do you blame Tom for leaving? Does he abandon his responsibilities? What do you think of Tom's priorities? Does he have a duty to take the place of his absent father? What would have happened if Tom had stayed? What would you do?

MAKING COMPARISONS

1. How does the play go beyond the short story to give us more of a social and political context within which we see the lives of Tom, Laura, and Amanda?

2. What difference does it make to you that in the play Williams changes Laura's disability from mental to physical?

3. Describe and explain the specific differences between the story's and the play's endings. Why, for example, does Williams change pieces of glass to candles?

WRITING ABOUT ISSUES

1. Argue that the social and political context developed in the play gives us a deeper appreciation for the choices that Tom makes.

2. Write a brief analysis of the re-visions Williams makes in moving from story to play, including the Chow dog alley to the dance hall, Laura's disabilities, Freckles to Jim, and so on.

3. Critics claim that the following thematic strands are present in *The Glass Menagerie*—tenderness, illusions, illness, fragility, transformation, emotion, nostalgia, and trap. Which seems the most important to you? Write a brief essay that explores the play's various themes.

4. Argue that we do or do not have a deeper responsibility to society to develop our own talents than to respond to the financial and emotional needs of our birth family.

A WEB ASSIGNMENT

The Internet can be an excellent resource for finding material to assist you in your critical analysis of specific works. Visit the Web Assignments section of the *Making Literature Matter* Web site to access the link to Bookrags.com. There, locate the segment that tracks topics and you will find three thematic focuses: Disappointment, Escape, and Expectation. Pick one and write a brief report on the ways such analysis helps us to understand the play.

Visit www.bedfordstmartins.com/makinglitmatter

GRANDPARENTS AND LEGACIES

NIKKI GIOVANNI, "Legacies"
WILLIAM CARLOS WILLIAMS, "The Last Words of My English Grandmother"
ALBERTO RÍOS, "Mi Abuelo"
LINDA HOGAN, "Heritage"
GARY SOTO, "Behind Grandma's House"

In contemporary middle-class America, the influence, even the presence, of our grandparents has waned. They often live elsewhere, perhaps in retirement communities or nursing homes. But this was not always the case. Grandparents in the past, and in traditional households even today, were active members of the family, exerting influence on the daily decisions of everyday life, from diet to childrearing. Some of this was beneficial: grandparents gave children a personal understanding of their cultural traditions as well as the benefit of their accumulated wisdom. But they could also create tension in families where change and progress conflict with the habits and attitudes of the past. The following five poets present us with different perspectives on their grandparents, some loving and proud, others less positive, and one quite funny.

BEFORE YOU READ

What specific memories do you have of your grandparents? What role do you think they should play in a family's life? What effects might the segregation of the elderly have on a society?

NIKKI GIOVANNI
Legacies

Raised near Cincinnati, Ohio, Nikki Giovanni (b. 1943) returned as a teenager to her birthplace and "spiritual" home in Knoxville, Tennessee, where she experienced the strong influence of her grandmother, Louvenia Watson. She studied at the University of Cincinnati from 1961–1963 and earned a B.A. at Fisk University in 1967. She also attended the University of Pennsylvania School of Social Work (1967) and Columbia University School of the Arts (1968). She has taught at a number of universities, since 1987 at Virginia Polytechnic Institute, where she is a professor of English. Her poetry, essays, and works for children reflect her commitment to African American community, family, and womanhood. Her latest book is Blues for All the Changes: New Poems *(1999). "Legacies" is from Giovanni's 1972 book,* My House.

her grandmother called her from the playground
   "yes, ma'am"
   "i want chu to learn how to make rolls," said the old

woman proudly
but the little girl didn't want
to learn how because she knew   5
even if she couldn't say it that
that would mean when the old one died she would be less
dependent on her spirit so
she said
     "i don't want to know how to make no rolls"   10
with her lips poked out
and the old woman wiped her hands on
her apron saying "lord
     these children"
and neither of them ever   15
said what they meant
and i guess nobody ever does   [1972]

THINKING ABOUT THE TEXT

1. Does the dialogue in Giovanni's poem reveal the true feelings of the grandmother and the girl? Be explicit about what is really going on in their minds. Is the girl superstitious?

2. Is it true that "nobody" (line 17) says what she really means? Do you? Is this an indication of honesty or something else — say, tact or convention? Are poets more likely to tell the truth?

3. What makes this piece a poem? Would you prefer more metaphors or similes, allusions, or flowery language? Is "proudly" (line 4) an important word here?

4. Change the grandmother's words to those that reflect more of what is in her heart. Might the girl respond differently if the grandmother were more forthright?

5. The title is only referred to obliquely. Why? What does it refer to? Is contemporary society concerned with legacies? Are you? Are they important or irrelevant?

WILLIAM CARLOS WILLIAMS
The Last Words of My English Grandmother

For most of his eighty years, William Carlos Williams (1883–1963) lived and practiced medicine in Rutherford, New Jersey, his birthplace, and in the nearby city of Paterson, the setting for his influential poetry sequence. He earned his medical degree at the University of Pennsylvania in 1906 and studied pediatrics in Germany. An important voice among modernist poets of the early twentieth century, Williams focused his theoretical prose on ideas and experiences that he saw as dis-

tinctly American and incorporated the rhythms and color of American speech into his poetry. Deceptively simple, his poems are crafted with deliberate precision. This poem appears in The Collected Poems of William Carlos Williams, 1909–1939.

There were some dirty plates
and a glass of milk
beside her on a small table
near the rank, disheveled bed —

Wrinkled and nearly blind   5
she lay and snored
rousing with anger in her tones
to cry for food,

Gimme something to eat —
They're starving me —   10
I'm all right I won't go
to the hospital. No, no, no

Give me something to eat
Let me take you
to the hospital, I said   15
and after you are well

you can do as you please.
She smiled, Yes
you do what you please first
then I can do what I please —   20

Oh, oh, oh! she cried
as the ambulance men lifted
her to the stretcher —
Is this what you call

making me comfortable?   25
By now her mind was clear —
Oh you think you're smart
you young people,

she said, but I'll tell you
you don't know anything.   30
Then we started.
On the way

we passed a long row
of elms. She looked at them
awhile out of   35
the ambulance window and said,

◆   ◆   ◆

What are all those
fuzzy-looking things out there?
Trees? Well, I'm tired
of them and rolled her head away.   [1924]   40

THINKING ABOUT THE TEXT

1. What is the speaker's attitude toward his grandmother? What is yours? Could you argue that the grandmother is brave and independent? Frightened and bitter?

2. What does the grandmother mean by saying young people "don't know anything" (line 30)? Do children "know anything" in your view?

3. Poets sometimes like to present concrete images that carry emotional weight instead of telling the reader what they intend. How do you respond to some of Williams's specific images? What do they suggest?

4. Rewrite "Well, I'm tired / of them" (lines 39–40) to something else, and explain how your change alters the meaning of the poem.

5. Should the grandmother's requests be honored? Is the speaker right to intervene? Are we responsible for how our grandparents want to act?

MAKING COMPARISONS

1. How would you describe the attitude of Giovanni's grandmother toward the young? Of Williams's grandmother?

2. How might the speaker in Williams's poem react if he had the grandmother of the first poem?

3. Would these two grandmothers get along?

ALBERTO RÍOS
Mi Abuelo°

Alberto Ríos (b. 1952) has said that being bilingual in English and Spanish is like going through life with a pair of binoculars; having at least two words for everything opens one's eyes to the world. Ríos is a person of the border in several ways: his father was from Chiapas, Mexico, and his mother from Lancashire, England. He grew up in the city of Nogales, Arizona, where he could stand with one foot in the United States and another in Mexico; and as a writer, he crosses the line between poetry and prose, having written seven books of poetry, three collections of short stories, and a memoir. He is an instructor of creative writing, since 1994 the Regents Professor of English at Arizona State University, where he has taught since 1982.

Mi Abuelo: My grandfather (Spanish).

He received his B.A. (1974) and his M.F.A. in creative writing (1979) from the University of Arizona. His work appears in 175 anthologies, including the Norton Anthology of Modern Poetry, *and his awards include fellowships from the Guggenheim Foundation and the National Endowment for the Arts and the 1982 Walt Whitman Award for* Whispering to Fool the Wind.

Where my grandfather is is in the ground
where you can hear the future
like an Indian with his ear at the tracks.
A pipe leads down to him so that sometimes
he whispers what will happen to a man   5
in town or how he will meet the best
dressed woman tomorrow and how the best
man at her wedding will chew the ground
next to her. Mi abuelo is the man
who speaks through all the mouths in my house.   10
An echo of me hitting the pipe sometimes
to stop him from saying *my hair is a*
sieve is the only other sound. It is a phrase
that among all others is the best,
he says, and *my hair is a sieve* is sometimes   15
repeated for hours out of the ground
when I let him, which is not often.
An abuelo should be much more than a man
like you! He stops then, and speaks: *I am a man*
who has served ants with the attitude   20
of a waiter, who has made each smile as only
an ant who is fat can, and they liked me best,
but there is nothing left. Yet I know he ground
green coffee beans as a child, and sometimes
he will talk about his wife, and sometimes   25
about when he was deaf and a man
cured him by mail and he heard groundhogs
talking, or about how he walked with a cane
he chewed on when he got hungry.
At best, mi abuelo is a liar.   30
I see an old picture of him at nani's with an
off-white yellow center mustache and sometimes
that's all I know for sure. He talks best
about these hills, *slowest waves,* and where this man
is going, and I'm convinced his hair is a sieve,   35
that his fever is cooled now underground.
Mi abuelo is an ordinary man.
I look down the pipe, sometimes, and see a
ripple-topped stream in its best suit, in the ground.   [1990]

THINKING ABOUT THE TEXT

1. The narrator seems ambivalent about his abuelo. What specific things does he know about him? Can you tell his attitude toward him? How do you read the line, "At best, mi abuelo is a liar" (line 30)? What might the worst be?

2. When the grandfather speaks from the grave (*"I am a man . . ."*) (lines 19–23), he seems odd indeed. Is he a bit crazy, or do you see meaning in his ant speech?

3. What does Ríos mean when he writes that his abuelo "speaks through all the mouths in my house" (line 10)? Could this be a positive notion?

4. Ríos seems convinced his grandfather's "fever is cooled now" (line 36). Should we take this literally?

5. Do you agree that Ríos wants to continue conversing with his dead abuelo? Why? Can we see this as a metaphor?

MAKING COMPARISONS

1. Do you agree that Ríos's poem is more indirect than Giovanni's or Williams's? Which poet's approach do you like better?

2. Ríos's speaker seems unsure about his grandfather's influence. Are Giovanni's and Williams's speakers more or less ambivalent than Ríos's? Say why.

3. Which poem of the three contains the most interesting images? Why?

LINDA HOGAN

Heritage

Born in 1947 in Denver, Colorado, Linda Hogan is a contemporary Native American poet who calls on her Chickasaw heritage to interpret environmental, antinuclear, and other spiritual and societal issues. Her published works include poems, stories, screenplays, essays, and novels. Her novel Power *(1998) has been praised for its beauty of language, mythical structure, and allegorical power. Her latest work is* The Woman Who Watches Over the World: A Native Memoir *(2001). Her many honors include an American Book Award for* Seeing Through the Sun *(1985), a Colorado Book Award and a Pulitzer nomination for* The Book of Medicines *(1993), fellowships from the Guggenheim Foundation and the National Endowment for the Arts, and a Lannan Award. Hogan received her M.A. from the University of Colorado at Boulder, where she currently teaches creative writing. "Heritage" is from her 1978 book titled* Calling Myself Home.

From my mother, the antique mirror
where I watch my face take on her lines.

She left me the smell of baking bread
to warm fine hairs in my nostrils,
she left the large white breasts that weigh down   5
my body.

From my father I take his brown eyes,
the plague of locusts that leveled our crops,
they flew in formation like buzzards.

From my uncle the whittled wood   10
that rattles like bones
and is white
and smells like all our old houses
that are no longer there. He was the man
who sang old chants to me, the words   15
my father was told not to remember.

From my grandfather who never spoke
I learned to fear silence.
I learned to kill a snake
when you're begging for rain.   20

And Grandmother, blue-eyed woman
whose skin was brown,
she used snuff.
When her coffee can full of black saliva
spilled on me   25
it was like the brown cloud of grasshoppers
that leveled her fields.
It was the brown stain
that covered my white shirt,
my whiteness a shame.   30
That sweet black liquid like the food
she chewed up and spit into my father's mouth
when he was an infant.
It was the brown earth of Oklahoma
stained with oil.   35
She said tobacco would purge your body of poisons.
It has more medicine than stones and knives
against your enemies.
That tobacco is the dark night that covers me.

She said it is wise to eat the flesh of deer   40
so you will be swift and travel over many miles.
She told me how our tribe has always followed a stick
that pointed west
that pointed east.
From my family I have learned the secrets   45
of never having a home.   [1978]

THINKING ABOUT THE TEXT

1. The last sentence seems to contain a contradiction. "From my family I have learned the secrets" might lead you to expect something positive. But maybe the last phrase is not meant to be positive. What is your reading of Hogan's conclusion?

2. What does the narrator learn from her mother? Her father? Her uncle? Her grandfather? Her grandmother? What kinds of things did you learn from your family members? Use concrete images.

3. Why does she say "my whiteness a shame" (line 30)? Is this a racial comment?

4. Examine the "black saliva" section in lines 21–39. Does it start off negatively? Does it change? Explain.

5. We all learn things from our families, both positive and negative. Is Hogan giving a balanced account? Should she? Would you? Do poets have any responsibility to the larger culture? Or should they just follow their own inner vision?

MAKING COMPARISONS

1. Does Hogan's poem seem more complex than those by Giovanni, Williams, and Ríos? Explain how.

2. Do you think that the last two stanzas in "Heritage" seem nonjudgmental, their tone flat? Describe the tone of the previous three poems.

3. Traditionally, as characters in fiction grow, they learn something from their interactions with others. How would you characterize the speakers in these four poems? Do they learn something?

GARY SOTO
Behind Grandma's House

Born in 1952 in Fresno, California, Gary Soto gives voice to San Joaquín Valley agricultural workers whose deprivations have been part of his experience and social awareness from an early age. After graduating with honors from California State University in 1974, Soto went on to earn an M.F.A. in creative writing from the University of California at Irvine in 1976 and to teach in the university system. He has received numerous writing awards, including the distinction of being the first writer identifying himself as Chicano to be nominated for a Pulitzer Prize. His most recent book is New and Selected Poems *(1995). His Mexican American heritage continues to be central to his work. The poem reprinted here is from Soto's 1985 book,* Black Hair.

At ten I wanted fame. I had a comb
And two Coke bottles, a tube of Bryl-creem.

I borrowed a dog, one with
Mismatched eyes and a happy tongue,
And wanted to prove I was tough   5
In the alley, kicking over trash cans,
A dull chime of tuna cans falling.
I hurled light bulbs like grenades
And men teachers held their heads,
Fingers of blood lengthening   10
On the ground. I flicked rocks at cats,
Their goofy faces spurred with foxtails.
I kicked fences. I shooed pigeons.
I broke a branch from a flowering peach
And frightened ants with a stream of spit.   15
I said "Shit," "Fuck you," and "No way
Daddy-O" to an imaginary priest
Until grandma came into the alley,
Her apron flapping in a breeze,
Her hair mussed, and said, "Let me help you,"   20
And punched me between the eyes.   [1985]

THINKING ABOUT THE TEXT

1. Were you glad or disturbed when the narrator's grandmother hit him? Does he deserve it? Are you angry or sympathetic to his attempts to be tough? Do you understand why he wants to appear older? Is this normal?

2. What did you want at ten? Did your grandparents know your desires? Did they support you? Did they ever set you straight? Are our grandparents' values too dated to matter?

3. Are the concrete details meaningful to you? Does the profanity help Soto achieve authenticity, or is it unnecessary?

4. Does the speaker learn something here, or is this just a snapshot of an event?

5. How would you describe our culture's ideas of the different roles of parents and grandparents? Do grandparents in today's culture have less influence than in the past? Is this a good thing or not?

MAKING COMPARISONS

1. Compare Soto's attitude here with that of the previous four poets. Is Soto less respectful or more?

2. Is this a gendered poem? That is, is it about male experience only, or could a female reader see herself in this or a comparable situation? Do any of the other four preceding poems seem gendered?

3. Do any of the five encounters with grandparents seem ideal to you? Which relationship comes closest to the one you would want?

WRITING ABOUT ISSUES

1. Pick one of the five preceding poems, and argue that it offers an appropriate view of grandparents.

2. Pick two of these poems, and argue that something of value is learned in each.

3. Which poem comes closest to your own experiences? Write a narrative that demonstrates this.

4. Do some research on retirement homes from a sociological point of view. Write a report about your findings. Include the import of such places on the family and on the larger culture. Do you think they are a positive development or not?

A FLAWED FAMILY:
A COLLECTION OF PLAYS BY SOPHOCLES

SOPHOCLES, *Oedipus the King*
SOPHOCLES, *Antigone*

"The bigger they are, the harder they fall" is literally true in sports such as boxing and football, where size can sometimes become a physical disadvantage. But the expression probably has its roots not in sports but in drama, where its meaning for those in power was not only metaphorical but painful. It was common in early Greek drama for great men and women to fall hard from positions of power and prestige. We are so used to plays and movies being about ordinary people that we forget that classic drama from the Greeks to Shakespeare and beyond was about the deeds of kings, queens, generals, and other significant people. It was thought that characters had to have some metaphorical weight for their lives to be of interest and for their success (comedies) or failures (tragedies) to be compelling enough to have dramatic meaning.

The tragic story of Oedipus, a king of Thebes and his family, would have been a familiar narrative for the audience in Athens in the fifth century B.C.E. Audience members would also have appreciated the idea that the sins of the father would be visited on the next generation. They would expect Oedipus's tragic story to be followed by the equally tragic story of his daughter, Antigone.

The Greeks were strongly influenced by notions of destiny and fate, a way of thinking that would have convinced early audiences that Oedipus, his wife Jocasta, as well as his daughter Antigone could not escape their fates. But they also believed that tragedy could not just randomly befall victims. They expected a powerful leader like Oedipus to cause his own downfall through a flaw in his character. This tragic flaw could not be something obvious, like cruelty, stupidity, or intolerance, but needed to be some positive attribute—like pride, commitment, dedication, or steadfastness—pushed too far. When simple curiosity about

(© Archivo Icono-
graphico, S.A./CORBIS.)

personal identity is transformed into an obsession, for example, audiences in Athens anticipated a hard fall, one that could bring down a whole family.

BEFORE YOU READ

Everybody has the potential to have a tragic flaw. As you think about famous people today, what potential tragic flaws do you imagine for them? What is your view of destiny? Does our culture have a view on fate and destiny?

SOPHOCLES
Oedipus the King

Translated by Robert Fagles

Along with Aeschylus and Euripides, Sophocles (496? B.C.E.–406? B.C.E.) is considered one of the greatest writers of tragedy in ancient Athens. During his lifetime, he was much respected in the city, often winning its dramatic competitions.

Evidently he wrote over a hundred plays, but only seven survive complete. As a practitioner of tragedy, Sophocles was innovative. Among other things, he increased the number of actors on stage from two to three, while reducing the chorus from fifty to fifteen. Productions of his plays did remain traditional in having the performers wear masks and be exclusively male. Oedipus the King and Antigone continue to be much performed today; moreover, through the centuries there have been numerous adaptations of them, such as Jean Anouilh's 1944 version of Antigone, a challenge to the Nazi occupiers of Paris.

Antigone was produced in 441 B.C.E., the first of three interrelated plays now known as the Oedipus cycle. Oedipus the King was produced between 430 and 427 B.C.E., and Oedipus at Colonus was posthumously produced in 401 B.C.E. Scholars know that the plots of these plays were familiar to Sophocles' audience. Less clear is whether that audience was familiar with the story of Antigone, which comes last in terms of plot chronology. The title character of Oedipus the King is Antigone's father, the ruler of Thebes. In the play, Oedipus blinds himself and leaves Thebes when he discovers that he has unknowingly fulfilled a terrible prophecy — that he would kill his own father and marry his mother. Oedipus at Colonus focuses on his death.

CHARACTERS

OEDIPUS, *king of Thebes*
A PRIEST of Zeus
CREON, brother of Jocasta
A CHORUS of Theban citizens and their *Leader*
TIRESIAS, a blind prophet
JOCASTA, the queen, wife of Oedipus
A MESSENGER from Corinth
A SHEPHERD
A MESSENGER from inside the palace
ANTIGONE, ISMENE, daughters of Oedipus and Jocasta
GUARDS and ATTENDANTS
PRIESTS OF THEBES

TIME AND SCENE: *The royal house of Thebes. Double doors dominate the facade; a stone altar stands at the center of the stage.*

Many years have passed since Oedipus solved the riddle of the Sphinx and ascended the throne of Thebes, and now a plague has struck the city. A procession of priests enters; suppliants, broken and despondent, they carry branches wound in wool and lay them on the altar.

The doors open. Guards assemble. Oedipus comes forward, majestic but for a telltale limp, and slowly views the condition of his people.

OEDIPUS: Oh my children, the new blood of ancient Thebes,
    why are you here? Huddling at my altar,

praying before me, your branches wound in wool.°
Our city reeks with the smoke of burning incense,
rings with cries for the Healer and wailing for the dead.   5
I thought it wrong, my children, to hear the truth
from others, messengers. Here I am myself—
you all know me, the world knows my fame:
I am Oedipus.

Helping a Priest to his feet.

                Speak up, old man. Your years,
your dignity—you should speak for the others.   10
Why here and kneeling, what preys upon you so?
Some sudden fear? some strong desire?
You can trust me; I am ready to help,
I'll do anything. I would be blind to misery
not to pity my people kneeling at my feet.   15
PRIEST: Oh Oedipus, king of the land, our greatest power!
You see us before you, men of all ages
clinging to your altars. Here are boys,
still too weak to fly from the nest,
and here the old, bowed down with the years,   20
the holy ones—a priest of Zeus° myself—and here
the picked, unmarried men, the young hope of Thebes.
And all the rest, your great family gathers now,
branches wreathed, massing in the squares,
kneeling before the two temples of queen Athena°   25
or the river-shrine where the embers glow and die
and Apollo sees the future in the ashes.
                    Our city—
look around you, see with your own eyes—
our ship pitches wildly, cannot lift her head
from the depths, the red waves of death . . .   30
Thebes is dying. A blight on the fresh crops
and the rich pastures, cattle sicken and die,
and the women die in labor, children stillborn,
and the plague, the fiery god of fever hurls down
on the city, his lightning slashing through us—   35
raging plague in all its vengeance, devastating
the house of Cadmus!° And Black Death luxuriates
in the raw, wailing miseries of Thebes.

Now we pray to you. You cannot equal the gods,
your children know that, bending at your altar.   40

---

3 wool: An offering to Apollo, god of poetry and the sun.   **21 Zeus:** The chief Olympian deity
and father of Apollo.   **25 Athena:** Goddess of wisdom.   **37 Cadmus:** Founder of Thebes.

But we do rate you first of men,
both in the common crises of our lives
and face-to-face encounters with the gods.
You freed us from the Sphinx; you came to Thebes
and cut us loose from the bloody tribute we had paid   45
that harsh, brutal singer. We taught you nothing,
no skill, no extra knowledge, still you triumphed.
A god was with you, so they say, and we believe it—
you lifted up our lives.
                              So now again,
Oedipus, king, we bend to you, your power—   50
we implore you, all of us on our knees:
find us strength, rescue! Perhaps you've heard
the voice of a god or something from other men,
Oedipus . . . what do you know?
The man of experience—you see it every day—   55
his plans will work in a crisis, his first of all.
Act now—we beg you, best of men, raise up our city!
Act, defend yourself, your former glory!
Your country calls you savior now
for your zeal, your action years ago.   60
Never let us remember of your reign:
you helped us stand, only to fall once more.
Oh raise up our city, set us on our feet.
The omens were good that day you brought us joy—
be the same man today!   65
Rule our land, you know you have the power,
but rule a land of the living, not a wasteland.
Ship and towered city are nothing, stripped of men
alive within it, living all as one.
OEDIPUS: My children,
I pity you. I see—how could I fail to see   70
what longings bring you here? Well I know
you are sick to death, all of you,
but sick as you are, not one is sick as I.
Your pain strikes each of you alone, each
in the confines of himself, no other. But my spirit   75
grieves for the city, for myself and all of you.
I wasn't asleep, dreaming. You haven't wakened me—
I've wept through the nights, you must know that,
groping, laboring over many paths of thought.
After a painful search I found one cure: 80
I acted at once. I sent Creon,
my wife's own brother, to Delphi° —

___

82 **Delphi:** The location of the oracle of Apollo.

Apollo the Prophet's oracle — to learn
what I might do or say to save our city.

Today's the day. When I count the days gone by   85
it torments me . . . what is he doing?
Strange, he's late, he's gone too long.
But once he returns, then, then I'll be a traitor
if I do not do all the god makes clear.
PRIEST: Timely words. The men over there   90
are signaling — Creon's just arriving.
OEDIPUS:

Sighting Creon, then turning to the altar.

                                          Lord Apollo,
let him come with a lucky word of rescue,
shining like his eyes!
PRIEST: Welcome news, I think — he's crowned, look,
and the laurel wreath is bright with berries.   95
OEDIPUS: We'll soon see. He's close enough to hear —

Enter Creon from the side; his face is shaded with a wreath.

Creon, prince, my kinsman, what do you bring us?
What message from the god?
CREON: Good news.
I tell you even the hardest things to bear,
if they should turn out well, all would be well.   100
OEDIPUS: Of course, but what were the god's *words?* There's no hope
and nothing to fear in what you've said so far.
CREON: If you want my report in the presence of these . . .

Pointing to the priests while drawing Oedipus toward the palace.

I'm ready now, or we might go inside.
OEDIPUS: Speak out,
speak to us all. I grieve for these, my people,   105
far more than I fear for my own life.
CREON: Very well,
I will tell you what I heard from the god.
Apollo commands us — he was quite clear —
"Drive the corruption from the land,
don't harbor it any longer, past all cure,   110
don't nurse it in your soil — root it out!"
OEDIPUS: How can we cleanse ourselves — what rites?
What's the source of the trouble?
CREON: Banish the man, or pay back blood with blood.
Murder sets the plague-storm on the city.
OEDIPUS: Whose murder?   115
Whose fate does Apollo bring to light?
CREON: Our leader,

 my lord, was once a man named Laius,
 before you came and put us straight on course.
OEDIPUS: I know—
 or so I've heard. I never saw the man myself.
CREON: Well, he was killed, and Apollo commands us now—   120
 he could not be more clear,
 "Pay the killers back—whoever is responsible."
OEDIPUS: Where on earth are they? Where to find it now,
 the trail of the ancient guilt so hard to trace?
CREON: "Here in Thebes," he said.   125
 Whatever is sought for can be caught, you know,
 whatever is neglected slips away.
OEDIPUS: But where,
 in the palace, the fields or foreign soil,
 where did Laius meet his bloody death?
CREON: He went to consult an oracle, he said,   130
 and he set out and never came home again.
OEDIPUS: No messenger, no fellow-traveler saw what happened?
 Someone to cross-examine?
CREON: No,
 they were all killed but one. He escaped,
 terrified, he could tell us nothing clearly,   135
 nothing of what he saw—just one thing.
OEDIPUS: What's that?
 One thing could hold the key to it all,
 a small beginning gives us grounds for hope.
CREON: He said thieves attacked them—a whole band,
 not single-handed, cut King Laius down.
OEDIPUS: A thief,   140
 so daring, wild, he'd kill a king? Impossible,
 unless conspirators paid him off in Thebes.
CREON: We suspected as much. But with Laius dead
 no leader appeared to help us in our troubles.
OEDIPUS: Trouble? Your *king* was murdered—royal blood!   145
 What stopped you from tracking down the killer
 then and there?
CREON: The singing, riddling Sphinx.
 She . . . persuaded us to let the mystery go
 and concentrate on what lay at our feet.
OEDIPUS: No,
 I'll start again—I'll bring it all to light myself!   150
 Apollo is right, and so are you, Creon,
 to turn our attention back to the murdered man.
 Now you have *me* to fight for you, you'll see:
 I am the land's avenger by all rights
 and Apollo's champion too.   155

But not to assist some distant kinsman, no,
for my own sake I'll rid us of this corruption.
Whoever killed the king may decide to kill me too,
with the same violent hand—by avenging Laius
I defend myself.

To the priests.

　　　　　　　　　Quickly, my children.　　　　　　　　160
Up from the steps, take up your branches now.

To the guards.

One of you summon the city here before us,
tell them I'll do everything. God help us,
we will see our triumph—or our fall.

Oedipus and Creon enter the palace, followed by the guards.

PRIEST:　Rise, my sons. The kindness we came for　　　　165
Oedipus volunteers himself.
Apollo has sent his word, his oracle—
Come down, Apollo, save us, stop the plague.

The priests rise, remove their branches, and exit to the side. Enter a Chorus, the citizens of Thebes, who have not heard the news that Creon brings. They march around the altar, chanting.

CHORUS:　　　　　　　　　　　　Zeus!
Great welcome voice of Zeus, what do you bring?
What word from the gold vaults of Delphi　　　　　170
comes to brilliant Thebes? I'm racked with terror—
　　　　　　　　　terror shakes my heart
and I cry your wild cries, Apollo, Healer of Delos
I worship you in dread . . . what now, what is your price?
some new sacrifice? some ancient rite from the past　　175
come round again each spring?—
　　　　　　　what will you bring to birth?
Tell me, child of golden Hope
　　　warm voice that never dies!

You are the first I call, daughter of Zeus　　　　　180
deathless Athena—I call your sister Artemis,°
heart of the market place enthroned in glory,
　　　　　　　　　　guardian of our earth—
I call Apollo astride the thunderheads of heaven—
O triple shield against death, shine before me now!　　185
If ever, once in the past, you stopped some ruin
launched against our walls
　　　　　you hurled the flame of pain

---

181 **Artemis:** Goddess of hunting, the moon, and chastity.

far, far from Thebes — you gods
    come now, come down once more!

                                      No, no   190
the miseries numberless, grief on grief, no end —
too much to bear, we are all dying
O my people . . .
        Thebes like a great army dying
and there is no sword of thought to save us, no   195
and the fruits of our famous earth, they will not ripen
no and the women cannot scream their pangs to birth —
screams for the Healer, children dead in the womb
          and life on life goes down
                  you can watch them go   200
    like seabirds winging west, outracing the day's fire
down the horizon, irresistibly
          streaking on to the shores of Evening
                        Death
so many deaths, numberless deaths on deaths, no end —
Thebes is dying, look, her children   205
stripped of pity . . .
        generations strewn on the ground
unburied, unwept, the dead spreading death
and the young wives and gray-haired mothers with them
cling to the altars, trailing in from all over the city —   210
Thebes, city of death, one long cortege
        and the suffering rises
              wails for mercy rise
and the wild hymn for the Healer blazes out
clashing with our sobs our cries of mourning —   215
        O golden daughter of god, send rescue
        radiant as the kindness in your eyes!
Drive him back! — the fever, the god of death
                  that raging god of war
not armored in bronze, not shielded now, he burns me,   220
battle cries in the onslaught burning on —
O rout him from our borders!
Sail him, blast him out to the Sea-queen's chamber
                the black Atlantic gulfs
    or the northern harbor, death to all   225
where the Thracian surf comes crashing.
Now what the night spares he comes by day and kills —
the god of death.

        O lord of the stormcloud,
you who twirl the lightning, Zeus, Father,
thunder Death to nothing!   230

Apollo, lord of the light, I beg you —
    whip your longbow's golden cord
showering arrows on our enemies — shafts of power
champions strong before us rushing on!

Artemis, Huntress,   235
torches flaring over the eastern ridges —
      ride Death down in pain!

God of the headdress gleaming gold, I cry to you —
your name and ours are one, Dionysus —
    come with your face aflame with wine   240
        your raving women's cries°
  your army on the march! Come with the lightning
come with torches blazing, eyes ablaze with glory!
Burn that god of death that all gods hate!

Oedipus enters from the palace to address the Chorus, as if addressing the entire city of Thebes.

OEDIPUS: You pray to the gods? Let me grant your prayers.   245
   Come, listen to me — do what the plague demands:
   you'll find relief and lift your head from the depths.

   I will speak out now as a stranger to the story,
   a stranger to the crime. If I'd been present then,
   there would have been no mystery, no long hunt   250
   without a clue in hand. So now, counted
   a native Theban years after the murder,
   to all of Thebes I make this proclamation:
   if any one of you knows who murdered Laius,
   the son of Labdacus, I order him to reveal   255
   the whole truth to me. Nothing to fear,
   even if he must denounce himself,
   let him speak up
   and so escape the brunt of the charge —
   he will suffer no unbearable punishment,   260
   nothing worse than exile, totally unharmed.

Oedipus pauses, waiting for a reply.

                       Next,
   if anyone knows the murderer is a stranger,
   a man from alien soil, come, speak up.
   I will give him a handsome reward, and lay up
   gratitude in my heart for him besides.   265

Silence again, no reply.

241 Dionysus . . . cries: God of fertility and wine who was attended by female orgiasts.

But if you keep silent, if anyone panicking,
trying to shield himself or friend or kin,
rejects my offer, then hear what I will do.
I order you, every citizen of the state
where I hold throne and power: banish this man —   270
whoever he may be — never shelter him, never
speak a word to him, never make him partner
to your prayers, your victims burned to the gods.
Never let the holy water touch his hands.
Drive him out, each of you, from every home.   275
He is the plague, the heart of our corruption,
as Apollo's oracle has revealed to me
just now. So I honor my obligations:
I fight for the god and for the murdered man.

Now my curse on the murderer. Whoever he is,   280
a lone man unknown in his crime
or one among many, let that man drag out
his life in agony, step by painful step —
I curse myself as well . . . if by any chance
he proves to be an intimate of our house,   285
here at my hearth, with my full knowledge,
may the curse I just called down on him strike me!

These are your orders: perform them to the last.
I command you, for my sake, for Apollo's, for this country
blasted root and branch by the angry heavens.   290
Even if god had never urged you on to act,
how could you leave the crime uncleansed so long?
A man so noble — your king, brought down in blood —
you should have searched. But I am the king now,
I hold the throne that he held then, possess his bed   295
and a wife who shares our seed . . . why, our seed
might be the same, children born of the same mother
might have created blood-bonds between us
if his hope of offspring hadn't met disaster —
but fate swooped at his head and cut him short.   300
So I will fight for him as if he were my father,
stop at nothing, search the world
to lay my hands on the man who shed his blood,
the son of Labdacus descended of Polydorus,
Cadmus of old and Agenor, founder of the line: 305
their power and mine are one.
                              Oh dear gods,
my curse on those who disobey these orders!
Let no crops grow out of the earth for them —
shrivel their women, kill their sons,

burn them to nothing in this plague   310
that hits us now, or something even worse.
But you, loyal men of Thebes who approve my actions,
may our champion, Justice, may all the gods
be with us, fight beside us to the end!

LEADER: In the grip of your curse, my king, I swear   315
I'm not the murderer, cannot point him out.
As for the search, Apollo pressed it on us—
he should name the killer.

OEDIPUS: Quite right,
but to force the gods to act against their will—
no man has the power.

LEADER: Then if I might mention   320
the next best thing . . .

OEDIPUS: The third best too—
don't hold back, say it.

LEADER: I still believe . . .
Lord Tiresias sees with the eyes of Lord Apollo.
Anyone searching for the truth, my king,
might learn it from the prophet, clear as day.   325

OEDIPUS: I've not been slow with that. On Creon's cue
I sent the escorts, twice, within the hour.
I'm surprised he isn't here.

LEADER: We need him—
without him we have nothing but old, useless rumors.

OEDIPUS: Which rumors? I'll search out every word.   330

LEADER: Laius was killed, they say, by certain travelers.

OEDIPUS: I know—but no one can find the murderer.

LEADER: If the man has a trace of fear in him
he won't stay silent long,
not with your curses ringing in his ears.   335

OEDIPUS: He didn't flinch at murder,
he'll never flinch at words.

Enter Tiresias, the blind prophet, led by a boy with escorts in attendance. He remains at a distance.

LEADER: Here is the one who will convict him, look,
they bring him on at last, the seer, the man of god.
The truth lives inside him, him alone.

OEDIPUS: O Tiresias,   340
master of all the mysteries of our life,
all you teach and all you dare not tell,
signs in the heavens, signs that walk the earth!
Blind as you are, you can feel all the more
what sickness haunts our city. You, my lord,   345
are the one shield, the one savior we can find.

We asked Apollo — perhaps the messengers
haven't told you — he sent his answer back:
"Relief from the plague can only come one way.
Uncover the murderers of Laius,   350
put them to death or drive them into exile."
So I beg you, grudge us nothing now, no voice,
no message plucked from the birds, the embers
or the other mantic ways within your grasp.
Rescue yourself, your city, rescue me —   355
rescue everything infected by the dead.
We are in your hands. For a man to help others
with all his gifts and native strength:
that is the noblest work.

TIRESIAS: How terrible — to see the truth
when the truth is only pain to him who sees!   360
I knew it well, but I put it from my mind,
else I never would have come.

OEDIPUS: What's this? Why so grim, so dire?

TIRESIAS: Just send me home. You bear your burdens,
I'll bear mine. It's better that way,   365
please believe me.

OEDIPUS: Strange response — unlawful,
unfriendly too to the state that bred and raised you;
you're withholding the word of god.

TIRESIAS: I fail to see
that your own words are so well-timed.
I'd rather not have the same thing said of me . . .   370

OEDIPUS: For the love of god, don't turn away,
not if you know something. We beg you,
all of us on our knees.

TIRESIAS: None of you knows —
and I will never reveal my dreadful secrets,
not to say your own.   375

OEDIPUS: What? You know and you won't tell?
You're bent on betraying us, destroying Thebes?

TIRESIAS: I'd rather not cause pain for you or me.
So why this . . . useless interrogation?
You'll get nothing from me.

OEDIPUS: Nothing! You,   380
you scum of the earth, you'd enrage a heart of stone!
You won't talk? Nothing moves you?
Out with it, once and for all!

TIRESIAS: You criticize my temper . . . unaware
of the one *you* live with, you revile me.   385

OEDIPUS: Who could restrain his anger hearing you?
What outrage — you spurn the city!

TIRESIAS: What will come will come.
    Even if I shroud it all in silence.
OEDIPUS: What will come? You're bound to *tell* me that.   390
TIRESIAS: I'll say no more. Do as you like, build your anger
    to whatever pitch you please, rage your worst—
OEDIPUS: Oh I'll let loose, I have such fury in me—
    now I see it all. You helped hatch the plot,
    you did the work, yes, short of killing him   395
    with your own hands—and given eyes I'd say
    you did the killing single-handed!
TIRESIAS: Is that so!
    I charge you, then, submit to that decree
    you just laid down: from this day onward
    speak to no one, not these citizens, not myself.   400
    You are the curse, the corruption of the land!
OEDIPUS: You, shameless—
    aren't you appalled to start up such a story?
    You think you can get away with this?
TIRESIAS: I have already.
    The truth with all its power lives inside me.   405
OEDIPUS: Who primed you for this? Not your prophet's trade.
TIRESIAS: You did, you forced me, twisted it out of me.
OEDIPUS: What? Say it again—I'll understand it better.
TIRESIAS: Didn't you understand, just now?
    Or are you tempting me to talk?   410
OEDIPUS: No, I can't say I grasped your meaning.
    Out with it, again!
TIRESIAS: I say you are the murderer you hunt.
OEDIPUS: That obscenity, twice—by god, you'll pay.
TIRESIAS: Shall I say more, so you can really rage?   415
OEDIPUS: Much as you want. Your words are nothing—futile.
TIRESIAS: You cannot imagine . . . . I tell you,
    you and your loved ones live together in infamy,
    you cannot see how far you've gone in guilt.
OEDIPUS: You think you can keep this up and never suffer?   420
TIRESIAS: Indeed, if the truth has any power.
OEDIPUS: It does
    but not for you, old man. You've lost your power,
    stone-blind, stone-deaf—senses, eyes blind as stone!
TIRESIAS: I pity you, flinging at me the very insults
    each man here will fling at you so soon.
OEDIPUS: Blind,   425
    lost in the night, endless night that nursed you!
    You can't hurt me or anyone else who sees the light—
    you can never touch me.
TIRESIAS: True, it is not your fate

to fall at my hands. Apollo is quite enough,
and he will take some pains to work this out.   430
OEDIPUS: Creon! Is this conspiracy his or yours?
TIRESIAS: Creon is not your downfall, no, you are your own.
OEDIPUS: O power—
wealth and empire, skill outstripping skill
in the heady rivalries of life,
what envy lurks inside you! Just for this,   435
the crown the city gave me—I never sought it,
they laid it in my hands—for this alone, Creon,
the soul of trust, my loyal friend from the start
steals against me . . . so hungry to overthrow me
he sets this wizard on me, this scheming quack,   440
this fortune-teller peddling lies, eyes peeled
for his own profit—seer blind in his craft!

Come here, you pious fraud. Tell me,
when did you ever prove yourself a prophet?
When the Sphinx, that chanting Fury kept her deathwatch here,   445
why silent then, not a word to set our people free?
There was a riddle, not for some passer-by to solve—
it cried out for a prophet. Where were you?
Did you rise to the crisis? Not a word,
you and your birds, your gods—nothing.   450
No, but I came by, Oedipus the ignorant,
I stopped the Sphinx! With no help from the birds,
the flight of my own intelligence hit the mark.

And this is the man you'd try to overthrow?
You think you'll stand by Creon when he's king?   455
You and the great mastermind—
you'll pay in tears, I promise you, for this,
this witch-hunt. If you didn't look so senile
the lash would teach you what your scheming means!
LEADER: I'd suggest his words were spoken in anger,   460
Oedipus . . . yours too, and it isn't what we need.
The best solution to the oracle, the riddle
posed by god—we should look for that.
TIRESIAS: You are the king no doubt, but in one respect,
at least, I am your equal: the right to reply.   465
I claim that privilege too.
I am not your slave. I serve Apollo.
I don't need Creon to speak for me in public.
                                           So,
you mock my blindness? Let me tell you this.
You with your precious eyes,   470
you're blind to the corruption of your life,

to the house you live in, those you live with —
who *are* your parents? Do you know? All unknowing
you are the scourge of your own flesh and blood,
the dead below the earth and the living here above,   475
and the double lash of your mother and your father's curse
will whip you from this land one day, their footfall
treading you down in terror, darkness shrouding
your eyes that now can see the light!

Soon, soon

you'll scream aloud — what haven won't reverberate?   480
What rock of Cithaeron° won't scream back in echo?
That day you learn the truth about your marriage,
the wedding-march that sang you into your halls,
the lusty voyage home to the fatal harbor!
And a load of other horrors you'd never dream   485
will level you with yourself and all your children.

There. Now smear us with insults — Creon, myself
and every word I've said. No man will ever
be rooted from the earth as brutally as you.

OEDIPUS: Enough! Such filth from him? Insufferable —   490
what, still alive? Get out —
faster, back where you came from — vanish!

TIRESIAS: I'd never have come if you hadn't called me here.

OEDIPUS: If I thought you'd blurt out such absurdities,
you'd have died waiting before I'd had you summoned.   495

TIRESIAS: Absurd, am I? To you, not to your parents:
the ones who bore you found me sane enough.

OEDIPUS: Parents — who? Wait . . . who is my father?

TIRESIAS: This day will bring your birth and your destruction.

OEDIPUS: Riddles — all you can say are riddles, murk and darkness.   500

TIRESIAS: Ah, but aren't you the best man alive at solving riddles?

OEDIPUS: Mock me for that, go on, and you'll reveal my greatness.

TIRESIAS: Your great good fortune, true, it was your ruin.

OEDIPUS: Not if I saved the city — what do I care?

TIRESIAS: Well then, I'll be going.

To his attendant.

Take me home, boy.   505

OEDIPUS: Yes, take him away. You're a nuisance here.
Out of the way, the irritation's gone.

Turning his back on Tiresias, moving toward the palace.

TIRESIAS: I will go,
once I have said what I came here to say.

---

481 Cithaeron: Where Oedipus was abandoned as an infant.

I'll never shrink from the anger in your eyes—
you can't destroy me. Listen to me closely: 510
the man you've sought so long, proclaiming,
cursing up and down, the murderer of Laius—
he is here. A stranger,
you may think, who lives among you,
he soon will be revealed a native Theban   515
but he will take no joy in the revelation.
Blind who now has eyes, beggar who now is rich,
he will grope his way toward a foreign soil,
a stick tapping before him step by step.

Oedipus enters the palace.

Revealed at last, brother and father both   520
to the children he embraces, to his mother
son and husband both—he sowed the loins
his father sowed, he spilled his father's blood!

Go in and reflect on that, solve that.
And if you find I've lied   525
from this day onward call the prophet blind.

Tiresias and the boy exit to the side.

CHORUS: Who—
who is the man the voice of god denounces
resounding out of the rocky gorge of Delphi?
    The horror too dark to tell,
whose ruthless bloody hands have done the work?   530
His time has come to fly
    to outrace the stallions of the storm
            his feet a streak of speed—
Cased in armor, Apollo son of the Father
lunges on him, lightning-bolts afire!   535
And the grim unerring Furies°
            closing for the kill.

                        Look,
the word of god has just come blazing
flashing off Parnassus'° snowy heights!
    That man who left no trace—   540
after him, hunt him down with all our strength!
Now under bristling timber
    up through rocks and caves he stalks
                like the wild mountain bull—
cut off from men, each step an agony, frenzied, racing blind   545

---

536 Furies: Three spirits who tormented evildoers.   **539 Parnassus:** A mountain in Greece associated with Apollo.

but he cannot outrace the dread voices of Delphi
ringing out of the heart of Earth,
    the dark wings beating around him shrieking doom
        the doom that never dies, the terror—

The skilled prophet scans the birds and shatters me with terror!   550
I can't accept him, can't deny him, don't know what to say,
I'm lost, and the wings of dark foreboding beating—
I cannot see what's come, what's still to come . . .
and what could breed a blood feud between
    Laius' house and the son of Polybus?°   555
I know of nothing, not in the past and not now,
no charge to bring against our king, no cause
to attack his fame that rings throughout Thebes—
    not without proof—not for the ghost of Laius,
    not to avenge a murder gone without a trace.   560

Zeus and Apollo know, they know, the great masters
    of all the dark and depth of human life.
But whether a mere man can know the truth,
whether a seer can fathom more than I—
there is no test, no certain proof   565
    though matching skill for skill
a man can outstrip a rival. No, not till I see
these charges proved will I side with his accusers.
We saw him then, when the she-hawk° swept against him,
saw with our own eyes his skill, his brilliant triumph—   570
    there was the test—he was the joy of Thebes!
    Never will I convict my king, never in my heart.

Enter Creon from the side.

CREON: My fellow-citizens, I hear King Oedipus
levels terrible charges at me. I had to come.
I resent it deeply. If, in the present crisis,   575
he thinks he suffers any abuse from me,
anything I've done or said that offers him
the slightest injury, why, I've no desire
to linger out this life, my reputation a shambles.
The damage I'd face from such an accusation   580
is nothing simple. No, there's nothing worse:
branded a traitor in the city, a traitor
to all of you and my good friends.
LEADER: True,
but a slur might have been forced out of him,
by anger perhaps, not any firm conviction.   585

---

555 Polybus: Thought to be Oedipus's father.   **569 she-hawk:** The Sphinx.

CREON: The charge was made in public, wasn't it?
    I put the prophet up to spreading lies?
LEADER: Such things were said . . .
    I don't know with what intent, if any.
CREON: Was his glance steady, his mind right   590
    when the charge was brought against me?
LEADER: I really couldn't say. I never look
    to judge the ones in power.

The doors open. Oedipus enters.

                              Wait,
    here's Oedipus now.
OEDIPUS: You—here? You have the gall
    to show your face before the palace gates?   595
    You, plotting to kill me, kill the king—
    I see it all, the marauding thief himself
    scheming to steal my crown and power!
                                        Tell me,
    in god's name, what did you take me for,
    coward or fool, when you spun out your plot?   600
    Your treachery—you think I'd never detect it
    creeping against me in the dark? Or sensing it,
    not defend myself? Aren't you the fool,
    you and your high adventure. Lacking numbers,
    powerful friends, out for the big game of empire—   605
    you need riches, armies to bring that quarry down!
CREON: Are you quite finished? It's your turn to listen
    for just as long as you've . . . instructed me.
    Hear me out, then judge me on the facts.
OEDIPUS: You've a wicked way with words, Creon,   610
    but I'll be slow to learn—from you.
    I find you a menace, a great burden to me.
CREON: Just one thing, hear me out in this.
OEDIPUS: Just one thing,
    don't tell me you're not the enemy, the traitor.
CREON: Look, if you think crude, mindless stubbornness   615
    such a gift, you've lost your sense of balance.
OEDIPUS: If you think you can abuse a kinsman,
    then escape the penalty, you're insane.
CREON: Fair enough, I grant you. But this injury
    you say I've done you, what is it?   620
OEDIPUS: Did you induce me, yes or no,
    to send for that sanctimonious prophet?
CREON: I did. And I'd do the same again.
OEDIPUS: All right then, tell me, how long is it now
    since Laius . . .
CREON: Laius—what did *he* do?

OEDIPUS: Vanished,   625
  swept from sight, murdered in his tracks.
CREON: The count of the years would run you far back . . .
OEDIPUS: And that far back, was the prophet at his trade?
CREON: Skilled as he is today, and just as honored.
OEDIPUS: Did he ever refer to me then, at that time?
CREON: No,   630
  never, at least, when I was in his presence.
OEDIPUS: But you did investigate the murder, didn't you?
CREON: We did our best, of course, discovered nothing.
OEDIPUS: But the great seer never accused me then — why not?
CREON: I don't know. And when I don't, *I* keep quiet.   635
OEDIPUS: You do know this, you'd tell it too —
  if you had a shred of decency.
CREON: What?
  If I know, I won't hold back.
OEDIPUS: Simply this:
  if the two of you had never put heads together,
  we'd never have heard about *my* killing Laius.   640
CREON: If that's what he says . . . well, you know best.
  But now I have a right to learn from you
  as you just learned from me.
OEDIPUS: Learn your fill,
  you never will convict me of the murder.
CREON: Tell me, you're married to my sister, aren't you?   645
OEDIPUS: A genuine discovery — there's no denying that.
CREON: And you rule the land with her, with equal power?
OEDIPUS: She receives from me whatever she desires.
CREON: And I am the third, all of us are equals?
OEDIPUS: Yes, and it's there you show your stripes —   650
  you betray a kinsman.
CREON: Not at all.
  Not if you see things calmly, rationally,
  as I do. Look at it this way first:
  who in his right mind would rather rule
  and live in anxiety than sleep in peace?   655
  Particularly if he enjoys the same authority.
  Not I, I'm not the man to yearn for kingship,
  not with a king's power in my hands. Who would?
  No one with any sense of self-control.
  Now, as it is, you offer me all I need,   660
  not a fear in the world. But if I wore the crown . . .
  there'd be many painful duties to perform,
  hardly to my taste.
       How could kingship
  please me more than influence, power
  without a qualm? I'm not that deluded yet,   665

to reach for anything but privilege outright,
profit free and clear.
Now all men sing my praises, all salute me,
now all who request your favors curry mine.
I'm their best hope: success rests in me.   670
Why give up that, I ask you, and borrow trouble?
A man of sense, someone who sees things clearly
would never resort to treason.
No, I've no lust for conspiracy in me,
nor could I ever suffer one who does.   675

Do you want proof? Go to Delphi yourself,
examine the oracle and see if I've reported
the message word-for-word. This too:
if you detect that I and the clairvoyant
have plotted anything in common, arrest me,   680
execute me. Not on the strength of one vote,
two in this case, mine as well as yours.
But don't convict me on sheer unverified surmise.

How wrong it is to take the good for bad,
purely at random, or take the bad for good.   685
But reject a friend, a kinsman? I would as soon
tear out the life within us, priceless life itself.
You'll learn this well, without fail, in time.
Time alone can bring the just man to light;
the criminal you can spot in one short day.

LEADER: Good advice,   690
my lord, for anyone who wants to avoid disaster.
Those who jump to conclusions may be wrong.

OEDIPUS: When my enemy moves against me quickly,
plots in secret, I move quickly too, I must,
I plot and pay him back. Relax my guard a moment,   695
waiting his next move — he wins his objective,
I lose mine.

CREON: What do you want?
You want me banished?

OEDIPUS: No, I want you dead.

CREON: Just to show how ugly a grudge can . . .

OEDIPUS: So,
still stubborn? you don't think I'm serious?   700

CREON: I think you're insane.

OEDIPUS: Quite sane — in my behalf.

CREON: Not just as much in mine?

OEDIPUS: You — my mortal enemy?

CREON: What if you're wholly wrong?

OEDIPUS: No matter — I must rule.

CREON: Not if you rule unjustly.
OEDIPUS: Hear him, Thebes, my city!
CREON: My city too, not yours alone!   705
LEADER: Please, my lords.

Enter Jocasta from the palace.

                         Look, Jocasta's coming,
     and just in time too. With her help
     you must put this fighting of yours to rest.
JOCASTA: Have you no sense? Poor misguided men,
     such shouting — why this public outburst?   710
     Aren't you ashamed, with the land so sick,
     to stir up private quarrels?

To Oedipus.

     Into the palace now. And Creon, you go home.
     Why make such a furor over nothing?
CREON: My sister, it's dreadful . . . Oedipus, your husband,   715
     he's bent on a choice of punishments for me,
     banishment from the fatherland or death.
OEDIPUS: Precisely. I caught him in the act, Jocasta,
     plotting, about to stab me in the back.
CREON: Never — curse me, let me die and be damned   720
     if I've done you any wrong you charge me with.
JOCASTA: Oh god, believe it, Oedipus,
     honor the solemn oath he swears to heaven.
     Do it for me, for the sake of all your people.

The Chorus begins to chant.

CHORUS: Believe it, be sensible   725
                    give way, my king, I beg you!
OEDIPUS: What do you want from me, concessions?
CHORUS: Respect him — he's been no fool in the past
     and now he's strong with the oath he swears to god.
OEDIPUS: You know what you're asking?
CHORUS: I do.
OEDIPUS: Then out with it!   730
CHORUS: The man's your friend, your kin, he's under oath —
     don't cast him out, disgraced
     branded with guilt on the strength of hearsay only.
OEDIPUS: Know full well, if that's what you want
     you want me dead or banished from the land.
CHORUS: Never —   735
     no, by the blazing Sun, first god of the heavens!
               Stripped of the gods, stripped of loved ones,
     let me die by inches if that ever crossed my mind.
     But the heart inside me sickens, dies as the land dies

and now on top of the old griefs you pile this,   740
 your fury—both of you!
OEDIPUS: Then let him go,
 even if it does lead to my ruin, my death
 or my disgrace, driven from Thebes for life.
 It's you, not him I pity—your words move me.
 He, wherever he goes, my hate goes with him.   745
CREON: Look at you, sullen in yielding, brutal in your rage—
 you'll go too far. It's perfect justice:
 natures like yours are hardest on themselves.
OEDIPUS: Then leave me alone—get out!
CREON: I'm going.
 You're wrong, so wrong. These men know I'm right.   750

Exit to the side. The Chorus turns to Jocasta.

CHORUS: Why do you hesitate, my lady
   why not help him in?
JOCASTA: Tell me what's happened first.
CHORUS: Loose, ignorant talk started dark suspicions
 and a sense of injustice cut deeply too.   755
JOCASTA: On both sides?
CHORUS: Oh yes.
JOCASTA: What did they say?
CHORUS: Enough, please, enough! The land's so racked already
 or so it seems to me . . .
 End the trouble here, just where they left it.
OEDIPUS: You see what comes of your good intentions now?   760
 And all because you tried to blunt my anger.
CHORUS: My king,
 I've said it once, I'll say it time and again—
  I'd be insane, you know it,
 senseless, ever to turn my back on you.
 You who set our beloved land—storm-tossed, shattered—   765
 straight on course. Now again, good helmsman,
 steer us through the storm!

The Chorus draws away, leaving Oedipus and Jocasta side by side.

JOCASTA: For the love of god,
 Oedipus, tell me too, what is it?
 Why this rage? You're so unbending.
OEDIPUS: I will tell you. I respect you, Jocasta,   770
 much more than these . . .

Glancing at the Chorus.

 Creon's to blame, Creon schemes against me.
JOCASTA: Tell me clearly, how did the quarrel start?
OEDIPUS: He says *I* murdered Laius—I am guilty.

JOCASTA: How does he know? Some secret knowledge
    or simple hearsay?

OEDIPUS: Oh, he sent his prophet in
    to do his dirty work. You know Creon,
    Creon keeps his own lips clean.

JOCASTA: A prophet?
    Well then, free yourself of every charge!
    Listen to me and learn some peace of mind:
    no skill in the world,
    nothing human can penetrate the future.
    Here is proof, quick and to the point.
    An oracle came to Laius one fine day
    (I won't say from Apollo himself
    but his underlings, his priests) and it said
    that doom would strike him down at the hands of a son,
    our son, to be born of our own flesh and blood. But Laius,
    so the report goes at least, was killed by strangers,
    thieves, at a place where three roads meet . . . my son—
    he wasn't three days old and the boy's father
    fastened his ankles, had a henchman fling him away
    on a barren, trackless mountain.
                      There, you see?
    Apollo brought neither thing to pass. My baby
    no more murdered his father than Laius suffered—
    his wildest fear—death at his own son's hands.
    That's how the seers and their revelations
    mapped out the future. Brush them from your mind.
    Whatever the god needs and seeks
    he'll bring to light himself, with ease.

OEDIPUS: Strange,
    hearing you just now . . . my mind wandered,
    my thoughts racing back and forth.

JOCASTA: What do you mean? Why so anxious, startled?

OEDIPUS: I thought I heard you say that Laius
    was cut down at a place where three roads meet.

JOCASTA: That was the story. It hasn't died out yet.

OEDIPUS: Where did this thing happen? Be precise.

JOCASTA: A place called Phocis, where two branching roads,
    one from Daulia, one from Delphi,
    come together—a crossroads.

OEDIPUS: When? How long ago?

JOCASTA: The heralds no sooner reported Laius dead
    than you appeared and they hailed you king of Thebes.

OEDIPUS: My god, my god—what have you planned to do to me?

JOCASTA: What, Oedipus? What haunts you so?

OEDIPUS: Not yet.

775

780

785

790

795

800

805

810

815

Laius—how did he look? Describe him.
Had he reached his prime?

JOCASTA: He was swarthy,
and the gray had just begun to streak his temples,
and his build . . . wasn't far from yours.

OEDIPUS: Oh no no,
I think I've just called down a dreadful curse 820
upon myself—I simply didn't know!

JOCASTA: What are you saying? I shudder to look at you.

OEDIPUS: I have a terrible fear the blind seer can see.
I'll know in a moment. One thing more—

JOCASTA: Anything,
afraid as I am—ask, I'll answer, all I can. 825

OEDIPUS: Did he go with a light or heavy escort,
several men-at-arms, like a lord, a king?

JOCASTA: There were five in the party, a herald among them,
and a single wagon carrying Laius.

OEDIPUS: Ai—
now I can see it all, clear as day. 830
Who told you all this at the time, Jocasta?

JOCASTA: A servant who reached home, the lone survivor.

OEDIPUS: So, could he still be in the palace—even now?

JOCASTA: No indeed. Soon as he returned from the scene
and saw you on the throne with Laius dead and gone, 835
he knelt and clutched my hand, pleading with me
to send him into the hinterlands, to pasture,
far as possible, out of sight of Thebes.
I sent him away. Slave though he was,
he'd earned that favor—and much more. 840

OEDIPUS: Can we bring him back, quickly?

JOCASTA: Easily. Why do you want him so?

OEDIPUS: I'm afraid,
Jocasta, I have said too much already.
That man—I've got to see him.

JOCASTA: Then he'll come.
But even I have a right, I'd like to think, 845
to know what's torturing you, my lord.

OEDIPUS: And so you shall—I can hold nothing back from you,
now I've reached this pitch of dark foreboding.
Who means more to me than you? Tell me,
whom would I turn toward but you 850
as I go through all this?

My father was Polybus, king of Corinth.
My mother, a Dorian, Merope. And I was held
the prince of the realm among the people there,
till something struck me out of nowhere, 855

something strange . . . worth remarking perhaps,
hardly worth the anxiety I gave it.
Some man at a banquet who had drunk too much
shouted out—he was far gone, mind you—
that I am not my father's son. Fighting words!   860
I barely restrained myself that day
but early the next I went to mother and father,
questioned them closely, and they were enraged
at the accusation and the fool who let it fly.
So as for my parents I was satisfied,   865
but still this thing kept gnawing at me,
the slander spread—I had to make my move.
                                            And so,
unknown to mother and father I set out for Delphi,
and the god Apollo spurned me, sent me away
denied the facts I came for,   870
but first he flashed before my eyes a future
great with pain, terror, disaster—I can hear him cry,
"You are fated to couple with your mother, you will bring
a breed of children into the light no man can bear to see—
you will kill your father, the one who gave you life!"   875
I heard all that and ran. I abandoned Corinth,
from that day on I gauged its landfall only
by the stars, running, always running
toward some place where I would never see
the shame of all those oracles come true.   880
And as I fled I reached that very spot
where the great king, you say, met his death.
Now, Jocasta, I will tell you all.
Making my way toward this triple crossroad
I began to see a herald, then a brace of colts   885
drawing a wagon, and mounted on the bench . . . a man,
just as you've described him, coming face-to-face,
and the one in the lead and the old man himself
were about to thrust me off the road—brute force—
and the one shouldering me aside, the driver,   890
I strike him in anger!—and the old man, watching me
coming up along his wheels—he brings down
his prod, two prongs straight at my head!
I paid him back with interest!
Short work, by god—with one blow of the staff   895
in this right hand I knock him out of his high seat,
roll him out of the wagon, sprawling headlong—
I killed them all—every mother's son!

Oh, but if there is any blood-tie
between Laius and this stranger . . .   900

what man alive more miserable than I?
More hated by the gods? *I* am the man
no alien, no citizen welcomes to his house,
law forbids it — not a word to me in public,
driven out of every hearth and home.   905
And all these curses I — no one but I
brought down these piling curses on myself!
And you, his wife, I've touched your body with these,
the hands that killed your husband cover you with blood.

Wasn't I born for torment? Look me in the eyes!   910
I am abomination — heart and soul!
I must be exiled, and even in exile
never see my parents, never set foot
on native earth again. Else I'm doomed
to couple with my mother and cut my father down . . .   915
Polybus who reared me, gave me life.
                                   But why, why?
Wouldn't a man of judgment say — and wouldn't he be right —
some savage power has brought this down upon my head?

Oh no, not that, you pure and awesome gods,
never let me see that day! Let me slip   920
from the world of men, vanish without a trace
before I see myself stained with such corruption,
stained to the heart.
LEADER: My lord, you fill our hearts with fear.
      But at least until you question the witness,   925
      do take hope.
OEDIPUS: Exactly. He is my last hope —
      I'm waiting for the shepherd. He is crucial.
JOCASTA: And once he appears, what then? Why so urgent?
OEDIPUS: I'll tell you. If it turns out that his story
      matches yours, I've escaped the worst.   930
JOCASTA: What did I say? What struck you so?
OEDIPUS: You said *thieves* —
      he told you a whole band of them murdered Laius.
      So, if he still holds to the same number,
      I cannot be the killer. One can't equal many.
      But if he refers to one man, one alone,   935
      clearly the scales come down on me:
      I am guilty.
JOCASTA: Impossible. Trust me,
      I told you precisely what he said,
      and he can't retract it now;
      the whole city heard it, not just I.   940
      And even if he should vary his first report
      by one man more or less, still, my lord,

he could never make the murder of Laius
truly fit the prophecy. Apollo was explicit:
my son was doomed to kill my husband . . . my son,   945
poor defenseless thing, he never had a chance
to kill his father. They destroyed him first.

So much for prophecy. It's neither here nor there.
From this day on, I wouldn't look right or left.
OEDIPUS: True, true. Still, that shepherd,   950
someone fetch him — now!
JOCASTA: I'll send at once. But do let's go inside.
I'd never displease you, least of all in this.

Oedipus and Jocasta enter the palace.

CHORUS: Destiny guide me always
Destiny find me filled with reverence   955
pure in word and deed.
Great laws tower above us, reared on high
born for the brilliant vault of heaven —
Olympian sky their only father,
nothing mortal, no man gave them birth,   960
their memory deathless, never lost in sleep:
within them lives a mighty god, the god does not grow old.

Pride breeds the tyrant
violent pride, gorging, crammed to bursting
with all that is overripe and rich with ruin —   965
clawing up to the heights, headlong pride
crashes down the abyss — sheer doom!
No footing helps, all foothold lost and gone,
But the healthy strife that makes the city strong —
I pray that god will never end that wrestling: 970
god, my champion, I will never let you go.

But if any man comes striding, high and mighty
in all he says and does,
no fear of justice, no reverence
for the temples of the gods —   975
let a rough doom tear him down,
repay his pride, breakneck, ruinous pride!
If he cannot reap his profits fairly
cannot restrain himself from outrage —
mad, laying hands on the holy things untouchable!   980

Can such a man, so desperate, still boast
he can save his life from the flashing bolts of god?
If all such violence goes with honor now
why join the sacred dance?

Never again will I go reverent to Delphi,   985
    the inviolate heart of Earth
or Apollo's ancient oracle at Abae
or Olympia of the fires—
    unless these prophecies all come true
for all mankind to point toward in wonder.   990
King of kings, if you deserve your titles
    Zeus, remember, never forget!
You and your deathless, everlasting reign.

    They are dying, the old oracles sent to Laius,
    now our masters strike them off the rolls.   995
      Nowhere Apollo's golden glory now—
      the gods, the gods go down.

Enter Jocasta from the palace, carrying a suppliant's branch wound in wool.

JOCASTA: Lords of the realm, it occurred to me,
just now, to visit the temples of the gods,
so I have my branch in hand and incense too.   1000
Oedipus is beside himself. Racked with anguish,
no longer a man of sense, he won't admit
the latest prophecies are hollow as the old—
he's at the mercy of every passing voice
if the voice tells of terror.   1005
I urge him gently, nothing seems to help,
so I turn to you, Apollo, you are nearest.

*Placing her branch on the altar, while an old herdsman enters from the side, not the
one just summoned by the king but an unexpected messenger from Corinth.*

I come with prayers and offerings . . . I beg you,
cleanse us, set us free of defilement!
Look at us, passengers in the grip of fear,   1010
watching the pilot of the vessel go to pieces.
MESSENGER:

Approaching Jocasta and the Chorus.

Strangers, please, I wonder if you could lead us
to the palace of the king . . . I think it's Oedipus.
Better, the man himself—you know where he is?
LEADER: This is his palace, stranger. He's inside.   1015
But here is his queen, his wife and mother
of his children.
MESSENGER: Blessings on you, noble queen,
queen of Oedipus crowned with all your family—
blessings on you always!
JOCASTA: And the same to you, stranger, you deserve it . . .   1020
such a greeting. But what have you come for?

Have you brought us news?
MESSENGER: Wonderful news —
for the house, my lady, for your husband too.
JOCASTA: Really, what? Who sent you?
MESSENGER: Corinth.
I'll give you the message in a moment.   1025
You'll be glad of it — how could you help it? —
though it costs a little sorrow in the bargain.
JOCASTA: What can it be, with such a double edge?
MESSENGER: The people there, they want to make your Oedipus
king of Corinth, so they're saying now.   1030
JOCASTA: Why? Isn't old Polybus still in power?
MESSENGER: No more. Death has got him in the tomb.
JOCASTA: What are you saying? Polybus, dead? — dead?
MESSENGER: If not,
if I'm not telling the truth, strike me dead too.
JOCASTA:

To a servant.

Quickly, go to your master, tell him this!   1035

You prophecies of the gods, where are you now?
This is the man that Oedipus feared for years,
he fled him, not to kill him — and now he's dead,
quite by chance, a normal, natural death,
not murdered by his son.
OEDIPUS:

Emerging from the palace.

                              Dearest,   1040
what now? Why call me from the palace?
JOCASTA:

Bringing the Messenger closer.

Listen to *him*, see for yourself what all
those awful prophecies of god have come to.
OEDIPUS: And who is he? What can he have for me?
JOCASTA: He's from Corinth, he's come to tell you   1045
your father is no more — Polybus — he's dead!
OEDIPUS:

Wheeling on the Messenger.

What? Let me have it from your lips.
MESSENGER: Well,
if that's what you want first, then here it is:
make no mistake, Polybus is dead and gone.
OEDIPUS: How — murder? sickness? — what? what killed him?   1050
MESSENGER: A light tip of the scales can put old bones to rest.

OEDIPUS: Sickness then — poor man, it wore him down.
MESSENGER: That,
       and the long count of years he'd measured out.
OEDIPUS: So!
       Jocasta, why, why look to the Prophet's hearth,
       the fires of the future? Why scan the birds   1055
       that scream above our heads? They winged me on
       to the murder of my father, did they? That was my doom?
       Well look, he's dead and buried, hidden under the earth,
       and here I am in Thebes, I never put hand to sword —
       unless some longing for me wasted him away,   1060
       then in a sense you'd say I caused his death.
       But now, all those prophecies I feared — Polybus
       packs them off to sleep with him in hell!
       They're nothing, worthless.
JOCASTA: There.
       Didn't I tell you from the start?   1065
OEDIPUS: So you did. I was lost in fear.
JOCASTA: No more, sweep it from your mind forever.
OEDIPUS: But my mother's bed, surely I must fear —
JOCASTA: Fear?
       What should a man fear? It's all chance,
       chance rules our lives. Not a man on earth   1070
       can see a day ahead, groping through the dark.
       Better to live at random, best we can.
       And as for this marriage with your mother —
       have no fear. Many a man before you,
       in his dreams, has shared his mother's bed.   1075
       Take such things for shadows, nothing at all —
       Live, Oedipus,
       as if there's no tomorrow!
OEDIPUS: Brave words,
       and you'd persuade me if mother weren't alive.
       But mother lives, so for all your reassurances   1080
       I live in fear, I must.
JOCASTA: But your father's death,
       that, at least, is a great blessing, joy to the eyes!
OEDIPUS: Great, I know . . . but I fear *her* — she's still alive.
MESSENGER: Wait, who is this woman, makes you so afraid?
OEDIPUS: Merope, old man. The wife of Polybus.   1085
MESSENGER: The queen? What's there to fear in her?
OEDIPUS: A dreadful prophecy, stranger, sent by the gods.
MESSENGER: Tell me, could you? Unless it's forbidden
       other ears to hear.
OEDIPUS: Not at all.
       Apollo told me once — it is my fate —   1090

I must make love with my own mother,
shed my father's blood with my own hands.
So for years I've given Corinth a wide berth,
and it's been my good fortune too. But still,
to see one's parents and look into their eyes   1095
is the greatest joy I know.
MESSENGER: You're afraid of that?
    That kept you out of Corinth?
OEDIPUS: My *father*, old man—
    so I wouldn't kill my father.
MESSENGER: So that's it.
    Well then, seeing I came with such good will, my king,
    why don't I rid you of that old worry now?   1100
OEDIPUS: What a rich reward you'd have for that.
MESSENGER: What do you think I came for, majesty?
    So you'd come home and I'd be better off.
OEDIPUS: Never, I will never go near my parents.
MESSENGER: My boy, it's clear, you don't know what you're doing.   1105
OEDIPUS: What do you mean, old man? For god's sake, explain.
MESSENGER: If you ran from *them*, always dodging home . . .
OEDIPUS: Always, terrified Apollo's oracle might come true—
MESSENGER: And you'd be covered with guilt, from both your parents.
OEDIPUS: That's right, old man, that fear is always with me.   1110
MESSENGER: Don't you know? You've really nothing to fear.
OEDIPUS: But why? If I'm their son—Merope, Polybus?
MESSENGER: Polybus was nothing to you, that's why, not in blood.
OEDIPUS: What are you saying—Polybus was not my father?
MESSENGER: No more than I am. He and I are equals.
OEDIPUS: My father—   1115
    how can my father equal nothing? You're nothing to me!
MESSENGER: Neither was he, no more your father than I am.
OEDIPUS: Then why did he call me his son?
MESSENGER: You were a gift,
    years ago—know for a fact he took you
    from my hands.
OEDIPUS: No, from another's hands?   1120
    Then how could he love me so? He loved me, deeply . . .
MESSENGER: True, and his early years without a child
    made him love you all the more.
OEDIPUS: And you, did you . . .
    buy me? find me by accident?
MESSENGER: I stumbled on you,
    down the woody flanks of Mount Cithaeron.
OEDIPUS: So close,   1125
    what were you doing here, just passing through?
MESSENGER: Watching over my flocks, grazing them on the slopes.

OEDIPUS: A herdsman, were you? A vagabond, scraping for wages?
MESSENGER: Your savior too, my son, in your worst hour.
OEDIPUS: Oh —
    when you picked me up, was I in pain? What exactly?   1130
MESSENGER: Your ankles . . . they tell the story. Look at them.
OEDIPUS: Why remind me of that, that old affliction?
MESSENGER: Your ankles were pinned together; I set you free.
OEDIPUS: That dreadful mark — I've had it from the cradle.
MESSENGER: And you got your name from that misfortune too,   1135
    the name's still with you.
OEDIPUS: Dear god, who did it? —
    mother? father? Tell me.
MESSENGER: I don't know.
    The one who gave you to me, he'd know more.
OEDIPUS: What? You took me from someone else?
    You didn't find me yourself?
MESSENGER: No sir,   1140
    another shepherd passed you on to me.
OEDIPUS: Who? Do you know? Describe him.
MESSENGER: He called himself a servant of . . .
    if I remember rightly — Laius.

Jocasta turns sharply.

OEDIPUS: The king of the land who ruled here long ago?   1145
MESSENGER: That's the one. That herdsman was *his* man.
OEDIPUS: Is he still alive? Can I see him?
MESSENGER: They'd know best, the people of these parts.

Oedipus and the Messenger turn to the Chorus.

OEDIPUS: Does anyone know that herdsman,
    the one he mentioned? Anyone seen him   1150
    in the fields, in town? Out with it!
    The time has come to reveal this once for all.
LEADER: I think he's the very shepherd you wanted to see,
    a moment ago. But the queen, Jocasta,
    she's the one to say.
OEDIPUS: Jocasta,   1155
    you remember the man we just sent for?
    Is *that* the one he means?
JOCASTA: That man . . .
    why ask? Old shepherd, talk, empty nonsense,
    don't give it another thought, don't even think —
OEDIPUS: What — give up now, with a clue like this?   1160
    Fail to solve the mystery of my birth?
    Not for all the world!
JOCASTA: Stop — in the name of god,
    if you love your own life, call off this search!

My suffering is enough.
OEDIPUS: Courage!
    Even if my mother turns out to be a slave,   1165
    and I a slave, three generations back,
    you would not seem common.
JOCASTA: Oh no,
    listen to me, I beg you, don't do this.
OEDIPUS: Listen to you? No more. I must know it all,
    see the truth at last.
JOCASTA: No, please —   1170
    for your sake — I want the best for you!
OEDIPUS: Your best is more than I can bear.
JOCASTA: You're doomed —
    may you never fathom who you are!
OEDIPUS:

To a servant.

    Hurry, fetch me the herdsman, now!
    Leave her to glory in her royal birth.   1175
JOCASTA: Aieeeeee —
              man of agony —
    that is the only name I have for you,
    that, no other — ever, ever, ever!

Flinging [herself] through the palace doors. A long, tense silence follows.

LEADER: Where's she gone, Oedipus?
    Rushing off, such wild grief . . .   1180
    I'm afraid that from this silence
    something monstrous may come bursting forth.
OEDIPUS: Let it burst! Whatever will, whatever must!
    I must know my birth, no matter how common
    it may be — must see my origins face-to-face.   1185
    She perhaps, she with her woman's pride
    may well be mortified by my birth,
    but I, I count myself the son of Chance,
    the great goddess, giver of all good things —
    I'll never see myself disgraced. She is my mother!   1190
    And the moons have marked me out, my blood-brothers,
    one moon on the wane, the next moon great with power.
    That is my blood, my nature — I will never betray it,
    never fail to search and learn my birth!
CHORUS: Yes — if I am a true prophet   1195
        if I can grasp the truth,
      by the boundless skies of Olympus,
    at the full moon of tomorrow, Mount Cithaeron
    you will know how Oedipus glories in you —
    you, his birthplace, nurse, his mountain-mother!   1200

And we will sing you, dancing out your praise —
you lift our monarch's heart!
    Apollo, Apollo, god of the wild cry
        may our dancing please you!
                Oedipus —
        son, dear child, who bore you?   1205
Who of the nymphs who seem to live forever
mated with Pan,° the mountain-striding Father?
Who was your mother? who, some bride of Apollo
the god who loves the pastures spreading toward the sun?
    Or was it Hermes, king of the lightning ridges?   1210
Or Dionysus, lord of frenzy, lord of the barren peaks —
did he seize you in his hands, dearest of all his lucky finds? —
    found by the nymphs, their warm eyes dancing, gift
to the lord who loves them dancing out his joy!

Oedipus strains to see a figure coming from the distance. Attended by palace guards, an old Shepherd enters slowly, reluctant to approach the king.

OEDIPUS: I never met the man, my friends . . . still,   1215
    if I had to guess, I'd say that's the shepherd,
    the very one we've looked for all along.
    Brothers in old age, two of a kind,
    he and our guest here. At any rate
    the ones who bring him in are my own men,   1220
    I recognize them.

Turning to the Leader.

                But you know more than I,
    you should, you've seen the man before.
LEADER: I know him, definitely. One of Laius' men,
    a trusty shepherd, if there ever was one.
OEDIPUS: You, I ask you first, stranger,   1225
    you from Corinth — is this the one you mean?
MESSENGER: You're looking at him. He's your man.
OEDIPUS:

To the Shepherd.

    You, old man, come over here —
    look at me. Answer all my questions.
    Did you ever serve King Laius?
SHEPHERD: So I did . . .   1230
    a slave, not bought on the block though,
    born and reared in the palace.
OEDIPUS: Your duties, your kind of work?
SHEPHERD: Herding the flocks, the better part of my life.
OEDIPUS: Where, mostly? Where did you do your grazing?

1207 Pan: God of shepherds.

SHEPHERD: Well,   1235
    Cithaeron sometimes, or the foothills round about.
OEDIPUS: This man — you know him? ever see him there?
SHEPHERD:

Confused, glancing from the Messenger to the King.

    Doing what — what man do you mean?
OEDIPUS:

Pointing to the Messenger.

    This one here — ever have dealings with him?
SHEPHERD: Not so I could say, but give me a chance,   1240
    my memory's bad . . .
MESSENGER: No wonder he doesn't know me, master.
    But let me refresh his memory for him.
    I'm sure he recalls old times we had
    on the slopes of Mount Cithaeron;   1245
    he and I, grazing our flocks, he with two
    and I with one — we both struck up together,
    three whole seasons, six months at a stretch
    from spring to the rising of Arcturus° in the fall,
    then with winter coming on I'd drive my herds   1250
    to my own pens, and back he'd go with his
    to Laius' folds.

To the Shepherd.

             Now that's how it was,
    wasn't it — yes or no?
SHEPHERD: Yes, I suppose . . .
    it's all so long ago.
MESSENGER: Come, tell me,
    you gave me a child back then, a boy, remember?   1255
    A little fellow to rear, my very own.
SHEPHERD: What? Why rake up that again?
MESSENGER: Look, here he is, my fine old friend —
    the same man who was just a baby then.
SHEPHERD: Damn you, shut your mouth — quiet!   1260
OEDIPUS: Don't lash out at him, old man —
    you need lashing more than he does.
SHEPHERD: Why,
    master, majesty — what have I done wrong?
OEDIPUS: You won't answer his question about the boy.
SHEPHERD: He's talking nonsense, wasting his breath.   1265
OEDIPUS: So, you won't talk willingly —
    then you'll talk with pain.

The guards seize the Shepherd.

1249 Arcturus: A star that whose rising marked the end of summer.

SHEPHERD: No, dear god, don't torture an old man!

OEDIPUS: Twist his arms back, quickly!

SHEPHERD: God help us, why? —
what more do you need to know? 1270

OEDIPUS: Did you give him that child? He's asking.

SHEPHERD: I did . . . I wish to god I'd died that day.

OEDIPUS: You've got your wish if you don't tell the truth.

SHEPHERD: The more I tell, the worse the death I'll die.

OEDIPUS: Our friend here wants to stretch things out, does he? 1275

Motioning to his men for torture.

SHEPHERD: No, no, I gave it to him — I just said so.

OEDIPUS: Where did you get it? Your house? Someone else's?

SHEPHERD: It wasn't mine, no, I got it from . . . someone.

OEDIPUS: Which one of them?

Looking at the citizens.

Whose house?

SHEPHERD: No —
god's sake, master, no more questions! 1280

OEDIPUS: You're a dead man if I have to ask again.

SHEPHERD: Then — the child came from the house . . .
of Laius.

OEDIPUS: A slave? or born of his own blood?

SHEPHERD: Oh no,
I'm right at the edge, the horrible truth — I've got to say it! 1285

OEDIPUS: And I'm at the edge of hearing horrors, yes, but I must hear!

SHEPHERD: All right! His son, they said it was — his son!
But the one inside, your wife,
she'd tell it best.

OEDIPUS: My wife — 1290
she gave it to you?

SHEPHERD: Yes, yes, my king.

OEDIPUS: Why, what for?

SHEPHERD: To kill it.

OEDIPUS: Her own child, 1295
how could she?

SHEPHERD: She was afraid —
frightening prophecies.

OEDIPUS: What?

SHEPHERD: They said —
he'd kill his parents. 1300

OEDIPUS: But you gave him to this old man — why?

SHEPHERD: I pitied the little baby, master,
hoped he'd take him off to his own country,
far away, but he saved him for this, this fate.
If you are the man he says you are, believe me, 1305

you were born for pain.
OEDIPUS: O god—
all come true, all burst to light!
O light—now let me look my last on you!
I stand revealed at last—
cursed in my birth, cursed in marriage,   1310
cursed in the lives I cut down with these hands!

Rushing through the doors with a great cry. The Corinthian Messenger, the Shepherd, and attendants exit slowly to the side.

CHORUS: O the generations of men
the dying generations—adding the total
of all your lives I find they come to nothing . . .
                              does there exist, is there a man on earth   1315
who seizes more joy than just a dream, a vision?
And the vision no sooner dawns than dies
blazing into oblivion.

You are my great example, you, your life,
your destiny, Oedipus, man of misery—   1320
I count no man blest.

                              You outranged all men!
                    Bending your bow to the breaking-point
you captured priceless glory, O dear god,
and the Sphinx came crashing down,
                              the virgin, claws hooked   1325
like a bird of omen singing, shrieking death—
like a fortress reared in the face of death
you rose and saved our land.

From that day on we called you king
we crowned you with honors, Oedipus, towering over all—   1330
mighty king of the seven gates of Thebes.

But now to hear your story—is there a man more agonized?
More wed to pain and frenzy? Not a man on earth,
the joy of your life ground down to nothing
O Oedipus, name for the ages—   1335
          one and the same wide harbor served you
                              son and father both
son and father came to rest in the same bridal chamber.
How, how could the furrows your father plowed
bear you, your agony, harrowing on   1340
in silence O so long?
                    But now for all your power
Time, all-seeing Time has dragged you to the light,
judged your marriage monstrous from the start—

the son and the father tangling, both one —
O child of Laius, would to god   1345
   I'd never seen you, never never!
      Now I weep like a man who wails the dead
and the dirge comes pouring forth with all my heart!
I tell you the truth, you gave me life
my breath leapt up in you   1350
and now you bring down night upon my eyes.

Enter a Messenger from the palace.

MESSENGER: Men of Thebes, always the first in honor,
   what horrors you will hear, what you will see,
   what a heavy weight of sorrow you will shoulder . . .
   if you are true to your birth, if you still have   1355
   some feeling for the royal house of Thebes.
   I tell you neither the waters of the Danube
   nor the Nile can wash this palace clean.
   Such things it hides, it soon will bring to light —
   terrible things, and none done blindly now,   1360
   all done with a will. The pains
   we inflict upon ourselves hurt most of all.
LEADER: God knows we have pains enough already.
   What can you add to them?
MESSENGER: The queen is dead.
LEADER: Poor lady — how?   1365
MESSENGER: By her own hand. But you are spared the worst,
   you never had to watch . . . I saw it all,
   and with all the memory that's in me
   you will learn what that poor woman suffered.

   Once she'd broken in through the gates,   1370
   dashing past us, frantic, whipped to fury,
   ripping her hair out with both hands —
   straight to her rooms she rushed, flinging herself
   across the bridal-bed, doors slamming behind her —
   once inside, she wailed for Laius, dead so long,   1375
   remembering how she bore his child long ago,
   the life that rose up to destroy him, leaving
   its mother to mother living creatures
   with the very son she'd borne.
   Oh how she wept, mourning the marriage-bed   1380
   where she let loose that double brood — monsters —
   husband by her husband, children by her child.
                And then —
   but how she died is more than I can say. Suddenly
   Oedipus burst in, screaming, he stunned us so
   we couldn't watch her agony to the end,   1385

our eyes were fixed on him. Circling
like a maddened beast, stalking, here, there
crying out to us —
　　　　　　　Give him a sword! His wife,
no wife, his mother, where can he find the mother earth
that cropped two crops at once, himself and all his children?　　　　　1390
He was raging — one of the dark powers pointing the way,
none of us mortals crowding around him, no,
with a great shattering cry — someone, something leading him on —
he hurled at the twin doors and bending the bolts back
out of their sockets, crashed through the chamber.　　　　　1395
And there we saw the woman hanging by the neck,
cradled high in a woven noose, spinning,
swinging back and forth. And when he saw her,
giving a low, wrenching sob that broke our hearts,
slipping the halter from her throat, he eased her down,　　　　　1400
in a slow embrace he laid her down, poor thing . . .
then, what came next, what horror we beheld!

He rips off her brooches, the long gold pins
holding her robes — and lifting them high,
looking straight up into the points,　　　　　1405
he digs them down the sockets of his eyes, crying, "You,
you'll see no more the pain I suffered, all the pain I caused!
Too long you looked on the ones you never should have seen,
blind to the ones you longed to see, to know! Blind
from this hour on! Blind in the darkness — blind!"　　　　　1410
His voice like a dirge, rising, over and over
raising the pins, raking them down his eyes.
And at each stroke blood spurts from the roots,
splashing his beard, a swirl of it, nerves and clots —
black hail of blood pulsing, gushing down.　　　　　1415

These are the griefs that burst upon them both,
coupling man and woman. The joy they had so lately,
the fortune of their old ancestral house
was deep joy indeed. Now, in this one day,
wailing, madness and doom, death, disgrace,　　　　　1420
all the griefs in the world that you can name,
all are theirs forever.

LEADER:　　　　　　　Oh poor man, the misery —
has he any rest from pain now?

A voice within, in torment.

MESSENGER:　　　　　　　He's shouting,
"Loose the bolts, someone, show me to all of Thebes!
My father's murderer, my mother's —"　　　　　1425

No, I can't repeat it, it's unholy.
Now he'll tear himself from his native earth,
not linger, curse the house with his own curse.
But he needs strength, and a guide to lead him on.
This is sickness more than he can bear.

The palace doors open.

                                    Look,   1430
he'll show you himself. The great doors are opening —
you are about to see a sight, a horror
even his mortal enemy would pity.

Enter Oedipus, blinded, led by a boy. He stands at the palace steps, as if surveying
his people once again.

CHORUS: O the terror —
        the suffering, for all the world to see,
        the worst terror that ever met my eyes.   1435
        What madness swept over you? What god,
        what dark power leapt beyond all bounds,
        beyond belief, to crush your wretched life? —
        godforsaken, cursed by the gods!
        I pity you but I can't bear to look.   1440
        I've much to ask, so much to learn,
        so much fascinates my eyes,
        but you . . . I shudder at the sight.
OEDIPUS: Oh, Ohhh —
        the agony! I am agony —
        where am I going? where on earth?   1445
                where does all this agony hurl me?
        where's my voice? —
                winging, swept away on a dark tide —
        My destiny, my dark power, what a leap you made!
CHORUS: To the depths of terror, too dark to hear, to see.   1450
OEDIPUS: Dark, horror of darkness
        my darkness, drowning, swirling around me
        crashing wave on wave — unspeakable, irresistible
                headwind, fatal harbor! Oh again,
        the misery, all at once, over and over   1455
        the stabbing daggers, stab of memory
        raking me insane.
CHORUS: No wonder you suffer
        twice over, the pain of your wounds,
        the lasting grief of pain.
OEDIPUS: Dear friend, still here?
        Standing by me, still with a care for me,   1460
                the blind man? Such compassion,
                loyal to the last. Oh it's you,

          I know you're here, dark as it is
              I'd know you anywhere, your voice —
      it's yours, clearly yours.
CHORUS: Dreadful, what you've done . . .   1465
      how could you bear it, gouging out your eyes?
      What superhuman power drove you on?
OEDIPUS: Apollo, friends, Apollo —
      he ordained my agonies — these, my pains on pains!
          But the hand that struck my eyes was mine,   1470
          mine alone — no one else —
              I did it all myself!
      What good were eyes to me?
      Nothing I could see could bring me joy.
CHORUS: No, no, exactly as you say.
OEDIPUS: What can I ever see?   1475
          What love, what call of the heart
      can touch my ears with joy? Nothing, friends.
          Take me away, far, far from Thebes,
              quickly, cast me away, my friends —
      this great murderous ruin, this man cursed to heaven,   1480
          the man the deathless gods hate most of all!
CHORUS: Pitiful, you suffer so, you understand so much . . .
      I wish you'd never known.
OEDIPUS: Die, die —
          whoever he was that day in the wilds
      who cut my ankles free of the ruthless pins,   1485
          he pulled me clear of death, he saved my life
          for this, this kindness —
                  Curse him, kill him!
      If I'd died then, I'd never have dragged myself,
          my loved ones through such hell.   1490
CHORUS: Oh if only . . . would to god.
OEDIPUS: I'd never have come to this,
          my father's murderer — never been branded
      mother's husband, all men see me now! Now,
          loathed by the gods, son of the mother I defiled
              coupling in my father's bed, spawning lives in the loins   1495
      that spawned my wretched life. What grief can crown this grief?
                  It's mine alone, my destiny — I am Oedipus!
CHORUS: How can I say you've chosen for the best?
      Better to die than be alive and blind.
OEDIPUS: What I did was best — don't lecture me,   1500
      no more advice. I, with *my* eyes,
      how could I look my father in the eyes
      when I go down to death? Or mother, so abused . . .
      I've done such things to the two of them,

crimes too huge for hanging.
                      Worse yet,   1505
the sight of my children, born as they were born,
how could I long to look into their eyes?
No, not with these eyes of mine, never.
Not this city either, her high towers,
the sacred glittering images of her gods —   1510
I am misery! I, her best son, reared
as no other son of Thebes was ever reared,
I've stripped myself, I gave the command myself.
All men must cast away the great blasphemer,
the curse now brought to light by the gods,   1515
the son of Laius — I, my father's son!

Now I've exposed my guilt, horrendous guilt,
could I train a level glance on you, my countrymen?
Impossible! No, if I could just block off my ears,
the springs of hearing, I would stop at nothing —   1520
I'd wall up my loathsome body like a prison,
blind to the sound of life, not just the sight.
Oblivion — what a blessing . . .
for the mind to dwell a world away from pain.

O Cithaeron, why did you give me shelter?   1525
Why didn't you take me, crush my life out on the spot?
I'd never have revealed my birth to all mankind.

O Polybus, Corinth, the old house of my fathers,
so I believed — what a handsome prince you raised —
under the skin, what sickness to the core.   1530
Look at me! Born of outrage, outrage to the core.

O triple roads — it all comes back, the secret,
dark ravine, and the oaks closing in
where the three roads join . . .
You drank my father's blood, my own blood   1535
spilled by my own hands — you still remember me?
What things you saw me do? Then I came here
and did them all once more!
                    Marriages! O marriage,
you gave me birth, and once you brought me into the world
you brought my sperm rising back, springing to light   1540
fathers, brothers, sons — one deadly breed —
brides, wives, mothers. The blackest things
a man can do, I have done them all!
                    No more —
it's wrong to name what's wrong to do. Quickly,
for the love of god, hide me somewhere,   1545

kill me, hurl me into the sea
where you can never look on me again.

Beckoning to the Chorus as they shrink away.

                                  Closer,
it's all right. Touch the man of sorrow.
Do. Don't be afraid. My troubles are mine
and I am the only man alive who can sustain them.   1550

Enter Creon from the palace, attended by palace guards.

LEADER: Put your requests to Creon. Here he is,
just when we need him. He'll have a plan, he'll act.
Now that he's the sole defense of the country
in your place.
OEDIPUS: Oh no, what can I say to him?
How can I ever hope to win his trust?   1555
I wronged him so, just now, in every way.
You must see that — I was so wrong, so wrong.
CREON: I haven't come to mock you, Oedipus,
or to criticize your former failings.

Turning to the guards.

                              You there,
have you lost all respect for human feeling?   1560
At least revere the Sun, the holy fire
that keeps us all alive. Never expose a thing
of guilt and holy dread so great it appalls
the earth, the rain from heaven, the light of day!
Get him into the halls — quickly as you can.   1565
Piety demands no less. Kindred alone
should see a kinsman's shame. This is obscene.
OEDIPUS: Please, in god's name . . . you wipe my fears away,
coming so generously to me, the worst of men.
Do one thing more, for your sake, not mine.   1570
CREON: What do you want? Why so insistent?
OEDIPUS: Drive me out of the land at once, far from sight,
where I can never hear a human voice.
CREON: I'd have done that already, I promise you.
First I wanted the god to clarify my duties.   1575
OEDIPUS: The god? His command was clear, every word:
death for the father-killer, the curse —
he said destroy me!
CREON: So he did. Still, in such a crisis
it's better to ask precisely what to do.   1580
OEDIPUS: You'd ask the oracle about a man like me?
CREON: By all means. And this time, I assume,
even you will obey the god's decrees.

OEDIPUS: I will,
    I will. And you, I command you — I beg you . . .
    the woman inside, bury her as you see fit.   1585
    It's the only decent thing,
    to give your own the last rites. As for me,
    never condemn the city of my fathers
    to house my body, not while I'm alive, no,
    let me live on the mountains, on Cithaeron,   1590
    my favorite haunt, I have made it famous.
    Mother and father marked out that rock
    to be my everlasting tomb — buried alive.
    Let me die there, where they tried to kill me.
    Oh but this I know: no sickness can destroy me,   1595
    nothing can. I would never have been saved
    from death — I have been saved
    for something great and terrible, something strange.
    Well let my destiny come and take me on its way!
    About my children, Creon, the boys at least,   1600
    don't burden yourself. They're men;
    wherever they go, they'll find the means to live.
    But my two daughters, my poor helpless girls,
    clustering at our table, never without me
    hovering near them . . . whatever I touched,   1605
    they always had their share. Take care of them,
    I beg you. Wait, better — permit me, would you?
    Just to touch them with my hands and take
    our fill of tears. Please . . . my king.
    Grant it, with all your noble heart.   1610
    If I could hold them, just once, I'd think
    I had them with me, like the early days
    when I could see their eyes.

Antigone and Ismene, two small children, are led in from the palace by a nurse.

                      What's that?
    O god! Do I really hear you sobbing? —
    my two children. Creon, you've pitied me?   1615
    Sent me my darling girls, my own flesh and blood!
    Am I right?
CREON: Yes, it's my doing.
    I know the joy they gave you all these years,
    the joy you must feel now.
OEDIPUS: Bless you, Creon!
    May god watch over you for this kindness,   1620
    better than he ever guarded me.
                    Children, where are you?
    Here, come quickly —

Groping for Antigone and Ismene, who approach their father cautiously, then embrace him.

                    Come to these hands of mine,
   your brother's hands, your own father's hands
   that served his once bright eyes so well—
   that made them blind. Seeing nothing, children,   1625
   knowing nothing, I became your father,
   I fathered you in the soil that gave me life.

   How I weep for you—I cannot see you now . . .
   just thinking of all your days to come, the bitterness,
   the life that rough mankind will thrust upon you.   1630
   Where are the public gatherings you can join,
   the banquets of the clans? Home you'll come,
   in tears, cut off from the sight of it all,
   the brilliant rites unfinished.
   And when you reach perfection, ripe for marriage,   1635
   who will he be, my dear ones? Risking all
   to shoulder the curse that weighs down my parents,
   yes and you too—that wounds us all together.
   What more misery could you want?
   Your father killed his father, sowed his mother,   1640
   one, one and the selfsame womb sprang you—
   he cropped the very roots of his existence.
   Such disgrace, and you must bear it all!
   Who will marry you then? Not a man on earth.
   Your doom is clear: you'll wither away to nothing,   1645
   single, without a child.

Turning to Creon.

                    Oh Creon,
   you are the only father they have now . . .
   we who brought them into the world
   are gone, both gone at a stroke—
   Don't let them go begging, abandoned,   1650
   women without men. Your own flesh and blood!
   Never bring them down to the level of my pains.
   Pity them. Look at them, so young, so vulnerable,
   shorn of everything—you're their only hope.
   Promise me, noble Creon, touch my hand.   1655

Reaching toward Creon, who draws back.

   You, little ones, if you were old enough
   to understand, there is much I'd tell you.
   Now, as it is, I'd have you say a prayer.
   Pray for life, my children,
   live where you are free to grow and season.   1660

Pray god you find a better life than mine,
the father who begot you.

CREON: Enough.
You've wept enough. Into the palace now.

OEDIPUS: I must, but I find it very hard.

CREON: Time is the great healer, you will see.   1665

OEDIPUS: I am going — you know on what condition?

CREON: Tell me. I'm listening.

OEDIPUS: Drive me out of Thebes, in exile.

CREON: Not I. Only the gods can give you that.

OEDIPUS: Surely the gods hate me so much —   1670

CREON: You'll get your wish at once.

OEDIPUS: You consent?

CREON: I try to say what I mean; it's my habit.

OEDIPUS: Then take me away. It's time.

CREON: Come along, let go of the children.

OEDIPUS: No —
don't take them away from me, not now! No no no!   1675

*Clutching his daughters as the guards wrench them loose and take them through
the palace doors.*

CREON: Still the king, the master of all things?
No more: here your power ends.
None of your power follows you through life.

*Exit Oedipus and Creon to the palace. The Chorus comes forward to address the
audience directly.*

CHORUS: People of Thebes, my countrymen, look on Oedipus.
He solved the famous riddle with his brilliance,   1680
he rose to power, a man beyond all power.
Who could behold his greatness without envy?
Now what a black sea of terror has overwhelmed him.
Now as we keep our watch and wait the final day,
count no man happy till he dies, free of pain at last.   1685

Exit in procession.   [c. 430 B.C.E.]

THINKING ABOUT THE TEXT

1. Do you think the search for the truth should be our highest priority?
   Might it depend on what you are trying to find out? Should Oedipus have
   been less driven? More adaptable? In what ways?

2. What do you think Oedipus's tragic flaw is? Do you see him as a victim of
   circumstances? As master of his fate? Are issues of free will involved in
   Oedipus's story? What if Oedipus's quest was for, say, a cure for cancer?
   Would you see his stubbornness differently?

3. Do you think Oedipus grows as a character? Besides his awful discovery, does he learn anything positive about himself or his place in the world?

4. According to Aristotle's theory of katharsis, Sophocles wants to arouse pity and fear in the audience. Did he in you? Explain. The final phase of katharsis is a purging of these two emotions as we watch Oedipus broken. Was this true for you? What did you feel reading the last few pages?

5. The Greeks had strong views about destiny and fate. Was your socialization influenced by such ideas? Why do people say, "What will be will be"? Did you ever hear anyone say that some event is "God's will"? How might ideas about free will or determinism influence social policy?

SOPHOCLES
Antigone
Translated by Robert Fagles

Antigone was first produced in 441 B.C.E., more than a decade before Oedipus the King *was first produced. Just before the action of* Antigone *begins, the heroine's two brothers have killed each other in battle. One, Eteocles, was defending Thebes; the other, Polynices, was leading an army against it. The current ruler of Thebes, Antigone's uncle Creon, now forbids burial of Polynices — a command that Antigone will defy.*

CHARACTERS

ANTIGONE, *daughter of Oedipus and Jocasta*
ISMENE, *sister of Antigone*
A CHORUS *of old Theban citizens and their* LEADER
CREON, *king of Thebes, uncle of Antigone and Ismene*
A SENTRY
HAEMON, *son of Creon and Eurydice*
TIRESIAS, *a blind prophet*
A MESSENGER
EURYDICE, *wife of Creon*
GUARDS, ATTENDANTS, AND A BOY

TIME AND SCENE: *The royal house of Thebes. It is still night, and the invading armies of Argos have just been driven from the city. Fighting on opposite sides, the sons of Oedipus, Eteocles and Polynices, have killed each other in combat. Their uncle, Creon, is now king of Thebes.*

Enter Antigone, slipping through the central doors of the palace. She motions to her sister, Ismene, who follows her cautiously toward an altar at the center of the stage.

ANTIGONE: My own flesh and blood—dear sister, dear Ismene,
            how many griefs our father Oedipus handed down!
            Do you know one, I ask you, one grief
            that Zeus° will not perfect for the two of us
            while we still live and breathe? There's nothing,   5
            no pain—our lives are pain—no private shame,
            no public disgrace, nothing I haven't seen
            in your griefs and mine. And now this:
            an emergency decree, they say, the Commander
            has just declared for all of Thebes.   10
            What, haven't you heard? Don't you see?
            The doom reserved for enemies
            marches on the ones we love the most.
ISMENE: Not I, I haven't heard a word, Antigone.
            Nothing of loved ones,   15
            no joy or pain has come my way, not since
            the two of us were robbed of our two brothers,
            both gone in a day, a double blow—
            not since the armies of Argos vanished,
            just this very night. I know nothing more,   20
            whether our luck's improved or ruin's still to come.
ANTIGONE: I thought so. That's why I brought you out here,
            past the gates, so you could hear in private.
ISMENE: What's the matter? Trouble, clearly . . .
            you sound so dark, so grim.   25
ANTIGONE: Why not? Our own brothers' burial!
            Hasn't Creon graced one with all the rites,
            disgraced the other? Eteocles, they say,
            has been given full military honors,
            rightly so—Creon's laid him in the earth   30
            and he goes with glory down among the dead.
            But the body of Polynices, who died miserably—
            why, a city-wide proclamation, rumor has it,
            forbids anyone to bury him, even mourn him.
            He's to be left unwept, unburied, a lovely treasure   35
            for birds that scan the field and feast to their heart's content.

            Such, I hear, is the martial law our good Creon
            lays down for you and me—yes, me, I tell you—
            and he's coming here to alert the uninformed
            in no uncertain terms,   40
            and he won't treat the matter lightly. Whoever
            disobeys in the least will die, his doom is sealed:
            stoning to death inside the city walls!

4 Zeus: The highest Olympian deity.

There you have it. You'll soon show what you are,
worth your breeding, Ismene, or a coward — 45
for all your royal blood.
ISMENE: My poor sister, if things have come to this,
who am I to make or mend them, tell me,
what good am I to you?
ANTIGONE: Decide.
Will you share the labor, share the work? 50
ISMENE: What work, what's the risk? What do you mean?
ANTIGONE:

Raising her hands.

Will you lift up his body with these bare hands
and lower it with me?
ISMENE: What? You'd bury him —
when a law forbids the city?
ANTIGONE: Yes!
He is my brother and — deny it as you will — 55
your brother too.
No one will ever convict me for a traitor.
ISMENE: So desperate, and Creon has expressly —
ANTIGONE: No,
he has no right to keep me from my own.
ISMENE: Oh my sister, think — 60
think how our own father died, hated,
his reputation in ruins, driven on
by the crimes he brought to light himself
to gouge out his eyes with his own hands —
then mother . . . his mother and wife, both in one, 65
mutilating her life in the twisted noose —
and last, our two brothers dead in a single day,
both shedding their own blood, poor suffering boys,
battling out their common destiny hand-to-hand.

Now look at the two of us, left so alone . . . 70
think what a death we'll die, the worst of all
if we violate the laws and override
the fixed decree of the throne, its power —
we must be sensible. Remember we are women,
we're not born to contend with men. Then too, 75
we're underlings, ruled by much stronger hands,
so we must submit in this, and things still worse.

I, for one, I'll beg the dead to forgive me —
I'm forced, I have no choice — I must obey
the ones who stand in power. Why rush to extremes? 80

It's madness, madness.
                              I won't insist,
ANTIGONE:
          no, even if you should have a change of heart,
          I'd never welcome you in the labor, not with me.
          So, do as you like, whatever suits you best —
          I'll bury him myself.   85
          And even if I die in the act, that death will be a glory.
          I'll lie with the one I love and loved by him —
          an outrage sacred to the gods! I have longer
          to please the dead than please the living here:
          in the kingdom down below I'll lie forever.   90
          Do as you like, dishonor the laws
          the gods hold in honor.
ISMENE: I'd do them no dishonor . . .
          but defy the city? I have no strength for that.
ANTIGONE: You have your excuses. I am on my way,
          I'll raise a mound for him, for my dear brother.   95
ISMENE: Oh Antigone, you're so rash — I'm so afraid for you!
ANTIGONE: Don't fear for me. Set your own life in order.
ISMENE: Then don't, at least, blurt this out to anyone.
          Keep it a secret. I'll join you in that, I promise.
ANTIGONE: Dear god, shout it from the rooftops. I'll hate you   100
          all the more for silence — tell the world!
ISMENE: So fiery — and it ought to chill your heart.
ANTIGONE: I know I please where I must please the most.
ISMENE: Yes, if you can, but you're in love with impossibility.
ANTIGONE: Very well then, once my strength gives out   105
          I will be done at last.
ISMENE: You're wrong from the start,
          you're off on a hopeless quest.
ANTIGONE: If you say so, you will make me hate you,
          and the hatred of the dead, by all rights,
          will haunt you night and day.   110
          But leave me to my own absurdity, leave me
          to suffer this — dreadful thing. I'll suffer
          nothing as great as death without glory.

Exit to the side.

ISMENE: Then go if you must, but rest assured,
          wild, irrational as you are, my sister,
          you are truly dear to the ones who love you.   115

*Withdrawing to the palace. Enter a Chorus, the old citizens of Thebes, chanting as
the sun begins to rise.*

CHORUS: Glory! — great beam of sun, brightest of all
          that ever rose on the seven gates of Thebes,

you burn through night at last!
                Great eye of the golden day,   120
mounting the Dirce's° banks you throw him back—
the enemy out of Argos, the white shield, the man of bronze—
he's flying headlong now
                the bridle of fate stampeding him with pain!

            And he had driven against our borders,   125
            launched by the warring claims of Polynices—
            like an eagle screaming, winging havoc
            over the land, wings of armor
            shielded white as snow,
            a huge army massing,   130
            crested helmets bristling for assault.

He hovered above our roofs, his vast maw gaping
closing down around our seven gates,
            his spears thirsting for the kill
                        but now he's gone, look,   135
before he could glut his jaws with Theban blood
or the god of fire put our crown of towers to the torch.
He grappled the Dragon none can master—Thebes—
            the clang of our arms like thunder at his back!

            Zeus hates with a vengeance all bravado,   140
            the mighty boasts of men. He watched them
            coming on in a rising flood, the pride
            of their golden armor ringing shrill—
            and brandishing his lightning
            blasted the fighter just at the goal,   145
            rushing to shout his triumph from our walls.

Down from the heights he crashed, pounding down on the earth!
And a moment ago, blazing torch in hand—
            mad for attack, ecstatic
he breathed his rage, the storm   150
            of his fury hurling at our heads!
But now his high hopes have laid him low
and down the enemy ranks the iron god of war
            deals his rewards, his stunning blows—Ares°
            rapture of battle, our right arm in the crisis.   155

            Seven captains marshaled at seven gates
            seven against their equals, gave
            their brazen trophies up to Zeus,
            god of the breaking rout of battle,

---

121 **the Dirce:** A river near Thebes.   154 **Ares:** God of war.

all but two: those blood brothers,   160
one father, one mother—matched in rage,
spears matched for the twin conquest—
clashed and won the common prize of death.

But now for Victory! Glorious in the morning,
joy in her eyes to meet our joy   165
    she is winging down to Thebes,
our fleets of chariots wheeling in her wake—
    Now let us win oblivion from the wars,
thronging the temples of the gods
in singing, dancing choirs through the night!   170
    Lord Dionysus,° god of the dance
    that shakes the land of Thebes, now lead the way!

Enter Creon from the palace, attended by his guard.

But look, the king of the realm is coming,
Creon, the new man for the new day,
whatever the gods are sending now . . .   175
what new plan will he launch?
Why this, this special session?
Why this sudden call to the old men
summoned at one command?

CREON: My countrymen,
the ship of state is safe. The gods who rocked her,   180
after a long, merciless pounding in the storm,
have righted her once more.
                  Out of the whole city
I have called you here alone. Well I know,
first, your undeviating respect
for the throne and royal power of King Laius.   185
Next, while Oedipus steered the land of Thebes,
and even after he died, your loyalty was unshakable,
you still stood by their children. Now then,
since the two sons are dead—two blows of fate
in the same day, cut down by each other's hands,   190
both killers, both brothers stained with blood—
as I am next in kin to the dead,
I now possess the throne and all its powers.

Of course you cannot know a man completely,
his character, his principles, sense of judgment,   195
not till he's shown his colors, ruling the people,
making laws. Experience, there's the test.
As I see it, whoever assumes the task,

---

171 **Dionysus:** God of fertility and wine.

the awesome task of setting the city's course,
and refuses to adopt the soundest policies   200
but fearing someone, keeps his lips locked tight,
he's utterly worthless. So I rate him now,
I always have. And whoever places a friend
above the good of his own country, he is nothing:
I have no use for him. Zeus my witness,   205
Zeus who sees all things, always—
I could never stand by silent, watching destruction
march against our city, putting safety to rout,
nor could I ever make that man a friend of mine
who menaces our country. Remember this: 210
our country *is* our safety.
Only while she voyages true on course
can we establish friendships, truer than blood itself.
Such are my standards. They make our city great.

Closely akin to them I have proclaimed,   215
just now, the following decree to our people
concerning the two sons of Oedipus.
Eteocles, who died fighting for Thebes,
excelling all in arms: he shall be buried,
crowned with a hero's honors, the cups we pour   220
to soak the earth and reach the famous dead.

But as for his blood brother, Polynices,
who returned from exile, home to his father-city
and the gods of his race, consumed with one desire—
to burn them roof to roots—who thirsted to drink   225
his kinsmen's blood and sell the rest to slavery:
that man—a proclamation has forbidden the city
to dignify him with burial, mourn him at all.
No, he must be left unburied, his corpse
carrion for the birds and dogs to tear,   230
an obscenity for the citizens to behold!

These are my principles. Never at my hands
will the traitor be honored above the patriot.
But whoever proves his loyalty to the state:
I'll prize that man in death as well as life.   235
LEADER: If this is your pleasure, Creon, treating
our city's enemy and our friend this way . . .
The power is yours, I suppose, to enforce it
with the laws, both for the dead and all of us,
the living.
CREON: Follow my orders closely then,   240
be on your guard.
           We're too old.

LEADER:
　　Lay that burden on younger shoulders.
CREON: No, no,
　　I don't mean the body—I've posted guards already.
LEADER:　　What commands for us then? What other service?
CREON:　　See that you never side with those who break my orders.　　　245
LEADER:　　Never. Only a fool could be in love with death.
CREON:　　Death is the price—you're right. But all too often
　　the mere hope of money has ruined many men.

A Sentry enters from the side.

SENTRY: My lord,
　　I can't say I'm winded from running, or set out
　　with any spring in my legs either—no sir,　　　　　　　　　　250
　　I was lost in thought, and it made me stop, often,
　　dead in my tracks, wheeling, turning back,
　　and all the time a voice inside me muttering,
　　"Idiot, why? You're going straight to your death."
　　Then muttering, "Stopped again, poor fool?　　　　　　　　255
　　If somebody gets the news to Creon first,
　　what's to save your neck?"
                                          And so,
　　mulling it over, on I trudged, dragging my feet,
　　you can make a short road take forever . . .
　　but at last, look, common sense won out,　　　　　　　　　260
　　I'm here, and I'm all yours,
　　and even though I come empty-handed
　　I'll tell my story just the same, because
　　I've come with a good grip on one hope,
　　what will come will come, whatever fate—　　　　　　　　265
CREON:　　Come to the point!
　　What's wrong—why so afraid?
SENTRY:　　First, myself, I've got to tell you,
　　I didn't do it, didn't see who did—
　　Be fair, don't take it out on me.　　　　　　　　　　　270
CREON:　　You're playing it safe, soldier,
　　barricading yourself from any trouble.
　　It's obvious, you've something strange to tell.
SENTRY:　　Dangerous too, and danger makes you delay
　　for all you're worth.　　　　　　　　　　　　　　275
CREON:　　Out with it—then dismiss!
SENTRY:　　All right, here it comes. The body—
　　someone's just buried it, then run off . . .
　　sprinkled some dry dust on the flesh,
　　given it proper rites.
CREON:　　　　　　　What?　　　　　　　　　　280
　　What man alive would dare—

SENTRY: I've no idea, I swear it.
   There was no mark of a spade, no pickaxe there,
   no earth turned up, the ground packed hard and dry,
   unbroken, no tracks, no wheelruts, nothing,
   the workman left no trace. Just at sunup   285
   the first watch of the day points it out—
   it was a wonder! We were stunned . . .
   a terrific burden too, for all of us, listen:
   you can't see the corpse, not that it's buried,
   really, just a light cover of road-dust on it,   290
   as if someone meant to lay the dead to rest
   and keep from getting cursed.
   Not a sign in sight that dogs or wild beasts
   had worried the body, even torn the skin.

   But what came next! Rough talk flew thick and fast,   295
   guard grilling guard—we'd have come to blows
   at last, nothing to stop it; each man for himself
   and each the culprit, no one caught red-handed,
   all of us pleading ignorance, dodging the charges,
   ready to take up red-hot iron in our fists,   300
   go through fire, swear oaths to the gods—
   "I didn't do it, I had no hand in it either,
   not in the plotting, not in the work itself!"

   Finally, after all this wrangling came to nothing,
   one man spoke out and made us stare at the ground,   305
   hanging our heads in fear. No way to counter him,
   no way to take his advice and come through
   safe and sound. Here's what he said:
   "Look, we've got to report the facts to Creon,
   we can't keep this hidden." Well, that won out,   310
   and the lot fell on me, condemned me,
   unlucky as ever, I got the prize. So here I am,
   against my will and yours too, well I know—
   no one wants the man who brings bad news.
LEADER: My king,
   ever since he began I've been debating in my mind,   315
   could this possibly be the work of the gods?
CREON: Stop—
   before you make me choke with anger—the gods!
   You, you're senile, must you be insane?
   You say—why it's intolerable—say the gods
   could have the slightest concern for that corpse?   320
   Tell me, was it for meritorious service
   they proceeded to bury him, prized him so? The hero
   who came to burn their temples ringed with pillars,
   their golden treasures—scorch their hallowed earth

and fling their laws to the winds.   325
Exactly when did you last see the gods
celebrating traitors? Inconceivable!

No, from the first there were certain citizens
who could hardly stand the spirit of my regime,
grumbling against me in the dark, heads together,   330
tossing wildly, never keeping their necks beneath
the yoke, loyally submitting to their king.
These are the instigators, I'm convinced—
they've perverted my own guard, bribed them
to do their work.
                    Money! Nothing worse   335
in our lives, so current, rampant, so corrupting.
Money—you demolish cities, root men from their homes,
you train and twist good minds and set them on
to the most atrocious schemes. No limit,
you make them adept at every kind of outrage,   340
every godless crime—money!
                    Everyone—
the whole crew bribed to commit this crime,
they've made one thing sure at least:
sooner or later they will pay the price.

Wheeling on the Sentry.

You—   345
I swear to Zeus as I still believe in Zeus,
if you don't find the man who buried that corpse,
the very man, and produce him before my eyes,
simple death won't be enough for you,
not till we string you up alive   350
and wring the immorality out of you.
Then you can steal the rest of your days,
better informed about where to make a killing.
You'll have learned, at last, it doesn't pay
to itch for rewards from every hand that beckons.   355
Filthy profits wreck most men, you'll see—
they'll never save your life.

SENTRY: Please,
    may I say a word or two, or just turn and go?
CREON: Can't you tell? Everything you say offends me.
SENTRY: Where does it hurt you, in the ears or in the heart?   360
CREON: And who are you to pinpoint my displeasure?
SENTRY: The culprit grates on your feelings,
    I just annoy your ears.
CREON: Still talking?
    You talk too much! A born nuisance—

SENTRY: Maybe so,
   but I never did this thing, so help me!
CREON: Yes you did—   365
   what's more, you squandered your life for silver!
SENTRY: Oh it's terrible when the one who does the judging
   judges things all wrong.
CREON: Well now,
   you just be clever about your judgments—
   if you fail to produce the criminals for me,   370
   you'll swear your dirty money brought you pain.

Turning sharply, reentering the palace.

SENTRY: I hope he's found. Best thing by far.
   But caught or not, that's in the lap of fortune;
   I'll never come back, you've seen the last of me.
   I'm saved, even now, and I never thought,   375
   I never hoped—
   dear gods, I owe you all my thanks!

Rushing out.

CHORUS: Numberless wonders
   terrible wonders walk the world but none the match for man—
   that great wonder crossing the heaving gray sea,
         driven on by the blasts of winter   380
   on through breakers crashing left and right,
      holds his steady course
   and the oldest of the gods he wears away—
   the Earth, the immortal, the inexhaustible—
   as his plows go back and forth, year in, year out   385
      with the breed of stallions turning up the furrows.

And the blithe, lightheaded race of birds he snares,
   the tribes of savage beasts, the life that swarms the depths—
         with one fling of his nets
   woven and coiled tight, he takes them all,   390
      man the skilled, the brilliant!
   He conquers all, taming with his techniques
   the prey that roams the cliffs and wild lairs,
   training the stallion, clamping the yoke across
      his shaggy neck, and the tireless mountain bull.   395

And speech and thought, quick as the wind
   and the mood and mind for law that rules the city—
      all these he has taught himself
   and shelter from the arrows of the frost
   when there's rough lodging under the cold clear sky   400
   and the shafts of lashing rain—
      ready, resourceful man!

Never without resources
never an impasse as he marches on the future —
only Death, from Death alone he will find no rescue   405
but from desperate plagues he has plotted his escapes.

Man the master, ingenious past all measure
past all dreams, the skills within his grasp —
he forges on, now to destruction
now again to greatness. When he weaves in   410
the laws of the land, and the justice of the gods
that binds his oaths together
he and his city rise high —
but the city casts out
that man who weds himself to inhumanity   415
thanks to reckless daring. Never share my hearth
never think my thoughts, whoever does such things.

Enter Antigone from the side, accompanied by the Sentry.

Here is a dark sign from the gods —
what to make of this? I know her,
how can I deny it? That young girl's Antigone!   420
Wretched, child of a wretched father,
Oedipus. Look, is it possible?
They bring you in like a prisoner —
why? did you break the king's laws?
Did they take you in some act of mad defiance?   425
SENTRY: She's the one, she did it single-handed —
we caught her burying the body. Where's Creon?

Enter Creon from the palace.

LEADER: Back again, just in time when you need him.
CREON: In time for what? What is it?
SENTRY: My king,
there's nothing you can swear you'll never do —   430
second thoughts make liars of us all.
I could have sworn I wouldn't hurry back
(what with your threats, the buffeting I just took),
but a stroke of luck beyond our wildest hopes,
what a joy, there's nothing like it. So,   435
back I've come, breaking my oath, who cares?
I'm bringing in our prisoner — this young girl —
we took her giving the dead the last rites.
But no casting lots this time; this is *my* luck,
my prize, no one else's.
                              Now, my lord,   440
here she is. Take her, question her,

cross-examine her to your heart's content.
But set me free, it's only right—
I'm rid of this dreadful business once for all.
CREON: Prisoner! Her? You took her—where, doing what?   445
SENTRY: Burying the man. That's the whole story.
CREON: What?
You mean what you say, you're telling me the truth?
SENTRY: She's the one. With my own eyes I saw her
bury the body, just what you've forbidden.
There. Is that plain and clear?   450
CREON: What did you see? Did you catch her in the act?
SENTRY: Here's what happened. We went back to our post,
those threats of yours breathing down our necks—
we brushed the corpse clean of the dust that covered it,
stripped it bare . . . it was slimy, going soft,   455
and we took to high ground, backs to the wind
so the stink of him couldn't hit us;
jostling, baiting each other to keep awake,
shouting back and forth—no napping on the job,
not this time. And so the hours dragged by   460
until the sun stood dead above our heads,
a huge white ball in the noon sky, beating,
blazing down, and then it happened—
suddenly, a whirlwind!
Twisting a great dust-storm up from the earth,   465
a black plague of the heavens, filling the plain,
ripping the leaves off every tree in sight,
choking the air and sky. We squinted hard
and took our whipping from the gods.

And after the storm passed—it seemed endless—   470
there, we saw the girl!
And she cried out a sharp, piercing cry,
like a bird come back to an empty nest,
peering into its bed, and all the babies gone . . .
Just so, when she sees the corpse bare   475
she bursts into a long, shattering wail
and calls down withering curses on the heads
of all who did the work. And she scoops up dry dust,
handfuls, quickly, and lifting a fine bronze urn,
lifting it high and pouring, she crowns the dead   480
with three full libations.
                              Soon as we saw
we rushed her, closed on the kill like hunters,
and she, she didn't flinch. We interrogated her,
charging her with offenses past and present—

she stood up to it all, denied nothing. I tell you,   485
it made me ache and laugh in the same breath.
It's pure joy to escape the worst yourself,
it hurts a man to bring down his friends.
But all that, I'm afraid, means less to me
than my own skin. That's the way I'm made.

CREON:

Wheeling on Antigone.

                                            You,   490
with your eyes fixed on the ground—speak up.
Do you deny you did this, yes or no?

ANTIGONE: I did it. I don't deny a thing.

CREON:

To the Sentry.

You, get out, wherever you please—
you're clear of a very heavy charge.   495

He leaves; Creon turns back to Antigone.

You, tell me briefly, no long speeches—
were you aware a decree had forbidden this?

ANTIGONE: Well aware. How could I avoid it? It was public.

CREON: And still you had the gall to break this law?

ANTIGONE: Of course I did. It wasn't Zeus, not in the least,   500
who made this proclamation—not to me.
Nor did that Justice, dwelling with the gods
beneath the earth, ordain such laws for men.
Nor did I think your edict had such force
that you, a mere mortal, could override the gods,   505
the great unwritten, unshakable traditions.
They are alive, not just today or yesterday:
they live forever, from the first of time,
and no one knows when they first saw the light.

These laws—I was not about to break them,   510
not out of fear of some man's wounded pride,
and face the retribution of the gods.
Die I must, I've known it all my life—
how could I keep from knowing?—even without
your death-sentence ringing in my ears.   515
And if I am to die before my time
I consider that a gain. Who on earth,
alive in the midst of so much grief as I,
could fail to find his death a rich reward?
So for me, at least, to meet this doom of yours   520
is precious little pain. But if I had allowed
my own mother's son to rot, an unburied corpse—

that would have been an agony! This is nothing.
And if my present actions strike you as foolish,
let's just say I've been accused of folly   525
by a fool.
LEADER: Like father like daughter,
passionate, wild . . .
she hasn't learned to bend before adversity.
CREON: No? Believe me, the stiffest stubborn wills
fall the hardest; the toughest iron,   530
tempered strong in the white-hot fire,
you'll see it crack and shatter first of all.
And I've known spirited horses you can break
with a light bit — proud, rebellious horses.
There's no room for pride, not in a slave,   535
not with the lord and master standing by.

This girl was an old hand at insolence
when she overrode the edicts we made public.
But once she'd done it — the insolence,
twice over — to glory in it, laughing,   540
mocking us to our face with what she'd done.
I'm not the man, not now: she is the man
if this victory goes to her and she goes free.

Never! Sister's child or closer in blood
than all my family clustered at my altar   545
worshiping Guardian Zeus — she'll never escape,
she and her blood sister, the most barbaric death.
Yes, I accuse her sister of an equal part
in scheming this, this burial.

To his attendants.

                        Bring her here!
I just saw her inside, hysterical, gone to pieces.   550
It never fails: the mind convicts itself
in advance, when scoundrels are up to no good,
plotting in the dark. Oh but I hate it more
when a traitor, caught red-handed,
tries to glorify his crimes.   555
ANTIGONE: Creon, what more do you want
than my arrest and execution?
CREON: Nothing. Then I have it all.
ANTIGONE: Then why delay? Your moralizing repels me,
every word you say — pray god it always will.   560
So naturally all I say repels you too.
                        Enough.
Give me glory! What greater glory could I win

than to give my own brother decent burial?
These citizens here would all agree,

To the Chorus.

    they'd praise me too   565
    if their lips weren't locked in fear.

Pointing to Creon.

    Lucky tyrants — the perquisites of power!
    Ruthless power to do and say whatever pleases *them*.
CREON: You alone, of all the people in Thebes,
    see things that way.
ANTIGONE: They see it just that way   570
    but defer to you and keep their tongues in leash.
CREON: And you, aren't you ashamed to differ so from them?
    So disloyal!
ANTIGONE: Not ashamed for a moment,
    not to honor my brother, my own flesh and blood.
CREON: Wasn't Eteocles a brother too — cut down, facing him?   575
ANTIGONE: Brother, yes, by the same mother, the same father.
CREON: Then how can you render his enemy such honors,
    such impieties in his eyes?
ANTIGONE: He'll never testify to that,
    Eteocles dead and buried.
CREON: He will —   580
    if you honor the traitor just as much as him.
ANTIGONE: But it was his brother, not some slave that died —
CREON: Ravaging our country! —
    but Eteocles died fighting in our behalf.
ANTIGONE: No matter — Death longs for the same rites for all.   585
CREON: Never the same for the patriot and the traitor.
ANTIGONE: Who, Creon, who on earth can say the ones below
    don't find this pure and uncorrupt?
CREON: Never. Once an enemy, never a friend,
    not even after death.   590
ANTIGONE: I was born to join in love, not hate —
    that is my nature.
CREON: Go down below and love,
    if love you must — love the dead! While I'm alive,
    no woman is going to lord it over me.

Enter Ismene from the palace, under guard.

CHORUS: Look,
    Ismene's coming, weeping a sister's tears,   595
    loving sister, under a cloud . . .
    her face is flushed, her cheeks streaming.
    Sorrow puts her lovely radiance in the dark.

CREON: You—
   in my house, you viper, slinking undetected,
   sucking my life-blood! I never knew   600
   I was breeding twin disasters, the two of you
   rising up against my throne. Come, tell me,
   will you confess your part in the crime or not?
   Answer me. Swear to me.
ISMENE: I did it, yes—
   if only she consents—I share the guilt,   605
   the consequences too.
ANTIGONE: No,
   Justice will never suffer that—not you,
   you were unwilling. I never brought you in.
ISMENE: But now you face such dangers . . . I'm not ashamed
   to sail through trouble with you,   610
   make your troubles mine.
ANTIGONE: Who did the work?
   Let the dead and the god of death bear witness!
   I've no love for a friend who loves in words alone.
ISMENE: Oh no, my sister, don't reject me, please,
   let me die beside you, consecrating   615
   the dead together.
ANTIGONE: Never share my dying,
   don't lay claim to what you never touched.
   My death will be enough.
ISMENE: What do I care for life, cut off from you?
ANTIGONE: Ask Creon. Your concern is all for him.   620
ISMENE: Why abuse me so? It doesn't help you now.
ANTIGONE: You're right—
   if I mock you, I get no pleasure from it,
   only pain.
ISMENE: Tell me, dear one,
   what can I do to help you, even now?
ANTIGONE: Save yourself. I don't grudge you your survival.   625
ISMENE: Oh no, no, denied my portion in your death?
ANTIGONE: You chose to live, I chose to die.
ISMENE: Not, at least,
   without every kind of caution I could voice.
ANTIGONE: Your wisdom appealed to one world—mine, another.
ISMENE: But look, we're both guilty, both condemned to death.   630
ANTIGONE: Courage! Live your life. I gave myself to death,
   long ago, so I might serve the dead.
CREON: They're both mad, I tell you, the two of them.
   One's just shown it, the other's been that way
   since she was born.
ISMENE: True, my king,   635
   the sense we were born with cannot last forever . . .

commit cruelty on a person long enough
and the mind begins to go.
CREON: Yours did,
when you chose to commit your crimes with her.
ISMENE: How can I live alone, without her?
CREON: Her?   640
Don't even mention her—she no longer exists.
ISMENE: What? You'd kill your own son's bride?
CREON: Absolutely:
there are other fields for him to plow.
ISMENE: Perhaps,
but never as true, as close a bond as theirs.
CREON: A worthless woman for my son? It repels me.   645
ISMENE: Dearest Haemon, your father wrongs you so!
CREON: Enough, enough—you and your talk of marriage!
ISMENE: Creon—you're really going to rob your son of Antigone?
CREON: Death will do it for me—break their marriage off.
LEADER: So, it's settled then? Antigone must die?   650
CREON: Settled, yes—we both know that.

To the guards.

Stop wasting time. Take them in.
From now on they'll act like women.
Tie them up, no more running loose;
even the bravest will cut and run,   655
once they see Death coming for their lives.

*The guards escort Antigone and Ismene into the palace. Creon remains while the
old citizens form their chorus.*

CHORUS: Blest, they are the truly blest who all their lives
have never tasted devastation. For others, once
the gods have rocked a house to its foundations
        the ruin will never cease, cresting on and on   660
from one generation on throughout the race—
like a great mounting tide
driven on by savage northern gales,
        surging over the dead black depths
roiling up from the bottom dark heaves of sand   665
and the headlands, taking the storm's onslaught full-force,
roar, and the low moaning
                        echoes on and on
                                    and now
as in ancient times I see the sorrows of the house,
the living heirs of the old ancestral kings,
piling on the sorrows of the dead   670
        and one generation cannot free the next—
some god will bring them crashing down,
the race finds no release.

And now the light, the hope
        springing up from the late last root   675
in the house of Oedipus, that hope's cut down in turn
by the long, bloody knife swung by the gods of death
by a senseless word
              by fury at the heart.
                       Zeus,
yours is the power, Zeus, what man on earth
can override it, who can hold it back?   680
Power that neither Sleep, the all-ensnaring
     no, nor the tireless months of heaven
can ever overmaster—young through all time,
mighty lord of power, you hold fast
     the dazzling crystal mansions of Olympus.   685
And throughout the future, late and soon
as through the past, your law prevails:
no towering form of greatness
        enters into the lives of mortals
                free and clear of ruin.
                         True,   690
our dreams, our high hopes voyaging far and wide
bring sheer delight to many, to many others
     delusion, blithe, mindless lusts
and the fraud steals on one slowly . . . unaware
till he trips and puts his foot into the fire.   695
     He was a wise old man who coined
the famous saying: "Sooner or later
foul is fair, fair is foul
to the man the gods will ruin"—
     He goes his way for a moment only   700
             free of blinding ruin.

Enter Haemon from the palace.

     Here's Haemon now, the last of all your sons.
     Does he come in tears for his bride,
     his doomed bride, Antigone—
     bitter at being cheated of their marriage?   705
CREON: We'll soon know, better than seers could tell us.

Turning to Haemon.

     Son, you've heard the final verdict on your bride?
     Are you coming now, raving against your father?
     Or do you love me, no matter what I do?
HAEMON: Father, I'm your *son* . . . you in your wisdom   710
     set my bearings for me—I obey you.
     No marriage could ever mean more to me than you,
     whatever good direction you may offer.
CREON: Fine, Haemon.

That's how you ought to feel within your heart,
subordinate to your father's will in every way.   715
That's what a man prays for: to produce good sons—
households full of them, dutiful and attentive,
so they can pay his enemy back with interest
and match the respect their father shows his friend.
But the man who rears a brood of useless children,   720
what has he brought into the world, I ask you?
Nothing but trouble for himself, and mockery
from his enemies laughing in his face.
                              Oh Haemon,
never lose your sense of judgment over a woman.
The warmth, the rush of pleasure, it all goes cold   725
in your arms, I warn you . . . a worthless woman
in your house, a misery in your bed.
What wound cuts deeper than a loved one
turned against you? Spit her out,
like a mortal enemy—let the girl go.   730
Let her find a husband down among the dead.

Imagine it: I caught her in naked rebellion,
the traitor, the only one in the whole city.
I'm not about to prove myself a liar,
not to my people, no, I'm going to kill her!   735
That's right—so let her cry for mercy, sing her hymns
to Zeus who defends all bonds of kindred blood.
Why, if I bring up my own kin to be rebels,
think what I'd suffer from the world at large.
Show me the man who rules his household well: 740
I'll show you someone fit to rule the state.
That good man, my son,
I have every confidence he and he alone
can give commands and take them too. Staunch
in the storm of spears he'll stand his ground,   745
a loyal, unflinching comrade at your side.

But whoever steps out of line, violates the laws
or presumes to hand out orders to his superiors,
he'll win no praise from me. But that man
the city places in authority, his orders   750
must be obeyed, large and small,
right and wrong.
                       Anarchy—
show me a greater crime in all the earth!
She, she destroys cities, rips up houses,
breaks the ranks of spearmen into headlong rout.   755

But the ones who last it out, the great mass of them
owe their lives to discipline. Therefore
we must defend the men who live by law,
never let some woman triumph over us.
Better to fall from power, if fall we must,   760
at the hands of a man—never be rated
inferior to a woman, never.

LEADER: To us,
    unless old age has robbed us of our wits,
    you seem to say what you have to say with sense.

HAEMON: Father, only the gods endow a man with reason,   765
    the finest of all their gifts, a treasure.
Far be it from me—I haven't the skill,
and certainly no desire, to tell you when,
if ever, you make a slip in speech . . . though
someone else might have a good suggestion.   770

Of course it's not for you,
in the normal run of things, to watch
whatever men say or do, or find to criticize.
The man in the street, you know, dreads your glance,
he'd never say anything displeasing to your face.   775
But it's for me to catch the murmurs in the dark,
the way the city mourns for this young girl.
"No woman," they say, "ever deserved death less,
and such a brutal death for such a glorious action.
She, with her own dear brother lying in his blood—   780
she couldn't bear to leave him dead, unburied,
food for the wild dogs or wheeling vultures.
Death? She deserves a glowing crown of gold!"
So they say, and the rumor spreads in secret,
darkly . . .
               I rejoice in your success, father—   785
nothing more precious to me in the world.
What medal of honor brighter to his children
than a father's growing glory? Or a child's
to his proud father? Now don't, please,
be quite so single-minded, self-involved,   790
or assume the world is wrong and you are right.
Whoever thinks that he alone possesses intelligence,
the gift of eloquence, he and no one else,
and character too . . . such men, I tell you,
spread them open—you will find them empty.
                      No,   795
it's no disgrace for a man, even a wise man,

to learn many things and not to be too rigid.
You've seen trees by a raging winter torrent,
how many sway with the flood and salvage every twig,
but not the stubborn — they're ripped out, roots and all.   800
Bend or break. The same when a man is sailing:
haul your sheets too taut, never give an inch,
you'll capsize, go the rest of the voyage
keel up and the rowing-benches under.

Oh give way. Relax your anger — change!   805
I'm young, I know, but let me offer this:
it would be best by far, I admit,
if a man were born infallible, right by nature.
If not — and things don't often go that way,
it's best to learn from those with good advice.   810
LEADER: You'd do well, my lord, if he's speaking to the point,
    to learn from him,

Turning to Haemon.

      and you, my boy, from him.
    You both are talking sense.
CREON: So,
    men our age, we're to be lectured, are we? —
    schooled by a boy his age?   815
HAEMON: Only in what is right. But if I seem young,
    look less to my years and more to what I do.
CREON: Do? Is admiring rebels an achievement?
HAEMON: I'd never suggest that you admire treason.
CREON: Oh? —
    isn't that just the sickness that's attacked her?   820
HAEMON: The whole city of Thebes denies it, to a man.
CREON: And is Thebes about to tell me how to rule?
HAEMON: Now, you see? Who's talking like a child?
CREON: Am I to rule this land for others — or myself?
HAEMON: It's no city at all, owned by one man alone.   825
CREON: What? The city *is* the king's — that's the law!
HAEMON: What a splendid king you'd make of a desert island —
    you and you alone.
CREON:

To the Chorus.

      This boy, I do believe,
    is fighting on her side, the woman's side.
HAEMON: If you are a woman, yes;   830
    my concern is all for you.
CREON: Why, you degenerate — bandying accusations,
    threatening me with justice, your own father!
HAEMON: I see my father offending justice — wrong.

CREON: Wrong?
    To protect my royal rights?
HAEMON: Protect your rights?   835
    When you trample down the honors of the gods?
CREON: You, you soul of corruption, rotten through —
    woman's accomplice!
HAEMON: That may be,
    but you'll never find me accomplice to a criminal.
CREON: That's what *she* is,   840
    and every word you say is a blatant appeal for her —
HAEMON: And you, and me, and the gods beneath the earth.
CREON: You'll never marry her, not while she's alive.
HAEMON: Then she'll die . . . but her death will kill another.
CREON: What, brazen threats? You go too far!
HAEMON: What threat?   845
    Combating your empty, mindless judgments with a word?
CREON: You'll suffer for your sermons, you and your empty wisdom!
HAEMON: If you weren't my father, I'd say you were insane.
CREON: Don't flatter me with Father — you woman's slave!
HAEMON: You really expect to fling abuse at me   850
    and not receive the same?
CREON: Is that so!
    Now, by heaven, I promise you, you'll pay —
    taunting, insulting me! Bring her out,
    that hateful — she'll die now, here,
    in front of his eyes, beside her groom!   855
HAEMON: No, no, she will never die beside me —
    don't delude yourself. And you will never
    see me, never set eyes on my face again.
    Rage your heart out, rage with friends
    who can stand the sight of you.   860

Rushing out.

LEADER: Gone, my king, in a burst of anger.
    A temper young as his . . . hurt him once,
    he may do something violent.
CREON: Let him do —
    dream up something desperate, past all human limit!
    Good riddance. Rest assured,   865
    he'll never save those two young girls from death.
LEADER: Both of them, you really intend to kill them both?
CREON: No, not her, the one whose hands are clean;
    you're quite right.
LEADER: But Antigone —
    what sort of death do you have in mind for her?   870
CREON: I'll take her down some wild, desolate path
    never trod by men, and wall her up alive

in a rocky vault, and set out short rations,
just a gesture of piety
to keep the entire city free of defilement.   875
There let her pray to the one god she worships:
Death — who knows? — may just reprieve her from death.
Or she may learn at last, better late than never,
what a waste of breath it is to worship Death.

Exit to the palace.

CHORUS: Love, never conquered in battle   880
      Love the plunderer laying waste the rich!
      Love standing the night-watch
                  guarding a girl's soft cheek,
      you range the seas, the shepherds' steadings off in the wilds —
      not even the deathless gods can flee your onset,   885
      nothing human born for a day —
      whoever feels your grip is driven mad.
                                          Love
      you wrench the minds of the righteous into outrage,
      swerve them to their ruin — you have ignited this,
      this kindred strife, father and son at war   890
                  and Love alone the victor —
      warm glance of the bride triumphant, burning with desire!
      Throned in power, side-by-side with the mighty laws!
      Irresistible Aphrodite,° never conquered —
      Love, you mock us for your sport.   895

Antigone is brought from the palace under guard.

      But now, even I'd rebel against the king,
      I'd break all bounds when I see this —
      I fill with tears, can't hold them back,
      not any more . . . I see Antigone make her way
      to the bridal vault where all are laid to rest.   900
ANTIGONE: Look at me, men of my fatherland,
            setting out on the last road
      looking into the last light of day
      the last I'll ever see . . .
      the god of death who puts us all to bed   905
      takes me down to the banks of Acheron° alive —
            denied my part in the wedding-songs,
      no wedding-song in the dusk has crowned my marriage —
      I go to wed the lord of the dark waters.
CHORUS: Not crowned with glory, crowned with a dirge,   910
            you leave for the deep pit of the dead.

---

894 Aphrodite: Goddess of love.   **906 Acheron:** A river in the underworld, to which the
dead go.

No withering illness laid you low,
  no strokes of the sword — a law to yourself,
  alone, no mortal like you, ever, you go down
  to the halls of Death alive and breathing.   915
ANTIGONE: But think of Niobe° — well I know her story —
  think what a living death she died,
Tantalus' daughter, stranger queen from the east:
there on the mountain heights, growing stone
binding as ivy, slowly walled her round   920
and the rains will never cease, the legends say
the snows will never leave her . . .
  wasting away, under her brows the tears
showering down her breasting ridge and slopes —
a rocky death like hers puts me to sleep.   925
CHORUS: But she was a god, born of gods,
  and we are only mortals born to die.
  And yet, of course, it's a great thing
  for a dying girl to hear, just hear
  she shares a destiny equal to the gods,   930
  during life and later, once she's dead.
ANTIGONE: O you mock me!
Why, in the name of all my fathers' gods
why can't you wait till I am gone —
  must you abuse me to my face?
O my city, all your fine rich sons!   935
And you, you springs of the Dirce,
holy grove of Thebes where the chariots gather,
     you at least, you'll bear me witness, look,
unmourned by friends and forced by such crude laws
I go to my rockbound prison, strange new tomb —   940
  always a stranger, O dear god,
I have no home on earth and none below,
  not with the living, not with the breathless dead.
CHORUS: You went too far, the last limits of daring —
  smashing against the high throne of Justice!   945
    Your life's in ruins, child — I wonder . . .
  do you pay for your father's terrible ordeal?
ANTIGONE: There — at last you've touched it, the worst pain
the worst anguish! Raking up the grief for father
   three times over, for all the doom   950
that's struck us down, the brilliant house of Laius.
O mother, your marriage-bed
the coiling horrors, the coupling there —

---

916 Niobe: A queen of Thebes who was punished by the gods for her pride and was turned into stone.

you with your own son, my father—doomstruck mother!
Such, such were my parents, and I their wretched child. 955
I go to them now, cursed, unwed, to share their home—
    I am a stranger! O dear brother, doomed
    in your marriage—your marriage murders mine,
      your dying drags me down to death alive!

Enter Creon.

CHORUS: Reverence asks some reverence in return— 960
    but attacks on power never go unchecked,
      not by the man who holds the reins of power.
    Your own blind will, your passion has destroyed you.

ANTIGONE: No one to weep for me, my friends,
    no wedding-song—they take me away 965
    in all my pain . . . the road lies open, waiting.
    Never again, the law forbids me to see
    the sacred eye of day. I am agony!
    No tears for the destiny that's mine,
    no loved one mourns my death.

CREON: Can't you see? 970
If a man could wail his own dirge *before* he dies,
he'd never finish.

To the guards.

            Take her away, quickly!
Wall her up in the tomb, you have your orders.
Abandon her there, alone, and let her choose—
death or a buried life with a good roof for shelter. 975
As for myself, my hands are clean. This young girl—
dead or alive, she will be stripped of her rights,
her stranger's rights, here in the world above.

ANTIGONE: O tomb, my bridal-bed—my house, my prison
cut in the hollow rock, my everlasting watch! 980
I'll soon be there, soon embrace my own,
the great growing family of our dead
Persephone° has received among her ghosts.
                     I,
the last of them all, the most reviled by far,
go down before my destined time's run out. 985
But still I go, cherishing one good hope:
my arrival may be dear to father,
dear to you, my mother,
dear to you, my loving brother, Eteocles—
When you died I washed you with my hands, 990
I dressed you all, I poured the cups

---

983 Persephone: Queen of the underworld.

across your tombs. But now, Polynices,
because I laid your body out as well,
this, this is my reward. Nevertheless
I honored you—the decent will admit it—   995
well and wisely too.
                Never, I tell you,
if I had been the mother of children
or if my husband died, exposed and rotting—
I'd never have taken this ordeal upon myself,
never defied our people's will. What law,   1000
you ask, do I satisfy with what I say?
A husband dead, there might have been another.
A child by another too, if I had lost the first.
But mother and father both lost in the halls of Death,
no brother could ever spring to light again.   1005

For this law alone I held you first in honor.
For this, Creon, the king, judges me a criminal
guilty of dreadful outrage, my dear brother!
And now he leads me off, a captive in his hands,
with no part in the bridal-song, the bridal-bed,   1010
denied all joy of marriage, raising children—
deserted so by loved ones, struck by fate,
I descend alive to the caverns of the dead.

What law of the mighty gods have I transgressed?
Why look to the heavens any more, tormented as I am?   1015
Whom to call, what comrades now? Just think,
my reverence only brands me for irreverence!
Very well: if this is the pleasure of the gods,
once I suffer I will know that I was wrong.
But if these men are wrong, let them suffer   1020
nothing worse than they mete out to me—
these masters of injustice!

LEADER: Still the same rough winds, the wild passion
    raging through the girl.

CREON:

To the guards.

                Take her away.
You're wasting time—you'll pay for it too.   1025

ANTIGONE: Oh god, the voice of death. It's come, it's here.

CREON: True. Not a word of hope—your doom is sealed.

ANTIGONE: Land of Thebes, city of all my fathers—
        O you gods, the first gods of the race!
        They drag me away, now, no more delay.   1030
        Look on me, you noble sons of Thebes—

the last of a great line of kings,
I alone, see what I suffer now
at the hands of what breed of men —
all for reverence, my reverence for the gods!   1035

She leaves under guard; the Chorus gathers.

CHORUS: Danaë, Danaë° —
   even she endured a fate like yours,
      in all her lovely strength she traded
   the light of day for the bolted brazen vault —
   buried within her tomb, her bridal-chamber,   1040
   wed to the yoke and broken.
         But she was of glorious birth
                     my child, my child
   and treasured the seed of Zeus within her womb,
   the cloudburst streaming gold!   1045
         The power of fate is a wonder,
         dark, terrible wonder —
         neither wealth nor armies
         towered walls nor ships
         black hulls lashed by the salt   1050
         can save us from that force.

The yoke tamed him too
      young Lycurgus° flaming in anger
   king of Edonia, all for his mad taunts
   Dionysus clamped him down, encased   1055
   in the chain-mail of rock
         and there his rage
                     his terrible flowering rage burst —
   sobbing, dying away . . . at last that madman
   came to know his god —   1060
         the power he mocked, the power
         he taunted in all his frenzy
         trying to stamp out
         the women strong with the god —
         the torch, the raving sacred cries —   1065
         enraging the Muses° who adore the flute.

And far north where the Black Rocks
      cut the sea in half
   and murderous straits
   split the coast of Thrace   1070

1036 Danaë: Locked in a cell by her father because it was prophesied that her son would kill him, but visited by Zeus in the form of a shower of gold. Their son was Perseus.   **1053 Lycurgus:** Punished by Dionysus because he would not worship him.   **1066 Muses:** Goddesses of the arts.

> a forbidding city stands
> where once, hard by the walls
> the savage Ares thrilled to watch
> a king's new queen, a Fury rearing in rage
> > against his two royal sons — 1075
> > her bloody hands, her dagger-shuttle
> stabbing out their eyes — cursed, blinding wounds —
> their eyes blind sockets screaming for revenge!
>
> They wailed in agony, cries echoing cries
> > the princes doomed at birth . . . 1080
> and their mother doomed to chains,
> walled off in a tomb of stone —
> > but she traced her own birth back
> to a proud Athenian line and the high gods
> and off in caverns half the world away, 1085
> born of the wild North Wind
> > she sprang on her father's gales,
> > > racing stallions up the leaping cliffs —
> child of the heavens. But even on her the Fates
> the gray everlasting Fates rode hard 1090
> my child, my child.

Enter Tiresias, the blind prophet, led by a boy.

TIRESIAS: Lords of Thebes,
I and the boy have come together,
hand in hand. Two see with the eyes of one . . .
so the blind must go, with a guide to lead the way.

CREON: What is it, old Tiresias? What news now? 1095

TIRESIAS: I will teach you. And you obey the seer.

CREON: I will,
I've never wavered from your advice before.

TIRESIAS: And so you kept the city straight on course.

CREON: I owe you a great deal, I swear to that.

TIRESIAS: Then reflect, my son: you are poised, 1100
once more, on the razor-edge of fate.

CREON: What is it? I shudder to hear you.

TIRESIAS: You will learn
when you listen to the warnings of my craft.
As I sat on the ancient seat of augury,°
in the sanctuary where every bird I know 1105
will hover at my hands — suddenly I heard it,
a strange voice in the wingbeats, unintelligible,
barbaric, a mad scream! Talons flashing, ripping,
they were killing each other — that much I knew —

1104 seat of augury: Where Tiresias looked for omens among birds.

the murderous fury whirring in those wings   1110
made that much clear!
                              I was afraid,
I turned quickly, tested the burnt-sacrifice,
ignited the altar at all points—but no fire,
the god in the fire never blazed.
Not from those offerings . . . over the embers   1115
slid a heavy ooze from the long thighbones,
smoking, sputtering out, and the bladder
puffed and burst—spraying gall into the air—
and the fat wrapping the bones slithered off
and left them glistening white. No fire!   1120
The rites failed that might have blazed the future
with a sign. So I learned from the boy here;
he is my guide, as I am guide to others.
                              And it's you—
your high resolve that sets this plague on Thebes.
The public altars and sacred hearths are fouled,   1125
one and all, by the birds and dogs with carrion
torn from the corpse, the doomstruck son of Oedipus!
And so the gods are deaf to our prayers, they spurn
the offerings in our hands, the flame of holy flesh.
No birds cry out an omen clear and true—   1130
they're gorged with the murdered victim's blood and fat.
Take these things to heart, my son, I warn you.
All men make mistakes, it is only human.
But once the wrong is done, a man
can turn his back on folly, misfortune too,   1135
if he tries to make amends, however low he's fallen,
and stops his bullnecked ways. Stubbornness
brands you for stupidity—pride is a crime.
No, yield to the dead!
Never stab the fighter when he's down.   1140
Where's the glory, killing the dead twice over?

I mean you well. I give you sound advice.
It's best to learn from a good adviser
when he speaks for your own good:
it's pure gain.
CREON: Old man—all of you! So,   1145
    you shoot your arrows at my head like archers at the target—
    I even have *him* loosed on me, this fortune-teller.
    Oh his ilk has tried to sell me short
    and ship me off for years. Well,
    drive your bargains, traffic—much as you like—   1150
    in the gold of India, silver-gold of Sardis.
    You'll never bury that body in the grave,

not even if Zeus's eagles rip the corpse
and wing their rotten pickings off to the throne of god!
Never, not even in fear of such defilement   1155
will I tolerate his burial, that traitor.
Well I know, we can't defile the gods —
no mortal has the power.
                         No,
reverend old Tiresias, all men fall,
it's only human, but the wisest fall obscenely   1160
when they glorify obscene advice with rhetoric —
all for their own gain.
TIRESIAS: Oh god, is there a man alive
who knows, who actually believes . . .
CREON: What now?
What earth-shattering truth are you about to utter?   1165
TIRESIAS: . . . just how much a sense of judgment, wisdom
is the greatest gift we have?
CREON: Just as much, I'd say,
as a twisted mind is the worst affliction going.
TIRESIAS: You are the one who's sick, Creon, sick to death.
CREON: I am in no mood to trade insults with a seer.   1170
TIRESIAS: You have already, calling my prophecies a lie.
CREON: Why not?
You and the whole breed of seers are mad for money!
TIRESIAS: And the whole race of tyrants lusts to rake it in.
CREON: This slander of yours —
are you aware you're speaking to the king?   1175
TIRESIAS: Well aware. Who helped you save the city?
CREON: You —
you have your skills, old seer, but you lust for injustice!
TIRESIAS: You will drive me to utter the dreadful secret in my heart.
CREON: Spit it out! Just don't speak it out for profit.
TIRESIAS: Profit? No, not a bit of profit, not for you.   1180
CREON: Know full well, you'll never buy off my resolve.
TIRESIAS: Then know this too, learn this by heart!
The chariot of the sun will not race through
so many circuits more, before you have surrendered
one born of your own loins, your own flesh and blood,   1185
a corpse for corpses given in return, since you have thrust
to the world below a child sprung for the world above,
ruthlessly lodged a living soul within the grave —
then you've robbed the gods below the earth,
keeping a dead body here in the bright air,   1190
unburied, unsung, unhallowed by the rites.

You, you have no business with the dead,
nor do the gods above — this is violence

you have forced upon the heavens.
And so the avengers, the dark destroyers late   1195
but true to the mark, now lie in wait for you,
the Furies sent by the gods and the god of death
to strike you down with the pains that you perfected!

There. Reflect on that, tell me I've been bribed.
The day comes soon, no long test of time, not now,   1200
that wakes the wails for men and women in your halls.
Great hatred rises against you—
cities in tumult, all whose mutilated sons
the dogs have graced with burial, or the wild beasts,
some wheeling crow that wings the ungodly stench of carrion   1205
back to each city, each warrior's hearth and home.

These arrows for your heart! Since you've raked me
I loose them like an archer in my anger,
arrows deadly true. You'll never escape
their burning, searing force.   1210

Motioning to his escort.

Come, boy, take me home.
So he can vent his rage on younger men,
and learn to keep a gentler tongue in his head
and better sense than what he carries now.

Exit to the side.

LEADER: The old man's gone, my king—   1215
terrible prophecies. Well I know,
since the hair on this old head went gray,
he's never lied to Thebes.
CREON: I know it myself—I'm shaken, torn.
It's a dreadful thing to yield . . . but resist now?   1220
Lay my pride bare to the blows of ruin?
That's dreadful too.
LEADER: But good advice,
Creon, take it now, you must.
CREON: What should I do? Tell me . . . I'll obey.
LEADER: Go! Free the girl from the rocky vault   1225
and raise a mound for the body you exposed.
CREON: That's your advice? You think I should give in?
LEADER: Yes, my king, quickly. Disasters sent by the gods
cut short our follies in a flash.
CREON: Oh it's hard.
giving up the heart's desire . . . but I will do it—   1230
no more fighting a losing battle with necessity.
LEADER: Do it now, go, don't leave it to others.

CREON: Now—I'm on my way! Come, each of you,
    take up axes, make for the high ground,
    over there, quickly! I and my better judgment   1235
    have come round to this—I shackled her,
    I'll set her free myself. I am afraid . . .
    it's best to keep the established laws
    to the very day we die.

Rushing out, followed by his entourage. The Chorus clusters around the altar.

CHORUS: God of a hundred names!
                        Great Dionysus—   1240
          Son and glory of Semele! Pride of Thebes—
    Child of Zeus whose thunder rocks the clouds—
    Lord of the famous lands of evening—
    King of the Mysteries!
                King of Eleusis, Demeter's plain°
    her breasting hills that welcome in the world—   1245
    Great Dionysus!
             Bacchus,° living in Thebes
    the mother-city of all your frenzied women—
                      Bacchus
        living along the Ismenus'° rippling waters
    standing over the field sown with the Dragon's teeth!

    You—we have seen you through the flaring smoky fires,   1250
        your torches blazing over the twin peaks
    where nymphs of the hallowed cave climb onward
                  fired with you, your sacred rage—
    we have seen you at Castalia's running spring°
    and down from the heights of Nysa° crowned with ivy   1255
    the greening shore rioting vines and grapes
        down you come in your storm of wild women
             ecstatic, mystic cries—
                    Dionysus—
    down to watch and ward the roads of Thebes!

    First of all cities, Thebes you honor first   1260
    you and your mother, bride of the lightning—
    come, Dionysus! now your people lie
    in the iron grip of plague,
    come in your racing, healing stride

1244 Demeter's plain: The goddess of grain was worshiped at Eleusis, near Athens.
1246 Bacchus: Another name for Dionysus.   **1248 Ismenus:** A river near Thebes where the
founders of the city were said to have sprung from a dragon's teeth.   **1254 Castalia's running
spring:** The sacred spring of Apollo's oracle at Delphi.   **1255 Nysa:** A mountain where Dionysus was worshiped.

              down Parnassus'° slopes   1265
or across the moaning straits.
                      Lord of the dancing —
dance, dance the constellations breathing fire!
Great master of the voices of the night!
Child of Zeus, God's offspring, come, come forth!
Lord, king, dance with your nymphs, swirling, raving   1270
arm-in-arm in frenzy through the night
       they dance you, Iacchus° —
                        Dance, Dionysus
giver of all good things!

Enter a Messenger from the side.

MESSENGER: Neighbors,
friends of the house of Cadmus° and the kings,
there's not a thing in this life of ours   1275
I'd praise or blame as settled once for all.
Fortune lifts and Fortune fells the lucky
and unlucky every day. No prophet on earth
can tell a man his fate. Take Creon:
there was a man to rouse your envy once,   1280
as I see it. He saved the realm from enemies;
taking power, he alone, the lord of the fatherland,
he set us true on course — flourished like a tree
with the noble line of sons he bred and reared . . .
and now it's lost, all gone.
                   Believe me,   1285
when a man has squandered his true joys,
he's good as dead, I tell you, a living corpse.
Pile up riches in your house, as much as you like —
live like a king with a huge show of pomp,
but if real delight is missing from the lot,   1290
I wouldn't give you a wisp of smoke for it,
not compared with joy.
LEADER: What now?
What new grief do you bring the house of kings?
MESSENGER: Dead, dead — and the living are guilty of their death!
LEADER: Who's the murderer? Who is dead? Tell us.   1295
MESSENGER: Haemon's gone, his blood spilled by the very hand —
LEADER: His father's or his own?
MESSENGER: His own . . .
raging mad with his father for the death —
LEADER: Oh great seer,

1265 Parnassus: A mountain in Greece that was sacred to Dionysus as well as other gods and goddesses. **1272 Iacchus:** Dionysus. **1274 Cadmus:** The legendary founder of Thebes.

you saw it all, you brought your word to birth!

MESSENGER: Those are the facts. Deal with them as you will.   1300

As he turns to go, Eurydice enters from the palace.

LEADER: Look, Eurydice. Poor woman, Creon's wife,
    so close at hand. By chance perhaps,
    unless she's heard the news about her son.

EURYDICE: My countrymen,
    all of you — I caught the sound of your words
    as I was leaving to do my part,   1305
    to appeal to queen Athena° with my prayers.
    I was just loosing the bolts, opening the doors,
    when a voice filled with sorrow, family sorrow,
    struck my ears, and I fell back, terrified,
    into the women's arms — everything went black.   1310
    Tell me the news, again, whatever it is . . .
    sorrow and I are hardly strangers;
    I can bear the worst.

MESSENGER: I — dear lady,
    I'll speak as an eye-witness. I was there.
    And I won't pass over one word of the truth.   1315
    Why should I try to soothe you with a story,
    only to prove a liar in a moment?
    Truth is always best.
                 So,
    I escorted your lord, I guided him
    to the edge of the plain where the body lay,   1320
    Polynices, torn by the dogs and still unmourned.
    And saying a prayer to Hecate of the Crossroads,
    Pluto° too, to hold their anger and be kind,
    we washed the dead in a bath of holy water
    and plucking some fresh branches, gathering . . .   1325
    what was left of him, we burned them all together
    and raised a high mound of native earth, and then
    we turned and made for that rocky vault of hers,
    the hollow, empty bed of the bride of Death.
    And far off, one of us heard a voice,   1330
    a long wail rising, echoing
    out of that unhallowed wedding-chamber;
    he ran to alert the master and Creon pressed on,
    closer — the strange, inscrutable cry came sharper,
    throbbing around him now, and he let loose   1335

1306 Athena: Goddess of wisdom and protector of Greek cities.   **1322–1323 Hecate, Pluto:** Gods of the underworld.

a cry of his own, enough to wrench the heart,
"Oh god, am I the prophet now? going down
the darkest road I've ever gone? My son —
it's *his* dear voice, he greets me! Go, men,
closer, quickly! Go through the gap,   1340
the rocks are dragged back —
right to the tomb's very mouth — and look,
see if it's Haemon's voice I think I hear,
or the gods have robbed me of my senses."

The king was shattered. We took his orders,   1345
went and searched, and there in the deepest,
dark recesses of the tomb we found her . . .
hanged by the neck in a fine linen noose,
strangled in her veils — and the boy,
his arms flung around her waist,   1350
clinging to her, wailing for his bride,
dead and down below, for his father's crimes
and the bed of his marriage blighted by misfortune.
When Creon saw him, he gave a deep sob,
he ran in, shouting, crying out to him,   1355
"Oh my child — what have you done? what seized you,
what insanity? what disaster drove you mad?
Come out, my son! I beg you on my knees!"
But the boy gave him a wild burning glance,
spat in his face, not a word in reply,   1360
he drew his sword — his father rushed out,
running as Haemon lunged and missed! —
and then, doomed, desperate with himself,
suddenly leaning his full weight on the blade,
he buried it in his body, halfway to the hilt.   1365
And still in his senses, pouring his arms around her,
he embraced the girl and breathing hard,
released a quick rush of blood,
bright red on her cheek glistening white.
And there he lies, body enfolding body . . .   1370
he has won his bride at last, poor boy,
not here but in the houses of the dead.

Creon shows the world that of all the ills
afflicting men the worst is lack of judgment.

Eurydice turns and reenters the palace.

LEADER: What do you make of that? The lady's gone,   1375
   without a word, good or bad.
MESSENGER: I'm alarmed too
   but here's my hope — faced with her son's death,

she finds it unbecoming to mourn in public.
Inside, under her roof, she'll set her women
to the task and wail the sorrow of the house.   1380
She's too discreet. She won't do something rash.
LEADER: I'm not so sure. To me, at least,
a long heavy silence promises danger,
just as much as a lot of empty outcries.
MESSENGER: We'll see if she's holding something back,   1385
hiding some passion in her heart.
I'm going in. You may be right — who knows?
Even too much silence has its dangers.

*Exit to the palace. Enter Creon from the side, escorted by attendants carrying
Haemon's body on a bier.*

LEADER: The king himself! Coming toward us,
look, holding the boy's head in his hands.   1390
Clear, damning proof, if it's right to say so —
proof of his own madness, no one else's,
no, his own blind wrongs.
CREON: Ohhh,
so senseless, so insane . . . my crimes,
my stubborn, deadly —   1395
Look at us, the killer, the killed,
father and son, the same blood — the misery!
My plans, my mad fanatic heart,
my son, cut off so young!
Ai, dead, lost to the world,   1400
not through your stupidity, no, my own.
LEADER: Too late,
too late, you see what justice means.
CREON: Oh I've learned
through blood and tears! Then, it was then,
when the god came down and struck me — a great weight
shattering, driving me down that wild savage path,   1405
ruining, trampling down my joy. Oh the agony,
the heartbreaking agonies of our lives.

Enter the Messenger from the palace.

MESSENGER: Master,
what a hoard of grief you have, and you'll have more.
The grief that lies to hand you've brought yourself —

Pointing to Haemon's body.

the rest, in the house, you'll see it all too soon.   1410
CREON: What now? What's worse than this?
MESSENGER: The queen is dead.
The mother of this dead boy . . . mother to the end —
poor thing, her wounds are fresh.

CREON: No, no,
          harbor of Death, so choked, so hard to cleanse! —
          why me? why are you killing me?   1415
          Herald of pain, more words, more grief?
          I died once, you kill me again and again!
          What's the report, boy . . . some news for me?
          My wife dead? O dear god!
          Slaughter heaped on slaughter?

The doors open; the body of Eurydice is brought out on her bier.

MESSENGER: See for yourself: 1420
     now they bring her body from the palace.
CREON: Oh no,
          another, a second loss to break the heart.
          What next, what fate still waits for me?
          I just held my son in my arms and now,
          look, a new corpse rising before my eyes —   1425
               wretched, helpless mother — O my son!
MESSENGER: She stabbed herself at the altar,
     then her eyes went dark, after she'd raised
     a cry for the noble fate of Megareus,° the hero
     killed in the first assault, then for Haemon,   1430
     then with her dying breath she called down
     torments on your head — you killed her sons.
CREON: Oh the dread,
          I shudder with dread! Why not kill me too? —
          run me through with a good sharp sword?
          Oh god, the misery, anguish —   1435
          I, I'm churning with it, going under.
MESSENGER: Yes, and the dead, the woman lying there,
     piles the guilt of all their deaths on you.
CREON: How did she end her life, what bloody stroke?
MESSENGER: She drove home to the heart with her own hand,   1440
     once she learned her son was dead . . . that agony.
CREON: And the guilt is all mine —
          can never be fixed on another man,
          no escape for me. I killed you,
          I, god help me, I admit it all!   1445

To his attendants.

          Take me away, quickly, out of sight.
          I don't even exist — I'm no one. Nothing.
LEADER: Good advice, if there's any good in suffering.
     Quickest is best when troubles block the way.

1429 **Megareus:** A son of Creon and Eurydice; he died when Thebes was attacked.

CREON:

Kneeling in prayer.

> Come, let it come! — that best of fates for me   1450
> that brings the final day, best fate of all.
> Oh quickly, now —
> so I never have to see another sunrise.

LEADER: That will come when it comes;
we must deal with all that lies before us.   1455
The future rests with the ones who tend the future.

CREON: That prayer — I poured my heart into that prayer!

LEADER: No more prayers now. For mortal men
there is no escape from the doom we must endure.

CREON: Take me away, I beg you, out of sight.   1460

> A rash, indiscriminate fool!
> I murdered you, my son, against my will —
> you too, my wife . . .
>   Wailing wreck of a man,
> whom to look to? where to lean for support?

Desperately turning from Haemon to Eurydice on their biers.

> Whatever I touch goes wrong — once more   1465
> a crushing fate's come down upon my head.

The Messenger and attendants lead Creon into the palace.

CHORUS: Wisdom is by far the greatest part of joy,
and reverence toward the gods must be safeguarded.
The mighty words of the proud are paid in full
with mighty blows of fate, and at long last   1470
those blows will teach us wisdom.

The old citizens exit to the side.   [c. 441 B.C.E.]

THINKING ABOUT THE TEXT

1. Is Antigone admirable in her steadfastness or just too stubborn? Are there principles worth dying for? Is Antigone a rebel fighting against injustice or a social misfit? Is there a middle ground?

2. Describe the argument between Antigone and Ismene. What point is Ismene making? Do you agree with her or with Antigone?

3. Some critics argue that Creon is the play's main character because he changes and Antigone doesn't. Does this argument have some credibility? What specifically does Creon learn?

4. How might you respond to this play if you were the mayor of a city? A religious leader of an orthodox faith with strict burial rituals? A feminist leader? A rebel? A conformist? How might your present context affect your reading?

5. Creon does not want to appear to be a weak leader, so he stays firm. Should he have bent the rules for his family? How would you have responded if he did so? Should contemporary leaders be strong, flexible, safe, and innovative?

MAKING COMPARISONS

1. Compare the tragic flaws of Oedipus and Antigone. Does Antigone seem like Oedipus's daughter?
2. Compare Creon and Oedipus as king. Who has more concern for the people? Who is a better leader? More just?
3. Compare the endings of each play in terms of justice.

WRITING ABOUT ISSUES

1. Argue for or against the idea that Antigone is the champion of the family against an unjust government and that she is a hero because she stands up for her principles.
2. Argue for or against the claim that Antigone was motivated by love and Creon by hate.
3. Write an essay that begins with this sentence: Oedipus is deeply committed to the search for truth, and his daughter, Antigone, is deeply committed to justice.
4. Would our present society benefit from the presence of people like Antigone and Oedipus? Would they be forces for good or for harm? Write a brief paper in which you set forth your position on these questions.

A WEB ASSIGNMENT

A number of Web sites are dedicated to various perspectives on Greek tragedy. Visit the Web Assignments section of the *Making Literature Matter* Web site to link to one of these sites where you will find history and discussion. Write a brief report of the ways both *Antigone* and *Oedipus* are tragic.

Visit www.bedfordstmartins.com/makinglitmatter

Not a Simple Decision:
Cultural Contexts for Gwendolyn Brooks's
"The Mother"

GWENDOLYN BROOKS, "The Mother"

Cultural Contexts
THURGOOD MARSHALL, "The Gestapo in Detroit"
LEON F. LITWACK, "Hellhounds"
RALPH GINZBURG, From *100 Years of Lynching*
PETER M. BERGMAN, "Snapshots from History"

The persona that Gwendolyn Brooks adopts in a poem written early in her career, "The Mother," is that of a woman who mourns the loss of the "children" (line 2) she might have had. Noting that "Abortions will not let you forget" (line 1), she seems to regret the loss of the joys of raising children. She seems haunted by their absence, hearing their "voices in the wind" (line 11). Speaking directly to them, she asks them to "Believe that even in my deliberateness I was not deliberate" (line 21). Even though the poem is filled with this kind of ambivalence, she seems to take responsibility for what was then an illegal act. Her idea is paradoxical, since the children she loves were never born. Her coda, "I loved you / All," seems to contradict her past actions. The modern reader can sympathize with her sense of loss, and yet we still wonder about her decision and why she claims to have "loved" fetuses that she aborted. Indeed, the grounds for her decision seem unclear. Although contemporary societies now see abortion as a woman's legal and personal choice, her public disclosure invites our speculation. There are undoubtedly a number of good reasons why a woman would make a decision that would cause such regret, but few women would make the decision lightly. It is interesting, therefore, that in her partial autobiography, *Report from Part One*, Gwendolyn Brooks writes about the persona created in this poem in the following way: "Hardly your crowned and praised and 'customary' Mother; but a Mother not unfamiliar, who decides that *she* rather than her World, will kill her children. The decision is not nice, not simple, and the emotional consequences are neither nice nor simple."

Since we know that many of the poems in her first collection, *A Street in Bronzeville* (1945), were attempts to enlighten an oblivious white America to the humanity of oppressed black America, cultural critics propose that one reasonable way to read the mother's choice is that she cannot ethically bring children into a world where they will be second-class citizens at best, discriminated against in almost all avenues of American society—from education and business, to sports, the military, and religion. (Indeed this decision is close to the reasoning of Ruth Younger in *A Raisin in the Sun*, written by a contemporary of Brooks, Lorraine Hansberry.) There were few safe havens for blacks in America in the era Brooks grew up in. Poverty was endemic, injustice was the rule, and official physical violence was not uncommon.

(The Granger Collection,
New York.)

While there are a number of interesting ways to read this complex poem, we
have chosen four texts that might help you perform a cultural analysis by filling
out the social, political, and economic contexts that the mother in the poem lives
in and that would probably influence her decision not to give birth. The first was
written by a future Supreme Court judge, the respected black jurist, Thurgood
Marshall. He talks of one of the largest race riots of the century, a catastrophe
Brooks would have been familiar with. The second essay is from an immensely
disturbing text, *Without Sanctuary: Lynching Photography in America,* and is followed by a series of brief headlines about lynchings collected in *100 Years of
Lynching.* The last selection is a series of historical observations taken from *The
Chronological History of the Negro in America* for the years 1935 through 1945.

BEFORE YOU READ

What factors would you consider before having children? Would the condition of the world be a factor? Would your economic status? Your psychological state? Might it matter if you were poor and living in Somalia? If you were
a Christian living under the Taliban?

GWENDOLYN BROOKS
The Mother

Gwendolyn Brooks (1917–2000) became the first African American to win the Pulitzer Prize, receiving it in 1950 for a book of poems entitled Annie Allen. *She garnered many other awards for her poetry, besides serving as poet laureate of Illinois and poetry consultant to the Library of Congress. In most of her work, Brooks was concerned with the lives of African Americans, including issues of civil rights. "The Mother" appeared in her first book of poetry,* A Street in Bronzeville *(1945). Other collections of her verse include* Selected Poems *(1963, 1999),* Blacks *(1987), and* Children Coming Home *(1992). Brooks also published a novel,* Maud Martha *(1953), and an autobiography,* Report from Part One *(1972).*

Abortions will not let you forget.
You remember the children you got that you did not get,
The damp small pulps with a little or with no hair,
The singers and workers that never handled the air.
You will never neglect or beat   5
Them, or silence or buy with a sweet.
You will never wind up the sucking-thumb
Or scuttle off ghosts that come.
You will never leave them, controlling your luscious sigh,
Return for a snack of them, with gobbling mother-eye.   10

I have heard in the voices of the wind the voices of my dim killed children
I have contracted. I have eased
My dim dears at the breasts they could never suck.
I have said, Sweets, if I sinned, if I seized
Your luck   15
And your lives from your unfinished reach,
If I stole your births and your names,
Your straight baby tears and your games,
Your stilted or lovely loves, your tumults, your marriages, aches, and your deaths,
If I poisoned the beginnings of your breaths,   20
Believe that even in my deliberateness I was not deliberate.
Though why should I whine,
Whine that the crime was other than mine? —
Since anyhow you are dead.
Or rather, or instead,   25
You were never made.
But that too, I am afraid,
Is faulty: oh, what shall I say, how is the truth to be said?
You were born, you had body, you died.
It is just that you never giggled or planned or cried.   30

◆ ◆ ◆

Believe me, I loved you all.
Believe me, I knew you, though faintly, and I loved, I loved you
All.   [1945]

THINKING ABOUT THE TEXT

1. What in the poem helps you (or doesn't help you) understand the narrator's decision? Are there specific questions you would still want to ask?

2. Why does the narrator use "you" instead of "me" throughout the poem?

3. What are the points at which Brooks seems to waver? Why does she?

4. Since the "children" were never born, how can she talk to them? How can she love them?

5. Is this a defense of abortion? An attack on abortion? A plea for understanding? An emotional snapshot of a regretful woman? How do you read the poem?

THURGOOD MARSHALL
The Gestapo in Detroit

Thurgood Marshall (1908–1993) graduated from Howard Law School in 1933 and in 1936 joined the legal staff of the National Association for the Advancement of Colored People. He argued more than thirty cases before the U.S. Supreme Court, successfully challenging racial segregation, most notably in higher education. His arguments against the "separate but equal" doctrine established in an earlier Supreme Court case (Plessey v. Ferguson, 1896) contributed to the landmark decision handed down in Brown v. Board of Education of Topeka *(1954). He was appointed to the U.S. Court of Appeals in 1962 and two years later was the first African American to sit on the Supreme Court, where he consistently supported the position taken by those challenging discrimination based on race or sex. This selection originally appeared in* The Crisis *in August 1943.*

Riots are usually the result of many underlying causes, yet no single factor is more important than the attitude and efficiency of the police. When disorder starts, it is either stopped quickly or permitted to spread into serious proportions, depending upon the actions of the local police.

Much of the blood spilled in the Detroit riot is on the hands of the Detroit police department. In the past the Detroit police have been guilty of both inefficiency and an attitude of prejudice against Negroes. Of course, there are several individual exceptions.

The citizens of Detroit, White and Negro, are familiar with the attitude of the police as demonstrated during the trouble in 1942 surrounding the Sojourner Truth housing project. At that time a mob of White persons armed with rocks, sticks and other weapons attacked Negro tenants who were attempting to move into the project. Police were called to the scene. Instead of dispersing the mob which was unlawfully on property belonging to the federal government and leased to Negroes, they directed their efforts toward dispersing the Negroes who were attempting to get into their own homes. All Negroes approaching the project were searched and their automobiles likewise searched. White people were neither searched nor disarmed by the police. This incident is typical of the one-sided law enforcement practiced by Detroit police. White hoodlums were justified in their belief that the police would act the same way in any further disturbances.

In the June riot of this year, the police ran true to form. The trouble reached riot proportions because the police once again enforced the law with an unequal hand. They used "persuasion" rather than firm action with White rioters, while against Negroes they used the ultimate in force: night sticks, revolvers, riot guns, submachine guns, and deer guns. As a result, twenty-five of the thirty-four persons killed were Negroes. Of the latter, seventeen were killed by police.

The excuse of the police department for the disproportionate number of Negroes killed is that the majority of them were shot while committing felonies; namely, the looting of stores on Hasting Street. On the other hand, the crimes of arson and felonious assaults are also felonies. It is true that some Negroes were looting stores and were shot while committing these crimes. It is equally true that White persons were turning over and burning automobiles on Woodward Avenue. This is arson. Others were beating Negroes with iron pipes, clubs, and rocks. This is felonious assault. Several Negroes were stabbed. This is assault with intent to murder.

All these crimes are matters of record; many were committed in the presence of police officers, several on the pavement around the City Hall. Yet the record remains: Negroes killed by police — seventeen; White persons killed by police — none. The entire record, both of the riot killings and of previous disturbances, reads like the story of the Nazi Gestapo.

Evidence of tension in Detroit has been apparent for months. The *Detroit Free Press* sent a reporter to the police department. When Commissioner Witherspoon was asked how he was handling the situation he told the reporter: "We have given orders to handle it with kid gloves. The policemen have taken insults to keep trouble from breaking out. I doubt if you or I could have put up with it." This weak-kneed policy of the police commissioner coupled with the anti-Negro attitude of many members of the force helped to make a riot inevitable.

SUNDAY NIGHT ON BELLE ISLE

Belle Isle is a municipal recreation park where thousands of White and Negro war workers and their families go on Sundays for their outings. There had been isolated instances of racial friction in the past. On Sunday night, June 20, there was trouble between a group of White and Negro people. The disturbance was under control by midnight. During the time of the disturbance and after it was under control, the police searched the automobiles of all Negroes and searched the Negroes as well. They did not search the white people. One Negro who was to be inducted into the army the following week was arrested because another person in the car had a small penknife. This youth was later sentenced to ninety days in jail before his family could locate him. Many Negroes were arrested during this period and rushed to local police stations. At the very beginning the police demonstrated that they would continue to handle racial disorders by searching, beating and arresting Negroes while using mere persuasion on White people.

THE RIOT SPREADS

A short time after midnight, disorder broke out in a White neighborhood near the Roxy theatre on Woodward Avenue. The Roxy is an all-night theatre attended by white and Negro patrons. Several Negroes were beaten and others were forced to remain in the theatre for lack of police protection. The rumor spread among the White people that a Negro had raped a White woman on Belle Island and that the Negroes were rioting.

At about the same time a rumor spread around Hastings and Adams Streets   10 in the Negro area that White sailors had thrown a Negro woman and her baby into the lake at Belle Isle and that the police were beating Negroes. This rumor was also repeated by an unidentified Negro at one of the night spots. Some Negroes began to attack White persons in the area. The police immediately began to use their sticks and revolvers against them. The Negroes began to break out the windows of stores of White merchants on Hastings Street.

The interesting thing is that when the windows in the stores on Hastings Street were first broken, there was no looting. An officer of the Merchants' Association walked the length of Hastings Street, starting at seven o'clock Monday morning and noticed that none of the stores with broken windows had been looted. It is thus clear that the original breaking of windows was not for the purpose of looting.

Throughout Monday the police, instead of placing men in front of the stores to protect them from looting, contented themselves with driving up and down Hastings Street from time to time, stopping in front of the stores. The usual procedure was to jump out of the squad cars with drawn revolvers and riot guns to shoot whoever might be in the store. The policemen would then tell the Negro bystanders to "run and not look back." On several occasions, persons running were shot in the back. In other instances, bystanders were clubbed by police. To the police, all Negroes on Hastings Street were "looters." This included war workers returning from work. There is no question that many Negroes were guilty of looting, just as there is always looting during earthquakes or as there was when English towns were bombed by the Germans.

CARS DETOURED INTO MOBS

Woodward Avenue is one of the main thoroughfares of the city of Detroit. Small groups of White people began to rove up and down Woodward beating Negroes, stoning cars containing Negroes, stopping streetcars and yanking Negroes from them, and stabbing and shooting Negroes. In no case did the police do more than try to "reason" with these mobs, many of which were, at this stage, quite small. The police did not draw their revolvers or riot guns, and never used any force to disperse these mobs. As a result of this, the mobs got larger and bolder and even attacked Negroes on the pavement of the City Hall in demonstration not only of their contempt for Negroes, but of their contempt for law and order as represented by the municipal government.

During this time, Mayor Jeffries was in his office in the City Hall with the door locked and the window shade drawn. The use of night sticks or the drawing of revolvers would have dispersed these White groups and saved the lives of many Negroes. It would not have been necessary to shoot, [as] it would have been sufficient to threaten to shoot into the White mobs. The use of a fire hose would have dispersed many of the groups. None of these things was done and the disorder took on the proportions of a major riot. The responsibility rests with the Detroit police.

At the height of the disorder on Woodward Avenue, Negroes driving north on Brush Street (a Negro street) were stopped at Vernor Highway by a policeman who forced them to detour to Woodward Avenue. Many of these cars are automobiles which appeared in the pictures released by several newspapers showing them overturned and burned on Woodward Avenue. 15

While investigating the riot, we obtained many affidavits from Negroes concerning police brutality during the riot. It is impossible to include the facts of all of these affidavits. However, typical instances may be cited. A Negro soldier in uniform who had recently been released from the army with a medical discharge, was on his way down Brush Street Monday morning, toward a theatre on Woodward Avenue. This soldier was not aware of the fact that the riot was still going on. While in the Negro neighborhood on Brush Street, he reached a corner where a squad car drove up and discharged several policemen with drawn revolvers who announced to a small group on the corner to run and not look back. Several of the Negroes who did not move quite fast enough for the police were struck with night sticks and revolvers. The soldier was yanked from behind by one policeman and struck in the head with a blunt instrument and knocked to the ground, where he remained in a stupor. The police then returned to their squad car and drove off. A Negro woman in the block noticed the entire incident from her window, and she rushed out with a cold, damp towel to bind the soldier's head. She then hailed two Negro postal employees who carried the soldier to a hospital where his life was saved.

There are many additional affidavits of similar occurrences involving obviously innocent civilians throughout many Negro sections in Detroit where there had been no rioting at all. It was characteristic of these cases that the policemen would drive up to a corner, jump out with drawn revolvers, striking at Negroes indiscriminately, ofttimes shooting at them, and in all cases forcing them to run. At the same time on Woodward Avenue, White civilians were seizing Negroes and telling them to "run, nigger, run." At least two Negroes, "shot while looting," were innocent persons who happened to be in the area at that time.

One Negro who had been an employee of a bank in Detroit for the past eighteen years was on his way to work on a Woodward Avenue streetcar when he was seized by one of the White mobs. In the presence of at least four policemen, he was beaten and stabbed in the side. He also heard several shots fired from the back of the mob. He managed to run to two of the policemen who proceeded to "protect" him from the mob. The two policemen, followed by two mounted policemen, proceeded down Woodward Avenue. While he was being escorted by these policemen, the man was struck in the face by at least eight of the mob, and at no time was any effort made to prevent him from being struck. After a short distance this man noticed a squad car parked on the other side of the street. In sheer desperation, he broke away from the two policemen who claimed to be protecting him and ran to the squad car, begging for protection. The officer in the squad car put him in the back seat and drove off, thereby saving his life.

During all this time, the fact that the man was either shot or stabbed was evident because of the fact that blood was spurting from his side. Despite this obvious felony, committed in the presence of at least four policemen, no effort was made at that time either to protect the victim or to arrest the persons guilty of the felony.   [1943]

THINKING ABOUT THE TEXT

1. What is your response to Marshall's account? What causes does he give for riots?

2. Does the writer seem balanced in his account? Is an argument being made? What are his claim and his warrants?

3. Does police brutality continue today? What is problematic about defining it? What do you think are the causes?

LEON F. LITWACK
Hellhounds

Leon F. Litwack (b. 1929) is Alexander F. and May T. Morrison Professor of American History at the University of California, Berkeley, where he has spent almost his entire career, earning a B.A. in 1951 and a Ph.D. in 1958 and teaching since 1964. Litwack's many publications include North of Slavery: The Free Negro in the Antebellum North *(1961),* Been in the Storm So Long: The Aftermath of Slavery *(1979; winner of both the Pulitzer Prize and National Book Award), and* Trouble in Mind: Black Southerners in the Age of Jim Crow *(1998). Litwack has received many honors in recognition of his distinguished and path-breaking scholarship, including the Pulitzer Prize in history, the Francis Parkman Prize, the American Book Award, and election to the presidency of the Organization of American Historians. The following selection is from* Without Sanctuary *(2000).*

The criminal justice system (the law, the courts, the legal profession) operated with ruthless efficiency in upholding the absolute power of whites to command the subordination and labor of blacks.

But even this overwhelming display of superiority did not afford white southerners the internal security they sought or relieve their fears of *"uppity," "troublesome,"* ambitious, and independent-minded black men and women who had not yet learned the rituals of deference and submission. The quality of the racial violence that gripped the South made it distinctive in this nation's history. In the late nineteenth and early twentieth century, two or three black southerners were hanged, burned at the stake, or quietly murdered every week. In the 1890s, lynchings claimed an average of 139 lives each year, 75 percent of them black. The numbers declined in the following decades, but the percentage of black victims rose to 90 percent. Between 1882 and 1968, an estimated 4,742 blacks met their deaths at the hands of lynch mobs. As many if not more blacks were victims of legal lynchings (speedy trials and executions), private white violence, and *"nigger hunts,"* murdered by a variety of means in isolated rural sections and dumped into rivers and creeks.

Even an accurate body count of black lynching victims could not possibly reveal how hate and fear transformed ordinary white men and women into mindless murderers and sadistic torturers, or the savagery that, with increasing regularity, characterized assaults on black men and women in the name of restraining their savagery and depravity. Nothing so dramatically or forcefully underscored the cheapness of black life in the South. The way one black Mississippian recalled white violence in the 1930s applied as accurately and even more pervasively to the late nineteenth and early twentieth centuries. *"Back in those days, to kill a Negro wasn't nothing. It was like killing a chicken or killing a snake. The whites would say, 'Niggers jest supposed to die, ain't no damn good anyway—so jest go on an' kill 'em.'"* Whatever their value as laborers, black people were clearly expendable and replaceable. "In those days it was *'Kill a mule, buy another. Kill a nigger, hire another,'*" a black southerner remembered. *"They had to have a license to kill anything but a nigger. We was always in season."*

The cheapness of black life reflected in turn the degree to which so many whites by the early twentieth century had come to think of black men and women as inherently and permanently inferior, as less than human, as little more than animals. *"We Southern people don't care to equal ourselves with animals,"* a white Floridian told a northern critic. *"The people of the South don't think any more of killing the black fellows than you would think of killing a flea . . . and if I was to live 1,000 years that would be my opinion and every other Southern man."* A former governor of Georgia, William J. Northern, after canvassing his state in the interest of law and order, found the same disregard for black life. *"I was amazed to find scores and hundreds of men who believed the Negro to be a brute, without responsibility to God, and his slaughter nothing more than the killing of a dog."*

Lynching was hardly a new phenomenon. For many decades, it had served 5 as a means of extra-legal justice in the Far West and Midwest, and most of the victims had been white, along with numbers of American Indians, Mexicans, Asians, and blacks. But in the 1890s, lynching and sadistic torture rapidly became exclusive public rituals of the South, with black men and women as the principal victims. During slavery, blacks had been exposed to violence on the plantations and farms where they worked and from the patrollers if they ventured off those plantations. The financial investment each slave represented had operated to some degree as a protective shield for blacks accused of crimes, but in the event of an insurrection — real or imagined — whites had used murder, decapitation, burning, and lynching to punish suspected rebels and impress upon all blacks the dangers of resistance.

The violence meted out to blacks after emancipation and during Reconstruction, including mob executions designed to underscore the limits of black freedom, anticipated to a considerable degree the wave of murder and terrorism that would sweep across the South two decades later and become one of its unmistakable trademarks. What was strikingly new and different in the late nineteenth and early twentieth century was the sadism and exhibitionism that characterized white violence. The ordinary modes of execution and punishment no longer satisfied the emotional appetite of the crowd. To kill the victim was not enough; the execution became public theater, a participatory ritual of torture and death, a voyeuristic spectacle prolonged as long as possible (once for seven hours) for the benefit of the crowd. Newspapers on a number of occasions announced in advance the time and place of a lynching, special "excursion" trains transported spectators to the scene, employers sometimes released their workers to attend, parents sent notes to school asking teachers to excuse their children for the event, and entire families attended, the children hoisted on their parents' shoulders to miss none of the action and accompanying festivities. Returning from one such occasion, a nine-year-old white youth remained unsatisfied. "*I have seen a man hanged*," he told his mother; "*now I wish I could see one burned.*"

The story of a lynching, then, is more than the simple fact of a black man or woman hanged by the neck. It is the story of slow, methodical, sadistic, often highly inventive forms of torture and mutilation. If executed by fire, it is the redhot poker applied to the eyes and genitals and the stench of burning flesh, as the body slowly roasts over the flames and the blood sizzles in the heat. If executed by hanging, it is the convulsive movement of the limbs. Whether by fire or rope, it is the dismemberment and distribution of severed bodily parts as favors and souvenirs to participants and the crowd: teeth, ears, toes, fingers, nails, kneecaps, bits of charred skin and bones. Such human trophies might reappear as watch fobs or be displayed conspicuously for public viewing. The severed knuckles of Sam Hose, for example, would be prominently displayed in the window of a grocery store in Atlanta.

The brutalities meted out in these years often exceeded the most vivid of imaginations. After learning of the lynching of her husband, Mary Turner — in her eighth month of pregnancy — vowed to find those responsible, swear out warrants against them, and have them punished in the courts. For making such a threat, a mob of several hundred men and women determined to "*teach her a lesson.*" After tying her ankles together, they hung her from a tree, head downward. Dousing her clothes with gasoline, they burned them from her body. While she was still alive, someone used a knife ordinarily reserved for splitting hogs to cut open the woman's abdomen. The infant fell from her womb to the ground and cried briefly, whereupon a member of this Valdosta, Georgia, mob crushed the baby's head beneath his heel. Hundreds of bullets were then fired into Mary Turner's body, completing the work of the mob. The Associated Press, in its notice of the affair, observed that Mary Turner had made *"unwise remarks"* about the execution of her husband, *"and the people, in their indignant mood, took exceptions to her remarks, as well as her attitude."* [2000]

THINKING ABOUT THE TEXT

1. Although this account is brutal, we left out material that was much more explicit and horrific. Should we have included this material? What is the effect of reading such material?

2. Did you know that hundreds of people who attended lynchings sent graphic postcards to their friends? Recently there was a controversial collection of these postcards on exhibit in New York City. Would you go to such an exhibition? What might be the value of such a show?

3. One of the most chilling aspects of the photographs of lynchings is the festive atmosphere. Nowhere in the hundreds of faces in the crowd do we see any guilt. How can you account for this?

RALPH GINZBURG
From *100 Years of Lynching*

Ralph Ginzburg (b. 1929) is a freelance writer and photographer. In 1963, he was indicted, tried, and convicted in Philadelphia for "pandering" salacious material in his advertising of Eros, a hardcover magazine of erotic art. The case was subsequently tried in the U.S. Supreme Court, which upheld the conviction but then granted him a retrial. Ginzburg has written a wide variety of articles in a number of newspapers and magazines. He has also published several books, including a daily pictorial chronicle of Manhattan, I Shot New York (1999). The book from which the following excerpts are taken was originally published in 1962 and is still considered one of the most important contributions to the study of lynching and hate crimes in America.

St. Louis Argus
June 8, 1926

NEGRO LYNCHED FOR "ATTACKING" CHILD HE ONLY STARTLED

OSCEOLA, Ark., June 2—Albert Blades, 22, a Negro visiting here from St. Louis, was hanged and his body was burned Wednesday morning for an alleged attack on a small white girl. Following the lynching, doctors who examined the child said that she had not been attacked.

There appears to be some question of whether the child wasn't merely frightened by the unexpected appearance of Blades in a picnic grounds where she and her classmates were playing. Blades pleaded his innocence to the last.

New York World-Telegram
November 29, 1933

CROWD CHEERED AND LAUGHED
AT NEGRO'S HORRIBLE DEATH

ST. JOSEPH, Nov. 29—They didn't hang Lloyd Warner. They burned him alive. Here's how it all happened, from start to finish.

The mob started to gather about 5 P.M., but they were good-natured then. The sheriff was kidding them and nothing would have happened had not three river workers taken charge of things. They didn't say much, except "get me that" or "do this" as they went about breaking into the jail. It was very business like.

Of course, excitement mounted and permeated the mob of at least 10,000.   5
There were lots of women along and many sightseers who didn't take part. There was at least a thousand from out of town.

About 9 o'clock the mob tried to enter the jail through the Court House next door. Through a passageway they got to the second floor of the jail, but were unable to go further. So they went back to batter their way in.

On the third floor were Sheriff Otto Theisen, his deputies, two newspaper men and national guardsmen. They were armed with tear gas and pistols, but not a shot was fired except by the mob.

The mob fired plenty, but the bullets only scarred the jail walls.

Guardsmen en route with three tanks were stopped. The mob yanked the soldiers out of the tanks and mauled them.

After a section of oilfield casing or water main pipe failed to batter in the out-   10
side door, two five-ton trucks were backed up. Log chains were attached and the doors pulled from the walls.

The second door inside was battered down and but one remained when the sheriff went out the back door, came around to the front and said to the mob:

"You are plenty of Irishmen and I am but one Dutchman. You are too many for me, boys. I'll turn him over to you."

The mob cheered and shouted.

The sheriff said he feared they would lynch all prisoners. He went for Warner, who was chattering in fear. Warner hung to his cell bars for life, until his fingers bled. He was pulled loose and taken downstairs. But the sheriff didn't show the prisoner yet.

"You fellows clear out," the sheriff said calmly. "Send four men in and I will   15
let them have him."

This was done.

The Negro, clinging to every object he could reach, tried to hold himself back. Warner was dragged a block toward the center of town to a small tree across from the Hotel Robidoux (the city's leading hotel).

They tied an inch and a half rope around his neck. But for a hanging the job was bungled.

It was tied so that it only threw his head back instead of forward so as to break his neck. He hung and struggled as the crowd yelled. Laughter rang out on all sides. Men and women leaned calmly against buildings, witnessing the horrible sight.

Warner wanted to talk but they wouldn't let him.   20

Then some one ran across the street, got seven gallons of gasoline from a filling station. Warner had on pants, shoes and socks which they drenched and set afire.

Warner was still alive.

He was burned alive.

He didn't cry out.

The fire went out. More gas was thrown on him and lighted again. Then the   25
rope burned in two.

As the body slumped, wood was piled around and the fire was lighted a third time.

The crowd cheered and laughed and made jokes.

Galveston (Texas) *Tribune*
June 21, 1934

WHITE GIRL IS JAILED,
NEGRO FRIEND IS LYNCHED

NEWTON, Tex., June 21 — A negro charged with associating with a white girl here was lynched last night by a mob of 200 armed men who over-powered two deputy sheriffs who were taking him to another city for safe keeping.

The nude body of the negro, John Griggs, was found at 2 A.M. today in front of a box factory. He had been hanged and shot.

The deputies were halted on the highway 27 miles south of here. The offi-   30
cers were disarmed and a noose was thrown around the negro's neck as he sat in the officers' car.

The negro was jerked from the car. The officers were told to "get going." They drove away immediately.

Deputy Sheriffs D. W. Smith and W. E. Davison were ordered by Sheriff T. S. Hughes to spirit the negro from the old Newton county jail last night when a howling mob of men and women gathered outside.

"We told the negro the jail was about to be stormed and that we were help-less," Smith said. "We asked him if he wanted to attempt to slip away and go to Orange with us.

"He accepted gladly."

The negro, crying frantically, was given a coat and hastened out the rear door   35
of the jail to an awaiting automobile.

Smith said that about 27 miles from Newton the road was blocked by a mob of men standing eight men deep.

They were all armed with shotguns, rifles and pistols, Smith said.

As soon as the auto was stopped, Smith said other men came from the side of the road and the car was surrounded.

"I tried to plead with the men not to take the negro," Smith said, "but they jerked me from the car and took my gun. Davison got the same treatment.

"After they took the negro from the car they told us to get moving. There was   40
nothing else we could do."

Griggs had been in jail for over a week on a charge of associating with a
white woman. The woman had also been arrested and is still in jail on a charge of
vagrancy. Her name is given as Joan Rivers, age 19.

Further details concerning the couple are vague. Some sources give Griggs'
age as 38, others as 20. Some say they both worked in a local box factory, others
say they attended the same Texas college.

Macon (Georgia) *Telegraph*
October 26, 1934

BIG PREPARATION MADE FOR
LYNCHING TONIGHT

GREENWOOD, Fla., Oct. 26—Local citizens have been preparing all day for
the lynching of a negro scheduled to take place here tonight. This morning a
mob seized Claude Neal, 23, from a jail in Brewton, Ala., where he had been
held in connection with the murder of a white girl which took place here several
days ago.

At noon a "Committee of Six" representing the mob announced a timetable
for the lynching which was given in newspapers and over the radio as follows:

At sundown the negro will be taken to the farm two miles from here where   45
Miss Lola Cannidy, the murder victim, lived. There he will be mutilated by the
girl's father.

Then he will be brought to a pig-pen in the middle of a cotton field nearby,
where the girl's body was found, and killed.

Finally his body will be brought to Marianna, the county seat, nine miles
from here, and hung in the court house square for all to see.

The negro is presently being held at an undisclosed location in a swamp
along the Chattahoochee River, not far from the Cannidy farm.

"All white folks are invited to the party," said the announcement issued by
the mob's Committee of Six.

As a result, thousands of citizens have been congregating all afternoon at the   50
Cannidy farm. Bonfires have been started, piles of sharp sticks have been prepared, knives have been sharpened and one woman has displayed a curry-comb
with which she promises to torture the negro.

The crowd is said to have been addressed by a member of the Florida State
Legislature who, in a humorous vein, promised that no one would be disappointed if the crowd maintained decorum.

Some misgivings are said to have been expressed by the Committee over the
fact that the crowd is heavily armed and highly intoxicated. It is feared that shots
aimed at the negro may go astray and injure innocent bystanders, who include
some women with babes in arms.

During the early afternoon a party of men broke off from the crowd at the
Cannidy farm and paid a visit to the cabin where Neal's family lives and burned it
to the ground.

Early announcement of the lynching has had its repercussions outside the community. At Tallahassee, the Florida Council of the Association of Southern Women for the Prevention of Lynching has issued a strong appeal to law enforcement officials to do all within their power to prevent the mob from carrying out its plan. In Washington the Attorney General of the United States said that he was powerless to invoke the federal kidnapping law to rescue Neal because no ransom was involved.

In New York, Walter White, Secretary of the National Association for the   55
Advancement of Colored People, sent a telegram to Florida's Governor David Sholtz urging him to "take immediate steps" to protect Neal. J. P. Newell, the Governor's Executive Secretary at Tallahassee, has replied that the Governor is "out of the capital" and can not be reached.

THINKING ABOUT THE TEXT

1. What might be the effect of reading such accounts on the black community?

2. What explanation might you offer for such behavior in America?

3. The number of lynchings in the twentieth century is often put at about 5,000, but that does not include countless unpunished murders, framings, beatings, and other form of violence. Have you read about this in your high-school history texts? Why, or why not?

PETER M. BERGMAN
Snapshots from History

The following excerpts are from a 1969 work by Peter M. Bergman entitled The Chronological History of the Negro in America, *which Bergman assembled with the assistance of Mort N. Bergman and a staff of compilers. These excerpts suggest some of the conditions of life for African Americans in the 1930s and 1940s.*

1935

Median incomes of Negroes and whites in selected cities were:

	Negroes	Whites	Negro Income Lower by
New York City	$980	$1,930	49.2%
Chicago	726	1,687	56.9%
Columbus, Ohio	831	1,622	48.7%
Atlanta, Ga.	632	1,876	66.3%
Columbia, S.C.	576	1,876	69.3%
Mobile, Ala.	481	1,419	66.1%

The 3,500,000 Negro families receiving relief represented 21.5% of the total Negro population. Of the white population 12.8% were on relief. . . .

In the urban North approximately 50% of Negro families were on relief (3 to 4 times more than whites). In nine cities in the urban South 25% of Negro families and 11% of white families were on relief. More whites with an income below $500 were on relief than Negroes.

In urban areas Negro relief grants were smaller than white relief grants. The average for Negroes was $24.18, and for whites, $29.05.

Of relief cases who found employment, 8.8% of the Negroes received less in wages than they did on relief, while only 2.7% of the whites did. . . .   5

Senators Wagner of New York and Costigan of Colorado reintroduced an NAACP-drafted Federal anti-lynching bill. A filibuster killed this bill. Negroes were lynched at the rate of one every three weeks in this year.

The NAACP withdrew its support from Roosevelt when he refused to give his practical support to their anti-lynching bill, and because no civil rights legislation had been proposed in his term. The 26th annual convention of the NAACP met in St. Louis, and asked Harry L. Hopkins, Federal Emergency Relief administrator, to appoint a Negro as deputy administrator in every state with a large Negro population. . . .

Ten Southern states spent an average $17.04 on each Negro pupil and $49.30 on each white student in elementary and secondary schools. Negro schools also had more pupils per teacher, less transportation, a shorter school term, and poorer facilities than the white schools. . . .

Despite the previous legal victories of the NAACP Negroes were still denied the ballot in the Texas Democratic primary. Supreme Court Justice Roberts upheld the Texas law which read: "Be it resolved that all white citizens of the state of Texas who are qualified to vote . . . shall be eligible to membership in the Democratic Party." . . .

In this year 18 Negroes were lynched.   10

A riot in Harlem on March 19 was set off when a Negro boy was caught stealing a small knife from a 125th Street store. He escaped, but rumors spread that he had been beaten to death. Amid accusations of police brutality and merchant employment discrimination, Negroes smashed windows and looted. Three Negroes were killed, 200 store windows were smashed and over $200,000,000 in damage was done. An interracial committee on conditions in Harlem headed by E. Franklin Frazier, the Negro sociologist, reported that the riot was caused by "resentments against racial discrimination and poverty in the midst of plenty." Just prior to the riot Harlem businessmen who had been forced through a boycott to hire Negroes had secured an injunction on the basis of the Sherman Anti-Trust Act, and subsequently had fired the Negroes. . . .

1936

. . . An average dwelling unit for a Negro family had 3 rooms; for a white family, 5 to 6 rooms.

A survey of housing in four small Southern cities among non-relief families found that 60% of white dwellings had hot and cold water in kitchen and bathroom. Only 10% of the Negro dwellings had no indoor water supply, but more than 60% had no indoor water supply for the kitchen. More than 75% had no indoor water supply for the bathroom. Of the white dwellings 88% had a drain in the kitchen sink, but only 26% of the Negroes had drains.

The National Health Survey revealed that 73% of white families and only 9% of Negro families in cities of less than 10,000 had indoor flush toilets. . . .

The platform of the Democratic, Prohibition, Socialist Labor and Union parties made no mention of the Negro. 15

At the Democratic National Convention, "Cotton Ed" Smith, South Carolina Senator, and Mayor Burnet Maybank of Charleston walked out while a Negro minister was opening a session with a prayer. Smith said he would not support "any political organization that looks upon the Negro and caters to him as a political and social equal." Smith later walked out on a speech of Negro Congressman Mitchell of Illinois. The South Carolina delegation officially protested the presence of Negroes. . . .

Eight Negroes were lynched in this year.

In the 1934 case of *Brown, Ellington, Sheilds v. State of Mississippi,* three Negro farm laborers had been sentenced to death for murder. The only evidence was a confession by Ellington made under torture. When asked how severely he had whipped Ellington, the deputy sheriff stated, "Not too much for a Negro; not as much as I would have done if it were left to me." The convictions were upheld by the Mississippi Supreme Court, but the NAACP brought the case to the U.S. Supreme Court, where the conviction was reversed. . . .

1937

In contrast to only 18% of white males, 26% of all Negro males were unemployed. 33% of Negro females were unemployed, as against 24% of white females. Of the male non-white labor force in Northern states 39% was unemployed. . . .

By this year, the Housing Division of the Public Works Administration had built 21,319 units in 49 projects. Of these 14 projects were for Negroes only, 17 were integrated. Negroes occupied 7,507 units, about a third of the total. Rents, however, were high, shutting out the Negro who could not pay $24 month for three rooms. . . . 20

1938

. . . While 9.8% of Federal employees were Negro, with few exceptions they held jobs as postal clerks, mailmen, unskilled laborers, and janitors. . . .

In Birmingham, Ala., Negroes and whites were segregated in the state relief offices. . . .

1939

. . . In July, the Ku Klux Klan in Greenville, S.C., issued a statement warning: "The Klan will ride again if Greenville Negroes continue to register and vote."

The Ku Klux Klan burned 25 crosses and paraded through the Negro section of Miami, Fla., the night before a municipal election carrying Negro effigies with signs saying "This Nigger Tried to Vote." Despite this, 1,000 of 1,500 registered Negroes voted the next day, led by Sam Solomon, a Negro businessman.

In this year two Negroes were lynched.   25

In April, Mississippi Senator Theodore C. Bilbo introduced a back-to-Africa bill in the Senate. . . .

In 13 Southern states, only 99 of the 774 public libraries were open to Negroes. . . .

1940

. . . Life expectancy of white males in the U.S. was 62.1 years, and for non-white males, 51.5 years; for white females, 66.6 years, and for non-white females, 54.9 years.

The infant mortality rate per 1,000 live births was 73.8 for Negroes and 43.2 for whites. . . .

In the border cities of St. Louis, Baltimore, and Washington, D.C., Negroes   30
were virtually excluded from the major part of the city. Most lived in areas which were 75–90% Negro.

In the school year 1939–40, in 9 Southern states, per capita expenditure for public education for Negroes was $18.82; for whites, $58.69. In Mississippi, 5 times as much was spent per white child as per Negro child. In Louisiana, Alabama and Georgia, somewhat over 3 times as much was spent for white children as for Negro children. . . .

Percentages of distribution for male Negro employment in the South were: professional, technical, etc., 1.6%; managers, officials, proprietors, 0.9%; clerical workers, 1.2%; craftsmen and foremen, 3.6%; operators, 10.9%; service workers, 11.2%; non-farm laborers, 20.6%; total non-farm, 50%; farmers and farm workers, 50%. The percentages for Negro females in Southern states were: professional and technical, 4.4%; managers, officials, proprietors, 0.6%; clerical and sales, 0.9%; craftsmen and foremen, 0.1%; operatives, 5%; service workers, 58%; service workers other than household, 8.9%; non-farm laborers, 0.9%; total non-farm, 79.6%; farm and farm workers, 20.4%.

Distribution of Negro workers among various types of occupations in the U.S. exclusive of the South was: professional and technical: male 3.1%, female 3.7%; managers, officials, proprietors: male 2.8%, female 1.1%; clerical and sales: male 5.6%, female 3%; craftsmen and foremen: male 7.7%, female 0.3%; operatives: male 19.6%, female 10.6%; service workers, private household: male 32.6%, female 64.6%; non-farm laborers: male 24.5%, female 0.8%; total non-farm: male 95.9%, female 99.8%; farm and farm workers: male 4.1%, female 0.2%. . . .

In October, President Roosevelt announced that Negro strength in the Army would be in proportion to the Negro percentage of the total population; the Negro groups would be organized in every major branch of the service, combatant as well as noncombatant; that Negroes would have the opportunity to become officers and attend Officers Training Schools; that Negroes would be trained as pilots, mechanics, and technical aviation specialists. However, Negroes and whites would not be mingled in the same regiments because that would "produce situations destructive to morale and detrimental to the preparation for national defense."

This year four Negroes were lynched. 35

In Brownsville, Tex., seven prominent Negroes were run out of town, and Ebert Williams, an NAACP leader, was murdered. These men had been leading a voting drive.

An Atlanta, Ga., ordinance segregated public parks except for "so much of Grant Park as is occupied by the zoo."

Atlanta also passed a city ordinance requiring Jim Crow taxis, with different colored signs to indicate the race they served. It required that white drivers carry white passengers, and Negro drivers carry Negro passengers.

A survey made by the Southern Regional Council indicated that only about 2% of the Negroes of voting age in 12 Southern states qualified to vote under the state election laws.

Only 5% of Southern Negroes of voting age were registered to vote. Of a 40 population of 3,651,256 Negroes, 80,000 to 90,000 voted in the 1940 election in Alabama, Georgia, Mississippi, Louisiana, Florida, Texas, South Carolina, and Arkansas. . . .

1941

. . . Immediately after the bombing of Pearl Harbor, the NAACP called on all Negroes to give wholehearted support to the war effort.

A study revealed five times as many Negroes draftees as whites were rejected. It also showed that 12.3% of the Negroes were rejected for lack of 4th grade reading ability, compared with 1.1% of whites.

The NAACP protested a War Department policy that white men needed a score of 15 on the Army Intelligence Test, while Negroes were required to score 39 to be admitted to the service.

By Nov. 30, there were 97,725 Negroes in the regular Army. During World War II, Negro anti-aircraft units fought in Burma, the Ryukyus, Normandy, Italy, and North Africa. Negro engineer troops helped to build the Ledo Road in Burma, the Stilwell Road in China, and the Alcan Highway in Alaska and Canada. Negro transport units were found supplying all battle fronts.

In December, Gen. George C. Marshall wrote to Secretary of War Stimson: 45 "The settlement of vexing racial problems cannot be permitted to complicate the tremendous task of the War Department, and thereby jeopardize discipline and morale."

The Department of War announced the formation of the first Army Air Corps squadron for Negroes on Jan. 16, one day after a Howard University student, Yancey Williams, filed suit against the Secretary of War to force consideration of his application to be a flying cadet in the Army Air Corps.

Negroes in the Navy were allowed to serve only as mess attendants and stewards. However, several noncombatant Negroes demonstrated such heroism under fire that they were awarded the Navy Cross or the Bronze Star medal.

Negro soldiers training in the South were subjected to discriminatory treatment throughout the entire World War II period. In Alexandria, La., 28 Negroes were shot down by white civilians and officers; race riots broke out in the Mobile Naval Yard, Fort Bragg, (N.C.), Camp Davis, and other Army camps.

In this year 4 Negroes were lynched.

More than 100 Negro officers were locked in the stockade at Freeman Field,   50
Ind., for entering a white-only officers' club. . . .

1942

. . . In Detroit, on Feb. 28, 1,200 persons armed with knives, clubs, rifles, and shotguns gathered to prevent three Negro families from moving into the 200-unit Sojourner Truth settlement, designated by the U.S. Housing Authority as Negro housing. The *New York Times* reported that scores of Negroes and whites were injured as police tried three times to disperse the crowd with tear gas. Shots were fired. About 18 people were taken to hospitals, and 104 rioters were arrested. Mayor Jeffries ordered the moving halted. Occupancy of the homes by Negroes was postponed until April, when 12 families moved in with 800 state troopers standing guard.

Six Negroes were lynched in this year.

Roland Haynes, a pioneer Negro concert singer who in the 1920s had been one of the foremost singers in the U.S., was struck by a policeman and taken to the city jail of Rome, Ga., because he spoke up for his wife when she sat in one of the "white places" in a shoe store.

The local office of the Federal Employment Service in Portsmouth, Va., in its advertising for workers specified that Negroes could apply only for unskilled and domestic jobs. . . .

1943

. . . In Detroit, in the spring, 26,000 white workers struck the Packard Motor   55
Plant in protest over the employment of Negroes. Walter White of the NAACP reported hearing one man scream to the assembly of strikers: "I'd rather see Hitler and Hirohito win the war than work beside a nigger on the assembly line." The riot began with a fistfight between a Negro and a white on the bridge leading from Belle Isle Park to the city. Rumors spread among both communities of various atrocities. White mobs attacked Negroes, dragging them from cars and entering Negro movie theaters. Negroes retaliated, smashing white-owned shops in Detroit's ghetto, Paradise Valley. In one day, 34 persons were killed. Of the Negroes killed, 17 were killed by the police. On the second day, at Walter White's request, President Roosevelt declared a Federal state of emergency and sent in 6,000 Federal troops and state troopers who established an uneasy peace. The NAACP set up relief headquarters, and Walter White remarked that the Negroes looked like the "bombed-out victims of Nazi terror in Europe." Thurgood Marshall reported on the looting and destruction of Negro property by the Detroit police, but no action was taken.

On May 25, a race riot began at a Mobile, Ala., shipyard when Negro workers were upgraded. Gov. Chauncey Sparks of Alabama ordered 7 companies of state guardsmen to be on the alert. Of the 8 men injured at the Atlanta Drydock & Shipbuilding Co., 7 were Negroes. The disturbance began when Negro welders were assigned to work on the same job with white welders. Police finally put down the riot, and the plant resumed operation after 7,000 Negroes were sent home from their jobs at the plant and throughout the city. . . .

In August, in Harlem, a Negro woman, Margie Polite, argued with a white policeman. A Negro soldier objected to the way the policeman spoke to her, and to his saying that she would be arrested for disorderly conduct. The policeman allegedly was knocked down by the soldier and, fearing a further attack, shot him. The woman then ran down the street screaming that the soldier had been killed. He had in fact only been wounded. A riot ensued. It took, according to the *New York Times*, 8,000 State Guard troops, 1,500 civilian volunteers (mostly Negro), and 6,600 members of the city police, military police and civil patrol units to quell the riot. Five persons were killed and 400 injured. Hundreds of stores were wrecked and looted. Property damage was estimated as high as $5 million. About 500 people were arrested, all Negroes, 100 of them women. The dead were all Negroes, and all but approximately 40 policemen of the injured.

William H. Hastie, a Negro civilian aide to Secretary of War Stimson, resigned on Jan. 6 in protest over continued segregation of training facilities in the Air Force and the Army. A few weeks later the Air Force announced a program for the expansion of Negro pilot training with Negroes being accepted "throughout the entire technical training command as well as at the Air Force Officers Training School at Miami, Fla.". . .

1944

. . . When Secretary of War Stimson was questioned about the use of Negro combat units for labor, he wrote: "It so happens that a relatively large percentage of the Negroes inducted in the Army have fallen within lower educational qualifications, and many Negro units accordingly have been unable to master efficiently the techniques of modern weapons." Stimson further stated: "I do not believe that they [the Negro 93rd Squadron] can be turned into a really effective combat troop without all officers being white.". . .

Negroes stationed on Guam were subject to discrimination, taunts and physical violence. On Christmas Eve the situation exploded when Negro soldiers on liberty were driven out of a white recreation area by gunfire. Shooting broke out on Christmas Day, and a Negro was killed and another wounded. Mass arrests of Negroes were made, but no whites were arrested. Of the Negroes 44 were sentenced to long prison terms, but the NAACP secured their release by appeals to the President and the War Department.

At Yerba Buena, 52 Negro sailors were charged with mutiny after racial trouble. The NAACP secured their return to duty. . . .

Two Negroes were lynched in this year.

Gunnar Myrdal, in his book *American Dilemma*, wrote: "Segregation is now becoming so complete that the white Southerner practically never sees a Negro except as his servant and in other standardized and formalized caste situations.". . .

1945

. . . The 370th Negro Regiment of the U.S. Army was joined with a Japanese-American regiment and an American white regiment to make up a reconstructed 92nd Division. In April, this division fought in the Northern Appenines in Italy and moved successfully to Genoa. Though the Negro 92nd Division was plagued by difficulties and was later called by Gen. Mark Clark before a Southern audience in 1956 "the worst division I had," by July 10, 1945, its members had received 542 Bronze Stars, 82 Silver Stars, 12 Legion of Merit Awards, 2 Distinguished Service Crosses, and 1 Distinguished Service Medal.

There were 165,000 Negro enlisted men in the Navy and 53 officers. There   65
were 17,000 Negroes in the Marine Corps. About 4,000 enlisted men and 4 officers in the Coast Guard were Negroes. By the end of the year, 95% of the Negroes in the Navy were still serving as messmen. . . .

Gwendolyn Brooks, a Negro, published *A Street in Bronzeville*, her first book of poems. . . .   [1969]

THINKING ABOUT THE TEXT

1. What specific items caught your attention? How do you think a pregnant, unmarried African American woman living in Chicago in the late 1930s and 1940s might react to the events described in this selection?

2. If you were an historian, what generalizations about race relations might you draw from reading this raw data?

3. Which, if any, historical injustices should be taught in American classrooms?

WRITING ABOUT ISSUES

1. Argue that there are (or are not) contextual reasons why a mother might decide not to bring children into the world.

2. Find other poems that deal with abortion (for example, Anne Sexton's "The Abortion," and Marge Piercy's "Right to Life"), and write an essay that compares them to "The Mother."

3. Do further research on lynchings in America. Argue that these deaths should (or should not) be seen as an American holocaust.

A WEB ASSIGNMENT

Numerous Web sites address the topic of lynching in America and many include graphic photos. Visit the Web Assignments section of the *Making Literature Matter* Web site to find the link to the site associated with *Without Sanctuary*. This site also posts viewer responses. After reviewing the site, write a response you could post to it. Or, write a response that analyzes your experience of looking at the lynching postcards.

Visit www.bedfordstmartins.com/makinglitmatter

FAMILY TRAGEDY

KATE BRAVERMAN, "Pagan Night"
T. CORAGHESSAN BOYLE, "The Love of My Life"

Ambitious politicians are not the only voices extolling the virtues of family life. We have all been so socialized by millennia of images and narratives to accept the naturalness of motherhood and fatherhood that parenthood has become a concept nearly beyond critique, beyond questioning. Indeed, we sometimes look askance at those who do not accept roles as loving, supportive parents. And since babies are almost universally seen as innocent, parents who harm them are usually demonized. We don't want to know why, perhaps because we don't want to forgive.

Writers do not shy away from the dark corners of human experience, and we can profitably turn to writers like Kate Braverman and T. Coraghessan Boyle to shine the artist's light on disturbing stories of family life gone awry. In his notes on "The Love of My Life" Boyle writes that at its essence the world "remains a dark and mysterious place. I write fiction in order to address and measure my response to that darkness and that mystery." With Boyle, we can try to sort out the inevitably conflicting feelings we have about the actions of the two sets of parents in the following stories.

BEFORE YOU READ

Respond to the following statement: "Neonaticide (the killing of an infant less than a day old) has been going on for centuries. Some societies have allowed the practice if done under extreme stress. Some modern philosophers also agree with this position."

KATE BRAVERMAN
Pagan Night

Kate Braverman writes fiction and poetry that are often termed "experimental," and her readers, a continually growing group since her first publications in the 1970s, have been called a "cult audience." She defines herself as an "unrepentant feminist" and remains a child of the 1960s. A native of California, educated at Berkeley, Braverman has set her three novels in Los Angeles, and most of her work reflects her western milieu. She says that "Pagan Night" was written one summer on the Snake River in Idaho. In addition to her novels, she has published numerous essays and short stories in magazines and two volumes of short stories, Squandering the Blue *(1990) and* Small Craft Warnings *(1998). "Pagan Night," which appeared in the 1995 volume of* The Best American Short Stories, *is also included in the latter collection of Braverman's stories.*

Sometimes they called him Forest or Sky. Sometimes they called him River or Wind. Once, during a week of storms when she could not leave the van at all, not for seven consecutive days, they called him Gray. The baby with the floating name and how she carries him and he keeps crying, has one rash after another, coughs, seems to shudder and choke. It is a baby of spasms, of a twisted face turning colors. You wouldn't want to put his picture on the baby-food jar. You wouldn't want to carry his picture in your wallet, even if you had his photograph and she doesn't.

Of course, Dalton never wanted this baby. Neither did she. The baby was just something that happened and there didn't seem to be the time to make it not happen. They were on tour, two months of one-nighters between San Diego and Seattle and when it was over the band broke up. When it was over, they got drunk and sold the keyboards and video cameras for heroin. Then they were in San Francisco and she still had the apartment. Later, they had Dalton's van.

Then they had to leave San Francisco. Something about the equipment, the amplifiers Dalton insisted were his, that they had accrued to him by a process of decision and sacrifice. Then they had to wind through California with her belly already showing and all they had left were their black leather jackets and the silver-and-turquoise jewelry they had somehow acquired in Gallup or Flagstaff. Dalton kept talking about the drummer's kit, which he claimed was actually his, and they sold it in Reno and lived on the fortieth floor of an old hotel with a view of the mountains. They had room service for three weeks and by then she had stopped throwing up. After that there was more of Nevada and the van broke again on the other side of the state. There was the slow entry into Idaho, after mountains and desert and Utah and the snow had melted and then the baby they had almost forgotten about was born.

Dalton can't stand the baby crying. That's why she leaves the van, walks three miles into town along the river. When she has a dollar-fifty, she buys an espresso in the café where the waitress has heard of her band.

Sunny stays away from the van as long as she can. Sometimes someone will offer her a ride to the park or the zoo or the shopping mall and she takes it. She's let her hair grow out, the purple and magenta streaks are nearly gone, seem an accident that could have happened to anyone, a mislabeled bottle, perhaps. Dalton says it's better to blend in. He's cut his hair, too, and wears a San Diego Padres baseball cap. He says it makes him feel closer to God.

Willow. Cottonwood. Creek. Eagle. She could call the baby Willow. But Dalton refuses to give it a name. He resists the gender, refers to the baby as it, not he. Just it, the creature that makes the noise. But it doesn't cost any money. She still feeds it from her body and the rashes come and go. It's because she doesn't have enough diapers. Sunny puts suntan lotion on the baby's sores, massage oil, whatever is left in her suitcase from the other life. Once she covered the baby's rash with layers of fluorescent orange lipstick, the last of her stage makeup.

Sunny has begun to realize that if she can't keep the baby quiet, Dalton will leave her. It won't always be summer here. There will come a season when she can't just walk all day, or sit in the mall or the lobby of the granite city hall, pretending to read a newspaper. She won't be able to spend the entire winter in the

5

basement of the museum where they have built a replica of the town as it was in the beginning, with its penny-candy store and nickel barber shop and baths for a quarter. She won't be able to spend five or six months attempting to transport herself through time telepathically. She could work in the saloon, find an Indian to watch the baby. Later she could marry the sheriff.

Today, walking by the river, it occurred to Sunny that this landscape was different from any other she had known. It wasn't the punched-awake, intoxicated glow of the tropics, seductive and inflamed. It didn't tease you and make you want to die for it. That's what she thought of Hawaii. And it wasn't the rancid gleam like spoiled lemons that coated everything in a sort of bad childhood waxy veneer flashback. That's what she thought of Los Angeles where they had lived for two years. In Los Angeles, afternoon smelled of ash and some enormous August you could not placate or forget. Los Angeles air reminded her of what happened to children in foster homes at dusk when they took their clothes off, things that were done in stucco added-on garages with ropes and pieces of metal and the freeway rushing in the background like a cheap sound track. It was in sync, but it had no meaning.

This Idaho was an entirely separate area of the spectrum. There was something unstable about it, as if it had risen from a core of some vast, failed caution. It was the end of restlessness. It was what happened when you stopped looking over your shoulder. It was what happened when you dared to catch your breath, when you thought you were safe.

Sunny feels there is some mean streak to this still raw, still frontier, place. 10
This land knows it gets cold, winter stays too long, crops rot, you starve. This land knows about wind, how after storms the clouds continue to assemble every afternoon over the plain, gather and recombine and rain again and this can go on for weeks. Her shoes are always damp. Her feet are encased in white blisters. Always, the thunderheads are congregating and mating and their spawn is a cold rain.

Somedays the clouds are in remission, ringing the plain but staying low. On such afternoons, the three of them go down to the Snake River. They follow a dirt road to another dirt road and they've been instructed where to turn, near the hit-by-lightning willow. They park on a rise above the channel. Dalton leaves his guitar in the van and padlocks it, walks ahead of her and the baby with the fishing pole over his shoulder. They walk beneath black branches, find the path of smooth rocks down to the bank leading to a railroad bridge. It's a trestle over the Snake made from railroad ties with gaps between them and the tracks running down the center. This is how they cross the Snake, reach the other bank where the fishing is supposed to be good. There are tiny grassy islands Dalton can roll up his black jeans and wade out to. Dalton traded somebody in town for a fly-fishing rod. He probably traded drugs for the rod, though she realizes she hasn't seen her black leather jacket for more than a week.

On Sundays yellow with orioles and tiger monarchs and a sun that turns the grasses soft, Dalton takes them fishing on the far bank of the river. One late afternoon he caught four trout. Sunny could see their rainbows when the sun struck their skin. They looked sewed with red sequins. They were supposed to be sixteen inches. That was the rule for the South Fork of the Snake. Their trout were smaller, seven and eight inches, but they kept them anyway, cooked them on a stick over a fire they made near the van. Dalton said the eyes were the best part and he gave her one and it was white as a pried-open moon and she ate it.

Now she is walking into a yellow that makes her feel both restless and invigorated. A yellow of simultaneity and symbols and some arcane celebration she can vaguely sense. When she ate the trout eyes, they were like crisp white stones. She thought of rituals, primitive people, the fundamental meaning of blood. If one mastered these elements, it might be possible to see better in the dark. She shakes her head as if to clear it, but nothing changes. Her entire life is a network of intuitions, the beginning of words, like neon and dome, pine, topaz, shadow, but then the baby starts crying.

Sunny knows it's all a matter of practice, even silence and erasure and absence. What it isn't is also a matter of practice. In the same way you can take piano or voice and train yourself to recognize and exploit your range, you can also teach yourself not to speak, not to remember. That's why when Dalton asks what's she thinking, she says, "Nothing." It's a kind of discipline. What she's really thinking about is what will happen when summer is over. What will happen if she can't make the baby stop crying?

Sometimes when she is frightened, it calms her to think about Marilyn Monroe. Sunny knows all about Marilyn's childhood, the foster homes, the uncles who fondled her breasts, kissed her seven-year-old nipples, and they got hard. Then Marilyn knew she was a bad girl. She would always be a bad girl. It was like being at a carnival, a private carnival, just for her. There were balloons and streamers, party hats and birthday cakes with chocolate frosting and her name written in a neon pink. And no one could tell her no. She had liked to think about Marilyn Monroe when they were driving in the van between gigs. The band was in its final incarnation then. Sunny was already pregnant and it was called Pagan Night.

When Dalton asks her what she's thinking and she says, "Nothing," she is really imagining winter and how she is certain there won't be enough to eat. Dalton says he'll shoot a cow. There are cows grazing outside of town, off half the dirt roads and along the banks of the river. Or he'll shoot a deer, an elk, he'll trap rabbits. He's been talking to people in town, at the Rio Bar. He's traded something for the fly-fishing rig, but he still has both guns and the rifle. He'll never trade the weapons, not even for heroin, even if they could find any here.

Today, on this cool morning, Sunny has walked from the river to the zoo. Admission is one dollar, but the woman in the booth knows her and has started to simply wave her in.

Sunny passes through a gate near a willow and she would like to name the baby Willow. It would be an omen and it would survive winter. Then she is entering the zoo, holding her baby without a name. She sits with her baby near the swan pond until someone gives her a quarter, a sandwich, a freshly purchased bag of popcorn. They simply hand it to her.

She has memorized each animal, bird, and fish in this miniature zoo. The birds stand by mossy waterfalls of the sort she imagines adorn the swimming pools of movie stars. She sits nursing her baby that she is pretending is named

15

Willow. If anyone asks, and she knows no one will, she is prepared to say, His name is Willow.

Later, she stands in a patch of sun by an exhibit featuring a glassed-in bluish pool that should contain a penguin or a seal, but is empty. It smells derelict, harsh and sour with something like the residue of trapped wind and the final thoughts of small mammals as they chew off their feet and bleed to death. You can walk down a flight of stairs and look through the glass, but nothing is swimming. She knows. She has climbed down twice.

Sunny likes to look at what isn't there, in the caged water whipped by sun. This is actually the grotto that is most full, with its battered streams of light like hieroglyphics, a language in flux, lost in shifting ripples.

She pauses in front of the golden eagle. It will not look at her, even when she whistles. The information stenciled to the cage says the golden eagle can live thirty years, longer than many movie stars, longer than Hendrix and Janis and Jim Morrison and James Dean. This particular bird will probably outlive her.

Sunny is thinking about how hungry she is, when someone offers her half a peanut butter and jelly sandwich. Actually, the woman has her child do this, reach out a baby arm to her as if she is now some declawed beast you could let your kid near.

Her own baby is wrapped in a shawl, the same shawl she had once laid across the sofa in the living room of her apartment in San Francisco. She had gone there to study modern dancing, tap, and ballet. Her father had wanted her to go to nursing school. If she went to nursing school, her father could believe she had finally forgotten. He could conclude that she was well and whole, and he could sleep without pills. His ulcer would disappear. He could take communion again.

Sunny took singing lessons and began to meet men with rock 'n' roll bands. Nursing school became white and distant. It became a sort of moon you could put between your teeth and swallow. She stopped envisioning herself in a starched cotton uniform with a stethoscope around her neck. What she wanted now was to smoke grass and hash and opium and stare out the window at Alcatraz. What she wanted to do was sniff powder drawn in lines across a wide square of mirror she kept on the side of the sofa, like a sort of magic screen where you could watch your face change forever.

Now, at the zoo, she stands on the wood slats surrounding the fish pond filled with keepers, twenty- and twenty-five- and thirty-inch rainbow trout. This is what keepers look like. On yellow Sundays, she and Dalton and the baby walk across the railroad trestle over the Snake River. But Dalton will never catch a fish this big.

She was afraid the first time they crossed the bridge. Dalton had to grab her hand. He hadn't touched her body since the baby was born. He had to pull her along. The bridge was higher than she had thought. The river was rushing underneath like a sequence of waves, but faster and sharper, without breath or cycles, and she was holding the baby. That day she was secretly calling the baby Sunday. And she was cradling Sunday with one arm and Dalton was holding her other hand, pulling her through the yellow. He was also holding the fishing rod he'd somehow procured at the Rio Bar, traded somebody something for, she is beginning to think it was her black leather jacket with the studs on the cuffs, the special studs sewed on by a woman who claimed she was a gypsy in Portland.

Dalton must think she won't need her leather jacket in winter. He isn't considering what she'll need in winter. Maybe they won't still be in Idaho. Maybe they won't still be together. And the bridge was wider than she had at first imagined. It was like a pier with its set of two railroad tracks down the center, one thinner, the other fatter, one unused set covered with rust. The bridge was made from railroad ties and there were gaps between them where a foot could get caught, something small could fall through. Dalton said, "Make a pattern. Step every other one. Don't look down." That's what she did, stepped every other one, didn't look down, but still she could hear the river in a kind of anguish beneath her and she was shaking.

"It's an abandoned bridge, isn't it?" she asked Dalton.

The first few times he said yes, but when they had crossed the fourth time, he said no. She stopped, found herself staring into sun. "What do you mean?" she demanded.

"Look at the rails. The larger set are clean. Trains do this." He pointed at the tracks. "Or they'd be covered with rust."

"What if the train came now? As we were crossing?" she finally asked.

"There are beams every twenty feet." Dalton pointed to a kind of metal girder. "We'd hang on the side until it passed."

She tries to imagine herself standing on the girder, holding the baby which in her mind is named Sunday in one of her arms. She cannot conceive of this. Instead she remembers, suddenly, a story Dalton once told her years ago, before they had gone on the road, when they first recited their secret information to each other, their collection of shame, where they were truly from, what had happened, what was irrevocable.

Dalton told her about a night in high school when he had been drinking beer with his friends. Perhaps it was spring. They had been drinking since dawn and now it was after midnight. It was Ohio. That's where Dalton was from. His friends had wandered down to the train station. His best friend had tried to hop a train. Johnny Mohawk. That's what they called him, Mohawk, because he said he was part Indian. Johnny Mohawk tried to hop a train and fell. It ran over him, amputating both legs, his right arm, and half of his left.

"He was so drunk, that's what saved him," Dalton explained. It must have been later. They were riding in a tour bus. They had an album out and the company had given them a roadie, a driver, and a bus. Outside was neon and wind and houses you didn't want to live in. "He was so drunk, he didn't feel it," Dalton was saying. "If he'd been more awake, the shock would have killed him."

Dalton glanced out the window, at some in-between stretch of California where there were waist-high grasses and wild flowers and a sense of too much sun, even in the darkness. She asked him what happened. She tried to imagine Johnny Mohawk, but she could not. Her mind refused to accommodate the brutal lack of symmetry, would produce only words like tunnel and agony, suffocate and scream. Even if she had gone to nursing school, even if she went right now, enrolled in the morning, she could do nothing about Johnny Mohawk. It would always be too late.

30

35

"It was the best thing ever happened to him," Dalton said. "He was on his way to becoming a professional drunk. Like his father, like his uncles and inbred cousins. After the accident, he got a scholarship to State. They gave him a tutor and a special car. Now he's an engineer for an oil company."

Sunny thinks about Johnny Mohawk as she stands in the zoo, in front of a grotto with grassy sides and a sleeping male and female lion. Their cage seems too small to contain them if they wanted to do anything other than sleep in the damp green grass. She wonders what would happen if she fell in, over the low metal bar.

Near her, a pregnant woman with three blond daughters, each with a differ-   40
ent colored ribbon in their long yellow hair, tells her two-year-old, "Don't you climb up on that bar now. You fall in, there'd be no way to get you out. That hungry old lion would eat you right up."

Sunny feels the baby in her arms, how heavy it is, how it could so easily slide from her, through the bar, into the grassy grotto. She could never retrieve it. No one would expect her to.

Then she is walking past the one zebra. When Dalton asks her if she wants to talk about anything, she shakes her head, no. She is considering how filled each no is, glittering and yellow. Each no is a miniature carnival, with curled smiles and balloons on strings and a profusion of names for babies. And in this no are syllables like willow and cottonwood and shadow and Johnny Mohawk. And in this no is the railroad trestle above one hundred thousand rainbow trout.

Sunny's favorite exhibit is the snow leopard. It is strange that a zoo in a tiny town should have such an animal. They are so rare. She reads what the snow leopard eats, mammals and birds. Its social life is solitary. How long does it live? Twenty-five years. Not quite long enough to see its first record go platinum. And it isn't really asleep on the green slope behind its grid of bars as much as it is simply turned away. Perhaps it is thinking about the past, and on its lip is something that isn't quite a smile. Or perhaps he is simply listening to birds.

There are always birds when they cross the railroad trestle on Sunday, the Snake below them, the bald eagles and blue herons and swallows and robins, orioles and magpies, in the air near their shoulders. And there is no schedule for the train. She's called Union Pacific five times, waited for the man in charge to come back from vacation, to come back from the flu, to be at his desk, and there is no way to predict when the train runs over this particular trestle. It's a local. It gets put together at the last moment, no one knows when.

When they cross the bridge on Sunday, she is obsessively listening for trains.   45
And there are so many birds, fat robins, unbelievably red, and orioles, the yellow of chalk from fourth grade when she got an A and her teacher let her write the entire spelling list for the week on the blackboard. And ducks and Canadian geese and loons, all of them stringing their syllables across the afternoon, hanging them near her face like a kind of party streamer. The baby is named Sunday or Sometimes and she feels how heavy it is, how it could just drop from her arms.

It's become obvious that these fishing Sundays are not about catching trout. It's a practice for something else entirely, for leaving, for erasure, silence, and absence. She understands now. It's the end of July. She won't be able to feed the baby from her body indefinitely or walk through town all day, looking for trash cans where she can deposit the diapers she has used over and over again.

Now it is time to rehearse. They are involved in a new show with an agenda they don't mention. It's a rehearsal for abandoning the baby. She practices leaving it on the bank, walking fifty steps away, smoking a cigarette. Then she rushes back to retrieve it, to press it against her. If she simply took a slightly longer path from the bank, permitted herself to smoke a joint, a third or fourth cigarette, she might not remember exactly where she placed the baby, not with all the foliage, the vines and brush, bushes and trees, the whole bank an ache of greenery. Something could have interceded, a sudden aberration in the river current or perhaps a hawk. She wouldn't be blamed.

In the children's petting zoo, a gray rabbit mounts a white one. Another white rabbit eats from a bowl. They eat and mate, eat and mate. In the winter, Dalton says he'll shoot a deer. He's made a deal with somebody at the Rio Bar, something about sharing and storing. There are always cattle, fish, rabbits, beavers, and otters that can be trapped.

During the day, Dalton says he's working on songs. He still has both guitars. He can only write music when the baby isn't crying or coughing. She wants to name the baby Music or Tears. Once she tells Dalton she wants to name the baby Bay. She remembers the apartment they had with the view of the bridge, the way at midnight the wind felt like a scalded blue. It was when everything seemed simultaneously anesthetized and hot. It was a moment she remembers as happy.

"It's not time to name it," Dalton said. He was strumming his twelve-string. 50 He said many African tribes didn't name a baby until it had survived a year. Dalton looked at her and smiled. His lips reminded her of Marilyn Monroe.

That's when she realized each day would have to be distinct and etched. She licks the baby's face. She sits on a bench in the sun at the zoo by a pond with a mossy waterfall in the center. There are swans in this pond. She closes her eyes and smells the baby and decides to name him Swan. She kisses his cheek and whispers in his ear, "Your name is Swan. Your name is Moss. Your name is Bye-Bye."

"What are you thinking?" Dalton asks. It was during the storm two weeks ago. He was drinking tequila. Rain struck the van and she thought of rocks and bullets and time travel.

"Nothing," she replied.

Wind. Hidden networks. The agenda that sparks. You know how night feels without candles, without light bulbs, maps, schedules. This is what we do not speak of Bye-bye-bye, baby. Bye-bye-bye.

Everyday, Dalton says he's going to write songs while she is gone. He has a 55 joint in his mouth, curled on his side in the back of the van on a ridge above the Snake River where they now live. He has a bottle of vodka tucked into his belt. The vodka is gone when she comes back. Sunny has to knock again and again on the side of the van, has to kick it with her foot, has to shout his name, until he wakes up.

Each day must be separate, an entity, like a species, a snow leopard, a zebra, or a rainbow trout. Each one with a distinct evolution and morphology, niches, complex accidents. Last Sunday, she smoked a joint and drank tequila. Then they crossed the river on the railroad ties. She has a pattern, left foot, skip one with the right, left foot, skip one with the right, don't look down.

She knows it will happen on a Sunday, perhaps next Sunday. Dalton will say, "Come over, look at this."

"I can't. I'm feeding the baby," she will answer.

"Put it down a second," he'll say. "You've got to see this."

She'll place the baby in the center of soft weeds: She'll follow the sound of 60 his voice, find Dalton on the bank with a great trout, twenty inches, thirty inches long. It will be their keeper and she will bend down, help him pull it in. Her feet will get wet. She will use her hat for a net, her red hat that says Wyoming Centennial 1990. The seconds will elongate, the minutes will spread into an afternoon, with no one counting or keeping track. When they've pulled the trout in, when they've finished the tequila, it will be dark. They will begin searching for the baby, but there will be only shadow. No one could say they were at fault. No one could say anything. No one knows about them or the baby, and the van has got at least five thousand miles left in it. They could be in New York or Florida in two days.

Perhaps it will be a Sunday when they are crossing the bridge. She'll be holding the baby named Sometimes or Swan or Willow, and they'll have to leap onto the steel girders as the train rushes by. The baby will drop from her arms into the Snake and it will be taken on the current like Moses.

They will never mention the falling. They will not speak of it, not once. It will just be something caught in the edge of their smile, like a private carnival that went through town and maybe you saw it once and too briefly and then it was gone.

She knows Dalton believes they are purer, more muscle and bone, closer to an archetypal winter beyond artifice. That was part of why they called the band Pagan Night. They are animals, barbarians, heathens. They are savage and recognize this, its possibilities and what it costs. In China and India, girl children are often drowned at birth. There are fashions of surviving famines engraved on the nerves.

Maybe this Sunday they will be crossing the bridge when the train erupts from a spoil of foliage and shadow, willows and heron and orioles. Dalton will have left his guitar in the van, padlocked with his paperback myths of primitive people. Perhaps it will be a Sunday after Dalton returned from the Rio Bar with heroin. They will have cooked it up and had it that night, all night, and the next day, all day, until it was finished and there was nothing left, not even in the cotton in the spoon.

When she stands on the Sunday railroad trestle, she will think about 65 ineluctable trajectories. There is a destiny to the direction and journey of all objects, stars and birds, babies and stones and rivers. Who can explain how or why that snow leopard came from Asia to reside in an obsolete grotto in a marginal farming town among barley and potato fields in southern Idaho? What shaped such a voyage, what miscalculations, what shift of wind or currents, what failure of which deity?

Sunny knows exactly what she will be thinking when it happens. There are always acres of sun and their fading. It is all a sequence of erasures and absences. Who is to say flesh into water or flesh into rock is not a form of perfection? What of Moses on the river with an ineluctable destiny to be plucked from reeds by a princess? Perhaps on some fishing Sunday when the baby is named Swallow or Tiger and falls from her arms, someone on a distant bank will look up and say they saw the sudden ascension of a god.   [1995]

THINKING ABOUT THE TEXT

1. Do you think Sunny will eventually abandon her baby? If so, is her love for Dalton the main reason? How would you describe her decision-making process?

2. Is Sunny's behavior understandable — that is, can you articulate what makes her tick, her motivations, her sense of herself? Does an analysis of her character make her more or less sympathetic to you?

3. Does the band's name have significance? Can you give specific examples of the author's attitude toward either Dalton or Sunny?

4. Do you see any significance in the story ending on a bridge? In calling the baby "Forest or Sky"? In mentioning Marilyn Monroe, the snow leopard, and Moses?

5. What has gone wrong in the lives of these young parents to lead them to this situation? Is society at fault? Could someone intervene in their lives to make a difference?

T. CORAGHESSAN BOYLE
The Love of My Life

T. Coraghessan Boyle, who says that his middle name is pronounced with the stress on the second syllable and that his friends call him Tom, has written fourteen books of fiction, the most recent of which are Friend of the Earth *(2000) and* After the Plague *(2001). After graduating from SUNY, Potsdam, with a B.A. in English and history, Boyle taught for several years at the high school that he had attended as a teenager, though he continued to follow his interests in creative writing. In the early 1970s, he attended the prestigious University of Iowa Writers' Workshop and went on to receive a Ph.D. in nineteenth-century British literature from Iowa in 1977. His list of awards and publications is long; most recently, he received the O. Henry Award 2001 for the short story reprinted here, "The Love of My Life." Boyle says that the story is based on a news event of a few years ago that "should break your heart. I know it broke mine."*

They wore each other like a pair of socks. He was at her house, she was at his. Everywhere they went — to the mall, to the game, to movies and shops and the classes that structured their days like a new kind of chronology — their fingers were entwined, their shoulders touching, their hips joined in the slow triumphant sashay of love. He drove her car, slept on the couch in the family room at her parents' house, played tennis and watched football with her father on the big, thirty-six-inch TV in the kitchen. She went shopping with his mother and hers, a triumvirate of tastes, and she would have played tennis with his father, if it came to it, but his father was dead. "I love you," he told her, because he did, because there was no feeling like this, no triumph, no high—it was like being immortal and unconquerable, like floating. And a hundred times a day she said it, too: "I love you. I love you."

They were together at his house one night when the rain froze on the streets and sheathed the trees in glass. It was her idea to take a walk and feel it in their hair and on the glistening shoulders of their parkas, an other-worldly drumming of pellets flung down out of the troposphere, alien and familiar at the same time, and they glided the length of the front walk and watched the way the power lines bellied and swayed. He built a fire when they got back, while she towelled her hair and made hot chocolate laced with Jack Daniel's. They'd rented a pair of slasher movies for the ritualized comfort of them—"Teens have sex," he said, "and then they pay for it in body parts"—and the maniac had just climbed out of the heating vent, with a meat hook dangling from the recesses of his empty sleeve, when the phone rang.

It was his mother, calling from the hotel room in Boston where she was curled up—shacked up?—for the weekend with the man she'd been dating. He tried to picture her, but he couldn't. He even closed his eyes a minute, to concentrate, but there was nothing there. Was everything all right? she wanted to know. With the storm and all? No, it hadn't hit Boston yet, but she saw on the Weather Channel that it was on its way. Two seconds after he hung up—before she could even hit the Start button on the VCR—the phone rang again, and this time it was her mother. Her mother had been drinking. She was calling from the restaurant, and China could hear a clamor of voices in the background. "Just stay put," her mother shouted into the phone. "The streets are like a skating rink. Don't you even think of getting in that car."

Well, she wasn't thinking of it. She was thinking of having Jeremy to herself, all night, in the big bed in his mother's room. They'd been having sex ever since they started going together at the end of their junior year, but it was always sex in the car or sex on a blanket or the lawn, hurried sex, nothing like she wanted it to be. She kept thinking of the way it was in the movies, where the stars ambushed each other on beds the size of small planets and then did it again and again until they lay nestled in a heap of pillows and blankets, her head on his chest, his arm flung over her shoulder, the music fading away to individual notes plucked softly on a guitar and everything in the frame glowing as if it had been sprayed with liquid gold. That was how it was supposed to be. That was how it was going to be. At least for tonight.

She'd been wandering around the kitchen as she talked, dancing with the phone in an idle slow saraband, watching the frost sketch a design on the window over the sink, no sound but the soft hiss of the ice pellets on the roof, and now she pulled open the freezer door and extracted a pint box of ice cream. She was in her socks, socks so thick they were like slippers, and a pair of black leggings under

5

an oversize sweater. Beneath her feet, the polished floorboards were as slick as the sidewalk outside, and she liked the feel of that, skating indoors in her big socks. "Uh-huh," she said into the phone. "Uh-huh. Yeah, we're watching a movie." She dug a finger into the ice cream and stuck it in her mouth.

"Come on," Jeremy called from the living room, where the maniac rippled menacingly over the Pause button. "You're going to miss the best part."

"O.K., Mom, O.K.," she said into the phone, parting words, and then she hung up. "You want ice cream?" she called, licking her finger.

Jeremy's voice came back at her, a voice in the middle range, with a congenital scratch in it, the voice of a nice guy, a very nice guy who could be the star of a TV show about nice guys: "What kind?" He had a pair of shoulders and pumped-up biceps, too, a smile that jumped from his lips to his eyes, and close-cropped hair that stood up straight off the crown of his head. And he was always singing — she loved that — his voice so true he could do any song, and there was no lyric he didn't know, even on the oldies station. She scooped ice cream and saw him in a scene from last summer, one hand draped casually over the wheel of his car, the radio throbbing, his voice raised in perfect synch with Billy Corgan's, and the night standing still at the end of a long dark street overhung with maples.

"Chocolate. Swiss-chocolate almond."

"O.K.," he said, and then he was wondering if there was any whipped cream, or maybe hot fudge — he was sure his mother had a jar stashed away somewhere, *Look behind the mayonnaise on the top row* — and when she turned around he was standing in the doorway.

She kissed him — they kissed whenever they met, no matter where or when, even if one of them had just stepped out of the room, because that was love, that was the way love was — and then they took two bowls of ice cream into the living room and, with a flick of the remote, set the maniac back in motion.

It was an early spring that year, the world gone green overnight, the thermometer twice hitting the low eighties in the first week of March. Teachers were holding sessions outside. The whole school, even the halls and the cafeteria, smelled of fresh-mowed grass and the unfolding blossoms of the fruit trees in the development across the street, and students — especially seniors — were cutting class to go out to the quarry or the reservoir or to just drive the backstreets with the sunroof and the windows open wide. But not China. She was hitting the books, studying late, putting everything in its place like pegs in a board, even love, even that. Jeremy didn't get it. "Look, you've already been accepted at your first-choice school, you're going to wind up in the top ten G.P.A.-wise, and you've got four years of tests and term papers ahead of you, and grad school after that. You'll only be a high-school senior once in your life. Relax. Enjoy it. Or at least *experience* it."

He'd been accepted at Brown, his father's alma mater, and his own G.P.A. would put him in the top ten percent of their graduating class, and he was content with that, skating through his final semester, no math, no science, taking art and music, the things he'd always wanted to take but never had time for — and Lit., of course, A.P. History, and Spanish 5. *"Tú eres el amor de mi vida,"* he would tell her when they met at her locker or at lunch or when he picked her up for a movie on Saturday nights.

"*Y tú también,*" she would say, "or is it '*yo también*'?" — French was her language. "But I keep telling you it really matters to me, because I know I'll never catch Margery Yu or Christian Davenport, I mean they're a lock for val and salut, but it'll kill me if people like Kerry Sharp or Jalapy Seegrand finish ahead of me — you should know that, you of all people — "

It amazed him that she actually brought her books along when they went   15
backpacking over spring break. They'd planned the trip all winter and through the long wind tunnel that was February, packing away freeze-dried entrées, PowerBars, Gore-Tex windbreakers, and matching sweatshirts, weighing each item on a handheld scale with a dangling hook at the bottom of it. They were going up into the Catskills, to a lake he'd found on a map, and they were going to be together, without interruption, without telephones, automobiles, parents, teachers, friends, relatives, and pets, for five full days. They were going to cook over an open fire, they were going to read to each other and burrow into the double sleeping bag with the connubial zipper up the seam he'd found in his mother's closet, a relic of her own time in the lap of nature. It smelled of her, of his mother, a vague scent of her perfume that had lingered there dormant all these years, and maybe there was the faintest whiff of his father, too, though his father had been gone so long he didn't even remember what he looked like, let alone what he might have smelled like. Five days. And it wasn't going to rain, not a drop. He didn't even bring his fishing rod, and that was love.

When the last bell rang down the curtain on Honors Math, Jeremy was waiting at the curb in his mother's Volvo station wagon, grinning up at China through the windshield while the rest of the school swept past with no thought for anything but release. There were shouts and curses, T-shirts in motion, slashing legs, horns bleating from the seniors' lot, the school buses lined up like armored vehicles awaiting the invasion — chaos, sweet chaos — and she stood there a moment to savor it. "Your mother's car?" she said, slipping in beside him and laying both arms over his shoulders to pull him to her for a kiss. He'd brought her jeans and hiking boots along, and she was going to change as they drove, no need to go home, no more circumvention and delay, a stop at McDonald's, maybe, or Burger King, and then it was the sun and the wind and the moon and the stars. Five days. Five whole days.

"Yeah," he said, in answer to her question, "my mother said she didn't want to have to worry about us breaking down in the middle of nowhere — "

"So she's got your car? She's going to sell real estate in your car?"

He just shrugged and smiled. "Free at last," he said, pitching his voice down low till it was exactly like Martin Luther King's. "Thank God Almighty, we are free at last."

It was dark by the time they got to the trailhead, and they wound up camping   20
just off the road in a rocky tumble of brush, no place on earth less likely or less comfortable, but they were together, and they held each other through the damp whispering hours of the night and hardly slept at all. They made the lake by noon the next day, the trees just coming into leaf, the air sweet with the smell of the sun

in the pines. She insisted on setting up the tent, just in case — it could rain, you never knew — but all he wanted to do was stretch out on a gray neoprene pad and feel the sun on his face. Eventually, they both fell asleep in the sun, and when they woke they made love right there, beneath the trees, and with the wide blue expanse of the lake giving back the blue of the sky. For dinner, it was étouffée and rice, out of the foil pouch, washed down with hot chocolate and a few squirts of red wine from Jeremy's bota bag.

The next day, the whole day through, they didn't bother with clothes at all. They couldn't swim, of course — the lake was too cold for that — but they could bask and explore and feel the breeze out of the south on their bare legs and the places where no breeze had touched before. She would remember that always, the feel of that, the intensity of her motions, the simple unrefined pleasure of living in the moment. Wood smoke. Duelling flashlights in the night. The look on Jeremy's face when he presented her with the bag of finger-size crayfish he'd spent all morning collecting.

What else? The rain, of course. It came midway through the third day, clouds the color of iron filings, the lake hammered to iron, too, and the storm that crashed through the trees and beat at their tent with a thousand angry fists. They huddled in the sleeping bag, sharing the wine and a bag of trail mix, reading to each other from a book of Donne's love poems (she was writing a paper for Mrs. Masterson called "Ocular Imagery in the Poetry of John Donne") and the last third of a vampire novel that weighed eighteen-point-one ounces.

And the sex. They were careful, always careful — *I will never, never be like those breeders that bring their puffed-up squalling little red-faced babies to class,* she told him, and he agreed, got adamant about it, even, until it became a running theme in their relationship, the breeders overpopulating an overpopulated world and ruining their own lives in the process — but she had forgotten to pack her pills and he had only two condoms with him, and it wasn't as if there were a drugstore around the corner.

In the fall — or the end of August, actually — they packed their cars separately and left for college, he to Providence and she to Binghamton. They were separated by three hundred miles, but there was the telephone, there was e-mail, and for the first month or so there were Saturday nights in a motel in Danbury, but that was a haul, it really was, and they both agreed that they should focus on their course work and cut back to every second or maybe third week. On the day they'd left — and no, she didn't want her parents driving her up there, she was an adult and she could take care of herself — Jeremy followed her as far as the Bear Mountain Bridge and they pulled off the road and held each other till the sun fell down into the trees. She had a poem for him, a Donne poem, the saddest thing he'd ever heard. It was something about the moon. *More than moon,* that was it, lovers parting and their tears swelling like an ocean till the girl — the woman, the female — had more power to raise the tides than the moon itself, or some such. *More than moon.* That's what he called her after that, because she was white and round and getting rounder, and it was no joke, and it was no term of endearment.

She was pregnant. Pregnant, they figured, since the camping trip, and it was   25
their secret, a new constant in their lives, a fact, an inescapable fact that never
varied no matter how many home-pregnancy kits they went through. Baggy
clothes, that was the key, all in black, cargo pants, flowing dresses, a jacket even
in summer. They went to a store in the city where nobody knew them and she got
a girdle, and then she went away to school in Binghamton and he went to Providence. "You've got to get rid of it," he told her in the motel room that had become
a prison. "Go to a clinic." he told her for the hundredth time, and outside it was
raining—or, no, it was clear and cold that night, a foretaste of winter. "I'll find the
money—you know I will."

She wouldn't respond. Wouldn't even look at him. One of the *Star Wars*
movies was on TV, great flat thundering planes of metal roaring across the
screen, and she was just sitting there on the edge of the bed, her shoulders
hunched and hair hanging limp. Someone slammed a car door—two doors in
rapid succession—and a child's voice shouted, "Me! Me first!"

"China," he said. "Are you listening to me?"

"I can't," she murmured, and she was talking to her lap, to the bed, to the
floor. "I'm scared. I'm so scared." There were footsteps in the room next door,
ponderous and heavy, then the quick tattoo of the child's feet and a sudden
thump against the wall. "I don't want anyone to know," she said.

He could have held her, could have squeezed in beside her and wrapped her
in his arms, but something flared in him. He couldn't understand it. He just
couldn't. "What are you thinking? Nobody'll know. He's a doctor, for Christ's
sake, sworn to secrecy, the doctor-patient compact and all that. What are you
going to do, keep it? Huh? Just show up for English 101 with a baby on your lap
and say, 'Hi, I'm the Virgin Mary'?"

She was crying. He could see it in the way her shoulders suddenly crumpled   30
and now he could hear it, too, a soft nasal complaint that went right through him.
She lifted her face to him and held out her arms and he was there beside her,
rocking her back and forth in his arms. He could feel the heat of her face against
the hard fibre of his chest, a wetness there, fluids, her fluids. "I don't want a doctor," she said.

And that colored everything, that simple negative: life in the dorms, roommates, bars, bullshit sessions, the smell of burning leaves and the way the light
fell across campus in great wide smoking bands just before dinner, the unofficial
skateboard club, films, lectures, pep rallies, football—none of it mattered. He
couldn't have a life. Couldn't be a freshman. Couldn't wake up in the morning
and tumble into the slow steady current of the world. All he could think of was
her. Or not simply her—her and him, and what had come between them.
Because they argued now, they wrangled and fought and debated, and it was no
pleasure to see her in that motel room with the queen-size bed and the big color
TV and the soaps and shampoos they made off with as if they were treasure. She
was pig-headed, stubborn, irrational. She was spoiled, he could see that now,
spoiled by her parents and their standard of living and the socioeconomic expectations of her class—of his class—and the promise of life as you like it, an

unscrolling vista of pleasure and acquisition. He loved her. He didn't want to turn his back on her. He would be there for her no matter what, but why did she have to be so *stupid*?

Big sweats, huge sweats, sweats that drowned and engulfed her, that was her campus life, sweats and the dining hall. Her dorm mates didn't know her, and so what if she was putting on weight? Everybody did. How could you shovel down all those carbohydrates, all that sugar and grease and the puddings and nachos and all the rest, without putting on ten or fifteen pounds the first semester alone? Half the girls in the dorm were waddling around like the Doughboy, their faces bloated and blotched with acne, with crusting pimples and whiteheads fed on fat. So she was putting on weight. Big deal. "There's more of me to love," she told her roommate, "and Jeremy likes it that way. And, really, he's the only one that matters." She was careful to shower alone, in the early morning, long before the light had begun to bump up against the windows.

On the night her water broke—it was mid-December, almost nine months, as best as she could figure—it was raining. Raining hard. All week she'd been having tense rasping sotto-voce debates with Jeremy on phone—arguments, fights—and she told him that she would die, creep out into the woods like some animal and bleed to death, before she'd go to a hospital. "And what am I supposed to do?" he demanded in a high childish whine, as if he were the one who'd been knocked up, and she didn't want to hear it, she didn't.

"Do you love me?" she whispered. There was a long hesitation, a pause you could have poured all the affirmation of the world into.

"Yes," he said finally, his voice so soft and reluctant it was like the last gasp of   35
a dying old man.

"Then you're going to have to rent the motel."

"And then what?"

"Then—I don't know." The door was open, her roommate framed there in the hall, a burst of rock and roll coming at her like an assault. "I guess you'll have to get a book or something."

By eight, the rain had turned to ice and every branch of every tree was coated with it, the highway littered with glistening black sticks, no moon, no stars, the tires sliding out from under her, and she felt heavy, big as a sumo wrestler, heavy and loose at the same time. She'd taken a towel from the dorm and put it under her, on the seat, but it was a mess, everything was a mess. She was cramping. Fidgeting with her hair. She tried the radio, but it was no help, nothing but songs she hated, singers that were worse. Twenty-two miles to Danbury and the first of the contractions came like a seizure, like a knife blade thrust into her spine. Her world narrowed to what the headlights would show her.

Jeremy was waiting for her at the door to the room, the light behind him   40
a pale rinse of nothing, no smile on his face, no human expression at all. They didn't kiss—they didn't even touch—and then she was on the bed, on her back, her face clenched like a fist. She heard the rattle of the sleet at the window, the murmur of TV: *I can't let you go like this,* a man protested, and she could picture him, angular and tall, a man in a hat and overcoat in a black-and-white

world that might have been another planet, *I just can't.* "Are you —?" Jeremy's voice drifted into the mix, and then stalled. "Are you ready? I mean, is it time? Is it coming now?"

She said one thing then, one thing only, her voice as pinched and hollow as the sound of the wind in the gutters: "Get it out of me."

It took a moment, and then she could feel his hands fumbling with her sweats.

Later, hours later, when nothing had happened but pain, a parade of pain with drum majors and brass bands and penitents crawling on their hands and knees till the streets were stained with their blood, she cried out and cried out again. "It's like *Alien*," she gasped, "like that thing in *Alien* when it, it —"

"It's O.K.," he kept telling her, "it's O.K.," but his face betrayed him. He looked scared, looked as if he'd been drained of blood in some evil experiment in yet another movie, and a part of her wanted to be sorry for him, but another part, the part that was so commanding and fierce it overrode everything else, couldn't begin to be.

He was useless, and he knew it. He'd never been so purely sick at heart and   45
terrified in all his life, but he tried to be there for her, tried to do his best, and when the baby came out, the baby girl all slick with blood and mucus and the lumped white stuff that was like something spilled at the bottom of a garbage can, he was thinking of the ninth grade and how close he'd come to fainting while the teacher went around the room to prick their fingers one by one so they each could smear a drop of blood across a slide. He didn't faint now. But he was close to it, so close he could feel the room dodging away under his feet. And then her voice, the first intelligible thing she'd said in an hour: "Get rid of it. Just get rid of it."

Of the drive back to Binghamton he remembered nothing. Or practically nothing. They took towels from the motel and spread them across the seat of her car, he could remember that much . . . and the blood, how could he forget the blood? It soaked through her sweats and the towels and even the thick cotton bathmat and into the worn fabric of the seat itself. And it all came from inside her, all of it, tissue and mucus and the shining bright fluid, no end to it, as if she'd been turned inside out. He wanted to ask her about that, if that was normal, but she was asleep the minute she slid out from under his arm and dropped into the seat. If he focused, if he really concentrated, he could remember the way her head lolled against the doorframe while the engine whined and the car rocked and the slush threw a dark blanket over the windshield every time a truck shot past in the opposite direction. That and the exhaustion. He'd never been so tired, his head on a string, shoulders slumped, his arms like two pillars of concrete. And what if he'd nodded off? What if he'd gone into a skid and hurtled over an embankment into the filthy gray accumulation of the worst day of his life? What then?

She made it into the dorm under her own power, nobody even looked at her, and, no, she didn't need his help. "Call me," she whispered, and they kissed, her lips so cold it was like kissing a steak through the plastic wrap, and then he parked her car in the student lot and walked to the bus station. He made Danbury late that night, caught a ride out to the motel, and walked right through the "Do Not

Disturb" sign on the door. Fifteen minutes. That was all it took. He bundled up everything, every trace, left the key in the box at the desk, and stood scraping the ice off the windshield of his car while the night opened up above him to a black glitter of sky. He never gave a thought to what lay discarded in the Dumpster out back, itself wrapped in plastic, so much meat, so much cold meat.

He was at the very pinnacle of his dream, the river dressed in its currents, the deep hole under the cutbank, and the fish like silver bullets swarming to his bait, when they woke him—when Rob woke him, Rob Greiner, his roommate, Rob with a face of crumbling stone and two policemen there at the door behind him and the roar of the dorm falling away to a whisper. And that was strange, police-men, a real anomaly in that setting, and at first—for the first thirty seconds, at least—he had no idea what they were doing there. Parking tickets? Could that be it? But then they asked him his name, just to confirm it, joined his hands together behind his back, and fitted two loops of naked metal over his wrists, and he began to understand. He saw McCaffrey and Tuttle from across the hall staring at him as if he were Jeffrey Dahmer or something, and the rest of them, all the rest, every head poking out of every door up and down the corridor, as the police led him away.

"What's all this about?" he kept saying, the cruiser nosing through the dark streets to the station house, the man at the wheel and the man beside him as incapable of speech as the seats or the wire mesh or the gleaming black dash-board that dragged them forward into the night. And then it was up the steps and into an explosion of light, more men in uniform, stand here, give me your hand, now the other one, and then the cage and the questions. Only then did he think of that thing in the garbage sack and the sound it had made—its body had made—when he flung it into the Dumpster like a sack of flour and the lid slammed down on it. He stared at the walls, and this was a movie, too. He'd never been in trouble before, never been inside a police station, but he knew his role well enough, because he'd seen it played out a thousand times on the tube: deny everything. Even as the two detectives settled in across from him at the bare wooden table in the little box of the overlit room he was telling himself just that: *Deny it, deny it all.*

The first detective leaned forward and set his hands on the table as if he'd   50 come for a manicure. He was in his thirties, or maybe his forties, a tired-looking man with the scars of the turmoil he'd witnessed gouged into the flesh under his eyes. He didn't offer a cigarette ("I don't smoke," Jeremy was prepared to say, giv-ing them that much at least), and he didn't smile or soften his eyes. And when he spoke his voice carried no freight at all, not outrage or threat or cajolery—it was just a voice, flat and tired. "Do you know a China Berkowitz?" he said.

And she. She was in the community hospital, where the ambulance had deposited her after her roommate had called 911 in a voice that was like a bone stuck in the back of her throat, and it was raining again. Her parents were there, her mother red-eyed and sniffling, her father looking like an actor who has forgot-ten his lines, and there was another woman there, too, a policewoman. The policewoman sat in an orange plastic chair in the corner, dipping her head to the knitting in her lap. At first, China's mother had tried to be pleasant to the woman, but pleasant wasn't what the circumstances called for, and now she ignored her, because the very unpleasant fact was that China was being taken into custody as soon as she was released from the hospital.

For a long while no one said anything—everything had already been said, over and over, one long flood of hurt and recrimination—and the antiseptic silence of the hospital held them in its grip while the rain beat at the windows and the machines at the foot of the bed counted off numbers. From down the hall came a snatch of TV dialogue, and for a minute China opened her eyes and thought she was back in the dorm. "Honey," her mother said, raising a purgatorial face to her, "are you all right? Can I get you anything?"

"I need to—I think I need to pee."

"Why?" her father demanded, and it was the perfect non sequitur. He was up out of the chair, standing over her, his eyes liked cracked porcelain. "Why didn't you tell us, or at least tell your mother—or Dr. Fredman? Dr. Fredman, at least. He's been—he's like a family member, you know that, and he could have, or he would have . . . What were you *thinking*, for Christ's sake?"

Thinking? She wasn't thinking anything, not then and not now. All she wanted—and she didn't care what they did to her, beat her, torture her, drag her weeping through the streets in a dirty white dress with "Baby Killer" stitched over her breast in scarlet letters—was to see Jeremy. Just that. Because what really mattered was what he was thinking.

The food at the Sarah Barnes Cooper Women's Correctional Institute was exactly what they served at the dining hall in college, heavy on the sugars, starches, and bad cholesterol, and that would have struck her as ironic if she'd been there under other circumstances—doing community outreach, say, or researching a paper for sociology class. But given the fact that she'd been locked up for more than a month now, the object of the other girls' threats, scorn, and just plain *nastiness*, given the fact that her life was ruined beyond any hope of redemption, and every newspaper in the country had her shrunken white face plastered across its front page under a headline that screamed "MOTEL MOM," she didn't have much use for irony. She was scared twenty-four hours a day. Scared of the present, scared of the future, scared of the reporters waiting for the judge to set bail so that they could swarm all over her the minute she stepped out the door. She couldn't concentrate on the books and magazines her mother brought her, or even on the TV in the rec room. She sat in her room—it was a room, just like a dorm room, except that they locked you in at night—and stared at the walls, eating peanuts, M&M's, sunflower seeds by the handful, chewing for the pure animal gratification of it. She was putting on more weight, and what did it matter?

Jeremy was different. He'd lost everything—his walk, his smile, the muscles of his upper arms and shoulders. Even his hair lay flat now, as if he couldn't bother with a tube of gel and a comb. When she saw him at the arraignment, saw him for the first time since she'd climbed out of the car and limped into the dorm with the blood wet on her legs, he looked like a refugee, like a ghost. The room they were in—the courtroom—seemed to have grown up around them, walls, windows, benches, lights, and radiators already in place, along with the judge, the American flag, and the ready-made spectators. It was hot. People coughed into their fists and shuffled their feet, every sound magnified. The judge presided, his arms like bones twirled in a bag, his eyes searching and opaque as he peered over the top of his reading glasses.

China's lawyer didn't like Jeremy's lawyer, that much was evident, and the state prosecutor didn't like anybody. She watched him—Jeremy, only him—as the reporters held their collective breath and the judge read off the charges and her mother bowed her head and sobbed into the bucket of her hands. And Jeremy was watching her, too, his eyes locked on hers as if he defied them all, as if nothing mattered in the world but her, and when the judge said *First-degree murder* and *Murder by abuse or neglect* he never flinched.

She sent him a note that day—"I love you, will always love you no matter what, More than Moon"—and in the hallway, afterward, while their lawyers fended off the reporters and the bailiffs tugged impatiently at them, they had a minute, just a minute, to themselves. "What did you tell them?" he whispered. His voice was a rasp, almost a growl; she looked at him, inches away, and hardly recognized him.

"I told them it was dead."   60

"My lawyer—Mrs. Teagues?—she says they're saying it was alive when we, when we put it in the bag." His face was composed, but his eyes were darting like insects trapped inside his head.

"It was dead."

"It looked dead," he said, and already he was pulling away from her and some callous shit with a camera kept annihilating them with flash after flash of light, "and we certainly didn't—I mean, we didn't slap it or anything to get it breathing. . . ."

And then the last thing he said to her, just as they were pulled apart, and it was nothing she wanted to hear, nothing that had any love in it, or even the hint of love: "You told me to get rid of it."

There was no elaborate name for the place where they were keeping him. It   65
was known as Drum Hill Prison, period. No reform-minded notions here, no verbal gestures toward rehabilitation or behavior modification, no benefactors, mayors, or role models to lend the place their family names, but then who in his right mind would want a prison named after him anyway? At least they kept him separated from the other prisoners, the gangbangers and dope dealers and sexual predators and the like. He was no longer a freshman at Brown, not officially, but he had his books and his course notes and he tried to keep up as best he could. Still, when the screams echoed through the cell block at night and the walls dripped with the accumulated breath of eight and a half thousand terminally angry sociopaths, he had to admit it wasn't the sort of college experience he'd bargained for.

And what had he done to deserve it? He still couldn't understand. That thing in the Dumpster—and he refused to call it human, let alone a baby—was nobody's business but his and China's. That's what he'd told his attorney, Mrs. Teagues, and his mother and her boyfriend, Howard, and he'd told them over and over again: *I didn't do anything wrong.* Even if it was alive, and it was, he knew in his heart that it was, even before the state prosecutor presented evidence of blunt-force trauma and death by asphyxiation and exposure, it didn't matter, or shouldn't have mattered. There was no baby. There was nothing but a mistake, a mistake clothed in blood and mucus. When he really thought about it, thought it through on its merits and dissected all his mother's pathetic arguments about where he'd be today if she'd felt as he did when she was pregnant herself, he hardened like a rock, like sand turning to stone under all the pressure the planet can bring to bear. Another unwanted child in an overpopulated world? They should have given him a medal.

It was the end of January before bail was set—three hundred and fifty thousand dollars his mother didn't have—and he was released to house arrest. He wore a plastic anklet that set off an alarm if he went out the door, and so did she, so did China, imprisoned like some fairy-tale princess at her parents' house. At first, she called him every day, but mostly what she did was cry—"I want to see it," she sobbed. "I want to see our daughter's *grave*." That froze him inside. He tried to picture her—her now, China, the love of his life—and he couldn't. What did she look like? What was her face like, her nose, her hair, her eyes and breasts and the slit between her legs? He drew a blank. There was no way to summon her the way she used to be or even the way she was in court, because all he could remember was the thing that had come out of her, four limbs and the equipment of a female, shoulders rigid and eyes shut tight, as if she were a mummy in a tomb . . . and the breath, the shuddering long gasping rattle of a breath he could feel ringing inside her even as the black plastic bag closed over her face and the lid of the Dumpster opened like a mouth.

He was in the den, watching basketball, a drink in his hand (7UP mixed with Jack Daniel's in a ceramic mug, so no one would know he was getting shit-faced at two o'clock on a Sunday afternoon), when the phone rang. It was Sarah Teagues. "Listen, Jeremy," she said in her crisp, equitable tones, "I thought you ought to know—the Berkowitzes are filing a motion to have the case against China dropped."

His mother's voice on the portable, too loud, a blast of amplified breath and static: "On what grounds?"

"She never saw the baby, that's what they're saying. She thought she had a miscarriage."   70

"Yeah, right," his mother said.

Sarah Teagues was right there, her voice as clear and present as his mother's. "Jeremy's the one that threw it in the Dumpster, and they're saying he acted alone. She took a polygraph test day before yesterday."

He could feel his heart pounding like it used to when he plodded up that last agonizing ridge behind the school with the cross-country team, his legs sapped, no more breath left in his body. He didn't say a word. Didn't even breathe.

"She's going to testify against him."

♦ ♦ ♦

Outside was the world, puddles of ice clinging to the lawn under a weak   75
afternoon sun, all the trees stripped bare, the grass dead, the azalea under the
window reduced to an armload of dead brown twigs. She wouldn't have wanted
to go out today anyway. This was the time of year she hated most, the long interval between the holidays and spring break, when nothing grew and nothing
changed—it didn't even seem to snow much anymore. What was out there for
her anyway? They wouldn't let her see Jeremy, wouldn't even let her talk to him
on the phone or write him anymore, and she wouldn't be able to show her face at
the mall or even the movie theater without somebody shouting out her name as if
she were a freak, as if she were another Monica Lewinsky or Heidi Fleiss. She
wasn't China Berkowitz, honor student, not anymore—she was the punch line to
a joke, a footnote to history.

She wouldn't mind going for a drive, though—that was something she
missed, just following the curves out to the reservoir to watch the way the ice
cupped the shore, or up to the turnout on Route 9 to look out over the river where
it oozed through the mountains in a shimmering coil of light. Or to take a walk in
the woods, just that. She was in her room, on her bed, posters of bands she'd outgrown staring down from the walls, her high-school books on two shelves in the
corner, the closet door flung open on all the clothes she'd once wanted so desperately she could have died for each individual pair of boots or the cashmere
sweaters that felt so good against her skin. At the bottom of her left leg, down
there at the foot of the bed, was the anklet she wore now, the plastic anklet with
the transmitter inside, no different, she supposed, than the collars they put on
wolves to track them across all those miles of barren tundra or the bears sleeping
in their dens. Except that hers had an alarm on it.

For a long while she just lay there gazing out the window, watching the
rinsed-out sun slip down into the sky that had no more color in it than a TV tuned
to an unsubscribed channel, and then she found herself picturing things the way
they were an eon ago, when everything was green. She saw the azalea bush in
bloom, the leaves knifing out of the trees, butterflies—or were they cabbage
moths?—hovering over the flowers. Deep green. That was the color of the world.
And she was remembering a night, summer before last, just after she and Jeremy
started going together, the crickets thrumming, the air thick with humidity, and
him singing along with the car radio, his voice so sweet and pure it was as if he'd
written the song himself, just for her. And when they got to where they were
going, at the end of that dark lane overhung with trees, to a place where it was private and hushed and the night fell in on itself as if it couldn't support the weight
of the stars, he was as nervous as she was. She moved into his arms and they
kissed, his lips groping for hers in the dark, his fingers trembling over the thin
yielding silk of her blouse. He was Jeremy. He was the love of her life. And she
closed her eyes and clung to him as if that were all that mattered.   [2000]

THINKING ABOUT THE TEXT

1. Both China and Jeremy are condemned by their peers in this story (and
   they were in real life). Is that your response, too? Did Boyle persuade you

to see how such an event is possible? Do you want to understand how such an event is possible? Or is there no explanation for such behavior?

2. After reading the first few pages of the exposition, what do you think Boyle's purpose is in this opening scene? Is the phrase "Teens have sex . . . and then they pay for it in body parts" (para. 2) clever or too ironic, perhaps even cruel?

3. Look again at the fourth paragraph. What does it tell you about China's frame of mind? Her sense of reality?

4. Is Boyle trying to make an argument about the power of the media? The obliviousness of teens? The power of first love?

5. Have China and Jeremy's lives been irreparably ruined? Boyle ends the story with China remembering a summer night shortly after she started dating Jeremy. Can this memory save the relationship, or is it proof of her blindness?

MAKING COMPARISONS

1. Compare Jeremy and Dalton. Why do they both refer to the baby as "it"? What are some other similarities? Differences?

2. Compare the titles of both stories. Can you sense the authors' attitudes toward the couples from these titles?

3. What part does love play in the problems of the couples in the two stories? What are other problems they have?

WRITING ABOUT ISSUES

1. Write a brief argument in favor of a light sentence for China and Jeremy.

2. Write a comparison of Sunny and China including the nature of their relationship to Dalton and Jeremy and your speculation about their futures.

3. In the conclusion Jeremy thinks: "And what had he done to deserve it? He still couldn't understand" (para. 66). Write a brief analysis of this position.

4. In *Intimate Reading,* her study of the memoir, Janet Ellerby claims that reading memoirs of women who keep secrets "will help those people who rush to damn unfortunate adolescent girls to understand why these desperate girls hide their pregnancies from their families . . . and themselves . . . and help others understand how a panicked and forsaken girl in unimaginable pain might hysterically abandon the newborn she has steadfastly denied, whether she gives birth in a delivery room or a high school bathroom . . . [and] will help our culture understand that we have not yet solved the physical and psychological obstacles that adolescent girls must brave when faced with unwanted pregnancies." Write an essay that agrees or disagrees with this position.

GAYS AND LESBIANS IN FAMILIES

ESSEX HEMPHILL, "Commitments"
KITTY TSUI, "A Chinese Banquet"
MINNIE BRUCE PRATT, "Two Small-Sized Girls"

The late Essex Hemphill was gay; Kitty Tsui and Minnie Bruce Pratt are lesbian. All three writers in this cluster remind their audience that families may have gay or lesbian members. Usually the media give a different impression. The families depicted in most literature, films, television shows, and songs are heterosexual. Indeed, much of American society prefers this image. Families that do have gay or lesbian members may refuse to admit the fact, let alone accept it. Throughout history, of course, plenty of gays and lesbians have concealed their sexual identities from their families in the first place, fearing rejection.

Nowadays, though, increasing numbers of gays and lesbians are not only "coming out of the closet" but are also publicly claiming the term *family*. Many seek acceptance by the families they were raised in. Many also seek the right to form and raise families of their own. Some are working to get same-sex marriage legalized. Note that in all these efforts, they have quite a few heterosexual allies, but they face heterosexual resistance too. As was demonstrated in the 1990s in the case of lesbian mother Sharon Bottoms, a parent who is not heterosexual can still lose custody of his or her children for that reason. Also, gays and lesbians are far from winning a universal right to adopt. When Hawaii seemed on the verge of permitting same-sex marriage, arguments about it raged throughout the United States, and the federal government sought to discourage it by passing the Defense of Marriage Act in 1996. Consider your own position on these matters as you read the following poems. Each refers to American society's widespread assumption that families are heterosexual; each also points out the suffering that can result from this belief.

BEFORE YOU READ

What, at present, is your attitude toward gays and lesbians? Try to identify specific people, experiences, and institutions that have shaped your view. If it has changed over the years, explain how. Finally, describe an occasion that made you quite conscious of the attitude you now hold.

ESSEX HEMPHILL
Commitments

Before his untimely death from AIDS-related complications, Essex Hemphill (1957–1995) explored through prose, poetry, and film what it meant to live as a black gay man. The following poem comes from his 1992 book Ceremonies: Prose and Poetry. *His other books include a collection he edited,* Brother to Brother:

New Writings by Black Gay Men *(1991). Hemphill also appeared in the docu-
mentaries* Looking for Langston *and* Tongues Untied.

I will always be there.
When the silence is exhumed.
When the photographs are examined
I will be pictured smiling
among siblings, parents,   5
nieces and nephews.

In the background of the photographs
the hazy smoke of barbecue,
a checkered red-and-white tablecloth
laden with blackened chicken,   10
glistening ribs, paper plates,
bottles of beer, and pop.

In the photos
the smallest children
are held by their parents.   15
My arms are empty, or around
the shoulders of unsuspecting aunts
expecting to throw rice at me someday.

Or picture tinsel, candles,
ornamented, imitation trees,   20
or another table, this one
set for Thanksgiving,
a turkey steaming the lens.

My arms are empty
in those photos, too,   25
so empty they would break
around a lover.

I am always there
for critical emergencies,
graduations,   30
the middle of the night.

I am the invisible son.
In the family photos
nothing appears out of character.
I smile as I serve my duty.   [1992]   35

THINKING ABOUT THE TEXT

1. The speaker begins with the announcement "I will always be there," and
   yet later he says "I am the invisible son" (line 32). How can these two

statements be reconciled? In the second line, he uses the word *exhumed*. Look up this word in a dictionary. What do you infer from the speaker's use of it?

2. Unlike the other stanzas, the second lacks verbs. Should Hemphill have included at least one verb there for the sake of consistency? Why, or why not? Is the scene described in the second stanza characteristic of your own family? Note similarities and differences.

3. What do you think the speaker means when he describes his arms in the photographs as "so empty they would break / around a lover" (lines 26–27)?

4. In line 34, the speaker refers to "character." How does he seem to define the term? He concludes the poem by noting, "I smile as I serve my duty." Should this line be taken as an indication of how he really feels about his family commitments? Why, or why not?

5. List some commitments that you think the speaker's family should be making toward him. What overall attitude of yours toward the family does your list suggest? What is your overall attitude toward the speaker?

KITTY TSUI
A Chinese Banquet

Born in Hong Kong in 1953, Kitty Tsui grew up there and in England before moving to the United States in 1969. Besides being a writer, she is an artist, an actor, and a bodybuilder. The following comes from her 1983 volume of poetry, The Words of a Woman Who Breathes Fire. *Her latest book is* Breathless *(1996), a collection of stories.*

for the one who was not invited

it was not a very formal affair but
all the women over twelve
wore long gowns and a corsage,
except for me.

it was not a very formal affair, just   5
the family getting together,
poa poa,° kuw fu° without kuw mow°
(her excuse this year is a headache).

aunts and uncles and cousins,
the grandson who is a dentist,   10

---

7 *poa poa:* Maternal grandmother.   **kuw fu:** Uncle.   **kuw mow:** Aunt.

the one who drives a mercedes benz,
sitting down for shark's fin soup.

they talk about buying a house and
taking a two week vacation in beijing.
i suck on shrimp and squab,   15
dreaming of the cloudscape in your eyes.

my mother, her voice beaded with sarcasm;
you're twenty six and not getting younger.
it's about time you got a decent job.
she no longer asks when i'm getting married.   20

you're twenty six and not getting younger.
what are you doing with your life?
you've got to make a living.
why don't you study computer programming?

she no longer asks when i'm getting married.   25
one day, wanting desperately to
bridge the boundaries that separate us,
wanting desperately to touch her,

tell her: mother, i'm gay,
mother i'm gay and so happy with her.   30
but she will not listen,
she shakes her head.

she sits across from me,
emotions invading her face.
her eyes are wet but   35
she will not let tears fall.

mother, i say,
you love a man.
i love a woman.
it is not what she wants to hear.   40

aunts and uncles and cousins,
very much a family affair.
but you are not invited,
being neither my husband nor my wife.

aunts and uncles and cousins   45
eating longevity noodles
fragrant with ham inquire:
sold that old car of yours yet?

i want to tell them: my back is healing,
i dream of dragons and water.   50
my home is in her arms,
our bedroom ceiling the wide open sky.   [1983]

THINKING ABOUT THE TEXT

1. How would you describe the speaker's relationship with her mother? Do you think the mother is wrong not to invite her daughter's lover? Identify specific values, principles, and experiences of yours that influence your answer.

2. How would you describe the conversations at the banquet? How familiar are such conversations to you? Where does the speaker contrast them with another kind of talk?

3. How helpful is the poem's title? Where specifically does the poem refer to Chinese culture? To what extent does ethnicity seem to matter in this text?

4. Note repetitions in the poem. What is their effect?

5. Tsui doesn't use capitalization. What is the effect of this move?

MAKING COMPARISONS

1. Do you sense that Hemphill's speaker, like Tsui's, is "wanting desperately to / bridge the boundaries that separate us" (lines 26–27)? Support your answer by referring to specific words in Hemphill's poem.

2. By focusing so much on photographs, Hemphill's poem emphasizes sight. Does Tsui's poem emphasize sight, or does it give at least as much attention to another sense? Support your answer by referring to details of the poem.

3. Tsui's poem addresses someone in particular; Hemphill's does not. Does this difference make for a significant difference in effect? Why, or why not?

MINNIE BRUCE PRATT
Two Small-Sized Girls

Minnie Bruce Pratt (b. 1946) has long been active in the women's movement. Her prose writings include Rebellion: Essays, 1980–1991 *(1991) and a 1995 volume of short pieces titled* S/HE. *As a poet, she has published* The Sound of One Fork *(1981);* Crime against Nature *(1990), which won the prestigious Lamont Prize of the American Academy of Poets; and* We Say We Love Each Other *(1992). Her latest book is* Walking Back Up Depot Street *(1999). In divorce proceedings, Pratt lost custody of her two sons because she is a lesbian. Many of the poems in* Crime against Nature, *including the following, refer to this experience.*

1.

Two small-sized girls, hunched in the corn crib,
skin prickly with heat and dust.   We rustle
in the corn husks and grab rough cobs gnawed

empty as bone.   We twist them with papery shreds.
Anyone passing would say we're making our dolls.   5

Almost sisters, like our mothers, we turn and shake
the shriveled beings.   We are not playing at babies.
We are doing, single-minded, what we've been watching
our grandmother do.   We are making someone.   We hunker
on splintered grey planks older than our mothers,   10
and ignore how the sun blazes across us, the straw husks,
the old door swung open for the new corn of the summer.

2.

Here's the cherry spool bed from her old room,
the white bedspread crocheted by Grandma,
rough straw baskets hanging on the blank wall,   15
snapshots from her last trip home, ramshackle
houses eaten up by kudzu.   The same past
haunts us.   We have ended up in the same present

where I sit crosslegged with advice on how to keep
her children from being seized by their father   20
ten years after I lost my own.   The charge then:
crime against nature, going too far with women,
and not going back to men.   And hers?   Wanting
to have her small garden the way she wanted it,
and wanting to go her own way.   The memory: 25

  Her father's garden, immense rows of corn,
  cantaloupe and melon squiggling, us squatting,
  late afternoon, cool in the four o'clocks;
  waiting for them to open, making up stories,
  anything might happen, waiting in the garden.   30

3.

So much for the power of my ideas about oppression
and her disinterest in them.   In fact we've ended
in the same place.   Made wrong, knowing we've done
nothing wrong:
            Like the afternoon we burned up   35
  the backyard, wanting to see some fire.
  The match's seed opened into straw, paper,
  then bushes, like enormous red and orange
  lantana flowers.   We chased the abrupt power
  blooming around us down to charred straw,   40
  and Grandma bathed us, scorched and ashy,
  never saying a word.

> Despite our raw hearts,
> guilt from men who used our going to take our children,
> we know we've done nothing wrong, to twist and search   45
> for the kernels of fire deep in the body's shaken husk.   [1990]

THINKING ABOUT THE TEXT

1. Do you think any behavior deserves to be called a "crime against nature" (line 22)? Explain your reasoning.

2. Ironically, one pattern in Pratt's poem is nature imagery. Do you consider some or all of this imagery to be symbolic, or do you accept the images simply as details of a physical scene? Refer to specific examples.

3. Compare the three sections of the poem. What are their common elements? How do they significantly differ from one another? Why does the speaker believe that she and her cousin have "ended / in the same place" (lines 32–33)?

4. How would you describe the two girls' relationship to their grandmother? Support your answer with specific details from the text.

5. Do you think this poem is an affirmation of family ties? A criticism of them? Both? Again, refer to specific details.

MAKING COMPARISONS

1. Both Tsui's speaker and Pratt's address another woman. In Tsui's poem, it is the "one who was not invited"; in Pratt's, it is the speaker's cousin. Are the speakers expressing pretty much the same message to these women? Support your answer with specific details from both poems.

2. Do you get the impression that all three speakers in this cluster are searching for Pratt's "kernels of fire deep in the body's shaken husk" (line 46)? Show how these words are or are not relevant in each case.

3. Do you sympathize with any of the three speakers more than the others? Why, or why not?

WRITING ABOUT ISSUES

1. Choose Hemphill's, Tsui's, or Pratt's poem, and write an essay arguing for or against a position held by someone in the poem. The person can be the speaker. Support your argument with specific details and examples.

2. Choose two of the poems in this cluster, and write an essay comparing how commitments figure in them. Be sure to cite specific words of each poem.

3. In the next week, observe and jot down things on your campus that you think might disturb a gay or lesbian student. (If you are a gay or lesbian student, you may have already thought about such matters.) Then write an essay addressing the issue of whether your campus is inviting to gay

and lesbian students. In arguing for your position on this issue, refer to some of the observations you made. If you wish, refer as well to one or more of the poems in this cluster.

4. Increasingly, the United States is grappling with whether same-sex marriage should be legalized. Another debate is whether gays and lesbians should lose child custody rights because of their sexual orientation. Choose one of these issues, and read at least three articles about it. Then write an essay in which you not only put forth and support your own position on the issue but also state whether and how the articles affected your thinking. If you wish, you may refer as well to one or more of the poems in this cluster.

13

Teaching and Learning

Philosophy, said Aristotle, begins in wonder. So does education.
— Mike Rose

It is noble to teach oneself, but still nobler to teach others — and less trouble.
— Mark Twain

Education must begin with the solution of the teacher-student contradiction, by reconciling the poles of the contradiction so that both are simultaneously teachers *and* students.
— Paulo Freire

How do we make ideals for ourselves, those success stories we try to live by? And secondly — and in some ways more problematic — how do we make them our own? How do we get to feel that to some extent we have chosen them — that they formulate what matters most to us — rather than had them imposed upon us? Ideals should feel like affinities, not impositions. . . . Clearly, these issues reach a kind of crisis around the initiation rite of going to university, and leaving it.
— Adam Phillips

Any classroom is a site of conflicting beliefs, values, affiliations, desires, class and gender identities, the tapping of which can offer opportunity for critical reflection.
— C. H. Knoblauch and Lil Brannon

Learning to make experience work both experientially and analytically in our day-to-day teaching and learning can unite teachers and students across the lines of race, class, gender, and sexual identity. We can mobilize our lived experiences of one form of discrimination to end social amnesia about other forms of discrimination. In that critical space, differences can and must engage one another.
— Min-Zhan Lu

634

Probably you are thinking a lot about teaching and learning as you read selections from this book because you are encountering it in a college course. But even if you were delving into the book entirely on your own, it might bring issues of teaching and learning to mind. Countless readers turn to literature hoping to learn things from it, and many writers see literature as a way to teach others their insights. In addition, a vast number of literary works depict situations of teaching and learning, sometimes explicitly labeling them as such. But these are not the only reasons we feature a chapter on teaching and learning. We do so also because teaching and learning involve many of the same *rhetorical* considerations you face as a writer of arguments. Much of the time, the student is an audience, and the student's teacher aims to persuade him or her to accept a certain idea, to try a certain line of inquiry, or to see a certain subject as interesting. Naturally, roles can wind up reversed, with the teacher learning things from the student. As you may find in this class, students also wind up teaching one another.

Teaching and learning can occur outside of officially designated classrooms. Indeed, teaching and learning are an integral part of everyday life. To emphasize this point, we begin with a cluster of poems by Cathy Song, Julia Alvarez, and Forrest Hamer in which the speakers recall lessons they learned elsewhere (p. 636). In the second cluster (p. 643), stories by James Agee and Toni Cade Bambara remind us that, whether inside or outside a classroom, adults must decide when, what, and how to teach young children about society. Of course, for better or worse, few adults manage to exert total control over a child's fate. In quite a few literary works, children move from innocence to experience without a caregiver's consistent guidance. Such is the case with the classic fairy tale "Little Red Riding Hood," and our third cluster (p. 666) invites you to compare three versions of this story: Charles Perrault's, Jacob and Wilhelm Grimm's, and a modern rendition by Angela Carter entitled "The Company of Wolves." You will see that with Perrault's version the loss of innocence is deadly; the heroine does not survive. But even when children live to acquire the worldly knowledge of an adult, their elders may mourn their lost naivete. Our next cluster (p. 682), a trio of poems by Louise Glück, Toi Derricotte, and Philip Levine, features speakers, presumably adults, who brood over the growing constraints faced by schoolchildren they observe.

Rarely do students completely accept these constraints; they seek to be more than just robots. In the poems by Langston Hughes, Linda Pastan, Henry Reed, Walt Whitman, and Rosemary Catacalos that comprise the fourth cluster (p. 688), a student resists, ignores, or at least carefully weighs a particular instructor's demands. In David Mamet's play *Oleanna*, the centerpiece of the next cluster (p. 697), a college student even charges her professor with sexual harassment. To help you examine their conflict and put it in a larger context, we include three background documents: an account of the Clarence Thomas–Anita Hill hearings, the case study of a college student who used informal mediation to deal with a teacher who had harassed her, and an article proposing changes in the way that many colleges deal with sexual harassment charges.

The next two clusters encourage you to consider how education and culture may relate. In the first (p. 751), Richard Rodriguez recalls the painful process he went through as he moved from the Mexican American heritage of his parents to the Anglo-American world of school. Rodriguez does conclude that this shift was ultimately necessary and desirable; we follow his essay, though, with comments from Hispanic Americans who disagree. The next cluster (p. 767) consists of two short stories and an essay by Jamaica Kincaid. Although she lives now in the United States, Kincaid was born and raised on the island of Antigua when it was a colony of England. Her short story "Girl" suggests the training in Antiguan gender roles she received within her family, while the other two works show how the island's schools tried to indoctrinate its children in British lore.

The next-to-last cluster (p. 786) reminds you that literature itself has served as a means of educating. The three poems we feature, by David Wagoner, Theodore Roethke, and Elizabeth Bishop, provide lessons on how to live one's life, but that is not to say you must simply accept whatever an author or character tries to teach. Consider, for example, how much you should trust the advice-giving narrators of Jonathan Swift's "A Modest Proposal," Daniel Orozco's "Orientation," and Pam Houston's "How to Talk to a Hunter." We conclude this chapter with these three pieces (p. 792) precisely because they force you to consider just how reliable a would-be teacher is.

RECALLING LESSONS OF CHILDHOOD

CATHY SONG, "The Grammar of Silk"
JULIA ALVAREZ, "How I Learned to Sweep"
FORREST HAMER, "Lesson"

Many people recall learning significant childhood lessons in settings other than school. Such is the case with the following three poems. In the first, the speaker values the time she spent in a Saturday sewing school. The speaker in the second poem recalls how she learned to sweep her home, although the reader is plainly encouraged to think about sweeping as a metaphor for other, more troubling acts. In the third poem, an African American man describes a family trip through Mississippi in the early 1960s, an experience that gave him certain ideas about his relationship with his father. As you read these poems, observe how each depicts a parent-child relationship. Consider whether each parent consciously intends the lesson emphasized in the poem. Furthermore, compare the adult speaker of each poem with his or her younger self. To what extent do they seem similar? In what ways might their perspectives differ?

BEFORE YOU READ

What are some things that your parents or other people who raised you intentionally taught you? What are some things that they unintentionally taught you?

CATHY SONG
The Grammar of Silk

Cathy Song (b. 1955) was born and raised in Honolulu, Hawaii, and currently teaches at the University of Hawaii at Manoa. Her first volume of poetry, Picture Bride, *won the 1982 Yale Series of Younger Poets Award and was nominated for the National Book Critics Circle Award. She has published three others:* Frameless Windows, Available Light *(1988);* School Figures *(1994), which includes the following poem; and* The Land of Bliss *(2001).*

On Saturdays in the morning
my mother sent me to Mrs. Umemoto's sewing school.
It was cool and airy in her basement,
pleasant — a word I choose
to use years later to describe   5
the long tables where we sat
and cut, pinned, and stitched,
the Singer's companionable whirr,
the crisp, clever bite of scissors
parting like silver fish a river of calico.   10

The school was in walking distance
to Kaimuki Dry Goods
where my mother purchased my supplies —
small cards of buttons,
zippers and rickrack packaged like licorice,   15
lifesaver rolls of thread
in fifty-yard lengths,
spun from spools, tough as tackle.
Seamstresses waited at the counters
like librarians to be consulted.   20
Pens and scissors dangled like awkward pendants
across flat chests,
a scarf of measuring tape flung across a shoulder,
time as a pincushion bristled at the wrist.
They deciphered a dress's blueprints   25
with an architect's keen eye.

This evidently was a sanctuary,
a place where women confined with children
conferred, consulted the oracle,
the stone tablets of the latest pattern books.   30
Here mothers and daughters paused in symmetry,
offered the proper reverence —
hushed murmurings for the shantung silk

which required a certain sigh,
as if it were a piece from the Ming Dynasty.   35

My mother knew there would be no shortcuts
and headed for the remnants,
the leftover bundles with yardage
enough for a heart-shaped pillow,
a child's dirndl, a blouse without darts.   40
Along the aisles
my fingertips touched the titles —
satin, tulle, velvet,
peach, lavender, pistachio,
sherbet-colored linings —   45
and settled for the plain brown-and-white composition
of polka dots on kettle cloth
my mother held up in triumph.

She was determined that I should sew
as if she knew what she herself was missing,   50
a moment when she could have come up for air —
the children asleep,
the dishes drying on the rack —
and turned on the lamp
and pulled back the curtain of sleep.   55
To inhabit the night,
the night as a black cloth, white paper,
a sheet of music in which she might find herself singing.

On Saturdays at Mrs. Umemoto's sewing school,
when I took my place beside the other girls,   60
bent my head and went to work,
my foot keeping time on the pedal,
it was to learn the charitable oblivion
of hand and mind as one —
a refuge such music affords the maker —   65
the pleasure of notes in perfectly measured time.   [1994]

THINKING ABOUT THE TEXT

1. How do you think Song defines the word *grammar*? Note that the word
   appears only in the poem's title and is not usually applied to silk. Why,
   then, do you think Song calls her poem "The Grammar of Silk"? Which
   lines seem related to this title?

2. Even as she uses the word *pleasant* to describe Mrs. Umemoto's basement, the speaker admits that it is "a word I choose / to use years later"
   (lines 4–5). What other lines seem to reflect the adult's perspective more
   than the child's?

3. Only the first and last stanzas describe the sewing school itself. What might Song's purpose be in including the four middle stanzas? How important do they seem compared with the first and last stanzas?

4. Describe the speaker's mother with three adjectives of your own. What, in your own words, does she seem to have been "missing" (line 50)? Do you mainly think of her as missing something, or are you more conscious of what she had?

5. Does the culture evoked in this poem seem different from your own? What specific aspects of the poem's culture and your own come to mind as you try to answer this question?

JULIA ALVAREZ
How I Learned to Sweep

Although born in New York City, Julia Alvarez (b. 1950) was raised in the Dominican Republic until she was ten. Her first novel, How the Garcia Girls Lost Their Accents *(1991), concerns Dominican immigrants living in Manhattan. Her second,* In the Time of the Butterflies *(1994), is based on real-life women who were murdered by the regime of the Dominican dictator Rafael Leonidas Trujillo. Her third novel,* Yo! *(1996), centers on a writer much like Alvarez herself. Alvarez has also published volumes of poetry, including* Homecoming *(1984; revised edition, 1996) and* The Other Side/El Otro Lado *(1995). The following poem appears in* Homecoming *as one of a series of thirteen poems collectively entitled "Housekeeping."*

My mother never taught me sweeping. . . .
One afternoon she found me watching
t.v. She eyed the dusty floor
boldly, and put a broom before
me, and said she'd like to be able	5
to eat her dinner off that table,
and nodded at my feet, then left.
I knew right off what she expected
and went at it. I stepped and swept;
the t.v. blared the news; I kept	10
my mind on what I had to do,
until in minutes, I was through.
Her floor was as immaculate
as a just-washed dinner plate.
I waited for her to return	15
and turned to watch the President,
live from the White House, talk of war:
in the Far East our soldiers were

landing in their helicopters
into jungles their propellers   20
swept like weeds seen underwater
while perplexing shots were fired
from those beautiful green gardens
into which these dragonflies
filled with little men descended.   25
I got up and swept again
as they fell out of the sky.
I swept all the harder when
I watched a dozen of them die . . .
as if their dust fell through the screen   30
upon the floor I had just cleaned.
She came back and turned the dial;
the screen went dark. *That's beautiful,*
she said, and ran her clean hand through
my hair, and on, over the window-   35
sill, coffee table, rocker, desk,
and held it up — I held my breath —
That's beautiful, she said, impressed,
she hadn't found a speck of death.   [1984]

THINKING ABOUT THE TEXT

1. In line 1, the speaker begins by announcing "My mother never taught me sweeping. . . ." How is it, then, that the speaker "knew right off what she expected" (line 8)?

2. Identify rhyming patterns in this poem. What is their effect? Identify sections where there is no rhyme. What is their effect?

3. How old do you think the speaker was when she learned how to sweep? Why do you think the sight of dying soldiers made her sweep "all the harder" (line 28)? What response to the war might reasonably have been expected of her?

4. What do you conclude about the speaker's mother from the last two lines?

5. What other things do children or parents like to sweep away?

MAKING COMPARISONS

1. Whereas Alvarez uses rhyme at various points, Song does not. Does this difference lead to a difference in the two poems' overall effect? Explain.

2. Song uses the words *sanctuary* and *oblivion*. Look these up in a dictionary. How might they be applied to Alvarez's poem? Do you think Alvarez would attach the same connotations to them as Song does? Why, or why not?

3. Compare the mothers in Alvarez's and Song's poems. Do you sympathize with one mother more than the other? Why, or why not?

FORREST HAMER
Lesson

Besides being a poet, Forrest Hamer (b. 1956) is a psychologist, a lecturer in psychology at the University of California at Berkeley, and a candidate at the San Francisco Psychoanalytic Institute. As a poet, he has published in several journals. "Lesson" appears in his first book of poems, Call & Response *(1996), much of which deals with his experiences growing up African American.*

It was 1963 or 4, summer,
and my father was driving our family
from Ft. Hood to North Carolina in our 56 Buick.
We'd been hearing about Klan attacks, and we knew

Mississippi to be more dangerous than usual.   5
Dark lay hanging from trees the way moss did,
and when it moaned light against the windows
that night, my father pulled off the road to sleep.

                 Noises
that usually woke me from rest afraid of monsters   10
kept my father awake that night, too,
and I lay in the quiet noticing him listen, learning
that he might not be able always to protect us

from everything and the creatures besides;
perhaps not even from the fury suddenly loud   15
through my body about this trip from Texas
to settle us home before he would go away

to a place no place in the world
he named Viet Nam. A boy needs a father
with him, I kept thinking, fixed against noise   20
from the dark.   [1996]

THINKING ABOUT THE TEXT

1. Hamer's title suggests there was only one lesson, yet there seem to be two. On the one hand, the child seems to have learned that his father "might not be able always to protect us/from everything and the creatures besides" (lines 13–14). On the other hand, the child seems to have learned that "A boy needs a father/with him" (lines 19–20). Consider whether these two lessons are compatible. Do you believe that the title applies to both? Why, or why not?

2. The speaker begins with "It was 1963 or 4, summer." What do you conclude from his uncertainty about the year his journey through Mississippi

took place? How does it affect you? What was going on in Mississippi from 1963 to 1964? (You may need to research this in the library.)

3. What is the effect of Hamer's visually isolating the word *Noises* in line 9? What other words in the poem can be linked to this one?

4. Was the child justified in resenting his father's departure for Vietnam? Should the father not have gone? Your answers to these questions are, in effect, claims. With what evidence and assumptions do you make them?

5. In the United States today, many children are raised without their fathers. This fact has led to much debate over social policy. People argue about whether and how fathers should be pushed to participate in their children's upbringing. At the same time, some feel that women should be discouraged from becoming single mothers, in part because sons need to have fathers around. What would you think if they used Hamer's claim "A boy needs a father / with him" (lines 19–20) in arguing for their position?

MAKING COMPARISONS

1. Think of the father in Hamer's poem and the mothers in Song's and Alvarez's poems. Do any of these parents seem like intentional teachers who consciously aim to impart certain lessons to their children? Support your answer by referring to specific details in each poem.

2. What might each of these poems have looked like if written by the parent involved? More specifically, what sorts of things might the parent have said?

3. Hamer's poem and Alvarez's share a historical context in that they both refer to the Vietnam war. What do you associate with this war? Compare how the children in these two poems think about it. Do they each regard the war in much the same way? Refer to specific lines in each text to support your answer. How historically specific is Song's poem in comparison?

WRITING ABOUT ISSUES

1. Choose Song's, Alvarez's, or Hamer's poem, and write an essay discussing the role gender plays in it. Does the poem focus on one gender? In what ways? How is the poem relevant to both men and women? Be sure to support your claim with specific details of the text.

2. Write an essay comparing the speakers in two of the poems in this cluster. Consider not only how the speakers thought and acted as youths but also what they may be like now as adults, including the attitudes they may have toward their younger selves. Refer to specific details of both texts.

3. Write a dialogue between your present self and the person you were at a particular age. Focus this dialogue on a specific historical event or development that your younger self was struggling to understand. Then write

at least three paragraphs comparing the two perspectives that emerged in your dialogue. What turned out to be the similarities and differences between your present and younger selves?

4. Think of a school you attended and a skill or principle that the school didn't teach but should have. Taking as your audience the school's current administrators, write an essay arguing for including this skill or principle in the school's curriculum now. While you may cite experiences of your own as evidence for your position, be sure to give additional reasons for adopting it.

TEACHING CHILDREN ABOUT SOCIETY

JAMES AGEE, "A Mother's Tale"
TONI CADE BAMBARA, "The Lesson"

In the first story here, a cow tells a group of calves about the horrors of the slaughterhouse. In the second story, an African American woman tries to convince some children of her race that whites unfairly control their society's wealth. In effect, both stories remind us that whether in or out of school, adults often try to teach young children about the society they are entering.

What specific aspects of their society, though, should young children learn about? What overall view of their society should they be taught to adopt? People give different answers to these questions. Often their responses vary because they have in mind their own social circumstances, including the treatment given their specific class, race, gender, religion, ethnic group, and sexual orientation. Furthermore, even people who respond similarly may disagree about other matters: in particular, about *how* and *when* a child should be taught whatever vision of society they think appropriate. The two stories here encourage you to ponder all these issues.

BEFORE YOU READ

In his memoir *Fatheralong* (1994), John Edgar Wideman notes that his father's attitude toward society differs from that of his late mother. "The first rule of my father's world," Wideman writes, "is that you stand alone. Alone, alone, alone. . . . Accept the bottom line, icy clarity, of the one thing you can rely on: nothing" (50). On the other hand, "My mother's first rule was love. She refused to believe she was alone. *Be not dismayed, what e'er betides / God will take care of you*" (51). What were you taught about society as you were growing up? What specific messages were you given about it by your parents or the people who raised you? How did they convey these messages to you?

JAMES AGEE
A Mother's Tale

Today, James Agee (1909–1955) is probably best known for his journalistic 1941 book Let Us Now Praise Famous Men, *in which he and photographer Walker Evans documented the hardships of sharecroppers during the Great Depression. Agee is also known for his Pulitzer Prize–winning novel* A Death in the Family (1957), *a fictionalized account of his father's death that was published posthumously. Agee wrote in several other genres, including short fiction, poetry, screenplays, and film criticism. "A Mother's Tale" was published in* Harper's Bazaar *magazine in 1951. Agee wrote it shortly after he had suffered a series of heart attacks; it was his last work of fiction published while he was alive.*

The calf ran up the little hill as fast as he could and stopped sharp.

"Mama!" he cried, all out of breath. "What *is* it! What are they *doing!* Where are they *going!*"

Other spring calves came galloping too.

They all were looking up at her and awaiting her explanation, but she looked out over their excited eyes. As she watched the mysterious and majestic thing they had never seen before, her own eyes became even more than ordinarily still, and during the considerable moment before she answered, she scarcely heard their urgent questioning.

Far out along the autumn plain, beneath the sloping light, an immense drove of cattle moved eastward. They went at a walk, not very fast, but faster than they could imaginably enjoy. Those in front were compelled by those behind; those at the rear, with few exceptions, did their best to keep up; those who were locked within the herd could no more help moving than the particles inside a falling rock. Men on horses rode ahead, and alongside, and behind, or spurred their horses intensely back and forth, keeping the pace steady, and the herd in shape; and from man to man a dog sped back and forth incessantly as a shuttle, barking, incessantly, in a hysterical voice. Now and then one of the men shouted fiercely, and this like the shrieking of the dog was tinily audible above a low and awesome sound which seemed to come not from the multitude of hooves but from the center of the world, and above the sporadic bawlings and bellowings of the herd.

From the hillside this tumult was so distant that it only made more delicate the prodigious silence in which the earth and sky were held; and, from the hill, the sight was as modest as its sound. The herd was virtually hidden in the dust it raised, and could be known, in general, only by the horns, which pricked this flat sunlit dust like little briars. In one place a twist of the air revealed the trembling fabric of many backs; but it was only along the near edge of the mass that individual animals were discernible, small in a driven frieze, walking fast, stumbling and recovering, tossing their armed heads, or opening their skulls heavenward in one of those cries which searched the hillside long after the jaws were shut.

5

From where she watched, the mother could not be sure whether there were any she recognized. She knew that among them there must be a son of hers; she had not seen him since some previous spring, and she would not be seeing him again. Then the cries of the young ones impinged on her bemusement: "Where are they going?"

She looked into their ignorant eyes.

"Away," she said.

"Where?" they cried. "Where? Where?" her own son cried again.   10

She wondered what to say.

"On a long journey."

"But where *to?*" they shouted. "Yes, where *to?*" her son exclaimed, and she could see that he was losing his patience with her, as he always did when he felt she was evasive.

"I'm not sure," she said.

Their silence was so cold that she was unable to avoid their eyes for long.   15

"Well, not *really* sure. Because, you see," she said in her most reasonable tone, "I've never seen it with my own eyes, and that's the only way to *be* sure; isn't it."

They just kept looking at her. She could see no way out.

"But I've *heard* about it," she said with shallow cheerfulness, "from those who *have* seen it, and I don't suppose there's any good reason to doubt them."

She looked away over them again, and for all their interest in what she was about to tell them, her eyes so changed that they turned and looked, too.

The herd, which had been moving broadside to them, was being turned   20 away, so slowly that like the turning of stars it could not quite be seen from one moment to the next; yet soon it was moving directly away from them, and even during the little while she spoke and they all watched after it, it steadily and very noticeably diminished, and the sounds of it as well.

"It happens always about this time of year," she said quietly while they watched. "Nearly all the men and horses leave, and go into the North and the West."

"Out on the range," her son said, and by his voice she knew what enchantment the idea already held for him.

"Yes," she said, "out on the range." And trying, impossibly, to imagine the range, they were touched by the breath of grandeur.

"And then before long," she continued, "everyone has been found, and brought into one place; and then . . . what you see, happens. All of them.

"Sometimes when the wind is right," she said more quietly, "you can hear   25 them coming long before you can see them. It isn't even like a sound, at first. It's more as if something were moving far under the ground. It makes you uneasy. You wonder, why, what in the world can *that* be! Then you remember what it is and then you can really hear it. And then, finally, there they all are."

She could see this did not interest them at all.

"But where are they *going?*" one asked, a little impatiently.

"I'm coming to that," she said; and she let them wait. Then she spoke slowly but casually.

"They are on their way to a railroad."

There, she thought; that's for that look you all gave me when I said I wasn't   30
sure. She waited for them to ask; they waited for her to explain.

"A railroad," she told them, "is great hard bars of metal lying side by side, or
so they tell me, and they go on and on over the ground as far as the eye can see. And
great wagons run on the metal bars on wheels, like wagon wheels but smaller,
and these wheels are made of solid metal too. The wagons are much bigger than
any wagon you've ever seen, as big as, big as sheds, they say, and they are pulled
along on the iron bars by a terrible huge dark machine, with a loud scream."

"Big as *sheds?*" one of the calves said skeptically.

"Big *enough*, anyway," the mother said. "I told you I've never seen it myself.
But those wagons are so big that several of us can get inside at once. And that's
exactly what happens."

Suddenly she became very quiet, for she felt that somehow, she could not
imagine just how, she had said altogether too much.

"Well, *what* happens," her son wanted to know. "What do you mean,   35
happens."

She always tried hard to be a reasonably modern mother. It was probably better, she felt, to go on, than to leave them all full of imaginings and mystification.
Besides, there was really nothing at all awful about what happened . . . if only one
could know *why*.

"Well," she said, "it's nothing much, really. They just—why, when they all
finally *get* there, why there are all the great cars waiting in a long line, and the big
dark machine is up ahead . . . smoke comes out of it, they say . . . and . . . well,
then, they just put us into the wagons, just as many as will fit in each wagon, and
when everybody is in, why . . ." She hesitated, for again, though she couldn't be
sure why, she was uneasy.

"Why then," her son said, "the train takes them away."

Hearing that word, she felt a flinching of the heart. Where had he picked it
up, she wondered, and she gave him a shy and curious glance. Oh dear, she
thought. I should never have even *begun* to explain. "Yes," she said, "when
everybody is safely in, they slide the doors shut."

They were all silent for a little while. Then one of them asked thoughtfully,   40
"Are they taking them somewhere they don't want to go?"

"Oh, I don't think so," the mother said. "I imagine it's very nice."

"*I* want to go," she heard her son say with ardor. "I want to go right now," he
cried. "Can I, Mama? *Can* I? *Please?*" And looking into his eyes, she was overwhelmed by sadness.

"Silly thing," she said, "there'll be time enough for that when you're grown
up. But what I very much hope," she went on, "is that instead of being chosen to
go out on the range and to make the long journey, you will grow up to be very
strong and bright so they will decide that you may stay here at home with Mother.
And you, too," she added, speaking to the other little males; but she could not
honestly wish this for any but her own, least of all for the eldest, strongest and
most proud, for she knew how few are chosen.

She could see that what she said was not received with enthusiasm.

"But I want to go," her son said.

"Why?" she asked. "I don't think any of you realize that it's a great *honor* to be chosen to stay. A great privilege. Why, it's just the most ordinary ones are taken out onto the range. But only the very pick are chosen to stay here at home. If you want to go out on the range," she said in hurried and happy inspiration, "all you have to do is be ordinary and careless and silly. If you want to have even a chance to be chosen to stay, you have to try to be stronger and bigger and braver and brighter than anyone else, and that takes *hard work. Every day.* Do you see?" And she looked happily and hopefully from one to another. "Besides," she added, aware that they were not won over, "I'm told it's a very rough life out there, and the men are unkind."

"Don't you see," she said again; and she pretended to speak to all of them, but it was only to her son.

But he only looked at her. "Why do you want me to stay home?" he asked flatly; in their silence she knew the others were asking the same question.

"Because it's safe here," she said before she knew better, and realized she had put it in the most unfortunate way possible. "Not safe, not just that," she fumbled. "I mean . . . because here we *know* what happens, and what's going to happen, and there's never any doubt about it, never any reason to wonder, to worry. Don't you see? It's just *Home*," and she put a smile on the word, "where we all know each other and are happy and well."

They were so merely quiet, looking back at her, that she felt they were neither won over nor alienated. Then she knew of her son that he, anyhow, was most certainly not persuaded, for he asked the question she most dreaded: "Where do they go on the train?" And hearing him, she knew that she would stop at nothing to bring that curiosity and eagerness, and that tendency toward skepticism, within safe bounds.

"Nobody knows," she said, and she added, in just the tone she knew would most sharply engage them, "Not for sure, anyway."

"What do you mean, *not for sure*," her son cried. And the oldest, biggest calf repeated the question, his voice cracking.

The mother deliberately kept silence as she gazed out over the plain, and while she was silent they all heard the last they would ever hear of all those who were going away: one last great cry, as faint almost as a breath; the infinitesimal jabbing vituperation of the dog; the solemn muttering of the earth.

"Well," she said, after even this sound was entirely lost, "there was one who came back." Their instant, trustful eyes were too much for her. She added, "Or so they say."

They gathered a little more closely around her, for now she spoke very quietly.

"It was my great-grandmother who told me," she said. "She was told it by *her* great-grandmother, who claimed she saw it with her own eyes, though of course I can't vouch for that. Because of course I wasn't even dreamed of then, and Great-grandmother was so very, very old, you see, that you couldn't always be sure she knew quite *what* she was saying."

Now that she began to remember it more clearly, she was sorry she had committed herself to telling it.

"Yes," she said, "the story is, there was one, *just* one, who ever came back, and he told what happened on the train, and where the train went and what happened after. He told it all in a rush, they say, the last things first and every which way, but as it was finally sorted out and gotten into order by those who heard it and those they told it to, this is more or less what happened:

"He said that after the men had gotten just as many of us as they could into the car he was in, so that their sides pressed tightly together and nobody could lie down, they slid the door shut with a startling rattle and a bang, and then there was a sudden jerk, so strong they might have fallen except that they were packed so closely together, and the car began to move. But after it had moved only a little way, it stopped as suddenly as it had started, so that they all nearly fell down again. You see, they were just moving up the next car that was joined on behind, to put more of us into it. He could see it all between the boards of the car, because the boards were built a little apart from each other, to let in air."

Car, her son said again to himself. Now he would never forget the word.   60

"He said that then, for the first time in his life, he became very badly frightened, he didn't know why. But he was sure, at that moment, that there was something dreadfully to be afraid of. The others felt this same great fear. They called out loudly to those who were being put into the car behind, and the others called back, but it was no use; those who were getting aboard were between narrow white fences and then were walking up a narrow slope and the man kept jabbing them as they do when they are in an unkind humor, and there was no way to go but on into the car. There was no way to get out of the car, either: he tried, with all his might, and he was the one nearest the door.

"After the next car behind was full, and the door was shut, the train jerked forward again, and stopped again, and they put more of us into still another car, and so on, and on, until all the starting and stopping no longer frightened anybody; it was just something uncomfortable that was never going to stop, and they began instead to realize how hungry and thirsty they were. But there was no food and no water, so they had to put up with this; and about the time they became resigned to going without their suppers (for by now it was almost dark), they heard a sudden and terrible scream which frightened them even more deeply than anything had frightened them before, and the train began to move again, and they braced their legs once more for the jolt when it would stop, but this time, instead of stopping, it began to go fast, and then even faster, so fast that the ground nearby slid past like a flooded creek and the whole country, he claimed, began to move too, turning slowly around a far mountain as if it were on one great wheel. And then there was a strange kind of disturbance inside the car, he said, or even inside his very bones. He felt as if everything in him was *falling*, as if he had been filled full of a heavy liquid that all wanted to flow one way, and all the others were leaning as he was leaning, away from this queer heaviness that was trying to pull them over, and then just as suddenly this leaning heaviness was gone and they nearly fell again before they could stop leaning against it. He could never understand what this was, but it too happened so many times that they all got used to it, just as they got used to seeing the country turn like a slow wheel, and just as they got used to the long cruel screams of the engine, and the steady iron noise beneath them which made the cold darkness so fearsome, and the hunger and the thirst and the continual standing up, and the moving on and on and on as if they would never stop."

"*Didn't* they ever stop?" one asked.

"Once in a great while," she replied. "Each time they did," she said, "he thought, Oh, now *at last!* At *last* we can get out and stretch our tired legs and lie down! *At last* we'll be given food and water! But they never let them out. And they never gave them food or water. They never even cleaned up under them. They had to stand in their manure and in the water they made."

"Why did the train stop?" her son asked, and with somber gratification; she   65
saw that he was taking all this very much to heart.

"He could never understand why," she said. "Sometimes men would walk up and down alongside the cars, and the more nervous and the more trustful of us would call out; but they were only looking around, they never seemed to do anything. Sometimes he could see many houses and bigger buildings together where people lived. Sometimes it was far out in the country and after they had stood still for a long time they would hear a little noise which quickly became louder, and then became suddenly a noise so loud it stopped their breathing and during this noise something black would go by, very close, and so fast it couldn't be seen. And then it was gone as suddenly as it had appeared, and the noise became small, and then in the silence their train would start up again.

"Once, he tells us, something very strange happened. They were standing still, and cars of a very different kind began to move slowly past. These cars were not red, but black, with many glass windows like those in a house; and he says they were as full of human beings as the car he was in was full of our kind. And one of these people looked into his eyes and smiled, as if he liked him, or as if he knew only too well how hard the journey was.

"So by his account it happens to them, too," she said, with a certain pleased vindictiveness. "Only they were sitting down at their ease, not standing. And the one who smiled was eating."

She was still, trying to think of something; she couldn't quite grasp the thought.

"But didn't they *ever* let them out?" her son asked.   70

The oldest calf jeered. "Of *course* they did. He came back, didn't he? How would he ever come back if he didn't get out?"

"They didn't let them out," she said, "for a long, long time."

"How long?"

"So long, and he was so tired, he could never quite be sure. But he said that it turned from night to day and from day to night and back again several times over, with the train moving nearly all of this time, and that when it finally stopped, early one morning, they were all so tired and so discouraged that they hardly even noticed any longer, let alone felt any hope that anything would change for them, ever again; and then all of a sudden men came up and put up a wide walk and unbarred the door and slid it open, and it was the most wonderful and happy moment of his life when he saw the door open, and walked into the open air with all his joints trembling, and drank the water and ate the delicious food they had ready for him; it was worth the whole terrible journey."

Now that these scenes came clear before her, there was a faraway shining in   75 her eyes, and her voice, too, had something in it of the faraway.

"When they had eaten and drunk all they could hold they lifted up their heads and looked around, and everything they saw made them happy. Even the trains made them cheerful now, for now they were no longer afraid of them. And though these trains were forever breaking to pieces and joining again with other broken pieces, with shufflings and clashings and rude cries, they hardly paid them attention any more, they were so pleased to be in their new home, and so surprised and delighted to find they were among thousands upon thousands of strangers of their own kind, all lifting up their voices in peacefulness and thanksgiving, and they were so wonderstruck by all they could see, it was so beautiful and so grand.

"For he has told us that now they lived among fences as white as bone, so many, and so spiderishly complicated, and shining so pure, that there's no use trying even to hint at the beauty and the splendor of it to anyone who knows only the pitiful little outfittings of a ranch. Beyond these mazy fences, through the dark and bright smoke which continually turned along the sunlight, dark buildings stood shoulder to shoulder in a wall as huge and proud as mountains. All through the air, all the time, there was an iron humming like the humming of the iron bar after it has been struck to tell the men it is time to eat, and in all the air, all the time, there was that same strange kind of iron strength which makes the silence before lightning so different from all other silence.

"Once for a little while the wind shifted and blew over them straight from the great buildings, and it brought a strange and very powerful smell which confused and disturbed them. He could never quite describe this smell, but he has told us it was unlike anything he had ever known before. It smelled like old fire, he said, and old blood and fear and darkness and sorrow and most terrible and brutal force and something else, something in it that made him want to run away. This sudden uneasiness and this wish to run away swept through every one of them, he tells us, so that they were all moved at once as restlessly as so many leaves in a wind, and there was great worry in their voices. But soon the leaders among them concluded that it was simply the way men must smell when there are a great many of them living together. Those dark buildings must be crowded very full of men, they decided, probably as many thousands of them, indoors, as there were of us, outdoors; so it was no wonder their smell was so strong and, to our kind, so unpleasant. Besides, it was so clear now in every other way that men were not as we had always supposed, but were doing everything they knew how to make us comfortable and happy, that we ought to just put up with their smell, which after all they couldn't help, any more than we could help our own. Very likely men didn't like the way we smelled, any more than we liked theirs. They passed along these ideas to the others, and soon everyone felt more calm, and then the wind changed again, and the fierce smell no longer came to them, and the smell of their own kind was back again, very strong of course, in such a crowd, but ever so homey and comforting, and everyone felt easy again.

"They were fed and watered so generously, and treated so well, and the majesty and the loveliness of this place where they had all come to rest was so far beyond anything they had ever known or dreamed of, that many of the simple and ignorant, whose memories were short, began to wonder whether that whole difficult journey, or even their whole lives up to now, had ever really been. Hadn't it all been just shadows, they murmured, just a bad dream?

"Even the sharp ones, who knew very well it had all really happened, began   80
to figure that everything up to now had been made so full of pain only so that all they had come to now might seem all the sweeter and the more glorious. Some of the oldest and deepest were even of a mind that all the puzzle and tribulation of the journey had been sent us as a kind of harsh trying or proving of our worthiness; and that it was entirely fitting and proper that we could earn our way through to such rewards as these, only through suffering, and through being patient under pain which was beyond our understanding; and that now at the last, to those who had borne all things well, all things were made known: for the mystery of suffering stood revealed in joy. And now as they looked back over all that was past, all their sorrows and bewilderments seemed so little and so fleeting that, from the simplest among them even to the most wise, they could feel only the kind of amused pity we feel toward the very young when, with the first thing that hurts them or they are forbidden, they are sure there is nothing kind or fair in all creation, and carry on accordingly, raving and grieving as if their hearts would break."

She glanced among them with an indulgent smile, hoping the little lesson would sink home. They seemed interested but somewhat dazed. I'm talking way over their heads, she realized. But by now she herself was too deeply absorbed in her story to modify it much. *Let* it be, she thought, a little impatient; it's over *my* head, for that matter.

"They had hardly before this even wondered that they were alive," she went on, "and now all of a sudden they felt they understood *why* they were. This made them very happy, but they were still only beginning to enjoy this new wisdom when quite a new and different kind of restiveness ran among them. Before they quite knew it they were all moving once again, and now they realized that they were being moved, once more, by men, toward still some other place and purpose they could not know. But during these last hours they had been so well that now they felt no uneasiness, but all moved forward calm and sure toward better things still to come; he has told us that he no longer felt as if he were being driven, even as it became clear that they were going toward the shade of those great buildings; but guided.

"He was guided between fences which stood ever more and more narrowly near each other among companions who were pressed ever more and more closely against one another; and now as he felt their warmth against him it was not uncomfortable, and his pleasure in it was not through any need to be close among others through anxiousness, but was a new kind of strong and gentle delight, at being so very close, so deeply of his own kind that it seemed as if the very breath and heartbeat of each one were being exchanged through all that multitude, and each was another, and others were each, and each was a multitude, and the multitude was one. And quieted and made mild within this melting, they now entered the cold shadow cast by the buildings, and now with every step the smell of the buildings grew stronger, and in the darkening air the glittering of the fences was ever more queer.

"And now as they were pressed ever more intimately together he could see ahead of him a narrow gate, and he was strongly pressed upon from either side and from behind, and went in eagerly, and now he was between two fences so narrowly set that he brushed either fence with either flank, and walked alone, seeing just one other ahead of him, and knowing of just one other behind him, and for a moment the strange thought came to him, that the one ahead was his father, and that the one behind was the son he had never begotten.

"And now the light was so changed that he knew he must have come inside one of the gloomy and enormous buildings, and the smell was so much stronger that it seemed almost to burn his nostrils, and the smell and the somber new light blended together and became some other thing again, beyond his describing to us except to say that the whole air beat with it like one immense heart and it was as if the beating of this heart were pure violence infinitely manifolded upon violence: so that the uneasy feeling stirred in him again that it would be wise to turn around and run out of this place just as fast and as far as ever he could go. This he heard, as if he were telling it to himself at the top of his voice, but it came from somewhere so deep and so dark inside him that he could only hear the shouting of it as less than a whisper, as just a hot and chilling breath, and he scarcely heeded it, there was so much else to attend to.

"For as he walked along in this sudden and complete loneliness, he tells us, this wonderful knowledge of being one with all his race meant less and less to him, and in its place came something still more wonderful: he knew what it was to be himself alone, a creature separate and different from any other, who had never been before, and would never be again. He could feel this in his whole weight as he walked, and in each foot as he put it down and gave his weight to it and moved above it, and in every muscle as he moved, and it was a pride which lifted him up and made him feel large, and a pleasure which pierced him through. And as he began with such wondering delight to be aware of his own exact singleness in this world, he also began to understand (or so he thought) just why these fences were set so very narrow, and just why he was walking all by himself. It stole over him, he tells us, like the feeling of a slow cool wind, that he was being guided toward some still more wonderful reward or revealing, up ahead, which he could not of course imagine, but he was sure it was being held in store for him alone.

"Just then the one ahead of him fell down with a great sigh, and was so quickly taken out of the way that he did not even have to shift the order of his hooves as he walked on. The sudden fall and the sound of that sigh dismayed him, though, and something within him told him that it would be wise to look up: and there he saw Him.

"A little bridge ran crosswise above the fences. He stood on this bridge with His feet as wide apart as He could set them. He wore spattered trousers but from the belt up He was naked and as wet as rain. Both arms were raised high above His head and in both hands He held an enormous Hammer. With a grunt which was hardly like the voice of a human being, and with all His strength, He brought this Hammer down onto the forehead of our friend: who, in a blinding blazing, heard from his own mouth the beginning of a gasping sigh; then there was only darkness."

Oh, this is *enough!* it's *enough!* she cried out within herself, seeing their terrible young eyes. How *could* she have been so foolish as to tell so much!

"What happened then?" she heard, in the voice of the oldest calf, and she was horrified. This shining in their eyes: was it only excitement? no pity? no fear?   90

"What happened?" two others asked.

Very well, she said to herself. I've gone so far; now I'll go the rest of the way. She decided not to soften it, either. She'd teach them a lesson they wouldn't forget in a hurry.

"Very well," she was surprised to hear herself say aloud.

"How long he lay in this darkness he couldn't know, but when he began to come out of it, all he knew was the most unspeakably dreadful pain. He was upside down and very slowly swinging and turning, for he was hanging by the tendons of his heels from great frightful hooks, and he has told us that the feeling was as if his hide were being torn from him inch by inch, in one piece. And then as he became more clearly aware he found that this was exactly what was happening. Knives would sliver and slice along both flanks, between the hide and the living flesh; then there was a moment of most precious relief; then red hands seized his hide and there was a jerking of the hide and a tearing of tissue which it was almost as terrible to hear as to feel, turning his whole body and the poor head at the bottom of it; and then the knives again.

"It was so far beyond anything he had ever known unnatural and amazing   95 that he hung there through several more such slicings and jerkings and tearings before he was fully able to take it all in: then, with a scream, and a supreme straining of all his strength, he tore himself from the hooks and collapsed sprawling to the floor and, scrambling right to his feet, charged the men with the knives. For just a moment they were so astonished and so terrified they could not move. Then they moved faster than he had ever known men could—and so did all the other men who chanced to be in his way. He ran down a glowing floor of blood and down endless corridors which were hung with the bleeding carcasses of our kind and with bleeding fragments of carcasses, among blood-clothed men who carried bleeding weapons, and out of that vast room into the open, and over and through one fence after another, shoving aside many an astounded stranger and shouting out warnings as he ran, and away up the railroad toward the West.

"How he ever managed to get away, and how he ever found his way home, we can only try to guess. It's told that he scarcely knew, himself, by the time he came to this part of his story. He was impatient with those who interrupted him to ask about that, he had so much more important things to tell them, and by then he was so exhausted and so far gone that he could say nothing very clear about the little he did know. But we can realize that he must have had really tremendous strength, otherwise he couldn't have outlived the Hammer; and that strength such as his—which we simply don't see these days, it's of the olden time—is capable of things our own strongest and bravest would sicken to dream of. But there was something even stronger than his strength. There was his righteous fury, which nothing could stand up against, which brought him out of that fearful place. And there was his high and burning and heroic purpose, to keep him safe along the way, and to guide him home, and to keep the breath of life in him until he could warn us. He did manage to tell us that he just followed the railroad, but how he chose one among the many which branched out from that place, he couldn't say. He told us, too, that from time to time he recognized shapes of mountains and other landmarks, from his journey by train, all reappearing backward and with a changed look and hard to see, too (for he was shrewd enough to travel mostly at night), but still recognizable. But that isn't enough to account for it. For he has told us, too, that he simply *knew* the way; that he didn't hesitate one moment in choosing the right line of railroad, or even think of it as choosing; and that the landmarks didn't really guide him, but just made him the more sure of what he was already sure of; and that whenever he *did* encounter human beings—and during the later stages of his journey, when he began to doubt he would live to tell us, he traveled day and night—they never so much as moved to make him trouble, but stopped dead in their tracks, and their jaws fell open.

"And surely we can't wonder that their jaws fell open. I'm sure yours would, if you had seen him as he arrived, and I'm very glad I wasn't there to see it, either, even though it is said to be the greatest and most momentous day of all the days that ever were or shall be. For we have the testimony of eyewitnesses, how he looked, and it is only too vivid, even to hear of. He came up out of the East as much staggering as galloping (for by now he was so worn out by pain and exertion and loss of blood that he could hardly stay upright), and his heels were so piteously torn by the hooks that his hooves doubled under more often than not, and in his broken forehead the mark of the Hammer was like the socket for a third eye.

"He came to the meadow where the great trees made shade over the water. 'Bring them all together!' he cried out, as soon as he could find breath. 'All!' Then he drank; and then he began to speak to those who were already there: for as soon as he saw himself in the water it was as clear to him as it was to those who watched him that there was no time left to send for the others. His hide was all gone from his head and his neck and his forelegs and his chest and most of one side and a part of the other side. It was flung backward from his naked muscles by the wind of his running and now it lay around him in the dust like a ragged garment. They say there is no imagining how terrible and in some way how grand the eyeball is when the skin has been taken entirely from around it: his eyes, which were bare in this way, also burned with pain, and with the final energies of his life, and with his desperate concern to warn us while he could: and he rolled his eyes wildly while he talked, or looked piercingly from one to another of the listeners, interrupting himself to cry out, '*Believe* me! Oh, *believe* me!' For it had evidently never occurred to him that he might not be believed, and must make this last great effort, in addition to all he had gone through for us, to *make* himself believed; so that he groaned with sorrow and with rage and railed at them without tact or mercy for their slowness to believe. He had scarcely what you could call a voice left, but with this relic of a voice he shouted and bellowed and bullied us and insulted us, in the agony of his concern. While he talked he bled from the mouth, and the mingled blood and saliva hung from his chin like the beard of a goat.

"Some say that with his naked face, and his savage eyes, and that beard and the hide lying off his bare shoulders like shabby clothing, he looked almost human. But others feel this is an irreverence even to think; and others, that it is a poor compliment to pay the one who told us, at such cost to himself, the true ultimate purpose of Man. Some did not believe he had ever come from our ranch in the first place, and of course he was so different from us in appearance and even in his voice, and so changed from what he might ever have looked or sounded like before, that nobody could recognize him for sure, though some were sure they did. Others suspected that he had been sent among us with his story for some mischievous and cruel purpose, and the fact that they could not imagine what this purpose might be, made them, naturally, all the more suspicious. Some believed he was actually a man, trying—and none too successfully, they said—to disguise himself as one of us; and again the fact that they could not imagine why a man would do this, made them all the more uneasy. There were quite a few who doubted that anyone who could get into such bad condition as he was in, was fit even to give reliable information, let alone advice, to those in good health. And some whispered, even while he spoke, that he had turned lunatic; and many came to believe this. It wasn't only that his story was so fantastic; there was good reason to wonder, many felt, whether anybody in his right mind would go to such trouble for others. But even those who did not believe him listened intently, out of curiosity to hear so wild a tale, and out of the respect it is only proper to show any creature who is in the last agony.

"What he told, was what I have just told you. But his purpose was away   100 beyond just the telling. When they asked questions, no matter how curious or suspicious or idle or foolish, he learned, toward the last, to answer them with all the patience he could and in all the detail he could remember. He even invited them to examine his wounded heels and the pulsing wound in his head as closely as they pleased. He even begged them to, for he knew that before everything else, he must be believed. For unless we could believe him, wherever could we find any reason, or enough courage, to do the hard and dreadful things he told us we must do!

"It was only these things, he cared about. Only for these, he came back."

Now clearly remembering what these things were, she felt her whole being quail. She looked at the young ones quickly and as quickly looked away.

"While he talked," she went on, "and our ancestors listened, men came quietly among us; one of them shot him. Whether he was shot in kindness or to silence him is an endlessly disputed question which will probably never be settled. Whether, even, he died of the shot, or through his own great pain and weariness (for his eyes, they say, were glazing for some time before the men came), we will never be sure. Some suppose even that he may have died of his sorrow and his concern for us. Others feel that he had quite enough to die of, without that. All these things are tangled and lost in the disputes of those who love to theorize and to argue. There is no arguing about his dying words, though; they were very clearly remembered:

"*Tell them! Believe!*"

After a while her son asked, "What did he tell them to do?"   105

She avoided his eyes. "There's a great deal of disagreement about that, too," she said after a moment. "You see, he was so very tired."

They were silent.

"So tired," she said, "some think that toward the end, he really *must* have been out of his mind."

"Why?" asked her son.

"Because he was so tired out and so badly hurt."   110

They looked at her mistrustfully.

"And because of what he told us to do."

"What did he tell us to do?" her son asked again.

Her throat felt dry. "Just . . . things you can hardly bear even to think of. That's all."

They waited. "Well, *what?*" her son asked in a cold, accusing voice.   115

"'*Each one is himself,*'" she said shyly. "'*Not of the herd. Himself alone.*' That's one."

"What else?"

"'*Obey nobody. Depend on none.*'"

"What else?"

She found that she was moved. "'*Break down the fences,*'" she said less shyly.   120
"'*Tell everybody, everywhere.*'"

"Where?"

"Everywhere. You see, he thought there must be ever so many more of us than we had ever known."

They were silent. "What else?" her son asked.

"'*For if even a few do not hear me, or disbelieve me, we are all betrayed.*'"

"Betrayed?"   125

"He meant, doing as men want us to. Not for ourselves, or the good of each other."

They were puzzled.

"Because, you see, he felt there was no other way." Again her voice altered:
"'*All who are put on the range are put onto trains. All who are put onto trains meet The Man With The Hammer. All who stay home are kept there to breed others to go onto the range, and so betray themselves and their kind and their children forever.*

"'*We are brought into this life only to be victims; and there is no other way for us unless we save ourselves.*'

"Do you understand?"   130

Still they were puzzled, she saw; and no wonder, poor things. But now the ancient lines rang in her memory, terrible and brave. They made her somehow proud. She began actually to want to say them.

"'*Never be taken,*'" she said. "'*Never be driven. Let those who can, kill Man. Let those who cannot, avoid him.*'"

She looked around at them.

"What else?" her son asked, and in his voice there was a rising valor.

She looked straight into his eyes. "'*Kill the yearlings,*'" she said very gently.   135
"'*Kill the calves.*'"

She saw the valor leave his eyes.

"Kill us?"

She nodded. "'*So long as Man holds dominion over us,*'" she said. And in
dread and amazement she heard herself add, "'*Bear no young.*'"

With this they all looked at her at once in such a way that she loved her
child, and all these others, as never before; and there dilated within her such a
sorrowful and marveling grandeur that for a moment she saw nothing, and heard
nothing except her own inward whisper, "Why, *I* am one alone. And of the herd,
too. Both at once. All one."

Her son's voice brought her back: "Did they do what he told them to?"   140

The oldest one scoffed, "Would we be here, if they had?"

"They say some did," the mother replied. "Some tried. Not all."

"What did the men do to them?" another asked.

"I don't know," she said. "It was such a very long time ago."

"Do you believe it?" asked the oldest calf.   145

"There are some who believe it," she said.

"Do *you?*"

"I'm told that far back in the wildest corners of the range there are some of
us, mostly very, very old ones, who have never been taken. It's said that they meet,
every so often, to talk and just to think together about the heroism and the terror
of two sublime Beings, The One Who Came Back, and The Man With The
Hammer. Even here at home, some of the old ones, and some of us who are just
old-fashioned, believe it, or parts of it anyway. I know there are some who say that
a hollow at the center of the forehead — a sort of shadow of the Hammer's blow —
is a sign of very special ability. And I remember how Great-grandmother used to
sing an old, pious song, let's see now, yes, 'Be not like dumb-driven cattle, be a
hero in the strife.' But there aren't many. Not any more."

"Do *you* believe it?" the oldest calf insisted; and now she was touched to realize that every one of them, from the oldest to the youngest, needed very badly to
be sure about that.

"Of course not, silly," she said; and all at once she was overcome by a curious   150
shyness, for it occurred to her that in the course of time, this young thing might
be bred to her. "It's just an old, old legend." With a tender little laugh she added,
lightly, "We use it to frighten children with."

By now the light was long on the plain and the herd was only a fume of
gold near the horizon. Behind it, dung steamed, and dust sank gently to the shattered ground. She looked far away for a moment, wondering. Something — it
was like a forgotten word on the tip of the tongue. She felt the sudden chill of the
late afternoon and she wondered what she had been wondering about. "Come,
children," she said briskly, "it's high time for supper." And she turned away; they
followed.

◆   ◆   ◆

The trouble was, her son was thinking, you could never trust her. If she said a thing was so, she was probably just trying to get her way with you. If she said a thing wasn't so, it probably was so. But you never could be sure. Not without seeing for yourself. I'm going to go, he told himself; I don't care *what* she wants. And if it isn't so, why then I'll live on the range and make a great journey and find out what *is* so. And if what she told was true, why then I'll know ahead of time and the one I will charge is The Man With The Hammer. I'll put Him and His Hammer out of the way forever, and that will make me an even better hero than The One Who Came Back.

So, when his mother glanced at him in concern, not quite daring to ask her question, he gave her his most docile smile, and snuggled his head against her, and she was comforted.

The littlest and youngest of them was doing double skips in his effort to keep up with her. Now that he wouldn't be interrupting her, and none of the big ones would hear and make fun of him, he shyly whispered his question, so warmly moistly ticklish that she felt as if he were licking her ear.

"What is it, darling?" she asked, bending down.   155

"What's a train?"   [1951]

THINKING ABOUT THE TEXT

1. In one sense, Agee's is not a realistic story. After all, it features animals that talk and engage in philosophical reflection. Do you find the story plausible in any respect, or is your reaction to it complete disbelief? Develop your response by referring to particular details of the text.

2. What historical events resemble the fictional events in this story — in particular, the transport and slaughter of the cows? Whom, if anyone, do you think of as you read about The One Who Came Back?

3. What are the mother cow's changing thoughts and feelings as she tells the story? How does her audience influence her way of telling it? Refer to specific passages.

4. Although she recounts the experiences of The One Who Came Back, the mother cow does not directly witness them. Moreover, the story that she tells about him has been passed down through the years; she is only the latest teller of it. What might have been Agee's purpose in having her lack direct evidence for the history she recalls?

5. What lessons does The One Who Came Back draw from his experiences? What does the mother cow seem to think of his views? What do you think of them?

TONI CADE BAMBARA
The Lesson

Toni Cade Bambara (1939–1995) taught at various colleges and worked as a community activist. She edited The Black Woman *(1970), a collection of essays that became a landmark of contemporary black feminism. Also a fiction writer, she received the American Book Award for her 1980 novel* The Salt Eaters *and has produced several collections of short stories. "The Lesson" comes from her first short-story collection,* Gorilla, My Love *(1972).*

Back in the days when everyone was old and stupid or young and foolish and me and Sugar were the only ones just right, this lady moved on our block with nappy hair and proper speech and no makeup. And quite naturally we laughed at her, laughed the way we did at the junk man who went about his business like he was some big-time president and his sorry-ass horse his secretary. And we kinda hated her too, hated the way we did the winos who cluttered up our parks and pissed on our handball walls and stank up our hallways and stairs so you couldn't halfway play hide-and-seek without a goddamn gas mask. Miss Moore was her name. The only woman on the block with no first name. And she was black as hell, cept for her feet, which were fish-white and spooky. And she was always planning these boring-ass things for us to do, us being my cousin, mostly, who lived on the block cause we all moved North the same time and to the same apartment then spread out gradual to breathe. And our parents would yank our heads into some kinda shape and crisp up our clothes so we'd be presentable for travel with Miss Moore, who always looked like she was going to church, though she never did. Which is just one of the things the grownups talked about when they talked behind her back like a dog. But when she came calling with some sachet she'd sewed up or some gingerbread she'd made or some book, why then they'd all be too embarrassed to turn her down and we'd get handed over all spruced up. She'd been to college and said it was only right that she should take responsibility for the young ones' education, and she not even related by marriage or blood. So they'd go for it. Specially Aunt Gretchen. She was the main gofer in the family. You got some ole dumb shit foolishness you want somebody to go for, you send for Aunt Gretchen. She been screwed into the go-along for so long, it's a blood-deep natural thing with her. Which is how she got saddled with me and Sugar and Junior in the first place while our mothers were in a la-de-da apartment up the block having a good ole time.

So this one day, Miss Moore rounds us all up at the mailbox and it's puredee hot and she's knockin herself out about arithmetic. And school suppose to let up in summer I heard, but she don't never let up. And the starch in my pinafore scratching the shit outta me and I'm really hating this nappy-head bitch and her goddamn college degree. I'd much rather go to the pool or to the show where it's cool. So me and Sugar leaning on the mailbox being surly, which is a Miss

Moore word. And Flyboy checking out what everybody brought for lunch. And Fat Butt already wasting his peanut-butter-and-jelly sandwich like the pig he is. And Junebug punchin on Q.T.'s arm for potato chips. And Rosie Giraffe shifting from one hip to the other waiting for somebody to step on her foot or ask her if she from Georgia so she can kick ass, preferably Mercedes'. And Miss Moore asking us do we know what money is, like we a bunch of retards. I mean real money, she say, like it's only poker chips or monopoly papers we lay on the grocer. So right away I'm tired of this and say so. And would much rather snatch Sugar and go to the Sunset and terrorize the West Indian kids and take their hair ribbons and their money too. And Miss Moore files that remark away for next week's lesson on brotherhood, I can tell. And finally I say we oughta get to the subway cause it's cooler and besides we might meet some cute boys. Sugar done swiped her mama's lipstick, so we ready.

So we heading down the street and she's boring us silly about what things cost and what our parents make and how much goes for rent and how money ain't divided up right in this country. And then she gets to the part about we all poor and live in the slums, which I don't feature. And I'm ready to speak on that, but she steps out in the street and hails two cabs just like that. Then she hustles half the crew in with her and hands me a five-dollar bill and tells me to calculate 10 percent tip for the driver. And we're off. Me and Sugar and Junebug and Flyboy hangin out the window and hollering to everybody, putting lipstick on each other cause Flyboy a faggot anyway, and making farts with our sweaty armpits. But I'm mostly trying to figure how to spend this money. But they all fascinated with the meter ticking and Junebug starts laying bets as to how much it'll read when Flyboy can't hold his breath no more. Then Sugar lays bets as to how much it'll be when we get there. So I'm stuck. Don't nobody want to go for my plan, which is to jump out at the next light and run off to the first bar-b-que we can find. Then the driver tells us to get the hell out cause we there already. And the meter reads eighty-five cents. And I'm stalling to figure out the tip and Sugar say give him a dime. And I decide he don't need it bad as I do, so later for him. But then he tries to take off with Junebug foot still in the door so we talk about his mama something ferocious. Then we check out that we on Fifth Avenue and everybody dressed up in stockings. One lady in a fur coat, hot as it is. White folks crazy.

"This is the place," Miss Moore say, presenting it to us in the voice she uses at the museum. "Let's look in the windows before we go in."

"Can we steal?" Sugar asks very serious like she's getting the ground rules   5
squared away before she plays. "I beg your pardon," say Miss Moore, and we fall out. So she leads us around the windows of the toy store and me and Sugar screamin, "This is mine, that's mine, I gotta have that, that was made for me, I was born for that," till Big Butt drowns us out.

"Hey, I'm goin to buy that there."

"That there? You don't even know what it is, stupid."

"I do so," he say punchin on Rosie Giraffe. "It's a microscope."

"Whatcha gonna do with a microscope, fool?"

"Look at things."   10

"Like what, Ronald?" ask Miss Moore. And Big Butt ain't got the first notion. So here go Miss Moore gabbing about the thousands of bacteria in a drop of water and the somethinorother in a speck of blood and the million and one living things in the air around us is invisible to the naked eye. And what she say that for? Junebug go to town on that "naked" and we rolling. Then Miss Moore ask what it cost. So we all jam into the window smudgin it up and the price tag say $300. So then she ask how long'd take for Big Butt and Junebug to save up their allowances. "Too long," I say. "Yeh," adds Sugar, "outgrown it by that time." And Miss Moore say no, you never outgrow learning instruments. "Why, even medical students and interns and," blah, blah, blah. And we ready to choke Big Butt for bringing it up in the first damn place.

"This here costs four hundred eighty dollars," says Rosie Giraffe. So we pile up all over her to see what she pointin out. My eyes tell me it's a chunk of glass cracked with something heavy, and different-color inks dripped into the splits, then the whole thing put into a oven or something. But for $480 it don't make sense.

"That's a paperweight made of semi-precious stones fused together under tremendous pressure," she explains slowly, with her hands doing the mining and all the factory work.

"So what's a paperweight?" asks Rosie Giraffe.

"To weigh paper with, dumbbell," say Flyboy, the wise man from the East.   15

"Not exactly," say Miss Moore, which is what she say when you warm or way off too. "It's to weigh paper down so it won't scatter and make your desk untidy." So right away me and Sugar curtsy to each other and then to Mercedes who is more the tidy type.

"We don't keep paper on top of the desk in my class," say Junebug, figuring Miss Moore crazy or lyin one.

"At home, then," she say. "Don't you have a calendar and pencil case and a blotter and a letter-opener on your desk at home where you do your homework?" And she know damn well what our homes look like cause she nosys around in them every chance she gets.

"I don't even have a desk," say Junebug. "Do we?"

"No. And I don't get no homework neither," says Big Butt.   20

"And I don't even have a home," say Flyboy like he do at school to keep the white folks off his back and sorry for him. Send this poor kid to camp posters, is his specialty.

"I do," says Mercedes. "I have a box of stationery on my desk and a picture of my cat. My godmother bought the stationery and the desk. There's a big rose on each sheet and the envelopes smell like roses."

"Who wants to know about your smelly-ass stationery," say Rosie Giraffe fore I can get my two cents in.

"It's important to have a work area all your own so that . . ."

"Will you look at this sailboat, please," say Flyboy, cuttin her off and pointin   25 to the thing like it was his. So once again we tumble all over each other to gaze at this magnificent thing in the toy store which is just big enough to maybe sail two kittens across the pond if you strap them to the posts tight. We all start reciting the price tag like we in assembly. "Handcrafted sailboat of fiberglass at one thousand one hundred ninety-five dollars."

"Unbelievable," I hear myself say and am really stunned. I read it again for myself just in case the group recitation put me in a trance. Same thing. For some reason this pisses me off. We look at Miss Moore and she lookin at us, waiting for I dunno what.

"Who'd pay all that when you can buy a sailboat set for a quarter at Pop's, a tube of glue for a dime, and a ball of string for eight cents? It must have a motor and a whole lot else besides," I say. "My sailboat cost me about fifty cents."

"But will it take water?" say Mercedes with her smart ass.

"Took mine to Alley Pond Park once," say Flyboy. "String broke. Lost it. Pity."

"Sailed mine in Central Park and it keeled over and sank. Had to ask my   30
father for another dollar."

"And you got the strap," laugh Big Butt. "The jerk didn't even have a string on it. My old man wailed on his behind."

Little Q.T. was staring hard at the sailboat and you could see he wanted it bad. But he too little and somebody'd just take it from him. So what the hell. "This boat for kids, Miss Moore?"

"Parents silly to buy something like that just to get all broke up," say Rosie Giraffe.

"That much money it should last forever," I figure.

"My father'd buy it for me if I wanted it."   35

"Your father, my ass," say Rosie Giraffe getting a chance to finally push Mercedes.

"Must be rich people shop here," say Q.T.

"You are a very bright boy," say Flyboy. "What was your first clue?" And he rap him on the head with the back of his knuckles, since Q.T. the only one he could get away with. Though Q.T. liable to come up behind you years later and get his licks in when you half expect it.

"What I want to know is," I says to Miss Moore though I never talk to her, I wouldn't give the bitch that satisfaction, "is how much a real boat costs? I figure a thousand'd get you a yacht any day."

"Why don't you check that out," she says, "and report back to the group?"   40
Which really pains my ass. If you gonna mess up a perfectly good swim day least you could do is have some answers. "Let's go in," she say like she got something up her sleeve. Only she don't lead the way. So me and Sugar turn the corner to where the entrance is, but when we get there I kinda hang back. Not that I'm scared, what's there to be afraid of, just a toy store. But I feel funny, shame. But what I got to be shamed about? Got as much right to go in as anybody. But somehow I can't seem to get hold of the door, so I step away from Sugar to lead. But she hangs back too. And I look at her and she looks at me and this is ridiculous. I mean, damn, I have never ever been shy about doing nothing or going nowhere. But then Mercedes steps up and then Rosie Giraffe and Big Butt crowd in behind and shove, and next thing we all stuffed into the doorway with only Mercedes squeezing past us, smoothing out her jumper and walking right down the aisle. Then the rest of us tumble in like a glued-together jigsaw done all wrong. And

people lookin at us. And it's like the time me and Sugar crashed into the Catholic church on a dare. But once we got in there and everything so hushed and holy and the candles and the bowin and the handkerchiefs on all the drooping heads, I just couldn't go through with the plan. Which was for me to run up to the altar and do a tap dance while Sugar played the nose flute and messed around in the holy water. And Sugar kept givin me the elbow. Then later teased me so bad I tied her up in the shower and turned it on and locked her in. And she'd be there till this day if Aunt Gretchen hadn't finally figured I was lying about the boarder takin a shower.

Same thing in the store. We all walkin on tiptoe and hardly touchin the games and puzzles and things. And I watched Miss Moore who is steady watchin us like she waitin for a sign. Like Mama Drewery watches the sky and sniffs the air and takes note of just how much slant is in the bird formation. Then me and Sugar bump smack into each other, so busy gazing at the toys, 'specially the sailboat. But we don't laugh and go into our fat-lady bump-stomach routine. We just stare at that price tag. Then Sugar run a finger over the whole boat. And I'm jealous and want to hit her. Maybe not her, but I sure want to punch somebody in the mouth.

"Watcha bring us here for, Miss Moore?"

"You sound angry, Sylvia. Are you mad about something?" Givin me one of them grins like she tellin a grown-up joke that never turns out to be funny. And she's lookin very closely at me like maybe she plannin to do my portrait from memory. I'm mad, but I won't give her that satisfaction. So I slouch around the store bein very bored and say, "Let's go."

Me and Sugar at the back of the train watchin the tracks whizzin by large then small then getting gobbled up in the dark. I'm thinkin about this tricky toy I saw in the store. A clown that somersaults on a bar then does chin-ups just cause you yank lightly at his leg. Cost $35. I could see me askin my mother for a $35 birthday clown. "You wanna who that costs what?" she'd say, cocking her head to the side to get a better view of the hole in my head. Thirty-five dollars could buy new bunk beds for Junior and Gretchen's boy. Thirty-five dollars and the whole household could go visit Grand-daddy Nelson in the country. Thirty-five dollars would pay for the rent and the piano bill too. Who are these people that spend that much for performing clowns and $1000 for toy sailboats? What kinda work they do and how they live and how come we ain't in on it? Where we are is who we are, Miss Moore always pointin out. But it don't necessarily have to be that way, she always adds then waits for somebody to say that poor people have to wake up and demand their share of the pie and don't none of us know what kind of pie she talking about in the first damn place. But she ain't so smart cause I still got her four dollars from the taxi and she sure ain't gettin it. Messin up my day with this shit. Sugar nudges me in my pocket and winks.

Miss Moore lines us up in front of the mailbox where we started from, seem like years ago, and I got a headache for thinkin so hard. And we lean all over each other so we can hold up under the draggy-ass lecture she always finishes us off with at the end before we thank her for borin us to tears. But she just looks at us like she readin tea leaves. Finally she say, "Well, what did you think of F. A. O. Schwarz?"

45

Rosie Giraffe mumbles, "White folks crazy."

"I'd like to go there again when I get my birthday money," says Mercedes, and we shove her out the pack so she has to lean on the mailbox by herself.

"I'd like a shower. Tiring day," say Flyboy.

Then Sugar surprises me by sayin, "You know, Miss Moore, I don't think all of us here put together eat in a year what that sailboat costs." And Miss Moore lights up like somebody goosed her. "And?" she say, urging Sugar on. Only I'm standin on her foot so she don't continue.

"Imagine for a minute what kind of society it is in which some people can   50 spend on a toy what it would cost to feed a family of six or seven. What do you think?"

"I think," say Sugar pushing me off her feet like she never done before, cause I whip her ass in a minute, "that this is not much of a democracy if you ask me. Equal chance to pursue happiness means an equal crack at the dough, don't it?" Miss Moore is beside herself and I am disgusted with Sugar's treachery. So I stand on her foot one more time to see if she'll shove me. She shuts up, and Miss Moore looks at me, sorrowfully I'm thinkin. And somethin weird is goin on, I can feel it in my chest.

"Anybody else learn anything today?" lookin dead at me. I walk away and Sugar has to run to catch up and don't even seem to notice when I shrug her arm off my shoulder.

"Well, we got four dollars anyway," she says.

"Uh hunh."

"We could go to Hascombs and get half a chocolate layer and then go to the   55 Sunset and still have plenty money for potato chips and ice cream sodas."

"Un hunh."

"Race you to Hascombs," she say.

We start down the block and she gets ahead which is O.K. by me cause I'm going to the West End and then over to the Drive to think this day through. She can run if she want to and even run faster. But ain't nobody gonna beat me at nuthin.   [1972]

THINKING ABOUT THE TEXT

1. Bambara's story begins with "Back in the days," which suggests that Sylvia is significantly older now than she was then. How much time do you think has passed since the events she recalls? Does it matter to you how old she is now? Why, or why not?

2. Miss Moore is not officially a teacher. Nor is she a relative of the children she instructs. Is it right, then, for her to "take responsibility for the young ones' education" (para. 1)? Make arguments for and against her doing so.

3. Consider Miss Moore herself as making an argument. What are her claims? Which of her strategies, if any, seem effective in persuading her audience? Which, if any, seem ineffective?

4. What statements by the children articulate the lesson that Miss Moore teaches? Are all these statements saying pretty much the same thing? At the end of the story is Sylvia ready to agree with all of them? Explain.

5. Do class and race seem equally important in this story, or does one seem more important than the other? Elaborate your reasoning.

MAKING COMPARISONS

1. In paragraph 92 of "A Mother's Tale," Agee writes, "Very well, she said to herself. I've gone so far; now I'll go the rest of the way. She decided not to soften it, either. She'd teach them a lesson they wouldn't forget in a hurry." Can this passage about the mother cow be applied to Miss Moore as well? Why, or why not? What would you think if a teacher of yours had this attitude?

2. Compare the lessons that the mother cow and Miss Moore teach. Do the lessons seem similar, or are you more struck by their differences?

3. Rewrite a paragraph of Agee's story as narrated by one of the young cows using a voice like Sylvia's. What does this exercise tell you about Agee's story? About Bambara's?

WRITING ABOUT ISSUES

1. Choose either "A Mother's Tale" or "The Lesson," and write an essay explaining how the story depicts children as learners. Refer to specific statements made by and about them. Whichever story you choose, feel free to make distinctions among its children.

2. At the end of Agee's story, the mother cow's son distrusts her account. Furthermore, he plans to "make a great journey" (para. 152) despite her wishes. At the end of Bambara's story, however, Sylvia evidently comes closer to sharing Miss Moore's view of society. Should we conclude that Miss Moore is a better teacher than the mother cow? Write an essay arguing your position on this issue of evaluation.

3. Write an essay explaining how a certain occasion changed, or came close to changing, your view of society. Give details of the occasion itself, identifying any "teachers" involved. Be specific, too, about the view you held before the occasion, why you had thought of your society that way, and how the occasion provided you with evidence for another view.

4. Today, cattle are still slaughtered for meat, and some people can afford expensive toys while others don't have much money at all. Think of eight-year-olds in your neighborhood. Choose one of these situations and write an essay identifying what and how you would teach the children about it. Be sure to justify the goals and methods you would adopt.

LOSING INNOCENCE: RE-VISIONS OF "LITTLE RED RIDING HOOD"

CHARLES PERRAULT, "Little Red Riding Hood"
JACOB AND WILHELM GRIMM, "Little Red Cap"
ANGELA CARTER, "The Company of Wolves"

The tale of Little Red Riding Hood is still told to children throughout the world. In a sense, her adventure is part of their education. What, though, do they learn from this narrative? Scholars have suggested various interpretations. Among the most well-known and provocative is that of psychoanalyst Bruno Bettelheim, who sees the tale as a symbolic treatment of a girl's effort to understand her sexual development. In this view, the story teaches girls to work through adolescent anxieties. But whatever decoding the tale receives, two aspects of it remain important. First, it depicts a child's move from innocence to experience, however these terms are defined. Little Red Riding Hood learns something, largely on her own. Second, more than one version of her story exists; by now, several do. Indeed, the story is worth analyzing in a chapter on Teaching and Learning precisely because it serves as an instrument of children's education, focuses on a child's discovery, and yet circulates in various forms. Hence, we devote a re-vision cluster to this ever-popular tale, inviting you to compare three particular versions of it: Charles Perrault's from the seventeenth century, the Brothers Grimm's from the nineteenth century, and Angela Carter's modern variation.

BEFORE YOU READ

Write down what you remember about the story of Little Red Riding Hood, and then compare your version with those of your classmates. What elements of the story do your class's various renditions of it have in common? What differences, if any, emerge? Why do you think the story has been so popular?

CHARLES PERRAULT
Little Red Riding Hood

Along with the Brothers Grimm, Charles Perrault (1628–1703) was the most influential teller of the fairy tales many of us learned as children. Born in Paris to a fairly wealthy family, Perrault was trained as a lawyer. For his literary and philosophical achievements, however, Perrault was elected to the prestigious Académie Française in 1671. During his lifetime, he and others were involved in a major cultural dispute over the relative merits of ancient authors and modern ones, with Perrault favoring the more up-to-date group. Later generations remember him best, though, for his 1697 book, Stories or Tales from Times Past, with Morals: Tales of Mother Goose. *This collection included "Le Petit Chaperon Rouge," which English-speaking*

(Jacob and Wilhelm Grimm. Culver Pictures, Inc.)

(Charles Perrault. The Granger Collection, New York.)

(Angela Carter. Miriam Berkley.)

readers have come to know as "Little Red Riding Hood." This story did not completely originate with Perrault; probably he had heard folktales containing some of its narrative elements. Nevertheless, his version became popular on publication and has remained so ever since.

Once upon a time there lived in a certain village a little country girl, the prettiest creature who was ever seen. Her mother was excessively fond of her, and her grandmother doted on her still more. This good woman had a little red riding hood made for her. It suited the girl so extremely well that everybody called her Little Red Riding Hood.

One day her mother, having made some cakes, said to her, "Go, my dear, and see how your grandmother is doing, for I hear she has been very ill. Take her a cake, and this little pot of butter."

Little Red Riding Hood set out immediately to go to her grandmother, who lived in another village.

As she was going through the wood, she met with a wolf, who had a very great mind to eat her up, but he dared not, because of some woodcutters working nearby in the forest. He asked her where she was going. The poor child, who did not know that it was dangerous to stay and talk to a wolf, said to him, "I am going to see my grandmother and carry her a cake and a little pot of butter from my mother."

"Does she live far off?" said the wolf. 5

"Oh I say," answered Little Red Riding Hood. "It is beyond that mill you see there, at the first house in the village."

"Well," said the wolf, "and I'll go and see her too. I'll go this way and go you that, and we shall see who will be there first."

The wolf ran as fast as he could, taking the shortest path, and the little girl took a roundabout way, entertaining herself by gathering nuts, running after butterflies, and gathering bouquets of little flowers. It was not long before the wolf arrived at the old woman's house. He knocked at the door: tap, tap.

"Who's there?"

"Your grandchild, Little Red Riding Hood," replied the wolf, counterfeiting 10 her voice, "who has brought you a cake and a little pot of butter sent you by Mother."

The good grandmother, who was in bed because she was somewhat ill, cried out, "Pull the bobbin, and the latch will go up."

The wolf pulled the bobbin, and the door opened, and then he immediately fell upon the good woman and ate her up in a moment, for it had been more than three days since he had eaten. He then shut the door and got into the grandmother's bed, expecting Little Red Riding Hood, who came some time afterwards and knocked at the door: tap, tap.

"Who's there?"

Little Red Riding Hood, hearing the big voice of the wolf, was at first afraid but, believing her grandmother had a cold and was hoarse, answered, "It is your grandchild Little Red Riding Hood, who has brought you a cake and a little pot of butter Mother sends you."

The wolf cried out to her, softening his voice as much as he could, "Pull the 15 bobbin, and the latch will go up."

Little Red Riding Hood pulled the bobbin, and the door opened.

The wolf, seeing her come in, said to her, hiding himself under the bedclothes, "Put the cake and the little pot of butter upon the stool, and come get into bed with me."

Little Red Riding Hood took off her clothes and got into bed. She was greatly amazed to see how her grandmother looked in her nightclothes and said to her, "Grandmother, what big arms you have!"

"All the better to hug you with, my dear."

"Grandmother, what big legs you have!" 20

"All the better to run with, my child."

"Grandmother, what big ears you have!"

"All the better to hear with, my child."

"Grandmother, what big eyes you have!"

"All the better to see with, my child." 25

"Grandmother, what big teeth you have got!"

"All the better to eat you up with."

And saying these words, this wicked wolf fell upon Little Red Riding Hood, and ate her all up.

Moral: Children, especially attractive, well bred young ladies, should never talk to strangers, for if they should do so, they may well provide dinner for a wolf. I say "wolf," but there are various kinds of wolves. There are also those who are charming, quiet, polite, unassuming, complacent, and sweet, who pursue young women at home and in the streets. And unfortunately, it is these gentle wolves who are the most dangerous ones of all.   [1697]

THINKING ABOUT THE TEXT

1. To what extent does it matter to the story that Little Red Riding Hood is pretty? Would your reaction be the same if you learned she was homely or if you did not know how she looked? Explain.

2. The two main female characters are Little Red Riding Hood and her grandmother. Although the girl's mother appears briefly at the start, she then disappears from the narrative. What purposes are served by Perrault's leaving her out?

3. How would you describe Little Red Riding Hood as Perrault depicts her? Refer to specific details of the text.

4. In this version, Little Red Riding Hood dies. Would you draw different ideas from the text if she had lived? If so, what?

5. Does Perrault's moral seem well connected to the preceding story? Why, or why not? What metaphoric wolves might this moral apply to?

JACOB AND WILHELM GRIMM

Little Red Cap

Jacob Grimm (1785–1863) and Wilhelm Grimm (1786–1859) were born in Hanau, Germany, and studied law at Marburg University. They served as linguistics professors at Gottingen University and made major contributions to the historical study of language. The Grimms began to collect folktales from various oral European traditions for their friends but later published their efforts for both children and adults. Their methods became a model for the scientific collection of folktales and folk songs. Today they are known best for their volume Children's and Household Tales, *which was first published in 1812 and went through six more editions, the last in 1857. Their book included their version of the Little Red Riding Hood story, although their title for it was (in English translation) "Little Red Cap."*

Once upon a time there was a sweet little girl. Everyone who saw her liked her, but most of all her grandmother, who did not know what to give the child next. Once she gave her a little cap made of red velvet. Because it suited her so well, and she wanted to wear it all the time, she came to be known as Little Red Cap.

One day her mother said to her, "Come Little Red Cap. Here is a piece of cake and a bottle of wine. Take them to your grandmother. She is sick and weak, and they will do her well. Mind your manners, and give her my greetings. Behave yourself on the way, and do not leave the path, or you might fall down and break the glass, and then there will be nothing for your grandmother. And when you enter her parlor, don't forget to say 'Good morning,' and don't peer into all the corners first."

"I'll do everything just right," said Little Red Cap, shaking her mother's hand.

The grandmother lived out in the woods, a half hour from the village. When Little Red Cap entered the woods, a wolf came up to her. She did not know what a wicked animal he was and was not afraid of him.

"Good day to you, Little Red Cap."   5

"Thank you, wolf."

"Where are you going so early, Little Red Cap?"

"To Grandmother's."

"And what are you carrying under your apron?"

"Grandmother is sick and weak, and I am taking her some cake and wine.   10
We baked yesterday, and they should be good for her and give her strength."

"Little Red Cap, just where does your grandmother live?"

"Her house is a good quarter hour from here in the woods, under the three large oak trees. There's a hedge of hazel bushes there. You must know the place," said Little Red Cap.

The wolf thought to himself, "Now that sweet young thing is a tasty bite for me. She will taste even better than the old woman. You must be sly, and you can catch them both."

He walked along a little while with Little Red Cap. Then he said, "Little Red Cap, just look at the beautiful flowers that are all around us. Why don't you go and take a look? And I don't believe you can hear how beautifully the birds are singing. You are walking along as though you were on your way to school. It is very beautiful in the woods."

Little Red Cap opened her eyes, and when she saw the sunbeams dancing to   15
and fro through the trees and how the ground was covered with beautiful flowers, she thought, "If I take a fresh bouquet to Grandmother, she will be very pleased. Anyway, it is still early, and I'll be home on time." And she ran off the path into the woods looking for flowers. Each time she picked one, she thought that she could see an even more beautiful one a little way off, and she ran after it, going farther and farther into the woods. But the wolf ran straight to the grandmother's house and knocked on the door.

"Who's there?"

"Little Red Cap. I'm bringing you some cake and wine. Open the door."

"Just press the latch," called out the grandmother. "I'm too weak to get up."

The wolf pressed the latch, and the door opened. He stepped inside, went straight to the grandmother's bed, and ate her up. Then he put on her clothes, put her cap on his head, got into her bed, and pulled the curtains shut.

Little Red Cap had run after the flowers. After she had gathered so many that she could not carry any more, she remembered her grandmother and then continued on her way to her house. She found, to her surprise, that the door was open. She walked into the parlor, and everything looked so strange that she thought, "Oh, my God, why am I so afraid? I usually like it at Grandmother's."

She called out, "Good morning!" but received no answer.

Then she went to the bed and pulled back the curtains. Grandmother was lying there with her cap pulled down over her face and looking very strange.

"Oh, Grandmother, what big ears you have!"

"All the better to hear you with."

"Oh, Grandmother, what big eyes you have!"

"All the better to see you with."

"Oh, Grandmother, what big hands you have!"

"All the better to grab you with!"

"Oh, Grandmother, what a horribly big mouth you have!"

"All the better to eat you with!"

The wolf had scarcely finished speaking when he jumped from the bed with a single leap and ate up poor Little Red Cap. As soon as the wolf had satisfied his desires, he climbed back into bed, fell asleep, and began to snore very loudly.

A huntsman was just passing by. He thought, "The old woman is snoring so loudly. You had better see if something is wrong with her."

He stepped into the parlor, and when he approached the bed, he saw the wolf lying there. "So here I find you, you old sinner," he said. "I have been hunting for you a long time."

He was about to aim his rifle when it occurred to him that the wolf might have eaten the grandmother and that she still might be rescued. So instead of shooting, he took a pair of scissors and began to cut open the wolf's belly. After a few cuts he saw the red cap shining through, and after a few more cuts the girl jumped out, crying, "Oh, I was so frightened! It was so dark inside the wolf's body!"

And then the grandmother came out as well, alive but hardly able to breathe. Then Little Red Cap fetched some large stones. She filled the wolf's body with them, and when he woke up and tried to run away, the stones were so heavy that he immediately fell down dead.

The three of them were happy. The huntsman skinned the wolf and went home with the pelt. The grandmother ate the cake and drank the wine that Little Red Cap had brought. And Little Red Cap thought, "As long as I live, I will never leave the path and run off into the woods by myself if Mother tells me not to."

They also tell how Little Red Cap was taking some baked things to her grandmother another time, when another wolf spoke to her and wanted her to leave the path. But Little Red Cap took care and went straight to Grandmother's. She told her that she had seen the wolf and that he had wished her a good day but had stared at her in a wicked manner. "If we hadn't been on a public road, he would have eaten me up," she said.

"Come," said the grandmother. "Let's lock the door, so he can't get in."

Soon afterward the wolf knocked on the door and called out, "Open up, Grandmother. It's Little Red Cap, and I'm bringing you some baked things."

They remained silent and did not open the door. Gray-Head crept around   40
the house several times and finally jumped onto the roof. He wanted to wait until Little Red Cap went home that evening and then follow her and eat her up in the darkness. But the grandmother saw what he was up to. There was a large stone trough in front of the house.

"Fetch a bucket, Little Red Cap," she said to the child. "Yesterday I cooked some sausage. Carry the water that I boiled them with to the trough." Little Red Cap carried water until the large, large trough was clear full. The smell of sausage arose into the wolf's nose. He sniffed and looked down, stretching his neck so long that he could no longer hold himself, and he began to slide. He slid off the roof, fell into the trough, and drowned. And Little Red Cap returned home happily, and no one harmed her.   [1857]

THINKING ABOUT THE TEXT

1. Why do you think that, at the beginning of the tale, the Grimms emphasize how sweet and likable Little Red Cap is?

2. To what extent do you blame Little Red Cap for being distracted by the beauty of nature? Explain your reasoning.

3. The Grimms have Little Red Cap and her grandmother rescued by a hunter. What would you say to someone who sees the Grimms as implying that women always need help from a man?

4. The wolf dies because Little Red Cap has filled his body with stones. Why do you think the Grimms did not have the huntsman simply shoot the wolf after freeing Little Red Cap and her grandmother?

5. Why do you think the Grimms added the second story? What is its effect?

MAKING COMPARISONS

1. Does Red Riding Hood seem basically the same in both Perrault's version and the Grimms' version? Refer to specific details of both texts.

2. In Perrault's tale, the wolf persuades Red Riding Hood to take off her clothes and get into bed with him. In the Grimms' account, the wolf jumps up from the bed and eats her. How significant is this difference between the two versions?

3. In Perrault's version, Red Riding Hood and her grandmother die. The Grimms, on the other hand, have them rescued. Do you therefore see these two versions as putting forth different views of life? Explain.

ANGELA CARTER

The Company of Wolves

A native of Sussex, England, Angela Carter (1940–1991) worked in various genres, writing novels, short stories, screenplays, essays, and newspaper articles. Her fiction is most known for imaginatively refashioning classic tales of fantasy, including supernatural and Gothic thrillers as well as fairy tales. Often, Carter rewrote these narratives from a distinctly female point of view, challenging what she saw as their patriarchal values and using them to explore the psychology of both genders. "The Company of Wolves," her version of the Little Red Riding Hood tale, was first published in the journal Bananas *in 1977. It then appeared in Carter's short story volume* The Bloody Chamber *(1979) and was reprinted in* Burning Our Boats *(1995), a posthumous collection of all her stories. This tale also served as the basis for a 1984 film of the same title, which Carter wrote with director Neil Jordan.*

One beast and only one howls in the woods by night.

The wolf is carnivore incarnate, and he's as cunning as he is ferocious; once he's had a taste of flesh then nothing else will do.

At night, the eyes of wolves shine like candle flames, yellowish, reddish, but that is because the pupils of their eyes fatten on darkness and catch the light from your lantern to flash it back to you — red for danger; if a wolf's eyes reflect only moonlight, then they gleam a cold and unnatural green, a mineral, a piercing color. If the benighted traveler spies those luminous, terrible sequins stitched suddenly on the black thickets, then he knows he must run, if fear has not struck him stock-still.

But those eyes are all you will be able to glimpse of the forest assassins as they cluster invisibly round your smell of meat as you go through the wood unwisely late. They will be like shadows, they will be like wraiths, gray members of a congregation of nightmare; hark! his long, wavering howl . . . an aria of fear made audible.

The wolfsong is the sound of the rending you will suffer, in itself a murdering.   5

It is winter and cold weather. In this region of mountain and forest, there is now nothing for the wolves to eat. Goats and sheep are locked up in the byre,° the deer departed for the remaining pasturage on the southern slopes — wolves grow lean and famished. There is so little flesh on them that you could count the starveling ribs through their pelts, if they gave you time before they pounced. Those slavering jaws; the lolling tongue; the rime of saliva on the grizzled chops — of all the teeming perils of the night and the forest, ghosts, hobgoblins, ogres that grill babies upon gridirons, witches that fatten their captives in cages for cannibal tables, the wolf is worst for he cannot listen to reason.

You are always in danger in the forest, where no people are. Step between the portals of the great pines where the shaggy branches tangle about you, trapping

byre: Barn or shed.

the unwary traveler in nets as if the vegetation itself were in a plot with the wolves who live there, as though the wicked trees go fishing on behalf of their friends — step between the gateposts of the forest with the greatest trepidation and infinite precautions, for if you stray from the path for one instant, the wolves will eat you. They are gray as famine, they are as unkind as plague.

The grave-eyed children of the sparse villages always carry knives with them when they go out to tend the little flocks of goats that provide the homesteads with acrid milk and rank, maggoty cheeses. Their knives are half as big as they are, the blades are sharpened daily.

But the wolves have ways of arriving at your own hearthside. We try and try but sometimes we cannot keep them out. There is no winter's night the cottager does not fear to see a lean, gray, famished snout questing under the door, and there was a woman once bitten in her own kitchen as she was straining the macaroni.

Fear and flee the wolf; for, worst of all, the wolf may be more than he seems.   10

There was a hunter once, near here, that trapped a wolf in a pit. This wolf had massacred the sheep and goats; eaten up a mad old man who used to live by himself in a hut halfway up the mountain and sing to Jesus all day; pounced on a girl looking after the sheep, but she made such a commotion that men came with rifles and scared him away and tried to track him into the forest but he was cunning and easily gave them the slip. So this hunter dug a pit and put a duck in it, for bait, all alive-oh; and he covered the pit with straw smeared with wolf dung. Quack, quack! went the duck and a wolf came slinking out of the forest, a big one, a heavy one, he weighed as much as a grown man, and the straw gave way beneath him — into the pit he tumbled. The hunter jumped down after him, slit his throat, cut off all his paws for a trophy.

And then no wolf at all lay in front of the hunter but the bloody trunk of a man, headless, footless, dying, dead.

A witch from up the valley once turned an entire wedding party into wolves because the groom had settled on another girl. She used to order them to visit her, at night, from spite, and they would sit and howl around her cottage for her, serenading her with their misery.

Not so very long ago, a young woman in our village married a man who vanished clean away on her wedding night. The bed was made with new sheets and the bride lay down in it; the groom said, he was going out to relieve himself, insisted on it, for the sake of decency, and she drew the coverlet up to her chin and she lay there. And she waited and she waited and then she waited again — surely he's been gone a long time? Until she jumps up in bed and shrieks to hear a howling, coming on the wind from the forest.

That long-drawn, wavering howl has, for all its fearful resonance, some   15
inherent sadness in it, as if the beasts would love to be less beastly if only they knew how and never cease to mourn their own condition. There is a vast melancholy in the canticles° of the wolves, melancholy infinite as the forest, endless as these long nights of winter and yet that ghastly sadness, that mourning for their own, irremediable appetites, can never move the heart for not one phrase in it

canticles: Songs or chants.

hints at the possibility of redemption; grace could not come to the wolf from its own despair, only through some external mediator, so that, sometimes, the beast will look as if he half welcomes the knife that despatches him.

The young woman's brothers searched the outhouses and the haystacks but never found any remains, so the sensible girl dried her eyes and found herself another husband not too shy to piss into a pot who spent the nights indoors. She gave him a pair of bonny babies and all went right as a trivet until, one freezing night, the night of the solstice, the hinge of the year when things do not fit together as well as they should, the longest night, her first good man came home again.

A great thump on the door announced him as she was stirring the soup for the father of her children, and she knew him the moment she lifted the latch to him although it was years since she'd worn black for him and now he was in rags and his hair hung down his back and never saw a comb, alive with lice.

"Here I am again, missus," he said. "Get me my bowl of cabbage and be quick about it."

Then her second husband came in with wood for the fire and when the first one saw she'd slept with another man and, worse, clapped his red eyes on her little children who'd crept into the kitchen to see what all the din was about, he shouted: "I wish I were a wolf again, to teach this whore a lesson!" So a wolf he instantly became and tore off the eldest boy's left foot before he was chopped up with the hatchet they used for chopping logs. But when the wolf lay bleeding and gasping its last, the pelt peeled off again and he was just as he had been, years ago, when he ran away from his marriage bed, so that she wept and her second husband beat her.

They say there's an ointment the Devil gives you that turns you into a wolf the minute you rub it on. Or that he was born feet first and had a wolf for his father and his torso is a man's but his legs and genitals are a wolf's. And he has a wolf's heart.

Seven years is a werewolf's natural span but if you burn his human clothing you condemn him to wolfishness for the rest of his life, so old wives hereabouts think it some protection to throw a hat or an apron at the werewolf, as if clothes made the man. Yet by the eyes, those phosphorescent eyes, you know him in all his shapes; the eyes alone unchanged by metamorphosis.

Before he can become a wolf, the lycanthrope° strips stark naked. If you spy a naked man among the pines, you must run as if the Devil were after you.

It is midwinter and the robin, the friend of man, sits on the handle of the gardener's spade and sings. It is the worst time in all the year for wolves, but this strong-minded child insists she will go off through the wood. She is quite sure the wild beasts cannot harm her although, well-warned, she lays a carving knife in the basket her mother has packed with cheeses. There is a bottle of harsh liquor distilled from brambles; a batch of flat oatcakes baked on the hearthstone; a pot or two of jam. The flaxen-haired girl will take these delicious gifts to a reclusive

---

lycanthrope: Werewolf.

grandmother so old the burden of her years is crushing her to death. Granny lives two hours' trudge through the winter woods; the child wraps herself up in her thick shawl, draws it over her head. She steps into her stout wooden shoes; she is dressed and ready and it is Christmas Eve. The malign door of the solstice still swings upon its hinges, but she has been too much loved ever to feel scared.

Children do not stay young for long in this savage country. There are no toys for them to play with, so they work hard and grow wise, but this one, so pretty and the youngest of her family, a little late-comer, had been indulged by her mother and the grandmother who'd knitted her the red shawl that, today, has the ominous if brilliant look of blood on snow. Her breasts have just begun to swell; her hair is like lint, so fair it hardly makes a shadow on her pale forehead; her cheeks are an emblematic scarlet and white and she has just started her woman's bleeding, the clock inside her that will strike, henceforward, once a month.

She stands and moves within the invisible pentacle° of her own virginity. She   25
is an unbroken egg; she is a sealed vessel; she has inside her a magic space the entrance to which is shut tight with a plug of membrane; she is a closed system; she does not know how to shiver. She has her knife and she is afraid of nothing.

Her father might forbid her, if he were home, but he is away in the forest, gathering wood, and her mother cannot deny her.

The forest closed upon her like a pair of jaws.

There is always something to look at in the forest, even in the middle of winter—the huddled mounds of birds, succumbed to the lethargy of the season, heaped on the creaking boughs and too forlorn to sing; the bright frills of the winter fungi on the blotched trunks of the trees; the cuneiform° slots of rabbits and deer, the herringbone tracks of the birds, a hare as lean as a rasher of bacon streaking across the path where the thin sunlight dapples the russet brakes of last year's bracken.

When she heard the freezing howl of a distant wolf, her practiced hand sprang to the handle of her knife, but she saw no sign of a wolf at all, nor of a naked man, neither, but then she heard a clattering among the brushwood and there sprang on to the path a fully clothed one, a very handsome young one, in the green coat and wide-awake hat of a hunter, laden with carcasses of game birds. She had her hand on her knife at the first rustle of twigs, but he laughed with a flash of white teeth when he saw her and made her a comic yet flattering little bow; she'd never seen such a fine fellow before, not among the rustic clowns of her native village. So on they went together, through the thickening light of the afternoon.

Soon they were laughing and joking like old friends. When he offered to   30
carry her basket, she gave it to him although her knife was in it because he told her his rifle would protect them. As the day darkened, it began to snow again; she felt the first flakes settle on her eyelashes, but now there was only half a mile to go and there would be a fire, and hot tea, and a welcome, a warm one, surely, for the dashing huntsman as well as for herself.

---

pentacle: Five-pointed star; also called a pentagram.   **cuneiform:** Wedge-shaped.

This young man had a remarkable object in his pocket. It was a compass. She looked at the little round glass face in the palm of his hand and watched the wavering needle with a vague wonder. He assured her this compass had taken him safely through the wood on his hunting trip because the needle always told him with perfect accuracy where the north was. She did not believe it; she knew she should never leave the path on the way through the wood or else she would be lost instantly. He laughed at her again; gleaming trails of spittle clung to his teeth. He said, if he plunged off the path into the forest that surrounded them, he could guarantee to arrive at her grandmother's house a good quarter of an hour before she did, plotting his way through the undergrowth with his compass, while she trudged the long way, along the winding path.

I don't believe you. Besides, aren't you afraid of the wolves?

He only tapped the gleaming butt of his rifle and grinned.

Is it a bet? he asked her. Shall we make a game of it? What will you give me if I get to your grandmother's house before you?

What would you like? she asked disingenuously.   35

A kiss.

Commonplaces of a rustic seduction; she lowered her eyes and blushed.

He went through the undergrowth and took her basket with him but she forgot to be afraid of the beasts, although now the moon was rising, for she wanted to dawdle on her way to make sure the handsome gentleman would win his wager.

Grandmother's house stood by itself a little way out of the village. The freshly falling snow blew in eddies about the kitchen garden, and the young man stepped delicately up the snowy path to the door as if he were reluctant to get his feet wet, swinging his bundle of game and the girl's basket and humming a little tune to himself.

There is a faint trace of blood on his chin; he has been snacking on his catch.   40

He rapped upon the panels with his knuckles.

Aged and frail, granny is three-quarters succumbed to the mortality the ache in her bones promises her and almost ready to give in entirely. A boy came out from the village to build up her hearth for the night an hour ago and the kitchen crackles with busy firelight. She has her Bible for company, she is a pious old woman. She is propped up on several pillows in the bed set into the wall peasant-fashion, wrapped up in the patchwork quilt she made before she was married, more years ago than she cares to remember. Two china spaniels with liver-colored blotches on their coats and black noses sit on either side of the fireplace. There is a bright rug of woven rags on the pantiles. The grandfather clock ticks away her eroding time.

We keep the wolves outside by living well.

He rapped upon the panels with his hairy knuckles.

It is your granddaughter, he mimicked in a high soprano.   45

Lift up the latch and walk in, my darling.

You can tell them by their eyes, eyes of a beast of prey, nocturnal, devastating eyes as red as a wound; you can hurl your Bible at him and your apron after, granny, you thought that was a sure prophylactic against these infernal vermin . . .

now call on Christ and his mother and all the angels in heaven to protect you but it won't do you any good.

His feral muzzle is sharp as a knife; he drops his golden burden of gnawed pheasant on the table and puts down your dear girl's basket, too. Oh, my God, what have you done with her?

Off with his disguise, that coat of forest-colored cloth, the hat with the feather tucked into the ribbon; his matted hair streams down his white shirt and she can see the lice moving in it. The sticks in the hearth shift and hiss; night and the forest has come into the kitchen with darkness tangled in its hair.

He strips off his shirt. His skin is the color and texture of vellum. A crisp   50
stripe of hair runs down his belly, his nipples are ripe and dark as poison fruit, but he's so thin you could count the ribs under his skin if only he gave you the time. He strips off his trousers and she can see how hairy his legs are. His genitals, huge. Ah! huge.

The last thing the old lady saw in all this world was a young man, eyes like cinders, naked as a stone, approaching her bed.

The wolf is carnivore incarnate.

When he had finished with her, he licked his chops and quickly dressed himself again, until he was just as he had been when he came through her door. He burned the inedible hair in the fireplace and wrapped the bones up in a napkin that he hid away under the bed in the wooden chest in which he found a clean pair of sheets. These he carefully put on the bed instead of the tell-tale stained ones he stowed away in the laundry basket. He plumped up the pillows and shook out the patchwork quilt, he picked up the Bible from the floor, closed it and laid it on the table. All was as it had been before except that grandmother was gone. The sticks twitched in the grate, the clock ticked and the young man sat patiently, deceitfully beside the bed in granny's nightcap.

Rat-a-tap-tap.

Who's there, he quavers in granny's antique falsetto.   55

Only your granddaughter.

So she came in, bringing with her a flurry of snow that melted in tears on the tiles, and perhaps she was a little disappointed to see only her grandmother sitting beside the fire. But then he flung off the blanket and sprang to the door, pressing his back against it so that she could not get out again.

The girl looked round the room and saw there was not even the indentation of a head on the smooth cheek of the pillow and how, for the first time she'd seen it so, the Bible lay closed on the table. The tick of the clock cracked like a whip. She wanted her knife from her basket, but she did not dare reach for it because his eyes were fixed upon her—huge eyes that now seemed to shine with a unique, interior light, eyes the size of saucers, saucers full of Greek fire, diabolic phosphorescence.

What big eyes you have.

All the better to see you with.   60

No trace at all of the old woman except for a tuft of white hair that had caught in the bark of an unburned log. When the girl saw that, she knew she was in danger of death.

Where is my grandmother?

There's nobody here but we two, my darling.

Now a great howling rose up all around them, near, very near, as close as the kitchen garden, the howling of a multitude of wolves; she knew the worst wolves are hairy on the inside and she shivered, in spite of the scarlet shawl she pulled more closely round herself as if it could protect her although it was as red as the blood she must spill.

Who has come to sing us carols, she said.   65

Those are the voices of my brothers, darling; I love the company of wolves. Look out of the window and you'll see them.

Snow half-caked the lattice and she opened it to look into the garden. It was a white night of moon and snow; the blizzard whirled round the gaunt, grey beasts who squatted on their haunches among the rows of winter cabbage, pointing their sharp snouts to the moon and howling as if their hearts would break. Ten wolves; twenty wolves — so many wolves she could not count them, howling in concert as if demented or deranged. Their eyes reflected the light from the kitchen and shone like a hundred candles.

It is very cold, poor things, she said; no wonder they howl so.

She closed the window on the wolves' threnody° and took off her scarlet shawl, the color of poppies, the color of sacrifices, the color of her menses, and, since her fear did her no good, she ceased to be afraid.

What shall I do with my shawl?   70

Throw it on the fire, dear one. You won't need it again.

She bundled up her shawl and threw it on the blaze, which instantly consumed it. Then she drew her blouse over her head; her small breasts gleamed as if the snow had invaded the room.

What shall I do with my blouse?

Into the fire with it, too, my pet.

The thin muslin went flaring up the chimney like a magic bird and now off   75
came her skirt, her woolen stockings, her shoes, and on to the fire they went, too, and were gone for good. The firelight shone through the edges of her skin; now she was clothed only in her untouched integument° of flesh. This dazzling, naked she combed out her hair with her fingers; her hair looked white as the snow outside. Then went directly to the man with red eyes in whose unkempt mane the lice moved; she stood up on tiptoe and unbuttoned the collar of his shirt.

What big arms you have.

All the better to hug you with.

Every wolf in the world now howled a prothalamion° outside the window as she freely gave the kiss she owed him.

What big teeth you have!

She saw how his jaw began to slaver and the room was full of the clamor of   80
the forest's Liebestod° but the wise child never flinched, even when he answered:

---

threnody: Lament or dirge.   **integument:** Outer covering, such as animal skin or seed coat.
prothalamion: Wedding song.   **Liebestod:** Final aria in Richard Wagner's opera *Tristan und Isolde*, in which Isolde sings over Tristan's dead body and ultimately dies herself.

All the better to eat you with.

The girl burst out laughing; she knew she was nobody's meat. She laughed at him full in the face, she ripped off his shirt for him and flung it into the fire, in the fiery wake of her own discarded clothing. The flames danced like dead souls on Walpurgisnacht,° and the old bones under the bed set up a terrible clattering, but she did not pay them any heed.

Carnivore incarnate, only immaculate flesh appeases him.

She will lay his fearful head on her lap and she will pick out the lice from his pelt and perhaps she will put the lice into her mouth and eat them, as he will bid her, as she would do in a savage marriage ceremony.

The blizzard will die down.   85

The blizzard died down, leaving the mountains as randomly covered with snow as if a blind woman had thrown a sheet over them, the upper branches of the forest pines limed, creaking, swollen with the fall.

Snowlight, moonlight, a confusion of paw-prints.

All silent, all still.

Midnight; and the clock strikes. It is Christmas Day, the werewolves' birthday, the door of the solstice stands wide open; let them all sink through.

See! sweet and sound she sleeps in granny's bed, between the paws of the   90
tender wolf.   [1977]

Walpurgisnacht: May Day eve, the medieval witches' sabbath.

THINKING ABOUT THE TEXT

1. The story begins with a section about wolves before it gets to the Red Riding Hood narrative. What image of wolves does this prologue convey? What in particular seems the purpose of the extended anecdote about the wife with two husbands?

2. Note places where Carter shifts tenses. Why do you suppose she does this?

3. Why does the girl not get to her grandmother's house before the wolf does? Be specific about her state of mind.

4. Bear in mind the story's title. What do you think is Carter's purpose in having the grandmother's house surrounded by a whole "company" of wolves? Note that Red Riding Hood is not mentioned in the title. Are wolves indeed more important than she is in Carter's story? Support your answer with details from the text.

5. What do you conclude about the girl from her behavior at the end of the story? To what extent is "savage marriage ceremony" (para. 84) indeed an apt term for what occurs?

MAKING COMPARISONS

1. To what extent is Carter's image of wolves different from Perrault's and the Grimms'? Refer to details of all three texts.

2. Several critics have described Carter's versions of fairy tales as feminist. To what extent can this term be applied to Perrault's and the Grimms' narratives as well as hers? Define what you mean by *feminist*.

3. Would you say Carter's writing style is more realistic than that of Perrault and the Grimms? Or is the term *realism* completely irrelevant in the case of fairy tales? Explain.

WRITING ABOUT ISSUES

1. Choose one of these versions of the Red Riding Hood story, and write an essay in which you elaborate a moral that modern *adults* might learn from it. Or write an essay in which you explain what a child might learn from Carter's version.

2. Does Carter's version radically depart from Perrault's and the Grimms', or does it basically resemble them? Write an essay that addresses this question by focusing on Carter's story and one of the other two.

3. Write an essay explaining what you think you learned from a fairy tale or other fictional story that you heard as a child. If you want to contrast your thinking about the story now with your thinking about it then, do so. Feel free to compare the story you focus on with any of the versions of Red Riding Hood in this cluster.

4. Write your own version of the story of Red Riding Hood, and on a separate piece of paper write the moral you think should be drawn from your text. Then give your version to a classmate, and see if he or she can guess your moral.

A WEB ASSIGNMENT

In the Web Assignments section of the *Making Literature Matter* Web site, you will find a link to The Red Riding Hood Project, developed by a class at the University of Southern Mississippi. The site contains sixteen versions of the Red Riding Hood tale, accompanied by visual images. Choose a version you have not read before, and write an essay comparing it to one of the three versions in this cluster. In particular, discuss the extent to which the version on the site significantly differs from the version you have selected from this cluster.

Visit www.bedfordstmartins.com/makinglitmatter

OBSERVING SCHOOLCHILDREN

LOUISE GLÜCK, "The School Children"
TOI DERRICOTTE, "Fears of the Eighth Grade"
PHILIP LEVINE, "Among Children"

Even writers who no longer attend school make schoolchildren a subject of their work. Indeed, many poems depict schoolchildren as symbols of innocence. Several of these suggest that such innocence is doomed to fade with adulthood, while others find that particular social trends threaten it. Of course, to decide whether a poem takes either position, you must first think about what you mean by *innocence*. As you read the following poems by Louise Glück, Toi Derricotte, and Philip Levine, consider your own definition of the term as well as the specific comments each poem makes about the schoolchildren it describes.

BEFORE YOU READ

Recall a class that you were part of in school. Imagine an older person observing that class in preparation for writing a poem about it. What are some specific aspects of the class that he or she might have observed? If you wish, try writing a poem about the class.

LOUISE GLÜCK
The School Children

For many years, Louise Glück (b. 1943) has taught creative writing at Goddard College in Vermont. She has also published several volumes of poetry, winning the Pulitzer Prize for The Wild Iris *(1992). In her poetry, Glück often deals with domestic life, though with mythic references that make it seem more mysterious than familiar. The following poem comes from her 1975 book,* The House on Marshland.

The children go forward with their little satchels.
And all morning the mothers have labored
to gather the late apples, red and gold,
like words of another language.

And on the other shore   5
are those who wait behind great desks
to receive these offerings.

How orderly they are — the nails
on which the children hang
their overcoats of blue or yellow wool.   10

◆　◆　◆

And the teachers shall instruct them in silence
and the mothers shall scour the orchards for a way out,
drawing to themselves the gray limbs of the fruit trees
bearing so little ammunition.   [1975]

THINKING ABOUT THE TEXT

1. Do you think Glück is commenting on a very particular group of school-children or on schoolchildren in general? Explain your reasoning.

2. The words "How orderly they are" (line 8) appear before Glück identifies the "they." Only afterward does she indicate that "they" refers to "the nails." Why do you think she delays? What is the effect?

3. Although the poem's title suggests that it will focus on the schoolchildren, the poem also refers to mothers and teachers. After reading it, do you think the schoolchildren are indeed its focus? Support your claim by referring to specific lines.

4. What roles do colors play in this poem? Identify each color mentioned and some things that a reader might associate with each.

5. What are some specific ways in which a teacher might instruct children "in silence" (line 11)? Has a teacher of yours ever done so? In what sense might the mothers of schoolchildren need "a way out" (line 12) and "ammunition" (line 14)?

TOI DERRICOTTE
Fears of the Eighth Grade

Toi Derricotte (b. 1941) is the professor of English at the University of Pittsburgh. She has published poetry in several journals and written four books of it. The following poem appears in her 1989 volume Captivity.

When I ask what things they fear,
their arms raise like soldiers volunteering for battle:
Fear of going into a dark room, my murderer is waiting.
Fear of taking a shower, someone will stab me.
Fear of being kidnapped, raped.   5
Fear of dying in war.
When I ask how many fear this,
all the children raise their hands.

I think of this little box of consecrated land,
the bombs somewhere else,   10
the dead children in their mothers' arms,
women crying at the gates of the bamboo palace.

♦   ♦   ♦

How thin the veneer!
The paper towels, napkins, toilet paper — everything
burned up in a day.   15

These children see the city after Armageddon°
The demons stand visible in the air
between their friends talking.
They see fire in a spring day
the instant before conflagration.   20
They feel blood through closed faucets,
the dead rising from boiling seas.   [1989]

16 **Armageddon:** In the Bible (Rev. 16:16), Armageddon is associated with the end of the
world; specifically, it is the place where the forces of good and evil fight their final battle.

THINKING ABOUT THE TEXT

1. Evidently the speaker is referring to a particular group of eighth graders
   whom she has interviewed. Do you think many other eighth graders
   would have the same fears? What else might the speaker have asked these
   children to learn how they view the world?

2. Does Derricotte's speaker seem to express a particular attitude toward the
   children's statements? Or do you see her as leaving you free to make your
   own judgment of them? Refer to specific lines.

3. Where, specifically, might the "somewhere else" in line 10 be? Think of
   particular countries.

4. Does the reference to Armageddon in line 16 make sense? Do you
   assume that the last stanza truly conveys what "These children see"?
   Again, support your answers by referring to specific lines.

5. What would you say to these children? In what ways would you address
   their fears if you were their teacher? In your view, to what extent does the
   typical eighth-grade curriculum address their concerns?

MAKING COMPARISONS

1. Both Glück's and Derricotte's poems end with images of violence. Glück
   refers to "ammunition," and Derricotte evokes Armageddon. Does the
   emphasis on violence seem appropriate in each case?

2. Both Glück's and Derricotte's poems are four stanzas long, with the
   middle two stanzas being shorter than the first and the last. Is the effect of
   this structure the same in each case?

3. While Glück's poem refers to teachers, Derricotte's doesn't. Is this a significant difference? Why, or why not?

PHILIP LEVINE
Among Children

Philip Levine (b. 1928) is a leading contemporary American poet. Much of his writing deals with his youth in the industrial city of Detroit, especially his work in various factories there. He won the National Book Award for his 1991 volume What Work Is. *We feature its title poem in Chapter 5, and the following poem comes from the same book.*

I walk among the rows of bowed heads—
the children are sleeping through fourth grade
so as to be ready for what is ahead,
the monumental boredom of junior high
and the rush forward tearing their wings   5
loose and turning their eyes forever inward.
These are the children of Flint, their fathers
work at the spark plug factory or truck
bottled water in 5 gallon sea-blue jugs
to the widows of the suburbs. You can see   10
already how their backs have thickened,
how their small hands, soiled by pig iron,
leap and stutter even in dreams. I would like
to sit down among them and read slowly
from *The Book of Job*° until the windows   15
pale and the teacher rises out of a milky sea
of industrial scum, her gowns streaming
with light, her foolish words transformed
into song, I would like to arm each one
with a quiver of arrows so that they might   20
rush like wind there where no battle rages

---

15 *The Book of Job:* In the Old Testament, Job is a virtuous man whose faith in God is tested when God allows horrible suffering to be inflicted on him. In Chapter 39, God speaks to Job about the vast differences in their knowledge and power. A particular passage from this speech seems especially pertinent to Levine's poem (Job 39:19–25, King James Version):

> Hast thou given the horse strength? Hast thou clothed his neck with thunder?
> Canst thou make him afraid as a grasshopper? The glory of his nostrils *is* terrible.
> He paweth in the valley, and rejoiceth in *his* strength; he goeth on to meet the armed men.
> He mocketh at fear, and is not affrighted; neither turneth he back from the sword.
> The quiver rattleth against him, the glittering spear and the shield.
> He swalloweth the ground with fierceness and rage; neither believeth he that *it* is the sound of the trumpet.
> He saith among the trumpets, Ha, ha; and he smelleth the battle afar off, the thunder of the captains, and the shouting.

shouting among the trumpets, Ha! Ha!
How dear the gift of laughter in the face
of the 8 hour day, the cold winter mornings
without coffee and oranges, the long lines　　　　　　　　　　　25
of mothers in old coats waiting silently
where the gates have closed. Ten years ago
I went among these same children, just born,
in the bright ward of the Sacred Heart and leaned
down to hear their breaths delivered that day,　　　　　　　　30
burning with joy. There was such wonder
in their sleep, such purpose in their eyes
closed against autumn, in their damp heads
blurred with the hair of ponds, and not one
turned against me or the light, not one　　　　　　　　　　35
said, I am sick, I am tired, I will go home,
not one complained or drifted alone,
unloved, on the hardest day of their lives.
Eleven years from now they will become
the men and women of Flint or Paradise,　　　　　　　　　40
the majors of a minor town, and I
will be gone into smoke or memory,
so I bow to them here and whisper
all I know, all I will never know.　　　　　　　　　　　　[1991]

THINKING ABOUT THE TEXT

1. Characterize the poem's speaker, using at least three adjectives of your own. What specific lines support your characterization?

2. The speaker describes these children at various stages in their lives. Besides discussing their present situation, he refers back to their births and forward to their adulthoods "Eleven years from now" (line 39). Do you find his comments about each stage plausible? Why, or why not?

3. In line 7, the speaker specifically identifies his subjects as "the children of Flint," an industrial city in Michigan. In what ways does their situation resemble that of schoolchildren in other places?

4. Do you find Levine's reference to the Book of Job (line 15) effective, or does it reduce your ability to understand and appreciate the poem? Explain.

5. At the end of the poem, the speaker reports that "I bow to them here and whisper / all I know, all I will never know" (lines 43–44). What would you say to someone who doubts that the speaker actually bows to these children and whispers such things to them? What would you say to someone who argues that the speaker should have taken more active steps to improve the children's lot?

MAKING COMPARISONS

1. Compared with Glück's and Derricotte's poems, Levine's more extensively uses "I." Does his reliance on it make his poem more or less effective than the other two? Why?

2. Of the three poems, Levine's most specifically identifies the schoolchildren it describes, announcing that they "are the children of Flint" (line 7). Does Levine's poem therefore seem less universal in its implications than the other two poems do? Why, or why not?

3. In describing schoolchildren, Glück and Derricotte focus on the present. Levine, however, refers to three stages in his subjects' lives: infancy, youth, and adulthood. Does his broader perspective amount to a significant difference? Explain.

WRITING ABOUT ISSUES

1. Each of the poems in this cluster uses biblical allusions. Besides Derricotte's reference to Armageddon and Levine's to the Book of Job, Glück's mention of apples can be linked with events in the Garden of Eden. Choose one of these poems, and write an essay explaining how echoes of the Bible function in it. How do these echoes contribute to the poem's overall meaning and effect?

2. Any of the poems in this cluster can be seen as being mainly about the schoolchildren it describes. But perhaps one or more of these poems should be seen as mainly about the speaker who does the describing. Then again, perhaps one or more of them should be seen as equally concerned with the schoolchildren and the speaker. Choose two of these poems, and write an essay explaining how each should be seen. Support your claims by referring to specific lines.

3. Choose a person you have known since he or she was a child. Write an essay examining the extent to which this person was an "innocent" child, as well as the extent to which he or she is "innocent" now. (You will have to define what you mean by *innocent*.) Be sure to support your claims about the person with specific details of his or her life.

4. What are the fears of schoolchildren today? Ask a group of them, or ask at least two precollege teachers, or read at least two articles on the subject. On the basis of your research, write an essay focusing on one of the fears you have discovered. Besides identifying the fear, propose and argue for one way of addressing it. (Feel free to admit that additional ways may be necessary.) If you wish, refer to one or more of the poems in this cluster.

Responding to Teachers

LANGSTON HUGHES, "Theme for English B"
LINDA PASTAN, "Ethics"
HENRY REED, "Naming of Parts"
WALT WHITMAN, "When I Heard the Learn'd Astronomer"
ROSEMARY CATACALOS, "David Talamántez on the Last Day of Second Grade"

Each of the following poems features a student responding to someone given institutional authority to teach him or her. In the first poem, the speaker is an African American college student writing an essay assigned by his white instructor. The speaker in the second poem remembers ethics classes she took as a youth, recalling in particular how she treated a certain question the teacher liked to ask. The third poem seems to feature two speakers: while a military officer teaches recruits how to use a rifle, one student mentally plays with his instructor's words. In the fourth poem, the speaker chooses to observe the heavens by himself rather than hear a "learn'd astronomer" lecture about them. The final poem focuses on a boy whose exultation on the last day of second grade defies his teacher's criticisms of him.

By this point in your life, you have had many people officially designated as your teachers. Probably you have seen their lectures, questions, assignments, and overall behavior as reflecting their particular educational philosophy. At the same time, your reactions to them have said something about what you consider worth learning and how you think those subjects should be taught. In some cases, perhaps, your view of teaching and learning coincided with your teacher's. At other times, though, you may have suffered an unfortunate mismatch. With each poem here, identify the teacher's assumptions about teaching and learning. Also consider those expressed by the student in his or her response.

BEFORE YOU READ

Think of a past or present writing assignment that you have found especially challenging. What specifically was the assignment? What do you believe was the educational philosophy behind it? Why did you find it a challenge? Was it a worthwhile assignment? Why, or why not? In what ways, if any, would you have changed it?

LANGSTON HUGHES
Theme for English B

Langston Hughes (1902–1967) has long been regarded as a major African American writer. He is increasingly seen today as an important contributor to American literature in general. Hughes worked in a wide range of genres, including fiction, drama, and autobiography. Nevertheless, he is primarily known for his poems. He

wrote "Theme for English B" in 1949, when he was twenty-five years older than the
poem's speaker. He himself, though, had attended "a college on the hill above
Harlem"—Columbia University.

The instructor said,
> Go home and write
> a page tonight.
> And let that page come out of you—
> Then, it will be true. 5

I wonder if it's that simple?
I am twenty-two, colored, born in Winston-Salem.
I went to school there, then Durham, then here
to this college on the hill above Harlem.
I am the only colored student in my class. 10
The steps from the hill lead down into Harlem,
through a park, then I cross St. Nicholas,
Eighth Avenue, Seventh, and I come to the Y,
the Harlem Branch Y, where I take the elevator
up to my room, sit down, and write this page: 15

It's not easy to know what is true for you or me
at twenty-two, my age. But I guess I'm what
I feel and see and hear, Harlem, I hear you:
hear you, hear me—we two—you, me, talk on this page.
(I hear New York, too.) Me—who? 20
Well, I like to eat, sleep, drink, and be in love.
I like to work, read, learn, and understand life.
I like a pipe for a Christmas present,
or records—Bessie,° bop, or Bach.
I guess being colored doesn't make me *not* like 25
the same things other folks like who are other races.
So will my page be colored that I write?
Being me, it will not be white.
But it will be
a part of you, instructor. 30
You are white—
yet a part of me, as I am part of you.
That's American.
Sometimes perhaps you don't want to be a part of me.
Nor do I often want to be a part of you. 35
But we are, that's true!
As I learn from you,
I guess you learn from me—

24 **Bessie:** Bessie Smith (1898?–1937), the famous American blues singer.

although you're older — and white —
and somewhat more free.   40

This is my page for English B.   [1949]

THINKING ABOUT THE TEXT

1. Write a page in which you respond to the teacher's assignment. In what respects has your page "come out of you" (line 4)? In what respects is it "true" (line 5)? Do you find the assignment reasonable? Why, or why not?

2. What seems to be the speaker's evaluation of the assignment? To what extent does he critique or challenge the assignment rather than merely submit to it? Support your answer by referring to specific lines.

3. What does Hughes's speaker mean by "You are . . . a part of me, as I am part of you" (lines 31–32)? Do you think that in today's historical and cultural context any white teacher of a black student is "somewhat more free" (line 40) than that student? Why, or why not?

4. Identify where the poem rhymes. What is the effect of this rhyming?

5. What might be the teacher's reaction to the speaker's page? What would you like the teacher's reaction to be?

LINDA PASTAN
Ethics

Raised in New York City, Linda Pastan (b. 1932) now lives in Potomac, Maryland. She has published many books of poetry, including The Five Stages of Grief *(1981);* Waiting for My Life *(1981), where "Ethics" originally appeared; and* PM/AM: New and Selected Poems *(1982). Much of Pastan's poetry deals with her own family life. Increasingly, she has been concerned as well with issues of aging and mortality.*

In ethics class so many years ago
our teacher asked this question every fall:
if there were a fire in a museum
which would you save, a Rembrandt painting
or an old woman who hadn't many   5
years left anyhow? Restless on hard chairs
caring little for pictures or old age
we'd opt one year for life, the next for art
and always half-heartedly. Sometimes
the woman borrowed my grandmother's face   10

leaving her usual kitchen to wander
some drafty, half-imagined museum.
One year, feeling clever, I replied
why not let the woman decide herself?
Linda, the teacher would report, eschews   15
the burdens of responsibility.
This fall in a real museum I stand
before a real Rembrandt, old woman,
or nearly so, myself. The colors
within this frame are darker than autumn,   20
darker even than winter — the browns of earth,
though earth's most radiant elements burn
through the canvas. I know now that woman
and painting and season are almost one
and all beyond saving by children.   [1981]   25

THINKING ABOUT THE TEXT

1. What specific topics would you expect to see addressed in a college-level ethics class? Which do you think are appropriate for an ethics class at the high-school level? Should students be required to take such a class in earlier grades? Why, or why not? (You may want to consult a dictionary definition of the word *ethics*.)

2. How would you respond to the teacher's question? Do you think it an appropriate one to ask? Why, or why not? Judging by Linda's behavior in the poem, what do you think the teacher should have said about her?

3. What do you usually associate with fall and winter? Does Pastan seem to encourage these associations? Explain.

4. Note the speaker's description of the actual Rembrandt painting. Do you find it an objective description? Why, or why not?

5. State in your own words the lesson articulated in the poem's last sentence. Do you agree with the argument made there against the teacher's question? Why, or why not? Do you think the speaker is rejecting the whole subject of ethics? Why, or why not?

MAKING COMPARISONS

1. Compare the teacher's question in Pastan's poem to the assignment given Hughes's speaker. Do you prefer one to the other? Explain.

2. Unlike Hughes's poem, Pastan's explicitly leaps to a later stage in the speaker's life. Is this a significant difference? Why, or why not?

3. Is it fair to say that Pastan's poem is pessimistic, while Hughes's is optimistic? Elaborate your reasoning.

HENRY REED
Naming of Parts

*The English writer Henry Reed (1914–1986) was primarily known as an author
and translator of plays for radio. But he also wrote two volumes of poetry,* A Map of
Verona: Poems *(1946) and* Lessons of the War *(1970). The following poem, which
appears in both volumes, is one in a series of poems collectively entitled "Naming of
the Parts."*

Today we have naming of parts. Yesterday,
We had daily cleaning. And tomorrow morning,
We shall have what to do after firing. But today,
Today we have naming of parts. Japonica
Glistens like coral in all of the neighboring gardens,   5
        And today we have naming of parts.

This is the lower sling swivel. And this
Is the upper sling swivel, whose use you will see,
When you are given your slings. And this is the piling swivel,
Which in your case you have not got. The branches   10
Hold in the gardens their silent, eloquent gestures,
        Which in our case we have not got.

This is the safety-catch, which is always released
With an easy flick of the thumb. And please do not let me
See anyone using his finger. You can do it quite easy   15
If you have any strength in your thumb. The blossoms
Are fragile and motionless, never letting anyone see
        Any of them using their finger.

And this you can see is the bolt. The purpose of this
Is to open the breech, as you see. We can slide it   20
Rapidly backwards and forwards: we call this
Easing the spring. And rapidly backwards and forwards
The early bees are assaulting and fumbling the flowers:
        They call it easing the Spring.

They call it easing the Spring: it is perfectly easy   25
If you have any strength in your thumb: like the bolt,
And the breech, and the cocking-piece, and the point of balance,
Which in our case we have not got; and the almond-blossom
Silent in all of the gardens and the bees going backwards and forwards,
        For today we have naming of parts.   [1946]   30

THINKING ABOUT THE TEXT

  1. Reed's poem features two voices. Identify the lines where each appears.
     What adjectives would you use to describe each?

2. Does this poem progress in any way, or does the situation it presents remain unchanged at the end? Refer to specific lines in supporting your response.

3. Do you take the poem to be antimilitary? Why, or why not?

4. The author visually isolates the last line of each stanza. Why do you think he does so?

5. The poem features a lot of repetition. What is its effect?

MAKING COMPARISONS

1. Does the scene of instruction that Reed presents seem very different from the classes evoked by Hughes and Pastan? From classes that you have taken? Explain.

2. The instructor in "Naming of Parts" speaks a lot more than the instructors in "Theme for English B" and "Ethics." Does this difference matter? Why, or why not?

3. Reed's poem seems very much concerned with language — specifically, the act of "naming" various things. Do the other two poems show similar concerns, or do they deal with largely different topics? Refer to specific lines in each text.

WALT WHITMAN
When I Heard the Learn'd Astronomer

Walt Whitman (1819–1892) became one of the United States' most famous and influential poets. He was especially known for celebrating the human body and democracy. His most important volume of poetry was Leaves of Grass *(1855). Although it originally consisted of a dozen poems, Whitman added to it and revised its format as it went through several more editions, the final one appearing in 1892. Besides being a poet, Whitman worked as a printer, newspaper editor, journalist, and government clerk. During the Civil War, he tended wounded Union soldiers. He wrote the following poem in 1865.*

When I heard the learn'd astronomer,
When the proofs, the figures, were ranged in columns before me,
When I was shown the charts and diagrams, to add, divide, and measure them,
When I sitting heard the astronomer where he lectured with much applause in
      the lecture-room,
How soon unaccountable I became tired and sick,   5
Till rising and gliding out I wandered off by myself,
In the mystical moist night-air, and from time to time,
Looked up in perfect silence at the stars.   [1865]

THINKING ABOUT THE TEXT

1. How does Whitman's speaker seem to define *learn'd*? Do you think he would apply this term to himself? If so, what definition of it would he have in mind?

2. The first four lines all begin with the word *when*, a technique known as anaphora. What is its effect?

3. Describe how the lines change in length as the poem moves along. Do you think Whitman is justified in making the fourth line as long as it is? Explain your reasoning. Note that the poem is actually just one sentence; what does Whitman achieve by making it so?

4. What distinctions does the speaker make between his behavior in the first line and his behavior in the last? Do you see him as proposing another method of education than the astronomer's, or do you take him to be rejecting education altogether? Explain. How much do you think a person can learn by simply gazing at the stars?

5. The poem ends by apparently endorsing "perfect silence." Yet Whitman *is not* silent; after all, he wrote this poem. Do you think Whitman is contradicting himself? Why, or why not?

MAKING COMPARISONS

1. Of the poems in this cluster so far, only in Whitman's does a student walk out on a teacher. Does this action make you regard the student in Whitman's poem differently than you do the students in the other poems? Why, or why not?

2. In each of the first three poems, we see a teacher's words quoted. Whitman's poem, however, does not actually quote the astronomer. Is this a significant difference? Why, or why not?

3. In what ways, if any, does Whitman's word *unaccountable* apply to the first three poems?

ROSEMARY CATACALOS

David Talamántez on the Last Day of Second Grade

Rosemary Catacalos (b. 1944) grew up in San Antonio, Texas. Formerly a reporter and arts columnist, she is now executive director of San Francisco State University's Poetry Center and American Poetry Archives. Her own books of poetry, both published in 1984, are As Long As It Takes *and* Again for the First Time. *The following poem appeared in a 1996 issue of* The Texas Observer *and was subsequently included in the collection* Best American Poetry 1996.

San Antonio, Texas 1988

David Talamántez, whose mother is at work, leaves his mark,
    everywhere in the schoolyard,
tosses pages from a thick sheaf of lined paper high in the air one by
    one, watches them

catch on the teachers' car bumpers, drift into the chalky narrow shade   5
    of the water fountain.
One last batch, stapled together, he rolls tight into a makeshift horn
    through which he shouts

David! and *David, yes!* before hurling it away hard and darting across
    Barzos Street against   10
the light, the little sag of head and shoulders when, safe on the other
    side, he kicks a can

in the gutter and wanders toward home. David Talamántez believes
    birds are warm blooded,
the way they are quick in the air and give out long strings of   15
    complicated music, different

all the time, not like cats and dogs. For this he was marked down in
    Science, and for putting
his name in the wrong place, on the right with the date instead on the
    left with Science   20

Questions, and for not skipping a line between his heading and
    answers. The X's for wrong
things are big, much bigger than Talamántez's tiny writing. *Write larger,*
    his teacher says

in red ink across the tops of many pages. *Messy!* she says on others   25
    where he has erased
and started over, erased and started over. Spelling, Language
    Expression, Sentences Using

the Following Words. *Neck. I have a neck name.* No! 20's, 30's. *Think
    again!* He's good   30
in Art, though, makes 70 on Reading Station Artist's Corner, where
    he's traced and colored

an illustration from *Henny Penny.* A goose with red-and-white striped
    shirt, a hen in a turquoise
dress. Points off for the birds, cloud and butterfly he's drawn in   35
    freehand. *Not in the original*

picture! Twenty-five points off for writing nothing in the blank after
    This is my favorite scene
in the book because . . . There's a page called Rules. *Listen! Always
    working! Stay in your seat!*   40

◆ ◆ ◆

Raise your hand before you speak! No fighting! Be quiet! Rules copied from
    the board, no grade,
only a huge red checkmark. Later there is a test on Rules. *Listen! Alay*
    ercng! Sast in ao snet!

Rars aone bfo your spek! No finagn! Be cayt! He gets 70 on Rules, 10 on   45
    Spelling. An old man
stoops to pick up a crumpled drawing of a large family crowded
    around a table, an apartment

with bars on the windows in Alazán Courts, a huge sun in one corner
    saying, *To mush noys!*   50
After correcting the spelling, the grade is 90. *Nice details!* And there's
    another mark, on this paper

and all the others, the one in the doorway of La Rosa Beauty Shop, the
    one that blew under
the pool table at La Tenampa, the ones older kids have wadded up like   55
    big spit balls, the ones run

over by cars. On every single page David Talamántez has crossed out
    the teacher's red numbers
and written in giant letters, blue ink, *Yes! David, yes!*   [1996]

THINKING ABOUT THE TEXT

1. In *Best American Poetry 1996,* Catacalos admits that "David Talamántez
   is a composite of many Chicano children in many times and places." As
   you read her poem, do you assume she based it on a real-life individual?
   Why, or why not? How conscious are you that the boy in this poem is Chicano? Do you think it could just as easily be about someone from a different ethnic background? Explain your reasoning.

2. Sum up and evaluate the teacher's judgments of David's writing and his
   other work. What are some of her values and assumptions?

3. What are some adjectives of your own for David? Note what he does with
   the papers he has gotten back. Is he engaging in significant acts of resistance? Explain your view.

4. Here is an issue of policy: What should be done about the kind of situation described in this poem? By whom?

5. Many sentences in this poem run from one line to the next—a technique
   called *enjambment.* What is the effect?

MAKING COMPARISONS

1. Of all the students in this cluster, David Talamántez is the only one
   shown merely as a child. Does he seem notably less mature than the other
   students you have encountered here? Why, or why not?

2. Whereas the students in the other four poems are also the speakers of the poems, David Talamántez is not. Does this difference produce a difference in effect? Explain.

3. David is tossing papers away. Is it fair, then, to say that he is more destructive than the students in the other poems? What details of the five texts do you have in mind as you answer this question?

WRITING ABOUT ISSUES

1. Choose any poem in this cluster, and write an essay describing and evaluating the relationship between student and teacher. Use specific lines to support your claims.

2. Choose two of the teachers in these poems, and write an essay comparing their educational philosophies. What do they think their students should know and do? What method of instruction might they think works best? What do you think of their approaches to teaching?

3. Think of a teacher whose style disturbed you at first. Did you eventually regard this person as a good teacher, or did you reach a different conclusion? Write an essay answering this question, making sure to define what you mean by *good*. Refer to specific interactions you had with the teacher and specific things that influenced your reactions to him or her. You may find it useful to refer to one or more poems in this cluster.

4. Ask five or more students not in this class the following questions: What basic goals should teachers have when they respond to their students' writing? What sorts of things should they comment on? How should they word their comments? How many comments should they make? Then write an essay presenting and arguing for your own answers to these questions, making reference to what your interviewees said.

CHARGING A TEACHER WITH SEXUAL HARASSMENT: CULTURAL CONTEXTS FOR DAVID MAMET'S *OLEANNA*

DAVID MAMET, *Oleanna*

CULTURAL CONTEXTS:
ANITA HILL AND CLARENCE THOMAS, *Statements to the United States Senate Judiciary Committee on October 11, 1991*
HOWARD GADLIN, From "Mediating Sexual Harassment"
ROBERT M. O'NEIL, "Protecting Free Speech When the Issue Is Sexual Harassment"

Many would say that for a college to be a truly educational community, it must be a community whose members treat one another with respect. Yet no campus is free from abuses of power. Consider, for example, sexual harassment.

(Brigitte Lacombe.)

The term is fairly new, dating to the early 1970s. But the forms of behavior it refers to have long occurred on campuses, even if only now prohibited by law. In the introduction to their 1997 book *Sexual Harassment on Campus: A Guide for Administrators, Faculty, and Students,* Bernice R. Sandler and Robert J. Shoop note that "most of the studies done at individual campuses document that 20 percent to 30 percent of undergraduate women have experienced some form of sexual harassment from faculty, administrators, or other staff" (13). In some cases, students have harassed faculty, other campus employees, and other students. Many people who experience sexual harassment fail to complain about it, often because their harassers are in positions of power and may very well proclaim innocence. Therefore, more and more colleges are developing means of encouraging victims of sexual harassment to report it. At the same time, these colleges need to define sexual harassment clearly for their communities and to decide what procedures to follow when someone is accused of it.

In the following play, David Mamet's *Oleanna,* a female student accuses a male professor of sexual harassment. As you might guess, this play incites controversy among its viewers. While some audiences sympathize with the accuser, others sympathize with the accused, and still others regard both characters with mixed feelings. Debate also arises over how fair Mamet is to each character. To help you think about the play and the issues it raises, we add background documents. We begin with a pair of statements, one by Anita Hill and the other by Clarence Thomas, that were made to the Judiciary Committee of the United States Senate on October 11, 1991. These statements are especially worth reading here because many audience members at the initial productions of *Oleanna* had the Hill-Thomas Senate Judiciary Committee hearings in mind. Thomas had been nominated to the United States Supreme Court, and Hill, who appeared as a witness at his confirmation hearings, accused him of repeatedly harassing her when she worked for him. The charges were heatedly denied by Thomas. The Hill-Thomas hearings, broadcast on TV, seized the nation's attention, with much debate ensuing over who was telling the truth. One effect of the proceedings was increased public awareness that sexual harassment can occur, whether or not Thomas was guilty of it.

The other two documents here analyze specific cases of sexual harassment on campus, each of which might be compared to the case that Mamet dramatizes. Howard Gadlin tells of a woman student who, feeling harassed by one of her professors, chooses to confront him in an informal proceeding supervised by a mediator. Law professor Robert O'Neil uses the case of another professor charged with sexual harassment to argue for new ways of defining and handling it.

BEFORE YOU READ

Have you experienced or observed sexual harassment? How widespread do you think it is on your campus? What kinds of behavior come to mind as you consider these questions?

DAVID MAMET
Oleanna

For much of his career as a playwright, David Mamet (b. 1947) worked in the theater world of Chicago. He has written over twenty plays, including American Buffalo *(1975),* Glengarry Glen Ross *(1984),* Speed the Plow *(1988), and* The Cryptogram *(1994). He has also worked in film. Besides writing the screenplays for* The Verdict *(1982) and* The Untouchables *(1987), he wrote and directed the movies* House of Games *(1987),* Things Change *(1988),* Homicide *(1991),* The Spanish Prisoner *(1997),* State and Main *(2000), and* Heist *(2001), as well as the film version of* Oleanna *(1994). The play premiered in Cambridge, Massachusetts, in May 1992 and then opened off Broadway the following October. Mamet directed both the Cambridge and the New York productions, with his wife Rebecca Pidgeon starring as Carol. You will notice that much of* Oleanna's *dialogue is fragmented with interrupted sentences. They are typical of Mamet's career-long effort to reproduce the discontinuities of everyday speech. You may find the play easier to follow if you read at least some of it aloud, either by yourself or with others.*

> The want of fresh air does not seem much to affect the happiness of children in a London alley: the greater part of them sing and play as though they were on a moor in Scotland. So the absence of a genial mental atmosphere is not commonly recognized by children who have never known it. Young people have a marvelous faculty of either dying or adapting themselves to circumstances. Even if they are unhappy—very unhappy—it is astonishing how easily they can be prevented from finding it out, or at any rate from attributing it to any other cause than their own sinfulness.
>
> — Samuel Butler, *The Way of All Flesh*

> "Oh, to be in *Oleanna,*
> That's where I would rather be.
> Than be bound in Norway
> And drag the chains of slavery."
> — folk song

CHARACTERS

CAROL, *a woman of twenty*
JOHN, *a man in his forties*

The play takes place in John's office.

ONE

John is talking on the phone. Carol is seated across the desk from him.

JOHN *(on the phone):*   And what about the land. *(Pause)* The land. And what about the land? *(Pause)* What about it? *(Pause)* No. I don't understand. Well, yes, I'm I'm . . . no, I'm *sure* it's signif . . . I'm sure it's significant. *(Pause)* Because it's significant to mmmmmm . . . did you call Jerry? *(Pause)* Because . . . no, no, no, no, no. What did they say . . . ? Did you speak to the *real* estate . . . where *is* she . . . ? Well, well, all right. Where are her notes? Where are the notes we took with her. *(Pause)* I thought you were? No. No, I'm sorry, I didn't mean that, I just thought that I saw you, when we were there . . . what . . . ? I thought I saw you with a *pencil.* WHY NOW? is what I'm say . . . well, that's why I say "call Jerry." Well, I can't right now, be . . . no, I *didn't* schedule any . . . Grace: I *didn't* . . . I'm well aware . . . Look: Look. Did you call Jerry? Will you call Jerry . . . ? Because I can't now. I'll be there, I'm sure I'll be there in fifteen, in twenty. I intend to. No, we aren't *going* to lose the, we aren't *going* to lose the house. Look: Look, I'm not minimizing it. The "easement." Did she say "easement"? *(Pause)* What did she *say;* is it a "term of art," are we *bound* by it . . . I'm sorry . . . *(Pause)* are: we: yes. *Bound* by . . . Look: *(He checks his watch.)* before the other side *goes home,* all right? "a term of art." Because: that's right *(Pause)* The yard for the boy. Well, that's the whole . . . Look: I'm going to meet you there . . . *(He checks his watch.)* Is the realtor there? All right, tell her to show you the basement again. Look at the *this* because . . . Bec . . . I'm leaving in,

I'm leaving in ten or fifteen . . . Yes. No, no, I'll meet you at the new . . . That's a good. If he thinks it's necc . . . you tell Jerry to meet . . . All right? We *aren't* going to lose the deposit. All right? I'm sure it's going to be . . . *(Pause)* I hope so. *(Pause)* I love you, too. *(Pause)* I love you, too. As soon as . . . I will.

　　　(He hangs up.) (He bends over the desk and makes a note.) (He looks up.) (To Carol:) I'm sorry . . .

CAROL:　*(Pause)* What is a "term of art"?

JOHN:　*(Pause)* I'm sorry . . . ?

CAROL:　*(Pause)* What is a "term of art"?

JOHN:　Is that what you want to talk about?

CAROL:　. . . to talk about . . . ?

JOHN:　Let's take the mysticism out of it, shall we? Carol? *(Pause)* Don't you think? I'll tell you: when you have some "thing." Which must be broached. *(Pause)* Don't you think . . . ? *(Pause)*

CAROL:　. . . don't I think . . . ?

JOHN:　Mmm?

CAROL:　. . . did I . . . ?

JOHN:　. . . what?

CAROL:　Did . . . did I . . . did I say something wr . . .

JOHN:　*(Pause)* No. I'm sorry. No. You're right. I'm very sorry. I'm somewhat rushed. As you see. I'm sorry. You're right. *(Pause)* What is a "term of art"? It seems to mean a *term*, which has come, through its use, to mean something *more specific* than the words would, to someone *not acquainted* with them . . . indicate. That, I believe, is what a "term of art," would mean. *(Pause)*

CAROL:　You don't know what it means . . . ?

JOHN:　I'm not sure that I know what it means. It's one of those things, perhaps you've had them, that, you look them up, or have someone explain them to you, and you say "aha," and, you immediately *forget* what . . .

CAROL:　You don't do that.

JOHN:　. . . I . . . ?

CAROL:　You don't do . . .

JOHN:　. . . I don't, what . . . ?

CAROL:　. . . for . . .

JOHN:　. . . I don't for . . .

CAROL:　. . . no . . .

JOHN:　. . . forget things? Everybody does that.

CAROL:　No, they don't.

JOHN:　They don't . . .

CAROL:　No.

JOHN:　*(Pause)* No. Everybody does that.

CAROL:　Why would they do that . . . ?

JOHN:　Because. I don't know. Because it doesn't interest them.

CAROL:　No.

JOHN:　I think so, though. *(Pause)* I'm sorry that I was distracted.

CAROL:　You don't have to say that to me.

JOHN:　You paid me the compliment, or the "obeisance" — all right — of coming in here . . . All right. *Carol.* I find that I am at a *standstill.* I find that I . . .

CAROL: . . . what . . .

JOHN: . . . one moment. In regard to your . . . to your . . .

CAROL: Oh, oh. You're buying a new house!

JOHN: No, let's get on with it.

CAROL: "get on"? *(Pause)*

JOHN: I know how . . . *believe* me. I know how . . . potentially *humiliating* these . . . I have no desire to . . . I have no desire other than to help you. But: *(He picks up some papers on his desk.)* I won't even say "but." I'll say that as I go back over the . . .

CAROL: I'm just, I'm just trying to . . .

JOHN: . . . no, it will not do.

CAROL: . . . what? What will . . . ?

JOHN: No. I see, I see what you, it . . . *(He gestures to the papers.)* but your work . . .

CAROL: I'm just: I sit in class I . . . *(She holds up her notebook.)* I take notes . . .

JOHN *(simultaneously with* "notes"*):*   Yes. I understand. What I am trying to *tell* you is that some, some basic . . .

CAROL: . . . I . . .

JOHN: . . . one moment: some basic miss communi . . .

CAROL: I'm doing what I'm told. I bought your book, I read your . . .

JOHN: No, I'm sure you . . .

CAROL: No, no, no. I'm doing what I'm told. It's *difficult* for me. It's *difficult* . . .

JOHN: . . . but . . .

CAROL: I don't . . . lots of the *language* . . .

JOHN: . . . please . . .

CAROL: The *language*, the "things" that you say . . .

JOHN: I'm sorry. No. I don't think that that's true.

CAROL: It *is* true. I . . .

JOHN: I think . . .

CAROL: It *is* true.

JOHN: . . . I . . .

CAROL: Why would I . . . ?

JOHN: I'll tell you why: you're an incredibly bright girl.

CAROL: . . . I . . .

JOHN: You're an incredibly . . . you have no problem with the . . . Who's kidding who?

CAROL: . . . I . . .

JOHN: No. No. I'll tell you why. I'll tell . . . I think you're *angry*, I . . .

CAROL: . . . why would I . . .

JOHN: . . . wait one moment. I . . .

CAROL: It *is* true. I have *problems* . . .

JOHN: . . . every . . .

CAROL: . . . I come from a different *social* . . .

JOHN: . . . ev . . .

CAROL: a different economic . . .

JOHN: . . . Look:

CAROL: No. I: when I *came* to this school:

JOHN: Yes. Quite . . . *(Pause)*

CAROL: . . . does that mean nothing . . . ?

JOHN: . . . but look: look . . .

CAROL: . . . I . . .

JOHN: *(Picks up paper.)* Here: Please: Sit down. *(Pause)* Sit down. *(Reads from her paper.)* "I think that the ideas contained in this work express the author's feelings in a way that he intended, based on his results." What can that mean? Do you see? What . . .

CAROL: I, the best that I . . .

JOHN: I'm saying, that perhaps this course . . .

CAROL: No, no, no, you can't, you can't . . . I have to . . .

JOHN: . . . how . . .

CAROL: . . . I have to pass it . . .

JOHN: Carol, I:

CAROL: I *have* to pass this course, I . . .

JOHN: Well.

CAROL: . . . don't you . . .

JOHN: Either the . . .

CAROL: . . . I . . .

JOHN: . . . either the, I . . . either the *criteria* for judging progress in the class are . . .

CAROL: No, no, no, no, I have to pass it.

JOHN: Now, look: I'm a human being, I . . .

CAROL: I did what you told me. I did, I did everything that, I read your *book*, you told me to buy your book and read it. Everything you *say* I . . . *(She gestures to her notebook.)* *(The phone rings.)* I do. . . . Ev . . .

JOHN: . . . look:

CAROL: . . . everything I'm told . . .

JOHN: Look. Look. I'm not your *father.* *(Pause)*

CAROL: What?

JOHN: I'm.

CAROL: Did I say you were my father?

JOHN: . . . no . . .

CAROL: Why did you say that . . . ?

JOHN: I . . .

CAROL: . . . why . . . ?

JOHN: . . . in class I . . . *(He picks up the phone.)* *(Into phone:)* Hello. I can't talk now. Jerry? Yes? I underst . . . I can't talk now. I know . . . I know . . . Jerry. I can't *talk* now. Yes, I. Call me back in . . . Thank you. *(He hangs up.)* *(To Carol:)* What do you want me to do? We are two people, all right? Both of whom have subscribed to . . .

CAROL: No, no . . .

JOHN: . . . certain arbitrary . . .

CAROL: No. You have to help me.

JOHN: Certain institutional . . . you tell me what you want me to do. . . . You tell me what you want me to . . .

CAROL: How can I go back and tell them the *grades* that I . . .

JOHN: . . . what can I do . . . ?
CAROL: *Teach* me. *Teach* me.
JOHN: . . . I'm trying to teach you.
CAROL: I read your book. I read it. I don't under . . .
JOHN: . . . you don't understand it.
CAROL: No.
JOHN: Well, perhaps it's not well *written* . . .
CAROL (*simultaneously with* "written"):   No. No. No. I want to *understand* it.
JOHN: What don't you understand? *(Pause)*
CAROL: *Any* of it. What you're trying to say. When you talk about . . .
JOHN: . . . yes . . . ? *(She consults her notes.)*
CAROL: "Virtual warehousing of the young" . . .
JOHN: "Virtual warehousing of the young." If we artificially prolong adoles-
          cence . . .
CAROL: . . . and about "The Curse of Modern Education."
JOHN: . . . well . . .
CAROL: I don't . . .
JOHN: Look. It's just a *course*, it's just a *book*, it's just a . . .
CAROL: No. No. There are *people* out there. People who came *here*. To know
          something they didn't *know*. Who *came* here. To be *helped*. To be *helped*. So
          someone would *help* them. To *do* something. To *know* something. To get,
          what do they say? "To get on in the world." How can I do that if I don't, if I
          fail? But I don't *understand*. I don't *understand*. I don't understand what any-
          thing means . . . and I walk around. From morning 'til night: with this one
          thought in my head. I'm *stupid*.
JOHN: No one thinks you're stupid.
CAROL: No? What am I . . . ?
JOHN: I . . .
CAROL: . . . what am I, then?
JOHN: I think you're angry. Many people are. I have a *telephone* call that I have
          to make. And an *appointment*, which is rather *pressing*; though I sympathize
          with your concerns, and though I wish I had the time, this was not a previ-
          ously scheduled meeting and I . . .
CAROL: . . . you think I'm nothing . . .
JOHN: . . . have an appointment with a *realtor*, and with my wife and . . .
CAROL: You think that I'm stupid.
JOHN: No. I certainly don't.
CAROL: You said it.
JOHN: No. I did not.
CAROL: You did.
JOHN: When?
CAROL: . . . you . . .
JOHN: No. I never did, or never would say that to a student, and . . .
CAROL: You said, "What can that mean?" *(Pause)* "What can that mean?" . . .
          (Pause)
JOHN: . . . and what did that mean to you . . . ?

CAROL: That meant I'm stupid. And I'll never learn. That's what that meant. And you're right.

JOHN: . . . I . . .

CAROL: But then. But then, what am I doing here . . . ?

JOHN: . . . if you thought that I . . .

CAROL: . . . when nobody wants me, and . . .

JOHN: . . . if you interpreted . . .

CAROL: Nobody *tells* me anything. And I *sit* there . . . in the *corner*. In the *back*. And everybody's talking about "this" all the time. And "concepts," and "precepts" and, and, and, and, and, WHAT IN THE WORLD ARE YOU *TALK-ING* ABOUT? And I read your book. And they said, "Fine, go in that class." Because you talked about responsibility to the young. I DON'T KNOW WHAT IT MEANS AND I'M *FAILING* . . .

JOHN: May . . .

CAROL: No, you're right. "Oh, hell." I failed. Flunk me out of it. It's garbage. Everything I do. "The ideas contained in this work express the author's feelings." That's right. That's right. I know I'm stupid. I know what I am. *(Pause)* I know what I am, Professor. You don't have to tell me. *(Pause)* It's pathetic. Isn't it?

JOHN: . . . Aha . . . *(Pause)* Sit down. Sit down. Please. *(Pause)* Please sit down.

CAROL: Why?

JOHN: I want to talk to you.

CAROL: Why?

JOHN: Just sit down. *(Pause)* Please. Sit down. Will you, please . . . ? *(Pause. She does so.)* Thank you.

CAROL: What?

JOHN: I want to tell you something.

CAROL: *(Pause)* What?

JOHN: Well, I know what you're talking about.

CAROL: No. You don't.

JOHN: I think I do. *(Pause)*

CAROL: How can you?

JOHN: I'll tell you a story about myself. *(Pause)* Do you mind? *(Pause)* I was raised to think myself stupid. That's what I want to tell you. *(Pause)*

CAROL: What do you mean?

JOHN: Just what I said. I was brought up, and my earliest, and most persistent memories are of being told that I was stupid. "You have such *intelligence*. Why must you behave so *stupidly*?" Or, "Can't you *understand*? Can't you *understand*?" And I could *not* understand. I could *not* understand.

CAROL: What?

JOHN: The simplest problem. Was beyond me. It was a mystery.

CAROL: What was a mystery?

JOHN: How people learn. How *I* could learn. Which is what I've been speaking of in class. And of *course* you can't hear it. Carol. Of *course* you can't. *(Pause)* I used to speak of "real people," and wonder what the *real* people did. The *real* people. Who were they? *They* were the people other than myself. The *good* people. The *capable* people. The people who could do the things, I could not do: learn, study, retain . . . all that *garbage*—which is what I have been talking

of in class, and that's *exactly* what I have been talking of—If you are told . . .
Listen to this. If the young child is told he cannot understand. Then he takes it
as a *description* of himself. What am I? I am *that which can not understand.*
And I saw you out there, when we were speaking of the concepts of . . .

CAROL: I can't understand any of them.

JOHN: Well, then, that's *my* fault. That's not your fault. And that is not verbiage.
That's what I firmly hold to be the truth. And I am sorry, and I owe you an
apology.

CAROL: Why?

JOHN: And I suppose that I have had some *things* on my mind. . . . We're buying
a *house,* and . . .

CAROL: People said that you were stupid . . . ?

JOHN: Yes.

CAROL: When?

JOHN: I'll tell you when. Through my life. In my childhood; and, perhaps, they
stopped. But I heard them continue.

CAROL: And what did they say?

JOHN: They said I was incompetent. Do you see? And when I'm tested the, the,
the *feelings* of my youth about the *very subject of learning* come up. And I . . .
I become, I feel "unworthy," and "unprepared." . . .

CAROL: . . . yes.

JOHN: . . . eh?

CAROL: . . . yes.

JOHN: And I feel that I must fail. *(Pause)*

CAROL: . . . but then you *do* fail. *(Pause)* You have to. *(Pause)* Don't you?

JOHN: A *pilot.* Flying a plane. The pilot is flying the plane. He thinks: Oh, my
God, my mind's been drifting! Oh, my God! What kind of a cursed imbecile
am I, that I, with this so precious cargo of *Life* in my charge, would allow my
attention to wander. Why was I born? How deluded are those who put their
trust in me, . . . et cetera, so on, and he crashes the plane.

CAROL: *(Pause)* He could just . . .

JOHN: That's right.

CAROL: He could say:

JOHN: My attention *wandered* for a moment . . .

CAROL: . . . uh huh . . .

JOHN: I had a *thought* I did not like . . . but now:

CAROL: . . . but now it's . . .

JOHN: That's what I'm telling you. It's time to put my attention . . . see: it is not:
this is what I learned. It is Not Magic. Yes. Yes. *You.* You are going to be
frightened. When faced with what may or may not be but which you are
going to perceive as a test. You will become frightened. And you will say: "I
am incapable of . . ." and everything *in* you will think these two things. "I
must. But I can't." And you will think: Why was I born to be the laughing-
stock of a world in which everyone is better than I? In which I am entitled to
nothing. Where I can not learn. *(Pause)*

CAROL: Is that . . . *(Pause)* Is that what I have . . . ?

JOHN: Well. I don't know if I'd put it that way. Listen: I'm talking to you as I'd talk to my son. Because that's what I'd like him to have that I never had. I'm talking to you the way I wish that someone had talked to me. I don't know how to do it, other than to be *personal*, . . . but . . .

CAROL: Why would you want to be personal with me?

JOHN: Well, you see? That's what I'm saying. We can only interpret the behavior of others through the screen we . . . *(The phone rings.)* Through . . . *(To phone:)* Hello . . . ? *(To Carol:)* Through the screen we create. *(To phone:)* Hello. *(To Carol:)* Excuse me a moment. *(To phone:)* Hello? No, I can't talk nnn . . . I know I did. In a few . . . I'm . . . is he coming to the . . . yes. I talked to him. We'll meet you at the No, because I'm with a *student*. It's going to be fff . . . This is important, too. I'm with a *student*, Jerry's going to . . . Listen: the sooner I get off, the sooner I'll be down, all right. I love you. Listen, listen, I said "I love you," it's going to work *out* with the, because I feel that it is, I'll be right down. All right? Well, then it's going to take as long as it takes. *(He hangs up.)* *(To Carol:)* I'm sorry.

CAROL: What was that?

JOHN: There are some problems, as there usually are, about the final agreements for the new house.

CAROL: You're buying a new house.

JOHN: That's right.

CAROL: Because of your promotion.

JOHN: Well, I suppose that that's right.

CAROL: Why did you stay here with me?

JOHN: Stay here.

CAROL: Yes. When you should have gone.

JOHN: Because I like you.

CAROL: You like me.

JOHN: Yes.

CAROL: Why?

JOHN: Why? Well? Perhaps we're similar. *(Pause)* Yes. *(Pause)*

CAROL: You said "everyone has problems."

JOHN: Everyone has problems.

CAROL: Do they?

JOHN: Certainly.

CAROL: You do?

JOHN: Yes.

CAROL: What are they?

JOHN: Well. *(Pause)* Well, you're perfectly right. *(Pause)* If we're going to take off the Artificial *Stricture*, of "Teacher," and "Student," why should *my* problems be any more a mystery than your own? Of *course* I have problems. As you saw.

CAROL: . . . with what?

JOHN: With my *wife* . . . with *work* . . .

CAROL: With work?

JOHN: Yes. And, and, perhaps my problems are, do you see? *Similar* to yours.

CAROL: Would you tell me?

JOHN: All right. *(Pause)* I came *late* to teaching. And I found it Artificial. The notion of "I know and you do not"; and I saw an *exploitation* in the education process. I told you. I hated school, I hated teachers. I hated everyone who was in the position of a "boss" because I *knew*—I didn't *think*, mind you, I *knew* I was going to fail. Because I was a fuckup. I was just no goddamned good. When I . . . late in life . . . *(Pause)* When I *got out from under* . . . when I worked my way out of the need to fail. When I . . .

CAROL: How do you do that? *(Pause)*

JOHN: You have to look at what you are, and what you feel, and how you act. And, finally, you have to look at how you act. And say: If that's what I *did*, that must be how I think of myself.

CAROL: I don't understand.

JOHN: If I fail all the time, it must be that I think of myself as a failure. If I do not want to think of myself as a failure, perhaps I should begin by *succeeding* now and again. Look. The tests, you see, which you encounter, in school, in college, in life, were designed, in the most part, for idiots. *By* idiots. There is no need to fail at them. They are not a test of your worth. They are a test of your ability to retain and spout back misinformation. Of *course* you fail them. They're *nonsense*. And I . . .

CAROL: . . . no . . .

JOHN: Yes. They're *garbage*. They're a *joke*. Look at me. Look at me. The Tenure Committee. The Tenure Committee. Come to judge me. The Bad Tenure Committee.

The "Test." Do you see? They put me to the test. Why, they had people voting on me I wouldn't employ to wax my car. And yet, I go before the Great Tenure Committee, and I have an urge, to *vomit*, to, to, to puke my *badness* on the table, to show them: "I'm no good. Why would you pick *me*?"

CAROL: They granted you tenure.

JOHN: Oh no, they announced it, but they haven't *signed*. Do you see? "At any moment . . ."

CAROL: . . . mmm . . .

JOHN: "They might not *sign*" . . . I might not . . . the *house* might not go through . . . Eh? Eh? They'll find out my "dark secret." *(Pause)*

CAROL: . . . what is it . . . ?

JOHN: There *isn't* one. But *they* will find an index of my badness . . .

CAROL: Index?

JOHN: A ". . . pointer." A "Pointer." You see? Do you see? I *understand* you. I. Know. That. Feeling. Am I entitled to my job, and my nice *home*, and my *wife*, and my *family*, and so on. This is what I'm saying: That theory of education which, that *theory*:

CAROL: I . . . I . . . *(Pause)*

JOHN: What?

CAROL: I . . .

JOHN: What?

CAROL: I want to know about my grade. *(Long pause)*

JOHN: Of course you do.

CAROL: Is that bad?

JOHN: No.

CAROL: Is it bad that I asked you that?

JOHN: No.

CAROL: Did I upset you?

JOHN: No. And I apologize. Of *course* you want to know about your grade. And, of course, you can't concentrate on anyth . . . *(The telephone starts to ring.)* Wait a moment.

CAROL: I should go.

JOHN: I'll make you a deal.

CAROL: No, you have to . . .

JOHN: Let it ring. I'll make you a deal. You stay here. We'll start the whole course over. I'm going to say it was not you, it was I who was not paying attention. We'll start the whole course over. Your grade is an "A." Your final grade is an "A." *(The phone stops ringing.)*

CAROL: But the class is only half over . . .

JOHN *(simultaneously with* "over"*):*   Your grade for the whole term is an "A." If you will come back and meet with me. A few more times. Your grade's an "A." Forget about the paper. You didn't like it, you didn't like writing it. It's not important. What's important is that I awake your interest, if I can, and that I answer your questions. Let's start over. *(Pause)*

CAROL: Over. With what?

JOHN: Say this is the beginning.

CAROL: The beginning.

JOHN: Yes.

CAROL: Of what?

JOHN: Of the class.

CAROL: But we can't start over.

JOHN: I say we can. *(Pause)* I say we can.

CAROL: But I don't believe it.

JOHN: Yes, I know that. But it's true. What is The Class but you and me? *(Pause)*

CAROL: There are rules.

JOHN: Well. We'll break them.

CAROL: How can we?

JOHN: We won't tell anybody.

CAROL: Is that all right?

JOHN: I say that it's fine.

CAROL: Why would you do this for me?

JOHN: I like you. Is that so difficult for you to . . .

CAROL: Um . . .

JOHN: There's no one here but you and me. *(Pause)*

CAROL: All right. I did not understand. When you referred . . .

JOHN: All right, yes?

CAROL: When you referred to hazing.

JOHN: Hazing.

CAROL: You wrote, in your book. About the comparative . . . the comparative . . . *(She checks her notes.)*

JOHN: Are you checking your notes . . . ?

CAROL: Yes.

JOHN: Tell me in your own . . .

CAROL: I want to make sure that I have it right.

JOHN: No. Of course. You want to be exact.

CAROL: I want to know everything that went on.

JOHN: . . . that's good.

CAROL: . . . so I . . .

JOHN: That's very good. But I was suggesting, many times, that that which we wish to retain is retained oftentimes, I think, *better* with less expenditure of effort.

CAROL: *(Of notes)* Here it is: you wrote of *hazing.*

JOHN: . . . that's correct. Now: I said "hazing." It means ritualized annoyance. We shove this book at you, we say read it. Now, you say you've read it? I think that you're *lying.* I'll *grill* you, and when I find you've lied, you'll be disgraced, and your life will be ruined. It's a sick game. Why do we do it? Does it educate? In no sense. Well, then, what is higher education? It is something-other-than-useful.

CAROL: What is "something-other-than-useful?"

JOHN: It has become a ritual, it has become an article of faith. That all must be subjected to, or to put it differently, that all are entitled to Higher Education. And my point . . .

CAROL: You disagree with that?

JOHN: Well, let's address that. What do you think?

CAROL: I don't know.

JOHN: What do you think, though? *(Pause)*

CAROL: I don't know.

JOHN: I spoke of it in class. Do you remember my example?

CAROL: Justice.

JOHN: Yes. Can you repeat it to me? *(She looks down at her notebook.)* Without your notes? I ask you as a favor to me, so that I can see if my idea was interesting.

CAROL: You said "justice" . . .

JOHN: Yes?

CAROL: . . . that all are entitled . . . *(Pause)* I . . . I . . . I . . .

JOHN: Yes. To a speedy trial. To a fair trial. But they needn't be given a trial *at all* unless they stand accused. Eh? Justice is their right, should they choose to avail themselves of it, they should have a fair trial. It does not follow, of necessity, a person's life is incomplete without a trial in it. Do you see?

My point is a confusion between equity and *utility* arose. So we confound the *usefulness* of higher education with our, granted, right to equal access to the same. We, in effect, create a *prejudice* toward it, completely independent of . . .

CAROL: . . . that it is prejudice that we should go to school?

JOHN: Exactly. *(Pause)*

CAROL: How can you say that? How . . .

JOHN: Good. Good. *Good.* That's right! Speak up! What is a prejudice? An unreasoned belief. We are all subject to it. None of us is not. When it is threatened, or opposed, we feel anger, and feel, do we not? As you do now. Do you not? Good.

CAROL: . . . but how can you . . .

JOHN: . . . let us examine. Good.

CAROL: How . . .

JOHN: Good. Good. When . . .

CAROL: I'M SPEAKING . . . *(Pause)*

JOHN: I'm sorry.

CAROL: How can you . . .

JOHN: . . . I beg your pardon.

CAROL: That's all right.

JOHN: I beg your pardon.

CAROL: That's all right.

JOHN: I'm sorry I interrupted you.

CAROL: That's all right.

JOHN: You were saying?

CAROL: I was saying . . . I was saying . . . *(She checks her notes.)* How can you say in a class. Say in a college class, that college education is prejudice?

JOHN: I said that our predilection for it . . .

CAROL: Predilection . . .

JOHN: . . . you know what that means.

CAROL: Does it mean "liking"?

JOHN: Yes.

CAROL: But how can you say that? That College . . .

JOHN: . . . that's my *job*, don't you know.

CAROL: What is?

JOHN: To provoke you.

CAROL: No.

JOHN: Oh. Yes, though.

CAROL: To provoke me?

JOHN: That's right.

CAROL: To make me mad?

JOHN: That's right. To force you . . .

CAROL: . . . to make me mad is your job?

JOHN: To force you to . . . listen: *(Pause)* Ah. *(Pause)* When I was young somebody told me, are you ready, the rich copulate less often than the poor. But when they do, they take more of their clothes off. Years. Years, mind you, I would compare experiences of my own to this dictum, saying, aha, this fits the norm, or ah, this is a variation from it. What did it mean? Nothing. It was some jerk thing, some school kid told me that took up room inside my head. *(Pause)*

Somebody told *you*, and you hold it as an article of faith, that higher education is an unassailable good. This notion is so dear to you that when I question it you become angry. Good. Good, I say. Are not those the very things which we should question? I say college education, since the war, has become so a matter of course, and such a fashionable necessity, for those either of or aspiring *to* to the new vast middle class, that we *espouse* it, as a matter of right, and have ceased to ask, "What is it good for?" *(Pause)*

What might be some reasons for pursuit of higher education?
One: A love of learning.
Two: The wish for mastery of a skill.
Three: For economic betterment.
(Stops. Makes a note.)

CAROL: I'm keeping you.

JOHN: One moment. I have to make a note . . .

CAROL: It's something that I said?

JOHN: No, we're buying a house.

CAROL: You're buying the new house.

JOHN: To go with the tenure. That's right. Nice *house,* close to the *private school* . . . *(He continues making his note.)* . . . We were talking of economic *betterment (Carol writes in her notebook.)* . . . I was thinking of the School Tax. *(He continues writing.) (To himself:)* . . . *where is it written* that I have to send my child to public school. . . . Is it a law that I have to improve the City Schools at the expense of my own interest? And, is this not simply *The White Man's Burden?* Good. And *(Looks up to Carol)* . . . does this interest you?

CAROL: No. I'm taking notes . . .

JOHN: You don't have to take notes, you know, you can just listen.

CAROL: I want to make sure I remember it. *(Pause)*

JOHN: I'm not lecturing you, I'm just trying to tell you some things I think.

CAROL: What do you think?

JOHN: Should all kids go to college? *Why* . . .

CAROL: *(Pause)* To learn.

JOHN: But if he does not learn.

CAROL: If the child does not learn?

JOHN: Then why is he in college? Because he was told it was his "right"?

CAROL: Some might find college instructive.

JOHN: I would hope so.

CAROL: But how do they feel? Being told they are wasting their time?

JOHN: I don't think I'm telling them that.

CAROL: You said that education was "prolonged and systematic hazing."

JOHN: Yes. It can be so.

CAROL: . . . if education is so *bad,* why do you do it?

JOHN: I do it because I love it. *(Pause)* Let's. . . . I suggest you look at the demographics, wage-earning capacity, college- and non-college-educated men and women, 1855 to 1980, and let's see if we can wring some worth from the statistics. Eh? And . . .

CAROL: No.

JOHN: What?

CAROL: I can't understand them.

JOHN: . . . you . . . ?

CAROL: . . . the "charts." The *Concepts*, the . . .

JOHN: "Charts" are simply . . .

CAROL: When I leave here . . .

JOHN: Charts, do you see . . .

CAROL: No, I can't . . .

JOHN: You can, though.

CAROL: NO, NO—I DON'T UNDERSTAND. DO YOU SEE??? I DON'T UNDERSTAND . . .

JOHN: What?

CAROL: *Any* of it. *Any* of it. I'm *smiling* in class, I'm *smiling,* the whole time. What are you *talking* about? What is everyone *talking* about? I don't *understand.* I don't know what it *means.* I don't know what it means to *be* here . . . you tell me I'm intelligent, and then you tell me I should not be *here,* what do you *want* with me? What does it *mean?* Who should I *listen* to . . . I . . .
(He goes over to her and puts his arm around her shoulder.)
NO! *(She walks away from him.)*

JOHN: Sshhhh.

CAROL: No, I don't under . . .

JOHN: Sshhhhh.

CAROL: I don't know what you're *saying* . . .

JOHN: Sshhhhh. It's all right.

CAROL: . . . I have to . . .

JOHN: Sshhhhh. Sshhhhh. Let it go a moment. *(Pause)* Sshhhhh . . . let it go. *(Pause)* Just let it go. *(Pause)* Just let it go. It's all right. *(Pause)* Sshhhhh. *(Pause)* I understand . . . *(Pause)* What do you feel?

CAROL: I feel bad.

JOHN: I know. It's all right.

CAROL: I . . . *(Pause)*

JOHN: What?

CAROL: I . . .

JOHN: What? Tell me.

CAROL: I don't understand you.

JOHN: I know. It's all right.

CAROL: I . . .

JOHN: What? *(Pause)* What? *Tell* me.

CAROL: I can't tell you.

JOHN: No, you must.

CAROL: I can't.

JOHN: No. Tell me. *(Pause)*

CAROL: I'm bad. *(Pause)* Oh, God. *(Pause)*

JOHN: It's all right.

CAROL: I'm . . .

JOHN: It's all right.

CAROL: I can't talk about this.

JOHN: It's all right. Tell me.

CAROL: Why do you want to know this?

JOHN: I don't want to know. I want to know whatever you . . .

CAROL: I always . . .

JOHN: . . . good . . .

CAROL: I always . . . all my life . . . I have never told anyone this . . .

JOHN: Yes. Go on. *(Pause)* Go on.

CAROL: All of my life . . . *(The phone rings.)* *(Pause. John goes to the phone and picks it up.)*

JOHN *(into phone):*   I can't talk now. *(Pause)* What? *(Pause)* Hmm. *(Pause)* All right, I . . . I. Can't. Talk. Now. No, no, no, I *Know* I did, but. . . . What? Hello. What? She *what?* She *can't*, she said the agreement is void? How, how is the agreement *void? That's Our House.*

I have the *paper;* when we come down, next week, with the payment, and the paper, that house is . . . wait, wait, wait, wait, wait, wait, wait: Did Jerry . . . is Jerry there? *(Pause)* Is *she* there . . . ? Does she have a *lawyer* . . . ? How the *hell,* how the *Hell.* That is . . . it's a question, you said, of the *easement.* I don't underst . . . it's not the *whole agreement.* It's just the *easement,* why would she? Put, put, put, *Jerry* on. *(Pause)* Jer, *Jerry:* What the *Hell* . . . that's my *house.* That's . . . Well, I'm no, no, no, I'm *not* coming ddd . . . List, *Listen, screw* her. You *tell* her. You, listen: I want you to take *Grace,* you take Grace, and get out of that house. You *leave* her there. Her and her lawyer, and you *tell* them, we'll see them in court next . . . no. No. Leave her there, leave her to *stew* in it: You tell her, we're *getting* that house, and we are going to . . . No. I'm *not* coming down. I'll be damned if I'll sit in the same rrr . . . the next, you tell her the next time I *see* her is in court . . . I . . . *(Pause)* What? *(Pause)* What? I don't understand. *(Pause)* Well, what about the house? *(Pause)* There isn't any problem with the hhh . . . *(Pause)* No, no, no, that's all right. All ri . . . All right . . . *(Pause)* Of course. Tha . . . Thank you. No, I will. Right away. *(He hangs up.)* *(Pause)*

CAROL: What is it? *(Pause)*

JOHN: It's a surprise party.

CAROL: It is.

JOHN: Yes.

CAROL: A party for you.

JOHN: Yes.

CAROL: Is it your birthday?

JOHN: No.

CAROL: What is it?

JOHN: The tenure announcement.

CAROL: The tenure announcement.

JOHN: They're throwing a party for us in our new house.

CAROL: Your new house.

JOHN: The house that we're buying.

CAROL: You have to go.

JOHN: It seems that I do.

CAROL: *(Pause)* They're proud of you.

JOHN: Well, there are those who would say it's a form of aggression.

CAROL: What is?

JOHN: A surprise.

TWO

John and Carol seated across the desk from each other.

JOHN: You see, *(pause)* I love to teach. And flatter myself I am *skilled* at it. And I love the, the aspect of *performance*. I think I must confess that.

When I found I loved to teach I swore that I would not become that cold, rigid automaton of an instructor which I had encountered as a child.

Now, I was not unconscious that it was given me to err upon the other side. And, so, I asked and *ask* myself if I engaged in heterodoxy, I will not say "gratuitously" for I do not care to posit orthodoxy as a given good—but, "to the detriment of, of my students." *(Pause)*

As I said. When the possibility of tenure opened, and, of course, I'd long pursued it, I was, of course *happy,* and *covetous* of it. I asked myself if I was wrong to covet it. And thought about it long, and, I hope, truthfully, and saw in myself several things in, I think, no particular order. *(Pause)*

That I *would* pursue it. That I *desired* it, that I was not pure of longing for security, and that that, perhaps, was not reprehensible in me. That I had duties *beyond* the school, and that my duty to my home, for instance, was, or should be, if it were not, of an equal weight. That tenure, and security, and yes, and *comfort*, were not, of themselves, to be scorned; and were even worthy of honorable pursuit. And that it was given me. Here, in this place, which I enjoy, and in which I find comfort, to assure myself of—as far as it rests in The Material—a continuation of that joy and comfort. In exchange for what? Teaching? Which I love.

What was the price of this security? To obtain *tenure.* Which tenure the committee is in the process of granting me. And on the basis of which I contracted to purchase a house. Now, as you don't have your own family, at this point, you may not know what that means. But to me it is important. A home. A Good Home. To raise my family. Now: The Tenure Committee will meet. This is the process, and a *good* process. Under which the school has functioned for quite a long time. They will meet, and hear your complaint— which you have the right to make; and they will dismiss it. They will *dismiss* your complaint; and, in the intervening period, I will lose my house. I will not be able to close on my house. I will lose my *deposit,* and the home I'd picked out for my wife and son will go by the boards. Now: I see I have angered you. I understand your anger at teachers. I was angry with mine. I felt hurt and humiliated by them. Which is one of the reasons that I went into education.

CAROL: What do you want of me?

JOHN: *(Pause)* I was hurt. When I received the report. Of the tenure committee. I was shocked. And I was hurt. No, I don't mean to subject you to my weak sensibilities. All right. Finally, I didn't understand. Then I thought: is it not always at those points at which we reckon ourselves unassailable that we are most vulnerable and . . . *(Pause)* Yes. All right. You find me pedantic. Yes. I am. By nature, by *birth*, by profession. I don't know . . . I'm always looking for a *paradigm* for . . .

CAROL: I don't know what a paradigm is.

JOHN: It's a model.

CAROL: Then why can't you use that word? *(Pause)*

JOHN: If it is important to you. Yes, all right. I was looking for a model. To continue: I feel that one point . . .

CAROL: I . . .

JOHN: One second . . . upon which I am unassailable is my unflinching concern for my students' dignity. I asked you here to . . . in the spirit of *investigation*, to ask you . . . to ask . . . *(Pause)* What have I done to you? *(Pause)* And, and, I suppose, how can I make amends. Can we not settle this now? It's pointless, really, and I want to know.

CAROL: What you can do to force me to retract?

JOHN: That is not what I meant at all.

CAROL: To bribe me, to convince me . . .

JOHN: . . . No.

CAROL: To retract . . .

JOHN: That is not what I meant at all. I think that you know it is not.

CAROL: That is not what I know. I *wish* I . . .

JOHN: I do not want to . . . you wish what?

CAROL: No, you said what amends can you make. To force me to retract.

JOHN: That is not what I said.

CAROL: I have my notes.

JOHN: Look. Look. The Stoics say . . .

CAROL: The Stoics?

JOHN: The Stoical Philosophers say if you remove the phrase "I have been injured," you have removed the injury. Now: Think: I know that you're upset. Just tell me. Literally. Literally: what wrong have I done you?

CAROL: Whatever you have done to me — to the extent that you've done it to *me*, do you know, rather than to me as a *student*, and, so, to the student body, is contained in my report. To the tenure committee.

JOHN: Well, all right. *(Pause)* Let's see. *(He reads.)* I find that I am sexist. That I am *elitist*. I'm not sure I know what that means, other than it's a derogatory word, meaning "bad." That I . . . That I insist on wasting time, in nonprescribed, in self-aggrandizing and theatrical *diversions* from the prescribed *text* . . . that these have taken both sexist and pornographic forms . . . here we find listed . . . *(Pause)* Here we find listed . . . instances " . . . closeted with a student" . . . "Told a rambling, sexually explicit story, in which the frequency and attitudes of fornication of the poor and rich are, it would seem, the central point . . . moved to *embrace* said student and . . . all part of a pattern . . ." *(Pause)*

(He reads.) That I used the phrase "The White Man's Burden" . . . that I told you how I'd asked you to my room because I quote like you. *(Pause)*

(He reads.) "He said he 'liked' me. That he 'liked being with me.' He'd let me write my examination paper over, if I could come back oftener to see him in his office." *(Pause)* *(To Carol:)* It's *ludicrous*. Don't you know that? It's not *necessary*. It's going to *humiliate* you, and it's going to cost me my *house*, and . . .

CAROL: It's "*ludicrous* . . ."?

John picks up the report and reads again.

JOHN: "He told me he had problems with his wife; and that he wanted to take off the artificial stricture of Teacher and Student. He put his arm around me . . ."

CAROL: Do you deny it? Can you deny it . . . ? Do you see? *(Pause)* Don't you see? You don't see, do you?

JOHN: I don't see . . .

CAROL: You think, you think you can deny that these things happened; or, if they *did*, if they *did*, that they meant what you *said* they meant. Don't you see? You drag me in here, you drag us, to listen to you "go on"; and "go on" about this, or that, or we don't "express" ourselves very well. We don't say what we mean. Don't we? Don't we? We *do* say what we mean. And you say that "I don't understand you . . .": Then *you* . . . *(Points.)*

JOHN: "Consult the Report"?

CAROL: . . . that's right.

JOHN: You see. You see. Can't you. . . . You see what I'm saying? Can't you tell me in your own words?

CAROL: Those are my own words. *(Pause)*

JOHN: *(He reads.)* "He told me that if I would stay alone with him in his office, he would change my grade to an A." *(To Carol:)* What have I done to you? Oh. My God, are you so hurt?

CAROL: What I "feel" is irrelevant. *(Pause)*

JOHN: Do you know that I tried to help you?

CAROL: What I know I have reported.

JOHN: I would like to help you now. I would. Before this escalates.

CAROL *(simultaneously with "escalates")*: You see. I don't think that I need your help. I don't think I need anything you have.

JOHN: I feel . . .

CAROL: I don't *care* what you feel. Do you see? DO YOU SEE? You can't *do* that anymore. You. Do. Not. Have. The. Power. Did you misuse it? *Someone* did. Are you part of that group? *Yes. Yes.* You Are. You've *done* these things. And to say, and to say, "Oh. Let me help you with your problem . . ."

JOHN: Yes. I understand. I understand. You're *hurt*. You're *angry*. Yes. I think your *anger* is *betraying* you. Down a path which helps no one.

CAROL: I don't *care* what you think.

JOHN: You don't? *(Pause)* But you talk of *rights*. Don't you see? *I* have rights too. Do you see? I have a *house* . . . part of the *real* world; and The Tenure Committee, Good Men and True . . .

CAROL: . . . Professor . . .

JOHN: . . . Please: *Also* part of that world: you understand? This is my *life*. I'm not a *bogeyman*. I don't "stand" for something, I . . .

CAROL: . . . Professor . . .

JOHN: . . . I . . .

CAROL: Professor. I came here as a *favor*. At your personal request. Perhaps I should not have done so. But I did. On my behalf, and on behalf of my group. And you speak of the tenure committee, one of whose members is a woman, as you know. And though you might call it Good Fun, or An Historical Phrase, or An Oversight, or, All of the Above, to refer to the committee as Good Men and True, it is a demeaning remark. It is a sexist remark, and to overlook it is to countenance continuation of that method of thought. It's a remark . . .

JOHN: OH COME ON. Come on. . . . Sufficient to deprive a family of . . .

CAROL: Sufficient? Sufficient? Sufficient? Yes. It is a *fact* . . . and that story, which I quote, is *vile* and *classist*, and *manipulative* and *pornographic*. It . . .

JOHN: . . . it's pornographic . . . ?

CAROL: What gives you the *right*. Yes. To speak to a *woman* in your private . . . Yes. Yes. I'm sorry. I'm sorry. You feel yourself empowered . . . you say so yourself. To *strut*. To *posture*. To "perform." To "Call me in here . . ." Eh? You say that higher education is a joke. And treat it as such, you *treat* it as such. And *confess* to a taste to play the *Patriarch* in your class. To grant *this*. To deny *that*. To embrace your students.

JOHN: How can you assert. How can you stand there and . . .

CAROL: How can you *deny* it. You did it to me. *Here*. You *did*. . . . You *confess*. You love the Power. To *deviate*. To *invent*, to transgress . . . to *transgress* whatever norms have been established for us. And you think it's charming to "question" in yourself this taste to mock and destroy. But you should question it. Professor. And you pick those things which you feel *advance* you: publication, *tenure*, and the steps to get them you call "harmless rituals." And you perform those steps. Although you say it is hypocrisy. But to the aspirations of your students. Of *hardworking students*, who come here, who *slave* to come here—you have no idea what it cost me to come to this school—you *mock* us. You call education "hazing," and from your so-protected, so-elitist seat you hold our confusion as a *joke*, and our hopes and efforts with it. Then you sit there and say "what have I done?" And ask me to understand that *you* have aspirations too. But I tell you. I tell you. That you are vile. And that you are exploitative. And if you possess one ounce of that inner honesty you describe in your book, you can look in yourself and see those things that I see. And you can find revulsion equal to my own. Good day. *(She prepares to leave the room.)*

JOHN: Wait a second, will you, just one moment. *(Pause)* Nice day today.

CAROL: What?

JOHN: You said "Good day." I think that it is a nice day today.

CAROL: *Is* it?

JOHN: Yes, I think it is.

CAROL: And why is that important?

JOHN: Because it is the essence of all human communication. I say something conventional, you respond, and the information we exchange is not about the "weather," but that we both agree to converse. In effect, we agree that we are both human. *(Pause)*

I'm not a . . . "exploiter," and you're not a . . . "deranged," what? *Revolutionary* . . . that we may, that we may have . . . positions, and that we may have . . . desires, which are in *conflict*, but that we're just human. *(Pause)* That means that sometimes we're *imperfect.* *(Pause)* Often we're in conflict . . . *(Pause) Much* of what we do, you're right, in the name of "principles" is *self-serving* . . . much of what we do is *conventional. (Pause)* You're right. *(Pause)* You said you came in the class because you wanted to learn about *education.* I don't know that I can teach you about education. But I know that I can tell you what I *think* about education, and then *you* decide. And you don't have to fight with me. *I'm* not the subject. *(Pause)* And where I'm *wrong* . . . perhaps it's not your job to "fix" me. I don't want to fix *you.* I would like to tell you what I *think,* because that *is* my job, conventional as it is, and flawed as I may be. And then, if you can show me some better *form,* then we can proceed from there. But, just like "nice day, isn't it . . . ?" I don't think we can proceed until we accept that each of us is human. *(Pause)* And we still can have difficulties. We *will* have them . . . that's all right too. *(Pause)* Now:

CAROL: . . . wait . . .

JOHN: Yes. I want to hear it.

CAROL: . . . the . . .

JOHN: Yes. Tell me frankly.

CAROL: . . . my position . . .

JOHN: I want to hear it. In your own words. What you want. And what you feel.

CAROL: . . . I . . .

JOHN: . . . yes . . .

CAROL: My Group.

JOHN: Your "Group" . . . ? *(Pause)*

CAROL: The people I've been talking to . . .

JOHN: There's no shame in that. Everybody needs advisers. Everyone needs to expose themselves. To various points of view. It's not wrong. It's essential. Good. Good. Now: You and I . . . *(The phone rings.)*

You and I . . .

(He hesitates for a moment, and then picks it up.) (Into phone) Hello. *(Pause)* Um . . . no, I know they do. *(Pause)* I know she does. Tell her that I . . . can I call you back? . . . Then tell her that I think it's going to be fine. *(Pause)* Tell her just, just hold on, I'll . . . can I get back to you? . . . Well . . .

no, no, no, we're *taking* the house . . . we're . . . no, no, nn . . . no, she will
nnn, it's not a *question* of refunding the dep . . . no . . . it's not a *question* of
the deposit . . . will you call Jerry? Babe, baby, will you just call Jerry? Tell
him, nnn . . . tell him they, well, they're to keep the deposit, because the
deal, be . . . because the deal is going to go *through* . . . because I know . . .
be . . . will you please? Just *trust* me. Be . . . well, I'm dealing with the complaint. Yes. Right *Now*. Which is why I . . . yes, no, no, it's really, I can't *talk*
about it now. Call Jerry, and I can't talk now. Ff . . . fine. Gg . . . good-bye.
(Hangs up.) (Pause) I'm sorry we were interrupted.

CAROL: No . . .
JOHN: I . . . I was saying:
CAROL: You said that we should agree to talk about my complaint.
JOHN: That's correct.
CAROL: But we *are* talking about it.
JOHN: Well, that's correct too. You see? This is the *gist* of education.
CAROL: No, no. I mean, we're talking about it at the Tenure Committee Hear-
         ing. *(Pause)*
JOHN: Yes, but I'm saying: we can talk about it *now*, as easily as . . .
CAROL: No. I think that we should stick to the process . . .
JOHN: . . . wait a . . .
CAROL: . . . the "conventional" process. As you said. *(She gets up.)* And you're
         right, I'm sorry if I was, um, if I was "discourteous" to you. You're right.
JOHN: Wait, wait a . . .
CAROL: I really should go.
JOHN: Now, look, granted. I have an interest. In the status quo. All right? Every-
         one does. But what I'm saying is that the *committee* . . .
CAROL: Professor, you're right. Just don't impinge on me. We'll take our differ-
         ences, and . . .
JOHN: You're going to make a . . . look, look, look, you're going to . . .
CAROL: I shouldn't have come here. They told me . . .
JOHN: One moment. No. No. There are *norms*, here, and there's no reason.
         Look: I'm trying to *save* you . . .
CAROL: No one *asked* you to . . . you're trying to save *me*? Do me the courtesy
         to . . .
JOHN: I *am* doing you the courtesy. I'm talking *straight* to you. We can settle this
         now. And I want you to sit *down* and . . .
CAROL: You must excuse me . . . *(She starts to leave the room.)*
JOHN: Sit down, it seems we each have a. . . . Wait one moment. Wait one
         moment . . . just do me the courtesy to . . .

He restrains her from leaving.

CAROL: LET ME GO.
JOHN: I have no desire to *hold* you, I just want to *talk* to you . . .
CAROL: LET ME GO. LET ME GO. WOULD SOMEBODY *HELP* ME?
         WOULD SOMEBODY *HELP* ME PLEASE . . . ?

THREE

At rise, Carol and John are seated.

JOHN: I have asked you here. *(Pause)* I have asked you here against, against my . . .

CAROL: I was most surprised you asked me.

JOHN: . . . against my better *judgment*, against . . .

CAROL: I was most surprised . . .

JOHN: . . . against the . . . yes. I'm sure.

CAROL: . . . If you would like me to leave, I'll leave. I'll go right now . . . *(She rises.)*

JOHN: Let us begin *correctly*, may we? I feel . . .

CAROL: That is what I wished to do. That's why I came here, but now . . .

JOHN: . . . I feel . . .

CAROL: But now perhaps you'd like me to leave . . .

JOHN: I don't want you to leave. I asked you to come . . .

CAROL: I didn't have to come here.

JOHN: No. *(Pause)* Thank you.

CAROL: All right. *(Pause) (She sits down.)*

JOHN: Although I feel that it *profits*, it would *profit* you something, to . . .

CAROL: . . . what I . . .

JOHN: If you would hear me out, if you would hear me out.

CAROL: I came here to, the court officers told me not to come.

JOHN: . . . the "court" officers . . . ?

CAROL: I was shocked that you asked.

JOHN: . . . wait . . .

CAROL: Yes. But I did *not* come here to hear what it "profits" me.

JOHN: The "court" officers . . .

CAROL: . . . no, no, perhaps I should leave . . . *(She gets up.)*

JOHN: Wait.

CAROL: No. I shouldn't have . . .

JOHN: . . . wait. Wait. Wait a moment.

CAROL: Yes? What is it you want? *(Pause)* What is it you want?

JOHN: I'd like you to stay.

CAROL: You want me to stay.

JOHN: Yes.

CAROL: You do.

JOHN: Yes. *(Pause)* Yes. I would like to have you hear me out. If you would. *(Pause)* Would you please? If you would do that I would be in your debt. *(Pause) (She sits.)* Thank you. *(Pause)*

CAROL: What is it you wish to tell me?

JOHN: All right. I cannot . . . *(Pause)* I cannot help but feel you are owed an apology. *(Pause) (Of papers in his hands)* I have read. *(Pause)* And reread these accusations.

CAROL: What "accusations"?

JOHN: The, the tenure comm . . . what other accusations . . . ?

CAROL: The tenure committee . . . ?

JOHN: Yes.

CAROL: Excuse me, but those are not accusations. They have been *proved*. They are facts.

JOHN: . . . I . . .

CAROL: No. Those are not "accusations."

JOHN: . . . those?

CAROL: . . . the committee *(The phone starts to ring.)* the committee has . . .

JOHN: . . . All right . . .

CAROL: . . . those are not accusations. The Tenure Committee.

JOHN: ALL RIGHT. ALL RIGHT. ALL RIGHT. *(He picks up the phone.)* Hello. Yes. No. I'm here. Tell Mister . . . No, I can't talk to him now . . . I'm sure he has, but I'm fff . . . I know . . . No, I have no time t . . . tell Mister . . . tell Mist . . . tell Jerry that I'm *fine* and that I'll call him right aw . . . *(Pause)* My wife . . . Yes. I'm sure she has. Yes, thank you. Yes, I'll call her too. I cannot talk to you now. *(He hangs up.) (Pause)* All right. It was good of you to come. Thank you. I have studied. I have spent some time studying the indictment.

CAROL: You will have to explain that word to me.

JOHN: An "indictment" . . .

CAROL: Yes.

JOHN: Is a "bill of particulars." A . . .

CAROL: All right. Yes.

JOHN: In which is alleged . . .

CAROL: No. I cannot allow that. I cannot allow that. Nothing is alleged. Everything is proved . . .

JOHN: Please, wait a sec . . .

CAROL: I cannot *come* to allow . . .

JOHN: If I may . . . If I may, from whatever you feel is "established," by . . .

CAROL: The issue here is not what I "feel." It is not my "feelings," but the feelings of women. And men. Your superiors, who've been "polled," do you see? To whom *evidence* has been presented, who have *ruled*, do you see? Who have weighed the testimony and the evidence, and have *ruled*, do you see? That you are *negligent*. That you are *guilty*, that you are found *wanting*, and in *error*; and are *not*, for the reasons so-told, to be given tenure. That you are to be disciplined. For facts. For *facts*. Not "alleged," what is the word? But *proved*. Do you see? *By your own actions.*

That is what the tenure committee has said. That is what my lawyer said. For what you did in class. For what you did *in this office.*

JOHN: They're going to discharge me.

CAROL: As full well they should. You don't understand? You're angry? What has *led* you to this place? Not your sex. Not your race. Not your class. YOUR OWN ACTIONS. And you're *angry*. You *ask* me here. What *do* you want? You want to "charm" me. You want to "convince" me. You want me to recant. I will *not* recant. Why should I . . . ? What I say is right. You tell me, you are going to tell me that you have a wife and child. You are going to say that you have a career and that you've worked for twenty years for this. Do you know what you've *worked* for? *Power*. For *power*. Do you understand? And you sit there, and you tell me *stories*. About your *house*, about all the private *schools*, and about *privilege*, and how you are entitled. To *buy*, to *spend*, to *mock*, to *summon*. All your stories. All your silly weak *guilt*, it's all about *privilege*; and you won't know it. Don't you see? You worked twenty years for the right to *insult* me. And you feel entitled to be *paid* for it. Your Home. Your Wife . . . Your sweet "deposit" on your house . . .

JOHN: Don't you have feelings?

CAROL: That's my point. You see? Don't you have feelings? Your final argument. What is it that has no feelings. *Animals*. I don't take your side, you question if I'm Human.

JOHN: Don't you have feelings?

CAROL: I have a responsibility. I . . .

JOHN: . . . to . . . ?

CAROL: To? This institution. To the *students*. To my *group*.

JOHN: . . . your "group." . . .

CAROL: Because I speak, yes, not for myself. But for the group; for those who suffer what I suffer. On behalf of whom, even if I, were, inclined, to what, forgive? Forget? What? Overlook your . . .

JOHN: . . . my behavior?

CAROL: . . . it would be wrong.

JOHN: Even if you were inclined to "forgive" me.

CAROL: It would be wrong.

JOHN: And what would transpire.

CAROL: Transpire?

JOHN: Yes.

CAROL: "Happen?"

JOHN: Yes.

CAROL: Then *say* it. For Christ's sake. Who the *hell* do you think that you are? You want a post. You want unlimited power. To do and to say what you want. As it pleases you — Testing, Questioning, Flirting . . .

JOHN: I never . . .

CAROL: Excuse me, one moment, will you?

(She reads from her notes.)

The twelfth: "Have a good day, dear."

The fifteenth: "Now, don't *you* look fetching . . ."

April seventeenth: "If you girls would come over here . . ." I saw you. I saw you, Professor. For two semesters sit there, stand there and exploit our, as you thought, "paternal prerogative," and what is that but rape; I swear to God. You asked me in here to explain something to me, as a child, that I did not understand. But I came to explain something to you. You Are Not God. You ask me why I came? I came here to instruct you.

(She produces his book.)

And your book? You think you're going to show me some "light"? You "*maverick.*" Outside of tradition. No, no, *(She reads from the book's liner notes.)* "*of that fine tradition of *inquiry*. Of Polite *skepticism*" . . . and you say you believe in free intellectual discourse. YOU BELIEVE IN NOTHING. YOU BELIEVE IN NOTHING AT ALL.

JOHN: I believe in freedom of thought.

CAROL: Isn't that fine. *Do* you?

JOHN: Yes. I do.

CAROL: Then why do you question, for one moment, the committee's decision refusing your tenure? Why do you question your suspension? You believe in what *you call* freedom of thought. Then, fine. *You* believe in freedom-of-thought *and* a home, and, *and* prerogatives for your kid, *and* tenure. And I'm going to tell you. You believe *not* in "freedom of thought," but in an elitist, in, in a protected hierarchy which rewards you. And for whom you are the clown. And you mock and exploit the system which pays your rent. You're wrong. I'm not wrong. You're wrong. You think that I'm full of hatred. I know what you think I am.

JOHN: Do you?

CAROL: You think I'm a, of course I do. You think I am a frightened, repressed, confused, I don't know, abandoned young thing of some doubtful sexuality, who wants, power and revenge. *(Pause) Don't* you? *(Pause)*

JOHN: Yes. I do. *(Pause)*

CAROL: Isn't that better? And I feel that that is the first moment which you've treated me with respect. For you told me the truth. *(Pause)* I did not come here, as you are assured, to gloat. Why would I want to gloat? I've profited nothing from your, your, as you say, your "misfortune." I came here, as you did me the honor to *ask* me here, I came here to *tell* you something.

(Pause) That I think . . . that I think you've been wrong. That I think you've been terribly wrong. Do you hate me now? *(Pause)*

JOHN: Yes.

CAROL: Why do you hate me? Because you think me wrong? No. Because I have, you think, *power* over you. Listen to me. Listen to me, Professor. *(Pause)* It is the power that you hate. So deeply that, that any atmosphere of free discussion is impossible. It's not "unlikely." It's *impossible*. Isn't it?

JOHN: Yes.

CAROL: Isn't it . . . ?

JOHN: Yes. I suppose.

CAROL: Now. The thing which you find so cruel is the self-same process of selection I, and my group, go through *every day of our lives*. In admittance to school. In our tests, in our class rankings. . . . Is it unfair? I can't tell you. But, if it is fair. Or even if it is "unfortunate but necessary" for us, then, by God, so must it be for you. *(Pause)* You write of your "responsibility to the young." Treat us with respect, and that will *show* you your responsibility. You write that education is just hazing. *(Pause)* But we worked to get to this school.

(*Pause*) And some of us. (*Pause*) Overcame prejudices. Economic, sexual, you cannot begin to imagine. And endured humiliations I *pray* that you and those you love never will encounter. (*Pause*) To gain admittance here. To pursue that same dream of security *you* pursue. We, who, who are, at any moment, in danger of being deprived of it. By . . .

JOHN: . . . by . . . ?

CAROL: By the administration. By the teachers. By *you*. By, say, one low grade, that keeps us out of graduate school; by one, say, one capricious or inventive answer on our parts, which, perhaps, you don't find amusing. Now you *know*, do you see? What it is to be subject to that power. (*Pause*)

JOHN: I don't understand. (*Pause*)

CAROL: My charges are not trivial. You see that in the haste, I think, with which they were accepted. A *joke* you have told, with a sexist tinge. The language you use, a verbal or physical caress, yes, yes, I know, you say that it is meaningless. I understand. I differ from you. To lay a hand on someone's shoulder.

JOHN: It was devoid of sexual content.

CAROL: I say it was not. I SAY IT WAS NOT. Don't you begin to *see* . . . ? Don't you begin to understand? IT'S NOT FOR YOU TO SAY.

JOHN: I take your point, and I see there is much good in what you refer to.

CAROL: . . . do you think so . . . ?

JOHN: . . . but, and this is not to say that I cannot change, in those things in which I am deficient . . . But, the . . .

CAROL: Do you hold yourself harmless from the charges of sexual exploitativeness . . . ? (*Pause*)

JOHN: Well, I . . . I . . . I . . . You know I, as I said, I . . . think I am not too old to *learn*, and I *can* learn, I . . .

CAROL: Do you hold yourself innocent of the charge of . . .

JOHN: . . . wait, wait, wait . . . All right, let's go back to . . .

CAROL: YOU FOOL. Who do you think I am? To come here and be taken in by a *smile*. You little yapping fool. You think I want "revenge." I don't want revenge. I WANT UNDERSTANDING.

JOHN: . . . *do* you?

CAROL: I do. (*Pause*)

JOHN: What's the use. It's over.

CAROL: Is it? What is?

JOHN: My job.

CAROL: Oh. Your job. That's what you want to talk about. (*Pause*) (*She starts to leave the room. She steps and turns back to him.*) All right. (*Pause*) What if it were possible that my Group withdraws its complaint. (*Pause*)

JOHN: What?

CAROL: That's right. (*Pause*)

JOHN: Why.

CAROL: Well, let's say as an act of friendship.

JOHN: An act of friendship.

CAROL: Yes. (*Pause*)

JOHN: In exchange for what.

CAROL: Yes. But I don't think, "exchange." Not "in exchange." For what do we derive from it? *(Pause)*

JOHN: "Derive."

CAROL: Yes.

JOHN: *(Pause)* Nothing. *(Pause)*

CAROL: That's right. We derive nothing. *(Pause)* Do you see that?

JOHN: Yes.

CAROL: That is a little word, Professor. "Yes." "I see that." But you will.

JOHN: And you might speak to the committee . . . ?

CAROL: To the committee?

JOHN: Yes.

CAROL: Well. Of course. That's on your mind. We might.

JOHN: "If" what?

CAROL: "Given" what. Perhaps. I think that that is more friendly.

JOHN: GIVEN WHAT?

CAROL: And, believe me, I understand your rage. It is not that I don't feel it. But I do not see that it is deserved, so I do not resent it. . . . All right. I have a list.

JOHN: . . . a list.

CAROL: Here is a list of books, which we . . .

JOHN: . . . a list of books . . . ?

CAROL: That's right. Which we find questionable.

JOHN: What?

CAROL: Is this so bizarre . . . ?

JOHN: I can't believe . . .

CAROL: It's not necessary you believe it.

JOHN: Academic freedom . . .

CAROL: Someone chooses the books. If you can choose them, others can. What are you, "God"?

JOHN: . . . no, no, the "dangerous." . . .

CAROL: You have an agenda, we have an agenda. I am not interested in your feelings or your motivation, but your actions. If you would like me to speak to the Tenure Committee, here is my list. You are a Free Person, you decide. *(Pause)*

JOHN: Give me the list. *(She does so. He reads.)*

CAROL: I think you'll find . . .

JOHN: I'm capable of reading it. Thank you.

CAROL: We have a number of *texts* we need re . . .

JOHN: I see that.

CAROL: We're amenable to . . .

JOHN: Aha. Well, let me look over the . . . *(He reads.)*

CAROL: I think that . . .

JOHN: LOOK. I'm reading your demands. All right?! *(He reads) (Pause)* You want to ban my book?

CAROL: We do not . . .

JOHN *(Of list):*   It says here . . .

CAROL: . . . We want it removed from inclusion as a representative example of the university.

JOHN: Get out of here.

CAROL: If you put aside the issues of personalities.

JOHN: Get the fuck out of my office.

CAROL: No, I think I would reconsider.

JOHN: . . . you think you can.

CAROL: We can and we *will.* Do you want our support? That is the only quest . . .

JOHN: . . . to ban my *book* . . . ?

CAROL: . . . that is correct . . .

JOHN: . . . this . . . this is a *university* . . . we . . .

CAROL: . . . and we have a statement . . . which we need you to . . . *(She hands him a sheet of paper.)*

JOHN: No, no. It's out of the question. I'm sorry. I don't know what I was thinking of. I want to tell you something. I'm a teacher. I am a teacher. Eh? It's my *name* on the door, and *I* teach the class, and that's what I do. I've got a book with my name on it. And my son will *see* that *book* someday. And I have a respon . . . No, I'm sorry I have a *responsibility* . . . to *myself,* to my *son,* to my *profession.* . . . I haven't been *home* for two days, do you know that? Thinking this out.

CAROL: . . . you haven't?

JOHN: I've been, no. If it's of interest to you. I've been in a *hotel. Thinking. (The phone starts ringing.) Thinking* . . .

CAROL: . . . you haven't been home?

JOHN: . . . *thinking,* do you see?

CAROL: Oh.

JOHN: And, and, I owe you a debt, I see that now. *(Pause)* You're *dangerous,* you're *wrong* and it's my *job* . . . to say no to you. That's my job. You are absolutely right. You want to ban my book? Go to *hell,* and they can do whatever they want to me.

CAROL: . . . you haven't been home in two days . . .

JOHN: I think I told you that.

CAROL: . . . you'd better get that phone. *(Pause)* I think that you should pick up the phone. *(Pause)*

John picks up the phone.

JOHN *(on phone):*   Yes. *(Pause)* Yes. Wh . . . I. I. I had to be away. All ri . . . did they wor . . . did they worry ab . . . No. I'm all right, now, Jerry. I'm f . . . I got a little turned *around,* but I'm *sitting* here and . . . I've got it figured out. I'm fine. I'm fine don't worry about me. I got a little bit mixed up. But I am not sure that it's not a blessing. It cost me my job? Fine. Then the job was not worth having. Tell Grace that I'm coming home and everything is fff . . . *(Pause)* What? *(Pause)* What? *(Pause)* What do you *mean?* WHAT? Jerry . . .

Jerry. They . . . Who, who, what can they do . . . ? *(Pause)* NO. *(Pause)* NO. They can't do th . . . What do you mean? *(Pause)* But how . . . *(Pause)* She's, she's, she's *here* with me. To . . . Jerry. I don't underst . . . *(Pause)* *(He hangs up.)* *(To Carol:)* What does this mean?

CAROL: I thought you knew.

JOHN: What. *(Pause)* What does it mean. *(Pause)*

CAROL: You tried to rape me. *(Pause)* According to the law. *(Pause)*

JOHN: . . . what . . . ?

CAROL: You tried to rape me. I was leaving this office, you "pressed" yourself into me. You "pressed" your body into me.

JOHN: . . . I . . .

CAROL: My Group has told your lawyer that we may pursue criminal charges.

JOHN: . . . no . . .

CAROL: . . . under the statute. I am told. It was battery.

JOHN: . . . no . . .

CAROL: Yes. And attempted rape. That's right. *(Pause)*

JOHN: I think that you should go.

CAROL: Of course. I thought you knew.

JOHN: I have to talk to my lawyer.

CAROL: Yes. Perhaps you should. *(The phone rings again.)* *(Pause)*

JOHN: *(Picks up phone. Into phone:)* Hello? I . . . Hello . . . ? I . . . Yes, he just called. No . . . I. I can't talk to you now, Baby. *(To Carol:)* Get out.

CAROL: . . . your wife . . . ?

JOHN: . . . who it is is no concern of yours. Get out. *(To phone:)* No, no, it's going to be all right. I. I can't talk now, Baby. *(To Carol:)* Get out of here.

CAROL: I'm going.

JOHN: Good.

CAROL *(exiting):*   . . . and don't call your wife "baby."

JOHN: What?

CAROL: Don't call your wife baby. You heard what I said.

Carol starts to leave the room. John grabs her and begins to beat her.

JOHN: You vicious little bitch. You think you can come in here with your political correctness and destroy my life?

He knocks her to the floor.

After how I treated you . . . ? You should be . . . *Rape you* . . . ? Are you kidding me . . . ?

He picks up a chair, raises it above his head, and advances on her.

I wouldn't touch you with a ten-foot pole. You little *cunt* . . .

She cowers on the floor below him. Pause. He looks down at her. He lowers the chair. He moves to his desk, and arranges the papers on it. Pause. He looks over at her.

. . . well . . .

Pause. She looks at him.

CAROL: Yes. That's right.

(She looks away from him, and lowers her head. To herself:) . . . yes. That's right.

End   [1992]

THINKING ABOUT THE TEXT

1. What are the main arguments that each character makes during the play? In particular, what are their respective views on education?

2. What should an audience consider in evaluating the characters' arguments? Do you sympathize with one character more than the other? When *Oleanna* was performed in Washington, D.C., the theater lobby featured a chalkboard on which audience members could "vote" for either John or Carol. Do you think Mamet encourages the audience to take sides? Why, or why not?

3. Near the end of the first scene, Carol says, "I have never told anyone this" (p. 714). What might she have been about to tell John? What should an audience consider in trying to resolve this issue of fact?

4. In the second and third scenes, Carol refers several times to her "group." Identify some places where she strikes you as relying especially on language worked out in this group. Should the audience be critical of Carol's reliance on the group's language? Why, or why not? How individualistic does John's language seem?

5. Should Mamet have had his characters speak in complete sentences more often? Why, or why not? At numerous moments in the play, Mamet has John speaking on the phone. Why might Mamet have done this? How do John's phone conversations conceivably affect Carol? How do they affect you?

ANITA HILL AND CLARENCE THOMAS
Statements to the United States Senate Judiciary Committee on October 11, 1991

The following statements come from the United States Senate Judiciary Committee hearings on the nomination of Clarence Thomas to the United States Supreme Court. The hearings were broadcast on nationwide television from October 11 to October 13, 1991. Actually, the Judiciary Committee had begun considering Thomas's nomination on September 10 and thought it was finished, but it reconvened when his former employee Anita Hill accused him of sexually harassing her earlier in their careers. Eventually, the Committee ended its inquiry into Hill's charges without determining their validity, and the entire Senate confirmed Thomas's nomination by a vote of 52 to 48. Nevertheless, debates aroused by the Hill-Thomas clash lingered.

Thomas's nomination had already been controversial because of his judicial philosophy. He was replacing one of the best-known figures in the history of civil rights in the United States and the first African American Supreme Court Justice, Thurgood Marshall. Though Thomas himself is black, he is notably more conservative than Marshall. Because Hill is African American, too, some people felt she should have supported Thomas in loyalty to their common race. Others were concerned about gender inequality, believing that this was a case of a man abusing a woman. Furthermore, disagreement arose over whether Hill was treated fairly by the Judiciary Committee, which consisted entirely of white middle-aged and elderly men. Whatever the differences in views, the hearings gave the topic of sexual harassment new public attention.

When Oleanna *premiered in Cambridge, Massachusetts, just six months after the hearings, and when it opened on Broadway in the fall of 1992, Hill's depiction of Thomas as a sexual harasser was still fresh in audiences' memories. Several reviewers explicitly noted this fact. Mamet himself discourages suggestions that the hearings influenced his writing of the play. He reports that he did not watch them and that he had written the first act before the hearings began. Still, he acknowledges that he resumed work on the play in the aftermath of the hearings so that perhaps they did affect him somewhat. Whatever his intentions, the hearings affected audiences' perceptions of the play.*

Each statement that follows is from October 11, 1991, the opening day of the Hill-Thomas hearings. In the morning session, then-Judge Thomas gives his first statement after Professor Hill's allegations. In the afternoon session, Hill makes her formal statement to the Senate Judiciary Committee.

FIRST STATEMENT OF JUDGE CLARENCE THOMAS AFTER PROFESSOR ANITA HILL'S ALLEGATIONS, U.S. SENATE JUDICIARY COMMITTEE, OCTOBER 11, 1991, MORNING SESSION

Mr. Chairman, Senator Thurmond, members of the committee:

As excruciatingly difficult as the last two weeks have been, I welcome the opportunity to clear my name today. No one other than my wife and Senator Danforth, to whom I read this statement at 6:30 A.M., has seen or heard the statement — no handlers, no advisors.

The first I learned of the allegations by Professor Anita Hill was on September 25, 1991, when the FBI came to my home to investigate her allegations. When informed by the FBI agent of the nature of the allegations and the person making them, I was shocked, surprised, hurt, and enormously saddened.

I have not been the same since that day. For almost a decade my responsibilities included enforcing the rights of victims of sexual harassment. As a boss, as a friend, and as a human being I was proud that I have never had such an allegation leveled against me, even as I sought to promote women and minorities into nontraditional jobs.

In addition, several of my friends, who are women, have confided in me   5
about the horror of harassment on the job or elsewhere. I thought I really understood the anguish, the fears, the doubts, the seriousness of the matter. But since
September 25th, I have suffered immensely as these very serious charges were
leveled against me.

I have been racking my brains and eating my insides out trying to think of
what I could have said or done to Anita Hill to lead her to allege that I was interested in her in more than a professional way and that I talked with her about
pornographic or X-rated films.

Contrary to some press reports, I categorically denied all of the allegations and
denied that I ever attempted to date Anita Hill, when first interviewed by the FBI. I
strongly reaffirm that denial. Let me describe my relationship with Anita Hill.

In 1981, after I went to the Department of Education as an Assistant Secretary
in the Office of Civil Rights, one of my closest friends, from both college and law
school, Gil Hardy, brought Anita Hill to my attention. As I remember, he indicated
that she was dissatisfied with her law firm and wanted to work in government. Based
primarily, if not solely, on Gil's recommendation, I hired Anita Hill.

During my tenure at the Department of Education, Anita Hill was an attorney-
advisor who worked directly with me. She worked on special projects, as well as
day-to-day matters. As I recall, she was one of two professionals working directly
with me at the time. As a result, we worked closely on numerous matters.

I recall being pleased with her work product and the professional but cordial   10
relationship which we enjoyed at work. I also recall engaging in discussions
about politics and current events.

Upon my nomination to become chairman of the Equal Employment
Opportunity Commission, Anita Hill, to the best of my recollection, assisted me
in the nomination and confirmation process. After my confirmation, she and
Diane Holt, then my secretary, joined me at EEOC. I do not recall that there was
any question or doubts that she would become a special assistant to me at EEOC,
although as a career employee she retained the option of remaining at the
Department of Education.

At EEOC our relationship was more distant. And our contacts less frequent,
as a result of the increased size of my personal staff and the dramatic increase and
diversity of my day-to-day responsibilities.

Upon reflection, I recall that she seemed to have had some difficulty adjusting to this change in her role. In any case, our relationship remained both cordial
and professional. At no time did I become aware, either directly or indirectly, that
she felt I had said or done anything to change the cordial nature of our relationship.

I detected nothing from her or from my staff or from Gil Hardy, our mutual
friend, with whom I maintained regular contact. I am certain that had any statement or conduct on my part been brought to my attention, I would remember it
clearly because of the nature and seriousness of such conduct, as well as my
adamant opposition to sex discrimination sexual harassment. But there were no
such statements.

In the spring of 1983, Mr. Charles Cothey contacted me to speak at the law   15
school at Oral Roberts University in Tulsa, Oklahoma. Anita Hill, who is from

Oklahoma, accompanied me on that trip. It was not unusual that individuals on my staff would travel with me occasionally. Anita Hill accompanied me on that trip primarily because this was an opportunity to combine business and a visit to her home.

As I recall, during our visit at Oral Roberts University, Mr. Cothey mentioned to me the possibility of approaching Anita Hill to join the faculty at Oral Roberts University Law School. I encouraged him to do so. I noted to him, as I recall, that Anita Hill would do well in teaching. I recommended her highly and she eventually was offered a teaching position.

Although I did not see Anita Hill often after she left EEOC, I did see her on one or two subsequent visits to Tulsa, Oklahoma. And on one visit I believe she drove me to the airport. I also occasionally received telephone calls from her. She would speak directly with me or with my secretary, Diane Holt. Since Anita Hill and Diane Holt had been with me at the Department of Education, they were fairly close personally, and I believe they occasionally socialized together.

I would also hear about her through Linda Jackson, then Linda Lambert, whom both Anita Hill and I met at the Department of Education. And I would hear of her from my friend Gil.

Throughout the time that Anita Hill worked with me, I treated her as I treated my other special assistants. I tried to treat them all cordially, professionally, and respectfully. And I tried to support them in their endeavors and be interested in and supportive of their success.

I had no reason or basis to believe my relationship with Anita Hill was anything but this way until the FBI visited me a little more than two weeks ago. I find it particularly troubling that she never raised any hint that she was uncomfortable with me. She did not raise or mention it when considering moving with me to EEOC from the Department of Education. And she never raised it with me when she left EEOC and was moving on in her life.

And to my fullest knowledge, she did not speak to any other women working with or around me, who would feel comfortable enough to raise it with me, especially Diane Holt, to whom she seemed closest on my personal staff. Nor did she raise it with mutual friends, such as Linda Jackson and Gil Hardy.

This is a person I have helped at every turn in the road, since we met. She seemed to appreciate the continued cordial relationship we had since day one. She sought my advice and counsel, as did virtually all of the members of my personal staff.

During my tenure in the executive branch as a manager, as a policy maker and as a person, I have adamantly condemned sex harassment. There is no member of this committee or this Senate who feels stronger about sex harassment than I do. As a manager, I made every effort to take swift and decisive action when sex harassment raised or reared its ugly head.

The fact that I feel so very strongly about sex harassment and spoke loudly about it at EEOC has made these allegations doubly hard on me. I cannot imagine anything that I said or did to Anita Hill that could have been mistaken for sexual harassment.

But with that said, if there is anything that I have said that has been misconstrued by Anita Hill or anyone else, to be sexual harassment, then I can say that I am so very sorry and I wish I had known. If I did know I would have stopped immediately and I would not, as I have done over the past two weeks, had to tear away at myself trying to think of what I could possibly have done. But I have not said or done the things that Anita Hill has alleged. God has gotten me through the days since September 25th and he is my judge. Mr. Chairman, something has happened to me in the dark days that have followed since the FBI agents informed me about these allegations. And the days have grown darker, as this very serious, very explosive, and very sensitive allegation or these sensitive allegations were selectively leaked in a distorted way to the media over the past weekend.

As if the confidential allegations, themselves, were not enough, this apparently calculated public disclosure has caused me, my family, and my friends enormous pain and great harm.

I have never, in all my life, felt such hurt, such pain, such agony. My family and I have been done a grave and irreparable injustice. During the past two weeks, I lost the belief that if I did my best all would work out. I called upon the strength that helped me get here from Pin Point, and it was all sapped out of me. It was sapped out of me because Anita Hill was a person I considered a friend, whom I admired and thought I had treated fairly and with the utmost respect. Perhaps I could have better weathered this if it were from someone else, but here was someone I truly felt I had done my best with.

Though I am, by no means, a perfect person, no means, I have not done what she has alleged, and I still do not know what I could possibly have done to cause her to make these allegations.

When I stood next to the President in Kennebunkport, being nominated to the Supreme Court of the United States, that was a high honor. But as I sit here, before you, 103 days later, that honor has been crushed. From the very beginning charges were leveled against me from the shadows — charges of drug abuse, anti-Semitism, wife-beating, drug use by family members, that I was a quota appointment, confirmation conversion, and much, much more, and now this.

I have complied with the rules. I responded to a document request that produced over 30,000 pages of documents. And I have testified for five full days, under oath. I have endured this ordeal for 103 days. Reporters sneaking into my garage to examine books I read. Reporters and interest groups swarming over divorce papers, looking for dirt. Unnamed people starting preposterous and damaging rumors. Calls all over the country specifically requesting dirt. This is not American. This is Kafka-esque. It has got to stop. It must stop for the benefit of future nominees and our country. Enough is enough.

I am not going to allow myself to be further humiliated in order to be confirmed. I am here specifically to respond to allegations of sex harassment in the work place. I am not here to be further humiliated by this committee, or anyone else, or to put my private life on display for a prurient interest or other reasons. I will not allow this committee or anyone else to probe into my private life. This is not what America is all about.

To ask me to do that would be to ask me to go beyond fundamental fairness. Yesterday, I called my mother. She was confined to her bed, unable to work, and unable to stop crying. Enough is enough.

Mr. Chairman, in my 43 years on this earth, I have been able, with the help of others and with the help of God, to defy poverty, avoid prison, overcome segregation, bigotry, racism, and obtain one of the finest educations available in this country. But I have not been able to overcome this process. This is worse than any obstacle or anything that I have ever faced. Throughout my life I have been energized by the expectation and the hope that in this country I would be treated fairly in all endeavors. When there was segregation, I hoped there would be fairness one day or some day. When there was bigotry and prejudice, I hoped that there would be tolerance and understanding some day.

Mr. Chairman, I am proud of my life, proud of what I have done, and what I have accomplished, proud of my family, and this process, this process is trying to destroy it all. No job is worth what I have been through, no job. No horror in my life has been so debilitating. Confirm me if you want, don't confirm me if you are so led, but let this process end. Let me and my family regain our lives. I never asked to be nominated. It was an honor. Little did I know the price, but it is too high.

I enjoy and appreciate my current position, and I am comfortable with the prospect of returning to my work as a judge on the U.S. Court of Appeals for the D.C. Circuit and to my friends there.   35

Each of these positions is public service, and I have given at the office. I want my life and my family's life back, and I want them returned expeditiously.

I have experienced the exhilaration of new heights from the moment I was called to Kennebunkport by the President to have lunch and he nominated me. That was the high point. At that time I was told eye-to-eye that, Clarence, you made it this far on merit, the rest is going to be politics, and it surely has been. There have been other highs. The out-pouring of support from my friends of long-standing, a bonding like I have never experienced with my old boss, Senator Danforth, the wonderful support of those who have worked with me.

There have been prayers said for my family and me by people I know and people I will never meet, prayers that were heard and that sustained not only me but also my wife and my entire family. Instead of understanding and appreciating the great honor bestowed upon me, I find myself, here today defending my name, my integrity, because somehow select portions of confidential documents, dealing with this matter were leaked to the public.

Mr. Chairman, I am a victim of this process, and my name has been harmed, my integrity has been harmed, my character has been harmed, my family has been harmed, my friends have been harmed. There is nothing this committee, this body, or this country can do to give me my good name back, nothing.

I will not provide the rope for my own lynching or for further humiliation. I   40 am not going to engage in discussions, nor will I submit to roving questions of what goes on in the most intimate parts of my private life or the sanctity of my bedroom. These are the most intimate parts of my privacy, and they will remain just that, private.

STATEMENT OF ANITA HILL
PROFESSOR OF LAW, UNIVERSITY OF OKLAHOMA,
NORMAN, OK, U.S. SENATE
JUDICIARY COMMITTEE,
OCTOBER 11, 1991, AFTERNOON SESSION

Mr. Chairman, Senator Thurmond, members of the committee: My name is Anita F. Hill, and I am a professor of law at the University of Oklahoma.

I was born on a farm in Okmulge County, Oklahoma, in 1956. I am the youngest of 13 children. I had my early education in Okmulge County. My father, Albert Hill, is a farmer in that area. My mother's name is Erma Hill. She is also a farmer and a housewife.

My childhood was one of a lot of hard work and not much money, but it was one of solid family affection as represented by my parents. I was reared in a religious atmosphere in the Baptist faith, and I have been a member of the Antioch Baptist Church, in Tulsa, Oklahoma, since 1983. It is a very warm part of my life at the present time.

For my undergraduate work, I went to Oklahoma State University and graduated from there in 1977. I am attaching to the statement a copy of my resume for further details of my education. . . .

I graduated from the university with academic honors and proceeded to the   45
Yale Law School, where I received my J.D. degree in 1980.

Upon graduation from law school, I became a practicing lawyer with the Washington, D.C., firm of Wald, Harkrader & Ross. In 1981, I was introduced to now Judge Thomas by a mutual friend. Judge Thomas told me that he was anticipating a political appointment and asked if I would be interested in working with him. He was, in fact, appointed as Assistant Secretary of Education for Civil Rights. After he had taken that post, he asked if I would become his assistant, and I accepted that position.

In my early period there, I had two major projects. First was an article I wrote for Judge Thomas's signature on the education of minority students. The second was the organization of a seminar on high-risk students, which was abandoned because Judge Thomas transferred to the EEOC, where he became the chairman of that office.

During this period at the Department of Education, my working relationship with Judge Thomas was positive. I had a good deal of responsibility and independence. I thought he respected my work and that he trusted my judgment.

After approximately three months of working there, he asked me to go out socially with him. What happened next and telling the world about it are the two most difficult things, experiences of my life. It is only after a great deal of agonizing consideration and a number of sleepless nights that I am able to talk of these unpleasant matters to anyone but my close friends.

I declined the invitation to go out socially with him and explained to him   50
that I thought it would jeopardize what at the time I considered to be a very good working relationship. I had a normal social life with other men outside of the office. I believed then, as now, that having a social relationship with a person who

was supervising my work would be ill-advised. I was very uncomfortable with the idea and told him so.

I thought that by saying no and explaining my reasons, my employer would abandon his social suggestions. However, to my regret, in the following few weeks he continued to ask me out on several occasions. He pressed me to justify my reasons for saying no to him. These incidents took place in his office or mine. They were in the form of private conversations which would not have been overheard by anyone else.

My working relationship became even more strained when Judge Thomas began to use work situations to discuss sex. On these occasions, he would call me into his office for reports on education issues and projects or he might suggest that because of the time pressures of his schedule, we go to lunch to a government cafeteria. After a brief discussion of work, he would turn the conversation to a discussion of sexual matters. His conversations were very vivid.

He spoke about acts that he had seen in pornographic films involving such matters as women having sex with animals and films showing group sex or rape scenes. He talked about pornographic materials depicting individuals with large penises or large breasts involved in various sex acts.

On several occasions Thomas told me graphically of his own sexual prowess. Because I was extremely uncomfortable talking about sex with him at all, and particularly in such a graphic way, I told him that I did not want to talk about these subjects. I would also try to change the subject to education matters or to nonsexual personal matters, such as his background or his beliefs. My efforts to change the subject were rarely successful.

Throughout the period of these conversations he also from time to time asked me for social engagements. My reactions to these conversations was to avoid them by limiting opportunities for us to engage in extended conversations. This was difficult because at the time I was his only assistant at the Office of Education or Office for Civil Rights.

During the latter part of my time at the Department of Education, the social pressures and any conversation of his offensive behavior ended. I began both to believe and hope that our working relationship could be a proper, cordial, and professional one.

When Judge Thomas was made chair of the EEOC, I needed to face the question of whether to go with him. I was asked to do so and I did. The work, itself, was interesting, and at that time it appeared that the sexual overtures, which had so troubled me, had ended.

I also faced the realistic fact that I had no alternative job. While I might have gone back to private practice, perhaps in my old firm or at another, I was dedicated to civil rights work, and my first choice was to be in that field. Moreover, at that time the Department of Education itself was a dubious venture. President Reagan was seeking to abolish the entire department.

For my first months at the EEOC, where I continued to be an assistant to Judge Thomas, there were no sexual conversations or overtures. However, during the fall and winter of 1982 these began again. The comments were random and ranged from pressing me about why I didn't go out with him to remarks about my

55

personal appearance. I remember him saying that "some day I would have to tell him the real reason that I wouldn't go out with him."

He began to show displeasure in his tone and voice and his demeanor in his continued pressure for an explanation. He commented on what I was wearing in terms of whether it made me more or less sexually attractive. The incidents occurred in his inner office at the EEOC. 60

One of the oddest episodes I remember was an occasion in which Thomas was drinking a Coke in his office. He got up from the table, at which we were working, went over to his desk to get the Coke, looked at the can, and asked, "Who has put pubic hair on my Coke?"

On other occasions he referred to the size of his own penis as being larger than normal, and he also spoke on some occasions of the pleasures he had given to women with oral sex. At this point, late 1982, I began to feel severe stress on the job. I began to be concerned that Clarence Thomas might take out his anger with me by degrading me or not giving me important assignments. I also thought that he might find an excuse for dismissing me.

In January of 1983, I began looking for another job. I was handicapped because I feared that if he found out, he might make it difficult for me to find other employment, and I might be dismissed from the job I had.

Another factor that made my search more difficult was that this was during a period of a hiring freeze in the government. In February of 1983, I was hospitalized for five days on an emergency basis for acute stomach pain, which I attributed to stress on the job. Once out of the hospital I became more committed to find other employment and sought further to minimize my contact with Thomas.

This became easier when Allyson Duncan became office director because most of my work was then funneled through her and I had contact with Clarence Thomas mostly in staff meetings. 65

In the spring of 1983, an opportunity to teach at Oral Roberts University opened up. I participated in a seminar, taught an afternoon session in a seminar at Oral Roberts University. The dean of the university saw me teaching and inquired as to whether I would be interested in pursuing a career in teaching, beginning at Oral Roberts University. I agreed to take the job, in large part because of my desire to escape the pressures I felt at the EEOC due to Judge Thomas.

When I informed him that I was leaving in July, I recall that his response was that now I would no longer have an excuse for not going out with him. I told him that I still preferred not to do so. At some time after that meeting, he asked if he could take me to dinner at the end of the term. When I declined, he assured me that the dinner was a professional courtesy only and not a social invitation. I reluctantly agreed to accept that invitation but only if it was at the very end of a working day.

On, as I recall, the last day of my employment at the EEOC in the summer of 1983, I did have dinner with Clarence Thomas. We went directly from work to a restaurant near the office. We talked about the work that I had done both at Education and at the EEOC. He told me that he was pleased with all of it except for an article and speech that I had done for him while we were at the Office fo:

Civil Rights. Finally, he made a comment that I will vividly remember. He said that if I ever told anyone of his behavior that it would ruin his career. This was not an apology, nor was it an explanation. That was his last remark about the possibility of our going out or reference to his behavior.

In July of 1983, I left the Washington, D.C., area and have had minimal contacts with Judge Clarence Thomas since. I am, of course, aware from the press that some questions have been raised about conversations I had with Judge Clarence Thomas after I left the EEOC.

From 1983 until today I have seen Judge Thomas only twice. On one occasion I needed to get a reference from him, and on another he made a public appearance at Tulsa. On one occasion he called me at home, and we had an inconsequential conversation. On one occasion he called me without reaching me, and I returned the call without reaching him, and nothing came of it. I have at least on three occasions been asked to act as a conduit to him for others.

I knew his secretary, Diane Holt. We had worked together both at EEOC and Education. There were occasions on which I spoke to her, and on some of these occasions, undoubtedly, I passed on some comment to then Chairman Thomas. There were a series of calls in the first three months of 1985, occasioned by a group in Tulsa which wished to have a civil rights conference. They wanted Judge Thomas to be the speaker and enlisted my assistance for this purpose.

I did call in January and February to no effect and finally suggested to the person directly involved, Susan Cahall, that she put the matter into her own hands and call directly. She did so in March of 1985.

In connection with that March invitation, Ms. Cahall wanted conference materials for the seminar, and some research was needed. I was asked to try and get the information and did attempt to do so. There was another call about another possible conference in July of 1985.

In August of 1987, I was in Washington, D.C., and I did call Diane Holt. In the course of this conversation she asked me how long I was going to be in town, and I told her. It is recorded in the messages as August 15th; it was, in fact, August 20th. She told me about Judge Thomas's marriage, and I did say congratulations.

It is only after a great deal of agonizing consideration that I am able to talk of these unpleasant matters to anyone except my closest friends, as I have said before. These last few days have been very trying and very hard for me, and it hasn't just been the last few days this week. It has actually been over a month now that I have been under the strain of this issue. Telling the world is the most difficult experience of my life, but it is very close to have to live through the experience that occasioned this meeting. I may have used poor judgment early on in my relationship with this issue. I was, however, that telling at any point in my career could adversely affect my future career. And I did not want, early on, to burn all the bridges to the EEOC.

As I said, I may have used poor judgment. Perhaps I should have taken angry or even militant steps, both when I was in the agency or after I had left it, but I must confess to the world that the course that I took seemed the better as well as the easier approach.

I declined any comment to newspapers, but later when Senate staff asked me about these matters, I felt that I had a duty to report. I have no personal vendetta against Clarence Thomas. I seek only to provide the committee with information which it may regard as relevant.

It would have been more comfortable to remain silent. I took no initiative to inform anyone. But when I was asked by a representative of this committee to report my experience, I felt that I had to tell the truth. I could not keep silent.

THINKING ABOUT THE TEXT

1. What image do you get of Clarence Thomas and Anita Hill after reading their respective statements? What strategies does each use to persuade people that he or she is telling the truth? Refer to particular words they use. If you had been a member of the Judiciary Committee, what questions would you have asked these two people after hearing their statements?

2. If people attending a production of *Oleanna* nowadays had just read these two statements, in what ways might the statements affect how they see the play? Would you expect an audience member's gender to be relevant in this instance? Why, or why not?

3. Anita Hill and Clarence Thomas are both African Americans, and their race has often figured in discussions of their clash. At the Cambridge and Broadway premieres of *Oleanna,* John and Carol were played by whites. Suppose you had been given the chance to cast these first productions with African Americans, which presumably would have encouraged audiences to think even more about Hill and Thomas as they watched the play. What factors would influence your decision about casting? What would you ultimately decide to do? Would it matter if John and Carol are played by whites or by African Americans? If so, how?

HOWARD GADLIN
From *"Mediating Sexual Harassment"*

Howard Gadlin (b. 1940) is university ombudsperson at the University of California at Los Angeles. He also codirects UCLA's Center for Interracial/Interethnic Conflict Resolution. In both these capacities, he mediates disputes among members of the university community, including cases of sexual harassment. The following case study is an excerpt from Gadlin's essay "Mediating Sexual Harassment," which appears in Bernice R. Sandler and Robert J. Shoop's 1997 book Sexual Harassment on Campus: A Guide for Administrators, Faculty, and Students.

When Joanna first called the office, she only wanted the answers to a few questions about the university's sexual harassment policy. "What does one do if she has a sexual harassment complaint about a teacher?" At that point it wasn't clear if she was calling for a friend or for herself. After a brief explanation from the secretary "she" became "I." "Where do I go? Who do I talk to? What happens to me? How much time would it take?" You could almost feel her poised to hang up the phone if the conversation went the wrong way, but you couldn't tell immediately which way was the wrong way.

We knew only that she didn't want to bring a charge; she didn't want to get him in trouble. She preferred not to give her name and, no, she didn't want to talk with one of the ombudspersons. The secretary reminded her that the Ombuds Office keeps these matters confidential and pointed out that it is often helpful to someone who has been harassed to at least come in and talk with us about the situation — there is no obligation to pursue a charge, no one would take her complaint away from her and act on it without her knowledge and permission.

The secretary also acknowledged that it must be a difficult experience to cope with on one's own. She finally said, "Well, maybe I should come in." "Why don't we set up an appointment, and if you don't come in, that's no problem?" Tentatively, Joanna agreed to come in the next day and she was even willing to leave her name. At this point, we knew only that her complaint had to do with a teacher.

When Joanna arrived, although somewhat tentative about being in the office, she relaxed as I repeated our pledge of confidentiality and our reassurance that we would not act without her knowledge and permission. I asked if she would be more comfortable if another woman were present or even if she would prefer meeting alone with the associate ombudsperson, a woman. Without hesitation she assured me that wasn't necessary. She was very bright, quite relaxed with herself, and her friendliness was apparent even when she was being cautious. Joanna's story was pretty straightforward:

> After receiving notification of her admission to several graduate schools (she was accepted everywhere she applied, all of them excellent schools), she had gone to the office of one of her professors to let him know of her success and to thank him for his letters of recommendation. She had taken two courses with Professor Toma and done very well. The professor had supported her interest in graduate school and there had never been any indication that he had any interest in her except as a student. After talking about her acceptance letters and graduate school choices, he suddenly shifted the focus of their conversation and began talking about how he was attracted to her and suggested that they find some way to get together off campus. There was no physical contact and he was polite, even charming, but she was totally taken off guard, and repulsed. [If faculty knew how many students find their advances either humorous or repulsive, there would be much less sexual harassment.] Joanna had managed to extricate herself from the situation without giving any indication of how upset she was. The only person she told about the incident was her boyfriend, and if it had not been for his insistence, she probably would not have pursued the matter.

Once we began talking her anger and disappointment came quickly to the surface. We reviewed the full range of formal and informal options available to her; she dismissed everything that would involve formal charges or investigations. As we talked, Joanna returned over and over again to two main concerns: She wanted Professor Toma to understand how inappropriate his advance had been and how upsetting it was for her; and she wanted to know that he would learn

5

enough from this that he wouldn't do the same to another student in the future. Of all the options, mediation seemed most appealing because it would allow her to speak for herself, but at the same time, mediation was daunting because she would have to meet with him face to face.

We talked about the concerns she had for a meeting—the ways in which he might be intimidating, his facility with language, the fact that he was the professor and she the student, and her uncertainty that she would be able to say the same things to his face that she was telling to me. I asked her to think about the kinds of things that could be done before and during the mediation to address these concerns so that it would not be a continuation of the harassment. From her perspective, she wanted a safe setting in which to confront him, one in which he could not intimidate her, throw around his status and power, or overwhelm her with smooth talk. Yet she felt very strongly that she wanted to be the person to confront him—shuttle diplomacy would not give her what she wanted from the process.

At that point we agreed that I would speak with him about her desire to address the incident in a nonadversarial manner, explain the process of mediation, and arrange for the three of us to meet. I urged her to approach the Woman's Resource Center for support and advocacy, explaining again that, as ombudsperson and mediator, I could not serve as her advocate. I encouraged her to bring someone who could serve as a support person with her to the mediation. Although appreciative of my suggestions, she decided to forgo having an advocate. She did, however, decide to meet with someone from the Woman's Resource Center. Without using her name, I made those arrangements so that she only had to mention that I had referred her.

The next step was to contact Professor Toma. When I identified myself on the phone, he seemed curious that I was calling him; but as soon as I mentioned that a student had come to see me, he said, "Oh, you must be calling about. . . ." We met within an hour of my call. At our initial meeting, after I explained the role of my office and the nature of mediation, he gave me an account of the events that differed very little from the one given by the student. Professor Toma was both remorseful and defensive—acknowledging that he had acted foolishly and reassuring me that, as a matter of principle, he did not get involved with undergraduates. (This was said in such a way as to imply, or at least so I inferred, that graduate students were another matter.) I reviewed with him the various options for handling sexual harassment complaints against faculty, reminded him again of the student's preference to resolve this without filing a formal charge, and asked him to take some time to think about how he wanted to respond before we went ahead with arrangements for mediation. We agreed to talk again before proceeding.

Over the years I have learned to be suspicious when someone accused of wrongdoing does not react with some self-righteous anger. This is especially so for people with status and power in an institution, and I knew he needed time to react to the accusation before I would risk letting the student be in the same room with him. It is important to note that this reaction has nothing to do with disputing the accuracy of the story told by the accuser. Sure enough, when he called back two days later, he was angry and much less apologetic than he had been in our first meeting. At that point I knew there was a chance that mediation, when we got to it, could be successful; without engaging his self-justification, there would be no hope of meaningful interaction between them at the mediation. Of course, the first step was to work through this stage with him, in private. To bring them together at this point would only mean subjecting her to his self-righteousness and intimidation.

We met for an hour and a half. Toma alternated between expressing rage   10
about her making so much of so little and asserting that he had not violated the sexual harassment policy: It was a single occurrence, she was no longer his student, there had been no physical contact, and so on. I was pretty certain he had spoken with a lawyer. Given that he was a tenured faculty member, it is most likely he was right — Toma would probably be cleared if there were a formal grievance and investigation. Much of the meaning of what had transpired between him and the student was implicit. His inclination was to take a legalistic stance and deny that what he had done was sexual harassment: Although not quite saying it, he implied he was being victimized here.

My role, beyond the usual active-listening restatements of feelings and positions, was to help him develop a framework for comparing the relative merits of sticking to this legalistic approach versus opening himself up to a more genuine engagement with the student in mediation. Several factors brought him around to mediation. First was the fact that he was preparing a formal defense against a charge that was not being posed in a formal way. The student, in asking for mediation, was asking for interaction rather than investigation. He was someone who took his role as a teacher seriously, and I believe it was difficult for him actually to be as adversarial as he was saying he was. Mediation could allow him to interact as a committed faculty member who had, tempted by the student's attractiveness and deluded by his own misreading of her gratitude, made a serious mistake and abused the power of his position. To defend his innocence in a formal investigation he would have to play a very different role — that of the misunderstood professor. And, most likely he would have had to lie. Second was his concern to not have the matter become public. I think he was especially concerned about his wife, but he was also aware that despite promises of confidentiality, formal charges usually become known. Certainly it would be difficult to keep his wife from learning he was under formal investigation for a charge of sexual harassment. Although he could probably be cleared in any formal proceeding, it was his reluctance to be involved in a formal proceeding that provided incentive for him to enter the mediation.

Those who would prefer that all sexual harassment cases be referred to a formal process must keep in mind how significant a factor formal proceedings are in mediation. It looms as an option for the victim, thereby influencing the decisions harassers make about being cooperative with mediation, and it lurks in the mediation sessions: Most of the time the person accused of harassment has no idea about the willingness or unwillingness of the person harassed to pursue a formal charge should the outcome of mediation be unsatisfactory. The existence of the possibility of a formal charge influences the person harassed as well, in part by reminding her of a potential source of leverage should the harasser be unresponsive to her concerns in the mediation. Although she may not want to go the formal route, that option is always available, and an especially recalcitrant harasser might well push the person he harassed over the edge into a decision to pursue a formal charge after all.

Of course we must be alert to the analogous risks to the person bringing the complaint as well. No doubt the harasser, especially when he is a person of some influence within the institution and in his field, is in a position to do irreparable harm to the reputation and career of the person he harassed. Should she not be responsive to his concerns during the course of mediation, or should she be too vociferous in the pursuit of her goals, he could easily create considerable difficulty for her.

In any event, by the time we had explored all the options available to him and the implications of pursuing each one, Professor Toma committed himself to the mediation although he remained convinced that he would be exonerated if a formal charge were to be brought against him. This was a wonderful illustration of the way formal and informal avenues of complaint work together. Without a formal mechanism, there would have been no leverage to move him toward mediation. Without an informal mechanism, either the student would not have come forward or he would have prevailed.

We scheduled the mediation session. However, before bringing them to-   15
gether, I met again with Joanna to report to her about the outcome of my session with the faculty member, to explore further her concerns now that she had met with a support person, and to prepare for the mediation itself. Despite my urging but not surprisingly, her preference was still to meet with me without the support person present and to attend the mediation session on her own as well. Acting autonomously was very important to her, and she felt it was important to confront him by herself, with only the mediator present. This is not to say that the support person was unhelpful or unimportant. She had helped her prioritize her goals and had given her an additional perspective from which to understand sexual harassment and its impact on those who are harassed. In my meeting with Joanna, we identified the conditions she felt would facilitate her ability to speak for herself, anticipated things he might say or do to throw her off, and clarified what she was hoping for as an outcome of the mediation. She was both apprehensive and eager for it to be over. We arranged to meet at the mediation session the next day.

The mediation itself was somewhat anticlimactic. Joanna spoke first and quite eloquently described her disappointment in the way he had misinterpreted her gratitude for his support. She pointed out that Professor Toma was older than her father and made it clear how his actions had dissolved her respect for him. She spoke about how her sense of academic accomplishment and achievement had been undermined by his actions, introducing an element of uncertainty in her response to other professors. She reviewed her actions to help him see what her friendliness meant, perhaps, from my point of view, with a bit too much implicit apology for what he might have imagined as her role in all this. Finally, Joanna expressed her concerns about future students and how he might approach them. While she reiterated her desire to not get him in trouble, she was unsure about what he could do to reassure her that he would not repeat his behavior with someone else.

I had been expecting Toma to put up some sort of defense, most likely in the form of the sort of explanation that recontextualized the whole event and gave it a different spin, making each statement and action more innocent than they probably were. I have heard such alternate accounts more times than I care to mention, often having to swallow my skepticism and remind myself about the importance of face-saving and the dynamics of embarrassment. But, he surprised me by beginning with an apology that was built around an acknowledgment of what he had done. He took full responsibility for any misinterpretations of her friendliness and made it clear that she had never given him reason to believe she was interested in him. It was, he owned up, a construction grounded in his own desire. He was defensive only when he tried to convince her that his support for her as a student had been based on his respect for her academic ability and achievement and not a strategy to flatter her. He insisted that until she returned to thank him, he had never paid attention to her attractiveness and although she probably didn't believe him completely he was specific enough in his praise of her work that she knew at least he remembered more about her than her appearance.

It was more complicated when it came to her concerns about the safety of other students. Although Toma attempted to assure her that he had never acted this way with undergraduates, she remained, quite reasonably, skeptical. Still, Joanna did not want to go to the department chair, or as some who have been harassed do, ask for a sealed letter to be placed in his file, to be opened only should a subsequent harassment charge be raised. It was almost as if she was asking him to give her a reason to believe him, but his harassment of her had made it unlikely that he could offer her adequate reassurance that it would not be happen again.

In the end she was left with his promises. Throughout the process she had been unwilling to have anyone else learn about the harassment incident. Because his account of why he had come on to her hadn't really made sense to her, his explanation about why he could be trusted not to repeat his actions was equally implausible. But he had understood her enough, she felt, to bring the matter to a close. Although I am often quite skeptical of agreements that address the possibility of recidivism only with promises of clean living, both my private sessions with the faculty member and his conduct during the mediation gave me reasons to trust his word here. This trust was borne out several months later when he called asking for some additional readings on sexual harassment to distribute among members of a newly formed committee whose function it would be to address sexual harassment in the department.

Nonetheless, the resolution of this case does point to one of the dilemmas facing mediators of sexual harassment cases—how to ensure that the harasser does not use the confidentiality of a mediated agreement as a cover for continuing his harassment. Although it is true that most people who have been harassed mention a concern about other possible victims among the reasons they chose to come forward, addressing that concern while preserving confidentiality is a complicated matter. To be sure, an agreement can include a clause about the possibility of future harassment, but in most cases we need more than promises. Some agreements specify that the grievant would come forward to present a formal

20

complaint should there be a later charge of harassment against the same person. Others involve depositing a sealed statement in a confidential file to be opened only should there be another harassment charge. Some policies protect the confidentiality of mediated agreements but allow the appropriate administrators to inquire of the ombudsperson about previous informally settled charges in the event of a later formal charge.

Although each of these options requires complex administrative manipulations, they can add teeth to clauses in agreements intended to protect others. My own preference is to conclude mediations with written agreements — they leave less room for differential recall about what exactly it was the parties agreed to. However, as is often the case with mediation, I am committed to tailoring the process to the needs and interests of the disputants. In circumstances where both parties prefer not to have a written agreement, I feel impelled, after exploring with them the implications of not having a written agreement, to honor their preferences. Of course, should they disagree about the form for expressing their agreement, then that too becomes an issue to be addressed in the mediation.

One of the ongoing debates among mediators is about whether and how to incorporate the interests of unrepresented parties in mediation. In the field of environmental and public policy mediation, concerns have been raised that agreements can have significant and long-term effects on large numbers of people who are not parties to the formal dispute. Some mediators advocate a very active role for the mediator to ensure that larger public interests are considered and argued for during the negotiations. At the very least, we should pose an analogous set of questions to those who mediate sexual harassment cases. It is not enough to reassure oneself that both parties agreed to the process, attended "voluntarily," and achieved a resolution that met both of their needs. As an ombudsperson, I have a certain latitude for raising concerns about institutional and individual interests that must be addressed in an agreement. Clearly this is one area that challenges the advocates of mediation.

No doubt those who are opposed, in principle, to the use of mediation for settling sexual harassment charges will not be satisfied by the arguments presented and the proposed modifications of the mediation method. But even if they cannot be persuaded, the objections raised point in the direction mediators must go to ensure that their method does not serve purposes that are the opposite of those that made mediation attractive to begin with — a prompt, confidential, creative, effective, humane, educational, and empowering alternative to formal processes for those who cannot or will not use them.

Having worked with literally hundreds of sexual harassment allegations, I am convinced that framing mediation and formal procedures as antithetical to one another undercuts efforts to address the problem effectively. In a well-designed system the availability of each approach strengthens the effectiveness of the other. I would never argue for a system that required mediation for sexual harassment, nor for one that permitted no options other than mediation. At the same time, I would be equally wary of a system that did not allow for the informal settlement of harassment charges, and mediation is one of the most effective means to informal settlement.

Formal justice systems can offer only punishment, retribution, and stigmatization of the offender. Although there are circumstances in which these are appropriate responses to harassment, formal procedures also take a tremendous toll on those who have been harassed and the organizations in which harassment occurs. Even though we have all assumed that punishment can reduce the frequency of sexual harassment, there is no reason to believe there is a connection between punishment and the need for healing required by either the person harassed or the organization. Anyone who has worked, taught, or studied in a department that has endured a formal sexual harassment case can testify to the fact that many more people than the two protagonists are affected by such cases. Relationships are strained, allegiances are polarized, and trust is diminished. Formal procedures cannot address these dynamics. Mediation can, both for the protagonists and for all those who care about the climates in their institutions. Mediation allows differences to be addressed without waging war. The potential effectiveness of mediation resides in the respect it affords both parties, the control it gives them over the resolution of their dispute, and its ability to construct a nonadversarial space in which "a remedial imagination," as my colleague, Carrie Menkel-Meadow calls it, can flourish.   [1997]

THINKING ABOUT THE TEXT

1. Joanna chose to go through mediation rather than lodge a formal complaint against Professor Toma. When does Gadlin indicate that it is nevertheless important for students to have the option of formally accusing someone of sexual harassment? What things did Joanna have to consider before she decided on mediation as her course of action?

2. After reading this case study, what do you think are the potential advantages and disadvantages of mediation?

3. Imagine that you were asked to serve as a mediator between Carol and John in *Oleanna*. What might you have said and to whom at the beginning of Act 2? At the beginning of Act 3? If you wish, try actually rewriting the beginning of these scenes, putting yourself in as mediator.

ROBERT M. O'NEIL
Protecting Free Speech When the Issue Is Sexual Harassment

The following article appeared in the September 13, 1996, issue of the Chronicle of Higher Education, *a weekly newspaper for college administrators and faculty. Author Robert M. O'Neil (b. 1934), a professor of constitutional law at the University of Virginia, founded and still directs the Thomas Jefferson Center for the Protection of Free Expression. In his article, O'Neil refers to Dean Cohen, a teacher*

whose college found him guilty of sexual harassment. When Cohen sued the college
for violating his freedom of speech, a federal district court ruled against him, but
subsequently an appeals court found in his favor. Like the appeals court, O'Neil
criticizes how the sexual harassment policy at Cohen's school was worded.

If sexually harassing speech is the least tolerable form of professorial speech,
it may also be the hardest to define and constrain. But now, in the first federal
appellate ruling on purely verbal harassment, the U.S. Court of Appeals for the
Ninth Circuit has provided some guidance to institutions that seek to curb such
expression. The ruling also offered some implicit warnings about policies that
contain excessively broad language.

The case arose at San Bernardino Valley College, when a grievance committee and the college's president found Dean Cohen, a longtime English teacher,
guilty of sexual harassment. A female student in his remedial English class had
complained that she found his teaching style and classroom materials offensive;
he conceded that he could be "abrasive" and "confrontational." The facts were
not in dispute: Mr. Cohen had used profanity and vulgarities, had occasionally
read articles from *Playboy* and *Hustler* aloud in class, and had discussed such topics as obscenity, cannibalism, and consensual sex with children. The student had
asked for an alternative exercise when Mr. Cohen assigned a paper asking students to "define pornography," but Mr. Cohen refused her request.

After he was found guilty of sexual harassment under San Bernardino Valley
College's newly adopted harassment policy, Mr. Cohen sued the college in federal court, claiming that his rights to free speech had been violated. The college's
policy included in its definition of sexual harassment speech or conduct that
unreasonably interferes "with an individual's academic performance" or that creates "an intimidating, hostile, or offensive learning environment." A district court
upheld the college's action, while recognizing that so broad a harassment policy
might give "the most sensitive and easily offended students . . . a veto power over
class content and methodology." The judge also upheld the college's order that
Mr. Cohen be required to attend sexual-harassment seminars, to "become sensitive to the particular needs of his students" and to "modify his teaching strategy
when it becomes apparent that his techniques create a climate which impedes
the students' ability to learn." The college also told Mr. Cohen that further violation of the policy could result in discipline "up to and including suspension or
termination."

The appeals court unanimously reversed the district judge, faulting the
vagueness of the college's policy. What especially troubled the court was that a
professor's "sexually oriented teaching methods" could be found to create a "hostile learning environment" and could lead to severe sanctions under the policy.
Invoking such imprecise terms, the court warned, would "trap the innocent by
not providing fair warning," and amounted to "legalistic ambush."

What does the Ninth Circuit's ruling mean for other harassment policies that
proscribe conduct that creates an offensive "climate" or "environment"? The
appeals court stopped short of declaring all "hostile environment" policies invalid.

5

The opinion left open, among other issues, whether classroom speech such as Mr. Cohen's might be punishable if a harassment policy, as the appeals court put it, "were more precisely construed by authoritative interpretive guidelines or if the College were to adopt a clearer and more precise policy."

Nonetheless, this judgment creates grave doubts about harassment policies that are aimed at classroom speech that produces an offensive environment. The court was concerned that such policies could penalize controversial or provocative pedagogical styles or the choice of teaching materials containing sexual themes — teaching styles and materials that might challenge or engage some students, even as they offended others. (Although the court stopped short of saying that Mr. Cohen's teaching constituted speech protected by the First Amendment, it did note that his style had long been deemed "pedagogically sound and within the bounds of teaching methodology permitted at the college.")

After the Cohen case, colleges should carefully review existing policies that attempt to deal with the presence of a hostile teaching environment. There are alternatives to the type of wording in San Bernardino's policy that would serve the same laudable goal — deterring unacceptable sexism in the college classroom — without falling afoul of the Constitution.

Last year, for example, The American Association of University Professors suggested a sexual-harassment policy for institutions' consideration. Under the terms of that policy, before it may be punished as harassment, speech "of a sexual nature . . . directed against another" must be shown to be "abusive" or "severely humiliating" or to have persisted despite the objection of the person or persons against whom it was directed. Alternatively, it must be speech that is "reasonably regarded as offensive and substantially impairs the academic or work opportunity of students, colleagues, or co-workers."

The latter option includes a critical stipulation. If a complaint is lodged   10
against speech of a sexual nature uttered in the context of teaching, to be found to be sexual harassment the speech must also be "persistent, pervasive, and not germane to the subject matter." Therein lies the key to the dilemma posed by the Cohen case. A harassment policy that is limited and qualified in this way would almost certainly meet the court's wish for "a clearer and more precise policy." Such a policy would also minimize the risk of punishing professorial speech that might offend some students, but nonetheless is "pedagogically sound" — for example, because it helps hold the attention of marginal students.

At the same time, such a policy would effectively address unacceptable harassment or exploitation of sexual themes in the classroom. It would clearly proscribe sexually oriented jibes, jokes, taunts, and the like that are addressed to another person, when they are abusive or severely humiliating or persist despite objection from the person addressed.

But what about speech not directed at a particular individual? Even though it creates a hostile climate or environment, speech that is not accompanied by physical harassment and that is not targeted at an individual should not be the sole reason for getting rid of a teacher. Something more clearly detrimental to basic academic values should be required for so severe a penalty, and such a situation also can be covered by a carefully bounded harassment policy. If, for example, a professor (save possibly in a course on twentieth-century American humor) begins each class with a round of sexist jokes, the conditions of the A.A.U.P.'s or similarly worded policies would seem to be met: The speech would be "persistent, pervasive, and not germane to the subject matter."

One other issue is important. Fair procedures are as essential in dealing with sexual harassment as they are in any other area of professorial misconduct. The intolerability of sexual harassment does not justify diluting the rigorous standards and safeguards that apply to the handling of other charges of misconduct. Informal procedures may, of course, be used to gather evidence or to facilitate the mediation of complaints, but when formal charges are filed and heard by campus officials, a faculty member's right to due process of law must be protected. Consistent with past legal precedents, the Ninth Circuit noted in the Cohen ruling that "Cohen was simply without any notice that the Policy would be applied in such a way as to punish his long-standing teaching style."

If classroom language creates a hostile climate but does not fall within the bounds of what the courts allow to be proscribed, the language still cannot be ignored by institutions. Indeed, the cases that have ended up in court would never have got that far if the academic system had been working properly. College teachers who create a hostile classroom climate, however acceptable their teaching styles may be to some students, must be warned of the corrosive effects of their behavior. They need to be guided by deans, department heads, and other colleagues in the quest for teaching methods and materials that enliven classes without offending or demeaning their students.

The first indication of students' concern about a professor's use of sexually sensitive material might, for example, warrant a classroom visit by someone designated by the department. Teaching-resource centers, which now exist on most campuses, should devote special attention to concerns about sexually sensitive material, so that faculty members become more aware of ways in which their teaching may unintentionally offend or alienate students. It also is clear that regular reviews of the classroom teaching of both tenured and non-tenured professors should include greater attention to practices that might impair the learning environment. It is such constructive approaches, not coercive sanctions or penalties, that constitute the most appropriate academic response.

While the Cohen decision leaves open many more issues than it settles or even addresses, it does, at the very least, warn us that in dealing with restrictions on speech in the classroom, vague and imprecise standards simply will not do. Precision of language and clarity of policy now are required in this realm, just as they have been for many years in policies dealing with other restraints on speech.

At the same time, the decision intensifies the need to make our campuses and classrooms more welcoming to all students. The issue is not whether sexual harassment in any form is tolerable, for surely it is not. Rather, the issue is how we define and address practices that we all agree have no place in the academy.

[1996]

THINKING ABOUT THE TEXT

1. In paragraph 17 O'Neil concludes his article by saying, "The issue is not whether sexual harassment in any form is tolerable, for surely it is not. Rather, the issue is how we define and address practices that we all agree have no place in the academy." Reread O'Neil's second paragraph, where he describes Dean Cohen's teaching methods. Would you grant Cohen's practices a place in the academy? Why, or why not? In reporting these practices, O'Neil states in the same paragraph that "the facts were not in dispute." Does he provide you with all the facts about Cohen's teaching that you would like to have? If not, what else would you like to know?

2. What are O'Neil's objections to the language that Cohen's college presently uses in its sexual harassment policy? What language would he like to see colleges use? Evaluate his recommendation.

3. In *Oleanna*, would Carol have a strong case against John if her college's policy on sexual harassment were phrased the way San Bernardino's policy was? Would she have a strong case against him if her college's policy used the language that O'Neil recommends? Explain your reasoning.

WRITING ABOUT ISSUES

1. At the end of *Oleanna*, argument degenerates into profanity and physical violence. Write an essay identifying at least three actions that, had they been taken well before then, might have prevented this outcome. Choose actions that you think would have been reasonable, productive, and fair. For each action you propose, identify who or what should have taken it. Throughout your essay, support your recommendations by referring to specific details of the actual text.

2. Write an essay comparing Carol with Anita Hill or Joanna (the student in Gadlin's case study), or comparing John with Dean Cohen (the professor that O'Neil discusses). Focus on whether the two people you discuss seem equally justified in feeling wronged. Support your position by referring to specific details of both cases.

3. Write an essay recalling a time when you were in conflict with a teacher and consulted another school official about it or considered doing so. Besides identifying the issue or issues involved in the conflict, explain why you considered bringing it to another official's attention and why you ultimately did, or did not, consult such an official. If you wish, compare your situation to Carol's.

4. Imagine that you have been asked to write an essay that will be included in the program for a new production of *Oleanna* on your own campus. More specifically, your notes are to relate Mamet's play to recent events and trends on the local and national scenes. If you had been assigned this essay for the play's first productions, most likely you would have referred to the Hill-Thomas hearings. Now write an essay that is more up to date.

────────── A WEB ASSIGNMENT ──────────

Visit the Web Assignments section of the *Making Literature Matter* Web site, where you will find a link to the current policies and procedures actually followed by one university, the University of Maryland, regarding sexual harassment. This online manual reflects changes in the law as of 1998, when a series of United States Supreme Court decisions in various ways increased an institution's liability for sexual harassment by its staff. Write an essay in which you consider whether Mamet's character John would probably be found innocent if he were accused by Carol at a university with these particular guidelines.

────────── **Visit www.bedfordstmartins.com/makinglitmatter** ──────────

COMPARING SCHOOL CULTURE WITH THE CULTURE OF HOME: CRITICAL COMMENTARIES ON RICHARD RODRIGUEZ'S "ARIA"

RICHARD RODRIGUEZ, "Aria"

CRITICAL COMMENTARIES:
RAMÓN SALDÍVAR, From *Chicano Narrative*
TOMÁS RIVERA, From "Richard Rodriguez's *Hunger of Memory* as Humanistic Antithesis"
VICTOR VILLANUEVA JR., From "Whose Voice Is It Anyway?"

For many American children, the culture of school differs greatly from the one they know at home. Children of immigrants to America may sense such a cultural divide, especially if their teachers speak English in the classroom while their parents speak another language at home. In his 1982 memoir *Hunger of Memory*, Richard Rodriguez recalls how he faced exactly this situation as the child of Mexican immigrants. Rodriguez uses his own experiences to argue that if the children of immigrants are to succeed in the United States, they must separate themselves from their home culture and immerse themselves in the English-oriented atmosphere of the American school. In making this argument, Rodriguez comes out against bilingual education and affirmative action. When it was first published, many people praised his book for its eloquence, honesty, and realism. Subsequently, however, the book received strong criticism, especially from Hispanic American educators. Several of them disagree with the positions it takes; moreover, they worry that Rodriguez will be seen as the authoritative guide to Hispanic American life. Here we include an excerpt from Rodriguez's book along with comments by three of his Hispanic critics. Although three of these texts are from the 1980s, the issues they examine are still very much alive. In the twenty-first century, people continue to debate how American immigrants and their children should be educated, arguing over such things as California's Proposition 209 (which outlawed racial preferences)

(Photograph by Robert Messick, Courtesy of David R. Godine Publishers Incorporated.)

and the English Only movement (which wants laws requiring government business to be conducted entirely in English).

BEFORE YOU READ

The following excerpt from Richard Rodriguez's *Hunger of Memory* ends with his claim that "the day I raised my hand in class and spoke loudly to an entire roomful of faces, my childhood started to end." When do you think your childhood started to end? Think of a particular moment or set of experiences.

RICHARD RODRIGUEZ
Aria

A native of San Francisco, California, Richard Rodriguez (b. 1944), is the son of Mexican immigrants. Until he entered school at the age of six, he spoke primarily Spanish. His 1982 memoir Hunger of Memory *describes how English language instruction distanced him from his parents' native culture. Rodriguez went on to attend Stanford University and the University of California at Berkeley, where he earned a doctorate in English Renaissance literature. He is also the author of* Days of Obligation: An Argument with My Mexican Father *(1992) and* Brown *(2002). Currently Rodriguez is a contributing editor for* Harper's *magazine and a commentator on public television's* NewsHour.

1

I remember to start with that day in Sacramento — a California now nearly thirty years past — when I first entered a classroom, able to understand some fifty stray English words.

The third of four children, I had been preceded to a neighborhood Roman Catholic school by an older brother and sister. But neither of them had revealed very much about their classroom experiences. Each afternoon they returned, as they left in the morning, always together, speaking in Spanish as they climbed the five steps of the porch. And their mysterious books, wrapped in shopping-bag paper, remained on the table next to the door, closed firmly behind them.

An accident of geography sent me to a school where all my classmates were white, many the children of doctors and lawyers and business executives. All my classmates certainly must have been uneasy on that first day of school — as most children are uneasy — to find themselves apart from their families in the first institution of their lives. But I was astonished.

The nun said, in a friendly but oddly impersonal voice, "Boys and girls, this is Richard Rodriguez." (I heard her sound out: *Rich-heard Road-ree-guess.*) It was the first time I had heard anyone name me in English. "Richard," the nun repeated more slowly, writing my name down in her black leather book. Quickly I turned to see my mother's face dissolve in a watery blur behind the pebbled glass door.

Many years later there is something called bilingual education — a scheme proposed in the late 1960s by Hispanic-American social activists, later endorsed by a congressional vote. It is a program that seeks to permit non-English-speaking children, many from lower-class homes, to use their family language as the language of school. (Such is the goal its supporters announce.) I hear them and am forced to say no: It is not possible for a child — any child — ever to use his family's language in school. Not to understand this is to misunderstand the public uses of schooling and to trivialize the nature of intimate life — a family's "language." 5

Memory teaches me what I know of these matters; the boy reminds the adult. I was a bilingual child, a certain kind — socially disadvantaged — the son of working-class parents, both Mexican immigrants.

In the early years of my boyhood, my parents coped very well in America. My father had steady work. My mother managed at home. They were nobody's victims. Optimism and ambition led them to a house (our home) many blocks from the Mexican south side of town. We lived among *gringos* and only a block from the biggest, whitest houses. It never occurred to my parents that they couldn't live wherever they chose. Nor was the Sacramento of the fifties bent on teaching them a contrary lesson. My mother and father were more annoyed than intimidated by those two or three neighbors who tried initially to make us unwelcome. ("Keep your brats away from my sidewalk!") But despite all they achieved, perhaps because they had so much to achieve, any deep feeling of ease, the confidence of "belonging" in public was withheld from them both. They regarded the people at work, the faces in crowds, as very distant from us. They were the others, *los gringos.* That term was interchangeable in their speech with another, even more telling, *los americanos.*

I grew up in a house where the only regular guests were my relations. For one day, enormous families of relatives would visit and there would be so many people that the noise and the bodies would spill out to the backyard and front porch. Then, for weeks, no one came by. (It was usually a salesman who rang the doorbell.) Our house stood apart. A gaudy yellow in a row of white bungalows. We were the people with the noisy dog. The people who raised pigeons and chickens. We were the foreigners on the block. A few neighbors smiled and waved. We waved back. But no one in the family knew the names of the old couple who lived next door; until I was seven years old, I did not know the names of the kids who lived across the street.

In public, my father and mother spoke a hesitant, accented, not always grammatical English. And they would have to strain — their bodies tense — to catch the sense of what was rapidly said by *los gringos.* At home they spoke Spanish. The language of their Mexican past sounded in counterpoint to the English of public society. The words would come quickly, with ease. Conveyed through those sounds was the pleasing, soothing, consoling reminder of being at home.

During those years when I was first conscious of hearing, my mother and father addressed me only in Spanish; in Spanish I learned to reply. By contrast, English (*inglés*), rarely heard in the house, was the language I came to associate with *gringos.* I learned my first words of English overhearing my parents speak to strangers. At five years of age, I knew just enough English for my mother to trust me on errands to stores one block away. No more.

10

I was a listening child, careful to hear the very different sounds of Spanish and English. Wide-eyed with hearing, I'd listen to sounds more than words. First, there were English (*gringo*) sounds. So many words were still unknown that when the butcher or the lady at the drugstore said something to me, exotic polysyllabic sounds would bloom in the midst of their sentences. Often, the speech of people in public seemed to me very loud, booming with confidence. The man behind the counter would literally ask, "What can I do for you?" But by being so firm and so clear, the sound of his voice said that he was a *gringo;* he belonged in public society.

I would also hear then the high nasal notes of middle-class American speech. The air stirred with sound. Sometimes, even now, when I have been traveling abroad for several weeks, I will hear what I heard as a boy. In hotel lobbies or airports, in Turkey or Brazil, some Americans will pass, and suddenly I will hear it again — the high sound of American voices. For a few seconds I will hear it with pleasure, for it is now the sound of *my* society — a reminder of home. But inevitably — already on the flight headed for home — the sound fades with repetition. I will be unable to hear it anymore.

When I was a boy, things were different. The accent of *los gringos* was never pleasing nor was it hard to hear. Crowds at Safeway or at bus stops would be noisy with sound. And I would be forced to edge away from the chirping chatter above me.

I was unable to hear my own sounds, but I knew very well that I spoke English poorly. My words could not stretch far enough to form complete thoughts. And the words I did speak I didn't know well enough to make into distinct sounds. (Listeners would usually lower their heads, better to hear what I was trying to say.) But it was one thing for *me* to speak English with difficulty. It was more troubling for me to hear my parents speak in public: their high-whining vowels and guttural consonants; their sentences that got stuck with "eh" and "ah" sounds; the confused syntax; the hesitant rhythm of sounds so different from the way *gringos* spoke. I'd notice, moreover, that my parents' voices were softer than those of *gringos* we'd meet.

I am tempted now to say that none of this mattered. In adulthood I am embarrassed by childhood fears. And in a way, it didn't matter very much that my parents could not speak English with ease. Their linguistic difficulties had no serious consequences. My mother and father made themselves understood at the county hospital clinic and at government offices. And yet, in another way, it mattered very much — it was unsettling to hear my parents struggle with English. Hearing them, I'd grow nervous, my clutching trust in their protection and power weakened.

There were many times like the night at a brightly lit gasoline station (a blaring white memory) when I stood uneasily, hearing my father. He was talking to a teenaged attendant. I do not recall what they were saying, but I cannot forget the sounds my father made as he spoke. At one point his words slid together to form one word — sounds as confused as the threads of blue and green oil in the puddle next to my shoes. His voice rushed through what he had left to say. And, toward the end, reached falsetto notes, appealing to his listener's understanding. I looked away to the lights of passing automobiles. I tried not to hear anymore. But I heard only too well the calm, easy tones in the attendant's reply. Shortly afterward, walking toward home with my father, I shivered when he put his hand on my shoulder. The very first chance that I got, I evaded his grasp and ran on ahead into the dark, skipping with feigned boyish exuberance.

But then there was Spanish. *Español:* my family's language. *Español:* the language that seemed to me a private language. I'd hear strangers on the radio and in the Mexican Catholic church across town speaking in Spanish, but I couldn't really believe that Spanish was a public language, like English. Spanish speakers, rather, seemed related to me, for I sensed that we shared — through our language — the experience of feeling apart from *los gringos*. It was thus a ghetto Spanish that I heard and I spoke. Like those whose lives are bound by a barrio, I was reminded by Spanish of my separateness from *los otros, los gringos* in power. But more intensely than for most barrio children — because I did not live in a barrio — Spanish seemed to me the language of home. (Most days it was only at home that I'd hear it.) It became the language of joyful return.

15

A family member would say something to me and I would feel myself specially recognized. My parents would say something to me and I would feel embraced by the sounds of their words. Those sounds said: *I am speaking with ease in Spanish. I am addressing you in words I never use with* los gringos. *I recognize you as someone special, close, like no one outside. You belong with us. In the family.*

(*Ricardo.*)

At the age of five, six, well past the time when most other children no longer   20
easily notice the difference between sounds uttered at home and words spoken in public, I had a different experience. I lived in a world magically compounded of sounds. I remained a child longer than most; I lingered too long, poised at the edge of language — often frightened by the sounds of *los gringos*, delighted by the sounds of Spanish at home. I shared with my family a language that was startlingly different from that used in the great city around us.

For me there were none of the gradations between public and private society so normal to a maturing child. Outside the house was public society; inside the house was private. Just opening or closing the screen door behind me was an important experience. I'd rarely leave home all alone or without reluctance. Walking down the sidewalk, under the canopy of tall trees, I'd warily notice the — suddenly — silent neighborhood kids who stood warily watching me. Nervously, I'd arrive at the grocery store to hear there the sounds of the *gringo* — foreign to me — reminding me that in this world so big, I was a foreigner. But then I'd return. Walking back toward our house, climbing the steps from the sidewalk, when the front door was open in summer, I'd hear voices beyond the screen door talking in Spanish. For a second or two, I'd stay, linger there, listening. Smiling, I'd hear my mother call out, saying in Spanish (words): "Is that you, Richard?" All the while her sounds would assure me: *You are home now; come closer; inside. With us.*

"*Sí,*" I'd reply.

Once more inside the house I would resume (assume) my place in the family. The sounds would dim, grow harder to hear. Once more at home, I would grow less aware of that fact. It required, however, no more than the blurt of the doorbell to alert me to listen to sounds all over again. The house would turn instantly still while my mother went to the door. I'd hear her hard English sounds. I'd wait to hear her voice return to soft-sounding Spanish, which assured me, as surely as did the clicking tongue of the lock on the door, that the stranger was gone.

Plainly, it is not healthy to hear such sounds so often. It is not healthy to distinguish public words from private sounds so easily. I remained cloistered by sounds, timid and shy in public, too dependent on voices at home. And yet it needs to be emphasized: I was an extremely happy child at home. I remember many nights when my father would come back from work, and I'd hear him call out to my mother in Spanish, sounding relieved. In Spanish, he'd sound light and free notes he never could manage in English. Some nights I'd jump up just at hearing his voice. With *mis hermanos* I would come running into the room where he was with my mother. Our laughing (so deep was the pleasure!) became screaming. Like others who know the pain of public alienation, we transformed the knowledge of our public separateness and made it consoling — the reminder of intimacy. Excited, we joined our voices in a celebration of sounds. *We are speaking now the way we never speak out in public. We are alone — together,* voices sounded, surrounded to tell me. Some nights, no one seemed willing to loosen the hold sounds had on us. At dinner, we invented new words. (Ours sounded Spanish, but made sense only to us.) We pieced together new words by taking, say, an English verb and giving it Spanish endings. My mother's instructions at bedtime would be lacquered with mock-urgent tones. Or a word like *sí* would become, in several notes, able to convey added measures of feeling. Tongues explored the edges of words, especially the fat vowels. And we happily sounded that military drum roll, the twirling roar of the Spanish *r*. Family language: my family's sounds. The voices of my parents and sisters and brother. Their voices insisting: *You belong here. We are family members. Related. Special to one another. Listen!* Voices singing and sighing, rising, straining, then surging, teeming with pleasure that burst syllables into fragments of laughter. At times it seemed there was steady quiet only when, from another room, the rustling whispers of my parents faded and I moved closer to sleep.

2

Supporters of bilingual education today imply that students like me miss a great deal by not being taught in their family's language. What they seem not to recognize is that, as a socially disadvantaged child, I considered Spanish to be a private language. What I needed to learn in school was that I had the right — and the obligation — to speak the public language of *los gringos.* The odd truth is that my first-grade classmates could have become bilingual, in the conventional sense of that word, more easily than I. Had they been taught (as upper-middle-class children are often taught early) a second language like Spanish or French, they could have regarded it simply as that: another public language. In my case such bilingualism could not have been so quickly achieved. What I did not believe was that I could speak a single public language.

Without question, it would have pleased me to hear my teachers address me in Spanish when I entered the classroom. I would have felt much less afraid. I would have trusted them and responded with ease. But I would have delayed — for how long postponed? — having to learn the language of public society. I would have evaded — and for how long could I have afforded to delay? — learning the great lesson of school, that I had a public identity.

Fortunately, my teachers were unsentimental about their responsibility. What they understood was that I needed to speak a public language. So their voices would search me out, asking me questions. Each time I'd hear them, I'd look up in surprise to see a nun's face frowning at me. I'd mumble, not really meaning to answer. The nun would persist, "Richard, stand up. Don't look at the floor. Speak up. Speak to the entire class, not just to me!" But I couldn't believe that the English language was mine to use. (In part, I did not want to believe it.) I continued to mumble. I resisted the teacher's demands. (Did I somehow suspect

25

that once I learned public language my pleasing family life would be changed?) Silent, waiting for the bell to sound, I remained dazed, diffident, afraid.

Because I wrongly imagined that English was intrinsically a public language and Spanish an intrinsically private one, I easily noted the difference between class-room language and the language of home. At school, words were directed to a general audience of listeners. ("Boys and girls.") Words were meaningfully ordered. And the point was not self-expression alone but to make oneself understood by many others. The teacher quizzed: "Boys and girls, why do we use that word in this sentence? Could we think of a better word to use there? Would the sentence change its meaning if the words were differently arranged? And wasn't there a better way of saying much the same thing?" (I couldn't say. I wouldn't try to say.)

Three months, Five. Half a year passed. Unsmiling, ever watchful, my teach-ers noted my silence. They began to connect my behavior with the difficult progress my older sister and brother were making. Until one Saturday morning three nuns arrived at the house to talk to our parents. Stiffly, they sat on the blue living room sofa. From the doorway of another room, spying the visitors, I noted the incongruity—the clash of two worlds, the faces and voices of school intruding upon the familiar setting of home. I overheard one voice gently wondering, "Do your children speak only Spanish at home, Mrs. Rodriguez?" While another voice added, "That Richard especially seems so timid and shy."

That Rich-heard!   30

With great tact the visitors continued, "Is it possible for you and your hus-band to encourage your children to practice their English when they are home?" Of course, my parents complied. What would they not do for their children's well-being? And how could they have questioned the Church's authority which those women represented? In an instant, they agreed to give up the language (the sounds) that had revealed and accentuated our family's closeness. The moment after the visitors left, the change was observed. *"Ahora,* speak to us *en inglés,"* my father and mother united to tell us.

At first, it seemed a kind of game. After dinner each night, the family gath-ered to practice "our" English. (It was still then *inglés,* a language foreign to us, so we felt drawn as strangers to it.) Laughing, we would try to define words we could not pronounce. We played with strange English sounds, often overanglicizing our pronunciations. And we filled the smiling gaps of our sentences with familiar Spanish sounds. But that was cheating, somebody shouted. Everyone laughed. In school, meanwhile, like my brother and sister, I was required to attend a daily tutoring session. I needed a full year of special attention. I also needed my teach-ers to keep my attention from straying in class by calling out, *Rich-heard*—their English voices slowly prying loose my ties to my other name, its three notes, *Ri-car-do.* Most of all I needed to hear my mother and father speak to me in a moment of seriousness in broken—suddenly heartbreaking—English. The scene was inevitable: One Saturday morning I entered the kitchen where my parents were talking in Spanish. I did not realize that they were talking in Spanish how-ever until, at the moment they saw me, I heard their voices change to speak En-glish. Those *gringo* sounds they uttered startled me. Pushed me away. In that moment of trivial misunderstanding and profound insight, I felt my throat twisted by unsounded grief. I turned quickly and left the room. But I had no place to escape to with Spanish. (The spell was broken.) My brother and sisters were speaking English in another part of the house.

Again and again in the days following, increasingly angry, I was obliged to hear my mother and father: "Speak to us *en inglés.*" (*Speak.*) Only then did I determine to learn classroom English. Weeks after, it happened: One day in school I raised my hand to volunteer an answer. I spoke out in a loud voice. And I did not think it remarkable when the entire class understood. That day, I moved very far from the disadvantaged child I had been only days earlier. The belief, the calming assurance that I belonged in public, had at last taken hold.

Shortly after, I stopped hearing the high and loud sounds of *los gringos.* A more and more confident speaker of English, I didn't trouble to listen to *how* strangers sounded, speaking to me. And there simply were too many English-speaking people in my day for me to hear American accents anymore. Conversations quickened. Listening to persons who sounded eccentrically pitched voices, I usually noted their sounds for an initial few seconds before I concentrated on *what* they were saying. Conversations became content-full. Transparent. Hearing someone's *tone* of voice — angry or questioning or sarcastic or happy or sad — I didn't distinguish it from the words it expressed. Sound and word were thus tightly wedded. At the end of a day, I was often bemused, always relieved, to realize how "silent," though crowded with words, my day in public had been. (This public silence measured and quickened the change in my life.)

At last, seven years old, I came to believe what had been technically true 35
since my birth: I was an American citizen.

But the special feeling of closeness at home was diminished by then. Gone was the desperate, urgent, intense feeling of being at home; rare was the experience of feeling myself individualized by family intimates. We remained a loving family, but one greatly changed. No longer so close; no longer bound tight by the pleasing and troubling knowledge of our public separateness. Neither my older brother nor sister rushed home after school anymore. Nor did I. When I arrived home there would often be neighborhood kids in the house. Or the house would be empty of sounds.

Following the dramatic Americanization of their children, even my parents grew more publicly confident. Especially my mother. She learned the names of all the people on our block. And she decided we needed to have a telephone installed in the house. My father continued to use the word *gringo.* But it was no longer charged with the old bitterness or distrust. (Stripped of any emotional content, the word simply became a name for those Americans not of Hispanic descent.) Hearing him, sometimes, I wasn't sure if he was pronouncing the Spanish word *gringo* or saying gringo in English.

Matching the silence I started hearing in public was a new quiet at home. The family's quiet was partly due to the fact that, as we children learned more and more English, we shared fewer and fewer words with our parents. Sentences needed to be spoken slowly when a child addressed his mother or father. (Often the parent wouldn't understand.) The child would need to repeat himself. (Still the parent misunderstood.) The young voice, frustrated, would end up saying,

"Never mind"—the subject was closed. Dinners would be noisy with the clinking of knives and forks against dishes. My mother would smile softly between her remarks; my father at the other end of the table would chew and chew at his food, while he stared over the heads of his children.

My *mother!* My *father!* After English became my primary language, I no longer knew what words to use in addressing my parents. The old Spanish words (those tender accents of sound) I had used earlier—*mamá* and *papá*—I couldn't use anymore. They would have been too painful reminders of how much had changed in my life. On the other hand, the words I heard neighborhood kids call *their* parents seemed equally unsatisfactory. *Mother* and *Father; Ma, Papa, Pa, Dad, Pop* (how I hated the all-American sound of that last word especially)—all these terms I felt were unsuitable, not really terms of address for *my* parents. As a result, I never used them at home. Whenever I'd speak to my parents, I would try to get their attention with eye contact alone. In public conversations, I'd refer to "my parents" or "my mother and father."

My mother and father, for their part, responded differently, as their children   40
spoke to them less. She grew restless, seemed troubled and anxious at the scarcity of words exchanged in the house. It was she who would question me about my day when I came home from school. She smiled at small talk. She pried at the edges of my sentences to get me to say something more. (What?) She'd join conversations she overheard, but her intrusions often stopped her children's talking. By contrast, my father seemed reconciled to the new quiet. Though his English improved somewhat, he retired into silence. At dinner he spoke very little. One night his children and even his wife helplessly giggled at his garbled English pronunciation of the Catholic Grace before Meals. Thereafter he made his wife recite the prayer at the start of each meal, even on formal occasions, when there were guests in the house. Hers became the public voice of the family. On official business, it was she, not my father, one would usually hear on the phone or in stores, talking to strangers. His children grew so accustomed to his silence that, years later, they would speak routinely of his shyness. (My mother would often try to explain: Both his parents died when he was eight. He was raised by an uncle who treated him like little more than a menial servant. He was never encouraged to speak. He grew up alone. A man of few words.) But my father was not shy, I realized, when I'd watch him speaking Spanish with relatives. Using Spanish, he was quickly effusive. Especially when talking with other men, his voice would spark, flicker, flare alive with sounds. In Spanish, he expressed ideas and feelings he rarely revealed in English. With firm Spanish sounds, he conveyed confidence and authority English would never allow him.

The silence at home, however, was finally more than a literal silence. Fewer words passed between parent and child, but more profound was the silence that resulted from my inattention to sounds. At about the time I no longer bothered to listen with care to the sounds of English in public, I grew careless about listening to the sounds family members made when they spoke. Most of the time I heard someone speaking at home and didn't distinguish his sounds from the words people uttered in public. I didn't even pay much attention to my parents' accented and ungrammatical speech. At least not at home. Only when I was with them in public would I grow alert to their accents. Though, even then, their sounds caused me less and less concern. For I was increasingly confident of my own public identity.

I would have been happier about my public success had I not sometimes recalled what it had been like earlier, when my family had conveyed its intimacy through a set of conveniently private sounds. Sometimes in public, hearing a stranger, I'd hark back to my past. A Mexican farmworker approached me downtown to ask directions to somewhere. "*¿Hijito . . . ?*" he said. And his voice summoned deep longing. Another time, standing beside my mother in the visiting room of a Carmelite convent, before the dense screen which rendered the nuns shadowy figures, I heard several Spanish-speaking nuns—their busy, singsong overlapping voices—assure us that yes, yes, we were remembered, all our family was remembered in their prayers. (Their voices echoed faraway family sounds.) Another day, a dark-faced old woman—her hand light on my shoulder—steadied herself against me as she boarded a bus. She murmured something I couldn't quite comprehend. Her Spanish voice came near, like the face of a never-before-seen relative in the instant before I was kissed. Her voice, like so many of the Spanish voices I'd hear in public, recalled the golden age of my youth. Hearing Spanish then, I continued to be a careful, if sad, listener to sounds. Hearing a Spanish-speaking family walking behind me, I turned to look. I smiled for an instant, before my glance found the Hispanic-looking faces of strangers in the crowd going by.

Today I hear bilingual educators say that children lose a degree of "individuality" by becoming assimilated into public society. (Bilingual schooling was popularized in the seventies, that decade when middle-class ethnics began to resist the process of assimilation—the American melting pot.) But the bilingualists simplistically scorn the value and necessity of assimilation. They do not seem to realize that there are *two* ways a person is individualized. So they do not realize that while one suffers a diminished sense of *private* individuality by becoming assimilated into public society, such assimilation makes possible the achievement of *public* individuality.

The bilingualists insist that a student should be reminded of his difference from others in mass society, his heritage. But they equate mere separateness with individuality. The fact is that only in private—with intimates—is separateness from the crowd a prerequisite for individuality. (An intimate draws me apart, tells me that I am unique, unlike all others.) In public, by contrast, full individuality is achieved, paradoxically, by those who are able to consider themselves members of the crowd. Thus it happened for me: Only when I was able to think of myself as an American, no longer an alien in *gringo* society, could I seek the rights and opportunities necessary for full public individuality. The social and political advantages I enjoy as a man result from the day that I came to believe that my name, indeed, is *Rich-heard Road-ree-guess*. It is true that my public society today is often impersonal. (My public society is usually mass society.) Yet despite the anonymity of the crowd and despite the fact that the individuality I achieve in public is often tenuous—because it depends on my being one in a crowd—I celebrate the day I acquired my new name. Those middle-class ethnics who scorn assimilation seem to me filled with decadent self-pity, obsessed by the burden of public life. Dangerously, they romanticize public separateness and they trivialize the dilemma of the socially disadvantaged.

My awkward childhood does not prove the necessity of bilingual education. My story discloses instead an essential myth of childhood — inevitable pain. If I rehearse here the changes in my private life after my Americanization, it is finally to emphasize the public gain. The loss implies the gain: The house I returned to each afternoon was quiet. Intimate sounds no longer rushed to the door to greet me. There were other noises inside. The telephone rang. Neighborhood kids ran past the door of the bedroom where I was reading my schoolbooks — covered with shopping-bag paper. Once I learned public language, it would never again be easy for me to hear intimate family voices. More and more of my day was spent hearing words. But that may only be a way of saying that the day I raised my hand in class and spoke loudly to an entire roomful of faces, my childhood started to end.   [1982]

THINKING ABOUT THE TEXT

1. What distinctions does Rodriguez make between the "private" and "public" worlds of his childhood? Ultimately, he brings up the possibility of "*public* individuality" (para. 43). What does he mean by this? Does this concept make sense to you?

2. What, according to Rodriguez, were the changes he experienced? With what tone does he recall these changes? Consider in particular the way he describes his changing relationship to his parents.

3. Do you agree with Rodriguez that the changes he went through were necessary? To what extent is your answer influenced by your own social position?

4. Rodriguez declares, "Those middle-class ethnics who scorn assimilation seem to me filled with decadent self-pity, obsessed by the burden of public life. Dangerously, they romanticize public separateness and they trivialize the dilemma of the socially disadvantaged" (para. 44). Evaluate this claim. Would you say that you are a "middle-class ethnic"? Why, or why not?

5. Rodriguez suggests that a student must speak up in class to succeed in school. Do you agree? Rodriguez indicates that matters of language play a crucial role in a child's education. Have you found this true? Be specific.

RAMÓN SALDÍVAR
From *Chicano Narrative*

Ramón Saldívar (b. 1949) is a professor of English and comparative literature at Stanford University. There he is also associate dean in the School of Humanities and Sciences as well as vice provost for undergraduate education. The following remarks about Hunger of Memory *come from Saldívar's 1990 book* Chicano Narrative.

Once Rodriguez learns a public language, he acquires a public identity. But he realizes that in his transformation from the private person of the home-centered Mexican culture to the public assimilated man of the Anglo society he has lost something. Each world's language brought out different emotions. Spanish radiated family intimacy but also provoked shame and embarrassment. English opened doors to society's networks, rewards, and recognitions, but also subverted the family's sense of intimacy. His life then becomes a tenuous attempt to hold off these contradictions, to accept the benefits of his Mexican-ness while rejecting its demands, until he must irrevocably choose between them.

And choose he does. He chooses with great anxiety and precious sadness to reject the duality of his working-class origins and his middle-class manners; he chooses to market his existential anguish to the most receptive audience imaginable: the right-wing establishment and the liberal academic intelligentsia. His writings against bilingual education [because it is a hindrance to the access to a "public" language] and against affirmative action [because it denigrates the achievements of those who have made it on their own merits] involve him, whether he admits it or not, in a political service to the Right. Rodriguez chooses to assimilate without ever considering whether he acted by will or merely submitted to an unquestioned grander scheme of political ideology.   [1990]

TOMÁS RIVERA

From *"Richard Rodriguez's* Hunger of Memory *as Humanistic Antithesis"*

Tomás Rivera (1935–1984) was chancellor of the University of California at the time he wrote the following comments. They appear in his article "Richard Rodriguez's Hunger of Memory *as Humanistic Antithesis," which was published posthumously in a 1984 issue of the journal* Melus.

[Rodriguez's] search for life and form in the literary form of autobiography has as a premise the basic core of family life. But then Richard Rodriguez struggles with the sense of dissociation from that basic culture. Clearly, he opts to dissociate, and, as a scholar, attempts to rationalize that only through dissociation from a native culture was he to gain and thus has gained the "other," that is, the "public" world. Without wisdom he almost forgets the original passions of human life. Is he well educated in literature? For literature above all gives and inculcates in the student and scholar the fundamental original elements of humanistic endeavor without regard to race or language, much less with regards to a public voice. The most important ideas that the study of the humanities relates are the fundamental values and elements of human beings, regardless of race and nationality. Ultimately, the study of the humanities teaches the idea that life is a relationship with the totality of people within its circumstance.

Then we come to the question of place and being. In Spanish there are two verbs meaning "to be," *ser* and *estar*. This is quite important to *Hunger of Memory*. Being born into a family is equal to being, *ser*. Education and instruction teaches us to be, *estar*. Both are fundamental verbs. *Ser* is an interior stage, and *estar* is an exterior one. To leave the *ser* only for the *estar* is a grievous error. Richard Rodriguez implies, at times explicitly, that the authentic being is and can be only in the *estar* (public voice) and only there is he/she complete. And further, he states that authenticity can only come by being an exterior being in English in the English speaking world. In the Hispanic world, the interior world of *ser* is ultimately more important than the world of *estar*. *Honra*, honesty, emanates from and is important to the *ser*. Richard Rodriguez opts for the *estar* world as the more important and does not give due importance to the world of *ser*. He has problems, in short, with the world from which he came. Surely this is an antithesis to a humanistic development

As with memory, the centrality of language is a constant pattern in the book. For the Hispanic reader the struggle quickly becomes English versus Spanish. His parents do not know the grand development of the Spanish language and its importance beyond their immediate family. However, Richard Rodriguez should, as an educated person, recognize this grand development. Surely, he could have given credit to the development of a language that has existed over six hundred years, which has elaborated a world literature, which has mixed with the many languages of the American continents, which is perhaps the most analytical of the romance languages, and which will be of such importance in the twenty-first century. Instead Richard Rodriguez flees, as a young man, from this previous human achievement. This fleeing is understandable as a symbol of the pressures of the Americanization process. Yet, as a formally educated scholar, reflecting upon that flight, he does not dare to signal the importance that the language has. Instead he sees it as an activity that has no redeeming value. He gives no value to the Hispanic language, its culture, its arts. It is difficult to believe that as an educated humanist he doesn't recognize the most important element of Hispanic culture — the context of the development of the distinct religions in the Spanish peninsula — the Judaic, the Christian, and the Moorish. These distinct cultures reached their apogees and clearly influenced Spanish. As a humanist, surely he must know this. The Hispanic world has elaborated and developed much in the history of ideas. Richard Rodriguez seems to indicate that the personal Spanish voice lacks the intelligence and ability to communicate beyond the sensibilities of the personal interactions of personal family life. This is intolerable. Hispanic culture has a historical tradition of great intellectual development.

[1984]

VICTOR VILLANUEVA JR.
From *"Whose Voice Is It Anyway?"*

Of Puerto Rican descent, Victor Villanueva Jr. (b. 1948) grew up in New York City. Currently he is a professor of English at Washington State University in Pullman, Washington. In 1993 he published an autobiography entitled Bootstraps: The Autobiography of an Academic of Color. *The following remarks come from his article "Whose Voice Is It Anyway? Rodriguez's Speech in Retrospect," which appeared in a 1987 issue of* English Journal. *As its title implies, Villanueva's article concerns not only* Hunger of Memory *but also a speech that Richard Rodriguez gave at a convention of English teachers.*

[Rodriguez] is a fine writer; of that there can be no doubt. But it is his message that has brought him fame, a message that states that the minority is no different than any other immigrant who came to this country not knowing its culture or its language, leaving much of the old country behind to become part of this new one, and in becoming part of America subtly changing what it means to be American. . . .

But choice hardly entered into most minorities' decisions to become American. Most of us recognize this when it comes to Blacks or American Indians. Slavery, forcible displacement, and genocide are fairly clear-cut. Yet the circumstances by which most minorities became Americans are no less clear-cut. The minority became an American almost by default, as part of the goods in big-time real-estate deals or as some of the spoils of war. What is true for the Native American applies to the Alaska Native, the Pacific Islander (including the Asian), Mexican Americans, Puerto Ricans. Puerto Rico was part of Christopher Columbus's great discovery, Arawaks and Boriquens among his "Indians," a real-estate coup for the Queen of Spain. Then one day in 1898, the Puerto Ricans who had for nearly four hundred years been made proud to be the offspring of Spain, so much so that their native Arawak and Boricua languages and ways were virtually gone, found themselves the property of the United States, property without the rights and privileges of citizenship until — conveniently — World War I. But citizenship notwithstanding, Puerto Rico remains essentially a colony today.

One day in 1845 and in 1848 other descendants of Spain who had all but lost their Indian identities found themselves Americans. These were the longtime residents and landowners of the Republic of Texas and the California Republic: the area from Texas to New Mexico, Arizona, Utah, and California. Residents in the newly established U.S. territories were given the option to relocate to Mexico or to remain on their native lands, with the understanding that should they remain they would be guaranteed American Constitutional rights. Those who stayed home saw their rights not very scrupulously guarded, falling victim over time to displacement, dislocation, and forced expatriation. There is something tragic in losing a long-established birthright, tragic but not heroic — especially not heroic to those whose ancestors had fled their homelands rather than acknowledge external rule.

The immigrant gave up much in the name of freedom — and for the sake of dignity. For the Spanish-speaking minority in particular, the freedom to be American without once again relinquishing one's ancestry is also a matter of dignity. . . .

Today I sport a doctorate in English from a major university, study and teach   5
rhetoric at another university, do research in and teach composition, continue to enjoy and teach English literature. I live in an all-American city in the heart of America. And I know I am not quite assimilated. In one weekend I was asked if I was Iranian one day and East Indian the next. "No," I said. "You have an accent," I was told. Yet tape recordings and passing comments throughout the years have told me that though there is a "Back East" quality to my voice, there isn't much of New York to it anymore, never mind the Black English of my younger years or the Spanish of my youngest. My "accent" was in my not sounding midwestern, which does have a discernible, though not usually a pronounced, regional quality. And my "accent," I would guess, was in my "foreign" features (which pale alongside the brown skin of Richard Rodriguez).

Friends think I make too much of such incidents. Minority hypersensitivity, they say. They desensitize me (and display their liberal attitudes) with playful jabs at Puerto Ricans: greasy-hair jokes, knife-in-pocket jokes, spicy-food jokes (and Puerto Ricans don't even eat hot foods, unless we're eating Mexican or East Indian foods). If language alone were the secret to assimilation, the rate of Puerto Rican and Mexican success would be greater, I think. So many Mexican Americans and Puerto Ricans remain in the barrios — even those who are monolingual, who have never known Spanish. If language alone were the secret, wouldn't the secret have gotten out long before Richard Rodriguez recorded his memoirs?

[1987]

MAKING COMPARISONS

1. Do you agree with Saldívar that Rodriguez's narrative serves the interests of political conservatives? Why, or why not?

2. To Rivera, Rodriguez fails to appreciate the rich cultural heritage behind Spanish as a language. Is it possible to value this heritage and yet still feel that the nuns were right to insist that his parents speak English at home? Explain.

3. How does Villanueva see minorities as different from immigrants? Does this distinction make sense to you? He argues that minorities need more than mastery of English if other Americans are to accept them. What do you think is required for such acceptance?

WRITING ABOUT ISSUES

1. Write an essay arguing for a particular characterization of the older Rodriguez, focusing on particular words that he uses as he recalls his childhood.

2. Should the young Rodriguez's school have been more respectful toward his home language and culture? Write an essay stating and arguing for your answer to this question. Refer to at least one of the critics quoted here. (Keep in mind that you don't have to agree with any of them.)

3. Write an essay recalling an experience that made you aware of the extent to which school had distanced you from the values and habits you knew at home. Perhaps you came to see the distance as vast; then again, perhaps you decided that it was minimal or nonexistent. Describe the experience with specific details and identify the conclusions it led you to. Also indicate whether you feel the same way as you look back on the experience now.

4. Write an essay arguing for your position on bilingual education or the English Only movement. Refer to at least two articles on your chosen topic. If you wish, refer to one or more of the selections in this cluster.

A WEB ASSIGNMENT

In the Web Assignments section of the *Making Literature Matter* Web site, you will find a link to the oral and visual "essays" that Richard Rodriguez has presented on PBS's *NewsHour*. Choose one of these pieces, and write an essay in which you relate it to "Aria." You may be especially interested in Rodriguez's essay for September 15, 1998, entitled "Language or Silence." (You can reach it by clicking the "Additional Essays" sign at the bottom of the original screen.) In this selection, Rodriguez examines issues surrounding the word *gay*. Furthermore, he states that he himself is gay and that he considers it important to acknowledge publicly his sexual orientation. In "Aria," however, and in the book *Hunger of Memory* from which it comes, Rodriguez did not reveal his homosexuality. In fact, many gays and lesbians have criticized him for this omission. If you wish, use your essay to explore how "Aria" nevertheless anticipates ideas he raises in "Language or Silence."

Visit www.bedfordstmartins.com/makinglitmatter

LEARNING IN A COLONIAL CONTEXT:
A COLLECTION OF WRITINGS BY JAMAICA KINCAID

JAMAICA KINCAID, "Girl"
JAMAICA KINCAID, "Columbus in Chains"
JAMAICA KINCAID, "On Seeing England for the First Time"

American public education has long aimed to ensure that students are proud of the United States and committed to its basic principles. Inevitably, much debate centers around what exactly America's basic principles are and around how they are best realized. Many people accuse American public education of insisting too much on cultural uniformity, while others argue that it does not pursue this goal enough. Such disagreement is evident in the previous cluster, where various commentators take issue with Richard Rodriguez's willingness to exchange his parents' Hispanic culture for the Anglo-American one of school.

Of course, citizens in many countries are taught in school to honor their nation's present rulers along with a particular cultural heritage. Children in countries dominated by others from a different culture often experience school as a place where the oppressor's culture is reinforced. The link between colonialism and indoctrination is a recurring concern of the writer Jamaica Kincaid, three of whose works we include here. Kincaid was born on Antigua, an island in the Caribbean that achieved full independence from Great Britain in 1981. Through her fiction and her nonfiction, she repeatedly reflects on what it means for a young woman to be educated in this political context. In her short story "Girl," the title character, presumably an Antiguan girl, gets instructed by a parental voice (her mother's?) in the supposed responsibilities of her gender. In the next story, "Columbus in Chains," and in her essay "On Seeing England for the First Time," Kincaid confronts her readers more directly with the practices and prejudices of the British-dominated schooling she experienced growing up. As you read all three texts, think about the political contexts of your own education and consider the various ways in which schooling is used to control as well as to liberate people.

BEFORE YOU READ

In what ways have the schools you attended affirmed a particular nation or culture? Try to recall at least a few examples. Do you think schools should encourage students to love their country? Another country? All countries? Explain your reasoning.

JAMAICA KINCAID

Girl

Originally named Elaine Potter Richardson, Jamaica Kincaid was born on the island of Antigua in the West Indies in 1949. At the time, Antigua was a British colony. Kincaid lived there until she was seventeen, when she emigrated to the United States. Soon after she arrived in this country, she became a nanny for the family of Michael Arlen, television critic of The New Yorker. *Eventually, her own short stories were published in that magazine, and during the early 1990s she wrote gardening columns for it as well. Although she continues to live in the United States, residing for the last several years in Vermont, almost all of her writing deals with her native land. In particular, she has written about Antiguan women growing up under British domination. "Girl" appeared in* The New Yorker *in 1978 and was later reprinted in Kincaid's first book, a 1984 collection of short stories entitled* At

(Mariana Cook.)

the Bottom of the River. *Subsequently, she has published the novels* Annie John *(1985),* Lucy *(1990), and* Autobiography of My Mother *(1996). Her books of non-fiction include* A Small Place, *an analysis of Antigua (1988); a memoir,* My Brother *(1997);* My Garden (Book) *(1999); and* Talk Stories *(2001), a collection of brief observations that she originally wrote for* The New Yorker.

Wash the white clothes on Monday and put them on the stone heap; wash the color clothes on Tuesday and put them on the clothesline to dry; don't walk bare-head in the hot sun; cook pumpkin fritters in very hot sweet oil; soak your little cloths right after you take them off; when buying cotton to make yourself a nice blouse, be sure that it doesn't have gum on it, because that way it won't hold up well after a wash; soak salt fish overnight before you cook it; is it true that you sing benna° in Sunday school?; always eat your food in such a way that it won't turn someone else's stomach; on Sundays try to walk like a lady and not like the slut you are so bent on becoming; don't sing benna in Sunday school; you mustn't speak to wharf-rat boys, not even to give directions; don't eat fruits on the street—flies will follow you; *but I don't sing benna on Sundays at all and never in Sunday school;* this is how to sew on a button; this is how to make a button-hole for the button you have just sewed on; this is how to hem a dress when you see the hem coming down and so to prevent yourself from looking like the slut I know you are so bent on becoming; this is how you iron your father's khaki shirt so that it doesn't

benna: Calypso music.

have a crease; this is how you iron your father's khaki pants so that they don't have a crease; this is how you grow okra — far from the house, because okra tree harbors red ants; when you are growing dasheen, make sure it gets plenty of water or else it makes your throat itch when you are eating it; this is how you sweep a corner; this is how you sweep a whole house; this is how you sweep a yard; this is how you smile to someone you don't like too much; this is how you smile to someone you don't like at all; this is how you smile to someone you like completely; this is how you set a table for tea; this is how you set a table for dinner; this is how you set a table for dinner with an important guest; this is how you set a table for lunch; this is how you set a table for breakfast; this is how to behave in the presence of men who don't know you very well, and this way they won't recognize immediately the slut I have warned you against becoming; be sure to wash every day, even if it is with your own spit; don't squat down to play marbles — you are not a boy, you know; don't pick people's flowers — you might catch something; don't throw stones at blackbirds, because it might not be a blackbird at all; this is how to make a bread pudding; this is how to make doukona;° this is how to make pepper pot; this is how to make a good medicine for a cold; this is how to make a good medicine to throw away a child before it even becomes a child; this is how to catch a fish; this is how to throw back a fish you don't like, and that way something bad won't fall on you; this is how to bully a man; this is how a man bullies you; this is how to love a man, and if this doesn't work there are other ways, and if they don't work don't feel too bad about giving up; this is how to spit up in the air if you feel like it, and this is how to move quick so that it doesn't fall on you; this is how to make ends meet; always squeeze bread to make sure it's fresh; *but what if the baker won't let me feel the bread?*; you mean to say that after all you are really going to be the kind of woman who the baker won't let near the bread?   [1978]

doukona: A spicy plantain pudding.

THINKING ABOUT THE TEXT

1. Is "Girl" really a story? What characteristics of a story come to mind as you consider this issue?

2. Describe the culture depicted in "Girl" as well as the role of females in that culture. Is either the culture or the role of females in it different from what you are familiar with? Explain.

3. Do you think that the instructions to this girl are all given on the same occasion? Why, or why not? Who do you suppose is giving the instructions? Would you say that the instructor is oppressive or domineering? Identify some of the assumptions or warrants behind your position.

4. What effect does Kincaid achieve by making this text a single long sentence? By having the girl speak at only two brief moments?

5. At one point, the girl is shown "how to make a good medicine to throw away a child before it even becomes a child." What do you think of the instructor's willingness to give such advice? What do you conclude from its position in the text between "how to make a good medicine for a cold"

and "how to catch a fish"? Does the order of the various pieces of advice matter? Could Kincaid have presented them in a different order without changing their effects?

JAMAICA KINCAID
Columbus in Chains

First published in The New Yorker *in 1983, the following short story later became a chapter in Jamaica Kincaid's 1985 novel* Annie John. *The book traces the early life of its title character, who is also the narrator. Like Kincaid, Annie John grows up on Antigua during its days as a British colony and ultimately leaves her native land. In "Columbus in Chains," which appears midway through the book, Annie recalls a day in her British-oriented education.*

Outside, as usual, the sun shone, the trade winds blew; on her way to put some starched clothes on the line, my mother shooed some hens out of her garden; Miss Dewberry baked the buns, some of which my mother would buy for my father and me to eat with our afternoon tea; Miss Henry brought the milk, a glass of which I would drink with my lunch, and another glass of which I would drink with the bun from Miss Dewberry; my mother prepared our lunch; my father noted some perfectly idiotic thing his partner in housebuilding, Mr. Oatie, had done, so that over lunch he and my mother could have a good laugh.

The Anglican church bell struck eleven o'clock—one hour to go before lunch. I was then sitting at my desk in my classroom. We were having a history lesson—the last lesson of the morning. For taking first place over all the other girls, I had been given a prize, a copy of a book called *Roman Britain*, and I was made prefect of my class. What a mistake the prefect part had been, for I was among the worst-behaved in my class and did not at all believe in setting myself up as a good example, the way a prefect was supposed to do. Now I had to sit in the prefect's seat—the first seat in the front row, the seat from which I could stand up and survey quite easily my classmates. From where I sat I could see out the window. Sometimes when I looked out, I could see the sexton going over to the minister's house. The sexton's daughter, Hilarene, a disgusting model of good behavior and keen attention to scholarship, sat next to me, since she took second place. The minister's daughter, Ruth, sat in the last row, the row reserved for all the dunce girls. Hilarene, of course, I could not stand. A girl that good would never do for me. I would probably not have cared so much for first place if I could be sure it would not go to her. Ruth I liked, because she was such a dunce and came from England and had yellow hair. When I first met her, I used to walk her home and sing bad songs to her just to see her turn pink, as if I had spilled hot water all over her.

Our books, *A History of the West Indies*, were open in front of us. Our day had begun with morning prayers, then a geometry lesson, then it was over to the science building for a lesson in "Introductory Physics" (not a subject we cared much for), taught by the most dingy-toothed Mr. Slacks, a teacher from Canada, then precious recess, and now this, our history lesson. Recess had the usual drama: this time, I coaxed Gwen out of her disappointment at not being allowed to join the junior choir. Her father—how many times had I wished he would become a leper and so be banished to a leper colony for the rest of my long and happy life with Gwen— had forbidden it, giving as his reason that she lived too far away from church, where choir rehearsals were conducted, and that it would be dangerous for her, a young girl, to walk home alone at night in the dark. Of course, all the streets had lamp-light, but it was useless to point that out to him. Oh, how it would have pleased us to press and rub our knees together as we sat in our pew while pretending to pay close attention to Mr. Simmons, our choirmaster, as he waved his baton up and down and across, and how it would have pleased us even more to walk home together, alone in the "early dusk" (the way Gwen had phrased it, a ready phrase always on her tongue), stopping, if there was a full moon, to lie down in a pasture and expose our bosoms in the moonlight. We had heard that full moonlight would make our breasts grow to a size we would like. Poor Gwen! When I first heard from her that she was one of ten children, right on the spot I told her that I would love only her, since her mother already had so many other people to love.

Our teacher, Miss Edward, paced up and down in front of the class in her usual way. In front of her desk stood a small table, and on it stood the dunce cap. The dunce cap was in the shape of a coronet, with an adjustable opening in the back, so that it could fit any head. It was made of cardboard with a shiny gold paper covering and the word "DUNCE" in shiny red paper on the front. When the sun shone on it, the dunce cap was all aglitter, almost as if you were being tricked into thinking it a desirable thing to wear. As Miss Edward paced up and down, she would pass between us and the dunce cap like an eclipse. Each Friday morn-ing, we were given a small test to see how well we had learned the things taught to us all week. The girl who scored lowest was made to wear the dunce cap all day the following Monday. On many Mondays, Ruth wore it—only, with her short yellow hair, when the dunce cap was sitting on her head she looked like a girl attending a birthday party in _The Schoolgirl's Own Annual_.

It was Miss Edward's way to ask one of us a question the answer to which she was sure the girl would not know and then put the same question to another girl who she was sure would know the answer. The girl who did not answer correctly would then have to repeat the correct answer in the exact words of the other girl. Many times, I had heard my exact words repeated over and over again, and I liked it especially when the girl doing the repeating was one I didn't care about very much. Pointing a finger at Ruth, Miss Edward asked a question the answer to which was "On the third of November 1493, a Sunday morning, Christopher Columbus discovered Dominica." Ruth, of course, did not know the answer, as she did not know the answer to many questions about the West Indies. I could hardly blame her. Ruth had come all the way from England. Perhaps she did not want to be in the West Indies at all. Perhaps she wanted to be in England, where no one would remind her constantly of the terrible things her ancestors had done; perhaps she had felt even worse when her father was a missionary in Africa. I could see how Ruth felt from looking at her face. Her ancestors had been the

5

masters, while ours had been the slaves. She had such a lot to be ashamed of, and by being with us every day she was always being reminded. We could look everybody in the eye, for our ancestors had done nothing wrong except just sit somewhere, defenseless. Of course, sometimes, what with our teachers and our books, it was hard for us to tell on which side we really now belonged — with the masters or the slaves — for it was all history, it was all in the past, and everybody behaved differently now; all of us celebrated Queen Victoria's birthday, even though she had been dead a long time. But we, the descendants of the slaves, knew quite well what had really happened, and I was sure that if the tables had been turned we would have acted differently; I was sure that if our ancestors had gone from Africa to Europe and come upon the people living there, they would have taken a proper interest in the Europeans on first seeing them, and said, "How nice," and then gone home to tell their friends about it.

I was sitting at my desk, having these thoughts to myself. I don't know how long it had been since I lost track of what was going on around me. I had not noticed that the girl who was asked the question after Ruth failed — a girl named Hyacinth — had only got a part of the answer correct. I had not noticed that after these two attempts Miss Edward had launched into a harangue about what a worthless bunch we were compared to girls of the past. In fact, I was no longer on the same chapter we were studying. I was way ahead, at the end of the chapter about Columbus's third voyage. In this chapter, there was a picture of Columbus that took up a whole page, and it was in color — one of only five color pictures in the book. In this picture, Columbus was seated in the bottom of a ship. He was wearing the usual three-quarter trousers and a shirt with enormous sleeves, both the trousers and shirt made of maroon-colored velvet. His hat, which was cocked up on one side of his head, had a gold feather in it, and his black shoes had huge gold buckles. His hands and feet were bound up in chains, and he was sitting there staring off into space, looking quite dejected and miserable. The picture had as a title "Columbus in Chains," printed at the bottom of the page. What had happened was that the usually quarrelsome Columbus had got into a disagreement with people who were even more quarrelsome, and a man named Bobadilla, representing King Ferdinand and Queen Isabella, had sent him back to Spain fettered in chains attached to the bottom of a ship. What just deserts, I thought, for I did not like Columbus. How I loved this picture — to see the usually triumphant Columbus, brought so low, seated at the bottom of a boat just watching things go by. Shortly after I first discovered it in my history book, I heard my mother read out loud to my father a letter she had received from her sister, who still lived with her mother and father in the very same Dominica, which is where my mother came from. Ma Chess was fine, wrote my aunt, but Pa Chess was not well. Pa Chess was having a bit of trouble with his limbs; he was not able to go about as he pleased; often he had to depend on someone else to do one thing or another for him. My mother read the letter in quite a state, her voice rising to a higher pitch with each sentence. After she read the part about Pa Chess's stiff limbs, she turned to my father and laughed as she said, "So the great man can no longer just get up and go. How I would love to see his face now!" When I next saw the picture of Columbus sitting there all locked up in his chains, I wrote under it the words "The Great Man Can No Longer Just Get Up and Go." I had written this out with my fountain pen, and in Old English lettering—a script I had recently mastered. As I sat there looking at the picture, I traced the words with my pen over and over, so that the letters grew big and you could read what I had written from not very far away. I don't know how long it was before I heard that my name, Annie John, was being said by this bellowing dragon in the form of Miss Edward bearing down on me.

I had never been a favorite of hers. Her favorite was Hilarene. It must have pained Miss Edward that I so often beat out Hilarene. Not that I liked Miss Edward and wanted her to like me back, but all my other teachers regarded me with much affection, would always tell my mother that I was the most charming student they had ever had, beamed at me when they saw me coming, and were very sorry when they had to write some version of this on my report card: "Annie is an unusually bright girl. She is well behaved in class, at least in the presence of her masters and mistresses, but behind their backs and outside the classroom quite the opposite is true." When my mother read this or something like it, she would burst into tears. She had hoped to display, with a great flourish, my report card to her friends, along with whatever prize I had won. Instead, the report card would have to take a place at the bottom of the old trunk in which she kept any important thing that had to do with me. I became not a favorite of Miss Edward's in the following way: Each Friday afternoon, the girls in the lower forms were given, instead of a last lesson period, an extra-long recess. We were to use this in ladylike recreation—walks, chats about the novels and poems we were reading, showing each other the new embroidery stitches we had learned to master in home class, or something just as seemly. Instead, some of the girls would play a game of cricket or rounders or stones, but most of us would go to the far end of the school grounds and play band. In this game, of which teachers and parents disapproved and which was sometimes absolutely forbidden, we would place our arms around each other's waist or shoulders, forming lines of ten or so girls, and then we would dance from one end of the school grounds to the other. As we danced, we would sometimes chant these words: "Tee la la la, come go. Tee la la la, come go." At other times we would sing a popular calypso song which usually had lots of unladylike words to it. Up and down the schoolyard, away from our teachers, we would dance and sing. At the end of recess—forty-five minutes—we were missing ribbons and other ornaments from our hair, the pleats of our linen tunics became unset, the collars of our blouses were pulled out, and we were soaking wet all the way down to our bloomers. When the school bell rang, we would make a whooping sound, as if in a great panic, and then we would throw ourselves on top of each other as we laughed and shrieked. We would then run back to our classes, where we prepared to file into the auditorium for evening prayers. After that, it was home for the weekend. But how could we go straight home after all that excitement? No sooner were we on the street than we would form little groups, depending on the direction we were headed in. I was never keen on joining them on the way home, because I was sure I would run into my mother. Instead, my friends and I would go to our usual place near the back of the churchyard and sit on the tombstones of people who had been buried there way before slavery was abolished, in 1833. We would sit and sing bad songs, use forbidden words, and, of course, show each other various parts of our bodies. While some of us watched, the others would walk up and down on the large tombstones showing off their legs. It was immediately a popular idea; everybody soon wanted to do it. It wasn't long before many girls — the ones whose mothers didn't pay strict attention to what they were doing — started to come to school on Fridays wearing not bloomers under their uniforms but underpants trimmed with lace and satin frills. It also wasn't long before an end came to all that. One Friday afternoon, Miss Edward, on her way home from school, took a shortcut through the churchyard. She must have heard the commotion we were making, because there she suddenly was, saying, "What is the meaning of this?" — just the very thing someone like her would say if she came unexpectedly on something like us. It was obvious that I was the ringleader. Oh, how I wished the ground would open up and take her in, but it did not. We all, shamefacedly, slunk home, I with Miss Edward at my side. Tears came to my mother's eyes when she heard what I had done. It was apparently such a bad thing that my mother couldn't bring herself to repeat my misdeed to my father in my presence. I got the usual punishment of dinner alone, outside under the breadfruit tree, but added on to that, I was not allowed to go to the library on Saturday, and on Sunday, after Sunday school and dinner, I was not allowed to take a stroll in the botanical gardens, where Gwen was waiting for me in the bamboo grove.

That happened when I was in the first form. Now here Miss Edward stood. Her whole face was on fire. Her eyes were bulging out of her head. I was sure that at any minute they would land at my feet and roll away. The small pimples on her face, already looking as if they were constantly irritated, now ballooned into huge, on-the-verge-of-exploding boils. Her head shook from side to side. Her strange bottom, which she carried high in the air, seemed to rise up so high that it almost touched the ceiling. Why did I not pay attention, she said. My impertinence was beyond endurance. She then found a hundred words for the different forms my impertinence took. On she went. I was just getting used to this amazing bellowing when suddenly she was speechless. In fact, everything stopped. Her eyes stopped, her bottom stopped, her pimples stopped. Yes, she had got close enough so that her eyes caught a glimpse of what I had done to my textbook. The glimpse soon led to closer inspection. It was bad enough that I had defaced my schoolbook by writing in it. That I should write under the picture of Columbus "The Great Man . . ." etc. was just too much. I had gone too far this time, defaming one of the great men in history, Christopher Columbus, discoverer of the island that was my home. And now look at me. I was not even hanging my head in remorse. Had my peers ever seen anyone so arrogant, so blasphemous?

I was sent to the headmistress, Miss Moore. As punishment, I was removed from my position as prefect, and my place was taken by the odious Hilarene. As an added punishment, I was ordered to copy Books I and II of *Paradise Lost,* by John Milton, and to have it done a week from that day. I then couldn't wait to get home to lunch and the comfort of my mother's kisses and arms. I had nothing to worry about there yet; it would be a while before my mother and father heard of my bad deeds. What a terrible morning! Seeing my mother would be such a tonic — something to pick me up.

When I got home, my mother kissed me absentmindedly. My father had got   10
home ahead of me, and they were already deep in conversation, my father regaling her with some unusually outlandish thing the oaf Mr. Oatie had done. I washed my hands and took my place at table. My mother brought me my lunch. I took one smell of it, and I could tell that it was the much hated breadfruit. My mother said not at all, it was a new kind of rice imported from Belgium, and not breadfruit, mashed and forced through a ricer, as I thought. She went back to talking to my father. My father could hardly get a few words out of his mouth before she was a jellyfish of laughter. I sat there, putting my food in my mouth. I could not believe that she couldn't see how miserable I was and so reach out a hand to comfort me and caress my cheek, the way she usually did when she sensed that something was amiss with me. I could not believe how she laughed at everything he said, and how bitter it made me feel to see how much she liked him. I ate my meal. The more I ate of it, the more I was sure that it was breadfruit. When I finished, my mother got up to remove my plate. As she started out the door, I said, "Tell me, really, the name of the thing I just ate."

My mother said, "You just ate some breadfruit. I made it look like rice so that you would eat it. It's very good for you, filled with lots of vitamins." As she said this, she laughed. She was standing half inside the door, half outside. Her body was in the shade of our house, but her head was in the sun. When she laughed, her mouth opened to show off big, shiny, sharp white teeth. It was as if my mother had suddenly turned into a crocodile.   [1983]

THINKING ABOUT THE TEXT

1. What adjectives would you use to describe Annie? List at least three. Do you trust her as a narrator? Why, or why not?

2. Evaluate the kind of education Annie is receiving. Would you say it is a good education? Why, or why not?

3. What do you make of the fact that Annie's caption for the picture of Columbus — "The Great Man Can No Longer Just Get Up and Go" (para. 6) — echoes what her mother said about Pa Chess? Do you admire Annie for writing this caption? Why, or why not? What image of Columbus do you think American children should be taught?

4. Although Miss Edward plays an important role in Kincaid's story, she speaks directly only once. What is the effect of this rarity?

5. At the end, Annie's mother lies to her. Given that so much of what comes before is about Annie's school relationships rather than about her relationship with her mother, how appropriate is this conclusion to the narrative? Explain your reasoning.

MAKING COMPARISONS

1. Considering what you know about Annie, how do you think she would react to the instructions given in "Girl"?

2. Compare the kinds of education presented in "Girl" and "Columbus in Chains." Does one kind seem better than the other? Support your reasoning by referring to specific details of each text.

3. Is gender equally important in "Girl" and "Columbus in Chains"? Again, refer to specific details of each.

JAMAICA KINCAID
On Seeing England for the First Time

In addition to her short stories and books, Jamaica Kincaid has written several essays, some of which have been gardening columns for The New Yorker. *Even in these, she has taken the opportunity to comment on England's political and cultural domination of her native island. But some of her essays very much focus on this subject. The following piece is an example. It was first published in a 1991 issue of* Transition, *a journal devoted to analyzing racial and ethnic relations around the world.*

When I saw England for the first time, I was a child in school sitting at a desk. The England I was looking at was laid out on a map gently, beautifully, delicately, a very special jewel; it lay on a bed of sky blue — the background of the map — its yellow form mysterious, because though it looked like a leg of mutton, it could not really look like anything so familiar as a leg of mutton because it was England — with shadings of pink and green, unlike any shadings of pink and green I had seen before, squiggly veins of red running in every direction. England was a special jewel all right, and only special people got to wear it. The people who got to wear England were English people. They wore it well and they wore it everywhere: in jungles, in deserts, on plains, on top of the highest mountains, on all the oceans, on all the seas, in places where they were not welcome, in places they should not have been. When my teacher had pinned this map up on the blackboard, she said, "This is England" — and she said it with authority, seriousness, and adoration, and we all sat up. It was as if she had said, "This is Jerusalem, the place you will go to when you die but only if you have been good." We understood then — we were meant to understand then — that England was to be our source of myth and the source from which we got our sense of reality, our sense of what was meaningful, our sense of what was meaningless — and much about our own lives and much about the very idea of us headed that last list.

At the time I was a child sitting at my desk seeing England for the first time, I was already very familiar with the greatness of it. Each morning before I left for school, I ate a breakfast of half a grapefruit, an egg, bread and butter and a slice of cheese, and a cup of cocoa; or half a grapefruit, a bowl of oat porridge, bread and butter and a slice of cheese, and a cup of cocoa. The can of cocoa was often left on the table in front of me. It had written on it the name of the company, the year the company was established, and the words "Made in England." Those words, "Made in England," were written on the box the oats came in too. They would also have been written on the box the shoes I was wearing came in; a bolt of gray linen cloth lying on the shelf of a store from which my mother had bought three yards to make the uniform that I was wearing had written along its edge those three words. The shoes I wore were made in England, so were my socks and cotton undergarments and the satin ribbons I wore tied at the end of two plaits of my hair. My father, who might have sat next to me at breakfast, was a carpenter and cabinet maker. The shoes he wore to work would have been made in England, as were his khaki shirt and trousers, his underpants and undershirt, his socks and brown felt hat. Felt was not the proper material from which a hat that was expected to provide shade from the hot sun should be made, but my father must have seen and admired a picture of an Englishman wearing such a hat in England, and this picture that he saw must have been so compelling that it caused him to wear the wrong hat for a hot climate most of his long life. And this hat — a brown felt hat — became so central to his character that it was the first thing he put on in the morning as he stepped out of bed and the last thing he took off before he stepped back into bed at night. As we sat at breakfast a car might go by. The car, a Hillman or a Zephyr, was made in England. The very idea of the meal itself, breakfast, and its substantial quality and quantity was an idea from England; we somehow knew that in England they began the day with this meal called breakfast and a proper breakfast was a big breakfast. No one I knew liked eating so much food so early in the day; it made us feel sleepy, tired. But this breakfast business was Made in England like almost everything else that surrounded us, the exceptions being the sea, the sky, and the air we breathed.

At the time I saw this map — seeing England for the first time — I did not say to myself, "Ah, so that's what it looks like," because there was no longing in me to put a shape to those three words that ran through every part of my life, no matter how small; for me to have had such a longing would have meant that I lived in a certain atmosphere, an atmosphere in which those three words were felt as a burden. But I did not live in such an atmosphere. My father's brown felt hat would develop a hole in its crown, the lining would separate from the hat itself, and six weeks before he thought that he could not be seen wearing it — he was a very vain man — he would order another hat from England. And my mother taught me to eat my food in the English way: the knife in the right hand, the fork in the left, my elbows held still close to my side, the food carefully balanced on my fork and then brought up to my mouth. When I had finally mastered it, I overheard her saying to a friend, "Did you see how nicely she can eat?" But I knew then that I enjoyed my food more when I ate it with my bare hands, and I continued to do so when she wasn't looking. And when my teacher showed us the map, she asked us to study it carefully, because no test we would ever take would be complete without this statement: "Draw a map of England."

I did not know then that the statement "Draw a map of England" was something far worse than a declaration of war, for in fact a flat-out declaration of war would have put me on alert, and again in fact, there was no need for war — I had long ago been conquered. I did not know then that this statement was part of a process that would result in my erasure, not my physical erasure, but my erasure all the same. I did not know then that this statement was meant to make me feel in awe and small whenever I heard the word "England": awe at its existence, small because I was not from it. I did not know very much of anything then—certainly not what a blessing it was that I was unable to draw a map of England correctly

After that there were many times of seeing England for the first time. I saw England in history. I knew the names of all the kings of England. I knew the names of their children, their wives, their disappointments, their triumphs, the names of people who betrayed them, I knew the dates on which they were born and the dates they died. I knew their conquests and was made to feel glad if I figured in them; I knew their defeats. I knew the details of the year 1066 (the Battle of Hastings, the end of the reign of the Anglo-Saxon kings) before I knew the details of the year 1832 (the year slavery was abolished). It wasn't as bad as I make it sound now; it was worse. I did like so much hearing again and again how Alfred the Great, traveling in disguise, had been left to watch cakes, and because he wasn't used to this the cakes got burned, and Alfred burned his hands pulling them out of the fire, and the woman who had left him to watch the cakes screamed at him. I loved King Alfred. My grandfather was named after him; his son, my uncle, was named after King Alfred; my brother is named after King Alfred. And so there are three people in my family named after a man they have never met, a man who died over ten centuries ago. The first view I got of England then was not unlike the first view received by the man who named my grandfather.

This view, though—the naming of the kings, their deeds, their disappointments—was the vivid view, the forceful view. There were other ones, subtler ones, softer, almost not there—but these were the ones that made the most lasting impression on me, these were the ones that made me really feel like nothing. "When morning touched the sky" was one phrase, for no morning touched the sky where I lived. The mornings where I lived came on abruptly, with a shock of heat and loud noises. "Evening approaches" was another, but the evenings where I lived did not approach; in fact, I had no evening—I had night and I had day and they came and went in a mechanical way: on, off; on, off. And then there were gentle mountains and low blue skies and moors over which people took walks for nothing but pleasure, when where I lived a walk was an act of labor, a burden, something only death or the automobile could relieve. And there were things that a small turn of a head could convey—entire worlds, whole lives would depend on this thing, a certain turn of a head. Everyday life could be quite tiring, more tiring than anything I was told not to do. I was told not to gossip, but they did that all the time. And they ate so much food, violating another of those rules they taught me: Do not indulge in gluttony. And the foods they ate actually: If only sometime I could eat cold cuts after theater, cold cuts of lamb and mint sauce, and Yorkshire pudding and scones, and clotted cream, and sausages that came from up-country (imagine, "up-country"). And having troubling thoughts at twilight, a good time to have troubling thoughts, apparently; and servants who stole and left in the middle of a crisis, who were born with a limp or some other kind of deformity, not nourished properly in their mother's womb (that last part I figured out for myself; the point was, oh to have an untrustworthy servant); and wonderful cobbled streets onto which solid front doors opened; and people whose eyes were blue and who had fair skins and who smelled only of lavender, or sometimes sweet pea or primrose. And those flowers with those names: delphiniums, foxgloves, tulips, daffodils, floribunda, peonies: in bloom, a striking display, being cut and placed in large glass bowls, crystal, decorating rooms so large twenty families the size of mine could fit in comfortably but used only for passing through. And the weather was so remarkable because the rain fell gently always, only occasionally in deep gusts, and it colored the air various shades of gray, each an appealing shade for a dress to be worn when a portrait was being painted; and when it rained at twilight, wonderful things happened: People bumped into each other unexpectedly and that would lead to all sorts of turns of events — a plot, the mere weather caused plots. I saw that people rushed: They rushed to catch trains, they rushed toward each other and away from each other; they rushed and rushed and rushed. That word: rushed! I did not know what it was to do that. It was too hot to do that, and so I came to envy people who would rush, even though it had no meaning to me to do such a thing. But there they are again. They loved their children; their children were sent to their own rooms as a punishment, rooms larger than my entire house. They were special, everything about them said so, even their clothes; their clothes rustled, swished, soothed. The world was theirs, not mine; everything told me so.

If now as I speak of all this I give the impression of someone on the outside looking in, nose pressed up against a glass window, that is wrong. My nose was pressed up against a glass window all right, but there was an iron vise at the back of my neck forcing my head to stay in place. To avert my gaze was to fall back into something from which I had been rescued, a hole filled with nothing, and that was the word for everything about me, nothing. The reality of my life was conquests, subjugation, humiliation, enforced amnesia. I was forced to forget. Just for instance, this: I lived in a part of St. John's, Antigua, called Ovals. Ovals was made up of five streets, each of them named after a famous English seaman — to be quite frank, an officially sanctioned criminal: Rodney Street (after George Rodney), Nelson Street (after Horatio Nelson), Drake Street (after Francis Drake), Hood Street, and Hawkins Street (after John Hawkins). But John Hawkins was knighted after a trip he made to Africa, opening up a new trade, the slave trade. He was then entitled to wear as his crest a Negro bound with a cord. Every single person living on Hawkins Street was descended from a slave. John Hawkins's ship, the one in which he transported the people he had bought and kidnapped, was called *The Jesus*. He later became the treasurer of the Royal Navy and rear admiral.

Again, the reality of my life, the life I led at the time I was being shown these views of England for the first time, for the second time, for the one-hundred-millionth time, was this: The sun shone with what sometimes seemed to be a deliberate cruelty; we must have done something to deserve that. My dresses did not rustle in the evening air as I strolled to the theater (I had no evening, I had no theater; my dresses were made of a cheap cotton, the weave of which would give way after not too many washings). I got up in the morning, I did my chores (fetched water from the public pipe for my mother, swept the yard), I washed myself, I went to a woman to have my hair combed freshly every day (because before we were allowed into our classroom our teachers would inspect us, and children who had not bathed that day, or had dirt under their fingernails, or whose hair had not been combed anew that day, might not be allowed to attend class). I ate that breakfast. I walked to school. At school we gathered in an auditorium and sang a hymn, "All Things Bright and Beautiful," and looking down on us as we sang were portraits of the Queen of England and her husband; they wore jewels and medals and they smiled. I was a Brownie. At each meeting we would form a little group around a flagpole, and after raising the Union Jack, we would say, "I promise to do my best, to do my duty to God and the Queen, to help other people every day and obey the scouts' law."

Who were these people and why had I never seen them, I mean really seen them, in the place where they lived? I had never been to England. No one I knew had ever been to England, or I should say, no one I knew had ever been and returned to tell me about it. All the people I knew who had gone to England had stayed there. Sometimes they left behind them their small children, never to see them again. England! I had seen England's representatives. I had seen the governor general at the public grounds at a ceremony celebrating the Queen's birthday. I had seen an old princess and I had seen a young princess. They had both been extremely not beautiful, but who of us would have told them that? I had never seen England, really seen it, I had only met a representative, seen a picture, read books, memorized its history. I had never set foot, my own foot, in it.

The space between the idea of something and its reality is always wide and deep and dark. The longer they are kept apart — idea of thing, reality of thing — the wider the width, the deeper the depth, the thicker and darker the darkness. This space starts out empty, there is nothing in it, but it rapidly becomes filled up with obsession or desire or hatred or love — sometimes all of these things, sometimes some of these things, sometimes only one of these things. The existence of the world as I came to know it was a result of this: idea of thing over here, reality of thing way, way over there. There was Christopher Columbus, an unlikable man, an unpleasant man, a liar (and so, of course, a thief) surrounded by maps and schemes and plans, and there was the reality on the other side of that width, the depth, that darkness. He became obsessed, he became filled with desire, the hatred came later, love was never a part of it. Eventually, his idea met the longed-for reality. That the idea of something and its reality are often two completely different things is something no one ever remembers; and so when they meet and find that they are not compatible, the weaker of the two, idea or reality, dies. That idea Christopher Columbus had was more powerful than the reality he met, and so the reality he met died.

And so finally, when I was a grown-up woman, the mother of two children, the wife of someone, a person who resides in a powerful country that takes up more than its fair share of a continent, the owner of a house with many rooms in it and of two automobiles, with the desire and will (which I very much act upon) to take from the world more than I give back to it, more than I deserve, more than I need, finally then, I saw England, the real England, not a picture, not a painting, not through a story in a book, but England, for the first time. In me, the space between the idea of it and its reality had become filled with hatred, and so when at last I saw it I wanted to take it into my hands and tear it into little pieces and then crumble it up as if it were clay, child's clay. That was impossible, and so I could only indulge in not-favorable opinions.

There were monuments everywhere; they commemorated victories, battles fought between them and the people who lived across the sea from them, all vile people, fought over which of them would have dominion over the people who looked like me. The monuments were useless to them now, people sat on them and ate their lunch. They were like markers on an old useless trail, like a piece of old string tied to a finger to jog the memory, like old decoration in an old house, dirty, useless, in the way. Their skins were so pale, it made them look so fragile, so weak, so ugly. What if I had the power to simply banish them from their land, send boat after boatload of them on a voyage that in fact had no destination, force them to live in a place where the sun's presence was a constant? This would rid them of their pale complexion and make them look more like me, make them look more like the people I love and treasure and hold dear, and more like the people who occupy the near and far reaches of my imagination, my history, my geography, and reduce them and everything they have ever known to figurines as evidence that I was in divine favor, what if all this was in my power? Could I resist it? No one ever has.

And they were rude, they were rude to each other. They didn't like each other very much. They didn't like each other in the way they didn't like me, and it occurred to me that their dislike for me was one of the few things they agreed on.

I was on a train in England with a friend, an English woman. Before we were in England she liked me very much. In England she didn't like me at all. She didn't like the claim I said I had on England, she didn't like the views I had of England. I didn't like England, she didn't like England, but she didn't like me not liking it too. She said, "I want to show you my England, I want to show you the England that I know and love." I had told her many times before that I knew England and I didn't want to love it anyway. She no longer lived in England; it was her own country, but it had not been kind to her, so she left. On the train, the conductor was rude to her; she asked something, and he responded in a rude way. She became ashamed. She was ashamed at the way he treated her; she was ashamed at the way he behaved. "This is the new England," she said. But I liked the conductor being rude; his behavior seemed quite appropriate. Earlier this had happened: We had gone to a store to buy a shirt for my husband; it was meant to be a special present, a special shirt to wear on special occasions. This was a store where the Prince of Wales has his shirts made, but the shirts sold in this store are beautiful all the same. I found a shirt I thought my husband would like and I wanted to buy him a tie to go with it. When I couldn't decide which one to choose, the salesman showed me a new set. He was very pleased with these, he said, because they bore the crest of the Prince of Wales, and the Prince of Wales had never allowed his crest to decorate an article of clothing before. There was something in the way he said it; his tone was slavish, reverential, awed. It made me feel angry; I wanted to hit him. I didn't do that. I said, my husband and I hate princes, my husband would never wear anything that had a prince's anything on it. My friend stiffened. The salesman stiffened. They both drew themselves in,

away from me. My friend told me that the prince was a symbol of her En-
glishness, and I could see that I had caused offense. I looked at her. She was an
English person, the sort of English person I used to know at home, the sort who
was nobody in England but somebody when they came to live among the people
like me. There were many people I could have seen England with; that I was seeing it with this particular person, a person who reminded me of the people who
showed me England long ago as I sat in church or at my desk, made me feel silent
and afraid, for I wondered if, all these years of our friendship, I had had a friend
or had been in the thrall of a racial memory.

I went to Bath — we, my friend and I, did this, but though we were together, I   15
was no longer with her. The landscape was almost as familiar as my own hand,
but I had never been in this place before, so how could that be again? And the
streets of Bath were familiar, too, but I had never walked on them before. It was
all those years of reading, starting with Roman Britain. Why did I have to know
about Roman Britain? It was of no real use to me, a person living on a hot,
drought-ridden island, and it is of no use to me now, and yet my head is filled
with this nonsense, Roman Britain. In Bath, I drank tea in a room I had read
about in a novel written in the eighteenth century. In this very same room, young
women wearing those dresses that rustled and so on danced and flirted and sometimes disgraced themselves with young men, soldiers, sailors, who were on their
way to Bristol or someplace like that, so many places like that where so many
adventures, the outcome of which was not good for me, began. Bristol, England.
A sentence that began "That night the ship sailed from Bristol, England" would
end not so good for me. And then I was driving through the countryside in an English motorcar, on narrow winding roads, and they were so familiar, though I had
never been on them before; and through little villages the names of which I
somehow knew so well though I had never been there before. And the countryside did have all those hedges and hedges, fields hedged in. I was marveling at all
the toil of it, the planting of the hedges to begin with and then the care of it, all
that clipping, year after year of clipping, and I wondered at the lives of the people
who would have to do this, because wherever I see and feel the hands that hold
up the world, I see and feel myself and all the people who look like me. And I
said, "Those hedges" and my friend said that someone, a woman named Mrs.
Rothchild, worried that the hedges weren't being taken care of properly; the
farmers couldn't afford or find the help to keep up the hedges, and often they
replaced them with wire fencing. I might have said to that, well if Mrs. Rothchild
doesn't like the wire fencing, why doesn't she take care of the hedges herself, but
I didn't. And then in those fields that were now hemmed in by wire fencing that a
privileged woman didn't like was planted a vile yellow flowering bush that produced an oil, and my friend said that Mrs. Rothchild didn't like this either; it
ruined the English countryside, it ruined the traditional look of the English
countryside.

It was not at that moment that I wished every sentence, everything I knew,
that began with England would end with "and then it all died; we don't know
how, it just all died." At that moment, I was thinking, who are these people who
forced me to think of them all the time, who forced me to think that the world I

knew was incomplete, or without substance, or did not measure up because it was not England; that I was incomplete, or without substance, and did not measure up because I was not English. Who were these people? The person sitting next to me couldn't give me a clue; no one person could. In any case, if I had said to her, I find England ugly, I hate England; the weather is like a jail sentence, the English are a very ugly people, the food in England is like a jail sentence, the hair of English people is so straight, so dead looking, the English have an unbearable smell so different from the smell of people I know, real people of course, she would have said that I was a person full of prejudice. Apart from the fact that it is I — that is, the people who look like me — who made her aware of the unpleasantness of such a thing, the idea of such a thing, prejudice, she would have been only partly right, sort of right: I may be capable of prejudice, but my prejudices have no weight to them, my prejudices have no force behind them, my prejudices remain opinions, my prejudices remain my personal opinion. And a great feeling of rage and disappointment came over me as I looked at England, my head full of personal opinions that could not have public, my public, approval. The people I come from are powerless to do evil on grand scale.

The moment I wished every sentence, everything I knew, that began with England would end with "and then it all died, we don't know how, it just all died" was when I saw the white cliffs of Dover. I had sung hymns and recited poems that were about a longing to see the white cliffs of Dover again. At the time I sang the hymns and recited the poems, I could really long to see them again because I had never seen them at all, nor had anyone around me at the time. But there we were, groups of people longing for something we had never seen. And so there they were, the white cliffs, but they were not that pearly majestic thing I used to sing about, that thing that created such a feeling in these people that when they died in the place where I lived they had themselves buried facing a direction that would allow them to see the white cliffs of Dover when they were resurrected, as surely they would be. The white cliffs of Dover, when finally I saw them, were cliffs, but they were not white; you would only call them that if the word "white" meant something special to you; they were dirty and they were steep; they were so steep, the correct height from which all my views of England, starting with the map before me in my classroom and ending with the trip I had just taken, should jump and die and disappear forever.   [1991]

THINKING ABOUT THE TEXT

1. Kincaid indicates that for her, "there were many times of seeing England for the first time" (para. 5). How does she develop this seemingly illogical claim?

2. What do you think Kincaid wants to make her audience believe and feel with this essay? Describe her tone. Is its effect on you the effect you think Kincaid wants it to have? Describe her characterization of herself. Do you think it is rhetorically effective? Why, or why not?

3. From what did the young Kincaid get her images of England? Look in particular at the images she reports in paragraph 6.

4. In paragraph 14, Kincaid recalls the incident in the clothing store after she describes her train trip, even though the incident in the store took place before the train trip. What does she gain by violating chronological order?

5. Does Kincaid learn anything from her trip to England? What? What would you say to someone who argued that she ought to have been more open-minded as a tourist?

MAKING COMPARISONS

1. Kincaid presents "Girl" and "Columbus in Chains" as works of fiction. As a reader, do you approach "On Seeing England for the First Time" differently because it is labeled nonfiction? Explain.

2. Compare the remarks about Columbus in "On Seeing England for the First Time" with Annie John's treatment of his picture in "Columbus in Chains." Do you think the two narrators have the same ideas about him? Refer to specific sentences in both texts.

3. "Girl" seems less explicitly concerned with colonialism than do the other two works. Is the world evoked in "Girl" quite different from the worlds of "Columbus in Chains" and "On Seeing England for the First Time"? Why, or why not? Using words from either or both of those texts, add a few sentences to "Girl" that more clearly establish the setting as colonial.

WRITING ABOUT ISSUES

1. Each of the three selections in this cluster either repeats certain words, refers to certain repeated acts, or both. Choose one of these selections, and write an essay explaining the role and function of repetition in it. Give specific examples of whatever repetitions you discuss.

2. Choose two of these selections and write an essay comparing the educational processes depicted in them. Do they depict the same kinds of teaching and learning or are there significant differences? Refer to specific details of both works.

3. Write your own version of "Girl," calling it either "Girl" or "Boy" and presenting in it advice that you were given as a youth. Exchange your version with a classmate's. After you read your classmate's version, add a paragraph or two to it in which you describe and evaluate the kind of education it depicts. Your classmate will do the same with your version. Return your classmate's version and get yours back. Finally, read your classmate's comments on your version and write a paragraph or two in which you state what you have learned from this exercise.

4. Midway through "On Seeing England for the First Time," Kincaid states the following: "The space between the idea of something and its reality is always wide and deep and dark. The longer they are kept apart—idea of thing, reality of thing—the wider the width, the deeper the depth, the thicker and darker the darkness. This space starts out empty, there is

nothing in it, but it rapidly becomes filled up with obsession or desire or hatred or love — sometimes all of these things, sometimes some of these things, sometimes only one of these things" (para. 10). In the rest of the paragraph, Kincaid gives the example of Columbus's relationship with the native inhabitants of the New World. Write an essay applying the passage quoted to another specific political situation, past or present. Focus on identifying who or what is responsible for "the space between the idea of something and its reality." Support your argument with facts drawn from library research.

A WEB ASSIGNMENT

In the Web Assignments section of the *Making Literature Matter* Web site, follow the link to a Web site about an emerging school of thought called *postcolonial studies*, which has been concerned with Jamaica Kincaid's writing among others. This site has been designed by Deepika Bahri, Peter Nowakowski, and Brian Cliff from the Department of English at Emory University in Atlanta, Georgia. Choose a work by Kincaid from the cluster you have just read, and then write an essay in which you relate it to one or more features of postcolonial studies identified by this site. Or follow the link this site provides to a separate page about Kincaid, written by Vanessa Pupello. In your essay, you can then connect your chosen work to one or more statements on this page.

Visit www.bedfordstmartins.com/makinglitmatter

TEACHING THROUGH LITERATURE

DAVID WAGONER, "The Singing Lesson"
THEODORE ROETHKE, "The Waking"
ELIZABETH BISHOP, "One Art"

Novelist and short-story writer Jane Smiley has observed that "every piece of fiction is in some degree also a how-to manual." Smiley could have said the same about any work of literature, not just stories. Through the centuries many readers have turned to literature for guidance, believing that within its pages lie valuable lessons. Furthermore, many writers of literature have seen it as a way of teaching. They have followed a recommendation made by the ancient philosopher Horace: he pointed out that art should both delight and instruct. In this cluster, we present works that associate literature with education. David Wagoner's poem has the word *lesson* in its very title, and Theodore Roethke's poem explicitly suggests how to learn. Elizabeth Bishop's poem gives instructions in "the art of losing," which supposedly "isn't hard to master." Can a poem be "poetic" when it resembles a lecture? Consider that question as you read the following texts.

BEFORE YOU READ

If you were asked to declare in a poem certain principles of living you have
come to adopt, what are some you might express? How controversial do you
think each would be?

DAVID WAGONER
The Singing Lesson

*David Wagoner (b. 1926) is a chancellor of the Academy of American Poets and
editor of the journal* Poetry Northwest. *The author of ten novels, he has also written
many volumes of poetry, the latest of which is* Walt Whitman Bathing *(1996). The
following poem appears in his 1974 book* Sleeping in the Woods.

You must stand erect but at your ease, a posture
Demanding a compromise
Between your spine and your head, your best face forward,
Your willful hands
Not beckoning or clenching or sweeping upward   5
But drawn in close:
A man with his arms spread wide is asking for it,
A martyred beggar,
A flightless bird on the nest dreaming of flying.
For your full resonance   10
You must keep your inspiring and expiring moments
Divided but equal,
Not locked like antagonists from breast to throat,
Choking toward silence.

If you have learned, with labor and luck, the measures   15
You were meant to complete,
You may find yourself before an audience
Singing into the light,
Transforming the air you breathe — that malleable wreckage,
That graveyard of shouts,   20
That inexhaustible pool of chatter and whimpers —
Into deathless music.
But remember, with your mouth wide open, eyes shut,
Some men will wonder,
When they look at you without listening, whether   25
You're singing or dying.
Take care to be heard. But even singing alone,
Singing for nothing,
Singing to empty space in no one's honor,

Keep time: it will tell   30
When you must give the final end-stopped movement
Your tacit approval.   [1974]

THINKING ABOUT THE TEXT

1. What words of Wagoner's poem might be used during an actual singing lesson? What words suggest that the poem is about more than singing? Does the poem do what the speaker is urging? In what ways?

2. Do you consider it significant that this singing lesson never uses rhyme? What do you think readers should conclude? What other verbal patterns does Wagoner use?

3. How might someone other than a singer or musician "Keep time" (line 30) and produce "deathless music" (line 22)?

4. At various points, the speaker refers to the singer's possible audience. How does the speaker characterize this audience? Refer to specific lines.

5. Evaluate the poem's advice. In what ways, if any, do you currently do what the poem recommends?

THEODORE ROETHKE
The Waking

Theodore Roethke (1908–1963) is regarded as one of the great modern American poets. The following poem appeared in his 1953 Pulitzer Prize–winning book entitled The Waking. *The poem is a* villanelle, *a centuries-old French form that is technically challenging for a writer. A villanelle is a nineteen-line poem consisting of five tercets (three-line stanzas) followed by a quatrain (four-line stanza); the first and third lines of the first tercet are used alternately to conclude each succeeding tercet, and they are joined to form a rhyme at the poem's end.*

I wake to sleep, and take my waking slow.
I feel my fate in what I cannot fear.
I learn by going where I have to go.

We think by feeling. What is there to know?
I hear my being dance from ear to ear.   5
I wake to sleep, and take my waking slow.

Of those so close beside me, which are you?
God bless the Ground! I shall walk softly there,
And learn by going where I have to go.

♦ ♦ ♦ ♦

Light takes the Tree; but who can tell us how? 10
The lowly worm climbs up a winding stair;
I wake to sleep, and take my waking slow.

Great Nature has another thing to do
To you and me; so take the lively air,
And, lovely, learn by going where to go. 15

This shaking keeps me steady. I should know.
What falls away is always. And is near.
I wake to sleep, and take my waking slow.
I learn by going where I have to go. [1953]

THINKING ABOUT THE TEXT

1. Explain how Roethke's poem is a villanelle, referring to the definition of this genre provided in the headnote about him. In Roethke's case, do you find the form effective? Why, or why not?

2. How would you respond to someone who is annoyed by the paradoxical phrase "I wake to sleep" (line 1)? Do you think the sentence "We think by feeling" (line 4) violates logic, too? Why, or why not?

3. At the end of the fifth tercet, Roethke departs a bit from the pattern of the villanelle by altering the line he is supposed to repeat. Instead of "I learn by going where I have to go" (line 3), he writes, "And, lovely, learn by going where to go" (line 15). Do you think this shift to explicit advice-giving is justifiable? Explain. Whom do you think "lovely" refers to? Is this fact important?

4. What philosophy of learning is expressed in this poem? Would you say that the line "I learn by going where I have to go" applies to you? What specific behavior do you think of in trying to answer this question? Do you believe the kind of learning described in the poem could take place in a college course? What assumptions are reflected in your answer to this question?

5. The first line of the fifth tercet seems to make "Great Nature" (line 13) an authority over human beings. What is your attitude toward this move? What does "take the lively air" (line 14) conceivably mean?

MAKING COMPARISONS

1. Because it is a villanelle, Roethke's poem can be described as highly formal. Is it much more formal than Wagoner's? Why, or why not?

2. Wagoner's is consistently a poem of advice or instruction. Is Roethke's? Support your answer by referring to specific lines of his.

3. Roethke's poem frequently uses the first person, but Wagoner's poem avoids it. Does this difference lead to a significant difference in the poems' effect?

ELIZABETH BISHOP
One Art

*Although she also wrote short stories, Elizabeth Bishop (1911–1979) became
known primarily for her poetry, winning both a Pulitzer Prize and a National Book
Award for it. Born in Worcester, Massachusetts, she spent much of her youth in
Nova Scotia. As an adult, she lived in various places, including New York City,
Florida, Mexico, and Brazil. Much of her poetry observes and reflects on a particu-
lar object or figure. "One Art" appeared in* Geography III *(1976), the last book that
Bishop published during her lifetime. Like Roethke's "The Waking," this poem is a
villanelle. (See the headnote to "The Waking" for a description of the form.)*

The art of losing isn't hard to master;
so many things seem filled with the intent
to be lost that their loss is no disaster.

Lose something every day. Accept the fluster
of lost door keys, the hour badly spent.   5
The art of losing isn't hard to master.

Then practice losing farther, losing faster:
places, and names, and where it was you meant
to travel. None of these will bring disaster.

I lost my mother's watch. And look! my last, or   10
next-to-last, of three loved houses went.
The art of losing isn't hard to master.

I lost two cities, lovely ones. And, vaster,
some realms I owned, two rivers, a continent.
I miss them, but it wasn't a disaster.   15

—Even losing you (the joking voice, a gesture
I love) I shan't have lied. It's evident
the art of losing's not too hard to master
though it may look like (*Write* it!) like disaster.   [1976]

THINKING ABOUT THE TEXT

1. What makes "One Art" a villanelle? Review the general definition of the
   form on page 788.

2. Describe the speaker's tone. Is it consistent? What do you conclude about
   the speaker's attitude toward "The art of losing" (lines 6, 12, 18)?

3. Look at the advice given in the third stanza. In what ways can it be considered useful? Would you argue that this advice shouldn't be heeded?
   Why, or why not?

4. In line 16, the word *you* is suddenly introduced. What is the effect?

5. The parenthetical expression "(*Write* it!)" in line 19 is a departure from the sheer repetition of lines characteristic of a villanelle. What do you make of this break? Do you think it appropriate, or do you find it merely jarring?

MAKING COMPARISONS

1. Compare Bishop's use of the villanelle form with Roethke's. Are you more aware of similarities or differences in their uses of it?

2. Both Wagoner and Bishop write about arts. For Wagoner, it's the art of singing; for Bishop, the art of losing. Do you see any resemblances between the two, judging by the poems? If so, what?

3. Does the implied listener seem equally important in all three poems? Explain.

WRITING ABOUT ISSUES

1. Choose Wagoner's, Roethke's, or Bishop's poem, and write an essay tracing how the poem develops. How, for instance, is the middle different from the beginning and the end different from earlier parts? Don't let yourself get stuck in merely repeating lines. While you should quote from the poem, focus on identifying in your own words the key stages it moves through.

2. Write an essay comparing the philosophies you see expressed in two of the poems in this cluster. Do these two poems appear to put forth similar philosophies, or are there important differences? As you explain the philosophy of each poem, be sure to cite specific lines.

3. Wagoner's poem elaborates a philosophy of life by focusing on the activity of singing. Roethke's poem does so by focusing on the activity of waking. Bishop's poem is about the activity of losing. Write an essay or poem expressing a philosophy of your own by focusing on a familiar activity. Feel free to bring in actual experiences of your own to develop your ideas.

4. Ask at least three students not in this class to tell you about a specific learning experience each has had recently. Write an essay discussing the extent to which each student apparently assumes that one must "Take care to be heard" (line 27) (Wagoner's words), or that "I learn by going where I have to go" (line 3) (Roethke's words), or that "loss is no disaster" (line 3) (Bishop's words). Support your claims about each student with specific details of the story he or she told you.

NARRATORS GIVING ADVICE

JONATHAN SWIFT, "A Modest Proposal"
DANIEL OROZCO, "Orientation"
PAM HOUSTON, "How to Talk to a Hunter"

The introduction to the previous cluster suggested that any work of literature can be considered a how-to manual. Each of the three works in this cluster has a narrator who dispenses advice. Yet in each case, you will be trying to determine whom the narrator is addressing, what situation is being described, how to evaluate the narrator's advice, and how to describe the narrator overall. These works belong to a specific literary tradition: that of the **unreliable narrator**. The term *unreliable* applies when you find yourself unable to accept a narrator's vision of life right away. Eventually, you may like and trust the narrator, but part of the process of reading the work is deciding whether you should.

BEFORE YOU READ

Recall an orientation you experienced. What were its goals? Its main activities? The key terms used during it? What did the people in charge seem to assume about their audience? What did you think of this orientation at the time? Why? Did your evaluation of it ever change? In what respect?

JONATHAN SWIFT
A Modest Proposal

FOR PREVENTING THE CHILDREN OF POOR PEOPLE
IN IRELAND FROM BEING A BURDEN TO THEIR PARENTS
OR COUNTRY, AND FOR MAKING THEM
BENEFICIAL TO THE PUBLIC

Jonathan Swift (1667–1745) was an eminent clergyman in his native Ireland, rising to the position of dean of St. Patrick's Cathedral in Dublin. But he also wrote many essays, political pamphlets, poems, and works of fiction, his best-known text being his 1726 prose satire Gulliver's Travels. *"A Modest Proposal," written in 1729, also continues to be widely read and much discussed. It reflects Swift's concern over the poverty and food shortages then afflicting Ireland. To him, the country suffered in part because of the narrow-minded policies of its ruler, England. Swift also faulted British owners of property in Ireland, many of whom were absentee landlords indifferent to their tenants' woes. Although "A Modest Proposal" is often classified as an essay, we think it can be called a short story because it contains a significant element of fiction: the real-life Swift surely did not agree with his narrator's remedy for Ireland. Indeed, this work is regarded as a classic example of irony.*

Through his narrator's absurd proposal, Swift aimed to shock readers into thinking about genuine solutions to his country's plight.

It is a melancholy object to those who walk through this great town or travel in the country, when they see the streets, the roads, and cabin doors, crowded with beggars of the female sex, followed by three, four, or six children, all in rags and importuning every passenger for an alms. These mothers, instead of being able to work for their honest livelihood, are forced to employ all their time in strolling to beg sustenance for their helpless infants: who as they grow up either turn thieves for want of work, or leave their dear native country to fight for the Pretender in Spain, or sell themselves to the Barbadoes.

I think it is agreed by all parties that this prodigious number of children in the arms, or on the backs, or at the heels of their mothers, and frequently of their fathers, is in the present deplorable state of the kingdom a very great additional grievance; and, therefore, whoever could find out a fair, cheap, and easy method of making these children sound, useful members of the commonwealth, would deserve so well of the public as to have his statue set up for a preserver of the nation.

But my intention is very far from being confined to provide only for the children of professed beggars; it is of a much greater extent, and shall take in the whole number of infants at a certain age who are born of parents in effect as little able to support them as those who demand our charity in the streets.

As to my own part, having turned my thoughts for many years upon this important subject, and maturely weighed the several schemes of our projectors,° have always found them grossly mistaken in their computation. It is true, a child just dropped from its dam may be supported by her milk for a solar year, with little other nourishment; at most not above the value of 2s.,° which the mother may certainly get, or the value in scraps, by her lawful occupation of begging; and it is exactly at one year old that I propose to provide for them in such a manner as instead of being a charge upon their parents or the parish, or wanting food and raiment for the rest of their lives, they shall on the contrary contribute to the feeding, and partly to the clothing, of many thousands.

There is likewise another great advantage in my scheme, that it will prevent those voluntary abortions, and that horrid practice of women murdering their bastard children, alas! too frequent among us! sacrificing the poor innocent babes I doubt more to avoid the expense than the shame, which would move tears and pity in the most savage and inhuman breast.

The number of souls in this kingdom being usually reckoned one million and a half, of these I calculate there may be about 200,000 couples whose wives are breeders; from which number I subtract 30,000 couples, who are able to maintain their own children (although I apprehend there cannot be so many, under the present distress of the kingdom); but this being granted, there will remain 170,000 breeders. I again subtract 50,000 for those women who miscarry, or whose children die by accident or disease within the year. There only remain 120,000

5

projectors: Those who devise plans.　**2s.:** Two shillings.

children of poor parents annually born. The question therefore is, how this number shall be reared and provided for? which, as I have already said, under the present situation of affairs, is utterly impossible by all the methods hitherto proposed. For we can neither employ them in handicraft or agriculture; we neither build houses (I mean in the country) nor cultivate land; they can very seldom pick up a livelihood by stealing, till they arrive at six years old, except where they are of towardly parts; although I confess they learn the rudiments much earlier; during which time they can, however, be properly looked upon only as probationers; as I have been informed by a principal gentleman in the county of Cavan, who protested to me that he never knew above one or two instances under the age of six, even in a part of the kingdom so renowned for the quickest proficiency in that art.

I am assured by our merchants, that a boy or a girl before twelve years old is no salable commodity; and even when they come to this age they will not yield above 3£.° or 3£. 2s. 6d.° at most on the exchange; which cannot turn to account either to the parents or kingdom, the charge of nutriment and rags having been at least four times that value.

I shall now therefore humbly propose my own thoughts, which I hope will not be liable to the least objection.

I have been assured by a very knowing American of my acquaintance in London, that a young healthy child well nursed is at a year old a most delicious, nourishing, and wholesome food, whether stewed, roasted, baked, or broiled; and I make no doubt that it will equally serve in a fricassee or a ragout.

I do therefore humbly offer it to public consideration that of the 120,000 children already computed, 20,000 may be reserved for breed, whereof only one-fourth part to be males; which is more than we allow to sheep, black cattle, or swine; and my reason is, that these children are seldom the fruits of marriage, a circumstance not much regarded by our savages; therefore one male will be sufficient to serve four females. That the remaining 100,000 may, at a year old, be offered in sale to the persons of quality and fortune through the kingdom; always advising the mother to let them suck plentifully in the last month, so as to render them plump and fat for a good table. A child will make two dishes at an entertainment for friends; and when the family dines alone, the fore or hind quarter will make a reasonable dish, and seasoned with a little pepper or salt will be very good boiled on the fourth day, especially in winter.

I have reckoned upon a medium that a child just born will weigh twelve pounds, and in a solar year, if tolerably nursed, will increase to twenty-eight pounds.

I grant this food will be somewhat dear, and therefore very proper for landlords, who, as they have already devoured most of the parents, seem to have the best title to the children.

Infant's flesh will be in season throughout the year, but more plentiful in March, and a little before and after: for we are told by a grave author, an eminent French physician, that fish being a prolific diet, there are more children born in Roman Catholic countries about nine months after Lent than at any other season; therefore, reckoning a year after Lent, the markets will be more glutted than usual,

10

3£.: Three pounds sterling. **6d.:** Six pence.

because the number of popish infants is at least three to one in this kingdom: and therefore it will have one other collateral advantage, by lessening the number of papists among us.

I have already computed the charge of nursing a beggar's child (in which list I reckon all cottagers, laborers, and four-fifths of the farmers) to be about 2s. per annum, rags included; and I believe no gentleman would repine to give 10s. for the carcass of a good fat child, which, as I have said, will make four dishes of excellent nutritive meat, when he has only some particular friend or his own family to dine with him. Thus the squire will learn to be a good landlord, and grow popular among the tenants; the mother will have 8s. net profit, and be fit for work till she produces another child.

Those who are more thrifty (as I must confess the times require) may flay the   15
carcass; the skin of which artificially dressed will make admirable gloves for ladies, and summer boots for fine gentlemen.

As to our city of Dublin, shambles° may be appointed for this purpose in the most convenient parts of it, and butchers we may be assured will not be wanting: although I rather recommend buying the children alive, and dressing them hot from the knife as we do roasting pigs.

A very worthy person, a true lover of his country, and whose virtues I highly esteem, was lately pleased in discoursing on this matter to offer a refinement upon my scheme. He said that many gentlemen of this kingdom, having of late destroyed their deer, he conceived that the want of venison might be well supplied by the bodies of young lads and maidens, not exceeding fourteen years of age nor under twelve; so great a number of both sexes in every country being now ready to starve for want of work and service; and these to be disposed of by their parents, if alive, or otherwise by their nearest relations. But with due deference to so excellent a friend and so deserving a patriot, I cannot be altogether in his sentiments; for as to the males, my American acquaintance assured me from frequent experience that their flesh was generally tough and lean, like that of our schoolboys by continual exercise, and their taste disagreeable; and to fatten them would not answer the charge. Then as to the females, it would, I think, with humble submission be a loss to the public, because they soon would become breeders themselves: and besides, it is not improbable that some scrupulous people might be apt to censure such a practice (although indeed very unjustly), as a little bordering upon cruelty; which, I confess, has always been with me the strongest objection against any project, how well soever intended.

But in order to justify my friend, he confessed that this expedient was put into his head by the famous Psalmanazar° a native of the island Formosa, who came from thence to London about twenty years ago: and in conversation told my friend, that in his country when any young person happened to be put to death, the executioner sold the carcass to persons of quality as a prime dainty; and that in his time the body of a plump girl of fifteen, who was crucified for an attempt to

---

shambles: Slaughterhouses. **Psalmanazar:** In 1704, the Frenchman George Psalmanazar (c. 1679–1763) wrote *An Historical and Geographical Description of Formosa* (now Taiwan). He claimed to be a Formosan native, but his hoax was exposed soon after the book's publication.

poison the emperor, was sold to his imperial majesty's prime minister of state, and other great mandarins of the court, in joints from the gibbet, at 400 crowns. Neither indeed, can I deny, that if the same use were made of several plump young girls in this town, who without one single groat to their fortunes cannot stir abroad without a chair, and appear at the playhouse and assemblies in foreign fineries which they never will pay for, the kingdom would not be the worse.

Some persons of a depending spirit are in great concern about the vast number of poor people, who are aged, diseased, or maimed, and I have been desired to employ my thoughts what course may be taken to ease the nation of so grievous an encumbrance. But I am not in the least pain upon that matter, because it is very well known that they are every day dying and rotting by cold and famine, and filth and vermin, as fast as can be reasonably expected. And as to the young laborers, they are now in as hopeful a condition: They cannot get work, and consequently pine away for want of nourishment, to a degree that if at any time they are accidentally hired to common labor, they have not strength to perform it; and thus the country and themselves are happily delivered from the evils to come.

I have too long digressed, and therefore shall return to my subject. I think the advantages by the proposal which I have made are obvious and many, as well as of the highest importance. 20

For first, as I have already observed, it would greatly lessen the number of papists, with whom we are yearly overrun, being the principal breeders of the nation as well as our most dangerous enemies; and who stay at home on purpose to deliver the kingdom to the Pretender, hoping to take their advantage by the absence of so many good Protestants, who have chosen rather to leave their country than stay at home and pay tithes against their conscience to an Episcopal curate.

Secondly, The poor tenants will have something valuable of their own, which by law may be made liable to distress and help to pay their landlord's rent, their corn and cattle being already seized, and money a thing unknown.

Thirdly, Whereas the maintenance of 100,000 children from two years old and upward, cannot be computed at less than 10s. a-piece per annum, the nation's stock will be thereby increased £50,000 per annum, beside the profit of a new dish introduced to the tables of all gentlemen of fortune in the kingdom who have any refinement in taste. And the money will circulate among ourselves, the goods being entirely of our own growth and manufacture.

Fourthly, The constant breeders beside the gain of 8s. sterling per annum by the sale of their children, will be rid of the charge of maintaining them after the first year.

Fifthly, This food would likewise bring great custom to taverns, where the vintners will certainly be so prudent as to procure the best receipts for dressing it to perfection, and consequently have their houses frequented by all the fine gentlemen, who justly value themselves upon their knowledge in good eating; and a skilful cook who understands how to oblige his guests, will contrive to make it as expensive as they please. 25

Sixthly, This would be a great inducement to marriage, which all wise nations have either encouraged by rewards or enforced by laws and penalties. It would increase the care and tenderness of mothers toward their children, when they were sure of a settlement for life to the poor babes, provided in some sort by the public, to their annual profit instead of expense. We should see an honest emulation among the married women, which of them would bring the fattest child to the market. Men would become as fond of their wives during the time of their pregnancy as they are now of their mares in foal, their cows in calf, their sows when they are ready to farrow; nor offer to beat or kick them (as is too frequent a practice) for fear of a miscarriage.

Many other advantages might be enumerated. For instance, the addition of some thousand carcasses in our exportation of barreled beef, the propagation of swine's flesh, and improvement in the art of making good bacon, so much wanted among us by the great destruction of pigs, too frequent at our table; which are no way comparable in taste or magnificence to a well-grown, fat, yearling child, which roasted whole will make a considerable figure at a lord mayor's feast or any other public entertainment. But this and many others I omit, being studious of brevity.

Supposing that 1,000 families in this city would be constant customers for infants' flesh, besides others who might have it at merry-meetings, particularly at weddings and christenings, I compute that Dublin would take off annually about 20,000 carcasses; and the rest of the kingdom (where probably they will be sold somewhat cheaper) the remaining 80,000.

I can think of no one objection that will possibly be raised against this proposal, unless it should be urged that the number of people will be thereby much lessened in the kingdom. This I freely own, and it was indeed one principal design in offering it to the world. I desire the reader will observe, that I calculate my remedy for this one individual kingdom of Ireland and for no other that ever was, is, or I think ever can be upon earth. Therefore let no man talk to me of other expedients: of taxing our absentees at 5s. a pound; of using neither clothes nor household furniture except what is of our own growth and manufacture; of utterly rejecting the materials and instruments that promote foreign luxury; of curing the expensiveness of pride, vanity, idleness, and gaming in our women; of introducing a vein of parsimony, prudence, and temperance; of learning to love our country, in the want of which we differ even from Laplanders and the inhabitants of Topinamboo; of quitting our animosities and factions, nor acting any longer like the Jews, who were murdering one another at the very moment their city was taken; of being a little cautious not to sell our country and conscience for nothing; of teaching landlords to have at least one degree of mercy toward their tenants; lastly, of putting a spirit of honesty, industry, and skill into our shopkeepers; who, if a resolution could now be taken to buy only our native goods, would immediately unite to cheat and exact upon us in the price the measure, and the goodness, nor could ever yet be brought to make one fair proposal of just dealing, though often and earnestly invited to it.

Therefore I repeat, let no man talk to me of these and the like expedients, till   30
he has at least some glimpse of hope that there will be ever some hearty and sincere attempt to put them in practice.

But as to myself, having been wearied out for many years with offering vain, idle, visionary thoughts, and at length utterly despairing of success, I fortunately fell upon this proposal; which, as it is wholly new, so it has something solid and real, of no expense and little trouble, full in our own power, and whereby we can incur no danger in disobliging England. For this kind of commodity will not bear exportation, the flesh being of too tender a consistence to admit a long continuance in salt, although perhaps I could name a country which would be glad to eat up our whole nation without it.

After all, I am not so violently bent upon my own opinion as to reject any offer proposed by wise men, which shall be found equally innocent, cheap, easy, and effectual. But before something of that kind shall be advanced in contradiction to my scheme, and offering a better, I desire the author or authors will be pleased maturely to consider two points. First, as things now stand, how they will be able to find food and raiment for 100,000 useless mouths and backs. And secondly, there being a round million of creatures in human figure throughout this kingdom, whose subsistence put into a common stock would leave them in debt 2,000,000£. sterling, adding those who are beggars by profession to the bulk of farmers, cottagers, and laborers, with the wives and children who are beggars in effect; I desire those politicians who dislike my overture, and may perhaps be so bold as to attempt an answer, that they will first ask the parents of these mortals, whether they would not at this day think it a great happiness to have been sold for food at a year old in the manner I prescribe, and thereby have avoided such a perpetual scene of misfortunes as they have since gone through by the oppression of landlords, the impossibility of paying rent without money or trade, the want of common sustenance, with neither house nor clothes to cover them from the inclemencies of the weather, and the most inevitable prospect of entailing the like or greater miseries upon their breed for ever.

I profess, in the sincerity of my heart, that I have not the least personal interest in endeavoring to promote this necessary work, having no other motive than the public good of my country, by advancing our trade, providing for infants, relieving the poor, and giving some pleasure to the rich. I have no children by which I can propose to get a single penny; the youngest being nine years old, and my wife past childbearing. [1729]

THINKING ABOUT THE TEXT

1. Analyze this essay as an argument that the narrator makes. What are his main claims? What support does he provide for them? What are some of his key warrants or assumptions?

2. What is the narrator's attitude toward the Irish poor? Identify various words he uses that indicate his judgments of them.

3. A word often associated with Swift's piece is *irony*. What are possible meanings of this term? What meaning of it seems most appropriate to Swift's work?

4. At what point in the piece do you realize that it is ironic? How would you describe the narrator's personality and tone before you get to this moment? List several adjectives for him.

5. Do you think Swift's piece would have succeeded in making many people more determined to solve Ireland's problems? Why, or why not?

DANIEL OROZCO
Orientation

Daniel Orozco (b. 1957) currently holds a writing fellowship at Stanford University. "Orientation" was selected for The Best American Short Stories 1995. *Originally, it appeared in a 1994 issue of* Seattle Review. *In a 1998 issue of the same journal, Orozco reports that since his story was published, "it has even been included in an employee orientation manual, which is either very funny or very disturbing."*

Those are the offices and these are the cubicles. That's my cubicle there, and this is your cubicle. This is your phone. Never answer your phone. Let the Voicemail System answer it. This is your Voicemail System Manual. There are no personal phone calls allowed. We do, however, allow for emergencies. If you must make an emergency phone call, ask your supervisor first. If you can't find your supervisor, ask Phillip Spiers, who sits over there. He'll check with Clarissa Nicks, who sits over there. If you make an emergency phone call without asking, you may be let go.

These are your IN and OUT boxes. All the forms in your IN box must be logged in by the date shown in the upper left-hand corner, initialed by you in the upper right-hand corner, and distributed to the Processing Analyst whose name is numerically coded in the lower left-hand corner. The lower right-hand corner is left blank. Here's your Processing Analyst Numerical Code Index. And here's your Forms Processing Procedures Manual.

You must pace your work. What do I mean? I'm glad you asked that. We pace our work according to the eight-hour workday. If you have twelve hours of work in your IN box, for example, you must compress that work into the eight-hour day. If you have one hour of work in your IN box, you must expand that work to fill the eight-hour day. That was a good question. Feel free to ask questions. Ask too many questions, however, and you may be let go.

That is our receptionist. She is a temp. We go through receptionists here. They quit with alarming frequency. Be polite and civil to the temps. Learn their names, and invite them to lunch occasionally. But don't get close to them, as it only makes it more difficult when they leave. And they always leave. You can be sure of that.

The men's room is over there. The women's room is over there. John LaFountaine, who sits over there, uses the women's room occasionally. He says it is accidental. We know better, but we let it pass. John LaFountaine is harmless, his forays into the forbidden territory of the women's room simply a benign thrill, a faint blip on the dull flat line of his life.

Russell Nash, who sits in the cubicle to your left, is in love with Amanda Pierce, who sits in the cubicle to your right. They ride the same bus together after work. For Amanda Pierce, it is just a tedious bus ride made less tedious by the idle nattering of Russell Nash. But for Russell Nash, it is the highlight of his day. It is the highlight of his life. Russell Nash has put on forty pounds, and grows fatter with each passing month, nibbling on chips and cookies while peeking glumly over the partitions at Amanda Pierce, and gorging himself at home on cold pizza and ice cream while watching adult videos on TV.

Amanda Pierce, in the cubicle to your right, has a six-year-old son named Jamie, who is autistic. Her cubicle is plastered from top to bottom with the boy's crayon artwork—sheet after sheet of precisely drawn concentric circles and ellipses, in black and yellow. She rotates them every other Friday. Be sure to comment on them. Amanda Pierce also has a husband, who is a lawyer. He subjects her to an escalating array of painful and humiliating sex games, to which Amanda Pierce reluctantly submits. She comes to work exhausted and freshly wounded each morning, wincing from the abrasions on her breasts, or the bruises on her abdomen, or the second-degree burns on the backs of her thighs.

But we're not supposed to know any of this. Do not let on. If you let on, you may be let go.

Amanda Pierce, who tolerates Russell Nash, is in love with Albert Bosch, whose office is over there. Albert Bosch, who only dimly registers Amanda Pierce's existence, has eyes only for Ellie Tapper, who sits over there. Ellie Tapper, who hates Albert Bosch, would walk through fire for Curtis Lance. But Curtis Lance hates Ellie Tapper. Isn't the world a funny place? Not in the ha-ha sense, of course.

Anika Bloom sits in that cubicle. Last year, while reviewing quarterly reports   10 in a meeting with Barry Hacker, Anika Bloom's left palm began to bleed. She fell into a trance, stared into her hand, and told Barry Hacker when and how his wife would die. We laughed it off. She was, after all, a new employee. But Barry Hacker's wife is dead. So unless you want to know exactly when and how you'll die, never talk to Anika Bloom.

Colin Heavey sits in that cubicle over there. He was new once, just like you. We warned him about Anika Bloom. But at last year's Christmas Potluck, he felt sorry for her when he saw that no one was talking to her. Colin Heavey brought her a drink. He hasn't been himself since. Colin Heavey is doomed. There's nothing he can do about it, and we are powerless to help him. Stay away from Colin Heavey. Never give any of your work to him. If he asks to do something, tell him you have to check with me. If he asks again, tell him I haven't gotten back to you.

This is the Fire Exit. There are several on this floor, and they are marked accordingly. We have a Floor Evacuation Review every three months, and an Escape Route Quiz once a month. We have our Biannual Fire Drill twice a year, and our Annual Earthquake Drill once a year. These are precautions only. These things never happen.

For your information, we have a comprehensive health plan. Any catastrophic illness, any unforeseen tragedy is completely covered. All dependents are completely covered. Larry Bagdikian, who sits over there, has six daughters. If anything were to happen to any of his girls, or to all of them, if all six were to simultaneously fall victim to illness or injury—stricken with a hideous degenerative muscle disease or some rare toxic blood disorder, sprayed with semiautomatic gunfire while on a class field trip, or attacked in their bunk beds by some prowling nocturnal lunatic—if any of this were to pass, Larry's girls would all be taken care of. Larry Bagdikian would not have to pay one dime. He would have nothing to worry about.

We also have a generous vacation and sick leave policy. We have an excellent disability insurance plan. We have a stable and profitable pension fund. We get group discounts for the symphony, and block seating at the ballpark. We get commuter ticket books for the bridge. We have Direct Deposit. We are all members of Costco.

This is our kitchenette. And this, this is our Mr. Coffee. We have a coffee 15 pool, into which we each pay two dollars a week for coffee, filters, sugar, and CoffeeMate. If you prefer Cremora or half-and-half to CoffeeMate, there is a special pool for three dollars a week. If you prefer Sweet 'n Low to sugar, there is a special pool for two-fifty a week. We do not do decaf. You are allowed to join the coffee pool of your choice, but you are not allowed to touch the Mr. Coffee.

This is the microwave oven. You are allowed to *heat* food in the microwave oven. You are not, however, allowed to *cook* food in the microwave oven.

We get one hour for lunch. We also get one fifteen-minute break in the morning, and one fifteen-minute break in the afternoon. Always take your breaks. If you skip a break, it is gone forever. For your information, your break is a privilege, not a right. If you abuse the break policy, we are authorized to rescind your breaks. Lunch, however, is a right, not a privilege. If you abuse the lunch policy, our hands will be tied, and we will be forced to look the other way. We will not enjoy that.

This is the refrigerator. You may put your lunch in it. Barry Hacker, who sits over there, steals food from this refrigerator. His petty theft is an outlet for his grief. Last New Year's Eve, while kissing his wife, a blood vessel burst in her brain. Barry Hacker's wife was two months pregnant at the time, and lingered in a coma for half a year before dying. It was a tragic loss for Barry Hacker. He hasn't been himself since. Barry Hacker's wife was a beautiful woman. She was also completely covered. Barry Hacker did not have to pay one dime. But his dead wife haunts him. She haunts all of us. We have seen her, reflected in the monitors of our computers, moving past our cubicles. We have seen the dim shadow of her face in our photocopies. She pencils herself in in the receptionist's appointment book, with the notation: To see Barry Hacker. She has left messages in the receptionist's Voicemail box, messages garbled by the electronic chirrups and buzzes in the phone line, her voice echoing from an immense distance within the ambient hum. But the voice is hers. And beneath her voice, beneath the tidal *whoosh* of static and hiss, the gurgling and crying of a baby can be heard.

In any case, if you bring a lunch, put a little something extra in the bag for Barry Hacker. We have four Barrys in this office. Isn't that a coincidence?

This is Matthew Payne's office. He is our Unit Manager, and his door is 20 always closed. We have never seen him, and you will never see him. But he is here. You can be sure of that. He is all around us.

This is the Custodian's Closet. You have no business in the Custodian's Closet.

And this, this is our Supplies Cabinet. If you need supplies, see Curtis Lance. He will log you in on the Supplies Cabinet Authorization Log, then give you a Supplies Authorization Slip. Present your pink copy of the Supplies Authorization Slip to Ellie Tapper. She will log you in on the Supplies Cabinet Key Log, then give you the key. Because the Supplies Cabinet is located outside the Unit

Manager's office, you must be very quiet. Gather your supplies quietly. The Supplies Cabinet is divided into four sections. Section One contains letterhead stationery, blank paper and envelopes, memo and note pads, and so on. Section Two contains pens and pencils and typewriter and printer ribbons, and the like. In Section Three we have erasers, correction fluids, transparent tapes, glue sticks, et cetera. And in Section Four we have paper clips and push pins and scissors and razor blades. And here are the spare blades for the shredder. Do not touch the shredder, which is located over there. The shredder is of no concern to you.

Gwendolyn Stich sits in that office there. She is crazy about penguins, and collects penguin knickknacks: penguin posters and coffee mugs and stationery, penguin stuffed animals, penguin jewelry, penguin sweaters and T-shirts and socks. She has a pair of penguin fuzzy slippers she wears when working late at the office. She has a tape cassette of penguin sounds which she listens to for relaxation. Her favorite colors are black and white. She has personalized license plates that read PEN GWEN. Every morning, she passes through all the cubicles to wish each of us a *good* morning. She brings Danish on Wednesdays for Hump Day morning break, and doughnuts on Fridays for TGIF afternoon break. She organizes the Annual Christmas Potluck, and is in charge of the Birthday List. Gwendolyn Stich's door is always open to all of us. She will always lend an ear, and put in a good word for you; she will always give you a hand, or the shirt off her back, or a shoulder to cry on. Because her door is always open, she hides and cries in a stall in the women's room. And John LaFountaine—who, enthralled when a woman enters, sits quietly in his stall with his knees to his chest—John LaFountaine has heard her vomiting in there. We have come upon Gwendolyn Stich huddled in the stairwell, shivering in the updraft, sipping a Diet Mr. Pibb and hugging her knees. She does not let any of this interfere with her work. If it interfered with her work, she might have to be let go.

Kevin Howard sits in that cubicle over there. He is a serial killer, the one they call the Carpet Cutter, responsible for the mutilations across town. We're not supposed to know that, so do not let on. Don't worry. His compulsion inflicts itself on strangers only, and the routine established is elaborate and unwavering. The victim must be a white male, a young adult no older than thirty, heavyset, with dark hair and eyes, and the like. The victim must be chosen at random, before sunset, from a public place; the victim is followed home, and must put up a struggle; et cetera. The carnage inflicted is precise: the angle and direction of the incisions; the layering of skin and muscle tissue; the rearrangement of the visceral organs; and so on. Kevin Howard does not let any of this interfere with his work. He is, in fact, our fastest typist. He types as if he were on fire. He has a secret crush on Gwendolyn Stich, and leaves a red-foil-wrapped Hershey's Kiss on her desk every afternoon. But he hates Anika Bloom, and keeps well away from her. In his presence, she has uncontrollable fits of shaking and trembling. Her left palm does not stop bleeding.

In any case, when Kevin Howard gets caught, act surprised. Say that he seemed like a nice person, a bit of a loner, perhaps, but always quiet and polite.

This is the photocopier room. And this, this is our view. It faces southwest. West is down there, toward the water. North is back there. Because we are on the seventeenth floor, we are afforded a magnificent view. Isn't it beautiful? It over-

25

looks the park, where the tops of those trees are. You can see a segment of the bay between those two buildings there. You can see the sun set in the gap between those two buildings over there. You can see this building reflected in the glass panels of that building across the way. There. See? That's you, waving. And look there. There's Anika Bloom in the kitchenette, waving back.

Enjoy this view while photocopying. If you have problems with the photocopier, see Russell Nash. If you have any questions, ask your supervisor. If you can't find your supervisor, ask Phillip Spiers. He sits over there. He'll check with Clarissa Nicks. She sits over there. If you can't find them, feel free to ask me. That's my cubicle. I sit in there.   [1994]

THINKING ABOUT THE TEXT

1. Does this orientation resemble other orientations with which you are familiar? In what ways? Consider the kinds of advice and the language used.

2. Does the office described here resemble other offices with which you are familiar? In what ways? At what points in the story does this office seem unusual?

3. List at least three adjectives that describe Orozco's narrator. What influences your evaluation of this narrator? What would you say to someone who claims that the story is more about the narrator than about the office?

4. What assumptions do you make about the narrator's audience, that is, the listener being oriented? Write a page or two from this person's point of view, stating his or her response to the orientation.

5. Does the order of the narrator's statements matter? Explain.

MAKING COMPARISONS

1. Does Swift's piece become outlandish more quickly than Orozco's story does? Explain.

2. Swift's narrator seems to address many people, whereas Orozco's narrator is evidently talking to one person. Do the two works differ in effect because of this difference in audience? Why, or why not?

3. If Swift's narrator worked in the office described in Orozco's story, what might be his job? What comments do you imagine him making about his coworkers?

PAM HOUSTON
How to Talk to a Hunter

A graduate of Denison University, Pam Houston (b. 1962) is completing a doctorate in English at the University of Utah. She is not a hunter, though she is a hunting guide and has edited the book Women on Hunting *(1994). The following story was published in a 1989 issue of the journal* Quarterly West. *It was then included in* The Best American Short Stories (1990), *in the paperback edition of* The Best American Short Stories of the Century (2000), *and in a 1992 volume of her own stories entitled* Cowboys Are My Weakness. *Houston's most recent books are another collection of her stories,* Waltzing the Cat (1998), *and a collection of essays,* A Little More about Me (1999).

When he says "Skins or blankets?" it will take you a moment to realize that he's asking which you want to sleep under. And in your hesitation he'll decide that he wants to see your skin wrapped in the big black moose hide. He carried it, he'll say, soaking wet and heavier than a dead man, across the tundra for two — was it hours or days or weeks? But the payoff, now, will be to see it fall across one of your white breasts. It's December, and your skin is never really warm, so you will pull the bulk of it around you and pose for him, pose for his camera, without having to narrate this moose's death.

You will spend every night in this man's bed without asking yourself why he listens to top-forty country. Why he donated money to the Republican Party. Why he won't play back his messages while you are in the room. You are there so often the messages pile up. Once you noticed the bright green counter reading as high as fifteen.

He will have lured you here out of a careful independence that you spent months cultivating; though it will finally be winter, the dwindling daylight and the threat of Christmas, that makes you give in. Spending nights with this man means suffering the long face of your sheepdog, who likes to sleep on your bed, who worries when you don't come home. But the hunter's house is so much warmer than yours, and he'll give you a key, and just like a woman, you'll think that means something. It will snow hard for thirteen straight days. Then it will really get cold. When it is sixty below there will be no wind and no clouds, just still air and cold sunshine. The sun on the windows will lure you out of bed, but he'll pull you back under. The next two hours he'll devote to your body. With his hands, with his tongue, he'll express what will seem to you like the most eternal of loves. Like the house key, this is just another kind of lie. Even in bed; especially in bed, you and he cannot speak the same language. The machine will answer the incoming calls. From under an ocean of passion and hide and hair you'll hear a woman's muffled voice between the beeps.

Your best female friend will say, "So what did you think? That a man who sleeps under a dead moose is capable of commitment?"

This is what you learned in college: A man desires the satisfaction of his desire; a woman desires the condition of desiring. 5

The hunter will talk about spring in Hawaii, summer in Alaska. The man who says he was always better at math will form the sentences so carefully it will be impossible to tell if you are included in these plans. When he asks you if you would like to open a small guest ranch way out in the country, understand that this is a rhetorical question. Label these conversations future perfect, but don't expect the present to catch up with them. Spring is an inconceivable distance from the December days that just keep getting shorter and gray.

He'll ask you if you've ever shot anything, if you'd like to, if you ever thought about teaching your dog to retrieve. Your dog will like him too much, will drop the stick at his feet every time, will roll over and let the hunter scratch his belly.

One day he'll leave you sleeping to go split wood or get the mail and his phone will ring again. You'll sit very still while a woman who calls herself something like Janie Coyote leaves a message on his machine: She's leaving work, she'll say, and the last thing she wanted to hear was the sound of his beautiful voice. Maybe she'll talk only in rhyme. Maybe the counter will change to sixteen. You'll look a question at the mule deer on the wall, and the dark spots on either side of his mouth will tell you he shares more with this hunter than you ever will. One night, drunk, the hunter told you he was sorry for taking that deer, that every now and then there's an animal that isn't meant to be taken, and he should have known that deer was one.

Your best male friend will say, "No one who needs to call herself Janie Coyote can hold a candle to you, but why not let him sleep alone a few nights, just to make sure?"

The hunter will fill your freezer with elk burger, venison sausage, organic potatoes, fresh pecans. He'll tell you to wear your seat belt, to dress warmly, to drive safely. He'll say you are always on his mind, that you're the best thing that's ever happened to him, that you make him glad that he's a man.

Tell him it don't come easy, tell him freedom's just another word for nothing left to lose.

These are the things you'll know without asking: The coyote woman wears her hair in braids. She uses words like "howdy." She's man enough to shoot a deer.

A week before Christmas you'll rent *It's a Wonderful Life* and watch it together, curled on your couch, faces touching. Then you'll bring up the word "monogamy." He'll tell you how badly he was hurt by your predecessor. He'll tell you he couldn't be happier spending every night with you. He'll say there's just a few questions he doesn't have the answers for. He'll say he's just scared and confused. Of course this isn't exactly what he means. Tell him you understand. Tell him you are scared too. Tell him to take all the time he needs. Know that you could never shoot an animal; and be glad of it.

Your best female friend will say, "You didn't tell him you loved him, did you?" Don't even tell her the truth. If you do you'll have to tell her that he said this: "I feel exactly the same way."

10

◆　◆　◆

Your best male friend will say, "Didn't you know what would happen when   15
you said the word 'commitment'?"

But that isn't the word that you said.

He'll say, "Commitment, monogamy, it all means just one thing."

The coyote woman will come from Montana with the heavier snows. The
hunter will call you on the day of the solstice to say he has a friend in town and
can't see you. He'll leave you hanging your Christmas lights; he'll give new
meaning to the phrase "longest night of the year." The man who has said he's not
so good with words will manage to say eight things about his friend without using
a gender-determining pronoun. Get out of the house quickly. Call the most
understanding person you know who will let you sleep in his bed.

Your best female friend will say, "So what did you think? That he was capable of living outside his gender?"

When you get home in the morning there's a candy tin on your pillow.   20
Santa, obese and grotesque, fondles two small children on the lid. The card will
say something like "From your not-so-secret admirer." Open it. Examine each
carefully made truffle. Feed them, one at a time, to the dog. Call the hunter's
machine. Tell him you don't speak chocolate.

Your best female friend will say, "At this point, what is it about him that you
could possibly find appealing?"

Your best male friend will say, "Can't you understand that this is a good sign?
Can't you understand that this proves how deep he's in with you?" Hug your best
male friend. Give him the truffles the dog wouldn't eat.

Of course the weather will cooperate with the coyote woman. The highways
will close, she will stay another night. He'll tell her he's going to work so he can
come and see you. He'll even leave her your number and write "Me at Work" on
the yellow pad of paper by his phone. Although you shouldn't, you'll have to be
there. It will be you and your nauseous dog and your half-trimmed tree all waiting for him like a series of questions.

This is what you learned in graduate school: In every assumption is contained the possibility of its opposite.

In your kitchen he'll hug you like you might both die there. Sniff him for   25
coyote. Don't hug him back.

He will say whatever he needs to to win. He'll say it's just an old friend. He'll
say the visit was all the friend's idea. He'll say the night away from you has given
him time to think about how much you mean to him. Realize that nothing short
of sleeping alone will ever make him realize how much you mean to him. He'll

say that if you can just be a little patient, some good will come out of this for the two of you after all. He still won't use a gender-specific pronoun.

Put your head in your hands. Think about what it means to be patient. Think about the beautiful, smart, strong, clever woman you thought he saw when he looked at you. Pull on your hair. Rock your body back and forth. Don't cry.

He'll say that after holding you it doesn't feel right holding anyone else. For "holding," substitute "fucking." Then take it as a compliment.

He will get frustrated and rise to leave. He may, or may not be bluffing. Stall for time. Ask a question he can't immediately answer. Tell him you want to make love on the floor. When he tells you your body is beautiful say, "I feel exactly the same way." Don't, under any circumstances, stand in front of the door.

Your best female friend will say, "They lie to us, they cheat on us, and we love them more for it." She'll say, "It's our fault; we raise them to be like that." 30

Tell her it can't be your fault. You've never raised anything but dogs.

The hunter will say it's late and he has to go home to sleep. He'll emphasize the last word in the sentence. Give him one kiss that he'll remember while he's fucking the coyote woman. Give him one kiss that ought to make him cry if he's capable of it, but don't notice when he does. Tell him to have a good night.

Your best male friend will say, "We all do it. We can't help it. We're self-destructive. It's the old bad-boy routine. You have a male dog, don't you?"

The next day the sun will be out and the coyote woman will leave. Think about how easy it must be for a coyote woman and a man who listens to top-forty country. The coyote woman would never use a word like "monogamy"; the coyote woman will stay gentle on his mind.

If you can, let him sleep alone for at least one night. If you can't, invite him over to finish trimming your Christmas tree. When he asks how you are, tell him you think it's a good idea to keep your sense of humor during the holidays. 35

Plan to be breezy and aloof and full of interesting anecdotes about all the other men you've ever known. Plan to be hotter than ever before in bed, and a little cold out of it. Remember that necessity is the mother of invention. Be flexible.

First, he will find the faulty bulb that's been keeping all the others from lighting. He will explain, in great detail, the most elementary electrical principles. You will take turns placing the ornaments you and other men, he and other women, have spent years carefully choosing. Under the circumstances, try to let this be a comforting thought.

He will thin the clusters of tinsel you put on the tree. He'll say something ambiguous like "Next year you should string popcorn and cranberries." Finally, his arm will stretch just high enough to place the angel on the top of the tree.

◆ ◆ ◆

Your best female friend will say, "Why can't you ever fall in love with a man who will be your friend?"

Your best male friend will say, "You ought to know this by now: Men always   40 cheat on the best women."

This is what you learned in the pop psychology book: Love means letting go of fear.

Play Willie Nelson's "Pretty Paper." He'll ask you to dance, and before you can answer he'll be spinning you around your wood stove, he'll be humming in your ear. Before the song ends he'll be taking off your clothes, setting you lightly under the tree, hovering above you with tinsel in his hair. Through the spread of the branches the all-white lights you insisted on will shudder and blur, outlining the ornaments he brought: a pheasant, a snow goose, a deer.

The record will end. Above the crackle of the wood stove and the rasp of the hunter's breathing you'll hear one long low howl break the quiet of the frozen night: your dog, chained and lonely and cold. You'll wonder if he knows enough to stay in his doghouse. You'll wonder if he knows that the nights are getting shorter now.   [1989]

THINKING ABOUT THE TEXT

1. Describe the narrator, listing at least three adjectives. What do you think of her? On what do you base your evaluation?

2. What would you say to someone who argued that this story engages in gender stereotypes? To someone who argued that it stereotypes hunters?

3. Do you think the "you" is the narrator herself? Why or why not? At any rate, Houston could have had the narrator dispense with references to "you" and just describe her own life. What are the possible purposes and effects of having the story be in the form of instructions? In what places does the narrator predict what the "you" will do rather than telling the "you" how to act?

4. Note the word *talk* in the title. In what ways does the story emphasize talking? What amount and kind of talk do you think should occur between the couple?

5. Would you say that the story has a happy ending? Why, or why not?

MAKING COMPARISONS

1. Both Orozco and Houston use humor, but do they use it in the same way? Does each of them use it to make a serious point? Support your answers with specific details from both texts. Would you say "A Modest Proposal" is humorous? Why, or why not?

2. Does Houston's narrator seem more focused on her own particular situation than Swift's and Orozco's narrators do? Explain.

3. Would you call all three works in this cluster ironic? Why, or why not? Identify what meanings of the term *ironic* you are applying.

WRITING ABOUT ISSUES

1. To what extent do Orozco's and Houston's stories stress gender differences? Write an essay in which you answer this question by focusing on one of the stories. Identify not only how much the story emphasizes gender differences but also the specific distinctions it seems to make. If you wish, you may also evaluate how the story treats gender differences, but provide support for your judgment.

2. Write an essay examining the extent to which Swift's, Orozco's, and Houston's narrators are independent people. How much do they serve others? How much individuality and freedom do they assert? In your essay, focus on comparing the three narrators. Does any one of them seem more independent than the others? Support your views by referring to specific details of the texts.

3. Imitating Swift, write a piece in which you calmly propose an outrageous solution to a current social problem. Or, imitating Orozco, write a piece in which you orient someone else to a group or community you know. Or, imitating Houston, write a piece in which you explain how to talk to a kind of person familiar to you. Whichever author you imitate, stick as much as possible to observations from your own experience.

4. Write an essay evaluating a proposal actually made to a group or community. Or write an essay evaluating a manual or other document meant to orient people. In either case, your audience is whoever produced what you are evaluating. Support your evaluation with specific details.

14

Loving

I came to Carthage where a whole frying pan full of abominable loves cracked about me on every side. I was not in love yet, yet I loved to be in love . . . I was looking for something to love, in love with love itself.
— Saint Augustine

Love, love, love—all the wretched cant of it, masking egotism, lust, masochism, fantasy under a mythology of sentimental postures, a welter of self-induced miseries and joys, blinding and masking the essential personalities in the frozen gestures of courtship, in the kissing and the dating and the desire, the compliments and the quarrels which verify its barrenness.
— Germaine Greer

There are very few people who are not ashamed of having loved one another once they have fallen out of love.
— La Rochefoucauld

The loss of love is a terrible thing; they lie who say that death is worse.
— Countee Cullen

Water may be older than light, diamonds crack in hot goat's blood, mountaintops give off cold fire, forests appear in mid-ocean, it may happen that a crab is caught with the shadow of a hand on its back, that the wind be imprisoned in a bit of knotted string. And it may be that love sometimes occurs without pain or misery.
— E. Annie Proulx

Of all forms of caution, caution in love is perhaps the most fatal to true happiness.
— Bertrand Russell

For you to ask advice on the rules of love is no better than to ask advice
on the rules of madness.

— Terence

Our culture makes many claims about love: Stories of the rejected lover who
dies of a broken heart abound. Modern kings give up the throne, ancient cities go
to war — all for love. Love is thought to be such a powerful emotion that its loss
may even make one want to die or to kill. (In some countries, finding one's wife
or husband in bed with a lover is a legal excuse for murder.) Men and women
seem willing to radically change their lives to be near their beloved. These are a
few examples of love's powerful influence on our behavior and our understanding of who we are.

Yet a serious discussion about the nature of love is often frustratingly difficult.
We can all make a list of things we love: a cold beer in summer, a great science-
fiction film, a new car, a quiet dinner with a good friend, a walk in fresh snow, a
football game when our favorite team comes from behind for a dramatic victory.
We love our parents, our siblings, our best friends. How can one word cover such
diversity?

When we try to generalize about love, we find ourselves relying on specific
incidents because giving examples is easier than giving definitions. If clarifying
the essence of love seems difficult, perhaps it is because our stories, myths, and
songs are filled with contradictions. Love conquers all, we say, but doesn't love
fade? We profess our undying love, but divorce statistics soar. Love is complex
and frustrating to pin down. Our culture even identifies different types of love:
true love, platonic love, maternal love, erotic love. Yet opinions about love are
strong; we all have evidence for what it is and isn't that we find persuasive.

But the evidence we find so convincing is influenced by cultural assumptions, probably more than we know. It would be naive to claim otherwise when
we are bombarded with so many movies, songs, and stories about love. Indeed,
some critics argue that romantic love is only a socially constructed illusion,
merely an elaborate rationalization for physical desire. Once the carnal attraction
fades, we get restless. At least, this is one argument, and probably not a popular
one among college students in search of love. Because we know what we feel
about those we love, we often grow impatient with other people's perspectives.
We are likely to ignore friends who say, "He wouldn't treat you like that if he
really loved you." Perhaps nothing arouses our interest more than a discussion of
our hopes and dreams about love.

Our engagement with stories and poems about love is equally complex and
ambivalent. Although the stories in this chapter often illuminate the sometimes
dark passageways we take in our romantic journeys, there is no consensus about
the final destination. Arguing about love stories engages us as much as it may also
baffle us. As you read, rely on your own experience, ethical positions, and literary
judgment in determining whether specific characters are indeed in love, whether
they should continue their relationship, whether they need more commitment or
less. The wise and the foolish seem equally perplexed in matters of the heart.

The first cluster (p. 812) deals with the poetic intensity of true love from five different perspectives. The next cluster (p. 820) focuses on three stories exploring the romantic illusions of dreams. Two essays comprise the next cluster (p. 838) as Diane Ackerman and Andrew Sullivan take opposing views on finding one's soul mate. Four poems on courtship follow (p. 846). We then focus on three startling love stories by Kate Chopin (p. 856). The sixth cluster (p. 869) presents a famous Anton Chekhov story and two modern variations. The next cluster examines the illusions of love by placing David Henry Hwang's play *M. Butterfly* in a cultural context (p. 908). Questions about the nature of love then concern three modern fiction writers (p. 968). The next-to-last two clusters deal with, first, Ann Sexton's, Robert Lowell's, and Denise Levertov's poetic takes on troubled marriages (p. 1003) and then Henrik Ibsen's popular and still controversial exploration of marriage and equality, *A Doll House* (p. 1008). Finally, we juxtapose a classic poem of love and world weariness, "Dover Beach," with "Night Ferry," a recent text with interesting, perhaps intentional, parallels to Matthew Arnold's poem (p. 1072).

TRUE LOVE

WILLIAM SHAKESPEARE, "Let me not to the marriage of true minds"
ANNE BRADSTREET, "To My Dear and Loving Husband"
E. E. CUMMINGS, "somewhere i have never travelled"
WISLAWA SZYMBORSKA, "True Love"
EDNA ST. VINCENT MILLAY, "Love Is Not All"

Think about the term *true love*. Why *true*? Does *love* need this modification? Isn't love supposed to be true? Is there a *false* love? Or is something else implied that *love* doesn't convey by itself? Might it be something like *the one-and-only*? Some writers seem committed to the idea that true love lasts forever, for better or worse, regardless of circumstances. Is this just a fantasy, something we hope will be true? Or is it a reality, delivered to those who are lucky or who work hard to make it true? See if you agree with the five poets in this cluster.

BEFORE YOU READ

Do you believe there is one perfect person in the world for you? Is it possible to love someone forever, even if both of you change over the years from young adulthood to retirement and beyond?

WILLIAM SHAKESPEARE

Let me not to the marriage of true minds

William Shakespeare (1564–1616) is best known to modern readers as a dramatist; however, there is evidence that both he and his contemporaries valued his poetry above the plays. In 1598, for example, a writer praised Shakespeare's "sugared sonnets among his private friends." As with other aspects of his life and work, questions about how much autobiographical significance to attach to Shakespeare's subject matter continue to arise. Regardless of the discussion, there can be no doubt that the sonnets attributed to Shakespeare, at times directed to a man and at others directed to a woman, address the subject of love. Sonnet 116, which was written in 1609 and proposes a "marriage of true minds," is no exception.

Let me not to the marriage of true minds,
Admit impediments. Love is not love
Which alters when it alteration finds,
Or bends with the remover to remove:
Oh, no! it is an ever-fixèd mark,   5
That looks on tempests and is never shaken;
It is the star to every wandering bark,
Whose worth's unknown, although his height be taken.
Love's not Time's fool, though rosy lips and cheeks
Within his bending sickle's compass come;   10
Love alters not with his brief hours and weeks,
But bears it out even to the edge of doom.
If this be error and upon me proved,
I never writ, nor no man ever loved.   [1609]

THINKING ABOUT THE TEXT

1. Would you be pleased if your beloved wrote you this sonnet? Is he professing his love or giving a definition of true love as unchanging?

2. What if love didn't last "even to the edge of doom" (line 12)? Would it then be ordinary?

3. Shakespeare uses images to describe true love. Which one strikes you as apt? Can you suggest an image of your own?

4. The concluding couplet seems to be saying something like, "I'm absolutely right." Do you think Shakespeare is? Can you think of a situation in which love should bend or alter?

5. The world seems to demonstrate that true love seldom lasts forever. Why then do writers of all kinds profess the opposite? If you really believe that true love does not exist, would you still marry? If your beloved asked you if your love would last forever, would you truthfully answer, "Only time will tell"?

ANNE BRADSTREET
To My Dear and Loving Husband

Anne Bradstreet (1612?–1672), one of the earliest poets in the canon of American literature, was born in England and came to the Massachusetts Bay Colony as the daughter of a governor; later she married another of the colony's governors. Her writings include an autobiographical sketch, several religious works, and a collection of wise sayings written for her son's moral education. Her poems were published in The Tenth Muse Lately Sprang Up in America *(London, 1650; second edition 1678), which has the distinction of being the first book of original verse written in what would become the United States. True to her Puritan milieu, her poems have their share of piety, but they also speak of married love.*

If ever two were one, then surely we.
If ever man were loved by wife, then thee;
If ever wife was happy in a man,
Compare with me, ye women, if you can.
I prize thy love more than whole mines of gold   5
Or all the riches that the East doth hold.
My love is such that rivers cannot quench,
Nor ought but love from thee, give recompense.
Thy love is such I can no way repay,
The heavens reward thee manifold, I pray.   10
Then while we live, in love let's so persevere
That when we live no more, we may live ever.   [1678]

THINKING ABOUT THE TEXT

1. Do you believe that the speaker means what she says? Why?
2. Do you agree that the goal of true love is to be one? What does this mean? Is there a danger in such a relationship?
3. Do you like Bradstreet's rhymes? Are they sophisticated? Subtle? Simple?
4. Why might she feel she has to repay her husband's love? Is true love based on reciprocity?
5. Does Bradstreet's concluding couplet suggest a link between persevering in love on earth and living forever in heaven? Does this connection make sense to you?

MAKING COMPARISONS

1. Would Bradstreet agree with Shakespeare's sonnet?
2. Compare Shakespeare's images with Bradstreet's. Which do you find more original? More appropriate? More sincere?
3. Why are these two poets so concerned with loving "forever"?

E. E. CUMMINGS
somewhere i have never travelled

Edward Estlin Cummings (1894–1962), who for many years preferred the lower-case e. e. cummings, was a highly innovative writer, willing to experiment with language on every level. Born in Cambridge, Massachusetts, and educated at Harvard, he tried his hand at essays, plays, and other types of prose; in fact, it was a novel based on a World War I concentration camp experience in France, The Enormous Room *(1922), that first brought cummings attention. It is his poetry, however, that most readers immediately recognize for its eccentric use of typography and punctuation, its wordplay and slang usage, its jazz rhythms, and its childlike foregrounding of the concrete above the abstract. Cummings hated pretension and would only agree to deliver the prestigious Eliot lectures at Harvard in 1953 if they were called* nonlectures. *His two large volumes of* The Complete Poems 1913–1962, *published in 1972, include humor, understated satire, and celebrations of love and sex.*

somewhere i have never travelled,gladly beyond
any experience,your eyes have their silence:
in your most frail gesture are things which enclose me,
or which i cannot touch because they are too near

your slightest look easily will unclose me   5
though i have closed myself as fingers,
you open always petal by petal myself as Spring opens
(touching skilfully,mysteriously)her first rose

or if your wish be to close me,i and
my life will shut very beautifully,suddenly,   10
as when the heart of this flower imagines
the snow carefully everywhere descending;

nothing which we are to perceive in this world equals
the power of your intense fragility:whose texture
compels me with the colour of its countries,   15
rendering death and forever with each breathing

(i do not know what it is about you that closes
and opens;only something in me understands
the voice of your eyes is deeper than all roses)
nobody,not even the rain,has such small hands   [1931] 20

THINKING ABOUT THE TEXT

1. In your own words, what is cummings saying about the effect love has on him? Is this hyperbolic? Why?
2. Does love open us up? In what ways? Can you give a personal example of what a strong feeling did to you?

3. Is this a poem about love or obsession or romantic infatuation? What is the difference?

4. What do you think "the power of your intense fragility" (line 14) might mean? Is this a contradiction?

5. When cummings says "something in me understands" (line 18), what might he mean? Is love located inside us somewhere? In our hearts? Our brains?

MAKING COMPARISONS

1. Is cummings's flower imagery more effective than the images that Shakespeare and Bradstreet use?

2. All the poets here use *forever*. What do they intend?

3. What do you imagine Shakespeare and Bradstreet would think about cummings's sentence structure? His images?

WISLAWA SZYMBORSKA
True Love

Translated by Stanislaw Baránczak and Clare Cavanagh

Wislawa Szymborska (b. 1923) was born in Poland and has lived in Krakow since 1931, studying literature at Jagiellonian University. She worked as a poetry editor for almost twenty years for a well-known literary journal in Krakow. She has published sixteen collections of poetry, many of which have been widely translated, and has won many prizes, including, most notably, the Nobel Prize for literature in 1996 "for poetry that with ironic precision allows the historical and biological context to come to light in fragments of human reality." The following poem is from View with a Grain of Sand *(1995).*

True love. Is it normal,
is it serious, is it practical?
What does the world get from two people
who exist in a world of their own?

Placed on the same pedestal for no good reason,   5
drawn randomly from millions, but convinced
it had to happen this way—in reward for what?
          For nothing.
The light descends from nowhere.
Why on these two and not on others?   10
Doesn't this outrage justice? Yes it does.
Doesn't it disrupt our painstakingly erected principles,
and cast the moral from the peak? Yes on both accounts.

◆ ◆ ◆

Look at the happy couple.
Couldn't they at least try to hide it,   15
fake a little depression for their friends' sake!
Listen to them laughing — it's an insult.
The language they use — deceptively clear.
And their little celebrations, rituals,
the elaborate mutual routines —   20
it's obviously a plot behind the human race's back!

It's hard even to guess how far things might go
if people start to follow their example.
What could religion and poetry count on?
What would be remembered? What renounced?   25
Who'd want to stay within bounds?

True love. Is it really necessary?
Tact and common sense tell us to pass over it in silence,
like a scandal in Life's highest circles.
Perfectly good children are born without its help.   30
It couldn't populate the planet in a million years,
it comes along so rarely.

Let the people who never find true love
keep saying that there's no such thing.

Their faith will make it easier for them to live and die.   [1972]   35

THINKING ABOUT THE TEXT

1. The tone of the poem seems to be crucial. Is Szymborska being ironic? Does it really matter to her if true love is practical?

2. Why does the poet ask a series of questions and then answer them? Would you have answered them in the same way she does?

3. Reading between the lines, what kind of behavior do those in "true love" exhibit? Is this true in your experience?

4. Can people just "follow their example" (line 23)? Is falling in love an act of will? Is it an accident? Does she really worry about "how far things might go" (line 22)?

5. How could this poem be seen as an argument against true love? As an argument for true love? Does the last line make you think the poet really does believe in true love? How would you explain the meaning of the last line?

MAKING COMPARISONS

1. How might Shakespeare, Bradstreet, and cummings respond to this poet's tone? Would they find it amusing? Annoying?

2. How might each of the poets respond to the question, Is true love necessary?

3. Do people "in true love" try to hide their emotions in public? Why?

EDNA ST. VINCENT MILLAY
Love Is Not All

Edna St. Vincent Millay (1892–1950) was born in Rockland, Maine. Her mother encouraged her to be ambitious and self-sufficient and taught her about literature at an early age. On the strength of her early poems Millay won a scholarship to Vassar where she became a romantic legend for breaking the "hearts of half the undergraduate class." She also soon became wildly famous for her love poetry, giving readings in large auditoriums across the country, much like a contemporary rock star. Openly bisexual, her fame, talent, beauty, and bohemian aura was said to drive her many admirers to distraction. A biography by Nancy Mitford, Savage Beauty *(2001), quotes from dozens of letters to Millay, whining, pleading, and groveling for her favors. Mitford writes that "she gave the Jazz Age its lyric voice." In fact, we still use a phrase that Salon.com says Millay "invented to describe a life of impudent abandon":*

> My candle burns at both ends;
>   It will not last the night;
> But oh, my foes, and oh, my friends —
>   It gives a lovely light!

Once called "the greatest female poet since Sappho," Millay's reputation in academic circles has fallen off somewhat. Perhaps compared to the cerebral and allusive free verse of poets like T. S. Eliot her work seems a bit obvious. But some critics still think of her as America's "most illustrious love poet." The title poem of Renascence and Other Poems *ranks as a landmark of modern literature, and the collection itself is ranked fifth on the New York Public Library's Books of the Century. The following poem is from* Fatal Interview *(1931).*

Love is not all: it is not meat nor drink
Nor slumber nor a roof against the rain;
Nor yet a floating spar to men that sink
And rise and sink and rise and sink again;
Love can not fill the thickened lung with breath,   5
Nor clean the blood, nor set the fractured bone;
Yet many a man is making friends with death
Even as I speak, for lack of love alone.
It well may be that in a difficult hour,
Pinned down by pain and moaning for release,   10
Or nagged by want past resolution's power,

I might be driven to sell your love for peace,
Or trade the memory of this night for food.
It well may be. I do not think I would.   [1931]

THINKING ABOUT THE TEXT

1. Would most people you know trade love for peace or the memory of a romantic night for food? Would you? What does it say about the narrator that she would not?

2. Do you think it is an exaggeration to say that "many a man is making friends with death / . . . for lack of love alone" (lines 7–8)?

3. When the narrator begins "Love is not all" followed by a colon, what expectations are raised? Are they satisfied?

4. What do you think of the rhyme scheme? Does it add to the poem's meaning? Would you rather read free verse than this sonnet form? Why, or why not?

5. Is this a poem about the tension between love and practicality? Explain.

MAKING COMPARISONS

1. Like Szymborska, Millay seems to use indirection to support her claim. What other similarities to "True Love" do you notice?

2. What claims for love do all five poems make?

3. Compare the tone of each of the narrators. Which do you prefer? Is sincerity an issue or authenticity or passion?

WRITING ABOUT ISSUES

1. Translate the cummings poem into concrete prose. Try not to use images; just explain the individual lines as simply as you can.

2. Write a comparison of the effects Bradstreet's, cummings's, and Millay's poems had on you.

3. Write a position paper arguing for or against the reality of true love. Make reference to three of the poems given here.

4. Look at a couple of love poems written at the same time as Shakespeare's sonnet (1609). Are there similarities? Differences? Do you think Shakespeare (or any great poet) can transcend his or her attitudes toward true love? Write an essay that tries to answer this question, using the poems you found.

Romantic Dreams

LESLIE MARMON SILKO, "Yellow Woman"
JAMES JOYCE, "Araby"
JOHN UPDIKE, "A & P"

Although centuries old, the cliché that the human heart is a mystery still seems valid. We still wonder if falling in love is natural: Is love our inborn impulse to seek romance, or is it simply a physical attraction spurred on by our evolutionary need to procreate? Perhaps Western culture has socialized us to believe in the power of romantic love and the often irrational behavior that follows. Might it serve some deep psychological need to find a substitute for a beloved parent? Is it a giving emotion? A selfish one? Is it a psychological malady or the one thing worth giving everything up for? Do we need to believe in it whether or not it exists? Since we are often driven to irrational behavior, delusions, and heartbreak might we be better off without romantic love? Or might life without it be intolerably flat?

In the following cluster, three fiction writers explore the ways romantic love can sometimes cloud judgment, encouraging us to act against our best interests.

Silko shows us a woman torn between myth and reality; Joyce shows us a boy in the throes of romantic idealism; and Updike gives us a memorable picture of how an indifferent world responds to romantic gestures.

BEFORE YOU READ

Can people be truly happy without being in love? Is there one person in the world who is your true love? Or are there only certain types of people you could love? If your love didn't make you "float on a cloud," would you be disappointed? Is true love unconditional? Have you ever been fooled by romantic dreams?

LESLIE MARMON SILKO
Yellow Woman

Leslie Marmon Silko (b. 1948) is a major figure in the American Indian Renaissance. Raised in "Old Laguna" on the Pueblo Reservation near Albuquerque, New Mexico, Silko weaves the mythology of her matrilineal society into stories that move freely through what she calls an "ocean of time." The Yellow Woman *character appears frequently in Silko's writing as both a traditional figure, closely connected with nature and heterosexuality, and as a female character awakening to her cultural and sexual identity. Silko writes both poetry and fiction, often synthesizing both genres into a single text. Her novels include* Storyteller *(1981), in which "Yellow Woman" appears;* Ceremony *(1977); and* Almanac of the Dead *(1991). She teaches at the University of Arizona at Tucson.*

1

My thigh clung to his with dampness, and I watched the sun rising up through the tamaracks and willows. The small brown water birds came to the river and hopped across the mud, leaving brown scratches in the alkali-white crust. They bathed in the river silently. I could hear the water, almost at our feet where the narrow fast channel bubbled and washed green ragged moss and fern leaves. I looked at him beside me, rolled in the red blanket on the white river sand. I cleaned the sand out of the cracks between my toes, squinting because the sun was above the willow trees. I looked at him for the last time, sleeping on the white river sand.

I felt hungry and followed the river south the way we had come the afternoon before, following our footprints that were already blurred by the lizard tracks and bug trails. The horses were still lying down, and the black one whinnied when he saw me but he did not get up—maybe it was because the corral was made out of thick cedar branches and the horses had not yet felt the sun like I had. I tried to look beyond the pale red mesas to the pueblo. I knew it was there, even if I could not see it, on the sand rock hill above the river, the same river that moved past me now and had reflected the moon last night.

The horse felt warm underneath me. He shook his head and pawed the sand. The bay whinnied and leaned against the gate trying to follow, and I remembered him asleep in the red blanket beside the river. I slid off the horse and tied him close to the other horse. I walked north with the river again, and the white sand broke loose in footprints over footprints.

"Wake up."

He moved in the blanket and turned his face to me with his eyes still closed.   5
I knelt down to touch him.

"I'm leaving."

He smiled now, eyes still closed. "You are coming with me, remember?" He sat up now with his bare dark chest and belly in the sun.

"Where?"

"To my place."

"And will I come back?"   10

He pulled his pants on. I walked away from him, feeling him behind me and smelling the willows.

"Yellow Woman," he said.

I turned to face him. "Who are you?" I asked.

He laughed and knelt on the low, sandy bank, washing his face in the river. "Last night you guessed my name, and you knew why I had come."

I stared past him at the shallow moving water and tried to remember the   15
night, but I could only see the moon in the water and remember his warmth around me.

"But I only said that you were him and that I was Yellow Woman—I'm not really her—I have my own name and I come from the pueblo on the other side of the mesa. Your name is Silva and you are a stranger I met by the river yesterday afternoon."

He laughed softly. "What happened yesterday has nothing to do with what you will do today, Yellow Woman."

"I know—that's what I'm saying—the old stories about the ka'tsina spirit° and Yellow Woman can't mean us."

My old grandpa liked to tell those stories best. There is one about Badger and Coyote who went hunting and were gone all day, and when the sun was going down they found a house. There was a girl living there alone, and she had light hair and eyes and she told them that they could sleep with her. Coyote wanted to be with her all night so he sent Badger into a prairie-dog hole, telling him he thought he saw something in it. As soon as Badger crawled in, Coyote blocked up the entrance with rocks and hurried back to Yellow Woman.

"Come here," he said gently.   20

He touched my neck and I moved close to him to feel his breathing and to hear his heart. I was wondering if Yellow Woman had known who she was—if she knew that she would become part of the stories. Maybe she'd had another name that her husband and relatives called her so that only the ka'tsina from the north and the storytellers would know her as Yellow Woman. But I didn't go on; I felt him all around me, pushing me down into the white river sand.

Yellow Woman went away with the spirit from the north and lived with him and his relatives. She was gone for a long time, but then one day she came back and she brought twin boys.

"Do you know the story?"

"What story?" He smiled and pulled me close to him as he said this. I was afraid lying there on the red blanket. All I could know was the way he felt, warm, damp, his body beside me. This is the way it happens in the stories, I was thinking, with no thought beyond the moment she meets the ka'tsina spirit and they go.

"I don't have to go. What they tell in stories was real only then, back in time   25
immemorial, like they say."

He stood up and pointed at my clothes tangled in the blanket. "Let's go," he said.

I walked beside him, breathing hard because he walked fast, his hand around my wrist. I had stopped trying to pull away from him, because his hand felt cool and the sun was high, drying the river bed into alkali. I will see someone, eventually I will see someone, and then I will be certain that he is only a man— some man from nearby—and I will be sure that I am not Yellow Woman. Because she is from out of time past and I live now and I've been to school and there are highways and pickup trucks that Yellow Woman never saw.

It was an easy ride north on horseback. I watched the change from the cottonwood trees along the river to the junipers that brushed past us in the foothills, and finally there were only piñons, and when I looked up at the rim of the mountain plateau I could see pine trees growing on the edge. Once I stopped to look down, but the pale sandstone had disappeared and the river was gone and the dark lava hills were all around. He touched my hand, not speaking, but always singing softly a mountain song and looking into my eyes.

ka'tsina spirit: A mountain spirit of the Laguna Pueblo Indians.

I felt hungry and wondered what they were doing at home now — my mother, my grandmother, my husband, and the baby. Cooking breakfast, saying, "Where did she go? — maybe kidnapped," and Al going to the tribal police with the details: "She went walking along the river."

The house was made with black lava rock and red mud. It was high above the   30
spreading miles of arroyos and long mesas. I smelled a mountain smell of pitch and buck brush. I stood there beside the black horse, looking down on the small, dim country we had passed, and I shivered.

"Yellow Woman, come inside where it's warm."

2

He lit a fire in the stove. It was an old stove with a round belly and an enamel coffeepot on top. There was only the stove, some faded Navajo blankets, and a bedroll and cardboard box. The floor was made of smooth adobe plaster, and there was one small window facing east. He pointed at the box.

"There's some potatoes and the frying pan." He sat on the floor with his arms around his knees pulling them close to his chest and he watched me fry the potatoes. I didn't mind him watching me because he was always watching me — he had been watching me since I came upon him sitting on the river bank trimming leaves from a willow twig with his knife. We ate from the pan and he wiped the grease from his fingers on his Levis.

"Have you brought women here before?" He smiled and kept chewing, so I said, "Do you always use the same tricks?"

"What tricks?" He looked at me like he didn't understand.   35

"The story about being a ka'tsina from the mountains. The story about Yellow Woman."

Silva was silent; his face was calm.

"I don't believe it. Those stories couldn't happen now," I said.

He shook his head and said softly, "But someday they will talk about us, and they will say, 'Those two lived long ago when things like that happened.' "

He stood up and went out. I ate the rest of the potatoes and thought about   40
things — about the noise the stove was making and the sound of the mountain wind outside. I remembered yesterday and the day before, and then I went outside.

I walked past the corral to the edge where the narrow trail cut through the black rim rock. I was standing in the sky with nothing around me but the wind that came down from the blue mountain peak behind me. I could see faint mountain images in the distance miles across the vast spread of mesas and valleys and plains. I wondered who was over there to feel the mountain wind on those sheer blue edges — who walks on the pine needles in those blue mountains.

"Can you see the pueblo?" Silva was standing behind me.

I shook my head. "We're too far away."

"From here I can see the world." He stepped out on the edge. "The Navajo reservation begins over there." He pointed to the east. "The Pueblo boundaries are over here." He looked below us to the south, where the narrow trail seemed to come from. "The Texans have their ranches over there, starting with that valley, the Concho Valley. The Mexicans run some cattle over there too."

"Do you ever work for them?"   45

"I steal from them," Silva answered. The sun was dropping behind us and shadows were filling the land below. I turned away from the edge that dropped forever into the valleys below.

"I'm cold," I said; "I'm going inside." I started wondering about this man who could speak the Pueblo language so well but who lived on a mountain and rustled cattle. I decided that this man Silva must be Navajo, because Pueblo men didn't do things like that.

"You must be a Navajo."

Silva shook his head gently. "Little Yellow Woman," he said, "you never give up, do you? I have told you who I am. The Navajo people know me, too." He knelt down and unrolled the bedroll and spread the extra blankets out on a piece of canvas. The sun was down, and the only light in the house came from outside — the dim orange light from sundown.

I stood there and waited for him to crawl under the blankets.   50

"What are you waiting for?" he said, and I lay down beside him. He undressed me slowly like the night before beside the river — kissing my face gently and running his hands up and down my belly and legs. He took off my pants and then he laughed.

"Why are you laughing?"

"You are breathing so hard."

I pulled away from him and turned my back to him.

He pulled me around and pinned me down with his arms and chest. "You   55
don't understand, do you, little Yellow Woman? You will do what I want."

And again he was all around me with his skin slippery against mine, and I was afraid because I understood that his strength could hurt me. I lay underneath him and I knew that he could destroy me. But later, while he slept beside me, I touched his face and I had a feeling — the kind of feeling for him that overcame me that morning along the river. I kissed him on the forehead and he reached out for me.

When I woke up in the morning he was gone. It gave me a strange feeling because for a long time I sat there on the blankets and looked around the little house for some object of his — some proof that he had been there or maybe that he was coming back. Only the blankets and the cardboard box remained. The .30–30° that had been leaning in the corner was gone, and so was the knife I had used the night before. He was gone, and I had my chance to go now. But first I had to eat, because I knew it would be a long walk home.

I found some dried apricots in the cardboard box, and I sat down on a rock at the edge of the plateau rim. There was no wind and the sun warmed me. I was surrounded by silence. I drowsed with apricots in my mouth, and I didn't believe that there were highways or railroads or cattle to steal.

When I woke up, I stared down at my feet in the black mountain dirt. Little black ants were swarming over the pine needles around my foot. They must have

.30–30: A rifle.

smelled the apricots. I thought about my family far below me. They would be
wondering about me, because this had never happened to me before. The tribal
police would file a report. But if old Grandpa weren't dead he would tell them
what happened—he would laugh and say, "Stolen by a ka'tsina, a mountain
spirit. She'll come home—they usually do." There are enough of them to handle
things. My mother and grandmother will raise the baby like they raised me. Al
will find someone else, and they will go on like before, except that there will be a
story about the day I disappeared while I was walking along the river. Silva had
come for me; he said he had. I did not decide to go. I just went. Moonflowers
blossom in the sand hills before dawn, just as I followed him. That's what I was
thinking as I wandered along the trail through the pine trees.

It was noon when I got back. When I saw the stone house I remembered that I   60
had meant to go home. But that didn't seem important any more, maybe because
there were little blue flowers growing in the meadow behind the stone house and
the gray squirrels were playing in the pines next to the house. The horses were
standing in the corral, and there was a beef carcass hanging on the shady side of a
big pine in front of the house. Flies buzzed around the clotted blood that hung
from the carcass. Silva was washing his hands in a bucket full of water. He must
have heard me coming because he spoke to me without turning to face me.

"I've been waiting for you."

"I went walking in the big pine trees."

I looked into the bucket full of bloody water with brown-and-white animal
hairs floating in it. Silva stood there letting his hand drip, examining me intently.

"Are you coming with me?"

"Where?" I asked him.   65

"To sell the meat in Marquez."

"If you're sure it's O.K."

"I wouldn't ask you if it wasn't," he answered.

He sloshed the water around in the bucket before he dumped it out and set
the bucket upside down near the door. I followed him to the corral and watched
him saddle the horses. Even beside the horses he looked tall, and I asked him
again if he wasn't Navajo. He didn't say anything; he just shook his head and kept
cinching up the saddle.

"But Navajos are tall."   70

"Get on the horse," he said, "and let's go."

The last thing he did before we started down the steep trail was to grab the
.30–30 from the corner. He slid the rifle into the scabbard that hung from his saddle.

"Do they ever try to catch you?" I asked.

"They don't know who I am."

"Then why did you bring the rifle?"   75

"Because we are going to Marquez where the Mexicans live."

3

The trail leveled out on a narrow ridge that was steep on both sides like an
animal spine. On one side I could see where the trail went around the rocky gray

hills and disappeared into the southeast where the pale sandrock mesas stood in the distance near my home. On the other side was a trail that went west, and as I looked far into the distance I thought I saw the little town. But Silva said no, that I was looking in the wrong place, that I just thought I saw houses. After that I quit looking off into the distance; it was hot and the wildflowers were closing up their deep-yellow petals. Only the waxy cactus flowers bloomed in the bright sun, and I saw every color that a cactus blossom can be; the white ones and the red ones were still buds, but the purple and the yellow were blossoms, open full and the most beautiful of all.

Silva saw him before I did. The white man was riding a big gray horse, coming up the trail toward us. He was traveling fast and the gray horse's feet sent rocks rolling off the trail into the dry tumbleweeds. Silva motioned for me to stop and we watched the white man. He didn't see us right away, but finally his horse whinnied at our horses and he stopped. He looked at us briefly before he loped the gray horse across the three hundred yards that separated us. He stopped his horse in front of Silva, and his young fat face was shadowed by the brim of his hat. He didn't look mad, but his small, pale eyes moved from the blood-soaked gunny sacks hanging from my saddle to Silva's face and then back to my face.

"Where did you get the fresh meat?" the white man asked.

"I've been hunting," Silva said, and when he shifted his weight in the saddle the leather creaked.   80

"The hell you have, Indian. You've been rustling cattle. We've been looking for the thief for a long time."

The rancher was fat, and sweat began to soak through his white cowboy shirt and the wet cloth stuck to the thick rolls of belly fat. He almost seemed to be panting from the exertion of talking, and he smelled rancid, maybe because Silva scared him.

Silva turned to me and smiled. "Go back up the mountain, Yellow Woman."

The white man got angry when he heard Silva speak in a language he couldn't understand. "Don't try anything, Indian. Just keep riding to Marquez. We'll call the state police from there."

The rancher must have been unarmed because he was very frightened and if   85 he had a gun he would have pulled it out then. I turned my horse around and the rancher yelled, "Stop!" I looked at Silva for an instant and there was something ancient and dark — something I could feel in my stomach — in his eyes, and when I glanced at his hand I saw his finger on the trigger of the .30–30 that was still in the saddle scabbard. I slapped my horse across the flank and the sacks of raw meat swung against my knees as the horse leaped up the trail. It was hard to keep my balance, and once I thought I felt the saddle slipping backward; it was because of this that I could not look back.

I didn't stop until I reached the ridge where the trail forked. The horse was breathing deep gasps and there was a dark film of sweat on its neck. I looked down in the direction I had come from, but I couldn't see the place. I waited. The wind came up and pushed warm air past me. I looked up at the sky, pale blue and full of thin clouds and fading vapor trails left by jets.

I think four shots were fired — I remember hearing four hollow explosions that reminded me of deer hunting. There could have been more shots after that, but I couldn't have heard them because my horse was running again and the loose rocks were making too much noise as they scattered around his feet.

Horses have a hard time running downhill, but I went that way instead of uphill to the mountain because I thought it was safer. I felt better with the horse running southeast past the round gray hills that were covered with cedar trees and black lava rock. When I got to the plain in the distance I could see the dark green patches of tamaracks that grew along the river; and beyond the river I could see the beginning of the pale sandrock mesas. I stopped the horse and looked back to see if anyone was coming; then I got off the horse and turned the horse around, wondering if it would go back to its corral under the pines on the mountain. It looked back at me for a moment and then plucked a mouthful of green tumbleweeds before it trotted back up the trail with its ears pointed forward, carrying its head daintily to one side to avoid stepping on the dragging reins. When the horse disappeared over the last hill, the gunny sacks full of meat were still swinging and bouncing.

4

I walked toward the river on a wood-hauler's road that I knew would eventually lead to the paved road. I was thinking about waiting beside the road for someone to drive by, but by the time I got to the pavement I had decided it wasn't very far to walk if I followed the river back the way Silva and I had come.

The river water tasted good, and I sat in the shade under a cluster of silvery willows. I thought about Silva, and I felt sad at leaving him; still, there was something strange about him, and I tried to figure it out all the way back home. 90

I came back to the place on the river bank where he had been sitting the first time I saw him. The green willow leaves that he had trimmed from the branch were still lying there, wilted in the sand. I saw the leaves and I wanted to go back to him — to kiss him and to touch him — but the mountains were too far away now. And I told myself, because I believe it, he will come back sometime and be waiting again by the river.

I followed the path up from the river into the village. The sun was getting low, and I could smell supper cooking when I got to the screen door of my house. I could hear their voices inside — my mother was telling my grandmother how to fix the Jell-O and my husband, Al, was playing with the baby. I decided to tell them that some Navajo had kidnapped me, but I was sorry that old Grandpa wasn't alive to hear my story because it was the Yellow Woman stories he liked to tell best. [1974]

THINKING ABOUT THE TEXT

1. Why does Yellow Woman run away with Silva? Does it have something to do with the coyote stories? What stories in your own culture have persuaded you to trust in romantic love?

2. How do myths and stories differ? Are either based on reality or fantasy? What are the social or cultural purposes of stories about love?

3. Do you trust the narrator's judgment? Sincerity? On what textual evidence are you basing this evaluation? What bearing does her cultural heritage have on your analysis of her?

4. What specific details of Silko's story do you remember? Is the narrator a careful observer? Explain. What effect does the narrator's "noticing little things" have on you as a reader?

5. Has Yellow Woman learned her lesson? Do societies change their views of romantic love? How?

JAMES JOYCE
Araby

James Joyce (1882–1941) is regarded as one of the most innovative and influential writers of the modernist movement of the early twentieth century. His use of interior monologue, wordplay, complex allusions, and other techniques variously delighted, offended, or puzzled readers. Joyce's work demanded attention and often received censorship during his lifetime. A Portrait of the Artist as a Young Man *(1916), set in Joyce's native Dublin, is largely autobiographical. Like his hero at the end of the novel, Joyce left Ireland at the age of twenty to spend the remainder of his life in Paris and other European cities. His long, complex novel* Ulysses *(1922), also set in Dublin, takes the reader through one day in the life of its protagonist and his city. In "Araby," published in* Dubliners *(1914), as in other stories in the collection, Joyce pictures the limited life of his character and leads him toward a sudden insight, or epiphany.*

North Richmond Street, being blind, was a quiet street except at the hour when the Christian Brothers' School set the boys free. An uninhabited house of two storeys stood at the blind end, detached from its neighbours in a square ground. The other houses of the street, conscious of decent lives within them, gazed at one another with brown imperturbable faces.

The former tenant of our house, a priest, had died in the back drawing-room. Air, musty from having been long enclosed, hung in all the rooms, and the waste room behind the kitchen was littered with old useless papers. Among these I found a few paper-covered books, the pages of which were curled and damp: *The Abbot*, by Walter Scott, *The Devout Communicant*, and *The Memoirs of Vidocq*. I liked the last best because its leaves were yellow. The wild garden behind the house contained a central apple-tree and a few straggling bushes under one of which I found the late tenant's rusty bicycle-pump. He had been a very charitable priest; in his will he had left all his money to institutions and the furniture of his house to his sister.

When the short days of winter came dusk fell before we had well eaten our dinners. When we met in the street the houses had grown sombre. The space of sky above us was the colour of ever-changing violet and towards it the lamps of the street lifted their feeble lanterns. The cold air stung us and we played till our bodies glowed. Our shouts echoed in the silent street. The career of our play brought us through the dark muddy lanes behind the houses where we ran the gauntlet of the rough tribes from the cottages, to the back doors of the dark dripping gardens where odours arose from the ashpits, to the dark odorous stables where a coachman smoothed and combed the horse or shook music from the buckled harness. When we returned to the street light from the kitchen windows had filled the areas. If my uncle was seen turning the corner we hid in the shadow until we had seen him safely housed. Or if Mangan's sister came out on the doorstep to call her brother in to his tea we watched her from our shadow peer up and down the street. We waited to see whether she would remain or go in and, if she remained, we left our shadow and walked up to Mangan's steps resignedly. She was waiting for us, her figure defined by the light from the half-opened door. Her brother always teased her before he obeyed and I stood by the railings looking at her. Her dress swung as she moved her body and the soft rope of her hair tossed from side to side.

Every morning I lay on the floor in the front parlour watching her door. The blind was pulled down to within an inch of the sash so that I could not be seen. When she came out on the doorstep my heart leaped. I ran to the hall, seized my books, and followed her. I kept her brown figure always in my eye and, when we came near the point at which our ways diverged, I quickened my pace and passed her. This happened morning after morning. I had never spoken to her, except for a few casual words, and yet her name was like a summons to all my foolish blood.

Her image accompanied me even in places the most hostile to romance. On 5
Saturday evenings when my aunt went marketing I had to go to carry some of the parcels. We walked through the flaring streets, jostled by drunken men and bargaining women, amid the curses of labourers, the shrill litanies of shop-boys who stood on guard by the barrel of pigs' cheeks, the nasal chanting of street-singers, who sang a *come-all-you* about O'Donovan Rossa,° or a ballad about the troubles in our native land. These noises converged in a single sensation of life for me: I imagined that I bore my chalice safely through a throng of foes. Her name sprang to my lips at moments in strange prayers and praises which I myself did not understand. My eyes were often full of tears (I could not tell why) and at times a flood from my heart seemed to pour itself out into my bosom. I thought little of the future. I did not know whether I would ever speak to her or not or, if I spoke to her, how I could tell her of my confused adoration. But my body was like a harp and her words and gestures were like fingers running upon the wires.

One evening I went into the back drawing-room in which the priest had died. It was a dark rainy evening and there was no sound in the house. Through one of the broken panes I heard the rain impinge upon the earth, the fine incessant needles of water playing in the sodden beds. Some distant lamp or lighted window gleamed below me. I was thankful that I could see so little. All my senses seemed to desire to veil themselves and, feeling that I was about to slip from them, I pressed the palms of my hands together until they trembled, murmuring: "O love! O love!" many times.

O'Donovan Rossa: Jeremiah O'Donovan (1831–1915) was nicknamed "Dynamite Rossa" for advocating violent means to achieve Irish independence.

At last she spoke to me. When she addressed the first words to me I was so confused that I did not know what to answer. She asked me was I going to *Araby*. I forgot whether I answered yes or no. It would be a splendid bazaar, she said she would love to go.

"And why can't you?" I asked.

While she spoke she turned a silver bracelet round and round her wrist. She could not go, she said, because there would be a retreat that week in her convent. Her brother and two other boys were fighting for their caps and I was alone at the railings. She held one of the spikes, bowing her head towards me. The light from the lamp opposite our door caught the white curve of her neck, lit up her hair that rested there and, falling, lit up the hand upon the railing. It fell over one side of her dress and caught the white border of a petticoat, just visible as she stood at ease.

"It's well for you," she said.   10

"If I go," I said, "I will bring you something."

What innumerable follies laid waste my waking and sleeping thoughts after that evening! I wished to annihilate the tedious intervening days. I chafed against the work of school. At night in my bedroom and by day in the classroom her image came between me and the page I strove to read. The syllables of the word *Araby* were called to me through the silence in which my soul luxuriated and cast an Eastern enchantment over me. I asked for leave to go to the bazaar on Saturday night. My aunt was surprised and hoped it was not some Freemason affair. I answered few questions in class. I watched my master's face pass from amiability to sternness; he hoped I was not beginning to idle. I could not call my wandering thoughts together. I had hardly any patience with the serious work of life which, now that it stood between me and my desire, seemed to me child's play, ugly monotonous child's play.

On Saturday morning I reminded my uncle that I wished to go to the bazaar in the evening. He was fussing at the hallstand, looking for the hat-brush, and answered me curtly:

"Yes, boy, I know."

As he was in the hall I could not go into the front parlour and lie at the window. I left the house in bad humour and walked slowly towards the school. The air was pitilessly raw and already my heart misgave me.   15

When I came home to dinner my uncle had not yet been home. Still it was early. I sat staring at the clock for some time and, when its ticking began to irritate me, I left the room. I mounted the staircase and gained the upper part of the house. The high cold empty gloomy rooms liberated me and I went from room to room singing. From the front window I saw my companions playing below in the street. Their cries reached me weakened and indistinct and, leaning my forehead against the cool glass, I looked over at the dark house where she lived. I may have stood there for an hour, seeing nothing but the brown-clad figure cast by my imagination, touched discreetly by the lamplight at the curved neck, at the hand upon the railings and at the border below the dress.

When I came downstairs again I found Mrs. Mercer sitting at the fire. She was an old garrulous woman, a pawnbroker's widow, who collected used stamps for some pious purpose. I had to endure the gossip of the tea-table. The meal was prolonged beyond an hour and still my uncle did not come. Mrs. Mercer stood up to go: she was sorry she couldn't wait any longer, but it was after eight o'clock and she did not like to be out late, as the night air was bad for her. When she had gone I began to walk up and down the room, clenching my fists. My aunt said:

"I'm afraid you may put off your bazaar for this night of Our Lord."

At nine o'clock I heard my uncle's latchkey in the halldoor. I heard him talking to himself and heard the hallstand rocking when it had received the weight of his overcoat. I could interpret these signs. When he was midway through his dinner I asked him to give me the money to go to the bazaar. He had forgotten.

"The people are in bed and after their first sleep now," he said.   20

I did not smile. My aunt said to him energetically:

"Can't you give him the money and let him go? You've kept him late enough as it is."

My uncle said he was very sorry he had forgotten. He said he believed in the old saying: "All work and no play makes Jack a dull boy." He asked me where I was going and, when I had told him a second time he asked me did I know *The Arab's Farewell to his Steed*. When I left the kitchen he was about to recite the opening lines of the piece to my aunt.

I held a florin° tightly in my hand as I strode down Buckingham Street towards the station. The sight of the streets thronged with buyers and glaring with gas recalled to me the purpose of my journey. I took my seat in a third-class carriage of a deserted train. After an intolerable delay the train moved out of the station slowly. It crept onward among ruinous houses and over the twinkling river. At Westland Row Station a crowd of people pressed to the carriage doors; but the porters moved them back, saying that it was a special train for the bazaar. I remained alone in the bare carriage. In a few minutes the train drew up beside an improvised wooden platform. I passed out on to the road and saw by the lighted dial of a clock that it was ten minutes to ten. In front of me was a large building which displayed the magical name.

I could not find any sixpenny entrance and, fearing that the bazaar would   25
be closed, I passed in quickly through a turnstile, handing a shilling to a weary-looking man. I found myself in a big hall girdled at half its height by a gallery. Nearly all the stalls were closed and the greater part of the hall was in darkness. I recognised a silence like that which pervades a church after a service. I walked into the centre of the bazaar timidly. A few people were gathered about the stalls which were still open. Before a curtain, over which the words *Café Chantant* were written in coloured lamps, two men were counting money on a salver. I listened to the fall of the coins.

Remembering with difficulty why I had come I went over to one of the stalls and examined porcelain vases and flowered tea-sets. At the door of the stall a young lady was talking and laughing with two young gentlemen. I remarked their English accents and listened vaguely to their conversation.

florin: A silver coin worth two shillings.

"O, I never said such a thing!"

"O, but you did!"

"O, but I didn't!"

"Didn't she say that?"

"Yes. I heard her."   30

"O, there's a . . . fib!"

Observing me the young lady came over and asked me did I wish to buy anything. The tone of her voice was not encouraging; she seemed to have spoken to me out of a sense of duty. I looked humbly at the great jars that stood like eastern guards at either side of the dark entrance to the stall and murmured:

"No, thank you."

The young lady changed the position of one of the vases and went back to   35
the two young men. They began to talk of the same subject. Once or twice the young lady glanced at me over her shoulder.

I lingered before her stall, though I knew my stay was useless, to make my interest in her wares seem the more real. Then I turned away slowly and walked down the middle of the bazaar. I allowed the two pennies to fall against the sixpence in my pocket. I heard a voice call from one end of the gallery that the light was out. The upper part of the hall was now completely dark.

Gazing up into the darkness I saw myself as a creature driven and derided by vanity; and my eyes burned with anguish and anger.   [1914]

THINKING ABOUT THE TEXT

1. Why do the boy's eyes burn with anguish and anger? Has he learned something about romantic love? Was he in love with Mangan's sister? Give evidence.

2. If this story is partly autobiographical, what is Joyce's attitude toward his younger self? Are you sympathetic or critical of your own initiations into the complexities of relationships?

3. Reread the first and last paragraph. In what ways might they be connected?

4. Find examples of religious imagery. What do you think is its purpose?

5. Do you think the boy's quest has symbolic meaning? Do you think cultures can also search for something?

MAKING COMPARISONS

1. Compare the growth of the boy with the wife in "Yellow Woman."

2. Make explicit the insight or epiphany the boy comes to at the end. What would be a comparable epiphany for the wife in "Yellow Woman"?

3. Is one ending more realistic than the other? Explain.

JOHN UPDIKE
A & P

John Updike was born in 1932 in Shillington, Pennsylvania, an only child of a father who taught high-school algebra and a mother who wrote short stories and novels. After graduating from Harvard, Updike studied art in England and later joined the staff of The New Yorker. *In 1959 he published his first novel,* The Poorhouse Fair, *and moved to Massachusetts, where he still lives. His many novels of contemporary American life are notable for their lyrical and accurate depiction of the details and concerns of modern America.* Rabbit Run *(1960) and the sequels* Rabbit Redux *(1971),* Rabbit Is Rich *(1981), and* Rabbit at Rest *(1990) are considered important and insightful records of American life. "A & P" comes from Updike's* Pigeon Feathers and Other Stories *(1962).*

In walks these three girls in nothing but bathing suits. I'm in the third checkout slot, with my back to the door, so I don't see them until they're over by the bread. The one that caught my eye first was the one in the plaid green two-piece. She was a chunky kid, with a good tan and a sweet broad soft-looking can with those two crescents of white just under it, where the sun never seems to hit, at the top of the backs of her legs. I stood there with my hand on a box of HiHo crackers trying to remember if I rang it up or not. I ring it up again and the customer starts giving me hell. She's one of these cash-register-watchers, a witch about fifty with rouge on her cheekbones and no eyebrows, and I know it made her day to trip me up. She'd been watching cash registers for fifty years and probably never seen a mistake before.

By the time I got her feathers smoothed and her goodies into a bag—she gives me a little snort in passing, if she'd been born at the right time they would have burned her over in Salem—by the time I get her on her way the girls had circled around the bread and were coming back, without a pushcart, back my way along the counters, in the aisle between the checkouts and the Special bins. They didn't even have shoes on. There was this chunky one, with the two-piece—it was bright green and the seams on the bra were still sharp and her belly was still pretty pale so I guessed she just got it (the suit)—there was this one, with one of those chubby berry-faces, the lips all bunched together under her nose, this one, and a tall one, with black hair that hadn't quite frizzed right, and one of these sunburns right across under the eyes, and a chin that was too long—you know, the kind of girl other girls think is very "striking" and "attractive" but never quite makes it, as they very well know, which is why they like her so much—and then the third one, that wasn't quite so tall. She was the queen. She kind of led them, the other two peeking around and making their shoulders round. She didn't look around, not this queen, she just walked straight on slowly, on these long white prima-donna legs. She came down a little hard on her heels, as if she didn't walk in her bare feet that much, putting down her heels and then letting the weight move along to her toes as if she was testing the floor with every step, putting a little deliberate extra action into it. You never know for sure how girls' minds work (do you really think it's a mind in there or just a little buzz like a bee in a glass jar?) but you got the idea she had talked the other two into coming in here with her, and now she was showing them how to do it, walk slow and hold yourself straight.

She had on a kind of dirty-pink — beige maybe, I don't know — bathing suit with a little nubble all over it, and what got me, the straps were down. They were off her shoulders looped loose around the cool tops of her arms, and I guess as a result the suit had slipped a little on her, so all around the top of the cloth there was this shining rim. If it hadn't been there you wouldn't have known there could have been anything whiter than those shoulders. With the straps pushed off, there was nothing between the top of the suit and the top of her head except just *her*, this clean bare plane of the top of her chest down from the shoulder bones like a dented sheet of metal tilted in the light. I mean, it was more than pretty.

She had sort of oaky hair that the sun and salt had bleached, done up in a bun that was unravelling, and a kind of prim face. Walking into the A & P with your straps down, I suppose it's the only kind of face you *can* have. She held her head so high her neck, coming up out of those white shoulders, looked kind of stretched, but I didn't mind. The longer her neck was, the more of her there was.

She must have felt in the corner of her eye me and over my shoulder Stoke- 5
sie in the second slot watching, but she didn't tip. Not this queen. She kept her eyes moving across the racks, and stopped, and turned so slow it made my stomach rub the inside of my apron, and buzzed to the other two, who kind of huddled against her for relief, and then they all three of them went up the cat-and-dog-food-breakfast-cereal-macaroni-rice-raisins-seasonings-spreads-spaghetti-soft-drinks-crackers-and-cookies aisle. From the third slot I look straight up this aisle to the meat counter, and I watched them all the way. The fat one with the tan sort of fumbled with the cookies, but on second thought she put the package back. The sheep pushing their carts down the aisle — the girls were walking against the usual traffic (not that we have one-way signs or anything) — were pretty hilarious. You could see them, when Queenie's white shoulders dawned on them, kind of jerk, or hop, or hiccup, but their eyes snapped back to their own baskets and on they pushed. I bet you could set off dynamite in an A & P and the people would by and large keep reaching and checking oatmeal off their lists and muttering "Let me see, there was a third thing, began with A, asparagus, no, ah, yes, applesauce!" or whatever it is they do mutter. But there was no doubt, this jiggled them. A few houseslaves in pin curlers even looked around after pushing their carts past to make sure what they had seen was correct.

You know, it's one thing to have a girl in a bathing suit down on the beach, where what with the glare nobody can look at each other much anyway, and another thing in the cool of the A & P, under the fluorescent lights, against all those stacked packages, with her feet paddling along naked over our checkboard green-and-cream rubber-tile floor.

"Oh Daddy," Stokesie said beside me. "I feel so faint."

"Darling," I said. "Hold me tight." Stokesie's married, with two babies chalked up on his fuselage already, but as far as I can tell that's the only difference. He's twenty-two, and I was nineteen this April.

"Is it done?" he asks, the responsible married man finding his voice. I forgot to say he thinks he's going to be manager some sunny day, maybe in 1990 when it's called the Great Alexandrov and Petrooshki Tea Company or something.

What he meant was, our town is five miles from a beach, with a big summer   10
colony out on the Point, but we're right in the middle of town, and the women generally put on a shirt or shorts or something before they get out of the car into the street. And anyway these are usually women with six children and varicose veins mapping their legs and nobody, including them, could care less. As I say, we're right in the middle of town, and if you stand at our front doors you can see two banks and the Congregational church and the newspaper store and three real-estate offices and about twenty-seven old freeloaders tearing up Central Street because the sewer broke again. It's not as if we're on the Cape; we're north of Boston and there's people in this town haven't seen the ocean for twenty years.

The girls had reached the meat counter and were asking McMahon something. He pointed, they pointed, and they shuffled out of sight behind a pyramid of Diet Delight peaches. All that was left for us to see was old McMahon patting his mouth and looking after them sizing up their joints. Poor kids, I began to feel sorry for them, they couldn't help it.

Now here comes the sad part of the story, at least my family says it's sad, but I don't think it's so sad myself. The store's pretty empty, it being Thursday afternoon, so there was nothing much to do except lean on the register and wait for the girls to show up again. The whole store was like a pinball machine and I didn't know which tunnel they'd come out of. After a while they come around out of the far aisle, around the light bulbs, records at discount of the Caribbean Six or Tony Martin Sings or some such gunk you wonder they waste the wax on, sixpacks of candy bars, and plastic toys done up in cellophane that fall apart when a kid looks at them anyway. Around they come, Queenie still leading the way, and holding a little gray jar in her hand. Slots Three through Seven are unmanned and I could see her wondering between Stokes and me, but Stokesie with his usual luck draws an old party in baggy gray pants who stumbles up with four giant cans of pineapple juice (what do these bums *do* with all that pineapple juice? I've often asked myself) so the girls come to me. Queenie puts down the jar and I take it into my fingers icy cold. Kingfish Fancy Herring Snacks in Pure Sour Cream: 49¢. Now her hands are empty, not a ring or a bracelet, bare as God made them, and I wonder where the money's coming from. Still with that prim look she lifts a folded dollar bill out of the hollow at the center of her nubbled pink top. The jar went heavy in my hand. Really, I thought that was so cute.

Then everybody's luck begins to run out. Lengel comes in from haggling with a truck full of cabbages on the lot and is about to scuttle into that door marked MANAGER behind which he hides all day when the girls touch his eye. Lengel's pretty dreary, teaches Sunday school and the rest, but he doesn't miss that much. He comes over and says, "Girls, this isn't the beach."

Queenie blushes, though maybe it's just a brush of sunburn I was noticing for the first time, now that she was so close. "My mother asked me to pick up a jar of herring snacks." Her voice kind of startled me, the way voices do when you see the people first, coming out so flat and dumb yet kind of tony, too, the way it ticked over "pick up" and "snacks." All of a sudden I slid right down her voice into her living room. Her father and the other men were standing around in ice-cream coats and bow ties and the women were in sandals picking up herring snacks on toothpicks off a big glass plate and they were all holding drinks the color of water with olives and sprigs of mint in them. When my parents have somebody over they get lemonade and if it's a real racy affair Schlitz in tall glasses with "They'll Do It Every Time" cartoons stencilled on.

"That's all right," Lengel said. "But this isn't the beach." His repeating this 15 struck me as funny, as if it had just occurred to him, and he had been thinking all these years the A & P was a great big sand dune and he was the head lifeguard. He didn't like my smiling — as I say he doesn't miss much — but he concentrates on giving the girls that sad Sunday-school–superintendent stare.

Queenie's blush is no sunburn now, and the plump one in plaid, that I liked better from the back — a really sweet can — pipes up, "We weren't doing any shopping. We just came in for the one thing."

"That makes no difference," Lengel tells her, and I could see from the way his eyes went that he hadn't noticed she was wearing a two-piece before. "We want you decently dressed when you come in here."

"We *are* decent," Queenie says suddenly, her lower lip pushing, getting sore now that she remembers her place, a place from which the crowd that runs the A & P must look pretty crummy. Fancy Herring Snacks flashed in her very blue eyes.

"Girls, I don't want to argue with you. After this come in here with your shoulders covered. It's our policy." He turns his back. That's policy for you. Policy is what the kingpins want. What the others want is juvenile delinquency.

All this while, the customers had been showing up with their carts but, you 20 know, sheep, seeing a scene, they had all bunched up on Stokesie, who shook open a paper bag as gently as peeling a peach, not wanting to miss a word. I could feel in the silence everybody getting nervous, most of all Lengel, who asks me, "Sammy, have you rung up their purchase?"

I thought and said "No" but it wasn't about that I was thinking. I go through the punches, 4, 9, GROC, TOT — it's more complicated than you think, and after you do it often enough, it begins to make a little song, that you hear words to, in my case "Hello (*bing*) there, you (*gung*) hap-py *pee*-pul (*splat*)!" — the *splat* being the drawer flying out. I uncrease the bill, tenderly as you may imagine, it just having come from between the two smoothest scoops of vanilla I had ever known were there, and pass a half and a penny into her narrow pink palm, and nestle the herrings in a bag and twist its neck and hand it over, all the time thinking.

The girls, and who'd blame them, are in a hurry to get out, so I say "I quit" to Lengel enough for them to hear, hoping they'll stop and watch me, their unsuspected hero. They keep right on going, into the electric eye; the door flies open and they flicker across the lot to their car, Queenie and Plaid and Big Tall Goony-Goony (not that as raw material she was so bad), leaving me with Lengel and a kink in his eyebrow.

"Did you say something, Sammy?"

"I said I quit."

"I thought you did."

"You didn't have to embarrass them."

"It was they who were embarrassing us."

I started to say something that came out "Fiddle-de-doo." It's a saying of my grandmother's, and I know she would have been pleased.

"I don't think you know what you're saying," Lengel said.

"I know you don't," I said. "But I do." I pull the bow at the back of my apron and start shrugging it off my shoulders. A couple customers that had been heading for my slot begin to knock against each other, like scared pigs in a chute.

Lengel sighs and begins to look very patient and old and gray. He's been a friend of my parents for years. "Sammy, you don't want to do this to your Mom and Dad," he tells me. It's true, I don't. But it seems to me that once you begin a gesture it's fatal not to go through with it. I fold the apron, "Sammy" stitched in red on the pocket, and put it on the counter, and drop the bow tie on top of it. The bow tie is theirs, if you've ever wondered. "You'll feel this for the rest of your life," Lengel says, and I know that's true, too, but remembering how he made that pretty girl blush makes me so scrunchy inside I punch the No Sale tab and the machine whirs "pee-pul" and the drawer splats out. One advantage to this scene taking place in summer, I can follow this up with a clean exit, there's no fumbling around getting your coat and galoshes, I just saunter into the electric eye in my white shirt that my mother ironed the night before, and the door heaves itself open, and outside the sunshine is skating around on the asphalt.

I look around for my girls, but they're gone, of course. There wasn't anybody but some young married screaming with her children about some candy they didn't get by the door of a powder-blue Falcon station wagon. Looking back in the big windows, over the bags of peat moss and aluminum lawn furniture stacked on the pavement, I could see Lengel in my place in the slot, checking the sheep through. His face was dark gray and his back stiff, as if he'd just had an injection of iron, and my stomach kind of fell as I felt how hard the world was going to be to me hereafter.   [1961]

THINKING ABOUT THE TEXT

1. Why do you think Sammy quits? Make a list of several plausible answers.

2. What would you do if you were in Sammy's position? What would your priorities be in this situation?

3. When Sammy hears Queenie's voice, he imagines an elegant cocktail party that he contrasts to his parents' "real racy affair" (para. 14) with lemonade and beer. What does this scene say about Sammy's attitude toward the girls? Toward his own social status?

4. Some critics have objected to Sammy's comment in the last sentence of paragraph 2 about "girls' minds." Is this a sexist observation? Does the time frame of the story figure in your opinion? Should it?

5. Comment on the last paragraph. What is the significance of the young married woman? Why does Sammy mention "sheep"? Why does Sammy think the world will be hard on him? Do you agree? What does "hard" mean?

MAKING COMPARISONS

1. Are the three main characters in this cluster wiser at each story's end? Are they happier?

2. Which character's views about romance are most compatible with yours when you were, say, thirteen? With yours presently?

3. Compare the last paragraphs of "Araby" and "A & P." What attitudes do they express?

WRITING ABOUT ISSUES

1. Choose either Yellow Woman, the boy in "Araby," or Sammy, and argue that this character was or was not really in love. Support your argument with references to the text and your own cultural experience.

2. Write an essay that defends or denies the idea that romantic love is irrational. Use two of the stories from this cluster.

3. Would any of the characters in this cluster have been comfortable in the cultural context you were raised in? (Consider movies, books, TV, family narratives, and so forth in analyzing your culture.) Write a brief analysis of how well one or more of these characters would "fit in."

4. Look up information about Native American culture and the coyote stories referred to in "Yellow Woman." Do they help to explain her attitudes? Do the same for the culture of Joyce's Ireland, especially religion and romance. How about the 1950s in middle America? In a brief essay argue that each story is understood more fully when the cultural context is provided.

COMPLETING THE SELF THROUGH LOVE

DIANE ACKERMAN, "Plato: The Perfect Union"
ANDREW SULLIVAN, "The Love Bloat"

Sometimes when you meet someone and fall in love, you feel like you have known your beloved for a long time. The intellectual, emotional, and physical connections are comfortable and authentic. You seem so compatible and seem to fit together so effortlessly that it feels almost mystical. Being in love is such a heady experience that few of those affected sit down to analyze the phenomenon. But some philosophers have. Several thousand years ago, Plato (c. 428–348 B.C.E.) wondered about the complexities of love. He wrote the *Symposium*, a version of drama called a *dialogue*, in which his mentor, Socrates, argues with various other philosophers. Socrates usually gets the best lines, and many critics think Plato's own thoughts are quite similar to those of Socrates. In the *Symposium*, Plato has Aristophanes tell an amazing story about the origins of the familiar "I found my one true love." Diane Ackerman's essay explains the dialogue and gives some interesting explanations. Andrew Sullivan's essay is a criticism of our expectations about romantic love. We suspect that Sullivan would probably disagree with Ackerman's belief that couples desire to become "one appetite, one struggle, one destiny," but it seems clear that he believes popular culture's obsession with romantic love leads to permanent disappointment.

BEFORE YOU READ

Does romantic love occur naturally, or is it mostly generated by novels, films, and other such narratives? Is romantic love an addiction? Do people you know hope to be madly in love? Do you know couples who are?

DIANE ACKERMAN
Plato: The Perfect Union

Diane Ackerman was born in 1948 in Waukegan, Illinois. She graduated from Pennsylvania State University and later received an M.F.A. and a Ph.D. from Cornell University. Ackerman has received the Academy of American Poets' Lavan Award as well as grants from the National Endowment for the Arts and the Rockefeller Foundation. Critics praised her book A Natural History of the Senses *(1990) for being wide-ranging, informed, and charming. She is the author of eighteen books of poetry and nonfiction, including the recent* Cultivating Delight: A Natural History of My Garden *(2001) and a book of poems,* I Praise My Destroyer *(2000). The following essay is from* A Natural History of Love *(1994). She has taught at Columbia and Cornell and is currently a staff writer for* The New Yorker.

Proust's *Remembrance of Things Past* begins with a child waiting in bed for his mother to come and give him a good-night kiss. Sensitive and lonely, he grows anxious and unhinged, and the rest of the novel (more the mosaic of a life than a work of fiction) chronicles his attempts to bridge the gap between himself and the rest of humanity. He could not feel more separate, isolated, and alone. The passage shows the eternal quest of the child, who must learn to be separate from his mother even while he longs to reunite with her. One of the keystones of romantic love—and also of the ecstatic religion practiced by mystics—is the powerful desire to become one with the beloved.

This vision of love has its wellsprings in ancient Greek thought. To Plato, lovers are incomplete halves of a single puzzle, searching for each other in order to become whole. They are a strength forged by two weaknesses. At some point, all lovers wish to lose themselves, to merge, to become one entity. By giving up their autonomy, they find their true selves. In a world ruled by myth, Plato tried to be rational, often using myths as allegories to make a point. His investigations of love in the *Symposium* are the oldest surviving attempts to systematically understand love. In the *Symposium*, he advises people to bridle their sexual urges, and also their need to give and receive love. They should concentrate all that energy on higher goals. He understood perfectly well that people would have to struggle hard to redirect such powerful instincts; it would produce much inner warfare. When, almost 3,000 years later, Freud talks of the same struggle, using words like "sublimation" and "resistance," he is harking back to Plato, for whom love was a great predicament and a riddle. This was no doubt in part because Plato was confused about his own sexual identity; as a younger man, he wrote in praise of homosexual love, and as an older man he condemned it as an unnatural crime.

At the *Symposium*'s banquet staged in honor of Eros, Socrates—who was a teacher and companion of Plato—and his friends exchange ideas about love. Actually, Socrates' job is to poke holes in everyone else's ideas. The banqueters are not present just to praise love, but to fathom it, to dive through its waves and plumb its depths. One of their first home truths is that love is a universal human need. Not just a mythic god, or a whim, or madness, but something integral to each person's life. When it is Aristophanes' turn, he relates a fable—one that has influenced people for thousands of years since. He explains that originally there were three sexes: men, women, and a hermaphroditic combination of man and woman. These primitive beings had two heads, two arms, two sets of genitals, and so on. Threatened by their potential power, Zeus divided each one of them in half, making individual lesbians, homosexual men, and heterosexuals. But each person longed for its missing half, which it sought out, tracked down, and embraced, so that it could become one again—and thereby Aristophanes arrives at an astonishing definition of love:

> Each of us when separated, having one side only, like a flat fish, is but the indenture of a man, and he is always looking for his other half. . . . And when one of them meets with his other half, the actual half of himself, whether he be a lover of youth or a lover of another sort, the pair are lost in an amazement of love and friendship and intimacy, and will not be out of the other's sight, as I may say, even for a moment: these are the people who pass their whole lives together; yet they could not explain what they desire of one another. For the intense yearning which each of them has towards the other does not appear to be the desire of lover's intercourse, but of something else which the soul of either evidently desires and cannot tell, and of which she has only a dark and doubtful presentiment. Suppose Hephaestus,° with his instruments, were to come to the pair who are lying side by side and say to them, "What do you people want of one another?" They would be unable to explain. And suppose further, that when he saw their

Hephaestus: Greek god of fire (also called Vulcan).

perplexity he said, "Do you desire to be wholly one; always day and night to be in one another's company, for if this is what you desire, I am ready to melt you into one and let you grow together . . ." There is not a man of them who when he heard the proposal would deny or would acknowledge that this meeting and melting into one another, this becoming one instead of two, was the very expression of his ancient need. And the reason is that human nature was originally one and we were a whole, and the desire and pursuit of the whole is called love.

It is an amazing fable, saying, in effect, that each person has an ideal love waiting somewhere to be found. Not "There's a lid for every pot," as my mother has sometimes said, but that each of us has a one-and-only, and finding that person makes us whole. This romantic ideal of the perfect partner was invented by Plato. It appealed so strongly to hearts and minds that people believed it in all the following centuries, and many still believe it today. As Freud discovered, Plato took his fable from India, where some gods were bisexual. Indeed, the original human in the Upanishads° is as lonely as Adam in the Bible, and like Adam he asks for company and is pleased when a female is made from his own body. In each case, all the people of the earth are born from their union. Evolutionary biologists tell us that our ultimate ancestor almost certainly was hermaphroditic, and something about that news feels right, not just in our reason but in the part of us that yearns for the other. John Donne° wrote magnificently about this passion for oneness, which takes on a special piquancy in his poem "The Flea." One day, sweetly loitering with his mistress, he notices a flea sucking a little blood from her arm and then from his. Joyously, he observes that their blood is married inside the flea.

Why should the idea of oneness be so compelling? Love changes all the physics in the known universe of one's emotions, and redraws the boundaries between what is real and what is possible. Children often believe in magic and miracles, and when they grow up they naturally believe in the miraculous power of love. Sometimes this is depicted in myths or legends by having the lovers drink a love potion, as Tristan and Isolde° do; be stung by Cupid's arrows; be enchanted by music as Eurydice° is; or receive a reviving kiss à la Sleeping Beauty.

In many eastern and western religions, the supplicants strive for a sense of unity with God. Although this is not supposed to be an erotic coupling, saints often describe it as if it were, dwelling in orgasmic detail on the sensuality of Christ's body. Religious ecstasy and the ecstasy of lovers have much in common — the sudden awareness, the taking of vows, the plighting of troths, the all-consuming fire in the heart and flesh, the rituals leading to bliss, and, for some Christians, a cannibalistic union with the godhead by symbolically drinking his blood and eating his flesh. Whether we fall in love with a human demigod or

5

Upanishads: Texts from circa 900 B.C.E. that form the basis of Hindu religion.
John Donne: British poet (1572–1631).
Tristan and Isolde: Characters in a German opera (1865) by Richard Wagner celebrating romantic love.
Eurydice: In Greek mythology Orpheus tries in vain to rescue his wife, Eurydice, from Hades.

with a deity, we feel that they can return us to a primordial state of oneness, that then our inner electric can run its full circuit, that we can at last be whole.

How bizarre it is to wish to blend blood and bones with someone. People cannot actually literally become one, of course; it's a physical impossibility. The idea is preposterous. We are separate organisms. Unless we are Siamese twins, we are not merged with another. Why should we feel incomplete, anyway? Why believe that uniting our body and thoughts and fate with another person's will cure our sense of loneliness? Wouldn't it make more sense to believe that when love brings two people together they are a community of two, not a compound of one? The idea of merging is so irrational, so contrary to common sense and observation, that its roots must strike deep into our psyche. Because a child is born of a mother, and lives as a separate entity, we think of the child as an individual. But in biological terms that is not precisely true. The child is an organic part of the mother that is expelled at birth, but it shares much of her biology, personality, even scent. The only and absolute perfect union of two is when a baby hangs suspended in its mother's womb, like a tiny madman in a padded cell, attached to her, feeling her blood and hormones and moods play through its body, feeling her feelings. After that perfect, pendent, dependent union, birth is an amputation, and the child like a limb looking to attach itself to the rest of its body. I am not saying this consciously occurs to anyone, but that it may explain the osmotic yearning we all feel, at one time or another, to blend our heart and body and fluids with someone else's. Only the thinnest rind of skin stands between us, only events slender as neurons. Only the fermenting mash of personality keeps us from crossing the boundary that organisms cherish to become one appetite, one struggle, one destiny. Then, when we finally reach that pinnacle, we feel more than whole: we feel limitless.   [1994]

THINKING ABOUT THE TEXT

1. Do you think Ackerman is making a claim about true love or the about the desire for wholeness? What support does she provide? Is there an opposition? Does she give it?

2. Ackerman suggests that the desire for wholeness is fairly common. Have you felt something similar to an "osmotic yearning" (para. 7)? Is it primarily physical or spiritual?

3. Ackerman begins with an anecdote from Marcel Proust's *Remembrance of Things Past*, which seems to describe something different from romantic love. Does she justify opening in this way?

4. Many of the essay's examples are from literature. Should Ackerman have given more factual examples? Should she have consulted scientists? Sociologists? Psychologists?

5. At the end, Ackerman suggests that the pinnacle can be, and is, reached. Do you agree? How can we account for so many failed relationships then? Should we keep trying to find our perfect mate no matter how disenchanted we are?

ANDREW SULLIVAN
The Love Bloat

A political conservative and a Roman Catholic who has written about having AIDS, Andrew Sullivan (b. 1963) defies political categorization. He has argued for full equality for homosexuals, especially in marriage and the military, and yet has received much criticism for arguing that the AIDS epidemic is over, although this may be an oversimplification of his views. Born and reared in England, he won a scholarship to Oxford University in the early 1980s. While at Oxford, he became the youngest ever president of the Oxford Debating Society. He subsequently came to the United States on an academic fellowship to Harvard University, where he earned graduate degrees in public administration and political science. While there he worked as an intern for New Republic *magazine, where he soon became its youngest ever full-time associate editor. He moved on to become editor-in-chief in 1991. Sullivan writes extensively and has earned numerous journalism awards. His books include* Virtually Normal: An Argument about Homosexuality *(1996),* Same-Sex Marriage: Pro and Con *(1997), and* Love Undetectable *(1998). The article reprinted here is from the* New York Times Magazine *in an issue published just before Valentine's Day in 2001.*

I know this isn't exactly the week to say it, but can we please ease up on our secular cult of romantic love?

As almost any serious person before the nineteenth century would have told you, the concept is a crock. To paraphrase Aristotle, it's a benighted attempt to found friendship on beauty. To quote Montaigne, it is "impetuous and fickle, a feverish flame." Shakespeare got this, too. His transcendent celebration of love, *Romeo and Juliet*, begins with Romeo's obsessive infatuation with a young woman he can barely let out of his sight. That woman is called Rosalind. Then Romeo meets Juliet, and Rosalind has about the longevity of an Internet start-up. Love is like that, Shakespeare seems to imply. It comes; it goes. If taken too seriously, it kills. Remember what happened to the star-crossed lovers? Compared with true friendship or patriotism or maternal love, romance is a joke of a feeling. Yet this joke, our culture tells us, is now the secret to true and lasting happiness.

For a while, there was reason to hope that we were recovering from this blight. The most innovative popular music of our time — hip-hop — has largely jettisoned the romantic premise of the bulk of the genre. The world learned a sobering lesson when the dreamy English princess turned into a bulimic neurotic before meeting an untimely death. Greater sex equality has helped discredit the idea that no woman is complete without a man. For good measure, our last president had a marriage that, whatever else it was founded on, had little to do with romance. But then the romance addiction returns. Britney clones go on dates in kindergarten. Boy pop groups parade as romantic fantasies for a new generation of screaming girls. The political quest for equal marriage rights for homosexuals merges into a cultural campaign for gay romance. Ronald Reagan's love letters sell briskly. *The Wedding Planner* does oddly well at the box office. As sex makes something of a comeback in the general culture—*Temptation Island*, anyone?—it needs the fig leaf of romance as much as it ever did to maintain a legitimate air.

But ever wonder why divorce rates are so high? The real culprit isn't some kind of moral collapse. It's excessive expectations, driven and fueled by the civic religion of romance. For a lucky few, infatuation sometimes does lead to lasting love, and love to family, and family to all the other virtues our preachers and politicians regularly celebrate. For the other 99 percent of us, relationships are, at best, useful economic bargains and, if we're lucky, successful sexual transactions—better than the alternative, which has long been close to social death. But thanks to the civic religion of romance, we constantly expect more and quit what we have in search of more. For the essence of romantic love is not the company of a lover but the pursuit. It's all promise with the delivery of the postal service.

O.K., so maybe I just broke up with someone, and that's why this year I feel   5
about Valentine's Day the way some people feel about Christmas. Its main effect is not to foster warm wonderful feelings in that minuscule number of people who happen to be in love this week but to engender abiding depression, jealousy, and loneliness in the rest of us who aren't.

That this cult should reach its most frenetic expression in modern democracies is no surprise. The elevation of romance into a soul-saving experience was devised by Rousseau. As Allan Bloom pointed out, Rousseau saw bourgeois love as a salve for the empty emotional center of restrained, law-bound societies. He wanted to substitute the passion of people for truth and honor and power with something just as absorbing but nowhere near as dangerous. Why not love? It flatters our narcissism. It diverts us with phony adrenaline, teases us with jealousy, hooks us with sex. It is the means by which our genes persuade our bodies to reproduce. It is so diverting that we tend to forget more pressing questions, like what to believe in or strive for. More important, in a culture in which sex is increasingly divorced from procreation, it gives copulation a new kind of purpose, apart from pleasure. It sacralizes it, dignifies it, elevates it. Love, we're told, conquers all.

The trouble is, of course, it doesn't. The love celebrated on Valentine's Day conquers nothing. It contains neither the friendship nor civility that makes marriage successful. It fulfills the way a drug fulfills—requiring new infusions to sustain the high. It prettifies sex, but doesn't remove sex's danger or lust. And by elevating it to a personal and cultural panacea, we suffer the permanent disappointment of excessive expectations, with all of their doleful social consequences. Less—affection, caring, friendship, the small favors of a husband for a wife after thirty years of marriage—is far more. And by knocking romance off its Hallmark pedestal, we might go some small way to restoring the importance and dignity of these less glamorous but more fulfilling relationships. "If love were all," Noel Coward once wrote, "I should be lonely." But it isn't. And nobody else's Valentine card should persuade you that loneliness is the only alternative.

[2001]

THINKING ABOUT THE TEXT

1. What is Sullivan's argument about romantic love? Do you agree with some of his provocative assertions, such as "If taken too seriously, it kills" (para. 2), "the civic religion of romance" fuels high divorce rates (para. 4), and it's all "promise with the delivery of the postal service" (para. 4)?

2. Is Sullivan's persona effective? Do you trust him? Does he give enough balanced attention to the opposition? Are you depressed, jealous, and lonely when you are not romantically involved?

3. How do you respond to such ideas that love is a blight, a joke, a salve for an empty emotional center, that it "diverts us with phony adrenaline, teases us with jealousy, hooks us with sex" (para. 6)?

4. How do you think Sullivan might imagine the ideal marriage? What is the "Hallmark pedestal" (para. 7)?

5. Would you rather have six good, long-standing friends or one good lover? Do you agree that "greater sex equality has helped discredit the idea that no woman is complete without a man" (para. 3)? If so, is this progress?

MAKING COMPARISONS

1. Is there a way Sullivan might agree with Ackerman's notion of our "passion for oneness" (para. 4)? Or is he unequivocally opposed to such an idea?

2. How would you compare the tone of each narrator's persona? Is one more effective than the other in persuading you? In making you think about your views?

3. Both writers refer to canonical writers and thinkers. Were you impressed? Are they effective allusions? Might it depend on the audience? Who is the audience for each piece?

WRITING ABOUT ISSUES

1. Argue against Sullivan's critique of romantic love by using some of the claims that Ackerman makes.

2. Argue that Sullivan is right in railing against Valentine's Day and the Hallmark pedestal.

3. Interview a dozen people your age, asking them if they would choose "affection, caring, and friendship" (para. 7) over a passionate, romantic relationship. Does the length of the relationship matter?

4. Using some novels and films you know, agree or disagree with Sullivan's "Love is like that. . . . It comes; it goes. If taken too seriously, it kills" (para. 2).

COURTSHIP

CHRISTOPHER MARLOWE, "The Passionate Shepherd to His Love"
SIR WALTER RALEIGH, "The Nymph's Reply to the Shepherd"
ANDREW MARVELL, "To His Coy Mistress"
T. S. ELIOT, "The Love Song of J. Alfred Prufrock"

Our language and literature are filled with references to the smooth talker, the charming seducer, the insincere young man with a good line hoping to get "lucky." But our plays, poems, novels, songs, and films are also filled with images of truly passionate lovers, Romeos and Juliets who act impulsively and follow their heart's desire without heeding the consequences. In matters of the heart, we seem ambivalent about following emotion or reason, impulse or logic. While often suspicious of idealized romantic longing, we also seem to root for those who risk all for love.

Telling the difference between an honest plea and a dishonest ploy is not easy. Even when we can tell the difference, knowing whether to respond positively or not is usually problematic. The first three poems deal with lovers facing this dilemma. The passionate shepherd is asking a young woman to be his lover. Is he sincere? Is he practical? In Raleigh's poem, the young woman responds with a highly conditional answer. Has she thrown away a choice for happiness or has she been judicious? Is Marvell interested in love or sex? Does he expect her to treat his "arguments" seriously? Is he madly in love or an opportunist? The last poem is a kind of modern counterpoint to these traditional love poems. Prufrock seems to have had lovers but is now wary and unsure of himself. He doesn't expect much, and, as a result, his heart will probably remain tentative.

BEFORE YOU READ

What decisions of the heart have you made that were not entirely logical? Do you feel that women are more susceptible to romantic promises than men, or is this just a stereotype?

CHRISTOPHER MARLOWE
The Passionate Shepherd to His Love

Best known for turning dramatic blank verse into high art in his play Doctor Faustus, *Marlowe (1564–1593) was also a major poet and one of the most learned and controversial writers of his time. He led a tempestuous and dangerous life and was often accused of being an atheist, a serious charge at the time. He was killed in a bar fight at the age of twenty-nine, the circumstances of which are still being debated. The official story that he was stabbed over the tavern bill is dubious given the informers, spies, and conspirators involved in the fight. Nevertheless, Marlowe's reputation as an Elizabethan dramatist is second only to Shakespeare's. The fol-*

*lowing poem, published posthumously, is his only surviving lyric and suggests his
impulsive attitude to live for the moment.*

Come live with me and be my love,
And we will all the pleasure prove
That valleys, groves, hills, and fields,
Woods, or steepy mountain yields.

And we will sit upon the rocks,   5
Seeing the shepherds feed their flocks,
By shallow rivers to whose falls
Melodious birds sing madrigals.

And I will make thee beds of roses
And a thousand fragrant posies,
A cap of flowers, and a kirtle°   10
Embroidered all with leaves of myrtle;

A gown made of the finest wool
Which from our pretty lambs we pull;
Fair lined slippers for the cold,
With buckles of the purest gold;   15

A belt of straw and ivy buds,
With coral clasps and amber studs:
And if these pleasures may thee move,
Come live with me, and be my love.   20

The shepherd swains shall dance and sing
For thy delight each May morning:
If these delights thy mind may move,
Then live with me and be my love.   [c. 1599]

11 **kirtle:** Dress or skirt.

THINKING ABOUT THE TEXT

1. As an argument, how persuasive do you think the shepherd's case is?
   Might his argument charm his listener? Might the speaker be more
   sophisticated than one would expect?

2. Marlowe is writing in the pastoral tradition, which highlights youth, optimism, and eternal love. Might Marlowe be dealing with a serious topic
   behind these idealized fancies?

3. What elements of reality or human nature does the speaker omit from his
   plea?

4. Carpe diem ("seize the day") was a popular attitude in Marlowe's day, as
   this poem suggests. Is it today? Can you give examples from popular culture? What are the advantages of adopting such an attitude? The disadvantages?

5. Do you think that love conquers all? Is sex a necessary prelude to love? Do you think love is more, or less, possible in certain settings — for example, at the beach, in the country, or perhaps in prison or a hospital? Does being in love depend on one's economic or psychological well-being?

SIR WALTER RALEIGH
The Nymph's Reply to the Shepherd

Sir Walter Raleigh (1554–1618) was an English soldier and explorer as well as a writer. He was a favorite of Elizabeth I, even though his outspokenness and interest in skeptical philosophy made him many enemies at court. In 1585, Raleigh sent the first of two groups of settlers to Roanoke Island, the second of which vanished without a trace by 1591. After he led an unsuccessful expedition to Guyana in search of gold, he was imprisoned in the Tower of London and eventually executed for trying to overthrow James I. The following poem exhibits his practical and skeptical bent.

If all the world and love were young,
And truth in every shepherd's tongue,
These pretty pleasures might me move
To live with thee and be thy love.

Time drives the flocks from field to fold   5
When rivers rage and rocks grow cold,
And Philomel° becometh dumb;
The rest complains of cares to come.

The flowers do fade, and wanton fields
To wayward winter reckoning yields;   10
A honey tongue, a heart of gall,
Is fancy's spring, but sorrow's fall.

Thy gowns, thy shoes, thy beds of roses,
Thy cap, thy kirtle, and thy posies
Soon break, soon wither, soon forgotten —   15
In folly ripe, in reason rotten.

Thy belt of straw and ivy buds,
Thy coral clasps and amber studs,
All these in me no means can move
To come to thee and be thy love.   20

But could youth last and love still breed,
Had joys no date° nor age no need,
Then these delights my mind might move
To live with thee and be thy love.   [1600]

7 **Philomel:** The nightingale.   22 **date:** End.

THINKING ABOUT THE TEXT

1. How might you consider this poem a refusal for a sexual affair? What arguments are put forth as a refutation?
2. Read between the lines. What might convince the speaker to be the shepherd's love? Or is that impossible?
3. What is the speaker's tone? Do you hear hostility or contempt?
4. What does Raleigh mean in line 16 by "In folly ripe, in reason rotten"?
5. What part does gender play in this poem? Is the speaker being stereotyped?

MAKING COMPARISONS

1. In what specific ways is Raleigh offering a refutation of Marlowe's poem? Is it effective?
2. What aspects of nature does Marlowe focus on? Raleigh?
3. How would you compare the attitudes of the two speakers in these poems? Is this a debate between man and woman? In what ways could this be both true and false?

ANDREW MARVELL
To His Coy Mistress

Andrew Marvell (1621–1678) was famous in his own time as an adroit politician and a writer of satire, but modern readers admire him for the style and content of his lyric, metaphysical poetry. Born into a Protestant family, Marvell was tolerant of Catholicism from a young age, and his willingness to somehow circumvent the religious prejudices of seventeenth-century England allowed his continued success. He traveled to Holland, France, Italy, and Spain — possibly to avoid the English civil war as a young man and undoubtedly to spy for England in later years. He tutored Cromwell's ward and later served on his Council of State, but was influential enough during the Restoration to get his fellow poet and mentor, John Milton, released from prison. Although admired by the Romantic poets of the early nineteenth century, Andrew Marvell's poetry (much of it published after his death) was revived in the twentieth century by T. S. Eliot and has been widely read for its ironic approach to the conventions of love.

Had we but world enough, and time,
This coyness, lady, were no crime.
We would sit down, and think which way
To walk, and pass our long love's day.
Thou by the Indian Ganges'° side   5

5 **Ganges:** A river in India sacred to the Hindus.

Shouldst rubies find; I by the tide
Of Humber° would complain.° I would
Love you ten years before the Flood,
And you should, if you please, refuse
Till the conversion of the Jews.   10
My vegetable love should grow°
Vaster than empires, and more slow;
An hundred years should go to praise
Thine eyes and on thy forehead gaze,
Two hundred to adore each breast,   15
But thirty thousand to the rest:
An age at least to every part,
And the last age should show your heart.
For, lady, you deserve this state,
Nor would I love at lower rate.   20
    But at my back I always hear
Time's wingèd chariot hurrying near;
And yonder all before us lie
Deserts of vast eternity.
Thy beauty shall no more be found,   25
Nor in thy marble vault shall sound
My echoing song; then worms shall try
That long preserved virginity,
And your quaint honor turn to dust,
And into ashes all my lust.   30
The grave's a fine and private place,
But none, I think, do there embrace.
    Now, therefore, while the youthful hue
Sits on thy skin like morning dew,
And while thy willing soul transpires°   35
At every pore with instant fires,
Now let us sport us while we may,
And now, like amorous birds of prey,
Rather at once our time devour
Than languish in his slow-chapped° power.   40
Let us roll all our strength and all
Our sweetness up into one ball,
And tear our pleasures with rough strife
Thorough° the iron gates of life.
Thus, though we cannot make our sun   45
Stand still, yet we will make him run.   [1681]

---

7 **Humber:** An estuary that flows through Marvell's native town, Hull.   **complain:** Sing love
songs.   11 **My vegetable love . . . grow:** A slow, insensible growth, like that of a vegetable.
35 **transpires:** Breathes forth.   40 **slow-chapped:** Slow-jawed.   44 **Thorough:** Through.

THINKING ABOUT THE TEXT

1. Considered as both an intellectual and an emotional argument, what is the narrator's goal and what specific claims does he make? Are they convincing? Do you think they were in 1681? Do you think women three hundred years ago worried about virginity? Why?

2. What does this poem say about the needs of Marvell's audience? What assumptions about women does the poem make?

3. How many sections does this poem have? What is the purpose of each? How is the concluding couplet in each related to that section? Is the rhyme scheme related to the meaning of these couplets?

4. Is the speaker passionate? Sincere? How do you make such a decision? Do you look at his language or his message?

5. Some feminist readers see in the last ten lines a kind of indirect threat, a suggestion of force through the use of violent images. Is this a plausible reading? If this is the case, what do you now think of the narrator's pleading?

MAKING COMPARISONS

1. Which of the male speakers seems the most trustworthy to you?

2. Do Marlowe and Marvell have the same goal?

3. How do you think the nymph would answer Marvell?

T. S. ELIOT

The Love Song of J. Alfred Prufrock

One of the most respected intellectuals of his time, Thomas Stearns Eliot (1888–1965) was a poet, playwright (Murder in the Cathedral)*, and critic* (The Sacred Wood)*. His poem "The Waste Land" (1922), considered a modernist masterpiece, is perhaps this century's most influential poem. The long-running Broadway play* Cats *is based on some of Eliot's lighter poems. Born in America and educated at Harvard, Eliot lived his mature life in England. He was awarded the Nobel Prize for literature in 1948.*

> *S'io credesse che mia risposta fosse*
> *A persona che mai tornasse al mondo,*
> *Questa fiamma staria senza più scosse.*
> *Ma perciocchè giammai di questo fondo*
> *Non tornò vivo alcun, s'i'odo il vero,*
> *Senza tema d'infamia ti rispondo.*°

EPIGRAPH: *S'io . . . rispondo:* In Dante's *Inferno,* a sufferer in hell says, "If I thought I was talking to someone who might return to earth, this flame would cease; but if what I have heard is true, no one does return; therefore, I can speak to you without fear of infamy."

Let us go then, you and I,
When the evening is spread out against the sky
Like a patient etherized upon a table;
Let us go, through certain half-deserted streets,
The muttering retreats   5
Of restless nights in one-night cheap hotels
And sawdust restaurants with oyster-shells:
Streets that follow like a tedious argument
Of insidious intent
To lead you to an overwhelming question . . .   10

Oh, do not ask, "What is it?"
Let us go and make our visit.

In the room the women come and go
Talking of Michelangelo.

    The yellow fog that rubs its back upon the window panes,   15
The yellow smoke that rubs its muzzle on the window panes
Licked its tongue into the corners of the evening,
Lingered upon the pools that stand in drains,
Let fall upon its back the soot that falls from chimneys,
Slipped by the terrace, made a sudden leap,   20
And seeing that it was a soft October night,
Curled once about the house, and fell asleep.

    And indeed there will be time°
For the yellow smoke that slides along the street,
Rubbing its back upon the window panes;   25
There will be time, there will be time
To prepare a face to meet the faces that you meet;
There will be time to murder and create,
And time for all the works and days° of hands
That lift and drop a question on your plate: 30
Time for you and time for me,
And time yet for a hundred indecisions,
And for a hundred visions and revisions,
Before the taking of a toast and tea.

In the room the women come and go   35
Talking of Michelangelo.

    And indeed there will be time
To wonder, "Do I dare?" and, "Do I dare?" —
Time to turn back and descend the stair,
With a bald spot in the middle of my hair —   40

---

23 there will be time: An allusion to Ecclesiastes 3:1–8: "To everything there is a season, and a time to every purpose under heaven." **29 works and days:** Hesiod's eighth century B.C.E. poem gave practical advice.

(They will say: "How his hair is growing thin!")
My morning coat, my collar mounting firmly to the chin,
My necktie rich and modest, but asserted by a simple pin —
(They will say: "But how his arms and legs are thin!")
Do I dare   45
Disturb the universe?
In a minute there is time
For decisions and revisions which a minute will reverse.

    For I have known them all already, known them all:
Have known the evenings, mornings, afternoons,   50
I have measured out my life with coffee spoons;
I know the voices dying with a dying fall
Beneath the music from a farther room.
    So how should I presume?

    And I have known the eyes already, known them all —   55
The eyes that fix you in a formulated phrase.
And when I am formulated, sprawling on a pin,
When I am pinned and wriggling on the wall,
Then how should I begin
To spit out all the butt-ends of my days and ways?   60
    And how should I presume?

    And I have known the arms already, known them all —
Arms that are braceleted and white and bare
(But in the lamplight, downed with light brown hair!)
    Is it perfume from a dress   65
    That makes me so digress?
Arms that lie along a table, or wrap about a shawl.
    And should I then presume?
    And how should I begin?

    Shall I say, I have gone at dusk through narrow streets,   70
And watched the smoke that rises from the pipes
Of lonely men in shirtsleeves, leaning out of windows? . . .

I should have been a pair of ragged claws
Scuttling across the floors of silent seas.

    And the afternoon, the evening, sleeps so peacefully!   75
Smoothed by long fingers,
Asleep . . . tired . . . or it malingers,
Stretched on the floor, here beside you and me.
Should I, after tea and cakes and ices,
Have the strength to force the moment to its crisis?   80
But though I have wept and fasted, wept and prayed,
Though I have seen my head (grown slightly bald) brought in upon a platter,°

---

82 **head . . . platter:** Like John the Baptist (Matt. 14:1–12).

I am no prophet — and here's no great matter;
I have seen the moment of my greatness flicker,
And I have seen the eternal Footman hold my coat, and snicker,   85
     And in short, I was afraid.

     And would it have been worth it, after all,
After the cups, the marmalade, the tea,
Among the porcelain, among some talk of you and me,
Would it have been worth while   90
To have bitten off the matter with a smile,
To have squeezed the universe into a ball°
To roll it toward some overwhelming question,
To say: "I am Lazarus,° come from the dead,
Come back to tell you all, I shall tell you all" —   95
If one, settling a pillow by her head,
     Should say: "That is not what I meant at all;
     That is not it, at all."

     And would it have been worth it, after all,
Would it have been worth while,   100
After the sunsets and the dooryards and the sprinkled streets,
After the novels, after the teacups, after the skirts that trail along the floor —
And this, and so much more? —
It is impossible to say just what I mean!
But as if a magic lantern threw the nerves in patterns on a screen: 105
Would it have been worth while
If one, settling a pillow or throwing off a shawl,
And turning toward the window, should say:
     "That is not it at all,
     That is not what I meant, at all."   110

No! I am not Prince Hamlet, nor was meant to be;
Am an attendant lord,° one that will do
To swell a progress,° start a scene or two
Advise the prince: withal, an easy tool,
Deferential, glad to be of use,   115
Politic, cautious, and meticulous;
Full of high sentence, but a bit obtuse;
At times, indeed, almost ridiculous —
Almost, at times, the Fool.

I grow old . . . I grow old . . .   120
I shall wear the bottoms of my trowsers rolled.

     Shall I part my hair behind?° Do I dare to eat a peach?

---

92 squeezed . . . ball: See lines 41–42 of Marvell's "To His Coy Mistress" (p. 850).   **94 I am
Lazarus:** Raised from the dead by Jesus.   **112 attendant lord:** Like Polonius in Shakespeare's
Hamlet.   **113 progress:** state procession.   **121–122 trowsers rolled . . . part my hair behind:**
The latest fashion.

I shall wear white flannel trowsers, and walk upon the beach.
I have heard the mermaids singing, each to each.

I do not think that they will sing to me.   125

I have seen them riding seaward on the waves,
Combing the white hair of the waves blown back
When the wind blows the water white and black.

We have lingered in the chambers of the sea
By seagirls wreathed with seaweed red and brown,   130
Till human voices wake us, and we drown.   [1917]

THINKING ABOUT THE TEXT

1. To what is Prufrock referring when he says, "Do I dare?" (line 38)? How about "that is not it, at all" (lines 98, 109)? What is Prufrock so anxious about?

2. Prufrock seems to characterize himself quite severely in lines 111 to 119. How would you describe him? Do you know people like him?

3. Do you think the imagery of the opening stanza sets the right tone for Prufrock's journey? How would you describe the tone — ironic, self-mocking, depressed, overly cautious, too self-conscious?

4. Is Prufrock making an argument against getting involved in a romance? What evidence does he use to support his argument?

5. Critics have given widely different interpretations of the two couplets, "In the room the women come and go / Talking of Michelangelo" (lines 13–14) and "I should have been a pair of ragged claws / Scuttling across the floors of silent seas" (lines 73–74). What do you think these lines mean?

MAKING COMPARISONS

1. What would Prufrock think of Marlowe's and Marvell's poems?

2. Some critics suggest that line 92 of "Prufrock" is an allusion to lines 41 and 42 of "To His Coy Mistress." Some critics also claim that line 26 refers to "To His Coy Mistress." Do you think so? What might be the point of referring to this famous poem?

3. Do you think Eliot's poem is a kind of modern refutation of romantic love à la Marlowe and Marvell?

WRITING ABOUT ISSUES

1. Some critics see Marlowe's poem as a representation of idealistic romanticism and Raleigh's poem as one of realism and practicality. Write a brief thematic comparison of these two poems arguing for the position that is more like your own.

2. Argue either that the speaker in Marlowe's or Marvell's poem has the right approach or that Prufrock's attitude is more typical and realistic.

3. Write a personal narrative about a time when you were (or were not) susceptible to a "carpe diem" argument.

4. There have been other replies to Marlowe's poem. Locate William Carlos Williams's "Raleigh Was Right," for example, and write a brief analysis of his refutations.

THE APPEARANCE OF LOVE: A COLLECTION OF WRITINGS BY KATE CHOPIN

KATE CHOPIN, "The Storm"
KATE CHOPIN, "The Story of an Hour"
KATE CHOPIN, "Désirée's Baby"

People at weddings often remark how happy and in love the bridal couple looks. But people can *appear* to be in love. Indeed, psychologists tell us that someone can play a loving role for years, at times actually believing the part he or she is playing. To a limited extent, this is true for all of us. We learn what it means to be in love from watching movies, reading books, and absorbing other clues from our culture. A man proposing marriage on one knee is just one cultural notion of how we should act when we are in love.

Suppose a woman acts lovingly toward her husband and then has a passionate sexual encounter with an old boyfriend. Which is her true self? Which is the appearance and which the reality? Sometimes a society's conventions about marriage are so strong that men and women have little choice but to conform. If we were to judge the behavior of a woman toward her husband a hundred years ago, we might not get an accurate reading of how much she loved him. Likewise, people can believe their lives to be quite harmonious until they find out that one of them has a surprising past. William Shakespeare wrote of love that would not change when difficulties arose, but such is not always the case. Does that mean that one's love is not deep enough? Or when a loved one does not live up to expectations, is it natural to readjust one's heart?

The following three stories take on controversial topics. Kate Chopin was not a conformist thinker, and her stories are filled with views of desire, love, and relationships meant to provoke her late-nineteenth-century readers. Indeed, they continue to provoke audiences today.

BEFORE YOU READ

Would you change your mind about loving someone if you found out he or she was having an affair? If they lied about their religion or their race? Is it possible to love someone and at the same time want to be free?

(Missouri Historical Society, St. Louis. Negative Por C-146. Kate Chopin carte de visite photograph by J. J. Scholten, 1869.)

KATE CHOPIN
The Storm

Kate Chopin (1851–1904) is known for her evocations of the unique, multiethnic Creole and Cajun societies of late-nineteenth-century Louisiana; however, her characters transcend the limitation of regional genre writing, striking a particularly resonant note among feminist readers. Born Katherine O'Flaherty in St. Louis, Missouri, she married Oscar Chopin in 1870 and went to live with him in New Orleans and on his Mississippi River plantation. Her short stories were collected in Bayou Folk *(1894) and* A Night in Acadie *(1897). Chopin's last novel,* The Awakening, *scandalized readers at the time of its publication in 1899 because of its frank portrayal of female sexuality in the context of an extramarital affair. Long ignored by readers and critics, her work was revived in the 1960s and continues to provoke heated discussion of her female characters: Are they women who seek freedom in the only ways available to them, or are they willing participants in their own victimhood?*

"The Storm" was written about 1898, but because of its provocative content,
Chopin probably did not even try to find a magazine that would risk the publicity.

1

The leaves were so still that even Bibi thought it was going to rain. Bobinôt,
who was accustomed to converse on terms of perfect equality with his little son,
called the child's attention to certain sombre clouds that were rolling with sinister
intention from the west, accompanied by a sullen, threatening roar. They were
at Friedheimer's store and decided to remain there till the storm had passed.
They sat within the door on two empty kegs. Bibi was four years old and looked
very wise.

"Mama'll be 'fraid, yes," he suggested with blinking eyes.

"She'll shut the house. Maybe she got Sylvie helpin' her this evenin'," Bobinôt responded reassuringly.

"No; she ent got Sylvie. Sylvie was helpin' her yistiday," piped Bibi.

Bobinôt arose and going across to the counter purchased a can of shrimps, of   5
which Calixta was very fond. Then he returned to his perch on the keg and sat
stolidly holding the can of shrimps while the storm burst. It shook the wooden
store and seemed to be ripping great furrows in the distant field. Bibi laid his little
hand on his father's knee and was not afraid.

2

Calixta, at home, felt no uneasiness for their safety. She sat at a side window
sewing furiously on a sewing machine. She was greatly occupied and did not
notice the approaching storm. But she felt very warm and often stopped to mop
her face on which the perspiration gathered in beads. She unfastened her white
sacque at the throat. It began to grow dark, and suddenly realizing the situation
she got up hurriedly and went about closing windows and doors.

Out on the small front gallery she had hung Bobinôt's Sunday clothes to air
and she hastened out to gather them before the rain fell. As she stepped outside,
Alcée Laballière rode in at the gate. She had not seen him very often since her
marriage, and never alone. She stood there with Bobinôt's coat in her hands, and
the big rain drops began to fall. Alcée rode his horse under the shelter of a side
projection where the chickens had huddled and there were plows and a harrow
piled up in the corner.

"May I come and wait on your gallery till the storm is over, Calixta?" he
asked.

"Come 'long in, M'sieur Alcée."

His voice and her own startled her as if from a trance, and she seized   10
Bobinôt's vest. Alcée, mounting to the porch, grabbed the trousers and snatched
Bibi's braided jacket that was about to be carried away by a sudden gust of wind.
He expressed an intention to remain outside, but it was soon apparent that he
might as well have been out in the open: the water beat in upon the boards in
driving sheets, and he went inside, closing the door after him. It was even necessary to put something beneath the door to keep the water out.

"My! what a rain! It's good two years sence it rain' like that," exclaimed Calixta as she rolled up a piece of bagging and Alcée helped her to thrust it beneath the crack.

She was a little fuller of figure than five years before when she married; but she had lost nothing of her vivacity. Her blue eyes still retained their melting quality; and her yellow hair, dishevelled by the wind and rain, kinked more stubbornly than ever about her ears and temples.

The rain beat upon the low, shingled roof with a force and clatter that threatened to break an entrance and deluge them there. They were in the dining room — the sitting room — the general utility room. Adjoining was her bed room, with Bibi's couch along side her own. The door stood open, and the room with its white, monumental bed, its closed shutters, looked dim and mysterious.

Alcée flung himself into a rocker and Calixta nervously began to gather up from the floor the lengths of a cotton sheet which she had been sewing.

"It this keeps up, *Dieu sait*° if the levees goin' to stan' it!" she exclaimed.   15

"What have you got to do with the levees?"

"I got enough to do! An' there's Bobinôt with Bibi out in that storm — if he only didn' left Friedheimer's!"

"Let us hope, Calixta, that Bobinôt's got sense enough to come in out of a cyclone."

She went and stood at the window with a greatly disturbed look on her face. She wiped the frame that was clouded with moisture. It was stiflingly hot. Alcée got up and joined her at the window, looking over her shoulder. The rain was coming down in sheets obscuring the view of far-off cabins and enveloping the distant wood in a gray mist. The playing of the lightning was incessant. A bolt struck a tall chinaberry tree at the edge of the field. It filled all visible space with a blinding glare and the crash seemed to invade the very boards they stood upon.

Calixta put her hands to her eyes, and with a cry, staggered backward. Alcée's   20
arm encircled her, and for an instant he drew her close and spasmodically to him.

"*Bonté!*"° she cried, releasing herself from his encircling arm and retreating from the window, "the house'll go next! If I only knew w'ere Bibi was!" She would not compose herself; she would not be seated. Alcée clasped her shoulders and looked into her face. The contact of her warm, palpitating body when he had unthinkingly drawn her into his arm, had aroused all the old-time infatuation and desire for her flesh.

"Calixta," he said, "don't be frightened. Nothing can happen. The house is too low to be struck, with so many tall trees standing about. There! aren't you going to be quiet? say, aren't you?" He pushed her hair back from her face that was warm and steaming. Her lips were as red and moist as pomegranate seed. Her white neck and a glimpse of her full, firm bosom disturbed him powerfully. As she glanced up at him the fear in her liquid blue eyes had given place to a drowsy gleam that unconsciously betrayed a sensuous desire. He looked down into her eyes and there was nothing for him to do but to gather her lips in a kiss. It reminded him of Assumption.

Dieu sait: God knows.   *Bonté:* Goodness.

"Do you remember—in Assumption, Calixta?" he asked in a low voice broken by passion. Oh! she remembered; for in Assumption he had kissed her and kissed and kissed her; until his senses would well nigh fail, and to save her he would resort to a desperate flight. If she was not an immaculate dove in those days, she was still inviolate; a passionate creature whose very defenselessness had made her defense, against which his honor forbade him to prevail. Now—well, now—her lips seemed in a manner free to be tasted, as well as her round, white throat and her whiter breasts.

They did not heed the crashing torrents, and the roar of the elements made her laugh as she lay in his arms. She was a revelation in that dim, mysterious chamber; as white as the couch she lay upon. Her firm, elastic flesh that was knowing for the first time its birthright, was like a creamy lily that the sun invites to contribute its breath and perfume to the undying life of the world.

The generous abundance of her passion, without guile or trickery, was like a   25
white flame which penetrated and found response in depths of his own sensuous nature that had never yet been reached.

When he touched her breasts they gave themselves up in quivering ecstasy, inviting his lips. Her mouth was a fountain of delight. And when he possessed her, they seemed to swoon together at the very borderland of life's mystery.

He stayed cushioned upon her, breathless, dazed, enervated, with his heart beating like a hammer upon her. With one hand she clasped his head, her lips lightly touching his forehead. The other hand stroked with a soothing rhythm his muscular shoulders.

The growl of the thunder was distant and passing away. The rain beat softly upon the shingles, inviting them to drowsiness and sleep. But they dared not yield.

The rain was over; and the sun was turning the glistening green world into a palace of gems. Calixta, on the gallery, watched Alcée ride away. He turned and smiled at her with a beaming face; and she lifted her pretty chin in the air and laughed aloud.

3

Bobinôt and Bibi, trudging home, stopped without at the cistern to make   30
themselves presentable.

"My! Bibi, w'at will yo' mama say! You ought to be ashame'. You oughtn' put on those good pants. Look at 'em! An' that mud on yo' collar! How you got that mud on yo' collar, Bibi? I never saw such a boy!" Bibi was the picture of pathetic resignation. Bobinôt was the embodiment of serious solicitude as he strove to remove from his own person and his son's the signs of their tramp over heavy roads and through wet fields. He scraped the mud off Bibi's bare legs and feet with a stick and carefully removed all traces from his heavy brogans. Then, prepared for the worst—the meeting with an over-scrupulous housewife, they entered cautiously at the back door.

Calixta was preparing supper. She had set the table and was dripping coffee at the hearth. She sprang up as they came in.

"Oh, Bobinôt! You back! My! but I was uneasy. W'ere you been during the rain? An' Bibi? he ain't wet? he ain't hurt?" She had clasped Bibi and was kissing

him effusively. Bobinôt's explanations and apologies which he had been composing all along the way, died on his lips as Calixta felt him to see if he were dry, and
seemed to express nothing but satisfaction at their safe return.

"I brought you some shrimps, Calixta," offered Bobinôt, hauling the can
from his ample side pocket and laying it on the table.

"Shrimps! Oh, Bobinôt! you too good fo' anything!" and she gave him a   35
smacking kiss on the cheek that resounded. "*J'vous réponds,*° we'll have a feas' tonight! umph-umph!"

Bobinôt and Bibi began to relax and enjoy themselves, and when the three
seated themselves at table they laughed much and so loud that anyone might
have heard them as far away as Laballière's.

4

Alcée Laballière wrote to his wife, Clarisse, that night. It was a loving letter,
full of tender solicitude. He told her not to hurry back, but if she and the babies
liked it at Biloxi, to stay a month longer. He was getting on nicely; and though he
missed them, he was willing to bear the separation a while longer—realizing that
their health and pleasure were the first things to be considered.

5

As for Clarisse, she was charmed upon receiving her husband's letter. She
and the babies were doing well. The society was agreeable; many of her old
friends and acquaintances were at the bay. And the first free breath since her marriage seemed to restore the pleasant liberty of her maiden days. Devoted as she
was to her husband, their intimate conjugal life was something which she was
more than willing to forego for a while.

So the storm passed and every one was happy.   [1898]

THINKING ABOUT THE TEXT

1. Does Calixta truly love Bobinôt? What explains the sudden passion of
   Calixta and Alcée? Are they in love?

2. Are you bothered by the happy ending? Are stories supposed to reinforce
   the dominant values of a society? What do you think would (or should)
   have happened in real life?

3. Can you recall other stories, novels, films, or television programs in
   which someone who is sexually transgressive is not punished?

4. Are the injured parties in this story really injured; that is, if they never find
   out, will they still suffer somehow?

5. Should extramarital affairs be illegal? Is Chopin suggesting that they are
   not so terrible, or is she simply saying something about passion?

J'vous réponds: I'm telling you.

KATE CHOPIN
The Story of an Hour

"The Story of an Hour" was first published in Bayou Folk *(1894). It is typical of Chopin's controversial works and caused a sensation among the reading public.*

Knowing that Mrs. Mallard was afflicted with a heart trouble, great care was taken to break to her as gently as possible the news of her husband's death.

It was her sister Josephine who told her, in broken sentences; veiled hints that revealed in half concealing. Her husband's friend Richards was there, too, near her. It was he who had been in the newspaper office when intelligence of the railroad disaster was received, with Brently Mallard's name leading the list of "killed." He had only taken the time to assure himself of its truth by a second telegram, and had hastened to forestall any less careful, less tender friend in bearing the sad message.

She did not hear the story as many women have heard the same, with a paralyzed inability to accept its significance. She wept at once, with sudden, wild abandonment, in her sister's arms. When the storm of grief had spent itself she went away to her room alone. She would have no one follow her.

There stood, facing the open window, a comfortable, roomy armchair. Into this she sank, pressed down by a physical exhaustion that haunted her body and seemed to reach into her soul.

She could see in the open square before her house the tops of trees that were all aquiver with the new spring life. The delicious breath of rain was in the air. In the street below a peddler was crying his wares. The notes of a distant song which some one was singing reached her faintly, and countless sparrows were twittering in the eaves.   5

There were patches of blue sky showing here and there through the clouds that had met and piled one above the other in the west facing her window.

She sat with her head thrown back upon the cushion of the chair, quite motionless, except when a sob came up into her throat and shook her, as a child who had cried itself to sleep continues to sob in its dreams.

She was young, with a fair, calm face, whose lines bespoke repression and even a certain strength. But now there was a dull stare in her eyes, whose gaze was fixed away off yonder on one of those patches of blue sky. It was not a glance of reflection, but rather indicated a suspension of intelligent thought.

There was something coming to her and she was waiting for it, fearfully. What was it? She did not know; it was too subtle and elusive to name. But she felt it, creeping out of the sky, reaching toward her through the sounds, the scents, the color that filled the air.

Now her bosom rose and fell tumultuously. She was beginning to recognize   10
this thing that was approaching to possess her, and she was striving to beat it back with her will — as powerless as her two white slender hands would have been.

When she abandoned herself a little whispered word escaped her slightly parted lips. She said it over and over under her breath: "free, free, free!" The vacant stare and the look of terror that had followed it went from her eyes. They stayed keen and bright. Her pulses beat fast, and the coursing blood warmed and relaxed every inch of her body.

She did not stop to ask if it were or were not a monstrous joy that held her. A clear and exalted perception enabled her to dismiss the suggestion as trivial.

She knew that she would weep again when she saw the kind, tender hands folded in death; the face that had never looked save with love upon her, fixed and gray and dead. But she saw beyond that bitter moment a long procession of years to come that would belong to her absolutely. And she opened and spread her arms out to them in welcome.

There would be no one to live for her during those coming years: she would live for herself. There would be no powerful will bending hers in that blind persistence with which men and women believe they have a right to impose a private will upon a fellow-creature. A kind intention or a cruel intention made the act seem no less a crime as she looked upon it in that brief moment of illumination.

And yet she had loved him — sometimes. Often she had not. What did it matter! What could love, the unsolved mystery, count for in face of this possession of self-assertion which she suddenly recognized as the strongest impulse of her being!

"Free! Body and soul free!" she kept whispering.

Josephine was kneeling before the closed door with her lips to the keyhole, imploring for admission. "Louise, open the door! I beg; open the door — you will make yourself ill. What are you doing, Louise? For heaven's sake open the door."

"Go away. I am not making myself ill." No; she was drinking in a very elixir of life through that open window.

Her fancy was running riot along those days ahead of her. Spring days, and summer days, and all sorts of days that would be her own. She breathed a quick prayer that life might be long. It was only yesterday she had thought with a shudder that life might be long.

She arose at length and opened the door to her sister's importunities. There was a feverish triumph in her eyes, and she carried herself unwittingly like a goddess of Victory. She clasped her sister's waist, and together they descended the stairs. Richards stood waiting for them at the bottom.

Some one was opening the front door with a latchkey. It was Brently Mallard who entered, a little travel-stained, composedly carrying his gripsack and umbrella. He had been far from the scene of accident, and did not even know there had been one. He stood amazed at Josephine's piercing cry; at Richards' quick motion to screen him from the view of his wife.

But Richards was too late.

When the doctors came they said she had died of heart disease — of joy that kills. [1894]

THINKING ABOUT THE TEXT

1. Is Louise Mallard really in love with her husband? Regardless of your answer, would she ever leave him? Is it possible to confuse love with duty?

2. Is it possible to assign blame for this tragedy? To Mr. Mallard? Mrs. Mallard? The culture?

3. Why did Chopin keep the story so brief? What would you like to know more about?

4. What specifically do you think Mrs. Mallard was thinking about in the room?

5. Do you think this situation was common during Chopin's time? Today?

MAKING COMPARISONS

1. Compare Mrs. Mallard and Calixta. Do you think Mrs. Mallard would have an extramarital affair?

2. Is Chopin sympathetic to Mrs. Mallard and Calixta? Is she judgmental?

3. Calixta and Alcée seem to be on more equal terms than Mr. and Mrs. Mallard. Do you think this is the case? Explain why this might be so.

KATE CHOPIN
Désirée's Baby

"Désirée's Baby" was written in 1892 and published in Bayou Folk *(1894). The story reflects her experience among the French Creoles in Louisiana.*

As the day was pleasant, Madame Valmondé drove over to L'Abri to see Désirée and the baby.

It made her laugh to think of Désirée with a baby. Why, it seemed but yesterday that Désirée was little more than a baby herself; when Monsieur in riding through the gateway of Valmondé had found her lying asleep in the shadow of the big stone pillar.

The little one awoke in his arms and began to cry for "Dada." That was as much as she could do or say. Some people thought she might have strayed there of her own accord, for she was of the toddling age. The prevailing belief was that she had been purposely left by a party of Texans, whose canvas-covered wagon, late in the day, had crossed the ferry that Coton Maïs kept, just below the plantation. In time Madame Valmondé abandoned every speculation but the one that Désirée had been sent to her by a beneficent Providence to be the child of her affection, seeing that she was without child of the flesh. For the girl grew to be beautiful and gentle, affectionate and sincere, — the idol of Valmondé.

It was no wonder, when she stood one day against the stone pillar in whose shadow she had lain asleep, eighteen years before, that Armand Aubigny riding by and seeing her there, had fallen in love with her. That was the way all the Aubignys fell in love, as if struck by a pistol shot. The wonder was that he had not loved her before; for he had known her since his father brought him home from

Paris, a boy of eight, after his mother died there. The passion that awoke in him that day, when he saw her at the gate, swept along like an avalanche, or like a prairie fire, or like anything that drives headlong over all obstacles.

Monsieur Valmondé grew practical and wanted things well considered: that is, the girl's obscure origin. Armand looked into her eyes and did not care. He was reminded that she was nameless. What did it matter about a name when he could give her one of the oldest and proudest in Louisiana? He ordered the *corbeille* from Paris, and contained himself with what patience he could until it arrived; then they were married.

Madame Valmondé had not seen Désirée and the baby for four weeks. When she reached L'Abri she shuddered at the first sight of it, as she always did. It was a sad looking place, which for many years had not known the gentle presence of a mistress, old Monsieur Aubigny having married and buried his wife in France, and she having loved her own land too well ever to leave it. The roof came down steep and black like a cowl, reaching out beyond the wide galleries that encircled the yellow stuccoed house. Big, solemn oaks grew close to it, and their thick-leaved, far-reaching branches shadowed it like a pall. Young Aubigny's rule was a strict one, too, and under it his negroes had forgotten how to be gay, as they had been during the old master's easy-going and indulgent lifetime.

The young mother was recovering slowly, and lay full length, in her soft white muslins and laces, upon a couch. The baby was beside her, upon her arm, where he had fallen sleep, at her breast. The yellow nurse woman sat beside a window fanning herself.

Madame Valmondé bent her portly figure over Désirée and kissed her, holding her an instant tenderly in her arms. Then she turned to the child.

"This is not the baby!" she exclaimed, in startled tones. French was the language spoken at Valmondé in those days.

"I knew you would be astonished," laughed Désirée, "at the way he has grown. The little *cochon de lait!*° Look at his legs, mamma, and his hands and fingernails, — real fingernails. Zandrine had to cut them this morning. Isn't it true, Zandrine?"

The woman bowed her turbaned head majestically, "Mais si, Madame."

"And the way he cries," went on Désirée, "is deafening. Armand heard him the other day as far away as La Blanche's cabin."

Madame Valmondé had never removed her eyes from the child. She lifted it and walked with it over to the window that was lightest. She scanned the baby narrowly, then looked as searchingly at Zandrine, whose face was turned to gaze across the fields.

"Yes, the child has grown, has changed," said Madame Valmondé, slowly, as she replaced it beside its mother. "What does Armand say?"

Désirée's face became suffused with a glow that was happiness itself.

"Oh, Armand is the proudest father in the parish, I believe, chiefly because it is a boy, to bear his name; though he says not, — that he would have loved a girl as well. But I know it isn't true. I know he says that to please me. And mamma," she

---

cochon de lait: French for "suckling pig"; an endearment.

added, drawing Madame Valmondé's head down to her and speaking in a whisper, "he hasn't punished one of them—not one of them—since baby is born. Even Négrillon, who pretended to have burnt his leg that he might rest from work—he only laughed, and said Négrillon was a great scamp. Oh, mamma, I'm so happy; it frightens me."

What Désirée said was true. Marriage, and later the birth of his son had softened Armand Aubigny's imperious and exacting nature greatly. This was what made the gentle Désirée so happy, for she loved him desperately. When he frowned she trembled, but loved him. When he smiled, she asked no greater blessing of God. But Armand's dark, handsome face had not often been disfigured by frowns since the day he fell in love with her.

When the baby was about three months old, Désirée awoke one day to the conviction that there was something in the air menacing her peace. It was at first too subtle to grasp. It had only been a disquieting suggestion; an air of mystery among the blacks; unexpected visits from far-off neighbors who could hardly account for their coming. Then a strange, an awful change in her husband's manner, which she dared not ask him to explain. When he spoke to her, it was with averted eyes, from which the old love-light seemed to have gone out. He absented himself from home; and when there, avoided her presence and that of her child, without excuse. And the very spirit of Satan seemed suddenly to take hold of him in his dealings with the slaves. Désirée was miserable enough to die.

She sat in her room, one hot afternoon, in her *peignoir*, listlessly drawing through her fingers the strands of her long, silky brown hair that hung about her shoulders. The baby, half naked, lay asleep upon her own great mahogany bed, that was like a sumptuous throne, with its satin-lined half-canopy. One of La Blanche's little quadroon boys—half naked too—stood fanning the child slowly with a fan of peacock feathers. Désirée's eyes had been fixed absently and sadly upon the baby, while she was striving to penetrate the threatening mist that she felt closing about her. She looked from her child to the boy who stood beside him, and back again; over and over. "Ah!" It was a cry that she could not help; which she was not conscious of having uttered. The blood turned like ice in her veins, and a clammy moisture gathered upon her face.

She tried to speak to the little quadroon boy; but no sound would come, at first. When he heard his name uttered, he looked up, and his mistress was pointing to the door. He laid aside the great, soft fan, and obediently stole away, over the polished floor, on his bare tiptoes.

She stayed motionless, with gaze riveted upon her child, and her face the picture of fright.

Presently her husband entered the room, and without noticing her, went to a table and began to search among some papers which covered it.

"Armand," she called to him, in a voice which must have stabbed him, if he was human. But he did not notice. "Armand," she said again. Then she rose and tottered towards him. "Armand," she panted once more, clutching his arm, "look at our child. What does it mean? tell me."

20

He coldly but gently loosened her fingers from about his arm and thrust the hand away from him. "Tell me what it means!" she cried despairingly.

"It means," he answered lightly, "that the child is not white; it means that you are not white." 25

A quick conception of all that this accusation meant for her nerved her with unwonted courage to deny it. "It is a lie; it is not true, I am white! Look at my hair, it is brown; and my eyes are gray, Armand, you know they are gray. And my skin is fair," seizing his wrist. "Look at my hand; whiter than yours, Armand," she laughed hysterically.

"As white as La Blanche's," he returned cruelly; and went away leaving her alone with their child.

When she could hold a pen in her hand, she sent a despairing letter to Madame Valmondé.

"My mother, they tell me I am not white. Armand has told me I am not white. For God's sake tell them it is not true. You must know it is not true. I shall die. I must die. I cannot be so unhappy, and live."

The answer that came was as brief: 30

"My own Désirée: Come home to Valmondé; back to your mother who loves you. Come with your child."

When the letter reached Désirée she went with it to her husband's study, and laid it open upon the desk before which he sat. She was like a stone image: silent, white, motionless after she placed it there.

In silence he ran his cold eyes over the written words. He said nothing. "Shall I go, Armand?" she asked in tones sharp with agonized suspense.

"Yes, go."

"Do you want me to go?" 35

"Yes, I want you to go."

He thought Almighty God had dealt cruelly and unjustly with him; and felt, somehow, that he was paying Him back in kind when he stabbed thus into his wife's soul. Moreover he no longer loved her, because of the unconscious injury she had brought upon his home and his name.

She turned away like one stunned by a blow, and walked slowly towards the door, hoping he would call her back.

"Good-by, Armand," she moaned.

He did not answer her. That was his last blow at fate. 40

Désirée went in search of her child. Zandrine was pacing the sombre gallery with it. She took the little one from the nurse's arms with no word of explanation, and descending the steps, walked away, under the live-oak branches.

It was an October afternoon; the sun was just sinking. Out in the still fields the negroes were picking cotton.

Désirée had not changed the thin white gàrment nor the slippers which she wore. Her hair was uncovered and the sun's rays brought a golden gleam from its brown meshes. She did not take the broad, beaten road which led to the far-off plantation of Valmondé. She walked across a deserted field, where the stubble bruised her tender feet, so delicately shod, and tore her thin gown to shreds.

She disappeared among the reeds and willows that grew thick along the banks of the deep, sluggish bayou; and she did not come back again.

Some weeks later there was a curious scene enacted at L'Abri. In the centre   45
of the smoothly swept back yard was a great bonfire. Armand Aubigny sat in the wide hallway that commanded a view of the spectacle; and it was he who dealt out to a half dozen negroes the material which kept this fire ablaze.

A graceful cradle of willow, with all its dainty furbishings, was laid upon the pyre, which had already been fed with the richness of a priceless *layette*. Then there were silk gowns, and velvet and satin ones added to these; laces, too, and embroideries; bonnets and gloves; for the *corbeille* had been of rare quality.

The last thing to go was a tiny bundle of letters; innocent little scribblings that Désirée had sent to him during the days of their espousal. There was the remnant of one back in the drawer from which he took them. But it was not Désirée's; it was part of an old letter from his mother to his father. He read it. She was thanking God for the blessing of her husband's love: —

"But, above all," she wrote, "night and day, I thank the good God for having so arranged our lives that our dear Armand will never know that his mother, who adores him, belongs to the race that is cursed with the brand of slavery."   [1892]

THINKING ABOUT THE TEXT

1. Does Armand really love Désirée? Explain.

2. Armand seems to have fallen in love "at first sight." Is this possible? Can love conquer all, even racial bias? Is Chopin skeptical?

3. What would you have done if you were Désirée? What will Armand do now that he knows?

4. Are we able to break free of our cultural heritage? What are the ways society tries to keep us in line? How do some people break free? Is there a danger in disregarding societal norms? Are there benefits?

5. Could this story happen this way today?

MAKING COMPARISONS

1. Which female character — Calixta, Louise, or Désirée — possesses true love for her husband? Do the husbands love their wives more? In different ways?

2. Which one of these marriages seems the strongest? Why?

3. Compare Chopin's attitude toward marriage in these three stories. Does she support all aspects of marriage? Since she wrote over a century ago, would she be pleased with the present state of marriage (including divorce)?

WRITING ABOUT ISSUES

1. Which ending seems more ethically questionable? Write a brief position paper suggesting that one of Chopin's endings should be changed (or remain the same) for moral reasons before junior high students read it.

2. Compare Alcée and Armand. Write a brief justification for or refutation of the behavior of one of them.

3. Do you think Louise Mallard should have admitted her feelings for her husband and left him? Would you? Why?

4. Chopin's works shocked American audiences. Research the ways sex, love, and relationships were dealt with in the 1880s in America. Write a brief explanation of why Chopin was ahead of her time.

A WEB ASSIGNMENT

E-journals have become a popular alternative for discussion forums. Visit the Web Assignments section of the *Making Literature Matter* Web site to find the link to *Domestic Goddesses*, a mediated e-journal site for information and discussions of nineteenth-century women writers. Read one of the essays on Chopin and her fiction. Write a report, making reference to how this piece applies to our three stories.

Visit www.bedfordstmartins.com/makinglitmatter

AFFAIRS OF LOVE: RE-VISIONS OF "THE LADY WITH THE DOG"

ANTON CHEKHOV, "The Lady with the Dog"
JOYCE CAROL OATES, "The Lady with the Pet Dog"
BETH LORDAN, "The Man with the Lapdog"

Cultural expectations can often be surprisingly contradictory, especially if an emotion such as love is involved. On the one hand, Western societies expect marriage to be based on love, not convenience. We dismiss the notion of arranged marriage because we think people should choose marriage partners that inspire them with feelings of passion and love. We have laws, conventions, and the weight of public opinion reinforcing these beliefs about the value of married life. On the other hand, we sometimes forgive married women or men for their affairs if they seem deeply and romantically committed to their lovers. We sometimes even value illicit love over marriage when the married couple seems to go through the motions of partnership without much real affection. We support marriage, but sometimes love matters more to us.

Writers (such as Nathaniel Hawthorne in his novel *The Scarlet Letter*) have long focused their attention on the charged drama of extramarital affairs, often detailing the tragic consequences of violating society's conventions. But writers can also surprise us with narratives of extramarital affairs that lead in surprising directions. Anton Chekhov's classic story of Dmitri and Anna appears for a while to be a predictable story of a womanizer deceiving yet another gullible woman,

(Anton Chekhov. The Granger Collection,
New York.)

(Joyce Carol Oates. Bernard Gotfryd.)

(Beth Lordan. Courtesy of Beth Lordan.)

but the story takes a turn that still surprises. Joyce Carol Oates's modern, more
ominous retelling of Chekhov's tale seems also to be an affirmation of love in
spite of convention. Beth Lordan's somber narrative draws on Chekhov's story in
a gentle, perhaps unacknowledged, infatuation complicated by age and illness.

BEFORE YOU READ

Undoubtedly you have seen movies and read novels involving married people
who have affairs. What is your response to these love triangles? Do you find
yourself hoping that the lovers will leave their spouses and live happily ever
after? What seems to determine your response to their infidelities?

ANTON CHEKHOV
The Lady with the Dog
Translated by Constance Garnett

Anton Chekhov (1860–1904), considered one of the great masters of short fiction, was born into a struggling family in a small port town in Russia. Although his childhood was absorbing and vivid, he remembers the experience as painful. To improve the family's economic situation, his father moved the family to Moscow, where Anton joined them in 1879, eventually graduating from Moscow University as a doctor in 1884. He sold some humorous sketches in school to pay his debts, and when two collections of his short stories were critically acclaimed in 1886 and 1887, he decided to devote himself to writing full time. Chekhov also wrote plays, including The Cherry Orchard, The Three Sisters, *and* Uncle Vanya, *which are still regularly performed. Many modern writers were influenced by Chekhov's laconic and precise prose style and his ability to get below the surface of human personality. The following story seems quite modern in its exploration of the psychological implications of sexual involvement, its lack of a neat solution, and its ability to intrigue us with what the characters leave unsaid.*

I

It was said that a new person had appeared on the sea front: a lady with a little dog. Dmitri Dmitritch Gurov, who had by then been a fortnight at Yalta, and so was fairly at home there, had begun to take an interest in new arrivals. Sitting in Verney's pavilion, he saw, walking on the sea-front, a fair-haired young lady of medium height, wearing a beret; a white Pomeranian dog was running behind her.

And afterwards he met her in the public gardens and in the square several times a day. She was walking alone, always wearing the same beret, and always with the same white dog; no one knew who she was, and every one called her simply "the lady with the dog."

"If she is here alone without a husband or friends, it wouldn't be amiss to make her acquaintance," Gurov reflected.

He was under forty, but he had a daughter already twelve years old, and two sons at school. He had been married young, when he was a student in his second year, and by now his wife seemed half as old again as he. She was a tall, erect woman with dark eyebrows, staid and dignified, and, as she said of herself, intellectual. She read a great deal, used phonetic spelling, called her husband, not Dmitri, but Dimitri, and he secretly considered her unintelligent, narrow, inelegant, was afraid of her, and did not like to be at home. He had begun being unfaithful to her long ago — had been unfaithful to her often, and, probably on that account, almost always spoke ill of women, and when they were talked about in his presence, used to call them "the lower race."

It seemed to him that he had been so schooled by bitter experience that he might call them what he liked, and yet he could not get on for two days together without "the lower race." In the society of men he was bored and not himself, with them he was cold and uncommunicative; but when he was in the company of women he felt free, and knew what to say to them and how to behave; and he was at ease with them even when he was silent. In his appearance, in his character, in his whole nature, there was something attractive and elusive which allured women and disposed them in his favor; he knew that, and some force seemed to draw him, too, to them.

Experience often repeated, truly bitter experience, had taught him long ago that with decent people, especially Moscow people—always slow to move and irresolute—every intimacy, which at first so agreeably diversifies life and appears a light and charming adventure, inevitably grows into a regular problem of extreme intricacy, and in the long run the situation becomes unbearable. But at every fresh meeting with an interesting woman this experience seemed to slip out of his memory, and he was eager for life, and everything seemed simple and amusing.

One evening he was dining in the gardens, and the lady in the beret came up slowly to take the next table. Her expression, her gait, her dress, and the way she did her hair told him that she was a lady, that she was married, that she was in Yalta for the first time and alone, and that she was dull there. . . . The stories told of the immorality in such places as Yalta are to a great extent untrue; he despised them, and knew that such stories were for the most part made up by persons who would themselves have been glad to sin if they had been able; but when the lady sat down at the next table three paces from him, he remembered these tales of easy conquests, of trips to the mountains, and the tempting thought of a swift, fleeting love affair, a romance with an unknown woman, whose name he did not know, suddenly took possession of him.

He beckoned coaxingly to the Pomeranian, and when the dog came up to him he shook his finger at it. The Pomeranian growled: Gurov shook his finger at it again.

The lady looked at him and at once dropped her eyes.

"He doesn't bite," she said, and blushed.

"May I give him a bone?" he asked; and when she nodded he asked courteously, "Have you been long in Yalta?"

"Five days."

"And I have already dragged out a fortnight here."

There was a brief silence.

"Time goes fast, and yet it is so dull here!" she said, not looking at him.

"That's only the fashion to say it is dull here. A provincial will live in Belyov or Zhidra and not be dull, and when he comes here it's 'Oh, the dulness! Oh, the dust!' One would think he came from Grenada."

She laughed. Then both continued eating in silence, like strangers, but after dinner they walked side by side; and there sprang up between them the light jesting conversation of people who are free and satisfied, to whom it does not matter where they go or what they talk about. They walked and talked of the strange light on the sea: the water was of a soft warm lilac hue, and there was a golden streak from the moon upon it. They talked of how sultry it was after a hot day. Gurov told her that he came from Moscow, that he had taken his degree in Arts, but had a post in a bank; that he had trained as an opera singer, but had given it up, that he owned two houses in Moscow. . . . And from her he learnt that she had grown up in Petersburg, but had lived in S—— since her marriage two years before, that she was staying another month in Yalta, and that her husband, who needed a holiday too, might perhaps come and fetch her. She was not sure whether her husband had a post in a Crown Department or under the Provincial Council—and was amused by her own ignorance. And Gurov learnt, too, that she was called Anna Sergeyevna.

Afterwards he thought about her in his room at the hotel—thought she would certainly meet him next day; it would be sure to happen. As he got into bed he thought how lately she had been a girl at school, doing lessons like his own daughter; he recalled the diffidence, the angularity, that was still manifest in her laugh and her manner of talking with a stranger. This must have been the first time in her life she had been alone in surroundings in which she was followed, looked at, and spoken to merely from a secret motive which she could hardly fail to guess. He recalled her slender, delicate neck, her lovely grey eyes.

"There's something pathetic about her, anyway," he thought, and fell asleep.

II

A week had passed since they had made acquaintance. It was a holiday. It was sultry indoors, while in the street the wind whirled the dust round and round, and blew people's hats off. It was a thirsty day, and Gurov often went into the pavilion, and pressed Anna Sergeyevna to have syrup and water or an ice. One did not know what to do with oneself.

In the evening when the wind had dropped a little, they went out on the groyne° to see the steamer come in. There were a great many people walking about the harbor; they had gathered to welcome some one, bringing bouquets. And two peculiarities of a well-dressed Yalta crowd were very conspicuous: the elderly ladies were dressed like young ones, and there were great numbers of generals.

Owing to the roughness of the sea, the steamer arrived late, after the sun had set, and it was a long time turning about before it reached the groyne. Anna Sergeyevna looked through her lorgnette at the steamer and the passengers as though looking for acquaintances, and when she turned to Gurov, her eyes were shining. She talked a great deal and asked disconnected questions, forgetting next moment what she had asked; then she dropped her lorgnette in the crush.

The festive crowd began to disperse; it was too dark to see people's faces. The wind had completely dropped, but Gurov and Anna Sergeyevna still stood as though waiting to see some one else come from the steamer. Anna Sergeyevna was silent now, and sniffed the flowers without looking at Gurov.

"The weather is better this evening," he said. "Where shall we go now? Shall we drive somewhere?"

groyne: A breakwater.

She made no answer.

Then he looked at her intently, and all at once put his arm round her and kissed her on the lips, and breathed in the moisture and the fragrance of the flowers; and he immediately looked round him, anxiously wondering whether any one had seen them.

"Let us go to your hotel," he said softly. And both walked quickly.

The room was close and smelt of the scent she had bought at the Japanese shop. Gurov looked at her and thought: "What different people one meets in the world!" From the past he preserved memories of careless, good-natured women, who loved cheerfully and were grateful to him for the happiness he gave them, however brief it might be; and of women like his wife who loved without any genuine feeling, with superfluous phrases, affectedly, hysterically, with an expression that suggested that it was not love nor passion, but something more significant; and of two or three others, very beautiful, cold women, on whose faces he had caught a glimpse of a rapacious expression—an obstinate desire to snatch from life more than it could give, and these were capricious, unreflecting, domineering, unintelligent women not in their first youth, and when Gurov grew cold to them their beauty excited his hatred, and the lace on their linen seemed to him like scales.

But in this case there was still the diffidence, the angularity of inexperienced youth, an awkward feeling; and there was a sense of consternation as though some one had suddenly knocked at the door. The attitude of Anna Sergeyevna— "the lady with the dog"—to what had happened was somehow peculiar, very grave, as though it were her fall—so it seemed, and it was strange and inappropriate. Her face dropped and faded, and on both sides of it her long hair hung down mournfully; she mused in a dejected attitude like "the woman who was a sinner" in an old-fashioned picture.

"It's wrong," she said. "You will be the first to despise me now."   30

There was a watermelon on the table. Gurov cut himself a slice and began eating it without haste. There followed at least half an hour of silence.

Anna Sergeyevna was touching; there was about her the purity of a good, simple woman who had seen little of life. The solitary candle burning on the table threw a faint light on her face, yet it was clear that she was very unhappy.

"How could I despise you?" asked Gurov. "You don't know what you are saying."

"God forgive me," she said, and her eyes filled with tears. "It's awful."

"You seem to feel you need to be forgiven."   35

"Forgiven? No. I am a bad, low woman; I despise myself and don't attempt to justify myself. It's not my husband but myself I have deceived. And not only just now; I have been deceiving myself for a long time. My husband may be a good, honest man, but he is a flunkey! I don't know what he does there, what his work is, but I know he is a flunkey! I was twenty when I was married to him. I have been tormented by curiosity; I wanted something better. 'There must be a different sort of life,' I said to myself. I wanted to live! To live, to live! . . . I was fired by curiosity . . . you don't understand it, but, I swear to God, I could not control myself; something happened to me: I could not be restrained. I told my husband

I was ill, and came here. . . . And here I have been walking about as though I were dazed, like a mad creature; . . . and now I have become a vulgar, contemptible woman whom any one may despise."

Gurov felt bored already, listening to her. He was irritated by the naive tone, by this remorse, so unexpected and inopportune; but for the tears in her eyes, he might have thought she was jesting or playing a part.

"I don't understand," he said softly. "What is it you want?"

She hid her face on his breast and pressed close to him.

"Believe me, believe me, I beseech you . . ." she said. "I love a pure, honest   40
life, and sin is loathsome to me. I don't know what I am doing. Simple people say: 'The Evil One has beguiled me.' And I may say of myself now that the Evil One has beguiled me."

"Hush, hush! . . ." he muttered.

He looked at her fixed, scared eyes, kissed her, talked softly and affectionately, and by degrees she was comforted, and her gaiety returned; they both began laughing.

Afterwards when they went out there was not a soul on the sea front. The town with its cypresses had quite a deathlike air, but the sea still broke noisily on the shore; a single barge was rocking on the waves, and a lantern was blinking sleepily on it.

They found a cab and drove to Oreanda.

"I found out your surname in the hall just now: it was written on the board —   45
Von Diderits," said Gurov. "Is your husband a German?"

"No; I believe his grandfather was a German, but he is an Orthodox Russian himself."

At Oreanda they sat on a seat not far from the church, looked down at the sea, and were silent. Yalta was hardly visible through the morning mist; white clouds stood motionless on the mountain-tops. The leaves did not stir on the trees, grasshoppers chirruped, and the monotonous hollow sound of the sea rising up from below, spoke of the peace, of the eternal sleep awaiting us. So it must have sounded when there was no Yalta, no Oreanda here; so it sounds now, and it will sound as indifferently and monotonously when we are all no more. And in this constancy, in this complete indifference to the life and death of each of us, there lies hid, perhaps, a pledge of our eternal salvation, of the unceasing movement of life upon earth, of unceasing progress toward perfection. Sitting beside a young woman who in the dawn seemed so lovely, soothed and spellbound in these magical surroundings — the sea, mountains, clouds, the open sky — Gurov thought how in reality everything is beautiful in this world when one reflects: everything except what we think or do ourselves when we forget our human dignity and the higher aims of our existence.

A man walked up to them — probably a keeper — looked at them and walked away. And this detail seemed mysterious and beautiful, too. They saw a steamer come from Theodosia, with its lights out in the glow of dawn.

"There is dew on the grass," said Anna Sergeyevna, after a silence.

"Yes. It's time to go home."   50

They went back to the town.

Then they met every day at twelve o'clock on the sea-front, lunched and dined together, went for walks, admired the sea. She complained that she slept badly, that her heart throbbed violently; asked the same questions, troubled now by jealousy and now by the fear that he did not respect her sufficiently. And often in the square or gardens, when there was no one near them, he suddenly drew her to him and kissed her passionately. Complete idleness, these kisses in broad daylight while he looked round in dread of some one's seeing them, the heat, the smell of the sea, and the continual passing to and fro before him of idle, well-dressed, well-fed people, made a new man of him; he told Anna Sergeyevna how beautiful she was, how fascinating. He was impatiently passionate, he would not move a step away from her, while she was often pensive and continually urged him to confess that he did not respect her, did not love her in the least, and thought of her as nothing but a common woman. Rather late almost every evening they drove somewhere out of town, to Oreanda or to the waterfall; and the expedition was always a success, the scenery invariably impressed them as grand and beautiful.

They were expecting her husband to come, but a letter came from him, saying that there was something wrong with his eyes, and he entreated his wife to come home as quickly as possible. Anna Sergeyevna made haste to go.

"It's a good thing I am going away," she said to Gurov. "It's the finger of destiny!"

She went by coach and he went with her. They were driving the whole day. When she had got into a compartment of the express, and when the second bell had rung, she said: 55

"Let me look at you once more . . . look at you once again. That's right."

She did not shed tears, but was so sad that she seemed ill, and her face was quivering.

"I shall remember you . . . think of you," she said. "God be with you; be happy. Don't remember evil against me. We are parting forever—it must be so, for we ought never to have met. Well, God be with you."

The train moved off rapidly, its lights soon vanished from sight, and a minute later there was no sound of it, as though everything had conspired together to end as quickly as possible that sweet delirium, that madness. Left alone on the platform, and gazing into the dark distance, Gurov listened to the chirrup of the grasshoppers and the hum of the telegraph wires, feeling as though he had only just waked up. And he thought, musing, that there had been another episode or adventure in his life, and it, too, was at an end, and nothing was left of it but a memory. . . . He was moved, sad, and conscious of a slight remorse. This young woman whom he would never meet again had not been happy with him; he was genuinely warm and affectionate with her, but yet in his manner, his tone, and his caresses there had been a shade of light irony, the coarse condescension of a happy man who was, besides, almost twice her age. All the time she had called him kind, exceptional, lofty; obviously he had seemed to her different from what he really was, so he had unintentionally deceived her. . . .

Here at the station was already a scent of autumn; it was a cold evening.   60

"It's time for me to go north," thought Gurov as he left the platform. "High time!"

III

At home in Moscow everything was in its winter routine; the stoves were heated, and in the morning it was still dark when the children were having breakfast and getting ready for school, and the nurse would light the lamp for a short time. The frosts had begun already. When the first snow has fallen, on the first day of sledge driving it is pleasant to see the white earth, the white roofs, to draw soft, delicious breath, and the season brings back the days of one's youth. The old limes and birches, white with hoar-frost, have a good-natured expression; they are nearer to one's heart than cypresses and palms, and near them one doesn't want to be thinking of the sea and the mountains.

Gurov was Moscow born; he arrived in Moscow on a fine frosty day, and when he put on his fur coat and warm gloves, and walked along Petrovka, and when on Saturday evening he heard the ringing of the bells, his recent trip and the places he had seen lost all charm for him. Little by little he became absorbed in Moscow life, greedily read three newspapers a day, and declared he did not read the Moscow papers on principle! He already felt a longing to go to restaurants, clubs, dinner parties, anniversary celebrations, and he felt flattered at entertaining distinguished lawyers and artists, and at playing cards with a professor at the doctors' club. He could already eat a whole plateful of salt fish and cabbage. . . .

In another month, he fancied, the image of Anna Sergeyevna would be shrouded in a mist in his memory and only from time to time would visit him in his dreams with a touching smile as others did. But more than a month passed, real winter had come, and everything was still clear in his memory as though he had parted with Anna Sergeyevna only the day before. And his memories glowed more and more vividly. When in the evening stillness he heard from his study the voices of his children, preparing their lessons, or when he listened to a song or the organ at the restaurant, or the storm howled in the chimney, suddenly everything would rise up in his memory: what had happened on the groyne, and the early morning with the mist on the mountains, and the steamer coming from Theodosia, and the kisses. He would pace a long time about his room, remembering it all and smiling; then his memories passed into dreams, and in his fancy the past was mingled with what was to come. Anna Sergeyevna did not visit him in dreams, but followed him about everywhere like a shadow and haunted him. When he shut his eyes, he saw her as though she were living before him, and she seemed to him lovelier, younger, tenderer than she was; and he imagined himself finer than he had been in Yalta. In the evenings she peeped out at him from the bookcase, from the fireplace, from the corner—he heard her breathing, the caressing rustle of her dress. In the street he watched the women, looking for someone like her.

He was tormented by an intense desire to confide his memories to some one. But in his home it was impossible to talk of his love, and he had no one outside; he could not talk to his tenants nor to any one at the bank. And what had he to talk of? Had he been in love, then? Had there been anything beautiful, poetical, or edifying or simply interesting in his relations with Anna Sergeyevna? And there was nothing for him but to talk vaguely of love, of woman, and no one guessed   65 what it meant; only his wife twitched her black eyebrows, and said: "The part of a lady killer does not suit you at all, Dimitri."

One evening, coming out of the doctors' club with an official with whom he had been playing cards, he could not resist saying:

"If only you knew what a fascinating woman I made the acquaintance of in Yalta!"

The official got into his sledge and was driving away, but turned suddenly and shouted:

"Dmitri Dmitritch!"

"What?"

"You were right this evening: the sturgeon was a bit too strong!"

These words, so ordinary, for some reason moved Gurov to indignation and struck him as degrading and unclean. What savage manners, what people! What senseless nights, what uninteresting, uneventful days! The rage for card playing, the gluttony, the drunkenness, the continual talk always about the same thing. Useless pursuits and conversations always about the same things absorb the better part of one's time, the better part of one's strength, and in the end there is left a life groveling and curtailed, worthless and trivial, and there is no escaping or getting away from it—just as though one were in a madhouse or a prison.

Gurov did not sleep all night and was filled with indignation. And he had a headache all next day. And the next night he slept badly; he sat up in bed, thinking, or paced up and down his room. He was sick of his children, sick of the bank; he had no desire to go anywhere or to talk of anything.

In the holidays in December he prepared for a journey, and told his wife he was going to Petersburg to do something in the interests of a young friend—and he set off for S——. What for? He did not very well know himself. He wanted to see Anna Sergeyevna and to talk with her—to arrange a meeting, if possible.

He reached S—— in the morning and took the best room at the hotel, in which the floor was covered with grey army cloth and on the table was an inkstand, grey with dust and adorned with a figure on horseback, with its hat in its hand and its head broken off. The hotel porter gave him the necessary information; Von Diderits lived in a house of his own in Old Gontcharny Street—it was not far from the hotel: he was rich and lived in good style, and had his own horses; every one in the town knew him. The porter pronounced the name "Dridirits."

Gurov went without haste to Old Gontcharny Street and found the house. Just opposite the house stretched a long grey fence adorned with nails.

"One would run away from a fence like that," thought Gurov, looking from the fence to the windows of the house and back again.

He considered: today was a holiday, and the husband would probably be at home. And in any case it would be tactless to go into the house and upset her. If he were to send her a note, it might fall into her husband's hands, and then it might ruin everything. The best thing was to trust to chance. And he kept walking up and down the street by the fence, waiting for the chance. He saw a beggar go in at the gate and dogs fly at him; then an hour later he heard a piano, and

70

75

the sounds were faint and indistinct. Probably it was Anna Sergeyevna playing. The front door suddenly opened, and an old woman came out, followed by the familiar white Pomeranian. Gurov was on the point of calling to the dog, but his heart began beating violently, and in his excitement he could not remember the dog's name.

He walked up and down and loathed the grey fence more and more, and by now he thought irritably that Anna Sergeyevna had forgotten him and was perhaps already amusing herself with some one else and that that was very natural in a young woman who had nothing to look at from morning till night but that confounded fence. He went back to his hotel room and sat for a long while on the sofa, not knowing what to do; then he had dinner and a long nap.

"How stupid and worrying it is!" he thought when he woke and looked at the   80
dark windows: it was already evening. "Here I've had a good sleep for some reason. What shall I do in the night?"

He sat on the bed, which was covered by a cheap grey blanket, such as one sees in hospitals, and he taunted himself in his vexation:

"So much for the lady with the dog . . . so much for the adventure. . . . You're in a nice fix. . . ."

That morning at the station a poster in large letters had caught his eye. *The Geisha* was to be performed for the first time. He thought of this and went to the theater.

"It's quite possible she may go to the first performance," he thought.

The theater was full. As in all provincial theaters, there was a fog above the   85
chandelier, the gallery was noisy and restless; in the front row the local dandies were standing up before the beginning of the performance, with their hands behind them; in the governor's box the governor's daughter, wearing a boa, was sitting in the front seat, while the governor himself lurked modestly behind the curtain with only his hands visible; the orchestra was a long time tuning up; the stage curtain swayed. All the time the audience were coming in and taking their seats, Gurov looked at them eagerly.

Anna Sergeyevna, too, came in. She sat down in the third row, and when Gurov looked at her, his heart contracted, and he understood clearly that for him there was in the whole world no creature so near, so precious, and so important to him; she, this little woman, in no way remarkable, lost in a provincial crowd, with a vulgar lorgnette in her hand, filled his whole life now, was his sorrow and his joy, the one happiness that he now desired for himself, and to the sounds of the inferior orchestra, of the wretched provincial violins, he thought how lovely she was. He thought and dreamed.

A young man with small side-whiskers, tall and stooping, came in with Anna Sergeyevna and sat down beside her; he bent his head at every step and seemed to be continually bowing. Most likely this was the husband whom at Yalta, in a rush of bitter feeling, she had called a flunkey. And there really was in his long figure, his side whiskers, and the small bald patch on his head, something of the flunkey's obsequiousness; his smile was sugary, and in his buttonhole there was some badge of distinction like the number on a waiter.

During the first interval the husband went away to smoke; she remained alone in her stall. Gurov, who was sitting in the stalls, too, went up to her and said in a trembling voice, with a forced smile:

"Good-evening."

She glanced at him and turned pale, then glanced again with horror, unable 90
to believe her eyes, and tightly gripped the fan and the lorgnette in her hands, evidently struggling with herself not to faint. Both were silent. She was sitting, he was standing, frightened by her confusion and not venturing to sit down beside her. The violins and the flute began tuning up. He felt suddenly frightened; it seemed as though all the people in the boxes were looking at them. She got up and went quickly to the door; he followed her, and both walked senselessly along passages, and up and down stairs, and figures in legal, scholastic, and civil service uniforms, all wearing badges, flitted before their eyes. They caught glimpses of ladies, of fur coats hanging on pegs; the draughts blew on them, bringing a smell of stale tobacco. And Gurov, whose heart was beating violently, thought:

"Oh, heavens! Why are these people here and this orchestra! . . ."

And at that instant he recalled how when he had seen Anna Sergeyevna off at the station, he had thought that everything was over and they would never meet again. But how far they were still from the end!

On the narrow, gloomy staircase over which was written "To the Amphitheater," she stopped.

"How you have frightened me!" she said, breathing hard, still pale and overwhelmed. "Oh, how you have frightened me! I am half dead. Why have you come? Why?"

"But do understand, Anna, do understand . . ." he said hastily in a low voice. 95
"I entreat you to understand. . . ."

She looked at him with dread, with entreaty, with love; she looked at him intently, to keep his features more distinctly in her memory.

"I am so unhappy," she went on, not heeding him. "I have thought of nothing but you all the time; I live only in the thought of you. And I wanted to forget, to forget you; but why, oh, why, have you come?"

On the landing above them two schoolboys were smoking and looking down, but that was nothing to Gurov; he drew Anna Sergeyevna to him and began kissing her face, her cheeks, and her hands.

"What are you doing, what are you doing!" she cried in horror, pushing him away. "We are mad. Go away today; go away at once. . . . I beseech you by all that is sacred, I implore you. . . . There are people coming this way!"

Some one was coming up the stairs. 100

"You must go away," Anna Sergeyevna went on in a whisper. "Do you hear, Dmitri Dmitritch? I will come and see you in Moscow. I have never been happy; I am miserable now, and I never, never shall be happy, never! Don't make me suffer still more! I swear I'll come to Moscow. But now let us part. My precious, good, dear one, we must part!"

She pressed his hand and began rapidly going downstairs, looking round at him, and from her eyes he could see that she really was unhappy. Gurov stood for a little while, listened, then, when all sound had died away, he found his coat and left the theater.

IV

And Anna Sergeyevna began coming to see him in Moscow. Once in two or three months she left S——, telling her husband that she was going to consult a doctor about an internal complaint—and her husband believed her and did not believe her. In Moscow she stayed at the Slaviansky Bazaar hotel, and at once sent a man in a red cap to Gurov. Gurov went to see her, and no one in Moscow knew of it.

Once he was going to see her in this way on a winter morning (the messenger had come the evening before when he was out). With him walked his daughter, whom he wanted to take to school: it was on the way. Snow was falling in big wet flakes.

"It's three degrees above freezing point, and yet it is snowing," said Gurov to his daughter. "The thaw is only on the surface of the earth; there is quite a different temperature at a greater height in the atmosphere." 105

"And why are there no thunderstorms in the winter, father?"

He explained that, too. He talked, thinking all the while that he was going to see *her*, and no living soul knew of it and probably never would know. He had two lives: one, open, seen and known by all who cared to know, full of relative truth and of relative falsehood, exactly like the lives of his friends and acquaintances; and another life running its course in secret. And through some strange, perhaps accidental, conjunction of circumstances, everything that was essential, of interest and of value to him, everything in which he was sincere and did not deceive himself, everything that made the kernel of his life, was hidden from other people; and all that was false in him, the sheath in which he hid himself to conceal the truth—such, for instance, as his work in the bank, his discussions at the club, his "lower race," his presence with his wife at anniversary festivities—all that was open. And he judged of others by himself, not believing in what he saw, and always believing that every man had his real, most interesting life under the cover of secrecy and under the cover of night. All personal life rested on secrecy, and possibly it was partly on that account that civilized man was so nervously anxious that personal privacy should be respected.

After leaving his daughter at school, Gurov went on to the Slaviansky Bazaar. He took off his fur coat below, went upstairs, and softly knocked at the door. Anna Sergeyevna, wearing his favorite grey dress, exhausted by the journey and the suspense, had been expecting him since the evening before. She was pale; she looked at him and did not smile, and he had hardly come in when she fell on his breast. Their kiss was slow and prolonged, as though they had not met for two years.

"Well, how are you getting on there?" he asked. "What news?"

"Wait; I'll tell you directly. . . . I can't talk." 110

She could not speak; she was crying. She turned away from him and pressed her handkerchief to her eyes.

"Let her have her cry out. I'll sit down and wait," he thought, and he sat down in an arm-chair.

Then he rang and asked for tea to be brought him, and while he drank his tea, she remained standing at the window with her back to him. She was crying from emotion, from the miserable consciousness that their life was so hard for them; they could only meet in secret, hiding themselves from people, like thieves! Was not their life shattered?

"Come, do stop!" he said.

It was evident to him that this love of theirs would not soon be over, that he 115 could not see the end of it. Anna Sergeyevna grew more and more attached to him. She adored him, and it was unthinkable to say to her that it was bound to have an end some day; besides, she would not have believed it!

He went up to her and took her by the shoulders to say something affectionate and cheering, and at that moment he saw himself in the looking-glass.

His hair was already beginning to turn grey. And it seemed strange to him that he had grown so much older, so much plainer during the last few years. The shoulders on which his hands rested were warm and quivering. He felt compassion for this life, still so warm and lovely, but probably already not far from beginning to fade and wither like his own. Why did she love him so much? He always seemed to women different from what he was, and they loved in him not himself but the man created by their imagination, whom they had been eagerly seeking all their lives; and afterwards, when they noticed their mistake, they loved him all the same. And not one of them had been happy with him. Time passed, he had made their acquaintance, got on with them, parted, but he had never once loved; it was anything you like, but not love.

And only now when his head was grey he had fallen properly, really in love — for the first time in his life.

Anna Sergeyevna and he loved each other like people very close and akin, like husband and wife, like tender friends; it seemed to them that fate itself had meant them for one another, and they could not understand why he had a wife and she a husband; and it was as though they were a pair of birds of passage, caught and forced to live in different cages. They forgave each other for what they were ashamed of in their past, they forgave everything in the present, and felt that this love of theirs had changed them both.

In moments of depression in the past he had comforted himself with any 120 arguments that came into his mind, but now he no longer cared for arguments; he felt profound compassion, he wanted to be sincere and tender. . . .

"Don't cry, my darling," he said. "You've had your cry; that's enough. . . . Let us talk now, let us think of some plan."

Then they spent a long while taking counsel together, talked of how to avoid the necessity for secrecy, for deception, for living in different towns and not seeing each other for long at a time. How could they be free from this intolerable bondage?

"How? How?" he asked, clutching his head. "How?"

And it seemed as though in a little while the solution would be found, and then a new and splendid life would begin; and it was clear to both of them that they had still a long, long road before them, and that the most complicated and difficult part of it was only just beginning. [1899]

THINKING ABOUT THE TEXT

1. When Dmitri surprises Anna in the theater, she says, "I live only in the thought of you. And I wanted to forget, to forget you" (para. 97). This seems to get at the classic tension or conflict in this story. Explain what conflict Anna is trying to articulate.

2. When Dmitri's memories of Anna "glowed more and more vividly" (para. 64), were you sympathetic? Why? What might be some alternative responses? Is Chekhov on Dmitri's side?

3. How do you explain Dmitri's strong reaction to the official who responds to Dmitri's declaration with "You were right this evening: the sturgeon was a bit too strong!" (para. 71)?

4. Some readers find the ending frustratingly vague; others think it strikes just the right note. Would you have preferred a happier or sadder ending? Something more conclusive and detailed?

5. Several issues seem to be at play in this story — issues of definition (what is love?), cause and effect (why does Dmitri fall in love?), evaluation (is the lovers' behavior acceptable?), historical context (what forces were important then and now?), social policy (is it indeed a sign of progress that divorce is easy today?). Choose the one that seems most relevant, and explain why.

JOYCE CAROL OATES
The Lady with the Pet Dog

Born as part of an Irish-Catholic family in Lockport, New York, Joyce Carol Oates (b. 1938) grew up in the sort of rural, working-class setting in which she sets much of her fiction. After earning a B.A. from Syracuse University in 1960 and an M.A. from the University of Wisconsin in 1961, she went on to teach at the University of Detroit and the University of Windsor, Ontario. A prolific writer who has produced at least a volume of work a year since 1965, Oates has published poetry, drama, novels, short stories, and essays on diverse topics. Her many honors include the National Book Award for them *(1969). She is currently writer-in-residence and the Roger S. Berlind Distinguished Professor in the Humanities at Princeton University. Recent works include* We Were the Mulvaneys *(1998),* Blonde *(2000), and* Faithless: Tales of Transgression *(2001). In 1999 Oates won the O. Henry Prize for continued achievement in the short story. This story was first published in the collection* Marriage and Infidelities *(1972).*

I

Strangers parted as if to make way for him.

There he stood. He was there in the aisle, a few yards away, watching her.

She leaned forward at once in her seat, her hand jerked up to her face as if to ward off a blow—but then the crowd in the aisle hid him, he was gone. She pressed both hands against her cheeks. He was not here, she had imagined him.

"My God," she whispered.

She was alone. Her husband had gone out to the foyer to make a telephone call; it was intermission at the concert, a Thursday evening.   5

Now she saw him again, clearly. He was standing there. He was staring at her. Her blood rocked in her body, draining out of her head . . . she was going to faint. . . . They stared at each other. They gave no sign of recognition. Only when he took a step forward did she shake her head *no—no—keep away*. It was not possible.

When her husband returned, she was staring at the place in the aisle where her lover had been standing. Her husband leaned forward to interrupt that stare.

"What's wrong?" he said. "Are you sick?"

Panic rose in her in long shuddering waves. She tried to get to her feet, panicked at the thought of fainting here, and her husband took hold of her. She stood like an aged woman, clutching the seat before her.

At home he helped her up the stairs and she lay down. Her head was like a   10 large piece of crockery that had to be held still, it was so heavy. She was still panicked. She felt it in the shallows of her face, behind her knees, in the pit of her stomach. It sickened her, it made her think of mucus, of something thick and gray congested inside her, stuck to her, that was herself and yet not herself—a poison.

She lay with her knees drawn up toward her chest, her eyes hotly open, while her husband spoke to her. She imagined that other man saying, *Why did you run away from me?* Her husband was saying other words. She tried to listen to them. He was going to call the doctor, he said, and she tried to sit up. "No, I'm all right now," she said quickly. The panic was like lead inside her, so thickly congested. How slow love was to drain out of her, how fluid and sticky it was inside her head!

Her husband believed her. No doctor. No threat. Grateful, she drew her husband down to her. They embraced, not comfortably. For years now they had not been comfortable together, in their intimacy and at a distance, and now they struggled gently as if the paces of this dance were too rigorous for them. It was something they might have known once, but had now outgrown. The panic in her thickened at this double betrayal: she drew her husband to her, she caressed him wildly, she shut her eyes to think about that other man.

A crowd of men and women parting, unexpectedly, and there he stood— there he stood—she kept seeing him, and yet her vision blotched at the memory. It had been finished between them, six months before, but he had come out here . . . and she had escaped him, now she was lying in her husband's arms, in his embrace, her face pressed against his. It was a kind of sleep, this lovemaking. She felt herself falling asleep, her body falling from her. Her eyes shut.

"I love you," her husband said fiercely, angrily.

She shut her eyes and thought of that other man, as if betraying him would   15 give her life a center.

"Did I hurt you? Are you—?" Her husband whispered.

Always this hot flashing of shame between them, the shame of her husband's near failure, the clumsiness of his love —

"You didn't hurt me," she said.

II

They had said good-by six months before. He drove her from Nantucket, where they had met, to Albany, New York, where she visited her sister. The hours of intimacy in the car had sealed something between them, a vow of silence and impersonality: she recalled the movement of the highways, the passing of other cars, the natural rhythms of the day hypnotizing her toward sleep while he drove. She trusted him, she could sleep in his presence. Yet she could not really fall asleep in spite of her exhaustion, and she kept jerking awake, frightened, to discover that nothing had changed — still the stranger who was driving her to Albany, still the highway, the sky, the antiseptic odor of the rented car, the sense of a rhythm behind the rhythm of the air that might unleash itself at any second. Everywhere on this highway, at this moment, there were men and women driving together, bonded together — what did that mean, to be together? What did it mean to enter into a bond with another person?

No, she did not really trust him; she did not really trust men. He would   20
glance at her with his small cautious smile and she felt a declaration of shame between them.

Shame.

In her head she rehearsed conversations. She said bitterly, "You'll be relieved when we get to Albany. Relieved to get rid of me." They had spent so many days talking, confessing too much, driven to a pitch of childish excitement, laughing together on the beach, breaking into that pose of laughter that seems to eradicate the soul, so many days of this that the silence of the trip was like the silence of a hospital — all these surface noises, these rattles and hums, but an interior silence, a befuddlement. She said to him in her imagination, "One of us should die." Then she leaned over to touch him. She caressed the back of his neck. She said, aloud, "Would you like me to drive for a while?"

They stopped at a picnic area where other cars were stopped — couples, families — and walked together, smiling at their good luck. He put his arm around her shoulders and she sensed how they were in a posture together, a man and a woman forming a posture, a figure, that someone might sketch and show to them. She said slowly, "I don't want to go back. . . ."

Silence. She looked up at him. His face was heavy with her words, as if she had pulled at his skin with her fingers. Children ran nearby and distracted him — yes, he was a father too, his children ran like that, they tugged at his skin with their light, busy fingers.

"Are you so unhappy?" he said.   25

"I'm not unhappy, back there. I'm nothing. There's nothing to me," she said.

They stared at each other. The sensation between them was intense, exhausting. She thought that this man was her savior, that he had come to her at a time in her life when her life demanded completion, an end, a permanent fixing of all that was troubled and shifting and deadly. And yet it was absurd to think this. No person could save another. So she drew back from him and released him.

A few hours later they stopped at a gas station in a small city. She went to the women's rest room, having to ask the attendant for a key, and when she came back her eye jumped nervously onto the rented car—why? did she think he might have driven off without her?—onto the man, her friend, standing in conversation with the young attendant. Her friend was as old as her husband, over forty, with lanky, sloping shoulders, a full body, his hair thick, a dark, burnished brown, a festive color that made her eye twitch a little—and his hands were always moving, always those rapid conversational circles, going nowhere, gestures that were at once a little aggressive and apologetic.

She put her hand on his arm, a claim. He turned to her and smiled and she felt that she loved him, that everything in her life had forced her to this moment and that she had no choice about it.

They sat in the car for two hours, in Albany, in the parking lot of a Howard   30
Johnson's restaurant, talking, trying to figure out their past. There was no future. They concentrated on the past, the several days behind them, lit up with a hot, dazzling August sun, like explosions that already belonged to other people, to strangers. Her face was faintly reflected in the green-tinted curve of the windshield, but she could not have recognized that face. She began to cry; she told herself: *I am not here, this will pass, this is nothing.* Still, she could not stop crying. The muscles of her face were springy, like a child's, unpredictable muscles. He stroked her arms, her shoulders, trying to comfort her. "This is so hard . . . this is impossible . . ." he said. She felt panic for the world outside this car, all that was not herself and this man, and at the same time she understood that she was free of him, as people are free of other people, she would leave him soon, safely, and within a few days he would have fallen into the past, the impersonal past. . . .

"I'm so ashamed of myself!" she said finally.

She returned to her husband and saw that another woman, a shadow-woman, had taken her place—noiseless and convincing, like a dancer performing certain difficult steps. Her husband folded her in his arms and talked to her of his own loneliness, his worries about his business, his health, his mother, kept tranquilized and mute in a nursing home, and her spirit detached itself from her and drifted about the rooms of the large house she lived in with her husband, a shadow-woman delicate and imprecise. There was no boundary to her, no edge. Alone, she took hot baths and sat exhausted in the steaming water, wondering at her perpetual exhaustion. All that winter she noticed the limp, languid weight of her arms, her veins bulging slightly with the pressure of her extreme weariness. *This is fate*, she thought, to be here and not there, to be one person and not another, a certain man's wife and not the wife of another man. The long, slow pain of this certainty rose in her, but it never became clear, it was baffling and imprecise. She could not be serious about it; she kept congratulating herself on her own good luck, to have escaped so easily, to have freed herself. So much love had gone into the first several years of her marriage that there wasn't much left, now, for another man. . . . She was certain of that. But the bath water made her dizzy, all that perpetual heat, and one day in January she drew a razor blade lightly across the inside of her arm, near the elbow, to see what would happen.

Afterward she wrapped a small towel around it, to stop the bleeding. The towel soaked through. She wrapped a bath towel around that and walked through the empty rooms of her home, lightheaded, hardly aware of the stubborn seeping of blood. There was no boundary to her in this house, no precise limit. She could flow out like her own blood and come to no end.

She sat for a while on a blue love seat, her mind empty. Her husband telephoned her when he would be staying late at the plant. He talked to her always about his plans, his problems, his business friends, his future. It was obvious that he had a future. As he spoke she nodded to encourage him, and her heartbeat quickened with the memory of her own, personal shame, the shame of this man's particular, private wife. One evening at dinner he leaned forward and put his head in his arms and fell asleep, like a child. She sat at the table with him for a while, watching him. His hair had gone gray, almost white, at the temples — no one would guess that he was so quick, so careful a man, still fairly young about the eyes. She put her hand on his head, lightly, as if to prove to herself that he was real. He slept, exhausted.

One evening they went to a concert and she looked up to see her lover there, 　35
in the crowded aisle, in this city, watching her. He was standing there, with his overcoat on, watching her. She went cold. That morning the telephone had rung while her husband was still home, and she had heard him answer it, heard him hang up — it must have been a wrong number — and when the telephone rang again, at 9:30, she had been afraid to answer it. She had left home to be out of the range of that ringing, but now, in this public place, in this busy auditorium, she found herself staring at that man, unable to make any sign to him, any gesture of recognition. . . .

He would have come to her but she shook her head. No. *Stay away.*

Her husband helped her out of the row of seats, saying, "Excuse us, please. Excuse us," so that strangers got to their feet, quickly, alarmed, to let them pass. Was that woman about to faint? What was wrong?

At home she felt the blood drain slowly back into her head. Her husband embraced her hips, pressing his face against her, in that silence that belonged to the earliest days of their marriage. She thought, *He will drive it out of me.* He made love to her and she was back in the auditorium again, sitting alone, now that the concert was over. The stage was empty; the heavy velvet curtains had not been drawn; the musicians' chairs were empty, everything was silent and expectant; in the aisle her lover stood and smiled at her — Her husband was impatient. He was apart from her, working on her, operating on her; and then, stricken, he whispered, "Did I hurt you?"

The telephone rang the next morning. Dully, sluggishly, she answered it. She recognized his voice at once — that "Anna?" with its lifting of the second syllable, questioning and apologetic and making its claim — "Yes, what do you want?" she said.

"Just to see you. Please —" 　40

"I can't."

"Anna, I'm sorry, I didn't mean to upset you —"

"I can't see you."

"Just for a few minutes — I have to talk to you —"

"But why, why now? Why now?" she said.   45

She heard her voice rising, but she could not stop it. He began to talk again, drowning her out. She remembered his rapid conversation. She remembered his gestures, the witty energetic circling of his hands.

"Please don't hang up!" he cried.

"I can't — I don't want to go through it again — "

"I'm not going to hurt you. Just tell me how you are."

"Everything is the same."   50

"Everything is the same with me."

She looked up at the ceiling, shyly. "Your wife? Your children?"

"The same."

"Your son?"

"He's fine — "   55

"I'm so glad to hear that. I — "

"Is it still the same with you, your marriage? Tell me what you feel. What are you thinking?"

"I don't know. . . ."

She remembered his intense, eager words, the movement of his hands, that impatient precise fixing of the air by his hands, the jabbing of his fingers.

"Do you love me?" he said.   60

She could not answer.

"I'll come over to see you," he said.

"No," she said.

What will come next, what will happen?

Flesh hardening on his body, aging. Shrinking. He will grow old, but not soft   65
like her husband. They are two different types: he is nervous, lean, energetic, wise. She will grow thinner, as the tension radiates out from her backbone, wearing down her flesh. Her collarbones will jut out of her skin. Her husband, caressing her in their bed, will discover that she is another woman — she is not there with him — instead she is rising in an elevator in a downtown hotel, carrying a book as a prop, or walking quickly away from that hotel, her head bent and filled with secrets. Love, what to do with it? . . . Useless as moths' wings, as moths' fluttering. . . . She feels the flutterings of silky, crazy wings in her chest.

He flew out to visit her every several weeks, staying at a different hotel each time. He telephoned her, and she drove down to park in an underground garage at the very center of the city.

She lay in his arms while her husband talked to her, miles away, one body fading into another. He will grow old, his body will change, she thought, pressing her cheek against the back of one of these men. If it was her lover, they were in a hotel room: always the propped-up little booklet describing the hotel's many services, with color photographs of its cocktail lounge and dining room and coffee shop. Grow old, leave me, die, go back to your neurotic wife and your sad, ordinary children, she thought, but still her eyes closed gratefully against his skin and she felt how complete their silence was, how they had come to rest in each other.

"Tell me about your life here. The people who love you," he said, as he always did.

One afternoon they lay together for four hours. It was her birthday and she was intoxicated with her good fortune, this prize of the afternoon, this man in her arms! She was a little giddy, she talked too much. She told him about her parents, about her husband. . . ."They were all people I believed in, but it turned out wrong. Now, I believe in you. . . ." He laughed as if shocked by her words. She did not understand. Then she understood. "But I believe truly in you. I can't think of myself without you," she said. . . . He spoke of his wife, her ambitions, her intelligence, her use of the children against him, her use of his younger son's blindness, all of his words gentle and hypnotic and convincing in the late afternoon peace of this hotel room . . . and she felt the terror of laughter, threatening laughter. Their words, like their bodies, were aging.

She dressed quickly in the bathroom, drawing her long hair up around the   70 back of her head, fixing it as always, anxious that everything be the same. Her face was slightly raw, from his face. The rubbing of his skin. Her eyes were too bright, wearily bright. Her hair was blond but not so blond as it had been that summer in the white Nantucket air.

She ran water and splashed it on her face. She blinked at the water. Blind. Drowning. She thought with satisfaction that soon, soon, he would be back home, in that house on Long Island she had never seen, with that woman she had never seen, sitting on the edge of another bed, putting on his shoes. She wanted nothing except to be free of him. Why not be free? *Oh,* she thought suddenly, *I will follow you back and kill you. You and her and the little boy. What is there to stop me?*

She left him. Everyone on the street pitied her, that look of absolute zero.

III

A man and a child, approaching her. The sharp acrid smell of fish. The crashing of waves. Anna pretended not to notice the father with his son — there was something strange about them. That frank, silent intimacy, too gentle, the man's bare feet in the water and the boy a few feet away, leaning away from his father. He was about nine years old and still his father held his hand.

A small yipping dog, a golden dog, bounded near them.

Anna turned shyly back to her reading; she did not want to have to speak to   75 these neighbors. She saw the man's shadow falling over her legs, then over the pages of her book, and she had the idea that he wanted to see what she was reading. The dog nuzzled her; the man called him away.

She watched them walk down the beach. She was relieved that the man had not spoken to her.

She saw them in town later that day, the two of them brown-haired and patient, now wearing sandals, walking with that same look of care. The man's white shorts were soiled and a little baggy. His pullover shirt was a faded green. His face was broad, the cheekbones wide, spaced widely apart, the eyes stark in their sockets, as if they fastened onto objects for no reason, ponderous and edgy. The little boy's face was pale and sharp; his lips were perpetually parted.

Anna realized that the child was blind.

The next morning, early, she caught sight of them again. For some reason she went to the back door of her cottage. She faced the sea breeze eagerly. Her heart hammered. . . . She had been here, in her family's old house, for three days, alone, bitterly satisfied at being alone, and now it was a puzzle to her how her soul strained to fly outward, to meet with another person. She watched the man with his son, his cautious, rather stooped shoulders above the child's small shoulders.

The man was carrying something, it looked like a notebook. He sat on the 80 sand, not far from Anna's spot of the day before, and the dog rushed up to them. The child approached the edge of the ocean, timidly. He moved in short jerky steps, his legs stiff. The dog ran around him. Anna heard the child crying out a word that sounded like "Ty"—it must have been the dog's name—and then the man joined in, his voice heavy and firm.

"Ty—"

Anna tied her hair back with a yellow scarf and went down to the beach.

The man glanced around at her. He smiled. She stared past him at the waves. To talk to him or not to talk—she had the freedom of that choice. For a moment she felt that she had made a mistake, that the child and the dog would not protect her, that behind this man's ordinary, friendly face there was a certain arrogant maleness—then she relented, she smiled shyly.

"A nice house you've got there," the man said.

She nodded her thanks. 85

The man pushed his sunglasses up on his forehead. Yes, she recognized the eyes of the day before—intelligent and nervous, the sockets pale, untanned.

"Is that your telephone ringing?" he said.

She did not bother to listen. "It's a wrong number," she said.

Her husband calling: she had left home for a few days, to be alone.

But the man, settling himself on the sand, seemed to misinterpret this. He 90 smiled in surprise, one corner of his mouth higher than the other. He said nothing. Anna wondered: *What is he thinking?* The dog was leaping about her, panting against her legs, and she laughed in embarrassment. She bent to pet it, grateful for its busyness. "Don't let him jump up on you," the man said. "He's a nuisance."

The dog was a small golden retriever, a young dog. The blind child, standing now in the water, turned to call the dog to him. His voice was shrill and impatient.

"Our house is the third one down—the white one," the man said.

She turned, startled. "Oh, did you buy it from Dr. Patrick? Did he die?"

"Yes, finally. . . ."

Her eyes wandered nervously over the child and the dog. She felt the ner- 95 vous beat of her heart out to the very tips of her fingers, the fleshy tips of her fingers: little hearts were there, pulsing. *What is he thinking?* The man had opened his notebook. He had a piece of charcoal and he began to sketch something.

Anna looked down at him. She saw the top of his head, his thick brown hair, the freckles on his shoulders, the quick, deft movement of his hand. Upside down, Anna herself being drawn. She smiled in surprise.

"Let me draw you. Sit down," he said.

She knelt awkwardly a few yards away. He turned the page of the sketch pad. The dog ran to her and she sat, straightening out her skirt beneath her, flinching from the dog's tongue. "Ty!" cried the child. Anna sat, and slowly the pleasure of the moment began to glow in her; her skin flushed with gratitude.

She sat there for nearly an hour. The man did not talk much. Back and forth the dog bounded, shaking itself. The child came to sit near them, in silence. Anna felt that she was drifting into a kind of trance while the man sketched her, half a dozen rapid sketches, the surface of her face given up to him. "Where are you from?" the man asked.

"Ohio. My husband lives in Ohio."   100

She wore no wedding band.

"Your wife — " Anna began.

"Yes?"

"Is she here?"

"Not right now."   105

She was silent, ashamed. She had asked an improper question. But the man did not seem to notice. He continued drawing her, bent over the sketch pad. When Anna said she had to go, he showed her the drawings — one after another of her, Anna, recognizably Anna, a woman in her early thirties, her hair smooth and flat across the top of her head, tied behind by a scarf. "Take the one you like best," he said, and she picked one of her with the dog in her lap, sitting very straight, her brows and eyes clearly defined, her lips girlishly pursed, the dog and her dress suggested by a few quick irregular lines.

"Lady with pet dog," the man said.

She spent the rest of that day reading, nearer her cottage. It was not really a cottage — it was a two-story house, large and ungainly and weathered. It was mixed up in her mind with her family, her own childhood, and she glanced up from her book, perplexed, as if waiting for one of her parents or her sister to come up to her. Then she thought of that man, the man with the blind child, the man with the dog, and she could not concentrate on her reading. Someone — probably her father — had marked a passage that must be important, but she kept reading and rereading it: *We try to discover in things, endeared to us on that account, the spiritual glamour which we ourselves have cast upon them; we are disillusioned, and learn that they are in themselves barren and devoid of the charm that they owed, in our minds, to the association of certain ideas.* . . .

She thought again of the man on the beach. She lay the book aside and thought of him: his eyes, his aloneness, his drawings of her.

They began seeing each other after that. He came to her front door in the   110
evening, without the child; he drove her into town for dinner. She was shy and extremely pleased. The darkness of the expensive restaurant released her; she heard herself chatter; she leaned forward and seemed to be offering her face up to him, listening to him. He talked about his work on a Long Island newspaper and she seemed to be listening to him, as she stared at his face, arranging her own face into the expression she had seen in that charcoal drawing. Did he see her

like that, then? — girlish and withdrawn and patrician? She felt the weight of his interest in her, a force that fell upon her like a blow. A repeated blow. Of course he was married, he had children — of course she was married, permanently married. This flight from her husband was not important. She had left him before, to be alone, it was not important. Everything in her was slender and delicate and not important.

They walked for hours after dinner, looking at the other strollers, the weekend visitors, the tourists, the couples like themselves. Surely they were mistaken for a couple, a married couple. *This is the hour in which everything is decided,* Anna thought. They had both had several drinks and they talked a great deal. Anna found herself saying too much, stopping and starting giddily. She put her hand to her forehead, feeling faint.

"It's from the sun — you've had too much sun — " he said.

At the door to her cottage, on the front porch, she heard herself asking him if he would like to come in. She allowed him to lead her inside, to close the door. *This is not important,* she thought clearly, *he doesn't mean it, he doesn't love me, nothing will come of it.* She was frightened, yet it seemed to her necessary to give in; she had to leave Nantucket with that act completed, an act of adultery, an accomplishment she would take back to Ohio and to her marriage.

Later, incredibly, she heard herself asking: "Do you . . . do you love me?"

"You're so beautiful!" he said, amazed.   115

She felt this beauty, shy and glowing and centered in her eyes. He stared at her. In this large, drafty house, alone together, they were like accomplices, conspirators. She could not think: how old was she? which year was this? They had done something unforgivable together, and the knowledge of it was tugging at their faces. A cloud seemed to pass over her. She felt herself smiling shrilly.

Afterward, a peculiar raspiness, a dryness of breath. He was silent. She felt a strange, idle fear, a sense of the danger outside this room and this old comfortable bed — a danger that would not recognize her as the lady in that drawing, the lady with the pet dog. There was nothing to say to this man, this stranger. She felt the beauty draining out of her face, her eyes fading.

"I've got to be alone," she told him.

He left, and she understood that she would not see him again. She stood by the window of the room, watching the ocean. A sense of shame overpowered her: it was smeared everywhere on her body, the smell of it, the richness of it. She tried to recall him, and his face was confused in her memory: she would have to shout to him across a jumbled space, she would have to wave her arms wildly. *You love me! You must love me!* But she knew he did not love her, and she did not love him; he was a man who drew everything up into himself, like all men, walking away, free to walk away, free to have his own thoughts, free to envision her body, all the secrets of her body. . . . And she lay down again in the bed, feeling how heavy this body had become, her insides heavy with shame, the very backs of her eyelids coated with shame.

"This is the end of one part of my life," she thought.   120

But in the morning the telephone rang. She answered it. It was her lover: they talked brightly and happily. She could hear the eagerness in his voice, the love in his voice, that same still, sad amazement—she understood how simple life was, there were no problems.

They spent most of their time on the beach, with the child and the dog. He joked and was serious at the same time. He said, once, "You have defined my soul for me," and she laughed to hide her alarm. In a few days it was time for her to leave. He got a sitter for the boy and took the ferry with her to the mainland, then rented a car to drive her up to Albany. She kept thinking: *Now something will happen. It will come to an end.* But most of the drive was silent and hypnotic. She wanted him to joke with her, to say again that she had defined his soul for him, but he drove fast, he was serious, she distrusted the hawkish look of his profile— she did not know him at all. At a gas station she splashed her face with cold water. Alone in the grubby little rest room, shaky and very much alone. In such places are women totally alone with their bodies. The body grows heavier, more evil, in such silence. . . . On the beach everything had been noisy with sunlight and gulls and waves; here, as if run to earth, everything was cramped and silent and dead.

She went outside, squinting. There he was, talking with the station attendant. She could not think as she returned to him whether she wanted to live or not.

She stayed in Albany for a few days, then flew home to her husband. He met her at the airport, near the luggage counter, where her three pieces of pale-brown luggage were brought to him on a conveyer belt, to be claimed by him. He kissed her on the cheek. They shook hands, a little embarrassed. She had come home again.

"How will I live out the rest of my life?" she wondered.   125

In January her lover spied on her: she glanced up and saw him, in a public place, in the DeRoy Symphony Hall. She was paralyzed with fear. She nearly fainted. In this faint she felt her husband's body, loving her, working its love upon her, and she shut her eyes harder to keep out the certainty of his love—some-times he failed at loving her, sometimes he succeeded, it had nothing to do with her or her pity or her ten years of love for him, it had nothing to do with a woman at all. It was a private act accomplished by a man, a husband, or a lover, in com-munion with his own soul, his manhood.

Her husband was forty-two years old now, growing slowly into middle age, getting heavier, softer. Her lover was about the same age, narrower in the shoul-ders, with a full, solid chest, yet lean, nervous. She thought, in her paralysis, of men and how they love freely and eagerly so long as their bodies are capable of love, love for a woman; and then, as love fades in their bodies, it fades from their souls and they become immune and immortal and ready to die.

Her husband was a little rough with her, as if impatient with himself. "I love you," he said fiercely, angrily. And then, ashamed, he said, "Did I hurt you? . . ."

"You didn't hurt me," she said.

Her voice was too shrill for their embrace.   130

While he was in the bathroom she went to her closet and took out that draw-ing of the summer before. There she was, on the beach at Nantucket, a lady with a pet dog, her eyes large and defined, the dog in her lap hardly more than a few snarls, a few coarse soft lines of charcoal . . . her dress smeared, her arms oddly limp . . . her hands not well drawn at all. . . . She tried to think: did she love the

man who had drawn this? did he love her? The fever in her husband's body had
touched her and driven her temperature up, and now she stared at the drawing
with a kind of lust, fearful of seeing an ugly soul in that woman's face, fearful of
seeing the face suddenly through her lover's eyes. She breathed quickly and
harshly, staring at the drawing.

And so, the next day, she went to him at his hotel. She wept, pressing against
him, demanding of him, "What do you want? Why are you here? Why don't you
let me alone?" He told her that he wanted nothing. He expected nothing. He
would not cause trouble.

"I want to talk about last August," he said.

"Don't—" she said.

She was hypnotized by his gesturing hands, his nervousness, his obvious agi-   135
tation. He kept saying, "I understand. I'm making no claims upon you."

They became lovers again.

He called room service for something to drink and they sat side by side on his
bed, looking through a copy of *The New Yorker*, laughing at the cartoons. It was so
peaceful in this room, so complete. They were on a holiday. It was a secret holiday. Four-thirty in the afternoon, on a Friday, an ordinary Friday: a secret holiday.

"I won't bother you again," he said.

He flew back to see her again in March, and in late April. He telephoned her
from his hotel—a different hotel each time—and she came down to him at once.
She rose to him in various elevators, she knocked on the doors of various rooms,
she stepped into his embrace, breathless and guilty and already angry with him,
pleading with him. One morning in May, when he telephoned, she pressed her
forehead against the doorframe and could not speak. He kept saying, "What's
wrong? Can't you talk? Aren't you alone?" She felt that she was going insane. Her
head would burst. Why, why did he love her, why did he pursue her? Why did he
want her to die?

She went to him in the hotel room. A familiar room: had they been here   140
before? "Everything is repeating itself. Everything is stuck," she said. He framed
her face in his hands and said that she looked thinner—was she sick?—what was
wrong? She shook herself free. He, her lover, looked about the same. There was a
small, angry pimple on his neck. He stared at her, eagerly and suspiciously. Did
she bring bad news?

"So you love me? You love me?" she asked.

"Why are you so angry?"

"I want to be free of you. The two of us free of each other."

"That isn't true—you don't want that—"

He embraced her. She was wild with that old, familiar passion for him, her   145
body clinging to his, her arms not strong enough to hold him. Ah, what
despair!—what bitter hatred she felt!—she needed this man for her salvation, he
was all she had to live for, and yet she could not believe in him. He embraced her
thighs, her hips, kissing her, pressing his warm face against her, and yet she could
not believe in him, not really. She needed him in order to live, but he was not
worth her love, he was not worth her dying. . . . She promised herself this: when

she got back home, when she was alone, she would draw the razor more deeply across her arm.

The telephone rang and he answered it: a wrong number.

"Jesus," he said.

They lay together, still. She imagined their posture like this, the two of them one figure, one substance; and outside this room and this bed there was a universe of disjointed, separate things, blank things, that had nothing to do with them. She would not be Anna out there, the lady in the drawing. He would not be her lover.

"I love you so much . . ." she whispered.

"Please don't cry! We have only a few hours, please. . . ." 150

It was absurd, their clinging together like this. She saw them as a single figure in a drawing, their arms and legs entwined, their heads pressing mutely together. Helpless substance, so heavy and warm and doomed. It was absurd that any human being should be so important to another human being. She wanted to laugh: a laugh might free them both.

She could not laugh.

Sometime later he said, as if they had been arguing, "Look. It's you. You're the one who doesn't want to get married. You lie to me—"

"Lie to you?"

"You love me but you won't marry me, because you want something left 155 over—Something not finished—All your life you can attribute your misery to me, to our not being married—you are using me—"

"Stop it! You'll make me hate you!" she cried.

"You can say to yourself that you're miserable because of *me*. We will never be married, you will never be happy, neither one of us will ever be happy—"

"I don't want to hear this!" she said.

She pressed her hands flatly against her face.

She went to the bathroom to get dressed. She washed her face and part of her 160 body, quickly. The fever was in her, in the pit of her belly. She would rush home and strike a razor across the inside of her arm and free that pressure, that fever.

The impatient bulging of the veins: an ordeal over.

The demand of the telephone's ringing: that ordeal over.

The nuisance of getting the car and driving home in all that five o'clock traffic: an ordeal too much for a woman.

The movement of this stranger's body in hers: over, finished.

Now, dressed, a little calmer, they held hands and talked. They had to talk 165 swiftly, to get all their news in: he did not trust the people who worked for him, he had faith in no one, his wife had moved to a textbook publishing company and was doing well, she had inherited a Ben Shahn painting from her father and wanted to "touch it up a little"—she was crazy!—his blind son was at another school, doing fairly well, in fact his children were all doing fairly well in spite of the stupid mistake of their parents' marriage—and what about her? what about her life? She told him in a rush the one thing he wanted to hear: that she lived with her husband lovelessly, the two of them polite strangers, sharing a bed, lying side by side in the night in that bed, bodies out of which souls had fled. There was no longer even any shame between them.

"And what about me? Do you feel shame with me still?" he asked.

She did not answer. She moved away from him and prepared to leave.

Then, a minute later, she happened to catch sight of his reflection in the bureau mirror — he was glancing down at himself, checking himself mechanically, impersonally, preparing also to leave. He too would leave this room: he too was headed somewhere else.

She stared at him. It seemed to her that in this instant he was breaking from her, the image of her lover fell free of her, breaking from her . . . and she realized that he existed in a dimension quite apart from her, a mysterious being. And suddenly, joyfully, she felt a miraculous calm. This man was her husband, truly — they were truly married, here in this room — they had been married haphazardly and accidentally for a long time. In another part of the city she had another husband, a "husband," but she had not betrayed that man, not really. This man, whom she loved above any other person in the world, above even her own self-pitying sorrow and her own life, was her truest lover, her destiny. And she did not hate him, she did not hate herself any longer; she did not wish to die; she was flooded with a strange certainty, a sense of gratitude, of pure selfless energy. It was obvious to her that she had, all along, been behaving correctly; out of instinct.

What triumph, to love like this in any room, anywhere, risking even the craziest of accidents!   170

"Why are you so happy? What's wrong?" he asked, startled. He stared at her. She felt the abrupt concentration in him, the focusing of his vision on her, almost a bitterness in his face, as if he feared her. What, was it beginning all over again? Their love beginning again, in spite of them? "How can you look so happy?" he asked. "We don't have any right to it. Is it because . . . ?"

"Yes," she said.   [1972]

THINKING ABOUT THE TEXT

1. Do you think that this story, told from a female point of view, captures a modern woman's consciousness in trying to negotiate the demands of her heart and her head?

2. What specific changes do you think would occur if Anna's lover became the central consciousness of the story? Does Anna have specific thoughts that make you sympathetic?

3. Psychologists tell us that in illicit love affairs our emotions are stretched to extremes. Can you give some examples of Anna's emotions being extreme? Do you think these are normal, given the context? What do they tell us about her?

4. Do you agree with Anna at the end when she claims, "What triumph, to love like this in any room, anywhere, risking even the craziest of accidents"? Is she saying love is the highest achievement, the ultimate goal, against all else?

MAKING COMPARISONS

1. Chekhov's story is told in linear time. Describe Oates's temporal strategy. Why, for example, do the characters, Anna and her lover, not meet until about the middle of the story?

2. Shame is mentioned several times in Oates's story. In what ways is shame a factor in Chekhov's story? How would you describe shame?

3. Is Oates's ending more or less satisfying than Chekhov's? How might you briefly describe the ending of each to a friend, putting your explicit spin on what you think is going on?

BETH LORDAN

The Man with the Lapdog

Beth Lordan (b. 1948) received her B.A. and M.F.A. from Cornell University. She has been teaching writing and literature at Southern Illinois University at Carbondale since 1991. Her first novel, August Heat, *was published in 1987. A collection of short stories,* And Both Shall Row, *was published in 1998. The following story was originally published in* The Atlantic Monthly *in February 1999 and won second prize in the 2000 O. Henry Awards. Not surprisingly, in her notes the author says her story implies "something about the connection between contemporary stories and previous literature."*

Almost every morning, as Lyle was getting ready to take the dog for a walk along the bay, his wife would ask, "Are ye down the prom, then?" They had met and married thirty years before, in Vermont, when she was Mary Curtin and he'd thought her a happy combination of exotic and domestic. At sixty, after their life in the States, she still called herself a Galway girl; at sixty-seven, after two years of retirement in Galway, Lyle still considered a prom a high school dance, not two miles of sidewalk beside the water.

So he would say, "We're going to walk along the bay," and hope she'd leave it at that. When they had first come to Ireland, the exchange had had a bit of a joke to it, but he felt it now as unwelcome pressure. He had no intention of taking up Irish idioms — he'd have felt foolish saying "half-five" instead of five-thirty, "Tuesday week" instead of next Tuesday, "ye" for you. "Toilet" instead of bathroom was unthinkable. He called things by their real names — "pubs" bars, "shops" stores, "chips" French fries, and "gardai" police.

He didn't love the talk, and he didn't love the Irish people, who always stood too close and talked too fast, and he had trouble, still, understanding what they said. He had frightened and embarrassed himself trying to drive on the wrong side of the road with the steering wheel on the wrong side of the car and had given it up. He disliked the weight of pound coins in his pocket, and he didn't care for Guinness.

And yet, somewhat to his surprise, he liked a lot about Ireland. He liked keeping the small garden in front of their house, the way things simply grew and thrived in the steady cool dampness. He liked the stone walls that surrounded every yard and separated one person's place from another's. He liked the little coal-burning fireplace in the sitting room. After forty years as an accountant for a hardware chain, he liked living in a place where people went for walks, and he liked going for walks. He liked the dog, a long-haired dachshund, a pretty, girlish little thing. He liked the opinionated newspapers, and he liked being a foreigner.

One day in early March, walking along the bay, he saw a couple he probably   5
wouldn't have noticed among the other tourists if it had been summer. They stood arm in arm looking out over the water, the woman dark-haired and attractive in an unglamorous way, the man thin and frail, apparently very ill. Lyle heard her say, "Yes, County Clare — I'm sure of it," her American accent clear; he nodded as he passed, and they nodded in response. The next day their walks crossed at about the same place, and all three smiled in recognition. That evening something on television about preseason tourists reminded him to say that he'd met an American couple.

"Have you?" his wife said. "Where are they from?"

"I don't know," he replied, sorry already that he'd said anything.

She tilted her head as if she was being playful and said, "So did ye talk about the weather, then?"

"Yes," he said. "We talked about the ugly weather."

On the third day, when they met again, Lyle gave the leash the small tug that   10
told the dog to sit and said, "It's a beautiful day, isn't it? — good to see the sun again."

Something rippled between the man and the woman and came out as a quick laugh in her answer. "It's glorious," she agreed. "And you're American!" she said.

"I am," he said.

The man, too, seemed amused as he put out his hand in introduction. "I'm Mark; this is my wife, Laura. And we, too, are Americans."

"Lyle," he said. He shook Mark's thin hand. "Are you here on vacation?"

"For three weeks," Laura said, as if three weeks were a long, luxurious season.   15
"And you?"

The dog was sitting patiently. "I'm retired, and my wife is Irish, so we came back here to live a couple of years ago."

They said where they were from, and how old their children were, and that this was their first trip to Ireland, long dreamed about, and then Laura reached out and put her hand lightly and briefly on the sleeve of Lyle's coat. "I have to tell you: we'd seen you walking here, and we made up a life for you —"

"We assumed you were Irish, of course," Mark said.

"I suppose it's because everything is so exactly as we expected it to be," Laura said. "The stone walls in the fields when we were coming over from Shannon, the pretty shops, the thatched roofs. We even saw a rainbow our first day here. So we just put you into the picture, the Galway gentleman, and when you turn out to be American, it's quite a joke on us." Her eyes sparkled.

Her eyes were very fine, her face strong, and Lyle admired even the simple   20
way she held her dark hair in her fist to keep it from blowing across her face. She

was coming into middle age with none of the artificiality of so many American women.

"So I've spoiled your postcard," he said, and all three of them laughed. When they parted, he kept the picture of himself her words had made: his overcoat and hat, his kindly aging face, the tidy small dog, obedient at the end of the leash. And he kept, too, the swift pleasure of her hand on his coat.

They met again the next day and the next, stopping to talk for a few minutes. Lyle would recognize them at some distance by Mark's brimmed hat and the bright shawl Laura wore over the shoulders of her coat. They walked in the mornings, she said, before the wind got too strong, because the wind tired Mark. He had lost his hair, and his face was swollen, but Lyle could see that in health he had been a handsome man. They always walked arm in arm, and she often seemed to be supporting him, more as a matter of balance than of strength, but something in the way they looked together led Lyle to believe that even before Mark's illness they had often walked this old-fashioned way, side by side, along streets or through parks. Lyle could almost remember the pleasure of that — the hand a warm pressure in the bend of his elbow, the wrist between his arm and his ribs eloquent and secret, the publicness of the linking.

The next evening his wife asked about his Americans, and he told her they were from Idaho, where Mark taught high school and Laura raised their four teenage children, who were with grandparents for these three weeks.

"A teacher," his wife said, wondering. "An expensive holiday for a teacher — and during the term."

"They have those deals," he said. "Two-for-ones. Off season." They were eating spaghetti, and he watched how she poked around among the strands, looking for something in particular.   25

"From the States to Ireland, do you think?" she said, doubtful.

"I don't know."

She chewed, and he could almost see her mind shifting. "If they did, Jimmy might be looking into it so."

Jimmy was their younger son, twenty-five years old without a dollar or a plan to his name. "He might," Lyle said cautiously.

She went on about fares and connections, and then safely into a story her sis-   30
ter Roisin had told her of a trip somebody had taken by bus from somewhere in Kerry to somewhere in Clare that sped along, if you counted all the time, at a rate of about six miles an hour. Lyle was relieved: they wouldn't have to talk about buying Jimmy a ticket, or how they weren't exactly rich themselves, or about his life-hating caution and how he'd always favored Kevin, and on and on. He finished his supper and waited for the end of the story, the ritual shake of her head, the "It's a terrible country." Back home she had told different stories about Ireland, ending them with "It's a grand country." Sometimes, now, he'd point this out to her, and ask why she had wanted to come back here if it was so damned terrible. But tonight, as he waited, in the noise of the long details of her telling, he thought of how simply Laura had spoken that morning.

She had asked about Saint Patrick's Day, how it would be celebrated, while Mark walked alone at a little distance, stooping unsteadily to pick up small shells.

Lyle told her that the parade would be small compared with American parades, the day a quiet family holiday, more like Labor Day than Mardi Gras.

"Maybe we'll try the parade, then," she said, watching Mark's slow progress back. "If it's not likely to be a big crowd. He gets tired."

"Is his recovery expected to be long?" Lyle had wondered for days how to ask and was pleased at how naturally the question came out.

"Oh, he won't recover," she said. "He's dying."

She put no drama into it at all, not into the words, not into the tone, not into   35
the way she raised her hand against the sudden emergence of the sun. "I'm sorry," Lyle said.

She nodded. "So are we." And then they had stood there quiet, waiting for Mark to come back and for their walks in opposite directions to continue.

He hadn't told his wife any of that, and now she had passed the end of the bus story and had come to something else. "It's not the traveling, I told her, it's the staying that's so dear, and she was saying that that's where the money is, in B-and-Bs. Why, the people in Kerry, half of them, in the summer move into caravans in their own back gardens and let all their rooms to the tourists. I couldn't do that, I told her—you know how I am about motels, sleeping in other people's beds, and it'd be the same thing but worse, having strangers in your bed and then going back to it in October so, knowing they'd been there. I'd be thinking I could feel the heat of those bodies in the mattress." She stood and gathered up the plates and silverware.

There, in something that wasn't quite his mind and wasn't quite his body, he felt the sweet warmth a woman left in a bed, and knew that the shape and smell of the warmth were Laura's. So when his wife asked, "They're at a B-and-B, I'd think, your Americans?" he responded, "Why—are you going to go ask what their damned tickets cost?"

She stopped in her work and stared at him. "That was nasty," she said, but he saw that her eyes were only alert, not wounded.

"Oh, give it a rest," he said, and went into the sitting room and turned on the   40
television and called the dog to his lap.

He discovered where they were staying by accident. The day before Saint Patrick's the rain was heavy, so he and the dog were trapped inside with the smell of damp coal ash and his wife's endless talk about the rain—lashing, she said, coming down in rods, she said, bucketing down, and how she hated rain in her face, she said, and, now, a soft day she didn't mind. But by midmorning the next day the rain had stopped, and he said he was going out. As he was putting on his overcoat, she came with a limp hank of shamrock and knelt on the kitchen floor to tie it to the dog's collar. "That looks pretty stupid," he said.

She patted the dog's head and stood up. "It looks lovely." She had two more bits, and he allowed her to pin one to the lapel of his coat. "Are you thinking of going to the parade, then?" she asked.

"It's not until noon." He hooked the leash onto the dog's collar. "Did you want to go?"

She made a wry face and pushed her hand in the air between them. "It's a poor excuse for a parade," she said. "Roisin's calling by for me to help her with her new curtains. I'll be back before tea."

Out of sight of the house, he stooped and adjusted the dog's greenery. The air was clean and cool. As he passed one of the schools, he could hear a few horns behind the building—kids preparing for the parade. Small family groups were slowly walking toward the parade route. Many people had small bunches of shamrock pinned to their coats. Children carried tricolors, and a few older boys had their faces painted green. He headed for the Salmon Weir Bridge, meaning to walk around the college and then circle back and maybe see the parade, maybe run into Mark and Laura. As he was waiting for the traffic to pass, he glanced down one of the side streets and saw Mark.

He was standing on the sidewalk, bareheaded, in jeans and a T-shirt, alone. Lyle had known he was thin, but there, coatless in the street, he was shockingly gaunt. As Lyle watched, Mark turned away, took two steps, and stopped. He put his arms up over his face and leaned against the building, like a child counting in a game of hide-and-seek. Farther up the street a door opened, and Laura came out. She hurried to Mark and put her hands on his shoulders. They spoke; Lyle could see that, and that Laura's hair was in a braid, and that her dark-green skirt rose and fell around her calves in the breeze, and that she was barefoot on the cold concrete. Then, slowly, she drew Mark from the wall and turned him to her. Still speaking, she took his hands and stepped backward, back toward the door she'd come out. He went with her a step, another step, and then she turned, pulling his arm around her waist. They walked together back inside, through the door of the Salmon Weir Hostel.

The rain began again.

Lyle was glad to find the house empty when he and the dog got home, empty and dim in the gray afternoon, with the glimmer of a coal fire in the sitting room. He threw away the shamrock, hung up his coat, and put the leash away. Mark would certainly die.

He jabbed at the fire with a small poker and put some more coal on, and then he sighed and sat down in his chair and watched the fire, listening to the coal whistling as it heated. He would die. She would stand as she had there on the sidewalk this morning and she would crumple, collapse in and down. Lyle rubbed his forehead with his fingertips.

The dog came and sat, alert, questioning, in front of him. "You're right," he said to her. "I forgot the treat. Come on." She followed him to the cupboard and gazed into his eyes as he gave her the little orange-colored biscuit.

Men would be lining up to take Mark's place, no doubt about it. The dog stayed in the kitchen to eat, as she always did, and Lyle went back to his chair. Poor bastard, knowing that. The idea of it was enough to send anybody out in shirtsleeves to grieve against the side of a building.

Then again. Maybe Laura would be one of those widows who didn't remarry. Maybe she'd dedicate herself to the children. Bring them back here in a year or two, show them where she and their father had spent these weeks. He would see her again, he thought, as the dog, her biscuit gone, trotted in; he lifted her into his lap, where she settled and fell immediately asleep. He'd see her, and she would be recovered from it.

He stroked the dog's smooth head. The wind was blowing across the chimney and making a low *hooing* sound; he had said before that sometimes he felt as if he were living in a jug, in this small room at the bottom of the chimney, but today he liked it. He relaxed into imagining Laura, in a few years, walking alone down by the Claddagh, and how he'd greet her, and how by then he'd have become, as he often did in dreams, younger and more attractive. Or he'd be in Idaho, somehow, and see her. At the edge of sleep, he imagined driving with her down the roads of his youth in rural Vermont, where small lanes branched off among the trees.

"Wrecked, are ye?" his wife said, chuckling, as his heart thudded two heavy strokes.

The next day Laura looked tired, but as they met, she smiled, her eyes bright, and she reached out and gripped his upper arm for an instant. He felt again that guilty lurch of his heart. "We're going adventuring," she said, releasing his arm. 55

"Adventuring?" He looked at Mark, whose smile seemed tight.

Laura said, "We're going to rent a car and drive the Ring of Kerry!"

"Drive it?" Lyle said, still to Mark. "Driving's a bit of a challenge here." Even to himself he sounded gruff, a spoilsport.

"She'll be doing it," Mark said, and Lyle heard the injury in his voice.

"I figure, if the other tourists can manage it, so can I," she said. 60

"Tourists are bad drivers," Lyle said, "especially on those narrow roads."

"You've been there, then," Mark said.

"Just once," Lyle said, and told hurriedly, gruffly, about the bus tour along the narrow roads, the number of tour buses, the hordes of rude Americans and Germans.

"But the car-rental man said that wouldn't be true now, this early in the year," Laura said, her eyes strained but her voice still gay. "And it would still be worth it—everybody says Kerry's beautiful."

You are beautiful, Lyle thought, before he could stop himself, and then his mouth went dry with the fear that he'd say it, make a fool of himself, and he lumbered on to say, "Oh, it is. It's very beautiful. The landscape." 65

Lyle's wife took her baths at bedtime, and sometimes talked to him through the half-closed door to their bedroom. Only watery sounds came from the bathroom tonight as he got into his pajamas, trying to think where that map of Kerry might have ended up. At one time, he was sure, the maps had all been in a drawer in the kitchen, but he had looked there earlier and found playing cards and string instead. So she'd reorganized at some point, and the maps could be anywhere. He opened the wardrobe door quietly and stared up at the stacks of shoe boxes on the top shelf. Where did you put the maps? he could say, and she'd say, Maps— and what'd you be wanting maps for and us with no car?

The bath water moved. "I've not seen that old dog outside Ward's shop all week," she said.

"No?" he said, to encourage her to go on, to cover the sound of the wardrobe door closing.

"John's had that dog for years on years, he has. A number of old dogs hereabout," she said. "Just past the school those two small dogs, the white one and the terrier, they're old. Judy down Canal Road, she's an old one, Maureen Ryder's dog. Oh—I dreamt of dogs," she said.

"Dogs?" he said, though encouragement wasn't really necessary now: she always told her dreams in endless detail.

"I'd the job of feeding them—big dogs on chains in a yard. I can still see two of them, these two bulldogs. The faces on them."

When he was a boy and something was lost, a shoe, say, or a hairbrush, his mother would stand in the kitchen and say, If I was a shoe, where would I be? So now Lyle stood beside the bed and closed his eyes and thought, If I was a road map, where would I be?

"I'd found this bright-blue plastic dish—half scoop, half dish, it was—and I'd filled it with dry dog food for the bulldogs." She gave a small laugh, and he heard the sound of dripping.

He bent and looked under the bed: four suitcases. If he were a road map, he might be in a suitcase, but he couldn't, certainly, get a suitcase out and open without her hearing, and he couldn't be sure the map was there, or if it was, that it would be in the first suitcase he opened.

"Pleased with myself, I was. And then your man comes up and he says, 'That's not enough,' he says, and then he says, 'Besides, they bite.'"

He stood up again, and knew that he was an aging man, with skinny legs inside the pajama pants that were snug around his bulging stomach, unfamiliar hair in his ears and nose. He stood still and heard his wife lifting herself from the bath water, and knew that the dream she was telling would go on in her rueful voice from behind the door until she'd finished it, and that when she came out, she'd get into bed behind him, damp in a way he'd once found so erotic that it nearly choked him. And maybe this would be one of the nights she'd put her moist hand on him.

"What the hell have you done with the damned road maps?" he said.

"Road maps?" she said. She pulled the bathroom door open and stood there in her worn nightgown, looking at him, the ends of her short gray hair dark and stringy with wet, dripping water down the sides of her neck. "And what'd you be wanting with road maps this time of night, cursing about it?"

"I wasn't cursing," he said.

"You were. You're cursing all the time now."

"I wouldn't be cursing if the damned maps had been where they belong."

"I'm not your housemaid," she said.

That was from an old, worn quarrel, almost a comfort, and he took up his part. "Just because I want to find things in my own God-damned house doesn't make me an ogre," he said.

"You should watch your language," she said. "And it wouldn't hurt to go to mass once in a while."

"Oh, mass! Sure—that's the answer to everything, isn't it? Maybe the priest could tell me where you've hidden the God-damned maps." He turned away ready for her to say it was his fault that neither of the boys went to mass and that Kevin would probably marry that Jewish girl, and he'd say he hoped so, better a whining Jew than a whining Catholic. While they were saying those things, he would put on his slippers and his robe, she would get into bed, and he'd go downstairs and have a drink. And when he came back up in half an hour, she'd be asleep.

But she didn't say that, and she didn't move toward the bed. "For your Americans, is it?" she said, so mildly that he stopped and turned to look at her. She took her robe from the hook on the door, and nodded as she pulled it on and tied the belt. "I may have them in the hall press," she said. "Will I look for them so?"

He nodded, still confused and suspicious, and he knew he should say thank you, but she was gone down the stairs, the dog trotting behind her, and then he heard her in the hall closet, and then he heard her talking to the dog. He stood beside the bed and tried to imagine what he could say to her if he went downstairs; he could imagine nothing. When he heard the television come on, he got into bed. For many years, maybe always, she had gone to bed first or they had gone to bed together, and he found the freedom of being the only body on the mattress so comfortable and novel that he fell asleep quickly.

When he woke in the morning, the first thing he knew was that he was still alone, and a quick jolt of fear made him thrust his hand onto her side of the bed. It was warm, and at the same moment he smelled the coffee and rashers, and so he was irritated with her before he was even out of bed. It was irrational, and he knew that: for thirty years he'd waked alone in bed to the smell of the breakfast she was cooking. And yet this morning it seemed to him that she had pretended a larger absence, and the charade had forced from him a reaction that he found embarrassing.

But maybe she'd found the maps, he thought as he went down the stairs and into the kitchen. There lay the maps, beside his plate.

"You found them," he said.

"Was it Donegal they were wanting?" she said. "That one's gone missing."

"No—Kerry," he said.

"Grand, then—Kerry's there," she said, sounding relieved and pleased.

After breakfast, as he was putting on his coat, she said, "I thought I'd walk along with ye this morning. I'm to meet Roisin at ten at the Franciscans, and a walk will just fill the time." She was putting on her coat as she spoke, so there was nothing he could say. "Don't forget your map," she said, and he pushed it into his coat pocket and went out the door ahead of her.

"It's a grand morning," she said approvingly as they crossed the street onto the prom, and it was—nearly windless, a hint of sun. He didn't answer, and they walked on, she with her hands in her pockets, he with one hand in his pocket and the other holding the leash.

He had little hope that they wouldn't meet Mark and Laura, and when he saw them at a distance, Mark sitting on a bench and Laura standing beside him, looking out toward Mutton Island, he pulled the map from his pocket, half thinking to make a quick gift of it and be gone.

90

95

His wife took a sharp breath and murmured, "He's thin."

"He's sick," Lyle snapped, and then Laura turned and saw them, and they were too close to say more.

Mark stood, with obvious effort, and smiled, and Laura smiled, and as Mark took off his hat, Lyle realized that he couldn't look at either of them, so he smiled into the air between them and said, "Good morning. This is my wife, Mary—Mark, Laura," his voice too hearty for the words.

They shook hands and said the things people say—I've heard so much about   100
you, a pleasure, how do you do, hello, Lyle smiling stupidly, helplessly, at the hotel across the road. Then his wife said, "How do ye find Galway?" and he could feel them hesitate and translate before Mark said, "It's a very friendly town. We'll be sorry to leave."

"But ye'll be back, then, after your trip to Kerry?"

Again a hesitation, in which Lyle heard the crying of the gulls, before Mark said, "Well—," and then Laura said, "Actually, we've been thinking about not going to Kerry after all. Given the roads."

Lyle looked down at the dog. Laura's voice was soft but strained. He wondered how obvious the map in his hand was, whether he could slide it back into his pocket without drawing attention.

"Ah, they're terrible, they are," his wife agreed, dismissing Kerry the Kingdom with a quick sigh as she sat on the bench. Mark sat beside her, his hat in his hand. "The thing ye might try is the Arans—have ye thought of that? There's a bus from town to Rossaveal, right to the ferry over, and then on the island there's the pony traps or the little buses, and back the same day." She laughed, comfortable, eager, sitting there with her purse on her lap as if this were a visit. "And, oh, the island's lovely, 'tis—it'll be gray here and the sun bright as Arizona over there."

"It sounds nice," Mark said.   105

"Ye might think of it," she went on. Lyle could see her thumbs on the purse, hidden from Mark and Laura, making rapid hard circles against the leather. "And Dublin, too—have ye been to Dublin?" She looked at Laura, who shook her head. "Oh, it's not to be missed, Dublin—just for a day, take the train over and back, the three museums and the Book of Kells. Of course, not all in a day, that'd be too much for anyone, it would, but just the National Museum, say, and they've a nice little tea shop there for your lunch." She stood up as if she'd settled something, but then she went on, hardly a breath between. "No, there's Ireland to see without Kerry, there is. Even right here in Galway. How much longer is your holiday?"

"Ten days?" Mark said, glancing at Laura.

"Or less," Laura said, "depending." She shrugged and drove her hands deep into her pockets. "The children," she said.

"I miss them," Mark said. His voice was quiet, but Lyle knew he was speaking to Laura. "I'd like to spend more time with them." His voice was like Mary's was when they fought about Jimmy—that soft tone, thinning with the threat of tears.

"Why, of course you would," Mary said. "Of course you would. But it takes a   110
bit to change the tickets, doesn't it?" The sympathy in her voice seemed all for the difficulty of ticket changes.

"Yes," Laura said. She turned her face to the bay for a second and let the breeze push her hair back, and then she took a step closer to Mark and touched his cheek with the backs of her fingers. "It may take some doing." Mark closed his eyes for a second, and when Laura took her hand away, he put his hat back on.

So this was the end of what he'd seen on the street: Laura and Ireland had failed and had surrendered. Mark would die, and Laura would not. They would not go together in joy to the edge of life.

"Well, then," Mary said, holding her purse over her stomach, smiling at Laura, "ye must come to tea, mustn't they, Lyle? Come to tea — let's see, could ye come today? No, wait — that won't work, will it? Maybe tomorrow?"

"That's very kind of you," Laura said.

Mark nodded to Lyle and said, "We'll meet again before then."   115

"Yes, of course — of course ye will, and you can tell Lyle, and we'll see about it, will we? It's grand by the fire on some of these days, it is, and ye should be in an Irish house before ye go back. It's lovely to have met ye so," she said, and shook Mark's hand again. Then she stepped in front of Lyle and put her arms around Laura and hugged her. Laura closed her eyes and for a second let her head touch Mary's.

Then they were apart, and the dog was up and ready to go, and Lyle found that he'd gotten the map back into his pocket somehow and had a hand free to shake Mark's. Then he and his wife were walking on, the dog trotting beside them, and after a few steps his wife slid her hand under his arm and his arm bent up to hold it, and so they walked on toward the Claddagh, the wind picking up at their backs.

"Coffee as well as tea, of course," she said, "since they're Americans, and tomorrow would be fine, it would, or Saturday."

"Let's make it Saturday," he said, because she was crying, and this was a decision they could make, although he didn't believe he'd ever see Mark or Laura again.

"Such lovely people," his wife said. "Such lovely people."   120

Lyle knew they were, and because his wife had said it, he wanted to say to her, So are we. He wanted to say that he wasn't a young man, but he wasn't dying, and that this hand on his arm was hers — that for them the end was still far off, with difficulties and complications still to come.

Instead he pressed her wrist against his side and said, "They are so. And it's a sad thing, it is."   [1999]

THINKING ABOUT THE TEXT

1. When Mary finally meets Laura and Mark, Lyle seems tense. How is this suggested? What small details suggest Mary's response? Much seems unspoken in this scene. How would you describe what is really happening?

2. Why is Lyle so cautious in telling his wife about Laura and Mark, especially about Mark's illness?

3. Were you surprised when Lyle starts fantasizing about Laura after he knows that "Mark would certainly die" (para. 48)? Are there hints of his attraction before this? Is this pure fantasy, or does he have real hope?

4. Comment on Lyle's searching for a map of the Ring of Kerry. Is this a symbolic device meant to suggest something about Lyle? Does his wife suspect something after this?

5. How do you read the ending here — as an affirmation of the marriage contract, as a recommitment of Lyle and Mary's love, as Lyle's resignation that his fantasies will never come true, or as something else?

MAKING COMPARISONS

1. Compare the center of consciousness in Lordan's story with the centers in Chekhov's and Oates's stories. What are the advantages and disadvantages to these perspectives?

2. What specifically seems to be the problem with the marriage of Lyle and Mary? How would you characterize the marital problems with the other two stories?

3. Describe the process of attraction that Lyle, Dmitri, and both Annas go through. Are there similarities? Differences?

WRITING ABOUT ISSUES

1. Argue that we do or do not have an obligation to ourselves to follow our hearts, even if it means that we end up breaking promises.

2. Are there heroes and villains in these three stories? Argue for making moral distinctions between two or three of the characters depicted here.

3. Each story has a specific historical and cultural context. Argue that understanding such placement in a particular time and place helps us know these fictional characters better.

4. All three stories end with all six marriages intact. Argue that each marriage will or will not survive. Include your position on making divorce easier or harder to obtain.

A WEB ASSIGNMENT

A number of reviews and articles about Joyce Carol Oates can be accessed via the Internet. Visit the Web Assignments section of the *Making Literature Matter* Web site to link to one of these sites. After reading several reviews and articles that look interesting, write a report noting the strengths and weaknesses that critics see in her work.

Visit www.bedfordstmartins.com/makinglitmatter

Romantic Illusions: Cultural Contexts for David Henry Hwang's *M. Butterfly*

DAVID HENRY HWANG, M. *Butterfly*

CULTURAL CONTEXTS:
PAUL GRAY, "What Is Love?"
ANASTASIA TOUFEXIS, "The Right Chemistry"
NATHANIEL BRANDEN, "Immature Love"

Our cultural assumptions are so pervasive that we may find it hard to question "the obvious." The reality of romantic love is such an assumption. We see and hear about it so often in movies, books, television shows, and songs that the reality of romantic love seems beyond question. We may search for the all-consuming, magical, "spiritual-emotional-sexual attachment" we often see in contemporary films. But does this love exist? Perhaps romantic love is just an illusion that has more to do with physical attraction and passion than with true love. How do we know the difference, especially if we believe totally that such love exists? Can the belief create the illusion of reality? Or can it so blind us that we fall in love with someone who turns out to be someone else entirely? How deceived can we be by the belief in romantic love? Perhaps some people want to be deceived and fall in love with the "wrong" person on purpose. The mysteries of love never seem more puzzling and surprising than when we try to explain why some people choose implausible loves.

BEFORE YOU READ

In the film *The Crying Game* (1992) the main character, a former IRA fighter, falls in love with a man who he thinks is an attractive woman. He is shocked at the discovery. Can you imagine this happening to someone? To you?

DAVID HENRY HWANG

M. Butterfly

David Henry Hwang (b. 1957) characterizes himself as "interested in the dust that settles when two worlds collide." Born in Los Angeles into an affluent, ethnically Chinese family, Hwang's earliest influences were multicultural: His banker father was born in Shanghai, and his mother, a pianist and music teacher, spent her early years in the Philippines. Hwang attended the elite Harvard School in North Hollywood, California, and later majored in English literature at Stanford University, graduating in 1979 with honors and a Phi Beta Kappa award. The same year, his first play FOB (for "fresh off the boat") was staged at the National Playwright's Conference. Hwang taught creative writing, studied playwriting at the Yale School

(Michele-Salmieri.)

of Drama, wrote television scripts, and saw several plays produced before achieving acclaim for M. Butterfly *in 1988. The play, with John Lithgow and B. D. Wong in the principal roles, broke box-office records and gained numerous honors, including the 1988 Tony Award for best play of the year.*

THE CHARACTERS

RENE GALLIMARD
SONG LILING
MARC/MAN NO. 2/CONSUL SHARPLESS
RENEE/WOMAN AT PARTY/PINUP GIRL
COMRADE CHIN/SUZUKI/SHU-FANG
HELGA
TOULON/MAN NO. 1/JUDGE
DANCERS

TIME AND PLACE

The action of the play takes place in a Paris prison in the present, and, in recall, during the decade 1960–1970 in Beijing, and from 1966 to the present in Paris.

PLAYWRIGHT'S NOTES

A former French diplomat and a Chinese opera singer have been sentenced to six years in jail for spying for China after a two-day trial that traced a story of clandestine love and mistaken sexual identity. . . .

Mr. Boursicot was accused of passing information to China after he fell in love with Mr. Shi, whom he believed for twenty years to be a woman.
— The New York Times, *May 11, 1986*

This play was suggested by international newspaper accounts of a recent espionage trial. For purposes of dramatization, names have been changed, characters created, and incidents devised or altered, and this play does not purport to be a factual record of real events or real people.

> *I could escape this feeling*
> *With my China girl . . .*
> — David Bowie & Iggy Pop

ACT 1, Scene 1

M. Gallimard's prison cell. Paris. 1988.
Lights fade up to reveal Rene Gallimard, sixty-five, in a prison cell. He wears a comfortable bathrobe and looks old and tired. The sparsely furnished cell contains a wooden crate, upon which sits a hot plate with a kettle and a portable tape recorder. Gallimard sits on the crate staring at the recorder, a sad smile on his face.
Upstage Song, who appears as a beautiful woman in traditional Chinese garb, dances a traditional piece from the Peking Opera, surrounded by the percussive clatter of Chinese music.
Then, slowly, lights and sound cross-fade; the Chinese opera music dissolves into a Western opera, the "Love Duet" from Puccini's Madame Butterfly. *Song continues dancing, now to the Western accompaniment. Though her movements are the same, the difference in music now gives them a balletic quality.*
Gallimard rises, and turns upstage towards the figure of Song, who dances without acknowledging him.

GALLIMARD: Butterfly, Butterfly . . .

He forces himself to turn away, as the image of Song fades out, and talks to us.

GALLIMARD: The limits of my cell are as such: four-and-a-half meters by five. There's one window against the far wall; a door, very strong, to protect me from autograph hounds. I'm responsible for the tape recorder, the hot plate, and this charming coffee table.

When I want to eat, I'm marched off to the dining room—hot, steaming slop appears on my plate. When I want to sleep, the light bulb turns itself off—the work of fairies. It's an enchanted space I occupy. The French—we know how to run a prison.

But, to be honest, I'm not treated like an ordinary prisoner. Why? Because I'm a celebrity. You see, I make people laugh.

I never dreamed this day would arrive. I've never been considered witty or clever. In fact, as a young boy, in an informal poll among my grammar school classmates, I was voted "least likely to be invited to a party." It's a title I managed to hold on to for many years. Despite some stiff competition.

But now, how the tables turn! Look at me: the life of every social function in Paris. Paris? Why be modest: My fame has spread to Amsterdam, London, New York. Listen to them! In the world's smartest parlors. I'm the one who lifts their spirits!

With a flourish, Gallimard directs our attention to another part of the stage.

Scene 2

A party. 1988.

Lights go up on a chic-looking parlor, where a well-dressed trio, two men and one woman, make conversation. Gallimard also remains lit; he observes them from his cell.

WOMAN: And what of Gallimard?

MAN 1: Gallimard?

MAN 2: Gallimard!

GALLIMARD *(to us):* You see? They're all determined to say my name, as if it were some new dance.

WOMAN: He still claims not to believe the truth.

MAN 1: What? Still? Even since the trial?

WOMAN: Yes. Isn't it mad?

MAN 2 *(laughing):* He says . . . it was dark . . . and she was very modest!

The trio break into laughter.

MAN 1: So—what? He never touched her with his hands?

MAN 2: Perhaps he did, and simply misidentified the equipment. A compelling case for sex education in the schools.

WOMAN: To protect the National Security—the Church can't argue with that.

MAN 1: That's impossible! How could he not know?

MAN 2: Simple ignorance.

MAN 1: For twenty years?

MAN 2: Time flies when you're being stupid.

WOMAN: Well, I thought the French were ladies' men.

MAN 2: It seems Monsieur Gallimard was overly anxious to live up to his national reputation.

WOMAN: Well, he's not very good-looking.

MAN 1: No, he's not.

MAN 2:   Certainly not.

WOMAN: Actually, I feel sorry for him.

MAN 2:   A toast! To Monsieur Gallimard!

WOMAN: Yes! To Gallimard!

MAN 1:   To Gallimard!

MAN 2:   *Vive la différence!*

They toast, laughing. Lights down on them.

Scene 3

M. Gallimard's cell.

GALLIMARD *(smiling):*   You see? They toast me. I've become a patron saint of the socially inept. Can they really be so foolish? Men like that—they should be scratching at my door, begging to learn my secrets! For I, Rene Gallimard, you see, I have known, and been loved by . . . the Perfect Woman.

    Alone in this cell, I sit night after night, watching our story play through my head, always searching for a new ending, one which redeems my honor, where she returns at last to my arms. And I imagine you—my ideal audience—who come to understand and even, perhaps just a little, to envy me.

He turns on his tape recorder. Over the house speakers, we hear the opening phrases of Madame Butterfly.

GALLIMARD: In order for you to understand what I did and why, I must introduce you to my favorite opera: *Madame Butterfly.* By Giacomo Puccini. First produced at La Scala, Milan, in 1904, it is now beloved throughout the Western world.

As Gallimard describes the opera, the tape segues in and out to sections he may be describing.

GALLIMARD: And why not? Its heroine, Cio-Cio-San, also known as Butterfly, is a feminine ideal, beautiful and brave. And its hero, the man for whom she gives up everything, is—*(He pulls out a naval officer's cap from under his crate, pops it on his head, and struts about.)*—not very good-looking, not too bright, and pretty much a wimp: Benjamin Franklin Pinkerton of the U.S. Navy. As the curtain rises, he's just closed on two great bargains: one on a house, the other on a woman—call it a package deal.

    Pinkerton purchased the rights to Butterfly for one hundred yen—in modern currency, equivalent to about . . . sixty-six cents. So, he's feeling pretty pleased with himself as Sharpless, the American consul, arrives to witness the marriage.

Marc, wearing an official cap to designate Sharpless, enters and plays the character.

SHARPLESS/MARC: Pinkerton!

PINKERTON/GALLIMARD: Sharpless! How's it hangin'? It's a great day, just great. Between my house, my wife, and the rickshaw ride in from town, I've saved nineteen cents just this morning.

SHARPLESS: Wonderful. I can see the inscription on your tombstone already: "I saved a dollar, here I lie." *(He looks around.)* Nice house.

PINKERTON: It's artistic. Artistic, don't you think? Like the way the shoji screens slide open to reveal the wet bar and disco mirror ball? Classy, huh? Great for impressing the chicks.

SHARPLESS: "Chicks"? Pinkerton, you're going to be a married man!

PINKERTON: Well, sort of.

SHARPLESS: What do you mean?

PINKERTON: This country — Sharpless, it is okay. You got all these geisha girls running around —

SHARPLESS: I know! I live here!

PINKERTON: Then, you know the marriage laws, right? I split for one month, it's annulled!

SHARPLESS: Leave it to you to read the fine print. Who's the lucky girl?

PINKERTON: Cio-Cio-San. Her friends call her Butterfly. Sharpless, she eats out of my hand!

SHARPLESS: She's probably very hungry.

PINKERTON: Not like American girls. It's true what they say about Oriental girls. They want to be treated bad!

SHARPLESS: Oh, please!

PINKERTON: It's true!

SHARPLESS: Are you serious about this girl?

PINKERTON: I'm marrying her, aren't I?

SHARPLESS: Yes — with generous trade-in terms.

PINKERTON: When I leave, she'll know what it's like to have loved a real man. And I'll even buy her a few nylons.

SHARPLESS: You aren't planning to take her with you?

PINKERTON: Huh? Where?

SHARPLESS: Home!

PINKERTON: You mean, America? Are you crazy? Can you see her trying to buy rice in St. Louis?

SHARPLESS: So, you're not serious.

Pause.

PINKERTON/GALLIMARD *(as Pinkerton):*   Consul, I am a sailor in port. *(As Gallimard.)* They then proceed to sing the famous duet, "The Whole World Over."

The duet plays on the speakers. Gallimard, as Pinkerton, lip-syncs his lines from the opera.

GALLIMARD: To give a rough translation: "The whole world over, the Yankee travels, casting his anchor wherever he wants. Life's not worth living unless he can win the hearts of the fairest maidens, then hotfoot it off the premises ASAP." *(He turns towards Marc.)* In the preceding scene, I played Pinkerton, the womanizing cad, and my friend Marc from school . . . *(Marc bows grandly for our benefit.)* played Sharpless, the sensitive soul of reason. In life, however, our positions were usually — no, always — reversed.

Scene 4

École Nationale.° Aix-en-Provence. 1947.

GALLIMARD: No, Marc, I think I'd rather stay home.

MARC: Are you crazy?! We are going to Dad's condo in Marseilles! You know what happened last time?

GALLIMARD: Of course I do.

MARC: Of course you don't! You never know. . . . They stripped, Rene!

GALLIMARD: Who stripped?

MARC: The girls!

GALLIMARD: Girls? Who said anything about girls?

MARC: Rene, we're a buncha university guys goin' up to the woods. What are we gonna do — talk philosophy?

GALLIMARD: What girls? Where do you get them?

MARC: Who cares? The point is, they come. On trucks. Packed in like sardines. The back flips open, babes hop out, we're ready to roll.

GALLIMARD: You mean, they just —?

MARC: Before you know it, every last one of them — they're stripped and splashing around my pool. There's no moon out, they can't see what's going on, their boobs are flapping, right? You close your eyes, reach out — it's grab bag, get it? Doesn't matter whose ass is between whose legs, whose teeth are sinking into who. You're just in there, going at it, eyes closed, on and on for as long as you can stand. *(Pause.)* Some fun, huh?

GALLIMARD: What happens in the morning?

MARC: In the morning, you're ready to talk some philosophy. *(Beat.)* So how 'bout it?

GALLIMARD: Marc, I can't . . . I'm afraid they'll say no — the girls. So I never ask.

MARC: You don't have to ask! That's the beauty — don't you see? They don't have to say yes. It's perfect for a guy like you, really.

GALLIMARD: You go ahead . . . I may come later.

MARC: Hey, Rene — it doesn't matter that you're clumsy and got zits — they're not looking!

GALLIMARD: Thank you very much.

MARC: Wimp.

Marc walks over to the other side of the stage, and starts waving and smiling at women in the audience.

GALLIMARD *(to us):*   We now return to my version of *Madame Butterfly* and the events leading to my recent conviction for treason.

Gallimard notices Marc making lewd gestures.

GALLIMARD: Marc, what are you doing?

MARC: Huh? *(Sotto voce.)* Rene, there're a lotta great babes out there. They're probably lookin' at me and thinking, "What a dangerous guy."

GALLIMARD: Yes — how could they help but be impressed by your cool sophistication?

°**École Nationale:** National School.

Gallimard pops the Sharpless cap on Marc's head, and points him offstage. Marc exits, leering.

Scene 5

M. Gallimard's cell.

GALLIMARD: Next, Butterfly makes her entrance. We learn her age — fifteen . . . but very mature for her years.

Lights come up on the area where we saw Song dancing at the top of the play. She appears there again, now dressed as Madame Butterfly, moving to the "Love Duet." Gallimard turns upstage slightly to watch, transfixed.

GALLIMARD: But as she glides past him, beautiful, laughing softly behind her fan, don't we who are men sigh with hope? We, who are not handsome, nor brave, nor powerful, yet somehow believe, like Pinkerton, that we deserve a Butterfly. She arrives with all her possessions in the folds of her sleeves, lays them all out, for her man to do with as he pleases. Even her life itself — she bows her head as she whispers that she's not even worth the hundred yen he paid for her. He's already given too much, when we know he's really had to give nothing at all.

Music and lights on Song out. Gallimard sits at his crate.

GALLIMARD: In real life, women who put their total worth at less than sixty-six cents are quite hard to find. The closest we come is in the pages of these magazines. (*He reaches into his crate, pulls out a stack of girlie magazines, and begins flipping through them.*) Quite a necessity in prison. For three or four dollars, you get seven or eight women.

   I first discovered these magazines at my uncle's house. One day, as a boy of twelve. The first time I saw them in his closet . . . all lined up — my body shook. Not with lust — no, with power. Here were women — a shelfful — who would do exactly as I wanted.

The "Love Duet" creeps in over the speakers. Special comes up, revealing, not Song this time, but a pinup girl in a sexy negligee, her back to us. Gallimard turns upstage and looks at her.

GIRL: I know you're watching me.

GALLIMARD: My throat . . . it's dry.

GIRL: I leave my blinds open every night before I go to bed.

GALLIMARD: I can't move.

GIRL: I leave my blinds open and the lights on.

GALLIMARD: I'm shaking. My skin is hot, but my penis is soft. Why?

GIRL: I stand in front of the window.

GALLIMARD: What is she going to do?

GIRL: I toss my hair, and I let my lips part . . . barely.

GALLIMARD: I shouldn't be seeing this. It's so dirty. I'm so bad.

GIRL: Then, slowly, I lift off my nightdress.

GALLIMARD: Oh, god. I can't believe it. I can't—

GIRL: I toss it to the ground.

GALLIMARD: Now, she's going to walk away. She's going to—

GIRL: I stand there, in the light, displaying myself.

GALLIMARD: No. She's—why is she naked?

GIRL: To you.

GALLIMARD: In front of a window? This is wrong. No—

GIRL: Without shame.

GALLIMARD: No, she must . . . like it.

GIRL: I like it.

GALLIMARD: She . . . she wants me to see.

GIRL: I want you to see.

GALLIMARD: I can't believe it! She's getting excited!

GIRL: I can't see you. You can do whatever you want.

GALLIMARD: I can't do a thing. Why?

GIRL: What would you like me to do . . . next?

Lights go down on her. Music off. Silence, as Gallimard puts away his magazines. Then he resumes talking to us.

GALLIMARD: Act Two begins with Butterfly staring at the ocean. Pinkerton's been called back to the U.S., and he's given his wife a detailed schedule of his plans. In the column marked "return date," he's written "when the robins nest." This failed to ignite her suspicions. Now, three years have passed without a peep from him. Which brings a response from her faithful servant, Suzuki.

Comrade Chin enters, playing Suzuki.

SUZUKI: Girl, he's a loser. What'd he ever give you? Nineteen cents and those ugly Day-Glo stockings? Look, it's finished! Kaput! Done! And you should be glad! I mean, the guy was a woofer! He tried before, you know—before he met you, he went down to geisha central and plunked down his spare change in front of the usual candidates—everyone else gagged! These are hungry prostitutes, and they were not interested, get the picture? Now, stop slathering when an American ship sails in, and let's make some bucks—I mean, yen! We are broke!

     Now, what about Yamadori? Hey, hey—don't look away—the man is a prince—figuratively, and, what's even better, literally. He's rich, he's handsome, he says he'll die if you don't marry him—and he's even willing to overlook the little fact that you've been deflowered all over the place by a foreign devil. What do you mean, "But he's Japanese"? What do you think you are? You think you've been touched by the whitey god? He was a sailor with dirty hands!

Suzuki stalks offstage.

GALLIMARD: She's also visited by Consul Sharpless, sent by Pinkerton on a minor errand.

Marc enters, as Sharpless.

SHARPLESS: I hate this job.

GALLIMARD: This Pinkerton—he doesn't show up personally to tell his wife he's abandoning her. No, he sends a government diplomat . . . at taxpayers' expense.

SHARPLESS: Butterfly? Butterfly? I have some bad — I'm going to be ill. Butterfly, I came to tell you —

GALLIMARD: Butterfly says she knows he'll return and if he doesn't she'll kill herself rather than go back to her own people. *(Beat.)* This causes a lull in the conversation.

SHARPLESS: Let's put it this way . . .

GALLIMARD: Butterfly runs into the next room, and returns holding —

Sound cue: a baby crying. Sharpless, "seeing" this, backs away.

SHARPLESS: Well, good. Happy to see things going so well. I suppose I'll be going now. Ta ta. Ciao. *(He turns away. Sound cue out.)* I hate this job. *(He exits.)*

GALLIMARD: At that moment, Butterfly spots in the harbor an American ship — the *Abramo Lincoln!*

Music cue: "The Flower Duet." Song, still dressed as Butterfly, changes into a wedding kimono, moving to the music.

GALLIMARD: This is the moment that redeems her years of waiting. With Suzuki's help, they cover the room with flowers —

Chin, as Suzuki, trudges onstage and drops a lone flower without much enthusiasm.

GALLIMARD: — and she changes into her wedding dress to prepare for Pinkerton's arrival.

Suzuki helps Butterfly change. Helga enters, and helps Gallimard change into a tuxedo.

GALLIMARD: I married a woman older than myself — Helga.

HELGA: My father was ambassador to Australia. I grew up among criminals and kangaroos.

GALLIMARD: Hearing that brought me to the altar —

Helga exits.

GALLIMARD: — where I took a vow renouncing love. No fantasy woman would ever want me, so, yes, I would settle for a quick leap up the career ladder. Passion, I banish, and in its place — practicality!

But my vows had long since lost their charm by the time we arrived in China. The sad truth is that all men want a beautiful woman, and the uglier the man, the greater the want.

Suzuki makes final adjustments of Butterfly's costume, as does Gallimard of his tuxedo.

GALLIMARD: I married late, at age thirty-one. I was faithful to my marriage for eight years. Until the day when, as a junior-level diplomat in puritanical Peking, in a parlor at the German ambassador's house, during the "Reign of a Hundred Flowers,"° I first saw her . . . singing the death scene from *Madame Butterfly.*

Suzuki runs offstage.

Reign of a Hundred Flowers: A brief period in 1957 when freedom of expression was allowed in China.

Scene 6

German ambassador's house. Beijing. 1960.

The upstage special area now becomes a stage. Several chairs face upstage, representing seating for some twenty guests in the parlor. A few "diplomats" — Renee, Marc, Toulon — in formal dress enter and take seats.

Gallimard also sits down, but turns towards us and continues to talk. Orchestral accompaniment on the tape is now replaced by a simple piano. Song picks up the death scene from the point where Butterfly uncovers the hara-kiri knife.

GALLIMARD: The ending is pitiful. Pinkerton, in an act of great courage, stays home and sends his American wife to pick up Butterfly's child. The truth, long deferred, has come up to her door.

Song, playing Butterfly, sings the lines from the opera in her own voice — which, though not classical, should be decent.

SONG: "Con onor muore / chi non puo serbar / vita con onore."

GALLIMARD *(simultaneously)*:   "Death with honor / Is better than life / Life with dishonor."

The stage is illuminated; we are now completely within an elegant diplomat's residence. Song proceeds to play out an abbreviated death scene. Everyone in the room applauds. Song, shyly, takes her bows. Others in the room rush to congratulate her. Gallimard remains with us.

GALLIMARD: They say in opera the voice is everything. That's probably why I'd never before enjoyed opera. Here . . . here was a Butterfly with little or no voice — but she had the grace, the delicacy . . . I believed this girl. I believed her suffering. I wanted to take her in my arms — so delicate, even I could protect her, take her home, pamper her until she smiled.

Over the course of the preceding speech, Song has broken from the upstage crowd and moved directly upstage of Gallimard.

SONG: Excuse me. Monsieur . . . ?

Gallimard turns upstage, shocked.

GALLIMARD: Oh! Gallimard. Mademoiselle . . . ? A beautiful . . .

SONG: Song Liling.

GALLIMARD: A beautiful performance.

SONG: Oh, please.

GALLIMARD: I usually —

SONG: You make me blush. I'm no opera singer at all.

GALLIMARD: I usually don't like *Butterfly*.

SONG: I can't blame you in the least.

GALLIMARD: I mean, the story —

SONG: Ridiculous.

GALLIMARD: I like the story, but . . . what?

SONG: Oh, you like it?

GALLIMARD: I . . . what I mean is, I've always seen it played by huge women in so much bad makeup.

SONG: Bad makeup is not unique to the West.

GALLIMARD: But, who can believe them?

SONG: And you believe me?

GALLIMARD: Absolutely. You were utterly convincing. It's the first time—

SONG: Convincing? As a Japanese woman? The Japanese used hundreds of our people for medical experiments during the war, you know. But I gather such an irony is lost on you.

GALLIMARD: No! I was about to say, it's the first time I've seen the beauty of the story.

SONG: Really?

GALLIMARD: Of her death. It's a . . . a pure sacrifice. He's unworthy, but what can she do? She loves him . . . so much. It's a very beautiful story.

SONG: Well, yes, to a Westerner.

GALLIMARD: Excuse me?

SONG: It's one of your favorite fantasies, isn't it? The submissive Oriental woman and the cruel white man.

GALLIMARD: Well, I didn't quite mean . . .

SONG: Consider it this way: what would you say if a blonde homecoming queen fell in love with a short Japanese businessman? He treats her cruelly, then goes home for three years, during which time she prays to his picture and turns down marriage from a young Kennedy. Then, when she learns he has remarried, she kills herself. Now, I believe you would consider this girl to be a deranged idiot, correct? But because it's an Oriental who kills herself for a Westerner—ah!—you find it beautiful.

Silence.

GALLIMARD: Yes . . . well . . . I see your point . . .

SONG: I will never do Butterfly again, Monsieur Gallimard. If you wish to see some real theater, come to the Peking Opera sometime. Expand your mind.

Song walks offstage. Other guests exit with her.

GALLIMARD *(to us):* So much for protecting her in my big Western arms.

Scene 7

M. Gallimard's apartment. Beijing. 1960.
Gallimard changes from his tux into a casual suit. Helga enters.

GALLIMARD: The Chinese are an incredibly arrogant people.

HELGA: They warned us about that in Paris, remember?

GALLIMARD: Even Parisians consider them arrogant. That's a switch.

HELGA: What is it that Madame Su says? "We are a very old civilization." I never know if she's talking about her country or herself.

GALLIMARD: I walk around here, all I hear every day, everywhere is how *old* this culture is. The fact that "old" may be synonymous with "senile" doesn't occur to them.

HELGA: You're not going to change them. "East is east, west is west, and . . ." whatever that guy said.

GALLIMARD: It's just that—silly. I met . . . at Ambassador Koening's tonight—
you should've been there.

HELGA: Koening? Oh god, no. Did he enchant you all again with the history of
Bavaria?

GALLIMARD: No. I met, I suppose, the Chinese equivalent of a diva. She's a
singer in the Chinese opera.

HELGA: They have an opera, too? Do they sing in Chinese? Or maybe—in
Italian?

GALLIMARD: Tonight, she did sing in Italian.

HELGA: How'd she manage that?

GALLIMARD: She must've been educated in the West before the Revolution. Her
French is very good also. Anyway, she sang the death scene from *Madame
Butterfly*.

HELGA: *Madame Butterfly!* Then I should have come. (*She begins humming,
floating around the room as if dragging long kimono sleeves.*) Did she have a
nice costume? I think it's a classic piece of music.

GALLIMARD: That's what *I* thought, too. Don't let her hear you say that.

HELGA: What's wrong?

GALLIMARD: Evidently the Chinese hate it.

HELGA: She hated it, but she performed it anyway? Is she perverse?

GALLIMARD: They hate it because the white man gets the girl. Sour grapes if you
ask me.

HELGA: Politics again? Why can't they just hear it as a piece of beautiful music?
So, what's in their opera?

GALLIMARD: I don't know. But, whatever it is, I'm sure it must be *old*.

Helga exits.

Scene 8

Chinese opera house and the streets of Beijing. 1960.
   The sound of gongs clanging fills the stage.

GALLIMARD: My wife's innocent question kept ringing in my ears. I asked
around, but no one knew anything about the Chinese opera. It took four
weeks, but my curiosity overcame my cowardice. This Chinese diva—this
unwilling Butterfly—what did she do to make her so proud?

   The room was hot, and full of smoke. Wrinkled faces, old women, teeth
missing—a man with a growth on his neck, like a human toad. All smiling,
pipes falling from their mouths, cracking nuts between their teeth, a live
chicken pecking at my foot—all looking, screaming, gawking . . . at her.

*The upstage area is suddenly hit with a harsh white light. It has become the stage
for the Chinese opera performance. Two dancers enter, along with Song. Gallimard
stands apart, watching. Song glides gracefully amidst the two dancers. Drums suddenly slam to a halt. Song strikes a pose, looking straight at Gallimard. Dancers
exit. Light change. Pause, then Song walks right off the stage and straight up to
Gallimard.*

SONG: Yes. You. White man. I'm looking straight at you.

GALLIMARD: Me?

SONG: You see any other white men? It was too easy to spot you. How often does a man in my audience come in a tie?

Song starts to remove her costume. Underneath, she wears simple baggy clothes. They are now backstage. The show is over.

SONG: So, you are an adventurous imperialist?

GALLIMARD: I . . . thought it would further my education.

SONG: It took you four weeks. Why?

GALLIMARD: I've been busy.

SONG: Well, education has always been undervalued in the West, hasn't it?

GALLIMARD *(laughing)*: I don't think that's true.

SONG: No, you wouldn't. You're a Westerner. How can you objectively judge your own values?

GALLIMARD: I think it's possible to achieve some distance.

SONG: Do you? *(Pause.)* It stinks in here. Let's go.

GALLIMARD: These are the smells of your loyal fans.

SONG: I love them for being my fans, I hate the smell they leave behind. I too can distance myself from my people. *(She looks around, then whispers in his ear.)* "Art for the masses" is a shitty excuse to keep artists poor. *(She pops a cigarette in her mouth.)* Be a gentleman, will you? And light my cigarette.

Gallimard fumbles for a match.

GALLIMARD: I don't . . . smoke.

SONG *(lighting her own)*: Your loss. Had you lit my cigarette, I might have blown a puff of smoke right between your eyes. Come.

They start to walk about the stage. It is a summer night on the Beijing streets. Sounds of the city play on the house speakers.

SONG: How I wish there were even a tiny café to sit in. With cappuccinos, and men in tuxedos and bad expatriate jazz.

GALLIMARD: If my history serves me correctly, you weren't even allowed into the clubs in Shanghai before the Revolution.

SONG: Your history serves you poorly, Monsieur Gallimard. True, there were signs reading "No dogs and Chinamen." But a woman, especially a delicate Oriental woman — we always go where we please. Could you imagine it otherwise? Clubs in China filled with pasty, big-thighed white women, while thousands of slender lotus blossoms wait just outside the door? Never. The clubs would be empty. *(Beat.)* We have always held a certain fascination for you Caucasian men, have we not?

GALLIMARD: But . . . that fascination is imperialist, or so you tell me.

SONG: Do you believe everything I tell you? Yes. It is always imperialist. But sometimes . . . sometimes, it is also mutual. Oh — this is my flat.

GALLIMARD: I didn't even —

SONG: Thank you. Come another time and we will further expand your mind.

Song exits. Gallimard continues roaming the streets as he speaks to us.

GALLIMARD: What was that? What did she mean, "Sometimes . . . it is mutual"? Women do not flirt with me. And I normally can't talk to them. But tonight, I held up my end of the conversation.

Scene 9

Gallimard's bedroom. Beijing. 1960.
    Helga enters.

HELGA: You didn't tell me you'd be home late.

GALLIMARD: I didn't intend to. Something came up.

HELGA: Oh? Like what?

GALLIMARD: I went to the . . . to the Dutch ambassador's home.

HELGA: Again?

GALLIMARD: There was a reception for a visiting scholar. He's writing a six-volume treatise on the Chinese revolution. We all gathered that meant he'd have to live here long enough to actually write six volumes, and we all expressed our deepest sympathies.

HELGA: Well, I had a good night too. I went with the ladies to a martial arts demonstration. Some of those men — when they break those thick boards — *(she mimes fanning herself)* whoo-whoo!

Helga exits. Lights dim.

GALLIMARD: I lied to my wife. Why? I've never had any reason to lie before. But what reason did I have tonight? I didn't do anything wrong. That night, I had a dream. Other people, I've been told, have dreams when angels appear. Or dragons, or Sophia Loren in a towel. In my dream, Marc from school appeared.

Marc enters, in a nightshirt and cap.

MARC: Rene! You met a girl!

Gallimard and Marc stumble down the Beijing streets. Night sounds over the speakers.

GALLIMARD: It's not that amazing, thank you.

MARC: No! It's so monumental, I heard about it halfway around the world in my sleep!

GALLIMARD: I've met girls before, you know.

MARC: Name one. I've come across time and space to congratulate you. *(He hands Gallimard a bottle of wine.)*

GALLIMARD: Marc, this is expensive.

MARC: On those rare occasions when you become a formless spirit, why not steal the best?

Marc pops open the bottle, begins to share it with Gallimard.

GALLIMARD: You embarrass me. She . . . there's no reason to think she likes me.

MARC: "Sometimes, it is mutual"?

GALLIMARD: Oh.

MARC: "Mutual"? "Mutual"? What does that mean?

GALLIMARD: You heard?

MARC: It means the money is in the bank, you only have to write the check!

GALLIMARD: I am a married man!

MARC: And an excellent one too. I cheated after . . . six months. Then again and again, until now — three hundred girls in twelve years.

GALLIMARD: I don't think we should hold that up as a model.

MARC: Of course not! My life — it is disgusting! Phooey! Phooey! But, you — you are the model husband.

GALLIMARD: Anyway, it's impossible. I'm a foreigner.

MARC: Ah, yes. She cannot love you, it is taboo, but something deep inside her heart . . . she cannot help herself . . . she must surrender to you. It is her destiny.

GALLIMARD: How do you imagine all this?

MARC: The same way you do. It's an old story. It's in our blood. They fear us, Rene. Their women fear us. And their men — their men hate us. And, you know something? They are all correct.

They spot a light in a window.

MARC: There! There, Rene!

GALLIMARD: It's her window.

MARC: Late at night — it burns. The light — it burns for you.

GALLIMARD: I won't look. It's not respectful.

MARC: We don't have to be respectful. We're foreign devils.

Enter Song, in a sheer robe, her face completely swathed in black cloth. The "One Fine Day" aria creeps in over the speakers. With her back to us, Song mimes attending to her toilette. Her robe comes loose, revealing her white shoulders.

MARC: All your life you've waited for a beautiful girl who would lay down for you. All your life you've smiled like a saint when it's happened to every other man you know. And you see them in magazines and you see them in movies. And you wonder, what's wrong with me? Will anyone beautiful ever want me? As the years pass, your hair thins and you struggle to hold on to even your hopes. Stop struggling, Rene. The wait is over. *(He exits.)*

GALLIMARD: Marc? Marc?

At that moment, Song, her back still towards us, drops her robe. A second of her naked back, then a sound cue: a phone ringing, very loud. Blackout, followed in the next beat by a special up on the bedroom area, where a phone now sits. Gallimard stumbles across the stage and picks up the phone. Sound cue out. Over the course of his conversation, area lights fill in the vicinity of his bed. It is the following morning.

GALLIMARD: Yes? Hello?

SONG *(offstage)*:   Is it very early?

GALLIMARD: Why, yes.

SONG *(offstage)*:   How early?

GALLIMARD: It's . . . it's 5:30. Why are you —?

SONG *(offstage)*:   But it's light outside. Already.

GALLIMARD: It is. The sun must be in confusion today.

Over the course of Song's next speech, her upstage special comes up again. She sits in a chair, legs crossed, in a robe, telephone to her ear.

SONG: I waited until I saw the sun. That was as much discipline as I could manage for one night. Do you forgive me?

GALLIMARD: Of course . . . for what?

SONG: Then I'll ask you quickly. Are you really interested in the opera?

GALLIMARD: Why, yes. Yes I am.

SONG: Then come again next Thursday. I am playing *The Drunken Beauty.* May I count on you?

GALLIMARD: Yes. You may.

SONG: Perfect. Well, I must be getting to bed. I'm exhausted. It's been a very long night for me.

Song hangs up; special on her goes off. Gallimard begins to dress for work.

Scene 10

Song Liling's apartment. Beijing. 1960.

GALLIMARD: I returned to the opera that next week, and the week after that . . . she keeps our meetings so short—perhaps fifteen, twenty minutes at most. So I am left each week with a thirst which is intensified. In this way, fifteen weeks have gone by. I am starting to doubt the words of my friend Marc. But no, not really. In my heart, I know she has . . . an interest in me. I suspect this is her way. She is outwardly bold and outspoken, yet her heart is shy and afraid. It is the Oriental in her at war with her Western education.

SONG *(offstage):*   I will be out in an instant. Ask the servant for anything you want.

GALLIMARD: Tonight, I have finally been invited to enter her apartment. Though the idea is almost beyond belief, I believe she is afraid of me.

Gallimard looks around the room. He picks up a picture in a frame, studies it. Without his noticing, Song enters, dressed elegantly in a black gown from the twenties. She stands in the doorway looking like Anna May Wong.°

SONG: That is my father.

GALLIMARD *(surprised):*   Mademoiselle Song . . .

She glides up to him, snatches away the picture.

SONG: It is very good that he did not live to see the Revolution. They would, no doubt, have made him kneel on broken glass. Not that he didn't deserve such a punishment. But he is my father. I would've hated to see it happen.

GALLIMARD: I'm very honored that you've allowed me to visit your home.

Song curtseys.

SONG: Thank you. Oh! Haven't you been poured any tea?

GALLIMARD: I'm really not—

Anna May Wong (1905–1961): Chinese American actor known for her exotic beauty and most often cast as a villain.

SONG (*to her offstage servant*):   Shu-Fang! Cha! Kwai-lah! (*To Gallimard.*) I'm
  sorry. You want everything to be perfect—
GALLIMARD: Please.
SONG: —and before the evening even begins—
GALLIMARD: I'm really not thirsty.
SONG: —it's ruined.
GALLIMARD (*sharply*):   Mademoiselle Song!

Song sits down.

SONG: I'm sorry.
GALLIMARD: What are you apologizing for now?

Pause; Song starts to giggle.

SONG: I don't know!

Gallimard laughs.

GALLIMARD: Exactly my point.
SONG: Oh, I am silly. Light-headed. I promise not to apologize for anything else
  tonight, do you hear me?
GALLIMARD: That's a good girl.

Shu-Fang, a servant girl, comes out with a tea tray and starts to pour.

SONG (*to Shu-Fang*):   No! I'll pour myself for the gentleman!

Shu-Fang, staring at Gallimard, exits.

GALLIMARD: You have a beautiful home.
SONG: No, I . . . I don't even know why I invited you up.
GALLIMARD: Well, I'm glad you did.

Song looks around the room.

SONG: There is an element of danger to your presence.
GALLIMARD: Oh?
SONG: You must know.
GALLIMARD: It doesn't concern me. We both know why I'm here.
SONG: It doesn't concern me either. No . . . well perhaps . . .
GALLIMARD: What?
SONG: Perhaps I am slightly afraid of scandal.
GALLIMARD: What are we doing?
SONG: I'm entertaining you. In my parlor.
GALLIMARD: In France, that would hardly—
SONG: France. France is a country living in the modern era. Perhaps even
  ahead of it. China is a nation whose soul is firmly rooted two thousand years
  in the past. What I do, even pouring the tea for you now . . . it has . . . impli-
  cations. The walls and windows say so. Even my own heart, strapped inside
  this Western dress . . . even it says things—things I don't care to hear.

*Song hands Gallimard a cup of tea. Gallimard puts his hand over both the teacup
and Song's hand.*

GALLIMARD: This is a beautiful dress.

SONG: Don't.

GALLIMARD: What?

SONG: I don't even know if it looks right on me.

GALLIMARD: Believe me —

SONG: You are from France. You see so many beautiful women.

GALLIMARD: France? Since when are the European women — ?

SONG: Oh! What am I trying to do, anyway?!

Song runs to the door, composes herself, then turns towards Gallimard.

SONG: Monsieur Gallimard, perhaps you should go.

GALLIMARD: But . . . why?

SONG: There's something wrong about this.

GALLIMARD: I don't see what.

SONG: I feel . . . I am not myself.

GALLIMARD: No. You're nervous.

SONG: Please. Hard as I try to be modern, to speak like a man, to hold a Western woman's strong face up to my own . . . in the end, I fail. A small, frightened heart beats too quickly and gives me away. Monsieur Gallimard, I'm a Chinese girl. I've never . . . never invited a man up to my flat before. The forwardness of my actions makes my skin burn.

GALLIMARD: What are you afraid of? Certainly not me, I hope.

SONG: I'm a modest girl.

GALLIMARD: I know. And very beautiful. *(He touches her hair.)*

SONG: Please — go now. The next time you see me, I shall again be myself.

GALLIMARD: I like you the way you are right now.

SONG: You are a cad.

GALLIMARD: What do you expect? I'm a foreign devil.

Gallimard walks downstage. Song exits.

GALLIMARD *(to us):* Did you hear the way she talked about Western women? Much differently than the first night. She does — she feels inferior to them — and to me.

Scene 11

The French embassy. Beijing. 1960.
Gallimard moves towards a desk.

GALLIMARD: I determined to try an experiment. In *Madame Butterfly*, Cio-Cio-San fears that the Western man who catches a butterfly will pierce its heart with a needle, then leave it to perish. I began to wonder: had I, too, caught a butterfly who would writhe on a needle?

Marc enters, dressed as a bureaucrat, holding a stack of papers. As Gallimard speaks, Marc hands papers to him. He peruses, then signs, stamps, or rejects them.

GALLIMARD: Over the next five weeks, I worked like a dynamo. I stopped going to the opera, I didn't phone or write her. I knew this little flower was waiting for me to call, and, as I wickedly refused to do so, I felt for the first time that rush of power — the absolute power of a man.

Marc continues acting as the bureaucrat, but he now speaks as himself.

MARC: Rene! It's me.

GALLIMARD: Marc—I hear your voice everywhere now. Even in the midst of work.

MARC: That's because I'm watching you—all the time.

GALLIMARD: You were always the most popular guy in school.

MARC: Well, there's no guarantee of failure in life like happiness in high school. Somehow I knew I'd end up in the suburbs working for Renault and you'd be in the Orient picking exotic women off the trees. And they say there's no justice.

GALLIMARD: That's why you were my friend?

MARC: I gave you a little of my life, so that now you can give me some of yours. *(Pause.)* Remember Isabelle?

GALLIMARD: Of course I remember! She was my first experience.

MARC: We all wanted to ball her. But she only wanted me.

GALLIMARD: I had her.

MARC: Right. You balled her.

GALLIMARD: You were the only one who ever believed me.

MARC: Well, there's a good reason for that. *(Beat.)* C'mon. You must've guessed.

GALLIMARD: You told me to wait in the bushes by the cafeteria that night. The next thing I knew, she was on me. Dress up in the air.

MARC: She never wore underwear.

GALLIMARD: My arms were pinned to the dirt.

MARC: She loved the superior position. A girl ahead of her time.

GALLIMARD: I looked up, and there was this woman . . . bouncing up and down on my loins.

MARC: Screaming, right?

GALLIMARD: Screaming, and breaking off the branches all around me, and pounding my butt up and down into the dirt.

MARC: Huffing and puffing like a locomotive.

GALLIMARD: And in the middle of all this, the leaves were getting into my mouth, my legs were losing circulation, I thought, "God. So this is *it?*"

MARC: You thought that?

GALLIMARD: Well, I was worried about my legs falling off.

MARC: You didn't have a good time?

GALLIMARD: No, that's not what I—I had a great time!

MARC: You're sure?

GALLIMARD: Yeah. Really.

MARC: 'Cuz I wanted you to have a good time.

GALLIMARD: I did.

Pause.

MARC: Shit. *(Pause.)* When all is said and done, she was kind of a lousy lay, wasn't she? I mean, there was a lot of energy there, but you never knew what she was doing with it. Like when she yelled "I'm coming!"—hell, it was so loud, you wanted to go, "Look, it's not that big a deal."

GALLIMARD: I got scared. I thought she meant someone was actually coming. *(Pause.)* But, Marc?

MARC: What?

GALLIMARD: Thanks.

MARC: Oh, don't mention it.

GALLIMARD: It was my first experience.

MARC: Yeah. You got her.

GALLIMARD: I got her.

MARC: Wait! Look at that letter again!

Gallimard picks up one of the papers he's been stamping, and rereads it.

GALLIMARD *(to us):*   After six weeks, they began to arrive. The letters.

Upstage special on Song, as Madame Butterfly. The scene is underscored by the "Love Duet."

SONG: Did we fight? I do not know. Is the opera no longer of interest to you? Please come — my audiences miss the white devil in their midst.

Gallimard looks up from the letter, towards us.

GALLIMARD *(to us):*   A concession, but much too dignified. *(Beat; he discards the letter.)* I skipped the opera again that week to complete a position paper on trade.

The bureaucrat hands him another letter.

SONG: Six weeks have passed since last we met. Is this your practice — to leave friends in the lurch? Sometimes I hate you, sometimes I hate myself, but always I miss you.

GALLIMARD *(to us):*   Better, but I don't like the way she calls me "friend." When a woman calls a man her "friend," she's calling him a eunuch or a homosexual. *(Beat; he discards the letter.)* I was absent from the opera for the seventh week, feeling a sudden urge to clean out my files.

Bureaucrat hands him another letter.

SONG: Your rudeness is beyond belief. I don't deserve this cruelty. Don't bother to call. I'll have you turned away at the door.

GALLIMARD *(to us):*   I didn't. *(He discards the letter; bureaucrat hands him another.)* And then finally, the letter that concluded my experiment.

SONG: I am out of words. I can hide behind dignity no longer. What do you want? I have already given you my shame.

Gallimard gives the letter back to Marc, slowly. Special on Song fades out.

GALLIMARD *(to us):*   Reading it, I became suddenly ashamed. Yes, my experiment had been a success. She was turning on my needle. But the victory seemed hollow.

MARC: Hollow?! Are you crazy?

GALLIMARD: Nothing, Marc. Please go away.

MARC *(exiting, with papers):*   Haven't I taught you anything?

GALLIMARD: "I have already given you my shame." I had to attend a reception that evening. On the way, I felt sick. If there is a God, surely he would punish me now. I had finally gained power over a beautiful woman, only to abuse it cruelly. There must be justice in the world. I had the strange feeling that the ax would fall this very evening.

Scene 12

Ambassador Toulon's residence. Beijing. 1960.

Sound cue: party noises. Light change. We are now in a spacious residence. Toulon, the French ambassador, enters and taps Gallimard on the shoulder.

TOULON: Gallimard? Can I have a word? Over here.

GALLIMARD *(to us)*: Manuel Toulon. French ambassador to China. He likes to think of us all as his children. Rather like God.

TOULON: Look, Gallimard, there's not much to say. I've liked you. From the day you walked in. You were no leader, but you were tidy and efficient.

GALLIMARD: Thank you, sir.

TOULON: Don't jump the gun. Okay, our needs in China are changing. It's embarrassing that we lost Indochina. Someone just wasn't on the ball there. I don't mean you personally, of course.

GALLIMARD: Thank you, sir.

TOULON: We're going to be doing a lot more information-gathering in the future. The nature of our work here is changing. Some people are just going to have to go. It's nothing personal.

GALLIMARD: Oh.

TOULON: Want to know a secret? Vice-Consul LeBon is being transferred.

GALLIMARD *(to us)*: My immediate superior!

TOULON: And most of his department.

GALLIMARD *(to us)*: Just as I feared! God has seen my evil heart—

TOULON: But not you.

GALLIMARD *(to us)*: —and he's taking her away just as . . . *(To Toulon.)* Excuse me, sir?

TOULON: Scare you? I think I did. Cheer up, Gallimard. I want you to replace LeBon as vice-consul.

GALLIMARD: You—? Yes, well, thank you, sir.

TOULON: Anytime.

GALLIMARD: I . . . accept with great humility.

TOULON: Humility won't be part of the job. You're going to coordinate the revamped intelligence division. Want to know a secret? A year ago, you would've been out. But the past few months, I don't know how it happened, you've become this new aggressive confident . . . thing. And they also tell me you get along with the Chinese. So I think you're a lucky man, Gallimard. Congratulations.

They shake hands. Toulon exits. Party noises out. Gallimard stumbles across a darkened stage.

GALLIMARD: Vice-consul? Impossible! As I stumbled out of the party, I saw it written across the sky: There is no God. Or, no—say that there is a God. But that God . . . understands. Of course! God who creates Eve to serve Adam,

who blesses Solomon with his harem but ties Jezebel to a burning bed° —
that God is a man. And he understands! At age thirty-nine, I was suddenly
initiated into the way of the world.

Scene 13

Song Liling's apartment. Beijing. 1960.
  Song enters, in a sheer dressing gown.

SONG: Are you crazy?
GALLIMARD: Mademoiselle Song —
SONG: To come here — at this hour? After . . . after eight weeks?
GALLIMARD: It's the most amazing —
SONG: You bang on my door? Scare my servants, scandalize the neighbors?
GALLIMARD: I've been promoted. To vice-consul.

Pause.

SONG: And what is that supposed to mean to me?
GALLIMARD: Are you my Butterfly?
SONG: What are you saying?
GALLIMARD: I've come tonight for an answer: are you my Butterfly?
SONG: Don't you know already?
GALLIMARD: I want you to say it.
SONG: I don't want to say it.
GALLIMARD: So, that is your answer?
SONG: You know how I feel about —
GALLIMARD: I do remember one thing.
SONG: What?
GALLIMARD: In the letter I received today.
SONG: Don't.
GALLIMARD: "I have already given you my shame."
SONG: It's enough that I even wrote it.
GALLIMARD: Well, then —
SONG: I shouldn't have it splashed across my face.
GALLIMARD: — if that's all true —
SONG: Stop!
GALLIMARD: Then what is one more short answer?
SONG: I don't want to!
GALLIMARD: Are you my Butterfly? (*Silence; he crosses the room and begins to
  touch her hair.*) I want from you honesty. There should be nothing false
  between us. No false pride.

Pause.

SONG: Yes, I am. I am your Butterfly.

God who creates Eve . . . burning bed: Eve, Adam, Solomon, and Jezebel are biblical characters. See Gen. 2:18–25; I Kings 11:1–8; and II Kings 9:11–37.

GALLIMARD: Then let me be honest with you. It is because of you that I was promoted tonight. You have changed my life forever. My little Butterfly, there
should be no more secrets: I love you.

He starts to kiss her roughly. She resists slightly.

SONG: No . . . no . . . gently . . . please, I've never . . .
GALLIMARD: No?
SONG: I've tried to appear experienced, but . . . the truth is . . . no.
GALLIMARD: Are you cold?
SONG: Yes. Cold.
GALLIMARD: Then we will go very, very slowly.

He starts to caress her; her gown begins to open.

SONG: No . . . let me . . . keep my clothes . . .
GALLIMARD: But . . .
SONG: Please . . . it all frightens me. I'm a modest Chinese girl.
GALLIMARD: My poor little treasure.
SONG: I am your treasure. Though inexperienced, I am not . . . ignorant. They
teach us things, our mothers, about pleasing a man.
GALLIMARD: Yes?
SONG: I'll do my best to make you happy. Turn off the lights.

*Gallimard gets up and heads for a lamp. Song, propped up on one elbow, tosses her
hair back and smiles.*

SONG: Monsieur Gallimard?
GALLIMARD: Yes, Butterfly?
SONG: *"Vieni, vieni!"*
GALLIMARD: "Come, darling."
SONG: *"Ah! Dolce notte!"*
GALLIMARD: "Beautiful night."
SONG: *"Tutto estatico d'amor ride il ciel!"*
GALLIMARD: "All ecstatic with love, the heavens are filled with laughter."

He turns off the lamp. Blackout.

ACT 2, Scene 1

M. Gallimard's cell. Paris. 1988.
  Lights up on Gallimard. He sits in his cell, reading from a leaflet.

GALLIMARD: This, from a contemporary critic's commentary on *Madame Butterfly:* "Pinkerton suffers from . . . being an obnoxious bounder whom every
man in the audience itches to kick." Bully for us men in the audience! Then,
in the same note: "Butterfly is the most irresistibly appealing of Puccini's
'Little Women.' Watching the succession of her humiliations is like watching a child under torture." *(He tosses the pamphlet over his shoulder.)* I suggest that, while we men may all want to kick Pinkerton, very few of us would
pass up the opportunity to *be* Pinkerton.

Gallimard moves out of his cell.

Scene 2

Gallimard and Butterfly's flat. Beijing. 1960.
   We are in a simple but well-decorated parlor. Gallimard moves to sit on a sofa, while Song, dressed in a cheongsam,° enters and curls up at his feet.

GALLIMARD *(to us):*   We secured a flat on the outskirts of Peking. Butterfly, as I was calling her now, decorated our "home" with Western furniture and Chinese antiques. And there, on a few stolen afternoons or evenings each week, Butterfly commenced her education.

SONG: The Chinese men — they keep us down.

GALLIMARD: Even in the "New Society"?

SONG: In the "New Society," we are all kept ignorant equally. That's one of the exciting things about loving a Western man. I know you are not threatened by a woman's education.

GALLIMARD: I'm no saint, Butterfly.

SONG: But you come from a progressive society.

GALLIMARD: We're not always reminding each other how "old" we are, if that's what you mean.

SONG: Exactly. We Chinese — once, I suppose, it is true, we ruled the world. But so what? How much more exciting to be part of the society ruling the world today. Tell me — what's happening in Vietnam?

GALLIMARD: Oh, Butterfly — you want me to bring my work home?

SONG: I want to know what you know. To be impressed by my man. It's not the particulars so much as the fact that you're making decisions which change the shape of the world.

GALLIMARD: Not the world. At best, a small corner.

Toulon enters, and sits at a desk upstage.

Scene 3

French embassy. Beijing. 1961.
   Gallimard moves downstage, to Toulon's desk. Song remains upstage, watching.

TOULON: And a more troublesome corner is hard to imagine.

GALLIMARD: So, the Americans plan to begin bombing?

TOULON: This is very secret, Gallimard: yes. The Americans don't have an embassy here. They're asking us to be their eyes and ears. Say Jack Kennedy signed an order to bomb North Vietnam, Laos. How would the Chinese react?

GALLIMARD: I think the Chinese will squawk —

TOULON: Uh-huh.

GALLIMARD: — but, in their hearts, they don't even like Ho Chi Minh.°

Pause.

---

cheongsam: A fitted dress with side slits in the skirt.   **Ho Chi Minh** (1890–1969): First president of North Vietnam (1945–1969).

TOULON: What a bunch of jerks. Vietnam was *our* colony. Not only didn't the Americans help us fight to keep them, but now, seven years later, they've come back to grab the territory for themselves. It's very irritating.

GALLIMARD: With all due respect, sir, why should the Americans have won our war for us back in fifty-four if we didn't have the will to win it ourselves?

TOULON: You're kidding, aren't you?

Pause.

GALLIMARD: The Orientals simply want to be associated with whoever shows the most strength and power. You live with the Chinese, sir. Do you think they like Communism?

TOULON: I live in China. Not with the Chinese.

GALLIMARD: Well, I—

TOULON: *You* live with the Chinese.

GALLIMARD: Excuse me?

TOULON: I can't keep a secret.

GALLIMARD: What are you saying?

TOULON: Only that I'm not immune to gossip. So, you're keeping a native mistress? Don't answer. It's none of my business. *(Pause.)* I'm sure she must be gorgeous.

GALLIMARD: Well . . .

TOULON: I'm impressed. You had the stamina to go out into the streets and hunt one down. Some of us have to be content with the wives of the expatriate community.

GALLIMARD: I do feel . . . fortunate.

TOULON: So, Gallimard, you've got the inside knowledge—what *do* the Chinese think?

GALLIMARD: Deep down, they miss the old days. You know, cappuccinos, men in tuxedos—

TOULON: So what do we tell the Americans about Vietnam?

GALLIMARD: Tell them there's a natural affinity between the West and the Orient.

TOULON: And that you speak from experience?

GALLIMARD: The Orientals are people too. They want the good things we can give them. If the Americans demonstrate the will to win, the Vietnamese will welcome them into a mutually beneficial union.

TOULON: I don't see how the Vietnamese can stand up to American firepower.

GALLIMARD: Orientals will always submit to a greater force.

TOULON: I'll note your opinions in my report. The Americans always love to hear how "welcome" they'll be. *(He starts to exit.)*

GALLIMARD: Sir?

TOULON: Mmmm?

GALLIMARD: This . . . rumor you've heard.

TOULON: Uh-huh?

GALLIMARD: How . . . widespread do you think it is?

TOULON: It's only widespread within this embassy. Where nobody talks because everybody is guilty. We were worried about you, Gallimard. We thought you

were the only one here without a secret. Now you go and find a lotus blossom . . . and top us all. *(He exits.)*

GALLIMARD *(to us):*   Toulon knows! And he approves! I was learning the benefits
of being a man. We form our own clubs, sit behind thick doors, smoke — and
celebrate the fact that we're still boys. *(He starts to move downstage, towards
Song.)* So, over the —

Suddenly Comrade Chin enters. Gallimard backs away.

GALLIMARD *(to Song):*   No! Why does she have to come in?

SONG: Rene, be sensible. How can they understand the story without her? Now,
don't embarrass yourself.

Gallimard moves down center.

GALLIMARD *(to us):*   Now, you will see why my story is so amusing to so many
people. Why they snicker at parties in disbelief. Please — try to understand
it from my point of view. We are all prisoners of our time and place. *(He
exits.)*

Scene 4

Gallimard and Butterfly's flat. Beijing. 1961.

SONG *(to us):*   1961. The flat Monsieur Gallimard rented for us. An evening
after he has gone.

CHIN: Okay, see if you can find out when the Americans plan to start bombing
Vietnam. If you can find out what cities, even better.

SONG: I'll do my best, but I don't want to arouse his suspicions.

CHIN: Yeah, sure, of course. So, what else?

SONG: The Americans will increase troops in Vietnam to 170,000 soldiers with
120,000 militia and 11,000 American advisors.

CHIN *(writing):*   Wait, wait, 120,000 militia and —

SONG: — 11,000 American —

CHIN: — American advisors. *(Beat.)* How do you remember so much?

SONG: I'm an actor.

CHIN: Yeah. *(Beat.)* Is that how come you dress like that?

SONG: Like what, Miss Chin?

CHIN: Like that dress! You're wearing a dress. And every time I come here,
you're wearing a dress. Is that because you're an actor? Or what?

SONG: It's a . . . disguise, Miss Chin.

CHIN: Actors, I think they're all weirdos. My mother tells me actors are like
gamblers or prostitutes or —

SONG: It helps me in my assignment.

Pause.

CHIN: You're not gathering information in any way that violates Communist
Party principles, are you?

SONG: Why would I do that?

CHIN: Just checking. Remember: when working for the Great Proletarian State,
you represent our Chairman Mao in every position you take.

SONG: I'll try to imagine the Chairman taking my positions.

CHIN: We all think of him this way. Good-bye, comrade. *(She starts to exit.)* Comrade?

SONG: Yes?

CHIN: Don't forget: there is no homosexuality in China!

SONG: Yes, I've heard.

CHIN: Just checking. *(She exits.)*

SONG *(to us):*   What passes for a woman in modern China.

Gallimard sticks his head out from the wings.

GALLIMARD: Is she gone?

SONG: Yes, Rene. Please continue in your own fashion.

Scene 5

Beijing. 1961–1963.

   Gallimard moves to the couch where Song still sits. He lies down in her lap, and she strokes his forehead.

GALLIMARD *(to us):*   And so, over the years 1961, '62, '63, we settled into our routine, Butterfly and I. She would always have prepared a light snack and then, ever so delicately, and only if I agreed, she would start to pleasure me. With her hands, her mouth . . . too many ways to explain, and too sad, given my present situation. But mostly we would talk. About my life. Perhaps there is nothing more rare than to find a woman who passionately listens.

Song remains upstage, listening, as Helga enters and plays a scene downstage with Gallimard.

HELGA: Rene, I visited Dr. Bolleart this morning.

GALLIMARD: Why? Are you ill?

HELGA: No, no. You see, I wanted to ask him . . . that question we've been discussing.

GALLIMARD: And I told you, it's only a matter of time. Why did you bring a doctor into this? We just have to keep trying — like a crapshoot, actually.

HELGA: I went, I'm sorry. But listen: he says there's nothing wrong with me.

GALLIMARD: You see? Now, will you stop —?

HELGA: Rene, he says he'd like you to go in and take some tests.

GALLIMARD: Why? So he can find there's nothing wrong with both of us?

HELGA: Rene, I don't ask for much. One trip! One visit! And then, whatever you want to do about it — you decide.

GALLIMARD: You're assuming he'll find something defective!

HELGA: No! Of course not! Whatever he finds — if he finds nothing, we decide what to do about nothing! But go!

GALLIMARD: If he finds nothing, we keep trying. Just like we do now.

HELGA: But at least we'll know! *(Pause.)* I'm sorry. *(She starts to exit.)*

GALLIMARD: Do you really want me to see Dr. Bolleart?

HELGA: Only if you want a child, Rene. We have to face the fact that time is running out. Only if you want a child. *(She exits.)*

GALLIMARD *(to Song)*: I'm a modern man, Butterfly. And yet, I don't want to go. It's the same old voodoo. I feel like God himself is laughing at me if I can't produce a child.

SONG: You men of the West—you're obsessed by your odd desire for equality. Your wife can't give you a child, and *you're* going to the doctor?

GALLIMARD: Well, you see, she's already gone.

SONG: And because this incompetent can't find the defect, you now have to subject yourself to him? It's unnatural.

GALLIMARD: Well, what is the "natural" solution?

SONG: In Imperial China, when a man found that one wife was inadequate, he turned to another—to give him his son.

GALLIMARD: What do you—? I can't . . . marry you, yet.

SONG: Please. I'm not asking you to be my husband. But I am already your wife.

GALLIMARD: Do you want to . . . have my child?

SONG: I thought you'd never ask.

GALLIMARD: But, your career . . . your—

SONG: Phooey on my career! That's your Western mind, twisting itself into strange shapes again. Of course I love my career. But what would I love most of all? To feel something inside me—day and night—something I know is yours. *(Pause.)* Promise me . . . you won't go to this doctor. Who is this Western quack to set himself as judge over the man I love? I know who is a man, and who is not. *(She exits.)*

GALLIMARD *(to us)*: Dr. Bolleart? Of course I didn't go. What man would?

Scene 6

Beijing. 1963.

Party noises over the house speakers. Renee enters, wearing a revealing gown.

GALLIMARD: 1963. A party at the Austrian embassy. None of us could remember the Austrian ambassador's name, which seemed somehow appropriate. *(To Renee.)* So, I tell the Americans, Diem° must go. The U.S. wants to be respected by the Vietnamese, and yet they're propping up this nobody seminarian as her president. A man whose claim to fame is his sister-in-law imposing fanatic "moral order" campaigns? Oriental women—when they're good, they're very good, but when they're bad, they're Christians.

RENEE: Yeah.

GALLIMARD: And what do you do?

RENEE: I'm a student. My father exports a lot of useless stuff to the Third World.

GALLIMARD: How useless?

RENEE: You know. Squirt guns, confectioner's sugar, Hula Hoops . . .

GALLIMARD: I'm sure they appreciate the sugar.

RENEE: I'm here for two years to study Chinese.

GALLIMARD: Two years!

Diem: Ngo Dinh Diem (1901–1963), president of South Vietnam (1955–1963), assassinated in a coup d'état supported by the United States.

RENEE: That's what everybody says.

GALLIMARD: When did you arrive?

RENEE: Three weeks ago.

GALLIMARD: And?

RENEE: I like it. It's primitive, but . . . well, this is the place to learn Chinese, so here I am.

GALLIMARD: Why Chinese?

RENEE: I think it'll be important someday.

GALLIMARD: You do?

RENEE: Don't ask me when, but . . . that's what I think.

GALLIMARD: Well, I agree with you. One hundred percent. That's very farsighted.

RENEE: Yeah. Well of course, my father thinks I'm a complete weirdo.

GALLIMARD: He'll thank you someday.

RENEE: Like when the Chinese start buying Hula Hoops?

GALLIMARD: There're a billion bellies out there.

RENEE: And if they end up taking over the world — well, then I'll be lucky to know Chinese too, right?

Pause.

GALLIMARD: At this point, I don't see how the Chinese can possibly take —

RENEE: You know what I *don't* like about China?

GALLIMARD: Excuse me? No — what?

RENEE: Nothing to do at night.

GALLIMARD: You come to parties at embassies like everyone else.

RENEE: Yeah, but they get out at ten. And then what?

GALLIMARD: I'm afraid the Chinese idea of a dance hall is a dirt floor and a man with a flute.

RENEE: Are you married?

GALLIMARD: Yes. Why?

RENEE: You wanna . . . fool around?

Pause.

GALLIMARD: Sure.

RENEE: I'll wait for you outside. What's your name?

GALLIMARD: Gallimard. Rene.

RENEE: Weird. I'm Renee too. (*She exits.*)

GALLIMARD (*to us*):   And so, I embarked on my first extra-extramarital affair. Renee was picture perfect. With a body like those girls in the magazines. If I put a tissue paper over my eyes, I wouldn't have been able to tell the difference. And it was exciting to be with someone who wasn't afraid to be seen completely naked. But is it possible for a woman to be *too* uninhibited, *too* willing, so as to seem almost too . . . masculine?

Chuck Berry° blares from the house speakers, then comes down in volume as Renee enters, toweling her hair.

Chuck Berry (b. 1926): Influential American rock 'n' roll musician whose first recording came out in 1955.

RENEE: You have a nice weenie.

GALLIMARD: What?

RENEE: Penis. You have a nice penis.

GALLIMARD: Oh. Well, thank you. That's very . . .

RENEE: What—can't take a compliment?

GALLIMARD: No, it's very . . . reassuring.

RENEE: But most girls don't come out and say it, huh?

GALLIMARD: And also . . . what did you call it?

RENEE: Oh. Most girls don't call it a "weenie," huh?

GALLIMARD: It sounds very—

RENEE: Small, I know.

GALLIMARD: I was going to say, "young."

RENEE: Yeah. Young, small, same thing. Most guys are pretty, uh, sensitive about that. Like, you know, I had a boyfriend back home in Denmark. I got mad at him once and called him a little weeniehead. He got so mad! He said at least I should call him a great big weeniehead.

GALLIMARD: I suppose I just say "penis."

RENEE: Yeah. That's pretty clinical. There's "cock," but that sounds like a chicken. And "prick" is painful, and "dick" is like you're talking about someone who's not in the room.

GALLIMARD: Yes. It's a . . . bigger problem than I imagined.

RENEE: I—I think maybe it's because I really don't know what to do with them—that's why I call them "weenies."

GALLIMARD: Well, you did quite well with . . . mine.

RENEE: Thanks, but I mean, really *do* with them. Like, okay, have you ever looked at one? I mean, really?

GALLIMARD: No, I suppose when it's part of you, you sort of take it for granted.

RENEE: I guess. But, like, it just hangs there. This little . . . flap of flesh. And there's so much fuss that we make about it. Like, I think the reason we fight wars is because we wear clothes. Because no one knows—between the men, I mean—who has the biggest . . . weenie. So, if I'm a guy with a small one, I'm going to build a really big building or take over a really big piece of land or write a really long book so the other men don't know, right? But, see, it never really works, that's the problem. I mean, you conquer the country, or whatever, but you're still wearing clothes, so there's no way to prove absolutely whose is bigger or smaller. And that's what we call a civilized society. The whole world run by a bunch of men with pricks the size of pins. (*She exits.*)

GALLIMARD (*to us*):   This was simply not acceptable.

A high-pitched chime rings through the air. Song, dressed as Butterfly, appears in the upstage special. She is obviously distressed. Her body swoons as she attempts to clip the stems of flowers she's arranging in a vase.

GALLIMARD: But I kept up our affair, wildly, for several months. Why? I believe because of Butterfly. She knew the secret I was trying to hide. But, unlike a Western woman, she didn't confront me, threaten, even pout. I remembered the words of Puccini's *Butterfly*:

SONG: "*Noi siamo gente avvezza / alle piccole cose / umili e silenziose.*"

GALLIMARD: "I come from a people / Who are accustomed to little / Humble and silent." I saw Pinkerton and Butterfly, and what she would say if he were unfaithful . . . nothing. She would cry, alone, into those wildly soft sleeves, once full of possessions, now empty to collect her tears. It was her tears and her silence that excited me, every time I visited Renee.

TOULON *(offstage)*: Gallimard!

Toulon enters. Gallimard turns towards him. During the next section, Song, up center, begins to dance with the flowers. It is a drunken, reckless dance, where she breaks small pieces off the stems.

TOULON: They're killing him.

GALLIMARD: Who? I'm sorry? What?

TOULON: Bother you to come over at this late hour?

GALLIMARD: No . . . of course not.

TOULON: Not after you hear my secret. Champagne?

GALLIMARD: Um . . . thank you.

TOULON: You're surprised. There's something that you've wanted, Gallimard. No, not a promotion. Next time. Something in the world. You're not aware of this, but there's an informal gossip circle among intelligence agents. And some of ours heard from some of the Americans —

GALLIMARD: Yes?

TOULON: That the U.S. will allow the Vietnamese generals to stage a coup . . . and assassinate President Diem.

The chime rings again. Toulon freezes. Gallimard turns upstage and looks at Butterfly, who slowly and deliberately clips a flower off its stem. Gallimard turns back towards Toulon.

GALLIMARD: I think . . . that's a very wise move!

Toulon unfreezes.

TOULON: It's what you've been advocating. A toast?

GALLIMARD: Sure. I consider this a vindication.

TOULON: Not exactly. "To the test. Let's hope you pass."

They drink. The chime rings again. Toulon freezes. Gallimard turns upstage, and Song clips another flower.

GALLIMARD *(to Toulon)*: The test?

TOULON *(unfreezing)*: It's a test of everything you've been saying. I personally think the generals probably will stop the Communists. And you'll be a hero. But if anything goes wrong, then your opinions won't be worth a pig's ear. I'm sure that won't happen. But sometimes it's easier when they don't listen to you.

GALLIMARD: They're your opinions too, aren't they?

TOULON: Personally, yes.

GALLIMARD: So we agree.

TOULON: But my opinions aren't on that report. Yours are. Cheers.

Toulon turns away from Gallimard and raises his glass. At that instant Song picks up the vase and hurls it to the ground. It shatters. Song sinks down amidst the shards of the vase, in a calm, childlike trance. She sings softly, as if reciting a child's nursery rhyme.

SONG *(repeat as necessary):*   "The whole world over, the white man travels, setting anchor, wherever he likes. Life's not worth living, unless he finds, the finest maidens, of every land . . ."

Gallimard turns downstage towards us. Song continues singing.

GALLIMARD: I shook as I left his house. That coward! That worm! To put the burden for his decisions on my shoulders!

     I started for Renee's. But no, that was all I needed. A schoolgirl who would question the role of the penis in modern society. What I wanted was revenge. A vessel to contain my humiliation. Though I hadn't seen her in several weeks, I headed for Butterfly's.

Gallimard enters Song's apartment.

SONG: Oh! Rene . . . I was dreaming!
GALLIMARD: You've been drinking?
SONG: If I can't sleep, then yes, I drink. But then, it gives me these dreams which — Rene, it's been almost three weeks since you visited me last.
GALLIMARD: I know. There's been a lot going on in the world.
SONG: Fortunately I am drunk. So I can speak freely. It's not the world, it's you and me. And an old problem. Even the softest skin becomes like leather to a man who's touched it too often. I confess I don't know how to stop it. I don't know how to become another woman.
GALLIMARD: I have a request.
SONG: Is this a solution? Or are you ready to give up the flat?
GALLIMARD: It may be a solution. But I'm sure you won't like it.
SONG: Oh well, that's very important. "Like it?" Do you think I "like" lying here alone, waiting, always waiting for your return? Please — don't worry about what I may not "like."
GALLIMARD: I want to see you . . . naked.

Silence.

SONG: I thought you understood my modesty. So you want me to — what — strip? Like a big cowboy girl? Shiny pasties on my breasts? Shall I fling my kimono over my head and yell "ya-hoo" in the process? I thought you respected my shame!
GALLIMARD: I believe you gave me your shame many years ago.
SONG: Yes — and it is just like a white devil to use it against me. I can't believe it. I thought myself so repulsed by the passive Oriental and the cruel white man. Now I see — we are always most revolted by the things hidden within us.
GALLIMARD: I just mean —
SONG: Yes?
GALLIMARD: — that it will remove the only barrier left between us.
SONG: No, Rene. Don't couch your request in sweet words. Be yourself — a cad — and know that my love is enough, that I submit — submit to the worst you can give me. *(Pause.)* Well, come. Strip me. Whatever happens, know that you have willed it. Our love, in your hands. I'm helpless before my man.

Gallimard starts to cross the room.

GALLIMARD: Did I not undress her because I knew, somewhere deep down, what I would find? Perhaps. Happiness is so rare that our mind can turn somersaults to protect it.

     At the time, I only knew that I was seeing Pinkerton stalking towards his Butterfly, ready to reward her love with his lecherous hands. The image sickened me, pulled me to my knees, so I was crawling towards her like a worm. By the time I reached her, Pinkerton . . . had vanished from my heart. To be replaced by something new, something unnatural, that flew in the face of all I'd learned in the world — something very close to love.

He grabs her around the waist; she strokes his hair.

GALLIMARD: Butterfly, forgive me.
SONG: Rene . . .
GALLIMARD: For everything. From the start.
SONG: I'm . . .
GALLIMARD: I want to —
SONG: I'm pregnant. *(Beat.)* I'm pregnant. *(Beat.)* I'm pregnant.

Beat.

GALLIMARD: I want to marry you!

Scene 7

Gallimard and Butterfly's flat. Beijing. 1963.

     Downstage, Song paces as Comrade Chin reads from her notepad. Upstage, Gallimard is still kneeling. He remains on his knees throughout the scene, watching it.

SONG: I need a baby.
CHIN *(from pad)*:   He's been spotted going to a dorm.
SONG: I need a baby.
CHIN: At the Foreign Language Institute.
SONG: I need a baby.
CHIN: The room of a Danish girl. . . . What do you mean, you need a baby?!
SONG: Tell Comrade Kang — last night, the entire mission, it could've ended.
CHIN: What do you mean?
SONG: Tell Kang — he told me to strip.
CHIN: Strip?!
SONG: Write!
CHIN: I tell you, I don't understand nothing about this case anymore. Nothing.
SONG: He told me to strip, and I took a chance. Oh, we Chinese, we know how to gamble.
CHIN *(writing)*:   ". . . told him to strip."
SONG: My palms were wet, I had to make a split-second decision.
CHIN: Hey! Can you slow down?!

Pause.

SONG: You write faster, I'm the artist here. Suddenly, it hit me — "All he wants is
for her to submit. Once a woman submits, a man is always ready to become
'generous.' "

CHIN: You're just gonna end up with rough notes.

SONG: And it worked! He gave in! Now, if I can just present him with a baby. A
Chinese baby with blond hair — he'll be mine for life!

CHIN: Kang will never agree! The trading of babies has to be a counterrevolutionary act!

SONG: Sometimes, a counterrevolutionary act is necessary to counter a counterrevolutionary act.

Pause.

CHIN: Wait.

SONG: I need one . . . in seven months. Make sure it's a boy.

CHIN: This doesn't sound like something the Chairman would do. Maybe
you'd better talk to Comrade Kang yourself.

SONG: Good. I will.

Chin gets up to leave.

SONG: Miss Chin? Why, in the Peking Opera, are women's roles played by men?

CHIN: I don't know. Maybe, a reactionary remnant of male —

SONG: No. *(Beat.)* Because only a man knows how a woman is supposed to act.

Chin exits. Song turns upstage, towards Gallimard.

GALLIMARD *(calling after Chin)*:   Good riddance! *(To Song.)* I could forget all
that betrayal in an instant, you know. If you'd just come back and become
Butterfly again.

SONG: Fat chance. You're here in prison, rotting in a cell. And I'm on a plane,
winging my way back to China. Your President pardoned me of our treason,
you know.

GALLIMARD: Yes, I read about that.

SONG: Must make you feel . . . lower than shit.

GALLIMARD: But don't you, even a little bit, wish you were here with me?

SONG: I'm an artist, Rene. You were my greatest . . . acting challenge. *(She
laughs.)* It doesn't matter how rotten I answer, does it? You still adore me.
That's why I love you, Rene. *(She points to us.)* So — you were telling your
audience about the night I announced I was pregnant.

*Gallimard puts his arms around Song's waist. He and Song are in the positions
they were in at the end of Scene 6.*

Scene 8

Same.

GALLIMARD: I'll divorce my wife. We'll live together here, and then later in
France.

SONG: I feel so . . . ashamed.

GALLIMARD: Why?

SONG: I had begun to lose faith. And now, you shame me with your generosity.

GALLIMARD: Generosity? No, I'm proposing for very selfish reasons.

SONG: Your apologies only make me feel more ashamed. My outburst a moment ago!

GALLIMARD: Your outburst? What about my request?!

SONG: You've been very patient dealing with my . . . eccentricities. A Western man, used to women freer with their bodies —

GALLIMARD: It was sick! Don't make excuses for me.

SONG: I have to. You don't seem willing to make them for yourself.

Pause.

GALLIMARD: You're crazy.

SONG: I'm happy. Which often looks like crazy.

GALLIMARD: Then make me crazy. Marry me.

Pause.

SONG: No.

GALLIMARD: What?

SONG: Do I sound silly, a slave, if I say I'm not worthy?

GALLIMARD: Yes. In fact you do. No one has loved me like you.

SONG: Thank you. And no one ever will. I'll see to that.

GALLIMARD: So what is the problem?

SONG: Rene, we Chinese are realists. We understand rice, gold, and guns. You are a diplomat. Your career is skyrocketing. Now, what would happen if you divorced your wife to marry a Communist Chinese actress?

GALLIMARD: That's not being realistic. That's defeating yourself before you begin.

SONG: We conserve our strength for the battles we can win.

GALLIMARD: That sounds like a fortune cookie!

SONG: Where do you think fortune cookies come from!

GALLIMARD: I don't care.

SONG: You do. So do I. And we should. That is why I say I'm not worthy. I'm worthy to love and even to be loved by you. But I am not worthy to end the career of one of the West's most promising diplomats.

GALLIMARD: It's not that great a career! I made it sound like more than it is!

SONG: Modesty will get you nowhere. Flatter yourself, and you flatter me. I'm flattered to decline your offer. *(She exits.)*

GALLIMARD *(to us):*   Butterfly and I argued all night. And, in the end, I left, knowing I would never be her husband. She went away for several months — to the countryside, like a small animal. Until the night I received her call.

A baby's cry from offstage. Song enters, carrying a child.

SONG: He looks like you.

GALLIMARD: Oh! *(Beat; he approaches the baby.)* Well, babies are never very attractive at birth.

SONG: Stop!

GALLIMARD: I'm sure he'll grow more beautiful with age. More like his mother.

SONG: *"Chi vide mai / a bimbo del Giappon . . . "*

GALLIMARD: "What baby, I wonder, was ever born in Japan" — or China, for that matter —

SONG: ". . . *occhi azzurrini?*"

GALLIMARD: "With azure eyes" — they're actually sort of brown, wouldn't you say?

SONG: "*E il labbro.*"

GALLIMARD: "And such lips!" (*He kisses Song.*) And such lips.

SONG: "*E i ricciolini d'oro schietto?*"

GALLIMARD: "And such a head of golden" — if slightly patchy — "curls?"

SONG: I'm going to call him "Peepee."

GALLIMARD: Darling, could you repeat that because I'm sure a rickshaw just flew by overhead.

SONG: You heard me.

GALLIMARD: "Song Peepee"? May I suggest Michael, or Stephan, or Adolph?

SONG: You may, but I won't listen.

GALLIMARD: You can't be serious. Can you imagine the time this child will have in school?

SONG: In the West, yes.

GALLIMARD: It's worse than naming him Ping Pong or Long Dong or —

SONG: But he's never going to live in the West, is he?

Pause.

GALLIMARD: That wasn't my choice.

SONG: It is mine. And this is my promise to you: I will raise him, he will be our child, but he will never burden you outside of China.

GALLIMARD: Why do you make these promises? I want to be burdened! I want a scandal to cover the papers!

SONG (*to us*): Prophetic.

GALLIMARD: I'm serious.

SONG: So am I. His name is as I registered it. And he will never live in the West.

Song exits with the child.

GALLIMARD (*to us*): Is it possible that her stubbornness only made me want her more? That drawing back at the moment of my capitulation was the most brilliant strategy she could have chosen? It is possible. But it is also possible that by this point she could have said, could have done . . . anything, and I would have adored her still.

Scene 9

Beijing. 1966.
   A driving rhythm of Chinese percussion fills the stage.

GALLIMARD: And then, China began to change. Mao became very old, and his cult became very strong. And, like many old men, he entered his second childhood. So he handed over the reins of state to those with minds like his own. And children ruled the Middle Kingdom° with complete caprice. The

---

Middle Kingdom: The royal domain of China during its feudal period.

doctrine of the Cultural Revolution° implied continuous anarchy. Contact between Chinese and foreigners became impossible. Our flat was confiscated. Her fame and my money now counted against us.

Two dancers in Mao suits and red-starred caps enter, and begin crudely mimicking revolutionary violence, in an agitprop fashion.

GALLIMARD: And somehow the American war went wrong too. Four hundred thousand dollars were being spent for every Viet Cong° killed; so General Westmoreland's° remark that the Oriental does not value life the way Americans do was oddly accurate. Why weren't the Vietnamese people giving in? Why were they content instead to die and die and die again?

Toulon enters. Percussion and dancers continue upstage.

TOULON: Congratulations, Gallimard.

GALLIMARD: Excuse me, sir?

TOULON: Not a promotion. That was last time. You're going home.

GALLIMARD: What?

TOULON: Don't say I didn't warn you.

GALLIMARD: I'm being transferred . . . because I was wrong about the American war?

TOULON: Of course not. We don't care about the Americans. We care about your mind. The quality of your analysis. In general, everything you've predicted here in the Orient . . . just hasn't happened.

GALLIMARD: I think that's premature.

TOULON: Don't force me to be blunt. Okay, you said China was ready to open to Western trade. The only thing they're trading out there are Western heads. And, yes, you said the Americans would succeed in Indochina. You were kidding, right?

GALLIMARD: I think the end is in sight.

TOULON: Don't be pathetic. And don't take this personally. You were wrong. It's not your fault.

GALLIMARD: But I'm going home.

TOULON: Right. Could I have the number of your mistress? *(Beat.)* Joke! Joke! Eat a croissant for me.

Toulon exits. Song, wearing a Mao suit, is dragged in from the wings as part of the upstage dance. They "beat" her, then lampoon the acrobatics of the Chinese opera, as she is made to kneel onstage.

GALLIMARD *(simultaneously)*: I don't care to recall how Butterfly and I said our hurried farewell. Perhaps it was better to end our affair before it killed her.

Gallimard exits. Percussion rises in volume. The lampooning becomes faster, more frenetic. At its height, Comrade Chin walks across the stage with a banner reading:

Cultural Revolution: The reform campaign of 1965–1967 to purge counterrevolutionary thought in China, that challenged Mao Zedong. **Viet Cong:** Member of the National Liberation Front of South Vietnam, against which U.S. forces were fighting. **General Westmoreland:** William Westmoreland (b. 1914), commander of American troops in Vietnam from 1964 to 1968.

"The Actor Renounces His Decadent Profession!" She reaches the kneeling Song. At the moment Chin touches Song's chin, percussion stops with a thud. Dancers strike poses.

CHIN: Actor-oppressor, for years you have lived above the common people and looked down on their labor. While the farmer ate millet—

SONG: I ate pastries from France and sweetmeats from silver trays.

CHIN: And how did you come to live in such an exalted position?

SONG: I was a plaything for the imperialists!

CHIN: What did you do?

SONG: I shamed China by allowing myself to be corrupted by a foreigner . . .

CHIN: What does this mean? The People demand a full confession!

SONG: I engaged in the lowest perversions with China's enemies!

CHIN: What perversions? Be more clear!

SONG: I let him put it up my ass!

Dancers look over, disgusted.

CHIN: Aaaa-ya! How can you use such sickening language?!

SONG: My language . . . is only as foul as the crimes I committed . . .

CHIN: Yeah. That's better. So—what do you want to do . . . now?

SONG: I want to serve the people!

Percussion starts up, with Chinese strings.

CHIN: What?

SONG: I want to serve the people!

Dancers regain their revolutionary smiles, and begin a dance of victory.

CHIN: What?!

SONG: I want to serve the people!!

Dancers unveil a banner: "The Actor Is Re-Habilitated!" Song remains kneeling before Chin, as the dancers bounce around them, then exit. Music out.

Scene 10

A commune. Hunan Province. 1970.

CHIN: How you planning to do that?

SONG: I've already worked four years in the fields of Hunan, Comrade Chin.

CHIN: So? Farmers work all their lives. Let me see your hands.

Song holds them out for her inspection.

CHIN: Goddamn! Still so smooth! How long does it take to turn you actors into good anythings? Hunh. You've just spent too many years in luxury to be any good to the Revolution.

SONG: I served the Revolution.

CHIN: Serve the Revolution? Bullshit! You wore dresses! Don't tell me—I was there. I saw you! You and your white vice-consul! Stuck up there in your flat, living off the People's Treasury! Yeah, I knew what was going on! You two . . . homos! Homos! Homos! *(Pause; she composes herself.)* Ah! Well . . . you will serve the people, all right. But not with the Revolution's money. This time, you use your own money.

SONG: I have no money.

CHIN: Shut up! And you won't stink up China anymore with your pervert stuff. You'll pollute the place where pollution begins—the West.

SONG: What do you mean?

CHIN: Shut up! You're going to France. Without a cent in your pocket. You find your consul's house, you make him pay your expenses—

SONG: No.

CHIN: And you give us weekly reports! Useful information!

SONG: That's crazy. It's been four years.

CHIN: Either that, or back to rehabilitation center!

SONG: Comrade Chin, he's not going to support me! Not in France! He's a white man! I was just his plaything—

CHIN: Oh yuck! Again with the sickening language? Where's my stick?

SONG: You don't understand the mind of a man.

Pause.

CHIN: Oh no? No I don't? Then how come I'm married, huh? How come I got a man? Five, six years ago, you always tell me those kind of things, I felt very bad. But not now! Because what does the Chairman say? He tells us *I'm* now the smart one, you're now the nincompoop! *You're* the blockhead, the harebrain, the nitwit! You think you're so smart? You understand "The Mind of a Man"? Good! Then *you* go to France and be a pervert for Chairman Mao!

Chin and Song exit in opposite directions.

Scene 11

Paris. 1968–1970.
Gallimard enters.

GALLIMARD: And what was waiting for me back in Paris? Well, better Chinese food than I'd eaten in China. Friends and relatives. A little accounting, regular schedule, keeping track of traffic violations in the suburbs.... And the indignity of students shouting the slogans of Chairman Mao at me—in French.

HELGA: Rene? Rene? *(She enters, soaking wet.)* I've had a . . . problem.

(She sneezes.)

GALLIMARD: You're wet.

HELGA: Yes, I . . . coming back from the grocer's. A group of students, waving red flags, they—

Gallimard fetches a towel.

HELGA: —they ran by, I was caught up along with them. Before I knew what was happening—

Gallimard gives her the towel.

HELGA: Thank you. The police started firing water cannons at us. I tried to shout, to tell them I was the wife of a diplomat, but—you know how it is . . .

(Pause.) Needless to say, I lost the groceries. Rene, what's happening to France?

GALLIMARD: What's —? Well, nothing, really.

HELGA: Nothing?! The storefronts are in flames, there's glass in the streets, buildings are toppling — and I'm wet!

GALLIMARD: Nothing! . . . that I care to think about.

HELGA: And is that why you stay in this room?

GALLIMARD: Yes, in fact.

HELGA: With the incense burning? You know something? I hate incense. It smells so sickly sweet.

GALLIMARD: Well, I hate the French. Who just smell — period!

HELGA: And the Chinese were better?

GALLIMARD: Please — don't start.

HELGA: When we left, this exact same thing, the riots —

GALLIMARD: No, no . . .

HELGA: Students screaming slogans, smashing down doors —

GALLIMARD: Helga —

HELGA: It was all going on in China, too. Don't you remember?!

GALLIMARD: Helga! Please! *(Pause.)* You have never understood China, have you? You walk in here with these ridiculous ideas, that the West is falling apart, that China was spitting in our faces. You come in, dripping of the streets, and you leave water all over my floor. *(He grabs Helga's towel, begins mopping up the floor.)*

HELGA: But it's the truth!

GALLIMARD: Helga, I want a divorce.

Pause; Gallimard continues mopping the floor.

HELGA: I take it back. China is . . . beautiful. Incense, I like incense.

GALLIMARD: I've had a mistress.

HELGA: So?

GALLIMARD: For eight years.

HELGA: I knew you would. I knew you would the day I married you. And now what? You want to marry her?

GALLIMARD: I can't. She's in China.

HELGA: I see. You know that no one else is ever going to marry me, right?

GALLIMARD: I'm sorry.

HELGA: And you want to leave. For someone who's not here, is that right?

GALLIMARD: That's right.

HELGA: You can't live with her, but still you don't want to live with me.

GALLIMARD: That's right.

Pause.

HELGA: Shit. How terrible that I can figure that out. *(Pause.)* I never thought I'd say it. But, in China, I was happy. I knew, in my own way, I knew that you were not everything you pretended to be. But the pretense — going on your arm to the embassy ball, visiting your office and the guards saying, "Good morning, good morning, Madame Gallimard" — the pretense . . . was very good indeed. *(Pause.)* I hope everyone is mean to you for the rest of your life. *(She exits.)*

GALLIMARD *(to us):*   Prophetic.

Marc enters with two drinks.

GALLIMARD *(to Marc):*   In China, I was different from all other men.

MARC: Sure. You were white. Here's your drink.

GALLIMARD: I felt . . . touched.

MARC: In the head? Rene, I don't want to hear about the Oriental love goddess. Okay? One night — can we just drink and throw up without a lot of conversation?

GALLIMARD: You still don't believe me, do you?

MARC: Sure I do. She was the most beautiful, et cetera, et cetera, blasé, blasé.

Pause.

GALLIMARD: My life in the West has been such a disappointment.

MARC: Life in the West is like that. You'll get used to it. Look, you're driving me away. I'm leaving. Happy, now? *(He exits, then returns.)* Look, I have a date tomorrow night. You wanna come? I can fix you up with —

GALLIMARD: Of course. I would love to come.

Pause.

MARC: Uh — on second thought, no. You'd better get ahold of yourself first.

He exits; Gallimard nurses his drink.

GALLIMARD *(to us):*   This is the ultimate cruelty, isn't it? That I can talk and talk and to anyone listening, it's only air — too rich a diet to be swallowed by a mundane world. Why can't anyone understand? That in China, I once loved, and was loved by, very simply, the Perfect Woman.

Song enters, dressed as Butterfly in wedding dress.

GALLIMARD *(to Song):*   Not again. My imagination is hell. Am I asleep this time? Or did I drink too much?

SONG: Rene!

GALLIMARD: God, it's too painful! That you speak?

SONG: What are you talking about? Rene — touch me.

GALLIMARD: Why?

SONG: I'm real. Take my hand.

GALLIMARD: Why? So you can disappear again and leave me clutching at the air? For the entertainment of my neighbors who — ?

Song touches Gallimard.

SONG: Rene?

Gallimard takes Song's hand. Silence.

GALLIMARD: Butterfly? I never doubted you'd return.

SONG: You hadn't . . . forgotten — ?

GALLIMARD: Yes, actually, I've forgotten everything. My mind, you see — there wasn't enough room in this hard head — not for the world *and* for you. No,

there was only room for one. *(Beat.)* Come, look. See? Your bed has been waiting, with the Klimt° poster you like, and—see? The *xiang lu*° you gave me?

SONG:　I . . . I don't know what to say.

GALLIMARD:　There's nothing to say. Not at the end of a long trip. Can I make
you some tea?

SONG:　But where's your wife?

GALLIMARD:　She's by my side. She's by my side at last.

Gallimard reaches to embrace Song. Song sidesteps, dodging him.

GALLIMARD:　Why?!

SONG *(to us)*:　So I did return to Rene in Paris. Where I found—

GALLIMARD:　Why do you run away? Can't we show them how we embraced that
evening?

SONG:　Please. I'm talking.

GALLIMARD:　You have to do what I say! I'm conjuring you up in *my* mind!

SONG:　Rene, I've never done what you've said. Why should it be any different in
your mind? Now split—the story moves on, and I must change.

GALLIMARD:　I welcomed you into my home! I didn't have to, you know! I
could've left you penniless on the streets of Paris! But I took you in!

SONG:　Thank you.

GALLIMARD:　So . . . please . . . don't change.

SONG:　You know I have to. You know I will. And anyway, what difference does it
make? No matter what your eyes tell you, you can't ignore the truth. You
already know too much.

Gallimard exits. Song turns to us.

SONG:　The change I'm going to make requires about five minutes. So I thought
you might want to take this opportunity to stretch your legs, enjoy a drink, or
listen to the musicians. I'll be here, when you return, right where you left me.

*Song goes to a mirror in front of which is a wash basin of water. She starts to remove
her makeup as stagelights go to half and houselights come up.*

ACT 3, Scene 1

A courthouse in Paris. 1986.

　　*As he promised, Song has completed the bulk of his transformation onstage by
the time the houselights go down and the stagelights come up full. As he speaks to
us, he removes his wig and kimono, leaving them on the floor. Underneath, he
wears a well-cut suit.*

SONG:　So I'd done my job better than I had a right to expect. Well, give him
some credit, too. He's right—I was in a fix when I arrived in Paris. I walked
from the airport into town, then I located, by blind groping, the Chinatown
district. Let me make one thing clear: whatever else may be said about the

---

Klimt: Gustav Klimt (1863–1918), Austrian painter in the art nouveau style, whose most
famous painting is *The Kiss.*　**xiang lu:** Incense burner.

Chinese, they are stingy! I slept in doorways three days until I could find a tailor who would make me this kimono on credit. As it turns out, maybe I didn't even need it. Maybe he would've been happy to see me in a simple shift and mascara. But . . . better safe than sorry.

That was 1970, when I arrived in Paris. For the next fifteen years, yes, I lived a very comfy life. Some relief, believe me, after four years on a fucking commune in Nowheresville, China. Rene supported the boy and me, and I did some demonstrations around the country as part of my "cultural exchange" cover. And then there was the spying.

Song moves upstage, to a chair. Toulon enters as a judge, wearing the appropriate wig and robes. He sits near Song. It's 1986, and Song is testifying in a courtroom.

SONG:　Not much at first. Rene had lost all his high-level contacts. Comrade Chin wasn't very interested in parking-ticket statistics. But finally, at my urging, Rene got a job as a courier, handling sensitive documents. He'd photograph them for me, and I'd pass them on to the Chinese embassy.

JUDGE:　Did he understand the extent of his activity?

SONG:　He didn't ask. He knew that I needed those documents, and that was enough.

JUDGE:　But he must've known he was passing classified information.

SONG:　I can't say.

JUDGE:　He never asked what you were going to do with them?

SONG:　Nope.

Pause.

JUDGE:　There is one thing that the court—indeed, that all of France—would like to know.

SONG:　Fire away.

JUDGE:　Did Monsieur Gallimard know you were a man?

SONG:　Well, he never saw me completely naked. Ever.

JUDGE:　But surely, he must've . . . how can I put this?

SONG:　Put it however you like. I'm not shy. He must've felt around?

JUDGE:　Mmmmm.

SONG:　Not really. I did all the work. He just laid back. Of course we did enjoy more . . . complete union, and I suppose he *might* have wondered why I was always on my stomach, but. . . . But what you're thinking is, "Of course a wrist must've brushed . . . a hand hit . . . over twenty years!" Yeah. Well, Your Honor, it was my job to make him think I was a woman. And chew on this: it wasn't all that hard. See, my mother was a prostitute along the Bundt before the Revolution. And, uh, I think it's fair to say she learned a few things about Western men. So I borrowed her knowledge. In service to my country.

JUDGE:　Would you care to enlighten the court with this secret knowledge? I'm sure we're all very curious.

SONG:　I'm sure you are. *(Pause.)* Okay, Rule One is: Men always believe what they want to hear. So a girl can tell the most obnoxious lies and the guys will believe them every time—"This is my first time"—"That's the biggest I've ever seen"—or *both*, which, if you really think about it, is not possible in a single lifetime. You've maybe heard those phrases a few times in your own life, yes, Your Honor?

JUDGE: It's not my life, Monsieur Song, which is on trial today.

SONG: Okay, okay, just trying to lighten up the proceedings. Tough room.

JUDGE: Go on.

SONG: Rule Two: As soon as a Western man comes into contact with the East — he's already confused. The West has sort of an international rape mentality towards the East. Do you know rape mentality?

JUDGE: Give us your definition, please.

SONG: Basically, "Her mouth says no, but her eyes say yes."

The West thinks of itself as masculine — big guns, big industry, big money — so the East is feminine — weak, delicate, poor . . . but good at art, and full of inscrutable wisdom — the feminine mystique.

Her mouth says no, but her eyes say yes. The West believes the East, deep down, *wants* to be dominated — because a woman can't think for herself.

JUDGE: What does this have to do with my question?

SONG: You expect Oriental countries to submit to your guns, and you expect Oriental women to be submissive to your men. That's why you say they make the best wives.

JUDGE: But why would that make it possible for you to fool Monsieur Gallimard? Please — get to the point.

SONG: One, because when he finally met his fantasy woman, he wanted more than anything to believe that she was, in fact, a woman. And second, I am an Oriental. And being an Oriental, I could never be completely a man.

Pause.

JUDGE: Your armchair political theory is tenuous, Monsieur Song.

SONG: You think so? That's why you'll lose in all your dealings with the East.

JUDGE: Just answer my question: did he know you were a man?

Pause.

SONG: You know, Your Honor, I never asked.

Scene 2

Same.

Music from the "Death Scene" from Butterfly *blares over the house speakers. It is the loudest thing we've heard in this play.*

Gallimard enters, crawling towards Song's wig and kimono.

GALLIMARD: Butterfly? Butterfly?

Song remains a man, in the witness box, delivering a testimony we do not hear.

GALLIMARD *(to us):* In my moment of greatest shame, here, in this courtroom — with that . . . person up there, telling the world. . . . What strikes me especially is how shallow he is, how glib and obsequious . . . completely . . . without substance! The type that prowls around discos with a gold medallion stinking of garlic. So little like my Butterfly.

Yet even in this moment my mind remains agile, flip-flopping like a man on a trampoline. Even now, my picture dissolves, and I see that . . . witness . . . talking to me.

Song suddenly stands straight up in his witness box, and looks at Gallimard.

SONG: Yes. You. White man.

Song steps out of the witness box, and moves downstage towards Gallimard. Light change.

GALLIMARD (*to Song*): Who? Me?

SONG: Do you see any other white men?

GALLIMARD: Yes. There're white men all around. This is a French courtroom.

SONG: So you are an adventurous imperialist. Tell me, why did it take you so long? To come back to this place?

GALLIMARD: What place?

SONG: This theater in China. Where we met many years ago.

GALLIMARD (*to us*): And once again, against my will, I am transported.

Chinese opera music comes up on the speakers. Song begins to do opera moves, as he did the night they met.

SONG: Do you remember? The night you gave your heart?

GALLIMARD: It was a long time ago.

SONG: Not long enough. A night that turned your world upside down.

GALLIMARD: Perhaps.

SONG: Oh, be honest with me. What's another bit of flattery when you've already given me twenty years' worth? It's a wonder my head hasn't swollen to the size of China.

GALLIMARD: Who's to say it hasn't?

SONG: Who's to say? And what's the shame? In pride? You think I could've pulled this off if I wasn't already full of pride when we met? No, not just pride. Arrogance. It takes arrogance, really—to believe you can will, with your eyes and your lips, the destiny of another. (*He dances.*) C'mon. Admit it. You still want me. Even in slacks and a button-down collar.

GALLIMARD: I don't see what the point of—

SONG: You don't? Well maybe, Rene, just maybe—I want you.

GALLIMARD: You do?

SONG: Then again, maybe I'm just playing with you. How can you tell? (*Reprising his feminine character, he sidles up to Gallimard.*) "How I wish there were even a small café to sit in. With men in tuxedos, and cappuccinos, and bad expatriate jazz." Now you want to kiss me, don't you?

GALLIMARD (*pulling away*): What makes you—?

SONG: —so sure? See? I take the words from your mouth. Then I wait for you to come and retrieve them. (*He reclines on the floor.*)

GALLIMARD: Why?! Why do you treat me so cruelly?

SONG: Perhaps I *was* treating you cruelly. But now—I'm being nice. Come here, my little one.

GALLIMARD: I'm not your little one!

SONG: My mistake. It's I who am *your* little one, right?

GALLIMARD: Yes, I—

SONG: So come get your little one. If you like, I may even let you strip me.

GALLIMARD: I mean, you were! Before . . . but not like this!

SONG: I was? Then perhaps I still am. If you look hard enough. (*He starts to remove his clothes.*)

GALLIMARD: What—what are you doing?

SONG: Helping you to see through my act.

GALLIMARD: Stop that! I don't want to! I don't—

SONG: Oh, but you asked me to strip, remember?

GALLIMARD: What? That was years ago! And I took it back!

SONG: No. You postponed it. Postponed the inevitable. Today, the inevitable has come calling.

From the speakers, cacophony: Butterfly mixed in with Chinese gongs.

GALLIMARD: No! Stop! I don't want to see!

SONG: Then look away.

GALLIMARD: You're only in my mind! All this is in my mind! I order you! To stop!

SONG: To what? To strip? That's just what I'm—

GALLIMARD: No! Stop! I want you—!

SONG: You want me?

GALLIMARD: To stop!

SONG: You know something, Rene? Your mouth says no, but your eyes say yes. Turn them away. I dare you.

GALLIMARD: I don't have to! Every night, you say you're going to strip, but then I beg you and you stop!

SONG: I guess tonight is different.

GALLIMARD: Why? Why should that be?

SONG: Maybe I've become frustrated. Maybe I'm saying "Look at me, you fool!" Or maybe I'm just feeling . . . sexy. (*He is down to his briefs.*)

GALLIMARD: Please. This is unnecessary. I know what you are.

SONG: You do? What am I?

GALLIMARD: A—a man.

SONG: You don't really believe that.

GALLIMARD: Yes I do! I knew all the time somewhere that my happiness was temporary, my love a deception. But my mind kept the knowledge at bay. To make the wait bearable.

SONG: Monsieur Gallimard—the wait is over.

Song drops his briefs. He is naked. Sound cue out. Slowly, we and Song come to the realization that what we had thought to be Gallimard's sobbing is actually his laughter.

GALLIMARD: Oh god! What an idiot! Of course!

SONG: Rene—what?

GALLIMARD: Look at you! You're a man! (*He bursts into laughter again.*)

SONG: I fail to see what's so funny!

GALLIMARD: "You fail to see—!" I mean, you never did have much of a sense of humor, did you? I just think it's ridiculously funny that I've wasted so much time on just a man!

SONG: Wait. I'm not "just a man."

GALLIMARD: No? Isn't that what you've been trying to convince me of?

SONG: Yes, but what I mean—

GALLIMARD: And now, I finally believe you, and you tell me it's not true? I think you must have some kind of identity problem.

SONG: Will you listen to me?

GALLIMARD: Why?! I've been listening to you for twenty years. Don't I deserve a vacation?

SONG: I'm not just any man!

GALLIMARD: Then, what exactly are you?

SONG: Rene, how can you ask—? Okay, what about this?

He picks up Butterfly's robes, starts to dance around. No music.

GALLIMARD: Yes, that's very nice. I have to admit.

Song holds out his arm to Gallimard.

SONG: It's the same skin you've worshipped for years. Touch it.

GALLIMARD: Yes, it does feel the same.

SONG: Now—close your eyes.

Song covers Gallimard's eyes with one hand. With the other, Song draws Galli-mard's hand up to his face. Gallimard, like a blind man, lets his hands run over Song's face.

GALLIMARD: This skin, I remember. The curve of her face, the softness of her cheek, her hair against the back of my hand . . .

SONG: I'm your Butterfly. Under the robes, beneath everything, it was always me. Now, open your eyes and admit it—you adore me. *(He removes his hand from Gallimard's eyes.)*

GALLIMARD: You, who knew every inch of my desires—how could you, of all people, have made such a mistake?

SONG: What?

GALLIMARD: You showed me your true self. When all I loved was the lie. A per-fect lie, which you let fall to the ground—and now, it's old and soiled.

SONG: So—you never really loved me? Only when I was playing a part?

GALLIMARD: I'm a man who loved a woman created by a man. Everything else—simply falls short.

Pause.

SONG: What am I supposed to do now?

GALLIMARD: You were a fine spy, Monsieur Song, with an even finer accom-plice. But now I believe you should go. Get out of my life!

SONG: Go where? Rene, you can't live without me. Not after twenty years.

GALLIMARD: I certainly can't live with you—not after twenty years of betrayal.

SONG: Don't be stubborn! Where will you go?

GALLIMARD: I have a date . . . with my Butterfly.

SONG: So, throw away your pride. And come . . .

GALLIMARD: Get away from me! Tonight, I've finally learned to tell fantasy from reality. And, knowing the difference, I choose fantasy.

SONG: *I'm* your fantasy!

GALLIMARD: You? You're as real as hamburger. Now get out! I have a date with my Butterfly and I don't want your body polluting the room! *(He tosses Song's suit at him.)* Look at these — you dress like a pimp.

SONG: Hey! These are Armani slacks and —! *(He puts on his briefs and slacks.)* Let's just say . . . I'm disappointed in you, Rene. In the crush of your adoration, I thought you'd become something more. More like . . . a woman.

But no. Men. You're like the rest of them. It's all in the way we dress, and make up our faces, and bat our eyelashes. You really have so little imagination!

GALLIMARD: You, Monsieur Song? Accuse me of too little imagination? You, if anyone, should know — I am pure imagination. And in imagination I will remain. Now get out!

Gallimard bodily removes Song from the stage, taking his kimono.

SONG: Rene! I'll never put on those robes again! You'll be sorry!

GALLIMARD *(to Song)*:   I'm already sorry! *(Looking at the kimono in his hands.)* Exactly as sorry . . . as a Butterfly.

Scene 3

M. Gallimard's prison cell. Paris. 1988.

GALLIMARD: I've played out the events of my life night after night, always searching for a new ending to my story, one where I leave this cell and return forever to my Butterfly's arms.

Tonight I realize my search is over. That I've looked all along in the wrong place. And now, to you, I will prove that my love was not in vain — by returning to the world of fantasy where I first met her.

He picks up the kimono; dancers enter.

GALLIMARD: There is a vision of the Orient that I have. Of slender women in cheongsams and kimonos who die for the love of unworthy foreign devils. Who are born and raised to be the perfect women. Who take whatever punishment we give them, and bounce back, strengthened by love, unconditionally. It is a vision that has become my life.

Dancers bring the washbasin to him and help him make up his face.

GALLIMARD: In public, I have continued to deny that Song Liling is a man. This brings me headlines, and is a source of great embarrassment to my French colleagues, who can now be sent into a coughing fit by the mere mention of Chinese food. But alone, in my cell, I have long since faced the truth.

And the truth demands a sacrifice. For mistakes made over the course of a lifetime. My mistakes were simple and absolute — the man I loved was a cad, a bounder. He deserved nothing but a kick in the behind, and instead I gave him . . . all my love.

Yes — love. Why not admit it all? That was my undoing, wasn't it? Love warped my judgment, blinded my eyes, rearranged the very lines on my face . . . until I could look in the mirror and see nothing but . . . a woman.

Dancers help him put on the Butterfly wig.

GALLIMARD: I have a vision. Of the Orient. That, deep within its almond eyes, there are still women. Women willing to sacrifice themselves for the love of a man. Even a man whose love is completely without worth.

Dancers assist Gallimard in donning the kimono. They hand him a knife.

GALLIMARD: Death with honor is better than life . . . life with dishonor. *(He sets himself center stage, in a seppuku position.)* The love of a Butterfly can withstand many things — unfaithfulness, loss, even abandonment. But how can it face the one sin that implies all others? The devastating knowledge that, underneath it all, the object of her love was nothing more, nothing less than . . . a man. *(He sets the tip of the knife against his body.)* It is 1988. And I have found her at last. In a prison on the outskirts of Paris. My name is Rene Gallimard — also known as Madame Butterfly.

Gallimard turns upstage and plunges the knife into his body, as music from the "Love Duet" blares over the speakers. He collapses into the arms of the dancers, who lay him reverently on the floor. The image holds for several beats. Then a tight special up on Song, who stands as a man, staring at the dead Gallimard. He smokes a cigarette; the smoke filters up through the lights. Two words leave his lips.

SONG: Butterfly? Butterfly?

Smoke rises as lights fade slowly to black.   [1988]

THINKING ABOUT THE TEXT

1. Gallimard says near the end of act 1, scene 5 that he married Helga for practicality. When he sees *Madame Butterfly,* he is changed. Does this make sense to you?

2. Is it hard to imagine falling in love with a person you think is one sex but is really another? How does the play try to explain Gallimard's mistake? Does it have something to do with his statement, "Happiness is so rare that our mind can turn somersaults to protect it" (act 2, scene 6)?

3. Why does Hwang tell this story mostly in flashback through Gallimard's eyes? Why not just do a straight play in linear time?

4. Look again at the court scene (act 3, scene 1). What do you think of Song's ideas about a fantasy woman? Is Gallimard any wiser at the end of the play, or does he still want the illusion?

5. Some critics also see a political allegory here concerning the West's view of the East. Does this make sense to you?

PAUL GRAY
What Is Love?

Paul Gray, a senior writer and book reviewer for Time, *joined the magazine in 1972 after an academic career, teaching at Princeton University through the 1960s. Currently, he reads five books a week and writes articles on a great variety of subjects, many of which appear as cover stories. "What Is Love?" was* Time's *lead article in the February 15, 1993, issue.*

What is this thing called love? What? Is this thing called love? What is this thing called? Love.

However punctuated, Cole Porter's simple question begs an answer. Love's symptoms are familiar enough: a drifting mooniness in thought and behavior, the mad conceit that the entire universe has rolled itself up into the person of the beloved, a conviction that no one on earth has ever felt so torrentially about a fellow creature before. Love is ecstasy and torment, freedom and slavery. Poets and songwriters would be in a fine mess without it. Plus, it makes the world go round.

Until recently, scientists wanted no part of it.

The reason for this avoidance, this reluctance to study what is probably life's most intense emotion, is not difficult to track down. Love is mushy; science is hard. Anger and fear, feelings that have been considerably researched in the field and the lab, can be quantified through measurements: pulse and breathing rates, muscle contractions, a whole spider web of involuntary responses. Love does not register as definitively on the instruments; it leaves a blurred fingerprint that could be mistaken for anything from indigestion to a manic attack. Anger and fear have direct roles — fighting or running — in the survival of the species. Since it is possible (a cynic would say commonplace) for humans to mate and reproduce without love, all the attendant sighing and swooning and sonnet writing have struck many pragmatic investigators as beside the evolutionary point.

So biologists and anthropologists assumed that it would be fruitless, even frivolous, to study love's evolutionary origins, the way it was encoded in our genes or imprinted in our brains. Serious scientists simply assumed that love — and especially Romantic Love — was really all in the head, put there five or six centuries ago when civilized societies first found enough spare time to indulge in flowery prose. The task of writing the book of love was ceded to playwrights, poets and pulp novelists.

But during the past decade, scientists across a broad range of disciplines have had a change of heart about love. The amount of research expended on the tender passion has never been more intense. Explanations for this rise in interest vary. Some cite the spreading threat of AIDS; with casual sex carrying mortal risks, it seems important to know more about a force that binds couples faithfully together. Others point to the growing number of women scientists and suggest that they may be more willing than their male colleagues to take love seriously. Says Elaine Hatfield, the author of *Love, Sex, and Intimacy: Their Psychology,*

5

Biology, and History, "When I was back at Stanford in the 1960s, they said study-ing love and human relationships was a quick way to ruin my career. Why not go where the real work was being done: on how fast rats could run?" Whatever the reasons, science seems to have come around to a view that nearly everyone else has always taken for granted: romance is real. It is not merely a conceit; it is bred into our biology.

Getting to this point logically is harder than it sounds. The love-as-cultural-delusion argument has long seemed unassailable. What actually accounts for the emotion, according to this scenario, is that people long ago made the mistake of taking fanciful literary tropes seriously. Ovid's *Ars Amatoria* is often cited as a major source of misreadings, its instructions followed, its ironies ignored. Other prime suspects include the twelfth-century troubadours in Provence who more or less invented the Art of Courtly Love, an elaborate, etiolated ritual for idle noblewomen and aspiring swains that would have been broken to bits by any hint of physical consummation.

Ever since then, the injunction to love and to be loved has hummed nonstop through popular culture; it is a dominant theme in music, films, novels, maga-zines and nearly everything shown on TV. Love is a formidable and thoroughly proved commercial engine; people will buy and do almost anything that promises them a chance at the bliss of romance.

But does all this mean that love is merely a phony emotion that we picked up because our culture celebrates it? Psychologist Lawrence Casler, author of *Is Marriage Necessary?*, forcefully thinks so, at least at first: "I don't believe love is part of human nature, not for a minute. There are social pressures at work." Then falls a shadow over this certainty. "Even if it is a part of human nature, like crime or violence, it's not necessarily desirable."

Well, love either is or is not intrinsic to our species; having it both ways leads nowhere. And the contention that romance is an entirely acquired trait—overly imaginative troubadours' revenge on muddled literalists—has always rested on some teetery premises.

For one thing, there is the chicken/egg dilemma. Which came first, sex or love? If the reproductive imperative was as dominant as Darwinians maintain, sex probably led the way. But why was love hatched in the process, since it was presum-ably unnecessary to get things started in the first place? Furthermore, what has sus-tained romance—that odd collection of tics and impulses—over the centuries? Most mass hallucinations, such as the seventeenth-century tulip mania in Holland, flame out fairly rapidly when people realize the absurdity of what they have been doing and, as the common saying goes, come to their senses. When people in love come to their senses, they tend to orbit with added energy around each other and look more helplessly loopy and self-besotted. If romance were purely a figment, unsupported by any rational or sensible evidence, then surely most folks would be immune to it by now. Look around. It hasn't happened. Love is still in the air.

And it may be far more widespread than even romantics imagined. Those who argue that love is a cultural fantasy have tended to do so from a Eurocentric and class-driven point of view. Romance, they say, arose thanks to amenities peculiar to the West: leisure time, a modicum of creature comforts, a certain

10

level of refinement in the arts and letters. When these trappings are absent, so is romance. Peasants mated; aristocrats fell in love.

But last year a study conducted by anthropologists William Jankowiak of the University of Nevada–Las Vegas and Edward Fischer of Tulane University found evidence of romantic love in at least 147 of the 166 cultures they studied. This discovery, if borne out, should pretty well wipe out the idea that love is an invention of the Western mind rather than a biological fact. Says Jankowiak: "It is, instead, a universal phenomenon, a panhuman characteristic that stretches across cultures. Societies like ours have the resources to show love through candy and flowers, but that does not mean that the lack of resources in other cultures indicates the absence of love."

Some scientists are not startled by this contention. One of them is anthropologist Helen Fisher, a research associate at the American Museum of Natural History and the author of *Anatomy of Love: The Natural History of Monogamy, Adultery and Divorce*, a recent book that is making waves among scientists and the general reading public. Says Fisher: "I've never *not* thought that love was a very primitive, basic human emotion, as basic as fear, anger or joy. It is so evident. I guess anthropologists have just been busy doing other things."

Among the things anthropologists—often knobby-kneed gents in safari shorts—tended to do in the past was ask questions about courtship and marriage rituals. This now seems a classic example, as the old song has it, of looking for love in all the wrong places. In many cultures, love and marriage do not go together. Weddings can have all the romance of corporate mergers, signed and sealed for family or territorial interests. This does not mean, Jankowiak insists, that love does not exist in such cultures; it erupts in clandestine forms, "a phenomenon to be dealt with."

Somewhere about this point, the specter of determinism begins once again   15
to flap and cackle. If science is going to probe and prod and then announce that we are all scientifically fated to love—and to love preprogrammed types—by our genes and chemicals, then a lot of people would just as soon not know. If there truly is a biological predisposition to love, as more and more scientists are coming to believe, what follows is a recognition of the amazing diversity in the ways humans have chosen to express the feeling. The cartoon images of cavemen bopping cavewomen over the head and dragging them home by their hair? Love. Helen of Troy, subjecting her adopted city to ten years of ruinous siege? Love. Romeo and Juliet? Ditto. Joe in Accounting making a fool of himself around the water cooler over Susan in Sales? Love. Like the universe, the more we learn about love, the more preposterous and mysterious it is likely to appear.   [1993]

THINKING ABOUT THE TEXT

1. Gray suggests that people will do almost anything that promises romance. Is this true of the people you know?

2. Gray claims scientists were looking for love in all the wrong places. Where were they looking, and why did they not find what they were looking for? Where should they have looked?

3. Does Gray's last sentence say something about the implausibility of
M. Butterfly?

ANASTASIA TOUFEXIS
The Right Chemistry

Anastasia Toufexis received a bachelor's degree in premedicine from Smith College in 1967. After several years as a writer for medical and pharmaceutical publications, she began writing for Time *magazine, where she has been an associate editor since 1978. This essay appeared in the February 15, 1993, issue.*

O.K., let's cut out all this nonsense about romantic love. Let's bring some scientific precision to the party. Let's put love under a microscope.

When rigorous people with Ph.D.s after their names do that, what they see is not some silly, senseless thing. No, their probe reveals that love rests firmly on the foundations of evolution, biology and chemistry. What seems on the surface to be irrational, intoxicated behavior is in fact part of nature's master strategy—a vital force that has helped humans survive, thrive and multiply through thousands of years. Says Michael Mills, a psychology professor at Loyola Marymount University in Los Angeles: "Love is our ancestors whispering in our ears."

It was on the plains of Africa about 4 million years ago, in the early days of the human species, that the notion of romantic love probably first began to blossom—or at least that the first cascades of neurochemicals began flowing from the brain to the bloodstream to produce goofy grins and sweaty palms as men and women gazed deeply into each other's eyes. When mankind graduated from scuttling around on all fours to walking on two legs, this change made the whole person visible to fellow human beings for the first time. Sexual organs were in full display, as were other characteristics, from the color of eyes to the span of shoulders. As never before, each individual had a unique allure.

When the sparks flew, new ways of making love enabled sex to become a romantic encounter, not just a reproductive act. Although mounting mates from the rear was, and still is, the method favored among most animals, humans began to enjoy face-to-face couplings; both looks and personal attraction became a much greater part of the equation.

Romance served the evolutionary purpose of pulling males and females into long-term partnership, which was essential to child rearing. On open grasslands, one parent would have a hard—and dangerous—time handling a child while foraging for food. "If a woman was carrying the equivalent of a twenty-pound bowling ball in one arm and a pile of sticks in the other, it was ecologically critical to pair up with a mate to rear the young," explains anthropologist Helen Fisher, author of *Anatomy of Love.*

While Western culture holds fast to the idea that true love flames forever (the movie *Bram Stoker's Dracula* has the Count carrying the torch beyond the

5

grave), nature apparently meant passions to sputter out in something like four years. Primitive pairs stayed together just "long enough to rear one child through infancy," says Fisher. Then each would find a new partner and start all over again.

What Fisher calls the "four-year itch" shows up unmistakably in today's divorce statistics. In most of the sixty-two cultures she has studied, divorce rates peak around the fourth year of marriage. Additional youngsters help keep pairs together longer. If, say, a couple have another child three years after the first, as often occurs, then their union can be expected to last about four more years. That makes them ripe for the more familiar phenomenon portrayed in the Marilyn Monroe classic *The Seven-Year Itch*.

If, in nature's design, romantic love is not eternal, neither is it exclusive. Less than 5 percent of mammals form rigorously faithful pairs. From the earliest days, contends Fisher, the human pattern has been "monogamy with clandestine adultery." Occasional flings upped the chances that new combinations of genes would be passed on to the next generation. Men who sought new partners had more children. Contrary to common assumptions, women were just as likely to stray. "As long as prehistoric females were secretive about their extramarital affairs," argues Fisher, "they could garner extra resources, life insurance, better genes and more varied DNA for their biological futures. Hence those who sneaked into the bushes with secret lovers lived on — unconsciously passing on through the centuries whatever it is in female spirit that motivates modern women to philander."

> Love is a romantic designation for a most ordinary biological — or, shall we say, chemical? — process. A lot of nonsense is talked and written about it.
> — Greta Garbo to Melvyn Douglas in *Ninotchka*

Lovers often claim that they feel as if they are being swept away. They're not mistaken; they are literally flooded by chemicals, research suggests. A meeting of eyes, a touch of hands or a whiff of scent sets off a flood that starts in the brain and races along the nerves and through the blood. The results are familiar: flushed skin, sweaty palms, heavy breathing. If love looks suspiciously like stress, the reason is simple: the chemical pathways are identical.

Above all, there is the sheer euphoria of falling in love — a not-so-surprising reaction, considering that many of the substances swamping the newly smitten are chemical cousins of amphetamines. They include dopamine, norepinephrine and especially phenylethylamine (PEA). Cole Porter knew what he was talking about when he wrote "I get a kick out of you." "Love is a natural high," observes Anthony Walsh, author of *The Science of Love: Understanding Love and Its Effects on Mind and Body*. "PEA gives you that silly smile that you flash at strangers. When we meet someone who is attractive to us, the whistle blows at the PEA factory."

But phenylethylamine highs don't last forever, a fact that lends support to arguments that passionate romantic love is short-lived. As with any amphetamine, the body builds up a tolerance to PEA; thus it takes more and more of the

10

substance to produce love's special kick. After two to three years, the body simply can't crank up the needed amount of PEA. And chewing on chocolate doesn't help, despite popular belief. The candy is high in PEA, but it fails to boost the body's supply.

Fizzling chemicals spell the end of delirious passion; for many people that marks the end of the liaison as well. It is particularly true for those whom Dr. Michael Liebowitz of the New York State Psychiatric Institute terms "attraction junkies." They crave the intoxication of falling in love so much that they move frantically from affair to affair just as soon as the first rush of infatuation fades.

Still, many romances clearly endure beyond the first years. What accounts for that? Another set of chemicals, of course. The continued presence of a partner gradually steps up production in the brain of endorphins. Unlike the fizzy amphetamines, these are soothing substances. Natural painkillers, they give lovers a sense of security, peace and calm. "That is one reason why it feels so horrible when we're abandoned or a lover dies," notes Fisher. "We don't have our daily hit of narcotics."

Researchers see a contrast between the heated infatuation induced by PEA, along with other amphetamine-like chemicals, and the more intimate attachment fostered and prolonged by endorphins. "Early love is when you love the way the other person makes you feel," explains psychiatrist Mark Goulston of the University of California, Los Angeles. "Mature love is when you love the person as he or she is." It is the difference between passionate and compassionate love, observes Walsh, a psychobiologist at Boise State University in Idaho. "It's Bon Jovi vs. Beethoven."

Oxytocin is another chemical that has recently been implicated in love. Produced by the brain, it sensitizes nerves and stimulates muscle contraction. In women it helps uterine contractions during childbirth as well as production of breast milk, and seems to inspire mothers to nuzzle their infants. Scientists speculate that oxytocin might encourage similar cuddling between adult women and men. The versatile chemical may also enhance orgasms. In one study of men, oxytocin increased to three to five times its normal level during climax, and it may soar even higher in women.

One mystery is the prevalence of homosexual love. Although it would seem to have no evolutionary purpose, since no children are produced, there is no denying that gays and lesbians can be as romantic as anyone else. Some researchers speculate that homosexuality results from a biochemical anomaly that occurs during fetal development. But that doesn't make romance among gays any less real. "That they direct this love toward their own sex," says Walsh, "does not diminish the value of that love one iota."

> A certain smile, a certain face.
> — Johnny Mathis

Chemicals may help explain (at least to scientists) the feelings of passion and compassion, but why do people tend to fall in love with one partner rather than a myriad of others? Once again, it's partly a function of evolution and biology. "Men are looking for maximal fertility in a mate," says Loyola Marymount's Mills. "That is in large part why females in the prime childbearing ages of seventeen to twenty-eight are so desirable." Men can size up youth and vitality in a glance, and studies indeed show that men fall in love quite rapidly. Women tumble more slowly, to a large degree because their requirements are more complex; they need more time to, check the guy out. "Age is not vital," notes Mills, "but the ability to provide security, father children, share resources, and hold a high status in society are all key factors."

Still, that does not explain why the way Mary walks and laughs makes Bill dizzy with desire while Marcia's gait and giggle leave him cold. "Nature has wired us for one special person," suggests Walsh, romantically. He rejects the idea that a woman or a man can be in love with two people at the same time. Each person carries in his or her mind a unique subliminal guide to the ideal partner, a "love map," to borrow a term coined by sexologist John Money of Johns Hopkins University.

Drawn from the people and experiences of childhood, the map is a record of whatever we found enticing and exciting — or disturbing and disgusting. Small feet, curly hair. The way our mothers patted our head or how our fathers told a joke. A fireman's uniform, a doctor's stethoscope. All the information gathered while growing up is imprinted in the brain's circuitry by adolescence. Partners never meet each and every requirement, but a sufficient number of matches can light up the wires and signal, "It's love." Not every partner will be like the last one, since lovers may have different combinations of the characteristics favored by the map.

O.K., that's the scientific point of view. Satisfied? Probably not. To most   20
people — with or without Ph.D.s — love will always be more than the sum of its natural parts. It's a commingling of body and soul, reality and imagination, poetry and phenylethylamine. In our deepest hearts, most of us harbor the hope that love will never fully yield up its secrets, that it will always elude our grasp.   [1993]

THINKING ABOUT THE TEXT

1. Toufexis's last paragraph asks, "Satisfied?" Were you impressed by these scientific claims?

2. Examine the last line carefully. Do you agree? Is this a possible "explanation" of what happens to Gallimard in M. *Butterfly*?

3. The author quotes Greta Garbo as saying "A lot of nonsense is talked and written about [romantic love.]" Do you agree? Give some examples from popular culture (movies, TV, MTV, and so forth).

NATHANIEL BRANDEN
Immature Love

Nathaniel Branden (b. 1930), a psychologist closely connected with the controversial novelist and philosopher Ayn Rand until 1968, conducts workshops and writes extensively on the subject of self-esteem. The following excerpt is taken from The Psychology of Romantic Love *(1980).*

"Maturity" and "immaturity" are concepts that refer to the success or failure of an individual's biological, intellectual, and psychological evolution to an adult stage of development.

In mature love relationships, "complementary differences" refers, predominately, to complementary *strengths*. In immature relationships, "complementary differences" tends to refer to complementary *weaknesses*. These weaknesses include needs, wants, and other personality traits that reflect some failure of healthy development, some failure of psychological maturation. As we shall see, we deal here, most essentially, with the issue of separation and individuation, with an individual's success or failure at the task of reaching an adult level of autonomy.

Many a person faces life with an attitude that, if translated into explicit speech, which it almost never is, would amount to the declaration, "When I was five years old, important needs of mine were not met—and until they are, I'm not moving on to six!" On a basic level these people are very passive, even though, on more superficial levels, they may sometimes appear active and "aggressive." At bottom, they are waiting, waiting to be rescued, waiting to be told they are good boys or good girls, waiting to be validated or confirmed by some outside source.

So their whole lives may be organized around the desire to please, to be taken care of, or, alternatively, to control and dominate, to manipulate and *coerce* the satisfaction of their needs and wants, because they don't trust the authenticity of anyone's love or caring. They have no confidence that what they are, without their facades and manipulations, is *enough*.

Whether their act is to be helpless and dependent, or to be controlling, over-protective, "responsible," "grown-up," there is an underlying sense of inadequacy, of nameless deficiency, that they feel only other human beings can correct. They are alienated from their own internal sources of strength and support; they are alienated from their own powers.

Whether they seek completion and fulfillment through domination or submission, through controlling or being controlled, through ordering or obeying, there is the same fundamental sense of emptiness, a void in the center of their being, a screaming hole where an autonomous self failed to develop. They have never assimilated and integrated the basic fact of human aloneness, individuation has not been attained to a level appropriate to their chronological development.

They have failed to transfer the source of their approval from others to self. They have failed to evolve into a state of self-responsibility. They have failed to make peace with the immutable fact of their ultimate aloneness—therefore they are crippled in their efforts to relate.

They view other human beings with suspicion, hostility, and feelings of alienation, or else see them as life belts by which they can stay afloat in the stormy sea of their own anxiety and insecurity. There is a tendency for immature persons to view others primarily, if not exclusively, as sources for the gratification of their own wants and needs, not as human beings in their own right, much as an infant views a parent. So their relationships tend to be dependent and manipulative, not the encounter of two autonomous selves who feel free to express themselves honestly and are able to appreciate and enjoy each other's being, but the encounter of two incomplete beings who look to love to solve the problem of their internal deficiencies, to finish magically the unfinished business of childhood, to fill up the holes in their personality, to make of "love" a substitute for evolution to maturity and self-responsibility.

These are some of the "basic similarities" shared by immature persons who fall in love. To understand why immature love is born is also to understand why it generally dies so swiftly.

An immature woman looks at her lover and, deep in her psyche, there is the 10 thought, "My father made me feel rejected, you will take his place and give me what he failed to give me. I will create a house for you, and cook your meals, and bear your children — I will be your good little girl."

Or a woman experiences herself as unloved or rejected by one or both parents. She fails to acknowledge the magnitude of her hurt and self-deprecatory feelings, and she passes into the *semblance* of adulthood. But the sense of unfinished business, the sense of incompleteness as a person, remains and continues to play a role in her motivation, beneath the surface of awareness. She "falls in love" with a man who, whatever his other virtues, shares important characteristics with her rejecting parent(s). Perhaps he is cold, unemotional, unable or unwilling to express love. Like a losing gambler who cannot resist returning to the table where past defeats were suffered, she feels compulsively drawn to him. *This time she will not lose.* She will melt him. She will find a way to melt him. She will find a way to inspire in him all the responses she longed for and failed to receive as a child. And in so doing, she feels, she will redeem her childhood — she will win the victory over her past.

What she does not realize is that, unless other factors intervene to generate a positive change in her psychology, the man is useful to her, is serviceable to her, in the drama she is playing only so long as he remains somewhat aloof, somewhat uncaring, somewhat distant from her. If he would become warm and loving, he no longer would be a suitable understudy for Mother or Father; he would no longer be appropriate for the role in which she has cast him. So at the same time that she cries for love, she takes careful measures to maintain the distance between them to prevent him from giving her the very things she asks for. If, somehow, in spite of her efforts, he does become loving and caring, the likelihood is that she will feel disoriented and will withdraw; probably she will fall out of love with him. "Why?" she cries to her psychotherapist, "do I always fall for men who don't know how to love?"

A man looks at his bride and there is the thought, "Now I am a married man; I am grown up; I have responsibilities — just like Father. I will work hard, I will be your protector, I will take care of you — just as Father did with Mother. Then he — and you — and everyone — will see that I am a good boy."

Or, when a man is a little boy his mother deserts her family to go off with her lover. The little boy feels betrayed and abandoned; it is *he* Mother has left, not Father. (This is the natural egocentricity of childhood.) He tells himself — perhaps with Father's help and encouragement — that "women are like that, not to be trusted." He resolves never to be vulnerable to such pain again. No woman will ever be allowed to make him suffer as Mother did. But years later he knows only two kinds of relationships with women; those in which he cares a good deal less than the woman, and it is he who hurts and betrays her; and those in which he has selected a woman who inevitably will not remain true to him, inevitably will make him suffer. Sooner or later, he almost always ends up with the second kind of woman — to complete the unfinished business of childhood (which he can never complete successfully in this manner, *because the woman is not his mother*, she is only a symbolic substitute). When the woman "lets him down," he professes to be shocked and bewildered. The intense "love affairs" of his life are of this second kind. He is disconnected from the original pain, from the source of the problem, from the feelings he disowned long ago; therefore he is powerless to deal with them effectively and to resolve them; he is the prisoner of that which he has failed to confront; but deep in his psyche, without a solution's ever being found, the drama continues. *Next* time he will beat the table. Meanwhile, for consolation, for rest, for recreation, for revenge, let him hurt as many women as he can. He asks, "Is romantic love a delusion? It never seems to work for me." . . .

On one level, it is true enough to say that a characteristic of immature love is   15
that the man or woman does not perceive his or her partner realistically; fantasies and projections take the place of clear vision. And yet, on a deeper level, on a level not ordinarily acknowledged, there is awareness, there is recognition, there is knowledge of whom they have chosen. They are not, in fact, blind, but the game in which they are engaged may require that they pretend, to themselves, to be blind. This allows them to go through the motions of being bewildered, hurt, outraged, shocked, when their partner behaves precisely as their own life scenario requires. Evidence for this lies in the consistency with which immature persons find precisely those immature other persons whose problems and style of being will complement and mesh with their own.   [1980]

THINKING ABOUT THE TEXT

1. Branden claims that some lovers are "waiting to be rescued" (para. 3). What does he mean by this? Might it apply to Gallimard?

2. According to Branden, the immature are dependent and manipulative and are trying "to finish magically the unfinished business of childhood" (para. 8). Explain.

3. Branden says that the immature often find compatible lovers. Is this true in your experience? In *M. Butterfly*?

WRITING ABOUT ISSUES

1. Argue that Gallimard's romantic attachment is either plausible or not. Use ideas from Gray, Toufexis, or Branden to enhance your claim.

2. Is Gallimard immature? Write an essay using your own experiences to support your claim.

3. Write a personal narrative about a strong attraction you had to someone who later turned out to be quite different than you imagined.

4. Research romantic love. Find experts who argue that it is simply a cultural illusion and write a position paper agreeing or disagreeing with them.

A WEB ASSIGNMENT

A number of sites focus on *M. Butterfly* and feature documents exploring the real-life models for Gallimard and Song. Visit the Web Assignments section of the *Making Literature Matter* Web site to find the link to one of these sites. There, you will find a full account of the actual events from *People Weekly* (8/8/88). Read this and/or other accounts and write a brief essay that explains the additions/deletions that Hwang made in adapting these events into *M. Butterfly*.

Visit www.bedfordstmartins.com/makinglitmatter

Is This Love?

WILLIAM FAULKNER, "A Rose for Emily"
RAYMOND CARVER, "What We Talk About When We Talk About Love"
F. SCOTT FITZGERALD, "Winter Dreams"

Although stories about those who die for love are not unknown, those about killing for love are much rarer. Can "killing for love" still be considered love, or is it something quite different, something dark and perverse? Can the world be so stressful, so unjust and cruel that someone batters a beloved in frustration? What if that person is looking to someone else to relieve the disappointments of the world? Is that love or just physical need? What if someone harbors violent fantasies about a person loved years before? These are not simple questions. Trying to understand our emotional contradictions and paradoxes never is. The following three writers grapple with these issues in creative and sometimes painful ways: Faulkner's story focuses on the interaction of tradition, madness, and love; Carver's looks at the complexity of discussing love; and Fitzgerald's poignant tale of young love and loss is a meditation on the ways love, social aspiration, beauty, and passion are complexly intertwined in America. See if you can decide if the characters in these stories are motivated by love or something more dangerous.

BEFORE YOU READ

Have you ever hurt somebody you love? Did you mean to? Has a loved one ever hurt you? Is it possible for an emotionally disturbed person to love?

WILLIAM FAULKNER
A Rose for Emily

William Faulkner (1897–1962) is recognized not only as one of the greatest American novelists and storytellers but as one of the major figures of world literature, having won the Nobel Prize in 1949. This acclaim failed to impress the people of his hometown, however, where his genteel poverty and peculiar ways earned him the title "Count No Count." Born in New Albany, Mississippi, and raised in Oxford, the home of the University of Mississippi, Faulkner briefly attended college there after World War I but was reduced to working odd jobs while continuing his writing. His fiction is most often set in Yoknapatawpha County, a created world whose history, geography, and complex genealogies parallel those of the American South. His many novels and stories blend the grotesquely comic with the appallingly tragic. The Sound and the Fury (1929) is often considered his finest work. In later years, Faulkner's "odd jobs" included scriptwriting for Hollywood movies, speaking at universities, and writing magazine articles. "A Rose for Emily," first published in Forum, presents a story of love as told by citizens of Yoknapatawpha County.

1

When Miss Emily Grierson died, our whole town went to her funeral: the men through a sort of respectful affection for a fallen monument, the women mostly out of curiosity to see the inside of her house, which no one save an old manservant—a combined gardener and cook—had seen in at least ten years.

It was a big, squarish frame house that had once been white, decorated with cupolas and spires and scrolled balconies in the heavily lightsome style of the seventies, set on what had once been our most select street. But garages and cotton gins had encroached and obliterated even the august names of that neighborhood; only Miss Emily's house was left, lifting its stubborn and coquettish decay above the cotton wagons and the gasoline pumps—an eyesore among eyesores. And now Miss Emily had gone to join the representatives of those august names where they lay in the cedar-bemused cemetery among the ranked and anonymous graves of Union and Confederate soldiers who fell at the battle of Jefferson.

Alive, Miss Emily had been a tradition, a duty, and a care; a sort of hereditary obligation upon the town, dating from that day in 1894 when Colonel Sartoris, the mayor—he who fathered the edict that no Negro woman should appear on the streets without an apron—remitted her taxes, the dispensation dating from the death of her father on into perpetuity. Not that Miss Emily would have accepted charity. Colonel Sartoris invented an involved tale to the effect that Miss Emily's father had loaned money to the town, which the town, as a matter of business, preferred this way of repaying. Only a man of Colonel Sartoris' generation and thought could have invented it, and only a woman could have believed it.

When the next generation, with its more modern ideas, became mayors and aldermen, this arrangement created some little dissatisfaction. On the first of the year they mailed her a tax notice. February came, and there was no reply. They wrote her a formal letter, asking her to call at the sheriff's office at her convenience. A week later the mayor wrote her himself, offering to call or to send his car for her, and received in reply a note on paper of an archaic shape, in a thin, flowing calligraphy in faded ink, to the effect that she no longer went out at all. The tax notice was also enclosed, without comment.

They called a special meeting of the Board of Aldermen. A deputation 5 waited upon her, knocked at the door through which no visitor had passed since she ceased giving china-painting lessons eight or ten years earlier. They were admitted by the old Negro into a dim hall from which a stairway mounted into still more shadow. It smelled of dust and disuse—a close, dank smell. The Negro led them into the parlor. It was furnished in heavy, leather-covered furniture. When the Negro opened the blinds of one window, they could see that the leather was cracked; and when they sat down, a faint dust rose sluggishly about their thighs, spinning with slow motes in the single sun-ray. On a tarnished gilt easel before the fireplace stood a crayon portrait of Miss Emily's father.

They rose when she entered—a small, fat woman in black, with a thin gold chain descending to her waist and vanishing into her belt, leaning on an ebony cane with a tarnished gold head. Her skeleton was small and spare; perhaps that was why what would have been merely plumpness in another was obesity in her. She looked bloated, like a body long submerged in motionless water, and of that pallid hue. Her eyes, lost in the fatty ridges of her face, looked like two small pieces of coal pressed into a lump of dough as they moved from one face to another while the visitors stated their errand.

She did not ask them to sit. She just stood in the door and listened quietly until the spokesman came to a stumbling halt. Then they could hear the invisible watch ticking at the end of the gold chain.

Her voice was dry and cold. "I have no taxes in Jefferson. Colonel Sartoris explained it to me. Perhaps one of you can gain access to the city records and satisfy yourselves."

"But we have. We are the city authorities, Miss Emily. Didn't you get a notice from the sheriff, signed by him?"

"I received a paper, yes," Miss Emily said. "Perhaps he considers himself the 10 sheriff. . . . I have no taxes in Jefferson."

"But there is nothing on the books to show that, you see. We must go by the—"

"See Colonel Sartoris. I have no taxes in Jefferson."

"But, Miss Emily—"

"See Colonel Sartoris." (Colonel Sartoris had been dead almost ten years.) "I have no taxes in Jefferson. Tobe!" The Negro appeared. "Show these gentlemen out."

2

So she vanquished them, horse and foot, just as she had vanquished their 15 fathers thirty years before about the smell. That was two years after her father's death and a short time after her sweetheart—the one we believed would marry her—had deserted her. After her father's death she went out very little; after her sweetheart went away, people hardly saw her at all. A few of the ladies had the temerity to call, but were not received, and the only sign of life about the place was the Negro man—a young man then—going in and out with a market basket.

"Just as if a man—any man—could keep a kitchen properly," the ladies said; so they were not surprised when the smell developed. It was another link between the gross, teeming world and the high and mighty Griersons.

A neighbor, a woman, complained to the mayor, Judge Stevens, eighty years old.

"But what will you have me do about it, madam?" he said.

"Why, send her word to stop it," the woman said. "Isn't there a law?"

"I'm sure that won't be necessary," Judge Stevens said. "It's probably just a   20 snake or a rat that nigger of hers killed in the yard. I'll speak to him about it."

The next day he received two more complaints, one from a man who came in diffident deprecation. "We really must do something about it, Judge. I'd be the last one in the world to bother Miss Emily, but we've got to do something." That night the Board of Aldermen met—three graybeards and one younger man, a member of the rising generation.

"It's simple enough," he said. "Send her word to have her place cleaned up. Give her a certain time to do it in, and if she don't. . . ."

"Dammit, sir," Judge Stevens said, "will you accuse a lady to her face of smelling bad?"

So the next night, after midnight, four men crossed Miss Emily's lawn and slunk about the house like burglars, sniffing along the base of the brickwork and at the cellar openings while one of them performed a regular sowing motion with his hand out of a sack slung from his shoulder. They broke open the cellar door and sprinkled lime there, and in all the outbuildings. As they recrossed the lawn, a window that had been dark was lighted and Miss Emily sat in it, the light behind her, and her upright torso motionless as that of an idol. They crept quietly across the lawn and into the shadow of the locusts that lined the street. After a week or two the smell went away.

That was when people had begun to feel really sorry for her. People in our   25 town, remembering how old lady Wyatt, her great-aunt, had gone completely crazy at last, believed that the Griersons held themselves a little too high for what they really were. None of the young men were quite good enough for Miss Emily and such. We had long thought of them as a tableau, Miss Emily a slender figure in white in the background, her father a spraddled silhouette in the foreground, his back to her and clutching a horsewhip, the two of them framed by the back-flung front door. So when she got to be thirty and was still single, we were not pleased exactly, but vindicated; even with insanity in the family she wouldn't have turned down all of her chances if they had really materialized.

When her father died, it got about that the house was all that was left to her; and in a way, people were glad. At last they could pity Miss Emily. Being left alone, and a pauper, she had become humanized. Now she too would know the old thrill and the old despair of a penny more or less.

The day after his death all the ladies prepared to call at the house and offer condolence and aid, as is our custom. Miss Emily met them at the door, dressed as usual and with no trace of grief on her face. She told them that her father was not dead. She did that for three days, with the ministers calling on her, and the doctors, trying to persuade her to let them dispose of the body. Just as they were about to resort to law and force, she broke down, and they buried her father quickly.

We did not say she was crazy then. We believed she had to do that. We remembered all the young men her father had driven away, and we knew that with nothing left, she would have to cling to that which had robbed her, as people will.

3

She was sick for a long time. When we saw her again, her hair was cut short, making her look like a girl, with a vague resemblance to those angels in colored church windows — sort of tragic and serene.

The town had just let the contracts for paving the sidewalks, and in the sum-   30
mer after her father's death they began the work. The construction company came with niggers and mules and machinery, and a foreman named Homer Bar- ron, a Yankee — a big, dark, ready man, with a big voice and eyes lighter than his face. The little boys would follow in groups to hear him cuss the niggers, and the niggers singing in time to the rise and fall of picks. Pretty soon he knew everybody in town. Whenever you heard a lot of laughing anywhere about the square, Homer Barron would be in the center of the group. Presently, we began to see him and Miss Emily on Sunday afternoons driving in the yellow-wheeled buggy and the matched team of bays from the livery stable.

At first we were glad that Miss Emily would have an interest, because the ladies all said, "Of course a Grierson would not think seriously of a Northerner, a day laborer." But there were still others, older people, who said that even grief could not cause a real lady to forget *noblesse oblige* — without calling it *noblesse oblige*. They just said, "Poor Emily. Her kinsfolk should come to her." She had some kin in Alabama; but years ago her father had fallen out with them over the estate of old lady Wyatt, the crazy woman, and there was no communication between the two families. They had not even been represented at the funeral.

And as soon as the old people said, "Poor Emily," the whispering began. "Do you suppose it's really so?" they said to one another. "Of course it is. What else could. . . ." This behind their hands; rustling of craned silk and satin behind jalousies closed upon the sun of Sunday afternoon as the thin, swift clop-clop-clop of the matched team passed: "Poor Emily."

She carried her head high enough — even when we believed that she was fallen. It was as if she demanded more than ever the recognition of her dignity as the last Grierson; as if it had wanted that touch of earthiness to reaffirm her imperviousness. Like when she bought the rat poison, the arsenic. That was over a year after they had begun to say "Poor Emily," and while the two female cousins were visiting her.

"I want some poison," she said to the druggist. She was over thirty then, still a slight woman, though thinner than usual, with cold, haughty black eyes in a face the flesh of which was strained across the temples and about the eyesockets as you imagine a lighthouse-keeper's face ought to look. "I want some poison," she said.

"Yes, Miss Emily. What kind? For rats and such? I'd recom——"   35

"I want the best you have. I don't care what kind."

The druggist named several. "They'll kill anything up to an elephant. But what you want is——"

"Arsenic," Miss Emily said. "Is that a good one?"

"Is . . . arsenic? Yes, ma'am. But what you want——"

"I want arsenic."   40

The druggist looked down at her. She looked back at him, erect, her face like a strained flag. "Why, of course," the druggist said. "If that's what you want. But the law requires you to tell what you are going to use it for."

Miss Emily just stared at him, her head tilted back in order to look him eye for eye, until he looked away and went and got the arsenic and wrapped it up. The Negro delivery boy brought her the package; the druggist didn't come back. When she opened the package at home there was written on the box, under the skull and bones: "For rats."

4

So the next day we all said, "She will kill herself"; and we said it would be the best thing. When she had first begun to be seen with Homer Barron, we had said, "She will marry him." Then we said, "She will persuade him yet," because Homer himself had remarked—he liked men, and it was known that he drank with the younger men in the Elks' Club—that he was not a marrying man. Later we said, "Poor Emily" behind the jalousies as they passed on Sunday afternoon in the glittering buggy, Miss Emily with her head high and Homer Barron with his hat cocked and a cigar in his teeth, reins and whip in a yellow glove.

Then some of the ladies began to say that it was a disgrace to the town and a bad example to the young people. The men did not want to interfere, but at last the ladies forced the Baptist minister—Miss Emily's people were Episcopal—to call upon her. He would never divulge what happened during that interview, but he refused to go back again. The next Sunday they again drove about the streets, and the following day the minister's wife wrote to Miss Emily's relations in Alabama.

So she had blood-kin under her roof again and we sat back to watch develop-   45
ments. At first nothing happened. Then we were sure that they were to be married. We learned that Miss Emily had been to the jeweler's and ordered a man's toilet set in silver, with the letters H.B. on each piece. Two days later we learned that she had bought a complete outfit of men's clothing, including a nightshirt, and we said, "They are married." We were really glad. We were glad because the two female cousins were even more Grierson than Miss Emily had ever been.

So we were not surprised when Homer Barron—the streets had been finished some time since—was gone. We were a little disappointed that there was not a public blowing-off, but we believed that he had gone on to prepare for Miss

Emily's coming, or to give her a chance to get rid of the cousins. (By that time it was a cabal, and we were all Miss Emily's allies to help circumvent the cousins.) Sure enough, after another week they departed. And, as we had expected all along, within three days Homer Barron was back in town. A neighbor saw the Negro man admit him at the kitchen door at dusk one evening.

And that was the last we saw of Homer Barron. And of Miss Emily for some time. The Negro man went in and out with the market basket, but the front door remained closed. Now and then we would see her at the window for a moment, as the men did that night when they sprinkled the lime, but for almost six months she did not appear on the streets. Then we knew that this was to be expected too; as if that quality of her father which had thwarted her woman's life so many times had been too virulent and too furious to die.

When we next saw Miss Emily, she had grown fat and her hair was turning gray. During the next few years it grew grayer and grayer until it attained an even pepper-and-salt iron-gray, when it ceased turning. Up to the day of her death at seventy-four it was still that vigorous iron-gray, like the hair of an active man.

From that time on her front door remained closed, save during a period of six or seven years, when she was about forty, during which she gave lessons in china-painting. She fitted up a studio in one of the downstairs rooms, where the daughters and granddaughters of Colonel Sartoris' contemporaries were sent to her with the same regularity and in the same spirit that they were sent to church on Sundays with a twenty-five-cent piece for the collection plate. Meanwhile her taxes had been remitted.

Then the newer generation became the backbone and the spirit of the town, and the painting pupils grew up and fell away and did not send their children to her with boxes of color and tedious brushes and pictures cut from the ladies' magazines. The front door closed upon the last one and remained closed for good. When the town got free postal delivery, Miss Emily alone refused to let them fasten the metal numbers above her door and attach a mailbox to it. She would not listen to them.

Daily, monthly, yearly we watched the Negro grow grayer and more stooped, going in and out with the market basket. Each December we sent her a tax notice, which would be returned by the post office a week later, unclaimed. Now and then we would see her in one of the downstairs windows — she had evidently shut up the top floor of the house — like the carven torso of an idol in a niche, looking or not looking at us, we could never tell which. Thus she passed from generation to generation — dear, inescapable, impervious, tranquil, and perverse.

And so she died. Fell ill in the house filled with dust and shadows, with only a doddering Negro man to wait on her. We did not even know she was sick; we had long since given up trying to get any information from the Negro. He talked to no one, probably not even to her, for his voice had grown harsh and rusty, as if from disuse.

She died in one of the downstairs rooms, in a heavy walnut bed with a curtain, her gray head propped on a pillow yellow and moldy with age and lack of sunlight.

50

5

The Negro met the first of the ladies at the front door and let them in, with their hushed, sibilant voices and their quick, curious glances, and then he disappeared. He walked right through the house and out the back and was not seen again.

The two female cousins came at once. They held the funeral on the second day, with the town coming to look at Miss Emily beneath a mass of bought flowers, with the crayon face of her father musing profoundly above the bier and the ladies sibilant and macabre; and the very old men — some in their brushed Confederate uniforms — on the porch and the lawn, talking of Miss Emily as if she had been a contemporary of theirs, believing that they had danced with her and courted her perhaps, confusing time with its mathematical progression, as the old do, to whom all the past is not a diminishing road but, instead, a huge meadow which no winter ever quite touches, divided from them now by the narrow bottleneck of the most recent decade of years.

Already we knew that there was one room in that region above stairs which no one had seen in forty years, and which would have to be forced. They waited until Miss Emily was decently in the ground before they opened it.

The violence of breaking down the door seemed to fill this room with pervading dust. A thin, acrid pall as of the tomb seemed to lie everywhere upon this room decked and furnished as for a bridal: upon the valance curtains of faded rose color, upon the rose-shaded lights, upon the dressing table, upon the delicate array of crystal and the man's toilet things backed with tarnished silver, silver so tarnished that the monogram was obscured. Among them lay a collar and tie, as if they had just been removed, which, lifted, left upon the surface a pale crescent in the dust. Upon a chair hung the suit, carefully folded; beneath it the two mute shoes and the discarded socks.

The man himself lay in the bed.

For a long while we just stood there, looking down at the profound and fleshless grin. The body had apparently once lain in the attitude of an embrace, but now the long sleep that outlasts love, that conquers even the grimace of love, had cuckolded him. What was left of him, rotted beneath what was left of the nightshirt, had become inextricable from the bed in which he lay; and upon him and upon the pillow beside him lay that even coating of the patient and biding dust.

Then we noticed that in the second pillow was the indentation of a head. One of us lifted something from it, and leaning forward, that faint and invisible dust dry and acrid in the nostrils, we saw a long strand of iron-gray hair.   [1931]

THINKING ABOUT THE TEXT

1. Do you think someone can love another so much they simply cannot bear for them to leave? Is it possible Emily was like this?

2. Can a disturbed person be in love? Does love have to be healthy? Is sanity culturally defined? Can you imagine a society that would accept Emily's behavior?

3. Who do you think the narrator of "A Rose for Emily" is? Why would Faulkner tell the story from this perspective? Why not from Emily's?

4. Look at the last sentence of paragraph 51. What do you make of the five adjectives used? Are they understandable in terms of the story?

5. Some critics think this story is not a love story but a political allegory about the South. Does this make sense to you? What else does the story suggest to you?

6. Comment on the various kinds of repression — social and psychological — that occur throughout the story. What connections can you draw, and what generalizations might you make about them?

7. Reread "A Rose for Emily." How does your knowledge of the ending of the story affect your second reading? What details of the narrative tend to stand out the second time around?

RAYMOND CARVER
What We Talk About When We Talk About Love

Raymond Carver (1938–1988) recreates in what has been called a "stripped-down and muscular prose style" the minutiae of everyday life in mid-twentieth-century America. Brought up in the Pacific Northwest in a working-class family, Carver began writing in high school and married early. While both he and his young wife worked at low-paying jobs, Carver took college courses and struggled to find time to write. In 1958, he studied fiction writing with John Gardner and graduated in 1963 from what is now the California State University at Humboldt. He received national recognition in 1967 when a story was included in the Best American Short Stories *annual anthology. Although Carver was a National Endowment for the Arts fellow in poetry in 1971, fiction has remained his primary genre, earning him numerous awards and fellowships, including O. Henry awards in 1974, 1975, and 1980. Despite his success as a writer, alcoholism plagued Carver for most of his life until with the help of Alcoholics Anonymous he stopped drinking in 1982, soon after his divorce. "What We Talk About When We Talk About Love" was the title story in his 1981 collection.*

My friend Mel McGinnis was talking. Mel McGinnis is a cardiologist, and sometimes that gives him the right.

The four of us were sitting around his kitchen table drinking gin. Sunlight filled the kitchen from the big window behind the sink. There were Mel and me and his second wife, Teresa—Terri, we called her—and my wife, Laura. We lived in Albuquerque then. But we were all from somewhere else.

There was an ice bucket on the table. The gin and the tonic water kept going around, and we somehow got on the subject of love. Mel thought real love was nothing less than spiritual love. He said he'd spent five years in a seminary before quitting to go to medical school. He said he still looked back on those years in the seminary as the most important years in his life.

Terri said the man she lived with before she lived with Mel loved her so much he tried to kill her. Then Terri said, "He beat me up one night. He dragged me around the living room by my ankles. He kept saying, 'I love you, I love you, you bitch.' He went on dragging me around the living room. My head kept knocking on things." Terri looked around the table. "What do you do with love like that?"

She was a bone-thin woman with a pretty face, dark eyes, and brown hair that hung down her back. She liked necklaces made of turquoise, and long pendant earrings. 5

"My God, don't be silly. That's not love, and you know it," Mel said. "I don't know what you'd call it, but I sure know you wouldn't call it love."

"Say what you want to, but I know it was," Terri said. "It may sound crazy to you, but it's true just the same. People are different, Mel. Sure, sometimes he may have acted crazy. Okay. But he loved me. In his own way maybe, but he loved me. There was love there, Mel. Don't say there wasn't."

Mel let out his breath. He held his glass and turned to Laura and me. "The man threatened to kill me," Mel said. He finished his drink and reached for the gin bottle. "Terri's a romantic. Terri's of the kick-me-so-I'll-know-you-love-me school. Terri, hon, don't look that way." Mel reached across the table and touched Terri's cheek with his fingers. He grinned at her.

"Now he wants to make up," Terri said.

"Make up what?" Mel said. "What is there to make up? I know what I know. That's all." 10

"How'd we get started on this subject, anyway?" Terri said. She raised her glass and drank from it. "Mel always has love on his mind," she said. "Don't you, honey?" She smiled, and I thought that was the last of it.

"I just wouldn't call Ed's behavior love. That's all I'm saying, honey," Mel said. "What about you guys?" Mel said to Laura and me. "Does that sound like love to you?"

"I'm the wrong person to ask," I said. "I didn't even know the man. I've only heard his name mentioned in passing. I wouldn't know. You'd have to know the particulars. But I think what you're saying is that love is an absolute."

Mel said, "The kind of love I'm talking about is. The kind of love I'm talking about, you don't try to kill people."

Laura said, "I don't know anything about Ed, or anything about the situation. But who can judge anyone else's situation?" 15

I touched the back of Laura's hand. She gave me a quick smile. I picked up Laura's hand. It was warm, the nails polished, perfectly manicured. I encircled the broad wrist with my fingers, and I held her.

"When I left, he drank rat poison," Terri said. She clasped her arms with her hands. "They took him to the hospital in Sante Fe. That's where we lived then, about ten miles out. They saved his life. But his gums went crazy from it. I mean they pulled away from his teeth. After that, his teeth stood out like fangs. My God," Terri said. She waited a minute, then let go of her arms and picked up her glass.

"What people won't do!" Laura said.

"He's out of the action now," Mel said. "He's dead."

Mel handed me the saucer of limes. I took a section, squeezed it over my   20
drink, and stirred the ice cubes with my finger.

"It gets worse," Terri said. "He shot himself in the mouth. But he bungled that too. Poor Ed," she said. Terri shook her head.

"Poor Ed nothing," Mel said. "He was dangerous."

Mel was forty-five years old. He was tall and rangy with curly soft hair. His face and arms were brown from the tennis he played. When he was sober, his gestures, all his movements, were precise, very careful.

"He did love me though, Mel. Grant me that," Terri said. "That's all I'm asking. He didn't love me the way you love me. I'm not saying that. But he loved me. You can grant me that, can't you?"

"What do you mean, he bungled it?" I said.   25

Laura leaned forward with her glass. She put her elbows on the table and held her glass in both hands. She glanced from Mel to Terri and waited with a look of bewilderment on her open face, as if amazed that such things happened to people you were friendly with.

"How'd he bungle it when he killed himself?" I said.

"I'll tell you what happened," Mel said. "He took this twenty-two pistol he'd bought to threaten Terri and me with. Oh, I'm serious, the man was always threatening. You should have seen the way we lived in those days. Like fugitives. I even bought a gun myself. Can you believe it? A guy like me? But I did. I bought one for self-defense and carried it in the glove compartment. Sometimes I'd have to leave the apartment in the middle of the night. To go to the hospital, you know? Terri and I weren't married then, and my first wife had the house and kids, the dog, everything, and Terri and I were living in this apartment here. Sometimes, as I say, I'd get a call in the middle of the night and have to go in to the hospital at two or three in the morning. It'd be dark out there in the parking lot, and I'd break into a sweat before I could even get to my car. I never knew if he was going to come up out of the shrubbery or from behind a car and start shooting. I mean, the man was crazy. He was capable of wiring a bomb, anything. He used to call my service at all hours and say he needed to talk to the doctor, and when I'd return the call, he'd say, 'Son of a bitch, your days are numbered.' Little things like that. It was scary, I'm telling you."

"I still feel sorry for him," Terri said.

"It sounds like a nightmare," Laura said. "But what exactly happened after he   30
shot himself?"

Laura is a legal secretary. We'd met in a professional capacity. Before we knew it, it was a courtship. She's thirty-five, three years younger than I am. In addition to being in love, we like each other and enjoy one another's company. She's easy to be with.

◆ ◆ ◆

"What happened?" Laura said.

Mel said, "He shot himself in the mouth in his room. Someone heard the shot and told the manager. They came in with a passkey, saw what had happened, and called an ambulance. I happened to be there when they brought him in, alive but past recall. The man lived for three days. His head swelled up to twice the size of a normal head. I'd never seen anything like it, and I hope I never do again. Terri wanted to go in and sit with him when she found out about it. We had a fight over it. I didn't think she should see him like that. I didn't think she should see him, and I still don't."

"Who won the fight?" Laura said.

"I was in the room with him when he died," Terri said. "He never came up   35
out of it. But I sat with him. He didn't have anyone else."

"He was dangerous," Mel said. "If you call that love, you can have it."

"It was love," Terri said. "Sure, it's abnormal in most people's eyes. But he was willing to die for it. He did die for it."

"I sure as hell wouldn't call it love," Mel said. "I mean, no one knows what he did it for. I've seen a lot of suicides, and I couldn't say anyone ever knew what they did it for."

Mel put his hands behind his neck and tilted his chair back. "I'm not interested in that kind of love," he said. "If that's love, you can have it."

Terri said, "We were afraid. Mel even made a will out and wrote to his   40
brother in California who used to be a Green Beret. Mel told him who to look for if something happened to him."

Terri drank from her glass. She said, "But Mel's right—we lived like fugitives. We were afraid. Mel was, weren't you, honey? I even called the police at one point, but they were no help. They said they couldn't do anything until Ed actually did something. Isn't that a laugh?" Terri said.

She poured the last of the gin into her glass and waggled the bottle. Mel got up from the table and went to the cupboard. He took down another bottle.

"Well, Nick and I know what love is," Laura said. "For us, I mean," Laura said. She bumped my knee with her knee. "You're supposed to say something now," Laura said, and turned her smile on me.

For an answer, I took Laura's hand and raised it to my lips. I made a big production out of kissing her hand. Everyone was amused.

"We're lucky," I said.   45

"You guys," Terri said. "Stop that now. You're making me sick. You're still on the honeymoon, for God's sake. You're still gaga, for crying out loud. Just wait. How long have you been together now? How long has it been? A year? Longer than a year?"

"Going on a year and a half," Laura said, flushed and smiling.

"Oh, now," Terri said. "Wait awhile."

She held her drink and gazed at Laura.

"I'm only kidding," Terri said.   50

Mel opened the gin and went around the table with the bottle.

"Here, you guys," he said. "Let's have a toast. I want to propose a toast. A toast to love. To true love," Mel said.

We touched glasses.

"To love," we said.

Outside in the backyard, one of the dogs began to bark. The leaves of the   55
aspen that leaned past the window ticked against the glass. The afternoon sun was like a presence in this room, the spacious light of ease and generosity. We could have been anywhere, somewhere enchanted. We raised our glasses again and grinned at each other like children who had agreed on something forbidden.

"I'll tell you what real love is," Mel said. "I mean, I'll give you a good example. And then you can draw your own conclusions." He poured more gin into his glass. He added an ice cube and a sliver of lime. We waited and sipped our drinks. Laura and I touched knees again. I put a hand on her warm thigh and left it there.

"What do any of us really know about love?" Mel said. "It seems to me we're just beginners at love. We say we love each other and we do, I don't doubt it. I love Terri and Terri loves me, and you guys love each other too. You know the kind of love I'm talking about now. Physical love, that impulse that drives you to someone special, as well as love of the other person's being, his or her essence, as it were. Carnal love and, well, call it sentimental love, the day-to-day caring about the other person. But sometimes I have a hard time accounting for the fact that I must have loved my first wife too. But I did, I know I did. So I suppose I am like Terri in that regard. Terri and Ed." He thought about it and then he went on. "There was a time when I thought I loved my first wife more than life itself. But now I hate her guts. I do. How do you explain that? What happened to that love? What happened to it, is what I'd like to know. I wish someone could tell me. Then there's Ed. Okay, we're back to Ed. He loves Terri so much he tries to kill her and he winds up killing himself." Mel stopped talking and swallowed from his glass. "You guys have been together eighteen months and you love each other. It shows all over you. You glow with it. But you both loved other people before you met each other. You've both been married before, just like us. And you probably loved other people before that too, even. Terri and I have been together five years, been married for four. And the terrible thing, the terrible thing is, but the good thing too, the saving grace, you might say, is that if something happened to one of us—excuse me for saying this—but if something happened to one of us tomorrow I think the other one, the other person, would grieve for a while, you know, but then the surviving party would go out and love again, have someone else soon enough. All this, all of this love we're talking about, it would just be a memory. Maybe not even a memory. Am I wrong? Am I way off base? Because I want you to set me straight if you think I'm wrong. I want to know. I mean, I don't know anything, and I'm the first one to admit it."

"Mel, for God's sake," Terri said. She reached out and took hold of his wrist. "Are you getting drunk? Honey? Are you drunk?"

"Honey, I'm just talking," Mel said. "All right? I don't have to be drunk to say what I think. I mean, we're all just talking, right?" Mel said. He fixed his eyes on her.

"Sweetie, I'm not criticizing," Terri said.

She picked up her glass.

"I'm not on call today," Mel said. "Let me remind you of that. I am not on call," he said.

"Mel, we love you," Laura said.

Mel looked at Laura. He looked at her as if he could not place her, as if she was not the woman she was.

"Love you too, Laura," Mel said. "And you, Nick, love you too. You know something?" Mel said. "You guys are our pals," Mel said.

He picked up his glass.

Mel said, "I was going to tell you about something. I mean, I was going to prove a point. You see, this happened a few months ago, but it's still going on right now, and it ought to make us feel ashamed when we talk like we know what we're talking about when we talk about love."

"Come on now," Terri said. "Don't talk like you're drunk if you're not drunk."

"Just shut up for once in your life," Mel said very quietly. "Will you do me a favor and do that for a minute? So as I was saying, there's this old couple who had this car wreck out on the interstate. A kid hit them and they were all torn to shit and nobody was giving them much chance to pull through."

Terri looked at us and then back at Mel. She seemed anxious, or maybe that's too strong a word.

Mel was handing the bottle around the table.

"I was on call that night," Mel said. "It was May or maybe it was June. Terri and I had just sat down to dinner when the hospital called. There'd been this thing out on the interstate. Drunk kid, teenager, plowed his dad's pickup into this camper with this old couple in it. They were up in their mid-seventies, that couple. The kid—eighteen, nineteen, something—he was DOA. Taken the steering wheel through his sternum. The old couple, they were alive, you understand. I mean, just barely. But they had everything. Multiple fractures, internal injuries, hemorrhaging, contusions, lacerations, the works, and they each of them had themselves concussions. They were in a bad way, believe me. And, of course, their age was two strikes against them. I'd say she was worse off than he was. Ruptured spleen along with everything else. Both kneecaps broken. But they'd been wearing their seatbelts and, God knows, that's what saved them for the time being."

"Folks, this is an advertisement for the National Safety Council," Terri said. "This is your spokesman, Dr. Melvin R. McGinnis, talking." Terri laughed. "Mel," she said, "sometimes you're just too much. But I love you, hon," she said.

"Honey, I love you," Mel said.

He leaned across the table. Terri met him halfway. They kissed.

"Terri's right," Mel said as he settled himself again. "Get those seatbelts on. But seriously, they were in some shape, those oldsters. By the time I got down there, the kid was dead, as I said. He was off in a corner, laid out on a gurney. I took one look at the old couple and told the ER nurse to get me a neurologist and an orthopedic man and a couple of surgeons down there right away."

He drank from his glass. "I'll try to keep this short," he said. "So we took the two of them up to the OR and worked like fuck on them most of the night. They had these incredible reserves, those two. You see that once in a while. So we did everything that could be done, and toward morning we're giving them a fifty-fifty chance, maybe less than that for her. So here they are, still alive the next morning. So, okay, we move them into the ICU, which is where they both kept plugging away at it for two weeks, hitting it better and better on all the scopes. So we transfer them out to their own room."

Mel stopped talking. "Here," he said, "let's drink this cheapo gin the hell up. Then we're going to dinner, right? Terri and I know a new place. That's where we'll go, to this new place we know about. But we're not going until we finish up this cut-rate, lousy gin."

Terri said, "We haven't actually eaten there yet. But it looks good. From the outside, you know."

"I like food," Mel said. "If I had it to do all over again, I'd be a chef, you		80
know? Right, Terri?" Mel said.

He laughed. He fingered the ice in his glass.

"Terri knows," he said. "Terri can tell you. But let me say this. If I could come back again in a different life, a different time and all, you know what? I'd like to come back as a knight. You were pretty safe wearing all that armor. It was all right being a knight until gunpowder and muskets and pistols came along."

"Mel would like to ride a horse and carry a lance," Terri said.

"Carry a woman's scarf with you everywhere," Laura said.

"Or just a woman," Mel said.		85

"Shame on you," Laura said.

Terri said, "Suppose you came back as a serf. The serfs didn't have it so good in those days," Terri said.

"The serfs never had it good," Mel said. "But I guess even the knights were vessels to someone. Isn't that the way it worked? But then everyone is always a vessel to someone. Isn't that right? Terri? But what I liked about knights, besides their ladies, was that they had that suit of armor, you know, and they couldn't get hurt very easy. No cars in those days, you know? No drunk teenagers to tear into your ass."

"Vassals," Terri said.

"What?" Mel said.		90

"Vassals," Terri said. "They were called vassals, not vessels."

"Vassals, vessels," Mel said, "what the fuck's the difference? You knew what I meant anyway. All right," Mel said. "So I'm not educated. I learned my stuff. I'm a heart surgeon, sure, but I'm just a mechanic. I go in and I fuck around and I fix things. Shit," Mel said.

"Modesty doesn't become you," Terri said.

"He's just a humble sawbones," I said. "But sometimes they suffocated in all that armor, Mel. They'd even have heart attacks if it got too hot and they were too tired and worn out. I read somewhere that they'd fall off their horses and not be able to get up because they were too tired to stand with all that armor on them. They got trampled by their own horses sometimes."

"That's terrible," Mel said. "That's a terrible thing, Nicky. I guess they'd just   95
lay there and wait until somebody came along and made a shish kebab out of
them."

"Some other vessel," Terri said.

"That's right," Mel said. "Some vassal would come along and spear the bastard in the name of love. Or whatever the fuck it was they fought over in those
days."

"Same things we fight over these days," Terri said.

Laura said, "Nothing's changed."

The color was still high in Laura's cheeks. Her eyes were bright. She brought   100
her glass to her lips.

Mel poured himself another drink. He looked at the label closely as if studying a long row of numbers. Then he slowly put the bottle down on the table and
slowly reached for the tonic water.

"What about the old couple?" Laura said. "You didn't finish that story you
started."

Laura was having a hard time lighting her cigarette. Her matches kept going
out.

The sunshine inside the room was different now, changing, getting thinner.
But the leaves outside the window were still shimmering, and I stared at the pattern they made on the panes and on the Formica counter. They weren't the same
patterns, of course.

"What about the old couple?" I said.   105

"Older but wiser," Terri said.

Mel stared at her.

Terri said, "Go on with your story, hon. I was only kidding. Then what happened?"

"Terri, sometimes," Mel said.

"Please, Mel," Terri said. "Don't always be so serious, sweetie. Can't you take   110
a joke?"

"Where's the joke?" Mel said.

He held his glass and gazed steadily at his wife.

"What happened?" Laura said.

Mel fastened his eyes on Laura. He said, "Laura, if I didn't have Terri and if I
didn't love her so much, and if Nick wasn't my best friend, I'd fall in love with
you, I'd carry you off, honey," he said.

"Tell your story," Terri said. "Then we'll go to that new place, okay?"   115

"Okay," Mel said. "Where was I?" he said. He stared at the table and then he
began again.

"I dropped in to see each of them every day, sometimes twice a day if I was
up doing other calls anyway. Casts and bandages, head to foot, the both of them.
You know, you've seen it in the movies. That's just the way they looked, just like
in the movies. Little eye-holes and nose-holes and mouth-holes. And she had to
have her legs slung up on top of it. Well, the husband was very depressed for the
longest while. Even after he found out that his wife was going to pull through, he
was still very depressed. Not about the accident, though. I mean, the accident was

one thing, but it wasn't everything. I'd get up to his mouth-hole, you know, and he'd say no, it wasn't the accident exactly but it was because he couldn't see her through his eye-holes. He said that was what was making him feel so bad. Can you imagine? I'm telling you, the man's heart was breaking because he couldn't turn his goddamn head and *see* his goddamn wife."

Mel looked around the table and shook his head at what he was going to say.

"I mean, it was killing the old fart just because he couldn't *look* at the fucking woman."

We all looked at Mel.   120

"Do you see what I'm saying?" he said.

Maybe we were a little drunk by then. I know it was hard keeping things in focus. The light was draining out of the room, going back through the window where it had come from. Yet nobody made a move to get up from the table to turn on the overhead light.

"Listen," Mel said. "Let's finish this fucking gin. There's about enough left here for one shooter all around. Then let's go eat. Let's go to the new place."

"He's depressed," Terri said. "Mel, why don't you take a pill?"

Mel shook his head. "I've taken everything there is."   125

"We all need a pill now and then," I said.

"Some people are born needing them," Terri said.

She was using her finger to rub at something on the table. Then she stopped rubbing.

"I think I want to call my kids," Mel said. "Is that all right with everybody? I'll call my kids," he said.

Terri said, "What if Marjorie answers the phone? You guys, you've heard us   130
on the subject of Marjorie? Honey, you know you don't want to talk to Marjorie. It'll make you feel even worse."

"I don't want to talk to Marjorie," Mel said. "But I want to talk to my kids."

"There isn't a day goes by that Mel doesn't say he wishes she'd get married again. Or else die," Terri said. "For one thing," Terri said, "she's bankrupting us. Mel says it's just to spite him that she won't get married again. She has a boy-friend who lives with her and the kids, so Mel is supporting the boyfriend too."

"She's allergic to bees," Mel said. "If I'm not praying she'll get married again, I'm praying she'll get herself stung to death by a swarm of fucking bees."

"Shame on you," Laura said.

"Bzzzzzzz," Mel said, turning his fingers into bees and buzzing them at   135
Terri's throat. Then he let his hands drop all the way to his sides.

"She's vicious," Mel said. "Sometimes I think I'll go up there dressed like a beekeeper. You know, that hat that's like a helmet with the plate that comes down over your face, the big gloves, and the padded coat? I'll knock on the door and let loose a hive of bees in the house. But first I'd make sure the kids were out, of course."

He crossed one leg over the other. It seemed to take him a lot of time to do it. Then he put both feet on the floor and leaned forward, elbows on the table, his chin cupped in his hands.

"Maybe I won't call the kids, after all. Maybe it isn't such a hot idea. Maybe we'll just go eat. How does that sound?"

"Sounds fine to me," I said. "Eat or not eat. Or keep drinking. I could head right on out into the sunset."

"What does that mean, honey?" Laura said.   140

"It just means what I said," I said. "It means I could just keep going. That's all it means."

"I could eat something myself," Laura said. "I don't think I've ever been so hungry in my life. Is there something to nibble on?"

"I'll put out some cheese and crackers," Terri said.

But Terri just sat there. She did not get up to get anything.

Mel turned his glass over. He spilled it out on the table.   145

"Gin's gone," Mel said.

Terri said, "Now what?"

I could hear my heart beating. I could hear everyone's heart. I could hear the human noise we sat there making, not one of us moving, not even when the room went dark.   [1981]

THINKING ABOUT THE TEXT

1. The argument between the couples seems to be about the nature of love. Which character's ideas make the most sense to you? What kinds of love are discussed? Are these demonstrated in the story? Do you think true love is an illusion?

2. Do you see similarities between Mel and Ed? Do any of the characters seem aware of any similarities? Is Mel a perceptive person? What are his problems? Is he in love with Terri? How do you interpret his fantasy with the bees and Marjorie?

3. Why does Mel seem so interested in knights? Is this symbolic? Are there other symbols here (light? dark? cardiologist?)? What do you make of the last paragraph? Why does it end with beating hearts and silence?

4. Is this story optimistic or pessimistic about true love? Is the old couple a positive or a negative example of true love? What about Nick and Laura? What about Ed? Could you argue that he was in love?

5. What does the title mean? Be specific, especially about the first word. Do you tell stories about love? Have you heard some recently? What lessons or information do they give about love?

MAKING COMPARISONS

1. Compare Ed to Emily Grierson in Faulkner's story. What similarities do you see in their behavior?

2. Have these stories complicated your idea of love?

3. Do you see Terri and Homer Barron as victims of love? Did they do something wrong?

F. SCOTT FITZGERALD
Winter Dreams

F. Scott Fitzgerald (1896–1940) was born into a financially unstable family in St. Paul, Minnesota. He attended Princeton University, writing more than studying. Before he graduated, he joined the army as an infantry lieutenant. While he was stationed in Alabama, he met and fell in love with a society belle, Zelda Sayre, who refused to marry poor. However, when This Side of Paradise *(1920) was well received and when his short stories started making money, Fitzgerald and Zelda were soon married. They lived an extravagant life as celebrities in Paris and on the Riviera. Although he was an alcoholic, he wrote sober. He was a skilled and serious craftsman, enough so that he wrote and revised* The Great Gatsby *(1925) during a period of wild parties. His personal excesses and the content of his fiction clearly identified him with the Jazz Age, which he wrote about in a clear, lyrical, and witty style. His themes, love and success, were informed by his own experiences. But he also wrote knowingly of loss and mutability. Indeed, he died of a heart attack at forty-four largely forgotten and believing himself a failure. Today, however, Gatsby, his classic novel of aspiration, is considered a masterpiece. "Winter Dreams" was published in 1922 in* Metropolitan *magazine.*

I

Some of the caddies were poor as sin and lived in one-room houses with a neurasthenic cow in the front yard, but Dexter Green's father owned the second best grocery-store in Black Bear — the best one was "The Hub," patronized by the wealthy people from Sherry Island — and Dexter caddied only for pocket-money.

In the fall when the days became crisp and gray, and the long Minnesota winter shut down like the white lid of a box, Dexter's skis moved over the snow that hid the fairways of the golf course. At these times the country gave him a feeling of profound melancholy — it offended him that the links should lie in enforced fallowness, haunted by ragged sparrows for the long season. It was dreary, too, that on the tees where the gay colors fluttered in summer there were now only the desolate sand-boxes knee-deep in crusted ice. When he crossed the hills the wind blew cold as misery, and if the sun was out he tramped with his eyes squinted up against the hard dimensionless glare.

In April the winter ceased abruptly. The snow ran down into Black Bear Lake scarcely tarrying for the early golfers to brave the season with red and black balls. Without elation, without an interval of moist glory, the cold was gone.

Dexter knew that there was something dismal about this Northern spring, just as he knew there was something gorgeous about the fall. Fall made him clinch his hands and tremble and repeat idiotic sentences to himself, and make brisk abrupt gestures of command to imaginary audiences and armies. October filled him with hope which November raised to a sort of ecstatic triumph, and in this mood the fleeting brilliant impressions of the summer at Sherry Island were ready grist to his mill. He became golf champion and defeated Mr. T. A. Hedrick in a marvellous match played a hundred times over the fairways of his imagination, a match each detail of which he changed about untiringly — sometimes he won with almost laughable ease, sometimes he came up magnificently from behind. Again, stepping from a Pierce-Arrow automobile, like Mr. Mortimer Jones, he strolled frigidly into the lounge of the Sherry Island Golf Club — or perhaps, surrounded by an admiring crowd, he gave an exhibition of fancy diving from the spring-board of the club raft. . . . Among those who watched him in open-mouthed wonder was Mr. Mortimer Jones.

And one day it came to pass that Mr. Jones — himself and not his ghost — came up to Dexter with tears in his eyes and said that Dexter was the — — best caddy in the club, and wouldn't he decide not to quit if Mr. Jones made it worth his while, because every other — — caddy in the club lost one ball a hole for him — regularly — 5

"No, sir," said Dexter decisively, "I don't want to caddy any more." Then, after a pause: "I'm too old."

"You're not more than fourteen. Why the devil did you decide just this morning that you wanted to quit? You promised that next week you'd go over to the State tournament with me."

"I decided I was too old."

Dexter handed in his "A Class" badge, collected what money was due him from the caddy master, and walked home to Black Bear Village.

"The best — — caddy I ever saw," shouted Mr. Mortimer Jones over a drink that afternoon. "Never lost a ball! Willing! Intelligent! Quiet! Honest! Grateful!" 10

The little girl who had done this was eleven — beautifully ugly as little girls are apt to be who are destined after a few years to be inexpressibly lovely and bring no end of misery to a great number of men. The spark, however, was perceptible. There was a general ungodliness in the way her lips twisted down at the corners when she smiled, and in the — Heaven help us — in the almost passionate quality of her eyes. Vitality is born early in such women. It was utterly in evidence now, shining through her thin frame in a sort of glow.

She had come eagerly out on to the course at nine o'clock with a white linen nurse and five small new golf-clubs in a white canvas bag which the nurse was carrying. When Dexter first saw her she was standing by the caddy house, rather ill at ease and trying to conceal the fact by engaging her nurse in an obviously unnatural conversation graced by startling and irrelevant grimaces from herself.

"Well, it's certainly a nice day, Hilda," Dexter heard her say. She drew down the corners of her mouth, smiled, and glanced furtively around, her eyes in transit falling for an instant on Dexter.

Then to the nurse:

"Well, I guess there aren't very many people out here this morning, are there?" 15

The smile again — radiant, blatantly artificial — convincing.

"I don't know what we're supposed to do now," said the nurse looking nowhere in particular.

"Oh, that's all right. I'll fix it up."

Dexter stood perfectly still, his mouth slightly ajar. He knew that if he moved forward a step his stare would be in her line of vision — if he moved backward he would lose his full view of her face. For a moment he had not realized how young she was. Now he remembered having seen her several times the year before — in bloomers.

Suddenly, involuntarily, he laughed, a short abrupt laugh — then, startled by   20
himself, he turned and began to walk quickly away.

"Boy!"

Dexter stopped.

"Boy — "

Beyond question he was addressed. Not only that, but he was treated to that absurd smile, that preposterous smile — the memory of which at least a dozen men were to carry into middle age.

"Boy, do you know where the golf teacher is?"   25

"He's giving a lesson."

"Well, do you know where the caddy-master is?"

"He isn't here yet this morning."

"Oh." For a moment this baffled her. She stood alternately on her right and left foot.

"We'd like to get a caddy," said the nurse. "Mrs. Mortimer Jones sent us out   30
to play golf, and we don't know how without we get a caddy."

Here she was stopped by an ominous glance from Miss Jones, followed immediately by the smile.

"There aren't any caddies here except me," said Dexter to the nurse, "and I got to stay here in charge until the caddy-master gets here."

"Oh."

Miss Jones and her retinue now withdrew, and at a proper distance from Dexter became involved in a heated conversation, which was concluded by Miss Jones taking one of the clubs and hitting it on the ground with violence. For further emphasis she raised it again and was about to bring it down smartly upon the nurse's bosom, when the nurse seized the club and twisted it from her hands.

"You damn little mean old *thing*!" cried Miss Jones wildly.   35

Another argument ensued. Realizing that the elements of comedy were implied in the scene, Dexter several times began to laugh, but each time restrained the laugh before it reached audibility. He could not resist the monstrous conviction that the little girl was justified in beating the nurse.

The situation was resolved by the fortuitous appearance of the caddy-master, who was appealed to immediately by the nurse.

"Miss Jones is to have a little caddy, and this one says he can't go."

"Mr. McKenna said I was to wait here till you came," said Dexter quickly.

"Well, he's here now." Miss Jones smiled cheerfully at the caddy-master.   40
Then she dropped her bag and set off at a haughty mince toward the first tee.

"Well?" The caddy-master turned to Dexter. "What you standing there like a dummy for? Go pick up the young lady's clubs."

"I don't think I'll go out to-day," said Dexter.

"You don't — "

"I think I'll quit."

The enormity of his decision frightened him. He was a favorite caddy, and   45
the thirty dollars a month he earned through the summer were not to be made
elsewhere around the lake. But he had received a strong emotional shock, and his
perturbation required a violent and immediate outlet.

It is not so simple as that, either. As so frequently would be the case in the
future, Dexter was unconsciously dictated to by his winter dreams.

II

Now, of course, the quality and the seasonability of these winter dreams varied, but the stuff of them remained. They persuaded Dexter several years later to
pass up a business course at the State university—his father, prospering now,
would have paid his way—for the precarious advantage of attending an older and
more famous university in the East, where he was bothered by his scanty funds.
But do not get the impression, because his winter dreams happened to be concerned at first with musings on the rich, that there was anything merely snobbish
in the boy. He wanted not association with glittering things and glittering people—
he wanted the glittering things themselves. Often he reached out for the best
without knowing why he wanted it—and sometimes he ran up against the mysterious denials and prohibitions in which life indulges. It is with one of those
denials and not with his career as a whole that this story deals.

He made money. It was rather amazing. After college he went to the city
from which Black Bear Lake draws its wealthy patrons. When he was only twenty-
three and had been there not quite two years, there were already people who
liked to say: "Now *there's* a boy—" All about him rich men's sons were peddling
bonds precariously, or investing patrimonies precariously, or plodding through
the two dozen volumes of the "George Washington Commercial Course," but
Dexter borrowed a thousand dollars on his college degree and his confident
mouth, and bought a partnership in a laundry.

It was a small laundry when he went into it, but Dexter made a specialty of
learning how the English washed fine woolen golf-stockings without shrinking
them, and within a year he was catering to the trade that wore knickerbockers.
Men were insisting that their Shetland hose and sweaters go to his laundry, just as
they had insisted on a caddy who could find golf-balls. A little later he was doing
their wives' lingerie as well—and running five branches in different parts of the
city. Before he was twenty-seven he owned the largest string of laundries in his
section of the country. It was then that he sold out and went to New York. But the
part of his story that concerns us goes back to the days when he was making his
first big success.

When he was twenty-three Mr. Hart—one of the gray-haired men who liked   50
to say "Now there's a boy"—gave him a guest card to the Sherry Island Golf Club
for a week-end. So he signed his name one day on the register, and that afternoon
played golf in a foursome with Mr. Hart and Mr. Sandwood and Mr. T. A.
Hedrick. He did not consider it necessary to remark that he had once carried
Mr. Hart's bag over this same links, and that he knew every trap and gully with his

eyes shut—but he found himself glancing at the four caddies who trailed them, trying to catch a gleam or gesture that would remind him of himself, that would lessen the gap which lay between his present and his past.

It was a curious day, slashed abruptly with fleeting, familiar impressions. One minute he had the sense of being a trespasser—in the next he was impressed by the tremendous superiority he felt toward Mr. T. A. Hedrick, who was a bore and not even a good golfer any more.

Then, because of a ball Mr. Hart lost near the fifteenth green, an enormous thing happened. While they were searching the stiff grasses of the rough there was a clear call of "Fore!" from behind a hill in their rear. And as they all turned abruptly from their search a bright new ball sliced abruptly over the hill and caught Mr. T. A. Hedrick in the abdomen.

"By Gad!" cried Mr. T. A. Hedrick, "they ought to put some of these crazy women off the course. It's getting to be outrageous."

A head and a voice came up together over the hill:

"Do you mind if we go through?"   55

"You hit me in the stomach!" declared Mr. Hedrick wildly.

"Did I?" The girl approached the group of men. "I'm sorry. I yelled 'Fore!'"

Her glance fell casually on each of the men—then scanned the fairway for her ball.

"Did I bounce into the rough?"

It was impossible to determine whether this question was ingenuous or mali-   60
cious. In a moment, however, she left no doubt, for as her partner came up over the hill she called cheerfully:

"Here I am! I'd have gone on the green except that I hit something."

As she took her stance for a short mashie shot, Dexter looked at her closely. She wore a blue gingham dress, rimmed at throat and shoulders with a white edging that accentuated her tan. The quality of exaggeration, of thinness, which had made her passionate eyes and down-turning mouth absurd at eleven, was gone now. She was arrestingly beautiful. The color in her cheeks was centred like the color in a picture—it was not a "high" color, but a sort of fluctuating and feverish warmth, so shaded that it seemed at any moment it would recede and disappear. This color and the mobility of her mouth gave a continual impression of flux, of intense life, of passionate vitality—balanced only partially by the sad luxury of her eyes.

She swung her mashie impatiently and without interest, pitching the ball into a sand-pit on the other side of the green. With a quick, insincere smile and a careless "Thank you!" she went on after it.

"That Judy Jones!" remarked Mr. Hedrick on the next tee, as they waited—some moments—for her to play on ahead. "All she needs is to be turned up and spanked for six months and then to be married off to an old-fashioned cavalry captain."

"My God, she's good-looking!" said Mr. Sandwood, who was just over thirty.   65

"Good-looking!" cried Mr. Hedrick contemptuously, "she always looks as if she wanted to be kissed! Turning those big cow-eyes on every calf in town!"

It was doubtful if Mr. Hedrick intended a reference to the maternal instinct.

"She'd play pretty good golf if she'd try," said Mr. Sandwood.

"She has no form," said Mr. Hedrick solemnly.

"She has a nice figure," said Mr. Sandwood. 70

"Better thank the Lord she doesn't drive a swifter ball," said Mr. Hart, winking at Dexter.

Later in the afternoon the sun went down with a riotous swirl of gold and varying blues and scarlets, and left the dry, rustling night of Western summer. Dexter watched from the veranda of the Golf Club, watched the even overlap of the waters in the little wind, silver molasses under the harvest-moon. Then the moon held a finger to her lips and the lake became a clear pool, pale and quiet. Dexter put on his bathing-suit and swam out to the farthest raft, where he stretched dripping on the wet canvas of the springboard.

There was a fish jumping and a star shining and the lights around the lake were gleaming. Over on a dark peninsula a piano was playing the songs of last summer and of summers before that—songs from "Chin-Chin" and "The Count of Luxemburg" and "The Chocolate Soldier"—and because the sound of a piano over a stretch of water had always seemed beautiful to Dexter he lay perfectly quiet and listened.

The tune the piano was playing at that moment had been gay and new five years before when Dexter was a sophomore at college. They had played it at a prom once when he could not afford the luxury of proms, and he had stood outside the gymnasium and listened. The sound of the tune precipitated in him a sort of ecstasy and it was with that ecstasy he viewed what happened to him now. It was a mood of intense appreciation, a sense that, for once, he was magnificently attuned to life and that everything about him was radiating a brightness and a glamour he might never know again.

A low, pale oblong detached itself suddenly from the darkness of the Island, 75 spitting forth the reverberated sound of a racing motorboat. Two white streamers of cleft water rolled themselves out behind it and almost immediately the boat was beside him, drowning out the hot tinkle of the piano in the drone of its spray. Dexter raising himself on his arms was aware of a figure standing at the wheel, of two dark eyes regarding him over the lengthening space of water—then the boat had gone by and was sweeping in an immense and purposeless circle of spray round and round in the middle of the lake. With equal eccentricity one of the circles flattened out and headed hack toward the raft.

"Who's that?" she called, shutting off her motor. She was so near now that Dexter could see her bathing-suit, which consisted apparently of pink rompers.

The nose of the boat bumped the raft, and as the latter tilted rakishly he was precipitated toward her. With different degrees of interest they recognized each other.

"Aren't you one of those men we played through this afternoon?" she demanded.

He was.

"Well, do you know how to drive a motor-boat? Because if you do I wish 80 you'd drive this one so I can ride on the surf-board behind. My name is Judy Jones"—she favored him with an absurd smirk—rather, what tried to be a smirk,

for, twist her mouth as she might, it was not grotesque, it was merely beautiful —
"and I live in a house over there on the Island, and in that house there is a man
waiting for me. When he drove up at the door I drove out of the dock because he
says I'm his ideal."

There was a fish jumping and a star shining and the lights around the lake
were gleaming. Dexter sat beside Judy Jones and she explained how her boat was
driven. Then she was in the water, swimming to the floating surf-board with a sin-
uous crawl. Watching her was without effort to the eye, watching a branch waving or a sea-gull flying. Her arms, burned to butternut, moved sinuously among
the dull platinum ripples, elbow appearing first, casting the forearm back with a
cadence of falling water, then reaching out and down, stabbing a path ahead.

They moved out into the lake; turning, Dexter saw that she was kneeling on
the low rear of the now uptilted surf-board.

"Go faster," she called, "fast as it'll go."

Obediently he jammed the lever forward and the white spray mounted at the
bow. When he looked around again the girl was standing up on the rushing
board, her arms spread wide, her eyes lifted toward the moon.

"It's awful cold," she shouted. "What's your name?"   85

He told her.

"Well, why don't you come to dinner to-morrow night?"

His heart turned over like the fly-wheel of the boat, and, for the second time,
her casual whim gave a new direction to his life.

III

Next evening while he waited for her to come down-stairs, Dexter peopled
the soft deep summer room and the sun-porch that opened from it with the men
who had already loved Judy Jones. He knew the sort of men they were — the men
who when he first went to college had entered from the great prep schools with
graceful clothes and the deep tan of healthy summers. He had seen that, in one
sense, he was better than these men. He was newer and stronger. Yet in acknowledging to himself that he wished his children to be like them he was admitting
that he was but the rough, strong stuff from which they eternally sprang.

When the time had come for him to wear good clothes, he had known who   90
were the best tailors in America, and the best tailors in America had made him
the suit he wore this evening. He had acquired that particular reserve peculiar
to his university, that set it off from other universities. He recognized the value to
him of such a mannerism and he had adopted it; he knew that to be careless in
dress and manner required more confidence than to be careful. But carelessness
was for his children. His mother's name had been Krimelich. She was a Bohemian of the peasant class and she had talked broken English to the end of her
days. Her son must keep to the set patterns.

At a little after seven Judy Jones came down-stairs. She wore a blue silk afternoon dress, and he was disappointed at first that she had not put on something
more elaborate. This feeling was accentuated when, after a brief greeting, she
went to the door of a butler's pantry and pushing it open called: "You can serve

dinner, Martha." He had rather expected that a butler would announce dinner, that there would be a cocktail. Then he put these thoughts behind him as they sat down side by side on a lounge and looked at each other.

"Father and mother won't be here," she said thoughtfully.

He remembered the last time he had seen her father, and he was glad the parents were not to be here to-night—they might wonder who he was. He had been born in Keeble, a Minnesota village fifty miles farther north, and he always gave Keeble as his home instead of Black Bear Village. Country towns were well enough to come from if they weren't inconveniently in sight and used as footstools by fashionable lakes.

They talked of his university, which she had visited frequently during the past two years, and of the near-by city which supplied Sherry Island with its patrons, and whither Dexter would return next day to his prospering laundries.

During dinner she slipped into a moody depression which gave Dexter a   95
feeling of uneasiness. Whatever petulance she uttered in her throaty voice worried him. Whatever she smiled at—at him, at a chicken liver, at nothing—it disturbed him that her smile could have no root in mirth, or even in amusement. When the scarlet corners of her lips curved down, it was less a smile than an invitation to a kiss.

Then, after dinner, she led him out on the dark sun-porch and deliberately changed the atmosphere.

"Do you mind if I weep a little?" she said.

"I'm afraid I'm boring you," he responded quickly.

"You're not. I like you. But I've just had a terrible afternoon. There was a man I cared about, and this afternoon he told me out of a clear sky that he was poor as a church-mouse. He'd never even hinted it before. Does this sound horribly mundane?"

"Perhaps he was afraid to tell you."   100

"Suppose he was," she answered. "He didn't start right. You see, if I'd thought of him as poor—well, I've been mad about loads of poor men, and fully intended to marry them all. But in this case, I hadn't thought of him that way, and my interest in him wasn't strong enough to survive the shock. As if a girl calmly informed her fiancé that she was a widow. He might not object to widows, but—

"Let's start right," she interrupted herself suddenly. "Who are you, anyhow?"

For a moment Dexter hesitated. Then:

"I'm nobody," he announced. "My career is largely a matter of futures."

"Are you poor?"   105

"No," he said frankly, "I'm probably making more money than any man my age in the Northwest. I know that's an obnoxious remark, but you advised me to start right."

There was a pause. Then she smiled and the corners of her mouth drooped and an almost imperceptible sway brought her closer to him, looking up into his eyes. A lump rose in Dexter's throat, and he waited breathless for the experiment, facing the unpredictable compound that would form mysteriously from the elements of their lips. Then he saw—she communicated her excitement to him, lavishly, deeply, with kisses that were not a promise but a fulfilment. They aroused in him not hunger demanding renewal but surfeit that would demand more surfeit . . . kisses that were like charity, creating want by holding back nothing at all.

It did not take him many hours to decide that he had wanted Judy Jones ever since he was a proud, desirous little boy.

IV

It began like that—and continued, with varying shades of intensity, on such a note right up to the dénouement. Dexter surrendered a part of himself to the most direct and unprincipled personality with which he had ever come in contact. Whatever Judy wanted, she went after with the full pressure of her charm. There was no divergence of method, no jockeying for position or premeditation of effects—there was a very little mental side to any of her affairs. She simply made men conscious to the highest degree of her physical loveliness. Dexter had no desire to change her. Her deficiencies were knit up with a passionate energy that transcended and justified them.

When, as Judy's head lay against his shoulder that first night, she whispered, "I don't know what's the matter with me. Last night I thought I was in love with a man and to-night I think I'm in love with you——"—it seemed to him a beautiful and romantic thing to say. It was the exquisite excitability that for the moment he controlled and owned. But a week later he was compelled to view this same quality in a different light. She took him in her roadster to a picnic supper, and after supper she disappeared, likewise in her roadster, with another man. Dexter became enormously upset and was scarcely able to be decently civil to the other people present. When she assured him that she had not kissed the other man, he knew she lying—yet he was glad that she had taken the trouble to lie to him. 110

He was, as he found before the summer ended, one of a varying dozen who circulated about her. Each of them had at one time been favored above all others—about half of them still basked in the solace of occasional sentimental revivals. Whenever one showed signs of dropping out through long neglect, she granted him a brief honeyed hour, which encouraged him to tag along for a year or so longer. Judy made these forays upon the helpless and defeated without malice, indeed half unconscious that there was anything mischievous in what she did.

When a new man came to town every one dropped out—dates were automatically cancelled.

The helpless part of trying to do anything about it was that she did it all herself. She was not a girl who could be "won" in the kinetic sense—she was proof against cleverness, she was proof against charm; if any of these assailed her too strongly she would immediately resolve the affair to a physical basis, and under the magic of her physical splendor the strong as well as the brilliant played her game and not their own. She was entertained only by the gratification of her desires and by the direct exercise of her own charm. Perhaps from so much youthful love, so many youthful lovers, she had come, in self-defense, to nourish herself wholly from within.

Succeeding Dexter's first exhilaration came restlessness and dissatisfaction. The helpless ecstasy of losing himself in her was opiate rather than tonic. It was fortunate for his work during the winter that those moments of ecstasy came infrequently. Early in their acquaintance it had seemed for a while that there was a deep and spontaneous mutual attraction—that first August, for example—three days of long evenings on her dusky veranda, of strange wan kisses through the late afternoon, in shadowy alcoves or behind the protecting trellises of the garden arbors, of mornings when she was fresh as a dream and almost shy at meeting him in the clarity of the rising day. There was all the ecstasy of an engagement about it, sharpened by his realization that there was no engagement. It was during those three days that, for the first time, he had asked her to marry him. She said "maybe some day," she said "kiss me," she said "I'd like to marry you," she said "I love you"—she said—nothing.

The three days were interrupted by the arrival of a New York man who vis- 115
ited at her house for half September. To Dexter's agony, rumor engaged them. The man was the son of the president of a great trust company. But at the end of a month it was reported that Judy was yawning. At a dance one night she sat all evening in a motor-boat with a local beau, while the New Yorker searched the club for her frantically. She told the local beau that she was bored with her visitor, and two days later he left. She was seen with him at the station, and it was reported that he looked very mournful indeed.

On this note the summer ended. Dexter was twenty-four, and he found himself increasingly in a position to do as he wished. He joined two clubs in the city and lived at one of them. Though he was by no means an integral part of the stag-lines at these clubs, he managed to be on hand at dances where Judy Jones was likely to appear. He could have gone out socially as much as he liked—he was an eligible young man, now, and popular with down-town fathers. His confessed devotion to Judy Jones had rather solidified his position. But he had no social aspirations and rather despised the dancing men who were always on tap for the Thursday or Saturday parties and who filled in at dinners with the younger married set. Already he was playing with the idea of going East to New York. He wanted to take Judy Jones with him. No disillusion as to the world in which she had grown up could cure his illusion as to her desirability.

Remember that—for only in the light of it can what he did for her be understood.

Eighteen months after he first met Judy Jones he became engaged to another girl. Her name was Irene Scheerer, and her father was one of the men who had always believed in Dexter. Irene was light-haired and sweet and honorable, and a little stout, and she had two suitors whom she pleasantly relinquished when Dexter formally asked her to marry him.

Summer, fall, winter, spring, another summer, another fall—so much he had given of his active life to the incorrigible lips of Judy Jones. She had treated him with interest, with encouragement, with malice, with indifference, with contempt. She had inflicted on him the innumerable little slights and indignities possible in such a case—as if in revenge for having ever cared for him at all. She had beckoned him and yawned at him and beckoned him again and he had responded often with bitterness and narrowed eyes. She had brought him ecstatic happiness and intolerable agony of spirit. She had caused him untold inconvenience and not a little trouble. She had insulted him, and she had ridden over him, and she had played his interest in her against his interest in his work—for fun. She had done everything to him except to criticise him—this she had not done—it seemed to him only because it might have sullied the utter indifference she manifested and sincerely felt toward him.

When autumn had come and gone again it occurred to him that he could   120
not have Judy Jones. He had to beat this into his mind but he convinced himself at last. He lay awake at night for a while and argued it over. He told himself the trouble and the pain she had caused him, he enumerated her glaring deficiencies as a wife. Then he said to himself that he loved her, and after a while he fell asleep. For a week, lest he imagined her husky voice over the telephone or her eyes opposite him at lunch, he worked hard and late, and at night he went to his office and plotted out his years.

At the end of a week he went to a dance and cut in on her once. For almost the first time since they had met he did not ask her to sit out with him or tell her that she was lovely. It hurt him that she did not miss these things—that was all. He was not jealous when he saw that there was a new man to-night. He had been hardened against jealousy long before.

He stayed late at the dance. He sat for an hour with Irene Scheerer and talked about books and about music. He knew very little about either. But he was beginning to be master of his own time now, and he had a rather priggish notion that he—the young and already fabulously successful Dexter Green—should know more about such things.

That was in October, when he was twenty-five. In January, Dexter and Irene became engaged. It was to be announced in June, and they were to be married three months later.

The Minnesota winter prolonged itself interminably, and it was almost May when the winds came soft and the snow ran down into Black Bear Lake at last. For the first time in over a year Dexter was enjoying a certain tranquillity of spirit. Judy Jones had been in Florida, and afterward in Hot Springs, and somewhere she had been engaged, and somewhere she had broken it off. At first, when Dexter had definitely given her up, it had made him sad that people still linked them together and asked for news of her, but when he began to be placed at dinner next to Irene Scheerer people didn't ask him about her any more—they told him about her. He ceased to be an authority on her.

May at last. Dexter walked the streets at night when the darkness was damp   125
as rain, wondering that so soon, with so little done, so much of ecstasy had gone from him. May one year back had been marked by Judy's poignant, unforgivable, yet forgiven turbulence—it had been one of those rare times when he fancied she had grown to care for him. That old penny's worth of happiness he had spent for this bushel of content. He knew that Irene would be no more than a curtain spread behind him, a hand moving among gleaming tea-cups, a voice calling to children . . . fire and loveliness were gone, the magic of nights and the wonder of

the varying hours and seasons . . . slender lips, down-turning, dropping to his lips and bearing him up into a heaven of eyes. . . . The thing was deep in him. He was too strong and alive for it to die lightly.

In the middle of May when the weather balanced for a few days on the thin bridge that led to deep summer he turned in one night at Irene's house. Their engagement was to be announced in a week now — no one would be surprised at it. And to-night they would sit together on the lounge at the University Club and look on for an hour at the dancers. It gave him a sense of solidity to go with her — she was so sturdily popular, so intensely "great."

He mounted the steps of the brownstone house and stepped inside.

"Irene," he called.

Mrs. Scheerer came out of the living-room to meet him.

"Dexter," she said, "Irene's gone up-stairs with a splitting headache. She 　130
wanted to go with you but I made her go to bed."

"Nothing serious, I —— "

"Oh, no. She's going to play golf with you in the morning. You can spare her for just one night, can't you, Dexter?"

Her smile was kind. She and Dexter liked each other. In the living-room he talked for a moment before he said good-night.

Returning to the University Club, where he had rooms, he stood in the doorway for a moment and watched the dancers. He leaned against the door-post, nodded at a man or two — yawned.

"Hello, darling."　135

The familiar voice at his elbow startled him. Judy Jones had left a man and crossed the room to him — Judy Jones, a slender enamelled doll in cloth of gold: gold in a band at her head, gold in two slipper points at her dress's hem. The fragile glow of her face seemed to blossom as she smiled at him. A breeze of warmth and light blew through the room. His hands in the pockets of his dinner-jacket tightened spasmodically. He was filled with a sudden excitement.

"When did you get back?" he asked casually.

"Come here and I'll tell you about it."

She turned and he followed her. She had been away — he could have wept at the wonder of her return. She had passed through enchanted streets, doing things that were like provocative music. All mysterious happenings, all fresh and quickening hopes, had gone away with her, come back with her now.

She turned in the doorway.　140

"Have you a car here? If you haven't, I have."

"I have a coupé."

In then, with a rustle of golden cloth. He slammed the door. Into so many cars she had stepped — like this — like that — her back against the leather, so — her elbow resting on the door — waiting. She would have been soiled long since had there been anything to soil her — except herself — but this was her own self outpouring.

With an effort he forced himself to start the car and back into the street. This was nothing, he must remember. She had done this before, and he had put her behind him, as he would have crossed a bad account from his books.

He drove slowly down-town and, affecting abstraction, traversed the deserted   145
streets of the business section, peopled here and there where a movie was giving
out its crowd or where consumptive or pugilistic youth lounged in front of pool
halls. The clink of glasses and the slap of hands on the bars issued from saloons,
cloisters of glazed glass and dirty yellow light.

She was watching him closely and the silence was embarrassing, yet in this
crisis he could find no casual word with which to profane the hour. At a convenient turning he began to zigzag back toward the University Club.

"Have you missed me?" she asked suddenly.

"Everybody missed you."

He wondered if she knew of Irene Scheerer. She had been back only a day —
her absence had been almost contemporaneous with his engagement.

"What a remark!" Judy laughed sadly — without sadness. She looked at him   150
searchingly. He became absorbed in the dashboard.

"You're handsomer than you used to be," she said thoughtfully. "Dexter, you
have the most rememberable eyes."

He could have laughed at this, but he did not laugh. It was the sort of thing
that was said to sophomores. Yet it stabbed at him.

"I'm awfully tired of everything, darling." She called every one darling,
endowing the endearment with careless, individual comraderie. "I wish you'd
marry me."

The directness of this confused him. He should have told her now that he
was going to marry another girl, but he could not tell her. He could as easily have
sworn that he had never loved her.

"I think we'd get along," she continued, on the same note, "unless probably   155
you've forgotten me and fallen in love with another girl."

Her confidence was obviously enormous. She had said, in effect, that she
found such a thing impossible to believe, that if it were true he had merely committed a childish indiscretion — and probably to show off. She would forgive him,
because it was not a matter of any moment but rather something to be brushed
aside lightly.

"Of course you could never love anybody but me," she continued, "I like the
way you love me. Oh, Dexter, have you forgotten last year?"

"No, I haven't forgotten."

"Neither have I!"

Was she sincerely moved — or was she carried along by the wave of her own   160
acting?

"I wish we could be like that again," she said, and he forced himself to
answer:

"I don't think we can."

"I suppose not. . . . I hear you're giving Irene Scheerer a violent rush."

There was not the faintest emphasis on the name, yet Dexter was suddenly
ashamed.

"Oh, take me home," cried Judy suddenly; "I don't want to go back to that   165
idiotic dance — with those children."

Then, as he turned up the street that led to the residence district, Judy began to cry quietly to herself. He had never seen her cry before.

The dark street lightened, the dwellings of the rich loomed up around them, he stopped his coupé in front of the great white bulk of the Mortimer Joneses' house, somnolent, gorgeous, drenched with the splendor of the damp moonlight. Its solidity startled him. The strong walls, the steel of the girders, the breadth and beam and pomp of it were there only to bring out the contrast with the young beauty beside him. It was sturdy to accentuate her slightness — as if to show what a breeze could be generated by a butterfly's wing.

He sat perfectly quiet, his nerves in wild clamor, afraid that if he moved he would find her irresistibly in his arms. Two tears had rolled down her wet face and trembled on her upper lip.

"I'm more beautiful than anybody else," she said brokenly, "why can't I be happy?" Her moist eyes tore at his stability — her mouth turned slowly downward with an exquisite sadness: "I'd like to marry you if you'll have me, Dexter. I suppose you think I'm not worth having, but I'll be so beautiful for you, Dexter."

A million phrases of anger, pride, passion, hatred, tenderness fought on his   170 lips. Then a perfect wave of emotion washed over him, carrying off with it a sediment of wisdom, of convention, of doubt, of honor. This was his girl who was speaking, his own, his beautiful, his pride.

"Won't you come in?" He heard her draw in her breath sharply.

Waiting.

"All right," his voice was trembling, "I'll come in."

V

It was strange that neither when it was over nor a long time afterward did he regret that night. Looking at it from the perspective of ten years, the fact that Judy's flare for him endured just one month seemed of little importance. Nor did it matter that by his yielding he subjected himself to a deeper agony in the end and gave serious hurt to Irene Scheerer and to Irene's parents, who had befriended him. There was nothing sufficiently pictorial about Irene's grief to stamp itself on his mind.

Dexter was at bottom hard-minded. The attitude of the city on his action was   175 of no importance to him, not because he was going to leave the city, but because any outside attitude on the situation seemed superficial. He was completely indifferent to popular opinion. Nor, when he had seen that it was no use, that he did not possess in himself the power to move fundamentally or to hold Judy Jones, did he bear any malice toward her. He loved her, and he would love her until the day he was too old for loving — but he could not have her. So he tasted the deep pain that is reserved only for the strong, just as he had tasted for a little while the deep happiness.

Even the ultimate falsity of the grounds upon which Judy terminated the engagement that she did not want to "take him away" from Irene — Judy, who had wanted nothing else — did not revolt him. He was beyond any revulsion or any amusement.

He went East in February with the intention of selling out his laundries and settling in New York—but the war came to America in March and changed his plans. He returned to the West, handed over the management of the business to his partner, and went into the first officers' training-camp in late April. He was one of those young thousands who greeted the war with a certain amount of relief, welcoming the liberation from webs of tangled emotion.

VI

This story is not his biography, remember, although things creep into it which have nothing to do with those dreams he had when he was young. We are almost done with them and with him now. There is only one more incident to be related here, and it happens seven years farther on.

It took place in New York, where he had done well—so well that there were no barriers too high for him. He was thirty-two years old, and, except for one flying trip immediately after the war, he had not been West in seven years. A man named Devlin from Detroit came into his office to see him in a business way, and then and there this incident occurred, and closed out, so to speak, this particular side of his life.

"So you're from the Middle West," said the man Devlin with careless curiosity. "That's funny—I thought men like you were probably born and raised on Wall Street. You know—wife of one of my best friends in Detroit came from your city. I was an usher at the wedding." 180

Dexter waited with no apprehension of what was coming.

"Judy Simms," said Devlin with no particular interest; "Judy Jones she was once."

"Yes, I knew her." A dull impatience spread over him. He had heard, of course, that she was married—perhaps deliberately he had heard no more.

"Awfully nice girl," brooded Devlin meaninglessly, "I'm sort of sorry for her."

"Why?" Something in Dexter was alert, receptive, at once. 185

"Oh, Lud Simms has gone to pieces in a way. I don't mean he ill-uses her, but he drinks and runs around——"

"Doesn't she run around?"

"No. Stays at home with her kids."

"Oh."

"She's a little too old for him," said Devlin. 190

"Too old!" cried Dexter. "Why, man, she's only twenty-seven."

He was possessed with a wild notion of rushing out into the streets and taking a train to Detroit. He rose to his feet spasmodically.

"I guess you're busy," Devlin apologized quickly. "I didn't realize——"

"No, I'm not busy," said Dexter, steadying his voice. "I'm not busy at all. Not busy at all. Did you say she was—twenty-seven? No, I said she was twenty-seven."

"Yes, you did," agreed Devlin dryly. 195

"Go on, then. Go on."

"What do you mean?"

"About Judy Jones."

Devlin looked at him helplessly.

"Well, that's—I told you all there is to it. He treats her like the devil. Oh, 200
they're not going to get divorced or anything. When he's particularly outrageous
she forgives him. In fact, I'm inclined to think she loves him. She was a pretty girl
when she first came to Detroit."

A pretty girl! The phrase struck Dexter as ludicrous.

"Isn't she—a pretty girl, any more?"

"Oh, she's all right."

"Look here," said Dexter, sitting down suddenly. "I don't understand. You
say she was a 'pretty girl' and now you say she's 'all right.' I don't understand what
you mean—Judy Jones wasn't a pretty girl, at all. She was a great beauty. Why, I
knew her, I knew her. She was——"

Devlin laughed pleasantly. 205

"I'm not trying to start a row," he said. "I think Judy's a nice girl and I like her.
I can't understand how a man like Lud Simms could fall madly in love with her,
but he did." Then he added: "Most of the women like her."

Dexter looked closely at Devlin, thinking wildly that there must be a reason
for this, some insensitivity in the man or some private malice.

"Lots of women fade just like *that*," Devlin snapped his fingers. "You must
have seen it happen. Perhaps I've forgotten how pretty she was at her wedding.
I've seen her so much since then, you see. She has nice eyes."

A sort of dullness settled down upon Dexter. For the first time in his life he
felt like getting very drunk. He knew that he was laughing loudly at something
Devlin had said, but he did not know what it was or why it was funny. When, in a
few minutes, Devlin went he lay down on his lounge and looked out the window
at the New York sky-line into which the sun was sinking in dull lovely shades of
pink and gold.

He had thought that having nothing else to lose he was invulnerable at last— 210
but he knew that he had just lost something more, as surely as if he had married
Judy Jones and seen her fade away before his eyes.

The dream was gone. Something had been taken from him. In a sort of
panic he pushed the palms of his hands into his eyes and tried to bring up a picture of the waters lapping on Sherry Island and the moonlit veranda, and gingham on the golf-links and the dry sun and the gold color of her neck's soft down.
And her mouth damp to his kisses and her eyes plaintive with melancholy and
her freshness like new fine linen in the morning. Why, these things were no
longer in the world! They had existed and they existed no longer.

For the first time in years the tears were streaming down his face. But they
were for himself now. He did not care about mouth and eyes and moving hands.
He wanted to care, and he could not care. For he had gone away and he could
never go back any more. The gates were closed, the sun was gone down, and
there was no beauty but the gray beauty of steel that withstands all time. Even the
grief he could have borne was left behind in the country of illusion, of youth, of
the richness of life, where his winter dreams had flourished.

"Long ago," he said, "long ago, there was something in me, but now that thing is gone. Now that thing is gone, that thing is gone. I cannot cry. I cannot care. That thing will come back no more."   [1922]

THINKING ABOUT THE TEXT

1. Is Dexter in love with Judy when he breaks off his engagement with Irene? When he first meets her on the golf course? At the story's end? Paragraph 175 says, "He loved her, and he would love her until the day he was too old for loving." Explain.

2. Judy brought Dexter "ecstatic happiness and intolerable agony of spirit" (para. 119). Is this what one might expect from passionate love? Would he have experienced these extremes with Irene? Is that good or bad?

3. Toward the end of the story it says, "The dream was gone" (para. 211). And then Dexter cries. What is he crying about? Is it his youth? Love? Illusions? Or something else? What does this last scene have to do with the story's title?

4. Do you agree with Dexter's comments in the last paragraph? How old is he? What does he think will not come back? Do you think he is right?

5. How much importance do issues of money and class have in this story? Would Dexter behave as he does if he were born into money? Would Judy be as desirable if she were from the middle class? Does money have an influence on your view of what is desirable in life?

MAKING COMPARISONS

1. Why do some people fall in love with dangerous people? Why does Terri? Dexter? Homer?

2. Have these stories complicated your idea of love?

3. Do you see Homer, Terri, and Dexter as victims of love? Did they do something wrong?

WRITING ABOUT ISSUES

1. What difficulties do you encounter when you try to define love? Write an essay in which you use Terri and Ed, Homer and Emily, and Dexter and Judy as examples that complicate the definition.

2. Argue that Dexter was or was not in love with Judy. Be sure to include opposing points of view.

3. Citing evidence from these and other stories, as well as novels, films, and your own experience, write an essay that explains your view of the necessary ingredients for a loving relationship.

4. Argue that because our culture overemphasizes romantic love, individuals feel pressured to find love, sometimes in all the wrong places.

TROUBLED MARRIAGES

ANNE SEXTON, "The Farmer's Wife"
ROBERT LOWELL, "To Speak of the Woe That Is in Marriage"
DENISE LEVERTOV, "The Ache of Marriage"

Through wedding vows, lovers pledge their everlasting devotion to each other. When they utter the words "until death do us part," most of them believe this will be true; others hope it will be. But the words or even the intensity of feeling does not guarantee longevity. Relations go sour, love fades, marriages fail. No one intends for this to happen. Most people want to be in a supportive, loving relationship. So why doesn't married love last? And what is to be done when a marriage is sliding fast into an emotional wasteland or coming to a standstill? As divorce rates indicate, the contemporary answer is to leave. That was not always possible, of course, and some experts wonder if that solution is best. The following three texts offer painful glimpses of marriages in trouble. How do such things happen, and what, if anything, can be done to alleviate the suffering of couples like these?

BEFORE YOU READ

Do you think a marriage should last forever? What should couples do in a bad marriage? Is open communication always a solution to problems in a relationship?

ANNE SEXTON
The Farmer's Wife

Anne Sexton (1928–1974) began writing poetry as therapy for repeated mental breakdowns and suicide attempts following the birth of her first child in 1951. Among the writers Robert Lowell, Sylvia Plath, Maxine Kumin, W. D. Snodgrass, and others often grouped as confessional poets, Sexton learned to use the intense, intimate materials of personal life in her poetry, maintaining little distance between herself and her readers. Her first collection of poetry, To Bedlam and Part Way Back *(1960), reflects this intensely confessional, female perspective, as do the later collections* All My Pretty Ones *(1962) and* Live or Die *(1966), which won the Pulitzer Prize. In the poems of* Transformations *(1971) Sexton retells Grimm fairy tales with a wry, bitter, feminist twist. Anne Sexton committed suicide in 1974. "The Farmer's Wife" is from* To Bedlam and Part Way Back.

From the hodge porridge
of their country lust,
their local life in Illinois,

where all their acres look
like a sprouting broom factory,   5
they name just ten years now
that she has been his habit;
as again tonight he'll say
honey bunch let's go
and she will not say how there   10
must be more to living
than this brief bright bridge
of the raucous bed or even
the slow braille touch of him
like a heavy god grown light,   15
that old pantomime of love
that she wants although
it leaves her still alone,
built back again at last,
minds apart from him, living   20
her own self in her own words
and hating the sweat of the house
they keep when they finally lie
each in separate dreams
and then how she watches him,   25
still strong in the blowzy bag
of his usual sleep while
her young years bungle past
their same marriage bed
and she wishes him cripple, or poet,   30
or even lonely, or sometimes,
better, my lover, dead.   [1960]

THINKING ABOUT THE TEXT

1. The last line seems to move in two directions. She calls him "my lover" but then says she sometimes wishes him dead. Does this make sense?

2. How can making love with her husband leave the farmer's wife "still alone" (line 18)? Is this her fault? His? Their fault? No one's fault?

3. Is the wife dissatisfied with sex? With her husband? With marriage itself? What do you think of her solution? What would you do?

4. Describe what you think the connotation of "his habit" is in line 7. How about "honey bunch" (line 9) and the "old pantomime of love" (line 16)?

5. Does Sexton's poem reflect marriages in general or only those in rural areas? Only ten-year-old marriages? Just this particular relationship?

ROBERT LOWELL
To Speak of the Woe
That Is in Marriage

Robert Lowell (1917–1977) spent much of his life as a poet reacting to cultural and historical influences that threatened to define him and to define American litera-ture as well. As the descendant of Mayflower New Englanders and the relative of poets James Russell Lowell and Amy Lowell, he struggled toward an individualistic vision and voice that greatly influenced his contemporaries in the 1950s and 1960s. Beginning at Harvard as a student of English literature, he moved to Kenyon Col-lege and later to Louisiana State University to study with various New Critics, thus placing himself in the midst of intellectual debates about literature. Lowell also found himself in conflict with tradition when he protested both World War II and the Vietnam War and as he wrestled with the place of religion in poetry, with the morality of capitalism, and with the vicissitudes of three marriages. Although the more formal verse of Lord Weary's Castle *(1946) won the Pulitzer Prize, he is best known for the confessional tone of* Life Studies *(1959), from which "To Speak of the Woe That Is in Marriage" is taken.*

> It is the future generation that presses into being by means of these exuber-ant feelings and supersensible soap bubbles of ours.
>
> —Schopenhauer

"The hot night makes us keep our bedroom windows open.
Our magnolia blossoms. Life begins to happen.
My hopped up husband drops his home disputes,
and hits the streets to cruise for prostitutes,
free-lancing out along the razor's edge.   5
This screwball might kill his wife, then take the pledge.
Oh the monotonous meanness of his lust. . . .
It's the injustice . . . he is so unjust—
whiskey-blind, swaggering home at five.
My only thought is how to keep alive.   10
What makes him tick? Each night now I tie
ten dollars and his car key to my thigh. . . .
Gored by the climacteric of his want,
he stalls above me like an elephant."   [1959]

THINKING ABOUT THE TEXT

1. What do you think the "home disputes" in line 3 are about? Why does he go to look for paid sex? Is the husband at fault here? Could he be the vic-tim instead of the wife?

2. The ten dollars tied to the wife's thigh seems symbolic and confusing. Is the money meant to provide him with an escape? Her with an escape? Is it meant to entice him? Is it possible to know?

3. The poem and its language are conversational in tone. What effect does this wife's monologue have on you? Is this intentional?

4. *Climacteric* (line 13) has a specific meaning. Look it up in a dictionary. Does this definition change your attitude toward the husband?

5. Since this poem was written in 1959, divorce has become quite common in America. Would Lowell be pleased? Are you?

MAKING COMPARISONS

1. Which poem seems more pessimistic about the couple's future together, Sexton's or Lowell's?

2. Do you agree that the wives in these two poems seem trapped? Why might this be so? Should they have other options? Such as?

3. Would you give these poems to a friend considering marriage? Why, or why not?

DENISE LEVERTOV
The Ache of Marriage

Denise Levertov (1923–1997) was born in England and educated entirely at home by literary parents. She claims to have decided to become a writer at age five, waiting until seventeen, however, to publish her first poem. She moved to the United States and became a citizen in 1956. Influenced by William Carlos Williams, she was associated with the Black Mountain poets of North Carolina. She later developed an open, experimental style, and her Here and Now *(1956) was considered an important avant-garde work. She published over twenty volumes of poetry and won a number of important awards. She spent the last decade of her life in Seattle. Her posthumous collection* This Great Unknowing: Last Poems *was published by New Directions in 1999. "The Ache of Marriage" is from* Poems, 1960–1967.

The ache of marriage:

thigh and tongue, beloved,
are heavy with it,
it throbs in the teeth

We look for communion
and are turned away, beloved,
each and each

♦ ♦ ♦

It is leviathan and we
in its belly
looking for joy, some joy   10
not to be known outside it

two by two in the ark of
the ache of it.   [1967]

THINKING ABOUT THE TEXT

1. What does comparing marriage to a leviathan suggest to you (line 8)? Why didn't she compare marriage to a whale? Is this comparison consistent with contemporary representations in films, novels, and TV?

2. What would you say is a good definition for *ache* (line 1)? What if she had used *pain*? How about *itch*?

3. If the narrator were more explicit and detailed, how might she amplify the phrase "We look for communion / and are turned away" (lines 5–6)?

4. One critic says the poet doesn't romanticize or lament. What do you think this means? Do you agree?

5. How would you explain the following phrases used by critics in discussing this poem: "inexorable separateness of lovers," "intentionally desperate and clumsy," "paradoxes of separateness-in-togetherness."

MAKING COMPARISONS

1. Is there more hope and more promise (less trouble) in this poem than in Sexton's or Lowell's?

2. In what ways are all three poems about being trapped?

3. One critic of the Levertov poem speaks of "unity and duality." Is this idea true of all three poems?

WRITING ABOUT ISSUES

1. Imagine you are the farmer's wife. Compose a letter to your husband explaining your feelings about your marriage.

2. Write an essay arguing that the liberalization of the divorce laws in the 1960s was either good or bad for American culture.

3. Write a personal essay narrating a relationship that began well but turned sour. Explain what went wrong. What is your present view about your decision to continue or end that relationship?

4. Try researching whether women in the 1920s and 1960s were more or less satisfied in marriages than they are today.

A MARRIAGE WORTH SAVING? CRITICAL COMMENTARIES ON HENRIK IBSEN'S A DOLL HOUSE

HENRIK IBSEN, A Doll House

CRITICAL COMMENTARIES:
HENRIETTA FRANCES LORD, From "The Life of Henrik Ibsen"
CLEMENT SCOTT, "Ibsen's Unlovely Creed"
HERMANN J. WEIGAND, From *The Modern Ibsen*
KATHERINE M. ROGERS, From "Feminism and *A Doll House*"
JOAN TEMPLETON, From "The *Doll House* Backlash:
Criticism, Feminism, and Ibsen"

The writer and scientist Loren Eiseley notes that "to grow is a gain, an enlargement of life. . . . Yet it is also a departure." Eiseley's seems a more sophisticated idea than one portraying personal and social progress as only positive. Life is more complicated than that. Most of us eagerly anticipate becoming adults and embracing adult responsibilities and privileges. But our literature is filled with nostalgia for the innocence and wonder of childhood. We have a sense that we have lost something as our culture, technology, and lifestyles have advanced. There is no going back, but to some the old ways sometimes seem simpler. Our grandparents longed to leave the limitations of small-town life, but fifty years later their urban grandchildren idealize small communities. Women agonized over the legal and personal restrictions of Victorian marriages, but contemporary women understand that divorce is often painful and difficult. No reasonable thinker would want women to return to the childlike position that wives were expected to inhabit a hundred years ago, but that does not mean we cannot acknowledge that divorce often comes with a steep emotional and practical price.

It appears that Henrik Ibsen understood this when he wrote *A Doll House* in 1879. It was an era of great political and social change, and Ibsen believed that writers could be instrumental in affecting the way people thought about the great issues of the day. His realistic problem plays confronted topical and controversial issues. Among the most debated was the status of women in society, especially their legal and emotional subjugation within marriage. To a contemporary audience, Nora, the main character of *A Doll House*, is treated like a child. Although that disturbs most women today, Ibsen's female audience tended not to sympathize with Nora. The play's unsettling conclusion outraged most men. Changes in accepted thinking are always contested. But although most critics today see Ibsen as a social visionary who championed equality in marriage, he was not naive enough to think that great sacrifice and pain would not also accompany freedom and equality. The solution of one problem often creates new problems. When Nora begins to question the old ways, her future starts to grow uncertain. Knowing what she knows, can she remain in her marriage?

BEFORE YOU READ

Do you think a woman is justified in leaving her children? Do you think absolute equality is necessary for love to exist in a marriage?

(National Library of Norway, Oslo Division, Picture Collection.)

HENRIK IBSEN
A Doll House

Translated by Rolf Fjelde

Henrik Ibsen (1828–1906) was born into a family with money in a small town in Norway, but his father soon went bankrupt. Ibsen later remembered this genteel poverty by writing about issues of social injustice that he experienced firsthand. At fifteen Ibsen was apprenticed to a pharmacist, a profession he had no interest in. He soon was drawn to the theater, working to establish a Norwegian national theater. But this led to frustration, and Ibsen spent almost thirty years in a self-imposed exile in Italy and Germany, where he wrote some of his most famous plays. Ibsen's plays are often performed today and still provoke controversy. They include

Ghosts *(1881),* An Enemy of the People *(1882),* Hedda Gabler *(1890), and* When We Dead Awaken *(1899).*

THE CHARACTERS

TORVALD HELMER, *a lawyer*
NORA, *his wife*
DR. RANK
MRS. LINDE
NILS KROGSTAD, *a bank clerk*
THE HELMERS' THREE SMALL CHILDREN
ANNE-MARIE, *their nurse*
HELENE, *a maid*
A DELIVERY BOY

SCENE: *The action takes place in Helmer's residence.*

ACT 1

A comfortable room, tastefully but not expensively furnished. A door to the right in the back wall leads to the entryway; another to the left leads to Helmer's study. Between these doors, a piano. Midway in the left-hand wall a door, and further back a window. Near the window a round table with an armchair and a small sofa. In the right-hand wall, toward the rear, a door, and nearer the foreground a porcelain stove with two armchairs and a rocking chair beside it. Between the stove and the side door, a small table. Engravings on the walls. An etagère with china figures and other small art objects; a small bookcase with richly bound books; the floor carpeted; a fire burning in the stove. It is a winter day.

A bell rings in the entryway; shortly after we hear the door being unlocked. Nora comes into the room, humming happily to herself; she is wearing street clothes and carries an armload of packages, which she puts down on the table to the right. She has left the hall door open; and through it a Delivery Boy is seen, holding a Christmas tree and a basket, which he gives to the Maid who let them in.

NORA: Hide the tree well, Helene. The children mustn't get a glimpse of it till this evening, after it's trimmed. *(To the Delivery Boy, taking out her purse.)* How much?
DELIVERY BOY: Fifty, ma'am.
NORA: There's a crown. No, keep the change. *(The Boy thanks her and leaves. Nora shuts the door. She laughs softly to herself while taking off her street things. Drawing a bag of macaroons from her pocket, she eats a couple, then steals over and listens at her husband's study door.)* Yes, he's home. *(Hums again as she moves to the table right.)*
HELMER *(from the study):* Is that my little lark twittering out there?
NORA *(busy opening some packages):* Yes, it is.
HELMER: Is that my squirrel rummaging around?
NORA: Yes!

HELMER: When did my squirrel get in?

NORA: Just now. *(Putting the macaroon bag in her pocket and wiping her mouth.)* Do come in, Torvald, and see what I've bought.

HELMER: Can't be disturbed. *(After a moment he opens the door and peers in, pen in hand.)* Bought, you say? All that there? Has the little spendthrift been out throwing money around again?

NORA: Oh, but Torvald, this year we really should let ourselves go a bit. It's the first Christmas we haven't had to economize.

HELMER: But you know we can't go squandering.

NORA: Oh yes, Torvald, we can squander a little now. Can't we? Just a tiny, wee bit. Now that you've got a big salary and are going to make piles and piles of money.

HELMER: Yes — starting New Year's. But then it's a full three months till the raise comes through.

NORA: Pooh! We can borrow that long.

HELMER: Nora! *(Goes over and playfully takes her by the ear.)* Are your scatter-brains off again? What if today I borrowed a thousand crowns, and you squandered them over Christmas week, and then on New Year's Eve a roof tile fell on my head and I lay there —

NORA *(putting her hand on his mouth)*: Oh! Don't say such things!

HELMER: Yes, but what if it happened — then what?

NORA: If anything so awful happened, then it just wouldn't matter if I had debts or not.

HELMER: Well, but the people I'd borrowed from?

NORA: Them? Who cares about them! They're strangers.

HELMER: Nora, Nora, how like a woman! No, but seriously, Nora, you know what I think about that. No debts! Never borrow! Something of freedom's lost — and something of beauty, too — from a home that's founded on borrowing and debt. We've made a brave stand up to now, the two of us; and we'll go right on like that the little while we have to.

NORA *(going toward the stove)*: Yes, whatever you say, Torvald.

HELMER *(following her)*: Now, now, the little lark's wings mustn't droop. Come on, don't be a sulky squirrel. *(Taking out his wallet.)* Nora, guess what I have here.

NORA *(turning quickly)*: Money!

HELMER: There, see. *(Hands her some notes.)* Good grief, I know how costs go up in a house at Christmastime.

NORA: Ten — twenty — thirty — forty. Oh, thank you, Torvald; I can manage no end on this.

HELMER: You really will have to.

NORA: Oh yes, I promise I will! But come here so I can show you everything I bought. And so cheap! Look, new clothes for Ivar here — and a sword. Here a horse and a trumpet for Bob. And a doll and a doll's bed here for Emmy; they're nothing much, but she'll tear them to bits in no time anyway. And here I have dress material and handkerchiefs for the maids. Old Anne-Marie really deserves something more.

HELMER: And what's in that package there?

NORA *(with a cry)*: Torvald, no! You can't see that till tonight!

HELMER: I see. But tell me now, you little prodigal, what have you thought of
for yourself?

NORA: For myself? Oh, I don't want anything at all.

HELMER: Of course you do. Tell me just what — within reason — you'd most like
to have.

NORA: I honestly don't know. Oh, listen, Torvald —

HELMER: Well?

NORA *(fumbling at his coat buttons, without looking at him)*:   If you want to give
me something, then maybe you could — you could —

HELMER: Come on, out with it.

NORA *(hurriedly)*:   You could give me money, Torvald. No more than you think
you can spare; then one of these days I'll buy something with it.

HELMER: But Nora —

NORA: Oh please, Torvald darling, do that! I beg you, please. Then I could hang
the bills in pretty gilt paper on the Christmas tree. Wouldn't that be fun?

HELMER: What are those little birds called that always fly through their fortunes?

NORA: Oh yes, spendthrifts: I know all that. But let's do as I say, Torvald; then I'll
have time to decide what I really need most. That's very sensible, isn't it?

HELMER *(smiling)*:   Yes, very — that is, if you actually hung onto the money I
give you, and you actually used it to buy yourself something. But it goes for
the house and for all sorts of foolish things, and then I only have to lay out
some more.

NORA: Oh, but Torvald —

HELMER: Don't deny it, my dear little Nora. *(Putting his arm around her waist.)*
Spendthrifts are sweet, but they use up a frightful amount of money. It's
incredible what it costs a man to feed such birds.

NORA: Oh, how can you say that! Really, I save everything I can.

HELMER *(laughing)*:   Yes, that's the truth. Everything you can. But that's nothing
at all.

NORA *(humming, with a smile of quiet satisfaction)*:   Hm, if you only knew what
expenses we larks and squirrels have, Torvald.

HELMER: You're an odd little one. Exactly the way your father was. You're never at
a loss for scaring up money; but the moment you have it, it runs right out
through your fingers; you never know what you've done with it. Well, one takes
you as you are. It's deep in your blood. Yes, these things are hereditary, Nora.

NORA: Ah, I could wish I'd inherited many of Papa's qualities.

HELMER: And I couldn't wish you anything but just what you are, my sweet
little lark. But wait; it seems to me you have a very — what should I call it? —
a very suspicious look today —

NORA: I do?

HELMER: You certainly do. Look me straight in the eye.

NORA *(looking at him)*:   Well?

HELMER *(shaking an admonitory finger)*:   Surely my sweet tooth hasn't been
running riot in town today, has she?

NORA: No. Why do you imagine that?

HELMER: My sweet tooth really didn't make a little detour through the confectioner's?

NORA: No, I assure you, Torvald—

HELMER: Hasn't nibbled some pastry?

NORA: No, not at all.

HELMER: Not even munched a macaroon or two?

NORA: No, Torvald, I assure you, really—

HELMER: There, there now. Of course I'm only joking.

NORA *(going to the table, right)*:   You know I could never think of going against you.

HELMER: No, I understand that; and you *have* given me your word. *(Going over to her.)* Well, you keep your little Christmas secrets to yourself, Nora darling. I expect they'll come to light this evening, when the tree is lit.

NORA: Did you remember to ask Dr. Rank?

HELMER: No. But there's no need for that: it's assumed he'll be dining with us. All the same, I'll ask him when he stops by here this morning. I've ordered some fine wine. Nora, you can't imagine how I'm looking forward to this evening.

NORA: So am I. And what fun for the children, Torvald!

HELMER: Ah, it's so gratifying to know that one's gotten a safe, secure job, and with a comfortable salary. It's a great satisfaction, isn't it?

NORA: Oh, it's wonderful!

HELMER: Remember last Christmas? Three whole weeks before, you shut yourself in every evening till long after midnight, making flowers for the Christmas tree, and all the other decorations to surprise us. Ugh, that was the dullest time I've ever lived through.

NORA: It wasn't at all dull for me.

HELMER *(smiling)*:   But the outcome *was* pretty sorry, Nora.

NORA: Oh, don't tease me with that again. How could I help it that the cat came in and tore everything to shreds.

HELMER: No, poor thing, you certainly couldn't. You wanted so much to please us all, and that's what counts. But it's just as well that the hard times are past.

NORA: Yes, it's really wonderful.

HELMER: Now I don't have to sit here alone, boring myself, and you don't have to tire your precious eyes and your fair little delicate hands—

NORA *(clapping her hands)*:   No, is it really true, Torvald, I don't have to? Oh, how wonderfully lovely to hear! *(Taking his arm.)* Now I'll tell you just how I've thought we should plan things. Right after Christmas—*(The doorbell rings.)* Oh, the bell. *(Straightening the room up a bit.)* Somebody would have to come. What a bore!

HELMER: I'm not home to visitors, don't forget.

MAID *(from the hall doorway)*:   Ma'am, a lady to see you—

NORA: All right, let her come in.

MAID *(to Helmer)*:   And the doctor's just come too.

HELMER: Did he go right to my study?

MAID: Yes, he did.

Helmer goes into his room. The Maid shows in Mrs. Linde, dressed in traveling clothes, and shuts the door after her.

MRS. LINDE *(in a dispirited and somewhat hesitant voice)*:   Hello, Nora.

NORA *(uncertain)*:   Hello—

MRS. LINDE: You don't recognize me.

NORA: No, I don't know — but wait, I think — *(Exclaiming.)* What! Kristine! Is it really you?

MRS. LINDE: Yes, it's me.

NORA: Kristine! To think I didn't recognize you. But then, how could I? *(More quietly.)* How you've changed, Kristine!

MRS. LINDE: Yes, no doubt I have. In nine — ten long years.

NORA: Is it so long since we met! Yes, it's all of that. Oh, these last eight years have been a happy time, believe me. And so now you've come in to town, too. Made the long trip in the winter. That took courage.

MRS. LINDE: I just got here by ship this morning.

NORA: To enjoy yourself over Christmas, of course. Oh, how lovely! Yes, enjoy ourselves, we'll do that. But take your coat off. You're not still cold? *(Helping her.)* There now, let's get cozy here by the stove. No, the easy chair there! I'll take the rocker here. *(Seizing her hands.)* Yes, now you have your old look again; it was only in that first moment. You're a bit more pale, Kristine — and maybe a bit thinner.

MRS. LINDE: And much, much older, Nora.

NORA: Yes, perhaps a bit older: a tiny, tiny bit; not much at all. *(Stopping short; suddenly serious.)* Oh, but thoughtless me, to sit here, chattering away. Sweet, good Kristine, can you forgive me?

MRS. LINDE: What do you mean, Nora?

NORA *(softly)*:   Poor Kristine, you've become a widow.

MRS. LINDE: Yes, three years ago.

NORA: Oh, I knew it, of course: I read it in the papers. Oh, Kristine, you must believe me; I often thought of writing you then, but I kept postponing it, and something always interfered.

MRS. LINDE: Nora dear, I understand completely.

NORA: No, it was awful of me, Kristine. You poor thing, how much you must have gone through. And he left you nothing?

MRS. LINDE: No.

NORA: And no children?

MRS. LINDE: No.

NORA: Nothing at all, then?

MRS. LINDE: Not even a sense of loss to feed on.

NORA *(looking incredulously at her)*:   But Kristine, how could that be?

MRS. LINDE *(smiling wearily and smoothing her hair)*:   Oh, sometimes it happens, Nora.

NORA: So completely alone. How terribly hard that must be for you. I have three lovely children. You can't see them now; they're out with the maid. But now you must tell me everything —

MRS. LINDE: No, no, no, tell me about yourself.

NORA: No, you begin. Today I don't want to be selfish. I want to think only of you today. But there *is* something I must tell you. Did you hear of the wonderful luck we had recently?

MRS. LINDE: No, what's that?

NORA: My husband's been made manager in the bank, just think!

MRS. LINDE: Your husband? How marvelous!

NORA: Isn't it? Being a lawyer is such an uncertain living, you know, especially if one won't touch any cases that aren't clean and decent. And of course Torvald would never do that, and I'm with him completely there. Oh, we're simply delighted, believe me! He'll join the bank right after New Year's and start getting a huge salary and lots of commissions. From now on we can live quite differently—just as we want. Oh, Kristine, I feel so light and happy! Won't it be lovely to have stacks of money and not a care in the world?

MRS. LINDE: Well, anyway, it would be lovely to have enough for necessities.

NORA: No, not just for necessities, but stacks and stacks of money!

MRS. LINDE (*smiling*):   Nora, Nora, aren't you sensible yet? Back in school you were such a free spender.

NORA (*with a quiet laugh*):   Yes, that's what Torvald still says. (*Shaking her finger.*) But "Nora, Nora" isn't as silly as you all think. Really, we've been in no position for me to go squandering. We've had to work, both of us.

MRS. LINDE: You too?

NORA: Yes, at odd jobs—needlework, crocheting, embroidery, and such— (*Casually.*) and other things too. You remember that Torvald left the department when we were married? There was no chance of promotion in his office, and of course he needed to earn more money. But that first year he drove himself terribly. He took on all kinds of extra work that kept him going morning and night. It wore him down, and then he fell deathly ill. The doctors said it was essential for him to travel south.

MRS. LINDE: Yes, didn't you spend a whole year in Italy?

NORA: That's right. It wasn't easy to get away, you know. Ivar had just been born. But of course we had to go. Oh, that was a beautiful trip, and it saved Torvald's life. But it cost a frightful sum, Kristine.

MRS. LINDE: I can well imagine.

NORA: Four thousand, eight hundred crowns it cost. That's really a lot of money.

MRS. LINDE: But it's lucky you had it when you needed it.

NORA: Well, as it was, we got it from Papa.

MRS. LINDE: I see. It was just about the time your father died.

NORA: Yes, just about then. And, you know, I couldn't make that trip out to nurse him. I had to stay here, expecting Ivar any moment, and with my poor sick Torvald to care for. Dearest Papa, I never saw him again, Kristine. Oh, that was the worst time I've known in all my marriage.

MRS. LINDE: I know how you loved him. And then you went off to Italy?

NORA: Yes. We had the means now, and the doctors urged us. So we left a month after.

MRS. LINDE: And your husband came back completely cured?

NORA: Sound as a drum!

MRS. LINDE: But—the doctor?

NORA: Who?

MRS. LINDE: I thought the maid said he was a doctor, the man who came in with me.

NORA: Yes, that was Dr. Rank—but he's not making a sick call. He's our closest friend, and he stops by at least once a day. No, Torvald hasn't had a sick moment since, and the children are fit and strong, and I am, too. *(Jumping up and clapping her hands.)* Oh, dear God, Kristine, what a lovely thing to live and be happy! But how disgusting of me—I'm talking of nothing but my own affairs. *(Sits on a stool close by Kristine, arms resting across her knees.)* Oh, don't be angry with me! Tell me, is it really true that you weren't in love with your husband? Why did you marry him, then?

MRS. LINDE: My mother was still alive, but bedridden and helpless—and I had my two younger brothers to look after. In all conscience, I didn't think I could turn him down.

NORA: No, you were right there. But was he rich at the time?

MRS. LINDE: He was very well off, I'd say. But the business was shaky, Nora. When he died, it all fell apart, and nothing was left.

NORA: And then—?

MRS. LINDE: Yes, so I had to scrape up a living with a little shop and a little teaching and whatever else I could find. The last three years have been like one endless workday without a rest for me. Now it's over, Nora. My poor mother doesn't need me, for she's passed on. Nor the boys, either; they're working now and can take care of themselves.

NORA: How free you must feel—

MRS. LINDE: No—only unspeakably empty. Nothing to live for now. *(Standing up anxiously.)* That's why I couldn't take it any longer out in that desolate hole. Maybe here it'll be easier to find something to do and keep my mind occupied. If I could only be lucky enough to get a steady job, some office work—

NORA: Oh, but Kristine, that's so dreadfully tiring, and you already look so tired. It would be much better for you if you could go off to a bathing resort.

MRS. LINDE *(going toward the window):*   I have no father to give me travel money, Nora.

NORA *(rising):*   Oh, don't be angry with me.

MRS. LINDE *(going to her):*   Nora dear, don't you be angry with me. The worst of my kind of situation is all the bitterness that's stored away. No one to work for, and yet you're always having to snap up your opportunities. You have to live; and so you grow selfish. When you told me the happy change in your lot, do you know I was delighted less for your sakes than for mine?

NORA: How so? Oh, I see. You think maybe Torvald could do something for you.

MRS. LINDE: Yes, that's what I thought.

NORA: And he will, Kristine! Just leave it to me; I'll bring it up so delicately— find something attractive to humor him with. Oh, I'm so eager to help you.

MRS. LINDE: How very kind of you, Nora, to be so concerned over me—doubly kind, considering you really know so little of life's burdens yourself.

NORA: I—? I know so little—?

MRS. LINDE *(smiling):*   Well, my heavens—a little needlework and such—Nora, you're just a child.

NORA *(tossing her head and pacing the floor):*   You don't have to act so superior.

MRS. LINDE: Oh?

NORA: You're just like the others. You all think I'm incapable of anything serious—

MRS. LINDE: Come now—

NORA: That I've never had to face the raw world.

MRS. LINDE: Nora dear, you've just been telling me all your troubles.

NORA: Hm! Trivia! *(Quietly.)* I haven't told you the big thing.

MRS. LINDE: Big thing? What do you mean?

NORA: You look down on me so, Kristine, but you shouldn't. You're proud that you worked so long and hard for your mother.

MRS. LINDE: I don't look down on a soul. But it *is* true: I'm proud—and happy, too—to think it was given to me to make my mother's last days almost free of care.

NORA: And you're also proud thinking of what you've done for your brothers.

MRS. LINDE: I feel I've a right to be.

NORA: I agree. But listen to this, Kristine—I've also got something to be proud and happy for.

MRS. LINDE: I don't doubt it. But whatever do you mean?

NORA: Not so loud. What if Torvald heard! He mustn't, not for anything in the world. Nobody must know, Kristine. No one but you.

MRS. LINDE: But what is it, then?

NORA: Come here. *(Drawing her down beside her on the sofa.)* It's true—I've also got something to be proud and happy for. I'm the one who saved Torvald's life.

MRS. LINDE: Saved—? Saved how?

NORA: I told you about the trip to Italy. Torvald never would have lived if he hadn't gone south—

MRS. LINDE: Of course; your father gave you the means—

NORA *(smiling):*   That's what Torvald and all the rest think, but—

MRS. LINDE: But—?

NORA: Papa didn't give us a pin. I was the one who raised the money.

MRS. LINDE: You? That whole amount?

NORA: Four thousand, eight hundred crowns. What do you say to that?

MRS. LINDE: But Nora, how was it possible? Did you win the lottery?

NORA *(disdainfully):*   The lottery? Pooh! No art to that.

MRS. LINDE: But where did you get it from then?

NORA *(humming, with a mysterious smile):*   Hmm, tra-la-la-la.

MRS. LINDE: Because you couldn't have borrowed it.

NORA: No? Why not?

MRS. LINDE: A wife can't borrow without her husband's consent.

NORA *(tossing her head):*   Oh, but a wife with a little business sense, a wife who knows how to manage—

MRS. LINDE: Nora, I simply don't understand—

NORA: You don't have to. Whoever said I *borrowed* the money? I could have gotten it other ways. *(Throwing herself back on the sofa.)* I could have gotten it from some admirer or other. After all, a girl with my ravishing appeal—

MRS. LINDE: You lunatic.

NORA: I'll bet you're eaten up with curiosity, Kristine.

MRS. LINDE: Now listen here, Nora—you haven't done something indiscreet?

NORA *(sitting up again):*   Is it indiscreet to save your husband's life?

MRS. LINDE: I think it's indiscreet that without his knowledge you—

NORA: But that's the point: he mustn't know! My Lord, can't you understand? He mustn't ever know the close call he had. It was to *me* the doctors came to say his life was in danger—that nothing could save him but a stay in the south. Didn't I try strategy then! I began talking about how lovely it would be for me to travel abroad like other young wives; I begged and I cried; I told him please to remember my condition, to be kind and indulge me; and then I dropped a hint that he could easily take out a loan. But at that, Kristine, he nearly exploded. He said I was frivolous, and it was his duty as man of the house not to indulge me in whims and fancies—as I think he called them. Aha, I thought, now you'll just have to be saved—and that's when I saw my chance.

MRS. LINDE: And your father never told Torvald the money wasn't from him?

NORA: No, never. Papa died right about then. I'd considered bringing him into my secret and begging him never to tell. But he was too sick at the time— and then, sadly, it didn't matter.

MRS. LINDE: And you've never confided in your husband since?

NORA: For heaven's sake, no! Are you serious? He's so strict on that subject. Besides—Torvald, with all his masculine pride—how painfully humiliating for him if he ever found out he was in debt to me. That would just ruin our relationship. Our beautiful, happy home would never be the same.

MRS. LINDE: Won't you ever tell him?

NORA *(thoughtfully, half smiling):*   Yes—maybe sometime, years from now, when I'm no longer so attractive. Don't laugh! I only mean when Torvald loves me less than now, when he stops enjoying my dancing and dressing up and reciting for him. Then it might be wise to have something in reserve— *(Breaking off.)* How ridiculous! That'll never happen—Well, Kristine, what do you think of my big secret? I'm capable of something too, hm? You can imagine, of course, how this thing hangs over me. It really hasn't been easy meeting the payments on time. In the business world there's what they call quarterly interest and what they call amortization, and these are always so terribly hard to manage. I've had to skimp a little here and there, wherever I could, you know. I could hardly spare anything from my house allowance, because Torvald has to live well. I couldn't let the children go poorly dressed; whatever I got for them, I felt I had to use up completely—the darlings!

MRS. LINDE: Poor Nora, so it had to come out of your own budget, then?

NORA: Yes, of course. But I was the one most responsible, too. Every time Torvald gave me money for new clothes and such, I never used more than half; always bought the simplest, cheapest outfits. It was a godsend that everything looks so well on me that Torvald never noticed. But it did weigh me down at times, Kristine. It *is* such a joy to wear fine things. You understand.

MRS. LINDE: Oh, of course.

NORA: And then I found other ways of making money. Last winter I was lucky enough to get a lot of copying to do. I locked myself in and sat writing every evening till late in the night. Ah, I was tired so often, dead tired. But still it was wonderful fun, sitting and working like that, earning money. It was almost like being a man.

MRS. LINDE: But how much have you paid off this way so far?

NORA: That's hard to say, exactly. These accounts, you know, aren't easy to figure. I only know that I've paid out all I could scrape together. Time and again I haven't known where to turn. (*Smiling.*) Then I'd sit here dreaming of a rich old gentleman who had fallen in love with me—

MRS. LINDE: What! Who is he?

NORA: Oh, really! And that he'd died, and when his will was opened, there in big letters it said, "All my fortune shall be paid over in cash, immediately, to that enchanting Mrs. Nora Helmer."

MRS. LINDE: But Nora dear—who *was* this gentleman?

NORA: Good grief, can't you understand? The old man never existed; that was only something I'd dream up time and again whenever I was at my wits' end for money. But it makes no difference now; the old fossil can go where he pleases for all I care; I don't need him or his will—because now I'm free. (*Jumping up.*) Oh, how lovely to think of that, Kristine! Carefree! To know you're carefree, utterly carefree; to be able to romp and play with the children, and to keep up a beautiful, charming home—everything just the way Torvald likes it! And think, spring is coming, with big blue skies. Maybe we can travel a little then. Maybe I'll see the ocean again. Oh yes, it *is* so marvelous to live and be happy!

The front doorbell rings.

MRS. LINDE (*rising*): There's the bell. It's probably best that I go.

NORA: No, stay. No one's expected. It must be for Torvald.

MAID (*from the hall doorway*): Excuse me, ma'am—there's a gentleman here to see Mr. Helmer, but I didn't know—since the doctor's with him—

NORA: Who is the gentleman?

KROGSTAD (*from the doorway*): It's me, Mrs. Helmer.

Mrs. Linde starts and turns away toward the window.

NORA (*stepping toward him, tense, her voice a whisper*): You? What is it? Why do you want to speak to my husband?

KROGSTAD: Bank business—after a fashion. I have a small job in the investment bank, and I hear now your husband is going to be our chief—

NORA: In other words, it's—

KROGSTAD: Just dry business, Mrs. Helmer. Nothing but that.

NORA: Yes, then please be good enough to step into the study. (*She nods indifferently as she sees him out by the hall door, then returns and begins stirring up the stove.*)

MRS. LINDE: Nora—who was that man?

NORA: That was a Mr. Krogstad—a lawyer.

MRS. LINDE: Then it really was him.

NORA: Do you know that person?

MRS. LINDE: I did once—many years ago. For a time he was a law clerk in our town.

NORA: Yes, he's been that.

MRS. LINDE: How he's changed.

NORA: I understand he had a very unhappy marriage.

MRS. LINDE: He's a widower now.

NORA: With a number of children. There now, it's burning. *(She closes the stove door and moves the rocker a bit to one side.)*

MRS. LINDE: They say he has a hand in all kinds of business.

NORA: Oh? That may be true; I wouldn't know. But let's not think about business. It's so dull.

Dr. Rank enters from Helmer's study.

RANK *(still in the doorway):*   No, no really—I don't want to intrude, I'd just as soon talk a little while with your wife. *(Shuts the door, then notices Mrs. Linde.)* Oh, beg pardon. I'm intruding here too.

NORA: No, not at all. *(Introducing him.)* Dr. Rank, Mrs. Linde.

RANK: Well now, that's a name much heard in this house. I believe I passed the lady on the stairs as I came.

MRS. LINDE: Yes, I take the stairs very slowly. They're rather hard on me.

RANK: Uh-hm, some touch of internal weakness?

MRS. LINDE: More overexertion, I'd say.

RANK: Nothing else? Then you're probably here in town to rest up in a round of parties?

MRS. LINDE: I'm here to look for work.

RANK: Is that the best cure for overexertion?

MRS. LINDE: One has to live, Doctor.

RANK: Yes, there's a common prejudice to that effect.

NORA: Oh, come on, Dr. Rank—you really do want to live yourself.

RANK: Yes, I really do. Wretched as I am, I'll gladly prolong my torment indefinitely. All my patients feel like that. And it's quite the same, too, with the morally sick. Right at this moment there's one of those moral invalids in there with Helmer—

MRS. LINDE *(softly):*   Ah!

NORA: Who do you mean?

RANK: Oh, it's a lawyer, Krogstad, a type you wouldn't know. His character is rotten to the root—but even he began chattering all-importantly about how he had to *live*.

NORA: Oh? What did he want to talk to Torvald about?

RANK: I really don't know. I only heard something about the bank.

NORA: I didn't know that Krog—that this man Krogstad had anything to do with the bank.

RANK: Yes, he's gotten some kind of berth down there. *(To Mrs. Linde.)* I don't know if you also have, in your neck of the woods, a type of person who scuttles about breathlessly, sniffing out hints of moral corruption, and then maneuvers his victim into some sort of key position where he can keep an eye on him. It's the healthy these days that are out in the cold.

MRS. LINDE: All the same, it's the sick who most need to be taken in.

RANK *(with a shrug):*   Yes, there we have it. That's the concept that's turning society into a sanatorium.

Nora, lost in her thoughts, breaks out into quiet laughter and claps her hands.

RANK: Why do you laugh at that? Do you have any real idea of what society is?

NORA: What do I care about dreary old society? I was laughing at something quite different — something terribly funny. Tell me, Doctor — is everyone who works in the bank dependent now on Torvald?

RANK: Is that what you find so terribly funny?

NORA *(smiling and humming):*   Never mind, never mind! *(Pacing the floor.)* Yes, that's really immensely amusing: that we — that Torvald has so much power now over all those people. *(Taking the bag out of her pocket.)* Dr. Rank, a little macaroon on that?

RANK: See here, macaroons! I thought they were contraband here.

NORA: Yes, but these are some that Kristine gave me.

MRS. LINDE: What? I — ?

NORA: Now, now, don't be afraid. You couldn't possibly know that Torvald had forbidden them. You see, he's worried they'll ruin my teeth. But hmp! Just this once! Isn't that so, Dr. Rank? Help yourself! *(Puts a macaroon in his mouth.)* And you too, Kristine. And I'll also have one, only a little one — or two, at the most. *(Walking about again.)* Now I'm really tremendously happy. Now there's just one last thing in the world that I have an enormous desire to do.

RANK: Well! And what's that?

NORA: It's something I have such a consuming desire to say so Torvald could hear.

RANK: And why can't you say it?

NORA: I don't dare. It's quite shocking.

MRS. LINDE: Shocking?

RANK: Well, then it isn't advisable. But in front of us you certainly can. What do you have such a desire to say so Torvald could hear?

NORA: I have such a huge desire to say — to hell and be damned!

RANK: Are you crazy?

MRS. LINDE: My goodness, Nora!

RANK: Go on, say it. Here he is.

NORA *(hiding the macaroon bag):*   Shh, shh, shh!

Helmer comes in from his study, hat in hand, overcoat over his arm.

NORA *(going toward him):*   Well, Torvald dear, are you through with him?

HELMER: Yes, he just left.

NORA: Let me introduce you — this is Kristine, who's arrived here in town.

HELMER: Kristine — ? I'm sorry, but I don't know —

NORA: Mrs. Linde, Torvald dear. Mrs. Kristine Linde.

HELMER: Of course. A childhood friend of my wife's, no doubt?

MRS. LINDE: Yes, we knew each other in those days.

NORA: And just think, she made the long trip down here in order to talk with you.

HELMER: What's this?

MRS. LINDE: Well, not exactly —

NORA: You see, Kristine is remarkably clever in office work, and so she's terribly eager to come under a capable man's supervision and add more to what she already knows —

HELMER: Very wise, Mrs. Linde.

NORA: And then when she heard that you'd become a bank manager — the story was wired out to the papers — then she came in as fast as she could and — Really, Torvald, for my sake you can do a little something for Kristine, can't you?

HELMER: Yes, it's not at all impossible. Mrs. Linde, I suppose you're a widow?

MRS. LINDE: Yes.

HELMER: Any experience in office work?

MRS. LINDE: Yes, a good deal.

HELMER: Well, it's quite likely that I can make an opening for you —

NORA (clapping her hands):   You see, you see!

HELMER: You've come at a lucky moment, Mrs. Linde.

MRS. LINDE: Oh, how can I thank you?

HELMER: Not necessary. (Putting his overcoat on.) But today you'll have to excuse me —

RANK: Wait, I'll go with you. (He fetches his coat from the hall and warms it at the stove.)

NORA: Don't stay out long, dear.

HELMER: An hour; no more.

NORA: Are you going too, Kristine?

MRS. LINDE (putting on her winter garments):   Yes, I have to see about a room now.

HELMER: Then perhaps we can all walk together.

NORA (helping her):   What a shame we're so cramped here, but it's quite impossible for us to —

MRS. LINDE: Oh, don't even think of it! Good-bye, Nora dear, and thanks for everything.

NORA: Good-bye for now. Of course you'll be back this evening. And you too, Dr. Rank. What? If you're well enough? Oh, you've got to be! Wrap up tight now.

In a ripple of small talk the company moves out into the hall; children's voices are heard outside on the steps.

NORA: There they are! There they are! (She runs to open the door. The children come in with their nurse, Anne-Marie.) Come in, come in! (Bends down and kisses them.) Oh, you darlings —! Look at them, Kristine. Aren't they lovely!

RANK: No loitering in the draft here.

HELMER: Come, Mrs. Linde — this place is unbearable now for anyone but mothers.

Dr. Rank, Helmer, and Mrs. Linde go down the stairs. Anne-Marie goes into the living room with the children. Nora follows, after closing the hall door.

NORA: How fresh and strong you look. Oh, such red cheeks you have! Like apples and roses. *(The children interrupt her throughout the following.)* And it was so much fun? That's wonderful. Really? You pulled both Emmy and Bob on the sled? Imagine, all together! Yes, you're a clever boy, Ivar. Oh, let me hold her a bit, Anne-Marie. My sweet little doll baby! *(Takes the smallest from the nurse and dances with her.)* Yes, yes, Mama will dance with Bob as well. What? Did you throw snowballs? Oh, if I'd only been there! No, don't bother, Anne-Marie—I'll undress them myself. Oh yes, let me. It's such fun. Go in and rest; you look half frozen. There's hot coffee waiting for you on the stove. *(The nurse goes into the room to the left. Nora takes the children's winter things off, throwing them about, while the children talk to her all at once.)* Is that so? A big dog chased you? But it didn't bite? No, dogs never bite little, lovely doll babies. Don't peek in the packages, Ivar! What is it? Yes, wouldn't you like to know. No, no, it's an ugly something. Well? Shall we play? What shall we play? Hide-and-seek? Yes, let's play hide-and-seek. Bob must hide first. I must? Yes, let me hide first. *(Laughing and shouting, she and the children play in and out of the living room and the adjoining room to the right. At last Nora hides under the table. The children come storming in, search, but cannot find her, then hear her muffled laughter, dash over to the table, lift the cloth up and find her. Wild shouting. She creeps forward as if to scare them. More shouts. Meanwhile, a knock at the hall door; no one has noticed it. Now the door half opens, and Krogstad appears. He waits a moment; the game goes on.)*

KROGSTAD: Beg pardon, Mrs. Helmer—

NORA *(with a strangled cry, turning and scrambling to her knees)*:   Oh! What do you want?

KROGSTAD: Excuse me. The outer door was ajar; it must be someone forgot to shut it—

NORA *(rising)*:   My husband isn't home, Mr. Krogstad.

KROGSTAD: I know that.

NORA: Yes—then what do you want here?

KROGSTAD: A word with you.

NORA: With—? *(To the children, quietly.)* Go in to Anne-Marie. What? No, the strange man won't hurt Mama. When he's gone, we'll play some more. *(She leads the children into the room to the left and shuts the door after them. Then, tense and nervous:)* You want to speak to me?

KROGSTAD: Yes, I want to.

NORA: Today? But it's not yet the first of the month—

KROGSTAD: No, it's Christmas Eve. It's going to be up to you how merry a Christmas you have.

NORA: What is it you want? Today I absolutely can't—

KROGSTAD: We won't talk about that till later. This is something else. You do have a moment to spare, I suppose?

NORA: Oh yes, of course—I do, except—

KROGSTAD: Good. I was sitting over at Olsen's Restaurant when I saw your husband go down the street—

NORA: Yes?

KROGSTAD: With a lady.

NORA: Yes. So?

KROGSTAD: If you'll pardon my asking: wasn't that lady a Mrs. Linde?

NORA: Yes.

KROGSTAD: Just now come into town?

NORA: Yes, today.

KROGSTAD: She's a good friend of yours?

NORA: Yes, she is. But I don't see —

KROGSTAD: I also knew her once.

NORA: I'm aware of that.

KROGSTAD: Oh? You know all about it. I thought so. Well, then let me ask you short and sweet: is Mrs. Linde getting a job in the bank?

NORA: What makes you think you can cross-examine me, Mr. Krogstad — you, one of my husband's employees? But since you ask, you might as well know — yes, Mrs. Linde's going to be taken on at the bank. And I'm the one who spoke for her, Mr. Krogstad. Now you know.

KROGSTAD: So I guessed right.

NORA *(pacing up and down):*   Oh, one does have a tiny bit of influence, I should hope. Just because I am a woman, don't think it means that — When one has a subordinate position, Mr. Krogstad, one really ought to be careful about pushing somebody who — hm —

KROGSTAD: Who has influence?

NORA: That's right.

KROGSTAD *(in a different tone):*   Mrs. Helmer, would you be good enough to use your influence on my behalf?

NORA: What? What do you mean?

KROGSTAD: Would you please make sure that I keep my subordinate position in the bank?

NORA: What does that mean? Who's thinking of taking away your position?

KROGSTAD: Oh, don't play the innocent with me. I'm quite aware that your friend would hardly relish the chance of running into me again; and I'm also aware now whom I can thank for being turned out.

NORA: But I promise you —

KROGSTAD: Yes, yes, yes, to the point: there's still time, and I'm advising you to use your influence to prevent it.

NORA: But Mr. Krogstad, I have absolutely no influence.

KROGSTAD: You haven't? I thought you were just saying —

NORA: You shouldn't take me so literally. I! How can you believe that I have any such influence over my husband?

KROGSTAD: Oh, I've known your husband from our student days. I don't think the great bank manager's more steadfast than any other married man.

NORA: You speak insolently about my husband, and I'll show you the door.

KROGSTAD: The lady has spirit.

NORA: I'm not afraid of you any longer. After New Year's, I'll soon be done with the whole business.

KROGSTAD *(restraining himself):*   Now listen to me, Mrs. Helmer. If necessary, I'll fight for my little job in the bank as if it were life itself.

NORA: Yes, so it seems.

KROGSTAD: It's not just a matter of income; that's the least of it. It's something else — All right, out with it! Look, this is the thing. You know, just like all the others, of course, that once, a good many years ago, I did something rather rash.

NORA: I've heard rumors to that effect.

KROGSTAD: The case never got into court; but all the same, every door was closed in my face from then on. So I took up those various activities you know about. I had to grab hold somewhere; and I dare say I haven't been among the worst. But now I want to drop all that. My boys are growing up. For their sakes, I'll have to win back as much respect as possible here in town. That job in the bank was like the first rung in my ladder. And now your husband wants to kick me right back down in the mud again.

NORA: But for heaven's sake, Mr. Krogstad, it's simply not in my power to help you.

KROGSTAD: That's because you haven't the will to — but I have the means to make you.

NORA: You certainly won't tell my husband that I owe you money?

KROGSTAD: Hm — what if I told him that?

NORA: That would be shameful of you. *(Nearly in tears.)* This secret — my joy and my pride — that he should learn it in such a crude and disgusting way — learn it from you. You'd expose me to the most horrible unpleasantness —

KROGSTAD: Only unpleasantness?

NORA *(vehemently):*   But go on and try. It'll turn out the worse for you, because then my husband will really see what a crook you are, and then you'll *never* be able to hold your job.

KROGSTAD: I asked if it was just domestic unpleasantness you were afraid of?

NORA: If my husband finds out, then of course he'll pay what I owe at once, and then we'd be through with you for good.

KROGSTAD *(a step closer):*   Listen, Mrs. Helmer — you've either got a very bad memory, or else no head at all for business. I'd better put you a little more in touch with the facts.

NORA: What do you mean?

KROGSTAD: When your husband was sick, you came to me for a loan of four thousand, eight hundred crowns.

NORA: Where else could I go?

KROGSTAD: I promised to get you that sum —

NORA: And you got it.

KROGSTAD: I promised to get you that sum, on certain conditions. You were so involved in your husband's illness, and so eager to finance your trip, that I guess you didn't think out all the details. It might just be a good idea to remind you. I promised you the money on the strength of a note I drew up.

NORA: Yes, and that I signed.

KROGSTAD: Right. But at the bottom I added some lines for your father to guarantee the loan. He was supposed to sign down there.

NORA:　　Supposed to? He did sign.

KROGSTAD:　　I left the date blank. In other words, your father would have dated his signature himself. Do you remember that?

NORA:　　Yes, I think—

KROGSTAD:　　Then I gave you the note for you to mail to your father. Isn't that so?

NORA:　　Yes.

KROGSTAD:　　And naturally you sent it at once—because only some five, six days later you brought me the note, properly signed. And with that, the money was yours.

NORA:　　Well, then; I've made my payments regularly, haven't I?

KROGSTAD:　　More or less. But—getting back to the point—those were hard times for you then, Mrs. Helmer.

NORA:　　Yes, they were.

KROGSTAD:　　Your father was very ill, I believe.

NORA:　　He was near the end.

KROGSTAD:　　He died soon after?

NORA:　　Yes.

KROGSTAD:　　Tell me, Mrs. Helmer, do you happen to recall the date of your father's death? The day of the month, I mean.

NORA:　　Papa died the twenty-ninth of September.

KROGSTAD:　　That's quite correct; I've already looked into that. And now we come to a curious thing—*(Taking out a paper.)* which I simply cannot comprehend.

NORA:　　Curious thing? I don't know—

KROGSTAD:　　This is the curious thing: that your father co-signed the note for your loan three days after his death.

NORA:　　How—? I don't understand.

KROGSTAD:　　Your father died the twenty-ninth of September. But look. Here your father dated his signature October second. Isn't that curious, Mrs. Helmer? *(Nora is silent.)* Can you explain it to me? *(Nora remains silent.)* It's also remarkable that the words "October second" and the year aren't written in your father's hand, but rather in one that I think I know. Well, it's easy to understand. Your father forgot perhaps to date his signature, and then someone or other added it, a bit sloppily, before anyone knew of his death. There's nothing wrong in that. It all comes down to the signature. And there's no question about *that*, Mrs. Helmer. It really *was* your father who signed his own name here, wasn't it?

NORA *(after a short silence, throwing her head back and looking squarely at him)*: No, it wasn't. *I* signed Papa's name.

KROGSTAD:　　Wait, now—are you fully aware that this is a dangerous confession?

NORA:　　Why? You'll soon get your money.

KROGSTAD:　　Let me ask you a question—why didn't you send the paper to your father?

NORA:　　That was impossible. Papa was so sick. If I'd asked him for his signature, I also would have had to tell him what the money was for. But I couldn't tell him, sick as he was, that my husband's life was in danger. That was just impossible.

KROGSTAD: Then it would have been better if you'd given up the trip abroad.

NORA: I couldn't possibly. The trip was to save my husband's life. I couldn't give that up.

KROGSTAD: But didn't you ever consider that this was a fraud against me?

NORA: I couldn't let myself be bothered by that. You weren't any concern of mine. I couldn't stand you, with all those cold complications you made, even though you knew how badly off my husband was.

KROGSTAD: Mrs. Helmer, obviously you haven't the vaguest idea of what you've involved yourself in. But I can tell you this: it was nothing more and nothing worse that I once did — and it wrecked my whole reputation.

NORA: You? Do you expect me to believe that you ever acted bravely to save your wife's life?

KROGSTAD: Laws don't inquire into motives.

NORA: Then they must be very poor laws.

KROGSTAD: Poor or not — if I introduce this paper in court, you'll be judged according to law.

NORA: This I refuse to believe. A daughter hasn't a right to protect her dying father from anxiety and care? A wife hasn't a right to save her husband's life? I don't know much about laws, but I'm sure that somewhere in the books these things are allowed. And you don't know anything about it — you who practice the law? You must be an awful lawyer, Mr. Krogstad.

KROGSTAD: Could be. But business — the kind of business we two are mixed up in — don't you think I know about that? All right. Do what you want now. But I'm telling you *this*: if I get shoved down a second time, you're going to keep me company. (*He bows and goes out through the hall.*)

NORA (*pensive for a moment, then tossing her head*):   Oh, really! Trying to frighten me! I'm not so silly as all that. (*Begins gathering up the children's clothes, but soon stops.*) But — ? No, but that's impossible! I did it out of love.

THE CHILDREN (*in the doorway, left*):   Mama, that strange man's gone out the door.

NORA: Yes, yes, I know it. But don't tell anyone about the strange man. Do you hear? Not even Papa!

THE CHILDREN: No, Mama. But now will you play again?

NORA: No, not now.

THE CHILDREN: Oh, but Mama, you promised.

NORA: Yes, but I can't now. Go inside; I have too much to do. Go in, go in, my sweet darlings. (*She herds them gently back in the room and shuts the door after them. Settling on the sofa, she takes up a piece of embroidery and makes some stitches, but soon stops abruptly.*) No! (*Throws the work aside, rises, goes to the hall door and calls out.*) Helene! Let me have the tree in here. (*Goes to the table, left, opens the table drawer, and stops again.*) No, but that's utterly impossible!

MAID (*with the Christmas tree*):   Where should I put it, ma'am?

NORA: There. The middle of the floor.

MAID: Should I bring anything else?

NORA: No, thanks. I have what I need.

The Maid, who has set the tree down, goes out.

NORA *(absorbed in trimming the tree)*: Candles here—and flowers here. That terrible creature! Talk, talk, talk! There's nothing to it at all. The tree's going to be lovely. I'll do anything to please you, Torvald. I'll sing for you, dance for you—

Helmer comes in from the hall, with a sheaf of papers under his arm.

NORA: Oh! You're back so soon?

HELMER: Yes. Has anyone been here?

NORA: Here? No.

HELMER: That's odd. I saw Krogstad leaving the front door.

NORA: So? Oh yes, that's true. Krogstad was here a moment.

HELMER: Nora, I can see by your face that he's been here, begging you to put in a good word for him.

NORA: Yes.

HELMER: And it was supposed to seem like your own idea? You were to hide it from me that he'd been here. He asked you that, too, didn't he?

NORA: Yes, Torvald, but—

HELMER: Nora, Nora, and you could fall for that? Talk with that sort of person and promise him anything? And then in the bargain, tell me an untruth?

NORA: An untruth—?

HELMER: Didn't you say that no one had been here? *(Wagging his finger.)* My little songbird must never do that again. A songbird needs a clean beak to warble with. No false notes. *(Putting his arm about her waist.)* That's the way it should be, isn't it? Yes, I'm sure of it. *(Releasing her.)* And so, enough of that. *(Sitting by the stove.)* Ah, how snug and cozy it is here. *(Leafing among his papers.)*

NORA *(busy with the tree, after a short pause)*: Torvald!

HELMER: Yes.

NORA: I'm so much looking forward to the Stenborgs' costume party, day after tomorrow.

HELMER: And I can't wait to see what you'll surprise me with.

NORA: Oh, that stupid business!

HELMER: What?

NORA: I can't find anything that's right. Everything seems so ridiculous, so inane.

HELMER: So my little Nora's come to *that* recognition?

NORA *(going behind his chair, her arms resting on its back)*: Are you very busy, Torvald?

HELMER: Oh—

NORA: What papers are those?

HELMER: Bank matters.

NORA: Already?

HELMER: I've gotten full authority from the retiring management to make all necessary changes in personnel and procedure. I'll need Christmas week for that. I want to have everything in order by New Year's.

NORA: So that was the reason this poor Krogstad—

HELMER: Hm.

NORA (*still leaning on the chair and slowly stroking the nape of his neck*): If you weren't so very busy, I would have asked you an enormous favor, Torvald.

HELMER: Let's hear. What is it?

NORA: You know, there isn't anyone who has your good taste—and I want so much to look well at the costume party. Torvald, couldn't you take over and decide what I should be and plan my costume?

HELMER: Ah, is my stubborn little creature calling for a lifeguard?

NORA: Yes, Torvald, I can't get anywhere without your help.

HELMER: All right—I'll think it over. We'll hit on something.

NORA: Oh, how sweet of you. (*Goes to the tree again. Pause.*) Aren't the red flowers pretty—? But tell me, was it really such a crime that this Krogstad committed?

HELMER: Forgery. Do you have any idea what that means?

NORA: Couldn't he have done it out of need?

HELMER: Yes, or thoughtlessness, like so many others. I'm not so heartless that I'd condemn a man categorically for just one mistake.

NORA: No, of course not, Torvald!

HELMER: Plenty of men have redeemed themselves by openly confessing their crimes and taking their punishment.

NORA: Punishment—?

HELMER: But now Krogstad didn't go that way. He got himself out by sharp practices, and that's the real cause of his moral breakdown.

NORA: Do you really think that would—?

HELMER: Just imagine how a man with that sort of guilt in him has to lie and cheat and deceive on all sides, has to wear a mask even with the nearest and dearest he has, even with his own wife and children. And with the children, Nora—that's where it's most horrible.

NORA: Why?

HELMER: Because that kind of atmosphere of lies infects the whole life of a home. Every breath the children take in is filled with the germs of something degenerate.

NORA (*coming closer behind him*): Are you sure of that?

HELMER: Oh, I've seen it often enough as a lawyer. Almost everyone who goes bad early in life has a mother who's a chronic liar.

NORA: Why just—the mother?

HELMER: It's usually the mother's influence that's dominant, but the father's works in the same way, of course. Every lawyer is quite familiar with it. And still this Krogstad's been going home year in, year out, poisoning his own children with lies and pretense; that's why I call him morally lost. (*Reaching his hands out toward her.)* So my sweet little Nora must promise me never to plead his cause. Your hand on it. Come, come, what's this? Give me your hand. There, now. All settled. I can tell you it'd be impossible for me to work alongside of him. I literally feel physically revolted when I'm anywhere near such a person.

NORA *(withdraws her hand and goes to the other side of the Christmas tree):* How hot it is here! And I've got so much to do.

HELMER *(getting up and gathering his papers):* Yes, and I have to think about getting some of these read through before dinner. I'll think about your costume, too. And something to hang on the tree in gilt paper, I may even see about that. *(Putting his hand on her head.)* Oh you, my darling little songbird. *(He goes into his study and closes the door after him.)*

NORA *(softly, after a silence):* Oh, really! It isn't so. It's impossible. It must be impossible.

ANNE-MARIE *(in the doorway, left):* The children are begging so hard to come in to Mama.

NORA: No, no, no, don't let them in to me! You stay with them, Anne-Marie.

ANNE-MARIE: Of course, ma'am. *(Closes the door.)*

NORA *(pale with terror):* Hurt my children —! Poison my home? *(A moment's pause; then she tosses her head.)* That's not true. Never. Never in all the world.

ACT 2

Same room. Beside the piano the Christmas tree now stands stripped of ornament, burned-down candle stubs on its ragged branches. Nora's street clothes lie on the sofa. Nora, alone in the room, moves restlessly about; at last she stops at the sofa and picks up her coat.

NORA *(dropping the coat again):* Someone's coming! *(Goes toward the door, listens.)* No — there's no one. Of course — nobody's coming today, Christmas Day — or tomorrow, either. But maybe — *(Opens the door and looks out.)* No, nothing in the mailbox. Quite empty. *(Coming forward.)* What nonsense! He won't do anything serious. Nothing terrible could happen. It's impossible. Why, I have three small children.

Anne-Marie, with a large carton, comes in from the room to the left.

ANNE-MARIE: Well, at last I found the box with the masquerade clothes.

NORA: Thanks. Put it on the table.

ANNE-MARIE *(does so):* But they're all pretty much of a mess.

NORA: Ahh! I'd love to rip them in a million pieces!

ANNE-MARIE: Oh, mercy, they can be fixed right up. Just a little patience.

NORA: Yes, I'll go get Mrs. Linde to help me.

ANNE-MARIE: Out again now? In this nasty weather? Miss Nora will catch cold — get sick.

NORA: Oh, worse things could happen. How are the children?

ANNE-MARIE: The poor mites are playing with their Christmas presents, but —

NORA: Do they ask for me much?

ANNE-MARIE: They're so used to having Mama around, you know.

NORA: Yes, but Anne-Marie, I *can't* be together with them as much as I was.

ANNE-MARIE: Well, small children get used to anything.

NORA: You think so? Do you think they'd forget their mother if she was gone for good?

ANNE-MARIE: Oh, mercy—gone for good!

NORA: Wait, tell me, Anne-Marie—I've wondered so often—how could you ever have the heart to give your child over to strangers?

ANNE-MARIE: But I had to, you know, to become little Nora's nurse.

NORA: Yes, but how could you *do* it?

ANNE-MARIE: When I could get such a good place? A girl who's poor and who's gotten in trouble is glad enough for that. Because that slippery fish, he didn't do a thing for me, you know.

NORA: But your daughter's surely forgotten you.

ANNE-MARIE: Oh, she certainly has not. She's written to me, both when she was confirmed and when she was married.

NORA *(clasping her about the neck)*:   You old Anne-Marie, you were a good mother for me when I was little.

ANNE-MARIE: Poor little Nora, with no other mother but me.

NORA: And if the babies didn't have one, then I know that you'd—What silly talk! *(Opening the carton.)* Go in to them. Now I'll have to—Tomorrow you can see how lovely I'll look.

ANNE-MARIE: Oh, there won't be anyone at the party as lovely as Miss Nora. *(She goes off into the room, left.)*

NORA *(begins unpacking the box, but soon throws it aside)*:   Oh, if I dared to go out. If only nobody would come. If only nothing would happen here while I'm out. What craziness—nobody's coming. Just don't think. This muff—needs a brushing. Beautiful gloves, beautiful gloves. Let it go. Let it go! One, two, three, four, five, six—*(With a cry.)* Oh, there they are! *(Poises to move toward the door, but remains irresolutely standing. Mrs. Linde enters from the hall, where she has removed her street clothes.)*

NORA: Oh, it's you, Kristine. There's no one else out there? How good that you've come.

MRS. LINDE: I hear you were up asking for me.

NORA: Yes, I just stopped by. There's something you really can help me with. Let's get settled on the sofa. Look, there's going to be a costume party tomorrow evening at the Stenborgs' right above us, and now Torvald wants me to go as a Neapolitan peasant girl and dance the tarantella that I learned in Capri.

MRS. LINDE: Really, are you giving a whole performance?

NORA: Torvald says yes, I should. See, here's the dress. Torvald had it made for me down there; but now it's all so tattered that I just don't know—

MRS. LINDE: Oh, we'll fix that up in no time. It's nothing more than the trimmings—they're a bit loose here and there. Needle and thread? Good, now we have what we need.

NORA: Oh, how sweet of you!

MRS. LINDE *(sewing):*   So you'll be in disguise tomorrow, Nora. You know what? I'll stop by then for a moment and have a look at you all dressed up. But listen, I've absolutely forgotten to thank you for that pleasant evening yesterday.

NORA *(getting up and walking about):*   I don't think it was as pleasant as usual yesterday. You should have come to town a bit sooner, Kristine — Yes, Torvald really knows how to give a home elegance and charm.

MRS. LINDE: And you do, too, if you ask me. You're not your father's daughter for nothing. But tell me, is Dr. Rank always so down in the mouth as yesterday?

NORA: No, that was quite an exception. But he goes around critically ill all the time — tuberculosis of the spine, poor man. You know, his father was a disgusting thing who kept mistresses and so on — and that's why the son's been sickly from birth.

MRS. LINDE *(lets her sewing fall to her lap):*   But my dearest Nora, how do you know about such things?

NORA *(walking more jauntily):*   Hmp! When you've had three children, then you've had a few visits from — from women who know something of medicine, and they tell you this and that.

MRS. LINDE *(resumes sewing; a short pause):*   Does Dr. Rank come here every day?

NORA: Every blessed day. He's Torvald's best friend from childhood, and *my* good friend, too. Dr. Rank almost belongs to this house.

MRS. LINDE: But tell me — is he quite sincere? I mean, doesn't he rather enjoy flattering people?

NORA: Just the opposite. Why do you think that?

MRS. LINDE: When you introduced us yesterday, he was proclaiming that he'd often heard my name in this house; but later I noticed that your husband hadn't the slightest idea who I really was. So how could Dr. Rank — ?

NORA: But it's all true, Kristine. You see, Torvald loves me beyond words, and, as he puts it, he'd like to keep me all to himself. For a long time he'd almost be jealous if I even mentioned any of my old friends back home. So of course I dropped that. But with Dr. Rank I talk a lot about such things, because he likes hearing about them.

MRS. LINDE: Now listen, Nora; in many ways you're still like a child. I'm a good deal older than you, with a little more experience. I'll tell you something: you ought to put an end to all this with Dr. Rank.

NORA: What should I put an end to?

MRS. LINDE: Both parts of it, I think. Yesterday you said something about a rich admirer who'd provide you with money —

NORA: Yes, one who doesn't exist — worse luck. So?

MRS. LINDE: Is Dr. Rank well off?

NORA: Yes, he is.

MRS. LINDE: With no dependents?

NORA: No, no one. But —

MRS. LINDE: And he's over here every day?

NORA: Yes, I told you that.

MRS. LINDE: How can a man of such refinement be so grasping?

NORA: I don't follow you at all.

MRS. LINDE: Now don't try to hide it, Nora. You think I can't guess who loaned you the forty-eight hundred crowns?

NORA: Are you out of your mind? How could you think such a thing! A friend of ours, who comes here every single day. What an intolerable situation that would have been!

MRS. LINDE: Then it really wasn't him.

NORA: No, absolutely not. It never even crossed my mind for a moment—And he had nothing to lend in those days; his inheritance came later.

MRS. LINDE: Well, I think that was a stroke of luck for you, Nora dear.

NORA: No, it never would have occurred to me to ask Dr. Rank—Still, I'm quite sure that if I had asked him—

MRS. LINDE: Which you won't, of course.

NORA: No, of course not. I can't see that I'd ever need to. But I'm quite positive that if I talked to Dr. Rank—

MRS. LINDE: Behind your husband's back?

NORA: I've got to clear up this other thing; *that's* also behind his back. I've *got* to clear it all up.

MRS. LINDE: Yes, I was saying that yesterday, but—

NORA (*pacing up and down*): A man handles these problems so much better than a woman—

MRS. LINDE: One's husband does, yes.

NORA: Nonsense. (*Stopping.*) When you pay everything you owe, then you get your note back, right?

MRS. LINDE: Yes, naturally.

NORA: And can rip it into a million pieces and burn it up—that filthy scrap of paper!

MRS. LINDE (*looking hard at her, laying her sewing aside, and rising slowly*): Nora, you're hiding something from me.

NORA: You can see it in my face?

MRS. LINDE: Something's happened to you since yesterday morning. Nora, what is it?

NORA (*hurrying toward her*): Kristine! (*Listening.*) Shh! Torvald's home. Look, go in with the children a while. Torvald can't bear all this snipping and stitching. Let Anne-Marie help you.

MRS. LINDE (*gathering up some of the things*): All right, but I'm not leaving here until we've talked this out. (*She disappears into the room, left, as Torvald enters from the hall.*)

NORA: Oh, how I've been waiting for you, Torvald dear.

HELMER: Was that the dressmaker?

NORA: No, that was Kristine. She's helping me fix up my costume. You know, it's going to be quite attractive.

HELMER: Yes, wasn't that a bright idea I had?

NORA: Brilliant! But then wasn't I good as well to give in to you?

HELMER: Good—because you give in to your husband's judgment? All right, you little goose, I know you didn't mean it like that. But I won't disturb you. You'll want to have a fitting, I suppose.

NORA: And you'll be working?

HELMER: Yes. *(Indicating a bundle of papers.)* See. I've been down to the bank. *(Starts toward his study.)*

NORA: Torvald.

HELMER *(stops)*:   Yes.

NORA: If your little squirrel begged you, with all her heart and soul, for something—?

HELMER: What's that?

NORA: Then would you do it?

HELMER: First, naturally, I'd have to know what it was.

NORA: Your squirrel would scamper about and do tricks, if you'd only be sweet and give in.

HELMER: Out with it.

NORA: Your lark would be singing high and low in every room—

HELMER: Come on, she does that anyway.

NORA: I'd be a wood nymph and dance for you in the moonlight.

HELMER: Nora—don't tell me it's that same business from this morning?

NORA *(coming closer)*:   Yes, Torvald, I beg you, please!

HELMER: And you actually have the nerve to drag that up again?

NORA: Yes, yes, you've got to give in to me; you *have* to let Krogstad keep his job in the bank.

HELMER: My dear Nora, I've slated his job for Mrs. Linde.

NORA: That's awfully kind of you. But you could just fire another clerk instead of Krogstad.

HELMER: This is the most incredible stubbornness! Because you go and give an impulsive promise to speak up for him, I'm expected to—

NORA: That's not the reason, Torvald. It's for your own sake. That man does writing for the worst papers; you said it yourself. He could do you any amount of harm. I'm scared to death of him—

HELMER: Ah, I understand. It's the old memories haunting you.

NORA: What do you mean by that?

HELMER: Of course, you're thinking about your father.

NORA: Yes, all right. Just remember how those nasty gossips wrote in the papers about Papa and slandered him so cruelly. I think they'd have had him dismissed if the department hadn't sent you up to investigate, and if you hadn't been so kind and open-minded toward him.

HELMER: My dear Nora, there's a notable difference between your father and me. Your father's official career was hardly above reproach. But mine is; and I hope it'll stay that way as long as I hold my position.

NORA: Oh, who can ever tell what vicious minds can invent? We could be so snug and happy now in our quiet, carefree home—you and I and the children, Torvald! That's why I'm pleading with you so—

HELMER: And just by pleading for him you make it impossible for me to keep him on. It's already known at the bank that I'm firing Krogstad. What if it's rumored around now that the new bank manager was vetoed by his wife —

NORA: Yes, what then — ?

HELMER: Oh yes — as long as our little bundle of stubbornness gets her way —! I should go and make myself ridiculous in front of the whole office — give people the idea I can be swayed by all kinds of outside pressure. Oh, you can bet I'd feel the effects of that soon enough! Besides — there's something that rules Krogstad right out at the bank as long as I'm the manager.

NORA: What's that?

HELMER: His moral failings I could maybe overlook if I had to —

NORA: Yes, Torvald, why not?

HELMER: And I hear he's quite efficient on the job. But he was a crony of mine back in my teens — one of those rash friendships that crop up again and again to embarrass you later in life. Well, I might as well say it straight out: we're on a first-name basis. And that tactless fool makes no effort at all to hide it in front of others. Quite the contrary — he thinks that entitles him to take a familiar air around me, and so every other second he comes booming out with his "Yes, Torvald!" and "Sure thing, Torvald!" I tell you, it's been excruciating for me. He's out to make my place in the bank unbearable.

NORA: Torvald, you can't be serious about all this.

HELMER: Oh no? Why not?

NORA: Because these are such petty considerations.

HELMER: What are you saying? Petty? You think I'm petty!

NORA: No, just the opposite, Torvald dear. That's exactly why —

HELMER: Never mind. You call my motives petty; then I might as well be just that. Petty! All right! We'll put a stop to this for good. (*Goes to the hall door and calls.*) Helene!

NORA: What do you want?

HELMER (*searching among his papers*):   A decision. (*The maid comes in.*) Look here; take this letter; go out with it at once. Get hold of a messenger and have him deliver it. Quick now. It's already addressed. Wait, here's some money.

MAID: Yes, sir. (*She leaves with the letter.*)

HELMER (*straightening his papers*):   There, now, little Miss Willful.

NORA (*breathlessly*):   Torvald, what was that letter?

HELMER: Krogstad's notice.

NORA: Call it back, Torvald! There's still time. Oh, Torvald, call it back! Do it for my sake — for your sake, for the children's sake! Do you hear, Torvald; do it! You don't know how this can harm us.

HELMER: Too late.

NORA: Yes, too late.

HELMER: Nora dear, I can forgive you this panic, even though basically you're insulting me. Yes, you are! Or isn't it an insult to think that I should be afraid of a courtroom hack's revenge? But I forgive you anyway, because this shows so beautifully how much you love me. (*Takes her in his arms.*) This is the way it should be, my darling Nora. Whatever comes, you'll see; when it really counts, I have strength and courage enough as a man to take on the whole weight myself.

NORA *(terrified)*:   What do you mean by that?

HELMER: The whole weight, I said.

NORA *(resolutely)*:   No, never in all the world.

HELMER: Good. So we'll share it, Nora, as man and wife. That's as it should be. *(Fondling her.)* Are you happy now? There, there, there—not these frightened dove's eyes. It's nothing at all but empty fantasies—Now you should run through your tarantella and practice your tambourine. I'll go to the inner office and shut both doors, so I won't hear a thing; you can make all the noise you like. *(Turning in the doorway.)* And when Rank comes, just tell him where he can find me. *(He nods to her and goes with his papers into the study, closing the door.)*

NORA *(standing as though rooted, dazed with fright, in a whisper)*:   He really could do it. He will do it. He'll do it in spite of everything. No, not that, never, never! Anything but that! Escape! A way out—*(The doorbell rings.)* Dr. Rank! Anything but that! *Anything*, whatever it is! *(Her hands pass over her face, smoothing it; she pulls herself together, goes over and opens the hall door. Dr. Rank stands outside, hanging his fur coat up. During the following scene, it begins getting dark.)*

NORA: Hello, Dr. Rank. I recognized your ring. But you mustn't go in to Torvald yet; I believe he's working.

RANK: And you?

NORA: For you, I always have an hour to spare—you know that. *(He has entered, and she shuts the door after him.)*

RANK: Many thanks. I'll make use of these hours while I can.

NORA: What do you mean by that? While you can?

RANK: Does that disturb you?

NORA: Well, it's such an odd phrase. Is anything going to happen?

RANK: What's going to happen is what I've been expecting so long—but I honestly didn't think it would come so soon.

NORA *(gripping his arm)*:   What is it you've found out? Dr. Rank, you have to tell me!

RANK *(sitting by the stove)*:   It's all over for me. There's nothing to be done about it.

NORA *(breathing easier)*:   Is it you—then—?

RANK: Who else? There's no point in lying to one's self. I'm the most miserable of all my patients, Mrs. Helmer. These past few days I've been auditing my internal accounts. Bankrupt! Within a month I'll probably be laid out and rotting in the churchyard.

NORA: Oh, what a horrible thing to say.

RANK: The thing itself is horrible. But the worst of it is all the other horror before it's over. There's only one final examination left; when I'm finished with that, I'll know about when my disintegration will begin. There's something I want to say. Helmer with his sensitivity has such a sharp distaste for anything ugly. I don't want him near my sickroom.

NORA: Oh, but Dr. Rank—

RANK: I won't have him in there. Under no condition. I'll lock my door to him—As soon as I'm completely sure of the worst, I'll send you my calling card marked with a black cross, and you'll know then the wreck has started to come apart.

NORA: No, today you're completely unreasonable. And I wanted you so much to be in a really good humor.

RANK: With death up my sleeve? And then to suffer this way for somebody else's sins. Is there any justice in that? And in every single family, in some way or another, this inevitable retribution of nature goes on—

NORA *(her hands pressed over her ears):*   Oh, stuff! Cheer up! Please—be gay!

RANK: Yes, I'd just as soon laugh at it all. My poor, innocent spine, serving time for my father's gay army days.

NORA *(by the table, left):*   He was so infatuated with asparagus tips and pâté de foie gras, wasn't that it?

RANK: Yes—and with truffles.

NORA: Truffles, yes. And then with oysters, I suppose?

RANK: Yes, tons of oysters, naturally.

NORA: And then the port and champagne to go with it. It's so sad that all these delectable things have to strike at our bones.

RANK: Especially when they strike at the unhappy bones that never shared in the fun.

NORA: Ah, that's the saddest of all.

RANK *(looks searchingly at her):*   Hm.

NORA *(after a moment):*   Why did you smile?

RANK: No, it was you who laughed.

NORA: No, it was you who smiled, Dr. Rank!

RANK *(getting up):*   You're even a bigger tease than I'd thought.

NORA: I'm full of wild ideas today.

RANK: That's obvious.

NORA *(putting both hands on his shoulders):*   Dear, dear Dr. Rank, you'll never die for Torvald and me.

RANK: Oh, that loss you'll easily get over. Those who go away are soon forgotten.

NORA *(looks fearfully at him):*   You believe that?

RANK: One makes new connections, and then—

NORA: Who makes new connections?

RANK: Both you and Torvald will when I'm gone. I'd say you're well under way already. What was that Mrs. Linde doing here last evening?

NORA: Oh, come—you can't be jealous of poor Kristine?

RANK: Oh yes, I am. She'll be my successor here in the house. When I'm down under, that woman will probably—

NORA: Shh! Not so loud. She's right in there.

RANK: Today as well. So you see.

NORA: Only to sew on my dress. Good gracious, how unreasonable you are. *(Sitting on the sofa.)* Be nice now, Dr. Rank. Tomorrow you'll see how beautifully I'll dance; and you can imagine then that I'm dancing only for you—yes, and of course for Torvald, too—that's understood. *(Takes various items out of the carton.)* Dr. Rank, sit over here and I'll show you something.

RANK *(sitting)*:   What's that?

NORA: Look here. Look.

RANK: Silk Stockings.

NORA: Flesh-colored. Aren't they lovely? Now it's so dark here, but tomorrow— No, no, no, just look at the feet. Oh well, you might as well look at the rest.

RANK: Hm—

NORA: Why do you look so critical? Don't you believe they'll fit?

RANK: I've never had any chance to form an opinion on that.

NORA *(glancing at him a moment)*:   Shame on you. *(Hits him lightly on the ear with the stockings.)* That's for you. *(Puts them away again.)*

RANK: And what other splendors am I going to see now?

NORA: Not the least bit more, because you've been naughty. *(She hums a little and rummages among her things.)*

RANK *(after a short silence)*:   When I sit here together with you like this, completely easy and open, then I don't know—I simply can't imagine—whatever would have become of me if I'd never come into this house.

NORA *(smiling)*:   Yes, I really think you feel completely at ease with us.

RANK *(more quietly, staring straight ahead)*:   And then to have to go away from it all—

NORA: Nonsense, you're not going away.

RANK *(his voice unchanged)*:   —and not even be able to leave some poor show of gratitude behind, scarcely a fleeting regret—no more than a vacant place that anyone can fill.

NORA: And if I asked you now for—? No—

RANK: For what?

NORA: For a great proof of your friendship—

RANK: Yes, yes?

NORA: No, I mean—for an exceptionally big favor—

RANK: Would you really, for once, make me so happy?

NORA: Oh, you haven't the vaguest idea what it is.

RANK: All right, then tell me.

NORA: No, but I can't, Dr. Rank—it's all out of reason. It's advice and help, too—and a favor—

RANK: So much the better. I can't fathom what you're hinting at. Just speak out. Don't you trust me?

NORA: Of course. More than anyone else. You're my best and truest friend, I'm sure. That's why I want to talk to you. All right, then, Dr. Rank: there's something you can help me prevent. You know how deeply, how inexpressibly dearly Torvald loves me; he'd never hesitate a second to give up his life for me.

RANK *(leaning close to her)*:   Nora—do you think he's the only one—

NORA *(with a slight start)*:   Who—?

RANK: Who'd gladly give up his life for you.

NORA *(heavily)*:   I see.

RANK: I swore to myself you should know this before I'm gone. I'll never find a better chance. Yes, Nora, now you know. And also you know now that you can trust me beyond anyone else.

NORA *(rising, natural and calm):*   Let me by.

RANK *(making room for her, but still sitting):*   Nora —

NORA *(in the hall doorway):*   Helene, bring the lamp in. *(Goes over to the stove.)* Ah, dear Dr. Rank, that was really mean of you.

RANK *(getting up):*   That I've loved you just as deeply as somebody else? Was *that* mean?

NORA: No, but that you came out and told me. That was quite unnecessary —

RANK: What do you mean? Have you known — ?

The Maid comes in with the lamp, sets it on the table, and goes out again.

RANK: Nora — Mrs. Helmer — I'm asking you: have you known about it?

NORA: Oh, how can I tell what I know or don't know? Really, I don't know what to say — Why did you have to be so clumsy, Dr. Rank! Everything was so good.

RANK: Well, in any case, you now have the knowledge that my body and soul are at your command. So won't you speak out?

NORA *(looking at him):*   After that?

RANK: Please, just let me know what it is.

NORA: You can't know anything now.

RANK: I have to. You mustn't punish me like this. Give me the chance to do whatever is humanly possible for you.

NORA: Now there's nothing you can do for me. Besides, actually, I don't need any help. You'll see — it's only my fantasies. That's what it is. Of course! *(Sits in the rocker, looks at him, and smiles.)* What a nice one you are, Dr. Rank. Aren't you a little bit ashamed, now that the lamp is here?

RANK: No, not exactly. But perhaps I'd better go — for good?

NORA: No, you certainly can't do that. You must come here just as you always have. You know Torvald can't do without you.

RANK: Yes, but *you?*

NORA: You know how much I enjoy it when you're here.

RANK: That's precisely what threw me off. You're a mystery to me. So many times I've felt you'd almost rather be with me than with Helmer.

NORA: Yes — you see, there are some people that one loves most and other people that one would almost prefer being with.

RANK: Yes, there's something to that.

NORA: When I was back home, of course I loved Papa most. But I always thought it was so much fun when I could sneak down to the maids' quarters, because they never tried to improve me, and it was always so amusing, the way they talked to each other.

RANK: Aha, so it's *their* place that I've filled.

NORA *(jumping up and going to him):*   Oh, dear, sweet Dr. Rank, that's not what I meant at all. But you can understand that with Torvald it's just the same as with Papa —

The Maid enters from the hall.

MAID: Ma'am—please! *(She whispers to Nora and hands her a calling card.)*

NORA *(glancing at the card):*   Ah! *(Slips it into her pocket.)*

RANK: Anything wrong?

NORA: No, no, not at all. It's only some—it's my new dress—

RANK: Really? But—there's your dress.

NORA: Oh, that. But this is another one—I ordered it—Torvald mustn't know—

RANK: Ah, now we have the big secret.

NORA: That's right. Just go in with him—he's back in the inner study. Keep him there as long as—

RANK: Don't worry. He won't get away. *(Goes into the study.)*

NORA *(to the Maid):*   And he's standing waiting in the kitchen?

MAID: Yes, he came up by the back stairs.

NORA: But didn't you tell him somebody was here?

MAID: Yes, but that didn't do any good.

NORA: He won't leave?

MAID: No, he won't go till he's talked with you, ma'am.

NORA: Let him come in, then—but quietly. Helene, don't breathe a word about this. It's a surprise for my husband.

MAID: Yes, yes, I understand—*(Goes out.)*

NORA: This horror—it's going to happen. No, no, no, it can't happen, it mustn't. *(She goes and bolts Helmer's door. The Maid opens the hall door for Krogstad and shuts it behind him. He is dressed for travel in a fur coat, boots, and a fur cap.)*

NORA *(going toward him):*   Talk softly. My husband's home.

KROGSTAD: Well, good for him.

NORA: What do you want?

KROGSTAD: Some information.

NORA: Hurry up, then. What is it?

KROGSTAD: You know, of course, that I got my notice.

NORA: I couldn't prevent it, Mr. Krogstad. I fought for you to the bitter end, but nothing worked.

KROGSTAD: Does your husband's love for you run so thin? He knows everything I can expose you to, and all the same he dares to—

NORA: How can you imagine he knows anything about this?

KROGSTAD: Ah, no—I can't imagine it either, now. It's not at all like my fine Torvald Helmer to have so much guts—

NORA: Mr. Krogstad, I demand respect for my husband!

KROGSTAD: Why, of course—all due respect. But since the lady's keeping it so carefully hidden, may I presume to ask if you're also a bit better informed than yesterday about what you've actually done?

NORA: More than you could ever teach me.

KROGSTAD: Yes, I *am* such an awful lawyer.

NORA: What is it you want from me?

KROGSTAD: Just a glimpse of how you are, Mrs. Helmer. I've been thinking about you all day long. A cashier, a night-court scribbler, a—well, a type like me also has a little of what they call a heart, you know.

NORA: Then show it. Think of my children.

KROGSTAD: Did you or your husband ever think of mine? But never mind. I simply wanted to tell you that you don't need to take this thing too seriously. For the present, I'm not proceeding with any action.

NORA: Oh no, really! Well—I knew that.

KROGSTAD: Everything can be settled in a friendly spirit. It doesn't have to get around town at all; it can stay just among us three.

NORA: My husband must never know anything of this.

KROGSTAD: How can you manage that? Perhaps you can pay me the balance?

NORA: No, not right now.

KROGSTAD: Or you know some way of raising the money in a day or two?

NORA: No way that I'm willing to use.

KROGSTAD: Well, it wouldn't have done you any good, anyway. If you stood in front of me with a fistful of bills, you still couldn't buy your signature back.

NORA: Then tell me what you're going to do with it.

KROGSTAD: I'll just hold onto it—keep it on file. There's no outsider who'll even get wind of it. So if you've been thinking of taking some desperate step—

NORA: I have.

KROGSTAD: Been thinking of running away from home—

NORA: I have!

KROGSTAD: Or even of something worse—

NORA: How could you guess that?

KROGSTAD: You can drop those thoughts.

NORA: How could you guess I was thinking of *that*?

KROGSTAD: Most of us think about *that* at first. I thought about it too, but I discovered I hadn't the courage—

NORA (lifelessly): I don't either.

KROGSTAD (relieved): That's true, you haven't the courage? You too?

NORA: I don't have it—I don't have it.

KROGSTAD: It would be terribly stupid, anyway. After that first storm at home blows out, why, then—I have here in my pocket a letter for your husband—

NORA: Telling everything?

KROGSTAD: As charitably as possible.

NORA (quickly): He mustn't ever get that letter. Tear it up. I'll find some way to get money.

KROGSTAD: Beg pardon, Mrs. Helmer, but I think I just told you—

NORA: Oh, I don't mean the money I owe you. Let me know how much you want from my husband, and I'll manage it.

KROGSTAD: I don't want money from your husband.

NORA: What do you want, then?

KROGSTAD: I'll tell you what. I want to recoup, Mrs. Helmer; I want to get on in the world—and there's where your husband can help me. For a year and a half I've kept myself clean of anything disreputable—all that time struggling with the worst conditions; but I was satisfied, working my way up step by step. Now I've been written right off, and I'm just not in the mood to come crawling back. I tell you, I want to move on. I want to get back in the bank—in a better position. Your husband can set up a job for me—

NORA: He'll never do that!

KROGSTAD: He'll do it. I know him. He won't dare breathe a word of protest. And once I'm in there together with him, you just wait and see! Inside of a year, I'll be the manager's right-hand man. It'll be Nils Krogstad, not Torvald Helmer, who runs the bank.

NORA: You'll never see the day!

KROGSTAD: Maybe you think you can—

NORA: I have the courage now—for *that*.

KROGSTAD: Oh, you don't scare me. A smart, spoiled lady like you—

NORA: You'll see; you'll see!

KROGSTAD: Under the ice, maybe? Down in the freezing coal-black water? There, till you float up in the spring, ugly, unrecognizable, with your hair falling out—

NORA: You don't frighten me.

KROGSTAD: Nor do you frighten me. One doesn't do these things, Mrs. Helmer. Besides, what good would it be? I'd still have him safe in my pocket.

NORA: Afterwards? When I'm no longer—?

KROGSTAD: Are you forgetting that *I'll* be in control then over your final reputation? *(Nora stands speechless, staring at him.)* Good; now I've warned you. Don't do anything stupid. When Helmer's read my letter, I'll be waiting for his reply. And bear in mind that it's your husband himself who's forced me back to my old ways. I'll never forgive him for that. Good-bye, Mrs. Helmer. *(He goes out through the hall.)*

NORA *(goes to the hall door, opens it a crack, and listens):* He's gone. Didn't leave the letter. Oh no, no, that's impossible too! *(Opening the door more and more.)* What's that? He's standing outside—not going downstairs. He's thinking it over? Maybe he'll—? (A letter falls in the mailbox; then Krogstad's footsteps are heard, dying away down a flight of stairs. Nora gives a muffled cry and runs over toward the sofa table. A short pause.)* In the mailbox. *(Slips warily over to the hall door.)* It's lying there. Torvald, Torvald—now we're lost!

MRS. LINDE *(entering with costume from the room, left):* There now, I can't see anything else to mend. Perhaps you'd like to try—

NORA *(in a hoarse whisper):* Kristine, come here.

MRS. LINDE *(tossing the dress on the sofa):* What's wrong? You look upset.

NORA: Come here. See that letter? *There!* Look—through the glass in the mailbox.

MRS. LINDE: Yes, yes, I see it.

NORA: That letter's from Krogstad—

MRS. LINDE: Nora—it's Krogstad who loaned you the money!

NORA: Yes, and now Torvald will find out everything.

MRS. LINDE: Believe me, Nora, it's best for both of you.

NORA: There's more you don't know. I forged a name.

MRS. LINDE: But for heaven's sake—?

NORA: I only want to tell you that, Kristine, so that you can be my witness.

MRS. LINDE: Witness? Why should I—?

NORA: If I should go out of my mind — it could easily happen —

MRS. LINDE: Nora!

NORA: Or anything else occurred — so I couldn't be present here —

MRS. LINDE: Nora, Nora, you aren't yourself at all!

NORA: And someone should try to take on the whole weight, all of the guilt, you follow me —

MRS. LINDE: Yes, of course, but why do you think — ?

NORA: Then you're the witness that it isn't true, Kristine. I'm very much myself; my mind right now is perfectly clear; and I'm telling you: nobody else has known about this; I alone did everything. Remember that.

MRS. LINDE: I will. But I don't understand all this.

NORA: Oh, how could you ever understand it? It's the miracle now that's going to take place.

MRS. LINDE: The miracle?

NORA: Yes, the miracle. But it's so awful, Kristine. It mustn't take place, not for anything in the world.

MRS. LINDE: I'm going right over and talk with Krogstad.

NORA: Don't go near him; he'll do you some terrible harm!

MRS. LINDE: There was a time once when he'd gladly have done anything for me.

NORA: He?

MRS. LINDE: Where does he live?

NORA: Oh, how do I know? Yes. *(Searches in her pocket.)* Here's his card. But the letter, the letter — !

HELMER *(from the study, knocking on the door):*   Nora!

NORA *(with a cry of fear):*   Oh! What is it? What do you want?

HELMER: Now, now, don't be so frightened. We're not coming in. You locked the door — are you trying on the dress?

NORA: Yes, I'm trying it. I'll look just beautiful, Torvald.

MRS. LINDE *(who has read the card):*   He's living right around the corner.

NORA: Yes, but what's the use? We're lost. The letter's in the box.

MRS. LINDE: And your husband has the key?

NORA: Yes, always.

MRS. LINDE: Krogstad can ask for his letter back unread; he can find some excuse —

NORA: But it's just this time that Torvald usually —

MRS. LINDE: Stall him. Keep him in there. I'll be back as quick as I can. *(She hurries out through the hall entrance.)*

NORA *(goes to Helmer's door, opens it, and peers in):*   Torvald!

HELMER *(from the inner study):*   Well — does one dare set foot in one's own living room at last? Come on, Rank, now we'll get a look — *(In the doorway.)* But what's this?

NORA: What, Torvald dear?

HELMER: Rank had me expecting some grand masquerade.

RANK *(in the doorway):*   That was my impression, but I must have been wrong.

NORA: No one can admire me in my splendor — not till tomorrow.

HELMER: But Nora dear, you look so exhausted. Have you practiced too hard?

NORA: No, I haven't practiced at all yet.

HELMER: You know, it's necessary —

NORA: Oh, it's absolutely necessary, Torvald. But I can't get anywhere without your help. I've forgotten the whole thing completely.

HELMER: Ah, we'll soon take care of that.

NORA: Yes, take care of me, Torvald, please! Promise me that? Oh, I'm so nervous. That big party — You must give up everything this evening for me. No business — don't even touch your pen. Yes? Dear Torvald, promise?

HELMER: It's a promise. Tonight I'm totally at your service — you little helpless thing. Hm — but first there's one thing I want to — (*Goes toward the hall door.*)

NORA: What are you looking for?

HELMER: Just to see if there's any mail.

NORA: No, no, don't do that, Torvald!

HELMER: Now what?

NORA: Torvald, please. There isn't any.

HELMER: Let me look, though. (*Starts out. Nora, at the piano, strikes the first notes of the tarantella. Helmer, at the door, stops.*) Aha!

NORA: I can't dance tomorrow if I don't practice with you.

HELMER (*going over to her*):   Nora dear, are you really so frightened?

NORA: Yes, so terribly frightened. Let me practice right now; there's still time before dinner. Oh, sit down and play for me, Torvald. Direct me. Teach me, the way you always have.

HELMER: Gladly, if it's what you want. (*Sits at the piano.*)

NORA (*snatches the tambourine up from the box, then a long, varicolored shawl, which she throws around herself, whereupon she springs forward and cries out*): Play for me now! Now I'll dance!

Helmer plays and Nora dances. Rank stands behind Helmer at the piano and looks on.

HELMER (*as he plays*):   Slower. Slow down.

NORA: Can't change it.

HELMER: Not so violent, Nora!

NORA: Has to be just like this.

HELMER (*stopping*):   No, no, that won't do at all.

NORA (*laughing and swinging her tambourine*):   Isn't that what I told you?

RANK: Let me play for her.

HELMER (*getting up*):   Yes, go on. I can teach her more easily then.

Rank sits at the piano and plays; Nora dances more and more wildly. Helmer has stationed himself by the stove and repeatedly gives her directions; she seems not to hear them; her hair loosens and falls over her shoulders; she does not notice, but goes on dancing. Mrs. Linde enters.

MRS. LINDE (*standing dumbfounded at the door*):   Ah —!

NORA (*still dancing*):   See what fun, Kristine!

HELMER: But Nora darling, you dance as if your life were at stake.

NORA: And it is.

HELMER: Rank, stop! This is pure madness. Stop it, I say!

Rank breaks off playing, and Nora halts abruptly.

HELMER *(going over to her):* I never would have believed it. You've forgotten everything I taught you.

NORA *(throwing away the tambourine):* You see for yourself.

HELMER: Well, there's certainly room for instruction here.

NORA: Yes, you see how important it is. You've got to teach me to the very last minute. Promise me that, Torvald?

HELMER: You can bet on it.

NORA: You mustn't, either today or tomorrow, think about anything else but me; you mustn't open any letters — or the mailbox —

HELMER: Ah, it's still the fear of that man —

NORA: Oh yes, yes, that too.

HELMER: Nora, it's written all over you — there's already a letter from him out there.

NORA: I don't know. I guess so. But you mustn't read such things now; there mustn't be anything ugly between us before it's all over.

RANK *(quietly to Helmer):* You shouldn't deny her.

HELMER *(putting his arms around her):* The child can have her way. But tomorrow night, after you've danced —

NORA: Then you'll be free.

MAID *(in the doorway, right):* Ma'am, dinner is served.

NORA: We'll be wanting champagne, Helene.

MAID: Very good, ma'am. *(Goes out.)*

HELMER: So — a regular banquet, hm?

NORA: Yes, a banquet — champagne till daybreak! *(Calling out.)* And some macaroons, Helene. Heaps of them — just this once.

HELMER *(taking her hands):* Now, now, now — no hysterics. Be my own little lark again.

NORA: Oh, I will soon enough. But go on in — and you, Dr. Rank. Kristine, help me put up my hair.

RANK *(whispering, as they go):* There's nothing wrong — really wrong, is there?

HELMER: Oh, of course not. It's nothing more than this childish anxiety I was telling you about. *(They go out, right.)*

NORA: Well?

MRS. LINDE: Left town.

NORA: I could see by your face.

MRS. LINDE: He'll be home tomorrow evening. I wrote him a note.

NORA: You shouldn't have. Don't try to stop anything now. After all, it's a wonderful joy, this waiting here for the miracle.

MRS. LINDE: What is it you're waiting for?

NORA: Oh, you can't understand that. Go in to them; I'll be along in a moment.

Mrs. Linde goes into the dining room. Nora stands a short while as if composing herself; then she looks at her watch.

NORA: Five. Seven hours to midnight. Twenty-four hours to the midnight after, and then the tarantella's done. Seven and twenty-four? Thirty-one hours to live.

HELMER *(in the doorway, right):*   What's become of the little lark?
NORA *(going toward him with open arms):*   Here's your lark!

ACT 3

Same scene. The table, with chairs around it, has been moved to the center of the room. A lamp on the table is lit. The hall door stands open. Dance music drifts down from the floor above. Mrs. Linde sits at the table, absently paging through a book, trying to read, but apparently unable to focus her thoughts. Once or twice she pauses, tensely listening for a sound at the outer entrance.

MRS. LINDE *(glancing at her watch):*   Not yet—and there's hardly any time left. If only he's not—*(Listening again.)* Ah, there he is. *(She goes out in the hall and cautiously opens the outer door. Quiet footsteps are heard on the stairs. She whispers:)* Come in. Nobody's here.

KROGSTAD *(in the doorway):*   I found a note from you at home. What's back of all this?

MRS. LINDE: I just *had* to talk to you.

KROGSTAD: Oh? And it just *had* to be here in this house?

MRS. LINDE: At my place it was impossible; my room hasn't a private entrance. Come in; we're all alone. The maid's asleep, and the Helmers are at the dance upstairs.

KROGSTAD *(entering the room):*   Well, well, the Helmers are dancing tonight? Really?

MRS. LINDE: Yes, why not?

KROGSTAD: How true—why not?

MRS. LINDE: All right, Krogstad, let's talk.

KROGSTAD: Do we two have anything more to talk about?

MRS. LINDE: We have a great deal to talk about.

KROGSTAD: I wouldn't have thought so.

MRS. LINDE: No, because you've never understood me, really.

KROGSTAD: Was there anything more to understand—except what's all too common in life? A calculating woman throws over a man the moment a better catch comes by.

MRS. LINDE: You think I'm so thoroughly calculating? You think I broke it off lightly?

KROGSTAD: Didn't you?

MRS. LINDE: Nils—is that what you really thought?

KROGSTAD: If you cared, then why did you write me the way you did?

MRS. LINDE: What else could I do? If I had to break off with you, then it was my job as well to root out everything you felt for me.

KROGSTAD *(wringing his hands):*   So that was it. And this—all this, simply for money!

MRS. LINDE: Don't forget I had a helpless mother and two small brothers. We couldn't wait for you, Nils; you had such a long road ahead of you then.

KROGSTAD: That may be; but you still hadn't the right to abandon me for some-body else's sake.

MRS. LINDE: Yes—I don't know. So many, many times I've asked myself if I did have that right.

KROGSTAD *(more softly)*:   When I lost you, it was as if all the solid ground dis-solved from under my feet. Look at me; I'm a half-drowned man now, hang-ing onto a wreck.

MRS. LINDE: Help may be near.

KROGSTAD: It was near—but then you came and blocked it off.

MRS. LINDE: Without my knowing it, Nils. Today for the first time I learned that it's you I'm replacing at the bank.

KROGSTAD: All right—I believe you. But now that you know, will you step aside?

MRS. LINDE: No, because that wouldn't benefit you in the slightest.

KROGSTAD: Not "benefit" me, hm! I'd step aside anyway.

MRS. LINDE: I've learned to be realistic. Life and hard, bitter necessity have taught me that.

KROGSTAD: And life's taught me never to trust fine phrases.

MRS. LINDE: Then life's taught you a very sound thing. But you do have to trust in actions, don't you?

KROGSTAD: What does that mean?

MRS. LINDE: You said you were hanging on like a half-drowned man to a wreck.

KROGSTAD: I've good reason to say that.

MRS. LINDE: I'm also like a half-drowned woman on a wreck. No one to suffer with; no one to care for.

KROGSTAD: You made your choice.

MRS. LINDE: There wasn't any choice then.

KROGSTAD: So—what of it?

MRS. LINDE: Nils, if only we two shipwrecked people could reach across to each other.

KROGSTAD: What are you saying?

MRS. LINDE: Two on one wreck are at least better off than each on his own.

KROGSTAD: Kristine!

MRS. LINDE: Why do you think I came into town?

KROGSTAD: Did you really have some thought of me?

MRS. LINDE: I have to work to go on living. All my born days, as long as I can remember, I've worked, and it's been my best and my only joy. But now I'm completely alone in the world; it frightens me to be so empty and lost. To work for yourself—there's no joy in that. Nils, give me something—some-one to work for.

KROGSTAD: I don't believe all this. It's just some hysterical feminine urge to go out and make a noble sacrifice.

MRS. LINDE: Have you ever found me to be hysterical?

KROGSTAD: Can you honestly mean this? Tell me—do you know everything about my past?

MRS. LINDE: Yes.

KROGSTAD: And you know what they think I'm worth around here.

MRS. LINDE: From what you were saying before, it would seem that with me you could have been another person.

KROGSTAD: I'm positive of that.

MRS. LINDE: Couldn't it happen still?

KROGSTAD: Kristine—you're saying this in all seriousness? Yes, you are! I can see it in you. And do you really have the courage, then—?

MRS. LINDE: I need to have someone to care for; and your children need a mother. We both need each other. Nils, I have faith that you're good at heart—I'll risk everything together with you.

KROGSTAD (*gripping her hands*): Kristine, thank you, thank you—Now I know I can win back a place in their eyes. Yes—but I forgot—

MRS. LINDE (*listening*): Shh! The tarantella. Go now! Go on!

KROGSTAD: Why? What is it?

MRS. LINDE: Hear the dance up there? When that's over, they'll be coming down.

KROGSTAD: Oh, then I'll go. But—it's all pointless. Of course, you don't know the move I made against the Helmers.

MRS. LINDE: Yes, Nils, I know.

KROGSTAD: And all the same, you have the courage to—?

MRS. LINDE: I know how far despair can drive a man like you.

KROGSTAD: Oh, if I only could take it all back.

MRS. LINDE: You easily could—your letter's still lying in the mailbox.

KROGSTAD: Are you sure of that?

MRS. LINDE: Positive. But—

KROGSTAD (*looks at her searchingly*): Is that the meaning of it, then? You'll save your friend at any price. Tell me straight out. Is that it?

MRS. LINDE: Nils—anyone who's sold herself for somebody else once isn't going to do it again.

KROGSTAD: I'll demand my letter back.

MRS. LINDE: No, no.

KROGSTAD: Yes, of course. I'll stay here till Helmer comes down; I'll tell him to give me my letter again—that it only involves my dismissal—that he shouldn't read it—

MRS. LINDE: No, Nils, don't call the letter back.

KROGSTAD: But wasn't that exactly why you wrote me to come here?

MRS. LINDE: Yes, in that first panic. But it's been a whole day and night since then, and in that time I've seen such incredible things in this house. Helmer's got to learn everything; this dreadful secret has to be aired; those two have to come to a full understanding; all these lies and evasions can't go on.

KROGSTAD: Well, then, if you want to chance it. But at least there's one thing I can do, and do right away—

MRS. LINDE (*listening*): Go now, go quick! The dance is over. We're not safe another second.

KROGSTAD: I'll wait for you downstairs.

MRS. LINDE: Yes, please do; take me home.

KROGSTAD: I can't believe it; I've never been so happy. (*He leaves by way of the outer door; the door between the room and the hall stays open.*)

MRS. LINDE (*straightening up a bit and getting together her street clothes*): How different now! How different! Someone to work for, to live for—a home to build. Well, it is worth the try! Oh, if they'd only come! (*Listening.*) Ah, there they are. Bundle up. (*She picks up her hat and coat. Nora's and Helmer's voices can be heard outside; a key turns in the lock, and Helmer brings Nora into the hall almost by force. She is wearing the Italian costume with a large black shawl about her; he has on evening dress, with a black domino open over it.*)

NORA (*struggling in the doorway*):   No, no, no, not inside! I'm going up again. I don't want to leave so soon.

HELMER: But Nora dear—

NORA: Oh, I beg you, please, Torvald. From the bottom of my heart, *please*— only an hour more!

HELMER: Not a single minute, Nora darling. You know our agreement. Come on, in we go; you'll catch cold out here. (*In spite of her resistance, he gently draws her into the room.*)

MRS. LINDE: Good evening.

NORA: Kristine!

HELMER: Why, Mrs. Linde—are you here so late?

MRS. LINDE: Yes, I'm sorry, but I did want to see Nora in costume.

NORA: Have you been sitting here, waiting for me?

MRS. LINDE: Yes. I didn't come early enough; you were all upstairs; and then I thought I really couldn't leave without seeing you.

HELMER (*removing Nora's shawl*):   Yes, take a good look. She's worth looking at, I can tell you that, Mrs. Linde. Isn't she lovely?

MRS. LINDE: Yes, I should say—

HELMER: A dream of loveliness, isn't she? That's what everyone thought at the party, too. But she's horribly stubborn—this sweet little thing. What's to be done with her? Can you imagine, I almost had to use force to pry her away.

NORA: Oh, Torvald, you're going to regret you didn't indulge me, even for just a half hour more.

HELMER: There, you see. She danced her tarantella and got a tumultuous hand—which was well earned, although the performance may have been a bit too naturalistic—I mean it rather overstepped the proprieties of art. But never mind—what's important is, she made a success, an overwhelming success. You think I could let her stay on after that and spoil the effect? Oh no; I took my lovely little Capri girl—my capricious little Capri girl, I should say—took her under my arm; one quick tour of the ballroom, a curtsy to every side, and then—as they say in novels—the beautiful vision disappeared. An exit should always be effective, Mrs. Linde, but that's what I can't get Nora to grasp. Phew, it's hot in here. (*Flings the domino on a chair and opens the door to his room.*) Why's it dark in here? Oh yes, of course. Excuse me. (*He goes in and lights a couple of candles.*)

NORA (*in a sharp, breathless whisper*):   So?

MRS. LINDE (*quietly*):   I talked with him.

NORA: And—?

MRS. LINDE: Nora—you must tell your husband everything.

NORA (*dully*): I knew it.

MRS. LINDE: You've got nothing to fear from Krogstad, but you have to speak out.

NORA: I won't tell.

MRS. LINDE: Then the letter will.

NORA: Thanks, Kristine. I know now what's to be done. Shh!

HELMER (*reentering*): Well, then, Mrs. Linde—have you admired her?

MRS. LINDE: Yes, and now I'll say good night.

HELMER: Oh, come, so soon? Is this yours, this knitting?

MRS. LINDE: Yes, thanks. I nearly forgot it.

HELMER: Do you knit, then?

MRS. LINDE: Oh yes.

HELMER: You know what? You should embroider instead.

MRS. LINDE: Really? Why?

HELMER: Yes, because it's a lot prettier. See here, one holds the embroidery so, in the left hand, and then one guides the needle with the right—so—in an easy, sweeping curve—right?

MRS. LINDE: Yes, I guess that's—

HELMER: But, on the other hand, knitting—it can never be anything but ugly. Look, see here, the arms tucked in, the knitting needles going up and down—there's something Chinese about it. Ah, that was really a glorious champagne they served.

MRS. LINDE: Yes, good night, Nora, and don't be stubborn anymore.

HELMER: Well put, Mrs. Linde!

MRS. LINDE: Good night, Mr. Helmer.

HELMER (*accompanying her to the door*): Good night, good night. I hope you get home all right. I'd be very happy to—but you don't have far to go. Good night, good night. (*She leaves. He shuts the door after her and returns.*) There, now, at last we got her out the door. She's a deadly bore, that creature.

NORA: Aren't you pretty tired, Torvald?

HELMER: No, not a bit.

NORA: You're not sleepy?

HELMER: Not at all. On the contrary, I'm feeling quite exhilarated. But you? Yes, you really look tired and sleepy.

NORA: Yes, I'm very tired. Soon now I'll sleep.

HELMER: See! You see! I was right all along that we shouldn't stay longer.

NORA: Whatever you do is always right.

HELMER (*kissing her brow*): Now my little lark talks sense. Say, did you notice what a time Rank was having tonight?

NORA: Oh, was he? I didn't get to speak with him.

HELMER: I scarcely did either, but it's a long time since I've seen him in such high spirits. (*Gazes at her a moment, then comes nearer her.*) Hm—it's marvelous, though, to be back home again—to be completely alone with you. Oh, you bewitchingly lovely young woman!

NORA: Torvald, don't look at me like that!

HELMER: Can't I look at my richest treasure? At all that beauty that's mine, mine alone — completely and utterly.

NORA (*moving around to the other side of the table*):   You mustn't talk to me that way tonight.

HELMER (*following her*):   The tarantella is still in your blood, I can see — and it makes you even more enticing. Listen. The guests are beginning to go. (*Dropping his voice.*) Nora — it'll soon be quiet through this whole house.

NORA: Yes, I hope so.

HELMER: You do, don't you, my love? Do you realize — when I'm out at a party like this with you — do you know why I talk to you so little, and keep such a distance away; just send you a stolen look now and then — you know why I do it? It's because I'm imagining then that you're my secret darling, my secret bride-to-be, and that no one suspects there's anything between us.

NORA: Yes, yes; oh, yes, I know you're always thinking of me.

HELMER: And then when we leave and I place the shawl over those fine young rounded shoulders — over that wonderful curving neck — then I pretend that you're my young bride, that we're just coming from the wedding, that for the first time I'm bringing you into my house — that for the first time I'm alone with you — completely alone with you, your trembling young beauty! All this evening I've longed for nothing but you. When I saw you turn and sway in the tarantella — my blood was pounding till I couldn't stand it — that's why I brought you down here so early —

NORA: Go away, Torvald! Leave me alone. I don't want all this.

HELMER: What do you mean? Nora, you're teasing me. You will, won't you? Aren't I your husband — ?

A knock at the outside door.

NORA (*startled*):   What's that?

HELMER (*going toward the hall*):   Who is it?

RANK (*outside*):   It's me. May I come in a moment?

HELMER (*with quiet irritation*):   Oh, what does he want now? (*Aloud.*) Hold on. (*Goes and opens the door.*) Oh, how nice that you didn't just pass us by!

RANK: I thought I heard your voice, and then I wanted so badly to have a look in. (*Lightly glancing about.*) Ah, me, these old familiar haunts. You have it snug and cozy in here, you two.

HELMER: You seemed to be having it pretty cozy upstairs, too.

RANK: Absolutely. Why shouldn't I? Why not take in everything in life? As much as you can, anyway, and as long as you can. The wine was superb —

HELMER: The champagne especially.

RANK: You noticed that too? It's amazing how much I could guzzle down.

NORA: Torvald also drank a lot of champagne this evening.

RANK: Oh?

NORA: Yes, and that always makes him so entertaining.

RANK: Well, why shouldn't one have a pleasant evening after a well-spent day?

HELMER: Well spent? I'm afraid I can't claim that.

RANK (*slapping him on the back*):   But I can, you see!

NORA: Dr. Rank, you must have done some scientific research today.

RANK: Quite so.

HELMER: Come now—little Nora talking about scientific research!

NORA: And can I congratulate you on the results?

RANK: Indeed you may.

NORA: Then they were good?

RANK: The best possible for both doctor and patient—certainty.

NORA (*quickly and searchingly*):   Certainty?

RANK: Complete certainty. So don't I owe myself a gay evening afterwards?

NORA: Yes, you're right, Dr. Rank.

HELMER: I'm with you—just so long as you don't have to suffer for it in the morning.

RANK: Well, one never gets something for nothing in life.

NORA: Dr. Rank—are you very fond of masquerade parties?

RANK: Yes, if there's a good array of odd disguises—

NORA: Tell me, what should we two go as at the next masquerade?

HELMER: You little featherhead—already thinking of the next!

RANK: We two? I'll tell you what: you must go as Charmed Life—

HELMER: Yes, but find a costume for *that*!

RANK: Your wife can appear just as she looks every day.

HELMER: That was nicely put. But don't you know what you're going to be?

RANK: Yes, Helmer, I've made up my mind.

HELMER: Well?

RANK: At the next masquerade I'm going to be invisible.

HELMER: That's a funny idea.

RANK: They say there's a hat—black, huge—have you never heard of the hat that makes you invisible? You put it on, and then no one on earth can see you.

HELMER (*suppressing a smile*):   Ah, of course.

RANK: But I'm quite forgetting what I came for. Helmer, give me a cigar, one of the dark Havanas.

HELMER: With the greatest pleasure. (*Holds out his case.*)

RANK: Thanks. (*Takes one and cuts off the tip.*)

NORA (*striking a match*):   Let me give you a light.

RANK: Thank you. (*She holds the match for him; he lights the cigar.*) And now good-bye.

HELMER: Good-bye, good-bye, old friend.

NORA: Sleep well, Doctor.

RANK: Thanks for that wish.

NORA: Wish me the same.

RANK: You? All right, if you like—Sleep well. And thanks for the light. (*He nods to them both and leaves.*)

HELMER (*his voice subdued*):   He's been drinking heavily.

NORA (*absently*):   Could be. (*Helmer takes his keys from his pocket and goes out in the hall.*) Torvald—what are you after?

HELMER: Got to empty the mailbox; it's nearly full. There won't be room for the morning papers.

NORA: Are you working tonight?

HELMER: You know I'm not. Why—what's this? Someone's been at the lock.

NORA: At the lock—?

HELMER: Yes, I'm positive. What do you suppose—? I can't imagine one of the maids—? Here's a broken hairpin. Nora, it's yours—

NORA *(quickly):*   Then it must be the children—

HELMER: You'd better break them of that. Hm, hm—well, opened it after all. *(Takes the contents out and calls into the kitchen.)* Helene! Helene, would you put out the lamp in the hall. *(He returns to the room shutting the hall door, then displays the handful of mail.)* Look how it's piled up. *(Sorting through them.)* Now what's this?

NORA *(at the window):*   The letter! Oh, Torvald, no!

HELMER: Two calling cards—from Rank.

NORA: From Dr. Rank?

HELMER *(examining them):*   "Dr. Rank, Consulting Physician." They were on top. He must have dropped them in as he left.

NORA: Is there anything on them?

HELMER: There's a black cross over the name. See? That's a gruesome notion. He could almost be announcing his own death.

NORA: That's just what he's doing.

HELMER: What! You've heard something? Something he's told you?

NORA: Yes. That when those cards came, he'd be taking his leave of us. He'll shut himself in now and die.

HELMER: Ah, my poor friend! Of course I knew he wouldn't be here much longer. But so soon—And then to hide himself away like a wounded animal.

NORA: If it has to happen, then it's best it happens in silence—don't you think so, Torvald?

HELMER *(pacing up and down):*   He'd grown right into our lives. I simply can't imagine him gone. He with his suffering and loneliness—like a dark cloud setting off our sunlit happiness. Well, maybe it's best this way. For him, at least. *(Standing still.)* And maybe for us too, Nora. Now we're thrown back on each other, completely. *(Embracing her.)* Oh you, my darling wife, how can I hold you close enough? You know what, Nora—time and again I've wished you were in some terrible danger, just so I could stake my life and soul and everything, for your sake.

NORA *(tearing herself away, her voice firm and decisive):*   Now you must read your mail, Torvald.

HELMER: No, no, not tonight. I want to stay with you, dearest.

NORA: With a dying friend on your mind?

HELMER: You're right. We've both had a shock. There's ugliness between us— these thoughts of death and corruption. We'll have to get free of them first. Until then—we'll stay apart.

NORA *(clinging about his neck):*   Torvald—good night! Good night!

HELMER (*kissing her on the cheek*):   Good night, little songbird. Sleep well, Nora. I'll be reading my mail now. (*He takes the letters into his room and shuts the door after him.*)

NORA (*with bewildered glances, groping about, seizing Helmer's domino, throwing it around her, and speaking in short, hoarse, broken whispers*):   Never see him again. Never, never. (*Putting her shawl over her head.*) Never see the children either—them, too. Never, never. Oh, the freezing black water! The depths—down—Oh, I wish it were over—He has it now; he's reading it— now. Oh no, no, not yet. Torvald, good-bye, you and the children—(*She starts for the hall; as she does, Helmer throws open his door and stands with an open letter in his hand.*)

HELMER: Nora!

NORA (*screams*):   Oh—!

HELMER: What is this? You know what's in this letter?

NORA: Yes, I know. Let me go! Let me out!

HELMER (*holding her back*):   Where are you going?

NORA (*struggling to break loose*):   You can't save me, Torvald!

HELMER (*slumping back*):   True! Then it's true what he writes? How horrible! No, no, it's impossible—it can't be true.

NORA: It *is* true. I've loved you more than all this world.

HELMER: Ah, none of your slippery tricks.

NORA (*taking one step toward him*):   Torvald—!

HELMER: What *is* this you've blundered into!

NORA: Just let me loose. You're not going to suffer for my sake. You're not going to take on my guilt.

HELMER: No more play-acting. (*Locks the hall door.*) You stay right here and give me a reckoning. You understand what you've done? Answer! You understand?

NORA (*looking squarely at him, her face hardening*):   Yes. I'm beginning to understand everything now.

HELMER (*striding about*):   Oh, what an awful awakening! In all these eight years—she who was my pride and joy—a hypocrite, a liar—worse, worse—a criminal! How infinitely disgusting it all is! The shame! (*Nora says nothing and goes on looking straight at him. He stops in front of her.*) I should have suspected something of the kind. I should have known. All your father's flimsy values—Be still! All your father's flimsy values have come out in you. No religion, no morals, no sense of duty—Oh, how I'm punished for letting him off! I did it for your sake, and you repay me like this.

NORA: Yes, like this.

HELMER: Now you've wrecked all my happiness—ruined my whole future. Oh, it's awful to think of. I'm in a cheap little grafter's hands; he can do anything he wants with me, ask for anything, play with me like a puppet—and I can't breathe a word. I'll be swept down miserably into the depths on account of a featherbrained woman.

NORA: When I'm gone from this world, you'll be free.

HELMER: Oh, quit posing. Your father had a mess of those speeches too. What good would that ever do me if you were gone from this world, as you say? Not the slightest. He can still make the whole thing known; and if he does, I could be falsely suspected as your accomplice. They might even think that I was behind it—that I put you up to it. And all that I can thank you for—you that I've coddled the whole of our marriage. Can you see now what you've done to me?

NORA *(icily calm):* Yes.

HELMER: It's so incredible, I just can't grasp it. But we'll have to patch up whatever we can. Take off the shawl. I said, take if off! I've got to appease him somehow or other. The thing has to be hushed up at any cost. And as for you and me, it's got to seem like everything between us is just as it was—to the outside world, that is. You'll go right on living in this house, of course. But you can't be allowed to bring up the children; I don't dare trust you with them—Oh, to have to say this to someone I've loved so much! Well, that's done with. From now on happiness doesn't matter; all that matters is saving the bits and pieces, the appearance—*(The doorbell rings. Helmer starts.)* What's that? And so late. Maybe the worst—? You think he'd—? Hide, Nora! Say you're sick. *(Nora remains standing motionless. Helmer goes and opens the door.)*

MAID *(half dressed, in the hall):* A letter for Mrs. Helmer.

HELMER: I'll take it. *(Snatches the letter and shuts the door.)* Yes, it's from him. You don't get it; I'm reading it myself.

NORA: Then read it.

HELMER *(by the lamp):* I hardly dare. We may be ruined, you and I. But—I've got to know. *(Rips open the letter, skims through a few lines, glances at an enclosure, then cries out joyfully.)* Nora! *(Nora looks inquiringly at him.)* Nora! Wait—better check it again—Yes, yes, it's true. I'm saved. Nora, I'm saved!

NORA: And I?

HELMER: You too, of course. We're both saved, both of us. Look. He's sent back your note. He says he's sorry and ashamed—that a happy development in his life—oh, who cares what he says! Nora, we're saved! No one can hurt you. Oh, Nora, Nora—but first, this ugliness all has to go. Let me see—*(Takes a look at the note.)* No, I don't want to see it; I want the whole thing to fade like a dream. *(Tears the note and both letters to pieces, throws them into the stove and watches them burn.)* There—now there's nothing left—He wrote that since Christmas Eve you—Oh, they must have been three terrible days for you, Nora.

NORA: I fought a hard fight.

HELMER: And suffered pain and saw no escape but—No, we're not going to dwell on anything unpleasant. We'll just be grateful and keep on repeating: it's over now, it's over! You hear me, Nora? You don't seem to realize—it's over. What's it mean—that frozen look? Oh, poor little Nora, I understand. You can't believe I've forgiven you. But I have, Nora; I swear I have. I know that what you did, you did out of love for me.

NORA: That's true.

HELMER: You loved me the way a wife ought to love her husband. It's simply the means that you couldn't judge. But you think I love you any the less for not knowing how to handle your affairs? No, no — just lean on me; I'll guide you and teach you. I wouldn't be a man if this feminine helplessness didn't make you twice as attractive to me. You mustn't mind those sharp words I said — that was all in the first confusion of thinking my world had collapsed. I've forgiven you, Nora; I swear I've forgiven you.

NORA: My thanks for your forgiveness. (*She goes out through the door, right.*)

HELMER: No, wait — (*Peers in.*) What are you doing in there?

NORA (*inside*):   Getting out of my costume.

HELMER (*by the open door*):   Yes, do that. Try to calm yourself and collect your thoughts again, my frightened little songbird. You can rest easy now; I've got wide wings to shelter you with. (*Walking about close by the door.*) How snug and nice our home is, Nora. You're safe here; I'll keep you like a hunted dove I've rescued out of a hawk's claws. I'll bring peace to your poor, shuddering heart. Gradually it'll happen, Nora; you'll see. Tomorrow all this will look different to you; then everything will be as it was. I won't have to go on repeating I forgive you; you'll feel it for yourself. How can you imagine I'd ever conceivably want to disown you — or even blame you in any way? Ah, you don't know a man's heart, Nora. For a man there's something indescribably sweet and satisfying in knowing he's forgiven his wife — and forgiven her out of a full and open heart. It's as if she belongs to him in two ways now: in a sense he's given her fresh into the world again, and she's become his wife and his child as well. From now on that's what you'll be to me — you little, bewildered, helpless thing. Don't be afraid of anything, Nora; just open your heart to me, and I'll be conscience and will to you both — (*Nora enters in her regular clothes.*) What's this? Not in bed? You've changed your dress?

NORA: Yes, Torvald, I've changed my dress.

HELMER: But why now, so late?

NORA: Tonight I'm not sleeping.

HELMER: But Nora dear —

NORA (*looking at her watch*):   It's still not so very late. Sit down, Torvald; we have a lot to talk over. (*She sits at one side of the table.*)

HELMER: Nora — what is this? That hard expression —

NORA: Sit down. This'll take some time. I have a lot to say.

HELMER (*sitting at the table directly opposite her*):   You worry me, Nora. And I don't understand you.

NORA: No, that's exactly it. You don't understand me. And I've never understood you either — until tonight. No, don't interrupt. You can just listen to what I say. We're closing out accounts, Torvald.

HELMER: How do you mean that?

NORA (*after a short pause*):   Doesn't anything strike you about our sitting here like this?

HELMER: What's that?

NORA: We've been married now eight years. Doesn't it occur to you that this is the first time we two, you and I, man and wife, have ever talked seriously together?

HELMER: What do you mean — seriously?

NORA: In eight whole years — longer even — right from our first acquaintance, we've never exchanged a serious word on any serious thing.

HELMER: You mean I should constantly go and involve you in problems you couldn't possibly help me with?

NORA: I'm not talking of problems. I'm saying that we've never sat down seriously together and tried to get to the bottom of anything.

HELMER: But dearest, what good would that ever do you?

NORA: That's the point right there: you've never understood me. I've been wronged greatly, Torvald — first by Papa, and then by you.

HELMER: What! By us — the two people who've loved you more than anyone else?

NORA *(shaking her head):*   You never loved me. You've thought it fun to be in love with me, that's all.

HELMER: Nora, what a thing to say!

NORA: Yes, it's true now, Torvald. When I lived at home with Papa, he told me all his opinions, so I had the same ones too; or if they were different I hid them, since he wouldn't have cared for that. He used to call me his doll-child, and he played with me the way I played with my dolls. Then I came into your house —

HELMER: How can you speak of our marriage like that?

NORA *(unperturbed):*   I mean, then I went from Papa's hands into yours. You arranged everything to your own taste, and so I got the same taste as you — or I pretended to; I can't remember. I guess a little of both, first one, then the other. Now when I look back, it seems as if I'd lived here like a beggar — just from hand to mouth. I've lived by doing tricks for you, Torvald. But that's the way you wanted it. It's a great sin what you and Papa did to me. You're to blame that nothing's become of me.

HELMER: Nora, how unfair and ungrateful you are! Haven't you been happy here?

NORA: No, never. I thought so — but I never have.

HELMER: Not — not happy!

NORA: No, only lighthearted. And you've always been so kind to me. But our home's been nothing but a playpen. I've been your doll-wife here, just as at home I was Papa's doll-child. And in turn the children have been my dolls. I thought it was fun when you played with me, just as they thought it fun when I played with them. That's been our marriage, Torvald.

HELMER: There's some truth in what you're saying — under all the raving exaggeration. But it'll all be different after this. Playtime's over; now for the schooling.

NORA: Whose schooling — mine or the children's?

HELMER: Both yours and the children's, dearest.

NORA: Oh, Torvald, you're not the man to teach me to be a good wife to you.

HELMER: And you can say that?

NORA: And I — how am I equipped to bring up children?

HELMER: Nora!

NORA: Didn't you say a moment ago that that was no job to trust me with?

HELMER: In a flare of temper! Why fasten on that?

NORA: Yes, but you were so very right. I'm not up to the job. There's another job I have to do first. I have to try to educate myself. You can't help me with that. I've got to do it alone. And that's why I'm leaving you now.

HELMER *(jumping up):*   What's that?

NORA: I have to stand completely alone, if I'm ever going to discover myself and the world out there. So I can't go on living with you.

HELMER: Nora, Nora!

NORA: I want to leave right away. Kristine should put me up for the night —

HELMER: You're insane! You've no right! I forbid you!

NORA: From here on, there's no use forbidding me anything. I'll take with me whatever is mine. I don't want a thing from you, either now or later.

HELMER: What kind of madness is this!

NORA: Tomorrow I'm going home — I mean, home where I came from. It'll be easier up there to find something to do.

HELMER: Oh, you blind, incompetent child!

NORA: I must learn to be competent, Torvald.

HELMER: Abandon your home, your husband, your children! And you're not even thinking what people will say.

NORA: I can't be concerned about that. I only know how essential this is.

HELMER: Oh, it's outrageous. So you'll run out like this on your most sacred vows.

NORA: What do you think are my most sacred vows?

HELMER: And I have to tell you that! Aren't they your duties to your husband and children?

NORA: I have other duties equally sacred.

HELMER: That isn't true. What duties are they?

NORA: Duties to myself.

HELMER: Before all else, you're a wife and mother.

NORA: I don't believe in that anymore. I believe that, before all else, I'm a human being, no less than you — or anyway, I ought to try to become one. I know the majority thinks you're right, Torvald, and plenty of books agree with you, too. But I can't go on believing what the majority says, or what's written in books. I have to think over these things myself and try to understand them.

HELMER: Why can't you understand your place in your own home? On a point like that, isn't there one everlasting guide you can turn to? Where's your religion?

NORA: Oh, Torvald, I'm really not sure what religion is.

HELMER: What — ?

NORA: I only know what the minister said when I was confirmed. He told me religion was this thing and that. When I get clear and away by myself, I'll go into that problem too. I'll see if what the minister said was right, or, in any case, if it's right for me.

HELMER: A young woman your age shouldn't talk like that. If religion can't move you, I can try to rouse your conscience. You do have some moral feeling? Or, tell me — has that gone too?

NORA: It's not easy to answer that, Torvald. I simply don't know. I'm all confused about these things. I just know I see them so differently from you. I find out, for one thing, that the law's not at all what I'd thought—but I can't get it through my head that the law is fair. A woman hasn't a right to protect her dying father or save her husband's life! I can't believe that.

HELMER: You talk like a child. You don't know anything of the world you live in.

NORA: No, I don't. But now I'll begin to learn for myself. I'll try to discover who's right, the world or I.

HELMER: Nora, you're sick; you've got a fever. I almost think you're out of your head.

NORA: I've never felt more clearheaded and sure in my life.

HELMER: And—clearheaded and sure—you're leaving your husband and children?

NORA: Yes.

HELMER: Then there's only one possible reason.

NORA: What?

HELMER: You no longer love me.

NORA: No. That's exactly it.

HELMER: Nora! You can't be serious!

NORA: Oh, this is so hard, Torvald—you've been so kind to me always. But I can't help it. I don't love you anymore.

HELMER (*struggling for composure*): Are you also clearheaded and sure about that?

NORA: Yes, completely. That's why I can't go on staying here.

HELMER: Can you tell me what I did to lose your love?

NORA: Yes, I can tell you. It was this evening when the miraculous thing didn't come—then I knew you weren't the man I'd imagined.

HELMER: Be more explicit; I don't follow you.

NORA: I've waited now so patiently eight long years—for, my Lord, I know miracles don't come every day. Then this crisis broke over me, and such a certainty filled me: *now* the miraculous event would occur. While Krogstad's letter was lying out there, I never for an instant dreamed that you could give in to his terms. I was so utterly sure you'd say to him: go on, tell your tale to the whole wide world. And when he'd done that—

HELMER: Yes, what then? When I'd delivered my own wife into shame and disgrace—

NORA: When he'd done that, I was so utterly sure that you'd step forward, take the blame on yourself and say: I am the guilty one.

HELMER: Nora—!

NORA: You're thinking I'd never accept such a sacrifice from you? No, of course not. But what good would my protests be against you? That was the miracle I was waiting for, in terror and hope. And to stave that off, I would have taken my life.

HELMER: I'd gladly work for you day and night, Nora—and take on pain and deprivation. But there's no one who gives up honor for love.

NORA: Millions of women have done just that.

HELMER: Oh, you think and talk like a silly child.

NORA: Perhaps. But you neither think nor talk like the man I could join myself to. When your big fright was over — and it wasn't from any threat against me, only for what might damage you — when all the danger was past, for you it was just as if nothing had happened. I was exactly the same, your little lark, your doll, that you'd have to handle with double care now that I'd turned out so brittle and frail. *(Gets up.)* Torvald — in that instant it dawned on me that for eight years I've been living here with a stranger, and that I've even conceived three children — oh, I can't stand the thought of it! I could tear myself to bits.

HELMER *(heavily):*   I see. There a gulf that's opened between us — that's clear. Oh, but Nora, can't we bridge it somehow?

NORA: The way I am now, I'm no wife for you.

HELMER: I have the strength to make myself over.

NORA: Maybe — if your doll gets taken away.

HELMER: But to part! To part from you! No, Nora no — I can't imagine it.

NORA *(going out, right):*   All the more reason why it has to be. *(She reenters with her coat and a small overnight bag, which she puts on a chair by the table.)*

HELMER: Nora, Nora, not now! Wait till tomorrow.

NORA: I can't spend the night in a strange man's room.

HELMER: But couldn't we live here like brother and sister —

NORA: You know very well how long that would last. *(Throws her shawl about her.)* Good-bye, Torvald. I won't look in on the children. I know they're in better hands than mine. The way I am now, I'm no use to them.

HELMER: But someday, Nora — someday — ?

NORA: How can I tell? I haven't the least idea what'll become of me.

HELMER: But you're my wife, now and wherever you go.

NORA: Listen, Torvald — I've heard that when a wife deserts her husband's house just as I'm doing, then the law frees him from all responsibility. In any case, I'm freeing you from being responsible. Don't feel yourself bound, any more than I will. There has to be absolute freedom for us both. Here, take your ring back. Give me mine.

HELMER: That too?

NORA: That too.

HELMER: There it is.

NORA: Good. Well, now it's all over. I'm putting the keys here. The maids know all about keeping up the house — better than I do. Tomorrow, after I've left town, Kristine will stop by to pack up everything that's mine from home. I'd like those things shipped up to me.

HELMER: Over! All over! Nora, won't you ever think about me?

NORA: I'm sure I'll think of you often, and about the children and the house here.

HELMER: May I write you?

NORA: No — never. You're not to do that.

HELMER: Oh, but let me send you —

NORA: Nothing. Nothing.

HELMER: Or help you if you need it.

NORA: No. I accept nothing from strangers.

HELMER: Nora—can I never be more than a stranger to you?

NORA *(picking up her overnight bag):*   Ah, Torvald—it would take the greatest miracle of all—

HELMER: Tell me the greatest miracle!

NORA: You and I both would have to transform ourselves to the point that—Oh, Torvald, I've stopped believing in miracles.

HELMER: But I'll believe. Tell me! Transform ourselves to the point that—?

NORA: That our living together could be a true marriage. *(She goes out down the hall.)*

HELMER *(sinks down on a chair by the door, face buried in his hands):*   Nora! Nora! *(Looking about and rising.)* Empty. She's gone. *(A sudden hope leaps in him.)* The greatest miracle—?

From below, the sound of a door slamming shut.   [1879]

THINKING ABOUT THE TEXT

1.   Critics disagree about the necessity for Nora's leaving. What would your advice to her be? One critic thinks she has to leave because Torvald is impossible. What do you think?

2.   Do you find credible the change in Nora's character from the first scene to the last? Do you know people who have transformed themselves?

3.   Is Torvald in love with Nora in the first act? Explain. Is Nora in love with him in the first act? What is your idea of love in a marriage?

4.   An early critic of the play claims that it is a comedy. Is this possible? How would you characterize it? Is it an optimistic or a pessimistic play? Is it tragic?

5.   A few critics think Nora will return. Do you think this is possible? Under what conditions would you counsel her to do so? Do you think the "door heard 'round the world" had a positive or negative effect on marriage?

HENRIETTA FRANCES LORD
From "The Life of Henrik Ibsen"

Henrietta Frances Lord was the first English translator of Ibsen's A Doll House. *The following excerpt is from the introductory essay to her 1882 translation, which she titled* Nora.

Some of the clearest light Ibsen has so far shed on marriage we get from *Nora.* The problem is set in its purest form; no unfavorable circumstances hinder the working out of marriage; nor does the temper of Nora or Helmer; both are well fitted for married life, and everything points to their being naturally suited to each other. The hindrance lies exclusively in the application of a false view of life, or—if some insist it once contained truth—a view that Western peoples have outlived. When Helmer said he would work night and day for his wife, his were no empty words. He had done it, he meant to do it; he had been faithfully working for eight years, and there is no sign that he meant to cease. His happiness lay in Nora's being unruffled. Nor would he dream of curtailing what *he* considers her wife's freedom, i.e., the happy play of her imagination. He would deprive her but of one thing—reality. How could he claim to be a "real man," he would say, if he gave it to her? And he so far succeeds in unfitting her for action, that when she takes upon herself to meddle in realities, she immediately commits a crime. He gives her everything but his confidence; not because he has anything to conceal, but because she is a woman. . . .

The idea in *Nora* is: the object of marriage is to make each human personality free. However incontrovertible this may be when laid down as an axiom, does that confer the power of giving it expression in real life, steering one's way among all the difficulties of deceit, inexperience, etc.? Doubtless not; but the poet's work tells us, until the relation between man and woman turns in this direction, the relation is not yet Love. This is the idea in *Nora*, freed from all side issues, and no other key will unlock it.   [1882]

CLEMENT SCOTT
Ibsen's Unlovely Creed

Clement Scott (1841–1904), the editor of the journal Theatre, *published "A Doll's House" in the July 1889 issue. This article was a lengthy attack on Ibsen's ten-year-old play.*

It is an unlovely, selfish creed—but let women hear it. Nora, when she finds her husband is not the ideal hero she imagined, determines to cap his egotism with her selfishness. It is to be an eye for an eye, a tooth for a tooth. Pardon she cannot grant, humiliation she will not recognise. The frivolous butterfly, the Swedish Frou-Frou, the spoiled plaything has mysteriously become an Ibsenite revivalist. There were no previous signs of her conversion, but she has exchanged playfulness for preaching. She, a loving, affectionate woman, forgets about the eight years' happy married life, forgets the nest of the little bird, forgets her duty, her very instinct as a mother, forgets the three innocent children who are asleep in the next room, forgets her responsibilities, and does a thing that one of the lower animals would not do. A cat or dog would tear any one who separated it from its offspring, but the socialistic Nora, the apostle of the new creed of humanity, leaves her children almost without a pang. She has determined to leave her home. . . .

It is all self, self, self! This is the ideal woman of the new creed; not a woman who is the fountain of love and forgiveness and charity, not the pattern woman we have admired in our mothers and our sisters, not the model of unselfishness and charity, but a mass of aggregate conceit and self-sufficiency, who leaves her home and deserts her friendless children because she has *herself* to look after. The "strange man" who is the father of her children has dared to misunderstand her; she will scorn his regrets and punish him. Why should the men have it all their own way, and why should women be bored with the love of their children when they have themselves to study? And so Nora goes out, delivers up her wedding-ring without a sigh, quits her children without a kiss, and bangs the door! And the husband cries, "A miracle! a miracle!" and well he may. It would be a miracle, if he could ever live again with so unnatural a creature.   [1889]

HERMANN J. WEIGAND
From *The Modern Ibsen*

Hermann J. Weigand (1892–1985) wrote one of the first full-length studies of Ibsen, The Modern Ibsen *(1925). To today's readers, Weigand's thesis that Ibsen wrote* A Doll House *as a comedy seems odd indeed. But in the 1920s, Weigand was a respected academic critic and his ideas were influential.*

If I have been successful in showing "A Doll's House" to be high comedy of the subtlest order up to this point, our vision will not be put to any particular strain to see the genius of comedy hovering over the scene of the settlement. If we see Torvald as neither a cad nor a villain, but as a worthy, honest citizen as citizens go, a careful provider, a doting husband, unimaginative, but scarcely a shade less so than the average male, self-complacent and addicted to heroic stage-play—a habit fostered by the uncritical adoration of his mate; if Nora is to us not the tragic heroine as which she is commonly pictured, but an irresistibly bewitching piece of femininity, an extravagant poet and romancer, utterly lacking in sense of fact, and endowed with a natural gift for play-acting which makes her instinctively dramatize her experiences:—how can the settlement fail of a fundamentally comic appeal? We can follow Nora's indictment of Torvald and conventional man-governed society with the most alert sympathy; we can be thrilled by her spirited gesture of emancipation; we can applaud her bravery; we can enjoy watching Torvald's bluffed expression turn gradually into a hangdog look of contrition as he winces under her trouncing and gets worsted in every phase of the argument: and we will be aware at the same time that Nora is enjoying the greatest moment of her life—the supreme thrill that is tantamount, in fact, to a fulfillment of her hunger for the miracle!

Not the least among the items contributing to the comedy is the fact that Nora scores with even the most questionable of her accusations, thanks to the dash of her unexpected invective. "You have never understood me," she charges. Nothing could be truer; but how was he to understand her, when she played the lark and the squirrel with such spontaneous zest? How was he to divine her capacity for devotion, when she delighted in acting the incorrigible spendthrift, when it amused her to make him believe that the money he gave her simply melted between her fingers, when she played a perpetual game of hide-and-seek—and played it so effectively because play-acting was second nature to her? Now she blames him for not having treated her as a serious, responsible person, whereas all her efforts had heretofore been bent on appearing charmingly irresponsible. Past master of the arts of feminine coquetry, she is fully persuaded that she has cultivated these little tricks only under the pressure of male egotism, as if they were not a fundamental part of her instinctive endowment. And she gravely distributes the blame for having made the desire to please the supreme rule of her conduct, between Torvald and her father. Incidentally, her charge that in all the years of their marriage they have never exchanged one serious word about serious things, is incorrect: she has quite forgotten how seriously Torvald lectured her on the subjects of forgery and lying less than three days ago. If what she means is rather that they have never discussed any of their domestic problems in the spirit of serious partnership, it would seem that she were at least as much to blame for this as Torvald. Similarly, when she claims that her tastes in all matters are nothing but a reflection of those of her husband, she is certainly deluding herself. She very cleverly inculcated the idea in Torvald that she was dependent on his counsel even in such matters as choosing a fancy dress costume; but to be convinced that it is in reality her taste which is reflected in the cozy interior of their flat, scarcely requires so direct a hint as her chatter in the first scene, where she says: "And now I'll tell you how I think we ought to plan things, Torvald. As soon as Christmas is over . . ." The ring at the door cuts her short, but we can wager that she had a whole bagful of suggestions on refurnishing and redecorating the apartment on a scale in keeping with their enlarged income; and Torvald would not be the man he is, if he did not follow the lead of his little charmer.

She has never been happy, she now discovers. She had thought herself happy for eight years, but now it appears that she has been only merry. You are mistaken, dear Nora, we are obliged to reply. If your happiness now turns out to have been based on an illusion, its present collapse can not touch feelings that have become part of the irrevocable past. As we see, Nora brings the same intense will-to-believe to the reinterpretation of her past, as had supported her so recently in her expectation of the miracle. She is the same play-acting, hysterical Nora she always was, only: she has now changed her dress.

There is melodrama in Nora's calm announcement that she is going to leave her husband. She extracts all the thrills she possibly can from the situation. She has lived with a strange man for eight years, and borne three children to a stranger; she will not stay another night under a stranger's roof; she will not take a cent of Torvald's money, for she accepts no gifts from strangers; he must not even write to her; she returns his ring and demands her own, as a symbol of the total severance of their relations. Even the thought of her children, to whom she is devotedly attached, can not budge her from her determination. "I know they are in better hands than mine," she says, referring evidently to the old nursemaid of whose educative talent Nora is herself the most striking product.

One miracle Nora has undeniably accomplished. She has seen her husband, strutting lately in a pose of self-complacent heroism, wilt under the withering fire of her words. She has seen his conceited pride shrink and dwindle and disappear altogether. She has seen his face register shame, contrition and abject humility.

5

The suggestive power of the words in which she voiced her sense of injury has been so intense as to turn his initial resistance into a complete rout. Succumbing to the hypnotic spell of her personality, he accepts her version of the facts as the truth. (And there is not a reader of "A Doll's House," I daresay, who has not equally succumbed to that spell at one time or other.) When Nora makes her dramatic exit, she is conscious of having scored a complete psychological victory. Torvald's final gesture is one of unconditional surrender.

The conclusion is skillfully timed. The drop of the curtain finds us in a state of comic elation; for, whatever we think of the logic of Nora's arguments, we enjoy the victory of the superior, if erratic individual over the representative of commonplace respectability. And we are the less inclined to begrudge Nora the completeness of her triumph, as our imagination leaps ahead to speculate on the reaction that is bound to set in on the next day.

I would not predict with dogmatic certainty what is going to happen. It is barely possible that not even Christina's sober counsels will succeed in dissuading Nora from leaving her home. In that case, granted that she succeeds in finding employment, will she find the tedium of the daily routine endurable? Working in earnest for a living will not provide any of the thrills of those nights of secret copy-work that made her remark to Christina: "Sometimes I was so tired, so tired. And yet it was so awfully amusing to work in that way and earn money. I almost felt as if I were a man." It is hard to picture Nora as a bank clerk or a telephone operator, but it is harder to think of her playing the part for more than three days at a time. Other possibilities come to mind, too. One can choose to think of Nora taking to the lecture platform, agitating for the emancipation of woman. Or, again, she may find a lover and weave new romances about a new hero.

But personally I am convinced that after putting Torvald through a sufficiently protracted ordeal of suspense, Nora will yield to his entreaties and return home — on her own terms. She will not bear the separation from her children very long, and her love for Torvald, which is not as dead as she thinks, will reassert itself. For a time the tables will be reversed: a meek and chastened husband will eat out of the hand of his squirrel; and Nora, hoping to make up by a sudden spurt of zeal for twenty-eight years of lost time, will be trying desperately hard to grow up. I doubt, however, whether her volatile enthusiasm will even carry her beyond the stage of resolutions. The charm of novelty worn off, she will tire of the new game very rapidly and revert, imperceptibly, to her role of song-bird and charmer, as affording an unlimited range to the exercise of her inborn talents of coquetry and play-acting.   [1925]

KATHERINE M. ROGERS
From "Feminism and A Doll House*"*

The following excerpt is from "Feminism and A Doll House," *an essay by Katherine M. Rogers (b. 1932) that was included in the collection* Approaches to Teaching Ibsen's A Doll House *(1985).*

. . . In the context of a women's studies course, the critical opinion that Ibsen was not concerned specifically with women's freedom in A *Doll House* has no credibility. Nevertheless, at some point we consider his famous declaration, in his "Speech at the Banquet of the Norwegian League for Women's Rights" (1898), that he never "consciously worked for the women's rights movement" and was "not even quite clear as to just what this women's rights movement really is." This statement can easily be explained by Ibsen's dislike for party affiliation, his objection to being reduced from an artist to a propagandist, and his belief that the important thing is human development rather than specific political rights. It is valuable to make this point in women's studies courses, which tend to become overpoliticized. Our students should also be reminded of the differences between their attitudes and those of the original audience of 1879, who would not have considered the Helmer marriage so obviously bad or Torvald's complacency self-evidently ludicrous. In fact, Ibsen was concerned lest the audience sympathize entirely with Torvald, and he therefore purposely overwrote Torvald's lines—with the result that Torvald seems a caricature today and Nora's admiration for him seems fatuous. Similarly, we must not let contemporary enthusiasm for liberation lead us to oversimplify the ending into a happy triumph. Thinking of Nora's painful disillusionment, her parting from her children, and the uncertainties of her future independent career, Ibsen called his play "the tragedy of modern times."

But most of our class time is spent exploring the major feminist issues raised in the play, first analyzing what Ibsen says about them and then evaluating his presentation in terms of our own experience. Looking beyond the differences in property laws and modes of speech between Ibsen's time and our own, we see how the economic dependency, patriarchal rationalizations, and chivalric illusions that Ibsen so brilliantly anatomized in the nineteenth-century Helmer marriage continue to influence men's and women's attitudes today.

Immediately in the opening dialogue, Torvald lectures Nora about squandering his money and doles out to her the amount he thinks proper; and Nora petitions and excuses her expenditures—just like the beggar she ultimately recognizes herself to be. Thus Ibsen shows us how economic dependence degrades women in a society where respect is based on earning power, where unpaid work in the home is not considered work. Ibsen goes on to slow the exhilarating freedom, traditionally denied women, of having one's own money—when Nora asks for money as a Christmas present (and Torvald would rather give her anything else) or when she confides that she enjoyed the copying work she did at night because it made her feel like a man. Kristine, who was forced to marry to support her family, and Anne-Marie, who was forced to give up her child to support herself, round out the picture of women's economic helplessness. Having explored what Ibsen said about economic oppression, we ask ourselves whether the conditions he exposed still prevail: To what extent do men still control money in the home and in society at large? Are women still thought to be doing nothing when they merely run their households? Are such women generally considered parasitic and extravagant? How many men are still more comfortable with dependent wives than with independent ones?

We then analyze the patriarchal rationalizations that govern Torvald's treatment of Nora—his assumption that logic and responsibility pertain to men, his belief that male honor is supremely important while female honor is too negligible to mention, his self-congratulation on the heroism with which he would defend her should the need arise. We note that he appreciates Nora's real or supposed deficiencies because he needs something to belittle her for. We proceed from there to the destructive interplay between Torvald and Nora—for of course he could not be what he is if she did not constantly feed his self-importance. When he orders her not to eat macaroons, she meekly agrees, then disobeys and lies to him like a naughty child (thus behaving in a way that would reinforce his feelings of superiority, if he should find out). When she wants something from him, she flatters and manipulates instead of asking directly, as an equal. She proves his charge that she does not understand the society she lives in when she declares her indifference to the well-being of anyone outside her family and defiantly asserts that the law would never prosecute the mother of three little children. Concealing her competence and strength, Nora makes every effort to appear the twittering lark Torvald believes and wants her to be.

Their relationship leads us to consider how couples reinforce each other's destructive behavior patterns and whether an oppressive or exploitative situation is possible without mutual connivance. We decide how much Nora's limitations are merely assumed by those who wish to patronize her (Torvald's assurance that she cannot deal with serious problems) and how much they are real (her blind confidence in her husband's strength and wisdom). To the extent that they are real, we look into their social causes—for example, limited education and experience confine one's sympathies; lack of authority encourages one to resort to lies and tricks to gain one's ends. We may contrast Nora with Kristine, a woman who has been forced to live in a hard world (and who also starts out patronizing Nora).

What my students find hardest to accept in Nora is her romantic illusion that Torvald will assume responsibility for her forgery; it strikes them as a ridiculously unwarranted expectation, as well as a humiliating admission of feminine weakness. We must recognize that Ibsen's deflation of romantic chivalry, which seems far-fetched and pointless now, was necessary in the nineteenth century, when chivalry was pervasively used to conceal the domination and exploitation of women. Having implied from the beginning the falsities of nineteenth-century patriarchal marriage, in which the husband protects his wife from life in return for her uncritical admiration and dependence, Ibsen clinches his point by subjecting masculine heroism to a test and showing that a woman cannot in fact trust it to protect her. Nora's longing for a romantic hero who will save her is not only demeaning; it cannot be fulfilled because it is false. Once required to sacrifice something to his grandiose ideals, Torvald dismisses love and heroics as irrelevant and chides Nora for her faith in them. Men teach women that love is all-important and pretend to believe it themselves, but they soon enough reveal their disbelief when put to the test. Nora, confined to private life, has simply taken at face value the myths she has been taught about romantic love. While the ideal of chivalry may no longer be sufficiently credited to be worth attacking. we can profitably discuss other aspects of idealized romantic love. What is the difference between

5

loving and being in love with? Must traditional romantic expectations be changed if marriage is to become egalitarian?

Having accounted for Nora's romantic illusions about her breach of the law, we concentrate on those aspects of her behavior that persist in ourselves. This can be a useful exercise in self-knowledge. I confess that on seeing *A Doll House* for the first time I was actually filled with rage — it must have been because I saw too much of myself in Nora, being patronized and acquiescing in that patronage. We would like to believe that we have nothing in common with the little lark, but how many of us are altogether liberated from traditional sexual role-playing? How effectively do we deal with men's assumptions of superiority? Don't we, in fact, sometimes confirm those assumptions by acting cute or use them to flatter men into giving us what we want? Do we always react appropriately to belittlement if the tone is playful? Are we not occasionally tempted to forgo equality for sexual tributes and chivalrous protectiveness, even though we are more aware than Nora of the diminution these imply?

Finally, our class discusses two general moral issues important to feminists. First, do we agree with Ibsen's opinion, stated in his preliminary notes and dramatized in the play, that women and men have completely different concepts of law and conscience? Or should we attribute it to sexual stereotyping, based on the fact that most of the women he knew were confined to private life? If there are differences, are they natural or acquired? Have the increased education and experience of women since Nora's day changed their concepts of justice? Men have defined justice in abstract and sociological terms, ignoring the values important to women and then finding women wanting. Should women disprove masculine sneers by proving they can understand abstract justice as clearly as men can? Or should they strive to realize a new standard where consideration for a sick husband or a dying father outweighs the letter of the law? Do women naturally respond more to the concrete, the personal, the familial? And if so, should they use this sensitivity to modify society's concept of justice?

Second, there is the even more fundamental issue of duty to oneself, an issue that becomes ever more acute as women become increasingly unwilling to sacrifice themselves to the family. If women put their self-realization first, as men have traditionally done, what will happen to dependent others? The conflict between Nora's duty to herself and her duty to her children (if not to Torvald) must not be minimized. Can women take care of their duty to their children by redividing responsibilities in the home? Is everyone's first duty, as Nora comes to feel, to think out his or her own values and face reality without illusions? Is this self-development, in fact, necessary for adequacy as a parent? Can a woman who is not a mature human being be a good mother? (In this connection I mention Ibsen's suggestion, in his notes for *A Doll House*, that many nineteenth-century mothers might well go away and die, like insects, once they had completed the work of physical propagation.) How can one reconcile necessary self-realization with fulfilling the obligations of conventional social roles? (Torvald, Nora says, must learn to live independently of her as she must of him.) How can one be independent in marriage? How is it that Kristine will apparently find fulfillment in the relationship that Nora must reject in order to find herself? What is the difference between the

Helmer marriage (and Kristine's first one, where she "sold herself" for her dependent mother and brothers) and the one she will make with Krogstad, since there
too she will be working for him and his children?

In short, I try to make my students see how Ibsen illuminates the way women   10
and men still interact, raises questions that still need to be asked, and suggests
answers that still apply. *A Doll House* continues to remind us that we are not as
liberated as we would like to believe.   [1985]

JOAN TEMPLETON

From *"The* Doll House *Backlash:*
Criticism, Feminism, and Ibsen"

Joan Templeton (b. 1940), a professor and critic, published "The Doll House *Backlash: Criticism, Feminism, and Ibsen" in the academic journal* PMLA *in January
1989. The following is an excerpt from that essay.*

The a priori dismissal of women's rights as the subject of *A Doll House* is a
gentlemanly backlash, a refusal to acknowledge the existence of a tiresome reality, "the hoary problem of women's rights," as Michael Meyer has it; the issue is
decidedly *vieux jeu*,° and its importance has been greatly exaggerated. In Ibsen's
timeless world of Everyman, questions of gender can only be tedious intrusions.

But for over a hundred years, Nora has been under direct siege as exhibiting
the most perfidious characteristics of her sex; the original outcry of the 1880s is
swollen now to a mighty chorus of blame. She is denounced as an irrational and
frivolous narcissist; an "abnormal" woman, a "hysteric"; a vain, unloving egoist
who abandons her family in a paroxysm of selfishness. The proponents of the last
view would seem to think Ibsen had in mind a housewife Medea, whose cruelty
to husband and children he tailored down to fit the framed, domestic world of
realist drama.

The first attacks were launched against Nora on moral grounds and against
Ibsen, ostensibly, on "literary" ones. The outraged reviewers of the premiere
claimed that *A Doll House* did not have to be taken as a serious statement about
women's rights because the heroine of Act III is an incomprehensible transformation of the heroine of Acts I and II. This reasoning provided an ideal way to dismiss Nora altogether; nothing she said needed to be taken seriously, and her door
slamming could be written off as silly theatrics.

The argument for the two Noras, which still remains popular, has had its
most determined defender in the Norwegian scholar Else Høst, who argues that
Ibsen's carefree, charming "lark" could never have become the "newly fledged,
feminist." In any case it is the "childish, expectant, ecstatic, broken-hearted
Nora" who makes *A Doll House* immortal; the other one, the unfeeling woman

vieux jeu: Old hat.

of Act III who coldly analyzes the flaws in her marriage, is psychologically uncon-
vincing and wholly unsympathetic.

The most unrelenting attempt on record to trivialize Ibsen's protagonist, and   5
a favorite source for Nora's later detractors, is Hermann Weigand's. In a classic
1925 study, Weigand labors through forty-nine pages to demonstrate that Ibsen
conceived of Nora as a silly, lovable female. At the beginning, Weigand confesses,
he was, like all men, momentarily shaken by the play: "Having had the misfortune to be born of the male sex, we slink away in shame, vowing to mend our
ways." The chastened critic's remorse is short-lived, however, as a "clear male
voice, irreverently breaking the silence," stuns with its critical acumen: " 'The
meaning of the final scene,' the voice says, 'is epitomized by Nora's remark: "Yes,
Torvald. Now I have changed my dress." ' " With this epiphany as guide, Weigand
spends the night poring over the "little volume." Dawn arrives, bringing with it
the return of "masculine self-respect." For there is only one explanation for the
revolt of "this winsome little woman" and her childish door slamming: Ibsen
meant *A Doll House* as comedy. Nora's erratic behavior at the curtain's fall leaves
us laughing heartily, for there is no doubt that she will return home to "revert,
imperceptibly, to her role of songbird and charmer," After all, since Nora is

> an irresistibly bewitching piece of femininity, an extravagant poet and
> romancer, utterly lacking in sense of fact, and endowed with a natural gift
> for play-acting which makes her instinctively dramatize her experiences:
> how can the settlement fail of a fundamentally comic appeal?

The most popular way to render Nora inconsequential has been to attack her
morality; whatever the vocabulary used, the arguments have remained much the
same for over a century. Oswald Crawford, writing in the *Fortnightly Review* in
1891, scolded that while Nora may be "charming as doll-women may be charming," she is "unprincipled." A half century later, after Freudianism had produced
a widely accepted "clinical" language of disapproval, Nora could be called
"abnormal." Mary McCarthy lists Nora as one of the "neurotic" women whom
Ibsen, she curiously claims, was the first playwright to put on stage. For Maurice
Valency, Nora is a case study of female hysteria, a willful, unwomanly woman:
"Nora is a carefully studied example of what we have come to know as the hysterical personality—bright, unstable, impulsive, romantic, quite immune from feelings of guilt, and, at bottom, not especially feminine."

More recent assaults on Nora have argued that her forgery to obtain the
money to save her husband's life proves her irresponsibility and egotism. Brian
Johnston condemns Nora's love as "unintelligent" and her crime as "a trivial act
which nevertheless turns to evil because it refused to take the universal ethical
realm into consideration at all"; Ibsen uses Torvald's famous pet names for
Nora—lark, squirrel—to give her a "strong 'animal' identity" and to underscore
her inability to understand the ethical issues faced by human beings. Evert Sprinchorn argues that Nora had only to ask her husband's kindly friends (entirely
missing from the play) for the necessary money: ". . . any other woman would
have done so. But Nora knew that if she turned to one of Torvald's friends for
help, she would have had to share her role of savior with someone else."

Even Nora's sweet tooth is evidence of her unworthiness, as we see her "surreptitiously devouring the forbidden [by her husband] macaroons," even "brazenly offer[ing] macaroons to Doctor Rank, and finally lying in her denial that the macaroons are hers"; eating macaroons in secret suggests that "Nora is deceitful and manipulative from the start" and that her exit thus "reflects only a petulant woman's irresponsibility." As she eats the cookies, Nora adds insult to injury by declaring her hidden wish to say "death and damnation" in front of her husband, thus revealing, according to Brian Downs, of Christ's College, Cambridge, "something a trifle febrile and morbid" in her nature.

Much has been made of Nora's relationship with Doctor Rank, the surest proof, it is argued, of her dishonesty. Nora is revealed as *la belle dame sans merci*° when she "suggestively queries Rank whether a pair of silk stockings will fit her"; she "flirts cruelly with [him] and toys with his affection for her, drawing him on to find out how strong her hold over him actually is."

Nora's detractors have often been, from the first, her husband's defenders. In an argument that claims to rescue Nora and Torvald from "the campaign for the liberation of women" so that they "become vivid and disturbingly real," Evert Sprinchorn pleads that Torvald "has given Nora all the material things and all the sexual attention that any young wife could reasonably desire. He loves beautiful things, and not least his pretty wife." Nora is incapable of appreciating her husband because she "is not a normal woman. She is compulsive, highly imaginative, and very much inclined to go to extremes." Since it is she who has acquired the money to save his life, Torvald, and not Nora, is really the "wife in the family," although he "has regarded himself as the breadwinner . . . the main support of his wife and children, as any decent husband would like to regard himself." In another defense, John Chamberlain argues that Torvald deserves our sympathy because he is no "mere common or garden chauvinist." If Nora were less the actress Weigand has proved her to be, "the woman in her might observe what the embarrassingly naive feminist overlooks or ignores, namely, the indications that Torvald, for all his faults, is taking her at least as seriously as he can — and perhaps even as seriously as she deserves." [1989]

10

la belle dame sans merci: The beautiful lady without mercy.

MAKING COMPARISONS

1. Lord argues that the purpose of marriage "is to make each human personality free" (para. 2). Without this axiom, she believes, there cannot be real love in a marriage. Would Templeton agree?

2. How did you respond to Weigand's last sentence about "inborn talents of coquetry and play-acting"? How do you think Rogers would respond?

3. Which comments from these five critics do you find the most useful in understanding Nora and Torvald? Which are the least useful? Outline a brief position paper citing the comments and explaining your reasoning.

WRITING ABOUT ISSUES

1. Argue that Nora will, or will not, return. Be specific about the implications of either decision. Refer to at least one of the critics.

2. Write a brief comparison of Weigand and Rogers, pointing out their basic disagreement about Nora, women, the purpose of the play, and anything else that seems relevant.

3. What is your idea of a real marriage? Write an essay in which you explain the elements of such a relationship.

4. Ibsen was practically forced to change his ending when the play was produced in other countries. In Germany, for example, Nora's last line is "Ah, though it is a sin against myself, I cannot leave them!" Do you like this ending better? Write an essay in which you rewrite the ending for a current audience. Explain your choice, noting both what you think the function of the writer should be in our culture and what the nature of a marriage should be.

A WEB ASSIGNMENT

Several Web sites are dedicated to the plays of Henrik Ibsen. Visit the Web Assignments section of the *Making Literature Matter* Web site to link to one of these sites. At the Ibsen Centre you will find a section on films based on his plays ("filmography"). Look up the reviews for *A Doll House* and write a brief report on the issues that concern these reviewers.

Visit www.bedfordstmartins.com/makinglitmatter

LOVE AS A HAVEN?

MATTHEW ARNOLD, "Dover Beach"
MARK DOTY, "Night Ferry"

Part of our cultural narrative about romance — circulating for centuries in novels, poems, and films — is that love will save us from the disappointments and frustrations of the world. If our society sometimes seems cruel or unfair, if our jobs are tedious, if the economy fails, if war, injustice, and racism persist, we can always find solace in the arms of our beloved. It is here in a loving relationship that one can escape the world's duplicity, finding instead loyalty, acceptance, intimacy, and comfort. It is a popular and widespread scenario. Is romantic love enough to keep the world at bay? Can it help us suffer, with Hamlet, the "slings and arrows of outrageous fortune" or endure "the heart-ache and the thousand natural shocks that flesh is heir to"? Is that putting perhaps too much pressure on romance?

Both poems in this cluster seem to have a fairly dark view of existence. Arnold's famous concluding stanza employs the metaphor "Where ignorant armies clash by night" to characterize life. And Doty's poem begins with a similar image, "We're launched into the darkness / . . . onto the indefinite / black surface." And both poets speak directly to their lovers, perhaps hoping for a respite from "The eternal note of sadness."

MATTHEW ARNOLD
Dover Beach

Victorian poet Matthew Arnold (1822–1889) was the eldest son of Thomas Arnold, an influential clergyman and historian and headmaster of one of England's most prestigious college preparatory schools, Rugby. He grew up in an educational milieu in which religious, political, and social issues were discussed in depth. He went on to Oxford, where he eventually achieved success despite his irreverence and eccentricity. In 1851, he became an inspector of schools and served in this capacity for thirty-five years. He drew on his experiences with people of diverse social classes to become a keen critic of British education and culture, and he expressed his views of society in critical essays on literary, social, and religious issues as well as in poems. Living during an age in which Charles Darwin published The Origin of Species *(1871) and religious dogma was being questioned in many ways, Arnold suggests in "Dover Beach" that human love becomes especially important in such a world. The poem may have been written during the months just before or just after Arnold's marriage and honeymoon, which included a ferry ride from Dover, England, to Calais, France.*

The sea is calm tonight.
The tide is full, the moon lies fair
Upon the straits;—on the French coast the light
Gleams and is gone; the cliffs of England stand,
Glimmering and vast, out in the tranquil bay.   5
Come to the window, sweet is the night-air!
Only, from the long line of spray
Where the sea meets the moon-blanched land,
Listen! you hear the grating roar
Of pebbles which the waves draw back, and fling,   10
At their return, up the high strand,
Begin, and cease, and then again begin,
With tremulous cadence slow, and bring
The eternal note of sadness in.

Sophocles long ago   15
Heard it on the Aegean, and it brought

Into his mind the turbid ebb and flow
Of human misery;° we
Find also in the sound a thought,
Hearing it by this distant northern sea.   20

The Sea of Faith
Was once, too, at the full, and round earth's shore
Lay like the folds of a bright girdle furled.
But now I only hear
Its melancholy, long, withdrawing roar,   25
Retreating, to the breath
Of the night-wind, down the vast edges drear
And naked shingles° of the world.

Ah, love, let us be true
To one another! for the world, which seems   30
To lie before us like a land of dreams,
So various, so beautiful, so new,
Hath really neither joy, nor love, nor light,
Nor certitude, nor peace, nor help for pain;
And we are here as on a darkling plain   35
Swept with confused alarms of struggle and flight,
Where ignorant armies clash by night.   [1867]

15–18 **Sophocles . . . misery:** In *Antigone*, Sophocles compares the disasters that beset the
house of Oedipus to a mounting tide.   28 **shingles:** Pebble beach.

THINKING ABOUT THE TEXT

1. In trying to recreate this scene—say, for a movie script—what would you
   have the lovers look like? Where would the couple be positioned? If you
   were the director, how would you explain the scene to the actors—that is,
   what is the speaker saying? Put another way, what argument is being made?

2. What does Arnold seem to be using the sea as a metaphor for? What other
   metaphors and similes are used? Are they effective in making his point?

3. Some feminist readers see this poem as yet another example of a man who
   hopes to escape temporarily from the troubles of the world by finding
   comfort and support from a woman. Is there some validity to this point?
   Why, for example, doesn't the woman speak?

4. In the recent film *The Anniversary Party*, Kevin Kline's character reads the
   last stanza of this poem to a couple celebrating their sixth wedding
   anniversary. Some critics saw it as an ironic joke, others as a parody of a
   "sweet" love poem. What is it about the poem that seems to make it inappropriate for such an occasion? Would you send it to your beloved? Why?

5. What specific reasons are given by the speaker for the lovers to be true to
   one another, beginning with "for the world" (line 30)? Is this an attitude
   you share? Do you know others who agree? Is this an extreme position?
   What would the opposite view be? Is this extreme, as well?

MARK DOTY
Night Ferry

Mark Doty (b. 1953) was born in Tennessee, but his father, who was a builder working for the Army Corps of Engineers, was a man who could not get along with supervisors and often moved the family. In the autobiographical Firebird *(1999), Doty describes growing up as "a sissy" in a Southern Gothic family. He attended high school in Tucson, Arizona, where he first developed an interest in writing, then briefly attended the University of Tucson, but dropped out and married when he was eighteen. He attended Drake University in Iowa in the 1970s, where he and his wife published chapbooks of poetry together. In 1981, he dissolved his marriage when he acknowledged his homosexuality. He received his M.F.A. at Goddard College in Vermont and taught there, eventually moving with his partner to Provincetown, Massachusetts. After his partner died from complications of AIDS in 1984, Doty's poetry took on a new intensity and significance. Doty has taught at several universities and now teaches at the University of Houston. He has published five poetry collections and two memoirs. His awards and fellowships include the National Book Critics Award and the T. S. Eliot Prize in 1993 for* My Alexandria. *His most recent book is* Still Life with Oysters and Lemons *(2001).*

We're launched into the darkness,
half a load of late passengers
    gliding onto the indefinite
        black surface, a few lights vague

and shimmering on the island shore.   5
Behind us, between the landing's twin flanks
    (wooden pylons strapped with old tires),
        the docklights shatter in our twin,

folding wakes, their colors
on the roughened surface combed   10
    like the patterns of Italian bookpaper,
        lustrous and promising. The narrative

of the ferry begins and ends brilliantly,
and its text is this moving out
    into what is soon before us   15
        and behind: the night going forward,

sentence by sentence, as if on faith,
into whatever takes place.
    It's strange how we say things *take place*,
        as if occurrence were a location—   20

         ◆   ◆   ◆   ◆

the dark between two shores,
for instance, where for a little while
    we're on no solid ground. Twelve minutes,
       precisely, the night ferry hurries

  across the lake. And what happens   25
is always the body of water,
    its skin like the wrong side of satin.
      I love to stand like this,

  where the prow pushes blunt into the future,
knowing, more than seeing, how   30
    the surface rushes and doesn't even break
      but simply slides under us.

  Lake melds into shoreline,
one continuous black moiré;
    the boatmen follow the one course they know   35
      toward a dock nearly the mirror

  of the first, mercury lamps vaporing
over the few late birds
    attending the pier. Even the bored men
      at the landing, who wave   40

  their flashlights for the last travelers,
steering us toward the road, will seem
    the engineers of our welcome,
      their red-sheathed lights marking

  the completion of our, or anyone's, crossing.   45
Twelve dark minutes. Love,
    we are between worlds, between
      unfathomed water and I don't know how much

  light-flecked black sky, the fogged circles
of island lamps. I am almost not afraid   50
    on this good boat, breathing its good smell
      of grease and kerosene,

  warm wind rising up the stairwell
from the engine's serious study.
    There's no beautiful binding   55
      for this story, only the temporary,

  liquid endpapers of the hurried water,
shot with random color. But in the gliding forward's
    a scent so quick and startling
      it might as well be blowing   60

             ♦   ♦   ♦   ♦

off the stars. Now, just before we arrive,
the wind carries a signal and a comfort,
lovely, though not really meant for us:
woodsmoke risen from the chilly shore. [1993]

THINKING ABOUT THE TEXT

1. The poem seems to be a sustained metaphor for life's journey. In what ways does this comparison make sense? What other significant metaphor is developed?

2. As symbols, what do the following images suggest—"a few lights vague / and shimmering" (lines 4–5), "like the patterns of Italian bookpaper, / lustrous and promising" (lines 11–12), "no beautiful binding / for this story, only the temporary, / liquid endpapers of the hurried water, / shot with random color" (lines 55–58)?

3. How did you evaluate the speaker's attitude when he says, "I am almost not afraid / on this good boat, breathing its good smell" (lines 50–51)?

4. Does the image of "a scent . . . / . . . blowing / off the stars" in lines 59 to 61 seem more mysterious than Doty's other images? What idea might the poet be after with such imagery?

5. Can we sustain the journey-of-life metaphor into the last stanza? Where might the passengers be arriving? What is the signal "not really meant for us" (line 63)? Why woodsmoke? Why "the chilly shore" (line 64)?

MAKING COMPARISONS

1. What specific images here of sea and shore seem to echo those in "Dover Beach"?

2. Does Doty mean something different than Arnold when he uses the words "faith" (line 17), "night" (lines 16, 24), and "love" (lines 28, 46)? What comparable phrases can you find in Arnold for Doty's "we're on no solid ground" (line 23) and "between / unfathomed water" (lines 47–48)?

3. Is Doty's poem more or less philosophically bleak than Arnold's? As direct or less? As poetic or more?

WRITING ABOUT ISSUES

1. Argue that Doty's image of a ferry crossing a lake at night is or is not a more appropriate metaphor for contemporary life than Arnold's "a darkling plain / Swept with confused alarm" (lines 35–36).

2. The poet Percy Shelley noted that our "sweetest songs are of saddest thought," perhaps commenting on the often melancholy nature of some of our best literature. Argue that this is or is not the case with these two poems. Try to include other favorite texts as examples to support your claim.

3. Doty seems less concerned than Arnold with love as an antidote to his problems. Argue that people do or do not put enough emphasis on love in their lives.

4. Do you think that one's outlook on life is directly related to age? Do middle-aged writers tend to have a darker vision and younger writers a sunnier perspective? You might examine several early and recent songs by well-established singers or bands that you know and like. Write a report in which you compare the early songs with the later songs and also analyze these songs as either typical or atypical of youth's optimistic view of life.

15

Doing Justice

It is not desirable to cultivate a respect for the law, so much as for the right.

— Henry David Thoreau

The subject judged knows a part of the world of reality which the judging spectator fails to see, knows more while the spectator knows less; and, wherever there is conflict of opinion and difference of vision, we are bound to believe that the truer side is the side that feels the more, and not the side that feels the less.

— William James

Injustice anywhere is a threat to justice everywhere. We are caught in an inescapable network of mutuality, tied in a single garment of destiny. Whatever affects one directly affects all indirectly.

— Martin Luther King Jr.

Justice is a continual balancing of competing visions, plural viewpoints, shifting histories, interests, and allegiances. To acknowledge that level of complexity is to require, to seek, and to value a multiplicity of knowledge systems, in pursuit of a more complete sense of the world in which we all live.

— Patricia J. Williams

Beyond our talk of rights we have each other, and the steady burden of learning to live together and apart.

— Martha Minow

Thinking about literature involves people making judgments about other people's views. Throughout your course, you have been making judgments as you interpret and evaluate written works, including the texts in this book and those produced by the class. You have been deciding also how you feel about positions expressed by your teacher and classmates. In all these acts of judgment, you have considered where you stand on general issues of aesthetics, ethics, politics, religion, and law.

Outside school, you judge things all the time, though you may not always be aware that you are doing so. You may be more conscious of your judgments when other people disagree with you, when you face multiple options, when you are trying to understand something complex, when your decisions will have significant consequences, or when you must review an act you have already committed. Some people are quite conscious that they make judgments because they have the political, professional, or institutional authority to enforce their will. Of course, these people may wind up being judged by whomever they dominate, and they may even face active revolt.

A term closely related to judgment is *justice*, which many people associate with judgments that are wise, fair, and sensitive to the parties involved. In this sense, justice is an ideal, which may not always be achieved in real life. Indeed, though communities hope their police departments and courts will act soundly, sometimes representatives of our legal institutions are accused of violating justice instead of upholding it. Much, of course, depends on how *justice* is defined in any particular case, and equally crucial is who defines it. Many works of literature have challenged laws of the society in which they were written, while others have at least questioned or complicated the notions of justice prevailing in their culture. Often, literature has probed the complexities of situations that in real life are resolved as clear victories for one particular party. In this respect, literature draws attention to issues that we may normally oversimplify or overlook.

The opening cluster in this chapter is a group of four poems (p. 1081), each of which features a speaker deciding how to treat a certain animal. The second cluster (p. 1091) moves completely into the world of human beings, presenting a pair of stories about the moral anguish that issues of military justice can provoke. Next, essays by Scott Russell Sanders, Joyce Carol Oates, and Maxine Hong Kingston ponder how a community's attempt at justice may be influenced by race, class, and cultural conditions (p. 1113). The two clusters that follow present works that, directly or indirectly, raise charges of injustice. Charlotte Perkins Gilman's 1892 short story "The Yellow Wallpaper" (p. 1148) suggests that women diagnosed as mad may actually be exhibiting the trauma of patriarchal domination. Gilman's story is followed by three documents that shed light on the era in which she wrote. Next is a set of four poems by African Americans who protest incidents of racial injustice in various time periods (p. 1173).

The following three clusters are concerned with how justice is or is not served by branding certain people criminals, chastising them, and even seeking revenge against them. Two plays (p. 1185), William Shakespeare's *Hamlet* and Susan Glaspell's *Trifles*, show how people tracking down murderers may suffer from their own internal dramas. Then four poems examine the responsibilities of people who witness or learn about punishments (p. 1302). Next is a trio of stories in which characters avenge what they see as wrongdoing (p. 1314), leaving you to decide whether they are right to take justice into their own hands.

The chapter concludes with three clusters in which characters seeking justice become outsiders to society. First come three stories by Nathaniel Hawthorne

(p. 1345), each of which chronicles a Puritan protagonist's growing obsession with sin. Then Flannery O'Connor's modern short story "A Good Man Is Hard to Find" (p. 1378) presents a character called The Misfit who gets downright homicidal in his effort to see religious justice done. Also in this cluster are O'Connor's explanation of her story and comments by three critics who are skeptical of her analysis. The final cluster (p. 1403) is two versions of "The Demon Lover," whose title character invades the human world to seize a woman who had pledged herself to him. One text is a centuries-old ballad, and the other is a modern short story by Elizabeth Bowen. In both works, the demon lover takes his idea of justice to a terrible extreme. Like the other texts in this chapter, both versions help you explore what justice means to you.

DOING JUSTICE TO ANIMALS

MAXINE KUMIN, "Woodchucks"
D. H. LAWRENCE, "Snake"
ELIZABETH BISHOP, "The Fish"
WILLIAM STAFFORD, "Traveling through the Dark"

You live in an age of nearly constant debate over how to treat nature. One controversy focuses on justice to animals. Do animals have rights? If so, what specifically are they? Literary works can dramatize and illustrate such issues, as you will see with the following poems. In each, the speaker must judge how to deal with a certain animal. As you read, compare not only the speakers' decisions but also the values that their choices reflect. Think, too, about the judgments you have made regarding animals, your overall sense of what justice to animals involves, and the forces influencing your view.

BEFORE YOU READ

Describe at least one encounter you have had with wildlife, noting how you behaved at the time and what influenced your conduct. What is your attitude toward people who like to hunt or fish? What forms of wildlife, if any, do you think people are justified in fearing or despising? Do you think the notion of animal rights has merit? Identify particular values that your answers reflect.

MAXINE KUMIN
Woodchucks

Maxine Kumin (b. 1925) is a Pulitzer Prize–winning poet. She writes in a range of genres, however; her work includes four novels, a short-story collection, two volumes of essays, and several children's books. "Woodchucks" comes from her 1971 collection of poems Our Ground Time Here Will Be Brief. *Like much of Kumin's writing, this poem deals with the world of nature. Kumin lives on a farm in New Hampshire, where she raises horses.*

Gassing the woodchucks didn't turn out right.
The knockout bomb from the Feed and Grain Exchange
was featured as merciful, quick at the bone
and the case we had against them was airtight,
both exits shoehorned shut with puddingstone,°   5
but they had a sub-sub-basement out of range.

Next morning they turned up again, no worse
for the cyanide than we for our cigarettes
and state-store Scotch, all of us up to scratch.
They brought down the marigolds as a matter of course   10
and then took over the vegetable patch
nipping the broccoli shoots, beheading the carrots.

The food from our mouths, I said, righteously thrilling
to the feel of the .22, the bullets' neat noses.
I, a lapsed pacifist fallen from grace   15
puffed with Darwinian° pieties for killing,
now drew a bead on the littlest woodchuck's face.
He died down in the everbearing roses.

Ten minutes later I dropped the mother. She
flipflopped in the air and fell, her needle teeth   20
still hooked in a leaf of early Swiss chard.
Another baby next. O one-two-three
the murderer inside me rose up hard,
the hawkeye killer came on stage forthwith.

There's one chuck left. Old wily fellow, he keeps   25
me cocked and ready day after day after day.
All night I hunt his humped-up form. I dream
I sight along the barrel in my sleep.
If only they'd all consented to die unseen
gassed underground the quiet Nazi way.   [1972]   30

5 puddingstone: Cement mixed with pebbles.   **16 Darwinian:** Charles Darwin (1809–1882), an English naturalist who first theorized about evolution and natural selection.

THINKING ABOUT THE TEXT

1. In line 4, the word *case* evidently refers to a method of entrapping the woodchucks, but probably it refers as well to the speaker's reasons for hunting them. Does the speaker have a good "case" for going after them?

What is important to consider in evaluating her behavior? In what ways does your experience with farms and gardens affect your view of her?

2. Identify the stages in the speaker's campaign to get rid of the woodchucks. What psychological changes does she go through? In particular, what attitude toward her behavior does she express in the third and fourth stanzas? Support your answer by referring to specific words of hers.

3. Rewrite stanzas 3, 4, or 5 using the third person rather than the first. What is the effect of such a change? What advantages, if any, does the poet gain by resorting to the first person?

4. Trace the poem's rhyme pattern. Where does Kumin use alliteration as well? What effect do her technical choices have?

5. Presumably the last line alludes to the mass exterminations of the Holocaust. What would you say to someone who argues that this is an inappropriate, even tasteless, way to end a poem about woodchucks?

D. H. LAWRENCE
Snake

David Herbert Lawrence (1885–1930) was a leading novelist and short-story writer in the first half of the twentieth century. The son of a coal miner and a former schoolteacher, he describes his English working-class upbringing in his autobiographical novel Sons and Lovers *(1913). Probably he remains best known for his 1928 novel* Lady Chatterley's Lover. *For many years, it was banned in England and the United States because it explicitly described the sexual relationship between an aristocratic woman and her husband's gamekeeper. In most of his work, Lawrence endorses human passion, although he argued that people needed to exist in harmony with nature as well as with one another. Besides writing fiction, he painted and wrote poetry. "Snake," published in 1913, is based on Lawrence's stay in Sicily, one of the many places he went as he searched for a land friendly to his ideals.*

A snake came to my water-trough
On a hot, hot day, and I in pyjamas for the heat,
To drink there.

In the deep, strange-scented shade of the great dark carob-tree
I came down the steps with my pitcher   5
And must wait, must stand and wait, for there he was at the trough before me.

He reached down from a fissure in the earth-wall in the gloom
And trailed his yellow-brown slackness soft-bellied down, over the edge of the
            stone trough
And rested his throat upon the stone bottom,
And where the water had dripped from the tap, in a small clearness,   10

He sipped with his straight mouth,
Softly drank through his straight gums, into his slack long body,
Silently.

Someone was before me at my water-trough,
And I, like a second comer, waiting.   15

He lifted his head from his drinking, as cattle do,
And looked at me vaguely, as drinking cattle do,
And flickered his two-forked tongue from his lips, and mused a moment,
And stooped and drank a little more,
Being earth-brown, earth-golden from the burning bowels of the earth   20
On the day of Sicilian July, with Etna smoking.

The voice of my education said to me
He must be killed,
For in Sicily the black, black snakes are innocent, the gold are venomous.

And voices in me said, If you were a man   25
You would take a stick and break him now, and finish him off.

But must I confess how I liked him,
How glad I was he had come like a guest in quiet, to drink at my water-trough
And depart peaceful, pacified, and thankless,
Into the burning bowels of this earth?   30

Was it cowardice, that I dared not kill him?
Was it perversity, that I longed to talk to him?
Was it humility, to feel so honoured?
I felt so honoured.

And yet those voices: 35
If you were not afraid, you would kill him!

And truly I was afraid, I was most afraid,
But even so, honoured still more
That he should seek my hospitality
From out the dark door of the secret earth.   40

He drank enough
And lifted his head, dreamily, as one who has drunken,
And flickered his tongue like a forked night on the air, so black;
Seeming to lick his lips,
And looked around like a god, unseeing, into the air,   45
And slowly turned his head,
And slowly, very slowly, as if thrice adream,
Proceeded to draw his slow length curving round
And climb again the broken bank of my wall-face.

And as he put his head into that dreadful hole,   50
And as he slowly drew up, snake-easing his shoulders, and entered farther,

A sort of horror, a sort of protest against his withdrawing into that horrid black
　　hole,
Deliberately going into the blackness, and slowly drawing himself after,
Overcame me now his back was turned.

I looked round, I put down my pitcher,　　　　　　　　　　　　　　　　　55
I picked up a clumsy log
And threw it at the water-trough with a clatter.

I think it did not hit him,
But suddenly that part of him that was left behind convulsed in undignified haste,
Writhed like lightning, and was gone　　　　　　　　　　　　　　　　　60
Into the black hole, the earth-lipped fissure in the wall-front,
At which, in the intense still noon, I stared with fascination.

And immediately I regretted it.
I thought how paltry, how vulgar, what a mean act!
I despised myself and the voices of my accursed human education.　　　　　65

And I thought of the albatross,°
And I wished he would come back, my snake.

For he seemed to me again like a king,
Like a king in exile, uncrowned in the underworld,
Now due to be crowned again.　　　　　　　　　　　　　　　　　　　70

And so, I missed my chance with one of the lords
Of life.
And I have something to expiate;
A pettiness.　　　　　　　　　　　　　　　　　　　　　　　　[1913]

66 **albatross:** In Samuel Taylor Coleridge's "Rime of the Ancient Mariner," a seaman brings
misfortune to the crew of his ship by killing an albatross, an ocean bird.

THINKING ABOUT THE TEXT

1. What did you associate with snakes before reading this poem? Does
   Lawrence push you to look at snakes differently, or does his poem endorse
   the view you already had? Develop your answer by referring to specific
   lines.

2. Discuss the poem as an argument involving various "voices." How do you
   think you would have reacted to the snake if you had been the speaker?
   What "voices" might you have heard inside your own mind? What people
   or institutions would these "voices" have come from?

3. Why does the speaker throw the log just as the snake is leaving? Note the
   explanation the speaker gives as well as the judgment he then makes
   about his act. Do both make sense to you? Why, or why not?

4. Lawrence begins many lines with the word *and.* What is the effect of his
   doing so?

5. In "Snake," Lawrence writes positively about an animal that is often feared. Think of a similar poem that you might write. What often-feared animal would you choose? What positive qualities would you point out or suggest in describing this animal? If you wish, try actually writing such a poem.

MAKING COMPARISONS

1. Here is an issue of evaluation: Do Kumin's and Lawrence's speakers seem equally guilty of pettiness? Consult a dictionary definition of the word.

2. Does one of these speakers seem more self-divided than the other? Explain.

3. Do Kumin's and Lawrence's poems seem equally poetic? What features of poetry do you have in mind as you address this issue of genre?

ELIZABETH BISHOP
The Fish

Although she also wrote short stories, Elizabeth Bishop (1911–1979) is primarily known for her poetry, winning both the Pulitzer Prize and the National Book Award for it. Born in Worcester, Massachusetts, she spent much of her youth in Nova Scotia. As an adult, she lived in various places, including New York City, Florida, Mexico, and Brazil. Much of her poetry observes and reflects on a particular object or figure. Such is the case with "The Fish," which Bishop wrote in 1940 and then included in her 1946 book North and South.

I caught a tremendous fish
and held him beside the boat
half out of water, with my hook
fast in a corner of his mouth.
He didn't fight.   5
He hadn't fought at all.
He hung a grunting weight,
battered and venerable
and homely. Here and there
his brown skin hung in strips   10
like ancient wall-paper,
and its pattern of darker brown
was like wall-paper:
shapes like full-blown roses
stained and lost through age.   15
He was speckled with barnacles,

fine rosettes of lime,
and infested
with tiny white sea-lice,
and underneath two or three   20
rags of green weed hung down.
While his gills were breathing in
the terrible oxygen
— the frightening gills,
fresh and crisp with blood,   25
that can cut so badly —
I thought of the coarse white flesh
packed in like feathers,
the big bones and the little bones,
the dramatic reds and blacks   30
of his shiny entrails,
and the pink swim-bladder
like a big peony.
I looked into his eyes
which were far larger than mine   35
but shallower, and yellowed,
the irises backed and packed
with tarnished tinfoil
seen through the lenses
of old scratched isinglass.   40
They shifted a little, but not
to return my stare.
— It was more like the tipping
of an object toward the light.
I admired his sullen face,   45
the mechanism of his jaw,
and then I saw
that from his lower lip
— if you could call it a lip —
grim, wet, and weapon-like,   50
hung five old pieces of fish-line,
or four and a wire leader
with the swivel still attached,
with all their five big hooks
grown firmly in his mouth.   55
A green line, frayed at the end
where he broke it, two heavier lines,
and a fine black thread
still crimped from the strain and snap
when it broke and he got away.   60
Like medals with their ribbons
frayed and wavering,

a five-haired beard of wisdom
trailing from his aching jaw.
I stared and stared   65
and victory filled up
the little rented boat,
from the pool of bilge
where oil had spread a rainbow
around the rusted engine   70
to the bailer rusted orange,
the sun-cracked thwarts,
the oarlocks on their strings,
the gunnels — until everything
was rainbow, rainbow, rainbow!   75
And I let the fish go.   [1946]

THINKING ABOUT THE TEXT

1. Does the speaker change her attitude toward the fish, or does it stay pretty much the same? Support your reasoning by referring to specific lines. Are you surprised that the speaker lets the fish go? Why, or why not? How effective a conclusion is her release of the fish?

2. To what extent is the speaker describing the fish objectively? In what ways, if any, does her description of him seem to reflect her own particular values? Refer to specific lines.

3. The speaker reports that "victory filled up / the little rented boat" (lines 66–67). Whose victory might she have in mind? Why might she use this word? Often, a victory for one is a defeat for another. Is that the case here?

4. Where does the poem refer to acts and instruments of seeing? What conclusions might be drawn from these references?

5. How significant is it that the fish is male?

MAKING COMPARISONS

1. What would you say to someone who argues that Bishop's speaker is more admirable than Kumin's and Lawrence's speakers because she lets the animal go free?

2. With each of these three poems, consider what you learn about the speaker's own state of mind. Does one of these poems tell you more about its speaker's thoughts than the other poems do? Support your answer by referring to specific lines.

3. Bishop's poem is one long, continuous stanza, whereas Kumin and Lawrence divide theirs into several stanzas. Does this difference in strategy lead to a significant difference in effect? Do you consider one of these strategies better than the other? Explain your reasoning.

WILLIAM STAFFORD
Traveling through the Dark

Besides being a poet himself, William Stafford (1914–1995) was a mentor to many others. During World War II, he was a conscientious objector. Later, he wrote and taught poetry at a variety of places in the United States, eventually settling in Oregon. The following poem was written in 1960 and subsequently appeared in a 1962 collection of Stafford's poems, also entitled Traveling through the Dark.

Traveling through the dark I found a deer
dead on the edge of the Wilson River road.
It is usually best to roll them into the canyon:
that road is narrow; to swerve might make more dead.

By glow of the tail-light I stumbled back of the car 5
and stood by the heap, a doe, a recent killing;
she had stiffened already, almost cold.
I dragged her off; she was large in the belly.

My fingers touching her side brought me the reason —
her side was warm; her fawn lay there waiting, 10
alive, still, never to be born.
Beside that mountain road I hesitated.

The car aimed ahead its lowered parking lights;
under the hood purred the steady engine.
I stood in the glare of the warm exhaust turning red; 15
around our group I could hear the wilderness listen.

I thought hard for us all — my only swerving —
then pushed her over the edge into the river. [1962]

THINKING ABOUT THE TEXT

1. At the end of the poem, the speaker says "I thought hard for us all." Who does "us" refer to? What might the speaker have said to defend what he did? What might be an argument against his act? What would you have done, and why?

2. "To swerve" appears in the first stanza, "swerving" in the last. How would you define these words as they appear in the poem? What does Stafford achieve by using them to frame it?

3. Note in the fourth stanza what verbs the speaker associates with the car and the engine. What is the effect of these verbs on you?

4. Note, too, the last line of the fourth stanza. What would you say to someone who criticized this line because it is impossible for someone to "hear" someone else "listen"?

5. Though Stafford begins his poem with the phrase "Traveling through the dark," the rest of the poem deals with what happened when the speaker stopped traveling for a moment. How appropriate, then, is the poem's title?

MAKING COMPARISONS

1. Do you believe that the four authors in this cluster are all making the same point about human beings' relationship to nature? Why, or why not?

2. Could the words "I thought hard for us all" apply to all four speakers in this cluster? Support your answer by referring to specific lines of each text.

3. Rank the four poems in this cluster according to their degree of artistic success, moving down from your most favorite to your least favorite. Then rank them according to their degree of clarity, moving down from the poem you find most clear to the one you find least clear. Looking over your rankings, would you say that your evaluation of each poem is influenced by its degree of clarity? Explain. What other things affect how you judge these poems?

WRITING ABOUT ISSUES

1. Choose one of the poems in this cluster, and write an essay describing and evaluating its speaker. As you develop your judgment, acknowledge and address at least one other possible way of looking at this person: that is, a different judgment that someone might make of him or her.

2. Write an essay suggesting what one of the speakers in these poems might say about another. What, for example, might Bishop's speaker say about Lawrence's? Support your conjecture with details from both texts.

3. Write an essay arguing for or against how you treated a certain animal in a certain situation. Choose a situation in which you did, in fact, consider acting differently at the time. If you wish, you can draw analogies between your experience and any of those depicted in this cluster.

4. Should hunting and fishing be encouraged? Should society recognize animal rights, even to the extent of disallowing the use of animals in scientific and medical experiments? Choose one of these issues, read at least two articles on it, and then write an essay presenting and supporting your position. At some point in your essay, tell whether and how the articles you read taught you something you hadn't known. As you make your case, you may also want to mention one or more of the poems in this cluster.

MILITARY JUSTICE

FRANK O'CONNOR, "Guests of the Nation"
HARUKI MURAKAMI, "Another Way to Die"

The following stories differ in setting. Frank O'Connor's focuses on the Irish-British conflict in the first decades of the twentieth century, while Haruki Murakami's deals with the Japanese occupation of Manchuria near the end of World War II. In both stories, however, characters must decide whether and how they will fulfill duties assigned them by the armies they serve. The decision is not easy because their duty requires them to assist in the destruction of people who have done them no personal harm. As you read, consider the conflicts you have felt between your "official" duty and other obligations.

BEFORE YOU READ

Think of an occasion when you were assigned a certain duty or task but were reluctant to perform it because you knew it would harm someone else. Identify the specific values that were in conflict, what you ultimately did, and why you decided to act that way. Do you think it is ever all right for soldiers to disobey orders or ignore rules they are supposed to enforce? Explain your reasoning.

FRANK O'CONNOR

Guests of the Nation

During the 1920s, Ireland was torn by various levels of armed conflict. The main opponents were England, who had been ruling the country, and Irish militants seeking to free it. Early in the decade, the southern part of Ireland did become semi-independent. Yet in many ways it remained under England's control, and Northern Ireland gained no freedom at all. Therefore, the Irish Republican Army and other groups initially fought against the new state as well as against the English government. One of the rebels was a clerk from Cork named Michael Donovan (1903–1955), who was eventually captured and sentenced to prison. After his release, he launched what became a long and distinguished career as a fiction writer, taking the pen name Frank O'Connor. Today, he is chiefly known for his short stories. The following one appeared in his first published collection, also entitled Guests of the Nation *(1931).*

1

At dusk the big Englishman, Belcher, would shift his long legs out of the ashes and say "Well, chums, what about it?" and Noble or me would say "All right, chum" (for we had picked up some of their curious expressions), and the little Englishman, Hawkins, would light the lamp and bring out the cards. Sometimes Jeremiah Donovan would come up and supervise the game and get excited over Hawkins's cards, which he always played badly, and shout at him as if he was one of our own "Ah, you divil, you, why didn't you play the tray?"

But ordinarily Jeremiah was a sober and contented poor devil like the big Englishman, Belcher, and was looked up to only because he was a fair hand at documents, though he was slow enough even with them. He wore a small cloth hat and big gaiters over his long pants, and you seldom saw him with his hands out of his pockets. He reddened when you talked to him, tilting from toe to heel and back, and looking down all the time at his big farmer's feet. Noble and me used to make fun of his broad accent, because we were from the town.

I couldn't at the time see the point of me and Noble guarding Belcher and Hawkins at all, for it was my belief that you could have planted that pair down anywhere from this to Claregalway and they'd have taken root there like a native weed. I never in my short experience seen two men to take to the country as they did.

They were handed on to us by the Second Battalion when the search for them became too hot, and Noble and myself, being young, took over with a natural feeling of responsibility, but Hawkins made us look like fools when he showed that he knew the country better than we did.

"You're the bloke they calls Bonaparte," he says to me. "Mary Brigid O'Connell told me to ask you what you done with the pair of her brother's socks you borrowed."

For it seemed, as they explained it, that the Second used to have little evenings, and some of the girls of the neighborhood turned in, and, seeing they were such decent chaps, our fellows couldn't leave the two Englishmen out of them. Hawkins learned to dance "The Walls of Limerick," "The Siege of Ennis," and "The Waves of Tory" as well as any of them, though, naturally, he couldn't return the compliment, because our lads at that time did not dance foreign dances on principle.

So whatever privileges Belcher and Hawkins had with the Second they just naturally took with us, and after the first day or two we gave up all pretense of keeping a close eye on them. Not that they could have got far, for they had accents you could cut with a knife and wore khaki tunics and overcoats with civilian pants and boots. But it's my belief that they never had any idea of escaping and were quite content to be where they were.

It was a treat to see how Belcher got off with the old woman of the house where we were staying. She was a great warrant to scold, and cranky even with us, but before ever she had a chance of giving our guests, as I may call them, a lick of her tongue, Belcher had made her his friend for life. She was breaking sticks, and Belcher, who hadn't been more than ten minutes in the house, jumped up from his seat and went over to her.

"Allow me, madam," he says, smiling his queer little smile, "please allow me"; and he takes the bloody hatchet. She was struck too paralytic to speak, and after that, Belcher would be at her heels, carrying a bucket, a basket, or a load of turf, as the case might be. As Noble said, he got into looking before she leapt, and

5

hot water, or any little thing she wanted, Belcher would have it ready for her. For such a huge man (and though I am five foot ten myself I had to look up at him) he had an uncommon shortness or should I say lack? of speech. It took us some time to get used to him, walking in and out, like a ghost, without a word. Especially because Hawkins talked enough for a platoon, it was strange to hear big Belcher with his toes in the ashes come out with a solitary "Excuse me, chum" or "That's right, chum." His one and only passion was cards, and I will say for him that he was a good card-player. He could have fleeced myself and Noble, but whatever we lost to him Hawkins lost to us, and Hawkins played with the money Belcher gave him.

Hawkins lost to us because he had too much old gab, and we probably lost to Belcher for the same reason. Hawkins and Noble would spit at one another about religion into the early hours of the morning, and Hawkins worried the soul out of Noble, whose brother was a priest, with a string of questions that would puzzle a cardinal. To make it worse even in treating of holy subjects, Hawkins had a deplorable tongue. I never in all my career met a man who could mix such a variety of cursing and bad language into an argument. He was a terrible man, and a fright to argue. He never did a stroke of work, and when he had no one else to talk to, he got stuck in the old woman.

He met his match in her, for one day when he tried to get her to complain profanely of the drought, she gave him a great come-down by blaming it entirely on Jupiter Pluvius (a deity neither Hawkins nor I have ever heard of, though Noble said that among the pagans it was believed that he had something to do with the rain). Another day he was swearing at the capitalists for starting the German war when the old lady laid down her iron, puckered up her little crab's mouth, and said: "Mr. Hawkins, you can say what you like about the war, and think you'll deceive me because I'm only a simple poor countrywoman, but I know what started the war. It was the Italian Count that stole the heathen divinity out of the temple in Japan. Believe me, Mr. Hawkins, nothing but sorrow and want can follow the people that disturb the hidden powers."

A queer old girl, all right.

2

We had our tea one evening, and Hawkins lit the lamp and we all sat into cards. Jeremiah Donovan came in too, and sat down and watched us for a while, and it suddenly struck me that he had no great love for the two Englishmen. It came as a great surprise to me, because I hadn't noticed anything about him before.

Late in the evening a really terrible argument blew up between Hawkins and Noble, about capitalists and priests and love of your country.

"The capitalists," says Hawkins with an angry gulp, "pays the priests to tell you about the next world so as you won't notice what the bastards are up to in this."

"Nonsense, man!" says Noble, losing his temper. "Before ever a capitalist was thought of, people believed in the next world."

Hawkins stood up as though he was preaching a sermon.

"Oh, they did, did they?" he says with a sneer. "They believed all the things you believe, isn't that what you mean? And you believe that God created Adam, and Adam created Shem, and Shem created Jehoshophat. You believe all that silly old fairytale about Eve and Eden and the apple. Well, listen to me, chum. If you're entitled to hold a silly belief—like that, I'm entitled to hold my silly belief which is that the first thing your God created was a bleeding capitalist, with morality and Rolls-Royce complete. Am I right, chum?" he says to Belcher.

"You're right, chum," says Belcher with his amused smile, and got up from the table to stretch his long legs into the fire and stroke his moustache. So, seeing that Jeremiah Donovan was going, and that there was no knowing when the argument about religion would be over, I went out with him. We strolled down to the village together, and then he stopped and started blushing and mumbling and saying I ought to be behind, keeping guard on the prisoners. I didn't like the tone he took with me, and anyway I was bored with life in the cottage, so I replied by asking him what the hell we wanted guarding them at all for. I told him I'd talked it over with Noble, and that we'd both rather be out with a fighting column.

"What use are those fellows to us?" says I.   20

He looked at me in surprise and said: "I thought you knew we were keeping them as hostages."

"Hostages?" I said.

"The enemy have prisoners belonging to us," he says, "and now they're talking of shooting them. If they shoot our prisoners, we'll shoot theirs."

"Shoot them?" I said.

"What else did you think we were keeping them for?" he says.   25

"Wasn't it very unforeseen of you not to warn Noble and myself of that in the beginning?" I said.

"How was it?" says he. "You might have known it."

"We couldn't know it, Jeremiah Donovan," says I. "How could we when they were on our hands so long?"

"The enemy have our prisoners as long and longer," says he.

"That's not the same thing at all," says I.   30

"What difference is there?" says he.

I couldn't tell him, because I knew he wouldn't understand. If it was only an old dog that was going to the vet's, you'd try and not get too fond of him, but Jeremiah Donovan wasn't a man that would ever be in danger of that.

"And when is this thing going to be decided?" says I.

"We might hear tonight," he says. "Or tomorrow or the next day at latest. So if it's only hanging round here that's a trouble to you, you'll be free soon enough."

It wasn't the hanging round that was a trouble to me at all by this time. I had   35
worse things to worry about. When I got back to the cottage the argument was still on. Hawkins was holding forth in his best style, maintaining that there was no next world, and Noble was maintaining that there was; but I could see that Hawkins had had the best of it.

"Do you know what, chum?" he was saying with a saucy smile. "I think you're just as big a bleeding unbeliever as I am. You say you believe in the next world, and you know just as much about the next world as I do, which is sweet damn-all. What's heaven? You don't know. Where's heaven? You don't know. You know sweet damn-all! I ask you again, do they wear wings?"

"Very well, then," says Noble, "they do. Is that enough for you? They do wear wings."

"Where do they get them, then? Who makes them? Have they a factory for wings? Have they a sort of store where you hands in your chit and takes your bleeding wings?"

"You're an impossible man to argue with," says Noble. "Now, listen to me —" And they were off again.

It was long after midnight when we locked up and went to bed. As I blew out the candle I told Noble what Jeremiah Donovan was after telling me. Noble took it very quietly. When we'd been in bed about an hour he asked me did I think we ought to tell the Englishmen. I didn't think we should, because it was more than likely that the English wouldn't shoot our men, and even if they did, the brigade officers, who were always up and down with the Second Battalion and knew the Englishmen well, wouldn't be likely to want them plugged. "I think so too," says Noble. "It would be great cruelty to put the wind up them now."

"It was very unforeseen of Jeremiah Donovan anyhow," says I.

It was next morning that we found it so hard to face Belcher and Hawkins. We went about the house all day scarcely saying a word. Belcher didn't seem to notice; he was stretched into the ashes as usual, with his usual look of waiting in quietness for something unforeseen to happen, but Hawkins noticed and put it down to Noble's being beaten in the argument of the night before.

"Why can't you take a discussion in the proper spirit?" he says severely. "You and your Adam and Eve! I'm a Communist, that's what I am. Communist or anarchist, it all comes to much the same thing." And for hours he went round the house, muttering when the fit took him. "Adam and Eve! Adam and Eve! Nothing better to do with their time than picking bleeding apples!"

3

I don't know how we got through that day, but I was very glad when it was over, the tea things were cleared away, and Belcher said in his peaceable way: "Well, chums, what about it?" We sat round the table and Hawkins took out the cards, and just then I heard Jeremiah Donovan's footstep on the path and a dark presentiment crossed my mind. I rose from the table and caught him before he reached the door.

"What do you want?" I asked.

"I want those two soldier friends of yours," he says, getting red.

"Is that the way, Jeremiah Donovan?" I asked.

"That's the way. There were four of our lads shot this morning, one of them a boy of sixteen."

"That's bad," I said.

At that moment Noble followed me out, and the three of us walked down the path together, talking in whispers. Feeney, the local intelligence officer, was standing by the gate.

"What are you going to do about it?" I asked Jeremiah Donovan.

"I want you and Noble to get them out; tell them they're being shifted again; that'll be the quietest way."

"Leave me out of that," says Noble under his breath.

Jeremiah Donovan looks at him hard.

"All right," he says. "You and Feeney get a few tools from the shed and dig a   55
hole by the far end of the bog. Bonaparte and myself will be after you. Don't let
anyone see you with the tools. I wouldn't like it to go beyond ourselves."

We saw Feeney and Noble go round to the shed and went in ourselves. I left
Jeremiah Donovan to do the explanations. He told them that he had orders to
send them back to the Second Battalion. Hawkins let out a mouthful of curses,
and you could see that though Belcher didn't say anything, he was a bit upset too.
The old woman was for having them stay in spite of us, and she didn't stop advising them until Jeremiah Donovan lost his temper and turned on her. He had a
nasty temper, I noticed. It was pitch-dark in the cottage by this time, but no one
thought of lighting the lamp, and in the darkness the two Englishmen fetched
their topcoats and said good-bye to the old woman.

"Just as a man makes a home of a bleeding place, some bastard at headquarters thinks you're too cushy and shunts you off," says Hawkins, shaking her hand.

"A thousand thanks, madam," says Belcher. "A thousand thanks for everything"—as though he'd made it up.

We went round to the back of the house and down towards the bog. It was
only then that Jeremiah Donovan told them. He was shaking with excitement.

"There were four of our fellows shot in Cork this morning and now you're to   60
be shot as a reprisal."

"What are you talking about?" snaps Hawkins. "It's bad enough being mucked
about as we are without having to put up with your funny jokes."

"It isn't a joke," says Donovan. "I'm sorry, Hawkins, but it's true," and begins
on the usual rigmarole about duty and how unpleasant it is.

I never noticed that people who talk a lot about duty find it much of a
trouble to them.

"Oh, cut it out!" says Hawkins.

"Ask Bonaparte," says Donovan, seeing that Hawkins isn't taking him seri-   65
ously. "Isn't it true, Bonaparte?"

"It is," I say, and Hawkins stops.

"Ah, for Christ's sake, chum!"

"I mean it, chum," I say.

"You don't sound as if you mean it."

"If he doesn't mean it, I do," says Donovan, working himself up.   70

"What have you against me, Jeremiah Donovan?"

"I never said I had anything against you. But why did your people take out
four of our prisoners and shoot them in cold blood?"

He took Hawkins by the arm and dragged him on, but it was impossible to
make him understand that we were in earnest. I had the Smith and Wesson in my
pocket and I kept fingering it and wondering what I'd do if they put up a fight for
it or ran, and wishing to God they'd do one or the other. I knew if they did run for

it, that I'd never fire on them. Hawkins wanted to know was Noble in it, and when we said yes, he asked us why Noble wanted to plug him. Why did any of us want to plug him? What had he done to us? Weren't we all chums? Didn't we understand him and didn't he understand us? Did we imagine for an instant that he'd shoot us for all the so-and-so officers in the so-and-so British Army?

By this time we'd reached the bog, and I was so sick I couldn't even answer him. We walked along the edge of it in the darkness, and every now and then Hawkins would call a halt and begin all over again, as if he was wound up, about our being chums, and I knew that nothing but the sight of the grave would convince him that we had to do it. And all the time I was hoping that something would happen; that they'd run for it or that Noble would take over the responsibility from me. I had the feeling that it was worse on Noble than on me.

4

At last we saw the lantern in the distance and made towards it. Noble was carrying it, and Feeney was standing somewhere in the darkness behind him, and the picture of them so still and silent in the bogland brought it home to me that we were in earnest, and banished the last bit of hope I had.

Belcher, on recognizing Noble, said: "Hallo, chum," in his quiet way, but Hawkins flew at him at once, and the argument began all over again, only this time Noble had nothing to say for himself and stood with his head down, holding the lantern between his legs.

It was Jeremiah Donovan who did the answering. For the twentieth time, as though it was haunting his mind, Hawkins asked if anybody thought he'd shoot Noble.

"Yes, you would," says Jeremiah Donovan.

"No, I wouldn't, damn you!"

"You would, because you'd know you'd be shot for not doing it."

"I wouldn't, not if I was to be shot twenty times over. I wouldn't shoot a pal. And Belcher wouldn't—isn't that right, Belcher?"

"That's right, chum," Belcher said, but more by way of answering the question than of joining in the argument. Belcher sounded as though whatever unforeseen thing he'd always been waiting for had come at last.

"Anyway, who says Noble would be shot if I wasn't? What do you think I'd do if I was in his place, out in the middle of a blasted bog?"

"What would you do?" asks Donovan.

"I'd go with him wherever he was going, of course. Share my last bob with him and stick by him through thick and thin. No one can ever say of me that I let down a pal."

"We had enough of this," says Jeremiah Donovan, cocking his revolver. "Is there any message you want to send?"

"No, there isn't."

"Do you want to say your prayers?"

Hawkins came out with a cold-blooded remark that even shocked me and turned on Noble again.

75

80

85

"Listen to me, Noble," he says. "You and me are chums. You can't come over   90
to my side, so I'll come over to your side. That show you I mean what I say? Give
me a rifle and I'll go along with you and the other lads."

Nobody answered him. We knew that was no way out.

"Hear what I'm saying?" he says. "I'm through with it. I'm a deserter or anything else you like. I don't believe in your stuff, but it's no worse than mine. That
satisfy you?"

Noble raised his head, but Donovan began to speak and he lowered it again
without replying.

"For the last time, have you any messages to send?" says Donovan in a cool,
excited sort of voice.

"Shut up, Donovan! You don't understand me, but these lads do. They're   95
not the sort to make a pal and kill a pal. They're not the tools of any capitalist."

I alone of the crowd saw Donovan raise his Webley to the back of
Hawkins's neck, and as he did so I shut my eyes and tried to pray. Hawkins had
begun to say something else when Donovan fired, and as I opened my eyes at the
bang, I saw Hawkins stagger at the knees and lie out flat at Noble's feet, slowly
and as quiet as a kid falling asleep, with the lantern-light on his lean legs and
bright farmer's boots. We all stood very still, watching him settle out in the last
agony.

Then Belcher took out a handkerchief and began to tie it about his own eyes
(in our excitement we'd forgotten to do the same for Hawkins), and, seeing it
wasn't big enough, turned and asked for the loan of mine. I gave it to him and he
knotted the two together and pointed with his foot at Hawkins.

"He's not quite dead," he says. "Better give him another."

Sure enough, Hawkins's left knee is beginning to rise. I bend down and put
my gun to his head; then, recollecting myself, I get up again. Belcher understands what's in my mind.

"Give him his first," he says. "I don't mind. Poor bastard, we don't know   100
what's happening to him now."

I knelt and fired. By this time I didn't seem to know what I was doing.
Belcher, who was fumbling a bit awkwardly with the handkerchiefs, came out
with a laugh as he heard the shot. It was the first time I heard him laugh and it
sent a shudder down my back; it sounded so unnatural.

"Poor bugger!" he said quietly. "And last night he was so curious about it all.
It's very queer, chums, I always think. Now he knows as much about it as they'll
ever let him know, and last night he was all in the dark."

Donovan helped him to tie the handkerchiefs about his eyes. "Thanks,
chum," he said. Donovan asked if there were any messages he wanted sent.

"No, chum," he says, "not for me. If any of you would like to write to
Hawkins's mother, you'll find a letter from her in his pocket. He and his mother
were great chums. But my missus left me eight years ago. Went away with another
fellow and took the kid with her. I like the feeling of a home, as you may have
noticed, but I couldn't start again after that."

It was an extraordinary thing, but in those few minutes Belcher said more   105
than in all the weeks before. It was just as if the sound of the shot had started a
flood of talk in him and he could go on the whole night like that, quite happily,

talking about himself. We stood round like fools now that he couldn't see us any longer. Donovan looked at Noble, and Noble shook his head. Then Donovan raised his Webley, and at that moment Belcher gives his queer laugh again. He may have thought we were talking about him, or perhaps he noticed the same thing I'd noticed and couldn't understand it.

"Excuse me, chums," he says. "I feel I'm talking the hell of a lot, and so silly, about my being so handy about a house and things like that. But this thing came on me suddenly. You'll forgive me, I'm sure."

"You don't want to say a prayer?" asks Donovan.

"No, chum," he says. "I don't think it would help. I'm ready, and you boys want to get it over."

"You understand that we're only doing our duty?" says Donovan.

Belcher's head was raised like a blind man's, so that you could only see his   110
chin and the tip of his nose in the lantern-light.

"I never could make out what duty was myself," he said. "I think you're all good lads, if that's what you mean. I'm not complaining."

Noble, just as if he couldn't bear any more of it, raised his fist at Donovan, and in a flash Donovan raised his gun and fired. The big man went over like a sack of meal, and this time there was no need of a second shot.

I don't remember much about the burying, but that it was worse than all the rest because we had to carry them to the grave. It was all mad lonely with nothing but a patch of lantern-light between ourselves and the dark, and birds hooting and screeching all round, disturbed by the guns. Noble went through Hawkins's belongings to find the letter from his mother, and then joined his hands together. He did the same with Belcher. Then, when we'd filled the grave, we separated from Jeremiah Donovan and Feeney and took our tools back to the shed. All the way we didn't speak a word. The kitchen was dark and cold as we'd left it, and the old woman was sitting over the hearth, saying her beads. We walked past her into the room, and Noble struck a match to light the lamp. She rose quietly and came to the doorway with all her cantankerousness gone.

"What did ye do with them?" she asked in a whisper, and Noble started so that the match went out in his hand.

"What's that?" he asked without turning around.   115

"I heard ye," she said.

"What did you hear?" asked Noble.

"I heard ye. Do ye think I didn't hear ye, putting the spade back in the houseen?"

Noble struck another match and this time the lamp lit for him.

"Was that what ye did to them?" she asked.   120

Then, by God, in the very doorway, she fell on her knees and began praying, and after looking at her for a minute or two Noble did the same by the fireplace. I pushed my way out past her and left them at it. I stood at the door, watching the stars and listening to the shrieking of the birds dying out over the bogs. It is so strange what you feel at times like that that you can't describe it. Noble says he saw everything ten times the size, as though there were nothing in the whole world but that little patch of bog with the two Englishmen stiffening into it, but with me it was as if the patch of bog where the Englishmen were was a million miles away, and even Noble and the old woman, mumbling behind me, and the birds and the bloody stars were all far away, and I was somehow very small and very lost and lonely like a child astray in the snow. And anything that happened to me afterwards, I never felt the same about again.   [1931, 1954]

THINKING ABOUT THE TEXT

1. What thoughts are expressed about duty in this story? What do these thoughts indicate to you about the characters who express them? Does the story lead you to conclude that *any* duty is worthwhile? If so, what specific duty or duties do you see it is as endorsing?

2. Do you think there is anything Bonaparte can and should have done that he didn't do? Explain. How does his response to the executions differ from Noble's and the woman's? State the difference in your own words.

3. Identify references to the "unforeseen." Which characters were surprised by the execution order? Which, if any, foresaw it? Did the ending surprise you? Why, or why not?

4. Through much of the story, Hawkins argues against religion and capitalism. What do you think of his arguments? Near the end, he argues against his own execution. Should readers agree with the case he makes? Why, or why not? Compare Hawkins and Belcher. Which ultimately strikes you more, their similarities or their differences?

5. Before you read the story, what did you know about conflicts between the English and the Irish? Does O'Connor provide enough historical background for you? If not, what additional sorts of details should he have incorporated into his story? Where in the world are there conflicts today that could produce situations like the one O'Connor depicts?

HARUKI MURAKAMI
Another Way to Die
Translated by Jay Rubin

Haruki Murakami (b. 1949) was born in Kobe, Japan, and for many Japanese readers he is now their country's leading fiction writer. Because his works are increasingly translated, he is becoming better known in the United States and other countries. Murakami has translated into Japanese the works of several American writers, and during the first half of the 1990s he taught at Princeton University. Recently, Murakami has studied terrorism. For his book Underground *(published in English in 2000), he interviewed survivors of a religious cult's 1995 poison gas attack on the Tokyo subway system. But political concerns are evident as well in the following story, a chapter from Murakami's novel* The Wind-Up Bird Chronicle *(published in English in 1997). The novel deals with the Japanese occupation of Manchuria, an area of China, beginning in the 1930s. The Japanese established a nation called Manchukuo, which was nominally headed by the former emperor of China until 1945, when Russian forces moved in and World War II ended overall. "Another Way to Die" takes place during this period.*

The Japanese veterinarian woke before 6 A.M. Most of the animals in the Hsin-ching zoo were already awake. The open window let in their cries and the breeze that carried their smells, which told him the weather without his having to look outside. This was part of his routine here in Manchuria: he would listen, then inhale the morning air, and so ready himself for each new day.

Today, however, should have been different from the day before. It *had* to be different. So many voices and smells had been lost! The tigers, the leopards, the wolves, the bears: all had been liquidated — eliminated — by a Japanese squad the previous afternoon to avoid the animals' escaping as the city came under Russian attack. Now, after some hours of sleep, those events seemed to him like part of a sluggish nightmare he had had long ago. But he knew they had actually happened. His ears still felt a dull ache from the roar of the soldiers' rifles; that could not be a dream. It was August now, the year 1945, and he was here in the city of Hsin-ching, in Japanese-held Manchuria; Soviet troops had burst across the border and were pressing closer every hour. This was reality — as real as the sink and toothbrush he saw in front of him.

The sound of the elephants' trumpeting gave him some sense of relief. Ah, yes — the elephants had survived. Fortunately, the young lieutenant in charge of yesterday's action had had enough normal human sensitivity to remove the elephants from the list, the veterinarian thought as he washed his face. Since coming to Manchuria, he had met any number of stiff-necked, fanatical young officers from his homeland, and the experience always left him shaken. Most of them were farmers' sons who had spent their youthful years in the depressed nineteen-thirties, steeped in the tragedies of poverty while a megalomaniac nationalism was hammered into their skulls. They would follow the orders of a superior without a second thought, no matter how outlandish. If they were commanded, in the name of the Emperor, to dig a hole through the earth to Brazil, they would grab a shovel and set to work. Some people called this "purity," but the veterinarian had other words for it. As an urban doctor's son, educated in the relatively liberal atmosphere of Japan in the twenties, the veterinarian could never understand those young officers. Shooting a couple of elephants should have been a simpler assignment than digging through the earth to Brazil, but yesterday's lieutenant, though he spoke with a slight country accent, seemed to be a more normal human being than other officers were — better educated and more reasonable. The veterinarian could sense this from the way the young man spoke and handled himself.

In any case, the elephants had not been killed, and the veterinarian told himself that he should probably be grateful. The soldiers, too, must have been glad to be spared the task. The Chinese workers may have regretted the omission — they had missed out on a lot of meat and ivory.

The veterinarian boiled water in a kettle, soaked his beard in a hot towel, and shaved. Then he ate breakfast alone: tea, toast, and butter. The food rations in

5

Manchuria were far from sufficient, but compared with those elsewhere they were still fairly generous. This was good news both for him and for the animals. The animals showed resentment at their reduced allotments of feed, but the situation here was better than in zoos back in the Japanese homeland, where food supplies had already bottomed out. No one could predict the future, but for now, at least, both animals and humans were spared the pain of extreme hunger.

He wondered how his wife and daughter were doing. They had left for Japan a few days earlier, and if all went according to plan their train should have reached the Korean coast by now. There they would board the transport ship that would carry them home to Japan. The doctor missed seeing them when he woke up in the morning. He missed hearing their lively voices as they prepared breakfast. A hollow quiet ruled the house. This was no longer the home he loved, the place where he belonged. And yet, at the same time, he could not help feeling a certain strange joy at being left alone in this empty official residence; now he was able to sense the implacable power of fate in his very bones and flesh.

Fate itself was the veterinarian's own fatal disease. From his youngest days, he had had a weirdly lucid awareness that "I, as an individual, am living under the control of some outside force." Most of the time, the power of fate played on like a quiet and monotonous ground bass, coloring only the edges of his life. Rarely was he reminded of its existence. But every once in a while the balance would shift and the force would increase, plunging him into a state of near-paralytic resignation. He knew from experience that nothing he could do or think would ever change the situation.

Not that he was a passive creature; indeed, he was more decisive than most, and he always saw his decisions through. In his profession, too, he was outstanding: a veterinarian of exceptional skill, a tireless educator. He was certainly no fatalist, as most people use the word. And yet never had he experienced the unshakable certainty that he had arrived at a decision entirely on his own. He always had the sense that fate had forced him to decide things to suit its own convenience. On occasion, after the momentary satisfaction of having decided something of his own free will, he would see that things had been decided beforehand by an external power cleverly camouflaged as free will, mere bait thrown in his path to lure him into behaving as he was meant to. He felt like a titular head of state who did nothing more than impress the royal seal on documents at the behest of a regent who wielded all true power in the realm—like the Emperor of this puppet empire of Manchukuo.

Now, left behind in his residence at the zoo, the veterinarian was alone with his fate. And it was fate above all, the gigantic power of fate, that held sway here— not the Kwantung Army, not the Soviet Army, not the troops of the Chinese Communists or of the Kuomintang.° Anyone could see that fate was the ruler here, and that individual will counted for nothing. It was fate that had spared the

---

not the ... the Kuomintang: The Kwantung Army was the Japanese-controlled military force in Manchukuo. In August 1945, when Murakami's story takes place, the Soviet Army was on the verge of defeating this force. The Kuomintang, led by General Chiang Kai-shek, was the controlling party in the overall Chinese government. The Chinese Communists managed to take over China in 1948, forcing Chiang Kai-shek and his allies to flee to Taiwan.

elephants and buried the tigers and leopards and wolves and bears the day before. What would it bury now, and what would it spare? These were questions that no one could answer.

The veterinarian left his residence to prepare for the morning feeding. He 10 assumed that no one would show up for work anymore, but he found two Chinese boys waiting for him in his office. He did not know them. They were thirteen or fourteen years old, dark-complexioned and skinny, with roving animal eyes. "They told us to help you," one boy said. The doctor nodded. He asked their names, but they made no reply. Their faces remained blank, as if they had not heard the question. These boys had obviously been sent by the Chinese people who had worked here until the day before. Those people had probably ended all contact with the Japanese now, in anticipation of a new regime, but assumed that children would not be held accountable. The boys had been sent as a sign of good will — the workers knew that he could not care for the animals alone.

The veterinarian gave each boy two cookies, then put them to work helping him feed the animals. They led a mule-drawn cart from cage to cage, providing each animal with its particular feed and changing its water. Cleaning the cages was out of the question. The best they could manage was a quick hose-down, to wash away the droppings.

They started the work at eight o'clock and finished after ten. The boys then disappeared without a word. The veterinarian felt exhausted from the hard physical labor. He went back to the office and reported to the zoo director that the animals had been fed.

Just before noon, the young lieutenant came back to the zoo leading the same eight soldiers he had brought the day before. Fully armed again, they walked with a metallic clinking that could be heard far in advance of their arrival. Their shirts were blackened with sweat. Cicadas were screaming in the trees, as they had been yesterday. Today, however, the soldiers had not come to kill animals. The lieutenant saluted the director and said, "We need to know the current status of the zoo's usable carts and draft animals." The director informed him that the zoo had exactly one mule and one wagon. "We contributed our only truck and two horses two weeks ago," he noted. The lieutenant nodded and announced that he would immediately commandeer the mule and wagon, as per orders of Kwantung Army Headquarters.

"Wait just a minute," the veterinarian interjected. "We need those to feed the animals twice a day. All our local people have disappeared. Without that mule and wagon, our animals will starve to death. Even with them, we can barely keep up."

"We're all just barely keeping up, sir," said the lieutenant, whose eyes were 15 red and whose face was covered with stubble. "Our first priority is to defend the city. You can always let the animals out of their cages if need be. We've taken care of the dangerous carnivores. The others pose no security risk. These are military orders, sir. You'll just have to manage as you see fit."

Cutting the discussion short, the lieutenant had his men take the mule and wagon. When they were gone, the veterinarian and the director looked at each other. The director sipped his tea, shook his head, and said nothing.

Four hours later, the soldiers were back with the mule and wagon, a filthy canvas tarpaulin covering the mounded contents of the wagon. The mule was panting, its hide foaming with the afternoon heat and the weight of the load. The eight soldiers marched four Chinese men ahead of them at bayonet point— young men, perhaps twenty years old, wearing baseball uniforms and with their hands tied behind their backs. Black-and-blue marks on their faces made it obvious that they had been severely beaten. The right eye of one man was swollen almost shut, and the bleeding lips of another had stained his baseball shirt bright red. The shirtfronts had nothing written on them, but there were small rectangles where the name patches had been torn off. The numbers on their backs were 1, 4, 7, and 9. The veterinarian could not begin to imagine why, at such a time of crisis, four young Chinese men would be wearing baseball uniforms or why they had been so badly beaten and dragged here by Japanese troops. The scene looked like something not of this world— a painting by a mental patient.

The lieutenant asked the zoo director if he had any picks and shovels he could let them use. The young officer looked even more pale and haggard than he had before. The veterinarian led him and his men to a toolshed behind the office. The lieutenant chose two picks and two shovels for his men. Then he asked the veterinarian to come with him and, leaving his men there, walked into a thicket beyond the road. The veterinarian followed. Wherever the lieutenant walked, huge grasshoppers scattered. The smell of summer grass hung in the air. Mixed in with the deafening screams of cicadas, the sharp trumpeting of elephants now and then seemed to sound a distant warning.

The lieutenant went on among the trees without speaking, until he found a kind of opening in the woods. The area had been slated for construction of a plaza for small animals that children could play with. The plan had been postponed indefinitely, however, when the worsening military situation made construction materials scarce. The trees had been cleared away to make a circle of bare ground, and the sun illuminated this one part of the woods like stage lighting. The lieutenant stood in the center of the circle and scanned the area. Then he dug at the ground with the heel of his boot.

"We're going to bivouac here for a while," he said, kneeling down and scoop- ing up a handful of dirt.   20

The veterinarian nodded in response. He had no idea why they had to bivouac in a zoo, but he decided not to ask. Here in Hsin-ching, experience had taught him never to question military men. Questions did nothing but make them angry, and they never gave you a straight answer in any case.

"First we dig a big hole here," the lieutenant said, speaking as if to himself. He stood up and took a pack of cigarettes from his shirt pocket. Putting a cigarette between his lips, he offered one to the doctor, then lit both with a match. The two concentrated on their smoking to fill the silence. Again the lieutenant began digging at the ground with his boot. He drew a kind of diagram in the earth, then rubbed it out. Finally, he asked the veterinarian, "Where were you born?"

"In Kanagawa," the doctor said. "In a town called Ofuna, near the sea, an hour or two from Tokyo."

The lieutenant nodded.

"And where were you born?" the veterinarian asked. 25

Instead of answering, the lieutenant narrowed his eyes and watched the smoke rising from between his fingers. No, it never pays to ask a military man questions, the veterinarian told himself again. They like to ask questions, but they'll never give you an answer. They wouldn't give you the time of day—literally.

"There's a movie studio there," the lieutenant said.

It took the veterinarian a few seconds to realize the lieutenant was talking about Ofuna. "That's right. A big studio. I've never been inside, though."

The lieutenant dropped what was left of his cigarette on the ground and crushed it out. "I hope you make it back there," he said. "Of course, there's an ocean to cross between here and Japan. We'll probably all die over here." He kept his eyes on the ground as he spoke. "Tell me, Doctor, are you afraid of death?"

"I guess it depends on how you die," the veterinarian said after a moment's 30 thought.

The lieutenant raised his eyes and looked at the veterinarian as if his curiosity had been aroused. He had apparently been expecting another answer. "You're right," he said. "It does depend on how you die."

The two remained silent for a time. The lieutenant looked as if he might just fall asleep there standing up. He was obviously exhausted. An especially large grasshopper flew over them like a bird and disappeared into a distant clump of grass with a noisy beating of wings. The lieutenant glanced at his watch.

"Time to get started," he said to no one in particular. Then he spoke to the veterinarian. "I'd like you to stay around for a while. I might have to ask you to do me a favor."

The veterinarian nodded.

The soldiers led the Chinese prisoners to the opening in the woods and 35 untied their hands. The corporal drew a large circle on the ground using a baseball bat—why a soldier would have a bat the veterinarian found another mystery—and ordered the prisoners, in Japanese, to dig a deep hole the size of the circle. With the picks and shovels, the four men in baseball uniforms started digging in silence. Half the Japanese squad stood guard over them while the other half stretched out beneath the trees. They seemed to be in desperate need of sleep; no sooner had they hit the ground in full gear than they began snoring. The four soldiers who remained awake kept watch over the digging nearby, rifles resting on their hips, bayonets fixed, ready for immediate use. The lieutenant and the corporal took turns overseeing the work and napping under the trees.

It took less than an hour for the four Chinese prisoners to dig a hole some twelve feet across and deep enough to come up to their necks. One of the men asked for water, speaking in Japanese. The lieutenant nodded, and a soldier brought a bucket full of water. The four Chinese took turns ladling water from the bucket and gulping it down with obvious relish. They drank almost the entire bucketful. Their uniforms were smeared black with blood, mud, and sweat.

The lieutenant had two of the soldiers pull the wagon over to the hole. The corporal yanked the tarpaulin off, to reveal four dead men piled in the wagon.

They wore the same baseball uniforms as the prisoners, and they, too, were obviously Chinese. They appeared to have been shot, and their uniforms were covered with black bloodstains. Large flies were beginning to swarm over the corpses. Judging from the way the blood had dried, the doctor guessed that they had been dead for close to twenty-four hours.

The lieutenant ordered the four Chinese who had dug the hole to throw the bodies into it. Without a word, faces blank, the men took the bodies out of the wagon and threw them, one at a time, into the hole. Each corpse landed with a dull thud. The numbers on the dead men's uniforms were 2, 5, 6, and 8. The veterinarian committed them to memory.

When the four Chinese had finished throwing the bodies into the hole, the soldiers tied each man to a nearby tree. The lieutenant held up his wrist and studied his watch with a grim expression. Then he looked up toward a spot in the sky for a while, as if searching for something there. He looked like a stationmaster standing on the platform and waiting for a hopelessly overdue train. But in fact he was looking at nothing at all. He was just allowing a certain amount of time to go by. Once he had accomplished that, he turned to the corporal and gave him curt orders to bayonet three of the four prisoners—Nos. 1, 7, and 9.

Three soldiers were chosen and took up their positions in front of the three   40
Chinese. The soldiers looked paler than the men they were about to kill. The Chinese looked too tired to hope for anything. The corporal offered each of them a smoke, but they refused. He put his cigarettes back into his shirt pocket.

Taking the veterinarian with him, the lieutenant went to stand somewhat apart from the other soldiers. "You'd better watch this," he said. "This is another way to die."

The veterinarian nodded. The lieutenant is not saying this to me, he thought. He's saying it to himself.

In a gentle voice, the lieutenant explained, "Shooting them would be the simplest and most efficient way to kill them, but we have orders not to waste a single bullet—and certainly not to waste bullets killing Chinese. We're supposed to save our ammunition for the Russians. We'll just bayonet them, I suppose, but that's not as easy as it sounds. By the way, Doctor, did they teach you how to use a bayonet in the Army?"

The doctor explained that, as a cavalry veterinarian, he had not been trained to use a bayonet.

"Well, the proper way to kill a man with a bayonet is this: First, you thrust it   45
in under the ribs—here." The lieutenant pointed to his own torso just above the stomach. "Then you drag the point in a big, deep circle inside him to scramble the organs. Then you thrust upward to puncture the heart. You can't just stick it in and expect him to die. We soldiers have this drummed into us. Hand-to-hand combat using bayonets ranks right up there along with night assaults as the pride of the Imperial Army—though mainly it's a lot cheaper than tanks and planes and cannons. Of course, you can train all you want, but finally what you're stabbing is a straw doll, not a live human being. It doesn't bleed or scream or spill its guts on the ground. These soldiers have never actually killed a human being that way. And neither have I."

The lieutenant looked at the corporal and gave him a nod. The corporal barked his order to the three soldiers, who snapped to attention. Then they took a half step back and thrust out their bayonets, each man aiming his blade at his prisoner. One of the young men (No. 7) growled something in Chinese that sounded like a curse and gave a defiant spit—which never reached the ground but dribbled down the front of his baseball uniform.

At the sound of the next order, the three soldiers thrust their bayonets into the Chinese men with tremendous force. Then, as the lieutenant had said, they twisted the blades so as to rip the men's internal organs, and thrust the tips upward. The cries of the Chinese men were not very loud—more like deep sobs than like screams, as if they were heaving out the breath left in their bodies all at once through a single opening. The soldiers pulled out their bayonets and stepped back. The corporal barked his order again, and the men repeated the procedure exactly as before—stabbing, twisting, thrusting upward, withdrawing. The veterinarian watched in numbed silence, overtaken by the sense that he was beginning to split in two. He became simultaneously the stabber and the stabbed. He could feel both the impact of the bayonet as it entered his victim's body and the pain of having his internal organs slashed to bits.

It took much longer than he would have imagined for the Chinese men to die. Their sliced-up bodies poured prodigious amounts of blood on the ground, but, even with their organs shredded, they went on twitching slightly for quite some time. The corporal used his own bayonet to cut the ropes that bound the men to the trees, and then he had the soldiers who had not participated in the killing help drag the fallen bodies to the hole and throw them in. These corpses also made a dull thud on impact, but the doctor couldn't help feeling that the sound was different from that made by the earlier corpses—probably because these were not entirely dead yet.

Now only the young Chinese prisoner with the number 4 on his shirt was left. The three pale-faced soldiers tore broad leaves from plants at their feet and proceeded to wipe their bloody bayonets. Not only blood but strange-colored body fluids and chunks of flesh adhered to the blades. The men had to use many leaves to return the bayonets to their original bare-metal shine.

The veterinarian wondered why only the one man, No. 4, had been left alive, but he was not going to ask questions. The lieutenant took out another cigarette and lit up. He then offered a smoke to the veterinarian, who accepted it in silence and, after putting it between his lips, struck his own match. His hand did not tremble, but it seemed to have lost all feeling, as if he were wearing thick gloves. 50

"These men were cadets in the Manchukuo Army Officer Candidate School," the lieutenant said. "They refused to participate in the defense of Hsin-ching. They killed two of their Japanese instructors last night and tried to run away. We caught them during night patrol, killed four of them on the spot, and captured the other four. Two more escaped in the dark." The lieutenant rubbed his beard with the palm of his hand. "They were trying to make their getaway in baseball uniforms. I guess they figured they'd be arrested as deserters if they wore their military uniforms. Or maybe they were afraid of what Communist troops would do to them if they were caught in their Manchukuo uniforms. Anyway, all they had in their barracks to wear besides their cadet outfits were uniforms of the O.C.S. baseball team. So they tore off the names and tried to get away wearing these. I don't know if you know, but the school had a great team. They used to go to Taiwan and Korea for friendship games. That guy"—and here the lieutenant motioned toward the man tied to the tree—"was captain of the team and batted cleanup. We think he was the one who organized the getaway, too. He killed the two instructors with a bat. The instructors knew there was trouble in the barracks and weren't going to distribute weapons to the cadets until it was an absolute emergency. But they forgot about the baseball bats. Both of them had their skulls cracked open. They probably died instantly. Two perfect home runs. This is the bat."

The lieutenant had the corporal bring the bat to him. He passed the bat to the veterinarian. The doctor took it in both hands and held it up in front of his face, the way a player stepping into the batter's box does. It was just an ordinary bat, not very well made, with a rough finish and an uneven grain. It was heavy, though, and well broken in. The handle was black with sweat. It didn't look like a bat that had been used recently to kill two human beings. After getting a feel for its weight, the veterinarian handed it back to the lieutenant, who gave it a few easy swings, handling it like an expert.

"Do you play baseball?" the lieutenant asked the veterinarian.

"All the time when I was a kid."

"Too grown up now?"

"No more baseball for me," the veterinarian said, and he was on the verge of asking "How about you, lieutenant?" but he swallowed the words.

"I've been ordered to beat this guy to death with the same bat he used," the lieutenant said in a dry voice as he tapped the ground with the tip of the bat. "An eye for an eye, a tooth for a tooth. Just between you and me, I think the order stinks. What the hell good is it going to do to kill these guys? We don't have any planes left, we don't have any warships, our best troops are dead. Just the other day some kind of special new bomb wiped out the whole city of Hiroshima in a split second. Either we're going to be swept out of Manchuria or we'll all be killed, and China will belong to the Chinese again. We've already killed a lot of Chinese, and adding a few bodies to the count isn't going to make any difference. But orders are orders. I'm a soldier and I have to follow orders. We killed the tigers and leopards yesterday, and today we have to kill these guys. So take a good look, Doctor. This is another way for people to die. You're a doctor, so you're probably used to knives and blood and guts, but you've probably never seen anyone beaten to death with a baseball bat."

The lieutenant ordered the corporal to bring player No. 4, the cleanup batter, to the edge of the hole. Once again they tied his hands behind his back, then blindfolded him and had him kneel down on the ground. He was a tall, strongly built young man with massive arms the size of most people's thighs. The lieutenant called over one young soldier and handed him the bat. "Kill him with this," he said. The young soldier stood at attention and saluted before taking the bat, but having taken it in his hands he just went on standing there as if stupefied. He seemed unable to grasp the concept of beating a Chinese man to death with a baseball bat.

55

"Have you ever played baseball?" the lieutenant asked the young soldier.

"No, sir, never," the soldier replied in a loud voice. Both the village in Hokkaido where he was born and the village in Manchuria where he grew up had been so poor that no family in either place could have afforded the luxury of a baseball or a bat. He had spent his boyhood running around the fields, catching dragonflies and playing at sword fighting with sticks. He had never in his life played baseball, or even seen a game. This was the first time he had ever held a bat.

The lieutenant showed him how to hold the bat and taught him the basics of the swing, demonstrating a few times himself. "See? It's all in the hips," he grunted through clenched teeth. "Starting from the backswing, you twist from the waist down. The tip of the bat follows through naturally. Understand? If you concentrate too much on swinging the bat, your arms do all the work and you lose power. Swing from the hips."

The soldier didn't seem fully to comprehend the lieutenant's instructions, but he took off his heavy gear as ordered and practiced his swing for a while. Everyone was watching him. The lieutenant placed his hands over the soldier's to help him adjust his grip. He was a good teacher. Before long, the soldier's swing, though somewhat awkward, was swishing through the air. What the young soldier lacked in skill he made up for in muscle power, having spent his days working on the farm.

"That's good enough," the lieutenant said, using his hat to wipe the sweat from his brow. "O.K., now try to do it in one good, clean swing. Don't let him suffer."

What he really wanted to say was "I don't want to do this any more than you do. Who the hell could have thought of anything so stupid? Killing a guy with a baseball bat . . ." But an officer could never say such a thing to an enlisted man.

The soldier stepped up behind the blindfolded Chinese man where he knelt on the ground. When the soldier raised the bat, the strong rays of the setting sun cast its long, thick shadow on the earth. This is so weird, the veterinarian thought. The lieutenant's right: I've never seen a man killed with a baseball bat. The young soldier held the bat aloft for a long time. The veterinarian saw its tip shaking.

The lieutenant nodded to the soldier. With a deep breath, the soldier took a backswing, then smashed the bat with all his strength into the back of the Chinese cadet's head. He did it amazingly well. He swung his hips exactly as the lieutenant had taught him to, the brand of the bat made a direct hit behind the man's ear, and the bat followed through perfectly. There was a dull crushing sound as the skull shattered. The man himself made no sound. His body hung in the air for a moment in a strange pose, then flopped forward. He lay with his cheek on the ground, blood flowing from one ear. He did not move. The lieutenant looked at his watch. Still gripping the bat, the young soldier stared off into space, his mouth agape.

The lieutenant was a person who did things with great care. He waited for a full minute. When he was certain that the Chinese man was not moving at all, he said to the veterinarian, "Could you do me a favor and check to see that he's really dead?"

The veterinarian nodded, walked over to where the young Chinese lay, and knelt down and removed his blindfold. The man's eyes were open wide, the pupils turned upward, and bright-red blood was flowing from his ear. His half-opened mouth revealed the tongue lying tangled inside. The impact had left his neck twisted at a strange angle. The man's nostrils had expelled thick gobs of blood, making black stains on the dry ground. One particularly alert—and large—fly had already burrowed its way into a nostril to lay eggs. Just to make sure, the veterinarian took the man's wrist and felt for a pulse. There was no pulse—certainly not where there was supposed to be one. The young soldier had ended this burly man's life with a single swing of a bat—indeed, his first-ever swing of a bat. The veterinarian glanced toward the lieutenant and nodded, to signal that the man was, without a doubt, dead. Having completed his assigned task, he was beginning slowly to rise to his full height when it seemed to him that the sun shining on his back suddenly increased in intensity.

At that very moment, the young Chinese batter in uniform No. 4 rose up into a sitting position as if he had just come fully awake. Without the slightest uncertainty or hesitation—or so it seemed to those watching—he grabbed the doctor's wrist. It all happened in a split second. The veterinarian could not understand; this man was dead, he was sure of it. But now, thanks to one last drop of life that seemed to well up out of nowhere, the man was gripping the veterinarian's wrist with the strength of a steel vise. Eyelids stretched open to the limit, pupils still glaring upward, the man fell forward into the hole, dragging the doctor in after him. The doctor fell in on top of him and heard the man's ribs crack as his weight came down. Still the Chinese ballplayer continued to grip his wrist. The soldiers saw all this happening, but they were too stunned to do anything more than stand and watch. The lieutenant recovered first and leaped into the hole. He drew his pistol from his holster, set the muzzle against the Chinese man's head, and pulled the trigger twice. Two sharp, overlapping cracks rang out, and a large black hole opened in the man's temple. Now his life was completely gone, but still he refused to release the doctor's wrist. The lieutenant knelt down and, pistol in one hand, began the painstaking process of prying open the corpse's fingers one at a time. The veterinarian lay there in the hole, surrounded by eight silent Chinese corpses in baseball uniforms. Down in the hole, the screeching of cicadas sounded very different from the way it sounded above ground.

Once the veterinarian had been freed from the dead man's grasp, the soldiers pulled him and the lieutenant out of the grave. The veterinarian squatted down on the grass and took several deep breaths. Then he looked at his wrist. The man's fingers had left five bright-red marks. On this hot August afternoon, the veterinarian felt chilled to the core of his body. I'll never get rid of this coldness again, he thought. That man was truly, seriously trying to take me with him wherever he was going.

The lieutenant reset the pistol's safety and carefully slipped the gun into its holster. This was the first time he had ever fired a gun at a human being. But he tried not to think about it. The war would continue for a little while at least, and people would continue to die. He could leave the deep thinking for later. He

70

wiped his sweaty right palm on his pants, then ordered the soldiers who had not participated in the execution to fill in the hole. A huge swarm of flies had already taken custody of the pile of corpses.

The young soldier went on standing where he was, stupefied, gripping the bat. He couldn't seem to make his hands let go. The lieutenant and the corporal left him alone. He had seemed to be watching the whole bizarre series of events—the "dead" Chinese suddenly grabbing the veterinarian by the wrist, their falling into the grave, the lieutenant's leaping in and finishing him off, and now the other soldiers' filling in the hole. But in fact he had not been watching any of it. He had been listening to a bird in a tree somewhere making a *"Creeeak! Creeeak!"* sound as if winding a spring. The soldier looked up, trying to pinpoint the direction of the cries, but he could see no sign of the windup bird. He felt a slight sense of nausea at the back of his throat.

As he listened to the winding of the spring, the young soldier saw one fragmentary image after another rise up before him and fade away. After the Japanese were disarmed by the Soviets, the lieutenant would be handed over to the Chinese and hanged for his responsibility in these executions. The corporal would die of the plague in a Siberian concentration camp: he would be thrown into a quarantine shed and left there until dead, though in fact he had merely collapsed from malnutrition and had not contracted the plague—not, at least, until he was thrown into the shed. The veterinarian would die in an accident a year later: a civilian, he would be taken by the Soviets for cooperating with the military and sent to another Siberian camp to do hard labor; he would be working in a deep shaft of a Siberian coal mine when a flood would drown him along with many soldiers. And I, thought the young soldier with the bat in his hands—but he could not see his own future. He could not even see as real the events that were happening before his very eyes. He closed his eyes now and listened to the call of the windup bird.

Then, all at once, he thought of the ocean—the ocean he had seen from the deck of the ship bringing him from Japan to Manchuria eight years earlier. He had never seen the ocean before, nor had he seen it since. He could still remember the smell of the salt air. The ocean was one of the greatest things he had ever seen in his life—bigger and deeper than anything he had imagined. It changed its color and shape and expression according to time and place and weather. It aroused a deep sadness in his heart, and at the same time it brought his heart peace and comfort. Would he ever see it again? He loosened his grip and let the bat fall to the ground. It made a dry sound as it struck the earth. After the bat left his hands, he felt a slight increase in his nausea.

The windup bird went on crying, but no one else could hear its call. [1997]   75

THINKING ABOUT THE TEXT

1. This story gets pretty violent. What would you say to someone who argues that it is too violent?

2. Review the veterinarian's reflections on fate in paragraphs 7 and 8. As the story proceeds, is it reasonable of him to believe that "as an individual, [he

is] living under the control of some outside force"? Evaluate his behavior. Do you believe he could and should have done something other than what he actually does?

3. What is the effect of setting this story in and near a zoo? What is the effect of making baseball equipment an important feature of the story?

4. At the end, the story shifts to the young soldier's point of view. Do you find this move effective, or do you consider it unreasonably jarring? Explain. Should readers assume that the soldier is correctly predicting what will happen to other characters? Why, or why not?

5. Do you expect a Japanese audience to look at this story much differently than an American audience would? Identify some of the warrants or assumptions behind your answer. Do you think there have ever been Americans capable of behaving as the Japanese characters in this story do? Again, identify some of your warrants or assumptions.

MAKING COMPARISONS

1. O'Connor's story is told in the first person, but Murakami's is told in the third person. O'Connor gives names to most of the characters in his story, but Murakami does not name any of the characters in his. Do you react to the stories differently for these reasons? Why, or why not?

2. In O'Connor's story, the prisoners become friends with their guards. This does not happen in Murakami's story, though. Is one of the stories more horrifying than the other because of this difference? Explain.

3. "And anything that happened to me afterwards," Bonaparte reports, "I never felt the same about again" (para. 121). After being freed from the clutch of the dead man, the veterinarian in Murakami's story thinks, "I'll never get rid of this coldness again" (para. 70). Are these statements signs that Bonaparte and the veterinarian are quite similar people? Why, or why not?

WRITING ABOUT ISSUES

1. Choose O'Connor's or Murakami's story, and write an essay comparing two of the characters in the story. Above all, consider whether they are more alike than different, and identify what their author conceivably accomplishes with the relationship he draws between them.

2. Do you consider the behavior of the Irish soldiers and the Japanese soldiers to be equally justifiable? Write an essay that addresses this question by focusing on both stories. Support your argument with specific details from both texts.

3. Choose a character from these stories who resembles you in some important way. Write a letter to this character that not only acknowledges the resemblance but also argues for or against the character's behavior. Be sure to give reasons for your position.

4. Throughout modern history, military personnel and revolutionary movements have either wrestled with moral dilemmas or engaged in morally debatable actions: examples include the behavior of Nazi and Japanese officers in World War II; the United States's dropping of the atomic bomb on Hiroshima and Nagasaki; the My Lai massacre during the Vietnam War; Irish Republican Army bombings in London; the U.S. Navy Tailhook scandal; and the treatment of gays and lesbians in the U.S. armed forces. Research one such case, and write an essay stating and defending the principles you think should apply to it. In making your argument, you can refer to stories in this cluster and other reading you have done.

COMMUNITY JUSTICE

SCOTT RUSSELL SANDERS, "Doing Time in the Thirteenth Chair"
JOYCE CAROL OATES, "I, the Juror"
MAXINE HONG KINGSTON, "No Name Woman"

Decisions about justice are often made in the name of an entire community. Even when rulers issue a policy that reflects merely their own mind, they may claim that it enacts their whole society's will. In the American legal system, people act as representatives of their community when they serve on a jury. Of course, jurors may disagree as they try to decide a case, revealing individual values in the process. Moreover, any particular version of community justice is subject to further debate. When the white police officers who were videotaped beating African American motorist Rodney King were initially acquitted by a jury from a predominantly white Los Angeles suburb, many people accused the jurors of racial prejudice. The verdicts delivered by juries in the criminal and civil trials of O. J. Simpson also produced divided opinions about how fair his two juries were.

The first two essays here encourage you to consider the relationship between jurors' social backgrounds and their ultimate decisions. Scott Russell Sanders and Joyce Carol Oates recall their own experiences as alternate juror and juror, respectively. Sanders evidently feels that the white middle-class people he served with fairly decided the fate of a working-class man. Oates, on the other hand, believes that race seriously influenced her jury's thinking.

Juries are not the only means through which communities express their sense of justice. Throughout the centuries, collective judgments have taken plenty of other forms. In the third essay here, the "no name woman" of the title is author Maxine Hong Kingston's aunt, who killed herself in her village in China after neighbors attacked her farm because of her adulterous pregnancy. Kingston's American family continued to punish the aunt by being silent about her life and death. Why and how do communities punish individuals? What criteria should we use in evaluating both formal and informal styles of justice?

BEFORE YOU READ

Have you ever served on a jury? If so, what was the experience like? If not, would you like to be on a jury? Why, or why not? In general, do you have faith in the jury system? What specifically comes to mind as you consider this question?

SCOTT RUSSELL SANDERS
Doing Time in the Thirteenth Chair

Scott Russell Sanders (b. 1945) spent much of his youth at a military munitions base, where his father worked. He describes this experience in the title essay of his 1987 book The Paradise of Bombs, *which also includes the following piece. Today, Sanders is a professor of English at Indiana University. Besides essays, he has published fiction, a study of the writer D. H. Lawrence, and book-length nonfictional works including* Staying Put: Making a Home in a Restless World *(1993) and* Hunting for Hope: A Father's Journeys *(1998).*

The courtroom is filled with the ticking of a clock and the smell of mold. Listening to the minutes click away, I imagine bombs or mechanical hearts sealed behind the limestone walls. Forty of us have been yanked out of our usual orbits and called to appear for jury duty in this ominous room, beneath the stained-glass dome of the county courthouse. We sit in rows like strangers in a theater, coats rumpled in our laps, crossing and uncrossing our legs, waiting for the show to start.

I feel sulky and rebellious, the way I used to feel when a grade-school teacher made me stay inside during recess. This was supposed to have been the first day of my Christmas vacation, and the plain, uncitizenly fact is that I don't want to be here. I want to be home hammering together some bookshelves for my wife. I want to be out tromping the shores of Lake Monroe with my eye cocked skyward for bald eagles and sharp-shinned hawks.

But the computer-printed letter said to report today for jury duty, and so here I sit. The judge beams down at us from his bench. Tortoise-shell glasses, twenty-dollar haircut, square boyish face: although probably in his early forties, he could pass for a student-body president. He reminds me of an owlish television know-it-all named Mr. Wizard who used to conduct scientific experiments (Magnetism! Litmus tests! Sulphur dioxide!) on a kids' show in the 1950s. Like Mr. Wizard, he lectures us in slow, pedantic speech: trial by one's peers, tradition stretching back centuries to England, defendant innocent until proven guilty beyond a reasonable doubt, and so abundantly on. I spy around for the clock. It must be overhead, I figure, up in the cupola above the dome, raining its ticktocks down on us.

When the lecture is finished, the judge orders us to rise, lift our hands, and swear to uphold the truth. There is a cracking of winter-stiff knees as we stand and again as we sit down. Then he introduces the principal actors: the sleek young prosecutor, who peacocks around like a politician on the hustings; the married pair of brooding, elegantly dressed defense lawyers; and the defendant. I don't want to look at this man who is charged with crimes against the "peace and dignity" of the State of Indiana. I don't want anything to do with his troubles. But I grab an image anyway, of a squat, slit-eyed man about my age, mid-thirties, stringy black hair parted in the middle and dangling like curtains across his face, sparse black beard. The chin whiskers and squinted-up eyes make him look faintly Chinese, and faintly grimacing.

Next the judge reads a list of twelve names, none of them mine, and twelve sworn citizens shuffle into the jury box. The lawyers have at them, darting questions. How do you feel about drugs? Would you say the defendant there looks guilty because he has a beard? Are you related to any police officers? Are you pregnant? When these twelve have finished answering, the attorneys scribble names on sheets of paper which they hand to the judge, and eight of the first bunch are sent packing. The judge reads eight more names, the jury box fills up with fresh bodies, the questioning resumes. Six of these get the heave-ho. And so the lawyers cull through the potential jurors, testing and chucking them like two men picking over apples in the supermarket. At length they agree on a dozen, and still my name has not been called. Hooray, I think. I can build those bookshelves after all, can watch those hawks.

Before setting the rest of us free, however, the judge consults his list. "I am calling alternate juror number one," he says, and then he pronounces my name.

Groans echo down my inmost corridors. For the first time I notice a thirteenth chair beside the jury box, and that is where the judge orders me to go.

"Yours is the most frustrating job," the judge advises me soothingly. "Unless someone else falls ill or gets called away, you will have to listen to all the proceedings without taking part in the jury's final deliberations or decisions."

I feel as though I have been invited to watch the first four acts of a five-act play. Never mind, I console myself: the lawyers will throw me out. I'm the only one in the courtroom besides the defendant who sports a beard or long hair. A backpack decorated with NO NUKES and PEACE NOW and SAVE THE WHALES buttons leans against my boots. How can they expect me, a fiction writer, to confine myself to facts? I am unreliable, a confessed fabulist, a marginal Quaker and Wobbly socialist, a man so out of phase with my community that I am thrown into fits of rage by the local newspaper. The lawyers will take a good look at me and race one another to the bench for the privilege of having the judge boot me out.

But neither Mr. Defense nor Mr. Prosecution quite brings himself to focus on my shady features. Each asks me a perfunctory question, the way vacationers will press a casual thumb against the spare tire before hopping into the car for a trip. If there's air in the tire, you don't bother about blemishes. And that is all I am, a spare juror stashed away in the trunk of the court, in case one of the twelve originals gives out during the trial.

Ticktock. The judge assures us that we should be finished in five days, just in time for Christmas. The real jurors exchange forlorn glances. Here I sit, number thirteen, and nobody looks my way. Knowing I am stuck here for the duration, I perk up, blink my eyes. Like the bear going over the mountain, I might as well see what I can see.

♦ ♦ ♦

What I see is a parade of mangled souls. Some of them sit on the witness stand and reveal their wounds; some of them remain offstage, summoned up only by the words of those who testify. The case has to do with the alleged sale, earlier this year, of hashish and cocaine to a confidential informer. First the prosecutor stands at a podium in front of the jury and tells us how it all happened, detail by criminal detail, and promises to prove every fact to our utter satisfaction. Next, one of the defense attorneys has a fling at us. It is the husband of the Mr.-and-Mrs. team, a melancholy-looking man with bald pate and mutton-chop sideburns, deep creases in the chocolate skin of his forehead. Leaning on the podium, he vows that he will raise a flock of doubts in our minds — grave doubts, reasonable doubts — particularly regarding the seedy character of the confidential informer. They both speak well, without hemming and hawing, without stumbling over syntactic cliffs, better than senators at a press conference. Thus, like rival suitors, they begin to woo the jury.

At mid-morning, before hearing from the first witness, we take a recess. (It sounds more and more like school.) Thirteen of us with peel-away JUROR tags stuck to our shirts and sweaters retreat to the jury room. We drink coffee and make polite chat. Since the only thing we have in common is this trial, and since the judge has just forbidden us to talk about that, we grind our gears trying to get a conversation started. I find out what everybody does in the way of work: a bar waitress, a TV repairman (losing customers while he sits here), a department store security guard, a dentist's assistant, an accountant, a nursing home nurse, a cleaning woman, a caterer, a mason, a boisterous old lady retired from rearing children (and married, she tells us, to a school-crossing guard), a meek college student with the demeanor of a groundhog, a teacher. Three of them right now are unemployed. Six men, six women, with ages ranging from twenty-one to somewhere above seventy. Chaucer could gather this bunch together for a literary pilgrimage, and he would not have a bad sampling of smalltown America.

Presently the bailiff looks in to see what we're up to. She is a jowly woman, fiftyish, with short hair the color and texture of buffed aluminum. She wears silvery half-glasses of the sort favored by librarians; in the courtroom she peers at us above the frames with a librarian's skeptical glance, as if to make sure we are awake. To each of us she now gives a small yellow pad and a ballpoint pen. We are to write our names on the back, take notes on them during the trial, and surrender them to her whenever we leave the courtroom. (School again.) Without saying so directly, she lets us know that we are her flock and she is our shepherd. Anything we need, any yen we get for traveling, we should let her know.

I ask her whether I can go downstairs for a breath of air, and the bailiff answers "sure." On the stairway I pass a teenage boy who is listlessly polishing with a rag the wrought-iron filigree that supports the banister. Old men sheltering from December slouch on benches just inside the ground-floor entrance of the courthouse. Their faces have been caved in by disappointment and the loss of teeth. Two-dollar cotton work gloves, the cheapest winter hand-covers, stick out

15

of their back pockets. They are veterans of this place; so when they see me coming with the blue JUROR label pasted on my chest, they look away. Don't tamper with jurors, especially under the very nose of the law. I want to tell them I'm not a real juror, only a spare, number thirteen. I want to pry old stories out of them, gossip about hunting and dogs, about their favorite pickup trucks, their worst jobs. I want to ask them when and how it all started to go wrong for them. Did they hear a snap when the seams of their life began to come apart? But they will not be fooled into looking at me, not these wily old men with the crumpled faces. They believe the label on my chest and stare down at their unlaced shoes.

I stick my head out the door and swallow some air. The lighted thermometer on the bank reads twenty-eight degrees. Schmaltzy Christmas organ music rebounds from the brick-and-limestone shopfronts of the town square. The Salvation Army bell rings and rings. Delivery trucks hustling through yellow lights blare their horns at jaywalkers.

The bailiff must finally come fetch me, and I feel like a wayward sheep. On my way back upstairs, I notice the boy dusting the same square foot of iron filigree, and realize that he is doing this as a penance. Some judge ordered him to clean the metalwork. I'd like to ask the kid what mischief he's done, but the bailiff, looking very dour, is at my heels.

In the hallway she lines us up in our proper order, me last. Everybody stands up when we enter the courtroom, and then, as if we have rehearsed these routines, we all sit down at once. Now come the facts.

The facts are a mess. They are full of gaps, chuckholes, switchbacks, and dead ends — just like life.

At the outset we are shown three small plastic bags. Inside the first is a wad of aluminum foil about the size of an earlobe; the second contains two white pills; the third holds a pair of stamp-sized, squarish packets of folded brown paper. A chemist from the state police lab testifies that he examined these items and found cocaine inside the brown packets, hashish inside the wad of aluminum foil. As for the white pills, they are counterfeits of a popular barbiturate, one favored by politicians and movie stars. They're depressants — downers — but they contain no "controlled substances."

There follows half a day's worth of testimony about how the bags were sealed, who locked them in the narcotics safe at the Bloomington police station, which officer drove them up to the lab in Indianapolis and which drove them back again, who carried them in his coat pocket and who carried them in his briefcase. Even the judge grows bored during this tedious business. He yawns, tips back in his chair, sips coffee from a mug, folds and unfolds with deft thumbs a square of paper about the size of the cocaine packets. The wheels of justice grind slowly. We hear from police officers in uniform, their handcuffs clanking, and from mustachioed officers in civvies, revolvers bulging under their suitcoats. From across the courtroom, the bailiff glares at us above her librarian's glasses, alert to catch us napping. She must be an expert at judging the degrees of tedium.

◆ ◆ ◆

"Do you have to go back and be in the jail again tomorrow?" my little boy asks me at supper.

"Not jail," I correct him. "*Jury*. I'm in the jury."

"With real police?"

"Yes."

"And guns?"

"Yes, real guns."

On the second day there is much shifting of limbs in the jury box when the confidential informer, whom the police call I90, takes the stand. Curly-haired, thirty-three years old, bear-built and muscular like a middle-range wrestler, slow of eye, calm under the crossfire of questions, I90 works — when he works — as a drywall finisher. (In other words, he gets plasterboard ready for painting. It's a dusty, blinding job; you go home powdered white as a ghost, and you taste the joint-filler all night.) Like roughly one-quarter of the construction workers in the county, right now he's unemployed.

The story he tells is essentially this: Just under a year ago, two cops showed up at his house. They'd been tipped off that he had a mess of stolen goods in his basement, stuff he'd swiped from over in a neighboring county. "Now look here," the cops said to him, "you help us out with some cases we've got going, and we'll see what we can do to help you when this here burglary business comes to court." "Like how?" he said. "Like tell us what you know about hot property, and maybe finger a drug dealer or so." He said yes to that, with the two cops sitting at his kitchen table, and — zap! — he was transformed into I90. (Hearing of this miraculous conversion, I am reminded of Saul on the road to Damascus, the devil's agent suddenly seeing the light and joining the angels.) In this new guise he gave information that led to several arrests and some prison terms, including one for his cousin and two or three for other buddies.

In this particular case, his story goes on, he asked a good friend of his where a guy could buy some, you know, drugs. The friend's brother led him to Bennie's trailer, where Bennie offered to sell I90 about any kind of drug a man's heart could desire. "All I want's some hash," I90 told him, "but I got to go get some money off my old lady first." "Then go get it," said Bennie.

Where I90 went was to the police station. There they fixed him up to make a "controlled buy": searched him, searched his car; strapped a radio transmitter around his waist; took his money and gave him twenty police dollars to make the deal. Back I90 drove to Bennie's place, and on his tail in an unmarked police car drove Officer B., listening over the radio to every burp and glitch sent out by I90's secret transmitter. On the way, I90 picked up a six-pack of Budweiser. ("If you walk into a suspect's house drinking a can of beer," Officer B. later tells us, "usually nobody'll guess you're working for the police.") Inside the trailer, the woman Bennie lives with was now fixing supper, and her three young daughters were playing cards on the linoleum floor. I90 bought a gram of blond Lebanese hashish from Bennie for six dollars. Then I90 said that his old lady was on him bad to get her some downers, and Bennie obliged by selling him a couple of 714's (the white pills favored by movie stars and politicians) at seven dollars for the pair.

They shot the bull awhile, Bennie bragging about how big a dealer he used to be (ten pounds of hash and five hundred hits of acid a week), I90 jawing along like an old customer. After about twenty minutes in the trailer, I90 drove to a secluded spot near the L & N railroad depot, and there he handed over the hash and pills to Officer B., who milked the details out of him.

Four days later, I90 went through the same routine, this time buying two packets of cocaine — two "dimes' " worth — from Bennie for twenty dollars. Inside the trailer were half a dozen or so of Bennie's friends, drinking whiskey and smoking pot and watching TV and playing backgammon and generally getting the most out of a Friday night. Again Officer B. tailed I90, listened to the secret radio transmission, and took it all down in a debriefing afterwards behind the Colonial Bakery.

The lawyers burn up a full day leading I90 through this story, dropping questions like breadcrumbs to lure him on, Mr. Prosecutor trying to guide him out of the labyrinth of memory and Mr. Defense trying to get him lost. I90 refuses to get lost. He tells and retells his story without stumbling, intent as a wrestler on a dangerous hold.

On the radio news I hear that U.S. ships have intercepted freighters bound out from Beirut carrying tons and tons of Lebanese hashish, the very same prize strain of hash that I90 claims he bought from Bennie. Not wanting to irk the Lebanese government, the radio says, our ships let the freighters through. Tons and tons sailing across the Mediterranean — into how many one-gram slugs could that cargo be divided?

Out of jail the defense lawyers subpoena one of I90's brothers, who is awaiting his own trial on felony charges. He has a rabbity look about him, face pinched with fear, ready to bolt for the nearest exit. His canary yellow T-shirt is emblazoned with a scarlet silhouette of the Golden Gate Bridge. The shirt and the fear make looking at him painful. He is one of seven brothers and four sisters. Hearing that total of eleven children — the same number as in my father's family — I wonder if the parents were ever booked for burglary or other gestures of despair.

This skittish gent tells us that he always buys his drugs from his brother, good old I90. And good old I90, he tells us further, has a special fondness for snorting cocaine. Glowing there on the witness stand in his yellow shirt, dear brother gives the lie to one after another of I90's claims. But just when I'm about ready, hearing all of this fraternal gossip, to consign I90 to the level of hell reserved by Dante for liars, the prosecutor takes over the questioning. He soon draws out a confession that there has been a bitter feud recently between the two brothers. "And haven't you been found on three occasions to be mentally incompetent to stand trial?" the prosecutor demands.

"Yessir," mutters the brother.

"And haven't you spent most of the past year in and out of mental institutions?"

"Yessir."

35

This second admission is so faint, like a wheeze, that I must lean forward to   40
hear it, even though I am less than two yards away. While the prosecutor lets this
damning confession sink into the jury, the rabbity brother just sits there, as if
exposed on a rock while the hawks dive, his eyes pinched closed.

By day three of the trial, we jurors are no longer strangers to one another.
Awaiting our entry into court, we exhibit wallet photos of our children, of nieces
and nephews. We moan in chorus about our Christmas shopping lists. The
caterer tells about serving 3,000 people at a basketball banquet. The boisterous
old lady, to whom we have all taken a liking, explains how the long hairs on her
white cats used to get on her husband's black suit pants until she put the cats out
in the garage with heating pads in their boxes.

"Where do you leave your car?" the accountant asks.

"On the street," explains the lady. "I don't want to crowd those cats. They're
particular as all get-out."

People compare their bowling scores, their insurance rates, their diets. The
mason, who now weighs about 300 pounds, recounts how he once lost 129
pounds in nine months. His blood pressure got so bad he had to give up dieting,
and inside of a year he'd gained all his weight back and then some. The nurse,
who wrestles the bloated or shriveled bodies of elderly paupers at the city's old
folks' home, complains about her leg joints, and we all sympathize. The security
guard entertains us with sagas about shoplifters. We compare notes on car wrecks,
on where to get a transmission overhauled, on the outgoing college football
coach and the incoming city mayor. We talk, in fact, about everything under the
sun except the trial.

In the hall, where we line up for our reentry into the courtroom, a sullen boy   45
sits at a table scrawling on a legal pad. Line after line he copies the same sentence: "I never will steal anything ever again." More penance. He's balancing on
the first rung of a ladder that leads up—or down—to the electric chair. Somewhere in the middle of the ladder is a good long prison sentence, and that, I calculate, is what is at stake in our little drug-dealing case.

On the third day of testimony, we learn that I90 has been hidden away
overnight by police. After he stepped down from the witness stand yesterday,
Bennie's mate, Rebecca, greeted the informant outside in the lobby and threatened to pull a bread knife out of her purse and carve him into mincemeat. I look
with new interest at the stolid, bulky, black-haired woman who has been sitting
since the beginning of the trial right behind the defendant. From time to time
she has leaned forward, touched Bennie on the shoulder, and bent close to whisper something in his good ear. She reminds me of the Amish farm wives of my
Ohio childhood—stern, unpainted, built stoutly for heavy chores, her face a
fortress against outsiders.

When Rebecca takes the stand, just half a dozen feet from where I sit in
chair thirteen, I sense a tigerish fierceness beneath her numb surface. She plods
along behind the prosecutor's questions until he asks her, rhetorically, whether
she would like to see Bennie X put in jail; then she lashes out. God no, she

doesn't want him locked away. Didn't he take her in when she had two kids already and a third in the oven, and her first husband run off, and the cupboards empty? And haven't they been living together just as good as married for eight years, except while he was in jail, and don't her three little girls call him Daddy? And hasn't he been working on the city garbage trucks, getting up at four in the morning, coming home smelling like other people's trash, and hasn't she been bagging groceries at the supermarket, her hands slashed with paper cuts, and her mother looking after the girls, all so they can keep off the welfare? Damn right she doesn't want him going to any prison.

What's more, Rebecca declares, Bennie don't deserve prison because he's clean. Ever since he got out of the slammer a year ago, he's quit dealing. He's done his time and he's mended his ways and he's gone straight. What about that sale of cocaine? the prosecutor wants to know. It never happened, Rebecca vows. She was there in the trailer the whole blessed night, and she never saw Bennie sell nobody nothing, least of all cocaine, which he never used because it's too expensive — it'll run you seventy-five dollars a day — and which he never sold even when he was dealing. The prosecutor needles her: How can she remember that particular night so confidently? She can remember, she flares at him, because early that evening she got a call saying her sister's ten-year-old crippled boy was fixing to die, and all the family was going to the children's hospital in Indianapolis to watch him pass away. That was a night she'll never forget as long as she lives.

When I was a boy, my friends and I believed that if you killed a snake, the mate would hunt you out in your very bed and strangle or gnaw or smother you. We held a similar belief regarding bears, wolves, and mountain lions, although we were much less likely to run into any of those particular beasts. I have gone years without remembering that bit of child's lore, until today, when Rebecca's tigerish turn on the witness stand revives it. I can well imagine her stashing a bread knife in her purse. And if she loses her man for years and stony years, and has to rear those three girls alone, the cupboards empty again, she might well jerk that knife out of her purse one night and use it on something other than bread.

During recess, we thirteen sit in the jury room and pointedly avoid talking about the bread knife. The mason tells how a neighbor kid's Ford Pinto skidded across his lawn and onto his front porch, blocking the door and nosing against the picture window. "I took the wheels off and chained the bumper to my maple tree until his daddy paid for fixing my porch."

Everyone, it seems, has been assaulted by a car or truck. Our vehicular yarns wind closer and closer about the courthouse. Finally, two of the women jurors — the cigarillo-smoking caterer and the elderly cat lady — laugh nervously. The two of them were standing just inside the plate-glass door of the courthouse last night, the caterer says, when along came a pickup truck, out poked an arm from the window, up flew a smoking beer can, and then BAM! the can exploded. "We jumped a yard in the air!" cries the old woman. "We thought it was some of Bennie's mean-looking friends," the caterer admits. Everybody laughs at the tableau of speeding truck, smoking can, exploding cherry bomb, leaping jurors. Then we choke into sudden silence, as if someone has grabbed each of us by the throat.

♦ ♦ ♦

Four of Bennie's friends—looking not so much mean as broken, like shell-shocked refugees—testify on his behalf during the afternoon of day three. Two of them are out-of-work men in their twenties, with greasy hair to their shoulders, fatigue jackets, and clodhopper boots: their outfits and world-weary expressions are borrowed from record jackets. They are younger versions of the old men with caved-in faces who crouch on benches downstairs, sheltering from December. The other two witnesses are young women with reputations to keep up, neater than the scruffy men; gold crosses dangle over their sweaters, and gum cracks between crooked teeth. All four speak in muttered monosyllables and orphaned phrases, as if they are breaking a long vow of silence and must fetch bits and pieces of language from the archives of memory. They were all at Bennie's place on the night of the alleged cocaine sale, and they swear in unison that no such sale took place.

Officer B., the puppetmaster who pulled the strings on 190, swears just as adamantly that both the sales, of cocaine and of hash, *did* take place, for he listened to the proceedings over the radio in his unmarked blue Buick. He is a sleepy-eyed man in his mid-thirties, about the age of the informant and the defendant, a law-upholding alter ego for those skewed souls.

Double-chinned, padded with the considerable paunch that seems to be issued along with the police badge, Officer B. answers Mr. Prosecutor and Mr. Defense in a flat, walkie-talkie drawl, consulting a sheaf of notes in his lap, never contradicting himself. Yes, he neglected to tape the opening few minutes of the first buy, the minutes when the exchange of hashish and money actually took place. Why? "I had a suspicion my batteries were weak, and I wanted to hold off." And, yes, he did erase the tape of the debriefing that followed buy number one. Why? "It's policy to reuse the old cassettes. Saves the taxpayers' money." And, yes, the tape of the second buy is raw, indecipherable noise, because a blaring TV in the background drowns out all human voices. (Listening to the tape, we can understand nothing in the scrawking except an ad for the American Express Card.) The tapes, in other words, don't prove a thing. What it all boils down to is the word of the law and of the unsavory informer versus the word of the many-times-convicted defendant, his mate, and his friends.

Toward the end of Officer B.'s testimony, there is a resounding clunk, like a muffled explosion, at the base of the witness stand. We all jump—witness, judge, jury, onlookers—and only relax when the prosecutor squats down and discovers that a pair of handcuffs has fallen out of Officer B.'s belt. Just a little reminder of the law's muscle. All of us were envisioning bombs. When Officer B. steps down, the tail of his sportcoat is hitched up over the butt of his gun.

55

The arrest: A squad car pulls up to the front of the trailer, and out the trailer's back door jumps Bennie, barefooted, wearing T-shirt and cut-off jeans. He dashes away between tarpaper shacks, through dog yards, over a stubbled field (his bare feet bleeding), through a patch of woods to a railroad cut. Behind him puffs a skinny cop (who recounts this scene in court), shouting, "Halt! Police!" But Bennie never slows down until he reaches that railroad cut, where he stumbles, falls, rolls down to the tracks like the sorriest hobo. The officer draws his gun.

Bennie lifts his hands for the familiar steel cuffs. The two of them trudge back to the squad car, where Officer B. reads the arrest warrant and Bennie blisters everybody with curses.

The judge later instructs us that flight from arrest may be regarded as evidence, not of guilt but of *consciousness* of guilt. Oh ho! A fine distinction! Guilt for what! Selling drugs? Playing hooky? Original sin? Losing his job at Coca-Cola? I think of those bleeding feet, the sad chase. I remember a drunken uncle who stumbled down a railroad cut, fell asleep between the tracks, and died of fear when a train passed over.

On day four of the trial, Bennie himself takes the stand. He is shorter than I thought, and fatter — too many months of starchy jail food and no exercise. With exceedingly long thumbnails he scratches his jaw. When asked a question, he rolls his eyes, stares at the ceiling, then answers in a gravelly country voice, the voice of a late-night disk jockey. At first he is gruffly polite, brief in his replies, but soon he gets cranked up and rants in a grating monologue about his painful history.

He graduated from high school in 1968, worked eight months at RCA and Coca-Cola, had a good start, had a sweetheart, then the Army got him, made him a cook, shipped him to Vietnam. After a few weeks in the kitchen, he was transferred to the infantry because the fodder-machine was short of foot soldiers. "Hey, listen, man, I ain't nothing but a cook," he told them. "I ain't been trained for combat." And they said, "Don't you worry; you'll get on-the-job training. Learn or die." The artillery ruined his hearing. (Throughout the trial he has held a hand cupped behind one ear, and has followed the proceedings like a grandfather.) Some of his buddies got shot up. He learned to kill people. "We didn't even know what we was there for." To relieve his constant terror, he started doing drugs: marijuana, opium, just about anything that would ease a man's mind. Came home from Vietnam in 1971 a wreck, got treated like dirt, like a babykiller, like a murdering scumbag, and found no jobs. His sweetheart married an insurance salesman.

Within a year after his return he was convicted of shoplifting and burglary. He was framed on the second charge by a friend, but couldn't use his only alibi because he had spent the day of the robbery in bed with a sixteen-year-old girl, whose father would have put him away for statutory rape. As it was, he paid out two years in the pen, where he sank deeper into drugs than ever before. "If you got anything to buy or trade with, you can score more stuff in the state prisons than on the streets of Indianapolis." After prison, he still couldn't find work, couldn't get any help for his drug-thing from the Veterans' Administration, moved in with Rebecca and her three girls, eventually started selling marijuana and LSD. "Everytime I went to somebody for drugs, I got ripped off. That's how I got into dealing. If you're a user, you're always looking for a better deal."

In 1979 he was busted for selling hash, in 1980 for possessing acid, betrayed in both cases by the man from whom he had bought his stock. "He's a snitch, just a filthy snitch. You can't trust nobody." Back to prison for a year, back out again in December 1981. No jobs, no jobs, no damn jobs; then part-time on the city garbage truck, up at four in the morning, minus five degrees and the wind blow-

60

ing and the streets so cold his gloves stuck to the trash cans. Then March came, and this I90 guy showed up, wanted to buy some drugs, and "I told him I wasn't dealing any more. I done my time and gone straight. I told him he didn't have enough money to pay me for no thirty years in the can." (The prosecutor bristles, the judge leans meaningfully forward: we jurors are not supposed to have any notion of the sentence that might follow a conviction on this drug charge.)

In his disk-jockey voice, Bennie denies ever selling anything to this I90 snitch. (He keeps using the word "snitch": I think of tattle-tales, not this adult betrayal.) It was I90, he swears, who tried to sell *him* the hash. Now the pills, why, those he had lying around for a friend who never picked them up, and so he just gave them to I90. "They was give to me, and so I couldn't charge him nothing. They wasn't for me anyway. Downers I do not use. To me, life is a downer. Just to cope with every day, that is way down low enough for me." And as for the cocaine, he never laid eyes on it until the man produced that little plastic bag in court. "I don't use coke. It's too expensive. That's for the bigwigs and the upstanding citizens, as got the money."

Sure, he admits, he ran when the police showed up at his trailer. "I'm flat scared of cops. I don't like talking to them about anything. Since I got back from Vietnam, every time they cross my path they put bracelets on me." (He holds up his wrists. They are bare now, but earlier this morning, when I saw a deputy escorting him into the courthouse, they were handcuffed.) He refuses to concede that he is a drug addict, but agrees he has a terrible habit, "a gift from my country in exchange for me going overseas and killing a bunch of strangers."

After the arrest, forced to go cold turkey on his dope, he begged the jail doctor — "He's no kind of doctor, just one of them that fixes babies" — to zonk him out on something. And so, until the trial, he has spent eight months drowsing under Valium and Thorazine. "You can look down your nose at me for that if you want, but last month another vet hung himself two cells down from me." (The other guy was a scoutmaster, awaiting trial for sexually molesting one of his boys. He had a record of severe depression dating from the war, and used his belt for the suicide.)

"The problem with my life," says Bennie, "is Vietnam." For awhile after coming home, he slept with a knife under his pillow. Once, wakened suddenly, thinking he was still in Vietnam, he nearly killed his best friend. During the week of our trial, another Vietnam vet up in Indianapolis shot his wife in the head, imagining she was a gook. Neighbors got to him before he could pull out her teeth, as he used to pull out the teeth of the enemies he bagged over in Vietnam.

When I look at Bennie, I see a double image. He was drafted during the same month in which I, studying in England, gave Uncle Sam the slip. I hated that war, and feared it, for exactly the reasons he describes — because it was foul slaughter, shameful, sinful, pointless butchery. While he was over there killing and dodging, sinking into the quicksand of drugs, losing his hearing, storing up a lifetime's worth of nightmares, I was snug in England, filling my head with words. We both came home to America in the same year, I to job and family, he to nothing. Ten years after that homecoming, we stare across the courtroom at one another as into a funhouse mirror.

♦   ♦   ♦

As the twelve jurors file past me into the room where they will decide on Bennie's guilt or innocence, three of them pat my arm in a comradely way. They withdraw beyond a brass-barred gate; I sit down to wait on a deacon's bench in the hallway outside the courtroom. I feel stymied, as if I have rocketed to the moon only to be left riding the ship round and round in idle orbit while my fellow astronauts descend to the moon's surface. At the same time I feel profoundly relieved, because, after the four days of testimony, I still cannot decide whether Bennie truly sold those drugs, or whether I90, to cut down on his own prison time, set up this ill-starred Bennie for yet another fall. Time, time — it always comes down to time: in jail, job, and jury box we are spending and hoarding our only wealth, the currency of days.

Even through the closed door of the courtroom, I still hear the ticking of the clock. The sound reminds me of listening to my daughter's pulse through a stethoscope when she was still riding, curled up like a stowaway, in my wife's womb. Ask not for whom this heart ticks, whispered my unborn daughter through the stethoscope: it ticks for thee. So does the courtroom clock. It grabs me by the ear and makes me fret about time — about how little there is of it, about how we are forever bumming it from one another as if it were cups of sugar or pints of blood ("You got a minute?" "Sorry, have to run, not a second to spare"). Seize the day, we shout, to cheer ourselves; but the day has seized us and flings us forward pell-mell toward the end of all days.

Now and again there is a burst of laughter from the jury room, but it is always squelched in a hurry. They are tense, and laugh to relieve the tension, and then feel ashamed of their giddiness. Lawyers traipse past me — the men smoking, striking poses, their faces like lollipops atop their ties; the women teetering on high heels. The bailiff walks into our judge's office carrying a bread knife. To slice her lunch? As evidence against Rebecca? A moment later she emerges bearing a piece of cake and licking her fingers. Christmas parties are breaking out all over the courthouse.

Rebecca herself paces back and forth at the far end of my hallway, her steps as regular as the clock's tick, killing time. Her bearded and cross-wearing friends sidle up to comfort her, but she shrugs them away. Once she paces down my way, glances at the barred door of the jury room, hears muffled shouts. This she must take for good news, because she throws me a rueful smile before turning back.   70

Evidently the other twelve are as muddled by the blurred and contradictory "facts" of the case as I am, for they spend from noon until five reaching their decision. They ask for lunch. They ask for a dictionary. They listen again to the tapes. Sullen teenagers, following in the footsteps of Bennie and I90, slouch into the misdemeanor office across the hall from me; by and by they slouch back out again, looking unrepentant. At length the 300-pound mason lumbers up to the gate of the jury room and calls the bailiff. "We're ready as we're going to be." He looks bone-weary, unhappy, and dignified. Raising his eyebrows at me, he shrugs. Comrades in uncertainty.

The cast reassembles in the courtroom, the judge asks the jury for its decision, and the mason stands up to pronounce Bennie guilty. I stare at my boots. Finally I glance up, not at Bennie or Rebecca or the lawyers, but at my fellow jurors. They look distraught, wrung-out and despairing, as if they have just crawled out of a mine after an explosion and have left some of their buddies behind. Before quitting the jury room, they composed and signed a letter to the judge pleading with him to get some help—drug help, mind help, any help—for Bennie.

The ticking of the clock sounds louder in my ears than the judge's closing recital. But I do, with astonishment, hear him say that we must all come back tomorrow for one last piece of business. He is sorry, he knows we are worn out, but the law has prevented him from warning us ahead of time that we might have to decide on one more question of guilt.

The legal question posed for us on the morning of day five is simple: Has Bennie been convicted, prior to this case, of two or more unrelated felonies? If so, then he is defined by Indiana state law as a "habitual offender," and we must declare him to be such. We are shown affidavits for those earlier convictions—burglary, sale of marijuana, possession of LSD—and so the answer to the legal question is clear.

But the moral and psychological questions are tangled, and they occupy the jury for nearly five more hours on this last day of the trial. Is it fair to sentence a person again, after he has already served time for his earlier offenses? How does the prosecutor decide when to apply the habitual offender statute, and does its use in this case have anything to do with the political ambitions of the sleek young attorney? Did Bennie really steal that $150 stereo, for which he was convicted a decade ago, or did he really spend the day in bed with his sixteen-year-old girlfriend? Did Vietnam poison his mind and blight his life?

Two sheriff's deputies guard the jury today; another guards me in my own little cell. The bailiff would not let me stay out on the deacon's bench in the hall, and so, while a plainclothes detective occupies my old seat, I sit in a room lined with file cabinets and stare out like a prisoner through the glass door. "I have concluded," wrote Pascal, "that the whole misfortune of men comes from a single thing, and that is their inability to remain at rest in a room." I agree with him; nothing but that cruising deputy would keep me here.

This time, when the verdict is announced, Rebecca has her daughters with her, three little girls frightened into unchildlike stillness by the courtroom. Their lank hair and washed-out eyes remind me of my childhood playmates, the children of dead-end, used-up West Virginia coalminers who'd moved to Ohio in search of work. The mother and daughter are surrounded by half a dozen rough customers, guys my age with hair down over their shoulders and rings in their ears, with flannel shirts, unfocused eyes. Doubtless they are the reason so many holstered deputies and upholstered detectives are patrolling the courthouse, and the reason I was locked safely away in a cell while the jury deliberated.

When the mason stands to pronounce another verdict of guilty, I glimpse what I do not want to glimpse: Bennie flinging his head back, Rebecca snapping hers forward into her palms, the girls wailing.

The judge accompanies all thirteen of us into the jury room, where he keeps us for an hour while the deputies clear the rough customers from the courthouse. We are not to be alarmed, he reassures us; he is simply being cautious, since so

75

much was at stake for the defendant. "How much?" the mason asks. "Up to twenty-four years for the drug convictions, plus a mandatory thirty years for the habitual offender charges," the judge replies. The cleaning woman, the nurse, and the TV repairman begin crying. I swallow carefully. For whatever it's worth, the judge declares comfortingly, he agrees with our decisions. If we knew as much about this Bennie as he knows, we would not be troubled. And that is just the splinter in the brain, the fact that we know so little—about Bennie, about Vietnam, about drugs, about ourselves—and yet we must grope along in our ignorance, pronouncing people guilty or innocent, squeezing out of one another that precious fluid, time.

And so I do my five days in the thirteenth chair. Bennie may do as many as   80
fifty-four years in prison, buying his drugs from meaner dealers, dreaming of land mines and of his adopted girls, checking the date on his watch, wondering at what precise moment the hinges of his future slammed shut.   [1987]

THINKING ABOUT THE TEXT

1. Trace the references to time in this essay. In what ways does Sanders make it a central subject? Note his references to bombs. What is the effect of his emphasis on them?

2. On the whole, is your impression of the jury positive? Negative? Somewhere in between? Identify some things that influence your opinion. Is there any other information about the jury that you wish Sanders had provided? If so, what sort of information?

3. Rather than being a full-fledged juror, Sanders was an alternate, occupying the thirteenth chair. What, if any, were the advantages of his position for him as an observer? What, if any, were the disadvantages?

4. At one point in his essay, Sanders compares himself to Bennie. Does this comparison make sense to you? Why, or why not? Throughout the essay, Sanders emphasizes the sense of community that developed among the jurors. To what extent does he call attention to Bennie's community— that is, Bennie's friends and family? Does he treat this community in a way you think appropriate? Explain.

5. Are you inclined to believe that justice was served in Bennie's case? Why, or why not? What additional sort of information, if any, would you need to be sure?

JOYCE CAROL OATES
I, the Juror

Since the early 1960s, Joyce Carol Oates (b. 1938) has published prolifically in all the genres represented in this book. In the 1990s alone, she wrote several well-regarded novels, including Because It Is Bitter, and Because It Is My Heart *(1990),*

Black Water *(1992)*, Foxfire *(1993)*, What I Lived For *(1994)*, *and* We Were the Mulvaneys *(1996)*. *In the genre of the essay, she is probably best known for her book* On Boxing *(1987)*, *whose subject has long fascinated her. At present, Oates teaches at Princeton University. The following essay was first published in a 1995 issue of the literary journal* Witness.

In pursuit of an abstract principle of Justice. In pursuit of that sense of community of which Justice is both the consequence and the catalyst. In pursuit of some wavering, insubstantial, indefinable expression of one's heart's desire — that, as citizens of a country, and not mere "individuals," we participate in an action that is unbiased, fair, equitable, *right*.

Yet — "Judge not, lest ye be judged." As if the very action through which Justice might be realized brings with it mortal risk.

When the pink, smudgily computer-printed summons from the Sheriff's Office, County of Mercer, Trenton, New Jersey, arrived in the mail for SMITH, JOYCE C., notifying that I was scheduled to serve as a petit juror for no less than five days in late August, in the Mercer County Courthouse, my feelings were ambivalent. Throughout adulthood I had always hoped to be called for jury duty — while living in Detroit, and more recently in Princeton — but I had never been selected; I did not think of it as a "duty" so much as a privilege, very likely an adventure. To live out one's life as an American citizen without having once served as a juror, no matter how minor the trial, would be a pity — wouldn't it? Like not being caught up, at least once, in the romance of a Presidential campaign; indeed, like never having voted. We who oscillate between idealism and skepticism, with the quicksilver instability of those sub-atomic particles that are now one thing and now its opposite, begin after all as idealists.

The very *impersonality* of the summons had an air of romance for me — for it was "Joyce C. Smith" and not "Joyce Carol Oates" who had been called. Rare for me now, thus the more precious, any public experience in which I can be invisible, as if bodiless: that fundamental necessity for the writer.

Strictly speaking, "Joyce C. Smith" has no existence except as a legal entity: a husband's wife in a patriarchal society. (One day, will the acquisition of a husband's name, and the eradication of one's maiden name, come to seem as curious a custom as its reverse would seem now?) This legal entity is duly registered as a property (co-)owner and voter. There are no publications indexed under "Joyce C. Smith" in any library, and there is no one on the faculty of Princeton University, where I teach, bearing that name. Since there was no provision in the questionnaire accompanying the summons for the explanation of a "career" name, and I feared a punitive misfiring in the unimaginative computer brain in Trenton, I thought it most pragmatic to identify "Joyce C. Smith" as a housewife and teacher. (Some years ago, in Detroit and Windsor, Ontario, "Joyce C. Smith" had in fact taught college.) This seemed to me to conform to the letter of the law, and to give me a fair chance to get onto a jury.

(I should explain that the local consensus is that Princeton residents are routinely dismissed from juries in Trenton, no matter our hope to serve. Prosecutors

5

OATES / *I, the Juror* **1129**

don't want us because we are collectively perceived as "liberals" likely to interpret crime in terms of societal pressures; defense attorneys don't want us because we are perceived as "intellectuals" likely to resist rhetorical manipulation.)

Any relationship with the law, as with any governmental bureaucracy, is qualified by a certain air of menace and threat; and so I did, for all my theoretical enthusiasm, feel ambivalent about the summons. To serve as a juror is not a volitional option: names are randomly selected from a merged list of registered voters and licensed drivers, and once your name is on such a list, stored in the computer, it is virtually impossible to get it off. And there is, in the New Jersey Statute, this inhospitable warning: *Every person summoned as a Grand or Petit Juror who shall either fail to appear or refuse, without reasonable excuse, to serve or be sworn, shall be fined by the Court and may be punished as for Contempt of Court.* (Meaning, bluntly, that you can be sent to jail for declining to participate in an action that may send another person to jail.)

Though, as a novelist, I have done extensive research into criminal law and into courtroom procedure, I had attended only a single trial in my life, and that not on a daily basis, long ago, in the 1950s, when I was a junior high school student in Lockport, New York. Two young men were being tried on charges of first-degree murder in a robbery slaying. Vivid as certain memories of that experience are — the old courthouse, the airlessness, the stiff, resigned postures of the accused men seated at the defense table, the elderly judge on his raised platform, in his somber judicial gown — I seem not to remember the verdict. (Probably I was not there for the verdict.) My general sense of the trial was its deliberate snail's pace, its lethargy. Its public display of an adult, and therefore an impenetrable ritual of which I had no clearer comprehension than an observer, say, of a gigantic grinding machine would have of its inner workings, seen from without. Your instinct is to know that you don't ever want to get caught in it.

One afternoon, during an interlude of fatiguing, seemingly pointless repetition, I must have surreptitiously opened a book to read, and a sheriff's deputy leaned toward me, to say in an undertone, "Better close that book. The judge will kick you out of the courtroom if he sees you reading." How startled I was, and how struck by the fact that in a courtroom, this highest expression of adult ritual, the judge, the emblem of all patriarchy, has the authority to determine where an individual's eyes might rest!

Fortunately, they can't see into our skulls. 10

The Mercer County Courthouse, built in 1903 in the generic American courthouse style, still exudes, from the street, a weatherworn dignity; its dank, antiquated interior exudes what might be called "atmosphere." We prospective jurors descended in a rambling herd into the basement, promptly at 8:30 A.M. on August 26, 1991, where we were crowded together in two low-ceilinged rooms, where we would sit on folding chairs while we waited to be called up to a courtroom on the fifth floor.

A prophetic sign was posted on a wall: *They also serve who only stand and wait. — John Milton.* The sign was yellowed with age.

And so we waited. Some of us tried to read or work, until the blaring television sets (game shows, soap operas) became too distracting; a few of us, the more restless, began to pace in the corridor immediately outside the jury assembly room, which was allowed by our overseers so long as it appeared, or could be made to appear, that we were really going to or coming from the restrooms. Other areas of the courthouse were forbidden to us (we were wearing white jurors' badges), and doors at the far end of two long corridors, opening to the outside, were conspicuously posted EMERGENCY ONLY—ALARM SET OFF IF OPENED. Already, by 11:00 A.M., I was tracing elongated figure eights in the corridors, with a hope of forestalling early glimmerings of panic.

I learned that, of the 599 citizens of Mercer County who had been summoned for jury duty that week, 500 had managed to exempt themselves. This in itself was certainly deflating; yet more deflating was it to be warned, by one of the assembly room overseers (they were all women, with a look of being prison matrons in disguise as office workers), that, should any of us leave the courthouse without authorization, an officer from the Mercer County Sheriff's Department was empowered to follow after us and arrest us—"This has been known to happen." Indeed, the bulletin boards in the assembly room were festooned with clippings celebrating the power of the state to arrest, fine, and confine: accounts of citizens who, having failed to comply with the summons to jury duty, were surprised and arrested in their homes or in their places of work, fined hundreds of dollars, jailed for three days and/or sentenced to one hundred hours of "community service."

I asked one of the administrators how long we might wait to be called up to a   15
courtroom, and the woman answered, curtly, "Until you're called." Was it possible, I asked, that we would not be called at all that day? "Yes, it's possible," she said. I approached another administrator, a woman of my approximate age, to ask why the system was so punitive, and so inefficient; and the woman stared at me with a hurt, swimming look, and said, "I'm sorry you find it so!" "But don't *you* find it so?" I asked reasonably, indicating the dreary room of glassy-eyed men and women, and the woman said angrily, "The way it used to be done, two hundred people were here for two solid weeks—and that was that." When I expressed dismay, she repeated, with an air of threat, "The way it used to be done, two hundred people were here for two solid weeks—*and that was that.*"

"I see," I said.

At last, shortly before noon, a panel of fifty men and women, including "Joyce C. Smith, Juror 552," was summoned to a courtroom on the fifth floor. Though I'd been warned that this part of the jury selection can be deadly—no reading material is allowed in the courtroom, and, of course, no pacing is permitted—it was impossible not to feel a hopeful anticipation.

We were welcomed to her courtroom by Judge Judith A. Yaskin, an attractive, highly articulate woman in her mid- or late forties, who presented the case to be tried and explained the jury selection process. The case was aggravated assault; the defendant, a thirty-year-old black man, and his attorney, and the prosecuting attorney, were in the room. Selecting the jury begins with sheer chance: pellets with numbers corresponding to jurors' numbers are shuffled and drawn by an officer of the court, as in a bingo game. In theory, the jury of fourteen (including two alternates) could be drawn from the first fourteen pellets, but during the voir

dire jurors are exempted for various reasons (admitted prejudices, prior knowledge of the case to be tried, connections with the defendant, law enforcement
officials, etc., as well as the peremptory challenge dismissals by the prosecuting
and defense attorneys) and new jurors have to be selected and questioned. The
procedure involves numberless repetitions and can be protracted for weeks in a
trial of major proportions; the case to be tried, here, fortunately, was a minor one,
and a jury was constituted by early afternoon.

To my surprise, number 552 was drawn from the lottery, and I took my seat in
the jury box as Juror Number Eleven. When Judge Yaskin questioned me I identified myself as a housewife and teacher, with the intention of explaining my professional career in more detail if required; but the judge had no further questions.
(As it would turn out at the trial's end, Judge Yaskin had recognized me as a
writer, but seemed to have thought that my writing career was not relevant to the
procedure. Neither the defense counsel nor the prosecuting attorney took the
slightest interest in me, except perhaps as a malleable presence on the jury. What
good fortune: I'd had a nightmare fantasy of being forced to explain to a gathering
of quizzical, bemused strangers that I was a "writer," of whom no one would have
heard — like the tragic Dorothy Richardson, in a nursing home at the end of her
life, believed delusional because she insisted she'd been a novelist.) The focus of
the voir dire was on jurors who had been victims of crimes: could they be impartial in judging a criminal case? How sobering to learn that so many jurors, most of
them residents of Trenton, were victims of multiple crimes. Burglary, vandalism,
assault. One woman had been burglarized five times in recent years, but insisted
she would be impartial as a juror. In each case Judge Yaskin asked if the criminals
had been apprehended, and in each case, remarkably, the answer was "No." A
message rippled through our midst: *Crime goes largely unpunished in Trenton;*
and, a variant, *Criminals lead charmed lives in certain regions of America.*

But here we were gathered, in a solemn ritual, to isolate, contemplate, and
pass judgment on a crime. One had to conclude that the defendant was sheerly
unlucky to have been caught.

Of course most of the crime victims were summarily rejected by the defense
counsel, as if their insistences upon being impartial were handily recognized as
lies. The defense counsel also rejected the only juror in the box to have acknowledged living in Princeton (I had not been asked where I lived), and the single
man, of the approximately fifty male prospective jurors in the courthouse that
day, to be wearing a suit.

(What of courtroom attire? To my surprise, the majority of my fellow jurors
were dressed extremely casually. Here and there a man conspicuous in sport
coat and tie, a few women in high heels and stockings, but, overall, the tide of
prospective jurors looked as if they'd wandered off from a tour bus, in quintessen-
tially American play clothes for adults. Blue jeans, slacks, T-shirts, shorts were in
colorful abundance, contrasting with the more formal, subdued attire of the officers of the court. One youngish man made a comical sight as, in brief nylon-blue
running shorts and T-shirt cut high on the shoulders, he came from the rear of
the courtroom when his number was called to enter the jury box, passing close
below the judge in her black robe. The death penalty is still on the statute in New

20

Jersey: I couldn't help but wonder if jurors in Mickey Mouse sweatshirts vote to send defendants to their deaths.)

Another startling development, for those of us new to courtroom procedure, was the mechanical rejection of certain jurors on the basis of skin pigmentation. Overt racial prejudice has become so anachronistic, we like to think, or, in any case, associated with marginal renegade behavior, it is both shocking and puzzling to encounter it in a public place; still more, in the churchy atmosphere of a courtroom. Since the defendant to be tried was black, however, the prosecuting attorney exercised his right of peremptory challenge to reject as many persons of color as possible. Here was the most crude, the most brainless, racial discrimination in action, entirely countenanced by law: "Your Honor, please thank and excuse Juror Number Two," the attorney said, and a light-skinned black, startled, was urged to leave the box. Another juror was called, a young Chinese-American woman, and again the attorney said, "Your Honor, please thank and excuse Juror Number Two," and she too left the box. Another lottery draw, another juror, everyone stared as another black man came forward, and again—"Your Honor, please thank and excuse Juror Number Two." And he too left. Was this a comic routine? The next juror, as an oddity of luck would have it (by far the majority of the prospective jurors were Caucasian), was also a black man—an undergraduate, as it would turn out, at Middlebury College; hardly was he seated when the prosecuting attorney said, in a flat, inflectionless voice, "Your Honor, please thank and excuse Juror Number Two." And the young man too was ushered out, with a look of surprise, disappointment, hurt, embarrassment. Perhaps he had never before experienced such crude racial discrimination so personally? so publicly? in a gathering of elders?

Finally, and ironically, Juror Number Two was in fact a black man. The prosecuting attorney must have run out of options.

There is a mystique, homey and comforting as Norman Rockwell paintings, of trial-by-jury in America. Trial-by-jury-of-one's-peers.   25

A mystique predicated upon not having contemplated one's peers very closely in a while.

There is a mystique, too, accruing to the dignity, the sanctity of the court, which is meant to resemble a church. Were we not all obliged to swear, on the Holy Bible, to truthfulness? (In fact, there were not enough Bibles for fourteen jurors, so we had to share them, awkwardly. I wondered at my integrity as, an atheist, I murmured with the others, "I do swear." Perhaps my fingers were not exactly touching the simulated-leather hide of the Holy Book?) Somewhere in our judicial tradition the separation of church and state, surely one of the great principles of American society, seems to have been overlooked.

The trial was not a complex one, though with interruptions and delays it stretched out over several days. There were only five witnesses, four for the prosecution, and the defendant himself, who testified last. The charge of aggravated assault had been brought against a thirty-year-old black man apparently involved in the drug trade who had beaten a young black woman who he believed had informed on him to the police after a drug raid in January 1990; one had the sense (as a juror, denied virtually any contextual information, and made, from time to time, to leave the courtroom, one is absorbed in trying to figure out what *really* happened, what the *real* story is) that the defendant was someone the Trenton police and the prosecutor's office hoped to send to prison since, perhaps, they had not succeeded in sending him away on other charges. Otherwise the case, in crime-afflicted Trenton, seemed an anomaly.

"I am the judge of the law," Judge Yaskin told the jury several times, with the patience of a grade school teacher, "— and you are the judge of the facts." Hearing witnesses' testimonies that often conflicted, forced to sift through such "facts" as are proffered by such testimony, and having to remember everything (jurors may not take notes in the courtroom), one quickly becomes bedazzled, confused. Why take the word of one witness over another, when all sound sincere and plausible? Is there a singular truth that *must* exist, and can be brought to bear against the exactitude of the New Jersey criminal statute? (We jurors were to decide whether aggravated assault had been committed — whether the defendant "knowingly, purposefully, and recklessly intended to inflict serious physical injury, or did inflict serious physical injury." As if there were no significant difference between act and intention.) The witnesses' testimonies gave us, all but one of us Caucasian, a painfully intimate look at the black Trenton underclass; I found myself close to tears during the victim's testimony, hearing of her life, her activities as a crack addict, forced to examine, with the other jurors, her slightly disfigured left eyelid — the claim of the prosecution being that the woman had suffered permanent damage as a result of the beating. And what irony — the woman had her right arm in a sling, and a badly bruised face, from what was apparently a very recent beating, unrelated to the case being tried. (Of course, the woman's present condition was never explained.)

There was much sorrow here, and sordidness; and hopelessness; yet an air 30 now and then of the farcical as well. As in a ghetto version of "Rashomon," witnesses supplied wildly varying details, each convinced he or she was remembering correctly. Did the alleged assault take place at noon of January 21, 1990? at 4:30 P.M.? at 7:30 P.M.? Was the defendant, charged with kicking the victim in the head, wearing yellow steel-toed boots, as the victim swore, or black leather boots, as his cousin swore, or, as the defendant swore, black sneakers? One eyewitness saw only kicks, not punches; another saw punches, but no kicks. All of the prosecution witnesses, it developed through cross-examination, had criminal records; yet, because of legal protocol, we were never told if the defendant had a criminal record. (Later, during the jury's deliberation, some of the jurors seemed actually to have thought that the defendant was "clean.") How frustrating the testimonies were, how tediously protracted by the defense counsel's cross-examination, how repetitive, stupefyingly dull — as we traced and retraced the same narrow terrain, like a snail with a motor imbalance. I wondered if, my eyes open, I might begin to hallucinate.

And then, of course, as in fictionalized trials, the attorneys quickly called out, "Your Honor, I object!" when questioning got interesting; when crucial matters arose, as often they did, the judge and the attorneys conferred out of earshot, while we jurors looked on deaf and mute; at any time court might be recessed, and we would be sent out to the jury room, forbidden to discuss the case, and with no knowledge of when we might be summoned back, or if we would be summoned back at all. (Trials often end abruptly, and jurors, to that moment flattered into believing themselves essential to the execution of justice, are summarily dismissed and sent home.) To experience the legal system as a layman is to discover yourself on a playing field in the midst of a bizarre, intricately structured game with unknown rules and a private language; the jury itself, though the fabled glory of our American criminal justice system, resembles nothing so much as a large, ungainly, anachronistic beast with one eye patched over, a gag in its mouth, cotton stuffed in an ear, a leg shackled. Yet the delusion persists, the jury judges "facts."

"She was fidgeting all the time, she was nervous."
"She said she was going *down* the stairs, not *up*."
"How can you believe her — she's a crack addict."
"People like that, Walnut Street, Trenton — that's how they live." 35
"Her eye didn't look like it was hurt that bad."
"I'd almost believe the defendant, over her."
"They're all a pack of liars."

So often, in recent years, has the reflex of blaming the victim been exposed by the media, some of us have been led to think it no longer presents much of a danger to impartial judgment in cases of assault and rape, especially cases of male defendant and female victims. Certainly, feminists would like to think that this is so, that some progress has been made. Yet, clearly, human instinct is conservative, even primitive: if you are a female victim pleading your case, and others can discover a way to blame you for your misfortune, they will do so. (After the St. John's University trial, in which white defendants were found not guilty of sexual assault against a young black woman, a commentator asked, "When have white men ever been found guilty of raping black women?") As if the victim, and not the defendant, were on trial. And especially, as in our case, if the victim is of another class and race, a self-confessed, if former, drug addict . . . The unvoiced judgment is: *She got what she deserved.*

The jury on which I served was very likely a representative cross-section of 40 area citizens, equally divided in gender, middle to lower-middle class incomes, eleven Caucasians and one black; and my experience in their midst left me shaken and depressed for days. So this is what a jury thinks, says, does! So this is the mystique in action! Certainly these men and women were not evil, nor even malicious. I am not suggesting that. I believe that most of them were well-intentioned and not racist, at least not consciously racist. But they were not thoughtful people; they were not, in a way, serious people. Among them, I was the only one to take notes during our recesses from the court; I was the only one, as it would turn out, who seemed to have considered the black witnesses, and especially the victim, as human beings like myself. (How vain this sounds! I wish there were some other way to express it.) When we were sequestered in our jury room and might have used the time to think quietly about the case (discussions are forbidden until a trial is over), most of the jurors chatted and laughed as if there were nothing of much import going on. Testimony that seemed to me self-evidently painful, heartrending in what it suggested of the profound distance between our worlds and theirs, slid off them as if uttered in a foreign language: a language that had nothing to do with them. (What of the single black juror? He was an older man, and probably said about five words during the discussion. Younger and possibly more assertive blacks had been bumped from the jury.) White jurors, reflecting the bias of their society, are notorious for not taking very seriously crimes by blacks committed against blacks, and this bias was borne out by our jury; if the victim had been, not black, but a young white woman, they would surely have seen the charge differently.

As it was, I was astonished by the ferocity of my fellow jurors' attack on the victim's testimony, which was not only pitiless but derisive, contemptuous. Men led the attack immediately, before we were even seated around the table — the most vociferous was, in fact, the man who had showed up on the first day in running shorts — but women joined in, too. Hours of earnest testimony were discounted by a wave of the hand, a "gut-level" opinion; inconsistencies in testimony were interpreted as evidence of falsehood even as the jurors themselves misremembered facts. There was no effort on the part of the jury foreman to assure an orderly discussion, and very likely this would not have made much of a difference in the quality of the discourse, which was on about the level of a group of people discussing where to go to eat.

Perhaps human beings have only a measure of sympathy for others, and little to spare. Perhaps there is a human instinct, a gene for survival, that shuts down identification with men and women in distress who are different from ourselves, and without power. I am trying to separate my own biases from those of my fellow jurors, who of course have a right to bias, and, as sworn jurors, the privilege of voting as intuition urged: they reacted swiftly, and they reacted without subtlety or ambiguity, and they reacted in near-unanimity in rejecting the prosecution's charge against the defendant. They simply did not take it, nor the world from which it sprang, seriously.

After deliberation, the twelve of us agreed upon a verdict of "guilty" for the lesser charge of simple assault. (Even the defense counsel acknowledged that something had been done to the victim to account for her injuries.) How many hours we jurors spent together, how many hours the protracted ceremony of the trial consumed, like an antique machine clanking and grinding and laboring to bring forth a verdict any Trenton judge might have handed down after a few hours' review of the case — multiply this by thousands, hundreds of thousands, adding in such cases as the child molestation trial in Los Angeles a few years ago that took two years — two years! — and you have a criminal justice system that not only fails to guarantee "justice" but is cumbersome, inefficient, outmoded. If jurors were really possessed of unique qualities of divination conferred upon them when they are sworn in, the archaic system might justify itself; but, as my personal experience suggests, this is not the case.

Moreover, verdicts of "guilty" handed down by petit juries are frequently of little real consequence. Judges do the actual sentencing, which might be a fine, or probation, or community service, or months in prison, or years; if years, the prison parole board determines the sentence. This is as it should be, since the idea of juries also determining sentences would be a nightmare.

In retrospect, I am grateful for my experience as a juror in Trenton, New Jersey, though it is not one I am eager to repeat. I came into contact with an estimable, indeed judicious judge; I experienced the procedure of a small, circumscribed criminal case; I was disabused, by my fellow jurors, of certain romantic illusions. And I was paid $5 a day by the State of New Jersey—which, considering the contribution we made, seems about right.

Afterword

I wrote this essay immediately after the conclusion of the trial. Months later, I am still haunted by the experience. What most distressed me was the assumption, so unexamined as to be chilling, on the part of the white jurors, that they belonged to a world, if not to a species, wholly distinct from the blacks of Trenton's underclass whom they were empowered to judge. There is *we*, and there is *they*—and an unbridgeable distance between.

In Richard Wright's classic novel *Native Son* (1940), the tragic argument is made that white racist America has so dehumanized Negro Americans that, like Bigger Thomas, the eponymous hero of the novel, some of the more aggressive are in danger of becoming primitive, brutalized, unfeeling killers (of Negroes as well as Caucasians: Bigger Thomas murders a young black woman as viciously and as gratuitously as he murders the white millionaire's daughter); these very Negroes are then loathed, repudiated, and sentenced to death, for being dehumanized. Bigger Thomas can have no "feeling" for his victims because he has been made incapable of human feeling.

Yet, as Wright says in his memoir *Black Boy* (1944):

> After I had learned other ways of life I used to brood upon the unconscious irony of those who felt that Negroes led so passional an existence! I saw that what had been taken as our emotional strength was our negative confusions, our flights, our frenzy under pressure.

In judging others, the burden is ours to transcend the limits of self; in terms of race, the limits, and blindnesses, of race. How is this possible? Who is qualified? Is the concept of human Justice a commonly held delusion, as readily served by, say, a lottery, as by human effort and collaboration? After so many weeks, I am still preoccupied with the experience of having been a juror, serving on that particular jury, in a representative American city of the present time. I hear again the smug assertions of certain of my fellow jurors; I see several faces with unwanted oneiric clarity; obsessively, I see the purse-lipped white-haired retiree who had denounced the blacks in the trial as a "pack of liars" sitting reading the New Testament, as he had done somewhat conspicuously during some of our sequestered time together. Though I am Caucasian, thus one of their own, the proposition unnerved me: *What if these people were entrusted with my life? What sympathy would they have for me? — or for one another?*

The shadow that falls upon us at such sobering moments is nothing less than 50 our estrangement from humanity, and surely there is no estrangement more profound and more corrosive. For juries too should submit to judgment. But in what court — and who to preside?   [1995]

THINKING ABOUT THE TEXT

1. What images do you get of Oates as you read her essay? Refer to details of the text that influence your impression of her. Overall, to what extent do you trust and respect her as a reporter?

2. In the second half of her essay, Oates focuses on the trial itself and the jury's subsequent deliberations. What do you sense her basically doing in the first half?

3. Oates seems to have been surprised by the behavior of the other jurors. Does the conduct she describes surprise you? Identify aspects of your past experiences that affect your answer. After Oates published her essay, the U.S. Supreme Court ruled that attorneys cannot exclude a potential juror on racial grounds. Evidently Oates believes that her jury would have behaved more responsibly if it had, in fact, included more African Americans. Do you agree? Why, or why not?

4. How do you think the jurors should have acted? Identify things you wish they had done.

5. Oates suggests that her experience as a juror reveals problems with the American criminal justice system as a whole. Do you think it is reasonable of her to generalize in this way? Explain.

MAKING COMPARISONS

1. Evidently Sanders believes that his jury behaved well, even though its members' social class apparently differed from the defendant's. Oates, on the other hand, suggests that her jurors were guilty of racism toward people involved in the case they judged. Are you convinced that the Indiana jury was, in fact, much better than the New Jersey one? Does Sanders lead you to think that the American criminal justice system is better than Oates suggests? Identify some of the warrants or assumptions behind your answers.

2. For the most part, Sanders and Oates use different tenses. He recounts his trial in present tense, while she uses the past. Do you like one of these rhetorical strategies more than the other? Why, or why not?

3. Is time as important a subject in Oates's essay as it is in Sanders's? Refer to specific details of both.

MAXINE HONG KINGSTON
No Name Woman

Born in Stockton, California, to Chinese immigrants, Maxine Hong Kingston's
(b. 1940) first language was Say Yup, a dialect of Cantonese. As a member of a
close-knit community, many of whose members came from the same village in
China, she was immersed in the storytelling tradition of her particular Chinese cul-
ture and soon became a gifted writer in her second language, English. Winning
eleven scholarships, Kingston began her education at the University of California
at Berkeley as an engineering major but soon moved into English literature, receiv-
ing her B.A. in 1962 and her teaching certificate in 1965. After teaching in Hawaii
for ten years, Kingston published her first book in 1976. The Woman Warrior:
Memoirs of a Girlhood among Ghosts, *the book from which our selection comes,*
won the National Book Critics Circle Award for nonfiction. This reinterpretation of
oral traditions is continued in Kingston's later books, including Tripmaster Monkey: His Fake Book *(1989). Her most recent work is a collection of critical essays,*
Hawai'i One Summer *(1998).*

"You must not tell anyone," my mother said, "what I am about to tell you. In
China your father had a sister who killed herself. She jumped into the family
well. We say that your father has all brothers because it is as if she had never
been born.

"In 1924 just a few days after our village celebrated seventeen hurry-up weddings—to make sure that every young man who went 'out on the road' would
responsibly come home—your father and his brothers and your grandfather and
his brothers and your aunt's new husband sailed for America, the Gold Mountain. It was your grandfather's last trip. Those lucky enough to get contracts
waved good-bye from the decks. They fed and guarded the stowaways and helped
them off in Cuba, New York, Bali, Hawaii. 'We'll meet in California next year,'
they said. All of them sent money home.

"I remember looking at your aunt one day when she and I were dressing; I
had not noticed before that she had such a protruding melon of a stomach. But I
did not think, 'She's pregnant,' until she began to look like other pregnant
women, her shirt pulling and the white tops of her black pants showing. She
could not have been pregnant, you see, because her husband had been gone for
years. No said anything. We did not discuss it. In early summer she was ready
to have the child, long after the time when it could have been possible.

"The village had also been counting. On the night the baby was to be born
the villagers raided our house. Some were crying. Like a great saw, teeth strung
with lights, files of people walked zigzag across our land, tearing the rice. Their
lanterns doubled in the disturbed black water, which drained away through the
broken bunds. As the villagers closed in, we could see that some of them, probably men and women we knew well, wore white masks. The people with long hair

hung it over their faces. Women with short hair made it stand up on end. Some had tied white bands around their foreheads, arms, and legs.

"At first they threw mud and rocks at the house. Then they threw eggs and 5 began slaughtering our stock. We could hear the animals scream their deaths — the roosters, the pigs, a last great roar from the ox. Familiar wild heads flared in our night windows; the villagers encircled us. Some of the faces stopped to peer at us, their eyes rushing like searchlights. The hands flattened against the panes, framed heads, and left red prints.

"The villagers broke in the front and the back doors at the same time, even though we had not locked the doors against them. Their knives dripped with the blood of our animals. They smeared blood on the doors and walls. One woman swung a chicken, whose throat she had slit, splattering blood in red arcs about her. We stood together in the middle of our house, in the family hall with the pictures and tables of the ancestors around us, and looked straight ahead.

"At that time the house had only two wings. When the men came back, we would build two more to enclose our courtyard and a third one to begin a second courtyard. The villagers pushed through both wings, even your grandparents' rooms, to find your aunt's, which was also mine until the men returned. From this room a new wing for one of the younger families would grow. They ripped up her clothes and shoes and broke her combs, grinding them underfoot. They tore her work from the loom. They scattered the cooking fire and rolled the new weaving in it. We could hear them in the kitchen breaking our bowls and banging the pots. They overturned the great waist-high earthenware jugs; duck eggs, pickled fruits, vegetables burst out and mixed in acrid torrents. The old woman from the next field swept a broom through the air and loosed the spirits-of-the-broom over our heads. 'Pig.' 'Ghost.' 'Pig,' they sobbed and scolded while they ruined our house.

"When they left, they took sugar and oranges to bless themselves. They cut pieces from the dead animals. Some of them took bowls that were not broken and clothes that were not torn. Afterward we swept up the rice and sewed it back up into sacks. But the smells from the spilled preserves lasted. Your aunt gave birth in the pigsty that night. The next morning when I went for the water, I found her and the baby plugging up the family well.

"Don't let your father know that I told you. He denies her. Now that you have started to menstruate, what happened to her could happen to you. Don't humiliate us. You wouldn't like to be forgotten as if you had never been born. The villagers are watchful."

Whenever she had to warn us about life, my mother told stories that ran like 10 this one, a story to grow up on. She tested our strength to establish realities. Those in the emigrant generations who could not reassert brute survival died young and far from home. Those of us in the first American generations have had to figure out how the invisible world the emigrants built around our childhoods fits in solid America.

The emigrants confused the gods by diverting their curses, misleading them with crooked streets and false names. They must try to confuse their offspring as well, who, I suppose, threaten them in similar ways — always trying to get things straight, always trying to name the unspeakable. The Chinese I know hide their names; sojourners take new names when their lives change and guard their real names with silence.

Chinese-Americans, when you try to understand what things in you are Chinese, how do you separate what is peculiar to childhood, to poverty, insanities, one family, your mother who marked your growing with stories, from what is Chinese? What is Chinese tradition and what is the movies?

If I want to learn what clothes my aunt wore, whether flashy or ordinary, I would have to begin, "Remember Father's drowned-in-the-well sister?" I cannot ask that. My mother has told me once and for all the useful parts. She will add nothing unless powered by Necessity, a riverbank that guides her life. She plants vegetable gardens rather than lawns; she carries the odd-shaped tomatoes home from the fields and eats food left for the gods.

Whenever we did frivolous things, we used up energy; we flew high kites. We children came up off the ground over the melting cones our parents brought home from work and the American movie on New Year's Day—*Oh, You Beautiful Doll* with Betty Grable one year, and *She Wore a Yellow Ribbon* with John Wayne another year. After the one carnival ride each, we paid in guilt; our tired father counted his change on the dark walk home.

Adultery is extravagance. Could people who hatch their own chicks and eat the embryos and the heads for delicacies and boil the feet in vinegar for party food, leaving only the gravel, eating even the gizzard lining—could such people engender a prodigal aunt? To be a woman, to have a daughter in starvation time was a waste enough. My aunt could not have been the lone romantic who gave up everything for sex. Women in the old China did not choose. Some man had commanded her to lie with him and be his secret evil. I wonder whether he masked himself when he joined the raid on her family.

15

Perhaps she had encountered him in the fields or on the mountain where the daughters-in-law collected fuel. Or perhaps he first noticed her in the marketplace. He was not a stranger because the village housed no strangers. She had to have dealings with him other than sex. Perhaps he worked an adjoining field, or he sold her the cloth for the dress she sewed and wore. His demand must have surprised, then terrified her. She obeyed him; she always did as she was told.

When the family found a young man in the next village to be her husband, she had stood tractably beside the best rooster, his proxy, and promised before they met that she would be his forever. She was lucky that he was her age and she would be the first wife, an advantage secure now. The night she first saw him, he had sex with her. Then he left for America. She had almost forgotten what he looked like. When she tried to envision him, she only saw the black and white face in the group photograph the men had had taken before leaving.

The other man was not, after all, much different from her husband. They both gave orders: she followed. "If you tell your family, I'll beat you. I'll kill you. Be here again next week." No one talked sex, ever. And she might have separated the rapes from the rest of living if only she did not have to buy her oil from him or gather wood in the same forest. I want her fear to have lasted just as long as rape lasted so that the fear could have been contained. No drawn-out fear. But women at sex hazarded birth and hence lifetimes. The fear did not stop but permeated everywhere. She told the man, "I think I'm pregnant." He organized the raid against her.

On nights when my mother and father talked about their life back home, sometimes they mentioned an "outcast table" whose business they still seemed to be settling, their voices tight. In a commensal tradition, where food is precious, the powerful older people made wrongdoers eat alone. Instead of letting them start separate new lives like the Japanese, who could become samurais and geishas, the Chinese family, faces averted but eyes glowering sideways, hung on to the offenders and fed them leftovers. My aunt must have lived in the same house as my parents and eaten at an outcast table. My mother spoke about the raid as if she had seen it, when she and my aunt, a daughter-in-law to a different household, should not have been living together at all. Daughters-in-law lived with their husbands' parents, not their own; a synonym for marriage in Chinese is "taking a daughter-in-law." Her husband's parents could have sold her, mortgaged her, stoned her. But they had sent her back to her own mother and father, a mysterious act hinting at disgraces not told me. Perhaps they had thrown her out to deflect the avengers.

She was the only daughter; her four brothers went with her father, husband, and uncles "out on the road" and for some years became western men. When the goods were divided among the family, three of the brothers took land, and the youngest, my father, chose an education. After my grandparents gave their daughter away to her husband's family, they had dispensed all the adventure and all the property. They expected her alone to keep the traditional ways, which her brothers, now among the barbarians, could fumble without detection. The heavy, deep-rooted women were to maintain the past against the flood, safe for returning. But the rare urge west had fixed upon our family, and so my aunt crossed boundaries not delineated in space.

20

The work of preservation demands that the feelings playing about in one's guts not be turned into action. Just watch their passing like cherry blossoms. But perhaps my aunt, my forerunner, caught in a slow life, let dreams grow and fade and after some months or years went toward what persisted. Fear at the enormities of the forbidden kept her desires delicate, wire and bone. She looked at a man because she liked the way the hair was tucked behind his ears, or she liked the question-mark line of a long torso curving at the shoulder and straight at the hip. For warm eyes or a soft voice or a slow walk — that's all — a few hairs, a line, a brightness, a sound, a pace, she gave up family. She offered us up for a charm that vanished with tiredness, a pigtail that didn't toss when the wind died. Why, the wrong lighting could erase the dearest thing about him.

It could very well have been, however, that my aunt did not take subtle enjoyment of her friend, but, a wild woman, kept rollicking company. Imagining her free with sex doesn't fit, though. I don't know any women like that, or men either. Unless I see her life branching into mine, she gives me no ancestral help.

To sustain her being in love, she often worked at herself in the mirror, guessing at the colors and shapes that would interest him, changing them frequently in order to hit on the right combination. She wanted him to look back.

On a farm near the sea, a woman who tended her appearance reaped a reputation for eccentricity. All the married women blunt-cut their hair in flaps about their ears or pulled it back in tight buns. No nonsense. Neither style blew easily into heart-catching tangles. And at their weddings they displayed themselves in their long hair for the last time. "It brushed the backs of my knees," my mother tells me. "It was braided, and even so, it brushed the backs of my knees."

At the mirror my aunt combined individuality into her bob. A bun could have been contrived to escape into black streamers blowing in the wind or in quiet wisps about her face, but only the older women in our picture album wear buns. She brushed her hair back from her forehead, tucking the flaps behind her ears. She looped a piece of thread, knotted into a circle between her index fingers and thumbs, and ran the double strand across her forehead. When she closed her fingers as if she were making a pair of shadow geese bite, the string twisted together catching the little hairs. Then she pulled the thread away from her skin, ripping the hairs out neatly, her eyes watering from the needles of pain. Opening her fingers, she cleaned the thread, then rolled it along her hairline and the tops of her eyebrows. My mother did the same to me and my sisters and herself. I used to believe that the expression "caught by the short hairs" meant a captive held with a depilatory string. It especially hurt at the temples, but my mother said we were lucky we didn't have to have our feet bound when we were seven. Sisters used to sit on their beds and cry together, she said, as their mothers or their slave removed the bandages for a few minutes each night and let the blood gush back into their veins. I hope that the man my aunt loved appreciated a smooth brow, that he wasn't just a tits-and-ass man.

Once my aunt found a freckle on her chin, at a spot that the almanac said predestined her for unhappiness. She dug it out with a hot needle and washed the wound with peroxide.

More attention to her looks than these pullings of hairs and pickings at spots would have caused gossip among the villagers. They owned work clothes and good clothes, and they wore good clothes for feasting the new seasons. But since a woman combing her hair hexes beginnings, my aunt rarely found an occasion to look her best. Women looked like great sea snails—the corded wood, babies, and laundry they carried were the whorls on their backs. The Chinese did not admire a bent back; goddesses and warriors stood straight. Still there must have been a marvelous freeing of beauty when a worker laid down her burden and stretched and arched.

Such commonplace loveliness, however, was not enough for my aunt. She dreamed of a lover for the fifteen days of New Year's, the time for families to exchange visits, money, and food. She plied her secret comb. And sure enough she cursed the year, the family, the village, and herself.

Even as her hair lured her imminent lover, many other men looked at her. Uncles, cousins, nephews, brothers would have looked, too, had they been home between journeys. Perhaps they had already been restraining their curiosity, and they left, fearful that their glances, like a field of nesting birds, might be startled and caught. Poverty hurt, and that was their first reason for leaving. But another, final reason for leaving the crowded house was the never-said.

She may have been unusually beloved, the precious only daughter, spoiled   30
and mirror gazing because of the affection the family lavished on her. When her
husband left, they welcomed the chance to take her back from the in-laws; she
could live like the little daughter for just a while longer. There are stories that my
grandfather was different from other people, "crazy ever since the little Jap bayo-
neted him in the head." He used to put his naked penis on the dinner table,
laughing. And one day he brought home a baby girl, wrapped up inside his
brown western-style greatcoat. He had traded one of his sons, probably my father,
the youngest, for her. My grandmother made him trade back. When he finally
got a daughter of his own, he doted on her. They must have all loved her, except
perhaps my father, the only brother who never went back to China, having once
been traded for a girl.

Brothers and sisters, newly men and women, had to efface their sexual color
and present plain miens. Disturbing hair and eyes, a smile like no other, threatened the ideal of five generations living under one roof. To focus blurs, people
shouted face to face and yelled from room to room. The immigrants I know
have loud voices, unmodulated to American tones even after years away from
the village where they called their friendships out across the fields. I have not
been able to stop my mother's screams in public libraries or over telephones.
Walking erect (knees straight, toes pointed forward, not pigeon-toed, which is
Chinese-feminine) and speaking in an inaudible voice, I have tried to turn myself
American-feminine. Chinese communication was loud, public. Only sick people
had to whisper. But at the dinner table, where the family members came nearest
one another, no one could talk, not the outcasts nor any eaters. Every word that
falls from the mouth is a coin lost. Silently they gave and accepted food with both
hands. A preoccupied child who took his bowl with one hand got a sideways
glare. A complete moment of total attention is due everyone alike. Children and
lovers have no singularity here, but my aunt used a secret voice, a separate atten-
tiveness.

She kept the man's name to herself throughout her labor and dying; she did
not accuse him that he be punished with her. To save her inseminator's name she
gave silent birth.

He may have been somebody in her own household, but intercourse with
a man outside the family would have been no less abhorrent. All the village
were kinsmen, and the titles shouted in loud country voices never let kinship be
forgotten. Any man within visiting distance would have been neutralized as a
lover — "brother," "younger brother," "older brother" — one hundred and fifteen
relationship titles. Parents researched birth charts probably not so much to assure
good fortune as to circumvent incest in a population that has but one hundred
surnames. Everybody has eight million relatives. How useless then sexual mannerisms, how dangerous.

As if it came from an atavism deeper than fear, I used to add "brother" silently
to boys' names. It hexed the boys, who would or would not ask me to dance, and
made them less scary and as familiar and deserving of benevolence as girls.

But, of course, I hexed myself also — no dates. I should have stood up, both   35
arms waving, and shouted out across libraries, "Hey, you! Love me back." I had

no idea, though, how to make attraction selective, how to control its direction and magnitude. If I made myself American-pretty so that the five or six Chinese boys in the class fell in love with me, everyone else — the Caucasian, Negro, and Japanese boys — would too. Sisterliness, dignified and honorable, made much more sense.

Attraction eludes control so stubbornly that whole societies designed to organize relationships among people cannot keep order, not even when they bind people to one another from childhood and raise them together. Among the very poor and the wealthy, brothers married their adopted sisters, like doves. Our family allowed some romance, paying adult brides' prices and providing dowries so that their sons and daughters could marry strangers. Marriage promises to turn strangers into friendly relatives — a nation of siblings.

In the village structure, spirits shimmered among the live creatures, balanced and held in equilibrium by time and land. But one human being flaring up into violence could open up a black hole, a maelstrom that pulled in the sky. The frightened villagers, who depended on one another to maintain the real, went to my aunt to show her a personal, physical representation of the break she had made in the "roundness." Misallying couples snapped off the future, which was to be embodied in true offspring. The villagers punished her for acting as if she could have a private life, secret and apart from them.

If my aunt had betrayed the family at a time of large grain yields and peace, when many boys were born, and wings were being built on many houses, perhaps, she might have escaped such severe punishment. But the men — hungry, greedy, tired of planting in dry soil — had been forced to leave the village in order to send food-money home. There were ghost plagues, bandit plagues, wars with the Japanese, floods. My Chinese brother and sister had died of an unknown sickness. Adultery, perhaps only a mistake during good times, became a crime when the village needed food.

The round moon cakes and round doorways, the round tables of graduated size that fit one roundness inside another, round windows and rice bowls — these talismans had lost their power to warn this family of the law: a family must be whole, faithfully keeping the descent line by having sons to feed the old and the dead, who in turn look after the family. The villagers came to show my aunt and her lover-in-hiding a broken house. The villagers were speeding up the circling of events because she was too shortsighted to see that her infidelity had already harmed the village, that waves of consequences would return unpredictably, sometimes in disguise, as now, to hurt her. This roundness had to be made coin-sized so that she would see its circumference: punish her at the birth of her baby. Awaken her to the inexorable. People who refused fatalism because they could invent small resources insisted on culpability. Deny accidents and wrest fault from the stars.

After the villagers left, their lanterns now scattering in various directions toward home, the family broke their silence and cursed her. "Aiaa, we're going to die. Death is coming. Death is coming. Look what you've done. You've killed us. Ghost! Dead ghost! Ghost! You've never been born." She ran out into the fields, 40 far enough from the house so that she could no longer hear their voices, and pressed herself against the earth, her own land no more. When she felt the birth coming, she thought that she had been hurt. Her body seized together. "They've hurt me too much," she thought. "This is gall, and it will kill me." With forehead and knees against the earth, her body convulsed and then relaxed. She turned on her back, lay on the ground. The black well of sky and stars went out and out and out forever; her body and her complexity seemed to disappear. She was one of the stars, a bright dot in blackness, without home, without a companion, in eternal cold and silence. An agoraphobia rose in her, speeding higher and higher, bigger and bigger; she would not be able to contain it; there would be no end to fear.

Flayed, unprotected against space, she felt pain return, focusing her body. This pain chilled her — a cold, steady kind of surface pain. Inside, spasmodically, the other pain, the pain of the child, heated her. For hours she lay on the ground, alternately body and space. Sometimes a vision of normal comfort obliterated reality: she saw the family in the evening gambling at the dinner table, the young people massaging their elders' backs. She saw them congratulating one another, high joy on the mornings the rice shoots came up. When these pictures burst, the stars drew yet further apart. Black space opened.

She got to her feet to fight better and remembered that old-fashioned women gave birth in their pigsties to fool the jealous, pain-dealing gods, who do not snatch piglets. Before the next spasms could stop her, she ran to the pigsty, each step a rushing out into emptiness. She climbed over the fence and knelt in the dirt. It was good to have a fence enclosing her, a tribal person alone.

Laboring, this woman who had carried her child as a foreign growth that sickened her every day, expelled it at last. She reached down to touch the hot, wet, moving mass, surely smaller than anything human, and could feel that it was human after all — fingers, toes, nails, nose. She pulled it up on to her belly, and it lay curled there, butt in the air, feet precisely tucked one under the other. She opened her loose shirt and buttoned the child inside. After resting, it squirmed and thrashed and she pushed it up to her breast. It turned its head this way and that until it found her nipple. There, it made little snuffling noises. She clenched her teeth at its preciousness, lovely as a young calf, a piglet, a little dog.

She may have gone to the pigsty as a last act of responsibility: she would protect this child as she had protected its father. It would look after her soul, leaving supplies on her grave. But how would this tiny child without family find her grave when there would be no marker for her anywhere, neither in the earth nor the family hall? No one would give her a family hall name. She had taken the child with her into the wastes. At its birth the two of them had felt the same raw pain of separation, a wound that only the family pressing tight could close. A child with no descent line would not soften her life but only trail after her, ghostlike, begging her to give it purpose. At dawn the villagers on their way to the fields would stand around the fence and look.

Full of milk, the little ghost slept. When it awoke, she hardened her breasts against the milk that crying loosens. Toward morning she picked up the baby and walked to the well.

45

Carrying the baby to the well shows loving. Otherwise abandon it. Turn its face into the mud. Mothers who love their children take them along. It was probably a girl; there is some hope of forgiveness for boys.

"Don't tell anyone you had an aunt. Your father does not want to hear her name. She has never been born." I have believed that sex was unspeakable and words so strong and fathers so frail that "aunt" would do my father mysterious harm. I have thought that my family, having settled among immigrants who had also been their neighbors in the ancestral land, needed to clean their name, and a wrong word would incite the kinspeople even here. But there is more to this silence: they want me to participate in her punishment. And I have.

In the twenty years since I heard this story I have not asked for details nor said my aunt's name; I do not know it. People who can comfort the dead can also chase after them to hurt them further—a reverse ancestor worship. The real punishment was not the raid swiftly inflicted by the villagers, but the family's deliberately forgetting her. Her betrayal so maddened them, they saw to it that she would suffer forever, even after death. Always hungry, always needing, she would have to beg food from other ghosts, snatch and steal it from those whose living descendants give them gifts. She would have to fight the ghosts massed at crossroads for the buns a few thoughtful citizens leave to decoy her away from village and home so that the ancestral spirits could feast unharassed. At peace, they could act like gods, not ghosts, their descent lines providing them with paper suits and dresses, spirit money, paper houses, paper automobiles, chicken, meat, and rice into eternity—essences delivered up in smoke and flames, steam and incense rising from each rice bowl. In an attempt to make the Chinese care for people outside the family, Chairman Mao encourages us now to give our paper replicas to the spirits of outstanding soldiers and workers, no matter whose ancestors they may be. My aunt remains forever hungry. Goods are not distributed evenly among the dead.

My aunt haunts me—her ghost drawn to me because now, after fifty years of neglect, I alone devote pages of paper to her, though not origamied into houses and clothes. I do not think she always means me well. I am telling on her, and she was a spite suicide, drowning herself in the drinking water. The Chinese are always very frightened of the drowned one, whose weeping ghost, wet hair hanging and skin bloated, waits silently by the water to pull down a substitute. [1976]

THINKING ABOUT THE TEXT

1. This cautionary tale is meant to persuade Kingston to conform to her parents' values. What is the argument behind the narrative the mother tells? Does it make sense to you? What might be a contemporary argument in a middle-class American family?

2. Were you ever put at an "outcast table" (para. 19) or anything comparable in your house or school? Did you ever hear of such a ritual? What did happen when you were punished? What kinds of things were you punished for? Why do you think these specific things were chosen?

3. Is this also a tale about gender inequality? How does Kingston suggest this? How are relations between men and women portrayed here?

4. How do ghosts and spirits function in this essay? Which parts of this piece seem true to you, and which seem fictional? Why do you suppose Kingston blends these elements?

5. Sexual mores change over time and from country to country. What specifically about the aunt's context made her transgression so severe? How would her "crime" be viewed in contemporary America? Why? What do you think an ideal response would be?

MAKING COMPARISONS

1. Whereas Sanders and Oates were involved in the cases they report, Kingston was only told a story about her aunt's death and heard it many years after the event. In what ways, if any, is this difference relevant?

2. Does the community that judged Kingston's aunt seem less rational than the juries discussed by Sanders and Oates? Define what you mean by *rational*.

3. To what extent do the judging groups in all three essays concern themselves with behavior that you consider private rather than public? Again, define what you mean by these terms.

WRITING ABOUT ISSUES

1. In effect, Sanders, Oates, and Kingston invite you to judge the community justice they describe. Choose one of the essays, and think of the questions you would ask to guide your evaluation of the community behavior that the author describes. Then write an essay in which you state whether and how the author addresses these questions.

2. Sanders, Oates, and Kingston tell you things about themselves. Choose two of these authors, and write an essay in which you compare their self-disclosures. Do you get pretty much the same impression of both authors, or do the images they project of themselves strike you as significantly different? Refer to specific details of their texts.

3. In 1991, four white police officers went on trial for various offenses related to their videotaped beating of an African American man, Rodney King, who was resisting arrest. The judge felt that the officers could not receive a fair trial in southeast Los Angeles, where the beating occurred. Therefore, the trial was moved to a suburb, Simi Valley. The jury's ten whites, one Hispanic, and one Asian reflected the predominantly white middle-class makeup of the town. Critics argued that a Los Angeles jury probably would have been partially or even predominantly black. The Simi Valley jurors proceeded to acquit the officers of almost every charge. Many Americans protested the outcome, believing that a more racially

diverse jury would have reached more responsible verdicts and that the trial should have taken place where the complaint was filed. In the *Washington Post*, however, a letter writer disagreed: "As for the change of venue, the Constitution guarantees us a jury of our peers. The Simi Valley jury was surely more representative of the officers' peers than a southeast Los Angeles jury would have been." Write an essay in which you identify and defend what you think should be meant by the phrase "a jury of one's peers." In arguing for your definition, refer to at least one actual case. Possibilities include the King case; the cases described by Sanders, Oates, or Kingston; the two O. J. Simpson trials; and cases in your local community.

4. Write an essay analyzing and evaluating the behavior of a particular jury. It might be a jury that you sat on or observed. Then again, it might be a jury that someone told you about or that you read about. Feel free to compare your chosen jury with any of the judging groups in this cluster's essays.

PSYCHIATRIC INJUSTICE: CULTURAL CONTEXTS FOR CHARLOTTE PERKINS GILMAN'S "THE YELLOW WALLPAPER"

CHARLOTTE PERKINS GILMAN, "The Yellow Wallpaper"

CULTURAL CONTEXTS:
CHARLOTTE PERKINS GILMAN, "Why I Wrote 'The Yellow Wallpaper' "
S. WEIR MITCHELL, From "The Evolution of the Rest Treatment"
JOHN HARVEY KELLOGG, From *The Ladies' Guide in Health and Disease*

When doctors make a medical or psychiatric diagnosis, they pinpoint their patient's condition but also often accept or reject their society's definition of *health*. The social context of diagnoses seems especially worth considering when a particular condition afflicts one gender much more than the other. Today, many more women than men appear to suffer from depression, anorexia, bulimia, and multiple personality disorder. Why? Perhaps traditional female roles encourage these illnesses; perhaps gender bias affects how doctors label and treat them. Charlotte Perkins Gilman raised both these possibilities in her 1892 short story "The Yellow Wallpaper." In her own life, Gilman suffered from what we now call postpartum depression after the birth of her daughter. Subsequently Gilman was ordered by her doctor, the well-known S. Weir Mitchell, to undergo a "rest cure" in which she did no work. For Gilman, the cure proved worse than the disease, and through "The Yellow Wallpaper" she suggested that women found to be mentally ill may actually be rebelling against patriarchal constraints. Besides Gilman's story, we include her account of why she wrote it, an excerpt from a lecture by Mitchell about his cure, and some advice about motherhood from John Kellogg, another influential doctor of the time.

(Charlotte Perkins Gilman. The Granger Collection, New York.)

BEFORE YOU READ

How is mental illness depicted in movies and television shows you have seen? Which representations of mental illness have you appreciated the most? Which have you especially disliked? State your criteria for these judgments.

CHARLOTTE PERKINS GILMAN
The Yellow Wallpaper

Charlotte Perkins Gilman (1860–1935) was a major activist and theorist in America's first wave of feminism. During her lifetime, she was chiefly known for her 1898 book Women and Economics. *In it she argued that women should not be confined to the household and made economically dependent on men. Gilman also advanced such ideas through her many public speaking appearances and her magazine* The Forerunner, *which she edited from 1909 to 1916. Gilman wrote many articles and works of fiction for* The Forerunner, *including a tale called* Herland

(1915) in which she envisioned an all-female utopia. Today, however, Gilman is best known for her short story "The Yellow Wallpaper," which she published first in an 1892 issue of the New England Magazine. *The story is based on Gilman's struggle with depression after the birth of her daughter Katharine in 1885. Seeking help for emotional turmoil, Gilman consulted the eminent neurologist Silas Weir Mitchell, who prescribed his famous "rest cure." This treatment, which forbade Gilman to work, actually worsened her distress. She improved only after she moved to California, divorced her husband, let him raise Katharine with his new wife, married someone else, and plunged fully into a literary and political career. As Gilman noted in her posthumously published autobiography,* The Living of Charlotte Perkins Gilman *(1935), she never fully recovered from the debilitation that had led her to Dr. Mitchell, but she ultimately managed to be enormously productive. Although "The Yellow Wallpaper" is a work of fiction rather than a factual account of her experience with Mitchell, Gilman used the story to criticize the doctor's patriarchal approach as well as society's efforts to keep women passive.*

It is very seldom that mere ordinary people like John and myself secure ancestral halls for the summer.

A colonial mansion, a hereditary estate, I would say a haunted house and reach the height of romantic felicity — but that would be asking too much of fate!

Still I will proudly declare that there is something queer about it.

Else, why should it be let so cheaply? And why have stood so long untenanted?

John laughs at me, of course, but one expects that in marriage. 5

John is practical in the extreme. He has no patience with faith, an intense horror of superstition, and he scoffs openly at any talk of things not to be felt and seen and put down in figures.

John is a physician, and *perhaps* — (I would not say it to a living soul, of course, but this is dead paper and a great relief to my mind) — *perhaps* that is one reason I do not get well faster.

You see, he does not believe I am sick!

And what can one do?

If a physician of high standing, and one's own husband, assures friends and 10 relatives that there is really nothing the matter with one but temporary nervous depression — a slight hysterical tendency — what is one to do?

My brother is also a physician, and also of high standing, and he says the same thing.

So I take phosphates or phosphites — whichever it is, and tonics, and journeys, and air, and exercise, and am absolutely forbidden to "work" until I am well again.

Personally, I disagree with their ideas.

Personally, I believe that congenial work, with excitement and change, would do me good.

But what is one to do? 15

I did write for a while in spite of them; but it *does* exhaust me a good deal —
having to be so sly about it, or else meet with heavy opposition.

I sometimes fancy that in my condition if I had less opposition and more
society and stimulus — but John says the very worst thing I can do is to think about
my condition, and I confess it always makes me feel bad.

So I will let it alone and talk about the house.

The most beautiful place! It is quite alone, standing well back from the road,
quite three miles from the village. It makes me think of English places that you
read about, for there are hedges and walls and gates that lock, and lots of separate
little houses for the gardeners and people.

There is a *delicious* garden! I never saw such a garden — large and shady, full   20
of box-bordered paths, and lined with long grape-covered arbors with seats under
them.

There were greenhouses, too, but they are all broken now.

There was some legal trouble, I believe, something about the heirs and co-
heirs; anyhow, the place has been empty for years.

That spoils my ghostliness, I am afraid, but I don't care — there is something
strange about the house — I can feel it.

I even said so to John one moonlight evening, but he said what I felt was a
draught, and shut the window.

I get unreasonably angry with John sometimes. I'm sure I never used to be so   25
sensitive. I think it is due to this nervous condition.

But John says if I feel so, I shall neglect proper self-control; so I take pains to
control myself — before him, at least, and that makes me very tired.

I don't like our room a bit. I wanted one downstairs that opened on the
piazza and had roses all over the window, and such pretty old-fashioned chintz
hangings! but John would not hear of it.

He said there was only one window and not room for two beds, and no near
room for him if he took another.

He is very careful and loving, and hardly lets me stir without special direction.

I have a schedule prescription for each hour in the day; he takes all care from   30
me, and so I feel basely ungrateful not to value it more.

He said we came here solely on my account, that I was to have perfect rest
and all the air I could get. "Your exercise depends on your strength, my dear,"
said he, "and your food somewhat on your appetite; but air you can absorb all the
time." So we took the nursery at the top of the house.

It is a big, airy room, the whole floor nearly, with windows that look all ways,
and air and sunshine galore. It was nursery first and then playroom and gymnasium, I should judge; for the windows are barred for little children, and there are
rings and things in the walls.

The paint and paper look as if a boys' school had used it. It is stripped off —
the paper — in great patches all around the head of my bed, about as far as I can
reach, and in a great place on the other side of the room low down. I never saw a
worse paper in my life.

One of those sprawling flamboyant patterns committing every artistic sin.

It is dull enough to confuse the eye in following, pronounced enough to constantly irritate and provoke study, and when you follow the lame uncertain curves for a little distance they suddenly commit suicide — plunge off at outrageous angles, destroy themselves in unheard of contradictions.

The color is repellant, almost revolting; a smouldering unclean yellow, strangely faded by the slow-turning sunlight.

It is a dull yet lurid orange in some places, a sickly sulphur tint in others.

No wonder the children hated it! I should hate it myself if I had to live in this room long.

There comes John, and I must put this away, — he hates to have me write a word.

We have been here two weeks, and I haven't felt like writing before, since that first day.

I am sitting by the window now, up in this atrocious nursery, and there is nothing to hinder my writing as much as I please, save lack of strength.

John is away all day, and even some nights when his cases are serious.

I am glad my case is not serious!

But these nervous troubles are dreadfully depressing.

John does not know how much I really suffer. He knows there is no *reason* to suffer, and that satisfies him.

Of course it is only nervousness. It does weigh on me so not to do my duty in any way!

I meant to be such a help to John, such a real rest and comfort, and here I am a comparative burden already!

Nobody would believe what an effort it is to do what little I am able, — to dress and entertain, and order things.

It is fortunate Mary is so good with the baby. Such a dear baby!

And yet I *cannot* be with him, it makes me so nervous.

I suppose John never was nervous in his life. He laughs at me so about this wall-paper!

At first he meant to repaper the room, but afterward he said that I was letting it get the better of me, and that nothing was worse for a nervous patient than to give way to such fancies.

He said that after the wall-paper was changed it would be the heavy bedstead, and then the barred windows, and then that gate at the head of the stairs, and so on.

"You know the place is doing you good," he said, "and really, dear, I don't care to renovate the house just for a three months' rental."

"Then do let us go downstairs," I said, "there are such pretty rooms there."

Then he took me in his arms and called me a blessed little goose, and said he would go down cellar, if I wished, and have it whitewashed into the bargain.

But he is right enough about the beds and windows and things.

It is an airy and comfortable room as anyone need wish, and, of course, I would not be so silly as to make him uncomfortable just for a whim.

I'm really getting quite fond of the big room, all but that horrid paper.

Out of one window I can see the garden, those mysterious deep-shaded arbors, the riotous old-fashioned flowers, and bushes and gnarly trees. 60

Out of another I get a lovely view of the bay and a little private wharf belonging to the estate. There is a beautiful shaded lane that runs down there from the house. I always fancy I see people walking in these numerous paths and arbors, but John has cautioned me not to give way to fancy in the least. He says that with my imaginative power and habit of story-making, a nervous weakness like mine is sure to lead to all manner of excited fancies, and that I ought to use my will and good sense to check the tendency. So I try.

I think sometimes that if I were only well enough to write a little it would relieve the press of ideas and rest me.

But I find I get pretty tired when I try.

It is so discouraging not to have any advice and companionship about my work. When I get really well, John says we will ask Cousin Henry and Julia down for a long visit; but he says he would as soon put fireworks in my pillow-case as to let me have those stimulating people about now.

I wish I could get well faster. 65

But I must not think about that. This paper looks to me as if it *knew* what a vicious influence it had!

There is a recurrent spot where the pattern lolls like a broken neck and two bulbous eyes stare at you upside down.

I get positively angry with the impertinence of it and the everlastingness. Up and down and sideways they crawl, and those absurd, unblinking eyes are everywhere. There is one place where two breadths didn't match, and the eyes go all up and down the line, one a little higher than the other.

I never saw so much expression in an inanimate thing before, and we all know how much expression they have! I used to lie awake as a child and get more entertainment and terror out of blank walls and plain furniture than most children could find in a toy-store.

I remember what a kindly wink the knobs of our big, old bureau used to 70 have, and there was one chair that always seemed like a strong friend.

I used to feel that if any of the other things looked too fierce I could always hop into that chair and be safe.

The furniture in this room is no worse than inharmonious, however, for we had to bring it all from downstairs. I suppose when this was used as a playroom they had to take the nursery things out, and no wonder! I never saw such ravages as the children have made here.

The wall-paper, as I said before, is torn off in spots, and it sticketh closer than a brother—they must have had perseverance as well as hatred.

Then the floor is scratched and gouged and splintered, the plaster itself is dug out here and there, and this great heavy bed, which is all we found in the room, looks as if it had been through the wars.

But I don't mind it a bit—only the paper. 75

There comes John's sister. Such a dear girl as she is, and so careful of me! I must not let her find me writing.

She is a perfect and enthusiastic housekeeper, and hopes for no better profession. I verily believe she thinks it is the writing which made me sick!

But I can write when she is out, and see her a long way off from these windows.

There is one that commands the road, a lovely shaded winding road, and one that just looks off over the country. A lovely country, too, full of great elms and velvet meadows.

This wallpaper has a kind of sub-pattern in a different shade, a particularly irritating one, for you can only see it in certain lights, and not clearly then.

But in the places where it isn't faded and where the sun is just so — I can see a strange, provoking, formless sort of figure, that seems to skulk about behind that silly and conspicuous front design.

There's sister on the stairs!

Well, the Fourth of July is over! The people are all gone and I am tired out. John thought it might do me good to see a little company, so we just had mother and Nellie and the children down for a week.

Of course I didn't do a thing. Jennie sees to everything now.

But it tired me all the same.

John says if I don't pick up faster he shall send me to Weir Mitchell° in the fall.

But I don't want to go there at all. I had a friend who was in his hands once, and she says he is just like John and my brother, only more so!

Besides, it is such an undertaking to go so far.

I don't feel as if it was worthwhile to turn my hand over for anything, and I'm getting dreadfully fretful and querulous.

I cry at nothing, and cry most of the time.

Of course I don't when John is here, or anybody else, but when I am alone.

And I am alone a good deal just now. John is kept in town very often by serious cases, and Jennie is good and lets me alone when I want her to.

So I walk a little in the garden or down that lovely lane, sit on the porch under the roses, and lie down up here a good deal.

I'm getting really fond of the room in spite of the wallpaper. Perhaps *because* of the wallpaper.

It dwells in my mind so!

I lie here on this great immovable bed — it is nailed down, I believe — and follow that pattern about by the hour. It is as good as gymnastics, I assure you. I start, we'll say, at the bottom, down in the corner over there where it has not been touched, and I determine for the thousandth time that I *will* follow that pointless pattern to some sort of a conclusion.

I know a little of the principle of design, and I know this thing was not arranged on any laws of radiation, or alternation, or repetition, or symmetry, or anything else that I ever heard of.

Weir Mitchell: Dr. S. Weir Mitchell (1829–1914) was an eminent Philadelphia neurologist who advocated "rest cures" for nervous disorders. He was the author of *Diseases of the Nervous System, Especially of Women* (1881).

It is repeated, of course, by the breadths, but not otherwise.

Looked at in one way each breadth stands alone, the bloated curves and flourishes—a kind of "debased Romanesque" with *delirium tremens*—go waddling up and down in isolated columns of fatuity.

But, on the other hand, they connect diagonally, and the sprawling outlines 100 run off in great slanting waves of optic horror, like a lot of wallowing seaweeds in full chase.

The whole thing goes horizontally, too, at least it seems so, and I exhaust myself in trying to distinguish the order of its going in that direction.

They have used a horizontal breadth for a frieze, and that adds wonderfully to the confusion.

There is one end of the room where it is almost intact, and there, when the crosslights fade and the low sun shines directly upon it, I can almost fancy radiation after all,—the interminable grotesques seem to form around a common centre and rush off in headlong plunges of equal distraction.

It makes me tired to follow it. I will take a nap I guess.

I don't know why I should write this. 105

I don't want to.

I don't feel able.

And I know John would think it absurd. But I *must* say what I feel and think in some way—it is such a relief!

But the effort is getting to be greater than the relief.

Half the time now I am awfully lazy, and lie down ever so much. 110

John says I mustn't lose my strength, and has me take cod liver oil and lots of tonics and things, to say nothing of ale and wine and rare meat.

Dear John! He loves me very dearly, and hates to have me sick. I tried to have a real earnest reasonable talk with him the other day, and tell him how I wish he would let me go and make a visit to Cousin Henry and Julia.

But he said I wasn't able to go, nor able to stand it after I got there; and I did not make out a very good case for myself, for I was crying before I had finished.

It is getting to be a great effort for me to think straight. Just this nervous weakness I suppose.

And dear John gathered me up in his arms, and just carried me upstairs and 115 laid me on the bed, and sat by me and read to me till it tired my head.

He said I was his darling and his comfort and all he had, and that I must take care of myself for his sake, and keep well.

He says no one but myself can help me out of it, that I must use my will and self-control and not let any silly fancies run away with me.

There's one comfort, the baby is well and happy, and does not have to occupy this nursery with the horrid wallpaper.

If we had not used it, that blessed child would have! What a fortunate escape! Why, I wouldn't have a child of mine, an impressionable little thing, live in such a room for worlds.

I never thought of it before, but it is lucky that John kept me here after all, I 120 can stand it so much easier than a baby, you see.

Of course I never mention it to them any more — I am too wise, but I keep watch of it all the same.

There are things in the wallpaper that nobody knows but me, or ever will.

Behind that outside pattern the dim shapes get clearer every day.

It is always the same shape, only very numerous.

And it is like a woman stooping down and creeping about behind that pat-   125
tern. I don't like it a bit. I wonder — I begin to think — I wish John would take me away from here!

It is so hard to talk with John about my case, because he is so wise, and because he loves me so.

But I tried it last night.

It was moonlight. The moon shines in all around just as the sun does.

I hate to see it sometimes, it creeps so slowly, and always comes in by one window or another.

John was asleep and I hated to waken him, so I kept still and watched the   130
moonlight on that undulating wallpaper till I felt creepy.

The faint figure behind seemed to shake the pattern, just as if she wanted to get out.

I got up softly and went to feel and see if the paper *did* move, and when I came back John was awake.

"What is it, little girl?" he said. "Don't go walking about like that — you'll get cold."

I thought it was a good time to talk, so I told him that I really was not gaining here, and that I wished he would take me away.

"Why, darling!" said he, "our lease will be up in three weeks, and I can't see   135
how to leave before.

"The repairs are not done at home, and I cannot possibly leave town just now. Of course if you were in any danger, I could and would, but you really are better, dear, whether you can see it or not. I am a doctor, dear, and I know. You are gaining flesh and color, your appetite is better, I feel really much easier about you."

"I don't weigh a bit more," said I, "nor as much; and my appetite may be better in the evening when you are here but it is worse in the morning when you are away!"

"Bless her little heart!" said he with a big hug, "she shall be as sick as she pleases! But now let's improve the shining hours by going to sleep, and talk about it in the morning!"

"And you won't go away?" I asked gloomily.

"Why, how can I, dear? It is only three weeks more and then we will take a   140
nice little trip of a few days while Jennie is getting the house ready. Really dear you are better!"

"Better in body perhaps —" I began, and stopped short, for he sat up straight and looked at me with such a stern, reproachful look that I could not say another word.

"My darling," said he, "I beg you, for my sake and for our child's sake, as well as for your own, that you will never for one instant let that idea enter your mind!

There is nothing so dangerous, so fascinating, to a temperament like yours. It is a false and foolish fancy. Can you trust me as a physician when I tell you so?"

So of course I said no more on that score, and we went to sleep before long. He thought I was asleep first, but I wasn't, and lay there for hours trying to decide whether that front pattern and the back pattern really did move together or separately.

On a pattern like this, by daylight, there is a lack of sequence, a defiance of law, that is a constant irritant to a normal mind.

The color is hideous enough, and unreliable enough, and infuriating   145
enough, but the pattern is torturing.

You think you have mastered it, but just as you get well underway in following, it turns a back-somersault and there you are. It slaps you in the face, knocks you down, and tramples upon you. It is like a bad dream.

The outside pattern is a florid arabesque, reminding one of a fungus. If you can imagine a toadstool in joints, an interminable string of toadstools, budding and sprouting in endless convolutions — why, that is something like it.

That is, sometimes!

There is one marked peculiarity about this paper, a thing nobody seems to notice but myself, and that is that it changes as the light changes.

When the sun shoots in through the east window — I always watch for that   150
first long, straight ray — it changes so quickly that I never can quite believe it.

That is why I watch it always.

By moonlight — the moon shines in all night when there is a moon — I wouldn't know it was the same paper.

At night in any kind of light, in twilight, candlelight, lamplight, and worst of all by moonlight, it becomes bars! The outside pattern I mean, and the woman behind it is as plain as can be.

I didn't realize for a long time what the thing was that showed behind, that dim sub-pattern, but now I am quite sure it is a woman.

By daylight she is subdued, quiet. I fancy it is the pattern that keeps her so   155
still. It is so puzzling. It keeps me quiet by the hour.

I lie down ever so much now. John says it is good for me, and to sleep all I can.

Indeed he started the habit by making me lie down for an hour after each meal.

It is a very bad habit I am convinced, for you see I don't sleep.

And that cultivates deceit, for I don't tell them I'm awake — O, no!

The fact is I am getting a little afraid of John.   160

He seems very queer sometimes, and even Jennie has an inexplicable look.

It strikes me occasionally, just as a scientific hypothesis, — that perhaps it is the paper!

I have watched John when he did not know I was looking, and come into the room suddenly on the most innocent excuses, and I've caught him several times *looking at the paper!* And Jennie too. I caught Jennie with her hand on it once.

She didn't know I was in the room, and when I asked her in a quiet, a very quiet voice, with the most restrained manner possible, what she was doing with the paper — she turned around as if she had been caught stealing, and looked quite angry — asked me why I should frighten her so!

Then she said that the paper stained everything it touched, that she had　165 found yellow smooches on all my clothes and John's, and she wished we would be more careful!

Did not that sound innocent? But I know she was studying that pattern, and I am determined that nobody shall find it out but myself!

Life is very much more exciting now than it used to be. You see I have something more to expect, to look forward to, to watch. I really do eat better, and am more quiet than I was.

John is so pleased to see me improve! He laughed a little the other day, and said I seemed to be flourishing in spite of my wall-paper.

I turned it off with a laugh. I had no intention of telling him it was *because* of the wall-paper — he would make fun of me. He might even want to take me away.

I don't want to leave now until I have found it out. There is a week more, and　170 I think that will be enough.

I'm feeling ever so much better! I don't sleep much at night, for it is so interesting to watch developments; but I sleep a good deal in the daytime.

In the daytime it is tiresome and perplexing.

There are always new shoots on the fungus, and new shades of yellow all over it. I cannot keep count of them, though I have tried conscientiously.

It is the strangest yellow, that wall-paper! It makes me think of all the yellow things I ever saw — not beautiful ones like buttercups, but old foul, bad yellow things.

But there is something else about that paper — the smell! I noticed it the　175 moment we came into the room, but with so much air and sun it was not bad. Now we have had a week of fog and rain, and whether the windows are open or not, the smell is here.

It creeps all over the house.

I find it hovering in the dining-room, skulking in the parlor, hiding in the hall, lying in wait for me on the stairs.

It gets into my hair.

Even when I go to ride, if I turn my head suddenly and surprise it — there is that smell!

Such a peculiar odor, too! I have spent hours in trying to analyze it, to find　180 what it smelled like.

It is not bad — at first, and very gentle, but quite the subtlest, most enduring odor I ever met.

In this damp weather it is awful, I wake up in the night and find it hanging over me.

It used to disturb me at first. I thought seriously of burning the house — to reach the smell.

But now I am used to it. The only thing I can think of that it is like is the *color* of the paper! A yellow smell.

There is a very funny mark on this wall, low down, near the mopboard. A   185
streak that runs round the room. It goes behind every piece of furniture, except
the bed, a long, straight, even *smooch*, as if it had been rubbed over and over.

I wonder how it was done and who did it, and what they did it for. Round and
round and round — round and round and round — it makes me dizzy!

I really have discovered something at last.

Through watching so much at night, when it changes so, I have finally
found out.

The front pattern *does* move — and no wonder! The woman behind shakes it!

Sometimes I think there are a great many women behind, and sometimes   190
only one, and she crawls around fast, and her crawling shakes it all over.

Then in the very bright spots she keeps still, and in the very shady spots she
just takes hold of the bars and shakes them hard.

And she is all the time trying to climb through. But nobody could climb
through that pattern — it strangles so; I think that is why it has so many heads.

They get through, and then the pattern strangles them off and turns them
upside down, and makes their eyes white!

If those heads were covered or taken off it would not be half so bad.

I think that woman gets out in the daytime!   195

And I'll tell you why — privately — I've seen her!

I can see her out of every one of my windows!

It is the same woman, I know, for she is always creeping, and most women do
not creep by daylight.

I see her in that long shaded lane, creeping up and down. I see her in those
dark grape arbors, creeping all around the garden.

I see her on that long road under the trees, creeping along, and when a car-   200
riage comes she hides under the blackberry vines.

I don't blame her a bit. It must be very humiliating to be caught creeping by
daylight!

I always lock the door when I creep by daylight. I can't do it at night, for I
know John would suspect something at once.

And John is so queer now, that I don't want to irritate him. I wish he would
take another room! Besides, I don't want anybody to get that woman out at night
but myself.

I often wonder if I could see her out of all the windows at once.

But, turn as fast as I can, I can only see out of one at one time.   205

And though I always see her, she *may* be able to creep faster than I can turn!

I have watched her sometimes away off in the open country, creeping as fast
as a cloud shadow in a high wind.

If only that top pattern could be gotten off from the under one! I mean to try
it, little by little.

I have found out another funny thing, but I shan't tell it this time! It does not
do to trust people too much.

There are only two more days to get this paper off, and I believe John is beginning to notice. I don't like the look in his eyes.

And I heard him ask Jennie a lot of professional questions, about me. She had a very good report to give.

She said I slept a good deal in the daytime.

John knows I don't sleep very well at night, for all I'm so quiet!

He asked me all sorts of questions too, and pretended to be very loving and kind.

As if I couldn't see through him!

Still, I don't wonder he acts so, sleeping under this paper for three months.

It only interests me, but I feel sure John and Jennie are secretly affected by it.

Hurrah! This is the last day, but it is enough. John to stay in town over night, and won't be out until this evening.

Jennie wanted to sleep with me — the sly thing! But I told her I should undoubtedly rest better for a night all alone.

That was clever, for really I wasn't alone a bit! As soon as it was moonlight and that poor thing began to crawl and shake the pattern, I got up and ran to help her.

I pulled and she shook, I shook and she pulled, and before morning we had peeled off yards of that paper.

A strip about as high as my head and half around the room.

And then when the sun came and that awful pattern began to laugh at me, I declared I would finish it to-day!

We go away to-morrow, and they are moving all my furniture down again to leave things as they were before.

Jennie looked at the wall in amazement, but I told her merrily that I did it out of pure spite at the vicious thing.

She laughed and said she wouldn't mind doing it herself, but I must not get tired.

How she betrayed herself that time!

But I am here, and no person touches this paper but me, — not *alive*!

She tried to get me out of the room — it was too patent! But I said it was so quiet and empty and clean now that I believed I would lie down again and sleep all I could, and not to wake me even for dinner — I would call when I woke.

So now she is gone, and the servants are gone, and the things are gone, and there is nothing left but that great bedstead nailed down, with the canvas mattress we found on it.

We shall sleep downstairs to-night, and take the boat home to-morrow.

I quite enjoy the room, now it is bare again.

How those children did tear about here!

This bedstead is fairly gnawed!

But I must get to work.

I have locked the door and thrown the key down into the front path.

I don't want to go out, and I don't want to have anybody come in, till John comes.

I want to astonish him.

I've got a rope up here that even Jennie did not find. If that woman does get out, and tries to get away, I can tie her!

But I forgot I could not reach far without anything to stand on!   240

This bed will *not* move!

I tried to lift and push it until I was lame, and then I got so angry I bit off a little piece at one corner — but it hurt my teeth.

Then I peeled off all the paper I could reach standing on the floor. It sticks horribly and the pattern just enjoys it! All those strangled heads and bulbous eyes and waddling fungus growths just shriek with derision!

I am getting angry enough to do something desperate. To jump out of the window would be admirable exercise, but the bars are too strong even to try.

Besides I wouldn't do it. Of course not. I know well enough that a step like   245
that is improper and might be misconstrued.

I don't like to *look* out of the windows even — there are so many of those creeping women, and they creep so fast.

I wonder if they all come out of that wall-paper as I did?

But I am securely fastened now by my well-hidden rope — you don't get *me* out in the road there!

I suppose I shall have to get back behind the pattern when it comes night, and that is hard!

It is so pleasant to be out in this great room and creep around as I please!   250

I don't want to go outside. I won't, even if Jennie asks me to.

For outside you have to creep on the ground, and everything is green instead of yellow.

But here I can creep smoothly on the floor, and my shoulder just fits in that long smooch around the wall, so I cannot lose my way.

Why, there's John at the door!

It is no use, young man, you can't open it!   255

How he does call and pound!

Now he's crying for an axe.

It would be a shame to break down that beautiful door!

"John dear!" said I in the gentlest voice, "the key is down by the front steps, under a plantain leaf!"

That silenced him for a few moments.   260

Then he said — very quietly indeed, "Open the door, my darling!"

"I can't," said I. "The key is down by the front door under a plantain leaf!"

And then I said it again, several times, very gently and slowly, and said it so often that he had to go and see, and he got it of course, and came in. He stopped short by the door.

"What is the matter?" he cried. "For God's sake, what are you doing!"

I kept on creeping just the same, but I looked at him over my shoulder.   265

"I've got out at last," said I, "in spite of you and Jane. And I've pulled off most of the paper, so you can't put me back!"

Now why should that man have fainted? But he did, and right across my path by the wall, so that I had to creep over him every time!   [1892]

THINKING ABOUT THE TEXT

1. What psychological stages does the narrator go through as the story progresses?

2. How does the wallpaper function as a symbol in this story? What do you conclude about the narrator when she becomes increasingly interested in the woman she finds there?

3. Explain your ultimate view of the narrator, by using specific details of the story and by identifying some of the warrants or assumptions behind your opinion. Do you admire her? Sympathize with her? Recoil from her? What would you say to someone who simply dismisses her as crazy?

4. The story is narrated in the present tense. Would its effect be different if it were narrated in the past? Why, or why not?

5. In real life, Gilman's husband and her doctor were two separate people. In the story, the narrator's husband is her doctor as well. Why do you think Gilman made this change? What is the effect of her combining husband and doctor?

CHARLOTTE PERKINS GILMAN
Why I Wrote "The Yellow Wallpaper"

Gilman published the following piece in the October 1913 issue of her magazine The Forerunner.

Many and many a reader has asked that. When the story first came out, in the *New England Magazine* about 1891, a Boston physician made protest in *The Transcript*. Such a story ought not to be written, he said; it was enough to drive anyone mad to read it.

Another physician, in Kansas I think, wrote to say that it was the best description of incipient insanity he had ever seen, and — begging my pardon — had I been there?

Now the story of the story is this:

For many years I suffered from a severe and continuous nervous breakdown tending to melancholia — and beyond. During about the third year of this trouble I went, in devout faith and some faint stir of hope, to a noted specialist in nervous diseases, the best known in the country. This wise man put me to bed and applied the rest cure, to which a still good physique responded so promptly that, he concluded there was nothing much the matter with me, and sent me home with solemn advice to "live as domestic a life as far as possible," to "have but two hours' intellectual life a day," and "never to touch pen, brush or pencil again as long as I lived." This was in 1887.

I went home and obeyed those directions for some three months, and came so near the border line of utter mental ruin that I could see over.

5

Then, using the remnants of intelligence that remained, and helped by a wise friend, I cast the noted specialist's advice to the winds and went to work again — work, the normal life of every human being; work, in which is joy and growth and service, without which one is a pauper and a parasite; ultimately recovering some measure of power.

Being naturally moved to rejoicing by this narrow escape, I wrote *The Yellow Wallpaper*, with its embellishments and additions to carry out the ideal (I never had hallucinations or objections to my mural decorations) and sent a copy to the physician who so nearly drove me mad. He never acknowledged it.

The little book is valued by alienists° and as a good specimen of one kind of literature. It has to my knowledge saved one woman from a similar fate — so terrifying her family that they let her out into normal activity and she recovered.

But the best result is this. Many years later I was told that the great specialist had admitted to friends of his that he had altered his treatment of neurasthenia since reading *The Yellow Wallpaper*.

It was not intended to drive people crazy, but to save people from being   10
driven crazy, and it worked.   [1913]

alienists: Nineteenth-century term for psychiatrists.

THINKING ABOUT THE TEXT

1. S. Weir Mitchell was the "noted specialist in nervous diseases" (para. 4) whom Gilman mentions. Yet she does not identify him by name. Why not, do you think? Some historians argue that, contrary to Gilman's claim here, Mitchell continued to believe his "rest cure" valid. Does this issue of fact matter to your judgment of her piece? Why, or why not?

2. Look again at Gilman's last sentence. Do you believe that her story could indeed "save people from being driven crazy"? Why, or why not?

3. Does this piece as a whole affect your interpretation and opinion of Gilman's story? Why, or why not? In general, how much do you think readers of a story should know about its author's life?

S. WEIR MITCHELL
From "The Evolution of the Rest Treatment"

Charlotte Perkins Gilman sought help from Silas Weir Mitchell (1829–1914) because he was a well-known and highly respected physician who had treated many women's mental problems. Mitchell developed his "rest cure" while serving as an army surgeon during the Civil War. Ironically, like Gilman he was also a writer. Besides producing numerous monographs on medical subjects, he published many short stories and novels. The following is an excerpt from a lecture that Mitchell gave to the Philadelphia Neurological Society in 1904, twelve years after "The

Yellow Wallpaper" appeared. As you will see, Mitchell was still enthusiastic about his "rest cure," although he had changed it in certain respects since devising it.

I have been asked to come here to-night to speak to you on some subject connected with nervous disease. I had hoped to have had ready a fitting paper for so notable an occasion, but have been prevented by public engagements and private business so as to make it quite impossible. I have, therefore, been driven to ask whether it would be agreeable if I should speak in regard to the mode in which the treatment of disease by rest was evolved. This being favorably received, I am here this evening to say a few words on that subject.

You all know full well that the art of cure rests upon a number of sciences, and that what we do in medicine, we cannot always explain, and that our methods are far from having the accuracy involved in the term scientific. Very often, however, it is found that what comes to us through some accident or popular use and proves of value, is defensible in the end by scientific explanatory research. This was the case as regards the treatment I shall briefly consider for you to-night.

The first indication I ever had of the great value of mere rest in disease, was during the Civil War, when there fell into the hands of Doctors Morehouse, Keen and myself, a great many cases of what we called acute exhaustion. These were men, who, being tired by much marching, gave out suddenly at the end of some unusual exertion, and remained for weeks, perhaps months, in a pitiable state of what we should call today, Neurasthenia. In these war cases, it came on with strange abruptness. It was more extreme and also more certainly curable than are most of the graver male cases which now we are called on to treat.

I have seen nothing exactly like it in civil experience, but the combination of malaria, excessive exertion, and exposure provided cases such as no one sees today. Complete rest and plentiful diet usually brought these men up again and in many instances enabled them to return to the front.

In 1872 I had charge of a man who had locomotor ataxia° with extreme pain in the extremities, and while making some unusual exertion, he broke his right thigh. This confined him to his bed for three months, and the day he got up, he broke his left thigh. This involved another three months of rest. At the end of that time he confessed with satisfaction that his ataxia was better, and that he was, as he remained thereafter, free from pain. I learned from this, and two other cases, that in ataxia the bones are brittle, and I learned also that rest in bed is valuable in a proportion of such cases. You may perceive that my attention was thus twice drawn towards the fact that mere rest had certain therapeutic values.

In 1874 Mrs. G., of B——, Maine, came to see me in the month of January. I have described her case elsewhere, so that it is needless to go into detail here, except to say that she was a lady of ample means, with no special troubles or annoyances, but completely exhausted by having had children in rapid succession and from having undertaken to do charitable and other work to an extent far beyond her strength. When first I saw this tall woman, large, gaunt, weighing

5

ataxia: An inability to control muscular movements that is symptomatic of some nervous diseases.

under a hundred pounds, her complexion pale and acneous, and heard her story, I was for a time in a state of such therapeutic despair as usually fell upon physicians of that day when called upon to treat such cases. She had been to Spas, to physicians of the utmost eminence, passed through the hands of gynecologists, worn spinal supporters, and taken every tonic known to the books. When I saw her she was unable to walk up stairs. Her exercise was limited to moving feebly up and down her room, a dozen times a day. She slept little and, being very intelligent, felt deeply her inability to read or write. Any such use of the eyes caused headache and nausea. Conversation tired her, and she had by degrees accepted a life of isolation. She was able partially to digest and retain her meals if she lay down in a noiseless and darkened room. Any disturbance or the least excitement, in short, any effort, caused nausea and immediate rejection of her meal. With care she could retain enough food to preserve her life and hardly to do more. Anemia, which we had then no accurate means of measuring, had been met by half a dozen forms of iron, all of which were said to produce headache, and generally to disagree with her. Naturally enough, her case had been pronounced to be hysteria, but calling names may relieve a doctor and comfort him in failure, but does not always assist the patient, and to my mind there was more of a general condition of nervous excitability due to the extreme of weakness than I should have been satisfied to label with the apologetic label hysteria.

I sat beside this woman day after day, hearing her pitiful story, and distressed that a woman, young, once handsome, and with every means of enjoyment in life should be condemned to what she had been told was a state of hopeless invalidism. After my third or fourth visit, with a deep sense that everything had been done for her that able men could with reason suggest, and many things which reason never could have suggested, she said to me that I appeared to have nothing to offer which had not been tried over and over again. I asked her for another day before she gave up the hope which had brought her to me. The night brought counsel. The following morning I said to her, if you are at rest you appear to digest your meals better. "Yes," she said. "I have been told that on that account I ought to lie in bed. It has been tried, but when I remain in bed for a few days, I lose all appetite, have intense constipation, and get up feeling weaker than when I went to bed. Please do not ask me to go to bed." Nevertheless, I did, and a week in bed justified her statements. She threw up her meals undigested, and was manifestly worse for my experiment. Sometimes the emesis° was mere regurgitation, sometimes there was nausea and violent straining, with consequent extreme exhaustion. She declared that unless she had the small exercise of walking up and down her room, she was infallibly worse. I was here between two difficulties. That she needed rest I saw, that she required some form of exercise I also saw. How could I unite the two?

As I sat beside her, with a keen sense of defeat, it suddenly occurred to me that some time before, I had seen a man, known as a layer on of hands, use very rough rubbing for a gentleman who was in a state of general paresis.° Mr. S. had asked me if I objected to this man rubbing him. I said no, and that I should like to

---

emesis: Vomiting.　**paresis:** Brain syphilis.

see him do so, as he had relieved, to my knowledge, cases of rheumatic stiffness. I was present at two sittings and saw this man rub my patient. He kept him sitting in a chair at the time and was very rough and violent like the quacks now known as osteopaths. I told him he had injured my patient by his extreme roughness, and that if he rubbed him at all he must be more gentle. He took the hint and as a result there was every time a notable but temporary gain. Struck with this, I tried to have rubbing used on spinal cases, but those who tried to do the work were inefficient, and I made no constant use of it. It remained, however, on my mind, and recurred to me as I sat beside this wreck of a useful and once vigorous woman. The thought was fertile. I asked myself why rubbing might not prove competent to do for the muscles and tardy circulation what voluntary exercise does. I said to myself, this may be exercise without exertion, and wondered why I had not long before had this pregnant view of the matter.

Suffice it to say that I brought a young woman to Mrs. G.'s bedside and told her how I thought she ought to be rubbed. The girl was clever, and developed talent in that direction, and afterwards became the first of that great number of people who have since made a livelihood by massage. I watched the rubbing two or three times, giving instructions, in fact developing out of the clumsy massage I had seen, the manual of a therapeutic means, at that time entirely new to me. A few days later I fell upon the idea of giving electric passive exercise and cautiously added this second agency. Meanwhile, as she had always done best when secluded, I insisted on entire rest and shut out friends, relatives, books and letters. I had some faith that I should succeed. In ten days I was sure the woman had found a new tonic, hope, and blossomed like a rose. Her symptoms passed away one by one. I was soon able to add to her diet, to feed her between meals, to give her malt daily, and, after a time, to conceal in it full doses of pyro-phosphates of iron. First, then, I had found two means which enabled me to use rest in bed without causing the injurious effects of unassisted rest; secondly, I had discovered that massage was a tonic of extraordinary value: thirdly, I had learned that with this combination of seclusion, massage and electricity, I could overfeed the patient until I had brought her into a state of entire health. I learned later the care which had to be exercised in getting these patients out of bed. But this does not concern us now. In two months she gained forty pounds and was a cheerful, blooming woman, fit to do as she pleased. She has remained, save for time's ravage, what I made her.

It may strike you as interesting that for a while I was not fully aware of the enormous value of a therapeutic discovery which employed no new agents, but owed its usefulness to a combination of means more or less well known.

Simple rest as a treatment had been suggested, but not in this class of cases. Massage has a long history. Used, I think, as a luxury by the Orientals for ages, it was employed by Ling in 1813. It never attained perfection in the hands of the Swedes, nor do they to-day understand the proper use of this agent. It was over and over recognized in Germany, but never generally accepted. In France, at a later period, Dreyfus, in 1841, wrote upon it and advised its use, as did Recamier and Lainé in 1868. Two at least of these authors thought it useful as a general agent, but no one seems to have accepted their views, nor was its value as a tonic spoken of in the books on therapeutics or recommended on any text-book as a powerful toning agent. It was used here in the Rest Treatment, and this, I think, gave it vogue and caused the familiar use of this invaluable therapeutic measure.

A word before I close. My first case left me in May, 1874, and shortly afterwards I began to employ the same method in other cases, being careful to choose only those which seemed best suited to it. My first mention in print of the treatment was in 1875, in the Sequin Lectures, Vol. 1., No. 4, "Rest in the Treatment of Disease." In that paper I first described Mrs. G.'s case. My second paper was in 1877, an address before the Medico-Chirurgical faculty of Maryland, and the same year I printed my book on "Rest Treatment." The one mistake in the book was the title. I was, however, so impressed at the time by the extraordinary gain in flesh and blood under this treatment that I made it too prominent in the title of the book. Let me say that for a long time the new treatment was received with the utmost incredulity. When I spoke in my papers of the people who had gained half a pound a day or more, my results were questioned and ridiculed in this city as approaching charlatanism. At a later date in England some physicians were equally wanting in foresight and courtesy. It seems incredible that any man who was a member of the British Medical Association could have said that he would rather see his patients not get well than have them cured by such a method as that. It was several years before it was taken up by Professor Goodell, and it was a longer time in making its way in Europe when by mere accident it came to be first used by Professor William Playfair.

I suffered keenly at that time from this unfair criticism, as any sensitive man must have done, for some who were eminent in the profession said of it and of me things which were most inconsiderate. Over and over in consultation I was rejected with ill-concealed scorn. I made no reply to my critics. I knew that time would justify me: I have added a long since accepted means of helping those whom before my day few helped. This is a sufficient reward for silence, patience and self-faith. I fancy that there are in this room many who have profited for themselves and their patients by the thought which evolved the Rest Treatment as I sat by the beside of my first rest case in 1874. Playfair said of it at the British Association that he had nothing to add to it and nothing to omit, and to this day no one has differed as to his verdict.

How fully the use of massage has been justified by the later scientific studies of Lauder Brunton, myself, and others you all know. It is one of the most scientific of remedial methods.   [1904]

THINKING ABOUT THE TEXT

1. How would you describe Mitchell's tone in this lecture? What self-image does he seem to cultivate? Support your answers by referring to specific words in the text.

2. Why does Mitchell consider Mrs. G.'s case significant? In what ways does she resemble Gilman and the narrator of Gilman's story?

3. Mitchell indicates that his patients have included male as well as female hysterics. Are we therefore justified in concluding that gender did not matter much in his application of the "rest cure"? Why, or why not?

JOHN HARVEY KELLOGG
From *The Ladies' Guide* in Health and Disease

John Harvey Kellogg (1852–1943) was an American physician who wrote much advice about how to discipline one's sexual desires and, in the case of women, how to be a good mother. As founder and superintendent of the Battle Creek Sanitarium in Michigan, Dr. Kellogg urged that his patients eat cereals as part of their treatment, and eventually his brother established the cereal company that bears their family name. Dr. Kellogg's keen interest in cereals and health foods is satirized in T. Coraghessan Boyle's 1993 novel The Road to Wellville *and the film based on that book. The following piece is an excerpt from Kellogg's 1882* Ladies' Guide in Health and Disease: Girlhood, Maidenhood, Wifehood, Motherhood. *In this selection, he virtually equates womanhood with motherhood and discusses what a woman must do to produce outstanding children. Kellogg's advice reflects the view that much of his society held about women — or at least about middle- and upper-class white women. His discussion of "puerperal mania" is especially relevant to Gilman's story.*

The special influence of the mother begins with the moment of conception. In fact it is possible that the mental condition at the time of the generative act has much to do with determining the character of the child, though it is generally conceded that at this time the influence of the father is greater than that of the mother. Any number of instances have occurred in which a drunken father has impressed upon his child the condition of his nervous system to such a degree as to render permanent in the child the staggering gait and maudlin manner which in his own case was a transient condition induced by the poisonous influence of alcohol. A child born as the result of a union in which both parents were in a state of beastly intoxication was idiotic.

Another fact might be added to impress the importance that the new being should be supplied from the very beginning of its existence with the very best conditions possible. Indeed, it is desirable to go back still further, and secure a proper preparation for the important function of maternity. The qualities which go to make up individuality of character are the result of the summing up of a long line of influences, too subtle and too varied to admit of full control, but still, to some degree at least, subject to management. The dominance of law is nowhere more evident than in the relation of ante-natal influences to character.

The hap-hazard way in which human beings are generated leaves no room for surprise that the race should deteriorate. No stock-breeder would expect anything but ruin should he allow his animals to propagate with no attention to their physical conditions or previous preparation.

Finding herself in a pregnant condition, the mother should not yield to the depressing influences which often crowd upon her. The anxieties and fears which women sometimes yield themselves to, grow with encouragement, until they become so absorbed as to be capable of producing a profoundly evil impression on the child. The true mother who is prepared for the functions of maternity, will welcome the evidence of pregnancy, and joyfully enter upon the Heaven-given task of molding a human character, of bringing into the world a new being whose life-history may involve the destinies of nations, or change the current of human thought for generations to come.

The pregnant mother should cultivate cheerfulness of mind and calmness of temper, but should avoid excitements of all kinds, such as theatrical performances, public contests of various descriptions, etc. Anger, envy, irritability of temper, and, in fact, all the passions and propensities should be held in check. The fickleness of desire and the constantly varying whims which characterize the pregnant state in some women should not be regarded as uncontrollable, and to be yielded to as the only means of appeasing them. The mother should be gently encouraged to resist such tendencies when they become at all marked, and to assist her in the effort, her husband should endeavor to engage her mind by interesting conversation, reading, and various harmless and pleasant diversions.

If it is desired that the child should possess a special aptitude for any particular art or pursuit, during the period of pregnancy the mother's mind should be constantly directed in this channel. If artistic taste or skill is the trait desired, the mother should be surrounded by works of art of a high order of merit. She should read art, think art, talk, and write about art, and if possible, herself engage in the close practical study of some one or more branches of art, as painting, drawing, etching, or modeling. If ability for authorship is desired, then the mother should devote herself assiduously to literature. It is not claimed that by following these suggestions any mother can make of her children great artists or authors at will; but it is certain that by this means the greatest possibilities in individual cases can be attained; and it is certain that decided results have been secured by close attention to the principles laid down. It should be understood, however, that not merely a formal and desultory effort on the part of the mother is what is required. The theme selected must completely absorb her mind. It must be the one idea of her waking thoughts and the model on which is formed the dreams of her sleeping hours.

The question of diet during pregnancy as before stated is a vitally important one as regards the interests of the child. A diet into which enters largely such unwholesome articles as mustard, pepper, hot sauces, spices, and other stimulating condiments, engenders a love for stimulants in the disposition of the infant. Tea and coffee, especially if used to excess, undoubtedly tend in the same direction. We firmly believe that we have, in the facts first stated, the key to the constant increase in the consumption of ardent spirits. The children of the present generation inherit from their condiment-consuming, tea-, coffee-, and liquor-drinking, and tobacco-using parents, not simply a readiness for the acquirement of the habits mentioned, but a propensity for the use of stimulants which in persons of weak will-power and those whose circumstances are not the most favorable, becomes irresistible.

The present generation is also suffering in consequence of the impoverished diet of its parents. The modern custom of bolting the flour from the different grains has deprived millions of infants and children of the necessary supply of bone-making material, thus giving rise to a greatly increased frequency of the various diseases which arise from imperfect bony structure, as rickets, caries, premature decay of the teeth, etc. The proper remedy is the disuse of fine-flour bread and all other bolted grain preparations. Graham-flour bread, oatmeal, cracked wheat, and similar preparations, should be relied upon as the leading articles of diet. Supplemented by milk, the whole-grain preparations constitute a complete form of nourishment, and render a large amount of animal food not only unnecessary but really harmful on account of its stimulating character. It is by no means so necessary as is generally supposed that meat, fish, fowl, and flesh in various forms should constitute a large element of the dietary of the pregnant or nursing mother in order to furnish adequate nourishment for the developing child. We have seen the happiest results follow the employment of a strictly vegetarian dietary, and do not hesitate to advise moderation in the use of flesh food, though we do not recommend the entire discontinuance of its use by the pregnant mother who has been accustomed to use it freely.

A nursing mother should at once suspend nursing if she discovers that pregnancy has again occurred. The continuance of nursing under such circumstances is to the disadvantage of three individuals, the mother, the infant at the breast, and the developing child.

Sexual indulgence during pregnancy may be suspended with decided benefit to both mother and child. The most ancient medical writers call attention to the fact that by the practice of continence° during gestation, the pains of childbirth are greatly mitigated. The injurious influences upon the child of the gratification of the passions during the period when its character is being formed, is undoubtedly much greater than is usually supposed. We have no doubt that this is a common cause of the transmission of libidinous tendencies to the child; and that the tendency to abortion is induced by sexual indulgence has long been a well established fact. The females of most animals resolutely resist the advances of the males during this period, being guided in harmony with natural law by their natural instincts which have been less perverted in them than in human beings. The practice of continence during pregnancy is also enforced in the harems of the East, which fact leads to the practice of abortion among women of this class who are desirous of remaining the special favorites of the common husband.

The general health of the mother must be kept up in every way. It is especially important that the regularity of the bowels should be maintained. Proper diet and as much physical exercise as can be taken are the best means for accomplishing this. When constipation is allowed to exist, the infant as well as the mother suffers. The effete products which should be promptly removed from the body, being long retained, are certain to find their way back into the system again, poisoning not only the blood of the mother but that of the developing fœtus. . . .

Puerperal Mania. — This form of mental disease is most apt to show itself about two weeks after delivery. Although, fortunately, of not very frequent occur-

10

---

continence: Chastity, abstinence, or restraint.

rence, it is a most serious disorder when it does occur, and hence we may with propriety introduce the following somewhat lengthy, but most graphic description of the disease from the pen of Dr. Ramsbotham, an eminent English physician:—

"In mania there is almost always, at the very commencement, a troubled, agitated, and hurried manner, a restless eye, an unnaturally anxious, suspicious, and unpleasing expression of face;—sometimes it is pallid, at others more flushed than usual;—an unaccustomed irritability of temper, and impatience of control or contradiction; a vacillation of purpose, or loss of memory; sometimes a rapid succession of contradictory orders are issued, or a paroxysm of excessive anger is excited about the merest trifle. Occasionally, one of the first indications will be a sullen obstinacy, or listlessness and stubborn silence. The patient lies on her back, and can by no means be persuaded to reply to the questions of her attendants, or she will repeat them, as an echo, until, all at once, without any apparent cause, she will break out into a torrent of language more or less incoherent, and her words will follow each other with surprising rapidity. These symptoms will sometimes show themselves rather suddenly, on the patient's awakening from a disturbed and unrefreshing sleep, or they may supervene more slowly when she has been harassed with wakefulness for three or four previous nights in succession, or perhaps ever since her delivery. She will very likely then become impressed with the idea that some evil has befallen her husband, or, what is still more usual, her child; that it is dead or stolen; and if it be brought to her, nothing can persuade her it is her own; she supposes it to belong to somebody else; or she will fancy that her husband is unfaithful to her, or that he and those about her have conspired to poison her. Those persons who are naturally the objects of her deepest and most devout affection, are regarded by her with jealousy, suspicion, and hatred. This is particularly remarkable with regard to her newly born infant; and I have known many instances where attempts have been made to destroy it when it has been incautiously left within her power. Sometimes, though rarely, may be observed a great anxiety regarding the termination of her own case, or a firm conviction that she is speedily about to die. I have observed upon occasions a constant movement of the lips, while the mouth was shut; or the patient is incessantly rubbing the inside of her lips with her fingers, or thrusting them far back into her mouth; and if questions are asked, particularly if she be desired to put out her tongue, she will often compress the lips forcibly together, as if with an obstinate determination of resistance. One peculiarity attending some cases of puerperal mania is the immorality and obscenity of the expressions uttered; they are often such, indeed, as to excite our astonishment that women in a respectable station of society could ever have become acquainted with such language."

The insanity of childbirth differs from that of pregnancy in that in the latter cases the patient is almost always melancholy,° while in the former there is active mania. Derangement of the digestive organs is a constant accompaniment of the disease.

---

melancholy: Mental state characterized by severe depression, somatic problems, and hallucinations or delusions.

If the patient has no previous or hereditary tendency to insanity, the prospect 15
of a quite speedy recovery is good. The result is seldom immediately fatal, but the
patient not infrequently remains in a condition of mental unsoundness for
months or even years, and sometimes permanently.

Treatment: When there is reason to suspect a liability to puerperal mania
from previous mental disease or from hereditary influence, much can be done to
ward off an attack. Special attention must be paid to the digestive organs, which
should be regulated by proper food and simple means to aid digestion. The tendency to sleeplessness must be combatted by careful nursing, light massage at
night, rubbing of the spine, alternate hot and cold applications to the spine, cool-
ing the head by cloths wrung out of cold water, and the use of the warm bath at
bed time. These measures are often successful in securing sleep when all other
measures fail.

The patient must be kept very quiet. Visitors, even if near relatives, must not
be allowed when the patient is at all nervous or disturbed, and it is best to exclude
nearly every one from the sick-room with the exception of the nurse, who should
be a competent and experienced person.

When the attack has really begun, the patient must have the most vigilant
watchcare, not being left alone for a moment. It is much better to care for the
patient at home, when possible to do so efficiently, than to take her to an asylum.

When evidences of returning rationality appear, the greatest care must be
exercised to prevent too great excitement. Sometimes a change of air, if the
patient is sufficiently strong, physically, will at this period prove eminently
beneficial. A visit from a dear friend will sometimes afford a needed stimulus to
the dormant faculties. Such cases as these of course require intelligent medical
supervision.   [1882]

THINKING ABOUT THE TEXT

1. What specific responsibilities does Kellogg assign to women? What are
   some key assumptions he makes about them?

2. Quite possibly Kellogg would have said that the narrator of Gilman's story
   suffers from puerperal mania. What details of the story would support this
   diagnosis? What significant details of the narrator's life, if any, would Kellogg be ignoring if he saw her as *merely* a case of puerperal mania?

3. If Kellogg's advice were published today, what parts of it do you think
   readers would accept? What parts do you think many readers would reject?

WRITING ABOUT ISSUES

1. "The Yellow Wallpaper" ends with the narrator creeping. Write an essay
   explaining how you think this act should be judged. What should readers
   take into consideration as they seek to put this act in context?

2. Write an essay discussing "The Yellow Wallpaper" as a response to the
   kind of thinking expressed in Mitchell's or Kellogg's selection. Refer to

specific details of both texts. If you wish, you may refer as well to Gilman's "Why I Wrote 'The Yellow Wallpaper.' "

3. Write an essay about an occasion when you, or someone you know, tried to challenge a medical or psychiatric diagnosis. Above all, analyze how doctor and patient behaved toward each other. (There may have been more than one doctor involved.) If you wish, imagine what Gilman would have said about this experience.

4. As we said in the introduction to this cluster, today many more women than men seek treatment for depression, anorexia, bulimia, and multiple personality disorder. Research one of these conditions, and then write an essay in which you try to explain why it seems to afflict mostly women. If you wish, refer to any of the texts in this cluster.

A WEB ASSIGNMENT

At the *Making Literature Matter* Web site, follow the link to the home page of the Charlotte Perkins Gilman Society. Once you arrive there, follow the link to an online reproduction of "The Yellow Wallpaper" as it first appeared in an 1892 issue of *New England Magazine*. You will notice that this version of the text includes three illustrations. Write an essay in which you speculate on how these illustrations might have affected readers' experience of the story. If you wish, you can suggest other moments of the story that you would like to have seen illustrated.

Visit www.bedfordstmartins.com/makinglitmatter

RACIAL INJUSTICE

COUNTEE CULLEN, "Incident"
LANGSTON HUGHES, "Let America Be America Again"
AUDRE LORDE, "Afterimages"
CORNELIUS EADY, "Who Am I?"

Throughout literary history, poets have written to protest social injustice. In the United States, many African American poets have especially denounced the white-dominated society's oppression of their race. While racism has not been these poets' sole concern, often it has drawn their attention. Even when addressing it, however, they have varied in their specific subjects and techniques, as you can see by comparing the four twentieth-century poems in this cluster. The earliest, Countee Cullen's "Incident," dates from the 1920s; the most recent, Cornelius Eady's "Who Am I?," first appeared in 1996. Although all four poems are concerned with injustices done against African Americans, each reflects in some way the particular historical circumstances of its writing. Moreover, although all four poems have a first-person speaker, they differ significantly in their use of this voice. Together, these texts show that while racial injustice has perpetually concerned African American poets, they have approached this topic through a wide range of means.

BEFORE YOU READ

If the topic is racial injustice, what specific types of incidents do you think an African American poet could have written about in the early twentieth century? What incidents do you think such a poet might write about in the early twenty-first century?

COUNTEE CULLEN
Incident

Countee Cullen (1903–1946) was one of the leading writers of the Harlem Renaissance, a New York–based movement of African American authors, artists, and intellectuals that flourished from World War I to the Great Depression. Cullen's place of birth may have been Baltimore, Louisville, or New York, but by 1918 he was living in New York as the adopted son of a Methodist minister. Cullen wrote poetry and received prizes for it even as he attended New York University. In 1925, while pursuing a master's degree from Harvard, he published his first book of poems, Color, *which contained "Incident." His later books included* Copper Sun *(1927),* The Black Christ and Other Poems *(1929), a translation of Euripides' play* Medea *(1935), and a children's book,* The Lost Zoo *(1940). Cullen gained much attention when, in 1928, he wed the daughter of famed African American writer and scholar W. E. B. DuBois, but their marriage ended just two years later. During the 1930s, Cullen's writing did not earn him enough to live on, so he taught English and French at Frederick Douglass High School. At the time of his death in 1946, he was collaborating on the Broadway musical* St. Louis Woman. *In part because he died relatively young, Cullen's reputation faded. Langston Hughes became much better known as a Harlem Renaissance figure. "Incident," however, has been consistently anthologized, and today Cullen is being rediscovered along with other contributors to African American literature.*

Once riding in old Baltimore
    Heart-filled, head-filled with glee,
I saw a Baltimorean
    Keep looking straight at me.

Now I was eight and very small,
    And he was no whit bigger, 5
And so I smiled, but he poked out
    His tongue and called me, "Nigger."

◆ ◆ ◆

I saw the whole of Baltimore
    From May until December:
Of all the things that happened there
    That's all that I remember.   [1925]

10

THINKING ABOUT THE TEXT

1. Why do you think the speaker calls attention to his heart *and* his head in the second line? Might referring to just one of these things have been enough?

2. "Baltimorean" (line 3) seems a rather unusual and abstract term for the boy that the speaker encountered. How do you explain its presence in the poem? How important is it that the speaker name the city where the incident occurred?

3. Although the incident that the speaker recalls must have been painful for him, why do you think he does not state his feelings about it more explicitly? What is the effect of his relative reticence about it?

4. The rhythm of this poem is rather sing-songy. Why do you think Cullen made it so?

5. The speaker states that he was eight at the time of the incident. How old might he be now? How important is his age?

LANGSTON HUGHES
Let America Be America Again

Langston Hughes (1902–1967) has long been regarded as a major African American writer and is increasingly seen as an important contributor to American literature in general. Like Countee Cullen, Hughes was actively involved in the 1920s movement called the Harlem Renaissance. Then and later, he worked in various genres, including fiction, drama, and autobiography. Nevertheless, he is primarily known for his poems. "Let America Be America Again" appeared in a 1938 pamphlet by Hughes entitled A New Song, *which was published by a socialist organization named the International Worker Order. At this point in his career, Hughes was critical of capitalism and sympathetic toward Communism, as were many other writers during the Great Depression. During the late 1930s, Communism in the United States entered a phase called the Popular Front, which linked Marxist principles to traditional American ideas and values. The title of Hughes's poem reflects this attempt at connection. Note, too, that within the poem Hughes sees African Americans as part of a larger population suffering from poverty and powerlessness. Indeed, the Depression led many writers to connect racism with other kinds of oppression, especially inequalities of class.*

Let America be America again.
Let it be the dream it used to be.
Let it be the pioneer on the plain
Seeking a home where he himself is free.

(America never was America to me.)　　　　　　　　　　　　　　　5

Let America be the dream the dreamers dreamed —
Let it be that great strong land of love
Where never kings connive nor tyrants scheme
That any man be crushed by one above.

(It never was America to me.)　　　　　　　　　　　　　　　10

O, let my land be a land where Liberty
Is crowned with no false patriotic wreath,
But opportunity is real, and life is free,
Equality is in the air we breathe.

(There's never been equality for me,　　　　　　　　　　　　　15
Nor freedom in this "homeland of the free.")

Say, who are you that mumbles in the dark?
And who are you that draws your veil across the stars?

I am the poor white, fooled and pushed apart,
I am the Negro bearing slavery's scars.　　　　　　　　　　　　20
I am the red man driven from the land,
I am the immigrant clutching the hope I seek —
And finding only the same old stupid plan
Of dog eat dog, of mighty crush the weak.

I am the young man, full of strength and hope,　　　　　　　　25
Tangled in that ancient endless chain
Of profit, power, gain, of grab the land!
Of grab the gold! Of grab the ways of satisfying need!
Of work the men! Of take the pay!
Of owning everything for one's own greed!　　　　　　　　　　30

I am the farmer, bondsman to the soil.
I am the worker sold to the machine.
I am the Negro, servant to you all.
I am the people, humble, hungry, mean —
Hungry yet today despite the dream.　　　　　　　　　　　　35
Beaten yet today — O, Pioneers!
I am the man who never got ahead,
The poorest worker bartered through the years.

Yet I'm the one who dreamt our basic dream
In that Old World while still a serf of kings,　　　　　　　　40
Who dreamt a dream so strong, so brave, so true,
That even yet its mighty daring sings

In every brick and stone, in every furrow turned
That's made America the land it has become.
O, I'm the man who sailed those early seas   45
In search of what I meant to be my home—
For I'm the one who left dark Ireland's shore,
And Poland's plain, and England's grassy lea,
And torn from Black Africa's strand I came
To build a "homeland of the free."   50

The free?

Who said the free? Not me?
Surely not me? The millions on relief today?
The millions shot down when we strike?
The millions who have nothing for our pay?   55
For all the dreams we've dreamed
And all the songs we've sung
And all the hopes we've held
And all the flags we've hung,
The millions who have nothing for our pay—   60
Except the dream that's almost dead today.

O, let America be America again—
The land that never has been yet—
And yet must be—the land where *every* man is free.
The land that's mine—the poor man's, Indian's, Negro's, ME—   65
Who made America,
Whose sweat and blood, whose faith and pain,
Whose hand at the foundry, whose plow in the rain,
Must bring back our mighty dream again.

Sure, call me any ugly name you choose—   70
The steel of freedom does not stain.
From those who live like leeches on the people's lives,
We must take back our land again,
America!

O, yes,   75
I say it plain,
America never was America to me,
And yet I swear this oath—
America will be!

Out of the rack and ruin of our gangster death,   80
The rape and rot of graft, and stealth, and lies,
We, the people, must redeem
The land, the mines, the plants, the rivers.
The mountains and the endless plain—
All, all the stretch of these great green states—   85
And make America again!   [1938]

THINKING ABOUT THE TEXT

1. In the title and in the first line comes the plea "Let America be America again." At several points in the poem, however, the speaker indicates that America has never lived up to its ideals. Identify these points. How can we reconcile them with the opening plea?
2. What are key repetitions in this poem? What is their effect?
3. What other oppressed peoples does the speaker refer to besides African Americans? Does he succeed in convincing you that all these groups belong together in the poem? What significant differences among them, if any, do you think he overlooks?
4. Although the speaker uses "I" a lot, sometimes he refers to "we." What is the effect of this shift? Should he have used one of these pronouns more than he does? Explain.
5. What lines of this poem seem to reflect the specific period of the Depression? What lines, if any, strike you as still relevant today?

MAKING COMPARISONS

1. Here is an issue of genre: The last word of Cullen's "Incident" is "remember." To what extent is it helpful to see both his poem and Hughes's as memory poems?
2. Here is another issue of genre: What would you say to someone who argues that Cullen's and Hughes's poems are best seen as protest poems?
3. Hughes's poem is significantly longer than Cullen's. Does Cullen nevertheless convey pretty much the same ideas, or does Hughes raise several altogether different points? Refer to specific details of both texts.

AUDRE LORDE
Afterimages

A prolific writer and speaker, Audre Lorde (1934–1992) was also active in the civil rights, women's, and gay and lesbian movements. She published several books of poetry, including Cables to Rage *(1970),* From a Land Where Other People Live *(1973),* The New York Head Shop and Museum *(1974),* Coal *(1976),* The Black Unicorn *(1978), and* Our Dead behind Us *(1986). In addition, she wrote several works of nonfiction, including a memoir,* Zami: A New Spelling of My Name *(1982); a collection of essays and speeches,* Sister Outsider *(1984); and an account of her struggle with breast cancer,* The Cancer Journals *(1980).*

The following poem, written in 1981, appears in Lorde's Chosen Poems: Old and New *(1st ed. 1982, 2nd ed. 1992). It deals with the 1955 murder of Emmett Till, a fifteen-year-old African American from Chicago who was killed while visiting*

*relatives in Mississippi. Till's beaten, shot, and mutilated body was discovered float-
ing decomposed in a river. Two white men, Roy Bryant and J. W. Milam, were tried
for the crime, their motive apparently being that Till had whistled at Bryant's wife.
The Till case aroused national attention, especially when Till's mother displayed
her son's body in an open casket to make public the atrocities done to him.
Although Bryant and Milam were acquitted by an all-white jury, the murder of
Emmett Till was a pivotal moment for the dawning civil rights movement. In her
poem, Lorde relates the river in which Till's body was found to a later flood in which
the homes and belongings of poor white Mississippians were destroyed.*

I

However the image enters
its force remains within
my eyes
rockstrewn caves where dragonfish evolve
wild for life, relentless and acquisitive   5
learning to survive
where there is no food
my eyes are always hungry
and remembering
however the image enters   10
its force remains.
A white woman stands bereft and empty
a black boy hacked into a murderous lesson
recalled in me forever
like a lurch of earth on the edge of sleep   15
etched into my visions
food for dragonfish that learn
to live upon whatever they must eat
fused images beneath my pain.

II

The Pearl River floods through the streets of Jackson   20
A Mississippi summer televised.
Trapped houses kneel like sinners in the rain
a white woman climbs from her roof to a passing boat
her fingers tarry for a moment on the chimney
now awash   25
tearless and no longer young, she holds
a tattered baby's blanket in her arms.
In a flickering afterimage of the nightmare rain
a microphone
thrust up against her flat bewildered words   30

"we jest come from the bank yestiddy
     borrowing money to pay the income tax
     now everything's gone. I never knew
     it could be so hard."
Despair weighs down her voice like Pearl River mud   35
caked around the edges
her pale eyes scanning the camera for help or explanation
unanswered
she shifts her search across the watered street, dry-eyed
     "hard, but not this hard."   40
Two tow-headed children hurl themselves against her
hanging upon her coat like mirrors
until a man with ham-like hands pulls her aside
snarling "She ain't got nothing more to say!"
and that lie hangs in his mouth   45
like a shred of rotting meat.

III

I inherited Jackson, Mississippi.
For my majority it gave me Emmett Till
his 15 years puffed out like bruises
on plump boy-cheeks   50
his only Mississippi summer
whistling a 21 gun salute to Dixie
as a white girl passed him in the street
and he was baptized my son forever
in the midnight waters of the Pearl.   55

His broken body is the afterimage of my 21st year
when I walked through a northern summer
my eyes averted
from each corner's photographies
newspapers protest posters magazines   60
Police Story, Confidential, True
the avid insistence of detail
pretending insight or information
the length of gash across the dead boy's loins
his grieving mother's lamentation   65
the severed lips, how many burns
his gouged out eyes
sewed shut upon the screaming covers
louder than life
all over   70
the veiled warning, the secret relish
of a black child's mutilated body

fingered by street-corner eyes
bruise upon livid bruise
and wherever I looked that summer 75
I learned to be at home with children's blood
with savored violence
with pictures of black broken flesh
used, crumpled, and discarded
lying amid the sidewalk refuse 80
like a raped woman's face.

A black boy from Chicago
whistled on the streets of Jackson, Mississippi
testing what he'd been taught was a manly thing to do
his teachers 85
ripped his eyes out his sex his tongue
and flung him to the Pearl weighted with stone
in the name of white womanhood
they took their aroused honor
back to Jackson 90
and celebrated in a whorehouse
the double ritual of white manhood
confirmed.

IV

> *"If earth and air and water do not judge them who are*
> *we to refuse a crust of bread?"*

Emmett Till rides the crest of the Pearl, whistling
24 years his ghost lay like the shade of a raped woman 95
and a white girl has grown older in costly honor
(what did she pay to never know its price?)
now the Pearl River speaks its muddy judgment
and I can withhold my pity and my bread.
     "Hard, but not this hard." 100
Her face is flat with resignation and despair
with ancient and familiar sorrows
a woman surveying her crumpled future
as the white girl besmirched by Emmett's whistle
never allowed her own tongue 105
without power or conclusion
unvoiced
she stands adrift in the ruins of her honor
and a man with an executioner's face
pulls her away. 110

♦   ♦   ♦

Within my eyes
the flickering afterimages of a nightmare rain
a woman wrings her hands
beneath the weight of agonies remembered
I wade through summer ghosts   115
betrayed by vision
hers and my own
becoming dragonfish to survive
the horrors we are living
with tortured lungs   120
adapting to breathe blood.

A woman measures her life's damage
my eyes are caves, chunks of etched rock
tied to the ghost of a black boy
whistling   125
crying and frightened
her tow-headed children cluster
like little mirrors of despair
their father's hands upon them
and soundlessly   130
a woman begins to weep.   [1981]

THINKING ABOUT THE TEXT

1. Early in the poem comes the image of dragonfish (line 17), and this image returns in the next-to-last stanza. What does it signify to you?

2. This poem is divided into four parts. What is the function of each?

3. What do you conclude about the white woman and her husband from their remarks in section II?

4. What does Lorde suggest is the relation between Emmett Till and the white woman who is being rescued from the flooding river?

5. How important is the "I" in this poem? Where are you especially conscious of the speaker's feelings? Would the poem's effect be the same if it were not written in the first person?

MAKING COMPARISONS

1. The title of Lorde's poem, "Afterimages," suggests that it emphasizes the visual. Does the poem do this more than Cullen's and Hughes's poems do? Refer to specific details of all three texts.

2. Compare the speakers in these three poems. Does one of the speakers seem more emotional than the other two?

3. Recall Cullen's and Hughes's titles. If Cullen's title "Incident" were applied to Lorde's poem, conceivably it would refer to the killing of Emmett Till.

What would you say to someone who argues, however, that this murder was far worse than the kind of event described in Cullen's poem and is therefore more worth writing about? Could Hughes's title "Let America Be America Again" be applied to Lorde's poem? Why, or why not?

CORNELIUS EADY
Who Am I?

Cornelius Eady (b. 1954) has published several books of poetry, including Victims of the Latest Dance Craze *(1986),* The Gathering of My Name *(1991),* You Don't Miss Your Water *(1995), and* The Autobiography of a Jukebox *(1997). He has also taught creative writing at several colleges, including the State University of New York at Stony Brook, City College of New York, and the New School. The following poem first appeared in a 1996 issue of the literary journal* Ploughshares *and was also included in Eady's most recent book,* Brutal Imagination *(2001). It deals with the 1994 case of Susan Smith, a Southern white woman who claimed that an African American man had kidnapped her two sons but was discovered to have drowned them herself, a crime for which she is now serving a life sentence. Throughout Eady's sequence, the speaker is the imaginary African American whom Smith blamed for her children's disappearance.*

Who are you, mister?
One of the boys asks
From the eternal backseat
And here is the one good thing:
If I am alive, then so, briefly, are they,   5
Two boys returned, three and one,
Quiet and scared, bunched together
Breathing like small beasts.
They can't place me, yet there's
Something familiar.   10
Though my skin and sex are different, maybe
It's the way I drive
Or occasionally glance back
With concern,
Maybe it's the mixed blessing   15
Someone, perhaps circumstance,
Has given us,
The secret thrill of hiding,
Childish, in plain sight,
Seen, but not seen,   20
As if suddenly given the power
To move through walls,

To know every secret without permission.
We roll sleepless through the dark streets, but inside
The cab is lit with brutal imagination.   [2001]   25

THINKING ABOUT THE TEXT

1. Why do you suppose Susan Smith claimed that her children's kidnapper was an African American man?

2. The title of this poem is a question. Does the poem answer it? If so, how?

3. Describe the speaker's relationship with the two boys. What, conceivably, does he have in mind when he says that they sense "Something familiar" (line 10) about him?

4. The word *secret* is repeated. What is its role in the poem?

5. What does the speaker apparently have in mind with his final phrase, "brutal imagination"? (This is also the title of the book where the poem appears.)

MAKING COMPARISONS

1. The speaker in Eady's poem is an imaginary man. Is the poem therefore less realistic than the poems by Cullen, Hughes, and Lorde? Define what you mean by *realistic*.

2. How might Eady's phrase "brutal imagination" be applied to the other three poems?

3. Eady's poem is the most recent of the four in this cluster. Do the other three poems seem less timely than his, or do you think that even they could have been written today?

WRITING ABOUT ISSUES

1. Choose one of the poems by Cullen, Hughes, Lorde, and Eady, and write an essay analyzing how it treats whatever white people it mentions.

2. Choose two of the poems in this cluster, and write an essay comparing their strategies for examining racial injustice. Do these poems seem mostly alike in their strategies, or do they use significantly different ones?

3. Write an essay recalling an incident in which you perceived racial injustice and were not immediately sure how to respond to it. Focus on what the incident helped you realize about yourself. Be sure to define what you mean by *racial injustice*.

4. Through research, identify an incident of racial injustice that received much attention. Be sure to note the incident's key details. Then write an essay identifying what you would emphasize in a poem about this incident. Or write the poem, and add a paragraph or two explaining why you emphasized certain things in it.

BRINGING MURDERERS TO JUSTICE

WILLIAM SHAKESPEARE, *Hamlet, Prince of Denmark*
SUSAN GLASPELL, *Trifles*

The title of this cluster, Bringing Murderers to Justice, describes the plot of many mystery thrillers that are not usually deemed artistic masterpieces. Back in the 1930s and 1940s, most literary critics classified Dashiell Hammett's *The Maltese Falcon,* Raymond Chandler's *The Big Sleep,* and James M. Cain's *Double Indemnity* as "pulp" fiction rather than genuine literature. Today, however, several critics esteem these particular books, feeling they shrewdly and stylishly probe human psychology even as their sleuths hunt killers. This new appreciation links the formerly separate realms of popular culture and literary art. Conversely, works long acclaimed as literary classics may nevertheless share elements of plot with the latest paperback thrillers. Take, for example, the play widely thought to be the greatest in the English language, William Shakespeare's *Hamlet.* Its hero acts as a detective as he attempts to expose and punish his uncle Claudius, who has slain Hamlet's father and wed his mother. Efforts to solve a murder are also key to Susan Glaspell's *Trifles,* one of the most famous twentieth-century plays by a woman. Glaspell's characters suspect John Wright's wife, Minnie, killed him, but they have difficulty locating evidence of her guilt and determining her motive. Both Shakespeare's and Glaspell's plays are psychologically, morally, and philosophically complex. Prince Hamlet and the two women in *Trifles* suffer torments as they pursue their quests; for them, solving a homicide does not mean peace of mind. Of course, these two plays were written centuries apart. Moreover, they vary greatly in length; next to *Hamlet, Trifles* may seem a trifle. Both plays demonstrate, however, that in bringing murderers to justice people may wind up grappling with themselves.

BEFORE YOU READ

Think of a detective story with which you are familiar. To what extent, and in what ways, is this story more than just a "whodunit"? Do you think it should be taught in a literature class? Why, or why not?

WILLIAM SHAKESPEARE
Hamlet, Prince of Denmark

William Shakespeare's reputation as the greatest dramatist in the English language is built on his five major tragedies: Romeo and Juliet *(1594),* Hamlet *(1600),* Othello *(1604),* Macbeth *(1605), and* King Lear *(1605). But he was also a master in other genres, including comedies (*As You Like It *in 1599), histories (*Henry IV *in 1597), and romances (*The Tempest *in 1611). And his collection of sonnets is considered art of the highest order.*

Very little is known about Shakespeare's personal life. He attended the grammar school at Stratford-upon-Avon, where he was born in 1564. He married Anne
Hathaway in 1582 and had three children. Around 1590 he moved to London, where
he became an actor and began writing plays. He was an astute businessperson,
becoming a shareholder in London's famous Globe Theatre. After writing thirty-
seven plays, he retired to Stratford in 1611. When he died in 1616, he left behind the
most respected body of work in literature. Shakespeare's ability to use artistic language to convey a wide range of humor and emotion is perhaps unsurpassed.

[DRAMATIS PERSONAE

CLAUDIUS, *King of Denmark*
HAMLET, *son to the late and nephew to the present king*
POLONIUS, *lord chamberlain*
HORATIO, *friend to Hamlet*
LAERTES, *son to Polonius*
VOLTIMAND ⎫
CORNELIUS ⎪
ROSENCRANTZ ⎬ *courtiers*
GUILDENSTERN ⎪
OSRIC ⎭
A GENTLEMAN
A PRIEST
MARCELLUS ⎫ *officers*
BERNARDO ⎭
FRANCISCO, *a soldier*
REYNALDO, *servant to Polonius*
PLAYERS
TWO CLOWNS, *grave-diggers*
FORTINBRAS, *Prince of Norway*
A CAPTAIN
ENGLISH AMBASSADORS
GERTRUDE, *Queen of Denmark, and mother to Hamlet*
OPHELIA, *daughter to Polonius*
LORDS, LADIES, OFFICERS, SOLDIERS, SAILORS, MESSENGERS, AND OTHER
     ATTENDANTS
GHOST *of Hamlet's Father*

SCENE: *Denmark.*]

[ACT 1, Scene 1]

Elsinore. A platform° before the castle.]
     Enter Bernardo and Francisco, two sentinels.

ACT 1, SCENE 1. **platform:** A level space on the battlements of the royal castle at Elsinore, a
Danish seaport; now Helsingör.

BERNARDO: Who's there?
FRANCISCO: Nay, answer me:° stand, and unfold yourself.
BERNARDO: Long live the king!°
FRANCISCO: Bernardo?
BERNARDO: He.   5
FRANCISCO: You come most carefully upon your hour.
BERNARDO: 'Tis now struck twelve; get thee to bed, Francisco.
FRANCISCO: For this relief much thanks: 'tis bitter cold,
     And I am sick at heart.
BERNARDO: Have you had quiet guard?
FRANCISCO: Not a mouse stirring.   10
BERNARDO: Well, good night.
     If you do meet Horatio and Marcellus,
     The rivals° of my watch, bid them make haste.

Enter Horatio and Marcellus.

FRANCISCO: I think I hear them. Stand, ho! Who is there?
HORATIO: Friends to this ground.
MARCELLUS: And liegemen to the Dane.   15
FRANCISCO: Give you° good night.
MARCELLUS: O, farewell, honest soldier:
     Who hath reliev'd you?
FRANCISCO: Bernardo hath my place.
     Give you good night.   *Exit Francisco.*
MARCELLUS: Holla! Bernardo!
BERNARDO: Say,
     What, is Horatio there?
HORATIO: A piece of him.
BERNARDO: Welcome, Horatio: welcome, good Marcellus.   20
MARCELLUS: What, has this thing appear'd again to-night?
BERNARDO: I have seen nothing.
MARCELLUS: Horatio says 'tis but our fantasy,
     And will not let belief take hold of him
     Touching this dreaded sight, twice seen of us: 25
     Therefore I have entreated him along
     With us to watch the minutes of this night;
     That if again this apparition come,
     He may approve° our eyes and speak to it.
HORATIO: Tush, tush, 'twill not appear.
BERNARDO: Sit down awhile;   30
     And let us once again assail your ears,
     That are so fortified against our story
     What we have two nights seen.

---

2 **me:** This is emphatic, since Francisco is the sentry.   3 **Long live the king:** Either a pass-
word or greeting; Horatio and Marcellus use a different one in line 15.   13 **rivals:** Partners.
16 **Give you:** God give you.   29 **approve:** Corroborate.

HORATIO: Well, sit we down,
    And let us hear Bernardo speak of this.
BERNARDO: Last night of all,   35
    When yond same star that's westward from the pole°
    Had made his course t' illume that part of heaven
    Where now it burns, Marcellus and myself,
    The bell then beating one, —

Enter Ghost.

MARCELLUS: Peace, break thee off; look, where it comes again!   40
BERNARDO: In the same figure, like the king that's dead.
MARCELLUS: Thou art a scholar;° speak to it, Horatio.
BERNARDO: Looks 'a not like the king? mark it, Horatio.
HORATIO: Most like: it harrows° me with fear and wonder.
BERNARDO: It would be spoke to.°
MARCELLUS: Speak to it, Horatio.   45
HORATIO: What art thou that usurp'st this time of night,
    Together with that fair and warlike form
    In which the majesty of buried Denmark°
    Did sometimes march? by heaven I charge thee, speak!
MARCELLUS: It is offended.
BERNARDO: See it stalks away!   50
HORATIO: Stay! speak, speak! I charge thee, speak!   *Exit Ghost.*
MARCELLUS: 'Tis gone, and will not answer.
BERNARDO: How now, Horatio! you tremble and look pale:
    Is not this something more than fantasy?
    What think you on 't?   55
HORATIO: Before my God, I might not this believe
    Without the sensible and true avouch
    Of mine own eyes.
MARCELLUS: Is it not like the king?
HORATIO: As thou art to thyself:
    Such was the very armour he had on   60
    When he the ambitious Norway combated;
    So frown'd he once, when, in an angry parle,
    He smote° the sledded Polacks° on the ice.
    'Tis strange.
MARCELLUS: Thus twice before, and jump° at this dead hour,   65
    With martial stalk hath he gone by our watch.
HORATIO: In what particular thought to work I know not;
    But in the gross and scope° of my opinion,
    This bodes some strange eruption to our state.

---

36 pole: Polestar.   **42 scholar:** Exorcisms were performed in Latin, which Horatio as an educated man would be able to speak.   **44 harrows:** Lacerates the feelings.   **45 It . . . to:** A ghost could not speak until spoken to.   **48 buried Denmark:** The buried king of Denmark.   **63 smote:** Defeated; **sledded Polacks:** Polanders using sledges.   **65 jump:** Exactly.   **68 gross and scope:** General drift.

MARCELLUS: Good now,° sit down, and tell me, he that knows,   70
  Why this same strict and most observant watch
  So nightly toils° the subject° of the land,
  And why such daily cast° of brazen cannon,
  And foreign mart° for implements of war;
  Why such impress° of shipwrights, whose sore task   75
  Does not divide the Sunday from the week;
  What might be toward, that this sweaty haste
  Doth make the night joint-labourer with the day:
  Who is't that can inform me?
HORATIO: That can I;
  At least, the whisper goes so. Our last king,   80
  Whose image even but now appear'd to us,
  Was, as you know, by Fortinbras of Norway,
  Thereto prick'd on° by a most emulate° pride,
  Dar'd to the combat; in which our valiant Hamlet—
  For so this side of our known world esteem'd him—   85
  Did slay this Fortinbras; who, by a seal'd compact,
  Well ratified by law and heraldry,°
  Did forfeit, with his life, all those his lands
  Which he stood seiz'd° of, to the conqueror:
  Against the which, a moiety competent°   90
  Was gaged by our king; which had return'd
  To the inheritance of Fortinbras,
  Had he been vanquisher; as, by the same comart,°
  And carriage° of the article design'd,
  His fell to Hamlet. Now, sir, young Fortinbras,   95
  Of unimproved° mettle hot and full,°
  Hath in the skirts of Norway here and there
  Shark'd up° a list of lawless resolutes,°
  For food and diet,° to some enterprise
  That hath a stomach in't; which is no other—   100
  As it doth well appear unto our state—
  But to recover of us, by strong hand
  And terms compulsatory, those foresaid lands
  So by his father lost: and this, I take it,
  Is the main motive of our preparations,   105
  The source of this our watch and the chief head
  Of this post-haste and romage° in the land.

---

70 **Good now:** An expression denoting entreaty or expostulation.   72 **toils:** Causes or makes to toil;   **subject:** People, subjects.   73 **cast:** Casting, founding.   74 **mart:** Buying and selling, traffic.   75 **impress:** Impressment.   83 **prick'd on:** Incited;   **emulate:** Rivaling.   87 **law and heraldry:** Heraldic law, governing combat.   89 **seiz'd:** Possessed.   90 **moiety competent:** Adequate or sufficient portion.   93 **comart:** Joint bargain.   94 **carriage:** Import, bearing.   96 **unimproved:** Not turned to account;   **hot and full:** Full of fight.   98 **Shark'd up:** Got together in haphazard fashion;   **resolutes:** Desperadoes.   99 **food and diet:** No pay but their keep.   107 **romage:** Bustle, commotion.

BERNARDO: I think it be no other but e'en so:
    Well may it sort° that this portentous figure
    Comes armed through our watch; so like the king   110
    That was and is the question of these wars.
HORATIO: A mote° it is to trouble the mind's eye.
    In the most high and palmy state° of Rome,
    A little ere the mightiest Julius fell,
    The graves stood tenantless and the sheeted dead   115
    Did squeak and gibber in the Roman streets:
    As stars with trains of fire° and dews of blood,
    Disasters° in the sun; and the moist star°
    Upon whose influence Neptune's empire° stands
    Was sick almost to doomsday with eclipse: 120
    And even the like precurse° of fear'd events,
    As harbingers preceding still the fates
    And prologue to the omen coming on,
    Have heaven and earth together demonstrated
    Unto our climatures and countrymen. —   125

Enter Ghost.

    But soft, behold! lo, where it comes again!
    I'll cross° it, though it blast me. Stay, illusion!
    If thou hast any sound, or use of voice,
    Speak to me!   *It° spreads his arms.*
    If there be any good thing to be done,   130
    That may to thee do ease and grace to me,
    Speak to me!
    If thou art privy to thy country's fate,
    Which, happily, foreknowing may avoid,
    O, speak!   135
    Or if thou hast uphoarded in thy life
    Extorted treasure in the womb of earth,
    For which, they say, you spirits oft walk in death,   *The cock crows.*
    Speak of it:° stay, and speak! Stop it, Marcellus.
MARCELLUS: Shall I strike at it with my partisan?°   140
HORATIO: Do, if it will not stand.
BERNARDO: 'Tis here!
HORATIO: 'Tis here!
MARCELLUS: 'Tis gone!   *[Exit Ghost.]*
    We do it wrong, being so majestical,

---

109 sort: Suit.   **112 mote:** Speck of dust.   **113 palmy state:** Triumphant sovereignty.
117 stars . . . fire: I.e., comets.   **118 Disasters:** Unfavorable aspects;   **moist star:** The moon,
governing tides.   **119 Neptune's empire:** The sea.   **121 precurse:** Heralding.   **127 cross:**
Meet, face, thus bringing down the evil influence on the person who crosses it.   **129 It:** The
Ghost, or perhaps Horatio.   **133–139 If . . . it:** Horatio recites the traditional reasons why
ghosts might walk.   **140 partisan:** Long-handled spear with a blade having lateral projections.

To offer it the show of violence;
For it is, as the air, invulnerable,   145
And our vain blows malicious mockery.

BERNARDO: It was about to speak, when the cock crew.°

HORATIO: And then it started like a guilty thing
Upon a fearful summons. I have heard,
The cock, that is the trumpet to the morn,   150
Doth with his lofty and shrill-sounding throat
Awake the god of day; and, at his warning,
Whether in sea or fire, in earth or air,
Th' extravagant and erring° spirit hies
To his confine:° and of the truth herein   155
This present object made probation.°

MARCELLUS: It faded on the crowing of the cock.
Some say that ever 'gainst° that season comes
Wherein our Saviour's birth is celebrated,
The bird of dawning singeth all night long: 160
And then, they say, no spirit dare stir abroad;
The nights are wholesome; then no planets strike,°
No fairy takes, nor witch hath power to charm,
So hallow'd and so gracious° is that time.

HORATIO: So have I heard and do in part believe it.   165
But, look, the morn, in russet mantle clad,
Walks o'er the dew of yon high eastward hill:
Break we our watch up; and by my advice,
Let us impart what we have seen to-night
Unto young Hamlet; for, upon my life,   170
This spirit, dumb to us, will speak to him.
Do you consent we shall acquaint him with it,
As needful in our loves, fitting our duty?

MARCELLUS: Let's do 't, I pray; and I this morning know
Where we shall find him most conveniently.   *Exeunt.*   175

[Scene 2]

[A room of state in the castle.]

    *Flourish. Enter Claudius, King of Denmark, Gertrude the Queen, Coun-
cilors, Polonius and his son Laertes, Hamlet, cum aliis° [including Voltimand and
Cornelius].*

KING: Though yet of Hamlet our dear brother's death
The memory be green, and that it us befitted

---

147 cock crew: According to traditional ghost lore, spirits returned to their confines at cock-
crow.   **154 extravagant and erring:** Wandering. Both words mean the same thing.
155 confine: Place of confinement.   **156 probation:** Proof, trial.   **158 'gainst:** Just before.
162 planets strike: It was thought that planets were malignant and might strike travelers by
night.   **164 gracious:** Full of goodness.   SCENE 2. **cum aliis:** With others.

To bear our hearts in grief and our whole kingdom
To be contracted in one brow of woe,
Yet so far hath discretion fought with nature   5
That we with wisest sorrow think on him,
Together with remembrance of ourselves.
Therefore our sometime sister, now our queen,
Th' imperial jointress° to this warlike state,
Have we, as 'twere with a defeated joy, —   10
With an auspicious and a dropping eye,
With mirth in funeral and with dirge in marriage,
In equal scale weighing delight and dole, —
Taken to wife: nor have we herein barr'd
Your better wisdoms, which have freely gone   15
With this affair along. For all, our thanks.
Now follows, that° you know, young Fortinbras,
Holding a weak supposal° of our worth,
Or thinking by our late dear brother's death
Our state to be disjoint° and out of frame,°   20
Colleagued° with this dream of his advantage,°
He hath not fail'd to pester us with message,
Importing° the surrender of those lands
Lost by his father, with all bands of law,
To our most valiant brother. So much for him.   25
Now for ourself and for this time of meeting:
Thus much the business is: we have here writ
To Norway, uncle of young Fortinbras, —
Who, impotent and bed-rid, scarcely hears
Of this his nephew's purpose, — to suppress   30
His further gait° herein; in that the levies,
The lists and full proportions, are all made
Out of his subject:° and we here dispatch
You, good Cornelius, and you, Voltimand,
For bearers of this greeting to old Norway;   35
Giving to you no further personal power
To business with the king, more than the scope
Of these delated° articles allow.
Farewell, and let your haste commend your duty.

CORNELIUS: ⎫
VOLTIMAND: ⎬ In that and all things will we show our duty.   40

KING: We doubt it nothing: heartily farewell.

                         [Exeunt Voltimand and Cornelius.]

---

9 jointress: Woman possessed of a jointure, or, joint tenancy of an estate.   **17 that:** That which.   **18 weak supposal:** Low estimate.   **20 disjoint:** Distracted, out of joint;   **frame:** Order.   **21 Colleagued:** Added to;   **dream . . . advantage:** Visionary hope of success.   **23 Importing:** Purporting, pertaining to.   **31 gait:** Proceeding.   **33 Out of his subject:** At the expense of Norway's subjects (collectively).   **38 delated:** Expressly stated.

And now, Laertes, what's the news with you?
You told us of some suit; what is 't, Laertes?
You cannot speak of reason to the Dane,°
And lose your voice:° what wouldst thou beg, Laertes,   45
That shall not be my offer, not thy asking?
The head is not more native° to the heart,
The hand more instrumental° to the mouth,
Than is the throne of Denmark to thy father.
What wouldst thou have, Laertes?
LAERTES: My dread lord,   50
Your leave and favour to return to France;
From whence though willingly I came to Denmark,
To show my duty in your coronation,
Yet now, I must confess, that duty done,
My thoughts and wishes bend again toward France   55
And bow them to your gracious leave and pardon.°
KING: Have you your father's leave? What says Polonius?
POLONIUS: He hath, my lord, wrung from me my slow leave
By laboursome petition, and at last
Upon his will I seal'd my hard consent: 60
I do beseech you, give him leave to go.
KING: Take thy fair hour, Laertes; time be thine,
And thy best graces spend it at thy will!
But now, my cousin° Hamlet, and my son, —
HAMLET [*aside*]:   A little more than kin, and less than kind!°   65
KING: How is it that the clouds still hang on you?
HAMLET: Not so, my lord; I am too much in the sun.°
QUEEN: Good Hamlet, cast thy nighted colour off,
And let thine eye look like a friend on Denmark.
Do not for ever with thy vailed lids   70
Seek for thy noble father in the dust:
Thou know'st 'tis common; all that lives must die,
Passing through nature to eternity.
HAMLET: Ay, madam, it is common.°
QUEEN: If it be,
Why seems it so particular with thee?   75

---

44 the Dane: Danish king.   **45 lose your voice:** Speak in vain.   **47 native:** Closely connected, related.   **48 instrumental:** Serviceable.   **56 leave and pardon:** Permission to depart.   **64 cousin:** Any kin not of the immediate family.   **65 A little . . . kind:** My relation to you has become more than kinship warrants; it has also become unnatural.   **67 I am . . . sun:** (1) I am too much out of doors, (2) I am too much in the sun of your grace (ironical), (3) I am too much of a son to you. Possibly an allusion to the proverb "Out of heaven's blessing into the warm sun"; i.e., Hamlet is out of house and home in being deprived of the kingship.   **74 Ay . . . common:** It is common, but it hurts nevertheless; possibly a reference to the commonplace quality of the queen's remark.

HAMLET: Seems, madam! nay, it is; I know not "seems."
　　　　'Tis not alone my inky cloak, good mother,
　　　　Nor customary suits° of solemn black,
　　　　Nor windy suspiration° of forc'd breath,
　　　　No, nor the fruitful river in the eye,   80
　　　　Nor the dejected 'haviour of the visage,
　　　　Together with all forms, moods, shapes of grief,
　　　　That can denote me truly: these indeed seem,
　　　　For they are actions that a man might play:
　　　　But I have that within which passeth show;   85
　　　　These but the trappings and the suits of woe.
KING: 'Tis sweet and commendable in your nature, Hamlet,
　　　　To give these mourning duties to your father:
　　　　But, you must know, your father lost a father;
　　　　That father lost, lost his, and the survivor bound   90
　　　　In filial obligation for some term
　　　　To do obsequious° sorrow: but to persever
　　　　In obstinate condolement° is a course
　　　　Of impious stubbornness; 'tis unmanly grief;
　　　　It shows a will most incorrect° to heaven,   95
　　　　A heart unfortified, a mind impatient,
　　　　An understanding simple and unschool'd:
　　　　For what we know must be and is as common
　　　　As any the most vulgar thing° to sense,
　　　　Why should we in our peevish opposition   100
　　　　Take it to heart? Fie! 'tis a fault to heaven,
　　　　A fault against the dead, a fault to nature,
　　　　To reason most absurd; whose common theme
　　　　Is death of fathers, and who still hath cried,
　　　　From the first corse till he that died to-day,   105
　　　　"This must be so." We pray you, throw to earth
　　　　This unprevailing° woe, and think of us
　　　　As of a father: for let the world take note,
　　　　You are the most immediate° to our throne;
　　　　And with no less nobility° of love   110
　　　　Than that which dearest father bears his son,
　　　　Do I impart° toward you. For your intent
　　　　In going back to school in Wittenberg,°
　　　　It is most retrograde° to our desire:
　　　　And we beseech you, bend you° to remain   115

78 customary suits: Suits prescribed by custom for mourning.　**79 windy suspiration:** Heavy sighing.　**92 obsequious:** Dutiful.　**93 condolement:** Sorrowing.　**95 incorrect:** Untrained, uncorrected.　**99 vulgar thing:** Common experience.　**107 unprevailing:** Unavailing. **109 most immediate:** Next in succession.　**110 nobility:** High degree.　**112 impart:** The object is apparently *love* (line 110).　**113 Wittenberg:** Famous German university founded in 1502.　**114 retrograde:** Contrary.　**115 bend you:** Incline yourself; imperative.

Here, in the cheer and comfort of our eye,
Our chiefest courtier, cousin, and our son.
QUEEN: Let not thy mother lose her prayers, Hamlet:
I pray thee, stay with us; go not to Wittenberg.
HAMLET: I shall in all my best obey you, madam.   120
KING: Why, 'tis a loving and a fair reply:
Be as ourself in Denmark. Madam, come;
This gentle and unforc'd accord of Hamlet
Sits smiling to my heart: in grace whereof,
No jocund health that Denmark drinks to-day,   125
But the great cannon to the clouds shall tell,
And the king's rouse° the heaven shall bruit again,°
Re-speaking earthly thunder. Come away.

Flourish. Exeunt all but Hamlet.

HAMLET: O, that this too too sullied flesh would melt,
Thaw and resolve itself into a dew!   130
Or that the Everlasting had not fix'd
His canon 'gainst self-slaughter! O God! God!
How weary, stale, flat and unprofitable,
Seem to me all the uses of this world!
Fie on't! ah fie! 'tis an unweeded garden,   135
That grows to seed; things rank and gross in nature
Possess it merely.° That it should come to this!
But two months dead: nay, not so much, not two:
So excellent a king; that was, to this,
Hyperion° to a satyr; so loving to my mother   140
That he might not beteem° the winds of heaven
Visit her face too roughly. Heaven and earth!
Must I remember? why, she would hang on him,
As if increase of appetite had grown
By what it fed on: and yet, within a month—   145
Let me not think on't—Frailty, thy name is woman!—
A little month, or ere those shoes were old
With which she followed my poor father's body,
Like Niobe,° all tears:—why she, even she—
O God! a beast, that wants discourse of reason,°   150
Would have mourn'd longer—married with my uncle,
My father's brother, but no more like my father
Than I to Hercules: within a month:

---

127 rouse: Draft of liquor; **bruit again:** Echo.   **137 merely:** Completely, entirely.
140 Hyperion: God of the sun in the older regime of ancient gods.   **141 beteem:** Allow.
149 Niobe: Tantalus's daughter, who boasted that she had more sons and daughters than Leto;
for this Apollo and Artemis slew her children. She was turned into stone by Zeus on Mount
Sipylus.   **150 discourse of reason:** Process or faculty of reason.

Ere yet the salt of most unrighteous tears
Had left the flushing in her galled° eyes,   155
She married. O, most wicked speed, to post
With such dexterity° to incestuous sheets!
It is not nor it cannot come to good:
But break, my heart; for I must hold my tongue.

Enter Horatio, Marcellus, and Bernardo.

HORATIO: Hail to your lordship!
HAMLET: I am glad to see you well: 160
    Horatio! — or I do forget myself.
HORATIO: The same, my lord, and your poor servant ever.
HAMLET: Sir, my good friend; I'll change that name with you:°
    And what make you from Wittenberg, Horatio?
    Marcellus?   165
MARCELLUS: My good lord—
HAMLET: I am very glad to see you. Good even, sir.
    But what, in faith, make you from Wittenberg?
HORATIO: A truant disposition, good my lord.
HAMLET: I would not hear your enemy say so,   170
    Nor shall you do my ear that violence,
    To make it truster of your own report
    Against yourself: I know you are no truant.
    But what is your affair in Elsinore?
    We'll teach you to drink deep ere you depart.   175
HORATIO: My lord, I came to see your father's funeral.
HAMLET: I prithee, do not mock me, fellow-student;
    I think it was to see my mother's wedding.
HORATIO: Indeed, my lord, it follow'd hard° upon.
HAMLET: Thrift, thrift, Horatio! the funeral bak'd meats°   180
    Did coldly furnish forth the marriage tables.
    Would I had met my dearest° foe in heaven
    Or ever I had seen that day, Horatio!
    My father! — methinks I see my father.
HORATIO: Where, my lord!
HAMLET: In my mind's eye, Horatio.   185
HORATIO: I saw him once; 'a° was a goodly king.
HAMLET: 'A was a man, take him for all in all,
    I shall not look upon his like again.
HORATIO: My lord, I think I saw him yesternight.
HAMLET: Saw? who?   190

---

155 **galled:** Irritated.   157 **dexterity:** Facility.   163 **I'll ... you:** I'll be your servant, you
shall be my friend; also explained as "I'll exchange the name of friend with you."   179 **hard:**
Close.   180 **bak'd meats:** Meat pies.   182 **dearest:** Direst. The adjective *dear* in Shakespeare has two different origins: O.E. *deore*, "beloved," and O.E. *deor*, "fierce." *Dearest* is the
superlative of the second.   186 **'a:** He.

HORATIO: My lord, the king your father.
HAMLET: The king my father!
HORATIO: Season your admiration° for a while
    With an attent ear, till I may deliver,
    Upon the witness of these gentlemen,
    This marvel to you.
HAMLET: For God's love, let me hear.   195
HORATIO: Two nights together had these gentlemen,
    Marcellus and Bernardo, on their watch,
    In the dead waste and middle of the night,
    Been thus encount'red. A figure like your father,
    Armed at point exactly, cap-a-pe,°   200
    Appears before them, and with solemn march
    Goes slow and stately by them: thrice he walk'd
    By their oppress'd° and fear-surprised eyes,
    Within his truncheon's° length; whilst they, distill'd°
    Almost to jelly with the act° of fear,   205
    Stand dumb and speak not to him. This to me
    In dreadful secrecy impart they did;
    And I with them the third night kept the watch:
    Where, as they had deliver'd, both in time,
    Form of the thing, each word made true and good,   210
    The apparition comes: I knew your father;
    These hands are not more like.
HAMLET: But where was this?
MARCELLUS: My lord, upon the platform where we watch'd.
HAMLET: Did you not speak to it?
HORATIO: My lord, I did;
    But answer made it none: yet once methought   215
    It lifted up it° head and did address
    Itself to motion, like as it would speak;
    But even then the morning cock crew loud,
    And at the sound it shrunk in haste away,
    And vanish'd from our sight.
HAMLET: 'Tis very strange.   220
HORATIO: As I do live, my honour'd lord, 'tis true;
    And we did think it writ down in our duty
    To let you know of it.
HAMLET: Indeed, indeed, sirs, but this troubles me.
    Hold you the watch to-night?
MARCELLUS: ⎫
                         We do, my lord.   225
BERNARDO: ⎭

---

192 **Season your admiration:** Restrain your astonishment.   200 **cap-a-pe:** From head to foot.
203 **oppress'd:** Distressed.   204 **truncheon:** Officer's staff;   **distill'd:** Softened, weakened.
205 **act:** Action.   216 **it:** Its.

HAMLET: Arm'd, say you?

MARCELLUS: ⎱
BERNARDO: ⎰   Arm'd, my lord.

HAMLET: From top to toe?

MARCELLUS: ⎱
BERNARDO: ⎰   My lord, from head to foot.

HAMLET: Then saw you not his face?

HORATIO: O, yes, my lord; he wore his beaver° up.

HAMLET: What, look'd he frowningly?

HORATIO: A countenance more   230
    In sorrow than in anger.

HAMLET: Pale or red?

HORATIO: Nay, very pale.

HAMLET: And fix'd his eyes upon you?

HORATIO: Most constantly.

HAMLET: I would I had been there.

HORATIO: It would have much amaz'd you.

HAMLET: Very like, very like. Stay'd it long?   235

HORATIO: While one with moderate haste might tell a hundred.

MARCELLUS: ⎱
BERNARDO: ⎰   Longer, longer.

HORATIO: Not when I saw't.

HAMLET: His beard was grizzled,—no?

HORATIO: It was, as I have seen it in his life,
    A sable° silver'd.

HAMLET: I will watch to-night;   240
    Perchance 'twill walk again.

HORATIO: I warr'nt it will.

HAMLET: If it assume my noble father's person,
    I'll speak to it, though hell itself should gape
    And bid me hold my peace. I pray you all,
    If you have hitherto conceal'd this sight,   245
    Let it be tenable in your silence still;
    And whatsoever else shall hap to-night,
    Give it an understanding, but no tongue:
    I will requite your loves. So, fare you well:
    Upon the platform, 'twixt eleven and twelve,   250
    I'll visit you.

ALL: Our duty to your honour.

HAMLET: Your loves, as mine to you: farewell.   *Exeunt [all but Hamlet].*
    My father's spirit in arms! all is not well;
    I doubt° some foul play: would the night were come!
    Till then sit still, my soul: foul deeds will rise,   255
    Though all the earth o'erwhelm them, to men's eyes.   *Exit.*

229 **beaver:** Visor on the helmet.   239 **sable:** Black color.   254 **doubt:** Fear.

[Scene 3]

[A room in Polonius's house.]
  Enter Laertes and Ophelia, his Sister.

LAERTES: My necessaries are embark'd: farewell:
    And, sister, as the winds give benefit
    And convoy is assistant,° do not sleep,
    But let me hear from you.

OPHELIA: Do you doubt that?

LAERTES: For Hamlet and the trifling of his favour,   5
    Hold it a fashion° and a toy in blood,°
    A violet in the youth of primy° nature,
    Forward,° not permanent, sweet, not lasting,
    The perfume and suppliance of a minute;°
    No more.

OPHELIA: No more but so?

LAERTES: Think it no more: 10
    For nature, crescent,° does not grow alone
    In thews° and bulk, but, as this temple° waxes,
    The inward service of the mind and soul
    Grows wide withal. Perhaps he loves you now,
    And now no soil° nor cautel° doth besmirch   15
    The virtue of his will: but you must fear,
    His greatness weigh'd,° his will is not his own;
    For he himself is subject to his birth:
    He may not, as unvalued persons do,
    Carve for himself; for on his choice depends   20
    The safety and health of this whole state;
    And therefore must his choice be circumscrib'd
    Unto the voice and yielding° of that body
    Whereof he is the head. Then if he says he loves you,
    It fits your wisdom so far to believe it   25
    As he in his particular act and place
    May give his saying deed;° which is no further
    Than the main voice of Denmark goes withal.
    Then weigh what loss your honour may sustain,
    If with too credent° ear you list his songs,   30
    Or lose your heart, or your chaste treasure open
    To his unmast'red° importunity.

SCENE 3. **3 convoy is assistant:** Means of conveyance are available.   **6 fashion:** Custom,
prevailing usage;   **toy in blood:** Passing amorous fancy.   **7 primy:** In its prime.   **8 Forward:**
Precocious.   **9 suppliance of a minute:** Diversion to fill up a minute.   **11 crescent:** Growing, waxing.   **12 thews:** Bodily strength;   **temple:** Body.   **15 soil:** Blemish;   **cautel:** Crafty
device.   **17 greatness weigh'd:** High position considered.   **23 voice and yielding:** Assent,
approval.   **27 deed:** Effect.   **30 credent:** Credulous.   **32 unmast'red:** Unrestrained.

Fear it, Ophelia, fear it, my dear sister,
And keep you in the rear of your affection,
Out of the shot and danger of desire.   35
The chariest° maid is prodigal enough,
If she unmask her beauty to the moon:
Virtue itself 'scapes not calumnious strokes:
The canker galls the infants of the spring,°
Too oft before their buttons° be disclos'd,°   40
And in the morn and liquid dew° of youth
Contagious blastments° are most imminent.
Be wary then; best safety lies in fear:
Youth to itself rebels, though none else near.

OPHELIA: I shall the effect of this good lesson keep,   45
As watchman to my heart. But, good my brother,
Do not, as some ungracious° pastors do,
Show me the steep and thorny way to heaven;
Whiles, like a puff'd° and reckless libertine,
Himself the primrose path of dalliance treads,   50
And recks° not his own rede.°

Enter Polonius.

LAERTES: O, fear me not.
I stay too long: but here my father comes.
A double° blessing is a double grace;
Occasion° smiles upon a second leave.

POLONIUS: Yet here, Laertes? aboard, aboard, for shame!   55
The wind sits in the shoulder of your sail,
And you are stay'd for. There; my blessing with thee!
And these few precepts° in thy memory
Look thou character.° Give thy thoughts no tongue,
Nor any unproportion'd° thought his act.   60
Be thou familiar, but by no means vulgar.°
Those friends thou hast, and their adoption tried,
Grapple them to thy soul with hoops of steel;
But do not dull thy palm with entertainment
Of each new-hatch'd, unfledg'd° comrade. Beware   65
Of entrance to a quarrel, but being in,
Bear't that th' opposed may beware of thee.
Give every man thy ear, but few thy voice;

---

36 chariest: Most scrupulously modest.   **39 The canker . . . spring:** The cankerworm destroys the young plants of spring.   **40 buttons:** Buds;   **disclos'd:** Opened.   **41 liquid dew:** I.e., time when dew is fresh.   **42 blastments:** Blights.   **47 ungracious:** Graceless.   **49 puff'd:** Bloated.   **51 recks:** Heeds;   **rede:** Counsel.   **53 double:** I.e., Laertes has already bade his father good-by.   **54 Occasion:** Opportunity.   **58 precepts:** Many parallels have been found to the series of maxims which follows, one of the closer being that in Lyly's *Euphues.*   **59 character:** Inscribe.   **60 unproportion'd:** Inordinate.   **61 vulgar:** Common.   **65 unfledg'd:** Immature.

Take each man's censure, but reserve thy judgement.
Costly thy habit as thy purse can buy,   70
But not express'd in fancy;° rich, not gaudy;
For the apparel oft proclaims the man,
And they in France of the best rank and station
Are of a most select and generous chief in that.°
Neither a borrower nor a lender be;   75
For loan oft loses both itself and friend,
And borrowing dulleth edge of husbandry.°
This above all: to thine own self be true,
And it must follow, as the night the day,
Thou canst not then be false to any man.   80
Farewell: my blessing season° this in thee!
LAERTES: Most humbly do I take my leave, my lord.
POLONIUS: The time invites you; go; your servants tend.
LAERTES: Farewell, Ophelia; and remember well
What I have said to you.
OPHELIA: 'Tis in my memory lock'd,   85
And you yourself shall keep the key of it.
LAERTES: Farewell.   *Exit Laertes.*
POLONIUS: What is 't, Ophelia, he hath said to you?
OPHELIA: So please you, something touching the Lord Hamlet.
POLONIUS: Marry, well bethought: 90
'Tis told me, he hath very oft of late
Given private time to you; and you yourself
Have of your audience been most free and bounteous:
If it be so, as so 'tis put on° me,
And that in way of caution, I must tell you,   95
You do not understand yourself so clearly
As it behooves my daughter and your honour.
What is between you? give me up the truth.
OPHELIA: He hath, my lord, of late made many tenders°
Of his affection to me.   100
POLONIUS: Affection! pooh! you speak like a green girl,
Unsifted° in such perilous circumstance.
Do you believe his tenders, as you call them?
OPHELIA: I do not know, my lord, what I should think.
POLONIUS: Marry, I will teach you: think yourself a baby;   105
That you have ta'en these tenders° for true pay,
Which are not sterling.° Tender° yourself more dearly;

---

71 **express'd in fancy:** Fantastical in design.   74 **Are . . . that:** *Chief* is usually taken as a
substantive meaning "head," "eminence."   77 **husbandry:** Thrift.   81 **season:** Mature.
94 **put on:** Impressed on.   99, 103 **tenders:** Offers.   102 **Unsifted:** Untried.   106 **tenders:** Promises to pay.   107 **sterling:** Legal currency;   **Tender:** Hold.

Or—not to crack the wind° of the poor phrase,
Running it thus—you'll tender me a fool.°
OPHELIA: My lord, he hath importun'd me with love   110
In honourable fashion.
POLONIUS: Ay, fashion° you may call it; go to, go to.
OPHELIA: And hath given countenance° to his speech, my lord,
With almost all the holy vows of heaven.
POLONIUS: Ay, springes° to catch woodcocks.° I do know,   115
When the blood burns, how prodigal the soul
Lends the tongue vows: these blazes, daughter,
Giving more light than heat, extinct in both,
Even in their promise, as it is a-making,
You must not take for fire. From this time   120
Be somewhat scanter of your maiden presence;
Set your entreatments° at a higher rate
Than a command to parley.° For Lord Hamlet,
Believe so much in him,° that he is young,
And with a larger tether may he walk   125
Than may be given you: in few,° Ophelia,
Do not believe his vows; for they are brokers;°
Not of that dye° which their investments° show,
But mere implorators of° unholy suits,
Breathing° like sanctified and pious bawds,   130
The better to beguile. This is for all:
I would not, in plain terms, from this time forth,
Have you so slander° any moment leisure,
As to give words or talk with the Lord Hamlet.
Look to 't, I charge you: come your ways.   135
OPHELIA: I shall obey, my lord.   *Exeunt.*

[Scene 4]

[The platform.]
Enter Hamlet, Horatio, and Marcellus.

HAMLET: The air bites shrewdly; it is very cold.
HORATIO: It is a nipping and an eager air.
HAMLET: What hour now?
HORATIO: I think it lacks of twelve.
MARCELLUS: No, it is struck.

---

108 **crack the wind:** I.e., run it until it is broken-winded.   109 **tender ... fool:** Show me a fool
(for a daughter).   112 **fashion:** Mere form, pretense.   113 **countenance:** Credit, support.
115 **springes:** Snares;   **woodcocks:** Birds easily caught, type of stupidity.   122 **entreatments:**
Conversations, interviews.   123 **command to parley:** Mere invitation to talk.   124 **so ...**
him: This much concerning him.   126 **in few:** Briefly.   127 **brokers:** Go-betweens, pro-
curers.   128 **dye:** Color or sort;   **investments:** Clothes.   129 **implorators of:** Solicitors of.
130 **Breathing:** Speaking.   133 **slander:** Bring disgrace or reproach upon.

HORATIO: Indeed? I heard it not: then it draws near the season   5
    Wherein the spirit held his wont to walk.

A flourish of trumpets, and two pieces go off.

    What does this mean, my lord?
HAMLET: The king doth wake° to-night and takes his rouse,°
    Keeps wassail,° and the swagg'ring up-spring° reels;°
    And, as he drains his draughts of Rhenish° down,   10
    The kettle-drum and trumpet thus bray out
    The triumph of his pledge.°
HORATIO: Is it a custom?
HAMLET: Ay, marry, is 't:
    But to my mind, though I am native here
    And to the manner born,° it is a custom   15
    More honour'd in the breach than the observance.
    This heavy-headed revel east and west
    Makes us traduc'd and tax'd of other nations:
    They clepe° us drunkards, and with swinish phrase°
    Soil our addition;° and indeed it takes   20
    From our achievements, though perform'd at height,
    The pith and marrow of our attribute.°
    So, oft it chances in particular men,
    That for some vicious mole of nature° in them,
    As, in their birth—wherein they are not guilty,   25
    Since nature cannot choose his origin—
    By the o'ergrowth of some complexion,
    Oft breaking down the pales° and forts of reason,
    Or by some habit that too much o'er-leavens°
    The form of plausive° manners, that these men,   30
    Carrying, I say, the stamp of one defect,
    Being nature's livery,° or fortune's star,°—
    Their virtues else—be they as pure as grace,
    As infinite as man may undergo—
    Shall in the general censure take corruption   35
    From that particular fault: the dram of eale°

SCENE 4. 8 **wake:** Stay awake, hold revel;   **rouse:** Carouse, drinking bout.   9 **wassail:** Carousal; **up-spring:** Last and wildest dance at German merry-makings;   **reels:** Reels through.   10 **Rhenish:** Rhine wine.   12 **triumph . . . pledge:** His glorious achievement as a drinker.   15 **to . . . born:** Destined by birth to be subject to the custom in question.   19 **clepe:** Call;   **with swinish phrase:** By calling us swine.   20 **addition:** Reputation.   22 **attribute:** Reputation.   24 **mole of nature:** Natural blemish in one's constitution.   28 **pales:** Palings (as of a fortification).   29 **o'er-leavens:** Induces a change throughout (as yeast works in bread).   30 **plausive:** Pleasing.   32 **nature's livery:** Endowment from nature;   **fortune's star:** The position in which one is placed by fortune, a reference to astrology. The two phrases are aspects of the same thing.   36–38 **the dram . . . scandal:** A famous crux: *dram of eale* has had various interpretations, the preferred one being probably, "a dram of evil."

Doth all the noble substance of a doubt
To his own scandal.°

Enter Ghost.

HORATIO: Look, my lord, it comes!
HAMLET: Angels and ministers of grace° defend us!
Be thou a spirit of health or goblin damn'd,   40
Bring with thee airs from heaven or blasts from hell,
Be thy intents wicked or charitable,
Thou com'st in such a questionable° shape
That I will speak to thee: I'll call thee Hamlet,
King, father, royal Dane: O, answer me!   45
Let me not burst in ignorance; but tell
Why thy canoniz'd° bones, hearsed° in death,
Have burst their cerements;° why the sepulchre,
Wherein we saw thee quietly interr'd,
Hath op'd his ponderous and marble jaws,   50
To cast thee up again. What may this mean,
That thou, dead corse, again in complete steel
Revisits thus the glimpses of the moon,°
Making night hideous; and we fools of nature°
So horridly to shake our disposition   55
With thoughts beyond the reaches of our souls?
Say, why is this? wherefore? what should we do?

[Ghost] beckons [Hamlet].

HORATIO: It beckons you to go away with it,
As if it some impartment° did desire
To you alone.
MARCELLUS: Look, with what courteous action   60
It waves you to a more removed° ground:
But do not go with it.
HORATIO: No, by no means.
HAMLET: It will not speak; then I will follow it.
HORATIO: Do not, my lord!
HAMLET: Why, what should be the fear?
I do not set my life at a pin's fee;   65
And for my soul, what can it do to that,
Being a thing immortal as itself?
It waves me forth again: I'll follow it.
HORATIO: What if it tempt you toward the flood, my lord,
Or to the dreadful summit of the cliff   70

---

39 **ministers of grace:** Messengers of God.   43 **questionable:** Inviting question or conversation.   47 **canoniz'd:** Buried according to the canons of the church; **hearsed:** Coffined.
48 **cerements:** Grave-clothes.   53 **glimpses of the moon:** The earth by night.   54 **fools of
nature:** Mere men, limited to natural knowledge.   59 **impartment:** Communication.
61 **removed:** Remote.

That beetles o'er° his base into the sea,
And there assume some other horrible form,
Which might deprive your sovereignty of reason°
And draw you into madness? think of it:
The very place puts toys of desperation,°   75
Without more motive, into every brain
That looks so many fathoms to the sea
And hears it roar beneath.
HAMLET: It waves me still.
    Go on; I'll follow thee.
MARCELLUS: You shall not go, my lord.
HAMLET: Hold off your hands!   80
HORATIO: Be rul'd; you shall not go.
HAMLET: My fate cries out,
    And makes each petty artere° in this body
    As hardy as the Nemean lion's° nerve.°
    Still am I call'd. Unhand me, gentlemen.
    By heaven, I'll make a ghost of him that lets° me!   85
    I say, away! Go on; I'll follow thee.   *Exeunt Ghost and Hamlet.*
HORATIO: He waxes desperate with imagination.
MARCELLUS: Let's follow; 'tis not fit thus to obey him.
HORATIO: Have after. To what issue° will this come?
MARCELLUS: Something is rotten in the state of Denmark.   90
HORATIO: Heaven will direct it.°
MARCELLUS: Nay, let's follow him.   *Exeunt.*

[Scene 5]

[Another part of the platform.]
    Enter Ghost and Hamlet.

HAMLET: Whither wilt thou lead me? speak; I'll go no further.
GHOST: Mark me.
HAMLET: I will.
GHOST: My hour is almost come,
    When I to sulphurous and tormenting flames
    Must render up myself.
HAMLET: Alas, poor ghost!

---

71 beetles o'er: Overhangs threateningly.   **73 deprive . . . reason:** Take away the sovereignty of your reason. It was thought that evil spirits would sometimes assume the form of departed spirits in order to work madness in a human creature.   **75 toys of desperation:** Freakish notions of suicide.   **82 artere:** Artery.   **83 Nemean lion's:** The Nemean lion was one of the monsters slain by Hercules;   **nerve:** Sinew, tendon. The point is that the arteries which were carrying the spirits out into the body were functioning and were as stiff and hard as the sinews of the lion.   **85 lets:** Hinders.   **89 issue:** Outcome.   **91 it:** I.e., the outcome.

GHOST: Pity me not, but lend thy serious hearing   5
    To what I shall unfold.
HAMLET: Speak; I am bound to hear.
GHOST: So art thou to revenge, when thou shalt hear.
HAMLET: What?
GHOST: I am thy father's spirit,
    Doom'd for a certain term to walk the night,   10
    And for the day confin'd to fast° in fires,
    Till the foul crimes done in my days of nature
    Are burnt and purg'd away. But that I am forbid
    To tell the secrets of my prison-house,
    I could a tale unfold whose lightest word   15
    Would harrow up thy soul, freeze thy young blood,
    Make thy two eyes, like stars, start from their spheres,°
    Thy knotted° and combined° locks to part
    And each particular hair to stand an end,
    Like quills upon the fretful porpentine:°   20
    But this eternal blazon° must not be
    To ears of flesh and blood. List, list, O, list!
    If thou didst ever thy dear father love —
HAMLET: O God!
GHOST: Revenge his foul and most unnatural° murder.   25
HAMLET: Murder!
GHOST: Murder most foul, as in the best it is;
    But this most foul, strange and unnatural.
HAMLET: Haste me to know't, that I, with wings as swift
    As meditation or the thoughts of love,   30
    May sweep to my revenge.
GHOST: I find thee apt;
    And duller shouldst thou be than the fat weed°
    That roots itself in ease on Lethe wharf,°
    Wouldst thou not stir in this. Now, Hamlet, hear:
    'Tis given out that, sleeping in my orchard,   35
    A serpent stung me; so the whole ear of Denmark
    Is by a forged process of my death
    Rankly abus'd: but know, thou noble youth,
    The serpent that did sting thy father's life
    Now wears his crown.

SCENE 5. **11 fast:** Probably, do without food. It has been sometimes taken in the sense of doing general penance. **17 spheres:** Orbits. **18 knotted:** Perhaps intricately arranged; **combined:** Tied, bound. **20 porpentine:** Porcupine. **21 eternal blazon:** Promulgation or proclamation of eternity, revelation of the hereafter. **25 unnatural:** I.e., pertaining to fratricide. **32 fat weed:** Many suggestions have been offered as to the particular plant intended, including asphodel; probably a general figure for plants growing along rotting wharves and piles. **33 Lethe wharf:** Bank of the river of forgetfulness in Hades.

HAMLET: O my prophetic soul!   40
    My uncle!
GHOST: Ay, that incestuous, that adulterate° beast,
    With witchcraft of his wit, with traitorous gifts,—
    O wicked wit and gifts, that have the power
    So to seduce!—won to his shameful lust   45
    The will of my most seeming-virtuous queen:
    O Hamlet, what a falling-off was there!
    From me, whose love was of that dignity
    That it went hand in hand even with the vow
    I made to her in marriage, and to decline   50
    Upon a wretch whose natural gifts were poor
    To those of mine!
    But virtue, as it never will be moved,
    Though lewdness court it in a shape of heaven,
    So lust, though to a radiant angel link'd,   55
    Will sate itself in a celestial bed,
    And prey on garbage.
    But, soft! methinks I scent the morning air;
    Brief let me be. Sleeping within my orchard,
    My custom always of the afternoon,   60
    Upon my secure° hour thy uncle stole,
    With juice of cursed hebona° in a vial,
    And in the porches of my ears did pour
    The leperous° distilment; whose effect
    Holds such an enmity with blood of man   65
    That swift as quicksilver it courses through
    The natural gates and alleys of the body,
    And with a sudden vigour it doth posset°
    And curd, like eager° droppings into milk,
    The thin and wholesome blood: so did it mine;   70
    And a most instant tetter bark'd about,
    Most lazar-like,° with vile and loathsome crust,
    All my smooth body.
    Thus was I, sleeping, by a brother's hand
    Of life, of crown, of queen, at once dispatch'd:°   75
    Cut off even in the blossoms of my sin,
    Unhous'led,° disappointed,° unanel'd,°
    No reck'ning made, but sent to my account
    With all my imperfections on my head:

---

42 adulterate: Adulterous. **61 secure:** Confident, unsuspicious. **62 hebona:** Generally supposed to mean henbane, conjectured *hemlock*; *ebenus*, meaning "yew." **64 leperous:** Causing leprosy. **68 posset:** Coagulate, curdle. **69 eager:** Sour, acid. **72 lazar-like:** Leperlike. **75 dispatch'd:** Suddenly bereft. **77 Unhous'led:** Without having received the sacrament; **disappointed:** Unready, without equipment for the last journey; **unanel'd:** Without having received extreme unction.

O, horrible! O, horrible! most horrible!°   80
If thou hast nature in thee, bear it not;
Let not the royal bed of Denmark be
A couch for luxury° and damned incest.
But, howsomever thou pursues this act,
Taint not thy mind,° nor let thy soul contrive   85
Against thy mother aught: leave her to heaven
And to those thorns that in her bosom lodge,
To prick and sting her. Fare thee well at once!
The glow-worm shows the matin° to be near,
And 'gins to pale his uneffectual fire:°   90
Adieu, adieu, adieu! remember me.   *[Exit.]*
HAMLET: O all you host of heaven! O earth! what else?
And shall I couple° hell? O, fie! Hold, hold, my heart;
And you, my sinews, grow not instant old,
But bear me stiffly up. Remember thee!   95
Ay, thou poor ghost, whiles memory holds a seat
In this distracted globe.° Remember thee!
Yea, from the table of my memory
I'll wipe away all trivial fond records,
All saws° of books, all forms, all pressures° past,   100
That youth and observation copied there;
And thy commandment all alone shall live
Within the book and volume of my brain,
Unmix'd with baser matter: yes, by heaven!
O most pernicious woman!   105
O villain, villain, smiling, damned villain!
My tables,°—meet it is I set it down,
That one may smile, and smile, and be a villain;
At least I am sure it may be so in Denmark: *[Writing.]*
So, uncle, there you are. Now to my word;°   110
It is "Adieu, adieu! remember me,"
I have sworn't.

Enter Horatio and Marcellus.

HORATIO: My lord, my lord—
MARCELLUS: Lord Hamlet,—
HORATIO: Heavens secure him!
HAMLET: So be it!
MARCELLUS: Hillo, ho, ho,° my lord!   115

---

80 **O . . . horrible:** Many editors give this line to Hamlet; Garrick and Sir Henry Irving spoke it in that part.   83 **luxury:** Lechery.   85 **Taint . . . mind:** Probably, deprave not thy character, do nothing except in the pursuit of a natural revenge.   89 **matin:** Morning.   90 **uneffectual fire:** Cold light.   93 **couple:** Add.   97 **distracted globe:** Confused head.   100 **saws:** Wise sayings; **pressures:** Impressions stamped.   107 **tables:** Probably a small portable writing-tablet carried at the belt.   110 **word:** Watchword.   115 **Hillo, ho, ho:** A falconer's call to a hawk in air.

HAMLET: Hillo, ho, ho, boy! come, bird, come.
MARCELLUS: How is't, my noble lord?
HORATIO: What news, my lord?
HAMLET: O, wonderful!
HORATIO: Good my lord, tell it.
HAMLET: No; you will reveal it.
HORATIO: Not I, my lord, by heaven.
MARCELLUS: Nor I, my lord.   120
HAMLET: How say you, then; would heart of man once think it?
     But you'll be secret?
HORATIO: ⎫
MARCELLUS: ⎭   Ay, by heaven, my lord.
HAMLET: There's ne'er a villain dwelling in all Denmark
     But he's an arrant° knave.
HORATIO: There needs no ghost, my lord, come from the grave   125
     To tell us this.
HAMLET: Why, right; you are in the right;
     And so, without more circumstance at all,
     I hold it fit that we shake hands and part:
     You, as your business and desire shall point you;
     For every man has business and desire,   130
     Such as it is; and for my own poor part,
     Look you, I'll go pray.
HORATIO: These are but wild and whirling words, my lord.
HAMLET: I am sorry they offend you, heartily;
     Yes, 'faith, heartily.
HORATIO: There's no offence, my lord.   135
HAMLET: Yes, by Saint Patrick,° but there is, Horatio,
     And much offence too. Touching this vision here,
     It is an honest° ghost, that let me tell you:
     For your desire to know what is between us,
     O'ermaster 't as you may. And now, good friends,   140
     As you are friends, scholars and soldiers,
     Give me one poor request.
HORATIO: What is 't, my lord? we will.
HAMLET: Never make known what you have seen to-night.
HORATIO: ⎫
MARCELLUS: ⎭   My lord, we will not.
HAMLET: Nay, but swear 't.
HORATIO: In faith,   145
     My lord, not I.
MARCELLUS: Nor I, my lord, in faith.

---

124 arrant: Thoroughgoing.   **136 Saint Patrick:** St. Patrick was keeper of Purgatory and patron saint of all blunders and confusion.   **138 honest:** I.e., a real ghost and not an evil spirit.

HAMLET: Upon my sword.°

MARCELLUS: We have sworn, my lord, already.

HAMLET: Indeed, upon my sword, indeed.   *Ghost cries under the stage.*

GHOST: Swear.

HAMLET: Ah, ha, boy! say'st thou so? art thou there, truepenny?°   150
    Come on — you hear this fellow in the cellarage —
    Consent to swear.

HORATIO: Propose the oath, my lord.

HAMLET: Never to speak of this that you have seen,
    Swear by my sword.

GHOST *[beneath]*:   Swear.   155

HAMLET: Hic et ubique?° then we'll shift our ground.
    Come hither, gentlemen,
    And lay your hands again upon my sword:
    Swear by my sword,
    Never to speak of this that you have heard.   160

GHOST *[beneath]*:   Swear by his sword.

HAMLET: Well said, old mole! canst work i' th' earth so fast?
    A worthy pioner!° Once more remove, good friends.

HORATIO: O day and night, but this is wondrous strange!

HAMLET: And therefore as a stranger give it welcome.   165
    There are more things in heaven and earth, Horatio,
    Than are dreamt of in your philosophy.
    But come;
    Here, as before, never, so help you mercy,
    How strange or odd soe'er I bear myself,   170
    As I perchance hereafter shall think meet
    To put an antic° disposition on,
    That you, at such times seeing me, never shall,
    With arms encumb'red° thus, or this head-shake,
    Or by pronouncing of some doubtful phrase,   175
    As "Well, well, we know," or "We could, an if we would,"
    Or "If we list to speak," or "There be, an if they might,"
    Or such ambiguous giving out,° to note°
    That you know aught of me: this not to do,
    So grace and mercy at your most need help you,   180
    Swear.

GHOST *[beneath]*:   Swear.

HAMLET: Rest, rest, perturbed spirit! *[They swear.]* So, gentlemen,
    With all my love I do commend me to you:
    And what so poor a man as Hamlet is   185
    May do, t' express his love and friending° to you,

---

147 **sword:** I.e., the hilt in the form of a cross.   150 **truepenny:** Good old boy, or the like.
156 **Hic et ubique?:** Here and everywhere?   163 **pioner:** Digger, miner.   172 **antic:** Fantastic.   174 **encumb'red:** Folded or entwined.   178 **giving out:** Profession of knowledge;
to note: To give a sign.   186 **friending:** Friendliness.

God willing, shall not lack. Let us go in together;
And still your fingers on your lips, I pray.
The time is out of joint: O cursed spite,
That ever I was born to set it right!   190
Nay, come, let's go together.   *Exeunt.*

[ACT 2, Scene 1]

[A room in Polonius's house.]
Enter old Polonius with his man [Reynaldo].

POLONIUS: Give him this money and these notes, Reynaldo.
REYNALDO: I will, my lord.
POLONIUS: You shall do marvellous wisely, good Reynaldo,
   Before you visit him, to make inquire
   Of his behaviour.
REYNALDO: My lord, I did intend it.   5
POLONIUS: Marry, well said; very well said. Look you, sir,
   Inquire me first what Danskers° are in Paris;
   And how, and who, what means, and where they keep,°
   What company, at what expense; and finding
   By this encompassment° and drift° of question   10
   That they do know my son, come you more nearer
   Than your particular demands will touch it:°
   Take° you as 'twere, some distant knowledge of him;
   As thus, "I know his father and his friends,
   And in part him": do you mark this, Reynaldo?   15
REYNALDO: Ay, very well, my lord.
POLONIUS: "And in part him; but" you may say "not well:
   But, if 't be he I mean, he's very wild;
   Addicted so and so": and there put on° him
   What forgeries° you please; marry, none so rank   20
   As may dishonour him; take heed of that;
   But, sir, such wanton,° wild and usual slips
   As are companions noted and most known
   To youth and liberty.
REYNALDO: As gaming, my lord.
POLONIUS: Ay, or drinking, fencing,° swearing, quarrelling,   25
   Drabbing;° you may go so far.
REYNALDO: My lord, that would dishonour him.

ACT 2, SCENE 1. **7 Danskers:** Danke was a common variant for "Denmark"; hence "Dane."
8 keep: Dwell.   **10 encompassment:** Roundabout talking;   **drift:** Gradual approach or course.
11–12 come . . . it: I.e., you will find out more this way than by asking pointed questions.
13 Take: Assume, pretend.   **19 put on:** Impute to.   **20 forgeries:** Invented tales.   **22 wanton:** Sportive, unrestrained.   **25 fencing:** Indicative of the ill repute of professional fencers and
fencing schools in Elizabethan times.   **26 Drabbing:** Associating with immoral women.

POLONIUS: 'Faith, no; as you may season it in the charge.
  You must not put another scandal on him,
  That he is open to incontinency;°   30
  That's not my meaning: but breathe his faults so quaintly°
  That they may seem the taints of liberty,°
  The flash and outbreak of a fiery mind,
  A savageness in unreclaimed° blood,
  Of general assault.°
REYNALDO: But, my good lord, —   35
POLONIUS: Wherefore should you do this?
REYNALDO: Ay, my lord,
  I would know that.
POLONIUS: Marry, sir, here's my drift;
  And, I believe, it is a fetch of wit:°
  You laying these slight sullies on my son,
  As 'twere a thing a little soil'd i' th' working,   40
  Mark you,
  Your party in converse, him you would sound,
  Having ever° seen in the prenominate° crimes
  The youth you breathe of guilty, be assur'd
  He closes with you in this consequence;°   45
  "Good sir," or so, or "friend," or "gentleman,"
  According to the phrase or the addition
  Of man and country.
REYNALDO: Very good, my lord.
POLONIUS: And then, sir, does 'a this — 'a does — what was I about to say? By the
  mass, I was about to say something: where did I leave?   50
REYNALDO: At "closes in the consequence," at "friend or so," and "gentle-
  man."
POLONIUS: At "closes in the consequence," ay, marry;
  He closes thus: "I know the gentleman;
  I saw him yesterday, or t' other day,   55
  Or then, or then; with such, or such; and, as you say,
  There was 'a gaming; there o'ertook in 's rouse;°
  There falling out at tennis": or perchance,
  "I saw him enter such a house of sale,"
  Videlicet,° a brothel, or so forth.   60
  See you now;
  Your bait of falsehood takes this carp of truth:
  And thus do we of wisdom and of reach,°

---

30 incontinency: Habitual   loose   behavior.   **31 quaintly:** Delicately,   ingeniously.
32 taints of liberty: Blemishes due to freedom.   **34 unreclaimed:** Untamed.   **35 general
assault:** Tendency that assails all untrained youth.   **38 fetch of wit:** Clever trick.   **43 ever:** At
any time;   **prenominate:** Before-mentioned.   **45 closes . . . consequence:** Agrees with you
in this conclusion.   **57 o'ertook in 's rouse:** Overcome by drink.   **60 Videlicet:** Namely.
63 reach: Capacity, ability.

With windlasses° and with assays of bias,° 65
By indirections° find directions° out:
So by my former lecture° and advice,
Shall you my son. You have me, have you not?
REYNALDO: My lord, I have.
POLONIUS: God bye ye;° fare ye well.
REYNALDO: Good my lord!
POLONIUS: Observe his inclination in yourself.° 70
REYNALDO: I shall, my lord.
POLONIUS: And let him ply his music.°
REYNALDO: Well, my lord.
POLONIUS: Farewell!   *Exit Reynaldo.*

Enter Ophelia.

                    How now, Ophelia! what's the matter?
OPHELIA: O, my lord, my lord, I have been so affrighted!
POLONIUS: With what, i' th' name of God? 75
OPHELIA: My lord, as I was sewing in my closet,°
Lord Hamlet, with his doublet° all unbrac'd;°
No hat upon his head; his stockings foul'd,
Ungart'red, and down-gyved° to his ankle;
Pale as his shirt; his knees knocking each other; 80
And with a look so piteous in purport
As if he had been loosed out of hell
To speak of horrors,—he comes before me.
POLONIUS: Mad for thy love?
OPHELIA: My lord, I do not know;
But truly, I do fear it.
POLONIUS: What said he? 85
OPHELIA: He took me by the wrist and held me hard;
Then goes he to the length of all his arm;
And, with his other hand thus o'er his brow,
He falls to such perusal of my face
As 'a would draw it. Long stay'd he so; 90
At last, a little shaking of mine arm
And thrice his head thus waving up and down,
He rais'd a sigh so piteous and profound
As it did seem to shatter all his bulk°
And end his being: that done, he lets me go: 95

---

64 windlasses: I.e., circuitous paths; **assays of bias:** Attempts that resemble the course of the bowl, which, being weighted on one side, has a curving motion. **65 indirections:** Devious courses; **directions:** Straight courses, i.e., the truth. **66 lecture:** Admonition. **68 bye ye:** Be with you. **70 Observe . . . yourself:** In your own person, not by spies; or conform your own conduct to his inclination; or test him by studying yourself. **72 ply his music:** Probably to be taken literally. **76 closet:** Private chamber. **77 doublet:** Close-fitting coat; **unbrac'd:** Unfastened. **79 down-gyved:** Fallen to the ankles (like gyves or fetters). **94 bulk:** Body.

And, with his head over his shoulder turn'd,
He seem'd to find his way without his eyes;
For out o' doors he went without their helps,
And, to the last, bended their light on me.

POLONIUS: Come, go with me: I will go seek the king. 100
This is the very ecstasy of love,
Whose violent property° fordoes° itself
And leads the will to desperate undertakings
As oft as any passion under heaven
That does afflict our natures. I am sorry. 105
What, have you given him any hard words of late?

OPHELIA: No, my good lord, but, as you did command,
I did repel his letters and denied
His access to me.

POLONIUS: That hath made him mad.
I am sorry that with better heed and judgement 110
I had not quoted° him: I fear'd he did but trifle,
And meant to wrack thee; but, beshrew my jealousy!°
By heaven, it is as proper to our age
To cast beyond° ourselves in our opinions
As it is common for the younger sort 115
To lack discretion. Come, go we to the king:
This must be known; which, being kept close, might move
More grief to hide than hate to utter love.°
Come. *Exeunt.*

[Scene 2]

[A room in the castle.]
Flourish. Enter King and Queen, Rosencrantz, and Guildenstern [with others].

KING: Welcome, dear Rosencrantz and Guildenstern!
Moreover that° we much did long to see you,
The need we have to use you did provoke
Our hasty sending. Something have you heard
Of Hamlet's transformation; so call it, 5
Sith° nor th' exterior nor the inward man
Resembles that it was. What it should be,
More than his father's death, that thus hath put him
So much from th' understanding of himself,
I cannot dream of: I entreat you both, 10

---

102 **property:** Nature; **fordoes:** Destroys.   111 **quoted:** Observed.   112 **beshrew my jealousy:** Curse my suspicions.   114 **cast beyond:** Overshoot, miscalculate.   117–118 **might . . .
love:** I.e., I might cause more grief to others by hiding the knowledge of Hamlet's love to Ophelia than hatred to me and mine by telling of it.   SCENE 2. 2 **Moreover that:** Besides the fact
that.   6 **Sith:** Since.

That, being of so young days° brought up with him,
And sith so neighbour'd to his youth and haviour,
That you vouchsafe your rest° here in our court
Some little time: so by your companies
To draw him on to pleasures, and to gather,   15
So much as from occasion you may glean,
Whether aught, to us unknown, afflicts him thus,
That, open'd, lies within our remedy.

QUEEN: Good gentlemen, he hath much talk'd of you;
And sure I am two men there are not living   20
To whom he more adheres. If it will please you
To show us so much gentry° and good will
As to expend your time with us awhile,
For the supply and profit° of our hope,
Your visitation shall receive such thanks   25
As fits a king's remembrance.

ROSENCRANTZ: Both your majesties
Might, by the sovereign power you have of us,
Put your dread pleasures more into command
Than to entreaty.

GUILDENSTERN: But we both obey,
And here give up ourselves, in the full bent°   30
To lay our service freely at your feet,
To be commanded.

KING: Thanks, Rosencrantz and gentle Guildenstern.

QUEEN: Thanks, Guildenstern and gentle Rosencrantz:
And I beseech you instantly to visit   35
My too much changed son. Go, some of you,
And bring these gentlemen where Hamlet is.

GUILDENSTERN: Heavens make our presence and our practices
Pleasant and helpful to him!

QUEEN: Ay, amen!
Exeunt Rosencrantz and Guildenstern [with some Attendants].

Enter Polonius.

POLONIUS: Th' ambassadors from Norway, my good lord,   40
Are joyfully return'd.

KING: Thou still hast been the father of good news.

POLONIUS: Have I, my lord? I assure my good liege,
I hold my duty, as I hold my soul,
Both to my God and to my gracious king: 45
And I do think, or else this brain of mine

---

11 of . . . days: From such early youth.   **13 vouchsafe your rest:** Please to stay.   **22 gentry:** Courtesy.   **24 supply and profit:** Aid and successful outcome.   **30 in . . . bent:** To the utmost degree of our mental capacity.

Hunts not the trail of policy so sure
As it hath us'd to do, that I have found
The very cause of Hamlet's lunacy.

KING: O, speak of that; that do I long to hear.   50

POLONIUS: Give first admittance to th' ambassadors;
My news shall be the fruit to that great feast.

KING: Thyself do grace to them, and bring them in.   *[Exit Polonius.]*
He tells me, my dear Gertrude, he hath found
The head and source of all your son's distemper.   55

QUEEN: I doubt° it is no other but the main;°
His father's death, and our o'erhasty marriage.

KING: Well, we shall sift him.

Enter Ambassadors [Voltimand and Cornelius, with Polonius.]

Welcome, my good friends!
Say, Voltimand, what from our brother Norway?

VOLTIMAND: Most fair return of greetings and desires.   60
Upon our first, he sent out to suppress
His nephew's levies; which to him appear'd
To be a preparation 'gainst the Polack;
But, better look'd into, he truly found
It was against your highness: whereat griev'd,   65
That so his sickness, age and impotence
Was falsely borne in hand,° sends out arrests
On Fortinbras; which he, in brief, obeys;
Receives rebuke from Norway, and in fine°
Makes vow before his uncle never more   70
To give th' assay° of arms against your majesty.
Whereon old Norway, overcome with joy,
Gives him three score thousand crowns in annual fee,
And his commission to employ those soldiers,
So levied as before, against the Polack: 75
With an entreaty, herein further shown,   *[Giving a paper.]*
That it might please you to give quiet pass
Through your dominions for this enterprise,
On such regards of safety and allowance°
As therein are set down.

KING: It likes° us well;   80
And at our more consider'd° time we'll read,
Answer, and think upon this business.
Meantime we thank you for your well-took labour:
Go to your rest; at night we'll feast together:

---

56 doubt: Fear;   **main:** Chief point, principal concern.   **67 borne in hand:** Deluded.
69 in fine: In the end.   **71 assay:** Assault, trial (of arms).   **79 safety and allowance:** Pledges
of safety to the country and terms of permission for the troops to pass.   **80 likes:** Pleases.
81 consider'd: Suitable for deliberation.

Most welcome home!   *Exeunt Ambassadors.*
POLONIUS: This business is well ended.   85
My liege, and madam, to expostulate
What majesty should be, what duty is,
Why day is day, night night, and time is time,
Were nothing but to waste night, day and time.
Therefore, since brevity is the soul of wit,°   90
And tediousness the limbs and outward flourishes,°
I will be brief: your noble son is mad:
Mad call I it; for, to define true madness
What is 't but to be nothing else but mad?
But let that go.
QUEEN: More matter, with less art.   95
POLONIUS: Madam, I swear I use no art at all.
That he is mad, 'tis true: 'tis true 'tis pity;
And pity 'tis 'tis true: a foolish figure;°
But farewell it, for I will use no art.
Mad let us grant him, then: and now remains   100
That we find out the cause of this effect,
Or rather say, the cause of this defect,
For this effect defective comes by cause:
Thus it remains, and the remainder thus.
Perpend.°   105
I have a daughter—have while she is mine—
Who, in her duty and obedience, mark,
Hath given me this: now gather, and surmise.
[Reads the letter.] "To the celestial and my soul's idol, the most beautified
Ophelia,"—   110
That's an ill phrase, a vile phrase; "beautified" is a vile phrase: but you shall
hear. Thus: *[Reads.]*
"In her excellent white bosom, these, & c."
QUEEN: Came this from Hamlet to her?
POLONIUS: Good madam, stay awhile; I will be faithful.   *[Reads.]* 115
                "Doubt thou the stars are fire;
                    Doubt that the sun doth move;
                "Doubt truth to be a liar;
                    But never doubt I love.
"O dear Ophelia, I am ill at these numbers;° I have not art to reckon°   120
my groans: but that I love thee best, O most best, believe it. Adieu.
    "Thine evermore, most dear lady, whilst this machine° is to him,
                                                                    HAMLET."

---

90 **wit:** Sound sense or judgment.   91 **flourishes:** Ostentation, embellishments.   98 **figure:**
Figure of speech.   105 **Perpend:** Consider.   120 **ill . . . numbers:** Unskilled at writing
verses;   **reckon:** Number metrically, scan.   122 **machine:** Bodily frame.

This, in obedience, hath my daughter shown me,
And more above,° hath his solicitings,   125
As they fell out° by time, by means° and place,
All given to mine ear.

KING: But how hath she
Receiv'd his love?

POLONIUS: What do you think of me?

KING: As of a man faithful and honourable.

POLONIUS: I would fain prove so. But what might you think,   130
When I had seen this hot love on the wing—
As I perceiv'd it, I must tell you that,
Before my daughter told me—what might you,
Or my dear majesty your queen here, think,
If I had play'd the desk or table-book,°   135
Or given my heart a winking,° mute and dumb,
Or look'd upon this love with idle sight;
What might you think? No, I went round to work,
And my young mistress thus I did bespeak:°
"Lord Hamlet is a prince, out of thy star;°   140
This must not be": and then I prescripts gave her,
That she should lock herself from his resort,
Admit no messengers, receive no tokens.
Which done, she took the fruits of my advice;
And he, repelled—a short tale to make—   145
Fell into a sadness, then into a fast,
Thence to a watch,° thence into a weakness,
Thence to a lightness,° and, by this declension,°
Into the madness wherein now he raves,
And all we mourn for.

KING: Do you think 'tis this?   150

QUEEN: It may be, very like.

POLONIUS: Hath there been such a time—I would fain know that—
That I have positively said " 'Tis so,"
When it prov'd otherwise?

KING: Not that I know.

POLONIUS [*pointing to his head and shoulder*]:   Take this from this, if this be
       otherwise: 155
If circumstances lead me, I will find
Where truth is hid, though it were hid indeed
Within the centre.°

KING: How may we try it further?

---

125 **more above:** Moreover.   126 **fell out:** Occurred;   **means:** Opportunities (of access).
135 **play'd . . . table-book:** I.e., remained shut up, concealed this information.   136 **given . . .
winking:** Given my heart a signal to keep silent.   139 **bespeak:** Address.   140 **out . . . star:**
Above thee in position.   147 **watch:** State of sleeplessness.   148 **lightness:** Lightheadedness;
declension: Decline, deterioration.   158 **centre:** Middle point of the earth.

POLONIUS: You know, sometimes he walks four hours together
    Here in the lobby.
QUEEN: So he does indeed.   160
POLONIUS: At such a time I'll loose my daughter to him:
    Be you and I behind an arras° then;
    Mark the encounter: if he love her not
    And be not from his reason fall'n thereon,°
    Let me be no assistant for a state,   165
    But keep a farm and carters.
KING: We will try it.

Enter Hamlet [reading on a book].

QUEEN: But, look, where sadly the poor wretch comes reading.
POLONIUS: Away, I do beseech you both, away:

                    Exeunt King and Queen [with Attendants].
    I'll board° him presently. O, give me leave.
    How does my good Lord Hamlet?   170
HAMLET: Well, God-a-mercy.
POLONIUS: Do you know me, my lord?
HAMLET: Excellent well; you are a fishmonger.°
POLONIUS: Not I, my lord.
HAMLET: Then I would you were so honest a man.   175
POLONIUS: Honest, my lord!
HAMLET: Ay, sir; to be honest, as this world goes, is to be one man picked out of
    ten thousand.
POLONIUS: That's very true, my lord.
HAMLET: For if the sun breed maggots in a dead dog, being a good kissing   180
    carrion,° — Have you a daughter?
POLONIUS: I have, my lord.
HAMLET: Let her not walk i' the sun:° conception° is a blessing: but as your
    daughter may conceive — Friend, look to 't.
POLONIUS *[aside]:* How say you by° that? Still harping on my daughter: yet he   185
    knew me not at first; 'a said I was a fishmonger: 'a is far gone, far gone: and
    truly in my youth I suffered much extremity for love; very near this. I'll speak
    to him again. What do you read, my lord?
HAMLET: Words, words, words.
POLONIUS: What is the matter,° my lord?   190
HAMLET: Between who?°
POLONIUS: I mean, the matter that you read, my lord.

---

162 arras: Hanging, tapestry.   **164 thereon:** On that account.   **169 board:** Accost.   **173 fishmonger:** An opprobrious expression meaning "bawd," "procurer."   **180–181 good kissing carrion:** I.e., a good piece of flesh for kissing (?).   **183 i' the sun:** In the sunshine of princely favors; **conception:** Quibble on "understanding" and "pregnancy."   **185 by:** Concerning.   **190 matter:** Substance.   **191 Between who:** Hamlet deliberately takes *matter* as meaning "basis of dispute."

HAMLET: Slanders, sir: for the satirical rogue says here that old men have grey
          beards, that their faces are wrinkled, their eyes purging° thick amber and
          plum-tree gum and that they have a plentiful lack of wit, together with most   195
          weak hams: all which, sir, though I most powerfully and potently believe, yet
          I hold it not honesty° to have it thus set down, for yourself, sir, should be old
          as I am, if like a crab you could go backward.

POLONIUS *[aside]*:   Though this be madness, yet there is method in 't. — Will
          you walk out of the air, my lord?   200

HAMLET: Into my grave.

POLONIUS: Indeed, that's out of the air. *(Aside.)* How pregnant sometimes his
          replies are! a happiness° that often madness hits on, which reason and sanity
          could not so prosperously° be delivered of. I will leave him, and suddenly
          contrive the means of meeting between him and my daughter. — My hon-   205
          ourable lord, I will most humbly take my leave of you.

HAMLET: You cannot, sir, take from me any thing that I will more willingly part
          withal: except my life, except my life, except my life.

Enter Guildenstern and Rosencrantz.

POLONIUS: Fare you well, my lord.

HAMLET: These tedious old fools!   210

POLONIUS: You go to seek the Lord Hamlet; there he is.

ROSENCRANTZ *[to Polonius]*:   God save you, sir!   *[Exit Polonius.]*

GUILDENSTERN: My honoured lord!

ROSENCRANTZ: My most dear lord!

HAMLET: My excellent good friends! How dost thou, Guildenstern? Ah, Rosen-   215
          crantz! Good lads, how do ye both?

ROSENCRANTZ: As the indifferent° children of the earth.

GUILDENSTERN: Happy, in that we are not over-happy;
          On Fortune's cap we are not the very button.

HAMLET: Nor the soles of her shoe?   220

ROSENCRANTZ: Neither, my lord.

HAMLET: Then you live about her waist, or in the middle of her favours?

GUILDENSTERN: 'Faith, her privates° we.

HAMLET: In the secret parts of Fortune? O, most true; she is a strumpet. What's
          the news?   225

ROSENCRANTZ: None, my lord, but that the world's grown honest.

HAMLET: Then is doomsday near: but your news is not true. Let me question
          more in particular: what have you, my good friends, deserved at the hands of
          Fortune, that she sends you to prison hither?

GUILDENSTERN: Prison, my lord!   230

HAMLET: Denmark's a prison.

ROSENCRANTZ: Then is the world one.

---

194 purging: discharging.   **197 honesty:** Decency.   **203 happiness:** Felicity of expression.
204 prosperously: Successfully.   **217 indifferent:** Ordinary.   **223 privates:** I.e., ordinary
men (sexual pun on *private parts*).

HAMLET: A goodly one; in which there are many confines,° wards and dungeons, Denmark being one o' the worst.

ROSENCRANTZ: We think not so, my lord.   235

HAMLET: Why, then, 'tis none to you; for there is nothing either good or bad,
but thinking makes it so: to me it is a prison.

ROSENCRANTZ: Why then, your ambition makes it one; 'tis too narrow for your
mind.

HAMLET: O God, I could be bounded in a nutshell and count myself a king of   240
infinite space, were it not that I have bad dreams.

GUILDENSTERN: Which dreams indeed are ambition, for the very substance of
the ambitious° is merely the shadow of a dream.

HAMLET: A dream itself is but a shadow.

ROSENCRANTZ: Truly, and I hold ambition of so airy and light a quality that it is   245
but a shadow's shadow.

HAMLET: Then are our beggars bodies, and our monarchs and outstretched
heroes the beggars' shadows. Shall we to the court? for, by my fay,° I cannot
reason.°

ROSENCRANTZ: ⎱
                    ⎰   We'll wait upon° you.   250
GUILDENSTERN: ⎰

HAMLET: No such matter: I will not sort° you with the rest of my servants, for, to
speak to you like an honest man, I am most dreadfully attended.° But, in the
beaten way of friendship,° what make you at Elsinore?

ROSENCRANTZ: To visit you, my lord: no other occasion.

HAMLET: Beggar that I am, I am ever poor in thanks; but I thank you: and sure,   255
dear friends, my thanks are too dear a° halfpenny. Were you not sent for? Is it
your own inclining? Is it a free visitation? Come, come, deal justly with me:
come, come; nay, speak.

GUILDENSTERN: What should we say, my lord?

HAMLET: Why, any thing, but to the purpose. You were sent for; and there is a   260
kind of confession in your looks which your modesties have not craft enough
to colour: I know the good king and queen have sent for you.

ROSENCRANTZ: To what end, my lord?

HAMLET: That you must teach me. But let me conjure° you, by the rights of our
fellowship, by the consonancy of our youth,° by the obligation of our ever-   265
preserved love, and by what more dear a better proposer° could charge you
withal, be even and direct with me, whether you were sent for, or no?

ROSENCRANTZ [*aside to Guildenstern*]:   What say you?

HAMLET [*aside*]:   Nay, then, I have an eye of you. — If you love me, hold not off.

GUILDENSTERN: My lord, we were sent for.   270

---

233 confines: Places of confinement.   **242–243 very . . . ambitious:** That seemingly most
substantial thing which the ambitious pursue.   **248 fay:** Faith.   **249 reason:** Argue.   **250 wait
upon:** Accompany.   **251 sort:** Class.   **252 dreadfully attended:** Poorly provided with servants.   **252–253 in the . . . friendship:** As a matter of course among friends.   **256 a:** I.e., at a.
264 conjure: Adjure, entreat.   **265 consonancy of our youth:** The fact that we are of the
same age.   **266 better proposer:** One more skillful in finding proposals.

HAMLET: I will tell you why; so shall my anticipation prevent your discovery,° and your secrecy to the king and queen moult no feather. I have of late — but wherefore I know not — lost all my mirth, forgone all custom of exercises; and indeed it goes so heavily with my disposition that this goodly frame, the earth, seems to me a sterile promontory, this most excellent canopy, the air,   275 look you, this brave o'erhanging firmament, this majestical roof fretted° with golden fire, why, it appeareth nothing to me but a foul and pestilent congregation of vapours. What a piece of work is a man! how noble in reason! how infinite in faculties!° in form and moving how express° and admirable! in action how like an angel! in apprehension° how like a god! the beauty of the   280 world! the paragon of animals! And yet, to me, what is this quintessence° of dust? man delights not me: no, nor woman neither, though by your smiling you seem to say so.

ROSENCRANTZ: My lord, there was no such stuff in my thoughts.

HAMLET: Why did you laugh then, when I said "man delights not me"?   285

ROSENCRANTZ: To think, my lord, if you delight not in man, what lenten° entertainment the players shall receive from you: we coted° them on the way; and hither are they coming, to offer you service.

HAMLET: He that plays the king shall be welcome; his majesty shall have tribute of me; the adventurous knight shall use his foil and target;° the lover shall   290 not sigh gratis; the humorous man° shall end his part in peace; the clown shall make those laugh whose lungs are tickle o' the sere;° and the lady shall say her mind freely, or the blank verse shall halt for 't.° What players are they?

ROSENCRANTZ: Even those you were wont to take delight in, the tragedians of   295 the city.

HAMLET: How chances it they travel? their residence,° both in reputation and profit, was better both ways.

ROSENCRANTZ: I think their inhibition° comes by the means of the late innovation.°   300

HAMLET: Do they hold the same estimation they did when I was in the city? are they so followed?

ROSENCRANTZ: No, indeed, are they not.

HAMLET: How° comes it? do they grow rusty?

---

271 **prevent your discovery:** Forestall your disclosure.   276 **fretted:** Adorned.   279 **faculties:** Capacity;   **express:** Well-framed (?), exact (?).   280 **apprehension:** Understanding. 281 **quintessence:** The fifth essence of ancient philosophy, supposed to be the substance of the heavenly bodies and to be latent in all things.   286 **lenten:** Meager.   287 **coted:** Overtook and passed beyond.   290 **foil and target:** Sword and shield.   291 **humorous man:** Actor who takes the part of the humor characters.   292 **tickle o' the sere:** Easy on the trigger. 292–293 **the lady . . . for 't:** The lady (fond of talking) shall have opportunity to talk, blank verse or no blank verse.   297 **residence:** Remaining in one place.   299 **inhibition:** Formal prohibition (from acting plays in the city or, possibly, at court).   299–300 **innovation:** The new fashion in satirical plays performed by boy actors in the "private" theaters.   304–322 **How . . . load:** The passage is the famous one dealing with the War of the Theatres (1599–1602); namely, the rivalry between the children's companies and the adult actors.

ROSENCRANTZ: Nay, their endeavour keeps in the wonted pace: but there is,   305
sir, an aery° of children, little eyases,° that cry out on the top of question,°
and are most tyrannically° clapped for 't: these are now the fashion, and so
berattle° the common stages°—so they call them—that many wearing
rapiers° are afraid of goose-quills° and dare scarce come thither.

HAMLET: What, are they children? who maintains 'em? how are they escoted?°   310
Will they pursue the quality° no longer than they can sing?° will they not say
afterwards, if they should grow themselves to common° players—as it is most
like, if their means are no better—their writers do them wrong, to make
them exclaim against their own succession?°

ROSENCRANTZ: 'Faith, there has been much to do on both sides; and the nation   315
holds it no sin to tarre° them to controversy: there was, for a while, no money
bid for argument,° unless the poet and the player went to cuffs° in the
question.°

HAMLET: Is 't possible?

GUILDENSTERN: O, there has been much throwing about of brains.   320

HAMLET: Do the boys carry it away?°

ROSENCRANTZ: Ay, that they do, my lord; Hercules and his load° too.

HAMLET: It is not very strange; for my uncle is king of Denmark, and those that
would make mows° at him while my father lived, give twenty, forty, fifty, a
hundred ducats° a-piece for his picture in little.° 'Sblood, there is something   325
in this more than natural, if philosophy could find it out.

A flourish [of trumpets within].

GUILDENSTERN: There are the players.

HAMLET: Gentlemen, you are welcome to Elsinore. Your hands, come then:
the appurtenance of welcome is fashion and ceremony: let me comply° with
you in this garb,° lest my extent° to the players, which, I tell you, must show   330
fairly outwards, should more appear like entertainment than yours. You are
welcome: but my uncle-father and aunt-mother are deceived.

GUILDENSTERN: In what, my dear lord?

HAMLET: I am but mad north-north-west:° when the wind is southerly I know a
hawk from a handsaw.°   335

---

306 aery: Nest; **eyases:** Young hawks; **cry . . . question:** Speak in a high key dominating conversation; clamor forth the height of controversy; probably "excel"; perhaps intended to decry leaders of the dramatic profession. **307 tyrannically:** Outrageously. **308 berattle:** Berate; **common stages:** Public theaters. **308–309 many wearing rapiers:** Many men of fashion, who were afraid to patronize the common players for fear of being satirized by the poets who wrote for the children. **309 goose-quills:** I.e., pens of satirists. **310 escoted:** Maintained. **311 quality:** Acting profession; **no longer . . . sing:** I.e., until their voices change. **312 common:** Regular, adult. **314 succession:** Future careers. **316 tarre:** Set on (as dogs). **317 argument:** Probably, plot for a play; **went to cuffs:** Came to blows. **318 question:** Controversy. **321 carry it away:** Win the day. **322 Hercules . . . load:** Regarded as an allusion to the sign of the Globe Theatre, which was Hercules bearing the world on his shoulder. **324 mows:** Grimaces. **325 ducats:** Gold coins worth 9s. 4d; **in little:** In miniature. **329 comply:** Observe the formalities of courtesy. **330 garb:** Manner; **extent:** Showing of kindness. **334 I am . . . north-north-west:** I am only partly mad, i.e., in only one point of the compass. **335 handsaw:** A proposed reading of *hernshaw* would mean "heron"; *handsaw* may be an early corruption of *hernshaw*. Another view regards *hawk* as the variant of *hack*, a tool of the pickax type, and *handsaw* as a saw operated by hand.

Enter Polonius.

POLONIUS: Well be with you, gentlemen!

HAMLET: Hark you, Guildenstern; and you too: at each ear a hearer: that great baby you see there is not yet out of his swaddling-clouts.°

ROSENCRANTZ: Happily he is the second time come to them; for they say an old man is twice a child.   340

HAMLET: I will prophesy he comes to tell me of the players; mark it. — You say right, sir: o' Monday morning;° 'twas then indeed.

POLONIUS: My lord, I have news to tell you.

HAMLET: My lord, I have news to tell you. When Roscius° was an actor in Rome, —   345

POLONIUS: The actors are come hither, my lord.

HAMLET: Buz, buz!°

POLONIUS: Upon my honour, —

HAMLET: Then came each actor on his ass, —

POLONIUS: The best actors in the world, either for tragedy, comedy, history,   350 pastoral, pastoral-comical, historical-pastoral, tragical-historical, tragical-comical-historical-pastoral, scene individable,° or poem unlimited:° Seneca° cannot be too heavy, nor Plautus° too light. For the law of writ and the liberty,° these are the only men.

HAMLET: O Jephthah, judge of Israel,° what a treasure hadst thou!   355

POLONIUS: What a treasure had he, my lord?

HAMLET: Why,

    "One fair daughter, and no more,
      The which he loved passing well."

POLONIUS *[aside]:* Still on my daughter.   360

HAMLET: Am I not i' the right, old Jephthah?

POLONIUS: If you call me Jephthah, my lord, I have a daughter that I love passing° well.

HAMLET: Nay, that follows not.

POLONIUS: What follows, then, my lord?   365

HAMLET: Why,

    "As by lot, God wot,"

and then, you know,

    "It came to pass, as most like° it was," —

the first row° of the pious chanson° will show you more; for look, where my   370 abridgement comes.°

---

338 swaddling-clouts: Cloths in which to wrap a newborn baby.   **342 o' Monday morning:** Said to mislead Polonius.   **344 Roscius:** A famous Roman actor.   **347 Buz, buz:** An interjection used at Oxford to denote stale news.   **352 scene individable:** A play observing the unity of place;   **poem unlimited:** A play disregarding the unities of time and place;   **Seneca:** Writer of Latin tragedies, model of early Elizabethan writers of tragedy.   **353 Plautus:** Writer of Latin comedy.   **353–354 law . . . liberty:** Pieces written according to rules and without rules, i.e., "classical" and "romantic" dramas.   **355 Jephthah . . . Israel:** Jephthah had to sacrifice his daughter; see Judges 11.   **363 passing:** Surpassingly.   **369 like:** Probable.   **370 row:** Stanza;   **chanson:** Ballad.   **371 abridgement comes:** Opportunity comes for cutting short the conversation.

Enter the Players.

You are welcome, masters; welcome, all. I am glad to see thee well. Welcome, good friends. O, old friend! why, thy face is valanced° since I saw thee last: comest thou to beard me in Denmark? What, my young lady and mistress! By'r lady, your ladyship is nearer to heaven than when I saw you last, by the   375
altitude of a chopine.° Pray God, your voice, like a piece of uncurrent° gold, be not cracked within the ring.° Masters, you are all welcome. We'll e'en to 't like French falconers, fly at any thing we see: we'll have a speech straight: come, give us a taste of your quality; come, a passionate speech.

FIRST PLAYER: What speech, my good lord?   380

HAMLET: I heard thee speak me a speech once, but it was never acted; or, if it was, not above once; for the play, I remember, pleased not the million; 'twas caviary to the general:° but it was — as I received it, and others, whose judgements in such matters cried in the top of° mine — an excellent play, well digested in the scenes, set down with as much modesty as cunning.° I remem-   385
ber, one said there were no sallets° in the lines to make the matter savoury, nor no matter in the phrase that might indict° the author of affectation; but called it an honest method, as wholesome as sweet, and by very much more handsome than fine.° One speech in 't I chiefly loved: 'twas Æneas' tale to Dido;° and thereabout of it especially, where he speaks of Priam's slaughter: if   390
it live in your memory, begin at this line: let me see, let me see —
"The rugged Pyrrhus,° like th' Hyrcanian beast,"° —
'tis not so: — it begins with Pyrrhus: —
"The rugged Pyrrhus, he whose sable arms,
Black as his purpose, did the night resemble   395
When he lay couched in the ominous horse,°
Hath now this dread and black complexion smear'd
With heraldry more dismal; head to foot
Now is he total gules;° horridly trick'd°
With blood of fathers, mothers, daughters, sons,   400
Bak'd and impasted° with the parching streets,
That lend a tyrannous and a damned light
To their lord's murder: roasted in wrath and fire,

---

373 valanced: Fringed (with a beard).   **376 chopine:** Kind of shoe raised by the thickness of the heel; worn in Italy, particularly at Venice;   **uncurrent:** Not passable as lawful coinage. **377 cracked within the ring:** In the center of coins were rings enclosing the sovereign's head; if the coin was cracked within this ring, it was unfit for currency.   **383 caviary to the general:** Not relished by the multitude.   **384 cried in the top of:** Spoke with greater authority than. **385 cunning:** Skill.   **386 sallets:** Salads: here, spicy improprieties.   **387 indict:** Convict. **388–389 as wholesome . . . fine:** Its beauty was not that of elaborate ornament, but that of order and proportion.   **389–390 Æneas' tale to Dido:** The lines recited by the player are imitated from Marlowe and Nashe's *Dido Queen of Carthage* (2.1.214 ff.). They are written in such a way that the conventionality of the play within a play is raised above that of ordinary drama. **392 Pyrrhus:** A Greek hero in the Trojan War;   **Hyrcanian beast:** The tiger; see Virgil, *Aeneid,* 4.266.   **396 ominous horse:** Trojan horse.   **399 gules:** Red, a heraldic term; **trick'd:** Spotted, smeared.   **401 impasted:** Made into a paste.

> And thus o'er-sized° with coagulate gore,
> With eyes like carbuncles, the hellish Pyrrhus   405
> Old grandsire Priam seeks."
> So, proceed you.
POLONIUS: 'Fore God, my lord, well spoken, with good accent and good discre-
> tion.
FIRST PLAYER: "Anon he finds him   410
> Striking too short at Greeks; his antique sword,
> Rebellious to his arm, lies where it falls,
> Repugnant° to command: unequal match'd,
> Pyrrhus at Priam drives; in rage strikes wide;
> But with the whiff and wind of his fell sword   415
> Th' unnerved father falls. Then senseless Ilium,°
> Seeming to feel this blow, with flaming top
> Stoops to his base, and with a hideous crash
> Takes prisoner Pyrrhus' ear: for, lo! his sword
> Which was declining on the milky head   420
> Of reverend Priam, seem'd i' th' air to stick:
> So, as a painted tyrant,° Pyrrhus stood,
> And like a neutral to his will and matter,°
> Did nothing.
> But, as we often see, against° some storm,   425
> A silence in the heavens, the rack° stand still,
> The bold winds speechless and the orb below
> As hush as death, anon the dreadful thunder
> Doth rend the region,° so, after Pyrrhus' pause,
> Aroused vengeance sets him new a-work;   430
> And never did the Cyclops' hammers fall
> On Mars's armour forg'd for proof eterne°
> With less remorse than Pyrrhus' bleeding sword
> Now falls on Priam.
> Out, out, thou strumpet, Fortune! All you gods,   435
> In general synod,° take away her power;
> Break all the spokes and fellies° from her wheel,
> And bowl the round nave° down the hill of heaven,
> As low as to the fiends!"
POLONIUS: This is too long.   440
HAMLET: It shall to the barber's, with your beard. Prithee, say on: he's for a jig°
> or a tale of bawdry,° or he sleeps: say on: come to Hecuba.°
FIRST PLAYER: "But who, ah woe! had seen the mobled° queen — "

---

404 **o'er-sized:** Covered as with size or glue.   413 **Repugnant:** Disobedient.   416 **Then senseless Ilium:** Insensate Troy.   422 **painted tyrant:** Tyrant in a picture.   423 **matter:** Task.   425
against: Before.   426 **rack:** Mass of clouds.   429 **region:** Assembly.   432 **proof eterne:** External resistance to assault.   436 **synod:** Assembly.   437 **fellies:** Pieces of wood forming the rim of
a wheel.   438 **nave:** Hub.   441 **jig:** Comic performance given at the end or in an interval of a
play.   442 **bawdry:** Indecency;   **Hecuba:** Wife of Priam, king of Troy.   443 **mobled:** Muffled.

HAMLET: "The mobled queen?"

POLONIUS: That's good; "mobled queen" is good.   445

FIRST PLAYER: "Run barefoot up and down, threat'ning the flames
With bisson rheum;° a clout° upon that head
Where late the diadem stood, and for a robe,
About her lank and all o'er-teemed° loins,
A blanket, in the alarm of fear caught up;   450
Who this had seen, with tongue in venom steep'd,
'Gainst Fortune's state would treason have pronounc'd:°
But if the gods themselves did see her then
When she saw Pyrrhus make malicious sport
In mincing with his sword her husband's limbs,   455
The instant burst of clamour that she made,
Unless things mortal move them not at all,
Would have made milch° the burning eyes of heaven,
And passion in the gods."

POLONIUS: Look, whe'r he has not turned° his colour and has tears in 's eyes.   460
Prithee, no more.

HAMLET: 'Tis well; I'll have thee speak out the rest soon. Good my lord, will you
see the players well bestowed? Do you hear, let them be well used; for they
are the abstract° and brief chronicles of the time: after your death you were
better have a bad epitaph than their ill report while you live.   465

POLONIUS: My lord, I will use them according to their desert.

HAMLET: God's bodykins,° man, much better: use every man after his desert,
and who shall 'scape whipping? Use them after your own honour and dignity: the less they deserve, the more merit is in your bounty. Take them in.

POLONIUS: Come, sirs.   470

HAMLET: Follow him, friends: we'll hear a play tomorrow.   *[Aside to First Player.]*
Dost thou hear me, old friend; can you play the Murder of Gonzago?

FIRST PLAYER: Ay, my lord.

HAMLET: We'll ha 't to-morrow night. You could, for a need, study a speech of
some dozen or sixteen lines,° which I would set down and insert in 't, could   475
you not?

FIRST PLAYER: Ay, my lord.

HAMLET: Very well. Follow that lord; and look you mock him not. — My good
friends, I'll leave you till night: you are welcome to Elsinore.

                                          Exeunt Polonius and Players.

ROSENCRANTZ: Good my lord!   *Exeunt [Rosencrantz and Guildenstern.]*   480

HAMLET: Ay, so, God bye to you. — Now I am alone.
O, what a rogue and peasant° slave am I!

---

447 bisson rheum: Blinding tears;   **clout:** Piece of cloth.   **449 o'er-teemed:** Worn out with
bearing children.   **452 pronounc'd:** Proclaimed.   **458 milch:** Moist with tears.   **460 turned:**
Changed.   **464 abstract:** Summary account.   **467 bodykins:** Diminutive form of the oath
"by God's body."   **475 dozen or sixteen lines:** Critics have amused themselves by trying to
locate Hamlet's lines. Lucianus's speech 3.2.222–227 is the best guess.   **482 peasant:** Base.

Is it not monstrous that this player here,
But in a fiction, in a dream of passion,
Could force his soul so to his own conceit   485
That from her working all his visage wann'd,°
Tears in his eyes, distraction in 's aspect,
A broken voice, and his whole function suiting
With forms to his conceit?° and all for nothing!
For Hecuba!   490
What's Hecuba to him, or he to Hecuba,
That he should weep for her? What would he do,
Had he the motive and the cue for passion
That I have? He would drown the stage with tears
And cleave the general ear with horrid speech,   495
Make mad the guilty and appall the free,
Confound the ignorant, and amaze indeed
The very faculties of eyes and ears.
Yet I,
A dull and muddy-mettled° rascal, peak,°   500
Like John-a-dreams,° unpregnant of° my cause,
And can say nothing; no, not for a king,
Upon whose property° and most dear life
A damn'd defeat was made. Am I a coward?
Who calls me villain? breaks my pate across?   505
Plucks off my beard, and blows it in my face?
Tweaks me by the nose? gives me the lie i' th' throat,
As deep as to the lungs? who does me this?
Ha!
'Swounds, I should take it: for it cannot be   510
But I am pigeon-liver'd° and lack gall
To make oppression bitter, or ere this
I should have fatted all the region kites°
With this slave's offal: bloody, bawdy villain!
Remorseless, treacherous, lecherous, kindless° villain!   515
O, vengeance!
Why, what an ass am I! This is most brave,
That I, the son of a dear father murder'd,
Prompted to my revenge by heaven and hell,
Must, like a whore, unpack my heart with words,   520

---

486 **wann'd:** Grew pale.   488–489 **his whole . . . conceit:** His whole being responded
with forms to suit his thought.   500 **muddy-mettled:** Dull-spirited;   **peak:** Mope, pine.
501 **John-a-dreams:** An expression occurring elsewhere in Elizabethan literature to indicate a
dreamer;   **unpregnant of:** Not quickened by.   503 **property:** Proprietorship (of crown and
life).   511 **pigeon-liver'd:** The pigeon was supposed to secrete no gall; if Hamlet, so he says,
had had gall, he would have felt the bitterness of oppression, and avenged it.   513 **region
kites:** Kites of the air.   515 **kindless:** Unnatural.

And fall a-cursing, like a very drab,°
A stallion!°
Fie upon 't! foh! About,° my brains! Hum, I have heard
That guilty creatures sitting at a play
Have by the very cunning of the scene   525
Been struck so to the soul that presently
They have proclaim'd their malefactions;
For murder, though it have no tongue, will speak
With most miraculous organ. I'll have these players
Play something like the murder of my father   530
Before mine uncle: I'll observe his looks:
I'll tent° him to the quick: if 'a do blench,°
I know my course. The spirit that I have seen
May be the devil:° and the devil hath power
T' assume a pleasing shape; yea, and perhaps   535
Out of my weakness and my melancholy,
As he is very potent with such spirits,°
Abuses me to damn me: I'll have grounds
More relative° than this:° the play's the thing
Wherein I'll catch the conscience of the king.   *Exit.*   540

[ACT 3, Scene 1]

[A room in the castle.]
Enter King, Queen, Polonius, Ophelia, Rosencrantz, Guildenstern, Lords.
KING: And can you, by no drift of conference,°
      Get from him why he puts on this confusion,
      Grating so harshly all his days of quiet
      With turbulent and dangerous lunacy?
ROSENCRANTZ: He does confess he feels himself distracted;   5
      But from what cause 'a will by no means speak.
GUILDENSTERN: Nor do we find him forward° to be sounded,
      But, with a crafty madness, keeps aloof,
      When we would bring him on to some confession
      Of his true state.
QUEEN: Did he receive you well?   10
ROSENCRANTZ: Most like a gentleman.
GUILDENSTERN: But with much forcing of his disposition.°

---

521 **drab:** Prostitute.   522 **stallion:** Prostitute (male or female).   523 **About:** About it,
or turn thou right about.   532 **tent:** Probe;   **blench:** Quail, flinch.   534 **May be the
devil:** Hamlet's suspicion is properly grounded in the belief of the time.   537 **spirits:** Humors.
539 **relative:** Closely related, definite;   **this:** I.e., the ghost's story.   **ACT 3, SCENE 1. 1 drift
of conference:** Device of conversation.   7 **forward:** Willing.   12 **forcing of his disposition:**
I.e., against his will.

ROSENCRANTZ: Niggard of question;° but, of our demands,
　　Most free in his reply.
QUEEN: Did you assay° him
　　To any pastime?   15
ROSENCRANTZ: Madam, it so fell out, that certain players
　　We o'er-raught° on the way: of these we told him;
　　And there did seem in him a kind of joy
　　To hear of it: they are here about the court,
　　And, as I think, they have already order   20
　　This night to play before him.
POLONIUS: 'Tis most true:
　　And he beseech'd me to entreat your majesties
　　To hear and see the matter.
KING: With all my heart; and it doth much content me
　　To hear him so inclin'd.   25
　　Good gentlemen, give him a further edge,°
　　And drive his purpose into these delights.
ROSENCRANTZ: We shall, my lord.   *Exeunt Rosencrantz and Guildenstern.*
KING: Sweet Gertrude, leave us too;
　　For we have closely° sent for Hamlet hither,
　　That he, as 'twere by accident, may here   30
　　Affront° Ophelia:
　　Her father and myself, lawful espials,°
　　Will so bestow ourselves that, seeing, unseen,
　　We may of their encounter frankly judge,
　　And gather by him, as he is behav'd,   35
　　If 't be th' affliction of his love or no
　　That thus he suffers for.
QUEEN: I shall obey you.
　　And for your part, Ophelia, I do wish
　　That your good beauties be the happy cause
　　Of Hamlet's wildness:° so shall I hope your virtues   40
　　Will bring him to his wonted way again,
　　To both your honours.
OPHELIA: Madam, I wish it may.   *[Exit Queen.]*
POLONIUS: Ophelia, walk you here. Gracious,° so please you,
　　We will bestow ourselves. *[To Ophelia.]* Read on this book;
　　That show of such an exercise° may colour°   45
　　Your loneliness. We are oft to blame in this, —
　　'Tis too much prov'd — that with devotion's visage

---

13 **Niggard of question**: Sparing of conversation.　14 **assay**: Try to win.　17 **o'er-raught**: Overtook.　26 **edge**: Incitement.　29 **closely**: Secretly.　31 **Affront**: Confront.　32 **lawful espials**: Legitimate spies.　40 **wildness**: Madness.　43 **Gracious**: Your grace (addressed to the king).　45 **exercise**: Act of devotion (the book she reads is one of devotion);　**colour**: Give a plausible appearance to.

And pious action we do sugar o'er
The devil himself.
KING: *[aside]* O, 'tis too true!
How smart a lash that speech doth give my conscience!   50
The harlot's cheek, beautied with plast'ring art,
Is not more ugly to° the thing° that helps it
Than is my deed to my most painted word:
O heavy burthen!
POLONIUS: I hear him coming: let's withdraw, my lord.   55

[Exeunt King and Polonius.]

Enter Hamlet.

HAMLET: To be, or not to be: that is the question:
Whether 'tis nobler in the mind to suffer
The slings and arrows of outrageous fortune,
Or to take arms against a sea° of troubles,
And by opposing end them? To die: to sleep;   60
No more; and by a sleep to say we end
The heart-ache and the thousand natural shocks
That flesh is heir to, 'tis a consummation
Devoutly to be wish'd. To die, to sleep;
To sleep: perchance to dream: ay, there's the rub;   65
For in that sleep of death what dreams may come
When we have shuffled° off this mortal coil,°
Must give us pause: there's the respect°
That makes calamity of so long life;°
For who would bear the whips and scorns of time,°   70
Th' oppressor's wrong, the proud man's contumely,
The pangs of despis'd° love, the law's delay,
The insolence of office° and the spurns°
That patient merit of th' unworthy takes,
When he himself might his quietus° make   75
With a bare bodkin?° who would fardels° bear,
To grunt and sweat under a weary life,
But that the dread of something after death,
The undiscover'd country from whose bourn°
No traveller returns, puzzles the will   80
And makes us rather bear those ills we have

---

52 to: Compared to;   **thing:** I.e., the cosmetic.   **59 sea:** The mixed metaphor of this speech has often been commented on; a later emendation *siege* has sometimes been spoken on the stage.   **67 shuffled:** Sloughed, cast;   **coil:** Usually means "turmoil"; here, possibly "body" (conceived of as wound about the soul like rope); *clay, soil, veil,* have been suggested as emendations.   **68 respect:** Consideration.   **69 of . . . life:** So long-lived.   **70 time:** The world.   **72 despis'd:** Rejected.   **73 office:** Office-holders;   **spurns:** Insults.   **75 quietus:** Acquittance; here, death.   **76 bare bodkin:** Mere dagger; *bare* is sometimes understood as "unsheathed";   **fardels:** Burdens.   **79 bourn:** Boundary.

Than fly to others that we know not of?
Thus conscience° does make cowards of us all;
And thus the native hue° of resolution
Is sicklied o'er° with the pale cast° of thought,   85
And enterprises of great pitch° and moment°
With this regard° their currents° turn awry,
And lose the name of action — Soft you now!
The fair Ophelia! Nymph, in thy orisons°
Be all my sins rememb'red.

OPHELIA: Good my lord,   90
How does your honour for this many a day?

HAMLET: I humbly thank you; well, well, well.

OPHELIA: My lord, I have remembrances of yours,
That I have longed long to re-deliver;
I pray you, now receive them.

HAMLET: No, not I;   95
I never gave you aught.

OPHELIA: My honour'd lord, you know right well you did;
And, with them, words of so sweet breath compos'd
As made the things more rich: their perfume lost,
Take these again; for to the noble mind   100
Rich gifts wax poor when givers prove unkind.
There, my lord.

HAMLET: Ha, ha! are you honest?°

OPHELIA: My lord?

HAMLET: Are you fair?   105

OPHELIA: What means your lordship?

HAMLET: That if you be honest and fair, your honesty° should admit no discourse to° your beauty.

OPHELIA: Could beauty, my lord, have better commerce° than with honesty?

HAMLET: Ay, truly; for the power of beauty will sooner transform honesty from   110
what it is to a bawd than the force of honesty can translate beauty into his
likeness: this was sometime a paradox, but now the time° gives it proof. I did
love you once.

OPHELIA: Indeed, my lord, you made me believe so.

HAMLET: You should not have believed me; for virtue cannot so inoculate° our   115
old stock but we shall relish of it:° I loved you not.

---

83 conscience: Probably, inhibition by the faculty of reason restraining the will from doing
wrong.   **84 native hue:** Natural color; metaphor derived from the color of the face.   **85 sicklied o'er:** Given a sickly tinge;   **cast:** Shade of color.   **86 pitch:** Height (as of a falcon's flight);
moment: Importance.   **87 regard:** Respect, consideration;   **currents:** Courses.   **89 orisons:**
Prayers.   **103–108 are you honest . . . beauty:** *Honest* meaning "truthful" and "chaste" and
fair meaning "just, honorable" (line 105) and "beautiful" (line 107) are not mere quibbles; the
speech has the irony of a *double entendre*.   **107 your honesty:** Your chastity.   **107–108 discourse to:** Familiar intercourse with.   **109 commerce:** Intercourse.   **112 the time:** The present age.   **115 inoculate:** Graft (metaphorical).   **116 but . . . it:** I.e., that we do not still
have about us a taste of the old stock; i.e., retain our sinfulness.

OPHELIA: I was the more deceived.

HAMLET: Get thee to a nunnery: why wouldst thou be a breeder of sinners? I am
myself indifferent honest;° but yet I could accuse me of such things that it
were better my mother had not borne me: I am very proud, revengeful,   120
ambitious, with more offences at my beck° than I have thoughts to put them
in, imagination to give them shape, or time to act them in. What should
such fellows as I do crawling between earth and heaven? We are arrant
knaves, all; believe none of us. Go thy ways to a nunnery. Where's your
father?   125

OPHELIA: At home, my lord.

HAMLET: Let the doors be shut upon him, that he may play the fool no where
but in 's own house. Farewell.

OPHELIA: O, help him, you sweet heavens!

HAMLET: If thou dost marry, I'll give thee this plague for thy dowry: be thou as   130
chaste as ice, as pure as snow, thou shalt not escape calumny. Get thee to a
nunnery, go: farewell. Or, if thou wilt needs marry, marry a fool; for wise
men know well enough what monsters° you make of them. To a nunnery, go,
and quickly too. Farewell.

OPHELIA: O heavenly powers, restore him!   135

HAMLET: I have heard of your° paintings too, well enough; God hath given you
one face, and you make yourselves another: you jig,° you amble, and you
lisp; you nick-name God's creatures, and make your wantonness your ignorance.° Go to, I'll no more on 't; it hath made me mad. I say, we will have no
moe marriage: those that are married already, all but one,° shall live; the rest   140
shall keep as they are. To a nunnery, go.   *Exit.*

OPHELIA: O, what a noble mind is here o'er-thrown!
The courtier's, soldier's, scholar's, eye, tongue, sword;
Th' expectancy and rose° of the fair state,
The glass of fashion and the mould of form,°   145
Th' observ'd of all observers,° quite, quite down!
And I, of ladies most deject and wretched,
That suck'd the honey of his music vows,
Now see that noble and most sovereign reason,
Like sweet bells jangled, out of time and harsh;   150
That unmatch'd form and feature of blown° youth
Blasted with ecstasy:° O, woe is me,
T' have seen what I have seen, see what I see!

---

119 **indifferent honest:** Moderately virtuous.   121 **beck:** Command.   133 **monsters:** An allusion to the horns of a cuckold.   136 **your:** Indefinite use.   137 **jig:** Move with jerky motion;
probably allusion to the *jig*, or song and dance, of the current stage.   138–139 **make . . . ignorance:** I.e., excuse your wantonness on the ground of your ignorance.   140 **one:** I.e., the king.
144 **expectancy and rose:** Source of hope.   145 **The glass . . . form:** The mirror of fashion
and the pattern of courtly behavior.   146 **observ'd . . . observers:** I.e., the center of attention
in the court.   151 **blown:** Blooming.   152 **ecstasy:** Madness.

Enter King and Polonius.

KING: Love! his affections do not that way tend;
    Nor what he spake, though it lack'd form a little,   155
    Was not like madness. There's something in his soul,
    O'er which his melancholy sits on brood;
    And I do doubt° the hatch and the disclose°
    Will be some danger: which for to prevent,
    I have in quick determination   160
    Thus set it down: he shall with speed to England,
    For the demand of our neglected tribute:
    Haply the seas and countries different
    With variable° objects shall expel
    This something-settled° matter in his heart,   165
    Whereon his brains still beating puts him thus
    From fashion of himself.° What think you on 't?
POLONIUS: It shall do well: but yet do I believe
    The origin and commencement of his grief
    Sprung from neglected love. How now, Ophelia!   170
    You need not tell us what Lord Hamlet said;
    We heard it all. My lord, do as you please;
    But, if you hold it fit, after the play
    Let his queen mother all alone entreat him
    To show his grief: let her be round° with him;   175
    And I'll be plac'd, so please you, in the ear
    Of all their conference. If she find him not,
    To England send him, or confine him where
    Your wisdom best shall think.
KING: It shall be so: 180
    Madness in great ones must not unwatch'd go.   *Exeunt.*

[Scene 2]

[A hall in the castle.]
    Enter Hamlet and three of the Players.

HAMLET: Speak the speech, I pray you, as I pronounced it to you, trippingly on
    the tongue: but if you mouth it, as many of your° players do, I had as lief the
    town-crier spoke my lines. Nor do not saw the air too much with your hand,
    thus, but use all gently; for in the very torrent, tempest, and, as I may say,
    whirlwind of your passion, you must acquire and beget a temperance that   5
    may give it smoothness. O, it offends me to the soul to hear a robustious°
    periwig-pated° fellow tear a passion to tatters, to very rags, to split the ears of

---

158 doubt: Fear; **disclose:** Disclosure or revelation (by chipping of the shell). **164 variable:** Various. **165 something-settled:** Somewhat settled. **167 From . . . himself:** Out of his natural manner. **175 round:** Blunt. SCENE 2. **2 your:** Indefinite use. **6 robustious:** Violent, boisterous. **7 periwig-pated:** Wearing a wig.

the groundlings,° who for the most part are capable of° nothing but inexplic-
able° dumb-shows and noise: I would have such a fellow whipped for o'er-
doing Termagant;° it out-herods Herod:° pray you, avoid it.   10
FIRST PLAYER: I warrant your honour.
HAMLET: Be not too tame neither, but let your own discretion be your tutor: suit
the action to the word, the word to the action; with this special observance,
that you o'er-step not the modesty of nature: for any thing so overdone is
from the purpose of playing, whose end, both at the first and now, was and is,   15
to hold, as 't were, the mirror up to nature; to show virtue her own feature,
scorn her own image, and the very age and body of the time his form and
pressure.° Now this overdone, or come tardy off,° though it make the unskil-
ful laugh, cannot but make the judicious grieve; the censure of the which
one° must in your allowance o'erweigh a whole theatre of others. O, there be   20
players that I have seen play, and heard others praise, and that highly, not to
speak it profanely, that, neither having the accent of Christians nor the gait
of Christian, pagan, nor man, have so strutted and bellowed that I have
thought some of nature's journeymen° had made men and not made them
well, they imitated humanity so abominably.   25
FIRST PLAYER: I hope we have reformed that indifferently° with us, sir.
HAMLET: O, reform it altogether. And let those that play your clowns speak no
more than is set down for them; for there be of° them that will themselves
laugh, to set on some quantity of barren° spectators to laugh too; though, in
the mean time, some necessary question of the play be then to be consid-   30
ered: that's villanous, and shows a most pitiful ambition in the fool that uses
it. Go, make you ready.   *[Exeunt Players.]*

Enter Polonius, Guildenstern, and Rosencrantz.

How now, my lord! will the king hear this piece of work?
POLONIUS: And the queen too, and that presently.
HAMLET: Bid the players make haste.   *[Exit Polonius.]*   35
Will you two help to hasten them?
ROSENCRANTZ: ⎫
GUILDENSTERN: ⎭ We will, my lord.   *Exeunt they two.*
HAMLET: What ho! Horatio!

Enter Horatio.

HORATIO: Here, sweet lord, at your service.

---

8 **groundlings:** Those who stood in the yard of the theater;   **capable of:** Susceptible of being
influenced by.   8–9 **inexplicable:** Of no significance worth explaining.   10 **Termagant:** A
god of the Saracens; a character in the St. Nicholas play, where one of his worshipers, leaving
him in charge of goods, returns to find them stolen; whereupon he beats the god (or idol), which
howls vociferously;   **Herod:** Herod of Jewry; a character in *The Slaughter of the Innocents* and
other cycle plays. The part was played with great noise and fury.   18 **pressure:** Stamp,
impressed character;   **come tardy off:** Inadequately done.   19–20 **the censure . . . one:** The
judgment of even one of whom.   24 **journeymen:** Laborers not yet masters in their trade.
26 **indifferently:** Fairly, tolerably.   28 **of:** I.e., some among them.   29 **barren:** I.e., of wit.

HAMLET: Horatio, thou art e'en as just° a man
    As e'er my conversation cop'd withal.   40
HORATIO: O, my dear lord, —
HAMLET: Nay, do not think I flatter;
    For what advancement may I hope from thee
    That no revenue hast but thy good spirits,
    To feed and clothe thee? Why should the poor be flatter'd?
    No, let the candied tongue lick absurd pomp,   45
    And crook the pregnant° hinges of the knee
    Where thrift° may follow fawning. Dost thou hear?
    Since my dear soul was mistress of her choice
    And could of men distinguish her election,
    S' hath seal'd thee for herself; for thou hast been   50
    As one, in suff'ring all, that suffers nothing,
    A man that fortune's buffets and rewards
    Hast ta'en with equal thanks: and blest are those
    Whose blood and judgement are so well commeddled,
    That they are not a pipe for fortune's finger   55
    To sound what stop° she please. Give me that man
    That is not passion's slave, and I will wear him
    In my heart's core, ay, in my heart of heart,
    As I do thee. — Something too much of this. —
    There is a play to-night before the king;   60
    One scene of it comes near the circumstance
    Which I have told thee of my father's death:
    I prithee, when thou seest that act afoot,
    Even with the very comment of thy soul°
    Observe my uncle: if his occulted° guilt   65
    Do not itself unkennel in one speech,
    It is a damned° ghost that we have seen,
    And my imaginations are as foul
    As Vulcan's stithy.° Give him heedful note;
    For I mine eyes will rivet to his face,   70
    And after we will both our judgements join
    In censure of his seeming.°
HORATIO: Well, my lord:
    If 'a steal aught the whilst this play is playing,
    And 'scape detecting, I will pay the theft.

Enter trumpets and kettledrums, King, Queen, Polonius, Ophelia, [Rosencrantz, Guildenstern, and others].

---

39 **just:** Honest, honorable.   46 **pregnant:** Pliant.   47 **thrift:** Profit.   56 **stop:** Hole in a wind instrument for controlling the sound.   64 **very . . . soul:** Inward and sagacious criticism. 65 **occulted:** Hidden.   67 **damned:** In league with Satan.   69 **stithy:** Smithy, place of *stiths* (anvils).   72 **censure . . . seeming:** Judgment of his appearance or behavior.

HAMLET: They are coming to the play; I must be idle:° Get you a place.   75
KING: How fares our cousin Hamlet?
HAMLET: Excellent, i' faith; of the chameleon's dish:° I eat the air, promise-crammed: you cannot feed capons so.
KING: I have nothing with° this answer, Hamlet; these words are not mine.°
HAMLET: No, nor mine now. *[To Polonius.]* My lord, you played once i' the uni-   80
versity, you say?
POLONIUS: That did I, my lord; and was accounted a good actor.
HAMLET: What did you enact?
POLONIUS: I did enact Julius Cæsar: I was killed i' the Capitol; Brutus killed me.
HAMLET: It was a brute part of him to kill so capital a calf there. Be the players   85
ready?
ROSENCRANTZ: Ay, my lord; they stay upon your patience.
QUEEN: Come hither, my dear Hamlet, sit by me.
HAMLET: No, good mother, here's metal more attractive.
POLONIUS *[to the king]*:   O, ho! do you mark that?   90
HAMLET: Lady, shall I lie in your lap?   *[Lying down at Ophelia's feet.]*
OPHELIA: No, my lord.
HAMLET: I mean, my head upon your lap?
OPHELIA: Ay, my lord.
HAMLET: Do you think I meant country° matters?   95
OPHELIA: I think nothing, my lord.
HAMLET: That's a fair thought to lie between maids' legs.
OPHELIA: What is, my lord?
HAMLET: Nothing.
OPHELIA: You are merry, my lord.   100
HAMLET: Who, I?
OPHELIA: Ay, my lord.
HAMLET: O God, your only° jig-maker.° What should a man do but be merry?
for, look you, how cheerfully my mother looks, and my father died within's
two hours.   105
OPHELIA: Nay, 'tis twice two months, my lord.
HAMLET: So long? Nay then, let the devil wear black, for I'll have a suit of
sables.° O heavens! die two months ago, and not forgotten yet? Then there's
hope a great man's memory may outlive his life half a year: but, by 'r lady, 'a
must build churches, then; or else shall 'a suffer not thinking on,° with the   110
hobbyhorse, whose epitaph is "For, O, for, O, the hobbyhorse is forgot."°

The trumpets sound. Dumb show follows.

75 idle: Crazy, or not attending to anything serious.   **77 chameleon's dish:** Chameleons were supposed to feed on air. (Hamlet deliberately misinterprets the king's "fares" as "feeds.")
79 have ... with: Make nothing of;   **are not mine:** Do not respond to what I ask.   **95 country:** With a bawdy pun.   **103 your only:** Only your;   **jig-maker:** Composer of jigs (song and dance).   **107–108 suit of sables:** Garments trimmed with the fur of the sable, with a quibble on *sable* meaning "black."   **110 suffer ... on:** Undergo oblivion.   **111 "For ... forgot":** Verse of a song occurring also in *Love's Labour's Lost*, 3.1.30. The hobbyhorse was a character in the Morris Dance.

Enter a King and a Queen [very lovingly]; the Queen embracing him, and he her. [She kneels, and makes show of protestation unto him.] He takes her up, and declines his head upon her neck: he lies him down upon a bank of flowers: she, seeing him asleep, leaves him. Anon comes in another man, takes off his crown, kisses it, pours poison in the sleeper's ears, and leaves him. The Queen returns; finds the King dead, makes passionate action. The Poisoner, with some three or four come in again, seem to condole with her. The dead body is carried away. The Poisoner woos the Queen with gifts: she seems harsh awhile, but in the end accepts love. [Exeunt.]

OPHELIA: What means this, my lord?

HAMLET: Marry, this is miching mallecho;° it means mischief.

OPHELIA: Belike this show imports the argument of the play.

Enter Prologue.

HAMLET: We shall know by this fellow: the players cannot keep counsel; they'll   115
tell all.

OPHELIA: Will 'a tell us what this show meant?

HAMLET: Ay, or any show that you'll show him: be not you ashamed to show,
he'll not shame to tell you what it means.

OPHELIA: You are naught, you are naught:° I'll mark the play.   120

PROLOGUE: For us, and for our tragedy,
Here stooping° to your clemency,
We beg your hearing patiently.   *[Exit.]*

HAMLET: Is this a prologue, or the posy° of a ring?

OPHELIA: 'Tis brief, my lord.   125

HAMLET: As woman's love.

Enter [two Players as] King and Queen.

PLAYER KING: Full thirty times hath Phoebus' cart gone round
Neptune's salt wash° and Tellus'° orbed ground,
And thirty dozen moons with borrowed° sheen
About the world have times twelve thirties been,   130
Since love our hearts and Hymen° did our hands
Unite commutual° in most sacred bands.

PLAYER QUEEN: So many journeys may the sun and moon
Make us again count o'er ere love be done!
But, woe is me, you are so sick of late,   135
So far from cheer and from your former state,
That I distrust° you. Yet, though I distrust,
Discomfort you, my lord, it nothing must:
For women's fear and love holds quantity;°

---

113 miching mallecho: Sneaking mischief.   **120 naught:** Indecent.   **122 stooping:** Bowing.   **124 posy:** Motto.   **128 salt wash:** The sea;   **Tellus:** Goddess of the earth (*orbed ground*).   **129 borrowed:** I.e., reflected.   **131 Hymen:** God of matrimony.   **132 commutual:** Mutually.   **137 distrust:** Am anxious about.   **139 holds quantity:** Keeps proportion between.

In neither aught, or in extremity.   140
Now, what my love is, proof hath made you know;
And as my love is siz'd, my fear is so:
Where love is great, the littlest doubts are fear;
Where little fears grow great, great love grows there.

PLAYER KING: 'Faith, I must leave thee, love, and shortly too;   145
My operant° powers their functions leave° to do:
And thou shalt live in this fair world behind,
Honour'd, belov'd; and haply one as kind
For husband shalt thou —

PLAYER QUEEN: O, confound the rest!
Such love must needs be treason in my breast: 150
In second husband let me be accurst!
None wed the second but who kill'd the first.

HAMLET *(aside):*   Wormwood, wormwood.

PLAYER QUEEN: The instances that second marriage move
Are base respects of thrift, but none of love: 155
A second time I kill my husband dead,
When second husband kisses me in bed.

PLAYER KING: I do believe you think what now you speak;
But what we do determine oft we break.
Purpose is but the slave to memory,   160
Of violent birth, but poor validity:
Which now, like fruit unripe, sticks on the tree;
But fall, unshaken, when they mellow be.
Most necessary 'tis that we forget
To pay ourselves what to ourselves is debt: 165
What to ourselves in passion we propose,
The passion ending, doth the purpose lose.
The violence of either grief or joy
Their own enactures° with themselves destroy:
Where joy most revels, grief doth most lament;   170
Grief joys, joy grieves, on slender accident.
This world is not for aye,° nor 'tis not strange
That even our loves should with our fortunes change;
For 'tis a question left us yet to prove,
Whether love lead fortune, or else fortune love.   175
The great man down, you mark his favourite flies;
The poor advanc'd makes friends of enemies.
And hitherto doth love on fortune tend;
For who° not needs shall never lack a friend,
And who in want a hollow friend doth try,   180

---

146 operant: Active; **leave:** Cease.   **169 enactures:** Fulfillments.   **172 aye:** Ever.   **179 who:**
Whoever.

Directly seasons° him his enemy.
But, orderly to end where I begun,
Our wills and fates do so contrary run
That our devices still are overthrown;
Our thoughts are ours, their ends° none of our own: 185
So think thou wilt no second husband wed;
But die thy thoughts when thy first lord is dead.

PLAYER QUEEN: Nor earth to me give food, nor heaven light!
 Sport and repose lock from me day and night!
 To desperation turn my trust and hope!   190
 An anchor's° cheer° in prison be my scope!
 Each opposite° that blanks° the face of joy
 Meet what I would have well and it destroy!
 Both here and hence pursue me lasting strife,
 If, once a widow, ever I be wife!   195

HAMLET: If she should break it now!

PLAYER KING: 'Tis deeply sworn. Sweet, leave me here awhile;
 My spirits grow dull, and fain I would beguile
 The tedious day with sleep.   *[Sleeps.]*

PLAYER QUEEN: Sleep rock thy brain;
 And never come mischance between us twain! *Exit.* 200

HAMLET: Madam, how like you this play?

QUEEN: The lady doth protest too much, methinks.

HAMLET: O, but she'll keep her word.

KING: Have you heard the argument? Is there no offence in 't?

HAMLET: No, no, they do but jest, poison in jest; no offence i' the world. 205

KING: What do you call the play?

HAMLET: The Mouse-trap. Marry, how? Tropically.° This play is the image of a
 murder done in Vienna: Gonzago° is the duke's name; his wife, Baptista:
 you shall see anon; 't is a knavish piece of work: but what o' that? your
 majesty and we that have free souls, it touches us not: let the galled jade° 210
 winch,° our withers° are unwrung.°

Enter Lucianus.

 This is one Lucianus, nephew to the king.

OPHELIA: You are as good as a chorus,° my lord.

---

181 seasons: Matures, ripens. **185 ends:** Results. **191 An anchor's:** An anchorite's;
cheer: Fare; sometimes printed as *chair.* **192 opposite:** Adverse thing; **blanks:** Causes to
blanch or grow pale. **207 Tropically:** Figuratively, *tropically* suggests a pun on *trap* in *Mouse-trap* (line 207). **208 Gonzago:** In 1538 Luigi Gonzago murdered the Duke of Urbano by
pouring poisoned lotion in his ears. **210 galled jade:** Horse whose hide is rubbed by saddle
or harness. **211 winch:** Wince; **withers:** The part between the horse's shoulder blades;
unwrung: Not wrung or twisted. **213 chorus:** In many Elizabethan plays the action was
explained by an actor known as the "chorus"; at a puppet show the actor who explained the
action was known as an "interpreter," as indicated by the lines following.

HAMLET: I could interpret between you and your love, if I could see the puppets
     dallying.°   215
OPHELIA: You are keen, my lord, you are keen.
HAMLET: It would cost you a groaning to take off my edge.
OPHELIA: Still better, and worse.°
HAMLET: So you mistake° your husbands. Begin, murderer; pox,° leave thy
     damnable faces, and begin. Come: the croaking raven doth bellow for   220
     revenge.
LUCIANUS: Thoughts black, hands apt, drugs fit, and time agreeing;
     Confederate° season, else no creature seeing;
     Thou mixture rank, of midnight weeds collected,
     With Hecate's° ban° thrice blasted, thrice infected,   225
     Thy natural magic and dire property,
     On wholesome life usurp immediately.

                    [Pours the poison into the sleeper's ears.]

HAMLET: 'A poisons him i' the garden for his estate. His name's Gonzago: the
     story is extant, and written in very choice Italian: you shall see anon how the
     murderer gets the love of Gonzago's wife.   230
OPHELIA: The king rises.
HAMLET: What, frighted with false fire!°
QUEEN: How fares my lord?
POLONIUS: Give o'er the play.
KING: Give me some light: away!   235
POLONIUS: Lights, lights, lights!   *Exeunt all but Hamlet and Horatio.*
HAMLET: Why, let the strucken deer go weep,
     The hart ungalled play;
     For some must watch, while some must sleep:
     Thus runs the world away.°   240
     Would not this,° sir, and a forest of feathers° — if the rest of my fortunes turn
     Turk with° me — with two Provincial roses° on my razed° shoes, get me a
     fellowship in a cry° of players,° sir?
HORATIO: Half a share.°
HAMLET: A whole one, I.   245

---

215 dallying: With sexual suggestion, continued in *keen* (sexually aroused), *groaning*
(i.e., in pregnancy), and *edge* (i.e., sexual desire or impetuosity).   **218 Still . . . worse:** More
keen, less decorous.   **219 mistake:** Err in taking;   **pox:** An imprecation.   **223 Confederate:**
Conspiring (to assist the murderer).   **225 Hecate:** The goddess of witchcraft;   **ban:**
Curse.   **232 false fire:** Fireworks, or a blank discharge.   **237–240 Why . . . away:** Probably
from an old ballad, with allusion to the popular belief that a wounded deer retires to weep and
die. Cf. *As You Like It*, 2.1.66.   **241 this:** I.e., the play;   **feathers:** Allusion to the plumes
which Elizabethan actors were fond of wearing.   **241–242 turn Turk with:** Go back on;   **two
Provincial roses:** Rosettes of ribbon like the roses of Provins near Paris, or else the roses of
Provence;   **razed:** Cut, slashed (by way of ornament).   **243 cry:** Pack (as of hounds);   **fellowship . . . players:** Partnership in a theatrical company.   **244 Half a share:** Allusion to the
custom in dramatic companies of dividing the ownership into a number of shares among the
householders.

For thou dost know, O Damon dear,
   This realm dismantled° was
Of Jove himself; and now reigns here
   A very, very° — pajock.°

HORATIO: You might have rhymed.   250

HAMLET: O good Horatio, I'll take the ghost's word for a thousand pound. Didst
perceive?

HORATIO: Very well, my lord.

HAMLET: Upon the talk of the poisoning?

HORATIO: I did very well note him.   255

HAMLET: Ah, ha! Come, some music! come, the recorders!°
For if the king like not the comedy,
Why then, belike, he likes it not, perdy.°
Come, some music!

Enter Rosencrantz and Guildenstern.

GUILDENSTERN: Good my lord, vouchsafe me a word with you.   260

HAMLET: Sir, a whole history.

GUILDENSTERN: The king, sir, —

HAMLET: Ay, sir, what of him?

GUILDENSTERN: Is in his retirement marvellous distempered.

HAMLET: With drink, sir?   265

GUILDENSTERN: No, my lord, rather with choler.°

HAMLET: Your wisdom should show itself more richer to signify this to his doctor; for, for me to put him to his purgation would perhaps plunge him into
far more choler.

GUILDENSTERN: Good my lord, put your discourse into some frame° and start   270
not so wildly from my affair.

HAMLET: I am tame, sir: pronounce.

GUILDENSTERN: The queen, your mother, in most great affliction of spirit, hath
sent me to you.

HAMLET: You are welcome.   275

GUILDENSTERN: Nay, good my lord, this courtesy is not of the right breed. If it
shall please you to make me a wholesome° answer, I will do your mother's
commandment; if not, your pardon and my return shall be the end of my
business.

HAMLET: Sir, I cannot.   280

GUILDENSTERN: What, my lord?

HAMLET: Make you a wholesome answer; my wit's diseased: but, sir, such
answer as I can make, you shall command; or, rather, as you say, my mother:
therefore no more, but to the matter:° my mother, you say, —

---

247 dismantled: Stripped, divested. **246–249 For . . . very:** Probably from an old ballad having
to do with Damon and Pythias. **249 pajock:** Peacock (a bird with a bad reputation). Possibly the
word was *patchock*, diminutive of *patch*, clown. **256 recorders:** Wind instruments of the flute
kind. **258 perdy:** Corruption of *par dieu*. **266 choler:** Bilious disorder, with quibble on the
sense "anger." **270 frame:** Order. **277 wholesome:** Sensible. **284 matter:** Matter in hand.

ROSENCRANTZ: Then thus she says; your behaviour hath struck her into amaze-   285
ment and admiration.

HAMLET: O wonderful son, that can so 'stonish a mother! But is there no sequel
at the heels of this mother's admiration? Impart.

ROSENCRANTZ: She desires to speak with you in her closet, ere you go to bed.

HAMLET: We shall obey, were she ten times our mother. Have you any further   290
trade with us?

ROSENCRANTZ: My lord, you once did love me.

HAMLET: And do still, by these pickers and stealers.°

ROSENCRANTZ: Good my lord, what is your cause of distemper? you do, surely,
bar the door upon your own liberty, if you deny your griefs to your friend.   295

HAMLET: Sir, I lack advancement.

ROSENCRANTZ: How can that be, when you have the voice° of the king himself
for your succession in Denmark?

HAMLET: Ay, sir, but "While the grass grows,"° — the proverb is something
musty.   300

Enter the Players with recorders.

O, the recorders! let me see one. To withdraw° with you: — why do you go
about to recover the wind° of me, as if you would drive me into a toil?°

GUILDENSTERN: O, my lord, if my duty be too bold, my love is too unmannerly.°

HAMLET: I do not well understand that. Will you play upon this pipe?   305

GUILDENSTERN: My lord, I cannot.

HAMLET: I pray you.

GUILDENSTERN: Believe me, I cannot.

HAMLET: I beseech you.

GUILDENSTERN: I know no touch of it, my lord.   310

HAMLET: 'Tis as easy as lying: govern these ventages° with your fingers and
thumb, give it breath with your mouth, and it will discourse most eloquent
music. Look you, these are the stops.

GUILDENSTERN: But these cannot I command to any utterance of harmony; I
have not the skill.   315

HAMLET: Why, look you now, how unworthy a thing you make of me! You
would play upon me; you would seem to know my stops; you would pluck
out the heart of my mystery; you would sound me from my lowest note to the
top of my compass:° and there is much music, excellent voice, in this little
organ;° yet cannot you make it speak. 'Sblood, do you think I am easier to be   320

---

293 pickers and stealers: Hands, so called from the catechism "to keep my hands from picking
and stealing." **297 voice:** Support. **299 "While . . . grows":** The rest of the proverb is "the
silly horse starves." Hamlet may be destroyed while he is waiting for the succession to the kingdom. **301 withdraw:** Speak in private. **302 recover the wind:** Get to the windward side;
toil: Snare. **303–304 if . . . unmannerly:** If I am using an unmannerly boldness, it is my love
which occasions it. **311 ventages:** Stops of the recorders. **319 compass:** Range of voice.
320 organ: Musical instrument, i.e., the pipe.

played on than a pipe? Call me what instrument you will, though you can fret° me, you cannot play upon me.

Enter Polonius.

God bless you, sir!

POLONIUS: My lord, the queen would speak with you, and presently.

HAMLET: Do you see yonder cloud that 's almost in shape of a camel? 325

POLONIUS: By the mass, and 'tis like a camel, indeed.

HAMLET: Methinks it is like a weasel.

POLONIUS: It is backed like a weasel.

HAMLET: Or like a whale?

POLONIUS: Very like a whale. 330

HAMLET: Then I will come to my mother by and by. *[Aside.]* They fool me to the top of my bent.° — I will come by and by.°

POLONIUS: I will say so.   *[Exit.]*

HAMLET: By and by is easily said.

Leave me, friends.   *[Exeunt all but Hamlet.]* 335

'Tis now the very witching time° of night,

When churchyards yawn and hell itself breathes out

Contagion to this world: now could I drink hot blood,

And do such bitter business as the day

Would quake to look on. Soft! now to my mother. 340

O heart, lose not thy nature; let not ever

The soul of Nero° enter this firm bosom:

Let me be cruel, not unnatural:

I will speak daggers to her, but use none;

My tongue and soul in this be hypocrites; 345

How in my words somever she be shent,°

To give them seals° never, my soul, consent!   *Exit.*

[Scene 3]

[A room in the castle.]

Enter King, Rosencrantz, and Guildenstern.

KING: I like him not, nor stands it safe with us

To let his madness range. Therefore prepare you;

I your commission will forthwith dispatch,°

And he to England shall along with you:

The terms° of our estate° may not endure 5

Hazard so near us as doth hourly grow

---

322 **fret:** Quibble on meaning "irritate" and the piece of wood, gut, or metal which regulates the fingering.   332 **top of my bent:** Limit of endurance, i.e., extent to which a bow may be bent; **by and by:** Immediately.   336 **witching time:** I.e., time when spells are cast. 342 **Nero:** Murderer of his mother, Agrippina.   346 **shent:** Rebuked.   347 **give them seals:** Confirm with deeds.   SCENE 3.   3 **dispatch:** Prepare.   5 **terms:** Condition, circumstances; **estate:** State.

Out of his brows.°
GUILDENSTERN: We will ourselves provide:
Most holy and religious fear it is
To keep those many many bodies safe
That live and feed upon your majesty.   10
ROSENCRANTZ: The single and peculiar° life is bound,
With all the strength and armour of the mind,
To keep itself from noyance;° but much more
That spirit upon whose weal depend and rest
The lives of many. The cess° of majesty   15
Dies not alone; but, like a gulf,° doth draw
What's near it with it: it is a massy wheel,
Fix'd on the summit of the highest mount,
To whose huge spokes ten thousand lesser things
Are mortis'd and adjoin'd; which, when it falls,   20
Each small annexment, petty consequence,
Attends° the boist'rous ruin. Never alone
Did the king sigh, but with a general groan.
KING: Arm° you, I pray you, to this speedy voyage;
For we will fetters put about this fear,   25
Which now goes too free-footed.
ROSENCRANTZ: We will haste us.
             Exeunt Gentlemen [Rosencrantz and Guildenstern].

Enter Polonius.

POLONIUS: My lord, he's going to his mother's closet:
Behind the arras° I'll convey° myself,
To hear the process;° I'll warrant she'll tax him home:°
And, as you said, and wisely was it said,   30
'Tis meet that some more audience than a mother,
Since nature makes them partial, should o'erhear
The speech, of vantage.° Fare you well, my liege:
I'll call upon you ere you go to bed,
And tell you what I know.
KING: Thanks, dear my lord.   *Exit [Polonius].*   35
O, my offence is rank, it smells to heaven;
It hath the primal eldest curse° upon't,
A brother's murder. Pray can I not,
Though inclination be as sharp as will:°

---

7 **brows:** Effronteries.   11 **single and peculiar:** Individual and private.   13 **noyance:** Harm.
15 **cess:** Decease.   16 **gulf:** Whirlpool.   22 **Attends:** Participates in.   24 **Arm:** Prepare.
28 **arras:** Screen of tapestry placed around the walls of household apartments;   **convey:** Implication of secrecy, *convey* was often used to mean "steal."   29 **process:** Proceedings;   **tax him home:** Reprove him severely.   33 **of vantage:** From an advantageous place.   37 **primal eldest curse:** The curse of Cain, the first to kill his brother.   39 **sharp as will:** I.e., his desire is as strong as his determination.

My stronger guilt defeats my strong intent;   40
And, like a man to double business bound,
I stand in pause where I shall first begin,
And both neglect. What if this cursed hand
Were thicker than itself with brother's blood,
Is there not rain enough in the sweet heavens   45
To wash it white as snow? Whereto serves mercy
But to confront° the visage of offence?
And what's in prayer but this two-fold force,
To be forestalled° ere we come to fall,
Or pardon'd being down? Then I'll look up;   50
My fault is past. But, O, what form of prayer
Can serve my turn? "Forgive me my foul murder"?
That cannot be: since I am still possess'd
Of those effects for which I did the murder,
My crown, mine own ambition° and my queen.   55
May one be pardon'd and retain th' offence?°
In the corrupted currents° of this world
Offence's gilded hand° may shove by justice,
And oft 'tis seen the wicked prize° itself
Buys out the law: but 'tis not so above;   60
There is no shuffling,° there the action lies°
In his true nature; and we ourselves compell'd,
Even to the teeth and forehead° of our faults,
To give in evidence. What then? what rests?°
Try what repentance can: what can it not?   65
Yet what can it when one can not repent?
O wretched state! O bosom black as death!
O limed° soul, that, struggling to be free,
Art more engag'd!° Help, angels! Make assay!°
Bow, stubborn knees; and, heart with strings of steel,   70
Be soft as sinews of the new-born babe!
All may be well.   [*He kneels.*]

Enter Hamlet.

HAMLET: Now might I do it pat,° now he is praying;
And now I'll do't. And so 'a goes to heaven;
And so am I reveng'd. That would be scann'd:°   75
A villain kills my father; and for that,

---

47 **confront:** Oppose directly.   49 **forestalled:** Prevented.   55 **ambition:** I.e., realization of ambition.   56 **offence:** Benefit accruing from offense.   57 **currents:** Courses.   58 **gilded hand:** Hand offering gold as a bribe.   59 **wicked prize:** Prize won by wickedness.   61 **shuffling:** Escape by trickery;   **lies:** Is sustainable.   63 **teeth and forehead:** Very face.   64 **rests:** Remains.   68 **limed:** Caught as with birdlime.   69 **engag'd:** Embedded;   **assay:** Trial.   73 **pat:** Opportunely.   75 **would be scann'd:** Needs to be looked into.

I, his sole son, do this same villain send
To heaven.
Why, this is hire and salary, not revenge.
'A took my father grossly, full of bread;° 80
With all his crimes broad blown,° as flush° as May;
And how his audit stands who knows save heaven?
But in our circumstance and course° of thought,
'Tis heavy with him: and am I then reveng'd,
To take him in the purging of his soul, 85
When he is fit and season'd for his passage?°
No!
Up, sword; and know thou a more horrid hent:°
When he is drunk asleep,° or in his rage,
Or in th' incestuous pleasure of his bed; 90
At game, a-swearing, or about some act
That has no relish of salvation in 't;
Then trip him, that his heels may kick at heaven,
And that his soul may be as damn'd and black
As hell, whereto it goes. My mother stays: 95
This physic° but prolongs thy sickly days. *Exit.*
KING: *[Rising]* My words fly up, my thoughts remain below:
Words without thoughts never to heaven go. *Exit.*

[Scene 4]

[The Queen's closet.]
Enter [Queen] Gertrude and Polonius.

POLONIUS: 'A will come straight. Look you lay° home to him:
Tell him his pranks have been too broad° to bear with,
And that your grace hath screen'd and stood between
Much heat° and him. I'll sconce° me even here.
Pray you, be round° with him. 5
HAMLET *(within):*   Mother, mother, mother!
QUEEN: I'll warrant you,
Fear me not: withdraw, I hear him coming.
                    [Polonius hides behind the arras.]
Enter Hamlet.

HAMLET: Now, mother, what's the matter?
QUEEN: Hamlet, thou hast thy father° much offended.

---

80 **full of bread:** Enjoying his worldly pleasures (see Ezekiel 16:49).   81 **broad blown:** In full bloom; **flush:** Lusty.   83 **in . . . course:** As we see it in our mortal situation.   86 **fit . . . passage:** I.e., reconciled to heaven by forgiveness of his sins.   88 **hent:** Seizing; or more probably, occasion of seizure.   89 **drunk asleep:** In a drunken sleep.   96 **physic:** Purging (by prayer). SCENE 4.   1 **lay:** Thrust.   2 **broad:** Unrestrained.   4 **Much heat:** I.e., the king's anger; **sconce:** Hide.   5 **round:** Blunt.   9–10 **thy father, my father:** I.e., Claudius, the elder Hamlet.

HAMLET: Mother, you have my father much offended.   10
QUEEN: Come, come, you answer with an idle tongue.
HAMLET: Go, go, you question with a wicked tongue.
QUEEN: Why, how now, Hamlet!
HAMLET: What's the matter now?
QUEEN: Have you forgot me?
HAMLET: No, by the rood,° not so:
    You are the queen, your husband's brother's wife;   15
    And—would it were not so!—you are my mother.
QUEEN: Nay, then, I'll set those to you that can speak.
HAMLET: Come, come, and sit you down; you shall not budge;
    You go not till I set you up a glass
    Where you may see the inmost part of you.   20
QUEEN: What wilt thou do? thou wilt not murder me?
    Help, help, ho!
POLONIUS [*behind*]:   What, ho! help, help; help!
HAMLET [*drawing*]:   How now! a rat? Dead, for a ducat, dead!
                                             [*Makes a pass through the arras.*]
POLONIUS [*behind*]:   O, I am slain!   [*Falls and dies.*]   25
QUEEN: O me, what hast thou done?
HAMLET: Nay, I know not:
    Is it the king?
QUEEN: O, what a rash and bloody deed is this!
HAMLET: A bloody deed! almost as bad, good mother,
    As kill a king, and marry with his brother.   30
QUEEN: As kill a king!
HAMLET: Ay, lady, it was my word.
                                  [*Lifts up the arras and discovers Polonius.*]
    Thou wretched, rash, intruding fool, farewell!
    I took thee for thy better: take thy fortune;
    Thou find'st to be too busy is some danger.
    Leave wringing of your hands: peace! sit you down,   35
    And let me wring your heart; for so I shall,
    If it be made of penetrable stuff,
    If damned custom have not braz'd° it so
    That it be proof and bulwark against sense.
QUEEN: What have I done, that thou dar'st wag thy tongue   40
    In noise so rude against me?
HAMLET: Such an act
    That blurs the grace and blush of modesty,
    Calls virtue hypocrite, takes off the rose
    From the fair forehead of an innocent love
    And sets a blister° there, makes marriage-vows   45

---

14 rood: Cross.   **38 braz'd:** Brazened, hardened.   **45 sets a blister:** Brands as a harlot.

As false as dicers' oaths: O, such a deed
As from the body of contraction° plucks
The very soul, and sweet religion° makes
A rhapsody° of words: heaven's face does glow
O'er this solidity and compound mass   50
With heated visage, as against the doom
Is thought-sick at the act.°
QUEEN: Ay me, what act,
That roars so loud, and thunders in the index?°
HAMLET: Look here, upon this picture, and on this.
The counterfeit presentment° of two brothers.   55
See, what a grace was seated on this brow;
Hyperion's° curls; the front° of Jove himself;
An eye like Mars, to threaten and command;
A station° like the herald Mercury
New-lighted on a heaven-kissing hill;   60
A combination and a form indeed,
Where every god did seem to set his seal,
To give the world assurance° of a man:
This was your husband. Look you now, what follows:
Here is your husband; like a mildew'd ear,°   65
Blasting his wholesome brother. Have you eyes?
Could you on this fair mountain leave to feed,
And batten° on this moor?° Ha! have you eyes?
You cannot call it love; for at your age
The hey-day° in the blood is tame, it's humble,   70
And waits upon the judgement: and what judgement
Would step from this to this? Sense, sure, you have,
Else could you not have motion;° but sure, that sense
Is apoplex'd;° for madness would not err,
Nor sense to ecstasy was ne'er so thrall'd°   75
But it reserv'd some quantity of choice,°
To serve in such a difference. What devil was't
That thus hath cozen'd° you at hoodman-blind?°
Eyes without feeling, feeling without sight,
Ears without hands or eyes, smelling sans° all,   80

---

47 contraction: The marriage contract.   **48 religion:** Religious vows.   **49 rhapsody:** Sense-
less string.   **49–52 heaven's . . . act:** Heaven's face blushes to look down on this world, and
Gertrude's marriage makes heaven feel as sick as though the day of doom were near.   **53 index:**
Prelude or preface.   **55 counterfeit presentment:** Portrayed representation.   **57 Hyperion's:**
The sun god's;   **front:** Brow.   **59 station:** Manner of standing.   **63 assurance:** Pledge, guarantee.   **65 mildew'd ear:** See Genesis 41:5–7.   **68 batten:** Grow fat;   **moor:** Barren upland.
70 hey-day: State of excitement.   **72–73 Sense . . . motion:** Sense and motion are functions
of the middle or sensible soul, the possession of sense being the basis of motion.   **74 apoplex'd:**
Paralyzed. Mental derangement was thus of three sorts: apoplexy, ecstasy, and diabolic possession.   **75 thrall'd:** Enslaved.   **76 quantity of choice:** Fragment of the power to choose.
78 cozen'd: Tricked, cheated;   **hoodman-blind:** Blindman's buff.   **80 sans:** Without.

Or but a sickly part of one true sense
Could not so mope.°
O shame! where is thy blush? Rebellious hell,
If thou canst mutine° in a matron's bones,
To flaming youth let virtue be as wax,   85
And melt in her own fire: proclaim no shame
When the compulsive ardour gives the charge,°
Since frost itself as actively doth burn
And reason pandars will.°

QUEEN: O Hamlet, speak no more:
Thou turn'st mine eyes into my very soul;   90
And there I see such black and grained° spots
As will not leave their tinct.

HAMLET: Nay, but to live
In the rank sweat of an enseamed° bed,
Stew'd in corruption, honeying and making love
Over the nasty sty, —

QUEEN: O, speak to me no more;   95
These words, like daggers, enter in mine ears;
No more, sweet Hamlet!

HAMLET: A murderer and a villain;
A slave that is not twentieth part the tithe
Of your precedent lord;° a vice of kings;°
A cutpurse of the empire and the rule,   100
That from a shelf the precious diadem stole,
And put it in his pocket!

QUEEN: No more!

Enter Ghost.

HAMLET: A king of shreds and patches,°—
Save me, and hover o'er me with your wings,
You heavenly guards! What would your gracious figure?   105

QUEEN: Alas, he's mad!

HAMLET: Do you not come your tardy son to chide,
That, laps'd in time and passion,° lets go by
Th' important° acting of your dread command?
O, say!   110

---

82 mope: Be in a depressed, spiritless state, act aimlessly. **84 mutine:** Mutiny, rebel.
87 gives the charge: Delivers the attack. **89 reason pandars will:** The normal and proper situation was one in which reason guided the will in the direction of good; here, reason is perverted and leads in the direction of evil. **91 grained:** Dyed in grain. **93 enseamed:** Loaded with grease, greased. **99 precedent lord:** I.e., the elder Hamlet; **vice of kings:** Buffoon of kings; a reference to the Vice, or clown, of the morality plays and interludes. **103 shreds and patches:** I.e., motley, the traditional costume of the Vice. **108 laps'd ... passion:** Having suffered time to slip and passion to cool; also explained as "engrossed in casual events and lapsed into mere fruitless passion, so that he no longer entertains a rational purpose."
109 important: Urgent.

GHOST: Do not forget: this visitation
   Is but to whet thy almost blunted purpose.
   But, look, amazement° on thy mother sits:
   O, step between her and her fighting soul:
   Conceit in weakest bodies strongest works: 115
   Speak to her, Hamlet.
HAMLET: How is it with you, lady?
QUEEN: Alas, how is 't with you,
   That you do bend your eye on vacancy
   And with th' incorporal° air do hold discourse?
   Forth at your eyes your spirits wildly peep;   120
   And, as the sleeping soldiers in th' alarm,
   Your bedded° hair, like life in excrements,°
   Start up, and stand an° end. O gentle son,
   Upon the heat and flame of thy distemper
   Sprinkle cool patience. Whereon do you look?   125
HAMLET: On him, on him! Look you, how pale he glares!
   His form and cause conjoin'd,° preaching to stones,
   Would make them capable. — Do not look upon me;
   Lest with this piteous action you convert
   My stern effects:° then what I have to do   130
   Will want true colour;° tears perchance for blood.
QUEEN: To whom do you speak this?
HAMLET: Do you see nothing there?
QUEEN: Nothing at all; yet all that is I see.
HAMLET: Nor did you nothing hear?
QUEEN: No, nothing but ourselves.
HAMLET: Why, look you there! look, how it steals away!   135
   My father, in his habit as he liv'd!
   Look, where he goes, even now, out at the portal!   *Exit Ghost.*
QUEEN: This is the very coinage of your brain:
   This bodiless creation ecstasy
   Is very cunning in.
HAMLET: Ecstasy!   140
   My pulse, as yours, doth temperately keep time,
   And makes as healthful music: it is not madness
   That I have utt'red: bring me to the test,
   And I the matter will re-word,° which madness
   Would gambol° from. Mother, for love of grace,   145

---

113 **amazement:** Frenzy, distraction.   119 **incorporal:** Immaterial.   122 **bedded:** Laid in smooth layers;   **excrements:** The hair was considered an excrement or voided part of the body. 123 **an:** On.   127 **conjoin'd:** United.   129–130 **convert . . . effects:** Divert me from my stern duty. For *effects*, possibly *affects* (affections of the mind).   131 **want true colour:** Lack good reason so that (with a play on the normal sense of *colour*) I shall shed tears instead of blood.   144 **re-word:** Repeat in words.   145 **gambol:** Skip away.

Lay not that flattering unction° to your soul,
That not your trespass, but my madness speaks:
It will but skin and film the ulcerous place,
Whiles rank corruption, mining° all within,
Infects unseen. Confess yourself to heaven;   150
Repent what's past; avoid what is to come;°
And do not spread the compost° on the weeds,
To make them ranker. Forgive me this my virtue;°
For in the fatness° of these pursy° times
Virtue itself of vice must pardon beg,   155
Yea, curb° and woo for leave to do him good.

QUEEN: O Hamlet, thou hast cleft my heart in twain.

HAMLET: O, throw away the worser part of it,
And live the purer with the other half.
Good night: but go not to my uncle's bed;   160
Assume a virtue, if you have it not.
That monster, custom, who all sense doth eat,
Of habits devil, is angel yet in this,
That to the use of actions fair and good
He likewise gives a frock or livery,   165
That aptly is put on. Refrain to-night,
And that shall lend a kind of easiness
To the next abstinence: the next more easy;
For use almost can change the stamp of nature,
And either . . . the devil, or throw him out°   170
With wondrous potency. Once more, good night:
And when you are desirous to be bless'd,°
I'll blessing beg of you. For this same lord,   *[Pointing to Polonius.]*
I do repent: but heaven hath pleas'd it so,
To punish me with this and this with me,   175
That I must be their scourge and minister.
I will bestow him, and will answer well
The death I gave him. So, again, good night.
I must be cruel, only to be kind:
Thus bad begins and worse remains behind.   180
One word more, good lady.

QUEEN: What shall I do?

HAMLET: Not this, by no means, that I bid you do:
Let the bloat° king tempt you again to bed;
Pinch wanton on your cheek; call you his mouse;

---

146 unction: Ointment used medicinally or as a rite; suggestion that forgiveness for sin may
not be so easily achieved.   **149 mining:** Working under the surface.   **151 what is to come:**
I.e., the sins of the future.   **152 compost:** Manure.   **153 this my virtue:** My virtuous talk in
reproving you.   **154 fatness:** Grossness;   **pursy:** Short-winded, corpulent.   **156 curb:** Bow,
bend the knee.   **170** Defective line usually emended by inserting *master* after *either*.   **172 be
bless'd:** Become blessed, i.e., repentant.   **183 bloat:** Bloated.

And let him, for a pair of reechy° kisses,   185
Or paddling in your neck with his damn'd fingers,
Make you to ravel all this matter out,
That I essentially° am not in madness,
But mad in craft. 'Twere good you let him know;
For who, that's but a queen, fair, sober, wise,   190
Would from a paddock,° from a bat, a gib,°
Such dear concernings° hide? who would do so?
No, in despite of sense and secrecy,
Unpeg the basket on the house's top,
Let the birds fly, and, like the famous ape,°   195
To try conclusions,° in the basket creep,
And break your own neck down.
QUEEN: Be thou assur'd, if words be made of breath,
           And breath of life, I have no life to breathe
           What thou hast said to me.   200
HAMLET: I must to England; you know that?
QUEEN: Alack,
           I had forgot: 'tis so concluded on.
HAMLET: There's letters seal'd: and my two schoolfellows,
           Whom I will trust as I will adders fang'd,
           They bear the mandate; they must sweep my way,°   205
           And marshal me to knavery. Let it work;
           For 'tis the sport to have the enginer°
           Hoist° with his own petar:° and 't shall go hard
           But I will delve one yard below their mines,
           And blow them at the moon: O, 'tis most sweet,   210
           When in one line two crafts° directly meet.
           This man shall set me packing:°
           I'll lug the guts into the neighbour room.
           Mother, good night. Indeed this counsellor
           Is now most still, most secret and most grave,   215
           Who was in life a foolish prating knave.
           Come, sir, to draw° toward an end with you.
           Good night, mother.   *Exeunt [severally; Hamlet dragging in Polonius.]*

---

185 reechy: Dirty, filthy.   **188 essentially:** In my essential nature.   **191 paddock:** Toad;
gib: Tomcat.   **192 dear concernings:** Important affairs.   **195 the famous ape:** A letter from
Sir John Suckling seems to supply other details of the story, otherwise not identified: "It is the
story of the jackanapes and the partridges; thou starest after a beauty till it is lost to thee, then
let'st out another, and starest after that till it is gone too."   **196 conclusions:** Experiments.
205 sweep my way: Clear my path.   **207 enginer:** Constructor of military works, or possibly,
artilleryman.   **208 Hoist:** Blown up;   **petar:** Defined as a small engine of war used to blow in
a door or make a breach, and as a case filled with explosive materials.   **211 two crafts:** Two
acts of guile, with quibble on the sense of "two ships."   **212 set me packing:** Set me to making
schemes, and set me to lugging (him), and, also, send me off in a hurry.   **217 draw:** Come,
with quibble on literal sense.

[ACT 4, Scene 1]

[A room in the castle.]
   Enter King and Queen, with Rosencrantz and Guildenstern.

KING: There's matter in these sighs, these profound heaves:
      You must translate: 'tis fit we understand them.
      Where is your son?
QUEEN: Bestow this place on us a little while.
                  [Exeunt Rosencrantz and Guildenstern.]
      Ah, mine own lord, what have I seen to-night!   5
KING: What, Gertrude? How does Hamlet?
QUEEN: Mad as the sea and wind, when both contend
      Which is the mightier: in his lawless fit,
      Behind the arras hearing something stir,
      Whips out his rapier, cries, "A rat, a rat!"   10
      And, in this brainish° apprehension,° kills
      The unseen good old man.
KING: O heavy deed!
      It had been so with us, had we been there:
      His liberty is full of threats to all;
      To you yourself, to us, to every one.   15
      Alas, how shall this bloody deed be answer'd?
      It will be laid to us, whose providence°
      Should have kept short,° restrain'd and out of haunt,°
      This mad young man: but so much was our love,
      We would not understand what was most fit;   20
      But, like the owner of a foul disease,
      To keep it from divulging,° let it feed
      Even on the pith of life. Where is he gone?
QUEEN: To draw apart the body he hath kill'd:
      O'er whom his very madness, like some ore   25
      Among a mineral° of metals base,
      Shows itself pure; 'a weeps for what is done.
KING: O Gertrude, come away!
      The sun no sooner shall the mountains touch,
      But we will ship him hence: and this vile deed   30
      We must, with all our majesty and skill,
      Both countenance and excuse. Ho, Guildenstern!

Enter Rosencrantz and Guildenstern.

      Friends both, go join you with some further aid:
      Hamlet in madness hath Polonius slain,

ACT 4, SCENE 1.   **11 brainish:** Headstrong, passionate;   **apprehension:** Conception, imagination.   **17 providence:** Foresight.   **18 short:** I.e., on a short tether;   **out of haunt:** Secluded.
22 divulging: Becoming evident.   **26 mineral:** Mine.

And from his mother's closet hath he dragg'd him: 35
Go seek him out; speak fair, and bring the body
Into the chapel. I pray you, haste in this.
                              [Exeunt Rosencrantz and Guildenstern.]
Come, Gertrude, we'll call up our wisest friends;
And let them know, both what we mean to do,
And what's untimely done . . .°   40
Whose whisper o'er the world's diameter,°
As level° as the cannon to his blank,°
Transports his pois'ned shot, may miss our name,
And hit the woundless° air. O, come away!
My soul is full of discord and dismay.   *Exeunt.*   45

[Scene 2]

[Another room in the castle.]
   Enter Hamlet.

HAMLET: Safely stowed.
ROSENCRANTZ:
                              (within) Hamlet! Lord Hamlet!
GUILDENSTERN:
HAMLET: But soft, what noise? who calls on Hamlet? O, here they come.

Enter Rosencrantz and Guildenstern.

ROSENCRANTZ: What have you done, my lord, with the dead body?
HAMLET: Compounded it with dust, whereto 'tis kin.
ROSENCRANTZ: Tell us where 'tis, that we may take it thence   5
   And bear it to the chapel.
HAMLET: Do not believe it.
ROSENCRANTZ: Believe what?
HAMLET: That I can keep your counsel° and not mine own. Besides, to be
   demanded of a sponge! what replication° should be made by the son of a king?   10
ROSENCRANTZ: Take you me for a sponge, my lord?
HAMLET: Ay, sir, that soaks up the king's countenance, his rewards, his authori-
   ties.° But such officers do the king best service in the end: he keeps them,
   like an ape an apple, in the corner of his jaw; first mouthed, to be last swal-
   lowed: when he needs what you have gleaned, it is but squeezing you, and,   15
   sponge, you shall be dry again.
ROSENCRANTZ: I understand you not, my lord.
HAMLET: I am glad of it: a knavish speech sleeps in a foolish ear.
ROSENCRANTZ: My lord, you must tell us where the body is, and go with us to
   the king.   20

---

40 Defective line; some editors add: *so, haply, slander;* others add: *for, haply, slander;* other
conjectures.   **41 diameter:** Extent from side to side.   **42 level:** Straight;   **blank:** White spot
in the center of a target.   **44 woundless:** Invulnerable.   **SCENE 2. 9 keep your counsel:**
Hamlet is aware of their treachery but says nothing about it.   **10 replication:** Reply.
12–13 authorities: Authoritative backing.

HAMLET: The body is with the king, but the king is not with the body.° The king
   is a thing—
GUILDENSTERN: A thing, my lord!
HAMLET: Of nothing: bring me to him. Hide fox, and all after.°   *Exeunt.*

[Scene 3]

[Another room in the castle.]
   Enter King, and two or three.

KING: I have sent to seek him, and to find the body.
   How dangerous is it that this man goes loose!
   Yet must not we put the strong law on him:
   He's lov'd of the distracted° multitude,
   Who like not in their judgement, but their eyes;   5
   And where 'tis so, th' offender's scourge° is weigh'd,°
   But never the offence. To bear all smooth and even,
   This sudden sending him away must seem
   Deliberate pause:° diseases desperate grown
   By desperate appliance are reliev'd,   10
   Or not at all.

Enter Rosencrantz, [Guildenstern,] and all the rest.

                       How now! what hath befall'n?
ROSENCRANTZ: Where the dead body is bestow'd, my lord,
   We cannot get from him.
KING: But where is he?
ROSENCRANTZ: Without, my lord; guarded, to know your pleasure.
KING: Bring him before us.   15
ROSENCRANTZ: Ho! bring in the lord.

They enter [with Hamlet].

KING: Now, Hamlet, where's Polonius?
HAMLET: At supper.
KING: At supper! where?
HAMLET: Not where he eats, but where 'a is eaten: a certain convocation of   20
   politic° worms° are e'en at him. Your worm is your only emperor for diet: we
   fat all creatures else to fat us, and we fat ourselves for maggots: your fat king
   and your lean beggar is but variable service,° two dishes, but to one table:
   that's the end.
KING: Alas, alas!   25

---

21 **The body . . . body:** There are many interpretations; possibly, "The body lies in death with
the king, my father; but my father walks disembodied"; or "Claudius has the bodily possession of
kingship, but kingliness, or justice of inheritance, is not with him."   24 **Hide . . . after:** An old
signal cry in the game of hide-and-seek.   SCENE 3.   4 **distracted:** I.e., without power of forming logical judgments.   6 **scourge:** Punishment;   **weigh'd:** Taken into consideration.
9 **Deliberate pause:** Considered action.   20–21 **convocation . . . worms:** Allusion to the
Diet of Worms (1521).   21 **politic:** Crafty.   23 **variable service:** A variety of dishes.

HAMLET: A man may fish with the worm that hath eat of a king, and eat of the
   fish that hath fed of that worm.
KING: What dost thou mean by this?
HAMLET: Nothing but to show you how a king may go a progress° through the
   guts of a beggar.   30
KING: Where is Polonius?
HAMLET: In heaven; send thither to see: if your messenger find him not there,
   seek him i' the other place yourself. But if indeed you find him not within
   this month, you shall nose him as you go up the stairs into the lobby.
KING [*to some Attendants*]:   Go seek him there.   35
HAMLET: 'A will stay till you come.   [*Exeunt Attendants.*]
KING: Hamlet, this deed, for thine especial safety, —
   Which we do tender,° as we dearly grieve
   For that which thou hast done, — must send thee hence
   With fiery quickness: therefore prepare thyself;   40
   The bark is ready, and the wind at help,
   Th' associates tend, and everything is bent
   For England.
HAMLET: For England!
KING: Ay, Hamlet.
HAMLET: Good.
KING: So is it, if thou knew'st our purposes.
HAMLET: I see a cherub° that sees them. But, come; for England! Farewell, dear   45
   mother.
KING: Thy loving father, Hamlet.
HAMLET: My mother: father and mother is man and wife; man and wife is one
   flesh; and so, my mother. Come, for England!   *Exit.*
KING: Follow him at foot;° tempt him with speed aboard;   50
   Delay it not; I'll have him hence to-night:
   Away! for every thing is seal'd and done
   That else leans on th' affair: pray you, make haste.
                                                   [*Exeunt all but the King.*]
   And, England, if my love thou hold'st at aught—
   As my great power thereof may give thee sense,   55
   Since yet thy cicatrice° looks raw and red
   After the Danish sword, and thy free awe°
   Pays homage to us—thou mayst not coldly set
   Our sovereign process; which imports at full,
   By letters congruing to that effect,   60
   The present death of Hamlet. Do it, England;
   For like the hectic° in my blood he rages,
   And thou must cure me: till I know 'tis done,
   Howe'er my haps,° my joys were ne'er begun.   *Exit.*

---

29 progress: Royal journey of state.   **38 tender:** Regard, hold dear.   **45 cherub:** Cherubim
are angels of knowledge.   **50 at foot:** Close behind, at heel.   **56 cicatrice:** Scar.   **57 free
awe:** Voluntary show of respect.   **62 hectic:** Fever.   **64 haps:** Fortunes.

[Scene 4]

[A plain in Denmark.]
Enter Fortinbras with his Army over the stage.

FORTINBRAS: Go, captain, from me greet the Danish king;
Tell him that, by his license,° Fortinbras
Craves the conveyance° of a promis'd march
Over his kingdom. You know the rendezvous.
If that his majesty would aught with us,   5
We shall express our duty in his eye;°
And let him know so.
CAPTAIN: I will do't, my lord.
FORTINBRAS: Go softly° on.   *[Exeunt all but Captain.]*

Enter Hamlet, Rosencrantz, [Guildenstern,] &c.

HAMLET: Good sir, whose powers are these?
CAPTAIN: They are of Norway, sir.   10
HAMLET: How purpos'd, sir, I pray you?
CAPTAIN: Against some part of Poland.
HAMLET: Who commands them, sir?
CAPTAIN: The nephew to old Norway, Fortinbras.
HAMLET: Goes it against the main° of Poland, sir,   15
Or for some frontier?
CAPTAIN: Truly to speak, and with no addition,
We go to gain a little patch of ground
That hath in it no profit but the name.
To pay five ducats, five, I would not farm it;°   20
Nor will it yield to Norway or the Pole
A ranker rate, should it be sold in fee.°
HAMLET: Why, then the Polack never will defend it.
CAPTAIN: Yes, it is already garrison'd.
HAMLET: Two thousand souls and twenty thousand ducats   25
Will not debate the question of this straw:°
This is th' imposthume° of much wealth and peace,
That inward breaks, and shows no cause without
Why the man dies. I humbly thank you, sir.
CAPTAIN: God be wi' you, sir.   *[Exit.]*
ROSENCRANTZ: Will 't please you go, my lord?   30
HAMLET: I'll be with you straight. Go a little before.
                                        [Exeunt all except Hamlet.]
How all occasions° do inform against° me,
And spur my dull revenge! What is a man,

SCENE 4.   2 **license:** Leave.   3 **conveyance:** Escort, convoy.   6 **in his eye:** In his presence.
8 **softly:** Slowly.   15 **main:** Country itself.   20 **farm it:** Take a lease of it.   22 **fee:** Fee simple.   26 **debate . . . straw:** Settle this trifling matter.   27 **imposthume:** Purulent abscess or
swelling.   32 **occasions:** Incidents, events;   **inform against:** Generally defined as "show,"
"betray" (i.e., his tardiness); more probably *inform* means "take shape," as in *Macbeth*, 2.1.48.

If his chief good and market of his time°
Be but to sleep and feed? a beast, no more.   35
Sure, he that made us with such large discourse,
Looking before and after, gave us not
That capability and god-like reason
To fust° in us unus'd. Now, whether it be
Bestial oblivion, or some craven scruple   40
Of thinking too precisely on th' event,
A thought which, quarter'd, hath but one part wisdom
And ever three parts coward, I do not know
Why yet I live to say "This thing 's to do";
Sith I have cause and will and strength and means   45
To do 't. Examples gross as earth exhort me:
Witness this army of such mass and charge
Led by a delicate and tender prince,
Whose spirit with divine ambition puff'd
Makes mouths at the invisible event,   50
Exposing what is mortal and unsure
To all that fortune, death and danger dare,
Even for an egg-shell. Rightly to be great
Is not to stir without great argument,
But greatly to find quarrel in a straw   55
When honour's at the stake. How stand I then,
That have a father kill'd, a mother stain'd,
Excitements of° my reason and my blood,
And let all sleep? while, to my shame, I see
The imminent death of twenty thousand men,   60
That, for a fantasy and trick° of fame,
Go to their graves like beds, fight for a plot°
Whereon the numbers cannot try the cause,
Which is not tomb enough and continent
To hide the slain? O, from this time forth,   65
My thoughts be bloody, or be nothing worth!   *Exit.*

[Scene 5]

[Elsinore. A room in the castle.]
    Enter Horatio, [Queen] Gertrude, and a Gentleman.

QUEEN: I will not speak with her.
GENTLEMAN: She is importunate, indeed distract:
    Her mood will needs be pitied.
QUEEN: What would she have?

---

34 market of his time: The best use he makes of his time, or, that for which he sells his time.
39 fust: Grow moldy.   **58 Excitements of:** Incentives to.   **61 trick:** Toy, trifle.   **62 plot:**
Piece of ground.

GENTLEMAN: She speaks much of her father; says she hears
   There's tricks° i' th' world; and hems, and beats her heart;°   5
   Spurns enviously at straws;° speaks things in doubt,
   That carry but half sense: her speech is nothing,
   Yet the unshaped° use of it doth move
   The hearers to collection;° they yawn° at it,
   And botch° the words up fit to their own thoughts;   10
   Which, as her winks, and nods, and gestures yield° them,
   Indeed would make one think there might be thought,
   Though nothing sure, yet much unhappily.°
HORATIO: 'Twere good she were spoken with: for she may strew
   Dangerous conjectures in ill-breeding minds.°   15
QUEEN: Let her come in.   *[Exit Gentleman.]*
   [Aside.] To my sick soul, as sin's true nature is,
   Each toy seems prologue to some great amiss:°
   So full of artless jealousy is guilt,
   It spills itself in fearing to be spilt.°   20

Enter Ophelia [distracted].

OPHELIA: Where is the beauteous majesty of Denmark?
QUEEN: How now, Ophelia!
OPHELIA *(she sings):*   How should I your true love know
     From another one?
  By his cockle hat° and staff,   25
     And his sandal shoon.°
QUEEN: Alas, sweet lady, what imports this song?
OPHELIA: Say you? nay, pray you mark.
  (Song) He is dead and gone, lady,
     He is dead and gone;   30
  At his head a grass-green turf,
     At his heels a stone.
  O, ho!
QUEEN: Nay, but, Ophelia—
OPHELIA: Pray you, mark   35
  [Sings.] White his shroud as the mountain snow,—

Enter King.

QUEEN: Alas, look here, my lord.

SCENE 5. **5 tricks:** Deceptions;   **heart:** I.e., breast.   **6 Spurns . . . straws:** Kicks spitefully at
small objects in her path.   **8 unshaped:** Unformed, artless.   **9 collection:** Inference, a guess
at some sort of meaning;   **yawn:** Wonder.   **10 botch:** Patch.   **11 yield:** Deliver, bring forth
(her words).   **13 much unhappily:** Expressive of much unhappiness.   **15 ill-breeding
minds:** Minds bent on mischief.   **18 great amiss:** Calamity, disaster.   **19–20 So . . . spilt:**
Guilt is so full of suspicion that it unskillfully betrays itself in fearing to be betrayed.
25 cockle hat: Hat with cockleshell stuck in it as a sign that the wearer has been a pilgrim to
the shrine of St. James of Compostella. The pilgrim's garb was a conventional disguise for
lovers.   **26 shoon:** Shoes.

OPHELIA *(Song):*   Larded° all with flowers;
    Which bewept to the grave did not go
      With true-love showers.   40
KING: How do you, pretty lady?
OPHELIA: Well, God 'ild° you! They say the owl° was a baker's daughter.
    Lord, we know what we are, but know not what we may be. God be at your
    table!
KING: Conceit upon her father.   45
OPHELIA: Pray let's have no words of this; but when they ask you what it means,
    say you this:
    (Song) To-morrow is Saint Valentine's day,
      All in the morning betime,
    And I a maid at your window,   50
      To be your Valentine.°
    Then up he rose, and donn'd his clothes,
      And dupp'd° the chamber-door;
    Let in the maid, that out a maid
      Never departed more.   55
KING: Pretty Ophelia!
OPHELIA: Indeed, la, without an oath, I'll make an end on 't:
    [Sings.] By Gis° and by Saint Charity,
      Alack, and fie for shame!
    Young men will do 't, if they come to 't;   60
      By cock,° they are to blame.
    Quoth she, before you tumbled me,
      You promis'd me to wed.
    So would I ha' done, by yonder sun,
      An thou hadst not come to my bed.   65
KING: How long hath she been thus?
OPHELIA: I hope all will be well. We must be patient: but I cannot choose
    but weep, to think they would lay him i' the cold ground. My brother
    shall know of it: and so I thank you for your good counsel. Come, my
    coach! Good night, ladies; good night, sweet ladies; good night, good   70
    night.   *[Exit.]*
KING: Follow her close; give her good watch, I pray you.   *[Exit Horatio.]*
    O, this is the poison of deep grief; it springs
    All from her father's death. O Gertrude, Gertrude,
    When sorrows come, they come not single spies,   75
    But in battalions. First, her father slain:
    Next your son gone; and he most violent author
    Of his own just remove: the people muddied,

---

38 Larded: Decorated.   **42 God 'ild:** God yield or reward;   **owl:** Reference to a monkish
legend that a baker's daughter was turned into an owl for refusing bread to the Savior.
51 Valentine: This song alludes to the belief that the first girl seen by a man on the morning of
this day was his valentine or true love.   **53 dupp'd:** Opened.   **58 Gis:** Jesus.   **61 cock:** Per-
version of "God" in oaths.

Thick and unwholesome in their thoughts and whispers,
For good Polonius' death; and we have done but greenly,°   80
In hugger-mugger° to inter him: poor Ophelia
Divided from herself and her fair judgement,
Without the which we are pictures, or mere beasts:
Last, and as much containing as all these,
Her brother is in secret come from France;   85
Feeds on his wonder, keeps himself in clouds,°
And wants not buzzers° to infect his ear
With pestilent speeches of his father's death;
Wherein necessity, of matter beggar'd,°
Will nothing stick° our person to arraign   90
In ear and ear.° O my dear Gertrude, this,
Like to a murd'ring-piece,° in many places
Gives me superfluous death.   *A noise within.*

QUEEN: Alack, what noise is this?
KING: Where are my Switzers?° Let them guard the door.

Enter a Messenger.

What is the matter?
MESSENGER: Save yourself, my lord: 95
The ocean, overpeering° of his list,°
Eats not the flats with more impiteous haste
Than young Laertes, in a riotous head,
O'erbears your officers. The rabble call him lord;
And, as the world were now but to begin,   100
Antiquity forgot, custom not known,
The ratifiers and props of every word,°
They cry "Choose we: Laertes shall be king":
Caps, hands, and tongues, applaud it to the clouds:
"Laertes shall be king, Laertes king!"   *A noise within.* 105
QUEEN: How cheerfully on the false trail they cry!
O, this is counter,° you false Danish dogs!
KING: The doors are broke.

Enter Laertes with others.

LAERTES: Where is this king? Sirs, stand you all without.
DANES: No, let's come in.
LAERTES: I pray you, give me leave.   110
DANES: We will, we will.   *[They retire without the door.]*
LAERTES: I thank you: keep the door. O thou vile king,

---

80 **greenly:** Foolishly.   81 **hugger-mugger:** Secret haste.   86 **in clouds:** Invisible.
87 **buzzers:** Gossipers.   89 **of matter beggar'd:** Unprovided with facts.   90 **nothing stick:**
Not hesitate.   91 **In ear and ear:** In everybody's ears.   92 **murd'ring-piece:** Small cannon or
mortar; suggestion of numerous missiles fired.   94 **Switzers:** Swiss guards, mercenaries.
96 **overpeering:** Overflowing;   **list:** Shore.   102 **word:** Promise.   107 **counter:** A hunting
term meaning to follow the trail in a direction opposite to that which the game has taken.

Give me my father!

QUEEN: Calmly, good Laertes.

LAERTES: That drop of blood that's calm proclaims me bastard,
Cries cuckold to my father, brands the harlot 115
Even here, between the chaste unsmirched brow
Of my true mother.

KING: What is the cause, Laertes,
That thy rebellion looks so giant-like?
Let him go, Gertrude; do not fear our person:
There's such divinity doth hedge a king, 120
That treason can but peep to° what it would,°
Acts little of his will. Tell me, Laertes,
Why thou art thus incens'd. Let him go, Gertrude.
Speak, man.

LAERTES: Where is my father?

KING: Dead.

QUEEN: But not by him. 125

KING: Let him demand his fill.

LAERTES: How came he dead? I'll not be juggled with:
To hell, allegiance! vows, to the blackest devil!
Conscience and grace, to the profoundest pit!
I dare damnation. To this point I stand,
That both the worlds I give to negligence,° 130
Let come what comes; only I'll be reveng'd
Most throughly° for my father.

KING: Who shall stay you?

LAERTES: My will,° not all the world's:
And for my means, I'll husband them so well, 135
They shall go far with little.

KING: Good Laertes,
If you desire to know the certainty
Of your dear father, is 't writ in your revenge,
That, swoopstake,° you will draw both friend and foe,
Winner and loser? 140

LAERTES: None but his enemies.

KING: Will you know them then?

LAERTES: To his good friends thus wide I'll ope my arms;
And like the kind life-rend'ring pelican,°
Repast° them with my blood.

KING: Why, now you speak
Like a good child and a true gentleman. 145

---

121 peep to: I.e., look at from afar off; **would:** Wishes to do. **131 give to negligence:** He despises both the here and the hereafter. **133 throughly:** thoroughly. **134 My will:** He will not be stopped except by his own will. **139 swoopstake:** Literally, drawing the whole stake at once, i.e., indiscriminately. **143 pelican:** Reference to the belief that the pelican feeds its young with its own blood. **144 Repast:** Feed.

That I am guiltless of your father's death,
And am most sensibly in grief for it,
It shall as level to your judgement 'pear
As day does to your eye.   *A noise within: "Let her come in."*

LAERTES: How now! what noise is that?   150

Enter Ophelia.

O heat,° dry up my brains! tears seven times salt,
Burn out the sense and virtue of mine eye!
By heaven, thy madness shall be paid with weight,
Till our scale turn the beam. O rose of May!
Dear maid, kind sister, sweet Ophelia!   155
O heavens! is 't possible, a young maid's wits
Should be as mortal as an old man's life?
Nature is fine in love, and where 'tis fine,
It sends some precious instance of itself
After the thing it loves.   160

OPHELIA *(Song):*   They bore him barefac'd on the bier;
Hey non nonny, nonny, hey nonny;
And in his grave rain'd many a tear: —
Fare you well, my dove!

LAERTES: Hadst thou thy wits, and didst persuade revenge,   165
It could not move thus.

OPHELIA *[sings]:*   You must sing a-down a-down,
An you call him a-down-a.
O, how the wheel° becomes it! It is the false steward,° that stole his master's
daughter.   170

LAERTES: This nothing's more than matter.

OPHELIA: There's rosemary,° that's for remembrance; pray you, love, remember: and there is pansies,° that's for thoughts.

LAERTES: A document° in madness, thoughts and remembrance fitted.

OPHELIA: There's fennel° for you, and columbines:° there's rue° for you; and   175
here's some for me: we may call it herb of grace o' Sundays: O, you must
wear your rue with a difference. There's a daisy:° I would give you some
violets,° but they withered all when my father died: they say 'a made a
good end, —
[Sings.] For bonny sweet Robin is all my joy.°   180

---

151 heat: Probably the heat generated by the passion of grief.   **169 wheel:** Spinning wheel as
accompaniment to the song refrain;   **false steward:** The story is unknown.   **172 rosemary:**
Used as a symbol of remembrance both at weddings and at funerals.   **173 pansies:** Emblems
of love and courtship (from the French *pensée*).   **174 document:** Piece of instruction or lesson.   **175 fennel:** Emblem of flattery;   **columbines:** Emblem of unchastity (?) or ingratitude
(?);   **rue:** Emblem of repentance. It was usually mingled with holy water and then known as
herb of grace. Ophelia is probably playing on the two meanings of *rue,* "repentant" and "even
for ruth (pity)"; the former signification is for the queen, the latter for herself.   **177 daisy:**
Emblem of dissembling, faithlessness.   **178 violets:** Emblems of faithfulness.   **180 For . . .
joy:** Probably a line from a Robin Hood ballad.

LAERTES: Thought° and affliction, passion, hell itself,
 She turns to favour and to prettiness.
OPHELIA *(Song):*   And will 'a not come again?°
 And will 'a not come again?
  No, no, he is dead: 185
  Go to thy death-bed:
 He never will come again.

 His beard was as white as snow,
 All flaxen was his poll:°
  He is gone, he is gone,   190
  And we cast away° moan:
 God ha' mercy on his soul!
 And of all Christian souls, I pray God. God be wi' you. *[Exit.]*
LAERTES: Do you see this, O God?
KING: Laertes, I must commune with your grief,   195
 Or you deny me right.° Go but apart,
 Make choice of whom your wisest friends you will,
 And they shall hear and judge 'twixt you and me:
 If by direct or by collateral° hand
 They find us touch'd,° we will our kingdom give,   200
 Our crown, our life, and all that we call ours,
 To you in satisfaction; but if not,
 Be you content to lend your patience to us,
 And we shall jointly labour with your soul
 To give it due content.
LAERTES: Let this be so;   205
 His means of death, his obscure funeral—
 No trophy, sword, nor hatchment° o'er his bones,
 No noble rite nor formal ostentation—
 Cry to be heard, as 'twere from heaven to earth,
 That I must call 't in question.
KING: So you shall;   210
 And where th' offence is let the great axe fall.
 I pray you, go with me.   *Exeunt.*

[Scene 6]

[Another room in the castle.]
 Enter Horatio and others.

HORATIO: What are they that would speak with me?
GENTLEMAN: Sea-faring men, sir: they say they have letters for you.

---

181 Thought: Melancholy thought. **183 And . . . again:** This song appeared in the song-books as "The Merry Milkmaids' Dumps." **189 poll:** Head. **191 cast away:** Shipwrecked. **196 right:** My rights. **199 collateral:** Indirect. **200 touch'd:** Implicated. **207 hatchment:** Tablet displaying the armorial bearings of a deceased person.

HORATIO: Let them come in.   *[Exit Gentleman.]*
     I do not know from what part of the world
     I should be greeted, if not from lord Hamlet.   5

Enter Sailors.

FIRST SAILOR: God bless you, sir.
HORATIO: Let him bless thee too.
FIRST SAILOR: 'A shall sir, an 't please him. There's a letter for you, sir; it comes
     from the ambassador that was bound for England; if your name be Horatio,
     as I am let to know it is.   10
HORATIO *[reads]*:   "Horatio, when thou shalt have overlooked this, give these fel-
     lows some means° to the king: they have letters for him. Ere we were two
     days old at sea, a pirate of very warlike appointment gave us chase. Finding
     ourselves too slow of sail, we put on a compelled valour, and in the grapple I
     boarded them: on the instant they got clear of our ship; so I alone became   15
     their prisoner. They have dealt with me like thieves of mercy:° but they knew
     what they did; I am to do a good turn for them. Let the king have the letters I
     have sent; and repair thou to me with as much speed as thou wouldest fly
     death. I have words to speak in thine ear will make thee dumb; yet are they
     much too light for the bore° of the matter. These good fellows will bring thee   20
     where I am. Rosencrantz and Guildenstern hold their course for England: of
     them I have much to tell thee. Farewell.
                    "He that thou knowest thine, HAMLET."
     Come, I will give you way for these your letters;
     And do 't the speedier, that you may direct me
     To him from whom you brought them.   *Exeunt.*   25

[Scene 7]

[Another room in the castle.]
Enter King and Laertes.

KING: Now must your conscience° my acquittance seal,
     And you must put me in your heart for friend,
     Sith you have heard, and with a knowing ear,
     That he which hath your noble father slain
     Pursued my life.
LAERTES: It well appears: but tell me   5
     Why you proceeded not against these feats,
     So criminal and so capital° in nature,
     As by your safety, wisdom, all things else,
     You mainly° were stirr'd up.
KING: O, for two special reasons;
     Which may to you, perhaps, seem much unsinew'd,°   10

SCENE 6.   12 **means:** Means of access.   16 **thieves of mercy:** Merciful thieves.   20 **bore:**
Caliber, importance.   SCENE 7.   1 **conscience:** Knowledge that this is true.   7 **capital:** Punishable by death.   9 **mainly:** Greatly.   10 **unsinew'd:** Weak.

But yet to me th' are strong. The queen his mother
Lives almost by his looks; and for myself—
My virtue or my plague, be it either which—
She's so conjunctive° to my life and soul,
That, as the star moves not but in his sphere,°   15
I could not but by her. The other motive,
Why to a public count° I might not go,
Is the great love the general gender° bear him;
Who, dipping all his faults in their affection,
Would, like the spring° that turneth wood to stone,   20
Convert his gyves° to graces; so that my arrows,
Too slightly timber'd° for so loud° a wind,
Would have reverted to my bow again,
And not where I had aim'd them.
LAERTES: And so have I a noble father lost;   25
A sister driven into desp'rate terms,°
Whose worth, if praises may go back° again,
Stood challenger on mount° of all the age°
For her perfections: but my revenge will come.
KING: Break not your sleeps for that: you must not think   30
That we are made of stuff so flat and dull
That we can let our beard be shook with danger
And think it pastime. You shortly shall hear more:
I lov'd your father, and we love ourself;
And that, I hope, will teach you to imagine—   35

Enter a Messenger with letters.

How now! what news?
MESSENGER: Letters, my lord, from Hamlet:
These to your majesty; this to the queen.°
KING: From Hamlet! who brought them?
MESSENGER: Sailors, my lord, they say; I saw them not:
They were given me by Claudio;° he receiv'd them   40
Of him that brought them.
KING: Laertes, you shall hear them.
Leave us.   *[Exit Messenger.]*
[Reads.] "High and mighty, You shall know I am set naked° on your king-
dom. Tomorrow shall I beg leave to see your kingly eyes: when I shall, first

---

14 conjunctive: Conformable (the next line suggesting planetary conjunction).   **15 sphere:**
The hollow sphere in which, according to Ptolemaic astronomy, the planets were supposed to
move.   **17 count:** Account, reckoning.   **18 general gender:** Common people.   **20 spring:**
I.e., one heavily charged with lime.   **21 gyves:** Fetters; here, faults, or possibly, punishments
inflicted (on him).   **22 slightly timber'd:** Light;   **loud:** Strong.   **26 terms:** State, condition.
27 go back: Return to Ophelia's former virtues.   **28 on mount:** Set up on high;   **mounted**
(on horseback);   **of all the age:** Qualifies *challenger* and not *mount*.   **37 to the queen:** One
hears no more of the letter to the queen.   **40 Claudio:** This character does not appear in the
play.   **43 naked:** Unprovided (with retinue).

asking your pardon thereunto, recount the occasion of my sudden and   45
more strange return.   "HAMLET."
What should this mean? Are all the rest come back?
Or is it some abuse, and no such thing?
LAERTES: Know you the hand?
KING: 'Tis Hamlet's character. "Naked!"
And in a postscript here, he says "alone."   50
Can you devise° me?
LAERTES: I'm lost in it, my lord. But let him come;
It warms the very sickness in my heart,
That I shall live and tell him to his teeth,
"Thus didst thou."
KING: If it be so, Laertes—   55
As how should it be so? how otherwise?° —
Will you be rul'd by me?
LAERTES: Ay, my lord;
So you will not o'errule me to a peace.
KING: To thine own peace. If he be now return'd,
As checking at° his voyage, and that he means   60
No more to undertake it, I will work him
To an exploit, now ripe in my device,
Under the which he shall not choose but fall:
And for his death no wind of blame shall breathe,
But even his mother shall uncharge the practice°   65
And call it accident.
LAERTES: My lord, I will be rul'd;
The rather, if you could devise it so
That I might be the organ.°
KING: It falls right.
You have been talk'd of since your travel much,
And that in Hamlet's hearing, for a quality   70
Wherein, they say, you shine: your sum of parts
Did not together pluck such envy from him
As did that one, and that, in my regard,
Of the unworthiest siege.°
LAERTES: What part is that, my lord?
KING: A very riband in the cap of youth,   75
Yet needful too; for youth no less becomes
The light and careless livery that it wears
Than settled age his sables° and his weeds,

---

51 devise: Explain to.   **56 As . . . otherwise?** How can this (Hamlet's return) be true? (yet) how otherwise than true (since we have the evidence of his letter)? Some editors read *How should it not be so*, etc., making the words refer to Laertes's desire to meet with Hamlet. **60 checking at:** Used in falconry of a hawk's leaving the quarry to fly at a chance bird; turn aside.   **65 uncharge the practice:** Acquit the stratagem of being a plot.   **68 organ:** Agent, instrument.   **74 siege:** Rank.   **78 sables:** Rich garments.

Importing health and graveness. Two months since,
Here was a gentleman of Normandy: —　　　　　　　　　　　　 80
I have seen myself, and serv'd against, the French,
And they can well° on horseback: but this gallant
Had witchcraft in 't; he grew unto his seat;
And to such wondrous doing brought his horse,
As had he been incorps'd and demi-natur'd°　　　　　　　　　 85
With the brave beast: so far he topp'd° my thought,
That I, in forgery° of shapes and tricks,
Come short of what he did.

LAERTES: 　　　　　　　　　　A Norman was 't?
KING: 　 A Norman.
LAERTES: 　 Upon my life, Lamord.°
KING: 　　　　　　　　　　　 The very same.　　　　　　　　　 90
LAERTES: 　 I know him well: he is the brooch indeed
And gem of all the nation.

KING: 　 He made confession° of you,
And gave you such a masterly report
For art and exercise° in your defence°　　　　　　　　　　　 95
And for your rapier most especial,
That he cried out, 'twould be a sight indeed,
If one could match you: the scrimers° of their nation,
He swore, had neither motion, guard, nor eye,
If you oppos'd them. Sir, this report of his　　　　　　　　　 100
Did Hamlet so envenom with his envy
That he could nothing do but wish and beg
Your sudden coming o'er, to play° with you.
Now, out of this, —

LAERTES: 　　　　　　　　What out of this, my lord?
KING: 　 Laertes, was your father dear to you?　　　　　　　　 105
Or are you like the painting of a sorrow,
A face without a heart?

LAERTES: 　　　　　　　　　Why ask you this?
KING: 　 Not that I think you did not love your father;
But that I know love is begun by time;
And that I see, in passages of proof,°　　　　　　　　　　　 110
Time qualifies the spark and fire of it.
There lives within the very flame of love
A kind of wick or snuff that will abate it;
And nothing is at a like goodness still;

---

82 can well: Are skilled.　**85 incorps'd and demi-natur'd:** Of one body and nearly of one nature (like the centaur).　**86 topp'd:** Surpassed.　**87 forgery:** Invention.　**90 Lamord:** This refers possibly to Pietro Monte, instructor to Louis XII's master of the horse.　**93 confession:** Grudging admission of superiority.　**95 art and exercise:** Skillful exercise; **defence:** Science of defense in sword practice.　**98 scrimers:** Fencers.　**103 play:** Fence.　**110 passages of proof:** Proved instances.

For goodness, growing to a plurisy,°   115
Dies in his own too much:° that we would do,
We should do when we would; for this "would" changes
And hath abatements° and delays as many
As there are tongues, are hands, are accidents;°
And then this "should" is like a spendthrift° sigh,   120
That hurts by easing. But, to the quick o' th' ulcer:° —
Hamlet comes back: what would you undertake,
To show yourself your father's son in deed
More than in words?
LAERTES: To cut his throat i' th' church.
KING: No place, indeed, should murder sanctuarize;°   125
Revenge should have no bounds. But, good Laertes,
Will you do this, keep close within your chamber.
Hamlet return'd shall know you are come home:
We'll put on those shall praise your excellence
And set a double varnish on the fame   130
The Frenchman gave you, bring you in fine together
And wager on your heads: he, being remiss,
Most generous and free from all contriving,
Will not peruse the foils; so that, with ease,
Or with a little shuffling, you may choose   135
A sword unbated,° and in a pass of practice°
Requite him for your father.
LAERTES: I will do 't:
And, for that purpose, I'll anoint my sword.
I bought an unction of a mountebank,°
So mortal that, but dip a knife in it,   140
Where it draws blood no cataplasm° so rare,
Collected from all simples° that have virtue
Under the moon,° can save the thing from death
That is but scratch'd withal: I'll touch my point
With this contagion, that, if I gall° him slightly,   145
It may be death.
KING: Let's further think of this;
Weigh what convenience both of time and means
May fit us to our shape:° if this should fail,

---

115 plurisy: Excess, plethora.   **116 in his own too much:** Of its own excess.   **118 abate-
ments:** Diminutions.   **119 accidents:** Occurrences, incidents.   **120 spendthrift:** An allusion to the belief that each sigh cost the heart a drop of blood.   **121 quick o' th' ulcer:** Heart
of the difficulty.   **125 sanctuarize:** Protect from punishment; allusion to the right of sanctuary
with which certain religious places were invested.   **136 unbated:** Not blunted, having no button;   **pass of practice:** Treacherous thrust.   **139 mountebank:** Quack doctor.   **141 cata-
plasm:** Plaster or poultice.   **142 simples:** Herbs.   **143 Under the moon:** I.e., when
collected by moonlight to add to their medicinal value.   **145 gall:** Graze, wound.
148 shape: Part we propose to act.

And that our drift look through our bad performance,°
'Twere better not assay'd: therefore this project   150
Should have a back or second, that might hold,
If this should blast in proof.° Soft! let me see:
We'll make a solemn wager on your cunnings:°
I ha 't:
When in your motion you are hot and dry —   155
As make your bouts more violent to that end —
And that he calls for drink, I'll have prepar'd him
A chalice° for the nonce, whereon but sipping,
If he by chance escape your venom'd stuck,°
Our purpose may hold there. But stay, what noise?   160

Enter Queen.

QUEEN: One woe doth tread upon another's heel,
    So fast they follow: your sister's drown'd, Laertes.
LAERTES: Drown'd! O, where?
QUEEN: There is a willow° grows askant° the brook,
    That shows his hoar° leaves in the glassy stream;   165
    There with fantastic garlands did she make
    Of crow-flowers,° nettles, daisies, and long purples°
    That liberal° shepherds give a grosser name,
    But our cold maids do dead men's fingers call them:
    There, on the pendent boughs her crownet° weeds   170
    Clamb'ring to hang, an envious sliver° broke;
    When down her weedy° trophies and herself
    Fell in the weeping brook. Her clothes spread wide;
    And, mermaid-like, awhile they bore her up:
    Which time she chanted snatches of old lauds;°   175
    As one incapable° of her own distress,
    Or like a creature native and indued°
    Upon that element: but long it could not be
    Till that her garments, heavy with their drink,
    Pull'd the poor wretch from her melodious lay   180
    To muddy death.
LAERTES: Alas, then, she is drown'd?
QUEEN: Drown'd, drown'd.
LAERTES: Too much of water hast thou, poor Ophelia,

---

149 drift . . . performance: Intention be disclosed by our bungling.   **152 blast in proof:**
Burst in the test (like a cannon).   **153 cunnings:** Skills.   **158 chalice:** Cup.   **159 stuck:**
Thrust (from *stoccado*).   **164 willow:** For its significance of forsaken love;   **askant:** Aslant.
165 hoar: White (i.e., on the underside).   **167 crow-flowers:** Buttercups;   **long purples:**
Early purple orchids.   **168 liberal:** Probably, free-spoken.   **170 crownet:** Coronet; made
into a chaplet.   **171 sliver:** Branch.   **172 weedy:** I.e., of plants.   **175 lauds:** Hymns.
176 incapable: Lacking capacity to apprehend.   **177 indued:** Endowed with qualities fitting
her for living in water.

And therefore I forbid my tears: but yet
It is our trick;° nature her custom holds,   185
Let shame say what it will: when these are gone,
The woman will be out.° Adieu, my lord:
I have a speech of fire, that fain would blaze,
But that this folly drowns it.   *Exit.*
KING: Let's follow, Gertrude:
How much I had to do to calm his rage!   190
Now fear I this will give it start again;
Therefore let 's follow.   *Exeunt.*

[ACT 5, Scene 1]

[A churchyard.]
   Enter two Clowns° [with spades, &c.].
FIRST CLOWN: Is she to be buried in Christian burial when she wilfully seeks
   her own salvation?
SECOND CLOWN: I tell thee she is; therefore make her grave straight:° the
   crowner° hath sat on her, and finds it Christian burial.
FIRST CLOWN: How can that be, unless she drowned herself in her own   5
   defence?
SECOND CLOWN: Why, 'tis found so.
FIRST CLOWN: It must be "se offendendo";° it cannot be else. For here lies the
   point: if I drown myself wittingly,° it argues an act: and an act hath three
   branches;° it is, to act, to do, and to perform: argal,° she drowned herself   10
   wittingly.
SECOND CLOWN: Nay, but hear you, goodman delver,° —
FIRST CLOWN: Give me leave. Here lies the water; good: here stands the man;
   good: if the man go to this water, and drown himself, it is, will he, nill he, he
   goes, — mark you that; but if the water come to him and drown him, he   15
   drowns not himself: argal, he that is not guilty of his own death shortens not
   his own life.
SECOND CLOWN: But is this law?
FIRST CLOWN: Ay, marry, is 't; crowner's quest° law.
SECOND CLOWN: Will you ha' the truth on 't? If this had not been a gentle-   20
   woman, she should have been buried out o' Christian burial.

---

185 trick: Way.   **186–187 when . . . out:** When my tears are all shed, the woman in me will
be satisfied.   **ACT 5, SCENE 1. Clowns:** The word *clown* was used to denote peasants as well as
humorous characters; here applied to the rustic type of clown.   **3 straight:** Straightway, immediately; some interpret "from east to west in a direct line, parallel with the church."
4 crowner: Coroner.   **8 "se offendendo":** For *se defendendo,* term used in verdicts of justifiable homicide.   **9 wittingly:** Intentionally.   **10 three branches:** Parody of legal phraseology;
argal: Corruption of *ergo,* therefore.   **12 delver:** Digger.   **19 quest:** Inquest.

FIRST CLOWN: Why, there thou say'st:° and the more pity that great folk should have countenance° in this world to drown or hang themselves, more than their even° Christian. Come, my spade. There is no ancient gentlemen but gardeners, ditchers, and grave-makers: they hold up° Adam's profession.   25

SECOND CLOWN: Was he a gentleman?

FIRST CLOWN: 'A was the first that ever bore arms.

SECOND CLOWN: Why, he had none.

FIRST CLOWN: What, art a heathen? How dost thou understand the Scripture?   30
The Scripture says "Adam digged": could he dig without arms? I'll put another question to thee: if thou answerest me not to the purpose, confess thyself° —

SECOND CLOWN: Go to.°

FIRST CLOWN: What is he that builds stronger than either the mason, the ship-   35
wright, or the carpenter?

SECOND CLOWN: The gallows-maker; for that frame outlives a thousand tenants.

FIRST CLOWN: I like thy wit well, in good faith: the gallows does well; but how does it well? it does well to those that do ill: now thou dost ill to say the gal-   40
lows is built stronger than the church: argal, the gallows may do well to thee. To 't again, come.

SECOND CLOWN: "Who builds stronger than a mason, a shipwright, or a carpenter?"

FIRST CLOWN: Ay, tell me that, and unyoke.°   45

SECOND CLOWN: Marry, now I can tell.

FIRST CLOWN: To 't.

SECOND CLOWN: Mass,° I cannot tell.

Enter Hamlet and Horatio [at a distance].

FIRST CLOWN: Cudgel thy brains no more about it, for your dull ass will not mend his pace with beating; and, when you are asked this question next, say   50
"a grave-maker": the houses he makes lasts till doomsday. Go, get thee in, and fetch me a stoup° of liquor.   *[Exit Second Clown.] Song. [He digs.]*

In youth, when I did love, did love,
    Methought it was very sweet,
To contract — O — the time, for — a — my behove,°   55
    O, methought, there — a — was nothing — a — meet.

HAMLET: Has this fellow no feeling of his business, that 'a sings at grave-making?

HORATIO: Custom hath made it in him a property of easiness.°

---

22 **there thou say'st:** That's right.   23 **countenance:** Privilege.   24 **even:** Fellow.   25 **hold up:** Maintain, continue.   32–33 **confess thyself:** "And be hanged" completes the proverb. 34 **Go to:** Perhaps, "begin," or some other form of concession.   45 **unyoke:** After this great effort you may unharness the team of your wits.   48 **Mass:** By the Mass.   52 **stoup:** Two-quart measure.   55 **behove:** Benefit.   59 **property of easiness:** A peculiarity that now is easy.

HAMLET: 'Tis e'en so: the hand of little employment hath the daintier sense.   60

FIRST CLOWN: *(Song.)* But age, with his stealing steps,
　　Hath claw'd me in his clutch,
And hath shipped me into the land
　　As if I had never been such.   *[Throws up a skull.]*

HAMLET: That skull had a tongue in it, and could sing once: how the knave   65
jowls° it to the ground, as if 'twere Cain's jaw-bone,° that did the first murder!
This might be the pate of a politician,° which this ass now o'er-reaches;° one
that would circumvent God, might it not?

HORATIO: It might, my lord.

HAMLET: Or of a courtier; which could say "Good morrow, sweet lord! How   70
dost thou, sweet lord?" This might be my lord such-a-one, that praised my
lord such-a-one's horse, when he meant to beg it; might it not?

HORATIO: Ay, my lord.

HAMLET: Why, e'en so: and now my Lady Worm's; chapless,° and knocked
about the mazzard° with a sexton's spade: here's fine revolution, an we had   75
the trick to see 't. Did these bones cost no more the breeding, but to play at
loggats° with 'em? mine ache to think on 't.

FIRST CLOWN: *(Song.)* A pick-axe, and a spade, a spade,
　　For and° a shrouding sheet:
O, a pit of clay for to be made   80
　　For such a guest is meet.   *[Throws up another skull.]*

HAMLET: There's another: why may not that be the skull of a lawyer? Where be
his quiddities° now, his quillities,° his cases, his tenures,° and his tricks? why
does he suffer this mad knave now to knock him about the sconce° with a
dirty shovel, and will not tell him of his action of battery? Hum! This fellow   85
might be in 's time a great buyer of land, with his statutes, his recognizances,° his fines, his double vouchers,° his recoveries:° is this the fine° of
his fines, and the recovery of his recoveries, to have his fine pate full of fine
dirt? will his vouchers vouch him no more of his purchases, and double ones
too, than the length and breadth of a pair of indentures?° The very con-   90
veyances of his lands will scarcely lie in this box; and must the inheritor°
himself have no more, ha?

HORATIO: Not a jot more, my lord.

HAMLET: Is not parchment made of sheep-skins?

HORATIO: Ay, my lord, and of calf-skins° too.   95

---

66 **jowls:** Dashes;　**Cain's jaw-bone:** Allusion to the old tradition that Cain slew Abel with the jawbone of an ass.　67 **politician:** Schemer, plotter;　**o'er-reaches:** Quibble on the literal sense and the sense "circumvent."　74 **chapless:** Having no lower jaw.　75 **mazzard:** Head.　77 **loggats:** A game in which six sticks are thrown to lie as near as possible to a stake fixed in the ground, or block of wood on a floor.　79 **For and:** And moreover.　83 **quiddities:** Subtleties, quibbles;　**quillities:** Verbal niceties, subtle distinctions;　**tenures:** The holding of a piece of property or office or the conditions or period of such holding.　84 **sconce:** Head.　86–87 **statutes, recognizances:** Legal terms connected with the transfer of land.　87 **vouchers:** Persons called on to warrant a tenant's title;　**recoveries:** Process for transfer of entailed estate;　**fine:** The four uses of this word are as follows: (1) end, (2) legal process, (3) elegant, (4) small.　90 **indentures:** Conveyances or contracts.　91 **inheritor:** Possessor, owner.　95 **calf-skins:** Parchments.

HAMLET: They are sheep and calves which seek out assurance in that.° I will
speak to this fellow. Whose grave's this, sirrah?

FIRST CLOWN: Mine, sir.

[Sings.] O, a pit of clay for to be made
For such a guest is meet.   100

HAMLET: I think it be thine, indeed; for thou liest in 't.

FIRST CLOWN: You lie out on 't, sir, and therefore 't is not yours: for my part, I do
not lie in 't, yet it is mine.

HAMLET: Thou dost lie in 't, to be in 't and say it is thine: 'tis for the dead, not for
the quick; therefore thou liest.   105

FIRST CLOWN: 'Tis a quick lie, sir; 'twill away again, from me to you.

HAMLET: What man dost thou dig it for?

FIRST CLOWN: For no man, sir.

HAMLET: What woman, then?

FIRST CLOWN: For none, neither.   110

HAMLET: Who is to be buried in 't?

FIRST CLOWN: One that was a woman, sir; but, rest her soul, she's dead.

HAMLET: How absolute° the knave is! we must speak by the card,° or equivoca-
tion° will undo us. By the Lord, Horatio, these three years I have taken note
of it; the age is grown so picked° that the toe of the peasant comes so near the   115
heel of the courtier, he galls° his kibe.° How long hast thou been a grave-
maker?

FIRST CLOWN: Of all the day i' the year, I came to 't that day that our last king
Hamlet overcame Fortinbras.

HAMLET: How long is that since?   120

FIRST CLOWN: Cannot you tell that? every fool can tell that: it was the very day
that young Hamlet was born; he that is mad, and sent into England.

HAMLET: Ay, marry, why was he sent into England?

FIRST CLOWN: Why, because 'a was mad: 'a shall recover his wits there; or, if 'a
do not, 'tis no great matter there.   125

HAMLET: Why?

FIRST CLOWN: 'Twill not be seen in him there; there the men are as mad as he.

HAMLET: How came he mad?

FIRST CLOWN: Very strangely, they say.

HAMLET: How strangely?   130

FIRST CLOWN: Faith, e'en with losing his wits.

HAMLET: Upon what ground?

FIRST CLOWN: Why, here in Denmark: I have been sexton here, man and boy,
thirty years.°

HAMLET: How long will a man lie i' the earth ere he rot?   135

---

96 **assurance in that:** Safety in legal parchments.   113 **absolute:** Positive, decided;   **by the
card:** With precision, i.e., by the mariner's card on which the points of the compass were
marked.   113–114 **equivocation:** Ambiguity in the use of terms.   115 **picked:** Refined, fas-
tidious.   116 **galls:** Chafes;   **kibe:** Chilblain.   134 **thirty years:** This statement with that in
line 122 shows Hamlet's age to be thirty years.

FIRST CLOWN: Faith, if 'a be not rotten before 'a die — as we have many pocky°
corses now-a-days, that will scarce hold the laying in — 'a will last you some
eight year or nine year: a tanner will last you nine year.

HAMLET: Why he more than another?

FIRST CLOWN: Why, sir, his hide is so tanned with his trade, that 'a will keep out   140
water a great while; and your water is a sore decayer of your whoreson dead
body. Here's a skull now hath lain you i' th' earth three and twenty years.

HAMLET: Whose was it?

FIRST CLOWN: A whoreson mad fellow's it was: whose do you think it was?

HAMLET: Nay, I know not.   145

FIRST CLOWN: A pestilence on him for a mad rogue! 'a poured a flagon of Rhenish on my head once. This same skull, sir, was Yorick's skull, the king's jester.

HAMLET: This?

FIRST CLOWN: E'en that.

HAMLET: Let me see. *[Takes the skull.]* Alas, poor Yorick! I knew him, Horatio: a   150
fellow of infinite jest, of most excellent fancy: he hath borne me on his back
a thousand times; and now, how abhorred in my imagination it is! my gorge
rises at it. Here hung those lips that I have kissed I know not how oft. Where
be your gibes now? your gambols? your songs? your flashes of merriment,
that were wont to set the table on a roar? Not one now, to mock your own   155
grinning? quite chap-fallen? Now get you to my lady's chamber, and tell her,
let her paint an inch thick, to this favour she must come; make her laugh at
that. Prithee, Horatio, tell me one thing.

HORATIO: What's that, my lord?

HAMLET: Dost thou think Alexander looked o' this fashion i' the earth?   160

HORATIO: E'en so.

HAMLET: And smelt so? pah!   *[Puts down the skull.]*

HORATIO: E'en so, my lord.

HAMLET: To what base uses we may return, Horatio! Why may not imagination
trace the noble dust of Alexander, till 'a find it stopping a bung-hole?   165

HORATIO: 'Twere to consider too curiously,° to consider so.

HAMLET: No, faith, not a jot; but to follow him thither with modesty enough,
and likelihood to lead it: as thus: Alexander died, Alexander was buried,
Alexander returneth into dust; the dust is earth; of earth we make loam;° and
why of that loam, whereto he was converted, might they not stop a beer-   170
barrel?

    Imperious° Cæsar, dead and turn'd to clay,
    Might stop a hole to keep the wind away:
    O, that that earth, which kept the world in awe,
    Should patch a wall t'expel the winter's flaw!°   175
But soft! but soft awhile! here comes the king,

*Enter King, Queen, Laertes, and the Corse of [Ophelia, in procession, with Priest,
Lords, etc.].*

---

136 pocky: Rotten, diseased.   **166 curiously:** Minutely.   **169 loam:** Clay paste for brick-
making.   **172 Imperious:** Imperial.   **175 flaw:** Gust of wind.

The queen, the courtiers: who is this they follow?
And with such maimed rites? This doth betoken
The corse they follow did with desp'rate hand
Fordo° it° own life: 'twas of some estate.   180
Couch° we awhile, and mark.   *[Retiring with Horatio.]*
LAERTES: What ceremony else?
HAMLET: That is Laertes,
    A very noble youth: mark.
LAERTES: What ceremony else?
FIRST PRIEST: Her obsequies have been as far enlarg'd°   185
    As we have warranty: her death was doubtful;
    And, but that great command o'ersways the order,
    She should in ground unsanctified have lodg'd
    Till the last trumpet; for charitable prayers,
    Shards,° flints and pebbles should be thrown on her: 190
    Yet here she is allow'd her virgin crants,°
    Her maiden strewments° and the bringing home
    Of bell and burial.°
LAERTES: Must there no more be done?
FIRST PRIEST: No more be done:
    We should profane the service of the dead   195
    To sing a requiem and such rest to her
    As to peace-parted° souls.
LAERTES: Lay her i' th' earth:
    And from her fair and unpolluted flesh
    May violets spring! I tell thee, churlish priest,
    A minist'ring angel shall my sister be,   200
    When thou liest howling.°
HAMLET: What, the fair Ophelia!
QUEEN: Sweets to the sweet: farewell!   *[Scattering flowers.]*
    I hop'd thou shouldst have been my Hamlet's wife;
    I thought thy bride-bed to have deck'd, sweet maid,
    And not have strew'd thy grave.
LAERTES: O, treble woe   205
    Fall ten times treble on that cursed head,
    Whose wicked deed thy most ingenious sense°
    Depriv'd thee of! Hold off the earth awhile,
    Till I have caught her once more in mine arms: *[Leaps into the grave.]*
    Now pile your dust upon the quick and dead,   210
    Till of this flat a mountain you have made,

---

180 **Fordo:** Destroy;   **it:** Its.   181 **Couch:** Hide, lurk.   185 **enlarg'd:** Extended, referring to the
fact that suicides are not given full burial rites.   190 **Shards:** Broken bits of pottery.   191 **crants:**
Garlands customarily hung upon the biers of unmarried women.   192 **strewments:** Traditional
strewing of flowers.   192–193 **bringing . . . burial:** The laying to rest of the body, to the sound of
the bell.   197 **peace-parted:** Allusion to the text "Lord, now lettest thou thy servant depart in
peace."   201 **howling:** I.e., in hell.   207 **ingenious sense:** Mind endowed with finest qualities.

T' o'ertop old Pelion,° or the skyish head
Of blue Olympus.
HAMLET: *[Advancing]* What is he whose grief
    Bears such an emphasis? whose phrase of sorrow
    Conjures the wand'ring stars,° and makes them stand   215
    Like wonder-wounded hearers? This is I,
    Hamlet the Dane.   *[Leaps into the grave.]*
LAERTES: The devil take thy soul!   *[Grappling with him.]*
HAMLET: Thou pray'st not well.
    I prithee, take thy fingers from my throat;
    For, though I am not splenitive° and rash,   220
    Yet have I in me something dangerous,
    Which let thy wisdom fear: hold off thy hand.
KING: Pluck them asunder.
QUEEN: Hamlet, Hamlet!
ALL: Gentlemen, —
HORATIO: Good my lord, be quiet.

[The Attendants part them, and they come out of the grave.]

HAMLET: Why, I will fight with him upon this theme   225
    Until my eyelids will no longer wag.°
QUEEN: O my son, what theme?
HAMLET: I lov'd Ophelia: forty thousand brothers
    Could not, with all their quantity° of love,
    Make up my sum. What wilt thou do for her?   230
KING: O, he is mad, Laertes.
QUEEN: For love of God, forbear° him.
HAMLET: 'Swounds,° show me what thou 'lt do:
    Woo 't° weep? woo 't fight? woo 't fast? woo 't tear thyself?
    Woo 't drink up eisel?° eat a crocodile?   235
    I'll do 't. Dost thou come here to whine?
    To outface me with leaping in her grave?
    Be buried quick with her, and so will I:
    And, if thou prate of mountains, let them throw
    Millions of acres on us, till our ground,   240
    Singeing his pate against the burning zone,°
    Make Ossa like a wart! Nay, an thou 'lt mouth,
    I'll rant as well as thou.
QUEEN: This is mere madness:
    And thus awhile the fit will work on him;

---

212 **Pelion:** Olympus, Pelion, and Ossa are mountains in the north of Thessaly.   215 **wand'ring stars:** Planets.   220 **splenitive:** Quick-tempered.   226 **wag:** Move (not used ludicrously).   229 **quantity:** Some suggest that the word is used in a deprecatory sense (little bits, fragments).   232 **forbear:** Leave alone.   233 **'Swounds:** Oath, "God's wounds."   234 **Woo 't:** Wilt thou.   235 **eisel:** Vinegar. Some editors have taken this to be the name of a river, such as the Yssel, the Weissel, and the Nile.   241 **burning zone:** Sun's orbit.

Anon, as patient as the female dove.   245
When that her golden couplets° are disclos'd,
His silence will sit drooping.
HAMLET: Hear you, sir;
What is the reason that you use me thus?
I lov'd you ever: but it is no matter;
Let Hercules himself do what he may,   250
The cat will mew and dog will have his day.
KING: I pray thee, good Horatio, wait upon him.   *Exit Hamlet and Horatio.*
[*To Laertes.*] Strengthen your patience in° our last night's speech;
We'll put the matter to the present push.°
Good Gertrude, set some watch over your son.   255
This grave shall have a living° monument:
An hour of quiet shortly shall we see;
Till then, in patience our proceeding be.   *Exeunt.*

[Scene 2]

[*A hall in the castle.*]
Enter Hamlet and Horatio.

HAMLET: So much for this, sir: now shall you see the other;
You do remember all the circumstance?
HORATIO: Remember it, my lord!
HAMLET: Sir, in my heart there was a kind of fighting,
That would not let me sleep: methought I lay   5
Worse than the mutines in the bilboes.° Rashly,°
And prais'd be rashness for it, let us know,
Our indiscretion sometime serves us well,
When our deep plots do pall:° and that should learn us
There's a divinity that shapes our ends,   10
Rough-hew° them how we will, —
HORATIO: That is most certain.
HAMLET: Up from my cabin,
My sea-gown° scarf'd about me, in the dark
Grop'd I to find out them; had my desire,
Finger'd° their packet, and in fine° withdrew   15
To mine own room again; making so bold,
My fears forgetting manners, to unseal
Their grand commission; where I found, Horatio, —

---

246 **golden couplets:** The pigeon lays two eggs; the young when hatched are covered with golden down.   253 **in:** By recalling.   254 **present push:** Immediate test.   256 **living:** Lasting; also refers (for Laertes's benefit) to the plot against Hamlet.   SCENE 2. 6 **mutines in the bilboes:** Mutineers in shackles;   **Rashly:** Goes with line 12.   9 **pall:** Fail.   11 **Rough-hew:** Shape roughly; it may mean "bungle."   13 **sea-gown:** "A sea-gown, or a coarse, high-collered, and short-sleeved gowne, reaching down to the mid-leg, and used most by seamen and saylors" (Cotgrave, quoted by Singer).   15 **Finger'd:** Pilfered, filched;   **in fine:** Finally.

O royal knavery! — an exact command,
Larded° with many several sorts of reasons   20
Importing Denmark's health and England's too,
With, ho! such bugs° and goblins in my life,°
That, on the supervise,° no leisure bated,°
No, not to stay the grinding of the axe,
My head should be struck off.
HORATIO: Is 't possible?   25
HAMLET: Here's the commission: read it at more leisure.
But wilt thou hear me how I did proceed?
HORATIO: I beseech you.
HAMLET: Being thus be-netted round with villanies, —
Ere I could make a prologue to my brains,   30
They had begun the play° — I sat me down,
Devis'd a new commission, wrote it fair:
I once did hold it, as our statists° do,
A baseness to write fair° and labour'd much
How to forget that learning, but, sir, now   35
It did me yeoman's° service: wilt thou know
Th' effect of what I wrote?
HORATIO: Ay, good my lord.
HAMLET: An earnest conjuration from the king,
As England was his faithful tributary,
As love between them like the palm might flourish,   40
As peace should still her wheaten garland° wear
And stand a comma° 'tween their amities,
And many such-like 'As'es° of great charge,°
That, on the view and knowing of these contents,
Without debatement further, more or less,   45
He should the bearers put to sudden death,
Not shriving-time° allow'd.
HORATIO: How was this seal'd?
HAMLET: Why, even in that was heaven ordinant.°
I had my father's signet in my purse,
Which was the model of that Danish seal;   50
Folded the writ up in the form of th' other,
Subscrib'd it, gave 't th' impression, plac'd it safely,
The changeling never known. Now, the next day

---

20 **Larded:** Enriched.   22 **bugs:** Bugbears;   **such . . . life:** Such imaginary dangers if I were
allowed to live.   23 **supervise:** Perusal;   **leisure bated:** Delay allowed.   **30–31 prologue . . .
play:** I.e., before I could begin to think, my mind had made its decision.   33 **statists:** States-
men.   34 **fair:** In a clear hand.   36 **yeoman's:** I.e., faithful.   41 **wheaten garland:** Symbol
of peace.   42 **comma:** Smallest break or separation. Here *amity* begins and *amity* ends the
period, and *peace* stands between like a dependent clause. The comma indicates continuity,
link.   43 **'As'es:** The "whereases" of a formal document, with play on the word *ass*;   **charge:**
Import, and burden.   47 **shriving-time:** Time for absolution.   48 **ordinant:** Directing.

Was our sea-fight; and what to this was sequent°
Thou know'st already.   55
HORATIO: So Guildenstern and Rosencrantz go to 't.
HAMLET: Why, man, they did make love to this employment;
They are not near my conscience; their defeat
Does by their own insinuation° grow:
'Tis dangerous when the baser nature comes   60
Between the pass° and fell incensed° points
Of mighty opposites.
HORATIO: Why, what a king is this!
HAMLET: Does it not, think thee, stand° me now upon —
He that hath kill'd my king and whor'd my mother,
Popp'd in between th' election° and my hopes,   65
Thrown out his angle° for my proper life,
And with such coz'nage° — is 't not perfect conscience,
To quit° him with this arm? and is 't not to be damn'd,
To let this canker° of our nature come
In further evil?   70
HORATIO: It must be shortly known to him from England
What is the issue of the business there.
HAMLET: It will be short: the interim is mine;
And a man's life's no more than to say "One."
But I am very sorry, good Horatio,   75
That to Laertes I forgot myself;
For, by the image of my cause, I see
The portraiture of his: I'll court his favours:
But, sure, the bravery° of his grief did put me
Into a tow'ring passion.
HORATIO: Peace! who comes here?   80

Enter a Courtier [Osric].

OSRIC: Your lordship is right welcome back to Denmark.
HAMLET: I humbly thank you, sir. *[To Horatio.]* Dost know this water-fly?°
HORATIO: No, my good lord.
HAMLET: Thy state is the more gracious; for 'tis a vice to know him. He hath
much land, and fertile: let a beast be lord of beasts,° and his crib shall stand   85
at the king's mess:° 'tis a chough;° but, as I say, spacious in the possession of
dirt.

---

54 sequent: Subsequent.   **59 insinuation:** Interference.   **61 pass:** Thrust;   **fell incensed:**
Fiercely angered.   **63 stand:** Become incumbent.   **65 election:** The Danish throne was
filled by election.   **66 angle:** Fishing line.   **67 coz'nage:** Trickery.   **68 quit:** Repay.
69 canker: Ulcer, or possibly the worm which destroys buds and leaves.   **79 bravery:**
Bravado.   **82 water-fly:** Vain or busily idle person.   **85 lord of beasts:** See Genesis 1:26, 28.
85–86 his crib . . . mess: He shall eat at the king's table and be one of the group of persons
(usually four) constituting a *mess* at a banquet.   **86 chough:** Probably, chattering jackdaw;
also explained as *chuff*, provincial boor or churl.

OSRIC: Sweet lord, if your lordship were at leisure, I should impart a thing to you from his majesty.

HAMLET: I will receive it, sir, with all diligence of spirit. Put your bonnet to his   90
right use; 'tis for the head.

OSRIC: I thank you lordship, it is very hot.

HAMLET: No, believe me, 'tis very cold; the wind is northerly.

OSRIC: It is indifferent° cold, my lord, indeed.

HAMLET: But yet methinks it is very sultry and hot for my complexion.   95

OSRIC: Exceedingly, my lord; it is very sultry, — as 'twere, — I cannot tell how.
But, my lord, his majesty bade me signify to you that 'a has laid a great wager
on your head: sir, this is the matter, —

HAMLET: I beseech you, remember° —   *[Hamlet moves him to put on his hat.]*

OSRIC: Nay, good my lord; for mine ease,° in good faith. Sir, here is newly come   100
to court Laertes; believe me, an absolute gentleman, full of most excellent
differences, of very soft° society and great showing:° indeed, to speak
feelingly° of him, he is the card° or calendar of gentry,° for you shall find in
him the continent of what part a gentleman would see.

HAMLET: Sir, his definement° suffers no perdition° in you; though, I know, to   105
divide him inventorially° would dozy° the arithmetic of memory, and yet but
yaw° neither, in respect of his quick sail. But, in the verity of extolment, I
take him to be a soul of great article;° and his infusion° of such dearth and
rareness,° as, to make true diction of him, his semblable° is his mirror; and
who else would trace° him, his umbrage,° nothing more.   110

OSRIC: Your lordship speaks most infallibly of him.

HAMLET: The concernancy,° sir? why do we wrap the gentleman in our more
rawer breath?°

OSRIC: Sir?

HORATIO *[aside to Hamlet]:*   Is 't not possible to understand in another tongue?°   115
You will do 't, sir, really.

HAMLET: What imports the nomination° of this gentleman?

OSRIC: Of Laertes?

Horatio [aside to Hamlet]:   His purse is empty already; all 's golden words are
spent.   120

HAMLET: Of him, sir.

---

94 indifferent: Somewhat.   **99 remember:** I.e., remember thy courtesy; conventional phrase
for "Be covered."   **100 mine ease:** Conventional reply declining the invitation of "Remember
thy courtesy."   **102 soft:** Gentle;   **showing:** Distinguished appearance.   **103 feelingly:**
With just perception;   **card:** Chart, map;   **gentry:** Good breeding.   **105 definement:** Definition;   **perdition:** Loss, diminution.   **106 divide him inventorially:** I.e., enumerate his
graces;   **dozy:** Dizzy.   **107 yaw:** To move unsteadily (of a ship).   **108 article:** Moment or
importance;   **infusion:** Infused temperament, character imparted by nature.
108–109 dearth and rareness: Rarity.   **109 semblable:** True likeness.   **110 trace:** Follow;
umbrage: Shadow.   **112 concernancy:** Import.   **113 breath:** Speech.   **115 Is 't . . . tongue?:**
I.e., can one converse with Osric only in this outlandish jargon?   **117 nomination:** Naming.

OSRIC: I know you are not ignorant—

HAMLET: I would you did, sir; yet, in faith, if you did, it would not much approve° me. Well, sir?

OSRIC: You are not ignorant of what excellence Laertes is— 125

HAMLET: I dare not confess that, lest I should compare with him in excellence; but, to know a man well, were to know himself.°

OSRIC: I mean, sir, for his weapon; but in the imputation° laid on him by them, in his meed° he's unfellowed.

HAMLET: What's his weapon? 130

OSRIC: Rapier and dagger.

HAMLET: That's two of his weapons: but, well.

OSRIC: The king, sir, hath wagered with him six Barbary horses: against the which he has impawned,° as I take it, six French rapiers and poniards, with their assigns, as girdle, hangers,° and so: three of the carriages, in faith, are 135 very dear to fancy,° very responsive° to the hilts, most delicate° carriages, and of very liberal conceit.°

HAMLET: What call you the carriages?

HORATIO [*aside to Hamlet*]: I knew you must be edified by the margent° ere you had done. 140

OSRIC: The carriages, sir, are the hangers.

HAMLET: The phrase would be more german° to the matter, if we could carry cannon by our sides: I would it might be hangers till then. But, on: six Barbary horses against six French swords, their assigns, and three liberal-conceited carriages; that's the French bet against the Danish. Why is this 145 "impawned," as you call it?

OSRIC: The king, sir, hath laid, that in a dozen passes between yourself and him, he shall not exceed you three hits: he hath laid on twelve for nine; and it would come to immediate trial, if your lordship would vouchsafe the answer. 150

HAMLET: How if I answer "no"?

OSRIC: I mean, my lord, the opposition of your person in trial.

HAMLET: Sir, I will walk here in the hall: if it please his majesty, it is the breathing time° of day with me; let the foils be brought, the gentleman willing, and the king hold his purpose, I will win for him as I can; if not, I will gain noth- 155 ing but my shame and the odd hits.

OSRIC: Shall I re-deliver you e'en so?

HAMLET: To this effect, sir; after what flourish your nature will.

OSRIC: I commend my duty to your lordship.

---

124 **approve:** Command.   127 **but . . . himself:** But to know a man as excellent were to know Laertes.   128 **imputation:** Reputation.   129 **meed:** Merit.   134 **he has impawned:** He has wagered.   135 **hangers:** Straps on the sword belt from which the sword hung. 136 **dear to fancy:** Fancifully made;   **responsive:** Probably, well balanced, corresponding closely;   **delicate:** Fine in workmanship.   137 **liberal conceit:** Elaborate design.   139 **margent:** Margin of a book, place for explanatory notes.   142 **german:** Germane, appropriate. 153–154 **breathing time:** Exercise period.

HAMLET: Yours, yours. *[Exit Osric.]* He does well to commend it himself; there   160
    are no tongues else for 's turn.
HORATIO: This lapwing° runs away with the shell on his head.
HAMLET: 'A did comply, sir, with his dug,° before 'a sucked it. Thus has hey —
    and many more of the same breed that I know the drossy° age dotes on —
    only got the tune° of the time and out of an habit of encounter;° a kind of   165
    yesty° collection, which carries them through and through the most fann'd
    and winnowed° opinions; and do but blow them to their trial, the bubbles
    are out.°

Enter a Lord.

LORD: My lord, his majesty commended him to you by young Osric, who
    brings back to him, that you attend him in the hall: he sends to know if your   170
    pleasure hold to play with Laertes, or that you will take longer time.
HAMLET: I am constant to my purposes; they follow the king's pleasure: if his fit-
    ness speaks, mine is ready; now or whensoever, provided I be so able as now.
LORD: The king and queen and all are coming down.
HAMLET: In happy time.°   175
LORD: The queen desires you to use some gentle entertainment to Laertes
    before you fall to play.
HAMLET: She well instructs me.   *[Exit Lord.]*
HORATIO: You will lose this wager, my lord.
HAMLET: I do not think so; since he went into France, I have been in continual   180
    practice; I shall win at the odds. But thou wouldst not think how ill all 's here
    about my heart: but it is no matter.
HORATIO: Nay, good my lord, —
HAMLET: It is but foolery; but it is such a kind of gain-giving,° as would perhaps
    trouble a woman.   185
HORATIO: If your mind dislike any thing, obey it: I will forestall their repair
    hither, and say you are not fit.
HAMLET: Not a whit, we defy augury: there's a special providence in the fall of a
    sparrow. If it be now, 'tis not to come; if it be not to come, it will be now; if it
    be not now, yet it will come: the readiness is all:° since no man of aught he   190
    leaves knows, what is 't to leave betimes? Let be.

A table prepared. [Enter] Trumpets, Drums, and Officers with cushions; King,
Queen, [Osric,] and all the State; foils, daggers, [and wine borne in;] and Laertes.

KING: Come, Hamlet, come, and take this hand from me.

[The King puts Laertes' hand into Hamlet's.]

---

162 **lapwing**: Peewit; noted for its wiliness in drawing a visitor away from its nest and its
supposed habit of running about when newly hatched with its head in the shell; possibly
an allusion to Osric's hat.   163 **did comply . . . dug**: Paid compliments to his mother's
breast.   164 **drossy**: Frivolous.   165 **tune**: Temper, mood;   **habit of encounter**: Demeanor
of social intercourse.   166 **yesty**: Frothy.   166–167 **fann'd and winnowed**: Select and refined.
167–168 **blow . . . out**: I.e., put them to the test, and their ignorance is exposed.   175 **In happy
time**: A phrase of courtesy.   184 **gain-giving**: Misgiving.   190 **all**: All that matters.

HAMLET: Give me your pardon, sir: I have done you wrong;
　　　　　But pardon 't as you are a gentleman.
　　　　　This presence° knows,   195
　　　　　And you must needs have heard, how I am punish'd
　　　　　With a sore distraction. What I have done,
　　　　　That might your nature, honour and exception°
　　　　　Roughly awake, I here proclaim was madness.
　　　　　Was 't Hamlet wrong'd Laertes? Never Hamlet: 200
　　　　　If Hamlet from himself be ta'en away,
　　　　　And when he's not himself does wrong Laertes,
　　　　　Then Hamlet does it not, Hamlet denies it.
　　　　　Who does it, then? His madness: if 't be so,
　　　　　Hamlet is of the faction that is wrong'd;   205
　　　　　His madness is poor Hamlet's enemy.
　　　　　Sir, in this audience,
　　　　　Let my disclaiming from a purpos'd evil
　　　　　Free me so far in your most generous thoughts,
　　　　　That I have shot mine arrow o'er the house,   210
　　　　　And hurt my brother.
LAERTES:　　　　　　　　I am satisfied in nature,°
　　　　　Whose motive, in this case, should stir me most
　　　　　To my revenge: but in my terms of honour
　　　　　I stand aloof; and will no reconcilement,
　　　　　Till by some elder masters, of known honour,   215
　　　　　I have a voice° and precedent of peace,
　　　　　To keep my name ungor'd. But till that time,
　　　　　I do receive your offer'd love like love,
　　　　　And will not wrong it.
HAMLET:　　　　　　　　I embrace it freely;
　　　　　And will this brother's wager frankly play.   220
　　　　　Give us the foils. Come on.
LAERTES:　　　　　　　　Come, one for me.
HAMLET: I'll be your foil,° Laertes: in mine ignorance
　　　　　Your skill shall, like a star i' th' darkest night,
　　　　　Stick fiery off° indeed.
LAERTES:　　　　　　　　You mock me, sir.
HAMLET: No, by this hand.   225
KING: Give them the foils, young Osric. Cousin Hamlet,
　　　　　You know the wager?
HAMLET:　　　　　　　　Very well, my lord;
　　　　　Your grace has laid the odds o' th' weaker side.

---

195 presence: Royal assembly.   **198 exception:** Disapproval.   **211 nature:** I.e., he is personally satisfied, but his honor must be satisfied by the rules of the code of honor.   **216 voice:** Authoritative pronouncement.   **222 foil:** Quibble on the two senses: "background which sets something off," and "blunted rapier for fencing."   **224 Stick fiery off:** Stand out brilliantly.

KING: I do not fear it; I have seen you both:
> But since he is better'd, we have therefore odds.   230
LAERTES: This is too heavy, let me see another.
HAMLET: This likes me well. These foils have all a length?

[They prepare to play.]

OSRIC: Ay, my good lord.
KING: Set me the stoups of wine upon that table.
> If Hamlet give the first or second hit,   235
> Or quit in answer of the third exchange,
> Let all the battlements their ordnance fire;
> The king shall drink to Hamlet's better breath;
> And in the cup an union° shall he throw,
> Richer than that which four successive kings   240
> In Denmark's crown have worn. Give me the cups;
> And let the kettle° to the trumpet speak,
> The trumpet to the cannoneer without,
> The cannons to the heavens, the heavens to earth,
> "Now the king drinks to Hamlet." Come begin: *Trumpets the while.*   245
> And you, the judges, bear a wary eye.
HAMLET: Come on, sir.
LAERTES: Come, my lord.   *[They play.]*
HAMLET: One.
LAERTES: No.
HAMLET: Judgement.
OSRIC: A hit, a very palpable hit.

Drum, trumpets, and shot. Flourish. A piece goes off.

LAERTES: Well; again.
KING: Stay; give me drink. Hamlet, this pearl° is thine;
> Here's to thy health. Give him the cup.   250
HAMLET: I'll play this bout first; set it by awhile.
> Come. *[They play.]* Another hit; what say you?
LAERTES: A touch, a touch, I do confess 't.
KING: Our son shall win.
QUEEN: He's fat,° and scant of breath.
> Here, Hamlet, take my napkin, rub thy brows: 255
> The queen carouses° to thy fortune, Hamlet.
HAMLET: Good madam!
KING: Gertrude, do not drink.
QUEEN: I will, my lord; I pray you, pardon me.   *[Drinks.]*
KING *[aside]*:   It is the poison'd cup: it is too late.

---

239 union: Pearl. **242 kettle:** Kettledrum. **249 pearl:** I.e., the poison. **254 fat:** Not physically fit, out of training. Some earlier editors speculated that the term applied to the corpulence of Richard Burbage, who originally played the part, but the allusion now appears unlikely. *Fat* may also suggest "sweaty." **256 carouses:** Drinks a toast.

HAMLET: I dare not drink yet, madam; by and by.   260
QUEEN: Come, let me wipe thy face.
LAERTES: My lord, I'll hit him now.
KING: I do not think 't.
LAERTES *[aside]*:   And yet 'tis almost 'gainst my conscience.
HAMLET: Come, for the third, Laertes: you but dally;
    I pray you, pass with your best violence;   265
    I am afeard you make a wanton° of me.
LAERTES: Say you so? come on.   *[They play.]*
OSRIC: Nothing, neither way.
LAERTES: Have at you now!

*[Laertes wounds Hamlet; then, in scuffling, they change rapiers,° and Hamlet
wounds Laertes.]*

KING: Part them; they are incens'd.
HAMLET: Nay, come again.   *[The Queen falls.]*
OSRIC: Look to the queen there, ho!   270
HORATIO: They bleed on both sides. How is it, my lord?
OSRIC: How is 't, Laertes?
LAERTES: Why, as a woodcock° to mine own springe,° Osric;
    I am justly kill'd with mine own treachery.
HAMLET: How does the queen?
KING: She swounds° to see them bleed.   275
QUEEN: No, no, the drink, the drink, — O my dear Hamlet, —
    The drink, the drink! I am poison'd.   *[Dies.]*
HAMLET: O villany! Ho! let the door be lock'd:
    Treachery! Seek it out.   *[Laertes falls.]*
LAERTES: It is here, Hamlet: Hamlet, thou art slain;   280
    No med'cine in the world can do thee good;
    In thee there is not half an hour of life;
    The treacherous instrument is in thy hand,
    Unbated° and envenom'd: the foul practice
    Hath turn'd itself on me; lo, here I lie,   285
    Never to rise again: thy mother's poison'd:
    I can no more: the king, the king's to blame.
HAMLET: The point envenom'd too!
    Then, venom, to thy work.   *[Stabs the King.]*
ALL: Treason! treason!   290
KING: O, yet defend me, friends; I am but hurt.
HAMLET: Here, thou incestuous, murd'rous, damned Dane,
    Drink off this potion. Is thy union here?
    Follow my mother.   *[King dies.]*

---

266 wanton: Spoiled child;   **in scuffling, they change rapiers:** According to a widespread
stage tradition, Hamlet receives a scratch, realizes that Laertes's sword is unbated, and accordingly forces an exchange.   **273 woodcock:** As type of stupidity or as decoy;   **springe:** Trap,
snare.   **275 swounds:** Swoons.   **284 Unbated:** Not blunted with a button.

LAERTES: He is justly serv'd;
  It is a poison temper'd° by himself.   295
  Exchange forgiveness with me, noble Hamlet:
  Mine and my father's death come not upon thee,
  Nor thine on me!   *[Dies.]*

HAMLET: Heaven make thee free of it! I follow thee.
  I am dead, Horatio. Wretched queen, adieu!   300
  You that look pale and tremble at this chance,
  That are but mutes° or audience to this act,
  Had I but time — as this fell sergeant,° Death,
  Is strict in his arrest — O, I could tell you —
  But let it be. Horatio, I am dead;   305
  Thou livest; report me and my cause aright
  To the unsatisfied.

HORATIO: Never believe it:
  I am more an antique Roman° than a Dane:
  Here 's yet some liquor left.

HAMLET: As th' art a man,
  Give me the cup: let go, by heaven, I'll ha 't.   310
  O God! Horatio, what a wounded name,
  Things standing thus unknown, shall live behind me!
  If thou didst ever hold me in thy heart,
  Absent thee from felicity awhile,
  And in this harsh world draw thy breath in pain,   315
  To tell my story.   *A march afar off.*
             What warlike noise is this?

OSRIC: Young Fortinbras, with conquest come from Poland,
  To the ambassadors of England gives
  This warlike volley.

HAMLET: O, I die, Horatio;
  The potent poison quite o'er-crows° my spirit: 320
  I cannot live to hear the news from England;
  But I do prophesy th' election lights
  On Fortinbras: he has my dying voice;
  So tell him, with th' occurrents,° more and less,
  Which have solicited.° The rest is silence.   *[Dies.]* 325

HORATIO: Now cracks a noble heart. Good night, sweet prince;
  And flights of angels sing thee to thy rest!
  Why does the drum come hither?   *[March within.]*

Enter Fortinbras, with the [English] Ambassadors [and others].

FORTINBRAS: Where is this sight?

---

295 **temper'd:** Mixed.   **302 mutes:** Performers in a play who speak no words.   **303 sergeant:** Sheriff's officer.   **308 Roman:** It was the Roman custom to follow masters in death.   **320 o'er-crows:** Triumphs over.   **324 occurrents:** Events, incidents.   **325 solicited:** Moved, urged.

HORATIO: What is it you would see?
    If aught of woe or wonder, cease your search.   330
FORTINBRAS: This quarry° cries on havoc.° O proud Death,
    What feast is toward in thine eternal cell,
    That thou so many princes at a shot
    So bloodily hast struck?
FIRST AMBASSADOR: The sight is dismal;
    And our affairs from England come too late: 335
    The ears are senseless that should give us hearing,
    To tell him his commandment is fulfill'd,
    That Rosencrantz and Guildenstern are dead:
    Where should we have our thanks?
HORATIO: Not from his mouth,°
    Had it th' ability of life to thank you: 340
    He never gave commandment for their death.
    But since, so jump° upon this bloody question,°
    You from the Polack wars, and you from England,
    Are here arriv'd, give order that these bodies
    High on a stage° be placed to the view;   345
    And let me speak to th' yet unknowing world
    How these things came about: so shall you hear
    Of carnal, bloody, and unnatural acts,
    Of accidental judgements, casual slaughters,
    Of deaths put on by cunning and forc'd cause,   350
    And, in this upshot, purposes mistook
    Fall'n on th' inventors' heads: all this can I
    Truly deliver.
FORTINBRAS: Let us haste to hear it,
    And call the noblest to the audience.
    For me, with sorrow I embrace my fortune: 355
    I have some rights of memory° in this kingdom,
    Which now to claim my vantage doth invite me.
HORATIO: Of that I shall have also cause to speak,
    And from his mouth whose voice will draw on more:°
    But let this same be presently perform'd,   360
    Even while men's minds are wild; lest more mischance,
    On° plots and errors, happen.
FORTINBRAS: Let four captains
    Bear Hamlet, like a soldier, to the stage;
    For he was likely, had he been put on,
    To have prov'd most royal: and, for his passage,°   365

---

331 quarry: Heap of dead;   **cries on havoc:** Proclaims a general slaughter.   **339 his mouth:** I.e.,
the king's.   **342 jump:** Precisely;   **question:** Dispute.   **345 stage:** Platform.   **356 of memory:**
Traditional, remembered.   **359 voice . . . more:** Vote will influence still others.   **362 On:** On
account of, or possibly, on top of, in addition to.   **365 passage:** Death.

The soldiers' music and the rites of war
Speak loudly for him.
Take up the bodies: such a sight as this
Becomes the field,° but here shows much amiss.
Go, bid the soldiers shoot.   370

Exeunt [marching, bearing off the dead bodies; after which a peal of ordnance is shot off].   [c. 1600]

369 **field:** I.e., of battle.

THINKING ABOUT THE TEXT

1. Hamlet takes a long time to act on his father's request. Why does he delay? Should he have acted sooner, for example, when Claudius is praying?

2. In act 3, scene 4, Hamlet confronts his mother. After rereading this scene, what is your view of Hamlet's feelings toward his mother? Why do you think he uses such lurid imagery?

3. Contrast the relationship of Laertes and Polonius with that of Hamlet and his father. Is Laertes a more loyal son? Is Hamlet less devoted?

4. Some critics think that Hamlet idealizes his father's memory because he unconsciously resents his father. They also suggest that he cannot attach himself emotionally to Ophelia because he has not fully transferred his affection from his mother. Do you agree with these psychological interpretations? Why, or why not?

5. Make a list of all the family relationships in the play and characterize them as positive or negative, as healthy or troubled. Which relationship seems to you to be the most modern? The most ambiguous?

SUSAN GLASPELL
Trifles

Susan Glaspell (1876–1948) is best known for her association with the avant-garde Provincetown Players. They premiered Trifles *in 1916, with the author and her husband, the novelist George Cram Cook, in the cast. Glaspell and Cook had founded the company a year earlier while vacationing in Provincetown, Massachusetts. Since its debut, the play has continued to be performed and read, in part because it is both a compelling detective story and an incisive analysis of relationships among women.*

CHARACTERS

GEORGE HENDERSON, *county attorney*
HENRY PETERS, *sheriff*
LEWIS HALE, *a neighboring farmer*

MRS. PETERS
MRS. HALE

SCENE: *The kitchen in the now abandoned farmhouse of John Wright, a gloomy kitchen, and left without having been put in order—the walls covered with a faded wall paper. Down right is a door leading to the parlor. On the right wall above this door is a built-in kitchen cupboard with shelves in the upper portion and drawers below. In the rear wall at right, up two steps is a door opening onto stairs leading to the second floor. In the rear wall at left is a door to the shed and from there to the outside. Between these two doors is an old-fashioned black iron stove. Running along the left wall from the shed door is an old iron sink and sink shelf, in which is set a hand pump. Downstage of the sink is an uncurtained window. Near the window is an old wooden rocker. Centerstage is an <u>unpainted wooden kitchen table</u> with straight <u>chairs on either side.</u> There is a small chair down <u>right. Unwashed</u> pans under the sink, a loaf of bread outside the breadbox, a dish towel on the table—other signs of incompleted work. At the rear the shed door opens and the Sheriff comes in followed by the County Attorney and Hale. The Sheriff and Hale are men in middle life, the County Attorney is a young man; all are much bundled up and go at once to the stove. They are followed by the two women—the Sheriff's wife, Mrs. Peters, first; she is a slight wiry woman, a thin nervous face. Mrs. Hale is larger and would ordinarily be called more comfortable looking, but she is disturbed now and looks fearfully about as she enters. The women have come in slowly, and stand close together near the door.*

COUNTY ATTORNEY *(at stove rubbing his hands)*:   This feels good. Come up to the fire, ladies.

MRS. PETERS *(after taking a step forward)*:   I'm not—cold.

SHERIFF *(unbuttoning his overcoat and stepping away from the stove to right of table as if to mark the beginning of official business)*:   Now, Mr. Hale, before we move things about, you explain to Mr. Henderson just what you saw when you came here yesterday morning.

COUNTY ATTORNEY *(crossing down to left of the table)*:   By the way, has anything been moved? Are things just as you left them yesterday?

SHERIFF *(looking about)*:   It's just about the same. When it dropped below zero last night I thought I'd better send Frank out this morning to make a fire for us—*(sits right of center table)* no use getting pneumonia with a big case on, but I told him not to touch anything except the stove—and you know Frank.

COUNTY ATTORNEY: Somebody should have been left here yesterday.

SHERIFF: Oh—yesterday. When I had to send Frank to Morris Center for that man who went crazy—I want you to know I had my hands full yesterday. I knew you could get back from Omaha by today and as long as I went over everything here myself——

COUNTY ATTORNEY: Well, Mr. Hale, tell just what happened when you came here yesterday morning.

HALE *(crossing down to above table)*:   Harry and I had started to town with a load of potatoes. We came along the road from my place and as I got here I said,

"I'm going to see if I can't get John Wright to go in with me on a party telephone." I spoke to Wright about it once before and he put me off, saying folks talked too much anyway, and all he asked was peace and quiet—I guess you know about how much he talked himself; but I thought maybe if I went to the house and talked about it before his wife, though I said to Harry that I didn't know as what his wife wanted made much difference to John——

COUNTY ATTORNEY: Let's talk about that later, Mr. Hale. I do want to talk about that, but tell now just what happened when you got to the house.

HALE: I didn't hear or see anything; I knocked at the door, and still it was all quiet inside. I knew they must be up, it was past eight o'clock. So I knocked again, and I thought I heard somebody say, "Come in." I wasn't sure, I'm not sure yet, but I opened the door—this door *(indicating the door by which the two women are still standing)* and there in that rocker—*(pointing to it)* sat Mrs. Wright. *(They all look at the rocker down left.)*

COUNTY ATTORNEY: What—was she doing?

HALE: She was rockin' back and forth. She had her apron in her hand and was kind of—pleating it.

COUNTY ATTORNEY: And how did she—look?

HALE: Well, she looked queer.

COUNTY ATTORNEY: How do you mean—queer?

HALE: Well, as if she didn't know what she was going to do next. And kind of done up.

COUNTY ATTORNEY *(takes out notebook and pencil and sits left of center table)*: How did she seem to feel about your coming?

HALE: Why, I don't think she minded—one way or other. She didn't pay much attention. I said, "How do, Mrs. Wright, it's cold, ain't it?" And she said, "Is it?"—and went on kind of pleating at her apron. Well, I was surprised; she didn't ask me to come up to the stove, or to set down, but just sat there, not even looking at me, so I said, "I want to see John." And then she—laughed. I guess you would call it a laugh. I thought of Harry and the team outside, so I said a little sharp: "Can't I see John?" "No," she says, kind o' dull like. "Ain't he home?" says I. "Yes," says she, "he's home." "Then why can't I see him?" I asked her, out of patience. " 'Cause he's dead," says she. *"Dead?"* says I. She just nodded her head, not getting a bit excited, but rockin' back and forth. "Why—where is he?" says I, not knowing what to say. She just pointed upstairs—like that. *(Himself pointing to the room above.)* I started for the stairs, with the idea of going up there. I walked from there to here—then I says, "Why, what did he die of?" "He died of a rope round his neck," says she, and just went on pleatin' at her apron. Well, I went out and called Harry. I thought I might—need help. We went upstairs and there he was lyin'——

COUNTY ATTORNEY: I think I'd rather have you go into that upstairs, where you can point it all out. Just go on now with the rest of the story.

HALE: Well, my first thought was to get that rope off. It looked . . . *(stops; his face twitches)* . . . but Harry, he went up to him, and he said, "No, he's dead all right, and we'd better not touch anything." So we went back downstairs. She was still sitting that same way. "Has anybody been notified?" I asked.

"No," says she, unconcerned. "Who did this, Mrs. Wright?" said Harry. He said it businesslike — and she stopped pleatin' of her apron. "I don't know," she says. "You don't *know?*" says Harry. "No," says she. "Weren't you sleepin' in the bed with him?" says Harry. "Yes," says she, "but I was on the inside." "Somebody slipped a rope round his neck and strangled him and you didn't wake up?" says Harry. "I didn't wake up," she said after him. We must 'a' looked as if we didn't see how that could be, for after a minute she said, "I sleep sound." Harry was going to ask her more questions but I said maybe we ought to let her tell her story first to the coroner, or the sheriff, so Harry went fast as he could to Rivers' place, where there's a telephone.

COUNTY ATTORNEY: And what did Mrs. Wright do when she knew that you had gone for the coroner?

HALE: She moved from the rocker to that chair over there *(pointing to a small chair in the down right corner)* and just sat there with her hands held together and looking down. I got a feeling that I ought to make some conversation, so I said I had come in to see if John wanted to put in a telephone, and at that she started to laugh, and then she stopped and looked at me — scared. *(The County Attorney, who has had his notebook out, makes a note.)* I dunno, maybe it wasn't scared. I wouldn't like to say it was. Soon Harry got back, and then Dr. Lloyd came and you, Mr. Peters, and so I guess that's all I know that you don't.

COUNTY ATTORNEY *(rising and looking around):* I guess we'll go upstairs first — and then out to the barn and around there. *(To the Sheriff.)* You're convinced that there was nothing important here — nothing that would point to any motive?

SHERIFF: Nothing here but kitchen things. *(The County Attorney, after again looking around the kitchen, opens the door of a cupboard closet in right wall. He brings a small chair from right — gets on it and looks on a shelf. Pulls his hand away, sticky.)*

COUNTY ATTORNEY: Here's a nice mess. *(The women draw nearer up center.)*

MRS. PETERS *(to the other woman):* Oh, her fruit; it did freeze. *(To the Lawyer.)* She worried about that when it turned so cold. She said the fire'd go out and her jars would break.

SHERIFF *(rises):* Well, can you beat the woman! Held for murder and worryin' about her preserves.

COUNTY ATTORNEY *(getting down from chair):* I guess before we're through she may have something more serious than preserves to worry about. *(Crosses down right center.)*

HALE: Well, women are used to worrying over trifles. *(The two women move a little closer together.)*

COUNTY ATTORNEY *(with the gallantry of a young politician):* And yet, for all their worries, what would we do without the ladies? *(The women do not unbend. He goes below the center table to the sink, takes a dipperful of water from the pail, and pouring it into a basin, washes his hands. While he is doing this the Sheriff and Hale cross to cupboard, which they inspect. The County Attorney starts to wipe his hands on the roller towel, turns it for a cleaner* place.) Dirty towels! (*Kicks his foot against the pans under the sink.*) Not much of a housekeeper, would you say, ladies?

MRS. HALE (*stiffly*):   There's a great deal of work to be done on a farm.

COUNTY ATTORNEY: To be sure. And yet (*with a little bow to her*) I know there are some Dickson County farmhouses which do not have such roller towels. (*He gives it a pull to expose its full-length again.*)

MRS. HALE: Those towels get dirty awful quick. Men's hands aren't always as clean as they might be.

COUNTY ATTORNEY: Ah, loyal to your sex, I see. But you and Mrs. Wright were neighbors. I suppose you were friends, too.

MRS. HALE (*shaking her head*):   I've not seen much of her of late years. I've not been in this house — it's more than a year.

COUNTY ATTORNEY (*crossing to women up center*):   And why was that? You didn't like her?

MRS. HALE: I liked her all well enough. Farmers' wives have their hands full, Mr. Henderson. And then ——

COUNTY ATTORNEY: Yes —— ?

MRS. HALE (*looking about*):   It never seemed a very cheerful place.

COUNTY ATTORNEY: No — it's not cheerful. I shouldn't say she had the home-making instinct.

MRS. HALE: Well, I don't know as Wright had, either.

COUNTY ATTORNEY: You mean that they didn't get on very well?

MRS. HALE: No, I don't mean anything. But I don't think a place'd be any cheer-fuller for John Wright's being in it.

COUNTY ATTORNEY: I'd like to talk more of that a little later. I want to get the lay of things upstairs now. (*He goes past the women to up right where steps lead to a stair door.*)

SHERIFF: I suppose anything Mrs. Peters does'll be all right. She was to take in some clothes for her, you know, and a few little things. We left in such a hurry yesterday.

COUNTY ATTORNEY: Yes, but I would like to see what you take, Mrs. Peters, and keep an eye out for anything that might be of use to us.

MRS. PETERS: Yes, Mr. Henderson. (*The men leave by up right door to stairs. The women listen to the men's steps on the stairs, then look about the kitchen.*)

MRS. HALE (*crossing left to sink*):   I'd hate to have men coming into my kitchen, snooping around and criticizing. (*She arranges the pans under sink which the lawyer had shoved out of place.*)

MRS. PETERS: Of course it's no more than their duty. (*Crosses to cupboard up right.*)

MRS. HALE: Duty's all right, but I guess that deputy sheriff that came out to make the fire might have got a little of this on. (*Gives the roller towel a pull.*) Wish I'd thought of that sooner. Seems mean to talk about her for not having things slicked up when she had to come away in such a hurry. (*Crosses right to Mrs. Peters at cupboard.*)

MRS. PETERS (*who has been looking through cupboard, lifts one end of towel that covers a pan*):   She had bread set. (*Stands still.*)

•

MRS. HALE (*eyes fixed on a loaf of bread beside the breadbox, which is on a low shelf of the cupboard*):   She was going to put this in there. (*Picks up loaf, abruptly drops it. In a manner of returning to familiar things.*) It's a shame about her fruit. I wonder if it's all gone. (*Gets up on the chair and looks.*) I think there's some here that's all right, Mrs. Peters. Yes — here; (*holding it toward the window*) this is cherries, too. (*Looking again.*) I declare I believe that's the only one. (*Gets down, jar in her hand. Goes to the sink and wipes it off on the outside.*) She'll feel awful bad after all her hard work in the hot weather. I remember the afternoon I put up my cherries last summer. (*She puts the jar on the big kitchen table, center of the room. With a sigh, is about to sit down in the rocking chair. Before she is seated realizes what chair it is; with a slow look at it, steps back. The chair which she has touched rocks back and forth. Mrs. Peters moves to center table and they both watch the chair rock for a moment or two.*)

MRS. PETERS (*shaking off the mood which the empty rocking chair has evoked. Now in a businesslike manner she speaks*):   Well I must get those things from the front room closet. (*She goes to the door at the right but, after looking into the other room, steps back.*) You coming with me, Mrs. Hale? You could help me carry them. (*They go in the other room; reappear, Mrs. Peters carrying a dress, petticoat, and skirt, Mrs. Hale following with a pair of shoes.*) My, it's cold in there. (*She puts the clothes on the big table and hurries to the stove.*)

MRS. HALE (*right of center table examining the skirt*):   Wright was close. I think maybe that's why she kept so much to herself. She didn't even belong to the Ladies' Aid. I suppose she felt she couldn't do her part, and then you don't enjoy things when you feel shabby. I heard she used to wear pretty clothes and be lively, when she was Minnie Foster, one of the town girls singing in the choir. But that — oh, that was thirty years ago. This all you want to take in?

MRS. PETERS: She said she wanted an apron. Funny thing to want, for there isn't much to get you dirty in jail, goodness knows. But I suppose just to make her feel more natural. (*Crosses to cupboard.*) She said they was in the top drawer in this cupboard. Yes, here. And then her little shawl that always hung behind the door. (*Opens stair door and looks.*) Yes, here it is. (*Quickly shuts door leading upstairs.*)

MRS. HALE (*abruptly moving toward her*):   Mrs. Peters?

MRS. PETERS: Yes, Mrs. Hale? (*At up right door.*)

MRS. HALE: Do you think she did it?

MRS. PETERS (*in a frightened voice*):   Oh, I don't know.

MRS. HALE: Well, I don't think she did. Asking for an apron and her little shawl. Worrying about her fruit.

MRS. PETERS (*starts to speak, glances up, where footsteps are heard in the room above. In a low voice*):   Mr. Peters says it looks bad for her. Mr. Henderson is awful sarcastic in a speech and he'll make fun of her sayin' she didn't wake up.

MRS. HALE: Well, I guess John Wright didn't wake when they was slipping that rope under his neck.

MRS. PETERS (*crossing slowly to table and placing shawl and apron on table with other clothing*):   No, it's strange. It must have been done awful crafty and

still. They say it was such a—funny way to kill a man, rigging it all up like
that.

MRS. HALE (*crossing to left of Mrs. Peters at table*): That's just what Mr. Hale
said. There was a gun in the house. He says that's what he can't understand.

MRS. PETERS: Mr. Henderson said coming out that what was needed for the case
was a motive; something to show anger, or—sudden feeling.

MRS. HALE (*who is standing by the table*): Well, I don't see any signs of anger
around here. (*She puts her hand on the dish towel, which lies on the table,
stands looking down at table, one-half of which is clean, the other half messy.*)
It's wiped to here. (*Makes a move as if to finish work, then turns and looks at
loaf of bread outside the breadbox. Drops towel. In that voice of coming back
to familiar things.*) Wonder how they are finding things upstairs. (*Crossing
below table to down right.*) I hope she had it a little more red-up up there.
You know, it seems kind of *sneaking*. Locking her up in town and then coming out here and trying to get her own house to turn against her!

MRS. PETERS: But, Mrs. Hale, the law is the law.

MRS. HALE: I s'pose 'tis. (*Unbuttoning her coat.*) Better loosen up your things,
Mrs. Peters. You won't feel them when you go out. (*Mrs. Peters takes off her
fur tippet, goes to hang it on chair back left of table, stands looking at the work
basket on floor near down left window.*)

MRS. PETERS: She was piecing a quilt. (*She brings the large sewing basket to the
center table and they look at the bright pieces, Mrs. Hale above the table and
Mrs. Peters left of it.*)

MRS. HALE: It's a log cabin pattern. Pretty, isn't it? I wonder if she was goin' to
quilt it or just knot it? (*Footsteps have been heard coming down the stairs. The
Sheriff enters followed by Hale and the County Attorney.*)

SHERIFF: They wonder if she was going to quilt it or just knot it! (*The men
laugh, the women look abashed.*)

COUNTY ATTORNEY (*rubbing his hands over the stove*): Frank's fire didn't do
much up there, did it? Well, let's go out to the barn and get that cleared up.
(*The men go outside by up left door.*)

MRS. HALE (*resentfully*): I don't know as there's anything so strange, our takin'
up our time with little things while we're waiting for them to get the evidence. (*She sits in chair right of table smoothing out a block with decision.*) I
don't see as it's anything to laugh about.

MRS. PETERS (*apologetically*): Of course they've got awful important things on
their minds. (*Pulls up a chair and joins Mrs. Hale at the left of the table.*)

MRS. HALE (*examining another block*): Mrs. Peters, look at this one. Here, this is
the one she was working on, and look at the sewing! All the rest of it has been
so nice and even. And look at this! It's all over the place! Why, it looks as if
she didn't know what she was about! (*After she has said this they look at each
other, then start to glance back at the door. After an instant Mrs. Hale has
pulled at a knot and ripped the sewing.*)

MRS. PETERS: Oh, what are you doing, Mrs. Hale?

MRS. HALE (*mildly*): Just pulling out a stitch or two that's not sewed very good.
(*Threading a needle.*) Bad sewing always made me fidgety.

MRS. PETERS *(with a glance at door, nervously):*   I don't think we ought to touch things.

MRS. HALE: I'll just finish up this end. *(Suddenly stopping and leaning forward.)* Mrs. Peters?

MRS. PETERS: Yes, Mrs. Hale?

MRS. HALE: What do you suppose she was so nervous about?

MRS. PETERS: Oh — I don't know. I don't know as she was nervous. I sometimes sew awful queer when I'm just tired. *(Mrs. Hale starts to say something, looks at Mrs. Peters, then goes on sewing.)* Well, I must get these things wrapped up. They may be through sooner than we think. *(Putting apron and other things together.)* I wonder where I can find a piece of paper, and string. *(Rises.)*

MRS. HALE: In that cupboard, maybe.

MRS. PETERS *(crosses right looking in cupboard):*   Why, here's a bird-cage. *(Holds it up.)* Did she have a bird, Mrs. Hale?

MRS. HALE: Why, I don't know whether she did or not — I've not been here for so long. There was a man around last year selling canaries cheap, but I don't know as she took one; maybe she did. She used to sing real pretty herself.

MRS. PETERS *(glancing around):*   Seems funny to think of a bird here. But she must have had one, or why would she have a cage? I wonder what happened to it?

MRS. HALE: I s'pose maybe the cat got it.

MRS. PETERS: No, she didn't have a cat. She's got that feeling some people have about cats — being afraid of them. My cat got in her room and she was real upset and asked me to take it out.

MRS. HALE: My sister Bessie was like that. Queer, ain't it?

MRS. PETERS *(examining the cage):*   Why, look at this door. It's broke. One hinge is pulled apart. *(Takes a step down to Mrs. Hale's right.)*

MRS. HALE *(looking too):*   Looks as if someone must have been rough with it.

MRS. PETERS: Why, yes. *(She brings the cage forward and puts it on the table.)*

MRS. HALE *(glancing toward up left door):*   I wish if they're going to find any evidence they'd be about it. I don't like this place.

MRS. PETERS: But I'm awful glad you came with me, Mrs. Hale. It would be lonesome for me sitting here alone.

MRS. HALE: It would, wouldn't it? *(Dropping her sewing.)* But I tell you what I do wish, Mrs. Peters. I wish I had come over sometimes when *she* was here. I — *(looking around the room)* — wish I had.

MRS. PETERS: But of course you were awful busy, Mrs. Hale — your house and your children.

MRS. HALE *(rises and crosses left):*   I could've come. I stayed away because it weren't cheerful — and that's why I ought to have come. I — *(looking out left window)* — I've never liked this place. Maybe because it's down in a hollow and you don't see the road. I dunno what it is, but it's a lonesome place and always was. I wish I had come over to see Minnie Foster sometimes. I can see now — *(Shakes her head.)*

MRS. PETERS *(left of table and above it):*   Well, you mustn't reproach yourself, Mrs. Hale. Somehow we just don't see how it is with other folks until — something turns up.

MRS. HALE: Not having children makes less work — but it makes a quiet house, and Wright out to work all day, and no company when he did come in. *(Turning from window.)* Did you know John Wright, Mrs. Peters?

MRS. PETERS: Not to know him; I've seen him in town. They say he was a good man.

MRS. HALE: Yes — good; he didn't drink, and kept his word as well as most, I guess, and paid his debts. But he was a hard man, Mrs. Peters. Just to pass the time of day with him — *(Shivers.)* Like a raw wind that gets to the bone. *(Pauses, her eye falling on the cage.)* I should think she would 'a' wanted a bird. But what do you suppose went with it?

MRS. PETERS: I don't know, unless it got sick and died. *(She reaches over and swings the broken door, swings it again, both women watch it.)*

MRS. HALE: You weren't raised round here, were you? *(Mrs. Peters shakes her head.)* You didn't know — her?

MRS. PETERS: Not till they brought her yesterday.

MRS. HALE: She — come to think of it, she was kind of like a bird herself — real sweet and pretty, but kind of timid and — fluttery. How — she — did — change. *(Silence: then as if struck by a happy thought and relieved to get back to everyday things. Crosses right above Mrs. Peters to cupboard, replaces small chair used to stand on to its original place down right.)* Tell you what, Mrs. Peters, why don't you take the quilt in with you? It might take up her mind.

MRS. PETERS: Why, I think that's a real nice idea, Mrs. Hale. There couldn't possibly be any objection to it could there? Now, just what would I take? I wonder if her patches are in here — and her things. *(They look in the sewing basket.)*

MRS. HALE *(crosses to right of table)*: Here's some red. I expect this has got sewing things in it. *(Brings out a fancy box.)* What a pretty box. Looks like something somebody would give you. Maybe her scissors are in here. *(Opens box. Suddenly puts her hand to her nose.)* Why — — *(Mrs. Peters bends nearer, then turns her face away.)* There's something wrapped up in this piece of silk.

MRS. PETERS: Why, this isn't her scissors.

MRS. HALE *(lifting the silk)*: Oh, Mrs. Peters — it's — — *(Mrs. Peters bends closer.)*

MRS. PETERS: It's the bird.

MRS. HALE: But, Mrs. Peters — look at it! Its neck! Look at its neck! It's all — other side *to.*

MRS. PETERS: Somebody — wrung — its — neck. *(Their eyes meet. A look of growing comprehension, of horror. Steps are heard outside. Mrs. Hale slips box under quilt pieces, and sinks into her chair. Enter Sheriff and County Attorney. Mrs. Peters steps down left and stands looking out of window.)*

COUNTY ATTORNEY *(as one turning from serious things to little pleasantries)*: Well, ladies, have you decided whether she was going to quilt it or knot it? *(Crosses to center above table.)*

MRS. PETERS: We think she was going to — knot it. *(Sheriff crosses to right of stove, lifts stove lid, and glances at fire, then stands warming hands at stove.)*

COUNTY ATTORNEY: Well, that's interesting, I'm sure. *(Seeing the bird-cage.)* Has the bird flown?

MRS. HALE *(putting more quilt pieces over the box)*:   We think the — cat got it.

COUNTY ATTORNEY *(preoccupied)*:   Is there a cat? *(Mrs. Hale glances in a quick covert way at Mrs. Peters.)*

MRS. PETERS *(turning from window takes a step in)*:   Well, not *now*. They're superstitious, you know. They leave.

COUNTY ATTORNEY *(to Sheriff Peters, continuing an interrupted conversation)*:   No sign at all of anyone having come from the outside. Their own rope. Now let's go up again and go over it piece by piece. *(They start upstairs.)* It would have to have been someone who knew just the —— *(Mrs. Peters sits down left of table. The two women sit there not looking at one another, but as if peering into something and at the same time holding back. When they talk now it is in the manner of feeling their way over strange ground, as if afraid of what they are saying, but as if they cannot help saying it.)*

Mrs. Hale *(hesitatively and in hushed voice)*:   She liked the bird. She was going to bury it in that pretty box.

MRS. PETERS *(in a whisper)*:   When I was a girl — my kitten — there was a boy took a hatchet, and before my eyes — and before I could get there —— *(Covers her face an instant.)* If they hadn't held me back I would have — *(catches herself, looks upstairs where steps are heard, falters weakly)* — hurt him.

MRS. HALE *(with a slow look around her)*:   I wonder how it would seem never to have had any children around. *(Pause.)* No, Wright wouldn't like the bird — a thing that sang. She used to sing. He killed that, too.

MRS. PETERS *(moving uneasily)*:   We don't know who killed the bird.

MRS. HALE: I knew John Wright.

MRS. PETERS: It was an awful thing was done in this house that night, Mrs. Hale. Killing a man while he slept, slipping a rope around his neck that choked the life out of him.

MRS. HALE: His neck. Choked the life out of him. *(Her hand goes out and rests on the bird-cage.)*

MRS. PETERS *(with rising voice)*:   We don't know who killed him. We don't *know*.

MRS. HALE *(her own feeling not interrupted)*:   If there'd been years and years of nothing, then a bird to sing to you, it would be awful — still, after the bird was still.

MRS. PETERS *(something within her speaking)*:   I know what stillness is. When we homesteaded in Dakota, and my first baby died — after he was two years old, and me with no other then ——

MRS. HALE *(moving)*:   How soon do you suppose they'll be through looking for the evidence?

MRS. PETERS: I know what stillness is. *(Pulling herself back.)* The law has got to punish crime, Mrs. Hale.

MRS. HALE *(not as if answering that)*:   I wish you'd seen Minnie Foster when she wore a white dress with blue ribbons and stood up there in the choir and sang. *(A look around the room.)* Oh, I *wish* I'd come over here once in a while! That was a crime! That was a crime! Who's going to punish that?

MRS. PETERS *(looking upstairs)*:   We mustn't — take on.

MRS. HALE: I might have known she needed help! I know how things can be—
for women. I tell you, it's queer, Mrs. Peters. We live close together and we
live far apart. We all go through the same things—it's all just a different kind
of the same thing. (*Brushes her eyes, noticing the jar of fruit, reaches out for
it.*) If I was you I wouldn't tell her her fruit was gone. Tell her it *ain't.* Tell her
it's all right. Take this in to prove it to her. She—she may never know
whether it was broke or not.

MRS. PETERS (*takes the jar, looks about for something to wrap it in; takes petticoat
from the clothes brought from the other room, very nervously begins winding
this around the jar. In a false voice*):   My, it's a good thing the men couldn't
hear us. Wouldn't they just laugh! Getting all stirred up over a little thing
like a—dead canary. As if that could have anything to do with—with—
wouldn't they *laugh!* (*The men are heard coming downstairs.*)

MRS. HALE (*under her breath*):   Maybe they would—maybe they wouldn't.

COUNTY ATTORNEY: No, Peters, it's all perfectly clear except a reason for doing
it. But you know juries when it comes to women. If there was some definite
thing. (*Crosses slowly to above table. Sheriff crosses down right. Mrs. Hale and
Mrs. Peters remain seated at either side of table.*) Something to show—something to make a story about—a thing that would connect up with this strange
way of doing it—— (*The women's eyes meet for an instant. Enter Hale from
outer door.*)

HALE (*remaining by door*):   Well, I've got the team around. Pretty cold out there.

COUNTY ATTORNEY: I'm going to stay awhile by myself. (*To the Sheriff.*) You can
send Frank out for me, can't you? I want to go over everything. I'm not satisfied that we can't do better.

SHERIFF: Do you want to see what Mrs. Peters is going to take in? (*The Lawyer
picks up the apron, laughs.*)

COUNTY ATTORNEY: Oh, I guess they're not very dangerous things the ladies
have picked out. (*Moves a few things about, disturbing the quilt pieces which
cover the box. Steps back.*) No, Mrs. Peters doesn't need supervising. For that
matter a sheriff's wife is married to the law. Ever think of it that way, Mrs.
Peters?

MRS. PETERS: Not—just that way.

SHERIFF (*chuckling*):   Married to the law. (*Moves to down right door to the other
room.*) I just want you to come in here a minute, George. We ought to take a
look at these windows.

COUNTY ATTORNEY (*scoffingly*):   Oh, windows!

SHERIFF: We'll be right out, Mr. Hale. (*Hale goes outside. The Sheriff follows the
County Attorney into the room. Then Mrs. Hale rises, hands tight together,
looking intensely at Mrs. Peters, whose eyes make a slow turn, finally meeting
Mrs. Hale's. A moment Mrs. Hale holds her, then her own eyes point the way
to where the box is concealed. Suddenly Mrs. Peters throws back quilt pieces
and tries to put the box in the bag she is carrying. It is too big. She opens box,
starts to take bird out, cannot touch it, goes to pieces, stands there helpless.
Sound of a knob turning in the other room. Mrs. Hale snatches the box and*

puts it in the pocket of her big coat. Enter County Attorney and Sheriff, who remains down right.)

COUNTY ATTORNEY *(crosses to up left door facetiously):*   Well, Henry, at least we found out that she was not going to quilt it. She was going to—what is it you call it, ladies?

MRS. HALE *(standing center below table facing front, her hand against her pocket):* We call it—knot it, Mr. Henderson.

Curtain.   [1916]

THINKING ABOUT THE TEXT

1. Although much of this play is about Minnie Wright, Glaspell keeps her offstage. Why, do you think?

2. What does Glaspell imply about differences between men and women? Support your inference with details of the text.

3. What do Mrs. Hale and Mrs. Peters realize about themselves during the course of the play? To what extent should they feel guilty about their own past behavior?

4. Ultimately, Mrs. Hale and Mrs. Peters cover up evidence to protect Minnie Wright. They seem to act out of loyalty to their sex. How sympathetic are you to their stand? Do you feel there are times when you should be someone's ally because that person is of the same gender as you?

5. Is justice done in *Trifles*? Define what you mean by *justice* in this context.

WRITING ABOUT ISSUES

1. Choose a line or stretch of dialogue from *Hamlet* or *Trifles*, and write an essay in which you explain how these words bring psychological, moral, or philosophical complexity to the subject of bringing murderers to justice.

2. Write an essay in which you compare Hamlet to the character in *Trifles* that you think he most resembles. Or write an essay in which you show how a line or stretch of dialogue from Shakespeare's play can be applied to Glaspell's. Whatever your topic, quote from both plays to support the connection you make.

3. Write an essay recalling an occasion when you thought justice would be better served if a particular person were not punished according to the law. This may be a case you read or heard about or one that you personally experienced. Focus on explaining the definitions of *justice* that this situation led you to consider.

4. In today's United States, much debate revolves around the death penalty as means of bringing murderers to justice. Imagine that either *Hamlet* or *Trifles* has been read by a group of people who have now gathered to

debate their different views about capital punishment. Write an essay directed toward this particular audience. In your essay, focus on Claudius or Minnie Wright, and argue for the fate you think the character would deserve if he or she committed the same murder today.

PUNISHMENTS

ROBERT BROWNING, "My Last Duchess"
CAROLYN FORCHÉ, "The Colonel"
SEAMUS HEANEY, "Punishment"
SHERMAN ALEXIE, "Capital Punishment"

Acts of punishment are also acts of judgment. Clearly a punishment reflects the decisions and values of the person ordering it. Similarly, it says something about the ethics of the person willing to carry it out. Even people who merely learn about a punishment wind up judging it. Consciously or unconsciously, they choose to praise it, criticize it, or passively tolerate it. Each of these four poems deals with judgments made by punishers and by those who are, in some sense, their audience. Think about the actions you are taking and the principles you are expressing as you judge the people you encounter here.

BEFORE YOU READ

Recall a particular punishment that you considered unjust. What were the circumstances? What experiences, values, and reasoning led you to disapprove of the punishment? Could you have done anything to prevent it or to see that similarly unfair punishments did not recur? If so, what?

ROBERT BROWNING
My Last Duchess

Today, Robert Browning (1812–1889) is regarded as one of the greatest poets of nineteenth-century England, but in his own time he was not nearly as celebrated as his wife, the poet Elizabeth Barrett Browning. He is chiefly known for his achievements with the dramatic monologue, *a genre of poetry that emphasizes the speaker's own distinct personality. Often Browning's speakers are his imaginative recreations of people who once existed in real life. He was especially interested in religious, political, and artistic figures from the Renaissance. The following poem, perhaps Browning's most famous, was written in 1842, and its speaker, Duke of Ferrara, was an actual man.*

Ferrara°

That's my last Duchess painted on the wall,
Looking as if she were alive. I call
That piece a wonder, now: Frà Pandolf's° hands
Worked busily a day, and there she stands.
Will't please you sit and look at her? I said   5
"Frà Pandolf" by design, for never read
Strangers like you that pictured countenance,
The depth and passion of its earnest glance,
But to myself they turned (since none puts by
The curtain I have drawn for you, but I)   10
And seemed as they would ask me, if they durst,
How such a glance came there; so, not the first
Are you to turn and ask thus. Sir, 'twas not
Her husband's presence only, called that spot
Of joy into the Duchess' cheek: perhaps   15
Frà Pandolf chanced to say "Her mantle laps
Over my lady's wrist too much," or "Paint
Must never hope to reproduce the faint
Half-flush that dies along her throat": such stuff
Was courtesy, she thought, and cause enough   20
For calling up that spot of joy. She had
A heart — how shall I say? — too soon made glad,
Too easily impressed; she liked whate'er
She looked on, and her looks went everywhere.
Sir, 'twas all one! My favor at her breast,   25
The dropping of the daylight in the West,
The bough of cherries some officious fool
Broke in the orchard for her, the white mule
She rode with round the terrace — all and each
Would draw from her alike the approving speech,   30
Or blush, at least. She thanked men, — good! but thanked
Somehow — I know not how — as if she ranked
My gift of a nine-hundred-years-old name
With anybody's gift. Who'd stoop to blame
This sort of trifling? Even had you skill   35
In speech — which I have not — to make your will
Quite clear to such an one, and say, "Just this
Or that in you disgusts me; here you miss,
Or there exceed the mark" — and if she let
Herself be lessoned so, nor plainly set   40
Her wits to yours, forsooth, and made excuse,

Epigraph Ferrara: In the sixteenth century, the duke of this Italian city arranged to marry a second time after the mysterious death of his very young first wife.   **3 Frà Pandolf:** A fictitious artist.

— E'en then would be some stooping; and I choose
Never to stoop. Oh sir, she smiled, no doubt,
Whene'er I passed her; but who passed without
Much the same smile? This grew; I gave commands; 45
Then all smiles stopped together. There she stands
As if alive. Will't please you rise? We'll meet
The company below, then. I repeat,
The Count your master's known munificence
Is ample warrant that no just pretense 50
Of mine for dowry will be disallowed;
Though his fair daughter's self, as I avowed
At starting, is my object. Nay, we'll go
Together down, sir. Notice Neptune, though,
Taming a sea-horse, thought a rarity, 55
Which Claus of Innsbruck° cast in bronze for me! [1842]

56 **Claus of Innsbruck:** A fictitious artist.

THINKING ABOUT THE TEXT

1. The duke offers a history of his first marriage. Summarize his story in your own words, including the reasons he gives for his behavior. How would you describe him? Do you admire anything about him? If so, what?

2. Try to reconstruct the rhetorical situation in which the duke is making his remarks. Who might be his audience? What might be his goals? What strategies is he using to accomplish them? Cite details that support your conjectures.

3. When you read the poem aloud, how conscious are you of its rhymes? What is its rhyme scheme? What is the effect of Browning's using just one stanza rather than breaking the poem into several?

4. Going by this example of the genre, what are the advantages of writing a poem as a dramatic monologue? What are the disadvantages?

5. Browning suggests that the setting of this poem is Renaissance Italy. What relevance might his poem have had for readers in mid-nineteenth-century England? What relevance might it have for audiences in the United States today?

CAROLYN FORCHÉ
The Colonel

In her poetry, Carolyn Forché (b. 1950) often addresses contemporary abuses of power. Her first book of poems, Gathering the Tribes *(1976), won the Yale Series of Younger Poets competition. The following poem is from her second,* The Coun-

try between Us *(1981), which won the Lamont Award from the Academy of Ameri-
can Poets. Much of this book is based on Forché's experiences during her stay in El
Salvador, which at the time was beset by civil war. Forché's latest book of poetry is*
The Angel of History *(1994), and she has also edited a collection entitled* Against
Forgetting: Twentieth-Century Poetry of Witness *(1993). She lives in Rockville,
Maryland, and teaches creative writing at George Mason University in Fairfax,
Virginia.*

What you have heard is true. I was in his house. His wife carried a tray of coffee
and sugar. His daughter filed her nails, his son went out for the night. There were
daily papers, pet dogs, a pistol on the cushion beside him. The moon swung bare
on its black cord over the house. On the television was a cop show. It was in
English. Broken bottles were embedded in the walls around the house to scoop   5
the kneecaps from a man's legs or cut his hands to lace. On the windows there
were gratings like those in liquor stores. We had dinner, rack of lamb, good wine,
a gold bell was on the table for calling the maid. The maid brought green man-
goes, salt, a type of bread. I was asked how I enjoyed the country. There was a
brief commercial in Spanish. His wife took everything away. There was some talk   10
then of how difficult it had become to govern. The parrot said hello on the terrace. The colonel told it to shut up, and pushed himself from the table. My
friend said to me with his eyes: say nothing. The colonel returned with a sack
used to bring groceries home. He spilled many human ears on the table. They
were like dried peach halves. There is no other way to say this. He took one of   15
them in his hands, shook it in our faces, dropped it into a water glass. It came
alive there. I am tired of fooling around he said. As for the rights of anyone, tell
your people they can go fuck themselves. He swept the ears to the floor with his
arm and held the last of his wine in the air. Something for your poetry, no? he
said. Some of the ears on the floor caught this scrap of his voice. Some of the ears   20
on the floor were pressed to the ground.   [1978]

THINKING ABOUT THE TEXT

1. How do you characterize the colonel? List a number of specific adjectives
   and supporting details. Does your impression of him change as you read,
   or does it stay pretty much the same? Explain.

2. Forché calls this text a poem, and yet it seems to consist of one long prose
   paragraph. Here is an issue of genre: Is it *really* a poem? Support your
   answer by identifying what you think are characteristics of poetry. What is
   the effect of Forché's presenting the text as a poem? Note what the colonel
   says about poetry. How might this text be considered a response to him?

3. Forché uses many short sentences here. What is the effect of this strategy?
   Even though she quotes the colonel, she does not use quotation marks.
   What is the effect of this choice?

4. The poem begins, "What you have heard is true." Do you think the situation it describes really occurred? Identify some warrants or assumptions

that influence your answer. Where else does the poem refer to hearing? How might it be seen as being about audiences and their responses?

5. Forché wrote "The Colonel" after a stay in El Salvador, and so it is reasonable for her audience to conclude that the poem is set in that country. Yet she does not actually specify the setting. Should she have done so? Why, or why not?

MAKING COMPARISONS

1. Does Browning's duke strike you as the kind of person who would do what Forché's colonel does? Why, or why not?

2. Do the listeners in these two poems both seem passive? Refer to specific details of both texts.

3. "My Last Duchess" is a single stanza; "The Colonel" is a single paragraph. Would you say their forms are basically the same and with similar effects? Or are you more conscious of differences?

SEAMUS HEANEY
Punishment

For his distinguished career as a poet, Seamus Heaney (b. 1939) won the Nobel Prize for literature in 1995. He was raised as a Catholic in Northern Ireland, where Protestants remained in the majority and frequently conflicted with Catholics. Until the Peace Accord of 1997, the region was controlled by the British government, whereas now it is ruled by a mixed body representing both religions. Several of Heaney's poems deal with Catholic resistance to the longtime British domination of his native land. Heaney moved to Dublin in the Republic of Ireland in the early 1970s, but he has often visited the United States, even holding an appointment as Boylston Professor of Rhetoric at Harvard University. The following poem appears in Heaney's 1975 book North. *It is part of a whole sequence of poems based on P. V. Glob's 1969 book* The Bog People. *Heaney was drawn to Glob's photographs of Iron Age people whose preserved bodies were discovered in bogs of Denmark and other European countries.*

I can feel the tug
of the halter at the nape
of her neck, the wind
on her naked front.

It blows her nipples   5
to amber beads,
it shakes the frail rigging
of her ribs.

* * * * *

I can see her drowned
body in the bog,
the weighing stone,
the floating rods and boughs.

Under which at first
she was a barked sapling
that is dug up
oak-bone, brain-firkin:

her shaved head
like a stubble of black corn,
her blindfold a soiled bandage,
her noose a ring

to store
the memories of love.
Little adulteress,
before they punished you

you were flaxen-haired,
undernourished, and your
tar-black face was beautiful.
My poor scapegoat,

I almost love you
but would have cast, I know,
the stones of silence.°
I am the artful voyeur

of your brain's exposed
and darkened combs,
your muscles' webbing
and all your numbered bones:

I who have stood dumb
when your betraying sisters,
cauled in tar,
wept by the railings,°

who would connive
in civilized outrage
yet understand the exact
and tribal, intimate revenge.

[1975]

30–31 would have cast . . . of silence: In John 8:7–9, Jesus confronts a mob about to stone an adulterous woman and makes the famous statement "He that is without sin among you, let him first cast a stone at her." The crowd retreats, "being convicted by their own conscience." **37–40 I who . . . by the railings:** In 1969, the British army became highly visible occupiers of Northern Ireland. In Heaney's native city of Belfast, the Irish Republican Army retaliated against Irish Catholic women who dated British soldiers. Punishments included shaving the women's heads, stripping and tarring them, and handcuffing them to the city's railings.

THINKING ABOUT THE TEXT

1. Summarize your impression of the bog woman. Where does the speaker begin directly addressing her? Why do you suppose Heaney has him refrain from addressing her right away?

2. Who is the main subject of this poem? The bog woman? The "betraying sisters" (line 38)? The speaker? Some combination of these people?

3. The speaker refers to himself as a "voyeur" (line 32). Consult a dictionary definition of this word. How might it apply to the speaker? Do you think it is ultimately the best label for him? Explain. Do you feel like a voyeur reading this poem? Why, or why not?

4. What are the speaker's thoughts in the last stanza? What connotation do you attach to the word *connive*? (You might want to consult a dictionary definition of it.) What is the speaker's attitude toward "the exact / and tribal, intimate revenge"? Do you see him as tolerating violence?

5. What words in this poem, if any, are unfamiliar to you? What is their effect on you? Each stanza has four lines. Does this pattern create steady rhythm or one more fragmented than harmonious? Try reading it aloud.

MAKING COMPARISONS

1. Do you find the punishments alluded to in Heaney's, Browning's, and Forché's poems equally disturbing? Note specific details that influence your impressions.

2. How does each of these three poems raise the subject of silence? Does each suggest that silence is bad?

3. Which, if any, of the situations referred to in these three poems could happen in the contemporary United States?

SHERMAN ALEXIE
Capital Punishment

Born in Spokane, Washington, Sherman Alexie (b. 1966) is a member of the Spokane/Coeur d'Alene tribe. His fiction includes two novels, Reservation Blues *(1996) and* Indian Killer *(1997). He has also produced two collections of short stories,* The Toughest Indian in the World *(2001) and* The Lone Ranger and Tonto Fistfight in Heaven *(1994), which he adapted for the acclaimed 1998 film* Smoke Signals. *Alexie is a poet, too, with his collections of verse including* The Business of Fancy Dancing *(1992),* Old Shirts and New Skins *(1993),* First Indian on the Moon *(1993),* Drums Like This *(1996), and* One Stick Song *(2000). "Capital Punishment" appeared in a 1996 issue of* Indiana Review *and, that same year, in Alexie's collection* The Summer of Black Widows. *It was also selected for the 1996 edition of the volume* Best American Poetry. *Alexie wrote the poem after reading media coverage of an actual execution in the state of Washington.*

I prepare the last meal
for the Indian man to be executed

but this killer doesn't want much:
baked potato, salad, tall glass of ice water.

(I am not a witness) 5

It's mostly the dark ones
who are forced to sit in the chair

especially when white people die.
It's true, you can look it up

and this Indian killer pushed 10
his fists all the way down

a white man's throat, just to win a bet
about the size of his heart.

Those Indians are always gambling.
Still, I season this last meal 15

with all I have. I don't have much
but I send it down the line

with the handsome guard
who has fallen in love

with the Indian killer. 20
I don't care who loves whom.

(I am not a witness)

I don't care if I add too much
salt or pepper to the warden's stew.

He can eat what I put in front of him. 25
I just cook for the boss

but I cook just right
for the Indian man to be executed.

The temperature is the thing.
I once heard a story 30

about a black man who was electrocuted
in that chair and lived to tell about it

◆　◆　◆

before the court decided to sit him back down
an hour later and kill him all over again.

I have an extra sandwich hidden away   35
in the back of the refrigerator

in case this Indian killer survives
that first slow flip of the switch

and gets hungry while he waits
for the engineers to debate the flaws.   40

(I am not a witness)

I prepare the last meal for free
just like I signed up for the last war.

I learned how to cook
by lasting longer than any of the others.   45

Tonight, I'm just the last one left
after the handsome guard takes the meal away.

I turn off the kitchen lights
and sit alone in the dark

because the whole damn prison dims   50
when the chair is switched on.

You can watch a light bulb flicker
on a night like this

and remember it too clearly
like it was your first kiss   55

or the first hard kick to your groin.
It's all the same

when I am huddled down here
trying not to look at the clock

look at the clock, no, don't   60
look at the clock, when all of it stops

making sense: a salad, a potato
a drink of water all taste like heat.

(I am not a witness)

I want you to know I tasted a little   65
of that last meal before I sent it away.

It's the cook's job, to make sure
and I was sure I ate from the same plate

◆ ◆ ◆

and ate with the same fork and spoon
that the Indian killer used later   70

in his cell. Maybe a little bit of me
lodged in his stomach, wedged between

his front teeth, his incisors, his molars
when he chewed down on the bit

and his body arced like modern art   75
curving organically, smoke rising

from his joints, wispy flames decorating
the crown of his head, the balls of his feet.

(I am not a witness)

I sit here in the dark kitchen   80
when they do it, meaning

when they kill him, kill
and add another definition of the word

to the dictionary. American fills
its dictionary. We write down *kill* and everybody   85

in the audience shouts out exactly how
they spell it, what it means to them

and all of the answers are taken down
by the pollsters and secretaries

who take care of the small details: 90
time of death, pulse rate, press release.

I heard a story once about some reporters
at a hanging who wanted the hood removed

from the condemned's head, so they could look
into his eyes and tell their readers   95

what they saw there. What did they expect?
All of the stories should be simple.

1 death + 1 death = 2 deaths.
But we throw the killers in one grave

and victims in another. We form sides   100
and have two separate feasts.

(I am a witness)

I prepared the last meal
for the Indian man who was executed

◆ ◆ ◆

and have learned this: If any of us   105
stood for days on top of a barren hill

during an electrical storm
then lightning would eventually strike us

and we'd have no idea for which of our sins
we were reduced to headlines and ash.   [1996]   110

THINKING ABOUT THE TEXT

1. Alexie reports that in writing this poem, he aimed "to call for the abolition of the death penalty." In reading the poem, do you sense that this is his aim? Why, or why not? In what respects might the poem be seen as arguing against the death penalty? State how you viewed capital punishment before and after you read it. Did Alexie affect your attitude? If so, how?

2. Why do you think Alexie cast the speaker as the condemned man's cook? How do you explain the speaker's shift from denying that he is a witness to acknowledging that he is one? Identify how he seems to define the term *witness*. What would you say to someone who argues that the speaker is unreasonably stretching the meaning of this word, because apparently he didn't directly observe the execution?

3. How does race figure in this poem? Should people consider race when discussing capital punishment? If so, what about race should they especially ponder? In examining Alexie's poem, should readers bear in mind that the author is Native American? Why, or why not?

4. The film *Dead Man Walking* (1995), which deals with arguments about capital punishment, shows in chilling detail an execution by injection. Yet at the moment the condemned man dies, the film also shows the faces of his two victims. By contrast, Alexie doesn't refer to the victims of the executed men he writes about. Should he have mentioned them? Identify some of the values reflected in your answer.

5. Summarize and evaluate the lesson delivered by the speaker at the end of the poem. What do you think headlines might say about you if you were killed in the manner he describes?

MAKING COMPARISONS

1. Forché's first sentence is "What you have heard is true." After noting that "It's mostly the dark ones / who are forced to sit in the chair / especially when white people die," Alexie's speaker declares "It's true, you can look it up" (line 9). What do these lines imply about each poem's readers?

2. Do you think Alexie would appreciate Heaney's use of the word *tribal*? Why, or why not? Could the word be applied to any of the other poems in this cluster? If so, how?

3. Unlike the other poems in this cluster, Alexie's is in one- and two-line stanzas. Does this difference in pattern lead to a significant difference in effect? Explain.

WRITING ABOUT ISSUES

1. Choose one of the poems in this cluster and write an essay explaining how it can be seen as a poem about witnessing. In your essay, note what definition(s) of "witnessing" seem relevant to the poem, as well as what the poem seems to be saying about ethical issues involved in this act.

2. The eighth amendment to the U.S. Constitution forbids "cruel and unusual punishment." People who argue about capital punishment often find themselves considering whether it is indeed "cruel and unusual." For several years the U.S. Supreme Court considered it so because it was arbitrarily imposed and therefore banned it. Write an essay in which you examine the phrase "cruel and unusual punishment" by choosing two poems from this cluster and discussing whether the phrase applies to anything mentioned in them.

3. Write an essay in which you discuss whether the phrase "cruel and unusual punishment" applies to the event described in this paragraph from the March 26, 1997, issue of the *Washington Post*:

> Moments after convicted killer Pedro Medina was strapped into Florida's electric chair and 2,000 volts of electricity surged into his body this morning, flames leapt from the inmate's head, filling the death chamber with smoke and horrifying two dozen witnesses.

Does Medina's execution amount to "cruel and unusual punishment"? If you need additional information before firmly deciding, what do you need to know?

4. Today, Amnesty International and PEN International, a writers' organization, regularly bring to the American public's attention cases of what they deem unjust punishment. In fact, Amnesty International has criticized all instances of capital punishment in the United States. Research one of the cases reported by these organizations. Then write an article for your school newspaper in which you (a) present the basic facts of the case, (b) identify values and principles you think your audience should apply to it, and (c) point out anything you believe can and should be done about it. If you wish, refer to any of the poems in this cluster.

REVENGE

EDGAR ALLAN POE, "The Cask of Amontillado"
LOUISE ERDRICH, "Fleur"
ANDRE DUBUS, "Killings"

Many people consider revenge abhorrent. They hold that wrongdoers should be forgiven, left to the judgment of God ("Vengeance is mine, saith the Lord"), or dealt with through the supposed fair and rational processes of the judicial system. Yet others believe in getting even. They may tolerate or encourage revenge taken by others or retaliate themselves against perceived offenders, in effect following the ancient Babylonian principle of "an eye for an eye, a tooth for a tooth." In each of the following stories, a character expresses a judgment of one or more other characters by engaging in an act of revenge. As you read each story here, consider the logic, morality, context, and effects of the vengeance described.

BEFORE YOU READ

Do you believe it is ever justifiable for someone to avenge a crime or wrongdoing by going outside the law? What specific cases do you think about as you address this issue?

EDGAR ALLAN POE
The Cask of Amontillado

The life of Edgar Allan Poe (1809–1849) was relatively brief, its end tragically hastened by his alcohol and drug abuse, but his contributions to literature were unique. As a book reviewer, he produced pieces of literary criticism and theory that are still widely respected. As a poet, he wrote such classics as "The Raven" (1845), "The Bells" (1849), and "Annabel Lee" (1849). Moreover, his short fiction was groundbreaking and continues to be popular, a source for many films and television shows. With works such as "The Murders in the Rue Morgue" (1841), "The Gold Bug" (1843), and "The Purloined Letter" (1944), he pioneered the modern detective story. Others of Poe's tales are masterpieces of horror, including "The Fall of the House of Usher" (1842), "The Pit and the Pendulum" (1842), and the following story, which he wrote in 1846.

The thousand injuries of Fortunato I had borne as I best could; but when he ventured upon insult, I vowed revenge. You, who so well know the nature of my soul, will not suppose, however, that I gave utterance to a threat. *At length* I would be avenged; this was a point definitely settled — but the very definitiveness with which it was resolved precluded the idea of risk. I must not only punish, but punish with impunity. A wrong is unredressed when retribution overtakes its redresser. It is equally unredressed when the avenger fails to make himself felt as such to him who has done the wrong.

It must be understood, that neither by word nor deed had I given Fortunato cause to doubt my good-will. I continued, as was my wont, to smile in his face, and he did not perceive that my smile *now* was at the thought of his immolation.

He had a weak point—this Fortunato—although in other regards he was a man to be respected and even feared. He prided himself on his connoisseurship in wine. Few Italians have the true virtuoso spirit. For the most part their enthusiasm is adopted to suit the time and opportunity—to practise imposture upon the British and Austrian *millionnaires.* In painting and gemmary Fortunato, like his countrymen, was a quack—but in the matter of old wines he was sincere. In this respect I did not differ from him materially: I was skilful in the Italian vintages myself, and bought largely whenever I could.

It was about dusk, one evening during the supreme madness of the carnival season, that I encountered my friend. He accosted me with excessive warmth, for he had been drinking much. The man wore motley. He had on a tight-fitting parti-striped dress, and his head was surmounted by the conical cap and bells. I was so pleased to see him, that I thought I should never have done wringing his hand.

I said to him: "My dear Fortunato, you are luckily met. How remarkably well   5
you are looking to-day! But I have received a pipe° of what passes for Amontillado, and I have my doubts."

"How?" said he. "Amontillado? A pipe? Impossible! And in the middle of the carnival!"

"I have my doubts," I replied; "and I was silly enough to pay the full Amontillado price without consulting you in the matter. You were not to be found, and I was fearful of losing a bargain."

"Amontillado!"

"I have my doubts."

"Amontillado!"   10

"And I must satisfy them."

"Amontillado!"

"As you are engaged, I am on my way to Luchesi. If any one has a critical turn, it is he. He will tell me——"

"Luchesi cannot tell Amontillado from Sherry."

"And yet some fools will have it that his taste is a match for your own."   15

"Come, let us go."

"Whither?"

"To your vaults."

"My friend, no; I will not impose upon your good nature. I perceive you have an engagement. Luchesi——"

"I have no engagement;—come."   20

---

pipe: A large cask.

"My friend, no. It is not the engagement, but the severe cold with which I perceive you are afflicted. The vaults are insufferably damp. They are encrusted with nitre."

"Let us go, nevertheless. The cold is merely nothing. Amontillado! You have been imposed upon. And as for Luchesi, he cannot distinguish Sherry from Amontillado."

Thus speaking, Fortunato possessed himself of my arm. Putting on a mask of black silk, and drawing a *roquelaire*° closely about my person, I suffered him to hurry me to my palazzo.

There were no attendants at home; they had absconded to make merry in honor of the time. I had told them that I should not return until the morning, and had given them explicit orders not to stir from the house. These orders were sufficient, I well knew, to insure their immediate disappearance, one and all, as soon as my back was turned.

I took from their sconces two flambeaux, and giving one to Fortunato, bowed   25
him through several suites of rooms to the archway that led into the vaults. I passed down a long and winding staircase, requesting him to be cautious as he followed. We came at length to the foot of the descent, and stood together on the damp ground of the catacombs of the Montresors.

The gait of my friend was unsteady, and the bells upon his cap jingled as he strode.

"The pipe?" said he.

"It is farther on," said I; "but observe the white web-work which gleams from these cavern walls."

He turned toward me, and looked into my eyes with two filmy orbs that distilled the rheum of intoxication.

"Nitre?" he asked, at length.   30

"Nitre," I replied. "How long have you had that cough?"

"Ugh! ugh! ugh! — ugh! ugh! ugh! — ugh! ugh! ugh! — ugh! ugh! ugh! — ugh! ugh! ugh!"

My poor friend found it impossible to reply for many minutes.

"It is nothing," he said, at last.

"Come," I said, with decision, "we will go back; your health is precious. You   35
are rich, respected, admired, beloved; you are happy, as once I was. You are a man to be missed. For me it is no matter. We will go back; you will be ill, and I cannot be responsible. Besides, there is Luchesi — "

"Enough," he said; "the cough is a mere nothing; it will not kill me. I shall not die of a cough."

"True — true," I replied; "and, indeed, I had no intention of alarming you unnecessarily; but you should use all proper caution. A draught of this Medoc will defend us from the damps."

Here I knocked off the neck of a bottle which I drew from a long row of its fellows that lay upon the mould.

"Drink," I said, presenting him the wine.

---

roquelaire: A short cloak.

He raised it to his lips with a leer. He paused and nodded to me familiarly, 40
while his bells jingled.

"I drink," he said, "to the buried that repose around us."

"And I to your long life."

He again took my arm, and we proceeded.

"These vaults," he said, "are extensive."

"The Montresors," I replied, "were a great and numerous family." 45

"I forget your arms."

"A huge human foot d'or,° in a field azure; the foot crushes a serpent rampant whose fangs are imbedded in the heel."

"And the motto?"

"*Nemo me impune lacessit.*"°

"Good!" he said. 50

The wine sparkled in his eyes and the bells jingled. My own fancy grew warm with the Medoc. We had passed through walls of piled bones, with casks and puncheons intermingling into the inmost recesses of the catacombs. I paused again, and this time I made bold to seize Fortunato by an arm above the elbow.

"The nitre!" I said; "see, it increases. It hangs like moss upon the vaults. We are below the river's bed. The drops of moisture trickle among the bones. Come, we will go back ere it is too late. Your cough——"

"It is nothing," he said; "let us go on. But first, another draught of the Medoc."

I broke and reached him a flagon of De Grâve. He emptied it at a breath. His eyes flashed with a fierce light. He laughed and threw the bottle upward with a gesticulation I did not understand.

I looked at him in surprise. He repeated the movement—a grotesque one. 55

"You do not comprehend?" he said.

"Not I," I replied.

"Then you are not of the brotherhood."

"How?"

"You are not of the masons." 60

"Yes, yes," I said; "yes, yes."

"You? Impossible! A mason?"

"A mason," I replied.

"A sign," he said.

"It is this," I answered, producing a trowel from beneath the folds of my 65
roquelaire.

"You jest," he exclaimed, recoiling a few paces. "But let us proceed to the Amontillado."

"Be it so," I said, replacing the tool beneath the cloak, and again offering him my arm. He leaned upon it heavily. We continued our route in search of the Amontillado. We passed through a range of low arches, descended, passed on,

d'or: Of gold.
Nemo me impune lacessit: "No one wounds me with impunity" is the motto on the royal arms of Scotland.

and descending again, arrived at a deep crypt, in which the foulness of the air caused our flambeaux rather to glow than flame.

At the most remote end of the crypt there appeared another less spacious. Its walls had been lined with human remains, piled to the vault overhead, in the fashion of the great catacombs of Paris. Three sides of this interior crypt were still ornamented in this manner. From the fourth the bones had been thrown down, and lay promiscuously upon the earth, forming at one point a mound of some size. Within the wall thus exposed by the displacing of the bones, we perceived a still interior recess, in depth about four feet, in width three, in height six or seven. It seemed to have been constructed for no especial use within itself, but formed merely the interval between two of the colossal supports of the roof of the catacombs, and was backed by one of their circumscribing walls of solid granite.

It was in vain that Fortunato, uplifting his dull torch, endeavored to pry into the depth of the recess. Its termination the feeble light did not enable us to see.

"Proceed," I said; "herein is the Amontillado. As for Luchesi —" 70

"He is an ignoramus," interrupted my friend, as he stepped unsteadily forward, while I followed immediately at his heels. In an instant he had reached the extremity of the niche, and finding his progress arrested by the rock, stood stupidly bewildered. A moment more and I had fettered him to the granite. In its surface were two iron staples, distant from each other about two feet, horizontally. From one of these depended a short chain, from the other a padlock. Throwing the links about his waist, it was but the work of a few seconds to secure it. He was too much astounded to resist. Withdrawing the key I stepped back from the recess.

"Pass your hand," I said, "over the wall; you cannot help feeling the nitre. Indeed it is *very* damp. Once more let me *implore* you to return. No? Then I must positively leave you. But I must first render you all the little attentions in my power."

"The Amontillado!" ejaculated my friend, not yet recovered from his astonishment.

"True," I replied; "the Amontillado."

As I said these words I busied myself among the pile of bones of which I have 75 before spoken. Throwing them aside, I soon uncovered a quantity of building stone and mortar. With these materials and with the aid of my trowel, I began vigorously to wall up the entrance of the niche.

I had scarcely laid the first tier of the masonry when I discovered that the intoxication of Fortunato had in a great measure worn off. The earliest indication I had of this was a low moaning cry from the depth of the recess. It was *not* the cry of a drunken man. There was then a long and obstinate silence. I laid the second tier, and the third, and the fourth; and then I heard the furious vibrations of the chain. The noise lasted for several minutes, during which, that I might hearken to it with the more satisfaction, I ceased my labors and sat down upon the bones. When at last the clanking subsided, I resumed the trowel, and finished without interruption the fifth, the sixth, and the seventh tier. The wall was now nearly upon a level with my breast. I again paused, and holding the flambeaux over the masonwork, threw a few feeble rays upon the figure within.

A succession of loud and shrill screams, bursting suddenly from the throat of the chained form, seemed to thrust me violently back. For a brief moment I hesitated—I trembled. Unsheathing my rapier, I began to grope with it about the recess; but the thought of an instant reassured me. I placed my hand upon the solid fabric of the catacombs, and felt satisfied. I reapproached the wall. I replied to the yells of him who clamored. I reechoed—I aided—I surpassed them in volume and in strength. I did this, and the clamorer grew still.

It was now midnight, and my task was drawing to a close. I had completed the eighth, the ninth, and the tenth tier. I had finished a portion of the last and the eleventh; there remained but a single stone to be fitted and plastered in. I struggled with its weight; I placed it partially in its destined position. But now there came from out the niche a low laugh that erected the hairs upon my head. It was succeeded by a sad voice, which I had difficulty in recognizing as that of the noble Fortunato. The voice said—

"Ha! ha! ha!—he! he!—a very good joke indeed—an excellent jest. We will have many a rich laugh about it at the palazzo—he! he! he!—over our wine—he! he! he!"

"The Amontillado!" I said.   80

"He! he! he!—he! he! he!—yes, the Amontillado. But is it not getting late? Will not they be awaiting us at the palazzo, the Lady Fortunato and the rest? Let us be gone."

"Yes," I said, "let us be gone."

"*For the love of God, Montresor!*"

"Yes," I said, "for the love of God!"

But to these words I hearkened in vain for a reply. I grew impatient. I called   85
aloud:

"Fortunato!"

No answer. I called again:

"Fortunato!"

No answer still, I thrust a torch through the remaining aperture and let it fall within. There came forth in return only a jingling of the bells. My heart grew sick—on account of the dampness of the catacombs. I hastened to make an end of my labor. I forced the last stone into its position; I plastered it up. Against the new masonry I re-erected the old rampart of bones. For the half of a century no mortal has disturbed them. *In pace requiescat!*°   [1846]

In pace requiescat: In peace may he rest (Latin).

THINKING ABOUT THE TEXT

1. Evidently Montresor is recounting the story of his revenge fifty years after it took place. To whom might he be speaking? With what purposes?

2. Montresor does not describe in detail any of the offenses that Fortunato has supposedly committed against him. In considering how to judge Montresor, do you need such information? Why, or why not? State in

your own words the principles of revenge he lays out in the first paragraph.

3. What, if anything, does Poe achieve by having this story take place during a carnival? By repeating the word *amontillado* so much?

4. What does Montresor mean when he echoes Fortunato's words "for the love of God" (para. 84)? What might Fortunato be attempting to communicate with his final "jingling of the bells" (para. 89)?

5. Do you sympathize with Montresor? With Fortunato? Explain. What emotion did you mainly feel as you read the story? Identify specific features of it that led to this emotion.

LOUISE ERDRICH
Fleur

Louise Erdrich (b. 1954) is of German American and Chippewa descent. She was raised in Wahpeton, North Dakota, where both of her parents worked for the Bureau of Indian Affairs. In 1976, she earned a degree in Native American Studies at Dartmouth College; a year later, she received a master's degree in creative writing from the Johns Hopkins University. Although she has published poetry, essays, and a nonfiction book entitled The Blue Jay's Dance: A Birth Year *(1995), Erdrich is chiefly known for her novels about Native American life. Several of these feature a continuing cast of characters, including* Love Medicine *(1984; revised and expanded edition 1993),* The Beet Queen *(1986),* Tracks *(1988),* The Bingo Palace *(1994), and* Tales of Burning Love *(1996). She and her late husband Michael Dorris also collaborated on a novel entitled* The Crown of Columbus *(1991). "Fleur" was first published in a 1986 issue of* Esquire, *and later it became a chapter in* Tracks.

The first time she drowned in the cold and glassy waters of Lake Turcot, Fleur Pillager was only a girl. Two men saw the boat tip, saw her struggle in the waves. They rowed over to the place she went down, and jumped in. When they dragged her over the gunwales, she was cold to the touch and stiff, so they slapped her face, shook her by the heels, worked her arms back and forth, and pounded her back until she coughed up lake water. She shivered all over like a dog, then took a breath. But it wasn't long afterward that those two men disappeared. The first wandered off, and the other, Jean Hat, got himself run over by a cart.

It went to show, my grandma said. It figured to her, all right. By saving Fleur Pillager, those two men had lost themselves.

The next time she fell in the lake, Fleur Pillager was twenty years old and no one touched her. She washed onshore, her skin a dull dead gray, but when George Many Women bent to look closer, he saw her chest move. Then her eyes spun open, sharp black riprock, and she looked at him. "You'll take my place," she hissed. Everybody scattered and left her there, so no one knows how she dragged herself home. Soon after that we noticed Many Women changed, grew afraid, wouldn't leave his house, and would not be forced to go near water. For his caution, he lived until the day that his sons brought him a new tin bathtub. Then the first time he used the tub he slipped, got knocked out, and breathed water while his wife stood in the other room frying breakfast.

Men stayed clear of Fleur Pillager after the second drowning. Even though she was good-looking, nobody dared to court her because it was clear that Misshepeshu, the waterman, the monster, wanted her for himself. He's a devil, that one, love-hungry with desire and maddened for the touch of young girls, the strong and daring especially, the ones like Fleur.

Our mothers warn us that we'll think he's handsome, for he appears with 　5 green eyes, copper skin, a mouth tender as a child's. But if you fall into his arms, he sprouts horns, fangs, claws, fins. His feet are joined as one and his skin, brass scales, rings to the touch. You're fascinated, cannot move. He casts a shell necklace at your feet, weeps gleaming chips that harden into mica on your breasts. He holds you under. Then he takes the body of a lion or a fat brown worm. He's made of gold. He's made of beach moss. He's a thing of dry foam, a thing of death by drowning, the death a Chippewa cannot survive.

Unless you are Fleur Pillager. We all knew she couldn't swim. After the first time, we thought she'd never go back to Lake Turcot. We thought she'd keep to herself, live quiet, stop killing men off by drowning in the lake. After the first time, we thought she'd keep the good ways. But then, after the second drowning, we knew that we were dealing with something much more serious. She was haywire, out of control. She messed with evil, laughed at the old women's advice, and dressed like a man. She got herself into some half-forgotten medicine, studied ways we shouldn't talk about. Some say she kept the finger of a child in her pocket and a powder of unborn rabbits in a leather thong around her neck. She laid the heart of an owl on her tongue so she could see at night, and went out, hunting, not even in her own body. We know for sure because the next morning, in the snow or dust, we followed the tracks of her bare feet and saw where they changed, where the claws sprang out, the pad broadened and pressed into the dirt. By night we heard her chuffing cough, the bear cough. By day her silence and the wide grin she threw to bring down our guard made us frightened. Some thought that Fleur Pillager should be driven off the reservation, but not a single person who spoke like this had the nerve. And finally, when people were just about to get together and throw her out, she left on her own and didn't come back all summer. That's what this story is about.

During that summer, when she lived a few miles south in Argus, things happened. She almost destroyed that town.

When she got down to Argus in the year of 1920, it was just a small grid of six streets on either side of the railroad depot. There were two elevators, one central, the other a few miles west. Two stores competed for the trade of the three hundred citizens, and three churches quarreled with one another for their souls. There was a frame building for Lutherans, a heavy brick one for Episcopalians, and a long narrow shingled Catholic church. This last had a tall slender steeple, twice as high as any building or tree.

No doubt, across the low, flat wheat, watching from the road as she came near Argus on foot, Fleur saw that steeple rise, a shadow thin as a needle. Maybe in that raw space it drew her the way a lone tree draws lightning. Maybe in the end, the Catholics are to blame. For if she hadn't seen that sign of pride, that slim prayer, that marker, maybe she would have kept walking.

But Fleur Pillager turned, and the first place she went once she came into town was to the back door of the priest's residence attached to the landmark church. She didn't go there for a handout, although she got that, but to ask for work. She got that too, or the town got her. It's hard to tell which came out worse, her or the men or the town, although the upshot of it all was that Fleur lived.

The four men who worked at the butcher's had carved up about a thousand carcasses between them, maybe half of that steers and the other half pigs, sheep, and game animals like deer, elk, and bear. That's not even mentioning the chickens, which were beyond counting. Pete Kozka owned the place, and employed Lily Veddar, Tor Grunewald, and my stepfather, Dutch James, who had brought my mother down from the reservation the year before she disappointed him by dying. Dutch took me out of school to take her place. I kept house half the time and worked the other in the butcher shop, sweeping floors, putting sawdust down, running a hambone across the street to a customer's bean pot or a package of sausage to the corner. I was a good one to have around because until they needed me, I was invisible. I blended into the stained brown walls, a skinny, big-nosed girl with staring eyes. Because I could fade into a corner or squeeze beneath a shelf, I knew everything, what the men said when no one was around, and what they did to Fleur.

Kozka's Meats served farmers for a fifty-mile area, both to slaughter, for it had a stock pen and chute, and to cure the meat by smoking it or spicing it in sausage. The storage locker was a marvel, made of many thicknesses of brick, earth insulation, and Minnesota timber, lined inside with sawdust and vast blocks of ice cut from Lake Turcot, hauled down from home each winter by horse and sledge.

A ramshackle board building, part slaughterhouse, part store, was fixed to the low, thick square of the lockers. That's where Fleur worked. Kozka hired her for her strength. She could lift a haunch or carry a pole of sausages without stumbling, and she soon learned cutting from Pete's wife, a string thin blonde who chain-smoked and handled the razor-sharp knives with nerveless precision, slicing close to her stained fingers. Fleur and Fritzie Kozka worked afternoons, wrapping their cuts in paper, and Fleur hauled the packages to the lockers. The meat was left outside the heavy oak doors that were only opened at 5:00 each afternoon, before the men ate supper.

Sometimes Dutch, Tor, and Lily ate at the lockers, and when they did I stayed too, cleaned floors, restoked the fires in the front smokehouses, while the men sat around the squat cast-iron stove spearing slats of herring onto hardtack bread. They played long games of poker or cribbage on a board made from the planed end of a salt crate. They talked and I listened, although there wasn't much to hear since almost nothing ever happened in Argus. Tor was married, Dutch had lost my mother, and Lily read circulars. They mainly discussed about the auctions to come, equipment, or women.

Every so often, Pete Kozka came out front to make a whist, leaving Fritzie to 15 smoke cigarettes and fry raised doughnuts in the back room. He sat and played a few rounds but kept his thoughts to himself. Fritzie did not tolerate him talking behind her back, and the one book he read was the New Testament. If he said something, it concerned weather or a surplus of sheep stomachs, a ham that smoked green or the markets for corn and wheat. He had a good-luck talisman, the opal-white lens of a cow's eye. Playing cards, he rubbed it between his fingers. That soft sound and the slap of cards was about the only conversation.

Fleur finally gave them a subject.

Her cheeks were wide and flat, her hands large, chapped, muscular. Fleur's shoulders were broad as beams, her hips fishlike, slippery, narrow. An old green dress clung to her waist, worn thin where she sat. Her braids were thick like the tails of animals, and swung against her when she moved, deliberately, slowly in her work, held in and half-tamed, but only half. I could tell, but the others never saw. They never looked into her sly brown eyes or noticed her teeth, strong and curved and very white. Her legs were bare, and since she padded around in bead-work moccasins they never saw that her fifth toes were missing. They never knew she'd drowned. They were blinded, they were stupid, they only saw her in the flesh.

And yet it wasn't just that she was a Chippewa, or even that she was a woman, it wasn't that she was good-looking or even that she was alone that made their brains hum. It was how she played cards.

Women didn't usually play with men, so the evening that Fleur drew a chair up to the men's table without being so much as asked, there was a shock of surprise.

"What's this," said Lily. He was fat, with a snake's cold pale eyes and precious 20 skin, smooth and lily-white, which is how he got his name. Lily had a dog, a stumpy mean little bull of a thing with a belly drum-tight from eating pork rinds. The dog liked to play cards just like Lily, and straddled his barrel thighs through games of stud, rum poker, vingt-un. The dog snapped at Fleur's arm that first night, but cringed back, its snarl frozen, when she took her place.

"I thought," she said, her voice soft and stroking, "you might deal me in."

There was a space between the heavy bin of spiced flour and the wall where I just fit. I hunkered down there, kept my eyes open, saw her black hair swing over the chair, her feet solid on the wood floor. I couldn't see up on the table where the cards slapped down, so after they were deep in their game I raised myself up in the shadows, and crouched on a sill of wood.

I watched Fleur's hands stack and ruffle, divide the cards, spill them to each player in a blur, rake them up and shuffle again. Tor, short and scrappy, shut one eye and squinted the other at Fleur. Dutch screwed his lips around a wet cigar.

"Gotta see a man," he mumbled, getting up to go out back to the privy. The others broke, put their cards down, and Fleur sat alone in the lamplight that glowed in a sheen across the push of her breasts. I watched her closely, then she paid me a beam of notice for the first time. She turned, looked straight at me, and grinned the white wolf grin a Pillager turns on its victims, except that she wasn't after me.

"Pauline there," she said, "how much money you got?" 25

We'd all been paid for the week that day. Eight cents was in my pocket.

"Stake me," she said, holding out her long fingers. I put the coins in her palm and then I melted back to nothing, part of the walls and tables. It was a long time before I understood that the men would not have seen me no matter what I did, how I moved. I wasn't anything like Fleur. My dress hung loose and my back was already curved, an old woman's. Work had roughened me, reading made my eyes sore, caring for my mother before she died had hardened my face. I was not much to look at, so they never saw me.

When the men came back and sat around the table, they had drawn together. They shot each other small glances, stuck their tongues in their cheeks, burst out laughing at odd moments, to rattle Fleur. But she never minded. They played their vingt-un, staying even as Fleur slowly gained. Those pennies I had given her drew nickels and attracted dimes until there was a small pile in front of her.

Then she hooked them with five-card draw, nothing wild. She dealt, discarded, drew, and then she sighed and her cards gave a little shiver. Tor's eye gleamed, and Dutch straightened in his seat.

"I'll pay to see that hand," said Lily Veddar. 30

Fleur showed, and she had nothing there, nothing at all.

Tor's thin smile cracked open, and he threw his hand in too.

"Well, we know one thing," he said, leaning back in his chair, "the squaw can't bluff."

With that I lowered myself into a mound of swept sawdust and slept. I woke up during the night, but none of them had moved yet, so I couldn't either. Still later, the men must have gone out again, or Fritzie come out to break the game, because I was lifted, soothed, cradled in a woman's arms and rocked so quiet that I kept my eyes shut while Fleur rolled me into a closet of grimy ledgers, oiled paper, balls of string, and thick files that fit beneath me like a mattress.

The game went on after work the next evening. I got my eight cents back five 35 times over, and Fleur kept the rest of the dollar she'd won for a stake. This time they didn't play so late, but they played regular, and then kept going at it night after night. They played poker now, or variations, for one week straight, and each time Fleur won exactly one dollar, no more and no less, too consistent for luck.

By this time, Lily and the other men were so lit with suspense that they got Pete to join the game with them. They concentrated, the fat dog sitting tense in Lily Veddar's lap, Tor suspicious, Dutch stroking his huge square brow, Pete steady. It wasn't that Fleur won that hooked them in so, because she lost hands too. It was rather that she never had a freak hand or even anything above a straight. She only took on her low cards, which didn't sit right. By chance, Fleur should have gotten a full or flush by now. The irritating thing was she beat with pairs and never bluffed, because she couldn't, and still she ended up each night with exactly one dollar. Lily couldn't believe, first of all, that a woman could be smart enough to play cards, but even if she was, that she would then be stupid enough to cheat for a dollar a night. By day I watched him turn the problem over, his hard white face dull, small fingers probing at his knuckles, until he finally thought he had Fleur figured out as a bit-time player, caution her game. Raising the stakes would throw her.

More than anything now, he wanted Fleur to come away with something but a dollar. Two bits less or ten more, the sum didn't matter, just so he broke her streak.

Night after night she played, won her dollar, and left to stay in a place that just Fritzie and I knew about. Fleur bathed in the slaughtering tub, then slept in the unused brick smokehouse behind the lockers, a windowless place tarred on the inside with scorched fats. When I brushed against her skin I noticed that she smelled of the walls, rich and woody, slightly burnt. Since that night she put me in the closet I was no longer afraid of her, but followed her close, stayed with her, became her moving shadow that the men never noticed, the shadow that could have saved her.

August, the month that bears fruit, closed around the shop, and Pete and Fritzie left for Minnesota to escape the heat. Night by night, running, Fleur had won thirty dollars, and only Pete's presence had kept Lily at bay. But Pete was gone now, and one payday, with the heat so bad no one could move but Fleur, the men sat and played and waited while she finished work. The cards sweat, limp in their fingers, the table was slick with grease, and even the walls were warm to the touch. The air was motionless. Fleur was in the next room boiling heads.

Her green dress, drenched, wrapped her like a transparent sheet. A skin of lakeweed. Black snarls of veining clung to her arms. Her braids were loose, half-unraveled, tied behind her neck in a thick loop. She stood in steam, turning skulls through a vat with a wooden paddle. When scraps boiled to the surface, she bent with a round tin sieve and scooped them out. She'd filled two dishpans.   40

"Ain't that enough now?" called Lily. "We're waiting." The stump of a dog trembled in his lap, alive with rage. It never smelled me or noticed me above Fleur's smoky skin. The air was heavy in my corner, and pressed me down. Fleur sat with them.

"Now what do you say?" Lily asked the dog. It barked. That was the signal for the real game to start.

"Let's up the ante," said Lily, who had been stalking this night all month. He had a roll of money in his pocket. Fleur had five bills in her dress. The men had each saved their full pay.

"Ante a dollar then," said Fleur, and pitched hers in. She lost, but they let her scrape along, cent by cent. And then she won some. She played unevenly, as if chance was all she had. She reeled them in. The game went on. The dog was stiff now, poised on Lily's knees, a ball of vicious muscle with its yellow eyes slit in concentration. It gave advice, seemed to sniff the lay of Fleur's cards, twitched and nudged. Fleur was up, then down, saved by a scratch. Tor dealt seven cards, three down. The pot grew, round by round, until it held all the money. Nobody folded. Then it all rode on one last card and they went silent. Fleur picked hers up and blew a long breath. The heat lowered like a bell. Her card shook, but she stayed in.

Lily smiled and took the dog's head tenderly between his palms.   45

"Say, Fatso," he said, crooning the words, "you reckon that girl's bluffing?"

The dog whined and Lily laughed. "Me too," he said, "let's show." He swept his bills and coins into the pot and then they turned their cards over.

Lily looked once, looked again, then he squeezed the dog up like a fist of dough and slammed it on the table.

Fleur threw her arms out and drew the money over, grinning that same wolf grin that she'd used on me, the grin that had them. She jammed the bills in her dress, scooped the coins up in waxed white paper that she tied with string.

"Let's go another round," said Lily, his voice choked with burrs. But Fleur opened her mouth and yawned, then walked out back to gather slops for the one big hog that was waiting in the stock pen to be killed.   50

The men sat still as rocks, their hands spread on the oiled wood table. Dutch had chewed his cigar to damp shreds, Tor's eye was dull. Lily's gaze was the only one to follow Fleur. I didn't move. I felt them gathering, saw my stepfather's veins, the ones in his forehead that stood out in anger. The dog had rolled off the table and curled in a knot below the counter, where none of the men could touch it.

Lily rose and stepped out back to the closet of ledgers where Pete kept his private stock. He brought back a bottle, uncorked and tipped it between his fingers. The lump in his throat moved, then he passed it on. They drank, quickly felt the whiskey's fire, and planned with their eyes things they couldn't say out loud.

When they left, I followed. I hid out back in the clutter of broken boards and chicken crates beside the stock pen, where they waited. Fleur could not be seen at first, and then the moon broke and showed her, slipping cautiously along the rough board chute with a bucket in her hand. Her hair fell, wild and coarse, to her waist, and her dress was a floating patch in the dark. She made a pig-calling sound, rang the tin pail lightly against the wood, froze suspiciously. But too late. In the sound of the ring Lily moved, fat and nimble, stepped right behind Fleur and put out his creamy hands. At his first touch, she whirled and doused him with the bucket of sour slops. He pushed her against the big fence and the package of coins split, went clinking and jumping, winked against the wood. Fleur rolled over once and vanished in the yard.

The moon fell behind a curtain of ragged clouds, and Lily followed into the dark muck. But he tripped, pitched over the huge flank of the pig, who lay mired to the snout, heavily snoring. I sprang out of the weeds and climbed the side of the pen, stuck like glue. I saw the sow rise to her neat, knobby knees, gain her balance, and sway, curious, as Lily stumbled forward. Fleur had backed into the angle of rough wood just beyond, and when Lily tried to jostle past, the sow tipped up on her hind legs and struck, quick and hard as a snake. She plunged her head into Lily's thick side and snatched a mouthful of his shirt. She lunged again, caught him lower, so that he grunted in pained surprise. He seemed to ponder, breathing deep. Then he launched his huge body in a swimmer's dive.

The sow screamed as his body smacked over hers. She rolled, striking out   55
with her knife-sharp hooves, and Lily gathered himself upon her, took her foot-long face by the ears and scraped her snout and cheeks against the trestles of the pen. He hurled the sow's tight skull against an iron post, but instead of knocking her dead, he merely woke her from her dream.

She reared, shrieked, drew him with her so that they posed standing upright. They bowed jerkily to each other, as if to begin. Then his arms swung and flailed. She sank her black fangs into his shoulder, clasping him, dancing him forward and backward through the pen. Their steps picked up pace, went wild. The two dipped as one, box-stepped, tripped each other. She ran her split foot through his hair. He grabbed her kinked tail. They went down and came up, the same shape and then the same color, until the men couldn't tell one from the other in that light and Fleur was able to launch herself over the gates, swing down, hit gravel.

The men saw, yelled, and chased her at a dead run to the smokehouse. And Lily too, once the sow gave up in disgust and freed him. That is where I should have gone to Fleur, saved her, thrown myself on Dutch. But I went stiff with fear and couldn't unlatch myself from the trestles or move at all. I closed my eyes and put my head in my arms, tried to hide, so there is nothing to describe but what I couldn't block out, Fleur's hoarse breath, so loud it filled me, her cry in the old language, and my name repeated over and over among the words.

The heat was still dense the next morning when I came back to work. Fleur was gone but the men were there, slack-faced, hung over. Lily was paler and softer than ever, as if his flesh had steamed on his bones. They smoked, took pulls off a bottle. It wasn't noon yet. I worked awhile, waiting shop and sharpening steel. But I was sick, I was smothered, I was sweating so hard that my hands slipped on the knives, and I wiped my fingers clean of the greasy touch of the customers' coins. Lily opened his mouth and roared once, not in anger. There was no meaning to the sound. His boxer dog, sprawled limp beside his foot, never lifted its head. Nor did the other men.

They didn't notice when I stepped outside, hoping for a clear breath. And then I forgot them because I knew that we were all balanced, ready to tip, to fly, to be crushed as soon as the weather broke. The sky was so low that I felt the weight of it like a yoke. Clouds hung down, witch teats, a tornado's green-brown cones, and as I watched one flicked out and became a delicate probing thumb. Even as I picked up my heels and ran back inside, the wind blew suddenly, cold, and then came rain.

Inside, the men had disappeared already and the whole place was trembling as if a huge hand was pinched at the rafters, shaking it. I ran straight through, screaming for Dutch or for any of them, and then I stopped at the heavy doors of the lockers, where they had surely taken shelter. I stood there a moment. Everything went still. Then I heard a cry building in the wind, faint at first, a whistle and then a shrill scream that tore through the walls and gathered around me, spoke plain so I understood that I should move, put my arms out, and slam down the great iron bar that fit across the hasp and lock.

Outside, the wind was stronger, like a hand held against me. I struggled forward. The bushes tossed, the awnings flapped off storefronts, the rails of porches rattled. The odd cloud became a fat snout that nosed along the earth and sniffled, jabbed, picked at things, sucked them up, blew them apart, rooted around as if it was following a certain scent, then stopped behind me at the butcher shop and bored down like a drill.

60

I went flying, landed somewhere in a ball. When I opened my eyes and looked, stranger things were happening.

A herd of cattle flew through the air like giant birds, dropping dung, their mouths opened in stunned bellows. A candle, still lighted, blew past, and tables, napkins, garden tools, a whole school of drifting eyeglasses, jackets on hangers, hams, a checkerboard, a lampshade, and at last the sow from behind the lockers, on the run, her hooves a blur, set free, swooping, diving, screaming as everything in Argus fell apart and got turned upside down, smashed, and thoroughly wrecked.

Days passed before the town went looking for the men. They were bachelors, after all, except for Tor, whose wife had suffered a blow to the head that made her forgetful. Everyone was occupied with digging out, in high relief because even though the Catholic steeple had been torn off like a peaked cap and sent across five fields, those huddled in the cellar were unhurt. Walls had fallen, windows were demolished, but the stores were intact and so were the bankers and shop owners who had taken refuge in their safes or beneath their cash registers. It was a fair-minded disaster, no one could be said to have suffered much more than the next, at least not until Fritzie and Pete came home.

Of all the businesses in Argus, Kozka's Meats had suffered worst. The boards of the front building had been split to kindling, piled in a huge pyramid, and the shop equipment was blasted far and wide. Pete paced off the distance the iron bathtub had been flung—a hundred feet. The glass candy case went fifty, and landed without so much as a cracked pane. There were other surprises as well, for the back rooms where Fritzie and Pete lived were undisturbed. Fritzie said the dust still coated her china figures, and upon her kitchen table, in the ashtray, perched the last cigarette she'd put out in haste. She lit it up and finished it, looking through the window. From there, she could see that the old smokehouse Fleur had slept in was crushed to a reddish sand and the stockpens were completely torn apart, the rails stacked helter-skelter. Fritzie asked for Fleur. People shrugged. Then she asked about the others and, suddenly, the town understood that three men were missing.

There was a rally of help, a gathering of shovels and volunteers. We passed boards from hand to hand, stacked them, uncovered what lay beneath the pile of jagged splinters. The lockers, full of the meat that was Pete and Fritzie's investment, slowly came into sight, still intact. When enough room was made for a man to stand on the roof, there were calls, a general urge to hack through and see what lay below. But Fritzie shouted that she wouldn't allow it because the meat would spoil. And so the work continued, board by board, until at last the heavy oak doors of the freezer were revealed and people pressed to the entry. Everyone wanted to be the first, but since it was my stepfather lost, I was let go in when Pete and Fritzie wedged through into the sudden icy air.

Pete scraped a match on his boot, lit the lamp Fritzie held, and then the three of us stood still in its circle. Light glared off the skinned and hanging carcasses, the crates of wrapped sausages, the bright and cloudy blocks of lake ice, pure as winter. The cold bit into us, pleasant at first, then numbing. We must

65

have stood there a couple of minutes before we saw the men, or more rightly, the humps of fur, the iced and shaggy hides they wore, the bearskins they had taken down and wrapped around themselves. We stepped closer and tilted the lantern beneath the flaps of fur into their faces. The dog was there, perched among them, heavy as a doorstop. The three had hunched around a barrel where the game was still laid out, and a dead lantern and an empty bottle, too. But they had thrown down their last hands and hunkered tight, clutching one another, knuckles raw from beating at the door they had also attacked with hooks. Frost stars gleamed off their eyelashes and the stubble of their beards. Their faces were set in concentration, mouths open as if to speak some careful thought, some agreement they'd come to in each other's arms.

Power travels in the bloodlines, handed out before birth. It comes down through the hands, which in the Pillagers were strong and knotted, big, spidery, and rough, with sensitive fingertips good at dealing cards. It comes through the eyes, too, belligerent, darkest brown, the eyes of those in the bear clan, impolite as they gaze directly at a person.

In my dreams, I look straight back at Fleur, at the men. I am no longer the watcher on the dark sill, the skinny girl.

The blood draws us back, as if it runs through a vein of earth. I've come home and, except for talking to my cousins, live a quiet life. Fleur lives quiet too, down on Lake Turcot with her boat. Some say she's married to the waterman, Misshepeshu, or that she's living in shame with white men or windigos, or that she's killed them all. I'm about the only one here who ever goes to visit her. Last winter, I went to help out in her cabin when she bore the child, whose green eyes and skin the color of an old penny made more talk, as no one could decide if the child was mixed blood or what, fathered in a smokehouse, or by a man with brass scales, or by the lake. The girl is bold, smiling in her sleep, as if she knows what people wonder, as if she hears the old men talk, turning the story over. It comes up different every time and has no ending, no beginning. They get the middle wrong too. They only know that they don't know anything. [1986]

70

THINKING ABOUT THE TEXT

1. Should this story be called "Pauline" since she is the narrator and commits the climactic act of revenge?

2. Repeatedly Pauline associates Fleur with supernatural forces. What is the effect of these associations on you? If Erdrich had omitted them, would the story's impact have been different? If so, how?

3. In the process of reading the story, did you expect that the men would violently turn on Fleur, or were you surprised when they did? Note specific things that affected your ability to predict what would happen.

4. How do racial differences figure in this story? What role do gender differences play? Are race and gender equally relevant here?

5. Before she closes the door on the men, Pauline evidently feels guilty because she didn't help Fleur fight them. Is Pauline right to feel this way? Why, or why not? Was Pauline justified in taking revenge? Identify some warrants or assumptions behind your answer.

MAKING COMPARISONS

1. In both Poe's and Erdrich's stories, the narrator takes revenge by entombing someone. Compare how the stories describe this act. Does one story present it in a more horrifying way?

2. Both Poe's story and Erdrich's end by giving you brief glimpses of the avenger's thoughts some time after the act of revenge. Do these leaps forward have the same effect on you? Identify how each contributes to the overall meaning.

3. At the end of "Fleur," Pauline refers to the old men's talking about the origins of Fleur's child. Her last sentence is "They only know that they don't know anything." Would you apply the same statement to yourself as someone analyzing Erdrich's story? As someone attempting to understand Poe's? Explain your reasoning.

ANDRE DUBUS
Killings

Andre Dubus (1936–1999) served five years in the Marine Corps, attaining the rank of captain before becoming a full-time writer of short stories. Dubus lived in Haverhill, Massachusetts, and much of his fiction is set in the Merrimack Valley north of Boston. This is true of the following story, which appeared in his collection Finding a Girl in America *(1980) and was reprinted in his* Selected Stories *(1988). In 1991, Dubus also published a collection of essays,* Broken Vessels. *In part, the book deals with a 1986 accident that changed his life. Getting out of his car to aid stranded motorists, he was struck by another car; he eventually lost most of one leg and power over the other. Though confined to a wheelchair, Dubus continued to work actively. In 1996, he published his last collection of stories,* Dancing After Hours, *and in 1998, another volume of essays entitled* Meditations from a Moveable Chair. *Two years after he died came a much-acclaimed film adaptation of "Killings," entitled* In the Bedroom *(2001).*

On the August morning when Matt Fowler buried his youngest son, Frank, who had lived for twenty-one years, eight months, and four days, Matt's older son, Steve, turned to him as the family left the grave and walked between their friends, and said: "I should kill him." He was twenty-eight, his brown hair starting to thin in front where he used to have a cowlick. He bit his lower lip, wiped his eyes, then said it again. Ruth's arm, linked with Matt's, tightened; he looked at her. Beneath her eyes there was swelling from the three days she had suffered. At the limousine Matt stopped and looked back at the grave, the casket, and the Congregationalist minister who he thought had probably had a difficult job with the eulogy though he hadn't seemed to, and the old funeral director who was saying something to the six young pallbearers. The grave was on a hill and overlooked the Merrimack, which he could not see from where he stood; he looked at the opposite bank, at the apple orchard with its symmetrically planted trees going up a hill.

Next day Steve drove with his wife back to Baltimore where he managed the branch office of a bank, and Cathleen, the middle child, drove with her husband back to Syracuse. They had left the grandchildren with friends. A month after the funeral Matt played poker at Willis Trottier's because Ruth, who knew this was the second time he had been invited, told him to go, he couldn't sit home with her for the rest of her life, she was all right. After the game Willis went outside to tell everyone good night and, when the others had driven away, he walked with Matt to his car. Willis was a short, silver-haired man who had opened a diner after World War II, his trade then mostly very early breakfast, which he cooked, and then lunch for the men who worked at the leather and shoe factories. He now owned a large restaurant.

"He walks the Goddamn streets," Matt said.

"I know. He was in my place last night, at the bar. With a girl."

"I don't see him. I'm in the store all the time. Ruth sees him. She sees him   5
too much. She was at Sunnyhurst today getting cigarettes and aspirin, and there he was. She can't even go out for cigarettes and aspirin. It's killing her."

"Come back in for a drink."

Matt looked at his watch. Ruth would be asleep. He walked with Willis back into the house, pausing at the steps to look at the starlit sky. It was a cool summer night; he thought vaguely of the Red Sox, did not even know if they were at home tonight; since it happened he had not been able to think about any of the small pleasures he believed he had earned, as he had earned also what was shattered now forever: the quietly harried and quietly pleasurable days of fatherhood. They went inside. Willis's wife, Martha, had gone to bed hours ago, in the rear of the large house which was rigged with burglar and fire alarms. They went downstairs to the game room: the television set suspended from the ceiling, the pool table, the poker table with beer cans, cards, chips, filled ashtrays, and the six chairs where Matt and his friends had sat, the friends picking up the old banter as though he had only been away on vacation; but he could see the affection and courtesy in their eyes. Willis went behind the bar and mixed them each a Scotch and soda; he stayed behind the bar and looked at Matt sitting on the stool.

"How often have you thought about it?" Willis said.

"Every day since he got out. I didn't think about bail. I thought I wouldn't have to worry about him for years. She sees him all the time. It makes her cry."

"He was in my place a long time last night. He'll be back."   10

"Maybe he won't."

"The band. He likes the band."

"What's he doing now?"

"He's tending bar up to Hampton Beach. For a friend. Ever notice even the worst bastard always has friends? He couldn't get work in town. It's just tourists and kids up to Hampton. Nobody knows him. If they do, they don't care. They drink what he mixes."

"Nobody tells me about him."   15

"I hate him, Matt. My boys went to school with him. He was the same then. Know what he'll do? Five at the most. Remember that woman about seven years ago? Shot her husband and dropped him off the bridge in the Merrimack with a hundred-pound sack of cement and said all the way through it that nobody helped her. Know where she is now? She's in Lawrence now, a secretary. And whoever helped her, where the hell is he?"

"I've got a .38 I've had for years, I take it to the store now. I tell Ruth it's for the night deposits. I tell her things have changed: we got junkies here now too. Lots of people without jobs. She knows though."

"What does she know?"

"She knows I started carrying it after the first time she saw him in town. She knows it's in case I see him, and there's some kind of a situation —"

He stopped, looked at Willis, and finished his drink. Willis mixed him   20
another.

"What kind of situation?"

"Where he did something to me. Where I could get away with it."

"How does Ruth feel about that?"

"She doesn't know."

"You said she does, she's got it figured out."   25

He thought of her that afternoon: when she went into Sunnyhurst, Strout was waiting at the counter while the clerk bagged the things he had bought; she turned down an aisle and looked at soup cans until he left.

"Ruth would shoot him herself, if she thought she could hit him."

"You got a permit?"

"No."

"I do. You could get a year for that."   30

"Maybe I'll get one. Or maybe I won't. Maybe I'll just stop bringing it to the store."

Richard Strout was twenty-six years old, a high school athlete, football scholarship to the University of Massachusetts where he lasted for almost two semesters before quitting in advance of the final grades that would have forced him not to return. People then said: Dickie can do the work; he just doesn't want to. He came home and did construction work for his father but refused his father's offer to learn the business; his two older brothers had learned it, so that Strout and Sons trucks going about town, and signs on construction sites, now slashed wounds into Matt Fowler's life. Then Richard married a young girl and became a bartender, his salary and tips augmented and perhaps sometimes matched by his father, who also posted his bond. So his friends, his enemies (he had those: fist fights or, more often, boys and then young men who had not fought him when they thought they should have), and those who simply knew him by face and name, had a series of images of him which they recalled when they heard of the killing: the high school running back, the young drunk in bars, the oblivious hard-hatted young man eating lunch at a counter, the bartender who could perhaps be called courteous but not more than that: as he tended bar, his dark eyes and dark, wide-jawed face appeared less sullen, near blank.

One night he beat Frank. Frank was living at home and waiting for September, for graduate school in economics, and working as a lifeguard at Salisbury Beach, where he met Mary Ann Strout, in her first month of separation. She spent most days at the beach with her two sons. Before ten o'clock one night Frank came home; he had driven to the hospital first, and he walked into the living room with stitches over his right eye and both lips bright and swollen.

"I'm all right," he said, when Matt and Ruth stood up, and Matt turned off the television, letting Ruth get to him first: the tall, muscled but slender suntanned boy. Frank tried to smile at them but couldn't because of his lips.

"It was her husband, wasn't it?" Ruth said. 35

"Ex," Frank said. "He dropped in."

Matt gently held Frank's jaw and turned his face to the light, looked at the stitches, the blood under the white of the eye, the bruised flesh.

"Press charges," Matt said.

"No."

"What's to stop him from doing it again? Did you hit him at all? Enough so 40 he won't want to next time?"

"I don't think I touched him."

"So what are you going to do?"

"Take karate," Frank said, and tried again to smile.

"That's not the problem," Ruth said.

"You know you like her," Frank said. 45

"I like a lot of people. What about the boys? Did they see it?"

"They were asleep."

"Did you leave her alone with him?"

"He left first. She was yelling at him. I believe she had a skillet in her hand."

"Oh for God's sake," Ruth said. 50

Matt had been dealing with that too: at the dinner table on evenings when Frank wasn't home, was eating with Mary Ann; or, on the other nights—and Frank was with her every night—he talked with Ruth while they watched television, or lay in bed with the windows open and he smelled the night air and imagined, with both pride and muted sorrow, Frank in Mary Ann's arms. Ruth didn't like it because Mary Ann was in the process of divorce, because she had two children, because she was four years older than Frank, and finally—she told this in bed, where she had during all of their marriage told him of her deepest feelings: of love, of passion, of fears about one of the children, of pain Matt had caused her or she had caused him—she was against it because of what she had heard: that the marriage had gone bad early, and for most of it Richard and Mary Ann had both played around.

"That can't be true," Matt said. "Strout wouldn't have stood for it."

"Maybe he loves her."

"He's too hot-tempered. He couldn't have taken that."

But Matt knew Strout had taken it, for he had heard the stories too. He won- 55
dered who had told them to Ruth; and he felt vaguely annoyed and isolated: living with her for thirty-one years and still not knowing what she talked about with
her friends. On these summer nights he did not so much argue with her as try to
comfort her, but finally there was no difference between the two: she had concrete objections, which he tried to overcome. And in his attempt to do this, he
neglected his own objections, which were the same as hers, so that as he spoke to
her he felt as disembodied as he sometimes did in the store when he helped a
man choose a blouse or dress or piece of costume jewelry for his wife.

"The divorce doesn't mean anything," he said. "She was young and maybe
she liked his looks and then after a while she realized she was living with a bastard. I see it as a positive thing."

"She's not divorced yet."

"It's the same thing. Massachusetts has crazy laws, that's all. Her age is no
problem. What's it matter when she was born? And that other business: even if it's
true, which it probably isn't, it's got nothing to do with Frank, and it's in the past.
And the kids are no problem. She's been married six years; she ought to have kids.
Frank likes them. He plays with them. And he's not going to marry her anyway, so
it's not a problem of money."

"Then what's he doing with her?"

"She probably loves him, Ruth. Girls always have. Why can't we just leave it 60
at that?"

"He got home at six o'clock Tuesday morning."

"I didn't know you knew. I've already talked to him about it."

Which he had: since he believed almost nothing he told Ruth, he went to
Frank with what he believed. The night before, he had followed Frank to the car
after dinner.

"You wouldn't make much of a burglar," he said.

"How's that?" 65

Matt was looking up at him; Frank was six feet tall, an inch and a half taller
than Matt, who had been proud when Frank at seventeen outgrew him; he had
only felt uncomfortable when he had to reprimand or caution him. He touched
Frank's bicep, thought of the young taut passionate body, believed he could sense
the desire, and again he felt the pride and sorrow and envy too, not knowing
whether he was envious of Frank or Mary Ann.

"When you came in yesterday morning, I woke up. One of these mornings
your mother will. And I'm the one who'll have to talk to her. She won't interfere
with you. Okay? I know it means —" But he stopped, thinking: I know it means
getting up and leaving that suntanned girl and going sleepy to the car, I know —

"Okay," Frank said, and touched Matt's shoulder and got into the car.

There had been other talks, but the only long one was their first one: a night
driving to Fenway Park, Matt having ordered the tickets so they could talk, and
knowing when Frank said yes, he would go, that he knew the talk was coming
too. It took them forty minutes to get to Boston, and they talked about Mary Ann
until they joined the city traffic along the Charles River, blue in the late sun.

Frank told him all the things that Matt would later pretend to believe when he told them to Ruth.

"It seems like a lot for a young guy to take on," Matt finally said. 70

"Sometimes it is. But she's worth it."

"Are you thinking about getting married?"

"We haven't talked about it. She can't for over a year. I've got school."

"I *do* like her," Matt said.

He did. Some evenings, when the long summer sun was still low in the sky, 75 Frank brought her home; they came into the house smelling of suntan lotion and the sea, and Matt gave them gin and tonics and started the charcoal in the back-yard, and looked at Mary Ann in the lawn chair: long and very light brown hair (Matt thinking that twenty years ago she would have dyed it blonde), and the long brown legs he loved to look at; her face was pretty; she had probably never in her adult life gone unnoticed into a public place. It was in her wide brown eyes that she looked older than Frank; after a few drinks Matt thought what he saw in her eyes was something erotic, testament to the rumors about her; but he knew it wasn't that, or all that: she had, very young, been through a sort of pain that his children, and he and Ruth, had been spared. In the moments of his recognizing that pain, he wanted to tenderly touch her hair, wanted with some gesture to give her solace and hope. And he would glance at Frank, and hope they would love each other, hope Frank would soothe that pain in her heart, take it from her eyes; and her divorce, her age, and her children did not matter at all. On the first two evenings she did not bring her boys, and then Ruth asked her to bring them the next time. In bed that night Ruth said, "She hasn't brought them because she's embarrassed. She shouldn't feel embarrassed."

Richard Strout shot Frank in front of the boys. They were sitting on the living room floor watching television, Frank sitting on the couch, and Mary Ann just returning from the kitchen with a tray of sandwiches. Strout came in the front door and shot Frank twice in the chest and once in the face with a 9 mm auto-matic. Then he looked at the boys and Mary Ann, and went home to wait for the police.

It seemed to Matt that from the time Mary Ann called weeping to tell him until now, a Saturday night in September, sitting in the car with Willis, parked beside Strout's car, waiting for the bar to close, that he had not so much moved through his life as wandered through it, his spirits like a dazed body bumping into furniture and corners. He had always been a fearful father: when his chil-dren were young, at the start of each summer he thought of them drowning in a pond or the sea, and he was relieved when he came home in the evenings and they were there; usually that relief was his only acknowledgment of his fear, which he never spoke of, and which he controlled within his heart. As he had when they were very young and all of them in turn, Cathleen too, were drawn to the high oak in the backyard, and had to climb it. Smiling, he watched them, imagining the fall: and he was poised to catch the small body before it hit the earth. Or his legs were poised; his hands were in his pockets or his arms were folded and, for the child looking down, he appeared relaxed and confident while his heart beat with the two words he wanted to call out but did not: *Don't fall.* In winter he was less afraid: he made sure the ice would hold him before they skated, and he brought or sent them to places where they could sled without ending in the street. So he and his children had survived their childhood, and he only worried about them when he knew they were driving a long distance, and then he lost Frank in a way no father expected to lose his son, and he felt that all the fears he had borne while they were growing up, and all the grief he had been afraid of, had backed up like a huge wave and struck him on the beach and swept him out to sea. Each day he felt the same and when he was able to forget how he felt, when he was able to force himself not to feel that way, the eyes of his clerks and customers defeated him. He wished those eyes were oblivious, even cold; he felt he was withering in their tenderness. And beneath his listless wandering, every day in his soul he shot Richard Strout in the face; while Ruth, going about town on errands, kept seeing him. And at night in bed she would hold Matt and cry, or sometimes she was silent and Matt would touch her tightening arm, her clenched fist.

As his own right fist was now, squeezing the butt of the revolver, the last of the drinkers having left the bar, talking to each other, going to their separate cars which were in the lot in front of the bar, out of Matt's vision. He heard their voices, their cars, and then the ocean again, across the street. The tide was in and sometimes it smacked the sea wall. Through the windshield he looked at the dark red side wall of the bar, and then to his left, past Willis, at Strout's car, and through its windows he could see the now-emptied parking lot, the road, the sea wall. He could smell the sea.

The front door of the bar opened and closed again and Willis looked at Matt then at the corner of the building; when Strout came around it alone Matt got out of the car, giving up the hope he had kept all night (and for the past week) that Strout would come out with friends, and Willis would simply drive away; thinking: *All right then. All right*; and he went around the front of Willis's car, and at Strout's he stopped and aimed over the hood at Strout's blue shirt ten feet away. Willis was aiming too, crouched on Matt's left, his elbow resting on the hood.

"Mr. Fowler," Strout said. He looked at each of them, and at the guns. "Mr. Trottier." 80

Then Matt, watching the parking lot and the road, walked quickly between the car and the building and stood behind Strout. He took one leather glove from his pocket and put it on his left hand.

"Don't talk. Unlock the front and back and get in."

Strout unlocked the front door, reached in and unlocked the back, then got in, and Matt slid into the back seat, closed the door with his gloved hand, and touched Strout's head once with the muzzle.

"It's cocked. Drive to your house."

When Strout looked over his shoulder to back the car, Matt aimed at his 85 temple and did not look at his eyes.

"Drive slowly," he said. "Don't try to get stopped."

They drove across the empty front lot and onto the road, Willis's headlights shining into the car; then back through town, the sea wall on the left hiding the beach, though far out Matt could see the ocean; he uncocked the revolver; on the right were the places, most with their neon signs off, that did so much business in summer: the lounges and cafés and pizza houses, the street itself empty of traffic, the way he and Willis had known it would be when they decided to take Strout at the bar rather than knock on his door at two o'clock one morning and risk that one insomniac neighbor. Matt had not told Willis he was afraid he could not be alone with Strout for very long, smell his smells, feel the presence of his flesh, hear his voice, and then shoot him. They left the beach town and then were on the high bridge over the channel: to the left the smacking curling white at the breakwater and beyond that the dark sea and the full moon, and down to his right the small fishing boats bobbing at anchor in the cove. When they left the bridge, the sea was blocked by abandoned beach cottages, and Matt's left hand was sweating in the glove. Out here in the dark in the car he believed Ruth knew. Willis had come to his house at eleven and asked if he wanted a nightcap; Matt went to the bedroom for his wallet, put the gloves in one trouser pocket and the .38 in the other and went back to the living room, his hand in his pocket covering the bulge of the cool cylinder pressed against his fingers, the butt against his palm. When Ruth said good night she looked at his face, and he felt she could see in his eyes the gun, and the night he was going to. But he knew he couldn't trust what he saw. Willis's wife had taken her sleeping pill, which gave her eight hours—the reason, Willis had told Matt, he had the alarms installed, for nights when he was late at the restaurant—and when it was all done and Willis got home he would leave ice and a trace of Scotch and soda in two glasses in the game room and tell Martha in the morning that he had left the restaurant early and brought Matt home for a drink.

"He was making it with my wife." Strout's voice was careful, not pleading.

Matt pressed the muzzle against Strout's head, pressed it harder than he wanted to, feeling through the gun Strout's head flinching and moving forward; then he lowered the gun to his lap.

"Don't talk," he said.

Strout did not speak again. They turned west, drove past the Dairy Queen closed until spring, and the two lobster restaurants that faced each other and were crowded all summer and were now also closed, onto the short bridge crossing the tidal stream, and over the engine Matt could hear through his open window the water rushing inland under the bridge; looking to his left he saw its swift moonlit current going back into the marsh which, leaving the bridge, they entered: the salt marsh stretching out on both sides, the grass tall in patches but mostly low and leaning earthward as though windblown, a large dark rock sitting as though it rested on nothing but itself, and shallow pools reflecting the bright moon.

Beyond the marsh they drove through woods, Matt thinking now of the hole he and Willis had dug last Sunday afternoon after telling their wives they were going to Fenway Park. They listened to the game on a transistor radio, but heard none of it as they dug into the soft earth on the knoll they had chosen because elms and maples sheltered it. Already some leaves had fallen. When the hole was

90

deep enough they covered it and the piled earth with dead branches, then cleaned their shoes and pants and went to a restaurant farther up in New Hampshire where they ate sandwiches and drank beer and watched the rest of the game on television. Looking at the back of Strout's head he thought of Frank's grave; he had not been back to it; but he would go before winter, and its second burial of snow.

He thought of Frank sitting on the couch and perhaps talking to the children as they watched television, imagined him feeling young and strong, still warmed from the sun at the beach, and feeling loved, hearing Mary Ann moving about in the kitchen, hearing her walking into the living room; maybe he looked up at her and maybe she said something, looking at him over the tray of sandwiches, smiling at him, saying something the way women do when they offer food as a gift, then the front door opening and this son of a bitch coming in and Frank seeing that he meant the gun in his hand, this son of a bitch and his gun the last person and thing Frank saw on earth.

When they drove into town the streets were nearly empty: a few slow cars, a policeman walking his beat past the darkened fronts of stores. Strout and Matt both glanced at him as they drove by. They were on the main street, and all the stoplights were blinking yellow. Willis and Matt had talked about that too: the lights changed at midnight, so there would be no place Strout had to stop and where he might try to run. Strout turned down the block where he lived and Willis's headlights were no longer with Matt in the back seat. They had planned that too, had decided it was best for just the one car to go to the house, and again Matt had said nothing about his fear of being alone with Strout, especially in his house: a duplex, dark as all the houses on the street were, the street itself lit at the corner of each block. As Strout turned into the driveway Matt thought of the one insomniac neighbor, thought of some man or woman sitting alone in the dark living room, watching the all-night channel from Boston. When Strout stopped the car near the front of the house, Matt said: "Drive it to the back."

He touched Strout's head with the muzzle.   95

"You wouldn't have it cocked, would you? For when I put on the brakes."

Matt cocked it, and said: "It is now."

Strout waited a moment; then he eased the car forward, the engine doing little more than idling, and as they approached the garage he gently braked. Matt opened the door, then took off the glove and put it in his pocket. He stepped out and shut the door with his hip and said: "All right."

Strout looked at the gun, then got out, and Matt followed him across the grass, and as Strout unlocked the door Matt looked quickly at the row of small backyards on either side, and scattered tall trees, some evergreens, others not, and he thought of the red and yellow leaves on the trees over the hole, saw them falling soon, probably in two weeks, dropping slowly, covering. Strout stepped into the kitchen.

"Turn on the light."   100

Strout reached to the wall switch, and in the light Matt looked at his wide back, the dark blue shirt, the white belt, the red plaid pants.

"Where's your suitcase?"

"My suitcase?"

"Where is it?"

"In the bedroom closet."

105

"That's where we're going then. When we get to a door you stop and turn on the light."

They crossed the kitchen, Matt glancing at the sink and stove and refrigerator: no dishes in the sink or even the dish rack beside it, no grease splashings on the stove, the refrigerator door clean and white. He did not want to look at any more but he looked quickly at all he could see: in the living room magazines and newspapers in a wicker basket, clean ashtrays, a record player, the records shelved next to it, then down the hall where, near the bedroom door, hung a color photograph of Mary Ann and the two boys sitting on a lawn — there was no house in the picture — Mary Ann smiling at the camera or Strout or whoever held the camera, smiling as she had on Matt's lawn this summer while he waited for the charcoal and they all talked and he looked at her brown legs and at Frank touching her arm, her shoulder, her hair; he moved down the hall with her smile in his mind, wondering: was that when they were both playing around and she was smiling like that at him and they were happy, even sometimes, making it worth it? He recalled her eyes, the pain in them, and he was conscious of the circles of love he was touching with the hand that held the revolver so tightly now as Strout stopped at the door at the end of the hall.

"There's no wall switch."

"Where's the light?"

"By the bed."

110

"Let's go."

Matt stayed a pace behind, then Strout leaned over and the room was lighted: the bed, a double one, was neatly made; the ashtray on the bedside table clean, the bureau top dustless, and no photographs; probably so the girl — who *was* she? — would not have to see Mary Ann in the bedroom she believed was theirs. But because Matt was a father and a husband, though never an ex-husband, he knew (and did not want to know) that this bedroom had never been theirs alone. Strout turned around; Matt looked at his lips, his wide jaw, and thought of Frank's doomed and fearful eyes looking up from the couch.

"Where's Mr. Trottier?"

"He's waiting. Pack clothes for warm weather."

"What's going on?"

115

"You're jumping bail."

"Mr. Fowler—"

He pointed the cocked revolver at Strout's face. The barrel trembled but not much, not as much as he had expected. Strout went to the closet and got the suitcase from the floor and opened it on the bed. As he went to the bureau, he said: "He was making it with my wife. I'd go pick up my kids and he'd be there. Sometimes he spent the night. My boys told me."

He did not look at Matt as he spoke. He opened the top drawer and Matt stepped closer so he could see Strout's hands: underwear and socks, the socks rolled, the underwear folded and stacked. He took them back to the bed, arranged them neatly in the suitcase, then from the closet he was taking shirts and trousers and a jacket; he laid them on the bed and Matt followed him to the bathroom and watched from the door while he packed those things a person accumulated and that became part of him so that at times in the store Matt felt he was selling more than clothes.

"I wanted to try to get together with her again." He was bent over the suit- 120 case. "I couldn't even talk to her. He was always with her. I'm going to jail for it; if I ever get out I'll be an old man. Isn't that enough?"

"You're not going to jail."

Strout closed the suitcase and faced Matt, looking at the gun. Matt went to his rear, so Strout was between him and the lighted hall; then using his handkerchief he turned off the lamp and said: "Let's go."

They went down the hall, Matt looking again at the photograph, and through the living room and kitchen, Matt turning off the lights and talking, frightened that he was talking, that he was telling this lie he had not planned: "It's the trial. We can't go through that, my wife and me. So you're leaving. We've got you a ticket, and a job. A friend of Mr. Trottier's. Out west. My wife keeps seeing you. We can't have that anymore."

Matt turned out the kitchen light and put the handkerchief in his pocket, and they went down the two brick steps and across the lawn. Strout put the suitcase on the floor of the back seat, then got into the front seat and Matt got in the back and put on his glove and shut the door.

"They'll catch me. They'll check passenger lists." 125

"We didn't use your name."

"They'll figure that out too. You think I wouldn't have done it myself if it was that easy?"

He backed into the street, Matt looking down the gun barrel but not at the profiled face beyond it.

"You were alone," Matt said. "We've got it worked out."

"There's no planes this time of night, Mr. Fowler." 130

"Go back through town. Then north on 125."

They came to the corner and turned, and now Willis's headlights were in the car with Matt.

"Why north, Mr. Fowler?"

"Somebody's going to keep you for a while. They'll take you to the airport." He uncocked the hammer and lowered the revolver to his lap and said wearily: "No more talking."

As they drove back through town, Matt's body sagged, going limp with his 135 spirit and its new and false bond with Strout, the hope his lie had given Strout. He had grown up in this town whose streets had become places of apprehension and pain for Ruth as she drove and walked, doing what she had to do; and for him too, if only in his mind as he worked and chatted six days a week in his store; he wondered now if his lie would have worked, if sending Strout away would have been enough; but then he knew that just thinking of Strout in Montana or whatever place lay at the end of the lie he had told, thinking of him walking the streets there, loving a girl there (who *was* she?) would be enough to slowly rot the rest of his days. And Ruth's. Again he was certain that she knew, that she was waiting for him.

They were in New Hampshire now, on the narrow highway, passing the shopping center at the state line, and then houses and small stores and sandwich shops. There were few cars on the road. After ten minutes he raised his trembling hand, touched Strout's neck with the gun, and said: "Turn in up here. At the dirt road."

Strout flicked on the indicator and slowed.

"Mr. Fowler?"

"They're waiting here."

Strout turned very slowly, easing his neck away from the gun. In the moon-light the road was light brown, lighter and yellowed where the headlights shone; weeds and a few trees grew on either side of it, and ahead of them were the woods. 140

"There's nothing back here, Mr. Fowler."

"It's for your car. You don't think we'd leave it at the airport, do you?"

He watched Strout's large, big-knuckled hands tighten on the wheel, saw Frank's face that night: not the stitches and bruised eye and swollen lips, but his own hand gently touching Frank's jaw, turning his wounds to the light. They rounded a bend in the road and were out of sight of the highway: tall trees all around them now, hiding the moon. When they reached the abandoned gravel pit on the left, the bare flat earth and steep pale embankment behind it, and the black crowns of trees at its top, Matt said: "Stop here."

Strout stopped but did not turn off the engine. Matt pressed the gun hard against his neck, and he straightened in the seat and looked in the rearview mir-ror, Matt's eyes meeting his in the glass for an instant before looking at the hair at the end of the gun barrel.

"Turn it off." 145

Strout did, then held the wheel with two hands, and looked in the mirror.

"I'll do twenty years, Mr. Fowler; at least. I'll be forty-six years old."

"That's nine years younger than I am," Matt said, and got out and took off the glove and kicked the door shut. He aimed at Strout's ear and pulled back the hammer. Willis's headlights were off and Matt heard him walking on the soft thin layer of dust, the hard earth beneath it. Strout opened the door, sat for a moment in the interior light, then stepped out onto the road. Now his face was pleading. Matt did not look at his eyes, but he could see it in the lips.

"Just get the suitcase. They're right up the road."

Willis was beside him now, to his left. Strout looked at both guns. Then he opened the back door, leaned in, and with a jerk brought the suitcase out. He was turning to face them when Matt said: "Just walk up the road. Just ahead." 150

Strout turned to walk, the suitcase in his right hand, and Matt and Willis fol-lowed; as Strout cleared the front of his car he dropped the suitcase and, ducking, took one step that was the beginning of a sprint to his right. The gun kicked in Matt's hand, and the explosion of the shot surrounded him, isolated him in a nimbus of sound that cut him off from all his time, all his history, isolated him standing absolutely still on the dirt road with the gun in his hand, looking down at Richard Strout squirming on his belly, kicking one leg behind him, pushing himself forward, toward the woods. Then Matt went to him and shot him once in the back of the head.

Driving south to Boston, wearing both gloves now, staying in the middle lane and looking often in the rearview mirror at Willis's headlights, he relived the suitcase dropping, the quick dip and turn of Strout's back, and the kick of the gun, the sound of the shot. When he walked to Strout, he still existed within the first shot, still trembled and breathed with it. The second shot and the burial seemed to be happening to someone else, someone he was watching. He and Willis each held an arm and pulled Strout face-down off the road and into the woods, his bouncing sliding belt white under the trees where it was so dark that when they stopped at the top of the knoll, panting and sweating, Matt could not see where Strout's blue shirt ended and the earth began. They pulled off the branches then dragged Strout to the edge of the hole and went behind him and lifted his legs and pushed him in. They stood still for a moment. The woods were quiet save for their breathing, and Matt remembered hearing the movements of birds and small animals after the first shot. Or maybe he had not heard them. Willis went down to the road. Matt could see him clearly out on the tan dirt, could see the glint of Strout's car and, beyond the road, the gravel pit. Willis came back up the knoll with the suitcase. He dropped it in the hole and took off his gloves and they went down to his car for the spades. They worked quietly. Sometimes they paused to listen to the woods. When they were finished Willis turned on his flashlight and they covered the earth with leaves and branches and then went down to the spot in front of the car, and while Matt held the light Willis crouched and sprinkled dust on the blood, backing up till he reached the grass and leaves, then he used leaves until they had worked up to the grave again. They did not stop. They walked around the grave and through the woods, using the light on the ground, looking up through the trees to where they ended at the lake. Neither of them spoke above the sounds of their heavy and clumsy strides through low brush and over fallen branches. Then they reached it: wide and dark, lapping softly at the bank, pine needles smooth under Matt's feet, moonlight on the lake, a small island near its middle, with black, tall evergreens. He took out the gun and threw for the island: taking two steps back on the pine needles, striding with the throw and going to one knee as he followed through, looking up to see the dark shapeless object arcing downward, splashing.

They left Strout's car in Boston, in front of an apartment building on Commonwealth Avenue. When they got back to town Willis drove slowly over the bridge and Matt threw the keys into the Merrimack. The sky was turning light. Willis let him out a block from his house, and walking home he listened for sounds from the houses he passed. They were quiet. A light was on in his living room. He turned it off and undressed in there, and went softly toward the bedroom; in the hall he smelled the smoke, and he stood in the bedroom doorway and looked at the orange of her cigarette in the dark. The curtains were closed. He went to the closet and put his shoes on the floor and felt for a hanger.

"Did you do it?" she said.

He went down the hall to the bathroom and in the dark he washed his hands   155
and face. Then he went to her, lay on his back, and pulled the sheet up to his
throat.

"Are you all right?" she said.

"I think so."

Now she touched him, lying on her side, her hand on his belly, his thigh.

"Tell me," she said.

He started from the beginning, in the parking lot at the bar; but soon with his   160
eyes closed and Ruth petting him, he spoke of Strout's house: the order, the
woman presence, the picture on the wall.

"The way she was smiling," he said.

"What about it?"

"I don't know. Did you ever see Strout's girl? When you saw him in town?"

"No."

"I wonder who she was."   165

Then he thought: *not was: is. Sleeping now she is his girl.* He opened his eyes,
then closed them again. There was more light beyond the curtains. With Ruth
now he left Strout's house and told again his lie to Strout, gave him again that
hope that Strout must have for a while believed, else he would have to believe
only the gun pointed at him for the last two hours of his life. And with Ruth he
saw again the dropping suitcase, the darting move to the right: and he told of the
first shot, feeling her hand on him but his heart isolated still, beating on the road
still in that explosion like thunder. He told her the rest, but the words had no
images for him, he did not see himself doing what the words said he had done; he
only saw himself on that road.

"We can't tell the other kids," she said. "It'll hurt them, thinking he got away.
But we mustn't."

"No."

She was holding him, wanting him, and he wished he could make love with
her but he could not. He saw Frank and Mary Ann making love in her bed, their
eyes closed, their bodies brown and smelling of the sea; the other girl was faceless,
bodiless, but he felt her sleeping now; and he saw Frank and Strout, their faces
alive; he saw red and yellow leaves falling on the earth, then snow: falling and
freezing and falling; and holding Ruth, his cheek touching her breast, he shuddered with a sob that he kept silent in his heart.   [1979]

THINKING ABOUT THE TEXT

1. Here is an issue of cause and effect: Why, evidently, does Matt kill Richard
   Strout? Consider the possibility that he has more than one reason. Here is
   an issue of evaluation: To what extent should the reader sympathize with
   Matt? Identify some things that readers should especially consider in addressing this question.

2. Identify the argument that Richard Strout makes as he tries to keep Matt
   from killing him. What warrants or assumptions does Strout use? How
   common is his way of thinking?

3. Why does Willis help Matt take revenge? To what extent does Ruth's thinking resemble her husband's?

4. What is Matt's view of Mary Ann, his late son's girlfriend?

5. After beginning with Frank's funeral, the story features several flashbacks. Only gradually does Dubus provide certain seemingly important facts, such as exactly how Matt's son died. ("Richard Strout shot Frank in front of the boys.") What do you think might have been Dubus's purpose(s) in refusing to be more straightforward? In the last several pages, the story is pretty straightforward, moving step by step through the night of Matt's revenge. Why do you suppose Dubus changed his method of storytelling?

MAKING COMPARISONS

1. Montresor and Matt carefully plan their revenge. But Pauline appears to commit revenge spontaneously, not carefully planning it beforehand. Does this difference matter to you as you judge these three acts of revenge? Why, or why not?

2. How guilty does each of these three avengers feel? Compare their degrees of guilt by citing specific details from each text to support your impressions.

3. Do Poe, Erdrich, and Dubus seem equally committed to making you feel that the settings they describe really exist? Again, support your answer by referring to specific details from each text.

WRITING ABOUT ISSUES

1. Choose one of the three stories in this cluster and write an essay identifying the extent to which readers ought to feel sorry for the victim or victims of revenge. Argue for your position by citing details of the text.

2. In her book *Bird by Bird: Some Instructions on Writing and Life,* Anne Lamott advises would-be fiction writers that a story must culminate in "a killing or a healing or a domination." She goes on to explain:

> It can be a real killing, a murder, or it can be a killing of the spirit, or of something terrible inside one's soul, or it can be a killing of a deadness within, after which the person becomes alive again. The healing may be about union, reclamation, the rescue of a fragile prize. But whatever happens, we need to feel that it was inevitable, that even though we may be amazed, it feels absolutely right, that of course things would come to this, of course they would shake down in this way.

Choose two of the stories in this cluster and write an essay discussing the extent to which they obey Lamott's advice. Refer to specific words in the passage from her, as well as to specific details of the stories. If you wish, feel free to evaluate Lamott's advice. Do you think fiction writers ought to follow it?

3. Gerald Murphy, a famous socialite of the 1920s, once said that "living well is the best revenge." Murphy did not identify whom it was revenge against. Still, his statement is thought-provoking in its suggestion that revenge is not always recognizable as such. "Living well" may be revenge in disguise. Write an essay showing how a specific action you are familiar with can be seen as an act of revenge, even though many people wouldn't realize this. In your essay, also evaluate the action. Do you approve of this act of revenge? Why, or why not?

4. Write an essay examining a real-life legal case that involved one or more of the acts depicted in these stories: for example, rape, sexual relations between employer and employee, racial discrimination, reactions to perceived insults, acts of revenge. To learn important facts about the case, you may have to do research in the library. In your essay, point out at least one issue raised by the case, identify your position on the issue, and support your position. If you wish, refer to any of the stories in this cluster.

CONFRONTING SIN: A COLLECTION OF WRITINGS BY NATHANIEL HAWTHORNE

NATHANIEL HAWTHORNE, "Young Goodman Brown"
NATHANIEL HAWTHORNE, "The Minister's Black Veil: A Parable"
NATHANIEL HAWTHORNE, "Ethan Brand: A Chapter from an Abortive Romance"

For many people, justice is often a religious issue. They strive to obey laws of their religious group as well as the laws of their society. Actually, history has seen many theocracies — governments that use their justice system to impose a particular religion on their people. Contemporary examples include Islamic nations such as Iran and Saudi Arabia. By contrast, the United States is officially committed to a legal system that enforces the separation of church and state. Nevertheless, certain American communities have combined the two. Probably the best-known example is the Puritan society of seventeenth-century New England, whose citizens were required to follow a version of Protestantism that emphasized, among other things, perpetual consciousness of the individual's potential for sin. An extreme form of Puritan justice surfaced when the notorious 1692 Salem witchcraft trials condemned people to death for conspiring with demons.

One of the presiding judges at the Salem trials was John Hathorne, an ancestor of the nineteenth-century American author Nathaniel Hawthorne. Two and a half centuries later, Hawthorne wrote fiction that critically examined Puritan visions of religious justice. The following are three of his best-known stories on this subject. The title character of each tale is bent on confronting sin but risks losing his humanity in the process. These works are similar, too, in their dream-like atmosphere, which forces readers to decide for themselves what actually happens in them and what moral lessons to take from them.

(Portrait by G. P. A.
Healy, New Hampshire
Historical Society.)

BEFORE YOU READ

How useful do you find the term *sin*? Do you think society would be better
off if it used this word more?

NATHANIEL HAWTHORNE
Young Goodman Brown

*Nathaniel Hawthorne (1804–1864) was born in Salem, Massachusetts, into a fam-
ily that was founded by New England's Puritan colonists. This lineage troubled
Hawthorne, especially because his ancestor John Hathorne was involved as a judge
in the Salem witch trials. After graduating from Maine's Bowdoin College in 1825,
Hawthorne returned to Salem and began his career as a writer. In 1832, he self-
published his first novel,* Fanshawe, *but considered it an artistic as well as commercial failure and tried to destroy all unsold copies of it. He was more successful with
his 1832 short-story collection* Twice-Told Tales *(reprinted and enlarged in 1842).
In the early 1840s, Hawthorne worked as a surveyor in the Boston Custom House,*

briefly joined the Utopian community of Brook Farm, and then moved to Concord. There he published several children's books and lived with his wife, Sophia, in writer Ralph Waldo Emerson's former home, the Old Manse. In 1846, he produced a second collection of short stories, Mosses from an Old Manse. *For the next three years, Hawthorne worked in a custom house in his home town of Salem before publishing his most famous analysis of Puritan culture,* The Scarlet Letter *(1850). Later novels included* The House of the Seven Gables *(1851),* The Blithedale Romance *(an 1852 satire on Brook Farm), and* The Marble Faun *(1860). When his friend Franklin Pierce became president of the United States, Hawthorne served as American consul in Liverpool, England, for four years, and then traveled in Italy for two more. At his death in 1864, he was already highly respected as a writer. Much of his fiction deals with conflicted characters whose hearts and souls are torn by sin, guilt, pride, and isolation. Indeed, his good friend Herman Melville, author of* Moby-Dick, *praised "the power of blackness" he found in Hawthorne's works. The allegorical story "Young Goodman Brown" is an especially memorable example of this power. Hawthorne wrote the tale in 1835 and later included it in* Mosses from an Old Manse.

Young Goodman Brown came forth at sunset into the street at Salem village; but put his head back, after crossing the threshold, to exchange a parting kiss with his young wife. And Faith, as the wife was aptly named, thrust her own pretty head into the street, letting the wind play with the pink ribbons of her cap while she called to Goodman Brown.

"Dearest heart," whispered she, softly and rather sadly, when her lips were close to his ear, "prithee put off your journey until sunrise and sleep in your own bed to-night. A lone woman is troubled with such dreams and such thoughts that she's afeared of herself sometimes. Pray tarry with me this night, dear husband, of all nights in the year."

"My love and my Faith," replied young Goodman Brown, "of all nights in the year, this one night must I tarry away from thee. My journey, as thou callest it, forth and back again, must needs be done 'twixt now and sunrise. What, my sweet, pretty wife, dost thou doubt me already, and we but three months married?"

"Then God bless you!" said Faith, with the pink ribbons; "and may you find all well when you come back."

"Amen!" cried Goodman Brown. "Say thy prayers, dear Faith, and go to bed at dusk, and no harm will come to thee."

So they parted; and the young man pursued his way until, being about to turn the corner by the meeting-house, he looked back and saw the head of Faith still peeping after him with a melancholy air, in spite of her pink ribbons.

"Poor little Faith!" thought he, for his heart smote him. "What a wretch⌐ to leave her on such an errand! She talks of dreams, too. Methought as sʰ there was trouble in her face, as if a dream had warned her what wᵉ done to-night. But no, no; 't would kill her to think it. Well, she's a ʰ on earth, and after this one night I'll cling to her skirts and follow hᵉ

5

With this excellent resolve for the future, Goodman Brown felt himself justified in making more haste on his present evil purpose. He had taken a dreary
road, darkened by all the gloomiest trees of the forest, which barely stood aside to
let the narrow path creep through, and closed immediately behind. It was all as
lonely as could be; and there is this peculiarity in such a solitude, that the traveller knows not who may be concealed by the innumerable trunks and the thick
boughs overhead; so that with lonely footsteps he may yet be passing through an
unseen multitude.

"There may be a devilish Indian behind every tree," said Goodman Brown to
himself; and he glanced fearfully behind him as he added, "What if the devil
himself should be at my very elbow!"

His head being turned back, he passed a crook of the road, and, looking for-   10
ward again, beheld the figure of a man, in grave and decent attire, seated at the
foot of an old tree. He arose at Goodman Brown's approach and walked onward
side by side with him.

"You are late, Goodman Brown," said he. "The clock of the Old South was
striking as I came through Boston, and that is full fifteen minutes agone."

"Faith kept me back a while," replied the young man, with a tremor in his
voice, caused by the sudden appearance of his companion, though not wholly
unexpected.

It was now deep dusk in the forest, and deepest in that part of it where these
two were journeying. As nearly as could be discerned, the second traveller was
about fifty years old, apparently in the same rank of life as Goodman Brown, and
bearing a considerable resemblance to him, though perhaps more in expression
than features. Still they might have been taken for father and son. And yet,
though the elder person was as simply clad as the younger, and as simple in manner too, he had an indescribable air of one who knew the world, and who would
not have felt abashed at the governor's dinner table or in King William's court,
were it possible that his affairs should call him thither. But the only thing about
him that could be fixed upon as remarkable was his staff, which bore the likeness
of a great black snake, so curiously wrought that it might almost be seen to twist
and wriggle itself like a living serpent. This, of course, must have been an ocular
deception, assisted by the uncertain light.

"Come, Goodman Brown," cried his fellow-traveller, "this is a dull pace for
the beginning of a journey. Take my staff, if you are so soon weary."

"Friend," said the other, exchanging his slow pace for a full stop, "having   15
kept covenant by meeting thee here, it is my purpose now to return whence I
came. I have scruples touching the matter thou wot'st of."

"Sayest thou so?" replied he of the serpent, smiling apart. "Let us walk on,
nevertheless, reasoning as we go; and if I convince thee not thou shalt turn back.
We are but a little way in the forest yet."

"Too far! too far!" exclaimed the goodman, unconsciously resuming his
walk. "My father never went into the woods on such an errand, nor his father
before him. We have been a race of honest men and good Christians since the
days of the martyrs; and shall I be the first of the name of Brown that ever took this
ɔath and kept" —

"Such company, thou wouldst say," observed the elder person, interpreting his pause. "Well said, Goodman Brown! I have been as well acquainted with your family as with ever a one among the Puritans; and that's no trifle to say. I helped your grandfather, the constable, when he lashed the Quaker woman so smartly through the streets of Salem; and it was I that brought your father a pitch-pine knot, kindled at my own hearth, to set fire to an Indian village, in King Philip's war.° They were my good friends, both; and many a pleasant walk have we had along this path, and returned merrily after midnight. I would fain be friends with you for their sake."

"If it be as thou sayest," replied Goodman Brown, "I marvel they never spoke of these matters; or, verily, I marvel not, seeing that the least rumor of the sort would have driven them from New England. We are a people of prayer, and good works to boot, and abide no such wickedness."

"Wickedness or not," said the traveller with the twisted staff, "I have a very   20
general acquaintance here in New England. The deacons of many a church have drunk the communion wine with me; the selectmen of divers towns make me their chairman; and a majority of the Great and General Court are firm supporters of my interest. The governor and I, too — But these are state secrets."

"Can this be so?" cried Goodman Brown, with a stare of amazement at his undisturbed companion. "Howbeit, I have nothing to do with the governor and council; they have their own ways, and are no rule for a simple husbandman like me. But, were I to go on with thee, how should I meet the eye of that good old man, our minister, at Salem village? Oh, his voice would make me tremble both Sabbath day and lecture day."

Thus far the elder traveller had listened with due gravity; but now burst into a fit of irrepressible mirth, shaking himself so violently that his snake-like staff actually seemed to wriggle in sympathy.

"Ha! ha! ha!" shouted he again and again; then composing himself, "Well, go on, Goodman Brown, go on; but, prithee, don't kill me with laughing."

"Well, then, to end the matter at once," said Goodman Brown, considerably nettled, "there is my wife, Faith. It would break her dear little heart; and I'd rather break my own."

"Nay, if that be the case," answered the other, "e'en go thy ways, Goodman   25
Brown. I would not for twenty old women like the one hobbling before us that Faith should come to any harm."

As he spoke he pointed his staff at a female figure on the path, in whom Goodman Brown recognized a very pious and exemplary dame, who had taught him his catechism in youth, and was still his moral and spiritual adviser, jointly with the minister and Deacon Gookin.

"A marvel, truly that Goody Cloyse should be so far in the wilderness at nightfall," said he. "But with your leave, friend, I shall take a cut through the woods until we have left this Christian woman behind. Being a stranger to you, she might ask whom I was consorting with and whither I was going."

King Philip's war: King Philip, a Wampanoag chief, waged a bloody war against the New England colonists from 1675 to 1676.

"Be it so," said his fellow-traveller. "Betake you to the woods, and let me keep the path."

Accordingly the young man turned aside, but took care to watch his companion, who advanced softly along the road until he had come within a staff's length of the old dame. She, meanwhile, was making the best of her way, with singular speed for so aged a woman, and mumbling some indistinct words—a prayer, doubtless—as she went. The traveller put forth his staff and touched her withered neck with what seemed the serpent's tail.

"The devil!" screamed the pious old lady.   30

"Then Goody Cloyse knows her old friend?" observed the traveller, confronting her and leaning on his writhing stick.

"Ah, forsooth, and is it your worship indeed?" cried the good dame. "Yea, truly is it, and in the very image of my old gossip, Goodman Brown, the grandfather of the silly fellow that now is. But—would your worship believe it?—my broomstick hath strangely disappeared, stolen, as I suspect, by that unhanged witch, Goody Cory, and that, too, when I was all anointed with the juice of smallage, and cinquefoil, and wolf's bane"—

"Mingled with fine wheat and the fat of a new-born babe," said the shape of old Goodman Brown.

"Ah, your worship knows the recipe," cried the old lady, cackling aloud. "So, as I was saying, being all ready for the meeting, and no horse to ride on, I made up my mind to foot it; for they tell me there is a nice young man to be taken into communion to-night. But now your good worship will lend me your arm, and we shall be there in a twinkling."

"That can hardly be," answered her friend. "I may not spare you my arm,   35
Goody Cloyse; but here is my staff, if you will."

So saying, he threw it down at her feet, where, perhaps, it assumed life, being one of the rods which its owner had formerly lent to the Egyptian magi. Of this fact, however, Goodman Brown could not take cognizance. He had cast up his eyes in astonishment, and, looking down again, beheld neither Goody Cloyse nor the serpentine staff, but his fellow-traveller alone, who waited for him as calmly as if nothing had happened.

"That old woman taught me my catechism," said the young man; and there was a world of meaning in this simple comment.

They continued to walk onward, while the elder traveller exhorted his companion to make good speed and persevere in the path, discoursing so aptly that his arguments seemed rather to spring up in the bosom of his auditor than to be suggested by himself. As they went, he plucked a branch of maple to serve for a walking stick, and began to strip it of the twigs and little boughs, which were wet with evening dew. The moment his fingers touched them they became strangely withered and dried up as with a week's sunshine. Thus the pair proceeded, at a good free pace, until suddenly, in a gloomy hollow of the road, Goodman Brown sat himself down on the stump of a tree and refused to go any farther.

"Friend," he said, stubbornly, "my mind is made up. Not another step will I budge on this errand. What if a wretched old woman do choose to go to the devil when I thought she was going to heaven: is that any reason why I should quit my dear Faith and go after her?"

"You will think better of this by and by," said his acquaintance, composedly.   40
"Sit here and rest yourself a while; and when you feel like moving again, there is
my staff to help you along."

Without more words, he threw his companion the maple stick, and was as
speedily out of sight as if he had vanished into the deepening gloom. The young
man sat a few moments by the roadside, applauding himself greatly, and thinking
with how clear a conscience he should meet the minister in his morning walk,
nor shrink from the eye of good old Deacon Gookin. And what calm sleep would
be his that very night, which was to have been spent so wickedly, but so purely
and sweetly now, in the arms of Faith! Amidst these pleasant and praiseworthy
meditations, Goodman Brown heard the tramp of horses along the road, and
deemed it advisable to conceal himself within the verge of the forest, conscious of
the guilty purpose that had brought him thither, though now so happily turned
from it.

On came the hoof tramps and the voices of the riders, two grave old voices,
conversing soberly as they drew near. These mingled sounds appeared to pass
along the road, within a few yards of the young man's hiding-place; but, owing
doubtless to the depth of the gloom at that particular spot, neither the travellers
nor their steeds were visible. Though their figures brushed the small boughs by
the wayside, it could not be seen that they intercepted, even for a moment, the
faint gleam from the strip of bright sky athwart which they must have passed.
Goodman Brown alternately crouched and stood on tiptoe, pulling aside the
branches and thrusting forth his head as far as he durst without discerning so
much as a shadow. It vexed him the more, because he could have sworn, were
such a thing possible, that he recognized the voices of the minister and Deacon
Gookin, jogging along quietly, as they were wont to do, when bound to some
ordination or ecclesiastical council. While yet within hearing, one of the riders
stopped to pluck a switch.

"Of the two, reverend sir," said the voice like the deacon's, "I had rather miss
an ordination dinner than to-night's meeting. They tell me that some of our community are to be here from Falmouth and beyond, and others from Connecticut
and Rhode Island, besides several of the Indian powwows, who, after their fashion, know almost as much deviltry as the best of us. Moreover, there is a goodly
young woman to be taken into communion."

"Mighty well, Deacon Gookin!" replied the solemn old tones of the minister. "Spur up, or we shall be late. Nothing can be done, you know, until I get on
the ground."

The hoofs clattered again; and the voices, talking so strangely in the empty   45
air, passed on through the forest, where no church had ever been gathered or
solitary Christian prayed. Whither, then, could these holy men be journeying so
deep into the heathen wilderness? Young Goodman Brown caught hold of a tree
for support, being ready to sink down on the ground, faint and overburdened with
the heavy sickness of his heart. He looked up to the sky, doubting whether there
really was a heaven above him. Yet there was the blue arch, and the stars brightening in it.

"With heaven above and Faith below, I will yet stand firm against the devil!"
cried Goodman Brown.

While he still gazed upward into the deep arch of the firmament and had lifted his hands to pray, a cloud, though no wind was stirring, hurried across the zenith and hid the brightening stars. The blue sky was still visible, except directly overhead, where this black mass of cloud was sweeping swiftly northward. Aloft in the air, as if from the depths of the cloud, came a confused and doubtful sound of voices. Once the listener fancied that he could distinguish the accents of towns-people of his own, men and women, both pious and ungodly, many of whom he had met at the communion table, and had seen others rioting at the tavern. The next moment, so indistinct were the sounds, he doubted whether he had heard aught but the murmur of the old forest, whispering without a wind. Then came a stronger swell of those familiar tones, heard daily in the sunshine at Salem village, but never until now from a cloud of night. There was one voice, of a young woman, uttering lamentations, yet with an uncertain sorrow, and entreating for some favor, which, perhaps, it would grieve her to obtain; and all the unseen multitude, both saints and sinners, seemed to encourage her onward.

"Faith!" shouted Goodman Brown, in a voice of agony and desperation; and the echoes of the forest mocked him, crying, "Faith! Faith!" as if bewildered wretches were seeking her all through the wilderness.

The cry of grief, rage, and terror was yet piercing the night, when the unhappy husband held his breath for a response. There was a scream, drowned immediately in a louder murmur of voices, fading into far-off laughter, as the dark cloud swept away, leaving the clear and silent sky above Goodman Brown. But something fluttered lightly down through the air and caught on the branch of a tree. The young man seized it, and beheld a pink ribbon.

"My Faith is gone!" cried he after one stupefied moment. "There is no good on earth; and sin is but a name. Come, devil; for to thee is this world given." 50

And, maddened with despair, so that he laughed loud and long, did Goodman Brown grasp his staff and set forth again, at such a rate that he seemed to fly along the forest path rather than to walk or run. The road grew wilder and drearier and more faintly traced, and vanished at length, leaving him in the heart of the dark wilderness, still rushing onward with the instinct that guides mortal man to evil. The whole forest was peopled with frightful sounds — the creaking of the trees, the howling of wild beasts, and the yell of Indians; while sometimes the wind tolled like a distant church bell, and sometimes gave a broad roar around the traveller, as if all Nature were laughing him to scorn. But he was himself the chief horror of the scene, and shrank not from its other horrors.

"Ha! ha! ha!" roared Goodman Brown when the wind laughed at him. "Let us hear which will laugh loudest. Think not to frighten me with your deviltry. Come witch, come wizard, come Indian powwow, come devil himself, and here comes Goodman Brown. You may as well fear him as he fear you."

In truth, all through the haunted forest there could be nothing more frightful than the figure of Goodman Brown. On he flew among the black pines, brandishing his staff with frenzied gestures, now giving vent to an inspiration of horrid blasphemy, and now shouting forth such laughter as set all the echoes of the forest laughing like demons around him. The fiend in his own shape is less hideous than when he rages in the breast of man. Thus sped the demoniac on his course, until, quivering among the trees, he saw a red light before him, as when the felled trunks and branches of a clearing have been set on fire, and throw up their lurid blaze against the sky, at the hour of midnight. He paused, in a lull of the tempest that had driven him onward, and heard the swell of what seemed a hymn, rolling solemnly from a distance with the weight of many voices. He knew the tune; it was a familiar one in the choir of the village meeting-house. The verse died heavily away, and was lengthened by a chorus, not of human voices, but of all the sounds of the benighted wilderness pealing in awful harmony together. Goodman Brown cried out, and his cry was lost to his own ear by its unison with the cry of the desert.

In the interval of silence he stole forward until the light glared full upon his eyes. At one extremity of an open space, hemmed in by the dark wall of the forest, arose a rock, bearing some rude, natural resemblance either to an altar or a pulpit, and surrounded by four blazing pines, their tops aflame, their stems untouched, like candles at an evening meeting. The mass of foliage that had overgrown the summit of the rock was all on fire, blazing high into the night and fitfully illuminating the whole field. Each pendent twig and leafy festoon was in a blaze. As the red light arose and fell, a numerous congregation alternately shone forth, then disappeared in shadow, and again grew, as it were, out of the darkness, peopling the heart of the solitary woods at once.

"A grave and dark-clad company," quoth Goodman Brown.   55

In truth they were such. Among them, quivering to and fro between gloom and splendor, appeared faces that would be seen next day at the council board of the province, and others which, Sabbath after Sabbath, looked devoutly heavenward, and benignantly over the crowded pews, from the holiest pulpits in the land. Some affirm that the lady of the governor was there. At least there were high dames well known to her, and wives of honored husbands, and widows, a great multitude, and ancient maidens, all of excellent repute, and fair young girls, who trembled lest their mothers should espy them. Either the sudden gleams of light flashing over the obscure field bedazzled Goodman Brown, or he recognized a score of the church members of Salem village famous for their especial sanctity. Good old Deacon Gookin had arrived, and waited at the skirts of that venerable saint, his revered pastor. But, irreverently consorting with these grave, reputable, and pious people, these elders of the church, these chaste dames and dewy virgins, there were men of dissolute lives and women of spotted fame, wretches given over to all mean and filthy vice, and suspected even of horrid crimes. It was strange to see that the good shrank not from the wicked, nor were the sinners abashed by the saints. Scattered also among their pale-faced enemies were the Indian priests, or powwows, who had often scared their native forest with more hideous incantations than any known to English witchcraft.

"But where is Faith?" thought Goodman Brown; and, as hope came into his heart, he trembled.

Another verse of the hymn arose, a slow and mournful strain, such as the pious love, but joined to words which expressed all that our nature can conceive of sin, and darkly hinted at far more. Unfathomable to mere mortals is the lore of

fiends. Verse after verse was sung; and still the chorus of the desert swelled
between like the deepest tone of a mighty organ; and with the final peal of that
dreadful anthem there came a sound, as if the roaring wind, the rushing streams,
the howling beasts, and every other voice of the unconcerted wilderness were
mingling and according with the voice of guilty man in homage to the prince of
all. The four blazing pines threw up a loftier flame, and obscurely discovered
shapes and visages of horror on the smoke wreaths above the impious assembly.
At the same moment the fire on the rock shot redly forth and formed a flowing
arch above its base, where now appeared a figure. With reverence be it spoken,
the figure bore no slight similitude, both in garb and manner, to some grave
divine of the New England churches.

"Bring forth the converts!" cried a voice that echoed through the field and
rolled into the forest.

At the word, Goodman Brown stepped forth from the shadow of the trees   60
and approached the congregation, with whom he felt a loathful brotherhood by
the sympathy of all that was wicked in his heart. He could have well-nigh sworn
that the shape of his own dead father beckoned him to advance, looking downward from a smoke wreath, while a woman, with dim features of despair, threw
out her hand to warn him back. Was it his mother? But he had no power to retreat
one step, nor to resist, even in thought, when the minister and good old Deacon
Gookin seized his arms and led him to the blazing rock. Thither came also the
slender form of a veiled female, led between Goody Cloyse, that pious teacher of
the catechism, and Martha Carrier, who had received the devil's promise to be
queen of hell. A rampant hag was she. And there stood the proselytes beneath the
canopy of fire.

"Welcome, my children," said the dark figure, "to the communion of your
race. Ye have found thus young your nature and your destiny. My children, look
behind you!"

They turned; and flashing forth, as it were, in a sheet of flame, the fiend worshippers were seen; the smile of welcome gleamed darkly on every visage.

"There," resumed the sable form, "are all whom ye have reverenced from
youth. Ye deemed them holier than yourselves and shrank from your own sin,
contrasting it with their lives of righteousness and prayerful aspirations heavenward. Yet here are they all in my worshipping assembly. This night it shall be
granted you to know their secret deeds: how hoary-bearded elders of the church
have whispered wanton words to the young maids of their households; how many
a woman, eager for widows' weeds, has given her husband a drink at bedtime and
let him sleep his last sleep in her bosom; how beardless youths have made haste
to inherit their fathers' wealth; and how fair damsels—blush not, sweet ones—
have dug little graves in the garden, and bidden me, the sole guest, to an infant's
funeral. By the sympathy of your human hearts for sin ye shall scent out all the
places—whether in church, bedchamber, street, field, or forest—where crime
has been committed, and shall exult to behold the whole earth one stain of guilt,
one mighty blood spot. Far more than this. It shall be yours to penetrate, in every
bosom, the deep mystery of sin, the fountain of all wicked arts, and which inex-
haustibly supplies more evil impulses than human power—than my power at its

utmost — can make manifest in deeds. And now, my children, look upon each other."

They did so; and, by the blaze of the hell-kindled torches, the wretched man beheld his Faith, and the wife her husband, trembling before that unhallowed altar.

"Lo, there ye stand, my children," said the figure, in a deep and solemn tone, almost sad with its despairing awfulness, as if his once angelic nature could yet mourn for our miserable race. "Depending upon one another's hearts, ye had still hoped that virtue were not all a dream. Now are ye undeceived. Evil is the nature of mankind. Evil must be your only happiness. Welcome again, my children, to the communion of your race." 65

"Welcome," repeated the fiend worshippers, in one cry of despair and triumph.

And there they stood, the only pair, as it seemed, who were yet hesitating on the verge of wickedness in this dark world. A basin was hallowed, naturally, in the rock. Did it contain water, reddened by the lurid light? or was it blood? or, perchance, a liquid flame? Herein did the shape of evil dip his hand and prepare to lay the mark of baptism upon their foreheads, that they might be partakers of the mystery of sin, more conscious of the secret guilt of others, both in deed and thought, than they could now be of their own. The husband cast one look at his pale wife, and Faith at him. What polluted wretches would the next glance show them to each other, shuddering alike at what they disclosed and what they saw!

"Faith! Faith!" cried the husband, "look up to heaven, and resist the wicked one."

Whether Faith obeyed he knew not. Hardly had he spoken when he found himself amid calm night and solitude, listening to a roar of the wind which died heavily away through the forest. He staggered against the rock, and felt it chill and damp; while a hanging twig, that had been all on fire, besprinkled his cheek with the coldest dew.

The next morning young Goodman Brown came slowly into the street of Salem village, staring around him like a bewildered man. The good old minister was taking a walk along the graveyard to get an appetite for breakfast and meditate his sermon, and bestowed a blessing, as he passed, on Goodman Brown. He shrank from the venerable saint as if to avoid an anathema. Old Deacon Gookin was at domestic worship, and the holy words of his prayer were heard through the open window. "What God doth the wizard pray to?" quoth Goodman Brown. Goody Cloyse, that excellent old Christian, stood in the early sunshine at her own lattice, catechizing a little girl who had brought her a pint of morning's milk. Goodman Brown snatched away the child as from the grasp of the fiend himself. Turning the corner by the meeting-house, he spied the head of Faith, with the pink ribbons, gazing anxiously forth, and bursting into such joy at sight of him that she skipped along the street and almost kissed her husband before the whole village. But Goodman Brown looked sternly and sadly into her face, and passed on without a greeting. 70

Had Goodman Brown fallen asleep in the forest and only dreamed a wild dream of a witch-meeting?

Be it so if you will; but, alas! it was a dream of evil omen for young Goodman Brown. A stern, a sad, a darkly meditative, a distrustful, if not a desperate man did he become from the night of that fearful dream. On the Sabbath day, when the congregation were singing a holy psalm, he could not listen because an anthem of sin rushed loudly upon his ear and drowned all the blessed strain. When the minister spoke from the pulpit with power and fervid eloquence, and, with his hand on the open Bible, of the sacred truths of our religion, and of saint-like lives and triumphant deaths, and of future bliss or misery unutterable, then did Goodman Brown turn pale, dreading lest the roof should thunder down upon the gray blasphemer and his hearers. Often, awaking suddenly at midnight, he shrank from the bosom of Faith; and at morning or eventide, when the family knelt down at prayer, he scowled and muttered to himself, and gazed sternly at his wife, and turned away. And when he had lived long, and was borne to his grave a hoary corpse, followed by Faith, an aged woman, and children and grandchildren, a goodly procession, besides neighbors not a few, they carved no hopeful verse upon his tombstone, for his dying hour was gloom.   [1835]

THINKING ABOUT THE TEXT

1. "Young Goodman Brown" seems quite allegorical with journeys in the night woods and statements like "my Faith is gone" (para. 50). How would you explain this allegorical story? What is Brown looking for? What does he find out? How does he deal with his discoveries?

2. If you were a good friend of Brown's, what might you tell him to try to save him from a life of gloom?

3. The devil suggests that there is more evil in the human heart "than my power at its utmost" (para. 63). Do you agree? If so, is this a message to despair about?

4. The devil says he is well acquainted with Brown's family. What has his family done? Is Brown innocent and naive, or perhaps stubborn and arrogant, in his refusal to admit that evil exists all around us?

5. Do you suspect that Brown merely dreamed or imagined his experience in the woods? Or do you think it really took place? Refer to specific details of the text.

NATHANIEL HAWTHORNE
The Minister's Black Veil
A PARABLE

"The Minister's Black Veil" (1837) appeared in Hawthorne's first collection, Twice-Told Tales. *He wrote the story about two years after "Young Goodman Brown," although that tale did not appear in a book until he included it in the 1846* Mosses from an Old Manse.

The sexton stood in the porch of Milford meeting-house, pulling lustily at the bell-rope. The old people of the village came stooping along the street. Children, with bright faces, tript merrily beside their parents, or mimicked a graver gait, in the conscious dignity of their Sunday clothes. Spruce bachelors looked sidelong at the pretty maidens, and fancied that the Sabbath sunshine made them prettier than on weekdays. When the throng had mostly streamed into the porch, the sexton began to toll the bell, keeping his eye on the Reverend Mr. Hooper's door. The first glimpse of the clergyman's figure was the signal for the bell to cease its summons.

"But what has good Parson Hooper got upon his face?" cried the sexton in astonishment.

All within hearing immediately turned about, and beheld the semblance of Mr. Hooper, pacing slowly his meditative way towards the meeting-house. With one accord they started, expressing more wonder than if some strange minister were coming to dust the cushions of Mr. Hooper's pulpit.

"Are you sure it is our parson?" inquired Goodman Gray of the sexton.

"Of a certainty it is good Mr. Hooper," replied the sexton. "He was to have   5
exchanged pulpits with Parson Shute of Westbury; but Parson Shute sent to excuse himself yesterday, being to preach a funeral sermon."

The cause of so much amazement may appear sufficiently slight. Mr. Hooper, a gentlemanly person of about thirty, though still a bachelor, was dressed with due clerical neatness, as if a careful wife had starched his band, and brushed the weekly dust from his Sunday's garb. There was but one thing remarkable in his appearance. Swathed about his forehead, and hanging down over his face, so low as to be shaken by his breath, Mr. Hooper had on a black veil. On a nearer view, it seemed to consist of two folds of crape, which entirely concealed his features, except the mouth and chin, but probably did not intercept his sight, farther than to give a darkened aspect to all living and inanimate things. With this gloomy shade before him, good Mr. Hooper walked onward, at a slow and quiet pace, stooping somewhat and looking on the ground, as is customary with abstracted men, yet nodding kindly to those of his parishioners who still waited on the meeting-house steps. But so wonder-struck were they, that his greeting hardly met with a return.

"I can't really feel as if good Mr. Hooper's face was behind that piece of crape," said the sexton.

"I don't like it," muttered an old woman, as she hobbled into the meeting-house. "He has changed himself into something awful, only by hiding his face."

"Our parson has gone mad!" cried Goodman Gray, following him across the threshold.

A rumor of some unaccountable phenomenon had preceded Mr. Hooper   10
into the meeting-house, and set all the congregation astir. Few could refrain from twisting their heads towards the door; many stood upright, and turned directly about; while several little boys clambered upon the seats, and came down again with a terrible racket. There was a general bustle, a rustling of the women's gowns and shuffling of the men's feet, greatly at variance with that hushed repose which should attend the entrance of the minister. But Mr. Hooper appeared not to

notice the perturbation of his people. He entered with an almost noiseless step, bent his head mildly to the pews on each side, and bowed as he passed his oldest parishioner, a white-haired great-grandsire, who occupied an arm-chair in the center of the aisle. It was strange to observe, how slowly this venerable man became conscious of something singular in the appearance of his pastor. He seemed not fully to partake of the prevailing wonder, till Mr. Hooper had ascended the stairs, and showed himself in the pulpit, face to face with his con-gregation, except for the black veil. That mysterious emblem was never once withdrawn. It shook with his measured breath as he gave out the psalm; it threw its obscurity between him and the holy page, as he read the Scriptures; and while he prayed, the veil lay heavily on his uplifted countenance. Did he seek to hide it from the dread Being whom he was addressing?

Such was the effect of this simple piece of crape, that more than one woman of delicate nerves was forced to leave the meeting-house. Yet perhaps the pale-faced congregation was almost as fearful a sight to the minister, as his black veil to them.

Mr. Hooper had the reputation of a good preacher, but not an energetic one: he strove to win his people heavenward, by mild persuasive influences, rather than to drive them thither, by the thunders of the Word. The sermon which he now delivered, was marked by the same characteristics of style and manner, as the general series of his pulpit oratory. But there was something, either in the sen-timent of the discourse itself, or in the imagination of the auditors, which made it greatly the most powerful effort that they had ever heard from their pastor's lips. It was tinged, rather more darkly than usual, with the gentle gloom of Mr. Hooper's temperament. The subject had reference to secret sin, and those sad mysteries which we hide from our nearest and dearest, and would fain conceal from our own consciousness, even forgetting that the Omniscient can detect them. A sub-tle power was breathed into his words. Each member of the congregation, the most innocent girl, and the man of hardened breast, felt as if the preacher had crept upon them, behind his awful veil, and discovered their hoarded iniquity of deed or thought. Many spread their clasped hands on their bosoms. There was nothing terrible in what Mr. Hooper said; at least, no violence; and yet, with every tremor of his melancholy voice, the hearers quaked. An unsought pathos came hand in hand with awe. So sensible were the audience of some unwonted attribute in their minister, that they longed for a breath of wind to blow aside the veil, almost believing that a stranger's visage would be discovered, though the form, gesture, and voice were those of Mr. Hooper.

At the close of the services, the people hurried out with indecorous confu-sion, eager to communicate their pent-up amazement, and conscious of lighter spirits, the moment they lost sight of the black veil. Some gathered in little cir-cles, huddled closely together, with their mouths all whispering in the center; some went homeward alone, wrapt in silent meditation; some talked loudly, and profaned the Sabbath-day with ostentatious laughter. A few shook their sagacious heads, intimating that they could penetrate the mystery; while one or two affirmed that there was no mystery at all, but only that Mr. Hooper's eyes were so weakened by the midnight lamp, as to require a shade. After a brief interval, forth came good Mr. Hooper also, in the rear of his flock. Turning his veiled face from one group to another, he paid due reverence to the hoary heads, saluted the middle-aged with kind dignity, as their friend and spiritual guide, greeted the young with mingled authority and love, and laid his hands on the little children's heads to bless them. Such was always his custom on the Sabbath-day. Strange and bewildered looks repaid him for his courtesy. None, as on former occasions, aspired to the honor of walking by their pastor's side. Old Squire Saunders, doubtless by an accidental lapse of memory, neglected to invite Mr. Hooper to his table, where the good clergyman had been wont to bless the food, almost every Sunday since his settlement. He returned, therefore, to the parsonage, and, at the moment of closing the door, was observed to look back upon the people, all of whom had their eyes fixed upon the minister. A sad smile gleamed faintly from beneath the black veil, and flickered about his mouth, glimmering as he disappeared.

"How strange," said a lady, "that a simple black veil, such as any woman might wear on her bonnet, should become such a terrible thing on Mr. Hooper's face!"

"Something must surely be amiss with Mr. Hooper's intellects," observed her husband, the physician of the village. "But the strangest part of the affair is the effect of this vagary, even on a sober-minded man like myself. The black veil, though it covers only our pastor's face, throws its influence over his whole person, and makes him ghost-like from head to foot. Do you not feel it so?"

"Truly do I," replied the lady; "and I would not be alone with him for the world. I wonder he is not afraid to be alone with himself!"

"Men sometimes are so," said her husband.

That afternoon service was attended with similar circumstances. At its conclusion, the bell tolled for the funeral of a young lady. The relatives and friends were assembled in the house, and the more distant acquaintances stood about the door, speaking of the good qualities of the deceased, when their talk was interrupted by the appearance of Mr. Hooper, still covered with his black veil. It was now an appropriate emblem. The clergyman stepped into the room where the corpse was laid, and bent over the coffin, to take a last farewell of his deceased parishioner. As he stooped, the veil hung straight down from his forehead, so that, if her eye-lids had not been closed for ever, the dead maiden might have seen his face. Could Mr. Hooper be fearful of her glance, that he so hastily caught back the black veil? A person, who watched the interview between the dead and living, scrupled not to affirm, that, at the instant when the clergyman's features were disclosed, the corpse had slightly shuddered, rustling the shroud and muslin cap, though the countenance retained the composure of death. A superstitious old woman was the only witness of this prodigy. From the coffin, Mr. Hooper passed into the chamber of the mourners, and thence to the head of the staircase, to make the funeral prayer. It was a tender and heart-dissolving prayer, full of sorrow, yet so imbued with celestial hopes, that the music of a heavenly harp, swept by the fingers of the dead, seemed faintly to be heard among the saddest accents of the minister. The people trembled, though they but darkly understood him, when he prayed that they, and himself, and all of mortal race, might be ready, as he trusted this young maiden had been, for the dreadful hour that should snatch the veil from their faces. The bearers went heavily forth, and the mourners followed, saddening all the street, with the dead before them, and Mr. Hooper in his black veil behind.

"Why do you look back?" said one in the procession to his partner.

"I had a fancy," replied she, "that the minister and the maiden's spirit were walking hand in hand." 20

"And so had I, at the same moment," said the other.

That night, the handsomest couple in Milford village were to be joined in wedlock. Though reckoned a melancholy man, Mr. Hooper had a placid cheerfulness for such occasions, which often excited a sympathetic smile, where livelier merriment would have been thrown away. There was no quality of his disposition which made him more beloved than this. The company at the wedding awaited his arrival with impatience, trusting that the strange awe, which had gathered over him throughout the day, would now be dispelled. But such was not the result. When Mr. Hooper came, the first thing that their eyes rested on was the same horrible black veil, which had added deeper gloom to the funeral, and could portend nothing but evil to the wedding. Such was its immediate effect on the guests, that a cloud seemed to have rolled duskily from beneath the black crape, and dimmed the light of the candles. The bridal pair stood up before the minister. But the bride's cold fingers quivered in the tremulous hand of the bridegroom, and her death-like paleness caused a whisper, that the maiden who had been buried a few hours before, was come from her grave to be married. If ever another wedding were so dismal, it was that famous one, where they tolled the wedding-knell. After performing the ceremony, Mr. Hooper raised a glass of wine to his lips, wishing happiness to the new-married couple, in a strain of mild pleasantry that ought to have brightened the features of the guests, like a cheerful gleam from the hearth. At that instant, catching a glimpse of his figure in the looking-glass, the black veil involved his own spirit in the horror with which it overwhelmed all others. His frame shuddered — his lips grew white — he spilt the untasted wine upon the carpet — and rushed forth into the darkness. For the Earth, too, had on her Black Veil.

The next day, the whole village of Milford talked of little else than Parson Hooper's black veil. That, and the mystery concealed behind it, supplied a topic for discussion between acquaintances meeting in the street, and good women gossiping at their open windows. It was the first item of news that the tavern-keeper told to his guests. The children babbled of it on their way to school. One imitative little imp covered his face with an old black handkerchief, thereby so affrighting his playmates, that the panic seized himself, and he well nigh lost his wits by his own waggery.

It was remarkable, that, of all the busy-bodies and impertinent people in the parish, not one ventured to put the plain question to Mr. Hooper, wherefore he did this thing. Hitherto, whenever there appeared the slightest call for such interference, he had never lacked advisers, nor shown himself averse to be guided by their judgment. If he erred at all, it was by so painful a degree of self-distrust, that even the mildest censure would lead him to consider an indifferent action as a crime. Yet, though so well acquainted with this amiable weakness, no individual among his parishioners chose to make the black veil a subject of friendly remonstrance. There was a feeling of dread, neither plainly confessed nor carefully concealed, which caused each to shift the responsibility upon another, till at length it was found expedient to send a deputation of the church, in order to deal with Mr. Hooper about the mystery, before it should grow into a scandal. Never did an embassy so ill discharge its duties. The minister received them with friendly courtesy, but became silent, after they were seated, leaving to his visitors the whole burthen of introducing their important business. The topic, it might be supposed, was obvious enough. There was the black veil, swathed round Mr. Hooper's forehead, and concealing every feature above his placid mouth, on which, at times, they could perceive the glimmering of a melancholy smile. But that piece of crape, to their imagination, seemed to hang down before his heart, the symbol of a fearful secret between him and them. Were the veil but cast aside, they might speak freely of it, but not till then. Thus they sat a considerable time, speechless, confused, and shrinking uneasily from Mr. Hooper's eye, which they felt to be fixed upon them with an invisible glance. Finally, the deputies returned abashed to their constituents, pronouncing the matter too weighty to be handled, except by a council of the churches, if, indeed, it might not require a general synod.

But there was one person in the village, unappalled by the awe with which   25
the black veil had impressed all beside herself. When the deputies returned without an explanation, or even venturing to demand one, she, with the calm energy of her character, determined to chase away the strange cloud that appeared to be settling round Mr. Hooper, every moment more darkly than before. As his plighted wife, it should be her privilege to know what the black veil concealed. At the minister's first visit, therefore, she entered upon the subject, with a direct simplicity, which made the task easier both for him and her. After he had seated himself, she fixed her eyes steadfastly upon the veil, but could discern nothing of the dreadful gloom that had so overawed the multitude: it was but a double fold of crape, hanging down from his forehead to his mouth, and slightly stirring with his breath.

"No," said she aloud, and smiling, "there is nothing terrible in this piece of crape, except that it hides a face which I am always glad to look upon. Come, good sir, let the sun shine from behind the cloud. First lay aside your black veil: then tell me why you put it on."

Mr. Hooper's smile glimmered faintly.

"There is an hour to come," said he, "when all of us shall cast aside our veils. Take it not amiss, beloved friend, if I wear this piece of crape till then."

"Your words are a mystery too," returned the young lady. "Take away the veil for them, at least."

"Elizabeth, I will," said he, "so far as my vow may suffer me. Know, then, this   30
veil is a type and a symbol, and I am bound to wear it ever, both in light and darkness, in solitude and before the gaze of multitudes, and as with strangers, so with my familiar friends. No mortal eye will see it withdrawn. This dismal shade must separate me from the world: even you, Elizabeth, can never come behind it!"

"What grievous affliction hath befallen you," she earnestly inquired, "that you should thus darken your eyes for ever?"

"If it be a sign of mourning," replied Mr. Hooper, "I, perhaps, like most other mortals, have sorrows dark enough to be typified by a black veil."

"But what if the world will not believe that it is the type of an innocent sorrow?" urged Elizabeth. "Beloved and respected as you are, there may be whispers, that you hide your face under the consciousness of secret sin. For the sake of your holy office, do away this scandal!"

The color rose into her cheeks, as she intimated the nature of the rumors that were already abroad in the village. But Mr. Hooper's mildness did not forsake him. He even smiled again — that same sad smile, which always appeared like a faint glimmering of light, proceeding from the obscurity beneath the veil.

"If I hide my face for sorrow, there is cause enough," he merely replied; "and if I cover it for secret sin, what mortal might not do the same?"

35

And with this gentle, but unconquerable obstinacy, did he resist all her entreaties. At length Elizabeth sat silent. For a few moments she appeared lost in thought, considering, probably, what new methods might be tried, to withdraw her lover from so dark a fantasy, which, if it had no other meaning, was perhaps a symptom of mental disease. Though of a firmer character than his own, the tears rolled down her cheeks. But, in an instant, as it were, a new feeling took the place of sorrow: her eyes were fixed insensibly on the black veil, when, like a sudden twilight in the air, its terrors fell around her. She arose, and stood trembling before him.

"And do you feel it then at last?" said he mournfully.

She made no reply, but covered her eyes with her hand, and turned to leave the room. He rushed forward and caught her arm.

"Have patience with me, Elizabeth!" cried he passionately. "Do not desert me, though this veil must be between us here on earth. Be mine, and hereafter there shall be no veil over my face, no darkness between our souls! It is but a mortal veil — it is not for eternity! Oh! you know not how lonely I am, and how frightened to be alone behind my black veil. Do not leave me in this miserable obscurity for ever!"

"Lift the veil but once, and look me in the face," said she.

40

"Never! It cannot be!" replied Mr. Hooper.

"Then, farewell!" said Elizabeth.

She withdrew her arm from his grasp, and slowly departed, pausing at the door, to give one long, shuddering gaze, that seemed almost to penetrate the mystery of the black veil. But, even amid his grief, Mr. Hooper smiled to think that only a material emblem had separated him from happiness, though the horrors which it shadowed forth, must be drawn darkly between the fondest of lovers.

From that time no attempts were made to remove Mr. Hooper's black veil, or, by a direct appeal, to discover the secret which it was supposed to hide. By persons who claimed a superiority to popular prejudice, it was reckoned merely an eccentric whim, such as often mingles with the sober actions of men otherwise rational, and tinges them all with its own semblance of insanity. But with the multitude, good Mr. Hooper was irreparably a bugbear. He could not walk the streets with any peace of mind, so conscious was he that the gentle and timid would turn aside to avoid him, and that others would make it a point of hardihood to throw themselves in his way. The impertinence of the latter class compelled him to give up his customary walk, at sunset, to the burial ground, for when he leaned pensively over the gate, there would always be faces behind the grave-stones, peeping at his black veil. A fable went the rounds that the stare of the dead people drove him thence. It grieved him, to the very depth of his kind heart, to observe how the children fled from his approach, breaking up their merriest sports, while his melancholy figure was yet afar off. Their instinctive dread caused him to feel, more strongly than aught else, that a preternatural horror was interwoven with the threads of the black crape. In truth, his own antipathy to the veil was known to be so great, that he never willingly passed before a mirror, nor stooped to drink at a still fountain, lest, in its peaceful bosom, he should be affrighted by himself. This was what gave plausibility to the whispers, that Mr. Hooper's conscience tortured him for some great crime, too horrible to be entirely concealed, or otherwise than so obscurely intimated. Thus, from beneath the black veil, there rolled a cloud into the sunshine, an ambiguity of sin or sorrow, which enveloped the poor minister, so that love or sympathy could never reach him. It was said, that ghost and fiend consorted with him there. With self-shudderings and outward terrors, he walked continually in its shadow, groping darkly within his own soul, or gazing through a medium that saddened the whole world. Even the lawless wind, it was believed, respected his dreadful secret, and never blew aside the veil. But still good Mr. Hooper sadly smiled, at the pale visages of the worldly throng as he passed by.

Among all its bad influences, the black veil had the one desirable effect, of   45
making its wearer a very efficient clergyman. By the aid of his mysterious emblem—for there was no other apparent cause—he became a man of awful power, over souls that were in agony for sin. His converts always regarded him with a dread peculiar to themselves, affirming, though but figuratively, that, before he brought them to celestial light, they had been with him behind the black veil. Its gloom, indeed, enabled him to sympathize with all dark affections. Dying sinners cried aloud for Mr. Hooper, and would not yield their breath till he appeared; though ever, as he stooped to whisper consolation, they shuddered at the veiled face so near their own. Such were the terrors of the black veil, even when Death had bared his visage! Strangers came long distances to attend service at his church, with the mere idle purpose of gazing at his figure, because it was forbidden them to behold his face. But many were made to quake ere they departed! Once, during Governor Belcher's administration, Mr. Hooper was appointed to preach the election sermon. Covered with his black veil, he stood before the chief magistrate, the council, and the representatives, and wrought so deep an impression, that the legislative measures of that year were characterized by all the gloom and piety of our earliest ancestral sway.

In this manner Mr. Hooper spent a long life, irreproachable in outward act, yet shrouded in dismal suspicions; kind and loving, though unloved, and dimly feared; a man apart from men, shunned in their health and joy, but ever summoned to their aid in mortal anguish. As years wore on, shedding their snows above his sable veil, he acquired a name throughout the New-England churches, and they called him Father Hooper. Nearly all his parishioners, who were of mature age when he was settled, had been borne away by many a funeral: he had one congregation in the church, and a more crowded one in the churchyard; and having wrought so late into the evening, and done his work so well, it was now good Father Hooper's turn to rest.

Several persons were visible by the shaded candlelight, in the death-chamber of the old clergyman. Natural connections he had none. But there was the decorously grave, though unmoved physician, seeking only to mitigate the last pangs of the patient whom he could not save. There were the deacons, and other eminently pious members of his church. There, also, was the Reverend Mr. Clark, of Westbury, a young and zealous divine, who had ridden in haste to pray by the bedside of the expiring minister. There was the nurse, no hired hand-maiden of death, but one whose calm affection had endured thus long, in secrecy, in solitude, amid the chill of age, and would not perish, even at the dying hour. Who, but Elizabeth! And there lay the hoary head of good Father Hooper upon the death-pillow, with the black veil still swathed about his brow and reaching down over his face, so that each more difficult gasp of his faint breath caused it to stir. All through life that piece of crape had hung between him and the world: it had separated him from cheerful brotherhood and woman's love, and kept him in that saddest of all prisons, his own heart; and still it lay upon his face, as if to deepen the gloom of his darksome chamber, and shade him from the sunshine of eternity.

For some time previous, his mind had been confused, wavering doubtfully between the past and the present, and hovering forward, as it were, at intervals, into the indistinctness of the world to come. There had been feverish turns, which tossed him from side to side, and wore away what little strength he had. But in his most convulsive struggles, and in the wildest vagaries of his intellect, when no other thought retained its sober influence, he still showed an awful solicitude lest the black veil should slip aside. Even if his bewildered soul could have forgotten, there was a faithful woman at his pillow, who, with averted eyes, would have covered that aged face, which she had last beheld in the comeliness of manhood. At length the death-stricken old man lay quietly in the torpor of mental and bodily exhaustion, with an imperceptible pulse, and breath that grew fainter and fainter, except when a long, deep, and irregular inspiration seemed to prelude the flight of his spirit.

The minister of Westbury approached the bedside.

"Venerable Father Hooper," said he, "the moment of your release is at hand. Are you ready for the lifting of the veil, that shuts in time from eternity?"   50

Father Hooper at first replied merely by a feeble motion of his head; then, apprehensive, perhaps, that his meaning might be doubtful, he exerted himself to speak.

"Yea," said he, in faint accents, "my soul hath a patient weariness until that veil be lifted."

"And is it fitting," resumed the Reverend Mr. Clark, "that a man so given to prayer, of such a blameless example, holy in deed and thought, so far as mortal judgment may pronounce; is it fitting that a father in the church should leave a shadow on his memory, that may seem to blacken a life so pure? I pray you, my venerable brother, let not this thing be! Suffer us to be gladdened by your triumphant aspect, as you go to your reward. Before the veil of eternity be lifted, let me cast aside this black veil from your face!"

And thus speaking, the Reverend Mr. Clark bent forward to reveal the mystery of so many years. But, exerting a sudden energy, that made all the beholders stand aghast, Father Hooper snatched both his hands from beneath the bed-clothes, and pressed them strongly on the black veil, resolute to struggle, if the minister of Westbury would contend with a dying man.

"Never!" cried the veiled clergyman. "On earth, never!"   55

"Dark old man!" exclaimed the affrighted minister, "with what horrible crime upon your soul are you now passing to the judgment?"

Father Hooper's breath heaved; it rattled in his throat; but, with a mighty effort, grasping forward with his hands, he caught hold of life, and held it back till he should speak. He even raised himself in bed; and there he sat, shivering with the arms of death around him, while the black veil hung down, awful, at that last moment, in the gathered terrors of a life-time. And yet the faint, sad smile, so often there, now seemed to glimmer from its obscurity, and linger on Father Hooper's lips.

"Why do you tremble at me alone?" cried he, turning his veiled face round the circle of pale spectators. "Tremble also at each other! Have men avoided me, and women shown no pity, and children screamed and fled, only for my black veil? What, but the mystery which it obscurely typifies, has made this piece of crape so awful? When the friend shows his inmost heart to his friend; the lover to his best-beloved; when man does not vainly shrink from the eye of his Creator, loathsomely treasuring up the secret of his sin; then deem me a monster, for the symbol beneath which I have lived, and die! I look around me, and, lo! on every visage a Black Veil!"

While his auditors shrank from one another, in mutual affright, Father Hooper fell back upon his pillow, a veiled corpse, with a faint smile lingering on the lips. Still veiled, they laid him in his coffin, and a veiled corpse they bore him to the grave. The grass of many years has sprung up and withered on that grave, the burial-stone is moss-grown, and good Mr. Hooper's face is dust; but awful is still the thought, that it moldered beneath the Black Veil!   [1837]

THINKING ABOUT THE TEXT

1. Why do you think Hooper wears the veil? Keep in mind that more than one reason is possible. How helpful are Hooper's own statements as you try to determine his motives? Refer to specific things he says.

2. What are the effects of the veil? Identify how various people react to it.

3. What about Hooper's face can people still see? What does this feature imply about him?

4. What seem to be Hooper's basic religious principles? Do you think he is more religious than the rest of his community? Why, or why not?

5. What do you think of Hooper's wearing of the veil? What factors shape your own judgment of him?

MAKING COMPARISONS

1. What would you say to someone who argues that Hooper is what Good-man Brown becomes after his nighttime experience in the forest?
2. Both stories end with the title character's death. How much self-awareness does each seem to die with?
3. Is "The Minister's Black Veil" a more realistic story than "Young Good-man Brown"? Define what you mean by *realistic*.

NATHANIEL HAWTHORNE
Ethan Brand
A CHAPTER FROM AN ABORTIVE ROMANCE

"Ethan Brand" is a relatively late tale by Hawthorne. It appeared in his third col-lection of short stories, The Snow-Image and Other Twice-Told Tales, *published in 1851.*

Bartram, the lime-burner, a rough, heavy-looking man, begrimed with char-coal, sat watching his kiln, at nightfall, while his little son played at building houses with the scattered fragments of marble; when, on the hill-side below them, they heard a roar of laughter, not mirthful, but slow, and even solemn, like a wind shaking the boughs of the forest.

"Father, what is that?" asked the little boy, leaving his play, and pressing betwixt his father's knees.

"Oh, some drunken man, I suppose," answered the lime-burner; — "some merry fellow from the bar-room in the village, who dared not laugh loud enough within doors, lest he should blow the roof of the house off. So here he is, shaking his jolly sides, at the foot of Graylock."

"But, father," said the child, more sensitive than the obtuse, middle-aged clown, "he does not laugh like a man that is glad. So the noise frightens me!"

"Don't be a fool, child!" cried his father, gruffly. "You will never make a man, I do believe; there is too much of your mother in you. I have known the rustling of a leaf startle you. Hark! Here comes the merry fellow now. You shall see that there is no harm in him." 5

Bartram and his little son, while they were talking thus, sat watching the same lime-kiln that had been the scene of Ethan Brand's solitary and meditative life, before he began his search for the Unpardonable Sin. Many years, as we have seen, had now elapsed, since that portentous night when the IDEA was first developed. The kiln, however, on the mountain-side, stood unimpaired, and was in nothing changed, since he had thrown his dark thoughts into the intense glow of its furnace, and melted them, as it were, into the one thought that took posses-sion of his life. It was a rude, round, tower-like structure, about twenty feet high, heavily built of rough stones, and with a hillock of earth heaped about the larger part of its circumference; so that blocks and fragments of marble might be drawn by cart-loads, and thrown in at the top. There was an opening at the bottom of the tower, like an oven-mouth, but large enough to admit a man in a stooping posture, and provided with a massive iron door. With the smoke and jets of flame issuing from the chinks and crevices of this door, which seemed to give admittance into the hill-side, it resembled nothing so much as the private entrance to the infernal regions, which the shepherds of the Delectable Mountains were accustomed to show to pilgrims.

There are many such lime-kilns in that tract of country, for the purpose of burning the white marble which composes a large part of the substance of the hills. Some of them, built years ago, and long deserted, with weeds growing in the vacant round of the interior, which is open to the sky, and grass and wild flowers rooting themselves into the chinks of the stones, look already like relics of antiquity, and may yet be overspread with the lichens of centuries to come. Others, where the lime-burner still feeds his daily and night-long fire, afford points of interest to the wanderer among the hills, who seats himself on a log of wood or a fragment of marble, to hold chat with the solitary man. It is a lonesome, and, when the character is inclined to thought, may be an intensely thoughtful occupation; as it proved in the case of Ethan Brand, who had mused to such strange purpose, in days gone by, while the fire in this very kiln was burning.

The man, who now watched the fire, was of a different order, and troubled himself with no thoughts save the very few that were requisite to his business. At frequent intervals he flung back the clashing weight of the iron door, and, turning his face from the insufferable glare, thrust in huge logs of oak, or stirred the immense brands with a long pole. Within the furnace, was seen the curling and riotous flames, and the burning marble, almost molten with the intensity of heat; while, without, the reflection of the fire quivered on the dark intricacy of the surrounding forest, and showed, in the foreground, a bright and ruddy little picture of the hut, the spring beside its door, the athletic and coal-begrimed figure of the lime-burner, and the half-frightened child, shrinking into the protection of his father's shadow. And when, again, the iron door was closed, then re-appeared the tender light of the half-full moon, which vainly strove to trace out the indistinct shapes of the neighboring mountains; and, in the upper sky, there was a flitting congregation of clouds, still faintly tinged with the rosy sunset, though, thus far down into the valley, the sunshine had vanished long and long ago.

The little boy now crept still closer to his father, as footsteps were heard ascending the hill-side, and a human form thrust aside the bushes that clustered beneath the trees.

"Halloo! who is it?" cried the lime-burner, vexed at his son's timidity, yet half-infected by it. "Come forward, and show yourself, like a man; or I'll fling this chunk of marble at your head!" 10

"You offer me a rough welcome," said a gloomy voice, as the unknown man drew nigh. "Yet I neither claim nor desire a kinder one, even at my own fireside."

To obtain a distincter view, Bartram threw open the iron door of the kiln, whence immediately issued a gush of fierce light, that smote full upon the stranger's face and figure. To a careless eye, there appeared nothing very remarkable in his aspect, which was that of a man in a coarse, brown, country-made suit of clothes, tall and thin, with the staff and heavy shoes of a wayfarer. As he advanced, he fixed his eyes, which were very bright, intently upon the brightness of the furnace, as if he beheld, or expected to behold, some object worthy of note within it.

"Good evening, stranger," said the lime-burner, "whence come you, so late in the day?"

"I come from my search," answered the wayfarer; "for, at last, it is finished."

"Drunk, or crazy!" muttered Bartram to himself. "I shall have trouble with   15
the fellow. The sooner I drive him away, the better."

The little boy, all in a tremble, whispered to his father, and begged him to shut the door of the kiln, so that there might not be so much light; for that there was something in the man's face which he was afraid to look at, yet could not look away from. And, indeed, even the lime-burner's dull and torpid sense began to be impressed by an indescribable something in that thin, rugged, thoughtful visage, with the grizzled hair hanging wildly about it, and those deeply sunken eyes, which gleamed like fires within the entrance of a mysterious cavern. But, as he closed the door, the stranger turned towards him, and spoke in a quiet, familiar way, that made Bartram feel as if he were a sane and sensible man, after all.

"Your task draws to an end, I see," said he. "This marble has already been burning three days. A few hours more will convert the stone to lime."

"Why, who are you?" exclaimed the lime-burner. "You seem as well acquainted with my business as I myself."

"And well I may be," said the stranger "for I followed the same craft, many a long year; and here, too, on this very spot. But you are a new comer in these parts. Did you never hear of Ethan Brand?"

"The man that went in search of the Unpardonable Sin?" asked Bartram,   20
with a laugh.

"The same," answered the stranger. "He has found what he sought, and therefore he comes back again."

"What! then you are Ethan Brand, himself?" cried the lime-burner in amazement. "I am a new comer here, as you say; and they call it eighteen years since you left the foot of Graylock. But, I can tell you, the good folks still talk about Ethan Brand, in the village yonder, and what a strange errand took him away from his lime-kiln. Well, and so you have found the Unpardonable Sin?"

"Even so!" said the stranger, calmly.

"If the question is a fair one," proceeded Bartram, "where might it be?"

Ethan Brand laid his finger on his own heart. "Here!" replied he.   25

And then, without mirth in his countenance, but as if moved by an involuntary recognition of the infinite absurdity of seeking throughout the world for what was the closest of all things to himself, and looking into every heart, save his own, for what was hidden in no other breast, he broke into a laugh of scorn. It was the same slow, heavy laugh, that had almost appalled the lime-burner, when it heralded the wayfarer's approach.

The solitary mountain-side was made dismal by it. Laughter, when out of place, mistimed, or bursting forth from a disordered state of feeling, may be the most terrible modulation of the human voice. The laughter of one asleep, even if it be a little child—the madman's laugh—the wild, screaming laugh of a born idiot, are sounds that we sometimes tremble to hear, and would always willingly forget. Poets have imagined no utterance of fiends or hobgoblins so fearfully appropriate as a laugh. And even the obtuse lime-burner felt his nerves shaken, as this strange man looked inward at his own heart, and burst into laughter that rolled away into the night, and was indistinctly reverberated among the hills.

"Joe," said he to his little son, "scamper down to the tavern in the village, and tell the jolly fellows there that Ethan Brand has come back, and that he has found the Unpardonable Sin!"

The boy darted away on his errand, to which Ethan Brand made no objection, nor seemed hardly to notice it. He sat on a log of wood, looking steadfastly at the iron door of the kiln. When the child was out of sight, and his swift and light footsteps ceased to be heard, treading first on the fallen leaves, and then on the rocky mountain-path, the lime-burner began to regret his departure. He felt that the little fellow's presence had been a barrier between his guest and himself, and that he must now deal, heart to heart, with a man who, on his own confession, had committed the only crime for which Heaven could afford no mercy. That crime, in its indistinct blackness, seemed to overshadow him. The lime-burner's own sins rose up within him, and made his memory riotous with a throng of evil shapes that asserted their kindred with the Master Sin, whatever it might be, which it was within the scope of man's corrupted nature to conceive and cherish. They were all of one family; they went to and fro between his breast and Ethan Brand's, and carried dark greetings from one to the other.

Then Bartram remembered the stories which had grown traditionary in ref-   30
erence to this strange man, who had come upon him like a shadow of the night, and was making himself at home in his old place, after so long absence that the dead people, dead and buried for years, would have had more right to be at home, in any familiar spot, than he. Ethan Brand, it was said, had conversed with Satan himself, in the lurid blaze of this very kiln. The legend had been matter of mirth heretofore, but looked grisly now. According to this tale, before Ethan Brand departed on his search, he had been accustomed to evoke a fiend from the hot furnace of the lime-kiln, night after night, in order to confer with him about the Unpardonable Sin; the Man and the Fiend each laboring to frame the image of some mode of guilt, which could neither be atoned for, nor forgiven. And, with the first gleam of light upon the mountain-top, the fiend crept in at the iron door, there to abide in the intensest element of fire, until again summoned forth to share in the dreadful task of extending man's possible guilt beyond the scope of Heaven's else infinite mercy.

While the lime-burner was struggling with the horror of these thoughts, Ethan Brand rose from the log and flung open the door of the kiln. The action was in such accordance with the idea in Bartram's mind, that he almost expected to see the Evil One issue forth, red-hot from the raging furnace.

"Hold, hold!" cried he, with a tremulous attempt to laugh; for he was ashamed of his fears, although they overmastered him. "Don't, for mercy's sake, bring out your devil now!"

"Man!" sternly replied Ethan Brand, "what need have I of the devil? I have left him behind me on my track. It is with such half-way sinners as you that he busies himself. Fear not, because I open the door. I do but act by old custom, and am going to trim your fire, like a lime-burner, as I was once."

He stirred the vast coals, thrust in more wood, and bent forward to gaze into the hollow prison-house of the fire, regardless of the fierce glow that reddened upon his face. The lime-burner sat watching him, and half suspected his strange guest of a purpose, if not to evoke a fiend, at least to plunge bodily into the flames, and thus vanish from the sight of man. Ethan Brand, however, drew quietly back, and closed the door of the kiln.

"I have looked," said he, "into many a human heart that was seven times hotter with sinful passions than yonder furnace is with fire. But I found not there what I sought. No; not the Unpardonable Sin!"   35

"What is the Unpardonable Sin?" asked the lime-burner; and then he shrank farther from his companion, trembling lest his question should be answered.

"It is a sin that grew within my own breast," replied Ethan Brand, standing erect, with the pride that distinguishes all enthusiasts of his stamp. "A sin that grew nowhere else! The sin of an intellect that triumphed over the sense of brotherhood with man, and reverence for God, and sacrificed everything to its own mighty claims! The only sin that deserves a recompense of immortal agony! Freely, were it to do again, would I incur the guilt. Unshrinkingly, I accept the retribution!"

"The man's head is turned," muttered the lime-burner to himself. "He may be a sinner, like the rest of us — nothing more likely — but I'll be sworn, he is a madman, too."

Nevertheless, he felt uncomfortable at his situation, alone with Ethan Brand on the wild mountain-side, and was right glad to hear the rough murmur of tongues, and the footsteps of what seemed a pretty numerous party, stumbling over the stones, and rustling through the underbrush. Soon appeared the whole lazy regiment that was wont to infest the village tavern, comprehending three or four individuals who had drunk flip beside the bar-room fire, through all the winters, and smoked their pipes beneath the stoop, through all the summers since Ethan Brand's departure. Laughing boisterously, and mingling all their voices together in unceremonious talk, they now burst into the moonshine and narrow streaks of fire-light that illuminated the open space before the lime-kiln. Bartram set the door ajar again, flooding the spot with light, that the whole company might get a fair view of Ethan Brand, and he of them.

There, among other old acquaintances, was a once ubiquitous man, now   40
almost extinct, but whom we were formerly sure to encounter at the hotel of every thriving village throughout the country. It was the stage-agent. The present specimen of the genus was a wilted and smoke-dried man, wrinkled and red-nosed, in a smartly cut, brown, bob-tailed coat, with brass buttons, who, for a length of time unknown, had kept his desk and corner in the bar-room, and was still puffing what seemed to be the same cigar that he had lighted twenty years before. He had great fame as a dry joker, though, perhaps, less on account of any intrinsic humor, than from a certain flavor of brandy-toddy and tobacco-smoke, which impregnated all his ideas and expressions, as well as his person. Another

well-remembered, though strangely-altered face was that of Lawyer Giles, as people still called him in courtesy; an elderly ragamuffin, in his soiled shirt-sleeves and tow-cloth trowsers. This poor fellow had been an attorney, in what he called his better days, a sharp practitioner, and in great vogue among the village litigants; but flip, and sling, and toddy, and cocktails, imbibed at all hours, morning, noon, and night, had caused him to slide from intellectual, to various kinds and degrees of bodily labor, till, at last, to adopt his own phrase, he slid into a soap-vat. In other words, Giles was now a soap-boiler, in a small way. He had come to be but the fragment of a human being, a part of one foot having been chopped off by an axe, and an entire hand torn away by the devilish gripe of a steam-engine. Yet, though the corporeal hand was gone, a spiritual member remained; for, stretching forth the stump, Giles steadfastly averred, that he felt an invisible thumb and fingers, with as vivid a sensation as before the real ones were amputated. A maimed and miserable wretch he was; but one, nevertheless, whom the world could not trample on, and had no right to scorn, either in this or any previous stage of his misfortunes, since he had still kept up the courage and spirit of a man, asked nothing in charity, and, with his one hand — and that the left one — fought a stern battle against want and hostile circumstances.

Among the throng, too, came another personage, who, with certain points of similarity to Lawyer Giles, had more of difference. It was the village Doctor, a man of some fifty years, whom, at an earlier period of his life, we should have introduced as paying a professional visit to Ethan Brand, during the latter's supposed insanity. He was now a purple-visaged, rude, and brutal, yet half-gentlemanly figure, with something wild, ruined, and desperate in his talk, and in all the details of his gesture and manners. Brandy possessed this man like an evil spirit, and made him as surly and savage as a wild beast, and as miserable as a lost soul; but there was supposed to be in him such wonderful skill, such native gifts of healing, beyond any which medical science could impart, that society caught hold of him, and would not let him sink out of its reach. So, swaying to and fro upon his horse, and grumbling thick accents at the bedside, he visited all the sick chambers for miles about among the mountain towns; and sometimes raised a dying man, as it were, by miracle, or, quite as often, no doubt, sent his patient to a grave that was dug many a year too soon. The Doctor had an everlasting pipe in his mouth, and, as somebody said, in allusion to his habit of swearing, it was always alight with hell-fire.

These three worthies pressed forward, and greeted Ethan Brand, each after his own fashion, earnestly inviting him to partake of the contents of a certain black bottle; in which, as they averred, he would find something far better worth seeking for, than the Unpardonable Sin. No mind, which has wrought itself, by intense and solitary meditation, into a high state of enthusiasm, can endure the kind of contact with low and vulgar modes of thought and feeling, to which Ethan Brand was now subjected. It made him doubt — and, strange to say, it was a painful doubt — whether he had indeed found the Unpardonable Sin, and found it within himself. The whole question on which he had exhausted life, and more than life, looked like a delusion.

"Leave me," he said bitterly, "ye brute beasts, that have made yourselves so, shrivelling up your souls with fiery liquors! I have done with you. Years and years ago, I groped into your hearts and found nothing there for my purpose. Get ye gone!"

"Why, you uncivil scoundrel," cried the fierce Doctor, "is that the way you respond to the kindness of your best friends? Then let me tell you the truth. You have no more found the Unpardonable Sin than yonder boy Joe has. You are but a crazy fellow — I told you so, twenty years ago — neither better nor worse than a crazy fellow, and the fit companion of old Humphrey, here!"

He pointed to an old man, shabbily dressed, with long white hair, thin vis- 45 age, and unsteady eyes. For some years past, this aged person had been wandering about among the hills, inquiring of all travellers whom he met, for his daughter. The girl, it seemed, had gone off with a company of circus-performers; and, occasionally, tidings of her came to the village, and fine stories were told of her glittering appearance, as she rode on horseback in the ring, or performed marvellous feats on the tight-rope.

The white-haired father now approached Ethan Brand, and gazed unsteadily into his face.

"They tell me you have been all over the earth," said he, wringing his hands with earnestness. "You must have seen my daughter; for she makes a grand figure in the world, and everybody goes to see her. Did she send any word to her old father, or say when she is coming back?"

Ethan Brand's eye quailed beneath the old man's. That daughter, from whom he so earnestly desired a word of greeting, was the Esther of our tale; the very girl whom, with such cold and remorseless purpose, Ethan Brand had made the subject of a psychological experiment, and wasted, absorbed, and perhaps annihilated her soul, in the process.

"Yes," murmured he, turning away from the hoary wanderer; "it is no delusion. There is an Unpardonable Sin!"

While these things were passing, a merry scene was going forward in the area 50 of cheerful light, besides the spring and before the door of the hut. A number of the youth of the village, young men and girls, had hurried up the hill-side, impelled by curiosity to see Ethan Brand, the hero of so many a legend familiar to their childhood. Finding nothing, however, very remarkable in his aspect — nothing but a sun-burnt wayfarer, in plain garb and dusty shoes, who sat looking into the fire, as if he fancied pictures among the coals — these young people speedily grew tired of observing him. As it happened, there was other amusement at hand. An old German Jew, travelling with a diorama on his back, was passing down the mountain-road towards the village, just as the party turned aside from it; and, in hopes of eking out the profits of the day, the showman had kept them company to the lime-kiln.

"Come, old Dutchman," cried one of the young men, "let us see your pictures, if you can swear they are worth looking at!"

"Oh, yes, Captain," answered the Jew — whether as a matter of courtesy or craft, he styled everybody Captain — "I shall show you, indeed, some very superb pictures!"

So, placing his box in a proper position, he invited the young men and girls to look through the glass orifices of the machine, and proceeded to exhibit a series of the most outrageous scratchings and daubings, as specimens of the fine arts, that ever an itinerant showman had the face to impose upon his circle of spectators. The pictures were worn out, moreover, tattered, full of cracks and wrinkles, dingy with tobacco-smoke, and otherwise in a most pitiable condition. Some purported to be cities, public edifices, and ruined castles, in Europe; others represented Napoleon's battles, and Nelson's sea-fights; and in the midst of these would be seen a gigantic, brown, hairy hand — which might have been mistaken for the Hand of Destiny, though, in truth, it was only the showman's — pointing its forefinger to various scenes of the conflict, while its owner gave historical illustrations. When, with much merriment at its abominable deficiency of merit, the exhibition was concluded, the German bade little Joe put his head into the box. Viewed through the magnifying glasses, the boy's round, rosy visage assumed the strangest imaginable aspect of an immense, Titanic child, the mouth grinning broadly, and the eyes, and every other feature, overflowing with fun at the joke. Suddenly, however, that merry face turned pale, and its expression changed to horror; for this easily impressed and excitable child had become sensible that the eye of Ethan Brand was fixed upon him through the glass.

"You make the little man to be afraid, Captain," said the German Jew, turning up the dark and strong outline of his visage, from his stooping posture. "But, look again; and, by chance, I shall cause you to see somewhat that is very fine, upon my word!"

Ethan Brand gazed into the box for an instant, and then starting back,   55
looked fixedly at the German. What had he seen? Nothing, apparently; for a curious youth, who had peeped in, almost at the same moment, beheld only a vacant space of canvass.

"I remember you now," muttered Ethan Brand to the showman.

"Ah, Captain," whispered the Jew of Nuremberg, with a dark smile, "I find it to be a heavy matter in my show-box — this Unpardonable Sin! By my faith, Captain, it has wearied my shoulders, this long day, to carry it over the mountain."

"Peace!" answered Ethan Brand, sternly, "or get thee into the furnace yonder!"

The Jew's exhibition had scarcely concluded, when a great, elderly dog — who seemed to be his own master, as no person in the company laid claim to him — saw fit to render himself the object of public notice. Hitherto, he had shown himself a very quiet, well-disposed old dog, going round from one to another, and, by way of being sociable, offering his rough head to be patted by any kindly hand that would take so much trouble. But, now, all of a sudden, this grave and venerable quadruped, of his own mere notion, and without the slightest suggestion from anybody else, began to run round after his tail, which, to heighten the absurdity of the proceeding, was a great deal shorter than it should have been. Never was seen such headlong eagerness in pursuit of an object that could not possibly be attained; never was heard such a tremendous outbreak of growling, snarling, barking, and snapping — as if one end of the ridiculous brute's body were at deadly and most unforgivable enmity with the other. Faster and faster, roundabout went the cur; and faster and still faster fled the unapproachable brevity of his tail; and louder and fiercer grew his yells of rage and animosity; until, utterly exhausted, and as far from the goal as ever, the foolish old dog ceased his performance as suddenly as he had begun it. The next moment, he was as mild, quiet, sensible, and respectable in his deportment, as when he first scraped acquaintance with the company.

As may be supposed, the exhibition was greeted with universal laughter,   60
clapping of hands, and shouts of encore; to which the canine performer responded by wagging all that there was to wag of his tail, but appeared totally unable to repeat his very successful effort to amuse the spectators.

Meanwhile, Ethan Brand had resumed his seat upon the log; and, moved, it might be, by a perception of some remote analogy between his own case and that of this self-pursuing cur, he broke into the awful laugh, which, more than any other token, expressed the condition of his inward being. From that moment, the merriment of the party was at an end; they stood aghast, dreading lest the inauspicious sound should be reverberated around the horizon, and that mountain would thunder it to mountain, and so the horror be prolonged upon their ears. Then, whispering one to another, that it was late — that the moon was almost down — that the August night was growing chill — they hurried homeward, leaving the lime-burner and little Joe to deal as they might with their unwelcome guest. Save for these three human beings, the open space on the hill-side was a solitude, set in a vast gloom of forest. Beyond that darksome verge, the fire-light glimmered on the stately trunks and almost black foliage of pines, intermixed with the lighter verdure of sapling oaks, maples, and poplars, while, here and there, lay the gigantic corpses of dead trees, decaying on the leaf-strewn soil. And it seemed to little Joe — a timorous and imaginative child — that the silent forest was holding its breath, until some fearful thing should happen.

Ethan Brand thrust more wood into the fire, and closed the door of the kiln; then looking over his shoulder at the lime-burner and his son, he bade, rather than advised, them to retire to rest.

"For myself I cannot sleep," said he. "I have matters that it concerns me to meditate upon. I will watch the fire, as I used to do in the old time."

"And call the devil out of the furnace to keep you company, I suppose," muttered Bartram, who had been making intimate acquaintance with the black bottle above-mentioned. "But watch, if you like, and call as many devils as you like! For my part, I shall be all the better for a snooze. Come, Joe!"

As the boy followed his father into the hut, he looked back to the wayfarer,   65
and the tears came into his eyes; for his tender spirit had an intuition of the bleak and terrible loneliness in which this man had enveloped himself.

When they had gone, Ethan Brand sat listening to the crackling of the kindled wood, and looking at the little spirts of fire that issued through the chinks of the door. These trifles, however, once so familiar, had but the slightest hold of his attention; while deep within his mind, he was reviewing the gradual, but marvellous change, that had been wrought upon him by the search to which he had devoted himself. He remembered how the night-dew had fallen upon him — how the dark forest had whispered to him — how the stars had gleamed upon him — a simple and loving man, watching his fire in the years gone by, and ever musing as it burned. He remembered with what tenderness, with what love and sympathy for mankind, and what pity for human guilt and wo, he had first begun to contemplate those ideas which afterwards became the inspiration of his life; with what reverence he had then looked into the heart of man, viewing it as a temple originally divine, and however desecrated, still to be held sacred by a brother; with what awful fear he had deprecated the success of his pursuit, and prayed that the Unpardonable Sin might never be revealed to him. Then ensued that vast intellectual development, which, in its progress, disturbed the counterpoise between his mind and heart. The Idea that possessed his life had operated as a means of education; it had gone on cultivating his powers to the highest point of which they were susceptible; it had raised him from the level of an unlettered laborer, to stand on a star-light eminence, whither the philosophers of the earth, laden with the lore of universities, might vainly strive to clamber after him. So much for the intellect! But where was the heart? That, indeed, had withered — had contracted — had hardened — had perished! It had ceased to partake of the universal throb. He had lost his hold of the magnetic chain of humanity. He was no longer a brother-man, opening the chambers or the dungeons of our common nature by the key of holy sympathy, which gave him a right to share in all its secrets; he was now a cold observer, looking on mankind as the subject of his experiment, and, at length, converting man and woman to be his puppets, and pulling the wires that moved them to such degrees of crime as were demanded for his study.

Thus Ethan Brand became a fiend. He began to be so from the moment that his moral nature had ceased to keep the pace of improvement with his intellect. And now, as his highest effort and inevitable development — as the bright and gorgeous flower, and rich, delicious fruit of his life's labor — he had produced the Unpardonable Sin!

"What more have I to seek? What more to achieve?" said Ethan Brand to himself. "My task is done, and well done!"

Starting from the log with a certain alacrity in his gait, and ascending the hillock of earth that was raised against the stone circumference of the lime-kiln, he thus reached the top of the structure. It was a space of perhaps ten feet across, from edge to edge, presenting a view of the upper surface of the immense mass of broken marble with which the kiln was heaped. All these innumerable blocks and fragments of marble were red-hot, and vividly on fire, sending up great spouts of blue flame, which quivered aloft and danced madly, as within a magic circle, and sank and rose again, with continual and multitudinous activity. As the lonely man bent forward over this terrible body of fire, the blasting heat smote up against his person with a breath that, it might be supposed, would have scorched and shrivelled him up in a moment.

Ethan Brand stood erect and raised his arms on high. The blue flames played upon his face, and imparted the wild and ghastly light which alone could have suited its expression; it was that of a fiend on the verge of plunging into his gulf of intensest torment.

"Oh, Mother Earth," cried he, "who art no more my Mother, and into whose bosom this frame shall never be resolved! Oh, mankind, whose brotherhood I

70

have cast off, and trampled thy great heart beneath my feet! Oh, stars of Heaven, that shone on me of old, as if to light me onward and upward! — farewell all, and forever! Come, deadly element of Fire — henceforth my familiar friend! Embrace me as I do thee!"

That night the sound of a fearful peal of laughter rolled heavily through the sleep of the lime-burner and his little son; dim shapes of horror and anguish haunted their dreams, and seemed still present in the rude hovel when they opened their eyes to the daylight.

"Up, boy, up!" cried the lime-burner, staring about him. "Thank Heaven, the night is gone at last; and rather than pass such another, I would watch my lime-kiln, wide awake, for a twelvemonth. This Ethan Brand, with his humbug of an Unpardonable Sin, has done me no such mighty favor in taking my place!"

He issued from the hut, followed by little Joe, who kept fast hold of his father's hand. The early sunshine was already pouring its gold upon the mountain-tops, and though the valleys were still in shadow, they smiled cheerfully in the promise of the bright day that was hastening onward. The village, completely shut in by hills, which swelled away gently about it, looked as if it had rested peacefully in the hollow of the great hand of Providence. Every dwelling was distinctly visible; the little spires of the two churches pointed upward, and caught a fore-glimmering of brightness from the sun-gilt skies upon their gilded weather-cocks. The tavern was astir, and the figure of the old, smoke-dried stage-agent, cigar in mouth, was seen beneath the stoop. Old Graylock was glorified with a golden cloud upon his head. Scattered, likewise, over the breasts of the surrounding mountains, there were heaps of hoary mist, in fantastic shapes, some of them far down into the valley, others high up towards the summits, and still others, of the same family of mist or cloud, hovering in the gold radiance of the upper atmosphere. Stepping from one to another of the clouds that rested on the hills, and thence to the loftier brotherhood that sailed in air, it seemed almost as if a mortal man might thus ascend into the heavenly regions. Earth was so mingled with sky that it was a daydream to look at it.

To supply that charm of the familiar and homely, which Nature so readily   75
adopts into a scene like this, the stage-coach was rattling down the mountain-road, and the driver sounded his horn; while echo caught up the notes and inter-twined them into a rich, and varied, and elaborate harmony, of which the original performer could lay claim to little share. The great hills played a concert among themselves, each contributing a strain of airy sweetness.

Little Joe's face brightened at once.

"Dear father," cried he, skipping cheerily to and fro, "that strange man is gone, and the sky and the mountains all seem glad of it!"

"Yes," growled the lime-burner with an oath, "but he has let the fire go down, and no thanks to him, if five hundred bushels of lime are not spoilt. If I catch the fellow hereabouts again I shall feel like tossing him into the furnace!"

With his long pole in his hand he ascended to the top of the kiln. After a moment's pause he called to his son.

"Come up here, Joe!" said he.   80

So little Joe ran up the hillock and stood by his father's side. The marble was all burnt into perfect, snow-white lime. But on its surface, in the midst of the circle — snow-white too, and thoroughly converted into lime — lay a human skeleton, in the attitude of a person who, after long toil, lies down to long repose. Within the ribs — strange to say — was the shape of a human heart.

"Was the fellow's heart made of marble?" cried Bartram, in some perplexity at this phenomenon. "At any rate, it is burnt into what looks like special good lime; and, taking all the bones together, my kiln is half a bushel the richer for him."

So saying, the rude lime-burner lifted his pole, and letting it fall upon the skeleton, the relics of Ethan Brand were crumbled into fragments.   [1851]

THINKING ABOUT THE TEXT

1. According to Ethan Brand, what is the Unpardonable Sin? Do you think this label indeed applies to the sin he designates? Why, or why not?
2. Why, evidently, does Brand laugh?
3. What is the function of the child in this story? Of his father? Of the other characters?
4. What does the story's final image of Brand's body imply?
5. Would Brand have been better off never leaving home? Explain your reasoning.

MAKING COMPARISONS

1. Both Goodman Brown and Ethan Brand go on journeys. To what extent do their experiences seem similar?
2. Can the term *unpardonable sin* apply to something in "Young Goodman Brown" or "The Minister's Black Veil"? If so, what?
3. How does Hawthorne create mystery and suspense in these three stories? Does he use basically the same strategies in each?

WRITING ABOUT ISSUES

1. Choose one of these three Hawthorne stories, and write an essay in which you identify the definition of *justice* that the story seems to support.
2. In each of these Hawthorne stories, the title character becomes alienated from his community. Choose two of these characters, and write an essay in which you compare the reasons for their alienation and evaluate their respective acts. Does one of these characters deserve more sympathy than the others?
3. Write an essay recalling an occasion when someone you knew or read about was intent on branding someone else a sinner or wrongdoer. Moreover, let this occasion be one that left you with mixed feelings. Then write an essay that not only identifies the issues you thought were at stake but also expresses and supports your view of the outcome.

4. Find at least two articles on Puritanism, and write an essay in which you relate these to "Young Goodman Brown," "The Minister's Black Veil," or "Ethan Brand." Focus on showing how these articles help you understand your chosen story better.

A WEB ASSIGNMENT

The *Making Literature Matter* Web site will link you to another site that is a gateway to various sources and documents concerning the 1692 Salem witchcraft trials. The trials were a manifestation of Puritanism that troubled Hawthorne, in part because his ancestor John Hathorne was involved as a presiding judge. Especially worth examining are documents that tell you about some of the specific trials. To reach them, click the Browse button beneath the listing for George Lincoln Burr's *Narratives of the Witch Cases*. On the page where you arrive, you will see listings for various trials reported in Cotton Mather's 1693 work *Wonders of the Invisible World*. Click the button for the trial of Martha Carrier, which will take you to selections from Mather's account of her case. After reading about Carrier's trial, write an essay on the religious beliefs it revealed, which led her judges to condemn her to death. More specifically, describe these beliefs, and identify the extent to which they surface in "Young Goodman Brown," "The Minister's Black Veil," or "Ethan Brand."

Visit www.bedfordstmartins.com/makinglitmatter

MISFIT JUSTICE:
CRITICAL COMMENTARIES ON FLANNERY O'CONNOR'S
"A GOOD MAN IS HARD TO FIND"

FLANNERY O'CONNOR, "A Good Man Is Hard to Find"

CRITICAL COMMENTARIES:
FLANNERY O'CONNOR, From *Mystery and Manners*
MARTHA STEPHENS, From *The Question of Flannery O'Connor*
MADISON JONES, From "A Good Man's Predicament"
STEPHEN BANDY, From "'One of My Babies': The Misfit and the Grandmother"

Most of us are social beings; we long to fit in. The communities we form sustain us, giving us our moral compasses and our psychological bearings. But sometimes people voluntarily remove themselves from all traditional communities. Indeed, literature is filled with misfits. Their decisions may intrigue us but also perplex and trouble us, perhaps because they represent antisocial impulses in all of us. Especially interesting are those literary misfits who demand that their own

(Flannery O'Connor Collection, Ina Dillard Russell Library, Georgia College and State University.)

sense of justice be satisfied. Probably the most notable example in post–World War II American fiction is a character in Flannery O'Connor's 1953 short story "A Good Man Is Hard to Find." This man actually calls himself The Misfit, and he turns violent as he challenges Christianity's belief in Jesus's ability to raise the dead. O'Connor's story has been widely read, in part because it is subject to various interpretations. Here, in addition to the story and O'Connor's own remarks about it, we present three critical commentaries that disagree with her analysis.

BEFORE YOU READ

What do you think you might find in a story by a practicing Roman Catholic author? What topics, themes, characters, and events might she write about?

FLANNERY O'CONNOR
A Good Man Is Hard to Find

Flannery O'Connor (1925–1964) spent most of her life in Milledgeville, Georgia, where she raised peacocks on a farm with her mother. She died of lupus at the age of thirty-nine, when she was at the peak of her creative powers. All of her fiction reflects her Roman Catholic faith and Southern heritage, as do her nonfiction writings, which were collected after her death in Mystery and Manners *(1969). Critics have often seen in her work Christian parables of grace and redemption in the face of random violence. Like other Southern writers such as William Faulkner and Carson McCullers, she uses grotesque characters to suggest our own morally flawed humanity. O'Connor's early stories won her a scholarship to the University of Iowa, where she received her M.F.A. She went on to produce two novels,* Wise Blood *(1952) and* The Violent Bear It Away *(1960), but she is known and admired mostly for her short fiction. The following story was first published in the volume* Modern Writing 1 *in 1953. O'Connor then included it in her 1955 collection entitled* A Good Man Is Hard to Find and Other Stories. *The book won her national acclaim, as did a later collection, the posthumously published* Everything That Rises Must Converge *(1965). These two volumes were combined in 1979 as* The Complete Stories of Flannery O'Connor, *which won the National Book Award for fiction.*

> The dragon is by the side of the road, watching those who pass. Beware lest he devour you. We go to the Father of Souls, but it is necessary to pass by the dragon.
>
> — St. Cyril of Jerusalem

The grandmother didn't want to go to Florida. She wanted to visit some of her connections in east Tennessee and she was seizing at every chance to change Bailey's mind. Bailey was the son she lived with, her only boy. He was sitting on the edge of his chair at the table, bent over the orange sports section of the *Journal.* "Now look here, Bailey," she said, "see here, read this," and she stood with one hand on her thin hip and the other rattling the newspaper at his bald head. "Here this fellow that calls himself The Misfit is aloose from the Federal Pen and headed toward Florida and you read here what it says he did to these people. Just you read it. I wouldn't take my children in any direction with a criminal like that aloose in it. I couldn't answer to my conscience if I did."

Bailey didn't look up from his reading so she wheeled around then and faced the children's mother, a young woman in slacks, whose face was as broad and innocent as a cabbage and was tied around with a green head-kerchief that had two points on the top like rabbit's ears. She was sitting on the sofa, feeding the baby his apricots out of a jar. "The children have been to Florida before," the old lady said. "You all ought to take them somewhere else for a change so they would see different parts of the world and be broad. They never have been to east Tennessee."

The children's mother didn't seem to hear her but the eight-year-old boy, John Wesley, a stocky child with glasses, said, "If you don't want to go to Florida, why dontcha stay at home?" He and the little girl, June Star, were reading the funny papers on the floor.

"She wouldn't stay at home to be queen for a day," June Star said without raising her yellow head.

"Yes and what would you do if this fellow, The Misfit, caught you?" the   5
grandmother asked.

"I'd smack his face," John Wesley said.

"She wouldn't stay at home for a million bucks," June Star said. "Afraid she'd
miss something. She has to go everywhere we go."

"All right, Miss," the grandmother said. "Just remember that the next time
you want me to curl your hair."

June Star said her hair was naturally curly.

The next morning the grandmother was the first one in the car, ready to go.   10
She had her big black valise that looked like the head of a hippopotamus in one
corner, and underneath it she was hiding a basket with Pitty Sing, the cat, in it.
She didn't intend for the cat to be left alone in the house for three days because
he would miss her too much and she was afraid he might brush against one of the
gas burners and accidentally asphyxiate himself. Her son, Bailey, didn't like to
arrive at a motel with a cat.

She sat in the middle of the back seat with John Wesley and June Star on
either side of her. Bailey and the children's mother and the baby sat in front and
they left Atlanta at eight forty-five with the mileage on the car at 55890. The
grandmother wrote this down because she thought it would be interesting to say
how many miles they had been when they got back. It took them twenty minutes
to reach the outskirts of the city.

The old lady settled herself comfortably, removing her white cotton gloves
and putting them up with her purse on the shelf in front of the back window. The
children's mother still had on slacks and still had her head tied up in a green kerchief, but the grandmother had on a navy blue straw sailor hat with a bunch of
white violets on the brim and a navy blue dress with a small white dot in the print.
Her collars and cuffs were white organdy trimmed with lace and at her neckline
she had pinned a purple spray of cloth violets containing a sachet. In case of an
accident, anyone seeing her dead on the highway would know at once that she
was a lady.

She said she thought it was going to be a good day for driving, neither too hot
nor too cold, and she cautioned Bailey that the speed limit was fifty-five miles an
hour and that the patrolmen hid themselves behind billboards and small clumps
of trees and sped out after you before you had a chance to slow down. She
pointed out interesting details of the scenery: Stone Mountain; the blue granite
that in some places came up to both sides of the highway; the brilliant red clay
banks slightly streaked with purple; and the various crops that made rows of green
lace-work on the ground. The trees were full of silver-white sunlight and the
meanest of them sparkled. The children were reading comic magazines and their
mother had gone back to sleep.

"Let's go through Georgia fast so we won't have to look at it much," John
Wesley said.

"If I were a little boy," said the grandmother, "I wouldn't talk about my native   15
state that way. Tennessee has the mountains and Georgia has the hills."

"Tennessee is just a hillbilly dumping ground," John Wesley said, "and Georgia is a lousy state too."

"You said it," June Star said.

"In my time," said the grandmother, folding her thin veined fingers, "children were more respectful of their native states and their parents and everything else. People did right then. Oh look at the cute little pickaninny!" she said and pointed to a Negro child standing in the door of a shack. "Wouldn't that make a picture, now?" she asked and they all turned and looked at the little Negro out of the back window. He waved.

"He didn't have any britches on," June Star said.

"He probably didn't have any," the grandmother explained. "Little niggers in   20
the country don't have things like we do. If I could paint, I'd paint that picture," she said.

The children exchanged comic books.

The grandmother offered to hold the baby and the children's mother passed him over the front seat to her. She set him on her knee and bounced him and told him about the things they were passing. She rolled her eyes and screwed up her mouth and stuck her leathery thin face into his smooth bland one. Occasionally he gave her a faraway smile. They passed a large cotton field with five or six graves fenced in the middle of it, like a small island. "Look at the graveyard!" the grandmother said, pointing it out. "That was the old family burying ground. That belonged to the plantation."

"Where's the plantation?" John Wesley asked.

"Gone with the Wind," said the grandmother. "Ha. Ha."

When the children finished all the comic books they had brought, they   25
opened the lunch and ate it. The grandmother ate a peanut butter sandwich and an olive and would not let the children throw the box and the paper napkins out the window. When there was nothing else to do they played a game by choosing a cloud and making the other two guess what shape it suggested. John Wesley took one the shape of a cow and June Star guessed a cow and John Wesley said, no, an automobile, and June Star said he didn't play fair, and they began to slap each other over the grandmother.

The grandmother said she would tell them a story if they would keep quiet. When she told a story, she rolled her eyes and waved her head and was very dramatic. She said once when she was a maiden lady she had been courted by a Mr. Edgar Atkins Teagarden from Jasper, Georgia. She said he was a very good-looking man and a gentleman and that he brought her a watermelon every Saturday afternoon with his initials cut in it, E. A. T. Well, one Saturday, she said, Mr. Teagarden brought the watermelon and there was nobody at home and he left it on the front porch and returned in his buggy to Jasper, but she never got the watermelon, she said, because a nigger boy ate it when he saw the initials, E. A. T.! This story tickled John Wesley's funny bone and he giggled and giggled but June Star didn't think it was any good. She said she wouldn't marry a man that just brought her a watermelon on Saturday. The grandmother said she would have done well to marry Mr. Teagarden because he was a gentleman and had bought Coca-Cola stock when it first came out and that he had died only a few years ago, a very wealthy man.

They stopped at The Tower for barbecued sandwiches. The Tower was a part stucco and part wood filling station and dance hall set in a clearing outside of Timothy. A fat man named Red Sammy Butts ran it and there were signs stuck here and there on the building and for miles up and down the highway saying, TRY RED SAMMY'S FAMOUS BARBECUE. NONE LIKE FAMOUS RED SAMMY'S! RED SAM! THE FAT BOY WITH THE HAPPY LAUGH. A VETERAN! RED SAMMY'S YOUR MAN!

Red Sammy was lying on the bare ground outside The Tower with his head under a truck while a gray monkey about a foot high, chained to a small chinaberry tree, chattered nearby. The monkey sprang back into the tree and got on the highest limb as soon as he saw the children jump out of the car and run toward him.

Inside, The Tower was a long dark room with a counter at one end and tables at the other and dancing space in the middle. They all sat down at a board table next to the nickelodeon and Red Sam's wife, a tall burnt-brown woman with hair and eyes lighter than her skin, came and took their order. The children's mother put a dime in the machine and played "The Tennessee Waltz," and the grandmother said that tune always made her want to dance. She asked Bailey if he would like to dance but he only glared at her. He didn't have a naturally sunny disposition like she did and trips made him nervous. The grandmother's brown eyes were very bright. She swayed her head from side to side and pretended she was dancing in her chair. June Star said play something she could tap to so the children's mother put in another dime and played a fast number and June Star stepped out onto the dance floor and did her tap routine.

"Ain't she cute?" Red Sam's wife said, leaning over the counter. "Would you like to come be my little girl?"   30

"No I certainly wouldn't," June Star said. "I wouldn't live in a broken-down place like this for a million bucks!" and she ran back to the table.

"Ain't she cute?" the woman repeated, stretching her mouth politely.

"Aren't you ashamed?" hissed the grandmother.

Red Sam came in and told his wife to quit lounging on the counter and hurry up with these people's order. His khaki trousers reached just to his hip bones and his stomach hung over them like a sack of meal swaying under his shirt. He came over and sat down at a table nearby and let out a combination sigh and yodel. "You can't win," he said. "You can't win," and he wiped his sweating red face off with a gray handkerchief. "These days you don't know who to trust," he said. "Ain't that the truth?"

"People are certainly not nice like they used to be," said the grandmother.   35

"Two fellers come in here last week," Red Sammy said, "driving a Chrysler. It was a old beat-up car but it was a good one and these boys looked all right to me. Said they worked at the mill and you know I let them fellers charge the gas they bought? Now why did I do that?"

"Because you're a good man!" the grandmother said at once.

"Yes'm, I suppose so," Red Sam said as if he were struck with this answer.

His wife brought the orders, carrying the five plates all at once without a tray, two in each hand and one balanced on her arm. "It isn't a soul in this green world of God's that you can trust," she said. "And I don't count nobody out of that, not nobody," she repeated, looking at Red Sammy.

"Did you read about that criminal, The Misfit, that's escaped?" asked the   40
grandmother.

"I wouldn't be a bit surprised if he didn't attact this place right here," said the woman. "If he hears about it being here, I wouldn't be none surprised to see him. If he hears it's two cent in the cash register, I wouldn't be a tall surprised if he . . ."

"That'll do," Red Sam said. "Go bring these people their Co'-Colas," and the woman went off to get the rest of the order.

"A good man is hard to find," Red Sammy said. "Everything is getting terrible. I remember the day you could go off and leave your screen door unlatched. Not no more."

He and the grandmother discussed better times. The old lady said that in her opinion Europe was entirely to blame for the way things were now. She said the way Europe acted you would think we were made of money and Red Sam said it was no use talking about it, she was exactly right. The children ran outside into the white sunlight and looked at the monkey in the lacy chinaberry tree. He was busy catching fleas on himself and biting each one carefully between his teeth as if it were a delicacy.

They drove off again into the hot afternoon. The grandmother took cat naps   45
and woke up every few minutes with her own snoring. Outside of Toombsboro she woke up and recalled an old plantation that she had visited in this neighborhood once when she was a young lady. She said the house had six white columns across the front and that there was an avenue of oaks leading up to it and two little wooden trellis arbors on either side in front where you sat down with your suitor after a stroll in the garden. She recalled exactly which road to turn off to get to it. She knew that Bailey would not be willing to lose any time looking at an old house, but the more she talked about it, the more she wanted to see it once again and find out if the little twin arbors were still standing. "There was a secret panel in this house," she said craftily, not telling the truth but wishing that she were, "and the story went that all the family silver was hidden in it when Sherman came through but it was never found . . ."

"Hey!" John Wesley said. "Let's go see it! We'll find it! We'll poke all the woodwork and find it! Who lives there? Where do you turn off at? Hey Pop, can't we turn off there?"

"We never have seen a house with a secret panel!" June Star shrieked. "Let's go to the house with the secret panel! Hey Pop, can't we go see the house with the secret panel!"

"It's not far from here, I know," the grandmother said. "It wouldn't take over twenty minutes."

Bailey was looking straight ahead. His jaw was as rigid as a horseshoe. "No," he said.

The children began to yell and scream that they wanted to see the house   50
with the secret panel. John Wesley kicked the back of the front seat and June Star hung over her mother's shoulder and whined desperately into her ear that they

never had any fun even on their vacation, that they could never do what THEY wanted to do. The baby began to scream and John Wesley kicked the back of the seat so hard that his father could feel the blows in his kidney.

"All right!" he shouted and drew the car to a stop at the side of the road. "Will you all shut up? Will you all just shut up for one second? If you don't shut up, we won't go anywhere."

"It would be very educational for them," the grandmother murmured.

"All right," Bailey said, "but get this: this is the only time we're going to stop for anything like this. This is the one and only time."

"The dirt road that you have to turn down is about a mile back," the grandmother directed. "I marked it when we passed."

"A dirt road," Bailey groaned.   55

After they had turned around and were headed toward the dirt road, the grandmother recalled other points about the house, the beautiful glass over the front doorway and the candle-lamp in the hall. John Wesley said that the secret panel was probably in the fireplace.

"You can't go inside this house," Bailey said. "You don't know who lives there."

"While you all talk to the people in front, I'll run around behind and get in a window," John Wesley suggested.

"We'll all stay in the car," his mother said.

They turned onto the dirt road and the car raced roughly along in a swirl of   60
pink dust. The grandmother recalled the times when there were no paved roads and thirty miles was a day's journey. The dirt road was hilly and there were sudden washes in it and sharp curves on dangerous embankments. All at once they would be on a hill, looking down over the blue tops of trees for miles around, then the next minute, they would be in a red depression with the dust-coated trees looking down on them.

"This place had better turn up in a minute," Bailey said, "or I'm going to turn around."

The road looked as if no one had traveled on it in months.

"It's not much farther," the grandmother said and just as she said it, a horrible thought came to her. The thought was so embarrassing that she turned red in the face and her eyes dilated and her feet jumped up, upsetting her valise in the corner. The instant the valise moved, the newspaper top she had over the basket under it rose with a snarl and Pitty Sing, the cat, sprang onto Bailey's shoulder.

The children were thrown to the floor and their mother, clutching the baby, was thrown out the door onto the ground; the old lady was thrown into the front seat. The car turned over once and landed right-side-up in a gulch off the side of the road. Bailey remained in the driver's seat with the cat—gray-striped with a broad white face and an orange nose—clinging to his neck like a caterpillar.

As soon as the children saw they could move their arms and legs, they   65
scrambled out of the car, shouting, "We've had an ACCIDENT!" The grandmother was curled up under the dashboard, hoping she was injured so that Bailey's wrath would not come down on her all at once. The horrible thought she had had before the accident was that the house she had remembered so vividly was not in Georgia but in Tennessee.

Bailey removed the cat from his neck with both hands and flung it out the window against the side of a pine tree. Then he got out of the car and started looking for the children's mother. She was sitting against the side of the red gutted ditch, holding the screaming baby, but she only had a cut down her face and a broken shoulder. "We've had an ACCIDENT!" the children screamed in a frenzy of delight.

"But nobody's killed," June Star said with disappointment as the grandmother limped out of the car, her hat still pinned to her head but the broken front brim standing up at a jaunty angle and the violet spray hanging off the side. They all sat down in the ditch, except the children, to recover from the shock. They were all shaking.

"Maybe a car will come along," said the children's mother hoarsely.

"I believe I have injured an organ," said the grandmother, pressing her side, but no one answered her. Bailey's teeth were clattering. He had on a yellow sport shirt with bright blue parrots designed in it and his face was as yellow as the shirt. The grandmother decided that she would not mention that the house was in Tennessee.

The road was about ten feet above and they could only see the tops of the trees on the other side of it. Behind the ditch they were sitting in there were more woods, tall and dark and deep. In a few minutes they saw a car some distance away on top of a hill, coming slowly as if the occupants were watching them. The grandmother stood up and waved both arms dramatically to attract their attention. The car continued to come on slowly, disappeared around a bend and appeared again, moving even slower, on top of the hill they had gone over. It was a big black battered hearse-like automobile. There were three men in it.

It came to a stop just over them and for some minutes, the driver looked down with a steady expressionless gaze to where they were sitting, and didn't speak. Then he turned his head and muttered something to the other two and they got out. One was a fat boy in black trousers and a red sweat shirt with a silver stallion embossed on the front of it. He moved around on the right side of them and stood staring, his mouth partly open in a kind of loose grin. The other had on khaki pants and a blue striped coat and a gray hat pulled very low, hiding most of his face. He came around slowly on the left side. Neither spoke.

The driver got out of the car and stood by the side of it, looking down at them. He was an older man than the other two. His hair was just beginning to gray and he wore silver-rimmed spectacles that gave him a scholarly look. He had a long creased face and didn't have on any shirt or undershirt. He had on blue jeans that were too tight for him and was holding a black hat and a gun. The two boys also had guns.

"We've had an ACCIDENT!" the children screamed.

The grandmother had the peculiar feeling that the bespectacled man was someone she knew. His face was as familiar to her as if she had known him all her life but she could not recall who he was. He moved away from the car and began to come down the embankment, placing his feet carefully so that he wouldn't slip. He had on tan and white shoes and no socks, and his ankles were red and thin. "Good afternoon," he said. "I see you all had you a little spill."

"We turned over twice!" said the grandmother.   75

"Oncet," he corrected. "We seen it happen. Try their car and see will it run, Hiram," he said quietly to the boy with the gray hat.

"What you got that gun for?" John Wesley asked. "Whatcha gonna do with that gun?"

"Lady," the man said to the children's mother, "would you mind calling them children to sit down by you? Children make me nervous. I want all you all to sit down right together there where you're at."

"What are you telling US what to do for?" June Star asked.

Behind them the line of woods gaped like a dark open mouth. "Come here,"   80
said the mother.

"Look here now," Bailey began suddenly, "we're in a predicament! We're in . . ."

The grandmother shrieked. She scrambled to her feet and stood staring. "You're The Misfit!" she said. "I recognized you at once!"

"Yes'm," the man said, smiling slightly as if he were pleased in spite of himself to be known, "but it would have been better for all of you, lady, if you hadn't of reckernized me."

Bailey turned his head sharply and said something to his mother that shocked even the children. The old lady began to cry and The Misfit reddened.

"Lady," he said, "don't you get upset. Sometimes a man says things he don't   85
mean. I don't reckon he meant to talk to you thataway."

"You wouldn't shoot a lady, would you?" the grandmother said and removed a clean handkerchief from her cuff and began to slap at her eyes with it.

The Misfit pointed the toe of his shoe into the ground and made a little hole and then covered it up again. "I would hate to have to," he said.

"Listen," the grandmother almost screamed, "I know you're a good man. You don't look a bit like you have common blood. I know you must come from nice people!"

"Yes mam," he said, "finest people in the world." When he smiled he showed a row of strong white teeth. "God never made a finer woman than my mother and my daddy's heart was pure gold," he said. The boy with the red sweat shirt had come around behind them and was standing with his gun at his hip. The Misfit squatted down on the ground. "Watch them children, Bobby Lee," he said. "You know they make me nervous." He looked at the six of them huddled together in front of him and he seemed to be embarrassed as if he couldn't think of anything to say. "Ain't a cloud in the sky," he remarked, looking up at it. "Don't see no sun but don't see no cloud neither."

"Yes, it's a beautiful day," said the grandmother. "Listen," she said, "you   90
shouldn't call yourself The Misfit because I know you're a good man at heart. I can just look at you and tell."

"Hush!" Bailey yelled. "Hush! Everybody shut up and let me handle this!" He was squatting in the position of a runner about to sprint forward but he didn't move.

"I pre-chate that, lady," The Misfit said and drew a little circle in the ground with the butt of his gun.

"It'll take a half a hour to fix this here car," Hiram called, looking over the raised hood of it.

"Well, first you and Bobby Lee get him and that little boy to step over yonder with you," The Misfit said, pointing to Bailey and John Wesley. "The boys want to ast you something," he said to Bailey. "Would you mind stepping back in them woods there with them?"

"Listen," Bailey began, "we're in a terrible predicament! Nobody realizes   95
what this is," and his voice cracked. His eyes were as blue and intense as the parrots in his shirt and he remained perfectly still.

The grandmother reached up to adjust her hat brim as if she were going to the woods with him but it came off in her hand. She stood staring at it and after a second she let it fall on the ground. Hiram pulled Bailey up by the arm as if he were assisting an old man. John Wesley caught hold of his father's hand and Bobby Lee followed. They went off toward the woods and just as they reached the dark edge, Bailey turned and supporting himself against a gray naked pine trunk, he shouted, "I'll be back in a minute, Mamma, wait on me!"

"Come back this instant!" his mother shrilled but they all disappeared into the woods.

"Bailey Boy!" the grandmother called in a tragic voice but she found she was looking at The Misfit squatting on the ground in front of her. "I just know you're a good man," she said desperately. "You're not a bit common!"

"Nome, I ain't a good man," The Misfit said after a second as if he had considered her statement carefully, "but I ain't the worst in the world neither. My daddy said I was a different breed of dog from my brothers and sisters. 'You know,' Daddy said, 'it's some that can live their whole life out without asking about it and it's others has to know why it is, and this boy is one of the latters. He's going to be into everything!' " He put on his black hat and looked up suddenly and then away deep into the woods as if he were embarrassed again. "I'm sorry I don't have on a shirt before you ladies," he said, hunching his shoulders slightly. "We buried our clothes that we had on when we escaped and we're just making do until we can get better. We borrowed these from some folks we met," he explained.

"That's perfectly all right," the grandmother said. "Maybe Bailey has an extra   100
shirt in his suitcase."

"I'll look and see terrectly," The Misfit said.

"Where are they taking him?" the children's mother screamed.

"Daddy was a card himself," The Misfit said. "You couldn't put anything over on him. He never got in trouble with the Authorities though. Just had the knack of handling them."

"You could be honest too if you'd only try," said the grandmother. "Think how wonderful it would be to settle down and live a comfortable life and not have to think about somebody chasing you all the time."

The Misfit kept scratching in the ground with the butt of his gun as if he   105
were thinking about it. "Yes'm, somebody is always after you," he murmured.

The grandmother noticed how thin his shoulder blades were just behind his hat because she was standing up looking down at him. "Do you ever pray?" she asked.

He shook his head. All she saw was the black hat wiggle between his shoulder blades. "Nome," he said.

There was a pistol shot from the woods, followed closely by another. Then silence. The old lady's head jerked around. She could hear the wind move through the tree tops like a long satisfied insuck of breath. "Bailey Boy!" she called.

"I was a gospel singer for a while," The Misfit said. "I been most everything. Been in the arm service, both land and sea, at home and abroad, been twict married, been an undertaker, been with the railroads, plowed Mother Earth, been in a tornado, seen a man burnt alive oncet," and he looked up at the children's mother and the little girl who were sitting close together, their faces white and their eyes glassy; "I even seen a woman flogged," he said.

"Pray, pray," the grandmother began, "pray, pray . . ."   110

"I never was a bad boy that I remember of," The Misfit said in an almost dreamy voice, "but somewheres along the line I done something wrong and got sent to the penitentiary. I was buried alive," and he looked up and held her attention to him by a steady stare.

"That's when you should have started to pray," she said. "What did you do to get sent to the penitentiary, that first time?"

"Turn to the right, it was a wall," The Misfit said, looking up again at the cloudless sky. "Turn to the left, it was a wall. Look up it was a ceiling, look down it was a floor. I forgot what I done, lady. I set there and set there, trying to remember what it was I done and I ain't recalled it to this day. Oncet in a while, I would think it was coming to me, but it never come."

"Maybe they put you in by mistake," the old lady said vaguely.

"Nome," he said. "It wasn't no mistake. They had the papers on me."   115

"You must have stolen something," she said.

The Misfit sneered slightly. "Nobody had nothing I wanted," he said. "It was a head-doctor at the penitentiary said what I had done was kill my daddy but I known that for a lie. My daddy died in nineteen ought nineteen of the epidemic flu and I never had a thing to do with it. He was buried in the Mount Hopewell Baptist churchyard and you can go there and see for yourself."

"If you would pray," the old lady said, "Jesus would help you."

"That's right," The Misfit said.

"Well then, why don't you pray?" she asked trembling with delight suddenly.   120

"I don't want no hep," he said. "I'm doing all right by myself."

Bobby Lee and Hiram came ambling back from the woods. Bobby Lee was dragging a yellow shirt with bright blue parrots in it.

"Thow me that shirt, Bobby Lee," The Misfit said. The shirt came flying at him and landed on his shoulder and he put it on. The grandmother couldn't name what the shirt reminded her of. "No, lady," The Misfit said while he was buttoning it up, "I found out the crime don't matter. You can do one thing or you can do another, kill a man or take a tire off his car, because sooner or later you're going to forget what it was you done and just be punished for it."

The children's mother had begun to make heaving noises as if she couldn't get her breath. "Lady," he asked, "would you and that little girl like to step off yonder with Bobby Lee and Hiram and join your husband?"

"Yes, thank you," the mother said faintly. Her left arm dangled helplessly and 125
she was holding the baby, who had gone to sleep, in the other. "Hep that lady up,
Hiram," The Misfit said as she struggled to climb out of the ditch, "and Bobby
Lee, you hold onto that little girl's hand."

"I don't want to hold hands with him," June Star said. "He reminds me of
a pig."

The fat boy blushed and laughed and caught her by the arm and pulled her
off into the woods after Hiram and her mother.

Alone with The Misfit, the grandmother found that she had lost her voice.
There was not a cloud in the sky nor any sun. There was nothing around her but
woods. She wanted to tell him that he must pray. She opened and closed her
mouth several times before anything came out. Finally she found herself saying,
"Jesus. Jesus," meaning, Jesus will help you, but the way she was saying it, it
sounded as if she might be cursing.

"Yes'm," The Misfit said as if he agreed. "Jesus thown everything off balance.
It was the same case with Him as with me except He hadn't committed any crime
and they could prove I had committed one because they had the papers on me.
Of course," he said, "they never shown me my papers. That's why I sign myself
now. I said long ago, you get you a signature and sign everything you do and keep
a copy of it. Then you'll know what you done and you can hold up the crime to
the punishment and see do they match and in the end you'll have something to
prove you ain't been treated right. I call myself The Misfit," he said, "because I
can't make what all I done wrong fit what all I gone through in punishment."

There was a piercing scream from the woods, followed closely by a pistol 130
report. "Does it seem right to you, lady, that one is punished a heap and another
ain't punished at all?"

"Jesus!" the old lady cried. "You've got good blood! I know you wouldn't
shoot a lady! I know you come from nice people! Pray! Jesus, you ought not to
shoot a lady. I'll give you all the money I've got!"

"Lady," The Misfit said, looking beyond her far into the woods, "there never
was a body that give the undertaker a tip."

There were two more pistol reports and the grandmother raised her head like
a parched old turkey hen crying for water and called, "Bailey Boy, Bailey Boy!" as
if her heart would break.

"Jesus was the only One that ever raised the dead," The Misfit continued,
"and He shouldn't have done it. He thown everything off balance. If He did what
He said, then it's nothing for you to do but thow away everything and follow Him,
and if He didn't, then it's nothing for you to do but enjoy the few minutes you got
left the best you can—by killing somebody or burning down his house or doing
some other meanness to him. No pleasure but meanness," he said and his voice
had become almost a snarl.

"Maybe He didn't raise the dead," the old lady mumbled, not knowing what 135
she was saying and feeling so dizzy that she sank down in the ditch with her legs
twisted under her.

"I wasn't there so I can't say He didn't," The Misfit said. "I wisht I had of been
there," he said, hitting the ground with his fist. "It ain't right I wasn't there because

if I had of been there I would of known. Listen lady," he said in a high voice, "if I had of been there I would of known and I wouldn't be like I am now." His voice seemed about to crack and the grandmother's head cleared for an instant. She saw the man's face twisted close to her own as if he were going to cry and she murmured, "Why you're one of my babies. You're one of my own children!" She reached out and touched him on the shoulder. The Misfit sprang back as if a snake had bitten him and shot her three times through the chest. Then he put his gun down on the ground and took off his glasses and began to clean them.

Hiram and Bobby Lee returned from the woods and stood over the ditch, looking down at the grandmother who half sat and half lay in a puddle of blood with her legs crossed under her like a child's and her face smiling up at the cloudless sky.

Without his glasses, The Misfit's eyes were red-rimmed and pale and defenseless-looking. "Take her off and thow her where you thown the others," he said, picking up the cat that was rubbing itself against his leg.

"She was a talker, wasn't she?" Bobby Lee said, sliding down the ditch with a yodel.

"She would of been a good woman," The Misfit said, "if it had been some- 140 body there to shoot her every minute of her life."

"Some fun!" Bobby Lee said.

"Shut up, Bobby Lee," The Misfit said. "It's no real pleasure in life."   [1955]

THINKING ABOUT THE TEXT

1. Although this story begins with comedy, ultimately it shocks many readers. Did it shock you? Why, or why not? What would you say to someone who argues that the shift in tone is a flaw in the story?

2. Note places where the word *good* comes up in this story. How is it defined? Do the definitions change? Do you think the author has in mind a definition that does not occur to the characters? If so, what might that definition be?

3. What in his life history is The Misfit unsure about? Why do you think he is hazy about these matters? Should O'Connor have resolved for us all the issues of fact that bother him? Why, or why not?

4. Does The Misfit have any redeeming qualities? Does the grandmother? Explain. What do you think the grandmother means when she murmurs, "Why you're one of my babies. You're one of my own children!" (para. 136)? Why do you think The Misfit responds as he does?

5. There is much talk about Jesus and Christianity in this story. Should O'Connor have done more to help non-Christian readers see the story as relevant to them? Explain your reasoning.

FLANNERY O'CONNOR
From *Mystery and Manners*

For public presentations at colleges and other places, Flannery O'Connor often chose to read and comment on "A Good Man Is Hard to Find." The following remarks come from her introduction to the story when she read it at Hollins College in Virginia in 1963. After her death, the introduction was published as "On Her Own Work" in Mystery and Manners, *a 1969 collection of O'Connor's nonfiction pieces. Her comments on "A Good Man Is Hard to Find" encourage a religious analysis of it. How helpful, though, is her own interpretation? Many critics who have subsequently written about the story have raised and addressed this issue.*

It is true that the old lady is a hypocritical old soul; her wits are no match for the Misfit's, nor is her capacity for grace equal to his; yet I think the unprejudiced reader will feel that the Grandmother has a special kind of triumph in this story which instinctively we do not allow to someone altogether bad.

I often ask myself what makes a story work and what makes it hold up as a story, and I have decided that it is probably some action, some gesture of a character that is unlike any other in the story, one which indicates where the real heart of the story lies. This would have to be an action or a gesture which was both totally right and totally unexpected; it would have to be one that was both in character and beyond character; it would have to suggest both the world and eternity. The action or gesture I'm talking about would have to be on the anagogical level, that is, the level which has to do with the Divine life and our participation in it. It would be a gesture that transcended any neat allegory that might have been intended or any pat moral categories a reader could make. It would be a gesture which somehow made contact with mystery.

There is a point in this story where such a gesture occurs. The Grandmother is at last alone, facing the Misfit. Her head clears for an instant and she realizes, even in her limited way, that she is responsible for the man before her and joined to him by ties of kinship which have their roots deep in the mystery she has been merely prattling about so far. And at this point, she does the right thing, she makes the right gesture.

I find that students are often puzzled by what she says and does here, but I think myself that if I took out this gesture and what she says with it, I would have no story. What was left would not be worth your attention. Our age not only does not have a very sharp eye for the almost imperceptible intrusions of grace, it no longer has much feeling for the nature of the violences which precede and follow them. The devil's greatest wile, Baudelaire has said, is to convince us that he does not exist.

I suppose the reasons for the use of so much violence in modern fiction will   5
differ with each writer who uses it, but in my own stories I have found that violence is strangely capable of returning my characters to reality and preparing them to accept their moment of grace. Their heads are so hard that almost noth-

ing else will do the work. This idea, that reality is something to which we must be returned at considerable cost, is one which is seldom understood by the casual reader, but it is one which is implicit in the Christian view of the world.

I don't want to equate the Misfit with the devil. I prefer to think that, however unlikely this may seem, the old lady's gesture, like the mustard-seed, will grow to be a great crow-filled tree in the Misfit's heart and will be enough of a pain to him there to turn him into the prophet he was meant to become. But that's another story.

This story has been called grotesque, but I prefer to call it literal. A good story is literal in the same sense that a child's drawing is literal. When a child draws, he doesn't intend to distort but to set down exactly what he sees, and as his gaze is direct, he sees the lines that create motion. Now the lines of motion that interest the writer are usually invisible. They are lines of spiritual motion. And in this story you should be on the lookout for such things as the action of grace in the Grandmother's soul, and not for the dead bodies.   [1963]

MARTHA STEPHENS
From *The Question of Flannery O'Connor*

Martha Stephens is an emeritus professor of English and comparative literature at the University of Cincinnati. After Flannery O'Connor's religious explanation of "A Good Man Is Hard to Find" was published in the 1969 volume Mystery and Manners, *other readers of the story began responding to her comments. Stephens's 1973 book* The Question of Flannery O'Connor *includes one of the earliest attempts to gauge the helpfulness of O'Connor's analysis. Stephens is disturbed by the story's apparent shift of tone as it moves from farce to violent tragedy. O'Connor's remarks clarify this shift, Stephens thinks, but the religious doctrine reflected in them is severe.*

An ordinary and undistinguished family, a family even comical in its dullness, ill-naturedness, and triviality, sets out on a trip to Florida and on an ordinary summer day meets with a terrible fate. In what would the interest of such a story normally lie? Perhaps, one might think, in something that is revealed about the family in the way it meets its death, in some ironical or interesting truth about the nature of those people or those relationships — something we had been prepared unbeknownst to see, at the end plainly dramatized by their final common travail and death. But obviously, as regards the family as a whole, no such thing happens. The family is shown to be in death just as ordinary and ridiculous as before. With the possible exception of the grandmother, we know them no better; nothing about them of particular significance is brought forth.

The grandmother, being as we have seen the last to die, suffers the deaths of all her family while carrying on the intermittent conversation with the Misfit, and any reader will have some dim sense that it is through this encounter that the story is trying to transform and justify itself. One senses that this conversation — even though our attention is in reality fastened upon the horrible acts that are taking place in the background (and apparently against the thrust of the story) — is meant to be the real center of the story and the part in which the "point," as it were, of the whole tale lies.

But what is the burden of that queer conversation between the Misfit and the grandmother; what power does it have, even when we retrospectively sift and weigh it line by line, to transform our attitude towards the seemingly gratuitous — in terms of the art of the tale — horror of the massacre? The uninitiated reader will not, most likely, be able to unravel the strange complaint of the killer without some difficulty, but when we see the convict's peculiar dilemma in the context of O'Connor's whole work and what is known of her religious thought, it is not difficult to explain.

The Misfit's most intriguing statement — the line that seemingly the reader must ponder, set as it is as the final pronouncement on the grandmother after her death — is from the final passage quoted above: "She would of been a good woman if it had been somebody there to shoot her every minute of her life." Certainly we know from the first half of the story that the grandmother has seen herself as a good woman — and a good woman in a day when good men and women are hard to find, when people are disrespectful and dishonest, when they are not nice like they used to be. The grandmother is not common but a lady; and at the end of the story we know that she will be found dead just as we know she wanted to be — in the costume of a lady. She was not common, and the Misfit, with his "scholarly spectacles," his courtly apology for not wearing a shirt, his yes ma'ams and no ma'ams, was not common either — she had believed, wanted to believe, or pretended to believe. "Why I can see you come from good people," she said, "not common at all." Yet the Misfit says of her that she *would* have been a good woman if somebody had been there to shoot her all her life. And if we take the Misfit's statement as the right one about the grandmother, how was she a good woman in her death?

A good woman, perhaps we are given to believe, is one who understands the worthlessness and emptiness of being or not being a "lady," of having or not having Coca-Cola stock, of "being broad" and seeing the world, of good manners and genteel attire. "Woe to them," said Isaiah, "that are wise in their own eyes, and prudent in their own sight." The futility of all the grandmother's values, the story strives to encapsulate in this image of her disarray after the car has overturned and she has recognized the Misfit: "The grandmother reached up to adjust her hat brim as if she were going to the woods with him but it came off in her hand. She stood staring at it and after a second she let it fall on the ground."

The Misfit is a figure that seems, one must say to the story's credit, to have fascinated more readers than any other single O'Connor character, and it is by contrast with the tormented spiritual state of this seeming monster that the nature of the grandmother's futile values becomes evident. We learn that the center of the Misfit's thought has always been Jesus Christ, and what becomes clear as we study over the final scene is that the Misfit has, in the eyes of the author, the enormous distinction of having at least faced up to the problem of Christian belief.

And everything he has done—everything he so monstrously does here—proceeds from his inability to accept Christ, to truly believe. This is the speech which opens the narrow and emotionally difficult route into the meaning of the story:

> "Jesus was the only One that ever raised the dead," The Misfit continued, "and He shouldn't have done it. He thown everything off balance. If He did what He said, then it's nothing for you to do but thow away everything and follow Him, and if He didn't, then it's nothing for you to do but enjoy the few minutes you got left the best way you can—by killing somebody or burning down his house or doing some other meanness to him. No pleasure but meanness," he said and his voice had become almost a snarl.

The Misfit has chosen, at least, whom he would serve—has followed the injunction of the prophet in I Kings 18:21: "And Elijah came unto all the people, and said, How long halt ye between two opinions? if the Lord be God, follow him: but if Baal, then follow him." The crucial modern text for the authorial view here, which belongs to a tradition in religio-literary thought sometimes referred to as the sanctification of the sinner, is T. S. Eliot's essay on Baudelaire, in which he states: "So far as we are human, what we do must be either evil or good; so far as we do evil or good, we are human; and it is better, in a paradoxical way, to do evil than to do nothing; at least, we exist. It is true that the glory of man is his capacity for salvation; it is also true to say that his glory is his capacity for damnation."

Thus observe how, in the context of these statements, "A Good Man Is Hard to Find" begins to yield its meaning. What O'Connor has done is to take, in effect, Eliot's maxim—"It is better, in a paradoxical way, to do evil than to do nothing"—and to stretch our tolerance of this idea to its limits. The conclusion that one cannot avoid is that the story depends, for its final effect, on our being able to appreciate—even to be startled by, to be pleasurably struck with—the notion of the essential moral superiority of the Misfit over his victims, who have lived without choice or commitment of any kind, who have in effect not "lived" at all.

But again, in what sense is the grandmother a "good woman" in her death, as the Misfit claims? Here even exegesis falters. Because in her terror she calls on the name of Jesus, because she exhorts the Misfit to pray? Is she "good" because as the old lady sinks fainting into the ditch, after the Misfit's Jesus speech recorded above, she mumbles, "Maybe he didn't raise the dead"? Are we to see her as at last beginning to face the central question of human existence: did God send his son to save the world? Perhaps there is a clue in the dead grandmother's final image: she is said to half lie and half sit "in a puddle of blood with her legs crossed under her like a child's and her face smiling up at the cloudless sky." For Christ said, after all, that "whosoever shall not receive the kingdom of God as a little child shall in no wise enter herein."

To see that the Misfit is really the one courageous and admirable figure in the story; that the grandmother was perhaps—even as he said—a better woman in her death than she had ever been; to see that the pain of the other members of the family, that any godless pain or pleasure that human beings may experience is, beside the one great question of existence, *unimportant*—to see all these things is to enter fully into the experience of the story. Not to see them is to find oneself pitted not only against the forces that torture and destroy the wretched subjects of the story, but against the story itself and its attitude of indifference to and contempt for human pain.

Now as it happens, "A Good Man Is Hard to Find" was a favorite story of O'Connor's. It was the story she chose to read whenever she was asked to read from her work, and clearly it held a meaning for her that was particularly important. Whenever she read the story, she closed by reading a statement giving her own explanation of it. (One version of that statement can now be read in the collection of O'Connor's incidental prose edited by Robert and Sally Fitzgerald titled *Mystery and Manners*.) She had come to realize that it was a story that readers found difficult, and she said in her statement that she felt that the reason the story was misunderstood was that the present age "not only does not have a very sharp eye for the almost imperceptible intrusions of grace, it no longer has much feeling for the nature of the violences which precede and follow them." The intrusion of grace in "A Good Man Is Hard to Find" comes, Miss O'Connor said, in that much-discussed passage in which the grandmother, her head suddenly clearing for a moment, murmurs to the Misfit, "Why, you're one of my babies. You're one of my own children!" and is shot just as she reaches out to touch him. The grandmother's gesture here is what, according to O'Connor, makes the story work; it shows that the grandmother realizes that "she is responsible for the man before her and joined to him by ties of kinship which have their roots deep in the mystery she has been merely prattling about so far," and it affords the grandmother "a special kind of triumph . . . which we instinctively do not allow to someone altogether bad."

This explanation does solve, in a sense, one of the riddles of this odd story— although, of course, one must say that while it is interesting to know the intent of the author, speaking outside the story and after the fact, such knowledge does not change the fact that the intent of the narrator manifested strictly within the story is damagingly unclear on this important point. And what is even more important here is that O'Connor's statement about the story, taken as a whole, only further confirms the fact that the only problem in this tale is really a function of our difficulty with O'Connor's formidable doctrine. About the Misfit, O'Connor says that while he is not to be seen as the hero of the story, yet his capacity for grace is far greater than the grandmother's and that the author herself prefers to think "that the old lady's gesture, like the mustard-seed, will grow to be a great crow-filled tree in the Misfit's heart, and will be enough of a pain to him there to turn him into the prophet he was meant to become." The capacity for grace of the other members of the family is apparently zero, and hence—Christian grace in O'Connor, one cannot help noting, is rather an expensive process—it is proper that their deaths should have no spiritual context whatever.   [1973]

MADISON JONES
From "A Good Man's Predicament"

Now retired from the English department at Auburn University in Alabama, Madison Jones (b. 1925) is himself a writer of fiction, including several novels. He discussed O'Connor's story in the article "A Good Man's Predicament," published in a 1984 issue of the Southern Review. *Noting how O'Connor explains the story's climax, Jones proposes another interpretation of it, though he thinks his view is compatible with the author's.*

What has driven the Misfit to his homicidal condition is his powerful but frustrated instinct for meaning and justice. It may be inferred that this same instinct is what has produced his tormenting thoughts about Christ raising the dead, making justice where there is none. If only he could have been there when it happened, then he could have believed.

> "I wisht I could have been there," he said, hitting the ground with his fist. "It ain't right I wasn't there because if I had of been there I would of known. Listen lady," he said in a high voice, "if I had of been there I would have known and I wouldn't be like I am now."

It is torment to think of what might have been, that under other circumstances he would have been able to believe and so escape from the self he has become. In light of this it is possible to read the Misfit's obscure statement that Jesus "thowed everything off balance," as meaning this: that it would have been better, for the world's peace and his own, if no haunting doubt about the awful inevitability of man's condition ever had been introduced. In any case it could only be that doubt has made its contribution to the blighting of the Misfit's soul.

But doubts like this are not enough to alter the Misfit's vision. In the modern manner he believes what he can see with his eyes only, and his eyes have a terrible rigor. It is this rigor that puts him at such a distance from the grandmother who is one of the multitude "that live their whole life without asking about it," that spend their lives immersed in a world of platitudes which they have never once stopped to scrutinize. This, his distinction from the vulgarians whom the grandmother represents, his honesty, is the source of the Misfit's pride. It is why, when the grandmother calls him a "good" man, he answers: "Nome, I ain't a good man,". . ."but I ain't the worst in the world neither." And it is sufficient reason for the violent response that causes him so suddenly and unexpectedly to shoot the grandmother. Here is what happens, beginning with the grandmother's murmured words to the Misfit:

> "Why, you're one of my babies. You're one of my own children." She reached out and touched him on the shoulder. The Misfit sprang back as if a snake had bitten him and shot her three times through the chest.

Given the Misfit's image of himself, her words and her touching, blessing him, amount to intolerable insult, for hereby she includes him among the world's family of vulgarians. One of her children, her kind, indeed!

This reason for the Misfit's action is, I believe, quite sufficient to explain it, even though Flannery O'Connor, discussing the story in *Mystery and Manners*, implies a different explanation. The grandmother's words to the Misfit and her touching him, O'Connor says, are a gesture representing the intrusion of a moment of grace. So moved, the grandmother recognizes her responsibility for this man and the deep kinship between them. O'Connor goes on to say that perhaps in time to come the Misfit's memory of the grandmother's gesture will become painful enough to turn him into the prophet he was meant to be. Seen this way, through the author's eyes, we must infer an explanation other than my own for the Misfit's action. This explanation would envision the Misfit's sudden violence as caused by his dismayed recognition of the presence in the grandmother of a phenomenon impossible to reconcile with his own view of what is real. Thus the Misfit's act can be seen as a striking out in defense of a version of reality to whose logic he has so appallingly committed himself.

Faced with mutually exclusive interpretations of a fictional event, a reader must accept the evidence of the text in preference to the testimonial of the author. And where the text offers a realistic explanation as opposed to one based on the supernatural, a reader must find the former the more persuasive. *If* the two are in fact mutually exclusive. And *if*, of course, it is true that the acceptability of the author's explanation does in fact depend upon the reader's belief in the supernatural. As to this second condition, it is a measure of O'Connor's great gift that the story offers a collateral basis for understanding grace that is naturalistic in character. This grace may be spelled in lower case letters but the fictional consequence is the same. For sudden insight is quite within the purview of rationalistic psychology, provided only that there are intelligible grounds for it. And such grounds are present in the story. They are implicit in the logic that connects the grandmother and the Misfit, that makes of the Misfit "one of my own children." In the hysteria caused by the imminence of her death, which strips her of those banalities by which she has lived, the grandmother quite believably discovers this connection. And so with the terms of the Misfit's sudden violence. His own tormenting doubt, figured in those preceding moments when he cries out and hits the ground, has prepared him. Supernatural grace or not, the Misfit in this moment sees it as such, and strikes.

These two, the author's and my own, are quite different explanations of the Misfit's sudden violence. Either, I believe, is reasonable, though surely the nod should go to the one that more enriches the story's theme. *If* the two are mutually exclusive. I believe, however, that they are not. Such a mixture of motives, in which self-doubt and offended pride both participate, should put no strain on the reader's imagination. And seen together each one may give additional dimension to the story.   [1984]

5

STEPHEN BANDY

From "'One of My Babies':
The Misfit and the Grandmother"

In an article published in a 1996 issue of Studies in Short Fiction, *Stephen Bandy strongly disagrees with O'Connor's interpretation of "A Good Man Is Hard to Find." In particular, he thinks that the grandmother is sentimental and vindictive, whereas O'Connor is sympathetic to the character and believes that she manifests grace. Following are excerpts from Bandy's analysis.*

Grasping at any appeal, and hardly aware of what she is saying, the Grandmother declares to the Misfit: "Why you're one of my babies. You're one of my own children!" As she utters these shocking words, "She reached out and touched him on the shoulder. The Misfit sprang back as if a snake had bitten him and shot her three times through the chest" (p. 1391).

Noting that some squeamish readers had found this ending too strong, O'Connor defended the scene in this way: "If I took out this gesture and what she says with it, I would have no story. What was left would not be worth your attention" (*Mystery and Manners* 112).[1] Certainly the scene is crucial to the story, and most readers, I think, grant its dramatic "rightness" as a conclusion. What is arguable is the meaning to the Grandmother's final words to the Misfit, as well as her "gesture," which seemed equally important to O'Connor. One's interpretation depends on one's opinion of the Grandmother.

What *are* we to think of this woman? At the story's beginning, she seems a harmless busybody, utterly self-absorbed but also amusing, in her way. And, in her way, she provides a sort of human Rorschach test of her readers. We readily forgive her so much, including her mindless racism — she points at the "cute little pickaninny" by the roadside, and entertains her grandchildren with a story in which a watermelon is devoured by "a nigger boy." She is filled with the prejudices of her class and her time. And so, some readers conclude, she is in spite of it all a "good" person. Somewhat more ominously, the Misfit — after he has fired three bullets into her chest — pronounces that she might have been "a good woman . . . if it had been somebody there to shoot her every minute of her life" (p. 1391). We surmise that in the universe of this story, the quality of what is "good" (which is after all the key word of the story's title) depends greatly on who is using the term. I do not think the Misfit is capable of irony — he truly means what he says about her, even though he finds it necessary to kill her. Indeed, the opposing categories of "good" and "evil" are very much in the air throughout this story. But like most supposed opposites, they have an alarming tendency to merge. It is probably worth noting that the second line of the once-popular song that gave O'Connor her title is "You always get the other kind."

[1] Flannery O'Connor, *Mystery and Manners: Occasional Prose, Selected and Edited by Sally and Robert Fitzgerald* (New York: Farrar, Straus, and Giroux, 1969).

Much criticism of the story appears to take a sentimental view of the Grand-mother largely because she *is* a grandmother. Flannery O'Connor herself, as we shall see shortly, found little to blame in this woman, choosing to wrap her in the comfortable mantle of elderly Southern womanhood. O'Connor applies this generalization so uncritically that we half suspect she is pulling our leg. In any case, we can be sure that such sentimentality (in the mind of either the writer or her character) is fatal to clear thinking. If the Grandmother is old (although she does not seem to be *that* old), grey-haired, and "respectable," it follows that she must be weak, gentle, and benevolent—precisely the Grandmother's opinion of herself, and she is not shy of letting others know it. Intentionally or not, O'Connor has etched the Grandmother's character with wicked irony, which makes it all the more surprising to read the author's response to a frustrated teacher whose (Southern) students persisted in favoring the Grandmother, despite his strenuous efforts to point out her flaws. O'Connor said,

> I had to tell him that they resisted . . . because they all had grandmothers or great-aunts just like her at home, and they knew, from personal experience, that the old lady lacked comprehension, but that she had a good heart.

O'Connor continued,

> The Southerner is usually tolerant of those weaknesses that proceed from innocence, and he knows that a taste for self-preservation can be readily combined with the missionary spirit. (*Mystery and Manners* 110)

What is most disappointing in this moral summary of the Grandmother, and her ilk, is its disservice to the spiky, vindictive woman of the story. There may be a purpose to O'Connor's betrayal of her own character: her phrase "missionary spirit" gives the game away. O'Connor is determined that the Grandmother shall be the Misfit's savior, even though she may not seem so in the story. 5

The Grandmother's role as grace-bringer is by now a received idea, largely because the author said it is so. But one must question the propriety of such tinkering with the character, after the fact. It reduces the fire-breathing woman who animates this story to nothing much more than a cranky maiden aunt. On the contrary, the Grandmother is a fierce fighter, never more so than in her final moments, nose-to-nose with the Misfit.

Granted, the Grandmother is not a homicidal monster like the Misfit, and she certainly does not deserve to die for her minor sins. And yet, does she quite earn absolution from any moral weakness beyond that of "a hypocritical old soul" (111)? For every reader who sees the image of his or her own grandmother printed on this character's cold face, as O'Connor suggested we might do, there are surely many others who can only be appalled by a calculating opportunist who is capable of embracing her family's murderer, to save her own skin. Where indeed is the "good heart" which unites this unprincipled woman with all those "grandmothers or great-aunts just like her at home"? The answer to that question can only be an affirmation of the "banality of evil," to use Hannah Arendt's well-known phrase. . . .

What does in fact happen in this part of the story is quite straightforward: the Grandmother, having exhausted all other appeals to the Misfit, resorts to her only remaining (though certainly imperfect) weapon: motherhood. Declaring to the Misfit that he is one of her babies, she sets out to conquer him. Perhaps she hopes that this ultimate flattery will melt his heart, and he will collapse in her comforting motherly embrace. Such are the stratagems of sentimentality. The moral shoddiness of her action is almost beyond description. If we had not already guessed the depths to which the Grandmother might sink, now we know. It is not easy to say who is the more evil, the Misfit or the Grandmother, and indeed that is the point. Her behavior is the manifest of her character.

It has been said that no action is without its redeeming aspect. Could this unspeakable act of selfishness carry within it the seeds of grace, acting, as it were, above the Grandmother? So Flannery O'Connor believed. But what is the precise movement of grace in this scene? It is surely straining the text to propose that the Grandmother has in this moment "seen the light." Are we to regard her as the unwitting agent of divine grace whose selfish intentions are somehow transfigured into a blessing? Such seems to have been O'Connor's opinion:

> . . . however unlikely this may seem, the old lady's gesture, like the mustard-seed, will grow to be a great crow-filled tree in the Misfit's heart, and will be enough of a pain to him there to turn him into the prophet he was meant to become. (*Mystery and Manners* 113)

We are almost persuaded to forget that none of this happens in the story itself. If this can be so, then we can just as easily attribute any interpretation we like to the scene. But in fact he is in no way changed. There is no "later on" in fiction. We do not, and will not, see "created grace" in the spirit of the Misfit.

But more important, this is not the way grace works. As we read in the *New Catholic Encyclopedia*:

> . . . the spiritual creature must respond to this divine self-donation freely. Hence, the doctrine of grace supposes a creature already constituted in its own being in such wise that it has the possibility of entering into a free and personal relationship with the Divine Persons or of rejecting that relationship. (6: 661)

If grace was extended to the Misfit, he refused it and that is the end. There can be no crow-filled tree, nor can there be the "lines of spiritual motion" leading to that tree, however attractive the image may be. Prudently, O'Connor added, "But that's another story" (*Mystery and Manners* 113).   [1996]

MAKING COMPARISONS

1. Stephens believes that her interpretation of "A Good Man Is Hard to Find" is compatible with O'Connor's. Do you accept both? Why, or why not?

2. Jones and Bandy suggest that you should not rely completely on O'Connor's explanation of her story. Do they succeed in making you question the author's account? In general, do you think readers should accept an author's interpretation of his or her own work? Explain your reasoning.

3. All of these commentaries on the story focus on religious aspects of it, though not all of them agree on how much of a role, and what kind of a

role, religion plays in it. Are you similarly inclined to put the story in a religious framework? Why, or why not?

WRITING ABOUT ISSUES

1. The Misfit says that the grandmother "would of been a good woman . . . if it had been somebody there to shoot her every minute of her life" (para. 140). Write an essay in which you argue for your own understanding of this claim. Is The Misfit right or just cruel? How should we define *good* in this context?

2. Choose one of the interpretations featured in this cluster, and write an essay in which you imagine how O'Connor would respond to its points. Feel free to express and support your own views, too.

3. The man in O'Connor's story calls himself The Misfit "because I can't make what all I done wrong fit what all I gone through in punishment" (para. 129). But plainly he is also a misfit in the sense that he has become alienated from society. Write an essay recalling someone you knew who seemed to be a misfit in this sense. More specifically, speculate on and try to describe this person's own perspective — what the person believed, how the person viewed the world, why he or she acted in certain ways. If you wish, your essay can be in the form of a letter to this person.

4. O'Connor promoted her version of Christianity in "A Good Man Is Hard to Find" and in her commentary on the story. On the basis of both texts, list various principles and concepts that she associates with her religion. Then do research on another religion, perhaps by reading two or three articles on it. Write an essay in which you compare O'Connor's theology with the religion you have researched. If you wish, you can focus your comparison by imagining what adherents to the other religion would say about "A Good Man Is Hard to Find."

A WEB ASSIGNMENT

Perhaps you make negative associations with the word *misfit*, especially after reading O'Connor's story. But plenty of people have proudly claimed this label and, furthermore, garnered lots of admirers. A contemporary example is The Misfits, a rock band celebrated on many Web sites. At the *Making Literature Matter* Web site, you will find a link to a site that features The Misfits' lyrics as well as cover art for their albums. After exploring this site, write an essay in which you compare O'Connor's Misfit with the band members' representations of themselves. You might examine, for instance, whether the band is affiliating with some sort of religion, just as O'Connor's character thinks about Christianity even as he continues to be troubled by it.

Visit www.bedfordstmartins.com/makinglitmatter

SUPERNATURAL JUSTICE:
RE-VISIONS OF "THE DEMON LOVER"

ANONYMOUS, "The Demon Lover"
ELIZABETH BOWEN, "The Demon Lover"

Much of humanity refuses to concede that death is final. Several religions believe in resurrection, reincarnation, or the possibility of communicating with ancestors, and quite a few people argue for the existence of ghosts. Moreover, someone who doubts that the dead truly return may still enjoy films, television shows, and works of literature in which they do come back. In part, their popularity derives from their sensationalism; their audiences love the sheer excitement of seeing a dead person revive. But many examples of the genre are also thought-provoking as they explore relations between the dead and the living. In fact, *Hamlet* and other plays by Shakespeare use ghosts to raise issues of justice in the earthly world. *Hamlet* is just one instance of a whole set of works about supernatural justice, in which a dead person returns to demand that mortals obey his or her notion of moral law. Popular for centuries has been another story in this vein, "The Demon Lover." We present this tale in one of its ancient ballad versions and then invite you to compare it with a twentieth-century version by Elizabeth Bowen.

BEFORE YOU READ

Recall an example of a supernatural justice story that you are familiar with — that is, a film, television show, or literary text in which a dead person returns to correct wrongdoing among the living. Does this work have psychological or philosophical substance? Or does it simply try to elicit certain sensations? How much do you sympathize with the dead person? What is your overall reaction to this work? Identify things that influence your response to it.

ANONYMOUS
The Demon Lover

"The Demon Lover" (also called "James Harris") is a well-known example of the centuries-old Scottish ballad tradition. Ballads are verse narratives that were orally transmitted long before they were recorded in print. Their authors are unknown; indeed, probably all of them were shaped and altered in the telling. Like many other works in the genre, "The Demon Lover" features stanzas of four lines each, repeats several words, includes question-and-answer exchanges, plunges right into the action, and packs it with supernatural events. This poem exists in multiple versions; the one we present was recited by Walter Grieve, transcribed by William Laidlaw, and published in the fifth (1812) edition of a book entitled Minstrelsy of the Scottish Border.

(Elizabeth Bowen. Courtesy of Knopf Publishers Inc.)

"O where have you been, my long, long love,
    This long seven years and mair?"
"O I'm come to seek my former vows
    Ye graunted me before."

"O hold your tongue of your former vows,   5
    For they will breed sad strife:
O hold your tongue of your former vows,
    For I am become a wife."

He turned him right and round about,
    And the tear blinded his ee: 10
"I wad never hae trodden on Irish ground,
    If it had not been for thee.

"I might hae had a king's daughter,
    Far, far beyond the sea;

I might have had a king's daughter,   15
      Had it not been for love o thee."

"If ye might have had a king's daughter,
      Yer sel ye had to blame;
Ye might have taken the king's daughter,
      For ye kend that I was nane.   20

"If I was to leave my husband dear,
      And my two babes also,
O what have you to take me to,
      If with you I should go?"

"I hae seven ships upon the sea —   25
      The eighth brought me to land —
With four-and-twenty bold mariners,
      And music on every hand."

She has taken up her two little babes,
      Kissd them baith cheek and chin: 30
"O fair ye weel, my ain two babes,
      For I'll never see you again."

She set her foot upon the ship,
      No mariners could she behold;
But the sails were o the taffetie,   35
      And the masts of the beaten gold.

She had not sailed a league, a league,
      A league but barely three,
When dismal grew his countenance
      And drumlie° grew his ee.   40

They had not sailed a league, a league,
      A league but barely three,
Until she espied his cloven foot,
      And she wept right bitterlie.

"O hold your tongue of your weeping," says he,   45
      "Of your weeping now let me be;
I will show you how the lilies grow
      On the banks of Italy.

"O what hills are yon, yon pleasant hills,
      That the sun shines sweetly on?"   50
"O yon are the hills of heaven," he said,
      "Where you will never win."

40 drumlie: Gloomy.

"O whaten a mountain is yon," she said,
    "All so dreary wi frost and snow?"
"O yon is the mountain of hell," he cried,   55
    "Where you and I will go."

He strack the tap-mast wi his hand,
    The fore-mast wi his knee,
And he brake that gallant ship in twain,
    And sank her in the sea.   [1812]   60

THINKING ABOUT THE TEXT

1. What ideas expressed directly or indirectly in the poem may have contributed to its popularity?
2. Why, evidently, did the woman board the demon lover's ship?
3. Do you sympathize with either of the two characters? Why, or why not?
4. Identify specific instances of repetition. What is their effect?
5. What, for you, are the strengths and limitations of the ballad form?

ELIZABETH BOWEN
The Demon Lover

Elizabeth Bowen (1899–1973) was born in Dublin and educated in England. She was the author of many novels, essays, and short stories, including several tales of the supernatural. The following story is Bowen's adaptation of the centuries-old ballad also entitled "The Demon Lover." Bowen wrote her version in 1941 during the period known as the Blitz. Nazi bombers were regularly attacking London, prompting many of its citizens to seek refuge elsewhere in England or in other countries. Bowen's character Mrs. Drover, having fled with her family to the English countryside, is now returning to her London house merely for the day—or so she thinks.

Towards the end of her day in London Mrs. Drover went round to her shut-up house to look for several things she wanted to take away. Some belonged to herself, some to her family, who were by now used to their country life. It was late August; it had been a steamy, showery day: at the moment the trees down the pavement glittered in an escape of humid yellow afternoon sun. Against the next batch of clouds, already piling up ink-dark, broken chimneys and parapets stood out. In her once familiar street, as in any unused channel, an unfamiliar queerness had silted up; a cat wove itself in and out of railings, but no human eye watched Mrs. Drover's return. Shifting some parcels under her arm, she slowly forced round her latchkey in an unwilling lock, then gave the door, which had warped, a push with her knee. Dead air came out to meet her as she went in.

The staircase window having been boarded up, no light came down into the hall. But one door, she could just see, stood ajar, so she went quickly through into the room and unshuttered the big window in there. Now the prosaic woman, looking about her, was more perplexed than she knew by everything that she saw, by traces of her long former habit of life — the yellow smoke-stain up the white marble mantelpiece, the ring left by a vase on the top of the escritoire; the bruise in the wallpaper where, on the door being thrown open widely, the china handle had always hit the wall. The piano, having gone away to be stored, had left what looked like claw-marks on its part of the parquet. Though not much dust had seeped in, each object wore a film of another kind; and, the only ventilation being the chimney, the whole drawing-room smelled of the cold hearth. Mrs. Drover put down her parcels on the escritoire and left the room to proceed upstairs; the things she wanted were in a bedroom chest.

She had been anxious to see how the house was — the part-time caretaker she shared with some neighbours was away this week on his holiday, known to be not yet back. At the best of times he did not look in often, and she was never sure that she trusted him. There were some cracks in the structure, left by the last bombing, on which she was anxious to keep an eye. Not that one could do anything —

A shaft of refracted daylight now lay across the hall. She stopped dead and stared at the hall table — on this lay a letter addressed to her.

She thought first — then the caretaker *must* be back. All the same, who, seeing the house shuttered, would have dropped a letter in at the box? It was not a circular, it was not a bill. And the post office redirected, to the address in the country, everything for her that came through the post. The caretaker (even if he *were* back) did not know she was due in London today — her call here had been planned to be a surprise — so his negligence in the manner of this letter, leaving it to wait in the dusk and the dust, annoyed her. Annoyed, she picked up the letter, which bore no stamp. But it cannot be important, or they would know . . . She took the letter rapidly upstairs with her, without a stop to look at the writing till she reached what had been her bedroom, where she let in light. The room looked over the garden and other gardens: the sun had gone in; as the clouds sharpened and lowered, the trees and rank lawns seemed already to smoke with dark. Her reluctance to look again at the letter came from the fact that she felt intruded upon — and by someone contemptuous of her ways. However, in the tenseness preceding the fall of rain she read it: it was a few lines.

> Dear Kathleen: You will not have forgotten that today is our anniversary, and the day we said. The years have gone by at once slowly and fast. In view of the fact that nothing has changed, I shall rely upon you to keep your promise. I was sorry to see you leave London, but was satisfied that you would be back in time. You may expect me, therefore, at the hour arranged.
> Until then . . .   K.

Mrs. Drover looked for the date: it was today's. She dropped the letter on to the bed-springs, then picked it up to see the writing again — her lips, beneath the remains of lipstick, beginning to go white. She felt so much the change in her own face that she went to the mirror, polished a clear patch in it and looked at once urgently and stealthily in. She was confronted by a woman of forty-four, with eyes starting out under a hat-brim that had been rather carelessly pulled down. She had not put on any more powder since she left the shop where she ate her solitary tea. The pearls her husband had given her on their marriage hung loose round her now rather thinner throat, slipping in the V of the pink wool jumper her sister knitted last autumn as they sat round the fire. Mrs. Drover's most normal expression was one of controlled worry, but of assent. Since the birth of the third of her little boys, attended by a quite serious illness, she had had an intermittent muscular flicker to the left of her mouth, but in spite of this she could always sustain a manner that was at once energetic and calm.

Turning from her own face as precipitately as she had gone to meet it, she went to the chest where the things were, unlocked it, threw up the lid and knelt to search. But as rain began to come crashing down she could not keep from looking over her shoulder at the stripped bed on which the letter lay. Behind the blanket of rain the clock of the church that still stood struck six—with rapidly heightening apprehension she counted each of the slow strokes. "The hour arranged . . . My God," she said, "*what* hour? How should I . . . ? After twenty-five years . . ."

The young girl talking to the soldier in the garden had not ever completely seen his face. It was dark; they were saying goodbye under a tree. Now and then—for it felt, from not seeing him at this intense moment, as though she had never seen him at all—she verified his presence for these few moments longer by putting out a hand, which he each time pressed, without very much kindness, and painfully, on to one of the breast buttons of his uniform. That cut of the button on the palm of her hand was, principally what she was to carry away. This was so near the end of a leave from France that she could only wish him already gone. It was August 1916. Being not kissed, being drawn away from and looked at intimidated Kathleen till she imagined spectral glitters in the place of his eyes. Turning away and looking back up the lawn she saw, through branches of trees, the drawing-room window alight: she caught a breath for the moment when she could go running back there into the safe arms of her mother and sister, and cry: "What shall I do, what shall I do? He has gone."

Hearing her catch her breath, her fiancé said, without feeling: "Cold?"

"You're going away such a long way."

"Not so far as you think."   10

"I don't understand?"

"You don't have to," he said. "You will. You know what we said."

"But that was—suppose you—I mean, suppose."

"I shall be with you," he said, "sooner or later. You won't forget that. You need do nothing but wait."

Only a little more than a minute later she was free to run up the silent lawn.   15
Looking in through the window at her mother and sister, who did not for the moment perceive her, she already felt that unnatural promise drive down between her and the rest of all human kind. No other way of having given herself could have made her feel so apart, lost and foresworn. She could not have plighted a more sinister troth.

Kathleen behaved well when, some months later, her fiancé was reported missing, presumed killed. Her family not only supported her but were able to praise her courage without stint because they could not regret, as a husband for her, the man they knew almost nothing about. They hoped she would, in a year or two, console herself—and had it been only a question of consolation things might have gone much straighter ahead. But her trouble, behind just a little grief, was a complete dislocation from everything. She did not reject other lovers, for these failed to appear: for years she failed to attract men—and with the approach of her 'thirties she became natural enough to share her family's anxiousness on this score. She began to put herself out, to wonder; and at thirty-two she was very greatly relieved to find herself being courted by William Drover. She married him, and the two of them settled down in this quiet, arboreal part of Kensington: in this house the years piled up, her children were born and they all lived till they were driven out by the bombs of the next war. Her movements as Mrs. Drover were circumscribed, and she dismissed any idea that they were still watched.

As things were—dead or living the letter-writer sent her only a threat. Unable, for some minutes, to go on kneeling with her back exposed to the empty room, Mrs. Drover rose from the chest to sit on an upright chair whose back was firmly against the wall. The desuetude of her former bedroom, her married London home's whole air of being a cracked cup from which memory, with its reassuring power, had either evaporated or leaked away, made a crisis—and at just this crisis the letter-writer had, knowledgeably, struck. The hollowness of the house this evening cancelled years on years of voices, habits and steps. Through the shut windows she only heard rain fall on the roofs around. To rally herself, she said she was in a mood—and for two or three seconds shutting her eyes, told herself that she had imagined the letter. But she opened them—there it lay on the bed.

On the supernatural side of the letter's entrance she was not permitting her mind to dwell. Who, in London, knew she meant to call at the house today? Evidently, however, this had been known. The caretaker, *had* he come back, had had no cause to expect her: he would have taken the letter in his pocket, to forward it, at his own time, through the post. There was no other sign that the caretaker had been in—but, if not? Letters dropped in at doors of deserted houses do not fly or walk to tables in halls. They do not sit on the dust of empty tables with the air of certainty that they will be found. There is needed some human hand— but nobody but the caretaker had a key. Under circumstances she did not care to consider, a house can be entered without a key. It was possible that she was not alone now. She might be being waited for, downstairs. Waited for—until when? Until "the hour arranged." At least that was not six o'clock: six has struck.

She rose from the chair and went over and locked the door.

The thing was, to get out. To fly? No, not that: she had to catch her train. As a woman whose utter dependability was the keystone of her family life she was not willing to return to the country, to her husband, her little boys and her sister, without the objects she had come up to fetch. Resuming work at the chest she set about making up a number of parcels in a rapid, fumbling-decisive way. These, with her shopping parcels, would be too much to carry; these meant a taxi—at

20

the thought of the taxi her heart went up and her normal breathing resumed. I will ring up the taxi now; the taxi cannot come too soon: I shall hear the taxi out there running its engine, till I walk calmly down to it through the hall. I'll ring up — But no: the telephone is cut off . . . She tugged at a knot she had tied wrong.

The idea of flight . . . He was never kind to me, not really. I don't remember him kind at all. Mother said he never considered me. He was set on me, that was what it was — not love. Not love, not meaning a person well. What did he do, to make me promise like that? I can't remember — But she found that she could.

She remembered with such dreadful acuteness that the twenty-five years since then dissolved like smoke and she instinctively looked for the weal left by the button on the palm of her hand. She remembered not only all that he said and did but the complete suspension of *her* existence during that August week. I was not myself — they all told me so at the time. She remembered — but with one white burning blank as where acid has dropped on a photograph: *under no conditions* could she remember his face.

So, wherever he may be waiting, I shall not know him. You have no time to run from a face you do not expect.

The thing was to get to the taxi before any clock struck what could be the hour. She would slip down the street and round the side of the square to where the square gave on the main road. She would return in the taxi, safe, to her own door, and bring the solid driver into the house with her to pick up the parcels from room to room. The idea of the taxi driver made her decisive, bold: she unlocked her door, went to the top of the staircase and listened down.

She heard nothing — but while she was hearing nothing the *passé* air of the staircase was disturbed by a draught that travelled up to her face. It emanated from the basement: down there a door or window was being opened by someone who chose this moment to leave the house. 25

The rain had stopped; the pavements steamily shone as Mrs. Drover let herself out by inches from her own front door into the empty street. The unoccupied houses opposite continued to meet her look with their damaged stare. Making towards the thoroughfare and the taxi, she tried not to keep looking behind. Indeed, the silence was so intense — one of those creeks of London silence exaggerated this summer by the damage of war — that no tread could have gained on hers unheard. Where her street debouched on the square where people went on living, she grew conscious of, and checked, her unnatural pace. Across the open end of the square two buses impassively passed each other: women, a perambulator, cyclists, a man wheeling a barrow signalized, once again, the ordinary flow of life. At the square's most populous corner should be — and was — the short taxi rank. This evening, only one taxi — but this, although it presented its blank rump, appeared already to be alertly waiting for her. Indeed, without looking round the driver started his engine as she panted up from behind and put her hand on the door. As she did so, the clock struck seven. The taxi faced the main road: to make the trip back to her house it would have to turn — she had settled back on the seat and the taxi *had* turned before she, surprised by its knowing movement, recollected that she had not "said where." She leaned forward to scratch at the glass panel that divided the driver's head from her own.

The driver braked to what was almost a stop, turned round, and slid the glass panel back: the jolt of this flung Mrs. Drover forward till her face was almost into the glass. Through the aperture driver and passenger, not six inches between them, remained for an eternity eye to eye. Mrs. Drover's mouth hung open for some seconds before she could issue her first scream. After that she continued to scream freely and to beat with her gloved hands on the glass all round as the taxi, accelerating without mercy, made off with her into the hinterland of deserted streets.   [1941]

THINKING ABOUT THE TEXT

1. What specific features of this story promote horror?
2. Here is an issue of fact: What do you feel able to say about the demon lover as he was when Mrs. Drover first knew him?
3. Why conceivably is Mrs. Drover having this experience now, after many years of *not* encountering her former fiancé? Do you sympathize with her as she goes through this experience? Why, or why not?
4. Why do you think Bowen includes the scene of Mrs. Drover looking at herself in the mirror?
5. At the end of the story, Bowen doesn't really describe the driver. Should she have done so? Why, or why not?

MAKING COMPARISONS

1. What elements does Bowen's story share with the ballad version of "The Demon Lover" you have read?
2. Unlike the ballad version, Bowen sets the story in a particular place (London) and a particular time period (the Blitz, which was occurring as she wrote). What difference, if any, does this specificity make?
3. In Bowen's story, the demon lover is not as much a physical presence as he is in the ballad version. What is the effect of this difference?

WRITING ABOUT ISSUES

1. Choose the ballad version of "The Demon Lover" or Bowen's story, and then write an essay in which you identify your chosen text's strategies for creating suspense. Organize your essay by ranking these strategies, moving from least to most significant.
2. To what extent, and in what ways, is Bowen's story a realistic re-vision of the ballad? Write an essay answering this question, making sure to explain what you mean by *realistic*.
3. Think of a person whom you have not seen in years but who continues to haunt you. (This may be someone whom you barely knew in the first place.) Then write an essay analyzing your continuing attachment to this

person. The essay can take the form of a letter to him or her. If you wish, refer to either of the texts in this cluster.

4. Write an essay in which you show how a film or TV show you have seen has significant "Demon Lover" elements. Refer to one or both of the texts in this cluster.

A WEB ASSIGNMENT

Several urban legends are modern-day counterparts of vengeful lover stories such as "The Demon Lover." Visit the *Making Literature Matter* Web site and follow its link to a wonderful repository of urban legends accompanied by analysis. At this archive, you will find urban legends grouped with various categories. If you click Love or Sex, you will find a subcategory of tales about vengeful lovers. Choose one of these tales, and write an essay in which you identify the extent to which it is indeed similar to the "Demon Lover" ballad or Bowen's story.

Visit www.bedfordstmartins.com/makinglitmatter

16

Confronting Mortality

> To every thing there is a season, and a time to every purpose under the heaven; a time to be born, and a time to die.
> — Ecclesiastes

> Death destroys a man. The idea of death saves him.
> — E. M. Forster

> In becoming forcibly and essentially aware of my mortality, and of what I wished and wanted for my life, however short it might be, priorities and omissions became strongly etched in a merciless light, and what I most regretted were my silences. Of what had I *ever* been afraid?
> — Audre Lorde

> When I was young, I admired clever people. As I grew old, I came to admire kind people.
> — Abraham Joshua Heschel

> Every loss recapitulates earlier losses, but every reaffirmation of identity echoes earlier moments of clarity.
> — Mary Catherine Bateson

> Nothing is absolutely dead. Every meaning will have its homecoming festival.
> — Mikhail Bakhtin

Much literature deals with human hopes and desires. But just as often, literature depicts constraints on them. Among other things, it portrays the human body as vulnerable, aging, destined to die. Perhaps the most interesting and significant works of literature are those that examine how people try to live meaningfully despite their mortality. Whether or not readers believe in an afterlife, literature offers stirring accounts of humans struggling with earthly limits.

Not every writer of literature views mortality as bad. Many suggest that be-cause people know they will die, they are more apt to value their time on earth, whereas they might waste it if they expected it to last forever. For each of the writers in this chapter, death is at least worth serious attention. After all, it is a part of life.

We begin with a cluster of poems (p. 1415) by John Keats, Gerard Manley Hopkins, A. E. Houseman, and Robin Becker that focus on the passage of time, which leads many of us to contemplate our mortality. Next, a pair of short stories (p. 1424) by Tim O'Brien and Jameson Currier show particular communities of men working to survive in the face of mortal danger. O'Brien's characters are fighting in the Vietnam War; Currier's are threatened by AIDS. The third cluster (p. 1448) features poems about death by Emily Dickinson, who is well known for her many imaginative and thought-provoking death scenes. Because she wrote about death so much, you may think Dickinson was obsessed with the subject, but each of these poems takes a fresh angle.

The death of a stranger can move people to reflect on mortality in the stories comprising the fourth cluster (p. 1454). Katherine Mansfield depicts a girl con-fronting the body of a dead laborer after a joyous garden party; Gabriel García Márquez details a group of villagers' fascination with an anonymous corpse; and Don DeLillo presents a man similarly fascinated with a killing he sees on video-tape. Of course, when people do think about death, a wide variety of positions is available for them to take. In the next cluster (p. 1475), poets John Donne, Dylan Thomas, and Wislawa Szymborska all express scorn toward it. In the trio of essays that follow (p. 1481), George Orwell, Annie Dillard, and Bruce Weigl reflect on the social differences that can affect how people view the act of killing an animal. The seventh cluster (p. 1496) features Marsha Norman's play *'night, Mother*, in which a woman seeks to kill herself while her mother tries to prevent her from doing so. Americans are increasingly debating whether suicide is ever appropriate; to help you consider Norman's handling of this issue, we include three commentaries on her play.

Next come two clusters that put entire lives in perspective. The first (p. 1535) consists of works in which the speaker reviews the life of another person — here, Richard Cory. We present Edwin Arlington Robinson's famous poem about him and then invite you to compare Robinson's text with Paul Simon's and W. D. Snodgrass's variations on it. In the second (p. 1542), poems by Percy Bysshe Shelley, Stevie Smith, and Carl Dennis will help you think about dif-ferent ways in which people might review their own existence.

In the story that is the focus of our next cluster (p. 1547), Bharati Mukher-jee's "The Management of Grief," the heroine Shaila must learn to live with the fact that her husband and sons will never return to her. Along with other mem-bers of her Indian Canadian community, they have perished in an airplane crash over the Irish Sea. We include Mukherjee's story because it illustrates the cul-tural negotiations that often occur with such disasters. As Shaila attempts to come to terms with her loss, she finds herself dealing with native Canadians, Indian immigrants to Canada, her parents in India, and even authorities in Ireland, where she goes in an effort to recover her family's bodies. Although the story is a work of fiction, Mukherjee based it on the real-life crash of an Air India flight in

1985. With her husband Clark Blaise, she has written a book about that actual event, and we include their chapter on the trip to Ireland made by relatives of the victims. Also, we present a 2001 newspaper article about the Air India case; it reports the arrest of alleged perpetrators and recalls how Mukherjee and Blaise had interviewed one of these men for their book. To conclude the cluster, we present a 1996 opinion piece that brings up the cultural context of disaster. In it, author Sam Husseini criticizes airlines suspicious of passengers who belong to particular ethnic groups.

The chapter's final cluster (p. 1577) deals with another real-life disaster, the September 11, 2001, attacks on the World Trade Center and the Pentagon. Struggling to cope with this tragedy, people were especially drawn to certain poems, which they exchanged personally and also circulated on the Internet. We present three of these — William Butler Yeats's "The Second Coming," W. H. Auden's "September 1, 1939," and Adam Zagajewski's "Try to Praise the Mutilated World." The new popularity of these texts proved once again that literature can indeed matter.

THE PASSAGE OF TIME

JOHN KEATS, "Ode on a Grecian Urn"
GERARD MANLEY HOPKINS, "Spring and Fall"
A. E. HOUSMAN, "Loveliest of trees, the cherry now"
ROBIN BECKER, "The Star Show"

People often forget about their mortality until an experience reminds them that their life is moving on. The passage of time is, however, one of literature's recurring concerns. Here we feature poems on this topic by a contemporary American, Robin Becker, and three British writers from earlier eras — John Keats, Gerard Manley Hopkins, and A. E. Housman. Keats's poem "Ode on a Grecian Urn" ponders how the urn's images seem frozen in time, indirectly reminding readers that, by contrast, flesh-and-blood humans age. To dramatize this process of change, the other three poets juxtapose youth with later life. Hopkins's speaker tells a girl that she will get older, Housman's speaker revels in the beauty of nature while aware that his own life will eventually fade, and Becker's speaker looks back at her childhood. Like many writers, all four of these poets analyze time by referring to seasons. What do you associate symbolically with spring, summer, fall, and winter?

BEFORE YOU READ

What sorts of occasions typically make people realize that the years are passing? Identify at least two occasions when, unexpectedly, you became quite aware that you are growing older.

JOHN KEATS
Ode on a Grecian Urn

Despite his early death from tuberculosis, John Keats (1795–1821) produced several poems still regarded as masterpieces of British Romanticism. The following poem is from a series of odes that Keats composed in 1819; others include "Ode to a Nightingale" and "Ode on Melancholy." At this period in his life, Keats was experiencing emotional turmoil. Already he was suffering from the disease that would kill him, while he also felt growing passion for a woman named Fanny Brawne. In turning to the genre of the ode, Keats was perpetuating a kind of poem that dates back to ancient Greece, where it adhered to a fixed structure involving three stanzas. By Keats's time, the ode's form had become more flexible. Often it featured more than three stanzas, which could vary in rhythm and length. In subject matter, the modern ode often dealt with topics that Keats addresses here: on the one hand, the speaker's desire for enduring beauty; on the other, the reality of a changing world.

1

Thou still unravished bride of quietness,
   Thou foster-child of silence and slow time,
Sylvan° historian, who canst thus express
   A flowery tale more sweetly than our rhyme:
What leaf-fringed legend haunts about thy shape   5
   Of deities or mortals, or of both,
      In Tempe or the dales of Arcady?°
What men or gods are these? What maidens loath?
   What mad pursuit? What struggle to escape?
      What pipes and timbrels? What wild ecstasy?   10

2

Heard melodies are sweet, but those unheard
   Are sweeter; therefore, ye soft pipes, play on;
Not to the sensual ear, but, more endeared,
   Pipe to the spirit ditties of no tone:
Fair youth, beneath the trees, thou canst not leave   15
   Thy song, nor ever can those trees be bare;
      Bold Lover, never, never canst thou kiss,
Though winning near the goal — yet, do not grieve;

---

3 Sylvan: Rustic; the urn is decorated with a forest scene.   **7 Tempe . . . Arcady:** Beautiful rural valleys in Greece.

She cannot fade, though thou hast not thy bliss,
    For ever wilt thou love, and she be fair!   20

3

Ah, happy, happy boughs! that cannot shed
    Your leaves, nor ever bid the Spring adieu;
And, happy melodist, unwearièd,
    For ever piping songs for ever new;
More happy love! more happy, happy love!   25
    For ever warm and still to be enjoyed,
        For ever panting, and for ever young;
All breathing human passion far above,
    That leaves a heart high-sorrowful and cloyed,
        A burning forehead, and a parching tongue.   30

4

Who are these coming to the sacrifice?
    To what green altar, O mysterious priest,
Lead'st thou that heifer lowing at the skies,
    And all her silken flanks with garlands drest?
What little town by river or sea shore,   35
    Or mountain-built with peaceful citadel,
        Is emptied of this folk, this pious morn?
And, little town, thy streets for evermore
    Will silent be; and not a soul to tell
        Why thou art desolate, can e'er return.   40

5

O Attic° shape! Fair attitude! with brede°
    Of marble men and maidens overwrought,
With forest branches and the trodden weed;
    Thou, silent form, dost tease us out of thought
As doth eternity: Cold Pastoral!   45
    When old age shall this generation waste,
        Thou shalt remain, in midst of other woe
Than ours, a friend to man, to whom thou say'st,
    Beauty is truth, truth beauty — that is all
        Ye know on earth, and all ye need to know.   [1819]   50

---

41 Attic: Possessing classic Athenian simplicity.   **brede:** Design.

THINKING ABOUT THE TEXT

1. Visualize the urn based on Keats's lines about it. (You might draw a picture of it and compare your drawing with a classmate's.) How objective does the speaker's description of this object seem?

2. Two of the poem's stanzas are packed with questions. In general, what are these questions about?

3. What image of love does the speaker describe the urn as presenting? To what extent is it an image that you believe should be treasured?

4. What is the effect of the speaker's reference to the deserted town in the fourth stanza? Why do you think the speaker focuses on such an image at this point?

5. Why do you think the speaker calls the urn "cold" in line 45? Critics have long debated how to interpret the poem's last two lines. Do you agree with the speaker's statement that "Beauty is truth, truth beauty" is "all ye need to know"? Explain your reasoning.

GERARD MANLEY HOPKINS
Spring and Fall

Gerard Manley Hopkins (1844–1889) was a Jesuit priest who published few of his poems during his lifetime; they became widely known only after the second collected edition of them appeared in 1930. Hopkins is now especially famous for his development of a technique he called sprung rhythm. *As "Spring and Fall" demonstrates, a poem that uses it may include several stressed syllables in each line, and the number of stresses per line may vary. Sprung rhythm allows a poet to emphasize words as he or she sees fit, without following a regular pattern. The following poem was written in 1880.*

To a Young Child

Márgarét áre you gríeving
Over Goldengrove unleaving?
Leáves, like the things of man, you
With your fresh thoughts care for, can you?
Áh! ás the heart grows older   5
It will come to such sights colder
By and by, nor spare a sigh
Though worlds of wanwood leafmeal lie;°

---

8 Though worlds of wanwood leafmeal lie: The trees have shed leaves that now lie in piecemeal fashion on the ground. Probably Hopkins is describing these trees as pale, the most common modern meaning of *wan*. He may, however, be seeking to create the opposite impression, for *wan* resembles an Old English word that means "dark."

And yet you wíll weep and know why.
Now no matter, child, the name: 10
Sórrow's spríngs áre the same.
Nor mouth had, no nor mind, expressed
What heart heard of, ghost° guessed:
It ís the blight man was born for,
it is Margaret you mourn for.   [1880]   15

13 ghost: Soul.

THINKING ABOUT THE TEXT

1. In what respects does the poem relate to its title, "Spring and Fall"? Refer to specific lines.

2. What do you take to be the reasoning behind the speaker's ultimate claim — "it is Margaret you mourn for" (line 15)? Why do you suppose the speaker addresses Margaret this way? Could a child actually benefit from hearing such a message? If so, how?

3. Suppose the poem had been about Margaret rather than addressed to Margaret. Might its effect on you have been different? If so, how?

4. As we pointed out in the headnote, Hopkins was a priest. Does the poem seem to have been written by a religious person? What words of the text should someone especially consider in answering this question? How do you define *religious*?

5. Identify places where Hopkins uses alliteration, rhyming, and unusual words. How effective is each of these devices?

MAKING COMPARISONS

1. Hopkins's speaker addresses the child Margaret, while Keats's speaker addresses images on the urn. Do you react to the poems differently because of this difference in audience? Explain.

2. In line 45 of his poem, Keats uses the word "Cold." In line 6 of "Spring and Fall," Hopkins uses the word "colder." Are they applying these words to different subjects or to the same one? Explain.

3. To what extent is each of these two poems about mourning?

A. E. HOUSMAN

Loveliest of trees, the cherry now

A native of Fockbury, England, Alfred Edward Housman (1859–1936) became an accomplished scholar of classics, teaching Latin at University College in London and at Cambridge University. Today, though, he is known primarily as a poet. The following poem appeared in his first book of verse, A Shropshire Lad *(1896), which grew increasingly popular during the twentieth century. Housman published another volume,* Last Poems, *in 1922, and in 1936 his* More Poems *appeared shortly after his death. Interest in his life was renewed with Tom Stoppard's 1997 play* The Invention of Love, *which imagines conversations between Housman's younger and older selves. The relationship between youth and age is, in fact, a central concern of Housman's poetry, as you will see in this poem.*

Loveliest of trees, the cherry now
Is hung with bloom along the bough,
And stands about the woodland ride
Wearing white for Eastertide.

Now, of my threescore years and ten,   5
Twenty will not come again,
And take from seventy springs a score,
It only leaves me fifty more.

And since to look at things in bloom
Fifty springs are little room,   10
About the woodlands I will go
To see the cherry hung with snow.   [1896]

THINKING ABOUT THE TEXT

1. The word "now" appears in the first line of the first two stanzas. Why do you think Housman makes it so prominent?

2. According to the second stanza, how old is the speaker? What is the effect of showing him engaged in calculations?

3. The last word of the poem could have been "white," which is evidently the present color of the cherry trees. Yet Housman concludes the poem with "snow," a word not usually associated with "Eastertide." Why do you think he chose this particular word to end with?

4. Does the reference to "Eastertide" lead you to assume that this poem is meant to have religious implications? Why, or why not?

5. What is the tone of this poem? How does the rhyme scheme contribute to the tone?

MAKING COMPARISONS

1. Compare Housman's, Hopkins's, and Keats's references to spring. Do you think that the three poems express the same attitude toward this season? Why, or why not?

2. To what extent do Housman's woodlands resemble Hopkins's Goldengrove?

3. Is Housman's poem more about the speaker than Hopkins's and Keats's poems are? Explain.

ROBIN BECKER
The Star Show

Robin Becker (b. 1951) is associate professor of English and women's studies at Pennsylvania State University. Her books of poetry include Backtalk *(1982),* Giacometti's Dog *(1990),* The Horse Fair *(2000), and* All-American Girl, *a 1992 volume in which the following poem appears.*

Though we're flat on our backs
at midnight
under the enormous sky, I know I'm really
in the Fels Planetarium
in Philadelphia, where I've come with the other   5
third-graders for the Star Show.
Tonight the trailing
blazes of white explode
across the darkness like firecrackers
and my companions *ooooh* and point   10
and say *over there*, though the words are too late
to be of use and hang
in the air much longer than light.

What I remember about the Star Show
is the commentator's calm voice,   15
the miracle spreading overhead
as he wooed us in plain English,
as if he didn't need special gear
to show us the sky's mysteries.
He needed only the reclining seats, the artificial   20
ceiling shuddering close with its countless stars,
our willingness to leave the known
earth, our parents, teachers, friends, ourselves
for this uncertain meeting in the dark.

He urged us to let our eyes adjust   25
for the journey, he asked us to relax
as the room began to spin and he whispered
in his knowledgeable voice about Jupiter.
Like my rabbi appearing suddenly in the dome
to discuss Moses, he explained with sorrow   30
that brilliant Galileo
had to retract his scientific
conclusions before the Inquisition.
This made us sad, for we already knew
that Galileo was right,   35
that four stars revolved around Jupiter
as the earth revolved around the sun.

❖ ❖ ❖

And then, as though someone were shaking out a bedspread,
someone shook the sky and all the stars
shifted, it was winter, night of the lean wolf.   40
His voice grew cold and we buttoned our sweaters
because the temperature was failing, and we wanted
to follow him wherever he was going,
which was December. •
                                    Across the mountain passes   45
we hunted bear; with the Hopis, we cured buffalo
hides and predicted the hour of sunrise.
Who didn't want to linger on that winter
mesa with the spotted ponies, so close to the stars?

There wasn't time. He was galloping toward   50
summer while I sat weeping for what I'd lost:
a glimpse of the sadness to come, the astronomer's
sure purpose. He guided the constellations
from early spring to June and then the sun
rose higher than we thought possible   55
and the longest day endured; he brought us into
a meadow drenched with light, but it was night,
we knew it, for now we could name every star.
How could he leave us here, now that we had become
his, now that he had asked us   60
to learn his heaven? As the chairs began to tilt
he threw the stars across the sky, flung meteors
carelessly and laughed a grown-up laugh.
He punctured the darkness with white bullets
and the kids began to shout.   65
The seats fell forward and the sun rose
in the auditorium, warming the air.
I sat bereft before the retreating stars.
Row by row we stood and blinked
into that autumn afternoon, as the ordinary jeers   70
and curses filled our mouths.   [1992]

THINKING ABOUT THE TEXT

1. The poem begins with the speaker's present situation. What apparently is
   going on? Consider whether the first stanza is really necessary. If Becker
   had omitted it and begun with the second stanza, would the poem's effect
   have been significantly different? Explain.

2. Where does Becker use the seasons for a framework? Where does she
   refer to changes in the day? Should she be criticized for using what are,
   after all, conventional signs of the passing of time? Why, or why not?

3. What psychological changes does the speaker recall going through during the star show? Do you think a child might really have these feelings, or do you suspect they belong more to the adult who is looking back? How important to you is it that the poem be realistic?

4. Describe the commentator as the speaker remembers him. What do you conclude about this figure? What should be made of the fact that the speaker compares him to a rabbi?

5. Trace the poem's references to language. What should readers think when it ends with children's "jeers / and curses"?

MAKING COMPARISONS

1. Compare what Hopkins and Becker imply about a child's state of mind. Do their portraits of childhood seem pretty much the same, or are there important differences?

2. Would you say that the poems by Keats, Hopkins, Housman, and Becker all end with a tone of despair? Why, or why not?

3. Can any words in Becker's description of the commentator be used to describe Keats's, Hopkins's, or Housman's speaker? Explain. Choose two or three particular moments in the star show that Becker describes, and imagine that Keats's, Hopkins's, or Housman's speaker was the commentator during these moments. What might the speaker have said to the children?

WRITING ABOUT ISSUES

1. Choose one of the four poems in this cluster, and write an essay identifying its dominant mood or emotion. Support your impression by referring to specific lines. Feel free to mention other moods or emotions at work in the poem as you discuss its main one.

2. Write an essay comparing the degrees to which two poems in this cluster encourage readers to accept the passage of time. Refer to specific words in each text.

3. Write an essay recalling a particular show or ceremony you attended when you were young, one that made you aware that time was passing. Note particular things that gave you this impression, and explain how you felt about it. If you wish, distinguish between the self you were then and the self you are now. Feel free to refer to one or more of the poems in this cluster.

4. Write an essay analyzing how the passage of time is represented in a particular artifact of popular culture, such as a film, a television show, a calendar, a greeting card, or a song. (Keep in mind that representation may take the form of pictures or sounds, not just words.) In your analysis, identify what you assume is the audience for this artifact. You may want to compare the artifact to one or more of the poems in this cluster.

FIGHTING FOR SURVIVAL

TIM O'BRIEN, "The Things They Carried"
JAMESON CURRIER, "What They Carried"

In much literature, characters strive to preserve their own lives or those of others. From Homer's *Iliad* on, one recurring setting for these efforts has been war. Contemporary literature is no exception. For example, even though the war in Vietnam ended more than two decades ago, many poets, playwrights, fiction writers, and essayists continue to chronicle and reflect on the struggles of its participants, in part because they recognize that Americans still argue about whether the war should ever have been fought. Naturally, the Vietnam conflict is particularly a concern for writers who served in it. Here we include a short story by one veteran of it, Tim O'Brien. As indicated by the title, "The Things They Carried," the story depicts the experiences of soldiers in Vietnam by focusing on equipment they used to survive. Though similar in title, Jameson Currier's story reminds readers that the contemporary world has been marked by other kinds of "warfare." It details how a group of gay men work together to help a friend of theirs suffering from AIDS. At the start, you might assume that what's principally carried in this story is the AIDS virus. But Currier emphasizes the resources, physical as well as spiritual, with which his characters fight it. As you read both of these stories, compare their depictions of communities—more precisely, male communities—struggling to survive.

BEFORE YOU READ

List the sorts of personalities, emotions, and events that you think might appear in a story about an American military unit in Vietnam. Then list the sorts that you think might appear in a story about gay men coping with AIDS. Finally, identify differences and similarities between your two lists.

TIM O'BRIEN

The Things They Carried

A native of Minnesota, Tim O'Brien (b. 1946) was drafted after he graduated from Macalester College. Subsequently, he served in the Vietnam War, during which he received a Purple Heart. In one way or another, practically all of his fiction deals with the war, although he has been repeatedly ambiguous about how and when his work incorporates his own Vietnam experiences. O'Brien's novels include If I Die in a Combat Zone *(1973),* Going After Cacciato *(which won the National Book Award in 1978),* In the Lake of the Woods *(a 1994 book that touches on the massacre at My Lai, and* Tomcat in Love *(1998). Originally published in* Esquire *magazine, the following story was reprinted in* The Best American Short Stories

1987. *It then appeared along with related stories by O'Brien in a 1990 book also entitled* The Things They Carried.

First Lieutenant Jimmy Cross carried letters from a girl named Martha, a junior at Mount Sebastian College in New Jersey. They were not love letters, but Lieutenant Cross was hoping, so he kept them folded in plastic at the bottom of his rucksack. In the late afternoon, after a day's march, he would dig his foxhole, wash his hands under a canteen, unwrap the letters, hold them with the tips of his fingers, and spend the last hour of light pretending. He would imagine romantic camping trips into the White Mountains in New Hampshire. He would some-times taste the envelope flaps, knowing her tongue had been there. More than anything, he wanted Martha to love him as he loved her, but the letters were mostly chatty, elusive on the matter of love. She was a virgin, he was almost sure. She was an English major at Mount Sebastian, and she wrote beautifully about her professors and roommates and midterm exams, about her respect for Chaucer and her great affection for Virginia Woolf. She often quoted lines of poetry; she never mentioned the war, except to say, Jimmy, take care of yourself. The letters weighed ten ounces. They were signed "Love, Martha," but Lieu-tenant Cross understood that "Love" was only a way of signing and did not mean what he sometimes pretended it meant. At dusk, he would carefully return the letters to his rucksack. Slowly, a bit distracted, he would get up and move among his men, checking the perimeter, then at full dark he would return to his hole and watch the night and wonder if Martha was a virgin.

The things they carried were largely determined by necessity. Among the necessities or near necessities were P-38 can openers, pocket knives, heat tabs, wrist watches, dog tags, mosquito repellant, chewing gum, candy, cigarettes, salt tablets, packets of Kool-Aid, lighters, matches, sewing kits, Military Payment Cer-tificates, C rations, and two or three canteens of water. Together, these items weighed between fifteen and twenty pounds, depending upon a man's habits or rate of metabolism. Henry Dobbins, who was a big man, carried extra rations; he was especially fond of canned peaches in heavy syrup over pound cake. Dave Jensen, who practiced field hygiene, carried a toothbrush, dental floss, and sev-eral hotel-size bars of soap he'd stolen on R&R in Sydney, Australia. Ted Laven-der, who was scared, carried tranquilizers until he was shot in the head outside the village of Than Khe in mid-April. By necessity, and because it was SOP,° they all carried steel helmets that weighed five pounds including the liner and camouflage cover. They carried the standard fatigue jackets and trousers. Very few carried underwear. On their feet they carried jungle boots—2.1 pounds— and Dave Jensen carried three pairs of socks and a can of Dr. Scholl's foot powder as a precaution against trench foot. Until he was shot, Ted Lavender carried six or seven ounces of premium dope, which for him was a necessity. Mitchell Sanders, the RTO,° carried condoms. Norman Bowker carried a diary. Rat Kiley carried comic books. Kiowa, a devout Baptist, carried an illustrated New Testament that

SOP: Standard operating procedure.   **RTO:** Radiotelephone operator.

had been presented to him by his father, who taught Sunday school in Oklahoma City, Oklahoma. As a hedge against bad times, however, Kiowa also carried his grandmother's distrust of the white man, his grandfather's old hunting hatchet. Necessity dictated. Because the land was mined and booby-trapped, it was SOP for each man to carry a steel-centered, nylon-covered flak jacket, which weighed 6.7 pounds, but which on hot days seemed much heavier. Because you could die so quickly, each man carried at least one large compress bandage, usually in the helmet band for easy access. Because the nights were cold, and because the monsoons were wet, each carried a green plastic poncho that could be used as a raincoat or ground sheet or makeshift tent. With its quilted liner, the poncho weighed almost two pounds, but it was worth every ounce. In April, for instance, when Ted Lavender was shot, they used his poncho to wrap him up, then to carry him across the paddy, then to lift him into the chopper that took him away.

They were called legs or grunts.

To carry something was to "hump" it, as when Lieutenant Jimmy Cross humped his love for Martha up the hills and through the swamps. In its intransitive form, "to hump" meant "to walk," or "to march," but it implied burdens far beyond the intransitive.

Almost everyone humped photographs. In his wallet, Lieutenant Cross carried two photographs of Martha. The first was a Kodachrome snapshot signed "Love," though he knew better. She stood against a brick wall. Her eyes were gray and neutral, her lips slightly open as she stared straight-on at the camera. At night, sometimes, Lieutenant Cross wondered who had taken the picture, because he knew she had boyfriends, because he loved her so much, and because he could see the shadow of the picture taker spreading out against the brick wall. The second photograph had been clipped from the 1968 Mount Sebastian yearbook. It was an action shot—women's volleyball—and Martha was bent horizontal to the floor, reaching, the palms of her hands in sharp focus, the tongue taut, the expression frank and competitive. There was no visible sweat. She wore white gym shorts. Her legs, he thought, were almost certainly the legs of a virgin, dry and without hair, the left knee cocked and carrying her entire weight, which was just over one hundred pounds. Lieutenant Cross remembered touching that left knee. A dark theater, he remembered, and the movie was *Bonnie and Clyde*, and Martha wore a tweed skirt, and during the final scene, when he touched her knee, she turned and looked at him in a sad, sober way that made him pull his hand back, but he would always remember the feel of the tweed skirt and the knee beneath it and the sound of the gunfire that killed Bonnie and Clyde, how embarrassing it was, how slow and oppressive. He remembered kissing her good night at the dorm door. Right then, he thought, he should've done something brave. He should've carried her up the stairs to her room and tied her to the bed and touched that left knee all night long. He should've risked it. Whenever he looked at the photographs, he thought of new things he should've done.

What they carried was partly a function of rank, partly of field specialty.

As a first lieutenant and platoon leader, Jimmy Cross carried a compass, maps, code books, binoculars, and a .45-caliber pistol that weighed 2.9 pounds fully loaded. He carried a strobe light and the responsibility for the lives of his men.

As an RTO, Mitchell Sanders carried the PRC-25 radio, a killer, twenty-six pounds with its battery.

As a medic, Rat Kiley carried a canvas satchel filled with morphine and plasma and malaria tablets and surgical tape and comic books and all the things a medic must carry, including M&M's for especially bad wounds, for a total weight of nearly twenty pounds.

As a big man, therefore a machine gunner, Henry Dobbins carried the M-60, which weighed twenty-three pounds unloaded, but which was almost always loaded. In addition, Dobbins carried between ten and fifteen pounds of ammunition draped in belts across his chest and shoulders.

As PFCs or Spec 4s, most of them were common grunts and carried the standard M-16 gas-operated assault rifle. The weapon weighed 7.5 pounds unloaded, 8.2 pounds with its full twenty-round magazine. Depending on numerous factors, such as topography and psychology, the riflemen carried anywhere from twelve to twenty magazines, usually in cloth bandoliers, adding on another 8.4 pounds at minimum, fourteen pounds at maximum. When it was available, they also carried M-16 maintenance gear — rods and steel brushes and swabs and tubes of LSA on — all of which weighed about a pound. Among the grunts, some carried the M-79 grenade launcher, 5.9 pounds unloaded, a reasonably light weapon except for the ammunition, which was heavy. A single round weighed ten ounces. The typical load was twenty-five rounds. But Ted Lavender, who was scared, carried thirty-four rounds when he was shot and killed outside Than Khe, and he went down under an exceptional burden, more than twenty pounds of ammunition, plus the flak jacket and helmet and rations and water and toilet paper and tranquilizers and all the rest, plus the unweighed fear. He was dead weight. There was no twitching or flopping. Kiowa, who saw it happen, said it was like watching a rock fall, or a big sandbag or something — just boom, then down — not like the movies where the dead guy rolls around and does fancy spins and goes ass over teakettle — not like that, Kiowa said, the poor bastard just flat-fuck fell. Boom. Down. Nothing else. It was a bright morning in mid-April. Lieutenant Cross felt the pain. He blamed himself. They stripped off Lavender's canteens and ammo, all the heavy things, and Rat Kiley said the obvious, the guy's dead, and Mitchell Sanders used his radio to report one U.S. KIA° and to request a chopper. Then they wrapped Lavender in his poncho. They carried him out to a dry paddy, established security, and sat smoking the dead man's dope until the chopper came. Lieutenant Cross kept to himself. He pictured Martha's smooth young face, thinking he loved her more than anything, more than his men, and now Ted Lavender was dead because he loved her so much and could not stop thinking about her. When the dust-off arrived, they carried Lavender aboard. Afterward they burned Than Khe. They marched until dusk, then dug their holes, and that night Kiowa kept explaining how you had to be there, how fast it was, how the poor guy just dropped like so much concrete. Boom-down, he said. Like cement.

KIA: Killed in action.

10

◆ ◆ ◆

In addition to the three standard weapons—the M-60, M-16, and M-79—they carried whatever presented itself, or whatever seemed appropriate as a means of killing or staying alive. They carried catch-as-catch-can. At various times, in various situations, they carried M-14s and CAR-15s and Swedish Ks and grease guns and captured AK-47s and Chi-Coms and RPGs and Simonov carbines and black-market Uzis and .38-caliber Smith & Wesson handguns and 66 mm LAWs and shotguns and silencers and blackjacks and bayonets and C-4 plastic explosives. Lee Strunk carried a slingshot; a weapon of last resort, he called it. Mitchell Sanders carried brass knuckles. Kiowa carried his grandfather's feathered hatchet. Every third or fourth man carried a Claymore antipersonnel mine—3.5 pounds with its firing device. They all carried fragmentation grenades—fourteen ounces each. They all carried at least one M-18 colored smoke grenade—twenty-four ounces. Some carried CS or tear-gas grenades. Some carried white-phosphorus grenades. They carried all they could bear, and then some, including a silent awe for the terrible power of the things they carried.

In the first week of April, before Lavender died, Lieutenant Jimmy Cross received a good-luck charm from Martha. It was a simple pebble, an ounce at most. Smooth to the touch, it was a milky-white color with flecks of orange and violet, oval-shaped, like a miniature egg. In the accompanying letter, Martha wrote that she had found the pebble on the Jersey shoreline, precisely where the land touched water at high tide, where things came together but also separated. It was this separate-but-together quality, she wrote, that had inspired her to pick up the pebble and to carry it in her breast pocket for several days, where it seemed weightless, and then to send it through the mail, by air, as a token of her truest feelings for him. Lieutenant Cross found this romantic. But he wondered what her truest feelings were, exactly, and what she meant by separate-but-together. He wondered how the tides and waves had come into play on that afternoon along the Jersey shoreline when Martha saw the pebble and bent down to rescue it from geology. He imagined bare feet. Martha was a poet, with the poet's sensibilities, and her feet would be brown and bare, the toenails unpainted, the eyes chilly and somber like the ocean in March, and though it was painful, he wondered who had been with her that afternoon. He imagined a pair of shadows moving along the strip of sand where things came together but also separated. It was phantom jealousy, he knew, but he couldn't help himself. He loved her so much. On the march, through the hot days of early April, he carried the pebble in his mouth, turning it with his tongue, tasting sea salts and moisture. His mind wandered. He had difficulty keeping his attention on the war. On occasion he would yell at his men to spread out the column, to keep their eyes open, but then he would slip away into daydreams, just pretending, walking barefoot along the Jersey shore, with Martha, carrying nothing. He would feel himself rising. Sun and waves and gentle winds, all love and lightness.

What they carried varied by mission.

When a mission took them to the mountains, they carried mosquito netting, machetes, canvas tarps, and extra bug juice.   15

If a mission seemed especially hazardous, or if it involved a place they knew to be bad, they carried everything they could. In certain heavily mined AOs,° where the land was dense with Toe Poppers and Bouncing Betties, they took turns humping a twenty-eight-pound mine detector. With its headphones and big sensing plate, the equipment was a stress on the lower back and shoulders, awkward to handle, often useless because of the shrapnel in the earth, but they carried it anyway, partly for safety, partly for the illusion of safety.

On ambush, or other night missions, they carried peculiar little odds and ends. Kiowa always took along his New Testament and a pair of moccasins for silence. Dave Jensen carried night-sight vitamins high in carotin. Lee Strunk carried his slingshot; ammo, he claimed, would never be a problem. Rat Kiley carried brandy and M&M's. Until he was shot, Ted Lavender carried the starlight scope, which weighed 6.3 pounds with its aluminum carrying case. Henry Dobbins carried his girlfriend's pantyhose wrapped around his neck as a comforter. They all carried ghosts. When dark came, they would move out single file across the meadows and paddies to their ambush coordinates, where they would quietly set up the Claymores and lie down and spend the night waiting.

Other missions were more complicated and required special equipment. In mid-April, it was their mission to search out and destroy the elaborate tunnel complexes in the Than Khe area south of Chu Lai. To blow the tunnels, they carried one-pound blocks of pentrite high explosives, four blocks to a man, sixty-eight pounds in all. They carried wiring, detonators, and battery-powered clackers. Dave Jensen carried earplugs. Most often, before blowing the tunnels, they were ordered by higher command to search them, which was considered bad news, but by and large they just shrugged and carried out orders. Because he was a big man, Henry Dobbins was excused from tunnel duty. The others would draw numbers. Before Lavender died there were seventeen men in the platoon, and whoever drew the number seventeen would strip off his gear and crawl in head first with a flashlight and Lieutenant Cross's .45-caliber pistol. The rest of them would fan out as security. They would sit down or kneel, not facing the hole, listening to the ground beneath them, imagining cobwebs and ghosts, whatever was down there — the tunnel walls squeezing in — how the flashlight seemed impossibly heavy in the hand and how it was tunnel vision in the very strictest sense, compression in all ways, even time, and how you had to wiggle in — ass and elbows — a swallowed-up feeling — and how you found yourself worrying about odd things — will your flashlight go dead? Do rats carry rabies? If you screamed, how far would the sound carry? Would your buddies hear it? Would they have the courage to drag you out? In some respects, though not many, the waiting was worse than the tunnel itself. Imagination was a killer.

On April 16, when Lee Strunk drew the number seventeen, he laughed and muttered something and went down quickly. The morning was hot and very still. Not good, Kiowa said. He looked at the tunnel opening, then out across a dry paddy toward the village of Than Khe. Nothing moved. No clouds or birds or people. As they waited, the men smoked and drank Kool-Aid, not talking much, feeling sympathy for Lee Strunk but also feeling the luck of the draw. You win

---

AOs: Areas of operations.

some, you lose some, said Mitchell Sanders, and sometimes you settle for a rain check. It was a tired line and no one laughed.

Henry Dobbins ate a tropical chocolate bar. Ted Lavender popped a tran-   20
quilizer and went off to pee.

After five minutes, Lieutenant Jimmy Cross moved to the tunnel, leaned down, and examined the darkness. Trouble, he thought — a cave-in maybe. And then suddenly, without willing it, he was thinking about Martha. The stresses and fractures, the quick collapse, the two of them buried alive under all that weight. Dense, crushing love. Kneeling, watching the hole, he tried to concentrate on Lee Strunk and the war, all the dangers, but his love was too much for him, he felt paralyzed, he wanted to sleep inside her lungs and breathe her blood and be smothered. He wanted her to be a virgin and not a virgin, all at once. He wanted to know her. Intimate secrets — why poetry? Why so sad? Why the grayness in her eyes? Why so alone? Not lonely, just alone — riding her bike across campus or sitting off by herself in the cafeteria. Even dancing, she danced alone — and it was the aloneness that filled him with love. He remembered telling her that one evening. How she nodded and looked away. And how, later, when he kissed her, she received the kiss without returning it, her eyes wide open, not afraid, not a virgin's eyes, just flat and uninvolved.

Lieutenant Cross gazed at the tunnel. But he was not there. He was buried with Martha under the white sand at the Jersey shore. They were pressed together, and the pebble in his mouth was her tongue. He was smiling. Vaguely, he was aware of how quiet the day was, the sullen paddies, yet he could not bring himself to worry about matters of security. He was beyond that. He was just a kid at war, in love. He was twenty-two years old. He couldn't help it.

A few moments later Lee Strunk crawled out of the tunnel. He came up grinning, filthy but alive. Lieutenant Cross nodded and closed his eyes while the others clapped Strunk on the back and made jokes about rising from the dead.

Worms, Rat Kiley said. Right out of the grave. Fuckin' zombie.

The men laughed. They all felt great relief.   25

Spook City, said Mitchell Sanders.

Lee Strunk made a funny ghost sound, a kind of moaning, yet very happy, and right then, when Strunk made that high happy moaning sound, when he went *Ahhooooo*, right then Ted Lavender was shot in the head on his way back from peeing. He lay with his mouth open. The teeth were broken. There was a swollen black bruise under his left eye. The cheekbone was gone. Oh shit, Rat Kiley said, the guy's dead. The guy's dead, he kept saying, which seemed profound — the guy's dead. I mean really.

The things they carried were determined to some extent by superstition. Lieutenant Cross carried his good-luck pebble. Dave Jensen carried a rabbit's foot. Norman Bowker, otherwise a very gentle person, carried a thumb that had been presented to him as a gift by Mitchell Sanders. The thumb was dark brown, rubbery to the touch, and weighed four ounces at most. It had been cut from a VC corpse, a boy of fifteen or sixteen. They'd found him at the bottom of an irrigation ditch, badly burned, flies in his mouth and eyes. The boy wore black shorts and sandals. At the time of his death he had been carrying a pouch of rice, a rifle, and three magazines of ammunition.

You want my opinion, Mitchell Sanders said, there's a definite moral here.

He put his hand on the dead boy's wrist. He was quiet for a time, as if counting a pulse, then he patted the stomach, almost affectionately, and used Kiowa's hunting hatchet to remove the thumb.   30

Henry Dobbins asked what the moral was.

Moral?

You know. *Moral*.

Sanders wrapped the thumb in toilet paper and handed it across to Norman Bowker. There was no blood. Smiling, he kicked the boy's head, watched the flies scatter, and said, It's like with that old TV show — Paladin. Have gun, will travel.

Henry Dobbins thought about it.   35

Yeah, well, he finally said. I don't see no moral.

There it *is*, man.

Fuck off.

They carried USO stationery and pencils and pens. They carried Sterno, safety pins, trip flares, signal flares, spools of wire, razor blades, chewing tobacco, liberated joss sticks and statuettes of the smiling Buddha, candles, grease pencils, *The Stars and Stripes*, fingernail clippers, Psy Ops° leaflets, bush hats, bolos, and much more. Twice a week, when the resupply choppers came in, they carried hot chow in green Mermite cans and large canvas bags filled with iced beer and soda pop. They carried plastic water containers, each with a two-gallon capacity. Mitchell Sanders carried a set of starched tiger fatigues for special occasions. Henry Dobbins carried Black Flag insecticide. Dave Jensen carried empty sandbags that could be filled at night for added protection. Lee Strunk carried tanning lotion. Some things they carried in common. Taking turns, they carried the big PRC-77 scrambler radio, which weighed thirty pounds with its battery. They shared the weight of memory. They took up what others could no longer bear. Often, they carried each other, the wounded or weak. They carried infections. They carried chess sets, basketballs, Vietnamese-English dictionaries, insignia of rank, Bronze Stars and Purple Hearts, plastic cards imprinted with the Code of Conduct. They carried diseases, among them malaria and dysentery. They carried lice and ringworm and leeches and paddy algae and various rots and molds. They carried the land itself — Vietnam, the place, the soil — a powdery orange-red dust that covered their boots and fatigues and faces. They carried the sky. The whole atmosphere, they carried it, the humidity, the monsoons, the stink of fungus and decay, all of it, they carried gravity. They moved like mules. By daylight they took sniper fire, at night they were mortared, but it was not battle, it was just the endless march, village to village, without purpose, nothing won or lost. They marched for the sake of the march. They plodded along slowly, dumbly, leaning forward against the heat, unthinking, all blood and bone, simple grunts, soldiering with their legs, toiling up the hills and down into the paddies and across the

Psy Ops: Psychological operations.

rivers and up again and down, just humping, one step and then the next and then another, but no volition, no will, because it was automatic, it was anatomy, and the war was entirely a matter of posture and carriage, the hump was everything, a kind of inertia, a kind of emptiness, a dullness of desire and intellect and conscience and hope and human sensibility. Their principles were in their feet. Their calculations were biological. They had no sense of strategy or mission. They searched the villages without knowing what to look for, not caring, kicking over jars of rice, frisking children and old men, blowing tunnels, sometimes setting fires and sometimes not, then forming up and moving on to the next village, then other villages, where it would always be the same. They carried their own lives. The pressures were enormous. In the heat of early afternoon, they would remove their helmets and flak jackets, walking bare, which was dangerous but which helped ease the strain. They would often discard things along the route of march. Purely for comfort, they would throw away rations, blow their Claymores and grenades, no matter, because by nightfall the resupply choppers would arrive with more of the same, then a day or two later still more, fresh watermelons and crates of ammunition and sunglasses and woolen sweaters—the resources were stunning—sparklers for the Fourth of July, colored eggs for Easter. It was the great American war chest—the fruits of science, the smokestacks, the canneries, the arsenals at Hartford, the Minnesota forests, the machine shops, the vast fields of corn and wheat—they carried like freight trains; they carried it on their backs and shoulders—and for all the ambiguities of Vietnam, all the mysteries and unknowns, there was at least the single abiding certainty that they would never be at a loss for things to carry.

After the chopper took Lavender away, Lieutenant Jimmy Cross led his men   40
into the village of Than Khe. They burned everything. They shot chickens and dogs, they trashed the village well, they called in artillery and watched the wreckage, then they marched for several hours through the hot afternoon, and then at dusk, while Kiowa explained how Lavender died, Lieutenant Cross found himself trembling.

He tried not to cry. With his entrenching tool, which weighed five pounds, he began digging a hole in the earth.

He felt shame. He hated himself. He had loved Martha more than his men, and as a consequence Lavender was now dead, and this was something he would have to carry like a stone in his stomach for the rest of the war.

All he could do was dig. He used his entrenching tool like an ax, slashing, feeling both love and hate, and then later, when it was full dark, he sat at the bottom of his foxhole and wept. It went on for a long while. In part, he was grieving for Ted Lavender, but mostly it was for Martha, and for himself, because she belonged to another world, which was not quite real, and because she was a junior at Mount Sebastian College in New Jersey, a poet and a virgin and uninvolved, and because he realized she did not love him and never would.

Like cement, Kiowa whispered in the dark. I swear to God—boom-down. Not a word.

I've heard this, said Norman Bowker.   45

A pisser, you know? Still zipping himself up. Zapped while zipping.

All right, fine. That's enough.

Yeah, but you had to see it, the guy just—

I *heard*, man. Cement. So why not shut the fuck *up?*

Kiowa shook his head sadly and glanced over at the hole where Lieutenant 　50
Jimmy Cross sat watching the night. The air was thick and wet. A warm, dense
fog had settled over the paddies and there was the stillness that precedes rain.

After a time Kiowa sighed.

One thing for sure, he said. The Lieutenant's in some deep hurt. I mean that
crying jag—the way he was carrying on—it wasn't fake or anything, it was real
heavy-duty hurt. The man cares.

Sure, Norman Bowker said.

Say what you want, the man does care.

We all got problems. 　55

Not Lavender.

No, I guess not, Bowker said. Do me a favor, though.

Shut up?

That's a smart Indian. Shut up.

Shrugging, Kiowa pulled off his boots. He wanted to say more, just to lighten 　60
up his sleep, but instead he opened his New Testament and arranged it beneath
his head as a pillow. The fog made things seem hollow and unattached. He tried
not to think about Ted Lavender, but then he was thinking how fast it was, no
drama, down and dead, and how it was hard to feel anything except surprise. It
seemed un-Christian. He wished he could find some great sadness, or even
anger, but the emotion wasn't there and he couldn't make it happen. Mostly he
felt pleased to be alive. He liked the smell of the New Testament under his
cheek, the leather and ink and paper and glue, whatever the chemicals were. He
liked hearing the sounds of night. Even his fatigue, it felt fine, the stiff muscles
and the prickly awareness of his own body, a floating feeling. He enjoyed not
being dead. Lying there, Kiowa admired Lieutenant Jimmy Cross's capacity for
grief. He wanted to share the man's pain, he wanted to care as Jimmy Cross
cared. And yet when he closed his eyes, all he could think was Boom-down, and
all he could feel was the pleasure of having his boots off and the fog curling in
around him and the damp soil and the Bible smells and the plush comfort of
night.

After a moment Norman Bowker sat up in the dark.

What the hell, he said. You want to talk, *talk*. Tell it to me.

Forget it.

No, man, go on. One thing I hate, it's a silent Indian.

For the most part they carried themselves with poise, a kind of dignity. Now 　65
and then, however, there were times of panic, when they squealed or wanted to
squeal but couldn't, when they twitched and made moaning sounds and covered their heads and said Dear Jesus and flopped around on the earth and fired
their weapons blindly and cringed and sobbed and begged for the noise to stop
and went wild and made stupid promises to themselves and to God and to their
mothers and fathers, hoping not to die. In different ways, it happened to all of

them. Afterward, when the firing ended, they would blink and peek up. They would touch their bodies, feeling shame, then quickly hiding it. They would force themselves to stand. As if in slow motion, frame by frame, the world would take on the old logic—absolute silence, then the wind, then sunlight, then voices. It was the burden of being alive. Awkwardly, the men would reassemble themselves, first in private, then in groups, becoming soldiers again. They would repair the leaks in their eyes. They would check for casualties, call in dust-offs, light cigarettes, try to smile, clear their throats and spit and begin cleaning their weapons. After a time someone would shake his head and say, No lie, I almost shit my pants, and someone else would laugh, which meant it was bad, yes, but the guy had obviously not shit his pants, it wasn't that bad, and in any case nobody would ever do such a thing and then go ahead and talk about it. They would squint into the dense, oppressive sunlight. For a few moments, perhaps, they would fall silent, lighting a joint and tracking its passage from man to man, inhaling, holding in the humiliation. Scary stuff, one of them might say. But then someone else would grin or flick his eyebrows and say, Roger-dodger, almost cut me a new asshole, *almost.*

There were numerous such poses. Some carried themselves with a sort of wistful resignation, others with pride or stiff soldierly discipline or good humor or macho zeal. They were afraid of dying but they were even more afraid to show it.

They found jokes to tell.

They used a hard vocabulary to contain the terrible softness. *Greased,* they'd say. *Offed, lit up, zapped while zipping.* It wasn't cruelty, just stage presence. They were actors and the war came at them in 3-D. When someone died, it wasn't quite dying, because in a curious way it seemed scripted, and because they had their lines mostly memorized, irony mixed with tragedy, and because they called it by other names, as if to encyst and destroy the reality of death itself. They kicked corpses. They cut off thumbs. They talked grunt lingo. They told stories about Ted Lavender's supply of tranquilizers, how the poor guy didn't feel a thing, how incredibly tranquil he was.

There's a moral here, said Mitchell Sanders.

They were waiting for Lavender's chopper, smoking the dead man's dope.   70

The moral's pretty obvious, Sanders said, and winked. Stay away from drugs. No joke, they'll ruin your day every time.

Cute, said Henry Dobbins.

Mind-blower, get it? Talk about wiggy—nothing left, just blood and brains.

They made themselves laugh.

There it is, they'd say, over and over, as if the repetition itself were an act of   75 poise, a balance between crazy and almost crazy, knowing without going. There it is, which meant be cool, let it ride, because oh yeah, man, you can't change what can't be changed, there it is, there it absolutely and positively and fucking well *is.*

They were tough.

They carried all the emotional baggage of men who might die. Grief, terror, love, longing—these were intangibles, but the intangibles had their own mass and specific gravity, they had tangible weight. They carried shameful memories.

They carried the common secret of cowardice barely restrained, the instinct to run or freeze or hide, and in many respects this was the heaviest burden of all, for it could never be put down, it required perfect balance and perfect posture. They carried their reputations. They carried the soldier's greatest fear, which was the fear of blushing. Men killed, and died, because they were embarrassed not to. It was what had brought them to the war in the first place, nothing positive, no dreams of glory or honor, just to avoid the blush of dishonor. They died so as not to die of embarrassment. They crawled into tunnels and walked point and advanced under fire. Each morning, despite the unknowns, they made their legs move. They endured. They kept humping. They did not submit to the obvious alternative, which was simply to close the eyes and fall. So easy, really. Go limp and tumble to the ground and let the muscles unwind and not speak and not budge until your buddies picked you up and lifted you into the chopper that would roar and dip its nose and carry you off to the world. A mere matter of falling, yet no one ever fell. It was not courage, exactly; the object was not valor. Rather, they were too frightened to be cowards.

By and large they carried these things inside, maintaining the masks of composure. They sneered at sick call. They spoke bitterly about guys who had found release by shooting off their own toes or fingers. Pussies, they'd say. Candyasses. It was fierce, mocking talk, with only a trace of envy or awe, but even so, the image played itself out behind their eyes.

They imagined the muzzle against flesh. They imagined the quick, sweet pain, then the evacuation to Japan, then a hospital with warm beds and cute geisha nurses.

They dreamed of freedom birds.

At night, on guard, staring into the dark, they were carried away by jumbo jets. They felt the rush of takeoff. *Gone!* they yelled. And then velocity, wings and engines, a smiling stewardess—but it was more than a plane, it was a real bird, a big sleek silver bird with feathers and talons and high screeching. They were flying. The weights fell off, there was nothing to bear. They laughed and held on tight, feeling the cold slap of wind and altitude, soaring, thinking *It's over, I'm gone!*—they were naked, they were light and free—it was all lightness, bright and fast and buoyant, light as light, a helium buzz in the brain, a giddy bubbling in the lungs as they were taken up over the clouds and the war, beyond duty, beyond gravity and mortification and global entanglements—*Sin loi!*° they yelled, *I'm sorry, motherfuckers, but I'm out of it, I'm goofed, I'm on a space cruise, I'm gone!*—and it was a restful, disencumbered sensation, just riding the light waves, sailing that big silver freedom bird over the mountains and oceans, over America, over the farms and great sleeping cities and cemeteries and highways and the golden arches of McDonald's. It was flight, a kind of fleeing, a kind of falling, falling higher and higher, spinning off the edge of the earth and beyond the sun and through the vast, silent vacuum where there were no burdens and where everything weighed exactly nothing. *Gone!* they screamed, *I'm sorry but I'm gone!*

80

Sin loi: "Sorry about that!"

And so at night, not quite dreaming, they gave themselves over to lightness, they were carried, they were purely borne.

On the morning after Ted Lavender died, First Lieutenant Jimmy Cross crouched at the bottom of his foxhole and burned Martha's letters. Then he burned the two photographs. There was a steady rain falling, which made it difficult, but he used heat tabs and Sterno to build a small fire, screening it with his body, holding the photographs over the tight blue flame with the tips of his fingers.

He realized it was only a gesture. Stupid, he thought. Sentimental, too, but mostly just stupid.

Lavender was dead. You couldn't burn the blame.

Besides, the letters were in his head. And even now, without photographs, 85 Lieutenant Cross could see Martha playing volleyball in her white gym shorts and yellow T-shirt. He could see her moving in the rain.

When the fire died out, Lieutenant Cross pulled his poncho over his shoulders and ate breakfast from a can.

There was no great mystery, he decided.

In those burned letters Martha had never mentioned the war, except to say, Jimmy, take care of yourself. She wasn't involved. She signed the letters "Love," but it wasn't love, and all the fine lines and technicalities did not matter.

The morning came up wet and blurry. Everything seemed part of everything else, the fog and Martha and the deepening rain.

It was a war, after all. 90

Half smiling, Lieutenant Jimmy Cross took out his maps. He shook his head hard, as if to clear it, then bent forward and began planning the day's march. In ten minutes, or maybe twenty, he would rouse the men and they would pack up and head west, where the maps showed the country to be green and inviting. They would do what they had always done. The rain might add some weight, but otherwise it would be one more day layered upon all the other days.

He was realistic about it. There was that new hardness in his stomach.

No more fantasies, he told himself.

Henceforth, when he thought about Martha, it would be only to think that she belonged elsewhere. He would shut down the daydreams. This was not Mount Sebastian, it was another world, where there were no pretty poems or midterm exams, a place where men died because of carelessness and gross stupidity. Kiowa was right. Boom-down, and you were dead, never partly dead.

Briefly, in the rain, Lieutenant Cross saw Martha's gray eyes gazing back 95 at him.

He understood.

It was very sad, he thought. The things men carried inside. The things men did or felt they had to do.

He almost nodded at her, but didn't.

Instead he went back to his maps. He was now determined to perform his duties firmly and without negligence. It wouldn't help Lavender, he knew that, but from this point on he would comport himself as a soldier. He would dispose of his good-luck pebble. Swallow it, maybe, or use Lee Strunk's slingshot, or just drop it along the trail. On the march he would impose strict field discipline. He would be careful to send out flank security, to prevent straggling or bunching up, to keep his troops moving at the proper pace and at the proper interval. He would insist on clean weapons. He would confiscate the remainder of Lavender's dope. Later in the day, perhaps, he would call the men together and speak to them plainly. He would accept the blame for what had happened to Ted Lavender. He would be a man about it. He would look them in the eyes, keeping his chin level, and he would issue the new SOPs in a calm, impersonal tone of voice, an officer's voice, leaving no room for argument or discussion. Commencing immediately, he'd tell them, they would no longer abandon equipment along the route of march. They would police up their acts. They would get their shit together, and keep it together, and maintain it neatly and in good working order.

He would not tolerate laxity. He would show strength, distancing himself.   100

Among the men there would be grumbling, of course, and maybe worse, because their days would seem longer and their loads heavier, but Lieutenant Cross reminded himself that his obligation was not to be loved but to lead. He would dispense with love; it was not now a factor. And if anyone quarreled or complained, he would simply tighten his lips and arrange his shoulders in the correct command posture. He might give a curt little nod. Or he might not. He might just shrug and say Carry on, then they would saddle up and form into a column and move out toward the villages of Than Khe.   [1986]

THINKING ABOUT THE TEXT

1. A significant pattern in this story is the repeated references to "the things they carried." How does this pattern affect you? What might O'Brien have hoped to accomplish with it? At what points in the story are there variations on this pattern—changes in the kinds of things that the narrator reports being carried?

2. Describe the structure of this story. Is there a central event? If so, what is it, and why do you consider it central?

3. Evaluate Lieutenant Cross's fascination with Martha, including his preoccupation with the issue of whether she is a virgin. How sympathetic are you to him? At the end of the story, Cross blames himself for Ted Lavender's death. Is this a fair self-evaluation, or is he too hard on himself? Identify some of the warrants or assumptions behind your answer.

4. Do the other members of the company seem mostly alike, or are there significant differences among them? Explain. What is your evaluation of the company as a whole? List some adjectives for it.

5. Does the war depicted in this story appear significantly different from other wars, such as World War II? If so, in what ways? Is this an antiwar story? Identify characteristics you associate with the genre.

JAMESON CURRIER
What They Carried

A native of Georgia and a graduate of Emory University in Atlanta, Jameson Currier (b. 1955) now lives in Manhattan. Besides writing fiction, he has published essays and written a documentary film, Living Proof: HIV and the Pursuit of Happiness *(1993). In 1998, Currier published his first novel,* Where the Rainbow Ends, *which traces a group of men through the years of the AIDS crisis. The subject is similar to that of the following piece, which appears in a 1993 collection of Currier's stories entitled* Dancing on the Moon: Short Stories about AIDS.

John had carried the flowers since Perry Street, long-stemmed irises wrapped together by a pale-pink tissue. Now he held them across his lap in the taxi; a patch of his khaki pants had turned dark brown from the beads of water which rolled down the stems. Danny thought John would have tired of flowers; once a week he had carried irises to Adam. This afternoon, on their way to Seventh Avenue, John had hesitated in front of the florist, and Danny, recognizing the confused look which had rushed across John's face, had instinctively scooped up the flowers from the white plastic bucket. Shifting the weight of the canvas gym bag he was carrying to his left shoulder, Danny went inside and paid a small Oriental woman, watching her eyes disappear into fine lines as she smiled and wrapped the irises together. Outside again, on the sidewalk, John raised his arms toward Danny, taking the flowers as though offering to hold a child. In the taxi, Danny lifted John's hand and smelled his wrist, wondering why the fragrance of flowers never lasted as long as cologne.

Adam had carried only his briefcase to the emergency room. Inside was his wallet, his address book, a bottle of aspirin, and the reviews of the play he had been publicizing. Adam had tried calling John first, but he was out of the office, so he called Danny, because he was worried and wanted help quickly. When Danny got to the hospital, Adam was already in a private room and had a temperature of 103. Danny took the keys to Adam's apartment and brought back to the hospital Adam's pajamas, bathrobe, slippers, razor, shaving cream, toothbrush, toothpaste, and pillow. By the time Danny returned, Adam was asleep and John was sitting in the chair beside the bed, watching the sun set through the windows that overlooked East 79th Street.

The next day the doctors began their tests. Nurses drew blood and took away urine samples, though nothing was done specifically about the pain in Adam's lower back, which was the reason he had gone to the emergency room in the first place, Adam told Danny. John had to ask the nurses several times about getting some sort of medication to relieve Adam's discomfort, and finally got a doctor to order a prescription for Percodan. While Adam was being examined by yet another doctor, John and Danny sat in the waiting room, and John mentioned it wasn't the pain that had driven Adam to the hospital. He had been working too hard, had been trying to cover for his boss, who was on vacation. The producers were worried because the play wasn't a hit. Stress and exhaustion, John said, were the reasons Adam was here. Danny slumped down in his chair and rested his elbows against his knees, cupping his chin in the palms of his hands. Danny could tell Adam was thinner since last week; the youthful complexion had disappeared from his face, leaving behind an impression of bones and angles. Danny shifted his head till his eyes rested at a point somewhere beyond John. I wish I could believe that was the reason, Danny said. But I know it's not. Don't forget, I've been here before.

The following day John took off work and brought Adam flowers. Adam had not showered or shaved in three days. Lying in bed, he held the flowers across his chest and then asked John to help rearrange the pillows behind his neck. That night, Danny came by after work and brought the fruit salad that Adam had called and said he wanted, because, he added, he could not even stand to smell the hospital food. Danny had stopped at the Korean grocery on Lexington Avenue and bought a container of sliced peaches, melons, and strawberries, as out-of-season as the flowers John had found. John brought a bottle of orange soda Adam had called and asked for. While Adam ate, slowly and uncomfortably, John and Danny sat near the bed and watched *Hollywood Squares* on the wall-mounted television set. Before they left, Adam threw up the food, and John helped Adam change into a clean T-shirt, while Danny wiped the floor and rinsed the soiled pajamas. In the hall outside Adam's room, John mentioned he was surprised Adam was getting worse. Don't people go into the hospital to get better? he asked. Adam had been in the hospital only last month, overnight, for a blood transfusion. Danny said nothing but shifted his feet so he could lean against the wall for support. Danny knew Adam had already passed the point; the virus had become a disease.

Adam told John he didn't want any visitors. Only John and Danny were   5 allowed to come by. I don't want anyone to see me like this, Adam said. They would be upset and hurt. Some would be angry, he explained to Danny. He would be better in a few days and then would go home. And Adam said no one could bring him anything personal other than clothing and toiletries, not even a book or a radio or a *TV Guide*, anything, he noted, which would suggest he might be in the hospital for a while. After all, he said, I'm not planning on staying here long, and then, lifting his eyes to the ceiling and assessing himself realistically, added, I just don't want it to feel like a long time. In four days, Adam had dropped five pounds. He hated the hospital. He thought the nurses were inept; they couldn't even tell the difference between aspirin and Valium. They won't help me, he said. They can't stop the pain in my back.

And the doctors continued their tests: X rays of his chest, abdomen, and skull. There were bone scans, T scans, CAT scans, spinal taps, and another blood transfusion. By the end of the week, when friends found out Adam had not been at work or at home, the phone beside his hospital bed began ringing, and Danny knew the visitors could not be stopped.

Wes brought a new pair of pajamas after John mentioned Adam had already thrown out three pairs and several hospital gowns. Cheryl, Adam's assistant, brought a bag of Pepperidge Farm Goldfish crackers, which at the moment she spoke with Adam on the phone was what Adam wanted, though they remained unopened in the top drawer of the hospital dresser. Roy brought current copies of *Spy* and *New York* magazines; Elliot brought Archie and Superman comic books. They all tried to smile, joke, catch Adam up on what was happening at work or in the news. They would clear their throats, change the subject, or avert their eyes when necessary, carrying their feelings inside, the way they knew they must, the way they knew Adam wanted. In the evenings, John and Danny would bring whatever food Adam wanted: lemon yogurt, canned peaches, pretzels, or taco chips. Most nights Danny stayed later than visiting hours, in case Adam threw up and needed to be changed.

And the tests continued. Steve brought an advance copy of the book he was editing on the Bloomsbury authors. Elliot brought scissors, which Adam used to clip his nails. Bob brought lip balm, which Adam wanted because he thought the hospital air was so dry. When the new pajamas found their way into the trash, John went to a discount store and bought six irregular large T-shirts, though Adam's favorite was the old gray shirt Danny pulled from his gym bag one night; Adam refused to wear it, instead keeping it rolled up next to his assortment of pillows. The office sent an arrangement of red and white columbines. Millie sent a basket of painted daisies. Roy brought yellow tulips. One night during the second week, Adam asked John to bring the bottle of cologne he kept underneath the towels in the closet of the apartment. If I'm not washing, he said, at least I can smell better than the flowers. When a postcard arrived at the hospital from London, from Harris, Adam spent an hour trying to calculate how long it had taken to arrive by overseas mail, how long he had been in the hospital, and what day Harris had heard he was sick.

Cheryl said to Danny she had never realized the small red bumps on Adam's cheeks were Kaposi's sarcoma; she had thought it was acne that wouldn't go away. After all, she commented softly while Adam was sleeping, he'll bring almost anything back to his desk to eat. Although I do, too, she moaned, but he never had to worry about his weight. Later that week, Adam told John food had lost its taste. It only has a meaning now, he said, and the next day he stopped eating altogether. The nurses began feeding him with a machine suspended on a pole which pumped solutions of fats and minerals and vitamins through plastic tubes connected to a vein in his right arm. Adam seldom moved from the bed now. When he couldn't manage to push the pump to the bathroom, the nurses brought urinals and bedpans but were still sluggish about bringing him medication. John began to have problems coping with Adam's illness. So Danny began to wash Adam at night with warm, wet cloths and brought cups and pans of water from the sink so he could brush his teeth. Adam said he still had the pain in his lower back and the doctors could not find the cause. It's not even a brain tumor, Adam remarked during a commercial between rounds of *Jeopardy*. He turned his head away from the TV set and began to cry. All I want to do is go out and see a movie, he said. At a theatre. With real popcorn and butter. The next day Adam had a biopsy of the lymph glands of his neck. Two days later a doctor brought the news he had Burkitt's lymphoma. Danny made Adam call his mother in New Jersey and tell her he was sick. She's the only family you have, and you have to tell her, Danny said. It's not right to keep it a secret any longer. On Saturday, his mother came to the hospital, stayed two hours, and cried. On Monday, Adam began chemotherapy. Adam told Danny he was honestly going to get better. Because now he was ready to go back home.

Danny was surprised three weeks had passed. Many days he could not find an order or sense of strategy to what had to be done, so he began to make lists: what to carry to the hospital, what he had to buy, whom he had to call, what he had to do when he got home. Danny carried the lists in his gym bag, pressed between the pages of his calendar. Inside, along with a bottle of ibuprofen, Danny carried antihistamine pills, decongestant tablets, and a box of cherry-flavored cough drops, because he never knew if the headaches he got in the late afternoons might actually be the start of the flu or a cold. There was also a comb, two ballpoint pens, a small scratch pad that Danny used to jot down notes, and a combination lock for his gym locker, though Danny had not made it to the gym since Adam first entered the hospital. Some days Danny worried the canvas bag would rip; when he added a book to read on the subway, and an umbrella or gloves because the weather could slip without warning between fall and winter, the weight would almost reach ten pounds.

The day Adam came home, John and Danny carried everything in duffel bags from the hospital to the fourth-floor apartment. Adam had been released and set up on a home-care program. A nurse would visit if needed; every night he would continue the intravenous fluids. Two delivery men from the home-care service carried up the stairs an infusion pump similar to the one that had stood next to the hospital bed, and three large boxes of supplies. Inside were vitamin, lipid, and insulin bottles, and an assortment of needles, syringes, and plastic tubing. Enough supplies for a month, a hospital representative told Danny. Danny cleaned the refrigerator to make room for the plastic bags of nutritional solution which Adam had to have for twelve hours each night. In his gym bag Danny now carried a change of clothing, in case he slept overnight at Adam's apartment; in his calendar he wrote every possible emergency number he might have to use. John made five extra sets of keys to the apartment, one for Danny, one for himself, others for Roy, Wes, and Elliot, so they could come and go as quickly and easily as necessary. Elliot went to the grocery store to get the things Adam wanted to eat: frozen turkey tetrazzini and pizza, potato chips, mocha-nut ice cream, milk, and mint-chocolate-chip cookies. Roy went to the pharmacy to get the medicine the doctor had prescribed: Halcion for sleep, Xanax for anxiety, Nizoral for thrush, Zovirax for the herpes sores in Adam's mouth, and prednisone, Bactrim, allopurinol, and AZT. Adam complained about taking so many pills. His least favorite were the large yellow capsules, which he said were difficult to swallow. His voice sounds so strange now, Danny said to John when they were alone in the kitchen. It sounds as raspy as if he'd spent a lifetime smoking, and he's always coughing to clear away the phlegm.

That night, John and Danny helped Adam hook up the infusion pump, following the instructions a nurse had written for them. Before he left the hospital, Adam had had surgery to implant a catheter in his chest, because his arms had

10

turned into long strands of bruises where the veins had collapsed from being punctured with too many needles. It took John and Danny over two hours to do what the nurse had demonstrated in less than twenty minutes. They injected insulin and liquid vitamins into the clear solution of a plastic bag, connected plastic tubing to the bag and a bottle of lipids, and then suspended them from the poles of the infusion pump. They washed their hands and ran the tubing through the machine, then wiped the end with gauzes soaked in isopropyl and povidone-iodine. John panicked at every step, convinced Adam would be murdered by an air bubble. Danny continued, steadying his hands by placing his arms on Adam's stomach till he had connected the liquid-filled tubing to the tubing that hung from Adam's chest. Adam, too, was anxious and nervous. I don't want to go back, he said, and could not fall asleep. He refused to take the Halcion or Xanax and stayed awake, sweating and worrying and rolling the pump to the bathroom because of his diarrhea.

The first week Adam spent at home, everyone carried the hope he was getting better. Roy picked up Adam's paychecks and did the best he could to sort through what bills could be sent to the insurance company. Cheryl carried more insurance forms to the apartment. John did more grocery shopping; there never seemed to be enough paper towels, tissues, or garbage bags. Bob came by and trimmed Adam's hair. Elliot did the laundry. Wes took afternoons off from work to take Adam to the doctor's office for chemotherapy treatments. Danny arranged a meal service to deliver lunches to Adam in the afternoon. In the evenings, friends brought him dinner. Steve brought Chinese, Millie brought Italian, Bob brought cream of broccoli soup and an omelet from the restaurant where he worked. Adam said there was more food than he would ever eat, even if he did have an appetite.

When Danny arrived in the evenings now, he hung a change of clothing in the bedroom closet. His overnight kit, which contained soap, shampoo, deodorant, shaving cream, and a razor, found a permanent place by the bathroom windowsill. Danny slept on the floor beside Adam's bed; he was afraid of sleeping in the bed with Adam, because he was certain he would become tangled in the plastic tubes. Adam has always been a restless sleeper, John said. Before he became sick, he would toss so violently he would twist the sheet around himself till he cut off his circulation. When Adam could no longer make it to the bathroom in the middle of the night, even with help, Danny bought a bedpan, and John found the large plastic Donald Duck glasses to use as urinals, the ones Adam had brought back from his trip to Disney World.

Adam said afternoons were always the worst. He would be alone in the apartment, watching TV, when the depression would hit. But if anyone called, he refused to answer the phone, afraid of having someone hear the way his voice sounded. There were moments when Danny actually thought Adam was getting better. At least his spirits seemed to rise. At least he was eating. Every evening Adam would describe for Danny what he had eaten, how many bites he had taken, and if it tasted good or bad. Adam had also started coughing in his sleep, so fitfully Danny thought he wasn't sleeping well; Danny was surprised, then, when

15

he asked Adam one morning how he had slept and Adam answered, I'm sleeping better than ever.

Danny learned Adam's thoughts went through a cycle. One day it was, Am I going to die? Another, it would be, Do you think I'm going to die? Danny was never sure how to answer Adam's questions. Once, when Danny decided to be honest and Adam asked, How do I look?, Danny responded by saying, OK. Adam lifted himself out of bed and walked to the mirror that hung on the back of the bedroom door, bracing himself by holding on to the doorknob. Just OK? he questioned, and began brushing his thinning hair. Please, he added, I still have my vanity, and he walked to the window and threw the brush outside.

The second week he was home, Roy and Danny took Adam to see a movie. Danny helped Adam walk down the four flights of stairs, his arms wrapped around Adam's waist so he would not fall because Adam refused to use the cane John had bought. Roy borrowed a car and dropped them off in front of the theatre on 59th Street. Danny found it difficult to concentrate on the movie, even though Adam felt certain it would be nominated for a number of Academy Awards. Roy bought popcorn and sodas, though Adam ate nothing, coughing and squirming in his seat the entire two hours. Afterward, riding in the car back to the apartment, Adam said he wanted to get tickets to see *The Phantom of the Opera* and take a cruise to the Bahamas in the spring. When Roy and Danny were alone in Adam's kitchen, Roy said Adam was setting himself up for disappointments. Danny replied, It's the way Adam has always lived. He needs to look forward to something. Later, in the bedroom, Adam told Danny, Today was the first time I was actually afraid of dying.

Danny was concerned that Adam was telling him things he told no one else. When Roy or John or Wes or Elliot was out of the room, Adam would talk about how he had not had sex since July because of the pain in his back. Adam said he felt safe when Danny slept on the floor, though he knew it was selfish to ask so much of him, but John was too impatient, Roy flustered easily, and they never knew what to do if there was a problem. Once, Adam said to Danny, I'm so afraid you'll be so disgusted you'll walk away. Danny promised him he wouldn't leave, though Danny knew there were moments when he wished Adam would die quickly. Adam himself could be impatient: Danny was too slow bringing the medication or could not pick up the tissues fast enough from the floor. The glass of water was too cloudy or cold, the TV was not loud enough or too loud, or Danny had left his fingerprints on the lens after cleaning Adam's eyeglasses. Adam had now dropped six more pounds; at night, he would stretch out his arms and remark in a rather wry tone, I'm beginning to look worse than a Biafra baby.

On Wednesday, Wes invited friends over to watch *The Wizard of Oz* on TV. Roy decorated the living room with a rainbow of crepe paper. Cheryl made green cookies to eat when Dorothy reached the Emerald City. Danny carried Adam to the couch in the living room a few minutes before the movie was to start. John remarked it was odd it wasn't Sunday. Remember, Bob added, it was always telecast on Sunday nights. Elliot said when he was a kid his parents always made sure they stayed late at church that night just to torture him. Adam said the worst punishment his mother ever gave him was not letting him watch it one year. He cried so hard she finally relented, letting him out of his bedroom just as the Wicked Witch disappeared in a puff of smoke on top of the thatched roof. Steve said, Remember when we watched it all in black and white? Or when we had to go to someone's house to watch it in color, John added. Roy said his favorite was still *Peter Pan*. Remember when Mary Martin sang about Never-Never Land?

The next morning Adam said to Danny, We can't go on like this, and   20
laughed weakly. How many men have said that to you in your lifetime? Still trying to shake the sleep from his body, Danny sat on the side of the bed and held Adam's hand. I should go back to the hospital, Adam said. This isn't fair to anyone.

The moment Adam said he felt better was the time he was the most helpless, strapped in a wheelchair whizzing through a hospital corridor. It was almost fun, he told Danny later, all dressed in white, letting people I didn't even know worry about only me for just a few minutes.

The doctors began more tests: EKGs, EEGs, X rays, specimens, and cultures. The reason he went back, Adam said, was because he needed stronger chemotherapy, and he wasn't able to function at home alone the day after the dosages. He got angry only once, when a nurse said he wasn't trying hard enough when he refused to take a pill right away. He yelled back at her that she wasn't his mother. In fact, he added, I don't even like you, and besides, I didn't even ask for your opinion. The next day the stitching that held the catheter tubing in place fell apart. The doctor said it was impossible to perform the surgery again to repair it. Adam was too weak; now he weighed a hundred pounds. And an X ray showed a small black spot on his right lung. Another doctor said Adam wouldn't be able to sustain the amount of chemotherapy he would need. By the end of the night, the nurses had set him up on a respiratory system; oxygen rushed through plastic tubing to his nose. The next morning, Danny arranged for twenty-four-hour nursing care so Adam could go home. Adam had decided it was time to die.

It's not like I'm giving up, he said to Danny and John and Roy. It's just that I'm going to die naturally. Without surgery or therapy or treatments which would only prolong my life by a couple of days.

This time, John and Danny carried Adam up the stairs in a wheelchair. Roy went and picked up more prescriptions: Duricef, Compazine, nystatin, propranolol, and dexamethasone. A nurse was always there to give Adam his medication and make sure he would eat. Danny told John he felt somewhat relieved. Now there is someone who knows what to do about the coughing, knows when he needs to drink liquids, knows what time he is supposed to take a pill, knows what to say and how to deal with the pain. Someone is there to help him be comfortable. John answered, It isn't like this is all new to us.

Danny told John, Adam always had a fascination with suicide. Didn't he   25
remember Adam reading *Last Wish* by Betty Rollin? The first time he was in the hospital, Adam had asked if Danny could find someone who could get him Nembutal—his doctor had refused to give him a prescription. Adam mentioned suicide first to Danny because he knew it would upset John. Adam said that he wanted to live, but the quality of his life had deteriorated beyond depression. I've

spent the last two months waiting, he said. Waiting for doctors and nurses and medicine and food and visits and friends. Roy cried when Danny told him Adam wanted to die swiftly and painlessly, but Danny knew that Adam would not kill himself, that Adam had carried himself with dignity for so long, he wouldn't want his life to end with disappointments. Roy told Adam he didn't want him to do it, but if that was his decision, then he would do his best to respect it. But no one would help Adam find the medication. Adam complained it had been easy in the book. When Adam asked Danny to just open the window and let him jump, Danny said no, and Adam said he would do it himself. Danny laughed and tried turning it into a joke: How could someone who has not moved from bed in over a week make it to the window and jump from the fire escape? I thought you were going to help me die, Adam replied. I'm sorry I'm disappointing you, Danny answered. Now you know exactly how selfish I am. I'm sorry you're more valuable to me alive than dead.

Five days after coming home from the hospital, Adam died. In the afternoon he began to have respiratory problems. The nurse hooked him up to the oxygen tank which had been placed by his bed. By the time Danny arrived, around 7:00 P.M., Adam was semiconscious, lying on his back, gasping for breath, his arms twitching as if he were asking for help. Danny reached for Adam's hand, thinking he might calm him, but he was shocked that Adam's skin felt as cold and lifeless as vinyl, so Danny rubbed his hands along Adam's arms, hoping it would help the circulation. Thirty minutes later, when the gasping subsided, the nurse rolled Adam over to rest on his side. She turned to Danny and said in a brisk whisper, Have any arrangements been made? Does he want last rites? Danny paced the floor till the breathing stopped.

The only time Danny cried was the day in the hospital when an orderly came into the room and shaved the hair on Adam's chest before the surgery to implant the catheter. John cried after his first visit to the hospital. Roy said he had cried while waiting in line to buy underwear. Cheryl cried when Adam called and said she could have the posters that hung over his desk. Wes said he cried in the steam room at the gym, when he knew no one was looking. Bob and Millie cried while having drinks together at the bar of a Japanese restaurant in the Village after they had tried to get Adam to eat the dinner Millie had brought. Elliot cried during the opening credits when *Auntie Mame* came on TV one night; he and Adam had seen it together on a double bill at the Regency. Steve didn't cry, or so he said, though Danny noticed he had started walking with his fists clenched.

In the hospital a doctor remarked to John that someone might carry this virus in his body for years before it began to deteriorate the immune system. Some people might not be affected at all. Danny turned to the doctor and replied rather sarcastically, Do you think we're all fools? We all know about this disease. Don't you know? Danny added. Haven't you heard? It's the fear every gay man carries today.

The hardest thing, Danny said to John during the ride in the taxi, was carrying the ashes. Danny had picked them up yesterday from the funeral home. They had been placed inside a cardboard box, small and rectangular, and the man at the funeral home had placed the box in a plastic bag. When Danny took the bag, he was surprised it was so heavy for something that small, estimating the weight he held was almost ten pounds. As Danny walked back to the apartment, the weight grew heavier, he couldn't shake the thought of what he carried.

John took the flowers to the kitchen of Wes's apartment, unwrapped them   30 from the tissue, and arranged them in a tall glass vase. He carried them to the dining table and placed them at the center. Around him Roy, Millie, and Elliot took their seats. The extra leaf Wes had added to the table made the room seem smaller; the air was warm and perfumed by the ginger he had used in cooking. Bob dimmed the overhead light, Cheryl lit the candles with the matches she found in her purse, and Steve circled the table, pouring glasses of wine. Danny asked Wes if there was anything he could do to help: Give me something to do, Danny said. Bring these to the table, Wes answered, pointing at two steaming plates of food.

As Danny brought the plates from the kitchen he paused at the window, noticing the way the rain bent the branches of a tree toward the sidewalk. This afternoon Adam's mother had called him. She had found the portrait which had been painted of Adam eight years ago, the summer when Adam was twenty-four. She described the picture, the way the artist had overlapped a sequence of pale-blue and green strokes, like a camera out of focus, yet had remarkably managed to capture the dimples on the left side of his mouth when Adam tried to hold back a smile. Then she apologized for not mentioning at the funeral that, when she saw Adam the day before he died, he had said, I feel so ashamed that it has to end this way. They've made it so much easier for me, and I've only made it harder for them. You know he loved you very much, she said to Danny. He wanted you to have the portrait. I'll send it to you soon, she added, and then said goodbye.

Danny had done everything he knew how to do; why, then, did he feel that wasn't enough? He straightened his shoulders to release the strain from his back and then carried the plates to the table.   [1993]

THINKING ABOUT THE TEXT

1. This story has a flashback structure. It begins just before the memorial dinner for Adam but then recalls the events leading up to his death, ending with the dinner. Would the story's effect have been different if its structure had been strictly chronological? If so, how?

2. List the things carried in this story. What subcategories can they be placed in? Which of these things are especially significant to you? Why?

3. Characterize Danny, Adam, and John. How sympathetic are you to each? What specific details of the story affect your response to each?

4. What are some things you don't learn about the characters in this story? Would the story have been better if Currier had provided more facts about them? If so, what additional information should he have included?

5. Describe the narrator's tone. How emotional is it? Does it seem appropriate? Note that although conversations are reported, there are no quotation marks. Why do you suppose Currier omitted them?

MAKING COMPARISONS

1. Currier quite possibly was aware of O'Brien's story when he wrote his. Suppose that he did indeed know it. How might Currier's story be considered a comment on O'Brien's? Which specific features of O'Brien's story might Currier be honoring? Which might he be seen as challenging or ignoring?

2. To what extent does each of these stories undercut stereotypical images of Vietnam veterans and gay men?

3. Do you have the same emotional reaction to each of these stories? Identify what influences your reaction in each case.

WRITING ABOUT ISSUES

1. Write an essay explaining the role of setting in O'Brien's or in Currier's story. If you choose to discuss O'Brien's story, consider how it matters that the setting is the Vietnam War. How does this context shape the characters' thinking and behavior? If you choose to discuss Currier's story, consider at least two key settings featured in it, focusing on how these bring out certain traits in the story's characters.

2. Are the men in O'Brien's story as close to one another as the men in Currier's? Write an essay addressing this issue, referring to specific details of both texts.

3. For the next couple of days, keep a list of the things you carry. Then write at least three paragraphs in which you identify what your list reveals about you. Next, exchange your list with a classmate's, and write at least a paragraph in which you indicate what your classmate's list suggests about him or her. Finally, return your classmate's list with your analysis of it, get your list back with your classmate's commentary on it, and write at least a paragraph in which you identify what you have learned from this exercise.

4. Find an article that describes a specific American military unit in the Vietnam War or a specific group of men dealing with AIDS. Write an essay comparing O'Brien's story to the military article or Currier's story to the AIDS article. Focus on the two works as pieces of writing. In what ways do they resemble each other? What does the article do that the story doesn't, and vice versa?

IMAGINING THE END: A COLLECTION OF WRITINGS BY EMILY DICKINSON

EMILY DICKINSON, "I like a look of Agony"
EMILY DICKINSON, "I've seen a Dying Eye"
EMILY DICKINSON, "I heard a Fly buzz — when I died — "
EMILY DICKINSON, "Because I could not stop for Death — "

Through the centuries, works of literature have depicted scenes of death, with all sorts of purposes, styles, and effects. Among the best-known death scenes in literature are those produced by Emily Dickinson (1830–1886), now regarded as one of the greatest American poets. Although Dickinson spent much of her adult life as a virtual recluse, rarely leaving the Amherst, Massachusetts, home where she was born, her poems constantly reveal a lively, passionate intelligence. Moreover, death was hardly her sole topic; she wrote hundreds of poems on other subjects. Her poems about death are wonderfully creative, even playful in their use of metaphor and detail and express a range of attitudes toward death, from sadness to curiosity to acceptance. They vary as well in the positions they accord the speaker: the "I" is sometimes the dying person, at other times a witness to someone else's death. The four poems included here illustrate just a few of the diverse approaches that Dickinson took to human mortality. They do have in common the large amount of room they leave for interpretation; see if you and your classmates agree on how to analyze them.

BEFORE YOU READ

Why do you think a poet might be interested in describing scenes of death? Do you assume there is something unhealthy about such a focus? Why, or why not?

EMILY DICKINSON
I like a look of Agony

Emily Dickinson was an avid reader and a prolific writer, producing almost two thousand poems. Only a few of them were published while she was alive, partly because male editors of her time had difficulty appreciating her sheer originality as a woman writer. Furthermore, posthumous editors of her work have not always reproduced her manuscripts faithfully. Often they have altered the spelling, punctuation, and overall form of her poems in an attempt to make them seem more conventional than they really are. Dickinson did not even give her poems titles. Following customary practice, we have identified the poems in this cluster by their first lines. The following poem was written around 1861.

(Amherst College
Archives and Special
Collections.)

I like a look of Agony,
Because I know it's true —
Men do not sham Convulsion,
Nor simulate, a Throe —

The Eyes glaze once — and that is Death — 5
Impossible to feign
The Beads upon the Forehead
By homely Anguish strung.   [c. 1861]

THINKING ABOUT THE TEXT

1. What would you say to someone who argues that the speaker is being sadistic in liking "a look of Agony," especially when many Americans were dying agonizing deaths in the Civil War? Do you share to any extent the speaker's values?

2. What is the effect of Dickinson's use of capitalization?

3. How does the second stanza of the poem relate to the first?

4. Look up the word *homely* in a dictionary. Is Dickinson using the word in any of the senses you find there? Should she?

5. Note the words *Beads* and *strung* at the end of the poem. What object do they normally suggest? How appropriate is this object as a concluding image for the poem?

EMILY DICKINSON
I've seen a Dying Eye

Dickinson wrote this poem around 1862.

I've seen a Dying Eye
Run round and round a Room —
In search of Something — as it seemed —
Then Cloudier become —
And then — obscure with Fog —
And then — be soldered down
Without disclosing what it be
'Twere blessed to have seen —

5

[c. 1862]

THINKING ABOUT THE TEXT

1. To what extent does this poem seem to be about the speaker rather than about the dying person? What adjectives would you use to describe each?

2. What would you say to someone who argues that the word *run* is too active a verb for someone who is dying?

3. Should readers try to guess what the dying person is searching for? Why, or why not? Do you get the impression that he or she was, in fact, "blessed"?

4. Trace the poem's pattern of *m* sounds. What is their effect?

5. What do you conclude from the fact that the word *seen* appears both at the beginning and at the end of the poem?

MAKING COMPARISONS

1. Do you get the impression that this poem depicts the "look of Agony" that the speaker in the first poem likes? Refer to specific lines in each text.

2. How vivid is the death scene in this poem compared to that in the first?

3. What words in this poem can be related to the word *glaze* in the first?

EMILY DICKINSON
I heard a Fly buzz — when I died —

Dickinson wrote the following poem, one of her most famous, around 1862.

I heard a Fly buzz—when I died—
The Stillness in the Room
Was like the Stillness in the Air—
Between the Heaves of Storm—

The Eyes around—had wrung them dry—   5
And Breaths were gathering firm
For that last Onset—when the King
Be witnessed—in the Room—

I willed my Keepsakes—Signed away
What portion of me be   10
Assignable—and then it was
There interposed a Fly—

With Blue—uncertain stumbling Buzz—
Between the light—and me—
And then the Windows failed—and then   15
I could not see to see—   [c. 1862]

THINKING ABOUT THE TEXT

1. Do you find this poem amusing? Horrifying? Both? Neither? Identify specific lines, as well as any experiences of yours, that influence your response.

2. Many might argue that the poem presents a logical impossibility: No one can recall when he or she died because death extinguishes thought. How would you respond to this charge?

3. Why do you think Dickinson repeats the word *Stillness* in the first stanza? Consult a dictionary definition of the word. Why do you think she repeats *see* in the last line?

4. Although Dickinson mentions the fly in the first line, she doesn't return to it until the last line of the third stanza. Why do you think she delays? What might she have been trying to achieve in the intervening lines?

5. Although Dickinson writes "And then the Windows failed," plainly it is the speaker's eyesight that is failing. Why do you think Dickinson states otherwise?

MAKING COMPARISONS

1. In the first two poems, the "I" is a witness to someone else's death. Here, the "I" dies. Do you therefore read this poem with different feelings? Why, or why not?

2. Note the reference to "the King" in the second stanza of this poem. Would someone be justified in concluding that "the King" is what the dying person is searching for in "I've seen a Dying Eye"? Why, or why not? Does the first poem have nothing to do with religion since it does not use expressions like "the King"?

3. The second stanza of this poem refers to "Eyes" and "Breaths" rather than whole people. Similarly, "I've seen a Dying Eye" refers just to an eye rather than explicitly mentioning a person. Moreover, the second stanza of "I like a look of Agony," focuses purely on the eyes and the forehead. What should readers conclude from Dickinson's emphasis on parts of bodies?

EMILY DICKINSON

Because I could not stop for Death —

This poem, also one of Dickinson's best known, was written about 1863.

Because I could not stop for Death —
He kindly stopped for me —
The Carriage held but just Ourselves —
And Immortality.

We slowly drove — He knew no haste   5
And I had put away
My labor and my leisure too,
For His Civility —

We passed the School, where Children strove
At Recess — in the Ring —   10
We passed the Fields of Gazing Grain —
We passed the Setting Sun —

Or rather — He passed Us —
The Dews drew quivering and chill —
For only Gossamer, my Gown —   15
My Tippet° — only Tulle —   *shawl*

We paused before a House that seemed
A Swelling of the Ground —
The Roof was scarcely visible —
The Cornice — in the Ground —   20

Since then — 'tis Centuries — and yet
Feels shorter than the Day
I first surmised the Horses' Heads
Were toward Eternity —   [c. 1863]

THINKING ABOUT THE TEXT

1. Describe the speaker's tone. What do you think he or she means by "I could not stop for Death"? How, exactly, might "He kindly stopped for me" refer to something different? In what other lines, if any, do you sense the speaker expressing his or her feelings?

2. The first stanza ends by noting that immortality is a passenger in the carriage. Should readers conclude that the speaker is now immortal? Why, or why not?

3. What image of death do you get from this poem? List at least three adjectives of your own.

4. Note the things passed in the third stanza. Why do you think Dickinson chose to include these rather than other things? What is the effect of her making the ultimate destination a house?

5. Do you find this poem comforting? Remember that Dickinson wrote it when she was about thirty-three. If she had identified the speaker as being only that old, would you have reacted to the poem differently?

MAKING COMPARISONS

1. Do the first two lines of this poem seem applicable to the deaths in the other three poems? Explain your reasoning. In general, this poem develops the idea of dying as a journey. Is such a metaphor compatible with the death scenes of the other three poems? Refer to specific lines in them.

2. Is this poem sunnier than the other three? Explain.

3. Rank the four poems in this cluster from the one you like most to the one you like least. Identify the criteria you are using to make your evaluations.

WRITING ABOUT ISSUES

1. Each of the poems in this cluster refers to one or more efforts to see something. Choose one of the poems, and write an essay considering what is and isn't accomplished by whatever attempts at vision the poem discusses. Refer to specific lines.

2. Write an essay comparing two of the speakers in this cluster. Focus on identifying the extent to which they resemble each other in their feelings and thoughts. Refer to specific lines in each poem.

3. Choose one of the poems in this cluster and write an essay discussing how you would present the poem to a particular person you know. What about the poem would you emphasize to this person? What about the person's own life would you be thinking of? What kind of response would you hope for? If you wish, your essay can take the form of a letter to the person.

4. Obtain a contemporary sympathy card that features a poem. Then write an essay comparing the card's poem to a poem by Dickinson from this cluster. Focus on just one or two bases of comparison: for example, the poems' attitudes toward death, their language, their potential functions in society, their relative artistic quality. Be sure to quote from each of the two poems you discuss.

──────── A WEB ASSIGNMENT ────────

Emily Dickinson produced several handwritten manuscripts of her poem "I heard a Fly buzz—when I died—". The *Making Literature Matter* Web site will link you to an electronic reproduction of one such manuscript, at a site designed by Meredith Bishop and Brian Dillard for a class at the University of Texas, Austin. Looking at the manuscript, do you think a typeset version of it (such as the one in this book) can provide the same reading experience? Write an essay addressing this question. Consider in particular how slanted Dickinson's handwriting is. How relevant is this quality to your experience of the poem?

──────── Visit www.bedfordstmartins.com/makinglitmatter ────────

CONFRONTING THE DEATH OF A STRANGER

KATHERINE MANSFIELD, "The Garden-Party"
GABRIEL GARCÍA MÁRQUEZ, "The Handsomest Drowned Man
in the World"
DON DELILLO, "Videotape"

When do people really ponder human mortality? For some, it's when someone close to them dies or when they themselves are in peril. For others, it's when they witness the deaths of strangers, as is the case in the following three stories. Encountering a workman's body right after her family's party, the well-to-do young heroine of Katherine Mansfield's story finds herself suddenly contemplating the nature of life as well as death. When "the handsomest drowned man in the world" washes up on their island, Gabriel García Márquez's characters are moved to reflect on various limitations of their own. In Don DeLillo's story, which is set in our own electronic era, the narrator repeatedly watches and broods about a child's videotape of a murder. Indeed, nowadays you can witness fatal violence quite easily if you have TV; just turn on the evening news. Precisely because death is a regular feature of television and other media, people may be more apt to consider what it means to them. On the other hand, they may become less sensitive to death and less inclined to consider how to live in the face of it. Try weighing both possibilities as you see how Mansfield's, García Márquez's, and DeLillo's characters treat the demise of someone unknown to them.

BEFORE YOU READ

Describe a death scene that you have read or one that you have seen depicted on television or film. What was your emotional reaction to this scene? What specific aspects of it influenced your reaction most? How realistic was the scene? In what ways, if any, could it have been done more realistically? Be sure to identify what you mean by these terms.

KATHERINE MANSFIELD
The Garden-Party

Katherine Mansfield (1888–1923) was one of the leading writers in English during the first decades of the twentieth century. She is chiefly known for her short stories and for her journal, a version of which was published posthumously. Mansfield was born in New Zealand and spent most of her youth there. Eventually, though, she lived in France, Germany, and especially England until her death from tuberculosis at the age of thirty-four. The following story appeared in a 1922 collection of her works, also entitled The Garden-Party.

And after all the weather was ideal. They could not have had a more perfect day for a garden-party if they had ordered it. Windless, warm, the sky without a cloud. Only the blue was veiled with a haze of light gold, as it is sometimes in early summer. The gardener had been up since dawn, mowing the lawns and sweeping them, until the grass and the dark flat rosettes where the daisy plants had been seemed to shine. As for the roses, you could not help feeling they understood that roses are the only flowers that impress people at garden-parties; the only flowers that everybody is certain of knowing. Hundreds, yes, literally hundreds, had come out in a single night; the green bushes bowed down as though they had been visited by archangels.

Breakfast was not yet over before the men came to put up the marquee.

"Where do you want the marquee put, mother?"

"My dear child, it's no use asking me. I'm determined to leave everything to you children this year. Forget I am your mother. Treat me as an honoured guest."

But Meg could not possibly go and supervise the men. She had washed her   5
hair before breakfast, and she sat drinking her coffee in a green turban, with a dark wet curl stamped on each cheek. Jose, the butterfly, always came down in a silk petticoat and a kimono jacket.

"You'll have to go, Laura; you're the artistic one."

Away Laura flew, still holding her piece of bread-and-butter. It's so delicious to have an excuse for eating out of doors, and besides, she loved having to arrange things; she always felt she could do it so much better than anybody else.

Four men in their shirt-sleeves stood grouped together on the garden path. They carried staves covered with rolls of canvas, and they had big tool-bags slung on their backs. They looked impressive. Laura wished now that she had not got the bread-and-butter, but there was nowhere to put it, and she couldn't possibly throw it away. She blushed and tried to look severe and even a little bit short-sighted as she came up to them.

"Good morning," she said, copying her mother's voice. But that sounded so fearfully affected that she was ashamed, and stammered like a little girl, "Oh — er — have you come — is it about the marquee?"

"That's right, miss," said the tallest of the men, a lanky, freckled fellow, and   10
he shifted his tool-bag, knocked back his straw hat and smiled down at her. "That's about it."

His smile was so easy, so friendly that Laura recovered. What nice eyes he had, small, but such dark blue! And now she looked at the others, they were smiling too. "Cheer up, we won't bite," their smile seemed to say. How very nice workmen were! And what a beautiful morning! She mustn't mention the morning; she must be businesslike. The marquee.

"Well, what about the lily-lawn? Would that do?"

And she pointed to the lily-lawn with the hand that didn't hold the bread-and-butter. They turned, they stared in the direction. A little fat chap thrust out his under-lip, and the tall fellow frowned.

"I don't fancy it," said he. "Not conspicuous enough. You see, with a thing like a marquee," and he turned to Laura in his easy way, "you want to put it somewhere where it'll give you a bang slap in the eye, if you follow me."

Laura's upbringing made her wonder for a moment whether it was quite   15
respectful of a workman to talk to her of bangs slap in the eye. But she did quite follow him.

"A corner of the tennis-court," she suggested. "But the band's going to be in one corner."

"H'm, going to have a band, are you?" said another of the workmen. He was pale. He had a haggard look as his dark eyes scanned the tennis-court. What was he thinking?

"Only a very small band," said Laura gently. Perhaps he wouldn't mind so much if the band was quite small. But the tall fellow interrupted.

"Look here, miss, that's the place. Against those trees. Over there. That'll do fine."

Against the karakas. Then the karaka-trees would be hidden. And they were   20
so lovely, with their broad, gleaming leaves, and their clusters of yellow fruit. They were like trees you imagined growing on a desert island, proud, solitary, lifting their leaves and fruits to the sun in a kind of silent splendour. Must they be hidden by a marquee?

They must. Already the men had shouldered their staves and were making for the place. Only the tall fellow was left. He bent down, pinched a sprig of lavender, put his thumb and forefinger to his nose and snuffed up the smell. When Laura saw that gesture she forgot all about the karakas in her wonder at him caring for things like that — caring for the smell of lavender. How many men that she knew would have done such a thing? Oh, how extraordinarily nice workmen were, she thought. Why couldn't she have workmen for friends rather than the silly boys she danced with and who came to Sunday night supper? She would get on much better with men like these.

It's all the fault, she decided, as the tall fellow drew something on the back of an envelope, something that was to be looped up or left to hang, of these absurd class distinctions. Well, for her part, she didn't feel them. Not a bit, not an atom. . . . And now there came the chock-chock of wooden hammers. Some one whistled, some one sang out, "Are you right there, matey?" "Matey!" The friendliness of it, the — the — Just to prove how happy she was, just to show the tall fellow how at home she felt, and how she despised stupid conventions, Laura took a big bite of her bread-and-butter as she stared at the little drawing. She felt just like a work-girl.

"Laura, Laura, where are you? Telephone, Laura!" a voice cried from the house.

"Coming!" Away she skimmed, over the lawn, up the path, up the steps, across the veranda, and into the porch. In the hall her father and Laurie were brushing their hats ready to go to the office.

"I say, Laura," said Laurie very fast, "you might just give a squiz at my coat   25
before this afternoon. See if it wants pressing."

"I will," said she. Suddenly she couldn't stop herself. She ran at Laurie and gave him a small, quick squeeze. "Oh, I do love parties, don't you?" gasped Laura.

"Ra-ther," said Laurie's warm, boyish voice, and he squeezed his sister too, and gave her a gentle push. "Dash off to the telephone, old girl."

The telephone. "Yes, yes; oh yes. Kitty? Good morning, dear. Come to lunch? Do, dear. Delighted of course. It will only be a very scratch meal — just the sandwich crusts and broken meringue-shells and what's left over. Yes, isn't it a perfect morning? Your white? Oh, I certainly should. One moment — hold the line. Mother's calling." And Laura sat back. "What, mother? Can't hear."

Mrs. Sheridan's voice floated down the stairs. "Tell her to wear that sweet hat she had on last Sunday."

"Mother says you're to wear that *sweet* hat you had on last Sunday. Good.   30
One o'clock. Bye-bye."

Laura put back the receiver, flung her arms over her head, took a deep breath, stretched and let them fall. "Huh," she sighed, and the moment after the sigh she sat up quickly. She was still, listening. All the doors in the house seemed to be open. The house was alive with soft, quick steps and running voices. The green baize door that led to the kitchen regions swung open and shut with a muffled thud. And now there came a long, chuckling absurd sound. It was the heavy piano being moved on its stiff castors. But the air! If you stopped to notice, was the air always like this? Little faint winds were playing chase, in at the tops of the windows, out at the doors. And there were two tiny spots of sun, one on the inkpot, one on a silver photograph frame, playing too. Darling little spots. Especially the one on the inkpot lid. It was quite warm. A warm little silver star. She could have kissed it.

The front door bell pealed, and there sounded the rustle of Sadie's print skirt on the stairs. A man's voice murmured; Sadie answered, careless, "I'm sure I don't know. Wait. I'll ask Mrs. Sheridan."

"What is it, Sadie?" Laura came into the hall.

"It's the florist, Miss Laura."

It was, indeed. There, just inside the door, stood a wide, shallow tray full of   35
pots of pink lilies. No other kind. Nothing but lilies — canna lilies, big pink flowers, wide open, radiant, almost frighteningly alive on bright crimson stems.

"O-oh Sadie!" said Laura, and the sound was like a little moan. She crouched down as if to warm herself at that blaze of lilies; she felt they were in her fingers, on her lips, growing in her breast.

"It's some mistake," she said faintly. "Nobody ever ordered so many. Sadie, go and find mother."

But at that moment Mrs. Sheridan joined them.

"It's quite right," she said calmly. "Yes, I ordered them. Aren't they lovely?" She pressed Laura's arm. "I was passing the shop yesterday, and I saw them in the window. And I suddenly thought for once in my life I shall have enough canna lilies. The garden-party will be a good excuse."

"But I thought you said you didn't mean to interfere," said Laura. Sadie had gone. The florist's man was still outside at his van. She put her arm round her mother's neck and gently, very gently, she bit her mother's ear.

"My darling child, you wouldn't like a logical mother, would you? Don't do that. Here's the man."

He carried more lilies still, another whole tray.

"Bank them up, just inside the door, on both sides of the porch, please," said Mrs. Sheridan. "Don't you agree, Laura?"

"Oh, I *do* mother."

In the drawing-room Meg, Jose and good little Hans had at last succeeded in moving the piano.

"Now, if we put this chesterfield against the wall and move everything out of the room except the chairs, don't you think?"

"Quite."

"Hans, move these tables into the smoking-room, and bring a sweeper to take these marks off the carpet and — one moment, Hans — " Jose loved giving orders to the servants, and they loved obeying her. She always made them feel they were taking part in some drama. "Tell mother and Miss Laura to come here at once."

"Very good, Miss Jose."

She turned to Meg. "I want to hear what the piano sounds like, just in case I'm asked to sing this afternoon. Let's try over 'This Life is Weary.' "

Pom! Ta-ta-ta *Tee*-ta! The piano burst out so passionately that Jose's face changed. She clasped her hands. She looked mournfully and enigmatically at her mother and Laura as they came in.

> This Life is *Wee*-ary,
> A Tear — a Sigh.
> A Love that *Chan*-ges,
>   This Life is *Wee*-ary,
> A Tear — a Sigh.
> A Love that *Chan*-ges,
> And then . . . *Good*-bye!

But at the word "Good-bye," and although the piano sounded more desperate than ever, her face broke into a brilliant, dreadfully unsympathetic smile.

"Aren't I in good voice, mummy?" she beamed.

> This Life is *Wee*-ary,
> Hope comes to Die.
> A Dream — a *Wa*-kening.

But now Sadie interrupted them. "What is it, Sadie?"

"If you please, m'm, cook says have you got the flags for the sandwiches?"

"The flags for the sandwiches, Sadie?" echoed Mrs. Sheridan dreamily. And the children knew by her face that she hadn't got them. "Let me see." And she said to Sadie firmly, "Tell cook I'll let her have them in ten minutes."

Sadie went.

"Now, Laura," said her mother quickly. "Come with me into the smoking-room. I've got the names somewhere on the back of an envelope. You'll have to write them out for me. Meg, go upstairs this minute and take that wet thing off your head. Jose, run and finish dressing this instant. Do you hear me, children, or shall I have to tell your father when he comes home to-night? And — and, Jose, pacify cook if you do go into the kitchen, will you? I'm terrified of her this morning."

The envelope was found at last behind the dining-room clock, though how it had got there Mrs. Sheridan could not imagine.

"One of you children must have stolen it out of my bag, because I remember   60
vividly — cream cheese and lemon-curd. Have you done that?"

"Yes."

"Egg and — " Mrs. Sheridan held the envelope away from her. "It looks like mice. It can't be mice, can it?"

"Olive, pet," said Laura, looking over her shoulder.

"Yes, of course, olive. What a horrible combination it sounds. Egg and olive."

They were finished at last, and Laura took them off to the kitchen. She found   65
Jose there pacifying the cook, who did not look at all terrifying.

"I have never seen such exquisite sandwiches," said Jose's rapturous voice. "How many kinds did you say there were, cook? Fifteen?"

"Fifteen, Miss Jose."

"Well, cook, I congratulate you."

Cook swept up crusts with the long sandwich knife, and smiled broadly.

"Godber's has come," announced Sadie, issuing out of the pantry. She had   70
seen the man pass the window.

That meant the cream puffs had come. Godber's were famous for their cream puffs. Nobody ever thought of making them at home.

"Bring them in and put them on the table, my girl," ordered cook.

Sadie brought them in and went back to the door. Of course Laura and Jose were far too grown-up to really care about such things. All the same, they couldn't help agreeing that the puffs looked very attractive. Very. Cook began arranging them, shaking off the extra icing sugar.

"Don't they carry one back to all one's parties?" said Laura.

"I suppose they do," said practical Jose, who never liked to be carried back.   75
"They look beautifully light and feathery, I must say."

"Have one each, my dears," said cook in her comfortable voice. "Yer ma won't know."

Oh, impossible. Fancy cream puffs so soon after breakfast. The very idea made one shudder. All the same, two minutes later Jose and Laura were licking their fingers with that absorbed inward look that only comes from whipped cream.

"Let's go into the garden, out by the back way," suggested Laura. "I want to see how the men are getting on with the marquee. They're such awfully nice men."

But the back door was blocked by cook, Sadie, Godber's man and Hans.

Something had happened.   80

"Tuk-tuk-tuk," clucked cook like an agitated hen. Sadie had her hand clapped to her cheek as though she had toothache. Hans's face was screwed up in the effort to understand. Only Godber's man seemed to be enjoying himself; it was his story.

"What's the matter? What's happened?"

"There's been a horrible accident," said Cook. "A man killed."

"A man killed! Where? How? When?"

But Godber's man wasn't going to have his story snatched from under his very nose.

"Know those little cottages just below here, miss?" Know them? Of course, she knew them. "Well, there's a young chap living there, name of Scott, a carter. His horse shied at a traction-engine, corner of Hawke Street this morning, and he was thrown out on the back of his head. Killed."

"Dead!" Laura stared at Godber's man.

"Dead when they picked him up," said Godber's man with relish. "They were taking the body home as I come up here." And he said to the cook, "He's left a wife and five little ones."

"Jose, come here." Laura caught hold of her sister's sleeve and dragged her through the kitchen to the other side of the green baize door. There she paused and leaned against it. "Jose!" she said, horrified, "however are we going to stop everything?"

"Stop everything, Laura!" cried Jose in astonishment. "What do you mean?"

"Stop the garden-party, of course." Why did Jose pretend?

But Jose was still more amazed. "Stop the garden-party? My dear Laura, don't be so absurd. Of course we can't do anything of the kind. Nobody expects us to. Don't be so extravagant."

"But we can't possibly have a garden-party with a man dead just outside the front gate."

That really was extravagant, for the little cottages were in a lane to themselves at the very bottom of a steep rise that led up to the house. A broad road ran between. True, they were far too near. They were the greatest possible eyesore, and they had no right to be in that neighbourhood at all. They were little mean dwellings painted a chocolate brown. In the garden patches there was nothing but cabbage stalks, sick hens and tomato cans. The very smoke coming out of their chimneys was poverty-stricken. Little rags and shreds of smoke, so unlike the great silvery plumes that uncurled from the Sheridans' chimneys. Washerwomen lived in the lane and sweeps and a cobbler, and a man whose house-front was studded all over with minute bird-cages. Children swarmed. When the Sheridans were little they were forbidden to set foot there because of the revolting language and of what they might catch. But since they were grown up, Laura and Laurie on their prowls sometimes walked through. It was disgusting and sordid. They came out with a shudder. But still one must go everywhere; one must see everything. So through they went.

"And just think of what the band would sound like to that poor woman," said Laura.

"Oh, Laura!" Jose began to be seriously annoyed. "If you're going to stop a band playing every time some one has an accident, you'll lead a very strenuous life. I'm every bit as sorry about it as you. I feel just as sympathetic." Her eyes hardened. She looked at her sister just as she used to when they were little and fighting together. "You won't bring a drunken workman back to life by being sentimental," she said softly.

"Drunk! Who said he was drunk?" Laura turned furiously on Jose. She said, just as they had used to say on those occasions, "I'm going straight up to tell mother."

"Do, dear," cooed Jose.

"Mother, can I come in your room?" Laura turned the big glass door-knob.

"Of course, child. Why, what's the matter? What's given you such a colour?" 100 And Mrs. Sheridan turned round from her dressing-table. She was trying on a new hat.

"Mother, a man's been killed," began Laura.

"*Not* in the garden?" interrupted her mother.

"No, no!"

"Oh, what a fright you gave me!" Mrs. Sheridan sighed with relief, and took off the big hat and held it on her knees.

"But listen, mother," said Laura. Breathless, half-choking, she told the dread- 105 ful story. "Of course, we can't have our party, can we?" she pleaded. "The band and everybody arriving. They'd hear us, mother; they're nearly neighbors!"

To Laura's astonishment her mother behaved just like Jose, it was harder to bear because she seemed amused. She refused to take Laura seriously.

"But, my dear child, use your common sense. It's only by accident we've heard of it. If some one had died there normally—and I can't understand how they keep alive in those poky little holes—we should still be having our party, shouldn't we?"

Laura had to say "yes" to that, but she felt it was all wrong. She sat down on her mother's sofa and pinched the cushion frill.

"Mother, isn't it really terribly heartless of us?" she asked.

"Darling!" Mrs. Sheridan got up and came over to her, carrying the hat. 110 Before Laura could stop her she had popped it on. "My child!" said her mother, "the hat is yours. It's made for you. It's much too young for me. I have never seen you look such a picture. Look at yourself!" And she held up her hand-mirror.

"But, mother," Laura began again. She couldn't look at herself; she turned aside.

This time Mrs. Sheridan lost patience just as Jose had done.

"You are being very absurd, Laura," she said coldly. "People like that don't expect sacrifices from us. And it's not very sympathetic to spoil everybody's enjoyment as you're doing now."

"I don't understand," said Laura, and she walked quickly out of the room into her own bedroom. There, quite by chance, the first thing she saw was this charming girl in the mirror, in her black hat trimmed with gold daisies, and a long black velvet ribbon. Never had she imagined she could look like that. Is mother right? she thought. And now she hoped her mother was right. Am I being extravagant? Perhaps it was extravagant. Just for a moment she had another glimpse of that poor woman and those little children, and the body being carried into the house. But it all seemed blurred, unreal, like a picture in the newspaper. I'll remember it again after the party's over, she decided. And somehow that seemed quite the best plan. . . .

Lunch was over by half-past one. By half-past two they were all ready for the   115
fray. The green-coated band had arrived and was established in a corner of the tennis-court.

"My dear!" trilled Kitty Maitland, "aren't they too like frogs for words? You ought to have arranged them round the pond with the conductor in the middle on a leaf."

Laurie arrived and hailed them on his way to dress. At the sight of him Laura remembered the accident again. She wanted to tell him. If Laurie agreed with the others, then it was bound to be all right. And she followed him into the hall.

"Laurie!"

"Hallo!" He was half-way upstairs, but when he turned round and saw Laura he suddenly puffed out his cheeks and goggled his eyes at her. "My word, Laura; You do look stunning," said Laurie. "What an absolutely topping hat!"

Laura said faintly, "Is it?" and smiled up at Laurie, and didn't tell him   120
after all.

Soon after that people began coming in streams. The band struck up; the hired waiters ran from the house to the marquee. Wherever you looked there were couples strolling, bending to the flowers, greeting, moving on over the lawn. They were like bright birds that had alighted in the Sheridans' garden for this one afternoon, on their way to—where? Ah, what happiness it is to be with people who all are happy, to press hands, press cheeks, smile into eyes.

"Darling Laura, how well you look!"

"What a becoming hat, child!"

"Laura, you look quite Spanish. I've never seen you look so striking."

And Laura, glowing, answered softly, "Have you had tea? Won't you have an   125
ice? The passion-fruit ices really are rather special." She ran to her father and begged him. "Daddy darling, can't the band have something to drink?"

And the perfect afternoon slowly ripened, slowly faded, slowly its petals closed.

"Never a more delightful garden-party . . ." "The greatest success . . ." "Quite the most . . ."

Laura helped her mother with the good-byes. They stood side by side in the porch till it was all over.

"All over, all over, thank heaven," said Mrs. Sheridan. "Round up the others, Laura. Let's go and have some fresh coffee. I'm exhausted. Yes, it's been very suc- cessful. But oh, these parties, these parties! Why will you children insist on giving parties!" And they all of them sat down in the deserted marquee.

"Have a sandwich, daddy dear. I wrote the flag."   130

"Thanks." Mr. Sheridan took a bite and the sandwich was gone. He took another. "I suppose you didn't hear of a beastly accident that happened to-day?" he said.

"My dear," said Mrs. Sheridan, holding up her hand, "we did. It nearly ruined the party. Laura insisted we should put it off."

"Oh, mother!" Laura didn't want to be teased about it.

"It was a horrible affair all the same," said Mr. Sheridan. "The chap was married too. Lived just below in the lane, and leaves a wife and half a dozen kiddies, so they say."

An awkward little silence fell. Mrs. Sheridan fidgeted with her cup. Really, it   135
was very tactless of father. . . .

Suddenly she looked up. There on the table were all those sandwiches, cakes, puffs, all uneaten, all going to be wasted. She had one of her brilliant ideas.

"I know," she said. "Let's make up a basket. Let's send that poor creature some of this perfectly good food. At any rate, it will be the greatest treat for the children. Don't you agree? And she's sure to have neighbours calling in and so on. What a point to have it all ready prepared. Laura!" She jumped up. "Get me the big basket out of the stairs cupboard."

"But, mother, do you really think it's a good idea?" said Laura.

Again, how curious, she seemed to be different from them all. To take scraps from their party. Would the poor woman really like that?

"Of course! What's the matter with you to-day? An hour or two ago you were   140
insisting on us being sympathetic, and now—"

Oh, well! Laura ran for the basket. It was filled, it was heaped by her mother.

"Take it yourself, darling," said she. "Run down just as you are. No, wait, take the arum lilies too. People of that class are so impressed by arum lilies."

"The stems will ruin her lace frock," said practical Jose.

So they would. Just in time. "Only the basket, then. And, Laura!"—her mother followed her out of the marquee—"don't on any account—"

"What, mother?"   145

No, better not put such ideas into the child's head! "Nothing! Run along."

It was just growing dusky as Laura shut their garden gates. A big dog ran by like a shadow. The road gleamed white, and down below in the hollow the little cottages were in deep shade. How quiet it seemed after the afternoon. Here she was going down the hill to somewhere where a man lay dead, and she couldn't realize it. Why couldn't she? She stopped a minute. And it seemed to her that kisses, voices, tinkling spoons, laughter, the smell of crushed grass were somehow inside her. She had no room for anything else. How strange! She looked up at the pale sky, and all she thought was, "Yes, it was the most successful party."

Now the broad road was crossed. The lane began, smoky and dark. Women in shawls and men's tweed caps hurried by. Men hung over the palings; the children played in the doorways. A low hum came from the mean little cottages. In some of them there was a flicker of light, and a shadow, crab-like, moved across the window. Laura bent her head and hurried on. She wished now she had put on a coat. How her frock shone! And the big hat with the velvet streamer—if only it was another hat! Were the people looking at her? They must be. It was a mistake to have come; she knew all along it was a mistake. Should she go back even now?

No, too late. This was the house. It must be. A dark knot of people stood outside. Beside the gate an old, old woman with a crutch sat in a chair, watching.

She had her feet on a newspaper. The voices stopped as Laura drew near. The group parted. It was as though she was expected, as though they had known she was coming here.

Laura was terribly nervous. Tossing the velvet ribbon over her shoulder, she   150
said to a woman standing by, "Is this Mrs. Scott's house?" and the woman, smiling queerly, said, "It is, my lass."

Oh, to be away from this! She actually said, "Help me, God," as she walked up the tiny path and knocked. To be away from those staring eyes, or to be covered up in anything, one of those women's shawls even. I'll just leave the basket and go, she decided. I shan't even wait for it to be emptied.

Then the door opened. A little woman in black showed in the gloom.

Laura said, "Are you Mrs. Scott?" But to her horror the woman answered, "Walk in please, miss," and she was shut in the passage.

"No," said Laura, "I don't want to come in. I only want to leave this basket. Mother sent—"

The little woman in the gloomy passage seemed not to have heard her. "Step   155
this way, please, miss," she said in an oily voice, and Laura followed her.

She found herself in a wretched little low kitchen, lighted by a smoky lamp. There was a woman sitting before the fire.

"Em," said the little creature who had let her in. "Em! It's a young lady." She turned to Laura. She said meaningly, "I'm 'er sister, Miss. You'll excuse 'er, won't you?"

"Oh, but of course!" said Laura. "Please, please don't disturb her. I—I only want to leave—"

But at that moment the woman at the fire turned round. Her face, puffed up, red, with swollen eyes and swollen lips, looked terrible. She seemed as though she couldn't understand why Laura was there. What did it mean? Why was this stranger standing in the kitchen with a basket? What was it all about? And the poor face puckered up again.

"All right, my dear," said the other. "I'll thenk the young lady."   160

And again she began, "You'll excuse her, miss, I'm sure," and her face, swollen too, tried an oily smile.

Laura only wanted to get out, to get away. She was back in the passage. The door opened. She walked straight through into the bedroom, where the dead man was lying.

"You'd like a look at 'im, wouldn't you?" said Em's sister, and she brushed past Laura over to the bed. "Don't be afraid, my lass,—" and now her voice sounded fond and sly, and fondly she drew down the sheet—" 'e looks a picture. There's nothing to show. Come along, my dear."

There lay a young man, fast asleep—sleeping so soundly, so deeply, that he was far, far away from them both. Oh, so remote, so peaceful. He was dreaming. Never wake him up again. His head was sunk in the pillow, his eyes were closed; they were blind under the closed eyelids. He was given up to his dream. What did garden-parties and baskets and lace frocks matter to him? He was far from all those things. He was wonderful, beautiful. While they were laughing and while the band was playing, this marvel had come to the lane. Happy . . . happy. . . . All is well, said that sleeping face. This is just as it should be. I am content.

But all the same you had to cry, and she couldn't go out of the room without   165
saying something to him. Laura gave a loud childish sob.

"Forgive my hat," she said.

And this time she didn't wait for Em's sister. She found her way out of the door, down the path, past all those dark people. At the corner of the lane she met Laurie.

He stepped out of the shadow. "Is that you, Laura?"

"Yes."

"Mother was getting anxious. Was it all right?"   170

"Yes, quite. Oh, Laurie!" She took his arm, she pressed up against him.

"I say, you're not crying, are you?" asked her brother.

Laura shook her head. She was.

Laurie put his arm round her shoulder. "Don't cry," he said in his warm, loving voice. "Was it awful?"

"No," sobbed Laura. "It was simply marvellous. But, Laurie —" She stopped,   175
she looked at her brother. "Isn't life," she stammered, "isn't life —" But what life was she couldn't explain. No matter. He quite understood.

"*Isn't* it, darling?" said Laurie.   [1922]

THINKING ABOUT THE TEXT

1. Describe in your own words Laura's initial reaction to the dead man. Does her response seem sound and appropriate, or do you find it shallow? Support your evaluation.

2. Earlier in the story, Laura wonders if her family is being "heartless" in having the party despite the man's death. How fair is it to call the family "heartless"? What warrants or assumptions are reflected in your answer?

3. What distinctions are there between the culture of Laura's family and the culture of the workers? Do these cultures have anything in common? If so, what?

4. Although Mansfield has entitled her story "The Garden-Party" and describes the preparations for that party at length, she barely describes the party itself. Why, do you suppose?

5. To what extent is the story told from Laura's point of view and with her kind of language? Refer to specific passages.

GABRIEL GARCÍA MÁRQUEZ
The Handsomest Drowned Man in the World

A TALE FOR CHILDREN

Translated by Gregory Rabassa

Gabriel García Márquez (b. 1928) has achieved international renown, certified by his 1982 Nobel Prize for literature. For several years, though, he lived in exile from his native Colombia because he opposed its dictatorship. García Márquez's fiction is often described as "magic realism" because it mixes everyday life and fantastic events. His several novels include the frequently taught One Hundred Years of Solitude *(1967). The following piece is from a 1973 book by García Márquez entitled* Leaf Storm and Other Stories.

The first children who saw the dark and slinky bulge approaching through the sea let themselves think it was an enemy ship. Then they saw it had no flags or masts and they thought it was a whale. But when it washed up on the beach, they removed the clumps of seaweed, the jellyfish tentacles, and the remains of fish and flotsam, and only then did they see that it was a drowned man.

They had been playing with him all afternoon, burying him in the sand and digging him up again, when someone chanced to see them and spread the alarm in the village. The men who carried him to the nearest house noticed that he weighed more than any dead man they had ever known, almost as much as a horse, and they said to each other that maybe he'd been floating too long and the water had got into his bones. When they laid him on the floor they said he'd been taller than all other men because there was barely enough room for him in the house, but they thought that maybe the ability to keep on growing after death was part of the nature of certain drowned men. He had the smell of the sea about him and only his shape gave one to suppose that it was the corpse of a human being, because the skin was covered with a crust of mud and scales.

They did not even have to clean off his face to know that the dead man was a stranger. The village was made up of only twenty-odd wooden houses that had stone courtyards with no flowers and which were spread about on the end of a desertlike cape. There was so little land that mothers always went about with the fear that the wind would carry off their children and the few dead that the years had caused among them had to be thrown off the cliffs. But the sea was calm and bountiful and all the men fit into seven boats. So when they found the drowned man they simply had to look at one another to see that they were all there.

That night they did not go out to work at sea. While the men went to find out if anyone was missing in neighboring villages, the women stayed behind to care for the drowned man. They took the mud off with grass swabs, they removed the underwater stones entangled in his hair, and they scraped the crust off with tools used for scaling fish. As they were doing that they noticed that the vegetation on him came from faraway oceans and deep water and that his clothes were in tatters, as if he had sailed through labyrinths of coral. They noticed too that he bore his death with pride, for he did not have the lonely look of other drowned men who came out of the sea or that haggard, needy look of men who drowned in rivers. But only when they finished cleaning him off did they become aware of the kind of man he was and it left them breathless. Not only was he the tallest, strongest, most virile, and best built man they had ever seen, but even though they were looking at him there was no room for him in their imagination.

They could not find a bed in the village large enough to lay him on nor was there a table solid enough to use for his wake. The tallest men's holiday pants   5 would not fit him, nor the fattest ones' Sunday shirts, nor the shoes of the one with the biggest feet. Fascinated by his huge size and his beauty, the women then decided to make him some pants from a large piece of sail and a shirt from some bridal Brabant linen so that he could continue through his death with dignity. As they sewed, sitting in a circle and gazing at the corpse between stitches, it seemed to them that the wind had never been so steady nor the sea so restless as on that night and they supposed that the change had something to do with the dead man. They thought that if that magnificent man had lived in the village, his house would have had the widest doors, the highest ceiling, and the strongest floor; his bedstead would have been made from a midship frame held together by iron bolts, and his wife would have been the happiest woman. They thought that he would have had so much authority that he could have drawn fish out of the sea simply by calling their names and that he would have put so much work into his land that springs would have burst forth from among the rocks so that he would have been able to plant flowers on the cliffs. They secretly compared him to their own men, thinking that for all their lives theirs were incapable of doing what he could do in one night, and they ended up dismissing them deep in their hearts as the weakest, meanest, and most useless creatures on earth. They were wandering through that maze of fantasy when the oldest woman, who as the oldest had looked upon the drowned man with more compassion than passion, sighed:

"He has the face of someone called Esteban."

It was true. Most of them had only to take another look at him to see that he could not have any other name. The more stubborn among them, who were the youngest, still lived for a few hours with the illusion that when they put his clothes on and he lay among the flowers in patent leather shoes his name might be Lautaro. But it was a vain illusion. There had not been enough canvas, the poorly cut and worse sewn pants were too tight, and the hidden strength of his heart popped the buttons on his shirt. After midnight the whistling of the wind died down and the sea fell into its Wednesday drowsiness. The silence put an end to any last doubts: he was Esteban. The women who had dressed him, who had combed his hair, had cut his nails and shaved him were unable to hold back a shudder of pity when they had to resign themselves to his being dragged along the ground. It was then that they understood how unhappy he must have been with that huge body since it bothered him even after death. They could see him in life, condemned to going through doors sideways, cracking his head on cross-beams, remaining on his feet during visits, not knowing what to do with his soft pink, sealion hands while the lady of the house looked for her most resistant chair and begged him, frightened to death, sit here, Esteban, please, and he, leaning against the wall, smiling, don't bother, ma'am, I'm fine where I am, his heels raw and his back roasted from having done the same thing so many times whenever he paid a visit, don't bother, ma'am, I'm fine where I am, just to avoid the embarrassment of breaking up the chair, and never knowing perhaps that the ones who said don't go, Esteban, at least wait till the coffee's ready, were the ones who later on would whisper the big boob finally left, how nice, the handsome fool has gone. That was what the women were thinking beside the body a little before dawn. Later, when they covered his face with a handkerchief so that the light would not bother him, he looked so forever dead, so defenseless, so much like their men that the first furrows of tears opened in their hearts. It was one of the younger ones who began the weeping. The others, coming to, went from sighs to wails, and the more they sobbed the more they felt like weeping, because the drowned man was becoming all the more Esteban for them, and so they wept so much, for he was the most destitute, most peaceful, and most obliging man on earth, poor Esteban. So when the men returned with the news that the drowned man was not from the neighboring villages either, the women felt an opening of jubilation in the midst of their tears.

"Praise the Lord," they sighed, "he's ours!"

The men thought the fuss was only womanish frivolity. Fatigued because of the difficult nighttime inquiries, all they wanted was to get rid of the bother of the newcomer once and for all before the sun grew strong on that arid, windless day. They improvised a litter with the remains of foremasts and gaffs, tying it together with rigging so that it would bear the weight of the body until they reached the cliffs. They wanted to tie the anchor from a cargo ship to him so that he would sink easily into the deepest waves, where fish are blind and divers die of nostalgia, and bad currents would not bring him back to shore, as had happened with other bodies. But the more they hurried, the more the women thought of ways to waste time. They walked about like startled hens, pecking with the sea charms on their breasts, some interfering on one side to put a scapular of the good wind on the drowned man, some on the other side to put a wrist compass on him, and after a great deal of *get away from there, woman, stay out of the way, look, you almost made me fall on top of the dead man*, the men began to feel mistrust in their livers and started grumbling about why so many main-altar decorations for a stranger, because no matter how many nails and holy-water jars he had on him, the sharks would chew him all the same, but the women kept on piling on their junk relics, running back and forth, stumbling, while they released in sighs what they did not in tears, so that the men finally exploded with *since when has there ever been such a fuss over a drifting corpse, a drowned nobody, a piece of cold Wednesday meat*. One of the women, mortified by so much lack of care, then removed the handkerchief from the dead man's face and the men were left breathless too.

He was Esteban. It was not necessary to repeat it for them to recognize him. If they had been told Sir Walter Raleigh, even they might have been impressed with his gringo accent, the macaw on his shoulder, his cannibal-killing blunderbuss, but there could be only one Esteban in the world and there he was, stretched out like a sperm whale, shoeless, wearing the pants of an undersized child, and with those stony nails that had to be cut with a knife. They had only to take the handkerchief off his face to see that he was ashamed, that it was not his fault that he was so big or so heavy or so handsome, and if he had known that this was going to happen, he would have looked for a more discreet place to drown in; seriously, I even would have tied the anchor off a galleon around my neck and staggered off a cliff like someone who doesn't like things in order not to be upsetting people now with this Wednesday dead body, as you people say, in order not to be bothering anyone with this filthy piece of cold meat that doesn't have anything to do with me. There was so much truth in his manner that even the most mistrustful men, the ones who felt the bitterness of endless nights at sea fearing

10

that their women would tire of dreaming about them and begin to dream of drowned men, even they and others who were harder still shuddered in the marrow of their bones at Esteban's sincerity.

That was how they came to hold the most splendid funeral they could conceive of for an abandoned drowned man. Some women who had gone to get flowers in the neighboring villages returned with other women who could not believe what they had been told, and those women went back for more flowers when they saw the dead man, and they brought more and more until there were so many flowers and so many people that it was hard to walk about. At the final moment it pained them to return him to the waters as an orphan and they chose a father and mother from among the best people, and aunts and uncles and cousins, so that through him all the inhabitants of the village became kinsmen. Some sailors who heard the weeping from a distance went off course, and people heard of one who had himself tied to the mainmast, remembering ancient fables about sirens. While they fought for the privilege of carrying him on their shoulders along the steep escarpment by the cliffs, men and women became aware for the first time of the desolation of their streets, the dryness of their courtyards, the narrowness of their dreams as they faced the splendor and beauty of their drowned man. They let him go without an anchor so that he could come back if he wished and whenever he wished, and they all held their breath for the fraction of centuries the body took to fall into the abyss. They did not need to look at one another to realize that they were no longer all present, that they would never be. But they also knew that everything would be different from then on, that their houses would have wider doors, higher ceilings, and stronger floors so that Esteban's memory could go everywhere without bumping into beams and so that no one in the future would dare whisper the big boob finally died, too bad, the handsome fool has finally died, because they were going to paint their house fronts gay colors to make Esteban's memory eternal and they were going to break their backs digging for springs among the stones and planting flowers on the cliffs so that in future years at dawn the passengers on great liners would awaken, suffocated by the smell of gardens on the high seas, and the captain would have to come down from the bridge in his dress uniform, with his astrolabe, his pole star, and his row of war medals and, pointing to the promontory of roses on the horizon, he would say in fourteen languages, look there, where the wind is so peaceful now that it's gone to sleep beneath the beds, over there, where the sun's so bright that the sunflowers don't know which way to turn, yes, over there, that's Esteban's village.   [1973]

THINKING ABOUT THE TEXT

1. The subtitle of this story is "A Tale for Children." Is García Márquez being ironic, or does his story indeed fit that genre? How do you think an audience of children might react to it?

2. Identify the villagers' various conceptions of the dead man. What gender differences emerge? What should a reader conclude from the fact that these conceptions change? What would you say to someone who argues that the villagers are being foolish in giving the dead man a name and making so much of him?

Confronting the Death of a Stranger

3. Do you find humor in this story? If so, in what specific passages?

4. What, if anything, seems realistic about this story? Where, if anywhere, does García Márquez strike you as departing from realism? Elaborate how you are defining *realism*.

5. Identify the various sentence lengths in this story, using specific examples. Note in particular where García Márquez's sentences get quite long. Are these long sentences effective, or should he have broken them into shorter ones? Explain your reasoning.

MAKING COMPARISONS

1. Both Laura and García Márquez's villagers find their respective dead men physically attractive. Is this response sensible in each case? Identify some warrants or assumptions behind your answer.

2. Do you think both Laura and the villagers will be permanently affected by their encounters with these dead men? Support your answer by referring to specific details of both texts.

3. Analyze the role of flowers in Mansfield's and García Márquez's stories. Do flowers have roughly the same function in both?

DON DELILLO
Videotape

Don DeLillo (b. 1936) is a contemporary American writer known mostly for his novels. These include End Zone *(1972),* The Names *(1982),* White Noise *(1985),* Libra *(1988), a fictionalized biography of Lee Harvey Oswald, and* Underworld *(1997). The following story first appeared in the literary journal* Antaeus *in 1994. Subsequently, it was included in* The Pushcart Prize, XX: Best of the Small Presses 1995–96 *and became part of* Underworld. *Like most of DeLillo's fiction, the story deals with the impact of new media technology on human thought.*

It shows a man driving a car. It is the simplest sort of family video. You see a man at the wheel of a medium Dodge.

It is just a kid aiming her camera through the rear window of the family car at the windshield of the car behind her.

You know about families and their video cameras. You know how kids get involved, how the camera shows them that every subject is potentially charged, a million things they never see with the unaided eye. They investigate the meaning of inert objects and dumb pets and they poke at family privacy. They learn to see things twice.

It is the kid's own privacy that is being protected here. She is twelve years old and her name is being withheld even though she is neither the victim nor the perpetrator of the crime but only the means of recording it.

It shows a man in a sport shirt at the wheel of his car. There is nothing else to see. The car approaches briefly, then falls back.

You know how children with cameras learn to work the exposed moments that define the family cluster. They break every trust, spy out the undefended space, catching mom coming out of the bathroom in her cumbrous robe and turbaned towel, looking bloodless and plucked. It is not a joke. They will shoot you sitting on the pot if they can manage a suitable vantage.

The tape has the jostled sort of noneventness that marks the family product. Of course the man in this case is not a member of the family but a stranger in a car, a random figure, someone who has happened along in the slow lane.

It shows a man in his forties wearing a pale shirt open at the throat, the image washed by reflections and sunglint, with many jostled moments.

It is not just another video homicide. It is a homicide recorded by a child who thought she was doing something simple and maybe halfway clever, shooting some tape of a man in a car.

He sees the girl and waves briefly, wagging a hand without taking it off the wheel — an underplayed reaction that makes you like him.

It is unrelenting footage that rolls on and on. It has an aimless determination, a persistence that lives outside the subject matter. You are looking into the mind of home video. It is innocent, it is aimless, it is determined, it is real.

He is bald up the middle of his head, a nice guy in his forties whose whole life seems open to the hand-held camera.

But there is also an element of suspense. You keep on looking not because you know something is going to happen — of course you do know something is going to happen and you do look for that reason but you might also keep on looking if you came across this footage for the first time without knowing the outcome. There is a crude power operating here. You keep on looking because things combine to hold you fast — a sense of the random, the amateurish, the accidental, the impending. You don't think of the tape as boring or interesting. It is crude, it is blunt, it is relentless. It is the jostled part of your mind, the film that runs through your hotel brain under all the thoughts you know you're thinking.

The world is lurking in the camera, already framed, waiting for the boy or girl who will come along and take up the device, learn the instrument, shooting old granddad at breakfast, all stroked out so his nostrils gape, the cereal spoon baby-gripped in his pale fist.

It shows a man alone in a medium Dodge. It seems to go on forever.

There's something about the nature of the tape, the grain of the image, the sputtering black-and-white tones, the starkness — you think this is more real, truer-to-life than anything around you. The things around you have a rehearsed and layered and cosmetic look. The tape is superreal, or maybe underreal is the way you want to put it. It is what lies at the scraped bottom of all the layers you have added. And this is another reason why you keep on looking. The tape has a searing realness.

It shows him giving an abbreviated wave, stiff-palmed, like a signal flag at a siding.

You know how families make up games. This is just another game in which the child invents the rules as she goes along. She likes the idea of videotaping a man in his car. She has probably never done it before and she sees no reason to vary the format or terminate early or pan to another car. This is her game and she is learning it and playing it at the same time. She feels halfway clever and inventive and maybe slightly intrusive as well, a little bit of brazenness that spices any game.

And you keep on looking. You look because this is the nature of the footage, to make a channeled path through time, to give things a shape and a destiny.

Of course if she had panned to another car, the right car at the precise time, she would have caught the gunman as he fired.

The chance quality of the encounter. The victim, the killer, and the child with a camera. Random energies that approach a common point. There's something here that speaks to you directly, saying terrible things about forces beyond your control, lines of intersection that cut through history and logic and every reasonable layer of human expectation.

She wandered into it. The girl got lost and wandered clear-eyed into horror. This is a children's story about straying too far from home. But it isn't the family car that serves as the instrument of the child's curiosity, her inclination to explore. It is the camera that puts her in the tale.

You know about holidays and family celebrations and how somebody shows up with a camcorder and the relatives stand around and barely react because they're numbingly accustomed to the process of being taped and decked and shown on the VCR with the coffee and cake.

He is hit soon after. If you've seen the tape many times you know from the hand wave exactly when he will be hit. It is something, naturally, that you wait for. You say to your wife, if you're at home and she is there, Now here is where he gets it. You say, Janet, hurry up, this is where it happens.

Now here is where he gets it. You see him jolted, sort of wire-shocked—then he seizes up and falls toward the door or maybe leans or slides into the door is the proper way to put it. It is awful and unremarkable at the same time. The car stays in the slow lane. It approaches briefly, then falls back.

You don't usually call your wife over to the TV set. She has her programs, you have yours. But there's a certain urgency here. You want her to see how it looks. The tape has been running forever and now the thing is finally going to happen and you want her to be here when he's shot.

Here it comes all right. He is shot, head-shot, and the camera reacts, the child reacts—there is a jolting movement but she keeps on taping, there is a sympathetic response, a nerve response, her heart is beating faster but she keeps the camera trained on the subject as he slides into the door and even as you see him die you're thinking of the girl. At some level the girl has to be present here, watching what you're watching, unprepared—the girl is seeing this cold and you have to marvel at the fact that she keeps the tape rolling.

It shows something awful and unaccompanied. You want your wife to see it because it is real this time, not fancy movie violence—the realness beneath the layers of cosmetic perception. Hurry up, Janet, here it comes. He dies so fast.

There is no accompaniment of any kind. It is very stripped. You want to tell her it is realer than real but then she will ask what that means.

The way the camera reacts to the gunshot—a startle reaction that brings pity and terror into the frame, the girl's own shock, the girl's identification with the victim.

You don't see the blood, which is probably trickling behind his ear and down [30] the back of his neck. The way his head is twisted away from the door, the twist of the head gives you only a partial profile and it's the wrong side, it's not the side where he was hit.

And maybe you're being a little aggressive here, practically forcing your wife to watch. Why? What are you telling her? Are you making a little statement? Like I'm going to ruin your day out of ordinary spite. Or a big statement? Like this is the risk of existing. Either way you're rubbing her face in this tape and you don't know why.

It shows the car drifting toward the guardrail and then there's a jostling sense of two other lanes and part of another car, a split-second blur, and the tape ends here, either because the girl stopped shooting or because some central authority, the police or the district attorney or the TV station, decided there was nothing else you had to see.

This is either the tenth or eleventh homicide committed by the Texas Highway Killer. The number is uncertain because the police believe that one of the shootings may have been a copycat crime.

And there is something about videotape, isn't there, and this particular kind of serial crime? This is a crime designed for random taping and immediate playing. You sit there and wonder if this kind of crime became more possible when the means of taping an event and playing it immediately, without a neutral interval, a balancing space and time, became widely available. Taping-and-playing intensifies and compresses the event. It dangles a need to do it again. You sit there thinking that the serial murderer has found its medium, or vice versa—an act of shadow technology, of compressed time and repeated images, stark and glary and unremarkable.

It shows very little in the end. It is a famous murder because it is on tape and [35] because the murderer has done it many times and because the crime was recorded by a child. So the child is involved, the Video Kid as she is sometimes called because they have to call her something. The tape is famous and so is she. She is famous in the modern manner of people whose names are strategically withheld. They are famous without names or faces, spirits living apart from their bodies, the victims and witnesses, the underage criminals, out there somewhere at the edges of perception.

Seeing someone at the moment he dies, dying unexpectedly. This is reason alone to stay fixed to the screen. It is instructional, watching a man shot dead as he drives along on a sunny day. It demonstrates an elemental truth, that every breath you take has two possible endings. And that's another thing. There's a joke locked away here, a note of cruel slapstick that you are willing to appreciate even if it makes you feel a little guilty. Maybe the victim's a chump, a sort of silent-movie dope, classically unlucky. He had it coming, in a sense, for letting himself be caught on camera. Because once the tape starts rolling it can only end one way. This is what the context requires.

You don't want Janet to give you any crap about it's on all the time, they show it a thousand times a day. They show it because it exists, because they have to show it, because this is why they're out there, to provide our entertainment.

The more you watch the tape, the deader and colder and more relentless it becomes. The tape sucks the air right out of your chest but you watch it every time.   [1994]

THINKING ABOUT THE TEXT

1. If asked to identify significant features of your own historical context, would you include the ability of people to videotape things? Or do you consider the technology of videotape a relatively insignificant aspect of your times?

2. Describe in your own words the narrator of this story. Does his fascination with the videotape of the murder strike you as legitimate? In general, do you tend to identify with him, or do you consider him quite different from you? What specific features of the story, and of your own experience, come to mind as you evaluate him?

3. Analyze the narrator's repeated references to "you." Who, specifically, might be his audience? How friendly is he toward this "you"? What might be his rhetorical purposes as he addresses this "you"?

4. What do you feel able to say about the child? DeLillo could have had the videotaper be an adult. What, if anything, does DeLillo achieve by making the videotaper so young?

5. What does the narrator apparently mean when he suggests that the murderer commits the crimes as if they were a form of taped-and-played event (para. 34)? Compare this story to a videotape. How does it resemble one? Differ from one?

MAKING COMPARISONS

1. Evidently, Mansfield's and García Márquez's stories both take place in a world without videotape. Are the settings of these two stories extremely different from DeLillo's setting as a result? Explain.

2. What would you say to someone who argues that García Márquez's sub-title, "A Tale for Children," applies more to Mansfield's and DeLillo's stories since children actually figure in them?

3. Each of these three stories features a dead man, but none of them tells much about his life. Why do you suppose the author in each case was so uninformative?

WRITING ABOUT ISSUES

1. Choose Mansfield's, García Márquez's, or DeLillo's story, and write an essay considering whether any of the characters proves capable of recognizing reality. If you want to argue that no one in the story is capable, spend most of your essay discussing a few specific examples of short-sightedness. In any case, be sure to indicate the particular behavior you have in mind when arguing that a character is or isn't being realistic.

2. Choose two of the stories in this cluster, and write an essay discussing each as a portrait of a whole society. Focus above all on the issue of whether one of these portraits is more negative than the other.

3. Probably there are several deceased people whom you admire but who are strangers to all or most of your classmates. Write an essay describing one such person for your classmates, aiming to persuade them that they, too, should admire him or her.

4. Write an essay evaluating how a recent article or television news story reported someone's death. In your essay, be sure to describe precisely how the death was presented and specify the criteria you are using to evaluate that presentation. Feel free to mention any of the stories in this cluster.

DISRESPECTING DEATH

JOHN DONNE, "Death Be Not Proud"
DYLAN THOMAS, "Do Not Go Gentle into That Good Night"
WISLAWA SZYMBORSKA, "On Death, without Exaggeration"

Through their works, writers of literature convey a wide range of attitudes toward death. Some take the opportunity to mourn the demise of a loved one, a friend, or a public figure. Others use the written word to stress that death is inevitable. Many literary works deal with death by expressing both sorrow and resignation. Each of the poems in this cluster expresses still another stance toward death: disrespect. Directly addressing death, John Donne's speaker virtually sneers at it. Addressing someone in danger of dying, Dylan Thomas's speaker portrays death as a force to resist. Finally, Wislawa Szymborska describes death in terms that considerably reduce its significance. As you read all three poems, think about whether disrespect toward death makes sense to you. Perhaps you feel that it is appropriate in certain circumstances but not others. If so, exactly when would you want death scorned? When would you call for acceptance of it, even reverence toward it?

BEFORE YOU READ

If you were to write a poem treating Death as a person and insulting him or her, what specific remarks might you make?

JOHN DONNE
Death Be Not Proud

Long regarded as a major English writer, John Donne (1572–1631) was also trained as a lawyer and clergyman. Around 1594, he converted from Catholicism to Anglicanism; in 1615, he was ordained; and in 1621, he was appointed to the prestigious position of dean of St. Paul's Cathedral in London. Today, his sermons continue to be studied as literature, yet he is more known for his poetry. When he was a young man, he often wrote about love, but later he focused on religious themes. The following poem, one of Donne's "holy sonnets," is from 1611.

Death be not proud, though some have callèd thee
Mighty and dreadful, for thou art not so;
For those whom thou think'st thou dost overthrow
Die not, poor Death, nor yet canst thou kill me.
From rest and sleep, which but thy pictures° be,   *images*   5
Much pleasure; then from thee much more must flow,
And soonest our best men with thee do go,
Rest of their bones, and soul's delivery.°   *deliverance*
Thou art slave to Fate, Chance, kings, and desperate men,
And dost with Poison, War, and Sickness dwell;   10
And poppy or charms can make us sleep as well,
And better than thy stroke; why swell'st° thou then?   *swell with pride*
One short sleep past, we wake eternally
And death shall be no more; Death, thou shalt die.   [1611]

THINKING ABOUT THE TEXT

1. In a sense, Death is the speaker's audience. But presumably Donne expected the living to read his poem. What reaction might he have wanted from this audience?

2. Is the speaker proud? Define what you mean by the term.

3. Evidently the speaker believes in an afterlife. What would you say to people who consider the speaker naive and the poem irrelevant because they don't believe that "we wake eternally"? How significant is this warrant or assumption? Do you share it?

4. Identify the rhyme patterns. How aware of them were you when you first read the poem?

5. Imagine Death writing a sonnet in response to the speaker. Perhaps it would be entitled "Life Be Not Proud." What might Death say in it?

DYLAN THOMAS

Do Not Go Gentle into That Good Night

Dylan Thomas (1914–1953) was a Welsh poet, short-story writer, and playwright. Among his most enduring works are his radio dramas Under Milk Wood *(1954) and* A Child's Christmas in Wales *(1955). A frequent visitor to the United States, Thomas built a devoted audience in this country through his electrifying public readings. Unfortunately, he was also well known for his alcoholism, which killed him at a relatively young age. He wrote the following poem in 1952, not long before his own death. It takes the form of a* villanelle, *which consists of nineteen lines: five tercets (three-line stanzas) followed by a quatrain (four-line stanza). The first and third lines of the opening tercet are used alternately to conclude each succeeding tercet, and they are joined to form a rhyme at the poem's end.*

Do not go gentle into that good night,
Old age should burn and rave at close of day;
Rage, rage against the dying of the light.

Though wise men at their end know dark is right,
Because their words had forked no lightning they   5
Do not go gentle into that good night.

Good men, the last wave by, crying how bright
Their frail deeds might have danced in a green bay,
Rage, rage against the dying of the light.

Wild men who caught and sang the sun in flight,   10
And learn, too late, they grieved it on its way,
Do not go gentle into that good night.

Grave men, near death, who see with blinding sight
Blind eyes could blaze like meteors and be gay,
Rage, rage against the dying of the light.   15

And you, my father, there on the sad height,
Curse, bless, me now with your fierce tears, I pray.
Do not go gentle into that good night.
Rage, rage against the dying of the light.   [1952]

THINKING ABOUT THE TEXT

1. In what sense could the night possibly be "good," given that people are supposed to "rage" at it?

2. Why do you think Thomas has his speaker refer to "the dying of the light" instead of simply to "dying"? What other parts of the poem relate to the word *light*?

3. The speaker refers to four kinds of "men." Restate in your own words the description given of each. Should Thomas's language about them have been less abstract? Why, or why not?

4. What is the effect of climaxing the poem with a reference to "you, my father" (line 16)? If the father had been introduced in the first or second stanzas, would the effect have been quite different? If so, how?

5. What is the effect of the villanelle form? Judging by Thomas's poem, do you think it is worthwhile for a poet to write in this way, despite the technical challenges of the form? Should teachers of poetry writing push their students to write a villanelle? Explain your reasoning.

WISLAWA SZYMBORSKA
On Death, without Exaggeration

Translated by Stanislaw Baranczak and Clare Cavanagh

Although she has written several volumes of poetry, Wislawa Szymborska (b. 1923) was little known outside of her native Poland until she won the Nobel Prize for literature in 1996. Since then, readers in various countries have come to admire the blend of simplicity, wit, and wisdom in her writing. The Polish version of the following poem appeared in Szymborska's 1986 book The People on the Bridge. *Subsequently, Stanislaw Baranczak and Clare Cavanagh included it in their 1995 English collection of Szymborska's poems,* View with a Grain of Sand. *We present their translation of the text.*

It can't take a joke,
find a star, make a bridge.
It knows nothing about weaving, mining, farming,
building ships, or baking cakes.

In our planning for tomorrow,   5
it has the final word,
which is always beside the point.

It can't even get the things done
that are part of its trade:
dig a grave,   10
make a coffin,
clean up after itself.

Preoccupied with killing,
it does the job awkwardly,
without system or skill.   15
As though each of us were its first kill.

◆ ◆ ◆

Oh, it has its triumphs,
but look at its countless defeats,
missed blows,
and repeat attempts!   20

Sometimes it isn't strong enough
to swat a fly from the air.
Many are the caterpillars
that have outcrawled it.

All those bulbs, pods,   25
tentacles, fins, tracheae,
nuptial plumage, and winter fur
show that it has fallen behind
with its halfhearted work.

Ill will won't help   30
and even our lending a hand with wars and coups d'état
is so far not enough.

Hearts beat inside eggs.
Babies' skeletons grow.
Seeds, hard at work, sprout their first tiny pair of leaves   35
and sometimes even tall trees fall away.

Whoever claims that it's omnipotent
is himself living proof
that it's not.

There's no life   40
that couldn't be immortal
if only for a moment.

Death
always arrives by that very moment too late.

In vain it tugs at the knob   45
of the invisible door.
As far as you've come
can't be undone.   [1986]

THINKING ABOUT THE TEXT

1. Although the word *death* appears in the title, it doesn't appear in the text
   of the poem until the next-to-last stanza. Up till then, death is repeatedly
   referred to as "it." What is the effect of this pronoun? What might be the
   effect had Szymborska referred to death more explicitly throughout the text?

2. Evidently the speaker is trying not to exaggerate death. What sorts of
   remarks about death might the speaker see as an exaggeration of it?
   Define what you mean by *exaggeration*.

3. What images of death does the speaker create? Refer to specific lines.

4. In the eighth stanza, the speaker mentions that human beings are "lending a hand" to death. Do you take the speaker to be criticizing humanity at this point? Why, or why not?

5. Does the order of the stanzas matter? Could the speaker's observations about death appear in any order and have the same effect? Explain your reasoning.

MAKING COMPARISONS

1. Do all three poems in this cluster speak of death "without exaggeration"? Define what you mean by the term.

2. Does Szymborska's poem strike you as lighter, less serious than Donne's and Thomas's? Refer to specific lines in each text.

3. Suppose that you didn't know who wrote these three poems and were told that only one of the authors was female. What specific aspects of these poems, if any, would you consider as you tried to guess the one written by a woman?

WRITING ABOUT ISSUES

1. Choose Donne's, Thomas's, or Szymborska's poem, and write an essay analyzing the poem as an argument for a certain position on death. Specify the main claim and the evidence given in support of it. Feel free to evaluate the argument you discuss, although keep in mind that the artistic success of the poem may or may not depend on whether its argument is fully developed.

2. Write an essay comparing two of the poems in this cluster, focusing on the issue of whether they are basically similar or significantly different in the ideas and feelings they express. Refer to specific lines from each text.

3. Write an essay recalling a specific occasion when you had difficulty deciding whether to accept something as inevitable. In your essay, give details of the occasion, the difficulty, and your ultimate reasoning. Indicate as well what your final decision revealed about you. Perhaps you will want to distinguish between the self you were then and the self you are now. If you wish, refer to any of the poems in this cluster.

4. Imagine that you are on the staff of a nursing home. At a staff meeting, the chief administrator asks you and your colleagues to consider framing and hanging Donne's, Thomas's, or Szymborska's poem in the recreation room. Write a letter to the administrator in which you favor one of these poems or reject them all as inappropriate. Be sure to give reasons for your view.

REFLECTING ON KILLING ANIMALS

GEORGE ORWELL, "Shooting an Elephant"
ANNIE DILLARD, "The Deer at Providencia"
BRUCE WEIGL, "Spike"

When you think about death, probably you think about your own fate or that of other people. But occasions may arise when you have to ponder the death of an animal. At such times, you may agonize, especially if you have witnessed the death or felt somehow responsible for it. Perhaps you have had to consider ending a sick pet's life. Or perhaps you have wondered whether to protest social practices deadly to animals, such as hunting, laboratory experiments with monkeys, and the slaughter of cattle for human consumption. Of course, your social context may greatly influence your attitude toward the killing of animals, as the following three essays show. George Orwell's essay, written in the mid-1930s, is an account of his service as a British colonial policeman in Burma. He recalls a day when he shot an elephant merely to preserve his status in the village he patrolled. In effect, Orwell reminds his readers that the killing of animals can occur within and be influenced by human power struggles. Annie Dillard's essay, which dates from the early 1980s, is about an expedition she made with other Americans to a village in Ecuador. While there, she and the rest of her group came face to face with the mortal suffering of a deer captured by their hosts. Like Orwell's account, Dillard's suggests that cultural differences can significantly affect people's responses when an animal is slain. Finally, Bruce Weigl recalls his boyhood in a 1950s Ohio mill town, particularly the time when his dog got rabies and had to be shot. Even now, Weigl seems pained by the death, for his pet had brightened the difficult life of Weigl's working-class family. This third piece, then, joins the other two in suggesting that social circumstances can influence human beings' attitudes toward an animal's demise.

GEORGE ORWELL
Shooting an Elephant

George Orwell was the pen name of Eric Arthur Blair (1903–1950). Although born in India, he traveled widely. After his schooling in England, he joined the Indian Imperial Police in Burma, where he served from 1922 to 1927. Later, Orwell lived in Paris and London, studied the lives of coal miners in the north of England, and fought on the Republican side in the Spanish Civil War against the fascist forces of General Francisco Franco. Probably Orwell is best known today for two novels he wrote as warnings against totalitarianism, Animal Farm *(1945) and* Nineteen Eighty-Four *(1949). But he also wrote much journalism and many essays, often exploring through these writings how political ideologies influence human thinking, language, and behavior. The following essay, which tells of an event during his service in Burma, was first published in 1936.*

In Moulmein, in Lower Burma, I was hated by large numbers of people — the only time in my life that I have been important enough for this to happen to me. I was sub-divisional police officer of the town, and in an aimless, petty kind of way anti-European feeling was very bitter. No one had the guts to raise a riot, but if a European woman went through the bazaars alone somebody would probably spit betel juice over her dress. As a police officer I was an obvious target and was baited whenever it seemed safe to do so. When a nimble Burman tripped me up on the football field and the referee (another Burman) looked the other way, the crowd yelled with hideous laughter. This happened more than once. In the end the sneering yellow faces of young men that met me everywhere, the insults hooted after me when I was at a safe distance, got badly on my nerves. The young Buddhist priests were the worst of all. There were several thousands of them in the town and none of them seemed to have anything to do except stand on street corners and jeer at Europeans.

All this was perplexing and upsetting. For at that time I had already made up my mind that imperialism was an evil thing and the sooner I chucked up my job and got out of it the better. Theoretically — and secretly, of course — I was all for the Burmese and all against their oppressors, the British. As for the job I was doing, I hated it more bitterly than I can perhaps make clear. In a job like that you see the dirty work of Empire at close quarters. The wretched prisoners huddling in the stinking cages of the lockups, the grey, cowed faces of the long-term convicts, the scarred buttocks of the men who had been flogged with bamboos — all these oppressed me with an intolerable sense of guilt. But I could get nothing into perspective. I was young and ill-educated and I had had to think out my problems in the utter silence that is imposed on every Englishman in the East. I did not even know that the British Empire is dying, still less did I know that it is a great deal better than the younger empires that are going to supplant it.° All I knew was that I was stuck between my hatred of the empire I served and my rage against the evil-spirited little beasts who tried to make my job impossible. With one part of my mind I thought of the British Raj° as an unbreakable tyranny, as something clamped down, in *saecula saeculorum,*° upon the will of prostrate peoples; with another part I thought that the greatest joy in the world would be to drive a bayonet into a Buddhist priest's guts. Feelings like these are the normal by-products of imperialism; ask any Anglo-Indian official, if you can catch him off duty.

One day something happened which in a roundabout way was enlightening. It was a tiny incident in itself, but it gave me a better glimpse than I had had before of the real nature of imperialism — the real motives for which despotic governments act. Early one morning the sub-inspector at a police station the other end of the town rang me up on the phone and said that an elephant was ravaging the bazaar. Would I please come and do something about it? I did not know what I could do, but I wanted to see what was happening and I got on to a pony and started out. I took my rifle, an old .44 Winchester and much too small to kill

---

younger empires . . . supplant it: In 1936, Hitler and Stalin were in power and World War II was only three years away. **Raj:** Sovereignty. *saecula saeculorum:* From time immemorial.

an elephant, but I thought the noise might be useful *in terrorem.*° Various Burmans stopped me on the way and told me about the elephant's doings. It was not, of course, a wild elephant, but a tame one which had gone "must."° It had been chained up, as tame elephants always are when their attack of "must" is due, but on the previous night it had broken its chain and escaped. Its mahout,° the only person who could manage it when it was in that state, had set out in pursuit, but had taken the wrong direction and was now twelve hours' journey away, and in the morning the elephant had suddenly reappeared in the town. The Burmese population had no weapons and were quite helpless against it. It had already destroyed somebody's bamboo hut, killed a cow, and raided some fruit-stalls and devoured the stock; also it had met the municipal rubbish van and, when the driver jumped out and took to his heels, had turned the van over and inflicted violences upon it.

The Burmese sub-inspector and some Indian constables were waiting for me in the quarter where the elephant had been seen. It was a very poor quarter, a labyrinth of squalid bamboo huts, thatched with palm-leaf, winding all over a steep hillside. I remember that it was a cloudy, stuffy morning at the beginning of the rains. We began questioning people as to where the elephant had gone, and, as usual, failed to get any definite information. That is invariably the case in the East; a story always sounds clear enough at a distance, but the nearer you get to the scene of events the vaguer it becomes. Some of the people said that the elephant had gone in one direction, some said that he had gone in another, some professed not even to have heard of an elephant. I had almost made up my mind that the whole story was a pack of lies, when we heard yells a little distance away. There was a loud, scandalized cry of "Go away, child! Go away this instant!" and an old woman with a switch in her hand came round the corner of a hut, violently shooing away a crowd of naked children. Some more women followed, clicking their tongues and exclaiming; evidently there was something that the children ought not to have seen. I rounded the hut and saw a man's dead body sprawling in the mud. He was an Indian, a black Dravidian coolie, almost naked, and he could not have been dead many minutes. The people said that the elephant had come suddenly upon him round the corner of the hut, caught him with its trunk, put its foot on his back, and ground him into the earth. This was the rainy season and the ground was soft, and his face had scored a trench a foot deep and a couple of yards long. He was lying on his belly with arms crucified and head sharply twisted to one side. His face was coated with mud, the eyes wide open, the teeth bared and grinning with an expression of unendurable agony. (Never tell me, by the way, that the dead look peaceful. Most of the corpses I have seen looked devilish.) The friction of the great beast's foot had stripped the skin from his back as neatly as one skins a rabbit. As soon as I saw the dead man I sent an orderly to a friend's house nearby to borrow an elephant rifle. I had already sent back the pony, not wanting it to go mad with fright and throw me if it smelled the elephant.

in terrorem: In terrorizing him. **must:** That is, gone into a state of frenzy. **mahout:** A keeper and driver of an elephant.

The orderly came back in a few minutes with a rifle and five cartridges, and meanwhile some Burmans had arrived and told us that the elephant was in the paddy fields below, only a few hundred yards away. As I started forward practically the whole population of the quarter flocked out of the houses and followed me. They had seen the rifle and were all shouting excitedly that I was going to shoot the elephant. They had not shown much interest in the elephant when he was merely ravaging their homes, but it was different now that he was going to be shot. It was a bit of fun to them, as it would be to an English crowd; besides they wanted the meat. It made me vaguely uneasy. I had no intention of shooting the elephant—I had merely sent for the rifle to defend myself if necessary—and it is always unnerving to have a crowd following you. I marched down the hill, looking and feeling a fool, with the rifle over my shoulder and an ever-growing army of people jostling at my heels. At the bottom, when you got away from the huts, there was a metalled road and beyond that a miry waste of paddy fields a thousand yards across, not yet ploughed but soggy from the first rains and dotted with coarse grass. The elephant was standing eight yards from the road, his left side towards us. He took not the slightest notice of the crowd's approach. He was tearing up bunches of grass, beating them against his knees to clean them and stuffing them into his mouth.

I had halted on the road. As soon as I saw the elephant I knew with perfect certainty that I ought not to shoot him. It is a serious matter to shoot a working elephant—it is comparable to destroying a huge and costly piece of machinery—and obviously one ought not to do it if it can possibly be avoided. And at that distance, peacefully eating, the elephant looked no more dangerous than a cow. I thought then and I think now that his attack of "must" was already passing off; in which case he would merely wander harmlessly about until the mahout came back and caught him. Moreover, I did not in the least want to shoot him. I decided that I would watch him for a little while to make sure that he did not turn savage again, and then go home.

But at that moment I glanced round at the crowd that had followed me. It was an immense crowd, two thousand at the least and growing every minute. It blocked the road for a long distance on either side. I looked at the sea of yellow faces above the garish clothes—faces all happy and excited over this bit of fun, all certain that the elephant was going to be shot. They were watching me as they would watch a conjurer about to perform a trick. They did not like me, but with the magical rifle in my hands I was momentarily worth watching. And suddenly I realized that I should have to shoot the elephant after all. The people expected it of me and I had got to do it; I could feel their two thousand wills pressing me forward, irresistibly. And it was at this moment, as I stood there with the rifle in my hands, that I first grasped the hollowness, the futility of the white man's dominion in the East. Here was I, the white man with his gun, standing in front of the unarmed native crowd—seemingly the leading actor of the piece; but in reality I was only an absurd puppet pushed to and fro by the will of those yellow faces behind. I perceived in this moment that when the white man turns tyrant it is his own freedom that he destroys. He becomes a sort of hollow, posing dummy, the conventionalized figure of a sahib.° For it is the condition of his rule that he shall spend his life in trying to impress the "natives," and so in every crisis he has got to do what the "natives" expect of him. He wears a mask, and his face grows to fit it. I had got to shoot the elephant. I had committed myself to doing it when I sent for the rifle. A sahib has got to act like a sahib; he has got to appear resolute, to know his own mind and do definite things. To come all that way, rifle in hand, with two thousand people marching at my heels, and then to trail feebly away, having done nothing — no, that was impossible. The crowd would laugh at me. And my whole life, every white man's life in the East, was one long struggle not to be laughed at.

But I did not want to shoot the elephant. I watched him beating his bunch of grass against his knees, with the preoccupied grandmotherly air that elephants have. It seemed to me that it would be murder to shoot him. At that age I was not squeamish about killing animals, but I had never shot an elephant and never wanted to. (Somehow it always seems worse to kill a *large* animal.) Besides, there was the beast's owner to be considered. Alive, the elephant was worth at least a hundred pounds; dead, he would only be worth the value of his tusks, five pounds, possibly. But I had got to act quickly. I turned to some experienced-looking Burmans who had been there when we arrived, and asked them how the elephant had been behaving. They all said the same thing: he took no notice of you if you left him alone, but he might charge if you went too close to him.

It was perfectly clear to me what I ought to do. I ought to walk up to within, say, twenty-five yards of the elephant and test his behavior. If he charged I could shoot, if he took no notice of me it would be safe to leave him until the mahout came back. But also I knew that I was going to do no such thing. I was a poor shot with a rifle and the ground was soft mud into which one would sink at every step. If the elephant charged and I missed him, I should have about as much chance as a toad under a steamroller. But even then I was not thinking particularly of my own skin, only of the watchful yellow faces behind. For at that moment, with the crowd watching me, I was not afraid in the ordinary sense, as I would have been if I had been alone. A white man mustn't be frightened in front of "natives"; and so, in general, he isn't frightened. The sole thought in my mind was that if any-thing went wrong those two thousand Burmans would see me pursued, caught, trampled on, and reduced to a grinning corpse like that Indian up the hill. And if that happened it was quite probable that some of them would laugh. That would never do. There was only one alternative. I shoved the cartridges into the maga-zine and lay down on the road to get a better aim.

The crowd grew very still, and a deep, low, happy sigh, as of people who   10
see the theater curtain go up at last, breathed from innumerable throats. They were going to have their bit of fun after all. The rifle was a beautiful German thing with cross-hair sights. I did not then know that in shooting an elephant one would shoot to cut an imaginary bar running from ear-hole to ear-hole. I ought, therefore, as the elephant was sideways on, to have aimed straight at his ear-hole;

sahib: Term used among Hindus and Muslims in Colonial India when speaking of an official.

actually I aimed several inches in front of this, thinking the brain would be further forward.

When I pulled the trigger I did not hear the bang or feel the kick — one never does when a shot goes home — but I heard the devilish roar of glee that went up from the crowd. In that instant, in too short a time, one would have thought, even for the bullet to get there, a mysterious, terrible change had come over the elephant. He neither stirred nor fell, but every line on his body had altered. He looked suddenly stricken, shrunken, immensely old, as though the frightful impact of the bullet had paralyzed him without knocking him down. At last, after what seemed a long time — it might have been five seconds, I dare say — he sagged flabbily to his knees. His mouth slobbered. An enormous senility seemed to have settled upon him. One could have imagined him thousands of years old. I fired again into the same spot. At the second shot he did not collapse but climbed with desperate slowness to his feet and stood weakly upright, with legs sagging and head drooping. I fired a third time. That was the shot that did for him. You could see the agony of it jolt his whole body and knock the last remnant of strength from his legs. But in falling he seemed for a moment to rise, for as his hind legs collapsed beneath him he seemed to tower upwards like a huge rock toppling, his trunk reaching skywards like a tree. He trumpeted, for the first and only time. And then down he came, his belly towards me, with a crash that seemed to shake the ground even where I lay.

I got up. The Burmans were already racing past me across the mud. It was obvious that the elephant would never rise again, but he was not dead. He was breathing very rhythmically with long rattling gasps, his great mound of a side painfully rising and falling. His mouth was wide open — I could see far down into the caverns of pale pink throat. I waited a long time for him to die, but his breathing did not weaken. Finally, I fired my two remaining shots into the spot where I thought his heart must be. The thick blood welled out of him like red velvet, but still he did not die. His body did not even jerk when the shots hit him, the tortured breathing continued without a pause. He was dying, very slowly and in great agony, but in some world remote from me where not even a bullet could damage him further. I felt that I had got to put an end to that dreadful noise. It seemed dreadful to see the great beast lying there, powerless to move and yet powerless to die, and not even to be able to finish him. I sent back for my small rifle and poured shot after shot into his heart and down his throat. They seemed to make no impression. The tortured gasps continued as steadily as the ticking of a clock.

In the end I could not stand it any longer and went away. I heard later that it took him half an hour to die. Burmans were bringing dahs° and baskets even before I left, and I was told they had stripped his body almost to the bones by the afternoon.

Afterwards, of course, there were endless discussions about the shooting of the elephant. The owner was furious, but he was only an Indian and could do nothing. Besides, legally I had done the right thing, for a mad elephant has to be killed, like a mad dog, if its owner fails to control it. Among the Europeans opin-

---

dahs: Large heavy knives.

ion was divided. The older men said I was right, the younger men said it was a damn shame to shoot an elephant for killing a coolie, because an elephant was worth more than any damn Coringhee coolie. And afterwards I was very glad that the coolie had been killed; it put me legally in the right and it gave me a sufficient pretext for shooting the elephant. I often wondered whether any of the others grasped that I had done it solely to avoid looking a fool.   [1936]

THINKING ABOUT THE TEXT

1. Why is the writer focusing on this particular day in his past? What is he using it to illustrate? What other kinds of significance might one find in this episode?

2. On the basis of this essay, how would you describe the younger Orwell's attitude toward the Burmese villagers? Cite specific statements that you find especially helpful in answering this question. Does the older Orwell who is writing the essay seem much different from his younger self? Again, identify specific statements that affect your thinking on this issue.

3. According to the essay, at what points might the shooting of the elephant have been avoided? Why at these points did the younger Orwell nevertheless find himself heading toward the act of killing?

4. Reread the description of the elephant's suffering after he is shot. How does the writer's language encourage you to compare the elephant's physical decline with the eventual decline of the British Empire?

5. "Shooting an Elephant" has appeared in many essay anthologies, especially those intended for composition classes. Why is it anthologized so much, do you think? Should it be? Identify some of your warrants or assumptions in addressing this issue of evaluation.

ANNIE DILLARD

The Deer at Providencia

Annie Dillard (b. 1945) teaches creative writing at Wesleyan University in Middletown, Connecticut. She first came to national attention with her 1975 Pulitzer Prize–winning book Pilgrim at Tinker Creek, *which chronicled her nature walks in Virginia's Roanoke Valley. Since then, she has published several full-length books, including* Holy the Firm *(1978),* Living by Fiction *(1982),* For the Time Being *(1999), an autobiography entitled* An American Childhood *(1987), and a novel called* The Living *(1982). She is also a poet, having produced the collections* Tickets for a Prayer Wheel *(1974) and* Mornings Like This *(1995). But many of her readers are most familiar with Dillard's essays, which often deal with her travels to various places, her explorations of nature, and her spiritual quests. The following piece appears in her 1982 volume of essays* Teaching a Stone to Talk.

There were four of us North Americans in the jungle, in the Ecuadorian jungle on the banks of the Napo River in the Amazon watershed. The other three North Americans were metropolitan men. We stayed in tents in one riverside village, and visited others. At the village called Providencia we saw a sight which moved us, and which shocked the men.

The first thing we saw when we climbed the riverbank to the village of Providencia was the deer. It was roped to a tree on the grass clearing near the thatch shelter where we would eat lunch.

The deer was small, about the size of a whitetail fawn, but apparently full-grown. It had a rope around its neck and three feet caught in the rope. Someone said that the dogs had caught it that morning and the villagers were going to cook and eat it that night.

This clearing lay at the edge of the little thatched-hut village. We could see the villagers going about their business, scattering feed corn for hens about their houses, and wandering down paths to the river to bathe. The village headman was our host; he stood beside us as we watched the deer struggle. Several village boys were interested in the deer; they formed part of the circle we made around it in the clearing. So also did four businessmen from Quito who were attempting to guide us around the jungle. Few of the very different people standing in this circle had a common language. We watched the deer, and no one said much.

The deer lay on its side at the rope's very end, so the rope lacked slack to let it   5
rest its head in the dust. It was "pretty," delicate of bone like all deer, and thin-skinned for the tropics. Its skin looked virtually hairless, in fact, and almost translucent, like a membrane. Its neck was no thicker than my wrist; it was rubbed open on the rope, and gashed. Trying to paw itself free of the rope, the deer had scratched its own neck with its hooves. The raw underside of its neck showed red stripes and some bruises bleeding inside the muscles. Now three of its feet were hooked in the rope under its jaw. It could not stand, of course, on one leg, so it could not move to slacken the rope and ease the pull on its throat and enable it to rest its head.

Repeatedly the deer paused, motionless, its eyes veiled, with only its rib cage in motion, and its breaths the only sound. Then, after I would think, "It has given up; now it will die," it would heave. The rope twanged; the tree leaves clattered; the deer's free foot beat the ground. We stepped back and held our breaths. It thrashed, kicking, but only one leg moved; the other three legs tightened inside the rope's loop. Its hip jerked; its spine shook. Its eyes rolled; its tongue, thick with spittle, pushed in and out. Then it would rest again. We watched this for fifteen minutes.

Once three young native boys charged in, released its trapped legs, and jumped back to the circle of people. But instantly the deer scratched up its neck with its hooves and snared its forelegs in the rope again. It was easy to imagine a third and then a fourth leg soon stuck, like Brer Rabbit and the Tar Baby.

♦   ♦   ♦

We watched the deer from the circle, and then we drifted on to lunch. Our palm-roofed shelter stood on a grassy promontory from which we could see the deer tied to the tree, pigs and hens walking under village houses, and black-and-white cattle standing in the river. There was even a breeze.

Lunch, which was the second and better lunch we had that day, was hot and fried. There was a big fish called *doncella*, a kind of catfish, dipped whole in corn flour and beaten egg, then deep fried. With our fingers we pulled soft fragments of it from its sides to our plates, and ate; it was delicate fish-flesh, fresh and mild. Someone found the roe, and I ate of that too — it was fat and stronger, like egg yolk, naturally enough, and warm.

There was also a stew of meat in shreds with rice and pale brown gravy. I had 10 asked what kind of deer it was tied to the tree; Pepe had answered in Spanish, "*Gama.*" Now they told us this was *gama* too, stewed. I suspect the word means merely game or venison. At any rate, I heard that the village dogs had cornered another deer just yesterday, and it was this deer which we were now eating in full sight of the whole article. It was good. I was surprised at its tenderness. But it is a fact that high levels of lactic acid, which builds up in muscle tissues during exertion, tenderizes.

After the fish and meat we ate bananas fried in chunks and served on a tray; they were sweet and full of flavor. I felt terrific. My shirt was wet and cool from swimming; I had had a night's sleep, two decent walks, three meals, and a swim — everything tasted good. From time to time each one of us, separately, would look beyond our shaded roof to the sunny spot where the deer was still convulsing in the dust. Our meal completed, we walked around the deer and back to the boats.

That night I learned that while we were watching the deer, the others were watching me.

We four North Americans grew close in the jungle in a way that was not the usual artificial intimacy of travelers. We liked each other. We stayed up all that night talking, murmuring, as though we rocked on hammocks slung above time. The others were from big cities: New York, Washington, Boston. They all said that I had no expression on my face when I was watching the deer — or at any rate, not the expression they expected.

They had looked to see how I, the only woman, and the youngest, was taking the sight of the deer's struggles. I looked detached, apparently, or hard, or calm, or focused, still. I don't know. I was thinking. I remember feeling very old and energetic. I could say like Thoreau that I have traveled widely in Roanoke, Virginia. I have thought a great deal about carnivorousness; I eat meat. These things are not issues; they are mysteries.

Gentlemen of the city, what surprises you? That there is suffering here, or 15 that I know it?

We lay in the tent and talked. "If it had been my wife," one man said with special vigor, amazed, "she wouldn't have cared *what* was going on; she would have dropped *everything* right at that moment and gone in the village from here to there, to there, she would not have *stopped* until that animal was out of its suffering one way or another. She couldn't *bear* to see a creature in agony like that."

I nodded.

Now I am home. When I wake I comb my hair before the mirror above my dresser. Every morning for the past two years I have seen in that mirror, beside my sleep-softened face, the blackened face of a burnt man. It is a wire-service photograph clipped from a newspaper and taped to my mirror. The caption reads: "Alan McDonald in Miami hospital bed." All you can see in the photograph is a smudged triangle of face from his eyelids to his lower lip; the rest is bandages. You cannot see the expression in his eyes; the bandages shade them.

The story, headed MAN BURNED FOR SECOND TIME, begins:

> "Why does God hate me?" Alan McDonald asked from his hospital bed.
> "When the gunpowder went off, I couldn't believe it," he said. "I just couldn't believe it. I said, 'No, God couldn't do this to me again.'"

He was in a burn ward in Miami, in serious condition. I do not even know if he lived. I wrote him a letter at the time, cringing.

He had been burned before, thirteen years previously, by flaming gasoline.	20
For years he had been having his body restored and his face remade in dozens of operations. He had been a boy, and then a burnt boy. He had already been stunned by what could happen, by how life could veer.

Once I read that people who survive bad burns tend to go crazy; they have a very high suicide rate. Medicine cannot ease their pain; drugs just leak away, soaking the sheets, because there is no skin to hold them in. The people just lie there and weep. Later they kill themselves. They had not known, before they were burned, that the world included such suffering, that life could permit them personally such pain.

This time a bowl of gunpowder had exploded on McDonald.

> "I didn't realize what had happened at first," he recounted. "And then I heard that sound from 13 years ago. I was burning. I rolled to put the fire out and I thought, 'Oh God, not again.'
> "If my friend hadn't been there, I would have jumped into a canal with a rock around my neck."

His wife concludes the piece, "Man, it just isn't fair."

I read the whole clipping again every morning. This is the Big Time here, every minute of it. Will someone please explain to Alan McDonald in his dignity, to the deer at Providencia in his dignity, what is going on? And mail me the carbon.

When we walked by the deer at Providencia for the last time, I said to Pepe, with a pitying glance at the deer, "*Pobrecito*" — "poor little thing." But I was trying out Spanish. I knew at the time it was a ridiculous thing to say.	[1982]

THINKING ABOUT THE TEXT

1. Why did the men with whom Dillard was traveling expect her to act differently than she did? How do you think she should have behaved when she saw the villagers tormenting the deer? How do you feel about the satisfaction she derived from the deer-meat stew? Identify some of the warrants or assumptions behind your answers.

2. What do you make of Dillard's obsession with Alan McDonald? Do you believe his case belongs in this essay? Why, or why not?

3. Dillard declares, "These things are not issues; they are mysteries" (para. 14). What distinction does she make between *issues* and *mysteries*? How does she define these terms? Do you agree that the things she reports are better viewed as mysteries than as issues? Explain your reasoning.

4. At the end of the essay, Dillard returns to a moment back in Ecuador; she could have described this moment in the first section of the essay. Why do you think she chooses to conclude with it?

5. What does the word *Providencia* signify? (You may need to consult a classmate or a Spanish-English dictionary.) Why do you suppose Dillard included the word in her title?

MAKING COMPARISONS

1. Does Dillard seem less narrow-minded than Orwell? Identify details of both texts that you think especially important for you to consider as you answer this question.

2. Orwell's essay is pretty much one continuous story, whereas Dillard begins with the story of the deer and then jumps to her ongoing obsession with Alan McDonald. Does Dillard's essay seem less dramatic or intense than Orwell's because it is less continuous? Why, or why not?

3. Obviously gender is relevant to Dillard's essay. Is it as relevant to Orwell's essay? Explain.

BRUCE WEIGL
Spike

The son of a mill worker, Bruce Weigl (b. 1949) grew up in Lima, Ohio. After graduating from high school in 1967, he joined the United States Army and was sent to Vietnam. Today, Weigl is chiefly known as a poet, the latest collections of his own verse being Archeology of the Circle: New and Selected Poems *and* After the Others *(both 1999). He has also edited and translated Vietnamese and Romanian poetry. Originally, "Spike" appeared in a 1995 issue of* Ohio Review, *but we present the slightly revised version featured in Weigl's memoir* The Circle of Hanh *(2000).*

When my father brought Spike home in a box, I was sitting near the coal stove with my sister. We came together there with our different lives and sat near the stove to keep warm. He put the box down on the kitchen table. I saw it move and shake.

I want to say that my sister cried, that she ran behind our mother at the sink and pulled at her skirts, but it was me who cried when the box moved. I cried because even then I had seen the veil lifted a time or two. Even then I knew to fear things that moved inside of boxes your father brought home from the mill.

Spike was my dog when I was five. A ratty rattailed terrier with bent ears and a crazy dog grin. Some old man couldn't handle him anymore, so he gave him to my father. We had a small apartment then next to St. Peter's church with its outdoor rock altar and its blue bottomed holy pond, a grim four-family building where you had to share the bathroom with the drunk who sometimes would piss on the radiator in winter, a smell you could not wash away. When the old drunk would piss there in his drunkenness, my mother would wake to scrub it with a rough brush and lye soap. Even in winter she would open the window to let out the smell of human acids.

Three rooms and a bathroom you shared with strangers. Not a bad life, though I have always known a longing there, an emptiness I dwelled in even then.

When Spike hit the light of our kitchen where the coal stove sang and the family came together, it was as if a whirlwind had been released, a water spout or perhaps a small tornado. He spun his small tight muscle of a body all through the three rooms with such speed he was a blur. He ran so fast he seemed at times to run up the very walls, and he flew through the rooms so wildly that his running made them bigger, made us pause in our lives that had been headed somewhere else that night, somewhere not as bright or easy. We had already seen an empty table in that house, already we had felt the cold through cracks in the wall, but Spike somehow raised us above that grim life, above the mill noise and the slag dust. He caused us to look away from the sorrow and from the not having.

For a long time that night we could only stare, amazed. I had never seen a dog behave this way before. Nor had my father, who twice almost rose, I think to knock him down. Twice he almost rose. But after supper, after the mill noise lowered like a voice is quieted in the evening, Spike began to slow down, and as if to calm himself, he came to each of us and put his head in our hands, and like that he was inside of us.

Spike was my dog, but this is not the boy-and-dog story we're wont to tell. Not the noble dog who's taken from the boy in the city by evil men and delivered to hard labor in the cold. Not the dog who saves the boy from the fire, or from the well, or from the wild animal, or from the abandoned cave, or from the escaped con. Not that boy, and not that dog.

In the bedroom I shared with my sister, one window faced the street. Light from the church streaked in too. Two small beds only inches apart. A small dresser. Some shelves. One small light on a table between us. One small box for some toys. Autumn dusk, some yellow slag air on the rise. I'm busy at the toy box with a broken thing I'm trying to fix, sitting down facing the door, when dust suddenly shimmers in the light through the window, suddenly fills the light, and I

5

see Spike between me and the door in a knot of shadows becoming something else. He begins to quiver and to jerk his head. He takes a wide stance and struts in the twelve-by-six-foot space between me and the door.

(I went back there once and troubled the poor people of those rooms to let me in. I stood in that room and felt it get smaller and smaller. They watched me shyly from the doorway. On the wall of the room where Spike had entered that other realm, they had a picture of Jesus Christ, glossy blood on his feet and hands; blood dripped from the crown of thorns, but no spirit of Spike, no boy, no residue of terror.)

Spike struts that wide stance and growls in a way I'd never heard him growl   10 before, almost a human word comes out, almost a begging for release, and he whines high and painfully, and he makes a strange yelp too from time to time, and he jumps with all four feet in the air. But I am not afraid. Spike has never hurt me. He would never bite or scratch or snap at me. Not his boy, not even when I'd smacked him. Not even when I'd bitten him and shook his neck in my own mouth. I am not afraid. I only wonder why he moves in this strange way, and why that movement freezes me in place, my brain shutting things down on its own. Only when I see my father's face at the door, looking down at Spike, and then at me, do I know to be afraid.

"Don't move," he shouts, and Spike yelps like a spirit and jumps with all four feet so he makes me laugh. "Don't move and don't say nothing," my father shouts, and he shakes his fist at me, or at Spike.

I can't tell if he's mad at me in my dumb fear, unmoving, or at the dog, whose body is shaking and twitchy and making ugly yelps that must be wrong and bad. I can't tell until I see my father move towards me through the threshold with a grace I didn't know he possessed. He wants to lift me away, he says with his eyes, but Spike is at him like the spinning wild dog he had been the night my father brought him home, with that wild uncontrollable need.

My father jerks back when Spike does this, which makes me know a different terror: the one where the father is mortal. The one where the floodgates open to the world's bright debris. My father can only stand back in the hall, Spike stopped in the doorway, almost stilled in a slow rocking into himself, making quiet, low whines I think sound a lot like crying; they sound a lot like crying to me.

I entered another world then. A world of two small and terrible continents. Two small islands. On one I float in strange light with Spike. Distempered. Rabid, they said in those days. 1953, where Spike will not come towards me when I call him in all the voices that would usually make him come to me or hop and dance, or whine in song for scraps. He only wags his tail a bit when he hears his name, an act that must take unfathomable dog courage to call up from the spinning tunnel of his sickness.

On the other island is my father, and the whole rest of the world as I know it   15 and care for it and want so badly to be among again. But Spike will not have it. I am his, and whenever my father tries to move towards me, Spike leaps, spit and snarl and yelp, from all fours like a toy dog, or like a dog in a cartoon, at my father's throat and drives him back into the hall. A ferocity like beauty.

"Don't move," my father says, and goes away.

◆ ◆ ◆

Sometimes I feel free and light and brave as that boy I was by my toy box on that island of my sweet life, kept and claimed by the rabid dog who would not let anyone near, who even in his frenzy thought to keep them all away from me, his brain gone wrong except for that. Sometimes I want only to lie down and let it all go.

The time it took for my father to leave and return with a policeman close behind, I can measure only with the weight of need. Mine to simply sit there in my dullness and be the boy I was. Spike's to guard me hard and to the end.

The policeman has a steel bar. I think he'll hit the dog and make him stop, but instead he jabs the bar from the doorway at Spike's head as if to tease. In the policeman's eyes I see his fearful wonder, like in my father's eyes, and this makes me choke and gag. The policeman jabs the bar again until Spike snaps and the policeman pulls the bar away, dragging Spike by his clamped jaw.

I don't remember making words come. I don't remember caring for words, but I remember screaming *Stop* until Spike wags his tail again and almost turns around as if to drag up one more speck of memoried light, before he clenches down hard one last time on the bar and holds it in his rat dog's jaw.

Things move quickly now. I don't search for resolution anymore. What's done is done. I don't know why we long so for the dead who can do us no good.

The policeman drags Spike down the flight of dark stairs. My father follows. I'm left in the room, alone. I can't seem to stand or move until I hear a ruckus on the stairs. Even now, even tonight, with snow like a blanket over the broken day lilies, all of these lives and lives later, even now, I hear that snarling, snapping spit of a dog fighting for his life, and I hear the voices of the men too high in their panic. I run from the room towards the stairs and find my father behind the policeman who has Spike in a noose at the end of a long pole. He pushes Spike down. I grab my father's startled arm and hang on tight. He doesn't even hold me.

"Stay back," is all he says, and he pushes me away.

Outside the policeman holds Spike at bay at the end of the long pole. *That's what kind of trouble you can get into,* I think. He drags Spike towards the back where the garbage is heaped and the broken cars commune. My father stands beside him when he takes his pistol out. No one looks to me on the porch. I watch the policeman take his pistol out, that lovely practiced move. No one looks to me on the porch. I am five years old, and I know enough. My father half turns his head away when the policeman draws the hammer back and squeezes off a round into the rat dog's brain.

This is the end of things, I think. Nothing can go on from this. No light would ever find us again. No peace could fill our hearts. No laughter near the coal stove with the wild dog who danced on his hind legs and turned a dancer's turn and fell and flew around the rooms for us. The end near the garbage heap. My ears ringing, I stand on the porch and let wash over me all the grief and fear and love that keeps blossoming, even now, inside me. World of hurt. Deepest, what remains.

[2000]

THINKING ABOUT THE TEXT

1. Where in the text does Weigl seem to express the perspective of his younger self? Where does he seem to express the perspective of the adult writer? Refer to specific passages.

2. What was Spike like before he turned rabid? Describe him in your own words. Why, apparently, did the young Weigl value him? Would you have enjoyed having him as a pet? Why, or why not?

3. Why do you think Weigl included the parenthetical paragraph about his returning to the apartment as an adult?

4. What is the effect when Weigl uses the present tense? Why do you suppose he begins with the past tense instead of using the present tense throughout?

5. What do you take Weigl's last sentence to mean?

MAKING COMPARISONS

1. Unlike Orwell and Dillard, Weigl owned the animal that is killed. How significant is this difference? Also unlike Orwell and Dillard, Weigl was a child when the animal was killed. Again, how significant is this difference?

2. Both Orwell and Dillard recall people watching them during the episodes they write about. Is someone else's gaze just as important in Weigl's essay? Explain.

3. Do all three writers strike you as remembering things objectively? Refer to specific passages that influence your answer.

WRITING ABOUT ISSUES

1. Choose Orwell's, Dillard's, or Weigl's piece, and write an essay explaining how appropriately you think the writer behaved when the animal was killed. Take into account the specific circumstances the writer was in. Also provide reasons for your judgment.

2. Choose Orwell's or Weigl's piece. Then write an essay determining how applicable to your chosen text is Dillard's statement "these things are not issues; they are mysteries." Make clear how Dillard seems to define *issues* and *mysteries*.

3. Write an essay analyzing your behavior at a time when you had to decide how much to endorse the killing of a certain animal or of a certain group of animals. What thoughts ran through your mind? What specific pressures did you face? How did you believe your conduct would be viewed by others? Indicate any significant differences between your younger self and the kind of person you are now.

4. Research a group that is against hunting, against the killing of animals in lab experiments, or against the killing of animals for human consumption. Find out especially about the rhetorical strategies this group uses to advance its cause. Then write an essay identifying and evaluating some of these methods of persuasion.

ESCAPING LIFE: CRITICAL COMMENTARIES ON MARSHA NORMAN'S *'NIGHT, MOTHER*

MARSHA NORMAN, *'night, Mother*

CRITICAL COMMENTARIES:
LISA J. MCDONNELL, From "Diverse Similitude: Beth Henley and Marsha Norman"
SALLY BROWDER, From " 'I Thought You Were Mine': Marsha Norman's *'night, Mother*"
JENNY S. SPENCER, From "Norman's *'night, Mother*: Psycho-drama of Female Identity"

Should people intent on suicide always be stopped from committing it? Is suicide ever justifiable? For the families and loved ones of those who have killed themselves, the act is usually an occasion for pain instead of rejoicing. But increasingly, Americans debate the first two questions. In large part, they do so because of the new prominence given physician-assisted suicide. Even as the Supreme Court considered whether state laws could ban this practice, doctors such as Jack Kevorkian and Timothy Quill publicly confessed to helping physically ill or incapacitated patients kill themselves. Is suicide appropriate if the reasons for it are purely psychological? This question confronts the two characters in Marsha Norman's 1983 play *'night, Mother*. Near the start, Jessie announces to her mother, Thelma, that she will kill herself later that evening, and Thelma does everything she can to change her daughter's mind. As you read the play, consider whether you approve of Jessie's plan or side with Thelma in her efforts to thwart it. To help you weigh their positions, we include three commentaries on their conflict. Lisa McDonnell sees Jessie as using death to achieve selfhood, Sally Browder examines the psychological dynamics of the play's mother-daughter relationship, and Jenny Spencer observes that women's responses to the play differ from men's.

BEFORE YOU READ

What influences your view of suicide? Would you ever approve of someone's committing it? If so, under what circumstances?

(Susan Johann © 1991.)

MARSHA NORMAN
'night, Mother

Marsha Norman (b. 1947) grew up in Louisville, Kentucky, and has long been associated with the Actors Theatre there. Her plays include Getting Out *(1977),* Traveler in the Dark *(1984), and, most recently,* Trudy Blue *(1995). In 1991, her script for the musical* The Secret Garden *won her a Tony Award. The play* 'night, Mother, *for which Norman won the Pulitzer Prize, premiered at the American Repertory Theatre in Cambridge, Massachusetts, in January 1983. In March of that year, it was produced on Broadway. Both of these productions featured Kathy Bates as Jessie and Anne Pitoniak as Thelma; in the 1986 film version, the roles were played by Sissy Spacek and Anne Bancroft. As a theater piece,* 'night, Mother *has aroused a lot of attention for its treatment of suicide. It is also distinctive in its time span. With plays and movies, hardly ever does the time span represented coincide with the work's actual running time. This play covers about ninety minutes in the lives of its characters and takes the same amount of time to perform. Indeed, in most productions of the play, the time shown by the clocks on the set is the same as the actual time when the play is performed in the evening.*

CHARACTERS

JESSIE CATES, *in her late thirties or early forties, is pale and vaguely unsteady physically. It is only in the last year that Jessie has gained control of her mind and body, and tonight she is determined to hold on to that control. She wears pants and a long black sweater with deep pockets, which contain scraps of paper, and there may be a pencil behind her ear or a pen clipped to one of the pockets of the sweater.*

    As a rule, Jessie doesn't feel much like talking. Other people have rarely found her quirky sense of humor amusing. She has a peaceful energy on this night, a sense of purpose, but is clearly aware of the time passing moment by moment. Oddly enough, Jessie has never been as communicative or as enjoyable as she is on this evening, but we must know she has not always been this way. There is a familiarity between these two women that comes from having lived together for a long time. There is a shorthand to the talk and a sense of routine comfort in the way they relate to each other physically. Naturally, there are also routine aggravations.

THELMA CATES, MAMA, *is Jessie's mother, in her late fifties or early sixties. She has begun to feel her age and so takes it easy when she can, or when it serves her purpose to let someone help her. But she speaks quickly and enjoys talking. She believes that things are what she says they are. Her sturdiness is more a mental quality than a physical one, finally. She is chatty and nosy, and this is* her house.

The play takes place in a relatively new house built way out on a country road, with a living room and connecting kitchen, and a center hall that leads off to the bedrooms. A pull cord in the hall ceiling releases a ladder which leads to the attic. One of these bedrooms opens directly onto the hall, and its entry should be visible to everyone in the audience. It should be, in fact, the focal point of the entire set, and the lighting should make it disappear completely at times and draw the entire set into it at others. It is a point of both threat and promise. It is an ordinary door that opens onto absolute nothingness. That door is the point of all the action, and the utmost care should be given to its design and construction.

    The living room is cluttered with magazines and needlework catalogues, ashtrays and candy dishes. Examples of Mama's needlework are everywhere — pillows, afghans, and quilts, doilies and rugs, and they are quite nice examples. The house is more comfortable than messy, but there is quite a lot to keep in place here. It is more personal than charming. It is not quaint. Under no circumstances should the set and its dressing make a judgment about the intelligence or taste of Jessie and Mama. It should simply indicate that they are very specific real people who happen to live in a particular part of the country. Heavy accents, which would further distance the audience from Jessie and Mama, are also wrong.

The time is the present, with the action beginning about 8:15. Clocks onstage in the kitchen and on a table in the living room should run throughout the performance and be visible to the audience.

There will be no intermission.

Mama stretches to reach the cupcakes in a cabinet in the kitchen. She can't see them, but she can feel around for them, and she's eager to have one, so she's working pretty hard at it. This may be the most serious exercise Mama ever gets. She finds a cupcake, the coconut-covered, raspberry-and-marshmallow-filled kind known as a snowball, but sees that there's one missing from the package. She calls to Jessie, who is apparently somewhere else in the house.

MAMA *(unwrapping the cupcake)*:   Jessie, it's the last snowball, sugar. Put it on the list, O.K.? And we're out of Hershey bars, and where's that peanut brittle? I think maybe Dawson's been in it again. I ought to put a big mirror on the refrigerator door. That'll keep him out of my treats, won't it? You hear me, honey? *(Then more to herself.)* I hate it when the coconut falls off. Why does the coconut fall off?

Jessie enters from her bedroom, carrying a stack of newspapers.

JESSIE: We got any old towels?

MAMA: There you are!

JESSIE *(holding a towel that was on the stack of newspapers)*:   Towels you don't want anymore. *(Picking up Mama's snowball wrapper.)* How about this swimming towel Loretta gave us? Beach towel, that's the name of it. You want it? *(Mama shakes her head no.)*

MAMA: What have you been doing in there?

JESSIE: And a big piece of plastic like a rubber sheet or something. Garbage bags would do if there's enough.

MAMA: Don't go making a big mess, Jessie. It's eight o'clock already.

JESSIE: Maybe an old blanket or towels we got in a soap box sometime?

MAMA: I said don't make a mess. Your hair is black enough, hon.

JESSIE *(continuing to search the kitchen cabinets, finding two or three more towels to add to her stack)*:   It's not for my hair, Mama. What about some old pillows anywhere, or a foam cushion out of a yard chair would be real good.

MAMA: You haven't forgot what night it is, have you? *(Holding up her fingernails.)* They're all chipped, see? I've been waiting all week, Jess. It's Saturday night, sugar.

JESSIE: I know. I got it on the schedule.

MAMA *(crossing to the living room)*:   You want me to wash 'em now or are you making your mess first? *(Looking at the snowball.)* We're out of these. Did I say that already?

JESSIE: There's more coming tomorrow. I ordered you a whole case.

MAMA *(checking the TV Guide)*:   A whole case will go stale, Jessie.

JESSIE: They can go in the freezer till you're ready for them. Where's Daddy's gun?

MAMA: In the attic.

JESSIE: Where in the attic? I looked your whole nap and couldn't find it anywhere.

MAMA: One of his shoeboxes, I think.

JESSIE: Full of shoes. I looked already.

MAMA: Well, you didn't look good enough, then. There's that box from the ones he wore to the hospital. When he died, they told me I could have them back, but I never did like those shoes.

JESSIE *(pulling them out of her pocket)*:   I found the bullets. They were in an old milk can.

MAMA *(as Jessie starts for the hall)*:   Dawson took the shotgun, didn't he? Hand me that basket, hon.

JESSIE *(getting the basket for her)*:   Dawson better not've taken that pistol.

MAMA *(stopping her again)*:   Now my glasses, please. *(Jessie returns to get the glasses.)* I told him to take those rubber boots, too, but he said they were for fishing. I told him to take up fishing.

Jessie reaches for the cleaning spray and cleans Mama's glasses for her.

JESSIE: He's just too lazy to climb up there, Mama. Or maybe he's just being smart. That floor's not very steady.

MAMA *(getting out a piece of knitting)*:   It's not a floor at all, hon, it's a board now and then. Measure this for me. I need six inches.

JESSIE *(as she measures)*:   Dawson could probably use some of those clothes up there. Somebody should have them. You ought to call the Salvation Army before the whole thing falls in on you. Six inches exactly.

MAMA: It's plenty safe! As long as you don't go up there.

JESSIE *(turning to go again)*:   I'm careful.

MAMA: What do you want the gun for, Jess?

JESSIE *(not returning this time. Opening the ladder in the hall.)*:   Protection. *(She steadies the ladder as Mama talks.)*

MAMA: You take the TV way too serious, hon. I've never seen a criminal in my life. This is way too far to come for what's out here to steal. Never seen a one.

JESSIE *(taking her first step up)*:   Except for Ricky.

MAMA: Ricky is mixed up. That's not a crime.

JESSIE: Get your hands washed. I'll be right back. And get 'em real dry. You dry your hands till I get back or it's no go, all right?

MAMA: I thought Dawson told you not to go up those stairs.

JESSIE *(going up)*:   He did.

MAMA: I don't like the idea of a gun, Jess.

JESSIE *(calling down from the attic)*:   Which shoebox, do you remember?

MAMA: Black.

JESSIE: The box was black?

MAMA: The shoes were black.

JESSIE: That doesn't help much, Mother.

MAMA: I'm not trying to help, sugar. *(No answer.)* We don't have anything anybody'd want, Jessie. I mean, I don't even want what we got, Jessie.

JESSIE: Neither do I. Wash your hands. *(Mama gets up and crosses to stand under the ladder.)*

MAMA: You come down from there before you have a fit. I can't come up and get you, you know.

JESSIE: I know.

MAMA: We'll just hand it over to them when they come, how's that? Whatever they want, the criminals.

JESSIE: That's a good idea, Mama.

MAMA: Ricky will grow out of this and be a real fine boy, Jess. But I have to tell you, I wouldn't want Ricky to know we had a gun in the house.

JESSIE: Here it is. I found it.

MAMA: It's just something Ricky's going through. Maybe he's in with some bad people. He just needs some time, sugar. He'll get back in school or get a job or one day you'll get a call and he'll say he's sorry for all the trouble he's caused and invite you out for supper someplace dress-up.

JESSIE *(coming back down the steps)*: Don't worry. It's not for him, it's for me.

MAMA: I didn't think you would shoot your own boy, Jessie. I know you've felt like it, well, we've all felt like shooting somebody, but we don't do it. I just don't think we need . . .

JESSIE *(interrupting)*: Your hands aren't washed. Do you want a manicure or not?

MAMA: Yes, I do, but . . .

JESSIE *(crossing to the chair)*: Then wash your hands and don't talk to me anymore about Ricky. Those two rings he took were the last valuable things *I* had, so now he's started in on other people, door to door. I hope they put him away sometime. I'd turn him in myself if I knew where he was.

MAMA: You don't mean that.

JESSIE: Every word. Wash your hands and that's the last time I'm telling you.

Jessie sits down with the gun and starts cleaning it, pushing the cylinder out, checking to see that the chambers and barrel are empty, then putting some oil on a small patch of cloth and pushing it through the barrel with the push rod that was in the box. Mama goes to the kitchen and washes her hands, as instructed, trying not to show her concern about the gun.

MAMA: I shoulda got you to bring down that milk can. Agnes Fletcher sold hers to somebody with a flea market for forty dollars apiece.

JESSIE: I'll go back and get it in a minute. There's a wagon wheel up there, too. There's even a churn. I'll get it all if you want.

MAMA *(coming over, now, taking over now)*: What are you doing?

JESSIE: The barrel has to be clean, Mama. Old powder, dust gets in it . . .

MAMA: What for?

JESSIE: I told you.

MAMA *(reaching for the gun)*: And I told you, we don't get criminals out here.

JESSIE *(quickly pulling it to her)*: And I told you . . . *(Then trying to be calm.)* The gun is for me.

MAMA: Well, you can have it if you want. When I die, you'll get it all, anyway.

JESSIE: I'm going to kill myself, Mama.

MAMA *(returning to the sofa)*: Very funny. Very funny.

JESSIE: I am.

MAMA: You are not! Don't even say such a thing, Jessie.

JESSIE: How would you know if I didn't say it? You want it to be a surprise? You're lying there in your bed or maybe you're just brushing your teeth and you hear this . . . noise down the hall?

MAMA: Kill yourself.

JESSIE: Shoot myself. In a couple of hours.

MAMA: It must be time for your medicine.

JESSIE: Took it already.

MAMA: What's the matter with you?

JESSIE: Not a thing. Feel fine.

MAMA: You feel fine. You're just going to kill yourself.

JESSIE: Waited until I felt good enough, in fact.

MAMA: Don't make jokes, Jessie. I'm too old for jokes.

JESSIE: It's not a joke, Mama.

Mama watches for a moment in silence.

MAMA: That gun's no good, you know. He broke it right before he died. He dropped it in the mud one day.

JESSIE: Seems O.K. (*She spins the chamber, cocks the pistol, and pulls the trigger. The gun is not yet loaded, so all we hear is the click, but it will definitely work. It's also obvious that Jessie knows her way around a gun. Mama cannot speak.*) I had Cecil's all ready in there, just in case I couldn't find this one, but I'd rather use Daddy's.

MAMA: Those bullets are at least fifteen years old.

JESSIE (*pulling out another box*): These are from last week.

MAMA: Where did you get those?

JESSIE: Feed store Dawson told me about.

MAMA: Dawson!

JESSIE: I told him I was worried about prowlers. He said he thought it was a good idea. He told me what kind to ask for.

MAMA: If he had any idea . . .

JESSIE: He took it as a compliment. He thought I might be taking an interest in things. He got through telling me all about the bullets and then he said we ought to talk like this more often.

MAMA: And where was I while this was going on?

JESSIE: On the phone with Agnes. About the milk can, I guess. Anyway, I asked Dawson if he thought they'd send me some bullets and he said he'd just call for me, because he knew they'd send them if he told them to. And he was absolutely right. Here they are.

MAMA: How could he do that?

JESSIE: Just trying to help, Mama.

MAMA: And then I told you where the gun was.

JESSIE (*smiling, enjoying this joke*): See? Everybody's doing what they can.

MAMA: You told me it was for protection!

JESSIE: It *is!* I'm still doing your nails, though. Want to try that new Chinaberry color?

MAMA: Well, I'm calling Dawson right now. We'll just see what he has to say about this little stunt.

JESSIE: Dawson doesn't have any more to do with this.

MAMA: He's your brother.

JESSIE: And that's all.

MAMA *(stands up, moves toward the phone)*:   Dawson will put a stop to this. Yes he will. He'll take the gun away.

JESSIE: If you call him, I'll just have to do it before he gets here. Soon as you hang up the phone, I'll just walk in the bedroom and lock the door. Dawson will get here just in time to help you clean up. Go ahead, call him. Then call the police. Then call the funeral home. Then call Loretta and see if *she'll* do your nails.

MAMA: You will not! This is crazy talk, Jessie!

Mama goes directly to the telephone and starts to dial, but Jessie is fast, coming up behind her and taking the receiver out of her hand, putting it back down.

JESSIE *(firm and quiet)*:   I said no. This is private. Dawson is not invited.

MAMA: Just me.

JESSIE: I don't want anybody else over here. Just you and me. If Dawson comes over, it'll make me feel stupid for not doing it ten years ago.

MAMA: I think we better call the doctor. Or how about the ambulance. You like that one driver, I know. What's his name, Timmy? Get you somebody to talk to.

JESSIE *(going back to her chair)*:   I'm through talking, Mama. You're it. No more.

MAMA: We're just going to sit around like every other night in the world and then you're going to kill yourself? *(Jessie doesn't answer.)* You'll miss. *(Again there is no response.)* You'll just wind up a vegetable. How would you like that? Shoot your ear off? You know what the doctor said about getting excited. You'll cock the pistol and have a fit.

JESSIE: I think I can kill myself, Mama.

MAMA: You're not going to kill yourself, Jessie. You're not even upset! *(Jessie smiles, or laughs quietly, and Mama tries a different approach.)* People don't really kill themselves, Jessie. No, mam, doesn't make sense, unless you're retarded or deranged, and you're as normal as they come, Jessie, for the most part. We're all *afraid* to die.

JESSIE: I'm not, Mama. I'm cold all the time, anyway.

MAMA: That's ridiculous.

JESSIE: It's exactly what I want. It's dark and quiet.

MAMA: So is the back yard, Jessie! Close your eyes. Stuff cotton in your ears. Take a nap! It's quiet in your room. I'll leave the TV off all night.

JESSIE: So quiet I don't know it's quiet. So nobody can get me.

MAMA: You don't know what dead is like. It might not be quiet at all. What if it's like an alarm clock and you can't wake up so you can't shut it off. Ever.

JESSIE: Dead is everybody and everything I ever knew, gone. Dead is dead quiet.

MAMA: It's a sin. You'll go to hell.

JESSIE: Uh-huh.

MAMA: You will!

JESSIE: Jesus was a suicide, if you ask me.

MAMA: You'll go to hell just for saying that. Jessie!

JESSIE *(with genuine surprise)*:   I didn't know I thought that.

MAMA: Jessie!

Jessie doesn't answer. She puts the now-loaded gun back in the box and crosses to the kitchen. But Mama is afraid she's headed for the bedroom.

MAMA *(in a panic)*:   You can't use my towels! They're my towels. I've had them for a long time. I like my towels.

JESSIE: I asked you if you wanted that swimming towel and you said you didn't.

MAMA: And you can't use your father's gun, either. It's mine now, too. And you can't do it in my house.

JESSIE: Oh, come on.

MAMA: No. You can't do it. I won't let you. The house is in my name.

JESSIE: I have to go in the bedroom and lock the door behind me so they won't arrest you for killing me. They'll probably test your hands for gunpowder, anyway, but you'll pass.

MAMA: Not in my house!

JESSIE: If I'd known you were going to act like this, I wouldn't have told you.

MAMA: How am I supposed to act? Tell you to go ahead? O.K. by me, sugar? Might try it myself. What took you so long?

JESSIE: There's just no point in fighting me over it, that's all. Want some coffee?

MAMA: Your birthday's coming up, Jessie. Don't you want to know what we got you?

JESSIE: You got me dusting powder, Loretta got me a new housecoat, pink probably, and Dawson got me new slippers, too small, but they go with the robe, he'll say. *(Mama cannot speak.)* Right? *(Apparently Jessie is right.)* Be back in a minute.

Jessie takes the gun box, puts it on top of the stack of towels and garbage bags, and takes them into her bedroom. Mama, alone for a moment, goes to the phone, picks up the receiver, looks toward the bedroom, starts to dial, and then replaces the receiver in its cradle as Jessie walks back into the room. Jessie wonders, silently. They have lived together for so long there is very rarely any reason for one to ask what the other was about to do.

MAMA: I started to, but I didn't. I didn't call him.

JESSIE: Good. Thank you.

MAMA *(starting over, a new approach)*:   What's this all about, Jessie?

JESSIE: About?

Jessie now begins the next task she had "on the schedule," which is refilling all the candy jars, taking the empty papers out of the boxes of chocolates, etc. Mama generally snitches when Jessie does this. Not tonight, though. Nevertheless, Jessie offers.

MAMA: What did I do?

JESSIE: Nothing. Want a caramel?

MAMA *(ignoring the candy)*:   You're mad at me.

JESSIE: Not a bit. I am worried about you, but I'm going to do what I can before I go. We're not just going to sit around tonight. I made a list of things.

MAMA: What things?

JESSIE: How the washer works. Things like that.

MAMA: I know how the washer works. You put the clothes in. You put the soap in. You turn it on. You wait.

JESSIE: You do something else. You don't just wait.

MAMA: Whatever else you find to do, you're still mainly waiting. The waiting's the worst part of it. The waiting's what you pay somebody else to do, if you can.

JESSIE *(nodding)*:   O.K. Where do we keep the soap?

MAMA: I could find it.

JESSIE: See?

MAMA: If you're mad about doing the wash, we can get Loretta to do it.

JESSIE: Oh now, that might be worth staying to see.

MAMA: She'd never in her life, would she?

JESSIE: Nope.

MAMA: What's the matter with her?

JESSIE: She thinks she's better than we are. She's not.

MAMA: Maybe if she didn't wear that yellow all the time.

JESSIE: The washer repair number is on a little card taped to the side of the machine.

MAMA: Loretta doesn't ever have to come over here again. Dawson can just leave her at home when he comes. And we don't ever have to see Dawson either if he bothers you. Does he bother you?

JESSIE: Sure he does. Be sure you clean out the lint tray every time you use the dryer. But don't ever put your house shoes in, it'll melt the soles.

MAMA: What does Dawson do, that bothers you?

JESSIE: He just calls me Jess like he knows who he's talking to. He's always wondering what I do all day. I mean, I wonder that myself, but it's my day, so it's mine to wonder about, not his.

MAMA: Family is just accident, Jessie. It's nothing personal, hon. They don't mean to get on your nerves. They don't even mean to be your family, they just are.

JESSIE: They know too much.

MAMA: About what?

JESSIE: They know things about you, and they learned it before you had a chance to say whether you wanted them to know it or not. They were there when it happened and it don't belong to them, it belongs to you, only they got it. Like my mail-order bra got delivered to their house.

MAMA: By accident!

JESSIE: All the same . . . they opened it. They saw the little rosebuds on it. *(Offering her another candy.)* Chewy mint?

MAMA *(shaking her head no)*:   What do they know about you? I'll tell them never to talk about it again. Is it Ricky or Cecil or your fits or your hair is falling out or you drink too much coffee or you never go out of the house or what?

JESSIE: I just don't like their talk. The account at the grocery is in Dawson's
name when you call. The number's on a whole list of numbers on the back
cover of the phone book.

MAMA: Well! Now we're getting somewhere. They're none of them ever setting
foot in this house again.

JESSIE: It's not them, Mother. I wouldn't kill myself just to get away from them.

MAMA: You leave the room when they come over, anyway.

JESSIE: I stay as long as I can. Besides, it's you they come to see.

MAMA: That's because I stay in the room when they come.

JESSIE: It's not them.

MAMA: Then what is it?

JESSIE *(checking the list on her note pad)*:   The grocery won't deliver on Saturday
anymore. And if you want your order the same day, you have to call before
ten. And they won't deliver less than fifteen dollars' worth. What I do is tell
them what we need and tell them to add on cigarettes until it gets to fifteen
dollars.

MAMA: It's Ricky. You're trying to get through to him.

JESSIE: If I thought I could do that, I would stay.

MAMA: Make him sorry he hurt you, then. That's it, isn't it?

JESSIE: He's hurt me, I've hurt him. We're about even.

MAMA: You'll be telling him killing is O.K. with you, you know. Want him to
start killing next? Nothing wrong with it. Mom did it.

JESSIE: Only a matter of time, anyway, Mama. When the call comes, you let
Dawson handle it.

MAMA: Honey, nothing says those calls are always going to be some new trouble
he's into. You could get one that he's got a job, that he's getting married, or
how about he's joined the army, wouldn't that be nice?

JESSIE: If you call the Sweet Tooth before you call the grocery, that Susie will
take your fudge next door to the grocery and it'll all come out together. Be
sure you talk to Susie, though. She won't let them put it in the bottom of a
sack like that one time, remember?

MAMA: Ricky could come over, you know. What if he calls us?

JESSIE: It's not Ricky, Mama.

MAMA: Or anybody could call us, Jessie.

JESSIE: Not on Saturday night, Mama.

MAMA: Then what is it? Are you sick? If your gums are swelling again, we can
get you to the dentist in the morning.

JESSIE: No. Can you order your medicine or do you want Dawson to? I've got a
note to him. I'll add that to it if you want.

MAMA: Your eyes don't look right. I thought so yesterday.

JESSIE: That was just the ragweed. I'm not sick.

MAMA: Epilepsy is sick, Jessie.

JESSIE: It won't kill me. *(A pause.)* If it would, I wouldn't have to.

MAMA: You don't *have* to.

JESSIE: No, I don't. That's what I like about it.

MAMA: Well, I won't let you!

JESSIE: It's not up to you.

MAMA: Jessie!

JESSIE: I want to hang a big sign around my neck, like Daddy's on the barn. GONE FISHING.

MAMA: You don't like it here.

JESSIE (smiling):   Exactly.

MAMA: I meant here in my house.

JESSIE: I know you did.

MAMA: You never should have moved back in here with me. If you'd kept your little house or found another place when Cecil left you, you'd have made some new friends at least. Had a life to lead. Had your own things around you. Give Ricky a place to come see you. You never should've come here.

JESSIE: Maybe.

MAMA: But I didn't force you, did I?

JESSIE: If it was a mistake, we made it together. You took me in. I appreciate that.

MAMA: You didn't have any business being by yourself right then, but I can see how you might want a place of your own. A grown woman should . . .

JESSIE: Mama . . . I'm just not having a very good time and I don't have any reason to think it'll get anything but worse. I'm tired. I'm hurt. I'm sad. I feel used.

MAMA: Tired of what?

JESSIE: It all.

MAMA: What does that mean?

JESSIE: I can't say it any better.

MAMA: Well, you'll have to say it better because I'm not letting you alone till you do. What were those other things? Hurt . . . (Before Jessie can answer.) You had this all ready to say to me, didn't you? Did you write this down? How long have you been thinking about this?

JESSIE: Off and on, ten years. On all the time, since Christmas.

MAMA: What happened at Christmas?

JESSIE: Nothing.

MAMA: So why Christmas?

JESSIE: That's it. On the nose.

A pause. Mama knows exactly what Jessie means. She was there, too, after all.

JESSIE (putting the candy sacks away):   See where all this is? Red hots up front, sour balls and horehound mixed together in this one sack. New packages of toffee and licorice right in back there.

MAMA: Go back to your list. You're hurt by what?

JESSIE (Mama knows perfectly well):   Mama . . .

MAMA: O.K. Sad about what? There's nothing real sad going on right now. If it was after your divorce or something, that would make sense.

JESSIE (looking at her list, then opening the drawer):   Now, this drawer has everything in it that there's no better place for. Extension cords, batteries for the radio, extra lighters, sandpaper, masking tape, Elmer's glue, thumbtacks, that kind of stuff. The mousetraps are under the sink, but you call Dawson if you've got one and let him do it.

MAMA: Sad about what?

JESSIE: The way things are.

MAMA: Not good enough. What things?

JESSIE: Oh, everything from you and me to Red China.

MAMA: I think we can leave the Chinese out of this.

JESSIE (*crosses back into the living room*): There's extra light bulbs in a box in the hall closet. And we've got a couple of packages of fuses in the fuse box. There's candles and matches in the top of the broom closet, but if the lights go out, just call Dawson and sit tight. But don't open the refrigerator door. Things will stay cool in there as long as you keep the door shut.

MAMA: I asked you a question.

JESSIE: I read the paper. I don't like how things are. And they're not any better out there than they are in here.

MAMA: If you're doing this because of the newspapers, I can sure fix that!

JESSIE: There's just more of it on TV.

MAMA (*kicking the television set*): Take it out, then!

JESSIE: You wouldn't do that.

MAMA: Watch me.

JESSIE: What would you do all day?

MAMA (*desperately*): Sing. (*Jessie laughs.*) I would, too. You want to watch? I'll sing till morning to keep you alive, Jessie, please!

JESSIE: No. (*Then affectionately.*) It's a funny idea, though. What do you sing?

MAMA (*has no idea how to answer this*): We've got a good life here!

JESSIE (*going back into the kitchen*): I called this morning and canceled the papers, except for Sunday, for your puzzles; you'll still get that one.

MAMA: Let's get another dog, Jessie! You liked a big dog, now, didn't you? That King dog, didn't you?

JESSIE (*washing her hands*): I did like that King dog, yes.

MAMA: I'm so dumb. He's the one run under the tractor.

JESSIE: That makes him dumb, not you.

MAMA: For bringing it up.

JESSIE: It's O.K. Handi-Wipes and sponges under the sink.

MAMA: We could get a new dog and keep him in the house. Dogs are cheap!

JESSIE (*getting big pill jars out of the cabinet*): No.

MAMA: Something for you to take care of.

JESSIE: I've had you, Mama.

MAMA (*frantically starting to fill pill bottles*): You do too much for me. I can fill pill bottles all day, Jessie, and change the shelf paper and wash the floor when I get through. You just watch me. You don't have to do another thing in this house if you don't want to. You don't have to take care of me, Jessie.

JESSIE: I know that. You've just been letting me do it so I'll have something to do, haven't you?

MAMA (*realizing this was a mistake*): I don't do it as well as you. I just meant if it tires you out or makes you feel used . . .

JESSIE: Mama, I know you used to ride the bus. Riding the bus and it's hot and bumpy and crowded and too noisy and more than anything in the world you want to get off and the only reason in the world you don't get off is it's still fifty blocks from where you're going? Well, I can get off right now if I want to, because even if I ride fifty more years and get off then, it's the same place when I step down to it. Whenever I feel like it, I can get off. As soon as I've had enough, it's my stop. I've had enough.

MAMA: You're feeling sorry for yourself!

JESSIE: The plumber's helper is under the sink, too.

MAMA: You're not having a good time! Whoever promised you a good time? Do you think I've had a good time?

JESSIE: I think you're pretty happy, yeah. You have things you like to do.

MAMA: Like what?

JESSIE: Like crochet.

MAMA: I'll teach you to crochet.

JESSIE: I can't do any of that nice work, Mama.

MAMA: Good time don't come looking for you, Jessie. You could work some puzzles or put in a garden or go to the store. Let's call a taxi and go to the A&P!

JESSIE: I shopped you up for about two weeks already. You're not going to need toilet paper till Thanksgiving.

MAMA (*interrupting*):   You're acting like some little brat, Jessie. You're mad and everybody's boring and you don't have anything to do and you don't like me and you don't like going out and you don't like staying in and you never talk on the phone and you don't watch TV and you're miserable and it's your own sweet fault.

JESSIE: And it's time I did something about it.

MAMA: Not something like killing yourself. Something like . . . buying us all new dishes! I'd like that. Or maybe the doctor would let you get a driver's license now, or I know what let's do right this minute, let's rearrange the furniture.

JESSIE: I'll do that. If you want. I always thought if the TV was somewhere else, you wouldn't get such a glare on it during the day. I'll do whatever you want before I go.

MAMA (*badly frightened by those words*):   You could get a job!

JESSIE: I took that telephone sales job and I didn't even make enough money to pay the phone bill, and I tried to work at the gift shop at the hospital and they said I made people real uncomfortable smiling at them the way I did.

MAMA: You could keep books. You kept your dad's books.

JESSIE: But nobody ever checked them.

MAMA: When he died, they checked them.

JESSIE: And that's when they took the books away from me.

MAMA: That's because without him there wasn't any business, Jessie!

JESSIE (*putting the pill bottles away*):   You know I couldn't work. I can't do anything. I've never been around people my whole life except when I went to the hospital. I could have a seizure any time. What good would a job do? The kind of job I could get would make me feel worse.

MAMA: Jessie!

JESSIE: It's true!

MAMA: It's what you think is true!

JESSIE *(struck by the clarity of that)*:   That's right. It's what I think is true.

MAMA *(hysterically)*:   But I can't do anything about that!

JESSIE *(quietly)*:   No. You can't. *(Mama slumps, if not physically, at least emotionally.)* And I can't do anything either, about my life, to change it, make it better, make me feel better about it. Like it better, make it work. But I can stop it. Shut it down, turn it off like the radio when there's nothing on I want to listen to. It's all I really have that belongs to me and I'm going to say what happens to it. And it's going to stop. And I'm going to stop it. So. Let's just have a good time.

MAMA: Have a good time.

JESSIE: We can't go on fussing all night. I mean, I could ask you things I always wanted to know and you could make me some hot chocolate. The old way.

MAMA *(in despair)*:   It takes cocoa, Jessie.

JESSIE *(gets it out of the cabinet)*:   I bought cocoa, Mama. And I'd like to have a caramel apple and do your nails.

MAMA: You didn't eat a bite of supper.

JESSIE: Does that mean I can't have a caramel apple?

MAMA: Of course not. I mean . . . *(Smiling a little.)* Of course you can have a caramel apple.

JESSIE: I thought I could.

MAMA: I make the best caramel apples in the world.

JESSIE: I know you do.

MAMA: Or used to. And you don't get cocoa like mine anywhere anymore.

JESSIE: It takes time, I know, but . . .

MAMA: The salt is the trick.

JESSIE: Trouble and everything.

MAMA *(backing away toward the stove)*:   It's no trouble. What trouble? You put it in the pan and stir it up. All right. Fine. Caramel apples. Cocoa. O.K.

Jessie walks to the counter to retrieve her cigarettes as Mama looks for the right pan. There are brief near-smiles, and maybe Mama clears her throat. We have a truce, for the moment. A genuine but nevertheless uneasy one. Jessie, who has been in constant motion since the beginning, now seems content to sit.

Mama starts looking for a pan to make the cocoa, getting out all the pans in the cabinets in the process. It looks like she's making a mess on purpose so Jessie will have to put them all away again. Mama is buying time, or trying to, and entertaining.

JESSIE: You talk to Agnes today?

MAMA: She's calling me from a pay phone this week. God only knows why. She has a perfectly good Trimline at home.

JESSIE *(laughing)*:   Well, how is she?

MAMA: How is she every day, Jessie? Nuts.

JESSIE: Is she really crazy or just silly?

MAMA: No, she's really crazy. She was probably using the pay phone because she had another little fire problem at home.

JESSIE: Mother . . .

MAMA: I'm serious! Agnes Fletcher's burned down every house she ever lived in. Eight fires, and she's due for a new one any day now.

JESSIE *(laughing)*:   No!

MAMA: Wouldn't surprise me a bit.

JESSIE *(laughing)*:   Why didn't you tell me this before? Why isn't she locked up somewhere?

MAMA: 'Cause nobody ever got hurt, I guess. Agnes woke everybody up to watch the fires as soon as she set 'em. One time she set out porch chairs and served lemonade.

JESSIE *(shaking her head)*:   Real lemonade?

MAMA: The houses they lived in, you knew they were going to fall down anyway, so why wait for it, is all I could ever make out about it. Agnes likes a feeling of accomplishment.

JESSIE: Good for her.

MAMA *(finding the pan she wants)*:   Why are you asking about Agnes? One cup or two?

JESSIE: One. She's your friend. No marshmallows.

MAMA *(getting the milk, etc.)*:   You have to have marshmallows. That's the old way, Jess. Two or three? Three is better.

JESSIE: Three, then. Her whole house burns up? Her clothes and pillows and everything? I'm not sure I believe this.

MAMA: When she was a girl, Jess, not now. Long time ago. But she's still got it in her, I'm sure of it.

JESSIE: She wouldn't burn her house down now. Where would she go? She can't get Buster to build her a new one, he's dead. How could she burn it up?

MAMA: Be exciting, though, if she did. You never know.

JESSIE: You do too know, Mama. She wouldn't do it.

MAMA *(forced to admit, but reluctant)*:   I guess not.

JESSIE: What else? Why does she wear all those whistles around her neck?

MAMA: Why does she have a house full of birds?

JESSIE: I didn't know she had a house full of birds!

MAMA: Well, she does. And she says they just follow her home. Well, I know for a fact she's still paying on the last parrot she bought. You gotta keep your life filled up, she says. She says a lot of stupid things. *(Jessie laughs, Mama continues, convinced she's getting somewhere.)* It's all that okra she eats. You can't just willy-nilly eat okra two meals a day and expect to get away with it. Made her crazy.

JESSIE: She really eats okra twice a day? Where does she get it in the winter?

MAMA: Well, she eats it a lot. Maybe not two meals, but . . .

JESSIE: More than the average person.

MAMA *(beginning to get irritated)*:   I don't know how much okra the average person eats.

JESSIE: Do you know how much okra Agnes eats?

MAMA: No.

JESSIE: How many birds does she have?

MAMA: Two.

JESSIE: Then what are the whistles for?

MAMA: They're not real whistles. Just little plastic ones on a necklace she won playing Bingo, and I only told you about it because I thought I might get a laugh out of you for once even if it wasn't the truth, Jessie. Things don't have to be true to talk about 'em, you know.

JESSIE: Why won't she come over here?

Mama is suddenly quiet, but the cocoa and milk are in the pan now, so she lights the stove and starts stirring.

MAMA: Well now, what a good idea. We should've had more cocoa. Cocoa is perfect.

JESSIE: Except you don't like milk.

MAMA (*another attempt, but not as energetic*):   I hate milk. Coats your throat as bad as okra. Something just downright disgusting about it.

JESSIE: It's because of me, isn't it?

MAMA: No, Jess.

JESSIE: Yes, Mama.

MAMA: O.K. Yes, then, but she's crazy. She's as crazy as they come. She's a lunatic.

JESSIE: What is it exactly? Did I say something, sometime? Or did she see me have a fit and's afraid I might have another one if she came over, or what?

MAMA: I guess.

JESSIE: You guess what? What's she ever said? She must've given you some reason.

MAMA: Your hands are cold.

JESSIE: What difference does that make?

MAMA: "Like a corpse," she says, "and I'm gonna be one soon enough as it is."

JESSIE: That's crazy.

MAMA: That's Agnes. "Jessie's shook the hand of death and I can't take the chance it's catching, Thelma, so I ain't comin' over, and you can understand or no, but I ain't comin'. I'll come up the driveway, but that's as far as I go."

JESSIE (*laughing, relieved*):   I thought she didn't like me! She's scared of me! How about that! Scared of me.

MAMA: I could make her come over here, Jessie. I could call her up right now and she could bring the birds and come visit. I didn't know you ever thought about her at all. I'll tell her she just has to come and she'll come, all right. She owes me one.

JESSIE: No, that's all right. I just wondered about it. When I'm in the hospital, does she come over here?

MAMA: Her kitchen is just a tiny thing. When she comes over here, she feels like . . . (*Toning it down a little.*) Well, we all like a change of scene, don't we?

JESSIE (*playing along*):   Sure we do. Plus there's no birds diving around.

MAMA: I hate those birds. She says I don't understand them. What's there to understand about birds?

JESSIE: Why Agnes likes them, for one thing. Why they stay with her when they could be outside with the other birds. What their singing means. How they fly. What they think Agnes is.

MAMA: Why do you have to know so much about things, Jessie? There's just not that much *to* things that I could ever see.

JESSIE: That you could ever *tell*, you mean. You didn't have to lie to me about Agnes.

MAMA: I didn't lie. You never asked before!

JESSIE: You lied about setting fire to all those houses and about how many birds she has and how much okra she eats and why she won't come over here. If I have to keep dragging the truth out of you, this is going to take all night.

MAMA: That's fine with me. I'm not a bit sleepy.

JESSIE: Mama . . .

MAMA: All right. Ask me whatever you want. Here.

They come to an awkward stop, as the cocoa is ready and Mama pours it into the cups Jessie has set on the table.

JESSIE *(as Mama takes her first sip)*:   Did you love Daddy?

MAMA: No.

JESSIE *(pleased that Mama understands the rules better now)*:   I didn't think so. Were you really fifteen when you married him?

MAMA: The way he told it? I'm sitting in the mud, he comes along, drags me in the kitchen, "She's been there ever since"?

JESSIE: Yes.

MAMA: No. It was a big fat lie, the whole thing. He just thought it was funnier that way. God, this milk in here.

JESSIE: The cocoa helps.

MAMA *(pleased that they agree on this, at least)*:   Not enough, though, does it? You can still taste it, can't you?

JESSIE: Yeah, it's pretty bad. I thought it was my memory that was bad, but it's not. It's the milk, all right.

MAMA: It's a real waste of chocolate. You don't have to finish it.

JESSIE *(putting her cup down)*:   Thanks, though.

MAMA: I should've known not to make it. I knew you wouldn't like it. You never did like it.

JESSIE: You didn't ever love him, or he did something and you stopped loving him, or what?

MAMA: He felt sorry for me. He wanted a plain country woman and that's what he married, and then he held it against me the rest of my life like I was supposed to change and surprise him somehow. Like I remember this one day he was standing on the porch and I told him to get a shirt on and he went in and got one and then he said, real peaceful, but to the point, "You're right, Thelma. If God had meant for people to go around without any clothes on, they'd have been born that way."

JESSIE *(sees Mama's hurt)*:   He didn't mean anything by that, Mama.

MAMA: He never said a word he didn't have to, Jessie. That was probably all he'd said to me all day, Jessie. So if he said it, there was something to it, but I never did figure that one out. What did that mean?

JESSIE: I don't know. I liked him better than you did, but I didn't know him any better.

MAMA: How could I love him, Jessie. I didn't have a thing he wanted. *(Jessie doesn't answer.)* He got his share, though. You loved him enough for both of us. You followed him around like some . . . Jessie, all the man ever did was farm and sit . . . and try to think of somebody to sell the farm to.

JESSIE: Or make me a boyfriend out of pipe cleaners and sit back and smile like the stick man was about to dance and wasn't I going to get a kick out of that. Or sit up with a sick cow all night and leave me a chain of sleepy stick elephants on my bed in the morning.

MAMA: Or just sit.

JESSIE: I liked him sitting. Big old faded blue man in the chair. Quiet.

MAMA: Agnes gets more talk out of her birds than I got from the two of you. He could've had that GONE FISHING sign around his neck in that chair. I saw him stare off at the water. I saw him look at the weather rolling in. I got where I could practically see the boat myself. But you, you knew what he was thinking about and you're going to tell me.

JESSIE: I don't know, Mama! His life, I guess. His corn. His boots. Us. Things. You know.

MAMA: No, I don't know, Jessie! You had those quiet little conversations after supper every night. What were you whispering about?

JESSIE: We weren't whispering, you were just across the room.

MAMA: What did you talk about?

JESSIE: We talked about why black socks are warmer than blue socks. Is that something to go tell Mother? You were just jealous because I'd rather talk to him than wash the dishes with you.

MAMA: I was jealous because you'd rather talk to him than anything! *(Jessie reaches across the table for the small clock and stars to wind it.)* If I had died instead of him, he wouldn't have taken you in like I did.

JESSIE: I wouldn't have expected him to.

MAMA: Then what would you have done?

JESSIE: Come visit.

MAMA: Oh, I see. He died and left you stuck with me and you're mad about it.

JESSIE *(getting up from the table)*:   Not anymore. He didn't mean to. I didn't have to come here. We've been through this.

MAMA: He felt sorry for you, too, Jessie, don't kid yourself about that. He said you were a runt and he said it from the day you were born and he said you didn't have a chance.

JESSIE *(getting the canister of sugar and starting to refill the sugar bowl)*:   I know he loved me.

MAMA: What if he did? It didn't change anything.

JESSIE: It didn't have to. I miss him.

MAMA: He never really went fishing, you know. Never once. His tackle box was full of chewing tobacco and all he ever did was drive out to the lake and sit in his car. Dawson told me. And Bennie at the bait shop, he told Dawson. They all laughed about it. And he'd come back from fishing and all he'd have to show for it was . . . a whole pipe-cleaner *family*—chickens, pigs, a dog with a bad leg—it was creepy strange. It made me sick to look at them and I hid his pipe cleaners a couple of times but he always had more somewhere.

JESSIE:　I thought it might be better for you after he died. You'd get interested in things. Breathe better. Change somehow.

MAMA:　Into what? The Queen? A clerk in a shoe store? Why should I? Because he said to? Because you said to? (*Jessie shakes her head.*) Well I wasn't here for his entertainment and I'm not here for yours either, Jessie. I don't know what I'm here for, but then I don't think about it. (*Realizing what all this means.*) But I bet you wouldn't be killing yourself if he were still alive. That's a fine thing to figure out, isn't it?

JESSIE (*filling the honey jar now*):　That's not true.

MAMA:　Oh no? Then what were you asking about him for? Why did you want to know if I loved him?

JESSIE:　I didn't think you did, that's all.

MAMA:　Fine then. You were right. Do you feel better now?

JESSIE (*cleaning the honey jar carefully*):　It feels good to be right about it.

MAMA:　It didn't matter whether I loved him. It didn't matter to me and it didn't matter to him. And it didn't mean we didn't get along. It wasn't important. We didn't talk about it. (*Sweeping the pots off the cabinet.*) Take all these pots out to the porch!

JESSIE:　What for?

MAMA:　Just leave me this one pan. (*She jerks the silverware drawer open.*) Get me one knife, one fork, one big spoon, and the can opener, and put them out where I can get them. (*Starts throwing knives and forks in one of the pans.*)

JESSIE:　Don't do that! I just straightened that drawer!

MAMA (*throwing the pan in the sink*):　And throw out all the plates and cups. I'll use paper. Loretta can have what she wants and Dawson can sell the rest.

JESSIE (*calmly*):　What are you doing?

MAMA:　I'm not going to cook. I never liked it, anyway. I like candy. Wrapped in plastic or coming in sacks. And tuna. I like tuna. I'll eat tuna, thank you.

JESSIE (*taking the pan out of the sink*):　What if you want to make apple butter? You can't make apple butter in that little pan. What if you leave carrots on cooking and burn up that pan?

MAMA:　I don't like carrots.

JESSIE:　What if the strawberries are good this year and you want to go picking with Agnes.

MAMA:　I'll tell her to bring a pan. You said you would do whatever I wanted! I don't want a bunch of pans cluttering up my cabinets I can't get down to, anyway. Throw them out. Every last one.

JESSIE (*gathering up the pots*):　I'm putting them all back in. I'm not taking them to the porch. If you want them, they'll be here. You'll bend down and get them, like you got the one for the cocoa. And if somebody else comes over here to cook, they'll have something to cook in, and that's the end of it!

MAMA:　Who's going to come cook here?

JESSIE:　Agnes.

MAMA:　In my pots. Not on your life.

JESSIE:　There's no reason why the two of you couldn't just live here together. Be cheaper for both of you and somebody to talk to. And if the birds bothered you, well, one day when Agnes is out getting her hair done, you could take them all for a walk!

MAMA *(as Jessie straightens the silverware)*:   So that's why you're pestering me about Agnes. You think you can rest easy if you get me a new babysitter? Well, I don't want to live with Agnes. I barely want to talk with Agnes. She's just around. We go back, that's all. I'm not letting Agnes near this place. You don't get off as easy as that, child.

JESSIE: O.K., then. It's just something to think about.

MAMA: I don't like things to think about. I like things to go on.

JESSIE *(closing the silverware drawer)*:   I want to know what Daddy said to you the night he died. You came storming out of his room and said I could wait it out with him if I wanted to, but you were going to watch *Gunsmoke*. What did he say to you?

MAMA: He didn't have *anything* to say to me, Jessie. That's why I left. He didn't say a thing. It was his last chance not to talk to me and he took full advantage of it.

JESSIE *(after a moment)*:   I'm sorry you didn't love him. Sorry for you, I mean. He seemed like a nice man.

MAMA *(as Jessie walks to the refrigerator)*:   Ready for your apple now?

JESSIE: Soon as I'm through here, Mama.

MAMA: You won't like the apple, either. It'll be just like the cocoa. You never liked eating at all, did you? Any of it! What have you been living on all these years, toothpaste?

JESSIE *(as she starts to clean out the refrigerator)*:   Now, you know the milkman comes on Wednesdays and Saturdays, and he leaves the order blank in an egg box, and you give the bills to Dawson once a month.

MAMA: Do they still make that orangeade?

JESSIE: It's not orangeade, it's just orange.

MAMA: I'm going to get some. I thought they stopped making it. You just stopped ordering it.

JESSIE: You should drink milk.

MAMA: Not anymore, I'm not. That hot chocolate was the last. Hooray.

JESSIE *(getting the garbage can from under the sink)*:   I told them to keep delivering a quart a week no matter what you said. I told them you'd run out of Cokes and you'd have to drink it. I told them I knew you wouldn't pour it on the ground . . .

MAMA *(finishing her sentence)*:   And you told them you weren't going to be ordering anymore?

JESSIE: I told them I was taking a little holiday and to look after you.

MAMA: And they didn't think something was funny about that? You who doesn't go to the front steps? You, who only sees the driveway looking down from a stretcher passed out cold?

JESSIE *(enjoying this, but not laughing)*:   They said it was about time, but why didn't I take you with me? And I said I didn't think you'd want to go, and they said, "Yeah, everybody's got their own idea of vacation."

MAMA: I guess you think that's funny.

JESSIE (*pulling jars out of the refrigerator*):   You know there never was any reason to call the ambulance for me. All they ever did for me in the emergency room was let me wake up. I could've done that here. Now, I'll just call them out and you say yes or no. I know you like pickles. Ketchup?

MAMA: Keep it.

JESSIE: We've had this since last Fourth of July.

MAMA: Keep the ketchup. Keep it all.

JESSIE: Are you going to drink ketchup from the bottle or what? How can you want your food and not want your pots to cook it in? This stuff will all spoil in here, Mother.

MAMA: Nothing I ever did was good enough for you and I want to know why.

JESSIE: That's not true.

MAMA: And I want to know why you've lived here this long feeling the way you do.

JESSIE: You have no earthly idea how I feel.

MAMA: Well, how could I? You're real far back there, Jessie.

JESSIE: Back where?

MAMA: What's it like over there, where you are? Do people always say the right thing or get whatever they want, or what?

JESSIE: What are you talking about?

MAMA: Why do you read the newspaper? Why don't you wear that sweater I made for you? Do you remember how I used to look, or am I just any old woman now? When you have a fit, do you see stars or what? How did you fall off the horse, really? Why did Cecil leave you? Where did you put my old glasses?

JESSIE (*stunned by Mama's intensity*):   They're in the bottom drawer of your dresser in an old Milk of Magnesia box. Cecil left me because he made me choose between him and smoking.

MAMA: Jessie, I know he wasn't that dumb.

JESSIE: I never understood why he hated it so much when it's so good. Smoking is the only thing I know that's always just what you think it's going to be. Just like it was the last time, right there when you want it and real quiet.

MAMA: Your fits made him sick and you know it.

JESSIE: Say seizures, not fits. Seizures.

MAMA: It's the same thing. A seizure in the hospital is a fit at home.

JESSIE: They didn't bother him at all. Except he did feel responsible for it. It *was* his idea to go horseback riding that day. It was his idea I could do *anything* if I just made up my mind to. I fell off the horse because I didn't know how to hold on. Cecil left for pretty much the same reason.

MAMA: He had a girl, Jessie. I walked right in on them in the toolshed.

JESSIE (*after a moment*):   O.K. That's fair. (*Lighting another cigarette.*) Was she very pretty?

MAMA: She was Agnes's girl, Carlene. Judge for yourself.

JESSIE (*as she walks to the living room*):   I guess you and Agnes had a good talk about that, huh?

MAMA: I never thought he was good enough for you. They moved here from Tennessee, you know.

JESSIE: What are you talking about? You liked him better than I did. You flirted him out here to build your porch or I'd never even met him at all. You thought maybe he'd help you out around the place, come in and get some coffee and talk to you. God knows what you thought. All that curly hair.

MAMA: He's the best carpenter I ever saw. That little house of yours will still be standing at the end of the world, Jessie.

JESSIE: You didn't need a porch, Mama.

MAMA: All right! I wanted you to have a husband.

JESSIE: And I couldn't get one on my own, of course.

MAMA: How were you going to get a husband never opening your mouth to a living soul?

JESSIE: So I was quiet about it, so what?

MAMA: So I should have let you just sit here? Sit like your daddy? Sit here?

JESSIE: Maybe.

MAMA: Well, I didn't think so.

JESSIE: Well, what did you know?

MAMA: I never said I knew much. How was I supposed to learn anything living out here? I didn't know enough to do half the things I did in my life. Things happen. You do what you can about them and you see what happens next. I married you off to the wrong man, I admit that. So I took you in when he left. I'm sorry

JESSIE: He wasn't the wrong man.

MAMA: He didn't love you, Jessie, or he wouldn't have left.

JESSIE: He wasn't the wrong man, Mama. I loved Cecil so much. And I tried to get more exercise and I tried to stay awake. I tried to learn to ride a horse. And I tried to stay outside with him, but he always knew I was trying, so it didn't work.

MAMA: He was a selfish man. He told me once he hated to see people move into his houses after he built them. He knew they'd mess them up.

JESSIE: I loved that bridge he built over the creek in back of the house. It didn't have to be anything special, a couple of boards would have been just fine, but he used that yellow pine and rubbed it so smooth . . .

MAMA: He had responsibilities here. He had a wife and son here and he failed you.

JESSIE: Or that baby bed he built for Ricky. I told him he didn't have to spend so much time on it, but he said it had to last, and the thing ended up weighing two hundred pounds and I couldn't move it. I said, "How long does a baby bed have to last, anyway?" But maybe he thought if it was strong enough, it might keep Ricky a baby.

MAMA: Ricky is too much like Cecil.

JESSIE: He is not. Ricky is as much like me as it's possible for any human to be. We even wear the same size pants. These are his, I think.

MAMA: That's just the same size. That's not you're the same person.

JESSIE: I see it on his face. I hear it when he talks. We look out at the world and we see the same thing: Not Fair. And the only difference between us is Ricky's out there trying to get even. And he knows not to trust anybody and he got it straight from me. And he knows not to try to get work, and guess where he got that. He walks around like there's loose boards in the floor, and you know who laid that floor, I did.

MAMA: Ricky isn't through yet. You don't know how he'll turn out!

JESSIE *(going back to the kitchen)*: Yes I do and so did Cecil. Ricky is the two of us together for all time in too small a space. And we're tearing each other apart, like always, inside that boy, and if you don't see it, then you're just blind.

MAMA: Give him time, Jess.

JESSIE: Oh, he'll have plenty of that. Five years for forgery, ten years for armed assault . . .

MAMA *(furious)*: Stop that! *(Then pleading.)* Jessie, Cecil might be ready to try it again, honey, that happens sometimes. Go downtown. Find him. Talk to him. He didn't know what he had in you. Maybe he sees things different now, but you're not going to know that till you go see him. Or call him up! Right now! He might be home.

JESSIE: And say what? Nothing's changed, Cecil, I'd just like to look at you, if you don't mind? No. He loved me, Mama. He just didn't know how things fall down around me like they do. I think he did the right thing. He gave himself another chance, that's all. But I did beg him to take me with him. I did tell him I would leave Ricky and you and everything I loved out here if only he would take me with him, but he couldn't and I understood that. *(Pause.)* I wrote that note I showed you. I wrote it. Not Cecil. I said "I'm sorry, Jessie, I can't fix it all for you." I said I'd always love me, not Cecil. But that's how he felt.

MAMA: Then he should've taken you with him!

JESSIE *(picking up the garbage bag she has filled)*: Mama, you don't pack your garbage when you move.

MAMA: You will not call yourself garbage, Jessie.

JESSIE *(taking the bag to the big garbage can near the back door)*: Just a way of saying it, Mama. Thinking about my list, that's all. *(Opening the can, putting the garbage in, then securing the lid.)* Well, a little more than that. I was trying to say it's all right that Cecil left. It was . . . a relief in a way. I never was what he wanted to see, so it was better when he wasn't looking at me all the time.

MAMA: I'll make your apple now.

JESSIE: No thanks. You get the manicure stuff and I'll be right there.

Jessie ties up the big garbage bag in the can and replaces the small garbage bag under the sink, all the time trying desperately to regain her calm. Mama watches, from a distance, her hand reaching unconsciously for the phone. Then she has a better idea. Or rather she thinks of the only other thing left and is willing to try it. Maybe she is even convinced it will work.

MAMA: Jessie, I think your daddy had little . . .

JESSIE *(interrupting her)*: Garbage night is Tuesday. Put it out as late as you can. The Davis's dogs get in it if you don't. *(Replacing the garbage bag in the can under the sink.)* And keep ordering the heavy black bags. It doesn't pay to buy the cheap ones. And I've got all the ties here with the hammers and all. Take them out of the box as soon as you open a new one and put them in this drawer. They'll get lost if you don't, and rubber bands or something else won't work.

MAMA: I think your daddy had fits, too. I think he sat in his chair and had little fits. I read this a long time ago in a magazine, how little fits go, just little blackouts where maybe their eyes don't even close and people just call them "thinking spells."

JESSIE (*getting the slipcover out of the laundry basket*):   I don't think you want this manicure we've been looking forward to. I washed this cover for the sofa, but it'll take both of us to get it back on.

MAMA: I watched his eyes. I know that's what it was. The magazine said some people don't even know they've had one.

JESSIE: Daddy would've known if he'd had fits, Mama.

MAMA: The lady in this story had kept track of hers and she'd had eighty thousand of them in the last eleven years.

JESSIE: Next time you wash this cover, it'll dry better if you put it on wet.

MAMA: Jessie, listen to what I'm telling you. This lady had anywhere between five and five hundred fits a day and they lasted maybe fifteen seconds apiece, so that out of her life, she'd only lost about two weeks altogether, and she had a full-time secretary job and an IQ of 120.

JESSIE (*amused by Mama's approach*):   You want to talk about fits, is that it?

MAMA: Yes. I do. I want to say . . .

JESSIE (*interrupting*):   Most of the time I wouldn't even know I'd had one, except I wake up with different clothes on, feeling like I've been run over. Sometimes I feel my head start to turn around or hear myself scream. And sometimes there *is* this dizzy stupid feeling a little before it, but if the TV's on, well, it's easy to miss.

As Jessie and Mama replace the slipcover on the sofa and the afghan on the chair, the physical struggle somehow mirrors the emotional one in the conversation.

MAMA: I can tell when you're about to have one. Your eyes get this big! But, Jessie, you haven't . . .

JESSIE (*taking charge of this*):   What do they look like? The seizures.

MAMA (*reluctant*):   Different each time, Jess.

JESSIE: O.K. Pick one, then. A good one. I think I want to know now.

MAMA: There's not much to tell. You just . . . crumple, in a heap, like a puppet and somebody cut the strings all at once, or like the firing squad in some Mexican movie, you just slide down the wall, you know. You don't know what happens? How can you not know what happens?

JESSIE: I'm busy.

MAMA: That's not funny.

JESSIE: I'm not laughing. My head turns around and I fall down and then what?

MAMA: Well, your chest squeezes in and out, and you sound like you're gagging, sucking air in and out like you can't breathe.

JESSIE: Do it for me. Make the sound for me.

MAMA: I will not. It's awful-sounding.

JESSIE: Yeah. It felt like it might be. What's next?

MAMA: Your mouth bites down and I have to get your tongue out of the way fast, so you don't bite yourself.

JESSIE: Or you. I bite you, too, don't I?

MAMA: You got me once real good. I had to get a tetanus! But I know what to watch for now. And then you turn blue and the jerks start up. Like I'm standing there poking you with a cattle prod or you're sticking your finger in a light socket as fast as you can . . .

JESSIE: Foaming like a mad dog the whole time.

MAMA: It's bubbling, Jess, not foam like the washer overflowed, for God's sake; it's bubbling like a baby spitting up. I go get a wet washcloth, that's all. And then the jerks slow down and you wet yourself and it's over. Two minutes tops.

JESSIE: How do I get to the bed?

MAMA: How do you think?

JESSIE: I'm too heavy for you now. How do you do it?

MAMA: I call Dawson. But I get you cleaned up before he gets here and I make him leave before you wake up.

JESSIE: You could just leave me on the floor.

MAMA: I want you to wake up someplace nice, O.K.? *(Then making a real effort.)* But, Jessie, and this is the reason I even brought this up! You haven't had a seizure for a solid year. A whole year, do you realize that?

JESSIE: Yeah, the phenobarb's about right now, I guess.

MAMA: You bet it is. You might never have another one, ever! You might be through with it for all time!

JESSIE: Could be.

MAMA: You are. I know you are!

JESSIE: I sure am feeling good. I really am. The double vision's gone and my gums aren't swelling. No rashes or anything. I'm feeling as good as I ever felt in my life. I'm even feeling like worrying or getting mad and I'm not afraid it will start a fit if I do, I just go ahead.

MAMA: Of course you do! You can even scream at me, if you want to. I can take it. You don't have to act like you're just visiting here, Jessie. This is your house, too.

JESSIE: The best part is, my memory's back.

MAMA: Your memory's always been good. When couldn't you remember things? You're always reminding me what . . .

JESSIE: Because I've made lists for everything. But now I remember what things mean on my lists. I see "dish towels," and I used to wonder whether I was supposed to wash them, buy them, or look for them because I wouldn't remember where I put them after I washed them, but now I know it means wrap them up, they're a present for Loretta's birthday.

MAMA *(finished with the sofa now):*   You used to go looking for your lists, too, I've noticed that. You always know where they are now! *(Then suddenly worried.)* Loretta's birthday isn't coming up, is it?

JESSIE: I made a list of all the birthdays for you. I even put yours on it. *(A small smile.)* So you can call Loretta and remind her.

MAMA: Let's take Loretta to Howard Johnson's and have those fried clams. I *know* you love that clam roll.

JESSIE *(slight pause)*:   I won't be here, Mama.

MAMA: What have we just been talking about? You'll be here. You're well, Jessie. You're starting all over. You said it yourself. You're remembering things and . . .

JESSIE: I won't be here. If I'd ever had a year like this, to think straight and all, before now, I'd be gone already.

MAMA *(not pleading, commanding)*:   No, Jessie.

JESSIE *(folding the rest of the laundry)*:   Yes, Mama. Once I started remembering, I could see what it all added up to.

MAMA: The fits are over!

JESSIE: It's not the fits, Mama.

MAMA: Then it's me for giving them to you, but I didn't do it!

JESSIE: It's not the fits! You said it yourself, the medicine takes care of the fits.

MAMA *(interrupting)*:   Your daddy gave you those fits, Jessie. He passed it down to you like your green eyes and your straight hair. It's not my fault!

JESSIE: So what if he had little fits? It's not inherited. I fell off the horse. It was an accident.

MAMA: The horse wasn't the first time, Jessie. You had a fit when you were five years old.

JESSIE: I did not.

MAMA: You did! You were eating a popsicle and down you went. He gave it to you. It's *his* fault, not mine.

JESSIE: Well, you took your time telling me.

MAMA: How do you tell that to a five-year-old?

JESSIE: What did the doctor say?

MAMA: He said kids have them all the time. He said there wasn't anything to do but wait for another one.

JESSIE: But I didn't have another one.

Now there is a real silence.

JESSIE: You mean to tell me I had fits all the time as a kid and you just told me I fell down or something and it wasn't till I had the fit when Cecil was looking that anybody bothered to find out what was the matter with me?

MAMA: It wasn't *all the time*, Jessie. And they changed when you started to school. More like your daddy's. Oh, that was some swell time, sitting here with the two of you turning off and on like light bulbs some nights.

JESSIE: How many fits did I have?

MAMA: You never hurt yourself. I never let you out of my sight. I caught you every time.

JESSIE: But you didn't tell anybody.

MAMA: It was none of their business.

JESSIE: You were ashamed.

MAMA: I didn't want anybody to know. Least of all you.

JESSIE: Least of all me. Oh, right. That was mine to know, Mama, not yours. Did Daddy know?

MAMA: He thought you were . . . you fell down a lot. That's what he thought. You were careless. Or maybe he thought I beat you. I don't know what he thought. He didn't think about it.

JESSIE: Because you didn't tell him!

MAMA: If I told him about you, I'd have to tell him about him!

JESSIE: I don't like this. I don't like this one bit.

MAMA: I didn't think you'd like it. That's why I didn't tell you.

JESSIE: If I'd known I was an epileptic, Mama, I wouldn't have ridden any horses.

MAMA: Make you feel like a freak, is that what I should have done?

JESSIE: Just get the manicure tray and sit down!

MAMA *(throwing it to the floor)*:   I don't want a manicure!

JESSIE: Doesn't look like you do, no.

MAMA: Maybe I did drop you, you don't know.

JESSIE: If you say you didn't, you didn't.

MAMA *(beginning to break down)*:   Maybe I fed you the wrong thing. Maybe you had a fever sometime and I didn't know it soon enough. Maybe it's a punishment.

JESSIE: For what?

MAMA: I don't know. Because of how I felt about your father. Because I didn't want any more children. Because I smoked too much or didn't eat right when I was carrying you. It has to be something I did.

JESSIE: It does not. It's just a sickness, not a curse. Epilepsy doesn't mean anything. It just is.

MAMA: I'm not talking about the fits here, Jessie! I'm talking about this killing yourself. It has to be me that's the matter here. You wouldn't be doing this if it wasn't. I didn't tell you things or I married you off to the wrong man or I took you in and let your life get away from you or all of it put together. I don't know what I did, but I did it, I know. This is all my fault, Jessie, but I don't know what to do about it now!

JESSIE *(exasperated at having to say this again)*:   It doesn't have anything to do with you!

MAMA: Everything you do has to do with me, Jessie. You can't do *anything*, wash your face or cut your finger, without doing it to me. That's right! You might as well kill me as you, Jessie, it's the same thing. This has to do with me, Jessie.

JESSIE: Then what if it does! What if it has everything to do with you! What if you are all I have and you're not enough? What if I could take all the rest of it if only I didn't have you here? What if the only way I can get away from you for good is to kill myself? What if it is? I can *still* do it!

MAMA *(in desperate tears)*:   Don't leave me, Jessie! *(Jessie stands for a moment, then turns for the bedroom.)* No! *(She grabs Jessie's arm.)*

JESSIE *(carefully taking her arm away)*:   I have a box of things I want people to have. I'm just going to go get it for you. You . . . just rest a minute.

Jessie is gone. Mama heads for the telephone, but she can't even pick up the receiver this time and, instead, stoops to clean up the bottles that have spilled out of the manicure tray.

Jessie returns, carrying a box that groceries were delivered in. It probably says Hershey Kisses or Starkist Tuna. Mama is still down on the floor cleaning up, hoping that maybe if she just makes it look nice enough, Jessie will stay.

MAMA: Jessie, how can I live here without you? I need you! You're supposed to tell me to stand up straight and say how nice I look in my pink dress, and drink my milk. You're supposed to go around and lock up so I know we're safe for the night, and when I wake up, you're supposed to be out there making the coffee and watching me get older every day, and you're supposed to help me die when the time comes. I can't do that by myself, Jessie. I'm not like you, Jessie. I hate the quiet and I don't want to die and I don't want you to go, Jessie. How can I . . . *(Has to stop a moment.)* How can I get up every day knowing you had to kill yourself to make it stop hurting and I was here all the time and I never even saw it. And then you gave me this chance to make it better, convince you to stay alive, and I couldn't do it. How can I live with myself after this, Jessie?

JESSIE: I only told you so I could explain it, so you wouldn't blame yourself, so you wouldn't feel bad. There wasn't anything you could say to change my mind. I didn't want you to save me. I just wanted you to know.

MAMA: Stay with me just a little longer. Just a few more years. I don't have that many more to go, Jessie. And as soon as I'm dead, you can do whatever you want. Maybe with me gone, you'll have all the quiet you want, right here in the house. And maybe one day you'll put in some begonias up the walk and get just the right rain for them all summer. And Ricky will be married by then and he'll bring your grandbabies over and you can sneak them a piece of candy when their daddy's not looking and then be real glad when they've gone home and left you to your quiet again.

JESSIE: Don't you see, Mama, everything I do winds up like this. How could I think you would understand? How could I think you would want a manicure? We could hold hands for an hour and then I could go shoot myself? I'm sorry about tonight, Mama, but it's exactly why I'm doing it.

MAMA: If you've got the guts to kill yourself, Jessie, you've got the guts to stay alive.

JESSIE: I know that. So it's really just a matter of where I'd rather be.

MAMA: Look, maybe I can't think of what you should do, but that doesn't mean there isn't something that would help. *You* find it. *You* think of it. You can keep trying. You can get brave and try some more. You don't have to give up!

JESSIE: I'm *not* giving up! This *is* the other thing I'm trying. And I'm sure there are some other things that might work, but *might* work isn't good enough anymore. I need something that *will* work. *This* will work. That's why I picked it.

MAMA: But something might happen. Something that could change everything. Who knows what it might be, but it might be worth waiting for! *(Jessie doesn't respond.)* Try it for two more weeks. We could have more talks like tonight.

JESSIE: No, Mama.

MAMA: I'll pay more attention to you. Tell the truth when you ask me. Let you have your say.

JESSIE: No, Mama! We wouldn't have more talks like tonight, because it's this next part that's made this last part so good, Mama. No, Mama. *This* is how I have my say. This is how I say what I thought about it *all* and I say no. To Dawson and Loretta and the Red Chinese and epilepsy and Ricky and Cecil and you. And me. And hope. I say no! *(Then going to Mama on the sofa.)* Just let me go easy, Mama.

MAMA: How can I let you go?

JESSIE: You can because you have to. It's what you've always done.

MAMA: You are my child!

JESSIE: I am what became of your child. *(Mama cannot answer.)* I found an old baby picture of me. And it was somebody else, not me. It was somebody pink and fat who never heard of sick or lonely, somebody who cried and got fed, and reached up and got held and kicked but didn't hurt anybody, and slept whenever she wanted to, just by closing her eyes. Somebody who mainly just laid there and laughed at the colors waving around over her head and chewed on a polka-dot whale and woke up knowing some new trick nearly every day, and rolled over and drooled on the sheet and felt your hand pulling my quilt back up over me. That's who I started out and this is who is left. *(There is no self-pity here.)* That's what this is about. It's somebody I lost, all right, it's my own self. Who I never was. Or who I tried to be and never got there. Somebody I waited for who never came. And never will. So, see, it doesn't much matter what else happens in the world or in this house, even. I'm what was worth waiting for and I didn't make it. Me . . . who might have made a difference to me . . . I'm not going to show up, so there's no reason to stay, except to keep you company, and that's . . . not reason enough because I'm not . . . very good company. *(Pause.)* Am I.

MAMA *(knowing she must tell the truth)*: No. And neither am I.

JESSIE: I had this strange little thought, well, maybe it's not so strange. Anyway, after Christmas, after I decided to do this, I would wonder, sometimes, what might keep me here, what might be worth staying for, and you know what it was? It was maybe if there was something I really liked, like maybe if I really liked rice pudding or cornflakes for breakfast or something, that might be enough.

MAMA: Rice pudding is good.

JESSIE: Not to me.

MAMA: And you're not afraid?

JESSIE: Afraid of what?

MAMA: I'm afraid of it, for me, I mean. When my time comes. I know it's coming, but . . .

JESSIE: You don't know when. Like in a scary movie.

MAMA: Yeah, sneaking up on me like some killer on the loose, hiding out in the back yard just waiting for me to have my hands full someday and how am I supposed to protect myself anyhow when I don't know what he looks like and I don't know how he sounds coming up behind me like that or if it will hurt or take very long or what I don't get done before it happens.

JESSIE: You've got plenty of time left.

MAMA: I forget what for, right now.

JESSIE: For whatever happens, I don't know. For the rest of your life. For Agnes burning down one more house or Dawson losing his hair or . . .

MAMA *(quickly)*:   Jessie, I can't just sit here and say O.K., kill yourself if you want to.

JESSIE: Sure you can. You just did. Say it again.

MAMA *(really startled)*:   Jessie! *(Quiet horror.)* How dare you! *(Furious.)* How dare you! You think you can just leave whenever you want, like you're watching television here? No, you can't, Jessie. You make me feel like a fool for being alive, child, and you are so wrong! I like it here, and I will stay here until they make me go, until they drag me screaming and I mean screeching into my grave, and you're real smart to get away before then because, I mean, honey, you've never heard noise like that in your life. *(Jessie turns away.)* Who am I talking to? You're gone already, aren't you? I'm looking right through you! I can't stop you because you're already gone! I guess you think they'll all have to talk about you now! I guess you think this will really confuse them. Oh yes, ever since Christmas you've been laughing to yourself and thinking, "Boy, are they all in for a surprise." Well, nobody's going to be a bit surprised, sweetheart. This is just like you. Do it the hard way, that's my girl, all right. *(Jessie gets up and goes into the kitchen, but Mama follows her.)* You know who they're going to feel sorry for? Me! How about that! Not you, me! They're going to be *ashamed* of you. Yes. *Ashamed!* If somebody asks Dawson about it, he'll change the subject as fast as he can. He'll talk about how much he has to pay to park his car these days.

JESSIE: Leave me alone.

MAMA: It's the truth!

JESSIE: I should've just left you a note!

MAMA *(screaming)*:   Yes! *(Then suddenly understanding what she has said, nearly paralyzed by the thought of it, she turns slowly to face Jessie, nearly whispering.)* No. No. I . . . might not have thought of all the things you've said.

JESSIE: It's O.K., Mama.

Mama is nearly unconscious from the emotional devastation of these last few moments. She sits down at the kitchen table, hurt and angry and desperately afraid. But she looks almost numb. She is so far beyond what is known as pain that she is virtually unreachable and Jessie knows this, and talks quietly, watching for signs of recovery.

JESSIE *(washes her hands in the sink)*:   I remember you liked that preacher who did Daddy's, so if you want to ask him to do the service, that's O.K. with me.

MAMA *(not an answer, just a word)*:   What.

JESSIE *(putting on hand lotion as she talks)*:   And pick some songs you like or let Agnes pick, she'll know exactly which ones. Oh, and I had your dress cleaned that you wore to Daddy's. You looked real good in that.

MAMA: I don't remember, hon.

JESSIE: And it won't be so bad once your friends start coming to the funeral home. You'll probably see people you haven't seen for years, but I thought about what you should say to get you over that nervous part when they first come in.

MAMA *(simply repeating)*:   Come in.

JESSIE: Take them up to see their flowers, they'd like that. And when they say, "I'm so sorry, Thelma," you just say, "I appreciate your coming, Connie." And then ask how their garden was this summer or what they're doing for Thanksgiving or how their children . . .

MAMA: I don't think I should ask about their children. I'll talk about what they have on, that's always good. And I'll have some crochet work with me.

JESSIE: And Agnes will be there, so you might not have to talk at all.

MAMA: Maybe if Connie Richards does come, I can get her to tell me where she gets that Irish yarn, she calls it. I know it doesn't come from Ireland. I think it just comes with a green wrapper.

JESSIE: And be sure to invite enough people home afterward so you get enough food to feed them all and have some left for you. But don't let anybody take anything home, especially Loretta.

MAMA: Loretta will get all the food set up, honey. It's only fair to let her have some macaroni or something.

JESSIE: No, Mama. You have to be more selfish from now on. *(Sitting at the table with Mama.)* Now, somebody's bound to ask you why I did it and you just say you don't know. That you loved me and you know I loved you and we just sat around tonight like every other night of our lives, and then I came over and kissed you and said, " 'night, Mother," and you heard me close my bedroom door and the next thing you heard was the shot. And whatever reasons I had, well, you guess I just took them with me.

MAMA *(quietly)*:   It was something personal.

JESSIE: Good. That's good, Mama.

MAMA: That's what I'll say, then.

JESSIE: Personal. Yeah.

MAMA: Is that what I tell Dawson and Loretta, too? We sat around, you kissed me, " 'night, Mother"? They'll want to know more, Jessie. They won't believe it.

JESSIE: Well, then, tell them what we did. I filled up the candy jars. I cleaned out the refrigerator. We made some hot chocolate and put the cover back on the sofa. You had no idea. All right? I really think it's better that way. If they know we talked about it, they really won't understand how you let me go.

MAMA: I guess not.

JESSIE: It's private. Tonight is private, yours and mine, and I don't want anybody else to have any of it.

MAMA: O.K., then.

JESSIE *(standing behind Mama now, holding her shoulders)*:   Now, when you hear the shot, I don't want you to come in. First of all, you won't be able to get in by yourself, but I don't want you trying. Call Dawson, then call the police, and then call Agnes. And then you'll need something to do till somebody gets here, so wash the hot-chocolate pan. You wash that pan till you hear the doorbell ring and I don't care if it's an hour, you keep washing that pan.

MAMA: I'll make my calls and then I'll just sit. I won't need something to do. What will the police say?

JESSIE: They'll do that gunpowder test, I guess, and ask you what happened, and by that time, the ambulance will be here and they'll come in and get me and you know how that goes. You stay out here with Dawson and Loretta. You keep Dawson out here. I want the police in the room first, not Dawson, O.K.?

MAMA: What if Dawson and Loretta want me to go home with them?

JESSIE (*returning to the living room*): That's up to you.

MAMA: I think I'll stay here. All they've got is Sanka.

JESSIE: Maybe Agnes could come stay with you for a few days.

MAMA (*standing up, looking into the living room*): I'd rather be by myself, I think. (*Walking toward the box Jessie brought in earlier.*) You want me to give people those things?

JESSIE (*they sit down on the sofa, Jessie holding the box on her lap*): I want Loretta to have my little calculator. Dawson bought it for himself, you know, but then he saw one he liked better and he couldn't bring both of them home with Loretta counting every penny the way she does, so he gave the first one to me. Be funny for her to have it now, don't you think? And all my house slippers are in a sack for her in my closet. Tell her I know they'll fit and I've never worn any of them, and make sure Dawson hears you tell her that. I'm glad he loves Loretta so much, but I wish he knew not everybody has her size feet.

MAMA (*taking the calculator*): O.K.

JESSIE (*reaching into the box again*): This letter is for Dawson, but it's mostly about you, so read it if you want. There's a list of presents for you for at least twenty more Christmases and birthdays, so if you want anything special you better add it to this list before you give it to him. Or if you want to be surprised, just don't read that page. This Christmas, you're getting mostly stuff for the house, like a new rug in your bathroom and needlework, but next Christmas, you're really going to cost him next Christmas. I think you'll like it a lot and you'd never think of it.

MAMA: And you think he'll go for it?

JESSIE: I think he'll feel like a real jerk if he doesn't. Me telling him to, like this and all. Now, this number's where you call Cecil. I called it last week and he answered, so I know he still lives there.

MAMA: What do you want me to tell him?

JESSIE: Tell him we talked about him and I only had good things to say about him, but mainly tell him to find Ricky and tell him what I did, and tell Ricky you have something for him, out here, from me, and to come get it. (*Pulls a sack out of the box.*)

MAMA (*the sack feels empty*): What is it?

JESSIE (*taking it off*): My watch. (*Putting it in the sack and taking a ribbon out of the sack to tie around the top of it.*)

MAMA: He'll sell it!

JESSIE: That's the idea. I appreciate him not stealing it already. I'd like to buy him a good meal.

MAMA: He'll buy dope with it!

JESSIE: Well, then, I hope he gets some good dope with it, Mama. And the rest of this is for you. (*Handing Mama the box now. Mama picks up the things and looks at them.*)

MAMA *(surprised and pleased)*:   When did you do all this? During my naps, I guess.

JESSIE: I guess. I tried to be quiet about it. *(As Mama is puzzled by the presents.)* Those are just little presents. For whenever you need one. They're not bought presents, just things I thought you might like to look at, pictures or things you think you've lost. Things you didn't know you had, even. You'll see.

MAMA: I'm not sure I want them. They'll make me think of you.

JESSIE: No they won't. They're just things, like a free tube of toothpaste I found hanging on the door one day.

MAMA: Oh. All right, then.

JESSIE: Well, maybe there's one present in there somewhere. It's Granny's ring she gave me and I thought you might like to have it, but I didn't think you'd wear it if I gave it to you right now.

MAMA *(taking the box to a table nearby)*:   No. Probably not. *(Turning back to face her.)* I'm ready for my manicure, I guess. Want me to wash my hands again?

JESSIE *(standing up)*:   It's time for me to go, Mama.

MAMA *(starting for her)*:   No, Jessie, you've got all night!

JESSIE *(as Mama grabs her)*:   No, Mama.

MAMA: It's not even ten o'clock.

JESSIE *(very calm)*:   Let me go, Mama.

MAMA: I can't. You can't go. You can't do this. You didn't say it would be so soon, Jessie. I'm scared. I love you.

JESSIE *(takes her hands away)*:   Let go of me, Mama. I've said everything I had to say.

MAMA *(standing still a minute)*:   You said you wanted to do my nails.

JESSIE *(taking a small step backward)*:   I can't. It's too late.

MAMA: It's not too late!

JESSIE: I don't want you to wake Dawson and Loretta when you call. I want them to still be up and dressed so they can get right over.

MAMA *(as Jessie backs up, Mama moves in on her, but carefully)*:   They wake up fast, Jessie, if they have to. They don't matter here, Jessie. You do. I do. We're not through yet. We've got a lot of things to take care of here. I don't know where my prescriptions are and you didn't tell me what to tell Dr. Davis when he calls or how much you want me to tell Ricky or who I call to rake the leaves or . . .

JESSIE: Don't try and stop me, Mama, you can't do it.

MAMA *(grabbing her again, this time hard)*:   I can too! I'll stand in front of this hall and you can't get past me. *(They struggle.)* You'll have to knock me down to get away from me, Jessie. I'm not about to let you . . .

Mama struggles with Jessie at the door and in the struggle Jessie gets away from her and—

JESSIE *(almost a whisper)*:   'Night, Mother. *(She vanishes into her bedroom and we hear the door lock just as Mama gets to it.)*

MAMA *(screams)*:   Jessie! *(Pounding on the door.)* Jessie, you let me in there. Don't you do this, Jessie. I'm not going to stop screaming until you open this door, Jessie. Jessie! Jessie! What if I don't do any of the things you told me to do! I'll tell Cecil what a miserable man he was to make you feel the way he did and I'll give Ricky's watch to Dawson if I feel like it and the only way you can make sure I do what you want is you come out here and make me, Jessie! *(Pounding again.)* Jessie! Stop this! I didn't know! I was here with you all the time. How could I know you were so alone?

And Mama stops for a moment, breathless and frantic, putting her ear to the door, and when she doesn't hear anything, she stands up straight again and screams once more.

Jessie! Please!

And we hear the shot, and it sounds like an answer, it sounds like No.

   Mama collapses against the door, tears streaming down her face, but not screaming anymore. In shock now.

Jessie, Jessie, child . . . Forgive me. *(Pause.)* I thought you were mine.

And she leaves the door and makes her way through the living room, around the furniture, as though she didn't know where it was, not knowing what to do. Finally, she goes to the stove in the kitchen and picks up the hot-chocolate pan and carries it with her to the telephone and holds on to it while she dials the number. She looks down at the pan, holding it tight like her life depended on it. She hears Loretta answer.

MAMA: Loretta, let me talk to Dawson, honey.   [1983]

THINKING ABOUT THE TEXT

1. Here is an issue of cause and effect: Why does Jessie want to kill herself? Does she make her reasons clear, or is the audience left to guess them at the end of the play? How important a role does her epilepsy seem to play in her thinking?

2. What are Thelma's main arguments against Jessie's committing suicide? What are Jessie's main arguments in return? Do you side with one character more than the other? Why, or why not?

3. What are the advantages and disadvantages for the playwright in restricting the time span covered by the play to the length of its performance? How surprised were you by the play's ending? In the course of your reading, what elements in the text did you especially consider as you thought about how it might end?

4. Jessie and Thelma refer to several absent characters. Do any of them seem more important than others? If so, which and why? Evaluate Norman's decision to keep all of these characters offstage. Should she have brought any of them on?

5. What would you say to people worried that Norman's play will encourage suicide?

LISA J. MCDONNELL

From *"Diverse Similitude: Beth Henley and Marsha Norman"*

Lisa J. McDonnell (b. 1949) teaches in the English department at Denison University in Granville, Ohio. The following excerpt is from an article that appeared in a 1985 issue of the journal Southern Quarterly. *As the title suggests, McDonnell compares Norman with another contemporary Southern woman playwright, Beth Henley.*

Disillusioned by life on a number of fronts, Jessie, an overweight, epileptic young woman who has been abandoned by her husband, disappointed by her delinquent son, and frustrated by her inability to hold a job, decides to say "no" to hope and to take charge of her own life, thereby reclaiming her dignity as a human being. Although many argue that her death is merely an act of desperation, Jessie's decision to take her own life displays a new confidence in herself; she knows that it is the right decision for her. She goes beyond family expectations to find her own meaning only in the "rest" afforded by death. Her mother's obviously loving feelings are not sufficient reason for Jessie to prolong her miserable life. Unlike Henley's characters, who find hope and some strength for survival in their families, Jessie finds neither, but does manage to find *herself* in the act of dying.

Like Henley, Norman delineates characters and relationships sensitively. The relationship between Jessie and her mother demonstrates Norman's ability, for in *'night, Mother* Norman accomplishes the difficult task of making the audience identify with adversarial characters — Mama, who pleads, "Don't leave me, Jessie," and Jessie, who knows that her peace and dignity as an individual can be achieved only through death. By the end of the play the audience understands that Mama and Jessie's relationship is loving but empty, like the stage set that looks warm and homey until harsh lighting illuminates its sterility and emptiness. Like Arlie,° Jessie removes herself from her family in order to save herself; this movement contrasts with that of Henley's characters, who at their moment of testing draw on the family as a source of strength.   [1985]

Arlie: A character in Norman's 1977 play *Getting Out.*

SALLY BROWDER

From " *'I Thought You Were Mine'*: Marsha Norman's *'night, Mother*"

Sally Browder is a clinical psychologist. The following excerpt is from an essay that appeared in the 1989 collection Mother Puzzle: Daughters and Mothers in Contemporary American Literature, *edited by Mickey Pearlman.*

At some point, most mothers and daughters recognize that they are pitted in an ageless struggle by their mutual efforts to maintain their relationship in its earliest form or to alter it. Like a complicated primitive dance, they perpetually pull together and move apart. The daughter resists her mother's attempts to control her life, yet at the same time resents the mother for what the mother has not been able to provide for her. The mother, on the other hand, simultaneously pushes her daughter away, in an effort to teach her not to expect nurturance but to give it and yet strives to protect and cling to her daughter, to claim her as an extension or possession. From this struggle emerges the opportunity for daughters to make their own choices, develop a sense of themselves, and participate in relationships as more equal partners.

For daughters, and thus for all women, the struggle is played out continuously in relationships. It is the choice between security and risk, loyalty and self-assertion, submission and power. They must choose to replay intricate patterns of dependency and need or courageously engage in equitable partnerships. Given the unique dynamics of this first important relationship, women are in greatest peril of failing to develop an adequate sense of meaning and autonomy when they confront the temptation to accept a sense of meaning assigned to them by others, assigned to them initially by their mothers.

This is the tragic realization to which Jessie comes too late. Jessie's isolation and exclusive reliance upon her mother as sole companion are insufficient to provide her with a sense of self, to provide her with a sense of power, a sense of meaning in life: "What if you are all I have and you're not enough?" "It's somebody I lost, all right, it's my own self. Who I never was, or who I tried to be and never got there. Somebody I waited for who never came. And never will."

The healthy course, to participate in relationships as an equal partner rather than as a dependent or recipient, requires giving up the security of an unequal relationship. It requires being strong and hopeful about one's own future while tolerating the pain of knowing the limitations and diminishment of the one with whom one may be most identified. It also implies staying around to confront the consequences of honesty, something of which Jessie's choice of suicide relieved her.

Honesty is a casualty of unequal relationships. The lack of honesty in mother-daughter relationships is not always intentional or malicious and usually arises out of a desire to protect. Mothers alter the truth in an effort to shield their daughters from what well may be a harsh reality. In doing so, however, they fail to equip their daughters to deal with reality, whatever it may be. I am reminded of a friend's story of how, as a young girl, she could not tolerate spending even one night away from home. When she called home, her mother always insisted that everything was fine in the same tone of voice she always used, even in the presence of disaster. The mother's reassurances became red flags that pitched the young girl into a frenzy of anxiety and fear.

If Thelma is at fault, it is only in believing she could provide everything for this daughter, that she alone could be enough. So pervasive is this expectation, that even Jessie shares it, only realizing the bitter consequences of it on the evening of her death. She says of the decision to return to live with her mother, "If it was a mistake, we made it together."

In the end, whatever this particular mother did would have been wrong, just as whatever any mother does is wrong. As long as she is made to feel ultimately responsible for her daughter's well-being, a mother is thrust into unyielding, conflicting expectations. She encourages her daughter's dependency and identification with her while struggling with her own ambivalence about rearing a child who may serve to remind her of her own limitations. She must enable the daughter to develop a sense of self-sufficiency while being charged by society to engender qualities that may not contribute to a sense of power or well-being. The qualities that we think of as characterizing a good mother are not necessarily qualities that enable young daughters to attain autonomy. Mothers either love their children too much or not enough. And their daughters either love or hate them whatever they do.   [1989]

JENNY S. SPENCER
From "*Norman's* 'night, Mother: Psycho-drama of Female Identity"

Jenny S. Spencer (b. 1951) teaches in the English department of the University of Massachusetts at Amherst. The following excerpt is from an article that appeared in a 1987 issue of the journal Modern Drama.

To say that male viewers can identify with neither the characters of this play nor its central experience would be inaccurate; many obviously have. But I suggest that the play is potentially more terrifying for the female viewer because she *must* identify at one and the same time with both characters on the stage, and moreover, do so in a gender-specific manner. If we assume that the avenues open to male response are similar to the avenues available in "real life," then more than a single possibility exists. Men may react to these characters as "human beings" rather than sexual objects and grant them as much subjective autonomy as men are willing and able to grant women in their own lives. But since the focus of the play is so sharply defined as "private," outside history, and in the normal sphere of women's domination (the home and the family), it presents a relatively unthreatening and possibly uninteresting avenue to the female psyche. Perceiving themselves as relatively detached or capable of objectivity about such matters (women, home and family), men may more easily approach the problems addressed in the play in broadly thematic or symbolic terms: as emblematic of human existential problems involving freedom, determination, and morality; or as a "limited" play about women who are subconsciously denied the kind of individual autonomy that men take for granted. Finally, male response may be affected by the fact that neither woman, as depicted, offers herself as a viable substitute for men's own attachment to women; in other words, men are not bound to the action through structures of desire. In reviews of the play, Stanley Kauffman and Richard Gilman both describe Norman's characters in a negative manner, Kauffman calling the mother, for example, "a dodo" and "a silly old self-indulgent woman." As a female heroine, Jessie may be too strong and rational to appeal to men's protective instincts and too unemotional, apathetic, sexless, depressed, and unattractive to appeal to male desire. Gilman describes her in three words: "heavyset, slow-moving and morose." Norman goes to great lengths to portray Mama as anything but ideal and Jessie as anything but sexy; but for the female viewer, the characters' sexual identity is simply never in question. Using T. J. Scheff's definition of cathartic effect as "crying, laughing and other emotional processes that occur when an unresolved emotional distress is re-awakened in a properly distanced context," one might suggest that Norman's *'night, Mother* is aesthetically over-distanced for men (producing indifference) and aesthetically under-distanced for women (producing pain). Indeed, the power of the play for women rests not only on the ways in which Norman self-consciously addresses a female audience through subject matter, language, and situation. The text also presents a psycho-dynamically charged situation that symbolically mirrors the female viewer's own — a narrative movement at least partly generated from the desires, fantasies, resentments, and fears originally connected with the very process of gender acquisition.   [1987]

MAKING COMPARISONS

1. Do you agree with McDonnell that Jessie "does manage to find *herself* in the act of dying"? Why, or why not? What would you say to someone who argues that if anything, suicide is a loss of self?

2. Do Browder's comments about mother-daughter relationships make sense to you? Identify some specific things that have influenced your own view of this subject. How does Browder's psychoanalytic approach to Norman's play affect your interpretation of it?

3. Are you surprised by Spencer's claim that men and women tend to react differently to Norman's play? Why, or why not?

WRITING ABOUT ISSUES

1. Write an essay comparing Jessie with Thelma by focusing on what you consider to be the most important statement made by each character. Explain why the statements are noteworthy. In your essay, you may certainly refer to other lines, but concentrate on one for Jessie and one for Thelma.

2. Imagine that the three critics featured in this cluster have all made their comments as part of a conference panel on "Family Relationships in *'night, Mother.*" Now you, as the final panelist, will speak on the same general subject. In your talk, however, you will address this subject by focusing on Jessie's relationship with a man in her family: that is, her father, her brother, her son, or her former husband. Write the talk you would give, referring at some point to at least one statement made by a previous panelist.

3. Write an essay recalling an occasion when you tried to talk a family member or friend out of doing something you considered horribly self-destructive. Identify the specific arguments each of you made and the outcome of the confrontation. If you wish, distinguish between your thinking then and your thinking now. Make comparisons to the conflict between Jessie and Thelma if you feel they are pertinent.

4. Should doctors ever help patients kill themselves? Write an essay arguing your position on physician-assisted suicide. Refer to at least two articles that express different views on the subject.

A WEB ASSIGNMENT

The *Making Literature Matter* Web site will link you to the site of the Hemlock Society, an organization that is dedicated to helping people who want to end their lives do so. Write an essay in which you compare this organization's site to Norman's play, especially addressing whether one of these texts makes you more accepting of suicide than the other does.

Visit www.bedfordstmartins.com/makinglitmatter

REVIEWING SOMEONE'S LIFE: RE-VISIONS OF "RICHARD CORY"

EDWIN ARLINGTON ROBINSON, "Richard Cory"
PAUL SIMON, "Richard Cory"
W. D. SNODGRASS, "Richer Quarry"

More than ever, the mass media investigate the lives of the famous and discover sordid facts behind celebrities' attractive facades. As consumers of scandal, we find ourselves curious about the dirty secrets of engaging figures. Yet throughout the ages, people have compensated for their own miseries by looking up to others who seem better off. Even now, we can be puzzled and chagrined when someone we admire turns out to be a troubled soul. The shock of such a discovery is evoked by Edwin Arlington Robinson's poem "Richard Cory," whose title character ultimately does something that forces his community—and the poem's readers—to reconsider his life. Like Richard Cory, Robinson's poem is itself well regarded, largely because of its surprise ending. In the mid-1960s, the poem caught the imagination of singer-writer Paul Simon, who did his own variation on it. More recently, poet W. D. Snodgrass has performed what he calls a "de/composition" of the poem in an effort to point out the original text's strengths. Here, compare Robinson's "Richard Cory" with Simon's and Snodgrass's re-visions of it.

(Edwin Arlington Robinson. Special Collections, Colby College, Waterville, Maine.)

(Paul Simon. Chris Walter/Retna Ltd. NYC.)

(W. D. Snodgrass. © Dorothy Alexander.)

BEFORE YOU READ

What celebrities, in any realm of life, have you stopped admiring because of something you discovered about their lives? What do your initial admiration and your subsequent dismay reveal about your own values?

EDWIN ARLINGTON ROBINSON
Richard Cory

Edwin Arlington Robinson (1869–1935) eventually gained fame through poems such as the following, but he spent much of his life in relative obscurity. Robinson was born in Head Tide, Maine, and educated at Harvard University, though he had to give up his college studies when his family went bankrupt and his mother grew ill. Living in the Maine town of Gardner, he began writing poems based on his community, which he fictionally renamed Tilbury Town. These works included "Richard Cory," which evidently was inspired by the shotgun suicide of a Gardner man. The poem appeared in Robinson's 1897 book The Children of the Night. *That same year, depressed when the woman he loved married his brother, Robinson moved to New York City. Far from being able to live as a poet, he wound up working as a checker of shale in the subway system then under construction. Fortunately, Robinson's poems came to the attention of President Theodore Roosevelt, who got him a job at the New York Customs House. Later, Robinson moved back to Gardner and in his remaining years saw his national reputation increase. He won the Pulitzer Prize for poetry three times.*

Whenever Richard Cory went down town,
We people on the pavement looked at him:
He was a gentleman from sole to crown,
Clean favored, and imperially slim.

And he was always quietly arrayed,   5
And he was always human when he talked;
But still he fluttered pulses when he said,
"Good-morning," and he glittered when he walked.

And he was rich — yes, richer than a king —
And admirably schooled in every grace: 10
In fine, we thought that he was everything
To make us wish that we were in his place.

So on we worked, and waited for the light,
And went without the meat, and cursed the bread;
And Richard Cory, one calm summer night,   15
Went home and put a bullet through his head.   [1897]

THINKING ABOUT THE TEXT

1. Were you surprised by the ending? Why, or why not? On reading the poem again, do you get any sense of why Richard Cory killed himself? If so, what?

2. What is the speaker's tone toward Richard Cory? Toward the townspeople? Toward himself?

1537

u think the speaker feels obliged to add "yes, richer than a
) instead of simply saying "he was rich"?

the rhyme scheme of this poem? What role, if any, does the
e scheme play in the poem's overall effect?

. What would you say to someone who argued that this poem's theme is
simply "Money can't buy happiness"?

PAUL SIMON
Richard Cory

*Though born in Newark, New Jersey, Paul Simon (b. 1941) grew up in the New
York City borough of Queens. In high school, he met Art Garfunkel, with whom he
went on to form one of the most successful partnerships in rock music. Simon's version of "Richard Cory," subtitled "(with apologies to Edwin Arlington Robinson),"
is featured on the duo's best-selling 1966 album* The Sounds of Silence. *Since
1972, Simon has largely pursued a solo career. In 2001, he was inducted into the
Rock and Roll Hall of Fame.*

They say that Richard Cory owns one half of this whole town,
With political connections to spread his wealth around.
Born into society, a banker's only child,
He had everything a man could want: power, grace, and style.

But I work in his factory   5
And I curse the life I'm living
And I curse my poverty
And I wish that I could be,
Oh, I wish that I could be,
Oh, I wish that I could be   10
Richard Cory.

The papers print his picture almost everywhere he goes:
Richard Cory at the opera, Richard Cory at a show.
And the rumor of his parties and the orgies on his yacht!
Oh, he surely must be happy with everything he's got.   15

But I work in his factory
And I curse the life I'm living
And I curse my poverty
And I wish that I could be,
Oh, I wish that I could be,   20
Oh, I wish that I could be
Richard Cory.

♦   ♦   ♦

He freely gave to charity, he had the common touch,
And they were grateful for his patronage and thanked him very much,
So my mind was filled with wonder when the evening headlines read:
"Richard Cory went home last night and put a bullet through his head."

But I work in his factory
And I curse the life I'm living
And I curse my poverty
And I wish that I could be,   30
Oh, I wish that I could be,
Oh, I wish that I could be
Richard Cory.   [1966]

THINKING ABOUT THE TEXT

1. The lyric begins with "They." Why do you think it does not use the word again?

2. Although the fifth stanza uses the past tense to report Richard Cory's death, the other stanzas use present tense, as if Richard Cory were still alive. How do you explain this inconsistency?

3. The second, fourth, and sixth stanzas are the same. What is the effect of this repetition? What is the effect of repetition *within* each of these stanzas?

4. Which of the things reported about Richard Cory seem to be fact? Which things are you less inclined to accept as true of him?

5. This text was actually written to be sung. Do you think it works as a poem? Why, or why not?

MAKING COMPARISONS

1. Whereas the speaker of Robinson's poem uses *we* a great deal and never uses *I*, the speaker in Simon's version says *I* a lot. How significant is this difference?

2. Robinson's and Simon's speakers tell different things about Richard Cory. How significant is this difference?

3. Simon does not stop with Richard Cory's death, as Robinson does. Instead, Simon ends with a stanza that repeats stanzas 2 and 4. What is the effect of this change?

W. D. SNODGRASS
Richer Quarry

W. D. Snodgrass (b. 1926) has published over twenty books of poetry, including the Pulitzer Prize–winning Heart's Needle *(1959) and, more recently, a collection about the Nazi regime entitled* The Fuehrer Bunker *(1995). The following version*

ppears in Snodgrass's 2001 book De/Compositions. *The vol-*
, a play on his own name: to his friends, Snodgrass is known as
also signifies that in this book, Snodgrass deliberately spoils well-
by changing their language and rhythm. Through his revisions, he
all attention to the virtues of the original texts. As you read his "Richer
ry," closely compare his poem to Edwin Arlington Robinson's and see if you
think Robinson's is indeed better.

Wherever Richard Cory chanced to go
The people he encountered looked at him:
He was a gentleman from top to toe,
Good-looking, in the height of style and slim.

He always dressed in tasteful hats and suits
And he was always friendly when he talked;
But hearts beat faster after his salutes,
"Hello, there!" or to see the way he walked.

He was so rich — yes, richer than a king —
And had an inborn sense of charm and grace: 10
In short, we thought that he had everything
And we should feel he filled an envied place.

So on we labored without heat or light,
Had rotten food so some grew sick or died;
While Richard Cory, one hot autumn night,   15
Amazed us by committing suicide.   [2001]

THINKING ABOUT THE TEXT

1. Considered by itself, what might the title refer to?

2. How do the townspeople seem to define the term *gentleman* (line 3)? To what extent does the poem help you imagine what Richard Cory actually looked like?

3. The word *we* does not appear until the third stanza. What do you make of this delay?

4. Do you think the townspeople will remain "Amazed" (line 16) at Richard Cory's suicide, or do you expect that they will come to understand it somehow? Explain.

5. Is this poem bad? Why, or why not?

MAKING COMPARISONS

1. What is the most significant difference between Snodgrass's and Robinson's poems? Between Snodgrass's and Simon's poems? Bear in mind that the difference may involve just a word or two.

2. Which re-vision of Robinson's poem seems more faithful to the original, and why?

3. How might Snodgrass decompose Simon's poem? Try decomposing it yourself.

WRITING ABOUT ISSUES

1. Choose Robinson's, Simon's, or Snodgrass's version of "Richard Cory," and write an essay in which you analyze what the author is *doing* with Richard Cory's death aside from simply reporting it. What does the death enable the author to demonstrate?

2. Write an essay in which you rank these three versions of "Richard Cory" in quality and defend your judgment.

3. Write an essay in which you recall how a person whom you and your friends envied behaved unexpectedly. Focus on trying to explain how the person's behavior eventually made sense after all. If you wish, refer to one or more of the texts in this cluster.

4. Find three people unfamiliar with Robinson's "Richard Cory." Show them Snodgrass's poem, and ask them what they think of it. Then show them Robinson's and Simon's version, asking their opinion of each. Finally, write an essay in which you summarize and interpret your findings.

A WEB ASSIGNMENT

When in real life people kill themselves unexpectedly, they are sometimes compared to Richard Cory. At the *Making Literature Matter* Web site, you will find a link to an article that makes such an analogy as it discusses the suicide of rock star Kurt Cobain. In this article entitled "Who Will Tell Generation X? A Eulogy for Nirvana's Kurt Cobain, 1967–1994," author Steven Hill refers to Cobain as "the Richard Cory of his times." After reading the article, write an essay in which you examine the extent to which some other famous suicide can be described as a Richard Cory. Choose a person about whom you already know a lot or whose life you are willing to research. If you wish, refer to Hill's analysis as you develop your own.

Visit www.bedfordstmartins.com/makinglitmatter

Reviewing Your Own Life

PERCY BYSSHE SHELLEY, "Ozymandias"
STEVIE SMITH, "Not Waving but Drowning"
CARL DENNIS, "The God Who Loves You"

The first poem in this cluster is from the early nineteenth century. The remaining two are more recent; the latest is from 2001. But all three poems show people judging lives: either their own life, others' lives, or both. Try as we may to avoid making such judgments, we often wind up making them anyway. Plenty of our judgments are automatic and unconscious. Only on certain occasions might we seriously ponder the nature of our own or someone else's existence. But a literature course such as the one you are taking is a wonderful forum for considering lives. While reading various works for the course, you develop opinions about their characters. Maybe literature is most valuable when it conveys the message that summarizing and evaluating a life is difficult, and should be. A literary work may not be worth reading if it endorses snap judgments about people. Consider whether and how these three poems encourage you to complicate the biographies and autobiographies you construct.

BEFORE YOU READ

According to the contemporary writer Reynolds Price, "No one under forty can believe how nearly everything's inherited." In effect, Price is making a claim about the ability of people under forty to judge their lives. What does Price mean? How do you react to his claim?

PERCY BYSSHE SHELLEY

Ozymandias

Before his untimely death by drowning, Percy Bysshe Shelley (1792–1822) composed many poems that are now regarded as masterpieces of British Romanticism. Shelley published the following poem in 1818 after a visit to the British Museum. On exhibit there were artifacts from the tomb of the ancient Egyptian pharaoh Rameses II, called Ozymandias by many of Shelley's contemporaries. These objects included a broken statue of the pharaoh.

I met a traveler from an antique land
Who said: Two vast and trunkless legs of stone
Stand in the desert. . . . Near them, on the sand,
Half sunk, a shattered visage lies, whose frown,
And wrinkled lip, and sneer of cold command,
Tell that its sculptor well those passions read

Which yet survive, stamped on these lifeless things,
The hand that mocked them, and the heart that fed:
And on the pedestal these words appear:
"My name is Ozymandias, King of Kings: 10
Look on my works, ye Mighty, and despair!"
Nothing beside remains. Round the decay
Of that colossal wreck, boundless and bare
The lone and level sands stretch far away.   [1818]

THINKING ABOUT THE TEXT

1. "Ozymandias" is a sonnet, a poem consisting of fourteen lines. Often there is a significant division in content between a sonnet's first eight lines and its last six. Is there such a division in Shelley's poem? Explain.

2. How is the poem a comment on the epitaph it quotes from the statue's pedestal? Describe Ozymandias by listing at least three adjectives for him, and identify the specific lines that make you think of them.

3. Although the poem begins by referring to "I," this is not the main speaker of the poem; soon we are presented with the report of the "traveler." Shelley could have had the traveler narrate the whole poem. Why might he have begun with the "I"?

4. Both Shelley and the sculptor are artists. To what extent do they resemble each other? Note that the poem describes the sculptor as someone who "well those passions read" (line 6). Why does Shelley associate him with the act of reading?

5. According to this poem, what survives? What does not?

STEVIE SMITH
Not Waving but Drowning

Stevie Smith was the pen name of Florence Martin Smith (1902–1971). For much of her adult life, she was anything but a public figure; rather, she spent much time taking care of her aunt in a London suburb. During the 1960s, however, Smith became increasingly known in England for her poetry; she even read from it aloud on numerous radio broadcasts. Her Collected Poems *was published posthumously in 1975. The following poem, Smith's best known, appeared in a 1957 book that was also entitled* Not Waving but Drowning.

Nobody heard him, the dead man,
But still he lay moaning:
I was much further out than you thought
And not waving but drowning.

◆   ◆   ◆

Poor chap, he always loved larking
And now he's dead
It must have been too cold for him his heart gave way,
They said.

Oh, no, no, no, it was too cold always
(Still the dead one lay moaning)
I was much too far out all my life
And not waving but drowning.   [1957]

THINKING ABOUT THE TEXT

1. In what senses might the dead man have been drowning? In what senses might he have been "too cold" and "much too far out"?

2. How do you think it was possible for "They" to misunderstand the dead man's real situation?

3. Smith might have ended the poem with the first stanza. What do the second and third stanzas contribute?

4. What, if anything, does the dead man hope to achieve through his moaning?

5. Is it unrealistic for Smith to have a dead man speak?

MAKING COMPARISONS

1. Compare the dead man's statements to what Ozymandias says about himself. Does Smith's character seem wiser than Ozymandias? Do you sympathize with him more? Explain.

2. Is it possible that the man in Smith's poem had the same social stature as Ozymandias? Why, or why not?

3. Is there any equivalent in Shelley's poem to the "They" in Smith's? Support your answer by referring to specific lines in both poems.

CARL DENNIS
The God Who Loves You

A native of St. Louis, Missouri, Carl Dennis (b. 1939) earned a doctorate at the University of California, Berkeley. He has produced eight volumes of poetry as well as a book of literary criticism entitled Poetry as Persuasion *(2001). For his work, Dennis received* Poetry *magazine's prestigious Ruth Lilly Poetry Prize in 2000. Dennis is a professor of English at the University of Buffalo in New York, where he has taught since 1966. The following is from his latest book of poetry,* Practical Gods *(2001), which won the Pulitzer Prize.*

It must be troubling for the god who loves you
To ponder how much happier you'd be today

Had you been able to glimpse your many futures.
It must be painful for him to watch you on Friday evenings
Driving home from the office, content with your week —   5
Three fine houses sold to deserving families —
Knowing as he does exactly what would have happened
Had you gone to your second choice for college,
Knowing the roommate you'd have been allotted
Whose ardent opinions on painting and music   10
Would have kindled in you a lifelong passion.
A life thirty points above the life you're living
On any scale of satisfaction. And every point
A thorn in the side of the god who loves you.
You don't want that, a large-souled man like you   15
Who tries to withhold from your wife the day's disappointments
So she can save her empathy for the children.
And would you want this god to compare your wife
With the woman you were destined to meet on the other campus?
It hurts you to think of him ranking the conversation   20
You'd have enjoyed over there higher in insight
Than the conversation you're used to.
And think how this loving god would feel
Knowing that the man next in line for your wife
Would have pleased her more than you ever will   25
Even on your best days, when you really try.
Can you sleep at night believing a god like that
Is pacing his cloudy bedroom, harassed by alternatives
You're spared by ignorance? The difference between what is
And what could have been will remain alive for him   30
Even after you cease existing, after you catch a chill
Running out in the snow for the morning paper,
Losing eleven years that the god who loves you
Will feel compelled to imagine scene by scene
Unless you come to the rescue by imagining him   35
No wiser than you are, no god at all, only a friend
No closer than the actual friend you made at college,
The one you haven't written in months. Sit down tonight
And write him about the life you can talk about
With a claim to authority, the life you've witnessed,   40
Which for all you know is the life you've chosen.   [2001]

THINKING ABOUT THE TEXT

1. What is the effect of addressing the poem to a particular "you"? What specific things do you learn about the actual life of this "you"? What do you
assume or suppose about the poem's speaker? With what tone does the
speaker address the "you"?

2. Describe the god evoked by the poem. In what ways, if any, does this god resemble whatever being(s) you have associated with the word *god*?

3. What is the effect of having this poem be one long continuous stanza, rather than two or more shorter stanzas? How does the content of the poem develop? Must the lines appear in the order they do?

4. The poem refers to "The difference between what is / And what could have been" (lines 29–30). At what age does a person begin to think about this difference? To what extent do you think about it? Is it a reasonable subject for someone to ponder? Explain.

5. Near the end of the poem comes a piece of advice ("Sit down tonight," line 38). Does this advice make sense to you, given the situation of the poem's "you"? Why, or why not?

MAKING COMPARISONS

1. Dennis concludes his poem by referring to "the life you can talk about / With a claim to authority, the life you've witnessed, . . . the life you've chosen." To what extent, and in what ways, do these phrases apply to Shelley's and Smith's poems?

2. Do you think the "you" of Dennis's poem is in danger of becoming Shelley's Ozymandias or Smith's drowned man? Why, or why not?

3. While Dennis's poem refers to a god, no god is mentioned in Shelley's or Smith's poems. Is this a significant difference? If so, why?

WRITING ABOUT ISSUES

1. Choose Shelley's, Smith's, or Dennis's poem, and write an essay in which you explain the importance of noting who is speaking to whom and how.

2. Choose two of the poems in this cluster, and write an essay in which you compare how much they are about what *other* people think of the person under review.

3. Dennis mentions "The difference between what is / And what could have been." Write an essay analyzing someone you know who, in reviewing his or her life, has pondered this difference. What was the outcome of the deliberation? In your view, how appropriate was it for the person to brood about such issues in the first place?

4. In recent newspapers and magazines, find obituaries that present detailed accounts of the deceased person's life. What, basically, do these obituaries suggest are the important aspects of a person's life? Write an essay in which you answer this question by referring to several examples. If you wish, focus on multiple obituaries about the same person. Also, feel free to refer to poems in this cluster.

WHEN DISASTER STRIKES: CULTURAL CONTEXTS FOR BHARATI MUKHERJEE'S "THE MANAGEMENT OF GRIEF"

BHARATI MUKHERJEE, "The Management of Grief"

CULTURAL CONTEXTS:

CLARK BLAISE AND BHARATI MUKHERJEE, From *The Sorrow and the Terror: The Haunting Legacy of the Air India Tragedy*

PAUL GESSELL, "Revealing the 'Family Man' Terrorist"

SAM HUSSEINI, "Profile in Unfairness"

The public grows conscious of death's reality when large numbers of human beings perish in a disaster. Attention is especially great when terrorism is the definite or possible cause. A recent example, of course, is the September 11, 2001, attacks on the World Trade Center Towers, the Pentagon, and United Airlines Flight 93, in which thousands of Americans and hundreds of people from other countries died. Later, the United States' effort to find and punish the guilty also spanned the globe. Indeed, disasters regularly result in cultures tangling with each other as people grieve over victims, investigate causes, search for those responsible, adopt new safety measures, and attempt to get on with their lives.

Bharati Mukherjee explores the cultural contexts of disaster in her short story "The Management of Grief," which we present here. Its main characters are a community of Indian immigrants in Canada whose loved ones have suddenly died in an airplane crash. Mukherjee based her story on a real-life incident that occurred on June 23, 1985. Heading from Toronto and Montreal toward New Delhi and Bombay, Air India Flight 182 exploded over the Irish Sea. All 329 people aboard were killed. They included a large number of Canadian citizens who had emigrated from India or who were of Indian descent. After a long investigation, Canadian and Indian authorities found that the explosion resulted from a bomb planted by certain members of India's Sikh religion. Like many, though not all Sikhs, they were agitating for the creation of a separate, independent Sikh state, commonly referred to as Khalistan.

In struggling to "manage" her grief, Mukherjee's narrator Shaila must decide how she will henceforth treat Sikhs. At the same time, she finds herself dealing with authorities in Canada and Ireland, as well as her Indian neighbors. In short, the story's cultural contexts are multiple. To help you think about them, we include a chapter from Mukherjee's 1987 book about the Air India bombing, which she wrote with her husband Clark Blaise. We also include two newspaper articles. The first, published in a May 2001 issue of the *Ottawa Citizen*, is reporter Paul Gessell's account of his recent interview with Blaise. A few months earlier, the Canadian government had finally charged two men with playing major roles in the Air India bombing. To Gessell, Blaise revealed that he and Mukherjee had interviewed one of the men for their book, thinking him guilty even back then. The second article, from 1996, is an opinion piece related to the crash of TWA's New York–Paris Flight 800 four months before. The cause of this disaster remains mysterious, but at the time it was widely attributed to Arab

(Bharati Mukherjee.
© Jerry Bauer.)

terrorists. Author Sam Husseini worries that the TWA Flight 800 crash will encourage airline officials to harass passengers of Arab descent, treating them as if they are more prone to terrorism than other groups. As you probably know, concerns over such practices arose again after the disaster of September 11, 2001. In effect, Husseini reminds us that racial and ethnic profiling at airports is hardly new.

BEFORE YOU READ

Aside from the disaster of September 11, 2001, what is another that took several lives and caught your attention? Why were you interested in it? What do you think the other members of this class should note about it?

BHARATI MUKHERJEE
The Management of Grief

A native of Calcutta, Bharati Mukherjee (b. 1942) grew up in India. She attended the universities of Calcutta and Boroda, earning a master's degree in English and ancient Indian culture. In 1961, she moved to the United States. There, she

attended the University of Iowa's renowned Writers Workshop, where she earned a
master of fine arts as well as a doctorate in English. From 1966 to 1980, Mukherjee
taught at McGill University in Canada; currently, she is a professor of English at
the University of California in Berkeley. Her novels include The Tiger's Daughter
(1971), Wife *(1972),* Jasmine *(1989), and* The Holder of the World *(1993). In*
addition, she has published two volumes of short stories, Darkness *(1985) and* The
Middleman and Other Stories *(1988). "The Management of Grief" appears in*
the latter volume, which won the National Book Critics Circle Award for fiction.
The story was also selected for The Best American Short Stories 1987. *With her*
husband Clark Blaise, Mukherjee has written two nonfiction books. In the first,
Days and Nights in Calcutta *(1979), they each give an account of a trip they made*
to India. In the second, The Sorrow and the Terror: The Haunting Legacy of the
Air India Tragedy *(1987), they examine the real-life disaster on which the following*
story is based.

A woman I don't know is boiling tea the Indian way in my kitchen. There are
a lot of women I don't know in my kitchen, whispering and moving tactfully.
They open doors, rummage through the pantry, and try not to ask me where
things are kept. They remind me of when my sons were small, on Mother's Day
or when Vikram and I were tired, and they would make big, sloppy omelets. I
would lie in bed pretending I didn't hear them.

Dr. Sharma, the treasurer of the Indo-Canada Society, pulls me into the hallway. He wants to know if I am worried about money. His wife, who has just come
up from the basement with a tray of empty cups and glasses, scolds him. "Don't
bother Mrs. Bhave with mundane details." She looks so monstrously pregnant
her baby must be days overdue. I tell her she shouldn't be carrying heavy things.
"Shaila," she says, smiling, "this is the fifth." Then she grabs a teenager by his
shirttails. He slips his Walkman off his head. He has to be one of her four children; they have the same domed and dented foreheads. "What's the official word
now?" she demands. The boy slips the headphones back on. "They're acting evasive, Ma. They're saying it could be an accident or a terrorist bomb."

All morning, the boys have been muttering, Sikh bomb, Sikh bomb. The
men, not using the word, bow their heads in agreement. Mrs. Sharma touches
her forehead at such a word. At least they've stopped talking about space debris
and Russian lasers.

Two radios are going in the dining room. They are tuned to different stations.
Someone must have brought the radios down from my boys' bedrooms. I haven't
gone into their rooms since Kusum came running across the front lawn in her
bathrobe. She looked so funny, I was laughing when I opened the door.

The big TV in the den is being whizzed through American networks and
cable channels.

"Damn!" some man swears bitterly. "How can these preachers carry on like
nothing's happened?" I want to tell him we're not that important. You look at the
audience, and at the preacher in his blue robe with his beautiful white hair, the
potted palm trees under a blue sky, and you know they care about nothing.

5

The phone rings and rings. Dr. Sharma's taken charge. "We're with her," he keeps saying. "Yes, yes, the doctor has given calming pills. Yes, yes, pills are having necessary effect." I wonder if pills alone explain this calm. Not peace, just a deadening quiet. I was always controlled, but never repressed. Sound can reach me, but my body is tensed, ready to scream. I hear their voices all around me. I hear my boys and Vikram cry, "Mommy, Shaila!" and their screams insulate me, like headphones.

The woman boiling water tells her story again and again. "I got the news first. My cousin called from Halifax before six A.M., can you imagine? He'd gotten up for prayers and his son was studying for medical exams and heard on a rock channel that something had happened to a plane. They said first it had disappeared from the radar, like a giant eraser just reached out. His father called me, so I said to him, what do you mean, 'something bad'? You mean a hijacking? And he said, *Behn*, there is no confirmation of anything yet, but check with your neighbors because a lot of them must be on that plane. So I called poor Kusum straightaway. I knew Kusum's husband and daughter were booked to go yesterday."

Kusum lives across the street from me. She and Satish had moved in less than a month ago. They said they needed a bigger place. All these people, the Sharmas and friends from the Indo-Canada Society, had been there for the housewarming. Satish and Kusum made tandoori on their big gas grill and even the white neighbors piled their plates high with that luridly red, charred, juicy chicken. Their younger daughter had danced, and even our boys had broken away from the Stanley Cup telecast to put in a reluctant appearance. Everyone took pictures for their albums and for the community newspapers — another of our families had made it big in Toronto — and now I wonder how many of those happy faces are gone. "Why does God give us so much if all along He intends to take it away?" Kusum asks me.

I nod. We sit on carpeted stairs, holding hands like children. "I never once   1(told him that I loved him," I say. I was too much the well-brought-up woman. I was so well brought up I never felt comfortable calling my husband by his first name.

"It's all right," Kusum says. "He knew. My husband knew. They felt it. Modern young girls have to say it because what they feel is fake."

Kusum's daughter Pam runs in with an overnight case. Pam's in her McDonald's uniform. "Mummy! You have to get dressed!" Panic makes her cranky. "A reporter's on his way here."

"Why?"

"You want to talk to him in your bathrobe?" She starts to brush her mother's long hair. She's the daughter who's always in trouble. She dates Canadian boys and hangs out in the mall, shopping for tight sweaters. The younger one, the goody-goody one according to Pam, the one with a voice so sweet that when she sang *bhajans* for Ethiopian relief even a frugal man like my husband wrote out a hundred-dollar check, *she* was on that plane. *She* was going to spend July and August with grandparents because Pam wouldn't go. Pam said she'd rather waitress at McDonald's. "If it's a choice between Bombay and Wonderland, I'm picking Wonderland," she'd said.

"Leave me alone," Kusum yells. "You know what I want to do? If I didn't   15
have to look after you now, I'd hang myself."

Pam's young face goes blotchy with pain. "Thanks," she says, "don't let me
stop you."

"Hush," pregnant Mrs. Sharma scolds Pam. "Leave your mother alone. Mr.
Sharma will tackle the reporters and fill out the forms. He'll say what has to be
said."

Pam stands her ground. "You think I don't know what Mummy's thinking?
Why her? That's what. That's sick! Mummy wishes my little sister were alive and I
were dead."

Kusum's hand in mine is trembly hot. We continue to sit on the stairs.

She calls before she arrives, wondering if there's anything I need. Her name   20
is Judith Templeton and she's an appointee of the provincial government. "Multi-
culturalism?" I ask, and she says "partially," but that her mandate is bigger. "I've
been told you knew many of the people on the flight," she says. "Perhaps if you'd
agree to help us reach the others . . . ?"

She gives me time at least to put on tea water and pick up the mess in the
front room. I have a few *samosas* from Kusum's housewarming that I could fry up,
but then I think, why prolong this visit?

Judith Templeton is much younger than she sounded. She wears a blue suit
with a white blouse and a polka-dot tie. Her blond hair is cut short, her only
jewelry is pearl-drop earrings. Her briefcase is new and expensive looking, a
gleaming cordovan leather. She sits with it across her lap. When she looks out the
front windows onto the street, her contact lenses seem to float in front of her light
blue eyes.

"What sort of help do you want from me?" I ask. She has refused the tea, out
of politeness, but I insist, along with some slightly stale biscuits.

"I have no experience," she admits. "That is, I have an M.S.W. and I've
worked in liaison with accident victims, but I mean I have no experience with a
tragedy of this scale — "

"Who could?" I ask.   25

" — and with the complications of culture, language, and customs. Someone
mentioned that Mrs. Bhave is a pillar — because you've taken it more calmly."

At this, perhaps, I frown, for she reaches forward, almost to take my hand. "I
hope you understand my meaning, Mrs. Bhave. There are hundreds of people in
Metro directly affected, like you, and some of them speak no English. There are
some widows who've never handled money or gone on a bus, and there are old
parents who still haven't eaten or gone outside their bedrooms. Some houses and
apartments have been looted. Some wives are still hysterical. Some husbands are
in shock and profound depression. We want to help, but our hands are tied in so
many ways. We have to distribute money to some people, and there are legal documents — these things can be done. We have interpreters, but we don't always
have the human touch, or maybe the right human touch. We don't want to make
mistakes, Mrs. Bhave, and that's why we'd like to ask you to help us."

"More mistakes, you mean," I say.

"Police matters are not in my hands," she answers.

"Nothing I can do will make any difference," I say. "We must all grieve in our own way."

"But you are coping very well. All the people said, Mrs. Bhave is the strongest person of all. Perhaps if the others could see you, talk with you, it would help them."

"By the standards of the people you call hysterical, I am behaving very oddly and very badly, Miss Templeton." I want to say to her, *I wish I could scream, starve, walk into Lake Ontario, jump from a bridge.* "They would not see me as a model. I do not see myself as a model."

I am a freak. No one who has ever known me would think of me reacting this way. This terrible calm will not go away.

She asks me if she may call again, after I get back from a long trip that we all must make. "Of course," I say. "Feel free to call, anytime."

Four days later, I find Kusum squatting on a rock overlooking a bay in Ireland. It isn't a big rock, but it juts sharply out over water. This is as close as we'll ever get to them. June breezes balloon out her sari and unpin her knee-length hair. She has the bewildered look of a sea creature whom the tides have stranded.

It's been one hundred hours since Kusum came stumbling and screaming across my lawn. Waiting around the hospital, we've heard many stories. The police, the diplomats, they tell us things thinking that we're strong, that knowledge is helpful to the grieving, and maybe it is. Some, I know, prefer ignorance, or their own versions. The plane broke into two, they say. Unconsciousness was instantaneous. No one suffered. My boys must have just finished their breakfasts. They loved eating on planes, they loved the smallness of plates, knives, and forks. Last year they saved the airline salt and pepper shakers. Half an hour more and they would have made it to Heathrow.

Kusum says that we can't escape our fate. She says that all those people — our husbands, my boys, her girl with the nightingale voice, all those Hindus, Christians, Sikhs, Muslims, Parsis, and atheists on that plane — were fated to die together off this beautiful bay. She learned this from a swami in Toronto.

I have my Valium.

Six of us "relatives" — two widows and four widowers — chose to spend the day today by the waters instead of sitting in a hospital room and scanning photographs of the dead. That's what they call us now: relatives. I've looked through twenty-seven photos in two days. They're very kind to us, the Irish are very understanding. Sometimes understanding means freeing a tourist bus for this trip to the bay, so we can pretend to spy our loved ones through the glassiness of waves or in sun-speckled cloud shapes.

I could die here, too, and be content.

"What is that, out there?" She's standing and flapping her hands, and for a moment I see a head shape bobbing in the waves. She's standing in the water, I on the boulder. The tide is low, and a round, black, head-sized rock has just risen from the waves. She returns, her sari end dripping and ruined, and her face is a twisted remnant of hope, the way mine was a hundred hours ago, still laughing but inwardly knowing that nothing but the ultimate tragedy could bring two women together at six o'clock on a Sunday morning. I watch her face sag into blankness.

"That water felt warm, Shaila," she says at length.

"You can't," I say. "We have to wait for our turn to come."

I haven't eaten in four days, haven't brushed my teeth.

"I know," she says. "I tell myself I have no right to grieve. They are in a better   45
place than we are. My swami says depression is a sign of our selfishness."

Maybe I'm selfish. Selfishly I break away from Kusum and run, sandals slapping against stones, to the water's edge. What if my boys aren't lying pinned under the debris? What if they aren't stuck a mile below that innocent blue chop? What if, given the strong currents. . . .

Now I've ruined my sari, one of my best. Kusum has joined me, knee deep in water that feels to me like a swimming pool. I could settle in the water, and my husband would take my hand and the boys would slap water in my face just to see me scream.

"Do you remember what good swimmers my boys were, Kusum?"

"I saw the medals," she says.

One of the widowers, Dr. Ranganathan from Montreal, walks out to us, car-   50
rying his shoes in one hand. He's an electrical engineer. Someone at the hotel mentioned his work is famous around the world, something about the place where physics and electricity come together. He has lost a huge family, something indescribable. "With some good luck," Dr. Ranganathan suggests to me, "a good swimmer could make it safely to some island. It is quite possible that there may be many, many microscopic islets scattered around."

"You're not just saying that?" I tell Dr. Ranganathan about Vinod, my elder son. Last year he took diving as well.

"It's a parent's duty to hope," he says. "It is foolish to rule out possibilities that have not been tested. I myself have not surrendered hope."

Kusum is sobbing once again. "Dear lady," he says, laying his free hand on her arm, and she calms down.

"Vinod is how old?" he asks me. He's very careful, as we all are. *Is*, not was.

"Fourteen. Yesterday he was fourteen. His father and uncle were going to   55
take him down to the Taj and give him a big birthday party. I couldn't go with them because I couldn't get two weeks off from my stupid job in June." I process bills for a travel agent. June is a big travel month.

Dr. Ranganathan whips the pockets of his suit jacket inside out. Squashed roses, in darkening shades of pink, float on the water. He tore the roses off creepers in somebody's garden. He didn't ask anyone if he could pluck the roses, but now there's been an article about it in the local papers. When you see an Indian person, it says, please give them flowers.

"A strong youth of fourteen," he says, "can very likely pull to safety a younger one."

My sons, though four years apart, were very close. Vinod wouldn't let Mithun drown. *Electrical engineering*, I think, foolishly perhaps: this man knows important secrets of the universe, things closed to me. Relief spins me lightheaded. No wonder my boys' photographs haven't turned up in the gallery of photos of the recovered dead. "Such pretty roses," I say.

"My wife loved pink roses. Every Friday I had to bring a bunch home. I used to say, Why? After twenty-odd years of marriage you're still needing proof positive of my love?" He has identified his wife and three of his children. Then others from Montreal, the lucky ones, intact families with no survivors. He chuckles as he wades back to shore. Then he swings around to ask me a question. "Mrs. Bhave, you are wanting to throw in some roses for your loved ones? I have two big ones left."

But I have other things to float: Vinod's pocket calculator; a half-painted model B-52 for my Mithun. They'd want them on their island. And for my husband? For him I let fall into the calm, glassy waters a poem I wrote in the hospital yesterday. Finally he'll know my feelings for him.

"Don't tumble, the rocks are slippery," Dr. Ranganathan cautions. He holds out a hand for me to grab.

Then it's time to get back on the bus, time to rush back to our waiting posts on hospital benches.

Kusum is one of the lucky ones. The lucky ones flew here, identified in multiplicate their loved ones, then will fly to India with the bodies for proper ceremonies. Satish is one of the few males who surfaced. The photos of faces we saw on the walls in an office at Heathrow and here in the hospital are mostly of women. Women have more body fat, a nun said to me matter-of-factly. They float better.

Today I was stopped by a young sailor on the street. He had loaded bodies, he'd gone into the water when — he checks my face for signs of strength — when the sharks were first spotted. I don't blush, and he breaks down. "It's all right," I say. "Thank you." I heard about the sharks from Dr. Ranganathan. In his orderly mind, science brings understanding, it holds no terror. It is the shark's duty. For every deer there is a hunter, for every fish a fisherman.

The Irish are not shy; they rush to me and give me hugs and some are crying. I cannot imagine reactions like that on the streets of Toronto. Just strangers, and I am touched. Some carry flowers with them and give them to any Indian they see.

After lunch, a policeman I have gotten to know quite well catches hold of me. He says he thinks he has a match for Vinod. I explain what a good swimmer Vinod is.

"You want me with you when you look at photos?" Dr. Ranganathan walks ahead of me into the picture gallery. In these matters, he is a scientist, and I am grateful. It is a new perspective. "They have performed miracles," he says. "We are indebted to them."

The first day or two the policemen showed us relatives only one picture at a time; now they're in a hurry, they're eager to lay out the possibles, and even the probables.

The face on the photo is of a boy much like Vinod; the same intelligent eyes, the same thick brows dipping into a V. But this boy's features, even his cheeks, are puffier, wider, mushier.

"No." My gaze is pulled by other pictures. There are five other boys who look   70
like Vinod.

The nun assigned to console me rubs the first picture with a fingertip.
"When they've been in the water for a while, love, they look a little heavier." The
bones under the skin are broken, they said on the first day—try to adjust your
memories. It's important.

"It's not him. I'm his mother. I'd know."

"I know this one!" Dr. Ranganathan cries out, and suddenly from the back of
the gallery. "And this one!" I think he senses that I don't want to find my boys.
"They are the Kutty brothers. They were also from Montreal." I don't mean to be
crying. On the contrary, I am ecstatic. My suitcase in the hotel is packed heavy
with dry clothes for my boys.

The policeman starts to cry. "I am so sorry. I am so sorry, ma'am. I really
thought we had a match."

With the nun ahead of us and the policeman behind, we, the unlucky ones   75
without our children's bodies, file out of the makeshift gallery.

From Ireland most of us go on to India. Kusum and I take the same direct
flight to Bombay, so I can help her clear customs quickly. But we have to argue
with a man in uniform. He has large boils on his face. The boils swell and glow
with sweat as we argue with him. He wants Kusum to wait in line and he refuses
to take authority because his boss is on a tea break. But Kusum won't let her
coffins out of sight, and I shan't desert her though I know that my parents, elderly
and diabetic, must be waiting in a stuffy car in a scorching lot.

"You bastard!" I scream at the man with the popping boils. Other passengers
press closer. "You think we're smuggling contraband in those coffins!"

Once upon a time we were well-brought-up women; we were dutiful wives
who kept our heads veiled, our voices shy and sweet.

In India, I become, once again, an only child of rich, ailing parents. Old
friends of the family come to pay their respects. Some are Sikh, and inwardly,
involuntarily, I cringe. My parents are progressive people; they do not blame
communities for a few individuals.

In Canada it is a different story now.   80

"Stay longer," my mother pleads. "Canada is a cold place. Why would you
want to be by yourself?" I stay.

Three months pass. Then another.

"Vikram wouldn't have wanted you to give up things!" they protest. They call
my husband by the name he was born with. In Toronto he'd changed to Vik so
the men he worked with at his office would find his name as easy as Rod or Chris.
"You know, the dead aren't cut off from us!"

My grandmother, the spoiled daughter of a rich zamindar,° shaved her head
with rusty razor blades when she was widowed at sixteen. My grandfather died of

---

zamindar: Feudal landlord in British India.

childhood diabetes when he was nineteen, and she saw herself as the harbinger of bad luck. My mother grew up without parents, raised indifferently by an uncle, while her true mother slept in a hut behind the main estate house and took her food with the servants. She grew up a rationalist. My parents abhor mindless mortification.

The zamindar's daughter kept stubborn faith in Vedic rituals; my parents   85
rebelled. I am trapped between two modes of knowledge. At thirty-six, I am too old to start over and too young to give up. Like my husband's spirit, I flutter between worlds.

Courting aphasia, we travel. We travel with our phalanx of servants and poor relatives. To hill stations and to beach resorts. We play contract bridge in dusty gymkhana clubs. We ride stubby ponies up crumbly mountain trails. At tea dances, we let ourselves be twirled twice round the ballroom. We hit the holy spots we hadn't made time for before. In Varanasi, Kalighat, Rishikesh, Hardwar, astrologers and palmists seek me out and for a fee offer me cosmic consolations.

Already the widowers among us are being shown new bride candidates. They cannot resist the call of custom, the authority of their parents and older brothers. They must marry; it is the duty of a man to look after a wife. The new wives will be young widows with children, destitute but of good family. They will make loving wives, but the men will shun them. I've had calls from the men over crackling Indian telephone lines. "Save me," they say, these substantial, educated, successful men of forty. "My parents are arranging a marriage for me." In a month they will have buried one family and returned to Canada with a new bride and partial family.

I am comparatively lucky. No one here thinks of arranging a husband for an unlucky widow.

Then, on the third day of the sixth month into this odyssey, in an abandoned temple in a tiny Himalayan village, as I make my offering of flowers and sweetmeats to the god of a tribe of animists, my husband descends to me. He is squatting next to a scrawny sadhu° in moth-eaten robes. Vikram wears the vanilla suit he wore the last time I hugged him. The sadhu tosses petals on a butter-fed flame, reciting Sanskrit mantras, and sweeps his face of flies. My husband takes my hands in his.

You're beautiful, he starts. Then, *What are you doing here?*   90

Shall I stay? I ask. He only smiles, but already the image is fading. *You must finish alone what we started together.* No seaweed wreathes his mouth. He speaks too fast, just as he used to when we were an envied family in our pink split-level. He is gone.

In the windowless altar room, smoky with joss sticks and clarified butter lamps, a sweaty hand gropes for my blouse. I do not shriek. The sadhu arranges his robe. The lamps hiss and sputter out.

When we come out of the temple, my mother says, "Did you feel something weird in there?"

My mother has no patience with ghosts, prophetic dreams, holy men, and cults.

---

sadhu: Ascetic or holy man.

"No," I lie. "Nothing."   95

But she knows that she's lost me. She knows that in days I shall be leaving.

Kusum's put up her house for sale. She wants to live in an ashram in Hardwar. Moving to Hardwar was her swami's idea. Her swami runs two ashrams, the
one in Hardwar and another here in Toronto.

"Don't run away," I tell her.

"I'm not running away," she says. "I'm pursuing inner peace. You think you
or that Ranganathan fellow are better off?"

Pam's left for California. She wants to do some modeling, she says. She says   100
when she comes into her share of the insurance money she'll open a yoga-cum-
aerobics studio in Hollywood. She sends me postcards so naughty I daren't leave
them on the coffee table. Her mother has withdrawn from her and the world.

The rest of us don't lose touch, that's the point. Talk is all we have, says Dr.
Ranganathan, who has also resisted his relatives and returned to Montreal and to
his job, alone. He says, Whom better to talk with than other relatives? We've been
melted down and recast as a new tribe.

He calls me twice a week from Montreal. Every Wednesday night and every
Saturday afternoon. He is changing jobs, going to Ottawa. But Ottawa is over a
hundred miles away, and he is forced to drive two hundred and twenty miles a
day from his home in Montreal. He can't bring himself to sell his house. The
house is a temple, he says; the king-sized bed in the master bedroom is a shrine.
He sleeps on a folding cot. A devotee.

There are still some hysterical relatives. Judith Templeton's list of those
needing help and those who've "accepted" is in nearly perfect balance. Acceptance means you speak of your family in the past tense and you make active plans
for moving ahead with your life. There are courses at Seneca and Ryerson we
could be taking. Her gleaming leather briefcase is full of college catalogues and
lists of cultural societies that need our help. She has done impressive work, I
tell her.

"In the textbooks on grief management," she replies—I am her confidante, I
realize, one of the few whose grief has not sprung bizarre obsessions—"there are
stages to pass through: rejection, depression, acceptance, reconstruction." She
has compiled a chart and finds that six months after the tragedy, none of us still
rejects reality, but only a handful are reconstructing. "Depressed acceptance" is
the plateau we've reached. Remarriage is a major step in reconstruction (though
she's a little surprised, even shocked, over *how* quickly some of the men have
taken on new families). Selling one's house and changing jobs and cities is
healthy.

How to tell Judith Templeton that my family surrounds me, and that like   105
creatures in epics, they've changed shapes? She sees me as calm and accepting
but worries that I have no job, no career. My closest friends are worse off than I. I
cannot tell her my days, even my nights, are thrilling.

She asks me to help with families she can't reach at all. An elderly couple in
Agincourt whose sons were killed just weeks after they had brought their parents

over from a village in Punjab. From their names, I know they are Sikh. Judith Templeton and a translator have visited them twice with offers of money for airfare to Ireland, with bank forms, power-of-attorney forms, but they have refused to sign, or to leave their tiny apartment. Their sons' money is frozen in the bank. Their sons' investment apartments have been trashed by tenants, the furnishings sold off. The parents fear that anything they sign or any money they receive will end the company's or the country's obligations to them. They fear they are selling their sons for two airline tickets to a place they've never seen.

The high-rise apartment is a tower of Indians and West Indians, with a sprinkling of Orientals. The nearest bus-stop kiosk is lined with women in saris. Boys practice cricket in the parking lot. Inside the building, even I wince a bit from the ferocity of onion fumes, the distinctive and immediate Indianness of frying ghee, but Judith Templeton maintains a steady flow of information. These poor old people are in imminent danger of losing their place and all their services.

I say to her, "They are Sikh. They will not open up to a Hindu woman." And what I want to add is, as much as I try not to, I stiffen now at the sight of beards and turbans. I remember a time when we all trusted each other in this new country, it was only the new country we worried about.

The two rooms are dark and stuffy. The lights are off, and an oil lamp sputters on the coffee table. The bent old lady has let us in, and her husband is wrapping a white turban over his oiled, hip-length hair. She immediately goes to the kitchen, and I hear the most familiar sound of an Indian home, tap water hitting and filling a teapot.

They have not paid their utility bills, out of fear and inability to write a check. The telephone is gone, electricity and gas and water are soon to follow. They have told Judith their sons will provide. They are good boys, and they have always earned and looked after their parents.

We converse a bit in Hindi. They do not ask about the crash and I wonder if I should bring it up. If they think I am here merely as a translator, then they may feel insulted. There are thousands of Punjabi speakers, Sikhs, in Toronto to do a better job. And so I say to the old lady, "I too have lost my sons, and my husband, in the crash."

Her eyes immediately fill with tears. The man mutters a few words which sound like a blessing. "God provides and God takes away," he says.

I want to say, But only men destroy and give back nothing. "My boys and my husband are not coming back," I say. "We have to understand that."

Now the old woman responds. "But who is to say? Man alone does not decide these things." To this her husband adds his agreement.

Judith asks about the bank papers, the release forms. With a stroke of the pen, they will have a provincial trustee to pay their bills, invest their money, send them a monthly pension.

"Do you know this woman?" I ask them.

The man raises his hand from the table, turns it over, and seems to regard each finger separately before he answers. "This young lady is always coming here, we make tea for her, and she leaves papers for us to sign." His eyes scan a pile of papers in the corner of the room. "Soon we will be out of tea, then will she go away?"

The old lady adds, "I have asked my neighbors and no one else gets *angrezi*° visitors. What have we done?"

"It's her job," I try to explain. "The government is worried. Soon you will have no place to stay, no lights, no gas, no water."

"Government will get its money. Tell her not to worry, we are honorable 　120 people."

I try to explain the government wishes to give money, not take. He raises his hand. "Let them take," he says. "We are accustomed to that. That is no problem."

"We are strong people," says the wife. "Tell her that."

"Who needs all this machinery?" demands the husband. "It is unhealthy, the bright lights, the cold air on a hot day, the cold food, the four gas rings. God will provide, not government."

"When our boys return," the mother says.

Her husband sucks his teeth. "Enough talk," he says. 　125

Judith breaks in. "Have you convinced them?" The snaps on her cordovan briefcase go off like firecrackers in that quiet apartment. She lays the sheaf of legal papers on the coffee table. "If they can't write their names, an X will do — I've told them that."

Now the old lady has shuffled to the kitchen and soon emerges with a pot of tea and two cups. "I think my bladder will go first on a job like this," Judith says to me, smiling. "If only there was some way of reaching them. Please thank her for the tea. Tell her she's very kind."

I nod in Judith's direction and tell them in Hindi, "She thanks you for the tea. She thinks you are being very hospitable but she doesn't have the slightest idea what it means."

I want to say, Humor her. I want to say, My boys and my husband are with me too, more than ever. I look in the old man's eyes and I can read his stubborn, peasant's message: *I have protected this woman as best I can. She is the only person I have left. Give to me or take from me what you will, but I will not sign for it. I will not pretend that I accept.*

In the car, Judith says, "You see what I'm up against? I'm sure they're lovely 　130 people, but their stubbornness and ignorance are driving me crazy. They think signing a paper is signing their sons' death warrants, don't they?"

I am looking out the window. I want to say, *In our culture, it is a parent's duty to hope.*

"Now Shaila, this next woman is a real mess. She cries day and night, and she refuses all medical help. We may have to — "

"Let me out at the subway," I say.

"I beg your pardon?" I can feel those blue eyes staring at me.

It would not be like her to disobey. She merely disapproves, and slows at 　135 a corner to let me out. Her voice is plaintive. "Is there anything I said? Anything I did?"

---

angrezi: English or Anglo.

I could answer her suddenly in a dozen ways, but I choose not to. "Shaila? Let's talk about it," I hear, then slam the door.

A wife and mother begins her life in a new country, and that life is cut short. Yet her husband tells her: Complete what we have started. We, who stayed out of politics and came half way around the world to avoid religious and political feuding, have been the first in the New World to die from it. I no longer know what we started, nor how to complete it. I write letters to the editors of local papers and to members of Parliament. Now at least they admit it was a bomb. One MP answers back, with sympathy, but with a challenge. You want to make a difference? Work on a campaign. Work on mine. Politicize the Indian voter.

My husband's old lawyer helps me set up a trust. Vikram was a saver and a careful investor. He had saved the boys' boarding school and college fees. I sell the pink house at four times what we paid for it and take a small apartment downtown. I am looking for a charity to support.

We are deep in the Toronto winter, gray skies, icy pavements. I stay indoors, watching television. I have tried to assess my situation, how best to live my life, to complete what we began so many years ago. Kusum has written me from Hardwar that her life is now serene. She has seen Satish and has heard her daughter sing again. Kusum was on a pilgrimage, passing through a village, when she heard a young girl's voice, singing one of her daughter's favorite *bhajans*. She followed the music through the squalor of a Himalayan village, to a hut where a young girl, an exact replica of her daughter, was fanning coals under the kitchen fire. When she appeared, the girl cried out, "Ma!" and ran away. What did I think of that?

I think I can only envy her.   140

Pam didn't make it to California, but writes me from Vancouver. She works in a department store, giving makeup hints to Indian and Oriental girls. Dr. Ranganathan has given up his commute, given up his house and job, and accepted an academic position in Texas, where no one knows his story and he has vowed not to tell it. He calls me now once a week.

I wait, I listen and I pray, but Vikram has not returned to me. The voices and the shapes and the nights filled with visions ended abruptly several weeks ago.

I take it as a sign.

One rare, beautiful, sunny day last week, returning from a small errand on Yonge Street, I was walking through the park from the subway to my apartment. I live equidistant from the Ontario Houses of Parliament and the University of Toronto. The day was not cold, but something in the bare trees caught my attention. I looked up from the gravel, into the branches and the clear blue sky beyond. I thought I heard the rustling of larger forms, and I waited a moment for voices. Nothing.

"What?" I asked.   145

Then as I stood in the path looking north to Queen's Park and west to the university, I heard the voices of my family one last time. *Your time has come*, they said. *Go, be brave.*

I do not know where this voyage I have begun will end. I do not know which direction I will take. I dropped the package on a park bench and started walking.

[1988]

THINKING ABOUT THE TEXT

1. In what sense does this story involve culture? Define the term.

2. In what ways does Shaila develop during the story? Does she go through the stages of grief that Judith Templeton mentions?

3. Consider the title. Can grief be managed? Define the term *manage*. What characters in the story, if any, attempt to manage grief? In what ways?

4. Evaluate Judith Templeton's words and actions. Does she deserve any sympathy?

5. Identify the role of gender in the story. If Shaila had been male, what other elements of the story, if any, might have been different?

CLARK BLAISE and BHARATI MUKHERJEE
From *The Sorrow and the Terror:*
The Haunting Legacy of the Air India Tragedy

As we pointed out in the introduction to this cluster, Mukherjee based "The Management of Grief" on the June 23, 1985, crash of Air India Flight 182. Bound for New Delhi and Bombay after leaving Toronto and Montreal, it exploded over the Irish Sea. All 329 people aboard perished. Many of them were, like Shaila, Canadian citizens of Indian descent. The explosion was caused by a bomb that was detonated as part of an effort by certain members of India's Sikh religion to win from that country a separate, independent state that would be called Khalistan. While not all Sikhs have participated in the campaign for Khalistan, it has raged for several years, and there has been other violence committed during it. For example, in 1984 Sikhs assassinated India's prime minister Indira Gandhi, largely because under her orders the Indian military had stormed a Sikh holy place, the Golden Temple of Amritsar.

Mukherjee and her husband Clark Blaise (b. 1942) wrote about the Air India incident in their 1987 book The Sorrow and the Terror: The Haunting Legacy of the Air India Tragedy. *Like Mukherjee, Blaise is the author of several books, including the novels* Lunar Attractions *(1979) and* Lusts *(1983) as well as the nonfiction works* I Had a Father: A Post-Modern Autobiography *(1993) and* Time Lord *(2001). Currently he teaches in the Writers Workshop at the University of Iowa. Here we present Chapter 6 of their book, which deals with the immediate aftermath of the Air India disaster. Numerous relatives of the passengers journeyed to Cork, Ireland, hoping to identify and repossess the bodies of their loved ones. In this effort, they found themselves dealing with Irish as well as Canadian officials, including the Gardai (Irish police).*

At the Cork Regional Hospital, the relatives were let off at the main entrance in the West Wing. Some local people were in the lobby; patients' visitors, nursing staff, ordinary citizens moved by the tragedy. The counselors escorted the relatives through the lobby—a short walk—to the stairs leading up to the Nurses' Residence, and upstairs down a corridor lined with glass cases of plaster models of human parts, cases now draped so their contents would not upset the bereaved, to the hall where special Gardai detectives were to talk to them.

The detectives explained the identification process. First, each relative would have to fill out a pink Interpol identification form with the help of the policeman assigned to her or him. Then the Gardai would try to match the physical characteristics listed on the pink form with their own photographs and lists. If the Gardai found a match, the relative would be led away to another room and shown a selection of photographs. If the relative made a positive identification in this photo gallery, the mini-family of mourner, counselor, and policeman would make the long walk to the East Wing. There the relative would be taken into a room and shown a plastic bag of wet, ripped clothes and jewelry. If the relative recognized the washed-up debris, then and then only, would he or she be led into another, smaller room and shown a coffined body.

The Gardai announced the procedure. The bodies were in their care, and they had to be sure that the right body went to the right relative. Besides, that first day, with the first batch of relatives—it was Wednesday, June 26th—the pathology teams were still working on the retrieved bodies.

The relatives thought they would get to see the bodies of their loved ones right away. They thought they would, at least, see the photographs. They thought they would arrive, claim their dead, and try to make sense out of abominable tragedy. They didn't know what they thought. There were no rules on how to behave well in circumstances like this. Nobody they knew had gone through what they were going through. They knew one thing: they were angry. They didn't want to fill out more forms listing shape of nose, length of playground scars, shade of black hair. They had already done this back home while they'd been kept waiting by the authorities. Agents for the Kenyon Group, the undertakers and the local police, had gone over all that with them. The men had lifted fingerprints from textbooks in neat, suburban homes. Those men had come with Yellow Identification Forms. Pink forms, yellow forms. The relatives wanted to fill out no more forms; they wanted to grieve over bodies.

The counselors calmed the relatives. The Gardai were patient, sympathetic. 5
They had to be sure, they said. Having the relatives on hand made the filling out of the Pink Identification Forms much easier. The relatives allowed themselves to be comforted. Like them, the Irish were family people, emotional and godfearing. They filled out the Pink Forms. Separate agencies had their separate forms. The Yellow Forms, not handled by the Irish, were lost, they suspected.

They waited. They told each other how and when they had heard the dreadful news. One man's nephew, a studious immigrant, had been cramming for college exams with the radio on and he'd heard at four in the morning. Nobody had believed the nephew. You fell asleep, they had scolded him.

The counselors encouraged the relatives to talk. They saw an extraordinary bond forming within that vast, mournful body in the hall of the Nurses' Residence. The bereaved comforted each other. The bereaved accepted solace from other bereaved. More arrived. From India, Canada, the United States, Britain. Here were the nearly three hundred relatives, but they were not screaming; they were demanding nothing. They were private, and noble, in their terrible grief.

The Gardai, the counselors, and beefed-up staff from consulates and embassies met each flight at Cork Airport. So did TV and print journalists. The Press followed the relatives to the hospital. Do you believe the plane was sabotaged, they asked. Are you satisfied with the hospital's arrangements? How well have Canadian officials handled this tragedy? On camera, one or two men blew up at what they perceived as consular callousness or white-Canadian coldness. "Where are those bastards?" one relative demanded. "Are they sitting tight in cozy chairs?" Back home in Toronto his astounded teenaged son witnessed his father's grief on TV. He had never heard his quiet, hard-working, very correct father use the word "bastard."

The Gardai read through their records. They had 131 bodies. One hundred and ninety-eight bodies were in the plane's wreckage at the bottom of the sea. Most relatives who had come to Cork would have no body to grieve over or to cremate. The Gardai had to be careful. They called in a relative as soon as they felt there was a fair chance of match-up. The relative called in felt "lucky." (Afterwards, John Laurence, the father of the young dancers, said, "Can you imagine how topsy-turvy those days were? We thought we were 'lucky' if the police came in saying that they thought they had a body for viewing!" His two daughters were beautiful. He had photographs of them, eighteen and sixteen, in their splendid dance costumes. Their bodies were not brought back in bodybags to be rephotographed in mutilation.)

In the photo gallery some relatives had trouble recognizing the marked faces and bloated bodies. These were not the faces of the people they had hugged at Pearson International Airport or at Mirabel in Montreal. They had an easier time recognizing the photographs of friends and neighbors. The Gardai was glad of that help. Whole families had been lost on that plane. This was a tight community. The mourners in Cork remembered what departing friends had worn for the vacation trip to India. Those who could identify the pictures went on to the East Wing for the rest of the sad, grim procedure. The others came back to the hall to wait for a change in "luck." 10

In the hall relatives who had flown in from India had a hard time filling out the forms. Two women, both wives and mothers, both naturalized Canadians, had gone on to India ahead of their families. They did not know what their loved ones had worn on the plane when they had taken off on Saturday. The Indian relatives of Canadian families that had perished without survivors had the hardest time. They had come to identify and mourn brothers or sisters they hadn't seen perhaps in years. The faces had thickened or maybe thinned; many of the women had cut their hair. The infants they had cradled years ago had grown into teenaged math whizzes and dance instructors. Some India-based relatives could not speak English and had a harder time still with the identification.

So the relatives helped each other. Do you remember any birthmarks? Did they write you of any surgery, any illnesses? They felt very close.

Some of the relatives from India had horror stories about the Canadian High Commission in New Delhi. They had tried to get visas to go on to Canada after Cork, so they could at least help look after a devastated brother or sister for a few months. The Canadian High Commission, some said, had not only refused them visas but had behaved badly, had treated them with unnecessary rudeness. They said that the Canadian visa officers had acted suspicious, as though this were not family rallying in time of monumental tragedy, but just one more immigration scam to sneak into Canada.

There was a lot of waiting around in the hall where the Gardai detectives had given their procedural talk. To make the wait a little easier, the Friends of the Hospital, a volunteer group, set themselves up in a corner of another hall. They poured tea, cut cake. Some relatives fell sick during the waiting, and four had to be treated — for assorted ailments such as hysteria, diabetes, bad heart — in the hospital.

The relatives waited and asked each other deep questions about Fate. What if their families had been booked to fly on an airline other than Air India? Would the 329 people on that Air India Flight 182 have all died precisely at the ordained moment on the morning of Sunday, June 23rd? Many had originally reserved tickets on other airlines: British Airways, Kuwait Airways. Some had planned to send their families a week earlier or a week later. Why and how had it happened? The journalists were full of stories of sabotage. The journalists played phrases by them: Sikh terrorists, bag-bombs. (The refinement of phrase from "Sikh" to "Khalistani" would be slow.) Was the destruction of family life, which meant their lives in Canada, the lives they had worked so hard and saved so hard for, caused by the individual wills of *saboteurs*? In those early days, when the pain was real but the loss not yet felt, the Hindu relatives consoled themselves with thoughts of Destiny. When one has fulfilled one's mission on earth, one is recalled by God. Atman, the individual soul, dissolves forever into the Brahman, and the cycle of reincarnation is stopped. This happy fusion is promised to "pure" souls. And their loved ones on that plane had been innocent, pure. They had hurt nobody. The children, in fact, had done good. Many were carrying back money from their piggy-banks to give away to the Indian poor.

Thoughts about Fate consoled the Hindus in Cork. And this fatalism was a temporary boon to government and insurance companies. Angry relatives making emotional remarks about Sikh-Hindu conflicts to the Indian press could set off dreadful communal riots. Delhi had gone through such communal riots the day Mrs. Gandhi was fatally shot. The plane crash, the Indian officials suspected, was an act of Khalistani terrorist revenge — innocent blood for innocent blood — for those very riots. The Canadians and Air India were thankful for the fatalism of these New Canadians, which delayed any ferocious complaints to the Press about Canadian laxity in securing its major airports.

The relatives who were still without bodies tried their best to change their "luck." One man, an engineer, shaved off his mourner's stubble and spruced himself up. "My wife wouldn't go out with me if I didn't shave," he told his nephew who had come from Toronto to look after him in Cork. "I haven't shaved since I heard the news. Who knows, if I shave maybe she'll show up." And his wife's body did. The engineer found the bodies of his wife and son. The son didn't look mangled. His father was told it would be better if he didn't look at the wife's face. He didn't find the body of his teenaged daughter. And he thought to himself that if it is God's will to take a life, then it is also God's will to save life. "Why a miracle can't happen and save her?" he said to his nephew. He remembered what the Gardai had said about ocean currents bearing bodies, very possibly, towards Spain or France. Why not, he thought. Maybe, by a miracle, the daughter was alive. (In India, where he went from Cork, two astrologers assured him that his daughter was still alive. So did a Canadian astrologer when he got back to work. Water was a miraculous medium. He had heard a story of a man drowning in an Indian river, and then returning home alive to his family a year later. There were other stories. He liked especially the one in which a man died in a plane crash in Kashmir, and then two years after the "death," the man walked in the door of his house as though he'd never died in the crash.) He had posters made from his daughter's picture — posters as for a Missing Person — and a year after the crash he went to Málaga, Spain, and put the posters on walls.

The engineer was not the only one who believed that a daughter had survived the terrible fall. One mother brought dry clothes to Cork for her two missing girls. The girls were excellent swimmers. They would swim ashore and need clothes. The daughters were not retrieved by the rescue squads, and for a long time, for months in fact, the mother believed that they had made their way to an island and were waiting to be found.

For some relatives the process of identifying bodies of loved ones they had seen off cheerfully in Toronto just days before was grimly swift and grimly smooth. The young parents of a teenaged dancer rushed into London as early as Monday the 24th, and, dazed, located their daughter's photograph in the Air India office at Heathrow Airport. Their inconsolable grief made gut-wrenching international headline news.

They arrived in Cork, sped through the police identification process, and 20 had the body released to them. Their daughter had loved Toronto. Toronto, not India, had been her home. Toronto was where her soul should rest. The parents wanted to fly back with her casket right away. But the Air India office in Cork had its own cost-effective casket-freighting schedule. The parents were advised to fly home by themselves and wait for the body, which would be freighted into Toronto separately within three days, maybe four. But they would not part with their daughter a second time. They tried Aer-Lingus; they would fly Aer-Lingus if Aer-Lingus could fly the casket and them on the same flight. Aer-Lingus had its own problems; in the middle of this swell of disaster traffic, the local airline was grounded by a strike.

The parents tried the Canadian Embassy as a last resort. Many relatives perceived the Canadian officials as insensitive to their grief and as unhelpful. These officials were correct, but how could they know what was needed. The Canadian Embassy did have an office on the second floor of the hospital, however, and that's where the determined parents went. The Canadian officials served these parents coffee, and confided that they had instructions from External Affairs to get in touch with Ottawa as soon as the family arrived in Cork. The parents sat in that second-floor office while the Canadians called, first Ottawa, then on Ottawa's advice, the Canadian Forces base in West Germany, so that space for the family of living and dead could be freed that evening on a Hercules transport aircraft.

Months later, in Mississauga, the father recalled the soothing words of the Canadian official. "The diplomat said to me, 'The Hercules will be at the airport by 7:30. Get ready. But please don't tell anyone. There are a hundred and fifty other Canadians out there. We can't help anyone else. Let's go. Please get in my car and I'll drive you back to your hotel.' So he took us to the hotel, and he packed up my little suitcase. Then he took us down to the airport, to a small room where nobody could see us, and he waited with us until the Hercules came. Our daughter was lucky. We knew she would have fame, and she did. Her picture was in the papers. She was treated special."

The relatives whose loved ones' descriptions had not yet been matched with photographs of bodies spent many hours by the shores of Bantry Bay. Tony Dawson arranged coach trips. By island standards, Cork to Bantry is a longish way. The mourners left early in the morning and got back to their hotels late in the evening. The ocean calmed them. They felt close to the people they had lost. The water at the bay was still, still enough for good swimmers to stay afloat. They couldn't visualize churning seas or sharks, and the sailors who had plucked or winched or hefted mutilated bodies had been instructed not to talk; at least not about the gory part of their heroic job. The Laurences spent their most peaceful hours at the coast. They remembered their daughters had loved roses. One girl had loved red roses, the other white. They wanted to offer the sea red and white rose petals. There were gardens with rose bushes in Bantry, so they asked the owner of one garden, could they please pluck a rose. And the owner and her neighbours told the Laurences to take not one, not a bunch, but gardensful. In spite of the horror, these were radiant times. Thank God the plane went down off Ireland, the Laurences said. The Irish were sincere people. Anywhere else, in London or Toronto or Delhi, for instance, the same grief would have been unbearable.

But when they came back to Cork, to their hotels, the loss became nightly more real. And there were pictures to see, descriptions to listen to. Just in case. The relatives and the Gardai wanted to be sure, absolutely, positively sure, before they let a relative leave Cork. The Laurences looked through ninety pictures.

One of the relatives, Dr. Bal Gupta, a calm, methodical man not known to be emotional except for one outburst at the invisibility of Canadian officials, had lost his wife in the crash. He came back from Bantry Bay on Saturday evening and found a message from the hospital. The Gardai thought they had a match for Mrs. Gupta. He took the bus back to the hospital at once.

He had left his older son in Toronto, and brought with him his younger, a thirteen-year-old who'd suddenly, mysteriously, developed an ulcer. The boy, though sick, had come to Cork to look after his father. Father and son had arrived on Wednesday night. On Thursday Dr. Gupta had filled out forms. Friday had been a nightmare of waiting, but the waiting hadn't been the hospital's fault. He praised John Martin's Group for its generous-spirited management of the mammoth disaster. He praised the counsellor and the policeman who had stayed with him through the long, slow days of ordeal. He praised Kiran and Razia Doshi, the official and the unofficial Indian ambassadors. He had no praise, however, for the staff representing Canada.

"Up through Thursday," he said, "we didn't see the Canadians' faces, nobody's. . . . What happened was on Thursday night all of us were being bused back to our hotels from the hospital. It was very late, and I was probably the last one to come out. I came out and reporters surrounded us. I don't know if they were local TV crews, or CTV or what. They kept asking questions, such as 'Are you satisfied with the arrangements?' I told them that I was disappointed that more bodies could not be identified that day but that I understood why the Gardai had to be slow and meticulous. But when they asked me about the Canadian representatives . . . I don't know, I just burst out. I used some very unparliamentary language right there on tape! That night some Canadian official called me at the hotel, and the next morning, Friday morning, some Canadians came and apologized and said that they were working behind the scenes."

Saturday he and his son had gone on the bus to Bantry Bay. He had prayed on the ride over — he was a licensed Hindu priest back in Toronto — and he had prayed at the shore, tossed flowers in the water and prayed, and prayed again on the ride back to Cork. And in Cork there was the message: come to the hospital.

Dr. Gupta left his sick child in the hotel and rushed to face whatever alien ordeal. This is how he remembers the rest of Saturday night:

"First of all they [the Gardai] sat down and read from the post-mortem report. There were some discrepancies: the height was off by an inch, and the weight was a little different. But those things were all right, I thought, because of water absorption, etc. The description was about right. The clothes they described sounded the same as the *kurta* and *salivar* she'd been wearing. She'd dressed in a long *kurta* dress and tight pyjamas. The design seemed the same. Then the Gardai brought me a bag of effects. They showed me ornaments. I said, 'They don't belong to my wife. She didn't own those.' And they said, 'Well, anyway, we may as well show you the picture.' Then they showed me the picture. I said, 'This isn't my wife. This is my friend's wife. This is Mrs. Sharma.' The Gardai said. 'Well, it hasn't been a waste then. At least a body has been identified.'

"So we — the policeman and counsellor and I — came back up to the hall in the Nurses' Residence in the West Wing. They told us to wait. They said they would call us one by one. There were others waiting. What they had done was put the pictures up in a room, and they were asking people in small batches. Then all of a sudden, I don't know if somebody goofed or what, they opened the door and we went in and we looked at the pictures.

"#2 was Mrs. Sharma. #40 was the Sharmas' elder boy. #96 was Mrs. Radhakrishna. And then #97 was my wife's picture. I had no difficulty in identifying. The face was in reasonable shape, except for a cut. We identified two of the Sharma boys. We had some doubts about the third.

30

"Then I went to the policeman, and I said. 'That's my wife's body.' It was the same policeman. That was very good, you always dealt with the same policeman.

"Around seven or eight in the evening, they came to us and took down our description. Then they led us downstairs [to the East Wing] and showed us a bag of belongings. There were two rings, nothing else. There was no clothing.

"Then they showed us the body. The bodies were very well kept. The Gardai were identifying first through pictures, then they were bringing in the body from the morgue.

"If you requested they would leave you alone with the body in a little room. Otherwise, there were nuns there all the time.

"Then there was a lot of paperwork involved. I made a declaration about my wife's body. Then about the other bodies I'd identified. They made notes. We finished around eleven o'clock. Probably I was the last one to leave the hospital.

"I phoned home that night. I have a brother in Toronto. My brother's opinion was that if the body has been found, it should be taken to India for funeral rites. He said that he would call India and let my in-laws know.

"On Sunday the hospital organized a mixed service in the chapel. It was very beautiful. The Laurences read from the Bible, I read from the Gita. There were Muslim prayers. After that we had to do paperwork for the transportation of the body. I spent the whole of Sunday on the paperwork, and still it wasn't completed. The body could only be released by the police authorities. And the police authorities had to make sure that the body could be released. I was told to come back on Monday. I was making all the arrangements for the Sharma family, too. I phoned Sharma's brother in India, but the brother was already on his way to Ireland. Sunday night I had to take care of my son. He had fever, and I gave him antibiotics. I finished my wife's paperwork by lunchtime on Monday."

There were only two cases of initial misidentification. One husband matched memory with photograph and identified his wife's body, but the dental records on his wife's Yellow Form did not match the dental records from that body's post-mortem. Another body, misidentified and shipped on to London, was recalled in time for correct identification. One man, who had lost his wife and two small children, found his wife's body fairly quickly, but not those of his children. He remembered a year later that towards the end of the identification week when only a few bodies were left and he was hysterical with grief, the nuns had let him into a room so he could view the unclaimed bodies of children. He remembered (or misremembered) the nuns urging him to take two bodies as his own. He peered into faces, but the faces were alien. In the end, all the bodies retrieved were positively identified. This is unique in the history of air-crash disasters of this magnitude.

But some identifications took a long time. The identifications, for instance, of Ms. Rama Paul's brother's family. The whole Bhat family—mother, father, and two daughters, Bina and Tina—was wiped out. Rama Paul is a nurse at the Princess Margaret Hospital (for cancer patients) in Toronto. Soothing people in pain and in fear of death is her job. She is a remarkable person, remarkable in the Toronto Indo-Canadian community for her energy, her frankness and her ability to live a happy life on her own as a single woman. In this community, women in their forties are invariably wives or widows. Rama Paul devoted herself to her brother's family and to her patients at the Princess Margaret Hospital. She was so devoted, and so capable, that she had packed the Bhat family's suit-cases the night before the Air India flight and labelled each one with waterproof markers: BHAT, DOWNSVIEW, ONTARIO. She'd told the family what to wear before they'd driven to the airport: the suit he had graduated in for her brother, bridal red for her sister-in-law, and smart Canadian clothes she herself had bought for her nieces, who slept over more often in her apartment than they did in their own. When tragedy struck — and she had had premonitions strong enough and recurrent enough to urge her family even at the airport not to go — she became an excellent filler of the Pink and Yellow Forms. She knew what each member had worn, what object was in which part of each suitcase. With her nurse's memory for minutiae, she knew about birthmarks and scars. But she did not want to go to Cork as soon as she heard the dreaded, pre-intimated news.

"Air India wanted me to go when it happened," Rama Paul said. "They told me how many bodies had been found. I said to them, 'What guarantee can you give me that of the 329 who died, I'll find even one from my family. No, I don't want to go.' But I told them I wanted them to keep in touch with me. So they used to ring me up. They were very good about that.

"Then one Sunday morning, at about a quarter to five, the phone rang. I thought it was probably my sister in Australia. She sometimes calls. I get up at five on Sundays. It's a work day for me, and there aren't that many buses, so if I miss my bus I have to wait another half-hour. It wasn't my sister on the phone; it was a policeman from Cork. He said that he wanted to ask me some questions. I said, 'Look, I'm going off to work. I have to get ready to catch my bus. I'll be late if I answer your questions.' But he kept on asking questions: what was your niece wearing, and so on. I told him.

"He said, 'Miss Paul, we want you to fly immediately to Cork.'

"I said, 'No way. I'm not flying to Cork. I am going to work.'

"The policeman said, 'You have no choice.'   45

"I said, 'Look, Monday is my day off. I can fly on Monday.' But he wouldn't agree to that. So I warned him, 'I'm going to work now, and don't call me at work.'

"It was my bus time already, and I hadn't brushed my teeth or had a wash. I just slipped on my uniform and rushed to catch that bus. When I got to the hospital the nursing officer could tell that I was in a panic. In no time there were five calls from Cork, and three from Air India. The girls on the floor were really worried, because the callers identified themselves as police officers and kept asking what kind of passport does Miss Paul hold? I think between 7:30 and 9:30 that morning there must have been ten calls.

"Around twelve noon a man from Air India brought me a ticket. And early that evening Chandra's brother and I were off to Cork.

"When we got to Cork, we were treated like VIPs. We were the last relatives   50 to arrive, you see. There were a lot of people there, because they were putting on a big ceremony. A very beautiful ceremony. I think that's why they were rushing to identify bodies."

Rama Paul found three bodies in Cork. She had Kenyons air-freight those coffined bodies to India. At least the souls would finish the trip home.

Of the 132 bodies recovered from the sea, 60 were shipped to India, 13 to Canada, 2 to England, and 1 to the United States. There were 52 bodies cremated in Dublin, 2 bodies buried in Dublin and 2 buried in the serene, green city of Cork. Many had to leave the bodies of their loved ones on the ocean bed. Some day, they promised themselves, they would rent a ship to carry them to the exact spot where the *Emperor Kanishka* had torn through the waves. They would chant the final prayers for their lost families from the ship's deck, and in that way, calm their own bereft, bewildered souls.   [1987]

THINKING ABOUT THE TEXT

1. Compare this chapter to the Ireland section of Mukherjee's story. Does her fictional work seem significantly different in emphasis from her nonfiction one? What specific features of each come most to your mind as you consider this question?

2. Describing the relatives who came to Ireland, Blaise and Mukherjee write that "they were private, and noble, in their terrible grief" (para. 7). Which characters in Mukherjee's short story, if any, fit this description?

3. What do you suppose the two authors want to emphasize with the particular details and anecdotes they report? Where in this chapter, if anywhere, do Blaise and Mukherjee let their personal feelings show? Should they have expressed them more often? Why, or why not?

PAUL GESSELL
Revealing the "Family Man" Terrorist

At the time they were in Cork, relatives of the Air India flight's passengers did not know who or what had blown up the plane. In fact, they could not be certain that a "family man" had caused the disaster. Even at the time Blaise and Mukherjee wrote their book, no culprits had been precisely identified, although it was clear by then that Sikh terrorists had been involved. Not until fifteen years later were people arrested as major perpetrators. When Paul Gessell interviewed Clark Blaise for this article, two men had been charged. Subsequently, another one was. As we write, none of the three have yet gone to trial.

The search for a terrorist brought two famous authors to a Vancouver home, where they were greeted by a "self-appointed prophet," a bearded, turbaned Sikh with his hand on his kirpan, seemingly ready for battle.

It was 1986. The authors were the husband-and-wife duo of Clark Blaise and Bharati Mukherjee, two writers renowned for pummeling Canadian complacency with guerrilla-like strikes across the forty-ninth parallel. The two were in Canada researching a book about the bombing of an Air India Boeing 747 jet on June 23, 1985, that killed 329 passengers and crew off the coast of Ireland. The flight had originated in Toronto, and most of the dead were Canadian. The authors' attempts to discover who was responsible had brought them to this Vancouver home, where children watched *Star Trek* on a television in a room off the kitchen, where this once wealthy man in a striped rugby jersey held fast to his kirpan, ready to uphold his beliefs.

For the purposes of the book, *The Sorrow and the Terror*, the man was code-named "Sardar," a term of respect in the Punjab. The authors had also characterized him as "Dostoyevskian," saying his arrogant, obsessive, tragic demeanor reminded them of some character in a Russian novel. In a recent interview with the *Citizen*, Blaise revealed the true identity of Sardar. He is Ripudaman Singh Malik, charged on October 27 last year [2000] with first-degree murder for bombing Air India Flight 182. To reread the profile of Sardar in *The Sorrow and the Terror*, knowing now that he is Malik, the alleged murderer, is a chilling experience.

Obviously, Blaise and Mukherjee had their suspicions fifteen years ago about Malik. Sardar also had his suspicions.

"I know what you're doing and who you are," Sardar-Malik told the authors   5
fifteen years ago that day at the door as he grabbed his kirpan.

Malik's gesture startled the authors. According to Blaise: "If a fundamentalist Sikh draws his knife, he must draw blood. Usually, they do that and then they cut their own hand. He had his hand on it, but he didn't draw it."

The memory of that day is still sharp for Blaise. He was discussing Malik over lunch at the Chateau Laurier during a whistlestop in Ottawa to promote his newest book, *Time Lord*. It's all about that great Canadian invention of standard time, the creation of orderly time zones across the globe in the late nineteenth century. Much of the credit must go to Sir Sandford Fleming, the chief engineer of the Canadian Pacific Railway in its early days and the time lord of the title.

Time Lord is a book about a remarkable Canadian achievement, although Blaise and his wife, Mukherjee, apart from their literary prowess, are best known for highlighting Canadian failures. In 1980, with considerable fanfare, the two abandoned Canada, claiming it was too racist, and moved to the United States. Then in 1987, with *The Sorrow and the Terror*, they lobbed another grenade, essentially attacking Canadian society for being racist in its handling of the Air India bombing. According to a widely held theory in the Indo-Canadian community, Canadian authorities would have found the perpetrators of this crime much faster if the downed jet had been from British Airways or Alitalia and the passengers had been white-skinned, not brown-skinned. In the end, it took fifteen years for charges to be laid.

Malik and another Vancouver man, Ajaib Singh Bagri, were charged last fall. Their trial is to begin next February. Malik, in his 1986 interview with the authors, made allusions to "the end" being very near. "The end" for Malik, however, might still be a long time coming.

The man nicknamed Sardar was described in the book as being so rich that once, when a flight was delayed in Montreal, he bought an apartment block there sight unseen rather than waste time at the airport. He is portrayed in the book as a man who loves the business climate in Canada but loathes the country for its obsessions with drugs and sex. He was also rumored to have close ties to such prominent Sikh extremists as Inderjit Singh Reyat.

Malik was born in West Punjab in 1947 and, while still an infant, fled with his family from the new Muslim state of Pakistan to India.

"He was shaped by the knowledge that a man, no matter how hard working and blameless he might be, could lose his job, his house, even his nation, overnight," Blaise and Mukherjee wrote in *The Sorrow and the Terror*. "A man could lose everything he had worked and saved for, except his Sikh faith. Allegiance to anything but purity leads only to betrayal."

Embittered, Malik came to Canada as a young man. Before his baptism, before the beard and turban, he was, in his own words, "a bad Sikh." But as he matured, he became more devout and more wealthy. The wealth, however, began to disappear mysteriously.

The authors cited rumors that he "spent his money on Khalistan," the homeland Sikhs want to carve out of the Punjab. Malik claimed he lost money when the Indian government refused to allow him to travel there and "some Hindu" was given his business.

Malik agreed to be interviewed by the authors while he babysat his children. His wife was away on business. Malik, the book states, called himself liberated for allowing his wife so much independence.

"It is a scene of the starkest, most profound irony," the authors wrote. "The terrorist as family man. We have spent a winter in Toronto interviewing other family men, now widowed and childless, sitting in their vast empty houses."

These other family men were the grieving relatives of the bombing victims, many of whom were children starting summer vacations.

Much of Malik's time in 1986, he claimed, was spent planning Khalsa Sikh community projects designed to help less fortunate Sikhs in British Columbia.

"I go like a computer," Malik is quoted as saying. "I'm a heartless person. I'm a brain. I am a machine for converting Sikhs. I can be softspoken if necessary, and I can be very harsh. I use whatever is necessary."

The authors had set up the interview claiming they were writing about financially successful Indo-Canadians. But within thirty minutes of their interview request, Malik had secretly checked them out and knew they were really hunting terrorists. He still let them in the door and talked for three hours.

"He has kept us here, though he senses we are enemies, because we can engage him in ideas," the book said. "The scene . . . is virtually Russian in its intensity, its overtones of zealous commitment to courses of action rooted in piety. If there is a word to describe Sardar, it is Dostoyevskian."

Fast forward to the present and the Chateau Laurier, where Blaise reminisces about that encounter with Malik. The memories animate Blaise more than the discussion of *Time Lord*. "He [Malik] said, 'I know I am finished. I know that I am washed up, but I know I have left my mark.'"

Blaise, too, wants to leave a mark but seems to fear that such novels as *Lunar Attractions* or his many collections of short stories about Quebec, Florida, India, and other places are not enough.

He is a Canadian who was born in North Dakota and raised in the United States but came to Canada as an adult to tap his French-Canadian roots. He still feels Canadian, despite leaving the country twenty-one years ago. His wife, originally from India, prefers the United States to Canada, where she was horrified by the "Paki-bashers" of the 1970s in Toronto. The couple now lives in San Francisco.

"She was under a lot of psychological stress and had no literary visibility here," says Blaise. "As soon as she got to the States, she became a major force and I lost whatever force I had."

25

But the publication of *Time Lord* by the large firm Alfred A. Knopf Canada has put Blaise back in the spotlight. The book is garnering positive reviews on both sides of the Atlantic and is opening the door to other publishing opportunities.

"This book is kind of a resurgence, literally a renaissance, for me," says Blaise as he sips a glass of white wine.

Finally, Blaise thinks he, too, will be able to leave his mark.   [2001]

THINKING ABOUT THE TEXT

1. Blaise admits that he and Mukherjee engaged in two acts of duplicity. They misled Malik about why they were interviewing him, and they disguised Malik's name in their book. Do both these acts seem ethical to you? Why, or why not?

2. Of all the details you learn about Malik, which do you think most significant? Why?

3. As Gessell notes, Blaise and Mukherjee have suggested that Canadian authorities' own racism limited the hunt for the bombers. Whatever the truth of this allegation, do you think racism has played or could play a similar role in American investigations of disasters? Explain.

SAM HUSSEINI
Profile in Unfairness

In "The Management of Grief," Shaila becomes more distrustful of Sikhs because the plane crash appears to have been caused by members of that religion. Similarly, in real life, particular groups have become objects of suspicion when terrorism occurs or seems possible. Immediately following the Oklahoma City bombing, for instance, many Americans assumed that Arabs were responsible. The same suspicion arose when TWA Flight 800 crashed in 1996. If terrorism is to be thwarted, must airlines subject people of certain cultures to special scrutiny? Is such treatment ethical? Sam

Husseini, a consultant to the American-Arab Anti-Discrimination Committee, addresses these issues in the following opinion piece. It was published in the November 24, 1996, issue of the Washington Post, *four months after the TWA crash.*

The Gore Commission on Aviation Safety and Security, formed in the wake of the TWA 800 crash, made twenty recommendations — virtually all of which deal with security issues. Most troubling, the commission recommended — and on October 9 Clinton signed into law — a computer passenger "profiling" system to be created by the FAA in conjunction with Northwest Airlines. This pilot program is supposed to serve as a model for other airlines to adopt. If your "profile" fits that of a terrorist, you will undergo more questions and search than other passengers. It's a law that could make institutionalized discrimination more prevalent.

There's an imbalance in the commission's work fueled by fear of terrorism. Most plane crashes are not the result of terrorist attack. The best available evidence on the TWA crash now suggests that mechanical failure, not a bomb, was responsible. The commission's rush to judgment after the events of last July has come at the expense of civil rights in general.

Last August Laura Fadil, a nursing student at Yale University, went to the Newark airport for a flight to visit her relatives in Haifa, Israel, for the first time. As she got to the ticket counter of El Al, the national airline of Israel, security personnel asked her what kind of name "Fadil" was. When she told them it was an Arab name, she was taken to a room and questioned for thirty minutes. She was asked "If you're a student, how could you afford the plane ticket?" and "What's the amount of your scholarship?" Finally, she was told, "You're a security risk." Fadil offered to let the El Al officials hand search her bags, but she was ignored. Instead, she was given a ticket with another airline for the next day. Outraged she came to the American-Arab Anti-Discrimination Committee, where I work, with her story.

"I was raised as an American — we're used to rights," she says. "The experience was so foreign to me — to be treated that way, not because of anything I did. It was extremely humiliating. I don't think I'll ever forget it."

This type of thing isn't supposed to happen any more. "In the past, security 5 officers have sometimes used a crude profile consisting mainly of one factor, race, to single out minorities for special searches," the *New York Times* recently editorialized, implying that profiling has been abandoned.

It hasn't been. After the Oklahoma City bombing in April 1995, Abraham Ahmad was traveling from Oklahoma to Jordan to visit family. He was deemed a suspect in the bombing because of his ethnicity and travel destination. Law enforcement authorities detained and questioned him repeatedly over three days. He was stopped in Chicago and handcuffed and unnecessarily paraded through the London airport. He was made to answer questions about his religious practices. He was strip searched. Eventually he got an apology and was allowed to go on his way

In June, within twenty-four hours after the bombing of the U.S. military residence in Saudi Arabia, Lilia Tawasil and her daughter Zee traveled from the

Philippines to San Francisco. On arrival, U.S. Customs officials asked them about the veils they were wearing, about their religion, about their prayer rug. Lilia Tawasil later told me that she and her daughter were asked for numerous forms of identification, then taken to a room where a security agent frisked her — a grandmother of three — all because she was a Muslim wearing a veil. The Customs Service later apologized for not explaining why she was searched.

I myself was singled out three times for baggage searches while traveling from the Mideast to the United States through Europe in the summer of 1993 on a U.S. carrier.

This is what happens when "profiling" is put in practice. The Customs Service denies that it uses profiling but acknowledges that it does "passenger analysis." Whatever you call it, the practice seems to result in searches based on stereotypes. As the American Civil Liberties Union recently put it, "at the airport ticket counter, passengers check only their luggage, not their rights to personal security, privacy, and equality."

The Gore Commission says it "will establish an advisory board on civil liber- 10 ties questions that arise from the development and use of profiling systems." But that sounds like these concerns will be at best an afterthought. The FAA recently stated that none of the criteria of a profiling system they are developing with Northwest Airlines are based on "race, religion, gender or personal appearance" — but declined to say whether place of birth or travel history would be factors. So, it's possible that anyone who was born in or has visited an Arab country could be singled out when they're trying to fly from Pittsburgh to Los Angeles. This would be de facto discrimination.

And while "profiling" is overly broad from a civil rights perspective, it is overly narrow from a security perspective. Profiling, for example, would probably not have zeroed in on the white seminarian who recently pled guilty to trying to board a plane in Tampa with hand grenades. He was caught at a metal detector.

Still, some are all too willing to toss away rights for a false sense of security. *New York Times* columnist Thomas Friedman recently complained that it was too easy for him to get his bags through security: "I was going to TEHERAN, IRAN," Friedman emphasized, as if it belonged on another planet, "and security agents let some yo-yo load my suitcase without a tag or a search. On top of that, I look like [convicted bomber] Ramzi Yousef's twin brother!"

USA Today headlined a recent story "Improving Airport Security: Profiling May Be as Important as Technology." El Al, the airline that developed profiling and refused to seat Laura Fadil, was singled out for praise. Former El Al security official Arik Arad was quoted as saying, "Profiling — asking specific questions to identify travelers who pose the highest security risks — is the most valuable weapon in the war against terrorism." The paper reported that the Israeli carrier's alumni "now teach the airline's methods to other carriers." Is that supposed to be a good thing — to emulate a country that has sacrificed civil liberties in pursuit of illusory security? Since the TWA 800 crash, Arad has been a media darling, appearing on such shows as "This Week with David Brinkley."

In covering the investigation of the cause of the TWA crash, the big media outlets have focused on the apparent precedent of the bombing of Pan Am flight 103 over Lockerbie, Scotland, in 1988. Given the inconclusive results of the TWA 800 inquiry so far, plane crashes related to mechanical failures seem more relevant. For example, a Boeing 747-100 plane—the same kind of plane as TWA 800—exploded and crashed near Madrid in 1976. The plane had previously been owned by TWA and sold to the Iranian Air Force. The *Seattle Times* reported this summer that investigators compiled evidence that a fuel leak ignited by an electrical spark may have caused the explosion but were never able to say definitively what caused the crash.

Of course, the fact that TWA 800 might have been the result of a mechanical failure doesn't mean that terrorist attacks aren't possible. But in seeking to protect ourselves from terrorism and mechanical failures, we should recall the words of Thurgood Marshall: "History teaches that grave threats to liberty often come in times of urgency, when constitutional rights seem too extravagant to endure."

That seems to have been too often forgotten since the crash of TWA 800. In a recent *NBC Nightly News* segment, reporter Martin Fletcher noted that one of El Al's criteria for a suspicious profile is "young, dark-skinned men." Still, Fletcher reported approvingly, "Any airline can be as safe as El Al, security experts said today. They just need the money and the commitment."

Not to mention the brazenness to single out people because of the color of their skin.   [1996]

THINKING ABOUT THE TEXT

1. At the end of his article, Husseini suggests that profiling amounts to "brazenness." What other terms might he use to label the practice he is criticizing? How does he support his argument? Evaluate the case he makes. Does he use anecdotes about specific people as effectively as Blaise and Mukherjee do? What would you say to someone who criticizes him for failing to suggest alternative methods of preventing terrorism?

2. Husseini works for the American-Arab Anti-Discrimination Committee and is presumably of Arab descent. In what ways, if any, does his background matter to you as he criticizes the Israeli airline El Al?

3. In Mukherjee's story, Shaila is more suspicious of Sikhs after the plane crash. Do you suppose Husseini would fault her for being so? Why, or why not? What would you say to someone who argues that the arrest of Sikhs for the real-life Air India disaster indicates that the airline should have profiled Sikhs more in the first place?

WRITING ABOUT ISSUES

1. Write an essay comparing Shaila with another character in Mukherjee's story who has lost a family member in the plane crash. Are the differences between these two characters or their similarities more striking? Refer to specific acts and words of each.

2. Imagine that you are the present-day assistant editor of a newspaper in your hometown. Your boss, the editor, asks your advice: Should the newspaper remind its readers of the 1985 Air India disaster? If so, what are some things about it that are important to emphasize? Write a memo to your boss addressing these questions by referring to at least two of the texts in this cluster.

3. At one point in "The Management of Grief," Shaila claims to "flutter between worlds" (para. 85). Write an essay discussing at least one specific way in which this phrase applies to you. Be sure to identify what you mean by *worlds*.

4. Write an essay explaining how a particular disaster brought a certain cultural issue to the fore and what your position on the issue is. Define what you mean by *culture*, and support the position you express. To discuss the disaster in detail, you may need to do research in the library. If you wish, refer in your essay to one or more of the texts in this cluster.

A WEB ASSIGNMENT

At the *Making Literature Matter* Web site, link to the site of the Sikh Mediawatch and Resource Task Force (SMART). Explore various features of the site, including some of the newspaper articles it links to. Determine what images of Sikhs this organization is trying to counter and what images of Sikhs it promotes. Then write an essay in which you speculate on what the organization might say about one of the texts in this cluster. Support your speculation by referring to specific details of the site and of the text.

Visit www.bedfordstmartins.com/makinglitmatter

MAKING LITERATURE MATTER
FOR SEPTEMBER 11, 2001

WILLIAM BUTLER YEATS, "The Second Coming"
W. H. AUDEN, "September 1, 1939"
ADAM ZAGAJEWSKI, "Try to Praise the Mutilated World"

The most conspicuous disaster of recent times is the September 11, 2001, attack on the World Trade Center and the Pentagon. With the sudden and violent death of thousands, the world had to confront mortality in its most horrifying light. For help in working through their shock and grief, many turned to literature. Certain poems were passed from friend to friend and circulated through cyberspace. We present three of these. The first two come from the first half of the twentieth century, and each broods about crises that afflicted the world then. The last poem is more recent and calls for optimism, but even this text reflects its Polish author's consciousness of his nation's long, troubled history. As you read these poems, think about why, after September 11, each one newly mattered.

BEFORE YOU READ

What are your memories of September 11, 2001? What helped you in your efforts to cope with the events of that day?

WILLIAM BUTLER YEATS
The Second Coming

William Butler Yeats (1865–1939) was one of the most revered and influential modern poets, winning the Nobel Prize for literature in 1923. He was born in Dublin, Ireland, and although he spent part of his childhood in London, he is closely associated with his native country. Besides writing poetry, he cofounded Dublin's Abbey Theatre and wrote books of literary criticism along with treatises on mystical philosophy. Yeats was also strongly involved in Irish politics. Both in his literary works and in his civic life, he was dedicated to resurrecting Irish folklore traditions and overthrowing British rule. In 1922, he was even elected as a senator for the newly established Irish Free Republic.

Some of Yeats's writing was more personal than political. Several of his poems mourn his troubled romantic relationship with the Irish rebel Maud Gonne, who eventually married another man. But certainly "The Second Coming" shows Yeats's interest in using poetry to comment on national and even international events. This particular poem, included in Yeats's 1921 book Michael Robartes and the Dancer, *reflects his concern over recent political violence, including World War I, the Russian Revolution of 1917, and of course Great Britain's efforts to keep Ireland under its control. To express his anguish, Yeats draws on Christian narratives of Jesus and the Apocalypse. But he borrows, too, from Eastern religions that see the history of the universe as cyclical, and he also refers to the Egyptian legend of the Sphinx. In the years since the poem's publication, several lines from it have become famous, serving as titles of literary works and as quotations appropriate for disastrous occasions. For many readers, the poem foreshadowed the rise of fascism in Europe during the 1920s and 1930s. With the September 11, 2001, attacks, "The Second Coming" struck many as relevant again.*

Turning and turning in the widening gyre°
The falcon cannot hear the falconer;
Things fall apart; the center cannot hold;
Mere anarchy is loosed upon the world,

gyre: Circle or spiral.

The blood-dimmed tide is loosed, and everywhere   5
The ceremony of innocence is drowned;
The best lack all conviction, while the worst
Are full of passionate intensity.

Surely some revelation is at hand;
Surely the Second Coming is at hand;   10
The Second Coming! Hardly are those words out
When a vast image out of *Spiritus Mundi*°
Troubles my sight: somewhere in sands of the desert
A shape with lion body and the head of a man,
A gaze blank and pitiless as the sun,   15
Is moving its slow thighs, while all about it
Reel shadows of the indignant desert birds.
The darkness drops again; but now I know
That twenty centuries of stony sleep
Were vexed to nightmare by a rocking cradle,   20
And what rough beast, its hour come round at last,
Slouches towards Bethlehem to be born?   [1921]

Spiritus Mundi: Spirit of the universe.

THINKING ABOUT THE TEXT

1. Many people associate the phrase "the second coming" with the return of Jesus, whom they see as the Messiah. In what ways, if any, does the poem reinforce this definition? In what ways, if any, does the poem complicate it?

2. The poem consists of just two stanzas. What are the key differences between them?

3. What does the speaker seem certain about? Uncertain about? What questions do *you* have after reading the poem? Do you think the poem would be more effective if it answered these questions? Explain.

4. One of the most quoted statements from the poem is "The best lack all conviction, while the worst / Are full of passionate intensity" (lines 7–8). What current situations could this statement be applied to?

5. Look up the word *apocalypse* in a dictionary or encyclopedia. To what extent, and in what ways, does it apply to the scenes described in this poem?

W. H. AUDEN
September 1, 1939

Wystan Hugh Auden (1907–1973) was born in England and is widely regarded as the finest English poet of the twentieth century. Yet he moved to the United States in 1939, became an American citizen, and spent his remaining years living alternately in this country and Austria. Auden's reputation as a poet soared in the 1930s, especially with the publication of his second book, Poems, *at the beginning of the decade. In this period of his career, he was much influenced by psychoanalysis and Marxism. During the late 1930s, his leftist sympathies led him to join what was ultimately a losing cause, the fight against Fascist rebels in Spain. The following poem, written in New York City, expresses Auden's despair over the September 1, 1939, Nazi invasion of Poland, which he saw as yet another triumph of Fascism. After World War II, Auden changed his thinking in various ways. For one thing, he looked more to Christianity; moreover, he altered or renounced several of his poems. These include the one you are about to read, which he revised a number of times and then decided to omit from collections of his verse. Nevertheless, many literary anthologies have featured it, and it circulated widely in the wake of the September 11, 2001, attack.*

I sit in one of the dives
On Fifty-second Street
Uncertain and afraid
As the clever hopes expire
Of a low dishonest decade: 5
Waves of anger and fear
Circulate over the bright
And darkened lands of the earth,
Obsessing our private lives;
The unmentionable odour of death   10
Offends the September night.

Accurate scholarship can
Unearth the whole offence
From Luther until now
That has driven a culture mad,   15
Find what occurred at Linz,
What huge imago made
A psychopathic god:
I and the public know
What all schoolchildren learn,   20
Those to whom evil is done
Do evil in return.

Exiled Thucydides knew
All that a speech can say
About Democracy,   25
And what dictators do,
The elderly rubbish they talk
To an apathetic grave;
Analysed all in his book,

The enlightenment driven away,   30
The habit-forming pain,
Mismanagement and grief:
We must suffer them all again.

Into this neutral air
Where blind skyscrapers use   35
Their full height to proclaim
The strength of Collective Man,
Each language pours its vain
Competitive excuse:
But who can live for long   40
In an euphoric dream;
Out of the mirror they stare,
Imperialism's face
And the international wrong.

Faces along the bar   45
Cling to their average day:
The lights must never go out,
The music must always play,
All the conventions conspire
To make this fort assume   50
The furniture of home;
Lest we should see where we are,
Lost in a haunted wood,
Children afraid of the night
Who have never been happy or good.   55

The windiest militant trash
Important Persons shout
Is not so crude as our wish:
What mad Nijinsky wrote
About Diaghilev   60
Is true of the normal heart;
For the error bred in the bone
Of each woman and each man
Craves what it cannot have,
Not universal love   65
But to be loved alone.

From the conservative dark
Into the ethical life
The dense commuters come,
Repeating their morning vow;   70
"I will be true to the wife,
I'll concentrate more on my work,"

And helpless governors wake
To resume their compulsory game:
Who can release them now,   7
Who can reach the deaf,
Who can speak for the dumb?

All I have is a voice
To undo the folded lie,
The romantic lie in the brain   8
Of the sensual man-in-the-street
And the lie of Authority
Whose buildings grope the sky:
There is no such thing as the State
And no one exists alone;   8
Hunger allows no choice
To the citizen or the police;
We must love one another or die.

Defenceless under the night
Our world in stupor lies;   9
Yet, dotted everywhere,
Ironic points of light
Flash out wherever the Just
Exchange their messages:
May I, composed like them   95
Of Eros and of dust,
Beleaguered by the same
Negation and despair,
Show an affirming flame.   [1940]

THINKING ABOUT THE TEXT

1. Auden wrote this poem in New York City. In fact, he begins it by mentioning a bar there: "I sit in one of the dives / On Fifty-second Street." How important to the poem is its urban setting? Refer to specific lines.

2. Auden felt moved to write the poem by the Nazi invasion of Poland. In what lines, if any, do you sense he is referring directly or indirectly to this event?

3. Which physical senses does this poem employ? Again, refer to specific lines. Does one of the senses come to figure more prominently than the others?

4. Why do you think Auden describes the "points of light" as "Ironic" (line 92)? You might need to look up the word *ironic* in a dictionary.

5. Do you agree that "We must love one another or die" (line 88)? Why, or why not?

MAKING COMPARISONS

1. Yeats's poem ends with a question, Auden's with a wish. How significant is this difference?
2. Does Auden's poem seem more hopeful than Yeats's? Refer to specific lines in each text.
3. Do Yeats and Auden seem equally concerned with establishing a large historical framework for their subjects? Again, refer to specific lines in each text.

ADAM ZAGAJEWSKI
Try to Praise the Mutilated World

Translated by Clare Cavanaugh

Born in the Ukraine, Adam Zagajewski (b. 1945) grew up in Poland and became one of that country's dissident writers during the last years of its Communist regime. Although he has kept a home in France since 1982 and has taught at the University of Houston since 1988, his writing continues to reflect his sensitivity to Polish history. Prose by Zagajewski available in English translation includes a memoir, Another Beauty (2000), *along with two collections of essays,* Solitude and Solidarity (1990) *and* Two Cities (1995). *English versions of his poetry volumes include* Tremor (1985), Canvas (1991), Mysticism for Beginners (1997), *and* Without End: New and Selected Poems (2002), *which features "Try to Praise the Mutilated World." Soon after the September 11, 2001, attacks, this poem drew much attention. When* New Yorker *poetry editor Alice Quinn put it on the last page of the magazine's issue about the disaster, it was widely read, and then it was broadly circulated on the Internet. Ironically, Zagajewski had written the poem two years before. "I was born into a mutilated world, right after World War II," he said in a* USA Today *interview, "and the feeling that we tread on a frail ground has never left me."*

Try to praise the mutilated world.
Remember June's long days,
and wild strawberries, drops of wine, the dew.
The nettles that methodically overgrow
the abandoned homesteads of exiles.   5
You must praise the mutilated world.
You watched the stylish yachts and ships;
one of them had a long trip ahead of it,
while salty oblivion awaited others.
You've seen the refugees heading nowhere,   10
you've heard the executioners sing joyfully.

You should praise the mutilated world.
Remember the moments when we were together
in a white room and the curtain fluttered.
Return in thought to the concert where music flared.   15
You gathered acorns in the park in autumn
and leaves eddied over the earth's scars.
Praise the mutilated world
and the gray feather a thrush lost,
and the gentle light that strays and vanishes   20
and returns.   [2001]

THINKING ABOUT THE TEXT

1. What is the effect of addressing the poem to a "you"? Can you identify with this "you"? Why, or why not?

2. What specific things does the poem identify as worthy of praise? What, if anything, do they have in common?

3. Where does Zagajewski repeat, and yet vary, the first line? How significant are the changes he makes in it?

4. The speaker declares, "You've seen the refugees heading nowhere, / you've heard the executioners sing joyfully" (lines 10–11). What would you say to readers who insist that they haven't seen or heard such people?

5. Near the start, the poem refers to June. Near the end, it refers to autumn. Why this shift of seasons, do you think?

MAKING COMPARISONS

1. Does the term *mutilated* seem equally applicable to the worlds evoked by Yeats, Auden, and Zagajewski? Refer to specific lines in each poem.

2. Do all three of these poems balance abstract language with concrete detail? Again, refer to specific lines in each.

3. Zagajewski wrote his poem many years after Yeats and Auden wrote theirs. Does Zagajewski's poem seem more contemporary than the other two? Explain.

WRITING ABOUT ISSUES

1. Choose Yeats's, Auden's, or Zagajewski's poem, and write an essay speculating on the reasons it had such wide appeal after the attack of September 11, 2001. What about this poem, do you suppose, made it matter to people then? Focus on one or two particular possibilities.

2. Imagine Zagajewski's title, "Try to Praise the Mutilated World," as advice he is giving to Yeats and Auden. Then write an essay in which you use Yeats's or Auden's poem to speculate on what its author's response to

Zagajewski might be. Support your speculation by referring to specific lines by Zagajewski and by your other chosen author.

3. Write an essay in which you recall an occasion when a particular piece of writing helped you deal with some sort of disaster, personal or social. Focus on explaining what, specifically, about this work proved helpful to you, and how. If possible, include a copy of the piece with your essay.

4. In the aftermath of the September 11, 2001, disaster, people circulated lots of poems besides the three presented here. Identify another poem in this book that you think would have been worth circulating at the time, and write an essay defending your choice.

APPENDIX 1

Critical Approaches
to Literature

Exploring the topics of literary criticism can help readers understand the various ways literature can matter. One popular way to investigate critical approaches to literature is to group critics into schools. Critics who are primarily concerned with equality for women, for example, are often classified as feminist critics, and those concerned with the responses of readers are classified as reader-response critics. Likewise, critics who focus on the unconscious are said to belong to the psychoanalytic school, and those who analyze class conflicts belong to the Marxist school.

Classifying critics in this way is probably more convenient than precise. Few critics like to be pigeonholed or thought predictable, and many professional readers tend to be eclectic — that is, they use ideas from various schools to help them illuminate the text. Nevertheless, knowing something about contemporary schools of criticism can make you a more informed reader and help literature matter to you even more.

There is a commonsense belief that words mean just what they say — that to understand a certain passage in a text a reader simply needs to know what the words mean. But meaning is rarely straightforward. Scholars have been arguing over the meaning of passages in the Bible, in the Constitution, and in Shakespeare's plays for centuries without reaching agreement. Pinning down the exact meaning of words like *sin, justice,* and *love* is almost impossible, but even more daunting is the unacknowledged theory of reading that each person brings to any text, including literature. Some people who read the Bible or the Constitution, for example, believe in the literal meaning of the words, and some think the real meaning lies in the original intention of the writer, while others believe that the only meaning we can be sure of is our own perspective. For these latter readers, there is no objective meaning, and no absolutely true meaning is possible.

Indeed, a good deal of what a text means depends on the perspective that readers bring with them. Passages can be read effectively from numerous points of view. A generation ago most English professors taught their students to pay attention to the internal aspects of a poem and not to the poem's larger social and political contexts. So oppositions, irony, paradox, and coherence — not gender equality or social justice — were topics of discussion. Proponents of this approach were said to belong to the New Critical school. In the last twenty years or so, however, professors have put much more emphasis on the external aspects of interpretation, stressing social, political, cultural, sexual, and gender-based perspectives. Each one of these perspectives can give us a valuable window on a text, helping us see the rich possibilities of literature. Even though each approach can provide insights into a text, it also is blind to other textual elements. When we read in too focused a way, we can sometimes miss the opportunity to see what others see. Part of the excitement and challenge of making literature matter is an appreciation of both the diversity of perspectives that readers bring to their task and the remarkable ways reading and writing about literature help us see ourselves and our world in new and illuminating ways.

Contemporary Schools of Criticism

The following seven approaches are just a few of the many different literary schools or perspectives a reader can use in engaging a text. Think of them as intellectual tools or informed lenses that you can employ to enhance your interpretation of a particular literary text:

- New Criticism
- Feminist criticism
- Psychoanalytic criticism
- Marxist criticism
- Deconstruction
- Reader-response criticism
- Postcolonial criticism

NEW CRITICISM

New Criticism was developed over fifty years ago as a way to focus on "the text itself." Although it is no longer as popular as it once was, some of its principles are still widely accepted, especially the use of specific examples from the text as evidence for a particular interpretation. Sometimes called *close reading*, this approach does not see either the writer's intention or the reader's personal response as relevant. It is also uninterested in the text's social context, the spirit of the age, or its relevance to issues of gender, social justice, or oppression. These critics are interested, for example, in a poem's internal structure, images, symbols, metaphors, point of view, plot, and characterizations. Emphasis is placed on literary language — on the ways connotation, ambiguity, irony, and paradox all reinforce the meaning. In fact, how a poem means is inseparable from what it means. The primary method for judging the worth of a piece of literature is its organic unity or the complex way all the elements of a text contribute to the poem's meaning.

FEMINIST CRITICISM

Feminist criticism developed during the 1970s as an outgrowth of a resurgent women's movement. The goals of the feminist critic and the feminist political activist are similar—to contest the patriarchal point of view as the standard for all moral, aesthetic, political, and intellectual judgments and to assert that gender roles are primarily learned, not universal. They hope to uncover and challenge essentialist attitudes that hold it is normal for women to be kept in domestic, secondary, and subservient roles, and they affirm the value of a woman's experiences and perspectives in understanding the world.

PSYCHOANALYTIC CRITICISM

Psychoanalytic criticism began with Sigmund Freud's theories of the unconscious, especially the numerous repressed wounds, fears, unresolved conflicts, and guilty desires from childhood that can significantly affect behavior and mental health in our adult lives. Freud developed the tripart division of the mind into the ego (the conscious self), the superego (the site of what our culture has taught us about good and bad), and the id (the primitive unconscious and source of our sexual drive). Psychoanalytic critics often see literature as a kind of dream filled with symbolic elements that often mask their real meaning. Freud also theorized that young males were threatened by their fathers in the competition for the affection of their mothers. Critics are alert to the complex ways this Oedipal drama unfolds in literature.

MARXIST CRITICISM

Marxist criticism is based on the political and economic theories of Karl Marx. Marxists think that a society is propelled by its economy, which is manipulated by a class system. Most people, especially blue-collar workers (the proletariat), do not understand the complex ways their lives are subject to economic forces beyond their control. This false consciousness about history and material well-being prevents workers from seeing that their values have been socially constructed to keep them in their place. What most interests contemporary Marxists is the way ideology shapes our consciousness. And since literature both represents and projects ideology, Marxist critics see it as a way to unmask our limited view of society's structures.

DECONSTRUCTION

Deconstruction is really more a philosophical movement than a school of literary criticism, but many of its techniques have been used by Marxist and feminist literary critics to uncover important concepts they believe are hidden in texts. Made famous by the French philosopher Jacques Derrida, deconstruction's main tenet is that Western thought has divided the world into binary opposites. To gain a semblance of control over the complexity of human experience, we have constructed a world view where good is clearly at one end of a continuum and bad at the other. Additional examples of binary opposites include masculine and feminine, freedom and slavery, objective and subjective, mind and body, and presence and absence. According to Derrida, however, this arbitrary and illusory construct simply reflects the specific ideology of one culture. Far from being opposed to one another, masculinity and femininity, for example, are intimately interconnected, and traces of the feminine are to be found within the masculine. The concepts need each other for meaning to occur, an idea referred to as *differance*. Derrida also notes that language, far from being a neutral medium of communication, is infused with our biases, assumptions, and values—which leads some of us to refer to sexually active women as sluts and men as studs. One term is marginalized, and the other is privileged because our culture grants men more power than women in shaping the language that benefits them.

Thus, language filters, distorts, and alters our perception of the world. For deconstructors or deconstructive critics, language is not stable or reliable, and when closely scrutinized, it becomes slippery and ambiguous, constantly overflowing with implications, associations, and contradictions. For Derrida, this endless freeplay of meaning suggests that language is always changing, always in flux—especially so when we understand that words can be viewed from almost endless points of view or contexts. That is why deconstructionists claim that texts (or individuals or systems of thought) have no fixed definition, no center, no absolute meaning. And so one way to deconstruct or lay bare the arbitrary construction of a text is to show that the oppositions in the text are not really absolutely opposed, that outsiders can be seen to be insiders, and that words that seem to mean one thing can mean many things.

READER-RESPONSE CRITICISM

Reader-response criticism is often misunderstood to be simply giving one's opinion about a text: "I liked it," "I hate happy endings," "I think the characters were unrealistic." But reader-response criticism is actually more interested in why readers have certain responses. The central assumption is that texts do not come alive and do not mean anything until active readers engage them with specific assumptions about what reading is. New Critics think a reader's response is irrelevant because a text's meaning is timeless. But response critics, including feminists and Marxists, maintain that what a text means cannot be separated from the reading process used by readers as they draw on personal and literary experiences to make meaning. In other words, the text is not an object but an event that occurs in readers over time.

Response criticism includes critics who think that the reader's contribution to the making of meaning is quite small as well as critics who think that readers play a primary role in the process. Louise Rosenblatt is a moderate response critic since she thinks the contributions are about equal. Her transactive theory claims that the text guides our response, like a printed musical score that we adjust as we move through the text. She allows for a range of acceptable meanings as long as she can find reasonable textual support in the writing.

Response critics like Stanley Fish downplay individual responses, focusing instead on how communities influence our responses to texts. We probably all belong to a number of these interpretive communities (such as churches, universities, neighborhoods, political parties, and social class) and have internalized their interpretive strategies, their discourse, or their way of reading texts of all kinds. Fish's point is that we all come to texts already predisposed to read them in a certain way: we do not interpret stories, but we create them by using the reading tools and cultural assumptions we bring with us. Our reading then reveals what is in us more than what is in the text. We find what we expect to see.

POSTCOLONIAL CRITICISM

Postcolonial criticism, like feminist criticism, has developed because of the dramatic shrinking of the world and the increasing multicultural cast of our own country. It is mainly interested in the ways nineteenth-century European political domination affects the lives of people living in former colonies, especially the way the dominant culture becomes the norm and those without power are portrayed as inferior. Postcolonial critics often look for stereotypes in texts as well as in characters whose self-image has been damaged by being forced to see themselves as Other, as less than. As oppressed people try to negotiate life in both the dominant and the oppressed cultures, they can develop a double consciousness that leads to feelings of alienation and deep conflicts.

Working with the Critical Approaches

Keep these brief descriptions of the critical approaches in mind as you read the following story by James Joyce, one of the most important writers of the twentieth century. Joyce (1882–1941) was born in Ireland, although he spent most of his life in self-imposed exile on the European continent. "Counterparts" is from *Dubliners* (1914), a collection of stories set in the Irish city of his childhood years. (For more on James Joyce, see his story "Araby" on p. 828.)

JAMES JOYCE
Counterparts

The bell rang furiously and, when Miss Parker went to the tube, a furious voice called out in a piercing North of Ireland accent:

— Send Farrington here!

Miss Parker returned to her machine, saying to a man who was writing at a desk:

— Mr Alleyne wants you upstairs.

The man muttered *Blast him!* under his breath and pushed back his chair to   5 stand up. When he stood up he was tall and of great bulk. He had a hanging face, dark wine-coloured, with fair eyebrows and moustache: his eyes bulged forward slightly and the whites of them were dirty. He lifted up the counter and, passing by the clients, went out of the office with a heavy step.

He went heavily upstairs until he came to the second landing, where a door bore a brass plate with the inscription *Mr Alleyne*. Here he halted, puffing with labour and vexation, and knocked. The shrill voice cried:

—Come in!

The man entered Mr Alleyne's room. Simultaneously Mr Alleyne, a little man wearing gold-rimmed glasses on a cleanshaven face, shot his head up over a pile of documents. The head itself was so pink and hairless that it seemed like a large egg reposing on the papers. Mr Alleyne did not lose a moment:

—Farrington? What is the meaning of this? Why have I always to complain of you? May I ask you why you haven't made a copy of that contract between Bodley and Kirwan? I told you it must be ready by four o'clock.

—But Mr Shelley said, sir—

—*Mr Shelley said, sir.* . . . Kindly attend to what I say and not to what *Mr Shelley says, sir.* You have always some excuse or another for shirking work. Let me tell you that if the contract is not copied before this evening I'll lay the matter before Mr Crosbie. . . . Do you hear me now?

—Yes, sir.

—Do you hear me now? . . . Ay and another little matter! I might as well be talking to the wall as talking to you. Understand once for all that you get a half an hour for your lunch and not an hour and a half. How many courses do you want, I'd like to know. . . . Do you mind me, now?

—Yes, sir.

Mr Alleyne bent his head again upon his pile of papers. The man stared fixedly at the polished skull which directed the affairs of Crosbie & Alleyne, gauging its fragility. A spasm of rage gripped his throat for a few moments and then passed, leaving after it a sharp sensation of thirst. The man recognised the sensation and felt that he must have a good night's drinking. The middle of the month was passed and, if he could get the copy done in time, Mr Alleyne might give him an order on the cashier. He stood still, gazing fixedly at the head upon the pile of papers. Suddenly Mr Alleyne began to upset all the papers, searching for something. Then, as if he had been unaware of the man's presence till that moment, he shot up his head again, saying:

—Eh? Are you going to stand there all day? Upon my word, Farrington, you take things easy!

—I was waiting to see . . .

—Very good, you needn't wait to see. Go downstairs and do your work.

The man walked heavily towards the door and, as he went out of the room, he heard Mr Alleyne cry after him that if the contract was not copied by evening Mr Crosbie would hear of the matter.

He returned to his desk in the lower office and counted the sheets which remained to be copied. He took up his pen and dipped it in the ink but he continued to stare stupidly at the last words he had written: *In no case shall the said Bernard Bodley be* . . . The evening was falling and in a few minutes they would be lighting the gas: then he could write. He felt that he must slake the thirst in his throat. He stood up from his desk and, lifting the counter as before, passed out of the office. As he was passing out the chief clerk looked at him inquiringly.

—It's all right, Mr Shelley, said the man, pointing with his finger to indicate the objective of his journey.

The chief clerk glanced at the hat-rack but, seeing the row complete, offered no remark. As soon as he was on the landing the man pulled a shepherd's plaid cap out of his pocket, put it on his head and ran quickly down the rickety stairs. From the street door he walked on furtively on the inner side of the path towards the corner and all at once dived into a doorway. He was now safe in the dark snug of O'Neill's shop, and, filling up the little window that looked into the bar with his inflamed face, the colour of dark wine or dark meat, he called out:

—Here, Pat, give us a g.p., like a good fellow.

The curate brought him a glass of plain porter. The man drank it at a gulp and asked for a caraway seed. He put his penny on the counter and, leaving the curate to grope for it in the gloom, retreated out of the snug as furtively as he had entered it.

Darkness, accompanied by a thick fog, was gaining upon the dusk of Febru- 25
ary and the lamps in Eustace Street had been lit. The man went up by the houses until he reached the door of the office, wondering whether he could finish his copy in time. On the stairs a moist pungent odour of perfumes saluted his nose: evidently Miss Delacour had come while he was out in O'Neill's. He crammed his cap back again into his pocket and re-entered the office assuming an air of absent-mindedness.

—Mr Alleyne has been calling for you, said the chief clerk severely. Where were you?

The man glanced at the two clients who were standing at the counter as if to intimate that their presence prevented him from answering. As the clients were both male the chief clerk allowed himself a laugh.

—I know that game, he said. Five times in one day is a little bit. . . . Well, you better look sharp and get a copy of our correspondence in the Delacour case for Mr Alleyne.

This address in the presence of the public, his run upstairs and the porter he had gulped down so hastily confused the man and, as he sat down at his desk to get what was required, he realised how hopeless was the task of finishing his copy of the contract before half past five. The dark damp night was coming and he longed to spend it in the bars, drinking with his friends amid the glare of gas and the clatter of glasses. He got out the Delacour correspondence and passed out of the office. He hoped Mr Alleyne would not discover that the last two letters were missing.

The moist pungent perfume lay all the way up to Mr Alleyne's room. Miss 30
Delacour was a middle-aged woman of Jewish appearance. Mr Alleyne was said to be sweet on her or on her money. She came to the office often and stayed a long time when she came. She was sitting beside his desk now in an aroma of perfumes, smoothing the handle of her umbrella and nodding the great black feather in her hat. Mr Alleyne had swivelled his chair round to face her and thrown his right foot jauntily upon his left knee. The man put the corre- spondence on the desk and bowed respectfully but neither Mr Alleyne nor Miss Delacour took any notice of his bow. Mr Alleyne tapped a finger on the

correspondence and then flicked it towards him as if to say: *That's all right: you can go.*

The man returned to the lower office and sat down again at his desk. He stared intently at the incomplete phrase: *In no case shall the said Bernard Bodley be* . . . and thought how strange it was that the last three words began with the same letter. The chief clerk began to hurry Miss Parker, saying she would never have the letters typed in time for post. The man listened to the clicking of the machine for a few minutes and then set to work to finish his copy. But his head was not clear and his mind wandered away to the glare and rattle of the public-house. It was a night for hot punches. He struggled on with his copy, but when the clock struck five he had still fourteen pages to write. Blast it! He couldn't finish it in time. He longed to execrate aloud, to bring his fist down on something violently. He was so enraged that he wrote *Bernard Bernard* instead of *Bernard Bodley* and had to begin again on a clean sheet.

He felt strong enough to clear out the whole office singlehanded. His body ached to do something, to rush out and revel in violence. All the indignities of his life enraged him. . . . Could he ask the cashier privately for an advance? No, the cashier was no good, no damn good: he wouldn't give an advance. . . . He knew where he would meet the boys: Leonard and O'Halloran and Nosey Flynn. The barometer of his emotional nature was set for a spell of riot.

His imagination had so abstracted him that his name was called twice before he answered. Mr Alleyne and Miss Delacour were standing outside the counter and all the clerks had turned round in anticipation of something. The man got up from his desk. Mr Alleyne began a tirade of abuse, saying that two letters were missing. The man answered that he knew nothing about them, that he had made a faithful copy. The tirade continued: it was so bitter and violent that the man could hardly restrain his fist from descending upon the head of the manikin before him.

— I know nothing about any other two letters, he said stupidly.

— You — know — nothing. Of course you know nothing, said Mr Alleyne. Tell   35 me, he added, glancing first for approval to the lady beside him, do you take me for a fool? Do you think me an utter fool?

The man glanced from the lady's face to the little egg-shaped head and back again; and, almost before he was aware of it, his tongue had found a felicitous moment:

— I don't think, sir, he said, that that's a fair question to put to me.

There was a pause in the very breathing of the clerks. Everyone was astounded (the author of the witticism no less than his neighbours) and Miss Delacour, who was a stout amiable person, began to smile broadly. Mr Alleyne flushed to the hue of a wild rose and his mouth twitched with a dwarf's passion. He shook his fist in the man's face till it seemed to vibrate like the knob of some electric machine:

— You impertinent ruffian! You impertinent ruffian! I'll make short work of you! Wait till you see! You'll apologise to me for your impertinence or you'll quit the office instanter! You'll quit this, I'm telling you, or you'll apologise to me!

◆   ◆   ◆

He stood in a doorway opposite the office watching to see if the cashier   40
would come out alone. All the clerks passed out and finally the cashier came out
with the chief clerk. It was no use trying to say a word to him when he was with
the chief clerk. The man felt that his position was bad enough. He had been
obliged to offer an abject apology to Mr Alleyne for his impertinence but he
knew what a hornet's nest the office would be for him. He could remember the
way in which Mr Alleyne had hounded little Peake out of the office in order to
make room for his own nephew. He felt savage and thirsty and revengeful,
annoyed with himself and with everyone else. Mr Alleyne would never give him
an hour's rest; his life would be a hell to him. He had made a proper fool of himself this time. Could he not keep his tongue in his cheek? But they had never
pulled together from the first, he and Mr Alleyne, ever since the day Mr Alleyne
had overheard him mimicking his North of Ireland accent to amuse Higgins and
Miss Parker: that had been the beginning of it. He might have tried Higgins for
the money, but sure Higgins never had anything for himself. A man with two
establishments to keep up, of course he couldn't. . . . .

He felt his great body again aching for the comfort of the public-house. The
fog had begun to chill him and he wondered could he touch Pat in O'Neill's. He
could not touch him for more than a bob—and a bob was no use. Yet he must get
money somewhere or other: he had spent his last penny for the g.p. and soon it
would be too late for getting money anywhere. Suddenly, as he was fingering his
watch-chain, he thought of Terry Kelly's pawn-office in Fleet Street. That was the
dart! Why didn't he think of it sooner?

He went through the narrow alley of Temple Bar quickly, muttering to himself that they could all go to hell because he was going to have a good night of it.
The clerk in Terry Kelly's said *A crown!* but the consignor held out for six
shillings; and in the end the six shillings was allowed him literally. He came out
of the pawn-office joyfully, making a little cylinder of the coins between his
thumb and fingers. In Westmoreland Street the footpaths were crowded with
young men and women returning from business and ragged urchins ran here and
there yelling out the names of the evening editions. The man passed through the
crowd, looking on the spectacle generally with proud satisfaction and staring
masterfully at the office-girls. His head was full of the noises of tram-gongs and
swishing trolleys and his nose already sniffed the curling fumes of punch. As he
walked on he preconsidered the terms in which he would narrate the incident to
the boys:

—So, I just looked at him—coolly, you know, and looked at her. Then I
looked back at him again—taking my time, you know. *I don't think that that's a
fair question to put to me,* says I.

Nosey Flynn was sitting up in his usual corner of Davy Byrne's and, when he
heard the story, he stood Farrington a half-one, saying it was as smart a thing as
ever he heard. Farrington stood a drink in his turn. After a while O'Halloran and
Paddy Leonard came in and the story was repeated to them. O'Halloran stood tailors of malt, hot, all round and told the story of the retort he had made to the chief
clerk when he was in Callan's of Fownes's Street; but, as the retort was after the
manner of the liberal shepherds in the eclogues, he had to admit that it was not so

clever as Farrington's retort. At this Farrington told the boys to polish off that and have another.

Just as they were naming their poisons who should come in but Higgins! Of   45
course he had to join in with the others. The men asked him to give his version of it, and he did so with great vivacity for the sight of five small hot whiskies was very exhilarating. Everyone roared laughing when he showed the way in which Mr Alleyne shook his fist in Farrington's face. Then he imitated Farrington, saying, *And here was my nabs, as cool as you please,* while Farrington looked at the company out of his heavy dirty eyes, smiling and at times drawing forth stray drops of liquor from his moustache with the aid of his lower lip.

When that round was over there was a pause. O'Halloran had money but neither of the other two seemed to have any; so the whole party left the shop somewhat regretfully. At the corner of Duke Street Higgins and Nosey Flynn bevelled off to the left while the other three turned back towards the city. Rain was drizzling down on the cold streets and, when they reached the Ballast Office, Farrington suggested the Scotch House. The bar was full of men and loud with the noise of tongues and glasses. The three men pushed past the whining match-sellers at the door and formed a little party at the corner of the counter. They began to exchange stories. Leonard introduced them to a young fellow named Weathers who was performing at the Tivoli as an acrobat and knockabout *artiste*. Farrington stood a drink all round. Weathers said he would take a small Irish and Apollinaris. Farrington, who had definite notions of what was what, asked the boys would they have an Apollinaris too; but the boys told Tim to make theirs hot. The talk became theatrical. O'Halloran stood a round and then Farrington stood another round, Weathers protesting that the hospitality was too Irish. He promised to get them in behind the scenes and introduce them to some nice girls. O'Halloran said that he and Leonard would go but that Farrington wouldn't go because he was a married man; and Farrington's heavy dirty eyes leered at the company in token that he understood he was being chaffed. Weathers made them all have just one little tincture at his expense and promised to meet them later on at Mulligan's in Poolbeg Street.

When the Scotch House closed they went round to Mulligan's. They went into the parlour at the back and O'Halloran ordered small hot specials all round. They were all beginning to feel mellow. Farrington was just standing another round when Weathers came back. Much to Farrington's relief he drank a glass of bitter this time. Funds were running low but they had enough to keep them going. Presently two young women with big hats and a young man in a check suit came in and sat at a table close by. Weathers saluted them and told the company that they were out of the Tivoli. Farrington's eyes wandered at every moment in the direction of one of the young women. There was something striking in her appearance. An immense scarf of peacock-blue muslin was wound round her hat and knotted in a great bow under her chin; and she wore bright yellow gloves, reaching to the elbow. Farrington gazed admiringly at the plump arm which she moved very often and with much grace; and when, after a little time, she answered his gaze he admired still more her large dark brown eyes. The oblique staring expression in them fascinated him. She glanced at him once or twice and, when the party was leaving the room, she brushed against his chair and said *O, pardon!* in a London accent. He watched her leave the room in the hope that she would look back at him, but he was disappointed. He cursed his want of money and cursed all the rounds he had stood, particularly all the whiskies and Apollinaris which he had stood to Weathers. If there was one thing that he hated it was a sponge. He was so angry that he lost count of the conversation of his friends.

When Paddy Leonard called him he found that they were talking about feats of strength. Weathers was showing his biceps muscle to the company and boasting so much that the other two had called on Farrington to uphold the national honour. Farrington pulled up his sleeve accordingly and showed his biceps muscle to the company. The two arms were examined and compared and finally it was agreed to have a trial of strength. The table was cleared and the two men rested their elbows on it, clasping hands. When Paddy Leonard said *Go!* each was to try to bring down the other's hand on to the table. Farrington looked very serious and determined.

The trial began. After about thirty seconds Weathers brought his opponent's hand slowly down on to the table. Farrington's dark wine-coloured face flushed darker still with anger and humiliation at having been defeated by such a stripling.

— You're not to put the weight of your body behind it. Play fair, he said.　　50

— Who's not playing fair? said the other.

— Come on again. The two best out of three.

The trial began again. The veins stood out on Farrington's forehead, and the pallor of Weathers' complexion changed to peony. Their hands and arms trembled under the stress. After a long struggle Weathers again brought his opponent's hand slowly on to the table. There was a murmur of applause from the spectators. The curate, who was standing beside the table, nodded his red head towards the victor and said with loutish familiarity:

— Ah! that's the knack!

— What the hell do you know about it? said Farrington fiercely, turning on　　55
the man. What do you put in your gab for?

— Sh, sh! said O'Halloran, observing the violent expression of Farrington's face. Pony up, boys. We'll have just one little smahan more and then we'll be off.

A very sullen-faced man stood at the corner of O'Connell Bridge waiting for the little Sandymount tram to take him home. He was full of smouldering anger and revengefulness. He felt humiliated and discontented; he did not even feel drunk; and he had only twopence in his pocket. He cursed everything. He had done for himself in the office, pawned his watch, spent all his money; and he had not even got drunk. He began to feel thirsty again and he longed to be back again in the hot reeking public-house. He had lost his reputation as a strong man, having been defeated twice by a mere boy. His heart swelled with fury and, when he thought of the woman in the big hat who had brushed against him and said *Pardon!* his fury nearly choked him.

His tram let him down at Shelbourne Road and he steered his great body along in the shadow of the wall of the barracks. He loathed returning to his home.

When he went in by the side-door he found the kitchen empty and the kitchen fire nearly out. He bawled upstairs:

—Ada! Ada!

His wife was a little sharp-faced woman who bullied her husband when he was sober and was bullied by him when he was drunk. They had five children. A little boy came running down the stairs.

—Who is that? said the man, peering through the darkness.

—Me, pa.

—Who are you? Charlie?

—No, pa. Tom.

—Where's your mother?

—She's out at the chapel.

—That's right. . . . Did she think of leaving any dinner for me?

—Yes, pa. I—

—Light the lamp. What do you mean by having the place in darkness? Are the other children in bed?

The man sat down heavily on one of the chairs while the little boy lit the lamp. He began to mimic his son's flat accent, saying half to himself: *At the chapel. At the chapel, if you please!* When the lamp was lit he banged his fist on the table and shouted:

—What's for my dinner?

—I'm going . . . to cook it, pa, said the little boy.

The man jumped up furiously and pointed to the fire.

—On that fire! You let the fire out! By God, I'll teach you to do that again!

He took a step to the door and seized the walking-stick which was standing behind it.

—I'll teach you to let the fire out! he said, rolling up his sleeve in order to give his arm free play.

The little boy cried O, *pa!* and ran whimpering round the table, but the man followed him and caught him by the coat. The little boy looked about him wildly but, seeing no way of escape fell upon his knees.

—Now, you'll let the fire out the next time! said the man, striking at him viciously with the stick. Take that, you little whelp!

The boy uttered a squeal of pain as the stick cut his thigh. He clasped his hands together in the air and his voice shook with fright.

—O, pa! he cried. Don't beat me, pa! And I'll . . . I'll say a *Hail Mary* for you. . . . I'll say a *Hail Mary* for you, pa, if you don't beat me. . . . I'll say a *Hail Mary*. . . .   [1914]

A thorough critical analysis of "Counterparts" using any one of these approaches would take dozens of pages. The following are brief suggestions for how such a reading might proceed.

NEW CRITICISM

A New Critic might want to demonstrate the multiple ways the title holds the narrative together, giving it unity and coherence—for example, Farrington and his son Tom are counterparts since Tom is the victim of his father's bullying just as Farrington is bullied by Mr. Alleyne at work. You can also probably spot other counterparts: Farrington and his wife, for example, trade off bullying each other and their means of escaping from the drudgery of their lives, the bar and the church, are also parallel. And naturally when Weathers, the acrobat, defeats the much larger Farrington in arm wrestling, we are reminded of the verbal beating Farrington must endure from his equally diminutive boss, Mr. Alleyne. New Critics are fond of finding the ways all the elements of a text reinforce each other, so they also pay attention to subtle repetitions in language. When Farrington is referred to as "the man" again and again, this repeated sentence pattern would be seen as suggesting his mechanical dullness and his crude masculinity, both themes developed throughout the text.

FEMINIST CRITICISM

Feminist critics and their first cousins, gender critics, would naturally be struck by the violent masculinity of Farrington, his fantasies of riot and abuse, his savage feelings of revenge, and his "smouldering anger" (para. 57). Farrington is depicted not only as crude and brutish but also as a kind of perverse stereotype of male vanity, self-centeredness, and irresponsibility. His obsession with obtaining money for drinking completely disregards his role as the provider for a large family, and, of course, the beatings of his son are a cruel parody of his role as paternal protector. And if he had not wasted his money on drink, Farrington would also be a womanizer ("Farrington's eyes wandered at every moment in the direction of one of the young women," para. 47). Gender critics would be interested in the social and cultural mechanisms that could construct such primitive masculinity. Although there might not be enough explicitly in the text to satisfy such an inquiry, the male-dominated workplace and bar scene would be a fruitful place to begin.

PSYCHOANALYTIC CRITICISM

A psychoanalytic critic would first notice the extreme pattern of behavior Farrington exhibits, as he repeatedly withdraws from his adult work responsibilities and as he fantasizes about being physically violent against his supervisors. Critics would suggest that such behavior is typical of Farrington's repressed wounds and his unresolved conflicts with his own father. Farrington seems to be playing out painful childhood experiences. Given the violent displacement (taking it out on someone else) visited on Tom, we can imagine that Farrington is beating not only his boss, Mr. Alleyne, but also perhaps his own abusive father. The fantasies at work in Farrington also suggest the psychological defense of projection, since Farrington is blaming his problems on Mr. Alleyne and his job. Although his tasks do seem to be tedious, they certainly cannot account for his "spasm of rage" (para. 15) nor his desire "to clear out the whole office single-handed" (para. 32). When Farrington feels "humiliated and discontented" (para. 57), it is only in part because of his immediate context. It is the return of the repressed that plagues Farrington, a resurfacing of a buried pain. These ideas should also be tied to Farrington's death wish, especially his stunningly self-destructive behavior at work. Freudian critics would also see these specific actions as related to other core issues that would include intense loss of self-esteem, fear of intimacy, and betrayal.

MARXIST CRITICISM

A Marxist critic would be interested in focusing on the specific historical moment of "Counterparts" and not on Farrington's individual psyche, which can only distract us from the real force that affects human experience — the economic system in which Farrington is trapped. Economic power — not the Oedipal drama or gender — is the crucial human motivator. Farrington's material circumstances and not timeless values are the key to understanding his behavior. The real battle lines are drawn between Crosbie and Alleyne (the "haves") and Farrington (a "have-not") — that is, between the bourgeoisie and the proletariat, between those who control economic resources and those who perform the labor that fills the coffers of the rich. Farrington in a Marxist analysis is a victim of class warfare. His desperation, his humiliation, his rage, his cruel violence are all traceable to classism — an ideology that determines people's worth according to their economic class. Although Farrington does appear shiftless and irresponsible, it is not because of his class; it is because of the meaninglessness of his work and the demeaning hierarchy that keeps him at the bottom. In his alienation, he reverts to a primitive physical masculinity, a false consciousness that only further diminishes his sense of his worth.

Marxists are often interested in what lies beneath the text in its political unconscious. Like a psychoanalytic critic, to get at the unconscious Marxists look for symptoms on the surface that suggest problems beneath. Typically, such symptomatic readings reveal class conflicts that authors are sometimes unaware of themselves. Marxists critics might debate whether Joyce himself understood that the root cause of Farrington's aberrant behavior was economic and not psychological. This makes sense since for Marxists both reader and writer are under the sway of the same ideological system that they see as natural.

DECONSTRUCTION

One of many possible deconstructions of "Counterparts" would involve focusing on a troubling or puzzling point called an *aporia*. Some deconstructive critics have looked at the incomplete phrase that Farrington copies, *"In no case shall the said Bernard Bodley be . . ."* as an aporia, an ambiguous and not completely understandable textual puzzle but one that might be a way into the story's meaning. The oppositions that are being deconstructed or laid bare here are *presence* and *absence*, *word* and *reality*. Working off the implications of the title

"Counterparts," Bernard Bodley can be seen as a double or counterpart for Farrington, a character like Bodley whose existence is in doubt. Although Farrington's size suggests that he is very much physically present, his behavior might suggest otherwise. He spends his time copying other people's words and has a compelling need to repeat the narrative of his encounter with Mr. Allyne, as if he must demonstrate his own existence through repetition. He does not have a viable inner life, an authentic identity. Farrington's essence is not present but absent. His identity is insubstantial. He tries to fill the emptiness at the center of his being with camaraderie and potency, but his efforts produce the opposite — escape, loneliness, and weakness. In other words, the said Farrington does not really exist and cannot be. In this way, we can deconstruct "Counterparts" as a story where presence is absence, where strength is weakness, where Farrington's actions lead only to paralysis and repetition, where Farrington's frustration with his impotence makes his oppressors more powerful.

READER-RESPONSE CRITICISM

Willa Ervinman, a student, was asked to respond to the story by using Stanley Fish's ideas and noting the conflicts between the interpretive or discourse communities Willa belonged to and those depicted in the story. The following are excerpts from her response journal:

```
    I was upset by Farrington's lack of responsibility at
work. He is completely unreliable and demonstrates very
little self-esteem. He must know that the people he works
with consider him a slacker and a fake. I was raised in a
middle-class home where both my parents worked hard in a
bank from 9 to 5. Just the idea that they would sneak out
of work to drink in dark bars is absurd. My belief in the
discourse of middle-class responsibility or perhaps the
Protestant work ethic makes it almost impossible for me
to see Farrington with sympathy even though I can see
that his work is probably completely mechanical and
unfulfilling. . . .
    Farrington's domestic violence against his son is
such a violation of the discourse of domesticity that it
is hard to understand any other response. Someone in my
response group thought that Farrington was a victim of
his working-class discourse of masculinity. I can see
how he was humiliated by the smaller men, Mr. Alleyne
and Weathers, but beating his innocent son as a kind
```

```
of revenge cannot be forgiven. My grandmother tells me
that it was common for children to be physically pun-
ished in her day, but in the interpretive community I
was raised in, there is no excuse for domestic violence.
It is more than a character flaw; it is criminal behav-
ior, and I judge Farrington to be a social menace, beyond
compassion.
```

POSTCOLONIAL CRITICISM

"Counterparts" was written in the early twentieth century at a time when the Ireland Joyce writes about was still a colony of the British empire. Farrington is, then, a colonial subject and subject to political domination. At the story's opening, Farrington, a Catholic from the south of Ireland, is summoned by a "furious voice" from Northern Ireland, a stronghold of British sympathy and Protestant domination. The tension is announced early because it is crucial to Farrington's behavior and his internalized and colonized mindset. Many colonials have a negative self-image because they are alienated from their own indigenous culture. Indeed, Farrington seems completely ill suited to the office copying task he is relegated to. He seems more suited to some physical endeavor, but given the difficult economics of Dublin, he probably has few career options.

Farrington is the Other in the discourse of colonialism, and he is made to seem inferior at every turn, from the verbal lashing of Mr. Alleyne to the physical defeat by Weathers, who is probably British. Symbolically, Farrington tries to resist his subjugation by the British establishment but fails. He is what postcolonial theorists refer to as *unhomed* or *displaced*. He is uncomfortable at work, in the bars where he seeks solace, and finally in his ultimate refuge, a place unprepared even to feed him. Indeed, in an act likely to perpetuate abuse upon future generations, Farrington turns on his own family, becoming, through his enraged attack on his child Tom, a metaphor for the conflicted, tormented, and defeated Ireland. When a colonial is not "at home" even in his own home, he is truly in psychological agony and exile. Joyce represents the trauma of British domination through one subject's self-destructive and self-hating journey, a journey made even more cruelly ironic by Farrington's attack — in a mimicry of British aggression and injustice — on his own subjected son.

A WRITING EXERCISE

After reading "Like a Winding Sheet," write a brief analysis of Ann Petry's story using at least three of the seven schools of literary criticism as your frame of reference.

ANN PETRY
Like a Winding Sheet

Ann Lane Petry (1908–1997) consciously wrote in a long tradition of African American storytellers; for this she has been recognized by writers like Toni Morrison, Alice Walker, and Gloria Naylor. Unlike most of her literary ancestors, however, she grew up with the advantages of the middle class, including access to education. Born in Old Saybrook, Connecticut, she earned a degree from the University of Connecticut in 1934 and worked in the family drugstore until her marriage in 1938. Petry then became a journalist for Harlem newspapers and began to see her short stories published in magazines. In 1945, she won a fellowship for work on her first novel, The Street, *which was published the next year. In 1946, the short story* "Like a Winding Sheet" *was included in the annual anthology* The Best American Short Stories, *which was also dedicated to Ann Petry. Her* Miss Muriel and Other Stories *(1971) was the first collection of short stories by a black woman published in the United States. Her last novel was* The Narrows *(1988). In addition to her novels and stories, she wrote children's literature.*

He had planned to get up before Mae did and surprise her by fixing breakfast. Instead he went back to sleep and she got out of bed so quietly he didn't know she wasn't there beside him until he woke up and heard the queer soft gurgle of water running out of the sink in the bathroom.

He knew he ought to get up but instead he put his arms across his forehead to shut the afternoon sunlight out of his eyes, pulled his legs up close to his body, testing them to see if the ache was still in them.

Mae had finished in the bathroom. He could tell because she never closed the door when she was in there and now the sweet smell of talcum powder was drifting down the hall and into the bedroom. Then he heard her coming down the hall.

"Hi, babe," she said affectionately.

"Hum," he grunted, and moved his arms away from his head, opened one eye.   5

"It's a nice morning."

"Yeah." He rolled over and the sheet twisted around him, outlining his thighs, his chest. "You mean afternoon, don't ya?"

Mae looked at the twisted sheet and giggled. "Looks like a winding sheet," she said. "A shroud—" Laughter tangled with her words and she had to pause for a moment before she could continue. "You look like a huckleberry—in a winding sheet—"

"That's no way to talk. Early in the day like this," he protested.

He looked at his arms silhouetted against the white of the sheets. They were   10
inky black by contrast and he had to smile in spite of himself and he lay there smiling and savoring the sweet sound of Mae's giggling.

"Early?" She pointed a finger at the alarm clock on the table near the bed and giggled again. "It's almost four o'clock. And if you don't spring up out of there, you're going to be late again."

"What do you mean 'again'?"

"Twice last week. Three times the week before. And once the week before and—"

"I can't get used to sleeping in the daytime," he said fretfully. He pushed his legs out from under the covers experimentally. Some of the ache had gone out of them but they weren't really rested yet. "It's too light for good sleeping. And all that standing beats the hell out of my legs."

"After two years you oughta be used to it," Mae said.   15

He watched her as she fixed her hair, powdered her face, slipped into a pair of blue denim overalls. She moved quickly and yet she didn't seem to hurry.

"You look like you'd had plenty of sleep," he said lazily. He had to get up but he kept putting the moment off, not wanting to move, yet he didn't dare let his legs go completely limp because if he did he'd go back to sleep. It was getting later and later but the thought of putting his weight on his legs kept him lying there.

When he finally got up he had to hurry, and he gulped his breakfast so fast that he wondered if his stomach could possibly use food thrown at it at such a rate of speed. He was still wondering about it as he and Mae were putting their coats on in the hall.

Mae paused to look at the calendar. "It's the thirteenth," she said. Then a faint excitement in her voice, "Why, it's Friday the thirteenth." She had one arm in her coat sleeve and she held it there while she stared at the calendar. "I oughta stay home," she said. "I shouldn't go outa the house."

"Aw, don't be a fool," he said. "Today's payday. And payday is a good luck day   20
everywhere, any way you look at it." And as she stood hesitating he said, "Aw, come on."

And he was late for work again because they spent fifteen minutes arguing before he could convince her she ought to go to work just the same. He had to talk persuasively, urging her gently, and it took time. But he couldn't bring himself to talk to her roughly or threaten to strike her like a lot of men might have done. He wasn't made that way.

So when he reached the plant he was late and he had to wait to punch the time clock because the day-shift workers were streaming out in long lines, in groups and bunches that impeded his progress.

Even now just starting his workday his legs ached. He had to force himself to struggle past the outgoing workers, punch the time clock, and get the little cart he pushed around all night, because he kept toying with the idea of going home and getting back in bed.

He pushed the cart out on the concrete floor, thinking that if this was his plant he'd make a lot of changes in it. There were too many standing-up jobs for one thing. He'd figure out some way most of 'em could be done sitting down and he'd put a lot more benches around. And this job he had—this job that forced him to walk ten hours a night, pushing this little cart, well, he'd turn it into a sitting-down job. One of those little trucks they used around railroad stations would be good for a job like this. Guys sat on a seat and the thing moved easily, taking up little room and turning in hardly any space at all, like on a dime.

He pushed the cart near the foreman. He never could remember to refer to her as the forelady even in his mind. It was funny to have a white woman for a boss in a plant like this one.

She was sore about something. He could tell by the way her face was red and her eyes were half-shut until they were slits. Probably been out late and didn't get enough sleep. He avoided looking at her and hurried a little, head down, as he passed her though he couldn't resist stealing a glance at her out of the corner of his eye. He saw the edge of the light-colored slacks she wore and the tip end of a big tan shoe.

"Hey, Johnson!" the woman said.

The machines had started full blast. The whirr and the grinding made the building shake, made it impossible to hear conversations. The men and women at the machines talked to each other but looking at them from just a little distance away, they appeared to be simply moving their lips because you couldn't hear what they were saying. Yet the woman's voice cut across the machine sounds—harsh, angry.

He turned his head slowly. "Good evenin', Mrs. Scott," he said, and waited.

"You're late again."

"That's right. My legs were bothering me."

The woman's face grew redder, angrier looking. "Half this shift comes in late," she said. "And you're the worst one of all. You're always late. Whatsa matter with ya?"

"It's my legs," he said. "Somehow they don't ever get rested. I don't seem to get used to sleeping days. And I just can't get started."

"Excuses. You guys always got excuses," her anger grew and spread. "Every guy comes in here late always has an excuse. His wife's sick or his grandmother died or somebody in the family had to go to the hospital," she paused, drew a deep breath. "And the niggers is the worse. I don't care what's wrong with your legs. You get in here on time. I'm sick of you niggers—"

"You got the right to get mad," he interrupted softly. "You got the right to cuss me four ways to Sunday but I ain't letting nobody call me a nigger."

He stepped closer to her. His fists were doubled. His lips were drawn back in a thin narrow line. A vein in his forehead stood out swollen, thick.

And the woman backed away from him, not hurriedly but slowly—two, three steps back.

"Aw, forget it," she said. "I didn't mean nothing by it. It slipped out. It was an accident." The red of her face deepened until the small blood vessels in her cheeks were purple. "Go on and get to work," she urged. And she took three more slow backward steps.

He stood motionless for a moment and then turned away from the sight of the red lipstick on her mouth that made him remember that the foreman was a woman. And he couldn't bring himself to hit a woman. He felt a curious tingling in his fingers and he looked down at his hands. They were clenched tight, hard, ready to smash some of those small purple veins in her face.

He pushed the cart ahead of him, walking slowly. When he turned his head, she was staring in his direction, mopping her forehead with a dark blue handkerchief. Their eyes met and then they both looked away.

He didn't glance in her direction again but moved past the long work benches, carefully collecting the finished parts, going slowly and steadily up and down, and back and forth the length of the building, and as he walked he forced himself to swallow his anger, get rid of it.

And he succeeded so that he was able to think about what had happened without getting upset about it. An hour went by but the tension stayed in his hands. They were clenched and knotted on the handles of the cart as though ready to aim a blow.

And he thought he should have hit her anyway, smacked her hard in the face, felt the soft flesh of her face give under the hardness of his hands. He tried to make his hands relax by offering them a description of what it would have been like to strike her because he had the queer feeling that his hands were not exactly a part of him anymore — they had developed a separate life of their own over which he had no control. So he dwelt on the pleasure his hands would have felt — both of them cracking at her, first one and then the other. If he had done that his hands would have felt good now — relaxed, rested.

And he decided that even if he'd lost his job for it, he should have let her have it and it would have been a long time, maybe the rest of her life, before she called anybody else a nigger.

The only trouble was he couldn't hit a woman. A woman couldn't hit back the same way a man did. But it would have been a deeply satisfying thing to have cracked her narrow lips wide open with just one blow, beautifully timed and with all his weight in back of it. That way he would have gotten rid of all the energy and tension his anger had created in him. He kept remembering how his heart had started pumping blood so fast he had felt it tingle even in the tips of his fingers.

With the approach of night, fatigue nibbled at him. The corners of his mouth drooped, the frown between his eyes deepened, his shoulders sagged; but his hands stayed tight and tense. As the hours dragged by he noticed that the women workers had started to snap and snarl at each other. He couldn't hear what they said because of the sound of machines but he could see the quick lip movements that sent words tumbling from the sides of their mouths. They gestured irritably with their hands and scowled as their mouths moved.

Their violent jerky motions told him that it was getting close on to quitting time but somehow he felt that the night still stretched ahead of him, composed of endless hours of steady walking on his aching legs. When the whistle finally blew he went on pushing the cart, unable to believe that it had sounded. The whirring of the machines died away to a murmur and he knew then that he'd really heard the whistle. He stood still for a moment, filled with a relief that made him sigh.

Then he moved briskly, putting the cart in the storeroom, hurrying to take his place in the line forming before the paymaster. That was another thing he'd change, he thought. He'd have the pay envelopes handed to the people right at their benches so there wouldn't be ten or fifteen minutes lost waiting for the pay.

He always got home about fifteen minutes late on payday. They did it better in the plant where Mae worked, brought the money right to them at their benches.

He stuck his pay envelope in his pants' pocket and followed the line of workers heading for the subway in a slow-moving stream. He glanced up at the sky. It was a nice night, the sky looked packed full to running over with stars. And he thought if he and Mae would go right to bed when they got home from work they'd catch a few hours of darkness for sleeping. But they never did. They fooled around — cooking and eating and listening to the radio and he always stayed in a big chair in the living room and went almost but not quite to sleep and when they finally got to bed it was five or six in the morning and daylight was already seeping around the edges of the sky.

He walked slowly, putting off the moment when he would have to plunge into the crowd hurrying toward the subway. It was a long ride to Harlem and tonight the thought of it appalled him. He paused outside an all-night restaurant to kill time, so that some of the first rush of workers would be gone when he reached the subway.

The lights in the restaurant were brilliant, enticing. There was life and motion inside. And as he looked through the window he thought that everything within range of his eyes gleamed — the long imitation marble counter, the tall stools, the white porcelain-topped tables and especially the big metal coffee urn right near the window. Steam issued from its top and a gas flame flickered under it — a lively, dancing, blue flame.

A lot of the workers from his shift — men and women — were lining up near the coffee urn. He watched them walk to the porcelain-topped tables carrying steaming cups of coffee and he saw that just the smell of the coffee lessened the fatigue lines in their faces. After the first sip their faces softened, they smiled, they began to talk and laugh.

On a sudden impulse he shoved the door open and joined the line in front of the coffee urn. The line moved slowly. And as he stood there the smell of the coffee, the sound of the laughter and of the voices, helped dull the sharp ache in his legs.

He didn't pay any attention to the white girl who was serving the coffee at the urn. He kept looking at the cups in the hands of the men who had been ahead of him. Each time a man stepped out of the line with one of the thick white cups the fragrant steam got in his nostrils. He saw that they walked carefully so as not to spill a single drop. There was a froth of bubbles at the top of each cup and he thought about how he would let the bubbles break against his lips before he actually took a big deep swallow.

Then it was his turn. "A cup of coffee," he said, just as he had heard the others say.

The white girl looked past him, put her hands up to her head and gently lifted her hair away from the back of her neck, tossing her head back a little. "No more coffee for a while," she said.

He wasn't certain he'd heard her correctly and he said "What?" blankly.

"No more coffee for a while," she repeated.

There was silence behind him and then uneasy movement. He thought someone would say something, ask why or protest, but there was only silence and

50

55

then a faint shuffling sound as though the men standing behind him had simultaneously shifted their weight from one foot to the other.

He looked at the girl without saying anything. He felt his hands begin to tingle and the tingling went all the way down to his finger tips so that he glanced down at them. They were clenched tight, hard, into fists. Then he looked at the girl again. What he wanted to do was hit her so hard that the scarlet lipstick on her mouth would smear and spread over her nose, her chin, out toward her cheeks, so hard that she would never toss her head again and refuse a man a cup of coffee because he was black.

He estimated the distance across the counter and reached forward, balancing his weight on the balls of his feet, ready to let the blow go. And then his hands fell back down to his sides because he forced himself to lower them, to unclench them and make them dangle loose. The effort took his breath away because his hands fought against him. But he couldn't hit her. He couldn't even now bring himself to hit a woman, not even this one, who had refused him a cup of coffee with a toss of her head. He kept seeing the gesture with which she had lifted the length of her blond hair from the back of her neck as expressive of her contempt for him.

When he went out the door he didn't look back. If he had he would have seen the flickering blue flame under the shiny coffee urn being extinguished. The line of men who had stood behind him lingered a moment to watch the people drinking coffee at the tables and then they left just as he had without having had the coffee they wanted so badly. The girl behind the counter poured water in the urn and swabbed it out and as she waited for the water to run out, she lifted her hair gently from the back of her neck and tossed her head before she began making a fresh lot of coffee.

But he had walked away without a backward look, his head down, his hands in his pockets, raging at himself and whatever it was inside of him that had forced him to stand quiet and still when he wanted to strike out.

The subway was crowded and he had to stand. He tried grasping an overhead strap and his hands were too tense to grip it. So he moved near the train door and stood there swaying back and forth with the rocking of the train. The roar of the train beat inside his head, making it ache and throb, and the pain in his legs clawed up into his groin so that he seemed to be bursting with pain and he told himself that it was due to all that anger-born energy that had piled up in him and not been used and so it had spread through him like a poison — from his feet and legs all the way up to his head.

Mae was in the house before he was. He knew she was home before he put the key in the door of the apartment. The radio was going. She had it tuned up loud and she was singing along with it.

"Hello, babe," she called out, as soon as he opened the door.

He tried to say "hello" and it came out half grunt and half sigh.

"You sure sound cheerful," she said.

She was in the bedroom and he went and leaned against the doorjamb. The denim overalls she wore to work were carefully draped over the back of a chair by

the bed. She was standing in front of the dresser, tying the sash of a yellow housecoat around her waist and chewing gum vigorously as she admired her reflection
in the mirror over the dresser.

"Whatsa matter?" she said. "You get bawled out by the boss or somep'n?"   70

"Just tired," he said slowly. "For God's sake, do you have to crack that gum
like that?"

"You don't have to lissen to me," she said complacently. She patted a curl in
place near the side of her head and then lifted her hair away from the back of her
neck, ducking her head forward and then back.

He winced away from the gesture. "What you got to be always fooling with
your hair for?" he protested.

"Say, what's the matter with you anyway?" She turned away from the mirror
to face him, put her hands on her hips. "You ain't been in the house two minutes
and you're picking on me."

He didn't answer her because her eyes were angry and he didn't want to   75
quarrel with her. They'd been married too long and got along too well and so he
walked all the way into the room and sat down in the chair by the bed and
stretched his legs out in front of him, putting his weight on the heels of his shoes,
leaning way back in the chair, not saying anything.

"Lissen," she said sharply. "I've got to wear those overalls again tomorrow.
You're going to get them all wrinkled up leaning against them like that."

He didn't move. He was too tired and his legs were throbbing now that he
had sat down. Besides the overalls were already wrinkled and dirty, he thought.
They couldn't help but be for she'd worn them all week. He leaned farther back
in the chair.

"Come on, get up," she ordered.

"Oh, what the hell," he said wearily, and got up from the chair. "I'd just as
soon live in a subway. There'd be just as much place to sit down."

He saw that her sense of humor was struggling with her anger. But her sense   80
of humor won because she giggled.

"Aw, come on and eat," she said. There was a coaxing note in her voice.
"You're nothing but an old hungry nigger trying to act tough and—" she paused
to giggle and then continued, "You—"

He had always found her giggling pleasant and deliberately said things that
might amuse her and then waited, listening for the delicate sound to emerge
from her throat. This time he didn't even hear the giggle. He didn't let her finish
what she was saying. She was standing close to him and that funny tingling
started in his finger tips, went fast up his arms and sent his fist shooting straight
for her face.

There was the smacking sound of soft flesh being struck by a hard object and
it wasn't until she screamed that he realized he had hit her in the mouth—so
hard that the dark red lipstick had blurred and spread over her full lips, reaching
up toward the tip of her nose, down toward her chin, out toward her cheeks.

The knowledge that he had struck her seeped through him slowly and he
was appalled but he couldn't drag his hands away from her face. He kept striking
her and he thought with horror that something inside him was holding him,

binding him to this act, wrapping and twisting about him so that he had to continue it. He had lost all control over his hands. And he groped for a phrase, a word, something to describe what this thing was like that was happening to him and he thought it was like being enmeshed in a winding sheet—that was it—like a winding sheet. And even as the thought formed in his mind, his hands reached for her face again and yet again.   [1946]

APPENDIX 2

Writing a Research Paper

You may imagine that writing a research paper for your English class is a significantly different, and perhaps more difficult, assignment than others you have had. Because more steps are involved in their writing (for example, additional reading and analysis of sources), research papers tend to be long-range projects. They also tend to be more formal than other kinds of papers because they involve integrating and documenting source material.

These differences, however, are essentially of magnitude and appearance, not of substance. Despite the common misconception (cause of much unnecessary anxiety) that writing a research paper requires a special set of knowledge and skills, it draws principally on the same kind of knowledge and skills needed to write other types of papers. A writer still needs to begin with an arguable **issue** and a **claim**, still needs to marshal **evidence** to defend that claim, and still needs to present that evidence persuasively to convince an audience that the claim has merit. The main difference between research papers and other papers that you will write for this course is that the evidence for a research paper comes from a wider variety of sources.

Writing about literature begins with a **primary research source**—the story, poem, play, or essay on which the paper is focused. In addition to this primary source, however, research papers call on **secondary research sources**—historical, biographical, cultural, and critical documents that writers use to support their claims.

Identifying an Issue and a Tentative Claim

Your first task in writing a research paper is to identify an issue that you genuinely want to think and to learn more about. The more interested you are in your issue, the better your paper will be. You may choose, for example, to write about issues of theme, symbolism, pattern, or genre, or you may prefer to explore contextual issues of social policy, or of the author's biography, culture, or historical period. Any of the types of issues described on pages 25–32 are potentially suitable for research. The type of secondary research materials you use will depend largely on the issue you choose to pursue.

First, read your primary source carefully, taking notes as you do so. If you work with the texts in this book, you will want to read the biographical and contextual information about the author and any questions or commentaries that follow the texts. Then ask questions of your own to figure out what really interests you about the literature. Do not look for simple issues or questions that can be easily answered with a few factual statements; instead, try to discover a topic that will challenge you to perform serious research and do some hard thinking.

Before you begin looking for secondary research sources for your paper, formulate a tentative claim, much like a scientist who begins research with a hypothesis to be tested and affirmed or refuted. Since this tentative claim is unlikely to find its way into your final paper, do not worry if it seems a little vague or obvious. You will have plenty of opportunities to refine it as your research proceeds. Having a tentative claim in mind — or, better still, on paper — will prevent you from becoming overwhelmed by the multitude of potential secondary sources available to you.

Rebecca Stanley, who wrote the research paper that begins on page 1627, chose to write on Kate Chopin. After reading the three Chopin stories included in this book, she found herself wondering about the racial issues raised by "Désirée's Baby" (p. 864). She was horrified by the racism depicted by Chopin but also fascinated by Chopin's unusual and apparently sensitive treatment of the topic. Still, she knew that she lacked a clear sense of direction for her paper and would have to do more reading and thinking. On her second reading of the story (now that she was no longer concentrating on what would happen next), she began to notice how Chopin's vivid, descriptive language, especially her use of light and dark imagery, seemed to create a mood and comment on the theme of racism. She decided on a tentative claim: that there is a connection between the imagery in "Désirée's Baby" and Chopin's attitude towards race relations in her society. Clearly this claim would need refining, but it gave Rebecca a starting point as she headed to the library to begin her research.

Finding and Using Secondary Sources

Once you have your topic in mind and have sketched a tentative claim, begin looking for secondary research sources. Many different types of sources for literary research are available, and the types you will need will depend largely on the type of claim you choose to defend. If your issue is primarily one of interpretation — about the theme, patterns, or symbolism of the text, for instance — you will most likely need to consult literary criticism to see what has been said in the past about the literature you are discussing. If your issue concerns historical or cultural context, including issues of social policy, you may need to consult newspapers, magazines, and similar sorts of cultural documents. Some topics, like Rebecca's, might require several different types of sources.

Researching your project divides into two main activities. First, you will need to identify several secondary sources and construct a **working bibliography**—that is, a list of the materials you might use. Most researchers find it useful to record this working bibliography on a stack of note cards, with one entry per card containing all the pertinent information to help find the source and later to list it in the paper's bibliography, called the **Works Cited.** (Some researchers who have notebook-style computers prefer to bring them to the library and record their working bibliographies on a computer file instead of a collection of cards.) Once you have compiled a working bibliography, you will be ready to move on to the second stage: tracking down the materials you have identified, reading and evaluating them, and writing notes from (and about) them as a preliminary step to writing your own paper.

As you make note of potentially useful sources, it is important that you include in your working bibliography all of the information—including names, titles, publication information, and page numbers—that will eventually be needed for your Works Cited list. An explanation of the Works Cited format for each type of source (from books and articles to CD-ROMs and Web sites) begins on page 1619. Acquaint yourself with this format before you begin compiling your working bibliography; otherwise, you may forget to record crucial information that you will need when you prepare the final version of your paper.

FINDING SOURCES IN THE LIBRARY

Not many years ago, for most people the word *research* was synonymous with hours spent in the library hunting for books and articles. For many students today, *research* has become synonymous with the Internet. We have quickly come to believe that "everything" is available online. When it comes to scholarly research on literary topics, though, this is simply not true. Many of the best and most reliable sources are still available only in old-fashioned print media. If you restrict yourself to sources available electronically—on the Internet, say, or in full-text articles on CD-ROMs—you do yourself a serious disservice as a researcher.

A good place to commence your research is your college or university library's computerized **catalog**. Be aware that scholarly books are often quite specialized, and that you may want to start with one or two fairly general titles to orient you before venturing into more sharply focused scholarship. Because Rebecca was interested in race relations in the South during Chopin's time, she searched the catalog using the very general key words *race relations* and *United States,* which turned up references to a number of books. Among the most interesting titles was Stetson Kennedy's *Jim Crow Guide,* which provided her with a good deal of useful information for her paper.

Perhaps an even better place than the library catalog to begin research for your paper is the **MLA International Bibliography,** published each year by the Modern Language Association. Most college and university libraries carry both the CD-ROM and print versions of this work, which lists scholarly books and articles on a wide range of topics in literary criticism and history. The CD-ROM version is a powerful and flexible tool that allows a researcher to enter a topic or the name of an author or work of literature and then to see on-screen a list of books and articles addressing that topic. These references can be copied by hand, printed out, or downloaded to a floppy disk for your working bibliography.

The print version of the *Bibliography* is also useful, though you must understand its organization to use it efficiently. The bibliographic references are subdivided first by the nationality of the literature, then by its date of publication, then by the author and title of the work. To find information from this source for her paper, Rebecca first located the most recent edition of the MLA *International Bibliography*, moved to the section devoted to American literature, found the section on literature of 1800 to 1899, and finally moved to Kate Chopin and the specific story, "Désirée's Baby." If you find few or no references to your topic in an edition of the bibliography, try the editions for the previous few years. Chances are your topic will show up.

Sources of cultural information other than literary criticism and history can be found by using other excellent options widely available in college and university libraries. These include *InfoTrac*, a user-friendly electronic index of academic and general-interest periodicals including scholarly journals, magazines, and several prominent newspapers. Many researchers also like to use the *Readers' Guide to Periodical Literature* (available in both print and CD-ROM versions), the *Newspaper Abstracts*, and the many specialized indexes devoted to particular fields of study, from science, to history, to education. Let your topic lead you to the information sources that will be most valuable to you. Your reference librarians will be happy to tell you what is available in your particular library as well as how to use any of these books and databases.

EVALUATING SOURCES

Whatever method you use to locate your research materials, remember that not all sources are created equal. Be sure to allot some time for **evaluating** the materials you find. In general, the best and most reliable sources of information for academic papers are (1) books published by academic and university presses; (2) articles appearing in scholarly and professional journals; and (3) articles in prominent, reputable newspapers, such as the *New York Times* or the *Washington Post*. Many other types of sources—from CD-ROMs to popular magazines—may prove useful to you as well, but if you have any hesitation about the trustworthiness of a source, approach it with healthy skepticism. Also, the more recent your information, the better (unless, of course, you are doing historical research).

In general, basic questions you should ask of your sources include: (1) Is the information recent, and if not, is the validity of the information likely to have changed significantly over time? (2) How credible is the author? Is he or she a recognized expert on the subject? (3) Is the source published by an established, respectable press, or does it appear in a well-respected journal or periodical (the *Los Angeles Times* has more credibility than the *National Enquirer*, for example) or Web site (one supported by a university or library, for instance)? (4) Based on what you've learned about responsible argument, do the arguments in your source seem sound, fair, and thoughtful? Is the evidence convincing? Is the development of the argument logical?

You increase your own credibility with your audience by using the most credible research materials available to you, so do not just settle for whatever comes to hand if you have the opportunity to find a stronger source.

FINDING SOURCES WITH A COMPUTER

These days, reliable information is widely and conveniently available on CD-ROMs, many of which may be found in college and university libraries. These include texts of literary works (often with commentaries on these works), bibliographies and indexes to help you locate more traditional sources of information, and even the texts of historical and cultural documents. (For example, a CD-ROM about Robert Frost includes not only the texts of his poems but also critical commentaries, relevant source materials, biographical and autobiographical passages, and recordings of Frost reading his own poetry.) In addition, standard reference works such as encyclopedias and dictionaries are often available on CD-ROM, where they can be efficiently searched for background information or factual corroboration (names, dates, spelling) for your paper. Keep in mind that you may need to rely on your librarian to tell you about your library's holdings, because many CD-ROMs are not yet indexed in the same way as traditional books and magazines.

A wealth of information is available on the Internet as well, and, as with the information in the library, your goal is to find useful information efficiently, evaluate it carefully, and make effective use of it in your paper. Unfortunately, and unlike a library's sources, the information on the Internet is not indexed and organized to make it easily accessible to researchers. You will need to do a certain amount of "surfing" if you are to find appropriate materials for your project. A number of **search engines** (programs for finding information) are designed to help you track down documents on the Web, and if you are an old hand on the Internet, you can probably depend on search engines that have served you well in the past. Rather than searching for keywords, it is often more effective to use the feature of a search engine that allows you continually to narrow a topic until you arrive at the information desired.

For example, to find information on Kate Chopin, Rebecca launched the Web browser on her computer and went to *Yahoo!* From the menu of categories, she chose the following path, clicking on each entry successively: Arts/Humanities/Literature/Authors/Literary Fiction/Chopin, Kate. *Yahoo!* then provided her with several Web sites she could choose to visit, one of which contained the complete text of Chopin's novel *The Awakening* and several of her short stories. Other sites on the list provided a wealth of biographical and critical information about Chopin and her work as well as contextual information about southern literature, Chopin's contemporaries, and her culture. Had she entered Kate Chopin's name for a keyword search, these sources would also have turned up, but they would have been more difficult to find, as they would have been mixed with many other, less useful references to Chopin, from course syllabi to high-school term papers. (Similar information exists online for many of the other authors whose works appear in this book.)

Special care is needed to evaluate online sources, since anyone can put information on the Net. It will be up to you to determine if you are reading a piece of professional criticism or a middle-school term paper. When using online sources for serious research, look especially for work that has been signed by the author and is hosted by a respectable site, such as a university or a library.

Taking Notes: Summarizing, Paraphrasing, Quoting, and Avoiding Plagiarism

Once you have identified a number of sources for your paper and tracked down the books, periodicals, or other materials, it is time to begin reading, analyzing, and taking notes. At this point, it is especially important to keep yourself well organized and to write down *everything* that may be of use to you later. No matter how good your memory, do not count on remembering a few days (or even hours) later which notes or quotations come from which sources. Scrupulously write down page numbers and Web addresses, and double-check facts and spellings.

Many researchers find it easier to stay organized if they take notes on large note cards, with each card containing just one key point from one source. The notes you take from sources will fall into one of three basic categories: summaries, paraphrases, and quotations. (A fourth category is notes of your own ideas, prompted by your research. Write these down as well, keeping them separate and clearly labeled, as you would any other notes.)

Student researchers often rely too heavily on **quotations**, copying verbatim large sections from their research sources. Do not make this mistake. Instead, start your note taking with a **summary** of the source in question—just one or two sentences indicating in your own words the author's main point. Such summaries guarantee that you understand the gist of an author's argument and (since they are your own words) can readily be incorporated in your paper. You might think of a summary as a restatement of the author's principal claim, perhaps with a brief indication of the types of supporting evidence he or she marshals. You can also write summaries of supporting points—subsections of an author's argument—if they seem applicable to your paper. A summary should not, however, include quotations, exhaustive detail about subpoints, or a list of all the evidence in a given source. A summary is meant to provide a succinct overview—to demonstrate that you have grasped a point and can convey it to your readers.

Chances are you will want to take more specific notes as well, ones that **paraphrase** the most germane passages in a particular source. Unlike a summary, a paraphrase does not condense an argument or leave out supporting evidence; instead it puts the information into new words. A paraphrase is generally no shorter than the material being paraphrased, but it still has two advantages over a quotation. First, as with a summary, an accurate paraphrase proves that you understand the material you've read. Second, again as with a summary, a paraphrase is easier to integrate into your paper than a quotation, since it is already written in your own words and style. When you include a paraphrase in your notes, indicate on the note the page numbers in the original source.

The rule of thumb about summarizing or paraphrasing is that you must always clearly indicate which ideas are yours and which are those of others. It is **plagiarism**—a serious violation of academic standards—to accept credit for another's ideas, even if you put them in your own words. Ideas in your paper that are not attributed to a source will be assumed to be your own, so to avoid plagiarism it is important to leave no doubt in your reader's mind about when you are summarizing or paraphrasing. Always cite the source.

An exception to the rule is **common knowledge**—factual information that the average reader can be expected to know or is readily available in many easily accessible sources—which need not be referenced. For example, it is common knowledge that Kate Chopin was an American writer. It is also common knowledge that her original name was Katherine O'Flaherty and that she was born in St. Louis in 1851 and died there in 1904, even though most people would have to look that information up in an encyclopedia or biographical dictionary to verify it.

Sometimes, of course, you will want to copy quotations directly from a source. Do so sparingly, copying quotations only when the author's own words are especially succinct and pertinent. When you write down a quotation, enclose it in quotation marks, and record the *exact* wording, right down to the punctuation. As with a paraphrase, make note of the original page numbers for the quotation, as you will need to indicate this in your final paper.

Each time you take a note, be it summary, paraphrase, or quotation, take a moment to think about why you wrote it down. Why is this particular note from this source important? Write a brief commentary about the note's importance, maybe just a sentence or a few words, perhaps on the back of the note card (if you are using note cards). When the time comes to draft your paper, such commentaries will help you remember why you bothered to take the note and may restart your train of thought if it gets stuck.

And do not forget: If something you read in a source sparks an original idea, write it down and label it clearly as your own. Keep these notes with your notes from the primary and secondary sources. Without your own ideas, your paper will be little more than a report, a record of what others have said. Your ideas will provide the framework for an argument that is your own.

Writing the Paper: Integrating Sources

With your research completed (at least for the moment), it is time to get down to drafting the paper. At this point, many students find themselves overwhelmed with information and wonder if they are really in any better shape to begin writing than they were before starting their research. But having read and thought about a number of authors' ideas and arguments, you are almost certainly more prepared to construct an argument of your own. You can, of course, use any method that has worked for you in the past to devise a first draft of your paper. If you are having trouble getting started, though, you might look to Chapters 3 through 7 of this book, which discuss general strategies for exploring, planning, and drafting papers as well as more specific ideas for working with individual literary genres.

Start by revisiting your tentative claim. Refine it to take into account what you have learned during your research. Rebecca Stanley began with the claim that there was a connection between Chopin's imagery and the attitudes she expressed towards race relations in her society. Having done some research, Rebecca was now ready to claim that the patterns of imagery Chopin uses indicate not only the racial heritage of the main characters in the story but also how guilty or innocent they are of racism. While this is still not quite the thesis of Rebecca's final paper, it reflects the major focus of her research.

With your revised and refined claim at hand, examine your assembled notes, and try to subdivide them into groups of related ideas, each of which can form a single section of your paper or even a single piece of supporting evidence for your claim. You can then arrange the groups of notes according to a logical developmental pattern—for example, from cause to effect or from weakest to strongest evidence—which may provide a structure for the body of your essay. As you write, avoid using your own comments as a kind of glue to hold together other people's ideas. Instead, you are constructing an argument of your own, using secondary sources to support your own structure of claims and evidence.

Anytime you summarize, paraphrase, or quote another author, it should be clear how this author's ideas or words relate to your own argument. Keep in mind that, in your final paper, it is quite unlikely that every note you took deserves a place. Be prepared to discard any notes that do not, in some fashion, support your claim and strengthen your argument. Remember also that direct quotations should be used sparingly for greatest effect; papers that rely too heavily on them make for choppy reading. By contrast, summaries and paraphrases are in your own words and should be a clean and easy fit with your prose style.

Notice how Rebecca uses both summary and paraphrase in her essay (p. 1627). For example, she summarizes two Supreme Court decisions on page 5 of her paper and paraphrases information from *The Jim Crow Guide* on pages 4 and 5. In both cases, her references clearly indicate that the information originated from a particular source. Notice also how smoothly she integrates these summaries and paraphrases into her own discussion of interracial relationships and shows how they connect to the Chopin story and to her claim. The following section on documenting sources (pp. 1619–26) demonstrates the proper format for acknowledging authors whose work you summarize or paraphrase.

When you quote directly from either primary or secondary sources, you will need to follow special conventions of format and style. When quoting up to four lines of prose or three lines of poetry, integrate the quotation directly into your paragraph, enclosing the quoted material in double quotation marks and checking to make sure that the quotation accurately reflects the original. Longer quotations are set off from the text by starting a new line and indenting one inch on the left margin only; these are called **block quotations**. For these, quotation marks are omitted since the indention is enough to indicate that the material is a quotation. Examples of the correct format for both long and short quotations appear in Rebecca's paper.

When a short quotation is from a poem, line breaks in the poem are indicated by slash marks, with single spaces on either side. The example below demonstrates this using a short quotation from William Shakespeare's sonnet, "Let me not to the marriage of true minds." The number in parentheses is a page reference, and the format for these is explained in the next section, "Documenting Sources."

```
Shakespeare tells us that "Love is not love / Which
alters when it alteration finds, / Or bends with the
remover to remove" (716).
```

While it is essential to quote accurately, sometimes you may need to alter a quotation slightly, either by deleting text for brevity, or by adding or changing text to incorporate it grammatically. If you delete words from a quotation, indicate the deletion by inserting an ellipsis (three periods with spaces between them) as demonstrated below with another quotation from the Shakespeare sonnet.

```
Love, Shakespeare tells us, is "not Time's fool . . . But
bears it out even to the edge of doom" (716).
```

If you need to change or add words for clarity or grammatical correctness, indicate the changes with square brackets. If, for instance, you wanted to clarify the meaning of "It" in Shakespeare's line "It is the star to every wandering bark," you could do so like this:

```
Shakespeare claims that "[Love] is the star to every wan-
dering bark" (716).
```

In addition to these format considerations, remember a few general rules of thumb as you deploy primary and secondary sources in your paper. First, without stinting on necessary information, keep quotations as short as possible — your argument will flow more smoothly if you do. Quotations long enough to be blocked should be relatively rare. Second, never assume that a quotation is self-sufficient or its meaning self-evident. Every time you put a quotation in your paper, take the time to introduce it clearly and comment on it to demonstrate why you chose to include it in the first place. Finally, quote fairly and accurately, and stick to a consistent format (such as the MLA style explained below) when giving credit to your sources.

Documenting Sources: MLA Format

Documentation is the means by which you give credit to the authors of all primary and secondary sources cited within a research paper. It serves two principal purposes: (1) it allows your readers to find out more about the origin of the ideas you present; and (2) it protects you from charges of plagiarism. Every academic discipline follows slightly different conventions for documentation, but the method most commonly used for writing about literature is the format devised by the Modern Language Association (MLA). This documentation method encompasses **in-text citations**, which briefly identify within the body of your paper the source of a particular quotation, summary, or paraphrase, and a bibliography, called **Works Cited**, which gives more complete publication information.

While mastering the precise requirements of MLA punctuation and format can be time-consuming and even frustrating, getting it right adds immeasurably to the professionalism of a finished paper. More detailed information, including special circumstances and documentation styles for types of sources not covered here, will be found in the *MLA Handbook for Writers of Research Papers*, Fifth Edition, by Joseph Gibaldi (New York: Modern Language Association, 1999). Of course, if your instructor requests that you follow a different documentation method, you should follow his or her instructions instead.

MLA IN-TEXT CITATION

Each time you include information from any outside source — whether in the form of a summary, a paraphrase, or a quotation — you must provide your reader with a brief reference indicating the author and page number of the original. This reference directs the reader to the Works Cited list, where more complete information is available.

There are two basic methods for in-text citation. The first, and usually preferable, method is to include the author's name in the text of your essay and note the page number in parentheses at the end of the citation. The following paraphrase and quotation from James Joyce's "Araby" (p. 828) show the format to be followed for this method. Note that the page number (without the abbreviation "pg." or additional punctuation) is enclosed within the parentheses, and that the final punctuation for the sentence occurs after the parenthetical reference, effectively making the reference part of the preceding sentence. For a direct quotation, the closing quotation marks come before the page reference, but the final period is still saved until after the reference.

```
Joyce's narrator recounts how he thought of Mangan's sis-
ter constantly, even at the most inappropriate times
(829).

Joyce's narrator claims that he thought of Mangan's sis-
ter "even in places the most hostile to romance" (829).
```

The method is similar for long quotations (those set off from the main text of your essay). The only difference, as you can see on page 3 of Rebecca's essay, is that the final punctuation comes before the parenthetical page reference.

In those cases where citing the author's name in your text would be awkward or difficult, you may include both the author's last name and the page reference in the parenthetical citation. The example below draws a quotation from Nathaniel Branden's commentary "Immature Love," which appears on page 964. As demonstrated, the last name of the author (or authors) and the page number (or numbers) are the only thing included in such a reference. No additional punctuation or information is needed.

> According to one psychologist, the relationships of imma-
> ture persons "tend to be dependent and manipulative, not
> the encounter of two autonomous selves who feel free to
> express themselves honestly" (Branden 965).

Knowing the last name of the author is enough to allow your reader to find out more about the reference in the Works Cited, and having the page number makes it easy to find the original of the quotation, summary, or paraphrase should your reader choose to. The only time more information is needed is if you cite more than one work by the same author. In this case, you will need to specify from which of the author's works a particular citation comes. Notice that since Rebecca includes more than one of Kate Chopin's works in her Works Cited list, she always makes clear, either in her lead-in to a citation or in the parenthetical reference, which story is the basis of a paraphrase or source of a quotation. Electronic sources, such as CD-ROMs and Internet sources, are generally not divided into numbered pages. If you cite from such a source, the parenthetical reference need only include the author's last name (or, if the work is anonymous, an identifying title).

MLA WORKS CITED

The second feature of the MLA format is the Works Cited list, or bibliography. This list should begin on a new page of your paper and should be double spaced throughout and use hanging indention, which means that all lines except the first are indented one half inch. The list is alphabetized by author's last name (or by the title in the case of anonymous works) and includes every primary and secondary source referred to in your paper. The format for the most common types of entries is given below. If any of the information called for is unavailable for a particular source, simply skip that element and keep the rest of the entry as close as possible to the given format. An anonymous work, for instance, skips the author's name and is alphabetized under the title. In addition to the explanations below, you can see examples of MLA bibliographic format in Rebecca's Works Cited.

Books

Entries in your Works Cited for books should contain as much of the following information as is available to you. Follow the order and format exactly as given, with a period after each numbered element below (between author and title, and so on). Not all of these elements will be needed for most books. Copy the information directly from the title and publication pages of the book, not from a library catalog or other reference, because these sources often leave out some information.

1. The name(s) of the author(s) (or editor, if no author is listed, or organization in the case of a corporate author), last name first.

2. The full title, underlined or in italics. If the book has a subtitle, put a colon between title and subtitle.
3. The name(s) of the editor(s), if the book has both an author and an editor, following the abbreviation "Ed."
4. The name(s) of the translator or compiler, following the abbreviation "Trans.," or "Comp," as appropriate.
5. The edition, if other than the first.
6. The volume(s) used, if the book is part of a multivolume set.
7. The name of any series to which the book belongs.
8. The city of publication (followed by a colon), name of the publisher (comma), and year.

The examples below cover the most common types of books you will encounter.

A book by a single author or editor. Simply follow the elements and format as listed above. The first example below is for a book by a single author; note also the abbreviation UP, for "University Press." The second example is a book by a single editor. The third is for a book with both author (Conrad) and an editor (Murfin); note also that it is a second edition and a book in a series, so these facts are listed as well.

```
Cima, Gay Gibson. Performing Women: Female Char-
     acters, Male Playwrights, and the Modern Stage.
     Ithaca, NY: Cornell UP, 1993.
Tucker, Robert C., ed. The Marx-Engels Reader. New
     York: Norton, 1972.
Conrad, Joseph. Heart of Darkness. Ed. Ross C Murfin.
     2nd ed. Case Studies in Contemporary Criticism.
     Boston: Bedford/St. Martin's, 1996.
```

A book with multiple authors or editors. If a book has two or three authors or editors , list all names, but note that only the first name is given last name first and the rest are in normal order. In cases where a book has four or more authors or editors, give only the first name listed on the title page, followed by a comma and the phrase *et al.* (Latin for "and others").

```
Leeming, David, and Jake Page. God: Myths of the Male
     Divine. New York: Oxford UP, 1996.
Arrow, Kenneth Joseph, et al., eds. Education in a
     Research University. Stanford: Stanford UP, 1996.
```

A book with a corporate author. When a book has a group, government agency, or other organization listed as its author, treat that organization in your Works Cited just as you would a single author.

```
National Conference on Undergraduate Research. Pro-
     ceedings of the National Conference on Under-
```

graduate Research. Asheville: U of North Carolina,

1995.

Short Works from Collections and Anthologies

Many scholarly books are collections of articles on a single topic by several different authors. When you cite an article from such a collection, include the information given below. The format is the same for works of literature that appear in an anthology, such as this one.

1. The name of the author(s) of the article or literary work.
2. The title of the short work, enclosed in quotation marks.
3. Name(s) of the editor(s) of the collection or anthology.
4. All relevant publication information, in the same order and format as it would appear in a book citation.
5. The inclusive page numbers for the shorter work.

A single work from a collection or anthology. If you are citing only one article or literary work from any given collection or anthology, simply follow the format outlined above and demonstrated in the following examples.

Kirk, Russell. "Eliot's Christian Imagination." The

Placing of T. S. Eliot. Ed. Jewel Spears Brooker.

Columbia: U of Missouri P, 1991. 136-44.

Silko, Leslie Marmon. "Yellow Woman." Making

Literature Matter: An Anthology for Readers and

Writers. Ed. John Schilb and John Clifford. 2nd

ed. Boston: Bedford/St. Martin's, 2003. 820-27.

Multiple works from the same collection or anthology. If you are citing more than one short work from a single collection or anthology, it is often more efficient to set up a **cross-reference**. This means first writing a single general entry that provides full publication information for the collection or anthology as a whole. The entries for the shorter works then contain only the author and title of the shorter work, the names of the editors of the book, and the page numbers of the shorter work. The example below shows an entry for a short story cross-referenced with a general entry for this book; note that the entries remain in alphabetical order in your Works Cited, regardless of whether the general or specialized entry comes first.

Faulkner, William. "A Rose for Emily." Schilb and

Clifford. 969-75.

Schilb, John, and John Clifford, eds. Making Liter-

ature Matter: An Anthology for Readers and

Writers. 2nd ed. Boston: Bedford/St. Martin's,

2003.

Works in Periodicals

The following information should be included, in the given order and format, when you cite articles and other short works from journals, magazines, or newspapers.

1. The name(s) of the author(s) of the short work.
2. The title of the short work, in quotation marks.
3. The title of the periodical, underlined or italicized.
4. All relevant publication information as explained in the examples below.
5. The inclusive page numbers for the shorter work.

A work in a scholarly journal.   Publication information for work from scholarly and professional journals should include the volume number (and also the issue number, if the journal paginates each issue separately), the year of publication in parentheses and followed by a colon, and the page numbers of the shorter work.

```
Charles, Casey. "Gender Trouble in Twelfth Night."
     Theatre Journal 49 (1997): 121-41.
```

An article in a magazine.   Publication information for articles in general-circulation magazines includes the month(s) of publication for a monthly (or bimonthly), and the date (day, month, then year) for a weekly or biweekly, followed by a colon and the page numbers of the article.

```
Cowley, Malcolm. "It Took a Village." Utne Reader
     Nov.-Dec. 1997: 48-49.
Levy, Steven. "On the Net, Anything Goes." Newsweek 7
     July 1997: 28-30.
```

An article in a newspaper.   When citing an article from a newspaper include the date (day, month, year) and the edition if one is listed on the masthead, followed by a colon and the page numbers (including the section number or letter, if applicable).

```
Cobb, Nathan. "How to Dig Up a Family Tree." The
     Boston Globe 9 Mar. 1998: C7.
```

CD-ROMs

CD-ROMs come in two basic types, those published in a single edition—including major reference works like dictionaries and encyclopedias—and those published serially on a regular basis. In a Works Cited list, the first type is treated like a book and the second like a periodical. Details of citation appear in the following examples.

Single-edition CD-ROMs.   An entry for a single-edition CD-ROM is formatted like one for a book, but with the word *CD-ROM* preceding publication information. Most CD-ROMs are divided into smaller subsections, and these should be treated like short works from anthologies.

```
"Realism." The Oxford English Dictionary. 2nd ed.
    CD-ROM. Oxford: Oxford UP, 1992.
```

Serial CD-ROMs. Treat information published on periodically released CD-ROMs just as you would articles in print periodical, but also include the title of the CD-ROM, underlined or italicized, the word *CD-ROM*, the name of the vendor distributing the CD-ROM, and the date of electronic publication. Many such CD-ROMs contain reprints and abstracts of print works, and in these cases, the publisher and date for the print version should be listed as well, preceding the information for the electronic version.

```
Brodie, James Michael, and Barbara K. Curry. Sweet
    Words So Brave: The Story of African American
    Literature. Madison, WI: Knowledge Unlimited,
    1996. ERIC CD-ROM. SilverPlatter. 1997.
```

The Internet

Internet sources fall into several categories—World Wide Web documents and postings to newsgroups, listservs, and so on. Documentation for these sources should include as much of the following information as is available, in the order and format specified.

1. The name of the author(s), last name first (as for a print publication).
2. The title of the section of the work accessed (the subject line for e-mails and postings) in quotation marks.
3. The title of the full document or site, underlined or in italics.
4. Date the material was published or updated.
5. The protocol used for access (World Wide Web, FTP, USENET news-group, listserv, and so on).
6. The electronic address or path followed for access, in angle brackets.
7. The date you access a site, or the date specified on an e-mail or posting, in parentheses.

The examples below show entries for a Web site and a newsgroup citation, two of the most common sorts of Internet sources.

```
Brandes, Jay. "Maya Angelou: A Bibliography of
    Literary Criticism." 20 Aug. 1997. <http://
    www.geocities.com/ResearchTriangle/1221/
    Angelou.htm> (10 Feb. 1998).
Broun, Mike. "Jane Austen Video Package Launched."
    1 Mar. 1998. <rec.arts.prose> (11 Mar. 1998).
```

Personal Communication

In some cases you may get information directly from another person, either by conducting an interview or by receiving correspondence. In this case, include in your Works Cited the name of the person who gave you the information, the type of communication you had with that person, and the date of the communication.

```
McCorkle, Patrick. Personal [or Telephone] interview.
    12 Mar. 2002.

Aburrow, Clare. Letter [or E-mail] to the author. 15
    Apr. 2002.
```

Multiple Works by the Same Author

If you cite more than one work (in any medium) by a single author, the individual works are alphabetized by title. The author's full name is given only for the first citation in the Works Cited, after which it is replaced by three hyphens. The rest of the citation follows whatever format is appropriate for the medium of the source. The two entries below are for a work in an anthology and a book, both by the same author.

```
Faulkner, William. "A Rose for Emily." Making Litera-
    ture Matter: An Anthology for Readers and Writers.
    Ed. John Schilb and John Clifford. 2nd ed. Boston:
    Bedford/St. Martin's, 2003. 969-75.
---. The Sound and the Fury. New York: Modern Li-
    brary, 1956.
```

Occasionally, you may have an idea or find a piece of information that seems important to your paper but that you just cannot work in smoothly without interrupting the flow of ideas. Such information can be included in the form of **endnotes**. A small superscript number in your text signals a note, and the notes themselves appear on a separate page at the end of your paper, before the Works Cited. Rebecca Stanley's paper includes an endnote, but for many research papers none will be needed.

Sample Student Research Paper

Of course, not all research follows exactly the pattern we have described; it varies from researcher to researcher and project to project. In working on your own research paper, you may find yourself taking more or less time on certain steps, doing the steps in a slightly different order, or looping back to further refine your claim or do more research. But if you take the time to think your project through, do the research right, and write and revise carefully, you should end up with a paper you can be proud of. Take a look at the paper Rebecca finally wrote, and note the annotations, which point out key features of her text and of the MLA format.

Stanley 1

Rebecca Stanley

Professor Gardner

English 102

15 April ----

       Racial Disharmony and "Désirée's Baby"

    The sensuous quality of Kate Chopin's works, as
well as the Creole and Cajun dialect that flavor
her diction, establish her as one of the nineteenth
century's foremost writers. Both her style and
themes have led to her being considered a precursor
to the "Southern Renaissance" of the 1920s (Evans).
In recent years, critics have especially focused on
the ground-breaking explorations of female autonomy
in her short novel <u>The Awakening</u> and in stories
like "The Story of an Hour." Another trait that
sets Chopin's writing ahead of her contemporaries'
is her advocacy of racial harmony, which is not
characteristic of early southern literature. The
racial issue is explored in "Désirée's Baby," in
which Chopin uses black and white imagery and an
ironic twist at the end to teach her audience a
profound truth about humanity. Rather than make
assumptions based upon appearance, individuals
should look beyond the exterior and notice the common humanity that binds all people together. Many
people in Chopin's audience had never learned this
lesson, and sadly enough, neither have many modern-
day Americans.

    "Désirée's Baby" tells the tragic story of a
young woman's suffering in the face of her society's condemnation of mixed marriages. The reader
is introduced to the main character, Désirée, early
in her life, when she is a vulnerable infant, lacking any familial ties. Désirée has been abandoned
at the Valmondé gates, and a kindhearted Madame
Valmondé takes pity and adopts the child as her

*Separate title page
unnecessary. First page
gives student name,
teacher's name, course,
and due date in upper
left corner. Centered
below is paper's title.
Student's last name
and page number
appear in upper right
corner.*

*Information cited from
World Wide Web
source; no page
number in
parenthetical
reference.*

*Rebecca immediately
introduces issue of race
and makes two related
claims—one about
Chopin's imagery and
one about American
society.*

                                        Stanley 2

own. Any doubts lurking in Madame Valmondé's mind
regarding the baby's obscure origin are assuaged as
the child blossoms into a "beautiful and gentle,
affectionate and sincere" young adult--"the idol of
Valmondé" (Chopin 864). This description is
Chopin's first association of Désirée with goodness, suggesting that the baby has been sent to
Madame Valmondé "by a beneficent Providence" (864).
Throughout the story, Chopin continually describes
Désirée as innately good, and she supports this
with imagery of light and undefiled whiteness.

   A character foil emerges when Armand Aubigny
enters the scene on horseback. A dark and handsome
knight of sorts, Armand's shadow falls across
Désirée's whiteness as she stands at the gate
of Valmondé. Eighteen years have passed since
Désirée's initial arrival at the gate, and she has
blossomed into an exquisite young woman. Their
encounter ignites a fiery passion in Armand's soul,
which "[sweeps] along like an avalanche, or like a
prairie fire, or like anything that drives headlong
over all obstacles" (865). The young girl's name-
lessness does not concern Armand, for his Aubigny
heritage--one of the oldest and proudest in
Louisiana (865)--will compensate for her lack
thereof. He hastily dismisses all differences,
marrying Désirée as soon as the corbeille arrives
from Paris.

   Désirée makes the symbolic transition from
undefiled light to darkness when she takes up residence in the Aubigny household, which, like the man
of the house, is immediately characterized by its
dark and somber presence:

   The roof came down steep and black like a cowl,
      reaching out beyond the wide galleries that
      encircled the yellow stuccoed house. Big,

Quotation cited with author's name and page number.

Square brackets indicate alteration to quoted text. With the author's name already known, only the page number appears in parenthetical citation.

Format for block quotation, indented one inch on left margin only. Ellipses indicate deletion from quotation. Note format for page reference.

solemn oaks grew close to it, and their thick-
leaved, far-reaching branches shadowed it like
a pall. Young Aubigny's rule was a strict
one . . . and under it his negroes had forgotten
how to be gay. (865)

Désirée's presence brings sunshine to Armand's previously lonely world, and a new addition to the
Aubigny family further multiplies his joy as the
couple become the proud parents of a baby boy soon
after they are married. Chopin uses light imagery
in the description of Désirée's countenance, which
is "suffused with a glow that [is] happiness itself" (865), when she confides in Madame
Valmondé that Armand has undergone a total character change since the baby's arrival. Désirée
observes that the child's birth has indeed "softened Armand Aubigny's imperious and exacting nature
greatly" (866), marveling at the fact that none of
the blacks have been punished by him since the
baby's arrival. It is obvious that Désirée and
the baby bring an uncharacteristic happiness to
Armand, whose dark, handsome face, "[has] not
often been disfigured by frowns since the day he
fell in love" (866).

As Désirée reclines upon a couch, glowing in
her soft white muslins and laces, she is a vision
of perfect happiness and purity. Unfortunately,
this idyllic existence is short-lived. Something is
wrong with the child, something which will ultimately break many hearts and split the family asunder. Désirée slowly realizes that her child does
not appear to be of entirely white heritage. "Look
at our child," she pleads with Armand. "What does
it mean? tell me" (866). She clutches her husband's
arm in desperation yet he, with his heart of
stone, pushes her hand away in disgust. Finally,

he replies that the child is not white because the mother is not white. Eventually, bitter that Désirée and the child are part black, he coldheartedly forces them both to leave.

Although Armand is guilty for harsh treatment of someone whom he suspects is of mixed heritage, the racism he demonstrates is common in the place and time in which he lives. In New Orleans, where "Désirée's Baby" takes place, personal relationships between the races were clearly forbidden by society's rules of etiquette, as well as by state law. Southern society abided by certain unspoken rules that governed every type of interracial encounter. Even the shaking of hands between members of different races, under any set of circumstances, was taboo (Kennedy 212). Racist groups, most notably the Ku Klux Klan, were constantly on the prowl for those who violated this code of etiquette. For those who dared to exceed the established limits of interracial contact, the social ramifications were great. Oftentimes, death by lynching was the punishment for such unacceptable behavior.

In Armand's society, association with members of another race was not merely a faux pas--it was a flagrant violation of the law. Racism was enforced by the state of Louisiana to the extent that both races were forbidden to occupy space in the same apartment building, even with the existence of walls separating the races and segregated entrances. The only legal exception to this clause existed where a member of one race was employed as a servant of the other (Kennedy 74). The legal system did its best to maintain a stratified class structure that relegated blacks to the lowest position in society, dehumanizing them in the process.

Connection established between original claims and the specifics of the story.

Stanley 5

Since the legal system forbade even such casual
physical contact as handshaking and was known to
punish perpetrators with flogging (Kennedy 212),
interracial sexual relations were clearly taboo.
The language of Louisiana's legislation forbade
"sexual intercourse, cohabitation, concubinage,
and marriage between whites and all 'persons of
color,'" who are "defined by the courts to include
anyone having one-sixteenth or more Negro blood"
(Kennedy 66). However, this racist legislation was
not limited to the state of Louisiana or even to
the deep South.

Quotation within a quotation: The phrase "persons of color" was in quotation marks in original source, and this is indicated by placing it in single quotation marks within the full quotation.

   Legislation that restricted relations between
the races were commonplace in state and federal
laws across the nation. The United States' racial
precedent was set early on when Article I, section
2, of the Constitution specified that each black
was to be counted as three-fifths of a white person
in the determination of the number of each state's
representatives in Congress. However, legalized
racism did not end with the addition of the Fourteenth Amendment to the Constitution, despite its
guarantee of "life, liberty, and property" to every
citizen. Before and after the Fourteenth Amendment
was added, the U.S. Supreme Court repeatedly con-
doned the dehumanization of blacks in its rulings,
as evidenced in such cases as the Dred Scott decision (1857) and Plessy v. Ferguson (1896). The earlier decision was an outright denial of the black
race's humanity, in which the Court sought to bar
the entire race from the benefits of citizenship
and withhold the rights which are guaranteed to all
through the Constitution (Scott v. Sandford). The
subsequent decision sanctioned the forced segregation of the races (Plessy v. Ferguson). As long
as the involved party rendered lip-service to the

Summaries of constitutional articles and court cases.

Stanley 6

Constitution by stipulating that the facilities
provided were "separate but equal," the U.S. government turned a blind eye to blatant racial injustices (Kennedy 167-69) and relegated blacks to
their inferior position in society.

*Brief summary of
multiple pages in
original source.*

Succumbing to pressure from a social structure
and legal system so permeated with racism, Armand
forces his wife and their child to leave. Countless
happy homes, such as that of the Aubigny family,
have been torn apart by this demon of racism
throughout history. Some individuals in today's
society argue that the problem of race relations,
as well as the controversial issue of racial identity, are merely past conflicts that have been
overcome by a more enlightened people. However,
Louisiana--the very state in which the Aubigny family lived--was the location of a recent racial controversy, proving that the issue of race still
divides American society.

In 1983, an individual named Susie Guillory
Phipps requested that the Louisiana Bureau of Vital
Records change her racial classification from black
to white and attempted to sue the bureau after its
refusal to do so. Since Phipps is a descendent of
an eighteenth-century white planter and a black
slave, her birth certificate automatically classified her as black in accordance with a 1970 state
law that declared anyone with at least one-thirty-
second "Negro" blood to be black (Omi and Winant
13). Although Phipps's attorney argued that most
whites have at least one-twentieth "Negro" ancestry, the Court maintained its support of the
quantification of racial identity, and "in so
doing, affirmed the legality of assigning individuals to specific racial groupings" (13). Even as
late as 1986, Louisiana passed another racially

*Specific evidence
provided to support a
debatable claim.*

divisive ruling in which a woman with "negligible African heritage" was legally defined as black (Cose 78).

These modern court rulings raise the specter of racism which has haunted the South, and the entire country to a lesser extent, since the country's inception. It is the very same system that exists in Chopin's world, where, according to Michele Birnbaum:

> The "black," the "mulatto," the "quadroon," and the "Griffe" are subtle indices to social status in the white community. Named according to the ratio of "Negro blood" in their veins, these representative figures function not as indictments of an arbitrary colorline, but as reminders and reinforcements of cultural tiering. (308)[1]

The legal system's recent support of classification based upon percentages of racial heritage only maintains the rift that has divided the races by stressing differences and has granted equality a lesser significance. Countless potential relationships have been thwarted, and even terminated, by the legal system and the social system's racial codes. At times, the grounds for interracial couples' painful separations have been entirely false.

The agony of rejection undoubtedly breaks Désirée's heart as she bids farewell to the husband who has brought her much joy and the happy home they once shared. The rays from the October sunset illuminate the golden strands in her tresses like a halo, and the thin white dress dances in the breeze like an angel's robe. It is appropriate that Chopin uses light imagery in her description of Désirée, for the young woman is truly the only

Superscript numeral refers reader to endnote.

sunshine that the miserable Armand has ever known.
Like the sun, the beautiful Désirée is as glorious
in her departure as she is in her arrival. However,
unlike the sun, there is no hope for her return
tomorrow.

A few weeks after Désirée's dramatic farewell,
the miserable Armand presides over a great bonfire
in the backyard of L'Abri. This scene conjures up
vivid images of the devil and is consistent with
the dark imagery that Chopin uses throughout
"Désirée's Baby" to describe Armand. As he sits
high above the spectacle, a half dozen blacks feed
the flames with every reminder of his love affair
and previously joyous existence. After the willow
cradle and the baby's layette as well as Désirée's
silk and velvet robes have been devoured by the
blaze, only the couple's love letters from their
days of espousal remain. Among them lingers a
curious scrap of paper scrawled in his own
mother's handwriting. In the note, she thanks God
for blessing her with the love of her husband. In
conclusion, she declares, "But, above all . . .
night and day, I thank the good God for having so
arranged our lives that our dear Armand will
never know that his mother, who adores him, belongs
to the race that is cursed with the brand of slavery" (868).

One may wish that Armand had only known in time
that it was he--not Désirée--who shared a common
heritage with the slaves! Chopin drops hints about
Armand's black ancestry throughout the story, fore-
shadowing the ending with dark and evil imagery
that mirrors common stereotypes of the black race.
However, the awareness of his own heritage eludes
Armand, who makes the mistake of a lifetime based

upon societal prejudices. That knowledge would also
save Désirée, and the blacks of L'Abri, from the
misery that Armand has inflicted upon their lives
by treating them as second-class citizens. Readers
may wish he had only realized the "negro blood"
coursing through his veins is no different than the
"white," because the ending would have turned out
so differently. The regrets will undoubtedly haunt
Armand forever.

It is easy for the reader to judge Armand for
rejecting someone he regards as an inferior, yet
countless American citizens and the legal system
are guilty of committing the same crime. American
society has relegated an entire people to second-
class status, while ignoring the fact that the
only difference between the races is skin color.
Most individuals regret America's dark past, if
only due to the selfish realization that a countless number of Mozarts, Einsteins, and Shakespeares
were branded with a stamp of inferiority and
silenced by the legal and social systems. However,
the daily paper reveals that acts of racism are
still being committed, and the lesson of racial
equality has yet to be learned. American society
has done itself an immense disservice by making an
issue of skin color in the past, and it continues
to do so in the present. Until the world is perceived through color-blind eyes, barriers will
divide the races and peace will remain an unattain-
able goal.

Endnote

[1] Birnbaum is referring here to racial classifica-
tions in Chopin's novel <u>The Awakening</u>, but clearly
the same system applies in "Désirée's Baby."

*Endnote provides
information that could
not be easily integrated
into text of paper.*

Stanley 10

Works Cited

Birnbaum, Michele A. "'Alien Hands': Kate Chopin and the Colonization of Race." American Literature 66 (1994): 301-23.

Chopin, Kate. The Awakening. 1899. Ed. Nancy A. Walker. Boston: Bedford/St. Martin's, 1993.

---. "Désirée's Baby." Making Literature Matter: An Anthology for Readers and Writers. Ed. John Schilb and John Clifford. 2nd ed. Boston: Bedford/St. Martin's, 2003. 864-68.

---. "The Story of an Hour." Making Literature Matter: An Anthology for Readers and Writers. Ed. John Schilb and John Clifford. Boston: Bedford/St. Martin's, 2003. 862-63.

Cose, Ellis. "One Drop of Bloody History." Newsweek 13 Feb. 1995: 78+.

Evans, Patricia. "Southern Women Writers, An Historical Overview." Literature of the South. World Wide Web. <http://falcon.jmu.edu/~ramseyil/southwomen.htm> (8 Mar. 1998).

Kennedy, Stetson. The Jim Crow Guide: The Way It Was. N.p.: Lawrence & Wishart, 1959. Boca Raton: Florida Atlantic U, 1990.

Omi, Michael, and Harold Winant. "Racial Formations." Race, Class, and Gender in the United States: An Integrated Study. Ed. Paula Rothenberg. New York: St. Martin's, 1995. 13-22.

Plessy v. Ferguson. 163 US 537. US Supr. Ct. 1896.

Scott v. Sandford. 60 US 393. US Supr. Ct. 1856.

US Const. Amend. XIV, sec. 1.

Citation for an article in a scholarly journal.

Citation for a work in an anthology. Note style for multiple works by the same author.

Citation for an article in a general-circulation periodical. Citation for a World Wide Web source.

Citation for a book.

Citation for a chapter in a book.

Citations for court cases.

Citation for a government document.

Contents by Genre

Poems

Plays

Essays

Acknowledgments continued from p. iv

W. H. Auden. "September 1, 1929." From *W. H. Auden: The Collected Poems* by W. H. Auden. Copyright © 1940 and renewed 1968 by W. H. Auden. Used by permission of Random House, Inc.

Steven Gould Axelrod. Excerpt from *Sylvia Plath: The Wound and the Cure of Words* by Steven Gould Axelrod. Copyright © 1990 by Steven Gould Axelrod. Reprinted by permission of the Johns Hopkins University Press.

James Baldwin. "Sonny's Blues." Originally published in *Partisan Review*. Copyright © 1965. Copyright renewed. Collected in *Going to Meet the Man* by James Baldwin. Published by Vintage Books. Reprinted by arrangement with the James Baldwin Estate.

Toni Cade Bambara. "The Lesson." From *Gorilla, My Love* by Toni Cade Bambara. Copyright © 1972 by Toni Cade Bambara. Reprinted by permission of Random House, Inc.

Stephen Bandy. Excerpt from " 'One of My Babies': The Misfit and the Grandmother." Copyright © 1996 by Stephen Bandy. Originally published in *Studies in Short Fiction*. Reprinted by permission.

Robin Becker. "The Star Show." From *All American Girl* by Robin Becker. Copyright © 1996. Reprinted by permission of the University of Pittsburgh Press.

Peter M. Bergman. "Snapshots from History." © 1969 by Peter Bergman. Reprinted by permission of the Estate of Peter M. Bergman. All rights reserved.

Elizabeth Bishop. "One Art" and "The Fish." From *The Complete Poems 1927–1979*. Copyright © 1979, 1983 by Alice Helen Methfessel. Reprinted by permission of Farrar, Straus and Giroux, LLC.

Clark Blaise and Bharati Mukherjee. Excerpt originally published in *The Sorrow and the Terror: The Haunting Legacy of the Air India Tragedy* by Clark Blaise and Bharati Mukherjee. Copyright © 1988 by Clark Blaise and Bharati Mukherjee. Reprinted with permission of the authors.

Marie Boroff. Excerpt from "Robert Frost: 'To Earthward' " in *Frost: Centennial Essays II*. Copyright © 1976 University of Mississippi Press. Reprinted by permission.

Elizabeth Bowen. "The Demon Lover." From *Collected Stories* by Elizabeth Bowen. Copyright © 1946 and renewed 1974 by Elizabeth Bowen. Reprinted by permission of Alfred A. Knopf, a division of Random House, Inc.

T. Coraghessan Boyle. "The Love of My Life." From *After the Plague* by T. Coraghessan Boyle. Copyright © 2001 by T. Coraghessan Boyle. Used by permission of Viking Penguin, a division of Penguin Putnam, Inc.

Nathaniel Branden. "Immature Love." From *The Psychology of Romantic Love* by Nathaniel Branden. Copyright © 1980 by Nathaniel Branden. Reprinted by permission.

Kate Braverman. "Pagan Night." From *Small Craft Warnings: Stories* by Kate Braverman. Copyright © 1998 by Kate Braverman. Reprinted by permission of the University of Nevada Press.

Mary Lynn Broe. Excerpt from *Protean Poetic: The Poetry of Sylvia Plath* by Mary Lynn Broe. Copyright © 1980 by the Curators of the University of Missouri Press. Reprinted by permission of the University of Missouri Press.

Gwendolyn Brooks. "The Mother." From *Blacks* by Gwendolyn Brooks. Copyright © 1991 by Gwendolyn Brooks Blakely. Published by Third World Press, 1991. Reprinted by permission.

Sally Browder. Excerpt from " 'I Thought You Were Mine': Marsha Norman's *'night, Mother*." Published in *Mother Puzzles: Daughters and Mothers in Contemporary American Literature*, edited by Mickey Pearlman. Reprinted with the permission of Greenwood Publishing Group, Inc., Westport, CT.

Rebecca Brown. "The Gift of Sweat." From *The Gifts of the Body* by Rebecca Brown. Copyright © 1994 by Rebecca Brown. Reprinted by permission of HarperCollins Publishers, Inc.

Lynda K. Bundtzen. Excerpt from *Plath's Incarnations: Woman and the Creative Process* by Lynda K. Bundtzen. Copyright © 1983 by Lynda K. Bundtzen. Reprinted by permission of the University of Michigan Press.

Angela Carter. "The Company of Wolves." From *Burning Your Boats: The Collected Short Stories* by Angela Carter. Copyright © Angela Carter 1979. Reprinted by permission of the Estate of Angela Carter, c/o Rogers, Coleridge & White Ltd., 20 Powis Mews, London W11 1JN.

Raymond Carver. "The Bath" and "What We Talk About When We Talk About Love." From *What We Talk About When We Talk About Love* by Raymond Carver. Copyright © 1981 by Raymond Carver. "A Small, Good Thing." From *Cathedral* by Raymond Carver. Copyright © 1983 by Raymond Carver. Used by permission of Alfred A. Knopf, a division of Random House, Inc.

Rosemary Catacolos. "David Talamántez on the Last Day of Second Grade." Originally in *The Texas Observer* (1995) and reprinted in *The Best American Poetry 1996*, edited by Adrienne Rich, and reproduced on the National Endowment for the Arts Web site, www.arts.endow.gov. Copyright © 1995 by Rosemary Catacalos. Reprinted by permission of the author.

Lucille Clifton. "forgiving my father." From *two-headed woman* by Lucille Clifton. Copyright © 1980 by Lucille Clifton. Now appears in *Good Woman* by Lucille Clifton. Reprinted by permission of Curtis Brown Ltd.

John J. Condor. " 'After Apple-Picking': Frost's Troubled Sleep." Excerpts from *Frost: Centennial Essays*. Copyright © 1974 University of Mississippi Press. Reprinted by permission.

The Crisis. "The Hansberrys of Chicago: They Join Business Acumen with Social Vision." From *The Crisis*, April 1941. Reprinted by permission of the publisher. The author wishes to thank The Crisis Publishing Co., Inc., the publisher of the magazine of the National Association for the Advancement of Colored People, for authorizing the use of this work.

Countee Cullen. "Incident." From the book *Color* by Countee Cullen. Copyright © 1925 by Harper & Brothers. Copyright renewed 1953 by Ida M. Cullen. Reprinted by permission of GRM Associates, Inc., Agents for the Estate of Ida M. Cullen.

e. e. cummings. "somewhere I have never travelled,gladly beyond." Copyright © 1931, © 1959, 1991 by the Trustees for the E. E. Cummings Trust. Copyright © 1979 by George James Firmage, from *Complete Poems: 1904–1962* by e. e. cummings, edited by George J. Firmage. Reprinted by permission of Liveright Publishing Corporation.

Jameson Currier. "What They Carried." From *Dancing on the Mountain* by Jameson Currier. Copyright © 1993 by Jameson Currier. Used by permission of Viking Penguin, a division of Penguin Putnam, Inc.

Don DeLillo. "Videotape." From *Underworld* by Don DeLillo. Copyright © 1997 by Don DeLillo. Reprinted with the permission of Scribner, a Division of Simon & Schuster.

Carl Dennis. "The God Who Loves You." From *Practical Gods* by Carl Dennis. Copyright © 2001 by Carl Dennis. Used by permission of Viking Penguin, a division of Penguin Putnam, Inc.

Toi Derricotte. "Fears of the Eighth Grade." From *Captivity* by Toi Derricotte. Copyright © 1989. Reprinted by permission of the University of Pittsburgh Press.

Emily Dickinson. "Because I could not stop for Death —," "I heard a Fly buzz — when I died —," "I like a look of Agony," and "I've seen a Dying Eye." From *The Poems of Emily Dickinson*, edited by Thomas H. Johnson (The Belknap Press of Harvard University Press). Copyright © 1951, 1955, 1979, 1983 by the President and Fellows of Harvard College. Reprinted by permission of the publishers and the Trustees of Amherst College.

Annie Dillard. "The Deer at Providencia." From *Teaching a Stone to Talk: Expeditions and Encounters* by Annie Dillard. Copyright © 1982 by Annie Dillard. Reprinted by permission of HarperCollins Publishers, Inc.

Mark Doty. "Night Ferry." From *My Alexandria: Poems*. Copyright © 1993 by Mark Doty. Used by permission of the poet and the University of Illinois Press.

Andre Dubus. "Killings." From *Finding a Girl in America* by Andre Dubus. Copyright © 1980 by Andre Dubus. Reprinted by permission of David R. Godine, Publishers, Inc.

Stephen Dunn. "Hard Work." From *New and Selected Poems: 1974–1994* by Stephen Dunn. Copyright © 1994 by Stephen Dunn. Reprinted by permission of the author and W.W. Norton & Company, Inc.

Cornelius Eady. "Who Am I?" From *Cornelius Eady: The Gathering of My Name* by Cornelius Eady. Copyright © 1991 by Cornelius Eady. By permission of Carnegie Mellon University Press.

Alan Ehrenhalt. Excerpt from *The Lost City* by Alan Ehrenhalt. Copyright © 1995 by Alan Ehrenhalt. Reprinted by permission of Basic Books, a member of Perseus Books, LLC.

Loren Eiseley. "The Running Man." From *All the Strange Hours* by Loren Eiseley. Copyright © 1975 by Loren Eiseley. Reprinted with permission of Scribner, a division of Simon & Schuster, Inc.

T. S. Eliot. "The Love Song of J. Alfred Prufrock." From *Collected Poems 1909–1962* by T. S. Eliot. Reprinted by permission of Faber & Faber, Ltd.

Louise Erdrich. "Fleur." From *Tracks* by Louise Erdrich. Copyright © 1988 by Louise Erdrich. Reprinted by permission of Henry Holt and Company, LLC.

Robert Faggen. Excerpt from *Robert Frost and Challenge of Darwin* by Robert Faggen. Copyright © 1997 by Robert Faggen. Reprinted by permission of the University of Michigan Press.

William Faulkner. "A Rose for Emily." From *Collected Stories of William Faulkner* by William Faulkner. Copyright © 1930 and renewed 1939 by William Faulkner. Reprinted by permission of Random House, Inc.

Carolyn Forché. The Colonel." From *The Country Between Us* by Carolyn Forché. Copyright © 1981 by Carolyn Forché. Originally appeared in *Women's International Resource Exchange.* Reprinted by permission of HarperCollins Publishers, Inc.

Charles Fort. "We Did Not Fear the Father." Originally appeared in *The Georgia Review,* Volume LIII, Number 2 (Summer 1999). © 1999 by The University of Georgia. Reprinted by permission of *The Georgia Review* and Charles Fort.

Howard Gadlin. "Mediating Sexual Harassment." From *Sexual Harassment on Campus,* edited by Bernice R. Sandler and Robert J. Shoop. Copyright © 1997 by Allyn & Bacon. Reprinted by permission.

Paul Gessell. "Revealing the 'Family Man' Terrorist." From *The Ottawa Citizen,* May 19, 2001. Copyright © 2001 Southam Inc. Reprinted by permission of the publisher.

Ralph Ginzburg. Excerpt from *100 Years of Lynching* by Ralph Ginzburg. Copyright © 1992 by Ralph Ginzburg. Reprinted by permission of Red Sea Press.

Nikki Giovanni. "Legacies." From *My House* by Nikki Giovanni. Copyright © 1972 by Nikki Giovanni. Reprinted by permission of HarperCollins Publishers, Inc.

Louise Glück. "The School Children." From *The First Four Book of Poems* by Louise Glück. Copyright © 1968, 1971, 1972, 1973, 1974, 1975, 1976, 1977, 1978, 1979, 1980, 1985, 1995 by Louise Glück. Reprinted by permission of HarperCollins Publishers, Inc.

Paul Gray. "What Is Love?" From *Time,* February 15, 1993. Copyright © 1993 Time Inc. Reprinted by permission.

Forrest Hamer. "Lesson." From *Call and Response* by Forrest Hamer. (Alice James Books, 1995). Reprinted by permission of the publisher.

Lorraine Hansberry. *A Raisin in the Sun* by Lorraine Hansberry. Copyright © 1958 by Robert Nemiroff, as an unpublished work. Copyright © 1959, 1966, 1984 by Robert Nemiroff. Reprinted by permission of Random House, Inc. "Letter to the *New York Times* editor, April 23, 1964." From *To Be Young, Gifted and Black: Lorraine Hansberry in Her Own Words,* adapted by Robert Nemiroff. © 1969 by Robert Nemiroff and Robert Nemiroff as Executor of the Estate of Lorraine Hansberry.

Robert Hayden. "Those Winter Sundays." From *Angel of Ascent: New and Selected Poems* by Robert Hayden. Copyright © 1966 by Robert Hayden. Reprinted by permission of Liveright Publishing Corporation.

Seamus Heaney. "Punishment." From *Opened Ground: Selected Poems 1966–1996* by Seamus Heaney. Copyright © 1966 by Seamus Heaney. Reprinted by permission of Farrar, Straus and Giroux, LLC. From *New Selected Poems 1966–1987* by Seamus Heaney. Reprinted by permission of Faber & Faber Limited.

Essex Hemphill. "Commitments." From *Ceremonies* by Essex Hemphill. Copyright © 1992 by Essex Hemphill. Used by permission of Dutton, a division of Penguin Putnam, Inc.

Linda Hogan. "Heritage." From *Calling Myself Home* by Linda Hogan. Copyright © 1991 by Linda Hogan. First appeared in *Red Clay* by Linda Hogan. Reprinted by permission of The Greenfield Review Press.

bell hooks. "Inspired Eccentricity: Sarah and Gus Oldman." Reprinted by permission of the author.

A. E. Housman. "Loveliest of trees, the cherry now." From *Collected Poems of A. E. Housman.* © 1939, 1949, 1965 by Holt, Rinehart & Winston. © 1967, 1968 by Robert E. Symons. Reprinted by permission of The Society of Authors, as literary representatives of the Estate of A. E. Housman.

Pam Houston. "How to Talk to a Hunter." From *Cowboys Are My Weakness* by Pam Houston. Copyright © 1992 by Pam Houston. Reprinted by permission of W.W. Norton & Company, Inc.

Langston Hughes. "Let America Be America Again" and "Theme for English B." From *Collected Poems* by Langston Hughes. Copyright © 1994 by the Estate of Langston Hughes. Reprinted by permission of Alfred A. Knopf, a division of Random House, Inc.

Lynda Hull. "Night Waitress." From *Ghost Money* by Lynda Hull. Copyright © 1986 by Lynda Hull. Reprinted by permission of the University of Massachusetts Press.

Sam Husseini. "Profile in Unfairness." From the *Washington Post*, November 24, 1996. Copyright © 1996 by Washington Post Writers Group. Reprinted by permission.

David Henry Hwang. *M. Butterfly*. Copyright © 1986, 1988 by David Henry Hwang. Used by permission of Dutton Signet, a division of Penguin Putnam, Inc.

Henrik Ibsen. *A Doll House*. From *The Complete Major Prose and Plays of Henrik Ibsen*, translated by Rolf Fjelde. Translation copyright © 1965, 1970, 1975 by Rolf Fjelde. Used by permission of Dutton Signet, a division of Penguin Putnam, Inc.

Madison Jones. Excerpt from *A Good Man's Predicament* by Madison Jones. © Madison Jones. Reprinted by permission of Louisiana State University Press.

June Jordan. "Many Rivers to Cross." From *On Call: Political Essays* by June Jordan. Copyright © 1985 by June Jordan. Reprinted with the permission of the author.

Tim Kendall. Excerpt from *Sylvia Path: A Critical Study*. By permission of Faber & Faber Ltd.

Jamaica Kincaid. "Columbus in Chains." From *Annie John* by Jamaica Kincaid. Copyright © 1985 by Jamaica Kincaid. Reprinted by permission of Farrar, Straus and Giroux, LLC. "Girl." From *At the Bottom of the River* by Jamaica Kincaid. Copyright © 1983 by Jamaica Kincaid. "On Seeing England for the First Time." From *Transitions* by Jamaica Kincaid. Copyright © 1993 by Jamaica Kincaid. Reprinted by permission.

Maxine Hong Kingston. "No Name Woman." From *The Woman Warrior* by Maxine Hong Kingston. Copyright © 1975, 1976 by Maxine Hong Kingston. Reprinted by permission of Alfred A. Knopf, a division of Random House, Inc.

Yusef Komunyakaa. "Blackberries." From *Magic City* by Yusef Komunyakaa. Copyright © 1992 by Yusef Komunyakaa. Reprinted by permission of Wesleyan University Press.

Ted Kooser. "Four Secretaries." From *Weather Central* by Ted Kooser. Copyright © 1994 by Ted Kooser. Reprinted by permission of the University of Pittsburgh Press.

Maxine Kumin. "Woodchucks." From *Selected Poems 1960–1990* by Maxine Kumin. Copyright © 1972 by Maxine Kumin. Reprinted by permission of W.W. Norton & Company, Inc.

Dorianne Laux. "What I Wouldn't Do." From *What We Carry* by Dorianne Laux. Copyright © 1994 by Dorianne Laux. Reprinted with the permission of BOA Editions, Ltd.

D. H. Lawrence. "Snake." From *Compete Poems of D. H. Lawrence*, edited by V. de Lola Pinto and F. W. Roberts. Copyright © 1964, 1971 by Angelo Ravagli and C. M. Weekey, Executors of the Estate of Frieda Lawrence Ravagh. Reprinted by permission of Farrar, Straus and Giroux, LLC, and by permission of Viking Penguin, a division of Penguin Putnam, Inc.

Denise Levertov. "The Ache of Marriage." From *Poems 1960–1967* by Denise Levertov. Copyright © 1961 by Denise Levertov. Reprinted by permission of New Directions Publishing Corp.

Philip Levine. "Among Children" and "What Work Is." From *What Work Is* by Philip Levine. Copyright © 1992 by Philip Levine. Used by permission of Alfred A. Knopf, a division of Random House, Inc.

Shirley Geok-lin Lim. "Father from Asia." From *Crossing the Peninsula* by Shirley Geok-lin Lim. Copyright © Shirley Geok-lin Lim. Reprinted by permission of the author.

Leon F. Littwack. "Hellhounds." Reprinted by permission of the author.

Michael Lohre. "Dear Michael, Love Pam." From *Doubletake* magazine. Reprinted by permission.

Beth Lordan. "The Man with the Lapdog." Copyright © 1999 by Beth Lordan. Reprinted by permission of International Creative Management.

Audre Lorde. "Afterimages." From "The Transformation of Silence into Language and Action" in *Sister Outsider: Essays and Speeches* by Audre Lorde. © 1984. Published by The Crossing Press, P.O. Box 1048, Freedom, CA 95019. Reprinted by permission.

Robert Lowell. "To Speak of the Woe That Is in Marriage." From *Life Studies* by Robert Lowell. Copyright © 1959 by Robert Lowell. Copyright renewed 1987 by Harriet Lowell, Sheridan Lowell, and Caroline Lowell. Reprinted by permission of Farrar, Straus and Giroux, LLC.

David Mamet. *Oleanna*. Copyright © 1992 by David Mamet. Reprinted by permission of Vintage Books, a division of Random House, Inc.

Katherine Mansfield. "The Garden-Party." From *The Short Stories of of Katherine Mansfield* by Katherine Mansfield. Copyright © 1922 by Alfred A. Knopf, Inc. Renewed 1950 by John Middleton Murry. Reprinted by permission of the publisher.

Gabriel García Márquez. "The Handsomest Drowned Man in the World: A Tale for Children." Translated by Gregory Rabassa. Copyright © 1972 by Gregory Rabassa. Reprinted by permission of HarperCollins Publishers, Inc.

Thurgood Marshall. "The Gestapo in Detroit." From *The Crisis*, August 1943, pp. 232–233, 246. Copyright © 1943 The Crisis Publishing Co., Inc., the publisher of the magazine of the National Association for the Advancement of Colored People.

Lisa J. McDonnell. Excerpt from *Diverse Similitude: Beth Henley and Marsha Norman*. From *Southern Quarterly*, 1985. Reprinted by permission.

Edna St. Vincent Millay. "Love Is Not All." Sonnet XXX of *Fatal Interview* by Edna St. Vincent Millay. From *Collected Poems*, HarperCollins. Copyright © 1931, 1958 Edna St. Vincent Millay and Norma Millay Ellis. All rights reserved. Reprinted by permission of Elizabeth Barnett, Literary Executor.

N. Scott Momaday. "The Way to Rainy Mountains." From *The Way to Rainy Mountain* by N. Scott Momaday. Copyright © 1969 by the University of New Mexico Press. Reprinted by permission of the University of New Mexico Press.

Bharati Mukherjee. "The Management of Grief." From *The Middleman and Other Stories* by Bharati Mukherjee. Copyright © 1988 by Bharati Mukherjee. Used by permission of Grove/Atlantic, Inc. and Penguin Books Canada Limited.

Haruki Murakami. "Another Way to Die." From *The Wind-Up Bird Chronicle* by Haruki Murakami, translated by Jay Rubin. Copyright © 1997 by Haruki Murakami. Reprinted by permission of Alfred A. Knopf, a division of Random House, Inc.

Marsha Norman. *'night, Mother*. A Play by Marsha Norman. Copyright © 1983 by Marsha Norman. Reprinted by permission of Hill & Wang, a division of Farrar, Straus and Giroux, LLC.

Joyce Carol Oates. "I, the Juror." Published in 1995 by *Witness*. Copyright © 1995 by The Ontario Review, Inc. Reprinted by permission of John Hawkins Associates, Inc. "The Lady with the Pet Dog." From *Marriage and Infidelities* by Joyce Carol Oates. Copyright © 1972 by Joyce Carol Oates.

Tim O'Brien. "The Things They Carried." From *The Things They Carried* by Tim O'Brien. Copyright © 1990 by Tim O'Brien. Reprinted by permission of Houghton Mifflin Company. All rights reserved.

Flannery O'Connor. "A Good Man is Hard to Find." From *A Good Man is Hard to Find and Other Stories* by Flannery O'Connor. Copyright © 1953 by Flannery O'Connor and renewed 1981 by Regina O'Connor. Reprinted by permission of Harcourt, Inc. "On Her Own Work." From *Mystery and Manners* by Flannery O'Connor. Copyright © 1969 by the Estate of Mary Flannery O'Connor. Reprinted by permission of Farrar, Straus and Giroux, LLC.

Frank O'Connor. "Guests of the Nation." From *The Collected Stories of Frank O'Connor* by Frank O'Connor. Copyright © 1981 by Harriet O'Donovan Sheehy, Executor of the Estate of Frank O'Connor. Used by permission of Alfred A. Knopf, a division of Random House, Inc., and Joan Daves/Writer's House, Inc. on behalf of the proprietor.

Mary Oliver. "Singapore." From *New and Selected Poems* by Mary Oliver. Copyright © 1992 by Mary Oliver. Reprinted by permission of Beacon Press, Boston.

Tillie Olsen. "I Stand Here Ironing." From *Tell Me a Riddle* by Tillie Olsen. Copyright © 1956, 1957, 1960, 1961 by Tillie Olsen. Introduction by John Leonard. Used by permission of Delacorte Press/Seymour Laurence, a division of Random House, Inc.

Robert M. O'Neil. "Protecting Free Speech When the Issue Is Sexual Harassment." Originally published in *The Chronicle of Higher Education*, September 13, 1996. Reprinted by permission of the author.

Daniel Orozco. "Orientation." Reprinted by permission of the author.

George Orwell. "Shooting an Elephant." From *Shooting an Elephant and Other Stories* by George Orwell. Copyright © 1950 by Sonia Brownell Orwell and renewed 1978 by Sonia Pitt-Rivers. Reprinted by permission of Harcourt, Inc. and by permission of Bill Hamilton as the Literary Executor of the Estate of the Late Sonia Brownell Orwell, and Martin Seeker & Warburg Ltd.

Linda Pastan. "Ethics." From *Waiting for My Life, Poems by Linda Pastan*. Copyright © 1981 by Linda Pastan. Reprinted by permission of W.W. Norton & Company, Inc.

Ann Petry. "Like a Winding Sheet." From *Miss Muriel and Other Stories* by Ann Petry. Originally appeared in *The Crisis*, November 1945. Copyright © 1945 by Ann Petry. Renewed 1973 by Ann Petry. Reprinted by the permission of Russell & Volkening as agents for the author.

Marge Piercy. "For Strong Women," "The Market Economy," "To Be of Use," and "What's That Smell in the Kitchen?" From *Circles on the Water* by Marge Piercy. Copyright © 1982 by Marge Piercy. Used by permission of Alfred A. Knopf, a division of Random House, Inc.

Sylvia Plath. "Daddy." From *Ariel* by Sylvia Plath. Copyright © 1963 by Ted Hughes. Reprinted by permission of HarperCollins Publishers, Inc. From *The Collected Poems* by Sylvia Plath, edited by Ted Hughes. Reprinted by permission of Faber & Faber, Ltd.

Sidney Poitier. Excerpt from *The Measure of a Man: A Spiritual Autobiography* by Sidney Poitier. Copyright © 2000 by Sidney Poitier. Reprinted by permission of HarperCollins Publishers, Inc.

Minnie Bruce Pratt. "Two Small-Sized Girls." From *Crime Against Nature* by Minnie Bruce Pratt. Copyright © 1990 by Minnie Bruce Pratt. Reprinted by permission of Firebrand Books.

Henry Reed. "Naming of Parts." From *Henry Reed: Collected Poems,* edited by Jon Stallworthy. Copyright © 1991 by the Executor of Henry Reed's Estate. Reprinted by permission.

Alberto Ríos. "Mi Abuela." First printed in *Whispering to Fool the Wind* by Alberto Ríos. © 1982 by Alberto Ríos. Published by Sheep Meadow Press, 1982. Reprinted by permission of the author.

Tomás Rivera. "Richard Rodriguez's *Hunger of Memory* as Humanistic Antithesis." Published in *Melus,* vol. II, 1984. Copyright © 1984 MELUS, The Society for the Study of Multi-Ethnic Literature of the United States. Reprinted by permission.

Richard Rodriguez. "Aria: Memoir of a Bilingual Childhood." Copyright © 1980 by Richard Rodriguez. Originally appeared in *The American Scholar.* Reprinted by permission of Georges Borchardt, Inc., Literary Agency, for the author.

Theodore Roethke. "My Papa's Waltz." Copyright © 1942 by Hearst Magazines, Inc. From *The Collected Poems of Theodore Roethke* by Theodore Roethke. Used by permission of Doubleday, a division of Random House, Inc.

Katherine M. Rogers. Excerpt from "Feminism and *A Doll's House*" by Katherine M. Rogers, in *Approaches to Teaching Ibsen's* Doll House, edited by Yvonne Shaffer. Copyright © 1985 by the Modern Language Association. Reprinted by permission.

Ramón Saldívar. Excerpt from *Chicano Narrative* by Ramón Saldívar. © 1990. Reprinted by permission of The University of Wisconsin Press.

Scott Russell Sanders. "Doing Time in the Thirteenth Chair." From *Paradise of Bombs* by Scott Russell Sanders. Copyright © 1983 by Scott Russell Sanders. Originally published in *The North American Review.* Reprinted by permission of the author and the Virginia Kidd Agency, Inc.

Anne Sexton. "The Farmer's Wife." From *To Bedlam and Part Way Back* by Anne Sexton. Copyright © 1960 by Anne Sexton. Renewed 1988 by Linda G. Sexton. Reprinted by permission of Houghton Mifflin Company. All rights reserved.

William Shakespeare. *Hamlet, Prince of Denmark,* including footnotes, from *The Complete Works of William Shakespeare,* 4th edition, edited by David Bevington. Copyright © 1997 by Addison-Wesley Educational Publishers, Inc. Reprinted by permission.

Leslie Marmon Silko. "Yellow Woman." Copyright © 1974 by Leslie Marmon Silko. Reprinted by permission of The Wylie Agency.

Paul Simon. "Richard Cory." Copyright © 1966 Paul Simon. Used by permission of the Publisher, Paul Simon Music.

Stevie Smith. "Not Waving but Drowning." From *Collected Poems of Stevie Smith* by Stevie Smith. Copyright © 1972 by Stevie Smith. Reprinted by permission of New Directions Publishing Corp.

W. D. Snodgrass. "Richer Quarry." From *De/Compositions* by W. D. Snodgrass. Copyright © 2001 by W. D. Snodgrass. Reprinted with the permission of Greywolf Press, Saint Paul, Minnesota.

Cathy Song. "The Grammar of Silk." From *School Figures* by Cathy Song. Copyright © 1994. Reprinted by permission of the University of Pittsburgh Press.

Sophocles. "Antigone" and "Oedipus the King." From *Three Theban Plays* by Sophocles, translated by Robert Fagles. Copyright © 1982 by Robert Fagles. Used by permission of Viking Penguin, a division of Penguin Putnam, Inc.

Gary Soto. "Behind Grandma's House." From *Gary Soto: New and Selected Poems* by Gary Soto. Copyright © 1995 by Gary Soto. Reprinted by permission of Chronicle Books, San Francisco.

Jenny S. Spencer. Excerpt from *Norman's 'night, Mother: Psychodrama of Female Identity.* In *Modern Drama,* 1987. Reprinted by permission of the University of Toronto Press.

William Stafford. "Travelling Through the Dark." From *The Way It Is: New and Selected Poems*. Copyright © 1962, 1998 by the Estate of William Stafford. Reprinted with the permission of Graywolf Press, Saint Paul, Minnesota.

Maura Stanton. "Shoplifters." From *Cries of Swimmers* by Maura Stanton. Copyright © 1984 by Maura Stanton. Reprinted by permission of the University of Utah Press.

Brent Staples. "The Runaway Son." From *Parallel Time* by Brent Staples. Copyright © 1994 by Brent Staples. Reprinted by permission of Pantheon Books, a division of Random House, Inc.

Martha Stephens. Excerpt from "The Question of Flannery O'Connor." By permission of Louisiana State University Press.

Andrew Sullivan. "The Love Bloat." From *The New York Times* magazine, February 2001. Copyright © 2001 by The New York Times Company, Inc. Reprinted by permission.

Wislawa Szymborska. "On Death Without Exaggeration" and "True Love." From *View with a Grain of Sand* by Wislawa Szymborska. Copyright © 1993 by Wislawa Szymborska. English translation by Stanislaw Baránczak and Clare Cavanagh. Copyright © 1995 by Harcourt, Inc. Reprinted by permission of the publisher.

Amy Tan. "Two Kinds." From *The Joy Luck Club* by Amy Tan. Copyright © 1989 by Amy Tan. Reprinted by permission of Putnam Berkley, a division of Penguin Putnam, Inc.

Joan Templeton. "Is *A Doll's House* a Feminist Text?" Excerpted from "The *Doll House* Backlash: Criticism, Feminism and Ibsen." From *Proceedings of the Modern Language Association* January 1989, pp. 28–40. Copyright © 1989 by The Modern Language Association. Reprinted by permission of the Modern Language Association.

Dylan Thomas. "Do Not Go Gentle Into That Good Night." From *Collected Poems* by Dylan Thomas (J.M. Dent, Publishers). Reprinted by permission of David Higham Associates. From *The Poems of Dylan Thomas*. Copyright © 1952 by Dylan Thomas. Reprinted by permission of New Directions Publishing Corp.

Anastasia Toufexis. "The Right Chemistry." From *Time*, February 15, 1993. Copyright © 1993 Time Inc. Reprinted by permission.

Kitty Tsui. "A Chinese Banquet." From *The Words of a Woman Who Breathes Fire* by Kitty Tsui. Reprinted by permission of the author.

John Updike. "A & P." From *Pigeon Feathers and Other Stories* by John Updike. Copyright © 1962 by John Updike. Reprinted by permission of Alfred A. Knopf, a division of Random House, Inc.

Victor Villanueva, Jr. Excerpt from "Whose Voice Is It Anyway? Rodriguez's Speech in Retrospect." From *English Journal*, 1987. Copyright © 1987 by the National Council of Teachers of English. Reprinted with permission.

David Wagoner. "The Singing Lesson." From *Traveling Light: Collected and New Poems* by David Wagoner. Copyright © 1999 by David Wagoner. Used with permission of the poet and the University of Illinois Press.

Alice Walker. "Everyday Use." From *In Love and Trouble: Stories of Black Women* by Alice Walker. Copyright © 1973 by Alice Walker. Reprinted by permission of Harcourt, Inc. "In Search of Our Mothers' Gardens." From *In Search of Our Mothers' Gardens: Womaist Prose* by Alice Walker. Copyright © 1974 by Alice Walker. "Women." From *Revolutionary Petunias & Other Poems* by Alice Walker. Copyright © 1970 by Alice Walker.

Robert Penn Warren. "The Themes of Robert Frost." From *New and Selected Essays* by Robert Penn Warren. Copyright © 1947, 1989 by Robert Penn Warren. Reprinted by permission of Random House, Inc.

Rosanna Warren. "In Creve Coeur, Missouri." From *Stained Glass* by Rosanna Warren. Copyright © 1993 by Rosanna Warren. Reprinted by permission of W.W. Norton & Company, Inc.

Hermann J. Weigand. Excerpt from *The Modern Ibsen: A Reconsideration* by Hermann J. Weigand. Copyright © 1925 by Holt, Rinehart & Winston. Copyright © 1953 by Hermann J. Weigand. Reprinted by permission of Henry Holt and Company, LLC.

Bruce Weigl. "Spike." From *The Circle of Hanh: A Memoir* by Bruce Weigl. Copyright © 2000 by Bruce Weigl. Used by permission of Grove/Atlantic, Inc.

Eudora Welty. "A Visit of Charity." From *A Curtain of Green and Other Stories* by Eudora Welty. Copyright © 1941 and renewed 1969 by Eudora Welty. Reprinted by permission of Harcourt, Inc.

Tennessee Williams. *The Glass Menagerie*. Copyright © 1945 by Tennessee Williams and Edwina D. Williams. Renewed 1973 by Tennessee Williams. Reprinted by permission of Random

House, Inc. "Portrait of a Girl in Glass." From *The Collected Stoires of Tennessee Williams*. Copyright © 1948 by The University of the South. Renewed 1976 by The University of the South. Reprinted by permission of New Directions Publishing Corporation.

William Carlos Williams. "The Last Words of My English Grandmother." From *Collected Poems: 1909–1939*, Volume I. Copyright © 1938 by New Directions Publishing Corp. "The Use of Force." From *The Collected Stories of William Carlos Williams*. Copyright © 1938 by William Carlos Williams. Reprinted by permission of New Directions Publishing Corp.

Tobias Wolff. "The Rich Brother." From *Back in the World* by Tobias Wolff. Copyright © 1985 by Tobias Wolff. Reprinted by permission of International Creative Management.

James Wright. "Lying in a Hammock at William Duffy's Farm in Pine Island, Minnesota." From *Above the River: The Complete Poems* by James Wright. Copyright © 1990 by Anne Wright. Reprinted by permission of Wesleyan University Press.

William Butler Yeats. "The Second Coming." From *The Collected Works of W. B. Yeats, Volume I: The Poems*, revised and edited by Richard J. Finneran. Copyright © 1924 by The Macmillan Company. Copyright renewed 1952 by Bertha Georgie Yeats, Michael Butler Yeats, and Anne Yeats. Reprinted by permission of Scribners, a division of Simon & Schuster, Inc.

Adam Zagajewski. "Try to Praise the Mutilated World." From *Without End: New and Selected Poems* by Adam Zagajewski, translated by Clare Cavanagh, Renata Gorczynski, Benjamin Ivry, and C. K. Williams. Copyright © 2002 by FSG, LLC. Reprinted by permission of Farrar, Straus & Giroux, LLC.

Index of Authors, Titles, First Lines, and Terms

The boldfaced page references indicate where a key term is highlighted in the text.

Index of Key Terms